AMERICAN LITERATURE SERIES

HARRY HAYDEN CLARK, GENERAL EDITOR

A COLLEGE BOOK OF

American Literature

BRIEFER COURSE

EDITED BY

Milton Ellis	*Louise Pound*	*George Weida Spohn*
PROFESSOR OF ENGLISH,	PROFESSOR OF ENGLISH,	PROFESSOR OF ENGLISH,
UNIVERSITY OF MAINE	UNIVERSITY OF NEBRASKA	ST. OLAF COLLEGE

&

Frederick J. Hoffman
ASSOCIATE PROFESSOR OF ENGLISH,
UNIVERSITY OF WISCONSIN

SECOND EDITION
AMERICAN BOOK COMPANY

New York *Cincinnati* *Chicago* *Boston* *Atlanta* *Dallas* *San Francisco*

COPYRIGHT ACKNOWLEDGMENTS

Grateful acknowledgment is made to the following publishers and individuals for permission to reprint material which is in copyright or of which they are the authorized publishers:

Appleton-Century-Crofts, Inc.: for chapters v and vi from *The Red Badge of Courage* by Stephen Crane, copyright, 1895, D. Appleton and Company, Reprinted by permission of Appleton-Century-Crofts, Inc.

Brandt and Brandt: for "God's World" from *Renascence and Other Poems* by Edna St. Vincent Millay, published by Harper & Brothers, copyright 1917, 1945 by Edna St. Vincent Millay; for "Justice Denied in Massachusetts" and "Sonnet to Gath" from *The Buck in the Snow* by Edna St. Vincent Millay, published by Harper & Brothers, copyright 1927, 1945 by Edna St. Vincent Millay; for "All in green went my love riding," "Always before your voice," "Buffalo Bill," and "The Cambridge Ladies" from *Collected Poems* by E. E. Cummings, published by Harcourt, Brace & Company, Inc., copyright 1923 by E. E. Cummings; for "Pity this busy Monster, manunkind" from *1×1* by E. E. Cummings, published by Henry Holt & Company, Inc., copyright 1944 by E. E. Cummings. All the above reprinted by permission of Brandt and Brandt.

John Dos Passos: for "Prologue" from *U. S. A.*, "Lover of Mankind" from *The 42nd Parallel* and three selections from *The Big Money*, by John Dos Passos.

Doubleday & Company, Inc.: for chapter X of *McTeague* and for "The Responsibilities of the Novelist" from *Essays in Authorship* by Frank Norris, copyright 1899 and 1901–1903 respectively by the publishers, and for all the selections from Walt Whitman.

iv

~ Preface ~

A College Book of American Literature, Briefer Course, is designed particularly for semester courses in American literature in colleges and normal schools. For the purpose of such courses it is recognized that most writings of the colonial and provincial periods of our history, while important from a historical viewpoint, are intrinsically inferior as literature; and that although the literary outpourings of our own time are vital and interesting to us, we lack the perspective to evaluate them and gauge their permanent significance. The proper materials for such a course, then, lie mainly between the time of the American Revolution and the World War of 1914–1919. During this century and a third, our literature budded into national consciousness, bloomed into transcendental Romanticism, mellowed into Victorian ripeness, and hardened into the tough husk of Realism in the Machine Age, in readiness for a new seed time and burgeoning with widened horizons in the twentieth century—a full cycle of development worthy of careful study by anyone interested in the character and achievement of the American people. As a prelude to this period a few significant authors of the eighteenth century have been included; and, at the nearer end, a few notable poets, story writers, and critics who point in definite directions for the future.

Within this period an effort has been made to include selections which treat all phases of our literary development and which combine reflections of the political and social history of the age with those of the authors' best literary art, without allowing either tendency to go to an extreme.

Long teaching experience has shown the editors the desirability of balanced variety and allowance for many different emphases. In accordance with the marked diversity of critical approaches to American literature, individual teachers like to emphasize widely different aspects of the subject, and provision has been made to this end. Whether it is wished to emphasize the reforming spirit of Puritanism, or the influence of the Frontier, or Romanticism, or Realism, and whatever one's critical preferences and approaches, it is believed that most teachers will find the present work adequate.

It is further designed, through editorial suggestions, to combine in one work anthology, literary history, and a comprehensive guide to interpretation and critical reading. The four longer introductions to the main sections deal chiefly with the backgrounds out of which the literature grew. The sketches of individual authors are full enough to present the essential biographical and critical facts. The bibliographies for each writer, in addition to listing the usual general authorities, call attention to many of the special investigations which have enriched the study of our literature. Many headnotes offer, in unobtrusive fashion, suggestions that will help in pointing the way to a better understanding of some particular selections. There is also a minimum of footnote material where such material has seemed of value.

An attempt has also been made to present the individual and distinctive literary theories and aims of authors as a basis for interpreting and judging their work. Paragraphs on literary theory are included as integral parts of many of the author-sketches, particularly after 1800, when writers became self-conscious craftsmen. The student is thus enabled to measure an author's artistic achievement and to appreciate him in the light of his own literary standards.

The date of publication is given in roman type at the end of selections; the date of writing, if earlier, is in italics.

The last section of the book has been revised and rearranged. Several of the authors in the 1940 printing have been dropped as no longer serving a representative selection of twentieth-century American writing; many new authors have been added. A new introduction is provided for section four, prefaces have been written for all new authors, and those revised for authors remaining from the earlier book. The form of the book remains the same in the revision; the extensive and helpful bibliographical notes have been retained, and to them have been added important references to criticism and scholarship in the years since 1940.

Contents

I. Colonial and Eighteenth-Century American Literature

INTRODUCTION, 1

JONATHAN EDWARDS (1703–1758), 16
Personal Narrative
  Boyhood Experiences, 19
  Transcendent Contemplations, 21
  Sense of Sinfulness, 23
Sarah Pierrepont, 24
Sinners in the Hands of an Angry God
  Application, 25

JOHN WOOLMAN (1720–1772), 31
Journal
  Sundry Exercises, 31
  Voyage to England, 34

MICHEL-GUILLAUME JEAN DE CRÈVE-
  CŒUR (1735–1813), 37
Letters from an American Farmer
  What Is an American? 38

BENJAMIN FRANKLIN (1706–1790), 49
Autobiography
  Reasons for Writing, 52
  Early Reading and Self-Cultivation, 53
  Journey to Philadelphia, 55
  Employed as Printer in Philadelphia, 58
  Trip to Boston and Back, 60
  Great Expectations, 62
  Why Franklin Seldom Went to Church
    Services, 63
  The Project of Attaining Moral Perfection,
    64
  Public-spirited Projects, 67
The Whistle, 71
Letters
  To Samuel Mather, 72
  To Mason Weems and Edward Gantt, 73
  To Mrs. Sarah Bache, 74
  To Ezra Stiles, 76

THOMAS PAINE (1737–1809), 77
The Crisis
  The Times That Try Men's Souls, 79
Common Sense
  Thoughts on the Present State of American
    Affairs, 81

THOMAS YOUNG AND ETHAN ALLEN, 84
Reason the Only Oracle of Man
  Of the Eternity and Infinitude of Divine
    Providence, 85
  Of the Importance of the Exercise of Reason
    and Practice of Morality, in Order to the
    Happiness of Mankind, 88

THOMAS JEFFERSON (1743–1826), 89
The Unanimous Declaration, 91
A Girl's Education, 92
Notes on the State of Virginia
  On Slavery, 92
On the Adoption of the Constitution, 93
First Inaugural Address, 94
On Agricultural Education, 96
A Letter of Reconciliation, 97
Thoughts in Old Age, 98
The Character of Washington, 99

THE FEDERALIST, 101
X. *Advantages of the Union*, by James Madison,
  102

PHILIP FRENEAU (1752–1832), 106
The Power of Fancy, 109
The Beauties of Santa Cruz, 110
To the Memory of the Brave Americans, 111
To Sir Toby, 112
The Hurricane, 113
The Wild Honey Suckle, 113
The Indian Burying Ground, 114
To an Author, 114
On the Anniversary of the Storming of the Bastille,
  115
Ode, 115
Stanzas, 116
On a Honey Bee, 117
To a Caty-did, 117
On the Uniformity and Perfection of Nature, 118
On the Religion of Nature, 118

JOEL BARLOW (1754–1812), 119
The Hasty Pudding, 120
The Columbiad
  A League of Nations, 125

II. The Earlier Nineteenth Century

INTRODUCTION, 129

WILLIAM ELLERY CHANNING (1780–
  1842), 144
The Moral Argument against Calvinism, 145

WASHINGTON IRVING (1783–1859), 150
A History of New York
  Wouter Van Twiller, 154
  The Capture of Fort Christina, 157

The Sketch Book
    Rip Van Winkle, 159
    English Writers on America, 168
Bracebridge Hall
    The Stout Gentleman, 172
The Life and Voyages of Christopher Columbus
    The Discovery of Land, 177

WILLIAM CULLEN BRYANT (1794–1878), 181
The Embargo, 185
Thanatopsis, 186
The Yellow Violet, 188
To a Waterfowl, 188
Inscription for the Entrance to a Wood, 189
I Cannot Forget with What Fervid Devotion, 190
Green River, 190
Oh Fairest of the Rural Maids, 191
A Winter Piece, 191
An Indian at the Burial-place of His Fathers, 193
The Murdered Traveller, 194
A Forest Hymn, 195
The Death of the Flowers, 196
June, 197
The Evening Wind, 197
To the Fringed Gentian, 198
Song of Marion's Men, 198
The Prairies, 199
The Battlefield, 201
The Antiquity of Freedom, 201
O Mother of a Mighty Race, 202
The Death of Lincoln, 203
The Poet, 203
The Right of Workmen to Strike, 204

JAMES FENIMORE COOPER (1789–1851), 205
The Pilot
    Chapter XVII, 209
    Chapter XVIII, 214
The American Democrat
    An Aristocrat and a Democrat, 219

RALPH WALDO EMERSON (1803–1882), 221
Thought, 225
Good-bye, 226
Written in Naples, 226
The Apology, 226
The Rhodora, 227
Concord Hymn, 227
Each and All, 227
The Problem, 228
Woodnotes, 229
The Snow-Storm, 231
Forbearance, 231
Grace, 231
Hamatreya, 232
Musketaquid, 233
Ode Inscribed to W. H. Channing, 234
Days, 235
Two Rivers, 235
The Romany Girl, 236
Brahma, 236
Terminus, 236
Nature
    I. Nature, 237
    III. Beauty, 238
The American Scholar, 241
Letter to the Reverend Henry Ware, Jr., 251

Self-Reliance, 252
The Over-Soul, 265
English Traits
    Character, 267
Biographical Sketch of Thoreau, 272

HENRY DAVID THOREAU (1817–1862), 278
Smoke, 280
Haze, 280
Independence, 281
Walden
    Economy, 281
    Where I Lived and What I Lived For, 288
    Solitude, 291
    The Pond, 291
    Brute Neighbors, 299
    Conclusion, 300
Civil Disobedience, 301

NATHANIEL HAWTHORNE (1804–1864), 304
Sights from a Steeple, 308
The Gray Champion, 311
Young Goodman Brown, 316
The Maypole of Merry Mount, 323
Dr. Heidegger's Experiment, 329
David Swan, 334
Ethan Brand, 337
Preface to Twice-Told Tales, 346
American Notebooks
    Hints for Stories, 348

JOHN GREENLEAF WHITTIER (1807–1892), 350
The Exile's Departure, 353
To William Lloyd Garrison, 354
Memories, 354
Massachusetts to Virginia, 355
Proem, 358
Songs of Labor
    Dedication, 358
    The Shoemakers, 359
Ichabod! 360
The Kansas Emigrants, 361
Burns, 361
Maud Muller, 363
The Barefoot Boy, 364
Skipper Ireson's Ride, 366
Telling the Bees, 367
My Playmate, 368
Laus Deo! 369
Snow-Bound, 370
Abraham Davenport, 379
Among the Hills
    Prelude, 380
The Eternal Goodness, 382
In School-Days, 383
The Trailing Arbutus, 383
The Lost Occasion, 384

JAMES RUSSELL LOWELL (1819–1891), 385
Sonnets
    III. "I would not have this perfect love of ours," 389
    IV. "For this true nobleness I seek in vain," 390
Stanzas on Freedom, 390
The Present Crisis, 390

To the Dandelion, 392
A Fable for Critics, 393
Beaver Brook, 402
She Came and Went, 402
Auf Wiedersehen, 403
After the Burial, 403
The Biglow Papers, First Series
    No. I, A Letter, 404
The Biglow Papers, Second Series
    The Courtin', 407
    No. II, Jonathan to John, 408
    No. VI, Sunthin' in the Pastoral Line, 410
The Washers of the Shroud, 414
Ode Recited at the Harvard Commemoration, 416
An Ode for the Fourth of July, 1876, 422
To Whittier, 426
Emerson the Lecturer, 426
New England Two Centuries Ago, 431

EDGAR ALLAN POE (1809–1849), 439
A Dream within a Dream, 444
Song from Al Aaraaf, 444
Sonnet—To Science, 445

To Helen, 445
The City in the Sea, 445
The Sleeper, 446
Lenore, 447
Israfel, 448
To One in Paradise, 448
The Conqueror Worm, 449
Dream-Land, 449
The Raven, 450
Ulalume, 452
The Bells, 454
Eldorado, 455
Annabel Lee, 456
The Fall of the House of Usher, 456
The Masque of the Red Death, 466
The Cask of Amontillado, 470
The Purloined Letter, 473
Hawthorne's "Twice-Told Tales," 483
The Philosophy of Composition, 487

RICHARD HENRY DANA, JR. (1815–1882), 494
Two Years Before the Mast
    Rounding the Horn, 495

III. The Later Nineteenth Century

INTRODUCTION, 503

HERMAN MELVILLE (1819–1891), 517
Moby Dick
    XLI. Moby Dick, 520
    CXXXIII. The Chase—First Day, 525
    CXXXIV. The Chase—Second Day, 530
    CXXXV. The Chase—Third Day, 534

HENRY WADSWORTH LONGFELLOW
    (1807–1882), 540
The Spirit of Poetry, 545
A Psalm of Life, 546
The Village Blacksmith, 547
The Wreck of the Hesperus, 547
The Skeleton in Armor, 549
The Slave's Dream, 551
The Warning, 552
Mezzo Cammin, 552
Nuremberg, 552
The Day Is Done, 554
The Arsenal at Springfield, 554
The Belfry of Bruges
    Carillon, 555
Seaweed, 556
The Old Clock on the Stairs, 557
The Bridge, 558
King Witlaf's Drinking-Horn, 559
Resignation, 559
Evangeline
    Prologue, 560
    Part the First, 561
The Building of the Ship, 568
My Lost Youth, 573
The Song of Hiawatha
    XVI. Pau-Puk-Keewis, 575
    XVII. The Hunting of Pau-Puk-Keewis, 577
The Children's Hour, 581

Tales of a Wayside Inn
    The Wayside Inn, 582
    Paul Revere's Ride, 585
Hawthorne, 587
Dante, 587
Divina Commedia, 588
Giotto's Tower, 589
The Three Silences of Molinos, 589
Morituri Salutamus, 590
Victor and Vanquished, 593
Nature, 593
The Cross of Snow, 594
Jugurtha, 594

OLIVER WENDELL HOLMES (1809–1894), 594
Old Ironsides, 598
The Last Leaf, 599
My Aunt, 599
On Lending a Punch-Bowl, 600
The Deacon's Masterpiece, 601
The Voiceless, 602
The Boys, 603
Brother Jonathan's Lament for Sister Caroline, 604
Dorothy Q., 605
At the Saturday Club, 606
The Autocrat of the Breakfast-Table
    From Section I, 608
    From Section II, 609
    From Section III, 612
    From Section IV, 613
    From Section VI, 615
Elsie Venner
    I. The Brahmin Caste of New England, 616

ABRAHAM LINCOLN (1809–1865), 618
Autobiography, 619

The Gettysburg Address, 620
The Second Inaugural Address, 620

CIVIL WAR SONGS AND LYRICS, 621
My Maryland, by James Ryder Randall, 624
Charleston, by Henry Timrod, 625
Battle-Hymn of the Republic, by Julia Ward Howe, 625
Little Giffen, by Francis Orray Ticknor, 626
Sheridan's Ride, by Thomas Buchanan Read, 626
The Blue and the Gray, by Francis Miles Finch, 627

WALT WHITMAN (1819–1892), 628
Song of Myself
  1. I celebrate myself, and sing myself, 632
  10. Alone far in the wilds and mountains I hunt, 632
  16. I am of old and young, of the foolish as much as the wise, 633
  21. I am the poet of the Body and I am the poet of the Soul, 634
  31. I believe a leaf of grass is no less than the journey-work of the stars, 634
  33. Space and Time! now I see it is true, what I guess'd at, 635
  35. Would you hear of an old-time sea-fight? 639
  36. Stretch'd and still lies the midnight, 640
  43. I do not despise you priests, all time, the world over, 640
  47. I am the teacher of athletes, 641
  48. I have said that the soul is not more than the body, 642
  52. The spotted hawk swoops by and accuses me, he complains of my gab and my loitering, 642
Miracles, 643
Crossing Brooklyn Ferry, 643
There Was a Child Went Forth, 647
Out of the Cradle Endlessly Rocking, 648
Me Imperturbe, 652
For You O Democracy, 652
I Saw in Louisiana a Live-Oak Growing, 652
I Hear America Singing, 653
Poets to Come, 653
From Paumanok Starting I Fly Like a Bird, 653
Bivouac on a Mountain Side, 654
An Army Corps on the March, 654
Reconciliation, 654
Cavalry Crossing a Ford, 654
Come Up from the Fields Father, 655
Pioneers! O Pioneers! 656
To a Certain Civilian, 658
Beat! Beat! Drums! 658
The Wound-Dresser, 659
O Captain! My Captain! 660
When Lilacs Last in the Dooryard Bloom'd, 661
Vigil Strange I Kept on the Field One Night, 666
One's-Self I Sing, 667
Darest Thou Now O Soul, 667
Passage to India, 668
Thou Mother with Thy Equal Brood, 674
A Prairie Sunset, 677
Good-bye My Fancy! 677
Democratic Vistas, 678
Specimen Days
  My Passion for Ferries, 680
  Broadway Sights, 680

Omnibus Jaunts and Drivers, 681
Some Specimen Cases, 681

SIDNEY LANIER (1842–1881), 683
Thar's More in the Man Than Thar Is in the Land, 686
Corn, 687
The Symphony, 689
From the Flats, 693
Evening Song, 694
The Stirrup-Cup, 694
The Revenge of Hamish, 694
Song of the Chattahoochee, 696
The Marshes of Glynn, 697
A Ballad of Trees and the Master, 699
Marsh Song—at Sunset, 699

EMILY DICKINSON (1830–1886), 700
Success, 703
The Snake, 703
Much Madness Is Divinest Sense, 704
The Soul Selects Her Own Society, 704
To Fight Aloud Is Very Brave, 704
The Show Is Not the Show, 704
Inebriate of Air, 704
The Brain, 704
The Locomotive, 704
A Thought Went Up My Mind Today, 705
Hunger, 705
Just Lost When I Was Saved, 705
There Is No Frigate Like a Book, 705
Self-Reliance, 706
Disillusioned, 706
What Soft, Cherubic Creatures, 706
To Hear an Oriole Sing, 706
The Hummingbird, 706
A Bird Came Down the Walk, 706
Keeping the Sabbath, 707
The Frost, 707
Indian Summer, 707
The Sky Is Low, 707
To Make a Prairie, 707
Elysium Is as Far, 707
Going to Him! Happy Letter, 707
A Letter Received, 708
Exultation Is the Going, 708
I Never Saw a Moor, 708
The Last Night That She Lived, 708
The Bustle in a House, 708
If I Shouldn't Be Alive, 709
I Heard a Fly Buzz When I Died, 709
For Charlotte Brontë, 709
Publication Is the Auction, 709
A Secret, 709
Revolution, 709
The Tint I Cannot Take Is Best, 710
I Took One Draught of Life, 710
So the Eyes Accost and Sunder, 710
It Was a Quiet Way, 710
I Make His Crescent Fill or Lack, 710
Forever at His Side to Walk, 711
Why Do I Love Thee? 711
Although I Put Away His Life, 711
So Well That I Can Live Without, 711
Bereaved, 712
After Great Pain a Formal Feeling Comes, 712
I Got So I Could Hear His Name, 712
"Till Death" Is Narrow Loving, 712
Savior! I've No One Else to Tell, 712

A Wife at Daybreak I Shall Be, 713
Not What We Did Shall Be the Test, 713
Letters to T. W. Higginson, 713

BRET HARTE (1836–1902), 714
Plain Language from Truthful James, 717
Her Letter, 718
The Luck of Roaring Camp, 719
The Outcasts of Poker Flat, 724

JOHN HAY (1838–1905), 730
Little Breeches, 731
Jim Bludso, of the Prairie Belle, 731

SAMUEL LANGHORNE CLEMENS
    (MARK TWAIN) (1835–1910), 732
The Celebrated Jumping Frog of Calaveras County,
    736

The Gilded Age
    VIII. Colonel Sellers, Financial Wizard, 739
Life on the Mississippi
    VI. A Cub-Pilot's Experience, 743
    VII. A Daring Deed, 746
    VIII. Perplexing Lessons, 749

WILLIAM DEAN HOWELLS (1837–1920),
    753
The Rise of Silas Lapham
    XIV. A Dinner Party, 756
Criticism and Fiction
    Jane Austen, 766
    Decency in American Fiction, 767

HENRY JAMES (1843–1916), 770
Greville Fane, 773

IV. LITERATURE OF THE TWENTIETH CENTURY

INTRODUCTION, 785

STEPHEN CRANE (1871–1900), 815
The Red Badge of Courage
    Chapter V, 817
    Chapter VI, 820
The Blue Hotel, 823
The Black Riders
    I saw a man pursuing the horizon, 837
    I met a seer, 837
War Is Kind
    Do not weep, maiden, for war is kind, 837
    A newspaper is a collection of half-injustices,
        838
    The wayfarer, 838
    A man said to the universe 838

FRANK NORRIS (1870–1902), 838
McTeague
    Chapter X, 840
Essays in Authorship
    The Responsibilities of the Novelist, 843

THEODORE DREISER (1871–1945), 846
The Hand, 849

EDITH WHARTON (1862–1937), 858
The Other Two, 861

EDWIN ARLINGTON ROBINSON (1869–
    1935), 871
The House on the Hill, 874
Richard Cory, 874
Calvary, 874
George Crabbe, 874
Credo, 875
The Town Down the River, 875
Flammonde, 876
Miniver Cheevy, 877
Eros Turannos, 878
Luke Havergal, 878

ROBERT FROST (1875–   ), 879
The Trial by Existence, 881

Mending Wall, 882
The Death of the Hired Man, 883
The Mountain, 885
The Black Cottage, 886
An Old Man's Winter Night, 888
Birches, 888
The Road Not Taken, 889
A Time to Talk, 889
Stopping by Woods on a Snowy Evening, 889
Our Singing Strength, 890
Two Look at Two, 890
Two Tramps in Mud Time, 891
The Figure a Poem Makes
    Preface to Collected Poems, 892

VACHEL LINDSAY (1879–1931), 893
General William Booth Enters into Heaven, 896
The Congo
    I. Their Basic Savagery, 897
    II. Their Irrepressible High Spirits, 898
    III. The Hope of Their Religion, 899
The Santa-Fé Trail (A Humoresque), 900
Abraham Lincoln Walks at Midnight, 904
The Ghost of the Buffaloes, 904
The Booker Washington Trilogy
    I. Simon Legree:—A Negro Sermon, 905

CARL SANDBURG (1878–   ), 906
Chicago, 908
The Harbor, 909
A Teamster's Farewell, 909
To a Contemporary Bunkshooter, 909
Fog, 910
Nocturne in a Deserted Brickyard, 910
Cool Tombs, 911
Work Gangs, 911
Death Snips Proud Men, 911
Four Preludes on Playthings of the Wind, 912
A.E.F., 912

WILLA CATHER (1876–1947), 913
The Sculptor's Funeral, 916

SINCLAIR LEWIS (1885–   ), 923
Babbitt
    Chapter I, 925

CONTENTS

SHERWOOD ANDERSON (1876–1941), 931
The Triumph of the Egg
  The Egg, 933

F. SCOTT FITZGERALD (1896–1940), 939
All the Sad Young Men
  The Rich Boy, 940

ERNEST HEMINGWAY (1898–   ), 959
Men Without Women
  The Killers, 962
    In Another Country, 967

EUGENE O'NEILL (1888–   ), 970
Emperor Jones, 973

AMY LOWELL (1874–1925), 987
Patterns, 989

H(ILDA) D(OOLITTLE) (1886–   ), 991
The Garden, 991
Song, 992
Orchard, 992

T. S. ELIOT (1888–   ), 992
The Love Song of J. Alfred Prufrock, 995
Preludes, 997
Morning at the Window, 998
Gerontion, 998
Journey of the Magi, 999

WALLACE STEVENS (1879–   ), 1000
Harmonium
  Sunday Morning, 1002
  Sea-Surface Full of Clouds, 1003

E. E. CUMMINGS (1894–   ), 1004
All in green went my love riding, 1006
Always before your voice my soul, 1006
Buffalo Bill, 1007
The Cambridge Ladies, 1007
Pity this busy monster, manunkind, 1007

(HAROLD) HART CRANE (1899–1932), 1008
The Bridge
  The River, 1009

ARCHIBALD MacLEISH (1892–   ), 1011
You, Andrew Marvell, 1013
Memorial Rain, 1013
. . . & Forty-Second Street, 1014

EDNA ST. VINCENT MILLAY (1892–   ),
  1015
God's World, 1016
Justice Denied in Massachusetts, 1016
Sonnet to Gath, 1016

ELINOR WYLIE (1885–1928), 1017
The Lion and the Lamb, 1018
Sunset on the Spire, 1018

Heroics, 1018
King Honor's Eldest Son, 1018
The Eagle and the Mole, 1019
Unfinished Portrait, 1019
Nameless Song, 1019

ROBINSON JEFFERS (1887–   ), 1019
Science, 1021
To a Young Artist, 1021
Hurt Hawks, 1022

WILLIAM FAULKNER (1897–   ), 1022
These 13
  A Rose for Emily, 1024

THOMAS WOLFE (1900–1938), 1029
Look Homeward, Angel
  Chapter Six, 1032
Of Time and the River
  Chapter vii, 1036

JOHN DOS PASSOS (1896–   ), 1039
U.S.A
  Prologue, 1041
The 42nd Parallel
  Lover of Mankind, 1042
The Big Money
  The American Plan, 1043
  Newsreel LXVI, 1045
  The Camera Eye (50), 1046

JOHN STEINBECK (1902–   ), 1047
The Long Valley
  The Chrysanthemums, 1049

KARL JAY SHAPIRO (1913–   ), 1055
Person, Place and Thing
  University, 1056
  Buick, 1056
  The Fly, 1057

IRVING BABBITT (1865–1933), 1057
On Being Original, 1060

HENRY LOUIS MENCKEN (1880–   ),
  1068
Prejudices, Third Series
  Footnote on Criticism, 1070

T. S. ELIOT (1888–   ), 1076
The Sacred Wood
  Tradition and the Individual Talent, 1078

ROBERT PENN WARREN (1905–   ), 1082
William Faulkner, 1083

GENERAL BIBLIOGRAPHY, 1093

GENERAL INDEX OF AUTHORS AND
  TITLES, 1101

--Alphabetical List of Authors--

Allen, Ethan, 84
Anderson, Sherwood, 931

Babbitt, Irving, 1057
Barlow, Joel, 119
Bryant, William Cullen, 181

Cather, Willa, 913
Channing, William Ellery, 144
Clemens, Samuel Langhorne (Mark Twain),
   732
Cooper, James Fenimore, 205
Crane, (Harold) Hart, 1008
Crane, Stephen, 815
Crèvecœur, Michel-Guillaume Jean de, 37
Cummings, E. E., 1004

Dana, Richard Henry, Jr., 494
Dickinson, Emily, 700
Doolittle, Hilda, 991
Dos Passos, John, 1039
Dreiser, Theodore, 846

Edwards, Jonathan, 16
Eliot, T. S., 992, 1076
Emerson, Ralph Waldo, 221

Faulkner, William, 1022
Finch, Francis Miles, 627
Fitzgerald, F. Scott, 939
Franklin, Benjamin, 49
Freneau, Philip, 106
Frost, Robert, 879

Harte, Bret, 714
Hawthorne, Nathaniel, 304
Hay, John, 730
Hemingway, Ernest, 959
Holmes, Oliver Wendell, 594
Howe, Julia Ward, 625
Howells, William Dean, 753

Irving, Washington, 150

James, Henry, 770

Jeffers, Robinson, 1019
Jefferson, Thomas, 89

Lanier, Sidney, 683
Lewis, Sinclair, 923
Lincoln, Abraham, 618
Lindsay, Vachel, 893
Longfellow, Henry Wadsworth, 540
Lowell, Amy, 987
Lowell, James Russell, 385

MacLeish, Archibald, 1011
Madison, James, 102
Melville, Herman, 517
Mencken, Henry Louis, 1068
Millay, Edna St. Vincent, 1015

Norris, Frank, 838

O'Neill, Eugene, 970

Paine, Thomas, 77
Poe, Edgar Allan, 439

Randall, James Ryder, 624
Read, Thomas Buchanan, 626
Robinson, Edwin Arlington, 871

Sandburg, Carl, 906
Shapiro, Karl Jay, 1055
Steinbeck, John, 1047
Stevens, Wallace, 1000

Thoreau, Henry David, 278
Ticknor, Francis Orray, 626
Timrod, Henry, 625

Warren, Robert Penn, 1082
Wharton, Edith, 858
Whitman, Walt, 628
Whittier, John Greenleaf, 350
Wolfe, Thomas, 1029
Woolman, John, 31
Wylie, Elinor, 1017

Young, Thomas, 84

~ I ~

Colonial and

Eighteenth-Century

American

Literature

Colonial and Eighteenth-Century American Literature

1608–1800

Though the writing done in the colonial and provincial periods of our history is important for a full understanding of the later thought and expression in America, its value as pure literature is relatively slight. The tasks and limitations of early colonial life allowed little time or opportunity for the production of literature of a high order, while as sharers of the cultural traditions of England, the colonists felt no incentive to create a rival literature of their own. Hence for the most part the colonial writings impress us with their "homemadeness," like a crudely constructed article of furniture.

During the first half century after the settlements at Jamestown and Plymouth, the writers were transplanted Englishmen sending home narratives of their successes and trials or engaging in argument or justification regarding the religious, political, and social ideals which were shaping the thought and life of their new undertaking. Such were, in the former group, the historical accounts of the leaders Captain John Smith of Virginia, William Bradford of Plymouth, and John Winthrop of Massachusetts Bay. The colonists, north and south, took their religious views seriously; hence it is not surprising that many books, from the Reverend Alexander Whitaker's *Good News from Virginia* (1613) on, deal with religious controversy or exhortation—Thomas Morton's satire, *The New English Canaan;* the spirited argument for toleration, *The Bloody Tenent of Persecution,* by Roger Williams of Rhode Island; and the quaint and intolerant *Simple Cobler of Aggawam* by Nathaniel Ward. The poetry of the period was chiefly religious, too, including pious and artificial elegies for departed ministers and the grimly realistic *Day of Doom* of Michael Wigglesworth. The best poet before the Revolution was Edward Taylor, minister at Westfield, in Massachusetts Bay, whose work, only recently brought to light, invites comparison with the best of the English metaphysical poets by its sweet earnestness and the effectiveness of its homely conceits.

It was perhaps significant for the future in America, in contrast with the negligible part played by early women writers in England, that the most admired poet of the colonial time was Mrs. Anne Bradstreet, "the Tenth Muse lately sprung up in America"; and that she was followed by Mrs. Mary Rowlandson, writer of the best narrative of Indian captivity; and Mrs. Sarah Kemble Knight, Boston schoolmistress, who wrote the most spirited of early travel journals in America.

As the seventeenth century wore on and the older colonies became better established, the writers continued to be chiefly theologians and chroniclers or journalists in prose or verse. Foremost among the former were a father and son of the

1

remarkable Mather family, Increase (1639–1723) and Cotton (1663–1728), ministers of Boston and voluminous writers of sermons, religious treatises, and histories. Active and influential in the intellectual, religious, and political life of New England, their leadership waned after their failure to check the outburst of popular fanaticism in 1692, when nineteen persons accused of witchcraft were hanged—not burned—at Salem. Cotton Mather's masterpiece was his history *Magnalia Christi Americana*, completed in 1702 and designed to show how the achievements of New England were due to the favors of God, merited through adherence to the true faith by the founders of the colonies. In Virginia appeared an anonymous history of Bacon's Rebellion, probably written by John Cotton of Queen's Creek, with an eloquent elegy on Nathaniel Bacon. Other historical writers, Mrs. Rowlandson, Major Daniel Gookin, and Benjamin Tompson, deal with the Indians and Indian warfare. Our best picture of New England life just before and after 1700 is the diary of Judge Samuel Sewall of Boston, rivaling that of Pepys in its fullness and frankness. Mrs. Knight's journal of her ride through Rhode Island and Connecticut to New York in 1704 and Ebenezer Cook's satirical account of his travels in Maryland in 1707 are other contemporary accounts.

It was during the provincial period (1700–1770) that literature in America became responsive to current changes in England—generally with a lapse of two or three decades between the rise of a new form or vogue there and its first appearance on this side of the water. In prose, the great advance in clearness and effectiveness made by Swift, Defoe, and the essayists Addison and Steele is reflected in the work of numerous youthful imitators like Franklin in America. Provincial poetry also improved greatly under the discipline imposed by the clear and incisive, if somewhat formal and rigid, heroic couplets of Dryden and Pope.

The Middle and Southern Provinces came more actively into the literary picture after 1700, with the readable accounts of contemporary Virginia by Hugh Jones and Robert Beverley; Colonel William Byrd's spicy *History of the Dividing Line;* the often-praised *Journal* of the Quaker John Woolman of New Jersey; the *Letters from an American Farmer* (not published until 1782) by Crèvecœur, the French colonist in New York; Richard Lewis's fresh "Description of Spring," written in Maryland; and the lyrics of the Philadelphians Francis Hopkinson, Nathaniel Evans, and Thomas Godfrey. The last-named was also our first dramatist of note, whose imitative tragedy, *The Prince of Parthia*, was staged at Philadelphia in 1767.

It may be remarked also that the two most notable writers from New England in this period, Franklin and Edwards, both migrated to the Middle Provinces, the former to Philadelphia as a youth, the latter to Princeton in 1757. Other writers of the time in New England were the scholarly Tory governor Thomas Hutchinson, author of a *History of Massachusetts Bay;* John Barnard, writer of an entertaining autobiography; the rival Boston satirists Mather Byles and Joseph Green; the Negro prodigy Phillis Wheatley; and Dr. Benjamin Church, perhaps the most facile writer of the heroic couplet in eighteenth-century America.

Four influences which were to affect the whole subsequent course of American literature made their appearance in the earliest colonial period: those of earlier and current English literary models, of the middle-class point of view, of puritanism, and of frontier living conditions. From the beginning, echoes of Raleigh and the travel books are evident in the pages of John Smith and William Strachey; of English divines in the sermons of John Cotton and the Mathers; of Spenser, Herbert, and Donne in the verses of Anne Bradstreet and Edward Taylor. Most pervasive of all was the influence of the English Bible, whose dignified rhythms and splendid imagery enriched the prose of Bradford and all his successors. If many families owned no other book, they possessed in this one a storehouse of religious and secular history and instruction, tales of intrigue and heroic adventure, primitive folklore and scandalous anecdote, proverbial wisdom, fine lyric poetry, and tender romance. Later potent influences were those of Milton's lyrics, Butler's Hudibrastic couplets, Locke, Shaftesbury, and the deists, Thomson's *Seasons*, Richardson, and Dr. Samuel Johnson.

The English middle class formed the predominant element in all the early colonies, and remained ascendant in most of them. Its members were prevailingly thrifty, industrious, and moral in character, with a leaning toward religious dissent. They were also independent and individualistic, tenacious of rights and impatient of restrictions, and essentially practical-minded. Cut off by the Protestant reformation alike from the tradition of the medieval church and the spirit of renaissance humanism, they had little appreciation for the fine arts, and esteemed literature mainly as a handmaid to theology or learning. Outside the realm of everyday affairs, to us they seem to show a literal-minded credulity, accepting the text of the Bible as final authority in all matters and seeing direct divine intervention or warnings in all unusual occurrences. This mingling of common sense and credulity appears in the pages of Winthrop, Ward, the Mathers, Sewall, and other writers in their period.

Puritanism as a formative influence has to be understood in two distinct senses. One—Puritanism with capital P[1]—refers to a definite religious and political movement of the sixteenth and seventeenth centuries, limited chiefly to Great Britain and the English colonies. Its primary purpose in England was to "purify" the English church by eliminating its episcopal organization and certain forms of worship still retained from Catholicism, but it became involved also in the political struggle to replace the irresponsible Stuart monarchs with a republic or commonwealth. In New England it strove to preserve a pure Calvinistic religion and a

---

[1] Throughout this volume the distinction between "Puritanism," the historical movement, and "puritanism," the general attitude toward life, has been preserved in the capitalization.

commonwealth free from royal or Anglican domination. This restricted historical movement was, of course, very important in connection with the colonial period in America.

The second meaning of puritanism—without the capital—applies to a permanent influence or tendency running throughout British and American thought and literature from the time of John Wyclif or earlier, to the present. When we describe one of our contemporaries as a puritan, or a movement or issue today as puritanical, the term clearly implies a permanent and positive attitude toward life. This may perhaps be defined as a practical moral idealism. Two fundamentals of the puritan's outlook in all ages seem to be: first, that he is disturbed by the presence of evils and imperfections in the world he inhabits; and second, that he feels a sense of personal responsibility for doing something to remedy them. He is not only a critic but a reformer. His besetting sin is not hypocrisy, which is a contradiction of his nature, but the narrowness and intolerance of which he is often accused. He pursues certain eminently desirable objectives—usually moral ones—with such single-mindedness that he loses sight of others perhaps equally desirable, such as beauty, good fellowship, and happiness. He is thus the opposite of the conformist or "cavalier," who is indifferent to deficiencies in a world with which he is in general satisfied, shifts any responsibility for improvement to other shoulders—the church's or the state's—, and has a more catholic attitude toward the arts and the enjoyment of life. Of the early colonial writers, the roistering Thomas Morton is almost the only one who is not somewhat touched by puritan earnestness and religious seriousness.

When the Puritan movement expired in the eighteenth century, the spirit of puritanism did not, of course, become extinct. Rather, it impregnated the new enthusiastic religions which arose in that century and continued as a living force in the nineteenth and twentieth centuries. The Northern abolitionists showed all the characteristics of puritanism, which have still been in evidence in the crusades for temperance reform, social uplift, and world peace in our own time.

Frontier living conditions—hardships, Indian attacks, sickness, and starvation—are from the beginning reflected in the pages of Smith, Bradford, and Winthrop. Later, as the coast settlements became more secure and more crowded, the lure of better farming land, the quest of furs and lumber, the pressure of debt, and disagreements and dissatisfaction with the social order at home drew many of the younger, poorer, and more restless into the interior. Here, a life exposed to constant danger and often lived under most primitive conditions developed a venturesome, self-reliant, and sometimes lawless frontier class. Real settlement advanced slowly in the hundred and fifty years after Jamestown, extending at only a few points farther than a hundred miles from the coast; but in the century from 1775 to 1875 it leaped from the Alleghenies to the Pacific. Beyond the edges of the first settlers' villages lurked the menace of the savage, stealthy, and misunderstood Indians; hence with its grim record of warfare and devastated settlements, the frontier implied to the colonial period less of adventure and opportunity than of danger and insecurity.

The colonial scene up to the Revolution was a narrow strip of English settlement along the coast, east of the Great Lakes and the Alleghenies, extending from the Penobscot to Spanish Florida. Aside from the Negroes, the Dutch in New York, and small groups of Huguenot French, Germans, and Swedes, the early population was British, and very largely English. Throughout the middle of the eighteenth century this stock was augmented by great numbers of new immigrants, the Scotch-Irish and the Germans. The former, descendants of Scotch colonists who had lived for a century in the province of Ulster in northern Ireland, spread up and down the Allegheny frontier, from New York to South Carolina. They were tenacious, vigorous, restless, and inured to hard and frugal living—the best type of pioneer stock—and contributed more than any other to pushing the frontier westward after the Revolution. In the South they formed not only a buffer against the Indians but also a democratic influence in opposition to the aristocracy of the tidewater belt. Presbyterian Calvinists in religion, they desired a learned clergy and helped the establishment of schools and colleges where they settled. The Germans were Lutherans and Protestants of other sects, from the upper Rhine, an area over-run by a century of religious and dynastic wars. The greater number settled in east central Pennsylvania, where they retained their German customs and speech. Clinging to the name *deitsch*, they were confused by their English neighbors with the Dutch and are still misnamed the "Pennsylvania Dutch." A smaller number filtered through the same frontier occupied by the Scotch-Irish. The intermarriage of these two races often fused the sturdiness, industry, and conservatism of the Germans and the more imaginative Celtic zest into an excellent amalgam.

The great majority of the people were agricultural, raising chiefly tobacco for export in Virginia and Maryland, rice and indigo in South Carolina, and grain and general produce in the Middle Colonies and New England. In New York and New England, furs purchased from the Indians were for some time the chief export. Shipbuilding and trading by sea rapidly sprang up in the north, and supplying the West Indian colonies with lumber, fish, and other products became a lucrative occupation. By 1775, over 2500 American-built ships were engaged in commerce with Great Britain. Economically, most colonial families were self-supporting, not only raising their own food but making their own clothing and shoes from home-grown wool and leather, and constructing their own crude furniture, tools, and household implements. A series of bloody conflicts with the chief Indian federations during the last third of the seventeenth century weakened their resistance to westward expansion, and a succession of foreign wars involving the English and French terminated in 1763 with the withdrawal of French forces from Canada. By 1775 the total population of the colonies had grown to about 2,500,000.

In Virginia, as in Maryland and the Carolinas, advantages of soil and climate and the contour of the land and rivers favored the development of a purely agricultural civilization. The adventurers of the first years were virtually wiped out by disease, starvation, and massacre. Their successors were mainly sturdy middle-class stock, not greatly different, even in religious predilections, from the New Englanders. Church attendance was required, a strict code of laws was enforced, and plans were made for an ill-fated college at Henrico as early as 1619. During the English Civil War, however, Virginia, strongly loyal to the King, excluded Puritans, Quakers, and other dissenters from the franchise, and many were banished or left the colony. During most of the seventeenth century the tobacco plantations, averaging less than 200 acres in size, were mainly cultivated by the owners and white indentured servants.[1] Living along navigable rivers, the planters loaded their wares directly on board ship, with the result that towns were few and unimportant. Little manufacture was carried on, and the colonists depended on the mother country and on Dutch and New England traders for supplies. The education of the children was entrusted to their parents and to the church. Governor Berkeley was wont to thank God that in Virginia "there are no free schools or printing presses, and I hope there will be none for a hundred years." A few royalist cavalier families sought refuge in the colony during the Commonwealth, but most of them returned after the Restoration, and the later plantation aristocracy was mainly of middle-class origin.

The restrictions of the Navigation Act, coupled with the competition of Negro slave labor after 1680, greatly hampered the yeoman planters. From that period date the large plantations, operated by slaves, and the emigration to North Carolina, Maryland, and Pennsylvania of great numbers of impoverished planters and released white servants. By the mid-eighteenth century there had developed in Virginia and South Carolina the aristocratic planter whom we associate traditionally with the Old South. He was largely the product of a somewhat feudal life on his great plantation, now served mainly by slave labor, whereas Hugh Jones's description of him earlier in the century is still that of the middle-class merchant-planter, quick at figures, and a shrewd bargainer. By the Revolution, however, the code of personal honor, chivalrous respect for womanhood, and fondness for generous entertainment, racing, and hunting had produced the class of gentlemen, statesmen, and soldiers who were to become leaders in that great conflict. To the Southern gentleman, literature was not a fitting vocation but might be indulged in as an avocation. William Byrd amused himself by elaborating his jottings on

---

[1] T. J. Wertenbaker, *The Planters of Colonial Virginia* (1922), 45-54.

the North Carolina boundary expedition into a finely bound volume. It would not have occurred to him to publish it.

It was in the pleasure-loving South that the drama gained its first uncertain foothold in the provinces. After feeble beginnings at Charleston as early as 1703, and about 1716 at Williamsburg, the colonial capital of Virginia, the latter town was ready by 1752 to become the headquarters of a dramatic troupe from London which, under the name of the American Company, was to stay alive until 1800. Banned in New England and little encouraged in Quaker Philadelphia and commercial New York, it subsisted chiefly in coastal towns in Virginia, Maryland, and South Carolina, with occasional sojourns in the British West Indies.

The Puritan colonies in Massachusetts and Connecticut were designed as commonwealths in which the lives of men should be ordered "in harmony with the will of God." Both Plymouth (1620) and Massachusetts Bay (1630), however, were carefully planned in advance to be self-sustaining through the fur trade and other industries. The colonies in Connecticut and Rhode Island grew partly by expansion and partly as a result of disagreement with Massachusetts Bay in religious or political views. For the latter colony, like Virginia, sought to maintain religious unity and exclude or suppress discordant factions. Accordingly, Roger Williams and Anne Hutchinson were exiled to Rhode Island and John Wheelwright to New Hampshire; and Quakers, Anglicans, and even Baptists were fined, deprived of common rights, and harshly treated. Our sympathies are with Williams, but this policy doubtless saved the colony from the confusion and disunion which caused the downfall of the Puritan republic in England.

Certain democratic ideas prevailed in New England, such as the congregational form of church government, the general meeting of freemen to decide local matters of government, and the distribution of free land to all settlers. The number of freemen was limited, however, by restrictions of church membership and qualifications of property and character, to a small minority of the adult male population. In addition, the early clergy, probably the most learned and able in all our history, exercised as advisers a great degree of control in social and governmental affairs. From these two circumstances originated the "social system" which, combining the "three professions"—the minister, the doctor, and the lawyer—with the richer merchants and landowners into a changing but continuing aristocracy, dominated New England community life for over two centuries. In the democratic New England town meeting everyone had his say, but the final say was generally that of the largest taxpayer.

Compactly settled, with a homogeneous population whose middle-class ambitions and religious devotion both prompted them to industry and frugality, the New England colonists early achieved solidarity and economic self-sufficiency. Mostly well educated, they desired their children to continue so; hence in 1636 the

Massachusetts Bay settlers founded a Latin grammar school in Boston and chartered a college—Harvard—in Cambridge, and eleven years later required each town of one hundred families to maintain a free grammar school. The poverty of the New England soil turned the attention of the inhabitants to the sea, the returns from which, in fish, shipbuilding, and commerce, were to provide their chief wealth. With prosperity came relaxation of religious fervor and strictness and a decline in the influence of the clergy. Thus in the eighteenth century the Puritan gave place to the Yankee type—capable, shrewd, honest except when dealing with rascals, neighborly, practical-minded, and at least outwardly religious.[1]

The eighteenth century saw the Middle Provinces advance rapidly in numbers, wealth, and importance. The industry and thrift of the Quakers and the Germans matched that of the New Englanders, and by 1750 Pennsylvania had outstripped all her neighbors except Virginia and Massachusetts in population and was soon to pass the latter. Philadelphia became not only the largest town in English America, but also the chief literary and cultural center, where were to be found the greatest number of men of distinction, like Franklin, Hopkinson, the naturalist William Bartram, and the scientist Rittenhouse. The Quaker capital led also in the development of hospitals and in humanitarian reform in general. Anthony Benezet not only tried, like his fellow-Quaker Woolman, to prevent the spread of slavery, but also introduced reforms in the education of children in his schools in Philadelphia.[2] Like New York, the city had from the beginning a cosmopolitan population and attracted men of talent and energy from many other places.

Differences in religious opinion played a part in seventeenth-century and eighteenth-century life and thought which is difficult for even religious persons of today to realize. In the Southern and some of the Middle colonies the Anglicans or Episcopalians became the state church, which included the wealthy and ruling classes and was supported by general taxation. Comparatively tolerant, they tended to take their religion for granted, assuming that all who conformed to the exercises of the church and lived rightly would enjoy the benefits of heaven.

Throughout all the colonies, however, and exercising the status of a state church in New England were members of the various Calvinist sects—Congregationalists in eastern New England, Presbyterians in Connecticut, New Jersey, and the western settlements farther south, the Dutch Reformed in New York, and the Huguenots in South Carolina. As the religious faith of the New England Puritans, Calvinism tempered most of seventeenth-century literature. According to the Calvinist conception, fallen man was inherently base and wicked, and consequently God perforce *elected* certain souls to enjoy an unmerited bliss in heaven, leaving the rest to their just punishment for their original transgression in Adam. Since the elect

[1] V. L. Parrington, *The Colonial Mind, 1620-1800* (1927), 88-90.
[2] For Benezet's activities, see G. S. Brookes, *Friend Anthony Benezet* (1937).

had been known to God from the beginning of time, and thus predestined, no one could by his own right living and faith be preserved from eternal torment. An incentive for upright conduct and religious devotion, however, was offered in the assurance that since the spirits of the elect act in harmony with God's will, those whose thought and behavior were most godlike were doubtless of the elect. In addition to these Calvinistic doctrines, the Puritans developed the Covenant theory, which "held that after the fall of man, God voluntarily condescended to treat with man as with an equal and to draw up a covenant or contract with His creature in which He laid down the terms and conditions of salvation, and pledged Himself to abide by them. The covenant did not alter the fact that those only are saved upon whom God sheds His grace, but it made very clear and reasonable how and why certain men are selected, and prescribed the conditions under which they might reach a fair assurance of their own standing." [1]

The original Friends, or Quakers, were regarded and treated by Anglicans and Puritans alike as dangerous and revolutionary radicals. Their chief tenet was the "inner light," the presence of direct inspiration from God within the human spirit, as their sufficient guide for conduct and belief. In accordance with this equalitarian tenet, they decried such accepted conventions of Christian society as a paid ministry, special buildings and ceremonies for worship, the special sanctity of the Sabbath, military service, capital punishment, reverence for magistrates, and distinctions of class in dress. By protesting against these things in such ways as denouncing ministers in their pulpits, or running unclothed through the streets, some of them shocked and alarmed the magistrates of Massachusetts Bay into severe and cruel repressive measures. After four Quakers had been hanged there, King Charles intervened; and as the stimulus of persecution was removed and able and thoughtful leaders like Penn joined their body, they became an exceptionally stable, orderly, and peaceful sect, noted in Pennsylvania for their philanthropy and their just dealings with the Indians. In literature, their spirit is best shown in the journal of the eighteenth-century Quaker preacher, John Woolman.

Maryland, colonized by Catholic English families, was soon overrun by Protestants from Virginia; and eventually Anglicanism became the state church, but religious toleration was retained there, as also in Rhode Island under the leadership of Roger Williams.

Governmental progress during the provincial period developed along nearly parallel lines in all the colonies. After 1730 all were royal provinces except Rhode Island and Connecticut, which retained their self-governing charters, and the

---

[1] Perry Miller, "The Puritan Way of Life," in Miller and Johnson, *The Puritans* (1938), 58. This essay is perhaps the best brief interpretation of the Puritan's intellectual, cultural, and religious character. For more extended discussions, see Miller's "The Marrow of Puritan Divinity," in *Publications* of the Colonial Society of Massachusetts, XXXII (1932), 247–300; *Orthodoxy in Massachusetts, 1630–1650* (1933); and *The New England Mind: The Seventeenth Century* (1939).

proprietary colonies, Maryland, Pennsylvania, and Delaware. At the top was the governor, appointed, in all but the charter colonies, by the King or the proprietors. Next was the council—royal appointees except in Massachusetts, Rhode Island, and Connecticut—serving variously as the governor's cabinet, as a legislative upper house, and in certain judicial capacities. The popular assembly, or lower house, representing the towns in New England and the counties elsewhere, was elected by citizens having the required religious, property, and other qualifications. In the seventeenth century, the governors, with the assistance of the council, acting in behalf of the wealthier classes, could generally dominate or exercise an effective veto over the acts of the lower house. With considerable uniformity, however, the assembly gained power through the entire provincial period, by means of its control of taxes, including those for the governor's salary. In Massachusetts, control of the council passed into the hands of the lower house, which elected the councillors from among its own number.

Cultural advance in the colonies was necessarily slow. Harvard College, as has been noted, was chartered in 1636, but no other followed until William and Mary, in Virginia, in 1692, and Yale in 1702. Between 1740 and 1770, however, six new colleges arose in the northern provinces: Pennsylvania in 1740, Princeton in 1746, King's College (Columbia) in 1754, Brown in 1764, Rutgers in 1766, and Dartmouth in 1769. The first newspaper, the *Boston News Letter*, was issued in 1704; and by 1771 twenty-five weeklies were being published. Two short-lived magazines appeared in Philadelphia in 1741, followed by a number of others, mainly there and in Boston. Both these types of periodical were poor and imitative, but they gave evidence of a quickening interest in matters of general information and literary culture and gave an opportunity for hopeful writers to find a medium of publication. The majority of the provincial population was literate, though a general system of public education prevailed only in New England. Elsewhere, church schools, private academies, and home instruction were depended upon. Travel throughout the seventeenth century was generally by boat or on horseback, but road and bridge building increased rapidly after 1700, at first as a private enterprise, and by 1770 stagecoaches connected most of the larger towns. Under Franklin's direction postal service became much more rapid and efficient.

Among the provincial writers, two stand out pre-eminently. Jonathan Edwards was Franklin's superior in intellectual power and spiritual sensitiveness. His youthful exaltation in the presence of nature and his scientific and psychological speculations anticipate the Transcendentalists and the scientific explorers of the nineteenth century; but his religious devotion and his metaphysical skill led him into otherworldly paths. Thus he is remembered vaguely as an enkindler of spiritual emotionalism and as the last great defender through incontrovertible logic of the Calvinistic system of theology. The Yankee Franklin looked outward and forward, as a product of the Enlightenment. There was no practical concern of his time which he did not touch helpfully. His was the genius of common sense, in politics, invention, and society. And though pure letters were to him an avocation, his proverbial sayings, his essay letters, and the earlier passages of his unfinished auto-biography are the best remembered literature of his time in America.

During the middle years of the eighteenth century, three new influences tended to undermine the stability of the religious, intellectual, and political status in the American colonies. These were the philosophical-religious spirit of deism, the religious revival called the "Great Awakening," and the growing urge for self-government and local independence.

Deism, somewhat like puritanism, was, as Dr. Gustaf Koch describes it, "an attitude of mind rather than a specific creed, rather like the scientific temper of our age, which is superimposed upon our religious beliefs and institutions."[1] Accord-ing to the older theologies, man was the chief concern of God, who intervened directly in his personal affairs. But the new physics of Newton had changed the Earth from the center about which all else revolved, to a small unit in an infinitely vast universe. Certain implications of this were uneasily sensed by Sewall, who re-corded in his diary, December 23, 1714, that "Dr. C. Mather preached excellently from Ps. 37. Trust in the Lord, etc., only spake of the Sun being in the centre. I think it inconvenient to assert such problems." The English deists pictured "a mechanically perfect universe, operating with admirable precision . . . and pre-sided over by . . . a Creator intelligent, immaterial, and benevolent, who executed his will through changeless laws rather than through special providences."[2] Man, at present maladjusted to this divine scheme, not through his original sin but through centuries of misunderstandings chiefly due to ecclesiasticism, could regain his share in the divine benevolence by returning to a rationally ordered life and by contemplation of the glories of God's creation in external nature.

Such conceptions of God, man, and the universe, at great variance with the ideas of Governor Winthrop and Jonathan Edwards, spread slowly in America, at first among intellectuals like Cotton Mather himself, whose *Christian Philosopher* (1721) seems to show their influence, and Franklin, whose whole philosophy was colored by them; and later on a lower level through the fraternizing of Colonial and British army officers during the French and Indian Wars. They were an influence in the preaching of liberal Congregationalists like Mayhew and Chauncy in Boston in the mid-century, and prepared the way for the later shift to Unitarianism. In lit-erature, the boldest of attacks of reason against the tradition of authority were *Reason the Only Oracle of Man*,[3] published in Vermont in 1784 as the work of

---

[1] G. A. Koch, *Republican Religion: The American Revolution and the Cult of Reason* (1933), p. xiv. See H. M. Morais, *Deism in 18th Century America* (1934), for a summary of deistic influences in America.

[2] Walter F. Taylor, *History of American Letters* (1936), 41 and 50.

[3] Available in the Scholars' Facsimiles and Reprints Series (1940).

General Ethan Allen; and the memorable *Age of Reason*, written in France in 1794–1796 by the English-born citizen of the United States, Thomas Paine.

While deism was undermining the older churches intellectually, the Great Awakening assailed them on the side of the emotions. This great religious revival, in full progress by 1741, paralleled the success of the Wesleyan movement among the lower classes in England. Preceded by lesser revivals such as that of Jonathan Edwards at Northampton in 1734, it received great impetus from the preaching of George Whitefield, who traveled throughout the provinces, addressing large audiences from Georgia to Maine. Its greatest hold was upon the newer, less stable population of the back country, but it penetrated the older towns as well, producing vexatious schisms, such as that between the conservative Old Light Calvinists and the evangelistic New Lights. The Awakening was an evangelical movement, holding out the promise of salvation to all who would accept divine grace, and stressing the spiritual experience of conversion. Edwards recorded its manifestations with eager interest, but the faculties of Harvard and Yale, and conservative preachers like Charles Chauncy, denounced its emotional excesses and questioned its permanent good effects. Whitefield favored no creed, but most of his converts joined either the newly formed Methodists or the Baptists. These two groups superseded in the interior areas the Anglicans, "Old Light" Congregationalists, and Presbyterians, followed the frontier in its western advance, and became the dominant Protestant sects of the United States. In contrast with the increasing decorum and rationalism of the older faiths, they contributed an element of optimism, enthusiasm, and democracy to our early national life.

One of the effects of the defeat and withdrawal of the French forces was an increasing self-confidence and independence on the part of the American provincials. Their own part in the victory had not been small, particularly in the brilliant capture of Louisbourg by the New Englanders in 1745; while the disasters at Fort Duquesne in 1755 and Ticonderoga in 1758 somewhat lessened respect for British military leadership and prowess. The Navigation Acts and customs imposts which had threatened to wipe out colonial commerce had for a century been nullified by large-scale smuggling and illegal trading with the French and Spanish colonies, extremely profitable to the shipowners and merchants of Boston, Philadelphia, and New York. Upon the free-and-easy methods of these gentry the British attempts at enforcement of the commercial laws fell most heavily. Besides the mercantile, professional, and official classes, there were the increasing class of laborers and mechanics, largely unfranchised, in the towns, who, after earning high wages while war was in progress, were now out of employment and in many cases reduced to poverty and desperate circumstances. Though the merchants and lawyers led in opposition to British legislation and coercion, it was the unattached artisans and laborers of Boston, New York, and other towns who made up the anti-Tory mobs and, with farmers' sons from the country, mainly filled the ranks of the Continental armies.

The chief economic and political grievances which within a decade converted the temper of the Americans from self-assertive loyalty to open defiance were the curbs upon colonial manufactures, currency, and freedom of legislation; attempts to enforce dead-letter trade and navigation laws; new measures of direct taxation, ostensibly for colonial protection but actually to reduce the heavy burden of taxation in England; the ban upon expansion in the Indian country; and the coercive measures, enforced by the courts and the army, to repress American protest and opposition. Widespread boycotts of British goods, the Boston Massacre, the "tea parties" at Boston, Annapolis, and elsewhere, the summoning of a Continental Congress, creation of Committees of Safety and Correspondence, tarring and feathering of crown officers and Tory sympathizers, raising of provincial militia— the Minute Men—and assembling of munitions of war, were phases of rising disaffection and disturbance, culminating in bloodshed at Lexington and Concord and such bold challenging of British authority as the Mecklenburg Resolutions in North Carolina, in 1775.

The work of organizing and implementing popular opposition passed from the hands of the merchants who first fomented it into those of a remarkable group of agitators, mostly young lawyers and publicists. The oratory of James Otis against the Writs of Assistance in 1761 and of Patrick Henry before the Virginia Convention of 1775; and in print the *Letters from a Pennsylvania Farmer* (1767) of John Dickinson, the *Full Vindication of the Measures of Congress* (1774) of the youthful Hamilton, and the *Novanglus* letters (1775) of John Adams overbore the remonstrances of loyalists like Samuel Seabury, Daniel Leonard, and Joseph Galloway. Most effective of all were the trenchant *Common Sense* (1776) of Thomas Paine, boldly advocating separation from England, and the indefatigable circular letters and addresses of Samuel Adams of Boston, one of the shrewdest and most successful propagandists and organizers that ever lived.

The American mind came slowly and with honest reluctance to the idea of independence. In fact, the two first important phases of the war, the expulsion of the British forces from New England and the brilliant but ill-fated invasion of Canada, preceded the official separation and declaration of a state of war. When the Declaration, penned mainly by Thomas Jefferson, was signed in 1776, it perhaps represented the views of a minority of Americans; and hundreds of thousands remained loyal to the British government throughout the war. The loyalists were in general of the "better sort," often persons of property, social standing, and prominence under the royal government, and their retainers. They regarded resistance to the crown as treasonable rebellion, certain to fail and bring summary punishment upon its participants. When they protested against measures of opposition, they suffered harsh treatment from patriotic mobs, as described by Trumbull in *M'Fingal*. Great numbers left in the early days of the conflict. Many settled in the Canadian provinces of Nova Scotia and New Brunswick, whose abstention from the revolutionary movement was thus made certain. Others were driven out and their estates confiscated by the states. Still others, especially in the Middle and Southern states, fought beside the royal troops, to the number, it is said, of over 50,000. The later phases of the war, the British campaigns first to cut the Union in two at the Hudson and later to subdue the Southern states, were strongly supported and prolonged through loyalist assistance. Though a few returned after the war, more than a hundred thousand persons, including much of the most stable and cultured stock in the provinces, were lost to the United States through the loyalist emigration.

Naturally, the great conflict was provocative of much outpouring of literature dealing with its spirit and issues. Besides the political arguments on both sides already mentioned, the most influential American utterance was Thomas Paine's *The Crisis*, a series of stirring appeals issued at crucial moments during the war to hearten the Americans' resistance. The loyalists about New York contributed also the spirited drinking songs of Odell and Stansbury, and Samuel Peters's *General History of Connecticut* (1782), with its gibes at his neighbors' politics and religion and its preposterous yarns anticipating the similar ones later recorded along the western frontier. The most spontaneous of the Revolutionary writings were the songs and ballads on both sides, many of them anonymous. Trumbull's spirited satire *M'Fingal* has been mentioned. Most active of poets on the patriot side was Philip Freneau. His longest serious poem of the Revolution pictured the horrors of his own confinement in British prison ships in New York harbor.

The success of the Revolution found the former ruling class partly swept away and the control of government in the hands of younger men, except for a few older leaders like Franklin and Washington. Though the people in the sections not harmed by the later campaigns were mostly in a prosperous condition, the government, a unicameral congress, established under the Articles of Confederation, 1777, found itself helpless in the face of an economic and political emergency. Chiefly an advisory body after the removal of the need for urgent national defense, it was unable to secure co-operation from the states in necessary financial and political measures. Great amounts of worthless Continental and state paper money created a more paralyzing financial situation than had prevailed before the Revolution. Interstate jealousies led to discriminating legislation and hampered the efforts of Congress to regulate trade and commerce. Conflicting claims to western lands, the supervision of settlers living already outside the limits of the several states, and difficulties with the Spaniards and Indians raised new problems. Worst of all, the disbanded army, whose struggles and sacrifices had won the war, had been paid only in worthless bills and was in many cases destitute and desperate. Ex-soldiers were leaders in the attempts to prevent suits for debts by seizing courthouses in Massachusetts in 1786—called Shays' Rebellion—which brought most plainly before the states the necessity of a strong central government and led to the Constitutional Convention of 1787.

Naturally, the new constitution did not meet with universal approval. Jefferson and Franklin had misgivings about it, and Patrick Henry and Governor Clinton attacked it openly. Hopkinson humorously defended it in "The New Roof," and Hamilton, Madison, and Jay produced a memorable interpretation of its advantages and scope in a series of newspaper essays entitled *The Federalist: or the New Constitution* in 1787–88. The mercantile and propertied classes generally supported it in the face of distrust on the part of the agrarian population. Out of the debate for and against its adoption arose our two basic national political parties. With the elimination of the royalist Tory party, there was a shift to the right on the part of the former Whigs. The more prosperous of them, with remnants of the Tories, the mercantile and professional groups, and the comfortable farmers and planters, argued for the proposed constitution since it promised stability and secured the interests of property. These, who assumed the name Federalist, were to continue through our history under various names as National Republicans, Whigs, and Republicans. Opposed to these were mainly the formerly unfranchised laborers and poorer farmers, jealous of centralization of power and possible encroachments upon the state assemblies which their votes could now control, who co-operated loosely as Anti-federalists and who were later to be welded together by the great political organizer Jefferson into the Democratic-Republican or Democratic party. With some difficulty, often by shrewd bargaining and hairbreadth majorities, the better organized Federalist group secured the adherence of the necessary two thirds of the states. With the Federal Union thus assured, the unanimous selection of General Washington as the first President momentarily harmonized all factions and inaugurated the new government not only in a wave of good feeling at home but also with some degree of respect and admiration abroad, where the name of Washington had come to be revered by many.

The later eighteenth-century writers reflect the influence both of the neoclassical tradition, reinforced by Dr. Samuel Johnson, and that of the English pre-romantic literature. The sentimentality of Richardson and Sterne in the novel, the wonder stories of the Gothic romance, the awakened nature interest of Thomson and Cooper, and the humanitarianism of Burns and Godwin reappear in the poetry of Freneau, the novels of Mrs. Rowson and C. B. Brown, and the plays of William Dunlap. Added to these borrowed traits was the American ingredient of enthusiastic acceptance of political independence and democratic republicanism as the best form of political government, which appears even in the writings of the Federalist conservatives. The group called the Connecticut Wits, of whom Timothy Dwight, John Trumbull, and Joel Barlow were the chief, labored consciously to create a national poetry, but their neoclassical output was turgid and mostly lacking in vitality.

Of greater importance were four outstanding figures in different fields: the poet Philip Freneau, the novelist Charles Brockden Brown, the essayist-critic Joseph Dennie, and the dramatist William Dunlap. The novel got a belated start with the slight and didactic *Power of Sympathy* of William Hill Brown in 1789, followed by the sentimental best sellers *Charlotte Temple* (1790), by Mrs. Susanna Rowson, and *The Coquette* (1797), by Mrs. Hannah Webster Foster. H. H. Brackenridge's *Modern Chivalry* (1792–1805) poked good-humored fun at the crudenesses of the country, especially in the frontier region of the Alleghenies. C. B. Brown, also using American settings for his *Wieland* (1798), *Arthur Mervyn* (1799–1800), and *Edgar Huntly* (1800), and his other three novels, combined the tendencies of Richardson, Anne Radcliffe, and William Godwin with considerable skill. In the field of drama, Royall Tyler's comedy *The Contrast* (1787) and Dunlap's tragedy *André* (1797) were decided successes. Dunlap, as author of fifty-odd other original plays and adaptations, and as manager of the New York theater, did much to give the drama a secure foothold in America.

1703 ~ *Jonathan Edwards* ~ 1758

JONATHAN EDWARDS, greatest of American theologians, was the son of the minister at East Winsor, Connecticut. As a boy of eleven he showed, in his essays on the flying spider and on thunder, an intellectual zest and acumen and accuracy of observation which promised greater achievement in natural science than that of his contemporary, Franklin. At Yale, seminary of orthodox Calvinism, he read Locke and Newton. Graduated at seventeen, he continued with two years' study of theology and underwent an ecstatic experience of conversion and conviction of his own election to be saved. His *Personal Narrative* records in this period moods of spiritual aliveness and rapt enjoyment of nature which show his partial kinship with such later transcendental spirits as Wordsworth, Emerson, and Thoreau. After a brief term as pastor of a Presbyterian church in New York, he returned to Yale for two years as tutor. In 1736 he became the colleague of his mother's father, Solomon Stoddard, pastor in Northampton, Massachusetts. The next year he married Sarah Pierrepont, whose singular sweetness and purity of mind he had recorded four years earlier.

Edwards was a scholarly pastor, rarely visiting his parishioners, and usually spending thirteen hours a day at his books and writing. His sermons, however, were eloquent and compelling. His preaching, while restrained in delivery, became increasingly evangelistic in spirit, in contrast with the customarily doctrinal sermons of his Calvinist associates. He anticipated the Great Awakening with a remarkable religious revival in his parish in 1734 and became one of its most powerful preachers. His own congregation gained three hundred members in six months. He defended the revival, based on an appeal to the emotions or "religious affections," in answer to attacks by the Reverend Charles Chauncy and others but admitted that in some cases the apparent evidences of conversion were "enthusiastic delusions," arising from the natural emotions rather than from the "supernatural sense" granted by God to the elect for their complete regeneration, as described in his *Treatise concerning Religious Affections* (1746).

Edwards's own parishioners, after their enthusiasm had cooled, became critical of their pastor's strictness, not in his picturing of hell, but in "the high level of religious emotion which he expected them to maintain in their daily lives." After two years of dissension, he delivered his "Farewell Sermon" in 1750 and withdrew with his numerous family to the frontier town of Stockbridge, where he acted as missionary to the Indians and preached in the local church. In his seclusion here, he had opportunity to devote himself to study and turned out the notable treatises *The Nature of True Virtue* (1788), *The End for Which God Created the World* (1788), and *The Great Christian Doctrine of Original Sin Defended* (1758), and his masterpiece, *The Freedom of the Will* (1754). In 1757 recognition of his intellectual leadership among the Calvinists took the form of an invitation to become president of the new College of New Jersey (now Princeton). Three months after his induction, he died of smallpox as the result of inoculation.

Edwards returned to a purer Calvinism than that of the early New England Puritans. The central idea in his preaching and writing was the ineffable power and majesty of God, the contemplation of which never failed to entrance his mind and fill it with joy. That the nature of humankind, in contrast with God's goodness and might, is deplorably black and weak, and that man can be saved only through the interposition of divine grace, are ideas inherent in the Calvinistic system. His participation in the Great Awakening arose not from the evangelical hope that all men could repent and save themselves but from the feeling that the religious exaltation which was stimulated, when genuine, expressed "the kind of religion toward which a recognition of the sovereignty of God would tend." In denying to man any control over his will or desires—as distinct from his actions —Edwards occupied a position close to that of Locke and Hobbes. His explanation of total depravity as resulting from domination by the sole motive of self-love, after God withdrew from Adam's nature the divine motive of disinterested benevolence, harmonizes again with the views of Hobbes and with those of Mandeville. His later identification of true virtue, possible only in the elect, with this benevolence, achieved through the divinely given sense of moral beauty, seems suggested by Francis Hutcheson's *Inquiry into the Original of Our Ideas of Beauty and Virtue* (1725).

The synthesis of these views made a virtually impregnable fortress of logic for the Calvinistic theology of total dependence upon God. But though most men found his conclusions inescapable, they also found them intolerable, with the ultimate result of the rejection of the premises on which they were founded. This rejection of the validity of the Calvinistic dogma left the way open for the later triumph of Unitarianism in New England.

Around his sixteenth year, Edwards set down a set of rules for writing, which reflect, in their emphasis on unaffected simplicity, the precepts for good prose by Hobbes and Thomas Sprat—"a close, naked, natural way of speaking"—and the practice of Defoe, Swift, Steele, and Addison:

> Let much modesty be seen in the style . . .
> To be very moderate in the use of terms of art. Let it not look as if I was much read, or was conversant with books, or with the learned world.

As he progressed, the language of those books of the Bible from which texts for his sermons were most frequently chosen—the Psalms, the Proverbs, the Song of Solomon, Ecclesiastes, and the New Testament gospels—shows its influence in his description of his emotional experiences and in his hortatory sermons. Late in his life, a reading of Richardson's *Sir Charles Grandison* prompted the remark that he regretted not having given more attention to his style. He was never unaware of its effects, however, and the almost lyrical beauty of the *Personal Narrative* and the clear and precise diction of his philosophical treatises rank him with Franklin as one of the two best prose writers in eighteenth-century America.

Edwards's chief works, besides those mentioned above, are *God Glorified in the Work of Redemption* (1731); *A Faithful Narrative* (1737); *Sinners in the Hands of an Angry God* (1741); *Some Thoughts Concerning the Present Revival of Religion in New England* (1742); and *Farewell Sermon* (1750).

The best of a number of editions of Edwards's works is the one edited by S. Austin in 8 vols. (1808–09) and reprinted with additions by R. Ogle in 1847. The first four volumes were reissued in 1843 and frequently since then. Excellent volumes of selections with valuable introductions are C. H. Faust and T. H. Johnson, *Jonathan Edwards: Representative Selections* (1935), and Carl Van Doren, *Benjamin Franklin and Jonathan Edwards: Selections from Their Writings* (1920). *Selected Sermons of Jonathan Edwards* was edited by H. N. Gardiner (1904). Faust and Johnson's

Edwards contains an extensive bibliography. There are also bibliographies in *CHAL*, I, 428–432 (Edwards's separate works), and in *DAB*.

The standard life is A. V. G. Allen (1890). Other full-length biographies are that by Sereno E. Dwight (1829); H. B. Parkes, *Jonathan Edwards, the Fiery Puritan* (1930); and A. C. McGiffert, *Jonathan Edwards* (1932). The *DAB* article by Francis A. Christie is an excellent summary. Other valuable material may be found in H. S. Canby, *Classic Americans* (1931); F. I. Carpenter, "The Radicalism of Jonathan Edwards," *New England Quarterly*, IV, 629–644 (Oct., 1931); John Dewitt, "Jonathan Edwards, a Study," *Princeton Theological Review*, II, 88–109 (Jan., 1904); F. H. Foster, *A Genetic History of the New England Theology* (1907); Joseph Haroutunian, "Jonathan Edwards, a Study in Godliness," *Journal of Religion*, XI, 400–419 (July, 1931), and *Piety versus Moralism: the Passing of the New England Theology* (1932); Theodore Hornberger, "The Effect of the New Science upon the Thought of Jonathan Edwards," *American Literature*, IX, 196–207 (May, 1937); T. H. Johnson, "Jonathan Edwards and the 'Young Folks' Bible,'" *New England Quarterly*, V, 37–54 (Jan., 1932), and "Jonathan Edwards's Background of Reading," *Publications of the Colonial Society of Massachusetts*, XXVIII, 193–222 (Dec., 1931); H. M. Jones, "American Prose Style: 1700–1770," *Huntington Library Bulletin*, No. 6 (Nov., 1934); E. W. Miller, "The Great Awakening," *Princeton Theological Review*, II, 545–562 (Oct., 1904); P. E. More, "Edwards," in *CHAL*, I; I. W. Riley, *American Philosophy: The Early Schools* (1907), *American Thought from Puritanism to Pragmatism* (1923), and "The Real Jonathan Edwards," *Open Court*, XXII, 705–715 (Dec., 1908); H. W. Schneider, *The Puritan Mind* (1930); H. G. Townsend, *Philosophical Ideas in the United States* (1934); Joseph Tracy, *The Great Awakening: A History of the Revival of Religion in the Time of Edwards and Whitefield* (1841); M. C. Tyler, *History of American Literature, 1676–1765*, II, 177–192; G. L. Walker, "Jonathan Edwards and the Half-Way Covenant," *New Englander*, XLIII, 601–614 (Sept., 1884); Williston Walker, *A History of the Congregational Church in the United States* (1894), and *Ten New England Leaders* (1901), 217–263.

PERSONAL NARRATIVE

The account of Edwards's own conversion, about 1723, was written about twenty years later. It will be helpful to compare Edwards's thoughts and experiences with Wordsworth's *Tintern Abbey* and passages in Emerson's *Nature* and Thoreau's *Journals*.

[Boyhood Experiences]

I HAD a variety of concerns and exercises about my soul from my childhood; but had two more remarkable seasons of awakening, before I met with that change by which I was brought to those new dispositions, and that new sense of things, that I have since had. The first time was when I was a boy, some years before I went to college, at a time of re-markable awakening in my father's congregation. I was then very much affected for many months, and concerned about the things of religion, and my soul's salvation; and was abundant in duties. I used to pray five times a day in secret, and to spend much time in re-ligious talk with other boys, and used to meet with them to pray together. I experienced I know not what kind of delight in religion. My mind was much engaged in it, and had much self-righteous pleasure; and it was my delight to abound in religious duties. I, with some of my schoolmates, joined together, and built a booth in a swamp, in a very re-tired spot, for a place of prayer. And besides, I had particular secret places of my own in the woods, where I used to retire by myself, and was from time to time much affected. My affections seemed to be lively and easily moved, and I seemed to be in my element when engaged in religious duties. And I am ready to think, many are deceived with such affections and such a kind of delight as I then had in religion, and mistake it for grace.

But in process of time, my convictions and

affections wore off, and I entirely lost all those affections and delights, and left off secret prayer, at least as to any constant performance of it, and returned like a dog to his vomit and went on in the ways of sin. Indeed, I was at times very uneasy, especially towards the latter part of my time at college, when it pleased God to seize me with a pleurisy, in which he brought me nigh to the grave and shook me over the pit of hell. And yet it was not long after my recovery before I fell again into my old ways of sin. But God would not suffer me to go on with any quietness; I had great and violent inward struggles, till, after many conflicts with wicked inclinations, repeated resolutions, and bonds that I laid myself under by a kind of vows to God, I was brought wholly to break off all former wicked ways and all ways of known outward sin, and to apply myself to seek salvation, and practise many religious duties, but without that kind of affection and delight which I had formerly experienced. My concern now wrought more by inward struggles and conflicts and self-reflections. I made seeking my salvation the main business of my life. But yet, it seems to me, I sought after a miserable manner, which has made me sometimes since to question whether ever it issued in that which was saving, being ready to doubt whether such miserable seeking ever succeeded. I was indeed brought to seek salvation in a manner that I never was before; I felt a spirit to part with all things in the world, for an interest in Christ. My concern continued and prevailed, with many exercising thoughts and inward struggles; but yet it never seemed to be proper to express that concern by the name of terror.

From my childhood up, my mind had been full of objections against the doctrine of God's sovereignty, in choosing whom he would to eternal life, and rejecting whom he pleased, leaving them eternally to perish and be everlastingly tormented in hell. It used to appear like a horrible doctrine to me. But I remember the time very well when I seemed to be convinced and fully satisfied, as to this sovereignty of God and his justice in thus eternally disposing of men according to his sovereign pleasure. But never could give an account how, or by what means, I was thus convinced, not in the least imagining at the time, nor a long time after, that there was any extraordinary influence of God's Spirit in it; but only that now I saw further, and my reason apprehended the justice and reasonableness of it. However, my mind rested in it, and it put an end to all those cavils and objections. And there has been a wonderful alteration in my mind in respect to the doctrine of God's sovereignty from that day to this, so that I scarce ever have found so much as the rising of an objection against it, in the most absolute sense, in God's showing mercy to whom he will show mercy, and hardening whom he will. God's absolute sovereignty and justice, with respect to salvation and damnation, is what my mind seems to rest assured of as much as of any thing that I see with my eyes; at least it is so at times. But I have often, since that first conviction, had quite another kind of sense of God's sovereignty than I had then. I have often since had not only a conviction, but a delightful conviction. The doctrine has very often appeared exceeding pleasant, bright, and sweet. Absolute sovereignty is what I love to ascribe to God. But my first conviction was not so.

The first instance that I remember of that sort of inward, sweet delight in God and divine things that I have lived much in since, was on reading those words, 1 Tim. i. 17. *Now unto the King eternal, immortal, invisible, the only wise God, be honour and glory for ever and ever, Amen.* As I read the words, there came into my soul, and was as it were diffused through it, a sense of the glory of the Divine Being; a new sense, quite different from any thing I ever experienced before. Never any words of Scripture seemed to me as these words did. I thought with myself how excellent a Being that was, and how happy I should be if I might enjoy that God and be rapt up to him in heaven, and be as it were swallowed up in him for ever! I kept saying, and as it were singing, over these words of Scripture to myself; and went to pray to God that I might enjoy him, and prayed in a manner quite different from what I used to do, with a new sort of affection. But it never came into my thought that there was any thing spiritual, or of a saving nature in this.

[*Transcendent Contemplations*]

From about that time, I began to have a new kind of apprehensions and ideas of Christ and the work of redemption and the glorious way of salvation by him. An inward, sweet sense of these things, at times, came into my heart; and my soul was led away in pleasant views and contemplations of them. And my mind was greatly engaged to spend my time in reading and meditating on Christ, on the beauty and excellency of his person, and the lovely way of salvation by free grace in him. I found no books so delightful to me as those that treated of these subjects. Those words Cant. ii. 1. used to be abundantly with me, *I am the Rose of Sharon, and the Lily of the valleys*. The words seemed to me sweetly to represent the loveliness and beauty of Jesus Christ. The whole book of Canticles used to be pleasant to me, and I used to be much in reading it, about that time; and found, from time to time, an inward sweetness that would carry me away in my contemplations. This I know not how to express otherwise than by a calm, sweet abstraction of soul from all the concerns of this world; and sometimes a kind of vision, or fixed ideas and imaginations, of being alone in the mountains or some solitary wilderness, far from all mankind, sweetly conversing with Christ and wrapt and swallowed up in God. The sense I had of divine things would often of a sudden kindle up, as it were, a sweet burning in my heart; an ardor of soul, that I know not how to express.

Not long after I first began to experience these things, I gave an account to my father of some things that had passed in my mind. I was pretty much affected by the discourse we had together; and when the discourse was ended, I walked abroad alone, in a solitary place in my father's pasture, for contemplation. And as I was walking there and looking upon the sky and clouds, there came into my mind so sweet a sense of the glorious *majesty* and *grace* of God that I know not how to express. I seemed to see them both in a sweet conjunction, majesty and meekness joined together; it was a sweet, and gentle, and holy majesty, and also a majestic meekness, an aw-ful sweetness, a high, and great, and holy gentleness.

After this my sense of divine things gradually increased and became more and more lively and had more of that inward sweetness. The appearance of every thing was altered; there seemed to be, as it were, a calm, sweet, cast or appearance of divine glory in almost every thing. God's excellency, his wisdom, his purity and love seemed to appear in every thing, in the sun, moon, and stars, in the clouds and blue sky, in the grass, flowers, trees, in the water and all nature, which used greatly to fix my mind. I often used to sit and view the moon for continuance; and in the day, spent much time in viewing the clouds and sky, to behold the sweet glory of God in these things, in the meantime singing forth, with a low voice, my contemplations of the Creator and Redeemer. And scarce any thing, among all the works of nature, was so sweet to me as thunder and lightning; formerly nothing had been so terrible to me. Before, I used to be uncommonly terrified with thunder, and to be struck with terror when I saw a thunder-storm rising; but now, on the contrary, it rejoiced me. I felt God, so to speak, at the first appearance of a thunder-storm, and used to take the opportunity, at such times, to fix myself in order to view the clouds and see the lightnings play and hear the majestic and awful voice of God's thunder, which oftentimes was exceedingly entertaining, leading me to sweet contemplations of my great and glorious God. While thus engaged, it always seemed natural for me to sing, or chant forth my meditations, or to speak my thoughts in soliloquies with a singing voice.

I felt then great satisfaction as to my good estate, but that did not content me. I had vehement longings of soul after God and Christ and after more holiness, wherewith my heart seemed to be full and ready to break, which often brought to my mind the words of the Psalmist, Psal. cxix. 28. *My soul breaketh for the longing it hath*. I often felt a mourning and lamenting in my heart, that I had not turned to God sooner, that I might have had more time to grow in grace. My mind was greatly fixed on divine things, almost perpetually in the contemplation of them. I spent most of my time in thinking of divine things year after year; often walking alone in the woods and solitary places, for meditation, soliloquy, and prayer, and converse with God; and it was always my manner, at such times, to sing forth my contemplations. I was almost constantly in ejaculatory prayer, wherever I was. Prayer seemed to be natural to me as the breath by which the inward burnings of my heart had vent. The delights which I now felt in the things of religion were of an exceedingly different kind from those beforementioned, that I had when a boy, and what I then had no more notion of than one born blind has of pleasant and beautiful colors. They were of a more inward, pure soul, animating and refreshing nature. Those former delights never reached the heart, and did not arise from any sight of the divine excellency of the things of God, or any taste of the soul-satisfying and life-giving good there is in them.

My sense of divine things seemed gradually to increase until I went to preach at New York, which was about a year and a half after they began; and while I was there, I felt them very sensibly, in a much higher degree than I had done before. My longings after God and holiness were much increased. Pure and humble, holy and heavenly Christianity appeared exceedingly amiable to me. I felt a burning desire to be, in every thing, a complete Christian, and conformed to the blessed image of Christ, and that I might live in all things according to the pure, sweet, and blessed rules of the Gospel. I had an eager thirsting after progress in these things, which put me upon pursuing and pressing after them. It was my continual strife day and night and constant inquiry how I should *be* more holy and *live* more holily, and more becoming a child of God, and a disciple of Christ. I now sought an increase of grace and holiness and a holy life with much more earnestness than ever I sought grace before I had it. I used to be continually examining myself and studying and contriving for likely ways and means how I should live holily, with far greater diligence and earnestness than ever I pursued any thing in my life, but yet with too great a dependence upon my own strength, which afterwards proved a great damage to me. My experience had not then

taught me, as it has done since, my extreme feebleness and impotence, every manner of way, and the bottomless depths of secret corruption and deceit there was in my heart. However, I went on with my eager pursuit after more holiness and conformity to Christ.

The heaven I desired was a heaven of holiness—to be with God and to spend my eternity in divine love and holy communion with Christ. My mind was very much taken up with contemplations on heaven and the enjoyments there, and living there in perfect holiness, humility, and love; and it used at that time to appear a great part of the happiness of heaven, that there the saints could express their love to Christ. It appeared to me a great clog and burden, that what I felt within, I could not express as I desired. The inward ardor of my soul seemed to be hindered and pent up and could not freely flame out as it would. I used often to think how in heaven this principle should freely and fully vent and express itself. Heaven appeared exceedingly delightful, as a world of love, and that all happiness consisted in living in pure, humble, heavenly, divine love.

I remember the thoughts I used then to have of holiness, and said sometimes to myself, "I do certainly know that I love holiness, such as the gospel prescribes." It appeared to me that there was nothing in it but what was ravishingly lovely, the highest beauty and amiableness—a *divine* beauty, far purer than any thing here upon earth and that every thing else was like mire and defilement, in comparison of it.

Holiness, as I then wrote down some of my contemplations on it, appeared to me to be of a sweet, pleasant, charming, serene, calm nature, which brought an inexpressible purity, brightness, peacefulness, and ravishment to the soul. In other words, that it made the soul like a field or garden of God, with all manner of pleasant flowers, all pleasant, delightful, and undisturbed, enjoying a sweet calm and the gently vivifying beams of the sun. The soul of a true Christian, as I then wrote my meditations, appeared like such a little white flower as we see in the spring of the year, low and humble on the ground, opening its bosom to receive the pleasant beams of the sun's glory, rejoicing, as it were, in a calm rapture, diffusing around a sweet fragrancy, standing peacefully and lovingly in the midst of other flowers round about, all in like manner opening their bosoms to drink in the light of the sun. There was no part of creature-holiness that I had so great a sense of its loveliness as humility, brokenness of heart, and poverty of spirit; and there was nothing that I so earnestly longed for. My heart panted after this, to lie low before God, as in the dust, that I might be nothing, and that God might be ALL, that I might become as a little child.

While at New York, I sometimes was much affected with reflections on my past life, considering how late it was before I began to be truly religious, and how wickedly I had lived till then, and once so as to weep abundantly and for a considerable time together.

On January 12, 1723, I made a solemn dedication of myself to God and wrote it down, giving up myself and all that I had to God, to be for the future in no respect my own, to act as one that had no right to himself in any respect. And solemnly vowed to take God for my whole portion and felicity, looking on nothing else as any part of my happiness nor acting as if it were, and his law for the constant rule of my obedience, engaging to fight with all my might against the world, the flesh, and the devil, to the end of my life. But I have reason to be infinitely humbled when I consider how much I have failed of answering my obligation . . .

Once as I rode out into the woods for my health, in 1737, having alighted from my horse in a retired place, as my manner commonly has been, to walk for divine contemplation and prayer, I had a view that for me was extraordinary, of the glory of the Son of God as Mediator between God and man and his wonderful, great, full, pure, and sweet grace and love, and meek and gentle condescension. This grace that appeared so calm and sweet, appeared also great above the heavens. The person of Christ appeared ineffably excellent with an excellency great enough to swallow up all thought and conception—which continued, as near as I can judge, about an hour, which kept me the greater part of the time in a flood of tears and weeping aloud. I felt

an ardency of soul to be, what I know not otherwise how to express, emptied and annihilated; to lie in the dust and to be full of Christ alone; to love him with a holy and pure love; to trust in him, to live upon him, to serve and follow him, and to be perfectly sanctified and made pure, with a divine and heavenly purity. I have, several other times, had views very much of the same nature and which have had the same effects.

I have many times had a sense of the glory of the third person in the Trinity, in his office of Sanctifier, in his holy operations, communicating divine light and life to the soul. God, in the communications of his Holy Spirit, has appeared as an infinite fountain of divine glory and sweetness, being full and sufficient to fill and satisfy the soul, pouring forth itself in sweet communications, like the sun in its glory, sweetly and pleasantly diffusing light and life. And I have sometimes had an affecting sense of the excellency of the word of God as a word of life, as the light of life, a sweet, excellent, life-giving word, accompanied with a thirsting after that word, that it might dwell richly in my heart.

[Sense of Sinfulness]

Often, since I lived in this town, I have had very affecting views of my own sinfulness and vileness; very frequently to such a degree as to hold me in a kind of loud weeping, sometimes for a considerable time together, so that I have often been forced to shut myself up. I have had a vastly greater sense of my own wickedness and the badness of my own heart than ever I had before my conversion. It has often appeared to me that if God should mark iniquity against me, I should appear the very worst of all mankind, of all that have been since the beginning of the world to this time, and that I should have by far the lowest place in hell. When others that have come to talk with me about their soul concerns have expressed the sense they have had of their own wickedness by saying that it seemed to them that they were as bad as the devil himself, I thought their expression seemed exceedingly faint and feeble to represent my wickedness.

My wickedness, as I am in myself, has long

appeared to me perfectly ineffable and swallowing up all thought and imagination, like an infinite deluge or mountain over my head. I know not how to express better what my sins appear to me to be than by heaping infinite upon infinite and multiplying infinite by infinite. Very often, for these many years, these expressions are in my mind and in my mouth, "Infinite upon infinite—Infinite upon infinite!" When I look into my heart and take a view of my wickedness, it looks like an abyss infinitely deeper than hell. And it appears to me that were it not for free grace, exalted and raised up to the infinite height of all the fulness and glory of the great Jehovah and the arm of his power and grace stretched forth in all the majesty of his power and in all the glory of his sovereignty, I should appear sunk down in my sins below hell itself, far beyond the sight of every thing but the eye of sovereign grace, that can pierce even down to such a depth. And yet, it seems to me that my conviction of sin is exceedingly small and faint; it is enough to amaze me that I have no more sense of my sin. I know certainly that I have very little sense of my sinfulness. When I have had turns of weeping and crying for my sins, I thought I knew at the time that my repentance was nothing to my sin.

I have greatly longed of late for a broken heart and to lie low before God, and when I ask for humility, I cannot bear the thoughts of being no more humble than other Christians. It seems to me that though their degrees of humility may be suitable for them, yet it would be a vile self-exaltation in me not to be the lowest in humility of all mankind. Others speak of their longing to be "humbled to the dust"; that may be a proper expression for them, but I always think of myself that I ought, and it is an expression that has long been natural for me to use in prayer, "to lie infinitely low before God." And it is affecting to think how ignorant I was, when a young Christian, of the bottomless, infinite depths of wickedness, pride, hypocrisy, and deceit left in my heart.

I have a much greater sense of my universal, exceeding dependence of God's grace and strength and mere good pleasure, of late, than I used formerly to have, and have experienced more of an abhorrence of my own righteousness. The very thought of any joy arising in me on any consideration of my own amiableness, performances, or experiences, or any goodness of heart or life, is nauseous and detestable to me. And yet I am greatly afflicted with a proud and self-righteous spirit, much more sensibly than I used to be formerly. I see that serpent rising and putting forth its head continually, every where, all around me. Though it seems to me that, in some respects, I was a far better Christian for two or three years after my first conversion than I am now, and lived in a more constant delight and pleasure, yet, of late years I have had a more full and constant sense of the absolute sovereignty of God and a delight in that sovereignty, and have had more of a sense of the glory of Christ as a Mediator revealed in the gospel. On one Saturday night, in particular, I had such a discovery of the excellency of the gospel above all other doctrines that I could not but say to myself, "This is my chosen light, my chosen doctrine," and of Christ, "This is my chosen Prophet." It appeared sweet, beyond all expression, to follow Christ and to be taught and enlightened and instructed by him, to learn of him and live to him. Another Saturday night (January, 1739), I had such a sense, how sweet and blessed a thing it was to walk in the way of duty, to do that which was right and meet to be done and agreeable to the holy mind of God, that it caused me to break forth into a kind of loud weeping, which held me some time, so that I was forced to shut myself up and fasten the doors. I could not but, as it were, cry out, "How happy are they which do that which is right in the sight of God! They are blessed indeed; they are the happy ones!" I had, at the same time a very affecting sense, how meet and suitable it was that God should govern the world and order all things according to his own pleasure; and I rejoiced in it, that God reigned and that his will was done.

c. 1740   1808

[SARAH PIERREPONT]

The following description was written, according to Sereno Dwight's *Life*, on a blank leaf in a book in 1723, when Edwards was twenty and Miss

Pierrepont was thirteen, four years before they were married.

THEY say there is a young lady in New Haven who is beloved of that Great Being who made and rules the world, and that there are certain seasons in which this Great Being, in some way or other invisible, comes to her and fills her mind with exceeding sweet delight, and that she hardly cares for anything, except to meditate on him—that she expects after a while to be received up where he is, to be raised up out of the world and caught up into heaven, being assured that he loves her too well to let her remain at a distance from him always. There she is to dwell with him and to be ravished with his love and delight forever. Therefore, if you present all the world before her with the richest of its treasures, she disregards and cares not for it and is unmindful of any pain or affliction. She has a strange sweetness in her mind and singular purity in her affections, is most just and conscientious in all her conduct, and you could not persuade her to do anything wrong or sinful if you would give her all the world, lest she should offend this Great Being. She is of a wonderful sweetness, calmness, and universal benevolence of mind, especially after this great God has manifested himself to her mind. She will sometimes go about from place to place, singing sweetly, and seems to be always full of joy and pleasure, and no one knows for what. She loves to be alone, walking in the fields and groves, and seems to have some one invisible always conversing with her.

1723

From SINNERS IN THE HANDS OF AN ANGRY GOD

This discourse, delivered at Enfield, Connecticut, July 8, 1741, is probably the most famous of American minatory sermons. Contrary to common opinion, the "hell-fire" sermon is not characteristic of seventeenth-century Calvinistic preaching, which regarded one's future existence as a matter of foredetermined "election" and concerned itself chiefly with expounding and applying its own theological doctrine. With the Great Awakening and the rise of the Methodist and other evangelical sects, with their emphasis upon the act of conversion, the type of sermon which pleaded with sinners to "accept salvation" or terrified them with threats of hell if they continued in their course of indifference became increasingly common. The audience at Enfield were so moved by this address, delivered without sensationalism but with intense earnestness, that their sighs and groans of agony caused the preacher to pause and request silence in order that he might continue.

Application

Deuteronomy xxxii, 35.—Their foot shall slide in due time.

THE use of this awful subject may be for *awakening* to unconverted persons in this congregation. This that you have heard is the case of every one of you that are out of Christ. That world of misery, that lake of burning brimstone, is extended abroad under you. *There* is the dreadful pit of the glowing flames of the wrath of God; there is hell's wide gaping mouth open; and you have nothing to stand upon, nor any thing to take hold of. There is nothing between you and hell but the air; 'tis only the power and mere pleasure of God that holds you up.

You probably are not sensible of this; you find you are kept out of hell, but do not see the hand of God in it, but look at other things, as the good state of your bodily constitution, your care of your own life, and the means you use for your own preservation. But indeed these things are nothing; if God should withdraw his hand, they would avail no more to keep you from falling than the thin air to hold up a person that is suspended in it.

Your wickedness makes you as it were heavy as lead, and to tend downwards with great weight and pressure towards hell; and if God should let you go, you would immediately sink and swiftly descend and plunge into the bottomless gulf, and your healthy constitution, and your own care and prudence, and best contrivance, and all your righteousness, would have no more influence to uphold you and keep you out of hell than a spider's web would have to stop a falling rock. Were it not that so is the sovereign pleasure of God, the earth would not bear you one moment; for you are a burden to it; the creation groans with you; the creature is made subject to the bondage of your corruption, not willingly; the sun does not willingly shine upon you to give you light to serve sin and Satan; the earth does not willingly yield her increase to satisfy your lusts; nor is it willingly a stage for your wickedness to be acted upon; the air does not willingly serve you for breath to maintain the flame of life in your vitals, while you spend your life in the service of God's enemies. God's creatures are good, and were made for men to serve God with, and do not willingly subserve to any other purpose, and groan when they are abused to purposes so directly contrary to their nature and end. And the world would spew you out, were it not for the sovereign hand of him who hath subjected it in hope. There are the black clouds of God's wrath now hanging directly over your heads, full of the dreadful storm, and big with thunder; and were it not for the restraining hand of God, it would immediately burst forth upon you. The sovereign pleasure of God, for the present, stays his rough wind; otherwise it would come with fury, and your destruction would come like a whirlwind, and you would be like the chaff of the summer threshing floor.

The wrath of God is like great waters that are dammed for the present; they increase more and more and rise higher and higher, till an outlet is given; and the longer the stream is stopped, the more rapid and mighty is its course when once it is let loose. 'Tis true that judgment against your evil work has not been executed hitherto; the floods of God's vengeance have been withheld; but your guilt in the mean time is constantly increasing, and you are every day treasuring up more wrath; the waters are continually rising and waxing more and more mighty; and there is nothing but the mere pleasure of God that holds the waters back, that are unwilling to be stopped, and press hard to go forward. If God should only withdraw his hand from the floodgate, it would immediately fly open, and the fiery floods of the fierceness and wrath of God would rush forth with inconceivable fury, and would come upon you with omnipotent power; and if your strength were ten thousand times greater than it is, yea, ten thousand times greater than the strength of the stoutest, sturdiest devil in hell, it would be nothing to withstand or endure it.

The bow of God's wrath is bent, and the arrow made ready on the string, and justice bends the arrow at your heart and strains the bow, and it is nothing but the mere pleasure of God, and that of an angry God, without any promise or obligation at all, that keeps the arrow one moment from being made drunk with your blood.

Thus are all you that never passed under a great change of heart by the mighty power of the Spirit of God upon your souls; all that were never born again and made new creatures, and raised from being dead in sin to a state of new and before altogether unexperienced light and life, (however you may have reformed your life in many things, and may have had religious affections, and may keep up a form of religion in your families and closets and in the house of God, and may be strict in it) you are thus in the hands of an angry God; 'tis nothing but his mere pleasure that keeps you from being this moment swallowed up in everlasting destruction.

However unconvinced you may now be of the truth of what you hear, by and by you will be fully convinced of it. Those that are gone from being in the like circumstances with you, see that it was so with them; for destruction came suddenly upon most of them; when they expected nothing of it, and while they were saying, Peace and safety: now they see that those things that they depended on for peace and safety were nothing but thin air and empty shadows.

The God that holds you over the pit of hell much as one holds a spider or some loathsome insect over the fire, abhors you, and is dreadfully provoked; his wrath towards you burns like fire; he looks upon you as worthy of nothing else but to be cast into the fire; he is of purer eyes than to bear to have you in his sight; you are ten thousand times so abominable in his eyes as the most hateful and venomous serpent is in ours. You have offended him infinitely more than ever a stubborn rebel did his prince: and yet it is nothing but his hand that holds you from falling into the fire every moment. 'Tis ascribed to nothing else, that you did not go to hell the last night; that you was suffered to awake again in this world after you closed your eyes to sleep; and there is no other reason to be given why you have not dropped into hell since you arose in the morning, but that God's hand has held you up. There is no other reason to be given why you have not gone to hell since you have sat here in the house of God, provoking his pure eyes by your sinful wicked manner of attending his solemn worship. Yea, there is nothing else that is to be given as a reason why you do not this very moment drop down into hell.

O sinner! Consider the fearful danger you are in. 'Tis a great furnace of wrath, a wide and bottomless pit, full of the fire of wrath, that you are held over in the hand of that God whose wrath is provoked and incensed as much against you as against many of the damned in hell. You hang by a slender thread, with the flames of divine wrath flashing about it, and ready every moment to singe it and burn it asunder; and you have no interest in any mediator, and nothing to lay hold of to save yourself, nothing to keep off the flames of wrath, nothing of your own, nothing that you ever have done, nothing that you can do, to induce God to spare you one moment.

And consider here more particularly several things concerning that wrath that you are in such danger of:

1. *Whose* wrath it is. It is the wrath of the infinite God. If it were only the wrath of man, though it were of the most potent prince, it would be comparatively little to be regarded. The wrath of kings is very much dreaded, especially of absolute monarchs, that have the possessions and lives of their subjects wholly in their power, to be disposed of at their mere will. *Prov.* xx. 2, "The fear of a king is as the roaring of a lion: whoso provoketh him to anger sinneth against his own soul." The subject that very much enrages an arbitrary prince is liable to suffer the most extreme torments that human art can invent, or human power can inflict. But the greatest earthly potentates, in their greatest majesty and strength, and when clothed in their greatest terrors, are but feeble, despicable worms of the dust, in comparison of the great and almighty Creator and King of heaven and earth: it is but little that they can do when most enraged, and when they have exerted the utmost of their fury. All the kings of the earth before God

are as grasshoppers; they are nothing, and less than nothing: both their love and their hatred is to be despised. The wrath of the great King of kings is as much more terrible than theirs, as his majesty is greater. *Luke* xii. 4, 5, "And I say unto you my friends, Be not afraid of them that kill the body, and after that have no more that they can do. But I will forewarn you whom you shall fear: Fear him, which after he hath killed hath power to cast into hell; yea, I say unto you, Fear him."

2. 'Tis the *fierceness* of his wrath that you are exposed to. We often read of the *fury* of God; as in *Isaiah* lix. 18: "According to their deeds, accordingly he will repay fury to his adversaries." So *Isaiah* lxvi. 15, "For, behold, the Lord will come with fire, and with his chariots like a whirlwind, to render his anger with fury, and his rebuke with flames of fire." And so in many other places. So we read of God's *fierceness*, *Rev.* xix. 15. There we read of "the wine-press of the fierceness and wrath of Almighty God." The words are exceeding terrible: if it had only been said, "the wrath of God," the words would have implied that which is infinitely dreadful: but 'tis not only said so, but "the fierceness and wrath of God." The fury of God! The fierceness of Jehovah! Oh, how dreadful must that be! Who can utter or conceive what such expressions carry in them! But it is not only said so, but "the fierceness and wrath of Almighty God." As though there would be a very great manifestation of his almighty power in what the fierceness of his wrath should inflict, as though omnipotence should be as it were enraged, and exerted, as men are wont to exert their strength in the fierceness of their wrath. Oh! then, what will be the consequence! What will become of the poor worm that shall suffer it! Whose hands can be strong! And whose heart endure! To what a dreadful, inexpressible, inconceivable depth of misery must the poor creature be sunk who shall be the subject of this!

Consider this, you that are here present, that yet remain in an unregenerate state. That God will execute the fierceness of his anger implies that he will inflict wrath without any pity. When God beholds the ineffable extremity of your case, and sees your torment so vastly disproportioned to your strength, and sees how your poor soul is crushed and sinks down, as it were, into an infinite gloom; he will have no compassion upon you, he will not forbear the executions of his wrath, or in the least lighten his hand; there shall be no moderation or mercy, nor will God then at all stay his rough wind; he will have no regard to your welfare nor be at all careful lest you should suffer too much in any other sense, than only that you should not suffer beyond what strict justice requires: nothing shall be withheld because it is so hard for you to bear. *Ezek.* viii. 18, "Therefore will I also deal in fury: mine eye shall not spare, neither will I have pity: and though they cry in mine ears with a loud voice, yet will I not hear them." Now God stands ready to pity you; this is a day of mercy; you may cry now with some encouragement of obtaining mercy; but when once the day of mercy is past, your most lamentable and dolorous cries and shrieks will be in vain; you will be wholly lost and thrown away of God, as to any regard to your welfare; God will have no other use to put you to, but only to suffer misery; you shall be continued in being to no other end; for you will be a vessel of wrath fitted to destruction; and there will be no other use of this vessel but only to be filled full of wrath: God will be so far from pitying you when you cry to him, that 'tis said he will only "laugh and mock," *Prov.* i. 25, 26, &c.

How awful are those words, *Isaiah* lxiii. 3, which are the words of the great God: "I will tread them in mine anger, and trample them in my fury; and their blood shall be sprinkled upon my garments, and I will stain all my raiment." 'Tis perhaps impossible to conceive of words that carry in them greater manifestations of these three things, viz., contempt and hatred and fierceness of indignation. If you cry to God to pity you, he will be so far from pitying you in your doleful case or showing you the least regard or favor that instead of that he'll only tread you under foot; and though he will know that you can't bear the weight of omnipotence treading upon you, yet he won't regard that, but he will crush you under his feet without mercy; he'll crush out your blood and make it fly, and it shall be sprinkled on his garments, so as to stain all his raiment. He will not only hate you, but he will have you in the utmost contempt; no place shall be thought fit for you but under his feet, to be trodden down as the mire of the streets.

3. The *misery* you are exposed to is that which God will inflict to that end, that he might show what that *wrath of Jehovah* is. God hath had it on his heart to show to angels and men, both how excellent his love is and also how terrible his wrath is. Sometimes earthly kings have a mind to show how terrible their wrath is, by the extreme punishments they would execute on those that provoke 'em. Nebuchadnezzar, that mighty and haughty monarch of the Chaldean empire, was willing to show his wrath when enraged with Shadrach, Meshech, and Abednego; and accordingly gave order that the burning fiery furnace should be heated seven times hotter than it was before; doubtless it was raised to the utmost degree of fierceness that human art could raise it; but the great God is also willing to show his wrath and magnify his awful majesty and mighty power in the extreme sufferings of his enemies. *Rom.* ix. 22, "What if God, willing to show his wrath, and to make his power known, endured with much long-suffering the vessels of wrath fitted to destruction?" And seeing this is his design, and what he has determined, to show how terrible the unmixed, unrestrained wrath, the fury and fierceness of Jehovah is, he will do it to effect. There will be something accomplished and brought to pass that will be dreadful with a witness. When the great and angry God hath risen up and executed his awful vengeance on the poor sinner, and the wretch is actually suffering the infinite weight and power of his indignation, then will God call upon the whole universe to behold that awful majesty and mighty power that is to be seen in it. *Isa.* xxxiii. 12, 13, 14, "And the people shall be as the burnings of lime, as thorns cut up shall they be burnt in the fire. Hear, ye that are far off, what I have done; and ye that are near, acknowledge my might. The sinners in Zion are afraid; fearfulness hath surprised the hypocrites," &c.

Thus it will be with you that are in an unconverted state, if you continue in it; the infinite might, and majesty, and terribleness, of the Omnipotent God shall be magnified upon you in the ineffable strength of your torments. You shall be tormented in the presence of the holy angels, and in the presence of the Lamb; and when you shall be in this state of suffering, the glorious inhabitants of heaven shall go forth and look on the awful spectacle, that they may see what the wrath and fierceness of the Almighty is; and when they have seen it, they will fall down and adore that great power and majesty. *Isa.* lxvi. 23, 24, "And it shall come to pass, that from one new moon to another, and from one sabbath to another, shall all flesh come to worship before me, saith the Lord. And they shall go forth, and look upon the carcasses of the men that have transgressed against me: for their worm shall not die, neither shall their fire be quenched; and they shall be an abhorring unto all flesh."

4. It is *everlasting* wrath. It would be dreadful to suffer this fierceness and wrath of Almighty God one moment; but you must suffer it to all eternity: there will be no end to this exquisite, horrible misery. When you look forward you shall see a long forever, a boundless duration before you, which will swallow up your thoughts and amaze your soul; and you will absolutely despair of ever having any deliverance, any end, any mitigation, any rest at all; you will know certainly that you must wear out long ages, millions of millions of ages, in wrestling and conflicting with this almighty, merciless vengeance; and then when you have so done, when so many ages have actually been spent by you in this manner, you will know that all is but a point to what remains. So that your punishment will indeed be infinite. Oh, who can express what the state of a soul in such circumstances is! All that we can possibly say about it gives but a very feeble, faint representation of it; it is inexpressible and inconceivable, for "who knows the power of God's anger?"

How dreadful is the state of those that are daily and hourly in danger of this great wrath and infinite misery! But this is the dismal case of every soul in this congregation that has not been born again, however moral and strict, sober and religious, they may otherwise be. Oh, that you would consider it, whether you be young or old! There is reason to think that there are many in this congregation now hearing this discourse, that will actually be the subjects of this very misery to all eternity. We know not who they are, or in what seats they sit, or what thoughts they now have. It may be they are now at ease and hear all these things without much disturbance, and are now flattering themselves that they are not the persons, promising themselves that they shall escape. If we knew that there was one person, and but one, in the whole congregation, that was to be the subject of this misery, what an awful thing it would be to think of! If we knew who it was, what an awful sight would it be to see such a person! How might all the rest of the congregation lift up a lamentable and bitter cry over him! But alas! instead of one, how many is it likely will remember this discourse in hell! And it would be a wonder, if some that are now present should not be in hell in a very short time, before this year is out. And it would be no wonder if some persons that now sit here in some seats of this meeting-house in health, and quiet and secure, should be there before tomorrow morning. Those of you that finally continue in a natural condition, that shall keep out of hell longest, will be there in a little time! Your damnation does not slumber; it will come swiftly and, in all probability, very suddenly upon many of you. You have reason to wonder that you are not already in hell. 'Tis doubtless the case of some that heretofore you have seen and known, that never deserved hell more than you and that heretofore appeared as likely to have been now alive as you. Their ease is past all hope; they are crying in extreme misery and perfect despair. But here you are in the land of the living and in the house of God, and have an opportunity to obtain salvation. What would not those poor, damned, hopeless souls give for one day's such opportunity as you now enjoy!

And now you have an extraordinary opportunity, a day wherein Christ has flung the door of mercy wide open, and stands in the door calling and crying with a loud voice to poor sinners; a day wherein many are flocking to him and pressing into the Kingdom of God. Many are daily coming from the east, west, north and south; many that were very likely in the same miserable condition that you are in, are in now a happy state, with their hearts filled with love to him that has loved them and washed them from their sins in his own blood, and rejoicing in hope of the glory of God. How awful is it to be left behind at such a day! To see so many others feasting, while you are pining and perishing! To see so many rejoicing and singing for joy of heart, while you have cause to mourn for sorrow of heart and howl for vexation of spirit! How can you rest for one moment in such a condition? Are not your souls as precious as the souls of the people at Suffield, where they are flocking from day to day to Christ?

Are there not many here that have lived long in the world that are not to this day born again, and so are aliens from the common-wealth of Israel and have done nothing ever since they have lived but treasure up wrath against the day of wrath? Oh, sirs, your case in an especial manner is extremely dangerous; your guilt and hardness of heart is extremely great. Don't you see how generally persons of your years are passed over and left in the present remarkable and wonderful dispensation of God's mercy? You had need to consider yourselves and wake thoroughly out of sleep; you cannot bear the fierceness and the wrath of the infinite God.

And you that are young men and young women, will you neglect this precious season that you now enjoy, when so many others of your age are renouncing all youthful vanities and flocking to Christ? You especially have now an extraordinary opportunity; but if you neglect it, it will soon be with you as it is with those persons that spent away all the precious days of youth in sin and are now come to such a dreadful pass in blindness and hardness.

And you children that are unconverted, don't you know that you are going down to hell to bear the dreadful wrath of that God that is now angry with you every day and every night? Will you be content to be the children of the devil, when so many other children in the land are converted and are become the holy and happy children of the King of kings?

And let every one that is yet out of Christ and hanging over the pit of hell, whether they be old men and women or middle-aged or young people or little children, now hearken to the loud calls of God's word and provi-dence. This acceptable year of the Lord that is a day of such great favor to some will doubtless be a day of as remarkable vengeance to others. Men's hearts harden and their guilt increases apace at such a day as this, if they neglect their souls. And never was there so great danger of such persons being given up to hardness of heart and blindness of mind. God seems now to be hastily gathering in his elect in all parts of the land; and probably the bigger part of adult persons that ever shall be saved will be brought in now in a little time, and that it will be as it was on that great outpouring of the Spirit upon the Jews in the Apostles' days, the election will obtain and the rest will be blinded. If this should be the case with you, you will eternally curse this day, and will curse the day that ever you was born to see such a season of the pouring out of God's Spirit, and will wish that you had died and gone to hell before you had seen it. Now undoubtedly it is as it was in the days of John the Baptist, the axe is in an extraor-dinary manner laid at the root of the trees, that every tree that bringeth not forth good fruit may be hewn down and cast into the fire.

Therefore let every one that is out of Christ now awake and fly from the wrath to come. The wrath of Almighty God is now undoubt-edly hanging over a great part of this congrega-tion. Let every one fly out of Sodom. *"Haste and escape for your lives, look not behind you, escape to the mountain, lest ye be consumed."*

1741

1720 ~ *John Woolman* ~ 1772

O UR BEST INSIGHT into the character and workings of the Quaker spirit, as differing from that of the Puritan and the Anglican, is derived from a reading of John Woolman. He was born in New Jersey and brought up in the ways of the Friends. As a young clerk in a country store, he was asked to draw up a bill of sale for a Negro slave, a circumstance which made a deep impression upon his conscience. Successful as a tailor and merchant, he gave up his business lest worldly affairs should engross him too much. He began preaching at twenty-one and after 1743 became an itinerant minister, speaking to congregations of Friends especially against the evils of slavery and capitalistic exploitation, and also preaching to the Indians. In 1772 he went to England as a delegate from the Quakers in Pennsylvania to members of their own sect there, and died at York in a smallpox epidemic.

Woolman's most important work, and the one for which he is remembered today, is the *Journal* (1774), begun when he was thirty-five and continued until his death. It is a beautiful account written with appealing simplicity and the directness of a life without guile but with a consuming sympathy for the lowly and distressed. Charles Lamb, of a very different personality in many ways, urged his friends to get Woolman's *Journal* by heart. Whittier, his fellow Quaker, edited the *Journal* and, in characterizing it as "a classic of the inner life," emphasized the Friends' cultivation of the spirit above regard for physical activity and well-being.

Woolman's writings include *Some Considerations on the Keeping of Negroes* (1754, 1762); *Considerations on Pure Wisdom and Human Policy; on Labor, on Schools, and on the Right Use of the Lord's Outward Gifts* (1758); *Considerations on the True Harmony of Mankind and How It Is to Be Maintained* (1770); *Journal* (1774); and *Caution to the Rich* (1793).

His *Works* appeared in two parts in 1774. John G. Whittier edited the *Journal* and wrote an introduction for it in 1871. The best edition of his works is the *Journal and Essays of John Woolman*, edited with biographical introduction by Amelia M. Gummere (1922).

H. S. Canby's *Classic Americans* (1931), 28–34, gives an enlightening estimate of the place of the Quakers in the thought and life of the United States. See also W. T. Shore, *John Woolman: His Life and Our Times* (1913); M. Kent, "John Woolman: Mystic and Reformer," *Hibbert Journal*, January, 1928; R. M. Jones, *The Quakers in the American Colonies* (1921); A. Sharpless, *John Woolman, a Pioneer in Labor Reform* (1920); and E. C. Wilson, "John Woolman: a Social Reformer of the Eighteenth Century," *Economic Review*, April, 1901.

From the JOURNAL

CHAPTER III

[Sundry Exercises]

In March, 1755, while Braddock's expedition was under way, a general meeting of Quaker ministers and elders at Philadelphia issued an epistle to Friends, including the assertion: "We . . . have found it to be our duty to cease from those national contests productive of misery and bloodshed, and submit our cause to him, the most high, whose tender love to his children exceeds the most warm affections of natural parents, and who hath promised to his seed throughout the earth, as to one individual, 'I will never leave thee, nor forsake thee.'"

HAVING found drawings in my mind to visit Friends on Long Island, after obtaining a certificate from our monthly-meeting, I set off on the twelfth day of the fifth month, in the year 1756. When I reached the island, I lodged the first night at the house of my dear friend, Richard Hallet; the next day, being the first of the week, I was at the meeting in Newtown; in which we experienced the renewed manifestations of the love of Jesus Christ, to the comfort of the honest-hearted. I went that night to Flushing; and the next day, in company with my beloved friend, Matthew Franklin, we crossed the ferry at Whitestone; were at three meetings on the main, and then returned to the island; where I spent the remainder of the week in visiting meetings. The Lord, I believe, hath a people in those parts, who are honestly inclined to serve Him; but many, I fear, are too much clogged with the things of this life, and do not come forward bearing the cross in such faithfulness as He calls for.

My mind was deeply engaged in this visit, both in public and private; and, at several places, observing that they had slaves, I found myself under a necessity in a friendly way, to labor with them on that subject; expressing, as way opened, the inconsistency of that practice with the purity of the Christian Religion, and the ill effects of it manifested amongst us.

The latter end of the week, their yearly-meeting began; at which were our friends John Scarborough, Jane Hoskins, and Susanna Brown, from Pennsylvania. The public meetings were large, and measurably favored with divine goodness.

The exercise of my mind, at this meeting, was chiefly on account of those who were considered as the foremost rank in the society; and, in a meeting of ministers and elders, way opened, that I expressed in some measure what lay upon me; and, at a time when Friends were met for transacting the affairs of the church, having set a while silent, I felt a weight on my mind, and stood up; and, through the gracious regard of our heavenly Father, strength was given fully to clear myself of a burthen, which, for some days, had been increasing upon me.

Through the humbling dispensations of divine Providence, men are sometimes fitted for His service. The messages of the prophet Jeremiah, were so disagreeable to the people, and so reverse to the spirit they lived in, that he became the object of their reproach; and, in the weakness of nature, thought of desisting from his prophetic office; but, saith he, "His Word was in my heart as a burning fire shut up in my bones; and I was weary with forbearing, and could not stay." I saw at this time, that if I was honest in declaring that which truth opened in me, I could not please all men; and labored to be content in the way of my duty, however disagreeable to my own inclination. After this I went homeward, taking Woodbridge, and Plainfield in my way; in both which meetings, the pure influence of divine love was manifested; in an humbling sense whereof I went home, having been out about twenty-four days, and rode about three hundred and sixteen miles.

While I was out on this journey, my heart was much affected with a sense of the state of the churches in our southern provinces; and, believing the Lord was calling me to some farther labor amongst them, I was bowed in reverence before Him, with fervent desires that I might find strength to resign myself up to His heavenly will.

Until this year, 1756, I continued to retail goods, besides following my trade as a tailor; about which time, I grew uneasy on account of my business growing too cumbersome: I had begun with selling trimmings for garments, and from thence proceeded to sell cloths and linens; and at length, having got a considerable shop of goods, my trade increased every year, and the road to large business appeared open; but I felt a stop in my mind.

Through the mercies of the Almighty, I had, in a good degree, learned to be content with a plain way of living. I had but a small family, and, on serious consideration, I believed truth did not require me to engage in much cumbering affairs. It had been my general practice to buy and sell things really useful; things that served chiefly to please the vain mind in people. I was not easy to trade in; seldom did it; and, whenever I did, I found it [to] weaken me as a Christian.

The increase of business became my burthen; for, though my natural inclination was toward merchandise, yet I believed truth required me to live more free from outward cumbers: and there was now a strife in my mind between the two; and in this exercise my prayers were put up to the Lord, who graciously heard me, 10 and gave me a heart resigned to his holy will: Then I lessened my outward business; and, as I had opportunity, told my customers of my intention, that they might consider what shop to turn to: and, in a while, wholly laid down merchandise, following my trade, as a tailor, myself only, having no apprentice. I also had a nursery of appletrees; in which I employed some of my time in hoeing, grafting, trimming, and inoculating. In merchandise it is 20 the custom, where I lived, to sell chiefly on credit, and poor people often get in debt; and when payment is expected, not having wherewith to pay, their creditors often sue for it at law. Having often observed occurrences of this kind, I found it good for me to advise poor people to take such goods as were most useful and not costly.

In the time of trading, I had an opportunity of seeing, that the too liberal use of spirituous 30 liquors, and the custom of wearing too costly apparel, led some people into great inconveniences; and these two things appear to be often connected; for, by not attending to that use of things which is consistent with universal righteousness, there is an increase of labor which extends beyond what our heavenly Father intends for us: and by great labor, and often by much sweating, there is, even among such as are not drunkards, a craving of 40 some liquors to revive the spirits; that, partly by the luxurious drinking of some, and partly by the drinking of others (led to it through immoderate labor), very great quantities of rum are every year expended in our colonies; the greater part of which we should have no need of, did we steadily attend to pure wisdom.

Where men take pleasure in feeling their minds elevated with strong drink, and so indulge their appetite as to disorder their un- 50 derstandings, neglect their duty as members in a family or civil society, and cast off all regard to religion, their case is much to be pitied; and where such, whose lives are for the most part regular, and whose examples have a strong influence on the minds of others, adhere to some customs which powerfully draw to the use of more strong liquor than pure wisdom allows; this also, as it hinders the spreading of the spirit of meekness, and strengthens the hands of the more excessive drinkers, is a case to be lamented.

As every degree of luxury hath some connection with evil, those who profess to be disciples of Christ, and are looked upon as leaders of the people, should have that mind in them which was also in Christ, and so stand separate from every wrong way, as a means of help to the weaker. As I have sometimes been much spent in the heat, and taken spirits to revive me, I have found, by experience, that in such circumstances the mind is not so calm, nor so fitly disposed for divine meditation, as when all such extremes are avoided; and I have felt an increasing care to attend to that holy spirit which sets bounds to our desires, and leads those, who faithfully follow it, to apply all the gifts of divine providence to the purposes for which they were intended. Did such, as have the care of great estates, attend with singleness of heart to this heavenly instructor, which so opens and enlarges the mind, that men love their neighbors as themselves, they would have wisdom given them to manage, without finding occasion to employ some people in the luxuries of life, or to make it necessary for others to labor too hard; but, for want of steadily regarding this principle of divine love, a selfish spirit takes place in the minds of people, which is attended with darkness and manifold confusion in the world.

Though trading in things useful is an honest employ; yet, through the great number of superfluities which are bought and sold, and through the corruption of the times, they, who apply to merchandise for a living, have great need to be well experienced in that precept which the prophet Jeremiah laid down for his scribe: "Seekest thou great things for thyself? seek them not."

In the winter, this year, I was engaged with

Friends in visiting families; and, through the goodness of the Lord, we had oftentimes experience of His heart-tendering presence amongst us.

CHAPTER XI

[Voyage to England]

Having been some time under a religious concern to prepare for crossing the seas, in order to visit Friends in the northern parts of England, and more particularly in Yorkshire, after consideration I thought it expedient to inform Friends of it at our Monthly Meeting at Burlington, who, having unity with me therein, gave me a certificate. I afterwards communicated the same to our Quarterly Meeting, and they likewise certified their concurrence. Some time after, at the General Spring Meeting of ministers and elders, I thought it my duty to acquaint them with the religious exercise which attended my mind; and they likewise signified their unity therewith by a certificate, dated the 24th of third month, 1772, directed to Friends in Great Britain.

In the fourth month following I thought the time was come for me to make some inquiry for a suitable conveyance; and as my concern was principally towards the northern parts of England, it seemed most proper to go in a vessel bound to Liverpool or Whitehaven. While I was at Philadelphia deliberating on this subject I was informed that my beloved friend Samuel Emlen, junior, intended to go to London, and had taken a passage for himself in the cabin of the ship called the Mary and Elizabeth, of which James Sparks was master, and John Head, of the city of Philadelphia, one of the owners; and feeling a draught in my mind towards the steerage of the same ship, I went first and opened to Samuel the feeling I had concerning it.

My beloved friend wept when I spake to him, and appeared glad that I had thoughts of going in the vessel with him, though my prospect was toward the steerage; and he offering to go with me, we went on board, first into the cabin,—a commodious room,—and then into the steerage, where we sat down on a chest, the sailors being busy about us. The owner of the ship also came and sat down with us. My mind was turned towards Christ, the Heavenly Counsellor, and feeling at this time my own will subjected, my heart was contrite before Him. A motion was made by the owner to go and sit in the cabin, as a place more retired; but I felt easy to leave the ship, and, making no agreement as to a passage in her, told the owner if I took a passage in the ship I believed it would be in the steerage; but did not say much as to my exercise in that case.

After I went to my lodgings, and the case was a little known in town, a Friend laid before me the great inconvenience attending a passage in the steerage, which for a time appeared very discouraging to me.

I soon after went to bed, and my mind was under a deep exercise before the Lord, whose helping hand was manifested to me as I slept that night, and His love strengthened my heart. In the morning I went with two Friends on board the vessel again, and after a short time spent therein, I went with Samuel Emlen to the house of the owner, to whom, in the hearing of Samuel only, I opened my exercise in relation to a scruple I felt with regard to a passage in the cabin, in substance as follows:—

"That on the outside of that part of the ship where the cabin was I observed sundry sorts of carved work and imagery; that in the cabin I observed some superfluity of workmanship of several sorts; and that according to the ways of men's reckoning, the sum of money to be paid for a passage in that apartment has some relation to the expense of furnishing it to please the minds of such as give way to a conformity to this world; and that in this, as in other cases, the moneys received from the passengers are calculated to defray the cost of these superfluities, as well as the other expenses of their passage. I therefore felt a scruple with regard to paying my money to be applied to such purposes."

As my mind was now opened, I told the owner that I had, at several times, in my travels, seen great oppressions on this continent, at which my heart had been much affected and brought into a feeling of the state of the sufferers; and having many times been engaged in the fear and love of God to labor with those under whom the oppressed have been borne down and afflicted, I have often perceived that with a view to get riches and to provide estates for children, that they may live conformably to the customs and honors of this world, many are entangled in the spirit of oppression, and the exercise of my soul had been such that I could not find peace in joining in anything which I saw was against that wisdom which is pure.

After this I agreed for a passage in the steerage; and hearing that Joseph White had desired to see me, I went to his house, and next day home, where I tarried two nights. Early the next morning I parted with my family under a sense of the humbling hand of God upon me, and, going to Philadelphia, had an opportunity with several of my beloved friends, who appeared to be concerned for me on account of the unpleasant situation of that part of the vessel in which I was likely to lodge. In these opportunities my mind, through the mercies of the Lord, was kept low in an inward waiting for His help; and Friends having expressed their desire that I might have a more convenient place than the steerage, did not urge it, but appeared disposed to leave me to the Lord.

Having stayed two nights at Philadelphia, I went the next day to Derby Monthly Meeting, where through the strength of Divine love my heart was enlarged towards the youth there present, under which I was helped to labor in some tenderness of spirit. I lodged at William Horn's and afterwards went to Chester, where I met with Samuel Emlen, and we went on board 1st of fifth month, 1772. As I sat alone on the deck I felt a satisfactory evidence that my proceedings were not in my own will, but under the power of the cross of Christ.

Seventh of fifth month.—We have had rough weather mostly since I came on board, and the passengers, James Reynolds, John Till Adams, Sarah Logan and her hired maid, and John Bispham, all sea-sick at times; from which sickness, through the tender mercies of my Heavenly Father, I have been preserved, my afflictions now being of another kind. There appeared an openness in the minds of the master of the ship and in the cabin passengers towards me. We are often together on the deck, and sometimes in the cabin. My mind, through the merciful help of the Lord, hath been preserved in a good degree watchful and quiet, for which I have great cause to be thankful.

As my lodging in the steerage, now near a week, hath afforded me sundry opportunities of seeing, hearing, and feeling with respect to the life and spirit of many poor sailors, an exercise of soul hath attended me in regard to placing out children and youth where they may be likely to be exampled and instructed in the pure fear of the Lord.

Being much among the seamen I have, from a motion of love, taken sundry opportunities with one of them at a time, and have in free conversation labored to turn their minds towards the fear of the Lord. This day we had a meeting in the cabin, where my heart was contrite under a feeling of Divine love.

I believe a communication with different parts of the world by sea is at times consistent with the will of our Heavenly Father, and to educate some youth in the practice of sailing, I believe may be right; but how lamentable is the present corruption of the world! How impure are the channels through which trade is conducted! How great is the danger to which poor lads are exposed when placed on shipboard to learn the art of sailing! Five lads training up for the seas were on board this ship. Two of them were brought up in our Society, and the other, by name James Naylor, is a member, to whose father James Naylor, mentioned in Sewel's history, appears to have been uncle. I often feel a tenderness of heart towards these poor lads, and at times look at them as though they were my children according to the flesh.

O that all may take heed and beware of covetousness! O that all may learn of Christ, who was meek and lowly of heart! Then in faithfully following him he will teach us to be content with food and raiment without respect to the customs or honors of this world. Men thus redeemed will feel a tender concern for their fellow-creatures, and a desire that those in the lowest stations may be assisted and encouraged, and where owners of ships attain to the perfect law of liberty and are doers of the Word, these will be blessed in their deeds.

A ship at sea commonly sails all night, and

the seamen take their watches four hours at a time. Rising to work in the night, it is not commonly pleasant in any case, but in dark rainy nights it is very disagreeable, even though each man were furnished with all conveniences. If, after having been on deck several hours in the night, they come down into the steerage soaking wet, and are so closely stowed that proper convenience for change of garments is not easily come at, but for want of proper room their wet garments are thrown in heaps, and sometimes, through much crowding, are trodden under foot in going to their lodgings and getting out of them, and it is difficult at times for each to find his own. Here are trials for the poor sailors.

Now, as I have been with them in my lodge, my heart hath often yearned for them, and tender desires have been raised in me that all owners and masters of vessels may dwell in the love of God and therein act uprightly, and by seeking less for gain and looking carefully to their ways they may earnestly labor to remove all cause of provocation from the poor seamen, so that they may neither fret nor use excess of strong drink; for, indeed, the poor creatures, in the wet and cold, seem to apply at times to strong drink to supply the want of other convenience. Great reformation is wanting in the world, and the necessity of it among those who do business on great waters hath at this time been abundantly opened before me.

Eighth of fifth month.—This morning the clouds gathered, the wind blew strong from the southeast, and before noon so increased that sailing appeared dangerous. The seamen then bound up some of their sails and took down others, and the storm increasing they put the deadlights, so called, into the cabin windows and lighted a lamp as at night. The wind now blew vehemently, and the sea wrought to that degree that an awful seriousness prevailed in the cabin, in which I spent, I believe, about seventeen hours, for the cabin passengers had given me frequent invitations, and I thought the poor wet toiling seamen had need of all the room in the crowded steerage. They now ceased from sailing and put the vessel in the posture called lying to.

My mind during this tempest, through the gracious assistance of the Lord, was preserved in a good degree of resignation; and at times I expressed a few words in his love to my shipmates in regard to the all-sufficiency of Him who formed the great deep, and whose care is so extensive that a sparrow falls not without his notice, and thus in a tender frame of mind I spoke to them of the necessity of our yielding in true obedience to the instructions of our Heavenly Father, who sometimes through adversities intendeth our refinement.

About eleven at night I went out on the deck. The sea wrought exceedingly, and the high, foaming waves round about had in some sort the appearance of fire, but did not give much if any light. The sailor at the helm said he lately saw a corposant at the head of the mast. I observed that the master of the ship ordered the carpenter to keep on the deck; and, though he said little, I apprehended his care was that the carpenter with his axe might be in readiness in case of any extremity. Soon after this the vehemency of the wind abated, and before morning they again put the ship under sail.

Tenth of fifth month.—It being the first day of the week and fine weather, we had a meeting in the cabin, at which most of the seamen were present; this meeting was to me a strengthening time. 13th.—As I continue to lodge in the steerage I feel an openness this morning to express something further of the state of my mind in respect to poor lads bound apprentice to learn the art of sailing. As I believe sailing is of use in the world, a labor of soul attends me that the pure counsel of truth may be humbly waited for in this case by all concerned in the business of the seas. A pious father whose mind is exercised for the everlasting welfare of his child may not with a peaceable mind place him out to an employment among a people whose common course of life is manifestly corrupt and profane. Great is the present defect among seafaring men in regard to virtue and piety; and, by reason of an abundant traffic and many ships being used for war, so many people are employed on the sea that the subject of placing lads to this employment appears very weighty.

When I remember the saying of the Most High through his prophet, "This people have

I formed for myself; they shall show forth my praise," and think of placing children among such to learn the practice of sailing, the consistency of it with a pious education seems to me like that mentioned by the prophet, "There is no answer from God."

Profane examples are very corrupting and very forcible. And as my mind day after day and night after night hath been affected with a sympathizing tenderness towards poor children who are put to the employment of sailors, I have sometimes had weighty conversation with the sailors in the steerage, who were mostly respectful to me and became more so the longer I was with them. They mostly appeared to take kindly what I said to them; but their minds were so deeply impressed with the almost universal depravity among sailors that the poor creatures in their answers to me have revived in my remembrance that of the degenerate Jews a little before the captivity, as repeated by Jeremiah the prophet, "There is no hope."

1756–1772   1774

1735 ~ *Michel-Guillaume*
        Jean de Crèvecœur ~ 1813

CRÈVECŒUR was born near Caen in Normandy in 1735. Although he was descended from a distinguished family, he chose almost from boyhood to be a wanderer and adventurer. After an education partly obtained in England, he served with Montcalm in Canada during the last part of the French and Indian War, explored the lands between the Great Lakes and the Ohio River, perhaps as a map maker, and after the peace traveled extensively in New York and Pennsylvania, and in other English colonies. In 1769 he married and settled on a farm in Orange County, New York. Here he greatly enjoyed a bucolic life and penned the essays later gathered in his two books.

This idyllic existence was broken by the Revolution, with which he did not sympathize. Refusing to join either party, he was suspected by both, and in 1780 he returned temporarily to Europe. His *Letters from an American Farmer* was published in London in 1782 under the pseudonym of J. Hector St. John, and was soon reprinted in France and America.

With the close of the Revolution he returned to New York as French consul, to find that Indians had burned his house and killed his wife. After recovering his children, he lived in New York, continuing his interest in American agriculture by introducing the cultivation of various plants, among them alfalfa and the vetches. In 1790 he returned to France, where he spent the remaining twenty-three years of his life.

Crèvecœur's *Letters from an American Farmer*, dedicated to the liberal French philosopher Raynal, manifests minute and curious observation of the details of nature and country life, combined with a romantic idealization of both. His praise of the simple life and his sensibility show him akin to Rousseau, Richardson, and Burns. A friend of Jefferson and Franklin, he shares the former's preference for a primarily agricultural state. He is also the earliest writer to stress the "melting-pot" conception of the American race. Occasionally eccentric in construction and style, his essays often mingle the vigor of good English prose with the clarity of French.

The best edition of *Letters from an American Farmer* is the reprint of the English edition of 1792 issued in 1904 with a preface by W. P. Trent and an introduction by Ludwig Lewisohn. The book also appears in Everyman's Library. Crèvecœur's other books are *Voyage dans la Haute Pensylvanie et dans l'État de New-York* (3 vols., Paris, 1801); and *Sketches of Eighteenth Century America*, edited by H. L. Bourdin, R. H. Gabriel, and S. T. Williams, and first issued in 1925. The best biography is by Julia Post Mitchell (1916). The article in *DAB* is by S. T. Williams. A careful critical study of his work is H. C. Rice's *Le Cultivateur Américain* (Paris, 1933). See also several studies by Bourdin and Williams: "Crèvecœur on the Susquehanna," *Yale Review*, April, 1925; "Crèvecœur the Loyalist," *Nation*, Sept. 23, 1925; "Unpublished Manuscripts of Crèvecœur," *Studies in Philology*, July, 1925; and "The American Farmer Returns," *North American Review*, Sept., 1925; and Robert de Crèvecœur's *Saint Jean de Crèvecœur: Sa Vie et Ses Ouvrages* (1883).

From LETTERS FROM AN AMERICAN FARMER

LETTER III

What Is an American?

I wish I could be acquainted with the feelings and thoughts which must agitate the heart and present themselves to the mind of an enlightened Englishman, when he first lands on this continent. He must greatly rejoice that he lived at a time to see this fair country discovered and settled; he must necessarily feel a share of national pride, when he views the chain of settlements which embellishes these extended shores. When he says to himself, this is the work of my countrymen, who, when convulsed by factions, afflicted by a variety of miseries and wants, restless and impatient, took refuge here. They brought along with them their national genius, to which they principally owe what liberty they enjoy and what substance they possess. Here he sees the industry of his native country displayed in a new manner and traces in their works the embryos of all the arts, sciences, and ingenuity which flourish in Europe. Here he beholds fair cities, substantial villages, extensive fields, an immense country filled with decent houses, good roads, orchards, meadows, and bridges, where a hundred years ago all was wild, woody, and uncultivated! What a train of pleasing ideas this fair spectacle must suggest; it is a prospect which must inspire a good citizen with the most heartfelt pleasure. The difficulty consists in the manner of viewing so extensive a scene. He is arrived on a new continent; a modern society offers itself to his contemplation, different from what he had hitherto seen. It is not composed, as in Europe, of great lords who possess everything and of a herd of people who have nothing. Here are no aristocratical families, no courts, no kings, no bishops, no ecclesiastical dominion, no invisible power giving to a few a very visible one; no great manufacturers employing thousands, no great refinements of luxury. The rich and the poor are not so far removed from each other as they are in Europe. Some few towns excepted, we are all tillers of the earth, from Nova Scotia to West Florida. We are a people of cultivators, scattered over an immense territory, communicating with each other by means of good roads and navigable rivers, united by the silken bands of mild government, all respecting the laws without dreading their power, because they are equitable. We are all animated with the spirit of an industry which is unfettered and unrestrained, because each person works for himself. If he travels through our rural districts, he views not the hostile castle and the haughty mansion, contrasted with the clay-built hut and miserable cabin where cattle and men help to keep each other warm and dwell in meanness, smoke, and indigence. A pleasing uniformity of decent competence appears throughout our habitations. The meanest of our log-houses is a dry and comfortable habitation. Lawyer or merchant are the fairest titles our towns afford; that of a farmer is the only appellation of the rural inhabitants of our country. It must take some time ere he can reconcile himself to our dictionary, which is but short in words of dignity and names of honor. There, on a Sunday, he sees a congregation of respectable farmers and their wives, all clad in neat homespun, well mounted or riding in their own humble wagons. There is not among them an esquire, saving the unlettered magistrate. There he sees a parson as simple as his flock, a farmer who does not riot on the labor of others. We have no princes, for whom we toil, starve, and bleed: we are the most perfect society now existing in the world. Here man is free as he ought to be; nor is this pleasing equality so transitory as many others are. Many ages will not see the shores of our great lakes replenished with inland nations, nor the unknown bounds of North America entirely peopled. Who can tell how far it extends? Who can tell the millions of men whom it will feed and contain? for no European foot has as yet traveled half the extent of this mighty continent!

The next wish of this traveler will be to know whence came all these people? They are a mixture of English, Scotch, Irish, French, Dutch, Germans, and Swedes. From this promiscuous breed, that race now called Americans have arisen. The eastern provinces must indeed be excepted as being the unmixed descendants of Englishmen. I have heard many wish that they had been more intermixed also: for my part, I am no wisher, and think it much better as it has happened. They exhibit a most conspicuous figure in this great and variegated picture; they too enter for a great share in the pleasing perspective displayed in these thirteen provinces. I know it is fashionable to reflect on them, but I respect them for what they have done; for the accuracy and wisdom with which they have settled their territory; for the decency of their manners; for their early love of letters; their ancient college, the first in this hemisphere; for their industry, which to me who am but a farmer, is the criterion of everything. There never was a people, situated as they are, who with so ungrateful a soil have done more in so short a time. Do you think that the monarchical ingredients which are more prevalent in other governments have purged them from all foul stains? Their histories assert the contrary.

In this great American asylum, the poor of Europe have by some means met together, and in consequence of various causes; to what purpose should they ask one another what countrymen they are? Alas, two thirds of them had no country. Can a wretch who wanders about, who works and starves, whose life is a continual scene of sore affliction or pinching penury; can that man call England or any other kingdom his country? A country that had no bread for him, whose fields procured him no harvest, who met with nothing but the frowns of the rich, the severity of the laws, with jails and punishments; who owned not a single foot of the extensive surface of this planet? No! urged by a variety of motives, here they came. Every thing has tended to regenerate them; new laws, a new mode of living, a new social system; here they are become men: in Europe they were as so many useless plants, wanting vegetative mold, and refreshing showers; they withered, and were mowed down by want, hunger, and war; but now by the power of transplantation, like all other plants they have taken root and flourished! Formerly they were not numbered in any civil lists of their country, except in those of the poor; here they rank as citizens. By what invisible power has this surprising metamorphosis been performed? By that of the laws and that of their industry. The laws, the indulgent laws, protect them as they arrive, stamping on them the symbol of adoption; they receive ample rewards for their labors; these accumulated rewards procure them lands; those lands confer on them the title of freemen, and to that title every benefit is affixed which men can possibly require. This is the great operation daily performed by our laws. From whence proceed these laws? From our government. Whence the government? It is derived from the original genius and strong desire of the people ratified and confirmed by the crown. This is the great chain which links us all, this is the picture which every province exhibits, Nova Scotia excepted. There the crown has done all; either there were no people who had genius, or it was not much attended to: the consequence is, that the province is very thinly inhabited indeed; the power of the crown in conjunction with the mosquitos has prevented men from settling there. Yet some parts of it flourished once, and it contained a mild, harmless set of people. But for the fault of a few leaders, the whole were banished. The greatest political error the crown ever committed in America was to cut off men from a country which wanted nothing but men!

What attachment can a poor European emigrant have for a country where he had nothing? The knowledge of the language, the love of a few kindred as poor as himself, were the only cords that tied him: his country is now that which gives him land, bread, protection, and consequence. *Ubi panis ibi patria*,[1] is the motto of all emigrants. What then is the American, this new man? He is either a European or the descendant of a European; hence that strange mixture of blood which you will find in no other country. I could point out to you a family whose grandfather was an Englishman, whose wife was Dutch, whose son married a French woman, and whose present four sons have now four wives of different nations. *He* is an American, who, leaving behind him all his ancient prejudices and manners, receives new ones from the new mode of life he has embraced, the new government he obeys, and the new rank he holds. He becomes an American by being received in the broad lap of our great *Alma Mater*. Here individuals of all nations are melted into a new race of men, whose labors and posterity will one day cause great changes in the world. Americans are the western pilgrims who are carrying along with them that great mass of arts, sciences, vigor, and industry which began long since in the east; they will finish the great circle. The Americans were

[1] Where one can get a living, there is his country.

once scattered all over Europe; here they are incorporated into one of the finest systems of population which has ever appeared, and which will hereafter become distinct by the power of the different climates they inhabit. The American ought therefore to love this country much better than that wherein either he or his forefathers were born. Here the rewards of his industry follow with equal steps the progress of his labor; his labor is founded on the basis of nature, *self-interest;* can it want a stronger allurement? Wives and children, who before in vain demanded of him a morsel of bread, now, fat and frolicsome, gladly help their father to clear those fields whence exuberant crops are to arise to feed and to clothe them all, without any part being claimed, either by a despotic prince, a rich abbot, or a mighty lord. Here religion demands but little of him; a small voluntary salary to the minister, and gratitude to God; can he refuse these? The American is a new man, who acts upon new principles; he must therefore entertain new ideas, and form new opinions. From involuntary idleness, servile dependence, penury, and useless labor, he has passed to toils of a very different nature, rewarded by ample subsistence.—This is an American.

British America is divided into many provinces, forming a large association, scattered along a coast 1500 miles [in] extent and about 200 wide. This society I would fain examine, at least such as it appears in the middle provinces; if it does not afford that variety of tinges and gradations which may be observed in Europe, we have colors peculiar to ourselves. For instance, it is natural to conceive that those who live near the sea must be very different from those who live in the woods; the intermediate space will afford a separate and distinct class.

Men are like plants; the goodness and flavor of the fruit proceeds from the peculiar soil and exposition in which they grow. We are nothing but what we derive from the air we breathe, the climate we inhabit, the government we obey, the system of religion we profess, and the nature of our employment. Here you will find but few crimes; these have acquired as yet no root among us. I wish I was able to trace all my ideas; if my ignorance prevents me from describing them properly, I hope I shall be able to delineate a few of the outlines, which are all I propose.

Those who live near the sea feed more on fish than on flesh and often encounter that boisterous element. This renders them more bold and enterprising; this leads them to neglect the confined occupations of the land. They see and converse with a variety of people; their intercourse with mankind becomes extensive. The sea inspires them with a love of traffic, a desire of transporting produce from one place to another, and leads them to a variety of resources which supply the place of labor. Those who inhabit the middle settlements, by far the most numerous, must be very different; the simple cultivation of the earth purifies them, but the indulgences of the government, the soft remonstrances of religion, the rank of independent freeholders, must necessarily inspire them with sentiments very little known in Europe among people of the same class. What do I say? Europe has no such class of men; the early knowledge they acquire, the early bargains they make, give them a great degree of sagacity. As freemen they will be litigious; pride and obstinacy are often the cause of lawsuits; the nature of our laws and governments may be another. As citizens it is easy to imagine that they will carefully read the newspapers, enter into every political disquisition, freely blame or censure governors and others. As farmers, they will be careful and anxious to get as much as they can, because what they get is their own. As northern men they will love the cheerful cup. As Christians, religion curbs them not in their opinions; the general indulgence leaves every one to think for themselves in spiritual matters; the laws inspect our actions, our thoughts are left to God. Industry, good living, selfishness, litigiousness, country politics, the pride of freemen, religious indifference,[1] are their characteristics. If you recede still farther from the sea, you will come into more modern [2] settlements; they exhibit the same strong lineaments, in a ruder appearance. Religion seems to have still less influence, and their manners are less improved.

Now we arrive near the great woods, near the last inhabited districts; there men seem to be placed still farther beyond the reach of government, which in some measure leaves them to themselves. How can it pervade every corner; as they were driven there by misfortunes, necessity of beginnings, desire of acquiring large tracts of land, idleness, frequent want of economy, ancient debts; the reunion of such people does not afford a very pleasing spectacle. When discord, want of unity and friendship; when either drunkenness or idleness prevail in such remote districts; contention, inactivity, and wretchedness must ensue. There are not the same remedies to these evils as in a long established community. The few magistrates they have are in general little better than the rest; they are often in a perfect state of war—that of man against man, sometimes decided by blows, sometimes by means of the law; that of man against every wild inhabitant of these venerable woods, of which they are come to dispossess them. There men appear to be no better than carnivorous animals of a superior rank, living on the flesh of wild animals when they can catch them, and when they are not able, they subsist on grain. He who would wish to see America in its proper light and have a true idea of its feeble beginnings and barbarous rudiments must visit our extended line of frontiers where the last settlers dwell, and where he may see the first labors of settlement, the mode of clearing the earth, in all their different appearances; where men are wholly left dependent on their native tempers, and on the spur of uncertain industry, which often fails when not sanctified by the efficacy of a few moral rules. There, remote from the power of example and check of shame, many families exhibit the most hideous parts of our society. They are a kind of forlorn hope, preceding by ten or twelve years the most respectable army of veterans which come after them. In that space, prosperity will polish some, vice and the law will drive off the rest, who uniting again with others like themselves will recede still farther, making room for more industrious people, who will finish their improvements, convert the loghouse into a convenient habitation, and rejoicing that the first heavy labors are finished, will change in a few years that hitherto barbarous country into a

---

[1] disregard of religious differences   [2] recent

fine, fertile, well regulated district. Such is our progress, such is the march of the Europeans toward the interior parts of this continent. In all societies there are offcasts; this impure part serves as our precursors or pioneers; my father himself was one of that class,[1] but he came upon honest principles, and was therefore one of the few who held fast; by good conduct and temperance, he transmitted to me his fair inheritance, when not above one in fourteen 10 of his contemporaries had the same good fortune.

Forty years ago this smiling country was thus inhabited; it is now purged, a general decency of manners prevails throughout, and such has been the fate of our best countries.

Exclusive of those general characteristics, each province has its own, founded on the government, climate, mode of husbandry, customs, and peculiarity of circumstances. Euro- 20 peans submit insensibly to these great powers, and become, in the course of a few generations, not only Americans in general, but either Pennsylvanians, Virginians, or provincials under some other name. Whoever traverses the continent must easily observe those strong differences, which will grow more evident in time. The inhabitants of Canada, Massachusetts, the middle provinces, the southern ones, will be as different as their climates; their only 30 points of unity will be those of religion and language.

As I have endeavored to show you how Europeans become Americans, it may not be disagreeable to show you likewise how the various Christian sects introduced wear out, and how religious indifference becomes prevalent. When any considerable number of a particular sect happen to dwell contiguous to each other, they immediately erect a temple 40 and there worship the Divinity agreeably to their own peculiar ideas. Nobody disturbs them. If any new sect springs up in Europe, it may happen that many of its professors will come and settle in America. As they bring their zeal with them, they are at liberty to make proselytes if they can and to build a meeting [house] and to follow the dictates of their consciences; for neither the government nor any other power interferes. If they are 50

peaceable subjects and are industrious, what is it to their neighbors how and in what manner they think fit to address their prayers to the Supreme Being? But if the sectaries are not settled close together, if they are mixed with other denominations, their zeal will cool for want of fuel and will be extinguished in a little time. Then the Americans become as to religion what they are as to country, allied to all. In them the name of Englishman, Frenchman, and European is lost, and, in like manner, the strict modes of Christianity as practiced in Europe are lost also. This effect will extend itself still farther hereafter, and though this may appear to you as a strange idea, yet it is a very true one. I shall be able perhaps hereafter to explain myself better; in the meanwhile, let the following example serve as my first justification.

Let us suppose you and I to be traveling; we observe that in this house, to the right, lives a Catholic who prays to God as he has been taught and believes in transubstantiation; he works and raises wheat, he has a large family of children, all hale and robust; his belief, his prayers offend nobody. About one mile farther on the same road, his next neighbor may be a good, honest, plodding German Lutheran who addresses himself to the same God, the God of all, agreeably to the modes he has been educated in and believes in consubstantiation; by so doing he scandalizes nobody; he also works in his fields, embellishes the earth, clears swamps, etc. What has the world to do with his Lutheran principles? He persecutes nobody, and nobody persecutes him; he visits his neighbors, and his neighbors visit him. Next to him lives a seceder,[1] the most enthusiastic of all sectaries; his zeal is hot and fiery, but separated as he is from others of the same complexion, he has no congregation of his own to resort to, where he might cabal and mingle religious pride with worldly obstinacy. He likewise raises good crops, his house is handsomely painted, his orchard is one of the fairest in the neighborhood. How does it concern the welfare of the country or of the province at large what this man's religious sentiments are, or really whether he has any at all? He is a good farmer, he is a

---

[1] a piece of literary fiction on Crèvecœur's part

[1] a member of an independent Calvinistic sect

sober, peaceable, good citizen; William Penn himself would not wish for more. This is the visible character, the invisible one is only guessed at and is nobody's business. Next again lives a Low Dutchman who implicitly believes the rules laid down by the synod of Dort.[1] He conceives no other idea of a clergyman than that of an hired man; if he does his work well he will pay him the stipulated sum; if not, he will dismiss him and do without his sermons, and let his church be shut up for years. But notwithstanding this coarse idea, you will find his house and farm to be the neatest in all the country; and you will judge by his wagon and fat horses that he thinks more of the affairs of this world than of those of the next. He is sober and laborious, therefore he is all he ought to be as to the affairs of this life; as for those of the next, he must trust to the great Creator. Each of these people instruct their children as well as they can, but these instructions are feeble compared to those which are given to the youth of the poorest class in Europe. Their children will therefore grow up less zealous and more indifferent in matters of religion than their parents. The foolish vanity, or rather the fury of making proselytes, is unknown here; they have no time, the seasons call for all their attention, and thus in a few years this mixed neighborhood will exhibit a strange religious medley that will be neither pure Catholicism nor pure Calvinism. A very perceptible indifference even in the first generation will become apparent; and it may happen that the daughter of the Catholic will marry the son of the seceder, and settle by themselves at a distance from their parents. What religious education will they give their children? A very imperfect one. If there happens to be in the neighborhood any place of worship—we will suppose a Quaker's meeting—rather than not show their fine clothes, they will go to it, and some of them may perhaps attach themselves to that society. Others will remain in a perfect state of indifference; the children of these zealous parents will not be able to tell what their religious principles are,

[1] The Synod of Dort, or Dordrecht, 1618–19, established the ecclesiastical canon of the Dutch Reformed Church.

and their grandchildren still less. The neighborhood of a place of worship generally leads them to it, and the action of going thither is the strongest evidence they can give of their attachment to any sect. The Quakers are the only people who retain a fondness for their own mode of worship; for be they ever so far separated from each other, they hold a sort of communion with the society and seldom depart from its rules, at least in this country. Thus all sects are mixed as well as all nations; thus religious indifference is imperceptibly disseminated from one end of the continent to the other, which is at present one of the strongest characteristics of the Americans. Where this will reach no one can tell; perhaps it may leave a vacuum fit to receive other systems. Persecution, religious pride, the love of contradiction, are the food of what the world commonly calls religion. These motives have ceased here; zeal in Europe is confined; here it evaporates in the great distance it has to travel; there it is a grain of powder inclosed; here it burns away in the open air and consumes without effect.

But to return to our back settlers. I must tell you that there is something in the proximity of the woods which is very singular. It is with men as it is with the plants and animals that grow and live in the forests; they are entirely different from those that live in the plains. I will candidly tell you all my thoughts, but you are not to expect that I shall advance any reasons. By living in or near the woods, their actions are regulated by the wildness of the neighborhood. The deer often come to eat their grain, the wolves to destroy their sheep, the bears to kill their hogs, the foxes to catch their poultry. This surrounding hostility immediately puts the gun into their hands; they watch these animals, they kill some; and thus by defending their property, they soon become professed hunters; this is the progress; once hunters, farewell to the plough. The chase renders them ferocious, gloomy, and unsociable; a hunter wants no neighbor; he rather hates them because he dreads the competition. In a little time their success in the woods makes them neglect their tillage. They trust to the natural fecundity of the earth, and therefore do little; carelessness in fencing often exposes what little they sow to destruction; they are not at home to watch; in order, therefore, to make up the deficiency, they go oftener to the woods. That new mode of life brings along with it a new set of manners which I cannot easily describe. These new manners, being grafted on the old stock, produce a strange sort of lawless profligacy, the impressions of which are indelible. The manners of the Indian natives are respectable compared with this European medley. Their wives and children live in sloth and inactivity; and having no proper pursuits, you may judge what education the latter receive. Their tender minds have nothing else to contemplate but the example of their parents; like them they grow up a mongrel breed, half civilized, half savage, except nature stamps on them some constitutional propensities. That rich, that voluptuous sentiment is gone that struck them so forcibly; the possession of their freeholds no longer conveys to their minds the same pleasure and pride. To all these reasons you must add their lonely situation, and you cannot imagine what an effect on manners the great distances they live from each other has! Consider one of the last settlements in its first view; of what is it composed? Europeans who have not that sufficient share of knowledge they ought to have, in order to prosper; people who have suddenly passed from oppression, dread of government, and fear of laws, into the unlimited freedom of the woods. This sudden change must have a very great effect on most men, and on that class particularly. Eating of wild meat, whatever you may think, tends to alter their temper; though all the proof I can adduce is, that I have seen it; and having no place of worship to resort to, what little society this might afford is denied them. The Sunday meetings, exclusive of religious benefits, were the only social bonds that might have inspired them with some degree of emulation in neatness. Is it then surprising to see men thus situated, immersed in great and heavy labors, degenerate a little? It is rather a wonder the effect is not more diffusive. The Moravians and the Quakers are the only instances in exception to what I have advanced. The first never settle singly; it is a colony of the society which emigrates; they

carry with them their forms, worship, rules, and decency; the others never begin so hard; they are always able to buy improvements, in which there is a great advantage, for by that time the country is recovered from its first barbarity. Thus our bad people are those who are half cultivators and half hunters; and the worst of them are those who have degenerated altogether into the hunting state. As old ploughmen and new men of the woods, as Europeans and new made Indians, they contract the vices of both; they adopt the moroseness and ferocity of a native, without his mildness or even his industry at home. If manners are not refined, at least they are rendered simple and inoffensive by tilling the earth; all our wants are supplied by it; our time is divided between labor and rest and leaves none for the commission of great misdeeds. As hunters, it is divided between the toil of the chase, the idleness of repose, or the indulgence of inebriation. Hunting is but a licentious idle life, and if it does not always pervert good dispositions, yet, when it is united with bad luck, it leads to want; want stimulates that propensity to rapacity and injustice, too natural to needy men, which is the fatal gradation. After this explanation of the effects which follow by living in the woods, shall we yet vainly flatter ourselves with the hope of converting the Indians? We should rather begin with converting our back-settlers; and now if I dare mention the name of religion, its sweet accents would be lost in the immensity of these woods. Men thus placed are not fit either to receive or remember its mild instructions; they want temples and ministers, but as soon as men cease to remain at home and begin to lead an erratic life, let them be either tawny or white, they cease to be its disciples.

Thus have I faintly and imperfectly endeavored to trace our society from the sea to our woods; yet you must not imagine that every person who moves back acts upon the same principles or falls into the same degeneracy. Many families carry with them all their decency of conduct, purity of morals, and respect of religion; but these are scarce; the power of example is sometimes irresistible. Even among these back-settlers, their depravity is greater or less, according to what nation or province they belong. Were I to adduce proofs of this, I might be accused of partiality. If there happen to be some rich intervals, some fertile bottoms, in those remote districts, the people will there prefer tilling the land to hunting, and will attach themselves to it; but even on these fertile spots you may plainly perceive the inhabitants to acquire a great degree of rusticity and selfishness.

It is in consequence of this straggling situation and the astonishing power it has on manners that the back-settlers of both the Carolinas, Virginia, and many other parts have been long a set of lawless people; it has been even dangerous to travel among them. Government can do nothing in so extensive a country; better it should wink at these irregularities than that it should use means inconsistent with its usual mildness. Time will efface those stains; in proportion as the great body of population approaches them they will reform and become polished and subordinate. Whatever has been said of the four New England provinces, no such degeneracy of manners has ever tarnished their annals; their back-settlers have been kept within the bounds of decency and government by means of wise laws and by the influence of religion. What a detestable idea such people [1] must have given to the natives of the Europeans! They trade with them; the worst of people are permitted to do that which none but persons of the best characters should be employed in. They get drunk with them and often defraud the Indians. Their avarice, removed from the eyes of their superiors, knows no bounds; and aided by the little superiority of knowledge, these traders deceive them, and even sometimes shed blood. Hence those shocking violations, those sudden devastations which have so often stained our frontiers when hundreds of innocent people have been sacrificed for the crimes of a few. It was in consequence of such behavior that the Indians took the hatchet against the Virginians in 1774. Thus are our first steps trod; thus are our first trees felled, in general, by the most vicious of our people; and thus the path is opened for the arrival of

[1] i.e., those described at the beginning of the paragraph

a second and better class, the true American freeholders; the most respectable set of people in this part of the world: respectable for their industry, their happy independence, the great share of freedom they possess, the good regulation of their families, and for extending the trade and the dominion of our mother country.

Europe contains hardly any other distinctions but lords and tenants; this fair country alone is settled by freeholders, the possessors of the soil they cultivate, members of the government they obey, and the framers of their own laws, by means of their representatives. This is a thought which you have taught me to cherish; our difference from Europe, far from diminishing, rather adds to our usefulness and consequence as men and subjects. Had our forefathers remained there, they would only have crowded it, and perhaps prolonged those convulsions which had shook it so long. Every industrious European who transports himself here may be compared to a sprout growing at the foot of a great tree; it enjoys and draws but a little portion of sap; wrench it from the parent roots, transplant it, and it will become a tree bearing fruit also. Colonists are therefore entitled to the consideration due to the most useful subjects; a hundred families, barely existing in some parts of Scotland, will here in six years cause an annual exportation of 10,000 bushels of wheat: 100 bushels being but a common quantity for an industrious family to sell, if they cultivate good land. It is here then that the idle may be employed, the useless become useful, and the poor become rich; but by riches I do not mean gold and silver; we have but little of those metals; I mean a better sort of wealth, cleared land, cattle, good houses, good clothes, and an increase of people to enjoy them.

There is no wonder that this country has so many charms and presents to Europeans so many temptations to remain in it. A traveller in Europe becomes a stranger as soon as he quits his own kingdom; but it is otherwise here. We know, properly speaking, no strangers; this is every person's country; the variety of our soils, situations, climates, governments, and produce, hath something which must please everybody. No sooner does an European arrive, no matter of what condition, than his eyes are opened upon the fair prospect; he hears his language spoken; he retraces many of his own country manners; he perpetually hears the names of families and towns with which he is acquainted; he sees happiness and prosperity in all places disseminated; he meets with hospitality, kindness, and plenty everywhere; he beholds hardly any poor; he seldom hears of punishments and executions; and he wonders at the elegance of our towns, those miracles of industry and freedom. He cannot admire enough our rural districts, our convenient roads, good taverns, and our many accommodations; he involuntarily loves a country where everything is so lovely. When in England, he was a mere Englishman; here he stands on a larger portion of the globe, not less than its fourth part, and may see the productions of the north in iron and naval stores; the provisions of Ireland, the grain of Egypt, the indigo, the rice of China. He does not find, as in Europe, a crowded society where every place is over-stocked; he does not feel that perpetual collision of parties, that difficulty of beginning, that contention which oversets so many. There is room for everybody in America; has he any particular talent or industry? He exerts it in order to procure a livelihood, and it succeeds. Is he a merchant? The avenues of trade are infinite. Is he eminent in any respect? He will be employed and respected. Does he love a country life? Pleasant farms present themselves; he may purchase what he wants, and thereby become an American farmer. Is he a laborer, sober and industrious? He need not go many miles nor receive many informations before he will be hired, well fed at the table of his employer, and paid four or five times more than he can get in Europe. Does he want uncultivated lands? Thousands of acres present themselves, which he may purchase cheap. Whatever be his talents or inclinations, if they are moderate, he may satisfy them. I do not mean that every one who comes will grow rich in a little time; no, but he may procure an easy, decent maintenance by his industry. Instead of starving he will be fed; instead of being idle he will have employment; and these are riches enough for such men as come over here. The rich

stay in Europe; it is only the middling and the poor that emigrate. Would you wish to travel in independent idleness from north to south, you will find easy access and the most cheerful reception at every house, society without ostentation, good cheer without pride, and every decent diversion which the country affords, with little expense. It is no wonder that the European who has lived here a few years is desirous to remain; Europe, with all its pomp, is not to be compared to this continent for men of middle stations or laborers.

A European, when he first arrives, seems limited in his intentions as well as in his views; but he very suddenly alters his scale; two hundred miles formerly appeared a very great distance; it is now but a trifle; he no sooner breathes our air than he forms schemes and embarks in designs he never would have thought of in his own country. There the plenitude of society confines many useful ideas and often extinguishes the most laudable schemes which here ripen into maturity. Thus Europeans become Americans.

But how is this accomplished in that crowd of low, indigent people who flock here every year from all parts of Europe? I will tell you; they no sooner arrive than they immediately feel the good effects of that plenty of provisions we possess; they fare on our best food, and they are kindly entertained; their talents, character, and peculiar industry are immediately inquired into; they find countrymen everywhere disseminated, let them come from whatever part of Europe. Let me select one as an epitome of the rest: he is hired, he goes to work, and works moderately; instead of being employed by a haughty person, he finds himself with his equal, placed at the substantial table of the farmer, or else at an inferior one as good; his wages are high, his bed is not like that bed of sorrow on which he used to lie; if he behaves with propriety and is faithful, he is caressed and becomes, as it were, a member of the family. He begins to feel the effects of a sort of resurrection; hitherto he had not lived, but simply vegetated; he now feels himself a man, because he is treated as such; the laws of his own country had overlooked him in his insignificancy; the laws of this cover him with their mantle. Judge what an alteration there must arise in the mind and thoughts of this man; he begins to forget his former servitude and dependence; his heart involuntarily swells and glows; this first swell inspires him with those new thoughts which constitute an American. What love can he entertain for a country where his existence was a burden to him; if he is a generous, good man, the love of this new adoptive parent will sink deep into his heart. He looks around and sees many a prosperous person, who but a few years before was as poor as himself. This encourages him much; he begins to form some little scheme, the first, alas, he ever formed in his life. If he is wise he thus spends two or three years, in which time he acquires knowledge, the use of tools, the modes of working the lands, felling trees, etc. This prepares the foundation of a good name, the most useful acquisition he can make. He is encouraged, he has gained friends; he is advised and directed, he feels bold, he purchases some land; he gives all the money he has brought over, as well as what he has earned, and trusts to the God of harvests for the discharge of the rest. His good name procures him credit. He is now possessed of the deed, conveying to him and his posterity the fee simple and absolute property of two hundred acres of land, situated on such a river. What an epoch in this man's life! He is become a freeholder, from perhaps a German boor—he is now an American, a Pennsylvanian, an English subject. He is naturalized, his name is enrolled with those of the other citizens of the province. Instead of being a vagrant, he has a place of residence; he is called the inhabitant of such a county, or of such a district, and for the first time in his life counts for something, for hitherto he has been a cipher. I only repeat what I have heard many say, and no wonder their hearts should glow and be agitated with a multitude of feelings not easy to describe. From nothing to start into being; from a servant to the rank of a master; from being the slave of some despotic prince, to become a free man, invested with lands, to which every municipal blessing is annexed! What a change indeed! It is in consequence of that change that he becomes an American. This great metamorphosis has a double effect; it extinguishes all his European prejudices; he forgets that mechanism of subordination, that servility of disposition which poverty had taught him; and sometimes he is apt to forget too much, often passing from one extreme to the other. If he is a good man, he forms schemes of future prosperity, he proposes to educate his children better than he has been educated himself; he thinks of future modes of conduct, feels an ardor to labor he never felt before. Pride steps in and leads him to everything that the laws do not forbid; he respects them; with a heartfelt gratitude he looks toward the east, toward that insular government from whose wisdom all his new felicity is derived, and under whose wings and protection he now lives. These reflections constitute him the good man and the good subject. Ye poor Europeans, ye who sweat and work for the great—ye who are obliged to give so many sheaves to the church, so many to your lords, so many to your government, and have hardly any left for yourselves—ye who are held in less estimation than favorite hunters or useless lapdogs—ye who only breathe the air of nature because it cannot be withheld from you; it is here that ye can conceive the possibility of those feelings I have been describing; it is here the laws of naturalization invite every one to partake of our great labors and felicity, to till unrented, untaxed lands! Many, corrupted beyond the power of amendment, have brought with them all their vices, and disregarding the advantages held to them, have gone on in their former career of iniquity until they have been overtaken and punished by our laws. It is not every emigrant who succeeds; no, it is only the sober, the honest, and industrious; happy those to whom this transition has served as a powerful spur to labor, to prosperity, and to the good establishment of children, born in the days of their poverty; and who had no other portion to expect but the rags of their parents, had it not been for their happy emigration. Others again have been led astray by this enchanting scene; their new pride, instead of leading them to the fields, has kept them in idleness; the idea of possessing lands is all that satisfies them—though surrounded with fertility, they have mouldered away their time in inactivity, misinformed husbandry, and ineffectual endeavors. How much wiser, in general, the honest Germans than almost all other Europeans; they hire themselves to some of their wealthy landsmen, and in that apprenticeship learn everything that is necessary. They attentively consider the prosperous industry of others, which imprints in their minds a strong desire of possessing the same advantages. This forcible idea never quits them, they launch forth, and by dint of sobriety, rigid parsimony, and the most persevering industry, they commonly succeed. Their astonishment at their first arrival from Germany is very great—it is to them a dream; the contrast must be powerful indeed; they observe their countrymen flourishing in every place; they travel through whole counties where not a word of English is spoken; and in the names and the language of the people, they retrace Germany. They have been a useful acquisition to this continent, and to Pennsylvania in particular; to them it owes some share of its prosperity; to their mechanical knowledge and patience it owes the finest mills in all America, the best teams of horses, and many other advantages. The recollection of their former poverty and slavery never quits them as long as they live.

The Scotch and the Irish might have lived in their own country perhaps as poor, but enjoying more civil advantages; the effects of their new situation do not strike them so forcibly, nor has it so lasting an effect. From whence the difference arises I know not, but out of twelve families of emigrants of each country, generally seven Scotch will succeed, nine German, and four Irish. The Scotch are frugal and laborious, but their wives cannot work so hard as German women, who, on the contrary, vie with husbands and often share with them the most severe toils of the field, which they understand better. They have therefore nothing to struggle against but the common casualties of nature. The Irish do not prosper so well; they love to drink and to quarrel; they are litigious and soon take to the gun, which is the ruin of everything; they seem beside to labor under a greater degree of ignorance in husbandry than the others; perhaps it is that their industry had less scope

and was less exercised at home. I have heard many relate how the land was parcelled out in that kingdom; their ancient conquest has been a great detriment to them by over-setting their landed property. The lands possessed by a few are leased down *ad infinitum*, and the occupiers often pay five guineas an acre. The poor are worse lodged there than anywhere else in Europe; their potatoes, which are easily raised, are perhaps an inducement to laziness; their wages are too low and their whisky too cheap.

There is no tracing observations of this kind, without making at the same time very great allowances, as there are everywhere to be found a great many exceptions. The Irish themselves, from different parts of that kingdom, are very different. It is difficult to account for this surprising locality; one would think on so small an island an Irishman must be an Irishman: yet it is not so: they are different in their aptitude to, and in their love of labor.

The Scotch on the contrary are all industrious and saving; they want nothing more than a field to exert themselves in, and they are commonly sure of succeeding. The only difficulty they labor under is that technical American knowledge which requires some time to obtain; it is not easy for those who seldom saw a tree to conceive how it is to be felled, cut up, and split into rails and posts. . . .

After a foreigner from any part of Europe is arrived and become a citizen, let him devoutly listen to the voice of our great parent, which says to him, "Welcome to my shores, distressed European; bless the hour in which thou didst see my verdant fields, my fair navigable rivers, and my green mountaines!— If thou wilt work, I have bread for thee; if thou wilt be honest, sober, and industrious, I have greater rewards to confer on thee— ease and independence. I will give thee fields to feed and clothe thee, a comfortable fireside to sit by and tell thy children by what means thou hast prospered, and a decent bed to repose on. I shall endow thee, besides, with the immunities of a freeman. If thou wilt carefully educate thy children, teach them gratitude to God and reverence to that government, that philanthropic government which has collected here so many men and made them happy. I will also provide for thy progeny; and to every good man this ought to be the most holy, the most powerful, the most earnest wish he can possibly form, as

c. 1770

well as the most consolatory prospect when he dies. Go thou and work and till; thou shalt prosper, provided thou be just, grateful, and industrious."

1782

1706 -- *Benjamin Franklin* -- 1790

BENJAMIN FRANKLIN was born in Boston and brought up "piously in a dissenting way." At the age of twelve he was apprenticed to his half-brother James, a printer of ability and initiative, who in 1721 started the fourth American newspaper, the *New England Courant*. During the next five years he read avidly in Locke, Shaftesbury, Defoe, Addison and Steele, Cotton Mather, Bunyan, and many other writers, cultivated the style of the *Spectator* in the *Silence Dogood* series of essays, and contributed anonymously to the *Courant*. In 1723, after a disagreement with his brother, he set out for Philadelphia, where he arrived with one Dutch dollar and a copper shilling in his pocket. An expert printer, he had no difficulty in finding work. He also found a patron in Governor Keith, who volunteered to set him up in business and in 1724 sent him to London to buy equipment. The promised letter of credit did not follow, however, and Franklin fell back upon his trade as his support during two instructive years in England. Back in Philadelphia in 1726, his unassisted rise was so rapid that by 1730 he was sole owner of the *Philadelphia Gazette*.

The next eighteen years he spent in building a fortune and a reputation. Landmarks in his career were the *Busy-Body* essays (1729), *Poor Richard's Almanac* (1732–1757), which sold widely and was much quoted for its homely, pungently expressed wisdom, and the *General Magazine and Historical Chronicle* (1741), the first magazine *projected* in the colonies. In the same years Franklin taught himself to read French, Spanish, Italian, and Latin, and aimed at "moral perfection" by listing thirteen principal virtues and pursuing each for four weeks at a time. In 1727 he started the Junto, a club which debated morals, politics, and natural philosophy, and in which he learned how to be tactfully persuasive. Meanwhile, as a public-spirited citizen, he helped establish in Philadelphia a circulating library, the American Philosophical Society, a city hospital, and the Academy for the Education of Youth, which became the University of Pennsylvania. He also served in the Assembly and was appointed to various offices, the most important being that of deputy postmaster of the colonies from 1753 to 1774, in which capacity he improved the service and made the post office a financial success, and familiarized himself with the country by visits of inspection which included every colony.

In his leisure he studied science, especially weather conditions, and invented the Franklin stove. By 1748 he was able to retire from business and devote himself to such pursuits as his important work on electricity, as a result of which he was elected a Fellow of the Royal Society. After six years, however, public affairs claimed him for the rest of his life.

In 1754 he secured the approval of a congress of delegates held at Albany for a union of the colonies, but his plan was rejected. From 1757 to 1762 he was in England as the agent of Pennsylvania on business arising from the French and Indian War. He had time, nevertheless, for travel, study, and experiment, time to know the great scientists, to correspond with Hume and Dr. Johnson, and to receive honorary degrees from St. Andrew's and from Oxford. His reputation as a diplomat and man of business increased, so that by 1770 he was again in London, representing not only Pennsylvania but Georgia, New Jersey, and Massachusetts also.

The decade 1770–1780, spent mainly in England and France, was the period of his most successful and enjoyable writing. To these years belong the earliest and best portion of his *Autobiography*, written in 1771; his humorous political satires, "An Edict by the King of Prussia" and "Rules by which a Great Empire may be Reduced to a Small One" (1773); his delightful "bagatelles," "The Ephemera" (1776) and "The Whistle" (1779); and his "Dialogue between Franklin and the Gout" (1780).

In 1775 he returned briefly to America to be a member of the Second Continental Congress, to sketch a Plan of Union, to reorganize the post office, and to help draft the Declaration of Independence. The next year he was sent to France as one of three commissioners to prevent France from joining with England against the colonies. Great was his popularity in that country, where he seemed a symbol in himself of the Age of Enlightenment. After concluding final treaties of commerce, he secured in 1778 the defensive alliance with France which was so very important in helping win the Revolution. Three years later Congress sent him with Adams and Jay to negotiate the treaty of peace with England, completed in 1783. His persuasion and tact were helpful at the Constitutional Convention of 1787, although several of his ideas were not adopted. His last public act before his death was to sign a memorial to Congress for the abolition of slavery.

The *Autobiography* rather definitely traces Franklin's literary and religious development. If, as is said, his first teacher was the witty, intelligent, and tart Madam Sarah Knight, he had a good induction to education. He was mainly, however, in the sense of owing little to formal schooling, self-educated, with the aid of sound counsel from his father and extensive and substantial reading. F. L. Mott and

Chester Jorgenson list seventy authors, "to suggest only the more prominent," whom he seems to have read. In the formation of his style, he tells of his rewriting of *Spectator* essays, his experiments with Socratic argument, his friendly rivalry with James Collins and the Junto members in writing and debating, and his long-continued training as a newspaper editor, who, he said, must have "great easiness and command of wit and relating things clearly and intelligently and in a few good words."

Overfed as a boy with religious exercises in his Presbyterian home, he turned rather eagerly, upon discovering it, to the rational system of the deists, as found in the writings of Anthony Collins and Shaftesbury, and adopted it as his own. Later, becoming convinced that deism did not furnish a sufficient moral basis for conduct, he abandoned it as a religious system for a creed of his own described in his letter to Ezra Stiles (p. 76), which, reduced to the simplest elements of the Christian belief, was in effect close to Unitarianism. The deistic emphasis upon the rule of reason, however, remained dominant in his thinking throughout life; as did his idea of doing good to one's fellows, early implanted in his mind by Cotton Mather's "Essays to Do Good," as a more fitting form of worship than church attendance.

Politically and economically, Franklin adhered to the Whig doctrine founded upon natural rights and the social contract theory as set forth by Locke, supported by Newton's physical rationalism. As long as it was possible for him, he worked energetically for the idea of the British empire in its largest scope. His hopes frustrated by a short-sighted ministry and by the turn of events in America, he changed to the support of the Revolution and the erection of a strong and independent American nation. Though agrarian in feeling, he was no doctrinaire democrat, insisting as much upon obedience to the government as upon the rights of the governed. As an imperialist, he was, like Adam Smith, an advocate of free trade, and as a Whig he held to the ideas of laissez-faire and a government of limited powers.

Franklin was a New Englander, emancipated from narrowness by transfer to the freer atmosphere of the Middle Colonies and later to that of European courts. His point of view is that of the Yankee, expanded by the urbanity and liberalized philosophy, and the intellectual curiosity of eighteenth-century England and France. His dominant traits were shrewdness, thrift, common sense, and public spirit. He had a part in every intellectual and social movement of his age in America, from the introduction of street sweeping to spelling reform and antislavery agitation. The importance of these activities has naturally overshadowed his accomplishments as our first noteworthy familiar essayist, perhaps our best master of ironical yet genial political satire, and the author of one of the best pieces of autobiography in English. His wit is rarely bitter although it leans to a cynicism hardly surprising in a man who had seen so much of the world in so many strata of society.

That world he accepted with intelligence, tranquillity, and common sense. As a writer, he was our first great realist.

The best editions of Franklin's works are *The Complete Works of Benjamin Franklin* (10 vols., 1887–1888), edited by John Bigelow; and *The Writings of Benjamin Franklin, Collected and Edited with Life and Introduction* (10 vols., 1905–1907), by A. H. Smythe. The best edition of the *Autobiography* is by John Bigelow (3 vols., 1874). Excellent representative selections of his work are F. L. Mott and C. E. Jorgenson's *Benjamin Franklin* (1936), with useful introduction and bibliography; and C. Van Doren's *Franklin and Edwards* (1920). P. L. Ford issued the *Franklin Bibliography* in 1889.

The following biographies are worth noting: James Parton, *The Life and Times of Benjamin Franklin* (2 vols., 1864); J. B. McMaster, *Benjamin Franklin as a Man of Letters* (1887); S. G. Fisher, *The True Benjamin Franklin* (1899); P. L. Ford, *The Many-Sided Franklin* (1899); J. C. Oswald, *Benjamin Franklin, Printer* (1917); W. C. Bruce, *Benjamin Franklin Self-Revealed* (2 vols., 1917); Bernard Faÿ, *Franklin, the Apostle of Modern Times* (1929); A. H. Smythe, *Life of Franklin*, Vol. X, 141–510, of *The Writings of Benjamin Franklin* (1907); Carl Van Doren, *Benjamin Franklin* (1938). The detailed article in *DAB* is by Carl L. Becker, and that in the *Encyclopædia Britannica*, 14th edition, by Bernard Faÿ.

See also A. W. Wetzel, *Benjamin Franklin as an Economist*, in *Johns Hopkins University Studies*, XIII (1895); J. M. Stifler, *The Religion of Benjamin Franklin* (1925); M. R. Eiselen, *Franklin's Political Theories* (1928); L. M. MacLaurin, *Franklin's Vocabulary* (1928); W. G. Bleyer, *Main Currents in the History of American Journalism* (1927), Chaps. I and II; S. P. Sherman, "Franklin and the Age of Enlightenment," in *Americans* (1922).

From the AUTOBIOGRAPHY

[*Reasons for Writing*]

Twyford, at the Bishop of St. Asaph's, 1771

DEAR SON, I have ever had a pleasure in obtaining any little anecdotes of my ancestors. You may remember the inquiries I made among the remains of my relations when you were with me in England, and the journey I undertook for that purpose. Now imagining it may be equally agreeable to you to know the circumstances of *my* life, many of which you are yet unacquainted with, and expecting a week's uninterrupted leisure in my present country retirement, I sit down to write them for you. To which I have besides some other inducements. Having emerged from the poverty and obscurity in which I was born and bred, to a state of affluence and some degree of reputation in the world, and having gone so far through life with a considerable share of felicity, the conducing means I made use of, which with the blessing of God so well succeeded, my posterity may like to know, as they may find some of them suitable to their own situations, and therefore fit to be imitated.

That felicity, when I reflected on it, has induced me sometimes to say that were it offered to my choice, I should have no objection to a repetition of the same life from its beginning, only asking the advantages authors have in a second edition to correct some faults of the first. So would I, if I might, besides correcting the faults, change some sinister accidents and events of it for others more favorable. But though this were denied, I should still accept the offer. However, since such a repetition is not to be expected, the next thing most like living one's life over again seems to be a *recollection* of that life, and to make that recollection as durable as possible, the putting it down in writing.

Hereby, too, I shall indulge the inclination so natural in old men, to be talking of themselves and their own past actions; and I shall indulge it without being troublesome to others, who, through respect to age, might think themselves obliged to give me a hearing, since this may be read or not as any one pleases.

And, lastly (I may as well confess it, since my denial of it will be believed by nobody), perhaps I shall a good deal gratify my own *vanity*. Indeed, I scarce ever heard or saw the introductory words, *Without vanity I may say*, &c., but some vain thing immediately followed. Most people dislike vanity in others, whatever share they have of it themselves; but I give it fair quarter wherever I meet with it, being persuaded that it is often productive of good to the possessor, and to others that are within his sphere of action; and therefore, in many cases, it would not be quite absurd if a man were to thank God for his vanity among the other comforts of life. . . .

[Early Reading and Self-Cultivation]

From a child I was fond of reading, and all the little money that came into my hands was ever laid out in books. Pleased with the *Pilgrim's Progress*, my first collection was of John Bunyan's works in separate little volumes. I afterward sold them to enable me to buy R. Burton's *Historical Collections;* they were small chapmen's books, and cheap, forty or fifty in all. My father's little library consisted chiefly of books in polemic divinity, most of which I read, and have since often regretted that, at a time when I had such a thirst for knowledge, more proper books had not fallen in my way, since it was now resolved I should not be a clergyman. *Plutarch's Lives* there was, in which I read abundantly, and I still think that time spent to great advantage. There was also a book of Defoe's, called an *Essay on Projects*, and another of Dr. Mather's, called *Essays to Do Good*, which perhaps gave me a turn of thinking that had an influence on some of the principal future events of my life.

This bookish inclination at length determined my father to make me a printer, though he had already one son (James) of that profession. In 1717 my brother James returned from England with a press and letters, to set up his business in Boston. I liked it much better than that of my father, but still had a hankering for the sea. To prevent the apprehended effect of such an inclination, my father was impatient to have me bound to my brother. I stood out some time, but at last was persuaded, and signed the indentures when I was yet but twelve years old. I was to serve as an apprentice till I was twenty-one years of age, only I was to be allowed journeyman's wages during the last year. In a little time I made great proficiency in the business, and became a useful hand to my brother. I now had access to better books. An acquaintance with the apprentices of booksellers enabled me sometimes to borrow a small one, which I was careful to return soon and clean. Often I sat up in my room reading the greatest part of the night, when the book was borrowed in the evening and to be returned early in the morning, lest it should be missed or wanted.

And after some time an ingenious tradesman, Mr. Matthew Adams, who had a pretty collection of books, and who frequented our printing-house, took notice of me, invited me to his library, and very kindly lent me such books as I chose to read. I now took a fancy to poetry, and made some little pieces; my brother, thinking it might turn to account, encouraged me, and put me on composing two occasional ballads. One was called *The Lighthouse Tragedy*, and contained an account of the drowning of Captain Worthilake, with his two daughters; the other was a sailor's song, on the taking of Teach (or Blackbeard), the pirate. They were wretched stuff, in the Grub Street ballad style; and when they were printed he sent me about the town to sell them. The first sold wonderfully, the event, being recent, having made a great noise. This flattered my vanity; but my father discouraged me by ridiculing my performances, and telling me verse-makers were generally beggars. So I escaped being a poet, most probably a very bad one; but as prose writing has been of great use to me in the course of my life, and was a principal means of my advancement, I shall tell you how, in such a situation, I acquired what little ability I have in that way.

There was another bookish lad in the town, John Collins by name, with whom I was intimately acquainted. We sometimes disputed, and very fond we were of argument, and very desirous of confuting one another, which disputatious turn, by the way, is apt to become a very bad habit, making people often extremely disagreeable in company by the contradiction that is necessary to bring it into practice; and thence, besides souring and spoiling the conversation, is productive of disgusts and perhaps enmities where you may have occasion for friendship. I had caught it by reading my father's books of dispute about religion. Persons of good sense, I have since observed, seldom fall into it, except lawyers, university men, and men of all sorts that have been bred at Edinburgh.

A question was once, somehow or other, started between Collins and me, of the propriety of educating the female sex in learning, and their abilities for study. He was of opinion that it was improper, and that they were naturally unequal to it. I took the contrary side, perhaps a little for dispute's sake. He was naturally more eloquent, had a ready plenty of words; and sometimes, as I thought, bore me down more by his fluency than by the strength of his reasons. As we parted without settling the point, and were not to see one another again for some time, I sat down to put my arguments in writing, which I copied fair and sent to him. He answered, and I replied. Three or four letters of a side had passed, when my father happened to find my papers and read them. Without entering into the discussion, he took occasion to talk to me about the manner of my writing; observed that, though I had the advantage of my antagonist in correct spelling and pointing (which I owed to the printing-house), I fell far short in elegance of expression, in method, and in perspicuity, of which he convinced me by several instances. I saw the justice of his remarks, and thence grew more attentive to the *manner* in writing, and determined to endeavor at improvement.

About this time I met with an odd volume of the *Spectator*. It was the third. I had never before seen any of them. I bought it, read it over and over, and was much delighted with it. I thought the writing excellent, and wished, if possible, to imitate it. With that view I took some of the papers, and making short hints of the sentiment in each sentence, laid them by a few days, and then, without looking at the book, tried to complete the papers again, by expressing each hinted sentiment at length, and as fully as it had been expressed before,

in any suitable words that should come to hand. Then I compared my *Spectator* with the original, discovered some of my faults, and corrected them. But I found I wanted a stock of words, or a readiness in recollecting and using them, which I thought I should have acquired before that time if I had gone on making verses; since the continual occasion for words of the same import, but of different length, to suit the measure, or of different sound for the rhyme, would have laid me under a constant necessity of searching for variety, and also have tended to fix that variety in my mind, and make me master of it. Therefore I took some of the tales and turned them into verse; and, after a time, when I had pretty well forgotten the prose, turned them back again. I also sometimes jumbled my collections of hints into confusion, and after some weeks endeavored to reduce them into the best order, before I began to form the full sentences and complete the paper. This was to teach me method in the arrangement of thoughts. By comparing my work afterwards with the original, I discovered many faults and amended them; but I sometimes had the pleasure of fancying that, in certain particulars of small import, I had been lucky enough to improve the method or the language, and this encouraged me to think I might possibly in time come to be a tolerable English writer, of which I was extremely ambitious. My time for these exercises and for reading was at night, after work, or before it began in the morning, or on Sundays, when I contrived to be in the printing-house alone, evading as much as I could the common attendance on public worship which my father used to exact of me when I was under his care, and which indeed I still thought a duty, though I could not, as it seemed to me, afford the time to practice it.

When about sixteen years of age I happened to meet with a book, written by one Tryon, recommending a vegetable diet, I determined to go into it. My brother, being yet unmarried, did not keep house, but boarded himself and his apprentices in another family. My refusing to eat flesh caused an inconveniency, and I was frequently chid for my singularity. I made myself acquainted with Tryon's manner of preparing some of his dishes, such as boiling potatoes or rice, making hasty pudding, and a few others, and then proposed to my brother that if he would give me, weekly, half the money he paid for my board, I would board myself. He instantly agreed to it, and I presently found that I could save half what he paid me. This was an additional fund for buying books. But I had another advantage in it. My brother and the rest going from the printing-house to their meals, I remained there alone, and dispatching presently my light repast, which often was no more than a biscuit or a slice of bread, a handful of raisins or a tart from the pastry-cook's, and a glass of water, had the rest of the time till their return for study, in which I made the greater progress, from that greater clearness of head and quicker apprehension which usually attend temperance in eating and drinking.

And now it was that, being on some occasion made ashamed of my ignorance in figures, which I had twice failed in learning when at school, I took Cocker's book of Arithmetic, and went through the whole by myself with great ease. I also read Seller's and Sturmy's books of Navigation, and became acquainted with the little geometry they contain; but never proceeded far in that science. And I read about this time Locke *On Human Understanding* and the *Art of Thinking* by Messrs. du Port Royal.

While I was intent on improving my language, I met with an English grammar (I think it was Greenwood's), at the end of which there were two little sketches of the arts of rhetoric and logic, the latter finishing with a specimen of a dispute in the Socratic method; and soon after I procured Xenophon's *Memorable Things of Socrates*, wherein there are many instances of the same method. I was charmed with it, adopted it, dropped my abrupt contradiction and positive argumentation, and put on the humble inquirer and doubter. And being then, from reading Shaftesbury and Collins, become a real doubter in many points of our religious doctrine, I found this method safest for myself and very embarrassing to those against whom I used it; therefore I took a delight in it, practiced it continually, and grew very artful and expert in drawing people, even of superior knowl-

edge, into concessions the consequences of which they did not foresee, entangling them in difficulties out of which they could not extricate themselves, and so obtaining victories that neither myself nor my cause always deserved. I continued this method some few years, but gradually left it, retaining only the habit of expressing myself in terms of modest diffidence; never using, when I advanced anything that may possibly be disputed, the words *certainly, undoubtedly,* or any others that give the air of positiveness to an opinion; but rather say, I conceive or I apprehend a thing to be so or so; it appears to me, or I should think it so or so, for such and such reasons; or I imagine it to be so; or it is so if I am not mistaken. This habit, I believe, has been of great advantage to me when I have had occasion to inculcate my opinions, and persuade men into measures that I have been from time to time engaged in promoting; and as the chief ends of conversation are to *inform* or to be *informed,* to *please* or to *persuade,* I wish well-meaning, sensible men would not lessen their power of doing good by a positive, assuming manner, that seldom fails to disgust, tends to create opposition, and to defeat every one of those purposes for which speech was given us, to wit, giving or receiving information or pleasure. For if you would inform, a positive, dogmatical manner in advancing your sentiments may provoke contradiction and prevent a candid attention. If you wish information and improvement from the knowledge of others, and yet at the same time express yourself as firmly fixed in your present opinions, modest, sensible men who do not love disputation will probably leave you undisturbed in possession of your error. And by such a manner you can seldom hope to recommend yourself in *pleasing* your hearers, or to persuade those whose concurrence you desire.

[*Journey to Philadelphia*]

I then thought of going to New York, as the nearest place where there was a printer; and I was rather inclined to leave Boston when I reflected that I had already made myself a little obnoxious to the governing party, and from the arbitrary proceedings of the

Assembly in my brother's case, it was likely I might, if I stayed, soon bring myself into scrapes; and further, that my indiscreet disputations about religion began to make me pointed at with horror by good people as an infidel or atheist. I determined on the point, but my father now siding with my brother, I was sensible that if I attempted to go openly, means would be used to prevent me. My friend Collins, therefore, undertook to manage a little for me. He agreed with the captain of a New York sloop for my passage, under the notion of my being a young acquaintance of his who had got a naughty girl with child, whose friends would compel me to marry her, and therefore I could not appear or come away publicly. So I sold some of my books to raise a little money, was taken on board privately, and as we had a fair wind, in three days I found myself in New York, near three hundred miles from home, a boy of but seventeen, without the least recommendation to, or knowledge of, any person in the place, and with very little money in my pocket.

My inclinations for the sea were by this time worn out, or I might now have gratified them. But, having a trade, and supposing myself a pretty good workman, I offered my service to the printer in the place, old Mr. William Bradford, who had been the first printer in Pennsylvania, but removed from thence upon the quarrel of George Keith. He could give me no employment, having little to do, and help enough already; but says he, "My son at Philadelphia has lately lost his principal hand, Aquila Rose, by death; if you go thither, I believe he may employ you." Philadelphia was a hundred miles further; I set out, however, in a boat for Amboy, leaving my chest and things to follow me round by sea.

In crossing the bay, we met with a squall that tore our rotten sails to pieces, prevented our getting into the Kill, and drove us upon Long Island. In our way, a drunken Dutchman, who was a passenger too, fell overboard; when he was sinking, I reached through the water to his shock pate, and drew him up, so that we got him in again. His ducking sobered him a little, and he went to sleep, taking first out of his pocket a book, which he desired I would dry for him. It proved to be my old favorite author, Bunyan's *Pilgrim's Progress*, in Dutch, finely printed on good paper, with copper cuts, a dress better than I had ever seen it wear in its own language. I have since found that it has been translated into most of the languages of Europe, and suppose it has been more generally read than any other book, except perhaps the Bible. Honest John was the first that I know of who mixed narration and dialogue; a method of writing very engaging to the reader, who in the most interesting parts finds himself, as it were, brought into the company and present at the discourse. Defoe in his *Crusoe*, his *Moll Flanders*, *Religious Courtship*, *Family Instructor*, and other pieces, has imitated it with success, and Richardson has done the same in his *Pamela*, etc.

When we drew near the island, we found it was at a place where there could be no landing, there being a great surf on the stony beach. So we dropped anchor, and swung round towards the shore. Some people came down to the water edge and hallooed to us, as we did to them; but the wind was so high, and the surf so loud, that we could not hear so as to understand each other. There were canoes on the shore, and we made signs, and hallooed that they should fetch us; but they either did not understand us or thought it impracticable, so they went away, and night coming on, we had no remedy but to wait till the wind should abate; and, in the meantime, the boatman and I concluded to sleep, if we could; and so crowded into the scuttle, with the Dutchman, who was still wet; and the spray beating over the head of our boat, leaked through to us, so that we were soon almost as wet as he. In this manner we lay all night, with very little rest; but the wind abating the next day, we made a shift to reach Amboy before night, having been thirty hours on the water, without victuals, or any drink but a bottle of filthy rum, the water we sailed on being salt.

In the evening I found myself very feverish, and went in to bed; but having read somewhere that cold water drunk plentifully was good for a fever, I followed the prescription, sweat plentifully most of the night, my fever left me, and in the morning, crossing the ferry, I proceeded on my journey on foot, having fifty miles to Burlington, where I was told I should find boats that would carry me the rest of the way to Philadelphia.

It rained very hard all the day; I was thoroughly soaked, and by noon a good deal tired; so I stopped at a poor inn, where I stayed all night, beginning now to wish that I had never left home. I cut so miserable a figure, too, that I found, by the questions asked me, I was suspected to be some runaway servant, and in danger of being taken up on that suspicion. However, I proceeded the next day, and got in the evening to an inn, within eight or ten miles of Burlington, kept by one Dr. Brown. He entered into conversation with me while I took some refreshment, and, finding I had read a little, became very sociable and friendly. Our acquaintance continued as long as he lived. He had been, I imagine, an itinerant doctor, for there was no town in England, or country in Europe, of which he could not give a very particular account. He had some letters, and was ingenious, but much of an unbeliever, and wickedly undertook, some years after, to travesty the Bible in doggerel verse, as Cotton had done Virgil. By this means he set many of the facts in a very ridiculous light, and might have hurt weak minds if his work had been published, but it never was.

At his house I lay that night, and the next morning reached Burlington, but had the mortification to find that the regular boats were gone a little before my coming, and no other expected to go before Tuesday, this being Saturday; wherefore I returned to an old woman in the town, of whom I had bought gingerbread to eat on the water, and asked her advice. She invited me to lodge at her house till a passage by water should offer; and being tired with my foot traveling, I accepted the invitation. She, understanding I was a printer, would have had me stay at that town and follow my business, being ignorant of the stock necessary to begin with. She was very hospitable, gave me a dinner of ox-cheek with great good will, accepting only a pot of ale in return; and I thought myself fixed till Tuesday should come. However, walking in the evening by the side of the river, a boat came by, which I found was going towards Philadelphia, with several people in her. They took me in, and, as there was no wind, we rowed all the way; and about midnight, not having yet seen the city, some of the company were confident we must have passed it, and would row no farther; the others knew not where we were; so we put toward the shore, got into a creek, landed near an old fence, with the rails of which we made a fire, the night being cold, in October, and there we remained till daylight. Then one of the company knew the place to be Cooper's Creek, a little above Philadelphia, which we saw as soon as we got out of the creek, and arrived there about eight or nine o'clock on the Sunday morning, and landed at the Market Street wharf.

I have been the more particular in this description of my journey, and shall be so of my first entry into that city, that you may in your mind compare such unlikely beginnings with the figure I have since made there. I was in my working-dress, my best clothes being to come round by sea. I was dirty from my journey; my pockets were stuffed out with shirts and stockings, and I knew no soul nor where to look for lodging. I was fatigued with traveling, rowing, and want of rest, I was very hungry; and my whole stock of cash consisted of a Dutch dollar, and about a shilling in copper. The latter I gave the people of the boat for my passage, who at first refused it on account of my rowing; but I insisted on their taking it. A man being sometimes more generous when he has but a little money than when he has plenty, perhaps through fear of being thought to have but little.

Then I walked up the street, gazing about, till, near the market-house, I met a boy with bread. I had made many a meal on bread, and, inquiring where he got it, I went immediately to the baker's he directed me to, in Second Street, and asked for biscuit, intending such as we had in Boston; but they, it seems, were not made in Philadelphia. Then I asked for a three-penny loaf, and was told they had none such. So, not considering or knowing the difference of money, and the greater cheapness nor the names of his bread, I bade him give me three-penny worth of any sort. He gave me, accordingly, three great puffy rolls. I was surprised at the quantity, but took it, and, having no room in my pockets, walked off with a roll under each arm, and eating the other. Thus I went up Market Street as far as Fourth Street, passing by the door of Mr. Read, my future wife's father; when she, standing at the door, saw me, and thought I made, as I certainly did, a most awkward, ridiculous appearance. Then I turned and went down 10 Chestnut Street, and part of Walnut Street, eating my roll all the way, and, coming round, found myself again at Market Street wharf, near the boat I came in, to which I went for a draught of the river water; and, being filled with one of my rolls, gave the other two to a woman and her child that came down the river in the boat with us, and were waiting to go farther.

Thus refreshed, I walked again up the 20 street, which by this time had many clean-dressed people in it, who were all walking the same way. I joined them, and thereby was led into the great meeting-house of the Quakers, near the market. I sat down among them, and, after looking round a while and hearing nothing said, being very drowsy through labor and want of rest the preceding night, I fell fast asleep, and continued so till the meeting broke up, when one was kind enough to rouse me. 30 This was, therefore, the first house I was in, or slept in, in Philadelphia.

[Employed as Printer in Philadelphia]

Walking down again toward the river, and looking in the faces of people, I met a young Quaker man, whose countenance I liked, and, accosting him, requested he would tell me where a stranger could get lodging. We were 40 then near the sign of the Three Mariners. "Here," says he, "is one place that entertains strangers, but it is not a reputable house; if thee wilt walk with me, I'll show thee a better." He brought me to the Crooked Billet in Water Street. Here I got a dinner; and while I was eating it, several sly questions were asked me, as it seemed to be suspected from my youth and appearance that I might be some run-away.

After dinner, my sleepiness returned, and 50

being shown to a bed, I lay down without undressing and slept till six in the evening, was called to supper, went to bed again very early, and slept soundly till next morning. Then I made myself as tidy as I could, and went to Andrew Bradford the printer's. I found in the shop the old man his father, whom I had seen at New York, and who, traveling on horseback, had got to Philadelphia before me. He introduced me to his son, who received me civilly, gave me a breakfast, but told me he did not at present want a hand, being lately supplied with one; but there was another printer in town, lately set up, one Keimer, who, perhaps, might employ me; if not, I should be welcome to lodge at his house and he would give me a little work to do now and then till fuller business should offer.

The old gentleman said he would go with me to the new printer; and when we found him, "Neighbor," says Bradford, "I have brought to see you a young man of your business; perhaps you may want such a one." He asked me a few questions, put a composing stick in my hand to see how I worked, and then said he would employ me soon, though he had just then nothing for me to do; and taking old Bradford, whom he had never seen before, to be one of the town's people that had a good will for him, entered into a conversation on his present undertaking and prospects; while Bradford, not discovering [1] that he was the other printer's father, on Keimer's saying he expected soon to get the greatest part of the business into his own hands, drew him on by artful questions, and starting little doubts, to explain all his views, what interests he relied on, and in what manner he intended to proceed. I, who stood by and heard all, saw immediately that one of them was a crafty old sophister, and the other a mere novice. Bradford left me with Keimer, who was greatly surprised when I told him who the old man was.

Keimer's printing-house, I found, consisted of an old shattered press, and one small, worn-out font of English, which he was then using himself, composing an Elegy on Aquila Rose, before mentioned, an ingenious young man of excellent character, much respected in the

[1] revealing

town, clerk of the Assembly, and a pretty poet. Keimer made verses too, but very indifferently. He could not be said to write them, for his manner was to compose them in the types directly out of his head. So there being no copy, but one pair of cases, and the Elegy likely to require all the letter,[1] no one could help him. I endeavored to put his press (which he had not yet used, and of which he understood nothing) into order fit to be worked with; and promising to come and print off his Elegy as soon as he should have got it ready, I returned to Bradford's, who gave me a little job to do for the present, and there I lodged and dieted. A few days after, Keimer sent for me to print off the Elegy. And now he had got another pair of cases, and a pamphlet to reprint, on which he set me to work.

These two printers I found poorly qualified for their business. Bradford had not been bred to it, and was very illiterate; and Keimer, though something of a scholar, was a mere compositor knowing nothing of presswork. He had been one of the French prophets, and could act their enthusiastic agitations. At this time he did not profess any particular religion, but something of all on occasion; was very ignorant of the world, and had, as I afterward found, a good deal of the knave in his composition. He did not like my lodging at Bradford's while I worked with him. He had a house indeed, but without furniture, so he could not lodge me; but he got me a lodging at Mr. Read's before mentioned, who was the owner of his house; and my chest and clothes being come by this time, I made rather a more respectable appearance in the eyes of Miss Read than I had done when she first happened to see me eating my roll in the street.

I began now to have some acquaintance among the young people of the town that were lovers of reading, with whom I spent my evenings very pleasantly; and gaining money by my industry and frugality, I lived very agreeably, forgetting Boston as much as I could, and not desiring that any there should know where I resided except my friend Collins, who was in my secret, and kept it when I wrote to him. At length, an incident happened that sent me back again much sooner

¹ type

than I had intended. I had a brother-in-law, Robert Holmes, master of a sloop that traded between Boston and Delaware. He being at Newcastle, forty miles below Philadelphia, heard there of me, and wrote me a letter mentioning the concern of my friends in Boston at my abrupt departure, assuring me of their good will to me, and that everything would be accommodated to my mind if I would return, to which he exhorted me very earnestly. I wrote an answer to his letter, thanked him for his advice, but stated my reasons for quitting Boston fully and in such a light as to convince him I was not so wrong as he had apprehended.

Sir William Keith, governor of the province, was then at Newcastle, and Captain Holmes, happening to be in company with him when my letter came to hand, spoke to him of me, and showed him the letter. The governor read it, and seemed surprised when he was told my age. He said I appeared a young man of promising parts, and therefore should be encouraged; the printers of Philadelphia were wretched ones; and, if I would set up there, he made no doubt I should succeed; for his part, he would procure me the public business, and do me every other service in his power. This my brother-in-law afterwards told me in Boston, but I knew as yet nothing of it; when, one day, Keimer and I being at work together near the window, we saw the governor and another gentleman (which proved to be Colonel French of Newcastle), finely dressed, come directly across the street to our house, and heard them at the door.

Keimer ran down immediately, thinking it a visit to him; but the governor inquired for me, came up, and with a condescension and politeness I had been quite unused to made me many compliments, desired to be acquainted with me, blamed me kindly for not having made myself known to him when I first came to the place, and would have me away with him to the tavern, where he was going with Colonel French to taste, as he said, some excellent Madeira. I was not a little surprised, and Keimer stared like a pig poisoned. I went, however, with the governor and Colonel French to a tavern, at the corner of Third Street, and over the Madeira he proposed my setting up my business, laid before me the probabilities of success, and both he and Colonel French assured me I should have their interest and influence in procuring the public business of both governments. On my doubting whether my father would assist me in it, Sir William said he would give me a letter to him, in which he would state the advantages, and he did not doubt of prevailing with him. So it was concluded I should return to Boston in the first vessel, with the governor's letter recommending me to my father. In the meantime the intention was to be kept a secret, and I went on working with Keimer as usual, the governor sending for me now and then to dine with him, a very great honor I thought it, and conversing with me in the most affable, familiar, and friendly manner imaginable.

[Trip to Boston and Back]

About the end of April, 1724, a little vessel offered for Boston. I took leave of Keimer as going to see my friends. The governor gave me an ample letter, saying many flattering things of me to my father, and strongly recommending the project of my setting up at Philadelphia as a thing that must make my fortune. We struck on a shoal in going down the bay, and sprung a leak; we had a blustering time at sea, and were obliged to pump almost continually, at which I took my turn. We arrived safe, however, at Boston in about a fortnight. I had been absent seven months, and my friends had heard nothing of me; for my brother Holmes was not yet returned and had not written about me. My unexpected appearance surprised the family; all were, however, very glad to see me, and made me welcome, except my brother. I went to see him at his printing-house. I was better dressed than ever while in his service, having a genteel new suit from head to foot, a watch, and my pockets lined with near five pounds sterling in silver. He received me not very frankly, looked me all over, and turned to his work again.

The journeymen were inquisitive where I had been, what sort of a country it was, and

how I liked it. I praised it much, and the happy life I led in it; expressing strongly my intention of returning to it; and one of them asking what kind of money we had there, I produced a handful of silver, and spread it before them, which was a kind of raree show they had not been used to, paper being the money of Boston. Then I took an opportunity of letting them see my watch; and, lastly (my brother still grum and sullen), I gave them a piece of eight to drink, and took my leave. This visit of mine offended him extremely; for, when my mother some time after spoke to him of a reconciliation, and of her wishes to see us on good terms together and that we might live for the future as brothers, he said I had insulted him in such a manner before his people that he could never forget or forgive it. In this, however, he was mistaken.

My father received the governor's letter with some apparent surprise, but said little of it to me for some days, when Captain Holmes returning he showed it to him, asked him if he knew Keith, and what kind of man he was; adding his opinion that he must be of small discretion to think of setting a boy up in business who wanted yet three years of being at man's estate. Holmes said what he could in favor of the project, but my father was clear in the impropriety of it, and at last gave a flat denial to it. Then he wrote a civil letter to Sir William, thanking him for the patronage he had so kindly offered me, but declining to assist me as yet in setting up, I being, in his opinion, too young to be trusted with the management of a business so important, and for which the preparation must be so expensive.

My friend and companion Collins, who was a clerk in the post office, pleased with the account I gave him of my new country, determined to go thither also; and, while I waited for my father's determination, he set out before me by land to Rhode Island, leaving his books, which were a pretty collection of mathematics and natural philosophy, to come with mine and me to New York, where he proposed to wait for me.

My father, though he did not approve Sir William's proposition, was yet pleased that I had been able to obtain so advantageous a character from a person of such note where I had resided, and that I had been so industrious and careful as to equip myself so handsomely in so short a time; therefore, seeing no prospect of an accommodation between my brother and me, he gave his consent to my returning again to Philadelphia, advised me to behave respectfully to the people there, endeavor to obtain the general esteem, and avoid lampooning and libelling, to which he thought I had too much inclination; telling me, that by steady industry and a prudent parsimony I might save enough by the time I was one-and-twenty to set me up; and that, if I came near the matter, he would help me out with the rest. This was all I could obtain, except some small gifts as tokens of his and my mother's love, when I embarked again for New York, now with their approbation and their blessing.

The sloop putting in at Newport, Rhode Island, I visited my brother John, who had been married and settled there some years. He received me very affectionately, for he always loved me. A friend of his, one Vernon, having some money due to him in Pennsylvania, about 35 pounds currency, desired I would receive it for him, and keep it till I had his directions what to remit it in. Accordingly he gave me an order. This afterwards occasioned me a good deal of uneasiness. At Newport we took in a number of passengers for New York, among which were two young women, companions, and a grave, sensible matron-like Quaker woman with her attendants. I had shown an obliging readiness to do her some little services which impressed her, I suppose, with a degree of good will towards me. Therefore when she saw a daily growing familiarity between me and the two young women, which they appeared to encourage, she took me aside and said, "Young man, I am concerned for thee, as thou hast no friend with thee, and seems not to know much of the world, or of the snares youth is exposed to; depend upon it, those are very bad women. I can see it in all their actions, and if thee art not upon thy guard, they will draw thee into some danger: they are strangers to thee, and I advise thee in a friendly concern for thy welfare, to have no acquaintance with them."

As I seemed at first not to think so ill of them as she did, she mentioned some things she had observed and heard that had escaped my notice, but now convinced me she was right. I thanked her for her kind advice, and promised to follow it. When we arrived at New York, they told me where they lived and invited me to come and see them; but I avoided it. And it was well I did, for the next day the Captain missed a silver spoon and some other things that had been taken out of his cabin, and knowing that these were a couple of strumpets, he got a warrant to search their lodgings, found the stolen goods, and had the thieves punished. So though we had escaped a sunken rock which we scraped upon in the passage, I thought this escape of rather more importance to me.

At New York I found my friend Collins, who had arrived there some time before me. We had been intimate from children, and had read the same books together; but he had the advantage of more time for reading and studying, and a wonderful genius for mathematical learning, in which he far outstripped me. While I lived in Boston most of my hours of leisure for conversation were spent with him, and he continued a sober as well as an industrious lad; was much respected for his learning by several of the clergy and other gentlemen, and seemed to promise making a good figure in life: but during my absence he had acquired a habit of sotting with brandy; and I found by his own account and what I heard from others, that he had been drunk every day since his arrival at New York, and behaved very oddly. He had gamed too and lost his money, so that I was obliged to discharge his lodgings and defray his expenses to and at Philadelphia, which proved extremely inconvenient to me. The then Governor of New York, Burnet, son of Bishop Burnet, hearing from the Captain that a young man, one of his passengers, had a great many books, desired he would bring me to see him. I waited upon him accordingly, and should have taken Collins with me but that he was not sober. The governor treated me with great civility, showed me his library, which was a very large one, and we had a good deal of conversation about books and authors. This was the second governor who had done me the honor to take notice of me, which to a poor boy like me was very pleasing.

We proceeded to Philadelphia. I received on the way Vernon's money, without which we could hardly have finished our journey. Collins wished to be employed in some counting house; but whether they discovered his dramming by his breath, or by his behavior, though he had some recommendations, he met with no success in any application, and continued lodging and boarding at the same house with me and at my expense. Knowing I had that money of Vernon's, he was continually borrowing of me, still promising repayment as soon as he should be in business. At length he had got so much of it that I was distressed to think what I should do, in case of being called on to remit it. His drinking continued, about which we sometimes quarreled, for when a little intoxicated he was very fractious. Once in a boat on the Delaware with some other young men, he refused to row in his turn. "I will be rowed home," says he. "We will not row you," says I. "You must or stay all night on the water," says he, "just as you please." The others said, "Let us row; what signifies it?" But my mind being soured with his other conduct, I continued to refuse. So he swore he would make me row, or throw me overboard; and coming along stepping on the thwarts towards me, when he came up and struck at me I clapt my hand under his crotch, and rising pitched him head foremost into the river. I knew he was a good swimmer, and so was under little concern about him; but before he could get round to lay hold of the boat, we had with a few strokes pulled her out of his reach. And ever when he drew near the boat, we asked if he would row, striking a few strokes to slide her away from him. He was ready to die with vexation, and obstinately would not promise to row; however, seeing him at last beginning to tire, we lifted him in, and brought him home dripping wet in the evening. We hardly exchanged a civil word afterwards; and a West India captain who had a commission to procure a tutor for the sons of a gentleman at Barbadoes, happening to meet with him, agreed to carry him thither. He left me then, promising to remit me the first money he should receive in order to discharge the debt. But I never heard of him after.

[Great Expectations]

The breaking into this money of Vernon's was one of the first great errata of my life. And this affair showed that my father was not much out in his judgment when he supposed me too young to manage business of importance. But Sir William, on reading his letter, said he was too prudent. There was great difference in persons, and discretion did not always accompany years, nor was youth always without it. "And since he will not set you up," says he, "I will do it myself. Give me an inventory of the things necessary to be had from England, and I will send for them. You shall repay me when you are able; I am resolved to have a good printer here, and I am sure you must succeed." This was spoken with such an appearance of cordiality that I had not the least doubt of his meaning what he said. I had hitherto kept the proposition of my setting up a secret in Philadelphia, and I still kept it. Had it been known that I depended on the governor, probably some friend that knew him better would have advised me not to rely on him, as I afterwards heard it as his known character to be liberal of promises which he never meant to keep. Yet unsolicited as he was by me, how could I think his generous offers insincere? I believed him one of the best men in the world.

I presented him an inventory of a little printing house, amounting by my computation to about £100 sterling. He liked it, but asked me if my being on the spot in England to choose the types and see that everything was good of the kind, might not be of some advantage. "Then," says he, "when there, you may make acquaintances and establish correspondences in the bookselling and stationery way." I agreed that this might be advantageous. "Then," says he, "get yourself ready to go with *Annis*," which was the annual ship, and the only one at that time usually passing between London and Philadelphia. But it would be some months before *Annis* sailed; so I continued working with Keimer, fretting about the money Collins had got from me; and in daily apprehensions of being called upon by Vernon, which however did not happen for some years after.

I believe I have omitted mentioning that in my first voyage from Boston, being becalmed off Block Island, our people set about catching cod and hauled up a great many. Hitherto I had stuck to my resolution of not eating animal food; and on this occasion, I considered with my master Tryon, the taking every fish as a kind of unprovoked murder, since none of them had or ever could do us any injury that might justify the slaughter. All this seemed very reasonable. But I had formerly been a great lover of fish, and when this came hot out of the frying pan, it smelt admirably well. I balanced some time between principle and inclination, till I recollected that when the fish were opened, I saw smaller fish taken out of their stomachs. Then thought I, "If you eat one another, I don't see why we mayn't eat you." So I dined upon cod very heartily and continued to eat with other people, returning only now and then occasionally to a vegetable diet. So convenient a thing it is to be a *reasonable creature*, since it enables one to find or make a reason for every thing one has a mind to do.

1771   1791

[*Why Franklin Seldom Went to Church Services*]

I had been religiously educated as a Presbyterian; and though some of the dogmas of that persuasion, such as *the eternal decrees of God, election, reprobation,* etc., appeared to me unintelligible, others doubtful, and I early absented myself from the public assemblies of the sect, Sunday being my studying day, I never was without some religious principles. I never doubted, for instance, the existence of the Deity; that he made the world, and governed it by his Providence; that the most acceptable service of God was the doing good to man; that our souls are immortal; and that all crime will be punished and virtue rewarded, either here or hereafter. These I esteemed the essentials of every religion; and, being to be found in all the religions we had in our country, I respected them all, though with different degrees of respect, as I found them more or less mixed with other articles, which, without any tendency to inspire, promote, or confirm morality, served principally to divide us, and make us unfriendly to one another. This respect to all, with an opinion that the worst had some good effects, induced me to avoid all discourse that might tend to lessen the good opinion another might have of his own religion; and as our province increased in people, and new places of worship were continually wanted, and generally erected by voluntary contribution, my mite for such purpose, whatever might be the sect, was never refused.

Though I seldom attended any public worship, I had still an opinion of its propriety, and of its utility when rightly conducted, and I regularly paid my annual subscription for the support of the only Presbyterian minister or meeting we had in Philadelphia. He used to visit me sometimes as a friend, and admonish me to attend his administrations, and I was now and then prevailed on to do so, once for five Sundays successively. Had he been in my opinion a good preacher, perhaps I might have continued, notwithstanding the occasion I had for the Sunday's leisure in my course of study; but his discourses were chiefly either polemic arguments, or explications of the peculiar doctrines of our sect, and were all to me very dry, uninteresting, and unedifying, since not a single moral principle was inculcated or enforced, their aim seeming to be rather to make us Presbyterians than good citizens.

At length he took for his text that verse of the fourth chapter of Philippians, "*Finally, brethren, whatsoever things are true, honest, just, pure, lovely, or of good report, if there be any virtue, or any praise, think on these things.*" And I imagined, in a sermon on such a text, we could not miss of having some morality. But he confined himself to five points only, as meant by the apostle, viz.: 1. Keeping holy the Sabbath day. 2. Being diligent in reading the holy Scriptures. 3. Attending duly the public worship. 4. Partaking of the Sacrament. 5. Paying a due respect to God's ministers. These might be all good things; but as they were not the kind of good things that I expected from that text, I despaired of ever meeting with them from any other, was disgusted, and attended his preaching no more. I had some years before composed a little liturgy, or form of prayer, for my own private use (viz., in 1728), entitled, *Articles of Belief and Acts of Religion*. I returned to the use of this, and went no more to the public assemblies. My conduct might be blamable, but I leave it, without attempting further to excuse it; my present purpose being to relate facts, and not to make apologies for them.

[*The Project of Attaining Moral Perfection*]

It was about this time I conceived the bold and arduous project of arriving at moral perfection. I wished to live without committing any fault at any time; I would conquer all that either natural inclination, custom, or company might lead me into. As I knew, or thought I knew, what was right and wrong, I did not see why I might not always do the one and avoid the other. But I soon found I had undertaken a task of more difficulty than I had imagined. While my care was employed in guarding against one fault, I was often surprised by another; habit took the advantage of attention; inclination was sometimes too strong for reason. I concluded, at length, that the mere speculative conviction that it was our interest to be completely virtuous was not sufficient to prevent our slipping; and that the contrary habits must be broken, and good ones acquired and established, before we can have any dependence on a steady, uniform rectitude of conduct. For this purpose I therefore contrived the following method.

In the various enumerations of the moral virtues I had met with in my reading, I found the catalogue more or less numerous, as different writers included more or fewer ideas under the same name. Temperance, for example, was by some confined to eating and drinking, while by others it was extended to mean the moderating every other pleasure, appetite, inclination, or passion, bodily or mental, even to our avarice and ambition. I proposed to myself, for the sake of clearness, to use rather more names, with fewer ideas annexed to each, than a few names with more ideas; and I included under thirteen names of virtues all that at that time occurred to me as necessary or desirable, and annexed to each a short precept, which fully expressed the extent I gave to its meaning.

These names of virtues, with their precepts were:—

1. TEMPERANCE.

Eat not to dulness; drink not to elevation.

2. SILENCE.

Speak not but what may benefit others or yourself; avoid trifling conversation.

3. ORDER.

Let all your things have their places; let each part of your business have its time.

4. RESOLUTION.

Resolve to perform what you ought; perform without fail what you resolve.

5. FRUGALITY.

Make no expense but to do good to others or yourself; *i.e.*, waste nothing.

6. INDUSTRY.

Lose no time; be always employed in something useful; cut off all unnecessary actions.

7. SINCERITY.

Use no hurtful deceit; think innocently and justly; and if you speak, speak accordingly.

8. JUSTICE.

Wrong none by doing injuries, or omitting the benefits that are your duty.

9. MODERATION.

Avoid extremes; forbear resenting injuries so much as you think they deserve.

10. CLEANLINESS.

Tolerate no uncleanliness in body, clothes, or habitation.

11. TRANQUILLITY.

Be not disturbed at trifles, or at accidents common or unavoidable.

12. CHASTITY.

Rarely use venery but for health or offspring, never to dulness, weakness, or the injury of your own or another's peace or reputation.

13. HUMILITY.

Imitate Jesus and Socrates.

My intention being to acquire the *habitude* of all these virtues, I judged it would be well not to distract my attention by attempting the whole at once, but to fix it on one of them at a time; and, when I should be master of that, then to proceed to another, and so on, till I should have gone through the thirteen; and as the previous acquisition of some might facilitate the acquisition of certain others, I arranged them with that view, as they stand above. *Temperance* first, as it tends to procure that coolness and clearness of head which is so necessary where constant vigilance was to be kept up, and guard maintained against the unremitting attraction of ancient habits and the force of perpetual temptations. This being acquired and established, *Silence* would be more easy; and my desire being to gain knowledge at the same time that I improved in virtue, and considering that in conversation it was obtained rather by the use of the ears than of the tongue, and therefore wishing to break a habit I was getting into of prattling, punning, and joking, which only made me acceptable to trifling company, I gave *Silence* the second place. This and the next, *Order*, I expected would allow me more time for attending to my project and my studies. *Resolution*, once become habitual, would keep me firm in my endeavors to obtain all the subsequent virtues; *Frugality* and *Industry* freeing me from my remaining debt, and producing affluence and independence, would make more easy the practice of *Sincerity* and *Justice*, etc., etc. Conceiving then, that, agreeably to the advice of Pythagoras in his *Golden Verses*, daily examination would be necessary, I contrived the following method for conducting that examination.

I made a little book, in which I allotted a page for each of the virtues. I ruled each page with red ink, so as to have seven columns, one for each day of the week, marking each column with a letter for the day. I crossed these columns with thirteen red lines, marking the beginning of each line with the first letter of one of the virtues, on which line, and in its proper column, I might mark, by a little black spot, every fault I found upon examination to have been committed respecting that virtue upon that day.

Form of the Pages

		S.	M.	T.	W.	T.	F.	S.
TEMPERANCE EAT NOT TO DULNESS; DRINK NOT TO ELEVATION.								
T.								
S.		*	*		*		*	
O.		* *	*	*		*	*	*
R.				*			*	
F.			*			*		
I.			*					
S.			•					
J.								
M.								
C.								
T.								
C.								
H.								

I determined to give a week's strict attention to each of the virtues successively. Thus, in the first week, my great guard was to avoid every the least offense against *Temperance*, leaving the other virtues to their ordinary chance, only marking every evening the faults of the day. Thus, if in the first week I could keep my first line, marked T, clear of spots, I supposed the habit of that virtue so much strengthened, and its opposite weakened, that I might venture extending my attention to include the next, and for the following week keep both lines clear of spots. Proceeding thus to the last, I could go through a course complete in thirteen weeks, and four courses in a year. And like him who, having a garden to weed, does not attempt to eradicate all the bad herbs at once, which would exceed his reach and his strength, but works on one of the beds at a time, and, having accomplished the first, proceeds to a second, so I should have, I hoped, the encouraging pleasure of seeing on my pages the progress I made in virtue, by clearing successively my lines of their spots, till in the end, by a number of courses, I should be happy in viewing a clean book, after a thirteen weeks' daily examination.

This my little book had for its motto these lines from Addison's *Cato:*—

"Here will I hold. If there's a power above us
(And that there is, all nature cries aloud
Through all her works), He must delight in
  virtue;
And that which He delights in must be
  happy."

Another from Cicero,

"O vitae Philosophia dux! O virtutum inda-
gatrix expultrixque vitiorum! Unus dies, bene
et ex praeceptis tuis actus, peccanti immor-
talitati est anteponendus." [1]

Another from the Proverbs of Solomon,
speaking of wisdom or virtue:—

"Length of days is in her right hand, and
in her left hand riches and honor. Her ways
are ways of pleasantness, and all her paths are
peace." iii. 16, 17.

And conceiving God to be the fountain of
wisdom, I thought it right and necessary to
solicit his assistance for obtaining it; to this
end I formed the following little prayer, which
was prefixed to my tables of examination, for
daily use.

*"O powerful Goodness! bountiful Father!
merciful Guide! Increase in me that wisdom
which discovers my truest interest. Strengthen
my resolutions to perform what that wisdom
dictates. Accept my kind offices to thy other
children as the only return in my power for thy
continual favors to me."*

I used also sometimes a little prayer which
I took from Thomson's Poems, viz.:—

"Father of light and life, thou Good Supreme!
O teach me what is good; teach me Thyself!
Save me from folly, vanity, and vice,
From every low pursuit; and fill my soul
With knowledge, conscious peace, and virtue
  pure;
Sacred, substantial, never-fading bliss!"

The precept of *Order* requiring that *every
part of my business should have its allotted time*,
one page in my little book contained the following scheme of employment for the twenty
four hours of a natural day.

[1] O Philosophy, guide of life! O investigator and ex-
peller of crimes! A single day, lived well and in accordance with your precepts, is to be preferred to sinful
immortality.

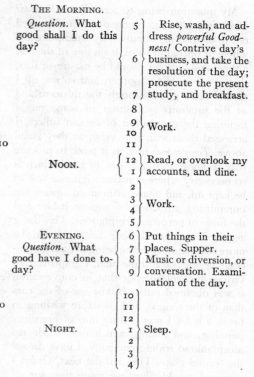

THE MORNING. *Question.* What good shall I do this day?	5 6 7	Rise, wash, and address *powerful Goodness!* Contrive day's business, and take the resolution of the day; prosecute the present study, and breakfast.
	8 9 10 11	Work.
NOON.	12 1	Read, or overlook my accounts, and dine.
	2 3 4 5	Work.
EVENING. *Question.* What good have I done to-day?	6 7	Put things in their places. Supper.
	8 9	Music or diversion, or conversation. Examination of the day.
NIGHT.	10 11 12 1 2 3 4	Sleep.

I entered upon the execution of this plan
for self-examination, and continued it with occasional intermissions for some time. I was
surprised to find myself so much fuller of
faults than I had imagined; but I had the satisfaction of seeing them diminish. To avoid the
trouble of renewing now and then my little
book, which, by scraping out the marks on
the paper of old faults to make room for new
ones in a new course, became full of holes, I
transferred my tables and precepts to the
ivory leaves of a memorandum book, on
which the lines were drawn with red ink that
made a durable stain, and on those lines I
marked my faults with a black-lead pencil,
which marks I could easily wipe out with a
wet sponge. After a while I went through one
course only in a year, and afterward only one
in several years, till at length I omitted them
entirely, being employed in voyages and business abroad, with a multiplicity of affairs that
interfered; but I always carried my little book
with me.

My scheme of ORDER gave me the most

trouble; and I found that, though it might be practicable where a man's business was such as to leave him the disposition of his time, that of a journeyman printer, for instance, it was not possible to be exactly observed by a master who must mix with the world and often receive people of business at their own hours. *Order*, too, with regard to places for things, papers, etc., I found extremely difficult to acquire. I had not been early accustomed to it, and having an exceeding good memory, I was not so sensible of the inconvenience attending want of method. This article, therefore cost me so much painful attention and my faults vexed me so much, and I made so little progress in amendment, and had such frequent relapses that I was almost ready to give up the attempt and content myself with a faulty character in that respect, like the man who, in buying an ax of a smith, my neighbor, desired to have the whole of its surface as bright as the edge. The smith consented to grind it bright for him if he would turn the wheel; he turned while the smith pressed the broad face of the ax hard and heavily on the stone, which made the turning of it very fatiguing. The man came every now and then from the wheel to see how the work went on and at length would take his ax as it was, without farther grinding. "No," said the smith, "turn on, turn on; we shall have it bright by and by; as yet, it is only speckled." "Yes," says the man, "*but I think I like a speckled ax best.*" And I believe this may have been the case with many who, having, for want of some such means as I employed, found the difficulty of obtaining good and breaking bad habits in other points of vice and virtue, have given up the struggle, and concluded that "*a speckled ax was best*"; for something that pretended to be reason, was every now and then suggesting to me that such extreme nicety as I exacted of myself might be a kind of foppery in morals, which, if it were known, would make me ridiculous; that a perfect character might be attended with the inconvenience of being envied and hated; and that a benevolent man should allow a few faults in himself, to keep his friends in countenance.

In truth, I found myself incorrigible with respect to Order; and now I am grown old and my memory bad, I feel very sensibly the want of it. But, on the whole, though I never arrived at the perfection I had been so ambitious of obtaining, but fell far short of it, yet I was, by the endeavor, a better and a happier man than I otherwise should have been if I had not attempted it; as those who aim at perfect writing by imitating the engraved copies, though they never reach the wished-for excellence of those copies, their hand is mended by the endeavor, and is tolerable while it continues fair and legible.

It may be well my posterity should be informed that to this little artifice, with the blessing of God, their ancestor owed the constant felicity of his life, down to his 79th year, in which this is written. What reverses may attend the remainder is in the hand of Providence; but if they arrive, the reflection on past happiness enjoyed ought to help his bearing them with more resignation. To Temperance he ascribes his long-continued health, and what is still left to him of a good constitution; to Industry and Frugality, the early easiness of his circumstances and acquisition of his fortune, with all that knowledge that enabled him to be a useful citizen, and obtained for him some degree of reputation among the learned: to Sincerity and Justice, the confidence of his country, and the honorable employs it conferred upon him; and to the joint influence of the whole mass of the virtues, even in the imperfect state he was able to acquire them, all that evenness of temper, and that cheerfulness in conversation which makes his company still sought for, and agreeable even to his younger acquaintance. I hope, therefore, that some of my descendants may follow the example and reap the benefit.

1784   1791

[*Public-spirited Projects*]

In 1751, Dr. Thomas Bond, a particular friend of mine, conceived the idea of establishing a hospital in Philadelphia (a very beneficent design, which has been ascribed to me, but was originally his) for the reception and cure of poor sick persons, whether inhabitants of the province or strangers. He was zealous and active in endeavoring to procure subscriptions for it, but the proposal being a novelty in America, and at first not well understood, he met with small success.

At length he came to me with the compliment that he found there was no such thing as carrying a public-spirited project through without my being concerned in it. "For," says he, "I am often asked by those to whom I propose subscribing, 'Have you consulted Franklin upon this business? And what does he think of it?' And when I tell them that I have not (supposing it rather out of your line), they do not subscribe, but say they will consider of it." I enquired into the nature and probable utility of his scheme, and receiving from him a very satisfactory explanation, I not only subscribed to it myself, but engaged heartily in the design of procuring subscriptions from others. Previously, however, to the solicitation, I endeavored to prepare the minds of the people by writing on the subject in newspapers, which was my usual custom in such cases but which he had omitted.

The subscriptions afterwards were more free and generous; but, beginning to flag, I saw they would be insufficient without some assistance from the Assembly, and therefore proposed to petition for it, which was done. The country members did not at first relish the project; they objected that it could only be serviceable to the city, and therefore the citizens alone should be at the expense of it; and they doubted whether the citizens themselves generally approved of it. My allegation on the contrary, that it met with such approbation as to leave no doubt of our being able to raise two thousand pounds by voluntary donations, they considered as a most extravagant supposition, and utterly impossible.

On this I formed my plan; and, asking leave to bring in a bill for incorporating the contributors according to the prayer of their petition and granting them a blank sum of money, which leave was obtained chiefly on the consideration that the House could throw the bill out if they did not like it, I drew it so as to make the important clause a conditional one, viz., "And be it enacted, by the authority aforesaid, that when the said contributors shall have met and chosen their managers and treasurer, *and shall have raised by their con-* *tributions a capital stock of —— value* (the yearly interest of which is to be applied to the accommodating of the sick poor in the said hospital, free of charge for diet, attendance, advice, and medicines), *and shall make the same appear to the satisfaction of the speaker of the Assembly for the time being*, that *then*, it shall and may be lawful for the said speaker, and he is hereby required, to sign an order on the provincial treasurer for the payment of two thousand pounds, in two yearly payments, to the treasurer of the said hospital, to be applied to the founding, building, and finishing of the same."

This condition carried the bill through; for the members who had opposed the grant, and now conceived they might have the credit of being charitable without the expense, agreed to its passage; and then, in soliciting subscriptions among the people, we urged the conditional promise of the law as an additional motive to give, since every man's donation would be doubled; thus the clause worked both ways. The subscriptions accordingly soon exceeded the requisite sum, and we claimed and received the public gift, which enabled us to carry the design into execution. A convenient and handsome building was soon erected; the institution has by constant experience been found useful, and flourishes to this day; and I do not remember any of my political manoeuvres, the success of which gave me at the time more pleasure, or wherein, after thinking of it, I more easily excused myself for having made some use of cunning.

It was about this time that another projector, the Rev. Gilbert Tennent, came to me with a request that I would assist him in procuring a subscription for erecting a new meeting-house. It was to be for the use of a congregation he had gathered among the Presbyterians, who were originally disciples of Mr. Whitefield. Unwilling to make myself disagreeable to my fellow-citizens by too frequently soliciting their contributions, I absolutely refused. He then desired I would furnish him with a list of the names of persons I knew by experience to be generous and public-spirited. I thought it would be unbecoming in me, after their kind compliance with my solicitations, to mark them out to be worried by other beggars, and therefore refused also to give such a list. He then desired I would at least give him my advice. "That I will readily do," said I; "and, in the first place, I advise you to apply to all those who you know will give something; next to those who you are uncertain whether they will give anything or not, and show them the list of those who have given; and, lastly, do not neglect those who you are sure will give nothing, for in some of them you may be mistaken." He laughed and thanked me, and said he would take my advice. He did so, for he asked of *everybody*, and he obtained a much larger sum than he expected, with which he erected the capacious and very elegant meeting-house that stands in Arch Street.

Our city, though laid out with a beautiful regularity, the streets large, straight, and crossing each other at right angles, had the disgrace of suffering those streets to remain long unpaved, and in wet weather the wheels of heavy carriages ploughed them into a quagmire, so that it was difficult to cross them; and in dry weather the dust was offensive. I had lived near what was called the Jersey Market, and saw with pain the inhabitants wading in mud while purchasing their provisions. A strip of ground down the middle of that market was at length paved with brick, so that, being once in the market, they had firm footing, but were often over shoes in dirt to get there. By talking and writing on the subject, I was at length instrumental in getting the street paved with stone between the market and the bricked foot pavement that was on each side next the houses. This, for some time, gave an easy access to the market dry-shod; but, the rest of the street not being paved, whenever a carriage came out of the mud upon this pavement, it shook off and left its dirt upon it, and it was soon covered with mire, which was not removed, the city as yet having no scavengers.

After some inquiry, I found a poor, industrious man who was willing to undertake keeping the pavement clean by sweeping it twice a week, carrying off the dirt from before all the neighbors' doors, for the sum of sixpence per month, to be paid by each house. I then wrote and printed a paper setting forth the advantages to the neighborhood that might be obtained by this small expense; the greater ease in keeping our houses clean, so much dirt not being brought in by people's feet; the benefit to the shops by more custom, etc., etc., as buyers could more easily get at them; and by not having, in windy weather, the dust blown in upon their goods, etc., etc. I sent one of these papers to each house and in a day or two went round to see who would subscribe an agreement to pay these sixpences. It was unanimously signed, and for a time well executed. All the inhabitants of the city were delighted with the cleanliness of the pavement that surrounded the market, it being a convenience to all, and this raised a general desire to have all the streets paved, and made the people more willing to submit to a tax for that purpose.

After some time I drew a bill for paving the city, and brought it into the Assembly. It was just before I went to England, in 1757, and did not pass till I was gone, and then with an alteration in the mode of assessment which I thought not for the better, but with an additional provision for lighting as well as paving the streets, which was a great improvement. It was by a private person, the late Mr. John Clifton, his giving a sample of the utility of lamps by placing one at his door, that the people were first impressed with the idea of enlighting all the city. The honor of this public benefit has also been ascribed to me, but it belongs truly to that gentleman. I did but follow his example, and have only some merit to claim respecting the form of our lamps, as differing from the globe lamps we were at first supplied with from London. Those we found inconvenient in these respects: they admitted no air below; the smoke, therefore, did not readily go out but circulated in the globe, lodged on its inside, and soon obstructed the light they were intended to afford; giving, besides, the daily trouble of wiping them clean; and an accidental stroke on one of them would demolish it, and render it totally useless. I therefore suggested the composing them of four flat panes, with a long funnel above to draw up the smoke and crevices admitting air below, to facilitate the ascent of the smoke; by this means they were kept clean, and did not grow dark in a few hours, as the London lamps do, but continued bright till morning, and an accidental stroke would generally break but a single pane, easily repaired.

I have sometimes wondered that the Londoners did not, from the effect holes in the bottom of the globe lamps used at Vauxhall have in keeping them clean, learn to have such holes in their street lamps. But these holes being made for another purpose, viz., to communicate flame more suddenly to the wick by a little flux hanging down through them, the other use, of letting in air, seems not to have been thought of; and therefore, after the lamps have been lit a few hours, the streets of London are very poorly illuminated.

The mention of these improvements puts me in mind of one I proposed, when in London, to Dr. Fothergill, who was among the best men I have known, and a great promoter of useful projects. I had observed that the streets, when dry, were never swept, and the light dust carried away; but it was suffered to accumulate till wet weather reduced it to mud, and then, after lying some days so deep on the pavement that there was no crossing but in paths kept clean by poor people with brooms, it was with great labor raked together and thrown up into carts open above, the sides of which suffered some of the slush at every jolt on the pavement to shake out and fall, sometimes to the annoyance of foot-passengers. The reason given for not sweeping the dusty streets was, that the dust would fly into the windows of shops and houses.

An accidental occurrence had instructed me how much sweeping might be done in a little time. I found at my door in Craven Street, one morning, a poor woman sweeping my pavement with a birch broom; she appeared very pale and feeble, as just come out of a fit of sickness. I asked who employed her to sweep there; she said, "Nobody; but I am very poor and in distress, and I sweeps before gentle-folkses's doors, and hopes they will give me something." I bid her sweep the whole street clean, and I would give her a shilling; this was at nine o'clock; at twelve she came for the shilling. From the slowness I saw at first in her working, I could scarce believe that the work was done so soon, and sent my servant to examine it, who reported that the whole street

was swept perfectly clean, and all the dust placed in the gutter, which was in the middle; and the next rain washed it quite away, so that the pavement and even the kennel were perfectly clean.

I then judged that if that feeble woman could sweep such a street in three hours, a strong, active man might have done it in half the time. And here let me remark the convenience of having but one gutter in such a narrow street, running down its middle, instead of two, one on each side, near the footway; for where all the rain that falls on a street runs from the sides and meets in the middle, it forms there a current strong enough to wash away all the mud it meets with; but when divided into two channels, it is often too weak to cleanse either, and only makes the mud it finds more fluid, so that the wheels of carriages and feet of horses throw and dash it upon the foot-pavement, which is thereby rendered foul and slippery, and sometimes splash it upon those who are walking. My proposal, communicated to the good doctor, was as follows:

"For the more effectual cleaning and keeping clean the streets of London and Westminster, it is proposed that the several watchmen be contracted with to have the dust swept up in dry seasons, and the mud raked up at other times, each in the several streets and lanes of his round; that they be furnished with brooms and other proper instruments for these purposes, to be kept at their respective stands ready to furnish the poor people they may employ in the service.

"That in the dry summer months the dust be all swept up into heaps at proper distances, before the shops and windows of houses are usually opened, when the scavengers, with close-covered carts, shall also carry it away.

"That the mud, when raked up, be not left in heaps to be spread abroad again by the wheels of carriages and trampling of horses, but that the scavengers be provided with bodies of carts, not placed high upon wheels, but low upon sliders, with lattice bottoms, which, being covered with straw, will retain the mud thrown into them, and permit the water to drain from it, whereby it will become much lighter, water making the greatest part of its weight; these bodies of carts to be placed at convenient distances, and the mud brought to them in wheelbarrows; they remaining where placed till the mud is drained, and then horses brought to draw them away."

I have since had doubts of the practicability of the latter part of this proposal, on account of the narrowness of some streets, and the difficulty of placing the draining-sled so as not to encumber too much the passage; but I am still of opinion that the former, requiring the dust to be swept up and carried away before the shops are open, is very practicable in the summer, when the days are long; for, in walking through the Strand and Fleet Street one morning at seven o'clock, I observed there was not one shop open though it had been daylight and the sun up above three hours; the inhabitants of London choosing voluntarily to live much by candle-light, and sleep by sunshine, and yet often complain, a little absurdly, of the duty on candles, and the high price of tallow.

Some may think these trifling matters not worth minding or relating; but when they consider that though dust blown into the eyes of a single person, or into a single shop on a windy day, is but of small importance, yet the great number of the instances in a populous city, and its frequent repetitions give it weight and consequence, perhaps they will not censure very severely those who bestow some attention to affairs of this seemingly low nature. Human felicity is produced not so much by great pieces of good fortune that seldom happen, as by little advantages that occur every day. Thus, if you teach a poor young man to shave himself, and keep his razor in order, you may contribute more to the happiness of his life than in giving him a thousand guineas. The money may be soon spent, the regret only remaining of having foolishly consumed it; but in the other case, he escapes the frequent vexation of waiting for barbers and of their sometimes dirty fingers, offensive breaths and dull razors; he shaves when most convenient to him and enjoys daily the pleasure of its being done with a good instrument. With these sentiments I have hazarded the few preceding pages, hoping they may afford hints which some time or other may be useful to a city I love, having lived many years in it very happily, and perhaps to some of our towns in America.

1788   1791

THE WHISTLE

TO MADAME BRILLON

This informal essay in letter form, sent to a cultured and witty acquaintance of Franklin's in Paris, is important for its literary influence in America during the next two decades. Its commonsense theme, its repetition of an axiomatic saying, and its series of brief illustrations are the basis of Noah Webster's "Prompter" essays and of Dennie's "Farrago" papers, a type which for a time competed with the Addison-Goldsmith stream of familiar essays.

Passy,[1] November 10, 1779

I RECEIVED my dear friend's two letters, one for Wednesday and one for Saturday. This is again Wednesday. I do not deserve one for today, because I have not answered the former. But, indolent as I am, and averse to writing, the fear of having no more of your pleasing epistles, if I do not contribute to the correspondence, obliges me to take up my pen; and as Mr. B. has kindly sent me word that he sets out tomorrow to see you, instead of spending this Wednesday evening as I have done its namesakes, in your delightful company, I sit down to spend it in thinking of you, in writing to you, and in reading over and over again your letters.

I am charmed with your description of Paradise, and with your plan of living there; and I approve much of your conclusion, that, in the meantime, we should draw all the good we can from this world. In my opinion, we might all draw more good from it than we do, and suffer less evil, if we would take care not to give too much for *whistles*. For it seems to me, that most of the unhappy people we meet with, are become so by neglect of that caution.

You ask what I mean? You love stories, and will excuse my telling one of myself.

When I was a child of seven years old, my friends, on a holiday, filled my pocket with coppers. I went directly to a shop where they sold toys for children; and, being charmed

[1] then a suburb of Paris

with the sound of a *whistle* that I met by the way in the hands of another boy, I voluntarily offered and gave all my money for one. I then came home, and went whistling all over the house, much pleased with my *whistle*, but disturbing all the family. My brothers, and sisters, and cousins, understanding the bargain I had made, told me I had given four times as much for it as it was worth; put me in mind what good things I might have bought with the rest of the money; and laughed at me so much for my folly, that I cried with vexation; and the reflection gave me more chagrin than the *whistle* gave me pleasure.

This however was afterwards of use to me, the impression continuing in my mind; so that often, when I was tempted to buy some unnecessary thing, I said to myself, *Don't give too much for the whistle;* and I saved my money.

As I grew up, came into the world, and observed the actions of men, I thought I met with many, very many, who *gave too much for the whistle.*

When I saw one too ambitious of court favor, sacrificing his time in attendance on levees, his repose, his liberty, his virtue, and perhaps his friends, to attain it, I have said to myself, *This man gives too much for his whistle.*

When I saw another fond of popularity, constantly employing himself in political bustles, neglecting his own affairs, and ruining them by that neglect, *He pays, indeed,* said I, *too much for his whistle.*

If I knew a miser, who gave up every kind of comfortable living, all the pleasure of doing good to others, all the esteem of his fellow-citizens, and the joys of benevolent friendship for the sake of accumulating wealth, *Poor man,* said I, *you pay too much for your whistle.*

When I met with a man of pleasure, sacrificing every laudable improvement of the mind, or of his fortune, to mere corporeal sensations, and ruining his health in their pursuit, *Mistaken man,* said I, *you are providing pain for yourself, instead of pleasure; you give too much for your whistle.*

If I see one fond of appearance, or fine clothes, fine houses, fine furniture, fine equipages, all above his fortune, for which he contracts debts, and ends his career in a prison, *Alas!* say I, *he has paid dear, very dear, for his whistle.*

When I see a beautiful, sweet-tempered girl married to an ill-natured brute of a husband, *What a pity,* say I, *that she should pay so much for a whistle!*

In short, I conceive that great part of the miseries of mankind are brought upon them by the false estimates they have made of the value of things, and by their *giving too much for their whistles.*

Yet I ought to have charity for these unhappy people, when I consider that, with all this wisdom of which I am boasting, there are certain things in the world so tempting, for example, the apples of King John, which happily are not to be bought; for if they were put to sale by auction, I might very easily be led to ruin myself in the purchase, and find that I had once more given too much for the *whistle.*

Adieu, my dear friend, and believe me ever yours very sincerely and with unalterable affection,

B. FRANKLIN

1779   1818

LETTERS

To Samuel Mather

Passy, May 12, 1784

REV^d SIR,

I received your kind letter, with your excellent advice to the people of the United States, which I read with great pleasure, and hope it will be duly regarded. Such writings, though they may be lightly passed over by many readers, yet, if they make a deep impression on one active mind in a hundred, the effects may be considerable. Permit me to mention one little instance, which, though it relates to myself, will not be quite uninteresting to you. When I was a boy, I met with a book, entitled "Essays to do Good," which I think was written by your father. It had been so little regarded by a former possessor, that several leaves of it were torn out; but the remainder gave me such a turn of thinking as to have an influence on my conduct through life; for I have always set a greater value on the character of a *doer of good* than on any other kind of reputation; and if I have been, as you seem to think, a useful citizen, the public owes the advantage of it to that book.

You mention your being in your 78th year; I am in my 79th; we are grown old together. It is now more than 60 years since I left Boston, but I remember well both your father and grandfather, having heard them both in the pulpit, and seen them in their houses. The last time I saw your father was in the beginning of 1724, when I visited him after my first trip to Pennsylvania. He received me in his library, and on my taking leave showed me a shorter way out of the house through a narrow passage, which was crossed by a beam over head. We were still talking as I withdrew, he accompanying me behind, and I turning partly towards him, when he said hastily, "Stoop, stoop!" I did not understand him, till I felt my head hit against the beam. He was a man that never missed any occasion of giving instruction, and upon this he said to me, "You are young, and have the world before you; *stoop* as you go through it, and you will miss many hard thumps." This advice, thus beat into my head, has frequently been of use to me; and I often think of it when I see pride mortified, and misfortunes brought upon people by their carrying their heads too high.

I long much to see again my native place, and to lay my bones there. I left it in 1723; I visited it in 1733, 1743, 1753, and 1763. In 1773 I was in England; in 1775 I had a sight of it, but could not enter, it being in possession of the enemy. I did hope to have been there in 1783, but could not obtain my dismission from this employment here; and now I fear I shall never have that happiness. My best wishes however attend my dear country. *Esto perpetua.* It is now blest with an excellent constitution; may it last for ever!

This powerful monarchy continues its friendship for the United States. It is a friendship of the utmost importance to our security, and should be carefully cultivated. Britain has not yet well digested the loss of its dominion over us, and has still at times some flattering hopes of recovering it. Accidents may increase those hopes, and encourage dangerous attempts. A breach between us and France would infallibly bring the English again upon our backs; and yet we have some wild heads among our countrymen, who are endeavoring to weaken that connection! Let us preserve our reputation by performing our engagements; our credit by fulfilling our contracts; and friends by gratitude and kindness; for we know not how soon we may again have occasion for all of them. With great and sincere esteem, I have the honor to be, &c.

B. FRANKLIN

To Mason Weems and Edward Gantt [1]

When, in March, 1783, the Episcopalian clergy of Connecticut, cut off by the Revolution from communion with their former spiritual head, the Bishop of London, met and elected Samuel Seabury as their bishop, they discovered that he could not be properly consecrated by the English Episcopacy without declaring allegiance to King George, as head of the Church of England. In this quandary, two Episcopalians applied for Franklin's good offices in the matter and received the following characteristic reply. Franklin's advice was in part followed when, after being rejected by the Archbishop of Canterbury, Seabury went to Aberdeen and was consecrated bishop by the "non-juring" bishops of Scotland. Thus the apostolic succession was established, and later the American Anglicans were organized as the independent Protestant Episcopal Church.

Passy, July 18, 1784

GENTLEMEN,

On receipt of your letter, acquainting me that the Archbishop would not permit you to be ordained, unless you took the Oath of Allegiance, I applied to a clergyman of my acquaintance for information on the subject of your obtaining ordination here. His opinion was, that it could not be done; and that, if it were done, you would be required to vow obedience to the Archbishop of Paris. I next inquired of the Pope's Nuncio, whether you might not be ordained by their bishop in America, powers being sent him for that purpose, if he has them not already. The answer was, "The thing is impossible, unless the gentlemen become Catholics."

[1] Mason Locke Weems (1760–1825), clergyman of Washington's parish in Virginia and later his biographer. Edward Gantt (1746–c. 1837), clergyman and physician in Maryland.

This is an affair of which I know very little, and therefore I may ask questions and purpose means that are improper or impracticable. But what is the necessity of your being connected with the Church of England? Would it not be as well, if you were of the Church of Ireland? The religion is the same, though there is the different set of bishops and archbishops. Perhaps if you were to apply to the Bishop of Derry, who is a man of liberal sentiments, he 10 might give you orders as of that church. If both Britain and Ireland refuse you, (and I am not sure that the Bishops of Denmark or Sweden would ordain you, unless you become Lutherans,) what is to be done? Next to becoming Presbyterians, the Episcopalian clergy of America, in my humble opinion, cannot do better than to follow the example of the first clergy of Scotland, soon after the conversion of that country to Chris- 20 tianity, who when their king had built the Cathedral of St. Andrew's, and requested the King of Northumberland for orders, and their request was refused; they assembled in the Cathedral; and, the miter, crosier, and robes of a bishop being laid upon the altar, they, after earnest prayers for direction in their choice, elected one of their own number; when the King said to him, "Arise, go to the 30 altar, and receive your office at the hand of God." His brethren led him to the altar, robed him, put the crosier in his hand, and the miter on his head, and he became the first Bishop of Scotland.

If the British Isles sunk in the sea (and the surface of this globe has suffered greater changes), you would probably take some such method as this; and if they persist in denying you ordination, 'tis the same thing. A hun- 40 dred years hence, when people are more enlightened, it will be wondered at, that men in America, qualified by their learning and piety to pray for and instruct their neighbors, should not be permitted to do it till they had made a voyage of six thousand miles out and home, to ask leave of a cross old gentleman at Canterbury; who seems, by your account, to have as little regard for the souls of the people of Maryland, as King William's attorney-general, Seymour, had for those of Virginia. 50 The Reverend Commissary Blair, who pro-

jected the College of that Province, and was in England to solicit benefactions and a charter, relates that the Queen, in the King's absence, having ordered Seymour to draw up the charter, which was to be given, with $2000 in money, he opposed the grant, saying that the nation was engaged in an expensive war, that the money was wanted for better purposes, and he did not see the least occasion for the college in Virginia. Blair represented to him, that its intention was to educate and qualify young men to be ministers of the Gospel, much wanted there; and begged Mr. Attorney would consider, that the people of Virginia had souls to be saved, as well as the people of England. "*Souls!*" says he, "*damn your souls. Make tobacco!*" I have the honor to be, Gentlemen, &c.

B. FRANKLIN

To Mrs. Sarah Bache

The Order of the Cincinnati (from Cincinnatus who left his plow in its furrow to go to the defense of Rome), an ancestor of the G.A.R., the American Legion, and similar groups, but much more exclusive in its nature, was organized in May, 1783, to comprise officers of three years' standing in the Revolutionary Army and their oldest male descendants in direct line. It was at once opposed by Adams, Jefferson, and others as tending to a hereditary military aristocracy and as a scheme for monopolizing the chief offices in the new Confederacy. Its chief legacy to the country was the rival Tammany Society, organized in 1789 to counteract its aristocratic influence. Franklin, in the following letter, jestingly satirizes the pretensions and elaborate insignia of the Order.

Passy, Jan. 26, 1784

MY DEAR CHILD,

Your care in sending me the newspapers is very agreeable to me. I received by Capt. Barney those relating to the *Cincinnati*. My opinion of the institution cannot be of much importance; I only wonder that, when the united wisdom of our nation had, in the Articles of Confederation, manifested their dislike of establishing ranks of nobility, by authority either of the Congress or of any particular state, a number of private persons should think proper to distinguish themselves and their posterity from their fellow citizens, and form an order of *hereditary Knights*, in direct opposition to the solemnly declared sense of their country! I imagine it must be likewise contrary to the good sense of most of those drawn into it by the persuasion of its projectors, who have been too much struck with the ribbons and crosses they have seen among them hanging to the buttonholes of foreign officers. And I suppose those, who disapprove of it, have not hitherto given it much opposition, from a principle somewhat like that of your good mother, relating to punctilious persons, who are always exacting little observances of respect; that, *"if people can be pleased with small matters, it is a pity but they should have them."*

In this view, perhaps, I should not myself, if my advice had been asked, have objected to their wearing their ribbon and badge according to their fancy, though I certainly should to the entailing it as an honor on their posterity. For honor, worthily obtained (as for example that of our officers), is in its nature a *personal* thing, and incommunicable to any but those who had some share in obtaining it. Thus among the Chinese, the most ancient, and from long experience the wisest of nations, honor does not *descend*, but *ascends*. If a man from his learning, his wisdom, or his valor, is promoted by the Emperor to the rank of mandarin, his parents are immediately entitled to all the same ceremonies of respect from the people, that are established as due to the mandarin himself; on the supposition that it must have been owing to the education, instruction, and good example afforded him by his parents, that he was rendered capable of serving the public.

This *ascending* honor is therefore useful to the state, as it encourages parents to give their children a good and virtuous education. But the *descending honor*, to posterity who could have no share in obtaining it, is not only groundless and absurd, but often hurtful to that posterity, since it is apt to make them proud, disdaining to the employed in useful arts, and thence falling into poverty, and all the meannesses, servility, and wretchedness attending it; which is the present case with much of what is called the *noblesse* in Europe. Or if, to keep up the dignity of the family,

estates are entailed entire on the eldest male heir, another pest to industry and improvement of the country is introduced, which will be followed by all the odious mixture of pride and beggary, and idleness, that have half depopulated Spain; occasioning continual extinction of families by the discouragements of marriage. . . .

The gentleman, who made the voyage to France to provide the ribbons and medals, has executed his commission. To me they seem tolerably done; but all such things are criticised. Some find fault with the Latin, as wanting classic elegance and correctness; and, since our nine universities were not able to furnish better Latin, it was pity, they say, that the mottos had not been in English. Others object to the title, as not properly assumable by any but Gen. Washington, who served without pay. Others object to the *bald eagle* as looking too much like a *dindon*, or turkey. For my own part, I wish the bald eagle had not been chosen as the representative of our country: he is a bird of bad moral character; he does not get his living honestly; you may have seen him perched on some dead tree near the river, where, too lazy to fish for himself, he watches the labor of the fishing-hawk; and, when that diligent bird has at length taken a fish, and is bearing it to his nest for the support of his mate and young ones, the bald eagle pursues him, and takes it from him. With all this injustice he is never in good case; but, like those among men who live by sharping and robbing, he is generally poor, and often very lousy. Besides, he is a rank coward; the little *Kingbird*, not bigger than a sparrow, attacks him boldly and drives him out of the district. He is therefore by no means a proper emblem for the brave and honest Cincinnati of America, who have driven all the *Kingbirds* from our country; though exactly fit for that order of knights which the French call *Chevaliers d'Industrie*.

I am, on this account, not displeased that the figure is not known as a bald eagle, but looks more like a turkey. For in truth, the turkey is in comparison a much more respectable bird, and withal a true original native of America. Eagles have been found in all countries, but the turkey was peculiar to ours, the first of the species seen in Europe being brought to France by the Jesuits from Canada, and served up at the wedding table of Charles the Ninth. He is a bird of courage, and would not hesitate to attack a grenadier of the British Guards, who should presume to invade his farmyard with a *red* coat on. . . .

B. FRANKLIN

To Ezra Stiles

This letter, written in the month before Franklin's death, gives his maturest religious views. The Reverend Ezra Stiles, president of Yale College from 1778 to 1795, was a religious liberal and interested in the advancement of natural science.

Philadᵃ, March 9, 1790

REVEREND AND DEAR SIR,

I received your kind letter of Jan'y 28, and am glad you have at length received the portrait of Gov'r Yale from his family, and deposited it in the College Library. He was a great and good man, and had the merit of doing infinite service to your country by his munificence to that institution. The honor you propose doing me by placing mine in the same room with his, is much too great for my deserts; but you always had a partiality for me, and to that it must be ascribed. I am, however, too much obliged to Yale College, the first learned society that took notice of me and adorned me with its honors, to refuse a request that comes from it through so esteemed a friend. But I do not think any one of the portraits you mention as in my possession worthy of the place and company you propose to place it in. You have an excellent artist lately arrived. If he will undertake to make one for you, I shall cheerfully pay the expense; but he must not delay setting about it, or I may slip through his fingers, for I am now in my eighty-fifth year, and very infirm.

I send with this a very learned work, as it seems to me, on the ancient Samaritan coins, lately printed in Spain, and at least curious for the beauty of the impression. Please to accept it for your College Library. I have subscribed for the Encyclopaedia now printing here, with the intention of presenting it to the College. I shall probably depart before the work is finished, but shall leave directions for its continuance to the end. With this you will receive some of the first numbers.

You desire to know something of my religion. It is the first time I have been questioned upon it. But I cannot take your curiosity amiss, and shall endeavor in a few words to gratify it. Here is my creed. I believe in one God, Creator of the Universe. That he governs it by his Providence. That he ought to be worshipped. That the most acceptable service we render to him is doing good to his other children. That the soul of man is immortal, and will be treated with justice in another life respecting its conduct in this. These I take to be the fundamental principles of all sound religion, and I regard them as you do in whatever sect I meet with them.

As to Jesus of Nazareth, my opinion of whom you particularly desire, I think the system of morals and his religion, as he left them to us, the best the world ever saw or is likely to see; but I apprehend it has received various corrupting changes, and I have, with most of the present Dissenters[1] in England, some doubts as to his divinity; though it is a question I do not dogmatize upon, having never studied it, and think it needless to busy myself with it now, when I expect soon an opportunity of knowing the truth with less trouble. I see no harm, however, in its being believed, if that belief has the good consequence, as probably it has, of making his doctrines more respected and better observed; especially as I do not perceive that the Supreme takes it amiss, by distinguishing the unbelievers in his government of the world with any peculiar marks of his displeasure.

I shall only add, respecting myself, that, having experienced the goodness of that Being in conducting me prosperously through a long life, I have no doubt of its continuance in the next, though without the smallest conceit of meriting such goodness. My sentiments on this head you will see in the copy of an old letter enclosed, which I wrote in answer to one from a zealous religionist, whom I had relieved

[1] The chief dissenting sect in England, the Presbyterians, had by the close of the eighteenth century largely become Unitarian in their religious views. Franklin carried on friendly correspondence with their great leader, Joseph Priestley, who migrated to Pennsylvania in 1794.

in a paralytic case by electricity, and who, being afraid I should grow proud upon it, sent me his serious though rather impertinent caution. I send you also the copy of another letter, which will show something of my disposition relating to religion. With great and sincere esteem and affection, I am, your obliged old friend and most obedient humble servant

B. FRANKLIN

1737 — *Thomas Paine* — 1809

THOMAS PAINE was born in England of a Quaker family, whose objections to organized religion and difference in social rank greatly affected his thinking throughout life. His education was gained not from schools but from a wide reading in books which increased his impatience with the structure of society, and from writing and debating in a men's literary club in London. He was middle-aged and had been unsuccessful as a sailor, corsetmaker, exciseman, schoolteacher, and tobacconist and grocer—and in matrimony—before he attracted the attention of Franklin, who suggested migration to America. He went to Philadelphia in 1774 and immediately established the *Pennsylvania Magazine*, which during its single year included a number of liberal articles on slavery, divorce, and politics. Enthusiastically adopting the colonists' quarrel, he published early in 1776, in a time of hesitation, his tract *Common Sense*, arguing the political necessity and economic desirability of separation from England. Half a million copies were circulated throughout the colonies, and its effect upon its readers, including the conservative Washington, was a great impetus in the direction of the Declaration of Independence. The ensuing *The Crisis* was a series of sixteen essays issued at moments of wavering and discouragement during the course of the war, to arouse and revive the spirits of the people. Together, *Common Sense* and *The Crisis* were two of the most influential propaganda documents in American history.

Paine came out of the war a national hero, with the liking and gratitude of the American people; Pennsylvania granted him a gift of £500, and New York, a confiscated estate in New Rochelle. In 1787 he returned to England, and the next fifteen years were spent abroad. In Europe he considered himself, like many Americans, a missionary for democratic ideas: in a later edition of *Common Sense* he asserted, "We have it in our power to make the world over again." To the young liberals in England, who welcomed the French Revolution, Paine addressed, in response to Burke's attacks in *Reflections on the Revolution in France* (1790), his indignant *The Rights of Man* (1791 and 1792), assailing the political theory of the British monarchy with its titled nobility and arguing for the welfare of the masses. As a result he was tried for treason and banished, but he was already in France.

At first he was welcomed with citizenship and a seat in the National Assembly, but during the Terror was imprisoned and in danger of death until released in 1794, through the intervention of Monroe. By his tactless *Letter to George Washington* (1796), in which he accused the President of duplicity and over-conservatism, he lost many friends in America.

Up to 1794 Paine's writings had chiefly been political and economic. In that year he began, in his famous work *The Age of Reason* (in two parts, 1794 and 1796), his assault upon "superstition," or organized religion, which he found everywhere interwoven with and helping to support governmental tyranny. On the positive side the book embodied his exposition of deistic theology. Discarding all respect for ecclesiastical tradition and viewing the authority of the Scriptures with the eyes of critical reason only, he undertook with merciless plainness and sarcasm to undermine the ground on which the established Christian, Jewish, and Mohammedan religious systems were founded. Upon their ruins he hoped to set up the religion of reason and nature, "lest in the general wreckage of superstition, of false systems of government, and false theology, we lose sight of morality, of humanity, and of the theology that is true." His ideas, drawn from Newtonian astronomy with its stress on a universe of immutable law and harmony, affected the thinking of many intellectuals, already stirred by currents of revolutionary thought, through its rational appeal, expressed in powerful phrase, as in the following:

Is it we that light up the sun, that pour down the rain, and fill the earth with abundance? Whether we sleep or wake, the vast machinery of the universe still goes on. Are these things, and the blessings they indicate in future, nothing to us? Can our gross feelings be excited by no other subjects than tragedy and suicide? Or is the gloomy pride of man become so intolerable that nothing can flatter it but a sacrifice of the Creator?

His religious views were actually not unlike those of many who consider themselves liberal Christians today, but he alienated many thoughtful readers by needless tactlessness and occasional scurrility regarding matters ordinarily held sacred. The orthodox clergy of all sects in the United States recognized the menace in his work, and Paine was denounced from the pulpits everywhere as an atheist, traitor, and drunkard. In 1802, when, broken by illness and intemperance, he returned to his New York farm at the invitation of President Jefferson, he was greeted with obloquy and intolerant abuse. He lived rather obscurely at New Rochelle until his death in 1809, and it was nearly a century before the real impulse that he had given to political and religious liberalism could be impartially estimated.

Moncure D. Conway has produced the standard edition of Paine's *Works* (4 vols., 1894–1896) and the standard *Life* (2 vols., 1892). See also the ten-volume *Life and Works* by W. M. Van der Weyde (1925) and the volume of selections by A. W. Peach (American Authors Series, 1928).

Other biographies include M. A. Best, *Thomas Paine, Prophet and Martyr of Democracy* (1927); and Ellery Sedgwick, *Thomas Paine* (1899). Good brief sketches are contained in the *DAB* and *DNB*.

Critical and interpretative studies are H. H. Clark, "An Historical Interpretation of Thomas Paine's Religion," *University of California Chronicle*, XXXV, 56–87 (January, 1933); "Thomas Paine's Theories of Rhetoric," *Transactions of the Wisconsin Academy of Sciences, Arts and Letters*, XXVIII, 307–339 (1933); and "Toward a Reinterpretation of Thomas Paine," *American Literature*, V, 133–145 (May, 1933); W. E. Dodd, "Tom Paine," *American Mercury*, XXI, 477–483 (December, 1930); C. E. Merriam, Jr., "Thomas Paine's Political Theories," *Political Science Quarterly*, XIV, 389–403 (September, 1899); D. S. Muzzey, "Thomas Paine and American Independence," *American Review*, IV, 278–288 (May–June, 1926); V. L. Parrington, *Main Currents in American Thought* (1927), I, 327–341; C. E. Persinger, "The Political Philosophy of Thomas Paine," *University of Nebraska Graduate Bulletin*, 6th ser., No. 3, 54–74 (July, 1901); Frank Smith, "New Light on Thomas Paine's First Year in America," *American Literature*, I, 347–371 (January, 1930); M. C. Tyler, *Literary History of the American Revolution* (1897), I, 451–474 and II, 35–49; Carl Van Doren, "Paine," in *American Writers on American Literature*, John Macy, ed., (1931), 25–35; and H. H. Clark, *Six New Letters of Thomas Paine* (1939).

From THE CRISIS

The Times That Try Men's Souls

The first number of *The American Crisis*, with its magnificent opening sentences, was written in camp, near the close of the first year of the war, when a series of military disasters had made it seem to many that the Revolution, despite Washington's skill and leadership, was doomed to swift failure. It was printed in the *Pennsylvania Journal*, Philadelphia, on December 19, 1776, and republished separately on December 23, the day before Washington's victory at Trenton, in which Paine participated.

THESE are the times that try men's souls. The summer soldier and the sunshine patriot will, in this crisis, shrink from the service of their country; but he that stands it *now*, deserves the love and thanks of man and woman. Tyranny, like hell, is not easily conquered; yet we have this consolation with us, that the harder the conflict, the more glorious the triumph. What we obtain too cheap, we esteem too lightly: it is dearness only that gives every thing its value. Heaven knows how to put a proper price upon its goods; and it would be strange indeed if so celestial an article as *freedom* should not be highly rated. Britain, with an army to enforce her tyranny, has declared that she has a right not only to tax but "to bind us in *all cases whatsoever*," and if being bound in that manner is not slavery, then there is not such a thing as slavery upon earth. Even the expression is impious; for so unlimited a power can belong only to God.

Whether the independence of the continent was declared too soon, or delayed too long, I will not now enter into as an argument; my own simple opinion is that had it been eight months earlier, it would have been much better. We did not make a proper use of last winter, neither could we, while we were in a dependent state. However, the fault, if it were one, was all our own; we have none to blame but ourselves. But no great deal is lost yet. All that Howe[1] has been doing for this month past, is rather a ravage than a conquest, which the spirit of the Jerseys, a year ago, would have quickly repulsed, and which time and a little resolution will soon recover.

I have as little superstition in me as any man living, but my secret opinion has ever been, and still is, that God Almighty will not give up a people to military destruction, or leave them unsupportedly to perish, who have so earnestly and so repeatedly sought to avoid the calamities of war, by every decent method which wisdom could invent. Neither have I

[1] Lord William Howe, general of the British forces at New York

so much of the infidel in me, as to suppose that He has relinquished the government of the world, and given us up to the care of devils; and as I do not, I cannot see on what grounds the king of Britain can look up to Heaven for help against us: a common murderer, a highwayman, or a housebreaker, has as good a pretence as he.

'Tis surprising to see how rapidly a panic will sometimes run through a country. All nations and ages have been subject to them: Britain has trembled like an ague at the report of a French fleet of flat-bottomed boats; and in the fourteenth century the whole English army, after ravaging the kingdom of France, was driven back like men petrified with fear; and this brave exploit was performed by a few broken forces collected and headed by a woman, Joan of Arc. Would that heaven might inspire some Jersey maid to spirit up her countrymen, and save her fair fellow sufferers from ravage and ravishment! Yet panics, in some cases, have their uses; they produce as much good as hurt. Their duration is always short; the mind soon grows through them, and acquires a firmer habit than before. But their peculiar advantage is, that they are the touchstones of sincerity and hypocrisy, and bring things and men to light, which might otherwise have lain forever undiscovered. In fact, they have the same effect on secret traitors which an imaginary apparition would have upon a private murderer. They sift out the hidden thoughts of man, and hold them up in public to the world. Many a disguised tory has lately shown his head, that shall penitentially solemnize with curses the day on which Howe arrived upon the Delaware.

As I was with the troops at Fort Lee, and marched with them to the edge of Pennsylvania, I am well acquainted with many circumstances, which those who live at a distance know but little or nothing of. Our situation there was exceedingly cramped, the place being a narrow neck of land between the North River and the Hackensack. Our force was inconsiderable, being not one fourth so great as Howe could bring against us. We had no army at hand to have relieved the garrison, had we shut ourselves up and stood on our defence. Our ammunition, light artillery, and the best part of our stores, had been removed, on the apprehension that Howe would endeavor to penetrate the Jerseys, in which case Fort Lee could be of no use to us; for it must occur to every thinking man, whether in the army or not, that these kind of field forts are only for temporary purposes, and last in use no longer than the enemy directs his force against the particular object which such forts are raised to defend. Such was our situation and condition at Fort Lee on the morning of the 20th of November, when an officer arrived with information that the enemy with 200 boats had landed about seven miles above. Major General Green, who commanded the garrison, immediately ordered them under arms, and sent express to General Washington at the town of Hackensack, distant by the way of the ferry, six miles. Our first object was to secure the bridge over the Hackensack, which laid up the river between the enemy and us, about six miles from us, and three from them. General Washington arrived in about three quarters of an hour, and marched at the head of the troops towards the bridge, which place I expected we should have a brush for; however, they did not choose to dispute it with us, and the greatest part of our troops went over the bridge, the rest over the ferry, except some which passed at a mill on a small creek, between the bridge and the ferry, and made their way through some marshy grounds up to the town of Hackensack, and there passed the river. We brought off as much baggage as the wagons could contain, the rest was lost. The simple object was to bring off the garrison, and march them on till they could be strengthened by the Jersey or Pennsylvania militia, so as to be enabled to make a stand. We stayed four days at Newark, collected our outposts with some of the Jersey militia, and marched out twice to meet the enemy, on being informed that they were advancing, though our numbers were greatly inferior to theirs. Howe, in my little opinion, committed a great error in generalship in not throwing a body of forces off from Staten Island through Amboy, by which means he might have seized all our stores at Brunswick, and intercepted our march into Pennsylvania; but if we believe the power of hell to be limited, we must likewise believe that their agents are under some providential control.

I shall not now attempt to give all the particulars of our retreat to the Delaware; suffice it for the present to say, that both officers and men, though greatly harassed and fatigued, frequently without rest, covering, or provision, the inevitable consequences of a long retreat, bore it with a manly and martial spirit. All their wishes centered in one, which 10 was, that the country would turn out and help them to drive the enemy back. Voltaire has remarked that King William [1] never appeared to full advantage but in difficulties and in action; the same remark may be made on General Washington, for the character fits him. There is a natural firmness in some minds which cannot be unlocked by trifles, but which, when unlocked, discovers a cabinet of fortitude; and I reckon it among those kind of 20 public blessings, which we do not immediately see, that God hath blessed him with uninterrupted health, and given him a mind that can even flourish upon care.

I shall conclude this paper with some miscellaneous remarks on the state of our affairs; and shall begin with asking the following question, Why is it that the enemy have left the New England provinces, and made these middle ones the seat of war? The answer is easy: 30 New England is not infested with tories, and we are. I have been tender in raising the cry against these men, and used numberless arguments to show them their danger, but it will not do to sacrifice a world either to their folly or their baseness. The period is now arrived, in which either they or we must change our sentiments, or one or both must fall. And what is a tory? Good God! what is he? I should not be afraid to go with a hundred 40 whigs against a thousand tories, were they to attempt to get into arms. Every tory is a coward; for servile, slavish, self-interested fear is the foundation of toryism; and a man under such influence, though he may be cruel, never can be brave.

But, before the line of irrecoverable separation be drawn between us, let us reason the matter together: Your conduct is an invitation

to the enemy, yet not one in a thousand of you has heart enough to join him. Howe is as much deceived by you as the American cause is injured by you. He expects you will all take up arms, and flock to his standard, with muskets on your shoulders. Your opinions are of no use to him, unless you support him personally, for 'tis soldiers, and not tories, that he wants.

I once felt all that kind of anger which a man ought to feel, against the mean principles that are held by the tories: a noted one, who kept a tavern at Amboy, was standing at his door, with as pretty a child in his hand, about eight or nine years old, as ever I saw, and after speaking his mind as freely as he thought was prudent, finished with this unfatherly expression. "*Well! give me peace in my day.*" Not a man lives on the continent but fully believes that a separation must some time or other finally take place, and a generous parent should have said, "*If there must be trouble, let it be in my day, that my child may have peace*"; and this single reflection, well applied, is sufficient to awaken every man to duty. Not a place upon earth might be so happy as America. Her situation is remote from all the wrangling world, and she has nothing to do but to trade with them. A man can distinguish himself between temper and principle, and I am as confident, as I am that God governs the world, that America will never be happy till she gets clear of foreign dominion. Wars, without ceasing, will break out till that period arrives, and the continent must in the end be conqueror; for though the flame of liberty may sometimes cease to shine, the coal can never expire. . . .

1776

From COMMON SENSE

Thoughts on the Present State of American Affairs

As early as October 18, 1775, Paine had prophesied the separation of the American colonies from England, in an article in the *Pennsylvania Journal*. Less than three months later, early in January, he published *Common Sense*, setting forth the reasons for and advantages of independence. The following extract is a portion of Part III of the pamphlet.

---

[1] William of Orange, later William III of England, defender of Holland against the French armies

IN the following pages I offer nothing more than simple facts, plain arguments, and common sense; and have no other preliminaries to settle with the reader, than that he will divest himself of prejudice and prepossession, and suffer his reason and his feelings to determine for themselves; that he will put on, or rather that he will not put off, the true character of a man, and generously enlarge his views beyond the present day.

Volumes have been written on the subject of the struggle between England and America. Men of all ranks have embarked in the controversy, from different motives, and with various designs; but all have been ineffectual, and the period of debate is closed. Arms, as the last resource, must decide the contest; the appeal was the choice of the King, and the continent hath accepted the challenge.

It has been reported of the late Mr. Pelham (who, though an able minister was not without his faults) that on his being attacked in the House of Commons, on the score that his measures were only of a temporary kind, replied, "they will last my time." Should a thought so fatal and unmanly possess the colonies in the present contest, the name of ancestors will be remembered by future generations with detestation.

The sun never shone on a cause of greater worth. 'Tis not the affair of a city, a county, a province, or a kingdom, but of a continent —of at least one eighth part of the habitable globe. 'Tis not the concern of a day, a year, or an age; posterity are virtually involved in the contest, and will be more or less affected even to the end of time, by the proceedings now. Now is the seedtime of continental union, faith, and honor. The least fracture now will be like a name engraved with the point of a pin on the tender rind of a young oak; the wound will enlarge with the tree, and posterity read it in full grown characters.

By referring the matter from argument to arms, a new area for politics is struck; a new method of thinking hath arisen. All plans, proposals, etc., prior to the nineteenth of April, i.e., to the commencement of hostilities, are like the almanacs of last year; which, though proper then, are superseded and useless now. Whatever was advanced by the advocates on either side of the question then, terminated in one and the same point, viz., a union with Great Britain; the only difference between the parties was the method of effecting it; the one proposing force, the other friendship; but it hath so far happened that the first has failed, and the second has withdrawn her influence.

As much hath been said of the advantages of reconciliation, which, like an agreeable dream, hath passed away and left us as we were, it is but right that we should examine the contrary side of the argument, and inquire into some of the many material injuries which these colonies sustain, and always will sustain, by being connected with and dependent on Great Britain. To examine that connection and dependence, on the principles of nature and common sense, to see what we have to trust to, if separated, and what we are to expect, if dependent.

I have heard it asserted by some, that as America has flourished under her former connection with Great Britain, the same connection is necessary towards her future happiness, and will always have the same effect. Nothing can be more fallacious than this kind of argument. We may as well assert that because a child has thrived upon milk, that it is never to have meat, or that the first twenty years of our lives is to become a precedent for the next twenty. But even this is admitting more than is true, for I answer roundly that America would have flourished as much, and probably much more, had no European power taken any notice of her. The articles of commerce by which she has enriched herself, are the necessaries of life, and will always have a market while eating is the custom of Europe.

But she has protected us, say some. That she hath engrossed us is true, and defended the continent at our expense as well as her own, is admitted; and she would have defended Turkey from the same motives, viz., for the sake of trade and dominion.

Alas! we have been long led away by ancient prejudices, and made large sacrifices to superstition. We have boasted the protection of Great Britain, without considering that her motive was interest not attachment; and that she did not protect us from our enemies on our account, but from her enemies on her own account, from those who had no quarrel with us on any other account, and who will always be our enemies on the same account. Let Britain waive her pretensions to the continent, or the continent throw off the dependence, and we should be at peace with France and Spain, were they at war with Britain. The miseries of Hanover's last war ought to warn us against connections.[1]

It hath lately been asserted in Parliament, that the colonies have no relation to each other but through the parent country, i.e., that Pennsylvania and the Jerseys, and so on for the rest, are sister colonies by the way of England; this is certainly a very roundabout way of proving relationship, but it is the nearest and only true way of proving enemyship, if I may so call it. France and Spain never were, nor perhaps ever will be, our enemies as Americans, but as our being the subjects of Great Britain.

But Britain is the parent country, say some. Then the more shame upon her conduct. Even brutes do not devour their young, nor savages make war upon their families; wherefore, the assertion, if true, turns to her reproach; but it happens not to be true, or only partly so, and the phrase, *parent* or *mother country*, hath been jesuitically adopted by the King and his parasites, with a low papistical[2] design of gaining an unfair bias on the credulous weakness of our minds. Europe and not England is the parent country of America. This new World hath been the asylum for the persecuted lovers of civil and religious liberty from *every part* of Europe. Hither have they fled, not from the tender embraces of the mother, but from the cruelty of the monster; and it is so far true of England, that the same tyranny which drove the first emigrants from home, pursues their descendants still.

In this extensive quarter of the Globe, we forget the narrow limits of three hundred and sixty miles (the extent of England) and carry our friendship on a larger scale; we claim brotherhood with every European Christian, and triumph in the generosity of the sentiment.

It is pleasant to observe by what regular gradations we surmount local prejudices, as we enlarge our acquaintance with the world. A man born in any town in England divided into parishes, will naturally associate most with his fellow parishioners (because their interests in many cases will be common) and distinguish him by the name of neighbor; if he meet him but a few miles from home, he drops the narrow idea of a street, and salutes him by the name of townsman; if he travel out of the county, and meets him in any other, he forgets the minor divisions of street and town, and calls him countryman, i.e., county-man; but if in their foreign excursions they should associate in France or any other part of Europe, their local remembrance would be enlarged into that of Englishmen. And by a just parity of reasoning, all Europeans meeting in America, or any other quarter of the globe, are countrymen; for England, Holland, Germany, or Sweden, when compared with the whole, stand in the same places on the larger scale which the divisions of street, town, and county do on the smaller one; distinctions too limited, for continental minds. Not one third of the inhabitants, even of this province,[1] are of English descent. Wherefore, I reprobate the phrase of parent or mother country applied to England only, as being false, selfish, narrow, and ungenerous.

But, admitting that we were all of English descent, what does it amount to? Nothing. Britain, being now an open enemy, extinguishes every other name and title, and to say that reconciliation is our duty, is truly farcical. The first king of England, of the present line (William the Conqueror) was a Frenchman, and half the peers of England are descendants from the same country; wherefore, by the same method of reasoning, England ought to be governed by France.

Much hath been said of the united strength of Britain and the colonies, that in conjunction they might bid defiance to the world. But this is mere presumption; the fate of war is uncertain, neither do the expressions mean anything; for this continent would never suffer

[1] The Kingdom of Hanover, in Germany, subject to the English Georges, was ravaged by the French armies during the French and Indian War, 1756–1763. [2] used in the sense of *crafty*

[1] Pennsylvania

itself to be drained of inhabitants, to support the British arms in either Asia, Africa, or Europe.

Besides, what have we to do with setting the world at defiance? Our plan is commerce, and that, well attended to, will secure us the peace and friendship of all Europe; because it is the interest of all Europe to have America a free port. Her trade will always be a protection, and her barrenness of gold and silver secure her from invaders.

I challenge the warmest advocate for reconciliation to show a single advantage that this continent can reap by being connected with Great Britain. I repeat the challenge; not a single advantage is derived. Our corn [1] will fetch its price in any market in Europe, and our imported goods must be paid for, buy them where we will.

But the injuries and disadvantages which we sustain by that connection, are without number; and our duty to mankind at large, as well as to ourselves, instructs us to renounce the alliance; because any submission to or dependence on Great Britain tends directly to involve this continent in European wars and quarrels; and sets us at variance with nations who would otherwise seek our friendship, and against whom we have neither anger nor complaint. As Europe is our market for trade, we ought to form no partial connection with any part of it. It is the true interest of America to steer clear of European contentions, which she never can do, while, by her dependence on Britain, she is made the make-weight in the scale of British politics.

Europe is too thickly planted with kingdoms to be long at peace, and whenever a war breaks out between England and any foreign power, the trade of America goes to ruin, because of her connection with Britain. The next war may not turn out like the last, and should it not, the advocates for reconciliation now will be wishing for separation then, because neutrality, in that case, would be a safer convoy than a man-of-war. Everything that is right or natural pleads for separation. The blood of the slain, the weeping voice of nature cries, "'Tis time to part." Even the distance at which the Almighty hath placed England and America is a strong and natural proof that the authority of the one over the other was never the design of Heaven. The time likewise at which the continent was discovered, adds weight to the argument, and the manner in which it was peopled increases the force of it. The Reformation was preceded by the discovery of America, as if the Almighty graciously meant to open a sanctuary to the persecuted in future years, when home should afford neither friendship nor safety. . . .

1776

[1] grain

Thomas Young and Ethan Allen

THE MOST NOTABLE deistic treatise written in eighteenth-century America, *Reason the Only Oracle of Man*, was published at Brattleboro, Vermont, in 1784, as the work of Colonel Ethan Allen (1738–1789), of Revolutionary fame. There seems to be good reason to believe, however, that Allen's part in the book was principally completing and seeing through the press a manuscript left by Dr. Thomas Young (1732–1777), though Allen may have collaborated in its early stages. Dr. Young, a native of New Windsor, New York, was for several years a physician in Dutchess County, New York, and from 1768 to 1774 in Boston, where he contributed to the *Royal Magazine*, was closely connected with Dr. Joseph Warren and Samuel Adams, and delivered the first anniversary address on the Boston Massacre. After a brief residence at Newport, he removed to Philadelphia. Here he served as a hospital surgeon until his early death and associated intimately with the patriot leaders, including Thomas Paine, to whom he may have shown the manuscript of *Reason the Only Oracle of Man*. This work, generally called the *Oracles of Reason*, had probably been undertaken as a challenge to orthodox Calvinistic theology as set forth in a number of "Questions" pronounced by Jonathan Edwards during his brief incumbency as president of Princeton in 1758. Ethan Allen, during the next few years, was living at Salisbury, Connecticut, not far from Dr. Young; was closely associated with him; and was actively sympathetic, as a youth of vigorous and inquiring mind, with his deistic views. After Young's death, Allen is said to have obtained the manuscript from his widow and, perhaps with the aid of a "young college graduate, a school-teacher," completed and published it. The few copies that survived a fire in the printer's shop did not win for Allen the literary fame which he hoped to gain, but provoked the New England clergy to charges of atheism. The fact that a bolt of lightning was the cause of the fire was regarded as a divine judgment.

The book was not merely a rationalistic attack upon religious orthodoxy but an ambitious design to set forth a systematized theology based upon deistic principles. Its influence was restricted by its limited circulation, but the later deists used it in their attempts to establish a deistic "church" in New York State.

Reason the Only Oracle of Man is available in Scholars' Facsimiles and Reprints, ed. John Pell (1939). For Dr. Young's life, see H. E. Edes, "Memoir of Dr. Thomas Young, 1731–1777," *Publications* of the Colonial Society of Massachusetts, XI, 2–54 (1910); the *DAB* article by G. P. Anderson; and J. S. Loring, *The Hundred Boston Orators* (1852). For Ethan Allen, see John Pell, *Ethan Allen* (1929); for bibliography, M. D. Gilman, *Bibliography of Vermont* (1897). See also G. P. Anderson, "Who Wrote Ethan Allen's Bible?" *New England Quarterly*, X, 685–696 (December, 1937); Dana Doten, "Ethan Allen's 'Orginal Something,'" *ibid.*, XI, 361–366 (June, 1938); G. A. Koch, *Republican Religion* (1933), 79 ff.; and B. T. Schantz, "Ethan Allen's Religious Ideas," *Journal of Religion*, XVIII, 183–217.

From REASON THE ONLY ORACLE
OF MAN

CHAPTER II, SECTION VII

*Of the Eternity and Infinitude of
Divine Providence*

WHEN we consider our solar system, attracted by its fiery center, and moving in its several orbits with regular, majestic, and periodical revolutions, we are charmed at the prospect and contemplation of those worlds of motion, and adore the wisdom and the power by which they are attracted, and their velocity regulated and perpetuated. And when we reflect that the blessings of life are derived from and dependent on the properties, qualities, constructions, proportions, and movements of that stupendous machine, we gratefully acknowledge the divine beneficence. When we extend our thoughts (through our external sensations) to the vast regions of the starry heavens, we are lost in the immensity of God's works; some stars appear fair and luminous, and others scarcely discernible to the eye, which by the help of glasses make a brilliant appearance, bringing the knowledge of others far remote within the verge of our feeble discoveries, which merely by the eye could not have been discerned or distinguished. These discoveries of the works of God naturally prompt the inquisitive mind to conclude that the author of this astonishing part of creation, which is displayed to our view, has still extended his creation; so that if it were possible that any of us could be transported to the farthest extended star which is perceptible to us here, we should from thence survey worlds as distant from that, as that is from this, and so on *ad infinitum*.

Furthermore, it is altogether reasonable to conclude that the heavenly bodies, *alias* worlds, which move or are situate within the circle of our knowledge, as well as all others throughout immensity, are each and every of them possessed or inhabited by some intelligent agents or other, however different their sensations or manner of receiving or communicating their ideas may be from ours, or however different from each other. For why would it not have been as wise or as consistent with the perfections which we adore in God, to have neglected giving being to intelligences in this world as in those other worlds, interspersed with either of various qualities in his immense creation? And inasmuch as this world is thus replenished, we may with the highest rational certainty infer that as God has given us to rejoice and adore him for our being, he has acted consistent with his goodness, in the display of his providence throughout the university of worlds.

To suppose that God Almighty has confined his goodness to this world, to the exclusion of all others, is much similar to the idle fancies of some individuals in this world, that they and those of their communion or faith are the favorites of heaven exclusively; but these are narrow and bigoted conceptions, which are degrading to a rational nature and utterly unworthy of God, of whom we should form the most exalted ideas. Furthermore, there could be no display of goodness or of any of the moral perfections of God, merely in repleting immensity with a stupid creation of elements or sluggish, senseless, and incogitative matter, which by nature may be supposed to be incapable of sensation, reflection, and enjoyment: undoubtedly elements and material compositions were designed by God to subserve rational beings, by constituting or supporting them in their respective modes of existence, in this or those other numerous worlds.

There may be in God's boundless empire of nature and providence as many different sorts of modified sensation as there are different worlds and temperatures in immensity, or at least sensation may more or less vary; but whether their sensations agree in any or many respects or not, or whether they agree with ours, or if in any part, how far, are matters unknown to us; but that there are intelligent orders of beings interspersed through the creation of God, is a matter of the highest degree of rational certainty of any thing that falls short of mathematical demonstration or of proofs which come within the reach of our outward sensations, called sensible demonstration. For if this is the only world that is replenished with life and reason, it includes the whole circumference of God's providence; and there would be no display of wisdom or goodness merely in governing rude elements and senseless matter, nor could there be any valuable end proposed by such a supposed government, or any happiness, instruction, or subserviency to being in general, for any reason assigned by such a creation (for it cannot be a providence) should have had the divine approbation; and consequently we may be morally certain that rational beings are interspersed co-extensive with the creation of God.

Although the various orders of intelligences throughout infinitude differ ever so much in their manner of sensation, and consequently in their manner of communication or of receiving ideas, yet reason and consciousness must be the same in all, but not the same with respect to the various objects of the several worlds, though in nature the same. For instance, a person born blind cannot possibly have an idea of colors, though his sensibility of sound and feeling may be as acute as ours;

and since there are such a variety of modes of sensation in this world, how vastly numerous may we apprehend them to be in immensity! We shall soon, by pondering on these things, feel the insufficiency of our imagination to conceive of the immense possibility of the variety of their modes of sensation and the manner of intercourse of cogitative beings.

It may be objected that a man cannot subsist in the sun; but does it follow from thence that God cannot or has not constituted a nature peculiar to that fiery region, and caused it to be as natural and necessary for it to suck in and breathe out flames of fire, as it is for us to do the like in air? Numerous are the kinds of fishy animals, which can no other way subsist but in the water, in which other animals would perish (amphibious ones excepted); while other animals, in a variety of forms, either swifter or slower, move on the surface of the earth or wing the air: of these there are sundry kinds which during the seasons of winter live without food; and many of the insects which are really possessed of animal life remain frozen, and as soon as they are let loose by the kind influence of the sun, they again assume their wonted animal life; and if animal life may differ so much in the same world, what inconceivable variety may be possible in worlds innumerable, as applicable to mental, cogitative, and organized beings! Certain it is, that any supposed obstructions concerning the quality or temperature of any or every of those worlds could not have been any bar in the way of God Almighty, with regard to his replenishing his universal creation with moral agents. The unlimited perfection of God could perfectly well adapt every part of his creation to the design of whatever rank or species of constituted beings his Godlike wisdom and goodness saw fit to impart existence to; so that as there is no deficiency of absolute perfection in God, it is rationally demonstrative that the immense creation is replenished with rational agents, and that it has been eternally so, and that the display of divine goodness must have been as perfect and complete in the antecedent, as it is possible to be in the subsequent eternity.

From this theological way of arguing on the creation and providence of God, it appears that the whole, which we denominate by the term *nature*, which is the same as creation perfectly regulated, was eternally connected together by the creator to answer the same all-glorious purpose, *to wit:* the display of the divine nature, the consequences of which are existence and happiness to being in general, so that creation, with all its productions, operates according to the laws of nature and is sustained by the self-existent eternal cause in perfect order and decorum, agreeable to the eternal wisdom, unalterable rectitude, impartial justice, and immense goodness of the divine nature, which is a summary of God's providence. It is from the established order of nature that summer and winter, rainy and fair seasons, monsoons, refreshing breezes, seed time and harvest, day and night, interchangeably succeed each other and diffuse their extensive blessings to man. Every enjoyment and support of life is from God, delivered to his creatures in and by the tendency, aptitude, disposition, and operation of those laws.— Nature is the medium or intermediate instrument through which God dispenses his benignity to mankind. The air we breathe in, the light of the sun, and the waters of the murmuring rills evince his providence; and well it is that they are given in so great profusion that they cannot by the monopoly of the rich be engrossed from the poor.

When we copiously pursue the study of nature, we are certain to be lost in the immensity of the works and wisdom of God; we may nevertheless, in a variety of things, discern their fitness, happifying tendency, and sustaining quality to us-ward, from all which, as rational and contemplative beings, we are prompted to infer that God is universally uniform and consistent in his infinitude of creation and providence; although we cannot comprehend all that consistency, by reason of infirmity, yet we are morally sure that of all possible plans, infinite wisdom must have eternally adopted the best, and infinite goodness have approved it, and infinite power have perfected it. And as the good of being in general must have been the ultimate end of God in his creation and government of his creatures, his omniscience could not fail to have it always present in his view. Universal nature must therefore be ultimately attracted to this single point, and infinite perfection must have eternally displayed itself in creation and providence. From hence we infer that God is as eternal and infinite in his goodness as his self-existent and perfect nature is omnipotently great.

CHAPTER XIV, SECTION III

Of the Importance of the Exercise of Reason and Practice of Morality, in Order to the Happiness of Mankind

The period of life is very uncertain, and at the longest is but short; a few years bring us from infancy to manhood, a few more to a dissolution; pain, sickness, and death are the necessary consequences of animal life. Through life we struggle with physical evils, which eventually are certain to destroy our earthly 20 composition; and well would it be for us did evils end here; but alas! moral evil has been more or less predominant in our agency; and though natural evil is unavoidable, yet moral evil may be prevented or remedied by the exercise of virtue. Morality is therefore of more importance to us than any or all other attainments, as it is a habit of mind which, from a retrospective consciousness of our agency in this life, we should carry with us into our 30 succeeding state of existence, as an acquired appendage of our rational nature and as the necessary means of our mental happiness. Virtue and vice are the only things in this world which, with our souls, are capable of surviving death; the former is the rational and only procuring cause of all intellectual happiness, and the latter of conscious guilt and misery; and therefore our indispensable duty and ultimate interest is to love, cultivate, and 40 improve the one, as the means of our greatest good, and to hate and abstain from the other, as productive of our greatest evil. And in order thereto, we should so far divest ourselves of the incumbrances of this world (which are too apt to engross our attention) as to enquire a consistent system of the knowledge of religious duty, and make it our constant endeavor in life to act conformably to it. The knowledge of the being, perfections, creation, 50 and providence of God, and of the immortality

of our souls, is the foundation of religion, which has been particularly illustrated in the four first chapters of this discourse. And as the pagan, Jewish, Christian, and Mahometan countries of the world have been overwhelmed with a multiplicity of revelations diverse from each other, and which, by their respective promulgators, are said to have been immediately inspired into their souls by the 10 spirit of God, or immediately communicated to them by the intervening agency of angels (as in the instance of the invisible Gabriel to Mahomet), and as those revelations have been received and credited by far the greater part of the inhabitants of the several countries of the world (on whom they have been obtruded) as supernaturally revealed by God or angels; and which, in doctrine and discipline, are in most respects repugnant to each other, it fully 20 evinces their imposture and authorizes us, without a lengthy course of arguing, to determine with certainty that not more than one, if any one, of them had their original from God, as they clash with each other, which is ground of high probability against the authenticity of each of them.

A revelation that may be supposed to be really of the institution of God must also be supposed to be perfectly consistent or uniform, and to be able to stand the test of truth; therefore such pretended revelations as are tendered to us as the contrivance of heaven, which do not bear that test, we may be morally certain, was [sic] either originally a deception or has since, by adulteration, become spurious. Furthermore, should we admit that among the numerous revelations on which the respective priests have given the stamp of divinity, some one of them was in reality of divine authority, 40 yet we could no otherwise, as rational beings, distinguish it from others, but by reason.

Reason therefore must be the standard by which we determine the respective claims of revelation; for otherwise we may as well subscribe to the divinity of the one as of the other, or to the whole of them, or to none at all. So likewise, on this thesis, if reason rejects the whole of those revelations, we ought to return to the religion of nature and reason.

Undoubtedly it is our duty, and for our 50 best good, that we occupy and improve the faculties with which our Creator has endowed us; but so far as prejudice or prepossession of opinion prevails over our minds, in the same proportion reason is excluded from our theory or practice. Therefore, if we would acquire useful knowledge, we must first divest ourselves of those impediments and sincerely endeavor to search out the truth and draw our conclusions from reason and just argument, which will never conform to our inclination, 10 interest, or fancy; but we must conform to that if we would judge rightly. As certain as we determine contrary to reason, we make a wrong conclusion; therefore, our wisdom is to conform to the nature and reason of things, as well in religious matters as in other sciences. Preposterously absurd would it be to negative the exercise of reason in religious concerns and yet be actuated by it in all other and less occurrences of life. All our knowledge of things 20 is derived from God, in and by the order of nature, out of which we cannot perceive, reflect, or understand anything whatsoever; our external senses are natural and so are our souls; by the instrumentality of the former we perceive the objects of sense, and with the latter we reflect on them. And those objects are also natural; so that ourselves, and all things about us, and our knowledge collected therefrom is natural, and not supernatural, as argued in the Sixth Chapter.

We may, and often do, connect or arrange our ideas together in a wrong or improper manner for the want of skill or judgment, or through mistake or the want of application, or through the influence of prejudice; but in all such cases the error does not originate from the ideas themselves but from the composer; for a system, or an arrangement of ideas justly composed, always contain[s] the truth, but an unjust composition never fails to contain error and falsehood. Therefore an unjust connection of ideas is not derived from nature but from the imperfect composition of man. Misconnection of ideas is the same as misjudging, and has no positive existence, being merely a creature of the imagination; but nature and truth are real and uniform, and the rational mind, by reasoning, discerns the uniformity and is thereby enabled to make a just composition of ideas which will stand the test of truth. But the fantastical illuminations of the credulous and superstitious part of mankind proceed from weakness, and as far as they take place in the world, subvert the religion of Reason and Truth.

1784

1743 -- *Thomas Jefferson* -- 1826

THE VERSATILITY so marked in many of the statesmen of the Revolution was amazingly conspicuous in Jefferson. He served his country in the House of Burgesses, the Continental Congress, and the Congress of the United States, and as Minister to France, Secretary of State, and President of the United States. Meanwhile he was concerned with the classics, with music, architecture, poetry, and science, besides developing a political theory which has largely dominated both the Democratic party and, in a measure, its successive rivals in this country. As a philosopher and lawyer, his writings stress both the abstract and the legal rights of man. The most important document associated with him is the Declaration of Independence, which he drafted.

Leagued by birth and marriage with the best Virginia families, the owner of 10,000 acres of land and over a hundred slaves, and an aristocrat in his tastes and culture, he was politically the advocate and spokesman of the independent small farmer class of the western counties of his state. Perhaps better acquainted than any other American with Greek, Roman, French, and other Continental political philosophies, he yet was actuated by the ideas of English theorists from Locke on, carried to their extreme application. He admitted that he professed "the same principles" that Tom Paine professed in *The Rights of Man*. As early as 1774, in his *Summary View of the Rights of British America*, on the basis of the rights of migration and conquest by the European settlers in America, as by the Anglo-Saxons in England, "he denied all parliamentary authority over the colonies and claimed that the only political tie with Great Britain was supplied by the King, to whom the colonists had voluntarily submitted." The Declaration of Independence therefore combines with an assertion of natural rights a long list of alleged injuries perpetrated by George III which justified the severing of this one tie of authority.

When, from his secretaryship in Washington's cabinet, he saw the new government, under Hamilton's influence, becoming more and more centralized in power and aristocratic in spirit—"galloping fast into monarchy"—he became alarmed and labored to organize the disunited agrarian and landless elements into an opposition party. By adroit leadership and the aid of devoted followers he succeeded, and within eight years was enabled to accomplish a peaceful revolution of power and re-direct the course of government toward popular sovereignty.

Jefferson envisaged an agricultural democracy composed mainly of and controlled by farmers and free laborers, and dreaded the growth of great industrial organizations in which the individual laborer has no voice or interest. Realizing the importance of education in such a scheme, he labored long and earnestly for the establishment of state-supported universities as opposed to church and private colleges. He planned for many years for the erection of the University of Virginia and regarded its establishment in 1819 as one of his greatest achievements.

The best edition of *The Writings of Thomas Jefferson* is by P. L. Ford (10 vols., with list of Jefferson's works in Vol. I, 1892–1899). *Thomas Jefferson's Correspondence* was edited by W. C. Ford (1916). G. Chinard edited *The Commonplace Book of Thomas Jefferson* (1926) and *The Literary Bible of Thomas Jefferson* (1928). The introduction in the latter discusses Jefferson's literary theories and tastes. F. C. Prescott's *Alexander Hamilton and Thomas Jefferson: Selections*, a very useful introduction, appeared in 1934.

Important biographies are those by G. Chinard (1929), W. E. Dodd (1911), A. J. Nock (1926), and C. G. Bowers, *Jefferson in Power* (1936). The article in *DAB* is by Dumas Malone; that in the *Encyclopædia Britannica*, by Francis S. Philbrick.

The background of Jefferson's work and special topics concerning it are discussed in the following: Henry Adams, *History of the United States . . . during the First and Second Administrations of Thomas Jefferson* (4 vols., 1889–1890); H. B. Adams, *Thomas Jefferson and the University of Virginia* (1888); J. T. Adams, *The Living Jefferson* (1936); C. F. Arrowood, *Thomas Jefferson and Education in a Republic* (1930); C. A. Beard, *Economic Origins of Jeffersonian Democracy*

(1915); C. G. Bowers, *Jefferson and Hamilton* (1925); E. Channing, *The Jeffersonian System, 1801–1811* (1906); J. H. Hazelton, *The Declaration of Independence* (1906); I. W. Riley, *American Philosophy, the Early Schools* (1907); and P. Wilstach, *Jefferson and Monticello* (1926).

THE UNANIMOUS DECLARATION

OF THE THIRTEEN UNITED
STATES OF AMERICA

WHEN, in the course of human events, it becomes necessary for one people to dissolve the political bands which have connected them with another, and to assume among the powers of the earth, the separate and equal station to which the laws of Nature and of Nature's God entitle them, a decent respect to the opinions of mankind requires that they should declare the causes which impel them to the separation.—We hold these truths to be self-evident, that all men are created equal, that they are endowed by their Creator with certain unalienable Rights, that among these are life, liberty and the pursuit of happiness. —That to secure these rights, governments are instituted among men, deriving their just powers from the consent of the governed.— That whenever any form of government becomes destructive of these ends, it is the right of the people to alter or abolish it, and to institute new government, laying its foundation on such principles, organizing its powers in such form as to them shall seem most likely to effect their safety and happiness. Prudence, indeed, will dictate that governments long established should not be changed for light and transient causes; and accordingly all experience hath shown that mankind are more disposed to suffer, while evils are sufferable, than to right themselves by abolishing the forms to which they are accustomed. But when a long train of abuses and usurpations, pursuing invariably the same object, evinces a design to reduce them under absolute despotism, it is their right, it is their duty, to throw off such government, and to provide new guards for their future security.—Such has been the patient sufferance of these Colonies; and such is now the necessity which constrains them to alter their former systems of government. The history of the present King of Great Britain is a history of repeated injuries and usurpations, all having in direct object the establishment of an absolute tyranny over these States. . . . In every stage of these oppressions we have petitioned for redress in the most humble terms. Our repeated petitions have been answered only by repeated injuries. A prince whose character is thus marked by every act which may define a tyrant is unfit to be the ruler of a free people. Nor have we been wanting in attentions to our British brethren. We have warned them from time to time of attempts by their legislature to extend an unwarrantable jurisdiction over us. We have reminded them of the circumstances of our emigration and settlement here. We have appealed to their native justice and magnanimity, and we have conjured them by the ties of our kindred to disavow these usurpations, which would inevitably interrupt our connection and correspondence. They too have been deaf to the voice of justice and of consanguinity. We must, therefore, acquiesce in the necessity which denounces our separation, and hold them, as we hold the rest of mankind, enemies in war, in peace friends.—

We, therefore, the Representatives of the UNITED STATES OF AMERICA, in General Congress Assembled, appealing to the Supreme Judge of the world for the rectitude of our intentions, do, in the name and by the authority of the good people of these Colonies, solemnly publish and declare that these United Colonies are, and of Right ought to be, FREE AND INDEPENDENT STATES; and that they are absolved from all allegiance to the British Crown, and that all political connection between them and the State of Great Britain is and ought to be totally dissolved; and that as free and independent states, they have full power to levy war, conclude peace, contract alliances, establish commerce, and to do all other acts and things which independent states may of right do.—And for the support of this Declaration, with a firm reliance on the protection of divine Providence, we mutually pledge to each other our lives, our fortunes and our sacred honor.

1776

[A GIRL'S EDUCATION]

LETTER TO MARTHA JEFFERSON

Annapolis, Nov. 28th, 1783

DEAR PATSY: After four days' journey, I arrived here without any accident, and in as good health as when I left Philadelphia. The conviction that you would be more improved in the situation I have placed you than if still with me has solaced me on my parting with you, which my love for you has rendered a difficult thing. The acquirements which I hope you will make under the tutors I have provided for you will render you more worthy of my love; and if they cannot increase it, they will prevent its diminution. Consider the good lady who has taken you under her roof, who has undertaken to see that you perform all your exercises, and to admonish you in all those wanderings from what is right or what is clever, to which your inexperience would expose you: consider her, I say, as your mother, as the only person to whom, since the loss with which Heaven has pleased to afflict you,[1] you can now look up; and that her displeasure or disapprobation, on any occasion, will be an immense misfortune, which should you be so unhappy as to incur by any unguarded act, think no concession too much to regain her good-will. With respect to the distribution of your time, the following is what I should approve:

From 8 to 10, practise music.

From 10 to 1, dance one day and draw another.

From 1 to 2, draw on the day you dance, and write a letter next day.

From 3 to 4, read French.

From 4 to 5, exercise yourself in music.

From 5 till bedtime, read English, write, etc.

Communicate this plan to Mrs. Hopkinson, and if she approves of it, pursue it. As long as Mrs. Trist remains in Philadelphia, cultivate her affection. She has been a valuable friend to you, and her good sense and good heart make her valued by all who know her, and by nobody on earth more than me. I expect you will write me by every post. Inform me what books you read, what tunes you learn, and

[1] Jefferson's wife, Martha Wayles Jefferson, had died in 1782.

enclose me your best copy of every lesson in drawing. Write also one letter a week either to your Aunt Eppes, your Aunt Skipwith, your Aunt Carr, or the little lady from whom I now enclose a letter, and always put the letter you so write under cover to me. Take care that you never spell a word wrong. Always before you write a word, consider how it is spelled, and, if you do not remember it, turn to a dictionary. It produces great praise to a lady to spell well. I have placed my happiness on seeing you good and accomplished; and no distress this world can now bring on me would equal that of your disappointing my hopes. If you love me, then strive to be good under every situation and to all living creatures, and to acquire those accomplishments which I have put in your power, and which will go far toward insuring you the warmest love of your affectionate father.

P.S.—Keep my letters and read them at times, that you may always have present in your mind those things which will endear you to me.

From NOTES ON THE STATE OF VIRGINIA

[On Slavery]

Notes on the State of Virginia, first published privately in 1784, was Jefferson's extended reply to a series of questions regarding his native state, its resources, inhabitants, etc., asked by the Marquis de Barbé-Marbois, Secretary of the French Legation at Philadelphia in 1781. The reply was written to inform the French people regarding their new allies.

THERE must doubtless be an unhappy influence on the manners of our people produced by the existence of slavery among us. The whole commerce between master and slave is a perpetual exercise of the most boisterous passions, the most unremitting despotism on the one part, and degrading submissions on the other. Our children see this and learn to imitate it, for man is an imitative animal. This quality is the germ of all education in him. From his cradle to his grave he is learning to do what he sees others do. If a parent could find no motive either in his philanthropy or his self-love for restraining the intemperance of passion toward his slave, it should always be a sufficient one that his child is present. But generally it is not sufficient. The parent storms, the child looks on, catches the lineaments of wrath, puts on the same airs in the circle of smaller slaves, gives a loose to the worst of passions, and thus nursed, educated, and daily exercised in tyranny, cannot but be stamped by it with odious peculiarities. The man must be a prodigy who can retain his manners and morals undepraved by such circumstances. And with what execration should the statesman be loaded who, permitting one-half the citizens thus to trample on the rights of the other, transforms those into despots, and these into enemies, destroys the morals of the one part, and the *amor patriae* of the other. For if a slave can have a country in this world, it must be any other in preference to that in which he is born to live and labor for another; in which he must lock up the faculties of his nature, contribute as far as depends on his individual endeavors to the evanishment of the human race, or entail his own miserable condition on the endless generations proceeding from him. With the morals of the people, their industry also is destroyed. For in a warm climate, no man will labor for himself who can make another labor for him. This is so true that, of the proprietors of slaves, a very small proportion indeed are ever seen to labor. And can the liberties of a nation be thought secure when we have removed their only firm basis, a conviction in the minds of the people that these liberties are of the gift of God? That they are not to be violated but with His wrath? Indeed, I tremble for my country when I reflect that God is just; that His justice cannot sleep forever; that considering numbers, nature, and natural means only, a revolution of the wheel of fortune, an exchange of situation, is among possible events; that it may become probable by supernatural interference! The Almighty has no attribute which can take side with us in such a contest. But it is impossible to be temperate and to pursue this subject through the various considerations of policy, of morals, of history natural and civil. We must be contented to hope they will force their way into everyone's mind. I think a

change already perceptible, since the origin of the present revolution. The spirit of the master is abating, that of the slave rising from the dust, his condition mollifying, the way, I hope, preparing, under the auspices of heaven, for a total emancipation, and that this is disposed, in the order of events, to be with the consent of the masters, rather than by their extirpation.

1784

[ON THE ADOPTION OF THE CONSTITUTION]

LETTER TO MR. ALEXANDER DONALD

During the debates on the Constitution, Jefferson was in France. The plan proposed in the following letter for insuring public rights is typical of his methods as a political leader. His fears, summarized here, are more fully outlined in his autobiography for this period.

February, 1788

DEAR SIR:

I wish with all my soul that the nine first conventions [1] may accept the new Constitution, because this will secure to us the good it contains, which I think great and important. But I equally wish that the four latest conventions, whichever they be, may refuse to accede to it till a declaration of rights be annexed. This would probably command the offer of such a declaration and thus give to the world fabric perhaps as much perfection as any one of that kind ever had. By a declaration of rights I mean one which shall stipulate freedom of religion, freedom of the press, freedom of commerce against monopolies, trial by juries in all cases, no suspensions of the habeas corpus, no standing armies. These are fetters against doing evil which no honest government should decline. There is another strong feature in the new Constitution which I as strongly dislike. That is, the perpetual re-eligibility of the President. [2] Of this I expect no amendment at present, because I do not see that anybody has objected to it on your side the water. But it will be productive of cruel

[1] the conventions held in the several states   [2] By an earlier vote, Jefferson says, the Convention had recommended, eight to two, a term of seven years, and, by a simple majority, only a single term of office for the President.

distress to our country, even in your day and mine. The importance to France and England, to have our government in the hands of a friend or a foe will occasion their interference by money, and even by arms. Our President will be of much more consequence to them than a King of Poland. We must take care, however, that neither this, nor any other objection to the new form, produces a schism 10 in our Union. That would be an incurable evil because near friends, falling out, never reunite cordially; whereas all of us going together, we shall be sure to cure the evils of our new Constitution, before they do great harm.

FIRST INAUGURAL ADDRESS

FRIENDS AND FELLOW-CITIZENS:—
Called upon to undertake the duties of the first executive office of our country, I avail 20 myself of the presence of that portion of my fellow-citizens which is here assembled, to express my grateful thanks for the favor with which they have been pleased to look towards me, to declare a sincere consciousness that the task is above my talents, and that I approach it with those anxious and awful presentiments which the greatness of the charge and the weakness of my powers so justly inspire. A rising nation spread over a wide and fruitful land, 30 traversing all the seas with the rich productions of their industry, engaged in commerce with nations who feel power and forget right, advancing rapidly to destinies beyond the reach of mortal eye; when I contemplate these transcendent objects, and see the honor, the happiness, and the hopes of this beloved country committed to the issue and the auspices of this day, I shrink from the contemplation, and humble myself before the magnitude of the 40 undertaking.

Utterly, indeed, should I despair, did not the presence of many whom I here see remind me that in the other high authorities provided by our constitution I shall find resources of wisdom, of virtue, and of zeal on which to rely under all difficulties. To you, then, gentlemen, who are charged with the sovereign functions of legislation, and to those associated with you, I look with encouragement for that guidance 50 and support which may enable us to steer with safety the vessel in which we are all embarked, amidst the conflicting elements of a troubled sea.

During the contest of opinion through which we have passed, the animation of discussions and of exertions has sometimes worn an aspect which might impose on strangers unused to think freely and to speak and to write what they think. But this being now decided by the voice of the nation, announced according to the rules of the constitution, all will, of course, arrange themselves under the will of the law, and unite in common efforts for the common good. All too will bear in mind this sacred principle, that though the will of the majority is in all cases to prevail, that will, to be rightful, must be reasonable; that the minority possess their equal rights, which equal laws must protect, and to violate would be oppression. Let us then, fellow-citizens, unite with one heart and one mind; let us restore to social intercourse that harmony and affection without which liberty, and even life itself, are but dreary things. And let us reflect that having banished from our land that religious intolerance under which mankind so long bled and suffered, we have yet gained little if we countenance a political intolerance as despotic, as wicked, and capable of as bitter and bloody persecutions. During the throes and convulsions of the ancient world, during the agonizing spasms of infuriated man, seeking through blood and slaughter his long-lost liberty, it was not wonderful that the agitation of the billows should reach even this distant and peaceful shore; that this should be more felt and feared by some and less by others; and should divide opinions as to measures of safety. But every difference of opinion is not a difference of principle. We have called by different names brethren of the same principle. We are all Republicans; we are all Federalists. If there be any among us who would wish to dissolve this Union, or to change its republican form, let them stand undisturbed as monuments of the safety with which error of opinion may be tolerated, where reason is left free to combat it. I know, indeed, that some honest men fear that a republican government cannot be strong; that this government is not strong enough. But would the honest patriot, in the full tide of successful experiment, abandon a government which has so far kept us free and firm, on the theoretic and visionary fear that this government, the world's best hope, may by possibility want energy to preserve itself? I trust not. I believe this, on the contrary, the strongest government on earth. I believe it the only one where every man, at the call of the law would fly to the standard of the law; would meet invasions of the public order as his own personal concern. Sometimes it is said that man cannot be trusted with the government of himself. Can he, then, be trusted with the government of others? Or have we found angels in the forms of kings to govern him? Let history answer this question.

Let us then, with courage and confidence, pursue our federal and republican principles; our attachment to union and representative government. Kindly separated by nature and a wide ocean from the exterminating havoc of one quarter of the globe; too high-minded to endure the degradation of the others, possessing a chosen country, with room enough for our descendants to the hundredth and thousandth generation, entertaining a due sense of our equal right to the use of our own faculties, to the acquisitions of our own industry, to honor and confidence from our fellow-citizens, resulting not from birth, but from our actions and their sense of them; enlightened by a benign religion, professed indeed and practised in various forms, yet all of them inculcating honesty, truth, temperance, gratitude, and the love of man; acknowledging and adoring an overruling Providence, which, by all its dispensations, proves that it delights in the happiness of man here, and his greater happiness hereafter; with all these blessings, what more is necessary to make us a happy and prosperous people? Still one thing more, fellow-citizens, a wise and frugal government, which shall restrain men from injuring one another, which shall leave them otherwise free to regulate their own pursuits of industry and improvement, and shall not take from the mouth of labor the bread it has earned. This is the sum of good government, and this is necessary to close the circle of our felicities.

About to enter, fellow-citizens, on the exercise of duties which comprehend everything dear and valuable to you, it is proper you should understand what I deem the essential principle of this government, and consequently those which ought to shape its administration. I will compress them in the narrowest compass they will bear, stating the general principle but not all its limitations. Equal and exact justice to all men, of whatever state or persuasion, religious or political; peace, commerce and honest friendship with all nations, entangling alliances with none; the support of the state governments in all their rights, as the most competent administrations for our domestic concerns and the surest bulwarks against anti-republican tendencies; the preservation of the general government in its whole constitutional vigor, as the sheet-anchor of our peace at home and safety abroad; a jealous care of the right of election by the people; a mild and safe corrective of abuses which are lopped by the sword of revolution, where peaceable remedies are unprovided; absolute acquiescence in the decisions of the majority, the vital principle of republics, from which [there] is no appeal but to force, the vital principle and immediate parent of despotism; a well-disciplined militia, our best reliance in peace and for the first moments of war, till regulars may relieve them; the supremacy of the civil over the military authority—economy in the public expense, that labor may be lightly burdened; the honest payment of our debts, and sacred preservation of the public faith; encouragement of agriculture, and of commerce as its handmaid; the diffusion of information and arraignment of all abuses at the bar of the public reason; freedom of religion, freedom of the press, and freedom of person, under the protection of the habeas corpus; and trial by juries impartially selected. These principles form the bright constellation which has gone before us, and guided our steps through an age of revolution and reformation. The wisdom of our sages and blood of our heroes have been devoted to their attainment; they should be the creed of our political faith, the text of civic instruction, the touchstone by which to try the services of those we trust; and should we wander from them in moments of error or alarm, let us hasten to retrace our steps and to regain the road which alone leads to peace, liberty, and safety.

I repair then, fellow-citizens, to the post which you have assigned me. With experience enough in subordinate stations to know the difficulties of this, the greatest of all, I have learned to expect that it will rarely fall to the lot of imperfect man to retire from this station with the reputation and the favor which bring him into it. Without pretensions to that high confidence you reposed in our first and greatest revolutionary character, whose preëminent services had entitled him to the first place in his country's love, and had destined for him the fairest page in the volume of faithful history, I ask so much confidence only as may give firmness and effect to the legal administration of your affairs. I shall often go wrong through defect of judgment. When right, I shall often be thought wrong by those whose positions will not command a view of the whole ground. I ask your indulgence for my own errors, which will never be intentional; and your support against the errors of others, who may condemn what they would not, if seen in all its parts. The approbation implied by your suffrage is a great consolation to me for the past; and my future solicitude will be to retain the good opinion of those who have bestowed it in advance, to conciliate that of others by doing them all the good in my power, and to be instrumental to the happiness and freedom of all.

Relying then on the patronage of your good-will, I advance with obedience to the work, ready to retire from it whenever you become sensible how much better choice it is in your power to make. And may that Infinite Power which rules the destinies of the universe lead our councils to what is best, and give them a favorable issue for your peace and prosperity.

1801

[ON AGRICULTURAL EDUCATION]

LETTER TO DAVID WILLIAMS

Jefferson's reliance upon an America chiefly devoted to agriculture and his distrust of commerce and particularly of large manufacturing industries was one of his chief tenets. In this letter he is one of the earliest advocates of advanced training for agriculturists.

Washington, November 14, 1803

SIR:

The greatest evils of populous society have ever appeared to me to spring from the vicious distribution of its members among the occupations called for. I have no doubt that those nations are essentially right which leave this to individual choice, as a better guide to an advantageous distribution than any other which could be devised. But when, by a blind concourse, particular occupations are ruinously overcharged, and others left in want of hands, the national authorities can do much toward restoring the equilibrium. On the revival of letters, learning became the universal favorite. And with reason, because there was not enough of it existing to manage the affairs of a nation to the best advantage, nor to advance its individuals to the happiness of which they were susceptible, by improvements in their minds, their morals, their health, and in those conveniences which contribute to the comfort and embellishment of life. All the efforts of the society, therefore, were directed to the increase of learning, and the inducements of respect, ease, and profit were held up for its encouragement. Even the charities of the nation forgot that misery was their object, and spent themselves in founding schools to transfer to science the hardy sons of the plough. To these incitements were added the powerful fascinations of great cities. These circumstances have long since produced an overcharge in the class of competitors for learned occupation and great distress among the supernumerary candidates; and the more, as their habits of life have disqualified them for reentering into the laborious class. The evil cannot be suddenly, nor perhaps ever, entirely cured; nor should I presume to say by what means it may be cured. Doubtless there are many engines which the nation might bring to bear on this object. Public opinion and public encouragement are among these. The class principally defective is that of agriculture. It is the first in utility, and ought to be the first in respect. The same artificial means which have been used to produce a competition in learning may be equally successful in restoring agriculture to its primary dignity in the eyes of men. It is a science of the very first order. It counts among its handmaids the most respectable sciences, such as Chemistry, Natural Philosophy, Mechanics, Mathematics generally, Natural History, Botany. In every college and university, a professorship of agriculture, and the class of its students, might be honored as the first. Young men closing their academical education with this, as the crown of all other sciences, fascinated with its solid charms, and at a time when they are to choose an occupation, instead of crowding the other classes, would return to the farms of their fathers, their own, or those of others, and replenish and invigorate a calling now languishing under contempt and oppression. The charitable schools, instead of storming their pupils with a lore which the present state of society does not call for, converted into schools of agriculture, might restore them to that branch qualified to enrich and honor themselves, and to increase the productions of the nation instead of consuming them. A gradual abolition of the useless offices so much accumulated in all governments might close this drain also from the labors of the field and lessen the burdens imposed on them. By these and the better means which will occur to others the surcharge of the learned might in time be drawn off to recruit the laboring class of citizens, the sum of industry be increased, and that of misery diminished.

Among the ancients, the redundance of population was sometimes checked by exposing infants. To the moderns, America has offered a more humane resource. Many who cannot find employment in Europe accordingly come here. Those who can labor do well, for the most part. Of the learned class of emigrants, a small portion find employments analogous to their talents. But many fail and return to complete their course of misery in the scenes where it began. Even here we find too strong a current from the country to the towns, and instances beginning to appear of that species of misery which you are so humanely endeavoring to relieve with you. Although we have in the old countries of Europe the lesson of their experience to warn us, yet I am not satisfied we shall have the firmness and wisdom to profit by it. The general desire of men to live by their heads rather than their hands, and the strong allurements of great cities to those who have any turn for dissipation, threaten to make them here, as in Europe, the sinks of voluntary misery. I perceive, however, that I have suffered my pen to run into a disquisition, when I had taken it up only to thank you for the volume you had been so kind as to send me, and to express my approbation of it. After apologizing, therefore, for having touched on a subject so much more familiar to you, and better understood, I beg leave to assure you of my high consideration and respect.

[A LETTER OF RECONCILIATION]

LETTER TO ABIGAIL ADAMS

This letter and that to John Adams, following, deal with the reconciliation of Adams and Jefferson after the defeat of the former in 1800 and explain Jefferson's attitude regarding their difference. Mrs. Adams had written a note of condolence on the death of Mary (Jefferson) Eppes but had carefully signed herself as one "who *once* took pleasure in subscribing herself your friend, Abigail Adams."

Washington, June 13, 1804

DEAR MADAM: The affectionate sentiments which you have had the goodness to express in your letter of May the 20th toward my dear departed daughter have awakened in me sensibilities natural to the occasion, and recalled your kindnesses to her, which I shall ever remember with gratitude and friendship. I can assure you with truth, they had made an indelible impression on her mind, and that to the last, on our meetings after long separations, whether I had heard lately of you and how you did were among the earliest of her inquiries. In giving you this assurance I perform a sacred duty for her, and at the same time am thankful for the occasion furnished me of expressing my regret that circumstances should have arisen which have seemed to draw a line of separation between us. The friendship with which you honored me has ever been valued and fully reciprocated; and although events have been passing which might be trying to some minds, I never believed yours to be of that kind, nor felt that my own was. Neither my estimate of your character, nor the esteem founded in that, has ever been lessened for a single moment, although doubts whether it would be acceptable may have forbidden manifestations of it.

Mr. Adams's friendship and mine began at an earlier date. It accompanied us through long and important scenes. The different conclusions we had drawn from our political reading and reflections were not permitted to lessen personal esteem, each party being conscious they were the result of an honest conviction in the other. Like differences of opinion existing among our fellow-citizens attached them to one or the other of us and produced a rivalship in their minds which did not exist in ours. We never stood in one another's way; for if either had been withdrawn at any time, his favorers would not have gone over to the other, but would have sought for someone of homogeneous opinions. This consideration was sufficient to keep down all jealousy between us, and to guard our friendship from any disturbance by sentiments of rivalship; and I can say with truth that one act of Mr. Adams's life, and one only, ever gave me a moment's personal displeasure. I did consider his last appointments to office as personally unkind.[1] They were from among my most ardent political enemies, from whom no faithful co-operation could ever be expected, and laid me under the embarrassment of acting through men whose views were to defeat mine, or to encounter the odium of putting others in their places. It seems but common justice to leave a successor free to act by instruments of his own choice. If my respect for him did not permit me to ascribe the whole blame to the influence of others, it left something for friendship to forgive, and after

brooding over it for some little time, and not always resisting the expression of it, I forgave it cordially and returned to the same state of esteem and respect for him which has so long subsisted. Having come into life a little later than Mr. Adams, his career has preceded mine, as mine is followed by some other; and it will probably be closed at the same distance after him which time originally placed between us.[1] I maintain for him, and shall carry into private life, an uniform and high measure of respect and good-will, and for yourself a sincere attachment.

I have thus, my dear Madam, opened myself to you without reserve, which I have long wished an opportunity of doing; and without knowing how it will be received, I feel relief from being unbosomed. And I have now only to entreat your forgiveness for this transition from a subject of domestic affliction, to one which seems of a different aspect. But though connected with political events, it has been viewed by me most strongly in its unfortunate bearings on my private friendships. The injury these have sustained has been a heavy price for what has never given me equal pleasure. That you may both be favored with health, tranquillity, and long life is the prayer of one who tenders you the assurance of his highest consideration and esteem.

[THOUGHTS IN OLD AGE]

LETTER TO JOHN ADAMS

Monticello, January 21, 1812

A LETTER from you calls up recollections very dear to my mind. It carries me back to the times when, beset with difficulties and dangers, we were fellow-laborers in the same cause, struggling for what is most valuable to man, his right of self-government. Laboring always at the same oar, with some wave ever ahead, threatening to overwhelm us, and yet passing harmless under our bark, we knew not how we rode through the storm with heart and hand, and made a happy port. Still, we did not expect to be without rubs and difficulties; and we have had them. First, the deten-

---

[1] "The last day of his political power, the last hours, and even beyond the midnight, were employed in filling all offices, and especially permanent ones, with the bitterest federalists, and providing for me the alternative, either to execute the government by my enemies, whose study it would be to thwart and defeat all my measures, or to incur the odium of such numerous removals from office as might bear me down." [From letter to Dr. Benjamin Rush (Jan. 16, 1811), who was instrumental in renewing the friendship of Adams and Jefferson.]

[1] The two old friends and political rivals died on the same day, July 4, 1826.

tion of the western posts, then the coalition of Pilnitz, outlawing our commerce with France, and the British enforcement of the outlawry. In your day, French depredations; in mine, English, and the Berlin and Milan decrees; now, the English orders of council, and the piracies they authorize. When these shall be over, it will be the impressment of our seamen or something else; and so we have gone on, and so we shall go on, puzzled and prospering 10 beyond example in the history of man. And I do believe we shall continue to grow, to multiply and prosper until we exhibit an association powerful, wise, and happy beyond what has yet been seen by men. As for France and England, with all their pre-eminence in science, the one is a den of robbers, and the other of pirates. And if science produces no better fruits than tyranny, murder, rapine, and destitution of national morality, I would rather 20 wish our country to be ignorant, honest, and estimable, as our neighboring savages are. But whither is senile garrulity leading me? Into politics, of which I have taken final leave. I think little of them and say less. I have given up newspapers in exchange for Tacitus and Thucydides, for Newton and Euclid, and I find myself much happier. Sometimes, indeed, I look back to former occurrences, in remembrance of our old friends and 30 fellow-laborers, who have fallen before us. Of the signers of the Declaration of Independence, I see now living not more than half a dozen on your side of the Potomac, and on this side, myself alone. You and I have been wonderfully spared, and myself with remarkable health, and a considerable activity of body and mind. I am on horseback three or four hours of every day; visit three or four times a year a possession I have ninety miles 40 distant, performing the winter journey on horseback. I walk little, however, a single mile being too much for me, and I live in the midst of my grandchildren, one of whom has lately promoted me to be a great-grandfather. I have heard with pleasure that you also retain good health and a greater power of exercise in walking than I do. But I would rather have heard this from yourself, and that, writing a letter like mine, full of egotisms, and details 50 of your health, your habits, occupations, and

enjoyments, I should have the pleasure of knowing that in the race of life you do not keep, in its physical decline, the same distance ahead of me which you have in political honors and achievements. No circumstances have lessened the interest I feel in these particulars respecting yourself; none have suspended for one moment my sincere esteem for you, and I now salute you with unchanged affection and respect.

[THE CHARACTER OF WASHINGTON]

LETTER TO DR. WALTER JONES

Monticello, Jan. 2, 1814

I THINK I knew General Washington intimately and thoroughly; and were I called on to delineate his character, it should be in terms like these:—

His mind was great and powerful, without being of the very first order; his penetration strong, though not so acute as that of a Newton, Bacon, or Locke; and as far as he saw, no judgment was ever sounder. It was slow in operation, being little aided by invention or imagination, but sure in conclusion. Hence the common remark of his officers, of the advantage he derived from councils of war, where, hearing all suggestions, he selected whatever was best; and certainly no general ever planned his battles more judiciously. But if deranged during the course of the action, if any member of his plan was dislocated by sudden circumstances, he was slow in a readjustment. The consequence was, that he often failed in the field, and rarely against an enemy in station, as at Boston and York.[1] He was incapable of fear, meeting personal dangers with the calmest unconcern. Perhaps the strongest feature in his character was prudence, never acting until every circumstance, every consideration, was maturely weighed; refraining if he saw a doubt; but when once decided, going through with his purpose, whatever obstacles opposed. His integrity was most pure, his justice the most inflexible I have ever known; no motives of interest, of consanguinity, of friendship, or hatred being

[1] Yorktown, in Virginia

able to bias his decision. He was, indeed, in every sense of the words, a wise, a good, and a great man. His temper was naturally irritable and high-toned; but reflection and resolution had obtained a firm and habitual ascendancy over it. If ever, however, it broke its bonds, he was most tremendous in his wrath. In his expenses he was honorable but exact; liberal in contributions to whatever promised utility, but frowning and unyielding on all visionary projects and all unworthy calls on his charity. His heart was not warm in its affections; but he exactly calculated every man's value, and gave him a solid esteem proportioned to it. His person, you know, was fine; his stature exactly what one would wish; his deportment easy, erect, and noble; the best horseman of his age, and the most graceful figure that could be seen on horseback. Although in the circle of his friends, where he might be unreserved with safety, he took a free share in conversation, his colloquial talents were not above mediocrity, possessing neither copiousness of ideas nor fluency of words. In public, when called on for a sudden opinion, he was unready, short, and embarrassed. Yet he wrote readily, rather diffusely, in an easy and correct style. This he had acquired by conversation with the world, for his education was merely reading, writing, and common arithmetic, to which he added surveying, at a later day. His time was employed in action chiefly, reading little, and that only in agriculture and English history. His correspondence became necessarily extensive, and with journalizing his agricultural proceedings, occupied most of his leisure hours within doors. On the whole, his character was in its mass perfect, in nothing bad, in few points indifferent; and it may truly be said that never did nature and fortune combine more perfectly to make a man great, and to place him in the same constellation with whatever worthies have merited from man an everlasting remembrance. For his was the singular destiny and merit, of leading the armies of his country successfully through an arduous war, for the establishment of its independence; of conducting its councils through the birth of a government new in its form and principles, until it had settled down into a quiet and orderly train; and of scrupu-

lously obeying the laws through the whole of his career, civil and military, of which the history of the world furnishes no other example.

How, then, can it be perilous for you to take such a man on your shoulders? I am satisfied the great body of republicans think of him as I do. We were, indeed, dissatisfied with him on his ratification of the British treaty. But this was short-lived. We knew his honesty, the wiles with which he was encompassed, and that age had already begun to relax the firmness of his purposes; and I am convinced he is more deeply seated in the love and gratitude of the republicans, than in the Pharisaical homage of the federal monarchists. For he was no monarchist from preference of his judgment. The soundness of that gave him correct views of the rights of man, and his severe justice devoted him to them. He has often declared to me that he considered our new Constitution as an experiment on the practicability of republican government, and with what dose of liberty man could be trusted for his own good; that he was determined the experiment should have a fair trial, and would lose the last drop of his blood in support of it. And these declarations he repeated to me the oftener and more pointedly because he knew my suspicions of Colonel Hamilton's views, and probably had heard from him the same declarations which I had, to wit, "that the British constitution, with its unequal representation, corruption, and other existing abuses, was the most perfect government which had ever been established on earth, and that a reformation of those abuses would make it an impracticable government." I do believe that General Washington had not a firm confidence in the durability of our government. He was naturally distrustful of men, and inclined to gloomy apprehensions; and I was ever persuaded that a belief that we must at length end in something like a British constitution had some weight in his adoption of the ceremonies of levees, birthdays, pompous meetings with Congress, and other forms of the same character, calculated to prepare us gradually for a change which he believed possible, and to let it come on with as little shock as might be to the public mind.

These are my opinions of General Washington, which I would vouch at the judgment seat of God, having been formed on an acquaintance of thirty years. I served with him in the Virginia legislature from 1769 to the Revolutionary war, and again a short time in Congress, until he left us to take command of the army. During the war and after it we corresponded occasionally, and in the four years of my continuance in the office of Secretary of State, our intercourse was daily, confidential, and cordial. After I retired from that office, great and malignant pains were taken by our federal monarchists, and not entirely without effect, to make him view me as a theorist, holding French principles of government, which would lead infallibly to licentiousness and anarchy. And to this he listened the more easily, from my known disapprobation of the British treaty. I never saw him afterwards, or these malignant insinuations should have been dissipated before his just judgment, as mists before the sun. I felt on his death, with my countrymen, that "verily a great man hath fallen this day in Israel."

More time and recollection would enable me to add many other traits of his character; but why add them to you who knew him well? And I cannot justify to myself a longer detention of your paper.

Vale, proprieque tuum, me esse tibi persuadeas.[1]

[1] "Adieu, and believe me to be sincerely yours."

The Federalist

THE COMPLETED TEXT of the proposed new Constitution, evolved in four months' secret deliberation and debate by the convention called for that purpose, was first made public on September 27, 1787. The new form of government was to become an effective reality as soon as nine of the thirteen states should ratify it in separate conventions. Geographically, in the crisis which followed, the state of New York occupied a commanding position, since her territories would effectually divide the new nation into two sections. This advantage Governor Clinton undertook to use by attacking the Constitution in a New York newspaper, in the hope of securing concessions favorable to his state. To counteract this disintegrating force, Alexander Hamilton (1757–1804), an able young New York lawyer and later Secretary of the Treasury from 1789 to 1795 in Washington's cabinet and chief leader of the extreme Federalists, designed an extended series of newspaper articles, to explain, interpret, and defend the proposed scheme of government. To assist in this arduous task, he called upon John Jay (1745–1829), secretary of foreign affairs under the old government and later Chief Justice, who, however, supplied only a few papers. Hamilton next enlisted the Virginian, James Madison (1751–1836), later Secretary of State and President, who was then in New York and who as a member of the Constitutional Convention had kept the shorthand notes which are our main source of information regarding its discussions. Madison wrote about thirty of the eighty-five numbers, Jay five, and Hamilton the rest. The authorship of a few is joint or disputed.

The entire series, issued between October, 1787, and April, 1788, and published in book form in the latter month, is not only a political document of the first importance but also a work of effectively reasoned and cogently written prose which challenged comparison with the best British documents of a similar nature. Its influence, beyond its direct assistance in adopting the Constitution, was great in clarifying and elaborating its functions and implications and also to a considerable degree in actually shaping them in accordance with the centralizing Federalist views of the authors.

Probably the best edition of *The Federalist* is that of P. L. Ford (1898), based upon the original newspaper versions. Henry Cabot Lodge's edition (1923) goes back to the same sources. Other easily available reprints are those in Everyman's Library (n. d.), J. S. Bassett's *Selections from the Federalist* (1921); and the complete edition of E. G. Bourne (1937). See also E. G. Bourne, "The Authorship of *The Federalist*," in *American Historical Review*, II, 443–460.

Hamilton's works are edited by H. C. Lodge (12 vols., 1904). An excellent sampling of his work, including several *Federalist* essays, is included in F. C. Prescott's *Alexander Hamilton and Thomas Jefferson, Representative Selections* (1934). Useful biographical and critical studies are those of J. C. Hamilton (1834); W. S. Culbertson (1911); C. G. Bowers, *Jefferson and Hamilton* (1925); and V. L. Parrington's chapter on Hamilton, in *Main Currents in American Thought*, I (1927), 292–307. For background of political theory, see J. S. Bassett, *The Federalist System, 1789–1801* (1906) and C. E. Merriam, *A History of American Political Theories* (1903).

Madison's *Writings* were edited by Gaillard Hunt (1900–1910), as was his important *Journal of the Debates in the Convention which Formed the Constitution* (1908). Biographies are those by W. C. Rives (3 vols., 1859–1868), Gaillard Hunt (1902), and A. E. Smith (1937). See also J. W. Pratt's article in *DAB*. The best account of Madison's later political life is given by Henry Adams in his *History of the United States, 1801–1817* (1889–1891).

[ADVANTAGES OF THE UNION]

THE FEDERALIST, NO. X

By James Madison

AMONG the numerous advantages promised by a well-constructed Union, none deserves to be more accurately developed than its tendency to break and control the violence of faction. The friend of popular governments never finds himself so much alarmed for their character and fate as when he contemplates their propensity to this dangerous vice. He will not fail, therefore, to set a due value on any plan which, without violating the principles to which he is attached, provides a proper cure for it. The instability, injustice, and confusion introduced into the public councils, have, in truth, been the mortal diseases under which popular governments have everywhere per-

ished; as they continue to be the favorite and fruitful topics from which the adversaries to liberty derive their most specious declamations. The valuable improvements made by the American constitutions on the popular models, both ancient and modern, cannot certainly be too much admired; but it would be an unwarrantable partiality, to contend that they have as effectually obviated the danger on this side, as was wished and expected. Complaints are everywhere heard from our most considerate and virtuous citizens, equally the friends of public and private faith, and of public and personal liberty, that our governments are too unstable, that the public good is disregarded in the conflicts of rival parties, and that measures are too often decided, not according to the rules of justice and the rights of the minor party, but by the superior force of interested and overbearing majority. However anxiously we may wish that these complaints had no foundation, the evidence of known facts will not permit us to deny that they are in some degree true. It will be found, indeed, on a candid review of our situation, that some of the distresses under which we labor have been erroneously charged on the operation of our governments; but it will be found, at the same time, that other causes will not alone account for many of our heaviest 10 misfortunes; and, particularly, for that prevailing and increasing distrust of public engagements, and alarm for private rights, which are echoed from one end of the continent to the other. These must be chiefly, if not wholly, effects of the unsteadiness and injustice with which a factious spirit has tainted our public administrations.

By a faction, I understand a number of citizens, whether amounting to a majority or 20 minority of the whole, who are united and actuated by some common impulse of passion, or of interest, adverse to the rights of other citizens, or to the permanent and aggregate interests of the community.

There are two methods of curing the mischiefs of faction: the one, by removing its causes; the other, by controlling its effects. There are again two methods of removing the causes of faction: the one, by destroying 30 the liberty which is essential to its existence; the other, by giving to every citizen the same opinions, the same passions, and the same interests.

It could never be more truly said than of the first remedy, that it was worse than the disease. Liberty is to faction what air is to fire, an aliment without which it instantly expires. But it could not be less folly to abolish liberty, which is essential to political life, because it 40 nourishes faction, than it would be to wish the annihilation of air, which is essential to animal life, because it imparts to fire its destructive agency.

The second expedient is as impracticable as the first would be unwise. As long as the reason of man continues fallible, and he is at liberty to exercise it, different opinions will be formed. As long as the connection subsists between his reason and his self-love, his opin- 50 ions and his passions will have a reciprocal

influence on each other; and the former will be objects to which the latter will attach themselves. The diversity in the faculties of men, from which the rights of property originate, is not less an insuperable obstacle to a uniformity of interests. The protection of these faculties is the first object of government. From the protection of different and unequal faculties of acquiring property, the possession of different degrees and kinds of property immediately results; and from the influence of these on the sentiments and views of the respective proprietors, ensues a division of the society into different interests and parties.

The latent causes of faction are thus sown in the nature of man; and we see them everywhere brought into different degrees of activity, according to the different circumstances of civil society. A zeal for different opinions concerning religion, concerning government, and many other points, as well of speculation as of practice; an attachment of different leaders ambitiously contending for pre-eminence and power; or to persons of other descriptions whose fortunes have been interesting to the human passions, have, in turn, divided mankind into parties, inflamed them with mutual animosity, and rendered them much more disposed to vex and oppress each other than to co-operate for their common good. So strong is this propensity of mankind to fall into mutual animosities, that where no substantial occasion presents itself, the most frivolous and fanciful distinctions have been sufficient to kindle their unfriendly passions and excite their most violent conflicts. But the most common and durable source of factions has been the various and unequal distribution of property. Those who hold and those who are without property have ever formed distinct interests in society. Those who are creditors, and those who are debtors, fall under a like discrimination. A landed interest, a manufacturing interest, a mercantile interest, a moneyed interest, with many lesser interests, grow up of necessity in civilized nations, and divide them into different classes, actuated by different sentiments and views. The regulation of these various and interfering interests forms the principal task of modern legislation, and involves the spirit of party and faction in the necessary and ordinary operations of the government.

No man is allowed to be a judge in his own cause, because his interest would certainly bias his judgment, and, not improbably, corrupt his integrity. With equal, nay, with greater reason, a body of men are unfit to be both judges and parties at the same time; yet what are many of the most important acts of legislation but so many judicial determinations, not indeed concerning the rights of single persons, but concerning the rights of large bodies of citizens? And what are the different classes of legislators but advocates and parties to the causes which they determine? Is a law proposed concerning private debts? It is a question to which the creditors are parties on one side and the debtors on the other. Justice ought to hold the balance between them. Yet the parties are, and must be, themselves the judges; and the most numerous party, or, in other words, the most powerful faction must be expected to prevail. Shall domestic manufactures be encouraged, and in what degree, by restrictions on foreign manufactures? are questions which would be differently decided by the landed and the manufacturing classes, and probably by neither with a sole regard to justice and the public good. The apportionment of taxes on the various descriptions of property is an act which seems to require the most exact impartiality; yet there is, perhaps, no legislative act in which greater opportunity and temptation are given to a predominant party to trample on the rules of justice. Every shilling with which they overburden the inferior number is a shilling saved to their own pockets.

It is in vain to say that enlightened statesmen will be able to adjust these clashing interests, and render them all subservient to the public good. Enlightened statesmen will not always be at the helm. Nor, in many cases, can such an adjustment be made at all without taking into view indirect and remote considerations, which will rarely prevail over the immediate interest which one party may find in disregarding the rights of another or the good of the whole.

The inference to which we are brought is, that the *causes* of faction cannot be removed,

and that relief is only to be sought in the means of controlling its *effects*.

If a faction consists of less than a majority, relief is supplied by the republican principle, which enables the majority to defeat its sinister views by regular vote. It may clog the administration, it may convulse the society; but it will be unable to execute and mask its violence under the forms of the Constitution. When a majority is included in a faction, the form of popular government, on the other hand, enables it to sacrifice to its ruling passion or interest both the public good and the rights of other citizens. To secure the public good and private rights against the danger of such a faction, and at the same time to preserve the spirit and the form of popular government, is then the great object to which our inquiries are directed. Let me add that it is the great desideratum by which this form of government can be rescued from the opprobrium under which it has so long labored, and be recommended to the esteem and adoption of mankind.

By what means is this object obtainable? Evidently by one of two only. Either the existence of the same passion or interest in a majority at the same time must be prevented, or the majority, having such co-existent passion or interest, must be rendered, by their number and local situation, unable to concert and carry into effect schemes of oppression. If the impulse and the opportunity be suffered to coincide, we well know that neither moral nor religious motives can be relied on as an adequate control. They are not found to be such on the injustice and violence of individuals, and lose their efficacy in proportion to the number combined together, that is, in proportion as their efficacy becomes needful.

From this view of the subject it may be concluded that a pure democracy, by which I mean a society consisting of a small number of citizens, who assemble and administer the government in person, can admit of no cure for the mischiefs of faction. A common passion or interest will, in almost every case, be felt by a majority of the whole; a communication and concert result from the form of government itself; and there is nothing to check the inducements to sacrifice the weaker party or an obnoxious individual. Hence it is that such democracies have ever been spectacles of turbulence and contention; have ever been found incompatible with personal security or the rights of property; and have in general been as short in their lives as they have been violent in their deaths. Theoretic politicians, who have patronized this species of government, have erroneously supposed that by reducing mankind to a perfect equality in their political rights, they would, at the same time, be perfectly equalized and assimilated in their possessions, their opinions, and their passions.

A republic, by which I mean a government in which the scheme of representation takes place, opens a different prospect, and promises the cure for which we are seeking. Let us examine the points in which it varies from pure democracy, and we shall comprehend both the nature of the cure and the efficacy which it must derive from the Union.

The two great points of difference between a democracy and a republic are: first, the delegation of the government, in the latter, to a small number of citizens elected by the rest; secondly, the greater number of citizens, and greater sphere of country, over which the latter may be extended.

The effect of the first difference is, on the one hand, to refine and enlarge the public views, by passing them through the medium of a chosen body of citizens, whose wisdom may best discern the true interest of their country, and whose patriotism and love of justice will be least likely to sacrifice it to temporary or partial considerations. Under such a regulation, it may well happen that the public voice, pronounced by the representatives of the people, will be more consonant to the public good than if pronounced by the people themselves, convened for the purpose. On the other hand, the effect may be inverted. Men of factious tempers, of local prejudices, or of sinister designs, may, by intrigue, by corruption, or by other means, first obtain the suffrages, and then betray the interests, of the people. The question resulting is, whether small or extensive republics are more favorable to the election of proper guardians of the public weal; and it is clearly decided in favor of the latter by two obvious considerations;

In the first place, it is to be remarked that, however small the republic may be, the representatives must be raised to a certain number, in order to guard against the cabals of a few; and that, however large it may be, they must be limited to a certain number, in order to guard against the confusion of a multitude. Hence the number of representatives in the two cases not being in proportion to that of the two constituents, and being proportionally greater in the small republic, it follows that, if the proportion of fit characters be not less in the large than in the small republic, the former will present a greater option, and consequently a greater probability of a fit choice.

In the next place, as each representative will be chosen by a greater number of citizens in the large than in the small republic, it will be more difficult for unworthy candidates to practise with success the vicious arts by which elections are too often carried; and the suffrages of the people being more free, will be more likely to center in men who possess the most attractive merit and the most diffusive and established character.

It must be confessed that in this, as in most other cases, there is a mean, on both sides of which inconveniences will be found to lie. By enlarging too much the number of electors, you render the representative too little acquainted with all their local circumstances and lesser interests; as by reducing it too much, you render him unduly attached to these, and too little fit to comprehend and pursue great and national objects. The federal Constitution forms a happy combination in this respect; the great and aggregate interests being referred to the national, the local and particular to the State legislatures.

The other point of difference is, the greater number of citizens and extent of territory which may be brought within the compass of republican than of democratic government; and it is this circumstance principally which renders factious combinations less to be dreaded in the former than in the latter. The smaller the society, the fewer probably will be the distinct parties and interests composing it; the fewer the distinct parties and interests, the more frequently will a majority be found of the same party; and the smaller the number of individuals composing a majority, and the smaller the compass within which they are placed, the more easily will they concert and execute their plans of oppression. Extend the sphere, and you take in a greater variety of parties and interests; you make it less probable that a majority of the whole will have a common motive to invade the rights of other citizens; or if such a common motive exists, it will be more difficult for all who feel it to discover their own strength, and to act in unison with each other. Besides other impediments, it may be remarked that, where there is a consciousness of unjust or dishonorable purposes, communication is always checked by distrust in proportion to the number whose concurrence is necessary.

Hence, it clearly appears, that the same advantage which a republic has over a democracy, in controlling the effects of faction, is enjoyed by a large over a small republic—is enjoyed by the Union over the States composing it. Does the advantage consist in the substitution of representatives whose enlightened views and virtuous sentiments render them superior to local prejudices and to schemes of injustice? It will not be denied that the representation of the Union will be most likely to possess these requisite endowments. Does it consist in the greater security afforded by a greater variety of parties, against the event of any one party being able to outnumber and op-

press the rest? In an equal degree does the increased variety of parties comprised within the Union increase this security? Does it, in fine, consist in the greater obstacles opposed to the concert and accomplishment of the secret wishes of an unjust and interested majority? Here, again, the extent of the Union gives it the most palpable advantage.

The influence of factious leaders may kindle a flame within their particular States, but will be unable to spread a general conflagration through the other States. A religious sect may degenerate into a political faction in a part of the Confederacy; but the variety of sects dispersed over the entire face of it must secure the national councils against any danger from that source. A rage for paper money, for an abolition of debts, for an equal division of property, or for any other improper or wicked project, will be less apt to pervade the whole body of the Union than a particular member of it; in the same proportion as such a malady is more likely to taint a particular county or district, than an entire State.

In the extent and proper structure of the Union, therefore, we behold a republican remedy for the diseases most incident to republican government. And according to the degree of pleasure and pride we feel in being republicans, ought to be our zeal in cherishing the spirit and supporting the character of Federalists.

1787

1752 ～ *Philip Freneau* ～ 1832

FRENEAU, the earliest important American poet, illustrates in his work virtually all the characteristics of English pre-romantic poetry, and in some of his poems dealing with nature and primitive life is even a forerunner of Wordsworth.

He was born of Huguenot and Scottish stock, at New York, but after his tenth year his home was chiefly the family estate, Mount Pleasant, near Matawan, New Jersey, where his father, a successful shipowner, lived in plantation fashion. At Princeton, then "a hotbed of Whiggism," Freneau won praise for several poems of considerable promise, and also joined heartily with his classmates James Madison and Hugh Henry Brackenridge, and with Aaron Burr and other fellow students, in organizations opposed to British repressive measures. His commencement poem (with Brackenridge) in 1771, "The Rising Glory of America," hopefully expresses these two interests. A third, after some experience in schoolteaching with Brackenridge and writing anti-British squibs for the New York papers, was supplied by a voyage to the West Indies and a two-year residence on the island of Santa Cruz. His "Beauties of Santa Cruz" and other poems of the period show how greatly the sea and the semi-tropical luxuriance of the islands had taken hold of his imagination.

Returning home by way of Bermuda in 1778, he apparently enlisted for service with Washington's army at Monmouth, contributed the Gothic "House of Night" and other Santa Cruz poems to Brackenridge's *United States Magazine*, and renewed his newspaper and broadside warfare with the hated British and Tories. This hatred was intensified by an imprisonment of two months in one of the prison hulks in New York harbor in the summer of 1780, when the American ship *Aurora*, on which he was sailing for the West Indies, was captured by the enemy. His satire, *The British Prison Ship*, published later in 1780, vigorously and realistically set forth the horrors and brutalities he underwent.

His first two collections of poems were published in 1786 and 1788, while he was at sea, on freighting voyages to Charleston and the West Indies. In 1790 he married Eleanor Forman and settled down at Mount Pleasant. In the following August he accepted from Jefferson, Secretary of State, an appointment as translator to the State Department. It was probably understood that he was to conduct an opposition newspaper to the Federalist party organ, the *Gazette of the United States*. Freneau's paper, the *National Gazette*, vigorously assailed the Federalist policies from October, 1791, to October, 1793. On account of this connection Freneau was bitterly censured by the Federalists, including Washington, but Jefferson credited him with having saved the Constitution when it was "galloping fast into monarchy." He resigned his post in October, 1793.

Between 1793 and 1803 he edited newspapers in New York and at home, still championing the Democrats and the revolutionists in France; published in 1795 his *Poems Written between the Years 1768 and 1794;* and made unsuccessful attempts at farming. From 1803 to 1807 he was again at sea, then came home to spend his last years in New Jersey. The War of 1812 again stirred his pen in the American cause. He also busied himself with two new editions of his poems in 1809 and 1815. The burning of his house and library at Mount Pleasant in the latter year rendered his family nearly destitute. They removed after a time to a farm near Freehold, left by one of Mrs. Freneau's brothers. Here the poet died, December 18, 1832, from the effects of exposure while returning from a tavern in a snowstorm at night.

Freneau's verse falls into two classes: patriotic and partisan songs, satires, and invectives; and imaginative lyrical, reflective, and descriptive poetry. In his time he was chiefly known for the former, which has the merits of vigor and spirit but is often hasty, ill-tempered, and incorrect. Of more permanent significance are the imaginative and romantic poems, which exhibit the late eighteenth-century themes of nature, humanitarianism, melancholy, interest in the remote and the super-natural, primitivism, and solitude, and the religious influence at first of deism and later of Unitarianism. Nearly all of these show real poetic talent and genuine imag-ination; but the same restlessness and impatience of restraint which kept him from success in business affairs make them suffer from lack of self-discipline and pruning. He missed the criticism and friendly rivalry of fellow writers, and cried,

> Thrice happy Dryden, who could meet
> Some rival bard in every street!
> When all were bent on writing well,
> It was some credit to excel.

His prose writings, though showing the same defects, have not received their due credit. While uneven in composition, his essays have the merits of pleasing senti-ment, humor, candid appreciation of contemporary faults and follies, and occasional bits of apt characterization. In Tomo Cheeki, the Creek Indian commentator on the white man's life and customs, he barely falls short of creating a lasting char-acter.

Freneau's early literary reputation suffered from his alignment with the Anti-federalists and Democrats, regarded as dangerous radicals by the Federalists, to whose ranks belonged most of the educated and leisured class who produced and encouraged letters and the arts; and he had later the misfortune to be surpassed in his own lifetime by Bryant, a far better poet, an experience not suffered by his fellow pioneers, the novelist Brown, the essayist Dennie, and the dramatist Dunlap, with whom he is to be ranked.

Editions of Freneau's works published in his lifetime, besides those named above, were: *Poems Written and Published during the American Revolutionary War* (2 vols., 1809), and *Poems on American Affairs* (2 vols., 1815). Recent collections are F. L. Pattee, *The Poems of Philip Freneau* (3 vols., 1902–07); H. H. Clark, *Poems of Freneau* (American Authors Series, 1929); L. F. Heart-man, *Unpublished Freneauana* (1918). V. H. Paltsits issued a *Bibliography of Philip Freneau* in 1903. For biography, consult F. L. Pattee's introduction to the *Poems*, Vol. I, and the sketch in *DAB;* M. S. Austin, *Philip Freneau, the Poet of the Revolution* (1901); and P. M. Marsh, "Philip Freneau and His Circle," *Pennsylvania Magazine of History and Biography*, LXIII, 37–59 (Jan., 1939).

For interpretation and criticism, see J. M. Beatty, "Churchill and Freneau," *American Liter-ature*, II, 121–130 (May, 1930); R. Brenner, *Twelve American Poets before 1900* (1933), 3–22; H. H. Clark, "Literary Influences on Philip Freneau," *Studies in Philology*, XXII, 1–33 (1925); and "What Made Freneau the Father of American Prose," *Wisconsin Academy of Sciences, Arts, and Letters*, XXV, 39–50 (1930); S. E. Forman, "The Political Activities of Philip Freneau," *Johns Hopkins University Studies in History and Political Science*, Ser. XX, No. 9–10 (1902); P. M. Marsh, "Was Freneau a Fighter?" *Proceedings of the New Jersey Historical Society*,

LVI, 211–218; V. L. Parrington, *Main Currents in American Thought* (1927), I, 368–381; F. L. Pattee, *Sidelights on American Literature* (1922), 250–292; and "Philip Freneau as a Postal Clerk," *American Literature*, IV, 61–62 (March, 1932); M. C. Tyler, *Literary History of the American Revolution*, I, 171–183, 413–425, and II, 246–276.

THE POWER OF FANCY

This early poem, written while Freneau was still in college, sums up many of the characteristics of pre-romantic poetry: the influence of Milton's "L'Allegro" and "Il Penseroso," which it parallels, love of nature, melancholy, fondness for distant scenes and remote times, contemplation of death and the tomb, praise of Ossian, and a suggestion of primitivism; mingled with a deistic definition of the universe.

WAKEFUL, vagrant, restless thing,
Ever wandering on the wing,
Who thy wondrous source can find,
Fancy, regent of the mind;
A spark from Jove's resplendent throne,
But thy nature all unknown.

This spark of bright, celestial flame,
From Jove's seraphic altar came,
And hence alone in man we trace,
Resemblance to the immortal race.   10

Ah! what is all this mighty whole,
These suns and stars that round us roll!
What are they all, where'er they shine,
But Fancies of the Power Divine!
What is this globe, these lands, and seas,
And heat, and cold, and flowers, and trees,
And life, and death, and beast, and man,
And time—that with the sun began—
But thoughts on reason's scale combin'd,
Ideas of the Almighty mind?   20

On the surface of the brain
Night after night she walks unseen;
Noble fabrics doth she raise
In the woods or on the seas,
On some high, steep, pointed rock,
Where the billows loudly knock
And the dreary tempests sweep
Clouds along the uncivil deep.

Lo! she walks upon the moon,
Listens to the chimy tune   30
Of the bright, harmonious spheres,
And the song of angels hears;
Sees this earth a distant star,
Pendant, floating in the air;
Leads me to some lonely dome,

Where Religion loves to come,
Where the bride of Jesus dwells,
And the deep ton'd organ swells
In notes with lofty anthems join'd,
Notes that half distract the mind.   40

Now like lightning she descends
To the prison of the fiends,
Hears the rattling of their chains,
Feels their never ceasing pains—
But, O never may she tell
Half the frightfulness of hell.

Now she views Arcadian rocks,
Where the shepherds guard their flocks,
And, while yet her wings she spreads,
Sees crystal streams and coral beds,   50
Wanders to some desert deep,
Or some dark, enchanted steep,
By the full moon light doth shew
Forests of a dusky blue,
Where, upon some mossy bed,
Innocence reclines her head.

Swift, she stretches o'er the seas
To the far off Hebrides,
Canvas on the lofty mast
Could not travel half so fast—   60
Swifter than the eagle's flight
Or instantaneous rays of light!
Lo! contemplative she stands
On Norwegia's rocky lands—
Fickle Goddess, set me down
Where the rugged winters frown
Upon Orca's howling steep,
Nodding o'er the northern deep,
Where the winds tumultuous roar,
Vext that Ossian sings no more.   70
Fancy, to that land repair,
Sweetest Ossian slumbers there;
Waft me far to southern isles
Where the soften'd winter smiles,
To Bermuda's orange shades,
Or Demarara's lovely glades;
Bear me o'er the sounding cape,
Painting death in every shape,
Where daring Anson spread the sail
Shatter'd by the stormy gale—   80

Lo! she leads me wide and far,
Sense can never follow her—
Shape thy course o'er land and sea,
Help me to keep pace with thee,
Lead me to yon chalky cliff,
Over rock and over reef,
Into Britain's fertile land,
Stretching far her proud command.
Look back and view, thro' many a year,
Caesar, Julius Caesar, there.   90
    Now to Tempe's verdant wood,
Over the mid ocean flood
Lo! the islands of the sea—
Sappho, Lesbos mourns for thee.
Greece, arouse thy humbled head,
Where are all thy mighty dead,
Who states to endless ruin hurl'd
And carried vengeance through the world?—
Troy, thy vanish'd pomp resume,
Or, weeping at thy Hector's tomb,   100
Yet those faded scenes renew,
Whose memory is to Homer due.
Fancy, lead me wandering still
Up to Ida's cloud-topt hill;
Not a laurel there doth grow
But in vision thou shalt show.
Every sprig on Virgil's tomb
Shall in livelier colors bloom,
And every triumph Rome has seen
Flourish on the years between.   110
    Now she bears me far away
In the east to meet the day,
Leads me over Ganges' streams,
Mother of the morning beams—
O'er the ocean hath she run,
Places me on Tinian;
Farther, farther in the east,
Till it almost meets the west,
Let us wandering both be lost
On Tahiti's sea-beat coast,   120
Bear me from that distant strand,
Over ocean, over land,
To California's golden shore—
Fancy, stop, and rove no more.
    Now, tho' late, returning home,
Lead me to Belinda's tomb;
Let me glide as well as you
Through the shroud and coffin too,
And behold, a moment, there,
All that once was good and fair—   130
Who doth here so soundly sleep?

Shall we break this prison deep?—
Thunders cannot wake the maid,
Lightnings cannot pierce the shade,
And tho' wintry tempests roar,
Tempests shall disturb no more.
    Yet must those eyes in darkness stay,
That once were rivals to the day?
Like heaven's bright lamp beneath the main
They are but set to rise again.   140
    Fancy, thou the muses' pride,
In thy painted realms reside
Endless images of things,
Fluttering each on golden wings,
Ideal objects, such a store,
The universe could hold no more:
Fancy, to thy power I owe
Half my happiness below;
By thee Elysian groves were made,
Thine were the notes that Orpheus play'd;   150
By thee was Pluto charm'd so well
While rapture seiz'd the sons of hell—
Come, O come—perceiv'd by none,
You and I will walk alone.

1770   1786

From THE BEAUTIES OF SANTA CRUZ

    Freneau, though genuinely patriotic, was by instinct a man of peace and gladly spent the first years of the Revolution in the West Indies. His sensuous enjoyment of the exotic beauty of the Danish island of St. Croix anticipates the spirit of Shelley in this respect.

Sick of thy northern glooms, come, shepherd, seek
More equal climes, and a serener sky:
Why shouldst thou toil amid thy frozen ground,
Where half-years' snows, a barren prospect, lie,

When thou mayst go where never frost was seen,
Or north-west winds with cutting fury blow,
Where never ice congealed the limpid stream,
Where never mountain tipt its head with snow?

Twice ten days prosperous gales thy barque shall bear
To isles that flourish in perpetual green,   10
Where richest herbage glads each fertile vale,
And ever verdant plants on every hill are seen.

Nor dread the dangers of the billowy deep,
Autumnal winds shall safely waft thee o'er;
Put off the timid heart, or, man unblest,
Ne'er shalt thou reach this gay enchanting
    shore.

Cool, woodland streams from shaded cliffs
    descend,
The dripping rock no want of moisture
    knows,
Supplied by springs that on the skies depend,
That fountain feeding as the current flows. 20

Such were the isles which happy Flaccus sung,
Where one tree blossoms while another bears,
Where spring forever gay, and ever young,
Walks her gay round through her unceasing
    years.

Such were the climes which youthful Eden
    saw
Ere crossing fates destroyed her golden reign—
Reflect upon thy loss, unhappy man,
And seek the vales of Paradise again.

No lowering skies are here—the neighboring
    sun   29
Clear and unveiled, his brilliant journey goes,
Each morn emerging from the ambient main,
And sinking there, each evening, to repose.

The native here, in golden plenty blest,
Bids from the soil the verdant harvests spring;
Feasts in the abundant dome, the joyous guest;
Time short,—life easy,—pleasure on the
    wing.

The smooth white cedar here delights the
    eye,
The bay-tree, with its aromatic green
The sea-side grapes, sweet natives of the sand,
And pulse, of various kinds, on trees are seen.

Here mingled vines their downward shadows
    cast,   41
Here, clustered grapes from loaded boughs
    depend,
Their leaves no frosts, their fruits no cold
    winds blast,
But, reared by suns, to time alone they bend.

The plantane and banana flourish here,
Of hasty growth, and love to fix their root
Where some soft stream of ambling water
    flows,
To yield full moisture to their clustered fruit.

No other trees so vast a leaf can boast,
So broad, so long—through these, refreshed,
    we stray,   50
And though the noon-sun all his radiance
    shed,
These friendly leaves shall shade me all the
    way,

And tempt the cooling breeze to hasten there,
With its sweet odorous breath to charm the
    grove;
High shades and verdant seats, while under-
    neath
A little stream by mossy banks doth rove,

Where once the Indian dames slept with their
    swains,
Or fondly kissed the moonlight eves away;—
The lovers fled, the tearful stream remains,
And only I console it with my lay!   60

Among the shades of yonder whispering grove
The green palmettos mingle, tall and fair,
That ever murmur, and forever move,
Fanning with wavy bough the ambient air.

O grant me, gods, if yet condemned to stray,
At least to spend life's sober evening here,
To plant a grove where winds yon sheltered
    bay,
And pluck these fruits, that frost nor winter
    fear.

1776   1779

TO THE MEMORY OF THE BRAVE AMERICANS

UNDER GENERAL GREENE, IN SOUTH CARO-
LINA, WHO FELL IN THE ACTION OF
SEPTEMBER 8, 1781

At Eutaw Springs the valiant died;
    Their limbs with dust are covered o'er—
Weep on, ye springs, your tearful tide;
    How many heroes are no more!

If in this wreck of ruin, they
  Can yet be thought to claim a tear,
O smite your gentle breast, and say
  The friends of freedom slumber here!

Thou, who shalt trace this bloody plain,
  If goodness rules thy generous breast, 10
Sigh for the wasted rural reign;
  Sigh for the shepherds, sunk to rest!

Stranger, their humble graves adorn;
  You too may fall, and ask a tear;
'Tis not the beauty of the morn
  That proves the evening shall be clear.—

They saw their injured country's woe;
  The flaming town, the wasted field;
Then rushed to meet the insulting foe;
  They took the spear—but left the shield. 20

Led by thy conquering genius, Greene,
  The Britons they compelled to fly;
None distant viewed the fatal plain,
  None grieved, in such a cause to die—

But, like the Parthian, famed of old,
  Who, flying, still their arrows threw,
These routed Britons, full as bold,
  Retreated, and retreating slew.

Now rest in peace, our patriot band;
  Though far from nature's limits thrown, 30
We trust they find a happier land,
  A brighter sunshine of their own.

              1781

TO SIR TOBY

A SUGAR PLANTER IN THE INTERIOR PARTS OF JAMAICA

Until after the Revolution, descriptions of the horrors of slavery in American literature are mainly confined to the West Indies, where Freneau's delight in exotic nature was marred with spectacles like those described in this poem.

IF there exists a hell—the case is clear—
Sir Toby's slaves enjoy that portion here:
Here are no blazing brimstone lakes, 'tis true;
But kindled rum too often burns as blue,

In which some fiend, whom nature must detest,
Steeps Toby's brand and marks poor Cudjoe's breast.
  Here whips on whips excite perpetual fears,
And mingled howlings vibrate on my ears;
Here nature's plagues abound, to fret and tease,
Snakes, scorpions, despots, lizards, centipedes.
No art, no care escapes the busy lash; 11
All have their dues—and all are paid in cash.
The eternal driver keeps a steady eye
On a black herd who would his vengeance fly,
But chained, imprisoned, on a burning soil,
For the mean avarice of a tyrant, toil!
The lengthy cart-whip guards this monster's reign,
And cracks, like pistols, from the fields of cane.
  Ye powers who formed these wretched tribes, relate,
What had they done, to merit such a fate! 20
Why were they brought from Eboe's sultry waste,
To see that plenty which they must not taste—
Food, which they cannot buy, and dare not steal,
Yams and potatoes—many a scanty meal!—
  One with a gibbet wakes his negro's fears,
One to the windmill nails him by the ears;
One keeps his slave in darkened dens, unfed,
One puts the wretch in pickle ere he's dead:
This, from a tree suspends him by the thumbs,
That, from his table grudges even the crumbs!
  O'er yond' rough hills a tribe of females go,
Each with her gourd, her infant, and her hoe;
Scorched by a sun that has no mercy here, 33
Driven by a devil, whom men call overseer.
In chains, twelve wretches to their labors haste;
Twice twelve I saw, with iron collars graced!—
  Are such the fruits that spring from vast domains?
Is wealth, thus got, Sir Toby, worth your pains!—
Who would your wealth on terms like these possess,
Where all we see is pregnant with distress—
Angola's natives scourged by ruffian hands, 41
And toil's hard product shipp'd to foreign lands?

Talk not of blossoms and your endless
    spring.
What joy, what smile, can scenes of misery
    bring?
Though Nature here has every blessing
    spread,
Poor is the laborer—and how meanly fed!—
  Here Stygian paintings light and shade
    renew,
Pictures of hell, that Virgil's pencil drew;
Here, surly Charons make their annual trip,
And ghosts arrive in every Guinea ship,   50
To find what beasts these western isles afford,
Plutonian scourges, and despotic lords:—
  Here they, of stuff determined to be free,
Must climb the rude cliffs of the Liguanee;
Beyond the clouds, in skulking haste repair,
And hardly safe from brother traitors there.

1784   *1792*

THE HURRICANE [1]

HAPPY the man who, safe on shore,
Now trims, at home, his evening fire;
Unmoved, he hears the tempests roar,
That on the tufted groves expire:
  Alas! on us they doubly fall,
  Our feeble barque must bear them all.

Now to their haunts the birds retreat,
The squirrel seeks his hollow tree,
Wolves in their shaded caverns meet,
All, all are blest but wretched we—   10
  Foredoomed a stranger to repose,
  No rest the unsettled ocean knows.

While o'er the dark abyss we roam,
Perhaps, with last departing gleam,
We saw the sun descend in gloom,
No more to see his morning beam;
  But buried low, by far too deep,
  On coral beds, unpitied, sleep!

But what a strange, uncoasted strand
Is that, where fate permits no day—   20
No charts have we to mark that land,
No compass to direct that way—
  What pilot shall explore that realm,
  What new Columbus take the helm!

[1] Near the east end of Jamaica, July 30, 1784.
[*Freneau's note.*]

While death and darkness both surround,
And tempests rage with lawless power,
Of friendship's voice I hear no sound,
No comfort in this dreadful hour—
  What friendship can in tempests be,
  What comforts on this raging sea?   30

The barque, accustomed to obey,
No more the trembling pilots guide:
Alone she gropes her trackless way,
While mountains burst on either side—
  Thus, skill and science both must fall;
  And ruin is the lot of all.

1784   *1785*

THE WILD HONEY SUCKLE

  This poem invites comparison, in form and
spirit, with Burns's "To a Mountain Daisy,"
written in 1786.

FAIR flower, that dost so comely grow,
Hid in this silent, dull retreat,
Untouched thy honied blossoms blow,
Unseen thy little branches greet:
  No roving foot shall crush thee here,
  No busy hand provoke a tear.

By Nature's self in white arrayed,
She bade thee shun the vulgar eye,
And planted here the guardian shade,
And sent soft waters murmuring by;   10
  Thus quietly thy summer goes,
  Thy days declining to repose.

Smit with those charms, that must decay,
I grieve to see your future doom;
They died—nor were those flowers more
    gay,
The flowers that did in Eden bloom;
  Unpitying frosts, and Autumn's power
  Shall leave no vestige of this flower.

From morning suns and evening dews
At first thy little being came: 20
If nothing once, you nothing lose,
For when you die you are the same;
  The space between, is but an hour,
  The frail duration of a flower.

                           1786

THE INDIAN BURYING GROUND

In spite of all the learned have said,
I still my old opinion keep;
The posture that we give the dead
Points out the soul's eternal sleep.

Not so the ancients of these lands—
The Indian, when from life released,
Again is seated with his friends,
And shares again the joyous feast.[1]

His imaged birds, and painted bowl,
And venison, for a journey dressed,　　　10
Bespeak the nature of the soul,
Activity, that knows no rest.

His bow, for action ready bent,
And arrows, with a head of stone,
Can only mean that life is spent,
And not the old ideas gone.

Thou, stranger, that shalt come this way,
No fraud upon the dead commit—
Observe the swelling turf, and say
They do not lie, but here they sit.　　　20

Here still a lofty rock remains,
On which the curious eye may trace
(Now wasted, half, by wearing rains)
The fancies of a ruder race.

Here still an aged elm aspires,
Beneath whose far-projecting shade
(And which the shepherd still admires)
The children of the forest played!

There oft a restless Indian queen
(Pale Shebah, with her braided hair)　　　30
And many a barbarous form is seen
To chide the man that lingers there.

By midnight moons, o'er moistening dews,
In habit for the chase arrayed,
The hunter still the deer pursues,
The hunter and the deer, a shade!

[1] The North American Indians bury their dead in
a sitting posture; decorating the corpse with wampum,
the images of birds, quadrupeds, etc.: and (if that of
a warrior) with bows, arrows, tomahawks, and other
military weapons. [*Freneau's note.*]

And long shall timorous fancy see
The painted chief, and pointed spear,
And Reason's self shall bow the knee
To shadows and delusions here.　　　40
　　　　　　　　　　　　　　　1788

TO AN AUTHOR

Your leaves bound up compact and fair,
In neat array at length prepare,
To pass their hour on learning's stage,
To meet the surly critic's rage;
The statesman's slight, the smatterer's sneer—
Were these, indeed, your only fear,
You might be tranquil and resigned:
What most should touch your fluttering mind
Is that few critics will be found
To sift your works, and deal the wound.　　　10

Thus, when one fleeting year is past
On some bye-shelf your book is cast—
Another comes, with something new,
And drives you fairly out of view:

With some to praise, but more to blame,
The mind returns to—whence it came;
And some alive, who scarce could read
Will publish satires on the dead.

Thrice happy Dryden, who could meet
Some rival bard in every street!　　　20
When all were bent on writing well
It was some credit to excel:—

Thrice happy Dryden, who could find
A Milbourne for his sport designed—
And Pope, who saw the harmless rage
Of Dennis bursting o'er his page
Might justly spurn the critic's aim,
Who only helped to swell his fame.

On these bleak climes by Fortune thrown,
Where rigid Reason reigns alone,　　　30
Where lovely Fancy has no sway,
Nor magic forms about us play—
Nor nature takes her summer hue
Tell me, what has the muse to do?—

An age employed in edging steel
Can no poetic raptures feel;
No solitude's attracting power,
No leisure of the noon day hour,
No shaded stream, no quiet grove
Can this fantastic century move,　　　40

The muse of love in no request—
Go—try your fortune with the rest,
One of the nine you should engage,
To meet the follies of the age:—

On one, we fear, your choice must fall—
The least engaging of them all—
Her visage stern—an angry style—
A clouded brow—malicious smile—
A mind on murdered victims placed—
She, only she, can please the taste!   50

· 1788

ON THE ANNIVERSARY

OF THE STORMING OF THE BASTILLE, AT PARIS, JULY 14TH, 1789

THE chiefs that bow to Capet's reign,
In mourning, now, their weeds display:
But we, that scorn a monarch's chain,
Combine to celebrate the day
    To Freedom's birth that put the seal,
    And laid in dust the proud Bastille.

To Gallia's rich and splendid crown,
This mighty day gave such a blow
As Time's recording hand shall own
No former age had power to do: 10
    No single gem some Brutus stole,
    But instant ruin seiz'd the whole.

Now tyrants rise, once more to bind
In royal chains a nation freed—
Vain hope! for they, to death consign'd,
Shall soon, like perjur'd Louis, bleed:
    O'er every king, o'er every queen
    Fate hangs the sword and guillotine.

"Plunged in a gulf of deep distress
France turns her back"—so traitors say.   20
Kings, priests, and nobles round her press,
Resolv'd to seize their destin'd prey:
    Thus Europe swears, in arms combin'd,
    "To Poland's doom is France consign'd."

Yet those who now are thought so low
From conquests that were basely gain'd,
Shall rise tremendous from the blow
And free two worlds, that still are chain'd,
    Restrict the Briton to his isle,
    And freedom plant in every soil.   30

Ye sons of this degenerate clime,[1]
Haste, arm the barque, expand the sail;
Assist to speed that golden time
When Freedom rules, and monarchs fail;
    All left to France—new powers may join
    And help to crush the cause divine.

Ah! while I write, dear France Allied,
My ardent wish I scarce restrain,
To throw these Sybil leaves aside,
And fly to join you on the main: 40
    Unfurl the topsail for the chase
    And help to crush the tyrant race!

1793

ODE [2]

No poem, perhaps, better portrays the zeal with which many Americans after the Revolution proclaimed their mission to make the entire world equally free. It greatly resembled that of the French after their revolution of 1789 and the Russians after theirs in 1917.

GOD save the Rights of Man!
Give us a heart to scan
Blessings so dear:
Let them be spread around
Wherever man is found,
And with the welcome sound
Ravish his ear.

Let us with France agree,
And bid the world be free,
While tyrants fall!   10
Let the rude savage host
Of their vast numbers boast—
Freedom's almighty trust
Laughs at them all!

Though hosts of slaves conspire
To quench fair Gallia's fire,
Still shall they fail:
Though traitors round her rise,
Leagued with her enemies,
To war each patriot flies,   20
And will prevail.

[1] a protest against Washington's neutrality policy, disregarding the defensive alliance between the United States and France   [2] sung to the tune of "God Save the King" (hence also of "America")

No more is valor's flame
Devoted to a name,
Taught to adore—
Soldiers of Liberty
Disdain to bow the knee,
But teach equality
To every shore.

The world at last will join
To aid thy grand design,   30
Dear Liberty!
To Russia's frozen lands
The generous flame expands:
On Afric's burning sands
Shall man be free!

In this our western world
Be Freedom's flag unfurl'd
Through all its shores!
May no destructive blast
Our heaven of joy o'ercast,   40
May Freedom's fabric last
While time endures.

If e'er her cause require!—
Should tyrants e'er aspire
To aim their stroke,
May no proud despot daunt—
Should he his standard plant,
Freedom will never want
Her hearts of oak!

1793   1795

STANZAS

OCCASIONED by certain absurd, extravagant,
and even blasphemous panegyrics and enco-
miums on the character of the late Gen. Washington, that appeared in several pamphlets,
journals, and other periodical publications, in
January, 1800.

No tongue can tell, no pen describe
The frenzy of a numerous tribe,
Who, by distemper'd fancy led,
Insult the memory of the dead.
Of old, there were in every age
Who stuff'd with gods the historian's page,
And raised beyond the human sphere
Some who, we know, were mortal here.

Such was the case, we know full well
When darkness spread her pagan spell;   10
Mere insects, born for tombs and graves,
They changed into celestial knaves;
Made some, condemn'd to tombs and shrouds,
Lieutenant generals in the clouds.

In journals meant to spread the news
From state to state—and we know whose—
We read a thousand idle things
That madness pens, or folly sings.

Was, Washington, your conquering sword
Condemn'd to such a base reward?   20
Was trash, like that we now review,
The tribute to your valor due?

One holds you *more than mortal kind*,
One holds you *all ethereal mind*,
This puts you in your Saviour's seat,
That makes you *dreadful in retreat*.

One says *you are become a star*,
One makes you *more resplendent, far*;
One sings, that, when to death you bow'd,
Old mother nature *shriek'd aloud*.   30

We grieve to see such pens profane
The first of chiefs, the first of men.—
To Washington—a man, who died—
Is *abba, father* well applied?

Absurdly, in a frantic strain,
Why ask him not for *sun* and *rain?*—
We sicken at the vile applause
That bids him *give the ocean laws*.

Ye patrons of the ranting strain,
What *temples have been rent in twain?*   40
What fiery chariots have been sent
To dignify the sad event?—

O ye profane, irreverent few,
Who reason's medium never knew,
On you she never glanced her beams;
You carry all things to extremes.

Shall they who spring from parent earth
Pretend to more than mortal birth?
Or, to the omnipotent allied,
Control his heaven, or join his side?   50

Or is there not some chosen curse,
Some vengeance due, with lightning's force,
That far and wide destruction spreads,
To burst on such irreverent heads!

Had they, in life, be-praised him so,
What would have been the event I know:
He would have spurn'd them, with disdain,
Or rush'd upon them with his cane.

He was no god, ye flattering knaves,
He *own'd no world, he ruled no waves;*   60
But—and exalt it, if you can,
He was the upright, *honest man.*

This was his glory; this outshone
Those attributes you dote upon:
On this strong ground he took his stand;
Such virtue saved a sinking land.

1800   1815

ON A HONEY BEE

DRINKING FROM A GLASS OF WINE AND DROWNED THEREIN

Thou, born to sip the lake or spring,
  Or quaff the waters of the stream,
Why hither come, on vagrant wing?
    Does Bacchus tempting seem,
      Did he for you this glass prepare?
      Will I admit you to a share?

Did storms harass or foes perplex,
  Did wasps or king-birds bring dismay,
Did wars distress, or labors vex,
    Or did you miss your way?   10
      A better seat you could not take
      Than on the margin of this lake.

Welcome!—I hail you to my glass:
  All welcome here you find;
Here let the cloud of trouble pass,
    Here be all care resigned.
      This fluid never fails to please,
      And drown the griefs of men or bees.

What forced you here we cannot know,
  And you will scarcely tell,—   20
But cheery we would have you go
  And bid a glad farewell:
      On lighter wings we bid you fly,
      Your dart will now all foes defy.

Yet take not, oh! too deep a drink,
  And in this ocean die;

Here bigger bees than you might sink,
  Even bees full six feet high.
    Like Pharaoh, then, you would be said
    To perish in a sea of red.   30

Do as you please, your will is mine;
  Enjoy it without fear,
And your grave will be this glass of wine,
  Your epitaph—a tear;
    Go, take your seat in Charon's boat;
    We'll tell the hive, you died afloat.

                      1809

TO A CATY-DID

In a branch of willow hid
Sings the evening Caty-did:
From the lofty locust bough
Feeding on a drop of dew,
In her suit of green arrayed
Hear her singing in the shade
    Caty-did, Caty-did, Caty-did!

While upon a leaf you tread,
Or repose your little head,
On your sheet of shadows laid,   10
All the day you nothing said:
Half the night your cheery tongue
Reveled out its little song,
    Nothing else but Caty-did.

From your lodgings on the leaf
Did you utter joy or grief?—
Did you only mean to say,
I have had my summer's day,
And am passing, soon, away
To the grave of Caty-did:—   20
    Poor, unhappy Caty-did!

But you would have uttered more
Had you known of nature's power—
From the world when you retreat,
And a leaf's your winding sheet,
Long before your spirit fled,
Who can tell but nature said,
Live again, my Caty-did!
    Live and chatter, Caty-did.

Tell me, what did Caty do?   30
Did she mean to trouble you?
Why was Caty not forbid
To trouble little Caty-did?
Wrong indeed at you to fling,
Hurting no one while you sing
    Caty-did! Caty-did! Caty-did!

Why continue to complain?
Caty tells me, she again
Will not give you plague or pain:—
Caty says you may be hid   40
Caty will not go to bed
While you sing us Caty-did.
    Caty-did! Caty-did! Caty-did!

But while singing, you forgot
To tell us what did Caty not:
Caty did not think of cold,
Flocks retiring to the fold,
Winter, with his wrinkles old,
Winter, that yourself foretold
    When you gave us Caty-did.   50

Stay securely in your nest;
Caty now will do her best,
All she can to make you blest;
But, you want no human aid—
Nature, when she formed you, said,
"Independent you are made,
My dear little Caty-did:
Soon yourself must disappear
With the verdure of the year,—"
And to go, we know not where,   60
    With your song of Caty-did.
                   1815

ON THE UNIFORMITY AND PER-
FECTION OF NATURE

This poem and the following, together with another entitled "On a Book Called *Unitarian Theology*" (1786), show Freneau's acceptance of contemporary deistic and Unitarian religious views.
In this he flouts the idea that in response to man's
petitions, eternal natural laws may be interrupted
in their normal course.

ON one fix'd point all nature moves,
Nor deviates from the track she loves;
Her system, drawn from reason's source,
She scorns to change her wonted course.

Could she descend from that great plan
To work unusual things for man,
To suit the insect of an hour—
This would betray a want of power,

Unsettled in its first design
And erring, when it did combine   10
The parts that form the vast machine,
The figures sketch'd on nature's scene.

Perfections of the great first cause
Submit to no contracted laws,
But all-sufficient, all-supreme,
Include no trivial views in them.

Who looks through nature with an eye
That would the scheme of heaven descry,
Observes her constant, still the same,
In all her laws, through all her frame.   20

No imperfection can be found
In all that is, above, around,—
All, nature made, in reason's sight
Is order all and all is right.
                   1815

ON THE RELIGION OF NATURE

THE power that gives with liberal hand
    The blessings man enjoys, while here,
And scatters through a smiling land
    The abundant products of the year;
      That power of nature, ever bless'd,
      Bestow'd religion with the rest.

Born with ourselves, her early sway
    Inclines the tender mind to take
The path of right, fair virtue's way
    Its own felicity to make.   10
      This universally extends
      And leads to no mysterious ends.

Religion, such as nature taught,
    With all divine perfection suits;
Had all mankind this system sought
    Sophists would cease their vain disputes,
      And from this source would nations know
      All that can make their heaven below.

This deals not curses on mankind,
    Or dooms them to perpetual grief,   20
If from its aid no joys they find,
    It damns them not for unbelief;
      Upon a more exalted plan
      Creatress nature dealt with man—

Joy to the day, when all agree
    On such grand systems to proceed,
From fraud, design, and error free,
    And which to truth and goodness lead:
      Then persecution will retreat
      And man's religion be complete.   30
                   1815

1754 ~ *Joel Barlow* ~ 1812

JOEL BARLOW, the son of a conservative Connecticut farmer, led a versatile and successful life both in his own country and in Europe. At Yale, he was tutored by Timothy Dwight, fought in the Revolution during a summer vacation, and at the public examination of his class in 1778, read his first long poem, *The Prospect of Peace*. In the next nine years he studied philosophy at Yale, taught school, managed a business, published a journal, wrote a new version of the Psalms, began to practice law, and worked on his epic, *The Vision of Columbus*, which appeared in nine books and more than five thousand lines in 1787.

In 1788 he went to Europe as agent for the Scioto Land Company. There he abandoned his Connecticut religion and politics, associated with Thomas Paine, enthusiastically supported the French Revolution, and in 1792 attacked the monarchical principle in *The Conspiracy of Kings* (1792), and the prose treatise *Advice to the Privileged Orders*, which was suppressed in England as being in a class with Paine's *Rights of Man*. He was made a citizen of France, acquired a considerable fortune in that country, and was appointed in 1795 United States minister to Algeria, where he made important treaties with Algeria, Tripoli, and Tunis. In 1805 he returned to America, built a mansion on the Potomac, and enlarged his *Vision of Columbus* into a grandiose epic, *The Columbiad*. In 1811 Madison assigned to him the difficult post of minister to France. In 1812, on a mission to confer with Napoleon during his Russian campaign, he became involved in the retreat from Moscow and died in Poland as a result of exposure.

In his two epic poems, a dream of the aged Columbus is used to summarize the whole history of the American continent to Barlow's own day. *The Columbiad* embodies his new political and religious radicalism, with prophecies for such a future federation of the world as Tennyson later foretold. His mock-epic *Hasty Pudding* (1793), in easy, witty verse, inspired by homesickness during a residence in Savoy, shows Barlow as his friends knew him better than does his serious verse.

Selections from Barlow's chief works, enumerated above, are included, with an introduction, in V. L. Parrington, *The Connecticut Wits* (1926). His life to 1787 is fully told in T. A. Zunder, *The Early Days of Joel Barlow* (1934). Other biographies are C. B. Todd, *Life and Letters of Joel Barlow* (1886) and M. C. Tyler, *Three Men of Letters* (1895), 129–180. See also *DAB;* V. L. Parrington, *Main Currents in American Thought* (1927), I, 382–389; V. P. Squires, "Joel Barlow—Patriot, Democrat, and Man of Letters," *Quarterly Journal of the University of North Dakota*, IX, 299–308; F. B. Dexter, *Biographical Sketches of the Graduates of Yale College* (1907), IV, 3–16; C. V. Miller, *Joel Barlow: Revolutionist, London, 1791–92* (1932); Maria dell' Isola, "Joel Barlow: Precurseur de la Société des Nations," *Revue de Littérature Com-*

parée, XIV, 283–296 (April–June, 1934); Leon Howard, *The Vision of Joel Barlow* (1937); and P. H. Boynton, "Joel Barlow Advises the Privileged Classes," *New England Quarterly*, III, 477–499 (Dec., 1939.)

THE HASTY PUDDING

CANTO I

YE Alps audacious, through the heavens that
    rise,
To cramp the day and hide me from the skies;
Ye Gallic flags, that o'er their heights unfurled,
Bear death to kings and freedom to the world,
I sing not you. A softer theme I choose,
A virgin theme, unconscious of the muse,
But fruitful, rich, well suited to inspire
The purest frenzy of poetic fire.

Despise it not, ye bards to terror steeled,
Who hurl your thunders round the epic field;
Nor ye who strain your midnight throats to
    sing   11
Joys that the vineyard and the stillhouse bring;
Or on some distant fair your notes employ,
And speak of raptures that you ne'er enjoy.
I sing the sweets I know, the charms I feel,
My morning incense, and my evening meal,—
The sweets of Hasty Pudding. Come, dear
    bowl,
Glide o'er my palate, and inspire my soul.
The milk beside thee, smoking from the kine,
Its substance mingled, married in with thine,
Shall cool and temper thy superior heat,   21
And save the pains of blowing while I eat.

Oh! could the smooth, the emblematic song
Flow like thy genial juices o'er my tongue,
Could those mild morsels in my numbers
    chime,
And, as they roll in substance, roll in rime,
No more thy awkward, unpoetic name
Should shun the muse or prejudice thy fame;
But, rising grateful to the accustomed ear,
All bards should catch it, and all realms re-
    vere!   30

Assist me first with pious toil to trace
Through wrecks of time, thy lineage and thy
    race;
Declare what lovely squaw, in days of yore,
(Ere great Columbus sought thy native shore)

First gave thee to the world; her works of
    fame
Have lived indeed, but lived without a name.
Some tawny Ceres, goddess of her days,
First learned with stones to crack the well-
    dried maize,
Through the rough sieve to shake the golden
    shower,
In boiling water stir the yellow flour: 40
The yellow flour, bestrewed and stirred with
    haste,
Swells in the flood and thickens to a paste,
Then puffs and wallops, rises to the brim,
Drinks the dry knobs that on the surface
    swim;
The knobs at last the busy ladle breaks,
And the whole mass its true consistence
    takes.

Could but her sacred name, unknown so
    long,
Rise, like her labors, to the son of song,
To her, to them I'd consecrate my lays,
And blow her pudding with the breath of
    praise.   50
If 'twas Oella [1] whom I sang before,
I here ascribe her one great virtue more.
Not through the rich Peruvian realms alone
The fame of Sol's sweet daughter should be
    known,
But o'er the world's wide climes should live
    secure,
Far as his rays extend, as long as they en-
    dure.

Dear Hasty Pudding, what unpromised joy
Expands my heart, to meet thee in Savoy!
Doomed o'er the world through devious paths
    to roam,
Each clime my country, and each house my
    home,   60
My soul is soothed, my cares have found an
    end;
I greet my long-lost, unforgotten friend.

[1] Peruvian princess in Barlow's *Vision of Columbus* (1787)

For thee through Paris, that corrupted town,
How long in vain I wandered up and down,
Where shameless Bacchus, with his drenching
    hoard,
Cold from his cave usurps the morning board.
London is lost in smoke and steeped in tea;
No Yankee there can lisp the name of thee;
The uncouth word, a libel on the town,
Would call a proclamation from the crown. 70
For climes oblique, that fear the sun's full rays,
Chilled in their fogs, exclude the generous
    maize:
A grain whose rich, luxuriant growth requires
Short, gentle showers, and bright, ethereal
    fires.

But here, though distant from our native
    shore,
With mutual glee, we meet and laugh once
    more.
The same! I know thee by that yellow face,
That strong complexion of true Indian race,
Which time can never change, nor soil impair,
Nor Alpine snows, nor Turkey's morbid air;
For endless years, through every mild do-
    main,   81
Where grows the maize, there thou art sure to
    reign.

But man, more fickle, the bold licence
    claims,
In different realms to give thee different names.
Thee the soft nations round the warm Levant
Polanta call; the French, of course, Polante.
E'en in thy native regions, how I blush
To hear the Pennsylvanians call thee Mush!
On Hudson's banks while men of Belgic
    spawn
Insult and eat thee by the name Suppawn. 90
All spurious appellations, void of truth;
I've better known thee from my earliest youth:
Thy name is Hasty Pudding! thus my sire
Was wont to greet thee fuming from his fire;
And while he argued in thy just defense
With logic clear he thus explained the sense:
"In haste the boiling caldron, o'er the blaze,
Receives and cooks the ready powdered maize,
In haste 'tis served, and then in equal haste,
With cooling milk, we make the sweet re-
    past.   100
No carving to be done, no knife to grate
The tender ear and wound the stony plate;

But the smooth spoon, just fitted to the lip,
And taught with art the yielding mass to dip,
By frequent journeys to the bowl well stored,
Performs the hasty honors of the board."
Such is thy name, significant and clear,
A name, a sound to every Yankee dear,
But most to me, whose heart and palate chaste
Preserve my pure, hereditary taste.   110

There are who strive to stamp with disre-
    pute
The luscious food, because it feeds the brute;
In tropes of high-strained wit, while gaudy
    prigs
Compare thy nursling, man, to pampered pigs;
With sovereign scorn I treat the vulgar jest,
Nor fear to share thy bounties with the beast.
What though the generous cow gives me to
    quaff
The milk nutritious: am I then a calf?
Or can the genius of the noisy swine,
Though nursed on pudding, thence lay claim
    to mine?   120
Sure the sweet song I fashion to thy praise,
Runs more melodious than the notes they
    raise.

My song, resounding in its grateful glee,
No merit claims: I praise myself in thee.
My father loved thee through his length of
    days!
For thee his fields were shaded o'er with maize;
From thee what health, what vigor he pos-
    sessed,
Ten sturdy freemen from his loins attest;
Thy constellation ruled my natal morn,
And all my bones were made of Indian corn.

Delicious grain, whatever form it take, 131
To roast or boil, to smother or to bake,
In every dish 'tis welcome still to me,
But most, my Hasty Pudding, most in thee.
Let the green succotash with thee contend;
Let beans and corn their sweetest juices blend;
Let butter drench them in its yellow tide,
And a long slice of bacon grace their side;
Not all the plate, how famed soe'er it be,
Can please my palate like a bowl of thee.   140
Some talk of hoe-cake, fair Virginia's pride!
Rich johnny-cake this mouth has often tried;
Both please me well, their virtues much the
    same,

Alike their fabric, as allied their fame,
Except in dear New England, where the last
Receives a dash of pumpkin in the paste,
To give it sweetness and improve the taste.
But place them all before me, smoking hot,
The big, round dumpling, rolling from the pot;
The pudding of the bag, whose quivering
    breast, 150
With suet lined, leads on the Yankee feast;
The charlotte brown, within whose crusty sides
A belly soft the pulpy apple hides;
The yellow bread whose face like amber glows
And all of Indian that the bakepan knows,—
You tempt me not; my favorite greets my eyes,
To that loved bowl my spoon by instinct flies.

CANTO II

To mix the food by vicious rules of art,
To kill the stomach and to sink the heart,
To make mankind to social virtue sour,
Cram o'er each dish, and be what they devour;
For this the kitchen muse first framed her book,
Commanding sweats to stream from every cook;
Children no more their antic gambols tried,
And friends to physic wondered why they died.

Not so the Yankee: his abundant feast,
With simples furnished and with plainness
    dressed, 10
A numerous offspring gathers round the board,
And cheers alike the servant and the lord;
Whose well-bought hunger prompts the joyous taste,
And health attends them from the short repast.

While the full pail rewards the milkmaid's toil,
The mother sees the morning caldron boil;
To stir the pudding next demands their care;
To spread the table and the bowls prepare;
To feed the household as their portions cool
And send them all to labor or to school. 20

Yet may the simplest dish some rules impart,
For nature scorns not all the aids of art.
E'en Hasty Pudding, purest of all food,
May still be bad, indifferent, or good,
As sage experience the short process guides,
Or want of skill, or want of care presides.
Whoe'er would form it on the surest plan,
To rear the child and long sustain the man;
To shield the morals while it mends the size,
And all the powers of every food supplies,—
Attend the lesson that the muse shall bring,
Suspend your spoons, and listen while I sing.

But since, O man! thy life and health demand 33
Not food alone, but labor from thy hand,
First, in the field, beneath the sun's strong rays,
Ask of thy mother earth the needful maize;
She loves the race that courts her yielding soil,
And gives her bounties to the sons of toil.

When now the ox, obedient to thy call,
Repays the loan that filled the winter stall, 40
Pursue his traces o'er the furrowed plain,
And plant in measured hills the golden grain.
But when the tender germ begins to shoot,
And the green spire declares the sprouting root,
Then guard your nursling from each greedy foe,
The insidious worm, the all-devouring crow.
A little ashes sprinkled round the spire,
Soon steeped in rain, will bid the worm retire;
The feathered robber with his hungry maw
Swift flies the field before your man of straw,
A frightful image, such as schoolboys bring
When met to burn the Pope or hang the King.

Thrice in the season, through each verdant
    row, 53
Wield the strong plowshare and the faithful hoe;
The faithful hoe, a double task that takes,
To till the summer corn and roast the winter cakes.

Slow springs the blade, while checked by chilling rains,
Ere yet the sun the seat of Cancer gains;
But when his fiercest fires emblaze the land,
Then start the juices, then the roots expand; 60
Then, like a column of Corinthian mold,
The stalk struts upward and the leaves unfold;

The bushy branches all the ridges fill,
Entwine their arms, and kiss from hill to hill.
Here cease to vex them; all your cares are
   done:
Leave the last labors to the parent sun;
Beneath his genial smiles, the well-dressed
   field,
When autumn calls, a plenteous crop shall
   yield.

Now the strong foliage bears the standards
   high,
And shoots the tall top-gallants to the sky;   70
The suckling ears their silky fringes bend,
And pregnant grown, their swelling coats dis-
   tend;
The loaded stalk, while still the burden grows,
O'erhangs the space that runs between the rows;
High as a hop-field waves the silent grove,
A safe retreat for little thefts of love,
When the pledged roasting-ears invite the maid
To meet her swain beneath the new-formed
   shade;
His generous hand unloads the cumbrous hill,
And the green spoils her ready basket fill;   80
Small compensation for the twofold bliss,
The promised wedding, and the present kiss.

Slight depredations these; but now the
   moon
Calls from his hollow tree the sly raccoon;
And while by night he bears his prize away,
The bolder squirrel labors through the day.
Both thieves alike, but provident of time,
A virtue rare, that almost hides their crime.
Then let them steal the little stores they can,
And fill their granaries from the toils of
   man;   90
We've one advantage where they take no
   part—
With all their wiles, they ne'er have found the
   art
To boil the Hasty Pudding; here we shine
Superior far to tenants of the pine;
This envied boon to man shall still belong,
Unshared by them in substance or in song.

At last the closing season browns the plain,
And ripe October gathers in the grain;
Deep-loaded carts the spacious corn-house
   fill;

The sack distended marches to the mill;   100
The laboring mill beneath the burden groans,
And showers the future pudding from the
   stones;
Till the glad housewife greets the powdered
   gold,
And the new crop exterminates the old.
Ah, who can sing what every wight must feel,
The joy that enters with the bag of meal,
A general jubilee pervades the house,
Wakes every child and gladdens every mouse!

CANTO III

The days grow short; but though the falling
   sun
To the glad swain proclaims his day's work
   done,
Night's pleasing shades his various tasks pro-
   long,
And yield new subjects to my various song.
For now, the corn-house filled, the harvest
   home,
The invited neighbors to the husking come;
A frolic scene, where work, and mirth, and
   play,
Unite their charms to chase the hours away.

Where the huge heap lies centered in the
   hall,
The lamp suspended from the cheerful wall,   10
Brown, corn-fed nymphs, and strong, hard-
   handed beaux;
Alternate ranged, extend in circling rows,
Assume their seats, the solid mass attack;
The dry husks rustle, and the corncobs crack;
The song, the laugh, alternate notes resound,
And the sweet cider trips in silence round.

The laws of husking every wight can tell;
And sure no laws he ever keeps so well:
For each red ear a general kiss he gains,
With each smut ear she smuts the luckless
   swains;   20
But when to some sweet maid a prize is cast,
Red as her lips and taper as her waist,
She walks the round and culls one favored
   beau,
Who leaps the luscious tribute to bestow.
Various the sport, as are the wits and brains
Of well-pleased lasses and contending swains;

Till the vast mound of corn is swept away,
And he that gets the last ear wins the day.

Meanwhile, the housewife urges all her care,
The well-earned feast to hasten and pre-
pare.   30
The sifted meal already waits her hand,
The milk is strained, the bowls in order stand,
The fire flames high; and as a pool—that
takes
The headlong stream that o'er the milldam
breaks—
Foams, roars, and rages with incessant toils,
So the vexed caldron rages, roars, and boils.

First with clean salt she seasons well the
food,
Then strews the flour and thickens all the
flood.
Long o'er the simmering fire she lets it stand—
To stir it well demands a stronger hand: 40
The husband takes his turn, and round and
round
The ladle flies; at last the toil is crowned;
When to the board the thronging huskers
pour,
And take their seats as at the corn before.

I leave them at their feast. There still belong
More useful matters to my faithful song;
For rules there are, though ne'er unfolded yet,
Nice rules and wise, how pudding should be
eat.

Some with molasses line the luscious treat,
And mix, like bards, the useful with the sweet.
A wholesome dish, and well deserving
praise,   51
A great resource in those bleak, wintry days,
When the chilled earth lies buried deep in
snow,
And raging Boreas dries the shivering cow.

Blest cow! thy praise shall still my notes
employ:
Great source of health, the only source of joy,
Mother of Egypt's god;—but sure for me,
Were I to leave my God I'd worship thee.
How oft thy teats these pious hands have
prest!
How oft thy bounties proved my only
feast!   60

How oft I've fed thee with my favorite grain,
And roared, like thee, to see thy children
slain!

Ye swains who know her various worth to
prize,
Ah! house her well from winter's angry skies.
Potatoes, pumpkins, should her sadness cheer,
Corn from your crib, and mashes from your
beer;
When spring returns, she'll well acquit the
loan,
And nurse at once your infants and her own.
Milk then with pudding I should always
choose,
To this in future I confine my muse,   70
Till she in haste some further hints unfold,
Well for the young, nor useless to the old.
First in your bowl the milk abundant take,
Then drop with care along the silver lake
Your flakes of pudding; these at first will hide
Their little bulk beneath the swelling tide;
But when their growing mass no more can sink,
When the soft island looms above the brink,
Then check your hand; you've got the portion
due;
So taught our sires, and what they taught is
true.   80

There is a choice in spoons. Though small
appear
The nice distinction, yet to me 'tis clear.
The deep-bowled Gallic spoon, contrived to
scoop
In ample draughts the thin, diluted soup,
Performs not well in those substantial things,
Whose mass adhesive to the metal clings;
Where the strong labial muscles must embrace
The gentle curve, and sweep the hollow space
With ease to enter and discharge the freight,
A bowl less concave, but still more dilate, 90
Becomes the pudding best. The shape, the size,
A secret rests, unknown to vulgar eyes.
Experienced feeders can alone impart
A rule so much above the lore of art.
These tuneful lips that thousand spoons have
tried,
With just precision could the point decide,
Though not in song; the muse but poorly
shines
In cones, and cubes, and geometric lines;

Yet the true form, as near as she can tell,
Is that small section of a goose-egg shell, 100
Which in two equal portions shall divide
The distance from the center to the side.

Fear not to slaver; 'tis no deadly sin.
Like the free Frenchman, from your joyous
    chin
Suspend the ready napkin; or, like me,
Poise with one hand your bowl upon your knee;
Just in the zenith your wise head project,
Your full spoon, rising in a line direct,
Bold as a bucket, heeds no drops that fall;
The wide-mouthed bowl will surely catch
    them all!   110

1792–93   1796

From THE COLUMBIAD

[*A League of Nations*]

EAGER he [1] looked: another train of years
Had rolled unseen and brighten'd still their
    spheres.
Earth, more resplendent in the floods of day,
Assumed new smiles and flush'd around him
    lay:
Green swell the mountains, calm the oceans
    roll,
Fresh beams of beauty kindle round the pole;
Through all the range where shores and seas
    extend,
In tenfold pomp the works of peace ascend.
Robed in the bloom of spring's eternal year,
And ripe with fruits, the same glad fields ap-
    pear;   10
O'er hills and vales perennial gardens run;
Cities unwalled stand sparkling in the sun;
The streams, all freighted from the bounteous
    plain,
Swell with the load and labor to the main,
Whose stormless waves command a steadier
    gale
And prop the pinions of a bolder sail;
Swayed with the weight, each ocean toils,
And joyous nature's full perfection smiles.
    Filled with unfolding fate, the visioned age
Now leads its actors on a broader stage;   20

[1] Columbus, whose vision embraced the history of
the American continent

When, clothed majestic in the robes of state,
Moved by one voice, in general congress meet
The legates of all empires. 'Twas the place [1]
Where wretched men first firmed their wander-
    ing pace,
Ere yet, beguiled, the dark, delirious hordes
Began to fight for altars and for lords;
Nile washes still the soil, and feels once more
The works of wisdom press his peopled shore.
    In this mid site, this monumental clime,
Reared by all realms to brave the wrecks of
    time   30
A spacious dome swells up, commodious
    great,
The last resort, the unchanging scene of state.
On rocks of adamant the walls ascend,
Tall columns heave, and sky-like arches bend;
Bright o'er the golden roofs the glittering
    spires
Far in the concave meet the solar fires;
Four blazing fronts, with gates unfolding high,
Look with immortal splendor round the sky.
Hither the delegated sires ascend,
And all the cares of every clime attend.   40
As the blest band, the guardian guides of
    heaven,
To whom the care of stars and suns is given,
When one great circuit shall have proved their
    spheres
And time well taught them how to wind their
    years,
Shall meet in general council, called to state
The laws and labors that their charge await,
To learn, to teach, to settle how to hold
Their course more glorious as their lights
    unfold;
From all the bounds of space (the mandate
    known)
They wing their passage to the eternal
    throne;   50
Each through his far dim sky illumes the
    road,
And sails and centres toward the mount of
    God,
There in mid universe their seats to rear,
Exchange their counsels and their works com-
    pare:
So, from all tracts of earth, this gathering
    throng
In ships and chariots shape their course along,

[1] Egypt, selected apparently for its central location

Reach with unwonted speed the place as-
signed,[1]
To hear and give the counsel of mankind.
  South of the sacred mansion, first resort
The assembled sires, and pass the spacious
court.   60
Here in his porch earth's figured Genius
stands,
Truth's mighty mirror poising in his hands.
Graved on the pedestal and chased in gold,
Man's noblest arts their symbol forms un-
fold:—
His tillage and his trade, with all the store
Of wondrous fabrics and of useful lore;
Labors that fashion to his sovereign sway
Earth's total powers, her soil and air and sea,
Force them to yield their fruits at his known
call,
And bear his mandates round the rolling
ball;   70
Beneath the footstool all destructive things,
The mask of priesthood and the mace of
kings,
Lie trampled in the dust; for here at last
Fraud, folly, error all their emblems cast.
Each envoy here unloads his wearied hand
Of some old idol from his native land:
One flings a pagod on the mingled heap,
One lays a crescent, one a cross to sleep [2];
Swords, sceptres, mitres, crowns and globes
and stars,
Codes of false fame and stimulants to wars   80

[1] Barlow anticipates the acceleration of travel but
does not foresee aerial navigation.   [2] Like Paine,
Barlow considers religious systems, as well as monarchical governments, as instruments for the enslave-
ment of mankind. Pagod (pagoda), crescent, and cross
symbolize the religions of the East, Mohammedanism,
and Christianity.

Sink in the settling mass; since guile began,
These are the agents of the woes of man.
  Now the full concourse, where the arches
bend,
Pour through by thousands and the seats
ascend.
Far as the centred eye can range around
Or the deep trumpet's solemn voice resound,
Long rows of reverent sires sublime extend,
And cares of worlds on every brow suspend.
High in the front, for soundest wisdom
known,
A sire elect in peerless grandeur shone: 90
He opened calm the universal cause,
To give each realm its limit and its laws,
Bid the last breath of tired contention cease
And bind all regions in the leagues of peace;
Till one confederate, condependent sway
Spread with the sun and bound the walks of
day,
One centred system, one all-ruling soul
Live through the parts to regulate the whole.
  "Here, then," said Hesper,[1] with a blissful
smile,
"Behold the fruits of thy long years of
toil.   100
To yon bright borders of Atlantic day
Thy swelling pinions led the trackless way,
And taught mankind such useful deeds to
dare,
To trace new seas and happy nations rear;
Till by fraternal hands their sails unfurled
Have waved at last in union o'er the world." [2]

[1] Spirit of the West; America   [2] Cf. Tennyson's
use of the same rhymes in "Locksley Hall":

"Till the war-drum throbbed no longer, and the battle-
flags were furled
  In the Parliament of man, the Federation of the
world."

~ II ~

*The
Earlier
Nineteenth
Century*

The Earlier Nineteenth Century
1800–1820

The period of approximately thirty years between the close of the Revolution and that of the War of 1812 saw a change from dominance by conservative aristocratic Federalism to that of blatant lower middle-class democracy, and from formality and respect in manners to loud and free self-assertiveness. It was a generation in which knee breeches were replaced by pantaloons, and powdered wigs and queues by short hair, an age of social instability and uncouthness and of coarse and bombastic newspaper style. Abroad, it was the generation in which the hope of the world was kindled by the French Revolution, to be blotted out by the Reign of Terror, the ensuing military dictatorship of Bonaparte, and the overthrow of the Napoleonic war machine by a coalition of European autocracies. At home, it saw the advance from uncertain participation in a new experiment in nationalism, through our first shift of political administration and our second major war, to assured unity and an Era of Good Feeling; and from an insecure position on the North American continent, shared with the powerful monarchies of France, Great Britain, and Spain, to the domination of that continent, through the Louisiana Purchase of 1803.

As the outstanding figure of the later provincial period was that of Franklin, and in the Revolutionary period, Washington, so Jefferson dominated the succeeding generation. While Secretary of State in Washington's first cabinet, alarmed by Hamilton's centralizing policy, he began quietly organizing opposition sentiment. After his retirement from the cabinet he devoted his energies to developing the scattered and disorganized dissent throughout the country into an effective party which was able to challenge the Federalists in the election of 1796; and four years later, aided by Federalist quarrels and the unpopularity of Jay's Treaty with England (1795) and the unwise Alien and Sedition Acts, to sweep into power in the new capital at Washington. Thus was brought about, without the disastrous effects predicted by the disappointed Federalists, the first of a series of orderly revolutions in party control throughout our political history, all accomplished peacefully except that of 1860.

The normal development of domestic prosperity, with the repeal of the obnoxious Alien and Sedition Acts, the reorganization of the treasury system, the defeat of the Barbary pirates, and the reduction of the national debt and taxes, increased Jefferson's popularity so greatly that in the election of 1804 he received all the electoral votes except those of Connecticut. When he withdrew in 1809 to return to his pursuit of science, philosophy, and education, his friend and Secretary of State, James Madison, was easily elected for two terms; and in 1816 the Federalists, discredited by their dubious dealings in the War of 1812, disappeared from the picture without the control of a single electoral vote. Meanwhile, the increasing tension of the conflict between Napoleon and his foes involved American shipping through the British blockade of France and Napoleon's counterdecrees. England, her naval personnel depleted by easy desertions to American vessels, assumed the right of search and removal of supposed British seamen. So offensive did this procedure become that when America was inevitably drawn into the world war, it was on the side of the Napoleonic military dictatorship, though against the sentiments of a large section of the country, expressed in the somewhat seditious Hartford Convention of 1814. The only end gained by this inglorious war, in which brilliant victories on the sea and at New Orleans were offset by the British capture and burning of the Capitol at Washington, was that henceforth the United States was never again menaced by attack from any European power. America now turned her face westward and, busied with the tasks of developing a continent, began a long era of international isolation.

The population and settled area of the country grew rapidly. The 3,900,000 people of the 1790 census had nearly doubled, rising to 7,300,000 by 1810. Virginia, with almost a million inhabitants, was nearly outstripped by New York, with Pennsylvania (800,000), North Carolina, and Massachusetts following in order. The largest city was now New York, with just under 100,000 population; Philadelphia followed with 53,000; Baltimore, 46,000; and Boston, 35,000. Three new states, Vermont, Kentucky, and Tennessee, were admitted to the Union before 1800, Ohio in 1803, and Louisiana in 1812. The boundary of settlement in 1810 crossed central Maine and northern New York, central Ohio and southern Indiana and Illinois to the area around St. Louis, skirted the Mississippi to Tennessee, and turned back through Alabama to the border of Florida, still a possession of Spain. The total area at least partially settled was nearly twice that of 1780. The vastness of the territory acquired by the Louisiana Purchase from Napoleon in 1803 for $11,000,000 almost staggered Jefferson, relieved as he was to be rid of a dangerous foreign neighbor west of the Mississippi.

When Jefferson's Embargo Act deprived the New England merchants and shipowners of their traditional source of income, they turned with great effectiveness to a reinvestment of their funds in mills built up along their rivers, for the manufacture of goods hitherto imported from England. By the end of the War of 1812, the capital invested in cotton factories alone had leaped from half a million dollars to nearly forty million dollars. The industry employed a hundred thousand men and women, mostly native New Englanders. Though the re-entry of British goods to American markets when peace was declared caused a temporary setback, these industries continued, aided by the Tariff of 1816, to make the United States independent of foreign manufacturers and to give New England an industrial supremacy that was greatly to augment her influence throughout the nineteenth century.

As has been seen, the Great Awakening had split the New England Congregationalist Church into the enthusiastic New Calvinists, following Edwards's example, and the more decorous and conservative Old Calvinists of the seaboard towns. The former combined a rigorous moralism and fundamentalist orthodoxy with an evangelistic attitude. The latter, during the eighteenth century, tended to become increasingly liberal. In the preaching of clergymen in Boston like Jonathan Mayhew (1720–1766) and Charles Chauncy (1705–1787), the innate wickedness of man's nature came to be questioned. This tendency was parallel to, though probably not necessarily prompted by, the ideas of Rousseau and of the deists in England and France.[1] As Barrett Wendell pointed out,[2] it had become difficult by that time for reasonable Boston folk to regard their decent and orderly neighbors as so inherently bad that only the sacrifice of a Son of God could avail to save them from eternal punishment; and accordingly this doctrine gradually lost its meaning for thoughtful liberals.

King's Chapel, at Boston, though Episcopalian in form, was tinctured strongly with Congregationalism, which was the ancestral religion of many of its members. After the Revolution, while Anglican ordination was still refused to the American clergy, the rector, James Freeman, and his vestrymen organized themselves in 1785 as an independent church with a revised American ritual. This, when adopted, omitted any reference to the Trinity—Father, Son, and Holy Ghost—and stressed the divine unity of God and the loving inspiration of God's word, and is generally taken as the first avowal in America of the liberal faith known as Unitarianism. William Ellery Channing, the chief exponent of the new faith, in his sermons and in his essay "The Moral Argument against Calvinism," stressed the kindly and forgiving nature of God and the necessity for interpreting the Scriptures according to the light of reason. The central idea of Unitarianism was not any of the things which it discarded—the literal infallibility of the Bible, including the story of the fall of Adam; the threefold nature of the Deity; the necessary divinity of Christ— but its positive affirmation of a conception of human nature not depraved but capable of almost infinite goodness and perfectibility, as witness the example of Jesus of Nazareth. By thus substituting an optimistic for a deterministic religious philosophy, it liberated, with surprising results, the active and energetic New England spirit from the inhibitions which Calvinism had imposed upon it for nearly

[1] G. A. Koch, *Republican Religion; The American Revolution and the Cult of Reason* (1933), 79 ff. Unitarianism included some ideas already associated with deism, such as reliance on reason, faith in "natural altruism," and parallelism between natural and spiritual laws.

[2] His chapter on Unitarianism in *A Literary History of America* (1901) is still the best brief interpretation of the movement in New England.

two centuries, and especially upon its self-expression in drama, secular painting, music, fiction, and philosophy.

By 1800, without a formal break, most of the older and more influential churches from Plymouth to Portland had embraced Unitarianism; and within a generation it had become, paralleled by the milder Universalism in the interior towns, the socially established religion of the New England seaboard. Though it never greatly expanded, because of its lack of proselyting zeal, its cultural influence was beyond all proportion to its numbers. It is largely through its liberalizing contacts that other American denominations, Protestant and Catholic alike, have come to place decreased emphasis upon credal differences and to stress social and intellectual values in religion. Its influence was magnified by the fine spiritual and intellectual stature of such early leaders as William Ellery Channing, James Freeman, Joseph Buckminster, Edward Everett Hale, the Emersons, Jared Sparks, Thomas Starr King, John Pierpont, Samuel F. Smith, Theodore Parker, and Sylvester Judd; and it is not surprising that the greater New England writers of the next century were almost without exception Unitarians.

1820–1850

I

The year 1820 may serve to mark the definite "arrival" of American literature, since in that and the following year were published Irving's completed masterpiece, *The Sketch Book*, Bryant's first volume of *Poems*, and Cooper's first successful novel, *The Spy*. These works, in three important fields, provided a prompt response to a part of Sydney Smith's sneering question in the *Edinburgh Review*, in January, 1820, "In the four quarters of the globe, who ever reads an American book, or goes to an American play, or looks at an American picture or statue?"

For the first time, literature in America was beginning to keep pace with its physical development, which was advancing with extraordinary swiftness. The fewer than ten million inhabitants in 1820 grew to more than twice as many in the next twenty-five years. In the meantime, Florida had been acquired from Spain in 1819, and the Texan republic was annexed in 1845. Further, the division of the Oregon territory in 1846, the conquest of California and the Southwest from Mexico in 1848, and the purchase of Alaska from Russia in 1867 brought the domain of the United States to over three million square miles, fourth largest in the world. The fast-moving boundary of actual settlement within this vast area had by 1850 reached a line extending across upper Michigan and Wisconsin, central Iowa, eastern Nebraska and Kansas, and central Texas and the Indian Territory, as the present Oklahoma was then called, newly set apart as a permanent refuge for the dispossessed eastern tribes.

It was fortunate, perhaps, that the pioneer settlement of the Ohio and Mississippi valleys was accomplished by a fairly homogeneous stock in race, language, religion, and social and political ideals, whose differences were readily assimilated. In general the westward advance was along two roughly parallel fronts. The larger, which traversed the country from the Ohio valley to the Gulf and the Rio Grande, was that of the pioneer stock originating mainly in Virginia and the Carolinas, which had led in crossing the Appalachian ridges into Kentucky and Tennessee. Rangy, restless, and unlettered, excellent huntsmen and fighters, they drove the tribesmen before them and developed an agricultural society in the Southwest and in the southern counties of Ohio, Indiana, and Illinois, and beyond the Mississippi in Missouri and Kansas. The later "Pike County" character, in John Hay's *Pike County Ballads* and the stories of Bret Harte, Mark Twain, and "John Phoenix," is perhaps rather a caricature than a portrait of this stock after its energy was mainly spent.

Slightly later, across the northern belt of the same Middle Western states and southern Michigan, Wisconsin, and Minnesota, poured a stream of migration originating chiefly in New England, through upstate New York, where much of it had paused for a generation.[1] Shrewd organizers and builders, these newcomers started the Lake cities, built up industries, banks, and commerce, and transplanted a New England civilization in the Middle West. Schools and libraries sprang up wherever they went, and in many places colleges, such as Oberlin, Knox, Beloit, Lawrence, Wabash, Carleton, and Grinnell.

Foreign immigration, which had been relatively small and mainly British in origin, received enormous impetus after 1845 from the suppression of popular revolutionary movements in central Europe and a series of disastrous famine years in Ireland. The Germans, farmers and artisans, generally pushed on into the interior, where their thrift and energy contributed greatly to the economic upbuilding of the new country. With additions from the older Pennsylvania German stock, they gave to many portions of the Middle West a Teutonic flavor, and helped culturally to make Cincinnati, Louisville, St. Louis, and Cleveland noteworthy musical centers. The Irish[2] settled in great numbers in Boston, New York, and other eastern industrial cities, of which they greatly altered the later political and religious character.

Of great importance in westward expansion was the improvement of communications. The federal highway known as the Cumberland Road reached Wheeling, on the Ohio, in 1818, and pushed on slowly to the Mississippi. The 1820's and 1830's were the great period of a projected network of canals, promoted by the construction of the Erie Canal across New York, 1817–1825. They were soon

[1] An excellent study of this migration is Lois K. Matthews' *The Expansion of New England* (Boston, 1909).
[2] Not to be confused with the Presbyterian Scotch-Irish of earlier immigration, from Northern Ireland.

superseded by the railroads, however, whose mileage by 1860 totalled 30,000, linking together all sections, but most effectively the industrial East and the grain- and cattle-producing West.

Manufactures, favored by fluctuating but continuous tariff protection, grew rapidly in the northeastern states as improved machinery and centralized plants increased their output. These factors, with the shift from native to foreign-born workers unprotected by labor laws, greatly changed the conditions in the early New England mills and partly justified unfavorable comparisons by slavery apologists with the labor system on the cotton plantations. By 1860 the value of manufactured products had caught up with that of agricultural products. Never- theless the southern cotton crop had grown to the enormous proportions of 5,000,- 000 bales exported in 1860, mainly by water to English and New England mills. For a time Yankee ships rivalled those of Great Britain in the carrying of this and other commerce, but the British, by first taking advantage of the shift to steam, re- gained the supremacy. During the clipper ship era, American commerce made great inroads into the Pacific trade with China and India, and after Commodore Perry's coup in 1854, with Japan.

II

Politically, the period from 1815 to 1860 was one of continued Democratic control based upon the common interests of the South and West, interrupted only by two brief and ineffectual Whig administrations. The unwieldy majority of the Era of Good Feeling soon split along natural lines of interest, and a faction calling itself the National Republicans, with the remnant of the Federalists, secured the election by Congress of John Quincy Adams in 1824. Adams, like his father an able, incorruptible, and unpopular statesman, was last in the series of presidents representing the aristocracy of Virginia and Massachusetts who had governed the new country for fifty years. His defeat in 1828 by General Andrew Jackson, hailed as champion of the common people against the aristocrats, was the greatest political overturn between 1800 and 1860. Swept into office by the extreme Democrats of the West and the poorer citizenry of the South and Northeast, Jackson displaced numerous officeholders, disrupted the National Bank, and governed as far as possible in favor of the unpropertied classes. The informality of manners, laxness of political appointments, and bitter social and party feuds of his regime left their marks on subsequent American politics. Himself a real leader of men, with little training for the presidency, Jackson's successors throughout the entire century were, with the exceptions of Lincoln and Cleveland, men of relatively mediocre ability.

Van Buren, who followed Jackson, inherited the disastrous financial panic of 1837; and the Whigs, as the opposition now called themselves, were able to defeat him for re-election by aping the Jacksonian campaign tactics. The Democrat Polk, however, secured the election of 1844 on a frankly expansionist policy; and during his administration the United States proper, through annexation, the Mexican War, and amicable negotiation with Great Britain, acquired practically its present area. With the return of prosperity, the Democrats, except for the Taylor-Fillmore administration, remained in power until 1860. Political lines were frequently obscured by crosscurrents—anti-Masonic, anti-immigration, anti-Catholic, and anti-slavery. Both the Missouri Compromise of 1820 and the Nebraska Compromise of 1850 were believed by Northern and Southern leaders to have "settled" the slavery issue, but like later nonpolitical issues, such as women's rights, prohibition, and old-age security, it could not be kept out of politics.

For several decades after 1789, the balance of population and representation in Congress between free and slave states remained fairly even. The South, however, proved to be a geographical unit, to which profitable slave labor and the plantation system were restricted by nature. The admission of Texas in 1845 virtually exhausted the possibilities of Southern—or at least, slave-state—expansion. But after 1830 the filling up of the Middle West and the West, enormously accelerated by German immigration and the discovery of gold in California in 1848, and the resulting clamor of the new territories for statehood, threw the old equilibrium out of balance. This, and the fact that the American System, with its protective tariff and "pork-barrel" appropriations for public improvements, chiefly communication, turned out greatly to the advantage of the North, while the exigencies of governing an increasing area and population tended to a centralization of government opposed to the Jeffersonian theory of states' rights, drew the South into a defensive solidarity which shut off its constructive contribution to American political history for nearly a century. A series of irritants, including the nullification agitation of the 1820's in South Carolina, the activities of abolitionist societies, the Fugitive Slave Law and the Underground Railroad, culminating in John Brown's raid on the arsenal at Harper's Ferry, led many Southerners and some Northerners to the conviction that secession and the formation of a separate union was the only ultimate solution. The most ominous sign of disunion, not fully appreciated at the time, was the division of the great Protestant sects into Southern and Northern branches, the Presbyterians in 1838, the Methodists in 1844, and the Baptists in 1845.

The period from 1820 to 1850, then, was one of futile attempts at adjustment of irreconcilable issues in rapidly changing conditions, in which the giant figures of Calhoun, Webster, and Clay were the chief protagonists. In the 1850's, the moribund Whig party effected a fusion with the American or Native Son and the Free-Soil elements in a new opposition party under the name Republican. By adroit management the mutually antagonistic German and anti-immigrant Know-Nothing votes were brought into alliance at the same time that Lincoln's political shrewdness alienated Southern support from Douglas, the Democratic leader;

and the former found himself elected, as a minority candidate with an electoral majority, to the presidency of a divided country. In the ensuing war the Confederacy, despite heroic resistance and superior leadership, was defeated by the greater weight of armies which included many German and Irish regiments and by the better industrial and communication systems of the Union. President Lincoln, at first inexperienced, hesitant, and distrusted, rose to heroic proportions with the success of Northern arms and the Emancipation Proclamation, and was spared by martyrdom the inevitable bickerings and obloquy suffered by Washington and Wilson in similar situations. At the same time his assassination was a tragedy to the South, left devastated by war and saddled with a bewildered and unproductive free Negro population at the mercy of a vindictive and rapacious reconstruction. Thereafter, the memory of common participation in the war, with skillful use of the memory of Lincoln, bound the agricultural West for fifty years in political alliance with the industrial East, not always to the equal interests of both sections.

III

As the introduction of power machines in industry stimulated manufactures, and steamboats, canals, and railroads took merchandise all over the country, the commercial class increased greatly in importance. Among influential inventions were the McCormick reaper in 1834 and Elias Howe's sewing machine, patented in 1846. The Morse electric telegraph was developed in 1844, and in 1866 Cyrus Field laid the Atlantic cable, establishing communication between the old and the new worlds. In the East greater differentiation of classes grew up as men were attracted from farms and small towns to the factory systems of large cities, where they no longer worked for themselves but for employers. Standards of living were raised, however, since manufactures made goods cheaper and more abundant. In the West, where farming was still the chief interest, less class cleavage appeared. Trading in land was profitable, and the discovery of gold caused a rush of adventurers to California and other regions. The South raised cotton and tobacco and remained preoccupied with these pursuits and with politics.

With the changing character of the population came changes in its interests. The new facilities for travel and intercommunication and the multiplication of newspapers and magazines served as civilizing agencies. Among leading reform movements of the period, the most absorbing was the abolition movement. Others concerned the prevention of war, the rights of the poor, the rights of women, prison reform, and temperance. The last-named movement was launched in 1826 in protest against the abuse of drinking and led to the formation of many "total abstinence" societies. The cultural life of the country was much influenced until after the Civil War by the lyceum, an institution that did much to spread knowledge. The earliest was established in Massachusetts in 1826, and in ten years the number increased to a thousand. The lyceum provided lectures, debates, concerts, and entertainments of other kinds, and enlightened its audiences on philosophical, literary, scientific, and educational matters. Through this agency Emerson broadcast his doctrine of self-reliance, which synchronized with the dominant individualism of the time.

Newspapers, magazines, and books played a larger and larger part in the life of the country as time passed. News features, diversified literary material, and humor broadened the old type of political journalism. Among leading newspapers the New York *Evening Post* was founded in 1801, the *Sun* in 1833, and the *Herald* in 1835, followed by the *Times* in 1841 and the *Tribune* in 1851. The *Springfield Republican*, most important of the smaller-city newspapers, was established in 1824. Weekly and monthly periodicals sprang up, addressed largely to feminine readers, over-sentimentalized in literary matter, and designed to foster elegance and refinement. *Godey's Lady's Book*, founded at Philadelphia in 1830, with its colored fashion plates as a feature, had a large circulation as late as 1876. The *North American Review*, patterned after the great English reviews, established as early as 1815, long ranked as the most important magazine in the country. *The Dial*, of interest as the organ of the American transcendentalists, was issued from 1840 till 1844. Many of its contributors continued to confer literary distinction upon the *Atlantic Monthly*, established in 1857. *Harper's Magazine* began in 1850, with New York City as its home.

Education gradually widened its range. From colonial times the New England schools had been supported by the communities as civil institutions. In the other colonies the schools had been largely private and under the oversight of the churches. As democracy advanced, more free public schools depending upon local or state support were instituted alongside the private and religious schools. Horace Mann (1798–1859) was a notable reformer, who did much to modernize and liberalize the school system of Massachusetts, and his influence spread to other states. Under his stimulus superintendents were trained, support and equipment improved, and normal schools fostered. In connection with elementary schools, mention may be made of *McGuffey's Readers*, made for the first and second grades in 1836 and later for more advanced classes. These readers had enormous influence and, in revised form, are still in use here and there. The first half of the century saw the establishment of many academies for those who could not attend college or for the preparation of those who could do so. Colleges and universities likewise multiplied. The backbone courses in higher institutions included Greek and Latin, and sometimes Hebrew, a little science, and usually some theology. The older eastern institutions prepared largely for the professions and derived their students chiefly from the superior classes. In the new West everybody was eager for educational advantages. Schools and libraries were started early, and state universities established, which eventually were opened to women as well as men. Distinguished scientists of the period were Louis Agassiz the naturalist and Asa Gray the botanist, both at Harvard, and Benjamin Silliman in chemistry, at Yale: Among notables in the humanities were President James Marsh of the University of Vermont, whose educational reforms have not yet been completely superseded; and Professor Karl Follen and President C. C. Felton of Harvard, who introduced German university methods into America. Eminent economists were Thomas Cooper of the University of South Carolina and his successor Francis Lieber, later professor at Columbia. Henry R. Schoolcraft took conspicuous rank for his interest in western exploration and in Indian lore.

The large publishing houses had their homes, as they still do, on the eastern coast. Both authors and publishers were long handicapped by the lack of an adequate copyright law. Popular European books might be republished by any houses that wished them; native writers thus had no protection against the competition of cheap pirated editions of works from abroad. No effective international copyright law protecting foreign and American books was passed until 1891.

Theaters and amusements gradually gained in popularity and standing. Stock companies arose in cities, and as traveling became easier, professional players, beginning about 1825, began to troupe through western circuits. Romantic dramas of European authorship were chiefly presented, but sometimes American plays, often dealing with historical figures and sometimes with Indian themes, were produced. Among the leading actors of the day were Edwin Booth, James H. Hackett, Edwin Forrest, William Macready, and Fanny Kemble. An English opera company sang in New Orleans in 1820, and Italian opera made its advent in New York City in 1825. As regards other forms of art, portrait painting and painting in the "grand style" continued, though artists of the distinction of Benjamin West, J. S. Copley, and Gilbert Stuart of the preceding period were lacking. The "back to nature" movement assumed considerable popularity among painters. Duncan Phyfe had deserved celebrity for beautiful craftsmanship in furniture, and Washington Allston won a name as a critic of art who promoted good taste. The architecture early favored was classical. Later a more decorated and elaborate type came into vogue.

IV

In an objective examination of pre-Civil War literature one is perhaps first struck with the fact that the ideas and points of view reflected are still primarily Anglo-Saxon. One is reminded that up to 1860, at least, the literate American population was still perhaps eighty per cent British in origin. A glance through Whitcomb's *Chronological Outlines of American Literature* reveals between 1820 and 1860 no name of importance in the field of pure letters that is not either British (English, Scottish, or Irish), Huguenot, or Dutch of several generations in an Anglo-Saxon environment. To deny to this literature the quality of being American or to brand it as imitative or colonial is accordingly simply to ignore the facts, particularly in view of the robust Americanism of Irving, Cooper, Bryant, and Emerson, to name no others. Nor do traces of influences that pervaded all literature in the English language, like that of Wordsworth, Byron, or Scott, indicate servile copying, any more than does any tradesman's fashioning his work to rival that of another workman more skillful in his own craft. Quite as common, in the generation after 1830, is imitation of the first three successful American writers, Irving, Cooper, and Bryant. In general, then, one finds in American literature of the time traits and ideas common to all other literature in English during the Romantic and early Victorian periods, with, to be sure, certain distinctive American features such as the implicit acceptance of democracy as the ideal political system, a certain expansiveness of physical outlook, a somewhat greater degree of puritanism than is found in Wordsworth, Crabbe, Tennyson, and Dickens, and the phenomenon of New England Transcendentalism—"Romanticism rooted in Puritan soil."

A second literary characteristic of the period is that widening of the American cultural horizon which has well been described as the Rediscovery of Europe. The self-consciousness of Americans between 1780 and 1830 is an evidence of the distance from European culture into which America had lapsed during a half-century of increasing national isolation. The eagerness with which American scholars and writers now sought and brought back the legendary lore, current thought, and artistic treasures of the Old World[1] is sometimes attributed to "escapism" or colonialism. Allowance must be made, of course, for the bareness and drabness of cultural life in a country busily engaged in material pursuits, but in what direction, one might ask, should the active American intellect have been expected to turn for enrichment? From the displaced Indian culture had been absorbed what it had to offer: the cultivation of maize, potatoes, and tobacco; the skirmish and ambush type of warfare; the powwow or convention method of conducting public business; emphasis upon outdoor life and organized physical prowess; and the habit of an unrevealing "poker-face" reserve in business and conversation. The Canadian and Spanish-American provinces and republics had little more to offer. Hence after the War of 1812 there was a zestful turning back to a rediscovered Europe. Ticknor, Everett, Bancroft, Motley, and Hedge studied at German universities; Emerson turned to Coleridge and the Orient; Irving went to England, Spain, and Germany; Cooper to France and Italy; Longfellow to Germany, Scandinavia, Italy, and Spain; Motley to the Netherlands; Hawthorne to England and Florence. In doing so they rendered pioneer service by enriching the American imagination; they re-established closer contact with European civilization, and in the end did much to break the fetters of cultural self-consciousness and inferiority.

[1] For an intelligent study of this phase of our national experience, see O. W. Long, *Literary Pioneers* (1935).

This awakened interest in Europe in no way lessened the pervasive influence of democratic theory. Perhaps mid-nineteenth century American literature is chiefly distinguished from European by its underlying accepted assumption that a democratic republic is the best of possible governments, and that social and political equality is the ideal state of society. Travelers who were enthusiastic over the art, literature, and legends of Europe did not fail to comment upon the advantages of American freedom and equality of opportunity. The victory of the Jacksonians in 1828, together with the gradual elimination of religious, property, and other qualifications upon general manhood suffrage, went far to give practical effect to the democratic theory; and the increasing immigrant population, fleeing tyranny and lack of social and economic opportunity in Europe, greatly intensified it. Cooper, vacationing in France, turned out a series of "republican novels"; and Bryant, Emerson, and Thoreau hailed with sympathetic interest the revolutions in Spanish America, Greece, and Italy, and less successful insurrectionary movements in Hungary, Poland, Cuba, and elsewhere. By 1823 the United States government felt sufficiently confident of its strength and of the success of the democratic system to assume, in the Monroe Doctrine, responsibility for forbidding further attempts by European monarchies to subjugate free peoples anywhere on the American continent, an attitude never challenged except by the French monarchy in Mexico while we were embroiled in internal war in 1861.

Another marked trait of American literature has been a certain expansiveness, the reflection of the consciousness of vast national areas and resources and of the unbounded expectancy of the future greatness of the country. Irving, hardly a chauvinist, exclaimed in his introduction to *The Sketch Book* (1820) about America's "mighty lakes, like oceans of liquid silver; . . . her valleys teeming with wild fertility; her tremendous cataracts thundering in her solitudes; her boundless plains, waving with spontaneous verdure; her broad, deep rivers, rolling in solemn silence to the ocean; her trackless forests, where vegetation puts forth all its magnificence." This feeling finds expression also in Bryant's "The Prairies" and "Thanatopsis," in Longfellow's *Evangeline* and *Hiawatha*, and in Cooper's romances of the forest and plain. The assumption of a great future, shared by Emerson, Lowell, and Whitman, naturally took in most minds the form of an expansionist policy, of which our war of conquest in Mexico was another manifestation. Schemes for the acquisition of Cuba, Haiti, and Nicaragua were promoted at different times; and down to the very end of the century many Americans looked forward to the "annexation" of Canada as the natural culmination of the "manifest destiny" of America.

Closely allied with this was the vitally important presence of the western frontier in the thinking of all Americans. The period under discussion was that in which the hugest strides of westward migration were made and the greatest areas brought under man's control. The West still appealed to the imagination of the East as an opportunity to the energetic, a lure to the ne'er-do-well, an asylum to the unsuccessful and discouraged. In the literature of the time, this effect upon the national imagination was more important than the actual frontier itself. The realities of life in the newer settlements were less often depicted by American writers, except in nonliterary forms, such as Bryant's personal letters, than by critical and often antagonistic foreigners, whose sarcastic comments served to make Americans, including Westerners like John Hay, only more sensitive and conscious of their newness and rawness.[1] As Lowell, himself a pioneer in handling the American scene and speech, commented regarding early New England life, there was a need of imaginative distance:

Everything is near, authentic, and petty. There is no mist of distance to soften outlines, no mirage of tradition to give characters and events an imaginative loom. So much downright work was perhaps never wrought on the earth's surface as during the first forty years after the settlement. But mere work is unpicturesque and devoid of sentiment.[2]

Cooper and Simms, in dealing with their pioneers, huntsmen, and Indian fighters, threw around them such a veil of imagination, just as Mrs. Stowe and Whittier, in their writings, romanticized the American Negro. Hence the result, as in the case of Brackenridge's earlier *Modern Chivalry*, that frontier conditions are most often effectively treated by the humorists, like Artemus Ward, Sut Lovingood, and John Phoenix, mainly men of eastern upbringing who saw the new country objectively. It remained for the western-born Mark Twain to combine fact, humor, and sentiment in exactly the right proportions.

Puritanism, in its insistent moral tone and in its concern with reform issues, continued to influence American literature of the mid-nineteenth century. The Revolution was succeeded by a second wave of religious revivals which rivalled the Great Awakening and strengthened throughout the country the hold of the younger sects, in which the puritan element was strong. On the negative side, probably no literature in any period was ever more scrupulously clean than that of the United States from 1820 to 1850. Poe, whose works were chaste enough, was condemned by a generation which exacted purity in the lives as well as the writings of its authors— a generation to whom Byron and Burns were wicked, and Moore and DeQuincey decidedly naughty. Later, despite their merits, the frankness of Melville and Whitman caused them to be effectively ignored throughout their lifetimes. On the positive side, the puritan moral earnestness is evident in the stories of Hawthorne as contrasted with those of Poe, in Bryant as compared with Irving, and in Whittier's

[1] For a discussion of British comment, consult Jane Mesick, *The British Traveler in America, 1785–1835* (1922).
[2] "New England Two Centuries Ago."

reforming zeal beside the quiet poise of Emerson. It was an era of social reforms in which the moral element was a dominating influence. The peace movement found Longfellow a quiet but sincere devotee. Margaret Fuller and Emerson championed the rights of women. Overshadowing all other issues was that of abolishing slavery, whose advocates, Whittier, Garrison, Lowell, and Mrs. Stowe, reveal in their intense moments all the moral fervor and often intolerant righteousness of the puritan in all ages.

After 1830 the literary ascendancy swung back from Philadelphia and New York to New England; and Boston, with neighboring Cambridge and Concord, became for half a century the nation's literary capital. In Massachusetts lived and wrote at the same time Emerson, Longfellow, Hawthorne, Thoreau, Whittier, Lowell, Emily Dickinson, Holmes, and for a time, Melville. Here flourished also the influential *North American Review* and *Atlantic Monthly*, the enterprising publishing house of Ticknor and Fields, and Harvard University, which was still in most fields the pre-eminent American seat of learning. Small wonder that poor Poe, competing with this literary galaxy, dubbed it the Mutual Admiration Society. The literary prestige of New England abroad was doubtless helped by the large number of colleges and other cultural institutions which had been started in the Middle West with New England encouragement and capital, and in the South by the host of Yankee schoolteachers and lawyers, building upon the established reputation of Noah Webster's blue-backed spelling books. The extraordinary predominance of this section, however, at a time when the center of population and national development in general were moving westward, is explainable only as a part of that New England renaissance whose industrial aspects have already been commented on.

American literature from 1820 to 1850 was of course a part of the general romantic movement, and shared its common characteristics, plus those separately discussed above. Its most distinctive contribution was perhaps the phenomenon called New England Transcendentalism. This may be loosely defined as a manifestation of practical idealism—in some cases more practical, in others more ideal—which matured in Cambridge and Concord about 1836, chiefly under the leadership of Ralph Waldo Emerson, who four years earlier had resigned his pastorate at the Second Church (Unitarian), Boston. Others of the transcendentalist group were also Unitarian clergymen who, like William Ellery Channing himself, unsatisfied with the religious liberation brought about by their sect, were eager for a greater degree of social amelioration, spiritual living, and intellectual cultivation. Another source of transcendentalism was the idealistic philosophy of the German Kant as transmitted in the writings and conversation of Coleridge and of Carlyle, the poetry of Wordsworth, and the eclectic philosophy of the Frenchman Cousin. The experimental freedom inherited from the American and French revolutions was also a factor in their thinking, and the frontier was not too distant for its vague suggestiveness to have a quickening effect upon the group. Along with these went some of the moral earnestness and zeal for reform of their puritan ancestors. The result was a spirit of enthusiastic receptivity and eagerness for spiritual and intellectual exploration beyond, or *transcending*, the bounds of ordinary concerns and accepted views of life, which either enkindled or mystified the minds of their contemporaries. Some of the transcendentalists, like Emerson and Thoreau, were chiefly interested in a freer and higher way of the inward life of the individual; others like Margaret Fuller, Curtis, and Ripley, in a better state of social living; others like Alcott and Elizabeth Peabody, in better ideals of education; others, like Hedge, Hawthorne, Brooks, and Dwight Sullivan, in advancement of the arts and literature; and still others on the edge of the group, like Channing and Sylvester Judd, in a more spiritual religion. All were eager, fresh, and individual in their views, and their combined effect was one of quickening and vitalizing the literature and thought of their time and broadening its cultural horizon. Lowell, never actually a transcendentalist, bears witness to this. Even after their joint undertakings, *The Dial* magazine and the community living at Brook Farm, were dispersed, they continued as individuals to contribute actively to the religious, social, political, and artistic life of their country.

New York City enjoyed a brief primacy in letters between the death of Dennie at Philadelphia in 1812 and the rise of the transcendentalists at Cambridge in 1836, with the Irvings, Cooper, Paulding, Halleck, and Drake, and the lesser Knickerbockers. Bryant and Willis joined the group and were its chief literary ornaments during the mid-century. Later, Melville, Whitman, and Poe were for a time associated with the city. Hartford witnessed a new group of Connecticut wits about 1830, including J. G. Percival, J. A. Hillhouse, Carlos Wilcox, and Lydia H. Sigourney. Philadelphia was important mainly as a dramatic center and as the seat of *Graham's*, *Sartain's*, and *Godey's*, with which Poe was connected. At Baltimore flourished a group comprising J. P. Kennedy, F. S. Key, W. C. Pinkney, the novelist John Neal, and others. West of the Alleghenies, Cincinnati and Lexington were the first cultural centers of importance.

Perhaps the most interesting group outside of Boston was that which flourished in the decade before the Civil War, in Charleston, South Carolina. This city was the literary capital of the lower Old South, whose brittle economic and social aristocracy rested upon Greek and Old Testament sanctions, while the chivalric romances of Sir Walter Scott furnished the external ideals for its spirit and manners. Here a coterie of writers of distinction kept alive the *Southern Review* and *Russell's Magazine* and created a considerable output of romantic verse and prose exhibiting the characteristics of lyrical sweetness, beauty, and delicate sentiment in dealing with themes of nature, chivalric adventure, and idealized womanhood, fused with a haunting melancholy which marks most Southern literature from Richard Henry Wilde to Lanier. Paul H. Hayne, Henry Timrod, and William G. Simms were the principal members of the group, whose hopes and activities were mainly snuffed out by the devastation resulting from the Civil War.

1780 -- *William Ellery Channing* -- 1842

BORN IN NEWPORT, Rhode Island, Channing was son of a father who represented the Presbyterianism of Princeton, but of a mother who came of liberal Harvard stock. After graduating at Harvard in 1798, he went as tutor to Richmond, Virginia, when overwork and ascetic habits undermined his health. Appointed a "regent" at Harvard, he studied theology and in 1803 was ordained minister of the Federal Street Church, Boston. Here, as his monument in the Boston Public Garden says, "He breathed into theology a humane spirit." His influential preaching, notably his famous sermon on Unitarian Christianity, at Baltimore in 1819, together with his "gracious, almost saintly character," made him a recognized leader among the Unitarian Congregational ministers of Boston. Although for over twenty years these ministers had filled the more influential pulpits in eastern New England, together with the seminary at Harvard, they objected to forming an independent sect. In 1808, however, the Trinitarian or Orthodox Congregationalists withdrew their support from Harvard and established their seminary at Andover; and in 1820 Channing organized the conference of liberal ministers, which in May, 1825, became the American Unitarian Association. The theological grounds for the separation of the Unitarians from Calvinistic orthodoxy are effectively set forth in his sermons and controversial writings, such as "The Moral Argument against Calvinism," first published in the *Christian Disciple*, in 1820.

Always a semi-invalid, in 1821 Channing took a long vacation, and on his return was assigned a colleague in his church. With greater freedom from then on, he was able to give more of his time to that diversity of spiritual and social reforms which accompanied the intellectual and artistic movement often called the New England Renaissance. Objecting to a critical and rationalistic tendency within his sect, he urged a greater degree of spirituality and, as a friend and follower of Coleridge, he was largely responsible for the Unitarian contribution to the Transcendental movement of the 1830's. He pleaded for "a poetry which pierces beneath the exterior of life to the depths of the soul, and which lays open its mysterious working, borrowing from the whole outward creation fresh images and correspondences, with which to illuminate the secrets of the world within us." In his "Remarks on

American Literature" (1830), he objected to the proneness of Americans to be influenced by English writers rather than being concerned with their own country. Always interested in politics as a moral issue, he helped to prepare New England for the abolition of slavery by a notable series of pamphlets. As a staunch pacifist, he preached against the War of 1812, and the Massachusetts branch of the American Peace Society was organized in his study. He was also a leader in the temperance movement in his century but believed its end should be accomplished by persuasion, not by legal enforcement.

Channing's works were published in 1903. Biographies are W. H. Channing's *Memoir* (1848, centenary edition 1880) and J. W. Chadwick's *William Ellery Channing, Minister of Religion* (1903). The *DAB* article is by Samuel McChord Crothers. For an excellent brief account of the Unitarian movement and Channing's part in it, see Barrett Wendell's *Literary History of America*, Book V, Chs. III and IV. For his connection with Transcendentalism see C. H. Goddard in *CHAL* and C. H. Gohdes's *The Periodicals of Transcendentalism*. See also C. W. Eliot, *Four American Leaders* (1906); Elizabeth P. Peabody, *Reminiscences of Reverend William Ellery Channing* (1880); R. E. Spiller, "A Case for W. E. Channing," *New England Quarterly*, III, 55–81 (Jan., 1930); and C. H. Faust, "The Background of the Unitarian Opposition to Transcendentalism," *Modern Philology*, XXXV, 297–324 (1938).

From THE MORAL ARGUMENT AGAINST CALVINISM

Though the Unitarian movement had its origin in the later decades of the eighteenth century and was definitely established and exerted its enormous influence upon American thought and literature by the beginning of the nineteenth, Channing's famous attack upon the early theology of New England was first published as a review in the *Christian Disciple* in 1820, seventeen years after he entered the ministry.

. . . THE principal argument against Calvinism, in *The General View of Christian Doctrines*,[1] is the *moral argument*, or that which is drawn from the inconsistency of the system with the divine perfections. It is plain that a doctrine which contradicts our best ideas of goodness and justice cannot come from the just and good God, or be a true representation of his character. This moral argument has always been powerful to the pulling down of the strongholds of Calvinism. Even in the dark period when this system was shaped and finished at Geneva, its advocates often writhed under the weight of it; and we cannot but deem it a mark of the progress of society that Calvinists are more and more troubled with the palpable repugnance of their doctrines to God's nature, and accordingly labor to soften and explain them until in many cases the name only is retained. If the stern reformer of Geneva could lift up his head and hear the mitigated tone in which some of his professed followers dispense his fearful doctrines, we fear that he could not lie down in peace until he had poured out his displeasure on their cowardice and degeneracy. He would tell them with a frown that *moderate Calvinism* was a solecism, a contradiction in terms, and would bid them in scorn to join their real friend, Arminius. Such is the power of public opinion and of an improved state of society on creeds that naked, undisguised Calvinism is not very fond of showing itself, and many of consequence know imperfectly what it means. What view of Christian doctrines is directed?

Calvinism teaches that, in consequence of Adam's sin in eating the forbidden fruit, God brings into life all his posterity with a nature wholly corrupt, so that they are utterly indisposed, disabled, and made opposite to all that is spiritually good, and wholly inclined to all evil, and that continually. It teaches that all

[1] *A General View of the Doctrines of Christianity* (Boston, 1809), which Channing is reviewing

mankind, having fallen in Adam, are under God's wrath and curse, and so made liable to all miseries in this life, to death itself, and to the pains of hell for ever. It teaches that from this ruined race God, out of his mere good pleasure, has elected a certain number to be saved by Christ, not induced to this choice by any foresight of their faith or good works, but wholly by his free grace and love; and that, having thus predestinated them to eternal life, he renews and sanctifies them by his almighty and special agency and brings them into a state of grace, from which they cannot fall and perish. It teaches that the rest of mankind he is pleased to pass over, and to ordain them to dishonor and wrath for their sins, to the honor of his justice and power; in other words, he leaves the rest to the corruption in which they were born, withholds the grace which is necessary to their recovery, and condemns them to "most grievous torments in soul and body without intermission in hellfire for ever." Such is Calvinism, as gathered from the most authentic records of the doctrine. Whoever will consult the famous Assembly's Catechisms and Confession will see the peculiarities of the system in all their length and breadth of deformity. A man of plain sense, whose spirit has not been broken to this creed by education or terror, will think that it is not necessary for us to travel to heathen countries, to learn how mournfully the human mind may misrepresent the Deity.

The moral argument against Calvinism, of which we have spoken, must seem irresistible to common and unperverted minds, after attending to the brief statement now given. It will be asked with astonishment, How is it possible that men can hold these doctrines and yet maintain God's goodness and equity? What principles can be more contradictory?—To remove the objection to Calvinism, which is drawn from its repugnance to the Divine perfections, recourse has been had, as before observed, to the distinction between natural and moral inability, and to other like subtleties. But a more common reply, we conceive, has been drawn from the weakness and imperfection of the human mind, and from its incapacity of comprehending God. Calvinists will tell us that because a doctrine opposes our convic-

tions of rectitude, it is not necessarily false; that apparent are not always real inconsistencies; that God is an infinite and incomprehensible being, and not to be tried by *our* ideas of fitness and morality; that we bring their system to an incompetent tribunal when we submit it to the decision of human reason and conscience; that we are weak judges of what is right and wrong, good and evil, in the Deity; that the happiness of the universe may require an administration of human affairs which is very offensive to limited understandings; that we must follow revelation, not reason or moral feeling, and must consider doctrines which shock us in revelation as awful mysteries, which are dark through our ignorance, and which time will enlighten. How little, it is added, can man explain or understand God's ways? How inconsistent the miseries of life appear with goodness in the Creator. How prone, too, have men always been to confound good and evil, to call the just unjust. How presumptuous is it in such a being to sit in judgment upon God, and to question the rectitude of the divine administration because it shocks *his* sense of rectitude. Such we conceive to be a fair statement of the manner in which the Calvinist frequently meets the objection that his system is at war with God's attributes. Such the reasoning by which the voice of conscience and nature is stifled, and men are reconciled to doctrines which, if tried by the established principles of morality, would be rejected with horror. On this reasoning we purpose to offer some remarks; and we shall avail ourselves of the opportunity to give our views of *the confidence which is due to our rational and moral faculties in religion.*

That God is infinite, and that man often errs, we affirm as strongly as our Calvinistic brethren. We desire to think humbly of ourselves, and reverently of our Creator. In the strong language of Scripture, "We cannot by searching find out God unto perfection. Clouds and darkness are round about him. His judgments are a great deep." God is great and good beyond utterance or thought. We have no disposition to idolize our own powers, or to penetrate the secret counsels of the Deity. But on the other hand, we think it ungrateful to disparage the powers which our Creator has given us, or to question the certainty or importance of the knowledge which he has seen fit to place within our reach. There is an affected humility, we think, as dangerous as pride. We may rate our faculties too meanly, as well as too boastingly. The worst error in religion, after all, is that of the skeptic, who records triumphantly the weaknesses and wanderings of the human intellect and maintains that no trust is due to the decisions of this erring reason. We by no means conceive that man's greatest danger springs from pride of understanding, though we think as badly of this vice as other Christians. The history of the church proves that men may trust their faculties too little as well as too much, and that the timidity which shrinks from investigation has injured the mind and betrayed the interests of Christianity as much as an irreverent boldness of thought.

It is an important truth, which, we apprehend, has not been sufficiently developed, that the ultimate reliance of a human being is and must be on his own mind. To confide in God, we must first confide in the faculties by which He is apprehended, and by which the proofs of His existence are weighed. A trust in our ability to distinguish between truth and falsehood is implied in every act of belief; for to question this ability would of necessity unsettle all belief. We cannot take a step in reasoning or action without a secret reliance on our own minds. Religion in particular implies that we have understandings endowed and qualified for the highest employments of intellect. In affirming the existence and perfections of God, we suppose and affirm the existence in ourselves of faculties which correspond to these sublime objects, and which are fitted to discern them. Religion is a conviction and an act of the human soul, so that, in denying confidence to the one, we subvert the truth and claims of the other. Nothing is gained to piety by degrading human nature, for in the competency of this nature to know and judge of God all piety has its foundation. Our proneness to err instructs us indeed to use our powers with great caution, but not to contemn and neglect them. The occasional abuse of our faculties, be it ever so enormous, does not prove them unfit for their highest end, which is to form clear and consistent views of God. Because our eyes sometimes fail or deceive us, would a wise man pluck them out, or cover them with a bandage, and choose to walk and work in the dark? Or because they cannot distinguish distant objects, can they discern nothing clearly in their proper sphere, and is sight to be pronounced a fallacious guide? Men who, to support a creed, would shake our trust in the calm, deliberate, and distinct decisions of our rational and moral powers endanger religion more than its open foes, and forge the deadliest weapon for the infidel.

It is true that God is an infinite being, and also true that his powers and perfections, his purposes and operations, his ends and means, being unlimited, are *incomprehensible*. In other words, they cannot be *wholly taken in* or *embraced* by the human mind. In the strong and figurative language of Scripture, we "know nothing" of God's ways; that is, we know *very few* of them. But this is just as true of the most advanced archangel as of man. In comparison with the vastness of God's system, the range of the highest created intellect is narrow; and in this particular, man's lot does not differ from that of his elder brethren in heaven. We are both confined in our observation and experience to a little spot in the creation. But are an angel's faculties worthy of no trust, or is his knowledge uncertain, because he learns and reasons from a small part of God's works? or are his judgments respecting the Creator to be charged with presumption because his views do not spread through the whole extent of the universe? We grant that our understandings cannot stretch beyond a very narrow sphere. But still the lessons which we learn within this sphere are just as sure as if it were indefinitely enlarged. Because much is explored, we are not to suspect what we have actually discovered. Knowledge is not the less real, because confined. The man who has never set foot beyond his native village knows its scenery and inhabitants as undoubtingly as if he had travelled to the poles. We indeed see very little, but that little is as true as if every thing else were seen, and our future discoveries must agree with and support it. Should the whole order and purposes of the universe be opened to us, it is certain that nothing would be disclosed which would in any degree shake our persuasion that the earth is inhabited by rational and moral beings, who are authorized to expect from their Creator the most benevolent and equitable government. No extent of observation can unsettle those primary and fundamental principles of moral truth which we derive from our highest faculties operating in the relations in which God had fixed us. In every region and period of the universe, it will be as true as it is now on the earth, that knowledge and power are the measures of responsibility, and that natural incapacity absolves from guilt. These and other moral verities, which are among our clearest perceptions, would, if possible, be strengthened in proportion as our powers should be enlarged; because harmony and consistency are the characters of God's administration, and all our researches into the universe only serve to manifest its unity, and to show a wider operation of the laws which we witness and experience on earth.

We grant that God is *incomprehensible*, in the sense already given. But he is not therefore *unintelligible;* and this distinction we conceive to be important. We do not pretend to know the *whole* nature and properties of God, but still we can form some *clear ideas* of him, and can reason from these ideas as justly as from any other. The truth is that we cannot be said to comprehend any being whatever, not the simplest plant or animal. All have hidden properties. Our knowledge of all is limited. But have we therefore no distinct ideas of the objects around us, and is all our reasoning about them unworthy of trust? Because God is infinite, his name is not therefore a mere sound. It is a representative of some distinct conceptions of our Creator; and these conceptions are as sure, and important, and as proper materials for the reasoning faculty as they would be if our views were indefinitely enlarged. We cannot indeed trace God's goodness and rectitude through the whole field of his operations; but we know the essential nature of these attributes, and therefore can often judge what accords with and opposes them. God's goodness, because infinite,

does not cease to be goodness, or essentially differ from the same attribute in man; nor does justice change its nature, so that it cannot be understood, because it is seated in an unbounded mind. There have indeed been philosophers, "falsely so called," who have argued from the unlimited nature of God that we cannot ascribe to him justice and other moral attributes, in any proper or definite sense of those words; and the inference is plain that all religion or worship wanting an intelligible object must be a misplaced, wasted offering. This doctrine from the infidel we reject with abhorrence; but something not very different too often reaches us from the mistaken Christian who, to save his creed, shrouds the Creator in utter darkness. In opposition to both, we maintain that God's attributes are intelligible, and that we can conceive as truly of his goodness and justice as of these qualities in men. In fact, these qualities are essentially the same in God and man, though differing in degree, in purity, and in extent of operation. We know not and we cannot conceive of any other justice or goodness than we learn from our own nature; and if God have not these, he is altogether unknown to us as a moral being; he offers nothing for esteem and love to rest upon; the objection of the infidel is just, that worship is wasted; "We worship we know not what."

It is asked, On what authority do we ascribe to God goodness and rectitude, in the sense in which these attributes belong to men, or how can we judge of the nature of attributes in the mind of the Creator? We answer by saying, How is it that we become acquainted with the mind of a fellow-creature? The last is as invisible, as removed from *immediate* inspection, as the first. Still we do not hesitate to speak of the justice and goodness of a neighbor; and how do we gain our knowledge? We answer, by witnessing the effects, operations, and expressions of these attributes. It is a law of our nature to argue from the effect to the cause, from the action to the agent, from the ends proposed and from the means of pursuing them, to the character and disposition of the being in whom we observe them. By these processes, we learn the invisible mind and character of man; and by the same we ascend to the mind of God, whose works, effects, operations, and ends are as expressive and significant of justice and goodness as the best and most decisive actions of men. If this reasoning be sound (and all religion rests upon it), then God's justice and goodness are intelligible attributes, agreeing essentially with the same qualities in ourselves. Their operation, indeed, is infinitely wider, and they are employed in accomplishing not only immediate but remote and unknown ends. Of consequence, we must expect that many parts of the divine administration will be *obscure*, that is, will not produce *immediate* good and an *immediate* distinction between virtue and vice. But still the unbounded operation of these attributes does not change their nature. They are still the same as if they acted in the narrowest sphere. We can still determine in many cases what does not accord with them. We are particularly sure that those essential principles of justice which enter into and even form our conception of this attribute, must pervade every province and every period of the administration of a just being, and that to suppose the Creator in any instance to forsake them, is to charge him directly with unrighteousness, however loudly the lips may compliment his equity.

"But is it not presumptuous in man," it is continually said, "to sit in judgment on God?" We answer that to "sit in judgment on God" is an ambiguous and offensive phrase, conveying to common minds the ideas of irreverence, boldness, familiarity. The question would be better stated thus:—Is it not presumptuous in man to judge concerning God and concerning what agrees or disagrees with his attributes? We answer confidently, No; for in many cases we are competent and even bound to judge. And we plead first in our defense the Scriptures. How continually does God in his word appeal to the understanding and moral judgment of man. "O inhabitants of Jerusalem and men of Judah, judge, I pray you, between me and my vineyard. What could have been done more to my vineyard that I have not done in it?" We observe, in the next place, that all religion supposes and is built on judgments passed by us on God and on his operations. Is it not, for example, our duty and a leading part of piety to *praise* God? And what is praising a being, but to adjudge and ascribe to him just and generous deeds and motives? And of what value is praise, except from those who are capable of distinguishing between actions which exalt and actions which degrade the character? Is it presumption to call God *excellent*? And what is this but to refer his character to a standard of excellence, to try it by the established principles of rectitude, and to pronounce its conformity to them; that is, to judge of God and his operations?

We are presumptuous, we are told, in judging of our Creator. But he himself has made this our duty, in giving us a moral faculty; and to decline it is to violate the primary law of our nature. Conscience, the sense of right, the power of perceiving moral distinctions, the power of discerning between justice and injustice, excellence and baseness, is the highest faculty given us by God, the whole foundation of our responsibility, and our sole capacity for religion. Now we are forbidden by this faculty to love a being who wants, or who fails to discover,[1] moral excellence. God, in giving us conscience, has implanted a principle within us which forbids us to prostrate ourselves before mere power, or to offer praise where we do not discover worth; a principle which challenges our supreme homage for supreme goodness, and which absolves us from guilt when we abhor a severe and unjust administration. Our Creator has consequently waived his own claims on our veneration and obedience, any farther than he discovers himself to us in characters of benevolence, equity, and righteousness. He rests his authority on the perfect coincidence of his will and government with those great and fundamental principles of morality written on our souls. He desires no worship but that which springs from the exercises of our moral faculties upon his character, from our discernment and persuasion of his rectitude and goodness. He asks, he accepts, no love or admiration but from those who can understand the nature and the proofs and moral excellence. . . .

1820

[1] lacks, or fails to exhibit

1783 ~ *Washington Irving* ~ 1859

WASHINGTON IRVING, the chief contribution of the city of New York to American literature, was born of British parents whose devotion to their adopted country, symbolized in his name, foreshadowed the combination in him of loyal American sentiment with a leavening of cosmopolitanism. A sunny but delicate lad, he was favored by his parents and talented older brothers; he roamed through the Hudson valley, attended Dunlap's playhouse surreptitiously, was excused from entering Columbia, studied law in a leisurely fashion, and enjoyed the privilege of a two years' journey to the Mediterranean countries and England in 1804–06. Already the author of a periodical essay series in the New York *Morning Chronicle* signed "Jonathan Oldstyle," he became on his return the leading spirit in a group of literary youths who turned out between January, 1807, and January, 1808, the twenty numbers of *Salmagundi*, the cleverest periodical papers yet produced in America. In 1809 he finished perhaps his most distinctive work, the comic *Knicker-bocker's History of New York*, begun with his brother Peter as a burlesque of a guidebook to New York. The next few rather aimless years were spent partly in desultory writing, associate-editing two literary magazines, and social visits to Washington, Baltimore, Philadelphia, and Albany, ostensibly to look after legal interests of the family cutlery business. In 1815, at the close of the war with England, he left New York to share the responsibility for the branch of the firm maintained by his brother Peter in England, not then expecting to remain long abroad. By 1818, when the bankruptcy of the firm threw him upon his own resources, his geniality, good manners, and eager interest in letters had made him intimate and welcome among English writers like Scott, Campbell, and Jeffrey. *The Sketch Book* of Geoffrey Crayon, Gent. (1819–1820), published simultaneously in England and America, won him popularity, financial competence, and literary reputation in both countries. The years from 1820 to 1826 were spent mainly in Germany, France, and Austria, while he continued the vein of *The Sketch Book* in *Bracebridge Hall* (1822) and *Tales of a Traveller* (1824). A sojourn of three years in Spain next produced *A History of the Life and Voyages of Columbus* (1828), *A Chronicle of the Conquest of Granada* (1829), and the later Spanish sketch book, *The Alhambra* (1832). After two more years as secretary to the American legation in London, he was ready in 1831 to return to enjoy the acclaim of his fellow countrymen. His remaining years were deservedly happy, spent after 1836 mainly at his residence, Sunnyside, at Tarrytown, on the Hudson. His early popularity was now augmented by the fact that more than any other American he had com-pelled a willing recognition of American literature in Europe. A tour of the south-

western states and territories in 1832 and a connection with the house of John Jacob
Astor resulted in three profitable books dealing with frontier America, *A Tour on
the Prairies* (1835), *Astoria* (1836), and *The Adventures of Captain Bonneville* (1837).
The literary work of his last years was largely biographical, including *Oliver
Goldsmith* (1849), *Mahomet and His Successors* (1849–1850), and *The Life of George
Washington* (1855–1859). In 1842 his leisure was interrupted by four years' service
as minister to Spain. He died at Sunnyside, November 28, 1859.

The importance of Irving's work as a writer is almost overshadowed by his
services as literary ambassador and as the foremost interpreter of England and the
Continent to Americans, in the nineteenth-century rediscovery of Europe. His
rare cosmopolitanism, by instinct as well as background, in a period of increasing
national isolation, fitted him well to be the spokesman to England of an America
which was still essentially Anglo-Saxon in most of its traditions and thinking. His
urbanity, friendly interest and curiosity, and frank reverence for everything that
was worthy of reverence in European tradition, combined with a proper degree of
national pride and self-respect free from bumptiousness, won him the warm friendship of Scott and other Englishmen. Thus he gained for his own works an unbiased
acceptance on their merits, and through them a reluctant recognition of the worth
of Bryant, Cooper, and later Americans. This service was most important because
of the generally contemptuous attitude of British criticism and the irritable sensitiveness of Americans which Irving deplored in "English Writers on America," and
also because of the fact that British criticism was necessarily to some extent a
yardstick for American cultural achievement.

In many ways Irving's spirit is that of late eighteenth-century English literature.
In him sentiment, melancholy, humanitarian sympathy, and interest in the past and
in nature were combined with and restrained by rationality and an active sense of
humor. In his early work the humor was rampant and attended with a robust vein
of coarseness, also native to the eighteenth century, which shows repeatedly in
Knickerbocker's History and is excellently blended with humor, sentiment, and intrigue in the comedy *Charles II* (with John Howard Payne). Nothing, perhaps, is
more characteristic of him than his handling of German romantic legend, in the
emergence of humor at the close of tales of horror and the supernatural like "The
Spectre Bridegroom" and "Adventure of the German Student."

His affections were instinctive rather than emotional, and his patriotism, while
loyal, was not ebullient. He was no party man. Belonging by class to the Federalist
group, he ridiculed the noisiness and bad manners of adherents of the popular
party, and the erudition and pacifism of President Jefferson; but he was friendly
with the Madisons and regarded himself as a "Jackson man" after his return to the
United States in 1832. Putting friendship always before politics, he wrote to his
friend Brevoort in 1811, "I have associated with both parties—and have found

worthy and intelligent men in both—with honest hearts, enlightened minds, generous feelings and bitter prejudices." His friendship with Southerners also kept him from taking an active stand regarding the current issues of nullification and slavery.

Irving was not a literary theorist, though he exaggerated when he wrote to Brevoort, "I do not read criticism, good or bad." To be a critic did not harmonize with Geoffrey Crayon, Gent.'s consistent pose of the detached observer, sympathetic but amused and somewhat languid, which had been passed on by many predecessors like the Spectator, the Looker-On, the Idler, and the American Lounger. Early in his career he wrote for the *Analectic Magazine* reviews of two American poets, R. T. Paine, Jr., and E. C. Holland, in the acid and reactionary vein of contemporary British criticism, but they were not written *con amore*, and he did not revert to the type. Usually, as in the six literary essays in *The Sketch Book*, he is "the honest bee, that extricates honey from the humblest weed," as he describes the sympathetic critic representing his ideal, in his late essay "Desultory Thoughts on Criticism" (1839). With himself, he was more exacting, discarding much manuscript and revising his grammar and diction rigorously. As to language, aside from his humorous work, he was a purist, objecting to the Wordsworthians' use in poetry of "common colloquial phrases and vulgar idioms, . . . coarse and commonplace," and to the "heterogeneous taste . . . gorgeous material . . . mingled up with . . . the most grotesque" in the prose of Leigh Hunt.

Irving was gifted with a prose style remarkable for ease, naturalness, and charm, already well developed in the Mustapha letters in *Salmagundi* (1807), and needing only maturing under the influence of his expanding interest in English and German romanticism and the setting, history, and legends of Spain and the Moors. He recognized that style was the chief quality of his work, writing in 1823, "I wish . . . to write in such a manner that my productions may have more than the mere interest of narrative to recommend them, . . . something, if I dare use the phrase, of classic merit, i.e., depending upon style, etc., which gives a production some chance for duration beyond the mere whim and fashion of the day." To the American short story he contributed several important tales but nothing by way of development. His most important piece of self-criticism, an oft-quoted letter to his friend Henry Brevoort, December 11, 1824, expresses both his concept of the type and his ideals of composition in it:

For my part I consider a story merely as a frame on which to stretch my materials. It is the play of thought and sentiment and language; the weaving in of characters, lightly yet expressively delineated; the familiar and faithful exhibition of scenes in common life; and the half-concealed vein of humor that is often playing through the whole—these are what I aim at, and upon which I felicitate myself in proportion as I think I succeed. . . . I have preferred a mode of sketches and short tales rather than long works, because I choose to take a line of writing peculiar to myself . . . and there is a constant activity of thought and nicety of execution required in writings of this kind, more than the world appears to imagine. . . . [In] these . . . every page must have its merit.

Sharing with Hawthorne and Longfellow a strong antiquarian interest, Irving felt the lack of historical background in America. The Hudson valley offered nearly two centuries of Dutch occupancy, but it was an alien and somewhat thin tradition, which he enjoyed but found difficult to take otherwise than humorously. The English Puritan tradition of New England which became Hawthorne's *milieu* he disliked heartily; and though he sentimentalized the "red man" much as Freneau and Cooper did, the forest and prairie devoid of human history did not appeal to him as a setting for story or essay. Hence his *Tour on the Prairies* is a piece of good reporting that lacks the underlying interest of "Rip Van Winkle" and "The Legend of Sleepy Hollow." Artistically he was more at home in the Moorish castles of Spain and in the manor houses of England, some of whose flavor he was able to instill into his residence, Sunnyside, where he spent his last years.

The standard edition is *The Works of Washington Irving* (21 vols., 1860–61). The twelve-volume Spuyten Duyvel Edition (1881) contains the same text and is more easily accessible. The best volume of selections, with a valuable introduction and bibliography, is H. A. Pochmann's *Washington Irving*, in the American Writers Series (1934). Editions of separate works include Edwin Greenlaw's (1919) and S. T. Williams and Tremaine McDowell's (1927) *Knickerbocker's History of New York;* W. R. Langfeld's *The Poems of Washington Irving* (1931); S. T. Williams and Barbara D. Simison's *Washington Irving on the Prairies: or A Narrative of a Tour in the Southwest* (1937). W. R. Langfeld and P. C. Blackburn have compiled *Washington Irving: A Bibliography* (1933), with descriptive annotations. For criticism and biography before 1917, see *CHAL*, I, 510–517.

The standard life is Stanley T. Williams, *Washington Irving* (2 vols., 1935). All the biographies go back in large part to Pierre M. Irving's *Life and Letters of Washington Irving, by his Nephew* (4 vols., 1862–64). A revised and condensed People's Edition of this work in 3 vols. was issued in 1869. Other biographies include G. S. Hellman, *Washington Irving, Esquire: Ambassador at Large from the New World to the Old* (1925); H. W. Mabie, *The Writers of Knickerbocker New York* (1912); and C. D. Warner, *Washington Irving*, in American Men of Letters Series (1881). The *Journals*, edited by W. P. Trent and G. S. Hellman (3 vols., 1919), do not include a considerable number of diaries and other manuscript notes subsequently edited by S. T. Williams in a number of separate volumes, for which see the current issues of the *PMLA* supplement. G. S. Hellman edited an important series of *Letters of Henry Brevoort to Irving* and *Letters from Irving to Henry Brevoort* (both 1918). The *DAB* article is by Stanley T. Williams; that in *CHAL* by G. H. Putnam.

For other critical and biographical studies, see Stockton Axson, "Washington Irving and the Knickerbocker Group," *Rice Institute Pamphlets*, XX, 178–195 (April, 1933); H. W. Boynton, "Irving," in *American Writers on American Literature*, edited by John Macy (1931); Wallace Bruce, *Along the Hudson with Washington Irving* (1913); W. B. Cairns, *British Criticism of American Writings, 1815–1833* (1922); H. S. Canby, *Classic Americans* (1931), 67–96, and *The Short Story in English* (1913); L. G. Clark, "Recollections of Washington Irving," *Lippincott's*

Magazine, III (1869); Edwin Greenlaw, "A Comedy in Politics," *Texas Review*, April, 1916 (satire on Jefferson in the *Knickerbocker History*); A. Keiser, *The Indian in American Literature*, 52–64 (1933); John Macy, *The Spirit of American Literature* (1913), 18–34; G. D. Morris, *Washington Irving's Fiction in the Light of French Criticism, Indiana University Studies*, No. 30 (May, 1916); V. L. Parrington, *The Romantic Revolution in America, 1800–1860* (1927), 203–212; F. L. Pattee, *The Development of the American Short Story* (1923), 1–26; H. A. Pochmann, "Irving's German Sources in the *Sketch Book*," *Studies in Philology*, XXVII, 477–507 (July, 1930), and "Irving's German Tour and Its Influence on His Tales," *PMLA*, XLV, 1150–1187 (December, 1930); F. P. Smith, "Washington Irving, the Fosters, and Some Poetry," *American Literature*, IX, 228–232 (May, 1937); R. E. Spiller, *The American in England* (see index, 1926); C. Webster, "Irving's Expurgations of the 1809 *History of New York*," *American Literature*, III, 293–305; Mary Zirkle, "Meeting in the West," *Christian Science Monitor*, XXIX, 14 (March 20, 1937).

Several important studies by S. T. Williams, not listed, are now embodied in his *Washington Irving* (2 vols., 1935).

From A HISTORY OF NEW YORK

The appearance of *Knickerbocker's History* was preceded by a series of mystifying advertisements in a New York paper, inquiring about the whereabouts of a mythical Dutch historian, Diedrich Knickerbocker, reported as having disappeared, leaving only his manuscript, which was to be published in the hope of defraying his bill for board and lodging. (See Irving's preface to "Rip Van Winkle," below.)

BOOK III, CHAPTER I

[*Wouter Van Twiller*]

GRIEVOUS and very much to be commiserated is the task of the feeling historian, who writes the history of his native land. If it fall to his lot to be the recorder of calamity or crime, the mournful page is watered with his tears; nor can he recall the most prosperous and blissful era without a melancholy sigh at the reflection that it has passed away forever! I know not whether it be owing to an immoderate love for the simplicity of former times, or to that certain tenderness of heart incident to all sentimental historians; but I candidly confess that I cannot look back on the happier days of our city, which I now describe, without great dejection of spirit. With faltering hand do I withdraw the curtain of oblivion that veils the modest merit of our venerable ancestors, and as their figures rise to my mental vision, humble myself before their mighty shades.

Such are my feelings when I revisit the family mansion of the Knickerbockers and spend a lonely hour in the chamber where hang the portraits of my forefathers, shrouded in dust, like the forms they represent. With pious reverence do I gaze on the countenances of those renowned burghers who have preceded me in the steady march of existence,— whose sober and temperate blood now meanders through my veins, flowing slower and slower in its feeble conduits, until its current shall soon be stopped forever!

These, I say to myself, are but frail memorials of the mighty men who flourished in the days of the patriarchs; but who, alas, have long since moldered in that tomb towards which my steps are insensibly and irresistibly hastening! As I pace the darkened chamber and lose myself in melancholy musings, the shadowy images around me almost seem to steal once more into existence—their countenances to assume the animation of life—their eyes to pursue me in every movement! Carried away by the delusions of fancy, I almost imagine myself surrounded by the shades of the departed, and holding sweet converse with the worthies of antiquity! Ah, hapless Diedrich! born in a degenerate age, abandoned to the buffetings of fortune—a stranger and a weary pilgrim in thy native land—blest with no weeping wife, nor family of helpless children, but doomed to wander neglected through those crowded streets, and elbowed by foreign upstarts from those fair abodes where once thine ancestors held sovereign empire!

Let me not, however, lose the historian in the man, nor suffer the doting recollections of age to overcome me, while dwelling with fond garrulity on the virtuous days of the patriarchs, —on those sweet days of simplicity and ease, which never more will dawn on the lovely island of Manna-hata.

These melancholy reflections have been forced from me by the growing wealth and importance of New Amsterdam, which, I plainly perceive, are to involve it in all kinds of perils and disasters. Already, as I observed at the close of my last book, they had awakened the attentions of the mother country. The usual mark of protection shown by mother countries to wealthy colonies was forthwith manifested; a governor being sent out to rule over the province, and squeeze out of it as much revenue as possible. The arrival of a governor of course put an end to the protectorate of Oloffe the Dreamer.[1] He appears, however, to have dreamt to some purpose during his sway, as we find him afterwards living as a patroon on a great landed estate on the banks of the Hudson; having virtually forfeited all right to his ancient appellation of Kortlandt or Lackland.

It was in the year of our Lord 1629 that Mynheer Wouter Van Twiller was appointed governor of the province of Nieuw Nederlandts, under the commission and control of their High Mightinesses the Lords States General of the United Netherlands, and the privileged West India Company.

This renowned old gentleman arrived at New Amsterdam in the merry month of June, the sweetest month in all the year; when Dan Apollo seems to dance up the transparent firmament—when the robin, the thrush, and a thousand other wanton songsters, make the woods to resound with amorous ditties, and the luxurious little boblincon[2] revels among the clover blossoms of the meadows,—all which happy coincidence persuaded the old dames of New Amsterdam, who were skilled in the art of foretelling events, that this was to be a happy and prosperous administration.

[1] in charge of the Dutch trading post at Manhattan before the appointment of a governor   [2] bobolink

The renowned Wouter (or Walter) Van Twiller was descended from a long line of Dutch burgomasters, who had successively dozed away their lives, and grown fat upon the bench of magistracy in Rotterdam; and who had comported themselves with such singular wisdom and propriety that they were never either heard or talked of—which, next to being universally applauded, should be the object of ambition of all magistrates and rulers. There are two opposite ways by which some men make a figure in the world: one, by talking faster than they think, and the other, by holding their tongues and not thinking at all. By the first, many a smatterer acquires the reputation of a man of quick parts; by the other, many a dunderpate, like the owl, the stupidest of birds, comes to be considered the very type of wisdom. This, by the way, is a casual remark, which I would not, for the universe, have it thought I apply to Governor Van Twiller. It is true he was a man shut up within himself, like an oyster, and rarely spoke, except in monosyllables; but then it was allowed he seldom said a foolish thing. So invincible was his gravity that he was never known to laugh or even to smile through the whole course of a long and prosperous life. Nay, if a joke were uttered in his presence that set light-minded hearers in a roar, it was observed to throw him into a state of perplexity. Sometimes he would deign to inquire into the matter, and when, after much explanation, the joke was made as plain as a pikestaff, he would continue to smoke his pipe in silence, and at length, knocking out the ashes, would exclaim, "Well! I see nothing in all that to laugh about."

With all his reflective habits, he never made up his mind on a subject. His adherents accounted for this by the astonishing magnitude of his ideas. He conceived every subject on so grand a scale that he had not room in his head to turn it over and examine both sides of it. Certain it is that, if any matter were propounded to him on which ordinary mortals would rashly determine at first glance, he would put on a vague, mysterious look, shake his capacious head, smoke some time in profound silence, and at length observe that "he had his doubts about the matter"; which gained him the reputation of a man slow of belief and not easily imposed upon. What is more, it gained him a lasting name; for to this habit of the mind has been attributed his surname of Twiller; which is said to be a corruption of the original Twijfler, or, in plain English, Doubter.

The person of this illustrious old gentleman was formed and proportioned as though it had been molded by the hands of some cunning 10 Dutch statuary, as a model of majesty and lordly grandeur. He was exactly five feet six inches in height, and six feet five inches in circumference. His head was a perfect sphere, and of such stupendous dimensions that Dame Nature, with all her sex's ingenuity, would have been puzzled to construct a neck capable of supporting it; wherefore, she wisely declined the attempt, and settled it firmly on the top of his backbone, just between the shoulders. 20 His body was oblong and particularly capacious at bottom; which was wisely ordered by Providence, seeing that he was a man of sedentary habits, and very averse to the idle labor of walking. His legs were short but sturdy in proportion to the weight they had to sustain; so that when erect he had not a little the appearance of a beer-barrel on skids. His face, that infallible index of the mind, presented a vast expanse, unfurrowed by any of 30 those lines and angles which disfigure the human countenance with what is termed expression. Two small gray eyes twinkled feebly in the midst like two stars of lesser magnitude in a hazy firmament, and his full-fed cheeks, which seemed to have taken toll of everything that went into his mouth, were curiously mottled and streaked with dusky red, like a spitzenburgh apple.

His habits were as regular as his person. He 40 daily took his four stated meals, appropriating exactly an hour to each; he smoked and doubted eight hours, and he slept the remaining twelve of the four-and-twenty. Such was the renowned Wouter Van Twiller—a true philosopher, for his mind was either elevated above, or tranquilly settled below, the cares and perplexities of this world. He had lived in it for years, without feeling the least curiosity to know whether the sun revolved round 50 it or it round the sun; and he had watched,

for at least half a century, the smoke curling from his pipe to the ceiling, without once troubling his head with any of those numerous theories by which a philosopher would have perplexed his brain, in accounting for its rising above the surrounding atmosphere.

In his council he presided with great state and solemnity. He sat in a huge chair of solid oak, hewn in the celebrated forest of the Hague, fabricated by an experienced timmerman [1] of Amsterdam, and curiously carved about the arms and feet, into exact imitations of gigantic eagle's claws. Instead of a scepter he swayed a long Turkish pipe, wrought with jasmin and amber, which had been presented to a stadtholder of Holland at the conclusion of a treaty with one of the petty Barbary powers. In this stately chair would he sit, and this magnificent pipe would he smoke, shaking his right knee with a constant motion, and fixing his eye for hours together upon a little print of Amsterdam which hung in a black frame against the opposite wall of the council-chamber. Nay, it has even been said, that when any deliberation of extraordinary length and intricacy was on the carpet, the renowned Wouter would shut his eyes for full two hours at a time, that he might not be disturbed by external objects; and at such times the internal commotion of his mind was evinced by certain regular guttural sounds which his admirers declared were merely the noise of conflict made by his contending doubts and opinions.

It is with infinite difficulty I have been enabled to collect these biographical anecdotes of the great man under consideration. The facts respecting him were so scattered and vague, and divers of them so questionable in point of authenticity, that I have had to give up the search after many, and decline the admission of still more, which would have tended to heighten the coloring of his portrait.

I have been the more anxious to delineate fully the person and habits of Wouter Van Twiller, from the consideration that he was not only the first, but also the best governor that ever presided over this ancient and respectable province; and so tranquil and benevolent was his reign that I do not find

[1] carpenter

throughout the whole of it a single instance of any offender being brought to punishment— a most indubitable sign of a merciful governor, and a case unparalleled, excepting in the reign of the illustrious King Log, from whom, it is hinted, the renowned Van Twiller was a lineal descendant.

The very outset of the career of this excellent magistrate was distinguished by an example of legal acumen that gave flattering presage of a wise and equitable administration. The morning after he had been installed in office, and at the moment that he was making his breakfast from a prodigious earthen dish filled with milk and Indian pudding, he was interrupted by the appearance of Wandle Schoonhoven, a very important old burgher of New Amsterdam, who complained bitterly of one Barent Bleecker, inasmuch as he refused to come to a settlement of accounts, seeing that there was a heavy balance in favor of the said Wandle. Governor Van Twiller, as I have already observed, was a man of few words; he was likewise a mortal enemy to multiplying writings—or being disturbed at his breakfast. Having listened attentively to the statement of Wandle Schoonhoven, giving an occasional grunt as he shoveled a spoonful of Indian pudding into his mouth,— either as a sign that he relished the dish or comprehended the story,—he called unto him his constable, and pulling out of his breeches-pocket a huge jackknife, dispatched it after the defendant as a summons, accompanied by his tobacco-box as a warrant.

This summary process was as effectual in those simple days as was the seal-ring of the great Haroun Alraschid [1] among the true believers. The two parties being confronted before him, each produced a book of accounts, written in a language and character that would have puzzled any but a High-Dutch commentator, or a learned decipherer of Egyptian obelisks. The sage Wouter took them one after the other, and having poised them in his hands, and attentively counted over the number of leaves, fell straightway into a very great doubt and smoked for half an hour without saying a word; at length, laying his finger beside his nose, and shutting his eyes for a moment, with

the air of a man who has just caught a subtle idea by the tail, he slowly took his pipe from his mouth, puffed forth a column of tobacco smoke, and with marvelous gravity and solemnity pronounced that, having carefully counted over the leaves and weighed the books, it was found that one was just as thick and as heavy as the other; therefore, it was the final opinion of the court that the accounts were equally balanced: therefore, Wandle should give Barent a receipt, and Barent should give Wandle a receipt, and the constable should pay the costs.

This decision, being straightway made known, diffused general joy throughout New Amsterdam, for the people immediately perceived that they had a very wise and equitable magistrate to rule over them. But its happiest effect was that not another lawsuit took place throughout the whole of his administration, and the office of constable fell into such decay that there was not one of those losel scouts [1] known in the province for many years. I am the more particular in dwelling on this transaction, not only because I deem it one of the most sage and righteous judgments on record, and well worthy the attention of modern magistrates, but because it was a miraculous event in the history of the renowned Wouter —being the only time he was ever known to come to a decision in the whole course of his life.

1809

BOOK VI, CHAPTER VIII

[The Capture of Fort Christina]

The bloodless capture of the Swedish trading post at Fort Christina, on the Delaware, in 1655, by a Dutch force under Governor Peter Stuyvesant is turned by Irving into a comic burlesque parodying the heroic style of the Greek and Roman epics. The fort was garrisoned by a small number of Swedes and Finns under Governor Jan Risingh.

The text is that of the original 1809 edition, modernized as to spelling and punctuation.

THE men of the Manhattoes plucked up new courage when they heard their leader—or rather they dreaded his fierce displeasure, of which they stood in more awe than of all the Swedes in Christendom—but the daring

Peter, not waiting for their aid, plunged sword in hand into the thickest of the foe. Then did he display some such incredible achievements as have never been known since the miraculous days of the giants. Wherever he went the enemy shrank before him—with fierce impetuosity he pushed forward, driving the Swedes, like dogs, into their own ditch— but as he fearlessly advanced, the foe, like rushing waves which close upon the scudding bark, thronged in his rear and hung upon his flank with fearful peril. One desperate Swede, who had a mighty heart almost as large as a peppercorn, drove his dastard sword full at the hero's heart. But the protecting power that watches over the safety of all great and good men turned aside the hostile blade, and directed it to a large side pocket, where reposed an enormous iron tobacco box, endowed like the shield of Achilles with supernatural powers—no doubt in consequence of its being piously decorated with a portrait of the blessed St. Nicholas. Thus was the dreadful blow repelled, but not without occasioning to the great Peter a fearful loss of wind.

Like as a furious bear, when gored by worrying curs, turns fiercely round, shows his dread teeth, and springs upon the foe, so did our hero turn upon the treacherous Swede. The miserable varlet sought in flight for safety—but the active Peter, seizing him by an immeasurable queue that dangled from his head—"Ah, whoreson caterpillar!" roared he, "here is what shall make dog's meat of thee!" So saying, he whirled his trusty sword and made a blow that would have decapitated him had he, like Briareus, half a hundred heads, but that the pitying steel struck short and shaved the queue forever from his crown. At this very moment a cunning arquebusier, perched on the summit of a neighboring mound, levelled his deadly instrument and would have sent the gallant Stuyvesant, a wailing ghost to haunt the Stygian shore— had not the watchful Minerva, who had just stopped to tie up her garter, saw [sic] the great peril of her favorite chief, and dispatched old Boreas with his bellows; who in the very nick of time, just as the direful match descended to the pan, gave such a lucky blast as blew all the priming from the touchhole!

Thus waged the horrid fight—when the stout Risingh, surveying the battle from the top of a little ravelin, perceived his faithful troops banged, beaten, and kicked by the invincible Peter. Language cannot describe the choler with which he was seized at the sight— he only stopped for a moment to disburden himself of five thousand anathemas; and then drawing his immeasurable cheese toaster, straddled down to the field of combat, with some such thundering strides as Jupiter is said by old Hesiod to have taken when he strode down the spheres, to play off his sky rockets at the Titans.

No sooner did these two rival heroes come face to face, than they each made a prodigious start of fifty feet (Flemish measure), such as is made by your most experienced stage champions. Then did they regard each other for a moment with bitter aspect, like two furious ram cats, on the very point of a clapper clawing. Then did they throw themselves in one attitude, then in another, striking their swords on the ground, first on the right side, then on the left; at last at it they went, like five hundred houses on fire! Words cannot tell the prodigies of strength and valor displayed in this direful encounter—an encounter compared to which the far famed battles of Ajax with Hector, of Eneas with Turnus, Orlando with Rodomont, Guy of Warwick with Colbrand the Dane, or of that renowned Welsh Knight Sir Owen of the mountains with the giant Guylon, were all gentle sports and holiday recreations. At length the valiant Peter, watching his opportunity, aimed a fearful blow with the full intention of cleaving his adversary to the very chine; but Risingh, nimbly raising his sword, warded it off so narrowly, that glancing on one side, it shaved away a huge canteen full of fourth proof brandy that he always carried swung on one side; thence pursuing its trenchant course, it severed off a deep coat pocket, stored with bread and cheese—all which dainties, rolling among the armies, occasioned a fearful scrambling between the Swedes and Dutchmen, and made the general battle to wax ten times more furious than ever.

Enraged to see his military stores thus woefully laid waste, the stout Risingh, collecting all his forces, aimed a mighty blow full at the hero's crest. In vain did his fierce little cocked hat oppose its course; the biting steel clove through the stubborn ram beaver, and would infallibly have cracked his gallant crown, but that the skull was of such adamantine hardness that the brittle weapon shivered into five and twenty pieces, shedding a thousand sparks, like beams of glory, round his grizzly visage.

Stunned with the blow, the valiant Peter reeled, turned up his eyes and beheld fifty thousand suns, besides moons and stars, dancing Scotch reels about the firmament—at length, missing his footing, by reason of his wooden leg, down he came on his seat of honor, with a crash that shook the surrounding hills, and would infallibly have wracked his anatomical system, had he not been received into a cushion softer than velvet, which Providence, or Minerva, or St. Nicholas, or some kindly cow, had benevolently prepared for his reception.

The furious Risingh, in despite of that noble maxim, cherished by all true knights, that "fair play is a jewel," hastened to take advantage of the hero's fall; but just as he was stooping to give the fatal blow, the ever vigilant Peter bestowed him a sturdy thwack over the sconce with his wooden leg, that set some dozen chimes of bells ringing triple bobmajors in his cerebellum. The bewildered Swede staggered with the blow, and in the mean time the wary Peter, espying a pocket pistol lying hard by (which had dropped from the wallet of his faithful squire and trumpeter Van Corlear during his furious encounter with the drummer) discharged it full at the head of the reeling Risingh—Let not my reader mistake—it was not a murderous weapon loaded with powder and ball, but a little sturdy stone pottle, charged to the muzzle with a double dram of true Dutch courage, which the knowing Van Corlear always carried about him by way of replenishing his valor. The hideous missive sung through the air, and true to its course, as was the mighty fragment of a rock discharged at Hector by bully Ajax, encountered the huge head of the gigantic Swede with matchless violence. This heaven-directed blow decided the

eventful battle. The ponderous pericranium of General Jan Risingh sunk upon his breast; his knees tottered under him; a deathlike torpor seized upon his Titan frame, and he tumbled to the earth with such tremendous violence that old Pluto started with affright, lest he should have broken through the roof of his infernal palace.

His fall, like that of Goliath, was the signal for defeat and victory—The Swedes gave way—the Dutch pressed forward; the former took to their heels, the latter hotly pursued—Some entered with them, pell mell, through the sally port—others stormed the bastion, and others scrambled over the curtain. Thus in a little while the impregnable fortress of Fort Christina, which like another Troy had stood a siege of full ten *hours*, was finally carried by assault, without the loss of a single man on either side. Victory, in the likeness of a gigantic ox fly, sat perched upon the little cocked hat of the gallant Stuyvesant, and it was universally declared by all the writers whom he hired to write the history of his expedition, that on this memorable day he gained a sufficient quantity of glory to immortalize a dozen of the greatest heroes in Christendom!

1809

RIP VAN WINKLE

A POSTHUMOUS WRITING OF DIEDRICH KNICKERBOCKER

By Woden, God of Saxons,
From whence comes Wensday, that is Wodensday,
Truth is a thing that ever I will keep
Unto thylke day in which I creep into
My sepulchre—

CARTWRIGHT

[The following Tale was found among the papers of the late Diedrich Knickerbocker, an old gentleman of New York, who was very curious in the Dutch history of the province, and the manners of the descendants from its primitive settlers. His historical researches, however, did not lie so much among books as among men; for the former are lamentably scanty on his favorite topics; whereas he found the old burghers, and still more their wives, rich in that legendary lore so invaluable to true history. Whenever, therefore, he happened upon a genuine Dutch family, snugly shut up in its low-roofed farmhouse under a spreading sycamore, he looked upon it as a little clasped volume of black-letter, and studied it with the zeal of a book-worm.

The result of all these researches was a history of the province during the reign of the Dutch governors, which he published some years since. There have been various opinions as to the literary character of his work, and, to tell the truth, it is not a whit better than it should be. Its chief merit is its scrupulous accuracy, which indeed was a little questioned on its first appearance, but has since been completely established; and it is now admitted into all historical collections as a book of unquestionable authority.

The old gentleman died shortly after the publication of his work, and now that he is dead and gone, it cannot do much harm to his memory to say that his time might have been much better employed in weightier labors. He, however, was apt to ride his hobby his own way; and though it did now and then kick up the dust a little in the eyes of his neighbors, and grieve the spirit of some friends, for whom he felt the truest deference and affection; yet his errors and follies are remembered "more in sorrow than in anger," and it begins to be suspected that he never intended to injure or offend. But however his memory may be appreciated by critics, it is still held dear by many folks whose good opinion is well worth having; particularly by certain biscuit-bakers, who have gone so far as to imprint his likeness on their new-year cakes; and have thus given him a chance for immortality, almost equal to the being stamped on a Waterloo Medal or a Queen Anne's Farthing.]

WHOEVER has made a voyage up the Hudson must remember the Kaatskill Mountains. They are a dismembered branch of the great Appalachian family, and are seen away to the west of the river, swelling up to a noble height, and lording it over the surrounding country. Every change of season, every change of weather, indeed, every hour of the day, produces some change in the magical hues and shapes of these mountains, and they are regarded by all the good wives, far and near, as perfect barometers. When the weather is fair and settled, they are clothed in blue and purple and print their bold outlines on the clear evening sky; but sometimes when the rest of the landscape is cloudless, they will gather a hood of gray vapors about their summits, which, in the last rays of the setting sun, will glow and light up like a crown of glory.

At the foot of these fairy mountains, the voyager may have descried the light smoke curling up from a village whose shingle-roofs gleam among the trees just where the blue tints of the upland melt away into the fresh green of the nearer landscape. It is a little village of great antiquity, having been founded by some of the Dutch colonists in the early times of the province, just about the beginning of the government of the good Peter Stuyvesant, (may he rest in peace!) and there were some of the houses of the original settlers standing within a few years, built of small yellow bricks brought from Holland, having latticed windows and gable fronts, surmounted with weather-cocks.

In that same village, and in one of these very houses (which, to tell the precise truth, was sadly time-worn and weather-beaten) there lived many years since, while the country was yet a province of Great Britain, a simple good-natured fellow, of the name of Rip Van Winkle. He was a descendant of the Van Winkles who figured so gallantly in the chivalrous days of Peter Stuyvesant, and accompanied him to the siege of Fort Christina. He inherited, however, but little of the martial character of his ancestors. I have observed that he was a simple good-natured man; he was, moreover, a kind neighbor, and an obedient, henpecked husband. Indeed, to the latter circumstance might be owing that meekness of spirit which gained him such universal popularity; for those men are most apt to be obsequious and conciliating abroad who are under the discipline of shrews at home. Their tempers, doubtless, are rendered pliant and malleable in the fiery furnace of domestic tribulation; and a curtain lecture is worth all the sermons in the world for teaching the virtues of patience and long-suffering. A termagant wife may, therefore, in some respects be considered a tolerable blessing; and if so, Rip Van Winkle was thrice blessed.

Certain it is, that he was a great favorite among all the good wives of the village, who, as usual with the amiable sex, took his part in all family squabbles; and never failed, whenever they talked those matters over in their evening gossipings, to lay all the blame on Dame Van Winkle. The children of the village, too, would shout with joy whenever he approached. He assisted at their sports, made their playthings, taught them to fly kites and shoot marbles, and told them long stories of ghosts, witches, and Indians. Whenever he went dodging about the village, he was surrounded by a troop of them, hanging on his skirts, clambering on his back, and playing a thousand tricks on him with impunity; and not a dog would bark at him throughout the neighborhood.

The great error in Rip's composition was an insuperable aversion to all kinds of profitable labor. It could not be from the want of assiduity or perseverance; for he would sit on a wet rock with a rod as long and heavy as a Tartar's lance and fish all day without a murmur even though he should not be encouraged by a single nibble. He would carry a fowling-piece on his shoulder for hours together, trudging through woods and swamps and up hill and down dale, to shoot a few squirrels or wild pigeons. He would never refuse to assist a neighbor, even in the roughest toil, and was a foremost man at all country frolics for husking Indian corn, or building stone-fences; the women of the village, too, used to employ him to run their errands and to do such little odd jobs as their less obliging husbands would not do for them. In a word, Rip was ready to attend to anybody's business but his own; but as to doing any family duty, and keeping his farm in order, he found it impossible.

In fact, he declared it was of no use to work on his farm; it was the most pestilent little piece of ground in the whole country; everything about it went wrong, and would go wrong, in spite of him. His fences were continually falling to pieces; his cow would either go astray or get among the cabbages; weeds were sure to grow quicker in his fields than anywhere else; the rain always made a point of setting in just as he had outdoor work to do; so that though his patrimonial estate had dwindled away under his management, acre by acre, until there was little more left than a mere patch of Indian corn and potatoes, yet it was the worst-conditioned farm in the neighborhood.

His children, too, were as ragged and wild as if they belonged to nobody. His son Rip, an urchin begotten in his own likeness, promised to inherit the habits, with the old clothes of his father. He was generally seen trooping like a colt at his mother's heels, equipped in a pair of his father's cast-off galligaskins, which he had much ado to hold up with one hand, as a fine lady does her train in bad weather.

Rip Van Winkle, however, was one of those happy mortals, of foolish, well-oiled dispositions, who take the world easy, eat white bread or brown, whichever can be got with least thought or trouble, and would rather starve on a penny than work for a pound. If left to himself, he would have whistled life away in perfect contentment; but his wife kept continually dinning in his ears about his idleness, his carelessness, and the ruin he was bringing on his family. Morning, noon, and night, her tongue was incessantly going, and everything he said or did was sure to produce a torrent of household eloquence. Rip had but one way of replying to all lectures of the kind, and that, by frequent use, had grown into a habit. He shrugged his shoulders, shook his head, cast up his eyes, but said nothing. This, however, always provoked a fresh volley from his wife; so that he was fain to draw off his forces, and take to the outside of the house—the only side which, in truth, belongs to a henpecked husband.

Rip's sole domestic adherent was his dog Wolf, who was as much henpecked as his master; for Dame Van Winkle regarded them as companions in idleness, and even looked upon Wolf with an evil eye, as the cause of his master's going so often astray. True it is, in all points of spirit befitting an honorable dog, he was as courageous an animal as ever scoured the woods—but what courage can withstand the ever-during and all-besetting terrors of a woman's tongue? The moment Wolf entered the house his crest fell, his tail drooped to the ground, or curled between his legs, he sneaked about with a gallows air, casting many a sidelong glance at Dame Van Winkle, and at the least flourish of a broomstick or ladle, he would fly to the door with yelping precipitation.

Times grew worse and worse with Rip Van Winkle as years of matrimony rolled on; a tart temper never mellows with age, and a sharp tongue is the only edged tool that grows keener with constant use. For a long while he used to console himself, when driven from home, by frequenting a kind of perpetual club of the sages, philosophers, and other idle personages of the village which held its sessions on a bench before a small inn, designated by a rubicund portrait of His Majesty George the Third. Here they used to sit in the shade through a long lazy summer's day, talking listlessly over village gossip, or telling endless sleepy stories about nothing. But it would have been worth any statesman's money to have heard the profound discussions that sometimes took place when, by chance, an 10 old newspaper fell into their hands from some passing traveler. How solemnly they would listen to the contents, as drawled out by Derrick Van Bummel, the schoolmaster, a dapper, learned little man, who was not to be daunted by the most gigantic word in the dictionary; and how sagely they would deliberate upon public events some months after they had taken place.

The opinions of this junto were completely 20 controlled by Nicholas Vedder, a patriarch of the village, and landlord of the inn, at the door of which he took his seat from morning till night, just moving sufficiently to avoid the sun and keep in the shade of a large tree; so that the neighbors could tell the hour by his movements as accurately as by a sun-dial. It is true he was rarely heard to speak, but smoked his pipe incessantly. His adherents, however, (for every great man has his ad- 30 herents) perfectly understood him and knew how to gather his opinions. When anything that was read or related displeased him, he was observed to smoke his pipe vehemently, and to send forth short, frequent, and angry puffs; but when pleased, he would inhale the smoke slowly and tranquilly, and emit it in light and placid clouds; and sometimes, taking the pipe from his mouth, and letting the fragrant vapor curl about his nose, would gravely nod his 40 head in token of perfect approbation.

From even this stronghold the unlucky Rip was at length routed by his termagant wife, who would suddenly break in upon the tranquillity of the assemblage and call the members all to naught; nor was that august personage, Nicholas Vedder himself, sacred from the daring tongue of this terrible virago, who charged him outright with encouraging her husband in habits of idleness.

Poor Rip was at last reduced almost to 50 despair; and his only alternative, to escape from the labor of the farm and clamor of his wife, was to take gun in hand and stroll away into the woods. Here he would sometimes seat himself at the foot of a tree and share the contents of his wallet with Wolf, with whom he sympathized as a fellow-sufferer in persecution. "Poor Wolf," he would say, "thy mistress leads thee a dog's life of it; but never mind, my lad, whilst I live thou shalt never want a friend to stand by thee!" Wolf would wag his tail, look wistfully in his master's face, and if dogs can feel pity, I verily believe he reciprocated the sentiment with all his heart.

In a long ramble of the kind on a fine autumnal day, Rip had unconsciously scrambled to one of the highest parts of the Kaatskill Mountains. He was after his favorite sport of squirrel shooting, and the still solitudes had echoed and reëchoed with the reports of his gun. Panting and fatigued, he threw himself, late in the afternoon, on a green knoll, covered with mountain herbage, that crowned the brow of a precipice. From an opening between the trees he could overlook all the lower country for many a mile of rich woodland. He saw at a distance the lordly Hudson, far, far below him, moving on its silent but majestic course, with the reflection of a purple cloud, or the sail of a lagging bark, here and there sleeping on its glassy bosom, and at last losing itself in the blue highlands.

On the other side he looked down into a deep mountain glen, wild, lonely, and shagged, the bottom filled with fragments from the impending cliffs and scarcely lighted by the reflected rays of the setting sun. For some time Rip lay musing on this scene; evening was gradually advancing; the mountains began to throw their long blue shadows over the valleys; he saw that it would be dark long before he could reach the village, and he heaved a heavy sigh when he thought of encountering the terrors of Dame Van Winkle.

As he was about to descend, he heard a voice from a distance, hallooing, "Rip Van Winkle! Rip Van Winkle!" He looked round, but could see nothing but a crow winging its solitary flight across the mountain. He thought his fancy must have deceived him, and turned again to descend, when he heard the same cry ring through the still evening air; "Rip Van Winkle! Rip Van Winkle!"—at the same time Wolf bristled up his back, and giving a low growl, skulked to his master's side, looking fearfully down into the glen. Rip now felt a vague apprehension stealing over him; he looked anxiously in the same direction, and perceived a strange figure slowly toiling up the rocks, and bending under the weight of something he carried on his back. He was surprised to see any human being in this lonely and unfrequented place; but supposing it to be someone of the neighborhood in need of his assistance, he hastened down to yield it.

On nearer approach he was still more surprised at the singularity of the stranger's appearance. He was a short, square-built old fellow, with thick bushy hair, and a grizzled beard. His dress was of the antique Dutch fashion: a cloth jerkin strapped round the waist, several pair of breeches, the outer one of ample volume, decorated with rows of buttons down the sides, and bunches at the knees. He bore on his shoulder a stout keg, that seemed full of liquor, and made signs for Rip to approach and assist him with the load. Though rather shy and distrustful of this new acquaintance, Rip complied with his usual alacrity; and mutually relieving one another, they clambered up a narrow gully, apparently the dry bed of a mountain torrent. As they ascended, Rip every now and then heard long rolling peals, like distant thunder, that seemed to issue out of a deep ravine, or rather cleft, between lofty rocks, toward which their rugged path conducted. He paused for an instant, but supposing it to be the muttering of one of those transient thunder-showers which often take place in mountain heights, he proceeded. Passing through the ravine, they came to a hollow like a small amphitheater, surrounded by perpendicular precipices, over the brinks of which impending trees shot their branches, so that you only caught glimpses of the azure sky and the bright evening cloud. During the whole time Rip and his companion had labored on in silence; for though the former marveled greatly what could be the object of carrying a keg of liquor up this wild mountain, yet there was something strange and incomprehensible about the unknown, that inspired awe and checked familiarity.

On entering the amphitheater, new objects of wonder presented themselves. On a level spot in the center was a company of odd-looking personages playing at ninepins. They were dressed in a quaint outlandish fashion; some wore short doublets, others jerkins, with long knives in their belts, and most of them had enormous breeches of similar style with that of the guide's. Their visages, too, were peculiar: one had a large beard, broad face, and small piggish eyes: the face of another seemed to consist entirely of nose, and was surmounted by a white sugar-loaf hat, set off with a little red cock's tail. They all had beards, of various shapes and colors. There was one who seemed to be the commander. He was a stout old gentleman, with a weather-beaten countenance; he wore a laced doublet, broad belt and hanger, high-crowned hat and feather, red stockings, and high-heeled shoes, with roses in them. The whole group reminded Rip of the figures in an old Flemish painting in the parlor of Dominie Van Shaick, the village parson, and which had been brought over from Holland at the time of the settlement.

What seemed particularly odd to Rip was, that though these folks were evidently amusing themselves, yet they maintained the gravest faces, the most mysterious silence, and were, withal, the most melancholy party of pleasure he had ever witnessed. Nothing interrupted the stillness of the scene but the noise of the balls, which, whenever they were rolled, echoed along the mountains like rumbling peals of thunder.

As Rip and his companion approached them, they suddenly desisted from their play, and stared at him with such fixed, statue-like gaze, and such strange, uncouth, lack-luster countenances, that his heart turned within him, and his knees smote together. His companion now emptied the contents of the keg into large flagons, and made signs to him to wait upon the company. He obeyed with fear and trembling; they quaffed the liquor in profound silence and then returned to their game.

By degrees Rip's awe and apprehension

subsided. He even ventured, when no eye was fixed upon him, to taste the beverage, which he found had much of the flavor of excellent Hollands. He was naturally a thirsty soul and was soon tempted to repeat the draught. One taste provoked another; and he reiterated his visits to the flagon so often that at length his senses were overpowered, his eyes swam in his head, his head gradually declined, and he fell into a deep sleep.

On waking, he found himself on the green knoll whence he had first seen the old man of the glen. He rubbed his eyes. It was a bright, sunny morning. The birds were hopping and twittering among the bushes, and the eagle was wheeling aloft, and breasting the pure mountain breeze. "Surely," thought Rip, "I have not slept here all night." He recalled the occurrences before he fell asleep—the strange man with a keg of liquor, the mountain ravine, the wild retreat among the rocks, the woe-begone party at ninepins, the flagon. "Oh! that flagon! that wicked flagon!" thought Rip, "What excuse shall I make to Dame Van Winkle?"

He looked round for his gun, but in place of the clean, well-oiled fowling-piece, he found an old firelock lying by him, the barrel incrusted with rust, the lock falling off, and the stock worm-eaten. He now suspected that the grave roisterers of the mountain had put a trick upon him, and, having dosed him with liquor, had robbed him of his gun. Wolf, too, had disappeared, but he might have strayed away after a squirrel or partridge. He whistled after him, and shouted his name, but all in vain; the echoes repeated his whistle and shout, but no dog was to be seen.

He determined to revisit the scene of the last evening's gambol, and if he met with any of the party, to demand his dog and gun. As he rose to walk, he found himself stiff in the joints, and wanting in his usual activity. "These mountain beds do not agree with me," thought Rip, "and if this frolic should lay me up with a fit of the rheumatism, I shall have a blessed time with Dame Van Winkle." With some difficulty he got down into the glen: he found the gully up which he and his companion had ascended the preceding evening; but to his astonishment a mountain stream was now foaming down it, leaping from rock to rock, and filling the glen with babbling murmurs. He, however, made shift to scramble up its sides, working his toilsome way through thickets of birch, sassafras, and witch-hazel, and sometimes tripped up or entangled by the wild grapevines that twisted their coils or tendrils from tree to tree, and spread a kind of network in his path.

At length he reached to where the ravine had opened through the cliffs to the amphitheater; but no traces of such opening remained. The rocks presented a high, impenetrable wall, over which the torrent came tumbling in a sheet of feathery foam, and fell into a broad, deep basin, black from the shadows of the surrounding forest. Here, then, poor Rip was brought to a stand. He again called and whistled after his dog; he was only answered by the cawing of a flock of idle crows, sporting high in air about a dry tree that overhung a sunny precipice; and who, secure in their elevation, seemed to look down and scoff at the poor man's perplexities. What was to be done? The morning was passing away and Rip felt famished for want of his breakfast. He grieved to give up his dog and gun; he dreaded to meet his wife; but it would not do to starve among the mountains. He shook his head, shouldered the rusty firelock, and, with a heart full of trouble and anxiety, turned his steps homeward.

As he approached the village he met a number of people, but none whom he knew, which somewhat surprised him, for he had thought himself acquainted with everyone in the country round. Their dress, too, was of a different fashion from that to which he was accustomed. They all stared at him with equal marks of surprise, and whenever they cast their eyes upon him, invariably stroked their chins. The constant recurrence of this gesture induced Rip, involuntarily, to do the same, when, to his astonishment, he found his beard had grown a foot long!

He had now entered the skirts of the village. A troop of strange children ran at his heels, hooting after him, and pointing at his gray beard. The dogs, too, not one of which he recognized for an old acquaintance, barked at him as he passed. The very village was altered; it was larger and more populous. There were rows of houses which he had never seen before, and those which had been his familiar haunts had disappeared. Strange names were over the doors—strange faces at the windows—everything was strange. His mind now misgave him; he began to doubt whether both he and the world around him were not bewitched. Surely this was his native village which he had left but the day before. There stood the Kaatskill Mountains. There ran the silver Hudson at a distance. There was every hill and dale precisely as it had always been. Rip was sorely perplexed. "That flagon last night," thought he, "has addled my poor head sadly!"

It was with some difficulty that he found the way to his own house, which he approached with silent awe, expecting every moment to hear the shrill voice of Dame Van Winkle. He found the house gone to decay— the roof fallen in, the windows shattered, and the doors off the hinges. A half-starved dog that looked like Wolf was skulking about it. Rip called him by name, but the cur snarled, showed his teeth, and passed on. This was an unkind cut indeed. "My very dog," sighed poor Rip, "has forgotten me!"

He entered the house, which, to tell the truth, Dame Van Winkle had always kept in neat order. It was empty, forlorn, and apparently abandoned. This desolateness overcame all his connubial fears. He called loudly for his wife and children. The lonely chambers rang for a moment with his voice, and then all again was silence.

He now hurried forth, and hastened to his old resort, the village inn. But it, too, was gone. A large, rickety wooden building stood in its place, with great gaping windows, some of them broken and mended with old hats and petticoats, and over the door was painted, "The Union Hotel, by Jonathan Doolittle."[1] Instead of the great tree that used to shelter the quiet little Dutch inn of yore, there now was reared a tall naked pole, with something on the top that looked like a red night-cap, and from it was fluttering a flag on which was a singular

assemblage of stars and stripes. All this was strange and incomprehensible. He recognized on the sign, however, the ruby face of King George, under which he had smoked so many a peaceful pipe; but even this was singularly metamorphosed. The red coat was changed for one of blue and buff, a sword was held in the hand instead of a scepter, the head was decorated with a cocked hat, and underneath was painted in large characters, *General Washington*.

There was, as usual, a crowd of folk about the door, but none that Rip recollected. The very character of the people seemed changed. There was a busy, bustling disputatious tone about it, instead of the accustomed phlegm and drowsy tranquillity. He looked in vain for the sage Nicholas Vedder, with his broad face, double chin, and fair long pipe, uttering clouds of tobacco smoke instead of idle speeches; or Van Bummel, the schoolmaster, doling forth the contents of an ancient newspaper. In place of these, a lean, bilious-looking fellow, with his pockets full of hand bills, was haranguing vehemently about rights of citizens, elections, members of Congress, liberty, Bunker's Hill, heroes of seventy-six, and other words which were a perfect Babylonish jargon to the bewildered Van Winkle.

The appearance of Rip, with his long grizzled beard, his rusty fowling-piece, his uncouth dress, and an army of women and children at his heels, soon attracted the attention of the tavern-politicians. They crowded round him, eyeing him from head to foot with great curiosity. The orator bustled up to him, and, drawing him partly aside, inquired on which side he voted? Rip stared in vacant stupidity. Another short but busy little fellow pulled him by the arm, and, rising on tiptoe, inquired in his ear, whether he was Federal or Democrat? Rip was equally at a loss to comprehend the question; when a knowing, self-important old gentleman, in a sharp cocked hat, made his way through the crowd, putting them to the right and left with his elbows as he passed, and planting himself before Van Winkle, with one arm akimbo, the other resting on his cane, his keen eyes and sharp hat penetrating, as it were, into his very soul, demanded in an austere tone, what brought him to the election with a

---

[1] an allusion, apparently, to the intrusion of New Englanders, whom Irving did not like as a class, into New York

gun on his shoulder, and a mob at his heels, and whether he meant to breed a riot in the village?

"Alas! gentlemen," cried Rip, somewhat dismayed, "I am a poor quiet man, a native of the place, and a loyal subject of the King, God bless him!"

Here a general shout burst from the bystanders. "A tory! a tory! a spy! a refugee! hustle him! away with him!" It was with great difficulty that the self-important man in the cocked hat restored order; and, having assumed a tenfold austerity of brow, demanded again of the unknown culprit what he came there for, and whom he was seeking? The poor man humbly assured him that he meant no harm, but merely came there in search of some of his neighbors, who used to keep about the tavern.

"Well, who are they? Name them."

Rip bethought himself a moment, and inquired, "Where's Nicholas Vedder?"

There was a silence for a little while, when an old man replied, in a thin, piping voice, "Nicholas Vedder! why, he is dead and gone these eighteen years! There was a wooden tombstone in the churchyard that used to tell all about him, but that's rotten and gone too."

"Where's Brom Dutcher?"

"Oh, he went off to the army in the beginning of the war; some say he was killed at the storming of Stony Point. Others say he was drowned in a squall at the foot of Antony's Nose. I don't know. He never came back again."

"Where's Van Bummel, the schoolmaster?"

"He went off to the wars, too, was a great militia general, and is now in Congress."

Rip's heart died away at hearing of these sad changes in his home and friends, and finding himself thus alone in the world. Every answer puzzled him, too, by treating such enormous lapses of time, and of matters which he could not understand: war, Congress, Stony Point; he had no courage to ask after any more friends, but cried out in despair, "Does nobody here know Rip Van Winkle?"

"Oh, Rip Van Winkle!" exclaimed two or three, "Oh, to be sure! that's Rip Van Winkle yonder, leaning against the tree."

Rip looked and beheld a precise counterpart of himself as he went up the mountain, apparently as lazy and certainly as ragged. The poor fellow was now completely confounded. He doubted his own identity. In the midst of his bewilderment, the man in the cocked hat demanded who he was, and what was his name?

"God knows," exclaimed he, at his wit's end; "I'm not myself. I'm somebody else. That's me yonder. No, that's somebody else got into my shoes. I was myself last night, but I fell asleep on the mountain, and they've changed my gun, and everything's changed, and I'm changed, and I can't tell what's my name, or who I am!"

The bystanders began now to look at each other, nod, wink significantly, and tap their fingers against their foreheads. There was a whisper, also, about securing the gun and keeping the old fellow from doing mischief, at the very suggestion of which the self-important man in the cocked hat retired with some precipitation. At this critical moment a fresh, comely woman pressed through the throng to get a peep at the gray-bearded man. She had a chubby child in her arms, which, frightened at his looks, began to cry. "Hush, Rip," cried she; "hush, you little fool; the old man won't hurt you."

The name of the child, the air of the mother, the tone of her voice, awakened a train of recollections in his mind. "What is your name, my good woman?" asked he.

"Judith Gardenier."

"And your father's name?"

"Ah, poor man, Rip Van Winkle was his name, but it's twenty years since he went away from home with his gun, and never has been heard of since. His dog came home without him; but whether he shot himself, or was carried away by the Indians, nobody can tell. I was then but a little girl."

Rip had but one question more to ask; but he put it with a faltering voice, "Where's your mother?"

"Oh, she too died but a short time since; she broke a blood-vessel in a fit of passion at a New England peddler."

There was a drop of comfort, at least, in this intelligence. The honest man could contain himself no longer. He caught his daughter and her child in his arms. "I am your father!" cried he. "Young Rip Van Winkle once—old Rip Van Winkle now! Does nobody know poor Rip Van Winkle?"

All stood amazed until an old woman, tottering out from among the crowd, put her hand to her brow, and peering under it in his face for a moment, exclaimed, "Sure enough! it is Rip Van Winkle. It is himself! Welcome home again, old neighbor. Why, where have 10 you been these twenty long years?"

Rip's story was soon told, for the whole twenty years had been to him but as one night. The neighbors stared when they heard it; some were seen to wink at each other and put their tongues in their cheeks; and the self-important man in the cocked hat, who, when the alarm was over, had returned to the field, screwed down the corners of his mouth and shook his head—upon which there was a 20 general shaking of the head throughout the assemblage.

It was determined, however, to take the opinion of old Peter Vanderdonk, who was seen slowly advancing up the road. He was a descendant of the historian of that name, who wrote one of the earliest accounts of the province. Peter was the most ancient inhabitant of the village and well versed in all the wonderful events and traditions of the neigh- 30 borhood. He recollected Rip at once and corroborated his story in the most satisfactory manner. He assured the company that it was a fact, handed down from his ancestor the historian, that the Kaatskill Mountains had always been haunted by strange beings. That it was affirmed that the great Hendrick Hudson, the first discoverer of the river and country, kept a kind of vigil there every twenty years with his crew of the *Half Moon;* 40 being permitted in this way to revisit the scenes of his enterprise and keep a guardian eye upon the river and the great city called by his name. That his father had once seen them in their old Dutch dresses playing at ninepins in a hollow of the mountain; and that he himself had heard, one summer afternoon, the sound of their balls, like distant peals of thunder.

To make a long story short, the company 50 broke up and returned to the more important concerns of the election. Rip's daughter took him home to live with her; she had a snug well-furnished house, and a stout, cheery farmer for a husband, whom Rip recollected for one of the urchins that used to climb upon his back. As to Rip's son and heir, who was the ditto of himself, seen leaning against the tree, he was employed to work on the farm, but evinced an hereditary disposition to attend to anything else but his business.

Rip now resumed his old walks and habits; he soon found many of his former cronies, though all rather the worse for the wear and tear of time, and preferred making friends among the rising generation, with whom he soon grew into great favor.

Having nothing to do at home, and being arrived at that happy age when a man can be idle with impunity, he took his place once more on the bench at the inn door and was reverenced as one of the patriarchs of the village and a chronicler of the old times "before the war." It was some time before he could get into the regular track of gossip or could be made to comprehend the strange events that had taken place during his torpor. How that there had been a revolutionary war, that the country had thrown off the yoke of old England, and that, instead of being a subject of His Majesty George the Third, he was now a free citizen of the United States. Rip, in fact, was no politician; the changes of states and empires made but little impression on him, but there was one species of despotism under which he had long groaned, and that was petticoat government. Happily that was at an end; he had got his neck out of the yoke of matrimony, and could go in and out whenever he pleased without dreading the tyranny of Dame Van Winkle. Whenever her name was mentioned, however, he shook his head, shrugged his shoulders, and cast up his eyes; which might pass either for an expression of resignation to his fate, or joy at his deliverance.

He used to tell his story to every stranger that arrived at Mr. Doolittle's hotel. He was observed, at first, to vary on some points every time he told it, which was doubtless owing to his having so recently awaked. It at last settled down precisely to the tale I have related, and not a man, woman, or child in the neighborhood but knew it by heart. Some always pretended to doubt the reality of it, and insisted that Rip had been out of his head, and that this was one point on which he always remained flighty. The old Dutch inhabitants, however, almost universally gave it full credit. Even to this day they never hear a thunderstorm of a summer afternoon about the Kaatskill, but they say Hendrick Hudson and his crew are at their game of ninepins; and it is a common wish of all henpecked husbands in the neighborhood, when life hangs heavy on their hands, that they might have a quieting draught out of Rip Van Winkle's flagon.

1819

ENGLISH WRITERS ON AMERICA

The "literary War of 1812," as it has been called, extended over a longer period than did the military hostilities between the United States and Great Britain. Its chief documents on the American side were Dr. Dwight's essay "On the [British] Review of *Inchiquin's Letters*" (1815), Robert Walsh's *An Appeal from the Judgments of Great Britain*, and the satirical parodies and arguments of Irving's friend, James Kirke Paulding: *The Diverting History of John Bull and Brother Jonathan, The Lay of the Scotch Fiddle* (both in 1813), and *The United States and England* (1815). The British contributions may be studied in W. B. Cairns, *British Criticisms of American Writings, 1783–1815* (1918) and *British Criticisms of American Writings, 1815–1833* (1922). Irving's essay in *The Sketch Book*, addressed to Americans but designed for English readers as well, sets forth the causes of international ill-will and gives sound advice to both.

"Methinks I see in my mind a noble and puissant nation, rousing herself like a strong man after sleep, and shaking her invisible locks: methinks I see her as an eagle, mewing her mighty youth, and kindling her endazzled eyes at the full mid-day beam."—MILTON ON THE LIBERTY OF THE PRESS.[1]

IT is with feelings of deep regret that I observe the literary animosity daily growing up between England and America. Great curiosity has been awakened of late with respect to the United States, and the London

[1] from Milton's *Areopagitica*, published in 1644

press has teemed with volumes of travels through the Republic; but they seem intended to diffuse error rather than knowledge; and so successful have they been, that, notwithstanding the constant intercourse between the nations, there is no people concerning whom the great mass of the British public have less pure information, or entertain more numerous prejudices.

English travellers are the best and the worst in the world. Where no motives of pride or interest intervene, none can equal them for profound and philosophical views of society, or faithful and graphical descriptions of external objects; but when either the interest or reputation of their own country comes in collision with that of another, they go to the opposite extreme, and forget their usual probity and candor in the indulgence of splenetic remark and an illiberal spirit of ridicule.

Hence, their travels are more honest and accurate, the more remote the country described. I would place implicit confidence in an Englishman's descriptions of the regions beyond the cataracts of the Nile; of unknown islands in the Yellow Sea; of the interior of India; or of any other tract which other travellers might be apt to picture out with the illusions of their fancies; but I would cautiously receive his account of his immediate neighbors and of those nations with which he is in habits of most frequent intercourse. However I might be disposed to trust his probity, I dare not trust his prejudices.

It has also been the peculiar lot of our country to be visited by the worst kind of English travellers. While men of philosophical spirit and cultivated minds have been sent from England to ransack the poles, to penetrate the deserts, and to study the manners and customs of barbarous nations, with which she can have no permanent intercourse of profit or pleasure; it has been left to the broken-down tradesman, the scheming adventurer, the wandering mechanic, the Manchester and Birmingham agent, to be her oracles respecting America. From such sources she is content to receive her information respecting a country in a singular state of moral and physical development; a country in which one of the greatest political experiments in the history of the world is now performing, and which presents the most profound and momentous studies to the statesman and philosopher.

That such men should give prejudiced accounts of America is not a matter of surprise. The themes it offers for contemplation are too vast and elevated for their capacities. The national character is yet in a state of fermentation: it may have its frothiness and sediment, but its ingredients are sound and wholesome: it has already given proofs of powerful and generous qualities; and the whole promises to settle down into something substantially excellent. But the causes which are operating to strengthen and ennoble it, and its daily indications of admirable properties, are all lost upon these purblind observers, who are only affected by the little asperities incident to its present situation. They are capable of judging only of the surface of things, of those matters which come in contact with their private interests and personal gratifications. They miss some of the snug conveniences and petty comforts which belong to an old, highly finished, and overpopulous state of society, where the ranks of useful labor are crowded, and many earn a painful and servile subsistence by studying the very caprices of appetite and self-indulgence. These minor comforts, however, are all-important in the estimation of narrow minds; which either do not perceive, or will not acknowledge, that they are more than counterbalanced among us by great and generally diffused blessings.

They may, perhaps, have been disappointed in some unreasonable expectation of sudden gain. They may have pictured America to themselves an El Dorado, where gold and silver abounded, and the natives were lacking in sagacity; and where they were to become strangely and suddenly rich, in some unforeseen but easy manner. The same weakness of mind that indulges absurd expectations produces petulance in disappointment. Such persons become embittered against the country on finding that there, as everywhere else, a man must sow before he can reap; must win wealth by industry and talent; and must contend with the common difficulties of nature and the shrewdness of an intelligent and enterprising people.

Perhaps, through mistaken, or ill-directed hospitality, or from the prompt disposition to cheer and countenance the stranger, prevalent among my countrymen, they may have been treated with unwonted respect in America; and having been accustomed all their lives to consider themselves below the surface of good society, and brought up in a servile feeling of inferiority, they become arrogant on the common boon of civility: they attribute to the lowliness of others their own elevation; and underrate a society where there are no artificial distinctions, and where, by any chance, such individuals as themselves can rise to consequence.

One would suppose, however, that information coming from such sources, on a subject where the truth is so desirable, would be received with caution by the censors of the press; that the motives of these men, their veracity, their opportunities of inquiry and observation, and their capacities for judging correctly, would be rigorously scrutinized before their evidence was admitted, in such sweeping extent, against a kindred nation. The very reverse, however, is the case, and it furnishes a striking instance of human inconsistency. Nothing can surpass the vigilance with which English critics will examine the credibility of the traveller who publishes an account of some distant, and comparatively unimportant country. How warily will they compare the measurements of a pyramid or the descriptions of a ruin; and how sternly will they censure any inaccuracy in these contributions of merely curious knowledge: while they will receive, with eagerness and unhesitating faith, the gross misrepresentations of coarse and obscure writers concerning a country with which their own is placed in the most important and delicate relations. Nay, they will even make these apocryphal volumes textbooks, on which to enlarge with a zeal and an ability worthy of a more generous cause.

I shall not, however, dwell on this irksome and hackneyed topic; nor should I have adverted to it, but for the undue interest apparently taken in it by my countrymen, and certain injurious effects which I apprehend it might produce upon the national feeling. We attach too much consequence to these attacks.

They cannot do us any essential injury. The tissue of misrepresentations attempted to be woven round us are like cobwebs woven round the limbs of an infant giant. Our country continually outgrows them. One falsehood after another falls off of itself. We have but to live on, and every day we live a whole volume of refutation. All the writers of England united, if we could for a moment suppose their great minds stooping to so unworthy a combination, could not conceal our rapidly growing importance and matchless prosperity. They could not conceal that these are owing, not merely to physical and local, but also to moral causes—to the political liberty, the general diffusion of knowledge, the prevalence of sound, moral, and religious principles which give force and sustained energy to the character of a people; and which, in fact, have been the acknowledged and wonderful supporters of their own national power, and glory.

But why are we so exquisitely alive to the aspersions of England? Why do we suffer ourselves to be so affected by the contumely she has endeavored to cast upon us? It is not in the opinion of England alone that honor lives, and reputation has its being. The world at large is the arbiter of a nation's fame; with its thousand eyes it witnesses a nation's deeds, and from their collective testimony is national glory or national disgrace established.

For ourselves, therefore, it is comparatively of but little importance whether England does us justice or not; it is, perhaps, of far more importance to herself. She is instilling anger and resentment into the bosom of a youthful nation, to grow with its growth, and strengthen with its strength. If in America, as some of her writers are laboring to convince her, she is hereafter to find an invidious rival and a gigantic foe, she may thank those very writers for having provoked rivalship and irritated hostility. Everyone knows the all-pervading influence of literature at the present day, and how much the opinions and passions of mankind are under its control. The mere contests of the sword are temporary; their wounds are but in the flesh, and it is the pride of the generous to forgive and forget them; but the slanders of the pen pierce to the heart; they rankle longest in the noblest spirits; they

dwell ever present in the mind, and render it morbidly sensitive to the most trifling collision. It is but seldom that any one overt act produces hostilities between two nations; there exists, most commonly, a previous jealousy and ill-wind, a predisposition to take offense. Trace these to their cause, and how often will they be found to originate in the mischievous effusions of mercenary writers, who, secure in their closets, and for ignominious bread, concoct and circulate the venom that is to inflame the generous and the brave.

I am not laying too much stress upon this point, for it applies most emphatically to our particular case. Over no nation does the press hold a more absolute control than over the people of America, for the universal education of the poorest classes makes every individual a reader. There is nothing published in England on the subject of our country, that does not circulate through every part of it. There is not a calumny dropped from an English pen, nor an unworthy sarcasm uttered by an English statesman, that does not go to blight good will and add to the mass of latent resentment. Possessing, then, as England does, the fountain-head from whence the literature of the language flows, how completely is it in her power, and how truly is it her duty, to make it the medium of amiable and magnanimous feeling—a stream where two nations meet together and drink in peace and kindness. Should she, however, persist in turning it to waters of bitterness, the time may come when she may repent her folly. The present friendship of America may be of but little moment to her, but the future destinies of that country do not admit of a doubt; over those of England, there lower some shadows of uncertainty. Should, then, a day of gloom arrive—should these reverses overtake her from which the proudest empires have not been exempt—she may look back with regret at her infatuation in repulsing from her side a nation she might have grappled to her bosom, and thus destroying her only chance for real friendship beyond the boundaries of her own dominions.

There is a general impression in England that the people of the United States are inimical to the parent country. It is one of the errors which have been diligently propagated by designing writers. There is, doubtless, considerable political hostility, and a general soreness at the illiberality of the English press; but, collectively speaking, the prepossessions of the people are strongly in favor of England. Indeed, at one time they amounted, in many parts of the Union, to an absurd degree of bigotry. The bare name of Englishman was a passport to the confidence and hospitality of every family, and too often gave a transient currency to the worthless and the ungrateful. Throughout the country there was something of enthusiasm connected with the idea of England. We looked to it with a hallowed feeling of tenderness and veneration, as the land of our forefathers—the august repository of the monuments and antiquities of our race —the birthplace and mausoleum of the sages and heroes of our paternal history. After our own country, there was none in whose glory we more delighted—none whose good opinion we were more anxious to possess—none towards which our hearts yearned with such throbbings of warm consanguinity. Even during the late war, whenever there was the least opportunity for kind feelings to spring forth, it was the delight of the generous spirits of our country to show that, in the midst of hostilities, they still kept alive the sparks of future friendship.

Is all this to be at an end? Is this golden band of kindred sympathies, so rare between nations, to be broken for ever?—Perhaps it is for the best—it may dispel an illusion which might have kept us in mental vassalage; which might have interfered occasionally with our true interests, and prevented the growth of proper national pride. But it is hard to give up the kindred tie! and there are feelings dearer than interest—closer to the heart than pride—that will still make us cast back a look of regret, as we wander farther and farther from the paternal roof, and lament the waywardness of the parent that would repel the affections of the child.

Shortsighted and injudicious, however, as the conduct of England may be in this system of aspersion, recrimination on our part would be equally ill-judged. I speak not of a prompt and spirited vindication of our country nor

the keenest castigation of her slanderers—but I allude to a disposition to retaliate in kind; to retort sarcasm and inspire prejudice, which seems to be growing widely among our writers. Let us guard particularly against such a temper, for it will redouble the evil instead of redressing the wrong. Nothing is so easy and inviting as the retort of abuse and sarcasm; but it is a paltry and unprofitable contest. It is the alternative of a morbid mind, fretted into petulance rather than warmed into indignation. If England is willing to permit the mean jealousies of trade or the rancorous animosities of politics to deprave the integrity of her press and poison the fountain of public opinion, let us beware of her example. She may deem it her interest to diffuse error and engender antipathy, for the purpose of checking emigration; we have no purpose of the kind to serve. Neither have we any spirit of national jealousy to gratify; for as yet, in all our rivalships with England, we are the rising and the gaining party. There can be no end to answer, therefore, but the gratification of resentment—a mere spirit of retaliation; and even that is impotent. Our retorts are never republished in England; they fall short, therefore, of their aim; but they foster a querulous and peevish temper among our writers; they sour the sweet flow of our early literature and sow thorns and brambles among its blossoms. What is still worse, they circulate through our own country, and, as far as they have effect, excite virulent national prejudices. This last is the evil most especially to be deprecated. Governed, as we are, entirely by public opinion, the utmost care should be taken to preserve the purity of the public mind. Knowledge is power, and truth is knowledge; whoever, therefore, knowingly propagates a prejudice willfully saps the foundation of his country's strength.

The members of a republic, above all other men, should be candid and dispassionate. They are, individually, portions of the sovereign mind and sovereign will, and should be enabled to come to all questions of national concern with calm and unbiased judgments. From the peculiar nature of our relations with England, we must have more frequent questions of a difficult and delicate character with her than with any other nation—questions that affect the most acute and excitable feelings; and as, in the adjusting of these, our national measures must ultimately be determined by popular sentiment, we cannot be too anxiously attentive to purify it from all latent passion or prepossession.

Opening, too, as we do, an asylum for strangers from every portion of the earth, we should receive all with impartiality. It should 10 be our pride to exhibit an example of one nation, at least, destitute of national antipathies and exercising not merely the overt acts of hospitality, but those more rare and noble courtesies which spring from liberality of opinion.

What have we to do with national prejudices? They are the inveterate diseases of old countries, contracted in rude and ignorant ages, when nations knew but little of each other, and 20 looked beyond their own boundaries with distrust and hostility. We, on the contrary, have sprung into national existence in an enlightened and philosophic age, when the different parts of the habitable world and the various branches of the human family have been indefatigably studied and made known to each other; and we forego the advantages of our birth if we do not shake off the national prejudices, as we would the local superstitions, 30 of the old world.

But above all let us not be influenced by any angry feelings so far as to shut our eyes to the perception of what is really excellent and amiable in the English character. We are a young people, necessarily an imitative one, and must take our examples and models, in a great degree, from the existing nations of Europe. There is no country more worthy of our study than England. The spirit of her 40 constitution is most analogous to ours. The manners of her people—their intellectual activity—their freedom of opinion—their habits of thinking on those subjects which concern the dearest interests and most sacred charities of private life, are all congenial to the American character, and, in fact, are all intrinsically excellent; for it is in the moral feeling of the people that the deep foundations of British prosperity are laid, and however the super- 50 structure may be timeworn or overrun by

abuses, there must be something solid in the basis, admirable in the materials, and stable in the structure of an edifice that so long has towered unshaken amidst the tempests of the world.

Let it be the pride of our writers, therefore, discarding all feelings of irritation, and disdaining to retaliate the illiberality of British authors, to speak of the English nation without prejudice and with determined candor. While they rebuke the indiscriminating bigotry with which some of our countrymen admire and imitate everything English, merely because it is English, let them frankly point out what is really worthy of approbation. We may thus place England before us as a perpetual volume of reference, wherein are recorded sound deductions from ages of experience; and while we avoid the errors and absurdities which may have crept into the page, we may draw thence golden maxims of practical wisdom, wherewith to strengthen and to embellish our national character.

1820

THE STOUT GENTLEMAN

A STAGECOACH ROMANCE

In contrast with the longer and more diffuse tales "Rip Van Winkle" and "The Legend of Sleepy Hollow," this narrative comes much closer, in its concentration, brevity, and fixed purpose, to the laws of short-story technique as later laid down by Poe.

I'll cross it though it blast me!—HAMLET

IT was a rainy Sunday in the gloomy month of November. I had been detained, in the course of a journey, by a slight indisposition, from which I was recovering, but was still feverish, and obliged to keep within doors all day in an inn of the small town of Derby. A wet Sunday in a country inn!—whoever has had the luck to experience one can alone judge of my situation. The rain pattered against the casements; the bells tolled for church with a melancholy sound. I went to the windows in quest of something to amuse the eye; but it seemed as if I had been placed completely out of the reach of all amusement. The windows of my bedroom looked out among tiled roofs and stacks of chimneys, while those of my sitting-room commanded a full view of the stable-yard. I know of nothing more calculated to make a man sick of this world than a stable-yard on a rainy day. The place was littered with wet straw that had been kicked about by travelers and stable-boys. In one corner was a stagnant pool of water, surrounding an island of muck; there were several half-drowned fowls crowded together under a cart among which was a miserable, crestfallen cock, drenched out of all life and spirit; his drooping tail matted, as it were, into a single feather, along which the water trickled from his back; near the cart was a half-dozing cow, chewing the cud, and standing patiently to be rained on, with wreaths of vapor rising from her reeking hide; a walleyed horse, tired of the loneliness of the stable, was poking his spectral head out of a window, with the rain dripping on it from the eaves; an unhappy cur, chained to a doghouse hard by, uttered something every now and then, between a bark and a yelp; a drab of a kitchen wench tramped backwards and forwards through the yard in pattens, looking as sulky as the weather itself; everything, in short, was comfortless and forlorn, excepting a crew of hardened ducks, assembled like boon companions round a puddle, and making a riotous noise over their liquor.

I was lonely and listless, and wanted amusement. My room soon became insupportable. I abandoned it and sought what is technically called the travelers'-room. This is a public room set apart at most inns for the accommodation of a class of wayfarers called travelers, or riders; a kind of commercial knightserrant, who are incessantly scouring the kingdom in gigs, on horseback, or by coach. They are the only successors, that I know of at the present day, to the knights-errant of yore. They lead the same kind of roving adventurous life, only changing the lance for a driving-whip, the buckler for a pattern-card, and the coat of mail for an upper Benjamin. Instead of vindicating the charms of peerless beauty, they rove about, spreading the fame and standing of some substantial tradesman, or manufacturer, and are ready at any time to bargain in his name, it being the fashion now-

adays to trade, instead of fight, with one another. As the room of the hostel, in the good old fighting times, would be hung round at night with the armor of wayworn warriors, such as coats of mail, falchions, and yawning helmets; so the travelers'-room is garnished with the harnessing of their successors, with box-coats, whips of all kinds, spurs, gaiters, and oilcloth covered hats.

I was in hopes of finding some of these worthies to talk with, but was disappointed. There were, indeed, two or three in the room; but I could make nothing of them. One was just finishing his breakfast, quarreling with his bread and butter, and huffing the waiter; another buttoned on a pair of gaiters, with many execrations at Boots for not having cleaned his shoes well; a third sat drumming on the table with his fingers and looking at the rain as it streamed down the window-glass; they all appeared infected by the weather and disappeared, one after the other, without exchanging a word.

I sauntered to the window, and stood gazing at the people, picking their way to church, with petticoats hoisted midleg high, and dripping umbrellas. The bell ceased to toll, and the streets became silent. I then amused myself with watching the daughters of a tradesman opposite, who, being confined to the house for fear of wetting their Sunday finery, played off their charms at the front windows to fascinate the chance tenants of the inn. They at length were summoned away by a vigilant vinegar-faced mother, and I had nothing further from without to amuse me.

What was I to do to pass away the long-lived day? I was sadly nervous and lonely; and everything about an inn seems calculated to make a dull day ten times duller. Old newspapers, smelling of beer and tobacco smoke, and which I had already read half a dozen times. Good for nothing books that were worse than rainy weather. I bored myself to death with an old volume of the *Lady's Magazine*. I read all the commonplace names of ambitious travelers scrawled on the panes of glass; the eternal families of the Smiths, and the Browns, and the Jacksons, and the Johnsons, and all the other sons, and I deciphered several scraps of fatiguing inn-window poetry which I have met with in all parts of the world.

The day continued lowering and gloomy; the slovenly, ragged, spongy clouds drifted heavily along; there was no variety even in the rain: it was one dull, continued, monotonous patter—patter—patter, excepting that now and then I was enlivened by the idea of a brisk shower, from the rattling of the drops upon a passing umbrella.

It was quite *refreshing* (if I may be allowed a hackneyed phrase of the day) when, in the course of the morning, a horn blew, and a stagecoach whirled through the street, with outside passengers stuck all over it, cowering under cotton umbrellas, and seethed together, and reeking with the steams of wet box-coats and upper Benjamins.

The sound brought out from their lurking-places a crew of vagabond boys, and vagabond dogs, and the carroty-headed hostler, and that nondescript animal ycleped Boots, and all the other vagabond race that infest the purlieus of an inn; but the bustle was transient; the coach again whirled on its way; and boy and dog, and hostler and Boots, all slunk back again to their holes; the street again became silent, and the rain continued to rain on. In fact, there was no hope of its clearing up; the barometer pointed to rainy weather; mine hostess' tortoise-shell cat sat by the fire washing her face, and rubbing her paws over her ears; and, on referring to the Almanac, I found a direful prediction stretching from the top of the page to the bottom through the whole month, "expect—much—rain—about —this—time!"

I was dreadfully hipped. The hours seemed as if they would never creep by. The very ticking of the clock became irksome. At length the stillness of the house was interrupted by the ringing of a bell. Shortly after I heard the voice of a waiter at the bar: "The stout gentleman in No. 13 wants his breakfast. Tea and bread and butter with ham and eggs, the eggs not to be too much done."

In such a situation as mine every incident is of importance. Here was a subject of speculation presented to my mind and ample exercise for my imagination. I am prone to paint pictures to myself, and on this occasion I had some materials to work upon. Had the guest up stairs been mentioned as Mr. Smith, or Mr. Brown, or Mr. Jackson, or Mr. Johnson, or merely as "the gentleman in No. 13," it would have been a perfect blank to me. I should have thought nothing of it; but "The stout gentleman!"—the very name had something in it of the picturesque. It at once gave the size; it embodied the personage to my mind's eye, and my fancy did the rest.

He was stout, or, as some term it, lusty; in all probability, therefore, he was advanced in life, some people expanding as they grow old. By his breakfasting rather late, and in his own room, he must be a man accustomed to live at his ease, and above the necessity of early rising, no doubt a round, rosy, lusty old gentleman.

There was another violent ringing. The stout gentleman was impatient for his breakfast. He was evidently a man of importance, "well to do in the world," accustomed to be promptly waited upon, of a keen appetite, and a little cross when hungry; "perhaps," thought I, "he may be some London Alderman, or who knows but he may be a Member of Parliament?" The breakfast was sent up, and there was a short interval of silence; he was, doubtless, making the tea. Presently there was a violent ringing; and before it could be answered, another ringing still more violent. "Bless me! what a choleric old gentleman!" The waiter came down in a huff. The butter was rancid, the eggs were overdone, the ham was too salt:—the stout gentleman was evidently nice in his eating—one of those who eat and growl, and keep the waiter on the trot, and live in a state militant with the household.

The hostess got into a fume. I should observe that she was a brisk, coquettish woman; a little of a shrew, and something of a slammerkin, but very pretty withal, with a nincompoop of a husband, as shrews are apt to have. She rated the servants roundly for their negligence in sending up so bad a breakfast, but said not a word against the stout gentleman; by which I clearly perceived that he must be a man of consequence, entitled to make a noise and to give trouble at a country inn. Other eggs, and ham, and bread and butter were sent up. They appeared to be more graciously received; at least there was no further complaint.

I had not made many turns about the travelers'-room when there was another ringing. Shortly afterwards there was a stir and an inquest about the house. The stout gentleman wanted the *Times* or the *Chronicle* newspaper. I set him down, therefore, for a whig; or rather, from his being so absolute and lordly where he had a chance, I suspected him of being a radical. Hunt, I had heard, was a large man; "who knows," thought I, "but it is Hunt himself!"[1]

My curiosity began to be awakened. I inquired of the waiter who was this stout gentleman that was making all this stir; but I could get no information: nobody seemed to know his name. The landlords of bustling inns seldom trouble their heads about the names or occupations of their transient guests. The color of a coat, the shape or size of the person, is enough to suggest a traveling name. It is either the tall gentleman, or the short gentleman, or the gentleman in black, or the gentleman in snuff-color; or, as in the present instance, the stout gentleman. A designation of the kind once hit on answers every purpose, and saves all further inquiry.

Rain—rain—rain! pitiless, ceaseless rain! No such thing as putting a foot out of doors and no occupation nor amusement within. By and by I heard some one walking over head. It was in the stout gentleman's room. He evidently was a large man by the heaviness of his tread, and an old man from his wearing such creaking soles. "He is doubtless," thought I, "some rich old square-toes of regular habits and is now taking exercise after breakfast."

I now read all the advertisements of coaches and hotels that were stuck about the mantelpiece. The *Lady's Magazine* had become an abomination to me; it was as tedious as the day itself. I wandered out, not knowing what to do, and ascended again to my room. I had not been there long, when there was a squall from a neighboring bedroom. A door opened and slammed violently; a chambermaid, that

I had remarked for having a ruddy, good-humored face, went down stairs in a violent flurry. The stout gentleman had been rude to her!

This sent a whole host of my deductions to the deuce in a moment. This unknown personage could not be an old gentleman, for old gentlemen are not apt to be so obstreperous to chambermaids. He could not be a young gentleman, for young gentlemen are not apt to inspire such indignation. He must be a middle-aged man and confounded ugly into the bargain, or the girl would not have taken the matter in such terrible dudgeon. I confess I was sorely puzzled.

In a few minutes I heard the voice of my landlady. I caught a glance of her as she came tramping up stairs, her face glowing, her cap flaring, her tongue wagging the whole way. "She'd have no such doings in her house, she'd warrant. If gentlemen did spend money freely, it was no rule. She'd have no servant-maids of hers treated in that way, when they were about their work, that's what she wouldn't."

As I hate squabbles, particularly with women, and above all with pretty women, I slunk back into my room and partly closed the door; but my curiosity was too much excited not to listen. The landlady marched intrepidly to the enemy's citadel and entered it with a storm. The door closed after her. I heard her voice in high windy clamor for a moment or two. Then it gradually subsided like a gust of wind in a garret; then there was a laugh; then I heard nothing more.

After a little while my landlady came out with an odd smile on her face, adjusting her cap, which was a little on one side. As she went down stairs I heard the landlord ask her what was the matter; she said, "Nothing at all, only the girl's a fool."—I was more than ever perplexed what to make of this unaccountable personage, who could put a good-natured chambermaid in a passion, and send away a termagant landlady in smiles. He could not be so old, nor cross, nor ugly either.

I had to go to work at his picture again, and to paint him entirely different. I now set him down for one of those stout gentlemen that are frequently met with swaggering about the doors of country inns. Moist, merry fellows,

[1] Leigh Hunt, English journalist, essayist, friend of Charles Lamb, regarded as a radical by his conservative contemporaries

in Belcher handkerchiefs, whose bulk is a little assisted by malt-liquors. Men who have seen the world, and been sworn at Highgate; who are used to tavern life; up to all the tricks of tapsters, and knowing in the ways of sinful publicans. Free-livers on a small scale; who are prodigal within the compass of a guinea; who call all the waiters by name, tousle the maids, gossip with the landlady at the bar, and prose over a pint of port or a glass of negus after dinner.

The morning wore away in forming these and similar surmises. As fast as I wove one system of belief, some movement of the unknown would completely overturn it, and throw all my thoughts again into confusion. Such are the solitary operations of a feverish mind. I was, as I have said, extremely nervous, and the continual meditation on the concerns of this invisible personage began to have its effect:—I was getting a fit of the fidgets.

Dinner-time came. I hoped the stout gentleman might dine in the travelers'-room and that I might at length get a view of his person; but no—he had dinner served in his own room. What could be the meaning of this solitude and mystery? He could not be a radical; there was something too aristocratical in thus keeping himself apart from the rest of the world and condemning himself to his own dull company throughout a rainy day. And then, too, he lived too well for a discontented politician. He seemed to expatiate on a variety of dishes, and to sit over his wine like a jolly friend of good living. Indeed, my doubts on this head were soon at an end; for he could not have finished his first bottle before I could faintly hear him humming a tune; and on listening, I found it to be "God save the King." 'Twas plain, then, he was no radical, but a faithful subject; one who grew loyal over his bottle, and was ready to stand by king and constitution, when he could stand by nothing else. But who could he be! My conjectures began to run wild. Was he not some personage of distinction traveling incog.? "God knows!" said I, at my wit's end; "it may be one of the royal family for aught I know, for they are all stout gentlemen!"

The weather continued rainy. The mysterious unknown kept his room, and, as far as I could judge, his chair, for I did not hear him move. In the meantime, as the day advanced, the travelers'-room began to be frequented. Some, who had just arrived, came in buttoned up in box-coats; others came home who had been dispersed about the town. Some took their dinners, and some their tea. Had I been in a different mood, I should have found entertainment in studying this peculiar class of men. There were two especially, who were regular wags of the road, and up to all the standing jokes of travelers. They had a thousand sly things to say to the waiting-maid, whom they called Louisa, and Ethelinda, and a dozen other fine names, changing the name every time, and chuckling amazingly at their own waggery. My mind, however, had become completely engrossed by the stout gentleman. He had kept my fancy in chase during a long day, and it was not now to be diverted from the scent.

The evening gradually wore away. The travelers read the papers two or three times over. Some drew round the fire and told long stories about their horses, about their adventures, their overturns, and breakings down. They discussed the credit of different merchants and different inns; and the two wags told several choice anecdotes of pretty chambermaids and kind landladies. All this passed as they were quietly taking what they called their night-caps, that is to say, strong glasses of brandy and water and sugar, or some other mixture of the kind; after which they one after another rang for "Boots" and the chambermaid, and walked off to bed in old shoes cut down into marvelously uncomfortable slippers.

There was now only one man left—a short-legged, long-bodied, plethoric fellow, with a very large, sandy head. He sat by himself, with a glass of port wine negus, and a spoon; sipping and stirring, and meditating and sipping, until nothing was left but the spoon. He gradually fell asleep bolt upright in his chair, with the empty glass standing before him; and the candle seemed to fall asleep too, for the wick grew long, and black, and cabbaged at the end, and dimmed the little light that remained in the chamber. The gloom that now prevailed was contagious. Around hung the shapeless, and almost spectral, box-coats of departed travelers, long since buried in deep sleep. I only heard the ticking of the clock, with the deep-drawn breathings of the sleeping topers, and the drippings of the rain, drop—drop—drop, from the eaves of the house. The church bells chimed midnight. All at once the stout gentleman began to walk over head, pacing slowly backwards and forwards. There was something extremely awful in all this, especially to one in my state of nerves. These ghastly great-coats, these guttural breathings, and the creaking footsteps of this mysterious being. His steps grew fainter and fainter, and at length died away. I could bear it no longer. I was wound up to the desperation of a hero of romance. "Be he who or what he may," said I to myself, "I'll have a sight of him!" I seized a chamber candle, and hurried up to No. 13. The door stood ajar. I hesitated —I entered. The room was deserted. There stood a large, broad-bottomed elbow-chair at a table, on which was an empty tumbler, and a *Times* newspaper, and the room smelt powerfully of Stilton cheese.

The mysterious stranger had evidently but just retired. I turned off, sorely disappointed, to my room, which had been changed to the front of the house. As I went along the corridor, I saw a large pair of boots, with dirty, waxed tops, standing at the door of a bed-chamber. They doubtless belonged to the unknown; but it would not do to disturb so redoubtable a personage in his den; he might discharge a pistol, or something worse, at my head. I went to bed, therefore, and lay awake half the night in a terribly nervous state; and even when I fell asleep, I was still haunted in my dreams by the idea of the stout gentleman and his wax-topped boots.

I slept rather late the next morning, and was awakened by some stir and bustle in the house, which I could not at first comprehend; until getting more awake, I found there was a mail coach starting from the door. Suddenly there was a cry from below, "The gentleman has forgot his umbrella! Look for the gentleman's umbrella in No. 13!" I heard an immediate scampering of a chambermaid along the passage, and a shrill reply as she ran, "Here it is! Here's the gentleman's umbrella!"

The mysterious stranger then was on the point of setting off. This was the only chance I should ever have of knowing him. I sprang out of bed, scrambled to the window, snatched aside the curtains, and just caught a glimpse of the rear of a person getting in at the coach-door. The skirts of a brown coat parted behind and gave me a full view of the broad disk of a pair of drab breeches. The door closed—"All right!" was the word—the coach whirled off;—and that was all I ever saw of the stout gentleman!

1822

From THE LIFE AND VOYAGES OF CHRISTOPHER COLUMBUS

BOOK III, CHAPTER IV

[*The Discovery of Land*]

THE situation of Columbus was daily becoming more and more critical. In proportion as he approached the regions where he expected to find land, the impatience of his crews augmented. The favorable signs which increased his confidence, were derided by them as delusive; and there was danger of their rebelling, and obliging him to turn back, when on the point of realizing the object of all his labors. They beheld themselves with dismay still wafted onward, over the boundless wastes of what appeared to them a mere watery desert, surrounding the habitable world. What was to become of them should their provisions fail? Their ships were too weak and defective even for the great voyage they had already made, but if they were still to press forward, adding at every moment to the immense expanse behind them, how should they ever be able to return, having no intervening port where they might victual and refit?

In this way they fed each other's discontents, gathering together in little knots, and fomenting a spirit of mutinous opposition: and when we consider the natural fire of the Spanish temperament and its impatience of control; and that a great part of these men were sailing on compulsion; we cannot wonder that there was imminent danger of their breaking forth into open rebellion and compelling Columbus to turn back. In their secret conferences they exclaimed against him as a desperado, bent, in a mad fantasy, upon doing something extravagant to render himself notorious. What were their sufferings and dangers to one evidently content to sacrifice his own life for the chance of distinction? What obligations bound them to continue on with him; or when were the terms of *their* agreement to be considered as fulfilled? They had already penetrated unknown seas, untraversed by a sail, far beyond where man had ever before ventured. They had done enough to gain themselves a character for courage and hardihood in undertaking such an enterprise and persisting in it so far. How much further were they to go in quest of a merely conjectured land? Were they to sail on until they perished, or until all return became impossible? In such case they would be the authors of their own destruction.

On the other hand, should they consult their safety, and turn back before too late, who would blame them? Any complaints made by Columbus would be of no weight; he was a foreigner without friends or influence; his schemes had been condemned by the learned, and discountenanced by people of all ranks. He had no party to uphold him, and a host of opponents whose pride of opinion would be gratified by his failure. Or, as an effectual means of preventing his complaints, they might throw him into the sea, and give out that he had fallen overboard while busy with his instruments contemplating the stars; a report which no one would have either the inclination or the means to controvert.

Columbus was not ignorant of the mutinous disposition of his crew; but he still maintained a serene and steady countenance, soothing some with gentle words, endeavoring to stimulate the pride or avarice of others, and openly menacing the refractory with signal punishment, should they do any thing to impede the voyage.

On the 25th of September, the wind again became favorable, and they were able to resume their course directly to the west. The airs being light, and the sea calm, the vessels sailed near to each other, and Columbus had much conversation with Martin Alonzo Pinzon on the subject of a chart, which the former had sent three days before on board of the *Pinta*. Pinzon thought that, according to the indications of the map, they ought to be in the neighborhood of Cipango, and the other islands which the admiral had therein delineated. Columbus partly entertained the same idea, but thought it possible that the ships might have been borne out of their track by the prevalent currents, or that they had not come so far as the pilots had reckoned. He desired that the chart might be returned, and Pinzon tying it to the end of a cord, flung it on board to him. While Columbus, his pilot, and several of his experienced mariners were studying the map, and endeavoring to make out from it their actual position, they heard a shout from the *Pinta*, and looking up, beheld Martin Alonzo Pinzon mounted on the stern of his vessel, crying "Land! land! Señor, I claim my reward!" He pointed at the same time to the southwest, where there was indeed an appearance of land at about twenty-five leagues' distance. Upon this Columbus threw himself on his knees and returned thanks to God; and Martin Alonzo repeated the *Gloria in excelsis*, in which he was joined by his own crew and that of the admiral.

The seamen now mounted to the masthead or climbed about the rigging, straining their eyes in the direction pointed out. The conviction became so general of land in that quarter, and the joy of the people so ungovernable, that Columbus found it necessary to vary from his usual course, and stand all night to the southwest. The morning light, however, put an end to all their hopes, as to a dream. The fancied land proved to be nothing but an evening cloud, and had vanished in the night. With dejected hearts they once more resumed their western course, from which Columbus would never have varied, but in compliance with their clamorous wishes.

For several days they continued on with the same propitious breeze, tranquil sea, and mild, delightful weather. The water was so calm that the sailors amused themselves with swimming about the vessel. Dolphins began to abound, and flying fish, darting into the air, fell upon the decks. The continued signs of land diverted the attention of the crews, and insensibly beguiled them onward.

On the 1st of October, according to the reckoning of the pilot of the admiral's ship, they had come five hundred and eighty leagues west since leaving the Canary islands. The reckoning which Columbus showed the crew, was five hundred and eighty-four, but the reckoning which he kept privately, was seven hundred and seven. On the following day, the weeds floated from east to west; and on the third day no birds were to be seen.

The crews now began to fear that they had passed between islands, from one to the other of which the birds had been flying. Columbus had also some doubts of the kind, but refused to alter his westward course. The people again uttered murmurs and menaces; but on the following day they were visited by such flights of birds, and the various indications of land became so numerous, that from a state of despondency they passed to one of confident expectation.

Eager to obtain the promised pension, the seamen were continually giving the cry of land, on the least appearance of the kind. To put a stop to these false alarms, which produced continual disappointments, Columbus declared that should any one give such notice, and land not be discovered within three days afterwards, he should thenceforth forfeit all claim to the reward.

On the evening of the 6th of October, Martin Alonzo Pinzon began to lose confidence in their present course, and proposed that they should stand more to the southward. Columbus, however, still persisted in steering directly west. Observing the difference of opinion in a person so important in his squadron as Pinzon, and fearing that chance or design might scatter the ships, he ordered that, should either of the caravels be separated from him, it should stand to the west, and endeavor as soon as possible to join company again: he directed, also, that the vessels should keep near to him at sunrise and sunset, as at these times the state of the atmosphere is most favorable to the discovery of distant land.

On the morning of the 7th of October, at sunrise, several of the admiral's crew thought they beheld land in the west, but so indistinctly that no one ventured to proclaim it, lest he should be mistaken, and forfeit all chance of the reward: the *Niña*, however, being a good sailer, pressed forward to ascertain the fact. In a little while a flag was hoisted at her masthead, and a gun discharged, being the preconcerted signals for land. New joy was awakened throughout the little squadron, and every eye was turned to the west. As they advanced, however, their cloud-built hopes faded away, and before evening the fancied land had again melted into air.

The crews now sank into a degree of dejection proportioned to their recent excitement; but new circumstances occurred to arouse them. Columbus, having observed great flights of small field-birds going towards the southwest, concluded they must be secure of some neighboring land, where they would find food and a resting-place. He knew the importance which the Portuguese voyagers attached to the flight of birds, by following which they had discovered most of their islands. He had now come seven hundred and fifty leagues, the distance at which he had computed to find the island of Cipango; as there was no appearance of it, he might have missed it through some mistake in the latitude. He determined, therefore, on the evening of the 7th of October to alter his course to the west-southwest, the direction in which the birds generally flew, and continue that direction for at least two days. After all, it was no great deviation from his main course, and would meet the wishes of the Pinzons, as well as be inspiriting to his followers generally.

For three days they stood in this direction, and the further they went the more frequent and encouraging were the signs of land. Flights of small birds of various colors, some of them such as sing in the fields, came flying about the ships, and then continued towards the southwest, and others were heard also flying by in the night. Tunny fish played about the smooth sea, and a heron, a pelican, and a duck, were seen, all bound in the same direction. The herbage which floated by was fresh and green, as if recently from land, and the air, Columbus observed, was sweet and fragrant as April breezes in Seville.

All these, however, were regarded by the crews as so many delusions beguiling them on to destruction; and when on the evening of the third day they beheld the sun go down upon a shoreless ocean, they broke forth into turbulent clamor. They exclaimed against this obstinacy in tempting fate by continuing on into a boundless sea. They insisted upon turning homeward, and abandoning the voyage as hopeless. Columbus endeavored to pacify them by gentle words and promises of large rewards; but finding that they only increased in clamor, he assumed a decided tone. He told them it was useless to murmur; the expedition had been sent by the sovereigns to seek the Indies, and, happen what might, he was determined to persevere, until, by the blessing of God, he should accomplish the enterprise.

Columbus was now at open defiance with his crew, and his situation became desperate. Fortunately the manifestations of the vicinity of land were such on the following day as no longer to admit a doubt. Besides a quantity of fresh weeds, such as grow in rivers, they saw a green fish of a kind which keeps about rocks; then a branch of thorn with berries on it, and recently separated from the tree, floated by them; then they picked up a reed, a small board, and, above all, a staff artificially carved. All gloom and mutiny now gave way to sanguine expectation; and throughout the day each one was eagerly on the watch, in hopes of being the first to discover the long-sought-for land.

In the evening, when, according to invariable custom on board of the admiral's ship, the mariners had sung the *salve regina*, or vesper hymn to the Virgin, he made an impressive address to his crew. He pointed out the goodness of God in thus conducting them by soft and favoring breezes across a tranquil ocean, cheering their hopes continually with fresh signs, increasing as their fears augmented, and thus leading and guiding them to a promised land. He now reminded them of the orders he had given on leaving the Canaries, that, after sailing westward seven hundred leagues, they should not make sail after midnight. Present appearances authorized such a precaution. He thought it probable they would make land that very night; he ordered, therefore, a vigilant lookout to be kept from the forecastle, promising to whomsoever should make the discovery, a doublet of velvet, in addition to the pension to be given by the sovereigns.

The breeze had been fresh all day, with more sea than usual, and they had made great progress. At sunset they had stood again to the west, and were ploughing the waves at a rapid rate, the *Pinta* keeping the lead, from her superior sailing. The greatest animation prevailed throughout the ships; not an eye was closed that night. As the evening darkened, Columbus took his station on the top of the castle or cabin on the high poop of his vessel, ranging his eye along the dusky horizon, and maintaining an intense and unremitting watch. About ten o'clock, he thought he beheld a light glimmering at a great distance. Fearing his eager hopes might deceive him, he called to Pedro Gutierrez, gentleman of the king's bedchamber, and inquired whether he saw such a light; the latter replied in the affirmative. Doubtful whether it might not yet be some delusion of the fancy, Columbus called Rodrigo Sanchez of Segovia, and made the same inquiry. By the time the latter had ascended the roundhouse, the light had disappeared. They saw it once or twice afterwards in sudden and passing gleams; as if it were a torch in the bark of a fisherman, rising and sinking with the waves; or in the hand of some person on shore, borne up and down as he walked from house to house. So transient and uncertain were these gleams, that few attached any importance to them; Columbus, however, considered them as certain signs of land, and moreover, that the land was inhabited.

They continued their course until two in the morning, when a gun from the *Pinta* gave the joyful signal of land. It was first descried by a mariner named Rodrigo de Triana; but the reward was afterwards adjudged to the admiral, for having previously perceived the light. The land was now clearly seen about two leagues distant, whereupon they took in sail, and laid to, waiting impatiently for the dawn.

The thoughts and feelings of Columbus in this little space of time must have been tumultuous and intense. At length in spite of every difficulty and danger, he had accomplished his object. The great mystery of the ocean was revealed; his theory, which had been the scoff of sages, was triumphantly established; he had secured to himself a glory durable as the world itself.

It is difficult to conceive the feelings of such a man, at such a moment; or the conjectures which must have thronged upon his mind, as to the land before him, covered with darkness. That it was fruitful, was evident from the vegetables which floated from its shores. He thought, too, that he perceived the fragrance of aromatic groves. The moving light he had beheld proved it the residence of man. But what were its inhabitants? Were they like those of the other parts of the globe; or were they some strange and monstrous race, such as the imagination was prone in those times to give to all remote and unknown regions? Had he come upon some wild island far in the Indian sea; or was this the famed Cipango itself, the object of his golden fancies? A thousand speculations of the kind must have swarmed upon him, as, with his anxious crews, he waited for the night to pass away; wondering whether the morning light would reveal a savage wilderness, or dawn upon spicy groves, and glittering fanes, and gilded cities, and all the splendor of oriental civilization.

1828

1794 ~ *William Cullen Bryant* ~ 1878

BRYANT is usually placed, for reasons of convenience, with his contemporaries Irving and Cooper in the New York group of writers (1815–1837), though he was essentially a product of New England environment and influences, and his best work as a poet was done before his removal to New York in 1825. His first thirty years, except a few months, were spent in the beautiful wooded Berkshire Hills region of western Massachusetts, where he was born on a farm in Cummington. At first a frail child, his precocious mind developed in an atmosphere of Calvinism and Federalism, modified by his own romantic devotion to the beauties of nature in his neighborhood. His father, Dr. Peter Bryant, physician of the town, a man of great physical and intellectual vigor, taught him to recognize the plants and herbs of the vicinity and their qualities, and encouraged his growing love of poetry. From the age of nine he wrote verses, first in the couplets of Pope, including *The Embargo, or a Sketch of the Times*, an ill-natured satire on Jefferson, which his proud father caused to be published in Boston in 1808. Later came acquaintance with the poetry of Thomson, Burns, Cowper, and the mid-eighteenth-century "graveyard poets."

After finishing at the Cummington school in 1808, he studied Latin and New Testament Greek with clergymen at North Brookfield and Plainfield, and entered the sophomore class at Williams College in 1811. His year there served chiefly to relax his Calvinism through acquaintance with the Greek poets and with French deistic views held by some of the students. Both influences are evident in his first draft of "Thanatopsis," written in the fall of 1811. Disappointed in his hope of transferring to Yale, Bryant spent the next four years in study in lawyers' offices in Worthington and Bridgewater, where he was admitted to the bar in August, 1815. Still a Federalist and opposed to the War of 1812, he volunteered for service in the militia, in expectation of being called upon to defend Massachusetts if she should secede from the Union. After a year in Plainfield, near home, he settled in Great Barrington for nine years' law practice, pursued successfully but with increasing distaste for the profession.

Recognition as a poet came in 1817, when his father gave to the editors of the new *North American Review* the manuscripts of "Thanatopsis" and "To a Waterfowl." After some incredulousness that so fine a poem as the former could be the work of an American, they printed it in the September issue. "To a Waterfowl" appeared in the *Review* in April, 1818, and the essay "Early American Poetry," decrying imitativeness and feebleness in American verse writers, in July. Further recognition came in the invitation to read the Phi Beta Kappa poem—"The Ages" —at Harvard in 1821. This was also the year of his first serious volume of verse, *Poems*, and of his marriage to Frances Fairchild, "fairest of the rural maids." His most creative period as a poet was 1824–1825, when he was actively writing for the *United States Literary Gazette*, of Boston. He had long desired to settle in that city, but in 1825, through the influence of the Sedgwick family, he accepted the co-editorship of the *New York Review* and of the reorganized *United States Review and Literary Gazette*, at New York. Two years later he became assistant editor of the *New York Evening Post* and in 1829 its editor, continuing, with a share in its ownership, for nearly fifty years. He had long since discarded Federalism for a democratic liberalism, and Calvinism for a conservative type of Unitarianism. Under his hand the *Evening Post* became one of the best and most influential of American newspapers. In its pages he advocated freedom of speech, free trade, the right of collective bargaining in labor, and the liberation of subject peoples abroad and of the slaves at home. The *Post* supported the Democratic administrations from Jackson to Pierce. When slavery became a paramount issue, Bryant joined the newly organized Republican party in 1855, helped to elect Lincoln, assailed the Southern seceders as traitors, and urged vigorous prosecution of the war. Later he retained his Republican affiliation, despite his objection to harsh reconstruction measures, the corruptness of the Grant administration, and his personal sympathy for Samuel J. Tilden.

In the editor, the poet was soon submerged, though Bryant retained his loyalty to verse, lectured on poets and poetry, and enjoyed an undimmed reputation as the first American to win achievement in that field. In his own output there was neither advance nor decline in quality. Occasionally, as in "The Prairies" (1832), celebrating his first trip to the West, "The Battlefield" (1842), and "The Death of Lincoln" (1865), he equalled his better earlier performances. His last long poem,

"The Flood of Years," in 1878, is the same kind of sober survey in noble blank verse as "The Ages" in 1821.

After 1832 he traveled extensively in America and abroad, somewhat enlarging the geographical scope of his poetry. Following the death of his wife in 1866, he turned seriously to a project, begun by 1863, of translating the *Iliad* and *Odyssey* into English blank verse. The two works, published in 1870 and 1872, respectively, are sometimes regarded as the most successful English versions of the Homeric epics. Though a wealthy man in his later life, he lived simply and retained his physical vigor beyond his eightieth year. His death on June 12, 1878, was hastened by exposure to the sun while delivering an address on the Italian patriot, Mazzini, in Central Park, New York.

Bryant's chief literary distinction is as a poet of unusual dignity and evenness in versification, and nobility and eloquence in language, dealing with a few elemental themes such as the beauty and harmony of nature, the sacredness of human freedom, the flow and ebb of human existence, and the power and beneficence of God. His realm is somewhat narrow, but he is supreme in it. As the first poet of his nation to earn distinction, his direct influence upon younger writers was naturally strong. Such early blank verse poems as Longfellow's "The Spirit of Poetry," Emerson's "The River," and Whittier's "The Past and Coming Year" attest this influence, sometimes needlessly attributed to Wordsworth. More important than any specific influence, however, is perhaps the general effect of his mastery of a wide range of metrical forms and the uniform high level of his technical excellence upon American versifiers, in a time of romantic stress upon inspired ideas rather than care for form.

Much of the course of development of English poetry is reflected in Bryant's career. Starting under the influence of Pope and the Augustans, he passed through that of the pre-romantics, Thomson, Cowper, Blair, and Kirke White, then emulated Byron and later felt the maturing influence of the kindred spirit of the Wordsworth of "Tintern Abbey" and the "Lucy" poems. In his most productive period, the middle 1820's, he was a versatile and almost exuberant romanticist, even exploring, like Irving, the realms of the German school of terror in such poems as "The Murdered Traveller." After 1835 he passed on to the more subdued romanticism of the Victorians, producing mostly serious, reflective, and generalizing poems like the noble "The Antiquity of Freedom," "The Death of Lincoln," and "The Poet." First and last, Bryant published a considerable amount of literary criticism, including his early essay "On the Use of Trisyllabic Feet in Iambic Verse" (1811), his review, "Early American Verse" (1818), his four "Lectures on Poetry" (1825), and editorial utterances in the *United States Literary Gazette*, the *Evening Post*, and his collections, *Selections from the American Poets* (1840), and *A Library of Poetry and Song* (1870). In all of these, the romantic theory is presented. He believed in originality rather than imitation. He maintained, in his "Lectures on Poetry," that the imagination—the "restless faculty . . . which is ever wandering from the combination of ideas directly presented to it to other combinations of its own"—and the emotions are the primary concerns of the literary artist.

In poetic practice, according to H. H. Clark, his chief tenets were (1) avoiding a "sickly and affected imitation" of the neo-classical poets of England, (2) avoiding affectations and conceits in language, (3) a preference for "a luminous style," (4) "a balanced harmony of emotion, understanding, and imagination," (5) images taken directly from nature, (6) a discriminating observation of the achievements and defects of other poets, (7) emphasis on the short lyric, (8) variation of meter, (9) concern with spiritual elevation and ethical beauty and elemental and universal themes. Genuine romanticist though he was in feeling, Bryant had a large share of the true classicist's appreciation of the value of restraint, dignity, and perfection of utterance.

Between 1827 and 1832, under the general influence of Irving's successes, Bryant tried his hand at a number of narrative sketches, but wisely decided to abandon this field, for which his imagination was not adapted. His other prose, largely in the form of editorials, critical essays, and travel sketches, shows the same sterling qualities of clearness, dignity, directness, and careful diction which distinguished his verse.

The Poetical Works of William Cullen Bryant (1876), supervised by Bryant, is the best edition of the poems included. The Poetical Works of William Cullen Bryant (2 vols., 1882, issued as vols. 3–4 of the Life and Writings) contains numerous other poems, with helpful notes by Parke Godwin. The Roslyn Edition of the Poetical Works (1903) is the best one-volume edition. It contains a memoir by R. H. Stoddard and the bibliography of H. C. Sturges (see below). The Prose Writings of William Cullen Bryant (2 vols., 1884, issued as vols. 5–6 of the Life and Writings) comprises essays, tales, addresses, editorials, travel sketches, and literary criticisms, edited by Parke Godwin. William Cullen Bryant: Representative Selections, by Tremaine McDowell (1935), contains—besides an excellent interpretative introduction, notes, and a bibliography brought up to date—a number of uncollected and unpublished poems and prose pieces.

Parke Godwin's A Biography of William Cullen Bryant, with Extracts from his Private Correspondence (1883), published as vols. 1 and 2 of the Life and Writings, is the standard biography. John Bigelow's William Cullen Bryant, American Men of Letters Series (1890), is based on personal association with Bryant as editor and man of affairs. See also W. A. Bradley, William Cullen Bryant, English Men of Letters Series (1905); G. W. Curtis, The Life, Character, and Writings of William Cullen Bryant (1879); Rica Brenner, Twelve American Poets before 1900 (1933), 23–47; "Bryant and the Sedgwick Family," Americana, XXXI, 626–38 (Oct., 1937); and "William Cullen Bryant and Fanny Wright," American Literature, VI, 427–32 (Jan., 1935); and a notable series of articles on Bryant's early life by Tremaine McDowell: "The Ancestry of William Cullen Bryant," Americana, XXII, 408–20 (Oct., 1928); "Cullen Bryant Prepares for College," South Atlantic Quarterly, XXX, 125–33 (April, 1931); "Cullen Bryant at Williams

College," *New England Quarterly*, I, 443–66 (Oct., 1928); "William Cullen Bryant and Yale," *New England Quarterly*, III, 706–16 (Oct., 1930); and "Bryant and the *North American Review*," *American Literature*, I, 14–26 (March, 1929).

Particularly useful general or specialized criticisms are Tremaine McDowell, introduction to *Bryant*, American Writers Series (1935), xiii–lxviii, a comprehensive treatment of the chief aspects of Bryant's work; and "Bryant's Practice in Composition and Revision," *PMLA*, LII, 474–502 (June, 1937); C. I. Glicksberg, "William Cullen Bryant, a Reinterpretation," *Revue Anglo-Américaine*, XI, 495–504 (Aug., 1934); G. W. Allen, *American Prosody* (1935), 27–55, on Bryant's verse; W. B. Cairns, *British Criticisms of American Writings, 1815–1833* (1922), 158–64 and *passim*, for contemporary criticism; Norman Foerster, *Nature in American Literature* (1923), 1–19, an excellent discussion of this subject; Allen Nevins, *The Evening Post: A Century of Journalism* (1922), indispensable for Bryant as an editor; and V. L. Parrington, *The Romantic Revolution in American Literature* (1927), 238–46, Bryant as a social and political liberal. See also contemporary judgments by Poe in the *Southern Literary Messenger* (Jan., 1837), *Burton's Gentleman's Magazine* (May, 1840), and *Godey's Lady's Book* (April, 1846); John Wilson in *Blackwood's* (April, 1832); the attacks by Harriet Monroe in *Poetry*, VI, 197–200 (July, 1915) and *Dial*, LIX, 314–15 and 479–80 (Oct. 14 and Nov. 25, 1915), and defense by J. L. Hervey, *Dial*, LIX, 92–3, 361–3, and 555–7 (Aug. 15, Oct. 28, and Dec. 9, 1915); studies of "Thanatopsis" by Carl Van Doren in the *Nation*, CI, 432–3 (Oct. 7, 1915) and by W. F. Johnson, *North American Review*, CCXXIV, 556–72 (Nov., 1927); the *CHAL* article on Bryant by W. E. Leonard, I, 260–78; and G. P. Voigt, *The Religious and Ethical Element in the Major American Poets* (1925), 13–27, an analysis of Bryant's religion.

From THE EMBARGO
OR SKETCHES OF THE TIMES

Bryant's boyhood satire on Jefferson, the sentiments of which he later disclaimed, gives evidence of his early mastery of the heroic couplet, of the inherited Federalist political views he held at that time, and the intolerant character of the anti-Jeffersonian campaigns.

BUT quit thy meaner game, indignant Muse,
And to thy country turn thy nobler views;
Ill-fated clime, condemned to feel th' extremes
Of a weak ruler's philosophic dreams;
Driven headlong on to ruin's fateful brink,
When will thy country feel—when will she think!
Satiric Muse, shall injured Commerce weep
Her ravished rights, and will thy thunders sleep;
Dart thy keen glances, knit thy threat'ning brows,
Call fire from heaven to blast thy country's foes.   10
Oh! let a youth thine inspiration learn—
Oh! give him, "words that breathe and thoughts that burn.". . .

E'en while I sing, see Faction urge her claim,
Mislead with falsehood, and with zeal inflame;
Lift her black banner, spread her empire wide,
And stalk triumphant with a Fury's stride.
She blows her brazen trump, and at the sound,
A motley throng, obedient, flock around;
A mist of changing hue o'er all she flings,
And darkness perches on her dragon wings! 20
As Johnson deep, as Addison refined,
And skill'd to pour conviction o'er the mind,
Oh might some patriot rise! the gloom dispel,
Chase Error's mist, and break her magic spell!

But vain the wish, for hark! the murmuring need
Of hoarse applause from yonder shed proceed;
Enter and view the thronging concourse there,
Intent, with gaping mouth and stupid stare;
While in their midst, their supple leader stands,
Harangues aloud, and flourishes his hands; 30
To adulation turns his servile throat,
And sues, successful, for each blockhead's vote. . . .

And thou, the scorn of every patriot name,
Thy country's ruin and thy council's shame!
Poor servile thing! derision of the brave!
Who erst from Tarleton fled to Carter's cave;
Thou, who, when menaced by perfidious
    Gaul,
Didst prostrate to her whisker'd minion fall;
And when our cash her empty bags supplied,
Didst meanly strive the foul disgrace to hide;

Go, wretch, resign the presidential chair, 41
Disclose thy secret measures, foul or fair.
Go, search with curious eyes for horned frogs,
Mid the wild wastes of Louisianian bogs;
Or, where the Ohio rolls his turbid stream,
Dig for huge bones, thy glory and thy theme.
Go, scan, Philosophist, thy Sally's charms,
And sink supinely in her sable arms;
But quit to abler hands the helm of state.

                1808

THANATOPSIS

The first column below and on pp. 187–8 contains the original version of "Thanatopsis" as it appeared in the *North American Review*, September, 1817. The four quatrains with which the original version begins obviously deal with the same theme as the ensuing blank verse, but may not have been intended to go with it. See Carl Van Doren, "The Growth of Thanatopsis," *Nation*, CI, 432–433 (Oct. 7, 1915).

Not that from life, and all its woes
The hand of death shall set me free;
Not that this head, shall then repose
In the low vale most peacefully.

Ah, when I touch time's farthest brink,
A kinder solace must attend;
It chills my very soul, to think
On that dread hour when life must end.

In vain the flatt'ring verse may breathe,
Of ease from pain, and rest from strife, 10
There is a sacred dread of death
Inwoven with the strings of life.

This bitter cup at first was given
When angry *justice* frown'd severe,
And 'tis th' eternal doom of heaven
That man must view the grave with fear.

—————Yet a few days, and thee,
The all-beholding sun, shall see no more,
In all his course; nor yet in the cold ground,
Where thy pale form was laid, with many
    tears, 20
Nor in th' embrace of ocean shall exist
Thy image. Earth, that nourished thee, shall
    claim
Thy growth, to be resolv'd to earth again;

THANATOPSIS

The revised version of "Thanatopsis," as it appeared in Bryant's *Poems* (1821), is printed in this second column. Whereas the original version was a subjective poem, Bryant's added introduction in the revision puts the discussion of death in the mouth of Nature. Aside from a remote suggestion of immortality in lines 77–78 of the new conclusion, the poem still contains no essential elements of Christianity.

To him who in the love of Nature holds
Communion with her visible forms, she speaks
A various language; for his gayer hours
She has a voice of gladness, and a smile
And eloquence of beauty, and she glides
Into his darker musings, with a mild
And healing sympathy, that steals away
Their sharpness, ere he is aware. When
    thoughts
Of the last bitter hour come like a blight
Over thy spirit, and sad images 10
Of the stern agony, and shroud, and pall,
And breathless darkness, and the narrow
    house,
Make thee to shudder, and grow sick at
    heart,—
Go forth, under the open sky, and list
To Nature's teachings, while from all around—
Earth and her waters, and the depths of air,—
Comes a still voice—

            Yet a few days, and thee
The all-beholding sun shall see no more
In all his course; nor yet in the cold ground,
Where thy pale form was laid, with many
    tears, 20
Nor in the embrace of ocean, shall exist
Thy image. Earth, that nourished thee, shall
    claim
Thy growth, to be resolved to earth again,

And, lost each human trace, surrend'ring up
Thine individual being, shalt thou go
To mix forever with the elements,
To be a brother to th' insensible rock
And to the sluggish clod, which the rude
   swain
Turns with his share, and treads upon. The
   oak
Shall send his roots abroad, and pierce thy
   mould. 30

Yet not to thy eternal resting place
Shalt thou retire alone—nor couldst thou wish
Couch more magnificent. Thou shalt lie down
With patriarchs of the infant world—with
   kings
The powerful of the earth—the wise, the good,
Fair forms, and hoary seers of ages past,
All in one mighty sepulchre.—The hills,
Rock-ribb'd and ancient as the sun,—the vales
Stretching in pensive quietness between;
The venerable woods—the floods that move
In majesty,—and the complaining brooks, 41
That wind among the meads, and make them
   green,
Are but the solemn decorations all,
Of the great tomb of man.—The golden
   sun,
The planets, all the infinite host of heaven
Are glowing on the sad abodes of death,
Through the still lapse of ages. All that tread
The globe are but a handful to the tribes
That slumber in its bosom.—Take the
   wings 49
Of morning—and the Borean desert[1] pierce—
Or lose thyself in the continuous woods
That veil Oregan,[2] where he hears no sound
Save his own dashings—yet—the dead are
   there,
And millions in those solitudes, since first
The flight of years began, have laid them down
In their last sleep—the dead reign there
   alone.—
So shalt thou rest—and what if thou shalt fall
Unnoticed by the living—and no friend 58
Take note of thy departure? Thousands more
Will share thy destiny.—The tittering world
Dance to the grave. The busy brood of care
Plod on, and each one chases as before

---

1 the Arctic wastes   2 really the Columbia: apparently pronounced like O'Regan by the boy poet

---

And, lost each human trace, surrendering up
Thine individual being, shalt thou go
To mix forever with the elements,
To be a brother to the insensible rock
And to the sluggish clod, which the rude
   swain
Turns with his share, and treads upon. The
   oak
Shall send his roots abroad, and pierce thy
   mould. 30

Yet not to thine eternal resting-place
Shalt thou retire alone, nor couldst thou wish
Couch more magnificent. Thou shalt lie down
With patriarchs of the infant world, with
   kings,
The powerful of the earth, the wise, the good,
Fair forms, and hoary seers of ages past,
All in one mighty sepulchre. The hills
Rock-ribbed and ancient as the sun, the vales
Stretching in pensive quietness between;
The venerable woods, rivers that move 40
In majesty, and the complaining brooks
That make the meadows green; and, poured
   round all,
Old Ocean's gray and melancholy waste,—
Are but the solemn decorations all
Of the great tomb of man. The golden sun,
The planets, all the infinite host of heaven,
Are shining on the sad abodes of death,
Through the still lapse of ages. All that tread
The globe are but a handful to the tribes
That slumber in its bosom.—Take the
   wings 50
Of morning, pierce the Barcan wilderness,
Or lose thyself in the continuous woods
Where rolls the Oregon, and hears no sound,
Save his own dashings—yet the dead are
   there:
And millions in those solitudes, since first
The flight of years began, have laid them down
In their last sleep—the dead reign there alone.
So shalt thou rest, and what if thou withdraw
In silence from the living, and no friend 59
Take note of thy departure? All that breathe
Will share thy destiny. The gay will laugh
When thou art gone, the solemn brood of care
Plod on, and each one as before will chase
His favorite phantom; yet all these shall leave
Their mirth and their employments, and shall
   come

His favourite phantom.—Yet all these shall
　　leave
Their mirth and their employments, and shall
　　come
And make their bed with thee!————[1]

1811　　　　　　　　　　　　　　　　　　*1817*

[1] Note that the poem was first written to suggest a
fragment, a favorite early device in Bryant's poetry. See
footnote to the conclusion of "Inscription for the Entrance to a Wood," p. 190.

And make their bed with thee. As the long train
Of ages glide away, the sons of men,
The youth in life's green spring, and he who
　　goes
In the full strength of years, matron and maid,
The speechless babe, and the gray-headed
　　man—　　　　　　　　　　　　　　　　70
Shall one by one be gathered to thy side,
By those, who in their turn shall follow them.

　So live, that when thy summons comes to
　　join
The innumerable caravan, which moves
To that mysterious realm, where each shall take
His chamber in the silent halls of death,
Thou go not, like the quarry-slave at night,
Scourged to his dungeon, but, sustained and
　　soothed　　　　　　　　　　　　　　78
By an unfaltering trust, approach thy grave,
Like one who wraps the drapery of his couch
About him, and lies down to pleasant dreams.

1811, 1821　　　　　　　　　　　　　　*1821*

THE YELLOW VIOLET

"The Yellow Violet" is one of the best examples
in Bryant's early work of the attempt to mix neo-
classical didacticism and formal circumlocutions—
"the genial hour" and "painted tribes of light"—
with real and appreciative description of the flowers and woods of Cummington.

WHEN beechen buds begin to swell,
　　And woods the bluebird's warble know,
The yellow violet's modest bell
　　Peeps from the last year's leaves below.

Ere russet fields their green resume,
　　Sweet flower, I love, in forest bare,
To meet thee, when thy faint perfume
　　Alone is in the virgin air.

Of all her train, the hands of Spring
　　First plant thee in the watery mold,　10
And I have seen thee blossoming
　　Beside the snow-bank's edges cold.

Thy parent sun, who bade thee view
　　Pale skies, and chilling moisture sip,
Has bathed thee in his own bright hue,
　　And streaked with jet thy glowing lip.

Yet slight thy form, and low thy seat,
　　And earthward bent thy gentle eye,
Unapt the passing view to meet,
　　When loftier flowers are flaunting nigh.　20

Oft, in the sunless April day,
　　Thy early smile has stayed my walk;
But midst the gorgeous blooms of May,
　　I passed thee on thy humble stalk.

So they who climb to wealth forget
　　The friends in darker fortunes tried.
I copied them—but I regret
　　That I should ape the ways of pride.

And when again the genial hour
　　Awakes the painted tribes of light,　30
I'll not o'erlook the modest flower
　　That made the woods of April bright.

1814　　　　　　　　　　　　　　　　*1821*

TO A WATERFOWL

Written at the end of a December day at Plainfield. While walking thither in a disconsolate frame
of mind to inquire about prospects of practicing
law there, he saw the flight of the solitary bird

against "one of those brilliant seas of chrysolite and opal which often flood the New England skies" (Godwin, *Biography*, I, 143–144). The student, in seeking an answer to the question why Matthew Arnold should have considered this the finest short poem in the English language, would do well to examine the means by which Bryant secures the effect of great space in his picture.

WHITHER, midst falling dew,
While glow the heavens with the last steps of
    day,
Far, through their rosy depths, dost thou
    pursue
      Thy solitary way?

      Vainly the fowler's eye
Might mark thy distant flight to do thee
    wrong,
As, darkly seen against the crimson sky,
      Thy figure floats along.

      Seek'st thou the plashy brink
Of weedy lake, or marge of river wide,   10
Or where the rocking billows rise and sink
      On the chafed ocean-side?

      There is a Power whose care
Teaches thy way along that pathless coast—
The desert and illimitable air—
      Lone wandering, but not lost.

      All day thy wings have fanned,
At that far height, the cold, thin atmosphere,
Yet stoop not, weary, to the welcome land,
      Though the dark night is near.   20

      And soon that toil shall end;
Soon shalt thou find a summer home, and rest,
And scream among thy fellows; reeds shall
    bend,
      Soon, o'er thy sheltered nest.

      Thou'rt gone, the abyss of heaven
Hath swallowed up thy form; yet, on my heart
Deeply hath sunk the lesson thou hast given,
      And shall not soon depart.

      He who, from zone to zone,
Guides through the boundless sky thy certain
    flight,   30
In the long way that I must tread alone
      Will lead my steps aright.

1815   1818

INSCRIPTION FOR THE ENTRANCE TO A WOOD

STRANGER, if thou hast learned a truth which
    needs
No school of long experience, that the world
Is full of guilt and misery, and hast seen
Enough of all its sorrows, crimes, and cares,
To tire thee of it, enter this wild wood
And view the haunts of Nature. The calm
    shade
Shall bring a kindred calm; and the sweet
    breeze,
That makes the green leaves dance, shall waft
    a balm
To thy sick heart.[1] Thou wilt find nothing
    here
Of all that pained thee in the haunts of men 10
And made thee loathe thy life. The primal
    curse [2]
Fell, it is true, upon the unsinning earth,
But not in vengeance. God hath yoked to
    guilt
Her pale tormentor, misery. Hence, these
    shades
Are still the abodes of gladness; the thick roof
Of green and stirring branches is alive
And musical with birds, that sing and sport
In wantonness of spirit; while, below,
The squirrel, with raised paws and form erect,
Chirps merrily. Throngs of insects in the
    shade   20
Try their thin wings and dance in the warm
    beam
That waked them into life. Even the green
    trees
Partake the deep contentment; as they bend
To the soft winds, the sun from the blue
    sky
Looks in and sheds a blessing on the scene.
Scarce less the cleft-born wild-flower seems to
    enjoy
Existence, than the wingèd plunderer
That sucks its sweets. The mossy rocks them-
    selves,

[1] Compare with lines 6–11 the passage in Wordsworth's "Lines Composed a Few Miles above Tintern Abbey," lines 22–31.   [2] Bryant said that as a young man he still supposed Calvinism "to be the accepted belief of the religious world." See Tremaine McDowell, "The Juvenile Verse of William Cullen Bryant," *Studies in Philology*, XXVI, 99–101.

And the old and ponderous trunks of pros-
trate trees
That lead from knoll to knoll a causey rude   30
Or bridge the sunken brook, and their dark
roots,
With all their earth upon them, twisting high,
Breathe fixed tranquillity. The rivulet
Sends forth glad sounds, and, tripping o'er its
bed
Of pebbly sands, or leaping down the rocks,
Seems with continuous laughter to rejoice
In its own being. Softly tread the marge,
Lest from her midway perch thou scare the
wren
That dips her bill in water.[1] The cool wind,
That stirs the stream in play, shall come to
thee,   40
Like one that loves thee nor will let thee
pass
Ungreeted, and shall give its light embrace.
1815   1817

I CANNOT FORGET WITH WHAT
FERVID DEVOTION

I CANNOT forget with what fervid devotion
    I worshiped the visions of verse and of
        fame;
Each gaze at the glories of earth, sky, and
        ocean,
    To my kindled emotions, was wind over
        flame.

And deep were my musings in life's early
        blossom,
    'Mid the twilight of mountain groves wan-
        dering along;
How thrilled my young veins, and how
        throbbed my full bosom,
    When o'er me descended the spirit of song!

'Mong the deep-cloven fells that for ages had
        listened
    To the rush of the pebble-paved river be-
        tween,   10
Where the kingfisher screamed and gray preci-
        pice glistened,
    All breathless with awe have I gazed on the
        scene;

[1] The earliest published version of the poem ended at
this point.

Till I felt the dark power o'er my reveries
        stealing,
    From the gloom of the thicket that over me
        hung,
And the thoughts that awoke, in that rapture
        of feeling,
    Were formed into verse as they rose to my
        tongue.

Bright visions! I mixed with the world, and ye
        faded,
    No longer your pure rural worshiper now;
In the haunts your continual presence per-
        vaded,
    Ye shrink from the signet of care on my
        brow.   20

In the old mossy groves on the breast of the
        mountains,
    In deep lonely glens where the waters com-
        plain,
By the shade of the rock, by the gush of the
        fountain,
    I seek your loved footsteps, but seek them
        in vain.

Oh, leave not forlorn and forever forsaken,
    Your pupil and victim to life and its tears!
But sometimes return, and in mercy awaken
    The glories ye showed to his earlier years.
1815   1826

GREEN RIVER

WHEN breezes are soft and skies are fair,
I steal an hour from study and care,
And hie me away to the woodland scene,
Where wanders the stream with waters of
        green,
As if the bright fringe of herbs on its brink
Had given their stain to the wave they drink;
And they, whose meadows it murmurs
        through,
Have named the stream from its own fair hue.

Yet pure its waters—its shallows are bright
With colored pebbles and sparkles of light,   10
And clear the depths where its eddies play,
And dimples deepen and whirl away,
And the plane-tree's speckled arms o'er-
        shoot
The swifter current that mines its root,

Through whose shifting leaves, as you walk
    the hill,
The quivering glimmer of sun and rill
With a sudden flash on the eye is thrown,
Like the ray that streams from the diamond-
    stone.
Oh, loveliest there the spring days come,
With blossoms, and birds, and wild-bees'
    hum;   20
The flowers of summer are fairest there,
And freshest the breath of the summer air;
And sweetest the golden autumn day
In silence and sunshine glides away.

Yet, fair as thou art, thou shunnest to glide,
Beautiful stream! by the village side;
But windest away from haunts of men,
To quiet valley and shaded glen;
And forest, and meadow, and slope of hill,
Around thee, are lonely, lovely, and still, 30
Lonely—save when, by thy rippling tides,
From thicket to thicket the angler glides;
Or the simpler comes, with basket and book,
For herbs of power on thy banks to look;
Or haply, some idle dreamer, like me,
To wander, and muse, and gaze on thee,
Still—save the chirp of birds that feed
On the river cherry and seedy reed,
And thy own wild music gushing out
With mellow murmur and fairy shout,   40
From dawn to the blush of another day,
Like traveler singing along his way.

That fairy music I never hear,
Nor gaze on those waters so green and clear,
And mark them winding away from sight,
Darkened with shade or flashing with light,
While o'er them the vine to its thicket clings,
And the zephyr stoops to freshen his wings,
But I wish that fate had left me free
To wander these quiet haunts with thee, 50
Till the eating cares of earth should depart,
And the peace of the scene pass into my
    heart;
And I envy thy stream, as it glides along
Through its beautiful banks in a trance of
    song.

Though forced to drudge for the dregs of
    men,
And scrawl strange words with the barbarous
    pen,

And mingle among the jostling crowd,
Where the sons of strife are subtle and loud—
I often come to this quiet place,
To breathe the airs that ruffle thy face, 60
And gaze upon thee in silent dream,
For in thy lonely and lovely stream
An image of that calm life appears
That won my heart in my greener years.
1819   *1821*

OH FAIREST OF THE RURAL
MAIDS

Oh fairest of the rural maids!
Thy birth was in the forest shades;
Green boughs, and glimpses of the sky,
Were all that met thine infant eye.

Thy sports, thy wanderings, when a child,
Were ever in the sylvan wild;
And all the beauty of the place
Is in thy heart and on thy face.

The twilight of the trees and rocks
Is in the light shade of thy locks;   10
Thy step is as the wind, that weaves
Its playful way among the leaves.

Thine eyes are springs, in whose serene [1]
And silent waters heaven is seen;
Their lashes are the herbs that look
On their young figures in the brook.

The forest depths, by foot unpressed,
Are not more sinless than thy breast;
The holy peace, that fills the air
Of those calm solitudes, is there.   20
1820   *1832*

A WINTER PIECE

The time has been that these wild solitudes,
Yet beautiful as wild, were trod by me
Oftener than now; and when the ills of life
Had chafed my spirit, when the unsteady pulse
Beat with strange flutterings, I would wander
    forth

[1] Poe, who regarded this lyric the most highly among
all Bryant's poems, particularly praised the figure in
lines 13–14, "for appropriateness, completeness, and
every perfect beauty of which imagery is susceptible."

And seek the woods. The sunshine on my
    path
Was to me as a friend. The swelling hills,
The quiet dells retiring far between
With gentle invitation to explore
Their windings, were a calm society   10
That talked with me and soothed me. Then the
    chant
Of birds, and chime of brooks, and soft caress
Of the fresh sylvan air, made me forget
The thoughts that broke my peace; and I
    began
To gather simples by the fountain's brink,
And lose myself in daydreams. While I stood
In Nature's loneliness, I was with one
With whom I early grew familiar, one
Who never had a frown for me, whose voice
Never rebuked me for the hours I stole   20
From cares I loved not, but of which the
    world
Deems highest, to converse with her. When
    shrieked
The bleak November winds, and smote the
    woods,
And the brown fields were herbless, and the
    shades
That met above the merry rivulet
Were spoiled, I sought, I loved them still,—
    they seemed
Like old companions in adversity.
Still there was beauty in my walks; the brook,
Bordered with sparkling frostwork, was as gay
As with its fringe of summer flowers. Afar,   30
The village with its spires, the path of streams,
And dim receding valleys, hid before
By interposing trees, lay visible
Through the bare grove, and my familiar
    haunts
Seemed new to me. Nor was I slow to come
Among them, when the clouds, from their still
    skirts
Had shaken down on earth the feathery snow,
And all was white. The pure keen air abroad,
Albeit it breathed no scent of herb, nor heard
Love-call of bird nor merry hum of bee,   40
Was not the air of death. Bright mosses crept
Over the spotted trunks, and the close buds
That lay along the boughs, instinct with life,
Patient, and waiting with the soft breath of
    Spring,
Feared not the piercing spirit of the North.

The snowbird twittered on the beechen
    bough;
And 'neath the hemlock, whose thick branches
    bent
Beneath its bright cold burden, and kept dry
A circle, on the earth, of withered leaves,
The partridge found a shelter. Through the
    snow   50
The rabbit sprang away. The lighter track
Of fox, and the raccoon's broad path were
    there,
Crossing each other. From his hollow tree,
The squirrel was abroad, gathering the nuts
Just fallen, that asked the winter cold and sway
Of winter blast, to shake them from their hold.

    But winter has yet brighter scenes,—he
    boasts
Splendors beyond what gorgeous Summer
    knows,
Or Autumn, with his many fruits, and woods
All flushed with many hues. Come, when the
    rains   60
Have glazed the snow, and clothed the trees
    with ice,
While the slant sun of February pours
Into the bowers a flood of light. Approach!
The incrusted surface shall upbear thy steps,
And the broad arching portals of the grove
Welcome thy entering. Look! the massy
    trunks
Are cased in the pure crystal; each light spray,
Nodding and tinkling in the breath of heaven,
Is studded with its trembling water-drops,
That glimmer with an amethystine light.   70
But round the parent stem the long low
    boughs
Bend in a glittering ring, and arbors hide
The glassy floor. Oh! you might deem the
    spot,
The spacious cavern of some virgin mine,
Deep in the womb of earth—where the gems
    grow,
And diamonds put forth radiant rods and bud
With amethyst and topaz—and the place
Lit up, most royally, with the pure beam
That dwells in them; or haply the vast hall
Of fairy palace, that outlasts the night   80
And fades not in the glory of the sun,
Where crystal columns send forth slender
    shafts

And crossing arches, and fantastic aisles
Wind from the sight in brightness and are lost
Among the crowded pillars. Raise thine eye:
Thou seest no cavern roof, no palace vault;
There the blue sky and the white drifting
  cloud
Look in. Again the wildered fancy dreams
Of spouting fountains, frozen as they rose,
And fixed, with all their branching jets, in
  air,   90
And all their sluices sealed. All, all is light;
Light without shade. But all shall pass away
With the next sun: from numberless vast
  trunks
Loosened, the crashing ice shall make a sound
Like the far roar of rivers, and the eve
Shall close o'er the brown woods as it was
  wont.

  And it is pleasant, when the noisy streams
Are just set free, and milder suns melt off
The plashy snow, save only the firm drift
In the deep glen or the close shade of pines, 100
'Tis pleasant to behold the wreaths of smoke
Roll up among the maples of the hill,
Where the shrill sound of youthful voices
  wakes
The shriller echo, as the clear pure lymph,
That from the wounded trees, in twinkling
  drops,
Falls, 'mid the golden brightness of the morn,
Is gathered in with brimming pails, and oft,
Wielded by sturdy hands, the stroke of ax
Makes the woods ring. Along the quiet air
Come and float calmly off the soft light
  clouds,   110
Such as you see in summer, and the winds
Scarce stir the branches. Lodged in sunny
  cleft,
Where the cold breezes come not, blooms
  alone
The little windflower, whose just opened eye
Is blue as the spring heaven it gazes at—
Startling the loiterer in the naked groves
With unexpected beauty, for the time
Of blossoms and green leaves is yet afar.
And ere it comes, the encountering winds
  shall oft
Muster their wrath again, and rapid clouds 120
Shade heaven, and, bounding on the frozen
  earth,

Shall fall their volleyed stores, rounded like
  hail,
And white like snow, and the loud North
  again
Shall buffet the vexed forest in his rage.
1820   *1821*

AN INDIAN AT THE BURIAL-PLACE OF HIS FATHERS

Like Freneau, Irving, and Cooper, Bryant took
a romantic interest in the vanishing Indian. "Monument Mountain," "The Indian Girl's Lament,"
and "The Prairies" are other poems in which this
interest also appears. Note the cosmic speculation
at the close, like that of "The Prairies" and "The
Flood of Years."

It is the spot I came to seek—
  My father's ancient burial-place,
Ere from these vales, ashamed and weak,
  Withdrew our wasted race.
It is the spot—I know it well—
Of which our old traditions tell.

For here the upland bank sends out
  A ridge toward the riverside;
I know the shaggy hills about,
  The meadows smooth and wide,   10
The plains, that, toward the southern sky,
Fenced east and west by mountains lie.

A white man, gazing on the scene,
  Would say a lovely spot was here,
And praise the lawns, so fresh and green,
  Between the hills so sheer.
I like it not—I would the plain
Lay in its tall old groves again.

The sheep are on the slopes around,
  The cattle in the meadows feed,   20
And laborers turn the crumbling ground,
  Or drop the yellow seed,
And prancing steeds, in trappings gay,
Whirl the bright chariot o'er the way.

Methinks it were a nobler sight
  To see these vales in woods arrayed,
Their summits in the golden light,
  Their trunks in grateful shade,
And herds of deer that bounding go
O'er hills and prostrate trees below.   30

And then to mark the lord of all,
  The forest hero, trained to wars,
Quivered and plumed, and lithe and tall,
  And seamed with glorious scars,
Walk forth, amid his reign, to dare
The wolf, and grapple with the bear.

This bank, in which the dead were laid,
  Was sacred when its soil was ours;
Hither the silent Indian maid
  Brought wreaths of beads and flowers, 40
And the gray chief and gifted seer
Worshipped the god of thunders here.

But now the wheat is green and high
  On clods that hid the warrior's breast,
And scattered in the furrows lie
  The weapons of his rest;
And there, in the loose sand, is thrown
Of his large arm the mouldering bone.

Ah, little thought the strong and brave
  Who bore their lifeless chieftain forth— 50
Or the young wife that weeping gave
  Her first-born to the earth,
That the pale race who waste us now
Among their bones should guide the plough.

They waste us—ay—like April snow
  In the warm noon, we shrink away;
And fast they follow, as we go
  Toward the setting day—
Till they shall fill the land, and we
Are driven into the Western sea. 60

But I behold a fearful sign,
  To which the white men's eyes are blind;
Their race may vanish hence, like mine,
  And leave no trace behind,
Save ruins o'er the region spread,
And the white stones above the dead.

Before these fields were shorn and tilled,
  Full to the brim our rivers flowed;
The melody of waters filled
  The fresh and boundless wood; 70
And torrents dashed and rivulets played,
And fountains spouted in the shade.

Those grateful sounds are heard no more,
  The springs are silent in the sun;
The rivers, by the blackened shore,
  With lessening current run;

The realm our tribes are crushed to get
  May be a barren desert yet.

1824

THE MURDERED TRAVELLER

WHEN Spring, to woods and wastes around,
  Brought bloom and joy again,
The murdered traveller's bones were found,
  Far down a narrow glen.

The fragrant birch, above him, hung
  Her tassels in the sky;
And many a vernal blossom sprung,
  And nodded careless by.

The redbird warbled, as he wrought
  His hanging nest o'er head, 10
And fearless, near the fatal spot,
  Her young the partridge led.

But there was weeping far away,
  And gentle eyes, for him,
With watching many an anxious day,
  Were sorrowful and dim.

They little knew, who loved him so,
  The fearful death he met,
When shouting o'er the desert snow,
  Unarmed, and hard beset;— 20

Nor how, when round the frosty pole
  The northern dawn was red,
The mountain wolf and wildcat stole
  To banquet on the dead;—

Nor how, when strangers found his bones,
  They dressed the hasty bier,
And marked his grave with nameless stones,
  Unmoistened by a tear.

But long they looked, and feared, and wept,
  Within his distant home; 30
And dreamed, and started as they slept,
  For joy that he was come.

Long, long they looked—but never spied
  His welcome step again,
Nor knew the fearful death he died
  Far down that narrow glen.

1824   1825

A FOREST HYMN

THE groves were God's first temples. Ere
    man learned
To hew the shaft, and lay the architrave,
And spread the roof above them—ere he
    framed
The lofty vault, to gather and roll back
The sound of anthems; in the darkling wood,
Amid the cool and silence, he knelt down,
And offered to the Mightiest solemn thanks
And supplication. For his simple heart
Might not resist the sacred influence
Which, from the stilly twilight of the place, 10
And from the gray old trunks that high in
    heaven
Mingled their mossy boughs, and from the
    sound
Of the invisible breath that swayed at once
All their green tops, stole over him, and
    bowed
His spirit with the thought of boundless
    power
And inaccessible majesty. Ah, why
Should we, in the world's riper years, neglect
God's ancient sanctuaries, and adore
Only among the crowd, and under roofs
That our frail hands have raised? Let me, at
    least, 20
Here, in the shadow of this aged wood,
Offer one hymn—thrice happy, if it find
Acceptance in His ear.

              Father, thy hand
Hath reared these venerable columns, thou
Didst weave this verdant roof. Thou didst
    look down
Upon the naked earth, and, forthwith, rose
All these fair ranks of trees. They, in thy
    sun,
Budded, and shook their green leaves in thy
    breeze,
And shot toward heaven. The century-living
    crow 30
Whose birth was in their tops, grew old and
    died
Among their branches, till, at last, they stood,
As now they stand, massy, and tall, and dark,
Fit shrine for humble worshiper to hold
Communion with his Maker. These dim
    vaults,

These winding aisles, of human pomp or
    pride
Report not. No fantastic carvings show
The boast of our vain race to change the form
Of thy fair works. But thou art here—thou
    fill'st
The solitude. Thou art in the soft winds 40
That run along the summit of these trees
In music; thou art in the cooler breath
That from the inmost darkness of the place
Comes, scarcely felt; the barky trunks, the
    ground,
The fresh moist ground, are all instinct with
    thee.
Here is continual worship;—Nature, here,
In the tranquillity that thou dost love,
Enjoys thy presence. Noiselessly, around,
From perch to perch, the solitary bird
Passes; and yon clear spring, that, midst its
    herbs, 50
Wells softly forth and wandering steeps the
    roots
Of half the mighty forest, tells no tale
Of all the good it does. Thou hast not left
Thyself without a witness, in the shades,
Of thy perfections. Grandeur, strength, and
    grace
Are here to speak of thee. This mighty oak—
By whose immovable stem I stand and seem
Almost annihilated—not a prince,
In all that proud old world beyond the deep,
E'er wore his crown as loftily as he 60
Wears the green coronal of leaves with
    which
Thy hand has graced him. Nestled at his root
Is beauty, such as blooms not in the glare
Of the broad sun. That delicate forest flower,
With scented breath and look so like a smile,
Seems, as it issues from the shapeless mold,
An emanation of the indwelling Life,
A visible token of the upholding Love,
That are the soul of this great universe.

    My heart is awed within me when I think
Of the great miracle that still goes on, 71
In silence, round me—the perpetual work
Of thy creation, finished, yet renewed
Forever. Written on thy works I read
The lesson of thy own eternity.
Lo! all grow old and die—but see again,
How on the faltering footsteps of decay

Youth presses—ever gay and beautiful youth
In all its beautiful forms. These lofty trees
Wave not less proudly that their ancestors 80
Molder beneath them. Oh, there is not lost
One of earth's charms: upon her bosom yet,
After the flight of untold centuries,
The freshness of her far beginning lies
And yet shall lie. Life mocks the idle hate
Of his arch-enemy Death—yea, seats him-
    self
Upon the tyrant's throne—the sepulcher,
And of the triumphs of his ghastly foe
Makes his own nourishment. For he came
    forth
From thine own bosom, and shall have no end.

There have been holy men who hid them-
    selves 91
Deep in the woody wilderness, and gave
Their lives to thought and prayer, till they
    outlived
The generation born with them, nor seemed
Less aged than the hoary trees and rocks
Around them;—and there have been holy
    men
Who deemed it were not well to pass life thus.
But let me often to these solitudes
Retire, and in thy presence reassure
My feeble virtue. Here its enemies, 100
The passions, at thy plainer footsteps shrink
And tremble and are still. O God! when
    thou
Dost scare the world with tempests, set on fire
The heavens with falling thunderbolts, or fill,
With all the waters of the firmament,
The swift dark whirlwind that uproots the
    woods
And drowns the villages; when, at thy call,
Uprises the great deep and throws himself
Upon the continent, and overwhelms
Its cities—who forgets not, at the sight 110
Of these tremendous tokens of thy power,
His pride, and lays his strifes and follies by?
Oh, from these sterner aspects of thy face
Spare me and mine, nor let us need the wrath
Of the mad unchained elements to teach
Who rules them. Be it ours to meditate,
In these calm shades, thy milder majesty,
And to the beautiful order of thy works
Learn to conform the order of our lives.

1824 1825

THE DEATH OF THE FLOWERS

An examination of the poems written before
1830 will show a surprising range of experimenta-
tion in verse forms, aside from the blank verse line
which was his most effective medium. Here the
combination of verse movement and sound effects
is finely suited to the tone of the poem.

THE melancholy days are come, the saddest
    of the year,
Of wailing winds and naked woods, and
    meadows brown and sere.
Heaped in the hollows of the grove, the au-
    tumn leaves lie dead;
They rustle to the eddying gust, and to the
    rabbit's tread;
The robin and the wren are flown, and from
    the shrubs the jay,
And from the wood-top calls the crow
    through all the gloomy day.

Where are the flowers, the fair young flowers,
    that lately sprang and stood
In brighter light and softer airs, a beauteous
    sisterhood?
Alas! they all are in their graves, the gentle
    race of flowers
Are lying in their lowly beds, with the fair
    and good of ours. 10
The rain is falling where they lie, but the cold
    November rain
Calls not from out the gloomy earth the
    lovely ones again.

The windflower and the violet, they perished
    long ago,
And the brier-rose and the orchis died amid
    the summer glow;
But on the hills the goldenrod, and the aster
    in the wood,
And the yellow sunflower by the brook in
    autumn beauty stood,
Till fell the frost from the clear cold heaven,
    as falls the plague on men,
And the brightness of their smile was gone,
    from upland, glade, and glen.

And now, when comes the calm mild day, as
    still such days will come,
To call the squirrel and the bee from out their
    winter home; 20

When the sound of dropping nuts is heard,
   though all the trees are still,
And twinkle in the smoky light the waters of
   the rill,
The south wind searches for the flowers whose
   fragrance late he bore,
And sighs to find them in the wood and by
   the stream no more.

And then I think of one who in her youthful
   beauty died,
The fair meek blossom that grew up and
   faded by my side.
In the cold moist earth we laid her, when the
   forests cast the leaf,
And we wept that one so lovely should have
   a life so brief:
Yet not unmeet it was that one, like that
   young friend of ours,
So gentle and so beautiful, should perish with
   the flowers.   30

1825

JUNE

I GAZED upon the glorious sky
   And the green mountains round,
And thought that when I came to lie
   At rest within the ground,
'Twere pleasant, that in flowery June,
   When brooks send up a cheerful tune,
And groves a joyous sound,
The sexton's hand, my grave to make,
The rich, green mountain-turf should break.

A cell within the frozen mould,   10
   A coffin borne through sleet,
And icy clods above it rolled,
   While fierce the tempests beat—
Away!—I will not think of these—
Blue be the sky and soft the breeze,
   Earth green beneath the feet,
And be the damp mould gently pressed
Into my narrow place of rest.

There through the long, long summer hours,
   The golden light should lie,   20
And thick young herbs and groups of flowers
   Stand in their beauty by.
The oriole should build and tell
His love-tale close beside my cell;

The idle butterfly
Should rest him there, and there be heard
The housewife bee and hummingbird.

And what if cheerful shouts at noon
   Come, from the village sent,
Or songs of maids, beneath the moon   30
   With fairy laughter blent?
And what if, in the evening light,
Betrothéd lovers walk in sight
   Of my low monument?
I would the lovely scene around
Might know no sadder sight nor sound.

I know that I no more should see
   The season's glorious show,
Nor would its brightness shine for me,
   Nor its wild music flow;   40
But if, around my place of sleep,
The friends I love should come to weep,
   They might not haste to go.
Soft airs, and song, and light, and bloom
Should keep them lingering by my tomb.

These to their softened hearts should bear
   The thought of what has been,
And speak of one who cannot share
   The gladness of the scene;
Whose part, in all the pomp that fills   50
The circuit of the summer hills,
   Is that his grave is green;
And deeply would their hearts rejoice
To hear again his living voice.

1825   *1826*

THE EVENING WIND

SPIRIT that breathest through my lattice, thou
   That cool'st the twilight of the sultry day,
Gratefully flows thy freshness round my
   brow;
   Thou hast been out upon the deep at play,
Riding all day the wild blue waves till now,
   Roughening their crests, and scattering
      high their spray,
And swelling the white sail. I welcome thee
To the scorched land, thou wanderer of the
   sea!

Nor I alone; a thousand bosoms round
   Inhale thee in the fulness of delight;   10
And languid forms rise up, and pulses bound
   Livelier, at coming of the wind of night;

And, languishing to hear thy grateful sound,
  Lies the vast inland stretched beyond the
      sight.
Go forth into the gathering shade; go forth,
God's blessing breathed upon the fainting
      earth!

Go, rock the little wood-bird in his nest,
  Curl the still waters, bright with stars, and
      rouse
The wide old wood from his majestic rest,
  Summoning from the innumerable boughs
The strange, deep harmonies that haunt his
      breast: 21
    Pleasant shall be thy way where meekly
      bows
The shutting flower, and darkling waters pass,
And where the o'ershadowing branches sweep
      the grass.

The faint old man shall lean his silver head
  To feel thee; thou shalt kiss the child asleep,
And dry the moistened curls that overspread
  His temples, while his breathing grows
      more deep;
And they who stand about the sick man's bed
  Shall joy to listen to thy distant sweep, 30
And softly part his curtains to allow
Thy visit, grateful to his burning brow.

Go—but the circle of eternal change,
  Which is the life of Nature, shall restore,
With sounds and scents from all thy mighty
      range,
    Thee to thy birthplace of the deep once
      more;   36
Sweet odors in the sea-air, sweet and strange,
  Shall tell the homesick mariner of the shore;
And, listening to thy murmur, he shall deem
He hears the rustling leaf and running stream.
1829   *1830*

TO THE FRINGED GENTIAN

It is interesting to contrast the language and
construction of this poem with those of the early
"The Yellow Violet."

THOU blossom bright with autumn dew,
And colored with the heaven's own blue,
That openest when the quiet light
Succeeds the keen and frosty night,

Thou comest not when violets lean
O'er wandering brooks and springs unseen,
Or columbines, in purple dressed,
Nod o'er the ground-bird's hidden nest.

Thou waitest late and com'st alone,
When woods are bare and birds are flown, 10
And frost and shortening days portend
The aged year is near his end.

Then doth thy sweet and quiet eye
Look through its fringes to the sky,
Blue—blue—as if that sky let fall
A flower from its cerulean wall.

I would that thus, when I shall see
The hour of death draw near to me,
Hope, blossoming within my heart,
May look to heaven as I depart. 20
1832

SONG OF MARION'S MEN

OUR band is few but true and tried,
  Our leader frank and bold;
The British soldier trembles
  When Marion's name is told.
Our fortress is the good greenwood,
  Our tent the cypress-tree;
We know the forest round us,
  As seamen know the sea.
We know its walls of thorny vines,
  Its glades of reedy grass, 10
Its safe and silent islands
  Within the dark morass.

Woe to the English soldiery
  That little dread us near!
On them shall light at midnight
  A strange and sudden fear:
When, waking to their tents on fire,
  They grasp their arms in vain,
And they who stand to face us
  Are beat to earth again; 20
And they who fly in terror deem
  A mighty host behind,
And hear the tramp of thousands
  Upon the hollow wind.

Then sweet the hour that brings release
  From danger and from toil:
We talk the battle over,
  And share the battle's spoil.

The woodland rings with laugh and shout,
  As if a hunt were up,   30
And woodland flowers are gathered
  To crown the soldier's cup.
With merry songs we mock the wind
  That in the pine-top grieves,
And slumber long and sweetly
  On beds of oaken leaves.

Well knows the fair and friendly moon
  The band that Marion leads—
The glitter of their rifles,
  The scampering of their steeds.   40
'Tis life to guide the fiery barb
  Across the moonlight plain;
'Tis life to feel the night-wind
  That lifts the tossing mane
A moment in the British camp—
  A moment—and away
Back to the pathless forest,
  Before the peep of day.

Grave men there are by broad Santee,
  Grave men with hoary hairs;   50
Their hearts are all with Marion,
  For Marion are their prayers.
And lovely ladies greet our band
  With kindliest welcoming,
With smiles like those of summer,
  And tears like those of spring.
For them we wear these trusty arms,
  And lay them down no more
Till we have driven the Briton,
  Forever, from our shore.   60

1831

THE PRAIRIES

Bryant's first visit to Illinois, where some of his brothers had settled, was made in 1832, and his impressions of the expanse of grassy plains are recorded in this poem.

THESE are the gardens of the Desert,[1] these
The unshorn fields, boundless and beautiful,
For which the speech of England has no
  name—
The Prairies. I behold them for the first,
And my heart swells while the dilated sight
Takes in the encircling vastness, Lo, they
  stretch
In airy undulations, far away,

[1] wilderness, uninhabited area, as regularly in eighteenth-century English

As if the Ocean, in his gentlest swell,
Stood still, with all his rounded billows fixed
And motionless forever. Motionless?   10
No, they are all unchained again: the clouds
Sweep over with their shadows, and beneath,
The surface rolls and fluctuates to the eye;
Dark hollows seem to glide along and chase
The sunny ridges. Breezes of the South,
Who toss the golden and the flame-like flow-
  ers,
And pass the prairie-hawk that, poised on
  high,
Flaps his broad wings, yet moves not, ye have
  played
Among the palms of Mexico and vines
Of Texas, and have crisped the limpid brooks
That from the fountains of Sonora glide   21
Into the calm Pacific: Have ye fanned
A nobler or a lovelier scene than this?
Man hath no part in all this glorious work:
The hand that built the firmament hath
  heaved
And smoothed these verdant swells, and sown
  their slopes
With herbage, planted them with island
  groves,
And hedged them round with forests. Fitting
  floor
For this magnificent temple of the sky,
With flowers whose glory and whose multi-
  tude   30
Rival the constellations! The great heavens
Seem to stoop down upon the scene in love—
A nearer vault, and of a tenderer blue,
Than that which bends above our Eastern
  hills.

As o'er the verdant waste I guide my steed,
Among the high rank grass that sweeps his
  sides,
The hollow beating of his footstep seems
A sacrilegious sound. I think of those
Upon whose rest he tramples: are they here,
The dead of other days? and did the dust   40
Of these fair solitudes once stir with life
And burn with passion? Let the mighty
  mounds[1]
That overlook the rivers, or that rise

[1] These great remains of a vanished race appealed greatly to the imagination of Bryant and his contemporary Americans.

In the dim forest crowded with old oaks,
Answer. A race that long has passed away
Built them; a disciplined and populous race
Heaped with long toil, the earth, while yet the
    Greek
Was hewing the Pentelicus to forms
Of symmetry, and rearing on its rock
The glittering Parthenon. These ample fields
Nourished their harvests; here their herds
    were fed,   51
When haply by their stalls the bison lowed,
And bowed his maned shoulder to the yoke.
All day this desert murmured with their toils,
Till twilight blushed, and lovers walked, and
    wooed
In a forgotten language, and old tunes,
From instruments of unremembered form,
Gave the soft winds a voice. The red man
    came,
The roaming hunter tribes, warlike and fierce,
And the mound-builders vanished from the
    earth.   60
The solitude of centuries untold
Has settled where they dwelt. The prairie-wolf
Hunts in their meadows, and his fresh-dug den
Yawns by my path. The gopher mines the
    ground
Where stood their swarming cities. All is
    gone:
All save the piles of earth that hold their bones;
The platforms where they worshiped un-
    known gods;
The barriers which they builded from the soil
To keep the foe at bay, till o'er the walls   69
The wild beleaguerers broke, and, one by one,
The strongholds of the plain were forced and
    heaped
With corpses. The brown vultures of the
    wood
Flocked to those vast uncovered sepulchers,
And sat, unscared and silent, at their feast.
Haply some solitary fugitive,
Lurking in marsh and forest, till the sense
Of desolation and of fear became
Bitterer than death, yielded himself to die.
Man's better nature triumphed then: kind
    words
Welcomed and soothed him; the rude con-
    querors   80
Seated the captive with their chiefs; he chose
A bride among the maidens, and at length

Seemed to forget—yet ne'er forgot—the wife
Of his first love, and her sweet little ones
Butchered amid their shrieks, with all his race.

Thus change the forms of being. Thus arise
Races of living things, glorious in strength,
And perish, as the quickening breath of God
Fills them or is withdrawn. The red man, too,
Has left the blooming wilds he ranged so
    long,   90
And, nearer to the Rocky Mountains, sought
A wilder hunting-ground. The beaver builds
No longer by these streams, but far away,
On waters whose blue surface ne'er gave back
The white man's face, among Missouri's
    springs,
And pools whose issues swell the Oregon,
He rears his little Venice. In these plains
The bison feeds no more: twice twenty
    leagues
Beyond remotest smoke of hunter's camp,
Roams the majestic brute, in herds that shake
The earth with thundering steps—yet here I
    meet   101
His ancient footprints stamped beside the pool.

Still this great solitude is quick with life.
Myriads of insects, gaudy as the flowers
They flutter over, gentle quadrupeds,
And birds that scarce have learned the fear of
    man,
Are here, and sliding reptiles of the ground,
Startlingly beautiful. The graceful deer
Bounds to the wood at my approach. The bee,
A more adventurous colonist than man,   110
With whom he came across the eastern deep,
Fills the savannas with his murmurings,
And hides his sweets, as in the golden age,
Within the hollow oak. I listen long
To his domestic hum, and think I hear
The sound of that advancing multitude
Which soon shall fill these deserts: from the
    ground
Comes up the laugh of children, the soft voice
Of maidens, and the sweet and solemn hymn
Of Sabbath worshipers; the low of herds   120
Blends with the rustling of the heavy grain
Over the dark-brown furrows. All at once
A fresher wind sweeps by and breaks my
    dream,
And I am in the wilderness alone.

1832   1833

THE BATTLEFIELD

This poem, like Longfellow's later "The Arsenal at Springfield," is a part of the first American agitation for world peace, most active in the eighteen-thirties and forties.

ONCE this soft turf, this rivulet's sands,
  Were trampled by a hurrying crowd,
And fiery hearts and armed hands
  Encountered in the battle-cloud.

Ah! never shall the land forget
  How gushed the lifeblood of her brave;
Gushed, warm with hope and valor yet,
  Upon the soil they fought to save.

Now all is calm, and fresh, and still;
  Alone the chirp of flitting bird,   10
And talk of children on the hill,
  And bell of wandering kine, are heard.

No solemn host goes trailing by
  The black-mouthed gun and staggering
    wain;
Men start not at the battle-cry,
  Oh, be it never heard again!

Soon rested those who fought; but thou
  Who minglest in the harder strife
For truths which men receive not now,
  Thy warfare only ends with life.   20

A friendless warfare! lingering long
  Through weary day and weary year,
A wild and many-weaponed throng
  Hang on thy front, and flank, and rear.

Yet nerve thy spirit to the proof,
  And blench not at thy chosen lot.
The timid good may stand aloof,
  The sage may frown—yet faint thou not.

Nor heed the shaft too surely cast,
  The foul and hissing bolt of scorn;   30
For with thy side shall dwell, at last,
  The victory of endurance born,

Truth, crushed to earth, shall rise again;
  Th' eternal years of God are hers;
But Error, wounded, writhes in pain,
  And dies among his worshipers.

Yea, though thou lie upon the dust,
  When those who helped thee flee in fear,
Die full of hope and manly trust,
  Like those who fell in battle here.   40

Another hand thy sword shall wield,
  Another hand the standard wave,
Till from the trumpet's mouth is pealed
  The blast of triumph o'er thy grave.

1837

THE ANTIQUITY OF FREEDOM

HERE are old trees, tall oaks, and gnarlèd
    pines,
That stream with gray-green mosses; here
    the ground
Was never trenched by spade, and flowers
    spring up
Unsown, and die ungathered. It is sweet
To linger here, among the flitting birds
And leaping squirrels, wandering brooks, and
    winds
That shake the leaves and scatter, as they pass,
A fragrance from the cedars, thickly set
With pale-blue berries. In these peaceful
    shades—
Peaceful, unpruned, immeasurably old—   10
My thoughts go up the long dim path of years,
Back to the earliest days of liberty.

O Freedom! thou art not, as poets dream,
A fair young girl, with light and delicate limbs,
And wavy tresses gushing from the cap [1]
With which the Roman master crowned his
    slave
When he took off the gyves. A bearded man,
Armed to the teeth, art thou; one mailèd hand
Grasps the broad shield, and one the sword;
    thy brow
Glorious in beauty though it be, is scarred   20
With tokens of old wars; thy massive limbs
Are strong with struggling. Power at thee
    has launched
His bolts, and with his lightnings smitten thee;
They could not quench the life thou hast
    from heaven;
Merciless Power has dug thy dungeon deep,

[1] the Liberty Cap, dating from the French Revolution, which adorns the head of Columbia on American coins

And his swart armorers, by a thousand fires,
Have forged thy chain; yet, while he deems
    thee bound,
The links are shivered, and the prison-walls
Fall outward; terribly thou springest forth,
As springs the flame above a burning pile,   30
And shoutest to the nations, who return
Thy shoutings, while the pale oppressor flies.

Thy birthright was not given by human
    hands:
Thou wert twinborn with man. In pleasant
    fields,
While yet our race was few, thou sat'st with
    him,
To tend the quiet flock and watch the stars,
And teach the reed to utter simple airs.
Thou by his side, amid the tangled wood,
Didst war upon the panther and the wolf,
His only foes; and thou with him didst draw
The earliest furrow on the mountain-side,   41
Soft with the deluge. Tyranny himself,
Thy enemy, although of reverend look,
Hoary with many years, and far obeyed,
Is later born than thou; and as he meets
The grave defiance of thine elder eye,
The usurper trembles in his fastnesses.

Thou shalt wax stronger with the lapse
    of years,
But he shall fade into a feebler age—
Feebler, yet subtler. He shall weave his
    snares,   50
And spring them on thy careless steps, and
    clap
His withered hands, and from their ambush
    call
His hordes to fall upon thee. He shall send
Quaint maskers, wearing fair and gallant
    forms
To catch thy gaze, and uttering graceful words
To charm thy ear; while his sly imps, by
    stealth,
Twine round thee threads of steel, light thread
    on thread,
That grow to fetters; or bind down thy arms
With chains concealed in chaplets. Oh! not
    yet
Mayst thou unbrace thy corslet, nor lay by   60
Thy sword; nor yet, O Freedom! close thy lids
In slumber; for thine enemy never sleeps,

And thou must watch and combat till the day
Of the new earth and heaven. But wouldst
    thou rest
Awhile from tumult and the frauds of men,
These old and friendly solitudes invite
Thy visit. They, while yet the forest-trees
Were young upon the unviolated earth,
And yet the moss-stains on the rock were
    new,   69
Beheld thy glorious childhood, and rejoiced.

                     1842

O MOTHER OF A MIGHTY RACE

Bryant's reaction on returning from a visit to
monarchical Europe just before the abortive revolutionary movements of 1848.

O MOTHER of a mighty race,
Yet lovely in thy youthful grace!
The elder dames, thy haughty peers,
Admire and hate thy blooming years.
    With words of shame
And taunts of scorn they join thy name.

For on thy cheeks the glow is spread
That tints thy morning hills with red;
Thy step—the wild-deer's rustling feet
Within thy woods are not more fleet;   10
    Thy hopeful eye
Is bright as thine own sunny sky.

Ay, let them rail—those haughty ones,
While safe thou dwellest with thy sons.
They do not know how loved thou art,
How many a fond and fearless heart
    Would rise to throw
Its life between thee and the foe.

They know not, in their hate and pride,
What virtues with thy children bide;   20
How true, how good, thy graceful maids
Make bright, like flowers, the valley-shades;
    What generous men
Spring, like thine oaks, by hill and glen;—

What cordial welcomes greet the guest
By thy lone rivers of the West;
How faith is kept, and truth revered,
And man is loved, and God is feared,
    In woodland homes,
And where the ocean border foams.   30

There's freedom at thy gates and rest
For Earth's downtrodden and opprest,
A shelter for the hunted head,
For the starved laborer toil and bread.
    Power, at thy bounds,
Stops and calls back his baffled hounds.

O fair young mother! on thy brow
Shall sit a nobler grace than now.
Deep in the brightness of the skies
The thronging years in glory rise,   40
    And, as they fleet,
Drop strength and riches at thy feet.

Thine eye, with every coming hour,
Shall brighten, and thy form shall tower;
And when thy sisters, elder born,
Would brand thy name with words of scorn,
    Before thine eye,
Upon their lips the taunt shall die.

1846   1847

THE DEATH OF LINCOLN

OH, slow to smite and swift to spare,
    Gentle and merciful and just!
Who, in the fear of God, didst bear
    The sword of power, a nation's trust!

In sorrow by thy bier we stand,
    Amid the awe that hushes all,
And speak the anguish of a land
    That shook with horror at thy fall.

Thy task is done; the bond are free:
    We bear thee to an honored grave,   10
Whose proudest monument shall be
    The broken fetters of the slave.

Pure was thy life; its bloody close
    Hath placed thee with the sons of light,
Among the noble host of those
    Who perished in the cause of Right.

1865   1866

THE POET

Bryant, like Milton, Wordsworth, and Whitman, regarded the poet's calling with earnest seriousness. The poet's self-analysis in these lines somewhat offsets James Russell Lowell's judgment of him in the "Fable for Critics."

THOU who wouldst wear the name
    Of poet 'mid thy brethren of mankind,

And clothe in words of flame
    Thoughts that shall live within the general
        mind!
Deem not the framing of a deathless lay
The pastime of a drowsy summer day.

But gather all thy powers
    And wreak them on the verse that thou dost
        weave,
And in thy lonely hours,
    At silent morning or at wakeful eve,   10
While the warm current tingles through thy
        veins
Set forth the burning words in fluent strains.

No smooth array of phrase,
    Artfully sought and ordered though it be,
Which the cold rhymer lays
    Upon his page with languid industry,
Can wake the listless pulse to livelier speed,
Or fill with sudden tears the eyes that read.

The secret wouldst thou know
    To touch the heart or fire the blood at will?
Let thine own eyes o'erflow;   21
    Let thy lips quiver with the passionate thrill;
Seize the great thought, ere yet its power be
        past,
And bind, in words, the fleet emotion fast.

Then, should thy verse appear
    Halting and harsh, and all unaptly wrought,
Touch the crude line with fear,
    Save in the moment of impassioned thought;
Then summon back the original glow, and
        mend
The strain with rapture that with fire was
        penned.   30

Yet let no empty gust
    Of passion find an utterance in thy lay,
A blast that whirls the dust
    Along the howling street and dies away;
But feelings of calm power and mighty sweep,
Like currents journeying through the windless
        deep.

Seek'st thou, in living lays,
    To limn the beauty of the earth and sky?
Before thine inner gaze
    Let all that beauty in clear vision lie;   40
Look on it with exceeding love, and write
The words inspired by wonder and delight.

Of tempests wouldst thou sing,
  Or tell of battles—make thyself a part
Of the great tumult; cling
  To the tossed wreck with terror in thy
    heart;
Scale, with the assaulting host, the rampart's
    height,
And strike and struggle in the thickest fight.

So shalt thou frame a lay
  That haply may endure from age to age,   50
And they who read shall say:
  "What witchery hangs upon this poet's
    page!
What art is his the written spells to find
That sway from mood to mood the willing
    mind!"

1863   1864

From THE RIGHT OF WORKMEN TO STRIKE

As editor of the New York *Evening Post*, Bryant won respect, and also hostility, for his courage and honesty in dealing with social and political issues at home and abroad. Readers who were surprised at vigorous and militant editorials from the pen of the nation's best-known poet failed to estimate properly the romantic humanitarian impulsiveness which here found freer and more [10] immediate play than in his more restrained utterances in verse. His defense a century ago of a group of New York tailors, heavily fined for forming a union and striking, was denounced as dangerous and radical.

SENTENCE was passed on Saturday on the twenty "men who had determined not to work." The punishment selected, on due consideration, by the judge was that officers appointed for the purpose should immediately [20] demand from each of the delinquents a sum of money which was named in the sentence of the court. The amount demanded would not have fallen short of the savings of many years. Either the offenders had not parted with these savings, or their brother workmen raised the ransom money for them on the spot. The fine was paid over as required. All is now well; justice has been satisfied. But if the expenses of their families had anticipated the law and left [30] nothing in their hands, or if friends had not been ready to buy the freedom of their comrades, they would have been sent to prison; and there they would have stayed until their wives and children, besides earning their own bread, had saved enough to redeem the captives from their cells. Such has been their punishment. What was their offense? They had committed the crime of unanimously declining to go to work at the wages offered [40] to them by their masters. They had said to one another, "Let us come out from the meanness and misery of our caste. Let us begin to do what every order more privileged and more honored is doing every day. By the means which we believe to be the best, let us raise ourselves and our families above the humbleness of our condition. We may be wrong, but we cannot help believing that we might do much if we were true brothers to each other, and would resolve not to sell the only thing which is our own, the cunning of our hands, for less than it is worth." What other things they may have done is nothing to the purpose: it was for this they were condemned; it is for this they are to endure the penalty of the law.

We call upon a candid and generous community to mark that the punishment inflicted upon these twenty "men who had determined not to work" is not directed against the offense of conspiring to prevent others by force from working at low wages, but expressly against the offense of settling by pre-concert the compensation which they thought they were entitled to obtain. It is certainly superfluous to repeat that this journal would be the very last to oppose a law levelled at any attempt to molest the laborer who chooses to work for less than the prices settled by the union. We have said, and to cut off cavil we say it now again, that a conspiracy to deter, by threats of violence, a fellow workman from arranging his own terms with his employers is a conspiracy to commit a felony—a conspiracy which, being a crime against liberty, we should be the first to condemn; a conspiracy which no strike should, for its own sake, countenance for a moment; a conspiracy already punishable by the statute and far easier to reach than the one of which "the twenty" stood accused; but a conspiracy, we must add, that has not a single feature in common with the base and barbarous prohibition under which the offenders were indicted and condemned.

They were condemned because they had determined not to work for the wages that were offered them! Can anything be imagined more abhorrent to every sentiment of generosity or justice than the law which arms the rich with the legal right to fix, by assize, the wages of the poor? If this is not SLAVERY, we have forgotten its definition. Strike the right of associating for the sale of labor from the privileges of a freeman, and you may as well at once bind him to a master, or ascribe him to the soil. If it be not in the color of his skin, and in the poor franchise of naming his own terms in a contract for his work, what advantage has the laborer of the North over the bondman of the South? Punish by human laws a "determination not to work," make it penal by any other penalty than idleness inflicts; and it matters little whether the taskmasters be one or many, an individual or an order, the hateful scheme of slavery will have gained a foothold in the land. And then the meanness of this law, which visits with its malice those who cling to it for protection, and shelters with all its fences those who are raised above its threats! A late solicitation for its aid against employers is treated with derision and contempt, but the moment the "masters" invoked its intervention, it came down from its high place with most indecent haste, and has now discharged its fury upon the naked heads of wretches so forlorn that their worst faults multiply their titles to a liberty which they must learn to win from livelier sensibilities than the barren benevolence of wealth or the tardy magnanimity of power. . . .

"Self-created societies," says Judge Edwards, "are unknown to the constitution and laws, and will not be permitted to rear their crest and extend their baneful influence over any portion of the community." If there is any sense in this passage, it means that self-created societies are unlawful, and must be put down by the courts. Down then with every literary, every religious, and every charitable association not incorporated! What nonsense is this! Self-created societies *are* known to the constitution and laws, for they are not prohibited, and the laws which allow them will, if justly administered, protect them. But suppose in charity that the reporter has put this absurdity into the mouth of Judge Edwards, and that he meant only those self-created societies which have an effect upon trade and commerce. Gather up then and sweep to the penitentiary all those who are confederated to carry on any business or trade in concert by fixed rules; see how many men you would leave at large in this city. The members of every partnership in the place will come under the penalties of the law, and not only these but every person pursuing any occupation whatever who governs himself by a mutual understanding with others that follow the same occupation. . . .

1836

1789 ~ *James Fenimore Cooper* ~ 1851

JAMES FENIMORE COOPER was born at Burlington, New Jersey. When he was two years old, his family moved to central New York. There the elder Cooper was a judge and owner of a large tract of land. Cooper spent his youth at Otsego Hall, his father's manor at Cooperstown, adjoining Lake Otsego, where, in an environment still retaining frontier conditions, the family lived in the state befitting a gentleman pioneer. Prepared for Yale by the rector of St. Peter's in Albany, he acquired a firm prejudice against New England and all Yankees. In his junior year at college, he was dismissed for a student prank, and shipped before the mast on a merchant vessel to train himself for the navy. Admitted as a midshipman, he served on the Atlantic, Lake Ontario, and Lake Champlain, settings he was later to use in his books. On his marriage in 1811, however, his bride, of the Tory De Lancey family, insisted on his giving up his profession, and he was satisfied to become a gentleman farmer. For the next eight years it seemed that he had found his vocation, managing three different farms, near enough to New York so that he could attend the theater and hobnob with the "Croakers" and other literary men of the town.

The story goes that one day he grew impatient with an English novel which he was reading aloud to his wife, and declared that he could write a better one. She challenged him to try, with the result that he published *Precaution* in 1820. It was a conventional novel of English manners in which he introduced a set balancing of characters that reappears in his later works. In his next book, *The Spy* (1821), he wisely shifted to the Westchester County that he knew well, and used for his hero a real Revolutionary spy, Harvey Birch. In this novel Cooper already shows his weakness and his strength. His language is stilted and affected, but the narrative is vigorous, and he arouses suspense by the use of flight and pursuit—soon to become a formula in his work. The book was at once successful in America and abroad. It was followed in 1823 by *The Pioneers*, important as a picture of Cooper's boyhood home, and as the first appearance of Natty Bumppo, the Leatherstocking who became his greatest creation. In the same year came *The Pilot*, a patriotic story of the sea, introducing John Paul Jones, and meant to show Scott, who had just published *The Pirate*, that a landsman could not do justice to an ocean tale.

These three successes established Cooper's position in New York. He founded—and controlled—the Bread and Cheese Club, a literary society. He served on the committee of welcome for Lafayette, and received an honorary degree from Columbia. Meanwhile he planned to write a story about each of the thirteen original states, but completed only *Lionel Lincoln* (1825), an accurate but dull account of Bunker's Hill. Instead he decided to go on with Natty Bumppo. In 1826 *The Last of the Mohicans* and in 1827 *The Prairie* not only continued the story of the great scout but introduced, in Chingachgook and Uncas, the Indian chiefs peculiar to Cooper's fiction, distinguished for nobility, eloquence, cunning, and romantic qualities.

In 1826 Cooper was appointed to the nominal position of consul at Lyons, France. For over seven years he lived with his family in Europe, traveling, spending much time in Paris, and meeting Scott, Lafayette, Moore, and other notables. Three of six novels published while there—*The Red Rover* (1828), *The Wept of Wish-ton-Wish* (1829), and *The Water-Witch* (1831)—deal with the American scene. Three others—*The Bravo* (1831), *The Heidenmauer* (1832), and *The Heads-*

man (1833)—are European historical romances, designed to "debunk" the glamour of monarchial and feudal tradition. In these and in *Notions of the Americans* (1828), he annoyed Europeans by finding fault with their character and institutions and eulogizing those of America.

Returning late in 1833 to New York, he was disappointed with his country and with his countrymen, concerned, as he thought, with "struggles for place, . . . jealousies of contending families, and the influence of mere money." At Cooperstown he and his neighbors quarreled. The tradition of the democratic feudal patroon and the frontier of his imagination were gone. For six years he abandoned fiction for historical and critical works, of which *A Letter to His Countrymen* (1834), *Gleanings in Europe* (1837–1838), *Homeward Bound* (1838), and *Home as Found* (1838) expressed and defended his views of Europeans and Americans. These culminated in *The American Democrat* (1838), "his most direct and comprehensive formulation of his social and political creed," maintaining that ideal democracy is not incompatible with true aristocracy—the "natural aristocracy" of Jefferson. These views brought him into partisan conflict with the editors of Whig newspapers, who assailed him acrimoniously, extending their attacks to his novels. Angered and embittered, Cooper retorted in kind with accusations of vulgarity, stupidity, and misrepresentation, which led to libel suits by which he gained legal vindication but lost popularity. Even his fair and accurate *History of the Navy of the United States* (1839) aroused recrimination and bitterness.

In 1840 he returned to fiction, though much of it is still critical in purpose. With *The Pathfinder* (1840) and *The Deerslayer* (1841) he rounded out the Leatherstocking Tales. Of his other novels the series consisting of *Satanstoe* (1845), *The Chainbearer* (1845), and *The Redskins* (1846)—in which he treated three generations of a New York family with some of the skill of his earlier series—are important because of the social views expressed in them. Of his last novels, *The Crater* (1848) and *The Ways of the Hour* (1850) are respectively a social allegory and a satire on trial by jury. Though his personal relations became somewhat calmer, and public appreciation of his work was returning, his prejudices remained strong and active.

Nevertheless Cooper's reputation as the earliest important American novelist is secure. His faults are inevitable in hurried production. Phrases and formulas recur annoyingly. Conversation is rarely lifelike. There are long passages of slow description. But his rapid work bears with it advantages as well. At his best Cooper has speed in narrative, characters that are convincing in their romantic backgrounds, and above all a sense of vitality and energy. The gusto with which he lived spills over into his books.

Though only his tales of adventure are well known, fully half of his novels deal with themes of social comment. It is worth noting also that the inadequacies of his style in narration tend to disappear in his argumentative and expository writing. In his personality and political and social views there was less of inconsistency than appears on the surface. He was sincerely devoted to freedom and opposed to tyranny of any sort. Freedom should allow the individual to develop clear-mindedness, nobility of character, and unselfishness—the qualities of a gentleman. When he found democratic Americans who were greedy, contentious, ignorant, and unmindful of others' rights, he assailed them in the name of democracy. By nature fearless, outspoken, and brusque, and brought up in a community of which his father was the first citizen and to a large degree the owner, he never learned to curb his tongue or pen, or to consider seriously the views of others.

Cooper believed that novels should have significance and an elevating purpose, beyond their value as entertainment. His conception of art, says Professor Quinn, "was to write about those things which are important, those scenes which are thrilling, those souls which have in them some flavor of nobility." He defended the idealizing of his heroes, white and red, as "the privilege of all writers of fiction, more particularly when their works aspire to the elevation of romances, to present the *beau-ideal* of their characters to the reader." He thought that a "rigid adhesion to truth, an indispensable requisite in history and travels, destroys the charm of fiction; for all that is necessary to be conveyed to the mind by the latter had better be done by delineation of principles, and of characters in their classes, than by a too fastidious attention to originals."

Cooper's great contribution to literature was the romance of the forest and the sea. Lack of American historical background was to him no handicap. In fact, only in isolation from ordinary civilization, perhaps, could he develop the unspoiled natural gentleman whom Leatherstocking portrays. This character, one of the few great personalities in world literature, is developed partly from an actual trapper of Cooper's childhood days, partly from the character and exploits of Daniel Boone, whose death in 1820 brought him back to public attention, partly from primitivistic fiction, and partly from his own ideas of true American character. His idealization of a few good Indians, partly derived from the Moravian Heckewelder's description of the Christian Indians of Pennsylvania, should be set off against the larger number in his books who share only their cunning and endurance, and are bloodthirsty and treacherous. In romances of the sea he had few predecessors—Smollett, John Davis, Scott in *The Pirate*—none of whom made the sea a living element in his stories; and he has had no peers. It is an inglorious tribute to Cooper's skill and excellence as a narrator in these two new fields that he should have been the progenitor of a flood of inferior thrillers of Wild West adventure and pirate stories in the later nineteenth and twentieth centuries.

The chief of many editions of Cooper's collected works are *J. Fenimore Cooper's Works* (32 vols., 1884–1890), edited by Susan F. Cooper, his daughter; and *The Works of James Fenimore Cooper*

(33 vols., 1895–1900). Editions of separate works with helpful introductions are *The Deerslayer*, in American Authors Series, F. L. Pattee, ed. (1927); *Last of the Mohicans*, in Modern Readers' Series, F. L. Pattee, ed. (1927); *The Pathfinder*, in Modern Readers' Series, R. A. Sharp, ed. (1926); *The Spy*, in Modern Student's Library, Tremaine McDowell, ed. (1931); *The American Democrat*, in Americana Deserta, H. L. Mencken, ed. (1931); *Gleanings in Europe*, R. E. Spiller, ed. (2 vols., 1928–1930). R. E. Spiller's *Cooper*, in the American Writers Series (1933), is an excellently edited volume of selections, with bibliography. Cooper directed his manuscripts to be destroyed. His remaining *Correspondence* was edited by his grandson, James F. Cooper (2 vols., 1922).

Noteworthy biographies are those by T. R. Lounsbury (1882); M. E. Phillips (1913); H. W. Boynton (1931); and R. E. Spiller, *Fenimore Cooper, Critic of His Times* (1931), in which emphasis is placed upon Cooper's social thought. Carl Van Doren is author of the *DAB* article and of the bibliography in *CHAL*, I, 350–54. R. E. Spiller and P. C. Blackburn have prepared *A Descriptive Bibliography of the Writings of James Fenimore Cooper* (1934). For further biography, see N. F. Adkins, "James Fenimore Cooper and the Bread and Cheese Club," *Modern Language Notes*, XLVII, 71–79 (Feb., 1932); R. Birdsall, *The Story of Cooperstown* (1917); Susan Fenimore Cooper, "A Glance Backward" and "A Second Glance Backward," *Atlantic Monthly* (Feb. and Oct., 1887); and "Fenimore Cooper and Lafayette: Friends of Polish Freedom," *American Literature*, VII, 56–75 (March, 1935).

Outstanding general criticisms are W. C. Brownell, *American Prose Masters* (1909), 3–60; H. S. Canby, *Classic Americans* (1931), 97–142; and V. L. Parrington, *The Romantic Revolution in America* (1927), 222–37 (on Cooper's political and social thought). See also S. L. Clemens, "Fenimore Cooper's Literary Offenses," *North American Review*, CLXI, 1–12 (July, 1895); John Erskine, *Leading American Novelists* (1910), 51–129; E. E. Hale, Jr., "American Scenery in Cooper's Novels," *Sewanee Review* (July, 1910); W. D. Howells, *Heroines of Fiction* (1901), I, 102–12; A. Keiser, *The Indian in American Literature* (1933), 101–43; "James Fenimore Cooper as Self-Critic," *Studies in Philology*, XXVII, 508–16 (July, 1930); and "The Identity of Harvey Birch," *American Literature*, II, 111–20 (May, 1930); E. R. Outland, *The Effingham Libels on Cooper* (1929); Gregory Paine, "Cooper and the *North American Review*," *Studies in Philology*, XXVIII, 799–809 (Oct., 1931); Louise Pound, "The Dialect of Cooper's Leatherstocking," *American Speech*, II, 479–88 (Sept., 1927); R. E. Spiller, "Fenimore Cooper, Critic of His Times: New Letters from Rome and Paris, 1830–1831," *American Literature*, I, 131–48 (May, 1929); "Fenimore Cooper's Defense of Slave-Owning America," *American Historical Review*, XXXV, 575–82 (April, 1930); introductions to *Gleanings in Europe: France* (1928), vii–xxi; *England* (1930), 7–23; Carl Van Doren, *The American Novel* (1940); A. H. Quinn, *American Fiction* (1936), 63–76; and Dorothy Waples, *The Whig Myth of James Fenimore Cooper* (1938).

From THE PILOT

The earliest and best of Cooper's sea-novels is *The Pilot* (1823), dealing with American naval adventures on the east coast of England during the Revolution. The events center about Cooper's customary two pairs of lovers, and there is plenty of opportunity for his usual chase and counter-chase as the contestants' fortunes shift. These are set against the larger exploits of the mysterious Pilot, John Paul Jones. The best character in the story is Long Tom Coffin, the Nantucket whale-man. The selection is an episode which occurs while Jones, Captain Griffith, and Manual, captain of marines, are reconnoitering on land.

CHAPTER XVII

"Pol. Very like a whale."

SHAKESPEARE

WHILE the young cornet still continued gazing at the whaleboat (for it was the party from the schooner that he saw), the hour expired for the appearance of Griffith and his

Companions; and Barnstable reluctantly determined to comply with the letter of his instructions, and leave them to their own sagacity and skill to regain the *Ariel*. The boat had been suffered to ride in the edge of the surf, since the appearance of the sun; and the eyes of her crew were kept anxiously fixed on the cliffs, though in vain, to discover the signal that was to call them to the place of landing. After looking at his watch for the twentieth time, and as often 10 casting glances of uneasy dissatisfaction toward the shore, the lieutenant exclaimed:

"A charming prospect this, Master Coffin, but rather too much poetry in it for your taste; I believe you relish no land that is of a harder consistency than mud!"

" I was born on the waters, sir," returned the cockswain, from his snug abode, where he was bestowed with his usual economy of room, "and it's according to all things for a 20 man to love his native soil. I'll not deny, Captain Barnstable, but I would rather drop my anchor on a bottom that won't broom a keel; though at the same time, I harbor no great malice against dry land."

"I shall never forgive it, myself, if any accident has befallen Griffith in this excursion," rejoined the lieutenant; "his pilot may be a better man on the water than on *terra firma*, Long Tom."

The cockswain turned his solemn visage, with an extraordinary meaning, toward his commander, before he replied:

"For as long a time as I have followed the waters, sir, and that has been ever since I've drawn my rations, seeing that I was born while the boat was crossing Nantucket shoals, I've never known a pilot come off in greater need than the one we fell in with when we made that stretch or two on the land, in the 40 dog-watch of yesterday."

"Ay! the fellow has played his part like a man; the occasion was great, and it seems that he was quite equal to his work."

"The frigate's people tell me, sir, that he handled the ship like a top," continued the cockswain; "but she is a ship that is a nateral inimy of the bottom!"

"Can you say as much for this boat, Master Coffin?" cried Barnstable; "keep her out of 50 the surf, or you'll have us rolling in upon the beach, presently, like an empty water-cask; you must remember that we cannot all wade like yourself, in two-fathom water."

The cockswain cast a cool glance at the crests of foam that were breaking over the tops of the billows, within a few yards of where their boat was riding, and called aloud to his men:

"Pull a stroke or two; away with her into dark water."

The drop of the oars resembled the movements of a nice machine, and the light boat skimmed along the water like a duck, that approaches to the very brink of some imminent danger, and then avoids it, at the most critical moment, apparently without an effort. While this necessary movement was making, Barnstable arose and surveyed the cliffs with keen eyes, and then, turning once more, in disappointment from his search, he said:

"Pull more from the land, and let her run down at an easy stroke to the schooner. Keep a lookout at the cliffs, boys; it is possible that they are stowed in some of the holes in the rocks, for it's no daylight business they are on."

The order was promptly obeyed, and they had glided along for nearly a mile in this manner, in the most profound silence, when suddenly the stillness was broken by a heavy rush of air, and a dash of the water, seemingly at no great distance from them.

"By Heaven, Tom," cried Barnstable, starting, "there is the blow of a whale!"

"Ay, ay, sir," returned the cockswain, with undisturbed composure; "here is his spout not half a mile to seaward; the easterly gale has driven the creater to leeward, and he begins to find himself in shoal water. He's been sleeping, while he should have been working to windward!"

"The fellow takes it coolly, too; he's in no hurry to get an offing!"

"I rather conclude, sir," said the cockswain, rolling over his tobacco in his mouth, very composedly, while his little sunken eyes began to twinkle with pleasure at the sight, "the gentleman has lost his reckoning, and don't know which way to head to take himself back into blue water."

"'Tis a finback!" exclaimed the lieutenant; "he will soon make headway, and be off."

"No, sir, 'tis a right whale," answered Tom; "I saw his spout; he threw up a pair of as pretty rainbows as a Christian would wish to look at. He's a raal oil-butt, that fellow!"

Barnstable laughed, turned himself away from the tempting sight, and tried to look at the cliffs; and then unconsciously bent his longing eyes again on the sluggish animal, who was throwing his huge carcass, at times, for many feet from the water, in idle gambols. The temptation for sport and the recollection of his early habits at length prevailed over his anxiety in behalf of his friends, and the young officer inquired of his cockswain:

"Is there any whale-line in the boat, to make fast to that harpoon which you bear about with you in fair weather or foul?"

"I never trust the boat from the schooner without part of a shot, sir," returned the cockswain; "there is something nateral in the sight of a tub to my old eyes."

Barnstable looked at his watch, and again at the cliffs, when he exclaimed, in joyous tones:

"Give strong way, my hearties! There seems nothing better to be done; let us have a stroke of a harpoon at this impudent rascal!"

The men shouted spontaneously, and the old cockswain suffered his solemn visage to relax into a small laugh, while the whaleboat sprang forward like a courser for the goal. During the few minutes they were pulling toward their game, Long Tom arose from his crouching attitude in the stern-sheets, and transferred his huge form to the bows of the boat, where he made such preparations to strike the whale as the occasion required. The tub, containing about half of a whale-line, was placed at the feet of Barnstable, who had been preparing an oar to steer with, in place of the rudder, which was unshipped, in order that if necessary the boat might be whirled round when not advancing.

Their approach was utterly unnoticed by the monster of the deep, who continued to amuse himself with throwing the water in two circular spouts high into the air, occasionally flourishing the broad flukes of his tail with a graceful but terrific force, until the hardy seamen were within a few hundred feet from him, when he suddenly cast his head downward, and, without an apparent effort, reared his immense body for many feet above the water, waving his tail violently, and producing a whizzing noise that sounded like the rushing of winds.

The cockswain stood erect, poising his harpoon, ready for the blow; but when he beheld the creature assume this formidable attitude, he waved his hand to his commander, who instantly signed to his men to cease rowing. In this situation the sportsmen rested for a few moments, while the whale struck several blows on the water in rapid succession, the noise of which re-echoed along the cliffs, like the hollow reports of so many cannon. After this wanton exhibition of his terrible strength, the monster sank again into his native element, and slowly disappeared from the eyes of his pursuers.

"Which way did he head, Tom?" cried Barnstable, the moment the whale was out of sight.

"Pretty much up and down, sir," returned the cockswain, whose eye was gradually brightening with the excitement of the sport; "he'll soon run his nose against the bottom if he stands long on that course, and will be glad to get another snuff of pure air. Send her a few fathoms to starboard, sir, and I promise we shall not be out of his track."

The conjecture of the experienced old seaman proved true; for in a few moments the water broke near them, and another spout was cast into the air, when the huge animal rushed for half his length in the same direction, and fell on the sea with a turbulence and foam equal to that which is produced by the launching of a vessel for the first time into its proper element. After this evolution the whale rolled heavily and seemed to rest from further efforts.

His slightest movements were closely watched by Barnstable and his cockswain, and when he was in a state of comparative rest, the former gave a signal to his crew to ply their oars once more. A few long and vigorous strokes sent the boat directly up to the broadside of the whale, with its bows pointing toward one of the fins, which was at times, as the animal yielded sluggishly to the action of the waves, exposed to view. The cockswain poised his harpoon with much precision, and then darted it from him with a violence that buried the iron in the blubber of their foe. The instant the blow was made Long Tom shouted with singular earnestness:

"Starn all!"

"Stern all!" echoed Barnstable; when the obedient seamen, by united efforts, forced the boat in a backward direction, beyond the reach of any blow from their formidable antagonist. The alarmed animal, however, meditated no such resistance; ignorant of his own power and of the insignificance of his enemies, he sought refuge in flight. One moment of stupid surprise succeeded the entrance of the iron, when he cast his huge tail into the air with a violence that threw the sea around him into increased commotion, and then disappeared with the quickness of lightning amid a cloud of foam.

"Snub him!" shouted Barnstable; "hold on, Tom, he rises already."

"Ay, ay, sir," replied the composed cockswain, seizing the line, which was running out of the boat with a velocity that rendered such a manoeuvre rather hazardous, and causing it to yield more gradually round the large loggerhead that was placed in the bows of the boat for that purpose. Presently the line stretched forward, and rising to the surface with tremulous vibrations, it indicated the direction in which the animal might be expected to reappear. Barnstable had cast the bows of the boat toward that point, before the terrified and wounded victim rose once more to the surface, whose time was, however, no longer wasted in his sports, but who cast the waters aside, as he forced his way with prodigious velocity along the surface. The boat was dragged violently in his wake, and cut through the billows with a terrific rapidity that at moments appeared to bury the slight fabric in the ocean. When Long Tom beheld his victim throwing his spouts on high again, he pointed with exultation to the jetting fluid, which was streaked with the deep red of blood, and cried:

"Ay, I've touched the fellow's life! it must be more than two foot of blubber that stops my iron from reaching the life of any whale that ever sculled the ocean!"

"I believe you have saved yourself the trouble of using the bayonet you have rigged for a lance," said his commander, who entered into the sport with all the ardor of one whose youth had been chiefly passed in such pursuits. "Feel your line, Master Coffin; can we haul alongside of our enemy? I like not the course he is steering, as he tows us from the schooner."

"'Tis the creater's way, sir," said the cockswain; "you know they need the air in their nostrils, when they run, the same as a man—but lay hold, boys, and let's haul up to him."

The seamen now seized the whale-line, and slowly drew their boat to within a few feet of the tail of the fish, whose progress became sensibly less rapid, as he grew weak with the loss of blood. In a few minutes he stopped running, and appeared to roll uneasily on the water, as if suffering the agony of death.

"Shall we pull in and finish him, Tom?" cried Barnstable; "a few sets from your bayonet will do it."

The cockswain stood examining his game with cool discretion, and replied to his interrogatory:

"No, sir, no—he's going into his flurry; there's no occasion for disgracing ourselves by using a soldier's weapon in taking a whale. Starn off, sir, starn off, the creater's in his flurry!"

The warning of the prudent cockswain was promptly obeyed, and the boat cautiously drew off to a distance, leaving to the animal a clear space while under its dying agonies. From a state of perfect rest, the terrible monster threw its tail on high, as when in sport, but its blows were trebled in rapidity and violence, till all was hid from view by a pyramid of foam that was deeply dyed with blood. The roarings of the fish were like the bellowing of a herd of bulls; and to one who was ignorant of the fact, it would have appeared as if a thousand monsters were engaged in deadly combat, behind the bloody mist that obstructed the view. Gradually, these efforts subsided, and when the discolored water again settled down to the long and regular swell of the ocean, the fish was seen, exhausted, and yielding passively to his fate. As life departed, the enormous black mass rolled to one side; and, when the white and glistening skin of the belly became apparent, the seamen well knew that their victory was achieved.

"What's to be done now?" said Barnstable, as he stood and gazed with a diminished excitement at their victim; "he will yield no food, and his carcass will probably drift to land, and furnish our enemies with the oil."

"If I had but the creater in Boston Bay," said the cockswain, "it would prove the making of me; but such is my luck forever! Pull up, at any rate, and let me get my harpoon and line—the English shall never get them while old Tom Coffin can blow."

"Don't speak too fast," said the strokesman of the boat, "whether he get your iron or not, here he comes in chase!"

"What mean you, fellow?" cried Barnstable.

"Captain Barnstable can look for himself," returned the seaman, "and tell whether I speak truth."

The young sailor turned and saw the *Alacrity* bearing down before the wind, with all her sails set, as she rounded a headland but a short half league to windward of the place where the boat lay.

"Pass that glass to me," said the captain, with steady composure. "This promises us work in one of two ways; if she be armed, it has become our turn to run; if not, we are strong enough to carry her."

A very brief survey made the experienced officer acquainted with the true character of the vessel in sight; and, replacing the glass with much coolness, he said:

"That fellow shows long arms and ten teeth, besides King George's pennant from his topmast-head. Now, my lads, you are to pull for your lives; for, whatever may be the notions of Master Coffin on the subject of his harpoon, I have no inclination to have my arms pinioned by John Bull, though his majesty himself put on the irons."

The men well understood the manner and meaning of their commander; and, throwing aside their coats, they applied themselves in earnest to their task. For half an hour a profound silence reigned in the boat, which made an amazing progress. But many circumstances conspired to aid the cutter; she had a fine breeze, with smooth water, and a strong tide

in her favor; and at the expiration of the time we have mentioned, it was but too apparent that the distance between the pursued and pursuers was lessened nearly half. Barnstable preserved his steady countenance, but there was an expression of care gathering around his dark brow, which indicated that he saw the increasing danger of their situation.

"That fellow has long legs, Master Coffin," he said, in a cheerful tone; "your whale-line must go overboard, and the fifty oar must be handled by your delicate hands."

Tom arose from his seat, and, proceeding forward, he cast the tub and its contents together into the sea, when he seated himself at the bow oar, and bent his athletic frame with amazing vigor to the task.

"Ah! there is much of your philosophy in that stroke, Long Tom," cried his commander. "Keep it up, boys; and if we gain nothing else, we shall at least gain time for deliberation.—Come, Master Coffin, what think you? We have three resources before us; let us hear which is your choice: first, we can turn and fight and be sunk; secondly, we can pull to the land, and endeavor to make good our retreat to the schooner in that manner; and, thirdly, we can head to the shore, and possibly, by running under the guns of that fellow, get the wind of him, and keep the air in our nostrils, after the manner of the whale. D—n the whale! but for the tow the black rascal gave us, we should have been out of sight of this rover!"

"If we fight," said Tom, with quite as much composure as his commander manifested, "we shall be taken or sunk; if we land, sir, I shall be taken, for one man, as I never could make any headway on dry ground, and if we try to get the wind of him by pulling under the cliffs, we shall be cut off by a parcel of lubbers that I can see running along their edges, hoping, I dare say, that they shall be able to get a skulking shot at a boat's crew of honest seafaring men."

"You speak with as much truth as philosophy, Tom," said Barnstable, who saw his slender hopes of success curtailed by the open appearance of the horse and foot on the cliffs. "These Englishmen have not slept the last night, and I fear Griffith and Manual will fare but badly. That fellow brings a capful of wind down with him—'tis just his play, and he walks like a race-horse. Ha! he begins to be in earnest!"

While Barnstable was speaking, a column of white smoke was seen issuing from the bows of the cutter; and as the report of a cannon was wafted to their ears, the shot was seen skipping from wave to wave, tossing the water in spray, and flying to a considerable distance beyond them. The seamen cast cursory glances in the direction of the passing ball, but it produced no manifest effect in either their conduct or appearance. The cockswain, who scanned its range with an eye of more practice than the rest, observed: "That's a lively piece for its metal, and it speaks with a good clear voice; but if they should hear it aboard the *Ariel*, the man who fired it will be sorry it wasn't born dumb."

"You are the prince of philosophers, Master Coffin!" cried Barnstable; "there is some hope in that; let the Englishmen talk away, and, my life on it, the Ariels don't believe it is thunder; hand me a musket—I'll draw another shot."

The piece was given to Barnstable, who discharged it several times, as if to taunt their enemies; and the scheme was completely successful. Goaded by the insults, the cutter discharged gun after gun at the little boat, throwing the shot frequently so near as to wet her crew with the spray, but without injuring them in the least. The failure of these attempts of the enemy excited the mirth of the reckless seamen, instead of creating any alarm; and whenever a shot came nearer than common, the cockswain would utter some such expression as:

"A ground swell, a long shot, and a small object make a clean target," or "A man must squint straight to hit a boat."

As, notwithstanding their unsuccessful gunnery, the cutter was constantly gaining on the whaleboat, there was a prospect of a speedy termination of the chase, when the report of a cannon was thrown back like an echo from one of the Englishman's discharges, and Barnstable and his companions had the pleasure of seeing the *Ariel* stretching slowly out from the little bay where she had passed

the night, with the smoke of the gun of defiance curling above her taper masts.

A loud and simultaneous shout of rapture was given by the lieutenant and all his boat's crew at this cheering sight, while the cutter took in all her light sails; and as she hauled up on a wind, she fired a whole broadside at the successful fugitives. Many stands of grape, with several round shot, flew by the boat and fell upon the water near them, raising a cloud of foam, but without doing any injury.

"She dies in a flurry," said Tom, casting his eyes at the little vortex into which the boat was then entering.

"If her commander be a true man," cried Barnstable, "he'll not leave us on so short an acquaintance. Give way, my souls! give way! I would see more of this loquacious cruiser."

The temptation for exertion was great, and it was not disregarded by the men; in a few minutes the whaleboat reached the schooner, when the crew of the latter received their commander and his companions with shouts and cheers that rang across the waters and reached the ears of the disappointed spectators on the verge of the cliffs.

CHAPTER XVIII

"Thus guided on their course they bore,
   Until they near'd the mainland shore;
When frequent on the hollow blast,
   Wild shouts of merriment were cast."
Lord of the Isles

The joyful shouts and hearty cheers of the *Ariel's* crew continued for some time after her commander had reached her deck. Barnstable answered the congratulations of his officers by cordial shakes of the hand; and after waiting for the ebullition of delight among the seamen to subside a little, he beckoned with an air of authority for silence.

"I thank you, my lads, for your good will," he said, when all were gathered around him in deep attention, "they have given us a tough chase, and if you had left us another mile to go, we had been lost. That fellow is a king's cutter; and though his disposition to run to leeward is a good deal mollified, yet he shows signs of fight. At any rate, he is stripping off some of his clothes, which looks as if he were game. Luckily for us, Captain Manual has taken all the marines ashore with him (though what he has done with them, or himself, is a mystery), or we should have had our decks lumbered with live cattle; but as it is, we have a good working breeze, tolerably smooth water, and a dead match! There is a sort of national obligation on us to whip that fellow; and therefore, without more words about the matter, let us turn to and do it, that we may get our breakfasts."

To this specimen of marine eloquence the crew cheered as usual, the young men burning for the combat, and the few old sailors who belonged to the schooner shaking their heads with infinite satisfaction, and swearing by sundry strange oaths that their captain "could talk, when there was need of such thing, like the best dictionary that ever was launched."

During this short harangue, and the subsequent comments, the *Ariel* had been kept, under a cloud of canvas, as near to the wind as she could lie; and as this was her best sailing, she had stretched swiftly out from the land to a distance whence the cliffs and the soldiers, who were spread along their summits, were plainly visible. Barnstable turned his glass repeatedly from the cutter to the shore, as different feelings predominated in his breast, before he again spoke.

"If Mr. Griffith is stowed away among those rocks," he at length said, "he shall see as pretty an argument, discussed in as few words, as he ever listened to, provided the gentlemen in yonder cutter have not changed their minds as to the road they intend to journey. What think you, Mr. Merry?"

"I wish with all my heart and soul, sir," returned the fearless boy, "that Mr. Griffith was safe aboard us; it seems the country is alarmed, and God knows what will happen if he is taken! As to the fellow to windward, he'll find it easier to deal with the *Ariel's* boat than with her mother; but he carries a broad sail; I question if he means to show play."

"Never doubt him, boy," said Barnstable; "he is working off the shore, like a man of sense, and besides, he has his spectacles on, trying to make out what tribe of Yankee Indians we belong to. You'll see him come to

the wind presently and send a few pieces of iron down this way, by way of letting us know where to find him. Much as I like your first lieutenant, Mr. Merry, I would rather leave him on the land this day than see him on my decks. I want no fighting captain to work this boat for me! But tell the drummer, sir, to beat to quarters."

The boy, who was staggering under the weight of his melodious instrument, had been expecting this command, and without waiting for the midshipman to communicate the order, he commenced that short rub-a-dub air that will at any time rouse a thousand men from the deepest sleep, and cause them to fly to their means of offence with a common soul. The crew of the *Ariel* had been collected in groups studying the appearance of the enemy, cracking their jokes, and waiting only for this usual order to repair to the guns; and at the first tap of the drum, they spread with steadiness to the different parts of the little vessel where their various duties called them. The cannon were surrounded by small parties of vigorous and athletic young men; the few marines were drawn up in array with muskets; the officers appeared in their boarding-caps, with pistols stuck in their belts and naked sabers in their hands. Barnstable paced his little quarter-deck with a firm tread, dangling a speaking-trumpet by its lanyard on his forefinger, or occasionally applying the glass to his eye, which, when not in use, was placed under one arm, while his sword was resting against the foot of the mainmast; a pair of heavy ship's pistols were thrust into his belt also; and piles of muskets, boarding-pikes, and naked sabers were placed on different parts of the deck. The laugh of the seamen was heard no longer, and those who spoke uttered their thoughts only in low and indistinct whispers.

The English cutter held her way from the land until she got an offing of more than two miles, when she reduced her sails to a yet smaller number; and heaving into the wind, she fired a gun in a direction opposite to that which pointed to the *Ariel*.

"Now I would wager a quintal [1] of codfish, Master Coffin," said Barnstable, "against the best cask of porter that was ever brewed in

[1] a hundredweight

England, that fellow believes a Yankee schooner can fly in the wind's eye! If he wishes to speak to us, why don't he give his cutter a little sheet and come down?"

The cockswain had made his arrangements for the combat with much more method and philosophy than any other man in the vessel. When the drum beat to quarters, he threw aside his jacket, vest, and shirt, with as little hesitation as if he stood under an American sun, and with all the discretion of a man who had engaged in an undertaking that required the free use of his utmost powers. As he was known to be a privileged individual in the *Ariel*, and one whose opinions, in all matters of seamanship, were regarded as oracles by the crew, and were listened to by his commander with no little demonstration of respect, the question excited no surprise. He was standing at the breech of his long gun with his brawny arms folded on a breast that had been turned to the color of blood by long exposure, his grizzled locks fluttering in the breeze, and his tall form towering far above the heads of all near him.

"He hugs the wind, sir, as if it was his sweetheart," was his answer; "but he'll let go his hold soon; and if he don't, we can find a way to make him fall to leeward."

"Keep a good full!" cried the commander in a stern voice; "and let the vessel go through the water.—That fellow walks well, Long Tom; but we are too much for him on a bowline [1]; though, if he continue to draw ahead in this manner, it will be night before we can get alongside him."

"Ay, ay, sir," returned the cockswain; "them cutters carries a press of canvas when they seem to have but little; their gaffs are all the same as young booms, and spread a broad head to their mainsails. But it's no hard matter to knock a few cloths out of their bolt-ropes, when she will both drop astarn and to leeward."

"I believe there is good sense in your scheme this time," said Barnstable; "for I am anxious about the frigate's people—though I hate a noisy chase. Speak to him, Tom, and let us see if he will answer."

"Ay, ay, sir," cried the cockswain, sinking his body in such a manner as to let his head

fall to a level with the cannon that he controlled, when, after divers orders, and sundry movements to govern the direction of the piece, he applied a match, with a rapid motion, to the priming. An immense body of white smoke rushed from the muzzle of the cannon, followed by a sheet of vivid fire, until, losing its power, it yielded to the wind, and as it rose from the water, spread like a cloud, and passing through the masts of the schooner, was driven far to leeward, and soon blended in the mists which were swiftly scudding before the fresh breezes of the ocean.

Although many curious eyes were watching this beautiful sight from the cliffs, there was too little of novelty in the exhibition to attract a single look of the crew of the schooner from the more important examination of the effect of the shot on their enemy. Barnstable sprang lightly on a gun, and watched the instant when the ball would strike with keen interest, while Long Tom threw himself aside from the line of the smoke with similar intention; holding one of his long arms extended toward his namesake, with a finger on the vent, and supporting his frame by placing the hand of the other on the deck, as his eyes glanced through an opposite port-hole, in an attitude that most men might have despaired of imitating with success.

"There go the chips!" cried Barnstable. "Bravo! Master Coffin, you never planted iron in the ribs of an Englishman with more judgment. Let him have another piece of it; and if he like the sport, we'll play a game of long bowls with him!"

"Ay, ay, sir," returned the cockswain, who, the instant he witnessed the effects of his shot, had returned to superintend the reloading of his gun; "if he holds on half an hour longer, I'll dub [1] him down to our own size, when we can close and make an even fight of it."

The drum of the Englishman was now, for the first time, heard rattling across the waters, and echoing the call to quarters, that had already proceeded from the *Ariel*.

"Ah! you have sent him to his guns!" said Barnstable; "we shall now hear more of it; wake him up, Tom—wake him up."

"We shall start him on end, or put him to

---

[1] close-hauled   [1] trim

sleep altogether, shortly," said the deliberate cockswain, who never allowed himself to be at all hurried, even by his commander. "My shot are pretty much like a shoal of porpoises, and commonly sail in each other's wake. Stand by—heave her breech forward—so; get out of that, you damned young reprobate, and let my harpoon alone!"

"What are you at there, Master Coffin?" cried Barnstable; "are you tongue-tied?"

"Here's one of the boys skylarking with my harpoon on the lee-scuppers, and by-and-by, when I shall want it most, there'll be a no-man's land to hunt for it in."

"Never mind the boy, Tom; send him aft here to me, and I'll polish his behavior; give the Englishman some more iron."

"I want the little villain to pass up my cartridges," returned the angry old seaman; "but if you'll be so good, sir, as to hit him a crack or two, now and then, as he goes by you to the magazine, the monkey will learn his manners, and the schooner's work will be all the better done for it.—A young herring-faced monkey! to meddle with a tool ye don't know the use of. If your parents had spent more of their money on your edication, and less on your outfit, you'd ha' been a gentleman to what ye are now."

"Hurrah! Tom, hurrah!" cried Barnstable, a little impatiently; "is your namesake never to open his throat again?"

"Ay, ay, sir; all ready," grumbled the cockswain; "depress a little; so—so; a damned young baboon-behaved curmudgeon; overhaul that forward fall [1] more; stand by with your match—but I'll pay him!—fire!" This was the actual commencement of the fight; for as the shot of Tom Coffin travelled, as he had intimated, very much in the same direction, their enemy found the sport becoming too hot to be endured in silence, and the report of the second gun from the *Ariel* was instantly followed by that of the whole broadside of the *Alacrity*. The shot of the cutter flew in a very good direction, but her guns were too light to give them efficiency at that distance, and as one or two were heard to strike against the bends [2] of the schooner and

fall back innocuously into the water, the cockswain, whose good humor became gradually restored as the combat thickened, remarked with his customary apathy:

"Them count for no more than love-taps—does the Englishman think that we are firing salutes?"

"Stir him up, Tom! every blow you give him will help to open his eyes," cried Barnstable, rubbing his hands with glee, as he witnessed the success of his efforts to close.

Thus far the cockswain and his crew had the fight, on the part of the *Ariel*, altogether to themselves, the men who were stationed at the smaller and shorter guns standing in perfect idleness by their sides; but in ten or fifteen minutes the commander of the *Alacrity*, who had been staggered by the weight of the shot that had struck him, found that it was no longer in his power to retreat if he wished it; when he decided on the only course that was left for a brave man to pursue, and steered boldly in such a direction as would soonest bring him in contact with his enemy without exposing his vessel to be raked by his fire. Barnstable watched each movement of his foe with eagle eyes, and when the vessel had got within a lessened distance, he gave the order for a general fire to be opened. The action now grew warm and spirited on both sides. The power of the wind was counteracted by the constant explosion of the cannon; and instead of driving rapidly to leeward, a white canopy of curling smoke hung above the *Ariel*, or rested on the water, lingering in her wake, so as to mark the path by which she was approaching to a closer and still deadlier struggle. The shouts of the young sailors as they handled their instruments of death became more animated and fierce, while the cockswain pursued his occupation with the silence and skill of one who labored in a regular vocation. Barnstable was unusually composed and quiet, maintaining the grave deportment of a commander on whom rested the fortunes of the contest, at the same time that his dark eyes were dancing with the fire of suppressed animation.

"Give it them!" he occasionally cried, in a voice that might be heard amid the bellowing

---

[1] tackle regulating the position of the cannon
[2] thick planks along the sides

of the cannon; "never mind their cordage, my lads; drive home their bolts, and make your marks below their ridge-ropes."[1]

In the meantime the Englishman played a manful game.

He had suffered a heavy loss by the distant cannonade, which no metal he possessed could retort upon his enemy; but he struggled nobly to repair the error in judgment with which he had begun the contest. The two vessels gradually drew nigher to each other, until they both entered into the common cloud created by their fire, which thickened and spread around them in such a manner as to conceal their dark hulls from the gaze of the curious and interested spectators on the cliffs. The heavy reports of the cannon were now mingled with the rattling of muskets and pistols, and streaks of fire might be seen glancing like flashes of lightning through the white cloud which enshrouded the combatants; and many minutes of painful uncertainty followed, before the deeply-interested soldiers who were gazing at the scene, discovered on whose banners victory had alighted.

We shall follow the combatants into their misty wreath, and display to the reader the events as they occurred.

The fire of the *Ariel* was much the most quick and deadly, both because she had suffered less, and her men were less exhausted; and the cutter stood desperately on to decide the combat, after grappling, hand to hand. Barnstable anticipated her intention, and well understood her commander's reason for adopting this course; but he was not a man to calculate coolly his advantages, when pride and daring invited him to a more severe trial. Accordingly, he met the enemy half-way, and as the vessels rushed together, the stern of the schooner was secured to the bows of the cutter, by the joint efforts of both parties. The voice of the English commander was now plainly to be heard, in the uproar, calling to his men to follow him.

"Away there, boarders! repel boarders on the starboard quarter!" shouted Barnstable through his trumpet.

This was the last order that the gallant young sailor gave with this instrument; for as he spoke, he cast it from him, and, seizing his saber, flew to the spot where the enemy was about to make his most desperate effort. The shouts, execrations, and tauntings of the combatants now succeeded to the roar of the cannon, which could be used no longer with effect, though the fight was still maintained with spirited discharges of the small-arms.

"Sweep him from his decks!" cried the English commander, as he appeared on his own bulwarks, surrounded by a dozen of his bravest men, "drive the rebellious dogs into the sea!"

"Away there, marines!" retorted Barnstable, firing his pistol at the advancing enemy, "leave not a man of them to sup his grog again."

The tremendous and close volley that succeeded this order nearly accomplished the command of Barnstable to the letter, and the commander of the *Alacrity*, perceiving that he stood alone, reluctantly fell back on the deck of his own vessel, in order to bring on his men once more.

"Board her! graybeards and boys, idlers and all!" shouted Barnstable, springing in advance of his crew—a powerful arm arrested the movement of the dauntless seaman, and before he had time to recover himself, he was drawn violently back to his own vessel by the irresistible grasp of his cockswain.

"The fellow's in his flurry," said Tom, "and it wouldn't be wise to go within reach of his flukes; but I'll just step ahead and give him a set with my harpoon."

Without waiting for a reply, the cockswain reared his tall frame on the bulwarks and was in the act of stepping on board of his enemy, when a sea separated the vessels, and he fell with a heavy dash of the waters into the ocean. As twenty muskets and pistols were discharged at the instant he appeared, the crew of the *Ariel* supposed his fall to be occasioned by his wounds and were rendered doubly fierce by the sight, and the cry of their commander to—

"Revenge Long Tom! board her! Long Tom or death!"

They threw themselves forward in irresistible numbers and forced a passage, with much bloodshed, to the forecastle of the *Alacrity*. The Englishman was overpowered but still remained undaunted—he rallied his crew and bore up most gallantly to the fray. Thrusts of pikes and blows of sabers were becoming close and deadly, while muskets and pistols were constantly discharged by those who were kept at a distance by the pressure of the throng of closer combatants.

Barnstable led his men in advance and became a mark of peculiar vengeance to his enemies, as they slowly yielded before his 10 vigorous assaults. Chance had placed the two commanders on opposite sides of the cutter's deck, and the victory seemed to incline toward either party, whenever these daring officers directed the struggle in person. But the Englishman, perceiving that the ground he maintained in person was lost elsewhere, made an effort to restore the battle by changing his position, followed by one or two of his best men. A marine, who preceded him, levelled 20 his musket within a few feet of the American commander, and was about to fire, when Merry glided among the combatants, and passed his dirk into the body of the man, who fell at the blow; shaking his piece with horrid imprecations, the wounded soldier prepared to deal his vengeance on his youthful assailant, when the fearless boy leaped within its muzzle,[1] and buried his own keen weapon in his heart.

"Hurrah!" shouted the unconscious Barn- 30 stable, from the edge of the quarter-deck, where, attended by a few men, he was driving all before him. "Revenge!—Long Tom and victory!"

"We have them!" exclaimed the Englishman; "handle your pikes! we have them between two fires."

The battle would probably have terminated very differently from what previous circumstances had indicated, had not a wild-looking 40 figure appeared in the cutter's channels at that moment, issuing from the sea, and gaining the deck at the same instant. It was Long Tom, with his iron visage rendered fierce by his previous discomfiture, and his grizzled locks drenched with the briny element from which he had risen, looking like Neptune with his trident. Without speaking, he poised his harpoon, and, with a powerful effort, pinned the

[1] i.e., too close to be harmed by discharge or a swing- 50 ing blow

unfortunate Englishman to the mast of his own vessel.

"Starn all!" cried Tom, by a sort of instinct, when the blow was struck; and, catching up the musket of the fallen marine, he dealt out terrible and fatal blows with its butt on all who approached him, utterly disregarding the use of the bayonet on its muzzle. The unfortunate commander of the *Alacrity* brandished his sword with frantic gestures, while his eyes rolled in horrid wildness, when he writhed for an instant in his passing agonies, and then, as his head dropped lifeless upon his gored breast, he hung against the spar, a spectacle of dismay to his crew. A few of the Englishmen stood chained to the spot in silent horror at the sight, but most of them fled to their lower deck, or hastened to conceal themselves in the secret parts of the vessel, leaving to the Americans the undisputed possession of the *Alacrity*.

1823

From THE AMERICAN DEMOCRAT

An Aristocrat and a Democrat

In his insistence upon the political theory of a democracy, Cooper did not lose sight of the fact, evident in his day as in ours, that it is a tendency of democracies to seek a level not above the average intelligence of the mass, and to emphasize achievement in the making and acquisition of things. (Compare Emerson's "Ode to Channing":

Things are in the saddle
And ride mankind.)

For the securing of a national achievement of more real value, there must be, Cooper maintains, an intellectual aristocracy, to the extent of complete freedom of following and cultivating one's individual tastes and gifts without jealousy and without interference by law or custom.

WE live in an age when the words aristocrat and democrat are much used, without regard to the real significations. An aristocrat is one of a few who possess the political power of a country; a democrat, one of the many. The words are also properly applied to those who entertain notions favorable to aristocratical or democratical forms of government. Such persons are not necessarily either aristocrats or democrats in fact, but merely so in opinion.

Thus a member of a democratical government may have an aristocratical bias, and vice versa.

To call a man who has the habits and opinions of a gentleman, an aristocrat from that fact alone, is an abuse of terms and betrays ignorance of the true principles of government, as well as of the world. It must be an equivocal freedom under which every one is not the master of his own innocent acts and associations; and he is a sneaking democrat indeed who will submit to be dictated to, in those habits over which neither law nor morality assumes a right of control.

Some men fancy that a democrat can only be one who seeks the level, social, mental and moral, of the majority, a rule that would at once exclude all men of refinement, education, and taste from the class. These persons are enemies of democracy, as they at once render it impracticable. They are usually great sticklers for their own associations and habits, too, though unable to comprehend any of a nature that are superior. They are, in truth, aristocrats in principle, though assuming a contrary pretension, the groundwork of all their feelings and arguments being self. Such is not the intention of liberty, whose aim is to leave every man to be the master of his own acts; denying hereditary honors, it is true, as unjust and unnecessary, but not denying the inevitable consequences of civilization.

The law of God is the only rule of conduct in this, as in other matters. Each man should do as he would be done by. Were the question put to the greatest advocate of indiscriminate association, whether he would submit to have his company and habits dictated to him, he would be one of the first to resist the tyranny; for they who are the most rigid in maintaining their own claims in such matters, are usually the loudest in decrying those whom they fancy to be better off than themselves. Indeed, it may be taken as a rule in social intercourse, that he who is the most apt to question the pretensions of others is the most conscious of the doubtful position he himself occupies; thus establishing the very claims he affects to deny, by letting his jealousy of it be seen. Manners, education, and refinement, are positive things, and they bring with them innocent tastes which are productive of high enjoyments; and it is as

unjust to deny their possessors their indulgence as it would be to insist on the less fortunate's passing the time they would rather devote to athletic amusements, in listening to operas for which they have no relish, sung in a language they do not understand.

All that democracy means, is as equal a participation in rights as is practicable; and to pretend that social equality is a condition of popular institutions is to assume that the latter are destructive of civilization, for, as nothing is more self-evident than the impossibility of raising all men to the highest standard of tastes and refinement, the alternative would be to reduce the entire community to the lowest. The whole embarrassment on this point exists in the difficulty of making men comprehend qualities they do not themselves possess. We can all perceive the difference between ourselves and our inferiors, but when it comes to a question of the difference between us and our superiors, we fail to appreciate merits of which we have no proper conceptions. In face of this obvious difficulty, there is the safe and just governing rule, already mentioned, or that of permitting every one to be the undisturbed judge of his own habits and associations, so long as they are innocent and do not impair the rights of others to be equally judges for themselves. It follows, that social intercourse must regulate itself, independently of institutions, with the exception that the latter, while they withhold no natural, bestow no factitious advantages beyond those which are inseparable from the rights of property, and general civilization.

In a democracy, men are just as free to aim at the highest attainable places in society, as to attain the largest fortunes; and it would be clearly unworthy of all noble sentiment to say that the grovelling competition for money shall alone be free, while that which enlists all the liberal acquirements and elevated sentiments of the race, is denied the democrat. Such an avowal would be at once a declaration of the inferiority of the system, since nothing but ignorance and vulgarity could be its fruits.

The democratic gentleman must differ in many essential particulars from the aristocratical gentleman, though in their ordinary habits and tastes they are virtually identical.

Their principles vary; and, to a slight degree, their deportment accordingly. The democrat, recognizing the right of all to participate in power, will be more liberal in his general sentiments, a quality of superiority in itself; but in conceding this much to his fellow man, he will proudly maintain his own independence of vulgar domination as indispensable to his personal habits. The same principles and manliness that would induce him to depose a royal despot would induce him to resist a vulgar tyrant.

There is no more capital, though more common error, than to suppose him an aristocrat who maintains his independence of habits; for democracy asserts the control of the majority, only in matters of law, and not in matters of custom. The very object of the institution is the utmost practicable personal liberty, and to affirm the contrary would be sacrificing the end to the means.

An aristocrat, therefore, is merely one who fortifies his exclusive privileges by positive institutions, and a democrat, one who is willing to admit of a free competition in all things. To say, however, that the last supposes this competition will lead to nothing is an assumption that means are employed without any reference to an end. He is the purest democrat who best maintains his rights, and no rights can be dearer to a man of cultivation than exemptions from unseasonable invasions on his time by the coarse-minded and ignorant.

1838

1803 -- *Ralph Waldo Emerson* -- 1882

EMERSON'S chief office for his day, as lecturer, essayist, and poet, was the enfranchisement and stimulation of the inward spirit of the individual. A liberated Puritan, he sought to emphasize the spiritual in life, and he exalted conscience and will. To the Calvinists, man had been innately evil; to the Unitarians, in opposition to Calvinism, man was innately good. Emerson, in the next stage, found divinity in him and in nature. He believed, because of this divinity, in the value of inner revelation rather than of formal argument. Nature he venerated for its spiritual content. He deferred to books only in so far as they showed by their spiritual inspiration that throughout history "the mind is one." He rarely read books as wholes. Neither did he defer to traditions of the past as such. He wished to give men the habit of thinking for themselves. His master idea was that man must rely on himself and develop to his own best. He taught the duty of self-development, self-culture, and "a self-trust which is a trust in God himself." Emerson felt the influence of the moral and ethical preoccupations of earlier New England and the new scientific interest in the contemporary world. He believed that "the laws of physics translate the laws of ethics."

Emerson led the quiet, uneventful life of a thinker and teacher. He was born May 25, 1803, in Boston, coming from a long line of pioneers, patriots, and ministers, the descendant of men who had founded the town of Concord, Massachusetts. His father, minister of the First Church, Boston, established the library of the Boston Athenaeum but died in 1811, leaving his widow with six children and no money. The mother, who, like most mothers of great men, seems to have been a superior woman, was obliged to take boarders to help educate and support her children. Emerson entered the Latin school at ten and at seventeen entered Harvard, obtaining his lodging free in return for carrying messages for the president, and earning three-fourths of the cost of his board by acting as waiter at the college commons. Later in the course he tutored backward students. His ability was soon noted and he took prizes for declamation and dissertations. Generally he preferred to devote more attention to his private reading than to the routine studies. In 1821 he was graduated somewhat above the middle of his class, and, after others had refused, he was made class poet, as later were Holmes and Lowell. After graduation Emerson taught in Boston from 1821 to 1825, paying debts and aiding his mother financially. He had been brought up a Unitarian and in 1825 entered the Unitarian divinity school at Harvard. In 1826, at the age of twenty-three, he was admitted to the ministry.

His early ecclesiastical career was brief. He spent the winter of 1826–1827 at St. Augustine, Florida, for the sake of his health. After preaching here and there, chiefly in Cambridge, he was made in 1829 an associate pastor of the Second Church in Boston, which had been the church of the Mathers, but was now Unitarian. In the same year he married Miss Ellen Tucker, who died in 1831. In 1832 a change in his religious views caused him to leave the pastorate. For one thing, he did not wish to administer the Lord's Supper, since it did not mean to him what it was supposed to mean; for another, he was disturbed at the thought of "praying to order." But especially he wished a hard and fast demarcation between the religious and the secular in daily life to be given up.

Soon after, urged by returning ill health, he sailed for Europe in a small brig, landing at Malta. He visited Italy, France, and England with A. H. Clough, the English poet. He sought out Wordsworth, Coleridge, and Carlyle, with the third of whom he formed a lasting friendship recorded in a famous correspondence. He was not Europeanized like Irving and Longfellow by his stay abroad, but the ideas he had from the English writers and from Goethe liberated him from old ways of thinking, and acquainted him with the idealistic philosophy of which Kant was the chief spokesman in Germany. Upon his return to America in 1833 he settled for the remainder of his life in Concord, also the home of Hawthorne, Alcott, and Thoreau. He had a small income from his first wife's estate and he did not need to work very hard or regularly.

In 1835 he married Lydia Jackson of Plymouth, and moved into a house of his own from the Old Manse, which had been the home of his grandfather and was later the home of Hawthorne. He preached occasionally and lectured frequently, at first on science and travel, and then on the topics treated in his essays. This was the day of the lyceum and Emerson had great success as a lecturer. He is described as having a "radiant presence," a serene and quiet manner, and a fascinating voice. An atmosphere of purity and candor is said to have hung about his discussion of transcendental subjects. The pay for lectures was not then very great. He received perhaps ten or twenty or fifty dollars at most for a lecture, but lecturing was the nearest thing to a profession that he had. His favorite books are easily determined from the abundant allusions and anecdotes in his lectures. They were the Greek classics, Plato especially, the Bible, Shakespeare, Montaigne, Milton, and Goethe.

Most of Emerson's writings, except for a few poems, come from his middle life. He published anonymously in 1836 his first work, *Nature*, in which he tried to present a better balanced form of religion. This, with his Phi Beta Kappa oration on "The American Scholar" (1837), called by O. W. Holmes "our intellectual Declaration of Independence," and the Harvard "Divinity School Address" (1838), made him widely known as one who declared a new doctrine of plain living and high thinking. It was not long before he became the intellectual leader of the so-called Transcendental movement, mainly the German eighteenth-century idealistic philosophy in American form. He was the editor for a time (1842–1844) of *The Dial*, magazine of the Transcendentalists, and was the indirect inspirer of many intellectual and social experiments, such as the Brook Farm enterprise (1841–1847) in which Hawthorne, G. W. Curtis, and Margaret Fuller joined, but from which Emerson held himself aloof.

In 1841 he issued *Essays, First Series*, and in 1844 his *Essays, Second Series*, from the material of many of his lectures. The latter had in their turn been made up from detached thoughts from his journals, in which he kept a diary of his intellectual life. In 1847 he issued the first volume of his poems containing his patriotic "Concord Hymn" and numerous poems of nature and human life. His verse, marked by a philosophic turn, often arose from meditations inspired by chance experience. Although he was an apostle of freedom in poetic form, which he deemed subordinate to thought, he hardly achieved it. Much of his verse follows conventions and is in regular meter and rhyme, though the rhymes are often careless and the lines harsh. His favorite form is the octosyllabic rhymed couplet. His poetry is condensed and thoughtful, but lacks artistic sense and controlling pattern, and he seems overaddicted to the ejaculatory. Those are not wanting, however, who think that his poetry will endure longer than his prose.

In 1847–1848 a second visit to Europe was spent in lecturing, in meeting distinguished people, and in studying men and manners in England and France. The lectures delivered in England were embodied later in *Representative Men* (1850) and his observations on English life in *English Traits* (1856), his most careful book.

New collections of essays, nearly all first composed as lectures, were *The Conduct of Life* (1860), *Society and Solitude* (1870), and *Letters and Social Aims* (1876).

These presented the values of spirit, mind, and expression characteristic of his earlier work. Emerson's prose style is condensed and carefully distilled, marked by a metaphysical texture of thought and by many illustrations and anecdotes. He had an especial gift for formulating aphorisms, maxims, and precepts.

Emerson's views of life changed but little as he advanced in years. In 1870 he delivered at Harvard a course of lectures published in 1893 as *Natural History of Intellect*. Having for years extended his lecture tours as far as the Mississippi, at sixty-eight he made a journey to California with a private party, and in the following year revisited England, France, and Italy, and journeyed as far as Egypt. On his return he was welcomed by his townsmen to a new home built by them after the destruction of his former home by fire. Again in Concord he continued his lecturing until he lost his memory. He died from pneumonia in his seventy-ninth year, April 27, 1882.

Emerson's personality carried authority. His audiences followed him intently even when they did not know what he meant. Something of his magic went with his death. Like others of the Transcendentalists, one of whose doctrines was that "being is better than doing," he was not active in practical politics or reform movements but preferred to remain self-dependent and aloof. Among his essays, however, there are many on political and social subjects, and Lowell said Emerson had great influence on those who fought in the Civil War.

To be a true poet, Emerson believed, one must live in harmony with divine law; he will thus become a medium for divine truth, which is universal. Genius is not eccentric but "a larger imbibing of the common heart," an "influx of the divine mind into our mind." The highest beauty "is the mark God sets upon virtue," and Beauty, Truth, and Goodness are "interchangeable," being "but different faces of the same All." "Expression is organic" not only with character but with thought. It is "not meters, but meter-making argument, that makes a poem,—a thought so passionate and alive, that . . . it has an architecture of its own." Attend to the thought, the inspiration, and the form will look out for itself. The poet should not imitate nature, the reports of the senses, but an ideal divinely inspired concept in his mind. Yet concrete facts are useful as symbols of spiritual ideas, and one may use the concrete American scene but only as a *means* of symbolizing the universal moral law transcending nationalities and time and space. The poet may be guided and inspired not only by the influx of the divine in his own individual mind but by the literature of the past in so far as it illustrates the fact that throughout history "the mind is One." Other poets reveal to him his own wealth, his own kinship with those who have been media of the oversoul. The poet should be a liberator and consoler. He should free us from bondage to matter by showing us that our distinctively human destiny is spiritual. He consoles us by teaching us to see particulars, including individual cases of suffering, in perspective; he teaches us to see "the permanent in the mutable and fleeting," to believe "what the years and the centuries say, against the hours."

The Centenary Edition, *The Complete Works of Ralph Waldo Emerson* (12 vols., 1903–1904), with a biographical introduction and notes by his son, E. W. Emerson, is the standard edition. Emerson's *Journals* were edited by E. W. Emerson and Waldo Emerson Forbes (1909–1914). Selections from these appear in Bliss Perry's *The Heart of Emerson's Journals* (1926). Later supplementations are *The Uncollected Writings: Essays, Addresses, Poems, Reviews, and Letters by Ralph Waldo Emerson*, edited by Charles C. Bigelow (1912), and the *Uncollected Lectures by Ralph Waldo Emerson*, edited by Clarence Gohdes (1932). Representative sermons may be found in *Young Emerson Speaks*, edited by A. C. McGiffert (1939). A comprehensive collection of the correspondence is *The Letters of Ralph Waldo Emerson*, edited by R. L. Rusk (6 vols., 1939).

Of the many biographies and works bearing on the life of Emerson, the following may be mentioned: Oliver Wendell Holmes, in the American Men of Letters Series (1884); F. I. Carpenter, *Ralph Waldo Emerson; Representative Selections*, in American Writers Series (1934); James E. Cabot, *A Memoir of Ralph Waldo Emerson* (2 vols., 1887), the most detailed life and still standard; E. W. Emerson, *Emerson in Concord* (1888), which tells of his father's home life; G. E. Woodberry, in the English Men of Letters Series (1907), a thoughtful literary treatment. O. W. Firkins, *Ralph Waldo Emerson* (1915), includes a discussion of Emerson's authorship and philosophy. Recent more or less popular treatments are by R. M. Gay (1928); and Régis Michaud, *Emerson: the Enraptured Yankee*, translated from the French by G. Boas (1930). Mark Van Doren wrote of Emerson in *DAB* (1931), and Van Wyck Brooks published *The Life of Emerson* (1932).

H. C. Goddard's *Studies in New England Transcendentalism* (1908) affords a good background for a study of Emerson. The following are among the best of the innumerable critical articles that concern Emerson: Matthew Arnold in his *Discourses in America* (1885); J. R. Lowell, "Emerson: The Lecturer" in *My Study Windows* (1871); George Santayana in *Interpretations of Poetry and Religion* (1900); W. C. Brownell in *American Prose Masters* (1909); P. E. More in the *Cambridge History of American Literature*, I, 1917; S. P. Sherman in *Americans* (1922); S. M. Crothers, *Ralph Waldo Emerson: How to Know Him* (1921); E. G. Sutcliffe, *Emerson's Theories of Literary Expression* (1923); Norman Foerster in *Nature in American Literature* (1923), also in *American Criticism* (1928); Bliss Perry in *The Praise of Folly* (1923), also *Emerson Today* (1931); Régis Michaud, *L'Esthétique d'Emerson* (1927), which treats Emerson's philosophy; V. L. Parrington, in *Main Currents of American Thought* (1927); A. Kreymborg, in *Our Singing Strength* (1929); H. H. Clark, "Emerson and Science," *Philological Quarterly*, X, 225–60 (July, 1931); Ludwig Lewisohn, in *Expression in America* (1932); H. R. Zink, *Emerson's Use of the Bible* (1935); G. W. Allen, in *American Prosody* (1935); N. Dillaway, *Prophet of America: Emerson and the Problems of Today* (1936).

For bibliographies, see G. W. Cooke, *A Bibliography of Ralph Waldo Emerson* (1908), and *CHAL*, I (1917). G. S. Hubbell's *A Concordance to the Poems of Ralph Waldo Emerson* (1932), is a useful reference work.

THOUGHT

In this early poem Emerson rejoices in his feeling of spiritual superiority over the "crowd," a recurrent note among the Old World romantic poets.

I AM not poor, but I am proud,
  Of one inalienable right,
Above the envy of the crowd,—
  Thought's holy light.

Better it is than gems or gold,
    And oh! it cannot die,
But thought will glow when the sun grows old,
    And mix with Deity.

1823   *1903*

GOOD-BYE

Written when the poet was a youth of twenty,
and first published in James Freeman Clarke's
Western Messenger. The "sylvan home" in which
he felt safe was the small house at Roxbury near
Boston in which his mother then lived. The poem
was written when he was teaching school in Boston.
It contains many of his cardinal doctrines concerning nature, self-reliance, and the superiority of
solitude over society. His son E. W. Emerson said
that Emerson hardly tolerated these boyish verses
in the later editions of his poems, thinking them
over-misanthropic (*Emerson in Concord*, 29).

GOOD-BYE, proud world! I'm going home:
Thou art not my friend, and I'm not thine.
Long through thy weary crowds I roam;
A river-ark on the ocean brine,
Long I've been tossed like the driven foam;
But now, proud world! I'm going home.

Good-bye to Flattery's fawning face;
To Grandeur with his wise grimace;
To upstart Wealth's averted eye;
To supple Office, low and high;   10
To crowded halls, to court and street;
To frozen hearts and hasting feet;
To those who go, and those who come;
Good-bye, proud world! I'm going home.

I am going to my own hearthstone,
Bosomed in yon green hills alone,—
A secret nook in a pleasant land,
Whose groves the frolic fairies planned,
Where arches green, the livelong day,
Echo the blackbird's roundelay,   20
And vulgar feet have never trod
A spot that is sacred to thought and God.

O, when I am safe in my sylvan home,
I tread on the pride of Greece and Rome;
And when I am stretched beneath the pines,
Where the evening star so holy shines,
I laugh at the lore and the pride of man,
At the sophist schools and the learned clan;
For what are they all, in their high conceit,
When man in the bush with God may meet? 30

1823   *1839*

WRITTEN IN NAPLES

The smooth flow and regularity of rhythm in
this poem are unusual with Emerson. His wife,
Ellen Tucker Emerson, referred to in the last line,
died in 1831.

WE are what we are made; each following day
Is the Creator of our human mould
Not less than was the first; the all-wise God
Gilds a few points in every several life,
And as each flower upon the fresh hillside,
And every colored petal of each flower,
Is sketched and dyed, each with a new design,
Its spot of purple, and its streak of brown,
So each man's life shall have its proper lights,
And a few joys, a few peculiar charms,   10
For him round-in the melancholy hours
And reconcile him to the common days.
Not many men see beauty in the fogs
Of close low pinewoods in a river town;
Yet unto me not morn's magnificence,
Nor the red rainbow of a summer eve,
Nor Rome, nor joyful Paris, nor the halls
Of rich men blazing hospitable light,
Nor wit, nor eloquence,—no, nor even the
    song
Of any woman that is now alive,—   20
Hath such a soul, such divine influence,
Such resurrection of the happy past,
As is to me when I behold the morn
Ope in such low moist roadside, and beneath
Peep the blue violets out of the black loam,
Pathetic silent poets that sing to me
Thine elegy, sweet singer, sainted wife.

1833   *1883*

THE APOLOGY

For its underlying thought, the superiority of
the lessons to be learned from nature over those to
be learned from man, this poem may be compared
with Wordsworth's "Expostulation and Reply"
and "The Tables Turned" (1798).

THINK me not unkind and rude
    That I walk alone in grove and glen;
I go to the god of the wood
    To fetch his word to men.

Tax not my sloth that I
    Fold my arms beside the brook;
Each cloud that floated in the sky
    Writes a letter in my book.

Chide me not, laborious band,
   For the idle flowers I brought;   10
Every aster in my hand
   Goes home loaded with a thought.

There was never mystery
   But 'tis figured in the flowers;
Was never secret history
   But birds tell it in the bowers.

One harvest from thy field
   Homeward brought the oxen strong;
A second crop thine acres yield,
   Which I gather in a song.   20

1834   *1847*

THE RHODORA

ON BEING ASKED, WHENCE IS THE FLOWER?

First published in the *Western Messenger*, July, 1839. Emerson, like Bryant in "The Yellow Violet" and "To the Fringed Gentian," replaces the rose or lily of older traditional poetry by an unhackneyed American flower. Unlike Bryant (or Lowell in "The Dandelion"), Emerson does not see the flower in his mind's eye, as if writing of it from a library; he comes upon it in a special place, at a special time, in a special mood. His line "Beauty is its own excuse for being," should be read with the realization that he admired Plato, who interfused Truth, Beauty, and Goodness, and held that the highest beauty must include the spiritual and the moral.

In May, when sea-winds pierced our solitudes,
I found the fresh Rhodora[1] in the woods,
Spreading its leafless blooms in a damp nook,
To please the desert and the sluggish brook.
The purple petals, fallen in the pool,
Made the black water with their beauty gay;
Here might the redbird come his plumes to cool,
And court the flower that cheapens his array.

Rhodora! if the sages ask thee why   9
This charm is wasted on the earth and sky,
Tell them, dear, that if eyes were made for
   seeing,
Then Beauty is its own excuse for being:
Why thou wert there, O rival of the rose!
I never thought to ask, I never knew:
But, in my simple ignorance, suppose
The selfsame Power that brought me there
   brought you.

1834   *1839*

[1] *Rhododendrum Rhodora* is the botanical name.

CONCORD HYMN

SUNG AT THE COMPLETION OF THE BATTLE
MONUMENT, JULY 4, 1837

The fight of the "embattled farmers" with the British at Concord was described by Emerson in his *Historical Discourse Delivered before the Citizens of Concord* (1835). In the *Selected Poems* of 1876, the hymn was given the title "Concord Fight." Emerson was not given to patriotic themes. The hymn is distinctively Emersonian only in the striking last line of the first quatrain. But it is a model of its kind in its flawless nobility of expression and sustained progress to its final lines. It is deservedly popular.

By the rude bridge that arched the flood,
   Their flag to April's breeze unfurled,
Here once the embattled farmers stood,
   And fired the shot heard round the world.

The foe long since in silence slept;
   Alike the conqueror silent sleeps;
And Time the ruined bridge has swept
   Down the dark stream which seaward
     creeps.

On this green bank, by this soft stream,
   We set today a votive stone;   10
That memory may their deed redeem,
   When, like our sires, our sons are gone.

Spirit, that made those heroes dare
   To die, and leave their children free,
Bid Time and Nature gently spare
   The shaft we raise to them and thee.

1836   *1837*

EACH AND ALL

The fundamental thought of this poem, which grew out of a casual outdoor experience, may be found in Emerson's *Nature* (iii): "Nature is a sea of forms radically alike and even unique. . . . Nothing is quite beautiful alone; nothing but is beautiful in the whole. A single object is only so far beautiful as it suggests this universal grace." Instead of placing it first, which would have been the clearer method, Emerson preceded his central thought by a number of illustrations. As a rule he does not plan out the structure of his poems carefully.

Little thinks, in the field, yon red-cloaked
   clown
Of thee from the hilltop looking down;

The heifer that lows in the upland farm,
Far-heard, lows not thine ear to charm;
The sexton, tolling his bell at noon,
Deems not that great Napoleon
Stops his horse, and lists with delight,
Whilst his files sweep round yon Alpine
    height;
Nor knowest thou what argument
Thy life to thy neighbor's creed has lent.   10
All are needed by each one;
Nothing is fair or good alone.
I thought the sparrow's note from heaven,
Singing at dawn on the alder bough;
I brought him home, in his nest, at even;
He sings the song, but it cheers not now,
For I did not bring home the river and
    sky;—
He sang to my ear,—they sang to my eye.
The delicate shells lay on the shore;
The bubbles of the latest wave   20
Fresh pearls to their enamel gave,
And the bellowing of the savage sea
Greeted their safe escape to me.
I wiped away the weeds and foam,
I fetched my sea-born treasures home;
But the poor, unsightly, noisome things
Had left their beauty on the shore
With the sun and the sand and the wild up-
    roar.
The lover watched his graceful maid,
As 'mid the virgin train she strayed,   30
Nor knew her beauty's best attire
Was woven still by the snow-white choir.
At last she came to his hermitage,
Like the bird from the woodlands to the
    cage;—
The gay enchantment was undone,
A gentle wife, but fairy none.
Then I said, "I covet truth;
Beauty is unripe childhood's cheat;
I leave it behind with the games of youth":—
As I spoke, beneath my feet   40
The ground-pine curled its pretty wreath,
Running over the club-moss burrs;
I inhaled the violet's breath;
Around me stood the oaks and firs;
Pine-cones and acorns lay on the ground;
Over me soared the eternal sky,
Full of light and of deity;
Again I saw, again I heard,
The rolling river, the morning bird;—

Beauty through my senses stole;   50
I yielded myself to the perfect whole.
                                        1839

THE PROBLEM

First published in *The Dial* for July, 1840. It
may be that the poet here presents his personal
problem, the conflict between his admiration and
reverence for a clergyman and his unwillingness to
be one. He resigned from the Unitarian ministry
when he felt that he could not sincerely perform
all that was expected of him. An entry in his
Journal for August 28, 1838, reads: "It is very
grateful to my feelings to go into a Roman cathedral, yet I look as my countrymen do at the
Roman priesthood. It is very grateful to me to go
into an English church and hear the liturgy read,
yet nothing would induce me to become an English priest." The main body of the poem, however,
seems to be the exposition of a thesis concerning
the relation of the formal and the spiritual rather
than the statement of a problem. Its underlying
thought is that all religions with their oracles,
litanies, temples, statues, prophets, priests, emerge
from the Divine in man. Man instinctively expresses his noblest ideals under the inspiration of
the Universal Mind, or Oversoul, or Deity. The
examples in the poem are cited as testifying to
this truth.

I LIKE a church; I like a cowl,
I love a prophet of the soul;
And on my heart monastic aisles
Fall like sweet strains, or pensive smiles:
Yet not for all his faith can see
Would I that cowlèd churchman be.

Why should the vest on him allure,
Which I could not on me endure?

Not from a vain or shallow thought
His awful Jove young Phidias brought;   10
Never from lips of cunning fell
The thrilling Delphic oracle[1];
Out from the heart of nature rolled
The burdens of the Bible old;
The litanies of nations came,
Like the volcano's tongue of flame,
Up from the burning core below,—
The canticles of love and woe:

[1] greatest of the Greek oracles, that of the Pythian
Apollo at Delphi

The hand that rounded Peter's dome
And groined the aisles of Christian Rome   20
Wrought in a sad sincerity;
Himself from God he could not free;
He builded better than he knew;—
The conscious stone to beauty grew.

Know'st thou what wove yon woodbird's
    nest
Of leaves, and feathers from her breast?
Or how the fish outbuilt her shell,
Painting with morn each annual cell?
Or how the sacred pine-tree adds
To her old leaves new myriads?   30
Such and so grew these holy piles,
Whilst love and terror laid the tiles.
Earth proudly wears the Parthenon,
As the best gem upon her zone,
And Morning opes with haste her lids
To gaze upon the Pyramids;
O'er England's abbeys bends the sky,
As on its friends, with kindred eye;
For out of Thought's interior sphere
These wonders rose to upper air;   40
And Nature gladly gave them place,
Adopted them into her race,
And granted them an equal date
With Andes and with Ararat.

These temples grew as grows the grass;
Art might obey, but not surpass.
The passive Master lent his hand
To the vast soul that o'er him planned;
And the same power that reared the shrine
Bestrode the tribes that knelt within.   50
Ever the fiery Pentecost[1]
Girds with one flame the countless host,
Trances the heart through chanting choirs,
And through the priest the mind inspires.
The word unto the prophet spoken
Was writ on tables yet unbroken;
The word by seers or sibyls[2] told,
In groves of oak, or fanes of gold,
Still floats upon the morning wind,
Still whispers to the willing mind.   60
One accent of the Holy Ghost
The heedless world hath never lost.
I know what say the fathers wise,—
The Book itself before me lies,

[1] fiftieth day after the Passover and the Crucifixion
(see Acts 2)   [2] prophetesses

Old *Chrysostom*, best Augustine,
And he who blent both in his line,
The younger *Golden Lips* or mines,
Taylor, the Shakspeare of divines,
His words are music in my ear,
I see his cowlèd portrait dear;   70
And yet, for all his faith could see,
I would not the good bishop be.

1839   *1840*

From WOODNOTES

First published in *The Dial*, 1840. A long poem
for Emerson. The second part is not included here.
The portrait of the "forest seer" seems so like
Thoreau as to have been inspired by him. Yet
E. W. Emerson said of his father that the portrait
was written before he came to know Thoreau
(*Emerson in Concord*, 111).

I

1

WHEN the pine tosses its cones
To the song of its waterfall tones,
Who speeds to the woodland walks?
To birds and trees who talks?
Caesar of his leafy Rome,
There the poet is at home.
He goes to the riverside,—
Not hook nor line hath he;
He stands in the meadows wide,—
Nor gun nor scythe to see.   10
Sure some god his eye enchants:
What he knows nobody wants.
In the wood he travels glad,
Without better fortune had,
Melancholy without bad.
Knowledge this man prizes best
Seems fantastic to the rest:
Pondering shadows, colors, clouds,
Grass-buds and caterpillar-shrouds,
Boughs on which the wild bees settle,   20
Tints that spot the violet's petal,
Why Nature loves the number five,
And why the star-form she repeats:
Lover of all things alive,
Wonderer at all he meets,
Wonderer chiefly at himself,
Who can tell him what he is?
Or how meet in human elf
Coming and past eternities?

2

And such I knew, a forest seer,   30
A minstrel of the natural year,
Foreteller of the vernal ides,
Wise harbinger of spheres and tides,
A lover true, who knew by heart
Each joy the mountain dales impart:
It seemed that Nature could not raise
A plant in any secret place,
In quaking bog, on snowy hill,
Beneath the grass that shades the rill,
Under the snow, between the rocks,   40
In damp fields known to bird and fox,
But he would come in the very hour
It opened in its virgin bower,
As if a sunbeam showed the place,
And tell its long-descended race.
It seemed as if the breezes brought him,
It seemed as if the sparrows taught him;
As if by secret sight he knew
Where, in far fields, the orchis grew.
Many haps fall in the field   50
Seldom seen by wishful eyes,
But all her shows did Nature yield,
To please and win this pilgrim wise.
He saw the partridge drum in the woods;
He heard the woodcock's evening hymn;
He found the tawny thrushes' broods;
And the shy hawk did wait for him;
What others did at distance hear,
And guessed within the thicket's gloom,
Was shown to this philosopher,   60
And at his bidding seemed to come.

3

In unploughed Maine he sought the lumberers'
     gang
Where from a hundred lakes young rivers
     sprang;
He trode the unplanted forest floor, whereon
The all-seeing sun for ages hath not shone;
Where feeds the moose, and walks the surly
     bear,
And up the tall mast[1] runs the woodpecker.
He saw beneath dim aisles, in odorous beds,
The slight Linnæa[2] hang its twinborn heads,
And blessed the monument of the man of
     flowers,   70

[1] tall pine tree   [2] a low prostrate vinelike plant,
sometimes called twinflower

Which breathes his sweet fame through the
     northern bowers;
He heard, when in the grove, at intervals,
With sudden roar the aged pine-tree falls,—
One crash, the death-hymn of the perfect
     tree,
Declares the close of its green century.
Low lies the plant to whose creation went
Sweet influence from every element;
Whose living towers the years conspired to
     build,
Whose giddy top the morning loved to gild.
Through these green tents, by eldest Nature
     dressed,   80
He roamed, content alike with man and
     beast.
Where darkness found him he lay glad at
     night;
There the red morning touched him with its
     light.
Three moons his great heart him a hermit
     made,
So long he roved at will the boundless shade.
The timid it concerns to ask their way,
And fear what foe in caves and swamps can
     stray,
To make no step until the event is known,
And ills to come as evils past bemoan.
Not so the wise; no coward watch he keeps   90
To spy what danger on his pathway creeps;
Go where he will, the wise man is at home,
His hearth the earth,—his hall the azure dome;
Where his clear spirit leads him, there's his
     road
By God's own light illumined and foreshowed.

4

'Twas one of the charmèd days
When the genius of God doth flow;
The wind may alter twenty ways,
A tempest cannot blow;
It may blow north, it still is warm;   100
Or south, it still is clear;
Or east, it smells like a clover-farm;
Or west, no thunder fear;
The musing peasant, lowly great,
Beside the forest water sate;
The rope-like pine-roots crosswise grown
Composed the network of his throne;
The wide lake, edged with sand and grass,
Was burnished to a floor of glass,

Painted with shadows green and proud 110
Of the tree and of the cloud.
He was the heart of all the scene;
On him the sun looked more serene;
To hill and cloud his face was known,—
It seemed the likeness of their own;
They knew by secret sympathy
The public child of earth and sky.
"You ask," he said, "what guide
Me through trackless thickets led,
Through thick-stemmed woodlands rough
    and wide. 120
I found the water's bed.
The watercourses were my guide;
I travelled grateful by their side,
Or through their channel dry;
They led me through the thicket damp,
Through brake and fern, the beavers' camp,
Through beds of granite cut my road,
And their resistless friendship showed.
The falling waters led me,
The foodful waters fed me, 130
And brought me to the lowest land,
Unerring to the ocean sand.
The moss upon the forest bark
Was polestar when the night was dark;
The purple berries in the wood
Supplied me necessary food;
For Nature ever faithful is
To such as trust her faithfulness.
When the forest shall mislead me,
When the night and morning lie, 140
When sea and land refuse to feed me,
'Twill be time enough to die;
Then will yet my mother yield
A pillow in her greenest field,
Nor the June flowers scorn to cover
The clay of their departed lover."

                        1840

THE SNOW–STORM

Whittier used lines from this poem as a motto for *Snow-Bound*. In content it is not distinctively Emersonian, not moral or philosophical, but mainly descriptive. Noteworthy are the felicitous lines ending the first and second paragraphs.

ANNOUNCED by all the trumpets of the sky,
Arrives the snow, and, driving o'er the fields,
Seems nowhere to alight: the whited air
Hides hills and woods, the river, and the
    heaven,

And veils the farmhouse at the garden's end.
The sled and traveler stopped, the courier's
    feet
Delayed, all friends shut out, the housemates
    sit
Around the radiant fireplace, enclosed
In a tumultuous privacy of storm.

    Come see the north wind's masonry. 10
Out of an unseen quarry evermore
Furnished with tile, the fierce artificer
Curves his white bastions with projected roof
Round every windward stake, or tree, or door.
Speeding, the myriad-handed, his wild work
So fanciful, so savage, nought cares he
For number or proportion. Mockingly,
On coop or kennel he hangs Parian [1] wreaths;
A swan-like form invests the hidden thorn;
Fills up the farmer's lane from wall to wall, 20
Maugre the farmer's sighs; and at the gate
A tapering turret overtops the work.
And when his hours are numbered, and the
    world
Is all his own, retiring, as he were not,
Leaves, when the sun appears, astonished Art
To mimic in slow structures, stone by stone,
Built in an age, the mad wind's nightwork,
The frolic architecture of the snow.

                        1841

FORBEARANCE

E. W. Emerson thought it probable that his father had Thoreau in mind in this poem. Its preference for the avoidance of praise, as inadequate or patronizing, is not usual.

HAST thou named all the birds without a gun?
Loved the wood-rose, and left it on its stalk?
At rich men's tables eaten bread and pulse?
Unarmed, faced danger with a heart of trust?
And loved so well a high behavior,
In man or maid, that thou from speech re-
    frained,
Nobility more nobly to repay?
O, be my friend, and teach me to be thine!

                        1842

GRACE

Although Emerson was the apostle of self-reliance, this poem testifies to his sense of the practical value of such curbs to freedom as he

[1] marble, noted for its fine quality and its whiteness, quarried in the island of Paros in the Aegean Sea

enumerates in line 3. The poem may be compared
with the "Ode to Duty" of Wordsworth, in which,
though his usual guides were high instincts and
intuitions, he welcomes the restraining forces of
conscience and duty.

How much, preventing God, how much I
    owe
To the defenses thou hast round me set;
Example, custom, fear, occasion slow,—
These scorned bondmen were my parapet.
I dare not peep over this parapet
To gauge with glance the roaring gulf below,
The depths of sin to which I had descended,
Had not these me against myself defended.

                       1842

HAMATREYA

    A poem on man's thirst to possess land and on
his transiency in the shadow of earth's might. The
earth is not owned by man, but he is the earth's
and he returns to it. The original idea on which
Emerson based the poem was Hindu, but his treatment gives it New England regionalization. The
names in the opening line are those of early Concord settlers. Peter Bulkeley was one of the poet's
own ancestors.

BULKELEY, Hunt, Willard, Hosmer, Meriam,
    Flint,
Possessed the land which rendered to their
    toil
Hay, corn, roots, hemp, flax, apples, wool,
    and wood.
Each of these landlords walked amidst his
    farm,
Saying, "'Tis mine, my children's and my
    name's.
How sweet the west wind sounds in my own
    trees!
How graceful climb those shadows on my
    hill!
I fancy these pure waters and the flags
Know me, as does my dog: we sympathize;
And, I affirm, my actions smack of the soil." 10

Where are these men? Asleep beneath their
    grounds:
And strangers, fond as they, their furrows
    plough.
Earth laughs in flowers, to see her boastful
    boys
Earth-proud, proud of the earth which is not
    theirs;

Who steer the plough, but cannot steer their
    feet
Clear of the grave.
They added ridge to valley, brook to pond,
And sighed for all that bounded their do-
    main;
"This suits me for a pasture; that's my park;
We must have clay, lime, gravel, granite-
    ledge,   20
And misty lowland, where to go for peat.
The land is well,—lies fairly to the south,
'Tis good, when you have crossed the sea and
    back,
To find the sitfast acres where you left them."
Ah! the hot owner sees not Death, who adds
Him to his land, a lump of mould the more.
Hear what the Earth says:—

EARTH-SONG

"Mine and yours;
    Mine, not yours.
Earth endures;
Stars abide—   30
Shine down in the old sea;
Old are the shores;
But where are old men?
I who have seen much,
Such have I never seen.

"The lawyer's deed
Ran sure,
In tail,[1]
To them and to their heirs   40
Who shall succeed,
Without fail,
Forevermore.

"Here is the land,
Shaggy with wood,
With its old valley,
Mound and flood.
But the heritors?—
Fled like the flood's foam.
The lawyer, and the laws,   50
And the kingdom,
Clean swept herefrom.

"They called me theirs,
Who so controlled me;
Yet every one
Wished to stay, and is gone.
How am I theirs,
If they cannot hold me,
But I hold them?"

[1] limitation of ownership, entailment

When I heard the Earth-song, 60
I was no longer brave;
My avarice cooled
Like lust in the chill of the grave.

1847

MUSKETAQUID

The accuracy and clearness of the details of
landscape in this poem may be noted. Musketaquid is the Indian name of the Concord River.

BECAUSE I was content with these poor fields,
Low, open meads, slender and sluggish
streams,
And found a home in haunts which others
scorned,
The partial wood-gods overpaid my love,
And granted me the freedom of their state,
And in their secret senate have prevailed
With the dear, dangerous lords that rule our
life,
Made moon and planets parties to their bond,
And through my rock-like, solitary wont 9
Shot million rays of thought and tenderness.
For me, in showers, in sweeping showers, the
spring
Visits the valley;—break away the clouds,—
I bathe in the morn's soft and silvered air,
And loiter willing by yon loitering stream.
Sparrows far off, and nearer, April's bird,
Blue-coated,—flying before from tree to tree,
Courageous sing a delicate overture
To lead the tardy concert of the year.
Onward and nearer rides the sun of May;
And wide around, the marriage of the plants
Is sweetly solemnized. Then flows amain[1] 21
The surge of summer's beauty; dell and crag,
Hollow and lake, hillside, and pine arcade,
Are touched with genius. Yonder ragged
cliff
Has thousand faces in a thousand hours.
Beneath low hills, in the broad interval
Through which at will our Indian rivulet
Winds mindful still of sannup[2] and of squaw,
Whose pipe and arrow oft the plough un-
buries, 29
Here in pine houses built of new fallen trees,
Supplanters of the tribe, the farmers dwell.
Traveller, to thee, perchance, a tedious road,
Or, it may be, a picture; to these men,

[1] with might   [2] warrior, Indian brave

The landscape is an armory of powers,
Which, one by one, they know to draw and
use.
They harness beast, bird, insect, to their
work;
They prove the virtues of each bed of rock,
And, like the chemist mid his loaded jars,
Draw from each stratum its adapted use
To drag their crops or weapon their arts
withal. 40
They turn the frost upon their chemic heap,
They set the wind to winnow pulse and grain,
They thank the spring-flood for its fertile
slime,
And, on cheap summit-levels of the snow,
Slide with the sledge to inaccessible woods
O'er meadows bottomless. So, year by year,
They fight the elements with elements,
(That one would say, meadow and forest
walked,
Transmuted in these men to rule their like,)
And by the order in the field disclose 50
The order regnant in the yeoman's brain.

What these strong masters wrote at large in
miles
I followed in small copy in my acre;
For there's no rood has not a star above it;
The cordial quality of pear or plum
Ascends as gladly in a single tree
As in broad orchards resonant with bees;
And every atom poises for itself,
And for the whole. The gentle deities 59
Showed me the lore of colors and of sounds,
The innumerable tenements of beauty,
The miracle of generative force,
Far-reaching concords of astronomy
Felt in the plants, and in the punctual birds;
Better, the linked purpose of the whole,
And, chiefest prize, found I true liberty
In the glad home plain-dealing nature gave.
The polite found me impolite; the great
Would mortify me, but in vain; for still
I am a willow of the wilderness, 70
Loving the wind that bent me. All my hurts
My garden spade can heal. A woodland walk,
A quest of river-grapes, a mocking thrush,
A wild-rose, or rock-loving columbine,
Salve my worst wounds.
For thus the wood-gods murmured in my
ear:

"Dost love our manners? Canst thou silent
    lie?
Canst thou, thy pride forgot, like nature
    pass
Into the winter night's extinguished mood?
Canst thou shine now, then darkle,   80
And being latent, feel thyself no less?
As, when the all-worshipped moon attracts
    the eye,
The river, hill, stems, foliage are obscure
Yet envies none, none are unenviable."

                      1847

ODE

INSCRIBED TO W. H. CHANNING

William Henry Channing, a Unitarian minister
of Boston, was deeply interested in experiments in
social reform, such as the Brook Farm experiment
with which Hawthorne associated himself. He was
a nephew of William Ellery Channing, the Unitarian leader. The ode reflects Emerson's attitude
toward reformers and humanitarian movements
and possibilities. A. T. Odell, *La Doctrine Sociale
d'Emerson* (1931), William Slater in the *International Journal of Ethics* (July, 1903), and
Van Wyck Brooks, *Harper's Magazine* (December,
1926), may be consulted concerning this phase of
Emerson's teaching. The poet expresses in "New
England Reformers" (*Works*, III), the fundamental thought of this ode, i.e., that outward
usages and attacks on existing institutions avail
society little when man, not himself renovated
through self-discipline, seeks to improve things
about him.

THOUGH loath to grieve
    The evil time's sole patriot,
I cannot leave
    My honied thought
        For the priest's cant,
        Or statesman's rant.

If I refuse
    My study for their politique,
Which at the best is trick,
    The angry Muse   10
    Puts confusion in my brain.

But who is he that prates
    Of the culture of mankind,
Of better arts and life?

Go, blindworm, go,
Behold the famous States
Harrying Mexico[1]
With rifle and with knife!

Or who, with accent bolder,
Dare praise the freedom-loving mountaineer?
I found by thee, O rushing Contoocook![2] 21
And in thy valleys, Agiochook![3]
The jackals of the negro-holder.

The God who made New Hampshire
    Taunted the lofty land
With little men;—
    Small bat and wren
House in the oak:—
    If earth-fire cleave
The upheaved land, and bury the folk, 30
    The southern crocodile would grieve.
Virtue palters; Right is hence;
    Freedom praised, but hid;
Funeral eloquence
    Rattles the coffin-lid.

What boots thy zeal,
    O glowing friend,
That would indignant rend
    The northland from the south?
Wherefore? to what good end? 40
Boston Bay and Bunker Hill
    Would serve things still;—
Things are of the snake.

The horseman serves the horse,
The neatherd serves the neat,[4]
    The merchant serves the purse,
The eater serves his meat;
    'Tis the day of the chattel,
Web to weave, and corn to grind;
    Things are in the saddle, 50
And ride mankind.

There are two laws discrete,
Not reconciled,—
Law for man, and law for thing;
The last builds town and fleet,
But it runs wild,
And doth the man unking.

---

[1] in the Mexican War (1846–1848), which inspired
the first series of Lowell's *Biglow Papers* [2] a New
Hampshire river flowing into the Merrimack [3] Indian
name for the White Mountains [4] old word for
cattle

'Tis fit the forest fall,
The steep be graded,
The mountain tunnelled, 60
The sand shaded,
The orchard planted,
The glebe tilled,
The prairie granted,
The steamer built.

Let man serve law for man;
Live for friendship, live for love,
For truth's and harmony's behoof;
The state may follow how it can,
As Olympus follows Jove. 70

Yet do not I implore
The wrinkled shopman to my sounding
    woods,
Nor bid the unwilling senator
Ask votes of thrushes in the solitudes.
Every one to his chosen work;—
Foolish hands may mix and mar;
Wise and sure the issues are.
Round they roll till dark is light,
Sex to sex, and even to odd;—
The over-god 80
Who marries Right to Might,
Who peoples, unpeoples,—
He who exterminates
Races by stronger races,
Black by white faces,—
Knows to bring honey
Out of the lion[1];
Grafts gentlest scion
On pirate and Turk.

The Cossack eats Poland,[2] 90
Like stolen fruit;
Her last noble is ruined,
Her last poet mute:
Straight, into double band
The victors divide;
Half for freedom strike and stand;—
The astonished Muse finds thousands at her
    side.

1847

[1] Judges 14:9   [2] Though a part of the Russian
Empire, Poland was constantly invaded by the Cossack cavalry of the Russian army.

DAYS

First printed in the *Atlantic Monthly*, November,
1857. It has been deservedly popular. Emerson
thought it perhaps his best poem. Its personifica-
tions are striking, and it has a well carried out
parable, simple dramatic expression, and vivid
final lines.

DAUGHTERS of Time, the hypocritic Days,
Muffled and dumb like barefoot dervishes,
And marching single in an endless file,
Bring diadems and fagots in their hands.
To each they offer gifts after his will,
Bread, kingdoms, stars, and sky that holds
    them all.
I, in my pleachèd garden, watched the pomp,
Forgot my morning wishes, hastily
Took a few herbs and apples, and the Day
Turned and departed silent. I, too late, 10
Under her solemn fillet saw the scorn.

1852 1857

TWO RIVERS

G. E. Woodberry (*Ralph Waldo Emerson*, 164)
terms this poem "admirable for the harmonizing
of the unseen river of the eye with the river of the
senses, so that the stream of eternity seems but the
immortalization of the stream of the meadows,
and to flow as it were out of it."

THY summer voice, Musketaquit,[1]
Repeats the music of the rain;
But sweeter rivers pulsing flit
Through thee, as thou through Concord Plain.

Thou in thy narrow banks art pent:
The stream I love unbounded goes
Through flood and sea and firmament;
Through light, through life, it forward flows.

I see the inundation sweet,
I hear the speeding of the stream 10
Through years, through men, through Nature
    fleet,
Through love and thought, through power
    and dream.

Musketaquit, a goblin strong,
Of shard and flint makes jewels gay;
They lose their grief who hear his song,
And where he winds is the day of day.

[1] another form of Musketaquid, the Indian name of
the Concord River

So forth and brighter fares my stream,—
Who drink it shall not thirst again;
No darkness stains its equal gleam,
And ages drop in it like rain.   20

1856   *1858*

THE ROMANY[1] GIRL

By Emerson's time the device of reproducing the
naïve comments of a more primitive person on
the manners and customs of the civilized was somewhat outworn. Goldsmith used it in *The Citizen of
the World; or Letters of a Chinese Philosopher* and
Swift used it in *Gulliver's Travels*. Writers are con-
ditioned by the age in which they live; but by the
middle of the century the romantic conception of
the superiority in integrity and simplicity of those
closer to nature was losing acceptance.

THE sun goes down, and with him takes
The coarseness of my poor attire;
The fair moon mounts, and aye the flame
Of gypsy beauty blazes higher.

Pale northern girls! you scorn our race;
You captives of your airtight halls,
Wear out indoors your sickly days,
But leave us the horizon walls.

And if I take you, dames, to task,
And say it frankly without guile,   10
Then you are gypsies in a mask,
And I the lady all the while.

If, on the heath, below the moon,
I court and play with paler blood,
Me false to mine dare whisper none,—
One sallow horseman knows me good.

Go, keep your cheek's rose from the rain,
For teeth and hair with shopmen deal;
My swarthy tint is in the grain,
The rocks and forest know it real.   20

The wild air bloweth in our lungs,
The keen stars twinkle in our eyes,
The birds gave us our wily tongues,
The panther in our dances flies.

You doubt we read the stars on high,
Nathless we read your fortunes true;
The stars may hide in the upper sky,
But without glass we fathom you.

1855   *1857*

[1] gypsy

BRAHMA

This poem emerged from Emerson's reading of
the sacred books of the East. Compare the following passages from the *Bhavagad-Gita:* "These finite
bodies have been said to belong to an eternal, indestructible, and infinite spirit . . . He who believes
that this spirit can kill, and he who thinks it can
be killed, both of these are wrong in judgment. It
neither kills nor is killed. It is not born nor dies at
any time. It has no origin nor will it ever have an
origin. Unborn, changeless, eternal both as to future and past time, it is not slain when the body
is killed" (chapter ii). Or: "I [Brahma] am the
origin of all gods . . . I am the soul . . . which
exists in the heart of all beings, and I am the beginning and the middle and also the end of existing
things . . . I am also eternal time . . . And I am
Death who seizes all, and the Birth of those to be"
(chapter ix).

IF the red slayer thinks he slays,
Or if the slain think he is slain,
They know not well the subtle ways
I keep, and pass, and turn again.

Far or forgot to me is near;
Shadow and sunlight are the same;
The vanished gods to me appear;
And one to me are shame and fame.

They reckon ill who leave me out;
When me they fly, I am the wings;   10
I am the doubter and the doubt,
And I the hymn the Brahmin sings.

The strong gods pine for my abode,
And pine in vain the sacred Seven;
But thou, meek lover of the good!
Find me, and turn thy back on heaven.

1856   *1857*

TERMINUS[1]

E. W. Emerson commented on this poem (Centenary Edition, 489): "In the last days of 1866 . . .
as I met my father in New York . . . we spent the
night together at the St. Denis Hotel, and as we
sat by the fire he read me two or three of his
poems . . . among them 'Terminus.' It almost
startled me. No thought of his ageing had ever
come to me, and there he sat, with no apparent
abatement of bodily vigor, and young in spirit,

[1] the god of boundaries in Roman mythology

recognizing with acquiescence his failing power; I
think he smiled as he read. He recognized, as none
of us did, that his working days were nearly done."
Emerson was not yet sixty-five when this poetic
renunciation of active life was written.

It is time to be old,
To take in sail:—
The god of bounds,
Who sets to seas a shore,
Came to me in his fatal rounds,
And said: "No more!
No farther shoot
Thy broad ambitious branches, and thy root.
Fancy departs: no more invent;
Contract thy firmament   10
To compass of a tent.
There's not enough for this and that,
Make thy option which of two;
Economize the failing river,
Not the less revere the Giver,
Leave the many and hold the few.
Timely wise accept the terms,
Soften the fall with wary foot;
A little while
Still plan and smile,   20

And, fault of novel germs,
Mature the unfallen fruit.
Curse, if thou wilt, thy sires,
Bad husbands of their fires,
Who, when they gave thee breath,
Failed to bequeath
The needful sinew stark as once,
The Baresark[1] marrow to thy bones,
But left a legacy of ebbing veins,
Inconstant heat and nerveless reins,—   30
Amid the Muses, left thee deaf and dumb,
Amid the gladiators, halt and numb."

As the bird trims her to the gale,
I trim myself to the storm of time,
I man the rudder, reef the sail,
Obey the voice at eve obeyed at prime:
"Lowly faithful, banish fear,
Right onward drive unharmed;
The port, well worth the cruise, is near,
And every wave is charmed."   40
1866   *1867*

[1] Given to wild violence. The more common form of
the word is *berserk*. In old Scandinavian lore the ber-
serks were savage heathen warriors.

From NATURE

Emerson's little book *Nature* was published
anonymously in 1836. It was reprinted, somewhat
revised, in *Nature, Addresses, and Lectures* (1849).
Emerson also had an essay on the subject in *Essays,
Second Series* (1844). Parts I and III are given here.
Emerson's Nature is that of the first half of the
century, when it was worshipped almost idola-
trously as a medium between God and man, the
three akin because of the spiritual element or   10
divinity in nature and man.

A subtle chain of countless rings
The next unto the farthest brings;
The eye reads omens where it goes,
And speaks all languages the rose;
And, striving to be man, the worm
Mounts through all the spires of form.

I. NATURE

To go into solitude, a man needs to retire   20
as much from his chamber as from society. I
am not solitary whilst I read and write, though
nobody is with me. But if a man would be

alone, let him look at the stars. The rays that
come from those heavenly worlds will separate between him and what he touches. One
might think the atmosphere was made transparent with this design, to give man, in the
heavenly bodies, the perpetual presence of the
sublime. Seen in the streets of cities, how
great they are! If the stars should appear one
night in a thousand years, how would men
believe and adore; and preserve for many
generations the remembrance of the city of
God which had been shown! But every night
come out these envoys of beauty, and light
the universe with their admonishing smile.

The stars awaken a certain reverence, because though always present, they are inaccessible; but all natural objects make a kindred
impression, when the mind is open to their
influence. Nature never wears a mean appearance. Neither does the wisest man extort
her secret, and lose his curiosity by finding
out all her perfection. Nature never became a
toy to a wise spirit. The flowers, the animals,
the mountains, reflected the wisdom of his

best hour, as much as they had delighted the simplicity of his childhood.

When we speak of nature in this manner, we have a distinct but most poetical sense in the mind. We mean the integrity of impression made by manifold natural objects. It is this which distinguishes the stick of timber of the woodcutter, from the tree of the poet. The charming landscape which I saw this morning, is indubitably made up of some twenty or thirty farms. Miller owns this field, Locke that, and Manning the woodland beyond. But none of them owns the landscape. There is a property in the horizon which no man has but he whose eye can integrate all the parts, that is, the poet. This is the best part of these men's farms, yet to this their warranty-deeds give no title.

To speak truly, few adult persons can see nature. Most persons do not see the sun. At least they have a very superficial seeing. The sun illuminates only the eye of the man, but shines into the eye and the heart of the child. The lover of nature is he whose inward and outward senses are still truly adjusted to each other; who has retained the spirit of infancy even into the era of manhood. His intercourse with heaven and earth, becomes part of his daily food. In the presence of nature, a wild delight runs through the man, in spite of real sorrows. Nature says—he is my creature, and maugre all his impertinent griefs, he shall be glad with me. Not the sun or the summer alone, but every hour and season yields its tribute of delight; for every hour and change corresponds to and authorizes a different state of the mind, from breathless noon to grimmest midnight. Nature is a setting that fits equally well a comic or a mourning piece. In good health, the air is a cordial of incredible virtue. Crossing a bare common, in snow puddles, at twilight, under a clouded sky, without having in my thoughts any occurrence of special good fortune, I have enjoyed a perfect exhilaration. I am glad to the brink of fear. In the woods too, a man casts off his years, as the snake his slough, and at what period soever of life, always is a child. In the woods, is perpetual youth. Within these plantations of God, a decorum and sanctity reign, a perennial festival is dressed, and the guest sees not how he should tire of them in a thousand years. In the woods, we return to reason and faith. There I feel that nothing can befall me in life—no disgrace, no calamity (leaving me my eyes), which nature cannot repair. Standing on the bare ground—my head bathed by the blithe air, and uplifted into infinite space—all mean egotism vanishes. I become a transparent eyeball; I am nothing; I see all; the currents of the Universal Being circulate through me; I am part or particle of God. The name of the nearest friend sounds then foreign and accidental: to be brothers, to be acquaintances—master or servant, is then a trifle and a disturbance. I am the lover of uncontained and immortal beauty. In the wilderness, I find something more dear and connate than in streets or villages. In the tranquil landscape, and especially in the distant line of the horizon, man beholds somewhat as beautiful as his own nature.

The greatest delight which the fields and woods minister, is the suggestion of an occult relation between man and the vegetable. I am not alone and unacknowledged. They nod to me, and I to them. The waving of the boughs in the storm, is new to me and old. It takes me by surprise, and yet is not unknown. Its effect is like that of a higher thought or a better emotion coming over me, when I deemed I was thinking justly or doing right.

Yet it is certain that the power to produce this delight, does not reside in nature, but in man, or in a harmony of both. It is necessary to use these pleasures with great temperance. For, nature is not always tricked in holiday attire, but the same scene which yesterday breathed perfume and glittered as for the frolic of the nymphs, is overspread with melancholy today. Nature always wears the colors of the spirit. To a man laboring under calamity, the heat of his own fire hath sadness in it. Then, there is a kind of contempt of the landscape felt by him who has just lost by death a dear friend. The sky is less grand as it shuts down over less worth in the population.

III. BEAUTY

A nobler want of man is served by nature, namely, the love of Beauty.

The ancient Greeks called the world κόσμος [kosmos], beauty. Such is the constitution of all things, or such the plastic power of the human eye, that the primary forms, as the sky, the mountain, the tree, the animal, give us a delight *in and for themselves;* a pleasure arising from outline, color, motion, and grouping. This seems partly owing to the eye itself. The eye is the best of artists. By the mutual action of its structure and of the laws of light, perspective is produced, which integrates every mass of objects, of what character soever, into a well colored and shaded globe, so that where the particular objects are mean and unaffecting, the landscape which they compose is round and symmetrical. And as the eye is the best composer, so light is the first of painters. There is no object so foul that intense light will not make beautiful. And the stimulus it affords to the sense, and a sort of infinitude which it hath, like space and time, make all matter gay. Even the corpse has its own beauty. But besides this general grace diffused over nature, almost all the individual forms are agreeable to the eye, as is proved by our endless imitations of some of them, as the acorn, the grape, the pine-cone, the wheat-ear, the egg, the wings and forms of most birds, the lion's claw, the serpent, the butterfly, sea-shells, flames, clouds, buds, leaves, and the forms of many trees, as the palm.

For better consideration, we may distribute the aspects of Beauty in a threefold manner.

1. First, the simple perception of natural forms is a delight. The influence of the forms and actions in nature is so needful to man, that, in its lowest functions, it seems to lie on the confines of commodity and beauty. To the body and mind which have been cramped by noxious work or company, nature is medicinal and restores their tone. The tradesman, the attorney comes out of the din and craft of the street and sees the sky and the woods, and is a man again. In their eternal calm, he finds himself. The health of the eye seems to demand a horizon. We are never tired, so long as we can see far enough.

But in other hours, Nature satisfies by its loveliness, and without any mixture of corporeal benefit. I see the spectacle of morning from the hilltop over against my house, from daybreak to sunrise, with emotions which an angel might share. The long slender bars of cloud float like fishes in the sea of crimson light. From the earth, as a shore, I look out into that silent sea. I seem to partake its rapid transformations; the active enchantment reaches my dust, and I dilate and conspire with the morning wind. How does Nature deify us with a few and cheap elements! Give me health and a day, and I will make the pomp of emperors ridiculous. The dawn is my Assyria; the sunset and moonrise my Paphos,[1] and unimaginable realms of faerie; broad noon shall be my England of the senses and the understanding; the night shall be my Germany of mystic philosophy and dreams.

Not less excellent, except for our less susceptibility in the afternoon, was the charm, last evening, of a January sunset. The western clouds divided and subdivided themselves into pink flakes modulated with tints of unspeakable softness, and the air had so much life and sweetness that it was a pain to come within doors. What was it that Nature would say? Was there no meaning in the live repose of the valley behind the mill, and which Homer or Shakespeare could not reform for me in words? The leafless trees become spires of flame in the sunset, with the blue east for their background, and the stars of the dead calices of flowers, and every withered stem and stubble rimed with frost, contribute something to the mute music.

The inhabitants of cities suppose that the country landscape is pleasant only half the year. I please myself with the graces of the winter scenery, and believe that we are as much touched by it as by the genial influences of summer. To the attentive eye, each moment of the year has its own beauty, and in the same field, it beholds, every hour, a picture which was never seen before, and which shall never be seen again. The heavens change every moment, and reflect their glory or gloom on the plains beneath. The state of the crop in the surrounding farms alters the expression of the earth from week to week. The succession of native plants in the pastures and roadsides, which makes the silent clock by which time tells the summer hours, will make even the

[1] ancient Paphos in the isle of Cyprus, chief seat of the worship of Venus

divisions of the day sensible to a keen observer. The tribes of birds and insects, like the plants punctual to their time, follow each other, and the year has room for all. By watercourses, the variety is greater. In July, the blue pontederia or pickerel-weed blooms in large beds in the shallow parts of our pleasant river, and swarms with yellow butterflies in continual motion. Art cannot rival this pomp of purple and gold. Indeed the river is a perpetual gala, and boasts each month a new ornament.

But this beauty of Nature which is seen and felt as beauty, is the least part. The shows of day, the dewy morning, the rainbow, mountains, orchards in blossom, stars, moonlight, shadows in still water, and the like, if too eagerly hunted, become shows merely, and mock us with their unreality. Go out of the house to see the moon, and 'tis mere tinsel; it will not please as when its light shines upon your necessary journey. The beauty that shimmers in the yellow afternoons of October, who ever could clutch it? Go forth to find it and it is gone; 'tis only a mirage as you look from the windows of diligence.

2. The presence of a higher, namely, of the spiritual element is essential to its perfection. The high and divine beauty which can be loved without effeminacy, is that which is found in combination with the human will. Beauty is the mark God sets upon virtue. Every natural action is graceful. Every heroic act is also decent, and causes the place and the bystanders to shine. We are taught by great actions that the universe is the property of every individual in it. Every rational creature has all nature for his dowry and estate. It is his, if he will. He may divest himself of it; he may creep into a corner, and abdicate his kingdom, as most men do, but he is entitled to the world by his constitution. In proportion to the energy of his thought and will, he takes up the world into himself. "All those things for which men plough, build, or sail, obey virtue," said Sallust. "The winds and waves," said Gibbon, "are always on the side of the ablest navigators." So are the sun and moon and all the stars of heaven. When a noble act is done,—perchance in a scene of great natural beauty; when Leonidas and his three hundred martyrs consume one day in dying, and the sun and moon come each and look at them once in the steep defile of Thermopylæ; when Arnold Winkelried, in the high Alps, under the shadow of the avalanche, gathers in his side a sheaf of Austrian spears to break the line for his comrades; are not these heroes entitled to add the beauty of the scene to the beauty of the deed? When the bark of Columbus nears the shore of America;—before it, the beach lined with savages, fleeing out of all their huts of cane; the sea behind; and the purple mountains of the Indian Archipelago around, can we separate the man from the living picture? Does not the New World clothe his form with her palm-groves and savannahs [1] as fit drapery? Ever does natural beauty steal in like air, and envelop great actions. When Sir Harry Vane was dragged up the Tower-hill, sitting on a sled, to suffer death as the champion of the English laws, one of the multitude cried out to him, "You never sate on so glorious a seat!" Charles II, to intimidate the citizens of London, caused the patriot Lord Russell to be drawn in an open coach through the principal streets of the city on his way to the scaffold. "But," his biographer says, "the multitude imagined they saw liberty and virtue sitting by his side." In private places, among sordid objects, an act of truth or heroism seems at once to draw to itself the sky as its temple, the sun as its candle. Nature stretches out her arms to embrace man, only let his thoughts be of equal greatness. Willingly does she follow his steps with the rose and the violet, and bend her lines of grandeur and grace to the decoration of her darling child. Only let his thoughts be of equal scope, and the frame will suit the picture. A virtuous man is in unison with her works, and makes the central figure of the visible sphere. Homer, Pindar, Socrates, Phocion, associate themselves fitly in our memory with the geography and climate of Greece. The visible heavens and earth sympathize with Jesus. And in common life whosoever has seen a person of powerful character and happy genius, will have remarked how easily he took all things along with him,—the persons, the opinions and the day, and nature became ancillary to a man.

3. There is still another aspect under which

---

[1] treeless plains

the beauty of the world may be viewed, namely, as it becomes an object of the intellect. Besides the relation of things to virtue, they have a relation to thought. The intellect searches out the absolute order of things as they stand in the mind of God, and without the colors of affection. The intellectual and the active powers seem to succeed each other, and the exclusive activity of the one generates the exclusive activity of the other. There is some- thing unfriendly in each to the other, but they are like the alternate periods of feeding and working in animals; each prepares and will be followed by the other. Therefore does beauty, which, in relation to actions, as we have seen, comes unsought, and comes because it is un- sought, remain for the apprehension and pursuit of the intellect; and then again, in its turn, of the active power. Nothing divine dies. All good is eternally reproductive. The beauty of nature re-forms itself in the mind, and not for barren contemplation, but for new creation.

All men are in some degree impressed by the face of the world; some men even to delight. This love of beauty is Taste. Others have the same love in such excess, that, not content with admiring, they seek to embody it in new forms. The creation of beauty is Art.

The production of a work of art throws a light upon the mystery of humanity. A work of art is an abstract or epitome of the world. It is the result or expression of nature, in minia- ture. For although the works of nature are innumerable and all different, the result or the expression of them all is similar and single. Nature is a sea of forms radically alike and even unique. A leaf, a sunbeam, a landscape, the ocean, make an analogous impression on the mind. What is common to them all,— that perfectness and harmony, is beauty. The standard of beauty is the entire circuit of natural forms,—the totality of nature; which the Italians expressed by defining beauty "il più nell' uno." [1] Nothing is quite beautiful alone; nothing but is beautiful in the whole. A single object is only so far beautiful as it sug- gests this universal grace. The poet, the painter, the sculptor, the musician, the archi- tect, seek each to concentrate this radiance of

[1] Translation follows.

the world on one point, and each in his several work to satisfy the love of beauty which stimulates him to produce. Thus is Art a nature passed through the alembic of man. Thus in art does Nature work through the will of a man filled with the beauty of her first works.

The world thus exists to the soul to satisfy the desire of beauty. This element I call an ultimate end. No reason can be asked or given why the soul seeks beauty. Beauty, in its larg- est and profoundest sense, is one expression for the universe. God is the all-fair. Truth, and goodness, and beauty, are but different faces of the same All. But beauty in nature is not ultimate. It is the herald of inward and eternal beauty, and is not alone a solid and satisfactory good. It must stand as a part, and not as yet the last or highest expression of the final cause of Nature.

1836

THE AMERICAN SCHOLAR

AN ORATION DELIVERED BEFORE THE PHI BETA KAPPA SOCIETY, AT CAMBRIDGE, AUGUST 31, 1837

For the stimulating effect of this speech when given as a Phi Beta Kappa address at Harvard, see Bliss Perry's *The Praise of Folly* (1923). It served as a declaration of principles on Emerson's part. He presents the scholar as Man Thinking, not merely man echoing other men's thoughts. The chief influences on him are Nature, which com- plements the soul, and Books, which typify the past, and of which each age must have its own. Action is better than books, and character higher than intellect, and labor is sacred. Emerson was the apostle of intellectual freedom, of self-trust, self-culture, and self-development. The peroration advocating American literary freedom from Europe is the high point of the speech. Shorn of Emerson's delivery, and its ideas somewhat obsolete with the passing of time, the speech cannot impress readers as it once did, but it holds its place as a landmark in American literary history; it was prophetic of a new era.

MR. PRESIDENT AND GENTLEMEN,

I greet you on the recommencement of our literary year. Our anniversary is one of hope, and, perhaps, not enough of labor. We do not meet for games of strength or skill, for the recitation of histories, tragedies, and odes, like the ancient Greeks; for parliaments of love and poesy, like the Troubadours[1]; nor for the advancement of science, like our contemporaries in the British and European capitals. Thus far, our holiday has been simply a friendly sign of the survival of the love of letters amongst a people too busy to give to letters any more. As such it is precious as the sign of an indestructible instinct. Perhaps the time is already come when it ought to be, and will be, something else; when the sluggard intellect of this continent will look from under its iron lids and fill the postponed expectation of the world with something better than the exertions of mechanical skill. Our day of dependence, our long apprenticeship to the learning of other lands, draws to a close. The millions that around us are rushing into life, cannot always be fed on the sere remains of foreign harvests. Events, actions arise, that must be sung, that will sing themselves. Who can doubt that poetry will revive and lead in a new age, as the star in the constellation Harp,[2] which now flames in our zenith, astronomers announce, shall one day be the polestar for a thousand years?

In this hope I accept the topic which not only usage but the nature of our association seem to prescribe to this day,—the AMERICAN SCHOLAR. Year by year we come up hither to read one more chapter of his biography. Let us inquire what light new days and events have thrown on his character and his hopes.

It is one of those fables which out of an unknown antiquity convey an unlooked-for wisdom, that the gods, in the beginning, divided Man into men, that he might be more helpful to himself; just as the hand was divided into fingers, the better to answer its end.

The old fable covers a doctrine ever new and sublime; that there is One Man,—present to all particular men only partially, or through one faculty; and that you must take the whole society to find the whole man. Man is not a farmer, or a professor, or an engineer, but he is

all. Man is priest, and scholar, and statesman, and producer, and soldier. In the *divided* or social state these functions are parcelled out to individuals, each of whom aims to do his stint of the joint work, whilst each other performs his. The fable implies that the individual, to possess himself, must sometimes return from his own labor to embrace all the other laborers. But, unfortunately, this original unit, this fountain of power, has been so distributed to multitudes, has been so minutely subdivided and peddled out, that it is spilled into drops, and cannot be gathered. The state of society is one in which the members have suffered amputation from the trunk, and strut about so many walking monsters,—a good finger, a neck, a stomach, an elbow, but never a man.

Man is thus metamorphosed into a thing, into many things. The planter, who is Man sent out into the field to gather food, is seldom cheered by any idea of the true dignity of his ministry. He sees his bushel and his cart, and nothing beyond, and sinks into the farmer, instead of Man on the farm. The tradesman scarcely ever gives an ideal worth to his work, but is ridden by the routine of his craft, and the soul is subject to dollars. The priest becomes a form; the attorney a statute-book; the mechanic a machine; the sailor a rope of the ship.

In this distribution of functions the scholar is the delegated intellect. In the right state he is *Man Thinking*. In the degenerate state, when the victim of society, he tends to become a mere thinker, or still worse, the parrot of other men's thinking.

In this view of him, as Man Thinking, the theory of his office is contained. Him Nature solicits with all her placid, all her monitory pictures; him the past instructs; him the future invites. Is not indeed every man a student, and do not all things exist for the student's behoof? And, finally, is not the true scholar the only true master? But the old oracle said, "All things have two handles: beware of the wrong one." In life, too often, the scholar errs with mankind and forfeits his privilege. Let us see him in his school, and consider him in reference to the main influences he receives.

I. The first in time and the first in importance of the influences upon the mind is

---

[1] medieval lyric poets of Southern France and Northern Italy, during the eleventh, twelfth, and thirteenth centuries, who often met in poetic contests
[2] the small northern constellation Lyra, toward which the solar system was thought to be moving

that of Nature. Every day, the sun; and, after sunset, Night and her stars. Ever the winds blow; ever the grass grows. Every day, men and women, conversing, beholding and beholden. The scholar is he of all men whom this spectacle most engages. He must settle its value in his mind. What is nature to him? There is never a beginning, there is never an end, to the inexplicable continuity of this web of God, but always circular power returning into itself. Therein it resembles his own spirit, whose beginning, whose ending, he never can find,—so entire, so boundless. Far too as her splendors shine, system on system shooting like rays, upward, downward, without center, without circumference,—in the mass and in the particle, Nature hastens to render account of herself to the mind. Classification begins. To the young mind every thing is individual, stands by itself. By and by, it finds how to join two things and see in them one nature; then three, then three thousand; and so, tyrannized over by its own unifying instinct, it goes on tying things together, diminishing anomalies, discovering roots running under ground whereby contrary and remote things cohere and flower out from one stem. It presently learns that since the dawn of history there has been a constant accumulation and classifying of facts. But what is classification but the perceiving that these objects are not chaotic, and are not foreign, but have a law which is also a law of the human mind? The astronomer discovers that geometry, a pure abstraction of the human mind, is the measure of planetary motion. The chemist finds proportions and intelligible method throughout matter; and science is nothing but the finding of analogy, identity, in the most remote parts. The ambitious soul sits down before each refractory fact; one after another reduces all strange constitutions, all new powers, to their class and their law, and goes on forever to animate the last fiber of organization, the outskirts of nature, by insight.

Thus to him, to this schoolboy under the bending dome of day, is suggested that he and it proceed from one root; one is leaf and one is flower; relation, sympathy, stirring in every vein. And what is that root? Is not that the soul of his soul? A thought too bold; a dream too

wild. Yet when this spiritual light shall have revealed the law of more earthly natures,—when he has learned to worship the soul, and to see that the natural philosophy that now is, is only the first gropings of its gigantic hand, he shall look forward to an ever expanding knowledge as to a becoming creator. He shall see that Nature is the opposite of the soul, answering to it part for part. One is seal and one is print. Its beauty is the beauty of his own mind. Its laws are the laws of his own mind. Nature then becomes to him the measure of his attainments. So much of Nature as he is ignorant of, so much of his own mind does he not yet possess. And, in fine, the ancient precept, "Know thyself," and the modern precept, "Study nature," become at last one maxim.

II. The next great influence into the spirit of the scholar is the mind of the Past,—in whatever form, whether of literature, of art, of institutions, that mind is inscribed. Books are the best type of the influence of the past, and perhaps we shall get at the truth,—learn the amount of this influence more conveniently,—by considering their value alone.

The theory of books is noble. The scholar of the first age received into him the world around; brooded thereon; gave it the new arrangement of his own mind, and uttered it again. It came into him life; it went out from him truth. It came to him shortlived actions; it went out from him immortal thoughts. It came to him business; it went from him poetry. It was dead fact; now, it is quick thought. It can stand, and it can go. It now endures, it now flies, it now inspires. Precisely in proportion to the depth of mind from which it issued, so high does it soar, so long does it sing.

Or, I might say, it depends on how far the process had gone, of transmuting life into truth. In proportion to the completeness of the distillation, so will the purity and imperishableness of the product be. But none is quite perfect. As no air-pump can by any means make a perfect vacuum, so neither can any artist entirely exclude the conventional, the local, the perishable from his book, or write a book of pure thought, that shall be as efficient, in all respects, to a remote posterity, as to contemporaries, or rather to the second age.

Each age, it is found, must write its own books; or rather, each generation for the next succeeding. The books of an older period will not fit this.

Yet hence arises a grave mischief. The sacredness which attaches to the act of creation, the act of thought, is transferred to the record. The poet chanting was felt to be a divine man: henceforth the chant is divine also. The writer was a just and wise spirit: henceforward it is settled the book is perfect; as love of the hero corrupts into worship of his statue. Instantly the book becomes noxious: the guide is a tyrant. The sluggish and perverted mind of the multitude, slow to open to the incursions of Reason, having once so opened, having once received this book, stands upon it, and makes an outcry if it is disparaged. Colleges are built on it. Books are written on it by thinkers, not by Man Thinking; by men of talent, that is, who start wrong, who set out from accepted dogmas, not from their own sight of principles. Meek young men grow up in libraries, believing it their duty to accept the views which Cicero, which Locke, which Bacon, have given; forgetful that Cicero, Locke, and Bacon were only young men in libraries when they wrote these books.

Hence, instead of Man Thinking, we have the bookworm. Hence the book-learned class, who value books, as such; not as related to nature and the human constitution, but as making a sort of Third Estate [1] with the world and the soul. Hence the restorers of readings, the emendators, the bibliomaniacs of all degrees.

Books are the best of things, well used; abused, among the worst. What is the right use? What is the one end which all means go to effect? They are for nothing but to inspire. I had better never see a book than to be warped by its attraction clean out of my own orbit, and made a satellite instead of a system. The one thing in the world, of value, is the active soul. This every man is entitled to; this every man contains within him, although in almost all men obstructed, and as yet unborn. The soul active sees absolute truth and utters truth,

[1] the common people, a phrase revived during the French Revolution from the class divisions of medieval France

or creates. In this action it is genius; not the privilege of here and there a favorite, but the sound estate of every man. In its essence it is progressive. The book, the college, the school of art, the institution of any kind, stop with some past utterance of genius. This is good, say they,—let us hold by this. They pin me down. They look backward and not forward. But genius looks forward: the eyes of man are set in his forehead, not in his hindhead; man hopes: genius creates. Whatever talents may be, if the man create not, the pure efflux of the Deity is not his;—cinders and smoke there may be, but not yet flame. There are creative manners, there are creative actions, and creative words; manners, actions, words, that is, indicative of no custom or authority, but springing spontaneous from the mind's own sense of good and fair.

On the other part, instead of being its own seer, let it receive from another mind its truth, though it were in torrents of light, without periods of solitude, inquest, and self-recovery, and a fatal disservice is done. Genius is always sufficiently the enemy of genius by overinfluence. The literature of every nation bears me witness. The English dramatic poets have Shakspearized now for two hundred years.

Undoubtedly there is a right way of reading, so it be sternly subordinated. Man Thinking must not be subdued by his instruments. Books are for the scholar's idle times. When he can read God directly, the hour is too precious to be wasted in other men's transcripts of their readings. But when the intervals of darkness come, as come they must,—when the sun is hid and the stars withdraw their shining,—we repair to the lamps which were kindled by their ray, to guide our steps to the East again, where the dawn is. We hear, that we may speak. The Arabian proverb says, "A fig tree, looking on a fig tree, becometh fruitful."

It is remarkable, the character of the pleasure we derive from the best books. They impress us with the conviction that one nature wrote and the same reads. We read the verses of one of the great English poets, of Chaucer, of Marvell, of Dryden, with the most modern joy,—with a pleasure, I mean, which is in great part caused by the abstraction of all *time* from their verses. There is some awe mixed with the joy of our surprise, when this poet, who lived in some past world, two or three hundred years ago, says that which lies close to my own soul, that which I also had well-nigh thought and said. But for the evidence thence afforded to the philosophical doctrine of the identity of all minds, we should suppose some preëstablished harmony, some foresight of souls that were to be, and some preparation of stores for their future wants, like the fact observed in insects, who lay up food before death for the young grub they shall never see.

I would not be hurried by any love of system, by any exaggeration of instincts, to underrate the Book. We all know, that as the human body can be nourished on any food, though it were boiled grass and the broth of shoes, so the human mind can be fed by any knowledge. And great and heroic men have existed who had almost no other information than by the printed page. I only would say that it needs a strong head to bear that diet. One must be an inventor to read well. As the proverb says, "He that would bring home the wealth of the Indies, must carry out the wealth of the Indies." There is then creative reading as well as creative writing. When the mind is braced by labor and invention, the page of whatever book we read becomes luminous with manifold allusion. Every sentence is doubly significant, and the sense of our author is as broad as the world. We then see, what is always true, that as the seer's hour of vision is short and rare among heavy days and months, so is its record, perchance, the least part of his volume. The discerning will read, in his Plato or Shakspeare, only that least part,—only the authentic utterances of the oracle;—all the rest he rejects, were it never so many times Plato's and Shakspeare's.

Of course there is a portion of reading quite indispensable to a wise man. History and exact science he must learn by laborious reading. Colleges, in like manner, have their indispensable office,—to teach elements. But they can only highly serve us when they aim not to drill, but to create; when they gather from far every ray of various genius to their hospitable halls, and by the concentrated fires, set the hearts of their youth on flame. Thought and knowledge are natures in which apparatus and pretension avail nothing. Gowns and pecuniary foundations, though of towns of gold, can never countervail the least sentence or syllable of wit. Forget this, and our American colleges will recede in their public importance, whilst they grow richer every year.

III. There goes in the world a notion that the scholar should be a recluse, a valetudinarian,—as unfit for any handiwork or public labor as a penknife for an ax. The so-called "practical men" sneer at speculative men, as if, because they speculate or *see*, they could do nothing. I have heard it said that the clergy,— who are always, more universally than any other class, the scholars of their day,—are addressed as women; that the rough, spontaneous conversation of men they do not hear, but only a mincing and diluted speech. They are often virtually disfranchised; and indeed there are advocates for their celibacy. As far as this is true of the studious classes, it is not just and wise. Action is with the scholar subordinate, but it is essential. Without it he is not yet man. Without it thought can never ripen into truth. Whilst the world hangs before the eye as a cloud of beauty, we cannot even see its beauty. Inaction is cowardice, but there can be no scholar without the heroic mind. The preamble of thought, the transition through which it passes from the unconscious to the conscious, is action. Only so much do I know, as I have lived. Instantly we know whose words are loaded with life, and whose not.

The world,—this shadow of the soul, or *other me*, lies wide around. Its attractions are the keys which unlock my thoughts and make me acquainted with myself. I run eagerly into this resounding tumult. I grasp the hands of those next me, and take my place in the ring to suffer and to work, taught by an instinct that so shall the dumb abyss be vocal with speech. I pierce its order; I dissipate its fear; I dispose of it within the circuit of my expanding life. So much only of life as I know by experience, so much of the wilderness have I vanquished and planted, or so far have I extended my being, my dominion. I do not see how any man can afford, for the sake of his nerves and his nap, to spare any action in which he can partake. It is pearls and rubies to his discourse. Drudgery, calamity, exasperation, want, are instructors in eloquence and wisdom. The true scholar grudges every opportunity of action past by, as a loss of power.

It is the raw material out of which the intellect molds her splendid products. A strange process, too, this by which experience is converted into thought, as a mulberry leaf [1] is converted into satin. The manufacture goes forward at all hours.

The actions and events of our childhood and youth are now matters of calmest observation. They lie like fair pictures in the air. Not so with our recent actions,—with the business which we now have in hand. On this we are quite unable to speculate. Our affections as yet circulate through it. We no more feel or know it than we feel the feet, or the hand, or the brain of our body. The new deed is yet a part of life,—remains for a time immersed in our unconscious life. In some contemplative hour it detaches itself from the life like a ripe fruit, to become a thought of the mind. Instantly it is raised, transfigured; the corruptible has put on incorruption.[2] Henceforth it is an object of beauty, however base its origin and neighborhood. Observe too the impossibility of antedating this act. In its grub state, it cannot fly, it cannot shine, it is a dull grub. But suddenly, without observation, the selfsame thing unfurls beautiful wings, and is an angel of wisdom. So is there no fact, no event, in our private history, which shall not, sooner or later, lose its adhesive, inert form, and astonish us by soaring from our body into the empyrean. Cradle and infancy, school and playground, the fear of boys, and dogs, and ferules, the love of little maids and berries, and many another fact that once filled the whole sky, are gone already; friend and relative, profession and party, town and country, nation and world, must also soar and sing.

Of course, he who has put forth his total strength in fit actions has the richest return of wisdom. I will not shut myself out of this globe of action, and transplant an oak into a flowerpot, there to hunger and pine; nor trust the revenue of some single faculty, and ex-

haust one vein of thought, much like those Savoyards,[1] who, getting their livelihood by carving shepherds, shepherdesses, and smoking Dutchmen, for all Europe, went out one day to the mountain to find stock, and discovered that they had whittled up the last of their pine-trees. Authors we have, in numbers, who have written out their vein, and who, moved by a commendable prudence, sail for Greece or Palestine, follow the trapper into the prairie, or ramble round Algiers, to replenish their merchantable stock.

If it were only for a vocabulary, the scholar would be covetous of action. Life is our dictionary. Years are well spent in country labors; in town; in the insight into trades and manufactures; in frank intercourse with many men and women; in science; in art; to the one end of mastering in all their facts a language by which to illustrate and embody our perceptions. I learn immediately from any speaker how much he has already lived, through the poverty or the splendor of his speech. Life lies behind us as the quarry from whence we get tiles and copestones for the masonry of today. This is the way to learn grammar. Colleges and books only copy the language which the field and the work-yard made.

But the final value of action, like that of books, and better than books, is that it is a resource. That great principle of Undulation in nature, that shows itself in the inspiring and expiring of the breath; in desire and satiety; in the ebb and flow of the sea; in day and night; in heat and cold; and, as yet more deeply ingrained in every atom and every fluid, is known to us under the name of Polarity,—these "fits of easy transmission and reflection," as Newton called them,—are the law of nature because they are the law of spirit.

The mind now thinks, now acts, and each fit reproduces the other. When the artist has exhausted his materials, when the fancy no longer paints, when thoughts are no longer apprehended and books are a weariness,—he has always the resource *to live*. Character is higher than intellect. Thinking is the function. Living is the functionary. The stream retreats to its source. A great soul will be strong to live, as well as strong to think. Does he lack

---

[1] the food of silkworms   [2] Corinthians 15:33   [1] inhabitants of Savoy in northwestern Italy

organ or medium to impart his truth? He can still fall back on this elemental force of living them. This is a total act. Thinking is a partial act. Let the grandeur of justice shine in his affairs. Let the beauty of affection cheer his lowly roof. Those "far from fame," who dwell and act with him, will feel the force of his constitution in the doings and passages of the day better than it can be measured by any public and designed display. Time shall teach him that the scholar loses no hour which the man lives. Herein he unfolds the sacred germ of his instinct, screened from influence. What is lost in seemliness is gained in strength. Not out of those on whom systems of education have exhausted their culture, comes the helpful giant to destroy the old or to build the new, but out of unhandselled[1] savage nature; out of terrible Druids[2] and Berserkers come at last Alfred and Shakspeare.

I hear therefore with joy whatever is beginning to be said of the dignity and necessity of labor to every citizen. There is virtue yet in the hoe and the spade, for learned as well as for unlearned hands. And labor is everywhere welcome; always we are invited to work; only be this limitation observed, that a man shall not for the sake of wider activity sacrifice any opinion to the popular judgments and modes of action.

I have now spoken of the education of the scholar by nature, by books, and by action. It remains to say somewhat of his duties.

They are such as become Man Thinking. They may all be comprised in self-trust. The office of the scholar is to cheer, to raise, and to guide men by showing them facts amidst appearances. He plies the slow, unhonored, and unpaid task of observation. Flamsteed and Herschel, in their glazed observatories, may catalogue the stars with the praise of all men, and the results being splendid and useful, honor is sure. But he, in his private observatory, cataloguing obscure and nebulous stars of the human mind, which as yet no man has thought of as such,—watching days and

months sometimes for a few facts; correcting still his old records;—must relinquish display and immediate fame. In the long period of his preparation he must betray often an ignorance and shiftlessness in popular arts, incurring the disdain of the able who shoulder him aside. Long he must stammer in his speech; often forego the living for the dead. Worse yet, he must accept,—how often!—poverty and solitude. For the ease and pleasure of treading the old road, accepting the fashions, the education, the religion of society, he takes the cross of making his own, and, of course, the self-accusation, the faint heart, the frequent uncertainty and loss of time, which are the nettles and tangling vines in the way of the self-relying and self-directed; and the state of virtual hostility in which he seems to stand to society, and especially to educated society. For all this loss and scorn, what offset? He is to find consolation in exercising the highest functions of human nature. He is one who raises himself from private considerations and breathes and lives on public and illustrious thoughts. He is the world's eye. He is the world's heart. He is to resist the vulgar prosperity that retrogrades ever to barbarism, by preserving and communicating heroic sentiments, noble biographies, melodious verse, and the conclusions of history. Whatsoever oracles the human heart, in all emergencies, in all solemn hours, has uttered as its commentary on the world of actions,—these he shall receive and impart. And whatsoever new verdict Reason from her inviolable seat pronounces on the passing men and events of to-day,—this he shall hear and promulgate.

These being his functions, it becomes him to feel all confidence in himself, and to defer never to the popular cry. He and he only knows the world. The world of any moment is the merest appearance. Some great decorum, some fetish of a government, some ephemeral trade, or war, or man, is cried up by half mankind and cried down by the other half, as if all depended on this particular up or down. The odds are that the whole question is not worth the poorest thought which the scholar has lost in listening to the controversy. Let him not quit his belief that a popgun is a popgun, though the ancient and honorable of the earth

---

[1] A handsel is a token given for good luck at the beginning of an enterprise; the negative adjective form used here means untried.   [2] ancient Celtic priests, who conducted mysterious rites of sacrifice

affirm it to be the crack of doom. In silence, in steadiness, in severe abstraction, let him hold by himself; add observation to observation, patient of neglect, patient of reproach, and bide his own time,—happy enough if he can satisfy himself alone that this day he has seen something truly. Success treads on every right step. For the instinct is sure that prompts him to tell his brother what he thinks. He then learns that in going down into the secrets of his own mind he has descended into the secrets of all minds. He learns that he who has mastered any law in his private thoughts, is master to that extent of all men whose language he speaks, and of all into whose language his own can be translated. The poet, in utter solitude remembering his spontaneous thoughts and recording them, is found to have recorded that which men in crowded cities find true for them also. The orator distrusts at first the fitness of his frank confessions, his want of knowledge of the persons he addresses, until he finds that he is the complement of his hearers;—that they drink his words because he fulfils for them their own nature; the deeper he dives into his privatest, secretest presentiment, to his wonder he finds this is the most acceptable, most public, and universally true. The people delight in it; the better part of every man feels, This is my music; this is myself.

In self-trust all the virtues are comprehended. Free should the scholar be,—free and brave. Free even to the definition of freedom, "without any hindrance that does not arise out of his own constitution." Brave; for fear is a thing which a scholar by his very function puts behind him. Fear always springs from ignorance. It is a shame to him if his tranquillity, amid dangerous times, arise from the presumption that like children and women his is a protected class; or if he seek a temporary peace by the diversion of his thoughts from politics or vexed questions, hiding his head like an ostrich in the flowering bushes, peeping into microscopes, and turning rhymes, as a boy whistles to keep his courage up. So is the danger a danger still; so is the fear worse. Manlike let him turn and face it. Let him look into its eye and search its nature, inspect its origin,—see the whelping of this lion,—which lies no great way back; he will then find in himself a perfect comprehension of its nature and extent; he will have made his hands meet on the other side, and can henceforth defy it and pass on superior. The world is his who can see through its pretension. What deafness, what stone-blind custom, what overgrown error you behold is there only by sufferance,—by your sufferance. See it to be a lie, and you have already dealt it its mortal blow.

Yes, we are the cowed,—we the trustless. It is a mischievous notion that we are come late into nature; that the world was finished a long time ago. As the world was plastic and fluid in the hands of God, so it is ever to so much of his attributes as we bring to it. To ignorance and sin, it is flint. They adapt themselves to it as they may; but in proportion as a man has anything in him divine, the firmament flows before him and takes his signet and form. Not he is great who can alter matter, but he who can alter my state of mind. They are the kings of the world who give the color of their present thought to all nature and all art, and persuade men by the cheerful serenity of their carrying the matter that this thing which they do is the apple which the ages have desired to pluck, now at last ripe, and inviting nations to the harvest. The great man makes the great thing. Wherever Macdonald sits,[1] there is the head of the table. Linnæus makes botany the most alluring of studies, and wins it from the farmer and the herb-woman; Davy, chemistry; and Cuvier, fossils. The day is always his who works in it with serenity and great aims. The unstable estimates of men crowd to him whose mind is filled with a truth, as the heaped waves of the Atlantic follow the moon.

For this self-trust, the reason is deeper than can be fathomed,—darker than can be enlightened. I might not carry with me the feeling of my audience in stating my own belief. But I have already shown the ground of my hope, in adverting to the doctrine that man is one. I believe man has been wronged; he has wronged himself. He has almost lost the light that can lead him back to his prerogatives. Men are become of no account. Men in history, men

---

[1] a proverbial saying of uncertain origin and appearing in various forms, emphasizing the fact that a man of strength and genius always makes his power felt

in the world of today, are bugs, are spawn, and are called "the mass" and "the herd." In a century, in a millennium, one or two men; that is to say, one or two approximations to the right state of every man. All the rest behold in the hero or the poet their own green and crude being,—ripened; yes, and are content to be less, so *that* may attain to its full stature. What a testimony, full of grandeur, full of pity, is borne to the demands of his own nature, by the poor clansman, the poor partisan, who rejoices in the glory of his chief. The poor and the low find some amends to their immense moral capacity, for their acquiescence in a political and social inferiority. They are content to be brushed like flies from the path of a great person, so that justice shall be done by him to that common nature which it is the dearest desire of all to see enlarged and glorified. They sun themselves in the great man's light, and feel it to be their own element. They cast the dignity of man from their downtrod selves upon the shoulders of a hero, and will perish to add one drop of blood to make that great heart beat, those giant sinews combat and conquer. He lives for us, and we live in him.

Men such as they are, very naturally seek money or power; and power because it is as good as money,—the "spoils," so called, "of office." And why not? for they aspire to the highest, and this, in their sleepwalking, they dream is highest. Wake them and they shall quit the false good and leap to the true, and leave governments to clerks and desks. This revolution is to be wrought by the gradual domestication of the idea of Culture. The main enterprise of the world for splendor, for extent, is the upbuilding of a man. Here are the materials strewn along the ground. The private life of one man shall be a more illustrious monarchy, more formidable to its enemy, more sweet and serene in its influence to its friend, than any kingdom in history. For a man, rightly viewed, comprehendeth the particular natures of all men. Each philosopher, each bard, each actor has only done for me, as by a delegate, what one day I can do for myself. The books which once we valued more than the apple of the eye, we have quite exhausted. What is that but saying that we have

come up with the point of view which the universal mind took through the eyes of one scribe; we have been that man, and have passed on. First, one, then another, we drain all cisterns, and waxing greater by all these supplies, we crave a better and more abundant food. The man has never lived that can feed us ever. The human mind cannot be enshrined in a person who shall set a barrier on any one side to this unbounded, unboundable empire. It is one central fire, which, flaming now out of the lips of Etna, lightens the capes of Sicily, and now out of the throat of Vesuvius, illuminates the towers and vineyards of Naples. It is one light which beams out of a thousand stars. It is one soul which animates all men.

But I have dwelt perhaps tediously upon this abstraction of the Scholar. I ought not to delay longer to add what I have to say of nearer reference to the time and to this country.

Historically, there is thought to be a difference in the ideas which predominate over successive epochs, and there are data for marking the genius of the Classic, of the Romantic, and now of the Reflective or Philosophical age. With the views I have intimated of the oneness or the identity of the mind through all individuals, I do not much dwell on these differences. In fact, I believe each individual passes through all three. The boy is a Greek; the youth, romantic; the adult, reflective. I deny not however that a revolution in the leading idea may be distinctly enough traced.

Our age is bewailed as the age of Introversion. Must that needs be evil? We, it seems, are critical; we are embarrassed with second thoughts; we cannot enjoy anything for hankering to know whereof the pleasure consists; we are lined with eyes; we see with our feet; the time is infected with Hamlet's unhappiness,—

"Sicklied o'er with the pale cast of thought."

It is so bad then? Sight is the last thing to be pitied. Would we be blind? Do we fear lest we should outsee nature and God, and drink truth dry? I look upon the discontent of the literary class as a mere announcement of the fact that they find themselves not in the state of mind of their fathers, and regret the coming state as untried; as a boy dreads the water before he has learned that he can swim. If there is any period one would desire to be born in, is it not the age of Revolution; when the old and the new stand side by side and admit of being compared; when the energies of all men are searched by fear and by hope; when the historic glories of the old can be compensated by the rich possibilities of the new era? This time, like all times, is a very good one, if we but know what to do with it.

I read with some joy of the auspicious signs of the coming days, as they glimmer already through poetry and art, through philosophy and science, through church and state.

One of these signs is the fact that the same movement which effected the elevation of what was called the lowest class in the state, assumed in literature a very marked and as benign an aspect. Instead of the sublime and beautiful, the near, the low, the common, was explored and poetized. That which had been negligently trodden under foot by those who were harnessing and provisioning themselves for long journeys into far countries, is suddenly found to be richer than all foreign parts. The literature of the poor, the feelings of the child, the philosophy of the street, the meaning of household life, are the topics of the time. It is a great stride. It is a sign,—is it not? —of new vigor when the extremities are made active, when currents of warm life run into the hands and the feet. I ask not for the great, the remote, the romantic; what is doing in Italy or Arabia; what is Greek art, or Provençal minstrelsy; I embrace the common, I explore and sit at the feet of the familiar, the low. Give me insight into today, and you may have the antique and future worlds. What would we really know the meaning of? The meal in the firkin; the milk in the pan; the ballad in the street; the news of the boat; the glance of the eye; the form and the gait of the body;—show me the ultimate reason of these matters; show me the sublime presence of the highest spiritual cause lurking, as always it does lurk, in these suburbs and extremities of Nature; let me see every trifle bristling with the polarity that ranges it instantly on an eternal law; and the shop, the plow, and the ledger referred to the like cause by which light undulates and poets sing;—and the world lies no longer a dull miscellany and lumber-room, but has form and order; there is no trifle, there is no puzzle, but one design unites and animates the farthest pinnacle and the lowest trench.

This idea has inspired the genius of Goldsmith, Burns, Cowper, and, in a newer time, of Goethe, Wordsworth, and Carlyle. This idea they have differently followed and with various success. In contrast with their writing, the style of Pope, of Johnson, of Gibbon, looks cold and pedantic. This writing is blood-warm. Man is surprised to find that things near are not less beautiful and wondrous than things remote. The near explains the far. The drop is a small ocean. A man is related to all nature. This perception of the worth of the vulgar is fruitful in discoveries. Goethe, in this very thing the most modern of the moderns, has shown us, as none ever did, the genius of the ancients.

There is one man of genius who has done much for this philosophy of life, whose literary value has never yet been rightly estimated;—I mean Emanuel Swedenborg. The most imaginative of men, yet writing with the precision of a mathematician, he endeavored to engraft a purely philosophical Ethics on the popular Christianity of his time. Such an attempt of course must have difficulty which no genius could surmount. But he saw and showed the connection between nature and the affections of the soul. He pierced the emblematic or spiritual character of the visible, audible, tangible world. Especially did his shade-loving muse hover over and interpret the lower parts of nature; he showed the mysterious bond that allies moral evil to the foul material forms, and has given in epical parables a theory of insanity, of beasts, of unclean and fearful things.

Another sign of our times, also marked by an analogous political movement, is the new importance given to the single person. Everything that tends to insulate the individual,— to surround him with barriers of natural respect, so that each man shall feel the world is his, and man shall treat with man as a sovereign state with a sovereign state,—tends to true union as well as greatness. "I learned," said the melancholy Pestalozzi, "that no man in God's wide earth is either willing or able to help any other man." Help must come from the bosom alone. The scholar is that man who must take up into himself all the ability of the time, all the contributions of the past, all the hopes of the future. He must be an university of knowledges. If there be one lesson more than another which should pierce his ear, it is, The world is nothing, the man is all; in yourself is the law of all nature, and you know not yet how a globule of sap ascends; in yourself slumbers the whole of Reason; it is for you to know all; it is for you to dare all. Mr. President and Gentlemen, this confidence in the unsearched might of man belongs, by all motives, by all prophecy, by all preparation, to the American Scholar. We have listened too long to the courtly muses of Europe. The spirit of the American freeman is already suspected to be timid, imitative, tame. Public and private avarice make the air we breathe thick and fat. The scholar is decent, indolent, complaisant. See already the tragic consequence. The mind of this country, taught to aim at low objects, eats upon itself. There is no work for any but the decorous and the complaisant. Young men of the fairest promise, who begin life upon our shores, inflated by the mountain winds, shined upon by all the stars of God, find the earth below not in unison with these, but are hindered from action by the disgust which the principles on which business is managed inspire, and turn drudges, or die of disgust, some of them suicides. What is the remedy? They did not yet see, and thousands of young men as hopeful now crowding to the barriers for the career do not yet see, that if the single man plant himself indomitably on his instincts, and there abide, the huge world will come round to him. Patience,—patience; with the shades of all the good and great for company; and for solace the perspective of your own infinite life; and for work the study and the communication of principles, the making those instincts prevalent, the conversion of the world. Is it not the chief disgrace in the world, not to be an unit;—not to be reckoned one character;—not to yield that peculiar fruit which each man was created to bear, but to be reckoned in the gross, in the hundred, or the thousand, of the party, the section, to which we belong; and our opinion predicted geographically, as the north, or the south? Not so, brothers and friends,—please God, ours shall not be so. We will walk on our own feet; we will work with our own hands; we will speak our own minds. The study of letters shall be no longer a name for pity, for doubt, and for sensual indulgence. The dread of man and the love of man shall be a wall of defense and a wreath of joy around all. A nation of men will for the first time exist, because each believes himself inspired by the Divine Soul which also inspires all men.

1837

TO THE REVEREND HENRY WARE, JR.

Henry Ware occupied the pulpit of the Second (Unitarian) Church in Boston. When he was appointed a professor in the Harvard Divinity School, Emerson, who had previously substituted for him, was made his successor. The letter is of interest as a confession on Emerson's part of his oracular inspiration and mode of writing. "I could not possibly give you . . . 'arguments' . . . I do not know what arguments mean in reference to any expression of a thought. I delight in telling what I think, but if you ask how . . . or why . . . I am the most helpless of mortal men."

Concord, October 8, 1838

MY DEAR SIR,—I ought sooner to have acknowledged your kind letter of last week, and the Sermon it accompanied. The letter was right manly and noble. The Sermon, too, I have read with attention. If it assails any doctrines of mine, perhaps I am not so quick to see it as writers generally—certainly I did not feel any disposition to depart from my habitual contentment that you should say your thought, whilst I say mine.

I believe I must tell you what I think of my new position. It strikes me very oddly that good and wise men at Cambridge and Boston should think of raising me into an object of criticism. I have always been, from my very incapacity of methodical writing, "a chartered

libertine," free to worship and free to rail;
lucky when I could make myself understood,
but never esteemed near enough to the institutions and mind of society to deserve the
notice of the masters of literature and religion.
I have appreciated fully the advantage of my
position; for I well know that there is no
scholar less willing or less able to be a polemic.
I could not give account of myself, if challenged. I could not possibly give you one of
the "arguments" you cruelly hint at, on which
any doctrine of mine stands. For I do not
know what arguments mean in reference to
any expression of a thought. I delight in telling what I think, but if you ask how I dare
say so, or why it is so, I am the most helpless
of mortal men. I do not even see that either
of these questions admits of an answer. So
that, in the present droll posture of my affairs, when I see myself suddenly raised into
the importance of a heretic, I am very uneasy
when I advert to the supposed duties of such
a personage, who is expected to make good
his thesis against all comers.

I certainly shall do no such thing. I shall
read what you and other good men write, as
I have always done,—glad when you speak
my thought, and skipping the page that has
nothing for me. I shall go on, just as before,
seeing whatever I can, and telling what I see;
and, I suppose, with the same fortune that has
hitherto attended me,—the joy of finding
that my abler and better brothers, who work
with the sympathy of society, loving and beloved, do now and then unexpectedly confirm my perceptions, and find my nonsense is
only their own thought in motley. And so I am
Your affectionate servant,
R. W. EMERSON

SELF–RELIANCE

This essay reflects Emerson's cardinal idea, the
self-sufficiency of the individual. It presents also his
attitude toward books and tradition, toward conformity and consistency, toward spontaneity, instinct, and intuition, toward travel and prayer.
There was no collectivism in Emerson. The influence of society seemed hampering to him. The
note of unsociability in this essay is recurrent in
his writing.

"Ne te quaesiveris extra."[1]

"Man is his own star and the soul that can
Render an honest and a perfect man,
Commands all light, all influence, all fate;
Nothing to him falls early or too late.
Our acts our angels are, or good or ill,
Our fatal shadows that walk by us still."
Epilogue to Beaumont and Fletcher's
Honest Man's Fortunes

Cast the bantling on the rocks,
Suckle him with the she-wolf's teat,
Wintered with the hawk and fox,
Power and speed be hands and feet.

I READ the other day some verses written
by an eminent painter which were original
and not conventional. The soul always hears
an admonition in such lines, let the subject be
what it may. The sentiment they instil is of
more value than any thought they may contain. To believe your own thought, to believe
that what is true for you in your private heart
is true for all men,—that is genius. Speak your
latent conviction, and it shall be the universal
sense; for the inmost in due time becomes the
outmost, and our first thought is rendered
back to us by the trumpets of the Last Judgment. Familiar as the voice of the mind is to
each, the highest merit we ascribe to Moses,
Plato, and Milton is that they set at naught
books and traditions, and spoke not what
men, but what *they* thought. A man should
learn to detect and watch that gleam of light
which flashes across his mind from within,
more than the luster of the firmament of bards
and sages. Yet he dismisses without notice
his thought, because it is his. In every work
of genius we recognize our own rejected
thoughts; they come back to us with a certain
alienated majesty. Great works of art have no
more affecting lesson for us than this. They
teach us to abide by our spontaneous impression with good-humored inflexibility then
most when the whole cry of voices is on the
other side. Else tomorrow a stranger will
say with masterly good sense precisely what
we have thought and felt all the time, and we
shall be forced to take with shame our own
opinion from another.

There is a time in every man's education
when he arrives at the conviction that envy

[1] "Do not seek beyond thyself."

is ignorance; that imitation is suicide; that he must take himself for better for worse as his portion; that though the wide universe is full of good, no kernel of nourishing corn can come to him but through his toil bestowed on that plot of ground which is given to him to till. The power which resides in him is new in nature, and none but he knows what that is which he can do, nor does he know until he has tried. Not for nothing one face, one character, one fact, makes much impression on him, and another none. This sculpture in the memory is not without preëstablished harmony. The eye was placed where one ray should fall, that it might testify of that particular ray. We but half express ourselves, and are ashamed of that divine idea which each of us represents. It may be safely intrusted as proportionate and of good issues, so it be faithfully imparted, but God will not have his work made manifest by cowards. A man is relieved and gay when he has put his heart into his work and done his best; but what he has said or done otherwise shall give him no peace. It is a deliverance which does not deliver. In the attempt his genius deserts him; no muse befriends; no invention, no hope.

Trust thyself: every heart vibrates to that iron string. Accept the place the divine providence has found for you, the society of your contemporaries, the connection of events. Great men have always done so, and confided themselves childlike to the genius of their age, betraying their perception that the absolutely trustworthy was seated at their heart, working through their hands, predominating in all their being. And we are now men, and must accept in the highest mind the same transcendent destiny; and not minors and invalids in a protected corner, not cowards fleeing before a revolution, but guides, redeemers and benefactors, obeying the Almighty effort and advancing on Chaos and the Dark.

What pretty oracles nature yields us on this text in the face and behavior of children, babes, and even brutes! That divided and rebel mind, that distrust of a sentiment because our arithmetic has computed the strength and means opposed to our purpose, these have not. Their mind being whole, their eye is as yet unconquered, and when we look in their faces we are disconcerted. Infancy conforms to nobody; all conform to it; so that one babe commonly makes four or five out of the adults who prattle and play to it. So God has armed youth and puberty and manhood no less with its own piquancy and charm, and made it enviable and gracious and its claims not to be put by, if it will stand by itself. Do not think the youth has no force, because he cannot speak to you and me. Hark! in the next room his voice is sufficiently clear and emphatic. It seems he knows how to speak to his contemporaries. Bashful or bold then, he will know how to make us seniors very unnecessary.

The nonchalance of boys who are sure of a dinner, and would disdain as much as a lord to do or say aught to conciliate one, is the healthy attitude of human nature. A boy is in the parlor what the pit [1] is in the playhouse; independent, irresponsible, looking out from his corner on such people and facts as pass by, he tries and sentences them on their merits, in the swift, summary way of boys, as good, bad, interesting, silly, eloquent, troublesome. He cumbers himself never about consequences, about interests; he gives an independent, genuine verdict. You must court him; he does not court you. But the man is as it were clapped into jail by his consciousness. As soon as he has once acted or spoken with éclat [2] he is a committed person, watched by the sympathy or the hatred of hundreds, whose affections must now enter into his account. There is no Lethe [3] for this. Ah, that he could pass again into his neutrality! Who can thus avoid all pledges and, having observed, observe again from the same unaffected, unbiased, unbribable, unaffrighted innocence,— must always be formidable. He would utter opinions on all passing affairs, which being seen to be not private but necessary, would sink like darts into the ear of men and put them in fear.

These are the voices which we hear in solitude, but they grow faint and inaudible as we enter into the world. Society everywhere is

---

[1] formerly where the cheapest seats in a theater were, just back of the orchestra, and from which might be heard the most outspoken judgments on play and players [2] brilliance [3] the river of forgetfulness in Hades

in conspiracy against the manhood of every one of its members. Society is a joint-stock company, in which the members agree, for the better securing of his bread to each share-holder, to surrender the liberty and culture of the eater. The virtue in most request is con-formity. Self-reliance is its aversion. It loves not realities and creators, but names and customs.

Whoso would be a man, must be a non-conformist. He who would gather immortal palms [1] must not be hindered by the name of goodness, but must explore if it be goodness. Nothing is at last sacred but the integrity of your own mind. Absolve you to yourself, and you shall have the suffrage of the world. I re-member an answer which when quite young I was prompted to make to a valued adviser who was wont to importune me with the dear old doctrines of the church. On my saying, "What have I to do with the sacredness of traditions, if I live wholly from within?" my friend suggested,—"But these impulses may be from below, not from above." I replied, "They do not seem to me to be such; but if I am the Devil's child, I will live then from the Devil." No law can be sacred to me but that of my nature. Good and bad are but names very readily transferable to that or this; the only right is what is after my constitution; the only wrong what is against it. A man is to carry himself in the presence of all opposition as if everything were titular [2] and ephemeral but he. I am ashamed to think how easily we capitulate to badges and names, to large societies and dead institutions. Every decent and well-spoken individual affects and sways me more than is right. I ought to go upright and vital, and speak the rude truth in all ways. If malice and vanity wear the coat of philan-thropy, shall that pass? If an angry bigot as-sumes this bountiful cause of Abolition, and comes to me with his last news from Barba-does, [3] why should I not say to him, "Go love thy infant; love thy wood-chopper; be good-natured and modest; have that grace; and never varnish your hard, uncharitable am-bition with this incredible tenderness for black folk a thousand miles off. Thy love afar is spite at home." Rough and graceless would be such greeting, but truth is handsomer than the affectation of love. Your goodness must have some edge to it,—else it is none. The doctrine of hatred must be preached, as the counteraction of the doctrine of love, when that pules and whines. I shun father and mother and wife and brother when my genius calls me. I would write on the lintels of the door-post, *Whim*. I hope it is somewhat better than whim at last, but we cannot spend the day in explanation. Expect me not to show cause why I seek or why I exclude company. Then again, do not tell me, as a good man did today, of my obligation to put all poor men in good situations. Are they *my* poor? I tell thee, thou foolish philanthropist, that I grudge the dollar, the dime, the cent I give to such men as do not belong to me and to whom I do not belong. There is a class of persons to whom by all spiritual affinity I am bought and sold; for them I will go to prison if need be; but your miscellaneous popular charities; the education at college of fools; the building of meeting-houses to the vain end to which many now stand; alms to sots, and the thou-sand-fold Relief Societies;—though I confess with shame I sometimes succumb and give the dollar, it is a wicked dollar, which by and by I shall have the manhood to withhold.

Virtues are, in the popular estimate, rather the exception than the rule. There is the man *and* his virtues. Men do what is called a good action, as some piece of courage or charity, much as they would pay a fine in expiation of daily non-appearance on parade. Their works are done as an apology or extenuation of their living in the world,—as invalids and the insane pay a high board. Their virtues are penances. I do not wish to expiate, but to live. My life is for itself and not for a spectacle. I much prefer that it should be of a lower strain, so it be genuine and equal, than that it should be glittering and unsteady. I wish it to be sound and sweet, and not to need diet and bleeding. I ask primary evidence that you are a man, and refuse this appeal from the man to his actions. I know that for myself it makes no difference whether I do or forbear those actions which are reckoned excellent. I cannot

[1] symbols of success   [2] existing in name or title only
[3] a British West Indian island from which slavery was officially abolished in 1834

consent to pay for a privilege where I have intrinsic right. Few and mean as my gifts may be, I actually am, and do not need for my own assurance or the assurance of my fellows any secondary testimony.

What I must do is all that concerns me, not what the people think. This rule, equally arduous in actual and in intellectual life, may serve for the whole distinction between greatness and meanness. It is the harder because you will always find those who think they know what is your duty better than you know it. It is easy in the world to live after the world's opinion; it is easy in solitude to live after our own; but the great man is he who in the midst of the crowd keeps with perfect sweetness the independence of solitude.

The objection to conforming to usages that have become dead to you is that it scatters your force. It loses your time and blurs the impression of your character. If you maintain a dead church, contribute to a dead Bible-society, vote with a great party either for the government or against it, spread your table like base housekeepers,—under all these screens I have difficulty to detect the precise man you are: and of course so much force is withdrawn from all your proper life. But do your work, and I shall know you. Do your work, and you shall reinforce yourself. A man must consider what a blindman's-buff is this game of conformity. If I know your sect I anticipate your argument. I hear a preacher announce for his text and topic the expediency of one of the institutions of his church. Do I not know beforehand that not possibly can he say a new and spontaneous word? Do I not know that with all this ostentation of examining the grounds of the institution he will do no such thing? Do I not know that he is pledged to himself not to look but at one side, the permitted side, not as a man, but as a parish minister? He is a retained attorney, and these airs of the bench are the emptiest affectation. Well, most men have bound their eyes with one or another handkerchief, and attached themselves to some one of these communities of opinion. This conformity makes them not false in a few particulars, authors of a few lies, but false in all particulars. Their every truth is not quite true. Their two is not

the real two, their four not the real four; so that every word they say chagrins us and we know not where to begin to set them right. Meantime Nature is not slow to equip us in the prison-uniform of the party to which we adhere. We come to wear one cut of face and figure, and acquire by degrees the gentlest asinine expression. There is a mortifying experience in particular, which does not fail to wreak itself also in the general history; I mean the "foolish face of praise,"[1] the forced smile which we put on in company where we do not feel at ease, in answer to conversation which does not interest us. The muscles, not spontaneously moved but moved by a low usurping wilfulness, grow tight about the outline of the face, with the most disagreeable sensation.

For nonconformity the world whips you with its displeasure. And therefore a man must know how to estimate a sour face. The bystanders look askance on him in the public street or in the friend's parlor. If this aversion had its origin in contempt and resistance like his own he might well go home with a sad countenance; but the sour faces of the multitude, like their sweet faces, have no deep cause, but are put on and off as the wind blows and a newspaper directs. Yet is the discontent of the multitude more formidable than that of the senate and the college. It is easy enough for a firm man who knows the world to brook the rage of the cultivated classes. Their rage is decorous and prudent, for they are timid, as being very vulnerable themselves. But when to their feminine rage the indignation of the people is added, when the ignorant and the poor are aroused, when the unintelligent brute force that lies at the bottom of society is made to growl and mow, it needs the habit of magnanimity and religion to treat it god-like as a trifle of no concernment.

The other terror that scares us from self-trust is our consistency; a reverence for our past act or word because the eyes of others have no other data for computing our orbit than our past acts, and we are loth to disappoint them.

But why should you keep your head over your shoulder? Why drag about this corpse

[1] from Pope's *Epistle to Arbuthnot*, line 212

of your memory, lest you contradict somewhat you have stated in this or that public place? Suppose you should contradict yourself; what then? It seems to be a rule of wisdom never to rely on your memory alone, scarcely even in acts of pure memory, but to bring the past for judgment into the thousand-eyed present, and live ever in a new day. In your metaphysics you have denied personality to the Deity, yet when the devout motions of the soul come, yield to them heart and life, though they should clothe God with shape and color. Leave your theory, as Joseph his coat in the hand of the harlot, and flee.[1]

A foolish consistency is the hobgoblin of little minds, adored by little statesmen and philosophers and divines. With consistency a great soul has simply nothing to do. He may as well concern himself with his shadow on the wall. Speak what you think now in hard words and tomorrow speak what tomorrow thinks in hard words again, though it contradict everything you said today.—"Ah, so you shall be sure to be misunderstood."—Is it so bad then to be misunderstood? Pythagoras was misunderstood, and Socrates, and Jesus, and Luther, and Copernicus, and Galileo, and Newton, and every pure and wise spirit that ever took flesh. To be great is to be misunderstood.

I suppose no man can violate his nature. All the sallies of his will are rounded in by the law of his being, as the inequalities of Andes and Himmaleh are insignificant in the curve of the sphere. Nor does it matter how you gage and try him. A character is like an acrostic or Alexandrian stanza[2];—read it forward, backward, or across, it still spells the same thing. In this pleasing contrite woodlife which God allows me, let me record day by day my honest thought without prospect or retrospect, and, I cannot doubt, it will be found symmetrical, though I mean it not and see it not. My book should smell of pines and resound with the hum of insects. The swallow over my window should interweave that thread or straw he carries in his bill into my web also. We pass for what we are. Character

teaches above our wills. Men imagine that they communicate their virtue or vice only by overt actions, and do not see that virtue or vice emit a breath every moment.

There will be an agreement in whatever variety of actions, so they be each honest and natural in their hour. For of one will, the actions will be harmonious, however unlike they seem. These varieties are lost sight of at a little distance, at a little height of thought. One tendency unites them all. The voyage of the best ship is a zigzag line of a hundred tacks. See the line from a sufficient distance, and it straightens itself to the average tendency. Your genuine action will explain itself and will explain your other genuine actions. Your conformity explains nothing. Act singly, and what you have already done singly will justify you now. Greatness appeals to the future. If I can be firm enough today to do right and scorn eyes, I must have done so much right before as to defend me now. Be it how it will, do right now. Always scorn appearances and you always may. The force of character is cumulative. All the foregone days of virtue work their health into this. What makes the majesty of the heroes of the senate and the field, which so fills the imagination? The consciousness of a train of great days and victories behind. They shed a united light on the advancing actor. He is attended as by a visible escort of angels. That is it which throws thunder into Chatham's voice, and dignity into Washington's port, and America into Adams's eye. Honor is venerable to us because it is no ephemera. It is always ancient virtue. We worship it today because it is not of today. We love it and pay it homage because it is not a trap for our love and homage, but is self-dependent, self-derived, and therefore of an old immaculate pedigree, even if shown in a young person.

I hope in these days we have heard the last of conformity and consistency. Let the words be gazetted[1] and ridiculous henceforward. Instead of the gong for dinner, let us hear a whistle from the Spartan fife.[2] Let us never bow and apologize more. A great man is com-

---

[1] Genesis 39:13   [2] Emerson means a palindrome, which is the same, read forward or backward, as "toot" or "Madam, I'm Adam."

[1] published to the world as the names of bankrupts were formerly   [2] the only musical instrument allowed to the Spartans

ing to eat at my house. I do not wish to please him; I wish that he would wish to please me. I will stand here for humanity, and though I would make it kind, I would make it true. Let us affront and reprimand the smooth mediocrity and squalid contentment of the times, and hurl in the face of custom and trade and office, the fact which is the upshot of all history, that there is a great responsible Thinker and Actor working wherever a man works; that a true man belongs to no other time or place, but is the center of things. Where he is there is Nature. He measures you and all men and all events. Ordinarily, everybody in society reminds us of somewhat else, or of some other person. Character, reality, reminds you of nothing else; it takes place [1] of the whole creation. The man must be so much that he must make all circumstances indifferent. Every true man is a cause, a country, and an age; requires infinite spaces and numbers and time fully to accomplish his design; —and posterity seem to follow his steps as a train of clients. A man Cæsar is born, and for ages after we have a Roman Empire. Christ is born, and millions of minds so grow and cleave to his genius that he is confounded with virtue and the possible of man. An institution is the lengthened shadow of one man; as, Monachism, of the Hermit Antony; the Reformation, of Luther; Quakerism, of Fox; Methodism, of Wesley; Abolition, of Clarkson. Scipio, Milton called "the height of Rome" [2]; and all history resolves itself very easily into the biography of a few stout and earnest persons.

Let a man then know his worth, and keep things under his feet. Let him not peep or steal, or skulk up and down with the air of a charity-boy, a bastard, or an interloper in the world which exists for him. But the man in the street, finding no worth in himself which corresponds to the force which built a tower or sculptured a marble god, feels poor when he looks on these. To him a palace, a statue, or a costly book have an alien and forbidding air, much like a gay equipage, and seem to say like that, "Who are you, Sir?" Yet they all are his, suitors for his notice, petitioners to his faculties that they will come out and take

possession. The picture waits for my verdict; it is not to command me, but I am to settle its claims to praise. That popular fable of the sot who was picked up dead-drunk in the street, carried to the duke's house, washed and dressed and laid in the duke's bed, and, on his waking, treated with all obsequious ceremony like the duke, and assured that he had been insane,[1] owes its popularity to the fact that it symbolizes so well the state of man who is in the world a sort of sot, but now and then wakes up, exercises his reason and finds himself a true prince.

Our reading is mendicant and sycophantic. In history our imagination plays us false. Kingdom and lordship, power and estate, are a gaudier vocabulary than private John and Edward in a small house and common day's work; but the things of life are the same to both; the sum total of both is the same. Why all this deference to Alfred and Scanderbeg and Gustavus? Suppose they were virtuous; did they wear out virtue? As great a stake depends on your private act today as followed their public and renowned steps. When private men shall act with original views, the luster will be transferred from the actions of kings to those of gentlemen.

The world has been instructed by its kings, who have so magnetized the eyes of nations. It has been taught by this colossal symbol the mutual reverence that is due from man to man. The joyful loyalty with which men have everywhere suffered the king, the noble, or the great proprietor to walk among them by law of his own, make his own scale of men and things and reverse theirs, pay for benefits not with money but with honor, and represent the law in his person, was the hieroglyphic by which they obscurely signified their consciousness of their own right and comeliness, the right of every man.

The magnetism which all original action exerts is explained when we inquire the reason of self-trust. Who is the Trustee? What is the aboriginal Self, on which a universal reliance may be grounded? What is the nature and power of that science-baffling star, without

[1] precedence   [2] *Paradise Lost*, IX, 510

[1] a story as old as the *Arabian Nights*, but best known as found in the introductory scene of Shakespeare's *The Taming of the Shrew*

parallax,[1] without calculable elements, which shoots a ray of beauty even into trivial and impure actions, if the least mark of independence appear? The inquiry leads us to that source, at once the essence of genius, of virtue, and of life, which we call Spontaneity or Instinct. We denote this primary wisdom as Intuition, whilst all later teachings are tuitions. In that deep force, the last fact behind which analysis cannot go, all things find their common origin. For the sense of being which in calm hours rises, we know not how, in the soul, is not diverse from things, from space, from light, from time, from man, but one with them and proceeds obviously from the same source whence their life and being also proceed. We first share the life by which things exist and afterwards see them as appearances in nature and forget that we have shared their cause. Here is the fountain of action and of thought. Here are the lungs of that inspiration which giveth man wisdom and which cannot be denied without impiety and atheism. We lie in the lap of immense intelligence, which makes us receivers of its truth and organs of its activity. When we discern justice, when we discern truth, we do nothing of ourselves, but allow a passage to its beams. If we ask whence this comes, if we seek to pry into the soul that causes, all philosophy is at fault. Its presence or its absence is all we can affirm. Every man discriminates between the voluntary acts of his mind and his involuntary perceptions, and knows that to his involuntary perceptions a perfect faith is due. He may err in the expression of them, but he knows that these things are so, like day and night, not to be disputed. My wilful actions and acquisitions are but roving;—the idlest reverie, the faintest native emotion, command my curiosity and respect. Thoughtless people contradict as readily the statement of perceptions as of opinions, or rather much more readily; for they do not distinguish between perception and notion. They fancy that I choose to see this or that thing. But perception is not whimsical, but fatal. If I see a trait, my children will see it after me, and in course of time all mankind,—

[1] the difference between the directions of a heavenly body as seen from two different standpoints

although it may chance that no one has seen it before me. For my perception of it is as much a fact as the sun.

The relations of the soul to the divine spirit are so pure that it is profane to seek to interpose helps. It must be that when God speaketh he should communicate, not one thing, but all things; should fill the world with his voice; should scatter forth light, nature, time, souls, from the center of the present thought; and new date and new create the whole. Whenever a mind is simple and receives a divine wisdom, old things pass away,—means, teachers, texts, temples fall; it lives now, and absorbs past and future into the present hour. All things are made sacred by relation to it,—one as much as another. All things are dissolved to their center by their cause, and in the universal miracle petty and particular miracles disappear. If therefore a man claims to know and speak of God and carries you backward to the phraseology of some old molded nation in another country, in another world, believe him not. Is the acorn better than the oak which is its fullness and completion? Is the parent better than the child into whom he has cast his ripened being? Whence then this worship of the past? The centuries are conspirators against the sanity and authority of the soul. Time and space are but physiological colors which the eye makes, but the soul is light: where it is, is day; where it was, is night; and history is an impertinence and an injury if it be anything more than a cheerful apologue or parable of my being and becoming.

Man is timid and apologetic; he is no longer upright; he dares not say "I think," "I am," but quotes some saint or sage. He is ashamed before the blade of grass or the blowing rose. These roses under my window make no reference to former roses or to better ones; they are for what they are; they exist with God today. There is no time to them. There is simply the rose; it is perfect in every moment of its existence. Before a leaf-bud has burst, its whole life acts; in the full-blown flower there is no more; in the leafless root there is no less. Its nature is satisfied and it satisfies Nature in all moments alike. But man postpones or remembers; he does not live in the present, but with reverted eye laments the past, or, heedless of the riches that surround him, stands on tiptoe to foresee the future. He cannot be happy and strong until he too lives with Nature in the present, above time.

This should be plain enough. Yet see what strong intellects dare not yet hear God himself unless he speak the phraseology of I know not what David, or Jeremiah, or Paul. We shall not always set so great a price on a few texts, on a few lives. We are like children who repeat by rote the sentences of grandames and tutors, and, as they grow older, of the men of talents and character they chance to see,— painfully recollecting the exact words they spoke; afterwards, when they come into the point of view which those had who uttered these sayings, they understand them and are willing to let the words go; for at any time they can use words as good when occasion comes. If we live truly, we shall see truly. It is as easy for the strong man to be strong, as it is for the weak to be weak. When we have new perception, we shall gladly disburden the memory of its hoarded treasures as old rubbish. When a man lives with God, his voice shall be as sweet as the murmur of the brook and the rustle of the corn.

And now at last the highest truth on this subject remains unsaid; probably cannot be said; for all that we say is the far-off remembering of the intuition. That thought by what I can now nearest approach to say it, is this. When good is near you, when you have life in yourself, it is not by any known or accustomed way; you shall not discern the footprints of any other; you shall not see the face of man; you shall not hear any name;—the way, the thought, the good, shall be wholly strange and new. It shall exclude example and experience. You take the way from man, not to man. All persons that ever existed are its forgotten ministers. Fear and hope are alike beneath it. There is somewhat low even in hope. In the hour of vision there is nothing that can be called gratitude, nor properly joy. The soul raised over passion beholds identity and eternal causation, perceives the self-existence of Truth and Right, and calms itself with knowing that all things go well. Vast spaces of nature, the Atlantic Ocean, the South Sea; long intervals of time, years, centuries, are of no account. This which I think and feel underlay every former state of life and circumstances, as it does underlie my present, and what is called life and what is called death.

Life only avails, not the having lived. Power ceases in the instant of repose; it resides in the moment of transition from a past to a new state, in the shooting of the gulf, in the darting to an aim. This one fact the world hates; that the soul *becomes;* for that forever degrades the past, turns all riches to poverty, all reputation to a shame, confounds the saint with the rogue, shoves Jesus and Judas equally aside. Why then do we prate of self-reliance? Inasmuch as the soul is present there will be power not confident but agent.[1] To talk of reliance is a poor external way of speaking. Speak rather of that which relies because it works and is. Who has more obedience than I masters me, though he should not raise his finger. Round him I must revolve by the gravitation of spirits. We fancy it rhetoric when we speak of eminent virtue. We do not yet see that virtue is Height, and that a man or a company of men, plastic and permeable to principles, by the law of nature must overpower and ride all cities, nations, kings, rich men, poets, who are not.

This is the ultimate fact which we so quickly reach on this, as on every topic, the resolution of all in the ever-blessed One. Self-existence is the attribute of the Supreme Cause, and it constitutes the measure of good by the degree in which it enters into all lower forms. All things real are so by so much virtue as they contain. Commerce, husbandry, hunting, whaling, war, eloquence, personal weight, are somewhat, and engage my respect as examples of its presence and impure action. I see the same law working in nature for conservation and growth. Power is, in nature, the essential measure of right. Nature suffers nothing to remain in her kingdoms which cannot help itself. The genesis and maturation of a planet, its poise and orbit, the bended tree recovering itself from the strong wind, the vital resources of every animal and vegetable, are demonstrations of the self-sufficing and therefore self-relying soul.

Thus all concentrates: let us not rove; let us

[1] active

sit at home with the cause. Let us stun and astonish the intruding rabble of men and books and institutions by a simple declaration of the divine fact. Bid the invaders take the shoes from off their feet, for God is here within. Let our simplicity judge them, and our docility to our own law demonstrate the poverty of nature and fortune beside our native riches.

But now we are a mob. Man does not stand in awe of man, nor is his genius admonished to stay at home, to put itself in communication with the internal ocean, but it goes abroad to beg a cup of water of the urns of other men. We must go alone. I like the silent church before the service begins, better than any preaching. How far off, how cool, how chaste the persons look, begirt each one with a precinct or sanctuary! So let us always sit. Why should we assume the faults of our friend, or wife, or father, or child, because they sit around our hearth, or are said to have the same blood? All men have my blood and I all men's. Not for that will I adopt their petulance or folly, even to the extent of being ashamed of it. But your isolation must not be mechanical, but spiritual, that is, must be elevation. At times the whole world seems to be in conspiracy to importune you with emphatic trifles. Friend, climate, child, sickness, fear, want, charity, all knock at once at thy closet door and say,—"Come out unto us." But keep thy state; come not into their confusion. The power men possess to annoy me I give them by a weak curiosity. No man can come near me but through my act. "What we love that we have, but by desire we bereave ourselves of the love."

If we cannot at once rise to the sanctities of obedience and faith, let us at least resist our temptations; let us enter into the state of war and wake Thor and Woden, courage and constancy, in our Saxon breasts. This is to be done in our smooth times by speaking the truth. Check this lying hospitality and lying affection. Live no longer to the expectation of these deceived and deceiving people with whom we converse. Say to them, "O father, O mother, O wife, O brother, O friend, I have lived with you after appearances hitherto. Henceforward I am the truth's. Be it known unto you that henceforward I obey no law

less than the eternal law. I will have no covenants but proximities. I shall endeavor to nourish my parents, to support my family, to be the chaste husband of one wife,—but these relations I must fill after a new and unprecedented way. I appeal from your customs. I must be myself. I cannot break myself any longer for you, or you. If you can love me for what I am, we shall be the happier. If you cannot, I will still seek to deserve that you should. I will not hide my tastes or aversions. I will so trust that what is deep is holy, that I will do strongly before the sun and moon whatever inly rejoices me and the heart appoints. If you are noble, I will love you; if you are not, I will not hurt you and myself by hypocritical attentions. If you are true, but not in the same truth with me, cleave to your companions; I will seek my own. I do this not selfishly but humbly and truly. It is alike your interest, and mine, and all men's, however long we have dwelt in lies, to live in truth. Does this sound harsh today? You will soon love what is dictated by your nature as well as mine, and if we follow the truth it will bring us out safe at last."—But so may you give these friends pain. Yes, but I cannot sell my liberty and my power, to save their sensibility. Besides, all persons have their moments of reason, when they look out into the region of absolute truth; then will they justify me and do the same thing.

The populace think that your rejection of popular standards is a rejection of all standard, and mere antinomianism[1]; and the bold sensualist will use the name of philosophy to gild his crimes. But the law of consciousness abides. There are two confessionals, in one or the other of which we must be shriven. You may fulfil your round of duties by clearing yourself in the *direct* or in the *reflex* way. Consider whether you have satisfied your relations to father, mother, cousin, neighbor, town, cat and dog—whether any of these can upbraid you. But I may also neglect this reflex standard and absolve me to myself. I have my own stern claims and perfect circle. It denies the name of duty to many offices that are called

[1] the belief that faith alone is enough to insure salvation, thus making it unnecessary to obey the moral law

duties. But if I can discharge its debts it enables me to dispense with the popular code. If any one imagines that this law is lax, let him keep its commandment one day.

And truly it demands something godlike in him who has cast off the common motives of humanity and has ventured to trust himself for a taskmaster. High be his heart, faithful his will, clear his sight, that he may in good earnest be doctrine, society, law, to himself, that a simple purpose may be to him as strong as iron necessity is to others!

If any man consider the present aspects of what is called by distinction *society*, he will see the need of these ethics. The sinew and heart of man seem to be drawn out, and we are become timorous, desponding whimperers. We are afraid of truth, afraid of fortune, afraid of death, and afraid of each other. Our age yields no great and perfect persons. We want men and women who shall renovate life and our social state, but we see that most natures are insolvent, cannot satisfy their own wants, have an ambition out of all proportion to their practical force and do lean and beg day and night continually. Our housekeeping is mendicant, our arts, our occupations, our marriages, our religion we have not chosen, but society has chosen for us. We are parlor soldiers. We shun the rugged battle of fate, where strength is born.

If our young men miscarry in their first enterprises they lose all heart. If the young merchant fails, men say he is *ruined*. If the finest genius studies at one of our colleges and is not installed in an office within one year afterwards in the cities or suburbs of Boston or New York, it seems to his friends and to himself that he is right in being disheartened and in complaining the rest of his life. A sturdy lad from New Hampshire or Vermont, who in turn tries all the professions, who *teams it*, *farms it*, *peddles*, keeps a school, preaches, edits a newspaper, goes to Congress, buys a township, and so forth, in successive years, and always like a cat falls on his feet, is worth a hundred of these city dolls. He walks abreast with his days and feels no shame in not "studying a profession," for he does not postpone his life, but lives already. He has not one chance, but a hundred chances. Let a Stoic open the resources of man and tell men they are not leaning willows, but can and must detach themselves; that with the exercise of self-trust, new powers shall appear; that a man is the word made flesh, born to shed healing to the nations; that he should be ashamed of our compassion, and that the moment he acts from himself, tossing the laws, the books, idolatries and customs out of the window, we pity him no more but thank and revere him;—and that teacher shall restore the life of man to splendor and make his name dear to all history.

It is easy to see that a greater self-reliance must work a revolution in all the offices and relations of men; in their religion; in their education; in their pursuits; their modes of living; their association; in their property; in their speculative views.

1. In what prayers do men allow themselves! That which they call a holy office is not so much as brave and manly. Prayer looks abroad and asks for some foreign addition to come through some foreign virtue, and loses itself in endless mazes of natural and supernatural, and mediatorial and miraculous. Prayer that craves a particular commodity, anything less than all good, is vicious. Prayer is the contemplation of the facts of life from the highest point of view. It is the soliloquy of a beholding and jubilant soul. It is the spirit of God pronouncing his works good. But prayer as a means to effect a private end is meanness and theft. It supposes dualism and not unity in nature and consciousness. As soon as the man is at one with God, he will not beg. He will then see prayer in all action. The prayer of the farmer kneeling in his field to weed it, the prayer of the rower kneeling with the stroke of his oar, are true prayers heard throughout nature, though for cheap ends. Caratach, in Fletcher's *Bonduca*, when admonished to inquire the mind of the god Andate, replies,—

"His hidden meaning lies in our endeavors;
Our valors are our best gods." [1]

Another sort of false prayers are our regrets. Discontent is the want of self-reliance: it is infirmity of will. Regret calamities if you can

[1] Act III, scene I, lines 80–81. The original reads "dwells" instead of "lies,"

thereby help the sufferer; if not, attend your own work and already the evil begins to be repaired. Our sympathy is just as base. We come to them who weep foolishly and sit down and cry for company, instead of imparting to them truth and health in rough electric shocks, putting them once more in communication with their own reason. The secret of fortune is joy in our hands. Welcome evermore to gods and men is the self-helping man. For him all doors are flung wide; him all tongues greet, all honors crown, all eyes follow with desire. Our love goes out to him and embraces him because he did not need it. We solicitously and apologetically caress and celebrate him because he held on his way and scorned our disapprobation. The gods love him because men hated him. "To the persevering mortal," said Zoroaster, "the blessed Immortals are swift."

As men's prayers are a disease of the will, so are their creeds a disease of the intellect. They say with those foolish Israelites, "Let not God speak to us, lest we die. Speak thou, speak any man with us, and we will obey." Everywhere I am hindered of meeting God in my brother, because he has shut his own temple doors and recites fables merely of his brother's, or his brother's brother's God. Every new mind is a new classification. If it prove a mind of uncommon activity and power, a Locke, a Lavoisier, a Hutton, a Bentham, a Fourier, it imposes its classification on other men, and lo! a new system! In proportion to the depth of the thought, and so to the number of the objects it touches and brings within reach of the pupil, is his complacency. But chiefly is this apparent in creeds and churches, which are also classifications of some powerful mind acting on the elemental thought of duty and man's relation to the Highest. Such is Calvinism, Quakerism, Swedenborgism. The pupil takes the same delight in subordinating everything to the new terminology as a girl who has just learned botany in seeing a new earth and new seasons thereby. It will happen for a time that the pupil will find his intellectual power has grown by the study of his master's mind. But in all unbalanced minds the classification is idolized, passes for the end and not for a speedily exhaustible means, so that the walls

of the system blend to their eye in the remote horizon with the walls of the universe; the luminaries of heaven seem to them hung on the arch their master built. They cannot imagine how you aliens have any right to see, —how you can see; "It must be somehow that you stole the light from us." They do not yet perceive that light, unsystematic, indomitable, will break into any cabin, even into theirs. Let them chirp awhile and call it their own. If they are honest and do well, presently their neat new pinfold [1] will be too strait and low, will crack, will lean, will rot and vanish, and the immortal light, all young and joyful, million-orbed, million-colored, will beam over the universe as on the first morning.

2. It is for want of self-culture that the superstition of Traveling, whose idols are Italy, England, Egypt, retains its fascination for all educated Americans. They who made England, Italy, or Greece venerable in the imagination, did so by sticking fast where they were, like an axis of the earth. In manly hours we feel that duty is our place. The soul is no traveler; the wise man stays at home, and when his necessities, his duties, on any occasion call him from his house, or into foreign lands, he is at home still and shall make men sensible by the expression of his countenance that he goes, the missionary of wisdom and virtue, and visits cities and men like a sovereign and not like an interloper or a valet.

I have no churlish objection to the circumnavigation of the globe for the purposes of art, of study, and benevolence, so that the man is first domesticated, or does not go abroad with the hope of finding somewhat greater than he knows. He who travels to be amused, or to get somewhat which he does not carry, travels away from himself, and grows old even in youth among old things. In Thebes, in Palmyra, his will and mind have become old and dilapidated as they. He carries ruins to ruins.

Traveling is a fool's paradise. Our first journeys discover to us the indifference of places. At home I dream that at Naples, at Rome, I can be intoxicated with beauty and lose my sadness. I pack my trunk, embrace

[1] an enclosure (pound) for stray animals

my friends, embark on the sea and at last wake up in Naples, and there beside me is the stern fact, the sad self, unrelenting, identical, that I fled from. I seek the Vatican and the palaces. I affect to be intoxicated with sights and suggestions, but I am not intoxicated. My giant goes with me wherever I go.

3. But the rage of traveling is a symptom of a deeper unsoundness affecting the whole intellectual action. The intellect is vagabond, and our system of education fosters restlessness. Our minds travel when our bodies are forced to stay at home. We imitate; and what is imitation but the traveling of the mind? Our houses are built with foreign taste; our shelves are garnished with foreign ornaments; our opinions, our tastes, our faculties lean, and follow the Past and the Distant. The soul created the arts wherever they have flourished. It was in his own mind that the artist sought his model. It was an application of his own thought to the thing to be done and the conditions to be observed. And why need we copy the Doric or the Gothic model?[1] Beauty, convenience, grandeur of thought and quaint expression are as near to us as to any, and if the American artist will study with hope and love the precise thing to be done by him, considering the climate, the soil, the length of the day, the wants of the people, the habit and form of the government, he will create a house in which all these will find themselves fitted, and taste and sentiment will be satisfied also.

Insist on yourself; never imitate. Your own gift you can present every moment with the cumulative force of a whole life's cultivation; but of the adopted talent of another you have only an extemporaneous half possession. That which each can do best, none but his Maker can teach him. No man yet knows what it is, nor can, till that person has exhibited it. Where is the master who could have taught Shakespeare? Where is the master who could have instructed Franklin, or Washington, or Bacon, or Newton? Every great man is a unique. The Scipionism of Scipio is precisely that part he could not borrow. Shakespeare will never be made by the study of Shakespeare. Do that which is assigned you, and you cannot hope too much or dare too much.

[1] styles of classic and medieval architecture

There is at this moment for you an utterance brave and grand as that of the colossal chisel of Phidias, or trowel of the Egyptians, or the pen of Moses or Dante, but different from all these. Not possibly will the soul, all rich, all eloquent, with thousand-cloven tongue, deign to repeat itself; but if you can hear what these patriarchs say, surely you can reply to them in the same pitch of voice; for the ear and the tongue are two organs of one nature. Abide in the simple and noble regions of thy life, obey thy heart, and thou shalt reproduce the Foreworld again.

4. As our Religion, our Education, our Art look abroad, so does our spirit of society. All men plume themselves on the improvement of society, and no man improves.

Society never advances. It recedes as fast on one side as it gains on the other. It undergoes continual changes; it is barbarous, it is civilized, it is christianized, it is rich, it is scientific; but this change is not amelioration. For everything that is given something is taken. Society acquires new arts and loses old instincts. What a contrast between the well-clad, reading, writing, thinking American, with a watch, a pencil and a bill of exchange in his pocket, and the naked New Zealander, whose property is a club, a spear, a mat and an undivided twentieth of a shed to sleep under! But compare the health of the two men and you shall see that the white man has lost his aboriginal strength. If the traveler tell us truly, strike the savage with a broadaxe and in a day or two the flesh shall unite and heal as if you struck the blow into soft pitch, and the same blow shall send the white to his grave.

The civilized man has built a coach, but has lost the use of his feet. He is supported on crutches, but lacks so much support of muscle. He has a fine Geneva watch, but he fails of the skill to tell the hour by the sun. A Greenwich nautical almanac he has, and so being sure of the information when he wants it, the man in the street does not know a star in the sky. The solstice he does not observe; the equinox he knows as little; and the whole bright calendar of the year is without a dial in his mind. His notebooks impair his memory; his libraries overload his wit; the insurance-office increases the number of accidents; and it may be a question whether machinery does not encumber; whether we have not lost by refinement some energy, by a Christianity, entrenched in establishments and forms, some vigor of wild virtue. For every Stoic was a Stoic; but in Christendom where is the Christian?

There is no more deviation in the moral standard than in the standard of height or bulk. No greater men are now than ever were. A singular equality may be observed between the great men of the first and of the last ages; nor can all the science, art, religion, and philosophy of the nineteenth century avail to educate greater men than Plutarch's heroes, three or four and twenty centuries ago. Not in time is the race progressive. Phocion, Socrates, Anaxagoras, Diogenes, are great men, but they leave no class. He who is really of their class will not be called by their name, but will be his own man, and in his turn the founder of a sect. The arts and inventions of each period are only its costume and do not invigorate men. The harm of the improved machinery may compensate its good. Hudson and Behring accomplished so much in their fishing-boats as to astonish Parry and Franklin, whose equipment exhausted the resources of science and art. Galileo, with an opera-glass, discovered a more splendid series of celestial phenomena than any one since. Columbus found the New World in an undecked boat. It is curious to see the periodical disuse and perishing of means and machinery which were introduced with loud laudation a few years or centuries before. The great genius returns to essential man. We reckoned the improvements of the art of war among the triumphs of science, and yet Napoleon conquered Europe by the bivouac, which consisted of falling back on naked valor and disencumbering it of all aids. The Emperor held it impossible to make a perfect army, says Las Casas, "without abolishing our arms, magazines, commissaries and carriages, until, in imitation of the Roman custom, the soldier should receive his supply of corn, grind it in his hand-mill and bake his bread himself."

Society is a wave. The wave moves onward, but the water of which it is composed does not. The same particle does not rise from the valley to the ridge. Its unity is only phenomenal. The persons who make up a nation today, next year die, and their experience dies with them.

And so the reliance on Property, including the reliance on governments which protect it, is the want of self-reliance. Men have looked away from themselves and at things so long that they have come to esteem the religious, learned and civil institutions as guards of property, and they deprecate assaults on these, because they feel them to be assaults on property. They measure their esteem of each other by what each has, and not by what each is. But a cultivated man becomes ashamed of his property, out of new respect for his nature. Especially he hates what he has if he see that it is accidental,—came to him by inheritance, or gift, or crime; then he feels that it is not having; it does not belong to him, has no root in him and merely lies there because no revolution or no robber takes it away. But that which a man is, does always by necessity acquire; and what the man acquires, is living property, which does not wait the beck of rulers, or mobs, or revolutions, or fire, or storm, or bankruptcies, but perpetually renews itself wherever the man breathes. "Thy lot or portion of life," said the Caliph Ali, "is seeking after thee; therefore be at rest from seeking after it." Our dependence on these foreign goods leads us to our slavish respect for numbers. The political parties meet in numerous conventions; the greater the concourse and with each new uproar of announcement, The delegation from Essex! The Democrats from New Hampshire! The Whigs of Maine! the young patriot feels himself stronger than before by a new thousand of eyes and arms. In like manner the reformers summon conventions and vote and resolve in multitude. Not so, O friends! will the God deign to enter and inhabit you, but by a method precisely the reverse. It is only as a man puts off all foreign support and stands alone that I see him to be strong and to prevail. He is weaker by every recruit to his banner. Is not a man better than a town? Ask nothing of men, and, in the endless mutation, thou only firm column must presently appear the upholder of all that surrounds thee. He who knows that power is inborn, that he is weak because he has looked for good out of him and elsewhere, and, so perceiving, throws himself unhesitatingly on his thought, instantly rights himself, stands in the erect position, commands his limbs, works miracles; just as a man who stands on his feet is stronger than a man who stands on his head.

So use all that is called Fortune. Most men gamble with her, and gain all, and lose all, as her wheel rolls. But do thou leave as unlawful 10 these winnings, and deal with Cause and Effect, the chancellors of God. In the Will work and acquire, and thou hast chained the wheel of Chance, and shall sit hereafter out of fear from her rotations. A political victory, a rise of rents, the recovery of your sick or the return of your absent friend, or some other favorable event raises your spirits, and you think good days are preparing for you. Do not believe it. Nothing can bring you peace 20 but yourself. Nothing can bring you peace but the triumph of principles.

1841

From THE OVER-SOUL

This essay appeared in the first series of Emerson's *Essays*, the volume that contained "The American Scholar" and "Self-Reliance." His mystical doctrine of the Over-Soul was a vital part of 30 Emerson's message. It has been praised by many, and by others, among them O. W. Holmes, scoffed at and termed over-difficult to understand. A suggestive list of the elements that entered into it is given in the Concord Edition, II, 426-48.

"But souls that of his own good life partake
He loves as his own self; dear as his eye
They are to Him: He'll never them forsake:
When they shall die, then God himself shall die:
They live, they live in blest eternity."

HENRY MORE 40

Space is ample, east and west,
But two cannot go abreast,
Cannot travel in it two:
Yonder masterful cuckoo
Crowds every egg out of the nest,
Quick or dead, except its own;
A spell is laid on sod and stone,
Night and Day 've been tampered with,
Every quality and pith
Surcharged and sultry with a power 50
That works its will on age and hour.

THERE is a difference between one and another hour of life in their authority and subsequent effect. Our faith comes in moments; our vice is habitual. Yet is there a depth in those brief moments, which constrains us to ascribe more reality to them than to all other experiences. For this reason, the argument, which is always forthcoming to silence those who conceive extraordinary hopes of man, namely, the appeal to experience, is forever invalid and vain. A mightier hope abolishes despair. We give up the past to the objector, and yet we hope. He must explain this hope. We grant that human life is mean; but how did we find out that it was mean? What is the ground of this uneasiness of ours, of this old discontent? What is the universal sense of want and ignorance, but the fine innuendo by which the great soul makes its enormous claim? Why do men feel that the natural history of man has never been written, but always he is leaving behind what you have said of him, and it becomes old, and books of metaphysics worthless? The philosophy of six thousand years has not searched the chambers and magazines of the soul. In its experiments there has always remained in the last analysis a residuum it could not resolve. Man is a stream whose source is hidden. Always our being is descending into us from we know not whence. The most exact calculator has no prescience that somewhat incalculable may not balk the very next moment. I am constrained every moment to acknowledge a higher origin for events than the will I call mine.

As with events, so is it with thoughts. When I watch that flowing river, which, out of regions I see not, pours for a season its streams into me,—I see that I am a pensioner,—not a cause, but a surprised spectator of this ethereal water; that I desire and look up, and put myself in the attitude of reception, but from some alien energy the visions come.

The Supreme Critic on all the errors of the past and the present, and the only prophet of that which must be, is that great nature in which we rest, as the earth lies in the soft arms of the atmosphere; that Unity, that Over-Soul, within which every man's particular being is contained and made one with all other; that common heart, of which all sincere conversation is the worship, to which all right action is submission; that overpowering reality which confutes our tricks and talents, and constrains every one to pass for what he is, and to speak from his character and not from his tongue; and which evermore tends and aims to pass into our thought and hand, and become wisdom, and virtue, and power, and beauty. We live in succession, in division, in parts, in particles. Meantime, within man is the soul of the whole; the wise silence; the universal beauty, to which every part and particle is equally related; the eternal ONE. And this deep power in which we exist, and whose beatitude is all accessible to us, is not only self-sufficing and perfect in every hour, but the act of seeing and the thing seen, the seer and the spectacle, the subject and the object, are one. We see the world piece by piece, as the sun, the moon, the animal, the tree; but the whole, of which these are the shining parts, is the soul. It is only by the vision of that Wisdom, that the horoscope of the ages can be read, and it is only by falling back on our better thoughts, by yielding to the spirit of prophecy which is innate in every man, that we can know what it saith. Every man's words, who speaks from that life, must sound vain to those who do not dwell in the same thought on their own part. I dare not speak for it. My words do not carry its august sense; they fall short and cold. Only itself can inspire whom it will, and, behold, their speech shall be lyrical, and sweet, and universal as the rising of the wind. Yet I desire, even by profane words, if sacred I may not use, to indicate the heaven of this deity, and to report what hints I have collected of the transcendent simplicity and energy of the Highest Law.

If we consider what happens in conversation, in reveries, in remorse, in times of passion, in surprises, in the instructions of dreams, wherein often we see ourselves in masquerade, —the droll disguises only magnifying and enhancing a real element, and forcing it on our distinct notice,—we shall catch many hints that will broaden and lighten into knowledge of the secret of nature. All goes to show that the soul in man is not an organ, but animates and exercises all the organs; is not a function, like the power of memory, of calculation, of comparison,—but uses these as hands and feet; is not a faculty, but a light; is not the intellect or the will, but the master of the intellect and the will; is the vast background of our being, in which they lie,—an immensity not possessed and that cannot be possessed. From within or from behind, a light shines through us upon things, and makes us aware that we are nothing, but the light is all. A man is the façade of a temple, wherein all wisdom and all good abide. What we commonly call man,—the eating, drinking, planting, counting man,—does not, as we know him, represent himself, but misrepresents himself. Him we do not respect; but the soul, whose organ he is, would he let it appear through his action, would make our knees bend. When it breathes through his intellect, it is genius; when it breathes through his will, it is virtue; when it flows through his affection, it is love. And the blindness of the intellect begins, when it would be something of itself. The weakness of the will begins, when the individual would be something of himself. All reform aims, in some one particular, to let the great soul have its way through us; in other words, to engage us to obey.

Of this pure nature every man is at some time sensible. Language cannot paint it with his colors. It is too subtle. It is undefinable, unmeasurable; but we know that it pervades and contains us. We know that all spiritual being is in man. A wise old proverb says, "God comes to see us without bell": that is, there is no screen or ceiling between our heads and the infinite heavens, so is there no bar or wall in the soul where man, the effect, ceases, and God, the cause, begins. The walls are taken away. We lie open on one side to the deeps of spiritual nature, to all the attributes of God. Justice we see and know, Love, Freedom, Power. These natures no man ever got above, but always they tower over us, and most in the moment when our interests tempt us to wound them.

The sovereignty of this nature whereof we speak is made known by its independency of those limitations which circumscribe us on every hand. The soul circumscribeth all things. As I have said, it contradicts all experience. In like manner it abolishes time and

space. The influence of the senses has, in most
men, overpowered the mind to that degree,
that the walls of time and space have come to
look solid, real, and insurmountable; and to
speak with levity of these limits is, in the
world, the sign of insanity. Yet time and space
are but inverse measures of the force of the
soul. A man is capable of abolishing them
both. The spirit sports with time—

"Can crowd eternity into an hour,
Or stretch an hour to eternity."

1841

From ENGLISH TRAITS

When he visited England in 1833 Emerson had
published nothing and was little known. His second
visit, in 1847-48, was preceded by the publication of *Nature* and the first and second volumes of
Essays. It was made in response to an invitation to
deliver courses of lectures in the larger English
towns. Much friendly hospitality was extended to
him and he met many celebrities, among them
Wordsworth and Carlyle whom he had known on
his first visit. He observed and pondered English
traits, and on his return to America he lectured
on England to his countrymen. In the course of
seven years he prepared these lectures for the press.
English Traits was published in 1856. Emerson
wrote of the English thoughtfully and without the
touches of harshness or derision usual in accounts
of a foreign country by a visitor. There are no
gossipy journalistic chroniclings in Emerson's
volume. His interest lay not in accounts of large
cities, social events and customs, or literary celebrities, but went deeper. Dr. Richard Garnett said of
the book, "Emerson is so little concerned with the
fashion of the day and so much with the solid
foundations of English life that his book should
endure as long as they do." Carlyle wrote to
Emerson of it, "I believe it to be worth all the
Books ever written by New England of the Old."

CHAPTER VIII

Character

THE English race are reputed morose. I do
not know that they have sadder brows than
their neighbors of northern climates. They are
sad by comparison with the singing and dancing nations: not sadder, but slow and staid,
as finding their joys at home. They, too, believe that where there is no enjoyment of life

there can be no vigor and art in speech or
thought; that your merry heart goes all the
way, your sad one tires in a mile. This trait
of gloom has been fixed on them by French
travelers, who, from Froissart, Voltaire, Le
Sage, Mirabeau, down to the lively journalists
of the *feuilletons*,[1] have spent their wit on the
solemnity of their neighbors. The French say,
gay conversation is unknown in their island.
The Englishman finds no relief from reflection, except in reflection. When he wishes for
amusement, he goes to work. His hilarity is
like an attack of fever. Religion, the theater,
and the reading the books of his country, all
feed and increase his natural melancholy. The
police does not interfere with public diver-
sions. It thinks itself bound in duty to respect
the pleasures and rare gayety of this incon-
solable nation; and their well-known courage
is entirely attributable to their disgust of life.

I suppose their gravity of demeanor and
their few words have obtained this reputation.
As compared with the Americans, I think them
cheerful and contented. Young people in this
country are much more prone to melancholy.
The English have a mild aspect and a ringing
cheerful voice. They are large-natured and not
so easily amused as the southerners, and are
among them as grown people among children,
requiring war, or trade, or engineering, or
science, instead of frivolous games. They are
proud and private, and even if disposed to
recreation, will avoid an open garden. They
sported sadly; *ils s'amusaient tristement, selon
la coutume de leur pays*,[2] said Froissart; and I
suppose never nation built their party-walls
so thick, or their garden-fences so high. Meat
and wine produce no effect on them. They
are just as cold, quiet and composed, at the
end, as at the beginning of dinner.

The reputation of taciturnity they have enjoyed for six or seven hundred years; and a
kind of pride in bad public speaking is noted
in the House of Commons, as if they were
willing to show that they did not live by their
tongues, or thought they spoke well enough
if they had the tone of gentlemen. In mixed
company they shut their mouths. A Yorkshire

---

[1] parts of French newspapers devoted to light literature, criticism, etc.   [2] "They sported sadly according to the custom of their country."

millowner told me he had ridden more than once all the way from London to Leeds, in the first-class carriage, with the same persons, and no word exchanged. The club-houses were established to cultivate social habits, and it is rare that more than two eat together, and oftenest one eats alone. Was it then a stroke of humor in the serious Swedenborg, or was it only his pitiless logic, that made him shut up the English souls in a heaven by them- [10] selves?

They are contradictorily described as sour, splenetic, and stubborn,—and as mild, sweet, and sensible. The truth is they have great range and variety of character. Commerce sends abroad multitudes of different classes. The choleric Welshman, the fervid Scot, the bilious resident in the East or West Indies, are wide of the perfect behavior of the edu- cated and dignified man of family. So is the [20] burly farmer; so is the country squire, with his narrow and violent life. In every inn is the Commercial-Room, in which "travelers," or bagmen who carry patterns and solicit orders for the manufacturers, are wont to be entertained. It easily happens that this class should characterize England to the foreigner, who meets them on the road and at every public house, whilst the gentry avoid the taverns, or seclude themselves whilst in them. [30]

But these classes are the right English stock, and may fairly show the national qualities, before yet art and education have dealt with them. They are good lovers, good haters, slow but obstinate admirers, and in all things very much steeped in their temperament, like men hardly awaked from deep sleep, which they enjoy. Their habits and instincts cleave to nature. They are of the earth, earthy; and of the sea, as the sea-kinds, attached to it for [40] what it yields them, and not from any senti- ment. They are full of coarse strength, rude exercise, butcher's meat and sound sleep; and suspect any poetic insinuation or any hint for the conduct of life which reflects on this animal existence, as if somebody were fumbling at the umbilical cord and might stop their sup- plies. They doubt a man's sound judgment if he does not eat with appetite, and shake their heads if he is particularly chaste. Take them [50] as they come, you shall find in the common

people a surly indifference, sometimes gruff- ness and ill temper; and in minds of more power, magazines of inexhaustible war, chal- lenging

"The ruggedest hour that time and spite dare bring
To frown upon the enraged Northumber- land." [1]

They are headstrong believers and defenders of their opinion, and not less resolute in main- taining their whim and perversity. Hezekiah Woodward wrote a book against the Lord's Prayer. And one can believe that Burton, the Anatomist of Melancholy, having predicted from the stars the hour of his death, slipped the knot himself round his own neck, not to falsify his horoscope.

Their looks bespeak an invincible stout- ness: they have extreme difficulty to run away, and will die game. Wellington said of the young coxcombs of the Life-Guards, deli- cately brought up, "But the puppies fight well"; and Nelson said of his sailors, "They really mind shot no more than peas." Of ab- solute stoutness no nation has more or better examples. They are good at storming re- doubts, at boarding frigates, at dying in the last ditch, or any desperate service which has daylight and honor in it; but not, I think, at enduring the rack, or any passive obedience, like jumping off a castle-roof at the word of a czar. Being both vascular and highly organ- ized, so as to be very sensible of pain; and intellectual, so as to see reason and glory in a matter.

Of that constitutional force which yields the supplies of the day, they have the more than enough; the excess which creates courage on fortitude, genius in poetry, invention in mechanics, enterprise in trade, magnificence in wealth, splendor in ceremonies, petulance and projects in youth. The young men have a rude health which runs into peccant humors. They drink brandy like water, cannot expend their quantities of waste strength on riding, hunting, swimming and fencing, and run into absurd frolics with the gravity of the Eumen- ides. They stoutly carry into every nook and corner of the earth their turbulent sense;

[1] from Shakespeare's *Henry IV*, Part II, I, 1

leaving no lie uncontradicted; no pretension unexamined. They chew hasheesh; cut themselves with poisoned creases; swing their hammock in the boughs of the Bohon Upas[1]; taste every poison; buy every secret; at Naples they put St. Januarius's blood in an alembic; they saw a hole into the head of the "winking Virgin," to know why she winks; measure with an English footrule every cell of the Inquisition, every Turkish caaba, every Holy of holies; translate and send to Bentley the arcanum bribed and bullied away from shuddering Bramins; and measure their own strength by the terror they cause. These travelers are of every class, the best and the worst; and it may easily happen that those of rudest behavior are taken notice of and remembered. The Saxon melancholy in the vulgar rich and poor appears as gushes of ill-humor, which every check exasperates into sarcasm and vituperation. There are multitudes of rude young English who have the self-sufficiency and bluntness of their nation, and who, with their disdain of the rest of mankind and with this indigestion and choler, have made the English traveler a proverb for uncomfortable and offensive manners. It was no bad description of the Briton generically, what was said two hundred years ago of one particular Oxford scholar: "He was a very bold man, uttered any thing that came into his mind, not only among his companions, but in public coffeehouses, and would often speak his mind of particular persons then accidentally present, without examining the company he was in; for which he was often reprimanded and several times threatened to be kicked and beaten."

The common Englishman is prone to forget a cardinal article in the bill of social rights, that every man has a right to his own ears. No man can claim to usurp more than a few cubic feet of the audibilities of a public room, or to put upon the company with the loud statement of his crotchets or personalities.

But it is in the deep traits of race that the fortunes of nations are written, and however derived,—whether a happier tribe or mixture of tribes, the air, or what circumstance that

mixed for them the golden mean of temperament,—here exists the best stock in the world, broad-fronted, broad-bottomed, best for depth, range and equability; men of aplomb and reserves, great range and many moods, strong instincts, yet apt for culture; war-class as well as clerks; earls and tradesmen; wise minority, as well as foolish majority; abysmal temperament, hiding wells of wrath, and glooms on which no sunshine settles, alternated with a common sense and humanity which hold them fast to every piece of cheerful duty; making this temperament a sea to which all storms are superficial; a race to which their fortunes flow, as if they alone had the elastic organization at once fine and robust enough for dominion; as if the burly inexpressive, now mute and contumacious, now fierce and sharp-tongued dragon, which once made the island light with his fiery breath, had bequeathed his ferocity to his conqueror. They hide virtues under vices, or the semblance of them. It is the misshapen hairy Scandinavian troll again, who lifts the cart out of the mire, or "threshes the corn that ten day-laborers could not end,"[1] but it is done in the dark and with muttered maledictions. He is a churl with a soft place in his heart, whose speech is a brash of bitter waters, but who loves to help you at a pinch. He says no, and serves you, and your thanks disgust him. Here was lately a cross-grained miser, odd and ugly, resembling in countenance the portrait of Punch with the laugh left out; rich by his own industry; sulking in a lonely house; who never gave a dinner to any man and disdained all courtesies; yet as true a worshipper of beauty in form and color as ever existed, and profusely pouring over the cold mind of his countrymen creations of grace and truth, removing the reproach of sterility from English art, catching from their savage climate every fine hint, and importing into their galleries every tint and trait of sunnier cities and skies; making an era in painting; and when he saw that the splendor of one of his pictures in the Exhibition dimmed his rival's that hung next it, secretly took a brush and blackened his own.[2]

---

[1] a Javanese tree the juice of which is used as an arrow poison

[1] quoted from Milton's *L'Allegro*, lines 108–9   [2] reference to a story about the English painter, Turner

They do not wear their heart in their sleeve for daws to peck at. They have that phlegm or staidness which it is a compliment to disturb. "Great men," said Aristotle, "are always of a nature originally melancholy." 'Tis the habit of a mind which attaches to abstractions with a passion which gives vast results. They dare to displease, they do not speak to expectation. They like the sayers of No, better than the sayers of Yes. Each of them has an opinion which he feels it becomes him to express all the more that it differs from yours. They are meditating opposition. This gravity is inseparable from minds of great resources.

There is an English hero superior to the French, the German, the Italian, or the Greek. When he is brought to the strife with fate, he sacrifices a richer material possession, and on more purely metaphysical grounds. He is there with his own consent, face to face with fortune, which he defies. On deliberate choice and from grounds of character, he has elected his part to live and die for, and dies with grandeur. This race has added new elements to humanity and has a deeper root in the world.

They have great range of scale, from ferocity to exquisite refinement. With larger scale, they have great retrieving power. After running each tendency to an extreme, they try another tack with equal heat. More intellectual than other races, when they live with other races they do not take their language, but bestow their own. They subsidize other nations, and are not subsidized. They proselyte, and are not proselyted. They assimilate other races to themselves, and are not assimilated. The English did not calculate the conquest of the Indies. It fell to their character. So they administer, in different parts of the world, the codes of every empire and race; in Canada, old French law; in the Mauritius, the Code Napoléon; in the West Indies, the edicts of the Spanish Cortés; in the East Indies, the Laws of Menu; in the Isle of Man, of the Scandinavian Thing; at the Cape of Good Hope, of the old Netherlands; and in the Ionian Islands, the Pandects of Justinian.

They are very conscious of their advantageous position in history. England is the lawgiver, the patron, the instructor, the ally. Compare the tone of the French and of the English press: the first querulous, captious, sensitive about English opinion; the English press never timorous about French opinion, but arrogant and contemptuous.

They are testy and headstrong through an excess of will and bias; churlish as men sometimes please to be who do not forget a debt, who ask no favors and who will do what they like with their own. With education and intercourse these asperities wear off and leave the good-will pure. If anatomy is reformed according to national tendencies, I suppose the spleen will hereafter be found in the Englishman, not found in the American, and differencing the one from the other. I anticipate another anatomical discovery, that this organ will be found to be cortical and caducous; that they are superficially morose, but at last tenderhearted, herein differing from Rome and the Latin nations. Nothing savage, nothing mean resides in the English heart. They are subject to panics of credulity and of rage, but the temper of the nation, however disturbed, settles itself soon and easily, as, in this temperate zone, the sky after whatever storms clears again, and serenity is its normal condition.

A saving stupidity masks and protects their perception, as the curtain of the eagle's eye. Our swifter Americans, when they first deal with English, pronounce them stupid; but, later, do them justice as people who wear well, or hide their strength. To understand the power of performance that is in their finest wits, in the patient Newton, or in the versatile transcendent poets, or in the Dugdales, Gibbons, Hallams, Eldons, and Peels, one should see how English day-laborers hold out. High and low, they are of an unctuous texture. There is an adipocere[1] in their constitution, as if they had oil also for their mental wheels and could perform vast amounts of work without damaging themselves.

Even the scale of expense on which people live, and to which scholars and professional men conform, proves the tension of their muscle, when vast numbers are found who can each lift this enormous load. I might even add, their daily feasts argue a savage vigor of body.

[1] waxy substance into which dead tissue is sometimes changed by continued moisture

No nation was ever so rich in able men; "Gentlemen," as Charles I said of Strafford, "whose abilities might make a prince rather afraid than ashamed in the greatest affairs of state"; men of such temper, that, like Baron Vere, "had one seen him returning from a victory, he would by his silence have suspected that he had lost the day; and, had he beheld him in a retreat, he would have collected him a conqueror by the cheerfulness 10 of his spirit." [1]

The following passage from the "Heimskringla" might almost stand as a portrait of the modern Englishman:—"Haldor was very stout and strong and remarkably handsome in appearances. King Harold gave him this testimony, that he, among all his men, cared least about doubtful circumstances, whether they betokened danger or pleasure; for, whatever turned up, he was never in higher nor in lower 20 spirits, never slept less nor more on account of them, nor ate nor drank but according to his custom. Haldor was not a man of many words, but short in conversation, told his opinion bluntly and was obstinate and hard: and this could not please the king, who had many clever people about him, zealous in his service. Haldor remained a short time with the king, and then came to Iceland, where he took up his abode in Hiardaholt and dwelt in 30 that farm to a very advanced age." [2]

The national temper, in the civil history, is not flashy or whiffling. The slow, deep English mass smoulders with fire, which at last sets all its borders in flame. The wrath of London is not French wrath, but has a long memory, and, in its hottest heat, a register and rule.

Half their strength they put not forth. They are capable of a sublime resolution, and if 40 hereafter the war of races, often predicted, and making itself a war of opinions also (a question of despotism and liberty coming from Eastern Europe), should menace the English civilization, these sea-kings may take once again to their floating castles and find a new home and a second millennium of power in their colonies.

[1] Fuller, *Worthies of England.* [*Emerson's note.*]
[2] *Heimskringla*, Laing's translation, vol. iii. p. 37. 50 [*Emerson's note.*]

The stability of England is the security of the modern world. If the English race were as mutable as the French, what reliance? But the English stand for liberty. The conservative, money-loving, lord-loving English are yet liberty-loving; and so freedom is safe: for they have more personal force than any other people. The nation always resist the immoral action of their government. They think humanely on the affairs of France, of Turkey, of Poland, of Hungary, of Schleswig Holstein, though overborne by the statecraft of the rulers at last.

Does the early history of each tribe show the permanent bias, which, though not less potent, is masked as the tribe spreads its activity into colonies, commerce, codes, arts, letters? The early history shows it, as the musician plays the air which he proceeds to conceal in a tempest of variations. In Alfred, in the Northmen, one may read the genius of the English society, namely that private life is the place of honor. Glory, a career, and ambition, words familiar to the longitude of Paris, are seldom heard in English speech. Nelson wrote from their hearts his homely telegraph, "England expects every man to do his duty."

For actual service, for the dignity of a profession, or to appease diseased or inflamed talent, the army and navy may be entered (the worst boys doing well in the navy); and the civil service in departments where serious official work is done; and they hold in esteem the barrister engaged in the severer studies of the law. But the calm, sound and most British Briton shrinks from public life as charlatanism, and respects an economy founded on agriculture, coal-mines, manufactures or trade, which secures an independence through the creation of real values.

They wish neither to command nor obey, but to be kings in their own houses. They are intellectual and deeply enjoy literature; they like well to have the world served up to them in books, maps, models, and every mode of exact information, and, though not creators in art, they value its refinement. They are ready for leisure, can direct and fill their own day, nor need so much as others the constraint of a necessity. But the history of the nation discloses, at every turn, this original predilection for private independence, and however this inclination may have been disturbed by the bribes with which their vast colonial power has warped men out of orbit, the inclination endures, and forms and reforms the laws, letters, manners and occupations. They choose that welfare which is compatible with the commonwealth, knowing that such alone is stable; as wise merchants prefer investments in the three per cents.

1856

BIOGRAPHICAL SKETCH OF THOREAU

First published in the *Atlantic Monthly*, August, 1862. Reprinted in *Lectures and Biographical Sketches* (1884). Written not long after the death of Thoreau. It is one of the most readable of Emerson's biographies. He writes detachedly of Thoreau, neither overpraising him nor speaking too critically. With the passing of time Thoreau has loomed larger than his contemporaries could well have foreseen. Emerson spoke of him more generously than did Lowell. See the latter's essay, "Thoreau," and, also, his *A Fable for Critics*.

A queen rejoices in her peers,
And wary Nature knows her own,
By court and city, dale and down,
And like a lover volunteers,
And to her son will treasures more,
And more to purpose, freely pour
In one wood talk, than learned men
Will find with glass in ten times ten.

It seemed as if the breezes brought him,
It seemed as if the sparrows taught him,
As if by secret sign he knew
Where in far fields the orchis grew.

HENRY DAVID THOREAU was the last male descendant of a French ancestor who came to this country from the Isle of Guernsey. His character exhibited occasional traits drawn from this blood, in singular combination with a very strong Saxon genius.

He was born in Concord, Massachusetts, on the 12th of July, 1817. He was graduated at Harvard College in 1837, but without any literary distinction. An iconoclast in literature, he seldom thanked colleges for their service to him, holding them in small esteem, whilst yet his debt to them was important.

After leaving the University, he joined his brother in teaching a private school, which he soon renounced. His father was a manufacturer of lead-pencils, and Henry applied himself for a time to this craft, believing he could make a better pencil than was then in use. After completing his experiments, he exhibited his work to chemists and artists in Boston, and having obtained their certificates to its excellence and to its equality with the best London manufacture, he returned home contented. His friends congratulated him that he had now opened his way to fortune. But he replied that he should never make another pencil. "Why should I? I would not do again what I have done once." He resumed his endless walks and miscellaneous studies, making every day some new acquaintance with Nature, though as yet never speaking of zoölogy or botany, since, though very studious of natural facts, he was incurious of technical and textual science.

At this time, a strong, healthy youth, fresh from college, whilst all his companions were choosing their profession, or eager to begin some lucrative employment, it was inevitable that his thoughts should be exercised on the same question, and it required rare decision to refuse all the accustomed paths and keep his solitary freedom at the cost of disappointing the natural expectations of his family and friends: all the more difficult that he had a perfect probity, was exact in securing his own independence, and in holding every man to the like duty. But Thoreau never faltered. He was a born protestant. He declined to give up his large ambition of knowledge and action for any narrow craft or profession, aiming at a much more comprehensive calling, the art of living well. If he slighted and defied the opinions of others, it was only that he was more intent to reconcile his practice with his own belief. Never idle or self-indulgent, he preferred, when he wanted money, earning it by some piece of manual labor agreeable to him, as building a boat or a fence, planting, grafting, surveying, or other short work, to any long engagements. With his hardy habits and few wants, his skill in woodcraft, and his powerful arithmetic, he was very competent to live in any part of the world. It would cost him less time to supply his wants than another. He was therefore secure of his leisure.

A natural skill for mensuration, growing out of his mathematical knowledge and his habit of ascertaining the measures and distances of objects which interested him, the size of trees, the depth and extent of ponds and rivers, the height of mountains, and the air-line distance of his favorite summits,—this, and his intimate knowledge of the territory about Concord, made him drift into the profession of land-surveyor. It had the advantage for him that it led him continually into new and secluded grounds, and helped his studies of Nature. His accuracy and skill in this work were readily appreciated, and he found all the employment he wanted.

He could easily solve the problems of the surveyor, but he was daily beset with graver questions, which he manfully confronted. He interrogated every custom, and wished to settle all his practice on an ideal foundation. He was a protestant *à outrance*,[1] and few lives contain so many renunciations. He was bred to no profession; he never married; he lived alone; he never went to church; he never voted; he refused to pay a tax to the State; he ate no flesh, he drank no wine, he never knew the use of tobacco; and, though a naturalist, he used neither trap nor gun. He chose, wisely no doubt for himself, to be the bachelor of thought and Nature. He had no talent for wealth, and knew how to be poor without the least hint of squalor or inelegance. Perhaps he fell into his way of living without forecasting it much, but approved it with later wisdom. "I am often reminded," he wrote in his journal, "that if I had bestowed on me the wealth of Croesus, my aims must be still the same, and my means essentially the same." He had no temptations to fight against,—no appetites, no passions, no taste for elegant trifles. A fine house, dress, the manners and talk of highly cultivated people, were all thrown away on him. He much preferred a good Indian, and considered these refinements as impediments to conversation, wishing to meet his companion on the simplest terms. He declined invitations to dinner-parties, because there each was in every one's way, and he

[1] "to the utmost"

could not meet the individuals to any purpose. "They make their pride," he said, "in making their dinner cost much; I make my pride in making my dinner cost little." When asked at table what dish he preferred, he answered, "The nearest." He did not like the taste of wine, and never had a vice in his life. He said, "I have a faint recollection of pleasure derived from smoking dried lily-stems, before I was a man. I had commonly a supply of these. I have never smoked anything more noxious."

He chose to be rich by making his wants few, and supplying them himself. In his travels, he used the railroad only to get over so much country as was unimportant to the present purpose, walking hundreds of miles, avoiding taverns, buying a lodging in farmers' and fishermen's houses, as cheaper, and more agreeable to him, and because there he could better find the men and the information he wanted.

There was somewhat military in his nature, not to be subdued, always manly and able, but rarely tender, as if he did not feel himself except in opposition. He wanted a fallacy to oppose, a blunder to pillory, I may say required a little sense of victory, a roll of the drum, to call his powers into full exercise. It cost him nothing to say No; indeed he found it much easier than to say Yes. It seemed as if his first instinct on hearing a proposition was to controvert it, so impatient was he of the limitations of our daily thought. This habit, of course, is a little chilling to the social affections; and though the companion would in the end acquit him of any malice or untruth, yet it mars conversation. Hence, no equal companion stood in affectionate relations with one so pure and guileless. "I love Henry," said one of his friends, "but I cannot like him; and as for taking his arm, I should as soon think of taking the arm of an elm-tree."

Yet, hermit and stoic as he was, he was really fond of sympathy, and threw himself heartily and childlike into the company of young people whom he loved, and whom he delighted to entertain, as he only could, with the varied and endless anecdotes of his experiences by field and river; and he was always ready to lead a huckleberry-party or a search for chestnuts or grapes. Talking, one day, of a public discourse, Henry remarked that whatever succeeded with the audience was bad. I said, "Who would not like to write something which all can read, like *Robinson Crusoe?* and who does not see with regret that his page is not solid with a right materialistic treatment, which delights everybody?" Henry objected, of course, and vaunted the better lectures which reached only a few persons. But, at supper, a young girl, understanding that he was to lecture at the Lyceum, sharply asked him "whether his lecture would be a nice, interesting story, such as she wished to hear, or whether it was one of those old philosophical things that she did not care about." Henry turned to her, and bethought himself, and, I saw, was trying to believe that he had matter that might fit her and her brother, who were to sit up and go to the lecture, if it was a good one for them.

He was a speaker and actor of the truth, born such, and was ever running into dramatic situations from this cause. In any circumstance it interested all bystanders to know what part Henry would take, and what he would say; and he did not disappoint expectation, but used an original judgment on each emergency. In 1845 he built himself a small framed house on the shores of Walden Pond, and lived there two years alone, a life of labor and study. This action was quite native and fit for him. No one who knew him would tax him with affectation. He was more unlike his neighbors in his thought than in his action. As soon as he had exhausted the advantages of that solitude, he abandoned it. In 1847, not approving some uses to which the public expenditure was applied, he refused to pay his town tax, and was put in jail. A friend paid the tax for him, and he was released. The like annoyance was threatened the next year. But as his friends paid the tax, notwithstanding his protest, I believe he ceased to resist. No opposition or ridicule had any weight with him. He coldly and fully stated his opinion without affecting to believe that it was the opinion of the company. It was of no consequence if every one present held the opposite opinion. On one occasion he went to the University Library to procure some books. The librarian refused to lend them. Mr. Thoreau repaired to the President, who stated to him the rules and usages, which permitted the loan of books to resident graduates, to clergymen who were alumni, and to some others resident within a circle of ten miles' radius from the College. Mr. Thoreau explained to the President that the railroad had destroyed the old scale of distances,—that the library was useless, yes, and President and College useless, on the terms of his rules,—that the one benefit he owed to the College was its library,—that, at this moment, not only his want of books was imperative but he wanted a large number of books, and assured him that he, Thoreau, and not the librarian, was the proper custodian of these. In short, the President found the petitioner so formidable, and the rules getting to look so ridiculous, that he ended by giving him a privilege which in his hands proved unlimited thereafter.

No truer American existed than Thoreau. His preference of his country and condition was genuine, and his aversation from English and European manners and tastes almost reached contempt. He listened impatiently to news or *bon-mots* gleaned from London circles; and though he tried to be civil, these anecdotes fatigued him. The men were all imitating each other, and on a small mould. Why can they not live as far apart as possible, and each be a man by himself? What he sought was the most energetic nature; and he wished to go to Oregon, not to London. "In every part of Great Britain," he wrote in his diary, "are discovered traces of the Romans, their funereal urns, their camps, their dwellings. But New England, at least, is not based on any Roman ruins. We have not to lay the foundations of our houses on the ashes of a former civilization."

But idealist as he was, standing for abolition of slavery, abolition of tariffs, almost for abolition of government, it is needless to say he found himself not only unrepresented in actual politics, but almost equally opposed to every class of reformers. Yet he paid the tribute of his uniform respect to the Antislavery party. One man, whose personal acquaintance he had formed, he honored with exceptional regard. Before the first friendly word had been spoken for Captain John

Brown, he sent notices to most houses in Concord that he would speak in a public hall on the condition and character of John Brown, on Sunday evening, and invited all people to come. The Republican Committee, the Abolitionist Committee, sent him word that it was premature and not advisable. He replied, —"I did not send to you for advice, but to announce that I am to speak." The hall was filled at an early hour by people of all parties, and his earnest eulogy of the hero was heard by all respectfully, by many with a sympathy that surprised themselves.

It was said of Plotinus that he was ashamed of his body, and 'tis very likely he had good reason for it,—that his body was a bad servant, and he had not skill in dealing with the material world, as happens often to men of abstract intellect. But Mr. Thoreau was equipped with a most adapted and serviceable body. He was of short stature, firmly built, of light complexion, with strong, serious blue eyes, and a grave aspect,—his face covered in the late years with a becoming beard. His senses were acute, his frame well-knit and hardy, his hands strong and skillful in the use of tools. And there was a wonderful fitness of body and mind. He could pace sixteen rods more accurately than another man could measure them with rod and chain. He could find his path in the woods at night, he said, better by his feet than his eyes. He could estimate the measure of a tree very well by his eye; he could estimate the weight of a calf or a pig, like a dealer. From a box containing a bushel or more of loose pencils, he could take up with his hands fast enough just a dozen pencils at every grasp. He was a good swimmer, runner, skater, boatman, and would probably outwalk most countrymen in a day's journey. And the relation of body to mind was still finer than we have indicated. He said he wanted every stride his legs made. The length of his walk uniformly made the length of his writing. If shut up in the house he did not write at all.

He had a strong commonsense, like that which Rose Flammock, the weaver's daughter in Scott's romance,[1] commends in her father, as resembling a yardstick, which, whilst it measures dowlas[2] and diaper, can equally well measure tapestry and cloth of gold. He had always a new resource. When I was planting forest trees, and had procured half a peck of acorns, he said that only a small portion of them would be sound, and proceeded to examine them and select the sound ones. But finding this took time, he said, "I think if you put them all into water the good ones will sink"; which experiment we tried with success. He could plan a garden or a house or a barn; would have been competent to lead a "Pacific Exploring Expedition"; could give judicious counsel in the gravest private or public affairs.

He lived for the day, not cumbered and mortified by his memory. If he brought you yesterday a new proposition, he would bring you today another not less revolutionary. A very industrious man, and setting, like all highly organized men, a high value on his time, he seemed the only man of leisure in town, always ready for any excursion that promised well, or for conversation prolonged into late hours. His trenchant sense was never stopped by his rules of daily prudence, but was always up to the new occasion. He liked and used the simplest food, yet, when some one urged a vegetable diet, Thoreau thought all diets a very small matter, saying that "the man who shoots the buffalo lives better than the man who boards at the Graham House." He said, "You can sleep near the railroad, and never be disturbed: Nature knows very well what sounds are worth attending to, and has made up her mind not to hear the railroad-whistle. But things respect the devout mind, and a mental ecstasy was never interrupted." He noted what repeatedly befell him, that, after receiving from a distance a rare plant, he would presently find the same in his own haunts. And those pieces of luck which happen only to good players happened to him. One day, walking with a stranger, who inquired where Indian arrow-heads could be found, he replied, "Everywhere," and, stooping forward, picked one on the instant from the ground. At Mount Washington, in Tuckerman's Ravine, Thoreau had a bad fall, and sprained his foot. As he was in the act of getting up from his fall, he saw for the first time the leaves of the *Arnica mollis.*

[1] *The Betrothed* (1825)   [2] a coarse linen cloth

His robust common sense, armed with stout hands, keen perceptions, and strong will, cannot yet account for the superiority which shone in his simple and hidden life. I must add the cardinal fact, that there was excellent wisdom in him, proper to a rare class of men, which showed him the material world as a means and symbol. This discovery, which sometimes yields to poets a certain casual and interrupted light, serving for the ornament of their writing, was in him an unsleeping insight; and whatever faults or obstructions of temperament might cloud it, he was not disobedient to the heavenly vision. In his youth, he said, one day, "The other world is all my art; my pencils will draw no other; my jackknife will cut nothing else; I do not use it as a means." This was the muse and genius that ruled his opinions, conversation, studies, work, and course of life. This made him a searching judge of men. At first glance he measured his companion, and, though insensible to some fine traits of culture, could very well report his weight and caliber. And this made the impression of genius which his conversation sometimes gave.

He understood the matter in hand at a glance, and saw the limitations and poverty of those he talked with, so that nothing seemed concealed from such terrible eyes. I have repeatedly known young men of sensibility converted in a moment to the belief that this was the man they were in search of, the man of men, who could tell them all they should do. His own dealing with them was never affectionate, but superior, didactic, scorning their petty ways,—very slowly conceding, or not conceding at all, the promise of his society at their houses, or even at his own. "Would he not walk with them?" "He did not know. There was nothing so important to him as his walk; he had no walks to throw away on company." Visits were offered him from respectful parties, but he declined them. Admiring friends offered to carry him at their own cost to the Yellowstone River,—to the West Indies,—to South America. But though nothing could be more grave or considerate than his refusals, they remind one, in quite new relations, of that fop Brummell's reply to the gentleman who offered him his carriage in a shower, "But where will *you* ride, then?"—and what accusing silences, and what searching and irresistible speeches, battering down all defenses, his companions can remember!

Mr. Thoreau dedicated his genius with such entire love to the fields, hills, and waters of his native town, that he made them known and interesting to all reading Americans, and to people over the sea. The river on whose banks he was born and died he knew from its springs to its confluence with the Merrimack. He had made summer and winter observations on it for many years, and at every hour of the day and night. The result of the recent survey of the Water Commissioners appointed by the State of Massachusetts he had reached by his private experiments, several years earlier. Every fact which occurs in the bed, on the banks, or in the air over it; the fishes, and their spawning and nests, their manners, their food; the shadflies which fill the air on a certain evening once a year, and which are snapped at by the fishes so ravenously that many of these die of repletion; the conical heaps of small stones on the river-shallows, the huge nests of small fishes, one of which will sometimes overfill a cart; the birds which frequent the stream, heron, duck, sheldrake, loon, osprey; the snake, muskrat, otter, woodchuck, and fox, on the banks; the turtle, frog, hyla, and cricket, which made the banks vocal,—were all known to him, and, as it were, townsmen and fellow-creatures; so that he felt an absurdity or violence in any narrative of one of these by itself apart, and still more of its dimensions on an inch-rule, or in the exhibition of its skeleton, or the specimen of a squirrel or a bird in brandy. He liked to speak of the manners of the river, as itself a lawful creature, yet with exactness, and always to an observed fact. As he knew the river, so the ponds in this region.

One of the weapons he used, more important to him than microscope or alcohol-receiver to other investigators, was a whim which grew on him by indulgence, yet appeared in gravest statement, namely, of extolling his own town and neighborhood as the most favored center for natural observation. He remarked that the Flora of Massachusetts embraced almost all the important plants of America,—most of the oaks, most of the willows, the best pines, the ash, the maple, the beech, the nuts. He returned Kane's "Arctic Voyage" to a friend of whom he had borrowed it, with the remark, that "most of the phenomena noted might be observed in Concord." He seemed a little envious of the Pole, for the coincident sunrise and sunset, or five minutes' day after six months: a splendid fact, which Annursnuc[1] had never afforded him. He found red snow in one of his walks, and told me that he expected to find yet the *Victoria regia*[2] in Concord. He was the attorney of the indigenous plants, and owned to a preference of the weeds to the imported plants, as of the Indian to the civilized man, and noticed, with pleasure, that the willow bean-poles of his neighbor had grown more than his beans. "See these weeds," he said, "which have been hoed at by a million farmers all spring and summer, and yet have prevailed, and just now come out triumphant over all lanes, pastures, fields, and gardens, such is their vigor. We have insulted them with low names, too,—as Pigweed, Wormwood, Chickweed, Shadblossom." He says, "They have brave names, too,—Ambrosia, Stellaria, Amelanchier, Amaranth, etc."

I think his fancy for referring everything to the meridian of Concord did not grow out of any ignorance or depreciation of other longitudes or latitudes, but was rather a playful expression of his conviction of the indifferency of all places, and that the best place for each is where he stands. He expressed it once in this wise: "I think nothing is to be hoped from you, if this bit of mould under your feet is not sweeter to you to eat than any other in this world, or in any world."

The other weapon with which he conquered all obstacles in science was patience. He knew how to sit immovable, a part of the rock he rested on, until the bird, the reptile, the fish, which had retired from him, should come back and resume its habits, nay, moved by curiosity, should come to him and watch him.

It was a pleasure and a privilege to walk with him. He knew the country like a fox or a bird, and passed through it as freely by paths of his own. He knew every track in the snow or on the ground, and what creature had taken this path before him. One must submit abjectly to such a guide, and the reward was great. Under his arm he carried an old music-book to press plants; in his pocket, his diary and pencil, a spyglass for birds, microscope, jackknife, and twine. He wore a straw hat, stout shoes, strong gray trousers, to brave scrub-oaks and smilax, and to climb a tree for a hawk's or a squirrel's nest. He waded into the pool for the water-plants, and his strong legs were no insignificant part of his armor. On the day I speak of he looked for the Menyanthes,[1] detected it across the wide pool, and, on examination of the florets, decided that it had been in flower five days. He drew out of his breast-pocket his diary, and read the names of all the plants that should bloom on this day, whereof he kept account as a banker when his notes fall due. The Cypripedium[2] not due till tomorrow. He thought that, if waked up from a trance, in this swamp, he could tell by the plants what time of the year it was within two days. The redstart was flying about, and presently the fine grosbeaks, whose brilliant scarlet "makes the rash gazer wipe his eye,"[3] and whose fine clear note Thoreau compared to that of a tanager which has got rid of its hoarseness. Presently he heard a note which he called that of the night-warbler, a bird he had never identified, had been in search of twelve years, which always, when he saw it, was in the act of diving down into a tree or bush, and which it was in vain to seek; the only bird which sings indifferently by night and by day. I told him he must beware of finding and booking it, lest life should have nothing more to show him. He said, "What you seek in vain for, half your life, one day you come full upon, all the family at dinner. You seek it like a dream, and as soon as you find it you become its prey."

1862

---

[1] a hill often visited by Thoreau, whose spelling for it is Annersnack   [2] a kind of water lily

[1] a genus of bog plants   [2] the lady's-slipper   [3] the sixth line of George Herbert's "Virtue"

1817 ~ *Henry David Thoreau* ~ 1862

THOREAU, the most individual of the transcendental group, came into recognition late, but permanently. He put into practice many of the ideas that Emerson preached. He preferred the simple life, questioned the desirability of wealth, and devoted himself to a search for the satisfying existence. He was a philosopher, with the naturalist's love of the open air, was something of a mystic, and had the Yankee's practical skill. He preceded William Morris and Ruskin in attacking industrial exploitation. Like them, he thought that "the only wealth is life."

Thoreau was the only one of the "Concord group" to be born in Concord. His father was a pencil maker, son of a Boston merchant who had emigrated from the island of Jersey. Thoreau was graduated at Harvard at the age of twenty in 1837. As a student he was not always tractable. He neglected studies he found unattractive, cared nothing for honors, and declared his diploma not worth the five dollars paid for it. For a few years he taught school, and at times in later years he lectured. But throughout his life he preferred to support himself mainly by the labor of his hands. He was an expert pencil maker, a carpenter, and an excellent surveyor. By the intermittent exercise of these employments as well as farm work, day labor, making gardens, and odd jobs such as whitewashing and building fences, he earned enough to supply his simple wants and those of the relatives at times dependent on him. Mostly he followed his own inclinations.

He was associated with the little band of transcendentalists, especially with Emerson, at whose house he lived (1841–1843) as tutor and gardener and whom he helped to edit *The Dial.* Though most persons thought him an imitator of Emerson, his mother thought the imitation the other way round, and it may be that Emerson's interest in nature and his nature lore came partly from Thoreau. Emerson, however, cultivated nature for its spiritual values while Thoreau liked it for its own sake. Much of his time was spent in the open air alone. He made himself thoroughly familiar with the woods, fields, and waters about his native place, and made longer journeys on several occasions to Cape Cod, the Maine woods, Minnesota, and Canada. He recorded his experiences and observations in his journals. His ruling passions—love of simplicity and independence and his love of nature—perhaps found completest expression when he spent more than two years in a little hut which he built in 1845 at Walden Pond near Concord, tilling a small plot of ground and depending for sustenance and enjoyment almost entirely on his own resources. Here he sought to demonstrate simple living and to get at elementary conditions. Although he was a man whose personal views and traits were carried out to the point of eccentricity, he was hardly a thoroughgoing hermit or recluse in these years, for he still met his friends at Walden, stayed for short periods at his mother's home, delivered occasional lectures, and heard other lectures at Concord. His life was blameless; he was honest, fearless, and original, and he was loved and respected by those who knew him. When but forty-five, he died of tuberculosis, as had his father and his brother.

Thoreau lived out Emerson's doctrines of nonconformity and self-reliance. He condemned the complex machinery of society and thought overmuch civilization a mistake. He prided himself on being a "mystic, a transcendentalist, and a natural philosopher." He took an antislavery stand when this was unpopular, championed John Brown as a hero, and would not pay his poll tax for the reason that it was used for the support of a government that countenanced war and slavery. He never voted, and he explained his political views in an essay on the duty of civil disobedience. His idea was transcendental individualism applied to government. Though turning against organized society, he was no communist, for he wished to foster not the masses but extreme individualism. He wanted to be governed by neither the majority nor the minority. His contemporaries refused to take him seriously, but his popularity has increased steadily since his death. The nature school, rising at the end of the century, turned to him as original and stimulating, and they, rather than the reformers, contributed to new interest in his life and his work.

Like Emerson and Carlyle, Thoreau distinguished between "two kinds" of writings, "one of genius, or the inspired, the other of intellect and taste, in the intervals of inspiration." He regarded expression as organic with thought and character; form would take care of itself. He paid great tribute to experience and action as giving vitality to style. "Steady labor with the hands . . . is unquestionably the best method of removing palaver and sentimentality out of one's style, both of speaking and writing." He valued "plainness, and vigor, and sincerity." "A sentence should read as if its author, had he held a plow instead of a pen, could have drawn a furrow deep and straight to the end." However, much as he was indebted to experience and nature, he insisted that they could be transmuted into literature only by being refracted through a sensitive mind and winnowed by retrospection and introspection. In all things he prided himself upon a sharp individuality.

The writings of Thoreau have a charm derived partly from the subject matter, but largely from his individual prose style. To his nature descriptions he brings a clarity of expression as well as a naturalist's care in observation; to his philosophical discussions, shrewdness and bits of humor. Although not given to making aphorisms as was Emerson, he makes occasional terse statements which, in their epigrammatic nature, resemble those of his friend. Momentarily, because of the independence of his thinking, his expression may become too subtle, but in the main he writes simply and lucidly. He revised his journals painstakingly and worked over his sentences with the care of a craftsman; yet there are few signs of labor in his style, which throughout many volumes keeps its quality of freshness and originality.

Thoreau's chief works published in his lifetime are *A Week on the Concord and Merrimac Rivers* (1849), a miscellany of essays, poems, and papers, translations from the classics, philosophy and nature notes, and *Walden, or Life in the Woods* (1854). *Excursions* (1863), *The Maine Woods* (1864), and *Cape Cod* (1865) appeared after his death. He contributed verse to *The Dial. The Writings of Henry David Thoreau* (10 vols., Riverside Edition) appeared in 1894. The body of his writing is now available in his *Collected Works*, Manuscript Edition, and (issued without the manuscript insertions) the standard Walden Edition (20 vols., 1906). These contain also his letters and journals. *The Heart of Thoreau's Journals* (1927) was edited by Odell Shepherd. Various minor omissions from the Walden Edition have been edited by F. B. Sanborn (1902, 1905, 1909) and others.

Articles of interest on Thoreau are by Emerson (above); by Lowell, in *My Study Windows* (1871); and by John Burroughs, in *Indoor Studies* (1889). See also Archibald MacMechan, in *CHAL*, II (1918); Norman Foerster, in *Nature in American Literature* (1923); V. L. Parrington, in *Main Currents in American Thought*, II (1927); H. S. Canby, in *Classic Americans* (1931); and Canby and Adams in *DAB*, XVIII (1936). André Bruel wrote *Emerson et Thoreau* (1929), and R. W. Adams discussed "Thoreau's Literary Apprenticeship," *Studies in Philology*, XXIX, October, 1932. A good general introduction is supplied in B. V. Crawford's *Thoreau*, in the American Writers Series (1934).

Books concerning Thoreau are a life by H. S. Salt, in the Great Writers Series (1890, 1896); F. B. Sanborn's *Thoreau*, in the American Men of Letters Series (1882, 1910), and his *The Life of Henry D. Thoreau* (1917). See also Mark Van Doren's *Henry David Thoreau, a Critical Study* (1916); Léon Bazalgette's fictionized biography, *Henry Thoreau, Bachelor of Nature* (1924); and J. B. Atkinson's *Henry D. Thoreau, the Cosmic Yankee* (1927).

A good bibliography of Thoreau is that of Francis H. Allen, *A Bibliography of Henry David Thoreau* (1908). See also the bibliography by Mark Van Doren in *CHAL*, II (1918), and by Harry Hartwick in W. F. Taylor's *A History of American Letters* (1936).

SMOKE

Thoreau, like Emerson, thought of himself as a poet; but his verse does not bulk large, the execution is uneven, and the lyrical quality not striking. Usually he treats abstract subjects or subjects from nature.

LIGHT-WINGED smoke, Icarian[1] bird,
Melting thy pinions in thy upward flight,
Lark without song, and messenger of dawn,
Circling above the hamlets as thy nest;
Or else, departing dream, and shadowy form
Of midnight vision, gathering up thy skirts;
By night star-veiling, and by day   7

[1] In Greek myth Daedalus and his son Icarus escaped from the labyrinth in Crete by means of artificial wings. Icarus flew too near the sun, the wax in his wings melted, and he was drowned in the sea named thereafter Icarian. This poem is antecedent to and suggestive of later imagist poems.

Darkening the light and blotting out the sun;
Go thou my incense upward from this hearth,
And ask the gods to pardon this clear flame.
                                    1843

HAZE

WOOF of the sun, ethereal gauze,
Woven of Nature's richest stuffs,
Visible heat, air-water, and dry sea,
Last conquest of the eye;
Toil of the day displayed, sun-dust,
Aerial surf upon the shores of earth,
Ethereal estuary, frith of light,
Breakers of air, billows of heat,
Fine summer spray on inland seas;
Bird of the sun, transparent-winged,   10
Owlet of noon, soft-pinioned,
From heath or stubble rising without song,—
Establish thy serenity o'er the fields.   1849

INDEPENDENCE

My life more civil is and free
    Than any civil polity.

Ye princes, keep your realms
    And circumscribèd power,
Not wide as are my dreams,
    Nor rich as is this hour.

What can ye give which I have not?
What can ye take which I have got?
    Can ye defend the dangerless?
    Can ye inherit nakedness? 10

To all true wants Time's ear is deaf,
Penurious States lend no relief
    Out of their pelf:
But a free soul—thank God—
    Can help itself.

Be sure your fate
Doth keep apart its state,—
Not linked with any band,
Even the noblest in the land,—

In tented fields with cloth of gold 20
    No place doth hold,
But is more chivalrous than they are,
    And sigheth for a nobler war;
    A finer strain its trumpet rings,
    A brighter gleam its armor flings.

The life that I aspire to live,
    No man proposeth me;
No trade upon the street
    Wears its emblazonry.

1841   *1863*

From WALDEN

Walden sets forth Thoreau's characteristic social
ideas and records his experiences as a recluse. It
is his most famous work. The original manuscript
was destroyed, but a second manuscript was recovered by F. B. Sanborn, near the end of the
century, and edited in 1909. It contains more
material than the 1854 edition; apparently the
earlier manuscript was cut down when printed.
Sanborn showed, further, that Thoreau trans- 10
ferred extracts from his journals, 1838–54, into
Walden, a work supposed to record his life in the
years 1845–47. *A Week on the Concord and
Merrimac Rivers* (1849) and *Walden* (1854) are
the only books published by Thoreau in his lifetime.

Economy

WHEN I wrote the following pages, or
rather the bulk of them, I lived alone, in the
woods, a mile from any neighbor, in a house 20
which I had built myself, on the shore of
Walden Pond, in Concord, Massachusetts,
and earned my living by the labor of my hands
only. I lived there two years and two months.
At present I am a sojourner in civilized life
again.

I should not obtrude my affairs so much on
the notice of my readers if very particular
inquiries had not been made by my townsmen concerning my mode of life, which some 30

would call impertinent, though they do not
appear to me at all impertinent, but, considering the circumstances, very natural and
pertinent. Some have asked what I got to
eat; if I did not feel lonesome; if I was not
afraid; and the like. Others have been curious
to learn what portion of my income I devoted
to charitable purposes; and some, who have
large families, how many poor children I
maintained. I will therefore ask those of my
readers who feel no particular interest in me to
pardon me if I undertake to answer some of
these questions in this book. In most books,
the *I*, or first person, is omitted; in this it will
be retained; that, in respect to egotism, is the
main difference. We commonly do not remember that it is, after all, always the first person
that is speaking. I should not talk so much
about myself if there were anybody else whom
I knew as well. Unfortunately, I am confined
to this theme by the narrowness of my experience. Moreover, I, on my side, require of
every writer, first or last, a simple and sincere
account of his own life, and not merely what
he has heard of other men's lives; some such
account as he would send to his kindred from a
distant land; for if he has lived sincerely, it
must have been in a distant land to me. Perhaps
these pages are more particularly addressed to
poor students. As for the rest of my readers,

they will accept such portions as apply to them. I trust that none will stretch the seams in putting on the coat, for it may do good service to him whom it fits.

I would fain say something, not so much concerning the Chinese and Sandwich Islanders, as you who read these pages, who are said to live in New England; something about your condition, especially your outward condition or circumstances in this world, in this town, what it is, whether it is necessary that it be as bad as it is, whether it cannot be improved as well as not. I have traveled a good deal in Concord; and everywhere, in shops, and offices, and fields, the inhabitants have appeared to me to be doing penance in a thousand remarkable ways. What I have heard of Brahmins sitting exposed to four fires and looking in the face of the sun; or hanging suspended, with their heads downward, over flames; or looking at the heavens over their shoulders "until it becomes impossible for them to resume their natural position, while from the twist of the neck nothing but liquids can pass into the stomach"; or dwelling, chained for life, at the foot of a tree; or measuring with their bodies, like caterpillars, the breadth of vast empires; or standing on one leg on the tops of pillars,— even these forms of conscious penance are hardly more incredible and astonishing than the scenes which I daily witness. The twelve labors[1] of Hercules were trifling in comparison with those which my neighbors have undertaken; for they were only twelve, and had an end; but I could never see that these men slew or captured any monster or finished any labor. They have no friend Iolas[2] to burn with a hot iron the root of the hydra's head, but as soon as one head is crushed, two spring up.

I see young men, my townsmen, whose misfortune it is to have inherited farms, houses, barns, cattle, and farming tools; for these are more easily acquired than got rid of. Better if they had been born in the open pasture and suckled by a wolf, that they might have seen with clearer eyes what field they were called to labor in. Who made them serfs of the soil? Why should they eat their sixty acres, when man is condemned to eat only his peck of dirt? Why should they begin digging their graves as soon as they are born? They have got to live a man's life, pushing all these things before them, and get on as well as they can. How many a poor immortal soul have I met well nigh crushed and smothered under its load, creeping down the road of life, pushing before it a barn seventy-five feet by forty, its Augean stables never cleansed, and one hundred acres of land tillage, mowing, pasture, and woodlot! The portionless, who struggle with no such unnecessary inherited encumbrances, find it labor enough to subdue and cultivate a few cubic feet of flesh. . . .

Near the end of March, 1845, I borrowed an axe and went down to the woods by Walden Pond, nearest to where I intended to build my house, and began to cut down some tall arrowy white pines, still in their youth, for timber. It is difficult to begin without borrowing, but perhaps it is the most generous course thus to permit your fellow-men to have an interest in your enterprise. The owner of the axe, as he released his hold on it, said that it was the apple of his eye; but I returned it sharper than I received it. It was a pleasant hillside where I worked, covered with pine woods, through which I looked out on the pond, and a small open field in the woods where pines and hickories were springing up. The ice in the pond was not yet dissolved, though there were some open spaces, and it was all dark colored and saturated with water. There were some slight flurries of snow during the days that I worked there; but for the most part when I came out on to the railroad, on my way home, its yellow sand heap stretched away gleaming in the hazy atmosphere, and the rails shone in the spring sun, and I heard the lark and pewee and other birds already come to commence another year with us. They were pleasant spring days, in which the winter of man's discontent[1] was thawing as well as the earth, and the life that had lain torpid began to stretch itself. One day, when my

---

[1] In the classical myth, these involved desperate undertakings, such as slaying the Nemean lion, the Hydra, and a water serpent, and cleansing the Augean stables in which 3000 oxen had been stabled for thirty years. Hercules turned the rivers Alpheus and Peneus through the stables and cleaned them in a day.   [2] the friend, companion, sometimes the charioteer of Hercules

[1] Richard III, I, 1

axe had come off and I had cut a green hickory for a wedge, driving it with a stone, and had placed the whole to soak in a pond hole in order to swell the wood, I saw a striped snake run into the water, and he lay on the bottom, apparently without inconvenience, as long as I stayed there, or more than a quarter of an hour; perhaps because he had not yet fairly come out of the torpid state. It appeared to me that for a like reason men remain in their present low and primitive condition; but if they should feel the influence of the spring of springs arousing them, they would of necessity rise to a higher and more ethereal life. I had previously seen the snakes in frosty mornings in my path with portions of their bodies still numb and inflexible, waiting for the sun to thaw them. On the 1st of April it rained and melted the ice, and in the early part of the day, which was very foggy, I heard a stray goose groping about over the pond and cackling as if lost, or like the spirit of the fog.

So I went on for some days cutting and hewing timber, and also studs and rafters, all with my narrow axe, not having many communicable or scholar-like thoughts, singing to myself,—

Men say they know many things;
But lo! they have taken wings,—
The arts and sciences,
And a thousand appliances;
The wind that blows
Is all that anybody knows.

I hewed the main timbers six inches square, most of the studs on two sides only, and the rafters and floor timbers on one side, leaving the rest of the bark on, so that they were just as straight and much stronger than sawed ones. Each stick was carefully mortised or tenoned by its stump, for I had borrowed other tools by this time. My days in the woods were not very long ones; yet I usually carried my dinner of bread and butter, and read the newspaper in which it was wrapped, at noon, sitting amid the green pine boughs which I had cut off, and to my bread was imparted some of their fragrance, for my hands were covered with a thick coat of pitch. Before I had done I was more the friend than the foe of the pine tree, though I had cut down some of them, having become better acquainted with

it. Sometimes a rambler in the wood was attracted by the sound of my axe, and we chatted pleasantly over the chips which I had made.

By the middle of April, for I made no haste in my work, but rather made the most of it, my house was framed and ready for the raising. I had already bought the shanty of James Collins, an Irishman who worked on the Fitchburg Railroad, for boards. James Collins' shanty was considered an uncommonly fine one. When I called to see it he was not at home. I walked about the outside, at first unobserved from within, the window was so deep and high. It was of small dimensions, with a peaked cottage roof, and not much else to be seen, the dirt being raised five feet all around as if it were a compost heap. The roof was the soundest part, though a good deal warped and made brittle by the sun. Doorsill there was none, but a perennial passage for the hens under the door board. Mrs. C. came to the door and asked me to view it from the inside. The hens were driven in by my approach. It was dark, and had a dirt floor for the most part, dank, clammy, and aguish, only here a board and there a board which would not bear removal. She lighted a lamp to show me the inside of the roof and the walls, and also that the board floor extended under the bed, warning me not to step into the cellar, a sort of dust hole two feet deep. In her own words, they were "good boards overhead, good boards all around, and a good window,"—of two whole squares originally, only the cat had passed out that way lately. There was a stove, a bed, and a place to sit, an infant in the house where it was born, a silk parasol, gilt-framed looking-glass, and a patent new coffeemill nailed to an oak sapling, all told. The bargain was soon concluded, for James had in the meanwhile returned. I to pay four dollars and twenty-five cents tonight, he to vacate at five tomorrow morning, selling to nobody else meanwhile: I to take possession at six. It were well, he said, to be there early, and anticipate certain indistinct but wholly unjust claims on the score of ground rent and fuel. This he assured me was the only encumbrance. At six I passed him and his family on the road. One large bundle held their all,—bed, coffeemill, looking-glass, hens,—all but the cat; she took to the woods and became a wild cat, and, as I learned afterward, trod in a trap set for woodchucks, and so became a dead cat at last.

I took down this dwelling the same morning, drawing the nails, and removed it to the pond side by small cartloads, spreading the boards on the grass there to bleach and warp back again in the sun. One early thrush gave me a note or two as I drove along the woodland path. I was informed treacherously by a young Patrick that neighbor Seeley, an Irishman, in the intervals of the carting, transferred the still tolerable straight, and drivable nails, staples, and spikes to his pocket, and then stood when I came back to pass the time of day, and look freshly up, unconcerned, with spring thoughts, at the devastation; there being a dearth of work, as he said. He was there to represent spectatordom, and help make this seemingly insignificant event one with the removal of the gods of Troy.[1]

I dug my cellar in the side of a hill sloping to the south, where a woodchuck had formerly dug his burrow, down through sumach and blackberry roots, and the lowest stain of vegetation, six feet square by seven deep, to a fine sand where potatoes would not freeze in any winter. The sides were left shelving, and not stoned; but the sun having never shone on them, the sand still keeps its place. It was but two hours' work. I took particular pleasure in this breaking of ground, for in almost all latitudes men dig into the earth for an equable temperature. Under the most splendid house in the city is still to be found the cellar where they store their roots as of old, and long after the superstructure has disappeared posterity remark its dent in the earth. The house is still but a sort of porch at the entrance of a burrow.

At length, in the beginning of May, with the help of some of my acquaintances,[2] rather to improve so good an occasion for neighborliness than from any necessity, I set up the frame of my house. No man was ever more honored in the character of his raisers than I. They are destined, I trust, to assist at the rais-

ing of loftier structures one day. I began to occupy my house on the 4th of July, as soon as it was boarded and roofed, for the boards were carefully featheredged and lapped, so that it was perfectly impervious to rain; but before boarding I laid the foundation of a chimney at one end, bringing two cartloads of stones up the hill from the pond in my arms. I built the chimney after my hoeing in the fall, before a fire became necessary for warmth, doing my cooking in the meanwhile out of doors on the ground, early in the morning: which mode I still think is in some respects more convenient and agreeable than the usual one. When it stormed before my bread was baked, I fixed a few boards over the fire, and sat under them to watch my loaf, and passed some pleasant hours in that way. In those days, when my hands were much employed, I read but little, but the least scraps of paper which lay on the ground, my holder, or tablecloth, afforded me as much entertainment, in fact answered the same purpose as the Iliad. . . .

Before winter I built a chimney, and shingled the sides of my house, which were already impervious to rain, with imperfect and sappy shingles made of the first slice of the log, whose edges I was obliged to straighten with a plane.

I have thus a tight shingled and plastered house, ten feet wide by fifteen long, and eight-feet posts, with a garret and a closet, a large window on each side, two trap doors, one door at the end, and a brick fireplace opposite. The exact cost of my house, paying the usual price for such materials as I used, but not counting the work, all of which was done by myself, was as follows; and I give the details because very few are able to tell exactly what their houses cost, and fewer still, if any, the separate cost of the various materials which compose them:—

Boards . . . . . . $8.03½, mostly shanty boards.
Refuse shingles for roof and sides . . . 4.00
Laths 1.25
Two second-hand windows with glass 2.43

---

[1] Virgil's *Aeneid*, II, 243–311. [2] Among these were Emerson, Ellery Channing, Bronson Alcott, and George William Curtis, then a Harvard student.

One thousand old brick ... 4.00	
Two casks of lime 2.40	That was high.
Hair .... .31	More than I needed.
Mantle-tree iron .... .15	
Nails........ 3.90	
Hinges and screws ..... .14	
Latch .... .10	
Chalk .... .01	
Transportation........ 1.40	I carried a good part
In all ...$28.12½	on my back.

These are all the materials excepting the timber, stones, and sand, which I claimed by squatter's right. I have also a small woodshed adjoining, made chiefly of the stuff which was left after building the house.

I intend to build me a house which will surpass any on the main street in Concord in grandeur and luxury, as soon as it pleases me as much and will cost me no more than my present one.

I thus found that the student who wishes for a shelter can obtain one for a lifetime at an expense not greater than the rent which he now pays annually. If I seem to boast more than is becoming, my excuse is that I brag for humanity rather than for myself; and my shortcomings and inconsistencies do not affect the truth of my statement. Notwithstanding much cant and hypocrisy,—chaff which I find it difficult to separate from my wheat, but for which I am as sorry as any man,—I will breathe freely and stretch myself in this respect, it is such a relief to both the moral and physical system; and I am resolved that I will not through humility become the devil's attorney. I will endeavor to speak a good word for the truth. At Cambridge College the mere rent of a student's room, which is only a little larger than my own, is thirty dollars each year, though the corporation had the advantage of building thirty-two side by side and under one roof, and the occupant suffers the inconvenience of many and noisy neighbors, and perhaps a residence in the fourth story. I cannot but think that if we had more true wisdom in these respects, not only less educa-

tion would be needed, because, forsooth, more would already have been acquired, but the pecuniary expense of getting an education would in a great measure vanish. Those conveniences which the student requires at Cambridge or elsewhere cost him or somebody else ten times as great a sacrifice of life as they would with proper management on both sides. Those things for which the most money is demanded are never the things which the student most wants. Tuition, for instance, is an important item in the term bill, while for the far more valuable education which he gets by associating with the most cultivated of his contemporaries no charge is made. The mode of founding a college is, commonly, to get up a subscription of dollars and cents, and then following blindly the principles of a division of labor to its extreme, a principle which should never be followed but with circumspection,—to call in a contractor who makes this a subject of speculation, and he employs Irishmen or other operatives actually to lay the foundations, while the students that are to be are said to be fitting themselves for it; and for these oversights successive generations have to pay. I think that it would be *better than this*, for the students, or those who desire to be benefited by it, even to lay the foundation themselves. The student who secures his coveted leisure and retirement by systematically shirking any labor necessary to man obtains but an ignoble and unprofitable leisure, defrauding himself of the experience which alone can make leisure fruitful. "But," says one, "you do not mean that the students should go to work with their hands instead of their heads?" I do not mean that exactly, but I mean something which he might think a good deal like that; I mean that they should not *play* life, or *study* it merely, while the community supports them at this expensive game, but earnestly *live* it from beginning to end. How could youths better learn to live than by at once trying the experiment of living? Methinks this would exercise their minds as much as mathematics. If I wished a boy to know something about the arts and sciences, for instance, I would not pursue the common course, which is merely to send him into the neighborhood of some professor, where anything is professed and practiced but the art of life;—to survey the world through a telescope or a microscope, and never with his natural eye; to study chemistry, and not learn how his bread is made, or mechanics, and not learn how it is earned; to discover new satellites to Neptune, and not detect the motes in his eyes, or to what vagabond he is a satellite himself; or to be devoured by the monsters that swarm all around him, while contemplating the monsters in a drop of vinegar. Which would have advanced the most at the end of a month,—the boy who had made his own jackknife from the ore which he had dug and smelted, reading as much as would be necessary for this,—or the boy who had attended the lectures on metallurgy at the Institute in the meanwhile, and had received a Rogers' penknife from his father? Which would be most likely to cut his fingers? . . . To my astonishment I was informed on leaving college that I had studied navigation!—why, if I had taken one turn down the harbor I should have known more about it. Even the *poor* student studies and is taught only *political* economy, while that economy of living which is synonymous with philosophy is not even sincerely professed in our colleges. The consequence is that while he is reading Adam Smith, Ricardo, and Say, he runs his father in debt irretrievably. . . .

Before I finished my house, wishing to earn ten or twelve dollars by some honest and agreeable method, in order to meet my unusual expenses, I planted about two acres and a half of light and sandy soil near it chiefly with beans, but also a small part with potatoes, corn, peas, and turnips. The whole lot contains eleven acres, mostly growing up to pines and hickories, and was sold the preceding season for eight dollars and eight cents an acre. One farmer said that it was "good for nothing but to raise cheeping squirrels on." I put no manure whatever on this land, not being the owner, but merely a squatter, and not expecting to cultivate so much again, and I did not quite hoe it all once. I got out several cords of stumps in plowing, which supplied me with fuel for a long time, and left small circles of virgin mold, easily distinguishable

through the summer by the greater luxuriance of the beans there. The dead and for the most part unmerchantable wood behind my house, and the driftwood from the pond, have supplied the remainder of my fuel. I was obliged to hire a team and a man for the plowing, though I held the plow myself. My farm outgoes for the first season were, for implements, seed, work, etc., $14.72½. The seed corn was given me. This never costs anything to speak of, unless you plant more than enough. I got twelve bushels of beans, and eighteen bushels of potatoes, besides some peas and sweet corn. The yellow corn and turnips were too late to come to anything. My whole income from the farm was

$$\$23.44$$

Deducting the outgoes 14.72½

There are left . . . . $ 8.71½

besides produce consumed and on hand at the time this estimate was made of the value of $4.50,—the amount on hand much more than balancing a little grass which I did not raise. All things considered, that is, considering the importance of a man's soul and of today, notwithstanding the short time occupied by my experiment, nay, partly even because of its transient character, I believe that that was doing better than any farmer in Concord did that year.

The next year I did better still, for I spaded up all the land which I required, about a third of an acre, and I learned from the experience of both years, not being in the least awed by many celebrated works on husbandry, Arthur Young among the rest, that if one would live simply and eat only the crop which he raised, and raise no more than he ate, and not exchange it for an insufficient quantity of more luxurious and expensive things, he would need to cultivate only a few rods of ground, and that it would be cheaper to spade up that than to use oxen to plow it, and to select a fresh spot from time to time than to manure the old, and he could do all his necessary farm work as it were with his left hand at odd hours in the summer; and thus he would not be tied to an ox, or horse, or cow, or pig, as at present. I desire to speak impartially on this point, and as one not interested in the success or failure

of the present economical and social arrangements. I was more independent than any
farmer in Concord, for I was not anchored to
a house or farm, but could follow the bent of
my genius, which is a very crooked one, every
moment. Besides being better off than they
already, if my house had been burned or my
crops had failed, I should have been nearly as
well off as before. . . .

By surveying, carpentry, and day-labor of
various other kinds in the village in the meanwhile, for I have as many trades as fingers, I
had earned $13.34. The expense of food for
eight months, namely, from July 4th to March
1st, the time when these estimates were made,
though I lived there more than two years,—
not counting potatoes, a little green corn, and
some peas, which I had raised, nor considering
the value of what was on hand at the last date,
was

Rice	....	$1.73½
Molasses	......	1.73	Cheapest form of the saccharine.
Rye meal	.....	1.04¾
Indian meal	...	.99¾	Cheaper than rye.
Pork	....	.22
Flour	....	.88	Costs more than Indian meal, both money and trouble.
Sugar	....	.80
Lard	....	.65
Apples	....	.25
Dried apples	..	.22
Sweet potatoes	.10
One pumpkin	.	.06
One watermelon	.02
Salt	....	.03

All experiments which failed.

Yes, I did eat $8.74, all told; but I should
not thus unblushingly publish my guilt, if I
did not know that most of my readers were
equally guilty with myself, and that their
deeds would look no better in print. The next
year I sometimes caught a mess of fish for
my dinner, and once I went so far as to
slaughter a woodchuck which ravaged my
beanfield,—effect his transmigration, as a
Tartar would say,—and devour him, partly
for experiment's sake; but though it afforded
me a momentary enjoyment, notwithstanding
a musky flavor, I saw that the longest use

would not make that a good practice, however it might seem to have your woodchucks
ready dressed by the village butcher.

Clothing and some incidental expenses within the same dates,
  though little can be inferred from
  this item, amounted to $8.40¾
Oil and some household utensils 2.00

So that all the pecuniary outgoes, excepting for washing and mending, which for the
most part were done out of the house, and
their bills have not yet been received,—and
these are all and more than all the ways by
which money necessarily goes out in this
part of the world,—were

House	....	$28.12½
Farm, one year	....	14.72½
Food eight months	....	8.74
Clothing, etc., eight months	....	8.40¾
Oil, etc., eight months	....	2.00
In all	....	$61.99¾

I address myself now to those of my readers
who have a living to get. And to meet this
I have for farm produce sold

		$23.44
Earned by day-labor	....	13.34
In all	....	$36.78

which subtracted from the sum of the outgoes leaves a balance of $25.21¾ on the one
side,—this being very nearly the means with
which I started, and the measure of expenses
to be incurred,—and on the other, besides the
leisure and independence and health thus secured, a comfortable house for me as long as
I choose to occupy it.

These statistics, however accidental and
therefore uninstructive they may appear, as
they have a certain completeness, have a certain value also. Nothing was given me of
which I have not rendered some account. It
appears from the above estimate, that my food
alone cost me in money about twenty-seven
cents a week. It was for nearly two years after
this, rye and Indian meal, without yeast,
potatoes, rice, a very little salt pork, molasses,
and salt, and my drink, water. It was fit that
I should live on rice, mainly, who loved so
well the philosophy of India. To meet the objections of some inveterate cavilers, I may as

well state that if I dined out occasionally, as I always had done, and I trust shall have opportunities to do again, it was frequently to the detriment of my domestic arrangements. But the dining out, being, as I have stated, a constant element, does not in the least affect a comparative statement like this.

I learned from my two years' experience that it would cost incredibly little trouble to obtain one's necessary food, even in this latitude; that a man may use as simple a diet as the animals, and yet retain health and strength. I have made a satisfactory dinner, satisfactory on several accounts, simply off a dish of purslane (*Portulaca oleracea*) which I gathered in my cornfield, boiled and salted. I give the Latin on account of the savoriness of the trivial name. And pray what more can a reasonable man desire, in peaceful times, in ordinary noons, than a sufficient number of ears of green sweet-corn boiled, with the addition of salt? Even the little variety that I used was a yielding to the demands of appetite, and not of health. Yet men have come to such a pass that they frequently starve, not for want of necessaries, but for want of luxuries; and I know a good woman who thinks that her son lost his life because he took to drinking water only. . . .

Where I Lived and What I Lived for

I was seated by the shore of a small pond, about a mile and a half south of the village of Concord and somewhat higher than it, in the midst of an extensive wood between that town and Lincoln, and about two miles south of that our only field known to fame, Concord Battle Ground; but I was so low in the woods that the opposite shore, half a mile off, like the rest, covered with wood, was my most distant horizon. For the first week, whenever I looked out on the pond it impressed me like a tarn high up on the side of a mountain, its bottom far above the surface of other lakes, and, as the sun arose, I saw it throwing off its nightly clothing of mist, and here and there, by degrees, its soft ripples or its smooth reflecting surface was revealed, while the mists, like ghosts, were stealthily withdrawing in every direction into the woods, as at the breaking up of some nocturnal conventicle. The very dew seemed to hang upon the trees later into the day than usual, as on the sides of mountains.

This small lake was of most value as a neighbor in the intervals of a gentle rain storm in August, when, both air and water being perfectly still, but the sky overcast, midafternoon had all the serenity of evening, and the wood-thrush sang around, and was heard from shore to shore. A lake like this is never smoother than at such a time; and the clear portion of the air above it being shallow and darkened by clouds, the water, full of light and reflections, becomes a lower heaven itself so much the more important. From a hilltop near by, where the wood had been recently cut off, there was a pleasing vista southward across the pond, through a wide indentation in the hills which form the shore there, where their opposite sides sloping toward each other suggested a stream flowing out in that direction through a wooded valley, but stream there was none. That way I looked between and over the near green hills to some distant and higher ones in the horizon, tinged with blue. Indeed, by standing on tiptoe I could catch a glimpse of some of the peaks of the still bluer and more distant mountain ranges in the northwest, those true-blue coins from heaven's own mint, and also of some portion of the village. But in other directions, even from this point, I could not see over or beyond the woods which surrounded me. It is well to have some water in your neighborhood, to give buoyancy to and float the earth. One value even of the smallest well is, that when you look into it you see that earth is not continent but insular. This is as important as that it keeps butter cool. When I looked across the pond from this peak toward the Sudbury meadows, which in time of flood I distinguished elevated perhaps by a mirage in their seething valley, like a coin in a basin, all the earth beyond the pond appeared like a thin crust insulated and floated even by this small sheet of intervening water, and I was reminded that this on which I dwelt was but *dry land*.

Though the view from my door was still more contracted, I did not feel crowded or confined in the least. There was pasture enough for my imagination. The low shrub-oak plateau to which the opposite shore arose, stretched away toward the prairies of the West and the steppes of Tartary, affording ample room for all the roving families of men. "There are none happy in the world but beings who enjoy freely a vast horizon,"—said Damodara,[1] when his herds required new and larger pastures.

Both place and time were changed, and I dwelt nearer to those parts of the universe and to those eras in history which had most attracted me. Where I lived was as far off as many a region viewed nightly by astronomers. We are wont to imagine rare and delectable places in some remote and more celestial corner of the system, behind the constellation of Cassiopeia's Chair, far from noise and disturbance. I discovered that my house actually had its site in such a withdrawn, but forever new and unprofaned, part of the universe. If it were worth the while to settle in those parts near to the Pleiades or the Hyades, to Aldebaran or Altair,[2] then I was really there, or at an equal remoteness from the life which I had left behind, dwindled and twinkling with as fine a ray to my nearest neighbor, and to be seen only in moonless nights by him. Such was that part of creation where I had squatted:

"There was a shepherd that did live,
  And held his thoughts as high
As were the mounts whereon his flocks
  Did hourly feed him by."

What should we think of the shepherd's life if his flocks always wandered to higher pastures than his thoughts?

Every morning was a cheerful invitation to make my life of equal simplicity, and I may say innocence, with Nature herself. I have been as sincere a worshiper of Aurora as the Greeks. I got up early and bathed in the pond; that was a religious exercise, and one of the best things which I did. They say that characters were engraven on the bathing tub of king Tching-thang to this effect: "Renew thyself completely each day; do it again, and again, and forever again." I can understand that. Morning brings back the heroic ages. I was as much affected by the faint hum of a mosquito making its invisible and unimaginable tour through my apartment at earliest dawn, when I was sitting with door and windows open, as I could be by any trumpet that ever sang of fame. It was Homer's requiem; itself an Iliad and Odyssey in the air, singing its own wrath and wanderings. There was something cosmical about it; a standing advertisement, till forbidden, of the everlasting vigor and fertility of the world. The morning, which is the most memorable season of the day, is the awakening hour. Then there is least somnolence in us; and for an hour, at least, some part of us awakes which slumbers all the rest of the day and night. Little is to be expected of that day, if it can be called a day, to which we are not awakened by our Genius, but by the mechanical nudgings of some servitor, are not awakened by our own newly-acquired force and aspirations from within, accompanied by the undulations of celestial music, instead of factory bells, and a fragrance filling the air—to a higher life than we fell asleep from; and thus the darkness bear its fruit, and prove itself to be good, no less than the light. That man who does not believe that each day contains an earlier, more sacred, and auroral hour than he has yet profaned, has despaired of life, and is pursuing a descending and darkening way. After a partial cessation of his sensuous life, the soul of man, or its organs rather, are reinvigorated each day, and his Genius tries again what noble life it can make. All memorable events, I should say, transpire in morning time and in a morning atmosphere. The Vedas[1] say, "All intelligences awake with the morning." Poetry and art, and the fairest and most memorable of the actions of men, date from such an hour. All poets and heroes, like Memnon,[2] are the children of Aurora, and emit their music at sunrise. To him whose elastic

---

[1] the Hindu divinity, Krishna   [2] The Pleiades and the Hyades are star groups. Aldebaran is the brightest star in the Hyades. Altair is a star of the first magnitude in the constellation Aquila.

[1] ancient sacred writings of the Hindus   [2] Memnon, son of Aurora and Tithonus, was king of the Ethiopians. Of a colossal statue near Thebes, Egypt, said to be Memnon's, it was reported that, when the first rays of the morning fell on it, a harplike sound was emitted, supposed to be Memnon's greeting to his mother.

and vigorous thought keeps pace with the sun, the day is a perpetual morning. It matters not what the clocks say or the attitudes and labors of men. Morning is when I am awake and there is a dawn in me. Moral reform is the effort to throw off sleep. Why is it that men give so poor an account of their day if they have not been slumbering? They are not such poor calculators. If they had not been overcome with drowsiness they would have performed something. The millions are awake enough for physical labor; but only one in a million is awake enough for effective intellectual exertion, only one in a hundred millions to a poetic or divine life. To be awake is to be alive. I have never yet met a man who was quite awake. How could I have looked him in the face? . . .

I went to the woods because I wished to live deliberately, to front only the essential facts of life, and see if I could not learn what it had to teach, and not, when I came to die, discover that I had not lived. I did not wish to live what was not life, living is so dear; nor did I wish to practice resignation, unless it was quite necessary. I wanted to live deep and suck out all the marrow of life, to live so sturdily and Spartan-like as to put to rout all that was not life, to cut a broad swath and shave close, to drive life into a corner, and reduce it to its lowest terms, and, if it proved to be mean, why then to get the whole and genuine meanness of it, and publish its meanness to the world; or if it were sublime, to know it by experience, and be able to give a true account of it in my next excursion. For most men, it appears to me, are in a strange uncertainty about it, whether it is of the devil or of God, and have *somewhat hastily* concluded that it is the chief end of man here to "glorify God and enjoy him forever."

Still we live meanly, like ants; though the fable tells us that we were long ago changed into men; like pygmies we fight with cranes[1]; it is error upon error, and clout upon clout, and our best virtue has for its occasion a superfluous and evitable wretchedness. Our life is frittered away by detail. An honest man has hardly need to count more than his ten fingers or in extreme cases he may add his ten toes, and lump the rest. Simplicity, simplicity, simplicity! I say, let your affairs be as two or three, and not a hundred or a thousand; instead of a million count half a dozen, and keep your accounts on your thumb nail. In the midst of this chopping sea of civilized life, such are the clouds and storms and quicksands and thousand-and-one items to be allowed for, that a man has to live, if he would not founder and go to the bottom and not make his port at all, by dead reckoning, and he must be a great calculator indeed who succeeds. Simplify, simplify. Instead of three meals a day, if it be necessary eat but one; instead of a hundred dishes, five; and reduce other things in proportion. Our life is like a German Confederacy, made up of petty states, with its boundary forever fluctuating, so that even a German cannot tell you how it is bounded at any moment. The nation itself, with all its so-called internal improvements, which, by the way are all external and superficial, is just such an unwieldy and overgrown establishment, cluttered with furniture and tripped up by its own traps, ruined by luxury and heedless expense, by want of calculation and a worthy aim, as the million households in the land; and the only cure for it as for them is in a rigid economy, a stern and more than Spartan simplicity of life and elevation of purpose. It lives too fast. Men think that it is essential that the *Nation* have commerce, and export ice, and talk through a telegraph, and ride thirty miles an hour, without a doubt, whether *they* do or not; but whether we should live like baboons or like men, is a little uncertain. If we do not get out sleepers, and forge rails, and devote days and nights to the work, but go to tinkering upon our *lives* to improve *them*, who will build railroads? And if railroads are not built, how shall we get to heaven in season? But if we stay at home and mind our business, who will want railroads? We do not ride on the railroad; it rides upon us. Did you ever think what those sleepers are that underlie the railroad? Each one is a man, an Irishman, or a Yankee man. The rails

[1] According to Homer's *Iliad* (III, 6) the pygmies, a nation of dwarfs, had to fight the cranes that migrated every winter to their country, attacking the cornfields.

are laid on them, and they are covered with sand, and the cars run smoothly over them. They are sound sleepers, I assure you. And every few years a new lot is laid down and run over; so that, if some have the pleasure of riding on a rail, others have the misfortune to be ridden upon. And when they run over a man that is walking in his sleep, a supernumerary sleeper in the wrong position, and wake him up, they suddenly stop the cars, and make a hue and cry about it, as if this were an exception. I am glad to know that it takes a gang of men for every five miles to keep the sleepers down and level in their beds as it is, for this is a sign that they may sometime get up again. . . .

Solitude

I find it wholesome to be alone the greater part of the time. To be in company, even with the best, is soon wearisome and dissipating. I love to be alone. I never found the companion that was so companionable as solitude. We are for the most part more lonely when we go abroad among men than when we stay in our chambers. A man thinking or working is always alone, let him be where he will. Solitude is not measured by the miles of space that intervene between a man and his fellows. The really diligent student in one of the crowded hives of Cambridge College is as solitary as a dervish in the desert. The farmer can work alone in the field or in the woods all day, hoeing or chopping, and not feel lonesome, because he is employed; but when he comes home at night he cannot sit down in a room alone, at the mercy of his thoughts, but must be where he can "see the folks," and recreate, and as he thinks remunerate, himself for his day's solitude; and hence he wonders how the student can sit alone in the house all night and most of the day without ennui and "the blues"; but he does not realize that the student, though in the house, is still at work in *his* field, and chopping in *his* woods, as the farmer in his, and in turn seeks the same recreation and society that the latter does, though it may be a more condensed form of it.

Society is commonly too cheap. We meet at very short intervals, not having had time to acquire any new value for each other. We meet at meals three times a day, and give each other a new taste of that musty old cheese that we are. We have had to agree on a certain set of rules called etiquette and politeness to make this frequent meeting tolerable, and that we need not come to open war. We meet at the post-office, and at the sociable, and about the fireside every night; we live thick and are in each other's way, and stumble over one another, and I think that we thus lose some respect for one another. Certainly less frequency would suffice for all important and heart communications. Consider the girls in a factory,—never alone, hardly in their dreams. It would be better if there were but one inhabitant to a square mile, as where I live. The value of a man is not in his skin, that we should touch him. . . .

I have a great deal of company in my house; especially in the morning, when nobody calls. Let me suggest a few comparisons, that some one may convey an idea of my situation. I am no more lonely than the loon in the pond that laughs so loud, or than Walden Pond itself. What company has that lonely lake, I pray? And yet it has not the blue devils, but the blue angels in it, in the azure tint of its waters. The sun is alone, except in thick weather, when there sometimes appear to be two, but one is a mock sun. God is alone— but the devil, he is far from being alone; he sees a great deal of company; he is legion. I am no more lonely than a single mullein or dandelion in a pasture, or a bean leaf, or sorrel, or a horse-fly, or a humble-bee. I am no more lonely than the Mill Brook, or a weathercock, or the north star, or an April shower, or a January thaw, or the first spider in a new house.

The Pond

In warm evenings I frequently sat in the boat playing the flute, and saw the perch, which I seemed to have charmed, hovering around me, and the moon travelling over the ribbed bottom, which was strewed with the wrecks of the forest. Formerly I had come to this pond adventurously, from time to time, in dark summer nights, with a companion, and making a fire close to the water's edge, which we thought attracted the fishes, we caught pouts with a bunch of worms strung on a thread, and when we had done, far in the night, threw the burning brands high into the air like skyrockets, which, coming down into the pond, were quenched with a loud hissing, and we were suddenly groping in total darkness. Through this, whistling a tune, we took our way to the haunts of men again. But now I had made my home by the shore.

Sometimes, after staying in a village parlor till the family had all retired, I have returned to the woods, and, partly with a view to the next day's dinner, spent the hours of midnight fishing from a boat by moonlight, serenaded by owls and foxes, and hearing, from time to time, the creaking note of some unknown bird close at hand. These experiences were very memorable and valuable to me—anchored in forty feet of water, and twenty or thirty rods from the shore, surrounded sometimes by thousands of small perch and shiners, dimpling the surface with their tails in the moonlight, and communicating by a long flaxen line with mysterious nocturnal fishes which had their dwelling forty feet below, or sometimes dragging sixty feet of line about the pond as I drifted in the gentle night breeze, now and then feeling a slight vibration along it, indicative of some life prowling about its extremity, of dull uncertain blundering purpose there, and slow to make up its mind. At length you slowly raise, pulling hand over hand, some horned pout squeaking and squirming to the upper air. It was very queer, especially in dark nights, when your thoughts had wandered to vast and cosmogonal themes in other spheres, to feel this faint jerk, which came to interrupt your dreams and link you to Nature again. It seemed as if I might next cast my line upward into the air, as well as downward into this element which was scarcely more dense. Thus I caught two fishes as it were with one hook.

The scenery of Walden is on a humble scale, and, though very beautiful, does not approach to grandeur, nor can it much concern one who has not long frequented it or lived by its shore; yet this pond is so remarkable for its depth and purity as to merit a particular description. It is a clear and deep green well, half a mile long and a mile and three quarters in circumference, and contains about sixty-one and a half acres; a perennial spring in the midst of pine and oak woods, without any visible inlet or outlet except by the clouds and evaporation. The surrounding hills rise abruptly from the water to the height of forty to eighty feet, though on the southeast and east they attain to about one hundred and one hundred and fifty feet respectively, within a quarter and a third of a mile. They are exclusively woodland. All our Concord waters have two colors at least, one when viewed at a distance, and another, more proper, close at hand. The first depends more on the light, and follows the sky. In clear weather, in summer, they appear blue at a little distance, especially if agitated, and at a great distance all appear alike. In stormy weather they are sometimes of a dark slate color. The sea, however, is said to be blue one day and green another without any perceptible change in the atmosphere. I have seen our river, when, the landscape being covered with snow, both water and ice were almost as green as grass. Some consider blue "to be the color of pure water, whether liquid or solid." But, looking directly down into our waters from a boat, they are seen to be of very different colors. Walden is blue at one time and green at another, even from the same point of view. Lying between the earth and the heavens, it partakes of the color of both. Viewed from a hilltop it reflects the color of the sky, but near at hand it is of a yellowish tint next the shore where you can see the sand, then a light green, which gradually deepens to a uniform dark green in the body of the pond. In some lights, viewed even from a hilltop, it is of a vivid green next the shore. Some have referred this to the reflection of the verdure; but it is equally green there against the railroad sand-bank, and in the spring, before the leaves are expanded, and it may be simply the result of the prevailing blue mixed with the yellow of the sand. Such is the color of its iris. This is that portion, also, where in the spring, the ice being warmed by the heat of the sun reflected from the bottom, and also transmitted through the earth, melts first and forms a narrow canal about the still frozen middle. Like the rest of our waters, when much agitated, in clear weather, so that the surface of the waves may reflect the sky at the right angle, or because there is more light mixed with it, it appears at a little distance of a darker blue than the sky itself; and at such a time, being on its surface, and looking with divided vision, so as to see the reflection, I have discerned a matchless and indescribable light blue, such as watered or changeable silks and sword blades suggest, more cerulean than the sky itself, alternating with the original dark green on the opposite sides of the waves, which last appeared but muddy in comparison. It is a vitreous greenish blue, as I remember it, like those patches of the winter sky seen through cloud vistas in the west before sundown. Yet a single glass of its water held up to the light is as colorless as an equal quantity of air. It is well known that a large plate of glass will have a green tint, owing, as the makers say, to its "body," but a small piece of the same will be colorless. How large a body of Walden water would be required to reflect a green tint I have never proved. The water of our river is black or a very dark brown to one looking directly down on it, and, like that of most ponds, imparts to the body of one bathing in it a yellowish tinge; but this water is of such crystalline purity that the body of the bather appears of an alabaster whiteness, still more unnatural, which, as the limbs are magnified and distorted withal, produces a monstrous effect, making fit studies for a Michael Angelo.

The water is so transparent that the bottom can easily be discerned at the depth of twenty-five or thirty feet. Paddling over it, you may see many feet beneath the surface the schools of perch and shiners, perhaps only an inch long, yet the former easily distinguished by their transverse bars, and you think that they must be ascetic fish that find a subsistence there. Once, in the winter, many years ago, when I had been cutting holes through the ice in order to catch pickerel, as I stepped ashore I tossed my axe back on to the ice, but, as if some evil genius had directed it, it slid four or five rods directly into one of the holes, where the water was twenty-five feet deep. Out of curiosity, I lay down on the ice and looked through the hole, until I saw the axe a little on one side, standing on its head, with its helve erect and gently swaying to and fro with the pulse of the pond; and there it might have stood erect and swaying till in the course of time the handle rotted off, if I had not disturbed it. Making another hole directly over it with an ice chisel which I had, and cutting down the longest birch which I could find in the neighborhood with my knife, I made a slip noose, which I attached to its end, and, letting it down carefully, passed it over the knob of the handle, and drew it by a line along the birch, and so pulled the axe out again.

The shore is composed of a belt of smooth rounded white stones like paving stones, excepting one or two short sand beaches, and is so steep that in many places a single leap will carry you into the water over your head; and were it not for its remarkable transparency, that would be the last to be seen of its bottom till it rose on the opposite side. Some think it is bottomless. It is nowhere muddy, and a casual observer would say that there were no weeds at all in it; and of noticeable plants, except in the little meadows recently overflowed, which do not properly belong to it, a closer scrutiny does not detect a flag nor a bulrush, nor even a lily, yellow or white, but only a few small heart-leaves and potamogetons,[1] and perhaps a water-target or two; all which however a bather might not perceive; and these plants are clean and bright like the element they grow in. The stones extend a rod or two into the water, and then the bottom is pure sand, except in the deepest parts, where there is usually a little sediment, probably from the decay of the leaves which have been wafted on to it so many successive falls; and a bright green weed is brought up on anchors even in midwinter. . . .

Yet perchance the first who came to this well have left some trace of their footsteps. I have been surprised to detect encircling the

[1] pondweeds, found in still waters of the temperate zones

pond, even where a thick wood has just been cut down on the shore, a narrow shelf-like path in the steep hillside, alternately rising and falling, approaching and receding from the water's edge, as old probably as the race of man here, worn by the feet of aboriginal hunters, and still from time to time unwittingly trodden by the present occupants of the land. This is particularly distinct to one standing on the middle of the pond in winter, just after a light snow has fallen, appearing as a clear undulating white line, unobscured by weeds and twigs, and very obvious a quarter of a mile off in many places where in summer it is hardly distinguishable close at hand. The snow reprints it, as it were, in clear white type alto-relievo.[1] The ornamented grounds of villas which will one day be built here may still preserve some trace of this.

The pond rises and falls, but whether regularly or not, and within what period, nobody knows, though, as usual, many pretend to know. It is commonly higher in the winter and lower in the summer, though not corresponding to the general wet and dryness. I can remember when it was a foot or two lower, and also when it was at least five feet higher, than when I lived by it. There is a narrow sand-bar running into it, with very deep water on one side, on which I helped boil a kettle of chowder, some six rods from the main shore, about the year 1824, which it has not been possible to do for twenty-five years; and on the other hand, my friends used to listen with incredulity when I told them, that a few years later I was accustomed to fish from a boat in a secluded cove in the woods, fifteen rods from the only shore they knew, which place was long since converted into a meadow. But the pond has risen steadily for two years, and now, in the summer of '52, is just five feet higher than when I lived there, or as high as it was thirty years ago, and fishing goes on again in the meadow. This makes a difference of level, at the outside, of six or seven feet; and yet the water shed by the surrounding hills is insignificant in amount, and this overflow must be referred to causes which

affect the deep springs. This same summer the pond has begun to fall again. It is remarkable that this fluctuation, whether periodical or not, appears thus to require many years for its accomplishment. I have observed one rise and a part of two falls, and I expect that a dozen or fifteen years hence the water will again be as low as I have ever known it. Flint's Pond, a mile eastward, allowing for the disturbance occasioned by its inlets and outlets, and the smaller intermediate ponds also, sympathize with Walden, and recently attained their greatest height at the same time with the latter. The same is true, as far as my observation goes, of White Pond.

This rise and fall of Walden at long intervals serves this use at least; the water standing at this great height for a year or more, though it makes it difficult to walk round it, kills the shrubs and trees which have sprung up about its edge since the last rise—pitch-pines, birches, alders, aspens, and others—and, falling again, leaves an unobstructed shore; for, unlike many ponds and all waters which are subject to a daily tide, its shore is cleanest when the water is lowest. On the side of the pond next my house a row of pitch-pines fifteen feet high has been killed and tipped over as if by a lever, and thus a stop put to their encroachments; and their size indicates how many years have elapsed since the last rise to this height. By this fluctuation the pond asserts its title to a shore, and thus the *shore* is *shorn*, and the trees cannot hold it by right of possession. These are the lips of the lake, on which no beard grows. It licks its chaps from time to time. When the water is at its height, the alders, willows, and maples send forth a mass of fibrous red roots several feet long from all sides of their stems in the water, and to the height of three or four feet from the ground, in the effort to maintain themselves; and I have known the high blueberry bushes about the shore, which commonly produce no fruit, bear an abundant crop under these circumstances.

Some have been puzzled to tell how the shore became so regularly paved. My townsmen have all heard the tradition—the oldest people tell me that they heard it in their

[1] a term used in sculpture, meaning that a figure stands out in "high relief," i.e., projects prominently from a background

youth—that anciently the Indians were holding a pow-wow upon a hill there, which rose as high into the heavens as the pond now sinks deep into the earth, and they used much profanity, as the story goes, though this vice is one of which the Indians were never guilty, and while they were thus engaged the hill shook and suddenly sank, and only one old squaw, named Walden, escaped, and from her the pond was named. It has been conjectured that when the hill shook, these stones rolled down its side and became the present shore. It is very certain, at any rate, that once there was no pond here, and now there is one; and this Indian fable does not in any respect conflict with the account of that ancient settler whom I have mentioned, who remembers so well when he first came here with his divining rod, saw a thin vapor rising from the sward, and the hazel pointed steadily downward, and he concluded to dig a well here. As for the stones, many still think that they are hardly to be accounted for by the action of the waves on these hills; but I observe that the surrounding hills are remarkably full of the same kind of stones, so that they have been obliged to pile them up in walls on both sides of the railroad cut nearest the pond; and, moreover, there are most stones where the shore is most abrupt; so that, unfortunately, it is no longer a mystery to me. I detect the paver. If the name was not derived from that of some English locality—Saffron Walden, for instance—one might suppose that it was called, originally, *Walled-in* Pond.

The pond was my well ready dug. For four months in the year its water is as cold as it is pure at all times; and I think that it is then as good as any, if not the best, in the town. In the winter, all water which is exposed to the air is colder than springs and wells which are protected from it. The temperature of the pond water which had stood in the room where I sat from five o'clock in the afternoon till noon the next day, the 6th of March, 1846, the thermometer having been up to 65° or 70° some of the time, owing partly to the sun on the roof, was 42°, or one degree colder than the water of one of the coldest wells in the village just drawn. The temperature of the

Boiling Spring the same day was 45°, or the warmest of any water tried, though it is the coldest that I know of in summer, when, beside, shallow and stagnant surface water is not mingled with it. Moreover, in summer, Walden never becomes so warm as most water which is exposed to the sun, on account of its depth. In the warmest weather I usually placed a pailful in my cellar, where it became cool in the night, and remained so during the day; though I also resorted to a spring in the neighborhood. It was as good when a week old as the day it was dipped, and had no taste of the pump. Whoever camps for a week in summer by the shore of a pond, needs only bury a pail of water a few feet deep in the shade of his camp to be independent of the luxury of ice.

There have been caught in Walden pickerel, one weighing seven pounds, to say nothing of another which carried off a reel with great velocity, which the fisherman safely set down at eight pounds because he did not see him, perch and pouts, some of each weighing over two pounds, shiners, chivins or roach (*Leuciscus pulchellus*), a very few breams, and a couple of eels, one weighing four pounds—I am thus particular because the weight of a fish is commonly its only title to fame, and these are the only eels I have heard of here;—also, I have a faint recollection of a little fish some five inches long, with silvery sides and a greenish back, somewhat dace-like in its character, which I mention here chiefly to link my facts to fable. Nevertheless, this pond is not very fertile in fish. Its pickerel, though not abundant, are its chief boast. I have seen at one time lying on the ice pickerel of at least three different kinds; a long and shallow one, steel-colored, most like those caught in the river; a bright golden kind, with greenish reflections and remarkably deep, which is the most common here; and another, golden-colored, and shaped like the last, but peppered on the sides with small dark brown or black spots, intermixed with a few faint blood-red ones, very much like a trout. The specific name *reticulatus* would not apply to this; it should be *guttatus* rather. These are all very firm fish, and weigh more than their size promises. The shiners, pouts, and perch also, and indeed all the fishes which inhabit this pond, are much cleaner, handsomer, and firmer fleshed than those in the river and most other ponds, as the water is purer, and they can easily be distinguished from them. Probably many ichthyologists would make new varieties of some of them. There are also a clean race of frogs and tortoises, and a few mussels in it; muskrats and minks leave their traces about it, and occasionally a travelling mud-turtle visits it. Sometimes, when I pushed off my boat in the morning, I disturbed a great mud-turtle which had secreted himself under the boat in the night. Ducks and geese frequent it in the spring and fall, the white-bellied swallows (*Hirundo bicolor*) skim over it, and the peetweets (*Totanus macularius*) "teter" along its stony shores all summer. I have sometimes disturbed a fish-hawk sitting on a white-pine over the water; but I doubt if it is ever profaned by the wing of a gull, like Fair Haven. At most, it tolerates one annual loon. These are all the animals of consequence which frequent it now.

You may see from a boat, in calm weather, near the sandy eastern shore, where the water is eight or ten feet deep, and also in some other parts of the pond, some circular heaps half a dozen feet in diameter by a foot in height, consisting of small stones less than a hen's egg in size, where all around is bare sand. At first you wonder if the Indians could have formed them on the ice for any purpose, and so, when the ice melted, they sank to the bottom; but they are too regular and some of them plainly too fresh for that. They are similar to those found in rivers; but as there are no suckers nor lampreys here, I know not by what fish they could be made. Perhaps they are the nests of the chivin. These lend a pleasing mystery to the bottom.

The shore is irregular enough not to be monotonous. I have in my mind's eye the western indented with deep bays, the bolder northern, and the beautifully scolloped southern shore, where successive capes overlap each other and suggest unexplored coves between. The forest has never so good a setting, nor is so distinctly beautiful, as when seen from the middle of a small lake amid hills which rise from the water's edge; for the

water in which it is reflected not only makes the best foreground in such a case, but, with its winding shore, the most natural and agreeable boundary to it. There is no rawness nor imperfection in its edge there, as where the axe has cleared a part, or a cultivated field abuts on it. The trees have ample room to expand on the water side, and each sends forth its most vigorous branch in that direction. There Nature has woven a natural selvage, and the eye rises by just gradations from the low shrubs of the shore to the highest trees. There are few traces of man's hand to be seen. The water laves the shore as it did a thousand years ago.

A lake is the landscape's most beautiful and expressive feature. It is earth's eye; looking into which the beholder measures the depth of his own nature. The fluviatile trees next the shore are the slender eyelashes which fringe it, and the wooded hills and cliffs around are its overhanging brows.

Standing on the smooth sandy beach at the east end of the pond, in a calm September afternoon, when a slight haze makes the opposite shore-line indistinct, I have seen whence came the expression, "the glassy surface of a lake." When you invert your head, it looks like a thread of finest gossamer stretched across the valley, and gleaming against the distant pine woods, separating one stratum of the atmosphere from another. You would think that you could walk dry under it to the opposite hills, and that the swallows which skim over might perch on it. Indeed, they sometimes dive below the line, as it were by mistake, and are undeceived. As you look over the pond westward you are obliged to employ both your hands to defend your eyes against the reflected as well as the true sun, for they are equally bright; and if, between the two, you survey its surface critically, it is literally as smooth as glass, except where the skater insects, at equal intervals scattered over its whole extent, by their motions in the sun produce the finest imaginable sparkle on it, or, perchance, a duck plumes itself, or, as I have said, a swallow skims so low as to touch it. It may be that in the distance a fish describes an arc of three or four feet in the air, and there is one bright flash where it emerges, and another where it strikes the water; sometimes the whole silvery arc is revealed; or here and there, perhaps, is a thistledown floating on its surface, which the fishes dart at and so dimple it again. It is like molten glass cooled but not congealed, and the few motes in it are pure and beautiful, like the imperfections in glass. You may often detect a yet smoother and darker water, separated from the rest as if by an invisible cobweb, boom of the water nymphs, resting on it. From a hilltop you can see a fish leap in almost any part; for not a pickerel or shiner picks an insect from this smooth surface but it manifestly disturbs the equilibrium of the whole lake. It is wonderful with what elaborateness this simple fact is advertised—this piscine murder will out—and from my distant perch I distinguish the circling undulations when they are half a dozen rods in diameter. You can even detect a water-bug (*Gyrinus*) ceaselessly progressing over the smooth surface a quarter of a mile off; for they furrow the water slightly, making a conspicuous ripple bounded by two diverging lines, but the skaters glide over it without rippling it perceptibly. When the surface is considerably agitated there are no skaters nor waterbugs on it, but apparently, in calm days, they leave their havens and adventurously glide forth from the shore by short impulses till they completely cover it. It is a soothing employment, on one of those fine days in the fall, when all the warmth of the sun is fully appreciated, to sit on a stump on such a height as this, overlooking the pond, and study the dimpling circles which are incessantly inscribed on its otherwise invisible surface amid the reflected skies and trees. Over this great expanse there is no disturbance but it is thus at once gently smoothed away and assuaged, as, when a vase of water is jarred, the trembling circles seek the shore, and all is smooth again. Not a fish can leap or an insect fall on the pond but it is thus reported in circling dimples, in lines of beauty, as it were the constant welling up of its fountain, the gentle pulsing of its life, the heaving of its breast. The thrills of joy and thrills of pain are undistinguishable. How peaceful the phenomena of the lake! Again

the works of man shine as in the spring, ay, every leaf and twig and stone and cobweb sparkles now at midafternoon as when covered with dew in a spring morning. Every motion of an oar or an insect produces a flash of light; and if an oar falls, how sweet the echo!

In such a day, in September or October, Walden is a perfect forest mirror, set round with stones as precious to my eye as if fewer or rarer. Nothing so fair, so pure, and at the same time so large, as a lake, perchance, lies on the surface of the earth. Sky water. It needs no fence. Nations come and go without defiling it. It is a mirror which no stone can crack, whose quicksilver will never wear off, whose gilding Nature continually repairs; no storms, no dust, can dim its surface ever fresh;—a mirror in which all impurity presented to it sinks, swept and dusted by the sun's hazy brush—this the light dust-cloth—which retains no breath that is breathed on it, but sends its own to float as clouds high above its surface, and be reflected in its bosom still.

A field of water betrays the spirit that is in the air. It is continually receiving new life and motion from above. It is intermediate in its nature between land and sky. On land only the grass and trees wave, but the water itself is rippled by the wind. I see where the breeze dashes across it by the streaks or flakes of light. It is remarkable that we can look down on its surface. We shall, perhaps, look down thus on the surface of air at length, and mark where a still subtler spirit sweeps over it.

The skaters and water-bugs finally disappear in the latter part of October, when the severe frosts have come; and then and in November, usually, in a calm day, there is absolutely nothing to ripple the surface. One November afternoon, in the calm at the end of a rain storm of several days' duration, when the sky was still completely overcast and the air was full of mist, I observed that the pond was remarkably smooth, so that it was difficult to distinguish its surface; though it no longer reflected the bright tints of October, but the somber November colors of the surrounding hills. Though I passed

over it as gently as possible, the slight undulations produced by my boat extended
almost as far as I could see, and gave a ribbed
appearance to the reflections. But, as I was
looking over the surface, I saw here and there
at a distance a faint glimmer, as if some skater
insects which had escaped the frosts might be
collected there, or, perchance, the surface,
being so smooth, betrayed where a spring
welled up from the bottom. Paddling gently
to one of these places, I was surprised to find
myself surrounded by myriads of small perch,
about five inches long, of a rich bronze color
in the green water, sporting there and constantly rising to the surface and dimpling it,
sometimes leaving bubbles on it. In such
transparent and seemingly bottomless water,
reflecting the clouds, I seemed to be floating
through the air as in a balloon, and their
swimming impressed me as a kind of flight or
hovering, as if they were a compact flock of
birds passing just beneath my level on the
right or left, their fins, like sails, set all around
them. There were many such schools in the
pond, apparently improving the short season
before winter would draw an icy shutter over
their broad skylight, sometimes giving to the
surface an appearance as if a slight breeze
struck it, or a few raindrops fell there. When I
approached carelessly and alarmed them, they
made a sudden plash and rippling with their
tails, as if one had struck the water with a
brushy bough, and instantly took refuge in
the depths. At length the wind rose, the mist
increased, and the waves began to run, and
the perch leaped much higher than before,
half out of water, a hundred black points,
three inches long, at once above the surface.
Even as late as the 5th of December, one year,
I saw some dimples on the surface, and
thinking it was going to rain hard immediately, the air being full of mist, I made
haste to take my place at the oars and row
homeward; already the rain seemed rapidly
increasing, though I felt none on my cheek,
and I anticipated a thorough soaking. But
suddenly the dimples ceased, for they were
produced by the perch, which the noise of
my oars had scared into the depths, and I saw
their schools dimly disappearing; so I spent a
dry afternoon after all.

An old man who used to frequent this
pond nearly sixty years ago, when it was
dark with surrounding forests, tells me that
in those days he sometimes saw it all alive
with ducks and other waterfowl, and that
there were many eagles about it. He came
here a-fishing, and used an old log canoe
which he found on the shore. It was made of
two white-pine logs dug out and pinned
together, and was cut off square at the ends.
It was very clumsy, but lasted a great many
years before it became water-logged and perhaps sank to the bottom. He did not know
whose it was; it belonged to the pond. He
used to make a cable for his anchor of strips
of hickory bark tied together. An old man, a
potter, who lived by the pond before the
Revolution, told him once that there was an
iron chest at the bottom, and that he had
seen it. Sometimes it would come floating up
to the shore; but when you went toward it, it
would go back into deep water and disappear.
I was pleased to hear of the old log canoe,
which took the place of an Indian one of the
same material but more graceful construction,
which perchance had first been a tree on the
bank, and then, as it were, fell into the water,
to float there for a generation, the most proper
vessel for the lake. I remember that when I
first looked into these depths there were
many large trunks to be seen indistinctly
lying on the bottom, which had either been
blown over formerly, or left on the ice at the
last cutting, when wood was cheaper; but now
they have mostly disappeared.

When I first paddled a boat on Walden, it
was completely surrounded by thick and
lofty pine and oak woods, and in some of its
coves grape vines had run over the trees
next the water and formed bowers under
which a boat could pass. The hills which
form its shores are so steep, and the woods
on them were then so high, that, as you
looked down from the west end, it had the
appearance of an amphitheater for some kind
of sylvan spectacle. I have spent many an
hour, when I was younger, floating over its
surface as the zephyr willed, having paddled
my boat to the middle, and lying on my back
across the seats, in a summer forenoon,
dreaming awake, until I was aroused by the

boat touching the sand, and I arose to see what shore my fates had impelled me to—days when idleness was the most attractive and productive industry. Many a forenoon have I stolen away, preferring to spend thus the most valued part of the day; for I was rich, if not in money, in sunny hours and summer days, and spent them lavishly; nor do I regret that I did not waste more of them in the workshop or the teacher's desk. But since I left those shores the wood choppers have still further laid them waste, and now for many a year there will be no more rambling through the aisles of the wood, with occasional vistas through which you see the water. My Muse may be excused if she is silent henceforth. How can you expect the birds to sing when their groves are cut down?

Now the trunks of trees on the bottom, and the old log canoe, and the dark surrounding woods, are gone, and the villagers, who scarcely know where it lies, instead of going to the pond to bathe or drink, are thinking to bring its water, which should be as sacred as the Ganges at least, to the village in a pipe, to wash their dishes with!—to earn their Walden by the turning of a cock or drawing of a plug! That devilish Iron Horse, whose ear-rending neigh is heard throughout the town, has muddied the Boiling Spring with his foot, and he it is that has browsed off all the woods on Walden shore; that Trojan horse, with a thousand men in his belly, introduced by mercenary Greeks! Where is the country's champion, the Moore of Moore Hall, to meet him at the Deep Cut and thrust an avenging lance between the ribs of the bloated pest?

Nevertheless, of all the characters I have known, perhaps Walden wears best, and best preserves its purity. Many men have been likened to it, but few deserve that honor. Though the wood choppers have laid bare first this shore and then that, and the Irish have built their sties by it, and the railroad has infringed on its border, and the ice-men have skimmed it once, it is itself unchanged, the same water which my youthful eyes fell on; all the change is in me. It has not acquired one permanent wrinkle after all its ripples. . . .

Brute Neighbors

As I was paddling along the north shore one very calm October afternoon, for such days especially they settle on to the lakes, like the milkweed down, having looked in vain over the pond for a loon, suddenly one, sailing out from the shore toward the middle a few rods in front of me, set up his wild laugh and betrayed himself. I pursued with a paddle and he dived, but when he came up I was nearer than before. He dived again, but I miscalculated the direction he would take, and we were fifty rods apart when he came to the surface this time, for I had helped to widen the interval; and again he laughed long and loud, with more reason than before. He manœuvred so cunningly that I could not get within half a dozen rods of him. Each time, when he came to the surface, turning his head this way and that, he coolly surveyed the water and the land, and apparently chose his course so that he might come up where there was the widest expanse of water and at the greatest distance from the boat. It was surprising how quickly he made up his mind and put his resolve into execution. He led me at once to the widest part of the pond, and could not be driven from it. While he was thinking one thing in his brain, I was endeavoring to divine his thought in mine. It was a pretty game, played on the smooth surface of the pond, a man against a loon. Suddenly your adversary's checker disappears beneath the board, and the problem is to place yours nearest to where his will appear again. Sometimes he would come up unexpectedly on the opposite side of me, having apparently passed directly under the boat. So long-winded was he and so unweariable, that when he had swum farthest he would immediately plunge again, nevertheless; and then no wit could divine where in the deep pond, beneath the smooth surface, he might be speeding his way like a fish, for he had time and ability to visit the bottom of the pond in its deepest part. It is said that loons have been caught in the New York lakes eighty feet beneath the surface, with hooks set for trout,—though Walden is deeper than that. How surprised must the fishes be to see this ungainly visitor from another sphere speeding his way amid their schools! Yet he appeared to know his course as surely under water as on the surface, and swum much faster there. Once or twice I saw a ripple where he approached the surface, just put his head out to reconnoitre, and instantly dived again. I found that it was as well for me to rest on my oars and wait his reappearing as to endeavor to calculate where he would rise; for again and again, when I was straining my eyes over the surface one way, I would suddenly be startled by his unearthly laugh behind me. But why, after displaying so much cunning, did he invariably betray himself the moment he came up by that loud laugh? Did not his white breast enough betray him? He was indeed a silly loon, I thought. I could commonly hear the plash of the water when he came up, and so also detected him. But after an hour he seemed as fresh as ever, dived as willingly, and swam yet farther than at first. It was surprising to see how serenely he sailed off with unruffled breast when he came to the surface, doing all the work with his webbed feet beneath. His usual note was this demoniac laughter, yet somewhat like that of a waterfowl; but occasionally, when he had balked me most successfully and come up a long way off, he uttered a long-drawn unearthly howl, probably more like that of a wolf than any bird; as when a beast puts his muzzle to the ground and deliberately howls. This was his looning—perhaps the wildest sound that is ever heard here, making the woods ring far and wide. I concluded that he laughed in derision of my efforts, confident of his own resources. Though the sky was by this time overcast, the pond was so smooth that I could see where he broke the surface when I did not hear him. His white breast, the stillness of the air, and the smoothness of the water were all against him. At length, having come up fifty rods off, he uttered one of those prolonged howls, as if calling on the god of loons to aid him, and immediately there came a wind from the east and rippled the surface, and filled the whole air with misty rain, and I was impressed as if it were the prayer of the loon answered, and his god was angry with me; and so I left him disappearing far away on the tumultuous surface.

For hours, in fall days, I watched the ducks cunningly tack and veer and hold the middle of the pond, far from the sportsman; tricks which they will have less need to practise in the Louisiana bayous. When compelled to rise they would sometimes circle round and round and over the pond at a considerable height from which they could easily see to other ponds and the river, like black motes in the sky; and, when I thought they had gone off thither long since, they would settle down by a slanting flight of a quarter of a mile on to a distant part which was left free; but what beside safety they get by sailing in the middle of Walden I do not know, unless they love its water for the same reason that I do.

Conclusion

I left the woods for as good a reason as I went there. Perhaps it seemed to me that I had several more lives to live, and could not spare any more time for that one. It is remarkable how easily and insensibly we fall into a particular route, and make a beaten track for ourselves. I had not lived there a week before my feet wore a path from my door to the pond-side; and though it is five or six years since I trod it, it is still quite distinct. It is true, I fear that others may have fallen into it, and so helped to keep it open. The surface of the earth is soft and impressible by the feet of men; and so with the paths which the mind travels. How worn and dusty, then, must be the highways of the world, how deep the ruts of tradition and conformity! I did not wish to take a cabin passage, but rather to go before the mast and on the deck of the world, for there I could best see the moonlight amid the mountains. I do not wish to go below now.

I learned this, at least, by my experiment; that if one advances confidently in the direction of his dreams, and endeavors to live the life which he has imagined, he will meet with a success unexpected in common hours. He will put some things behind, will pass an invisible boundary; new, universal, and more liberal laws will begin to establish themselves around and within him; or the old laws be expanded, and interpreted in his favor in a more liberal sense, and he will live with the license of a higher order of beings. In proportion as he simplifies his life, the laws of the universe will appear less complex, and solitude will not be solitude, nor poverty poverty, nor weakness weakness. If you have built castles in the air, your work need not be lost; that is where they should be. Now put the foundations under them.

1854

From CIVIL DISOBEDIENCE

Underlying "Civil Disobedience," like Lowell's *Biglow Papers*, was fear of the growing slave power and disapproval of the Mexican War. Thoreau's characteristic individualism made him loath to support a government that countenanced slavery and war. Gandhi is said to have liked "Civil Disobedience" and printed it as a tract.

I HEARTILY accept the motto,—"That government is best which governs least"; and I should like to see it acted up to more rapidly and systematically. Carried out, it finally amounts to this, which also I believe,—"That government is best which governs not at all"; and when men are prepared for it, that will be the kind of government which they will have. Government is at best but an expedient; but most governments are usually, and all governments are sometimes, inexpedient. The objections which have been brought against a standing army, and they are many and weighty, and deserve to prevail, may also at last be brought against a standing government. The standing army is only an arm of the standing government. The government itself, which is only the mode which the people have chosen to execute their will, is equally liable to be abused and perverted before the people can act through it. Witness the present Mexican war, the work of comparatively a few individuals using the standing government as their tool; for, in the outset, the people would not have consented to this measure.

This American government,—what is it but a tradition, though a recent one, endeavoring to transmit itself unimpaired to posterity, but each instant losing some of its integrity? It has not the vitality and force of a single living man; for a single man can bend it to his will. It is a sort of wooden gun to the people themselves. But it is not the less necessary for this; for the people must have some complicated machinery or other, and hear its din, to satisfy that idea of government which they have. Governments show thus how successfully men can be imposed on, even impose on themselves, for their own advantage. It is excellent, we must all allow. Yet this government never of itself furthered any enterprise, but by the alacrity with which it got out of its way. *It* does not keep the country free. *It* does not settle the West. *It* does not educate. The character inherent in the American people has done all that has been accomplished; and it would have done somewhat more, if the government had not sometimes got in its way. For government is an expedient by which men would fain succeed in letting one another alone; and, as has been said, when it is most expedient, the governed are most let alone by it. Trade and commerce, if they were not made of India-rubber, would never manage to bounce over the obstacles which legislators are continually putting in their way; and, if one were to judge these men wholly by the effects of their actions and not partly by their intentions, they would deserve to be classed and punished with those mischievous persons who put obstructions on the railroads.

But, to speak practically and as a citizen, unlike those who call themselves no-government men, I ask for, not at once no government, but *at once* a better government. Let every man make known what kind of government would command his respect, and that will be one step toward obtaining it. . . .

I have paid no poll-tax for six years. I was put into jail once on this account, for one night; and, as I stood considering the walls of solid stone, two or three feet thick, the door of wood and iron, a foot thick, and the iron grating which strained the light, I could not help being struck with the foolishness of that institution which treated me as if I were mere flesh and blood and bones, to be locked up. I wondered that it should have concluded at length that this was the best use it could put me to, and had never thought to avail itself of my services in some way. I saw that, if there was a wall of stone between me and my townsmen, there was a still more difficult one to climb or break through before they could get to be as free as I was. I did not for a moment feel confined, and the walls seemed a great waste of stone and mortar. I felt as if I alone of all my townsmen had paid my tax. They plainly did not know how to treat me, but behaved like persons who are underbred. In every threat and in every compliment there was a blunder; for they thought that my chief desire was to stand the other side of that stone wall. I could not but smile to see how industriously they locked the door on my meditations, which followed them out again without let or hindrance, and *they* were really all that was dangerous. As they could not reach me, they had resolved to punish my body; just as boys, if they cannot come at some person against whom they have a spite, will abuse his dog. I saw that the State was half-witted, that it was timid as a lone woman with her silver spoons, and that it did not know its friends from its foes, and I lost all my remaining respect for it, and pitied it.

Thus the State never intentionally confronts a man's sense, intellectual or moral, but only his body, his senses. It is not armed with superior wit or honesty, but with superior physical force. I was not born to be forced. I will breathe after my own fashion. Let us see who is the strongest. What force has a multitude? They only can force me who obey a higher law than I. They force me to become like themselves. I do not hear of *men* being *forced* to live this way or that by masses of men. What sort of life were that to live? When I meet a government which says to me, "Your money or your life," why should I be in haste to give it my money? It may be in a great strait, and not know what to do: I cannot help that. It must help itself; do as I do. It is not worth the while to snivel about it. I am not responsible for the successful working of the machinery of society. I am not the son of the engineer. I perceive that, when an acorn and a chestnut fall side by side, the one does not remain inert to make way for the other, but both obey their own laws, and spring and grow

and flourish as best they can, till one, perchance, overshadows and destroys the other. If a plant cannot live according to its nature, it dies; and so a man.

The night in prison was novel and interesting enough. The prisoners in their shirtsleeves were enjoying a chat and the evening air in the doorway, when I entered. But the jailer said, "Come, boys, it is time to lock up"; and so they dispersed, and I heard the sound of their steps returning into the hollow apartments. My roommate was introduced to me by the jailer as "a first-rate fellow and a clever man." When the door was locked, he showed me where to hang my hat, and how he managed matters there. The rooms were whitewashed once a month; and this one, at least, was the whitest, most simply furnished, and probably the neatest apartment in the town. He naturally wanted to know where I came from, and what brought me there; and, when I had told him, I asked him in my turn how he came there, presuming him to be an honest man, of course; and, as the world goes, I believe he was. "Why," said he, "they accuse me of burning a barn; but I never did it." As near as I could discover, he had probably gone to bed in a barn when drunk, and smoked his pipe there; and so a barn was burnt. He had the reputation of being a clever man, had been there some three months waiting for his trial to come on, and would have to wait as much longer; but he was quite domesticated and contented, since he got his board for nothing, and thought that he was well treated.

He occupied one window, and I the other; and I saw that if one stayed there long, his principal business would be to look out the window. I had soon read all the tracts that were left there, and examined where former prisoners had broken out, and where a grate had been sawed off, and heard the history of the various occupants of that room; for I found that even here there was a history and a gossip which never circulated beyond the walls of the jail. Probably this is the only house in the town where verses are composed, which are afterward printed in a circular form, but not published. I was shown quite a long list of verses which were composed by some young men who had been detected in an attempt to escape, who avenged themselves by singing them.

I pumped my fellow-prisoner as dry as I could, for fear I should never see him again; but at length he showed me which was my bed, and left me to blow out the lamp.

It was like traveling into a far country, such as I had never expected to behold, to lie there for one night. It seemed to me that I never had heard the town-clock strike before, nor the evening sounds of the village; for we slept with the windows open, which were inside the grating. It was to see my native village in the light of the Middle Ages, and our Concord was turned into a Rhine stream, and visions of knights and castles passed before me. They were the voices of old burghers that I heard in the streets. I was an involuntary spectator and auditor of whatever was done and said in the kitchen of the adjacent village-inn,—a wholly new and rare experience to me. It was a closer view of my native town. I was fairly inside of it. I never had seen its institutions before. This is one of its peculiar institutions; for it is a shire town. I began to comprehend what its inhabitants were about.

In the morning, our breakfasts were put through the hole in the door, in small oblong-square tin pans, made to fit, and holding a pint of chocolate, with brown bread, and an iron spoon. When they called for the vessels again, I was green enough to return what bread I had left; but my comrade seized it, and said that I should lay that up for lunch or dinner. Soon after he was let out to work at haying in a neighboring field, whither he went every day, and would not be back till noon; so he bade me good-day, saying that he doubted if he should see me again.

When I came out of prison,—for some one interfered, and paid that tax,—I did not perceive that great changes had taken place on the common, such as he observed who went in a youth and emerged a tottering and gray-headed man; and yet a change had to my eyes come over the scene,—the town, and State, and country,—greater than any that mere time could effect. I saw yet more distinctly the State in which I lived. I saw to what extent the people among whom I lived could be trusted as good neighbors and friends; that

their friendship was for summer weather only; that they did not greatly propose to do right; that they were a distinct race from me by their prejudices and superstitions, as the Chinamen and Malays are; that in their sacrifices to humanity they ran no risks, not even to their property; that after all they were not so noble but they treated the thief as he had treated them, and hoped, by a certain outward observance and a few prayers, and by walking in a particular straight though useless path from time to time, to save their souls. This may be to judge my neighbors harshly; for I believe that many of them are not aware that they have such an institution as the jail in their village.

It was formerly the custom in our village, when a poor debtor came out of jail, for his acquaintances to salute him, looking through their fingers, which were crossed to represent the grating of a jail window, "How do ye do?" My neighbors did not thus salute me, but first looked at me, and then at one another, as if I had returned from a long journey. I was put in jail as I was going to the shoemaker's to get a shoe which was mended. When I was let out the next morning, I proceeded to finish my errand, and, having put on my mended shoe, joined a huckleberry party, who were impatient to put themselves under my conduct; and in half an hour,—for the horse was soon tackled,—was in the midst of a huckleberry field, on one of our highest hills, two miles off, and then the State was nowhere to be seen.

This is the whole history of "My Prisons.". . .

The authority of government, even such as I am willing to submit to,—for I will cheerfully obey those who know and can do better than I, and in many things even those who neither know nor can do so well,—is still an impure one: to be strictly just, it must have the sanction and consent of the governed. It can have no pure right over my person and property but what I concede to it. The progress from an absolute to a limited monarchy, from a limited monarchy to a democracy, is a progress toward a true respect for the individual. Even the Chinese philosopher was wise enough to regard the individual as the basis of the empire. Is a democracy, such as we know it, the last improvement possible in government? Is it not possible to take a step further towards recognizing and organizing the rights of man? There will never be a really free and enlightened State until the State comes to recognize the individual as a higher and independent power, from which all its own power and authority are derived, and treats him accordingly. I please myself with imagining a State at last which can afford

to be just to all men, and to treat the individual with respect as a neighbor; which even would not think it inconsistent with its own repose if a few were to live aloof from it, not meddling with it, nor embraced by it, who fulfilled all the duties of neighbors and fellowmen. A State which bore this kind of fruit, and suffered it to drop off as fast as it ripened, would prepare the way for a still more perfect and glorious State, which also I have imagined, but not yet anywhere seen.

1849

1804 -- *Nathaniel Hawthorne* -- 1864

HAWTHORNE brought depth and, like Poe, intensity to American fiction, and he freed it from sentimentality. As an artist he far outranks his predecessors. He was concerned with the inner life and the effects of sin and evil on the conscience and character. C. B. Brown had preceded him in emphasis on the psychological, and he owes something to Irving's essays, but he found a new field in the borderland between the colonial and the modern. In his day, seventeenth-century Puritanism had receded far enough to be available as literary material. He knew its spirit, ideas, psychology, and superstitions, and he became its best interpreter, without definitely aligning himself either as a defender or condemner of it. No other author illustrates as clearly as does Hawthorne the complexity and subtlety of that motivating force in American literature that we call puritanism. Ethical considerations loom larger than happenings in his stories. It is the human soul that he studied. So distinctive were his gifts that his works will remain landmarks in the history of American fiction.

Nathaniel Hawthorne (the name was spelled Hathorne until the author inserted the *w*) was born at Salem, Massachusetts, July 4, 1804. The history of Salem, once a leading New England port, dated far back, and various legends clustered about it. It was the scene of Quaker persecutions and witchcraft tragedies. Many staunch Puritan characters, including the novelist's ancestors, were associated with it. Major William Hathorne had come to Massachusetts in 1630. He was an Indian fighter, a persecutor of Quakers, and a speaker in the General Court. Another of the author's ancestors was a magistrate, soldier, and statesman; and another, on whose head tradition said that a curse had been called down, was a judge in the witchcraft trials. The author's grandfather was an officer and a sea captain. His father, also a sea captain, died at Surinam when Nathaniel was four years old. By this time the family had outgrown its puritan severity, but had kept the puritan conscience.

Hawthorne's uncle provided for his education. He was fitted for college by Joseph Worcester, the author of Worcester's *Dictionary*, which was perhaps auspicious for the boy's vocabulary. At fourteen he spent many months in seclusion in the Maine woods on a half-developed tract of land that belonged to the family. He entered Bowdoin College in 1821 at the age of seventeen. He was in the same class (1825) with Longfellow. Franklin Pierce, who was to become President of the United States and who proved a good friend, was a member of the Class of 1824. Hawthorne's college life on the whole was uneventful. He was rather shy, given to pondering and dreaming, and did not rank especially high in scholarship, though he did good work in English composition.

After graduation, although without means, for his family was not well-to-do, Hawthorne seems to have had no impulse to adopt a profession. Temperamentally a recluse, he could never enter whole-heartedly into the life about him. He had grown up in solitary habits, for the Hawthorne family had a peculiar home life. They were rarely together even at meals, for after the death of the father, the mother withdrew somewhat from the world and at Salem, lived much of the time in her own room. During the years 1825–33, Hawthorne remained at Salem, reading and writing but making few acquaintances. His residence there was broken by journeys to different parts of New England and New York, but his type of life left him rather provincial. In these years at Salem, he drifted into the determination to be a writer and served his apprenticeship in romance. He wrote much and burned much. A number of tales and sketches appeared in obscure periodicals and newspapers. Many were later collected and published in 1837 under the title *Twice-Told Tales*, i.e., tales that had already been printed once. Although Salem was the home of seafarers, he never wrote a romance of the sea or of sea life.

For two years, 1836–1838, Hawthorne served as editor of a juvenile periodical in Boston. In 1838 he became engaged to Sophia Peabody of Salem. From 1839 to 1841 he acted as weigher and gauger in the Boston Custom House. He lost his position through a political change and invested his savings in the Brook Farm experiment. He was not enthusiastic, however, over his experiences with community life. The next year he married Miss Peabody and went to Concord, where he lived happily at the Old Manse for four years. His *Mosses from an Old Manse* was published in 1846.

From 1846 to 1849 he was a surveyor at the Salem Custom House, a position obtained for him by Pierce. He was paid fairly well and worked but three or four hours daily; but though he had much leisure, he was not productive as a writer. In 1849 he was removed from office through the political spoils system and gave his energies to the shaping of a romance, *The Scarlet Letter*, his first long work. It at once had extraordinary success. He was indignant at all of Salem for his removal from office and lampooned his associates there in the introductions to *The Scarlet Letter* and *The*

House of the Seven Gables. From 1850 to 1853 he lived successively at Lenox, West Newton, and Concord, where he purchased The Wayside in 1852. This remained his home. In this period he wrote *The House of the Seven Gables*, in which Judge Pyncheon was made to suggest the politician instrumental in his loss of office. He also wrote here *The Blithedale Romance* and *Tanglewood Tales.*

In 1853 he was appointed consul at Liverpool by his old college friend, President Pierce. This was one of the highest salaried posts open to award. Hawthorne held this office for four years and resigned in 1856. He spent the next three years in foreign travel, mainly in Italy, of which *The Marble Faun* (1860) was the chief product. Unlike Irving and Lowell, Hawthorne did not enjoy his stay in England, for he shared his countrymen's anti-English prejudice and he had a sense of banishment and aloofness while he was there. His English residence had little influence on his work. Perhaps his European experiences came too late in life. His remaining years were passed at The Wayside in Concord. He died at Plymouth, N.H., while setting out with President Pierce on a tour to the White Mountains, May 18, 1864.

Hawthorne was of impressive appearance and physique, erect, and slender. He had, perhaps, rather low vitality, for he showed a constitutional lassitude about work. His family was not affluent, but he tried only once for a systematic literary appointment. His positions were political. Yet although he lacked somewhat in energy and a sense of independence, he kept the admiration of his friends.

Hawthorne never found inspiration in externals. He was not concerned with the abolitionist movement, or with economics, humanitarian tendencies, books, or systems of thought. He showed little interest in philosophy and scholarship, and none in adventure and crime. He turned constantly to the shadowy world within, especially to the theme of solitude arising from egotism, self-isolation, or pride of intellect, and he brooded over the sinister problems of destiny. A sure sense of artistry marks his work. His style is rich in suggestion and symbolism, graceful, flowing, and lucid. The phrasing is literary yet suffused with emotion. He wrote carefully, striving for good technique and for unity of tone as in a poem. He liked the half-light or mirage, and suggestions and hints rather than direct treatment. Atmosphere appealed to him more than solid reality, but he never took his reader quite away from the actual world. The element of the extravagant and improbable so often present in his work is subordinated, never the leading theme. He introduced few characters, often making much of symbols that he associated with them, such as the scarlet letter and the minister's black veil, and he often endowed his characters with tricks of manner. He made much, too, of small scenes and single figures. A rich fancy and imagination play over materials often thin in themselves. The short story was his characteristic form of writing. In it he dealt with New England legends, allegories, parables, and moralistic themes. His longer works are like his short stories, only built on larger dimensions.

Among the authors Hawthorne read were Homer, Aesop, Dante, Rabelais, Cervantes, Milton, Rousseau, Byron, and Coleridge. He had a good reading knowledge of French and drew many French classics from the library of the Salem Athenaeum. He was especially attracted to Spenser and Bunyan (from whom derives probably his allegorical bent) and to Walter Scott and William Godwin. Among American writers he knew the early annalists, the Mathers, Freneau, C. B. Brown, the Connecticut Wits, Irving, and Cooper, and after 1850 he knew and admired Melville. Hawthorne termed himself no critic; indeed he expressed doubt of the value of "review articles on the old established model." He leaned if anything to impressionism. "I know well enough what I like but am always at a loss to render a reason." He thought "sensibility" and "deep appreciation" essential in criticism of art. He believed, too, that more attention should be given to writers' opinions of their own work. In prefaces like those to *Twice-Told Tales* and *The Scarlet Letter* he left a record of his fictional views. Apropos of Simms, whose writings he did not rank very high, he remarked in 1846 that it was time to break away from historical novels of "the same worn out mould that has been in use these thirty years." He admired Longfellow's *Evangeline* unreservedly, and admitted to a liking for Whittier's *The Supernaturalism of New England*. Though his own themes and his handling of them do not show it, he seems really to have admired and perhaps preferred stern realism. H. H. Clark says summarizingly of him: "What were Hawthorne's aims and ideals as a creator of fiction? . . . Just as in the ethical realm Hawthorne's thought was a somewhat unstable compound of the differing doctrines of Puritanism and Romanticism, so his literary doctrines represent an unstable compound of stern ethicism based on the moral law and capricious, fantastic romance. Devoted as he is to the sternest problems of the universal moral world, such as the psychological effects of wrongdoing, his treatment of these problems, and his artistic elaboration, are often . . . removed from the normal, the representative, and the probable. Indeed, a just appraisal of Hawthorne as a creator of literature depends in large measure upon a full understanding of his double aspect as at once a romancer and a moralist."

The authorized and standard edition of Hawthorne's works is *The Complete Works of Nathaniel Hawthorne*, with introductory notes by George Parsons Lathrop (Riverside Edition, 12 vols., 1883). The Lenox (14 vols., 1902) is a good later edition. *Hawthorne's First Diary* (1897) was edited by S. T. Pickard. Its authenticity was rejected by Hawthorne's son, Julian; but G. P. Lathrop, his son-in-law, and later writers have accepted it as genuine. His letters to Sophia Peabody, 1839–63, with a preface by Roswell Field, were printed at Chicago (2 vols., 1907), and his letters to W. D. Ticknor, 1851–64, were printed at Newark, N.J. (2 vols., 1910). Most of the latter were reprinted in C. Ticknor's *Hawthorne and His Publisher* (1913). *The Heart of Hawthorne's Journals* was edited by N. Arvin (1929). "Hawthorne's 'Spectator,'" edited by Elizabeth L. Chandler, appeared in the *New England Quarterly*, April, 1931. Randall Stewart edited and annotated *The American Notebooks* (1932); and also "Hawthorne and Politics: Unpublished Letters to William B. Pike" for the *New England Quarterly*, April, 1932. See also *Hawthorne in the American Writers Series*, Austin Warren, ed. (1934).

Leading biographical works on Hawthorne are James T. Field, *Yesterdays with Authors* (1871); George Parsons Lathrop, *A Study of Hawthorne* (1876); Henry James, *Hawthorne*, in English Men of Letters Series (1879); Julian Hawthorne, *Nathaniel Hawthorne and His Wife* (2 vols., 1884); Moncure D. Conway, *Life of Nathaniel Hawthorne*, in Great Writers Series (1890); Horatio Bridge, *Personal Recollections of Nathaniel Hawthorne*, which includes Hawthorne's letters to the author (1893); George E. Woodberry, *Nathaniel Hawthorne*, in American Men of Letters Series (1902), an excellent approach to Hawthorne; L. Dhaleine, *N. Hawthorne, sa Vie et son Œuvre* (1905), a critical work of importance; Lloyd Morris, *The Rebellious Puritan: Portrait of Mr. Hawthorne* (1927); Newton Arvin, *Hawthorne* (1929); and Carl Van Doren in *DAB*, VIII. Manning Hawthorne, "Parental and Family Influences on Hawthorne," *Essex Institute Collections*, LXXVI, 1–13, corrects misconceptions regarding his home life.

For criticism of Hawthorne see E. P. Whipple, in *Character and Characteristic Men* (1866); Lewis E. Gates, in *Studies and Appreciations* (1900); P. E. More, in *Shelburne Essays*, First Series (1904), and Second Series (1905); W. C. Brownell, in *American Prose Masters* (1909); John Erskine, in *CHAL*, II (1918); Carl Van Doren, in *The American Novel* (1921); F. L. Pattee, in *Development of the American Short Story* (1923); Elizabeth L. Chandler, *A Study of the Sources of the Tales and Romances Written by Nathaniel Hawthorne before 1853* (1926); Amy Louise Reed, "Self-Portraiture in the Work of Nathaniel Hawthorne," *Studies in Philology* (Jan., 1926); V. L. Parrington, in *The Romantic Revolution in America* (1927); H. S. Canby, in *Classic Americans* (1931); Ludwig Lewisohn, in *Expression in America* (1932); and Austin Warren, introduction to *Hawthorne*, in American Writers Series.

For bibliography consult Nina E. Browne, *A Bibliography of Nathaniel Hawthorne* (1905); *CHAL*, II; and H. Hartwick, in W. F. Taylor's *A History of American Letters* (1936).

SIGHTS FROM A STEEPLE

Published in *The Token*, an annual for 1831. The monologue of an observer at Salem who views from above the contemporary scene. He looks at the skies, the life of the town, its streets, shores, wharves, vessels, citizens, and the horizon. Hawthorne suggests, in a string of meditations and descriptions, both the outer and the inner life of the place. He liked the role of a detached observer, and wrote several other sketches or tales centering around single spots.

So! I have climbed high, and my reward is small. Here I stand, with wearied knees, earth, indeed, at a dizzy depth below, but heaven far, far beyond me still. O, that I could soar up into the very zenith, where man never breathed, nor eagle ever flew, and where the ethereal azure melts away from the eye, and appears only a deepened shade of nothingness! And yet I shiver at that cold and solitary thought. What clouds are gathering in the golden west, with direful intent against the brightness and warmth of this summer afternoon! They are ponderous air ships, black as death, and freighted with the tempest; and at intervals their thunder, the signal guns of that unearthly squadron, rolls distant along the deep of heaven. These nearer heaps of fleecy vapor—methinks I could roll and toss upon them the whole day long!—seem scattered here and there for the repose of tired pilgrims through the sky. Perhaps—for who can tell?—beautiful spirits are disporting themselves there, and will bless my mortal eye with the brief appearance of their curly locks of golden light, and laughing faces, fair and faint as the people of a rosy dream. Or, where the floating mass so imperfectly obstructs the color of the firmament, a slender foot and fairy limb, resting too heavily upon the frail support, may be thrust through, and suddenly withdrawn, while longing fancy follows them in vain. Yonder again is an airy archipelago, where the sunbeams love to linger in their journeyings through space. Every one of those little clouds has been dipped and steeped in radiance, which the slightest pressure might disengage in silvery profusion, like water wrung from a seamaid's hair. Bright they are as a young man's visions, and, like them, would be realized in chilliness, obscurity, and tears. I will look on them no more.

In three parts of the visible circle, whose center is this spire, I discern cultivated fields, villages, white countryseats, the waving lines of rivulets, little placid lakes, and here and there a rising ground, that would fain be termed a hill. On the fourth side is the sea, stretching away towards a viewless boundary, blue and calm, except where the passing anger of a shadow flits across its surface, and is gone. Hitherward, a broad inlet penetrates far into the land; on the verge of the harbor, formed by its extremity, is a town; and over it am I, a watchman, all-heeding and unheeded. O, that the multitude of chimneys could speak, like those of Madrid, and betray, in smoky whispers, the secrets of all who, since their first foundation, have assembled at the hearths within! O, that the Limping Devil[1] of Le Sage would perch beside me here, extend his wand over this contiguity of roofs, uncover every chamber, and make me familiar with their inhabitants! The most desirable mode of existence might be that of a spiritual Paul Pry,[2] hovering invisible round man and woman, witnessing their deeds, searching into their hearts, borrowing brightness from their felicity and shade from their sorrow, and retaining no emotion peculiar to himself. But none of these things are possible; and if I would know the interior of brick walls, or the mystery of human bosoms, I can but guess.

Yonder is a fair street, extending north and south. The stately mansions are placed each on its carpet of verdant grass, and a long flight of steps extends from every door to the pavement. Ornamental trees—the broad-leafed horse-chestnut, the elm so lofty and bending, the graceful but infrequent willow, and others whereof I know not the names—grow thrivingly among brick and stone. The oblique rays of the sun are intercepted by these green

citizens, and by the houses, so that one side of the street is a shaded and pleasant walk. On its whole extent there is now but a single passenger, advancing from the upper end; and he, unless distance and the medium of a pocket spyglass do him more than justice, is a fine young man of twenty. He saunters slowly forward, slapping his left hand with his folded gloves, bending his eyes upon the pavement, and sometimes raising them to throw a glance before him. Certainly, he has a pensive air. Is he in doubt, or in debt? Is he, if the question be allowable, in love? Does he strive to be melancholy and gentleman-like? Or, is he merely overcome by the heat? But I bid him farewell for the present. The door of one of the houses—an aristocratic edifice, with curtains of purple and gold waving from the windows, is now opened, and down the steps come two ladies, swinging their parasols, and lightly arrayed for a summer ramble. Both are young, both are pretty, but methinks the left-hand lass is the fairer of the twain; and, though she be so serious at this moment, I could swear that there is a treasure of gentle fun within her. They stand talking a little while upon the steps, and finally proceed up the street. Meantime, as their faces are now turned from me, I may look elsewhere.

Upon that wharf, and down the corresponding street, is a busy contrast to the quiet scene which I have just noticed. Business evidently has its center there, and many a man is wasting the summer afternoon in labor and anxiety, in losing riches or in gaining them, when he would be wiser to flee away to some pleasant country village, or shaded lake in the forest, or wild and cool sea-beach. I see vessels unloading at the wharf, and precious merchandise strewn upon the ground, abundantly as at the bottom of the sea, the market whence no goods return, and where there is no captain nor supercargo to render an account of sales. Here the clerks are diligent with their paper and pencils, and sailors ply the block and tackle that hang over the hold, accompanying their toil with cries, long drawn and roughly melodious, till the bales and puncheons ascend to upper air. At a little distance a group of gentlemen are assembled round the door of a warehouse. Grave seniors be they, and I

---

[1] a reference to Le Sage's *Le diable boiteux* ("The Devil on Two Sticks") [2] the meddlesome title character in one of John Poole's English comedies

would wager—if it were safe in these times to be responsible for any one—that the least eminent among them might vie with the old Vicentio,[1] that incomparable trafficker of Pisa. I can even select the wealthiest of the company. It is the elderly personage, in somewhat rusty black, with powdered hair, the superfluous whiteness of which is visible upon the cape of his coat. His twenty ships are wafted on some of their many courses by every breeze that blows, and his name—I will venture to say, though I know it not—is a familiar sound among the far separated merchants of Europe and the Indies.

But I bestow too much of my attention in this quarter. On looking again to the long and shady walk, I perceive that the two fair girls have encountered the young man. After a sort of shyness in the recognition, he turns back with them. Moreover, he has sanctioned my taste in regard to his companions by placing himself on the inner side of the pavement, nearest the Venus to whom I—enacting, on a steeple-top, the part of Paris on the top of Ida—adjudged the golden apple.[2]

In two streets, converging at right angles towards my watchtower, I distinguish three different processions. One is a proud array of voluntary soldiers, in bright uniform, resembling, from the height whence I look down, the painted veterans that garrison the windows of a toyshop. And yet, it stirs my heart; their regular advance, their nodding plumes, the sun-flash on their bayonets and musket barrels, the roll of their drums ascending past me, and the fife ever and anon piercing through—these things have wakened a warlike fire, peaceful though I be. Close to their rear marches a battalion of schoolboys, ranged in crooked and irregular platoons, shouldering sticks, thumping a harsh and unripe clatter from an instrument of tin, and ridiculously aping the intricate maneuvers of the foremost band. Nevertheless, as slight differences are scarcely perceptible from a church spire, one might be tempted to ask, "Which are the boys?"—or rather, "Which the men?"

But, leaving these, let us turn to the third procession, which, though sadder in outward show, may excite identical reflections in the thoughtful mind. It is a funeral. A hearse, drawn by a black and bony steed, and covered by a dusty pall; two or three coaches rumbling over the stones, their drivers half asleep; a dozen couple of careless mourners in their everyday attire; such was not the fashion of our fathers, when they carried a friend to his grave. There is now no doleful clang of the bell to proclaim sorrow to the town. Was the King of Terrors more awful in those days than in our own, that wisdom and philosophy have been able to produce this change? Not so. Here is a proof that he retains his proper majesty. The military men and the military boys are wheeling round the corner, and meet the funeral full in the face. Immediately the drum is silent, all but the tap that regulates each simultaneous footfall. The soldiers yield the path to the dusty hearse and unpretending train, and the children quit their ranks, and cluster on the sidewalks, with timorous and instinctive curiosity. The mourners enter the churchyard at the base of the steeple, and pause by an open grave among the burial stones; the lightning glimmers on them as they lower down the coffin, and the thunder rattles heavily while they throw the earth upon its lid. Verily, the shower is near, and I tremble for the young man and the girls, who have now disappeared from the long and shady street.

How various are the situations of the people covered by the roofs beneath me, and how diversified are the events at this moment befalling them! The newborn, the aged, the dying, the strong in life, and the recent dead are in the chambers of these many mansions. The full of hope, the happy, the miserable, and the desperate dwell together within the circle of my glance. In some of the houses over which my eyes roam so coldly, guilt is entering into hearts that are still tenanted by a debased and trodden virtue,—guilt is on the very edge of commission, and the impending deed might be averted; guilt is done, and the criminal wonders if it be irrevocable. There are broad thoughts struggling in my mind, and, were I able to give them distinctness,

---

[1] Vincentio, in *The Taming of the Shrew*   [2] In classic story, the Apple of Discord, labeled to the fairest, was tossed among the guests at a wedding. Paris, on Mt. Ida, awarded it to Venus.

they would make their way in eloquence. Lo! the raindrops are descending.

The clouds, within a little time, have gathered over all the sky, hanging heavily, as if about to drop in one unbroken mass upon the earth. At intervals, the lightning flashes from their brooding hearts, quivers, disappears, and then comes the thunder, traveling slowly after its twinborn flame. A strong wind has sprung up, howls through the darkened streets, and raises the dust in dense bodies, to rebel against the approaching storm. The disbanded soldiers fly, the funeral has already vanished like its dead, and all people hurry homeward—all that have a home; while a few lounge by the corners, or trudge on desperately, at their leisure. In a narrow lane, which communicates with the shady street, I discern the rich old merchant, putting himself to the top of his speed, lest the rain should convert his hair powder to a paste. Unhappy gentleman! By the slow vehemence and painful moderation wherewith he journeys, it is but too evident that Podagra[1] has left its thrilling tenderness in his great toe. But yonder, at a far more rapid pace, come three other of my acquaintance, the two pretty girls and the young man, unseasonably interrupted in their walk. Their footsteps are supported by the risen dust,—the wind lends them its velocity, —they fly like three sea-birds driven landward by the tempestuous breeze. The ladies would not thus rival Atalanta,[2] if they but knew that anyone were at leisure to observe them. Ah! as they hasten onward, laughing in the angry face of nature, a sudden catastrophe has chanced. At the corner where the narrow lane enters the street, they come plump against the old merchant, whose tortoise motion has just brought him to that point. He likes not the sweet encounter; the darkness of the whole air gathers speedily upon his visage, and there is a pause on both sides. Finally, he thrusts aside the youth with little courtesy, seizes an arm of each of the two girls, and plods onward, like a magician with a prize of captive fairies. All this is easy to be understood. How disconsolate the poor lover stands! regardless of the rain that threatens an exceeding damage to his well-fashioned habiliments, till he catches a backward glance of mirth from a bright eye, and turns away with whatever comfort it conveys.

The old man and his daughters are safely housed, and now the storm lets loose its fury. In every dwelling I perceive the faces of the chambermaids as they shut down the windows, excluding the impetuous shower, and shrinking away from the quick, fiery glare. The large drops descend with force upon the slated roofs, and rise again in smoke. There is a rush and roar, as of a river through the air, and muddy streams bubble majestically along the pavement, whirl their dusky foam into the kennel, and disappear beneath iron grates. Thus did Arethusa[1] sink. I love not my station here aloft, in the midst of the tumult which I am powerless to direct or quell, with the blue lightning wrinkling on my brow, and the thunder muttering its first awful syllables in my ear. I will descend. Yet let me give another glance to the sea, where the foam breaks out in long white lines upon a broad expanse of blackness, or boils up in far distant points, like snowy mountaintops in the eddies of a flood; and let me look once more at the green plain and little hills of the country, over which the giant of the storm is striding in robes of mist, and at the town, whose obscured and desolate streets might beseem a city of the dead; and turning a single moment to the sky, now gloomy as an author's prospects, I prepare to resume my station on lower earth. But stay! A little speck of azure has widened in the western heavens; the sunbeams find a passage, and go rejoicing through the tempest; and on yonder darkest cloud, born, like hallowed hopes, of the glory of another world and the troubles and tears of this, brightens forth the Rainbow!

1831

THE GRAY CHAMPION

First published in the *New England Magazine*, January, 1835, then in *Twice-Told Tales* (1837). Another of Hawthorne's sketches that recreates

---

[1] the gout [2] a maiden swift of foot and winner of many races in classic story

[1] In Greek myth, a woodland nymph, turned by Diana into an underground stream so that she might escape from a river god. The stream rose again as a fountain in Sicily.

the atmosphere of the past. It is a dramatic scene or tableau rather than a story; to some it seems allegorical of Truth resisting Tyranny. The Gray Champion is one of the regicides emerging from his hiding place to defend liberty. Hawthorne seems to have derived his striking incident from the story of the "Angel of Hadley" (Stiles, *A History of Three of the Judges of Charles I*, 1794), telling of a congregation of colonists who, in 1675, were surprised and thrown into consternation by Indians. Suddenly there appeared a man of venerable aspect who rallied them and took command, and under his direction they repelled the Indians and saved the town. He then vanished and the inhabitants supposed him to be an angel sent from God. The mystery was explained after 1688, when it was less dangerous to have it known that a regicide judge (Col. William Goffe, 1605–1679) was a fugitive in Hadley at that time. Goffe fled to America in 1660, lived in concealment in New Haven, 1661–1664, then went to Hadley, Massachusetts.

THERE was once a time when New England groaned under the actual pressure of heavier wrongs than those threatened ones which brought on the Revolution. James II, the bigoted successor of Charles the Voluptuous, had annulled the charters of all the colonies, and sent a harsh and unprincipled soldier to take away our liberties and endanger our religion. The administration of Sir Edmund Andros[1] lacked scarcely a single characteristic of tyranny: a Governor and Council, holding office from the King, and wholly independent of the country; laws made and taxes levied without concurrence of the people, immediate or by their representatives; the rights of private citizens violated, and the titles of all landed property declared void; the voice of complaint stifled by restrictions on the press; and, finally, disaffection overawed by the first band of mercenary troops that ever marched on our free soil. For two years our ancestors were kept in sullen submission by that filial love which had invariably secured their allegiance to the mother country, whether its head chanced to be a Parliament, Protector, or Popish Monarch. Till these evil times, however, such allegiance had been merely nominal, and the colonists had ruled themselves, enjoying far more freedom than

is even yet the privilege of the native subjects of Great Britain.

At length a rumor reached our shores that the Prince of Orange[1] had ventured on an enterprise, the success of which would be the triumph of civil and religious rights and the salvation of New England. It was but a doubtful whisper; it might be false, or the attempt might fail; and, in either case, the man that stirred against King James would lose his head. Still the intelligence produced a marked effect. The people smiled mysteriously in the streets, and threw bold glances at their oppressors; while far and wide there was a subdued and silent agitation, as if the slightest signal would rouse the whole land from its sluggish despondency. Aware of their danger, the rulers resolved to avert it by an imposing display of strength, and perhaps to confirm their despotism by yet harsher measures. One afternoon in April, 1689, Sir Edmund Andros and his favorite councillors, being warm with wine, assembled the redcoats of the Governor's Guard, and made their appearance in the streets of Boston. The sun was near setting when the march commenced.

The roll of the drum at that unquiet crisis seemed to go through the streets, less as the martial music of the soldiers, than as a muster-call to the inhabitants themselves. A multitude, by various avenues, assembled in King Street, which was destined to be the scene, nearly a century afterwards, of another encounter[2] between the troops of Britain and a people struggling against her tyranny. Though more than sixty years had elapsed since the Pilgrims came, this crowd of their descendants still showed the strong and somber features of their character perhaps more strikingly in such a stern emergency than on happier occasions. There were the sober garb, the general severity of mien, the gloomy but undismayed expression, the scriptural forms of speech, and the confidence in Heaven's blessing on a righteous cause, which would have marked a band of the original Puritans, when threatened by some peril of the wilderness. Indeed, it was not yet time for the old spirit

[1] appointed governor of the northern colonies in 1686

[1] became joint sovereign of England with Queen Mary in 1689   [2] the "Boston Massacre," March 5, 1770

to be extinct; since there were men in the streets that day who had worshipped there beneath the trees, before a house was reared to the God for whom they had become exiles. Old soldiers of the Parliament were here, too, smiling grimly at the thought that their aged arms might strike another blow against the house of Stuart. Here, also, were the veterans of King Philip's war,[1] who had burned villages and slaughtered young and old, with pious fierceness, while the godly souls throughout the land were helping them with prayer. Several ministers were scattered among the crowd, which, unlike all other mobs, regarded them with such reverence, as if there were sanctity in their very garments. These holy men exerted their influence to quiet the people, but not to disperse them. Meantime, the purpose of the Governor, in disturbing the peace of the town at a period when the slightest commotion might throw the country into a ferment, was almost the universal subject of inquiry, and variously explained.

"Satan will strike his master-stroke presently," cried some, "because he knoweth that his time is short. All our godly pastors are to be dragged to prison! We shall see them at a Smithfield[2] fire in King Street!"

Hereupon the people of each parish gathered closer round their minister, who looked calmly upwards and assumed a more apostolic dignity, as well befitted a candidate for the highest honor of his profession, the crown of martyrdom. It was actually fancied, at that period, that New England might have a John Rogers of her own to take the place of that worthy in the Primer.

"The Pope of Rome has given orders for a new St. Bartholomew!"[3] cried others. "We are to be massacred, man and male child!"

Neither was this rumor wholly discredited, although the wiser class believed the Governor's object somewhat less atrocious. His predecessor under the old charter, Bradstreet, a venerable companion of the first settlers, was known to be in town. There were grounds for conjecturing that Sir Edmund Andros intended at once to strike terror by a parade of military force, and to confound the opposite faction by possessing himself of their chief.

"Stand firm for the old charter Governor!" shouted the crowd, seizing upon the idea. "The good old Governor Bradstreet!"

While this cry was at the loudest, the people were surprised by the well-known figure of Governor Bradstreet himself, a patriarch of nearly ninety, who appeared on the elevated steps of a door, and, with characteristic mildness, besought them to submit to the constituted authorities.

"My children," concluded this venerable person, "do nothing rashly. Cry not aloud, but pray for the welfare of New England, and expect[1] patiently what the Lord will do in this matter!"

The event was soon to be decided. All this time, the roll of the drum had been approaching through Cornhill, louder and deeper, till with reverberations from house to house, and the regular tramp of martial footsteps, it burst into the street. A double rank of soldiers made their appearance, occupying the whole breadth of the passage, with shouldered matchlocks, and matches burning, so as to present a row of fires in the dusk. Their steady march was like the progress of a machine, that would roll irresistibly over everything in its way. Next, moving slowly, with a confused clatter of hoofs on the pavement, rode a party of mounted gentlemen, the central figure being Sir Edmund Andros, elderly, but erect and soldier-like. Those around him were his favorite councillors, and the bitterest foes of New England. At his right hand rode Edward Randolph, our arch-enemy, that "blasted wretch," as Cotton Mather calls him, who achieved the downfall of our ancient government, and was followed with a sensible curse, through life and to his grave. On the other side was Bullivant, scattering jests and mockery as he rode along. Dudley came behind, with a downcast look, dreading, as well he might, to meet the indignant gaze of the people, who beheld him, their only countryman by birth, among the oppressors of his native land.

[1] Last of the New England Indian wars, 1676. King Philip (Metacomet) was sachem of Pokanoket.
[2] Formerly a place of execution, outside the walls of London. John Rogers, mentioned in the next paragraph, was burnt at the stake there in 1555.   [3] a reference to the massacre of several thousand Huguenots in Paris on St. Bartholomew's Day, August 24, 1572

[1] await

The captain of a frigate in the harbor, and two or three civil officers under the Crown, were also there. But the figure which most attracted the public eye, and stirred up the deepest feeling, was the Episcopal clergyman of King's Chapel, riding haughtily among the magistrates in his priestly vestments, the fitting representative of prelacy and persecution, the union of church and state, and all those abominations which had driven the Puritans to the wilderness. Another guard of soldiers, in double rank, brought up the rear.

The whole scene was a picture of the condition of New England, and its moral, the deformity of any government that does not grow out of the nature of things and the character of the people. On one side the religious multitude, with their sad visages and dark attire, and on the other, the group of despotic rulers, with the high churchman in the midst, and here and there a crucifix at their bosoms, all magnificently clad, flushed with wine, proud of unjust authority, and scoffing at the universal groan. And the mercenary soldiers, waiting but the word to deluge the street with blood, showed the only means by which obedience could be secured.

"O Lord of Hosts," cried a voice among the crowd, "provide a Champion for thy people!"

This ejaculation was loudly uttered, and served as a herald's cry, to introduce a remarkable personage. The crowd had rolled back, and were now huddled together nearly at the extremity of the street, while the soldiers had advanced no more than a third of its length. The intervening space was empty —a paved solitude, between lofty edifices, which threw almost a twilight shadow over it. Suddenly, there was seen the figure of an ancient man, who seemed to have emerged from among the people, and was walking by himself along the centre of the street, to confront the armed band. He wore the old Puritan dress, a dark cloak and a steeple-crowned hat, in the fashion of at least fifty years before, with a heavy sword upon his thigh, but a staff in his hand to assist the tremulous gait of age.

When at some distance from the multitude, the old man turned slowly round, displaying a face of antique majesty, rendered doubly venerable by the hoary beard that descended on his breast. He made a gesture at once of encouragement and warning, then turned again, and resumed his way.

"Who is this gray patriarch?" asked the young men of their sires.

"Who is this venerable brother?" asked the old men among themselves.

But none could make reply. The fathers of the people, those of fourscore years and upwards, were disturbed, deeming it strange that they should forget one of such evident authority, whom they must have known in their early days, the associate of Winthrop, and all the old councillors, giving laws, and making prayers, and leading them against the savage. The elderly men ought to have remembered him, too, with locks as gray in their youth, as their own were now. And the young! How could he have passed so utterly from their memories—that hoary sire, the relic of long-departed times, whose awful benediction had surely been bestowed on their uncovered heads, in childhood?

"Whence did he come? What is his purpose? Who can this old man be?" whispered the wondering crowd.

Meanwhile, the venerable stranger, staff in hand, was pursuing his solitary walk along the centre of the street. As he drew near the advancing soldiers, and as the roll of their drum came full upon his ear, the old man raised himself to a loftier mien, while the decrepitude of age seemed to fall from his shoulders, leaving him in gray but unbroken dignity. Now, he marched onward with a warrior's step, keeping time to the military music. Thus the aged form advanced on one side, and the whole parade of soldiers and magistrates on the other, till, when scarcely twenty yards remained between, the old man grasped his staff by the middle, and held it before him like a leader's truncheon.[1]

"Stand!" cried he.

The eye, the face, and attitude of command; the solemn, yet warlike peal of that voice, fit either to rule a host in the battlefield or be raised to God in prayer, were irresistible. At the old man's word and outstretched arm, the roll of the drum was hushed at once, and the

[1] a sign of authority

advancing line stood still. A tremulous enthusiasm seized upon the multitude. That stately form, combining the leader and the saint, so gray, so dimly seen, in such an ancient garb, could only belong to some old champion of the righteous cause, whom the oppressor's drum had summoned from his grave. They raised a shout of awe and exultation, and looked for the deliverance of New England.

The Governor, and the gentlemen of his party, perceiving themselves brought to an unexpected stand, rode hastily forward, as if they would have pressed their snorting and affrighted horses right against the hoary apparition. He, however, blenched not a step, but glancing his severe eye round the group, which half encompassed him, at last bent it sternly on Sir Edmund Andros. One would have thought that the dark old man was chief ruler there, and that the Governor and Council, with soldiers at their back, representing the whole power and authority of the Crown, had no alternative but obedience.

"What does this old fellow here?" cried Edward Randolph, fiercely. "On, Sir Edmund! Bid the soldiers forward, and give the dotard the same choice that you give all his countrymen—to stand aside or be trampled on!"

"Nay, nay, let us show respect to the good grandsire," said Bullivant, laughing. "See you not, he is some old round-headed dignitary, who hath lain asleep these thirty years, and knows nothing of the change of times? Doubtless, he thinks to put us down with a proclamation in Old Noll's[1] name!"

"Are you mad, old man?" demanded Sir Edmund Andros, in loud and harsh tones. "How dare you stay the march of King James's Governor?"

"I have stayed the march of a King himself, ere now," replied the gray figure, with stern composure. "I am here, Sir Governor, because the cry of an oppressed people hath disturbed me in my secret place; and beseeching this favor earnestly of the Lord, it was vouchsafed me to appear once again on earth, in the good old cause of his saints. And what speak

[1] a nickname applied contemptuously to Oliver Cromwell by his enemies

ye of James? There is no longer a Popish tyrant on the throne of England, and by to-morrow noon, his name shall be a byword in this very street, where ye would make it a word of terror. Back, thou that wast a Governor, back! With this night thy power is ended—tomorrow, the prison!—back, lest I foretell the scaffold!"

The people had been drawing nearer and nearer, and drinking in the words of their champion, who spoke in accents long disused, like one unaccustomed to converse, except with the dead of many years ago. But his voice stirred their souls. They confronted the soldiers, not wholly without arms, and ready to convert the very stones of the street into deadly weapons. Sir Edmund Andros looked at the old man; then he cast his hard and cruel eye over the multitude, and beheld them burning with that lurid wrath, so difficult to kindle or to quench; and again he fixed his gaze on the aged form, which stood obscurely in an open space, where neither friend nor foe had thrust himself. What were his thoughts, he uttered no word which might discover. But whether the oppressor were overawed by the Gray Champion's look, or perceived his peril in the threatening attitude of the people, it is certain that he gave back, and ordered his soldiers to commence a slow and guarded retreat. Before another sunset, the Governor, and all that rode so proudly with him, were prisoners, and long ere it was known that James had abdicated, King William was proclaimed throughout New England.

But where was the Gray Champion? Some reported that, when the troops had gone from King Street, and the people were thronging tumultuously in their rear, Bradstreet, the aged Governor, was seen to embrace a form more aged than his own. Others soberly affirmed, that while they marvelled at the venerable grandeur of his aspect, the old man had faded from their eyes, melting slowly into the hues of twilight, till, where he stood, there was an empty space. But all agreed that the hoary shape was gone. The men of that generation watched for his reappearance, in sunshine and in twilight, but never saw him more, nor knew when his funeral passed, nor where his gravestone was.

And who was the Gray Champion? Perhaps his name might be found in the records of that stern Court of Justice, which passed a sentence, too mighty for the age, but glorious in all aftertimes, for its humbling lesson to the monarch and its high example to the subject. I have heard, that whenever the descendants of the Puritans are to show the spirit of their sires, the old man appears again. When eighty years had passed, he walked once more in King Street. Five years later, in the twilight of an April morning, he stood on the green beside the meetinghouse, at Lexington, where now the obelisk of granite, with a slab of slate inlaid, commemorates the first fallen of the Revolution. And when our fathers were toiling at the breastwork on Bunker's Hill, all through that night the old warrior walked his rounds. Long, long may it be, ere he comes again! His hour is one of darkness, and adversity, and peril. But should domestic tyranny oppress us, or the invader's step pollute our soil, still may the Gray Champion come, for he is the type of New England's hereditary spirit; and his shadowy march, on the eve of danger, must ever be the pledge that New England's sons will vindicate their ancestry.

1835

YOUNG GOODMAN BROWN

Published in the *New England Magazine*, April, 1835. Reprinted in *Mosses from an Old Manse* (1846). When Hawthorne was in the Salem Custom House, his interest as a writer of fiction was in brooding over the past of the historic old place. He turned not to the active sea life of the town but to the Salem of witchcraft days. He re-created, with a psychologist's interest, the hysterical condition of a community when anybody and everybody, even the elect, might come under suspicion. Hawthorne does not say whether Young Goodman Brown had fallen asleep and dreamed what is narrated, or whether it had actuality. For the materials of the tale he is indebted to Cotton Mather's *Wonders of the Invisible World*.

YOUNG Goodman Brown came forth at sunset into the street at Salem village; but put his head back, after crossing the threshold, to exchange a parting kiss with his young wife. And Faith, as the wife was aptly named, thrust her own pretty head into the street, letting the wind play with the pink ribbons of her cap while she called to Goodman Brown.

"Dearest heart," whispered she, softly and rather sadly, when her lips were close to his ear, "prithee put off your journey until sunrise and sleep in your own bed tonight. A lone woman is troubled with such dreams and such thoughts that she's afeard of herself sometimes. Pray tarry with me this night, dear husband, of all nights in the year."

"My love and my Faith," replied young Goodman Brown, "of all nights in the year, this one night must I tarry away from thee. My journey, as thou callest it, forth and back again, must needs be done 'twixt now and sunrise. What, my sweet, pretty wife, dost thou doubt me already, and we but three months married?"

"Then God bless you!" said Faith, with the pink ribbons; "and may you find all well when you come back."

"Amen!" cried Goodman Brown. "Say thy prayers, dear Faith, and go to bed at dusk, and no harm will come to thee."

So they parted; and the young man pursued his way until, being about to turn the corner by the meetinghouse, he looked back and saw the head of Faith still peeping after him with a melancholy air, in spite of her pink ribbons.

"Poor little Faith!" thought he, for his heart smote him. "What a wretch am I to leave her on such an errand! She talks of dreams, too. Methought as she spoke there was trouble in her face, as if a dream had warned her what work is to be done tonight. But no, no; 'twould kill her to think it. Well, she's a blessed angel on earth; and after this one night I'll cling to her skirts and follow her to heaven."

With this excellent resolve for the future, Goodman Brown felt himself justified in making more haste on his present evil purpose. He had taken a dreary road, darkened by all the gloomiest trees of the forest, which barely stood aside to let the narrow path creep through, and closed immediately behind. It was all as lonely as could be; and there is this peculiarity in such a solitude, that the traveler knows not who may be concealed by the innumerable trunks and the thick boughs overhead; so that with lonely footsteps he may yet be passing through an unseen multitude.

"There may be a devilish Indian behind every tree," said Goodman Brown to himself; and he glanced fearfully behind him as he added, "What if the devil himself should be at my very elbow!"

His head being turned back, he passed a crook of the road, and looking forward again, beheld the figure of a man, in grave and decent attire, seated at the foot of an old tree. He arose at Goodman Brown's approach and walked onward side by side with him.

"You are late, Goodman Brown," said he. "The clock of the Old South was striking as I came through Boston, and that is full fifteen minutes agone."

"Faith kept me back a while," replied the young man, with a tremor in his voice, caused by the sudden appearance of his companion, though not wholly unexpected.

It was now deep dusk in the forest, and deepest in that part of it where these two were journeying. As nearly as could be discerned, the second traveler was about fifty years old, apparently in the same rank of life as Goodman Brown, and bearing a considerable resemblance to him, though perhaps more in expression than features. Still they might have been taken for father and son. And yet, though the elder person was as simply clad as the younger, and as simple in manner too, he had an indescribable air of one who knew the world, and who would not have felt abashed at the governor's dinner table or in King William's court, were it possible that his affairs should call him thither. But the only thing about him that could be fixed upon as remarkable was his staff, which bore the likeness of a great black snake, so curiously wrought that it might almost be seen to twist and wriggle itself like a living serpent. This, of course, must have been an ocular deception, assisted by the uncertain light.

"Come, Goodman Brown," cried his fellow-traveler, "this is a dull pace for the beginning of a journey. Take my staff, if you are so soon weary."

"Friend," said the other, exchanging his slow pace for a full stop, "having kept covenant by meeting thee here, it is my purpose now to return whence I came. I have scruples touching the matter thou wot'st of."

"Sayest thou so?" replied he of the serpent, smiling apart. "Let us walk on, nevertheless, reasoning as we go; and if I convince thee not thou shalt turn back. We are but a little way in the forest yet."

"Too far! too far!" exclaimed the goodman, unconsciously resuming his walk. "My father never went into the woods on such an errand, nor his father before him. We have been a race of honest men and good Christians since the days of the martyrs; and shall I be the first of the name of Brown that ever took this path and kept"—

"Such company, thou wouldst say," observed the elder person, interpreting his pause. "Well said, Goodman Brown! I have been as well acquainted with your family as with ever a one among the Puritans; and that's no trifle to say. I helped your grandfather, the constable, when he lashed the Quaker woman so smartly through the streets of Salem; and it was I that brought your father a pitch-pine knot, kindled at my own hearth, to set fire to an Indian village, in King Philip's war. They were my good friends, both; and many a pleasant walk have we had along this path, and returned merrily after midnight. I would fain be friends with you for their sake."

"If it be as thou sayest," replied Goodman Brown, "I marvel they never spoke of these matters; or, verily, I marvel not, seeing that the least rumor of the sort would have driven them from New England. We are a people of prayer, and good works to boot, and abide no such wickedness."

"Wickedness or not," said the traveler with the twisted staff, "I have a very general acquaintance here in New England. The deacons of many a church have drunk the communion wine with me; the selectmen of divers towns make me their chairman; and a majority of the Great and General Court[1] are firm supporters of my interest. The governor and I, too—but these are state secrets."

"Can this be so?" cried Goodman Brown, with a stare of amazement at his undisturbed companion. "Howbeit, I have nothing to do

[1] the colonial lawmaking body

with the governor and council; they have their own ways, and are no rule for a simple husbandman like me. But, were I to go on with thee, how should I meet the eye of that good old man, our minister, at Salem village? Oh, his voice would make me tremble both Sabbath day and lecture day."

Thus far the elder traveler had listened with due gravity; but now burst into a fit of irrepressible mirth, shaking himself so violently that his snakelike staff actually seemed to wriggle in sympathy.

"Ha! ha! ha!" shouted he again and again; then composing himself, "Well, go on, Goodman Brown, go on; but, prithee, don't kill me with laughing."

"Well, then, to end the matter at once," said Goodman Brown, considerably nettled, "there is my wife, Faith. It would break her dear little heart; and I'd rather break my own."

"Nay, if that be the case," answered the other, "e'en go thy ways, Goodman Brown. I would not for twenty old women like the one hobbling before us that Faith should come to any harm."

As he spoke he pointed his staff at a female figure on the path, in whom Goodman Brown recognized a very pious and exemplary dame, who had taught him his catechism in youth, and was still his moral and spiritual adviser, jointly with the minister and Deacon Gookin.

"A marvel, truly, that Goody Cloyse[1] should be so far in the wilderness at nightfall," said he. "But with your leave, friend, I shall take a cut through the woods until we have left this Christian woman behind. Being a stranger to you, she might ask whom I was consorting with and whither I was going."

"Be it so," said his fellow-traveler. "Betake you to the woods, and let me keep the path."

Accordingly the young man turned aside, but took care to watch his companion, who advanced softly along the road until he had come within a staff's length of the old dame. She, meanwhile, was making the best of her way, with singular speed for so aged a woman,

and mumbling some indistinct words—a prayer, doubtless—as she went. The traveler put forth his staff and touched her withered neck with what seemed the serpent's tail.

"The devil!" screamed the pious old lady.

"Then Goody Cloyse knows her old friend?" observed the traveler, confronting her and leaning on his writhing stick.

"Ah, forsooth, and is it your worship indeed?" cried the good dame. "Yea, truly is it, and in the very image of my old gossip, Goodman Brown, the grandfather of the silly fellow that now is. But—would your worship believe it?—my broomstick hath strangely disappeared, stolen, as I suspect, by that unhanged witch, Goody Cory, and that, too, when I was all anointed with the juice of smallage, and cinquefoil, and wolf's bane—"[1]

"Mingled with fine wheat and the fat of a newborn babe," said the shape of old Goodman Brown.

"Ah, your worship knows the recipe," cried the old lady, cackling aloud. "So, as I was saying, being all ready for the meeting, and no horse to ride on, I made up my mind to foot it; for they tell me there is a nice young man to be taken into communion tonight. But now your good worship will lend me your arm, and we shall be there in a twinkling."

"That can hardly be," answered her friend. "I may not spare you my arm, Goody Cloyse; but here is my staff, if you will."

So saying, he threw it down at her feet, where, perhaps, it assumed life, being one of the rods which its owner had formerly lent to the Egyptian magi. Of this fact, however, Goodman Brown could not take cognizance. He had cast up his eyes in astonishment, and, looking down again, beheld neither Goody Cloyse nor the serpentine staff, but his fellow-traveler alone, who waited for him as calmly as if nothing had happened.

"That old woman taught me my catechism," said the young man; and there was a world of meaning in this simple comment.

They continued to walk onward, while the elder traveler exhorted his companion to make good speed and persevere in the path, discoursing so aptly that his arguments seemed

---

[1] Goody Cloyse, Goody Cory, and Martha Carrier, all mentioned in this story, were women sentenced to death for witchcraft in 1692 by one of Hawthorne's remote ancestors.

[1] The more familiar names of the plants mentioned are wild celery, five-finger, and monkshood.

rather to spring up in the bosom of his auditor than to be suggested by himself. As they went, he plucked a branch of maple to serve for a walking stick, and began to strip it of the twigs and little boughs, which were wet with evening dew. The moment his fingers touched them they became strangely withered and dried up as with a week's sunshine. Thus the pair proceeded, at a good free pace, until suddenly, in a gloomy hollow of the road, Goodman Brown sat himself down on the stump of a tree and refused to go any farther.

"Friend," said he, stubbornly, "my mind is made up. Not another step will I budge on this errand. What if a wretched old woman do choose to go to the devil when I thought she was going to heaven: is that any reason why I should quit my dear Faith and go after her?"

"You will think better of this by and by," said his acquaintance, composedly. "Sit here and rest yourself a while; and when you feel like moving again, there is my staff to help you along."

Without more words, he threw his companion the maple stick, and was as speedily out of sight as if he had vanished into the deepening gloom. The young man sat a few moments by the roadside, applauding himself greatly, and thinking with how clear a conscience he should meet the minister in his morning walk, nor shrink from the eye of good old Deacon Gookin. And what calm sleep would be his that very night, which was to have been spent so wickedly, but so purely and sweetly now, in the arms of Faith! Amidst these pleasant and praiseworthy meditations, Goodman Brown heard the tramp of horses along the road, and deemed it advisable to conceal himself within the verge of the forest, conscious of the guilty purpose that had brought him thither, though now so happily turned from it.

On came the hoof tramps and the voices of the riders, two grave old voices, conversing soberly as they drew near. These mingled sounds appeared to pass along the road, within a few yards of the young man's hiding-place; but, owing doubtless to the depth of the gloom at that particular spot, neither the travelers nor their steeds were visible. Though their figures brushed the small boughs by the wayside, it could not be seen that they intercepted, even for a moment, the faint gleam from the strip of bright sky athwart which they must have passed. Goodman Brown alternately crouched and stood on tiptoe, pulling aside the branches and thrusting forth his head as far as he durst without discerning so much as a shadow. It vexed him the more, because he could have sworn, were such a thing possible, that he recognized the voices of the minister and Deacon Gookin, jogging along quietly, as they were wont to do, when bound to some ordination or ecclesiastical council. While yet within hearing, one of the riders stopped to pluck a switch.

"Of the two, reverend sir," said the voice like the deacon's, "I had rather miss an ordination dinner than tonight's meeting. They tell me that some of our community are to be here from Falmouth and beyond, and others from Connecticut and Rhode Island, besides several of the Indian powwows, who, after their fashion, know almost as much deviltry as the best of us. Moreover, there is a goodly young woman to be taken into communion."

"Mighty well, Deacon Gookin!" replied the solemn old tones of the minister. "Spur up, or we shall be late. Nothing can be done, you know, until I get on the ground."

The hoofs clattered again; and the voices, talking so strangely in the empty air, passed on through the forest, where no church had ever been gathered or solitary Christian prayed. Whither, then, could these holy men be journeying so deep into the heathen wilderness? Young Goodman Brown caught hold of a tree for support, being ready to sink down on the ground, faint and overburdened with the heavy sickness of his heart. He looked up to the sky, doubting whether there really was a heaven above him. Yet there was the blue arch, and the stars brightening in it.

"With heaven above and Faith below, I will yet stand firm against the devil!" cried Goodman Brown.

While he still gazed upward into the deep arch of the firmament and had lifted his hands to pray, a cloud, though no wind was stirring, hurried across the zenith and hid the brightening stars. The blue sky was still visible, except directly overhead, where this black mass of cloud was sweeping swiftly northward. Aloft in the air, as if from the depths of the cloud, came a confused and doubtful sound of voices. Once the listener fancied that he could distinguish the accents of townspeople of his own, men and women, both pious and ungodly, many of whom he had met at the communion table, and had seen others rioting at the tavern. The next moment, so indistinct were the sounds, he doubted whether he had heard aught but the murmur of the old forest, whispering without a wind. Then came a stronger swell of those familiar tones, heard daily in the sunshine at Salem village, but never until now from a cloud of night. There was one voice, of a young woman, uttering lamentations, yet with an uncertain sorrow, and entreating for some favor, which, perhaps it would grieve her to obtain; and all the unseen multitude, both saints and sinners, seemed to encourage her onward.

"Faith!" shouted Goodman Brown, in a voice of agony and desperation; and the echoes of the forest mocked him, crying, "Faith! Faith!" as if bewildered wretches were seeking her all through the wilderness.

The cry of grief, rage, and terror was yet piercing the night, when the unhappy husband held his breath for a response. There was a scream, drowned immediately in a louder murmur of voices, fading into far-off laughter, as the dark cloud swept away, leaving the clear and silent sky above Goodman Brown. But something fluttered lightly down through the air and caught on the branch of a tree. The young man seized it, and beheld a pink ribbon.

"My Faith is gone!" cried he, after one stupefied moment. "There is no good on earth; and sin is but a name. Come, devil; for to thee is this world given."

And, maddened with despair, so that he laughed loud and long, did Goodman Brown grasp his staff and set forth again, at such a rate that he seemed to fly along the forest path rather than to walk or run. The road grew wilder and drearier and more faintly traced, and vanished at length, leaving him in the heart of the dark wilderness, still rushing onward with the instinct that guides mortal man to evil. The whole forest was peopled with frightful sounds—the creaking of the trees,

the howling of wild beasts, and the yell of Indians; while sometimes the wind tolled like a distant church bell, and sometimes gave a broad roar around the traveler, as if all Nature were laughing him to scorn. But he was himself the chief horror of the scene, and shrank not from its other horrors.

"Ha! ha! ha!" roared Goodman Brown when the wind laughed at him. "Let us hear which will laugh loudest. Think not to frighten me with your deviltry. Come witch, come wizard, come Indian powwow, come devil himself, and here comes Goodman Brown. You may as well fear him as he fear you."

In truth, all through the haunted forest there could be nothing more frightful than the figure of Goodman Brown. On he flew among the black pines, brandishing his staff with frenzied gestures, now giving vent to an inspiration of horrid blasphemy, and now shouting forth such laughter as set all the echoes of the forest laughing like demons around him. The fiend in his own shape is less hideous than when he rages in the breast of man. Thus sped the demoniac on his course, until, quivering among the trees, he saw a red light before him, as when the felled trunks and branches of a clearing have been set on fire, and throw up their lurid blaze against the sky, at the hour of midnight. He paused, in a lull of the tempest that had driven him onward, and heard the swell of what seemed a hymn, rolling solemnly from a distance with the weight of many voices. He knew the tune; it was a familiar one in the choir of the village meetinghouse. The verse died heavily away, and was lengthened by a chorus, not of human voices, but of all the sounds of the benighted wilderness pealing in awful harmony together. Goodman Brown cried out, and his cry was lost to his own ear by its unison with the cry of the desert.

In the interval of silence he stole forward until the light glared full upon his eyes. At one extremity of an open space, hemmed in by the dark wall of the forest, arose a rock, bearing some rude, natural resemblance either to an altar or a pulpit, and surrounded by four blazing pines, their tops aflame, their stems untouched, like candles at an evening meeting. The mass of foliage that had overgrown the summit of the rock was all on fire, blazing high into the night and fitfully illuminating the whole field. Each pendent twig and leafy festoon was in a blaze. As the red light arose and fell, a numerous congregation alternately shone forth, then disappeared in shadow, and again grew, as it were, out of the darkness, peopling the heart of the solitary woods at once.

"A grave and dark-clad company," quoth Goodman Brown.

In truth they were such. Among them, quivering to and fro between gloom and splendor, appeared faces that would be seen next day at the council board of the province, and others which, Sabbath after Sabbath, looked devoutly heavenward, and benignantly over the crowded pews, from the holiest pulpits in the land. Some affirm that the lady of the governor was there. At least there were high dames well known to her, and wives of honored husbands, and widows, a great multitude, and ancient maidens, all of excellent repute, and fair young girls, who trembled lest their mothers should espy them. Either the sudden gleams of light flashing over the obscure field bedazzled Goodman Brown, or he recognized a score of the church members of Salem village famous for their special sanctity. Good old Deacon Gookin had arrived, and waited at the skirts of that venerable saint, his revered pastor. But, irreverently consorting with these grave, reputable, and pious people, these elders of the church, these chaste dames and dewy virgins, there were men of dissolute lives and women of spotted fame, wretches given over to all mean and filthy vice, and suspected even of horrid crimes. It was strange to see that the good shrank not from the wicked, nor were the sinners abashed by the saints. Scattered also among their pale-faced enemies were the Indian priests, or powwows, who had often scared their native forest with more hideous incantations than any known to English witchcraft.

"But where is Faith?" thought Goodman Brown; and, as hope came into his heart, he trembled.

Another verse of the hymn arose, a slow and mournful strain, such as the pious love, but joined to words which expressed all that our nature can conceive of sin, and darkly hinted at far more. Unfathomable to mere mortals is the lore of fiends. Verse after verse was sung; and still the chorus of the desert swelled between like the deepest tone of a mighty organ; and with the final peal of that dreadful anthem there came a sound, as if the roaring wind, the rushing streams, the howling beasts, and every other voice of the unconcerted wilderness were mingling and according with the voice of guilty man in homage to the prince of all. The four blazing pines threw up a loftier flame, and obscurely discovered shapes and visages of horror on the smoke wreaths above the impious assembly. At the same moment the fire on the rock shot redly forth and formed a glowing arch above its base, where now appeared a figure. With reverence be it spoken, the figure bore no slight similitude, both in garb and manner, to some grave divine of the New England churches.

"Bring forth the converts!" cried a voice that echoed through the field and rolled into the forest.

At the word, Goodman Brown stepped forth from the shadow of the trees and approached the congregation, with whom he felt a loathful brotherhood by the sympathy of all that was wicked in his heart. He could have well-nigh sworn that the shape of his own dead father beckoned him to advance, looking downward from a smoke wreath, while a woman, with dim features of despair, threw out her hand to warn him back. Was it his mother? But he had no power to retreat one step, nor to resist, even in thought, when the minister and good old Deacon Gookin seized his arms and led him to the blazing rock. Thither came also the slender form of a veiled female, led between Goody Cloyse, that pious teacher of the catechism, and Martha Carrier, who had received the devil's promise to be queen of hell. A rampant hag was she. And there stood the proselytes beneath the canopy of fire.

"Welcome, my children," said the dark figure, "to the communion of your race. Ye have found thus young your nature and your destiny. My children, look behind you!"

They turned; and flashing forth, as it were,

in a sheet of flame, the fiend worshippers were seen; the smile of welcome gleamed darkly on every visage.

"There," resumed the sable form, "are all whom ye have reverenced from youth. Ye deemed them holier than yourselves, and shrank from your own sin, contrasting it with their lives of righteousness and prayerful aspirations heavenward. Yet here are they all in my worshipping assembly. This night it shall be granted you to know their secret deeds; how hoary-bearded elders of the church have whispered wanton words to the young maids of their households; how many a woman, eager for widows' weeds, has given her husband a drink at bedtime and let him sleep his last sleep in her bosom; how beardless youths have made haste to inherit their fathers' wealth; and how fair damsels—blush not, sweet ones—have dug little graves in the garden, and bidden me, the sole guest, to an infant's funeral. By the sympathy of your human hearts for sin ye shall scent out all the places—whether in church, bedchamber, street, field, or forest—where crime has been committed, and shall exult to behold the whole earth one stain of guilt, one mighty blood spot. Far more than this. It shall be yours to penetrate, in every bosom, the deep mystery of sin, the fountain of all wicked arts, and which inexhaustibly supplies more evil impulses than human power—than my power at its utmost—can make manifest in deeds. And now, my children, look upon each other."

They did so; and by the blaze of the hell-kindled torches, the wretched man beheld his Faith, and the wife her husband, trembling before that unhallowed altar.

"Lo, there ye stand, my children," said the figure, in a deep and solemn tone, almost sad with its despairing awfulness, as if his once angelic nature could yet mourn for our miserable race. "Depending upon one another's hearts, ye had still hoped that virtue were not all a dream. Now are ye undeceived. Evil is the nature of mankind. Evil must be your only happiness. Welcome again, my children, to the communion of your race."

"Welcome," repeated the fiend worshippers, in one cry of despair and triumph.

And there they stood, the only pair, as it seemed, who were yet hesitating on the verge of wickedness in this dark world. A basin was hollowed, naturally, in the rock. Did it contain water, reddened by the lurid light? or was it blood? or, perchance, a liquid flame? Herein did the shape of evil dip his hand and prepare to lay the mark of baptism upon their foreheads, that they might be partakers of the mystery of sin, more conscious of the secret guilt of others, both in deed and thought, than they could now be of their own. The husband cast one look at his pale wife, and Faith at him. What polluted wretches would the next glance show them to each other, shuddering alike at what they disclosed and what they saw!

"Faith! Faith!" cried the husband, "look up to heaven, and resist the wicked one."

Whether Faith obeyed he knew not. Hardly had he spoken when he found himself amid calm night and solitude, listening to a roar of the wind which died heavily away through the forest. He staggered against the rock, and felt it chill and damp; while a hanging twig, that had been all on fire, besprinkled his cheek with the coldest dew.

The next morning young Goodman Brown came slowly into the street of Salem village, staring around him like a bewildered man. The good old minister was taking a walk along the graveyard to get an appetite for breakfast and meditate his sermon, and bestowed a blessing, as he passed, on Goodman Brown. He shrank from the venerable saint as if to avoid an anathema. Old Deacon Gookin was at domestic worship, and the holy words of his prayer were heard through the open window. "What God doth the wizard pray to?" quoth Goodman Brown. Goody Cloyse, that excellent old Christian, stood in the early sunshine at her own lattice, catechizing a little girl who had brought her a pint of morning's milk. Goodman Brown snatched away the child as from the grasp of the fiend himself. Turning the corner by the meetinghouse, he spied the head of Faith, with the pink ribbons, gazing anxiously forth, and bursting into such joy at sight of him that she skipped along the street and almost kissed her husband before the whole village. But

Goodman Brown looked sternly and sadly into her face, and passed on without a greeting.

Had Goodman Brown fallen asleep in the forest and only dreamed a wild dream of a witch-meeting?

Be it so if you will; but, alas! it was a dream of evil omen for young Goodman Brown. A stern, a sad, a darkly meditative, a distrustful, if not a desperate man did he become from the night of that fearful dream. On the Sabbath day, when the congregation were singing a holy psalm, he could not listen because an anthem of sin rushed loudly upon his ear and drowned all the blessed strain. When the minister spoke from the pulpit with power and fervid eloquence, and, with his hand on the open Bible, of the sacred truths of our religion, and of saint-like lives and triumphant deaths, and of future bliss or misery unutterable, then did Goodman Brown turn pale, dreading lest the roof should thunder down upon the gray blasphemer and his hearers. Often, awaking suddenly at midnight, he shrank from the bosom of Faith; and at morning or eventide, when the family knelt down at prayer, he scowled and muttered to himself, and gazed sternly at his wife, and turned away. And when he had lived long, and was borne to his grave a hoary corpse, followed by Faith, an aged woman, and children and grandchildren, a goodly procession, besides neighbors not a few, they carved no hopeful verse upon his tombstone, for his dying hour was gloom.

1835

THE MAYPOLE OF MERRY MOUNT

Published in *The Token*, 1836. Colonial material has now become literary material. Captain Wollaston founded a colony near Plymouth village in 1625. When he went to Virginia, Thomas Morton, a seller of firearms and spirits to the Indians, succeeded him as director of Merry Mount. John Endicott and men from Salem visited the colony in Morton's absence, cut down the "idoll Maypole," admonished the colonists to become more sober in behavior, and renamed the place Mount Dagon. For a discussion of the sources of this tale, a dramatic pageant presenting the Merry-mounters as the expression of the happy acceptance of life and the Puritans as the sober rejection of it, see G. H. Orians, *Modern Language Notes*, LIII, 159–167 (March, 1938). The incident was made the subject of an opera by Howard Hanson, given at the Metropolitan Opera House in New York, February, 1934, with Lawrence Tibbett, baritone, in the leading role.

There is an admirable foundation for a philosophic romance in the curious history of the early settlement of Mount Wollaston, or Merry Mount. In the slight sketch here attempted, the facts, recorded on the grave pages of our New England annalists, have wrought themselves, almost spontaneously, into a sort of allegory. The masques, mummeries, and festive customs, described in the text, are in accordance with the manners of the age. Authority on these points may be found in Strutt's *Book of English Sports and Pastimes*.

[*Hawthorne's note.*]

BRIGHT were the days at Merry Mount, when the Maypole was the banner staff of that gay colony! They who reared it, should their banner be triumphant, were to pour sunshine over New England's rugged hills, and scatter flower seeds throughout the soil. Jollity and gloom were contending for an empire. Midsummer eve[1] had come, bringing deep verdure to the forest, and roses in her lap, of a more vivid hue than the tender buds of Spring. But May, or her mirthful spirit, dwelt all the year round at Merry Mount, sporting with the Summer months, and revelling with Autumn, and basking in the glow of Winter's fireside. Through a world of toil and care she flitted with a dreamlike smile, and came hither to find a home among the lightsome hearts of Merry Mount.

Never had the Maypole been so gayly decked as at sunset on midsummer eve. This venerated emblem was a pine-tree, which had preserved the slender grace of youth, while it equalled the loftiest height of the old wood monarchs. From its top streamed a silken banner, colored like the rainbow. Down nearly to the ground the pole was dressed with birchen boughs, and others of the liveliest green, and some with silvery leaves, fastened by ribbons that fluttered in fantastic knots of

[1] June 23, same date as St. John's Eve, referred to later in the story.

twenty different colors, but no sad ones. Garden flowers, and blossoms of the wilderness, laughed gladly forth amid the verdure, so fresh and dewy that they must have grown by magic on that happy pine-tree. Where this green and flowery splendor terminated, the shaft of the Maypole was stained with the seven brilliant hues of the banner at its top. On the lowest green bough hung an abundant wreath of roses, some that had been gathered in the sunniest spots of the forest, and others, of still richer blush, which the colonists had reared from English seed. O, people of the Golden Age, the chief of your husbandry was to raise flowers!

But what was the wild throng that stood hand in hand about the Maypole? It could not be that the fauns and nymphs, when driven from their classic groves and homes of ancient fable, had sought refuge, as all the persecuted did, in the fresh woods of the West. These were Gothic monsters, though perhaps of Grecian ancestry. On the shoulders of a comely youth uprose the head and branching antlers of a stag; a second, human in all other points, had the grim visage of a wolf; a third, still with the trunk and limbs of a mortal man, showed the beard and horns of a venerable he-goat. There was the likeness of a bear erect, brute in all but his hind legs, which were adorned with pink silk stockings. And here again, almost as wondrous, stood a real bear of the dark forest, lending each of his forepaws to the grasp of a human hand, and as ready for the dance as any in that circle. His inferior nature rose halfway, to meet his companions as they stooped. Other faces wore the similitude of man or woman, but distorted or extravagant, with red noses pendulous before their mouths, which seemed of awful depth, and stretched from ear to ear in an eternal fit of laughter. Here might be seen the Salvage Man, well known in heraldry, hairy as a baboon, and girdled with green leaves. By his side, a noble figure, but still a counterfeit, appeared an Indian hunter, with feathery crest and wampum belt. Many of this strange company wore fools-caps, and had little bells appended to their garments, tinkling with a silvery sound, responsive to the inaudible music of their gleesome spirits.

Some youths and maidens were of soberer garb, yet well maintained their places in the irregular throng by the expression of wild revelry upon their features. Such were the colonists of Merry Mount, as they stood in the broad smile of sunset round their venerated Maypole.

Had a wanderer, bewildered in the melancholy forest, heard their mirth, and stolen a half-affrighted glance, he might have fancied them the crew of Comus,[1] some already transformed to brutes, some midway between man and beast, and the others rioting in the flow of tipsy jollity that foreran the change. But a band of Puritans, who watched the scene, invisible themselves, compared the masques to those devils and ruined souls with whom their superstition peopled the black wilderness.

Within the ring of monsters appeared the two airiest forms that had ever trodden on any more solid footing than a purple and golden cloud. One was a youth in glistening apparel, with a scarf of the rainbow pattern crosswise on his breast. His right hand held a gilded staff, the ensign of high dignity among the revellers, and his left grasped the slender fingers of a fair maiden, not less gayly decorated than himself. Bright roses glowed in contrast with the dark and glossy curls of each, and were scattered round their feet, or had sprung up spontaneously there. Behind this lightsome couple, so close to the Maypole that its boughs shaded his jovial face, stood the figure of an English priest, canonically dressed, yet decked with flowers, in heathen fashion, and wearing a chaplet of the native vine leaves. By the riot of his rolling eye, and the pagan decorations of his holy garb, he seemed the wildest monster there, and the very Comus of the crew.

"Votaries of the Maypole," cried the flower-decked priest, "merrily, all day long, have the woods echoed to your mirth. But be this your merriest hour, my hearts! Lo, here stand the Lord and Lady of the May, whom I, a clerk of Oxford, and high priest of Merry Mount, am presently to join in holy matrimony. Up with your nimble spirits, ye morris-

[1] The god of festive joy and mirth in Milton's *Comus* (lines 92 ff.) is represented as the son of Circe and Bacchus.

dancers, green men, and glee maidens, bears and wolves, and horned gentlemen! Come; a chorus now, rich with the old mirth of Merry England, and the wilder glee of this fresh forest; and then a dance, to show the youthful pair what life is made of, and how airily they should go through it! All ye that love the Maypole, lend your voices to the nuptial song of the Lord and Lady of the May!"

This wedlock was more serious than most affairs of Merry Mount, where jest and delusion, trick and fantasy, kept up a continual carnival. The Lord and Lady of the May, though their titles must be laid down at sunset, were really and truly to be partners for the dance of life, beginning the measure that same bright eve. The wreath of roses, that hung from the lowest green bough of the Maypole, had been twined for them, and would be thrown over both their heads, in symbol of their flowery union. When the priest had spoken, therefore, a riotous uproar burst from the rout of monstrous figures.

"Begin you the stave, reverend Sir," cried they all; "and never did the woods ring to such a merry peal as we of the Maypole shall send up!"

Immediately a prelude of pipe, cithern, and viol, touched with practiced minstrelsy, began to play from a neighboring thicket, in such a mirthful cadence that the boughs of the Maypole quivered to the sound. But the May Lord, he of the gilded staff, chancing to look into his Lady's eyes, was wonder struck at the almost pensive glance that met his own.

"Edith, sweet Lady of the May," whispered he reproachfully, "is yon wreath of roses a garland to hang above our graves, that you look so sad? O, Edith, this is our golden time! Tarnish it not by any pensive shadow of the mind; for it may be that nothing of futurity will be brighter than the mere remembrance of what is now passing."

"That was the very thought that saddened me! How came it in your mind too?" said Edith, in a still lower tone than he, for it was high treason to be sad at Merry Mount. "Therefore do I sigh amid this festive music. And besides, dear Edgar, I struggle as with a dream, and fancy that these shapes of our jovial friends are visionary, and their mirth unreal, and that we are no true Lord and Lady of the May. What is the mystery in my heart?"

Just then, as if a spell had loosened them, down came a little shower of withering rose leaves from the Maypole. Alas, for the young lovers! No sooner had their hearts glowed with real passion than they were sensible of something vague and unsubstantial in their former pleasures, and felt a dreary presentiment of inevitable change. From the moment that they truly loved, they had subjected themselves to earth's doom of care and sorrow, and troubled joy, and had no more a home at Merry Mount. That was Edith's mystery. Now leave we the priest to marry them, and the masquers to sport round the Maypole, till the last sunbeam be withdrawn from its summit, and the shadows of the forest mingle gloomily in the dance. Meanwhile, we may discover who these gay people were.

Two hundred years ago, and more, the old world and its inhabitants became mutually weary of each other. Men voyaged by thousands to the West: some to barter glass beads, and such like jewels, for the furs of the Indian hunter; some to conquer virgin empires; and one stern band to pray. But none of these motives had much weight with the colonists of Merry Mount. Their leaders were men who had sported so long with life, that when Thought and Wisdom came, even these unwelcome guests were led astray by the crowd of vanities which they should have put to flight. Erring Thought and perverted Wisdom were made to put on masques, and play the fool. The men of whom we speak, after losing the heart's fresh gayety, imagined a wild philosophy of pleasure, and came hither to act out their latest daydream. They gathered followers from all that giddy tribe whose whole life is like the festal days of soberer men. In their train were minstrels, not unknown in London streets: wandering players, whose theaters had been the halls of noblemen; mummers, rope-dancers, and mountebanks, who would long be missed at wakes, church ales,[1] and fairs; in a word, mirth makers

---

[1] festivals, named from the liquor drunk on such occasions

of every sort, such as abounded in that age, but now began to be discountenanced by the rapid growth of Puritanism. Light had their footsteps been on land, and as lightly they came across the sea. Many had been maddened by their previous troubles into a gay despair; others were as madly gay in the flush of youth, like the May Lord and his Lady; but whatever might be the quality of their mirth, old and young were gay at Merry Mount. The young deemed themselves happy. The elder spirits, if they knew that mirth was but the counterfeit of happiness, yet followed the false shadow wilfully, because at least her garments glittered brightest. Sworn triflers of a lifetime, they would not venture among the sober truths of life not even to be truly blest.

All the hereditary pastimes of Old England were transplanted hither. The King of Christmas was duly crowned, and the Lord of Misrule[1] bore potent sway. On the Eve of St. John, they felled whole acres of the forest to make bonfires, and danced by the blaze all night, crowned with garlands, and throwing flowers into the flame. At harvest time, though their crop was of the smallest, they made an image with the sheaves of Indian corn, and wreathed it with autumnal garlands, and bore it home triumphantly. But what chiefly characterized the colonists of Merry Mount was their veneration for the Maypole. It has made their true history a poet's tale. Spring decked the hallowed emblem with young blossoms and fresh green boughs; Summer brought roses of the deepest blush, and the perfected foliage of the forest; Autumn enriched it with that red and yellow gorgeousness which converts each wildwood leaf into a painted flower; and Winter silvered it with sleet, and hung it round with icicles, till it flashed in the cold sunshine, itself a frozen sunbeam. Thus each alternate season did homage to the Maypole, and paid it a tribute of its own richest splendor. Its votaries danced round it, once, at least, in every month; sometimes they called it their religion, or their altar; but always, it was the banner staff of Merry Mount.

Unfortunately, there were men in the new world of a sterner faith than these Maypole worshippers. Not far from Merry Mount was a settlement of Puritans, most dismal wretches, who said their prayers before daylight, and then wrought in the forest or the cornfield till evening made it prayer time again. Their weapons were always at hand to shoot down the straggling savage. When they met in conclave, it was never to keep up the old English mirth, but to hear sermons three hours long, or to proclaim bounties on the heads of wolves and the scalps of Indians. Their festivals were fast days, and their chief pastime the singing of psalms. Woe to the youth or maiden who did but dream of a dance! The selectman nodded to the constable; and there sat the light-heeled reprobate in the stocks; or if he danced, it was round the whipping-post, which might be termed the Puritan Maypole.

A party of these grim Puritans, toiling through the difficult woods, each with a horseload of iron armor to burden his footsteps, would sometimes draw near the sunny precincts of Merry Mount. There were the silken colonists, sporting round their Maypole; perhaps teaching a bear to dance, or striving to communicate their mirth to the grave Indian; or masquerading in the skins of deer and wolves, which they had hunted for that especial purpose. Often, the whole colony were playing at blindman's buff, magistrates and all, with their eyes bandaged, except a single scapegoat, whom the blinded sinners pursued by the tinkling of the bells at his garments. Once, it is said, they were seen following a flower-decked corpse, with merriment and festive music, to his grave. But did the dead man laugh? In their quietest times, they sang ballads and told tales, for the edification of their pious visitors; or perplexed them with juggling tricks; or grinned at them through horse collars; and when sport itself grew wearisome, they made game of their own stupidity, and began a yawning match. At the very least of these enormities, the men of iron shook their heads and frowned so darkly that the revellers looked up, imagining that a momentary cloud had overcast the sunshine, which was to be perpetual there. On the other hand, the Puritans affirmed that, when a psalm was pealing from their place of

[1] the master of the Christmas revels

worship, the echo which the forest sent them back seemed often like the chorus of a jolly catch, closing with a roar of laughter. Who but the fiend, and his bond slaves, the crew of Merry Mount, had thus disturbed them? In due time, a feud arose, stern and bitter on one side, and as serious on the other as anything could be among such light spirits as had sworn allegiance to the Maypole. The future complexion of New England was involved in this important quarrel. Should the grizzly saints establish their jurisdiction over the gay sinners, then would their spirits darken all the clime and make it a land of clouded visages, of hard toil, of sermon and psalm forever. But should the banner staff of Merry Mount be fortunate, sunshine would break upon the hills, and flowers would beautify the forest, and late posterity do homage to the Maypole.

After these authentic passages from history, we return to the nuptials of the Lord and Lady of the May. Alas! we have delayed too long, and must darken our tale too suddenly. As we glance again at the Maypole, a solitary sunbeam is fading from the summit, and leaves only a faint, golden tinge blended with the hues of the rainbow banner. Even that dim light is now withdrawn, relinquishing the whole domain of Merry Mount to the evening gloom, which has rushed so instantaneously from the black surrounding woods. But some of these black shadows have rushed forth in human shape.

Yes, with the setting sun, the last day of mirth had passed from Merry Mount. The ring of gay masquers was disordered and broken; the stag lowered his antlers in dismay; the wolf grew weaker than a lamb; the bells of the morris-dancers tinkled with tremulous affright. The Puritans had played a characteristic part in the Maypole mummeries. Their darksome figures were intermixed with the wild shapes of their foes, and made the scene a picture of the moment, when waking thoughts start up amid the scattered fantasies of a dream. The leader of the hostile party stood in the center of the circle, while the rout of monsters cowered around him, like evil spirits in the presence of a dread magician. No fantastic foolery could look him in the face. So stern was the energy of his aspect,

that the whole man, visage, frame, and soul, seemed wrought of iron, gifted with life and thought, yet all of one substance with his headpiece and breastplate. It was the Puritan of Puritans; it was Endicott himself!

"Stand off, priest of Baal!" said he, with a grim frown, and laying no reverent hand upon the surplice. "I know thee, Blackstone![1] Thou art the man who couldst not abide the rule even of thine own corrupted church, and hast come hither to preach iniquity, and to give example of it in thy life. But now shall it be seen that the Lord hath sanctified this wilderness for his peculiar people. Woe unto them that would defile it! And first, for this flower-decked abomination, the altar of thy worship!"

And with his keen sword Endicott assaulted the hallowed Maypole. Nor long did it resist his arm. It groaned with a dismal sound; it showered leaves and rosebuds upon the remorseless enthusiast; and finally, with all its green boughs and ribbons and flowers, symbolic of departed pleasures, down fell the banner staff of Merry Mount. As it sank, tradition says, the evening sky grew darker, and the woods threw forth a more somber shadow.

"There," cried Endicott, looking triumphantly on his work, "there lies the only Maypole in New England! The thought is strong within me that, by its fall, is shadowed forth the fate of light and idle mirth makers, amongst us and our posterity. Amen, saith John Endicott."

"Amen!" echoed his followers.

But the votaries of the Maypole gave one groan for their idol. At the sound, the Puritan leader glanced at the crew of Comus, each a figure of broad mirth, yet, at this moment, strangely expressive of sorrow and dismay.

"Valiant captain," quoth Peter Palfrey, the Ancient[2] of the band, "what order shall be taken with the prisoners?"

"I thought not to repent me of cutting

[1] Did Governor Endicott speak less positively, we should suspect a mistake here. The Rev. Mr. Blackstone, though an eccentric, is not known to have been an immoral man. We rather doubt his identity with the priest of Merry Mount. [*Hawthorne's note.*]

[2] standard-bearer

down a Maypole," replied Endicott, "yet now I could find in my heart to plant it again, and give each of these bestial pagans one other dance round their idol. It would have served rarely for a whipping-post!"

"But there are pine-trees enow," suggested the lieutenant.

"True, good Ancient," said the leader. "Wherefore, bind the heathen crew, and bestow on them a small matter of stripes apiece, as earnest of our future justice. Set some of the rogues in the stocks to rest themselves, so soon as Providence shall bring us to one of our own well-ordered settlements, where such accommodations may be found. Further penalties, such as branding and cropping of ears, shall be thought of hereafter."

"How many stripes for the priest?" inquired Ancient Palfrey.

"None as yet," answered Endicott, bending his iron frown upon the culprit. "It must be for the Great and General Court to determine, whether stripes and long imprisonment, and other grievous penalty, may atone for his transgressions. Let him look to himself! For such as violate our civil order, it may be permitted us to show mercy. But woe to the wretch that troubleth our religion!"

"And this dancing bear," resumed the officer. "Must he share the stripes of his fellows?"

"Shoot him through the head!" said the energetic Puritan. "I suspect witchcraft in the beast."

"Here be a couple of shining ones," continued Peter Palfrey, pointing his weapon at the Lord and Lady of the May. "They seem to be of high station among these misdoers. Methinks their dignity will not be fitted with less than a double share of stripes."

Endicott rested on his sword, and closely surveyed the dress and aspect of the hapless pair. There they stood, pale, downcast, and apprehensive. Yet there was an air of mutual support, and of pure affection, seeking aid and giving it, that showed them to be man and wife, with the sanction of priest upon their love. The youth, in the peril of the moment, had dropped his gilded staff, and thrown his arm about the Lady of the May, who leaned against his breast, too lightly to

burden him, but with weight enough to express that their destinies were linked together, for good or evil. They looked first at each other, and then into the grim captain's face. There they stood, in the first hour of wedlock, while the idle pleasures, of which their companions were the emblems, had given place to the sternest cares of life, personified by the dark Puritans. But never had their youthful beauty seemed so pure and high as when its glow was chastened by adversity.

"Youth," said Endicott, "ye stand in an evil case, thou and thy maiden wife. Make ready presently, for I am minded that ye shall both have a token to remember your wedding day!"

"Stern man," cried the May Lord, "how can I move thee? Were the means at hand, I would resist to the death. Being powerless, I entreat! Do with me as thou wilt, but let Edith go untouched!"

"Not so," replied the immitigable zealot. "We are not wont to show an idle courtesy to that sex which requireth the stricter discipline. What sayest thou, maid? Shall thy silken bridegroom suffer thy share of the penalty, besides his own?"

"Be it death," said Edith, "and lay it all on me!"

Truly, as Endicott had said, the poor lovers stood in a woeful case. Their foes were triumphant, their friends captive and abased, their home desolate, the benighted wilderness around them, and a rigorous destiny, in the shape of the Puritan leader, their only guide. Yet the deepening twilight could not altogether conceal that the iron man was softened; he smiled at the fair spectacle of early love; he almost sighed for the inevitable blight of early hopes.

"The troubles of life have come hastily on this young couple," observed Endicott. "We will see how they comport themselves under their present trials ere we burden them with greater. If, among the spoil, there be any garments of a more decent fashion, let them be put upon this May Lord and his Lady, instead of their glistening vanities. Look to it, some of you."

"And shall not the youth's hair be cut?" asked Peter Palfrey, looking with abhorrence at the lovelock and long glossy curls of the young man.

"Crop it forthwith, and that in the true pumpkin-shell fashion," answered the captain. "Then bring them along with us, but more gently than their fellows. There be qualities in the youth, which may make him valiant to fight, and sober to toil, and pious to pray; and in the maiden, that may fit her to become a mother in our Israel, bringing up babes in better nurture than her own hath been. Nor think ye, young ones, that they are the happiest, even in our lifetime of a moment, who misspend it in dancing round a Maypole!"

And Endicott, the severest Puritan of all who laid the rock foundation of New England, lifted the wreath of roses from the ruin of the Maypole, and threw it, with his own gauntleted hand, over the heads of the Lord and Lady of the May. It was a deed of prophecy. As the moral gloom of the world overpowers all systematic gayety, even so was their home of wild mirth made desolate amid the sad forest. They returned to it no more. But as their flowery garland was wreathed of the brightest roses that had grown there, so, in the tie that united them, were intertwined all the purest and best of their early joys. They went heavenward, supporting each other along the difficult path which it was their lot to tread, and never wasted one regretful thought on the vanities of Merry Mount.

1836

DR. HEIDEGGER'S EXPERIMENT

Called "The Fountain of Youth" in the *Knickerbocker Magazine*, January, 1837. Renamed when reprinted in *Twice-Told Tales*. Its leading idea is the restoration of youth and its effect on the actions of four old persons who temporarily regain it, yet show no betterment of character. The moral it suggests is the futility of endeavor to escape from the common lot. The drinking of an elixir bringing immortal youth, which he had perhaps from William Godwin's *St. Leon*, is a favorite subject with Hawthorne. There are entries on the subject in the *Notebooks* and it plays a part in "A Virtuoso's Collection" (1842), "The Birthmark" (1843), and in *Dr. Grimshawe's Secret* which he left unfinished at his death.

THAT very singular man, old Dr. Heidegger, once invited four venerable friends to meet him in his study. There were three white-bearded gentlemen, Mr. Medbourne, Colonel Killigrew, and Mr. Gascoigne, and a withered gentlewoman, whose name was the Widow Wycherly. They were all melancholy old creatures, who had been unfortunate in life, and whose greatest misfortune it was that they were not long ago in their graves. Mr. Medbourne, in the vigor of his age, had been a prosperous merchant, but had lost his all by a frantic speculation, and was now little better than a mendicant. Colonel Killigrew had wasted his best years, and his health and substance, in the pursuit of sinful pleasures which had given birth to a brood of pains, such as the gout, and divers other torments of soul and body. Mr. Gascoigne was a ruined politician, a man of evil fame, or at least had been so, till time had buried him from the knowledge of the present generation, and made him obscure instead of infamous. As for the Widow Wycherly, tradition tells us that she was a great beauty in her day; but, for a long while past, she had lived in deep seclusion, on account of certain scandalous stories which had prejudiced the gentry of the town against her. It is a circumstance worth mentioning, that each of these three old gentlemen, Mr. Medbourne, Colonel Killigrew, and Mr. Gascoigne, were early lovers of the Widow Wycherly, and had once been on the point of cutting each other's throats for her sake. And, before proceeding farther, I will merely hint that Dr. Heidegger and all his four guests were sometimes thought to be a little beside themselves; as is not unfrequently the case with old people, when worried either by present troubles or woeful recollections.

"My dear old friends," said Dr. Heidegger, motioning them to be seated, "I am desirous of your assistance in one of those little experiments with which I amuse myself here in my study."

If all stories were true, Dr. Heidegger's study must have been a very curious place. It was a dim, old-fashioned chamber, festooned with cobwebs, and besprinkled with antique dust. Around the walls stood several oaken bookcases, the lower shelves of which were filled with rows of gigantic folios and black-letter quartos, and the upper with little parchment-covered duodecimos. Over the central bookcase was a bronze bust of Hippocrates, with which, according to some authorities, Dr. Heidegger was accustomed to hold consultations in all difficult cases of his practice. In the obscurest corner of the room stood a tall and narrow oaken closet, with its door ajar, within which doubtfully appeared a skeleton. Between two of the bookcases hung a looking-glass, presenting its high and dusty plate within a tarnished gilt frame. Among many wonderful stories related of this mirror, it was fabled that the spirits of all the doctor's deceased patients dwelt within its verge, and would stare him in the face whenever he looked thitherward. The opposite side of the chamber was ornamented with the full-length portrait of a young lady, arrayed in the faded magnificence of silk, satin, and brocade, and with a visage as faded as her dress. Above half a century ago, Dr. Heidegger had been on the point of marriage with this young lady; but, being affected with some slight disorder, she had swallowed one of her lover's prescriptions, and died on the bridal evening. The greatest curiosity of the study remains to be mentioned; it was a ponderous folio volume, bound in black leather, with massive silver clasps. There were no letters on the back, and nobody could tell the title of the book. But it was well known to be a book of magic; and once, when a chambermaid had lifted it, merely to brush away the dust, the skeleton had rattled in its closet, the picture of the young lady had stepped one foot upon the floor, and several ghastly faces had peeped forth from the mirror; while the brazen head of Hippocrates frowned, and said,—"Forbear."

Such was Dr. Heidegger's study. On the summer afternoon of our tale, a small round table, as black as ebony, stood in the center of the room, sustaining a cut-glass vase of beautiful form and elaborate workmanship. The sunshine came through the window, between the heavy festoons of two faded damask curtains, and fell directly across this vase; so that a mild splendor was reflected from it on the ashen visages of the five old people who sat around. Four champagne glasses were also on the table.

"My dear old friends," repeated Dr. Heidegger, "may I reckon on your aid in performing an exceedingly curious experiment?"

Now Dr. Heidegger was a very strange old gentleman, whose eccentricity had become the nucleus for a thousand fantastic stories. Some of these fables, to my shame be it spoken, might possibly be traced back to mine own veracious self; and if any passages of the present tale should startle the reader's faith, I must be content to bear the stigma of a fictionmonger.

When the doctor's four guests heard him talk of his proposed experiment, they anticipated nothing more wonderful than the murder of a mouse in an air pump, or the examination of a cobweb by the microscope, or some similar nonsense, with which he was constantly in the habit of pestering his intimates. But without waiting for a reply, Dr. Heidegger hobbled across the chamber, and returned with the same ponderous folio, bound in black leather, which common report affirmed to be a book of magic. Undoing the silver clasps, he opened the volume, and took from among its black-letter pages a rose, or what was once a rose, though now the green leaves and crimson petals had assumed one brownish hue, and the ancient flower seemed ready to crumble to dust in the doctor's hands.

"This rose," said Dr. Heidegger, with a sigh, "this same withered and crumbling flower, blossomed five-and-fifty years ago. It was given me by Sylvia Ward, whose portrait hangs yonder; and I meant to wear it in my bosom at our wedding. Five-and-fifty years it has been treasured between the leaves of this old volume. Now, would you deem it possible that this rose of half a century could ever bloom again?"

"Nonsense!" said the Widow Wycherly, with a peevish toss of her head. "You might as well ask whether an old woman's wrinkled face could ever bloom again."

"See!" answered Dr. Heidegger.

He uncovered the vase, and threw the faded rose into the water which it contained.

At first, it lay lightly on the surface of the fluid, appearing to imbibe none of its moisture. Soon, however, a singular change began to be visible. The crushed and dried petals stirred, and assumed a deepening tinge of crimson, as if the flower were reviving from a deathlike slumber; the slender stalk and twigs of foliage became green; and there was the rose of half a century, looking as fresh as when Sylvia Ward had first given it to her lover. It was scarcely full blown; for some of its delicate red leaves curled modestly around its moist bosom, within which two or three dewdrops were sparkling.

"That is certainly a very pretty deception," said the doctor's friends; carelessly, however, for they had witnessed greater miracles at a conjurer's show; "pray how was it effected?"

"Did you never hear of the 'Fountain of Youth?'" asked Dr. Heidegger, "which Ponce De Leon, the Spanish adventurer, went in search of two or three centuries ago?"

"But did Ponce De Leon ever find it?" said the Widow Wycherly.

"No," answered Dr. Heidegger, "for he never sought it in the right place. The famous Fountain of Youth, if I am rightly informed, is situated in the southern part of the Floridian peninsula, not far from Lake Macaco. Its source is overshadowed by several gigantic magnolias, which, though numberless centuries old, have been kept as fresh as violets by the virtues of this wonderful water. An acquaintance of mine, knowing my curiosity in such matters, has sent me what you see in the vase."

"Ahem!" said Colonel Killigrew, who believed not a word of the doctor's story; "and what may be the effect of this fluid on the human frame?"

"You shall judge for yourself, my dear Colonel," replied Dr. Heidegger; "and all of you, my respected friends, are welcome to so much of this admirable fluid as may restore to you the bloom of youth. For my own part, having had much trouble in growing old, I am in no hurry to grow young again. With your permission, therefore, I will merely watch the progress of the experiment."

While he spoke, Dr. Heidegger had been filling the four champagne glasses with the water of the Fountain of Youth. It was apparently impregnated with an effervescent gas, for little bubbles were continually ascending from the depths of the glasses, and bursting in silvery spray at the surface. As the liquor diffused a pleasant perfume, the old people doubted not that it possessed cordial and comfortable properties; and, though utter skeptics as to its rejuvenescent power, they were inclined to swallow it at once. But Dr. Heidegger besought them to stay a moment.

"Before you drink, my respectable old friends," said he, "it would be well that, with the experience of a lifetime to direct you, you should draw up a few general rules for your guidance, in passing a second time through the perils of youth. Think what a sin and a shame it would be, if with your peculiar advantages, you should not become patterns of virtue and wisdom to all the young people of the age!"

The doctor's four venerable friends made him no answer, except by a feeble and tremulous laugh; so very ridiculous was the idea, that, knowing how closely repentance treads behind the steps of error, they should ever go astray again.

"Drink, then," said the doctor, bowing: "I rejoice that I have so well selected the subjects of my experiment."

With palsied hands, they raised the glasses to their lips. The liquor, if it really possessed such virtues as Dr. Heidegger imputed to it, could not have been bestowed on four human beings who needed it more wofully. They looked as if they had never known what youth or pleasure was, but had been the offspring of Nature's dotage, and always the gray, decrepit, sapless, miserable creatures, who now sat stooping round the doctor's table, without life enough in their souls or bodies to be animated even by the prospect of growing young again. They drank off the water, and replaced their glasses on the table.

Assuredly there was an almost immediate improvement in the aspect of the party, not unlike what might have been produced by a glass of generous wine, together with a sudden glow of cheerful sunshine brightening over all their visages at once. There was a healthful suffusion on their cheeks, instead of the ashen hue that had made them look so corpse-like. They gazed at one another, and fancied that some magic power had really begun to smooth away the deep and sad inscriptions which Father Time had been so long engraving on their brows. The Widow Wycherly adjusted her cap, for she felt almost like a woman again.

"Give us more of this wondrous water!" cried they, eagerly. "We are younger—but we are still too old! Quick—give us more!"

"Patience, patience!" quoth Dr. Heidegger, who sat watching the experiment with philosophic coolness. "You have been a long time growing old. Surely, you might be content to grow young in half an hour! But the water is at your service."

Again he filled their glasses with the liquor of youth, enough of which still remained in the vase to turn half the old people in the city to the age of their own grandchildren. While the bubbles were yet sparkling on the brim, the doctor's four guests snatched their glasses from the table, and swallowed the contents at a single gulp. Was it delusion? Even while the draught was passing down their throats, it seemed to have wrought a change on their whole systems. Their eyes grew clear and bright; a dark shade deepened among their silvery locks, they sat around the table, three gentlemen of middle age, and a woman hardly beyond her buxom prime.

"My dear widow, you are charming!" cried Colonel Killigrew, whose eyes had been fixed upon her face, while the shadows of age were flitting from it like darkness from the crimson daybreak.

The fair widow knew, of old, that Colonel Killigrew's compliments were not always measured by sober truth; so she started up and ran to the mirror, still dreading that the ugly visage of an old woman would meet her gaze. Meanwhile, the three gentlemen behaved in such a manner as proved that the water of the Fountain of Youth possessed some intoxicating qualities; unless, indeed, their exhilaration of spirits were merely a lightsome dizziness caused by the sudden removal of the weight of years. Mr. Gascoigne's mind seemed to run on political topics, but whether relating to the past, present, or future, could not easily be determined, since the same ideas and phrases have been in vogue these fifty years. Now he rattled forth full-throated sentences about patriotism, national glory, and the people's right; now he muttered some perilous stuff or other, in a sly and doubtful whisper, so cautiously that even his own conscience could scarcely catch the secret; and now again he spoke in measured accents, and a deeply deferential tone, as if a royal ear were listening to his well-turned periods. Colonel Killigrew all this time had been trolling forth a jolly bottle-song, and ringing his glass in symphony with the chorus, while his eyes wandered towards the buxom figure of the Widow Wycherly. On the other side of the table, Mr. Medbourne was involved in a calculation of dollars and cents, with which was strangely intermingled a project for supplying the East Indies with ice, by harnessing a team of whales to the polar icebergs.

As for the Widow Wycherly, she stood before the mirror curtsying and simpering to her own image, and greeting it as the friend whom she loved better than all the world beside. She thrust her face close to the glass, to see whether some long-remembered wrinkle or crow's-foot had indeed vanished. She examined whether the snow had so entirely melted from her hair, that the venerable cap could be safely thrown aside. At last, turning briskly away, she came with a sort of dancing step to the table.

"My dear old doctor," cried she, "pray favor me with another glass!"

"Certainly, my dear madam, certainly!" replied the complaisant doctor; "see! I have already filled the glasses."

There, in fact, stood the four glasses, brimful of this wonderful water, the delicate spray of which, as it effervesced from the surface, resembled the tremulous glitter of diamonds. It was now so nearly sunset that the chamber had grown duskier than ever; but a mild and moonlike splendor gleamed from within the vase, and rested alike on the four guests, and on the doctor's venerable figure. He sat in a high-backed, elaborately carved, oaken arm-chair, with a gray dignity of aspect that might have well befitted that very Father Time whose power had never been disputed save by this fortunate company. Even while quaffing the third draught of the Fountain of Youth, they were almost awed by the expression of his mysterious visage.

But, the next moment, the exhilarating gush of young life shot through their veins. They were now in the happy prime of youth. Age, with its miserable train of cares, and sorrows, and diseases, was remembered only as the trouble of a dream from which they had joyously awoke. The fresh gloss of the soul, so early lost, and without which the world's successive scenes had been but a gallery of faded pictures, again threw its enchantment over all their prospects. They felt like new-created beings in a new-created universe.

"We are young! We are young!" they cried exultingly.

Youth, like the extremity of age, had effaced the strongly-marked characteristics of middle life, and mutually assimilated them all. They were a group of merry youngsters, almost maddened with the exuberant frolicsomeness of their years. The most singular effect of their gayety was an impulse to mock the infirmity and decrepitude of which they had so lately been the victims. They laughed loudly at their old-fashioned attire, the wide-skirted coats and flapped waistcoats of the young men, and the ancient cap and gown of the blooming girl. One limped across the floor like a gouty grandfather; one set a pair of spectacles astride of his nose, and pretended to pore over the black-letter pages of the book of magic; a third seated himself in an arm-chair, and strove to imitate the venerable dignity of Dr. Heidegger. Then all shouted mirthfully, and leaped about the room. The Widow Wycherly—if so fresh a damsel could be called a widow—tripped up to the doctor's chair, with a mischievous merriment in her rosy face.

"Doctor, you dear old soul," cried she, "get up and dance with me!" And then the four young people laughed louder than ever, to think what a queer figure the poor old doctor would cut.

"Pray excuse me," answered the doctor quietly. "I am old and rheumatic, and my dancing days were over long ago. But either

of these gay young gentlemen will be glad of so pretty a partner."

"Dance with me, Clara!" cried Colonel Killigrew.

"No, no, I will be her partner!" shouted Mr. Gascoigne.

"She promised me her hand, fifty years ago!" exclaimed Mr. Medbourne.

They all gathered round her. One caught both her hands in his passionate grasp—another threw his arm about her waist—the third buried his hand among the glossy curls that clustered beneath the widow's cap. Blushing, panting, struggling, chiding, laughing, her warm breath fanning each of their faces by turns, she strove to disengage herself, yet still remained in their triple embrace. Never was there a livelier picture of youthful rivalship, with bewitching beauty for the prize. Yet, by a strange deception, owing to the duskiness of the chamber, and the antique dresses which they still wore, the tall mirror is said to have reflected the figures of the three old, gray, withered grandsires, ridiculously contending for the skinny ugliness of a shriveled grandam.

But they were young: their burning passions proved them so. Inflamed to madness by the coquetry of the girl-widow, who neither granted nor quite withheld her favors, the three rivals began to interchange threatening glances. Still keeping hold of the fair prize, they grappled fiercely at one another's throats. As they struggled to and fro, the table was overturned, and the vase dashed into a thousand fragments. The precious Water of Youth flowed in a bright stream across the floor, moistening the wings of a butterfly, which, grown old in the decline of summer, had alighted there to die. The insect fluttered lightly through the chamber, and settled on the snowy head of Dr. Heidegger.

"Come, come, gentlemen!—come, Madame Wycherly," exclaimed the doctor, "I really must protest against this riot."

They stood still, and shivered; for it seemed as if gray Time were calling them back from their sunny youth, far down into the chill and darksome vale of years. They looked at old Dr. Heidegger, who sat in his carved arm-chair, holding the rose of half a century, which he had rescued from among the fragments of the shattered vase. At the motion of his hand, the four rioters resumed their seats; the more readily, because their violent exertions had wearied them, youthful though they were.

"My poor Sylvia's rose!" ejaculated Dr. Heidegger, holding it in the light of the sunset clouds; "it appears to be fading again."

And so it was. Even while the party were looking at it, the flower continued to shrivel up, till it became as dry and fragile as when the doctor had first thrown it into the vase. He shook off the few drops of moisture which clung to its petals.

"I love it as well thus as in its dewy freshness," observed he, pressing the withered rose to his withered lips. While he spoke, the butterfly fluttered down from the doctor's snowy head, and fell upon the floor.

His guests shivered again. A strange chilliness, whether of the body or spirit they could not tell, was creeping gradually over them all. They gazed at one another, and fancied that each fleeting moment snatched away a charm, and left a deepening furrow where none had been before. Was it an illusion? Had the changes of a lifetime been crowded into so brief a space, and were they now four aged people, sitting with their old friend, Dr. Heidegger?

"Are we grown old again, so soon?" cried they, dolefully.

In truth they had. The Water of Youth possessed merely a virtue more transient than that of wine. The delirium which it created had effervesced away. Yes! they were old again. With a shuddering impulse, that showed her a woman still, the widow clasped her skinny hands before her face, and wished that the coffin lid were over it, since it could be no longer beautiful.

"Yes, friends, ye are old again," said Dr. Heidegger, "and lo! the Water of Youth is all lavished on the ground. Well—I bemoan it not; for if the fountain gushed at my very doorstep, I would not stoop to bathe my lips in it—no, though its delirium were for years instead of moments. Such is the lesson ye have taught me!"

But the doctor's four friends had taught no such lesson to themselves. They resolved forthwith to make a pilgrimage to Florida, and quaff at morning, noon, and night, from the Fountain of Youth.

1837

DAVID SWAN

A FANTASY

First published in *The Token*, 1837. This sketch, centering about a single spot, like "Sights from a Steeple" or "A Rill from the Town Pump," concerns a sleeper who nearly has adventures. It is allegorical of the various fates that hover about human beings but may pass them by.

WE can be but partially acquainted even with the events which actually influence our course through life, and our final destiny. There are innumerable other events—if such they may be called—which come close upon us, yet pass away without actual results, or even betraying their near approach, by the reflection of any light or shadow across our minds. Could we know all the vicissitudes of our fortunes, life would be too full of hope and fear, exultation or disappointment, to afford us a single hour of true serenity. This idea may be illustrated by a page from the secret history of David Swan.

We have nothing to do with David until we find him, at the age of twenty, on the high road from his native place to the city of Boston, where his uncle, a small dealer in the grocery line, was to take him behind the counter. Be it enough to say that he was a native of New Hampshire, born of respectable parents, and had received an ordinary school education, with a classic finish by a year at Gilmanton Academy. After journeying on foot from sunrise till nearly noon of a summer's day, his weariness and the increasing heat determined him to sit down in the first convenient shade, and await the coming up of the stagecoach. As if planted on purpose for him, there soon appeared a little tuft of maples, with a delightful recess in the midst, and such a fresh, bubbling spring that it seemed never to have sparkled for any wayfarer but David Swan. Virgin or not, he kissed it with his thirsty lips, and then flung himself along the brink, pillowing his head upon some shirts and a pair of pantaloons, tied up in a striped cotton handkerchief. The sunbeams could not reach him; the dust did not yet arise from the road after the heavy rain of yesterday; and his grassy lair suited the young man better than a bed of down. The spring murmured drowsily beside him; the branches waved dreamily across the blue sky overhead; and a deep sleep, perchance hiding dreams within its depths, fell upon David Swan. But we are to relate events which he did not dream of.

While he lay sound asleep in the shade, other people were wide awake, and passed to and fro, afoot, or horseback, and in all sorts of vehicles, along the sunny road by his bed-chamber. Some looked neither to the right hand nor the left, and knew not that he was there; some merely glanced that way, without admitting the slumberer among their busy thoughts; some laughed to see how soundly he slept; and several, whose hearts were brimming full of scorn, ejected their venomous super-fluity on David Swan. A middle-aged widow, when nobody else was near, thrust her head a little way into the recess, and vowed that the young fellow looked charming in his sleep. A temperance lecturer saw him, and wrought poor David into the texture of his evening's discourse, as an awful instance of dead drunkenness by the roadside. But censure, praise, merriment, scorn, and indifference were all one, or rather all nothing, to David Swan.

He had slept only a few moments when a brown carriage, drawn by a handsome pair of horses, bowled easily along, and was brought to a standstill nearly in front of David's resting place. A linchpin had fallen out, and permitted one of the wheels to slide off. The damage was slight, and occasioned merely a momentary alarm to an elderly merchant and his wife, who were returning to Boston in the carriage. While the coachman and a servant were re-placing the wheel, the lady and gentleman sheltered themselves beneath the maple-trees, and there espied the bubbling fountain, and David Swan asleep beside it. Impressed with the awe which the humblest sleeper usually sheds around him, the merchant trod as lightly as the gout would allow; and his spouse took heed not to rustle her silk gown, lest David should start up all of a sudden.

"How soundly he sleeps!" whispered the old gentleman. "From what a depth he draws that easy breath! Such sleep as that, brought on without an opiate, would be worth more to me than half my income; for it would suppose health and an untroubled mind."

"And youth, besides," said the lady. "Healthy and quiet age does not sleep thus. Our slumber is no more like his than our wakefulness."

The longer they looked, the more did this elderly couple feel interested in the unknown youth, to whom the wayside and the maple shade were as a secret chamber, with the rich gloom of damask curtains brooding over him. Perceiving that a stray sunbeam glimmered down upon his face, the lady contrived to twist a branch aside, so as to intercept it. And having done this little act of kindness, she began to feel like a mother to him.

"Providence seems to have laid him here," whispered she to her husband, "and to have brought us hither to find him, after our dis-appointment in our cousin's son. Methinks I can see a likeness to our departed Henry. Shall we waken him?"

"To what purpose?" said the merchant, hesitating. "We know nothing of the youth's character."

"That open countenance!" replied his wife in the same hushed voice, yet earnestly. "This innocent sleep!"

While these whispers were passing, the sleeper's heart did not throb, nor his breath become agitated, nor his features betray the least token of interest. Yet Fortune was bend-ing over him, just ready to let fall a burden of gold. The old merchant had lost his only son, and had no heir to his wealth except a distant relative, with whose conduct he was dissatis-fied. In such cases people sometimes do stranger things than to act the magician, and awaken a young man to splendor who fell asleep in poverty.

"Shall we not waken him?" repeated the lady persuasively.

"The coach is ready, sir," said the servant, behind.

The old couple started, reddened, and hurried away, mutually wondering that they should ever have dreamed of doing anything so very ridiculous. The merchant threw him-self back in the carriage, and occupied his mind with the plan of a magnificent asylum for unfortunate men of business. Meanwhile, David Swan enjoyed his nap.

The carriage could not have gone above a mile or two, when a pretty young girl came along with a tripping pace, which showed precisely how her little heart was dancing in her bosom. Perhaps it was this merry kind of motion that caused—is there any harm in saying it?—her garter to slip its knot. Conscious that the silken girth—if silk it were—was relaxing its hold, she turned aside into the shelter of the maple-trees, and there found a young man asleep by the spring! Blushing as red as any rose that she should have intruded into a gentleman's bedchamber, and for such a purpose, too, she was about to make her escape on tiptoe. But there was peril near the sleeper. A monster of a bee had been wandering overhead—buzz, buzz, buzz—now among the leaves, now flashing through the strips of sunshine, and now lost in the dark shade, till finally he appeared to be settling on the eyelid of David Swan. The sting of a bee is sometimes deadly. As freehearted as she was innocent, the girl attacked the intruder with her handkerchief, brushed him soundly, and drove him from beneath the maple shade. How sweet a picture! This good deed accomplished, with quickened breath, and a deeper blush, she stole a glance at the youthful stranger for whom she had been battling with a dragon in the air.

"He is handsome!" thought she, and blushed redder yet.

How could it be that no dream of bliss grew so strong within him, that, shattered by its very strength, it should part asunder, and allow him to perceive the girl among its phantoms? Why, at least, did no smile of welcome brighten upon his face? She was come, the maid whose soul, according to the old and beautiful idea, had been severed from his own, and whom, in all his vague but passionate desires, he yearned to meet. Her, only, could he love with a perfect love; him, only, could she receive into the depths of her heart; and now her image was faintly blushing in the fountain by his side; should it pass away, its happy luster would never gleam upon his life again.

"How sound he sleeps!" murmured the girl.

She departed, but did not trip along the road so lightly as when she came.

Now, this girl's father was a thriving country merchant in the neighborhood, and happened, at that identical time, to be looking out for just such a young man as David Swan. Had David formed a wayside acquaintance with the daughter, he would have become the father's clerk, and all else in natural succession. So here, again, had good fortune—the best of fortunes—stolen so near that her garments brushed against him; and he knew nothing of the matter.

The girl was hardly out of sight when two men turned aside beneath the maple shade. Both had dark faces, set off by cloth caps, which were drawn down aslant over their brows. Their dresses were shabby, yet had a certain smartness. These were a couple of rascals who got their living by whatever the devil sent them, and now, in the interim of other business, had staked the joint profits of their next piece of villany on a game of cards, which was to have been decided here under the trees. But, finding David asleep by the spring, one of the rogues whispered to his fellow,—

"Hist!—Do you see that bundle under his head?"

The other villain nodded, winked, and leered.

"I'll bet you a horn of brandy," said the first, "that the chap has either a pocketbook, or a snug little hoard of small change, stowed away amongst his shirts. And if not there, we shall find it in his pantaloons pocket."

"But how if he wakes?" said the other.

His companion thrust aside his waistcoat, pointed to the handle of a dirk, and nodded.

"So be it!" muttered the second villain.

They approached the unconscious David, and, while one pointed the dagger towards his heart, the other began to search the bundle beneath his head. Their two faces, grim, wrinkled, and ghastly with guilt and fear, bent over their victim, looking horrible enough to be mistaken for fiends, should he suddenly awake. Nay, had the villains glanced aside into the spring, even they would hardly have known themselves as reflected there. But

David Swan had never worn a more tranquil aspect, even when asleep on his mother's breast.

"I must take away the bundle," whispered one.

"If he stirs, I'll strike," muttered the other.

But, at this moment, a dog, scenting along the ground, came in beneath the maple-trees, and gazed alternately at each of these wicked men, then at the quiet sleeper. He then lapped out of the fountain.

"Pshaw!" said one villain. "We can do nothing now. The dog's master must be close behind."

"Let's take a drink and be off," said the other.

The man with the dagger thrust back the weapon into his bosom, and drew forth a pocket pistol, but not of that kind which kills by a single discharge. It was a flask of liquor, with a block-tin tumbler screwed upon the mouth. Each drank a comfortable dram, and left the spot, with so many jests, and such laughter at their unaccomplished wickedness, that they might be said to have gone on their way rejoicing. In a few hours they had forgotten the whole affair, nor once imagined that the recording angel had written down the crime of murder against their souls, in letters as durable as eternity. As for David Swan, he still slept quietly, neither conscious of the shadow of death when it hung over him, nor of the glow of renewed life when that shadow was withdrawn.

He slept, but no longer so quietly as at first. An hour's repose had snatched from his elastic frame the weariness with which many hours of toil had burdened it. Now, he stirred —now, moved his lips, without a sound— now, talked, in an inward tone, to the noon-day specters of his dream. But a noise of wheels came rattling louder and louder along the road, until it dashed through the dispersing mist of David's slumber—and there was the stagecoach. He started up with all his ideas about him.

"Halloo, driver!—take a passenger?" shouted he.

"Room on top!" answered the driver.

Up mounted David, and bowled away merrily towards Boston, without so much as a parting glance at that fountain of dreamlike vicissitude. He knew not that a phantom of Wealth had thrown a golden hue upon its waters—nor that one of Love had sighed softly to their murmur—nor that one of Death had threatened to crimson them with his blood—all, in the brief hour since he lay down to sleep. Sleeping or waking, we hear not the airy footsteps of the strange things that almost happen. Does it not argue a superintending Providence that, while viewless and unexpected events thrust themselves continually athwart our path, there should still be regularity enough in mortal life to render foresight even partially available?

1837

ETHAN BRAND

A CHAPTER FROM AN ABORTIVE ROMANCE

Written probably in 1848. Published in the *Boston Museum*, January 5, 1850, and in the *Dollar Magazine*, May, 1851, then in *The Snow Image and Other Twice-Told Tales*, 1851. One of the most powerful and most perfectly executed of Hawthorne's tales. Its germ may be found in passages in the *American Notebooks*. In an entry of 1844 Hawthorne wrote, "The search of an investigator for the Unpardonable Sin — he at last finds it in his own heart." Hawthorne spent the weeks from July 29 to Sept. 9, 1838, at North Adams, Mass. In unrelated entries in his notebooks may be found the description of Graylock, and mention of the limekiln, the lime burner, the one-armed soapmaker, the diorama, and the incident of the dog. The descriptions in the story, drawn from reality, help to make it convincing despite its supernatural touches. Noteworthy in its structure is the observance of all three of the so-called dramatic unities, with their limitations of time and place and action.

BARTRAM the lime-burner, a rough, heavy-looking man, begrimed with charcoal, sat watching his kiln, at nightfall, while his little son played at building houses with the scattered fragments of marble, when, on the hillside below them, they heard a roar of laughter, not mirthful, but slow, and even solemn, like a wind shaking the boughs of the forest.

"Father, what is that?" asked the little boy, leaving his play, and pressing betwixt his father's knees.

"O, some drunken man, I suppose," answered the lime-burner; "some merry fellow from the barroom in the village, who dared not laugh loud enough within doors lest he should blow the roof of the house off. So here he is, shaking his jolly sides at the foot of Graylock."

"But, father," said the child, more sensitive than the obtuse, middle-aged clown, "he does not laugh like a man that is glad. So the noise frightens me!"

"Don't be a fool, child!" cried his father, gruffly. "You will never make a man, I do believe; there is too much of your mother in you. I have known the rustling of a leaf startle you. Hark! Here comes the merry fellow now. You shall see that there is no harm in him."

Bartram and his little son, while they were talking thus, sat watching the same limekiln that had been the scene of Ethan Brand's solitary and meditative life, before he began his search for the Unpardonable Sin. Many years, as we have seen, had now elapsed, since that portentous night when the IDEA was first developed. The kiln, however, on the mountainside, stood unimpaired, and was in nothing changed since he had thrown his dark thoughts into the intense glow of its furnace, and melted them, as it were, into the one thought that took possession of his life. It was a rude, round, tower-like structure, about twenty feet high, heavily built of rough stones, and with a hillock of earth heaped about the larger part of its circumference; so that the blocks and fragments of marble might be drawn by cartloads, and thrown in at the top. There was an opening at the bottom of the tower, like an oven-mouth, but large enough to admit a man in a stooping posture, and provided with a massive iron door. With the smoke and jets of flame issuing from the chinks and crevices of this door, which seemed to give admittance into the hillside, it resembled nothing so much as the private entrance to the infernal regions, which the shepherds of the Delectable Mountains were accustomed to show to pilgrims.

There are many such limekilns in that tract of country, for the purpose of burning the white marble which composes a large part of the substance of the hills. Some of them, built years ago, and long deserted, with weeds growing in the vacant round of the interior, which is open to the sky, and grass and wildflowers rooting themselves into the chinks of the stones, look already like relics of antiquity, and may yet be overspread with the lichens of centuries to come. Others, where the limeburner still feeds his daily and nightlong fire, afford points of interest to the wanderer among the hills, who seats himself on a log of wood or a fragment of marble, to hold a chat with the solitary man. It is a lonesome, and, when the character is inclined to thought, may be an intensely thoughtful occupation; as it proved in the case of Ethan Brand, who had mused to such strange purpose, in days gone by, while the fire in this very kiln was burning.

The man who now watched the fire was of a different order, and troubled himself with no thoughts save the very few that were requisite to his business. At frequent intervals, he flung back the clashing weight of the iron door, and, turning his face from the insufferable glare, thrust in huge logs of oak, or stirred the immense brands with a long pole. Within the furnace were seen the curling and riotous flames, and the burning marble, almost molten with the intensity of heat; while without, the reflection of the fire quivered on the dark intricacy of the surrounding forest, and showed in the foreground a bright and ruddy little picture of the hut, the spring beside its door, the athletic and coal-begrimed figure of the lime-burner, and the half-frightened child, shrinking into the protection of his father's shadow. And when again the iron door was closed, then reappeared the tender light of the half-full moon, which vainly strove to trace out the indistinct shapes of the neighboring mountains; and, in the upper sky, there was a flitting congregation of clouds, still faintly tinged with the rosy sunset, though thus far down into the valley the sunshine had vanished long and long ago.

The little boy now crept still closer to his father, as footsteps were heard ascending the hillside, and a human form thrust aside the bushes that clustered beneath the trees.

"Halloo! who is it?" cried the lime-burner, vexed at his son's timidity, yet half infected by it. "Come forward, and show yourself, like a man, or I'll fling this chunk of marble at your head!"

"You offer me a rough welcome," said a gloomy voice, as the unknown man drew nigh. "Yet I neither claim nor desire a kinder one, even at my own fireside."

To obtain a distincter view, Bartram threw open the iron door of the kiln, whence immediately issued a gush of fierce light, that smote full upon the stranger's face and figure. To a careless eye there appeared nothing very remarkable in his aspect, which was that of a man in a coarse, brown, country-made suit of clothes, tall and thin, with the staff and heavy shoes of a wayfarer. As he advanced, he fixed his eyes—which were very bright—intently upon the brightness of the furnace, as if he beheld, or expected to behold, some object worthy of note within it.

"Good evening, stranger," said the lime-burner; "whence come you, so late in the day?"

"I come from my search," answered the wayfarer; "for, at last, it is finished."

"Drunk!—or crazy!" muttered Bartram to himself. "I shall have trouble with the fellow. The sooner I drive him away, the better."

The little boy, all in a tremble, whispered to his father, and begged him to shut the door of the kiln, so that there might not be so much light; for that there was something in the man's face which he was afraid to look at, yet could not look away from. And, indeed, even the lime-burner's dull and torpid sense began to be impressed by an indescribable something in that thin, rugged, thoughtful visage, with the grizzled hair hanging wildly about it, and those deeply sunken eyes, which gleamed like fires within the entrance of a mysterious cavern. But, as he closed the door, the stranger turned towards him, and spoke in a quiet, familiar way, that made Bartram feel as if he were a sane and sensible man, after all.

"Your task draws to an end, I see," said he. "This marble has already been burning three days. A few hours more will convert the stone to lime."

"Why, who are you?" exclaimed the lime-burner. "You seem as well acquainted with my business as I am myself."

"And well I may be," said the stranger; "for I followed the same craft many a long year, and here, too, on this very spot. But you are a newcomer in these parts. Did you never hear of Ethan Brand?"

"The man that went in search of the Unpardonable Sin?" asked Bartram, with a laugh.

"The same," answered the stranger. "He has found what he sought, and therefore he comes back again."

"What! then you are Ethan Brand himself?" cried the lime-burner, in amazement. "I am a newcomer here, as you say, and they call it eighteen years since you left the foot of Graylock. But, I can tell you, the good folks still talk about Ethan Brand, in the village yonder, and what a strange errand took him away from his limekiln. Well, and so you have found the Unpardonable Sin?"

"Even so!" said the stranger, calmly.

"If the question is a fair one," proceeded Bartram, "Where might it be?"

Ethan Brand laid his finger on his own heart. "Here!" replied he.

And then, without mirth in his countenance, but as if moved by an involuntary recognition of the infinite absurdity of seeking throughout the world for what was the closest of all things to himself, and looking into every heart, save his own, for what was hidden in no other breast, he broke into a laugh of scorn. It was the same slow, heavy laugh, that had almost appalled the lime-burner when it heralded the wayfarer's approach.

The solitary mountainside was made dismal by it. Laughter, when out of place, mistimed, or bursting forth from a disordered state of feeling, may be the most terrible modulation of the human voice. The laughter of one asleep, even if it be a little child,—the madman's laugh,—the wild, screaming laugh of a born idiot,—are sounds that we sometimes tremble to hear, and would always willingly forget. Poets have imagined no utterance of fiends or hobgoblins so fearfully appropriate as a laugh. And even the obtuse lime-burner felt his nerves shaken, as this strange man looked inward at his own heart, and burst into laughter that rolled away into the night, and was indistinctly reverberated among the hills.

"Joe," said he to his little son, "scamper down to the tavern in the village, and tell the jolly fellows there that Ethan Brand has come back, and that he has found the Unpardonable Sin!"

The boy darted away on his errand, to which Ethan Brand made no objection, nor seemed hardly to notice it. He sat on a log of wood, looking steadfastly at the iron door of the kiln. When the child was out of sight, and his swift and light footsteps ceased to be heard treading first on the fallen leaves and then on the rocky mountain-path, the lime-burner began to regret his departure. He felt that the little fellow's presence had been a barrier between his guest and himself, and that he must now deal, heart to heart, with a man who, on his own confession, had committed the one only crime for which Heaven could afford no mercy. That crime, in its indistinct blackness, seemed to overshadow him. The lime-burner's own sins rose up within him, and made his memory riotous with a throng of evil shapes that asserted their kindred with the Master Sin, whatever it might be, which it was within the scope of man's corrupted nature to conceive and cherish. They were all of one family; they went to and fro between his breast and Ethan Brand's, and carried dark greetings from one to the other.

Then Bartram remembered the stories which had grown traditionary in reference to this strange man, who had come upon him like a shadow of the night, and was making himself at home in his old place, after so long absence that the dead people, dead and buried for years, would have had more right to be at home, in any familiar spot, than he. Ethan Brand, it was said, had conversed with Satan himself in the lurid blaze of this very kiln. The legend had been matter of mirth heretofore, but looked grisly now. According to this tale, before Ethan Brand departed on his search, he had been accustomed to evoke a fiend from the hot furnace of the limekiln, night after night, in order to confer with him about the Unpardonable Sin; the man and the fiend each laboring to frame the image of some mode of guilt which could neither be atoned for nor forgiven. And, with the first gleam of light upon the mountain-top, the fiend crept in at the iron door, there to abide the intensest element of fire, until again summoned forth to share in the dreadful task of extending man's possible guilt beyond the scope of Heaven's else infinite mercy.

While the lime-burner was struggling with the horror of these thoughts, Ethan Brand rose from the log, and flung open the door of the kiln. The action was in such accordance with the idea in Bartram's mind, that he almost expected to see the Evil One issue forth, red-hot from the raging furnace.

"Hold! hold!" cried he, with a tremulous attempt to laugh; for he was ashamed of his fears, although they overmastered him. "Don't, for mercy's sake, bring out your Devil now!"

"Man!" sternly replied Ethan Brand, "what need have I of the Devil? I have left him behind me, on my track. It is with such halfway sinners as you that he busies himself. Fear not, because I open the door. I do but act by old custom, and am going to trim your fire, like a lime-burner, as I was once."

He stirred the vast coals, thrust in more wood, and bent forward to gaze into the hollow prison-house of the fire, regardless of the fierce glow that reddened upon his face. The lime-burner sat watching him, and half suspected his strange guest of a purpose, if not to evoke a fiend, at least to plunge bodily into the flames, and thus vanish from the sight of man. Ethan Brand, however, drew quietly back, and closed the door of the kiln.

"I have looked," said he, "into many a human heart that was seven times hotter with sinful passions than yonder furnace is with fire. But I found not there what I sought. No, not the Unpardonable Sin!"

"What is the Unpardonable Sin?" asked the lime-burner; and then he shrank farther from his companion, trembling lest his question should be answered.

"It is a sin that grew within my own breast," replied Ethan Brand, standing erect, with a pride that distinguishes all enthusiasts of his stamp. "A sin that grew nowhere else! The sin of an intellect that triumphed over the sense of brotherhood with man and reverence for God, and sacrificed everything to its own mighty claims! The only sin that deserves a recompense of immortal agony! Freely, were it to do again, would I incur the guilt. Unshrinkingly I accept the retribution!"

"The man's head is turned," muttered the lime-burner to himself. "He may be a sinner, like the rest of us,—nothing more likely,—but, I'll be sworn, he is a madman too."

Nevertheless, he felt uncomfortable at his situation, alone with Ethan Brand on the wild mountainside, and was right glad to hear the rough murmur of tongues, and the footsteps of what seemed a pretty numerous party, stumbling over the stones and rustling through the underbrush. Soon appeared the whole lazy regiment that was wont to infest the village tavern, comprehending three or four individuals who had drunk flip beside the barroom fire through all the winters, and smoked their pipes beneath the stoop through all the summers, since Ethan Brand's departure. Laughing boisterously, and mingling all their voices together in unceremonious talk, they now burst into the moonshine and narrow streaks of firelight that illuminated the open space before the limekiln. Bartram set the door ajar again, flooding the spot with light, that the whole company might get a fair view of Ethan Brand, and he of them.

There, among other old acquaintances, was a once ubiquitous man, now almost extinct, but whom we were formerly sure to encounter at the hotel of every thriving village throughout the country. It was the stage-agent. The present specimen of the genus was a wilted and smoke-dried man, wrinkled and red-nosed, in a smartly cut, brown, bobtailed coat, with brass buttons, who, for a length of time unknown, had kept his desk and corner in the barroom, and was still puffing what seemed to be the same cigar that he had lighted twenty years before. He had great fame as a dry joker, though, perhaps, less on account of any intrinsic humor than from a certain flavor of brandy-toddy and tobacco-smoke, which impregnated all his ideas and expressions, as well as his person. Another well-remembered though strangely altered face was that of Lawyer Giles, as people still called him in courtesy; an elderly ragamuffin,

in his soiled shirt-sleeves and tow-cloth trousers. This poor fellow had been an attorney, in what he called his better days, a sharp practitioner, and in great vogue among the village litigants; but flip, and sling, and toddy, and cocktails, imbibed at all hours, morning, noon, and night, had caused him to slide from intellectual to various kinds and degrees of bodily labor, till, at last, to adopt his own phrase, he slid into a soap-vat. In other words, Giles was now a soap-boiler, in a small way. He had come to be but the fragment of a human being, a part of one foot having been chopped off by an axe, and an entire hand torn away by the devilish grip of a steam-engine. Yet, though the corporeal hand was gone, a spiritual member remained; for, stretching forth the stump, Giles steadfastly averred that he felt an invisible thumb and fingers with as vivid a sensation as before the real ones were amputated. A maimed and miserable wretch he was; but one, nevertheless, whom the world could not trample on, and had no right to scorn, either in this or any previous stage of his misfortunes, since he had still kept up the courage and spirit of a man, asked nothing in charity, and with his one hand—and that the left one—fought a stern battle against want and hostile circumstances.

Among the throng too, came another personage, who, with certain points of similarity to Lawyer Giles, had many more of difference. It was the village doctor; a man of some fifty years, whom, at an earlier period of his life, we introduced as paying a professional visit to Ethan Brand during the latter's supposed insanity. He was now a purple-visaged, rude, and brutal, yet half-gentlemanly figure, with something wild, ruined, and desperate in his talk, and in all the details of his gesture and manners. Brandy possessed this man like an evil spirit, and made him as surly and savage as a wild beast, and as miserable as a lost soul; but there was supposed to be in him such wonderful skill, such native gifts of healing, beyond any which medical science could impart, that society caught hold of him, and would not let him sink out of its reach. So, swaying to and fro upon his horse, and grumbling thick accents at the bedside, he visited all the sick-chambers for miles about among the mountain towns, and sometimes raised a dying man, as it were, by miracle, or quite as often, no doubt, sent his patient to a grave that was dug many a year too soon. The doctor had an everlasting pipe in his mouth, and, as somebody said, in allusion to his habit of swearing, it was always alight with hell-fire.

These three worthies pressed forward, and greeted Ethan Brand each after his own fashion, earnestly inviting him to partake of the contents of a certain black bottle, in which, as they averred, he would find something far better worth seeking for than the Unpardonable Sin. No mind, which has wrought itself by intense and solitary meditation into a high state of enthusiasm, can endure the kind of contact with low and vulgar modes of thought and feeling to which Ethan Brand was now subjected. It made him doubt—and, strange to say, it was a painful doubt—whether he had indeed found the Unpardonable Sin and found it within himself. The whole question on which he had exhausted life, and more than life, looked like a delusion.

"Leave me," he said bitterly, "ye brute beasts, that have made yourselves so, shrivelling up your souls with fiery liquors! I have done with you. Years and years ago, I groped into your hearts, and found nothing there for my purpose. Get ye gone!"

"Why, you uncivil scoundrel," cried the fierce doctor, "is that the way you respond to the kindness of your best friends? Then let me tell you the truth. You have no more found the Unpardonable Sin than yonder boy Joe has. You are but a crazy fellow,—I told you so twenty years ago,—neither better nor worse than a crazy fellow, and the fit companion of old Humphrey, here!"

He pointed to an old man, shabbily dressed, with long white hair, thin visage, and unsteady eyes. For some years past this aged person had been wandering about among the hills, inquiring of all travelers whom he met for his daughter. The girl, it seemed, had gone off with a company of circus-performers; and occasionally tidings of her came to the village, and fine stories were told of her glittering appearance as she rode on horseback in the

ring, or performed marvelous feats on the tightrope.

The white-haired father now approached Ethan Brand, and gazed unsteadily into his face.

"They tell me you have been all over the earth," said he, wringing his hands with earnestness. "You must have seen my daughter, for she makes a grand figure in the world, and everybody goes to see her. Did she send any word to her old father, or say when she was coming back?"

Ethan Brand's eye quailed beneath the old man's. That daughter, from whom he so earnestly desired a word of greeting, was the Esther of our tale, the very girl whom, with such cold and remorseless purpose, Ethan Brand had made the subject of a psychological experiment, and wasted, absorbed, and perhaps annihilated her soul, in the process.

"Yes," murmured he, turning away from the hoary wanderer; "it is no delusion. There is an Unpardonable Sin!"

While these things were passing, a merry scene was going forward in the area of cheerful light, beside the spring and before the door of the hut. A number of the youth of the village, young men and girls, had hurried up the hillside, impelled by curiosity to see Ethan Brand, the hero of so many a legend familiar to their childhood. Finding nothing, however, very remarkable in his aspect,—nothing but a sunburnt wayfarer, in plain garb and dusty shoes, who sat looking into the fire, as if he fancied pictures among the coals,—these young people speedily grew tired of observing him. As it happened, there was other amusement at hand. An old German Jew, traveling with a diorama on his back, was passing down the mountain-road towards the village just as the party turned aside from it, and, in hopes of eking out the profits of the day, the showman had kept them company to the limekiln.

"Come, old Dutchman," cried one of the young men, "let us see your pictures, if you can swear they are worth looking at!"

"O yes, Captain," answered the Jew,—whether as a matter of courtesy or craft, he styled everybody Captain,—"I shall show you, indeed, some very superb pictures!"

So, placing his box in a proper position, he invited the young men and girls to look through the glass orifices of the machine, and proceeded to exhibit a series of the most outrageous scratchings and daubings, as specimens of the fine arts, that ever an itinerant showman had the face to impose upon his circle of spectators. The pictures were worn out, moreover, tattered, full of cracks and wrinkles, dingy with tobacco-smoke, and otherwise in a most pitiable condition. Some purported to be cities, public edifices, and ruined castles in Europe; others represented Napoleon's battles and Nelson's sea-fights; and in the midst of these would be seen a gigantic, brown, hairy hand,—which might have been mistaken for the Hand of Destiny, though in truth, it was only the showman's,— pointing its forefinger to various scenes of the conflict, while its owner gave historical illustrations. When, with much merriment at its abominable deficiency of merit, the exhibition was concluded, the German bade little Joe put his head into the box. Viewed through the magnifying-glasses, the boy's round, rosy visage assumed the strangest imaginable aspect of an immense Titanic child, the mouth grinning broadly, and the eyes and every other feature overflowing with fun at the joke. Suddenly, however, that merry face turned pale, and its expression changed to horror, for this easily impressed and excitable child had become sensible that the eye of Ethan Brand was fixed upon him through the glass.

"You make the little man to be afraid, Captain," said the German Jew, turning up the dark and strong outline of his visage, from his stooping posture. "But look again, and, by chance, I shall cause you to see somewhat that is very fine, upon my word!"

Ethan Brand gazed into the box for an instant, and then starting back, looked fixedly at the German. What had he seen? Nothing, apparently; for a curious youth, who had peeped in almost at the same moment, beheld only a vacant space of canvas.

"I remember you now," muttered Ethan Brand to the showman.

"Ah, Captain," whispered the Jew of Nuremberg, with a dark smile, "I find it to be a heavy matter in my showbox,—this Unpardonable Sin! By my faith, Captain, it has wearied my shoulders, this long day, to carry it over the mountain."

"Peace," answered Ethan Brand, sternly, "or get thee into the furnace yonder!"

The Jew's exhibition had scarcely concluded, when a great, elderly dog—who seemed to be his own master, as no person in the company laid claim to him—saw fit to render himself the object of public notice. Hitherto, he had shown himself a very quiet, well-disposed old dog, going round from one to another, and by way of being sociable, offering his rough head to be patted by any kindly hand that would take so much trouble. But now, all of a sudden, this grave and venerable quadruped of his own mere motion, and without the slightest suggestion from anybody else, began to run round after his tail, which, to heighten the absurdity of the proceeding, was a great deal shorter than it should have been. Never was seen such headlong eagerness in pursuit of an object that could not possibly be attained; never was heard such a tremendous outbreak of growling, snarling, barking, and snapping,—as if one end of the ridiculous brute's body were at deadly and most unforgivable enmity with the other. Faster and faster, round about went the cur; and faster and still faster fled the unapproachable brevity of his tail; and louder and fiercer grew his yells of rage and animosity; until, utterly exhausted, and as far from the goal as ever, the foolish old dog ceased his performance as suddenly as he had begun it. The next moment he was as mild, quiet, sensible, and respectable in his deportment, as when he first scraped acquaintance with the company.

As may be supposed, the exhibition was greeted with universal laughter, clapping of hands, and shouts of encore, to which the canine performer responded by wagging all that there was to wag of his tail, but appeared totally unable to repeat his very successful effort to amuse the spectators.

Meanwhile, Ethan Brand had resumed his seat upon the log, and moved, it might be, by a perception of some remote analogy between his own case and that of this self-pursuing cur, he broke into the awful laugh, which, more than any other token, expressed the condition of his inward being. From that moment, the merriment of the party was at an end; they stood aghast, dreading lest the inauspicious sound should be reverberated around the horizon, and that mountain would thunder it to mountain, and so the horror be prolonged upon their ears. Then, whispering one to another that it was late,—that the moon was almost down,—that the August night was growing chill,—they hurried homewards, leaving the lime-burner and little Joe to deal as they might with their unwelcome guest. Save for these three human beings, the open space on the hillside was a solitude, set in a vast gloom of forest. Beyond that darksome verge, the firelight glimmered on the stately trunks and almost black foliage of pines, intermixed with the lighter verdure of sapling oaks, maples, and poplars, while here and there lay the gigantic corpses of dead trees, decaying on the leaf-strewn soil. And it seemed to little Joe—a timorous and imaginative child—that the silent forest was holding its breath, until some fearful thing should happen.

Ethan Brand thrust more wood into the fire, and closed the door of the kiln; then looking over his shoulder at the lime-burner and his son, he bade, rather than advised, them to retire to rest.

"For myself, I cannot sleep," said he. "I have matters that it concerns me to meditate upon. I will watch the fire, as I used to do in the old time."

"And call the Devil out of the furnace to keep you company, I suppose," muttered Bartram who had been making intimate acquaintance with the black bottle above mentioned. "But watch, if you like, and call as many devils as you like! For my part, I shall be all the better for a snooze. Come, Joe!"

As the boy followed his father into the hut, he looked back at the wayfarer, and the tears came into his eyes, for his tender spirit had an intuition of the bleak and terrible loneliness in which this man had enveloped himself.

When they had gone, Ethan Brand sat listening to the crackling of the kindled wood, and looking at the little spirts of fire that issued through the chinks of the door. These trifles, however, once so familiar, had but the slightest hold of his attention, while deep within his mind he was reviewing the gradual but marvelous change that had been wrought upon him by the search to which he had devoted himself. He remembered how the night dew had fallen upon him,—how the dark forest had whispered to him,—how the stars had gleamed upon him,—a simple and loving man, watching his fire in the years gone by, and ever musing as it burned. He remembered with what tenderness, with what love and sympathy for mankind, and what pity for human guilt and woe, he had first begun to contemplate those ideas which afterwards became the inspiration of his life; with what reverence he had then looked into the heart of man, viewing it as a temple originally divine, and, however desecrated, still to be held sacred by a brother; with what awful fear he had deprecated the success of his pursuit, and prayed that the Unpardonable Sin might never be revealed to him. Then ensued that vast intellectual development, which, in its progress, disturbed the counterpoise between his mind and heart. The Idea that possessed his life had operated as a means of education; it had gone on cultivating his powers to the highest point of which they were susceptible; it had raised him from the level of an unlettered laborer to stand on a star-lit eminence, whither the philosophers of the earth, laden with the lore of universities, might vainly strive to clamber after him. So much for the intellect! But where was the heart? That, indeed, had withered,—had contracted,—had hardened,—had perished! It had ceased to partake of the universal throb. He had lost his hold of the magnetic chain of humanity. He was no longer a brother-man, opening the chambers of the dungeons of our common nature by the key of holy sympathy, which gave him a right to share in all its secrets; he was now a cold observer, looking on mankind as the subject of his experiment, and, at length, converting man and woman to be his puppets, and pulling the wires that moved them to such degrees of crime as were demanded for his study.

Thus Ethan Brand became a fiend. He began to be so from the moment that his moral nature had ceased to keep the pace of improvement with his intellect. And now, as his highest effort and inevitable development,—as the bright and gorgeous flower, and rich, delicious fruit of his life's labor,—he had produced the Unpardonable Sin!

"What more have I to seek? what more to achieve?" said Ethan Brand to himself. "My task is done, and well done!"

Starting from the log with a certain alacrity in his gait and ascending the hillock of earth that was raised against the stone circumference of the limekiln, he thus reached the top of the structure. It was a space of perhaps ten feet across, from edge to edge, presenting a view of the upper surface of the immense mass of broken marble with which the kiln was heaped. All these innumerable blocks and fragments of marble were red-hot and vividly on fire, sending up great spouts of blue flame, which quivered aloft and danced madly, as within a magic circle, and sank and rose again, with continual and multitudinous activity. As the lonely man bent forward over this terrible body of fire, the blasting heat smote up against his person with a breath that, it might be supposed, would have scorched and shrivelled him up in a moment.

Ethan Brand stood erect, and raised his arms on high. The blue flames played upon his face, and imparted the wild and ghastly light which alone could have suited its expression; it was that of a fiend on the verge of plunging into his gulf of intensest torment.

"O Mother Earth," cried he, "who art no more my Mother, and into whose bosom this frame shall never be resolved! O mankind, whose brotherhood I have cast off, and trampled thy great heart beneath my feet! O stars of heaven, that shone on me of old, as if to light me onward and upward!—farewell all, and forever. Come, deadly element of Fire,— henceforth my familiar frame! Embrace me, as I do thee!"

That night the sound of a fearful peal of laughter rolled heavily through the sleep of the lime-burner and his little son; dim shapes of horror and anguish haunted their dreams, and seemed still present in the rude hovel, when they opened their eyes to the day-light.

"Up, boy, up!" cried the lime-burner, staring about him. "Thank Heaven, the night is gone, at last; and rather than pass such another, I would watch my limekiln, wide awake, for a twelvemonth. This Ethan Brand, with his humbug of an Unpardonable Sin, has done me no such mighty favor, in taking my place!"

He issued from the hut, followed by little Joe, who kept fast hold of his father's hand. The early sunshine was already pouring its gold upon the mountain-tops; and though the valleys were still in shadow, they smiled cheerfully in the promise of the bright day that was hastening onward. The village, completely shut in by hills, which swelled away gently about it, looked as if it had rested peacefully in the hollow of the great hand of Providence. Every dwelling was distinctly visible; the little spires of the two churches pointed upwards, and caught a fore-glimmering of brightness from the sun-gilt skies upon their gilded weathercocks. The tavern was astir, and the figure of the old, smoke-dried stage-agent, cigar in mouth, was seen beneath the stoop. Old Graylock was glorified with a golden cloud upon his head. Scattered likewise over the breasts of the surrounding mountains, there were heaps of hoary mist, in fantastic shapes, some of them far down into the valley, others high up towards the summits, and still others, of the same family of mist or cloud, hovering in the gold radiance of the upper atmosphere. Stepping from one to another of the clouds that rested on the hills, and thence to the loftier brotherhood that sailed in air, it seemed almost as if a mortal man might thus ascend into the heavenly regions. Earth was so mingled with sky that it was a daydream to look at it.

To supply that charm of the familiar and homely, which Nature so readily adopts into a scene like this, the stagecoach was rattling down the mountain-road, and the driver sounded his horn, while echo caught up the notes, and intertwined them into a rich and varied and elaborate harmony, of which the original performer could lay claim to little share. The great hills played a concert among themselves, each contributing a strain of airy sweetness.

Little Joe's face brightened at once.

"Dear father," cried he, skipping cheerily

to and fro, "that strange man is gone, and the sky and the mountains all seem glad of it!"

"Yes," growled the lime-burner, with an oath, "but he has let the fire go down, and no thanks to him if five hundred bushels of lime are not spoiled. If I catch the fellow hereabouts again, I shall feel like tossing him into the furnace!"

With his long pole in his hand, he ascended to the top of the kiln. After a moment's pause, he called to his son.

"Come up here, Joe!" said he.

So little Joe ran up the hillock, and stood by his father's side. The marble was all burnt into perfect, snow-white lime. But on its surface, in the midst of the circle,—snow-white too, and thoroughly converted into lime,—lay a human skeleton, in the attitude of a person who, after long toil, lies down to long repose. Within the ribs—strange to say—was the shape of a human heart.

"Was the fellow's heart made of marble?" cried Bartram, in some perplexity at this phenomenon. "At any rate, it is burnt into what looks like special good lime; and, taking all the bones together, my kiln is half a bushel the richer for him."

So saying, the rude lime-burner lifted his pole, and, letting it fall upon the skeleton, the relics of Ethan Brand were crumbled into fragments.

1850, 1851

PREFACE TO *TWICE-TOLD TALES*

In this preface, prefixed to the edition of 1851, Hawthorne comments on his own writing of fiction. The preface has autobiographical interest also.

THE Author of *Twice-Told Tales* has a claim to one distinction, which, as none of his literary brethren will care about disputing it with him, he need not be afraid to mention. He was, for a good many years, the obscurest man of letters in America.

These stories were published in magazines and annuals, extending over a period of ten or twelve years, and comprising the whole of the writer's young manhood, without making (so far as he has ever been aware) the slightest

impression on the public. One or two among them, the "Rill from the Town Pump," in perhaps a greater degree than any other, had a pretty wide newspaper circulation; as for the rest, he had no grounds for supposing that, on their first appearance, they met with the good or evil fortune to be read by anybody. Throughout the time above specified, he had no incitement to literary effort in a reasonable prospect of reputation or profit, nothing but the pleasure itself of composition —an enjoyment not at all amiss in its way, and perhaps essential to the merit of the work in hand, but which, in the long run, will hardly keep the chill out of a writer's heart, or the numbness out of his fingers. To this total lack of sympathy, at the age when his mind would naturally have been most effervescent, the public owe it (and it is certainly an effect not to be regretted on either part) that the Author can show nothing for the thought and industry of that portion of his life, save the forty sketches, or thereabouts, included in these volumes.

Much more, indeed, he wrote; and some very small part of it might yet be rummaged out (but it would not be worth the trouble) among the dingy pages of fifteen-or-twenty-year-old periodicals, or within the shabby morocco covers of faded souvenirs. The remainder of the works alluded to had a very brief existence, but, on the score of brilliancy, enjoyed a fate vastly superior to that of their brotherhood, which succeeded in getting through the press. In a word, the Author burned them without mercy or remorse, and, moreover, without any subsequent regret, and had more than one occasion to marvel that such very dull stuff, as he knew his condemned manuscripts to be, should yet have possessed inflammability enough to set the chimney on fire!

After a long while the first collected volume of the *Tales* was published. By this time, if the Author had ever been greatly tormented by literary ambition (which he does not remember or believe to have been the case), it must have perished, beyond resuscitation, in the dearth of nutriment. This was fortunate; for the success of the volume was not such as would have gratified a craving desire for notoriety. A moderate edition was "got rid of" (to use the publisher's very significant phrase) within a reasonable time, but apparently without rendering the writer or his productions much more generally known than before. The great bulk of the reading public probably ignored the book altogether. A few persons read it, and liked it better than it deserved. At an interval of three or four years, the second volume was published, and encountered much the same sort of kindly, but calm, and very limited reception. The circulation of the two volumes was chiefly confined to New England; nor was it until long after this period, if it even yet be the case, that the Author could regard himself as addressing the American public, or, indeed, any public at all. He was merely writing to his known or unknown friends.

As he glances over these long-forgotten pages, and considers his way of life while composing them, the Author can very clearly discern why all this was so. After so many sober years, he would have reason to be ashamed if he could not criticize his own work as fairly as another man's; and, though it is little his business, and perhaps still less his interest, he can hardly resist a temptation to achieve something of the sort. If writers were allowed to do so, and would perform the task with perfect sincerity and unreserve, their opinions of their own productions would often be more valuable and instructive than the works themselves.

At all events, there can be no harm in the Author's remarking that he rather wonders how the *Twice-Told Tales* should have gained what vogue they did than that it was so little and so gradual. They have the pale tint of flowers that blossomed in too retired a shade,—the coolness of a meditative habit, which diffuses itself through the feeling and observation of every sketch. Instead of passion there is sentiment; and, even in what purport to be pictures of actual life, we have allegory, not always so warmly dressed in its habiliments of flesh and blood as to be taken into the reader's mind without a shiver. Whether from lack of power, or an unconquerable reserve, the Author's touches have often an effect of tameness; the merriest man can hardly contrive to laugh at his broadest humor; the tenderest woman, one would suppose, will hardly shed warm tears at his deepest pathos. The book, if you would see anything in it, requires to be read in the clear, brown, twilight atmosphere in which it was written; if opened in the sunshine, it is apt to look exceedingly like a volume of blank pages.

With the foregoing characteristics, proper to the production of a person in retirement (which happened to be the Author's category at the time), the book is devoid of others that we should quite as naturally look for. The sketches are not, it is hardly necessary to say, profound; but it is rather more remarkable that they so seldom, if ever, show any design on the writer's part to make them so. They have none of the abstruseness of idea, or obscurity of expression, which mark the written communications of a solitary mind with itself. They never need translation. It is, in fact, the style of a man of society. Every sentence, so far as it embodies thought or sensibility, may be understood and felt by anybody who will give himself the trouble to read it, and will take up the book in a proper mood.

This statement of apparently opposite peculiarities leads us to a perception of what the sketches truly are. They are not the talk of a secluded man with his own mind and heart (had it been so, they could hardly have failed to be more deeply and permanently valuable), but his attempts, and very imperfectly successful ones, to open an intercourse with the world.

The Author would regret to be understood as speaking sourly or querulously of the slight mark made by his earlier literary efforts on the Public at large. It is so far the contrary, that he has been moved to write this Preface chiefly as affording him an opportunity to express how much enjoyment he has owed to these volumes, both before and since their publication. They are the memorials of very tranquil and not unhappy years. They failed, it is true,—nor could it have been otherwise,—in winning an extensive popularity. Occasionally, however, when he deemed them entirely forgotten, a paragraph or an article, from a native or foreign critic, would gratify his instincts of authorship with unexpected praise,—too generous praise, indeed, and too little alloyed with censure, which, therefore, he learned the better to inflict upon himself. And, by the bye, it is a very suspicious symptom of a deficiency of the popular element in a book when it calls forth no harsh criticism. This has been particularly the fortune of the *Twice-Told Tales*. They made no enemies, and were so little known and talked about that those who read, and chanced to like them, were apt to conceive the sort of kindness for the book which a person naturally feels for a discovery of his own.

This kindly feeling (in some cases, at least) extended to the Author, who, on the internal evidence of his sketches, came to be regarded as a mild, shy, gentle, melancholic, exceedingly sensitive, and not very forcible man, hiding his blushes under an assumed name, the quaintness of which was supposed, somehow or other, to symbolize his personal and literary traits. He is by no means certain that some of his subsequent productions have not been influenced and modified by a natural desire to fill up so amiable an outline, and to act in consonance with the character assigned to him; nor, even now, could he forfeit it without a few tears of tender sensibility. To conclude, however: these volumes have opened the way to most agreeable associations, and to the formation of imperishable friendships; and there are many golden threads interwoven with his present happiness, which he can follow up more or less directly, until he finds their commencement here; so that his pleasant pathway among realities seems to proceed out of the Dreamland of his youth, and to be bordered with just enough of its shadowy foliage to shelter him from the heat of the day. He is therefore satisfied with what the *Twice-Told Tales* have done for him, and feels it to be far better than fame.

LENOX, *January 11, 1851*

From AMERICAN NOTEBOOKS

The *American Notebooks* of Hawthorne were revised by Mrs. Hawthorne when she published passages from them in 1868, after his death. Dr. Randall Stewart's completer edition (1932), was made from the original manuscript in the J. Pierpont Morgan Library. The notebooks show Hawthorne to have been a very keen observer. They contain journalistic records of his life, and they show, too, that he was conscious of what lay behind the facts observed. Apparently he often started from some germinal idea entered in his notebooks and elaborated it into a story.

[*Hints for Stories*]

On the road to Northampton, we passed a tame crow, which was sitting on the peak of a barn. This crow flew down from its perch, and followed us a great distance, hopping along the road, and flying with its large, black, flapping wings, from post to post of the fence, or from tree to tree. At last, he gave up the pursuit with a croak of disappointment. The driver said, perhaps correctly, that the crow had scented some salmon which was in a basket under the seat, and that this was the secret of his pursuing us. This would be a terrific incident, if it were a dead body that the crow scented, instead of a basket of salmon. Suppose, for instance, in a coach traveling along, that one of the passengers suddenly should die, and that one of the indications of his death would be this deportment of the crow.

A sketch to be given of a modern reformer, —a type of the extreme doctrines on the subject of slaves, cold water, and other such topics. He goes about the streets haranguing most eloquently, and is on the point of making many converts, when his labors are suddenly interrupted by the appearance of the keeper of a madhouse, whence he has escaped.

A change from a gay young girl to an old woman; the melancholy events, the effects of which have clustered around her character, and gradually imbued it with their influence, till she becomes a lover of sick-chambers, taking pleasure in receiving dying breaths and in laying out the dead; also having her mind full of funeral reminiscences, and possessing more acquaintances beneath the burial turf than above it.

The scene of a story or sketch to be laid within the light of a street-lantern; the time, when the lamp is near going out; and the catastrophe to be simultaneous with the last flickering gleam.

A fellow without money, having a hundred and seventy miles to go, fastened a chain and padlock to his legs, and lay down to sleep in a field. He was apprehended, and carried gratis to a jail in the town whither he desired to go.

It is a singular thing, that, at the distance, say, of five feet, the work of the greatest dunce looks just as well as that of the greatest genius, —that little space being all the distance between genius and stupidity.

A series of strange, mysterious, dreadful events to occur, wholly destructive of a person's happiness. He to impute them to various persons and causes, but ultimately finds that he is himself the sole agent. Moral, that our welfare depends on ourselves.

A perception, for a moment, of one's eventual and moral self, as if it were another person,—the observant faculty being separated, and looking intently at the qualities of the character. There is a surprise when this happens,—this getting out of one's self,—and then the observer sees how queer a fellow he is.

Character of a man who, in himself and his external circumstances, shall be equally and totally false: his fortune resting on baseless credit,—his patriotism assumed,—his domestic affections, his honor and honesty, all a sham. His own misery in the midst of it,— it making the whole universe, heaven and earth alike, an unsubstantial mockery to him.

The semblance of a human face to be formed on the side of a mountain, or in the fracture of a small stone, by a *lusus naturae*. The face is an object of curiosity for years or centuries, and by and by a boy is born, whose features gradually assume the aspect of that portrait. At some critical juncture, the resemblance is found to be perfect. A prophecy may be connected.

Some man of powerful character to command a person, morally subjected to him, to perform some act. The commanding person to suddenly die; and, for all the rest of his life, the subjected one continues to perform that act.

To trace out the influence of a frightful and disgraceful crime in debasing and destroying a character naturally high and noble—the guilty person being alone conscious of the crime.

A man, virtuous in his general conduct, but committing habitually some monstrous crime —as murder—and doing this without the sense of guilt, but with a peaceful conscience— habit, probably, reconciling him to it; but something (for instance, discovery) occurs to make him sensible of his enormity. His horror then.

A Father Confessor—his reflections on character and the contrast of the inward man with the outward, as he looks round on his congregation—all whose secret sins are known to him.

A person with an ice-cold hand—his right hand; which people ever afterwards remember when once they have grasped it.

To make a story out of a scarecrow, giving it odd attributes. From different points of view, it should appear to change,—now an old man, now an old woman,—a gunner, a farmer, or the Old Nick.

1807 ~ *John Greenleaf Whittier* ~ 1892

WHITTIER'S LIFE and experiences are in strong contrast with those of his more cosmopolitan contemporaries. Whittier knew mainly New England and lived a very quiet life. He was influenced by the puritan background of his home region, as well as by the Quaker tradition that appeared in Woolman. He was involved deeply in reform, especially in the antislavery movement. His was an austere life of meager opportunities but effective accomplishment. Much of his poetry is autobiographical, born of his own activities and convictions.

Whittier was the descendant of Quaker farmers, and was bred in the Quaker faith. He was born in 1807 in the same house in Haverhill, Massachusetts, that had been built by his American ancestor, Thomas Whittier, in 1688. His early life was that of the typical farm boy—full of hard physical toil for which his frail constitution was ill-suited. His education was confined to a few weeks at a district school during the winters and to two terms at Haverhill Academy. He earned his own expenses at the Academy by shoemaking and by teaching. Only once in his boyhood did he journey so far from his home as Boston. The few books that were available in his household were chiefly almanacs, the lives of Quaker worthies, and the Bible. When he was about fourteen, he came to know Burns, who had a strong influence over him and whose life had some points of resemblance with his own.

Whittier's first printed verses appeared in a local paper edited by William Lloyd Garrison. They brought him to the attention of Garrison, who urged him to complete his education. His short stay at the Haverhill Academy followed in 1827. He spent the next year teaching. But a college education was not possible for him. Perhaps this is not to be regretted, for it might have traditionalized him as it did Longfellow and Lowell. Through the help of Garrison, he began his journalistic career as an editor of a Boston trade journal in 1829, but he was forced to return to Haverhill to take charge of the farm because of the illness of his father and his own uncertain health. He was editor of the *Essex Gazette* in 1830, and then of the *New England Review* at Hartford. In 1836 the old farm was sold, and he removed to the village of Amesbury, which became his permanent home.

Through Garrison's influence, Whittier became an abolitionist in the days when the abolitionists were a small and derided band championing an unpopular cause. In 1833 he was a delegate to an antislavery convention in Philadelphia. For the next thirty years he gave his best strength to the cause of the liberation of the slaves. In doing so, he seemed to sacrifice once for all his literary ambitions and his political future. It even changed the character of his writing. His early poems had been somewhat in the manner of Scott and Byron. His *Legends of New England* (1831) and his long narrative poem, "Moll Pitcher" (1832), indicate to what his tastes might have led him had he not given his strongest efforts to active work for emancipation. He conducted for a short time an abolitionist paper, the *Pennsylvania Freeman*, but he discontinued it when he was threatened by a mob and his office burned as a penalty for his alignment with the abolitionist cause. He wrote much prose in his lifetime, most of it on controversial topics, particularly antislavery propaganda. He was willing to undertake hard political drudgery, for alongside his benevolence and ideality he was endowed with patience, common sense, and practicality. He was a good journalist and rhetorician, and in his protests he made his issues plain in straightforward, conversational language.

At the close of the war he became less the propagandist and more the man of letters. His income was meager indeed until after the publication of *Snow-Bound* (1866), the poem which gave him permanent rank among American poets. He had been able to earn but little by his writing in earlier life and had been forced to practice rigid economy. *Snow-Bound*, however, and his later works brought him large returns.

Whittier found recognition first as the rhyming champion of the abolitionist movement. His antislavery poems, spontaneous and intense, form a large part of his work. These pieces were timely and therefore comparatively transient. They survive mainly for their historic interest. Yet when we read them today, "The Hunters of Men," "Massachusetts to Virginia," and "Ichabod" bring realization of the indignation and the loathing of wrong that stirred Whittier and his contemporaries. His slavery poems make too much, perhaps, of physical suffering, chains, and scourgings, but such emphasis counted in enlisting converts. He owes his lasting place among American poets to the important group of poems in which he writes of nature and simple country life in New England. He had good powers of description and the knack of storytelling, and he is at his best in short and simple ballads. In his later narrative verse he deals chiefly with historic or legendary materials, as in "Barbara Frietchie" or "Skipper Ireson's Ride." He was rooted in his native soil, and much of the bygone life and spirit of New England has been preserved in his work. In *Songs of Labor* (1850) he treats the dignity and independence of labor. Apparently he had past times in mind, however, for such workers as the shoemaker seemed to him like the master craftsmen of old. His outmoded economics did not fit the New England of his day, which had to do not with master craftsmen but with rising capitalism and industrialism. Late in life he wrote religious verse, and he still ranks as our chief religious poet.

Whittier's literary theories, as interpreted by H. H. Clark, evolved through three periods in which he wrote about fifty critical essays and book reviews. Up to 1833 he advocated either romance—fanciful, dreamy, or sensational—or nationalistic localism, as in his prefaces to *Legends of New England* and to the *Literary Remains of J. G. C. Brainard.* Then, from 1833 to 1858, he aimed to make "his rustic reed of song a weapon in the war with wrong," especially slavery, as in "Proem," "Dedication to Songs of Labor," and "Ego." He admired a friend's poems because "to their intrinsic beauty is added the holier aim of philanthropy." In this period also, as his tribute to Burns indicates, he was coming to see the beauty of "simple truth of fact and feeling." Thirdly, from 1858 on, he developed the view presaged in his essay on "The Beautiful" (1846), according to which beauty is not a matter of romantic escape or nationalistic reform but a spiritual quality of the inward life, a timeless and placeless "beauty of holiness." In "An Artist of the Beautiful," he concludes that "Beauty is goodness; ugliness is sin"; and in "The Tent on the Beach" he came to feel that

> Art no other sanction needs
> Than beauty for its own fair sake.

These three successive ideals are illustrated in "The Demon's Cave," "Massachusetts to Virginia," and "Skipper Ireson's Ride."

Whittier was not a great artist or a finished craftsman. Only the poetry of Bryant and Poe shows the same limitations of range. He restricted himself to few and simple meters. His style is often diffuse, his rhymes are careless. His artistic conscience was less strong than his moral, but his work is forceful and intense.

In appearance, Whittier was tall, erect, and slender. His nature is described as gentle, lovable, magnanimous, and kind, and he was genuinely modest about his own work. He never married, perhaps because he lacked the rugged health of his ancestors, or because of his poverty and obligations to his mother and sister, or of the conviction of the Quakers that they should not marry outside their own sect. His seventieth and eightieth birthdays were celebrated by his readers all over the United States. He died at the age of eighty-five, on September 7, 1892, during a visit to New Hampshire.

The standard edition of Whittier's writings is the Riverside, *The Complete Poetical and Prose Works of John Greenleaf Whittier* (7 vols., 1888–1889). The best single-volume edition of his poetry is the Cambridge Edition, edited by Horace E. Scudder (1894). *Whittier Correspondence from the Oak Knoll Collection* was edited by John Albree (1911). F. M. Pray's *A Study of Whittier's Apprenticeship as a Poet* (1930) contains most of his uncollected early poems.

Early lives of Whittier are those by F. H. Underwood (1884), by W. S. Kennedy (1884; revised and enlarged, 1892), and by W. J. Linton in the Great Writers Series (1893). Others are by T. W. Higginson in the English Men of Letters Series (1902); and G. R. Carpenter in the American Men of Letters Series (1903). The most extended life, still the standard one, is that by S. T. Pickard, *The Life and Letters of John Greenleaf Whittier* (2 vols., 1894; revised ed., 1907). Later biographies are G. K. Lewis's *J. G. Whittier, His Life and Work* (1913), and A. Mordell's *Quaker Militant: John Greenleaf Whittier* (1933). The latter is too Freudian to be wholly dependable.

Among critical articles and works may be mentioned those by the following authors: Barrett Wendell, in *Stelligeri and Other Essays* (1893); G. E. Woodberry, in *Makers of Literature* (1900); P. E. More, in *Shelburne Essays*, Third Series (1907); Bliss Perry, in *Park Street Papers* (1908); John Macy, in *The Spirit of American Literature* (1913); I. K. Eastburn, *Whittier's Relation to German Life and Thought* (1915); W. M. Payne, in *CHAL*, II (1918); E. J. Bailey, in *Religious Thought in the Greater American Poets* (1922); N. Foerster, in *Nature in American Literature* (1923); V. L. Parrington, in *Main Currents in American Thought*, II (1927); Alfred Kreymborg, in *Our Singing Strength* (1929); J. S. Stevens, *Whittier's Use of the Bible* (1930); A. Christy, "The Orientalism of Whittier," *American Literature* (Nov., 1933); R. Brenner, in *Twelve American Poets before 1900* (1933); A. T. Murray, *Religious Poems by J. G. Whittier* (1934); G. W. Allen, in *American Prosody* (1935); and B. M. Stearns, "Whittier as an Editor," *New England Quarterly*, XIII, 3 (June, 1940).

For bibliography, see T. F. Currier, *Bibliography of John Greenleaf Whittier* (1937); F. H. Ristine, in *CHAL*, II (1918); and Harry Hartwick, in W. F. Taylor's *A History of American Letters* (1935).

THE EXILE'S DEPARTURE

Whittier's first poem. Published June 9, 1826, in Garrison's Newburyport *Free Press*. It shows the influence of Thomas Moore, author of *Irish Melodies*. Whittier early liked romantic European themes, local settings, and the "Gothic" or weird supernatural. Then his interest shifted to themes of political and social reform, and still later to religious themes. Over a hundred of his early pieces have been printed by Frances M. Pray, *A Study of Whittier's Apprenticeship* (1930). Many show the influence of Scott and Byron.

FOND scenes which delighted my youthful
    existence,
  With feelings of sorrow I bid ye adieu—
A lasting adieu! for now, dim in the distance,
  The shores of Hibernia recede from my
    view.
Farewell to the cliffs, tempest-beaten and
    gray,
  Which guard the lov'd shores of my own
    native land;
Farewell to the village and sail-shadow'd bay,
  The forest-crown'd hill and water-wash'd
    strand.

I've fought for my country—I've brav'd all
    the dangers
  That throng round the path of the warrior
    in strife;   10
I now must depart to a nation of strangers,
  And pass in seclusion the remnant of life:
Far, far from the friends to my bosom most
    dear

With none to support me in peril and pain,
  And none but the stranger to drop the sad
    tear
  On the grave where the heart-broken Exile
    is lain.

Friends of my youth! I must leave you forever,
  And hasten to dwell in a region unknown:—
Yet time cannot change, nor the broad ocean
    sever,
  Hearts firmly united and tried as our
    own.   20
Ah no! though I wander, all sad and forlorn,
  In a far distant land, yet shall memory
    trace,
When far o'er the ocean's white surges I'm
    borne,
  The scene of past pleasures,—my own
    native place.

Farewell, shores of Erin, green land of my
    fathers:—
  Once more, and forever, a mournful adieu!
For round thy dim headlands the ocean mist
    gathers,
  And shrouds the fair isle I no longer can
    view.
I go—but wherever my footsteps I bend,
  For freedom and peace to my own native
    isle,   30
And contentment and joy to each warm-
    hearted friend
  Shall be the heart's prayer of the lonely
    Exile.

1826

TO WILLIAM LLOYD GARRISON

Read at an antislavery convention at Philadelphia, December, 1833. Whittier wrote an essay on Garrison in 1879 (*Works*, VII, 189–192). "My acquaintance with him," he said, "commenced in boyhood. My father was a subscriber to his first paper, the *Free Press*, and the humanitarian tone of his editorials awakened a deep interest in our little household, which was increased by a visit that he made us. When he afterwards edited the *Journal of the Times*, at Bennington, Vermont, I ventured to write him a letter of encouragement and sympathy, urging him to continue his labors against slavery, and assuring him that he could 'do great things,' an unconscious prophecy which has been fulfilled beyond the dream of my boyish enthusiasm. The friendship thus commenced has remained unbroken through half a century, confirming my early confidence in his zeal and devotion, and in the great intellectual and moral strength which he brought to the cause with which his name is identified."

CHAMPION of those who groan beneath
   Oppression's iron hand:
In view of penury, hate, and death,
   I see thee fearless stand.
Still bearing up thy lofty brow,
   In the steadfast strength of truth,
In manhood sealing well the vow
   And promise of thy youth.

Go on, for thou hast chosen well;
   On in the strength of God!   10
Long as one human heart shall swell
   Beneath the tyrant's rod.
Speak in a slumbering nation's ear,
   As thou hast ever spoken,
Until the dead in sin shall hear,
   The fetter's link be broken!

I love thee with a brother's love,
   I feel my pulses thrill,
To mark thy spirit soar above
   The cloud of human ill.   20
My heart hath leaped to answer thine,
   And echo back thy words,
As leaps the warrior's at the shine
   And flash of kindred swords!

They tell me thou art rash and vain,
   A searcher after fame;
That thou art striving but to gain
   A long-enduring name;

That thou hast nerved the Afric's hand
   And steeled the Afric's heart,   30
To shake aloft his vengeful brand,
   And rend his chain apart.

Have I not known thee well, and read
   Thy mighty purpose long?
And watched the trials which have made
   Thy human spirit strong?
And shall the slanderer's demon breath
   Avail with one like me,
To dim the sunshine of my faith
   And earnest trust in thee?   40

Go on, the dagger's point may glare
   Amid thy pathway's gloom;
The fate which sternly threatens there
   Is glorious martyrdom!
Then onward with a martyr's zeal;
   And wait thy sure reward
When man to man no more shall kneel,
   And God alone be Lord!

1832

MEMORIES

According to Pickard (*Life*, I, 276), "It was not without thought and deliberation that in 1888 he directed this poem to be placed at the head of his Poems Subjective and Reminiscent. He had never before publicly acknowledged how much of his heart was wrapped up in this delightful play of poetic fancy. . . . To a friend who told him that "Memories" was her favorite poem, he said 'I love it too; but I hardly knew whether to publish it, it was so personal and so near my heart.'" Among the qualities for which he praises its heroine are timidity (line 30) and artlessness (line 40). In lines 55–63 he refers to his Quakerism. Albert Mordell says that the girl of the poem was Mary Emerson Smith, a distant relative of the poet (*Quaker Militant*, 39–53).

A BEAUTIFUL and happy girl,
   With step as light as summer air,
Eyes glad with smiles, and brow of pearl,
Shadowed by many a careless curl
   Of unconfined and flowing hair;
A seeming child in everything,
   Save thoughtful brow and ripening charms,
As Nature wears the smile of Spring
   When sinking into Summer's arms.

A mind rejoicing in the light 10
  Which melted through its graceful bower,
Leaf after leaf, dew-moist and bright,
And stainless in its holy white,
  Unfolding like a morning flower:
A heart, which, like a fine-toned lute,
  With every breath of feeling woke,
And, even when the tongue was mute,
  From eye and lip in music spoke.

How thrills once more the lengthening chain
  Of memory, at the thought of thee! 20
Old hopes which long in dust have lain,
Old dreams, come thronging back again,
  And boyhood lives again in me;
I feel its glow upon my cheek,
  Its fulness of the heart is mine,
As when I leaned to hear thee speak,
  Or raised my doubtful eye to thine.

I hear again thy low replies,
  I feel thy arm within my own,
And timidly again uprise 30
The fringèd lids of hazel eyes,
  With soft brown tresses overblown.
Ah! memories of sweet summer eves,
  Of moonlit wave and willowy way,
Of stars and flowers, and dewy leaves,
  And smiles and tones more dear than
    they!

Ere this, thy quiet eye hath smiled
  My picture of thy youth to see,
When, half a woman, half a child,
Thy very artlessness beguiled, 40
  And folly's self seemed wise in thee;
I too can smile, when o'er that hour
  The lights of memory backward stream,
Yet feel the while that manhood's power
  Is vainer than my boyhood's dream.

Years have passed on, and left their trace
  Of graver care and deeper thought;
And unto me the calm, cold face
Of manhood, and to thee the grace
  Of woman's pensive beauty brought. 50
More wide, perchance, for blame than praise,
  The schoolboy's humble name has flown;
Thine, in the green and quiet ways
  Of unobtrusive goodness known.

And wider yet in thought and deed
  Diverge our pathways, one in youth;
Thine the Genevan's[1] sternest creed,
While answers to my spirit's need
  The Derby dalesman's simple truth.
For thee, the priestly rite and prayer, 60
  And holy day, and solemn psalm;
For me, the silent reverence where
  My brethren gather, slow and calm.

Yet hath thy spirit left on me
  An impress Time has worn not out,
And something of myself in thee,
A shadow from the past, I see,
  Lingering, even yet, thy way about;
Not wholly can the heart unlearn
  That lesson of its better hours, 70
Nor yet has Time's dull footstep worn
  To common dust that path of flowers.

Thus, while at times before our eyes
  The shadows melt, and fall apart,
And, smiling through them, round us lies
The warm light of our morning skies,—
  The Indian Summer of the heart!—
In secret sympathies of mind,
  In founts of feeling which retain
Their pure, fresh flow, we yet may find 80
  Our early dreams not wholly vain!
1841   1843, 1850

MASSACHUSETTS TO VIRGINIA

Written on reading an account of the proceedings of the citizens of Norfolk, Va., in reference to George Latimer, the alleged fugitive slave, who was seized in Boston without warrant at the request of James B. Grey, of Norfolk, claiming to be his master. The case caused great excitement North and South, and led to the presentation of a petition to Congress, signed by more than fifty thousand citizens of Massachusetts, calling for such laws and proposed amendments to the Constitution as should relieve the Commonwealth from all further participation in the crime of oppression. George Latimer himself was finally given free papers for the sum of four hundred dollars. [*Whittier's note.*]

[1] The Genevan was John Calvin, the Protestant theologian and reformer of the sixteenth century, who lived in Geneva. The "Derby dalesman" (line 59) refers to George Fox, who founded the Society of Friends of which Whittier was a member.

THE blast from Freedom's Northern hills,
  upon its Southern way,
Bears greeting to Virginia from Massachusetts
  Bay;
No word of haughty challenging, nor battle
  bugle's peal,
Nor steady tread of marching files, nor clang
  of horsemen's steel.

No trains of deep-mouthed cannon along our
  highways go;
Around our silent arsenals untrodden lies the
  snow;
And to the land-breeze of our ports, upon
  their errands far,
A thousand sails of commerce swell, but none
  are spread for war.

We hear thy threats, Virginia! thy stormy
  words and high
Swell harshly on the Southern winds which
  melt along our sky;   10
Yet, not one brown, hard hand foregoes its
  honest labor here,
No hewer of our mountain oaks suspends his
  axe in fear.

Wild are the waves which lash the reefs along
  St. George's bank;
Cold on the shores of Labrador the fog lies
  white and dank;
Through storm, and wave, and blinding mist,
  stout are the hearts which man
The fishing-smacks of Marblehead, the sea-
  coasts of Cape Ann.

The cold north light and wintry sun glare on
  their icy forms,
Bent grimly o'er their straining lines or
  wrestling with the storms;
Free as the winds they drive before, rough as
  the waves they roam,
They laugh to scorn the slaver's threat against
  their rocky home.   20

What means the Old Dominion? Hath she
  forgot the day
When o'er her conquered valleys swept the
  Briton's steel array?
How side by side, with sons of hers, the
  Massachusetts men
Encountered Tarleton's charge of fire, and
  stout Cornwallis, then?

Forgets she how the Bay State, in answer to
  the call
Of her old House of Burgesses, spoke out
  from Faneuil Hall?
When, echoing back her Henry's cry, came
  pulsing in each breath
Of Northern winds the thrilling sounds of
  "Liberty or Death!" [1]

What asks the Old Dominion? If now her
  sons have proved
False to their fathers' memory, false to the
  faith they loved;   30
If she can scoff at Freedom, and its great
  charter [2] spurn,
Must we of Massachusetts from truth and
  duty turn?

We hunt your bondmen, flying from Slavery's
  hateful hell;
Our voices, at your bidding, take up the
  bloodhound's yell;
We gather, at your summons, above our
  fathers' graves,
From Freedom's holy altar-horns [3] to tear your
  wretched slaves!

Thank God! not yet so vilely can Massachusetts bow;
The spirit of her early time is with her even
  now;
Dream not because her Pilgrim blood moves
  slow and calm and cool,
She thus can stoop her chainless neck, a
  sister's slave and tool!   40

All that a sister State should do, all that a free
  State may,
Heart, hand, and purse we proffer, as in our
  early day;
But that one dark loathsome burden ye must
  stagger with alone,
And reap the bitter harvest which ye your-
  selves have sown!

[1] Massachusetts followed Virginia by adopting resolutions of Virginia legislators in 1769 and 1774. Faneuil
Hall, in Boston, became conspicuous for its association
with patriotic meetings of the century. Patrick Henry's
noted speech was delivered in March, 1775.   [2] the
Declaration of Independence   [3] I Kings 1:50

Hold, while ye may, your struggling slaves,
  and burden God's free air
With woman's shriek beneath the lash, and
  manhood's wild despair;
Cling closer to the "cleaving curse"[1] that
  writes upon your plains
The blasting of Almighty wrath against a
  land of chains.

Still shame your gallant ancestry, the cavaliers
  of old,
By watching round the shambles where
  human flesh is sold;   50
Gloat o'er the newborn child, and count his
  market value, when
The maddened mother's cry of woe shall
  pierce the slaver's den!

Lower than plummet soundeth, sink the Virginia name;
Plant, if ye will, your fathers' graves with
  rankest weeds of shame;
Be, if ye will, the scandal of God's fair universe;
We wash our hands forever of your sin and
  shame and curse.

A voice from lips whereon the coal from
  Freedom's shrine hath been,
Thrilled, as but yesterday, the hearts of
  Berkshire's[2] mountain men:
The echoes of that solemn voice are sadly
  lingering still
In all our sunny valleys, on every wind-swept
  hill.   60

And when the prowling man-thief came hunt-
  ing for his prey
Beneath the very shadow of Bunker's shaft
  of gray,
How, through the free lips of the son, the
  father's warning spoke;
How, from its bonds of trade and sect, the
  Pilgrim city broke!

A hundred thousand right arms were lifted
  up on high,
A hundred thousand voices sent back their
  loud reply;

Through the thronged towns of Essex the
  startling summons rang,
And up from bench and loom and wheel her
  young mechanics sprang!

The voice of free, broad Middlesex, of thousands as of one,
The shaft of Bunker calling to that of Lexington;   70
From Norfolk's ancient villages, from Plym-
  outh's rocky bound
To where Nantucket feels the arms of ocean
  close her round;

From rich and rural Worcester, where through
  the calm repose
Of cultured vales and fringing woods the
  gentle Nashua flows,
To where Wachuset's wintry blasts the moun-
  tain larches stir,
Swelled up to Heaven the thrilling cry of
  "God save Latimer!"

And sandy Barnstable rose up, wet with the
  salt sea spray;
And Bristol sent her answering shout down
  Narragansett Bay!
Along the broad Connecticut old Hampden
  felt the thrill,
And the cheer of Hampshire's woodmen
  swept down from Holyoke Hill.   80

The voice of Massachusetts! Of her free sons
  and daughters,
Deep calling unto deep aloud, the sound of
  many waters!
Against the burden of that voice what tyrant
  power shall stand?
No fetters in the Bay State! No slave upon her
  land!

Look to it well, Virginians! In calmness we
  have borne,
In answer to our faith and trust, your insult
  and your scorn;
You've spurned our kindest counsels; you've
  hunted for our lives;
And shaken round our hearths and homes
  your manacles and gyves!

We wage no war, we lift no arm, we fling no
  torch within
The fire-damps of the quaking mine beneath
  your soil of sin;   90

---

[1] Genesis 4:11–12   [2] Here and in the five stanzas
that follow eleven of the fourteen counties in Massachusetts are specifically mentioned.

We leave ye with your bondmen, to wrestle,
 while ye can,
With the strong upward tendencies and godlike soul of man!

But for us and for our children, the vow which
 we have given
For freedom and humanity is registered in
 heaven;
No slave-hunt in our borders,—no pirate on
 our strand!
No fetters in the Bay State,—no slave upon
 our land!

            1843

PROEM

Introduction to his first volume of collected
poems (1849). Of interest is the validity of Whittier's view of his own poetry. He admires Sidney,
Spenser, Marvell, and Milton, and recognizes his
own limitations in craftsmanship and profundity
of insight. His ambition is to be the poet of Freedom. His moral sense and social idealism are
stronger than his artistic endowments.

I LOVE the old melodious lays
Which softly melt the ages through,
 The songs of Spenser's golden days,
 Arcadian Sidney's silvery phrase,
Sprinkling our noon of time with freshest
 morning dew.

Yet, vainly in my quiet hours
To breathe their marvelous notes I try;
 I feel them, as the leaves and flowers
 In silence feel the dewy showers,
And drink with glad, still lips the blessing of
 the sky.   10

The rigor of a frozen clime,
The harshness of an untaught ear,
 The jarring words of one whose rime
 Beat often Labor's hurried time,
Or Duty's rugged march through storm and
 strife, are here.

Of mystic beauty, dreamy grace,
No rounded art the lack supplies;
 Unskilled the subtle lines to trace,
 Or softer shades of Nature's face,
I view her common forms with unanointed
 eyes.   20

Nor mine the seer-like power to show
The secrets of the heart and mind;
 To drop the plummet-line below
 Our common world of joy and woe,
A more intense despair or brighter hope to
 find.

Yet here at least an earnest sense
Of human right and weal is shown;
 A hate of tyranny intense,
 And hearty in its vehemence,
As if my brother's pain and sorrow were my
 own.   30

O Freedom! if to me belong
Nor mighty Milton's gift divine,
 Nor Marvell's wit and graceful song,
 Still with a love as deep and strong
As theirs, I lay, like them, my best gifts on
 thy shrine!

1847   1849

From SONGS OF LABOR

Dedication

This dedication should be read in connection
with "Proem" for the light it throws on Whittier's
poetic ideals. He knows his deficiencies as an artist.
The value of his "simple lays of homely toil" lies
in his sympathy with labor, his zeal against injustice, and his manly performance of duty.

I WOULD the gift I offer here
 Might graces from thy favor take,
And, seen through Friendship's atmos-
 phere,
 On softened lines and coloring, wear
The unaccustomed light of beauty, for thy
 sake.

Few leaves of Fancy's spring remain:
 But what I have I give to thee,
The o'er-sunned bloom of summer's plain,
 And paler flowers, the latter rain
Calls from the westering slope of life's
 autumnal lea.   10

Above the fallen groves of green,
 Where youth's enchanted fountain stood,
Dry root and mossèd trunk between,
 A sober aftergrowth is seen,
As springs the pine where falls the gay-leafed
 maple wood.

Yet birds will sing, and breezes play
  Their leaf-harps in the somber tree;
And through the bleak and wintry day
  It keeps its steady green alway.—
So, even my afterthoughts may have a
    charm for thee.   20

Art's perfect forms no moral need,
  And beauty is its own excuse;
But for the dull and flowerless weed
  Some healing virtue still must plead,
And the rough ore must find its honors in its
    use.

So haply these, my simple lays
  Of homely toil, may serve to show
The orchard bloom and tasselled maize
  That skirt and gladden duty's ways,
The unsung beauty hid life's common things
    below.   30

Haply from them the toiler, bent
  Above his forge or plow may gain
A manlier spirit of content,
  And feel that life is wisest spent
Where the strong working hand makes strong
    the working brain.

The doom which to the guilty pair
  Without the walls of Eden came,
Transforming sinless ease to care
  And rugged toil, no more shall bear
The burden of old crime, or mark of primal
    shame.   40

A blessing now, a curse no more;
  Since He, whose name we breathe with
    awe,
The coarse mechanic vesture wore,
  A poor man toiling with the poor,
In labor as in prayer, fulfilling the same law.
                                         1850

The Shoemakers

This poem has especial interest from Whittier's
early experience in shoemaking. Factories were
beginning to produce shoes in vast quantities in
Whittier's day, but he is conscious, in his poem,
rather of the master craftsmen of medieval times
than of rising industrialism.

Ho! workers of the old time styled
  The Gentle Craft of Leather!
Young brothers of the ancient guild,
  Stand forth once more together!
Call out again your long array,
  In the olden merry manner!
Once more, on gay St. Crispin's day,[1]
  Fling out your blazoned banner!

Rap, rap! upon the well-worn stone
  How falls the polished hammer!   10
Rap, rap! the measured sound has grown
  A quick and merry clamor.
Now shape the sole! now deftly curl
  The glossy vamp around it,
And bless the while the bright-eyed girl
  Whose gentle fingers bound it!

For you, along the Spanish main
  A hundred keels are ploughing;
For you, the Indian[2] on the plain
  His lasso-coil is throwing;   20
For you, deep glens with hemlock dark
  The woodman's fire is lighting;
For you, upon the oak's gray bark,
  The woodman's axe is smiting.

For you, from Carolina's pine
  The rosin-gum is stealing;
For you, the dark-eyed Florentine
  Her silken skein is reeling;
For you, the dizzy goatherd roams
  His rugged Alpine ledges;   30
For you, round all her shepherd homes,
  Bloom England's thorny hedges.

The foremost still, by day or night,
  On moated mound or heather,
Where'er the need of trampled right
  Brought toiling men together;
Where the free burghers from the wall
  Defied the mail-clad master,
Than yours, at Freedom's trumpet-call,
  No craftsman rallied faster.   40

Let foplings sneer, let fools deride,
  Ye heed no idle scorner;
Free hands and hearts are still your pride,
  And duty done your honor.

[1] October 25, commemorating the martyrdom, in the
third century, of Crispin, a shoemaker   [2] a reference
to the Indian cowboys of the pampas in Argentina,
which was the chief source of cowhides at the time
Whittier was writing

Ye dare to trust, for honest fame,
　　The jury Time empanels,
And leave to truth each noble name
　　Which glorifies your annals.

Thy songs, Hans Sachs, are living yet,
　　In strong and hearty German;　　　　50
And Bloomfield's lay, and Gifford's wit,
　　And patriot fame of Sherman;
Still from his book, a mystic seer,
　　The soul of Behmen teaches,
And England's priestcraft shakes to hear
　　Of Fox's leathern breeches.

The foot is yours; where'er it falls,
　　It treads your well-wrought leather,
On earthen floor, in marble halls,
　　On carpet, or on heather.　　　　60
Still there the sweetest charm is found
　　Of matron grace or vestal's,
As Hebe's[1] foot bore nectar round
　　Among the old celestials!

Rap, rap!—your stout and bluff brogan,
　　With footsteps slow and weary,
May wander where the sky's blue span
　　Shuts down upon the prairie.
On Beauty's foot your slippers glance,
　　By Saratoga's fountains,[2]　　　　70
Or twinkle down the summer dance
　　Beneath the Crystal Mountains!

The red brick to the mason's hand,
　　The brown earth to the tiller's,[3]
The shoe in yours shall wealth command,
　　Like fairy Cinderella's!
As they who shunned the household maid
　　Beheld the crown upon her,
So all shall see your toil repaid
　　With hearth and home and honor.　　　　80

Then let the toast be freely quaffed,
　　In water cool and brimming,—
"All honor to the good old Craft,
　　Its merry men and women!"
Call out again your long array,
　　In the old time's pleasant manner:
Once more, on gay St. Crispin's day,
　　Fling out his blazoned banner!

1845　　　　　　　　　　　　　　*1850*

[1] cupbearer of the gods in Greek mythology
[2] Saratoga Springs, popular summer resort in the nineteenth century　[3] lines 74 and 76, 82 and 84, instances of the faulty rhymes into which Whittier often lapses

ICHABOD![1]

First published in the *National Era*, May 2, 1850. Later in his collected edition Whittier grouped it among "Personal Poems" and explained its writing in these words:

"This poem was the outcome of the surprise and grief and forecast of evil consequences which I felt on reading the seventh of March speech of Daniel Webster in support of the 'compromise' and the Fugitive Slave Bill. No partisan or personal enmity dictated it. On the contrary my admiration of the splendid personality and intellectual power of the great senator was never stronger than when I laid down his speech, and, in one of the saddest moments of my life, penned my protest. I saw, as I wrote, with painful clearness its sure results,—the Slave Power arrogant and defiant, strengthened and encouraged to carry out its scheme for the extension of its baleful system, or the dissolution of the Union, the guarantees of personal liberty in the free States broken down, and the whole country made the hunting-ground of slave-catchers. In the horror of such a vision, so soon fearfully fulfilled, if one spoke at all, he could speak only in tones of stern and sorrowful rebuke."

Whittier was roused to a white heat of lyric wrath and scorn when he wrote this poem. Webster, who thought it wisest to try to save the Union by a compromise, has been somewhat exonerated by later historians. Many years after writing "Ichabod," Whittier returned to the same subject in "The Lost Occasion" (see page 384), but the severity of his condemnation had now been tempered by the "consciousness of a common inheritance of frailty and weakness." He expressed regret that Webster had not lived until the great climax of the struggle over slavery, thinking that he might then have "made his last days glorious in defence of 'Liberty and Union, one and inseparable.'"

So fallen! so lost! the light withdrawn
　　Which once he wore!
The glory from his gray hairs gone
　　Forevermore!

Revile him not,—the Tempter hath
　　A snare for all;
And pitying tears, not scorn and wrath,
　　Befit his fall!

[1] See I Samuel 4:21

Oh, dumb be passion's stormy rage,
  When he who might   10
Have lighted up and led his age,
  Falls back in night.

Scorn! would the angels laugh, to mark
  A bright soul driven,
Fiend-goaded, down the endless dark,
  From hope and heaven!

Let not the land once proud of him
  Insult him now,
Nor brand with deeper shame his dim,
  Dishonored brow.   20

But let its humbled sons, instead,
  From sea to lake,
A long lament, as for the dead,
  In sadness make.

Of all we loved and honored, naught
  Save power remains,—
A fallen angel's pride of thought,
  Still strong in chains.

All else is gone; from those great eyes
  The soul has fled: 30
When faith is lost, when honor dies,
  The man is dead!

Then, pay the reverence of old days
  To his dead fame;
Walk backward, with averted gaze,
  And hide the shame!

    1850

THE KANSAS EMIGRANTS

This poem was written in the year that the
Kansas-Nebraska Bill was passed.

WE cross the prairie as of old
  The Pilgrims crossed the sea,
To make the West, as they the East,
  The homestead of the free.

We go to rear a wall of men
  On Freedom's southern line,
And plant beside the cotton-tree
  The rugged Northern pine!

We're flowing from our native hills
  As our free rivers flow: 10
The blessing of our Mother-land
  Is on us as we go.

We go to plant her common schools
  On distant prairie swells,
And give the Sabbaths of the wild
  The music of her bells.

Upbearing, like the Ark of old,
  The Bible in our van,
We go to test the truth of God
  Against the fraud of man.   20

No pause, nor rest, save where the streams
  That feed the Kansas run,
Save where our Pilgrim gonfalon
  Shall flout the setting sun!

We'll tread the prairie as of old
  Our fathers sailed the sea,
And make the West, as they the East,
  The homestead of the free!

    1854

BURNS

ON RECEIVING A SPRIG OF HEATHER
IN BLOSSOM

For awaking a lasting interest in Burns's poetry,
Whittier gives credit to his first schoolmaster,
Joshua Coffin, who brought to the Whittier home
a volume of Burns's poems, from which he read,
greatly to the delight of the boy of fourteen. "I
begged him to leave the book with me, and set
myself at once to the task of mastering the glossary of the Scottish dialect at the close. This was
about the first poetry I had ever read (with the
exception of that of the Bible, of which I had been
a close student), and it had a lasting influence
upon me. I began to make rhymes myself, and to
imagine stories and adventures." In "Yankee
Gypsies" (*Prose Works*, I, 336–37), Whittier says
that he owed his introduction to Burns's songs to
a wandering old Scotchman with a rich full voice
who sang "Bonny Doon," "Highland Mary," and
"Auld Lang Syne," after eating bread and cheese
and drinking cider in the old farmhouse kitchen.

No more these simple flowers belong
  To Scottish maid and lover;
Sown in the common soil of song,
  They bloom the wide world over.

In smiles and tears, in sun and showers,
  The minstrel and the heather,
The deathless singer and the flowers
  He sang of live together.

Wild heather-bells and Robert Burns!
  The moorland flower and peasant!   10
How, at their mention, memory turns
  Her pages old and pleasant!

The gray sky wears again its gold
  And purple of adorning,
And manhood's noonday shadows hold
  The dews of boyhood's morning.

The dews that washed the dust and soil
  From off the wings of pleasure,
The sky, that flecked the ground of toil
  With golden threads of leisure.   20

I call to mind the summer day,
  The early harvest mowing,
The sky with sun and clouds at play,
  And flowers with breezes blowing.

I hear the blackbird in the corn,
  The locust in the haying;
And, like the fabled hunter's horn,
  Old tunes my heart is playing.

How oft that day, with fond delay,
  I sought the maple's shadow,   30
And sang with Burns the hours away,
  Forgetful of the meadow!

Bees hummed, birds twittered, overhead
  I heard the squirrels leaping,
The good dog listened while I read,
  And wagged his tail in keeping.

I watched him while in sportive mood
  I read "The Twa Dogs'" story,
And half believed he understood
  The poet's allegory.   40

Sweet day, sweet songs! The golden hours
  Grew brighter for that singing,
From brook and bird and meadow flowers
  A dearer welcome bringing.

New light on home-seen Nature beamed,
  New glory over Woman;
And daily life and duty seemed
  No longer poor and common.

I woke to find the simple truth
  Of fact and feeling better   50
Than all the dreams that held my youth
  A still repining debtor:

That Nature gives her handmaid, Art,
  The themes of sweet discoursing;
The tender idyls of the heart
  In every tongue rehearsing.

Why dream of lands of gold and pearl,
  Of loving knight and lady,
When farmer boy and barefoot girl
  Were wandering there already?   60

I saw through all familiar things
  The romance underlying;
The joys and griefs that plume the wings
  Of Fancy skyward flying.

I saw the same blithe day return,
  The same sweet fall of even,
That rose on wooded Craigie-burn,
  And sank on crystal Devon.

I matched with Scotland's heathery hills
  The sweetbrier and the clover;   70
With Ayr and Doon, my native rills,
  Their wood hymns chanting over.

O'er rank and pomp, as he had seen,
  I saw the Man uprising;
No longer common or unclean,
  The child of God's baptizing!

With clearer eyes I saw the worth
  Of life among the lowly;
The Bible at his Cotter's hearth[1]
  Had made my own more holy.   80

And if at times an evil strain,
  To lawless love appealing,
Broke in upon the sweet refrain
  Of pure and healthful feeling,

It died upon the eye and ear,
  No inward answer gaining;
No heart had I to see or hear
  The discord and the staining.

Let those who never erred forget
  His worth, in vain bewailings;   90
Sweet Soul of Song! I own my debt
  Uncanceled by his failings!

Lament who will the ribald line
  Which tells his lapse from duty,
How kissed the maddening lips of wine
  Or wanton ones of beauty;

[1] stanzas 14–15 of Burns's "The Cotter's Saturday Night"

But think, while falls that shade between
  The erring one and Heaven,
That he who loved like Magdalen,[1]
  Like her may be forgiven.   100

Not his the song whose thunderous chime
  Eternal echoes render;
The mournful Tuscan's[2] haunted rhyme,
  And Milton's starry splendor!

But who his human heart has laid
  To Nature's bosom nearer?
Who sweetened toil like him, or paid
  To love a tribute dearer?

Through all his tuneful art, how strong
  The human feeling gushes!   110
The very moonlight of his song
  Is warm with smiles and blushes!

Give lettered pomp to teeth of Time,
  So "Bonnie Doon" but tarry;
Blot out the Epic's stately rhyme,
  But spare his "Highland Mary"!

            1854

MAUD MULLER

Whittier once said that the suggestion for this poem might have come from an incident in a journey with his sister along the Maine seaboard. They saw a beautiful young girl at work in a hayfield, who blushed as they talked with her and tried to cover her bare feet by raking hay over them.

MAUD MULLER, on a summer's day,
Raked the meadow sweet with hay.

Beneath her torn hat glowed the wealth
Of simple beauty and rustic health.

Singing she wrought, and her merry glee
The mock-bird echoed from his tree.

But when she glanced to the far-off town,
White from its hill-slope looking down,

The sweet song died, and a vague unrest 9
And a nameless longing filled her breast,—

A wish, that she hardly dared to own,
For something better than she had known.

      [1] Luke 7:37-50   [2] Dante

The Judge rode slowly down the lane,
Smoothing his horse's chestnut mane.

He drew his bridle in the shade
Of the apple-trees, to greet the maid,

And asked a draught from the spring that flowed
Through the meadow across the road.

She stooped where the cool spring bubbled up,
And filled for him her small tin cup, 20

And blushed as she gave it, looking down
On her feet so bare, and her tattered gown.

"Thanks!" said the Judge; "a sweeter draught
From a fairer hand was never quaffed."

He spoke of the grass and flowers and trees,
Of the singing birds and the humming bees;

Then talked of the haying, and wondered whether
The cloud in the west would bring foul weather.

And Maud forgot her brier-torn gown,
And her graceful ankles bare and brown; 30

And listened, while a pleased surprise
Looked from her long-lashed hazel eyes.

At last, like one who for delay
Seeks a vain excuse, he rode away.

Maud Muller looked and sighed: "Ah me!
That I the Judge's bride might be!

"He would dress me up in silks so fine,
And praise and toast me at his wine.

"My father should wear a broadcloth coat;
My brother should sail a painted boat. 40

"I'd dress my mother so grand and gay,
And the baby should have a new toy each day.

"And I'd feed the hungry and clothe the poor,
And all should bless me who left our door."

The Judge looked back as he climbed the hill,
And saw Maud Muller standing still.

"A form more fair, a face more sweet,
Ne'er hath it been my lot to meet.

"And her modest answer and graceful air
Show her wise and good as she is fair.   50

"Would she were mine, and I, to-day,
Like her, a harvester of hay:

"No doubtful balance of rights and wrongs,
Nor weary lawyers with endless tongues,

"But low of cattle and song of birds,
And health and quiet and loving words."

But he thought of his sisters proud and cold,
And his mother vain of her rank and gold.

So, closing his heart, the Judge rode on,
And Maud was left in the field alone.   60

But the lawyers smiled that afternoon,
When he hummed in court an old love-tune;

And the young girl mused beside the well
Till the rain on the unraked clover fell.

He wedded a wife of richest dower,
Who lived for fashion, as he for power.

Yet oft, in his marble hearth's bright glow,
He watched a picture come and go;

And sweet Maud Muller's hazel eyes
Looked out in their innocent surprise.   70

Oft, when the wine in his glass was red,
He longed for the wayside well instead:

And closed his eyes on his garnished rooms
To dream of meadows and clover-blooms.

And the proud man sighed, with a secret
    pain,
"Ah, that I were free again!

"Free as when I rode that day,
Where the barefoot maiden raked her hay."

She wedded a man unlearned and poor,
And many children played round her door.

But care and sorrow, and childbirth pain,   81
Left their traces on heart and brain.

And oft, when the summer sun shone hot
On the new-mown hay in the meadow lot,

And she heard the little spring brook fall
Over the roadside, through the wall,

In the shade of the apple-tree again
She saw a rider draw his rein.

And, gazing down with timid grace,
She felt his pleased eyes read her face.   90

Sometimes her narrow kitchen walls
Stretched away into stately halls;

The weary wheel to a spinnet turned,
The tallow candle an astral burned,

And for him who sat by the chimney lug,[1]
Dozing and grumbling o'er pipe and mug,

A manly form at her side she saw,
And joy was duty and love was law.

Then she took up her burden of life again,
Saying only, "It might have been."   100

Alas for maiden, alas for Judge,
For rich repiner and household drudge!

God pity them both! and pity us all,
Who vainly the dreams of youth recall.

For all of sad words of tongue or pen,
The saddest are these: "It might have been!"[2]

Ah, well! for us all some sweet hope lies
Deeply buried from human eyes;

And, in the hereafter, angels may
Roll the stone from its grave away!   110
                                          1854

THE BAREFOOT BOY

This poem of a happy rural childhood is probably in part autobiographical. The number,
variety, and accuracy of the details of landscape,
those of Whittier's own region, should be noted.

[1] Whittier said that "chimney lug" was a reference
"to the old custom in New England of hanging a pole
with hooks attached to it down the chimney, to hang
pots and kettles on."   [2] a rustic pronunciation of
"been," which in standard American English rhymes
with "pin" and in British English with "seen"

BLESSINGS on thee, little man,
Barefoot boy, with cheek of tan!
With thy turned-up pantaloons,
And thy merry whistled tunes;
With thy red lip, redder still
Kissed by strawberries on the hill;
With the sunshine on thy face,
Through thy torn brim's jaunty grace;
From my heart I give thee joy,—
I was once a barefoot boy! 10
Prince thou art,—the grown-up man
Only is republican.
Let the million-dollared ride!
Barefoot, trudging at his side,
Thou hast more than he can buy
In the reach of ear and eye,—
Outward sunshine, inward joy:
Blessings on thee, barefoot boy!

Oh for boyhood's painless play,
Sleep that wakes in laughing day, 20
Health that mocks the doctor's rules,
Knowledge never learned of schools,
Of the wild bee's morning chase,
Of the wild-flower's time and place,
Flight of fowl and habitude
Of the tenants of the wood;
How the tortoise bears his shell,
How the woodchuck digs his cell,
And the ground-mole sinks his well;
How the robin feeds her young, 30
How the oriole's nest is hung;
Where the whitest lilies blow,
Where the freshest berries grow,
Where the ground-nut trails its vine,
Where the wood-grape's clusters shine;
Of the black wasp's cunning way,
Mason of his walls of clay,
And the architectural plans
Of gray hornet artisans!
For, eschewing books and tasks, 40
Nature answers all he asks;
Hand in hand with her he walks,
Face to face with her he talks,
Part and parcel of her joy,—
Blessings on the barefoot boy!

Oh for boyhood's time of June,
Crowding years in one brief moon,
When all things I heard or saw,
Me, their master, waited for.

I was rich in flowers and trees, 50
Humming-birds and honey-bees;
For my sport the squirrel played,
Plied the snouted mole his spade;
For my taste the blackberry cone
Purpled over hedge and stone;
Laughed the brook for my delight
Through the day and through the night,
Whispering at the garden wall,
Talked with me from fall to fall;
Mine the sand-rimmed pickerel pond, 60
Mine the walnut slopes beyond,
Mine, on bending orchard trees,
Apples of Hesperides![1]
Still as my horizon grew,
Larger grew my riches too;
All the world I saw or knew
Seemed a complex Chinese toy,
Fashioned for a barefoot boy!

Oh for festal dainties spread,
Like my bowl of milk and bread; 70
Pewter spoon and bowl of wood,
On the door-stone, gray and rude!
O'er me, like a regal tent,
Cloudy-ribbed, the sunset bent,
Purple-curtained, fringed with gold,
Looped in many a wind-swung fold;
While for music came the play
Of the pied frogs' orchestra;
And, to light the noisy choir,
Lit the fly his lamp of fire. 80
I was monarch: pomp and joy
Waited on the barefoot boy!

Cheerily, then, my little man,
Live and laugh, as boyhood can!
Though the flinty slopes be hard,
Stubble-speared the new-mown sward,
Every morn shall lead thee through
Fresh baptisms of the dew;
Every evening from thy feet
Shall the cool wind kiss the heat: 90
All too soon these feet must hide
In the prison cells of pride,
Lose the freedom of the sod,
Like a colt's for work be shod,

[1] In classical mythology the golden apples given to
Hera on her marriage to Zeus were guarded by four or
five nymphs, helped by a dragon. Both the nymphs and
the garden where the apples grew were called the
Hesperides. It was one of the labors of Hercules to get
some of these apples.

Made to tread the mills of toil,
Up and down in ceaseless moil:
Happy if their track be found
Never on forbidden ground;
Happy if they sink not in
Quick and treacherous sands of sin.   100
Ah! that thou couldst know thy joy,
Ere it passes, barefoot boy!

1855

SKIPPER IRESON'S RIDE

Whittier wrote to Lowell, then editor of the newly established *Atlantic Monthly*, "I send . . . a bit of a Yankee ballad, the spirit of which pleases me more than the execution . . . The incident occurred sometime in the last century. The refrain is the actual song of the women on the march. To relish it one must understand the peculiar tone and dialect of the ancient Marbleheaders." Lowell answered, "I like it all the better for its provincialism . . . I am familiar with Marblehead and its dialect, and as the burthen is intentionally provincial I have taken the liberty to print it in such a way as shall give the peculiar accent. . . ."

The incident on which this poem is based took place in 1807. Whittier heard a bit of rhyme about it when at Haverhill Academy, from a schoolmate from Marblehead, and thought the occurrence much older. In reality Captain Ireson was blameless. The crew were responsible for abandoning the disabled vessel but charged him with the crime, and he was tarred and feathered. See Samuel Roads, Jr., *History of Marblehead* (1879).

OF all the rides since the birth of time,
Told in story or sung in rhyme,—
On Apuleius's Golden Ass,[1]
Or one-eyed Calender's horse of brass,[2]
Witch astride of a human back,
Islam's prophet on Al-Borák,—[3]
The strangest ride that ever was sped
Was Ireson's, out from Marblehead!

[1] Lucius Apuleius, a Roman satirical writer of the second century, tells in his *Metamorphoses* (generally called *The Golden Ass*) of the many adventures of a young man who had been transformed by magic into an ass. The word "golden" in the title refers to the excellence of the story, and not to the ass as Whittier's words seem to imply.   [2] This is a reference to the story told by the third calender in the *Arabian Nights*.   [3] According to legend, Mohammed was carried to the seventh heaven on the back of a strange winged, white mule.

Old Floyd Ireson, for his hard heart,
Tarred and feathered and carried in a cart
By the women of Marblehead!   11

Body of turkey, head of owl,
Wings a-droop like a rained-on fowl,
Feathered and ruffled in every part,
Captain Ireson stood in the cart.
Scores of women, old and young,
Strong of muscle, and glib of tongue,
Pushed and pulled up the rocky lane,
Shouting and singing the shrill refrain:
    "Here's Flud Oirson, fur his horrd horrt,   20
    Torr'd an' futherr'd an' corr'd in a corrt
        By the women o' Morble'ead!"

Wrinkled scolds with hands on hips,
Girls in bloom of cheek and lips,
Wild-eyed, free-limbed, such as chase
Bacchus round some antique vase,
Brief of skirt, with ankles bare,
Loose of kerchief and loose of hair,
With conch-shells blowing and fish-horns'
        twang,
Over and over the Maenads[1] sang: 30
    "Here's Flud Oirson, fur his horrd horrt,
    Torr'd an' futherr'd an' corr'd in a corrt
        By the women o' Morble'ead!"

Small pity for him!—He sailed away
From a leaking ship in Chaleur Bay,—
Sailed away from a sinking wreck,
With his own town's-people on her deck!
"Lay by! lay by!" they called to him.
Back he answered, "Sink or swim!
Brag of your catch of fish again!"   40
And off he sailed through the fog and rain!
    Old Floyd Ireson, for his hard heart,
    Tarred and feathered and carried in a cart
        By the women of Marblehead!

Fathoms deep in dark Chaleur
That wreck shall lie forevermore.
Mother and sister, wife and maid,
Looked from the rocks of Marblehead
Over the moaning and rainy sea,—
Looked for the coming that might not be!   50
What did the winds and the sea-birds say
Of the cruel captain who sailed away?—

[1] The frenzied women followers of Bacchus. To Whittier's mind the excited women of Marblehead seemed to resemble the Maenads pictured in relief on "some antique vase."

Old Floyd Ireson, for his hard heart,
Tarred and feathered and carried in a cart
  By the women of Marblehead!

Through the street, on either side,
Up flew windows, doors swung wide;
Sharp-tongued spinsters, old wives gray,
Treble lent the fish-horn's bray.
Sea-worn grandsires, cripple-bound,   60
Hulks of old sailors run aground,
Shook head, and fist, and hat, and cane,
And cracked with curses the hoarse refrain:
  "Here's Flud Oirson, fur his horrd horrt,
  Torr'd an' futherr'd an' corr'd in a corrt
  By the women o' Morble'ead!"

Sweetly along the Salem road
Bloom of orchard and lilac showed.
Little the wicked skipper knew
Of the fields so green and the sky so blue.   70
Riding there in his sorry trim,
Like an Indian idol glum and grim,
Scarcely he seemed the sound to hear
Of voices shouting, far and near:
  "Here's Flud Oirson, fur his horrd horrt,
  Torr'd an' futherr'd an' corr'd in a corrt
  By the women o' Morble'ead!"

"Hear me, neighbors!" at last he cried,—
"What to me is this noisy ride?
What is the shame that clothes the skin   80
To the nameless horror that lives within?
Waking or sleeping, I see a wreck,
And hear a cry from a reeling deck!
Hate me and curse me,—I only dread
The hand of God and the face of the dead!"
  Said old Floyd Ireson, for his hard heart,
  Tarred and feathered and carried in a cart
  By the women of Marblehead!

Then the wife of the skipper lost at sea
Said, "God has touched him! why should
    we!"   90
Said an old wife mourning her only son,
"Cut the rogue's tether and let him run!"
So with soft relentings and rude excuse,
Half scorn, half pity, they cut him loose,
And gave him a cloak to hide him in,
And left him alone with his shame and sin.
  Poor Floyd Ireson, for his hard heart,
  Tarred and feathered and carried in a cart
  By the women of Marblehead!

1828, 1857   1857

TELLING THE BEES

It was a folk custom brought from the Old
Country to New England to "tell the bees" by
dressing their hives in mourning when there was a
death in the family. This was supposed to keep the
swarms from seeking a new home.

Originally named "The Bees of Fernside." This
poem, narrating a sad story, is thought by critics
to be one of Whittier's best. The local details, the
gap in the wall, the stepping stones in the brook,
the barn, the white horns of the cattle, describe
faithfully the boyhood scenes of the old farm that
was the poet's birthplace.

HERE is the place; right over the hill
  Runs the path I took;
You can see the gap in the old wall still,
  And the stepping-stones in the shallow
    brook.

There is the house, with the gate red-barred,
  And the poplars tall;
And the barn's brown length, and the cattle-
    yard,
  And the white horns tossing above the wall.

There are the beehives ranged in the sun;
  And down by the brink   10
Of the brook are her poor flowers, weed
    o'errun,
  Pansy and daffodil, rose and pink.

A year has gone, as the tortoise goes,
  Heavy and slow;
And the same rose blows, and the same sun
    glows,
  And the same brook sings of a year ago.

There's the same sweet clover-smell in the
    breeze;
  And the June sun warm
Tangles his wings of fire in the trees,
  Setting, as then, over Fernside farm.   20

I mind me how with a lover's care
  From my Sunday coat
I brushed off the burrs, and smoothed my
    hair,
  And cooled at the brookside my brow and
    throat.

Since we parted, a month had passed,—
  To love, a year;
Down through the beeches I looked at last
  On the little red gate and the well-sweep
    near.

I can see it all now,—the slantwise rain
  Of light through the leaves,   30
The sundown's blaze on her window-pane,
  The bloom of her roses under the eaves.

Just the same as a month before,—
  The house and the trees,
The barn's brown gable, the vine by the
    door,—
  Nothing changed but the hives of bees.

Before them, under the garden wall,
  Forward and back,
Went drearily singing the chore-girl small,
  Draping each hive with a shred of black. 40

Trembling, I listened: the summer sun
  Had the chill of snow;
For I knew she was telling the bees of one
  Gone on the journey we all must go!

Then I said to myself, "My Mary weeps
  For the dead today:
Haply her blind old grandsire sleeps
  The fret and the pain of his age away."

But her dog whined low; on the doorway sill,
  With his cane to his chin,   50
The old man sat; and the chore-girl still
  Sung to the bees stealing out and in.

And the song she was singing ever since
  In my ear sounds on:—
"Stay at home, pretty bees, fly not hence!
  Mistress Mary is dead and gone!"

                                         1858

MY PLAYMATE

First published in the *Atlantic Monthly*. The
original title was "Eleanor." Tennyson admired
this gentle, pensive poem. T. W. Higginson gave
it high praise, pointing out, among other features,
the majority of monosyllables in the lines, the
occasional use of telling polysyllables, and the
harmonious combinations of sounds. Mordell
affirms that the girl of this poem is that of
"Memories," Mary Emerson Smith.

The pines were dark on Ramoth hill,[1]
  Their song was soft and low;
The blossoms in the sweet May wind
  Were falling like the snow.

The blossoms drifted at our feet,
  The orchard birds sang clear;
The sweetest and the saddest day
  It seemed of all the year.

For, more to me than birds or flowers,
  My playmate left her home,   10
And took with her the laughing spring,
  The music and the bloom.

She kissed the lips of kith and kin,
  She laid her hand in mine:
What more could ask the bashful boy
  Who fed her father's kine?

She left us in the bloom of May:
  The constant years told o'er
Their seasons with as sweet May morns,
  But she came back no more.   20

I walk, with noiseless feet, the round
  Of uneventful years;
Still o'er and o'er I sow the spring
  And reap the autumn ears.

She lives where all the golden year
  Her summer roses blow;
The dusky children of the sun
  Before her come and go.

There haply with her jeweled hands
  She smooths her silken gown,—   30
No more the homespun lap wherein
  I shook the walnuts down.

The wild grapes wait us by the brook,
  The brown nuts on the hill,
And still the May-day flowers make sweet
  The woods of Follymill.

The lilies blossom in the pond,
  The bird builds in the tree,
The dark pines sing on Ramoth hill
  The slow song of the sea.   40

---

[1] About two miles from the Whittier home at Amesbury. The woods of Follymill (line 36), noted for may-
flowers, were near by.

I wonder if she thinks of them,
  And how the old time seems,—
If ever the pines of Ramoth wood
  Are sounding in her dreams.

I see her face, I hear her voice.
  Does she remember mine?
And what to her is now the boy
  Who fed her father's kine?

What cares she that the orioles build
  For other eyes than ours,—   50
That other hands with nuts are filled,
  And other laps with flowers?

O playmate in the golden time!
  Our mossy seat is green,
Its fringing violets blossom yet,
  The old trees o'er it lean.

The winds so sweet with birch and fern
  A sweeter memory blow;
And there in spring the veeries sing
  The song of long ago.   60

And still the pines of Ramoth wood
  Are moaning like the sea,—
The moaning of the sea of change
  Between myself and thee!

1859–1860   1860

LAUS DEO!

The Latin title, "Praise be to God," is from
the Vulgate, the medieval Latin version of the
Scriptures. As first published the poem had the
subtitle: "On hearing the bells ring for the constitutional amendment abolishing slavery in the
United States." The ratification by the required
number of states was announced Dec. 18, 1865.
Whittier was sitting in the Friends' meetinghouse
at Amesbury when the bells rang out.

  IT is done!
  Clang of bell and roar of gun
Send the tidings up and down.
  How the belfries rock and reel!
  How the great guns, peal on peal,
Fling the joy from town to town!

  Ring, O Bells!
  Every stroke exulting tells
Of the burial hour of crime.

Loud and long, that all may hear,   10
  Ring for every listening ear
Of Eternity and Time!

  Let us kneel:
  God's own voice is in that peal,
And this spot is holy ground.
  Lord, forgive us! What are we,
  That our eyes this glory see,
That our ears have heard the sound!

  For the Lord
  On the whirlwind[1] is abroad;   20
In the earthquake He has spoken;
  He has smitten with His thunder
  The iron walls asunder,
And the gates of brass are broken!

  Loud and long
  Lift the old exulting song;
Sing with Miriam by the sea,[2]
  He has cast the mighty down;
  Horse and rider sink and drown;
"He hath triumphed gloriously!"   30

  Did we dare,
  In our agony of prayer,
Ask for more than He has done?
  When was ever His right hand
  Over any time or land
Stretched as now beneath the sun?

  How they pale,
  Ancient myth and song and tale,
In this wonder of our days,
  When the cruel rod of war   40
  Blossoms white with righteous law,
And the wrath of man is praise!

  Blotted out!
  All within and all about
Shall a fresher life begin;
  Freer breathe the universe
  As it rolls its heavy curse
On the dead and buried sin!

  It is done!
  In the circuit of the sun   50
Shall the sound thereof go forth.
  It shall bid the sad rejoice,
  It shall give the dumb a voice,
It shall belt with joy the earth!

---

[1] Job 28 ff.   [2] Exodus 15:21

Ring and swing,
　Bells of joy! On morning's wing
Send the song of praise abroad!
　With a sound of broken chains
　Tell the nations that He reigns,
Who alone is Lord and God!　　　60
　　　　　　　　　　　　　　1865

SNOW-BOUND

A WINTER IDYL

Whittier's *Snow-Bound* is very generally regarded as his masterpiece. It is chiefly a poem of description and character, a beautiful picture of a family circle and home. A record of a type of life that has vanished, or all but vanished, this poem of a New England farmhouse in midwinter, and the group about its fireside, is a social document of high value.

　　　　　　────────

As the Spirits of Darkness be stronger in the dark, so Good Spirits which be Angels of Light are augmented not only by the Divine light of the Sun, but also by our common VVood Fire: and as the Celestial Fire drives away dark spirits, so also this our Fire of VVood doth the same.—COR. AGRIPPA, *Occult Philosophy*, Book I, ch. v.

Announced by all the trumpets of the sky,
Arrives the snow, and, driving o'er the fields,
Seems nowhere to alight: the whited air
Hides hills and woods, the river, and the heaven,
And veils the farm-house at the garden's end.
The sled and traveler stopped, the courier's feet
Delayed, all friends shut out, the housemates sit
Around the radiant fireplace, enclosed
In a tumultuous privacy of storm.
　　　　　　EMERSON, *The Snow-Storm*

THE sun that brief December day
Rose cheerless over hills of gray,
And, darkly circled, gave at noon
A sadder light than waning moon.
Slow tracing down the thickening sky
Its mute and ominous prophecy,
A portent seeming less than threat,
It sank from sight before it set.
A chill no coat, however stout,
Of homespun stuff could quite shut out,　　10
A hard, dull bitterness of cold,
　That checked, mid-vein, the circling race
　Of life-blood in the sharpened face,
The coming of the snow-storm told.

The wind blew east[1]: we heard the roar
Of Ocean on his wintry shore,
And felt the strong pulse throbbing there
Beat with low rhythm our inland air.

Meanwhile we did our nightly chores,—
Brought in the wood from out of doors,　　20
Littered the stalls, and from the mows
Raked down the herd's-grass for the cows;
Heard the horse whinnying for his corn;
And, sharply clashing horn on horn,
Impatient down the stanchion rows
The cattle shake their walnut bows[2];
While, peering from his early perch
Upon the scaffold's pole of birch,
The cock his crested helmet bent
And down his querulous challenge sent.　　30
Unwarmed by any sunset light
The gray day darkened into night,
A night made hoary with the swarm
And whirl-dance of the blinding storm,
As zigzag wavering to and fro,
Crossed and recrossed the winged snow:
And ere the early bedtime came
The white drift piled the window-frame,
And through the glass the clothes-line posts
Looked in like tall and sheeted ghosts.　　40

So all night long the storm roared on:
The morning broke without a sun;
In tiny spherule traced with lines
Of Nature's geometric signs,
In starry flake and pellicle,
All day the hoary meteor fell;
And, when the second morning shone,
We looked upon a world unknown,
On nothing we could call our own.
Around the glistening wonder bent　　50
The blue walls of the firmament,
No cloud above, no earth below,—
A universe of sky and snow!
The old familiar sights of ours
Took marvelous shapes; strange domes and
　　towers
Rose up where sty or corn-crib stood,
Or garden-wall, or belt of wood;

────────

[1] That is, the wind blew from the east. The Whittier home was about fifteen miles from the Atlantic and under the conditions described the sound of the sea beating upon the shore could be faintly heard.　[2] The stanchions were upright bars with walnut bows attached by which cattle were held in their stalls.

A smooth white mound the brush-pile
   showed,
A fenceless drift what once was road;
The bridle-post an old man sat   60
With loose-flung coat and high cocked hat;
The well-curb had a Chinese roof [1];
And even the long sweep, high aloof,
In its slant splendor, seemed to tell
Of Pisa's leaning miracle. [2]

A prompt, decisive man, no breath
Our father wasted: "Boys, a path!"
Well pleased, (for when did farmer boy
Count such a summons less than joy?)
Our buskins on our feet we drew;   70
  With mittened hands, and caps drawn low,
  To guard our necks and ears from snow,
We cut the solid whiteness through.
And, where the drift was deepest, made
A tunnel walled and overlaid
With dazzling crystal: we had read
Of rare Aladdin's wondrous cave, [3]
And to our own his name we gave,
With many a wish the luck were ours
To test his lamp's supernal powers.   80
We reached the barn with merry din,
And roused the prisoned brutes within.
The old horse thrust his long head out,
And grave with wonder gazed about;
The cock his lusty greeting said,
And forth his speckled harem led;
The oxen lashed their tails, and hooked,
And mild reproach of hunger looked;
The hornèd patriarch of the sheep,
Like Egypt's Amun [4] roused from sleep,   90
Shook his sage head with gesture mute,
And emphasized with stamp of foot.

All day the gusty north-wind bore
The loosening drift its breath before;
Low circling round its southern zone,
The sun through dazzling snow-mist shone.

No church-bell lent its Christian tone
To the savage air, no social smoke
Curled over woods of snow-hung oak.
A solitude made more intense   100
By dreary-voicèd elements,
The shrieking of the mindless wind,
The moaning tree-boughs swaying blind,
And on the glass the unmeaning beat
Of ghostly finger-tips of sleet.
Beyond the circle of our hearth
No welcome sound of toil or mirth
Unbound the spell, and testified
Of human life and thought outside.
We minded that the sharpest ear   110
The buried brooklet could not hear,
The music of whose liquid lip
Had been to us companionship,
And, in our lonely life, had grown
To have an almost human tone.

As night drew on, and, from the crest
Of wooded knolls that ridged the west,
The sun, a snow-blown traveler, sank
From sight beneath the smothering bank,
We piled with care our nightly stack   120
Of wood against the chimney-back,—
The oaken log, green, huge, and thick,
And on its top the stout backstick;
The knotty forestick laid apart,
And filled between with curious art
The ragged brush; then, hovering near,
We watched the first red blaze appear,
Heard the sharp crackle, caught the gleam
On whitewashed wall and sagging beam,
Until the old, rude-furnished room   130
Burst, flower-like, into rosy bloom;
While radiant with a mimic flame
Outside the sparkling drift became,
And through the bare-boughed lilac-tree
Our own warm hearth seemed blazing
   free.
The crane and pendent trammels [1] showed,
The Turks' heads on the andirons [2] glowed;
While childish fancy, prompt to tell
The meaning of the miracle,
Whispered the old rhyme: "*Under the tree* 140

When fire outdoors burns merrily,
There the witches are making tea." [1]

The moon above the eastern wood
Shone at its full; the hill-range stood
Transfigured in the silver flood,
Its blown snows flashing cold and keen,
Dead white, save where some sharp ravine
Took shadow, or the somber green
Of hemlocks turned to pitchy black
Against the whiteness at their back.   150
For such a world and such a night
Most fitting that unwarming light,
Which only seemed where'er it fell
To make the coldness visible.

Shut in from all the world without,
We sat the clean-winged hearth about,
Content to let the north-wind roar
In baffled rage at pane and door,
While the red logs before us beat
The frost-line back with tropic heat;   160
And ever, when a louder blast
Shook beam and rafter as it passed,
The merrier up its roaring draught
The great throat of the chimney laughed;
The house-dog on his paws outspread
Laid to the fire his drowsy head,
The cat's dark silhouette on the wall
A couchant tiger's seemed to fall;
And, for the winter fireside meet,
Between the andirons' straddling feet,   170
The mug of cider simmered slow,
The apples sputtered in a row,
And, close at hand, the basket stood
With nuts from brown October's wood.

What matter how the night behaved?
What matter how the north-wind raved?
Blow high, blow low, not all its snow
Could quench our hearth-fire's ruddy glow.
O Time and Change!—with hair as gray
As was my sire's that winter day,   180
How strange it seems, with so much gone
Of life and love, to still live on!
Ah, brother! [2] only I and thou
Are left of all that circle now,—

The dear home faces whereupon
That fitful firelight paled and shone.
Henceforward, listen as we will,
The voices of that hearth are still;
Look where we may, the wide earth o'er,
Those lighted faces smile no more.   190
We tread the paths their feet have worn,
   We sit beneath their orchard-trees,
   We hear, like them, the hum of bees
And rustle of the bladed corn;
We turn the pages that they read,
   Their written words we linger o'er,
But in the sun they cast no shade,
No voice is heard, no sign is made,
   No step is on the conscious floor!
Yet Love will dream, and Faith will trust,   200
(Since He who knows our need is just,)
That somehow, somewhere, meet we must.
Alas for him who never sees
The stars shine through his cypress-trees!
Who, hopeless, lays his dead away,
Nor looks to see the breaking day
Across the mournful marbles play!
Who hath not learned, in hours of faith,
   The truth to flesh and sense unknown,
That Life is ever lord of Death,   210
   And Love can never lose its own!

We sped the time with stories old,
Wrought puzzles out, and riddles told,
Or stammered from our school-book lore
"The chief of Gambia's golden shore." [1]
How often since, when all the land
Was clay in Slavery's shaping hand,
As if a trumpet called, I've heard,
Dame Mercy Warren's rousing word:
"Does not the voice of reason cry,   220
   Claim the first right which Nature gave,
From the red scourge of bondage fly,
   Nor deign to live a burdened slave!"
Our father [2] rode again his ride
On Memphremagog's wooded side;

---

[1] According to an old superstition, the reflection of the fire on the snow outside was the witches' fire and it was not safe to go out of doors and to stand in the reflection.   [2] Whittier's younger brother Matthew died in 1883 at the age of seventy-one.

[1] From the third stanza of "The African Chief," by Sarah Wentworth Morton. The four lines (220–223) quoted below are from the same poem, forming the fourth stanza. Whittier's memory was at fault in attributing them to Dame Mercy Warren. In later editions lines 218–219 were changed to read:

   As if a far-blown trumpet stirred
      The languorous sin-sick air, I heard.

[2] John Whittier, the poet's father, died in 1830. As a young man, he had made the trips into Canada of which he tells in these lines.

Sat down again to moose and samp
In trapper's hut and Indian camp;
Lived o'er the old idyllic ease
Beneath St. François' hemlock trees;
Again for him the moonlight shone   230
On Norman cap and bodiced zone;

Again he heard the violin play
Which led the village dance away,
And mingled in its merry whirl
The grandam and the laughing girl.
Or, nearer home, our steps he led
Where Salisbury's level marshes spread
  Mile-wide as flies the laden bee;
Where merry mowers, hale and strong,
Swept, scythe on scythe, their swaths
    along   240
  The low green prairies of the sea.
We shared the fishing off Boar's Head,
  And round the rocky Isles of Shoals
  The hake-broil on the driftwood coals;
The chowder on the sand-beach made,
Dipped by the hungry, steaming hot,
With spoons of clam-shell from the pot.
We heard the tales of witchcraft old,
And dream and sign and marvel told
To sleepy listeners as they lay   250
Stretched idly on the salted hay
Adrift along the winding shores,
When favoring breezes deigned to blow
The square sail of the gundalow,
And idle lay the useless oars.

Our mother,[1] while she turned her wheel
Or run the new-knit stocking-heel,
Told how the Indian hordes came down
At midnight on Cocheco town,
And how her own great-uncle bore   260
His cruel scalp-mark to fourscore.
Recalling, in her fitting phrase,
  So rich and picturesque and free,
  (The common unrimed poetry
Of simple life and country ways)
The story of her early days,—
She made us welcome to her home;
Old hearths grew wide to give us room;
We stole with her a frightened look
At the gray wizard's conjuring-book,[2]   270

The fame whereof went far and wide
Through all the simple country-side;
We heard the hawks at twilight play,
The boat-horn on Piscataqua,
The loon's weird laughter far away;
We fished her little trout-brook, knew
What flowers in wood and meadow grew,
What sunny hillsides autumn-brown
She climbed to shake the ripe nuts down,
Saw where in sheltered cove and bay   280
The ducks' black squadron anchored lay,
And heard the wild-geese calling loud
Beneath the gray November cloud.

Then, haply, with a look more grave,
And soberer tone, some tale she gave
From painful Sewel's ancient tome,[1]
Beloved in every Quaker home,
Of faith fire-winged by martyrdom,
Or Chalkley's Journal,[2] old and quaint,—
Gentlest of skippers, rare sea-saint!—   290
Who, when the dreary calms prevailed,
And water-butt and bread-cask failed,
And cruel, hungry eyes pursued
His portly presence, mad for food,
With dark hints muttered under breath
Of casting lots for life or death,
Offered, if Heaven withheld supplies,
To be himself the sacrifice.
Then, suddenly, as if to save
The good man from his living grave,   300
A ripple on the water grew,
A school of porpoise flashed in view.
"Take, eat," he said, "and be content;
These fishes in my stead are sent
By Him who gave the tangled ram[3]
To spare the child of Abraham."

Our uncle,[4] innocent of books,
Was rich in lore of fields and brooks,
The ancient teachers never dumb
Of Nature's unhoused lyceum.   310
In moons and tides and weather wise,
He read the clouds as prophecies,
And foul or fair could well divine,
By many an occult hint and sign,

---

[1] Abigail Hussey Whittier, who died in 1857
[2] This was a copy of Cornelius Agrippa's *Three Books of Occult Philosophy* from which Whittier quoted in his note at the beginning of *Snow-Bound*.

[1] William Sewel's *History of the Quakers* was "painful" (i.e., painstaking) rather than enlivening.
[2] Thomas Chalkley, a traveling Quaker preacher, tells the story substantially as remembered by Whittier's mother.   [3] Genesis 23:13   [4] Moses Whittier, bachelor uncle, died in 1824.

Holding the cunning-warded keys[1]
To all the woodcraft mysteries;
Himself to Nature's heart so near
That all her voices in his ear
Of beast or bird had meanings clear,
Like Apollonius of old,   320
Who knew the tales the sparrows told,
Or Hermes, who interpreted
What the sage cranes of Nilus said;
A simple, guileless, childlike man,
Content to live where life began;
Strong only on his native grounds,
The little world of sights and sounds
Whose girdle was the parish bounds,
Whereof his fondly partial pride
The common features magnified,   330
As Surrey hills to mountains grew
In White of Selborne's loving view,—
He told how teal and loon he shot,
And how the eagle's eggs he got,
The feats on pond and river done,
The prodigies of rod and gun;
Till, warming with the tales he told,
Forgotten was the outside cold,
The bitter wind unheeded blew,
From ripening corn the pigeons flew,   340
The partridge drummed i' the wood, the mink
Went fishing down the river-brink.
In fields with bean or clover gay,
The woodchuck, like a hermit gray,
    Peered from the doorway of his cell;
The muskrat plied the mason's trade,
And tier by tier his mud-walls laid;
And from the shagbark overhead
    The grizzled squirrel dropped his shell.

Next, the dear aunt,[2] whose smile of cheer   350
And voice in dreams I see and hear,—
The sweetest woman ever Fate
Perverse denied a household mate,
Who, lonely, homeless, not the less
Found peace in love's unselfishness,
And welcome whereso'er she went,
A calm and gracious element,
Whose presence seemed the sweet income
And womanly atmosphere of home,—
Called up her girlhood memories,   360

The huskings and the apple-bees,
The sleigh-rides and the summer sails,
Weaving through all the poor details
And homespun warp of circumstance
A golden woof-thread of romance.
For well she kept her genial mood
And simple faith of maidenhood;
Before her still a cloud-land lay,
The mirage loomed across her way;
The morning dew, that dries so soon   370
With others, glistened at her noon;
Through years of toil and soil and care,
From glossy tress to thin gray hair,
All unprofaned she held apart
The virgin fancies of the heart.
Be shame to him of woman born
Who hath for such but thought of scorn.

There, too, our elder sister[1] plied
Her evening task the stand beside;
A full, rich nature, free to trust,   380
Truthful and almost sternly just,
Impulsive, earnest, prompt to act,
And make her generous thought a fact,
Keeping with many a light disguise
The secret of self-sacrifice.
O heart sore-tried! thou hast the best
That Heaven itself could give thee,—rest,
Rest from all bitter thoughts and things!
    How many a poor one's blessing went
    With thee beneath the low green tent   390
Whose curtain never outward swings!

As one who held herself a part
Of all she saw, and let her heart
    Against the household bosom lean,
Upon the motley-braided mat
Our youngest[2] and our dearest sat,
Lifting her large, sweet, asking eyes,
    Now bathed within the fadeless green
And holy peace of Paradise.
Oh, looking from some heavenly hill,   400
    Or from the shade of saintly palms,
    Or silver reach of river calms,
Do those large eyes behold me still?
With me one little year ago:—
The chill weight of the winter snow
    For months upon her grave has lain;

[1] The wards of a key are the notches that allow it, when turned, to pass the projections in the lock. Whittier's compound word suggests an intricately made key.
[2] Mercy Hussey, sister of Whittier's mother, died in 1846.

[1] Mary, later married to Jacob Caldwell, died in 1860.
[2] Whittier's sister Elizabeth died in 1864, the year before Snow-Bound was written.

And now, when summer south-winds blow
  And brier and harebell bloom again,
I tread the pleasant paths we trod,
I see the violet-sprinkled sod   410
Whereon she leaned, too frail and weak
The hillside flowers she loved to seek,
Yet following me where'er I went
With dark eyes full of love's content.
The birds are glad; the brier-rose fills
The air with sweetness; all the hills
Stretch green to June's unclouded sky;
But still I wait with ear and eye
For something gone which should be nigh,
A loss in all familiar things,   420
In flower that blooms, and bird that sings.
And yet, dear heart! remembering thee,
  Am I not richer than of old?
Safe in thy immortality,
  What change can reach the wealth I hold?
  What chance can mar the pearl and gold
Thy love hath left in trust with me?
And while in life's late afternoon,
  Where cool and long the shadows grow,
I walk to meet the night that soon   430
  Shall shape and shadow overflow,
I cannot feel that thou art far,
Since near at need the angels are;
And when the sunset gates unbar,
  Shall I not see thee waiting stand,
And, white against the evening star,
  The welcome of thy beckoning hand?

Brisk wielder of the birch and rule,[1]
The master of the district school
Held at the fire his favored place,   440
Its warm glow lit a laughing face
Fresh-hued and fair, where scarce appeared
The uncertain prophecy of beard.
He teased the mitten-blinded cat,[2]
Played cross-pins on my uncle's hat,
Sang songs, and told us what befalls
In classic Dartmouth's college halls.
Born the wild Northern hills among,
From whence his yeoman father wrung
By patient toil subsistence scant,   450
Not competence and yet not want,
He early gained the power to pay
His cheerful, self-reliant way;

Could doff at ease his scholar's gown
To peddle wares from town to town;
Or through the long vacation's reach
In lonely lowland districts teach,
Where all the droll experience found
At stranger hearths in boarding round,
The moonlit skater's keen delight,   460
The sleigh-drive through the frosty night,
The rustic party, with its rough
Accompaniment of blind-man's-buff,
And whirling plate, and forfeits paid,
His winter task a pastime made.
Happy the snow-locked homes wherein
He tuned his merry violin,
Or played the athlete in the barn,
Or held the good dame's winding yarn,
Or mirth-provoking versions told   470
Of classic legends rare and old,
Wherein the scenes of Greece and Rome
Had all the commonplace of home,
And little seemed at best the odds
'Twixt Yankee pedlers and old gods;
Where Pindus-born Araxes took
The guise of any grist-mill brook,
And dread Olympus at his will
Became a huckleberry hill.

A careless boy that night he seemed;   480
  But at his desk he had the look
And air of one who wisely schemed,
  And hostage from the future took[1]
  In trainèd thought and lore of book.
Large-brained, clear-eyed,—of such as he
Shall Freedom's young apostles be,
Who, following in War's bloody trail,
Shall every lingering wrong assail;
All chains from limb and spirit strike,
Uplift the black and white alike;   490
Scatter before their swift advance
The darkness and the ignorance,
The pride, the lust, the squalid sloth,
Which nurtured Treason's monstrous growth,
Made murder pastime, and the hell
Of prison-torture possible;
The cruel lie of caste refute,
Old forms remold, and substitute
For Slavery's lash the freeman's will,
For blind routine, wise-handed skill;   500

---

[1] George Haskell, Dartmouth student [2] An old trick in teasing a cat was to slip a mitten over its head.

[1] Being wise enough to foresee the future trend of events, he could use that insight as a guide in the affairs of the present.

A school-house plant on every hill,
Stretching in radiate nerve-lines thence
The quick wires of intelligence;
Till North and South together brought
Shall own the same electric thought,
In peace a common flag salute,
And, side by side in labor's free
And unresentful rivalry,
Harvest the fields wherein they fought.

Another guest[1] that winter night   510
Flashed back from lustrous eyes the light.
Unmarked by time, and yet not young,
The honeyed music of her tongue
And words of meekness scarcely told
A nature passionate and bold,
Strong, self-concentered, spurning guide,
Its milder features dwarfed beside
Her unbent will's majestic pride.
She sat among us, at the best,
A not unfeared, half-welcome guest,   520
Rebuking with her cultured phrase
Our homeliness of words and ways.
A certain pard-like, treacherous grace
    Swayed the lithe limbs and drooped the
        lash,
    Lent the white teeth their dazzling flash;
    And under low brows, black with night,
    Rayed out at times a dangerous light;
The sharp heat-lightnings of her face
    Presaging ill to him whom Fate
Condemned to share her love or hate.   530
A woman tropical, intense
In thought and act, in soul and sense,
She blended in a like degree
The vixen and the devotee,
Revealing with each freak or feint
    The temper of Petruchio's Kate,[2]
The raptures of Siena's saint.[3]
Her tapering hand and rounded wrist
Had facile power to form a fist;
The warm, dark languish of her eyes   540
Was never safe from wrath's surprise.

Brows saintly calm and lips devout
Knew every change of scowl and pout;
And the sweet voice had notes more high
And shrill for social battle-cry.

Since then what old cathedral town
Has missed her pilgrim staff and gown,
What convent-gate has held its lock
Against the challenge of her knock!
Through Smyrna's plague-hushed thor-
    oughfares,   550
Up sea-set Malta's rocky stairs,
Gray olive slopes of hills that hem
Thy tombs and shrines, Jerusalem,
Or startling on her desert throne
The crazy Queen of Lebanon[1]
With claims fantastic as her own,
Her tireless feet have held their way;
And still, unrestful, bowed, and gray,
She watches under Eastern skies,
    With hope each day renewed and fresh, 560
    The Lord's quick coming in the flesh,
Whereof she dreams and prophesies!

Where'er her troubled path may be,
    The Lord's sweet pity with her go!
The outward wayward life we see,
    The hidden springs we may not know.
Nor is it given us to discern
    What threads the fatal sisters[2] spun,
    Through what ancestral years has run
The sorrow with the woman born,   570
What forged her cruel chain of moods,
What set her feet in solitudes,
    And held the love within her mute,
What mingled madness in the blood,
    A life-long discord and annoy,
    Water of tears with oil of joy,
And hid within the folded bud
    Perversities of flower and fruit.
It is not ours to separate
The tangled skein of will and fate,   580
To show what metes and bounds should stand
Upon the soul's debatable land,

---

[1] Whittier said this was "Harriet Livermore, daughter of Judge Livermore, of New Hampshire, a young woman of fine natural ability, enthusiastic, eccentric, with slight control over her violent temper, which sometimes made her religious profession doubtful."   [2] the high-tempered heroine of Shakespeare's *The Taming of the Shrew*   [3] Saint Catherine of Siena, noted for her mildness and charity

[1] Lady Hester Stanhope, eccentric religious enthusiast, who established herself on the slope of Mt. Lebanon, where she awaited the second coming of Christ. Miss Livermore lived with her for some time, but the two finally quarreled.   [2] in Greek mythology, the three Fates, Clotho, Lachesis, and Atropos, who respectively spun the thread of life, drew it out to its destined length, and snipped it off

And between choice and Providence
Divide the circle of events;
But He who knows our frame is just,
   Merciful and compassionate,
And full of sweet assurances
And hope for all the language is,
That He remembereth we are dust!

At last the great logs, crumbling low,   590
Sent out a dull and duller glow,
The bull's-eye watch that hung in view,
Ticking its weary circuit through,
Pointed with mutely-warning sign
Its black hand to the hour of nine.
That sign the pleasant circle broke:
My uncle ceased his pipe to smoke,
Knocked from its bowl the refuse gray
And laid it tenderly away,
Then roused himself to safely cover   600
The dull red brands with ashes over.
And while, with care, our mother laid
The work aside, her steps she stayed
One moment, seeking to express
Her grateful sense of happiness
For food and shelter, warmth and health,
And love's contentment more than wealth,
With simple wishes (not the weak,
Vain prayers which no fulfilment seek,
But such as warm the generous heart,   610
O'er-prompt to do with Heaven its part)
That none might lack, that bitter night,
For bread and clothing, warmth and light.

Within our beds awhile we heard
The wind that round the gables roared,
With now and then a ruder shock,
Which made our very bedsteads rock.
We heard the loosened clapboards tost,
The board-nails snapping in the frost;
And on us, through the unplastered wall,   620
Felt the light-sifted snow-flakes fall;
But sleep stole on, as sleep will do
When hearts are light and life is new;
Faint and more faint the murmurs grew,
Till in the summer-land of dreams
They softened to the sound of streams,
Low stir of leaves, and dip of oars,
And lapsing waves on quiet shores.

Next morn we wakened with the shout
Of merry voices high and clear;   630

And saw the teamsters drawing near
To break the drifted highways out.
Down the long hillside treading slow
We saw the half-buried oxen go,
Shaking the snow from heads uptost,
Their straining nostrils white with frost.
Before our door the straggling train
Drew up, an added team to gain.
The elders threshed their hands a-cold,
   Passed, with the cider-mug, their jokes 640
   From lip to lip; the younger folks
Down the loose snow-banks, wrestling, rolled,
Then toiled again the cavalcade
   O'er windy hill, through clogged ravine,
   And woodland paths that wound between
Low drooping pine-boughs winter-weighed.
From every barn a team afoot,
At every house a new recruit,
Where, drawn by Nature's subtlest law,
Haply the watchful young men saw   650
Sweet doorway pictures of the curls
And curious eyes of merry girls,
Lifting their hands in mock defense
Against the snow-ball's compliments,
And reading in each missive tost
The charm with Eden never lost.

We heard once more the sleigh-bells' sound;
   And, following where the teamsters led,
The wise old Doctor[1] went his round,
Just pausing at our door to say,   660
In the brief autocratic way
Of one who, prompt at Duty's call,
Was free to urge her claim on all,
   That some poor neighbor sick abed
At night our mother's aid would need.
For, one in generous thought and deed,
   What mattered in the sufferer's sight
   The Quaker matron's inward light,
The Doctor's mail of Calvin's creed?
All hearts confess the saints elect   670
   Who, twain in faith, in love agree,
And melt not in an acid sect
   The Christian pearl of charity!

So days went on: a week had passed
Since the great world was heard from last.
The almanac we studied o'er,
Read and reread our little store

[1] Dr. Elias Weld of Rocks Village

Of books and pamphlets, scarce a score;
One harmless novel, mostly hid
From younger eyes, a book forbid,   680
And poetry, (or good or bad,
A single book was all we had,)
Where Ellwood's meek, drab-skirted Muse,
    A stranger to the heathen Nine,
    Sang, with a somewhat nasal whine,
The wars of David and the Jews.
At last the floundering carrier bore
The village paper to our door.
Lo! broadening outward as we read,
To warmer zones the horizon spread;   690
In panoramic length unrolled
We saw the marvels that it told.[1]
Before us passed the painted Creeks,
    And daft McGregor on his raids
    In Costa Rica's everglades.
And up Taygetos winding slow
Rode Ypsilanti's Mainote Greeks,
A Turk's head at each saddle bow!
Welcome to us its week-old news,
Its corner for the rustic Muse,   700
    Its monthly gauge of snow and rain,
Its record, mingling in a breath
The wedding bell and dirge of death;
Jest, anecdote, and love-lorn tale,
The latest culprit sent to jail;
Its hue and cry of stolen and lost,
Its vendue sales and goods at cost,
    And traffic calling loud for gain.
We felt the stir of hall and street,
The pulse of life that round us beat;   710
The chill embargo of the snow
Was melted in the genial glow;
Wide swung again our ice-locked door,
And all the world was ours once more!

Clasp, Angel of the backward look
    And folded wings of ashen gray
    And voice of echoes far away,
The brazen covers of thy book;
The weird palimpsest[2] old and vast,

Wherein thou hid'st the spectral past;   720
Where, closely mingling, pale and glow
The characters of joy and woe;
The monographs of outlived years,
Or smile-illumed or dim with tears,
    Green hills of life that slope to death,
And haunts of home, whose vistaed trees
Shade off to mournful cypresses
    With the white amaranths underneath.
Even while I look, I can but heed
    The restless sands' incessant fall,   730
Importunate hours that hours succeed,
Each clamorous with its own sharp need,
    And duty keeping pace with all.
Shut down and clasp the heavy lids;
I hear again the voice that bids
The dreamer leave his dream midway
For larger hopes and graver fears:
Life greatens in these later years,
The century's aloe[1] flowers today!
Yet, haply, in some lull of life,   740
Some Truce of God which breaks its strife
The worldling's eyes shall gather dew,
    Dreaming in throngful city ways
Of winter joys his boyhood knew;
And dear and early friends—the few
Who yet remain—shall pause to view
    These Flemish pictures[2] of old days;
Sit with me by the homestead hearth,
And stretch the hands of memory forth
    To warm them at the wood-fire's blaze!   750
And thanks untraced to lips unknown
Shall greet me like the odors blown
From unseen meadows newly mown,
Or lilies floating in some pond,
Wood-fringed, the wayside gaze beyond;
The traveler owns the grateful sense
Of sweetness near, he knows not whence,
And, pausing, takes with forehead bare
The benediction of the air.

1865   1866

[1] The contents of the village paper indicate that the scenes described in *Snow-Bound* took place when Whittier was about fifteen years of age. The Creek Indians were removed to Indian Territory in 1821, Sir Gregor McGregor was attempting to form a colony in Costa Rica in 1822, and the struggle of the Greeks for their independence from Turkey was going on then.   [2] a parchment which has been written over more than once, former writings having been erased

[1] The century plant was formerly supposed to bloom only once in a century. The finest achievement of the first century of America's independence, to Whittier's mind, was the abolition of slavery, with its promise for the future.   [2] The originators of the Flemish school were the brothers Hubert and Jan van Eyck. Its greatest later artists were Rubens, Van Dyck, and Teniers the younger. It was noted for its realism, attention to detail, and domestic subjects.

ABRAHAM DAVENPORT

Whittier's note, prefixed to this poem, reads: "The famous Dark Day of New England, May 19, 1780, was a physical puzzle for many years to our ancestors, but its occurrence brought something more than philosophical speculation into the minds of those who passed through it. Abraham Davenport's sturdy protest is a matter of history." For the occurrence, see J. W. Barber, *Connecticut Historical Collections* (1836), 407.

In the old days (a custom laid aside
With breeches and cocked hats) the people sent
Their wisest men to make the public laws.
And so, from a brown homestead, where the Sound
Drinks the small tribute of the Mianas,[1]
Waved over by the woods of Rippowams,
And hallowed by pure lives and tranquil deaths,
Stamford sent up to the councils of the State
Wisdom and grace in Abraham Davenport.

'Twas on a May-day of the far old year   10
Seventeen hundred eighty, that there fell
Over the bloom and sweet life of the Spring,
Over the fresh earth and the heaven of noon,
A horror of great darkness, like the night
In day of which the Norland sagas[2] tell,—
The Twilight of the Gods. The low-hung sky
Was black with ominous clouds, save where its rim
Was fringed with a dull glow, like that which climbs
The crater's sides from the red hell below.
Birds ceased to sing, and all the barn-yard fowls   20
Roosted; the cattle at the pasture bars
Lowed, and looked homeward; bats on leathern wings
Flitted abroad; the sounds of labor died;
Men prayed, and women wept; all ears grew sharp
To hear the doom-blast of the trumpet shatter
The black sky, that the dreadful face of Christ
Might look from the rent clouds, not as he looked

---

[1] Mianas and Rippowams, small streams in Connecticut near Stamford   [2] the Norse heroic tales of the final destruction of the world in the warfare between the gods and the giants

A loving guest at Bethany, but stern
As Justice and inexorable Law.

Meanwhile in the old State House, dim as ghosts,   30
Sat the lawgivers of Connecticut,
Trembling beneath their legislative robes.
"It is the Lord's Great Day! Let us adjourn,"
Some said; and then, as if with one accord,
All eyes were turned to Abraham Davenport.
He rose, slow cleaving with his steady voice
The intolerable hush. "This well may be
The Day of Judgment which the world awaits;
But be it so or not, I only know
My present duty, and my Lord's command
To occupy till He come. So at the post   41
Where He hath set me in His providence,
I choose, for one, to meet Him face to face,—
No faithless servant frightened from my task,
But ready when the Lord of the harvest calls;
And therefore, with all reverence, I would say,
Let God do His work, we will see to ours.
Bring in the candles." And they brought them in.

Then by the flaring lights the Speaker read,
Albeit with husky voice and shaking hands,   50
An act to amend an act to regulate
The shad and alewive fisheries. Whereupon
Wisely and well spake Abraham Davenport,
Straight to the question, with no figures of speech
Save the ten Arab signs, yet not without
The shrewd dry humor natural to the man:
His awe-struck colleagues listening all the while,
Between the pauses of his argument,
To hear the thunder of the wrath of God   59
Break from the hollow trumpet of the cloud.

And there he stands in memory to this day,
Erect, self-poised, a rugged face, half seen
Against the background of unnatural dark,
A witness to the ages as they pass,
That simple duty hath no place for fear.

1866   1867

From AMONG THE HILLS

Originally planned as a companion piece to *Snow-Bound*, under the name "A Summer Idyl." The story itself, not printed here, concerns the winning of "a city's fair, pale daughter" to his rustic life and region by a "sun-brown farmer." Touches of realism in the "Prelude" show that Whittier, had he wished, could have emphasized the hard monotonous sides of country life as do present-day writers. Instead he delights in honest labor; his characters perform their daily tasks gladly, not complainingly.

Prelude

ALONG the roadside, like the flowers of gold
That tawny Incas[1] for their gardens wrought,
Heavy with sunshine droops the goldenrod,
And the red pennons of the cardinal-flowers
Hang motionless upon their upright staves.
The sky is hot and hazy, and the wind,
Wing-weary with its long flight from the
    south,
Unfelt; yet, closely scanned, yon maple leaf
With faintest motion, as one stirs in dreams,
Confesses it. The locust by the wall   10
Stabs the noon-silence with his sharp alarm.
A single hay-cart down the dusty road
Creaks slowly, with its driver fast asleep
On the load's top. Against the neighboring
    hill,
Huddled along the stone wall's shady side,
The sheep show white, as if a snowdrift still
Defied the dog-star. Through the open door
A drowsy smell of flowers—gray heliotrope,
And white sweet clover, and shy mignon-
    ette—
Comes faintly in, and silent chorus lends   20
To the pervading symphony of peace.

No time is this for hands long over-worn
To task their strength: and (unto Him be
    praise
Who giveth quietness!) the stress and strain
Of years that did the work of centuries
Have ceased, and we can draw our breath
    once more
Freely and full.[2] So, as yon harvesters
Make glad their nooning underneath the elms
With tale and riddle and old snatch of song,
I lay aside grave themes, and idly turn   30
The leaves of memory's sketch-book, dream-
ing o'er

[1] the predominant tribe of Indians in Peru, a people
unusually advanced in civilization at the time of the
Spanish conquest in the sixteenth century   [2] written
soon after the close of the Civil War

Old summer pictures of the quiet hills,
And human life, as quiet, at their feet.

And yet not idly all. A farmer's son,
Proud of field-lore and harvest craft, and
    feeling
All their fine possibilities, how rich
And restful even poverty and toil
Become when beauty, harmony, and love
Sit at their humble hearth as angels sat
At evening in the patriarch's tent, when man 40
Makes labor noble, and his farmer's frock
The symbol of a Christian chivalry
Tender and just and generous to her
Who clothes with grace all duty; still, I know
Too well the picture has another side,—
How wearily the grind of toil goes on
Where love is wanting, how the eye and ear
And heart are starved amidst the plenitude
Of nature, and how hard and colorless
Is life without an atmosphere. I look   50
Across the lapse of half a century,
And call to mind old homesteads, where no
    flower
Told that the spring had come, but evil
    weeds,
Nightshade and rough-leaved burdock in the
    place
Of the sweet doorway greeting of the rose
And honeysuckle, where the house walls
    seemed
Blistering in sun, without a tree or vine
To cast the tremulous shadow of its leaves
Across the curtainless windows, from whose
    panes
Fluttered the signal rags of shiftlessness. 60
Within, the cluttered kitchen floor, unwashed
(Broom-clean I think they called it); the best
    room
Stifling with cellar-damp, shut from the air
In hot midsummer, bookless, pictureless
Save the inevitable sampler[1] hung
Over the fireplace, or a mourning piece,
A green-haired woman, peony-cheeked, be-
    neath
Impossible willows; the wide-throated hearth
Bristling with faded pine-boughs half con-
    cealing
The piled-up rubbish at the chimney's back; 70

[1] piece of decorative needlework, especially one showing embroidered letters or verses

And, in sad keeping with all things about
  them,
Shrill, querulous women, sour and sullen
  men,
Untidy, loveless, old before their time,
With scarce a human interest save their own
Monotonous round of small economies,
Or the poor scandal of the neighborhood;
Blind to the beauty everywhere revealed,
Treading the May-flowers with regardless
  feet;
For them the song-sparrow and the bobolink
Sang not, nor winds made music in the
  leaves;   80
For them in vain October's holocaust
Burned, gold and crimson, over all the hills,
The sacramental mystery of the woods.
Church-goers, fearful of the unseen Powers,
But grumbling over pulpit-tax and pew-
  rent,
Saving, as shrewd economists, their souls
And winter pork with the least possible out-
  lay
Of salt and sanctity; in daily life
Showing as little actual comprehension
Of Christian charity and love and duty   90
As if the Sermon on the Mount had been
Outdated like a last year's almanac:
Rich in broad woodlands and in half-tilled
  fields,
And yet so pinched and bare and comfort-
  less,
The veriest straggler limping on his rounds,
The sun and air his sole inheritance,
Laughed at a poverty that paid its taxes,
And hugged his rags in self-complacency!

Not such should be the homesteads of a land
Where whoso wisely wills and acts may
  dwell   100
As king and lawgiver, in broad-acred state,
With beauty, art, taste, culture, books, to
  make
His hour of leisure richer than a life
Of fourscore to the barons of old time.
Our yeoman should be equal to his home
Set in the fair, green valleys, purple walled,
A man to match his mountains, not to creep
Dwarfed and abased below them. I would
  fain
In this light way (of which I needs must own

With the knife-grinder[1] of whom Canning
  sings,   110
"Story, God bless you! I have none to tell
  you!")
Invite the eye to see and heart to feel
The beauty and the joy within their reach,—
Home, and home loves, and the beatitudes
Of nature free to all. Haply in years
That wait to take the places of our own,
Heard where some breezy balcony looks
  down
On happy homes, or where the lake in the
  moon
Sleeps dreaming of the mountains, fair as Ruth,
In the old Hebrew pastoral, at the feet   120
Of Boaz, even this simple lay of mine
May seem the burden of a prophecy,
Finding its late fulfilment in a change
Slow as the oak's growth, lifting manhood up
Through broader culture, finer manners, love,
And reverence, to the level of the hills.

O Golden Age whose light is of the dawn,
And not of sunset, forward, not behind,
Flood the new heavens and earth, and with
  thee bring
All the old virtues, whatsoever things   130
Are pure and honest and of good repute,
But add thereto whatever bard has sung
Or seer has told of when in trance and dream
They saw the Happy Isles of prophecy!
Let Justice hold her scale, and Truth divide
Between the right and wrong; but give the heart
The freedom of its fair inheritance;
Let the poor prisoner, cramped and starved
  so long,
At Nature's table feast his ear and eye
With joy and wonder; let all harmonies   140
Of sound, form, color, motion, wait upon
The princely guest, whether in soft attire
Of leisure clad, or the coarse frock of toil,
And, lending life to the dead forms of faith,
Give human nature reverence for the sake
Of One who bore it, making it divine
With the ineffable tenderness of God;
Let common need, the brotherhood of prayer,
The heirship of an unknown destiny,   149

---

[1] "The Friend of Humanity and the Knife Grinder,"
from which the quotation in line 111 was taken, was a
parody on one of Southey's poems, written by George
Canning.

The unsolved mystery round about us, make
A man more precious than the gold of Ophir.
Sacred, inviolate, unto whom all things
Should minister, as outward types and signs
Of the eternal beauty which fulfils
The one great purpose of creation, Love,
The sole necessity of Earth and Heaven!

1867–1868   1868

THE ETERNAL GOODNESS

The best known of Whittier's religious poems.
It contrasts with the old Calvinistic pieces with
their "iron creeds." The poem reflects the poet's
sense of humility, of the futility of question, his
concern with the goodness of God (his favorite
doctrine), and the inner peace of his Quaker faith.

O FRIENDS! with whom my feet have trod
　　The quiet aisles of prayer,
Glad witness to your zeal for God
　　And love of man I bear.

I trace your lines of argument;
　　Your logic linked and strong
I weigh as one who dreads dissent,
　　And fears a doubt as wrong.

But still my human hands are weak
　　To hold your iron creeds: 10
Against the words ye bid me speak
　　My heart within me pleads.

Who fathoms the Eternal Thought?
　　Who talks of scheme and plan?
The Lord is God! He needeth not
　　The poor device of man.

I walk with bare, hushed feet the ground
　　Ye tread with boldness shod;
I dare not fix with mete and bound
　　The love and power of God.   20

Ye praise His justice; even such
　　His pitying love I deem:
Ye seek a king; I fain would touch
　　The robe that hath no seam.

Ye see the curse which overbroods
　　A world of pain and loss;
I hear our Lord's beatitudes
　　And prayer upon the cross.

More than your schoolmen teach, within
　　Myself, alas! I know: 30
Too dark ye cannot paint the sin,
　　Too small the merit show.

I bow my forehead to the dust,
　　I veil mine eyes for shame,
And urge, in trembling self-distrust,
　　A prayer without a claim.

I see the wrong that round me lies,
　　I feel the guilt within;
I hear, with groan and travail-cries,
　　The world confess its sin.   40

Yet, in the maddening maze of things,
　　And tossed by storm and flood,
To one fixed trust my spirit clings;
　　I know that God is good!

Not mine to look where cherubim
　　And seraphs may not see,
But nothing can be good in Him
　　Which evil is in me.

The wrong that pains my soul below
　　I dare not throne above,   50
I know not of His hate,—I know
　　His goodness and His love.

I dimly guess from blessings known
　　Of greater out of sight,
And, with the chastened Psalmist,[1] own
　　His judgments too are right.

I long for household voices gone,
　　For vanished smiles I long,
But God hath led my dear ones on,
　　And He can do no wrong.   60

I know not what the future hath
　　Of marvel or surprise,
Assured alone that life and death
　　His mercy underlies.

And if my heart and flesh are weak
　　To bear an untried pain,
The bruisèd reed He will not break,
　　But strengthen and sustain.

No offering of my own I have,
　　Nor works my faith to prove;   70
I can but give the gifts He gave,
　　And plead His love for love.

[1] David. See Psalms 19:9.

And so beside the Silent Sea
  I wait the muffled oar;
No harm from Him can come to me
  On ocean or on shore.

I know not where His islands lift
  Their fronded palms in air;
I only know I cannot drift
  Beyond His love and care.   80

O brothers! if my faith is vain,
  If hopes like these betray,
Pray for me that my feet may gain
  The sure and safer way.

And Thou, O Lord! by whom are seen
  Thy creatures as they be,
Forgive me if too close I lean
  My human heart on Thee!

1865   1867

IN SCHOOL–DAYS

STILL sits the school-house by the road,
  A ragged beggar sleeping;
Around it still the sumachs grow,
  And blackberry vines are creeping.

Within, the master's desk is seen,
  Deep scarred by raps official;
The warping floor, the battered seats,
  The jack-knife's carved initial;

The charcoal frescoes on its wall;
  Its door's worn sill, betraying   10
The feet that, creeping slow to school,
  Went storming out to playing!

Long years ago a winter sun
  Shone over it at setting;
Lit up its western window-panes,
  And low eaves' icy fretting.

It touched the tangled golden curls,
  And brown eyes full of grieving,
Of one who still her steps delayed
  When all the school were leaving.   20

For near her stood the little boy
  Her childish favor singled:
His cap pulled low upon a face
  Where pride and shame were mingled.

Pushing with restless feet the snow
  To right and left, he lingered;—
As restlessly her tiny hands
  The blue-checked apron fingered.

He saw her lift her eyes; he felt
  The soft hand's light caressing,   30
And heard the tremble of her voice,
  As if a fault confessing.

"I'm sorry that I spelt the word:
  I hate to go above you,
Because,"—the brown eyes lower fell,—
  "Because, you see, I love you!"

Still memory to a gray-haired man
  That sweet child-face is showing.
Dear girl! the grasses on her grave
  Have forty years been growing!   40

He lives to learn, in life's hard school,
  How few who pass above him
Lament their triumph and his loss,
  Like her,—because they love him.

1869   1870

THE TRAILING ARBUTUS

This poem follows a familiar pattern in flower
poetry. The stanzas concerning the trailing arbutus are followed by a personal passage in which
Whittier finds a lesson for himself as he bends
over the flower. Bryant also added personal passages in "The Yellow Violet" and "To the Fringed
Gentian," and the same type of moralizing close
may be found in his "To a Waterfowl" and in
Longfellow's "The Village Blacksmith."

I WANDERED lonely where the pine-trees made
Against the bitter East their barricade,
  And, guided by its sweet
Perfume, I found, within a narrow dell,
The trailing spring flower tinted like a shell
  Amid dry leaves and mosses at my feet.

From under dead boughs, for whose loss the
    pines
Moaned ceaseless overhead, the blossoming
    vines
  Lifted their glad surprise,
While yet the bluebird smoothed in leafless
    trees   10
His feathers ruffled by the chill sea-breeze,
  And snow-drifts lingered under April skies.

As, pausing o'er the lonely flower I bent,
I thought of lives thus lowly, clogged and pent,
    Which yet find room,
Through care and cumber, coldness and decay,
To lend a sweetness to the ungenial day,
    And make the sad earth happier for their
      bloom.

1879

THE LOST OCCASION

See the headnote for "Ichabod" on page 360.

Some die too late and some too soon,
At early morning, heat of noon,
Or the chill evening twilight, Thou,
Whom the rich heavens did so endow
With eyes of power and Jove's own brow,
With all the massive strength that fills
Thy home-horizon's granite hills,
With rarest gifts of heart and head
From manliest stock inherited,
New England's stateliest type of man,   10
In port and speech Olympian;
Whom no one met, at first, but took
A second awed and wondering look
(As turned, perchance the eyes of Greece
On Phidias' unveiled masterpiece[1]);
Whose words in simplest homespun clad,
The Saxon strength of Caedmon's had,
With power reserved at need to reach
The Roman forum's loftiest speech,
Sweet with persuasion, eloquent   20
In passion, cool in argument,
Or, ponderous, falling on thy foes
As fell the Norse god's hammer blows,
Crushing as if with Talus' flail
Through Error's logic-woven mail,
And failing only when they tried
The adamant of the righteous side,—
Thou, foiled in aim and hope, bereaved
Of old friends, by the new deceived,
Too soon for us, too soon for thee,   30
Beside thy lonely Northern sea,
Where long and low the marsh-lands spread,
Laid wearily down thy august head.

Thou shouldst have lived to feel below
Thy feet Disunion's fierce upthrow;
The late-sprung mine that underlaid
Thy sad concessions vainly made.

[1] the colossal statue of Jove at Olympia: "unveiled" because all trace of it has been lost except some inscriptions on Greek coins

Thou shouldst have seen from Sumter's wall
The star-flag of the Union fall,
And armed rebellion pressing on   40
The broken lines of Washington!
No stronger voice than thine had then
Called out the utmost might of men,
To make the Union's charter free
And strengthen law by liberty.
How had that stern arbitrament
To thy gray age youth's vigor lent,
Shaming ambition's paltry prize
Before thy disillusioned eyes;
Breaking the spell about thee wound   50
Like the green withes that Samson bound;
Redeeming in one effort grand,
Thyself and thy imperiled land!
Ah, cruel fate, that closed to thee,
O sleeper by the Northern sea,
The gates of opportunity!
God fills the gaps of human need,
Each crisis brings its word and deed.
Wise men and strong we did not lack;
But still, with memory turning back,   60
In the dark hours we thought of thee,
And thy lone grave beside the sea.

Above that grave the east winds blow,
And from the marsh-lands drifting slow
The sea-fog comes, with evermore
The wave-wash of a lonely shore,
And sea-bird's melancholy cry,
As Nature fain would typify
The sadness of a closing scene,
The loss of that which should have been.   70
But, where thy native mountains bare
Their foreheads to diviner air,
Fit emblem of enduring fame,
One lofty summit keeps thy name.
For thee the cosmic forces did
The rearing of that pyramid,
The prescient ages shaping with
Fire, flood, and frost thy monolith.
Sunrise and sunset lay thereon
With hands of light their benison,   80
The stars of midnight pause to set
Their jewels in its coronet.
And evermore that mountain mass
Seems climbing from the shadowy pass
To light, as if to manifest
Thy nobler self, thy life at best!

1880

O F THE Concord and Cambridge groups, the former was the more original and radical, the latter more academic and its literary work of a more traditional type. James Russell Lowell was thought by his contemporaries to be the ablest of the Cambridge group.

The youngest of six children, Lowell was born February 22, 1819, in Cambridge, Massachusetts, at "Elmwood," a house of Revolutionary fame. His family belonged to the lettered class of New England and was one of unusual distinction. Many of his ancestors were clergymen. His grandfather, a prominent judge, was instrumental in ending slavery in Massachusetts. An uncle introduced cotton spinning into the United States and founded the city of Lowell. Another uncle established at Boston the Lowell Institute of free lectures on science, religion, and art. The poet's father, an eminent Unitarian clergyman for more than fifty years, was pastor of the West Church of Boston. President A. Lawrence Lowell of Harvard, his brother Percival Lowell, the astronomer, and their sister, the poet, Amy Lowell, were of the same ancestral stock.

From infancy Lowell was familiar with books, for the Lowell library was made up of the accumulations of several generations of scholarly men. He was early acquainted with Spenser and Shakespeare. He prepared for college at the school of an Englishman under whom Dr. Holmes and Colonel Higginson also studied. In 1834 he entered Harvard, but he was not a very serious undergraduate. In those days when miscellaneous reading was not so common as it is now, he read "nearly everything," he said, "except the books prescribed by the faculty." While Lowell was a sophomore, Longfellow came to Cambridge to succeed Ticknor as professor of modern languages, and his coming gave great stimulus to literary interests. In his junior year, Lowell was elected to write a college poem. As a senior, he was made editor of *Harvardiana*, the college magazine. Some of the verses he wrote for it were good enough to be included in the final editions of his poems. He was elected poet for his class, that of 1835, but his poem was read for him at the graduation exercises in August, since he had been "rusticated" to Concord for six weeks for neglect of college duties and such minor delinquencies as not attending chapel. Here he studied with the original of Parson Wilbur of the *Biglow Papers* and came to know Emerson.

After his graduation, Lowell began the study of law and took his degree from the Law School in 1840. He soon became engaged to Maria White of Watertown, who was an ardent abolitionist and a mild transcendentalist, and who was devoted to poetry. Stimulated by her interests, Lowell soon formed a more definite idea of what he wanted to do. He continued to write, and at twenty-two published his first volume of verse, *A Year's Life* (1841). In 1843 he founded with a friend the *Pioneer*, a magazine of literature and art, which was discontinued after a few issues, leaving its editors in debt. At the end of the year he issued another volume of poems. He married in 1844. After a winter in Philadelphia, he returned to Elmwood, his home for almost all the rest of his life.

The next six years were the most productive of his career. As a youth he was relatively radical and associated himself with reformers and romantic idealists. In 1845 he began to write for various antislavery papers. His first volume of prose, *Conversations on Some of the Old Poets*, appeared in 1846. In 1848 he published another volume of his poems and also his first and most distinctive masterpiece, the *Biglow Papers*, First Series, a satire in New England dialect which seems likely to live in American political history. In it he set forth his criticism of the conduct of the national government in the Mexican War. An elaborate setting was added when the various poems were collected and placed together, and the Yankee idyl, "The Courtin'," appeared with them in an appendix. The year 1848 was, in fact, his great poetic year. The literary satire, *A Fable for Critics*, containing humorous estimates of his contemporaries, was published then and also his best-known imaginative poem, *The Vision of Sir Launfal*. The latter is not notable in comparison with other Arthurian poems of the century, but it has been a moral force in the schools. About this same time he began his long and successful career as a public speaker on social and academic themes.

Mrs. Lowell died in 1853. Two years later Lowell gave the Lowell lectures, on the English poets, and as a result was appointed to succeed Longfellow in the Smith Professorship of modern languages at Harvard. He went alone to Europe, 1855–56, and then assumed his position of professor of French, Spanish, and Belles-Lettres, engaging in the direction of the department for twenty years. After he joined the Harvard faculty he rather disowned his early radicalism, and in his maturer years became increasingly conservative. Lowell was described by his students as not a typical professor. He was less formal and less methodical than Longfellow. Endowed with encyclopedic learning, he had also a sense of humor, a real gift for poetry, and a stimulating imagination.

In 1857, Lowell was made editor of the newly established *Atlantic Monthly*, which had Emerson, Motley, Holmes, and other members of the famous Saturday Club as contributors. He achieved eminence at once as an admirable editor, and the magazine exerted influence politically and in matters of taste. Lowell contributed to it much of his own critical writing and other prose and verse as well. That same year he returned again to Elmwood, after having married Miss Frances Dunlap (died 1885), who had been his daughter's governess. After two years, he resigned the direction of the *Atlantic* and two years later, in 1864, became editor with Professor Charles Eliot Norton of the *North American Review*, a post he held until his resignation in 1872.

During the Civil War period he wrote the second series of *Biglow Papers*, less spontaneous than the first. Issued in 1862–66, they reflected his views concerning the War. His "Commemoration Ode," composed in memory of the Harvard men who had fallen in the struggle, was first printed in the *Atlantic*. During his professorship he collected into volumes his various prose pieces, many of them made over from classroom lectures. Among them were his once famous essays on Dante, Spenser, Shakespeare, Wordsworth, and Keats. He was given an honorary degree by Oxford in 1873 and by Cambridge in 1874.

During a two years' vacation in Europe following his resignation from the *North American Review*, Lowell became interested in the contrasting problems of American public life and those in Europe. He soon became known as a political thinker, and as a reward for party service, he was appointed United States minister to Spain in 1877. Here his already great sympathy with the Spanish people and their literature deepened. Three years later he was made minister to England, 1880–85, where he came in contact with distinguished persons and made a strong impression as a statesman, a man of letters, and an interpreter of America to Europe. He was much in demand as a lecturer for special public events. His speeches were spiced with wit and fitted to the occasion, and he had genuine subject matter besides. He returned to America in 1885. The remaining six years of his life were devoted to public speaking, editing the collected edition of his poetry and prose, and publishing a few more poems, essays, and addresses. Among them was "Democracy," an address delivered in England, and "The Independent in Politics," delivered on his return to America. In 1887 he again gave the Lowell lectures. He published *Heartsease and Rue* in 1888. His political essays appeared in 1891. Little was left of the young radical in these later discussions of public affairs, and he had lost much of his enthusiasm for democracy. He died at Elmwood on August 12, 1891, at the age of seventy-two. His last volume, *Old English Dramatists*, was published the year following his death.

Part of Lowell's apparent inconsistency is the result of the fact that his mind developed and changed as he grew older, a fact that is reflected in the history of his literary theories and ideals as interpreted by H. H. Clark. Up to 1850 he thought that "any literature, as far as it is national, is diseased," and during that period he condemned traditionalism and exalted the universal moral sentiment as a corrective of social and local wrongs such as slavery. In his second period, from 1850 to 1867, he urged that our literature should be nationalistic, preferably in local dialect. And after 1867, becoming more respectful of traditionalism, he turned to a universality which includes and begins with nationalism but transcends it. He summed up his ideal in his essay on Spenser (1875): "All great poetry must smack of the soil, for it is rooted in it, must suck life and substance from it, but it must do so with the aspiring instinct of the pine that climbs forever toward diviner air, and not in the grovelling fashion of the potato. Any verse that makes you and me foreigners is not only not great poetry, but no poetry at all." As Norman Foerster has shown, Lowell thought that form should be organic and distinguished for unity, design, proportion, clearness, economy, repose, and impersonality. To him the ideal representation of life, which constitutes great literature, was to be achieved by the spiritual imagination, guided by reason and our cultural heritage, which finds in the chaos of experience an ordered ethical meaning and significance. The function of literature is to further the delight and happiness which derives from the joyful exercise of all the faculties of the mind and spirit working in harmony. In his own writing he seldom succeeded in practicing fully his own theories, but they provided criteria for his own critical essays which did much to interpret and evaluate the great European masters for a frontier people.

Lowell was a poet, author, teacher, public servant, man of the world, man of letters, wit, scholar, orator, critic, essayist, editor, diplomat, and professor. Some have termed him the "largest, best rounded personality in our literature," the "most representative of the Cambridge group," and "our noblest patriot and most completely rounded man." But though he dealt with a wide range of ideas and was influenced by various intellectual and social movements, he was a leader in none. He was too much a man of the library, and he suffered perhaps from his very versatility. He put forward no definite body of ideas and left no *magnum opus*. His work is so miscellaneous that it has little unity of effect.

As a poet, Lowell has worn less well than others of the Cambridge and Concord groups. He composed no one poem as popular as Holmes's "The Chambered Nautilus." His early verse followed conventional sources of inspiration. As the years passed, he tried many fields. A rough grouping of his verse includes poems of love and sentiment; personal and social verse; patriotic poems and poems of contemporary life and thought; nature poems descriptive of the flora and fauna of his own region; dialect poems and political satires (the only group in which he achieved a distinctive manner); and a narrative poem, "The Vision of Sir Launfal." His poetry was written principally from 1840 to 1870 and his prose from 1869 to 1890.

Lowell's prose, a literary miscellany, reflects his broad reading, resources of vocabulary, exuberant fancy, and the interests of a lecturer and editor. As a literary critic he ranked high in his own day, and he still ranks as our most distinguished critic-scholar. Some of his judgments, like those on Thoreau, Darwin, and Taine, seem now to require modification; but he had historical background, he understood the nature of criticism, and he outlined sound criteria. He left an impressive series of studies of great writers of the past, English and European. His political essays, too, now seem better reading than they did earlier in the present century.

When Lowell died, American romanticism was past. French and Russian realism were shaping the taste of a new generation. Individualism had triumphed and older literary traditions were being rapidly discarded.

Lowell's collected works were published in the Riverside Edition (10 vols., 1891). Another volume was added in the following year and the two volumes of H. E. Scudder's *Life* in 1902. The Elmwood Edition of Lowell's *Complete Writings* was published in 16 volumes in 1904. The *Letters*, edited by C. E. Norton, appeared in 1894 (enlarged, 1904). *New Letters*, edited by M. A. De Wolfe Howe, was issued in 1932.

Scudder's remains the standard biography of Lowell. Ferris Greenslet, *J. R. Lowell: His Life and Work*, is a brief but valuable account in the American Men of Letters Series (1905). M. A. De Wolfe Howe wrote of Lowell in *DAB*, XI (1933). E. E. Hale's *J. R. Lowell and His Friends* (1899) and E. W. Emerson's *The Early Years of the Saturday Club* (1918) are of interest to students of Lowell.

For selected critical discussion, see Poe's "Poems by James Russell Lowell," *Graham's Magazine* (March, 1844), and his review of "A Fable for Critics," *Southern Literary Messenger* (Feb., 1849); E. C. Stedman, in *Poets of America* (1885); Henry James, in the *Atlantic*, LIX (Jan., 1892), Barrett Wendell, in *Stelligeri and Other Essays* (1893); C. E. Norton, in *Harper's Magazine*, LXXXVI (May, 1893); J. V. Cheney, in *That Dome in Air* (1895); G. E. Woodberry, in *Makers of Literature* (1900); W. C. Brownell, in *American Prose Masters* (1909); Van Wyck Brooks, in *America's Coming of Age* (1915); J. J. Reilly, *J. R. Lowell as a Critic* (1915); E. M. Chapman, "The Biglow Papers Fifty Years After," *Yale Review*, N.S. VI (Oct., 1916); A. H. Thorndike, in *CHAL*, II (1918); W. R. Thayer, "Lowell as a Teacher," *Scribner's Magazine*, LXVIII (Oct., 1920); Bliss Perry, in *The Praise of Folly* (1923); N. Foerster, in *Nature in American Literature* (1923), and in *American Criticism* (1928); H. H. Clark, "Lowell's Criticism of Romantic Literature," *PMLA*, XLI (March, 1926), and "Lowell—Humanitarian, Nationalist, or Humanist?" *Studies in Philology*, XXVIII (1930); V. L. Parrington, in *Main Currents in American Thought*, II (1927); Alfred Kreymborg, in *Our Singing Strength* (1929); R. M. Lovett, in Macy's *American Writers on American Literature* (1931); R. Brenner, in *Twelve American Poets before 1900* (1933).

For bibliography see G. W. Cooke, *A Bibliography of James Russell Lowell* (1906); Killis Campbell, "Bibliographical Notes on Lowell," *University of Texas Studies in English*, IV (1924); L. S. Livingston, *A Bibliography of the First Editions in Book Form of the Writings of J. R. Lowell* (1914); Irita Van Doren, in *CHAL*, II (1918); and Harry Hartwick, in W. F. Taylor's *A History of American Letters* (1936).

From SONNETS

Lowell's early sonnets are well and smoothly executed. There were thirty-five in his first book. He commented on this lyric type when praising Longfellow's sonnets, on the occasion of the unveiling of a bust of that poet at Westminster Abbey, March 2, 1884: "I have been struck particularly with this quality of style in some of my late friend's sonnets, which seem to me in unity and evenness of flow among the most beautiful and perfect we have in the language. They remind one of those cabinets in which all the drawers are opened at once by the turn of a key in a single lock, whereas we all have seen sonnets with a lock in every line with a different key to each, and the added conundrums of secret drawers."

III

I WOULD not have this perfect love of ours
Grow from a single root, a single stem,
Bearing no goodly fruit, but only flowers
That idly hide life's iron diadem:
It should grow alway like that Eastern tree
Whose limbs take root and spread forth constantly;
That love for one, from which there doth not spring
Wide love for all, is but a worthless thing.

Not in another world, as poets prate,
Dwell we apart above the tide of things,   10
High floating o'er earth's clouds on faery
    wings;
But our pure love doth ever elevate
Into a holy bond of brotherhood
All earthly things, making them pure and
    good.

                                        1840

IV

"For this true nobleness I seek in vain,
In woman and in man I find it not;
I almost weary of my earthly lot,
My life-springs are dried up with burning
    pain."
Thou find'st it not? I pray thee look again,
Look *inward* through the depths of thine own
    soul.
How is it with thee? Art thou sound and
    whole?
Doth narrow search show thee no earthly
    stain?
BE NOBLE! and the nobleness that lies
In other men, sleeping, but never dead,   10
Will rise in majesty to meet thine own;
Then wilt thou see it gleam in many eyes,
Then will pure light around thy path be shed,
And thou wilt nevermore be sad and lone.

                                        1840

STANZAS ON FREEDOM

Lowell early showed humanitarian interest.
He was active as an abolitionist for some years
after 1840. These verses were sung at an antislavery picnic in Dedham, on the anniversary of
the West Indian emancipation, Aug. 1, 1843. In a
letter to a friend, 1846, Lowell told that when he
was printing his second volume of verse, he was
urged to suppress this poem. "My only answer
was—'Let all the others be suppressed if you
will—*that* I will never suppress.'" The last two
lines of the poem have been widely quoted.

    MEN! whose boast it is that ye
    Come of fathers brave and free,
    If there breathe on earth a slave,
    Are ye truly free and brave?
    If ye do not feel the chain,
    When it works a brother's pain,
    Are ye not base slaves indeed,
    Slaves unworthy to be freed?

Women! who shall one day bear
Sons to breathe New England air,   10
If ye hear, without a blush,
Deeds to make the roused blood rush
Like red lava through your veins,
For your sisters now in chains,—
Answer! are ye fit to be
Mothers of the brave and free?

Is true Freedom but to break
Fetters for our own dear sake,
And, with leathern hearts, forget
That we owe mankind a debt?   20
No! true freedom is to share
All the chains our brothers wear,
And, with heart and hand, to be
Earnest to make others free!

They are slaves who fear to speak
For the fallen and the weak;
They are slaves who will not choose
Hatred, scoffing, and abuse,
Rather than in silence shrink
From the truths they needs must think;   30
They are slaves who dare not be
In the right with two or three.

                                        1843

THE PRESENT CRISIS

Printed in the Boston *Courier*, Dec. 11, 1848,
under the title "Verses Suggested at the Present
Crisis." The crisis concerned the question of the
annexation of Texas and the extension of slave
territory. The long lines of the verse form may
have been suggested by Tennyson's "Locksley
Hall" (1842). Underlying the poem is the idea of
the onward sweep of progress and of the necessity of
action. The poem was at once popular and it was
widely quoted for years in public speeches by
such men as G. W. Curtis, Wendell Phillips, and
Charles Sumner.

WHEN a deed is done for Freedom, through
    the broad earth's aching breast
Runs a thrill of joy prophetic, trembling on
    from east to west,
And the slave, where'er he cowers, feels the
    soul within him climb
To the awful verge of manhood, as the energy
    sublime
Of a century bursts full-blossomed on the
    thorny stem of Time.

Through the walls of hut and palace shoots
the instantaneous throe,
When the travail of the Ages wrings earth's
systems to and fro;
At the birth of each new Era, with a recognizing start,
Nation wildly looks at nation, standing with
mute lips apart,
And glad Truth's yet mightier man-child
leaps beneath the Future's heart.   10

So the Evil's triumph sendeth, with a terror
and a chill,
Under continent to continent, the sense of
coming ill,
And the slave, where'er he cowers, feels his
sympathies with God
In hot tear-drops ebbing earthward, to be
drunk up by the sod,
Till a corpse crawls round unburied, delving
in the nobler clod.

For mankind are one in spirit, and an instinct bears along,
Round the earth's electric circle, the swift
flash of right or wrong;
Whether conscious or unconscious, yet Humanity's vast frame
Through its ocean-sundered fibres feels the
gush of joy or shame;—
In the gain or loss of one race all the rest have
equal claim.   20

Once to every man and nation comes the
moment to decide,
In the strife of Truth with Falsehood, for
the good or evil side;
Some great cause, God's new Messiah, offering each the bloom or blight,
Parts the goats upon the left hand, and the
sheep upon the right,
And the choice goes by forever 'twixt that
darkness and that light.

Hast thou chosen, O my people, on whose
party thou shalt stand,
Ere the Doom from its worn sandals shakes
the dust against our land?
Though the cause of Evil prosper, yet 'tis
Truth alone is strong,

And, albeit she wander outcast now, I see
around her throng
Troops of beautiful, tall angels, to enshield
her from all wrong.   30

Backward look across the ages and the
beacon-moments see,
That, like peaks of some sunk continent, jut
through Oblivion's sea;
Not an ear in court or market for the low
foreboding cry
Of those Crises, God's stern winnowers,
from whose feet earth's chaff must fly;
Never shows the choice momentous till the
judgment hath passed by.

Careless seems the great Avenger; history's
pages but record
One death-grapple in the darkness 'twixt old
systems and the Word;
Truth forever on the scaffold, Wrong forever on the throne,—
Yet that scaffold sways the future, and, behind the dim unknown,
Standeth God within the shadow, keeping
watch above his own.   40

We see dimly in the Present what is small
and what is great,
Slow of faith how weak an arm may turn the
iron helm of fate,
But the soul is still oracular; amid the market's
din,
List the ominous stern whisper from the
Delphic cave within,—
"They enslave their children's children who
make compromise with sin."

Slavery, the earth-born Cyclops,[1] fellest of
the giant brood,
Sons of brutish Force and Darkness, who
have drenched the earth with blood,
Famished in his self-made desert, blinded by
our purer day,
Gropes in yet unblasted regions for his
miserable prey;—
Shall we guide his gory fingers where our
helpless children play?   50

[1] one of a fabled race of one-eyed giants, said to
have lived in Sicily

Then to side with Truth is noble when we
    share her wretched crust,
Ere her cause bring fame and profit, and 'tis
    prosperous to be just;
Then it is the brave man chooses, while the
    coward stands aside,
Doubting in his abject spirit, till his Lord is
    crucified,
And the multitude make virtue of the faith
    they had denied.

Count me o'er earth's chosen heroes,—they
    were souls that stood alone,
While the men they agonized for hurled the
    contumelious stone,
Stood serene, and down the future saw the
    golden beam incline
To the side of perfect justice, mastered by
    their faith divine,
By one man's plain truth to manhood and
    to God's supreme design.   60

By the light of burning heretics Christ's
    bleeding feet I track,
Toiling up new Calvaries ever with the cross
    that turns not back,
And these mounts of anguish number how
    each generation learned
One new word of that grand *Credo* which in
    prophet-hearts hath burned
Since the first man stood God-conquered with
    his face to heaven upturned.

For Humanity sweeps onward: where to-
    day the martyr stands,
On the morrow crouches Judas with the
    silver in his hands;
Far in front the cross stands ready and the
    crackling fagots burn,
While the hooting mob of yesterday in silent
    awe return
To glean up the scattered ashes into His-
    tory's golden urn.   70

'Tis as easy to be heroes as to sit the idle slaves
Of a legendary virtue carved upon our
    father's graves,
Worshippers of light ancestral make the
    present light a crime;—
Was the Mayflower launched by cowards,
    steered by men behind their time?
Turn those tracks toward Past or Future, that
    make Plymouth Rock sublime?

They were men of present valor, stalwart old
    iconoclasts,
Unconvinced by axe or gibbet that all virtue
    was the Past's;
But we make their truth our falsehood, think-
    ing that hath made us free,
Hoarding it in mouldy parchments, while
    our tender spirits flee
The rude grasp of that great Impulse which
    drove them across the sea.   80

They have rights who dare maintain them;
    we are traitors to our sires,
Smothering in their holy ashes Freedom's
    new-lit altar-fires;
Shall we make their creed our jailer? Shall we,
    in our haste to slay,
From the tombs of the old prophets steal the
    funeral lamps away
To light up the martyr-fagots round the
    prophets of to-day?

New occasions teach new duties; Time makes
    ancient good uncouth;
They must upward still, and onward, who
    would keep abreast of Truth;
Lo, before us gleam her camp-fires! we our-
    selves must Pilgrims be,
Launch our Mayflower, and steer boldly
    through the desperate winter sea,
Nor attempt the Future's portal with the
    Past's blood-rusted key.   90

1844   1845

TO THE DANDELION

Published in *Graham's Magazine*, January, 1845.
It follows the standard pattern of old-world
flower poems, from which Emerson broke loose in
"The Rhodora" as Wordsworth had in "I Wandered Lonely." The flower is not an individual
flower, blooming in some special spot. The poet
apostrophizes it in the abstract, and finds a lesson
for himself as he contemplates it. The rich allu-
siveness of the poem is noteworthy.

DEAR common flower, that grow'st beside
    the way,
Fringing the dusty road with harmless gold,
    First pledge of blithesome May,
Which children pluck, and, full of pride, up-
    hold,

High-hearted buccaneers, o'erjoyed that
  they
An Eldorado[1] in the grass have found,
  Which not the rich earth's ample round
May match in wealth,—thou art more dear
  to me
Than all the prouder summer-blooms may
  be.

Gold such as thine ne'er drew the Spanish
  prow   10
Through the primeval hush of Indian seas,
  Nor wrinkled the lean brow
Of age, to rob the lover's heart of ease,
'Tis the spring's largess,[2] which she scat-
  ters now
To rich and poor alike, with lavish hand,
  Though most hearts never understand
To take it at God's value, but pass by
The offered wealth with unrewarded eye.

Thou art my tropics and mine Italy;
To look at thee unlocks a warmer clime;   20
  The eyes thou givest me
Are in the heart, and heed not space or time:
Not in mid June the golden-cuirassed[3] bee
Feels a more summer-like warm ravishment
  In the white lily's breezy tent,
His fragrant Sybaris,[4] than I, when first
From the dark green thy yellow circles
  burst.

Then think I of deep shadows on the grass,
Of meadows where in sun the cattle graze,
  Where, as the breezes pass,   30
The gleaming rushes lean a thousand ways,
Of leaves that slumber in a cloudy mass,
Or whiten in the wind, of waters blue
  That from the distance sparkle through
Some woodland gap, and of a sky above,
  Where one white cloud like a stray lamb
  doth move.

My childhood's earliest thoughts are linked
  with thee;
The sight of thee calls back the robin's song,
  Who, from the dark old tree
Beside the door, sang clearly all day long, 40
  And I, secure in childish piety,

Listened as if I heard an angel sing
  With news from heaven, which he could
  bring
Fresh every day to my untainted ears,
  When birds and flowers and I were happy
  peers.

How like a prodigal doth nature seem,
When thou, for all thy gold, so common
  art!
  Thou teachest me to deem
More sacredly of every human heart,
  Since each reflects in joy its scanty gleam 50
Of heaven and, could some wondrous secret
  show
  Did we but pay the love we owe,
And with a child's undoubting wisdom
  look
On all these living pages of God's book.

1845

From A FABLE FOR CRITICS

Pope's *Dunciad*, Byron's *English Bards and
Scotch Reviewers*, and Leigh Hunt's *The Feast of
the Poets*, all satirizing contemporary men of
letters, may have suggested to Lowell the rollick-
ing, effervescent verse criticism of his *Fable for
Critics*. The rhymed title page of the first edition
reads: "Reader! walk up at once (it will soon be too
late), and buy at a perfectly ruinous rate A FABLE
FOR CRITICS: or, better, (I like, as a thing that the
reader's first fancy may strike, an old-fashioned
title-page, such as presents a tabular view of
the volume's contents,) A Glance at a Few of
Our Literary Progenies (Mrs. Malaprop's word)
from the Tub of Diogenes; a vocal and musical
melody, that is, a series of jokes by a Wonderful
Quiz, who accompanies himself with a rub-a-dub-
dub, full of spirit and grace, on the top of the
tub. Set forth in October, the 31st day, in the
year '48, G. P. Putnam, Broadway." In the introduction Lowell said: "One word to such
readers (judicious and wise) as read books with
something behind the mere eyes, of whom in this
country, perhaps, there are two, including myself,
gentle reader, and you. All the characters sketched
in this slight *jeu d'esprit*, though, it may be, they
seem, here and there, rather free, and drawn from
a somewhat too cynical standpoint, are *meant* to
be faithful, for that is the grand point, and none
but an owl would feel sore at a rub from a jester

[1] a fabled land of gold, thought by early Spanish
explorers to be in South America   [2] free and liberal
gift   [3] with a breastplate of gold   [4] ancient Southern
Italian town, noted for its luxury

who tells you, without any subterfuge, that he sits
in Diogenes' tub."

.   .   .   .

"THERE comes Emerson first, whose rich
    words, every one,
Are like gold nails in temples[1] to hang tro-
    phies on,
Whose prose is grand verse, while his verse,
    the Lord knows,
Is some of it pr—— No, 'tis not even prose;
I'm speaking of meters; some poems have
    welled
From those rare depths of soul that have ne'er
    been excelled;
They're not epics, but that doesn't matter a
    pin,
In creating, the only hard thing's to begin;
A grass-blade's no easier to make than an
    oak,
If you've once found the way, you've achieved
    the grand stroke;   10
In the worst of his poems are mines of rich
    matter,
But thrown in a heap with a crash and a clatter;
Now it is not one thing nor another alone
Makes a poem, but rather the general tone,
The something pervading, uniting the whole,
The before unconceived, unconceivable soul,
So that just in removing this trifle or that,
    you
Take away, as it were, a chief limb of the
    statue;
Roots, wood, bark, and leaves, singly per-
    fect may be,
But, clapt hodge-podge together, they don't
    make a tree.   20

    "But to come back to Emerson (whom by
        the way,
I believe we left waiting),—his is, we may
    say,
A Greek head on right Yankee shoulders,
    whose range
Has Olympus for one pole, for t'other the
    Exchange[2];
He seems, to my thinking, (although I'm
    afraid

[1] Ecclesiastes 12:11   [2] Lowell says that Emerson
combined spirituality and idealism (Olympus was the
home of the gods in Greek mythology) with Yankee
shrewdness and practicality (the Exchange is the business mart, the Stock Exchange).

The comparison must, long ere this, have
    been made),
A Plotinus-Montaigne, where the Egyptian's
    gold mist
And the Gascon's shrewd wit cheek-by-jowl
    coexist;
All admire, and yet scarcely six converts he's
    got
To I don't (nor they either) exactly know
    what;   30
For though he builds glorious temples, 'tis
    odd
He leaves never a doorway to get in a god.
'Tis refreshing to old-fashioned people like
    me,
To meet such a primitive Pagan as he,
In whose mind all creation is duly respected
As parts of himself—just a little projected;
And who's willing to worship the stars and
    the sun,
A convert to—nothing but Emerson.
So perfect a balance there is in his head,
That he talks of things sometimes as if they
    were dead;   40
Life, nature, love, God, and affairs of that
    sort,
He looks at as merely ideas; in short,
As if they were fossils stuck round in a cab-
    inet,
Of such vast extent that our earth's a mere
    dab in it;
Composed just as he is inclined to conjec-
    ture her,
Namely, one part pure earth, ninety-nine
    parts pure lecturer;
You are filled with delight at his clear dem-
    onstration,
Each figure, word, gesture, just fits the occa-
    sion,
With the quiet precision of science he'll sort
    'em,
But you can't help suspecting the whole a
    post mortem.   50

    "There are persons, mole-blind to the soul's
        make and style,
Who insist on a likeness 'twixt him and
    Carlyle;
To compare him with Plato would be vastly
    fairer,
Carlyle's the more burly, but E. is the rarer;

He sees fewer objects, but clearlier, truelier,
If C.'s as original, E.'s more peculiar;
That he's more of a man you might say of
    the one,
Of the other he's more of an Emerson;
C.'s the Titan, as shaggy of mind as of limb,—
E. the clear-eyed Olympian, rapid and slim; 60
The one's two-thirds Norseman, the other half
    Greek,
Where the one's most abounding, the other's
    to seek;
C.'s generals [1] require to be seen in the mass—
E.'s specialties [2] gain if enlarged by the glass;
C. gives nature and God his own fits of the
    blues,
And rims common-sense things with mystical
    hues,—
E. sits in a mystery calm and intense,
And looks coolly around him with sharp
    common sense;
C. shows you how everyday matters unite
With the dim transdiurnal recesses of night,—
While E., in a plain, preternatural way,   71
Makes mysteries matters of mere every day;
C. draws all his characters quite à la Fuseli,—
Not sketching their bundles of muscles and
    thews illy,
But he paints with a brush so untamed and
    profuse,
They seem nothing but bundles of muscles
    and thews;
E. is rather like Flaxman, lines strait and
    severe,
And a colorless outline, but full, round, and
    clear;—
To the men he thinks worthy he frankly
    accords
The design of a white marble statue in words.
C. labors to get at the center, and then   81
Take a reckoning from there of his actions
    and men;
E. calmly assumes the said center as granted,
And, given himself, has whatever is wanted.

"He has imitators in scores, who omit
No part of the man but his wisdom and wit,—
Who go carefully o'er the sky-blue of his
    brain,
And when he has skimmed it once, skim it
    again;

If at all they resemble him, you may be sure
    it is
Because their shoals mirror his mists and ob-
    scurities,   90
As a mud-puddle seems deep as heaven for a
    minute,
While a cloud that floats o'er is reflected
    within it.

. . . .

"There is Bryant, as quiet, as cool, and as
    dignified,
As a smooth, silent iceberg, that never is
    ignified,
Save when by reflection 'tis kindled o' nights
With a semblance of flame by the chill
    Northern Lights.
He may rank (Griswold says so) first bard of
    your nation,
(There's no doubt that he stands in supreme
    iceolation),
Your topmost Parnassus [1] he may set his heel
    on,
But no warm applauses come, peal follow-
    ing peal on,—   100
He's too smooth and too polished to hang
    any zeal on:
Unqualified merits, I'll grant, if you choose,
    he has 'em,
But he lacks the one merit of kindling en-
    thusiasm;
If he stir you at all, it is just, on my soul,
Like being stirred up with the very North
    Pole.

"He is very nice reading in summer, but
    inter
Nos,[2] we don't want extra freezing in winter;
Take him up in the depth of July, my advice is,
When you feel an Egyptian devotion to ices,
But, deduct all you can, there's enough that's
    right good in him,   110
He has a true soul for field, river, and wood
    in him;
And his heart, in the midst of brick walls, or
    where'er it is,
Glows, softens, and thrills with the tenderest
    charities—

[1] generalizations   [2] specific points

[1] Grecian mountain, sacred to Apollo and the muses;
hence, the home of music and poetry   [2] among ourselves

To you mortals that delve in this trade-ridden planet?

No, to old Berkshire's hills, with their lime-stone and granite.

If you're one who *in loco* (add *foco* here) *desipis*,[1]

You will get of his outermost heart (as I guess) a piece;

But you'd get deeper down if you came as a precipice,

And would break the last seal of its inwardest fountain,

If you only could palm yourself off for a mountain. 120

Mr. Quivis,[2] or somebody quite as discerning,

Some scholar who's hourly expecting his learning,

Calls B. the American Wordsworth; but Wordsworth

Is worth near as much as your whole tuneful herd's worth.

No, don't be absurd, he's an excellent Bryant;

But, my friends, you'll endanger the life of your client,

By attempting to stretch him up into a giant:

If you choose to compare him, I think there are two persons fit for a parallel—Thomson and Cowper[3];

I don't mean exactly,—there's something of each, 130

There's T.'s love of nature, C.'s penchant to preach;

Just mix up their minds so that C.'s spice of craziness

Shall balance and neutralize T.'s turn for laziness,

And it gives you a brain cool, quite friction-less, quiet,

Whose internal police nips the buds of all riot,—

A brain like a permanent strait-jacket put on

The heart which strives vainly to burst off a button,—

A brain which, without being slow or me-chanic,

Does more than a larger less drilled, more volcanic;

He's a Cowper condensed, with no craziness bitten, 140

And the advantage that Wordsworth before him had written.

"But, my dear little bardlings, don't prick up your ears,

Nor suppose I would rank you and Bryant as peers;

If I call him an iceberg, I don't mean to say

There is nothing in that which is grand, in its way;

He is almost the one of your poets that knows

How much grace, strength, and dignity lie in Repose;

If he sometimes fall short, he is too wise to mar

His thought's modest fulness by going too far;

'Twould be well if your authors should all make a trial 150

Of what virtue there is in severe self-denial,

And measure their writings by Hesiod's staff,

Which teaches that all has less value than half.

"There is Whittier, whose swelling and vehement heart

Strains the strait-breasted drab of the Quaker apart,

And reveals the live Man, still supreme and erect,

Underneath the bemummying wrappers of sect;

There was ne'er a man born who had more of the swing

Of the true lyric bard and all that kind of thing;

And his failures arise (though he seem not to know it) 160

From the very same cause that has made him a poet,—

A fervor of mind which knows no separation

'Twixt simple excitement and pure inspiration,

As my Pythoness[1] erst sometimes erred from not knowing

---

[1] "If you're one who 'on suitable occasion can be foolish.'" Lowell adds a punning allusion to the Loco-focos, a radical wing of the Democratic party, who held a convention by the light of the newly invented locofoco matches. [2] anyone; cf. "Mr. Whosit"

[3] "To demonstrate quickly and easily how per--versely absurd 'tis to sound this name *Cowper*,
As people in general call him named *super*,
I remark that he rhymes it himself with horse-trooper." [*Lowell's note*.]

[1] the oracular priestess at Delphi

If 'twere I or mere wind through her tripod
    was blowing;
Let his mind once get head in its favorite
    direction
And the torrent of verse bursts the dams of
    reflection,
While, borne with the rush of the meter
    along,
The poet may chance to go right or go wrong,
Content with the whirl and delirium of
    song;   170
Then his grammar's not always correct, nor
    his rhymes,
And he's prone to repeat his own lyrics some-
    times,
Not his best, though, for those are struck off
    at white-heats
When the heart in his breast like a trip-ham-
    mer beats,
And can ne'er be repeated again any more
Than they could have been carefully plotted
    before:
Like old what's-his-name [1] there at the battle
    of Hastings
(Who, however, gave more than mere
    rhythmical bastings),
Our Quaker leads off metaphorical fights
For reform and whatever they call human
    rights,   180
Both singing and striking in front of the war
And hitting his foes with the mallet of Thor;
Anne haec, one exclaims, on beholding his
    knocks,
Vestis filii tui,[2] O, leather-clad Fox?
Can that be thy son, in the battle's mid din,
Preaching brotherly love and then driving it
    in
To the brain of the tough old Goliath of sin,
With the smoothest of pebbles from Cas-
    taly's spring,[3]
Impressed on his hard moral sense with a
    sling?

"All honor and praise to the right-hearted
    bard   190
Who was true to The Voice when such
    service was hard,

[1] The Norman minstrel, Taillefer, who was reputed
to have struck the first blow in the battle   [2] Latin
version of Genesis 37:32   [3] fountain of poetic inspiration on Parnassus

Who himself was so free he dared sing for
    the slave
When to look but a protest in silence was
    brave;
All honor and praise to the women and men
Who spoke out for the dumb and the down-
    trodden then!
I need not to name them, already for each
I see History preparing the statue and niche;
They were harsh, but shall *you* be so shocked
    at hard words
Who have beaten your pruning-hooks up
    into swords,
Whose rewards and hurrahs men are surer to
    gain   200
By the reaping of men and of women than
    grain?
Why should *you* stand aghast at their fierce
    wordy war, if
You scalp one another for Bank or for Tariff?[1]
Your calling them cut-throats and knaves all
    day long
Doesn't prove that the use of hard language
    is wrong;
While the World's heart beats quicker to
    think of such men
As signed Tyranny's doom with a bloody
    steel-pen,
While on Fourth-of-Julys beardless orators
    fright one
With hints at Harmodius and Aristogeiton,
You need not look shy at your sisters and
    brothers   210
Who stab with sharp words for the freedom
    of others;—
No, a wreath, twine a wreath for the loyal and
    true
Who, for sake of the many, dared stand with
    the few,
Not of blood-spattered laurel for enemies
    braved,
But of broad, peaceful oak-leaves for citizens
    saved!

"There is Hawthorne, with genius so
    shrinking and rare
That you hardly at first see the strength that
    is there;

[1] Questions of the constitutionality of a national
bank and of the tariff were much under discussion at
the time this poem was written.

A frame so robust, with a nature so sweet,
So earnest, so graceful, so lithe and so fleet,
Is worth a descent from Olympus to meet; 220
'Tis as if a rough oak that for ages had stood,
With his gnarled bony branches like ribs of
the wood,
Should bloom, after cycles of struggle and
scathe,
With a single anemone trembly and rathe;
His strength is so tender, his wildness so
meek,
That a suitable parallel sets one to seek,—
He's a John Bunyan Fouqué, a Puritan
Tieck;
When Nature was shaping him, clay was not
granted
For making so full-sized a man as she wanted,
So, to fill out her model, a little she spared 230
From some finer-grained stuff for a woman
prepared,
And she could not have hit a more excellent
plan
For making him fully and perfectly man.
The success of her scheme gave her so much
delight,
That she tried it again, shortly after, in
Dwight;
Only, while she was kneading and shaping
the clay,
She sang to her work in her sweet childish
way,
And found, when she'd put the last touch to
his soul,
That the music had somehow got mixed with
the whole.

"Here's Cooper, who's written six vol-
umes to show 240
He's as good as a lord: well, let's grant that
he's so;
If a person prefer that description of praise,
Why, a coronet's certainly cheaper than
bays;
But he need take no pains to convince us he's
not
(As his enemies say) the American Scott.
Choose any twelve men, and let C. read aloud
That one of his novels of which he's most
proud,
And I'd lay any bet that, without ever quit-
ting

Their box, they'd be all, to a man, for acquit-
ting.
He has drawn you one character, though, that
is new, 250
One wildflower he's plucked that is wet with
the dew
Of this fresh Western world, and, the thing
not to mince,
He has done naught but copy it ill ever since;
His Indians, with proper respect be it said,
Are just Natty Bumppo daubed over with
red,
And his very Long Toms are the same useful
Nat,
Rigged up in duck pants and a sou'-wester
hat,
(Though once in a Coffin, a good chance was
found
To have slipt the old fellow away under-
ground).
All his other men-figures are clothes upon
sticks, 260
The *dernière chemise* [1] of a man in a fix,
(As a captain besieged, when his garrison's
small,
Sets up caps upon poles to be seen o'er the
wall);
And the women he draws from one model
don't vary,
All sappy as maples and flat as a prairie.
When a character's wanted, he goes to the
task
As a cooper would do in composing a cask;
He picks out the staves, of their qualities
heedful,
Just hoops them together as tight as is need-
ful,
And, if the best fortune should crown the
attempt, he 270
Has made at the most something wooden and
empty.

"Don't suppose I would underrate Cooper's
abilities,
If I thought you'd do that, I should feel very
ill at ease;
The men who have given to *one* character life
And objective existence, are not very rife,
You may number them all, both prose-
writers and singers,

[1] "last shirt"

Without overrunning the bounds of your
    fingers,
And Natty won't go to oblivion quicker
Than Adams the parson or Primrose the
    vicar.[1]

"There is one thing in Cooper I like, too,
    and that is   280
That on manners he lectures his countrymen
    gratis,
Not precisely so either, because, for a rarity,
He is paid for his tickets in unpopularity.
Now he may overcharge his American pic-
    tures,
But you'll grant there's a good deal of truth in
    his strictures;
And I honor the man who is willing to sink
Half his present repute for the freedom to
    think,
And, when he has thought, be his cause strong
    or weak,
Will risk t'other half for the freedom to speak,
Caring naught for what vengeance the mob
    has in store,   290
Let that mob be the upper ten thousand or
    lower.

"There are truths you Americans need to be
    told,
And it never'll refute them to swagger and
    scold;
John Bull, looking o'er the Atlantic, in choler
At your aptness for trade, says you worship
    the dollar;
But to scorn such eye-dollar-try's what very
    few do,
And John goes to that church as often as you
    do.
No matter what John says, don't try to out-
    crow him,
'Tis enough to go quietly on and outgrow
    him;
Like most fathers, Bull hates to see Number
    One   300
Displacing himself in the mind of his son,
And detests the same faults in himself he'd
    neglected
When he sees them again in his child's glass
    reflected;

[1] Parson Adams is a character in Fielding's *Joseph
Andrews;* Dr. Primrose is the vicar in Goldsmith's *The
Vicar of Wakefield.*

To love one another you're too like by half.
If he is a bull, you're a pretty stout calf,
And tear your own pasture for naught but to
    show
What a nice pair of horns you're beginning to
    grow.

"There are one or two things I should just
    like to hint,
For you don't often get the truth told you in
    print;
The most of you (this is what strikes all
    beholders)   310
Have a mental and physical stoop in the
    shoulders;
Though you ought to be free as the winds and
    the waves,
You've the gait and the manners of run-
    away slaves;
Tho' you brag of your New World, you don't
    half believe in it,
And as much of the Old as is possible weave
    in it;
Your goddess of freedom, a tight, buxom girl,
With lips like a cherry and teeth like a pearl,
With eyes bold as Herè's,[1] and hair floating
    free,
And full of the sun as the spray of the sea,
Who can sing at a husking or romp at a
    shearing,   320
Who can trip through the forests alone with-
    out fearing,
Who can drive home the cows with a song
    through the grass,
Keeps glancing aside into Europe's cracked
    glass,
Hides her red hands in gloves, pinches up her
    lithe waist,
And makes herself wretched with transmarine
    taste;
She loses her fresh country charm when she
    takes
Any mirror except her own rivers and lakes.

"You steal Englishmen's books[2] and think
    Englishmen's thought,
With their salt on her tail your wild eagle is
    caught;
Your literature suits its each whisper and
    motion   330

[1] Juno, wife of Jupiter   [2] There was no international copyright law until much later.

To what will be thought of it over the ocean;
The cast clothes of Europe your statesman-
    ship tries
And mumbles again the old blarneys and
    lies;—
Forget Europe wholly, your veins throb with
    blood,
To which the dull current in hers is but
    mud;
Let her sneer, let her say your experiment
    fails,
In her voice there's a tremble e'en now while
    she rails,
And your shore will soon be in the nature of
    things
Covered thick with gilt driftwood of cast-
    away kings,
Where alone, as it were in a Longfellow's
    Waif [1]   340
Her fugitive pieces will find themselves safe.
O, my friends, thank your God, if you have
    one, that he
'Twixt the Old World and you set the gulf of
    a sea;
Be strong-backed, brown-handed, upright as
    your pines,
By the scale of a hemisphere shape your
    designs,
Be true to yourselves and this new nineteenth
    age,
As a statue by Powers, or a picture by Page,
Plow, sail, forge, build, carve, paint, make all
    over new,
To your own New-World instincts contrive
    to be true,
Keep your ears open wide to the Future's first
    call,   350
Be whatever you will, but yourselves first of
    all,
Stand fronting the dawn on Toil's heaven-
    scaling peaks,
And become my new race of more practical
    Greeks.—
Hem! your likeness at present I shudder to
    tell o't,
Is that you have your slaves, and the Greek
    had his helot." [2]

"There comes Poe, with his raven, like
    Barnaby Rudge,[1]
Three-fifths of him genius and two-fifths
    sheer fudge,
Who talks like a book of iambs and pen-
    tameters,
In a way to make people of common-sense
    damn meters,
Who has written some things quite the best
    of their kind,   360
But the heart somehow seems all squeezed
    out by the mind,
Who—but hey-day! What's this? Messieurs
    Mathews and Poe,
You mustn't fling mud-balls at Longfellow so,
Does it make a man worse that his character's
    such
As to make his friends love him (as you think)
    too much?
Why, there is not a bard at this moment alive
More willing than he that his fellows should
    thrive,
While you are abusing him thus, even now
He would help either one of you out of a
    slough;
You may say that he's smooth and all that till
    you're hoarse,   370
But remember that elegance also is force;
After polishing granite as much as you will,
The heart keeps its tough old persistency still;
Deduct all you can, that still keeps you at bay;
Why, he'll live till men weary of Collins and
    Gray.
I'm not overfond of Greek meters in English,
To me rhyme's a gain, so it be not too jinglish,
And your modern hexameter verses are no
    more
Like Greek ones than sleek Mr. Pope is like
    Homer;
As the roar of the sea to the coo of a pigeon
    is,   380
So, compared to your moderns, sounds old
    Melesigenes [2];
I may be too partial, the reason, perhaps, o't is
That I've heard the old blind man recite his
    own rhapsodies,

---

[1] *The Waif* (1845), a collection of fugitive verse,
edited by Longfellow   [2] a serf, or bondsman, of ancient Sparta

[1] a half-witted youth, always accompanied by his
pet raven, who appears in Dickens's novel of the same
name   [2] "Meles-born," an epithet applied to Homer
who, according to one story, was born near the Meles
River in Asia Minor

And my ear with that music impregnate may
  be,
Like the poor exiled shell with the soul of the
  sea,
Or as one can't bear Strauss when his nature is
  cloven
To its deeps within deeps by the stroke of
  Beethoven;
But, set that aside, and 'tis truth that I speak,
Had Theocritus written in English, not Greek,
I believe that his exquisite sense would scarce
  change a line   390
In that rare, tender, virgin-like pastoral
  Evangeline.
That's not ancient nor modern, its place is
  apart
Where time has no sway, in the realm of pure
  Art,
'Tis a shrine of retreat from Earth's hubbub
  and strife
As quiet and chaste as the author's own life.

. . . .

"What! Irving? thrice welcome, warm heart
  and fine brain,
You bring back the happiest spirit from Spain,
And the gravest sweet humor, that ever were
  there
Since Cervantes met death in his gentle
  despair;
Nay, don't be embarrassed, nor look so
  beseeching,—   400
I shan't run directly against my own preaching,
And, having just laughed at their Raphaels and
  Dantes,
Go to setting you up beside matchless Cer-
  vantes;
But allow me to speak what I honestly feel,—
To a true poet-heart add the fun of Dick
  Steele,
Throw in all of Addison, *minus* the chill,
With the whole of that partnership's stock and
  good-will,
Mix well, and while stirring, hum o'er, as a
  spell,
The fine *old* English Gentleman, simmer it
  well,
Sweeten just to your own private liking, then
  strain,   410
That only the finest and clearest remain,
Let it stand out of doors till a soul it receives

From the warm lazy sun loitering down
  through green leaves,
And you'll find a choice nature, not wholly
  deserving
A name either English or Yankee,—just
  Irving.

. . . .

"There's Holmes, who is matchless among
  you for wit;
A Leyden-jar always full-charged, from which
  flit
The electrical tingles of hit after hit;
In long poems 'tis painful sometimes and
  invites
A thought of the way the new Telegraph
  writes,   420
Which pricks down its little sharp sentences
  spitefully
As if you got more than you'd title to right-
  fully,
And you find yourself hoping its wild father
  Lightning
Would flame in for a second and give you a
  fright'ning.
He has perfect sway of what *I* call a sham
  meter,
But many admire it, the English pentameter,
And Campbell, I think, wrote most com-
  monly worse,
With less nerve, swing, and fire in the same
  kind of verse,
Nor e'er achieved aught in't so worthy of
  praise
As the tribute of Holmes to the grand *Mar-
  seillaise.*[1]   430
You went crazy last year over Bulwer's New
  Timon[2];
Why, if B. to the day of his dying, should
  rime on,
Heaping verses on verses and tomes upon
  tomes,
He could ne'er reach the best point and vigor
  of Holmes.
His are just the fine hands, too, to weave you a
  lyric

[1] in "Poetry: A Metrical Essay," read before the
Harvard chapter of Phi Beta Kappa, 1836   [2] a poem
in which Bulwer satirized the work of other poets,
including Tennyson (see Tennyson's "Literary
Squabbles" for his reply)

Full of fancy, fun, feeling, or spiced with
   satiric
In a measure so kindly, you doubt if the toes
That are trodden upon are your own or your
   foes'.

"There is Lowell, who's striving Parnassus
   to climb
With a whole bale of *isms* tied together with
   rhyme,   440
He might get on alone, spite of brambles and
   boulders,
But he can't with that bundle he has on his
   shoulders,
The top of the hill he will ne'er come nigh
   reaching
Till he learns the distinction 'twixt singing and
   preaching;
His lyre has some chords that would ring
   pretty well,
But he'd rather by half make a drum of the
   shell,
And rattle away till he's old as Methusalem,
At the head of a march to the last new Jerusalem."

                    1848

From BEAVER BROOK

Printed in the *Standard*, January 4, 1849.
Beaver Brook was within walking distance of Elmwood. Lowell wrote in 1849, "The little mill
stands in a valley between one of the spurs of
Wellington Hill and the main summit, just on
the edge of Waltham. It is surely one of the loveliest spots in the world. It is one of my lions, and
if you will make me a visit this spring I will take
you up to hear it roar, and I will show you 'the
oaks'—the largest, I fancy, left in the country"
(*Letters*, I, 149).

HUSHED with broad sunlight lies the hill,
And, minuting[1] the long day's loss,
The cedar's shadow, slow and still,
Creeps o'er its dial of gray moss.

Warm noon brims full the valley's cup,
The aspen's leaves are scarce astir,
Only the little mill sends up
Its busy, never-ceasing burr.

[1] recording by minutes

Climbing the loose-piled wall that hems
The road along the millpond's brink,   10
From 'neath the arching barberry-stems,
My footstep scares the shy chewink.

Beneath a bony buttonwood
The mill's red door lets forth the din;
The whitened miller, dust-imbued,
Flits past the square of dark within.

No mountain torrent's strength is here;
Sweet Beaver, child of forest still,
Heaps its small pitcher to the ear,
And gently waits the miller's will.   20

Swift slips Undine[1] along the race
Unheard, and then, with flashing bound,
Floods the dull wheel with light and grace,
And, laughing, hunts the loath drudge round.

The miller dreams not at what cost
The quivering millstones hum and whirl,
Nor how for every turn, are tost
Armfuls of diamond and of pearl. . . .

                    1849

SHE CAME AND WENT

Lowell's little daughter Blanche died in 1847.
His "The Changeling" and "The First Snow-Fall"
are other poems concerning her.

As a twig trembles, which a bird
   Lights on to sing, then leaves unbent,
So is my memory thrilled and stirred;—
   I only know she came and went.

As clasps some lake, by gusts unriven,
   The blue dome's measureless content,
So my soul held that moment's heaven;—
   I only know she came and went.

As, at one bound, our swift spring heaps
   The orchards full of bloom and scent,   10
So clove her May my wintry sleeps;—
   I only know she came and went.

An angel stood and met my gaze,
   Through the low doorway of my tent;
The tent is struck, the vision stays;—
   I only know she came and went.

[1] the water sprite in Fouqué's *Undine* (1811)

Oh, when the room grows slowly dim,
　And life's last oil is nearly spent,
One gush of light these eyes will brim,
　Only to think she came and went. 　20

1849

AUF WIEDERSEHEN[1]

Published in *Putnam's Magazine*, December,
1854. Composed after the death of Mrs. Lowell
(Maria White), October 27, 1853. See Longfellow's poem, "The Two Angels"; also Scudder's *Life*, I, 356–63, and *The Poems of Maria
White Lowell* (1855).

SUMMER

THE little gate was reached at last,
　Half hid in lilacs down the lane;
She pushed it wide, and, as she past,
A wistful look she backward cast,
　And said,—"*Auf wiedersehen!*"

With hand on latch, a vision white
　Lingered reluctant, and again
Half doubting if she did aright,
Soft as the dews that fell that night,
　She said,—"*Auf wiedersehen!*" 　10

The lamp's clear gleam flits up the stair;
　I linger in delicious pain;
Ah, in that chamber, whose rich air
To breathe in thought I scarcely dare,
　Thinks she,—"*Auf wiedersehen?*"

'Tis thirteen years; once more I press
　The turf that silences the lane;
I hear the rustle of her dress,
I smell the lilacs, and—ah, yes,
　I hear,—"*Auf wiedersehen!*" 　20

Sweet piece of bashful maiden art!
　The English words had seemed too fain,
But these—they drew us heart to heart,
Yet held us tenderly apart;
　She said,—"*Auf wiedersehen!*"

1854

AFTER THE BURIAL

Printed in the *Atlantic Monthly*, May, 1868.
Lowell suffered many bereavements in this period
of his life. Six stanzas of the poem were written
in 1850, the year of the death of his second little
daughter, Rose. The poem was completed in 1868,

[1] "Till we meet again."

when his mother and his only son, as well as his
daughters and his wife, were dead, and his father
invalided.

YES, faith is a goodly anchor;
　When skies are sweet as a psalm,
At the bows it lolls so stalwart,
　In bluff, broad-shouldered calm.

And when over breakers to leeward
　The tattered surges are hurled,
It may keep our head to the tempest,
　With its grip on the base of the world.

But, after the shipwreck, tell me
　What help in its iron thews, 　10
Still true to the broken hawser,
　Deep down among seaweed and ooze?

In the breaking gulfs of sorrow,
　When the helpless feet stretch out
And find in the deeps of darkness
　No footing so solid as doubt,

Then better one spar of Memory,
　One broken plank of the Past,
That our human heart may cling to,
　Though hopeless of shore at last! 　20

To the spirit its splendid conjectures,
　To the flesh its sweet despair,
Its tears o'er the thin-worn locket
　With its anguish of deathless hair!

Immortal? I feel it and know it,
　Who doubts it of such as she?
But that is the pang's very secret,—
　Immortal away from me.

There's a narrow ridge in the graveyard
　Would scarce stay a child in his race, 　30
But to me and my thought it is wider
　Than the star-sown vague of Space.

Your logic, my friend, is perfect,
　Your morals most drearily true;
But, since the earth clashed on *her* coffin,
　I keep hearing that, and not you.

Console if you will, I can bear it;
　'Tis a well-meant alms of breath;
But not all the preaching since Adam
　Has made Death other than Death. 　40

It is pagan; but wait till you feel it,—
That jar of our earth, that dull shock
When the ploughshare of deeper passion
Tears down to our primitive rock.

Communion in spirit! Forgive me,
But I, who am earthy and weak,

Would give all my incomes from dreamland
For a touch of her hand on my cheek.

That little shoe in the corner,
So worn and wrinkled and brown,   50
With its emptiness confutes you,
And argues your wisdom down.

1868

From THE BIGLOW PAPERS, FIRST SERIES

In these papers Lowell broke away from European models and from romance. The first number was printed in the Boston *Courier*, June 17, 1846. Its success led Lowell to write eight more numbers. These he published in book form in 1848. To the character Ezekiel Biglow, who introduces his son Hosea as a poet, Lowell added the Rev. Homer Wilbur, the learned minister of the town of Jaalam, who appended introductions, comments, and prose annotations. Lowell also prefixed to the book imaginary eulogistic comments, "Notices of an Independent Press." Among them he inserted stanzas of another poem by Hosea, later expanded into "The Courtin'" of the second series. A glossary of New England dialect words was added also. The poem had astonishing success and influenced political opinion. "When . . . I wrote the first of the series," Lowell said in the introduction to the second series, "I had no definite plan and no intention of ever writing another. Thinking the Mexican War, as I think it still, a national crime committed in behoof of slavery, our common sin, and wishing to put the feeling of those who thought as I did in a way that would tell, I imagined to myself such an up-country man as I had often seen at antislavery gatherings, capable of district school English, but always instinctively falling back into the natural stronghold of his homely dialect when heated to the point of self-forgetfulness. . . . I needed on occasion to rise above the level of mere *patois*, and for this purpose conceived the Rev. Mr. Wilbur. . . ."

No. I
A Letter

FROM MR. EZEKIEL BIGLOW OF JAALAM TO THE HON. JOSEPH T. BUCKINGHAM, EDITOR OF THE BOSTON *COURIER*, ENCLOSING A POEM OF HIS SON, MR. HOSEA BIGLOW.

JAYLEM, june 1846.

MISTER EDDYTER:—Our Hosea wuz down to Boston last week, and he see a cruetin

Sarjunt a struttin round as popler as a hen with 1 chicking, with 2 fellers a drummin and fifin arter him like all nater. the sarjunt he thout Hosea hedn't gut his i teeth cut cos he looked a kindo's though he'd jest com down, so he cal'lated to hook him in, but Hosy woodn't take none o' his sarse for all he hed much as 20 Rooster's tales stuck onto his hat and eenamost enuf brass a bobbin up and down on his shoulders and figureed onto his coat and trousis, let alone wut nater hed sot in his featers, to make a 6 pounder out on.

wal, Hosea he com home considerabal riled, and arter I'd gone to bed I heern Him a thrashin round like a short-tailed Bull in fli-time. The old Woman ses she to me ses she, Zekle, ses she, our Hosee's gut the chollery or suthin anuther ses she, don't you Bee skeered, ses I, he's oney amakin pottery [*Aut insanit, aut versos facit.*[1]—H. W.] ses i, he's ollers on hand at that ere busynes like Da & martin,[2] and shure enuf, cum mornin, Hosy he cum down stares full chizzle, hare on eend and cote tales flyin, and sot rite of to go reed his varses to Parson Wilbur bein he haint aney grate shows o' book larnin himself, bimeby he cum back and sed the parson wuz dreffle tickled with 'em as i hoop you will Be, and said they wuz True grit.

Hosea ses taint hardly fair to call 'em hisn now, cos the parson kind o' slicked off sum o' the last varses, but he told Hosee he didn't want to put his ore in to tetch to the Rest on 'em, bein they wuz verry well As thay wuz, and then Hosy ses he sed suthin a nuther about Simplex Mundishes[3] or sum sech feller, but I

---

[1] "Either he goes mad or he composes verses." "H. W." is Homer Wilbur, the parson who edits Ezekiel's writing, and who is quoting here from the second satire of Horace. [2] Day and Martin used rhymes in advertising their shoeblacking. [3] Parson Wilbur's expression was another quotation from Horace—*simplex munditiis*—which means "plain in [thy] neatness."

guess Hosea kind o' didn't hear him, for I never hearn o' nobody o' that name in this villadge, and I've lived here man and boy 76 year cum next tater diggin, and thair aint no wheres a kitting spryer'n I be.

If you print 'em I wish you'd jest let folks know who hosy's father is, cos my ant Keziah used to say it's nater to be curus ses she, she aint livin though and he's a likely kind o' lad.

EZEKIEL BIGLOW.

Thrash away, you'll *hev* to rattle
  On them kittle-drums o' yourn,—
'Taint a knowin' kind o' cattle
  Thet is ketched with moldy corn;
Put in stiff, you fifer feller,
  Let folks see how spry you be,—
Guess you'll toot till you are yeller
  'Fore you git ahold o' me!

Thet air flag's a leetle rotten,
  Hope it aint your Sunday's best;— 10
Fact! it takes a sight o' cotton
  To stuff out a soger's chest:
Sence we farmers hev to pay fer't,
  Ef you must wear humps like these,
Sposin' you should try salt hay fer't,
  It would du ez slick ez grease.

'Twouldn't suit them Southun fellers,
  They're a dreffle graspin' set,
We must ollers blow the bellers
  Wen they want their irons het; 20
May be it's all right ez preachin',
  But *my* narves it kind o' grates,
Wen I see the overreachin'
  O' them nigger-drivin' States.

Them thet rule us, them slave-traders,
  Haint they cut a thunderin' swarth,
(Helped by Yankee renegaders,)
  Thru the vartu o' the North!
We begin to think it's nater
  To take sarse an' not be riled;— 30
Who'd expect to see a tater
  All on eend at bein' biled?

Ez fer war, I call it murder,—
  There you hev it plain an' flat;
I don't want to go no furder
  Than my Testyment fer that;

God hez sed so plump an' fairly,
  It's ez long ez it is broad,
An' you've gut to git up airly
  Ef you want to take in God. 40

'Taint your eppyletts an' feathers
  Make the thing a grain more right;
'Taint afollerin' your bell-wethers
  Will excuse ye in His sight;
Ef you take a sword an' dror it,
  An' go stick a feller thru,
Guv'ment aint to answer for it,
  God'll send the bill to you.

Wut's the use o' meetin'-goin'
  Every Sabbath, wet or dry, 50
Ef it's right to go amowin'
  Feller-men like oats an' rye?
I dunno but wut it's pooty
  Trainin' round in bobtail coats,—
But it's curus Christian dooty
  This 'ere cuttin' folks's throats.

They may talk o' Freedom's airy[1]
  Tell they're pupple in the face,—
It's a grand gret cemetary
  Fer the barthrights of our race; 60
They jest want this Californy
  So's to lug new slave-states in
To abuse ye, an' to scorn ye,
  An' to plunder ye like sin.

Aint it cute to see a Yankee
  Take sech everlastin' pains,
All to git the Devil's thankee,
  Helpin' on 'em weld their chains?
Wy, it's jest ez clear ez figgers,
  Clear ez one an' one make two, 70
Chaps thet make black slaves o' niggers
  Want to make wite slaves o' you.

Tell ye jest the eend I've come to
  Arter cipherin' plaguy smart,
An' it makes a handy sum, tu,
  Any gump could larn by heart;
Laborin' man an' laborin' woman
  Hev one glory an' one shame,
Ev'y thin' thet's done inhuman
  Injers all on 'em the same. 80

[1] area

'Taint by turnin' out to hack folks
　You're agoin' to git your right,
Nor by lookin' down on black folks
　Coz you're put upon by wite;
Slavery aint o' nary color,
　'Taint the hide thet makes it wus,
All it keers fer in a feller
　'S jest to make him fill its pus.

Want to tackle *me* in, du ye?
　I expect you'll hev to wait; 　　90
Wen cold lead puts daylight thru ye
　You'll begin to kal'late;
'Spose the crows wun't fall to pickin'
　All the carkiss from your bones,
Coz you helped to give a lickin'
　To them poor half-Spanish drones?

Jest go home an' ask our Nancy
　Wether I'd be sech a goose
Ez to jine ye,—guess you'd fancy
　The etarnal bung was loose! 　　100
She wants me fer home consumption,
　Let alone the hay's to mow,—
Ef you're arter folks o' gumption,
　You've a darned long row to hoe.

Take them editors thet's crowin'
　Like a cockerel three months old,—
Don't ketch any on 'em goin',
　Though they *be* so blasted bold;
Aint they a prime lot o' fellers? 　　109
　'Fore they think on't guess they'll
　　　sprout,
(Like a peach thet's got the yellers)
　With the meanness bustin' out.

Wal, go 'long to help 'em stealin'
　Bigger pens to cram with slaves,
Help the men thet's ollers dealin'
　Insults on your fathers' graves;
Help the strong to grind the feeble,
　Help the many agin the few,
Help the men thet call your people 　　119
　Witewashed slaves an' peddlin' crew!

Massachusetts, God forgive her,
　She's akneeling with the rest,
She thet ough' to ha' clung ferever
　In her grand old eagle-nest;

She thet ough' to stand so fearless
　Wile the wracks are round her hurled,
Holdin' up a beacon peerless
　To the oppressed of all the world!

Ha'n't they sold your colored seamen?
　Ha'n't they made your env'ys w'iz? 　130
Wut'll make ye act like free men?
　Wut'll git your dander riz?
Come, I'll tell ye wut I'm thinkin'
　Is our dooty in this fix,
They'd ha' done 't ez quick ez winkin'
　In the days o' seventy-six.

Clang the bells in every steeple,
　Call all true men to disown
The tradoocers of our people,
　The enslavers o' their own; 　　140
Let our dear old Bay State proudly
　Put the trumpet to her mouth,
Let her ring this messidge loudly
　In the ears of all the South:—

"I'll return ye good for evil
　Much ez we frail mortils can,
But I won't go help the Devil
　Makin' man the cus o' man;
Call me coward, call me traiter,
　Jest ez suits your mean idees,— 　　150
Here I stand a tyrant-hater,
　An' the friend o' God an' Peace!"

Ef I'd *my* way I hed ruther
　We should go to work an' part,—
They take one way, we take t'other,—
　Guess it wouldn't break my heart;
Man hed ough' to put asunder
　Them thet God has noways jined;
An' I shouldn't gretly wonder
　Ef there's thousands o' my mind. 　160

[The first recruiting sergeant on record I conceive to have been that individual who is mentioned in the Book of Job as *going to and fro in the earth, and walking up and down in it.* Bishop Latimer will have him to have been a bishop, but to me that other calling would appear more congenial. The sect of Cainites is not yet extinct, who esteemed the first-born of Adam to be the most worthy, not only because of that privilege of primogeniture, but inasmuch as he was able to overcome and slay his younger brother. That was a wise saying of the famous Marquis Pescara to the Papal Legate, that *it was impossible for men to serve Mars and Christ at the same time.* Yet in time past the profession of arms was judged to be κατ ἐξοχήν that of a gentleman, nor does this opinion want for strenuous upholders even in our day. Must we suppose, then, that the profession of Christianity was only intended for losels, or, at best, to afford an opening for plebeian ambition? Or shall we hold with that nicely metaphysical Pomeranian, Captain Vratz, who was Count Königsmark's chief instrument in the murder of Mr. Thynne, that the Scheme of Salvation had been arranged with an especial eye to the necessities of the upper classes, and that "God would consider *a gentleman* and deal with him suitably to the condition and profession he had placed him in"? It may be said of us all, *Exemplo plus quam ratione vivimus.*—H. W.]

From THE BIGLOW PAPERS, SECOND SERIES

The first poem of the second series of *The Biglow Papers* was written early in December, 1861, and appeared in January, 1862, fourteen years after the launching of the first series. This second series of eleven numbers dealt with problems and events connected with the Civil War.

The Courtin'

In its first and briefer form this poem appeared in the "Notices of an Independent Press" in the first series of *The Biglow Papers*. In a later edition Lowell added more stanzas. The final text of the poem was first published at the end of the introduction to the second series. Lowell explained in his introduction how the poem happened to appear there:

The only attempt I had ever made at anything like a pastoral (if that may be called an attempt which was the result almost of pure accident) was in "The Courtin'". While the introduction to the First Series was going through the press, I received word from the printer that there was a blank page left which must be filled. I sat down at once and improvised another fictitious "notice of the press," in which, because verse would fill up space more cheaply than prose, I inserted an extract from a supposed ballad of Mr. Biglow. I kept no copy of it, and the printer, as directed, cut it off when the gap was filled. Presently I began to receive letters asking for the rest of it, sometimes for the *balance* of it. I had none, but to answer such demands, I patched a conclusion upon it in a later edition. Those who had only the first continued to importune me. Afterward, being asked to write it out as an autograph for the Baltimore Sanitary Commission Fair, I added other verses, into some of which I infused a little more sentiment in a homely way, and after a fashion completed it by sketching in the characters and making a connected story. Most likely I have spoiled it, but I shall put it at the end of this introduction, to answer once for all those kindly importunings.

God makes sech nights, all white an' still
    Fur 'z you can look or listen,
Moonshine an' snow on field an' hill,
    All silence an' all glisten.

Zekle crep' up quite unbeknown
    An' peeked in thru' the winder,
An' there sot Huldy all alone,
    'ith no one nigh to hender.

A fireplace filled the room's one side
    With half a cord o' wood in—   10
There warn't no stoves (tell comfort died)
    To bake ye to a puddin'.

The wa'nut logs shot sparkles out
    Towards the pootiest, bless her,
An' leetle flames danced all about
    The chiny on the dresser.

Agin the chimbley crook-necks hung,
    An' in amongst 'em rusted
The ole queen's-arm thet gran'ther Young
    Fetched back from Concord busted.   20

The very room, coz she was in,
    Seemed warm from floor to ceilin',
An' she looked full ez rosy agin
    Ez the apples she was peelin'.

'Twas kin' o' kingdom-come to look
    On sech a blessed cretur,
A dogrose blushin' to a brook
    Ain't modester nor sweeter.

He was six foot o' man, A1,
    Clear grit an' human natur';   30
None couldn't quicker pitch a ton
    Nor dror a furrer straighter.

He'd sparked it with full twenty gals,
    Hed squired 'em, danced 'em, druv 'em,
Fust this one, an' then thet, by spells—
    All is, he couldn't love 'em.

But long o' her his veins 'ould run
  All crinkly like curled maple,
The side she breshed felt full o' sun
  Ez a south slope in Ap'il.   40

She thought no v'ice hed sech a swing
  Ez hisn in the choir;
My! when he made Ole Hunderd ring,
  She *knowed* the Lord was nigher.

An' she'd blush scarlit, right in prayer,
  When her new meetin'-bunnet
Felt somehow thru' its crown a pair
  O' blue eyes sot upun it.

Thet night, I tell ye, she looked *some!*
  She seemed to've gut a new soul,   50
For she felt sartin-sure he'd come,
  Down to her very shoe-sole.

She heered a foot, an' knowed it tu,
  A-raspin' on the scraper,—
All ways to once her feelin's flew
  Like sparks in burnt-up paper.

He kin' o' l'itered on the mat
  Some doubtfle o' the sekle,
His heart kep' goin' pity-pat,
  But hern went pity Zekle.   60

An' yet she gin her cheer a jerk
  Ez though she wished him furder,
An' on her apples kep' to work,
  Parin' away like murder.

"You want to see my Pa, I s'pose?"
  "Wal . . . no . . . I come dasignin'"—
"To see my Ma? She's sprinklin' clo'es
  Agin to-morrer's i'nin'."

To say why gals acts so or so,
  Or don't, 'ould be presumin';   70
Mebby to mean *yes* an' say *no*
  Comes nateral to women.

He stood a spell on one foot fust,
  Then stood a spell on t'other,
An' on which one he felt the wust
  He couldn't ha' told ye nuther.

Says he, "I'd better call agin";
  Says she, "Think likely, Mister":
Thet last word pricked him like a pin,
  An' . . . Wal, he up an' kist her.   80

When Ma bimeby upon 'em slips,
  Huldy sot pale ez ashes,
All kin' o' smily roun' the lips
  An' teary roun' the lashes.

For she was jes' the quiet kind
  Whose naturs never vary,
Like streams that keep a summer mind
  Snowhid in Jenooary.

The blood clost roun' her heart felt glued
  Too tight for all expressin',   90
Tell mother see how metters stood,
  An' gin 'em both her blessin'.

Then her red come back like the tide
  Down to the Bay o' Fundy,
An' all I know is they was cried[1]
  In meetin' come nex' Sunday.

                  1861

From No. II

Jonathan to John

  The second number of the second series of *The Biglow Papers*, bearing the title "Mason and Slidell: a Yankee Idyll," had prefixed to it a letter to the editors of the *Atlantic Monthly*. The letter discusses the nature of the "Idyll" and mentions the case of the Confederate agents Mason and Slidell. These men, sent by the South to represent its cause in England and France, were removed from an English vessel by a Unionist captain. The British government proclaimed the act an "outrage," asked for the release of the prisoners and reparation, and prepared for hostilities. Lowell resented England's tendency to take the side of the South in the Civil War. "Jonathan to John" followed a dialogue between Concord Bridge, representing a protest at England's attitude, and the Bunker Hill monument, representing those favoring tolerance of it.

    It don't seem hardly right, John,
      When both my hands was full,
    To stump me to a fight, John,—
      Your cousin, tu, John Bull!
      Ole Uncle S. sez he, "I guess
        We know it now," sez he,
    "The lion's paw is all the law,
        Accordin' to J. B.,
        Thet's fit for you an' me!"

[1] i.e., the marriage banns were announced

You wonder why we're hot, John? 10
  Your mark wuz on the guns,
The neutral guns, thet shot, John,
  Our brothers an' our sons:
    Old Uncle S. sez he, "I guess
    There's human blood," sez he,
  "By fits an' starts, in Yankee hearts,
    Though 't may surprise J. B.
    More'n it would you an' me."

Ef *I* turned mad dogs loose, John,
  On *your* front-parlor stairs, 20
Would it jest meet your views, John,
  To wait an' sue their heirs?
    Ole Uncle S. sez he, "I guess,
    I on'y guess," sez he,
  "Thet ef Vattel on *his* toes fell,
    'Twould kind o' rile J. B.,
    Ez wal ez you an' me!"

Who made the law thet hurts, John,
  Heads I win,—ditto tails?
"*J. B.*" was on his shirts, John, 30
  Onless my memory fails.
    Ole Uncle S. sez he, "I guess
    (I'm good at thet)," sez he,
  "Thet sauce for goose ain't *jest* the juice
    For ganders with J. B.,
    No more'n with you or me!"

When your rights was our wrongs, John,
  You didn't stop for fuss,—
Britanny's trident prongs, John,
  Was good 'nough law for us. 40
    Ole Uncle S. sez he, "I guess,
    Though physic's good," sez he,
  "It doesn't foller thet he can swaller
    Prescriptions signed 'J. B.,'
    Put up by you and me!"

We own the ocean, tu, John:
  You mus'n' take it hard,
Ef we can't think with you, John.
  It's jest your own back-yard.
    Ole Uncle S. sez he, "I guess, 50
    Ef *thet's* his claim," sez he,
  "The fencin'-stuff'll cost enough
    To bust up friend J. B.,
    Ez wal ez you an' me!"

Why talk so dreffle big, John,
  Of honor when it meant

You didn't care a fig, John,
  But jest for *ten per cent?*
    Ole Uncle S. sez he, "I guess
    He's like the rest," sez he: 60
  "When all is done, it's number one
    Thet's nearest to J. B.,
    Ez wal ez t' you an' me!"

We give the critters back, John,
  Cos Abram thought 'twas right;
It warn't your bullyin' clack, John,
  Provokin' us to fight.
    Ole Uncle S. sez he, "I guess
    We've a hard row," sez he,
  "To hoe jest now; but thet somehow, 70
    May happen to J. B.,
    Ez wal ez you an' me!"

We ain't so weak an' poor, John,
  With twenty million people,
An' close to every door, John,
  A school-house an' a steeple.
    Ole Uncle S. sez he, "I guess,
    It is a fact," sez he,
  "The surest plan to make a Man
    Is, think him so, J. B., 80
    Ez much ez you or me!"

Our folks believe in Law, John;
  An' it's for her sake, now,
They've left the axe an' saw, John,
  The anvil an' the plough.
    Ole Uncle S. sez he, "I guess,
    Ef 't warn't for law," sez he,
  "There'd be one shindy[1] from here to Indy;
    An' thet don't suit J. B.
    (When 't ain't 'twixt you an' me!)" 90

We know we've got a cause, John,
  Thet's honest, just, an' true;
We thought 'twould win applause, John,
  Ef nowheres else, from you.
    Ole Uncle S. sez he, "I guess
    His love of right," sez he,
  "Hangs by a rotten fibre o' cotton:
    There's natur' in J. B.,
    Ez wal ez you an' me!"

The South says, "*Poor folks down!*" John,
  An' "*All men up!*" say we,— 101
White, yaller, black, an' brown, John:
  Now which is your idee?

[1] uproar, brawl

Ole Uncle S. sez he, "I guess,
    John preaches wal," sez he;
"But, sermon thru, an' come to *du*,
    Why, there's the old J. B.
    A crowdin' you an' me!"

Shall it be love, or hate, John?
    It's you thet's to decide;   110
Ain't *your* bonds held by Fate, John,
    Like all the world's beside?
    Ole Uncle S. sez he, "I guess
    Wise men forgive," sez he,
"But not forget; an' some time yet
    Thet truth may strike J. B.,
    Ez wal ez you an' me!"

God means to make this land, John,
    Clear thru, from sea to sea,
Believe an' understand, John,   120
    The *wuth* o' bein' free.
    Ole Uncle S. sez he, "I guess,
    God's price is high," sez he;
"But nothin' else than wut He sells
    Wears long, an' thet J. B.
    May larn, like you an' me!"

1861   1862

No. VI

Sunthin' in the Pastoral Line

This was a very popular number in the second
series of *The Biglow Papers.* It is a description of
spring in Yankee dialect, and an expression of
Lowell's marked delight in nature. For Lowell's
treatment of nature, consult Foerster's *Nature in
American Literature.*

Once git a smell o' musk into a draw,
An' it clings hold like precerdents in law:
Your gra'ma'am put it there,—when, good-
    ness knows—
To jes' this-worldify her Sunday-clo'es;
But the old chist wun't sarve her gran'-
    son's wife
(For, 'thout new funnitoor, wut good in life?),
An' so ole clawfoot, from the precinks dread
O' the spare chamber, slinks into the shed,
Where, dim with dust, it fust or last subsides
To holdin' seeds an' fifty things besides;   10
But better days stick fast in heart an' husk,
An' all you keep in't gits a scent o' musk.

Jes' so with poets: wut they've airly read
Gits kind o' worked into their heart an' head,
So 's 't they can't seem to write but jest on
    sheers
With furrin countries or played-out ideers,
Nor hev a feelin', ef it doosn't smack
O' wut some critter chose to feel 'way back:
This makes 'em talk o' daisies, larks, an'
    things,
Ez though we'd nothin' here that blows an'
    sings   20
(Why, I'd give more for one live bobolink
Than a square mile o' larks in printer's ink),—
This makes 'em think our fust o' May is May,
Which 'tain't, for all the almanicks can say.

O little city-gals, don't never go it
Blind on the word o' noospaper or poet!
They're apt to puff, an' May-day seldom looks
Up in the country ez it doos in books;
They're no more like than hornets'-nests an'
    hives,
Or printed sarmons be to holy lives.   30
I, with my trouses perched on cowhide boots,
Tuggin' my foundered feet out by the roots,
Hev seen ye come to fling on April's hearse
Your muslin nosegays from the milliner's,
Puzzlin' to find dry ground your queen to
    choose,
An' dance your throats sore in morocker
    shoes:
I've seen ye an' felt proud, thet, come wut
    would,
Our Pilgrim stock wuz pethed with hardi-
    hood.
Pleasure doos make us Yankees kind o'
    winch,
Ez though 'twuz sunthin' paid for by the
    inch;   40
But yit we du contrive to worry thru,
Ef Dooty tells us thet the thing's to du,
An' kerry a hollerday, if we set out,
Ez stiddily ez though 'twuz a redoubt.

I, country-born an' bred, know where to find
Some blooms thet make the season suit the
    mind,
An' seem to metch the doubtin' bluebird's
    notes,—
Half-vent'rin' liverworts in furry coats,
Bloodroots, whose rolled-up leaves ef you
    oncurl,

Each on 'em's cradle to a baby-pearl,—   50
But these are jes' Spring's pickets; sure ez sin,
The rebble frosts 'll try to drive 'em in;
For half our May's so awfully like Mayn't,
'twould rile a Shaker or an evrige saint;
Though I own up I like our back'ard springs
Thet kind o' haggle with their greens an'
     things,
An' when you 'most give up, 'uthout more
     words
Toss the fields full o' blossoms, leaves, an'
     birds:
Thet's Northun natur', slow an' apt to doubt,
But when it *doos* git stirred, ther' 's no gin-
     out!   60

Fust come the blackbirds clatt'rin' in tall trees,
An' settlin' things in windy Congresses,—
Queer politicians, though, for I'll be skinned
Ef all on 'em don't head aginst the wind.
'fore long the trees begin to show belief,—
The maple crimsons to a coral-reef,
Then saffern swarms swing off from all the
     willers
So plump they look like yaller caterpillars,
Then gray hossches'nuts leetle hands unfold
Softer 'n a baby's be at three days old: 70
Thet's robin-redbreast's almanick; he knows
Thet arter this ther' 's only blossom-snows;
So, choosin' out a handy crotch an' spouse,
He goes to plast'rin' his adobe house.

Then seems to come a hitch,—things lag be-
     hind,
Till some fine mornin' Spring makes up her
     mind,
An' ez, when snow-swelled rivers cresh their
     dams
Heaped-up with ice thet dovetails in an' jams,
A leak comes spirtin' thru some pin-hole
     cleft,
Grows stronger, fercer, tears out right an'
     left,   80
Then all the waters bow themselves an' come,
Suddin, in one gret slope o' shedderin' foam,
Jes' so our Spring gits everythin' in tune
An' gives one leap from Aperl into June:
Then all comes crowdin' in; afore you think,
Young oak-leaves mist the side-hill woods
     with pink;
The catbird in the laylock-bush is loud;
The orchards turn to heaps o' rosy cloud;

Red-cedars blossom tu, though few folks
     know it,
An' look all dipt in sunshine like a poet;   90
The lime-trees pile their solid stacks o' shade
An' drows'ly simmer with the bees' sweet
     trade;
In ellum-shrouds the flashin' hangbird clings
An' for the summer vy'ge his hammock
     slings;
All down the loose-walled lanes in archin'
     bowers
The barb'ry droops its strings o' golden
     flowers,
Whose shrinkin' hearts the school-gals love
     to try
With pins,—they'll worry yourn so, boys,
     bimeby!
But I don't love your cat'logue style,—do
     you?—
Ez ef to sell off Natur' by vendoo;   100
One word with blood in't's twice ez good ez
     two:
'nuff sed, June's bridesman, poet o' the year,
Gladness on wings, the bobolink, is here;
Half-hid in tip-top apple-blooms he swings,
Or climbs aginst the breeze with quiverin'
     wings,
Or, givin' way to't in a mock despair,
Runs down, a brook o' laughter, thru the air.

I ollus feel the sap start in my veins
In Spring, with curus heats an' prickly pains,
Thet drive me, when I git a chance, to walk
Off by myself to hev a privit talk   111
With a queer critter thet can't seem to 'gree
Along o' me like most folks,—Mister Me.
Ther' 's times when I'm unsoshle ez a stone,
An' sort o' suffercate to be alone,—
I'm crowded jes' to think thet folks are
     nigh,
An' can't bear nothin' closer than the sky;
Now the wind's full ez shifty in the mind
Ez wut it is ou'-doors, ef I ain't blind,
An' sometimes, in the fairest sou'west weather,
My innard vane pints east for weeks to-
     gether,
My natur' gits all goose-flesh, an' my sins   121
Come drizzlin' on my conscience sharp ez
     pins:
Wal, et sech times I jes' slip out o' sight
An' take it out in a fair stan'-up fight

With the one cuss I can't lay on the shelf,
The crook'dest stick in all the heap,— Myself.

'Twuz so las' Sabbath arter meetin'-time:
Findin' my feelin's wouldn't noways rhyme
With nobody's, but off the hendle flew   130
An' took things from an east-wind pint o'
    view,
I started off to lose me in the hills
Where the pines be, up back o' 'Siah's Mills:
Pines, ef you're blue, are the best friends I
    know,
They mope an' sigh an' sheer your feelin's
    so,—
They hesh the ground beneath so, tu, I swan,
You half-forgit you've gut a body on.
Ther' 's a small school'us' there where four
    roads meet,
The door-steps hollered out by little feet,
An' side-posts carved with names whose
    owners grew   140
To gret men, some on 'em, an' deacons, tu;
'tain't used no longer, coz the town hez gut
A high-school, where they teach the Lord
    knows wut:
Three-story larnin' 's pop'lar now; I guess
We thriv' ez wal on jes' two stories less,
For it strikes me ther' 's sech a thing ez sin-
    nin'
By overloadin' children's underpinnin':
Wal, here it wuz I larned my A B C,
An' it's a kind o' favorite spot with me.

We're curus critters: Now ain't jes' the
    minute   150
Thet ever fits us easy while we're in it;
Long ez 'twuz futur', 'twould be perfect
    bliss,—
Soon ez it's past, *thet* time's wuth ten o' this;
An' yit there ain't a man thet need be told
Thet Now's the only bird lays eggs o' gold.
A knee-high lad, I used to plot an' plan
An' think 'twuz life's cap-sheaf to be a man;
Now, gittin' gray, there's nothin' I enjoy
Like dreamin' back along into a boy:
So the ole school'us' is a place I choose   160
Afore all others, ef I want to muse;
I set down where I used to set, an' git
My boyhood back, an' better things with
    it,—
Faith, Hope, an' sunthin', ef it isn't Cherrity,

It's want o' guile, an' thet's ez gret a rerrity,—
While Fancy's cushin', free to Prince and
    Clown,
Makes the hard bench ez soft ez milkweed-
    down.

Now, 'fore I knowed, thet Sabbath arter-
    noon
When I sot out to tramp myself in tune,
I found me in the school'us' on my seat,   170
Drummin' the march to No-wheres with
    my feet.
Thinkin' o' nothin', I've heerd ole folks say
Is a hard kind o' dooty in its way:
It's thinkin' everythin' you ever knew,
Or ever hearn, to make your feelin's blue.
I sot there tryin' thet on for a spell:
I thought o' the Rebellion, then o' Hell,
Which some folks tell ye now is jest a metter-
    for
(A the'ry, p'raps, it wun't *feel* none the better
    for);   179
I thought o' Reconstruction, wut we'd win
Patchin' our patent self-blow-up agin:
I thought ef this 'ere milkin' o' the wits,
So much a month, warn't givin' Natur' fits,—
Ef folks warn't druv, findin' their own milk
    fail,
To work the cow thet hez an iron tail,
An' ef idees 'thout ripenin' in the pan
Would send up cream to humor ary man:
From this to thet I let my worryin' creep,
Till finally I must ha' fell asleep.

Our lives in sleep are some like streams thet
    glide   190
'twixt flesh an' sperrit boundin' on each side,
Where both shores' shadders kind o' mix an'
    mingle
In sunthin' thet ain't jes' like either single;
An' when you cast off moorin's from To-
    day,
An' down towards To-morrer drift away,
The imiges thet tengle on the stream
Make a new upside-down'ard world o' dream:
Sometimes they seem like sunrise-streaks an'
    warnin's
O' wut 'll be in Heaven on Sabbath-mornin's,
An', mixed right in ez ef jest out o' spite,
Sunthin' thet says your supper ain't gone
    right.   201

I'm gret on dreams, an' often when I wake,
I've lived so much it makes my mem'ry ache,
An' can't skurce take a cat-nap in my cheer
'thout hevin' 'em, some good, some bad, all
     queer.

Now I wuz settin' where I'd ben, it seemed,
An' ain't sure yit whether I r'ally dreamed,
Nor, ef I did, how long I might ha' slep',
When I hearn some un stompin' up the
     step,
An' lookin' round, ef two an' two make
     four,   210
I see a Pilgrim Father in the door.
He wore a steeple-hat, tall boots, an' spurs
With rowels to 'em big ez ches'nut-burs,
An' his gret sword behind him sloped away
Long 'z a man's speech thet dunno wut to
     say.—
"Ef your name's Biglow, an' your given-
     name
Hosee," sez he, "it's arter you I came;
I'm your gret-gran'ther multiplied by
     three."—
"My *wut?*" sez I.—"Your gret-gret-gret,"
     sez he:
"You wouldn't ha' never ben here but for
     me.   220
Two hundred an' three year ago this May
The ship I come in sailed up Boston Bay;
I'd been a cunnle in our Civil War,—
But wut on airth hev *you* gut up one for?
Coz we du things in England, 'tain't for you
To git a notion you can du 'em tu:
I'm told you write in public prints: ef true,
It's nateral you should know a thing or
     two."—
"Thet air's an argymunt I can't endorse,—
'twould prove, coz you wear spurs, you kep'
     a horse: 230
For brains," sez I, "wutever you may think,
Ain't boun' to cash the drafs o' pen-an'-ink,—
Though mos' folks write ez ef they hoped
     jes' quickenin'
The churn would argoo skim-milk into
     thickenin';
But skim-milk ain't a thing to change its
     view
O' wut it's meant for more'n a smoky flue.
But du pray tell me, 'fore we furder go,
How in all Natur' did you come to know

'bout our affairs," sez I, "in Kingdom-
     Come?"—
"Wal, I worked round at sperrit-rappin'
     some,   240
An' danced the tables till their legs wuz
     gone,
In hopes o' larnin' wut wuz goin' on,"
Sez he, "but mejums lie so like all-split
Thet I concluded it wuz best to quit.
But, come now, ef you wun't confess to
     knowin',
You've some conjectures how the thing's
     a-goin'."—
"Gran'ther," sez I, "a vane warn't never
     known
Nor asked to hev a jedgment of its own;
An' yit, ef 'tain't gut rusty in the jints,
It's safe to trust its say on certin pints: 250
It knows the wind's opinions to a T,
An' the wind settles wut the weather'll be."
"I never thought a scion of our stock
Could grow the wood to make a weather-
     cock;
When I wuz younger'n you, skurce more'n
     a shaver,
No airthly wind," sez he, "could make me
     waver!"
(Ez he said this, he clinched his jaw an' fore-
     head,
Hitchin' his belt to bring his sword-hilt for-
     rard.)—
"Jes so it wuz with me," sez I, "I swow,
When *I* wuz younger'n wut you see me
     now,—   260
Nothin' from Adam's fall to Huldy's bonnet,
Thet I warn't full-cocked with my jedgment
     on it;
But now I'm gittin' on in life, I find
It's a sight harder to make up my mind,—
Nor I don't often try tu, when events
Will du it for me free of all expense.
The moral question's ollus plain enough,—
It's jes' the human-natur' side thet's tough;
Wut's best to think mayn't puzzle me nor
     you,—
The pinch comes in decidin' wut to *du;*   270
Ef you *read* History, all runs smooth ez
     grease,
Coz there the men ain't nothin' more'n
     idees,—
But come to *make* it, ez we must to-day,

Th' idees hev arms an' legs an' stop the way:
It's easy fixin' things in facts an' figgers,—
They can't resist, nor warn't brought up with
    niggers;
But come to try your the'ry on,—why, then
Your facts an' figgers change to ign'ant men
Actin' ez ugly—" —"Smite 'em hip an'
    thigh!"   279
Sez gran'ther, "and let every man-child die!
Oh for three weeks o' Cromwle an' the Lord!
Up, Isr'el, to your tents an' grind the
    sword!"—

"Thet kind o' thing worked wal in ole Judee,
But you forgit how long it's ben A.D.;
You think thet's ellerkence,—I call it shoddy,
A thing," sez I, "wun't cover soul nor body;
I like the plain all-wool o' commonsense,
Thet warms ye now, an' will a twelve month
    hence.
You took to follerin' where the Prophets
    beckoned,
An', fust you knowed on, back come Charles
    the Second;   290
Now wut I want's to hev all *we* gain stick,
An' not to start Millennium too quick;
We hain't to punish only, but to keep,
An' the cure's gut to go a cent'ry deep."
"Wal, milk-an'-water ain't the best o' glue,"
Sez he, "an' so you'll find before you're
    thru;
Ef reshness venters sunthin,' shilly-shally
Loses ez often wut's ten times the vally.
Thet ex of ourn, when Charles's neck gut split,
Opened a gap thet ain't bridged over yit: 300
Slav'ry's your Charles, the Lord hez gin the
    ex—"
"Our Charles," sez I, "hez gut eight million
    necks.
The hardest question ain't the black man's
    right,
The trouble is to 'mancipate the white;
One's chained in body an' can be sot free,
But t'other's chained in soul to an idee:
It's a long job, but we shall worry thru it;
Ef bagnets fail, the spellin'-book must du it."
"Hosee," sez he, "I think you're goin' to
    fail: 309
The rettlesnake ain't dangerous in the tail;
This 'ere rebellion's nothin' but the rettle,—
You'll stomp on thet an' think you've won
    the bettle;

It's Slavery thet's the fangs an' thinkin' head,
An' ef you want selvation, cresh it dead,—
An' cresh it suddin, or you'll larn by waitin'
Thet Chance wun't stop to listen to de-
    batin'!'"—
"God's truth!" sez I,—"an' ef *I* held the club,
An' knowed jes' where to strike,—but there's
    the rub!"—
"Strike soon," sez he, "or you'll be dedly
    ailin',—   319
Folks thet's afeared to fail are sure o' failin';
God hates your sneakin' creturs thet believe
He'll settle things they run away an' leave!"
He brought his foot down fercely, ez he spoke,
An' give me sech a startle thet I woke.
    1862

THE WASHERS OF THE SHROUD

Published in the *Atlantic Monthly*, November,
1861. These were the days after Fort Sumter had
surrendered and the Union troops had met defeat
at Bull Run. Lowell was an impassioned nationalist. He felt deeply that America's future as a
democracy depended not on voting—"opinion's
wind"—but on submission to the Law:

"Three roots bear up Dominion: Knowledge,
    Will—
  These twain are strong, but stronger yet the third,
    Obedience."

Lowell stated to Charles Eliot Norton that the
hint for the poem came from a book on Breton
legends, by Souvestre. Probably he referred to the
tale, "The Washerwomen of Night," in *Le Foyer
Breton* (1844).

ALONG a riverside, I know not where,
I walked one night in mystery of dream;
A chill creeps curdling yet beneath my hair,
To think what chanced me by the pallid gleam
Of a moon-wraith that waned through
    haunted air.

Pale fireflies pulsed within the meadow-mist
Their halos, wavering thistledowns of light;
The loon, that seemed to mock some goblin
    tryst,
Laughed; and the echoes, huddling in affright,
Like Odin's hounds, fled baying down the
    night.   10

Then all was silent, till there smote my ear
A movement in the stream that checked my
    breath:

Was it the slow plash of a wading deer?
But something said, "This water is of Death!
The Sisters[1] wash a shroud,—ill thing to
    hear!"

I, looking then, beheld the ancient Three
Known to the Greeks and to the Norseman's
    creed,
That sit in shadow of the mystic Tree,
Still crooning as they weave their endless
    brede,
One song: "Time was, Time is, and Time
    shall be."   20

No wrinkled crones were they, as I had
    deemed,
But fair as yesterday, today, tomorrow,
To mourner, lover, poet, ever seemed:
Something too deep for joy, too high for
    sorrow,
Thrilled in their tones, and from their faces
    gleamed.

"Still men and nations reap as they have
    strawn,"
So sang they, working at their task the
    while,—
"The fatal raiment must be cleansed ere
    dawn:
For Austria? Italy? The Sea-Queen's isle?
O'er what quenched grandeur must our
    shroud be drawn?   30

"Or is it for a younger, fairer corse,
That gathered States like children round his
    knees,
That tamed the wave to be his posting-horse,
Feller of forests, linker of the seas,
Bridge builder, hammerer, youngest son of
    Thor's?

"What make we, murmur'st thou? and what
    are we?
When empires must be wound, we bring the
    shroud,
The time-old web of the implacable Three:
Is it too coarse for him, the young and proud?
Earth's mightiest deigned to wear it,—why
    not he?"   40

[1] the Norns or Fates of Norse mythology who tend
the roots of the "mystic Tree," Yggdrasil, which supports the universe

"Is there no hope?" I moaned, "so strong, so
    fair!
Our Fowler whose proud bird would brook
    erewhile
No rival's swoop in all our western air!
Gather the ravens, then, in funeral file
For him, life's morn yet golden in his hair?

"Leave me not hopeless, ye unpitying dames!
I see, half seeing: tell me, ye who scanned
The stars, Earth's elders, still must noblest
    aims
Be traced upon oblivious ocean-sands?   49
Must Hesper join the wailing ghosts of names?"

"When grass-blades stiffen with red battle-
    dew,
Ye deem we choose the victor and the slain:
Say, choose we them that shall be leal and
    true
To the heart's longing, the high faith of
    brain?
Yet there the victory lies, if ye but knew.

"Three roots bear up Dominion: Knowledge,
    Will,—
These twain are strong, but stronger yet the
    third,
Obedience,—'tis the great taproot that still,
Knit round the rock of Duty, is not stirred,
Though Heaven-loosed tempests spend their
    utmost skill.   60

"Is the doom sealed for Hesper? 'Tis not we
Denounce it, but the Law before all time:
The brave makes danger opportunity;
The waverer, paltering with the chance sub-
    lime,
Dwarfs it to peril: which shall Hesper be?

"Hath he let vultures climb his eagle's seat
To make Jove's bolts purveyors of their
    maw?
Hath he the Many's plaudits found more sweet
Than Wisdom? held Opinion's wind for
    law?   69
Then let him hearken for the doomster's feet!

"Rough are the steps, slow-hewn in flintiest
    rock,
States climb to power by; slippery those with
    gold

Down which they stumble to eternal mock:
No chafferer's hand shall long the scepter
   hold,
Who, given a Fate to shape, would sell the
   block.

"We sing old sagas, songs of weal and woe,
Mystic because too cheaply understood;
Dark sayings are not ours: men hear and
   know,
See Evil weak, see strength alone in Good,
Yet hope to stem God's fire with walls of
   tow.   80

"Time Was unlocks the riddle of Time Is,
That offers choice of glory or of gloom;
The solver makes Time Shall Be surely his.
But hasten, Sisters! for even now the tomb
Grates its slow hinge and calls from the
   abyss."

"But not for him," I cried, "not yet for him,
Whose large horizon, westering, star by star
Wins from the void to where on ocean's
   rim
The sunset shuts the world with golden bar,—
Not yet his thews shall fail, his eye grow
   dim!   90

"His shall be larger manhood, saved for those
That walk unblenching through the trial-
   fires;
Not suffering, but faint heart, is worst of
   woes,
And he no base-born son of craven sires,
Whose eye need blench confronted with his
   foes.

"Tears may be ours, but proud, for those
   who win
Death's royal purple in the foeman's lines;
Peace, too, brings tears; and mid the battle-
   din,
The wiser ear some text of God divines;
For the sheathed blade may rust with darker
   sin.   100

"God, give us peace! not such as lulls to
   sleep,
But sword on thigh, and brow with purpose
   knit!

And let our Ship of State to harbor sweep,
Her ports all up, her battle-lanterns lit,
And her leashed thunders gathering for their
   leap!"

So said I with clenched hands and passionate
   pain,
Thinking of dear ones by Potomac's side;
Again the loon laughed mocking, and again
The echoes bayed far down the night and
   died,   109
While, waking, I recalled my wandering brain.
                                        1861

ODE RECITED AT THE HAR-
VARD COMMEMORATION

Published in the *Atlantic Monthly*, September,
1865. Read on July 21, 1865, at services in memory of the Harvard students who had been killed
in the Civil War. The famous stanza concerning
President Lincoln was not recited when the poem
was delivered but was written immediately afterward. The ninth strophe was added only after
magazine publication. Lowell wrote at length concerning the metrical problems in his composition
of the ode, January 14, 1877, to J. B. Thayer
(*Letters*, II, 189-90). Many years later he wrote to
Richard Watson Gilder: "The ode itself was an
improvisation. Two days before the commemoration I had told my friend Child that it was impossible—that I was dull as door-mat. But the
next day something gave me a jog, and the whole
thing came out of me with a rush. I sat up all
night writing it out clear, and took it on the morning of the day to Child." F. H. Underwood has
given a vivid account of the occasion:

"The Commemoration services took place in
the open air, in the presence of a great assembly.
Prominent among the speakers were Major-Gen-
eral Meade, the hero of Gettysburg, and Major-
General Devens. The wounds of the war were
still fresh and bleeding, and the interest of the
occasion was deep and thrilling. The summer afternoon was drawing to its close when the poet began
the recital of the ode. No living audience could
for the first time follow with intelligent appreciation the delivery of such a poem. To be sure, it
had its obvious strong points and its sonorous
charms; but, like all the later poems of the author,
it is full of condensed thought and requires study.
The reader today finds many passages whose force
and beauty escaped him during the recital, yet
the effect of the poem at the time was overpowering. The face of the poet, always singularly expressive, was on this occasion almost transfigured,
—glowing, as if with an inward light. It was
impossible to look away from it. Our age has fur-

nished many great historic scenes, but this Commemoration combined the elements of grandeur and pathos, and produced an impression as lasting as life."

I

Weak-winged is song,
Nor aims at that clear-ethered height
Whither the brave deed climbs for light:
  We seem to do them wrong,
Bringing our robin's-leaf to deck their hearse
Who in warm life-blood wrote their nobler
    verse,
Our trivial song to honor those who come
With ears attuned to strenuous trump and
    drum,
And shaped in squadron-strophes[1] their de-
    sire,
Live battle-odes whose lines were steel and
    fire: 10
Yet sometimes feathered words are strong,
A gracious memory to buoy up and save
From Lethe's dreamless ooze, the common
    grave
  Of the unventurous throng.

II

Today our Reverend Mother welcomes back
  Her wisest Scholars, those who under-
    stood
The deeper teaching of her mystic tome,
  And offered their fresh lives to make it
    good:
    No lore of Greece or Rome,
No science peddling with the names of
    things, 20
Or reading stars to find inglorious fates,
  Can lift our life with wings
Far from Death's idle gulf that for the many
    waits,
  And lengthen out our dates
With that clear fame whose memory sings
In manly hearts to come, and nerves them and
    dilates:
Nor such thy teaching, Mother of us all!
  Not such the trumpet-call
  Of thy diviner mood,
  That could thy sons entice 30
From happy homes and toils, the fruitful
    nest

Of those half-virtues which the world calls
    best,
  Into War's tumult rude;
  But rather far that stern device
The sponsors chose that round thy cradle
    stood
  In the dim, unventured wood,
  The Veritas[1] that lurks beneath
  The letter's unprolific sheath,
Life of whate'er makes life worth living,
Seed-grain of high emprise, immortal food, 40
  One heavenly thing whereof earth hath the
    giving.

III

Many loved Truth, and lavished life's best oil
  Amid the dust of books to find her,
Content at last, for guerdon of their toil,
  With the cast mantle she hath left behind
    her.
Many in sad faith sought for her,
Many with crossed hands sighed for her;
But these, our brothers, fought for her,
At life's dear peril wrought for her,
So loved her that they died for her, 50
  Tasting the raptured fleetness
  Of her divine completeness:
    Their higher instinct knew
Those love her best who to themselves are
    true,
And what they dare to dream of dare to do;
  They followed her and found her
  Where all may hope to find,
Not in the ashes of the burnt-out mind,
But beautiful, with danger's sweetness round
    her.
  Where faith made whole with deed 60
  Breathes its awakening breath
  Into the lifeless creed,
  They saw her plumed and mailed,
  With sweet, stern face unveiled,
And all-repaying eyes, look proud on them
    in death.

IV

Our slender life runs rippling by, and glides
  Into the silent hollow of the past;
    What is there that abides
  To make the next age better for the last?

---

[1] The *strophe* or turn was sung by one part of the Greek chorus in the delivery of a choral ode; the antistrophe or response by the other part of the chorus.

[1] the motto, meaning "Truth," on the seal of Harvard University

Is earth too poor to give us   70
Something to live for here that shall out-
    live us?
Some more substantial boon
Than such as flows and ebbs with Fortune's
    fickle moon?
The little that we see
From doubt is never free;
The little that we do
Is but half-nobly true;
With our laborious hiving
What men call treasure, and the gods call
    dross,
Life seems a jest of Fate's contriving,   80
Only secure in every one's conniving,
A long account of nothings paid with loss,
Where we poor puppets, jerked by unseen
    wires,
After our little hour of strut and rave,
With all our pasteboard passions and desires,
Loves, hates, ambitions, and immortal fires,
Are tossed pell-mell together in the grave.
But stay! no age was e'er degenerate,
Unless men held it at too cheap a rate,
For in our likeness still we shape our fate.
Ah, there is something here   91
Unfathomed by the cynic's sneer,
Something that gives our feeble light
A high immunity from Night,
Something that leaps life's narrow bars
To claim its birthright with the hosts of
    heaven;
A seed of sunshine that can leaven
Our earthly dulness with the beams of stars,
And glorify our clay
With light from fountains elder than the Day;
A conscience more divine than we,   101
A gladness fed with secret tears,
A vexing, forward-reaching sense
Of some more noble permanence;
A light across the sea,
Which haunts the soul and will not let it be,
Still beaconing from the heights of unde-
    generate years.

V

Whither leads the path
To ampler fates that leads?
Not down through flowery meads,   110
    To reap an aftermath
Of youth's vainglorious weeds,

But up the steep, amid the wrath
And shock of deadly-hostile creeds,
Where the world's best hope and stay
By battle's flashes gropes a desperate way,
And every turf the fierce foot clings to bleeds.
    Peace hath her not ignoble wreath,
    Ere yet the sharp, decisive word   119
Light the black lips of cannon, and the sword
    Dreams in its easeful sheath;
But some day the live coal behind the thought,
    Whether from Bäal's stone obscene,
    Or from the shrine serene
    Of God's pure altar brought,
Bursts up in flame; the war of tongue and pen
Learns with what deadly purpose it was
    fraught,
And, helpless in the fiery passion caught,
Shakes all the pillared state with shock of men:
Some day the soft Ideal that we wooed   130
Confronts us fiercely, foe-beset, pursued,
And cries reproachful: "Was it, then, my
    praise,
And not myself was loved? Prove now thy
    truth;
I claim of thee the promise of thy youth;
Give me thy life, or cower in empty phrase,
The victim of thy genius, not its mate!"
    Life may be given in many ways,
    And loyalty to Truth be sealed
As bravely in the closet as the field,
    So bountiful is Fate;   140
    But then to stand beside her,
    When craven churls deride her,
To front a lie in arms and not to yield,
    This shows, methinks, God's plan
    And measure of a stalwart man,
    Limbed like the old heroic breeds,
Who stands self-poised on manhood's solid
    earth,
Not forced to frame excuses for his birth,
    Fed from within with all the strength he
    needs.

VI

Such was he, our Martyr-Chief,   150
    Whom late the Nation he had led,
    With ashes on her head,
Wept with the passion of an angry grief:
Forgive me, if from present things I turn
To speak what in my heart will beat and
    burn,

And hang my wreath on his world-honored
    urn.
    Nature, they say, doth dote,
    And cannot make a man
    Save on some worn-out plan,
    Repeating us by rote: 160
For him her Old-World moulds aside she
    threw,
    And, choosing sweet clay from the breast
    Of the unexhausted West,
With stuff untainted shaped a hero new,
Wise, steadfast in the strength of God, and
    true.
    How beautiful to see
Once more a shepherd of mankind indeed,
Who loved his charge but never loved to lead;
One whose meek flock the people joyed to
    be,
    Not lured by any cheat of birth,   170
    But by his clear-grained human worth,
And brave old wisdom of sincerity!
    They knew that outward grace is dust;
    They could not choose but trust
In that sure-footed mind's unfaltering skill,
    And supple-tempered will
That bent like perfect steel to spring again
    and thrust.
    His was no lonely mountain-peak of
    mind,
    Thrusting to thin air o'er our cloudy
    bars,
    A sea-mark now, now lost in vapors
    blind;   180
    Broad prairie rather, genial, level-lined,
    Fruitful and friendly for all human kind,
Yet also nigh to heaven and loved of loftiest
    stars.
    Nothing of Europe here,
Or, then, of Europe fronting mornward still,
    Ere any names of Serf and Peer
    Could Nature's equal scheme deface
    And thwart her genial will;
    Here was a type of the true elder race,
And one of Plutarch's men talked with us
    face to face.   190
I praise him not; it were too late;
And some innative weakness there must be
In him who condescends to victory
Such as the Present gives, and cannot wait,
    Safe in himself as in a fate.
    So always firmly he:

He knew to bide his time,
    And can his fame abide,
Still patient in his simple faith sublime,
    Till the wise years decide.   200
    Great captains, with their guns and drums,
    Disturb our judgment for the hour,
    But at last silence comes;
    These all are gone, and, standing like a
    tower,
    Our children shall behold his fame,
    The kindly-earnest, brave, foreseeing
    man,
Sagacious, patient, dreading praise, not
    blame,
    New birth of our new soil, the first Ameri-
    can.

VII

Long as man's hope insatiate can discern
    Or only guess some more inspiring
    goal   210
    Outside of Self, enduring as the pole,
Along whose course the flying axles burn
Of spirits bravely-pitched, earth's manlier
    brood;
    Long as below we cannot find
    The meed that stills the inexorable mind;
So long this faith to some ideal Good,
    Under whatever mortal names it masks,
    Freedom, Law, Country, this ethereal
    mood
That thanks the Fates for their severer
    tasks,
    Feeling its challenged pulses leap   220
    While others skulk in subterfuges cheap,
And, set in Danger's van, has all the boon it
    asks,
    Shall win man's praise and woman's love,
    Shall be a wisdom that we set above
All other skills and gifts to culture dear,
    A virtue round whose forehead we en-
    wreathe
    Laurels that with a living passion breathe
When other crowns grow, while we twine
    them, sear.
    What brings us thronging these high rites
    to pay,
    And seal these hours the noblest of our
    year,   230
    Save that our brothers found this better
    way?

VIII

We sit here in the Promised Land
That flows with Freedom's honey and milk;
But 'twas they won it, sword in hand,
Making the nettle danger soft for us as silk.
  We welcome back our bravest and our
     best—
Ah me! not all! some come not with the
     rest,
Who went forth brave and bright as any
     here!
I strive to mix some gladness with my strain,
  But the sad strings complain,   240
  And will not please the ear:
I sweep them for a pæan, but they wane
  Again and yet again
Into a dirge and die away in pain.
In these brave ranks I only see the gaps,
Thinking of dear ones whom the dumb turf
     wraps,
Dark to the triumph which they died to gain:
  Fitlier may others greet the living,
  For me the past is unforgiving;
  I with uncovered head   250
  Salute the sacred dead,
Who went, and who return not.—Say not so!
'Tis not the grapes of Canaan that repay,
But the high faith that failed not by the way;
Virtue treads paths that end not in the grave;
No ban of endless night exiles the brave;
  And to the saner mind
We rather seem the dead that stayed behind.
Blow, trumpets, all your exultations blow!
For never shall their aureoled presence lack:
I see them muster in a gleaming row,   261
With ever-youthful brows that nobler show;
We find in our dull road their shining track;
. In every nobler mood
We feel the orient of their spirit glow,
Part of our life's unalterable good,
Of all our saintlier aspiration;
  They come transfigured back,
Secure from change in their high-hearted
     ways,
Beautiful evermore, and with the rays   270
Of morn on their white Shields of Expecta-
     tion!

IX

But is there hope to save
Even this ethereal essence from the grave?

Whatever 'scaped Oblivion's subtle wrong
Save a few clarion names, or golden threads
     of song?
  Before my musing eye
  The mighty ones of old sweep by,
Disvoicèd now and insubstantial things,
As noisy once as we; poor ghosts of kings,
Shadows of empire wholly gone to dust,
And many races, nameless long ago,   281
To darkness driven by that imperious gust
Of ever-rushing Time that here doth blow:
O visionary world, condition strange,
Where naught abiding is but only Change,
Where the deep-bolted stars themselves still
     shift and range!
Shall we to more continuance make pre-
     tence?
Renown builds tombs; a life-estate is Wit;
  And, bit by bit,
The cunning years steal all from us but
     woe;   290
Leaves are we, whose decays no harvest
     sow.
  But, when we vanish hence,
Shall they lie forceless in the dark below,
Save to make green their little length of
     sods,
Or deepen pansies for a year or two,
Who now to us are shining-sweet as gods?
Was dying all they had the skill to do?
That were not fruitless: but the Soul
     resents
Such short-lived service, as if blind events
Ruled without her, or earth could so en-
     dure;   300
She claims a more divine investiture
Of longer tenure than Fame's airy rents;
Whate'er she touches doth her nature share;
Her inspiration haunts the ennobled air,
  Gives eyes to mountains blind,
Ears to the deaf earth, voices to the wind,
And her clear trump sings succor every-
     where
By lonely bivouacs to the wakeful mind;
For soul inherits all that soul could dare:
  Yea, Manhood hath a wider span   310
And larger privilege of life than man.
The single deed, the private sacrifice,
So radiant now through proudly-hidden
     tears,
Is covered up erelong from mortal eyes

With thoughtless drift of the deciduous
  years;
But that high privilege that makes all men
  peers,
That leap of heart whereby a people rise
  Up to a noble anger's height,
And, flamed on by the Fates, not shrink,
  but grow more bright,
That swift validity in noble veins,   320
Of choosing danger and disdaining shame,
  Of being set on flame
By the pure fire that flies all contact base
But wraps its chosen with angelic might,
  These are imperishable gains,
  Sure as the sun, medicinal as light,
  These hold great futures in their lusty reins
And certify to earth a new imperial race.

X

Who now shall sneer?
Who dare again to say we trace   330
  Our lines to a plebeian race?
  Roundhead and Cavalier!
Dumb are those names erewhile in battle loud;
Dream-footed as the shadow of a cloud,
  They flit across the ear:
That is best blood that hath most iron in't
To edge resolve with, pouring without stint
  For what makes manhood dear.
Tell us not of Plantagenets,
Hapsburgs, and Guelfs, whose thin bloods
  crawl   340
Down from some victor in a border-brawl!
  How poor their outworn coronets,
Matched with one leaf of that plain civic
  wreath
Our brave for honor's blazon shall bequeath,
  Through whose desert a rescued Nation sets
Her heel on treason, and the trumpet hears
Shout victory, tingling Europe's sullen ears
  With vain resentments and more vain re-
  grets!

XI

Not in anger, not in pride,
  Pure from passion's mixture rude   350
  Ever to base earth allied,
  But with far-heard gratitude,
  Still with heart and voice renewed,
To heroes living and dear martyrs dead,

The strain should close that consecrates our
  brave.
Lift the heart and lift the head!
  Lofty be its mood and grave,
  Not without a martial ring,
  Not without a prouder tread
  And a peal of exultation: 360
  Little right has he to sing
  Through whose heart in such an hour
  Beats no march of conscious power,
  Sweeps no tumult of elation!
  'Tis no Man we celebrate,
  By his country's victories great,
A hero half, and half the whim of Fate,
  But the pith and marrow of a Nation
  Drawing force from all her men,
  Highest, humblest, weakest, all,   370
  For her time of need, and then
  Pulsing it again through them,
Till the basest can no longer cower,
  Feeling his soul spring up divinely tall,
  Touched but in passing by her mantle-hem.
Come back, then, noble pride, for 'tis her
  dower!
  How could poet ever tower,
  If his passions, hopes, and fears,
  If his triumphs and his tears,
  Kept not measure with his people?   380
Boom, cannon, boom to all the winds and
  waves!
Clash out, glad bells, from every rocking
  steeple!
Banners, advance with triumph, bend your
  staves!
  And from every mountain-peak
  Let beacon-fire to answering beacon speak,
Katahdin tell Monadnock, Whiteface he,
And so leap on in light from sea to sea,
  Till the glad news be sent
  Across a kindling continent,
Making earth feel more firm and air breathe
  braver: 390
"Be proud! for she is saved, and all have
  helped to save her!
She that lifts up the manhood of the poor,
She of the open soul and open door,
  With room about her hearth for all man-
  kind!
The fire is dreadful in her eyes no more;
From her bold front the helm she doth
  unbind,

Sends all her handmaid armies back to spin,
And bids her navies, that so lately hurled
Their crashing battle, hold their thunders in,
Swimming like birds of calm along the un-
     harmful shore.   400
No challenge sends she to the elder world,
That looked askance and hated; a light
     scorn
Plays on her mouth, as round her mighty
     knees
She calls her children back, and waits the
     morn
Of nobler day, enthroned between her sub-
     ject seas."

XII

Bow down, dear Land, for thou hast found
     release!
   Thy God, in these distempered days,
Hath taught thee the sure wisdom of His ways,
And through thine enemies hath wrought thy
     peace!
     Bow down in prayer and praise!   410
No poorest in thy borders but may now
Lift to the juster skies a man's enfranchised
     brow.
O Beautiful! my Country! ours once more!
Smoothing thy gold of war-dishevelled hair
O'er such sweet brows as never other wore,
     And letting thy set lips,
     Freed from wrath's pale eclipse,
The rosy edges of their smile lay bare,
What words divine of lover or of poet   419
Could tell our love and make thee know it,
Among the Nations bright beyond compare?
     What were our lives without thee?
     What all our lives to save thee?
     We reck not what we gave thee;
     We will not dare to doubt thee,
But ask whatever else, and we will dare!

                                        1865

AN ODE

FOR THE FOURTH OF JULY, 1876

Published in the *Atlantic Monthly*, December,
1876. Lowell's nationalistic feeling is shown again
in this poem. The first section concerns the war
for independence and the birth of the American
republic. The second contrasts American con-

ditions and civilization with ancient civilizations,
such as those of Greece and Rome. The third section sounds a note of disillusionment. The poet is
disappointed in present conditions but retains his
faith in his country and its future. In the fourth
he praises the founders of New England,

     "The undaunted few
     Who changed the Old World for the New, . . .
     . . . conceived a deeper-rooted state, . . .
     By making man sole sponsor of himself."

I

I

ENTRANCED I saw a vision in the cloud
That loitered dreaming in yon sunset sky,
Full of fair shapes, half creatures of the eye,
Half chance-evoked by the wind's fantasy
In golden mist, an ever-shifting crowd:
There, mid unreal forms that came and went
In robes air-spun, of evanescent dye,
A woman's semblance shone pre-eminent;
Not armed like Pallas, not like Hera proud,
But, as on household diligence intent,   10
Beside her visionary wheel she bent
Like Aretë or Bertha, nor than they
Less queenly in her port: about her knee
Glad children clustered confident in play:
Placid her pose, the calm of energy;
And over her broad brow in many a round
(That loosened would have gilt her garment's
     hem),
Succinct, as toil prescribes, the hair was wound
In lustrous coils, a natural diadem.
The cloud changed shape, obsequious to the
     whim   20
Of some transmuting influence felt in me,
And, looking now, a wolf I seemed to see
Limned in that vapor, gaunt and hunger-bold,
Threatening her charge: resolve in every
     limb,
Erect she flamed in mail of sun-wove gold,
Penthesilea's self for battle dight;
One arm uplifted braced a flickering spear,
And one her admantine shield made light;
Her face, helm-shadowed, grew a thing to fear,
And her fierce eyes, by danger challenged,
     took   30
Her trident-sceptred mother's dauntless look.
"I know thee now, O goddess-born!" I cried,
And turned with loftier brow and firmer
     stride;
For in that spectral cloud-work I had seen

Her image, bodied forth by love and pride,
The fearless, the benign, the mother-eyed,
The fairer world's toil-consecrated queen.

2

What shape by exile dreamed elates the mind
Like hers whose hand, a fortress of the poor,
No blood in vengeance spilt, though lawful,
    stains?   40
Who never turned a suppliant from her
    door?
Whose conquests are the gains of all man-
    kind?
Today her thanks shall fly on every wind,
Unstinted, unrebuked, from shore to shore,
One love, one hope, and not a doubt behind!
Cannon to cannon shall repeat her praise,
Banner to banner flap it forth in flame;
Her children shall rise up to bless her name,
And wish her harmless length of days,
The mighty mother of a mighty brood,   50
Blessed in all tongues and dear to every blood,
The beautiful, the strong, and, best of all, the
    good!

3

Seven years long was the bow
Of battle bent, and the heightening
Storm-heaps convulsed with the throe
Of their uncontainable lightning;
Seven years long heard the sea
Crash of navies and wave-borne thunder;
Then drifted the cloud-rack alee,
And new stars were seen, a world's wonder; 60
Each by her sisters made bright,
All binding all to their stations,
Cluster of manifold light
Startling the old constellations:
Men looked up and grew pale:
Was it a comet or star,
Omen of blessing or bale,
Hung o'er the ocean afar?

4

Stormy the day of her birth:
Was she not born of the strong,   70
She, the last ripeness of earth,
Beautiful, prophesied long?
Stormy the days of her prime:
Hers are the pulses that beat
Higher for perils sublime,
Making them fawn at her feet.

Was she not born of the strong?
Was she not born of the wise?
Daring and counsel belong
Of right to her confident eyes: 80
Human and motherly they,
Careless of station or race:
Hearken! her children today
Shout for the joy of her face.

II

1

No praises of the past are hers,
No fanes by hallowing time caressed,
No broken arch that ministers
To some sad instinct in the breast:
She has not gathered from the years
Grandeur of tragedies and tears,   90
Nor from long leisure the unrest
That finds repose in forms of classic grace:
These may delight the coming race
Who haply shall not count it to our crime
That we who fain would sing are here before
    our time.
She also hath her monuments;
Not such as stand decrepitly resigned
To ruin-mark the path of dead events
That left no seed of better days behind,
The tourist's pensioners that show their
    scars   100
And maunder of forgotten wars;
She builds not on the ground, but in the mind,
Her open-hearted palaces
For larger-thoughted men with heaven and
    earth at ease:
Her march the plump mow marks, the sleep-
    less wheel,
The golden sheaf, the self-swayed common-
    weal;
The happy homesteads hid in orchard trees
Whose sacrificial smokes through peaceful air
Rise lost in heaven, the household's silent
    prayer;
What architect hath bettered these?   110
With softened eye the westward traveller sees
A thousand miles of neighbors side by side,
Holding by toil-won titles fresh from God
The lands no serf or seigneur ever trod,
With manhood latent in the very sod,
Where the long billow of the wheat-field's tide
Flows to the sky across the prairie wide,

A sweeter vision than the castled Rhine,
Kindly with thoughts of Ruth and Bible-days
    benign.

2

O ancient commonwealths, that we revere 120
Haply because we could not know you near,
Your deeds like statues down the aisles of
    Time
Shine peerless in memorial calm sublime,
And Athens is a trumpet still, and Rome;
Yet which of your achievements is not foam
Weighted with this one of hers (below you
    far
In fame, and born beneath a milder star),
That to Earth's orphans, far as curves the
    dome,
Of death-deaf sky, the bounteous West
    means home,
With dear precedency of natural ties 130
That stretch from roof to roof and made men
    gently wise?
And if the nobler passions wane,
Distorted to base use, if the near goal
Of insubstantial gain
Tempt from the proper racecourse of the soul
That crowns their patient breath
Whose feet, song-pinioned, are too fleet for
    Death,
Yet may she claim one privilege urbane
And haply first upon the civic roll,
That none can breathe her air nor grow
    humane. 140

3

O, better far the briefest hour
Of Athens self-consumed, whose plastic
    power
Hid Beauty safe from Death in words or
    stone;
Of Rome, fair quarry where those eagles
    crowd
Whose fulgurous vans about the world had
    blown
Triumphant storm and seeds of polity;
Of Venice, fading o'er her shipless sea,
Last iridescence of a sunset cloud;
Than this inert prosperity,
This bovine comfort in the sense alone! 150
Yet art came slowly even to such as those,
Whom no past genius cheated of their own

With prudence of o'ermastering precedent;
Petal by petal spreads the perfect rose,
Secure of the divine event;
And only children rend the bud half-blown
To forestall Nature in her calm intent:
Time hath a quiver full of purposes
Which miss not of their aim, to us unknown,
And brings about the impossible with ease: 160
Haply for us the ideal dawn shall break
From where in legend-tinted line
The peaks of Hellas drink the morning's
    wine,
To tremble on our lids with mystic sign
Till the drowsed ichor in our veins awake
And set our pulse in tune with moods di-
    vine:
Long the day lingered in its sea-fringed nest,
Then touched the Tuscan hills with golden
    lance
And paused; then on to Spain and France
The splendor flew, and Albion's misty
    crest: 170
Shall Ocean bar him from his destined West?
Or are we, then arrived too late,
Doomed with the rest to grope disconsolate,
Foreclosed of Beauty by our modern date?

III

1

Poets, as their heads grow gray,
Look from too far behind the eyes,
Too long-experienced to be wise
In guileless youth's diviner way;
Life sings not now, but prophesies;
Time's shadows they no more behold, 180
But, under them, the riddle old
That mocks, bewilders, and defies:
In childhood's face the seed of shame,
In the green tree an ambushed flame,
In Phosphor a vaunt-guard of Night,
They, though against their will, divine,
And dread the care-dispelling wine
Stored from the Muse's vintage bright,
By age imbued with second-sight.
From Faith's own eyelids there peeps out, 190
Even as they look, the leer of doubt;
The festal wreath their fancy loads
With care that whispers and forebodes:
Nor this our triumph-day can blunt Megaera's
    goads.

2

Murmur of many voices in the air
Denounces us degenerate,
Unfaithful guardians of a noble fate,
And prompts indifference or despair:
Is this the country that we dreamed in youth,
Where wisdom and not numbers should have
    weight,   200
Seed-field of simpler manners, braver truth,
Where shams should cease to dominate
In household, church, and state?
Is this Atlantis? This the unpoisoned soil,
Sea-whelmed for ages and recovered late,
Where parasitic greed no more should coil
Round Freedom's stem to bend awry and
    blight
What grew so fair, sole plant of love and light?
Who sit where once in crowned seclusion sate
The long-proved athletes of debate   210
Trained from their youth, as none thinks
    needful now?
Is this debating-club where boys dispute,
And wrangle o'er their stolen fruit,
The Senate, erewhile cloister of the few,
Where Clay once flashed and Webster's
    cloudy brow
Brooded those bolts of thought that all the
    horizon knew?

3

O, as this pensive moonlight blurs my pines,
Here while I sit and meditate these lines,
To gray-green dreams of what they are by
    day,
So would some light, no reason's sharp-edged
    ray,   220
Trance me in moonshine as before the flight
Of years had won me this unwelcome right
To see things as they are, or shall be soon,
In the frank prose of undissembling noon!

4

Back to my breast, ungrateful sigh!
Whoever fails, whoever errs,
The penalty be ours, not hers!
The present still seems vulgar, seen too nigh;
The golden age is still the age that's past:
I ask no drowsy opiate   230
To dull my vision of that only state
Founded on faith in man, and therefore sure
    to last.

For, O, my country, touched by thee,
The gray hairs gather back their gold;
Thy thought sets all my pulses free;
The heart refuses to be old;
The love is all that I can see.
Not to thy natal-day belong
Time's prudent doubt or age's wrong,
But gifts of gratitude and song: 240
Unsummoned crowd the thankful words,
As sap in springtime floods the tree,
Foreboding the return of birds,
For all that thou hast been to me!

IV

1

Flawless his heart and tempered to the core
Who, beckoned by the forward-leaning wave,
First left behind him the firm-footed shore,
And, urged by every nerve of sail and oar,
Steered for the Unknown which gods to
    mortals gave,
Of thought and action the mysterious door,
Bugbear of fools, a summons to the brave: 251
Strength found he in the unsympathizing
    sun,
And strange stars from beneath the horizon
    won,
And the dumb ocean pitilessly grave:
High hearted surely he;
But bolder they who first off-cast
Their moorings from the habitable Past
And ventured chartless on the sea
Of storm-engendering Liberty:
For all earth's width of waters is a span,   260
And their convulsed existence mere repose,
Matched with the unstable heart of man,
Shoreless in wants, mist-girt in all it knows,
Open to every wind of sect or clan,
And sudden-passionate in ebbs and flows.

2

They steered by stars the elder shipmen
    knew,
And laid their courses where the currents
    draw
Of ancient wisdom channelled deep in law,
The undaunted few
Who changed the Old World for the New,
And more devoutly prized   271
Than all perfection theorized
The more imperfect that had roots and grew.

They founded deep and well,
Those danger-chosen chiefs of men
Who still believed in Heaven and Hell,
Nor hoped to find a spell,
In some fine flourish of a pen,
To make a better man
That long-considering Nature will or can,
Secure against his own mistakes,   281
Content with what life gives or takes,
And acting still on some fore-ordered plan,
A cog of iron in an iron wheel,
Too nicely poised to think or feel,
Dumb motor in a clock-like commonweal.
They wasted not their brain in schemes
Of what man might be in some bubble-
    sphere,
As if he must be other than he seems
Because he was not what he should be here,
Postponing Time's slow proof to petulant
    dreams: 291
Yet herein they were great
Beyond the incredulous lawgivers of yore,
And wiser than the wisdom of the shelf,
That they conceived a deeper-rooted state,
Of hardier growth, alive from rind to core,
By making man sole sponsor of himself.

3

God of our fathers, Thou who wast,
Art, and shalt be when those eye-wise who
    flout
Thy secret presence shall be lost   300
In the great light that dazzles them to doubt,
We, sprung from loins of stalwart men
Whose strength was in their trust

That Thou wouldst make thy dwelling in their
    dust
And walk with those a fellow-citizen
Who build a city of the just,
We, who believe Life's bases rest
Beyond the probe of chemic test,
Still, like our fathers, feel Thee near,
Sure that, while lasts the immutable decree,
The land to Human Nature dear   311
Shall not be unbeloved of Thee.

                                    1876

TO WHITTIER

ON HIS SEVENTY-FIFTH BIRTHDAY

NEW ENGLAND'S poet, rich in love as years,
Her hills and valleys praise thee, her swift
    brooks
Dance in thy verse; to her grave sylvan nooks
Thy steps allure us, which the wood-thrush
    hears
As maids their lovers', and no treason fears;
Through thee her Merrimacs and Agiochooks
And many a name uncouth win gracious looks,
Sweetly familiar to both Englands' ears:

Peaceful by birthright as a virgin lake,   9
The lily's anchorage, which no eyes behold
Save those of stars, yet for thy brother's
    sake
That lay in bonds, thou blewst a blast as
    bold
As that wherewith the heart of Roland brake,
Far heard across the New World and the Old.

                                    1882

EMERSON THE LECTURER

Published as a review of Emerson's *The Conduct of Life* in the *Atlantic Monthly*, February, 1861, and revised in 1868. When in his junior year at Harvard, Lowell heard Emerson lecture. Later he made Emerson's acquaintance at Concord, and the older man took the youth with him on some of his walks. Lowell's account of Emerson as a speaker and teacher is of great interest.

IT is a singular fact that Mr. Emerson is the most steadily attractive lecturer in America. Into that somewhat cold-waterish region

adventurers of the sensational kind come down now and then with a splash, to become disregarded King Logs[1] before the next season. But Mr. Emerson always draws. A lecturer now for something like a third of a century, one of the pioneers of the lecturing system, the charm of his voice, his manner, and his matter has never lost its power over his earlier hearers, and continually winds new ones in its

[1] Aesop related that when the frogs petitioned Jupiter for a king he sent them down a log, which ruled satisfactorily until they discovered its true nature and rejected it.

enchanting meshes. What they do not fully understand they take on trust, and listen, saying to themselves, as the old poet[1] of Sir Philip Sidney,—

> "A sweet, attractive, kind of grace,
>   A full assurance given by looks,
>   Continual comfort in a face,
>   The lineaments of gospel books."

We call it a singular fact, because we Yankees are thought to be fond of the spread-eagle style, and nothing can be more remote from that than his. We are reckoned a practical folk, who would rather hear about a new air-tight stove than about Plato; yet our favorite teacher's practicality is not in the least of the Poor Richard variety. If he have any Buncombe constituency, it is that unrealized commonwealth of philosophers which Plotinus proposed to establish; and if he were to make an almanac, his directions to farmers would be something like this: "OCTOBER: *Indian Summer;* now is the time to get in your early Vedas." What, then, is his secret? Is it not that he out-Yankees us all? that his range includes us all? that he is equally at home with the potato-disease and original sin, with pegging shoes and the Over-Soul? that, as we try all trades, so has he tried all cultures? and above all, that his mysticism gives us a counterpoise to our super-practicality?

There is no man living to whom, as a writer, so many of us feel and thankfully acknowledge so great an indebtedness for ennobling impulses,—none whom so many cannot abide. What does he mean? ask these last. Where is his system? What is the use of it all? What the deuce have we to do with Brahma? I do not propose to write an essay on Emerson at this time. I will only say that one may find grandeur and consolation in a starlit night without caring to ask what it means, save grandeur and consolation; one may like Montaigne, as some ten generations before us have done, without thinking him so systematic as some more eminently tedious (or shall we say tediously eminent?) authors; one may

think roses as good in their way as cabbages, though the latter would make a better show in the witness-box, if cross-examined as to their usefulness; and as for Brahma, why, he can take care of himself, and won't bite us at any rate.

The bother with Mr. Emerson is, that, though he writes in prose, he is essentially a poet. If you undertake to paraphrase what he says, and to reduce it to words of one syllable for infant minds, you will make as sad work of it as the good monk with his analysis of Homer in the *Epistolæ Obscurorum Virorum.*[1] We look upon him as one of the few men of genius whom our age has produced, and there needs no better proof of it than his masculine faculty of fecundating other minds. Search for his eloquence in his books and you will perchance miss it, but meanwhile you will find that it has kindled all your thoughts. For choice and pith of language he belongs to a better age than ours, and might rub shoulders with Fuller and Browne,—though he does use that abominable word *reliable.* His eye for a fine, telling phrase that will carry true is like that of a backwoodsman for a rifle; and he will dredge you up a choice word from the mud of Cotton Mather himself. A diction at once so rich and so homely as his I know not where to match in these days of writing by the page; it is like homespun cloth-of-gold. The many cannot miss his meaning, and only the few can find it. It is the open secret of all true genius. It is wholesome to angle in those profound pools, though one be rewarded with nothing more than the leap of a fish that flashes his freckled side in the sun and as suddenly absconds in the dark and dreamy waters again. There is keen excitement, though there be no ponderable acquisition. If we carry nothing home in our baskets, there is ample gain in dilated lungs and stimulated blood. What does he mean, quotha? He means inspiring hints, a divining-rod to your deeper nature. No doubt, Emerson, like all original men, has his peculiar audience, and yet I know none that can hold a promiscuous crowd in pleased attention so long as he. As in all original men, there is

---

[1] Matthew Roydon, whose "Elegie," paying tribute to Sidney, appeared in the poetical miscellany, *The Phoenix Nest* (1593).

[1] "Letters of Obscure Men," a work of uncertain authorship which appeared early in the sixteenth century

something for every palate. "Would you know," says Goethe, "the ripest cherries? Ask the boys and the blackbirds."

The announcement that such a pleasure as a new course of lectures by him is coming, to people as old as I am, is something like those forebodings of spring that prepare us every year for a familiar novelty, none the less novel, when it arrives, because it is familiar. We know perfectly well what we are to expect [10] from Mr. Emerson, and yet what he says always penetrates and stirs us, as is apt to be the case with genius, in a very unlooked-for fashion. Perhaps genius is one of the few things which we gladly allow to repeat itself,— one of the few that multiply rather than weaken the force of their impression by iteration? Perhaps some of us hear more than the mere words, are moved by something deeper than the thoughts? If it be so, [20] we are quite right, for it is thirty years and more of "plain living and high thinking"[1] that speak to us in this altogether unique lay-preacher. We have shared in the beneficence of this varied culture, this fearless impartiality in criticism and speculation, this masculine sincerity, this sweetness of nature which rather stimulates than cloys, for a generation long. If ever there was a standing testimonial to the cumulative power and value of Char- [30] acter (and we need it sadly in these days), we have it in this gracious and dignified presence. What an antiseptic is a pure life! At sixty-five (or two years beyond his grand climacteric, as he would prefer to call it) he has that privilege of soul which abolishes the calendar, and presents him to us always the unwasted contemporary of his own prime. I do not know if he seem old to his younger hearers, but we who have known him so long wonder at the [40] tenacity with which he maintains himself even in the outposts of youth. I suppose it is not the Emerson of 1868 to whom we listen. For us the whole life of the man is distilled in the clear drop of every sentence, and behind each word we divine the force of a noble character, the weight of a large capital of thinking and being. We do not go to hear what Emerson says so much as to hear Emer-

son. Not that we perceive any falling-off in anything that ever was essential to the charm of Mr. Emerson's peculiar style of thought or phrase. The first lecture, to be sure, was more disjointed even than common. It was as if, after vainly trying to get his paragraphs into sequence and order, he had at last tried the desperate expedient of *shuffling* them. It was chaos come again, but it was a chaos full of shooting-stars, a jumble of creative forces. The second lecture, on "Criticism and Poetry," was quite up to the level of old times, full of that power of strangely subtle association whose indirect approaches startle the mind into almost painful attention, of those flashes of mutual understanding between speaker and hearer that are gone ere one can say it lightens. The vice of Emerson's criticism seems to be, that while no man is so sensitive to what is poetical, few men are less sensible than he of what makes a poem. He values the solid meaning of thought above the subtler meaning of style. He would prefer Donne, I suspect, to Spenser, and sometimes mistakes the queer for the original.

To be young is surely the best, if the most precarious, gift of life; yet there are some of us who would hardly consent to be young again, if it were at the cost of our recollection of Mr. Emerson's first lectures during the consulate[1] of Van Buren. We used to walk in from the country to the Masonic Temple (I think it was), through the crisp winter night, and listen to that thrilling voice of his, so charged with subtle meaning and subtle music, as ship-wrecked men on a raft to the hail of a ship that came with unhoped-for food and rescue. Cynics might say what they liked. Did our own imaginations transfigure dry remainder-biscuit[2] into ambrosia? At any rate, he brought us *life*, which, on the whole, is no bad thing. Was it all transcendentalism? magic-lantern pictures on mist? As you will. Those, then, were just what we wanted. But it was not so. The delight and the benefit were that he put us in communication with a larger style of thought, sharpened our wits with a more

[1] from Wordsworth's sonnet, "Written in London, 1802"

[1] i.e., presidency. Lowell is here, like Thoreau in the account of the battle of the ants, parodying the Roman historians' method of dating by consulships.
[2] Shakespeare's *As You Like It*, II, VII, 39

pungent phrase, gave us ravishing glimpses of an ideal under the dry husk of our New England; made us conscious of the supreme and everlasting originality of whatever bit of soul might be in any of us; freed us, in short, from the stocks of prose in which we had sat so long that we had grown well-nigh contented in our cramps. And who that saw the audience will ever forget it, where every one still capable of fire, or longing to renew in himself the half-forgotten sense of it, was gathered? Those faces, young and old, agleam with pale intellectual light, eager with pleased attention, flash upon me once more from the deep recesses of the years with an exquisite pathos. Ah, beautiful young eyes, brimming with love and hope, wholly vanished now in that other world we call the Past, or peering doubtfully through the pensive gloaming of memory, your light impoverishes these cheaper days! I hear again that rustle of sensation, as they turned to exchange glances over some pithier thought, some keener flash of that humor which always played about the horizon of his mind like heat-lightning, and it seems now like the sad whisper of the autumn leaves that are whirling around me. But would my picture be complete if I forgot that ample and vegete[1] countenance of Mr. R—— of W——,—how, from its regular post at the corner of the front bench, it turned in ruddy triumph to the profaner audience as if he were the inexplicably appointed fugleman of appreciation? I was reminded of him by those hearty cherubs in Titian's Assumption[2] that look at you as who should say, "Did you ever see a Madonna like *that*? Did you ever behold one hundred and fifty pounds of womanhood mount heavenward before like a rocket?"

To some of us that long-past experience remains as the most marvellous and fruitful we have ever had. Emerson awakened us, saved us from the body of this death. It is the sound of the trumpet that the young soul longs for, careless what breath may fill it. Sidney heard it in the ballad of "Chevy Chase,"[1] and we in Emerson. Nor did it blow retreat, but called to us with assurance of victory. Did they say he was disconnected? So were the stars, that seemed larger to our eyes, still keen with that excitement, as we walked homeward with prouder stride over the creaking snow. And were *they* not knit together by a higher logic than our mere sense could master? Were we enthusiasts? I hope and believe we were, and am thankful to the man who made us worth something for once in our lives. If asked what was left? what we carried home? we should not have been careful for an answer. It would have been enough if we had said that something beautiful had passed that way. Or we might have asked in return what one brought away from a symphony of Beethoven? Enough that he had set that ferment of wholesome discontent at work in us. There is one, at least, of those old hearers, so many of whom are now in the fruition of that intellectual beauty of which Emerson gave them both the desire and the foretaste, who will always love to repeat:—

"Che in la mente m' ê fitta, ed or m' accuora
La cara e buona immagine paterna
Di voi, quando nel mondo ad ora ad ora
M' insegnavaste come l' uom s' eterna."[2]

I am unconsciously thinking, as I write, of the third lecture of the present course, in which Mr. Emerson gave some delightful reminiscences of the intellectual influences in whose movement he had shared. It was like hearing Goethe read some passages of the *Wahrheit aus seinem Leben*.[3] Not that there was not a little *Dichtung*,[4] too, here and there, as the lecturer built up so lofty a pedestal under certain figures as to lift them into a prominence of obscurity, and seem to masthead them there. Everybody was asking his neighbor who this or that recondite great man was,

---

[1] ruddy, healthy.   [2] This famous painting depicts the Virgin ascending toward the throne on glowing clouds and surrounded by rejoicing angels. The amazed apostles look upward from below.

[1] Sidney wrote in his *Defense of Poetry* (1595): "Certainly I must confess mine own barbarousness; I never heard the old song of Percy and Douglas that I found not my heart moved more than by a trumpet."
[2] Dante's *Inferno*, XV, 82–85. Longfellow's translation reads:

"For in my mind is fixed, and touches now
My heart, the dear and good paternal image
Of you, when in the world from hour to hour
You taught me how a man becomes eternal."

[3] "Truth from His Life"   [4] "Poetry"

in the faint hope that somebody might once have heard of him. There are those who call Mr. Emerson cold. Let them revise their judgment in presence of this loyalty of his that can keep warm for half a century, that never forgets a friendship, or fails to pay even a fancied obligation to the uttermost farthing. This substantiation of shadows was but incidental, and pleasantly characteristic of the man to those who know and love him. The greater part of the lecture was devoted to reminiscences of things substantial in themselves. He spoke of Everett, fresh from Greece and Germany; of Channing; of the translations of Margaret Fuller, Ripley, and Dwight; of the *Dial* and Brook Farm. To what he said of the latter an undertone of good-humored irony gave special zest. But what every one of his hearers felt was that the protagonist in the drama was left out. The lecturer was no Æneas to babble the *quorum magna pars fui,*[1] and, as one of his listeners, I cannot help wishing to say how each of them was commenting the story as it went along, and filling up the necessary gaps in it from his own private store of memories. His younger hearers could not know how much they owed to the benign impersonality, the quiet scorn of everything ignoble, the never-sated hunger of self-culture, that were personified in the man before them. But the older knew how much the country's intellectual emancipation was due to the stimulus of his teaching and example, how constantly he had kept burning the beacon of an ideal life above our lower region of turmoil. To him more than to all other causes together did the young martyrs of our civil war owe the sustaining strength of thoughtful heroism that is so touching in every record of their lives. Those who are grateful to Mr. Emerson, as many of us are, for what they feel to be most valuable in their culture, or perhaps I should say their impulse, are grateful not so much for any direct teachings of his as for that inspiring lift which only genius can give, and without which all doctrine is chaff.

This was something like the *caret* which some of us older boys wished to fill up on the margin of the master's lecture. Few men have been so much to so many, and through so

large a range of aptitudes and temperaments and this simply because all of us value manhood beyond any or all other qualities of character. We may suspect in him, here and there, a certain thinness and vagueness of quality, but let the waters go over him as they list, this masculine fibre of his will keep its lively color and its toughness of texture. I have heard some great speakers and some accomplished orators, but never any that so moved and persuaded men as he. There is a kind of undertow in that rich baritone of his that sweeps our minds from their foothold into deeper waters with a drift we cannot and would not resist. And how artfully (for Emerson is a long-studied artist in these things) does the deliberate utterance, that seems waiting for the fit word, appear to admit us partners in the labor of thought and make us feel as if the glance of humor were a sudden suggestion, as if the perfect phrase lying written there on the desk were as unexpected to him as to us! In that closely filed speech of his at the Burns centenary dinner, every word seemed to have just dropped down to him from the clouds. He looked far away over the heads of his hearers, with a vague kind of expectation, as into some private heaven of invention, and the winged period came at last obedient to his spell. "My dainty Ariel!"[1] he seemed murmuring to himself as he cast down his eyes as if in deprecation of the frenzy of approval and caught another sentence from the Sibylline leaves that lay before him, ambushed behind a dish of fruit and seen only by nearest neighbors. Every sentence brought down the house, as I never saw one brought down before,—and it is not so easy to hit Scotsmen with a sentiment that has no hint of native brogue in it. I watched, for it was an interesting study, how the quick sympathy ran flashing from face to face down the long tables, like an electric spark thrilling as it went, and then exploded in a thunder of plaudits. I watched till tables and faces vanished, for I, too, found myself caught up in the common enthusiasm, and my excited fancy set me under the *bema*[2] listening to him

[1] "Of which things I was a great part" (*Aeneid*, II, 6)

[1] Shakespeare's *Tempest*, V, 1, 95   [2] "rostrum"; probably a reference to Lowell's enthusiasm for Demosthenes

who fulmined over Greece. I can never help applying to him what Ben Jonson said of Bacon: "There happened in my time one noble speaker, who was full of gravity in his speaking. His language was nobly censorious. No man ever spake more neatly, more pressly, more weightily, or suffered less emptiness, less idleness, in what he uttered. No member of his speech but consisted of his own graces. His hearers could not cough, or look aside from him, without loss. He commanded where he spoke." Those who heard him while their natures were yet plastic, and their mental nerves trembled under the slightest breath of divine air, will never cease to feel and say:—

"Was never eye did see that face,
    Was never ear did hear that tongue,
Was never mind did mind his grace,
    That ever thought the travail long;
But eyes, and ears, and every thought,
    Were with his sweet perfections caught." [1]

1861

From NEW ENGLAND TWO
CENTURIES AGO

Printed in the *North American Review*, January, 1865. Included later in *Among My Books* (1870), and to be found now in *Prose Works*, II. Ostensibly a review of the third volume of J. G. Palfrey's *History of England During the Stuart Dynasty* and of four volumes of *Collections* of the Massachusetts Historical Society. Lowell's nationalism appears in this article. He is concerned with the nature of freedom and with the principles of democracy, their historic genesis and development. The essay views in retrospect the people of New England, their region, history, and political faith. The author is concerned, too, with the relations of England and the new nation. He derives New England democracy from the Puritan tradition of civil liberty in the mother country.

THE history of New England is written imperishably on the face of a continent, and in characters as beneficent as they are enduring. In the Old World national pride feeds itself with the record of battles and conquests;— battles which proved nothing and settled nothing; conquests which shifted a boundary on the map, and put one ugly head instead of another on the coin which the people paid to the tax-gatherer. But wherever the New-Englander travels among the sturdy commonwealths which have sprung from the seed of the Mayflower, churches, schools, colleges, tell him where the men of his race have been, or their influence penetrated; and an intelligent freedom is the monument of conquests whose results are not to be measured in square miles. Next to the fugitives whom Moses led out of Egypt, the little ship-load of outcasts who landed at Plymouth two centuries and a half ago are destined to influence the future of the world. The spiritual thirst of mankind has for ages been quenched at Hebrew fountains; but the embodiment in human institutions of truths uttered by the Son of man eighteen centuries ago was to be mainly the work of Puritan thought and Puritan self-devotion. Leave New England out in the cold! While you are plotting it, she sits by every fireside in the land where there is piety, culture, and free thought.

Faith in God, faith in man, faith in work,— this is the short formula in which we may sum up the teaching of the founders of New England, a creed ample enough for this life and the next. If their municipal regulations smack somewhat of Judaism, yet there can be no nobler aim or more practical wisdom than theirs; for it was to make the law of man a living counterpart of the law of God, in their highest conception of it. Were they too earnest in the strife to save their souls alive? That is still the problem which every wise and brave man is lifelong in solving. If the Devil take a less hateful shape to us than to our fathers, he is as busy with us as with them; and if we cannot find it in our hearts to break with a gentleman of so much worldly wisdom, who gives such admirable dinners, and whose manners are so perfect, so much the worse for us.

Looked at on the outside, New England history is dry and unpicturesque. There is no rustle of silks, no waving of plumes, no clink of golden spurs. Our sympathies are not awakened by the changeful destinies, the rise and fall, of great families, whose doom was in their blood. Instead of all this, we have the homespun fates of Cephas and Prudence repeated in an infinite series of peaceable same-

---

[1] Lowell quotes a second time from Roydon's "Elegie."

ness, and finding space enough for record in the family Bible; we have the noise of axe and hammer and saw, an apotheosis[1] of dogged work, where, reversing the fairy-tale, nothing is left to luck, and, if there be any poetry, it is something that cannot be helped,—the waste of the water over the dam. Extrinsically, it is prosaic and plebeian; intrinsically, it is poetic and noble; for it is, perhaps, the most perfect incarnation of an idea the world has ever seen. That idea was not to found a democracy, nor to charter the city of New Jerusalem by an act of the General Court, as gentlemen seem to think whose notions of history and human nature rise like an exhalation from the good things at a Pilgrim Society dinner. Not in the least. They had no faith in the Divine institution of a system which gives Teague, because he can dig, as much influence as Ralph, because he can think, nor in personal at the expense of general freedom. Their view of human rights was not so limited that it could not take in human relations and duties also. They would have been likely to answer the claim, "I am as good as anybody," by a quiet "Yes, for some things, but not for others; as good, doubtless, in your place, where all things are good." What the early settlers of Massachusetts *did* intend, and what they accomplished, was the founding here of a *new* England, and a better one, where the political superstitions and abuses of the old should never have leave to take root. So much, we may say, they deliberately intended. No nobles, either lay or cleric, no great landed estates, and no universal ignorance as the seed-plot of vice and unreason; but an elective magistracy and clergy, land for all who would till it, and reading and writing, will ye nill ye, instead. Here at last, it would seem, simple manhood is to have a chance to play his stake against Fortune with honest dice, uncogged[2] by those three hoary sharpers, Prerogative, Patricianism, and Priestcraft. Whoever has looked into the pamphlets published in England during the Great Rebellion cannot but have been struck by the fact, that the principles and practice of the Puritan Colony had begun to react with considerable force on the

mother country; and the policy of the retrograde party there, after the Restoration, in its dealings with New England, finds a curious parallel as to its motives (time will show whether as to its results) in the conduct of the same party towards America during the last four years.[1] This influence and this fear alike bear witness to the energy of the principles at work here.

We have said that the details of New England history were essentially dry and unpoetic. Everything is near, authentic, and petty. There is no mist of distance to soften outlines, no mirage of tradition to give characters and events an imaginative loom. So much downright work was perhaps never wrought on the earth's surface in the same space of time as during the first forty years after the settlement. But mere work is unpicturesque, and void of sentiment. Irving instinctively divined and admirably illustrated in his "Knickerbocker" the humorous element which lies in this nearness of view, this clear, prosaic daylight of modernness, and this poverty of stage properties, which makes the actors and the deeds they were concerned in seem ludicrously small when contrasted with the semimythic grandeur in which we have clothed them, as we look backward from the crowned result, and fancy a cause as majestic as our conception of the effect. There was, indeed, one poetic side to the existence otherwise so narrow and practical; and to have conceived this, however partially, is the one original and American thing in Cooper. This diviner glimpse illumines the lives of our Daniel Boones, the man of civilization and old-world ideas confronted with our forest solitudes,—confronted, too, for the first time, with his real self, and so led gradually to disentangle the original substance of his manhood from the artificial results of culture. Here was our new Adam of the wilderness, forced to name anew, not the visible creation of God, but the invisible creation of man, in those forms that lie at the base of social institutions, so insensibly moulding personal character and controlling individual action. Here is the protagonist of our New World epic, a figure as poetic as that of Achilles, as ideally

[1] glorification   [2] uncontrolled by trickery, not "loaded"

[1] i.e., 1860–1864

representative as that of Don Quixote, as romantic in its relation to our homespun and plebeian mythus as Arthur in his to the mailed and plumed cycle of chivalry. We do not mean, of course, that Cooper's "Leatherstocking" is all this or anything like it, but that the character typified in him is ideally and potentially all this and more.

But whatever was poetical in the lives of the early New-Englanders had something shy, if not somber, about it. If their natures flowered, it was out of sight, like the fern. It was in the practical that they showed their true quality, as Englishmen are wont. It has been the fashion lately with a few feebleminded persons to undervalue the New England Puritans, as if they were nothing more than gloomy and narrow-minded fanatics. But all the charges brought against these large-minded and far-seeing men are precisely those which a really able fanatic, Joseph de Maistre, lays at the door of Protestantism. Neither a knowledge of human nature nor of history justifies us in confounding, as is commonly done, the Puritans of Old and New England, or the English Puritans of the third with those of the fifth decade of the seventeenth century. Fanaticism, or, to call it by its milder name, enthusiasm, is only powerful and active so long as it is aggressive. Establish it firmly in power, and it becomes conservatism, whether it will or no. A scepter once put in the hand, the grip is instinctive; and he who is firmly seated in authority soon learns to think security, and not progress, the highest lesson of statecraft. From the summit of power men no longer turn their eyes upward, but begin to look about them. Aspiration sees only one side of every question; possession, many. And the English Puritans, after their revolution was accomplished, stood in even a more precarious position than most successful assailants of the prerogative of whatever *is* to continue in being. They had carried a political end by means of a religious revival. The fulcrum on which they rested their lever to overturn the existing order of things (as history always placidly calls the particular forms of *dis*order for the time being) was in the soul of man. They could not renew the fiery gush of enthusiasm, when once

the molten metal had begun to stiffen in the mould of policy and precedent. The religious element of Puritanism became insensibly merged in the political; and, its one great man taken away, it died, as passions have done before, of possession. It was one thing to shout with Cromwell before the battle of Dunbar, "Now, Lord, arise, and let thine enemies be scattered!" and to snuffle, "Rise, Lord, and keep us safe in our benefices, our sequestered estates, and our five per cent!" Puritanism meant something when Captain Hodgson,[1] riding out to battle through the morning mist, turns over the command of his troop to a lieutenant, and stays to hear the prayer of a cornet, there was "so much of God in it." Become traditional, repeating the phrase without the spirit, reading the present backward as if it were written in Hebrew, translating Jehovah by "I was" instead of "I am,"—it was no more like its former self than the hollow drum made of Ziska's skin[2] was like the grim captain whose soul it had once contained. Yet the change was inevitable, for it is not safe to confound the things of Caesar with the things of God. Some honest republicans, like Ludlow, were never able to comprehend the chilling contrast between the ideal aim and the material fulfilment, and looked askance on the strenuous reign of Oliver,—that rugged boulder of primitive manhood lying lonely there on the dead level of the century,—as if some crooked changeling had been laid in the cradle instead of that fair babe of the Commonwealth they had dreamed. Truly there is a tide in the affairs of men, but there is no gulf-stream setting forever in one direction; and those waves of enthusiasm on whose crumbling crests we sometimes see nations lifted for a gleaming moment are wont to have a gloomy trough before and behind.

[1] This story may be found in Carlyle's account of the day before the battle of Dunbar in his *Oliver Cromwell's Letters and Speeches*, Part VI. [2] When John Ziska was near death, legend tells that he gave instructions that his skin should be tanned and used to make a drum to be carried at the head of the Bohemian armies, with the idea that it might produce the same consternation in the ranks of his country's enemies as had always been caused by the presence of the great general himself.

But the founders of New England, though they must have sympathized vividly with the struggles and triumphs of their brethren in the mother country, were never subjected to the same trials and temptations, never hampered with the same lumber of usages and tradition. They were not driven to win power by doubtful and desperate ways, nor to maintain it by any compromises of the ends which make it worth having. From the outset they were builders, without need of first pulling down, whether to make room or to provide material. For thirty years after the colonization of the Bay, they had absolute power to mould as they would the character of their adolescent commonwealth. During this time a whole generation would have grown to manhood who knew the Old World only by report, in whose habitual thought kings, nobles, and bishops would be as far away from all present and practical concern as the figures in a fairy-tale, and all whose memories and associations, all their unconscious training by eye and ear, were New English only. Nor were the men whose influence was greatest in shaping the framework and the policy of the Colony, in any true sense of the word, fanatics. Enthusiasts, perhaps, they were, but with them the fermentation had never gone further than the ripeness of the vinous stage. Disappointment had never made it acetous, nor had it ever putrefied into the turbid zeal of Fifth Monarchism and sectarian whimsey. There is no better ballast for keeping the mind steady on its keel, and saving it from all risk of *crankiness*, than business. And they were business men, men of facts and figures no less than of religious earnestness. The sum of two hundred thousand pounds had been invested in their undertaking,—a sum, for that time, truly enormous as the result of private combination for a doubtful experiment. That their enterprise might succeed, they must show a balance on the right side of the counting-house ledger, as well as in their private accounts with their own souls. The liberty of praying when and how they would, must be balanced with an ability of paying when and as they ought. Nor is the resulting fact in this case at variance with the *a priori* theory. They succeeded in making their thought the life and soul of a body politic, still powerful, still benignly operative, after two centuries; a thing which no mere fanatic ever did or ever will accomplish. Sober, earnest, and thoughtful men, it was no Utopia, no New Atlantis, no realization of a splendid dream, which they had at heart, but the establishment of the divine principle of Authority on the common interest and the common consent; the making, by a contribution from the free-will of all, a power which should curb and guide the free-will of each for the general good. If they were stern in their dealings with sectaries, it should be remembered that the Colony was in fact the private property of the Massachusetts Company, that unity was essential to its success, and that John of Leyden had taught them how unendurable by the nostrils of honest men is the corruption of the right of private judgment in the evil and selfish hearts of men when no thorough mental training has developed the understanding and given the judgment its needful means of comparison and correction. They knew that liberty in the hands of feeble-minded and unreasoning persons (and all the worse if they are honest) means nothing more than the supremacy of their particular form of imbecility; means nothing less, therefore, than downright chaos, a Bedlam-chaos of monomaniacs and bores. What was to be done with men and women, who bore conclusive witness to the fall of man by insisting on walking up the broadaisle of the meeting-house in a costume which that event had put forever out of fashion? About their treatment of witches, too, there has been a great deal of ignorant babble. Puritanism had nothing whatever to do with it. They acted under a delusion, which, with an exception here and there (and those mainly medical men, like Wierus and Webster), darkened the understanding of all Christendom. Dr. Henry More was no Puritan; and his letter to Glanvil, prefixed to the third edition of the *Sadducismus Triumphatus*, was written in 1678, only fourteen years before the trials at Salem. Bekker's *Beʒauberte Welt*[1] was published in 1693; and in the Preface he speaks of the difficulty of overcoming "the prejudices in which not only

[1] *The Enchanted World*

ordinary men, but the learned also, are obstinate." In Hathaway's case, 1702, Chief-Justice Holt, in charging the jury, expresses no disbelief in the possibility of witchcraft, and in the indictment implies its existence. Indeed, the natural reaction from the Salem mania of 1692 put an end to belief in devilish compacts and demoniac possessions sooner in New England than elsewhere. The last we hear of it there is in 1720, when Rev. Mr. Turell of Medford detected and exposed an attempted cheat by two girls. Even in 1692, it was the foolish breath of Cotton Mather and others of the clergy that blew the dying embers of this ghastly superstition into a flame; and they were actuated partly by a desire to bring about a religious revival, which might stay for a while the hastening lapse of their own authority, and still more by that credulous scepticism of feeble-minded piety which dreads the cutting away of an orthodox tumor of misbelief, as if the life-blood of faith would follow, and would keep even a stumbling-block in the way of salvation, if only enough generations had tripped over it to make it venerable. The witches were condemned on precisely the same grounds that in our day led to the condemnation of *Essays and Reviews*.[1]

But Puritanism was already in the decline when such things were possible. What had been a wondrous and intimate experience of the soul, a flash into the very crypt and basis of man's nature from the fire of trial, had become ritual and tradition. In prosperous times the faith of one generation becomes the formality of the next. "The necessity of reformation," set forth by order of the Synod which met at Cambridge in 1679, though no doubt overstating the case, shows how much even at that time the ancient strictness had been loosened. The country had grown rich, its commerce was large, and wealth did its natural work in making life softer and more worldly, commerce in deprovincializing the minds of

those engaged in it. But Puritanism had already done its duty. As there are certain creatures whose whole being seems occupied with an egg-laying errand they are sent upon, incarnate ovipositors, their bodies but bags to hold this precious deposit, their legs of use only to carry them where they may safeliest get rid of it, so sometimes a generation seems to have no other end than the conception and ripening of certain germs. Its blind stirrings, its apparently aimless seeking hither and thither, are but the driving of an instinct to be done with its parturient function toward these principles of future life and power. Puritanism, believing itself quick with the seed of religious liberty, laid, without knowing it, the egg of democracy. The English Puritans pulled down church and state to rebuild Zion on the ruins, and all the while it was not Zion, but America, they were building. But if their millennium went by, like the rest, and left men still human; if they, like so many saints and martyrs before them, listened in vain for the sound of that trumpet which was to summon all souls to a resurrection from the body of this death which men call life,— it is not for us, at least, to forget the heavy debt we owe them. It was the drums of Naseby and Dunbar that gathered the minute-men on Lexington Common; it was the red dint of the axe on Charles's block that marked One in our era. The Puritans had their faults. They were narrow, ungenial; they could not understand the text, "I have piped to you and ye have not danced," nor conceive that saving one's soul should be the cheerfullest, and not the dreariest, of businesses. Their preachers had a way, like the painful Mr. Perkins, of pronouncing *damn* with such an emphasis as left a doleful echo in their auditors' ears a good while after. And it was natural that men who captained or accompanied the exodus from existing forms and associations into the doubtful wilderness that led to the promised land, should find more to their purpose in the Old Testament than in the New. As respects the New England settlers, however visionary some of their religious tenets may have been, their political ideas savored of the reality, and it was no Nephelococcygia[1] of which they

---

[1] A volume, published in 1860, made up of seven essays on religious subjects, each by a very distinguished English liberal or broad-church thinker. *Replies to Essays and Reviews* appeared a year later, but time has settled the matter largely in favor of the liberals. One essay in *Essays and Reviews* is still of importance to present-day scholars, Mark Pattison's "Tendencies of Religious Thought in England, 1688–1750."

[1] "Cloud-cuckoo-town" in *The Birds* of Aristophanes

drew the plan, but of a commonwealth whose foundation was to rest on solid and familiar earth. If what they did was done in a corner, the results of it were to be felt to the ends of the earth; and the figure of Winthrop should be as venerable in history as that of Romulus is barbarously grand in legend.

I am inclined to think that many of our national characteristics, which are sometimes attributed to climate and sometimes to institutions, are traceable to the influences of Puritan descent. We are apt to forget how very large a proportion of our population is descended from emigrants who came over before 1660. Those emigrants were in great part representatives of that element of English character which was most susceptible of religious impressions; in other words, the most earnest and imaginative. Our people still differ from their English cousins (as they are fond of calling themselves when they are afraid we may do them a mischief) in a certain capacity for enthusiasm, a devotion to abstract principle, an openness to ideas, a greater aptness for intuitions than for the slow processes of the syllogism, and, as derivative from this, in minds of looser texture, a light-armed, skirmishing habit of thought, and positive preference of the birds in the bush,—an excellent quality of character *before* you have your bird in the hand.

There have been two great distributing centers of the English race on this continent, Massachusetts and Virginia. Each has impressed the character of its early legislators on the swarms it has sent forth. Their ideas are in some fundamental respects the opposites of each other, and we can only account for it by an antagonism of thought beginning with the early framers of their respective institutions. New England abolished caste; in Virginia they still talk of "quality folks." But it was in making education not only common to all, but in some sense compulsory on all, that the destiny of the free republics of America was practically settled. Every man was to be trained, not only to the use of arms, but of his wits also; and it is these which alone make the other effective weapons for the maintenance of freedom. You may disarm the hands, but not the brains, of a people, and to

know what should be defended is the first condition of successful defense. Simple as it seems, it was a great discovery that the key of knowledge could turn both ways, that it could open, as well as lock, the door of power to the many. The only things a New-Englander was ever locked out of were the jails. It is quite true that our Republic is the heir of the English Commonwealth; but as we trace events backward to their causes, we shall find it true also, that what made our Revolution a foregone conclusion was that act of the General Court, passed in May, 1647, which established the system of common schools. "To the end that learning may not be buried in the graves of our forefathers in Church and Commonwealth, the Lord assisting our endeavors, it is therefore ordered by this Court and authority thereof, that every township in this jurisdiction, after the Lord hath increased them to fifty householders, shall then forthwith appoint one within their towns to teach all such children as shall resort to him to write and read."

Passing through some Massachusetts village, perhaps at a distance from any house, it may be in the midst of a piece of woods where four roads meet, one may sometimes even yet see a small square one-story building, whose use would not be long doubtful. It is summer, and the flickering shadows of forest-leaves dapple the roof of the little porch, whose door stands wide, and shows, hanging on either hand, rows of straw hats and bonnets, that look as if they had done good service. As you pass the open windows, you hear whole platoons of high-pitched voices discharging words of two or three syllables with wonderful precision and unanimity. Then there is a pause, and the voice of the officer in command is heard reproving some raw recruit whose vocal musket hung fire. Then the drill of the small infantry begins anew, but pauses again because some urchin—who agrees with Voltaire that the superfluous is a very necessary thing—insists on spelling "subtraction" with an *s* too much.

If you had the good fortune to be born and bred in the Bay State, your mind is thronged with half-sad, half-humorous recollections. The a-b abs of little voices long since hushed in the mould, or ringing now in the pulpit, at the bar, or in the Senate-chamber, come back to the ear of memory. You remember the high stool on which culprits used to be elevated with the tall paper fool's-cap on their heads, blushing to the ears; and you think with wonder how you have seen them since as men climbing the world's penance-stools of ambition without a blush, and gladly giving everything for life's cap and 10 bells. And you have pleasanter memories of going after pond-lilies, of angling for horn-pouts,—that queer bat among the fishes,—of nutting, of walking over the creaking snow-crust in winter, when the warm breath of every household was curling up silently in the keen blue air. You wonder if life has any rewards more solid and permanent than the Spanish dollar that was hung around your neck to be restored again next day, and con- 20 clude sadly that it was but too true a prophecy and emblem of all worldly success. But your moralizing is broken short off by a rattle of feet and the pouring forth of the whole swarm,—the boys dancing and shouting,— the mere effervescence of the fixed air of youth and animal spirits uncorked,—the sedater girls in confidential twos and threes decanting secrets out of the mouth of one cape-bonnet into that of another. Times have 30 changed since the jackets and trousers used to draw up on one side of the road, and the petticoats on the other, to salute with bow and courtesy the white neckcloth of the par-son or the squire, if it chanced to pass during intermission.

Now this little building, and others like it, were an original kind of fortification invented by the founders of New England. They are the martello-towers that protect our coast. 40 This was the great discovery of our Puritan forefathers. They were the first lawgivers who saw clearly and enforced practically the simple moral and political truth, that knowl-edge was not an alms to be dependent on the chance charity of private men or the pre-carious pittance of a trust-fund, but a sacred debt which the Commonwealth owed to every one of her children. The opening of the first grammar-school was the opening of the 50 first trench against monopoly in church and state; the first row of trammels and pothooks which the little Shearjashubs and Elkanahs blotted and blubbered across their copy-books, was the preamble to the Declaration of Independence. The men who gave every man the chance to become a landholder, who made the transfer of land easy, and put knowledge within the reach of all, have been called narrow-minded, because they were intolerant. But intolerant of what? Of what they believed to be dangerous nonsense, which, if left free, would destroy the last hope of civil and religious freedom. They had not come here that every man might do that which seemed good in his own eyes, but in the sight of God. Toleration, moreover, is something which is won, not granted. It is the equilibrium of neutralized forces. The Puritans had no notion of tolerating mischief. They looked upon their little commonwealth as upon their private estate and homestead, as they had a right to do, and would no more allow the Devil's religion of unreason to be preached therein, than we should permit a prize-fight in our gardens. They were narrow; in other words they had an edge to them, as men that serve in great emergencies must; for a Gordian knot is settled sooner with a sword than a beetle.

The founders of New England are com-monly represented in the after-dinner oratory of their descendants as men "before their time," as it is called; in other words, delib-erately prescient of events resulting from new relations of circumstances, or even from circumstances new in themselves, and there-fore altogether alien from their own ex-perience. Of course, such a class of men is to be reckoned among those non-existent human varieties so gravely catalogued by the ancient naturalists. If a man could shape his action with reference to what should happen a century after his death, surely it might be asked of him to call in the help of that easier foreknowledge which reaches from one day to the next,—a power of prophecy whereof we have no example. I do not object to a wholesome pride of ancestry, though a little mythical, if it be accompanied with the feeling that *noblesse oblige*,[1] and do not result merely

[1] "nobility obligates"

in a placid self-satisfaction with our own mediocrity, as if greatness, like righteousness, could be imputed. We can pardon it even in conquered races, like the Welsh and Irish, who make up to themselves for present degradation by imaginary empires in the past whose boundaries they can extend at will, carrying the bloodless conquests of fancy over regions laid down upon no map, and concerning which authentic history is enviously dumb. Those long beadrolls of Keltic kings cannot tyrannize over us, and we can be patient so long as our own crowns are uncracked by the shillalah scepters of their actual representatives. In our own case, it would not be amiss, perhaps, if we took warning by the example of Teague and Taffy. At least, I think it would be wise in our orators not to put forward so prominently the claim of the Yankee to universal dominion, and his intention to enter upon it forthwith. If we do our duties as honestly and as much in the fear of God as our forefathers did, we need not trouble ourselves much about other titles to empire. The broad foreheads and long heads will win the day at last in spite of all heraldry, and it will be enough if we feel as keenly as our Puritan founders did that those organs of empire may be broadened and lengthened by culture.[1] That our self-complacency should not increase the complacency of outsiders is not to be wondered at. As *we* sometimes take credit to ourselves (since all commendation of our ancestry is indirect self-flattery) for what the Puritan fathers never were, so there are others who, to gratify a spite against their descendants, blame them for not having been what they could not be; namely, before their time in such matters as slavery, witchcraft, and the like. The view, whether of friend or foe, is equally unhistorical, nay, without the faintest notion of all that make history worth having as a teacher. That our grandfathers shared in the prejudices of their day is all that makes them human to us; and that never-

theless they could act bravely and wisely on occasion makes them only the more venerable. If certain barbarisms and superstitions disappeared earlier in New England than elsewhere, not by the decision of exceptionally enlightened or humane judges, but by force of public opinion, that is the fact that is interesting and instructive for us. I never thought it an abatement of Hawthorne's genius that he came lineally from one who sat in judgment on the witches in 1692; it was interesting rather to trace something hereditary in the somber character of his imagination, continually vexing itself to account for the origin of evil, and baffled for want of that simple solution in a personal Devil.

* * *

I have little sympathy with declaimers about the Pilgrim Fathers, who look upon them all as men of grand conceptions and superhuman foresight. An entire ship's company of Columbuses is what the world never saw. It is not wise to form any theory and fit our facts to it, as a man in a hurry is apt to cram his travelling-bag, with a total disregard of shape or texture. But perhaps it may be found that the facts will only fit comfortably together on a single plan, namely, that the fathers did have a conception (which those will call grand who regard simplicity as a necessary element of grandeur) of founding here a commonwealth on those two eternal bases of Faith and Work; that they had, indeed, no revolutionary ideas of universal liberty, but yet, what answered the purpose quite as well, an abiding faith in the brotherhood of man and the fatherhood of God; and that they did not so much propose to make all things new, as to develop the latent possibilities of English law and English character, by clearing away the fences by which the abuse of the one was gradually discommoning the other from the broad fields of natural right. They were not in advance of their age, as it is called, for no one who is so can ever work profitably in it; but they were alive to the highest and most earnest thinking of their time.

[1] "It is curious, that, when Cromwell proposed to transfer a colony from New England to Ireland, one of the conditions insisted on in Massachusetts was that a college should be established." [*Lowell's note.*]

1864   1865

1809 -- *Edgar Allan Poe* -- 1849

THE LIFE of Edgar Allan Poe, like those of the storm-and-stress geniuses of the Old World, such as Byron, De Musset, or Heine, contrasts strongly with the well-regulated lives of our other men of letters. Not a derivative of the Puritans like Bryant and Hawthorne, not a Yankee like Franklin, no product of or laureate of the country like Whittier, he was the spokesman of no region. There was no other genius of his type. He was of nervous mentality, super-sensitive, and lacking in self-control. His heredity was not one that promised much health or strength of resistance, and his environment was not favorable for the artistic ambition. His life was tragic and frustrated. Yet with Whitman, he is one of the two American poets acclaimed by Europeans.

Poe was born in Boston, January 19, 1809, the second son of poor strolling players. His father was of a Baltimore family; his mother, Elizabeth Arnold, an English actress of considerable talent. Young and delicately beautiful, she held leading parts in her theatrical troupe, and was the main support of the family. After Poe was born, the troupe remained in Boston to complete an engagement, then wandered off on a Southern circuit. Poe's father disappeared after July, 1810, within a few weeks of the birth of a third child, a daughter, and the mother was left in abject poverty with three small children. She died in Richmond, December 8, 1811, while still in her early twenties.

Almost from the start Poe was without real parental sympathy and guidance. At his mother's death it was his fortune to be taken into the family of John Allan at the wish of his wife. The boy was treated as a son for some years, though he was never formally adopted. Allan was later, when an inheritance was left him, to become a wealthy tobacco merchant in Richmond. Poe was made much of by Mrs. Allan and perhaps rather pampered by her. When Allan attempted to establish a branch of his tobacco business in England, 1815–1820, Poe was taken with him and was sent to several schools in England and Scotland, especially to the Manor House School, at Stoke-Newington. The influence of these years is perhaps responsible for Poe's recurrent references to castles, old tombs, mists, and isles in the sea.

The six years following 1820 were spent in Richmond, where Poe led the life of a youth of social standing, reading, studying, and being tutored. He became liked less and less by Allan, who was perhaps indulgent and exacting by turns. That the boy's temperament was scarcely normal is hinted in an early romance of this period. He had a schoolboy adoration for an older woman, the mother of a classmate, and when she died in 1824 he haunted her grave. This idolatry is recorded in the poem

"To Helen." There was perhaps another sentimental attachment during these years in a boyish engagement to a girl slightly younger than himself.

In February, 1826, when he was seventeen, Poe matriculated at the newly established University of Virginia, of which Thomas Jefferson was the special patron. Some of its principal courses were in ancient and modern languages, courses which then included ancient history and geography. Poe was a brilliant student, winning firsts in both French and Latin, and he was good in debate; but he seems to have had something of a name for drinking. At Christmas, 1827, he was withdrawn from school by Mr. Allan, who was angered at his large number of unpaid bills, especially gambling debts, said to have totalled more than two thousand dollars. Poe explained his gambling as a desperate attempt to remain in school, brought on by Allan's parsimony toward him. It is possible that Allan, wishing to get rid of him, sent him little or no money. After a quarrel with Allan in March, 1827, Poe left home, apparently taking with him a bundle of poems. In April he was in Boston, where he published anonymously *Tamerlane and Other Poems* from the press of a young friend. The little volume, the publication of a boy of eighteen, made no great stir. On May 26, under the name of Edgar A. Perry, Poe enlisted in a United States battery of artillery, in which he made a good record. His battery was sent that year to Fort Moultrie, South Carolina, and thence to Fortress Monroe, in Virginia. In 1829 he was promoted to be sergeant-major, the highest grade he could reach.

The death of Mrs. Allan in February of that year brought him again to Richmond, where he tried with partial success for a reconciliation with Mr. Allan. He was released from the army, April 15, 1829, and Allan seems to have tried next to have him appointed at West Point. Meanwhile Poe went to Baltimore, where he lived at the house of his father's sister, Mrs. Maria Clemm. He continued to write, and published in this year *Al Aaraaf, Tamerlane, and Minor Poems*. Again in Richmond for a short time, he had a violent quarrel with Allan and left him to enter West Point, July 1, 1830. After the death of the first Mrs. Allan, Poe's chances with Allan became less and less. They had never been very compatible and the second Mrs. Allan, married in 1830, was Poe's bitter critic. Because of Poe's unstable temperament there was undoubtedly much to be said on Allan's side as well as his.

Poe found the life at West Point too disciplined and austere. Interested in his writing, he neglected his duties and deliberately acquired demerits. He was court-martialed on the charge of remissness from duty and disobedience, and discharged March, 1831. Henceforth he was disowned by Allan, who died in 1834 without making any provision for Poe.

The rest of his life was a long struggle with poverty and want. He was often in desperate plight. For seventeen years he managed to live by his pen the uncertain, irregular life of a struggling writer, editor, and literary hack. A little later it might have been easier for him, with his powers and industry, to do well, but his day was not very favorable for the aesthetic life. It is possible, too, that his unstable nature might always have prevented him from keeping positions.

He published a second edition of his poems in New York in 1831, and in 1833 the first real stimulus to a literary career came when his "MS. Found in a Bottle" won a prize of fifty dollars offered by a Baltimore paper for the best prose tale. Some time later (1835), with the assistance of a friend, he got an appointment on the *Southern Literary Messenger*, and in 1836 he married his cousin Virginia Clemm, then aged thirteen or fourteen. He lost his position in 1837, but in 1839 he became the editor for a short time of *Burton's Gentleman's Magazine*, published in Philadelphia. His *Narrative of A. Gordon Pym* appeared in 1838, and two volumes of *Tales of the Grotesque and Arabesque* in 1839. In 1841–1842 he was on the staff of *Graham's Magazine*, and later tried unsuccessfully to establish a magazine of his own. A removal to New York followed in 1844, and there he did hack work for N. P. Willis's *New York Evening Mirror*. "The Raven," published in 1845 in the *Mirror*, was a great popular success and won fame for him, but brought him only ten dollars. In 1845–1846 he worked on the *Broadway Journal*, and in these years published *Tales* and *The Raven and Other Poems*.

Poe gained positions easily, at least at first, but his occasional lapses to inebriety made him incapable of work at times and hampered his success. He was never habitually intemperate but was constantly tempted by social usages and was susceptible to the least quantity, even a spoonful, of alcohol. It was hard for him to work steadily although his brilliancy was appreciated by his employers, and his friends sought to do much on his behalf. N. P. Willis said of him that he was industrious, quiet, patient, and gentlemanly. It is certain that he was a very hard worker, writing irregularly but rapidly.

More difficulties were added to his life by the failing health of his wife Virginia. Never very strong, she spent the last six years of her life as an invalid wasting away with tuberculosis. The family moved to Fordham in 1846, and the following year Virginia died. An attractive side of Poe's life is his tender care of her and his devotion to his mother-in-law, Mrs. Clemm, who lived with them and looked after them, and whose practical efforts kept the three together when they were in the greatest straits. Poe's domestic life was exemplary.

After Virginia's death Poe collapsed rapidly. *Eureka, a Prose Poem* was published in 1848 and was his last important work. He indulged more and more in intoxicants and had several mistaken love affairs. Among the women with whom he entered into sentimental romantic relations was Sarah Helen Whitman, a poet. Later, when in Richmond, he became engaged to a well-to-do widow, Mrs. Shelton (born Sarah Elmira Royster), whom he had known in his youth. On his way north he lapsed into drinking at Baltimore. He was found there in the street, helpless and insensible, and was taken to a hospital, where he died, October 7, 1849.

Poe summed up his ideals of poetry in "The Poetic Principle," and he illustrated his deductive tendency to create poems such as "The Raven" in the light of such ideals in "The Philosophy of Composition." In a didactic era he regarded poetry as the rhythmical creation of beauty,—goodness and truth being sharply subordinated. All details and imagery must harmonize so as to achieve a unity of effect on the mind of the reader, preferably an effect of melancholy which Poe regarded as "the most legitimate of all the poetic tones." To him the lyric, not over a hundred lines long, was the only true poem. He emphasized music, and hence prosodic technique, as of supreme importance in producing "a suggestive indefiniteness of meaning" and "novel moods of beauty in form, in color, in sound, in sentiment." In prosody Poe was an arch conservative; poetry depends not on accent but on time or "quantity," and he opposed substitutions of feet, contractions, elisions, "harsh consonants," and identical, light, or inexact rhymes. Although he opposed flat didacticism, he saw the essence of poetry as "an elevating excitement of the Soul" and he found beauty in "all noble thoughts—in all unworldly motives— in all holy impulses"; beauty resides in the ideal and "is not afforded the soul by any existing collocation of earth's forms."

Poe left only a small but distinctive body of verse. His poems are not to be read intellectually but for sound and suggestion. They are marked by intensity and by magic of expression. He was much occupied with technique and gained his effects on the borderland of music, without seeking to convey profound ideas. His poetry does not concern itself with patriotic themes or ethical abstractions, and it lacks a real human or a real nature element.

Poe's nearest predecessor in the writing of his type of fiction is Charles Brockden Brown. He was far more of an artist, however, than Brown. He did not create the short story, a relatively new form of art, for short tales had been written in Europe; but he did compact it, give it standards of structure for America, and rid it of the sentimental and meditative elements then common in tales. He summed up his ideals of the short story in his review of Hawthorne's *Twice-Told Tales*. A story must be short enough to be read at one sitting, so as to gain "the immense force derivable from totality." It should aim at a single and unique effect, all details being excluded which do not further "the one pre-established design." He also emphasized the need for verisimilitude and finality. In practice, his stories, with their carefully established backgrounds, strange heroes, and effects of horror, are a landmark in the development of American fiction. Poe's tales fall into several classes. They may be grouped into analytical tales or tales of ratiocination, such as "The Gold Bug" or "Murders in the Rue Morgue"; tales of mystery and occultism or horror and death, such as "The Fall of the House of Usher" and "Ligeia"; pseudo-scientific tales or tales of marvelous adventure, such as "MS. Found in a Bottle" or "The Descent into the Maelstrom"; tales of fantasy and extravaganza, such as "Eleanora" or

"The Domain of Arnheim"; and tales of humor, such as "The Devil in the Belfry," a class in which Poe is not at his best.

In still a third field, that of American literary criticism, Poe is of importance. He was especially interested in artistic analysis and left a definite body of critical ideas. When others emphasized spontaneity, he viewed and practiced logical concentration as a principle of art and sought to show how he reached his effects by conscious processes. In his own day he was known chiefly as a critic—a critic who sought not to explain or interpret or appreciate but to render sharply worded judgments. He thought American criticism was led astray by irrelevant patriotic or moralistic opinions, and as a corrective he advocated and practiced "an absolutely independent criticism . . . guiding itself only by the purest rules of Art; analyzing and urging these rules as it applies them; holding itself aloof from all personal bias: acknowledging no fear save that of outraging the right." (These ideals are set forth in his prospectus for *The Penn Magazine*, and they are amplified in his "Exordium.") His criticism is distinctive in its very "particular and methodical application" of his principles of the poem and short story already sketched. Doubtless Poe's quest as a journalist for sensationalism accentuated his rather harsh doctrine that "in pointing out frankly the errors of a work, we do nearly all that is critically necessary in displaying its merits." In his larger ideas of the function of a critic, the nature of genius and of imagination, and the extent to which poetry may deal with truth, Poe was in debt to Coleridge, as Stovall has shown. Margaret Alterton and Hardin Craig, interesting themselves in his "prose poem," *Eureka*, with its vision of a universe of ordered harmony, believe that in its Newtonian emphasis on natural law and harmony may be found the basis of his theory and practice of composition and his quest of unity and totality of effect in literature.

The Complete Works of Edgar Allan Poe (17 vols., 1902), edited by James A. Harrison (known as the Virginia Edition) is usually considered the best. Others include that by J. H. Ingram (1874–75), and the good but incomplete ten-volume edition by E. C. Stedman and G. E. Woodberry (1894–95, 1914). The *Poems* were edited separately by Andrew Lang in 1892, and by G. E. Woodberry in 1907. The best edition is *The Complete Poems of Edgar Allan Poe*, collected and edited by J. H. Whitty, and arranged with memoirs and notes and a bibliography (1911; second edition, 1917). There is also an excellent critical edition (1917) by Killis Campbell, who also edited Poe's short stories (1927). Poe's letters to Sarah Helen Whitman have been edited by J. A. Harrison (1909); the letters to George W. Eveleth, by James Southall Wilson, in *Alumni Bulletin*, University of Virginia, Jan., 1924; *Letters Till Now Unpublished* (in the Valentine Museum, Richmond, Virginia), by Mary Newton Stanard (1925). The "Poe-Chivers Papers" were edited by G. E. Woodberry, *Century Magazine*, XLIII, Jan.–Feb., 1903.

A factual biography of Poe is James A. Harrison's *Life and Letters of Edgar Allan Poe* (2 vols., 1903). Hervey Allen's *Israfel* (2 vols., 1926; rev., 1934) is a romantic biography which is readable but not wholly firsthand or reliable. He also treated Poe in the *DAB*, XV (1935). Similarly, J. W. Krutch's *Edgar Allan Poe, a Study in Genius* (1926) is not wholly trustworthy because of its slant toward a pathological hypothesis. *Edgar Allan Poe—The Man* (2 vols., 1926), by Mary E. Phillips, though not a finished piece of work, is based on original and valuable research. The best literary biography of Poe is G. E. Woodberry's *Edgar Allan Poe* (2 vols., 1909), which supersedes the author's briefer work of 1885. J. H. Ingram's *Life* (2 vols., 1880), and Una Pope-Hennessey's straightforward biography (1934), both deserve mention.

Critical articles and studies concerning Poe by Killis Campbell are included in *CHAL*, II (1918), and in learned periodicals. He is also the author of *The Mind of Poe* (1933). Other helpful studies are those by Charles F. Richardson, in *American Literature, 1607–1885*, II (1889); L. E. Gates, in *Studies and Appreciations* (1900); W. C. Brownell, in *American Prose Masters* (1909); Arthur Ransome, *Edgar Allan Poe, a Critical Study* (1910); Norman Foerster, in *American Criticism* (1928); Alfred Kreymborg, in *Our Singing Strength* (1929); Margaret Alterton, *Origin of Poe's Critical Theory* (1925); also the introduction to Alterton and Craig's *Poe: Representative Selections* (1935); C. P. Cambiare, *The Influence of Edgar Allan Poe in France* (1927); Gay W. Allen, in *American Prosody* (1935); and Edward Shanks, *Edgar Allan Poe* (1937). G. R. Graham, who knew Poe, offered contemporary criticism in *Graham's Magazine* for Feb., 1854, as did R. W. Griswold, who included a memoir, famous for its unfairness, in his edition of Poe's works mentioned above.

The best bibliographies of Poe may be found in *CHAL*, II (1918), in J. W. Robertson's *A Bibliography of the Writings of Edgar Allan Poe* (2 vols., 1934), and in the Craig-Alterton *Poe*.

A DREAM WITHIN A DREAM

The earliest title of this poem was "Imitation," changed to "To ——" in 1829. The present title was given it in 1839. First published in the 1827 volume, it underwent modifications in 1831 and 1849. At the time of his death, Poe was said to have been contemplating still further changes (Whitty, *Complete Poems*, viii–ix). The autobiographical element in the earlier texts was lessened in the later ones.

Take this kiss upon the brow!
And, in parting from you now,
Thus much let me avow—
You are not wrong who deem
That my days have been a dream;
Yet if hope has flown away
In a night, or in a day,
In a vision, or in none,
Is it therefore the less *gone?*
All that we see or seem   10
Is but a dream within a dream.

I stand amid the roar
Of a surf-tormented shore,
And I hold within my hand
Grains of the golden sand—
How few! yet how they creep
Through my fingers to the deep,
While I weep—while I weep!

O God! can I not grasp
Them with a tighter clasp?   20
O God! can I not save
One from the pitiless wave?
Is *all* that we see or seem
But a dream within a dream?

1827, 1829, 1849   1827

Song from AL AARAAF

"Spirit! that dwellest where,
In the deep sky,
The terrible and fair,
In beauty vie!
Beyond the line of blue—
The boundary of the star
Which turneth at the view
Of thy barrier and thy bar—
Of the barrier overgone
By the comets who were cast   10
From their pride and from their throne,
To be drudges till the last—
To be carriers of fire
(The red fire of their heart)
With speed that may not tire
And with pain that shall not part—
Who livest—*that* we know—
In Eternity—we feel—
But the shadow of whose brow
What spirit shall reveal?   20

Tho' the beings whom thy Nesace,
Thy messenger, hath known,
Have dream'd for thy Infinity
A model of their own—
Thy will is done, oh, God!
The star hath ridden high
Thro' many a tempest, but she rode
Beneath thy burning eye;
And here, in thought, to thee—
In thought that can alone   30
Ascend thy empire and so be
A partner of thy throne—
By winged Fantasy,
My embassy is given,
Till secrecy shall knowledge be
In the environs of Heaven."

1827–1829   1829

SONNET—TO SCIENCE

Though it was of later composition, Poe always
printed this sonnet just before *Al Aaraaf*, to which
it served as an introduction. The underlying idea,
that science curbs imaginative flights and so ends
poetry, was much discussed in Poe's day. Compare Keats's *Lamia*, II, 229–38.

SCIENCE! true daughter of Old Time thou art!
Who alterest all things with thy peering eyes,
Why preyest thou thus upon the poet's
     heart,
Vulture, whose wings are dull realities?
How should he love thee? or how deem thee
     wise,
Who wouldst not leave him in his wandering
To seek for treasure in the jewelled skies,
Albeit he soared with an undaunted wing?
Hast thou not dragged Diana from her car?
And driven the Hamadryad from the wood   10
To seek a shelter in some happier star?
Hast thou not torn the Naiad from her flood,
The Elfin from the green grass, and from me
The summer dream beneath the tamarind tree?

     1829

TO HELEN

Some think this Poe's best poem. If his statement is to be believed, it commemorates his devotion to a lady kind to him in his boyhood,
Mrs. Jane Stith Stanard of Richmond, who died
in 1824. A poem in a dream mood, it is marked by
grace and beauty of sound and suggestion, created in a minimum of words. The type of beauty
suggested for the heroine seems to shift from that
which soothes the "wayworn wanderer," in the
first stanza, to a classic type in the second, and to
a type associated with Psyche (the soul) in the
last.

HELEN, thy beauty is to me
Like those Nicéan barks of yore,
That gently, o'er a perfumed sea,
The weary, wayworn wanderer bore
To his own native shore.

On desperate seas long wont to roam,
Thy hyacinth hair, thy classic face,
Thy Naiad airs, have brought me home
To the glory that was Greece
And the grandeur that was Rome.   10

Lo! in yon brilliant window-niche
How statue-like I see thee stand,
The agate lamp within thy hand!
Ah, Pysche, from the regions which
Are Holy Land!

     1831

THE CITY IN THE SEA

The original title was "The Doomed City,"
changed to "The City of Sin" in 1836 and to the
present title in 1845. Poe's phantom city in its
stagnant sea is a pagan city. Blending with the
poet's scriptural memories of Babylon, and perhaps a beautiful Gomorrah, doomed also, was
the memory of a city engulfed by water (see
L. Pound, *American Literature*, March, 1934).
There is a vast lore of sunken cities, ancient and
modern. In *American Literature*, March, 1936, the
suggestion was made that Tyre (Ezekiel 26–28),
often referred to from the pulpit as "the city in
the sea," may have been in Poe's mind.

Lo! Death has reared himself a throne
In a strange city lying alone
Far down within the dim West,
Where the good and the bad and the worst
     and the best
Have gone to their eternal rest.
There shrines and palaces and towers
(Time-eaten towers that tremble not)
Resemble nothing that is ours.
Around, by lifting winds forgot,
Resignedly beneath the sky   10
The melancholy waters lie.

No rays from the holy heaven come down
On the long night-time of that town;
But light from out the lurid sea
Streams up the turrets silently,
Gleams up the pinnacles far and free:
Up domes, up spires, up kingly halls,
Up fanes, up Babylon-like walls,
Up shadowy long-forgotten bowers
Of sculptured ivy and stone flowers,   20
Up many and many a marvelous shrine
Whose wreathèd friezes intertwine
The viol, the violet, and the vine.

Resignedly beneath the sky
The melancholy waters lie.
So blend the turrets and shadows there
That all seem pendulous in air,
While from a proud tower in the town
Death looks gigantically down.

There open fanes and gaping graves   30
Yawn level with the luminous waves;
But not the riches there that lie
In each idol's diamond eye,—
Not the gayly-jeweled dead,
Tempt the waters from their bed;
For no ripples curl, alas,
Along that wilderness of glass;
No swellings tell that winds may be
Upon some far-off happier sea;
No heavings hint that winds have been   40
On seas less hideously serene!

But lo, a stir is in the air!
The wave—there is a movement there!
As if the towers had thrust aside,
In slightly sinking, the dull tide;
As if their tops had feebly given
A void within the filmy Heaven!
The waves have now a redder glow,
The hours are breathing faint and low;
And when, amid no earthly moans,   50
Down, down that town shall settle hence,
Hell, rising from a thousand thrones,
Shall do it reverence.

1831

THE SLEEPER

First published under the title "Irene." Striking are its lulling cadences and the magic of its

moonlit midnight. Poe liked it among the best of
his poems. He said in a letter cited in Ingram's
Life, "Your appreciation of 'The Sleeper' delights
me. In the higher qualities of poetry it is better
than 'The Raven'; but there is not one man in a
million who could be brought to agree with me in
this opinion. 'The Raven,' of course, is far better
as a work of art; but in the true basis of all art,
'The Sleeper' is the superior. I wrote the latter
when quite a boy."

At midnight, in the month of June,
I stand beneath the mystic moon.
An opiate vapor, dewy, dim,
Exhales from out her golden rim,
And, softly dripping, drop by drop,
Upon the quiet mountain-top,
Steals drowsily and musically
Into the universal valley.
The rosemary nods upon the grave;
The lily lolls upon the wave;   10
Wrapping the fog about its breast,
The ruin molders into rest;
Looking like Lethe, see! the lake
A conscious slumber seems to take,
And would not, for the world, awake.
All beauty sleeps!—and lo! where lies
Irene, with her destinies!

O lady bright! can it be right,
This window open to the night?
The wanton airs, from the tree-top,   20
Laughingly through the lattice drop;
The bodiless airs, a wizard rout,
Flit through thy chamber in and out,
And wave the curtain canopy
So fitfully, so fearfully,
Above the closed and fringèd lid
'Neath which thy slumb'ring soul lies
     hid,
That, o'er the floor and down the wall,
Like ghosts the shadows rise and fall.
O lady dear, hast thou no fear?   30
Why and what art thou dreaming here?
Sure thou art come o'er far-off seas,
A wonder to these garden trees!
Strange is thy pallor! strange thy dress!
Strange, above all, thy length of tress,
And this all solemn silentness!

The lady sleeps. Oh, may her sleep,
Which is enduring, so be deep!

Heaven have her in its sacred keep!
This chamber changed for one more holy,   40
This bed for one more melancholy,
I pray to God that she may lie
Forever with unopened eye,
While the pale sheeted ghosts go by.

My love, she sleeps. Oh, may her sleep,
As it is lasting, so be deep!
Soft may the worms about her creep!
Far in the forest, dim and old,
For her may some tall vault unfold:
Some vault that oft hath flung its black   50
And wingéd panels fluttering back,
Triumphant, o'er the crested palls
Of her grand family funerals—
Some sepulcher, remote, alone,
Against whose portal she hath thrown,
In childhood many an idle stone—
Some tomb from out whose sounding door
She ne'er shall force an echo more,
Thrilling to think, poor child of sin,
It was the dead who groaned within!   60

1831

LENORE

This poem in semidramatic form underwent revisions through many stages, from the short ballad stanzas of the original to the long lines with internal rhymes introduced in 1845. The name Lenore, liked by Poe for its sound, was perhaps suggested to him by Bürger's eighteenth-century German ballad of the supernatural of that name. When reviewing a volume of poems in 1844, Poe wrote: "Her tone ... is not so much the tone of passion, as of a gentle and melancholy regret, interwoven with a pleasant sense of the natural loveliness surrounding the lost in the tomb, and a memory of her beauty while alive.—Elegiac poems should either assume this character, or dwell purely on the beauty (moral or physical) of the departed, or better still, utter the note of triumph. I have endeavored to carry out this idea in some verses which I have called 'Lenore.'"

Ah, broken is the golden bowl[1]—the spirit flown forever!
Let the bell toll!—a saintly soul floats on the Stygian river;

And, Guy De Vere, hast *thou* no tear?— weep now or never more!
See! on yon drear and rigid bier low lies thy love, Lenore!
Come! let the burial rite be read—the funeral song be sung!—
An anthem for the queenliest dead that ever died so young—
A dirge for her the doubly dead in that she died so young.

"Wretches![1] ye loved her for her wealth and hated her for her pride,
And when she fell in feeble health, ye blessed her—that she died!
How *shall* the ritual, then, be read?—the requiem how be sung   10
By you—by yours, the evil eye,—by yours, the slanderous tongue
That did to death the innocence that died, and died so young?"

Peccavimus[2]; yet rave not thus! but let a Sabbath song
Go up to God so solemnly the dead may feel no wrong!
The sweet Lenore hath gone before, with Hope, that flew beside,
Leaving thee wild for the dear child that should have been thy bride—
For her, the fair and debonair, that now so lowly lies,
The life upon her yellow hair, but not within her eyes—
The life still there upon her hair, the death upon her eyes.

"Avaunt!—avaunt! to friends from fiends the indignant ghost is riven—   20
From Hell unto a high estate within the utmost Heaven—
From moan and groan to a golden throne beside the King of Heaven:—
Let *no* bell toll, then, lest her soul, amid its hallowed mirth,
Should catch the note as it doth float up from the damnéd Earth!

[1] The false friends of Lenore, who speak the first and third stanzas. The second and fourth stanzas are spoken by the bereaved lover.   [2] "We have sinned," a widely used phrase of confession.

[1] Ecclesiastes 12:6

And I—tonight my heart is light:—no dirge
    will I upraise,
But waft the angel on her flight with a Pæan
    of old days!"

                        1831

ISRAFEL

This lyric is unusual for Poe. It expresses rejoicing or exaltation, embodied in verse of up-
springing lightness. Of interest are the ideas of the
poet that it conveys. The ideal poet writes, from
his heart, impassioned melodious verse, and he is
endowed with superior wisdom and fervor. At the
end Poe recognizes regretfully how his environment influences or limits the poet.

———

And the angel Israfel, whose heart-strings are
a lute, and who has the sweetest voice of all God's
creatures.—KORAN.[1]

In Heaven a spirit doth dwell
    "Whose heart-strings are a lute"[2];
None sing so wildly well
As the angel Israfel,
And the giddy stars (so legends tell)
Ceasing their hymns, attend the spell
    Of his voice, all mute.

Tottering above
    In her highest noon,
The enamored moon   10
Blushes with love,
    While, to listen, the red levin
    (With the rapid Pleiads, even,
    Which were seven)
Pauses in Heaven.

And they say (the starry choir
    And the other listening things)
That Israfeli's fire
Is owing to that lyre
By which he sits and sings—   20
    The trembling living wire
    Of those unusual strings.

[1] Poe's motto is based upon a passage in Sale's
"Preliminary Discourse" to his translation of the
Koran. It is not in the Koran itself. Poe varied the
motto from edition to edition of his poems. [2] This
quotation, according to Professor Killis Campbell, is
based upon a passage in Le Rufus, by the French lyric
poet Béranger.

But the skies that angel trod,
Where deep thoughts are a duty,
Where Love's a grown-up God,
    Where the Houri[1] glances are
Imbued with all the beauty
    Which we worship in a star.

Therefore, thou art not wrong,
    Israfeli, who despisest   30
An unimpassioned song;
To thee the laurels belong,
    Best bard, because the wisest!
Merrily live, and long!

The ecstasies above
    With thy burning measures suit—
Thy grief, thy joy, thy hate, thy love,
    With the fervor of thy lute—
    Well may the stars be mute!

Yes, Heaven is thine; but this   40
    Is a world of sweets and sours;
Our flowers are merely—flowers,
And the shadow of thy perfect bliss
    Is the sunshine of ours.

If I could dwell
Where Israfel
    Hath dwelt, and he where I,
He might not sing so wildly well
    A mortal melody,
While a bolder note than this might
    swell   50
From my lyre within the sky.

                        1831

TO ONE IN PARADISE

First printed in Godey's Lady's Book, January,
1834, as a part of Poe's story "The Visionary,"
later renamed "The Assignation."

THOU wast all that to me, love,
    For which my soul did pine:
A green isle in the sea, love,
    A fountain and a shrine,
All wreathed with fairy fruits and
    flowers,
    And all the flowers were mine.

[1] The houris are beautiful black-eyed nymphs that
inhabit the paradise of the Mohammedans.

Ah, dream too bright to last!
  Ah, starry Hope, that didst arise
But to be overcast!
  A voice from out the Future cries,   10
"On! on!"—but o'er the Past
  (Dim gulf!) my spirit hovering lies
Mute, motionless, aghast!

For, alas! alas! with me
  The light of Life is o'er!
No more—no more—no more—
  (Such language holds the solemn sea
    To the sands upon the shore)
Shall bloom the thunder-blasted tree,
  Or the stricken eagle soar!   20

And all my days are trances,
  And all my nightly dreams
Are where thy gray eye glances,
  And where thy footstep gleams—
In what ethereal dances,
  By what eternal streams.

1834

THE CONQUEROR WORM

Published in *Graham's Magazine*, January, 1843.
It was later (1845) incorporated in the short
story "Ligeia." The poem is a miniature allegory
of human life. C. W. Kent (*Poems by Poe*) noted
that its five stanzas correspond to the five acts
of a tragedy.

Lo! 'tis a gala night
  Within the lonesome latter years.
An angel throng, bewinged, bedight
  In veils, and drowned in tears,
Sit in a theater to see
  A play of hopes and fears,
While the orchestra breathes fitfully
  The music of the spheres.

Mimes, in the form of God on high,
  Mutter and mumble low,   10
And hither and thither fly—
  Mere puppets they, who come and go
At bidding of vast formless things
  That shift the scenery to and fro,
Flapping from out their Condor wings
  Invisible Wo.

That motley drama—oh, be sure
  It shall not be forgot!
With its Phantom chased for evermore
  By a crowd that seize it not,   20
Through a circle that ever returneth in
  To the self-same spot,
And much of Madness, and more of Sin,
  And Horror the soul of the plot.

But see amid the mimic rout
  A crawling shape intrude!
A blood-red thing that writhes from out
  The scenic solitude!
It writhes!—it writhes!—with mortal pangs
  The mimes become its food,   30
And seraphs sob at vermin fangs
  In human gore imbued.

Out—out are the lights—out all!
  And, over each quivering form,
The curtain, a funeral pall,
  Comes down with the rush of a storm,
While the angels, all pallid and wan,
  Uprising, unveiling, affirm
That the play is the tragedy, "Man,"
  And its hero, the Conqueror Worm.   40

1843

DREAM–LAND

In theme this poem is related to Poe's earlier
"Spirits of the Dead" and "Fairy-Land." The
poet's manner in "The Raven" and "Ulalume"
is foreshadowed in this piece, especially his
abundant use of repetition.

By a route obscure and lonely,
Haunted by ill angels only,
Where an Eidolon,[1] named NIGHT,
On a black throne reigns upright,
I have reached these lands but newly
From an ultimate dim Thule[2]—
From a wild weird clime that lieth, sublime,
  Out of SPACE—out of TIME.

Bottomless vales and boundless floods,
And chasms, and caves, and Titan woods,

[1] A phantom or image. Night seems here to be a
symbol of death, as in "The Raven" (line 47).
[2] This mythical land was supposed by the ancients
to be the most northerly part of Europe.

With forms that no man can discover   11
For the tears that drip all over;
Mountains toppling evermore
Into seas without a shore;
Seas that restlessly aspire,
Surging, unto skies of fire;
Lakes that endlessly outspread
Their lone waters, lone and dead,—
Their still waters, still and chilly
With the snows of the lolling lily.   20

By the lakes that thus outspread
Their lone waters, lone and dead,—
Their sad waters, sad and chilly
With the snows of the lolling lily,—
By the mountains—near the river
Murmuring lowly, murmuring ever,—
By the grey woods,—by the swamp
Where the toad and the newt encamp,—
By the dismal tarns and pools
    Where dwell the Ghouls,—   30
By each spot the most unholy—
In each nook most melancholy,—
There the traveller meets, aghast,
Sheeted Memories of the Past—
Shrouded forms that start and sigh
As they pass the wanderer by—
White-robed forms of friends long given,
In agony, to the Earth—and Heaven.

For the heart whose woes are legion
'Tis a peaceful, soothing region—   40
For the spirit that walks in shadow
'Tis—oh, 'tis an Eldorado!
But the traveller, travelling through it,
May not—dare not openly view it;
Never its mysteries are exposed
To the weak human eye unclosed;
So wills its King, who hath forbid
The uplifting of the fringèd lid;
And thus the sad Soul that here passes
Beholds it but through darkened glasses.   50

By a route obscure and lonely,
Haunted by ill angels only,
Where an Eidolon, named NIGHT,
On a black throne reigns upright,
I have wandered home but newly
From this ultimate dim Thule.

1844

THE RAVEN

The best known of Poe's poems and that upon which his fame most securely rests. Originally published in the New York *Evening Mirror*, January 29, 1845, it underwent many though not extensive revisions. Its subject is a favorite with Poe, the grief of a bereaved lover for his lost love. Poe had reviewed Dickens's *Barnaby Rudge*, which began to appear in 1841, and perhaps derived from it his raven, through which the speaker receives the same answer to his questions concerning his despairing mood, hope of reunion, and of forgetfulness. Poe had also reviewed Mrs. Browning's *Lady Geraldine's Courtship* (1844), and there are indebtednesses of meter and expression to the Southern poet, T. H. Chivers. In "The Philosophy of Composition" Poe professes to tell exactly how "The Raven" was written, demonstrating the steps as in a mathematical problem. The account may not be accepted literally, but surely there is much truth in it. A great deal of critical thinking, analysis, and arrangement went into the composition of the poem. The technical procedure set forth is the same as that in his tales. Rossetti said that his "The Blessed Damozel" was inspired by "The Raven": "I saw that Poe had done the utmost it was possible to do with the grief of the lover on earth, and I determined to reverse the conditions, and give utterance to the yearning of the loved one in heaven." "The Raven" was reproduced widely, and translated into foreign languages.

ONCE upon a midnight dreary, while I pon-
    dered, weak and weary,
Over many a quaint and curious volume of
    forgotten lore—
While I nodded, nearly napping, suddenly
    there came a tapping,
As of some one gently rapping, rapping at
    my chamber door.
" 'Tis some visitor," I muttered, "tapping at
    my chamber door—
    Only this and nothing more."

Ah, distinctly I remember it was in the bleak
    December,
And each separate dying ember wrought its
    ghost upon the floor.
Eagerly I wished the morrow;—vainly I had
    sought to borrow
From my books surcease of sorrow—sorrow
    for the lost Lenore—   10

For the rare and radiant maiden whom the
angels name Lenore—
Nameless *here* for evermore.

And the silken sad uncertain rustling of each
purple curtain
Thrilled me—filled me with fantastic terrors
never felt before;
So that now, to still the beating of my heart,
I stood repeating
" 'Tis some visitor entreating entrance at my
chamber door,
Some late visitor entreating entrance at my
chamber door:
This it is and nothing more."

Presently my soul grew stronger; hesitating
then no longer,
"Sir," said I, "or Madam, truly your forgiveness I implore: 20
But the fact is I was napping, and so gently
you came rapping,
And so faintly you came tapping, tapping at
my chamber door,
That I scarce was sure I heard you"—here I
opened wide the door:—
Darkness there and nothing more.

Deep into that darkness peering, long I stood
there wondering, fearing,
Doubting, dreaming dreams no mortals ever
dared to dream before:
But the silence was unbroken, and the stillness gave no token,
And the only word there spoken was the
whispered word, "Lenore?"
This I whispered, and an echo murmured
back the word, "Lenore!"
Merely this and nothing more.   30

Back into the chamber turning, all my soul
within me burning,
Soon again I heard a tapping somewhat
louder than before.
"Surely," said I, "surely that is something at
my window lattice;
Let me see, then, what thereat is, and this
mystery explore;
Let my heart be still a moment and this
mystery explore:
'Tis the wind and nothing more!"

Open here I flung the shutter, when, with
many a flirt and flutter,
In there stepped a stately Raven of the
saintly days of yore;
Not the least obeisance made he; not a minute
stopped or stayed he;
But, with mien of lord or lady, perched above
my chamber door,   40
Perched upon a bust of Pallas just above my
chamber door:
Perched, and sat, and nothing more.

Then this ebony bird beguiling my sad fancy
into smiling
By the grave and stern decorum of the coun-
tenance it wore,
"Though thy crest be shorn and shaven,
thou," I said, "art sure no craven,
Ghastly grim and ancient Raven wandering
from the Nightly shore—
Tell me what thy lordly name is on the
Night's Plutonian shore!"
Quoth the Raven, "Nevermore."

Much I marveled this ungainly fowl to hear
discourse so plainly,
Though its answer little meaning—little rele-
vancy bore;   50
For we cannot help agreeing that no living
human being
Ever yet was blessed with seeing bird above
his chamber door,
Bird or beast upon the sculptured bust above
his chamber door,
With such name as "Nevermore."

But the Raven, sitting lonely on the placid
bust, spoke only
That one word, as if his soul in that one word
he did outpour,
Nothing further then he uttered, not a feather
then he fluttered,
Till I scarcely more than muttered,—
"Other friends have flown before;
On the morrow *he* will leave me, as my Hopes
have flown before."
Then the bird said, "Nevermore."   60

Startled at the stillness broken by reply so
aptly spoken,
"Doubtless," said I, "what it utters is its only
stock and store,

Caught from some unhappy master whom
    unmerciful Disaster
Followed fast and followed faster till his
    songs one burden bore—
Till the dirges of his Hope that melancholy
    burden bore
    Of 'Never—nevermore.'"

But the Raven still beguiling all my fancy into
    smiling,
Straight I wheeled a cushioned seat in front
    of bird and bust and door;
Then, upon the velvet sinking, I betook my-
    self to linking
Fancy unto fancy, thinking what this ominous
    bird of yore,   70
What this grim, ungainly, ghastly, gaunt, and
    ominous bird of yore
    Meant in croaking "Nevermore."

This I sat engaged in guessing, but no syllable
    expressing
To the fowl whose fiery eyes now burned into
    my bosom's core;
This and more I sat divining, with my head
    at ease reclining
On the cushion's velvet lining that the lamp-
    light gloated o'er,
But whose velvet violet lining with the lamp-
    light gloating o'er
    She shall press, ah, nevermore!

Then, methought, the air grew denser, per-
    fumed from an unseen censer
Swung by seraphim whose footfalls tinkled
    on the tufted floor.   80
"Wretch," I cried, "thy God hath lent thee
    —by these angels he hath sent thee
Respite—respite and nepenthe[1] from thy
    memories of Lenore!
Quaff, oh quaff this kind nepenthe, and for-
    get this lost Lenore!"
    Quoth the Raven, "Nevermore."

"Prophet!" said I, "thing of evil! prophet
    still, if bird or devil!
Whether Tempter sent, or whether tempest
    tossed thee here ashore,
Desolate yet all undaunted, on this desert
    land enchanted—

On this home by Horror haunted—tell me
    truly, I implore:
Is there—*is* there balm in Gilead?—tell me—
    tell me, I implore!"
    Quoth the Raven, "Nevermore."   90

"Prophet!" said I, "thing of evil—prophet
    still, if bird or devil!
By that Heaven that bends above us, by that
    God we both adore,
Tell this soul with sorrow laden if, within
    the distant Aidenn,[1]
It shall clasp a sainted maiden whom the
    angels name Lenore—
Clasp a rare and radiant maiden whom the
    angels name Lenore!"
    Quoth the Raven, "Nevermore."

"Be that word our sign of parting, bird or
    fiend!" I shrieked, upstarting:
"Get thee back into the tempest and the
    Night's Plutonian shore!
Leave no black plume as a token of that lie
    thy soul hath spoken!
Leave my loneliness unbroken! quit the bust
    above my door!   100
Take thy beak from out my heart, and take
    thy form from off my door!"
    Quoth the Raven, "Nevermore."

And the Raven, never flitting, *still* is sitting,
    still is sitting
On the pallid bust of Pallas just above my
    chamber door;
And his eyes have all the seeming of a demon's
    that is dreaming,
And the lamplight o'er him streaming throws
    his shadow on the floor:
And my soul from out that shadow that lies
    floating on the floor
    Shall be lifted—nevermore!

1845

ULALUME

Composed not long after the death of Poe's
wife. It used to be termed by critics "semi-
delirious," in its strange geography and its strange
content. The poem is indefinite; but it should be

---

[1] oblivion of grief

[1] variant of Eden

recalled that Poe held indefiniteness, the giving of pleasure, and beauty, to be the essentials of poetry. The speaker has much in common with the hero of "The Raven," who might take such a journey, in imagination, for his lost Lenore, a journey ending at the door of a tomb. The poet communes with his soul, though autobiographical interpretation is not to be insisted upon. S. Foster Damon has pointed out (*T. H. Chivers*, 214–15) indebtedness to Chivers's *Nacoochee*. There is a good discussion of the poem and its problems in the Craig-Alterton *Poe*, cxiii–cxv. Whitty (*Complete Poems*, 247) states that Poe, on transcribing "Ulalume" for a friend, wrote to her: "I would endeavor to explain to you what I really meant—or what I fancied I meant by the poem, if it were not that I remembered Dr. Johnson's bitter and rather just remark about the folly of explaining what, if worth explanation, would explain itself. He has a happy witticism, too, about some book which he calls 'as obscure as a explanatory note.'"

The skies they were ashen and sober;
 The leaves they were crispèd and sere,
 The leaves they were withering and sere;
It was night in the lonesome October
 Of my most immemorial year;
It was hard by the dim lake of Auber,[1]
 In the misty mid region of Weir:
It was down by the dank tarn of Auber,
 In the ghoul-haunted woodland of Weir.

Here once, through an alley Titanic 10
 Of cypress, I roamed with my Soul—
 Of cypress, with Psyche, my Soul.
These were days when my heart was volcanic
 As the scoriac rivers that roll,
 As the lavas that restlessly roll
Their sulphurous currents down Yaanek
 In the ultimate climes of the Pole,
That groan as they roll down Mount Yaanek
 In the realms of the Boreal Pole.

Our talk had been serious and sober, 20
 But our thoughts they were palsied and
  sere,
 Our memories were treacherous and sere,
For we knew not the month was October,
 And we marked not the night of the year,
 (Ah, night of all nights in the year!)

[1] Auber, Weir, and Yaanek are not definite geographical names but are examples of Poe's coinage of names for romantic suggestion.

We noted not the dim lake of Auber
 (Though once we had journeyed down
  here),
Remembered not the dank tarn of Auber,
 Nor the ghoul-haunted woodland of Weir.

And now, as the night was senescent 30
 And star-dials pointed to morn,
 As the star-dials hinted of morn,
At the end of our path a liquescent
 And nebulous lustre was born,
Out of which a miraculous crescent
 Arose, with a duplicate horn,
Astarte's bediamonded crescent
 Distinct with its duplicate horn.

And I said—"She is warmer than Dian:
 She rolls through an ether of sighs, 40
 She revels in a region of sighs:
She has seen that the tears are not dry on
 These cheeks, where the worm never dies,
And has come past the stars of the Lion
 To point us the path to the skies,
 To the Lethean peace of the skies:
Come up, in despite of the Lion,
 To shine on us with her bright eyes:
Come up through the lair of the Lion,
 With love in her luminous eyes." 50

But Psyche, uplifting her finger,
 Said—"Sadly this star I mistrust,
 Her pallor I strangely mistrust:
Oh, hasten!—oh, let us not linger!
 Oh, fly!—let us fly!—for we must."
In terror she spoke, letting sink her
 Wings till they trailed in the dust;
In agony sobbed, letting sink her
 Plumes till they trailed in the dust,
 Till they sorrowfully trailed in the dust. 60

I replied—"This is nothing but dreaming:
 Let us on by this tremulous light!
 Let us bathe in this crystalline light!
Its sibyllic splendor is beaming
 With hope and in beauty tonight:
 See, it flickers up the sky through the night!
Ah, we safely may trust to its gleaming,
 And be sure it will lead us aright:
We safely may trust to a gleaming
 That cannot but guide us aright, 70
 Since it flickers up to Heaven through the
  night."

Thus I pacified Psyche and kissed her,
  And tempted her out of her gloom,
  And conquered her scruples and gloom;
And we passed to the end of the vista,
  But were stopped by the door of a tomb,
  By the door of a legended tomb;
And I said—"What is written, sweet sister,
  On the door of this legended tomb?"
She replied—"Ulalume—Ulalume—   80
  'Tis the vault of thy lost Ulalume!"

Then my heart it grew ashen and sober
  As the leaves that were crispèd and sere,
  As the leaves that were withering and sere,
And I cried—"It was surely October
  On this very night of last year
  That I journeyed—I journeyed down
    here!—
  That I brought a dread burden down
    here—
  On this night of all nights in the year,
  Ah, what demon has tempted me here?   90
Well I know, now, this dim lake of Auber,
  This misty mid region of Weir:
Well I know, now, this dank tarn of Auber,
  This ghoul-haunted woodland of Weir.

1847

THE BELLS

This poem is said to have grown out of a suggestion made to the author by Mrs. L. M. Shew
in the summer of 1848. The first draft consisted
of but eighteen lines. In second and third drafts
the poem grew in length, and finally in a fourth
revision took the form given here. It has had great
praise as one of the finest examples of onomat-
opoeia in the language. It is, says Professor Harrison, "the most perfect imitation in word, sound,
and rhythm, in suggestion, in exquisite mimicry,
of its theme ever written."

I

HEAR the sledges with the bells,
  Silver bells!
What a world of merriment their melody
    foretells!
  How they tinkle, tinkle, tinkle,
    In the icy air of night!
  While the stars, that oversprinkle
  All the heavens, seem to twinkle
    With a crystalline delight;

Keeping time, time, time,
  In a sort of Runic rhyme.   10
To the tintinnabulation that so musically
    wells
  From the bells, bells, bells, bells,
    Bells, bells, bells—
From the jingling and the tinkling of the
    bells.

II

Hear the mellow wedding bells,
  Golden bells!
What a world of happiness their harmony
    foretells!
  Through the balmy air of night
  How they ring out their delight!
    From the molten-golden notes,   20
      And all in tune,
    What a liquid ditty floats
To the turtledove that listens, while she
    gloats
      On the moon!
  Oh, from out the sounding cells,
What a gush of euphony voluminously wells!
    How it swells!
    How it dwells
    On the Future! how it tells
    Of the rapture that impels   30
  To the swinging and the ringing
    Of the bells, bells, bells,
    Of the bells, bells, bells, bells,
      Bells, bells, bells—
To the rhyming and the chiming of the
    bells!

III

Hear the loud alarum bells,
  Brazen bells!
What a tale of terror, now, their turbulency
    tells!
  In the startled ear of night
  How they scream out their affright!   40
    Too much horrified to speak,
    They can only shriek, shriek,
      Out of tune,
In a clamorous appealing to the mercy of the
    fire,
In a mad expostulation with the deaf and
    frantic fire,
    Leaping higher, higher, higher,
    With a desperate desire,

And a resolute endeavor
  Now—now to sit or never,
By the side of the pale-faced moon.   50
  Oh, the bells, bells, bells!
  What a tale their terror tells
    Of Despair!
How they clang, and clash, and roar!
What a horror they outpour
On the bosom of the palpitating air!
  Yet the ear it fully knows,
    By the twanging
    And the clanging,
  How the danger ebbs and flows;   60
Yet the ear distinctly tells,
    In the jangling
    And the wrangling,
How the danger sinks and swells,
By the sinking or the swelling in the anger of
    the bells,
    Of the bells,
Of the bells, bells, bells, bells,
  Bells, bells, bells—
In the clamor and the clangor of the bells!

IV

  Hear the tolling of the bells,   70
    Iron bells!
What a world of solemn thought their mon-
    ody compels!
  In the silence of the night
  How we shiver with affright
At the melancholy menace of their tone!
  For every sound that floats
From the rust within their throats
    Is a groan.
  And the people—ah, the people,
  They that dwell up in the steeple,   80
    All alone,
  And who tolling, tolling, tolling
    In that muffled monotone,
  Feel a glory in so rolling
    On the human heart a stone——
They are neither man nor woman,
They are neither brute nor human,
    They are Ghouls:
  And their king it is who tolls;
  And he rolls, rolls, rolls,   90
    Rolls
  A pæan from the bells;
  And his merry bosom swells
With the pæan of the bells,

And he dances, and he yells:
  Keeping time, time, time,
  In a sort of Runic rhyme,
    To the pæan of the bells,
      Of the bells:
Keeping time, time, time,   100
  In a sort of Runic rhyme,
    To the throbbing of the bells,
    Of the bells, bells, bells—
    To the sobbing of the bells;
Keeping time, time, time,
    As he knells, knells, knells,
  In a happy Runic rhyme,
    To the rolling of the bells,
    Of the bells, bells, bells:
    To the tolling of the bells,   110
Of the bells, bells, bells, bells,
    Bells, bells, bells—
To the moaning and the groaning of the
    bells.

        1849

ELDORADO

"Poe writes of the search for the golden land as
the quest of human happiness in which man never
tires. 'Eldorado' is simple and beautiful, a noble
expression of the ideal as Poe had sought it, and
as all men, to some extent at least, also seek it"
(Alterton and Craig, *Poe*, 507).

  GAYLY bedight,
    A gallant knight,
In sunshine and in shadow,
    Had journeyed long,
    Singing a song,
In search of Eldorado.

    But he grew old,
    This knight so bold,
And o'er his heart a shadow
    Fell as he found   10
    No spot of ground
That looked like Eldorado.

    And, as his strength
    Failed him at length,
He met a pilgrim shadow—
    "Shadow," said he,
    "Where can it be,
This land of Eldorado?"

"Over the Mountains
Of the Moon, 20
Down the Valley of the Shadow,
Ride, boldly ride,"
The shade replied,
"If you seek for Eldorado!"

1849

ANNABEL LEE

This poem is commonly believed to have been written in memory of Poe's wife Virginia. However, to quote Alterton and Craig (*Poe*, 509), "A number of different ladies have been put forward as being inspiration for 'Annabel Lee.' It really does not matter, for Poe would not be the poet he is if it did. The poem is expressive of grief at bereavement as that grief may be sublimated by the recollection of true love and unforgettable beauty."

IT was many and many a year ago,
In a kingdom by the sea,
That a maiden there lived, whom you may know
By the name of Annabel Lee;—
And this maiden she lived with no other thought
Than to love, and be loved by me.

She was a child and *I* was a child,
In this kingdom by the sea;
But we loved with a love that was more than love,
I and my Annabel Lee— 10
With a love that the wingèd seraphs of heaven
Coveted her and me.

And this was the reason that, long ago,
In this kingdom by the sea,
A wind blew out of a cloud by night
Chilling my Annabel Lee;
So that her highborn kinsmen came
And bore her away from me,
To shut her up in a sepulcher
In this kingdom by the sea. 20

The angels, not half so happy in heaven,
Went envying her and me;
Yes! that was the reason (as all men know,
In this kingdom by the sea)
That the wind came out of the cloud, chilling
And killing my Annabel Lee.

But our love it was stronger by far than the love
Of those who were older than we,
Of many far wiser than we;
And neither the angels in heaven above, 30
Nor the demons down under the sea,
Can ever dissever my soul from the soul
Of the beautiful Annabel Lee:

For the moon never beams without bringing me dreams
Of the beautiful Annabel Lee;
And the stars never rise but I feel the bright eyes
Of the beautiful Annabel Lee;
And so, all the night-tide, I lie down by the side
Of my darling—my darling—my life and my bride,
In her sepulcher there by the sea, 40
In her tomb by the side of the sea.

1849

THE FALL OF THE HOUSE OF USHER

This story has been variously characterized as a "prose poem," "study in monotone," and "prose lyric of fear." Poe's "House," stands for an ancient degenerating family and its old decaying family seat, both approaching dissolution. Walpole's *The Castle of Otranto* preceded Poe's story and Hawthorne's *The House of the Seven Gables* followed it in giving the *locale* the prominence of the characters, even in the title. An atmosphere of desolation and disintegration is established at the opening, and maintained till the final effect of total collapse, toward which all the strands of the story converge. In Roderick Usher, the neuropath of impotent will, reserved for a horrible experience, is illustrated a frequent type of hero in Poe's tales.

Son cœur est un luth suspendu;
Sitôt qu'on le touche il résonne.[1]

Béranger

DURING the whole of a dull, dark, and soundless day in the autumn of the year, when the clouds hung oppressively low in the

[1] "His heart is a suspended lute; as soon as it is touched it resounds." Cf. "Israfel," line 2.

heavens, I had been passing alone, on horseback, through a singularly dreary tract of country; and at length found myself, as the shades of the evening drew on, within view of the melancholy House of Usher. I know not how it was, but, with the first glimpse of the building, a sense of insufferable gloom pervaded my spirit. I say insufferable; for the feeling was unrelieved by any of that half pleasurable, because poetic, sentiment with which the mind usually receives even the sternest natural images of the desolate or terrible. I looked upon the scene before me— upon the mere house, and the simple landscape features of the domain, upon the bleak walls, upon the vacant eyelike windows, upon a few rank sedges, and upon a few white trunks of decayed trees—with an utter depression of soul which I can compare to no earthly sensation more properly than to the afterdream of the reveler upon opium: the bitter lapse into everyday life, the hideous dropping off of the veil. There was an iciness, a sinking, a sickening of the heart, an unredeemed dreariness of thought, which no goading of the imagination could torture into aught of the sublime. What was it—I paused to think—what was it that so unnerved me in the contemplation of the House of Usher? It was a mystery all insoluble; nor could I grapple with the shadowy fancies that crowded upon me as I pondered. I was forced to fall back upon the unsatisfactory conclusion that while, beyond doubt, there *are* combinations of very simple natural objects which have the power of thus affecting us, still the analysis of this power lies among considerations beyond our depth. It was possible, I reflected, that a mere different arrangement of the particulars of the scene, of the details of the picture, would be sufficient to modify, or perhaps to annihilate, its capacity for sorrowful impression, and, acting upon this idea, I reined my horse to the precipitous brink of a black and lurid tarn that lay in unruffled luster by the dwelling, and gazed down—but with a shudder even more thrilling than before— upon the remodeled and inverted images of the gray sedge, and the ghastly tree-stems, and the vacant and eyelike windows.

Nevertheless, in this mansion of gloom I now proposed to myself a sojourn of some weeks. Its proprietor, Roderick Usher, had been one of my boon companions in boyhood; but many years had elapsed since our last meeting. A letter, however, had lately reached me in a distant part of the country— a letter from him—which in its wildly importunate nature had admitted of no other than a personal reply. The MS. gave evidence of nervous agitation. The writer spoke of acute bodily illness, of a mental disorder which oppressed him, and of an earnest desire to see me, as his best and indeed his only personal friend, with a view of attempting, by the cheerfulness of my society, some alleviation of his malady. It was the manner in which all this, and much more, was said—it was the apparent *heart* that went with his request— which allowed me no room for hesitation; and I accordingly obeyed forthwith what I still considered a very singular summons.

Although as boys we had been even intimate associates, yet I really knew little of my friend. His reserve had been always excessive and habitual. I was aware, however, that his very ancient family had been noted, time out of mind, for a peculiar sensibility of temperament, displaying itself, through long ages, in many works of exalted art, and manifested of late in repeated deeds of munificent yet unobtrusive charity, as well as in a passionate devotion to the intricacies, perhaps even more than to the orthodox and easily recognizable beauties, of musical science. I had learned, too, the very remarkable fact that the stem of the Usher race, all time-honored as it was, had put forth at no period any enduring branch; in other words, that the entire family lay in the direct line of descent, and had always, with a very trifling and very temporary variation, so lain. It was this deficiency, I considered, while running over in thought the perfect keeping of the character of the premises with the accredited character of the people, and while speculating upon the possible influence which the one, in the long lapse of centuries, might have exercised upon the other—it was this deficiency, perhaps, of collateral issue, and the consequent undeviating transmission from sire to son of the patrimony with the name, which had at length so identified the two as to merge the original title of the estate in the quaint and equivocal appellation of the "House of Usher"—an appellation which seemed to include, in the minds of the peasantry who used it, both the family and the family mansion.

I have said that the sole effect of my somewhat childish experiment, that of looking down within the tarn, had been to deepen the first singular impression. There can be no doubt that the consciousness of the rapid increase of my superstition—for why should I not so term it?—served mainly to accelerate the increase itself. Such, I have long known, is the paradoxical law of all sentiments having terror as a basis. And it might have been for this reason only, that, when I again uplifted my eyes to the house itself from its image in the pool, there grew in my mind a strange fancy—a fancy so ridiculous, indeed, that I but mention it to show the vivid force of the sensations which oppressed me. I had so worked upon my imagination as really to believe that about the whole mansion and domain there hung an atmosphere peculiar to themselves and their immediate vicinity: an atmosphere which had no affinity with the air of heaven, but which had reeked up from the decayed trees, and the gray wall, and the silent tarn; a pestilent and mystic vapor, dull, sluggish, faintly discernible, and leaden-hued.

Shaking off from my spirit what *must* have been a dream, I scanned more narrowly the real aspect of the building. Its principal feature seemed to be that of an excessive antiquity. The discoloration of ages had been great. Minute fungi overspread the whole exterior, hanging in a fine tangled webwork from the eaves. Yet all this was apart from any extraordinary dilapidation. No portion of the masonry had fallen; and there appeared to be a wild inconsistency between its still perfect adaptation of parts and the crumbling condition of the individual stones. In this there was much that reminded me of the specious totality of old woodwork which has rotted for long years in some neglected vault, with no disturbance from the breath of the external air. Beyond this indication of extensive decay, however, the fabric gave little token of instability. Perhaps the eye of a scrutinizing observer might have discovered a barely perceptible fissure, which, extending from the roof of the building in front, made its way down the wall in a zigzag direction, until it became lost in the sullen waters of the tarn.

Noticing these things, I rode over a short causeway to the house. A servant in waiting took my horse, and I entered the Gothic archway of the hall. A valet, of stealthy step, thence conducted me in silence through many dark and intricate passages in my progress to the *studio* of his master. Much that I encountered on the way contributed, I know not how, to heighten the vague sentiments of which I have already spoken. While the objects around me—while the carvings of the ceiling, the somber tapestries of the walls, the ebon blackness of the floors, and the phantasmagoric armorial trophies which rattled as I strode, were but matters to which, or to such as which, I had been accustomed from my infancy,—while I hesitated not to acknowledge how familiar was all this, I still wondered to find how unfamiliar were the fancies which ordinary images were stirring up. On one of the staircases I met the physician of the family. His countenance, I thought, wore a mingled expression of low cunning and perplexity. He accosted me with trepidation and passed on. The valet now threw open a door and ushered me into the presence of his master.

The room in which I found myself was very large and lofty. The windows were long, narrow, and pointed, and at so vast a distance from the black oaken floor as to be altogether inaccessible from within. Feeble gleams of encrimsoned light made their way through the trellised panes, and served to render sufficiently distinct the more prominent objects around; the eye, however, struggled in vain to reach the remoter angles of the chamber, or the recesses of the vaulted and fretted ceiling. Dark draperies hung upon the walls. The general furniture was profuse, comfortless, antique, and tattered. Many books and musical instruments lay scattered about, but failed to give any vitality to the scene. I felt that I breathed an atmosphere of sorrow. An air of stern, deep, and irredeemable gloom hung over and pervaded all.

Upon my entrance, Usher arose from a sofa on which he had been lying at full length, and greeted me with a vivacious warmth which had much in it, I at first thought, of an overdone cordiality—of the constrained effort of the *ennuyé* [1] man of the world. A glance, however, at his countenance, convinced me of his perfect sincerity. We sat down; and for some moments, while he spoke not, I gazed upon him with a feeling half of pity, half of 10 awe. Surely man had never before so terribly altered, in so brief a period, as had Roderick Usher! It was with difficulty that I could bring myself to admit the identity of the wan being before me with the companion of my early boyhood. Yet the character of his face had been at all times remarkable. A cadaverousness of complexion; an eye large, liquid, and luminous beyond comparison; lips somewhat thin and very pallid, but of a surpassingly 20 beautiful curve; a nose of a delicate Hebrew model, but with a breadth of nostril unusual in similar formations; a finely-molded chin, speaking, in its want of prominence, of a want of moral energy; hair of a more than weblike softness and tenuity,—these features, with an inordinate expansion above the regions of the temple, made up altogether a countenance not easily to be forgotten. And now in the mere exaggeration of the prevailing character of 30 these features, and of the expression they were wont to convey, lay so much of change that I doubted to whom I spoke. The now ghastly pallor of the skin, and the now miraculous luster of the eye, above all things startled and even awed me. The silken hair, too, had been suffered to grow all unheeded, and as, in its wild gossamer texture, it floated rather than fell about the face, I could not, even with effort, connect its arabesque expression with 40 any idea of simple humanity.

In the manner of my friend I was at once struck with an incoherence, an inconsistency; and I soon found this to arise from a series of feeble and futile struggles to overcome an habitual trepidancy, an excessive nervous agitation. For something of this nature I had indeed been prepared, no less by his letter than by reminiscences of certain boyish traits, and by conclusions deduced from his peculiar 50

[1] "bored"

physical conformation and temperament. His action was alternately vivacious and sullen. His voice varied rapidly from a tremulous indecision (when the animal spirits seemed utterly in abeyance) to that species of energetic concision—that abrupt, weighty, unhurried, and hollow-sounding enunciation, that leaden, self-balanced, and perfectly modulated guttural utterance—which may be observed in the lost drunkard, or the irreclaimable eater of opium, during the periods of his most intense excitement.

It was thus that he spoke of the object of my visit, of his earnest desire to see me, and of the solace he expected me to afford him. He entered at some length into what he conceived to be the nature of his malady. It was, he said, a constitutional and a family evil, and one for which he despaired to find a remedy— a mere nervous affection, he immediately added, which would undoubtedly soon pass off. It displayed itself in a host of unnatural sensations. Some of these, as he detailed them, interested and bewildered me; although, perhaps, the terms and the general manner of the narration had their weight. He suffered much from a morbid acuteness of the senses; the most insipid food was alone endurable; he could wear only garments of certain texture; the odors of all flowers were oppressive; his eyes were tortured by even a faint light; and there were but peculiar sounds, and these from stringed instruments, which did not inspire him with horror.

To an anomalous species of terror I found him a bounden slave. "I shall perish," said he, "I *must* perish in this deplorable folly. Thus, thus, and not otherwise, shall I be lost. I dread the events of the future, not in themselves, but in their results. I shudder at the thought of any, even the most trivial, incident, which may operate upon this intolerable agitation of soul. I have, indeed, no abhorrence of danger, except in its absolute effect,—in terror. In this unnerved, in this pitiable condition, I feel that the period will sooner or later arrive when I must abandon life and reason together in some struggle with the grim phantasm, FEAR."

I learned moreover at intervals, and through broken and equivocal hints, another singular feature of his mental condition. He was enchained by certain superstitious impressions in regard to the dwelling which he tenanted, and whence for many years he had never ventured forth, in regard to an influence whose supposititious force was conveyed in terms too shadowy here to be restated,—an influence which some peculiarities in the mere form and substance of his family mansion had, by dint of long sufferance, he said, obtained over his spirit; an effect which the *physique* of the gray walls and turrets, and of the dim tarn into which they all looked down, had at length brought about upon the *morale* of his existence.

He admitted, however, although with hesitation, that much of the peculiar gloom which thus afflicted him could be traced to a more natural and far more palpable origin,—to the severe and long-continued illness, indeed to the evidently approaching dissolution, of a tenderly beloved sister, his sole companion for long years, his last and only relative on earth. "Her decease," he said, with a bitterness which I can never forget, "would leave him (him, the hopeless and the frail) the last of the ancient race of the Ushers." While he spoke, the lady Madeline (for so was she called) passed slowly through a remote portion of the apartment, and, without having noticed my presence, disappeared. I regarded her with an utter astonishment not unmingled with dread, and yet I found it impossible to account for such feelings. A sensation of stupor oppressed me, as my eyes followed her retreating steps. When a door, at length, closed upon her, my glance sought instinctively and eagerly the countenance of the brother; but he had buried his face in his hands, and I could only perceive that a far more than ordinary wanness had overspread the emaciated fingers through which trickled many passionate tears.

The disease of the lady Madeline had long baffled the skill of her physicians. A settled apathy, a gradual wasting away of the person, and frequent although transient affections of a partially cataleptical character, were the unusual diagnosis. Hitherto she had steadily borne up against the pressure of her malady, and had not betaken herself finally to bed;

but, on the closing-in of the evening of my arrival at the house, she succumbed (as her brother told me at night with inexpressible agitation) to the prostrating power of the destroyer; and I learned that the glimpse I had obtained of her person would thus probably be the last I should obtain,—that the lady, at least while living, would be seen by me no more.

For several days ensuing, her name was unmentioned by either Usher or myself; and during this period I was busied in earnest endeavors to alleviate the melancholy of my friend. We painted and read together; or I listened, as if in a dream, to the wild improvisations of his speaking guitar. And thus, as a closer and still closer intimacy admitted me more unreservedly into the recesses of his spirit, the more bitterly did I perceive the futility of all attempt at cheering a mind from which darkness, as if an inherent positive quality, poured forth upon all objects of the moral and physical universe, in one unceasing radiation of gloom.

I shall ever bear about me a memory of the many solemn hours I thus spent alone with the master of the House of Usher. Yet I should fail in any attempt to convey an idea of the exact character of the studies, or of the occupations, in which he involved me, or led me the way. An excited and highly distempered ideality threw a sulphureous luster over all. His long, improvised dirges will ring forever in my ears. Among other things, I hold painfully in mind a certain singular perversion and amplification of the wild air of the last waltz of Von Weber. From the paintings over which his elaborate fancy brooded, and which grew, touch by touch, into vaguenesses at which I shuddered the more thrillingly because I shuddered knowing not why,—from these paintings (vivid as their images now are before me) I would in vain endeavor to educe more than a small portion which should lie within the compass of merely written words. By the utter simplicity, by the nakedness of his designs, he arrested and overawed attention. If ever mortal painted an idea, that mortal was Roderick Usher. For me at least, in the circumstances then surrounding me, there arose, out of the pure abstractions which the hypochondriac contrived to throw upon his canvas, an intensity of intolerable awe, no shadow of which felt I ever yet in the contemplation of the certainly glowing yet too concrete reveries of Fuseli.

One of the phantasmagoric conceptions of my friend, partaking not so rigidly of the spirit of abstraction, may be shadowed forth, although feebly, in words. A small picture presented the interior of an immensely long 10 and rectangular vault or tunnel, with low walls, smooth, white, and without interruption or device. Certain accessory points of the design served well to convey the idea that this excavation lay at an exceeding depth below the surface of the earth. No outlet was observed in any portion of its vast extent, and no torch, or other artificial source of light, was discernible; yet a flood of intense rays rolled throughout, and bathed the whole in a ghastly 20 and inappropriate splendor.

I have just spoken of that morbid condition of the auditory nerve which rendered all music intolerable to the sufferer, with the exception of certain effects of stringed instruments. It was, perhaps, the narrow limits to which he thus confined himself upon the guitar, which gave birth, in great measure, to the fantastic character of his performances. But the fervid *facility* of his *impromptus* could 30 not be so accounted for. They must have been, and were, in the notes as well as in the words of his wild fantasias (for he not unfrequently accompanied himself with rimed verbal improvisations), the result of that intense mental collectedness and concentration to which I have previously alluded as observable only in particular moments of the highest artificial excitement. The words of one of these rhapsodies I have easily remembered. I was, 40 perhaps, the more forcibly impressed with it as he gave it, because, in the under or mystic current of its meaning, I fancied that I perceived, and for the first time, a full consciousness, on the part of Usher, of the tottering of his lofty reason upon her throne. The verses, which were entitled "The Haunted Palace,"[1] ran very nearly, if not accurately, thus:—

[1] "By 'The Haunted Palace,'" Poe said to Griswold, "I mean to imply a mind haunted by phantoms— a disordered brain."

I

In the greenest of our valleys
  By good angels tenanted,
Once a fair and stately palace—
  Radiant palace—reared its head.
In the monarch Thought's dominion,
  It stood there;
Never seraph spread a pinion
  Over fabric half so fair.

II

Banners yellow, glorious, golden,
  On its roof did float and flow
(This—all this—was in the olden
  Time long ago),
And every gentle air that dallied,
  In that sweet day,
Along the ramparts plumed and pallid,
  A wingèd odor went away.

III

Wanderers in that happy valley
  Through two luminous windows saw
Spirits moving musically
  To a lute's well-tunèd law,
Round about a throne, where sitting,
  Porphyrogene,[1]
In state his glory well befitting,
  The ruler of the realm was seen.

IV

And all with pearl and ruby glowing
  Was the fair palace door,
Through which came flowing, flowing, flowing,
  And sparkling evermore,
A troop of Echoes, whose sweet duty
  Was but to sing,
In voices of surpassing beauty,
  The wit and wisdom of their king.

V

But evil things, in robes of sorrow,
  Assailed the monarch's high estate;
(Ah, let us mourn, for never morrow
  Shall dawn upon him, desolate!)
And, round about his home, the glory
  That blushed and bloomed
Is but a dim-remembered story
  Of the old time entombed.

VI

And travelers now within that valley
  Through the red-litten windows see

[1] a name which means "born to the purple"

Vast forms that move fantastically
  To a discordant melody;
While, like a ghastly rapid river,
  Through the pale door,
A hideous throng rush out forever,
  And laugh—but smile no more.

I well remember that suggestions arising from this ballad led us into a train of thought, wherein there became manifest an opinion of Usher's which I mention, not so much on account of its novelty (for other men[1] have thought thus) as on account of the pertinacity with which he maintained it. This opinion, in its general form, was that of the sentience of all vegetable things. But in his disordered fancy, the idea had assumed a more daring character, and trespassed, under certain conditions, upon the kingdom of inorganization. I lack words to express the full extent or the earnest *abandon* of his persuasion. The belief, however, was connected (as I have previously hinted) with the gray stones of the home of his forefathers. The conditions of the sentience had been here, he imagined, fulfilled in the method of collocation of these stones,—in the order of their arrangement, as well as in that of the many fungi which overspread them, and of the decayed trees which stood around; above all, in the long undisturbed endurance of this arrangement, and in its reduplication in the still waters of the tarn. Its evidence—the evidence of the sentience—was to be seen, he said (and I here started as he spoke), in the gradual yet certain condensation of an atmosphere of their own about the waters and the walls. The result was discoverable, he added, in that silent yet importunate and terrible influence which for centuries had molded the destinies of his family, and which made *him* what I now saw him,—what he was. Such opinions need no comment, and I will make none.

Our books—the books which for years had formed no small portion of the mental existence of the invalid—were, as might be supposed, in strict keeping with this character of phantasm. We pored together over such works as the Ververt and Chartreuse of Gresset; the Belphegor of Machiavelli; the Heaven and Hell of Swedenborg; the Subterranean Voyage of Nicholas Klimm by Holberg; the Chiromancy of Robert Flud, of Jean D'Indaginé, and of De la Chambre; the Journey into the Blue Distance of Tieck; and the City of the Sun of Campanella. One favorite volume was a small octavo edition of the *Directorium Inquisitorum*, by the Dominican Eymeric de Gironne; and there were passages in Pomponius Mela, about the old African Satyrs and Ægipans, over which Usher would sit dreaming for hours. His chief delight, however, was found in the perusal of an exceedingly rare and curious book in quarto Gothic,—the manual of a forgotten church,—the *Vigiliæ Mortuorum secundum Chorum Ecclesiæ Maguntinæ.*[1]

I could not help thinking of the wild ritual of this work, and of its probable influence upon the hypochondriac, when one evening, having informed me abruptly that the lady Madeline was no more, he stated his intention of preserving her corpse for a fortnight, (previously to its final interment) in one of the numerous vaults within the main walls of the building. The worldly reason, however, assigned for this singular proceeding was one which I did not feel at liberty to dispute. The brother had been led to his resolution (so he told me) by consideration of the unusual character of the malady of the deceased, of certain obtrusive and eager inquiries on the part of her medical men, and of the remote and exposed situation of the burial ground of the family. I will not deny that when I called to mind the sinister countenance of the person whom I met upon the staircase, on the day of my arrival at the house, I had no desire to oppose what I regarded as at best but a harmless, and by no means an unnatural, precaution.

At the request of Usher, I personally aided him in the arrangements for the temporary entombment. The body having been encoffined, we two alone bore it to its rest. The vault in which we placed it (and which had been so long unopened that our torches, half smothered in its oppressive atmosphere, gave us little opportunity for investigation) was small, damp, and entirely without means of

---

[1] Watson, Dr. Percival, Spallanzani, and especially the Bishop of Llandaff.—See "Chemical Essays," vol. v. [*Poe's note.*]

[1] "The Watches of the Dead according to the Choir of the Church of Mayence"

admission for light; lying, at great depth, immediately beneath that portion of the building in which was my own sleeping apartment. It had been used apparently, in remote feudal times, for the worst purposes of a donjon keep, and in later days as a place of deposit for powder, or some other highly combustible substance, as a portion of its floor, and the whole interior of a long archway through which we reached it, were carefully sheathed with copper. The door, of massive iron, had been also similarly protected. Its immense weight caused an unusually sharp grating sound as it moved upon its hinges.

Having deposited our mournful burden upon tressels within this region of horror, we partially turned aside the yet unscrewed lid of the coffin, and looked upon the face of the tenant. A striking similitude between the brother and sister now first arrested my attention; and Usher, divining, perhaps, my thoughts, murmured out some few words from which I learned that the deceased and himself had been twins, and that sympathies of a scarcely intelligible nature had always existed between them. Our glances, however, rested not long upon the dead, for we could not regard her unawed. The disease which had thus entombed the lady in the maturity of youth, had left, as usual in all maladies of a strictly cataleptical character, the mockery of a faint blush upon the bosom and the face, and that suspiciously lingering smile upon the lip which is so terrible in death. We replaced and screwed down the lid, and having secured the door of iron, made our way, with toil, into the scarcely less gloomy apartments of the upper portion of the house.

And now, some days of bitter grief having elapsed, an observable change came over the features of the mental disorder of my friend. His ordinary manner had vanished. His ordinary occupations were neglected or forgotten. He roamed from chamber to chamber with hurried, unequal, and objectless step. The pallor of his countenance had assumed, if possible, a more ghastly hue, but the luminousness of his eye had utterly gone out. The once occasional huskiness of his tone was heard no more; and a tremulous quaver, as if of extreme terror, habitually characterized his utterance. There were times, indeed, when I thought his unceasingly agitated mind was laboring with some oppressive secret, to divulge which he struggled for the necessary courage. At times, again, I was obliged to resolve all into the mere inexplicable vagaries of madness, for I beheld him gazing upon vacancy for long hours, in an attitude of the profoundest attention, as if listening to some imaginary sound. It was no wonder that his condition terrified—that it infected me. I felt creeping upon me, by slow yet certain degrees, the wild influences of his own fantastic yet impressive superstitions.

It was, especially, upon retiring to bed late in the night of the seventh or eighth day after the placing of the lady Madeline within the donjon, that I experienced the full power of such feelings. Sleep came not near my couch, while the hours waned and waned away. I struggled to reason off the nervousness which had dominion over me. I endeavored to believe that much if not all of what I felt was due to the bewildering influence of the gloomy furniture of the room,—of the dark and tattered draperies which, tortured into motion by the breath of a rising tempest, swayed fitfully to and fro upon the walls, and rustled uneasily about the decorations of the bed. But my efforts were fruitless. An irrepressible tremor gradually pervaded my frame; and at length there sat upon my very heart an incubus of utterly causeless alarm. Shaking this off with a gasp and a struggle, I uplifted myself upon the pillows, and, peering earnestly within the intense darkness of the chamber, hearkened—I know not why, except that an instinctive spirit prompted me—to certain low and indefinite sounds which came, through the pauses of the storm, at long intervals, I knew not whence. Overpowered by an intense sentiment of horror, unaccountable yet unendurable, I threw on my clothes with haste (for I felt that I should sleep no more during the night), and endeavored to arouse myself from the pitiable condition to which I had fallen, by pacing rapidly to and fro through the apartment.

I had taken but few turns in this manner, when a light step on an adjoining staircase arrested my attention. I presently recognized it as that of Usher. In an instant afterward he rapped with a gentle touch at my door, and entered, bearing a lamp. His countenance was, as usual, cadaverously wan—but, moreover, there was a species of mad hilarity in his eyes,—an evidently restrained hysteria in his whole demeanor. His air appalled me—but any- thing was preferable to the solitude which I had so long endured, and I even welcomed his presence as a relief.

"And you have not seen it?" he said abruptly, after having stared about him for some moments in silence,—"you have not then seen it?—but, stay! you shall." Thus speaking, and having carefully shaded his lamp, he hurried to one of the casements, and threw it freely open to the storm.

The impetuous fury of the entering gust nearly lifted us from our feet. It was, indeed, a tempestuous yet sternly beautiful night, and one wildly singular in its terror and its beauty. A whirlwind had apparently collected its force in our vicinity, for there were frequent and violent alterations in the direction of the wind; and the exceeding density of the clouds (which hung so low as to press upon the turrets of the house) did not prevent our perceiving the lifelike velocity with which they flew careering from all points against each other, without passing away into the distance. I say that even their exceeding density did not pre- vent our perceiving this; yet we had no glimpse of the moon or stars, nor was there any flashing forth of the lightning. But the under surfaces of the huge masses of agitated vapor, as well as all terrestrial objects immediately around us, were glowing in the unnatural light of a faintly luminous and distinctly visible gaseous exhalation which hung about and enshrouded the mansion.

"You must not—you shall not behold this!" said I shudderingly, to Usher, as I led him with a gentle violence from the window to a seat. "These appearances, which bewilder you, are merely electrical phenomena not un- common—or it may be that they have their ghastly origin in the rank miasma of the tarn. Let us close this casement; the air is chilling and dangerous to your frame. Here is one of your favorite romances. I will read, and you shall listen;—and so we will pass away this terrible night together."

The antique volume which I had taken up was the "Mad Trist"[1] of Sir Launcelot Can- ning, but I had called it a favorite of Usher's more in sad jest than in earnest; for, in truth, there is little in its uncouth and unimaginative prolixity which could have had interest for the lofty and spiritual ideality of my friend. It was, however, the only book immediately at hand; and I indulged a vague hope that the excite- ment which now agitated the hypochondriac might find relief (for the history of mental disorder is full of similar anomalies) even in the extremeness of the folly which I should read. Could I have judged, indeed, by the wild, overstrained air of vivacity with which he hearkened, or apparently hearkened, to the words of the tale, I might well have con- gratulated myself upon the success of my design.

I had arrived at that well-known portion of the story where Ethelred, the hero of the Trist, having sought in vain for peaceable admission into the dwelling of the hermit, proceeds to make good an entrance by force. Here, it will be remembered, the words of the narrative run thus:—

"And Ethelred, who was by nature of a doughty heart, and who was now mighty withal on account of the powerfulness of the wine which he had drunken, waited no longer to hold parley with the hermit, who, in sooth, was of an obstinate and maliceful turn, but, feeling the rain upon his shoulders, and fearing the rising of the tempest, uplifted his mace outright, and with blows made quickly room in the plankings of the door for his gauntleted hand; and now, pulling therewith sturdily, he so cracked, and ripped, and tore all asunder, that the noise of the dry and hollow-sounding wood alarumed and reverberated throughout the forest."

At the termination of this sentence I started, and for a moment paused; for it appeared to me (although I at once concluded that my excited fancy had deceived me)—it appeared to me that from some very remote portion of the mansion there came, indistinctly, to my ears, what might have been in its exact

[1] The names both of the volume and the author were apparently invented by Poe.

similarity of character the echo (but a stifled and dull one certainly) of the very cracking and ripping sound which Sir Launcelot had so particularly described. It was, beyond doubt, the coincidence alone which had arrested my attention; for, amid the rattling of the sashes of the casements, and the ordinary commingled noises of the still increasing storm, the sound, in itself, had nothing, surely, which should have interested or disturbed me. I continued the story:—

"But the good champion Ethelred, now entering within the door, was sore enraged and amazed to perceive no signal of the maliceful hermit; but, in the stead thereof, a dragon of a scaly and prodigious demeanor, and of a fiery tongue, which sate in guard before a palace of gold with a floor of silver; and upon the wall there hung a shield of shining brass with this legend enwritten:—

Who entereth herein, a conqueror hath bin;
Who slayeth the dragon, the shield he shall win.

And Ethelred uplifted his mace, and struck upon the head of the dragon, which fell before him, and gave up his pesty breath, with a shriek so horrid and harsh, and withal so piercing, that Ethelred had fain to close his ears with his hands against the dreadful noise of it, the like whereof was never before heard."

Here again I paused abruptly, and now with a feeling of wild amazement, for there could be no doubt whatever that, in this instance, I did actually hear (although from what direction it proceeded I found it impossible to say) a low and apparently distant, but harsh, protracted, and most unusual screaming or grating sound,—the exact counterpart of what my fancy had already conjured up for the dragon's unnatural shriek as described by the romancer.

Oppressed as I certainly was, upon the occurrence of this second and most extraordinary coincidence, by a thousand conflicting sensations, in which wonder and extreme terror were predominant, I still retained sufficient presence of mind to avoid exciting, by any observation, the sensitive nervousness of my companion. I was by no means certain that he had noticed the sounds in question; although, assuredly, a strange alteration had during the last few minutes taken place in his demeanor. From a position fronting my own, he had gradually brought round his chair, so as to sit with his face to the door of the chamber; and thus I could but partially perceive his features, although I saw that his lips trembled as if he were murmuring inaudibly. His head had dropped upon his breast; yet I knew that he was not asleep, from the wide and rigid opening of the eyes as I caught a glance of it in profile. The motion of his body, too, was at variance with this idea, for he rocked from side to side with a gentle yet constant and uniform sway. Having rapidly taken notice of all this, I resumed the narrative of Sir Launcelot, which thus proceeded:—

"And now the champion, having escaped from the terrible fury of the dragon, bethinking himself of the brazen shield, and of the breaking up of the enchantment which was upon it, removed the carcass from out of the way before him, and approached valorously over the silver pavement of the castle to where the shield was upon the wall; which in sooth tarried not for his full coming, but fell down at his feet upon the silver floor, with a mighty great and terrible ringing sound."

No sooner had these syllables passed my lips than—as if a shield of brass had indeed, at the moment, fallen heavily upon a floor of silver—I became aware of a distinct, hollow, metallic, and clangorous yet apparently muffled reverberation. Completely unnerved, I leaped to my feet; but the measured rocking movement of Usher was undisturbed. I rushed to the chair in which he sat. His eyes were bent fixedly before him, and throughout his whole countenance there reigned a stony rigidity. But, as I placed my hand upon his shoulder, there came a strong shudder over his whole person; a sickly smile quivered about his lips; and I saw that he spoke in a low, hurried, and gibbering murmur, as if unconscious of my presence. Bending closely over him, I at length drank in the hideous import of his words.

"Not hear it?—yes, I hear it, and *have* heard it. Long—long—long—many minutes, many hours, many days, have I heard it, yet I dared not—oh, pity me, miserable wretch that I am!—I dared not—I *dared* not speak! *We have put her living in the tomb!* Said I not that my senses were acute? I *now* tell you that I heard her first feeble movements in the hollow coffin. I heard them—many, many days ago— yet I dared not—*I dared not speak!* And now —tonight—Ethelred—ha! ha!—the break- ing of the hermit's door, and the death- cry of the dragon, and the clangor of the shield!—say, rather, the rending of her coffin, and the grating of the iron hinges of her prison, and her struggles within the coppered arch- way of the vault! Oh, whither shall I fly? Will she not be here anon? Is she not hurrying to upbraid me for my haste? Have I not heard her footstep on the stair? Do I not distinguish that heavy and horrible beating of her heart? Madman!"—here he sprang furiously to his feet, and shrieked out his syllables, as if in the effort he were giving up his soul—"*Madman! I tell you that she now stands without the door!*"

As if in the superhuman energy of his utterance there had been found the potency of a spell, the huge antique panels to which the speaker pointed threw slowly back, upon the instant, their ponderous and ebony jaws. It was the work of the rushing gust—but then without those doors there *did* stand the lofty and enshrouded figure of the lady Madeline of Usher! There was blood upon her white robes, and the evidence of some bitter struggle upon every portion of her emaciated frame. For a moment she remained trembling and reeling to and fro upon the threshold—then, with a low moaning cry, fell heavily inward upon the person of her brother, and, in her violent and now final death agonies, bore him to the floor a corpse, and a victim to the terrors he had anticipated.

From that chamber and from that mansion I fled aghast. The storm was still abroad in all its wrath as I found myself crossing the old causeway. Suddenly there shot along the path a wild light, and I turned to see whence a gleam so unusual could have issued; for the vast house and its shadows were alone behind me. The radiance was that of the full, setting, and blood-red moon, which now shone vividly through that once barely discernible fissure, of which I have before spoken as extending from the roof of the building, in a zigzag direction, to the base. While I gazed, this fissure rapidly widened—there came a fierce breath of the whirlwind—the entire orb of the satellite burst at once upon my sight—my brain reeled as I saw the mighty walls rushing asunder—there was a long, tumultuous shouting sound like the voice of a thousand waters—and the deep and dank tarn at my feet closed sullenly and silently over the fragments of the "*House of Usher.*"

1839

THE MASQUE OF THE RED DEATH

Poe was at his best in the composition of spectral fantasies. The structure of this story is as carefully wrought as that of "The Fall of the House of Usher," and, like the latter, it presents a single episode in a skilfully manipulated setting. In this story it is that bizarre, rich environment that he so often imagines. Striking features are the de- scription of the sequence of rooms, with their "Gothic" properties, the figures in the masquer- ade, and the culminating encounter in the last room, for which all the preceding details have prepared. The language of the tale is rhythmic and poetic.

THE "Red Death" had long devastated the country. No pestilence had ever been so fatal, or so hideous. Blood was its avatar[1] and its seal—the redness and the horror of blood. There were sharp pains, and sudden dizziness, and then profuse bleeding at the pores, with dissolution. The scarlet stains upon the body, and especially upon the face, of the victim were the pest ban which shut him out from the aid and from the sympathy of his fellow- men. And the whole seizure, progress, and termination of the disease were the incidents of half an hour.

But the Prince Prospero was happy and dauntless and sagacious. When his dominions were half depopulated, he summoned to his presence a thousand hale and lighthearted friends from among the knights and dames of his court, and with these retired to the deep seclusion of one of his castellated abbeys. This was an extensive and magnificent structure, the creation of the Prince's own eccentric yet august taste. A strong and lofty wall girdled it

[1] reincarnation, symbol

in. This wall had gates of iron. The courtiers, having entered, brought furnaces and massy hammers, and welded the bolts. They resolved to leave means neither of ingress or egress to the sudden impulses of despair or of frenzy from within. The abbey was amply provisioned. With such precautions the courtiers might bid defiance to contagion. The external world could take care of itself. In the mean time it was folly to grieve, or to think. The Prince had provided all the appliances of pleasure. There were buffoons, there were improvisatori,[1] there were ballet dancers, there were musicians, there was Beauty, there was wine. All these and security were within. Without was the "Red Death."

It was toward the close of the fifth or sixth month of his seclusion, and while the pestilence raged most furiously abroad, that the Prince Prospero entertained his thousand friends at a masked ball of the most unusual magnificence.

It was a voluptuous scene, that masquerade. But first let me tell of the rooms in which it was held. There were seven—an imperial suite. In many palaces, however, such suites form a long and straight vista, while the folding-doors slide back nearly to the walls on either hand, so that the view of the whole extent is scarcely impeded. Here the case was very different, as might have been expected from the Prince's love of the bizarre. The apartments were so irregularly disposed that the vision embraced but little more than one at a time. There was a sharp turn at every twenty or thirty yards, and at each turn a novel effect. To the right and left, in the middle of each wall, a tall and narrow Gothic window looked out upon a closed corridor which pursued the windings of the suite. These windows were of stained glass, whose color varied in accordance with the prevailing hue of the decorations of the chamber into which it opened. That at the eastern extremity was hung, for example, in blue—and vividly blue were its windows. The second chamber was purple in its ornaments and tapestries, and here the panes were purple. The third was green throughout, and so were the casements. The fourth was furnished and lighted with

[1] those who compose and sing extempore

orange, the fifth with white, the sixth with violet. The seventh apartment was closely shrouded in black velvet tapestries that hung all over the ceiling and down the walls, falling in heavy folds upon a carpet of the same material and hue. But, in this chamber only, the color of the windows failed to correspond with the decorations. The panes here were scarlet—a deep blood-color. Now in no one of the seven apartments was there any lamp or candelabrum, amid the profusion of golden ornaments that lay scattered to and fro or depended from the roof. There was no light of any kind emanating from lamp or candle within the suite of chambers. But in the corridors that followed the suite there stood, opposite to each window, a heavy tripod, bearing a brazier of fire, that projected its rays through the tinted glass and so glaringly illumined the room. And thus were produced a multitude of gaudy and fantastic appearances. But in the western or black chamber the effect of the firelight that streamed upon the dark hangings through the blood-tinted panes was ghastly in the extreme, and produced so wild a look upon the countenances of those who entered that there were few of the company bold enough to set foot within its precincts at all.

It was in this apartment, also, that there stood against the western wall a gigantic clock of ebony. Its pendulum swung to and fro with a dull, heavy, monotonous clang; and when the minute hand made the circuit of the face, and the hour was to be stricken, there came from the brazen lungs of the clock a sound which was clear and loud and deep and exceedingly musical, but of so peculiar a note and emphasis that, at each lapse of an hour, the musicians of the orchestra were constrained to pause, momentarily, in their performance, to hearken to the sound; and thus the waltzers perforce ceased their evolutions; and there was a brief disconcert of the whole gay company; and, while the chimes of the clock yet rang, it was observed that the giddiest grew pale, and the more aged and sedate passed their hands over their brows as if in confused revery or meditation. But when the echoes had fully ceased, a light laughter at once pervaded the assembly; the musicians looked at each other and smiled as if at their own nervousness and folly, and made whispering vows, each to the other, that the next chiming of the clock should produce in them no similar emotion; and then, after the lapse of sixty minutes (which embrace three thousand and six hundred seconds of the Time that flies) there came yet another chiming of the clock, and then were the same disconcert and tremulousness and meditation as before.

But, in spite of these things, it was a gay and magnificent revel. The tastes of the Prince were peculiar. He had a fine eye for colors and effects. He disregarded the *decora*[1] of mere fashion. His plans were bold and fiery, and his conceptions glowed with barbaric luster. There are some who would have thought him mad. His followers felt that he was not. It was necessary to hear and see and touch him to be *sure* that he was not.

He had directed, in great part, the movable embellishments of the seven chambers, upon occasion of this great *fête;* and it was his own guiding taste which had given character to the masqueraders. Be sure they were grotesque. There were much glare and glitter and piquancy and phantasm—much of what has been since seen in *Hernani*.[2] There were arabesque figures with unsuited limbs and appointments. There were delirious fancies such as the madman fashions. There was much of the beautiful, much of the wanton, much of the bizarre, something of the terrible, and not a little of that which might have excited disgust. To and fro in the seven chambers there stalked, in fact, a multitude of dreams. And these—the dreams—writhed in and about, taking hue from the rooms, and causing the wild music of the orchestra to seem as the echo of their steps. And, anon, there strikes the ebony clock which stands in the hall of the velvet. And then, for a moment, all is still, and all is silent save the voice of the clock. The dreams are stiff-frozen as they stand. But the echoes of the chime die away—they have endured but an instant—and a light, half-subdued laughter floats after them as they depart. And now again the music swells, and the dreams live, and writhe to and fro more merrily than ever, taking hue from the many tinted windows through which stream the rays from the tripods. But to the chamber which lies most westwardly of the seven, there are now none of the maskers who venture; for the night is waning away, and there flows a ruddier light through the blood-colored panes; and the blackness of the sable drapery appalls; and to him whose foot falls upon the sable carpet, there comes from the near clock of ebony a muffled peal more solemnly emphatic than any which reaches *their* ears who indulge in the more remote gayeties of the other apartments.

But these other apartments were densely crowded, and in them beat feverishly the heart of life. And the revel went whirlingly on, until at length there commenced the sounding of midnight upon the clock. And then the music ceased, as I have told; and the evolutions of the waltzers were quieted; and there was an uneasy cessation of all things as before. But now there were twelve strokes to be sounded by the bell of the clock; and thus it happened, perhaps, that more of thought crept, with more of time, into the meditations of the thoughtful among those who reveled. And thus, too, it happened, perhaps, that before the last echoes of the last chime had utterly sunk into silence, there were many individuals in the crowd who had found leisure to become aware of the presence of a masked figure which had arrested the attention of no single individual before. And the rumor of this new presence having spread itself whisperingly around, there arose at length from the whole company a buzz, or murmur, expressive of disapprobation and surprise—then, finally, of terror, of horror, and of disgust.

In an assembly of phantasms such as I have painted, it may well be supposed that no ordinary appearance could have excited such sensation. In truth the masquerade license of the night was nearly unlimited; but the figure in question had out-Heroded Herod,[1] and gone beyond the bounds of even the Prince's in-

---

[1] decorations   [2] the famous tragedy produced in 1830 by Victor Hugo, usually regarded as the beginning in France of the nineteenth-century romantic drama

[1] an expression in Hamlet's speech to the players (*Hamlet*, III, II)

definite decorum. There are chords in the hearts of the most reckless which cannot be touched without emotion. Even with the utterly lost, to whom life and death are equally jests, there are matters of which no jest can be made. The whole company, indeed, seemed now deeply to feel that in the costume and bearing of the stranger neither wit nor propriety existed. The figure was tall and gaunt, and shrouded from head to foot in the habiliments of the grave. The mask which concealed the visage was made so nearly to resemble the countenance of a stiffened corpse that the closest scrutiny must have had difficulty in detecting the cheat. And yet all this might have been endured, if not approved, by the mad revelers around. But the mummer had gone so far as to assume the type of the Red Death. His vesture was dabbled in *blood*— and his broad brow, with all the features of the face, was besprinkled with the scarlet horror.

When the eyes of Prince Prospero fell upon this spectral image (which with a slow and solemn movement, as if more fully to sustain its *rôle*, stalked to and fro among the waltzers) he was seen to be convulsed, in the first moment, with a strong shudder either of terror or distaste; but, in the next, his brow reddened with rage.

"Who dares?" he demanded hoarsely of the courtiers who stood near him—"who dares insult us with this blasphemous mockery? Seize him and unmask him—that we may know whom we have to hang at sunrise, from the battlements!"

It was in the eastern or blue chamber in which stood the Prince Prospero as he uttered these words. They rang throughout the seven rooms loudly and clearly—for the Prince was a bold and robust man, and the music had become hushed at the waving of his hand.

It was in the blue room where stood the Prince, with a group of pale courtiers by his side. At first, as he spoke, there was a slight rushing movement of this group in the direction of the intruder, who at the moment was also near at hand, and now, with deliberate and stately step, made closer approach to the speaker. But from a certain nameless awe with which the mad assumptions of the mummer had inspired the whole party, there were found none who put forth hand to seize him; so that, unimpeded, he passed within a yard of the Prince's person; and while the vast assembly, as if with one impulse, shrank from the centers of the rooms to the walls, he made his way uninterruptedly, but with the same solemn and measured step which had distinguished him from the first, through the blue chamber to the purple—through the purple to the green—through the green to the orange—through this again to the white —and even thence to the violet, ere a decided movement had been made to arrest him. It was then, however, that the Prince Prospero, maddening with rage and the shame of his own momentary cowardice, rushed hurriedly through the six chambers, while none followed him, on account of a deadly terror that had seized upon all. He bore aloft a drawn dagger, and had approached, in rapid impetuosity, to within three or four feet of the retreating figure, when the latter, having attained the extremity of the velvet apartment, turned suddenly and confronted his pursuer. There was a sharp cry—and the dagger dropped gleaming upon the sable carpet, upon which, instantly afterwards, fell prostrate in death the Prince Prospero. Then, summoning the wild courage of despair, a throng of the revelers at once threw themselves into the black apartment, and, seizing the mummer, whose tall figure stood erect and motionless within the shadow of the ebony clock, gasped in unutterable horror at finding the grave cerements and corpse-like mask, which they handled with so violent a rudeness, untenanted by any tangible form.

And now was acknowledged the presence of the Red Death. He had come like a thief in the night. And one by one dropped the revelers in the blood-bedewed halls of their revel, and died each in the despairing posture of his fall. And the life of the ebony clock went out with that of the last of the gay. And the flames of the tripods expired. And Darkness and Decay and the Red Death held illimitable dominion over all.

1842

THE CASK OF AMONTILLADO

This tale of vengeful spirit and thrilling malignity was published in an unexpected place, *Godey's
Lady's Book*, November, 1846. Poe's "Murders in
the Rue Morgue" has been criticized as slow in
opening. This tale in dialogue form could hardly
move more quickly or be more condensed. It
shows that Poe could present his stories dramatically, as well as in the usual mode of his day. The
background is the Roman catacombs, the period
not that of the Borgias and the Medicis, but Rome
of the nineteenth century, in the carnival season.
The tone and the suspense are maintained till
the end. Poe does not supply the motivation
of his central character; what it was that urged
him to his diabolic revenge remains unexplained.

THE thousand injuries of Fortunato I had
borne as I best could; but when he ventured
upon insult, I vowed revenge. You, who so
well know the nature of my soul, will not
suppose, however, that I gave utterance to a
threat. *At length* I would be avenged; this
was a point definitively settled—but the very
definitiveness with which it was resolved pre-
cluded the idea of risk. I must not only punish, but punish with impunity. A wrong is
unredressed when retribution overtakes its
redresser. It is equally unredressed when the
avenger fails to make himself felt as such to
him who has done the wrong.

It must be understood that neither by word
nor deed had I given Fortunato cause to doubt
my good will. I continued, as was my wont,
to smile in his face, and he did not perceive
that my smile *now* was at the thought of his
immolation.

He had a weak point—this Fortunato—
although in other regards he was a man to be
respected and even feared. He prided himself
on his connoisseurship in wine. Few Italians
have the true virtuoso[1] spirit. For the most
part their enthusiasm is adopted to suit the
time and opportunity—to practice imposture
upon the British and Austrian millionaires. In
painting and gemmary,[2] Fortunato, like his
countrymen, was a quack—but in the matter
of old wines he was sincere. In this respect I
did not differ from him materially: I was
skillful in the Italian vintages myself, and
bought largely whenever I could.

[1] skilled in critical taste   [2] love of gems

It was about dusk, one evening during the
supreme madness of the carnival season, that
I encountered my friend. He accosted me
with excessive warmth, for he had been
drinking much. The man wore motley. He
had on a tight-fitting parti-striped dress, and
his head was surmounted by the conical cap
and bells. I was so pleased to see him that I
thought I should never have done wringing
his hand.

I said to him, "My dear Fortunato, you are
luckily met. How remarkably well you are
looking today! But I have received a pipe of
what passes for Amontillado, and I have my
doubts."

"How?" said he. "Amontillado? A pipe?
Impossible! And in the middle of the carnival!"

"I have my doubts," I replied; "and I was
silly enough to pay the full Amontillado price
without consulting you in the matter. You
were not to be found, and I was fearful of
losing a bargain."

"Amontillado!"

"I have my doubts."

"Amontillado!"

"And I must satisfy them."

"Amontillado!"

"As you are engaged, I am on my way to
Luchesi. If any one has a critical turn, it is
he. He will tell me—"

"Luchesi cannot tell Amontillado from
Sherry."

"And yet some fools will have it that his
taste is a match for your own."

"Come, let us go."

"Whither?"

"To your vaults."

"My friend, no; I will not impose upon
your good nature. I perceive you have an
engagement. Luchesi—"

"I have no engagement;—come."

"My friend, no. It is not the engagement,
but the severe cold with which I perceive you
are afflicted. The vaults are insufferably damp.
They are incrusted with niter."

"Let us go, nevertheless. The cold is merely
nothing. Amontillado! You have been imposed upon. And as for Luchesi, he cannot
distinguish Sherry from Amontillado."

Thus speaking, Fortunato possessed himself of my arm. Putting on a mask of black

silk, and drawing a *roquelaire*[1] closely about my person, I suffered him to hurry me to my palazzo.

There were no attendants at home; they had absconded to make merry in honor of the time. I had told them that I should not return until the morning, and had given them explicit orders not to stir from the house. These orders were sufficient, I well knew, to insure their immediate disappearance, one and all, as soon as my back was turned.

I took from their sconces two flambeaus, and giving one to Fortunato, bowed him through several suites of rooms to the archway that led into the vaults. I passed down a long and winding staircase, requesting him to be cautious as he followed. We came at length to the foot of the descent, and stood together on the damp ground of the catacombs of the Montresors.

The gait of my friend was unsteady, and the bells upon his cap jingled as he strode.

"The pipe," said he.

"It is farther on," said I; "but observe the white webwork which gleams from these cavern walls."

He turned towards me, and looked into my eyes with two filmy orbs that distilled the rheum of intoxication.

"Niter?" he asked at length.

"Niter," I replied. "How long have you had that cough?"

"Ugh! ugh! ugh!—ugh! ugh! ugh!—ugh! ugh! ugh!—ugh! ugh! ugh!—ugh! ugh! ugh!"

My poor friend found it impossible to reply for many minutes.

"It is nothing," he said, at last.

"Come," I said, with decision, "we will go back; your health is precious. You are rich, respected, admired, beloved; you are happy, as once I was. You are a man to be missed. For me it is no matter. We will go back; you will be ill, and I cannot be responsible. Besides, there is Luchesi—"

"Enough," he said; "the cough is a mere nothing; it will not kill me. I shall not die of a cough."

"True—true," I replied; "and, indeed, I had no intention of alarming you unnecessarily—but you should use all proper cau-

[1] a cloak reaching about to the knees

tion. A draught of this Medoc will defend us from the damps."

Here I knocked off the neck of a bottle which I drew from a long row of its fellows that lay upon the mold.

"Drink," I said, presenting him the wine.

He raised it to his lips with a leer. He paused and nodded to me familiarly, while his bells jingled.

"I drink," he said, "to the buried that repose around us."

"And I to your long life."

He again took my arm, and we proceeded.

"These vaults," he said, "are extensive."

"The Montresors," I replied, "were a great and numerous family."

"I forget your arms."

"A huge human foot d'or, in a field azure[1]; the foot crushes a serpent rampant whose fangs are embedded in the heel."

"And the motto?"

"Nemo me impune lacessit."[2]

"Good!" he said.

The wine sparkled in his eyes and the bells jingled. My own fancy grew warm with the Medoc. We had passed through walls of piled bones, with casks and puncheons intermingling, into the inmost recesses of the catacombs. I paused again, and this time I made bold to seize Fortunato by an arm above the elbow.

"The niter!" I said; "see, it increases. It hangs like moss upon the vaults. We are below the river's bed. The drops of moisture trickle among the bones. Come, we will go back ere it is too late. Your cough—"

"It is nothing," he said; "let us go on. But first, another draught of the Medoc."

I broke and reached him a flagon of De Grâve. He emptied it at a breath. His eyes flashed with a fierce light. He laughed and threw the bottle upwards with a gesticulation I did not understand.

I looked at him in surprise. He repeated the movement—a grotesque one.

"You do not comprehend?" he said.

"Not I," I replied.

"Then you are not of the brotherhood."

"How?"

[1] a foot of gold on a blue field   [2] "No one attacks me with impunity."

"You are not of the masons."

"Yes, yes," I said, "yes, yes."

"You? Impossible! A mason?"

"A mason," I replied.

"A sign," he said.

"It is this," I answered, producing a trowel from beneath the folds of my *roquelaire*.

"You jest," he exclaimed, recoiling a few paces. "But let us proceed to the Amontillado."

"Be it so," I said, replacing the tool beneath the cloak, and again offering him my arm. He leaned upon it heavily. We continued our route in search of the Amontillado. We passed through a range of low arches, descended, passed on, and, descending again, arrived at a deep crypt, in which the foulness of the air caused our flambeaus rather to glow than flame.

At the most remote end of the crypt there appeared another less spacious. Its walls had been lined with human remains, piled to the vault overhead, in the fashion of the great catacombs of Paris. Three sides of this interior crypt were still ornamented in this manner. From the fourth the bones had been thrown down, and lay promiscuously upon the earth, forming at one point a mound of some size. Within the wall thus exposed by the displacing of the bones, we perceived a still interior recess, in depth about four feet, in width three, in height six or seven. It seemed to have been constructed for no especial use within itself, but formed merely the interval between two of the colossal supports of the roof of the catacombs, and was backed by one of their circumscribing walls of solid granite.

It was in vain that Fortunato, uplifting his dull torch, endeavored to pry into the depth of the recess. Its termination the feeble light did not enable us to see.

"Proceed," I said; "herein is the Amontillado. As for Luchesi—"

"He is an ignoramus," interrupted my friend, as he stepped unsteadily forward, while I followed immediately at his heels. In an instant he had reached the extremity of the niche, and finding his progress arrested by the rock stood stupidly bewildered. A moment more and I had fettered him to the granite. In its surface were two iron staples, distant from each other about two feet, horizontally. From one of these depended a short chain, from the other a padlock. Throwing the links about his waist, it was but the work of a few seconds to secure it. He was too much astounded to resist. Withdrawing the key, I stepped back from the recess.

"Pass your hand," I said, "over the wall; you cannot help feeling the niter. Indeed it is *very* damp. Once more let me *implore* you to return. No? Then I must positively leave you. But I must first render you all the little attentions in my power."

"The Amontillado!" ejaculated my friend, not yet recovered from his astonishment.

"True," I replied; "the Amontillado."

As I said these words I busied myself among the pile of bones of which I have before spoken. Throwing them aside, I soon uncovered a quantity of building stone and mortar. With these materials and with the aid of my trowel, I began vigorously to wall up the entrance of the niche.

I had scarcely laid the first tier of the masonry when I discovered that the intoxication of Fortunato had in a great measure worn off. The earliest indication I had of this was a low moaning cry from the depth of the recess. It was *not* the cry of a drunken man. There was then a long and obstinate silence. I laid the second tier, and the third, and the fourth; and then I heard the furious vibrations of the chain. The noise lasted for several minutes, during which, that I might hearken to it with the more satisfaction, I ceased my labors and sat down upon the bones. When at last the clanking subsided, I resumed the trowel, and finished without interruption the fifth, the sixth, and the seventh tier. The wall was now nearly upon a level with my breast. I again paused, and holding the flambeaus over the mason work, threw a few feeble rays upon the figure within.

A succession of loud and shrill screams, bursting suddenly from the throat of the chained form, seemed to thrust me violently back. For a brief moment I hesitated—I trembled. Unsheathing my rapier, I began to grope with it about the recess; but the thought of an instant reassured me. I placed my hand upon the solid fabric of the catacombs, and felt satisfied. I reapproached the wall. I replied to the yells of him who clamored. I re-echoed—I aided—I surpassed them in volume and in strength. I did this, and the clamorer grew still.

It was now midnight, and my task was drawing to a close. I had completed the eighth, the ninth, and the tenth tier. I had finished a portion of the last and the eleventh; there remained but a single stone to be fitted and plastered in. I struggled with its weight; I placed it partially in its destined position. But now there came from out the niche a low laugh that erected the hairs upon my head. It was succeeded by a sad voice, which I had difficulty in recognizing as that of the noble Fortunato. The voice said—

"Ha! ha! ha!—he! he! he!—a very good joke indeed—an excellent jest. We will have many a rich laugh about it at the palazzo— he! he! he!—over our wine—he! he! he!"

"The Amontillado!" I said.

"He! he! he!—he! he! he!—yes, the Amontillado. But is it not getting late? Will not they be awaiting us at the palazzo,—the Lady Fortunato and the rest? Let us be gone."

"Yes," I said, "let us be gone."

"*For the love of God, Montresor!*"

"Yes," I said, "for the love of God!"

But to these words I hearkened in vain for a reply. I grew impatient. I called aloud—

"Fortunato!"

No answer. I called again—

"Fortunato!"

No answer still. I thrust a torch through the remaining aperture and let it fall within. There came forth in return only a jingling of the bells. My heart grew sick—on account of the dampness of the catacombs. I hastened to make an end of my labor. I forced the last stone into its position; I plastered it up. Against the new masonry I re-erected the old rampart of bones. For the half of a century no mortal has disturbed them. *In pace requiescat.*

1846

THE PURLOINED LETTER

This narrative well illustrates Poe's tales of reasoning, of which "The Murders in the Rue Morgue" is another example and "The Gold Bug"

perhaps the best. It also illustrates Poe's second type of hero, who is little more than a disembodied intellect, interested not in ideas but in the detection of fact. The plot proportions are unusual; but, granting the type of structure, the method is successful. In the middle of the story the complication ends and the explication begins. Poe's tales of Dupin started the tradition of the Master Mind who solves mysteries and of the colorless, almost impersonal confidant or narrator, prototypes of Conan Doyle's Sherlock Holmes and Dr. Watson. The tradition begins also of the stupid police, whose futile efforts need outside supplementation.

Nil sapientiæ odiosius acumine nimio.[1]

SENECA

AT Paris, just after dark one gusty evening in the autumn of 18—, I was enjoying the twofold luxury of meditation and a meerschaum, in company with my friend, C. Auguste Dupin, in his little back library, or book closet, *au troisième,*[2] No. 33 Rue Dunôt, Faubourg St. Germain. For one hour at least we had maintained a profound silence; while each, to any casual observer, might have seemed intently and exclusively occupied with the curling eddies of smoke that oppressed the atmosphere of the chamber. For myself, however, I was mentally discussing certain topics which had formed matter for conversation between us at an earlier period of the evening; I mean the affair of the Rue Morgue, and the mystery attending the murder of Marie Rogêt. I looked upon it, therefore, as something of a coincidence, when the door of our apartment was thrown open and admitted our old acquaintance, Monsieur G——, the Prefect of the Parisian police.

We gave him a hearty welcome; for there was nearly half as much of the entertaining as of the contemptible about the man, and we had not seen him for several years. We had been sitting in the dark, and Dupin now arose for the purpose of lighting a lamp, but sat down again, without doing so, upon G——'s saying that he had called to consult us, or rather to ask the opinion of my friend, about some official business which had occasioned a great deal of trouble.

[1] "Nothing more hateful to wisdom than over-cleverness."   [2] on the third floor, i.e., the third floor above the ground floor

"If it is any point requiring reflection," observed Dupin, as he forbore to enkindle the wick, "we shall examine it to better purpose in the dark."

"That is another of your odd notions," said the Prefect, who had a fashion of calling everything "odd" that was beyond his comprehension, and thus lived amid an absolute legion of "oddities."

"Very true," said Dupin, as he supplied his visitor with a pipe, and rolled towards him a comfortable chair.

"And what is the difficulty now?" I asked. "Nothing more in the assassination way, I hope?"

"Oh, no; nothing of that nature. The fact is, the business is *very* simple indeed, and I make no doubt that we can manage it sufficiently well ourselves; but then I thought Dupin would like to hear the details of it, because it is so excessively *odd*."

"Simple and odd," said Dupin.

"Why, yes; and not exactly that, either. The fact is, we have all been a good deal puzzled because the affair *is* so simple, and yet baffles us altogether."

"Perhaps it is the very simplicity of the thing which puts you at fault," said my friend.

"What nonsense you *do* talk!" replied the Prefect, laughing heartily.

"Perhaps the mystery is a little *too* plain," said Dupin.

"Oh, good heavens! who ever heard of such an idea?"

"A little *too* self evident."

"Ha! ha! ha!—ha! ha! ha!—ho! ho! ho!" roared our visitor, profoundly amused, "oh, Dupin, you will be the death of me yet!"

"And what, after all, *is* the matter on hand?" I asked.

"Why, I will tell you," replied the Prefect, as he gave a long, steady, and contemplative puff, and settled himself in his chair. "I will tell you in a few words; but, before I begin, let me caution you that this is an affair demanding the greatest secrecy, and that I should most probably lose the position I now hold were it known that I confided it to any one."

"Proceed," said I.

"Or not," said Dupin.

"Well, then; I have received personal information from a very high quarter that a certain document of the last importance has been purloined from the royal apartments. The individual who purloined it is known; this beyond a doubt; he was seen to take it. It is known, also, that it still remains in his possession."

"How is this known?" asked Dupin.

"It is clearly inferred," replied the Prefect, "from the nature of the document, and from the nonappearance of certain results which would at once arise from its passing *out* of the robber's possession; that is to say, from his employing it as he must design in the end to employ it."

"Be a little more explicit," I said.

"Well, I may venture so far as to say that the paper gives its holder a certain power in a certain quarter where such power is immensely valuable." The Prefect was fond of the cant of diplomacy.

"Still I do not quite understand," said Dupin.

"No? Well; the disclosure of the document to a third person, who shall be nameless, would bring in question the honor of a personage of most exalted station; and this fact gives the holder of the document an ascendancy over the illustrious personage whose honor and peace are so jeopardized."

"But this ascendancy," I interposed, "would depend upon the robber's knowledge of the loser's knowledge of the robber. Who would dare"—

"The thief," said G——, "is the Minister D——, who dares all things, those unbecoming as well as those becoming a man. The method of the theft was not less ingenious than bold. The document in question—a letter, to be frank—had been received by the personage robbed while alone in the royal *boudoir*. During its perusal she was suddenly interrupted by the entrance of the other exalted personage, from whom especially it was her wish to conceal it. After a hurried and vain endeavor to thrust it in a drawer, she was forced to place it, open as it was, upon a table. The address, however, was uppermost, and, the contents thus unexposed, the letter escaped notice. At this juncture enters the

Minister D——. His lynx eye immediately perceives the paper, recognizes the handwriting of the address, observes the confusion of the personage addressed, and fathoms her secret. After some business transactions, hurried through in his ordinary manner, he produces a letter somewhat similar to the one in question, opens it, pretends to read it, and then places it in close juxtaposition to the other. Again he converses for some fifteen minutes upon the public affairs. At length in taking leave he takes also from the table the letter to which he had no claim. Its rightful owner saw, but of course dared not call attention to the act, in the presence of the third personage, who stood at her elbow. The Minister decamped, leaving his own letter—one of no importance—upon the table."

"Here, then," said Dupin to me, "you have precisely what you demand to make the ascendancy complete—the robber's knowledge of the loser's knowledge of the robber."

"Yes," replied the Prefect; "and the power thus attained has, for some months past, been wielded, for political purposes, to a very dangerous extent. The personage robbed is more thoroughly convinced, every day, of the necessity of reclaiming her letter. But this, of course, cannot be done openly. In fine, driven to despair, she has committed the matter to me."

"Than whom," said Dupin, amid a perfect whirlwind of smoke, "no more sagacious agent could, I suppose, be desired, or even imagined."

"You flatter me," replied the Prefect; "but it is possible that some such opinion may have been entertained."

"It is clear," said I, "as you observe, that the letter is still in possession of the Minister; since it is this possession, and not any employment of the letter, which bestows the power. With the employment the power departs."

"True," said G——; "and upon this conviction I proceeded. My first care was to make thorough search of the Minister's Hotel; and here my chief embarrassment lay in the necessity of searching without his knowledge. Beyond all things, I have been warned of the danger which would result from giving him reason to suspect our design."

"But," said I, "you are quite *au fait*[1] in these investigations. The Parisian police have done this thing often before."

"Oh, yes; and for this reason I did not despair. The habits of the Minister gave me, too, a great advantage. He is frequently absent from home all night. His servants are by no means numerous. They sleep at a distance from their master's apartment, and, being chiefly Neapolitans, are readily made drunk. I have keys, as you know, with which I can open any chamber or cabinet in Paris. For three months a night has not passed, during the greater part of which I have not been engaged, personally, in ransacking the D—— Hotel. My honor is interested, and, to mention a great secret, the reward is enormous. So I did not abandon the search until I had become fully satisfied that the thief is a more astute man than myself. I fancy that I have investigated every nook and corner of the premises in which it is possible that the paper can be concealed."

"But is it not possible," I suggested, "that although the letter may be in possession of the Minister, as it unquestionably is, he may have concealed it elsewhere than upon his own premises?"

"This is barely possible," said Dupin. "The present peculiar condition of affairs at court, and especially of those intrigues in which D—— is known to be involved, would render the instant availability of the document—its susceptibility of being produced at a moment's notice—a point of nearly equal importance with its possession."

"Its susceptibility of being produced?" said I.

"That is to say, of being *destroyed*," said Dupin.

"True," I observed; "the paper is clearly then upon the premises. As for its being upon the person of the Minister, we may consider that as out of the question."

"Entirely," said the Prefect. "He has been twice waylaid, as if by footpads, and his person rigorously searched under my own inspection."

[1] expert.

"You might have spared yourself this trouble," said Dupin. "D——, I presume, is not altogether a fool, and, if not, must have anticipated these waylayings as a matter of course."

"Not *altogether* a fool," said G——, "but then he's a poet, which I take to be only one remove from a fool."

"True," said Dupin, after a long and thoughtful whiff from his meerschaum, "although I have been guilty of certain doggerel myself."

"Suppose you detail," said I, "the particulars of your search."

"Why, the fact is, we took our time, and we searched *everywhere*. I have had long experience in these affairs. I took the entire building, room by room, devoting the nights of a whole week to each. We examined, first, the furniture of each apartment. We opened every possible drawer; and I presume you know that, to a properly trained police agent, such a thing as a *secret* drawer is impossible. Any man is a dolt who permits a 'secret' drawer to escape him in a search of this kind. The thing is *so* plain. There is a certain amount of bulk—of space—to be accounted for in every cabinet. Then we have accurate rules. The fiftieth part of a line could not escape us. After the cabinets we took the chairs. The cushions we probed with the fine long needles you have seen me employ. From the tables we removed the tops."

"Why so?"

"Sometimes the top of a table, or other similarly arranged piece of furniture, is removed by the person wishing to conceal an article; then the leg is excavated, the article deposited within the cavity, and the top replaced. The bottoms and tops of bedposts are employed in the same way."

"But could not the cavity be detected by sounding?" I asked.

"By no means, if, when the article is deposited, a sufficient wadding of cotton be placed around it. Besides, in our case we were obliged to proceed without noise."

"But you could not have removed—you could not have taken to pieces *all* articles of furniture in which it would have been possible to make a deposit in the manner you mention. A letter may be compressed into a thin spiral roll, not differing much in shape or bulk from a large knitting needle, and in this form it might be inserted into the rung of a chair, for example. You did not take to pieces all the chairs?"

"Certainly not; but we did better—we examined the rungs of every chair in the Hotel, and indeed, the jointings of every description of furniture, by the aid of a most powerful microscope. Had there been any traces of recent disturbance we should not have failed to detect it instantly. A single grain of gimlet-dust, for example, would have been as obvious as an apple. Any disorder in the gluing—any unusual gaping in the joints—would have sufficed to insure detection."

"I presume you looked to the mirrors, between the boards and the plates, and you probed the beds and the bedclothes, as well as the curtains and carpets?"

"That, of course; and when we had absolutely completed every particle of the furniture in this way, then we examined the house itself. We divided its entire surface into compartments, which we numbered, so that none might be missed; then we scrutinized each individual square inch throughout the premises, including the two houses immediately adjoining, with the microscope, as before."

"The two houses adjoining!" I exclaimed; "you must have had a great deal of trouble."

"We had; but the reward offered is prodigious."

"You include the *grounds* about the houses?"

"All the grounds are paved with brick. They gave us comparatively little trouble. We examined the moss between the bricks, and found it undisturbed."

"You looked among D——'s papers, of course, and into the books of the library?"

"Certainly; we opened every package and parcel; we not only opened every book, but we turned over every leaf in each volume, not contenting ourselves with a mere shake, according to the fashion of some of our police officers. We also measured the thickness of every book *cover*, with the most accurate admeasurement, and applied to each the most jealous scrutiny of the microscope. Had any of the bindings been recently meddled with, it would have been utterly impossible that the fact should have escaped observation. Some five or six volumes, just from the hands of the binder, we carefully probed, longitudinally, with the needles."

"You explored the floors beneath the carpets?"

"Beyond doubt. We removed every carpet, and examined the boards with the microscope."

"And the paper on the walls?"

"Yes."

"You looked into the cellars?"

"We did."

"Then," I said, "you have been making a miscalculation, and the letter is *not* upon the premises, as you suppose."

"I fear you are right there," said the Prefect. "And now, Dupin, what would you advise me to do?"

"To make a thorough re-search of the premises."

"That is absolutely needless," replied G——. "I am not more sure that I breathe than I am that the letter is not at the Hotel."

"I have no better advice to give you," said Dupin. "You have, of course, an accurate description of the letter?"

"Oh, yes!"—And here the Prefect, producing a memorandum-book, proceeded to read aloud a minute account of the internal, and especially of the external appearance of the missing document. Soon after finishing the perusal of this description, he took his departure, more entirely depressed in spirits than I had ever known the good gentleman before.

In about a month afterwards he paid us another visit, and found us occupied very nearly as before. He took a pipe and a chair, and entered into some ordinary conversation. At length I said,—

"Well, but G——, what of the purloined letter? I presume you have at last made up your mind that there is no such thing as over-reaching the Minister?"

"Confound him, say I—yes; I made the re-examination, however, as Dupin suggested—but it was all labor lost, as I knew it would be."

"How much was the reward offered, did you say?" asked Dupin.

"Why, a very great deal—a *very* liberal reward—I don't like to say how much precisely; but one thing I *will* say, that I wouldn't mind giving my individual check for fifty thousand francs to any one who could obtain me that letter. The fact is, it is becoming of more and more importance every day; and the reward has been lately doubled. If it were trebled, however, I could do no more than I have done."

"Why, yes," said Dupin, drawlingly, between the whiffs of his meerschaum, "I really —think, G——, you have not exerted yourself—to the utmost in this matter. You might —do a little more, I think, eh?"

"How?—in what way?"

"Why—puff, puff—you might—puff, puff —employ counsel in the matter, eh?—puff, puff, puff—Do you remember the story they tell of Abernethy?"

"No; hang Abernethy!"

"To be sure! hang him and welcome. But, once upon a time, a certain rich miser conceived the design of sponging upon this Abernethy for a medical opinion. Getting up, for this purpose, an ordinary conversation in a private company, he insinuated his case to the physician, as that of an imaginary individual.

"'We will suppose,' said the miser, 'that his symptoms are such and such; now, doctor, what would *you* have directed him to take?'"

"'Take!' said Abernethy, 'why, take *advice*, to be sure.'"

"But," said the Prefect, a little discomposed, "*I* am *perfectly* willing to take advice, and to pay for it. I would *really* give fifty thousand francs to any one who would aid me in the matter."

"In that case," replied Dupin, opening a drawer, and producing a checkbook, "you may as well fill me up a check for the amount mentioned. When you have signed it, I will hand you the letter."

I was astounded. The Prefect appeared absolutely thunderstricken. For some minutes he remained speechless and motionless, looking incredulously at my friend with open mouth, and eyes that seemed starting from their sockets; then, apparently recovering himself in some measure, he seized a pen, and after several pauses and vacant stares, finally filled up and signed a check for fifty thousand francs, and handed it across the table to Dupin. The latter examined it carefully and deposited it in his pocketbook; then, unlocking an escritoire, took thence a letter and gave it to the Prefect. This functionary grasped it in a perfect agony of joy, opened it with a trembling hand, cast a rapid glance at its contents, and then, scrambling and struggling to the door, rushed at length unceremoniously from the room and from the house, without having uttered a syllable since Dupin had requested him to fill up the check.

When he had gone, my friend entered into some explanations.

"The Parisian police," he said, "are exceedingly able in their way. They are persevering, ingenious, cunning, and thoroughly versed in the knowledge which their duties seem chiefly to demand. Thus, when G—— detailed to us his mode of searching the premises at the Hotel D——, I felt entire confidence in his having made a satisfactory investigation—so far as his labors extended."

"So far as his labors extended?" said I.

"Yes," said Dupin. "The measures adopted were not only the best of their kind, but carried out to absolute perfection. Had the letter been deposited within the range of their search, these fellows would, beyond a question, have found it."

I merely laughed—but he seemed quite serious in all that he said.

"The measures, then," he continued, "were good in their kind, and well executed; their defect lay in their being inapplicable to the case, and to the man. A certain set of highly ingenious resources are, with the Prefect, a sort of Procrustean bed[1] to which he forcibly adapts his designs. But he perpetually errs by being too deep or too shallow, for the matter in hand; and many a schoolboy is a better reasoner than he. I knew one about eight years of age, whose success at guessing in the game of 'even and odd' attracted universal admiration. This game is simple, and is played with marbles. One player holds in his hand a number of these toys, and demands of another whether that number is even or odd. If the guess is right, the guesser wins one; if wrong, he loses one. The boy to whom I allude won all the marbles of the school. Of course he had some principle of guessing; and this lay in mere observation and admeasurement of the astuteness of his opponents. For example, an arrant simpleton is his opponent, and, holding up his closed hand, asks, 'Are they even or odd?' Our schoolboy replies, 'Odd,' and loses; but upon the second trial he wins, for he then says to himself, 'The simpleton had them even upon the first trial, and his amount of cunning is just sufficient to make him have them odd upon the second; I will therefore guess odd'; he guesses odd, and wins. Now, with a simpleton a degree above the first he would have reasoned thus: 'This fellow finds that in the first instance I guessed odd, and in the second he will propose to himself, upon the first impulse, a simple variation from even to odd, as did the first simpleton; but then a second thought will suggest that this is too simple a variation, and finally he will decide upon putting it even as before. I will therefore guess even'; he guesses even, and wins. Now, this mode of reasoning in the schoolboy, whom his fellows termed 'lucky'— what, in its last analysis, is it?"

"It is merely," I said, "an identification of the reasoner's intellect with that of his opponent."

"It is," said Dupin; "and, upon inquiring of the boy by what means he effected the *thorough* identification in which his success consisted, I received answer as follows: 'When I wish to find out how wise, or how stupid, or how good, or how wicked is anyone, or what are his thoughts at the moment, I fashion the expression of my face, as accurately as possible, in accordance with the expression of his, and then wait to see what thoughts or sentiments arise in my mind or heart, as if to match or correspond with the expression.' This response of the schoolboy lies at the bottom of all the spurious pro-

---

[1] the famous bed to which the legendary Greek robber, Procrustes, made his victims fit, by stretching them if too short, and by cutting off portions of their limbs if they were too long

fundity which has been attributed to Roche-foucauld, to La Bruyère, to Machiavelli, and to Campanella.''

"And the identification," I said, "of the reasoner's intellect with that of his opponent, depends, if I understand you aright, upon the accuracy with which the opponent's intellect is admeasured."

"For its practical value it depends upon this," replied Dupin, "and the Prefect and his cohort fail so frequently, first, by default of this identification, and secondly, by ill-admeasurement, or rather through nonad-measurement, of the intellect with which they are engaged. They consider only their *own* ideas of ingenuity; and, in searching for any-thing hidden, advert only to the modes in which *they* would have hidden it. They are right in this much—that their own ingenuity is a faithful representative of that of *the mass:* but when the cunning of the individual felon is diverse in character from their own, the felon foils them, of course. This always hap-pens when it is above their own, and very usually when it is below. They have no varia-tion of principle in their investigations; at best, when urged by some unusual emergency —by some extraordinary reward—they ex-tend or exaggerate their old modes of *practice*, without touching their principles. What, for example, in this case of D——, has been done to vary the principle of action? What is all this boring, and probing, and sounding, and scrutinizing with the microscope, and divid-ing the surface of the building into registered square inches—what is it all but an exaggera-tion *of the application* of the one principle or set of principles of search, which are based upon the one set of notions regarding human ingenuity, to which the Prefect, in the long routine of his duty, has been accustomed? Do you not see he has taken it for granted that *all* men proceed to conceal a letter,—not exactly in a gimlet hole bored in a chair-leg— but, at least, in *some* out-of-the-way hole or corner suggested by the same tenor of thought which would urge a man to secrete a letter in a gimlet-hole bored in a chair leg? And do you not see, also, that such *recherchés*[1] nooks for concealment are adapted only for ordinary

[1] hidden, to be sought out with care

occasions and would be adopted only by ordinary intellects; for, in all cases of con-cealment, a disposal of the article concealed —a disposal of it in this *recherché* manner— is, in the very first instance, presumable and presumed; and thus its discovery depends, not at all upon the acumen, but altogether upon the mere care, patience, and determina-tion of the seekers; and where the case is of importance—or, what amounts to the same thing in the policial eyes, when the reward is of magnitude—the qualities in question have *never* been known to fail. You will now under-stand what I meant in suggesting that, had the purloined letter been hidden anywhere within the limits of the Prefect's examination—in other words, had the principle of its conceal-ment been comprehended within the principles of the Prefect—its discovery would have been a matter altogether beyond question. This functionary, however, has been thoroughly mystified; and the remote source of his defeat lies in the supposition that the Minister is a fool because he has acquired renown as a poet. All fools are poets; this the Prefect *feels;* and he is merely guilty of a *non distributio medii*[1] in thence inferring that all poets are fools."

"But is this really the poet?" I asked. "There are two brothers, I know; and both have attained reputation in letters. The Min-ister, I believe, has written learnedly on the Differential Calculus. He is a mathematician and no poet."

"You are mistaken; I know him well; he is both. As poet *and* mathematician he would reason well; as mere mathematician he could not have reasoned at all, and thus would have been at the mercy of the Prefect."

"You surprise me," I said, "by these opin-ions, which have been contradicted by the voice of the world. You do not mean to set at naught the well-digested idea of centuries. The mathematical reason has long been re-garded as *the* reason *par excellence.*"

" '*Il y a à parier*,' " replied Dupin, quoting from Chamfort, " '*que toute idée publique, toute convention reçue, est une sottise, car elle a*

[1] a term used in logic to mean an undistributed middle of a syllogism, thus leading to a wrong conclu-sion

convenu au plus grand nombre.' [1] The mathematicians, I grant you, have done their best to promulgate the popular error to which you allude, and which is none the less an error for its promulgation as truth. With an art worthy a better cause, for example, they have insinuated the term 'analysis' into application to algebra. The French are the originators of this particular deception; but if a term is of any importance—if words derive any value from applicability—then 'analysis' conveys 'algebra,' about as much as, in Latin, *'ambitus'* implies 'ambition,' *'religio,'* 'religion,' or *'homines honesti,'* a set of honorable men." [2]

"You have a quarrel on hand, I see," said I, "with some of the algebraists of Paris; but proceed."

"I dispute the availability, and thus the value of that reason which is cultivated in any especial form other than the abstractly logical. I dispute, in particular, the reason educed by mathematical study. The mathematics are the science of form and quantity; mathematical reasoning is merely logic applied to observation upon form and quantity. The great error lies in supposing that even the truths of what is called *pure* algebra are abstract or general truths. And this error is so egregious that I am confounded at the universality with which it has been received. Mathematical axioms are *not* axioms of general truth. What is true of *relation*—of form and quantity—is often grossly false in regard to morals, for example. In this latter science it is very usually *untrue* that the aggregated parts are equal to the whole. In chemistry, also, the axiom fails. In the consideration of motive it fails; for two motives, each of a given value, have not, necessarily, a value when united equal to the sum of their values apart. There are numerous other mathematical truths which are only truths within the limits of *relation*. But the mathematician argues, from his *finite truths*, through habit, as if they were of an absolutely general applicability—as the world indeed imagines them to be. Bryant, in his very

learned 'Mythology,' mentions an analogous source of error, when he says that 'although the Pagan fables are not believed, yet we forget ourselves continually, and make inferences from them as existing realities.' With the algebraists, however, who are Pagans themselves, the 'Pagan fables' *are* believed and the inferences are made, not so much through lapse of memory as through an unaccountable addling of the brains. In short I never yet encountered the mere mathematician who could be trusted out of equal roots, or one who did not clandestinely hold it as a point of his faith that $x^2 + px$ was absolutely and unconditionally equal to q. Say to one of these gentlemen, by way of experiment, if you please, that you believe occasions may occur where $x^2 + px$ is *not* altogether equal to q, and, having made him understand what you mean, get out of his reach as speedily as convenient, for, beyond doubt, he will endeavor to knock you down.

"I mean to say," continued Dupin, while I merely laughed at his last observations, "that if the Minister had been no more than a mathematician, the Prefect would have been under no necessity of giving me this check. I knew him, however, as both mathematician and poet, and my measures were adapted to his capacity with reference to the circumstances by which he was surrounded. I knew him as courtier, too, and as a bold *intriguant*.[1] Such a man, I considered, could not fail to be aware of the ordinary policial modes of action. He could not have failed to anticipate—and events have proved that he did not fail to anticipate—the waylayings to which he was subjected. He must have foreseen, I reflected, the secret investigations of his premises. His frequent absences from home at night, which were hailed by the Prefect as certain aids to his success, I regarded only as ruses, to afford opportunity for thorough search to the police, and thus the sooner to impress them with the conviction to which G——, in fact, did finally arrive,—the conviction that the letter was not upon the premises. I felt, also, that the whole train of thought, which I was at some pains in detailing to you just now, concerning the invariable principle of policial

---

[1] "It is safe to bet that every common notion, every received convention, is nonsense, since it has found favor with the majority."   [2] The general point of this discussion is that the derivatives of a word do not necessarily include its original meaning.

[1] "intriguer"

action in searches for articles concealed—I felt that this whole train of thought would necessarily pass through the mind of the Minister. It would imperatively lead him to despise all the ordinary *nooks* of concealment. *He* could not, I reflected, be so weak as not to see that the most intricate and remote recess of his Hotel would be as open as his commonest closets to the eyes, to the probes, to the gimlets, and to the microscopes of the Prefect. I saw, in fine, that he would be driven, as a matter of course, to *simplicity*, if not deliberately induced to it as a matter of choice. You will remember, perhaps, how desperately the Prefect laughed when I suggested, upon our first interview, that it was just possible this mystery troubled him so much on account of its being so *very* self-evident."

"Yes," said I, "I remember his merriment well. I really thought he would have fallen into convulsions."

"The material world," continued Dupin, "abounds with very strict analogies to the immaterial; and thus some color of truth has been given to the rhetorical dogma, that metaphor, or simile, may be made to strengthen an argument, as well as to embellish a description. The principle of the *vis inertiæ*,[1] for example, seems to be identical in physics and metaphysics. It is not more true in the former, that a large body is with more difficulty set in motion than a smaller one, and that its subsequent momentum is commensurate with this difficulty, than it is, in the latter, that intellects of the vaster capacity, while more forcible, more constant, and more eventful in their movements than those of inferior grade, are yet the less readily moved, and more embarrassed and full of hesitation in the first few steps of their progress. Again: have you ever noticed which of the street signs over the shop doors are the most attractive of attention?"

"I have never given the matter a thought," I said.

"There is a game of puzzles," he resumed, "which is played upon a map. One party playing requires another to find a given word, —the name of town, river, state, or empire, —any word, in short, upon the motley and perplexed surface of the chart. A novice in the game generally seeks to embarrass his opponents by giving them the most minutely lettered names; but the adept selects such words as stretch in large characters, from one end of the chart to the other. These, like the over-largely lettered signs and placards of the street, escape observation by dint of being excessively obvious; and here the physical oversight is precisely analogous with the moral inapprehension by which the intellect suffers to pass unnoticed those considerations which are too obtrusively and too palpably self-evident. But this is a point, it appears, somewhat above or beneath the understanding of the Prefect. He never once thought it probable, or possible, that the Minister had deposited the letter immediately beneath the nose of the whole world by way of best preventing any portion of that world from perceiving it.

"But the more I reflected upon the daring, dashing, and discriminating ingenuity of D——; upon the fact that the document must always have been *at hand*, if he intended to use it to good purpose; and upon the decisive evidence, obtained by the Prefect, that it was not hidden within the limits of that dignitary's ordinary search—the more satisfied I became that, to conceal this letter, the Minister had resorted to the comprehensive and sagacious expedient of not attempting to conceal it at all.

"Full of these ideas, I prepared myself with a pair of green spectacles, and called one fine morning, quite by accident, at the Ministerial Hotel. I found D—— at home, yawning, lounging, and dawdling, as usual, and pretending to be in the last extremity of *ennui*.[1] He is, perhaps, the most really energetic human being now alive—but that is only when nobody sees him.

"To be even with him, I complained of my weak eyes, and lamented the necessity of the spectacles, under cover of which I cautiously and thoroughly surveyed the whole apartment, while seemingly intent only upon the conversation of my host.

"I paid especial attention to a large writing table near which he sat, and upon which

---

[1] "force of inertia"

[1] "boredom"

lay confusedly some miscellaneous letters and other papers, with one or two musical instruments and a few books. Here, however, after a long and very deliberate scrutiny, I saw nothing to excite particular suspicion.

"At length my eyes, in going the circuit of the room, fell upon a trumpery filigree card-rack of pasteboard, that hung, dangling, by a dirty blue ribbon, from a little brass knob just beneath the middle of the mantelpiece. In this rack, which had three or four compartments, were five or six visiting cards and a solitary letter. This last was much soiled and crumpled. It was torn nearly in two, across the middle—as if a design, in the first instance, to tear it entirely up as worthless had been altered, or stayed, in the second. It had a large black seal, bearing the D—— cipher *very* conspicuously, and was addressed, in a diminutive female hand, to D——, the Minister himself. It was thrust carelessly, and even, as it seemed, contemptuously, into one of the upper divisions of the rack.

"No sooner had I glanced at this letter than I concluded it to be that of which I was in search. To be sure, it was, to all appearance, radically different from the one of which the Prefect had read us so minute a description. Here the seal was large and black, with the D—— cipher; there it was small and red, with the ducal arms of the S—— family. Here, the address, to the Minister, was diminutive and feminine; there, the superscription, to a certain royal personage, was markedly bold and decided; the size alone formed a point of correspondence. But, then, the *radicalness* of these differences, which was excessive; the dirt; the soiled and torn condition of the paper, so inconsistent with the *true* methodical habits of D——, and so suggestive of a design to delude the beholder into an idea of the worthlessness of the document; these things, together with the hyper-obtrusive situation of this document, full in the view of every visitor, and thus exactly in accordance with the conclusions to which I had previously arrived; these things, I say, were strongly corroborative of suspicion, in one who came with the intention to suspect.

"I protracted my visit as long as possible, and while I maintained a most animated discussion with the Minister, upon a topic which I knew well had never failed to interest and excite him, I kept my attention really riveted upon the letter. In this examination, I committed to memory its external appearance and arrangement in the rack; and also fell, at length, upon a discovery which set at rest whatever trivial doubt I might have entertained. In scrutinizing the edges of the paper, I observed them to be more *chafed* than seemed necessary. They presented the *broken* appearance which is manifested when a stiff paper, having been once folded and pressed with a folder, is refolded in a reversed direction, in the same creases or edges which had formed the original fold. This discovery was sufficient. It was clear to me that the letter had been turned, as a glove, inside out, redirected, and resealed. I bade the Minister good morning, and took my departure at once, leaving a gold snuffbox upon the table.

"The next morning I called for the snuffbox, when we resumed, quite eagerly, the conversation of the preceding day. While thus engaged, however, a loud report, as if of a pistol, was heard immediately beneath the windows of the Hotel, and was succeeded by a series of fearful screams, and the shoutings of a terrified mob. D—— rushed to a casement, threw it open, and looked out. In the meantime, I stepped to the card-rack, took the letter, put it in my pocket, and replaced it by a facsimile (so far as regards externals) which I had carefully prepared at my lodgings—imitating the D—— cipher very readily by means of a seal formed of bread.

"The disturbance in the street had been occasioned by the frantic behavior of a man with a musket. He had fired it among a crowd of women and children. It proved, however, to have been without ball, and the fellow was suffered to go his way as a lunatic or a drunkard. When he had gone, D—— came from the window, whither I had followed him immediately upon securing the object in view. Soon afterwards I bade him farewell. The pretended lunatic was a man in my own pay."

"But what purpose had you," I asked, "in replacing the letter by a facsimile? Would it not have been better, at the first visit, to have seized it openly and departed?"

"D——," replied Dupin, "is a desperate man, and a man of nerve. His Hotel, too, is not without attendants devoted to his interest. Had I made the wild attempt you suggest, I might never have left the Ministerial presence alive. The good people of Paris might have heard of me no more. But I had an object apart from these considerations. You know my political prepossessions. In this matter I act as a partisan of the lady concerned. For eighteen months the Minister has had her in his power. She has now him in hers——since, being unaware that the letter is not in his possession, he will proceed with his exactions as if it was. Thus will he inevitably commit himself at once to his political destruction. His downfall, too, will not be more precipitate than awkward. It is all very well to talk about the *facilis descensus Averni*,[1] but in all kinds of climbing, as Catalani said of singing, it is far more easy to get up than to come down. In the present instance I have no sympathy——at least no pity——for him who descends. He is that *monstrum horrendum*,[2] an unprincipled man of genius. I confess, however, that I should like very well to know the precise character of his thoughts, when, being defied by her whom the Prefect terms 'a certain personage,' he is reduced to opening the letter which I left for him in the card-rack."

"How? Did you put anything particular in it?"

"Why——it did not seem altogether right to leave the interior blank——that would have been insulting. D——, at Vienna once, did me an evil turn, which I told him, quite good-humoredly, that I should remember. So, as I knew he would feel some curiosity in regard to the identity of the person who had out-witted him, I thought it a pity not to give him a clew. He is well acquainted with my MS., and I just copied into the middle of the blank sheet the words:——

'——Un dessein si funeste,
S'il n'est digne d'Atrée, est digne de Thyeste.'[3]

They are to be found in Crébillon's *Atrée*."

1845

[1] "Easy is the descent into Avernus," the infernal regions. A much quoted passage from the *Aeneid*, VI, 126   [2] "dreadful monster"   [3] "A design so fatal, if it is not worthy of Atreus, is worthy of Thyestes."

HAWTHORNE'S "TWICE-TOLD TALES"

This review of the second edition of *Twice-Told Tales* was first published in *Graham's Magazine*, May, 1842. Poe was among the first to see Hawthorne's genius. The article, much more than a review, is an aesthetic treatise embodying the ideas of literary art that rule in Poe's own creations. It sets forth especially his views on the short story. Poe's contemporaries rated his critical articles, book reviews and essays, more highly than his fiction and verse.

WE said a few hurried words about Mr. Hawthorne in our last number, with the design of speaking more fully in the present. We are still, however, pressed for room, and must necessarily discuss his volumes more briefly and more at random than their high merits deserve.

The book professes to be a collection of *tales*, yet is, in two respects, misnamed. These pieces are now in their third republication, and, of course, are thrice-told. Moreover, they are by no means *all* tales either in the ordinary or in the legitimate understanding of the term. Many of them are pure essays; for example, "Sights from a Steeple," "Sunday at Home," "Little Annie's Ramble," "A Rill from the Town Pump," "The Toll-Gatherer's Day," "The Haunted Mind," "The Sister Years," "Snow-Flakes," "Night Sketches," and "Foot-Prints on the Sea-Shore." We mention these matters chiefly on account of their discrepancy with that marked precision and finish by which the body of the work is distinguished.

Of the essays just named, we must be content to speak in brief. They are each and all beautiful, without being characterized by the polish and adaptation so visible in the tales proper. A painter would at once note their leading or predominant feature, and style it *repose*. There is no attempt at effect. All is quiet, thoughtful, subdued. Yet this repose may exist simultaneously with high original-ity of thought; and Mr. Hawthorne has dem-onstrated the fact. At every turn we meet with novel combinations; yet these combina-tions never surpass the limits of the quiet. We are soothed as we read; and withal is a calm astonishment that ideas so apparently obvious have never occurred or been presented to us before. Herein our author differs materially from Lamb or Hunt or Hazlitt—who, with vivid originality of manner and expression, have less of the true novelty of thought than is generally supposed, and whose originality, at best, has an uneasy and meretricious quaintness, replete with startling effects unfounded in nature, and inducing trains of reflection which lead to no satisfactory result. The Essays of Hawthorne have much of the character of Irving, with more of originality, and less of finish; while, compared with the *Spectator*, they have a vast superiority at all points. The *Spectator*, Mr. Irving, and Mr. Hawthorne have in common that tranquil and subdued manner which we have chosen to denominate *repose;* but, in the case of the two former, this repose is attained rather by the absence of novel combination, or of originality, than otherwise, and consists chiefly in the calm, quiet, unostentatious expression of commonplace thoughts, in an unambitious, unadulterated Saxon. In them, by strong effort, we are made to conceive the absence of all. In the essays before us the absence of effort is too obvious to be mistaken, and a strong undercurrent of *suggestion* runs continuously beneath the upper stream of the tranquil thesis. In short, these effusions of Mr. Hawthorne are the product of a truly imaginative intellect, restrained, and in some measure repressed, by fastidiousness of taste, by constitutional melancholy, and by indolence.

But it is of his tales that we desire principally to speak. The tale proper, in our opinion, affords unquestionably the fairest field for the exercise of the loftiest talent, which can be afforded by the wide domains of mere prose. Were we bidden to say how the highest genius could be most advantageously employed for the best display of its own powers, we should answer, without hesitation—in the composition of a rhymed poem, not to exceed in length what might be perused in an hour. Within this limit alone can the highest order of true poetry exist. We need only here say, upon this topic, that, in almost all classes of composition, the unity of effect or impression is a point of the greatest importance. It is clear, moreover, that this unity cannot be thoroughly preserved in productions whose perusal cannot be completed at one sitting. We may continue the reading of a prose composition, from the very nature of prose itself, much longer than we can persevere, to any good purpose, in the perusal of a poem. This latter, if truly fulfilling the demands of the poetic sentiment, induces an exaltation of the soul which cannot be long sustained. All high excitements are necessarily transient. Thus a long poem is a paradox. And, without unity of impression, the deepest effects cannot be brought about. Epics were the offspring of an imperfect sense of Art, and their reign is no more. A poem *too* brief may produce a vivid, but never an intense or enduring impression. Without a certain continuity of effort—without a certain duration or repetition of purpose—the soul is never deeply moved. There must be the dropping of the water upon the rock. De Béranger has wrought brilliant things—pungent and spirit-stirring—but, like all immassive bodies, they lack *momentum*, and thus fail to satisfy the Poetic Sentiment. They sparkle and excite, but, from want of continuity, fail deeply to impress. Extreme brevity will degenerate into epigrammatism; but the sin of extreme length is even more unpardonable. *In medio tutissimus ibis.*[1]

Were we called upon, however, to designate that class of composition which, next to such a poem as we have suggested, should best fulfill the demands of high genius—should offer it the most advantageous field of exertion—we should unhesitatingly speak of the prose tale, as Mr. Hawthorne has here exemplified it. We allude to the short prose narrative, requiring from a half hour to one or two hours in its perusal. The ordinary novel is objectionable, from its length, for reasons already stated in substance. As it cannot be read at one sitting, it deprives itself, of course, of the immense force derivable from *totality*. Worldly interests intervening during the pauses of perusal, modify, annul, or counteract, in a greater or less degree, the impressions of the book. But simple cessation

---

[1] "You will go most safely in the middle."

in reading would, of itself, be sufficient to destroy the true unity. In the brief tale, however, the author is enabled to carry out the fullness of his intention, be it what it may. During the hour of perusal the soul of the reader is at the writer's control. There are no external or extrinsic influences—resulting from weariness or interruption.

A skillful literary artist has constructed a tale. If wise, he has not fashioned his thoughts to accommodate his incidents; but having conceived, with deliberate care, a certain unique or single *effect* to be wrought out, he then invents such incidents—he then combines such events as may best aid him in establishing this preconceived effect. If his very initial sentence tend not to the outbringing of this effect, then he has failed in his first step. In the whole composition there should be no word written, of which the tendency, direct or indirect, is not to the one pre-established design. And by such means, with such care and skill, a picture is at length painted which leaves in the mind of him who contemplates it with a kindred art, a sense of the fullest satisfaction. The idea of the tale has been presented unblemished, because undisturbed: and this is an end unattainable by the novel. Undue brevity is just as exceptionable here as in the poem; but undue length is yet more to be avoided.

We have said that the tale has a point of superiority even over the poem. In fact, while the *rhythm* of this latter is an essential aid in the development of the poem's highest idea—the idea of the Beautiful—the artificialities of this rhythm are an inseparable bar to the development of all points of thought or expression which have their basis in *Truth*. But Truth is often, and in very great degree, the aim of the tale. Some of the finest tales are tales of ratiocination. Thus the field of this species of composition, if not in so elevated a region on the mountain of Mind, is a tableland of far vaster extent than the domain of the mere poem. Its products are never so rich, but infinitely more numerous, and more appreciable by the mass of mankind. The writer of the prose tale, in short, may bring to his theme a vast variety of modes or inflections of thought and expression—(the ratiocinative,

for example, the sarcastic, or the humorous) which are not only antagonistical to the nature of the poem, but absolutely forbidden by one of its most peculiar and indispensable adjuncts; we allude, of course, to rhythm. It may be added here, *par parenthèse*, that the author who aims at the purely beautiful in a prose tale is laboring at a great disadvantage. For Beauty can be better treated in the poem. Not so with terror, or passion, or horror, or a multitude of such other points. And here it will be seen how full of prejudice are the usual animadversions against those *tales of effect*, many fine examples of which were found in the earlier numbers of *Blackwood*. The impressions produced were wrought in a legitimate sphere of action, and constituted a legitimate although sometimes an exaggerated interest. They were relished by every man of genius: although there were found many men of genius who condemned them without just ground. The true critic will but demand that the design intended be accomplished, to the fullest extent, by the means most advantageously applicable.

We have very few American tales of real merit—we may say, indeed, none, with the exception of *The Tales of a Traveler* of Washington Irving, and these *Twice-Told Tales* of Mr. Hawthorne. Some of the pieces of Mr. John Neal abound in vigor and originality; but, in general, his compositions of this class are excessively diffuse, extravagant, and indicative of an imperfect sentiment of Art. Articles at random are, now and then, met with in our periodicals which might be advantageously compared with the best effusions of the British Magazines; but, upon the whole, we are far behind our progenitors in this department of literature.

Of Mr. Hawthorne's Tales we would say, emphatically, that they belong to the highest region of Art—an Art subservient to genius of a very lofty order. We had supposed, with good reason for so supposing, that he had been thrust into his present position by one of the impudent *cliques* which beset our literature, and whose pretensions it is our full purpose to expose at the earliest opportunity; but we have been most agreeably mistaken. We know of few compositions which the critic can more honestly commend than these *Twice-Told Tales*. As Americans, we feel proud of the book.

Mr. Hawthorne's distinctive trait is invention, creation, imagination, originality—a trait which, in the literature of fiction, is positively worth all the rest. But the nature of the originality, so far as regards its manifestation in letters, is but imperfectly understood. The inventive or original mind as frequently displays itself in novelty of *tone* as in novelty of matter. Mr. Hawthorne is original at *all* points.

It would be a matter of some difficulty to designate the best of these tales; we repeat that, without exception, they are beautiful. "Wakefield" is remarkable for the skill with which an old idea—a well-known incident—is worked up or discussed. A man of whims conceives the purpose of quitting his wife and residing *incognito*, for twenty years, in her immediate neighborhood. Something of this kind actually happened in London. The force of Mr. Hawthorne's tale lies in the analysis of the motives which must or might have impelled the husband to such folly, in the first instance, with the possible causes of his perseverance. Upon this thesis a sketch of singular power has been constructed.

"The Wedding Knell" is full of the boldest imagination—an imagination fully controlled by taste. The most captious critic could find no flaw in this production.

"The Minister's Black Veil" is a masterly composition, of which the sole defect is that to the rabble its exquisite skill will be *caviare*. The *obvious* meaning of this article will be found to smother its insinuated one. The *moral* put into the mouth of the dying minister will be supposed to convey the *true* import of the narrative; and that a crime of dark dye (having reference to the "young lady") has been committed is a point which only minds congenial with that of the author will perceive.

"Mr. Higginbotham's Catastrophe" is vividly original, and managed most dexterously.

"Dr. Heidegger's Experiment" is exceedingly well imagined, and executed with surpassing ability. The artist breathes in every line of it.

"The White Old Maid" is objectionable even more than the "Minister's Black Veil," on the score of its mysticism. Even with the thoughtful and analytic, there will be much trouble in penetrating its entire import.

"The Hollow of the Three Hills" we would quote in full had we space;—not as evincing higher talent than any of the other pieces, but as affording an excellent example of the author's peculiar ability. The subject is commonplace. A witch subjects the Distant and the Past to the view of a mourner. It has been the fashion to describe, in such cases, a mirror in which the images of the absent appear; or a cloud of smoke is made to arise, and thence the figures are gradually unfolded. Mr. Hawthorne has wonderfully heightened his effect by making the ear, in place of the eye, the medium by which the fantasy is conveyed. The head of the mourner is enveloped in the cloak of the witch, and within its magic folds there arise sounds which have an all-sufficient intelligence. Throughout this article also, the artist is conspicuous—not more in positive than in negative merits. Not only is all done that should be done, but (what perhaps is an end with more difficulty attained) there is nothing done which should not be. Every word *tells*, and there is not a word which does *not* tell.

In "Howe's Masquerade" we observe something which resembles plagiarism—but which *may be* a very flattering coincidence of thought. We quote the passage in question:

"*With a dark flush of wrath* upon his brow, they saw the General *draw his sword* and *advance to meet* the figure *in the cloak* before the latter had stepped one pace upon the floor. '*Villain, unmuffle yourself,*' cried he. 'You pass no farther!' The figure, without blenching a hair's breadth from the sword which was pointed at his breast, made a solemn pause, and *lowered the cape of the cloak* from about his face, yet not sufficiently for the spectators to catch a glimpse of it. But Sir William Howe had evidently seen enough. The sternness of his countenance gave place to a look of wild amazement, if not horror, while he recoiled several steps from the figure, *and let fall his sword* upon the floor.*"

The idea here is, that the figure in the cloak is the phantom or reduplication of Sir William Howe; but in an article called "William Wilson," one of the *Tales of the Grotesque and Arabesque*, we have not only the same idea, but the same idea similarly presented in several respects. We quote two paragraphs, which our readers may compare with what has been already given. We have italicized, above, the immediate particulars of resemblance.

"The brief moment in which I averted my eyes had been sufficient to produce, appar- 10 ently, a material change in the arrangement at the upper or farther end of the room. A large mirror, it appeared to me, now stood where none had been perceptible before: and as I stepped up to it in extremity of terror, mine own image, but with features all pale and dabbled in blood, *advanced* with a feeble and tottering gait to meet me. Thus it appeared I say, but was not. It was Wilson, who then stood before me in the agonies of dis- 20 solution. Not a line in all the marked and singular lineaments of that face which was not even identically mine own. *His mask and cloak lay where he had thrown them, upon the floor.*"

Here it will be observed that, not only are the two general conceptions identical, but there are various *points* of similarity. In each case the figure seen is the wraith or duplication of the beholder. In each case the scene is a 30 masquerade. In each case the figure is cloaked. In each, there is a quarrel—that is to say, angry words pass between the parties. In each the beholder is enraged. In each the cloak and sword fall upon the floor. The "villain, unmuffle yourself," of Mr. H. is precisely paralleled by a passage at page 56 of "William Wilson."

In the way of objection we have scarcely a word to say of these tales. There is, perhaps, 40 a somewhat too general or prevalent *tone*— a tone of melancholy and mysticism. The subjects are insufficiently varied. There is not so much of *versatility* evinced as we might well be warranted in expecting from the high powers of Mr. Hawthorne. But beyond these trivial exceptions we have really none to make. The style is purity itself. Force abounds. High imagination gleams from every page. Mr. Hawthorne is a man of the truest genius. 50 We only regret that the limits of our Maga-

zine will not permit us to pay him that full tribute of commendation, which, under other circumstances, we should be so eager to pay.

1842

THE PHILOSOPHY OF COM-POSITION

Published in *Graham's Magazine*, April, 1846. Poe called this essay "my best specimen of analysis." Another contribution to aesthetic theory, it illustrates his critical development and his poetic ideas. Especially, it sets forth his method of composing "The Raven" (see headnote on that poem). An excellent discussion of the essay may be found in the Craig-Alterton *Poe*, lix–lxv.

CHARLES DICKENS, in a note now lying before me, alluding to an examination I once made of the mechanism of *Barnaby Rudge*, says—"By the way, are you aware that Godwin wrote his *Caleb Williams* backward? He first involved his hero in a web of difficulties, forming the second volume, and then, for the first, cast about him for some mode of accounting for what had been done."

I cannot think this the *precise* mode of procedure on the part of Godwin—and indeed what he himself acknowledges, is not altogether in accordance with Mr. Dickens's idea—but the author of *Caleb Williams* was too good an artist not to perceive the advantage derivable from at least a somewhat similar process. Nothing is more clear than that every plot, worth the name, must be elaborated to its *dénouement* before anything be attempted with the pen. It is only with the *dénouement* constantly in view that we can give a plot its indispensable air of consequence, or causation, by making the incidents, and especially the tone at all points, tend to the development of the intention.

There is a radical error, I think, in the usual mode of constructing a story. Either history affords a thesis—or one is suggested by an incident of the day—or, at best, the author sets himself to work in the combination of striking events to form merely the basis of his narrative—designing, generally, to fill in with description, dialogue, or authorial comment, whatever crevices of fact, or action, may, from page to page, render themselves apparent.

I prefer commencing with the consideration of an *effect*. Keeping originality *always* in view—for he is false to himself who ventures to dispense with so obvious and so easily attainable a source of interest—I say to myself, in the first place, "Of the innumerable effects, or impressions, of which the heart, the intellect, or (more generally) the soul is susceptible, what one shall I, on the present occasion, select?" Having chosen a novel, first, and secondly a vivid effect, I consider whether it can be best wrought by incident or tone—whether by ordinary incidents and peculiar tone, or the converse, or by peculiarity both of incident and tone—afterward looking about me (or rather within) for such combinations of event, or tone, as shall best aid me in the construction of the effect.

I have often thought how interesting a magazine paper might be written by any author who would—that is to say who could—detail, step by step, the processes by which any one of his compositions attained its ultimate point of completion. Why such a paper has never been given to the world, I am much at a loss to say—but, perhaps, the authorial vanity has had more to do with the omission than any one other cause. Most writers—poets in especial—prefer having it understood that they compose by a species of fine frenzy—an ecstatic intuition—and would positively shudder at letting the public take a peep behind the scenes, at the elaborate and vacillating crudities of thought—at the true purposes seized only at the last moment—at the innumerable glimpses of idea that arrived not at the maturity of full view—at the fully matured fancies discarded in despair as unmanageable—at the cautious selections and rejections—at the painful erasures and interpolations—in a word, at the wheels and pinions—the tackle for scene-shifting—the stepladders and demon-traps—the cock's feathers, the red paint, and the black patches, which, in ninety-nine cases out of the hundred, constitute the properties of the literary *histrio*.

I am aware, on the other hand, that the case is by no means common, in which an author is at all in condition to retrace the steps by which his conclusions have been attained. In general, suggestions, having arisen pell-mell, are pursued and forgotten in a similar manner.

For my own part, I have neither sympathy with the repugnance alluded to, nor at any time the least difficulty in recalling to mind the progressive steps of any of my compositions; and, since the interest of an analysis, or reconstruction, such as I have considered a *desideratum*, is quite independent of any real or fancied interest in the thing analyzed, it will not be regarded as a breach of decorum on my part to show the *modus operandi*[1] by which some one of my own works was put together. I select *The Raven*, as most generally known. It is my design to render it manifest that no one point in its composition is referrible either to accident or intuition—that the work proceeded, step by step, to its completion with the precision and rigid consequence of a mathematical problem.

Let us dismiss, as irrelevant to the poem, *per se*, the circumstance—or say the necessity—which, in the first place, gave rise to the intention of composing *a* poem that should suit at once the popular and the critical taste.

We commence, then, with this intention.

The initial consideration was that of extent. If any literary work is too long to be read at one sitting, we must be content to dispense with the immensely important effect derivable from unity of impression—for, if two sittings be required, the affairs of the world interfere, and every thing like totality is at once destroyed. But since, *ceteris paribus*,[2] no poet can afford to dispense with *any thing* that may advance his design, it but remains to be seen whether there is, in extent, any advantage to counterbalance the loss of unity which attends it. Here I say no, at once. What we term a long poem is, in fact, merely a succession of brief ones—that is to say, of brief poetical effects. It is needless to demonstrate that a poem is such, only inasmuch as it intensely excites, by elevating, the soul; and all intense excitements are, through a psychal necessity, brief. For this reason, at least one half of the *Paradise*

[1] "method of working"   [2] "other things being equal"

Lost is essentially prose—a succession of poetical excitements interspersed, *inevitably*, with corresponding depressions—the whole being deprived, through the extremeness of its length, of the vastly important artistic element, totality, or unity, of effect.

It appears evident, then, that there is a distinct limit, as regards length, to all works of literary art—the limit of a single sitting—and that, although in certain classes of prose composition, such as *Robinson Crusoe* (demanding no unity) this limit may be advantageously overpassed, it can never properly be overpassed in a poem. Within this limit, the extent of a poem may be made to bear mathematical relation to its merit—in other words, to the excitement or elevation—again in other words, to the degree of the true poetical effect which it is capable of inducing; for it is clear that the brevity must be in direct ratio of the intensity of the intended effect:—this, with one proviso—that a certain degree of duration is absolutely requisite for the production of any effect at all.

Holding in view these considerations, as well as that degree of excitement which I deemed not above the popular, while not below the critical, taste, I reached at once what I conceived the proper *length* for my intended poem—a length of about one hundred lines. It is, in fact, a hundred and eight.

My next thought concerned the choice of an impression, or effect, to be conveyed; and here I may as well observe that, throughout the construction, I kept steadily in view the design of rendering the work *universally* appreciable. I should be carried too far out of my immediate topic were I to demonstrate a point upon which I have repeatedly insisted, and which, with the poetical, stands not in the slightest need of demonstration—the point, I mean, that Beauty is the sole legitimate province of the poem. A few words, however, in elucidation of my real meaning, which some of my friends have evinced a disposition to misrepresent. That pleasure which is at once the most intense, the most elevating, and the most pure, is, I believe, found in the contemplation of the beautiful. When, indeed, men speak of Beauty, they mean, precisely, not a quality, as is supposed, but an effect—they refer, in short, just to that intense and pure elevation of *soul*—*not* of intellect, or of heart—upon which I have commented, and which is experienced in consequence of contemplating "the beautiful." Now I designate Beauty as the province of the poem, merely because it is an obvious rule of Art that effects should be made to spring from direct causes—that objects should be attained through means best adapted for their attainment—no one as yet having been weak enough to deny that the peculiar elevation alluded to is *most readily* attained in the poem. Now the object, Truth, or the satisfaction of the intellect, and the object Passion, or the excitement of the heart, are, although attainable, to a certain extent, in poetry, far more readily attainable in prose. Truth, in fact, demands a precision, and Passion a *homeliness* (the truly passionate will comprehend me) which are absolutely antagonistic to that Beauty which, I maintain, is the excitement, or pleasurable elevation, of the soul. It by no means follows from any thing here said, that passion, or even truth, may not be introduced, and even profitably introduced, into a poem—for they may serve in elucidation, or aid the general effect, as do discords in music, by contrast—but the true artist will always contrive, first, to tone them into proper subservience to the predominant aim, and, secondly, to enveil them, as far as possible, in that Beauty which is the atmosphere and the essence of the poem.

Regarding, then, Beauty as my province, my next question referred to the *tone* of its highest manifestation—and all experience has shown that this tone is one of *sadness*. Beauty of whatever kind, in its supreme development, invariably excites the sensitive soul to tears. Melancholy is thus the most legitimate of all the poetical tones.

The length, the province, and the tone, being thus determined, I betook myself to ordinary induction, with the view of obtaining some artistic piquancy which might serve me as a keynote in the construction of the poem—some pivot upon which the whole structure might turn. In carefully thinking over all the usual artistic effects—or more properly *points*, in the theatrical sense—I did not fail to perceive immediately that no one had been so universally employed as that of the *refrain*. The universality of its employment sufficed to assure me of its intrinsic value, and spared me the necessity of submitting it to analysis. I considered it, however, with regard to its susceptibility of improvement, and soon saw it to be in a primitive condition. As commonly used, the *refrain*, or burden, not only is limited to lyric verse, but depends for its impression upon the force of monotone—both in sound and thought. The pleasure is deduced solely from the sense of identity—of repetition. I resolved to diversify, and so heighten, the effect, by adhering, in general, to the monotone of sound, while I continually varied that of thought: that is to say, I determined to produce continuously novel effects, by the variation of the *application* of the refrain—the refrain itself remaining, for the most part, unvaried.

These points being settled, I next bethought me of the *nature* of my refrain. Since its application was to be repeatedly varied, it was clear that the refrain itself must be brief, for there would have been an insurmountable difficulty in frequent variations of application in any sentence of length. In proportion to the brevity of the sentence, would, of course, be the facility of the variation. This led me at once to a single word as the best refrain.

The question now arose as to the *character* of the word. Having made up my mind to a refrain, the division of the poem into stanzas was, of course, a corollary: the refrain forming the close of each stanza. That such a close, to have force, must be sonorous and susceptible of protracted emphasis, admitted no doubt; and these considerations inevitably led me to the long *o* as the most sonorous vowel, in connection with *r* as the most producible consonant.

The sound of the refrain being thus determined, it became necessary to select a word embodying this sound, and at the same time in the fullest possible keeping with that melancholy which I had predetermined as the tone of the poem. In such a search it would have been absolutely impossible to overlook the word "Nevermore." In fact, it was the very first which presented itself.

The next *desideratum* was a pretext for the continuous use of the one word "Nevermore." In observing the difficulty which I at once found in inventing a sufficiently plausible reason for its continuous repetition, I did not fail to perceive that this difficulty arose solely from the preassumption that the word was to be so continuously or monotonously spoken by a *human* being—I did not fail to perceive, in short, that the difficulty lay in the reconciliation of this monotony with the exercise of reason on the part of the creature repeating the word. Here, then, immediately arose the idea of a *nonreasoning* creature capable of speech; and, very naturally, a parrot, in the first instance, suggested itself, but was superseded forthwith by a Raven, as equally capable of speech, and infinitely more in keeping with the intended *tone*.

I had now gone so far as the conception of a Raven—the bird of ill omen—monotonously repeating the one word, "Nevermore" at the conclusion of each stanza, in a poem of melancholy tone, and in length about one hundred lines. Now, never losing sight of the object *supremeness*, or perfection, at all points, I asked myself—"Of all melancholy topics, what, according to the *universal* understanding of mankind, is the *most* melancholy?" "Death" —was the obvious reply. "And when," I said, "is this most melancholy of topics most poetical?" From what I have already explained at some length, the answer, here also, is obvious —"When it most closely allies itself to *Beauty*." The death, then, of a beautiful woman is, unquestionably, the most poetical topic in the world—and equally is it beyond doubt that the lips best suited for such topic are those of a bereaved lover.

I had now to combine the two ideas, of a lover lamenting his deceased mistress, and a Raven continuously repeating the word "Nevermore." I had to combine these, bearing in mind my design of varying, at every turn, the *application* of the word repeated; but the only intelligible mode of such combination is that of imagining the Raven employing the word in answer to the queries of the lover. And here it was that I saw at once the opportunity afforded for the effect on which I had been depending—that is to say, the effect of the *variation of application*. I saw that I could make the first query propounded by the lover—the first query to which the Raven should reply "Nevermore"—that I could make this first query a commonplace one—the second less so—the third still less, and so on—until at length the lover, startled from his original *nonchalance* by the melancholy character of the word itself—by its frequent repetition—and by a consideration of the ominous reputation of the fowl that uttered it—is at length excited to superstition, and wildly propounds queries of a far different character—queries whose solution he has passionately at heart—propounds them half in superstition and half in that species of despair which delights in self-torture—propounds them not altogether because he believes in the prophetic or demoniac character of the bird (which, reason assures him, is merely repeating a lesson learned by rote) but because he experiences a phrenzied pleasure in so modeling his questions as to receive from the *expected* "Nevermore" the most delicious because the most intolerable of sorrow. Perceiving the opportunity thus afforded me—or, more strictly, thus forced upon me in the progress of the construction—I first established in mind the climax, or concluding query—that query to which "Nevermore" should be in the last place an answer—that in reply to which this word "Nevermore" should involve the utmost conceivable amount of sorrow and despair.

Here then the poem may be said to have its beginning—at the end, where all works of art should begin—for it was here, at this point of my preconsiderations, that I first put pen to paper in the composition of the stanza:

"Prophet!" said I, "thing of evil—prophet still, if bird or devil!
By that Heaven that bends above us, by that God we both adore,
Tell this soul with sorrow laden if, within the distant Aidenn,
It shall clasp a sainted maiden whom the angels name Lenore—
Clasp a rare and radiant maiden whom the angels name Lenore!"
Quoth the Raven, "Nevermore."

I composed this stanza, at this point, first, that by establishing the climax, I might the better vary and graduate, as regards seriousness and importance, the preceding queries of the lover; and secondly, that I might definitely settle the rhythm, the meter, and the length and general arrangement of the stanza, —as well as graduate the stanzas which were to precede, so that none of them might surpass this in rhythmical effect. Had I been able, in the subsequent composition, to construct more vigorous stanzas, I should, without scruple, have purposely enfeebled them, so as not to interfere with the climacteric effect.

And here I may as well say a few words of the versification. My first object (as usual) was originality. The extent to which this has been neglected, in versification, is one of the most unaccountable things in the world. Admitting that there is little possibility of variety in mere *rhythm*, it is still clear that the possible varieties of meter and stanza are absolutely infinite—and yet, *for centuries, no man, in verse, has ever done, or ever seemed to think of doing, an original thing.* The fact is, that originality (unless in minds of very unusual force) is by no means a matter, as some suppose, of impulse or intuition. In general, to be found, it must be elaborately sought, and although a positive merit of the highest class, demands in its attainment less of invention than negation.

Of course, I pretend to no originality in either the rhythm or meter of *The Raven*. The former is trochaic—the latter is octameter acatelectic, alternating with heptameter catalectic repeated in the refrain of the fifth verse, and terminating with tetrameter catalectic. Less pedantically—the feet employed throughout (trochees) consist of a long syllable followed by a short: the first line of the stanza consists of eight of these feet—the second of seven and a half (in effect two thirds)—the third of eight—the fourth of seven and a half—the fifth the same—the sixth three and a half. Now, each of these lines, taken individually, has been employed before; and what originality *The Raven* has, is in their *combination into stanza;* nothing even remotely approaching this combination has ever been attempted. The effect of this originality of combination is aided by other unusual, and some altogether novel effects, arising from an extension of the application of the principles of rhyme and alliteration.

The next point to be considered was the mode of bringing together the lover and the Raven—and the first branch of this consideration was the *locale*. For this the most natural suggestion might seem to be a forest, or the fields—but it has always appeared to me that a close *circumscription of space* is absolutely necessary to the effect of insulated incident:— it has the force of a frame to a picture. It has an indisputable moral power in keeping concentrated the attention, and, of course, must not be confounded with mere unity of place.

I determined, then, to place the lover in his chamber—in a chamber rendered sacred to him by memories of her who had frequented it. The room is represented as richly furnished —this in mere pursuance of the ideas I have already explained on the subject of Beauty, as the sole true poetical thesis.

The *locale* being thus determined, I had now to introduce the bird—and the thought of introducing him through the window, was inevitable. The idea of making the lover suppose, in the first instance, that the flapping of the wings of the bird against the shutter, is a "tapping" at the door, originated in a wish to increase, by prolonging, the reader's curiosity, and in a desire to admit the incidental effect arising from the lover's throwing open the door, finding all dark, and thence adopting the half-fancy that it was the spirit of his mistress that knocked.

I made the night tempestuous, first, to account for the Raven's seeking admission, and secondly, for the effect of contrast with the (physical) serenity within the chamber.

I made the bird alight on the bust of Pallas, also for the effect of contrast between the marble and the plumage—it being understood that the bust was absolutely *suggested* by the bird—the bust of *Pallas* being chosen, first, as most in keeping with the scholarship of the lover, and secondly, for the sonorousness of the word, *Pallas*, itself.

About the middle of the poem, also, I have availed myself of the force of contrast, with a view of deepening the ultimate impression. For example, an air of the fantastic—approaching as nearly to the ludicrous as was admissible—is given to the Raven's entrance. He comes in "with many a flirt and flutter."

Not the *least obeisance made he;* not a moment
    stopped or stayed he;
But with mien of lord or lady, perched above
    my chamber door.

In the two stanzas which follow, the design is more obviously carried out:

Then this ebony bird beguiling my sad fancy
    into smiling
By the *grave and stern decorum of the counte-*
    nance it wore,
"Though thy *crest be shorn and shaven* thou,"
    I said, "art sure no craven,
Ghastly grim and ancient Raven wandering
    from the nightly shore—
Tell me what thy lordly name is on the Night's
    Plutonian shore?"
    Quoth the Raven, "Nevermore."

Much I marveled *this ungainly fowl* to hear
    discourse so plainly
Though its answer little meaning—little
    relevancy bore;
For we cannot help agreeing that no living
    human being
Ever yet was blessed with seeing bird above his
    chamber door,
Bird or beast upon the sculptured bust above his
    chamber door,
    With such name as "Nevermore."

The effect of the *dénouement* being thus provided for, I immediately drop the fantastic for a tone of the most profound seriousness—this tone commencing in the stanza directly following the one last quoted, with the line,

But the Raven, sitting lonely on that placid
    bust, spoke only, etc.

From this epoch the lover no longer jests— no longer sees anything even of the fantastic in the Raven's demeanor. He speaks of him as a "grim, ungainly, ghastly, gaunt, and ominous bird of yore," and feels the "fiery eyes" burning into his "bosom's core." This revolution of thought, or fancy, on the lover's part, is intended to induce a similar one on the part of the reader—to bring the mind into a proper frame for the *dénouement*—which is now brought about as rapidly and as *directly* as possible.

With the *dénouement* proper—with the Raven's reply, "Nevermore," to the lover's final demand if he shall meet his mistress in another world—the poem, in its obvious phase, that of a simple narrative, may be said to have its completion. So far, every thing is within the limits of the accountable—of the real. A raven, having learned by rote the single word "Nevermore," and having escaped from the custody of its owner, is driven at midnight, through the violence of a storm, to seek admission at a window from which a light still gleams—the chamber window of a student, occupied half in poring over a volume, half in dreaming of a beloved mistress deceased. The casement being thrown open at the fluttering of the bird's wings, the bird itself perches on the most convenient seat out of the immediate reach of the student, who, amused by the incident and the oddity of the visitor's demeanor, demands of it, in jest and without looking for a reply, its name. The raven addressed, answers with its customary word, "Nevermore"—a word which finds immediate echo in the melancholy heart of the student, who, giving utterance aloud to certain thoughts suggested by the occasion, is again startled by the fowl's repetition of "Nevermore." The student now guesses the state of the case, but is impelled, as I have before explained, by the human thirst for self-torture, and in part by superstition, to propound such queries to the bird as will bring him, the lover, the most of the luxury of sorrow, through the anticipated answer "Nevermore." With the indulgence, to the extreme, of this self-torture, the narration, in what I have termed its first or obvious phase, has a natural termination, and so far there has been no overstepping of the limits of the real.

But in subjects so handled, however skillfully, or with however vivid an array of incident, there is always a certain hardness or nakedness, which repels the artistical eye. Two things are invariably required—first, some amount of complexity, or more properly, adaptation; and, secondly, some amount of suggestiveness—some undercurrent, however indefinite, of meaning. It is this latter, in especial, which imparts to a work of art so much of that *richness* (to borrow from colloquy a forcible term) which we are too fond of confounding with *the ideal.* It is the *excess* of the suggested meaning—it is the rendering this the upper instead of the under current of the theme—which turns into prose (and that of the very flattest kind) the so-called poetry of the so-called transcendentalists.

Holding these opinions, I added the two concluding stanzas of the poem—their suggestiveness being thus made to pervade all the narrative which has preceded them. The undercurrent of meaning is rendered first apparent in the lines—

"Take thy beak from out *my heart,* and take
    thy form from off my door!"
  Quoth the Raven, "Nevermore!"

It will be observed that the words, "from out my heart," involve the first metaphorical expression in the poem. They, with the answer, "Nevermore," dispose the mind to seek a moral in all that has been previously narrated. The reader begins now to regard the Raven as emblematical—but it is not until the very last line of the very last stanza, that the intention of making him emblematical of *Mournful and Never-ending Remembrance* is permitted distinctly to be seen:

And the Raven, never flitting, *still* is sitting,
    still is sitting,
On the pallid bust of Pallas, just above my
    chamber door;
And his eyes have all the seeming of a demon's
    that is dreaming,
And the lamplight o'er him streaming throws
    his shadow on the floor;
And my soul *from out that shadow* that lies
    floating on the floor
  Shall be lifted—nevermore!

1846

1815 ~ *Richard Henry Dana Jr.* ~ 1882

THE AUTHOR of the classic of the sea, *Two Years Before the Mast*, was born in Cambridge, Massachusetts, the son of Richard Henry Dana, critic, journalist, and editor of the *North American Review*. Like Jonathan Edwards and Oliver Wendell Holmes, he was a descendant of Anne Bradstreet. The younger Dana attended Harvard, but because of weak health and eyesight, he was directed by his physician to take a sea voyage after his junior year. At nineteen he shipped as an ordinary seaman "before the mast" on the brig *Pilgrim*, sailing with a miscellaneous cargo from Boston to California via Cape Horn. These were the days of the highest development of the sailor's calling; after the middle of the century there were great changes in the condition of the merchant marine. Dana started homeward from San Diego in the *Alert* with a cargo of hides, May 18, 1836. Returning vigorous and ambitious after twenty-five months, he finished his course at Harvard and was graduated in 1837. He published his famous narrative of sea adventure in 1840, the year in which he was admitted to practice law. It is his one literary work, although he wrote for legal periodicals, played a political role as an abolitionist, and became a distinguished member of the Massachusetts bar. He died of pneumonia in 1882 at Rome.

His truthful autobiographical account of a sailor's life, perhaps the best of its kind, was written partly with a humanitarian intent. It accomplished what he hoped, and helped to ameliorate the life of sailors by exhibiting the occasional brutality of officers toward their men. He writes of his two years' adventure directly and accurately and with charm of style. Distinct personalities emerge as he pictures the crew, and nautical matters are made intelligible to land readers. He was brought up on romantic literature and liked in his youth Spenser, Byron, and Scott, and his narrative has something of the charm of romance. Mostly, however, its fundamental truthfulness, its dramatic incidents, and the author's good sense and modesty have made it one of our most famous narratives of adventure at sea.

Two Years Before the Mast is available in many special editions, as in Everyman's Library and in the Riverside Literature Series. For Dana's biography consult Charles Francis Adams's *Richard Henry Dana* (2 vols., 1890), and Bliss Perry's excellent essay, "Dana's Magical Chance," in *The Praise of Folly* (1923). E. F. Edgett wrote of Dana in the *DAB* (1930). See also G. Y. Smalley in *Anglo-American Memories* (1911), E. W. Emerson, *The Early Years of the Saturday Club* (1918), and J. D. Hart, "The Other Writings of Richard Henry Dana," *Colophon*, Part 19 (1934). Other articles may be found in the *Nation*, CI, Oct. 21, 1915; and in the *Outlook*, XCIX, Nov. 1911.

From TWO YEARS BEFORE THE MAST

The *Pilgrim* sailed from Boston, August 14, 1834. Dana tells of his duties and experiences as a member of the crew and of the dangers of the voyage about Cape Horn, which was rounded by the middle of November. The brig anchored at Santa Barbara, January 14, 1835. The author's account of life on the California coast includes details of trading at Monterey, of landing hides at San Diego, of hide-curing, and of "good times on shore." He went as far north as San Francisco. The homeward trip involved the rounding again of Cape Horn in the passage from the Pacific into the Atlantic, and the northward journey back to Boston.

CHAPTER V

[*Rounding the Horn*]

WEDNESDAY, *November 5th*. The weather was fine during the previous night, and we had a clear view of the Magellan Clouds and of the Southern Cross. The Magellan Clouds consist of three small nebulae in the southern part of the heavens—two bright, like the Milky Way, and one dark. They are first seen, just above the horizon, soon after crossing the southern tropic. The Southern Cross begins to be seen at 18° N., and, when off Cape Horn, is nearly overhead. It is composed of four stars in that form, and is one of the brightest constellations in the heavens.

During the first part of this day (Wednesday) the wind was light, but after noon it came on fresh, and we furled the royals. We still kept the studding sails out, and the captain said he should go round with them if he could. Just before eight o'clock (then about sundown, in that latitude) the cry of "All hands ahoy!" was sounded down the fore scuttle and the after hatchway, and, hurrying upon deck, we found a large black cloud rolling on toward us from the southwest, and darkening the whole heavens. "Here comes Cape Horn!" said the chief mate; and we had hardly time to haul down and clew up before it was upon us. In a few minutes a heavier sea was raised than I had ever seen, and as it was directly ahead, the little brig, which was no better than a bathing-machine, plunged into it, and all the forward part of her was under water; the sea pouring in through the bow-ports and hawseholes and over the knight-heads, threatening to wash everything overboard. In the lee scuppers it was up to a man's waist. We sprang aloft and double-reefed the topsails, and furled the other sails, and made all snug. But this would not do; the brig was laboring and straining against the head sea, and the gale was growing worse and worse. At the same time sleet and hail were driving with all fury against us. We clewed down, and hauled out the reef-tackles again, and close-reefed the fore-topsail, and furled the main, and hove her to, on the starboard tack. Here was an end to our fine prospects. We made up our minds to head winds and cold weather; sent down the royal yards, and unrove the gear; but all the rest of the top hamper remained aloft, even to the skysail masts and studding-sail booms.

Throughout the night it stormed violently, —rain, hail, snow, and sleet beating upon the vessel,—the wind continuing ahead, and the sea running high. At daybreak (about three A.M.) the deck was covered with snow. The captain sent up the steward with a glass of grog to each of the watch; and all the time that we were off the Cape, grog was given to the morning watch, and to all hands whenever we reefed topsails. The clouds cleared away at sunrise, and, the wind becoming more fair, we again made sail and stood nearly up to our course.

Thursday, November 6th. It continued more pleasant through the first part of the day, but at night we had the same scene over again. This time we did not heave to, as on the night before, but endeavored to beat to windward under close-reefed topsails, balance-reefed trysail, and fore topmast staysail. This night it was my turn to steer, or, as the sailors say, my *trick* at the helm, for two hours. Inexperienced as I was, I made out to steer to the satisfaction of the officer, and neither Stimson nor I gave up our tricks, all the time that we were off the Cape. This was something to boast of, for it requires a good deal of skill and watchfulness to steer a vessel close hauled, in a gale of wind, against a heavy head sea. "Ease her when she pitches," is the word; and a little carelessness in letting her ship a heavy sea might sweep the decks, or take a mast out of her.

Friday, November 7th. Towards morning the wind went down, and during the whole forenoon we lay tossing about in a dead calm, and in the midst of a thick fog. The calms here are unlike those in most parts of the world, for here there is generally so high a sea running, with periods of calm so short that it has no time to go down; and vessels, being under no command of sails or rudder, lie like logs upon the water. We were obliged to steady the booms and yards by guys and braces, and to lash everything well below. We now found our top hamper of some use, for though it is liable to be carried away or sprung by the sudden "bringing up" of a vessel when pitching in a chopping sea, yet it is a great help in steadying a vessel when rolling in a long swell, —giving more slowness, ease, and regularity to the motion.

The calm of the morning reminds me of a scene which I forgot to describe at the time of its occurrence, but which I remember from its being the first time that I had heard the near breathing of whales. It was on the night that we passed between the Falkland Islands and Staten Land. We had the watch from twelve to four, and, coming upon deck, found the little brig lying perfectly still, enclosed in a thick fog, and the sea as smooth as though oil had been poured upon it; yet now and then a long, low swell rolling under its surface, slightly lifting the vessel, but without breaking the glassy smoothness of the water. We were surrounded far and near by shoals of sluggish whales and grampuses, which the fog prevented our seeing, rising slowly to the surface, or perhaps lying out at length, heaving out those lazy, deep, and long-drawn breathings which give such an impression of supineness and strength. Some of the watch were asleep, and the others were quiet, so that there was nothing to break the illusion, and I stood leaning over the bulwarks, listening to the slow breathings of the mighty creatures,—now one breaking the water just alongside, whose black body I almost fancied that I could see through the fog; and again another, which I could just hear in the distance,—until the low and regular swell seemed like the heaving of the ocean's mighty bosom to the sound of its own heavy and long-drawn respirations.

Towards the evening of this day (Friday, 7th) the fog cleared off, and we had every appearance of a cold blow; and soon after sundown it came on. Again it was clew up and haul down, reef and furl, until we had got her down to close-reefed topsails, double-reefed trysail, and reefed fore-spencer. Snow, hail, and sleet were driving upon us most of the night, and the sea was breaking over the bows and covering the forward part of the little vessel; but, as she would lay her course, the captain refused to heave her to.

Saturday, November 8th. This day began with calm and thick fog, and ended with hail, snow, a violent wind, and close-reefed topsails.

Sunday, November 9th. Today the sun rose clear and continued so until twelve o'clock, when the captain got an observation. This was very well for Cape Horn, and we thought it a little remarkable that, as we had not had one unpleasant Sunday during the whole voyage, the only tolerable day here should be a Sunday. We got time to clear up the steerage and forecastle, and set things to rights, and to overhaul our wet clothes a little. But this did not last very long. Between five and six—the sun was then nearly three hours high—the cry of "All Starbowlines[1] ahoy?" summoned our watch on deck, and immediately all hands were called. A true specimen of Cape Horn was coming upon us. A great cloud of a dark slate-color was driving on us from the southwest; and we did our best to take in sail (for the light sails had been set during the first part of the day) before we were in the midst of it. We had got the light sails furled, the courses hauled up, and the topsail reef-tackles hauled out, and were just mounting the fore-rigging when the storm struck us. In an instant the sea, which had been comparatively quiet, was running higher and higher; and it became almost as dark as night. The hail and sleet were harder than I had yet felt them; seeming almost to pin us down to the rigging. We were longer taking in sail than ever before; for the sails were stiff and wet, the ropes and rigging covered with snow and sleet, and we ourselves cold and nearly blinded with the violence of the

[1] It is the fashion to call the respective watches Starbowlines and Larbowlines. [*Dana's note.*]

storm. By the time we had got down upon deck again, the little brig was plunging madly into a tremendous head sea, which at every drive rushed in through the bow-ports and over the bows, and buried all the forward part of the vessel. At this instant the chief mate, who was standing on the top of the windlass, at the foot of the spencermast, called out, "Lay out there and furl the jib!" This was no agreeable or safe duty, yet it must be done. John, a Swede (the best sailor on board), who belonged on the forecastle, sprang out upon the bowsprit. Another one must go. It was a clear case of holding back. I was near the mate, but sprang past several, threw the downhaul over the windlass, and jumped between the night-heads out upon the bowsprit. The crew stood abaft the windlass and hauled the jib down, while John and I got out upon the weather side of the jib boom, our feet on the foot-ropes, holding on by the spar, the great jib flying off to leeward and *slatting*[1] so as almost to throw us off the boom. For some time we could do nothing but hold on, and the vessel, diving into two huge seas, one after the other, plunged us twice into the water up to our chins. We hardly knew whether we were on or off; when, the boom lifting us up dripping from the water, we were raised high into the air and then lunged below again. John thought the boom would go every moment, and called out to the mate to keep the vessel off, and haul down the staysail; but the fury of the wind and the breaking of the seas against the bows defied every attempt to make ourselves heard, and we were obliged to do the best we could in our situation. Fortunately no other seas so heavy struck her, and we succeeded in furling the jib "after a fashion"; and, coming in over the staysail nettings, were not a little pleased to find that all was snug, and the watch gone below; for we were soaked through, and it was very cold. John admitted that it had been a post of danger, which good sailors seldom do when the thing is over. The weather continued nearly the same through the night.

Monday, November 10th. During a part of this day we were hove to, but the rest of the time were driving on, under close-reefed sails, with a heavy sea, a strong gale, and frequent squalls of hail and snow.

Tuesday, November 11th. The same.

Wednesday. The same.

Thursday. The same.

We had now got hardened to Cape weather, the vessel was under reduced sail, and everything secured on deck and below, so that we had little to do but to steer and to stand our watch. Our clothes were all wet through, and the only change was from wet to more wet. There is no fire in the forecastle, and we cannot dry clothes at the galley.[1] It was in vain to think of reading or working below, for we were too tired, the hatchways were closed down, and everything was wet and uncomfortable, black and dirty, heaving and pitching. We had only to come below when the watch was out, wring our wet clothes, hang them up to chafe against the bulkheads, and turn in and sleep as soundly as we could, until our watch was called again. A sailor can sleep anywhere, —no sound of wind, water, canvas, rope, wood, or iron can keep him awake,—and we were always fast asleep when three blows on the hatchway, and the unwelcome cry of "All Starbowlines ahoy! eight bells there below! do you hear the news?" (the usual formula of calling the watch) roused us up from our berths upon the cold, wet decks. The only time when we could be said to take any pleasure was at night and morning, when we were allowed a tin pot full of hot tea (or, as the sailors significantly call it, "water be-witched") sweetened with molasses. This, bad as it was, was still warm and comforting, and, together with our sea biscuit and cold salt beef, made a meal. Yet even this meal was attended with some uncertainty. We had to go ourselves to the galley and take our kid[2] of beef and tin pots of tea, and run the risk of losing them before we could get below. Many a kid of beef have I seen rolling in the scuppers, and the bearer lying at his length on the decks. I remember an English lad who was the life of the crew—whom we afterwards lost overboard—standing for nearly ten minutes at the galley, with his pot of tea in his hand, waiting for a chance to get down into the fore-

---

[1] flapping violently   [2] a deep wooden dish or mess tub for holding rations

[1] kitchen

castle; and, seeing what he thought was a "smooth spell," started to go forward. He had just got to the end of the windlass, when a great sea broke over the bows, and for a moment I saw nothing of him but his head and shoulders; and at the next instant, being taken off his legs, he was carried aft with the sea, until her stern lifting up, and sending the water forward, he was left high and dry at the side of the longboat, still holding on to his tin pot, which had now nothing in it but salt water. But nothing could ever daunt him, or overcome, for a moment, his habitual good-humor. Regaining his legs, and shaking his fist at the man at the wheel, he rolled below, saying, as he passed, "A man's no sailor, if he can't take a joke." The ducking was not the worst of such an affair, for, as there was an allowance of tea, you could get no more from the galley; and though the others would never suffer a man to go without, but would always turn in a little from their own pots to fill up his, yet this was at best but dividing the loss among all hands.

Something of the same kind befell me a few days after. The cook had just made for us a mess of hot "scouse,"—that is, biscuit pounded fine, salt beef cut into small pieces, and a few potatoes, boiled up together and seasoned with pepper. This was a rare treat, and I, being the last at the galley, had it put in my charge to carry down for the mess. I got along very well as far as the hatchway, and was just going down the steps, when a heavy sea, lifting the stern out of water, and, passing forward, dropping it again, threw the steps from their place, and I came down into the steerage a little faster than I meant to, with the kid on top of me, and the whole precious mess scattered over the floor. Whatever your feelings may be, you must make a joke of everything at sea; and if you were to fall from aloft and be caught in the belly of a sail, and thus saved from instant death, it would not do to look at all disturbed, or to treat it as a serious matter.

Friday, November 14th. We were now well to the westward of the Cape, and were changing our course to northward as much as we dared, since the strong southwest winds, which prevailed then, carried us in towards Patagonia. At two P.M. we saw a sail on our larboard beam, and at four we made it out to be a large ship, steering our course, under single-reefed topsails. We at that time had shaken the reefs out of our topsails, as the wind was lighter, and set the main topgallant sail. As soon as our captain saw what sail she was under, he set the fore topgallant sail and flying jib; and the old whaler—for such his boats and short sail showed him to be—felt a little ashamed, and shook the reefs out of his topsails, but could do no more, for he had sent down his topgallant masts off the Cape. He ran down for us, and answered our hail as the whale-ship *New England*, of Poughkeepsie, one hundred and twenty days from New York. Our captain gave our name, and added, ninety-two days from Boston. They then had a little conversation about longitude, in which they found that they could not agree. The ship fell astern, and continued in sight during the night. Toward morning, the wind having become light, we crossed our royal and sky-sail yards, and at daylight we were seen under a cloud of sail, having royals and skysails fore and aft. The "spouter," as the sailors call a whaleman, had sent up his main topgallant mast and set the sail, and made signal for us to heave to. About half past seven their whale-boat came alongside, and Captain Job Terry sprang on board, a man known in every port and by every vessel in the Pacific Ocean. "Don't you know Job Terry? I thought everybody knew Job Terry," said a green hand, who came in the boat, to me, when I asked him about his captain. He was indeed a singular man. He was six feet high, wore thick cowhide boots, and brown coat and trousers, and, except a sunburnt complexion, had not the slightest appearance of a sailor; yet he had been forty years in the whale-trade, and, as he said himself, had owned ships, built ships, and sailed ships. His boat's crew were a pretty raw set, just out of the bush, and, as the sailor's phrase is, "hadn't got the hayseed out of their hair." Captain Terry convinced our captain that our reckoning was a little out, and, having spent the day on board, put off in his boat at sunset for his ship, which was now six or eight miles astern. He began a "yarn" when he came aboard, which lasted, with but little intermission, for four hours. It was all about himself, and the Peruvian government, and the Dublin frigate, and her captain, Lord James Townshend, and President Jackson, and the ship *Ann M'Kim*, of Baltimore. It would probably never have come to an end, had not a good breeze sprung up, which sent him off to his own vessel. One of the lads who came in his boat, a thoroughly countrified-looking fellow, seemed to care very little about the vessel, rigging, or anything else, but went round looking at the live stock, and leaned over the pigsty, and said he wished he was back again tending his father's pigs.

A curious case of dignity occurred here. It seems that in a whale-ship there is an intermediate class, called boat-steerers. One of them came in Captain Terry's boat, but we thought he was cockswain of the boat, and a cockswain is only a sailor. In the whaler, the boat-steerers are between the officers and crew, a sort of petty officers; keep by themselves in the waist,[1] sleep amidships, and eat by themselves, either at a separate table, or at the cabin table, after the captain and mates are done. Of all this hierarchy we were entirely ignorant, so the poor boat-steerer was left to himself. The second mate would not notice him, and seemed surprised at his keeping amidships, but his pride of office would not allow him to go forward. With dinner-time came the *experimentum crucis*. What would he do? The second mate went to the second table without asking him. There was nothing for him but famine or humiliation. We asked him into the forecastle, but he faintly declined. The whaleboat's crew explained it to us, and we asked him again. Hunger got the victory over pride of rank,

[1] middle of the ship

and his boat-steering majesty had to take his grub out of our kid, and eat with his jackknife. Yet the man was ill at ease all the time, was sparing of his conversation, and kept up the notion of a condescension under stress of circumstances. One would say that, instead of a tendency to equality in human beings, the tendency is to make the most of inequalities, natural or artificial.

At eight o'clock we altered our course to the northward, bound for Juan Fernandez.[1]

This day we saw the last of the albatrosses, which had been our companions a great part of the time off the Cape. I had been interested in the bird from descriptions, and Coleridge's poem,[2] and was not at all disappointed. We caught one or two with a baited hook which we floated astern upon a shingle. Their long, flapping wings, long·legs, and large, staring eyes, give them a very peculiar appearance. They look well on the wing; but one of the finest sights that I have ever seen was an albatross asleep upon the water, during a calm, off Cape Horn, when a heavy sea was running. There being no breeze, the surface of the water was unbroken, but a long, heavy swell was rolling, and we saw the fellow, all white, directly ahead of us, asleep upon the waves, with his head under his wing; now rising on the top of one of the big billows, and then falling slowly until he was lost in the hollow between. He was undisturbed for some time, until the noise of our bows, gradually approaching, roused him, when, lifting his head, he stared upon us for a moment, and then spread his wide wings and took his flight.

[1] island group in the South Pacific about 400 miles off the coast of Chile   [2] "The Rime of the Ancient Mariner," published in 1798

~III~

*The
Later
Nineteenth
Century*

The Later Nineteenth Century

1850–1890

I

After the Civil War a new America emerged, marked by internal reconstruction as well as by external growth and material changes. Some review of social and political conditions [1] is needed for comprehension of the new after-war literature, since these affect all forms of writing. Chief determining factors for the period were the sweeping westward movement of population, the growth of expansive industrial organization, the discoveries of mechanistic and other science, and changes in agriculture, these combining to transform conditions of living and to modify the national temper. The era as a whole was marked by political corruption, feverish speculation, the exploitation of natural resources, and a somewhat rococo taste in art and architecture. The bad days of post-war disillusionment proved to be no very auspicious time for culture and the intellectual life. The dominance of New England in the field of letters persisted, chiefly in the magazines, which dictated even more than they reflected the literary taste of the country; but it was a nerveless and imitative dominance, and this region did not regain its earlier prestige. The leading literary phenomenon of the later century was the rise of realism, which came partly as an outgrowth of Western humor and of the new emphasis on local color, and partly from the influence of fiction writers of continental Europe, such as Balzac, Zola, Flaubert, Turgenev, and others.

The Civil War was a definite turning point in American history. Signs of change had been evident before the armed conflict broke out, but the significance of the signs was not always fully recognized. The North and the South, as though caught in the clutches of malevolent fate, had drawn farther and farther apart because of sectional differences, real or imagined, and sometimes exaggerated, until they had drifted to the brink of war. Among these sectional differences was the increasing confidence of the South in its economic system as a result of the successful weathering of the Panic of 1857, which had been disastrous in the North. The semi-feudal traditions which were deeply rooted in Southern society, the clear-cut demarcations between the different social strata topped by the planters' aristocracy, had no counterpart in the industrial North and were not regarded there with understanding or sympathy. Educational and cultural ideals in the respective sections had little in common. Even the church and its teachings were affected by sectional

[1] The best comprehensive accounts are Allan Nevins's *The Emergence of Modern America, 1865–1878* (1927), and A. M. Schlesinger's *The Rise of the City, 1878–1898* (1933). Both have fine bibliographies which will serve as guides to further reading in the many-sided life of the period.

prejudices. With characteristic pride many Southerners looked upon themselves as descendants of superior stock and resented the prospect of being dominated by the socially inferior "Puritans" of the North. By 1861 the situation resembled that of two suspicious nations watching each other across the line of the frontier. Although the signs became clearer as the conflict progressed, their implications for the future were only vaguely understood, and at the time of Lee's surrender at Appomattox no one could anticipate precisely in what direction the new course would tend. It is doubtful whether even the most thoughtful men realized how completely past conditions were to fade.

As is true for most wars, the issues were confused. In the North one heard much about free and slave labor and the preservation of the Union; in the South, about federal power and states' rights. Controversy over the status of new states and territories contributed to the cleavage. Basically the war was a struggle between two fundamentally different economic systems: the democratic agrarianism of the Southern planters on the one hand, and the rapidly developing industrialism of the republican North—a struggle that involved the change from a land economy to a money economy as the foundation of the coming economic set-up. The shift of the Western farmers, under Lincoln, from their natural affiliation with the Southern agrarians to a sixty-year alliance with the industrial East assured the victory of the North over the South in the war. The results [1] of these changes were far-reaching, extending beyond the bounds of industry, commerce, and other economic enterprises, into the realm of the cultural and spiritual life of the nation. Ultimately the optimistic, idealistic, romantic view of life which had characterized the first half of the nineteenth century yielded to the realistic spirit, with its increasing pessimism, a spirit still dominant in the first half of the present century.

II

The steady westward movement of population with its shifting frontier was to be a factor of major national significance. The tide of emigration moved over the plains till the frontier had receded beyond the Rocky Mountains to the Pacific. The movement had begun before the Civil War. Some of the best blood had been drained from New England and other Eastern states before the Confederate guns had opened on Fort Sumter. Henceforth the role of the New Englander decreased in importance. The discovery of gold in California made it the Mecca of thousands, men of all races, types, and conditions, who endured all manner of hardships in the hope of sharing the new source of wealth. While the gold-seekers were concentrating on a mad rush to the west coast, the land-grabbers were threading their way across the Alleghenies to take possession of the intervening territory, especially the fertile valley of the Mississippi. After the war, new land, made available by the

---

[1] Consult Paul Buck's *The Road to Reunion* (1937).

Homestead Act of 1862 as well as by easy purchase from the railroads to which the Government made vast grants, attracted thousands of discharged soldiers and other restless spirits with the lure of quick prosperity. The scramble for and speculation in new land lasted until free land was exhausted. The period was characterized also by the building of railroads. The first continental railway was completed in 1869. Four railroads crossed the continent by 1880, and soon railroads entered everywhere. Means of communication became easier, and travel increased.[1]

Another factor which helped to change the national temper was the tide of immigration which swept into the country following the Civil War. Because of the rapid expansion of industrial enterprise native labor was inadequate for the demand, and the sure prospect of work, together with the activity of the steamship lines, induced immigrants from many lands to come to America. According to André Siegfried,[2] some 2,356,000 were admitted in the decade from 1860 to 1870, and 4,273,000 in that from 1880 to 1890. Among them were Irish, Scandinavians, Germans, Russians, and a sprinkling of others. It was only after strict immigration laws were passed (1907, 1924) that the flow ceased. The population, native and foreign, increased from thirty-one millions in 1860 to seventy-five millions in 1900.

This diffusion of diversified national blood had the inevitable result of changing the complexion of the American scene. At first the various groups remained largely by themselves, like patches of alien texture dotting the landscape, and continued to live for the most part in accordance with the folkways and culture which they had brought from their native lands. This clannish isolating tendency gradually disappeared as the immigrants became more and more used to American ways, but many of them remained and still remain conscious of their national origin. It was through this persisting loyalty to ancestral customs and culture that they were enabled to contribute their spiritual heritage to their adopted country and thereby to enrich American civilization. Many have risen to positions of leadership in politics, art, literature, science, and education. The record of American progress since 1865 is generously sprinkled with non-English names. Another phase of the enriching process is seen in the expansion of the social fabric, bringing greater and greater diversification of character and experience, a matter of great significance to the literary artist, as a comparison of two such novels as Hawthorne's *The Scarlet Letter* and Sinclair Lewis's *Main Street* will show.

III

Many economic changes were brought about by the Civil War. During the colonial period of our history agrarian interests were predominant. By the time of

[1] See William H. Clark's *Railroads and Rivers* (1939).
[2] *America Comes of Age* (1927). Translated from French by H. H. and Doris Hemming.

the Revolution, however, a mercantile group, although an inconsiderable minority, had developed sufficient power to influence the Constitution itself. But it was not until the newly born sovereign nation had passed the infantile period that industrialism, as such, began to challenge seriously the agrarian interests as an economic rival. Before 1850 it was evident that the economic future of the North lay in the realm of manufacture and industry, while the South remained more and more doggedly agricultural. Apparently the divergent economic interests could not be reduced to a common denominator.

The war left both sides in a seriously impaired condition. As an effect of the almost continuous campaigning within its territory and of later maltreatment, the South was prostrate; even the victorious North felt the pinch of strained finances and the temporary disruption of its industrial system. When peace finally came about, the most pressing task was the restoration of normal industrial activity in order to satisfy the peacetime demand for goods, and to begin as soon as possible to liquidate the enormous war debt. The dual task was made easier because of the industrial stimulus and development which resulted from wartime demands. It has been said that the war was won in Northern factories. The use of steadily improved machinery in turn made possible a steadily increasing rate of production. The wartime impetus and the peacetime demands carried a vigorous industrial program into the new era, and marked the beginning of almost unprecedented expansion. Once the strain and uncertainty of conflict lifted, all energies were focused upon economic rehabilitation. The stage was set for the next period, a period often referred to by a name coined by Mark Twain, the Gilded Age, though it also goes by others such as the Diffusive Period, the Frontier Period, the Age of Innocence, the Great Barbecue, the Wasted Generation, the Tragic Era, none of which is very satisfactory.

The Gilded Age extended, roughly speaking, from 1865 to 1890. It was a period marked by vast industrial expansion and further characterized by reckless and often inexcusably wasteful exploitation of natural resources, by huge investment of capital, the increasing use of machinery, and an ever-mounting speed of production. Companies were formed for great undertakings. Nation-wide corporations grew up. With an eye to profitable enterprise, the country set to work with every available means to convert all known resources into usable and therefore profit-producing commodities. The nation's resources of forest, coal, iron, copper, and oil were exploited.

From one standpoint the period might be called the age of steel and lumber, for these lay at the heart of the industrial enterprise and prosperity. With the discovery of oil in western Pennsylvania in 1859, the constantly improved methods of refining it and the growing multiplicity of its uses, as well as those of its by-products ranging from quack medicine to illumination and power, the oil industry rapidly assumed national proportions. Before the Civil War the manufacture of steel was a slow and expensive process. For this reason production was limited, and its use confined largely to cutlery and high-grade tools. With the invention of the Bessemer process, introduced into America in 1864, both the production and the use of steel were revolutionized. The large scale output and less costly process were able to meet the insistent demands for steel caused by the rapid expansion of railroad lines and the growing use of machinery in manufacturing plants. As a result of this response to the requirements of a new age, mining and the conversion of crude ore into usable iron and steel also became a major industry. And while drilling machines and pumping towers dotted sections of the landscape in ever increasing numbers, and blast furnaces threw their lurid glare against the night sky throughout the cities and countryside of the East, the lumber industry was taking its toll of virgin forests, especially in the north Mississippi valley. Vast stretches of timberland were denuded with a reckless abandon and wastefulness which cannot be justified in the face even of a limitless plenty, a wastefulness so improvident that signs of depletion early pointed in the direction of an inescapable conservation program, if this resource is to meet the demands of the future. Among the new enterprises should be mentioned also the meat-packing industry, which took its place beside the oil, steel, and lumber interests; likewise the improved industries such as the manufacture of shoes and clothing on a scale that impressed foreign observers. The present purpose is not, however, to recount details of industrial and economic history, but rather to examine the effect which this period of industrialization had upon the temper and spirit of the people.

While industry was booming and laying the foundation of an unprecedented prosperity, the farmers of the West and South fared less well. They were menaced by discriminative freight rates giving them unfair competition, were dependent on Eastern tradesmen and financiers regarding the prices of goods they produced and consumed, were without the advantages of such a tariff as protected manufactured articles, and were harassed by the foreclosure of mortgages. The Southern farmers, their land devastated by military campaigns, hampered by the lack of labor, victimized by reconstruction agencies, found rehabilitation slow and sometimes frustrated. To recapitalize their individual enterprises, to re-establish their shattered markets, and to secure the means of a respectable livelihood or a measure of economic security seemed nearly hopeless. A few attempts to assist the farmer were made, however. The Grange movement, begun in 1867, spread with rapidity, and endeavors were made through concerted effort to obtain legislation favorable to the farmer. During the nineties, a third party movement growing out of the widespread organization of the Farmers' Alliance resulted in the formation of the Populist Party,[1] which brought considerable pressure to bear upon national affairs.

[1] See J. D. Hicks, *The Populist Revolt* (1931).

IV

The rapid expansion of industrial enterprise and the ready market for the ever-increasing variety of manufactured commodities made possible the acquisition of large profits. Aside from many legitimate methods of money-making, get-rich-quick schemes, speculation, and financial manipulation on a gigantic scale were resorted to. Instances are the Erie Railroad scandal, involving the watering of stock, and the Crédit Mobilier, a joint stock company organized in 1863 under the laws of Pennsylvania and reorganized in 1867 to build up the Union Pacific Railroad. It collapsed through scandal from charges of bribery of members of Congress. There was more than the usual friction between capital and labor. Strikes gave stimulus to the organization of labor unions. A group of men in 1881 formed a labor union which, five years later, was reorganized as the American Federation of Labor.[1] The movement was complicated by the tendency toward socialism and anarchism which in the Haymarket Riot in Chicago in 1886 resulted in the killing and wounding of several policemen and the subsequent hanging of a number of the rioters. The industrializing era is also responsible for the concentration of vast numbers of people in the cities and the consequent urbanization of a large part of the population. Since the factory system made it necessary that the workers live in centers of production, a steady drift of people from country to city, in place of the earlier exodus of town dwellers to the frontier, accompanied the industrial expansion. Thus cities became more numerous and larger. In 1860 the neighboring cities of New York and Brooklyn had a population of a million. Chicago, outstripping St. Louis, had by 1900 a population of upward of a million seven hundred thousand.

Along with the change from rural to urban environment there came also a change in the spiritual outlook and temper. Shorter and more regular hours of work, comforts and conveniences which only cities could provide, greater opportunities for social intercourse, means of entertainment, cultural advantages such as music and the drama, and a gradually growing sophistication gave the newly inducted city dwellers advantages over their country cousins, who continued to live the same restricted lives that their ancestors had lived for generations. Rural and small-town life was looked upon as narrow, culturally barren, and provincial. Further, the rise of capitalistic industrialism with its factory system resulted in the demarcation of classes and the growth of class feeling.

V

Since the days of Franklin and Edwards, American scientists have made notable contributions to the organized knowledge of physical nature. Men like Asa Gray

---

[1] See J. R. Commons and Others, *History of Labor in the United States* (1918); F. T. Carlton, *Organized Labor in American History* (1920); and A. Bimba, *The History of the American Working Class* (1927).

the botanist, 1810–1888, won a permanent place in the annals of scientific achievement. As inhabitants of a new continent, beset with problems thrust upon them by a strange environment, Americans were intellectually hospitable to any and all increase of knowledge which might have a bearing upon the vicissitudes of life. They received gratefully the application of scientific principles to industry, the invention of devices to lighten human toil. The discoveries of mechanistic and other science and greater wealth improved standards of living. Use of the telegraph increased, and electric lighting, the telephone, steam heat, matches, elevators, and paved streets appeared or had wider use. On the other hand, when scientific studies challenged and apparently undermined long-held views, the acceptance of their conclusions was not so immediate or enthusiastic. Some of the implications suggested by the study of biology and geology which had a direct bearing upon human origins and destiny caused considerable perturbation. Darwin's *On the Origin of Species* (1859), which conflicted with orthodoxy, was read hesitantly and rejected or feared by many because of its implied attitude toward the traditional teachings of the church. Herbert Spencer applied the Darwinian theory of evolution to the study of sociology and psychology. Through his interpretations of various aspects, John Fiske, 1842–1901, philosopher and historian, presented a confident optimism grounded upon a new view of man's biological past and an expanding vision of his future, an optimism yielding later to a more pessimistic outlook. These two men and Edward Youmans, 1821–1887, who was the chief promoter of Spencer's publications in the United States, and who secured the establishment of the *Popular Science Monthly* in 1872, were largely instrumental in making the American mind science-conscious.[1]

The Gilded Age was not marked by high artistic or aesthetic taste. Domestic architecture implied lavish expenditure and sought impressiveness through size and ornamentation. A house built on massive proportions was looked on as a sign of financial stability, if not as a guarantee of social respectability. In many instances expenditure was carried to the point of absurdity. Exterior ornamentations, sometimes of wood, sometimes of metal, often of intricate pattern and design and exhibiting a multiplicity of pointless detail, deserved the name given them of "gingerbread decoration." In contrast with the beauty of simplicity and orderliness which characterized early American architecture and which has been to some extent restored in our day, although on different lines, these creations of the Gilded Age are masterpieces of ill-advised complexity and disorder.

Not all its achievements were accepted without protest. Such books as Mark Twain's *The Gilded Age* (1873) and W. D. Howells's *The Rise of Silas Lapham* (1885), read in the light of later perspective, are not mere representations of life

[1] See B. J. Loewenberg, "The Controversy over Evolution in New England, 1859–1873," *New England Quarterly*, VIII, 232–257; "Reaction of American Scientists to Darwinism," *American Historical Review*, XXXVIII, 687–701.

but are as well rather pointed criticism of some of its tendencies. Henry George, 1839–1897, and Henry Adams, 1838–1918, were the professed critics of the period and the philosophy of life which characterized it. In his *Progress and Poverty* (1879–1880) George attacked it from the economic side. The tendency in American life as he viewed it made inevitable an ever-widening gap between wealth and poverty, as civilization advances. His contention was that land with all that it provides for the well-being of man belonged to the people as a gift of nature and that every human being has a right to as much of this gift as is necessary for his happiness and well-being. Henry Adams, writing somewhat later, felt keenly the smothering influence of the time upon the cultural and intellectual life of the nation. Scion of a renowned New England family, an intellectual by heritage and preference, he found the atmosphere of his age hostile to his ideals. In his bewilderment he sought to find a satisfying philosophy of history and of life in various ways, such as the study of American history and biography, and the interpretation of medieval French mysticism as represented in *Mont-Saint-Michel and Chartres.*

Two other trends deserve mention. Education gained in importance in the later century. Schools and colleges existed no longer merely for the clerical and learned professions but became more scientific and sought to give more emphasis to the practical, if not yet to the vocational. Education for women gained acceptance also. Oberlin opened its doors to women in 1835 and to coeducation on the college level in 1837, and it was the first institution to do so. Its example was followed in time by the state universities, and distinctive colleges for women, such as Vassar (1865) and Wellesley (1870), were founded.[1] By the end of the century the principle of feminine education was well established. Newspapers and popular magazines for home reading, for which this was a flourishing period, sprang into existence. *Harper's Magazine* (1850), the *Atlantic Monthly* (1857), *Scribner's Monthly* (1870), and the *Century* (1881), devoted to articles, essays, fiction, and travel sketches, competed in popularity and influence. The higher forms of literature became somewhat subordinated to science, popular interests, and the dissemination of news. The influence of the editorial, however, waned.

In the wake of great economic changes it was inevitable that the spirit of the people should change as well. Gone were the spacious idealistic pre-war days. The national mind tended as a whole toward continued and re-emphasized practicality. The measurement of industrial achievement in terms of profit focused attention on things rather than man. As interest in things became more pronounced, from romantic idealism with its confident optimism the pendulum slowly swung in the direction of artistic earthliness.

[1] See E. P. Cubberley, *Public Education in the United States* (1919, 1934), and Thomas Woody, *History of Women's Education in the United States* (1929).

VI

The new age was to be chiefly an age of prose; the age-old ascendancy of poetry was broken at last. It was marked by the entrance of unconventional, sometimes unliterary new work, much of it humorous. Changes in social and agricultural conditions were accompanied by literary changes and shifts of emphasis. New patterns of thought and new moods appeared and new topics displaced the old. After 1870 fiction became a more and more important form of literary art as it groped toward new subjects and a new technique. The literary frontier was extended beyond the Alleghenies over the Middle Border to the Pacific,[1] with Mark Twain and Bret Harte as leading pioneers in regional writing, local color, and the frontier spirit. The realistic movement got consciously under way in the 1880's, with W. D. Howells its avowed champion, though his proved to be the mild realism of the commonplace rather than the stern brand of European novelists like Zola, Flaubert, Turgenev, or Tolstoi. Later came naturalism, with Stephen Crane as its first exponent. Humanitarianism continued to have emphasis, and more attention was given to sociological problems and externalities. New political and other novels dealt with the phenomena of cities and with economic realism and psychology. A literature of protest[2] made its appearance, mirroring disillusionment and skepticism and exhibiting a new sense of political injustice, coercive regimentation, and class division. The passion for individual liberty dimmed. Romantic optimism, which had been a dominant trend from about 1850 to the Civil War, became outdated. Though the old authors continued to write, for the most part they merely echoed their earlier work. Culture still meant Europe and the past, but a new national culture struggled upward.[3] Preoccupation with fact, reality, things as they are, assumed the lead over sentimentality and the extravagant. The new realism was to influence all types of writing, fiction, drama, poetry, criticism, history.

The romanticism persisting in poetry was a paling romanticism of convention, its subject matter outworn. A group of younger poets, R. H. Stoddard, Bayard Taylor, E. R. Sill, E. C. Stedman, T. B. Aldrich, who came to maturity after the war, continued the declining tradition. Reared as they were in pre-war days, they did not realize the changed order and left unsung the beginnings of the new life. The bulk of the poetry continuing the Genteel Tradition is intellectually thin and devoid of ideas, emotionally somewhat forced and colorless, seeming at times artificial and insincere. Exotic old-world themes were preferred by these writers to native subject matter, and some of their best work dealt with foreign material. Keats and Tennyson strongly influenced several members of the group during

[1] See Dorothy Dondore, *The Prairie and the Making of Middle America* (1926).

[2] See C. C. Regier, *The Era of the Muckrakers* (1932).

[3] Consult H. H. Clark, "Nationalism in American Literature," *University of Toronto Quarterly*, II, 492–519 (July, 1933), and B. T. Spencer, "A National Literature, 1837–1855," *American Literature*, VIII (May, 1936), for discussions of growing nationalism.

their formative years, notably Taylor and Aldrich. Mere aestheticism, the striving for effects that are pretty and sentimental rather than beautiful or moving, almost assumed the proportions of a cult. Lanier, a romantic, though he was conscious of economic change, mainly continued to treat old themes. Post-war romanticism could not thrive long, however, in the new spiritual climate. The genteel tradition of sentimental cultured conformity to European models, a tradition often result-ing in a false refinement,[1] was to end with Walt Whitman and Emily Dickinson.

The major poetic figure of the after-war period is Whitman, who broke loose from convention in both matter and form. Neither departure proved acceptable to his contemporaries, but both were to inspire later literature. Whitman realized that new form was necessary for the new indigenous democratic material he aspired to treat. He wished to be the laureate of democracy and to teach equality and comrade-ship. He was impressed, too, by the vast American scene, stretching from coast to coast and from Canada to Florida; and he left a sort of general canvas of its wide spaces and varied life. Whitman was a child of the transcendentalists, especially Emerson, to whom he owed the suggestion of the need of a newer, freer verse form. He had their optimism and their self-confidence. In common with the ro-manticists of the earlier period he had faith in the goodness and perfectibility of the people, in idealistic philosophy, and in the worship of a beautiful and edifying pre-Darwinian nature permeated with divinity; although, unlike them, he did not profess to prefer solitude to society but felt drawn to crowds. Whitman belonged with the realists, on the other hand, in his sympathy with laborers, artisans, pi-oneers, with the life of the farm and the life of the city, in his realistic treatment of sex, and when picturing American harbors, ferryboats, and the American country-side. Through identifying himself in his peculiar manner with persons and ob-jects, and through his mannerism of addressing his readers as though face to face with them, he achieved extraordinary effects of intensity and reality. Whitman's democracy now seems more of the past than of the roseate future he prophesied; but such was the originality and force of his work that he will remain an outstand-ing literary personality of his day. His contribution to the growth of realism should not be minimized or overlooked.

The second salient poetic figure of the period is Emily Dickinson. Her work was preserved to us more or less by accident; only a few of her pieces were published in her lifetime, and not till the twentieth century did her recognition come. Her po-etic ideas and comments belong, in any case, to no special era but are independent of time. She too rejected conventions, cared for no set technique, no formulas of versification, no fastidious rhyming. She was free from conventions of matter as well. There is no European imitation in her work, no consciousness of Keats or

---

[1] See, however, W. F. Taylor, "The Gilded Age," *Sewanee Review*, January–March, 1937, who points out aspects of this age that modify the usual interpretations and criticisms of it.

Tennyson. Nor did she need outside experience to inspire her. Her recluse life with its narrow opportunities seemed to be enough. She found her themes in her household duties, her flowers, the weather, and in her inner life. She concerned herself with abstractions regarding the age-old subjects: life, death, love, nature, eternity. She must be read for her thought, for audacious daring bits spontaneously presented, comments on life, flights of the imagination, and sudden transcendental glimpses. The usual conception of her as a blighted soul, shunning human contacts because of her thwarted love affair, is probably mistaken. Rather does her poetry leave an effect of gaiety, joy, and utter independence.

VII

Much the same shifts of emphasis appear in the field of fiction as in the field of poetry. No one came forward to carry on the tradition of Cooper, Poe, and Hawthorne. In fiction, too, the romantic temper had lost its freshness and power and seemed to linger as a static aftermath. Even before Hawthorne's death in 1864 the stream of the novel began to thin. *The Lamplighter* (1854), by Maria S. Cummins, outsold *The Scarlet Letter* (1850), but is now forgotten. The so-called "domestic sentimentalists," Mrs. E. D. E. N. Southworth, Mary J. Holmes, Augusta Evans Wilson, produced a flood of lachrymose classics. The "evangelical sentimentalists," Dr. J. G. Holland, the first editor of *Scribner's Magazine*, and the Reverend E. P. Roe, one-time army chaplain, composed moralizing tales which conformed to the popular conception of poetic justice. Since the novel was forced to vindicate itself against popular prejudice by its emphasis on moral and religious sentiment [1] it is not hard to understand why Lew Wallace's *Ben Hur* (1880), a well-written story of the time of Christ, became one of the most widely read novels of the post-war period. In reality these writers represented the transition from the older romance to a new type of novel, the nature of which was yet undetermined. As romances, many were pallid reflections of a type that is past, love stories bathed in sweetness and sentimentalism and conveying moral lessons, but seldom penetrating beneath the surface of life and hence throwing little light upon its meaning and significance. Aside from touches of realism here and there, they were indifferent and unprophetic as omens of the novel that was to come.

Two definite phases of post-war literary development are mainly traceable to the western migration. One is the emergence of humor, culminating in Mark Twain; the other is the rise of local color, involving faithful details of region and scene, the "here and now," under the influence of Bret Harte.

Humor [2] has always been regarded as one of America's peculiar contributions to

---

[1] See A. H. Quinn, *American Fiction* (1936), and F. L. Pattee, *The Development of the American Short Story* (1923).

[2] See Constance M. Rourke, *American Humor* (1931), and Walter Blair, *Native American Humor* (1937). The latter has representative selections, with an extensive introduction and bibliography.

literature. It is essentially the product of the frontier—of the frontier after it moved far enough west to escape the inhibiting hand of the Puritan tradition. New England had produced genuine native Yankee humor, seen in such works as Samuel Peters's "lying history" of Connecticut (1781), Royall Tyler's *The Contrast* (1787), and at a much later date Lowell's *The Biglow Papers;* but the fact should be emphasized that the humor which has persisted and which is in the direct line of development sprang largely from the colorful westward-moving frontier. The eastern frontier was relatively homogeneous, the settlers being largely of Anglo-Saxon stock and showing a limited variety of human types. When different racial stocks were thrown together, as Dutch and English were in New York, Irving could write his humorous *Knickerbocker History* (1809). As the frontier moved westward it became more and more picturesque. Contrasts became sharper and sharper, and humor thrives on contrasts. It is not surprising therefore that Artemus Ward, Josh Billings, and Petroleum V. Nasby, natives of the East, sought contact with the moving frontier, Ward traveling all the way to the Pacific coast, Billings and Nasby visiting the Mississippi valley. They brought to their writings freshness and freedom, a release from convention and restraint, and considerable democratic irreverence, qualities which a more settled state of culture could hardly have inspired or stimulated. In fact, the humor of an eastern writer like Seba Smith, whose *Letters of Major Jack Downing* (1839) were very popular in their day, seems thin and pale beside that of the more virile writers who drew material and inspiration from the West.

Mark Twain is in the direct line of development of this western humor, and became its most famous exponent. Born in Missouri he moved as a young man to the Pacific coast where he was in turn prospector, miner, and newspaper man, and emerged as a professional humorist, making use of the contrasts, exaggeration, and burlesque suggested to him by frontier life. But Mark Twain was more than a humorist and professional laughter-smith. He was a critic and satirist as well. The failure of his generation to recognize his serious purposes became in later life a real tragedy to him. As a document in social history, *Life on the Mississippi* (1883) is an accurate and vivid record of the steamboat era. *The Gilded Age* (1873) is a rather sharp attack against the crass materialism of the get-rich-quick variety of money-makers who dominated the seventies and eighties. *The Prince and the Pauper* (1882) is a venture into English history, with an anti-monarchical slant. *A Connecticut Yankee at King Arthur's Court* (1889) is not merely a burlesque staged in the Middle Ages but a pitiless exposure of what the author regarded as a highly inferior civilization, and incidentally an implied defense of American democratic institutions. *The Mysterious Stranger* (1916), published after his death, deals cynically with the problem of man's origin and destiny. Mark Twain's life seems to have been an unfolding disillusionment, leading to unmitigated pessimism, both of which find in this posthumous book pointed and bitter expression. His fame has rested hitherto on such more purely humorous books as *The Adventures of Tom Sawyer* (1876) and *The Adventures of Huckleberry Finn* (1884) rather than upon the more serious books just mentioned. Upon which it will ultimately rest it is too early to conjecture. Recent studies, however, indicate that many of his writings once superficially regarded as humorous only now are seen to carry a purpose beyond the mere provocation of laughter, and that the admittedly critical aspect of his thought is at the moment of paramount interest. He looms as one of the great figures in our literature, from whatever angle he is approached.

Bret Harte, who had coached Mark Twain, was one of the original "Argonauts" to journey from the East to the shores of the Pacific. Here he found employment in a variety of occupations and finally established himself as a writer of a new type of prose. He took the western scene as subject matter for his work and endeavored to represent it with meticulous regard to immediate local conditions, such as character, dialect, and setting. These he overlaid with something of the sentimentalism of Dickens, of whose novels he was a lifelong sympathetic reader. In "The Luck of Roaring Camp" (1868) and "The Outcasts of Poker Flat" and "Tennessee's Partner" (1869), he is generally credited with beginning the local-color school of American fiction. As over against his fiction, Harte's verse is mediocre and at times descends to doggerel. He achieved great vogue during his lifetime, but he did not seem to be able to maintain the pace he had set for himself in his earlier writings and his work gradually lost favor. During his later years he lived in Europe, in lonely isolation from family, friends, home, and country.

Western poetry of this period is represented further by the work and colorful personality of Cincinnatus Hiner Miller, who later adopted the name of Joaquin. Born in Indiana, he was taken as a child to Oregon, where he grew up. The influence of Byron, whose works he read eagerly, is noticeable in his personality as well as in his poetry. Discouraged by the neglect of his own people, he went to London and found himself lionized by London society. His poetry, uneven in quality, rises on occasion to lyrical heights. The themes are largely western and the best passages are mainly inspired by the poet's love of the western scene.

The two realists who dominated American fiction until the end of the century are William Dean Howells and Henry James. Howells grew up in Ohio but lived for the greater part of his life in Boston and New York. In his *Criticism and Fiction* (1891) and other critical writings he assailed the practices of the romanticists and extolled the virtues of realism; as a novelist he put his critical theories into practice. Because of very definite religious convictions and a high sense of ethical responsibility he closed his eyes to much that seeing life steadily and seeing it whole would naturally have prompted him to notice, and which later novelists saw and reported. He was careful not to offend popular taste or the moral sensitivity of his readers.

He aimed to portray life as it unfolded itself in ordinary routine experiences, and avoided for the most part themes that are unpleasant and problematical. This does not mean that Howells was a man of timid or lackluster thought. He treated socialistic ideals in fictionized form in *A Traveller from Altruria* (1894), really a tract, and *Through the Eye of the Needle* (1907). He dulled the controversial edge of his liberal thought by his mild-mannered treatment and thus escaped many of the dangers which befell some of the later realists. In *The Rise of Silas Lapham* (1885) and *A Hazard of New Fortunes* (1889) he not merely sets changing social conditions in contrast but is at the same time definitely critical of them. He was influenced by some of the continental realists, notably Tolstoi, Turgenev, and Zola, whose general attitude he shared but whose extremes he avoided with zealous care. To such persons as enjoy the calm unfolding of the panorama of life in its quieter phases, some of Howells's novels are still vitally interesting. For the moment, however, his reputation is dimmed by the work of his more audacious successors.

Henry James, the internationalist, is pre-eminently a psychologist. Educated mostly abroad, he came to look upon his native land as essentially crude and uncultured. The mellow atmosphere of old-world centers of culture was more conducive to his spiritual development and peace of mind than that of America with its multiplicity of enterprises, most of which were culturally undirected and therefore, it seemed to him, largely wasted. The scenes of many of his novels are laid, in whole or in part, in foreign lands. In many of them American and foreign characters are confronted, and the contrasts do not always reflect credit upon his fellow countrymen. James probes deep into the spiritual experiences and motives of his characters and reveals with extraordinary meticulousness their mental processes.

The essay did not play a very conspicuous or important role in the after-war period. Perhaps the nature writers,[1] John Burroughs and John Muir, deserve leading mention. Nor was the drama very distinctive. The leaders in stage literature were Augustin Daly, James A. Herne, Bronson Howard, William Gillette, Augustus Thomas, Clyde Fitch—none of these of salient importance.

In general the decades from the 1830's till the Civil War have remained the Golden Age of American literature. In the last part of the century the literary product bulked large and the level of execution was high. Printing presses turned out masses of reading matter and more persons wrote than ever before. Nevertheless the more significant names came, as in England, in the first half of the century. Except for a few poets and fiction writers, the work of the later authors was less distinctive and original and achieved less recognition in other countries.

---

[1] Consult P. M. Hicks, *Development of the Natural History Essay in American Literature* (1924).

1819 -- *Herman Melville* -- 1891

IT WAS not until the twentieth century that Melville found acknowledgment as a major writer. His significance was suddenly recognized in the wake of a rising interest in the South Seas, fostered by Robert Louis Stevenson's residence in Samoa and Tahiti. It was Melville who first pointed out the romance of the islands of the South Pacific. He was an independent genius, owing little to the writers of New England or to the Knickerbocker school. Neither Hawthorne nor Poe had his vigor, breadth, and prodigality as a writer of fiction. His *Moby Dick* now ranks as one of our great works of fiction.

Herman Melville, a grandson of the old man of Holmes's "The Last Leaf," took pride in his New England ancestry. His family had been one of distinction in Scotland and had taken a prominent part in the Revolutionary War. He was born in New York on August 1, 1819. His father was a well-to-do merchant who traveled extensively. He died when Melville was still very young but not before the boy had developed a strong interest in foreign places and peoples. The family had reverses before his father died, and his mother was left with little or no support for herself and her small children. Melville was educated at the public schools and attended the Albany Academy until he was fifteen. He then tried clerking in a bank and teaching school, but he did not like teaching. In 1837 he ran off to sea and shipped on a boat that sailed to England. He tried once more to teach school but again gave it up. This was the age of fast sailing vessels, "clipper ships," and the spirit of the sea was strong within him.

The next years of his life were years of romance and adventure. In 1841, when he was twenty-one, he took ship for the South Pacific on the whaler *Acushnet* and remained on it for eighteen months. Because of the hardships of the life, he deserted, and with a comrade lived for four months among friendly cannibals, the Typees of the Marquesas Islands. He was rescued by an Australian whaler and put ashore at Tahiti, where he hired out for some time. He escaped once more and returned in an American ship to Boston. His "travel romances" or "sketch books of the South Seas" record these experiences. *Typee* (1846) gives an idyllic picture, probably influenced by Rousseau, of life in the Pacific Isles; and *Omoo* (1847) has its scenes laid in Tahiti and the Marquesas. In these tales of sea adventures, and in the later *Moby Dick*, both reality and imagination are relied upon as a basis for the incidents. *Redburn* (1849) and *White Jacket* (1850), books which belong to our naval history, are more or less autobiographical and tell of his life as a seaman on board a United States frigate. These early books brought him both celebrity and condemnation;

for he was censured for his arraignment of missionaries and soldiers, and his account of the ill effects that the bringing of the white man's civilization had upon the islands.

Once more in America, Melville was conspicuous as the "man who had escaped from the cannibals." In 1847, he married the daughter of the chief justice of Massachusetts. He lived for a while in New York and continued to write. In 1849 he traveled in London and Paris; and *Mardi*, a medley of travel sketches, philosophy, and satire, was published. After his return to America, he moved to Arrowhead Farm at Pittsfield, Massachusetts. Here he came to know Hawthorne at Lenox and in 1851 dedicated *Moby Dick* to him. After the publication of *Pierre* (1852) his work declined in interest and power, and his later books, such as *Israel Potter* (1855) and *Piazza Tales* (1856), are little known. He printed some poetry and tried lecturing; but as he grew older, he withdrew more and more from society. In 1866 he was made customs inspector at New York City and held the post for nineteen years. He died on September 29, 1891, an almost forgotten author.

Moby Dick, an amazing prose-epic masterpiece, did not succeed when it first appeared. This sea classic, then termed "Bedlam literature," enshrines the bygone life of the whaling ship with its technicalities and dangers, doing for it what Cooper had done for the frontier and what Mark Twain was to do for the steamboat age of the Mississippi. It contains two memorable characters: the monomaniac Captain Ahab, who ruled over a grim, wild crew, and the gigantic, malevolent white whale, Moby Dick. The struggle between them has been termed an allegory, for the fierce pursuit of the white whale seems symbolic of the unremitting hatred and hunting down of the vast moral evil of the world; but the author said that no allegory had been intended. Writing to Hawthorne, he also hinted quite broadly just the opposite. His depiction of sea life and its exciting action has never been surpassed. For Melville, the sea is terrific and tremendous, and he treats it with the mystical, intense, and bitter quality that is seen in all his writings. The book is emotional and pictorial, not logical, and its style is extravagant. But its gusto and strength are unmistakable.

Melville read much as a youth in his father's carefully selected library, and he continued to read, with the zest of a booklover, in later life. Some of the authors influencing him were Sir Thomas Browne, whom he greatly admired, Robert Burton, and Carlyle. On his return voyage from the South Seas he read the Elizabethan dramatists, Marlowe of the "mighty line," and Ben Jonson. Others he mentions are Beaumont and Fletcher, Milton, Rousseau, Chesterfield, Byron, Moore, and Scott, and he was interested in the German metaphysicians. Cooper he knew among American writers. Dana's *Two Years before the Mast*, which appeared in 1840, may have given him the urge to sea adventure. Before his first books were written he read everything he could lay his hands on about the South Seas, accounts of voyages, missionaries' reports, and travelers' descriptions. For *Moby Dick* he read everything available to him about whales and whaling, making notes and collecting allusions. If much in his books comes from his personal experience, much too comes from his reading, especially in his earlier ones. Professor C. R. Anderson (*Melville in the South Seas*, 1939) cites from Melville's *Redburn*, ". . . for materials they use odds and ends of old rigging called *junk*, the yarns of which are picked to pieces and then twisted into new combinations," adding that this is something like the manner in which "most books are manufactured." Professor Anderson believes that Melville's books about the South Seas were put together in much this way. In these his style is simple and direct. In *Moby Dick* and elsewhere his unique manner of expression comes to its own. It is not an orderly or disciplined style. It has vehemence, emotional quality, is of prodigal richness, and often rises to great power. There is realism of detail, and, since Melville has an ear for rhythm, there are frequent passages of beautiful lavish music.

Melville was more conscious of his artistic powers and problems than has been believed of one who wrote so copiously and so easily. This is clear from a reading of his *Pierre*. He wanted complete freedom in fiction writing, to be frank and truthful and to cut athwart accepted conventions of composition. He cared little for conforming to the orthodox in themes, or handling, or in his characters. He was no advocate of consistency in every character in fiction. Distinctive of him was his liking for lone mighty figures, such as Ahab or Pierre, "originals" of striking stature. He seems to have wished to select a "mighty theme," and to produce a "mighty book." This he did in *Moby Dick*.

There is a collected edition, *The Works of Herman Melville*, 16 vols., London, 1922–24. Many separate editions of *Moby Dick*, *Typee*, and *Pierre* are available. V. G. Paltsits edited *The Family Correspondence of Herman Melville, 1830–1904*, in *Bulletin of the N. Y. Public Library*, XXXIII, July and August, 1929; and M. Minnegerode, *Some Personal Letters of Herman Melville, and a Bibliography* (1922). Chief references for Melville are Raymond Weaver, *Herman Melville, Mariner and Mystic* (1921); John Freeman, *Herman Melville*, in English Men of Letters Series (1926); and Lewis Mumford, *Herman Melville* (1929). Van Wyck Brooks wrote of Melville in the *DAB*, 1933. Some of the more important critical discussions of Melville are those by Carl Van Doren, in *CHAL*, I (1917); Henry S. Canby, in *Definitions, First Series* (1922); P. H. Boynton, in *More Contemporary Americans* (1927); V. L. Parrington, in *Main Currents of American Thought*, I (1927); Van Wyck Brooks, in *Emerson and Others* (1927); Raymond Weaver, in Macy's *American Writers on American Literature* (1931); Willard Thorp, introduction to his *Melville* in the American Writers Series (1938); and C. R. Anderson, in *Melville in the South Seas* (1939). Among periodical articles are F. J. Mather, Jr., "Herman Melville," *Review*, I (August 9 and 16, 1919); E. L. G. Watson, "Moby Dick," *London Mercury*, III (Dec., 1920); F. L. Pattee, "Herman Melville," *American Mercury*, X (Jan., 1927); René Galland, "Herman Melville and 'Moby Dick,'" in *Revue Anglo-Américaine*, V (Oct., 1927); and G. C. Homans, "The Dark Angel: The Tragedy of Herman Melville," *New England Quarterly*, V (Oct., 1932).

From MOBY DICK

Melville's masterpiece, one of the great sea tales of the world, and the world's greatest whaling story. It may be read as a treatise telling everything to be known of whales and the whaling of the period, or it may be read as an adventure story of the sea. To critics it suggests the allegory of man's pursuit of evil in the world, although Melville once said that he did not see the allegory in the book till it was pointed out to him. There are three leading *dramatis personae*. The monomaniac Captain Ahab, in command of a strange, sinister crew, sets forth on his last voyage, ostensibly on an ordinary whaling expedition, but really to track down and destroy the gigantic malevolent White Whale that in an earlier encounter had mutilated him. He pursues the whale with avenging energy, pouring on it rage and hate, until he and his ship are finally destroyed by it. The last chapters tell of the terrible three-day chase in which these two well-matched characters are involved. The third character is the Sea, which is far more than mere setting or background. "In that wild beautiful romance," says Masefield in an often quoted passage, "Melville seems to have spoken the very secret of the sea, and to have drawn into his tale all the magic, all the wild joy of many waters." It too can be ferocious and violent in its malign moments, like Captain Ahab and the White Whale. In structure the book is more carefully planned than at first appears. It abounds in interruptions, digressions, rhapsodies, and denunciations; but, if it is prodigal in its wealth of material, it is also singularly original and powerful.

CHAPTER XLI

Moby Dick

I, ISHMAEL, was one of that crew; my shouts had gone up with the rest; my oath had been welded with theirs; and stronger I shouted, and more did I hammer and clinch my oath, because of the dread in my soul. A wild, mystical, sympathetical feeling was in me; Ahab's quenchless feud seemed mine. With greedy ears I learned the history of that murderous monster against whom I and all the others had taken our oaths of violence and revenge.

For some time past, though at intervals only, the unaccompanied, secluded White Whale had haunted those uncivilized seas mostly frequented by the Sperm Whale fishermen; but not all of them knew of his existence; only a few of them, comparatively, had knowingly seen him; while the number who as yet had actually and knowingly given battle to him, was small indeed. For, owing to the large number of whale-cruisers; the disorderly way they were sprinkled over the entire watery circumference, many of them adventurously pushing their quest along solitary latitudes, so as seldom or never for a whole twelvemonth or more on a stretch, to encounter a single news-telling sail of any sort; the inordinate length of each separate voyage; the irregularity of the times of sailing from home; all these, with other circumstances, direct and indirect, long obstructed the spread through the whole world-wide whaling fleet of the special individualizing tidings concerning Moby Dick. It was hardly to be doubted, that several vessels reported to have encountered, at such or such a time, or on such or such a meridian, a Sperm Whale of uncommon magnitude and malignity, which whale, after doing great mischief to his assailants, had completely escaped them; to some minds it was not an unfair presumption, I say, that the whale in question must have been no other than Moby Dick. Yet as of late the Sperm Whale fishery had been marked by various and not unfrequent instances of great ferocity, cunning, and malice in the monster attacked; therefore it was, that those who by accident ignorantly gave battle to Moby Dick; such hunters, perhaps, for the most part, were content to ascribe the peculiar terror he bred, more, as it were, to the perils of the Sperm Whale fishery at large, than to the individual cause. In that way, mostly, the disastrous encounter between Ahab and the whale had hitherto been popularly regarded.

And as for those who, previously hearing of the White Whale, by chance caught sight of him; in the beginning of the thing they had every one of them, almost, as boldly and fearlessly lowered for him, as for any other whale of that species. But at length, such calamities did ensue in these assaults—not restricted to sprained wrists and ankles, broken limbs, or devouring amputations—but fatal to the last degree of fatality; those repeated disastrous repulses, all accumulating and piling their terrors upon Moby Dick those things had gone far to shake the fortitude of many brave hunters, to whom the story of the White Whale had eventually come.

Nor did wild rumors of all sorts fail to exaggerate, and still the more horrify the true histories of these deadly encounters. For not only do fabulous rumors naturally grow out of the very body of all surprising terrible events,—as the smitten tree gives birth to its fungi; but, in maritime life, far more than in that of *terra firma*, wild rumors abound, wherever there is any adequate reality for them to cling to. And as the sea surpasses the land in this matter, so the whale-fishery surpasses every other sort of maritime life, in the wonderfulness and fearfulness of the rumors which sometimes circulate there. For not only are whalemen as a body unexempt from that ignorance and superstitiousness hereditary to all sailors; but of all sailors, they are by all odds the most directly brought into contact with whatever is appallingly astonishing in the sea; face to face they not only eye its greatest marvels, but, hand to jaw, give battle to them. Alone, in such remotest waters, that though you sailed a thousand miles, and passed a thousand shores, you would not come to any chiseled hearthstone, or aught hospitable beneath that part of the sun; in such latitudes and longitudes, pursuing too such a calling as he does, the whaleman is wrapped by influences all tending to make his fancy pregnant with many a mighty birth.

No wonder, then, that ever gathering volume from the mere transit over the wildest watery spaces, the outblown rumors of the White Whale did in the end incorporate with themselves all manner of morbid hints, and half-formed foetal suggestions of supernatural agencies, which eventually invested Moby Dick with new terrors unborrowed from anything that visibly appears. So that in many cases such a panic did he finally strike, that few who by those rumors, at least, had heard of the White Whale, few of those hunters were willing to encounter the perils of his jaw.

But there were still other and more vital practical influences at work. Not even at the present day has the original prestige of the Sperm Whale, as fearfully distinguished from all other species of the leviathan, died out of the minds of the whalemen as a body. There are those this day among them, who, though intelligent and courageous enough in offering battle to the Greenland or Right Whale, would perhaps—either from professional inexperience, or incompetency, or timidity, decline a contest with the Sperm Whale. At any rate, there are plenty of whalemen, especially among those whaling nations not sailing under the American flag, who have never hostilely encountered the Sperm Whale, but whose sole knowledge of the leviathan is restricted to the ignoble monster primitively pursued in the North. Seated on their hatches, these men will harken with a childish fireside interest and awe, to the wild, strange tales of Southern whaling. Nor is the pre-eminent tremendousness of the great Sperm Whale anywhere more feelingly comprehended, than on board of those prows which stem[1] him.

And as if the now tested reality of his might had in former legendary times thrown its shadow before it; we find some book naturalists—Olassen and Povelson—declaring the Sperm Whale not only to be a consternation to every other creature in the sea, but also to be so incredibly ferocious as continually to be athirst for human blood. Nor even down to so late a time as Cuvier's, were these or almost similar impressions effaced. For in his Natural History, the Baron himself affirms that at sight of the Sperm Whale, all fish (sharks included) are "struck with the most lively terrors," and "often in the precipitancy of their flight dash themselves against the rocks with such violence as to cause instantaneous death." And however the general experiences in the fishery may amend such reports as these; yet in their full terribleness, even to the bloodthirsty item of Povelson, the superstitious belief in them is, in some vicissitudes of their vocation, revived in the minds of the hunters.

So that overawed by the rumors and portents concerning him, not a few of the fisher-

[1] make headway against

men recalled, in reference to Moby Dick, the earlier days of the Sperm Whale fishery, when it was oftentimes hard to induce long practiced Right whalemen to embark in the perils of this new and daring warfare; such men protesting that although other leviathans might be hopefully pursued, yet to chase and point lances at such an apparition as the Sperm Whale was not for mortal man—that to attempt it, would be inevitably to be torn into a quick eternity. On this head, there are some remarkable documents that may be consulted.

Nevertheless, some there were, who even in the face of these things were ready to give chase to Moby Dick; and a still greater number who, chancing only to hear of him distantly and vaguely, without the specific details of any certain calamity, and without superstitious accompaniments, were sufficiently hardy not to flee from the battle if offered.

One of the wild suggestions referred to, as at last coming to be linked with the White Whale in the minds of the superstitiously inclined, was the unearthly conceit that Moby Dick was ubiquitous; that he had actually been encountered in opposite latitudes at one and the same instant of time.

Nor, credulous as such minds must have been, was this conceit altogether without some faint show of superstitious probability. For as the secrets of the currents in the seas have never yet been divulged, even to the most erudite research; so the hidden ways of the Sperm Whale when beneath the surface remain, in great part, unaccountable to his pursuers; and from time to time have originated the most curious and contradictory speculations regarding them, especially concerning the mystic modes whereby, after sounding to a great depth, he transports himself with such vast swiftness to the most widely distant points.

It is a thing well known to both American and English whale ships, and as well a thing placed upon authoritative record years ago by Scoresby, that some whales have been captured far north in the Pacific, in whose bodies have been found the barbs of harpoons darted in the Greenland seas. Nor is it to be gainsaid, that in some of these instances it has been declared that the interval of time between the two assaults could not have exceeded very many days. Hence, by inference, it has been believed by some whalemen, that the Nor'-West Passage, so long a problem to man, was never a problem to the whale. So that here, in the real living experience of living men, the prodigies related in old times of the inland Strello mountain in Portugal (near whose top there was said to be a lake in which the wrecks of ships floated up to the surface); and that still more wonderful story of the Arethusa fountain near Syracuse (whose waters were believed to have come from the Holy Land by an underground passage); these fabulous narrations are almost fully equaled by the realities of the whalemen.

Forced into familiarity, then, with such prodigies as these; and knowing that after repeated, intrepid assaults, the White Whale had escaped alive; it cannot be much matter of surprise that some whalemen should go still further in their superstitions; declaring Moby Dick not only ubiquitous, but immortal (for immortality is but ubiquity in time); that though groves of spears should be planted in his flanks, he would still swim away unharmed; or if indeed he should ever be made to spout thick blood, such a sight would be but a ghastly deception; for again in unensanguined billows hundreds of leagues away, his unsullied jet would once more be seen.

But even stripped of these supernatural surmisings, there was enough in the earthly make and incontestable character of the monster to strike the imagination with unwonted power. For, it was not so much his uncommon bulk that so much distinguished him from other sperm whales, but, as was elsewhere thrown out—a peculiar snow-white wrinkled forehead, and a high, pyramidical white hump. These were his prominent features; the tokens whereby, even in the limitless, uncharted seas, he revealed his identity, at a long distance, to those who knew him.

The rest of his body was so streaked, and spotted, and marbled with the same shrouded hue, that, in the end, he had gained his distinctive appellation of the White Whale; a name, indeed, literally justified by his vivid aspect, when seen gliding at high noon through a dark blue sea, leaving a milky-way wake of creamy foam, all spangled with golden gleaming. Nor was it his unwonted magnitude, nor his remarkable hue, nor yet his deformed lower jaw, that so much invested the whale with natural terror, as that unexampled, intelligent malignity which, according to specific accounts, he had over and over again evinced in his assaults. More than all, his treacherous retreats struck more of dismay than perhaps aught else. For, when swimming before his exulting pursuers, with every apparent symptom of alarm, he had several times been known to turn round suddenly, and, bearing down upon them, either stave their boats to splinters, or drive them back in consternation to their ship.

Already several fatalities had attended his chase. But though similar disasters, however little bruited[1] ashore, were by no means unusual in the fishery, yet in most instances, such seemed the White Whale's infernal forethought of ferocity, that every dismembering or death that he caused, was not wholly regarded as having been inflicted by an unintelligent agent.

Judge, then, to what pitches of inflamed, distracted fury the minds of his more desperate hunters were impelled, when amid the chips of chewed boats, and the sinking limbs of torn comrades, they swam out of the white curds of the whale's direful wrath into the serene, exasperating sunlight, that smiled on, as if at a birth or a bridal.

His three boats stove around him, and oars and men both whirling in the eddies, one captain, seizing the line-knife from his broken prow, had dashed at the whale, as an Arkansas duelist at his foe, blindly seeking with a six-inch blade to reach the fathom-deep life of the whale. That captain was Ahab. And then it was, that suddenly sweeping his sickle-shaped lower jaw beneath him, Moby Dick had reaped away Ahab's leg, as a mower a blade of grass in the field. No turbaned Turk, no hired Venetian or Malay, could have smote him with more seeing malice. Small reason was there to doubt, then, that ever since that almost fatal encounter, Ahab had cherished a wild vindictiveness against the whale, all the

more fell, for that in his frantic morbidness he at last came to identify with him, not only all his bodily woes, but all his intellectual and spiritual exasperations. The White Whale swam before him as the monomaniac incarnation of all those malicious agencies which some deep men feel eating in them, till they are left living on with half a heart and half a lung. That intangible malignity which has been from the beginning; which the ancient Ophites[1] of the east reverenced in their statue devil;—Ahab did not fall down and worship it like them; but deliriously transferring its ideas to the abhorred White Whale, he pitted himself, all mutilated, against it. All that most maddens and torments; all that stirs up the lees of things; all truth with malice in it; all that cracks the sinews and cakes the brain; all the subtle demonisms of life and thought; all evil, to crazy Ahab, were visibly personified, and made practically assailable in Moby Dick. He piled upon the whale's white hump the sum of all the general rage and hate felt by his whole race from Adam down; and then, as if his chest had been a mortar, he burst his hot heart's shell upon it.

It is not probable that this monomania in him took its instant rise at the precise time of his bodily dismemberment. Then, in darting at the monster, knife in hand, he had but given loose to a sudden, passionate, corporal animosity; and when he received the stroke that tore him, he probably felt the agonising bodily laceration, but nothing more. Yet, when by this collision forced to turn towards home, and for long months of days and weeks, Ahab and anguish lay stretched together in one hammock, rounding in midwinter that dreary, howling Patagonian Cape; then it was, that his torn body and gashed soul bled into one another; and so interfusing, made him mad. That it was only then, on the homeward voyage, after the encounter, that the final monomania seized him, seems all but certain from the fact that, at intervals during the passage, he was a raving lunatic; and, though unlimbed of a leg, yet such vital strength yet

[1] talked about

[1] Group of sects who revered the serpent (Ophis) by which Eve was tempted as the embodiment of divine wisdom. They were especially prominent in the second century and existed into the sixth.

lurked in his Egyptian chest, and was more-over intensified by his delirium, that his mates were forced to lace him fast, even there, as he sailed, raving in his hammock. In a strait-jacket, he swung to the mad rockings of the gales. And, when running into more sufferable latitudes, the ship, with mild stunsails spread, floated across the tranquil tropics, and, to all appearances, the old man's delirium seemed left behind him with the Cape Horn swells, and he came forth from his dark den into the blessed light and air; even then, when he bore that firm, collected front, however pale, and issued his calm orders once again; and his mates thanked God the direful madness was now gone; even then, Ahab, in his hidden self, raved on. Human madness is oftentimes a cunning and most feline thing. When you think it fled, it may have but become trans-figured into some still subtler form. Ahab's full lunacy subsided not, but deepeningly con-tracted; like the unabated Hudson, when that noble Northman flows narrowly, but un-fathomably through the Highland gorge. But, as in his narrow-flowing monomania, not one jot of Ahab's broad madness had been left be-hind; so in that broad madness, not one jot of his great natural intellect had perished. That before living agent, now became the living instrument. If such a furious trope may stand, his special lunacy stormed his general sanity, and carried it, and turned all its concentered cannon upon its own mad mark; so that far from having lost his strength, Ahab, to that one end, did now possess a thousand-fold more potency than ever he had sanely brought to bear upon any one reasonable object.

This is much; yet Ahab's larger, darker, deeper part remains unhinted. But vain to popularize profundities, and all truth is pro-found. Winding far down from within the very heart of this spiked Hotel de Cluny where we here stand—however grand and wonderful, now quit it;—and take your way, ye nobler, sadder souls, to those vast Roman halls of Thermes[1]; where far beneath the fan-tastic towers of man's upper earth, his root of grandeur, his whole awful essence sits in bearded state; an antique buried beneath an-tiquities, and throned on torsos! So with a broken throne, the great gods mock that captive king; so like a Caryatid,[1] he patient sits, upholding on his frozen brow the piled entablatures of ages. Wind ye down there, ye prouder, sadder souls! question that proud, sad king! A family likeness! aye, he did beget ye, ye young exiled royalties; and from your grim sire only will the old State-secret come.

Now, in his heart, Ahab had some glimpse of this, namely, all my means are sane, my motive and my object mad. Yet without power to kill, or change, or shun the fact; he likewise knew that to mankind he did long dissemble; in some sort, did still. But that thing of his dissembling was only subject to his perceptibility, not to his will determinate. Nevertheless, so well did he succeed in that dissembling, that when with ivory leg he stepped ashore at last, no Nantucketer thought him otherwise than but naturally grieved, and that to the quick, with the terrible casualty which had overtaken him.

The report of his undeniable delirium at sea was likewise popularly ascribed to a kindred cause. And so too, all the added moodiness which always afterwards, to the very day of sailing in the *Pequod* on the present voyage, sat brooding on his brow. Nor is it so very unlikely, that far from dis-trusting his fitness for another whaling voy-age, on account of such dark symptoms, the calculating people of that prudent isle were inclined to harbor the conceit, that for those very reasons he was all the better qualified and set on edge, for a pursuit so full of rage and wildness as the bloody hunt of whales. Gnawed within and scorched without, with the infixed, unrelenting fangs of some in-curable idea; such an one, could he be found, would seem the very man to dart his iron and lift his lance against the most appalling of all brutes. Or, if for any reason thought to be corporeally incapacitated for that, yet such an one would seem superlatively competent to cheer and howl on his underlings to the attack. But be all this as it may, certain it is, that with the mad secret of his unabated rage bolted up and keyed in him, Ahab had pur-

---

[1] a reference to the ruins of Roman baths, above which the Cluny Museum in Paris now stands

[1] a supporting column in architecture in the form of a draped female figure

posely sailed upon the present voyage with the one only and all-engrossing object of hunting the White Whale. Had any one of his old acquaintances on shore but half dreamed of what was lurking in him then, how soon would their aghast and righteous souls have wrenched the ship from such a fiendish man! They were bent on profitable cruises, the profit to be counted down in dollars from the mint. He was intent on an audacious, immitigable, and supernatural revenge.

Here, then, was this gray-headed, ungodly old man, chasing with curses a Job's whale[1] round the world, at the head of a crew, too, chiefly made up of mongrel renegades, and castaways, and cannibals—morally enfeebled also, by the incompetence of mere unaided virtue of right-mindedness in Starbuck, the invulnerable jollity of indifference and recklessness in Stubb, and the pervading mediocrity in Flask. Such a crew, so officered, seemed specially picked and packed by some infernal fatality to help him to his monomaniac revenge. How it was that they so aboundingly responded to the old man's ire— by what evil magic their souls were possessed, that at times his hate seemed almost theirs; the White Whale as much their insufferable foe as his; how all this came to be—what the White Whale was to them, or how to their unconscious understandings, also, in some dim, unsuspected way, he might have seemed the gliding great demon of the seas of life,— all this to explain, would be to dive deeper than Ishmael can go. The subterranean miner that works in us all, how can one tell whither leads his shaft by the ever shifting, muffled sound of his pick? Who does not feel the irresistible arm drag? What skiff in tow of a seventy-four can stand still? For one, I gave myself up to the abandonment of the time and the place; but while yet all a-rush to encounter the whale, could see naught in that brute but the deadliest ill.

CHAPTER CXXXIII

The Chase—First Day

That night, in the mid-watch, when the old man—as his wont at intervals—stepped

[1] Job 41

forth from the scuttle in which he leaned, and went to his pivot-hole,[1] he suddenly thrust out his face fiercely, snuffing up the sea air as a sagacious ship's dog will, in drawing nigh to some barbarous isle. He declared that a whale must be near. Soon that peculiar odor, sometimes to a great distance given forth by the living Sperm Whale, was palpable to all the watch; nor was any mariner surprised when, after inspecting the compass, and then the dog-vane, and then ascertaining the precise bearing of the odor as nearly as possible, Ahab rapidly ordered the ship's course to be slightly altered, and the sail to be shortened.

The acute policy dictating these movements was sufficiently vindicated at daybreak by the sight of a long sleek on the sea directly and lengthwise ahead, smooth as oil, and resembling in the pleated watery wrinkles bordering it, the polished metallic-like marks of some swift tide-rip, at the mouth of a deep, rapid stream.

"Man the mastheads! Call all hands!"

Thundering with the butts of three clubbed handspikes on the forecastle deck, Daggoo roused the sleepers with such judgment claps that they seemed to exhale from the scuttle, so instantaneously did they appear with their clothes in their hands.

"What d'ye see?" cried Ahab, flattening his face to the sky.

"Nothing, nothing, sir!" was the sound hailing down in reply.

"T'gallant-sails! stunsails alow and aloft, and on both sides!"

All sail being set, he now cast loose the life-line, reserved for swaying him to the mainroyal masthead; and in a few moments they were hoisting him thither, when, while but two-thirds of the way aloft, and while peering ahead through the horizontal vacancy between the maintopsail and topgallant-sail, he raised a gull-like cry in the air, "There she blows!—there she blows! A hump like a snowhill! It is Moby Dick!"

Fired by the cry which seemed simultaneously taken up by the three lookouts, the men on deck rushed to the rigging to behold the famous whale they had so long been

[1] where Ahab's ivory leg stood when not in use

pursuing. Ahab had now gained his final perch, some feet above the other lookouts, Tashtego standing just beneath him on the cap of the topgallant-mast, so that the Indian's head was almost on a level with Ahab's heel. From this height the whale was now seen some mile or so ahead, at every roll of the sea revealing his high sparkling hump, and regularly jetting his silent spout into the air. To the credulous mariners it seemed the same silent spout they had so long ago beheld in the moonlit Atlantic and Indian Oceans.

"And did none of ye see it before?" cried Ahab, hailing the perched men all around him.

"I saw him almost that same instant, sir, that Captain Ahab did, and I cried out," said Tashtego.

"Not the same instant; not the same—no, the doubloon[1] is mine. Fate reserved the doubloon for me. _I_ only; none of ye could have raised the White Whale first. There she blows! there she blows!—there she blows! There again!—there again!" he cried, in long-drawn, lingering, methodic tones, attuned to the gradual prolongings of the whale's visible jets. "He's going to sound! In stunsails! Down topgallant-sails! Stand by three boats. Mr. Starbuck, remember, stay on board, and keep the ship. Helm there! Luff, luff a point! So; steady, man, steady! There go flukes! No, no; only black water! All ready the boats there? Stand by, stand by! Lower me, Mr. Starbuck; lower, lower,—quick, quicker!" and he slid through the air to the deck.

"He is heading straight to leeward, sir," cried Stubb; "right away from us; cannot have seen the ship yet."

"Be dumb, man! Stand by the braces! Hard down the helm!—brace up! Shiver her!—shiver her! So; well that! Boats, boats!"

Soon all the boats but Starbuck's were dropped; all the boat-sails set—all the paddles plying; with rippling swiftness, shooting to leeward; and Ahab heading the onset. A pale, death-glimmer lit up Fedallah's sunken eyes; a hideous motion gnawed his mouth.

Like noiseless nautilus shells, their light

prows sped through the sea; but only slowly they neared the foe. As they neared him, the ocean grew still more smooth; seemed drawing a carpet over its waves; seemed a noon-meadow, so serenely it spread. At length the breathless hunter came so nigh his seemingly unsuspecting prey, that his entire dazzling hump was distinctly visible, sliding along the sea as if an isolated thing, and continually set in a revolving ring of finest, fleecy, greenish foam. He saw the vast involved wrinkles of the slightly projecting head beyond. Before it, far out on the soft Turkish-rugged waters, went the glistening white shadow from his broad, milky forehead, a musical rippling playfully accompanying the shade; and behind, the blue waters interchangeably flowed over into the moving valley of his steady wake; and on either hand bright bubbles arose and danced by his side. But these were broken again by the light toes of hundreds of gay fowls softly feathering the sea, alternate with their fitful flight; and like to some flagstaff rising from the painted hull of an argosy, the tall but shattered pole of a recent lance projected from the White Whale's back; and at intervals one of the cloud of soft-toed fowls hovering, and to and fro skimming like a canopy over the fish, silently perched and rocked on this pole, the long tail feathers streaming like pennons.

A gentle joyousness—a mighty mildness of repose in swiftness, invested the gliding whale. Not the white bull Jupiter swimming away with ravished Europa[1] clinging to his graceful horns; his lovely, leering eyes sideways intent upon the maid; with smooth bewitching fleetness, rippling straight for the nuptial bower in Crete; not Jove, not that great majesty Supreme! did surpass the glorified White Whale as he so divinely swam.

On each soft side—coincident with the parted swell, that but once laving him, then flowed so wide away—on each bright side, the whale shed off enticings. No wonder there had been some among the hunters who,

---

[1] the account of the doubloon is in Chapter XLVI of _Moby Dick_

[1] The story of how the maiden Europa was carried away to Crete by Jupiter, who had taken the form of a white bull, was told by the poet Moschus of about the second century, and may be found retold in Gayley's _Classic Myths_ and other books of classic mythology.

namelessly transported and allured by all this serenity, had ventured to assail it; but had fatally found that quietude but the vesture of tornadoes. Yet calm, enticing calm, oh, whale! thou glidest on, to all who for the first time eye thee, no matter how many in that same way thou may'st have bejuggled and destroyed before.

And thus, through the serene tranquillities of the tropical sea, among waves whose hand-clappings were suspended by exceeding rapture, Moby Dick moved on, still withholding from sight the full terrors of his submerged trunk, entirely hiding the wrenched hideousness of his jaw. But soon the fore part of him slowly rose from the water; for an instant his whole marbleized body formed a high arch, like Virginia's Natural Bridge, and warningly waving his bannered flukes in the air, the grand god revealed himself, sounded, and went out of sight. Hoveringly halting, and dipping on the wing, the white sea-fowls longingly lingered over the agitated pool that he left.

With oars apeak, and paddles down, the sheets of their sails adrift, the three boats now stilly floated, awaiting Moby Dick's reappearance.

"An hour," said Ahab, standing rooted in his boat's stern; and he gazed beyond the whale's place, towards the dim blue spaces and wide wooing vacancies to leeward. It was only an instant; for again his eyes seemed whirling round in his head as he swept the watery circle. The breeze now freshened; the sea began to swell.

"The birds!—the birds!" cried Tashtego.

In long Indian file, as when herons take wing, the white birds were now all flying towards Ahab's boat; and when within a few yards began fluttering over the water there, wheeling round and round, with joyous, expectant cries. Their vision was keener than man's; Ahab could discover no sign in the sea. But suddenly as he peered down and down into its depths, he profoundly saw a white living spot no bigger than a white weasel, with wonderful celerity uprising, and magnifying as it rose, till it turned, and then there were plainly revealed two long crooked rows of white, glistening teeth, floating up from the undiscoverable bottom. It was Moby Dick's open mouth and scrolled jaw; his vast, shadowed bulk still half blending with the blue of the sea. The glittering mouth yawned beneath the boat like an open-doored marble tomb; and giving one sidelong sweep with his steering oar, Ahab whirled the craft aside from this tremendous apparition. Then, calling upon Fedallah to change places with him, went forward to the bows, and seizing Perth's harpoon, commanded his crew to grasp their oars and stand by to stern.

Now, by reason of this timely spinning round the boat upon its axis, its bow, by anticipation, was made to face the whale's head while yet under water. But as if perceiving this stratagem, Moby Dick, with that malicious intelligence ascribed to him, sidelingly transplanted himself, as it were, in an instant, shooting his pleated head lengthwise beneath the boat.

Through and through; through every plank and each rib, it thrilled for an instant, the whale obliquely lying on his back, in the manner of a biting shark, slowly and feelingly taking its bows full within his mouth, so that the long, narrow, scrolled lower jaw curled high up into the open air, and one of the teeth caught in a rowlock. The bluish pearl-white of the inside of the jaw was within six inches of Ahab's head, and reached higher than that. In this attitude the White Whale now shook the slight cedar as a mildly cruel cat her mouse. With unastonished eyes Fedallah gazed, and crossed his arms; but the tiger-yellow crew were tumbling over each other's heads to gain the uttermost stern.

And now, while both elastic gunwales were springing in and out, as the whale dallied with the doomed craft in this devilish way; and from his body being submerged beneath the boat, he could not be darted at from the bows, for the bows were almost inside of him, as it were; and while the other boats involuntarily paused, as before a quick crisis impossible to withstand, then it was that monomaniac Ahab, furious with this tantalizing vicinity of his foe, which placed him all alive and helpless in the very jaws he hated; frenzied with all this, he seized the long bone with his naked hands, and wildly strove to wrench it from its gripe. As now he thus vainly strove, the jaw slipped from him; the frail gunwales bent in, collapsed, and snapped, as both jaws, like an enormous shears, sliding further aft, bit the craft completely in twain, and locked themselves fast again in the sea, midway between the two floating wrecks. These floated aside, the broken ends drooping, the crew at the stern-wreck clinging to the gunwales, and striving to hold fast to the oars to lash them across.

At that preluding moment, ere the boat was yet snapped, Ahab, the first to perceive the whale's intent, by the crafty upraising of his head, a movement that loosed his hold for the time; at that moment his hand had made one final effort to push the boat out of the bite. But only slipping further into the whale's mouth, and tilting over sideways as it slipped, the boat had shaken off his hold on the jaw; spilled him out of it, as he leaned to the push; and so he fell flat-faced upon the sea.

Ripplingly withdrawing from his prey, Moby Dick now lay at a little distance, vertically thrusting his oblong white head up and down in the billows; and at the same time slowly revolving his whole spindled body; so that when his vast wrinkled forehead rose—some twenty or more feet out of the water—the now rising swells, with all their confluent waves, dazzlingly broke against it; vindictively tossing their shivered spray still higher into the air. So, in a gale, the but half-baffled Channel billows only recoil from the base of the Eddystone, triumphantly to overleap its summit with their scud.

But soon resuming his horizontal attitude, Moby Dick swam swiftly round and round the wrecked crew; sideways churning the water in his vengeful wake, as if lashing himself up to still another and more deadly assault. The sight of the splintered boat seemed to madden him, as the blood of grapes and mulberries cast before Antiochus's elephants in the book of Maccabees.[1] Meanwhile Ahab half smothered in the foam of the whale's insolent tail and too much of a cripple to swim,—though he could still keep afloat, even in the heart of such a whirlpool as that; helpless Ahab's head was seen, like a tossed

[1] See First Maccabees vi : 34.

bubble which the least chance shock might burst. From the boat's fragmentary stern, Fedallah incuriously and mildly eyed him; the clinging crew, at the other drifting end, could not succor him; more than enough was it for them to look to themselves. For so revoltingly appalling was the White Whale's aspect, and so planetarily swift the ever-contracting circles he made, that he seemed horizontally swooping upon them. And though the other boats, unharmed, still hovered hard by, still they dared not pull into the eddy to strike, lest that should be the signal for the instant destruction of the jeopardized castaways, Ahab and all; nor in that case could they themselves hope to escape. With straining eyes, then, they remained on the outer edge of the direful zone, whose center had now become the old man's head.

Meantime, from the beginning all this had been descried from the ship's mastheads; and squaring her yards, she had borne down upon the scene; and was now so nigh, that Ahab in the water hailed her:—"Sail on the"—but that moment a breaking sea dashed on him from Moby Dick, and whelmed him for the time. But struggling out of it again, and chancing to rise on a towering crest, he shouted,—"Sail on the whale!—Drive him off!"

The *Pequod's* prows were pointed; and breaking up the charmed circle, she effectually parted the White Whale from his victim. As he sullenly swam off, the boats flew to the rescue.

Dragged into Stubb's boat with bloodshot, blinded eyes, the white brine caking in his wrinkles; the long tension of Ahab's bodily strength did crack, and helplessly he yielded to his body's doom for a time, lying all crushed in the bottom of Stubb's boat, like one trodden under foot of herds of elephants. Far inland, nameless wails came from him, as desolate sounds from out ravines.

But this intensity of his physical prostration did but so much the more abbreviate it. In an instant's compass, great hearts sometimes condense to one deep pang, the sum total of those shallow pains kindly diffused through feebler men's whole lives. And so, such hearts, though summary in each one suffering; still, if the gods decree it, in their lifetime aggregate a whole age of woe, wholly made up of instantaneous intensities; for even in their pointless centers, those noble natures contain the entire circumferences of inferior souls.

"The harpoon," said Ahab, halfway rising, and draggingly leaning on one bended arm —"is it safe?"

"Aye, sir, for it was not darted; this is it," said Stubb, showing it.

"Lay it before me;—any missing men?"

"One, two, three, four, five;—there were five oars, sir, and here are five men."

"That's good.—Help me, man; I wish to stand. So, so, I see him! there! there! going to leeward still; what a leaping spout!—Hands off from me! The eternal sap runs up in Ahab's bones again! Set the sail; out oars; the helm!"

It is often the case that when a boat is stove, its crew, being picked up by another boat, help to work that second boat; and the chase is thus continued with what is called double-banked oars. It was thus now. But the added power of the boat did not equal the added power of the whale, for he seemed to have treble-banked his every fin; swimming with a velocity which plainly showed, that if now, under these circumstances, pushed on, the chase would prove an indefinitely prolonged, if not a hopeless one; nor could any crew endure for so long a period, such an unintermitted, intense straining at the oar; a thing barely tolerable only in some one brief vicissitude. The ship itself, then, as it sometimes happens, offered the most promising intermediate means of overtaking the chase. Accordingly, the boats now made for her, and were soon swayed up to their cranes— the two parts of the wrecked boat having been previously secured by her—and then hoisting everything to her side, and stacking her canvas high up, and sideways outstretching it with stunsails, like the double-jointed wings of an albatross; the *Pequod* bore down in the leeward wake of Moby Dick. At the well-known, methodic intervals, the whale's glittering spout was regularly announced from the manned mastheads; and when he would be reported as just gone down, Ahab would take the time, and then pacing the deck, binnacle-watch in hand, so soon as the last second of the allotted hour expired, his voice was heard.—"Whose is the doubloon now? D'ye see him?" and if the reply was, "No, sir!" straightway he commanded them to lift him to his perch. In this way the day wore on; Ahab, now aloft and motionless; anon, unrestingly pacing the planks.

As he was thus walking, uttering no sound, except to hail the men aloft, or to bid them hoist a sail still higher, or to spread one to a still greater breadth—thus to and fro pacing, beneath his slouched hat, at every turn he passed his own wrecked boat, which had been dropped upon the quarter-deck, and lay there reversed; broken bow to shattered stern. At last he paused before it; and as in an already over-clouded sky fresh troops of clouds will sometimes sail across, so over the old man's face there now stole some such added gloom as this.

Stubb saw him pause; and perhaps intending, not vainly, though, to evince his own unabated fortitude, and thus keep up a valiant place in his Captain's mind, he advanced, and eyeing the wreck exclaimed—"The thistle the ass refused; it pricked his mouth too keenly, sir; ha! ha!"

"What soulless thing is this that laughs before a wreck? Man, man! did I not know thee brave as fearless fire (and as mechanical) I could swear thou wert a poltroon. Groan nor laugh should be heard before a wreck."

"Aye, sir," said Starbuck, drawing near, "'tis a solemn sight; an omen, and an ill one."

"Omen? omen?—the dictionary! If the gods think to speak outright to man, they will honorably speak outright; not shake their heads, and give an old wives' darkling hint.— Begone! Ye two are the opposite poles of one thing; Starbuck is Stubb reversed, and Stubb is Starbuck; and ye two are all mankind; and Ahab stands alone among the millions of the peopled earth, nor gods nor men his neighbors! Cold, cold—I shiver!—How now? Aloft there! D'ye see him? Sing out for every spout, though he spout ten times a second!"

The day was nearly done; only the hem of his golden robe was rustling. Soon, it was almost dark, but the lookout men still remained unset.

"Can't see the spout now, sir;—too dark"—cried a voice from the air.

"How heading when last seen?"

"As before, sir,—straight to leeward."

"Good! he will travel slower now 'tis night. Down royals and topgallant stunsails, Mr. Starbuck. We must not run over him before morning; he's making a passage now, and may heave-to a while. Helm there! Keep her full before the wind!—Aloft! come down!—Mr. Stubb, send a fresh hand to the foremast head, and see it manned till morning."—Then advancing towards the doubloon in the mainmast—"Men, this gold is mine, for I earned it; but I shall let it abide here till the White Whale is dead; and then, whosoever of ye first raises him, upon the day he shall be killed, this gold is that man's; and if on that day I shall again raise him, then, ten times its sum shall be divided among all of ye! Away now!—the deck is thine, sir."

And so saying, he placed himself halfway within the scuttle, and slouching his hat, stood there till dawn, except when at intervals rousing himself to see how the night wore on.

CHAPTER CXXXIV
The Chase—Second Day

At daybreak, the three mastheads were punctually manned afresh.

"D'ye see him?" cried Ahab, after allowing a little space for the light to spread.

"See nothing, sir."

"Turn up all hands and make sail! he travels faster than I thought for;—the top-gallant-sails!—aye, they should have been kept on her all night. But no matter—'tis but resting for the rush."

Here be it said, that this pertinacious pursuit of one particular whale, continued through day into night, and through night into day, is a thing by no means unprecedented in the South Sea fishery. For such is the wonderful skill, prescience of experience, and invincible confidence acquired by some great natural geniuses among the Nantucket commanders, that from the simple observation of a whale when last descried, they will, under certain given circumstances, pretty accurately foretell both the direction in which he

will continue to swim for a time, while out of sight, as well as his probable rate of progression during that period. And in these cases, somewhat as a pilot, when about losing sight of a coast, whose general trending he well knows, and which he desires shortly to return to again, but at some further point; like as this pilot stands by his compass, and takes the precise bearing of the cape at present visible, in order the more certainly to hit aright the remote, unseen headland, eventually to be visited: so does the fisherman, at his compass, with the whale; for after being chased, and diligently marked, through several hours of delight, then, when night obscures the fish, the creature's future wake through the darkness is almost as established to the sagacious mind of the hunter, as the pilot's coast is to him. So that to this hunter's wondrous skill, the proverbial evanescence of a thing writ in water, a wake, is to all desired purposes well-nigh as reliable as the steadfast land. And as the mighty iron Leviathan of the modern railway is so familiarly known in its every pace, that, with watches in their hands, men time his rate as doctors that of a baby's pulse; and lightly say of it, "the up train or the down train will reach such or such a spot, at such or such an hour," even so, almost, there are occasions when these Nantucketers time that other Leviathan of the deep, according to the observed humor of his speed; and say to themselves, "so many hours hence this whale will have gone two hundred miles, will have about reached this or that degree of latitude or longitude." But to render this acuteness at all successful in the end, the wind and the sea must be the whaleman's allies; for of what present avail to the becalmed or windbound mariner is the skill that assures him he is exactly ninety-three leagues and a quarter from his port? Inferable from these statements are many collateral subtile matters touching the chase of whales.

The ship tore on; leaving such a furrow in the sea as when a cannon-ball, missent, becomes a ploughshare and turns up the level field.

"By salt and hemp!" cried Stubb, "but this swift motion of the deck creeps up one's legs and tingles at the heart. This ship and I are two brave fellows!—Ha! ha! Some one take me up, and launch me, spine-wise, on the sea,—for by live-oaks! my spine's a keel. Ha, ha! we go the gait that leaves no dust behind!"

"There she blows—she blows!—she blows! —right ahead!" was now the masthead cry.

"Aye, aye!" cried Stubb; "I knew it—ye can't escape—blow on and split your spout, O whale! the mad fiend himself is after ye! blow your trump—blister your lungs!— Ahab will dam off your blood, as a miller shuts his water-gate upon the stream!"

And Stubb did but speak out for well-nigh all that crew. The frenzies of the chase had by this time worked them bubblingly up, like old wine worked anew. Whatever pale fears and forebodings some of them might have felt before; these were not only now kept out of sight through the growing awe of Ahab, but they were broken up, and on all sides routed, as timid prairie hares that scatter before the bounding bison. The hand of Fate had snatched all their souls; and by the stirring perils of the previous day; the rack of the past night's suspense; the fixed, unfearing, blind, reckless way in which their wild craft went plunging towards its flying mark; by all these things, their hearts were bowled along. The wind that made great bellies of their sails, and rushed the vessel on by arms invisible as irresistible; this seemed the symbol of that unseen agency which so enslaved them to the race.

They were one man, not thirty. For as the one ship that held them all; though it was put together of all contrasting things—oak, and maple, and pine wood; iron, and pitch, and hemp—yet all these ran into each other in the one concrete hull, which shot on its way, both balanced and directed by the long central keel; even so, all the individualities of the crew, this man's valor, that man's fear; guilt and guiltiness, all varieties were welded into oneness, and were all directed to that fatal goal which Ahab their one lord and keel did point to.

The rigging lived. The mastheads, like the tops of tall palms, were outspreadingly tufted with arms and legs. Clinging to a spar with one hand, some reached forth the other with impatient wavings; others, shading their eyes from the vivid sunlight, sat far out on the rocking yards; all the spars in full bearing of mortals, ready and ripe for their fate. Ah! how they still strove through that infinite blueness to seek out the thing that might destroy them!

"Why sing ye not out for him, if ye see him?" cried Ahab, when, after the lapse of some minutes since the first cry, no more had been heard. "Sway me up, men; ye have been deceived; not Moby Dick casts one odd jet that way, and then disappears."

It was even so; in their headlong eagerness, the men had mistaken some other thing for the whale-spout, as the event itself soon proved; for hardly had Ahab reached his perch; hardly was the rope belayed to its pin on deck, when he struck the keynote to an orchestra, that made the air vibrate as with the combined discharges of rifles. The triumphant halloo of thirty buckskin lungs was heard, as—much nearer to the ship than the place of the imaginary jet, less than a mile ahead—Moby Dick bodily burst into view! For not by any calm and indolent spoutings; not by the peaceable gush of that mystic fountain in his head, did the White Whale now reveal his vicinity; but by the far more wondrous phenomenon of breaching. Rising with his utmost velocity from the furthest depths, the Sperm Whale thus booms his entire bulk into the pure element of air, and piling up a mountain of dazzling foam, shows his place to the distance of seven miles and more. In those moments, the torn, enraged waves he shakes off seem his mane; in some cases this breaching is his act of defiance.

"There she breaches! there she breaches!" was the cry, as in his immeasurable bravadoes the White Whale tossed himself salmon-like to Heaven. So suddenly seen in the blue plain of the sea, and relieved against the still bluer margin of the sky, the spray that he raised, for the moment, intolerably glittered and glared like a glacier; and stood there gradually fading and fading away from its first sparkling intensity, to the dim mistiness of an advancing shower in a vale.

"Aye, breach your last to the sun, Moby Dick!" cried Ahab, "thy hour and thy harpoon are at hand!—Down! down all of ye, but one man at the fore. The boats!—stand by!"

Unmindful of the tedious rope-ladders of the shrouds, the men, like shooting stars, slid to the deck, by the isolated backstays and halyards, while Ahab, less dartingly, but still rapidly, was dropped from his perch.

"Lower away," he cried, so soon as he had reached his boat—a spare one, rigged the afternoon previous. "Mr. Starbuck, the ship is thine—keep away from the boats, but keep near them. Lower, all!"

As if to strike a quick terror into them, by this time being the first assailant himself, Moby Dick had turned, and was now coming for the three crews. Ahab's boat was central; and cheering his men, he told them he would take the whale head-and-head,—that is, pull straight up to his forehead,—a not uncommon thing; for when within a certain limit, such a course excludes the coming onset from the whale's sidelong vision. But ere that close limit was gained, and while yet all three boats were plain as the ship's three masts to his eye; the White Whale churning himself into furious speed, almost in an instant as it were, rushing among the boats with open jaws, and a lashing tail, offered appalling battle on every side; and heedless of the irons darted at him from every boat, seemed only intent on annihilating each separate plank of which those boats were made. But skillfully maneuvered, incessantly wheeling like trained chargers in the field; the boats for a while eluded him; though, at times, but by a plank's breadth; while all the time, Ahab's unearthly slogan tore every other cry but his to shreds.

But at last in his untraceable evolutions, the White Whale so crossed and recrossed, and in a thousand ways entangled the slack of the three lines now fast to him, that they foreshortened, and, of themselves, warped the devoted boats towards the planted irons in him; though now for a moment the whale drew aside a little, as if to rally for a more tremendous charge. Seizing that opportunity, Ahab first paid out more line; and then was rapidly hauling and jerking in upon it again— hoping that way to disencumber it of some snarls—when lo!—a sight more savage than the embattled teeth of sharks!

Caught and twisted—corkscrewed in the mazes of the line—loose harpoons and lances, with all their bristling barbs and points, came flashing and dripping up to the chocks in the bows of Ahab's boat. Only one thing could be done. Seizing the boat-knife, he critically reached within—through—and then, without —the rays of steel; dragged in the line beyond, passed it, inboard, to the bowsman, and then, twice sundering the rope near the chocks— dropped the intercepted fagot of steel into the sea; and was all fast again. That instant, the White Whale made a sudden rush among the remaining tangles of the other lines; by so doing, irresistibly dragged the more involved boats of Stubb and Flask towards his flukes; dashed them together like two rolling husks on a surf-beaten beach, and then, diving down into the sea, disappeared in a boiling maelstrom, in which, for a space, the odorous cedar chips of the wrecks danced round and round, like the grated nutmeg in a swiftly stirred bowl of 'punch.

While the two crews were yet circling in the waters, reaching out after the revolving linetubs, oars, and other floating furniture, while aslope little Flask bobbed up and down like an empty vial, twitching his legs upwards to escape the dreaded jaws of sharks; and Stubb was lustily singing out for some one to ladle him up; and while the old man's line—now parting—admitted of his pulling into the creamy pool to rescue whom he could;—in that wild simultaneousness of a thousand concerted perils,—Ahab's yet unstricken boat seemed drawn up towards Heaven by invisible wires,—as, arrow-like, shooting perpendicularly from the sea, the White Whale dashed his broad forehead against its bottom, and sent it, turning over and over, into the air; till it fell again—gunwale downwards— and Ahab and his men struggled out from under it, like seals from a seaside cave.

The first uprising momentum of the whale —modifying its direction as he struck the surface—involuntarily launched him along it, to a little distance from the center of the destruction he had made; and with his back to it, he now lay for a moment slowly feeling with his flukes from side to side; and whenever a stray oar, bit of plank, the least chip or crumb of the boats touched his skin, his tail swiftly drew back, and came sideways, smiting the sea. But soon, as if satisfied that his work for that time was done, he pushed his pleated forehead through the ocean, and trailing after him the intertangled lines, continued his leeward way at a traveler's methodic pace.

As before, the attentive ship having descried the whole fight, again came bearing down to the rescue, and dropping a boat, picked up the floating mariners, tubs, oars, and whatever else could be caught at, and safely landed them on her decks. Some sprained shoulders, wrists, and ankles; livid contusions; wrenched harpoons and lances; inextricable intricacies of rope; shattered oars and planks; all these were there; but no fatal or even serious ill seemed to have befallen any one. As with Fedallah the day before, so Ahab was now found grimly clinging to his boat's broken half, which afforded a comparatively easy float; nor did it so exhaust him as the previous day's mishap.

But when he was helped to the deck, all eyes were fastened upon him; as instead of standing by himself he still half-hung upon the shoulder of Starbuck, who had thus far been the foremost to assist him. His ivory leg had been snapped off, leaving but one short sharp splinter.

"Aye, aye, Starbuck, 'tis sweet to lean sometimes, be the leaner who he will; and would old Ahab had leaned oftener than he has."

"The ferrule has not stood, sir," said the carpenter, now coming up; "I put good work into that leg."

"But no bones broken, sir, I hope," said Stubb with true concern.

"Aye! and all splintered to pieces, Stubb!—d'ye see it.—But even with a broken bone, old Ahab is untouched; and I account no living bone of mine one jot more me, than this dead one that's lost; Nor White Whale, nor man, nor fiend, can so much as graze old Ahab in his own proper and inaccessible being. Can any lead touch yonder floor, any mast scrape yonder roof?—Aloft there! which way?"

"Dead to leeward, sir."

"Up helm, then; pile on the sail again, ship-keepers! down the rest of the spare boats and rig them—Mr. Starbuck, away, and muster the boats' crews."

"Let me first help thee towards the bulwarks, sir."

"Oh, oh, oh! how this splinter gores me now! Accursed fate! that the unconquerable captain in the soul should have such a craven mate!"

"Sir?"

"My body, man, not thee. Give me something for a cane—there, that shivered lance will do. Muster the men. Surely I have not seen him yet. By heaven, it cannot be!—missing?—quick! call them all."

The old man's hinted thought was true. Upon mustering the company, the Parsee[1] was not there.

"The Parsee!" cried Stubb—"he must have been caught in——"

"The black vomit wrench thee!—run all of ye above, alow, cabin, forecastle—find him—not gone—not gone!"

But quickly they returned to him with the tidings that the Parsee was nowhere to be found.

"Aye, sir," said Stubb—"caught among the tangles of your line—I thought I saw him dragging under."

"*My* line? *my* line? Gone?—gone?—What means that little word?—What death-knell rings in it, that old Ahab shakes as if he were the belfry. The harpoon, too!—toss over the litter there,—d'ye see it?—the forged iron, men, the White Whale's—no, no, no,—blistered fool! this hand did dart it!—'tis in the fish!—Aloft there! Keep him nailed—Quick!—all hands to the rigging of the boats—collect the oars—harpooners! the irons, the irons!—hoist the royals higher—a pull on all the sheets!—helm there! steady, steady

[1] "The mysterious Fedallah whom Ahab had stowed away to be a member of his own boat-crew. He exercised a strange power over his master. A secret, potent spell seemed to join them. 'At times, for longest hours, without a single hail, they stood far parted in the starlight; Ahab in his scuttle, the Parsee by the mainmast; but still fixedly gazing upon each other; as if in the Parsee Ahab saw his forethrown shadow, in Ahab the Parsee his abandoned substance' (Chapter CXXX)." [*Note quoted from Thorp's Melville.*]

A parsee is a member of the fire-worshippers of India, descendants of the old Persian Zoroastrians.

for your life! I'll ten times girdle the un-measured globe; yea and dive straight through it, but I'll slay him yet!"

"Great God! but for one single instant show thyself," cried Starbuck; "never, never wilt thou capture him, old man.—In Jesus' name no more of this, that's worse than devil's madness. Two days chased; twice stove to splinters; thy very leg once more snatched from under thee; thy evil shadow gone—all good angels mobbing thee with warnings:— what more wouldst thou have?—Shall we keep chasing this murderous fish till he swamps the last man? Shall we be dragged by him to the bottom of the sea? Shall we be towed by him to the infernal world? Oh, oh!—Impiety and blasphemy to hunt him more!"

"Starbuck, of late I've felt strangely moved to thee; ever since that hour we both saw— thou know'st what, in one another's eyes. But in this matter of the whale, be the front of thy face to me as the palm of this hand—a lipless, unfeatured blank. Ahab is for ever Ahab, man. This whole act's immutably decreed. 'Twas rehearsed by thee and me a billion years before this ocean rolled. Fool! I am the Fates' lieutenant; I act under orders. Look thou, underling! that thou obeyest mine. —Stand round me, men. Ye see an old man cut down to the stump; leaning on a shivered lance; propped up on a lonely foot. 'Tis Ahab —his body's part; but Ahab's soul's a centi-pede, that moves upon a hundred legs. I feel strained, half stranded, as ropes that tow dis-masted frigates in a gale; and I may look so. But ere I break, ye'll hear me crack; and till ye hear *that*, know that Ahab's hawser tows his purpose yet. Believe ye, men, in the things called omens? Then laugh aloud, and cry encore! For ere they drown, drowning things will twice rise to the surface; then rise again, to sink for evermore. So with Moby Dick— two days he's floated—to-morrow will be the third. Aye, men, he'll rise once more—but only to spout his last! D'ye feel brave men, brave?"

"As fearless fire," cried Stubb.

"And as mechanical," muttered Ahab. Then as the men went forward, he muttered on:— "The things called omens! And yesterday I talked the same to Starbuck there, concerning my broken boat. Oh! how valiantly I seek to drive out of others' hearts what's clinched so fast in mine!—The Parsee—the Parsee!— gone, gone? and he was to go before:—but still was to be seen again ere I could perish— How's that?—There's a riddle now might baffle all the lawyers backed by the ghosts of the whole line of judges:—like a hawk's beak it pecks my brain. *I'll, I'll* solve it, though!"

When dusk descended, the whale was still in sight to leeward.

So once more the sail was shortened, and everything passed nearly as on the previous night; only, the sound of hammers, and the hum of the grindstone was heard till nearly daylight, as the men toiled by lanterns in the complete and careful rigging of the spare boats and sharpening their fresh weapons for the morrow. Meantime, of the broken keel of Ahab's wrecked craft the carpenter made him another leg; while still as on the night before, slouched Ahab stood fixed within his scuttle; his hid heliotrope glance anticipatingly gone backward on its dial; set due eastward for the earliest sun.

CHAPTER CXXXV
The Chase—Third Day

The morning of the third day dawned fair and fresh, and once more the solitary night-man at the fore-masthead was relieved by crowds of the daylight lookouts, who dotted every mast and almost every spar.

"D'ye see him?" cried Ahab; but the whale was not yet in sight.

"In his infallible wake, though; but follow that wake, that's all. Helm there; steady, as thou goest, and hast been going. What a lovely day again! were it a new-made world, and made for a summer-house to the angels, and this morning the first of its throwing open to them, a fairer day could not dawn upon that world. Here's food for thought, had Ahab time to think; but Ahab never thinks; he only feels, feels, feels, *that's* tingling enough for mortal man! to think's audacity. God only has that right and privilege. Think-ing is, or ought to be, a coolness and a calm-ness; and our poor hearts throb, and our poor brains beat too much for that. And yet, I've sometimes thought my brain was very calm—frozen calm, this old skull cracks so, like a glass in which the contents turn to ice, and shiver it. And still this hair is growing now; this moment growing, and heat must breed it; but no, it's like that sort of common grass that will grow anywhere, between the earthly clefts of Greenland ice or in Vesuvius lava. How the wild winds blow it; they whip it about me as the torn shreds of split sails lash the tossed ship they cling to. A vile wind that has no doubt blown ere this through prison corridors and cells, and wards of hospitals, and ventilated them, and now comes blowing hither as innocent as fleeces. Out upon it!—it's tainted. Were I the wind, I'd blow no more on such a wicked, miserable world. I'd crawl somewhere to a cave, and slink there. And yet, 'tis a noble and heroic thing, the wind! who ever conquered it? In every fight it has the last and bitterest blow. Run tilting at it, and you but run through it. Ha! a coward wind that strikes stark naked men, but will not stand to receive a single blow. Even Ahab is a braver thing—a nobler thing than *that*. Would now the wind but had a body; but all the things that most exasperate and outrage mortal man, all these things are bodiless, but only bodiless as objects, not as agents. There's a most special, a most cunning, oh, a most malicious difference! And yet, I say again, and swear it now, that there's something all glorious and gracious in the wind. These warm Trade Winds, at least, that in the clear heavens blow straight on, in strong and steadfast, vigorous mildness; and veer not from their mark, however the baser currents of the sea may turn and tack, and mightiest Mississippis of the land shift and swerve about, uncertain where to go at last. And by the eternal Poles! these same Trades that so directly blow my good ship on; these Trades, or something like them—something so unchangeable, and full as strong, blow my keeled soul along! To it! Aloft there! What d'ye see?"

"Nothing, sir."

"Nothing! and noon at hand! The doubloon goes a-begging! See the sun! Aye, aye, it must be so. I've oversailed him. How, got the start? Aye, he's chasing *me* now; not I, *him*—that's bad; I might have known it, too. Fool! the lines—the harpoons he's towing. Aye, aye, I have run him by last night. About! about! Come down, all of ye, but the regular lookouts! Man the braces!"

Steering as she had done, the wind had been somewhat on the *Pequod's* quarter, so that now being pointed in the reverse direction, the braced ship sailed hard upon the breeze as she rechurned the cream in her now white wake.

"Against the wind he now steers for the open jaw," murmured Starbuck to himself, as he coiled the new-hauled main-brace upon the rail. "God keep us, but already my bones feel damp within me, and from the inside wet my flesh. I misdoubt me that I disobey my God in obeying him!"

"Stand by to sway me up!" cried Ahab, advancing to the hempen basket. "We should meet him soon."

"Aye, aye, sir," and straightway Starbuck did Ahab's bidding, and once more Ahab swung on high.

A whole hour now passed; gold-beaten out to ages. Time itself now held long breaths with keen suspense. But at last, some three points off the weather-bow, Ahab descried the spout again, and instantly from the three mastheads three shrieks went up as if the tongues of fire had voiced it.

"Forehead to forehead I meet thee, this third time, Moby Dick! On deck there!—brace sharper up; crowd her into the wind's eye. He's too far off to lower yet, Mr. Starbuck. The sails shake! Stand over that helmsman with a topmaul! So, so; he travels fast, and I must down. But let me have one more good round look aloft here at the sea; there's time for that. An old, old sight, and yet somehow so young; aye, and not changed a wink since I first saw it, a boy, from the sandhills of Nantucket! The same!—the same!—the same to Noah as to me. There's a soft shower to leeward. Such lovely leewardings! They must lead somewhere—to something else than common land, more palmy than the palms. Leeward! the white whale goes that way; look to windward, then; the better if the bitterer quarter. But good-bye, good-bye, old masthead! What's this?—green? ay, tiny mosses in these warped cracks. No such green weather stains on Ahab's head! There's the difference now between man's old age and matter's. But aye, old mast, we both grow old together; sound in our hulls, though, are we not, my ship? Aye, minus a leg, that's all. By heaven! this dead wood has the better of my live flesh every way. I can't compare with it; and I've known some ships made of dead trees outlast 10 the lives of men made of the most vital stuff of vital fathers. What's that he said? he should still go before me, my pilot; and yet to be seen again? But where? Shall I have eyes at the bottom of the sea, supposing I descend those endless stairs? and all night I've been sailing from him, wherever he did sink to. Aye, aye, like many more thou told'st direful truth as touching thyself, O Parsee; but, Ahab, there thy shot fell short. Good-bye, 20 masthead—keep a good eye upon the whale, the while I'm gone. We'll talk tomorrow, nay, tonight, when the White Whale lies down there, tied by head and tail."

He gave the word; and still gazing round him, was steadily lowered through the cloven blue air to the deck.

In due time the boats were lowered; but as standing in his shallop's stern, Ahab just hovered upon the point of the descent, he 30 waved to the mate,—who held one of the tackle-ropes on deck—and bade him pause.

"Starbuck!"

"Sir?"

"For the third time my soul's ship starts upon this voyage, Starbuck."

"Aye, sir, thou wilt have it so."

"Some ships sail from their ports, and ever afterwards are missing, Starbuck!"

"Truth, sir: saddest truth."

"Some men die at ebb tide; some at low 40 water; some at the full of the flood;—and I feel now like a billow that's all one crested comb, Starbuck. I am old;—shake hands with me, man."

Their hands met; their eyes fastened; Starbuck's tears the glue.

"Oh, my captain, my captain!—noble heart—go not—go not!—see, it's a brave man that weeps; how great the agony of the 50 persuasion then!"

"Lower away!"—cried Ahab, tossing the mate's arm from him. "Stand by the crew!"

In an instant the boat was pulling round close under the stern.

"The sharks! the sharks!" cried a voice from the low cabin-window there; "O master, my master, come back!"

But Ahab heard nothing; for his own voice was high-lifted then; and the boat leaped on.

Yet the voice spake true; for scarce had he pushed from the ship, when numbers of sharks, seemingly rising from out the dark waters beneath the hull, maliciously snapped at the blades of the oars, every time they dipped in the water; and in this way accompanied the boat with their bites. It is a thing not uncommonly happening to the whale-boats in those swarming seas; the sharks at times apparently following them in the same prescient way that vultures hover over the banners of marching regiments in the east. But these were the first sharks that had been observed by the *Pequod* since the White Whale had been first descried; and whether it was that Ahab's crew were all such tiger-yellow barbarians, and therefore their flesh more musky to the senses of the sharks—a matter sometimes well known to affect them,—however it was, they seemed to follow that one boat without molesting the others.

"Heart of wrought steel!" murmured Starbuck, gazing over the side, and following with his eyes the receding boat—"canst thou yet ring boldly to that sight?—lowering thy keel among ravening sharks, and followed by them, open-mouthed, to the chase; and this the critical third day?—For when three days flow together in one continuous intense pursuit; be sure the first is the morning, the second the noon, and the third the evening and the end of that thing—be that end what it may. Oh! my God! what is this that shoots through me, and leaves me so deadly calm, yet expectant,—fixed at the top of a shudder! Future things swim before me, as in empty outlines and skeletons; all the past is somehow grown dim. Mary, girl! thou fadest in pale glories behind me; boy! I seem to see but thy eyes grown wondrous blue. Strangest problems of life seem clearing; but clouds sweep between—Is my journey's end coming?

My legs feel faint; like his who has footed it all day. Feel thy heart,—beats it yet?—Stir thyself, Starbuck!—stave it off—move, move, speak aloud!—Masthead there! See ye my boy's hand on the hill?—Crazed;—aloft there!—keep thy keenest eye upon the boats: —mark well the whale!—Ho! again!—drive off that hawk! see! he pecks—he tears the vane"—pointing to the red flag flying at the main-truck—"Ha! he soars away with it!— Where's the old man now? sees't thou that sight, oh Ahab!—shudder, shudder!"

The boats had not gone very far, when by a signal from the mastheads—a downward pointed arm, Ahab knew that the whale had sounded; but intending to be near him at the next rising, he held on his way a little sideways from the vessel; the becharmed crew maintaining the profoundest silence, as the headbeat waves hammered and hammered against the opposing bow.

"Drive, drive in your nails, oh ye waves! to their uttermost heads drive them in! ye but strike a thing without a lid; and no coffin and no hearse can be mine;—and hemp only can kill me! Ha! ha!"

Suddenly the waters around them slowly swelled in broad circles; then quickly upheaved, as if sideways sliding from a submerged berg of ice, swiftly rising to the surface. A low rumbling sound was heard; a subterraneous hum; and then all held their breaths; as bedraggled with trailing ropes, and harpoons, and lances, a vast form shot lengthwise, but obliquely from the sea. Shrouded in a thin drooping veil of mist, it hovered for a moment in the rainbowed air; and then fell swamping back into the deep. Crushed thirty feet upwards, the waters flashed for an instant like heaps of fountains, then brokenly sank in a shower of flakes, leaving the circling surface creamed like new milk round the marble trunk of the whale.

"Give way!" cried Ahab to the oarsmen, and the boats darted forward to the attack; but maddened by yesterday's fresh irons that corroded in him, Moby Dick seemed combinedly possessed by all the angels that fell from heaven. The wide tiers of welded tendons overspreading his broad white forehead, beneath the transparent skin, looked knitted together; as head on, he came churning his tail among the boats; and once more flailed them apart; spilling out the irons and lances from the two mates' boats, and dashing in one side of the upper part of their bows, but leaving Ahab's almost without a scar.

While Daggoo and Queequeg were stopping the strained planks; and as the whale swimming out from them, turned, and showed one entire flank as he shot by them again; at that moment a quick cry went up. Lashed round and round to the fish's back; pinioned in the turns upon turns in which, during the past night, the whale had reeled the involutions of the lines around him, the half torn body of the Parsee was seen; his sable raiment frayed to shreds; his distended eyes turned full upon old Ahab.

The harpoon dropped from his hand.

"Befooled, befooled!"—drawing in a long lean breath—"Aye, Parsee! I see thee again.— Aye, and thou goest before; and this, *this* then is the hearse that thou didst promise. But I hold thee to the last letter of thy word. Where is the second hearse? Away, mates, to the ship! those boats are useless now; repair them if ye can in time, and return to me; if not, Ahab is enough to die—Down, men! the first thing that but offers to jump from this boat I stand in, that thing I harpoon. Ye are not other men, but my arms and my legs; and so obey me.— Where's the whale? gone down again?"

But he looked too nigh the boat; for as if bent upon escaping with the corpse he bore, and as if the particular place of the last encounter had been but a stage in his leeward voyage, Moby Dick was now again steadily swimming forward; and had almost passed the ship,—which thus far had been sailing in the contrary direction to him, though for the present her headway had been stopped. He seemed swimming with his utmost velocity, and now only intent upon pursuing his own straight path in the sea.

"Oh! Ahab," cried Starbuck, "not too late is it, even now, the third day, to desist. See! Moby Dick seeks thee not. It is thou, thou, that madly seekest him!"

Setting sail to the rising wind, the lonely boat was swiftly impelled to leeward, by both oars and canvas. And at last when Ahab was sliding by the vessel, so near as plainly to distinguish Starbuck's face as he leaned over the rail, he hailed him to turn the vessel about, and follow him, not too swiftly, at a judicious interval. Glancing upwards, he saw Tashtego, Queequeg, and Daggoo, eagerly mounting to the three mastheads; while the oarsmen were rocking in the two staved boats which had just been hoisted to the side, and were busily at work in repairing them. One after the other, through the port-holes, as he sped, he also caught flying glimpses of Stubb and Flask, busying themselves on deck among bundles of new irons and lances. As he saw all this; as he heard the hammers in the broken boats; far other hammers seemed driving a nail into his heart. But he rallied. And now marking that the vane or flag was gone from the main masthead, he shouted to Tashtego, who had just gained that perch, to descend again for another flag, and a hammer and nails, and so nail it to the mast.

Whether fagged by the three days' running chase, and the resistance to his swimming in the knotted hamper he bore; or whether it was some latent deceitfulness and malice in him: whichever was true, the White Whale's way now began to abate, as it seemed, from the boat so rapidly nearing him once more; though indeed the whale's last start had not been so long a one as before. And still as Ahab glided over the waves the unpitying sharks accompanied him; and so pertinaciously stuck to the boat; and so continually bit at the plying oars, that the blades became jagged and crunched, and left small splinters in the sea, at almost every dip.

"Heed them not! those teeth but give new rowlocks to your oars. Pull on! 'tis the better rest, the shark's jaw than the yielding water."

"But at every bite, sir, the thin blades grow smaller and smaller!"

"They will last long enough! pull on!— But who can tell"—he muttered—"whether these sharks swim to feast on the whale or on Ahab?—But pull on! Aye, all alive, now—we near him. The helm! take the helm; let me pass,"—and so saying, two of the oarsmen helped him forward to the bows of the still flying boat.

At length as the craft was cast to one side, and ran ranging along with the White Whale's flank, he seemed strangely oblivious of its advance—as the whale sometimes will—and Ahab was fairly within the smoky mountain mist, which, thrown off from the whale's spout, curled round his great Monadnock hump. He was even thus close to him; when, with body arched back, and both arms lengthwise high-lifted to the poise, he darted his fierce iron, and his far fiercer curse into the hated whale. As both steel and curse sank to the socket, as if sucked into a morass, Moby Dick sideways writhed; spasmodically rolled his nigh flank against the bow, and, without staving a hole in it, so suddenly canted the boat over, that had it not been for the elevated part of the gunwale to which he then clung, Ahab would once more have been tossed into the sea. As it was, three of the oarsmen—who foreknew not the precise instant of the dart, and were therefore unprepared for its effects—these were flung out; but so fell, that, in an instant two of them clutched the gunwale again, and rising to its level on a combing wave, hurled themselves bodily inboard again; the third man helplessly dropping astern, but still afloat and swimming.

Almost simultaneously, with a mighty volition of ungraduated, instantaneous swiftness, the White Whale darted through the weltering sea. But when Ahab cried out to the steersman to take new turns with the line, and hold it so; and commanded the crew to turn round on their seats, and tow the boat up to the mark; the moment the treacherous line felt that double strain and tug, it snapped in the empty air!

"What breaks in me? Some sinew cracks!— 'tis whole again; oars! oars! Burst in upon him!"

Hearing the tremendous rush of the sea-crashing boat, the whale wheeled round to present his blank forehead at bay; but in that evolution, catching sight of the nearing black hull of the ship; seemingly seeing in it the source of all his persecutions; bethinking it —it may be—a larger and nobler foe; of a sudden, he bore down upon its advancing prow, smiting his jaws amid fiery showers of foam.

Ahab staggered; his hand smote his forehead. "I grow blind; hands! stretch out before me that I may yet grope my way. Is't night?"

"The whale! The ship!" cried the cringing oarsmen.

"Oars! oars! Slope downwards to thy depths, O sea, that ere it be for ever too late, Ahab may slide this last, last time upon his mark! I see: the ship! the ship! Dash on, my men! Will ye not save my ship?"

But as the oarsmen violently forced their boat through the sledge-hammering seas, the before whale-smitten bow-ends of two planks burst through, and in an instant almost, the temporarily disabled boat lay nearly level with the waves; its half-wading, splashing crew, trying hard to stop the gap and bale out the pouring water.

Meantime, for that one beholding instant, Tashtego's masthead hammer remained suspended in his hand; and the red flag, half-wrapping him as with a plaid, then streamed itself straight out from him, as his own forward-flowing heart; while Starbuck and Stubb, standing upon the bowsprit beneath, caught sight of the down-coming monster just as soon as he.

"The whale, the whale! Up helm, up helm! Oh, all ye sweet powers of air, now hug me close! Let not Starbuck die, if die he must, in a woman's fainting fit. Up helm, I say—ye fools, the jaw! the jaw! Is this the end of all my bursting prayers? All my life-long fidelities? Oh, Ahab, Ahab, lo, they work. Steady! helmsman, steady. Nay, nay! Up helm again! He turns to meet us! Oh, his unappeasable brow drives on towards one, whose duty tells him he cannot depart. My God, stand by me now!

"Stand not by me, but stand under me, whoever you are that will now help Stubb; for Stubb, too, sticks here. I grin at thee, thou grinning whale! Whoever helped Stubb, or kept Stubb awake, but Stubb's own unwinking eye? And now poor Stubb goes to bed upon a mattress that is all too soft; would it were stuffed with brushwood! I grin at thee, thou grinning whale! Look ye, sun, moon, and stars! I call ye assassins of as good a fellow as ever spouted up his ghost. For all that, I would yet ring glasses with ye, would ye but hand the cup! Oh, oh, oh, oh! thou grinning whale, but there'll be plenty of gulping soon! Why fly ye not, O Ahab? For me, off shoes and jacket to it; let Stubb die in his drawers! A most mouldy and over-salted death, though;—cherries! cherries! cherries! Oh, Flask, for one red cherry ere we die!"

"Cherries? I only wish that we were where they grow. Oh, Stubb, I hope my poor mother's drawn my part-pay ere this; if not, a few coppers will come to her now, for the voyage is up."

From the ship's bows, nearly all the seamen now hung inactive; hammers, bits of plank, lances, and harpoons, mechanically retained in their hands, just as they had darted from their various employments; all their enchanted eyes intent upon the whale, which from side to side strangely vibrating his predestinating head, sent a broad band of overspreading semicircular foam before him as he rushed. Retribution, swift vengeance, eternal malice were in his whole aspect, and spite of all that mortal man could do, the solid white buttress of his forehead smote the ship's starboard bow, till men and timbers reeled. Some fell flat upon their faces. Like dislodged trucks, the heads of the harpooneers aloft shook on their bull-like necks. Through the breach, they heard the waters pour, as mountain torrents down a flume.

"The ship! The hearse!—the second hearse!" cried Ahab from the boat; "its wood could only be American!"

Diving beneath the settling ship, the whale ran quivering along its keel; but turning under water, swiftly shot to the surface again, far off the other bow, but within a few yards of Ahab's boat, where, for a time, he lay quiescent.

"I turn my body from the sun. What ho, Tashtego! let me hear thy hammer. Oh! ye three unsurrendered spires of mine; thou uncracked keel; the only god-bullied hull; thou firm deck, and haughty helm, and Pole-pointed prow,—death-glorious ship! must ye then perish, and without me? Am I cut off from the last fond pride of meanest shipwrecked captains? Oh, lonely death on lonely life! Oh, now I feel my topmost greatness lies in my topmost grief. Ho, ho! from all your furthest bounds, pour ye now in, ye bold billows of my whole foregone life, and top this one piled comber[1] of my death! Towards thee I roll, thou all-destroying but unconquering whale; to the last I grapple with thee; from hell's heart I stab at thee; for hate's sake I spit my last breath at thee. Sink all coffins and all hearses to one common pool! and since neither can be mine let me then tow to pieces, while still chasing thee, though tied to thee, thou damned whale! *Thus*, I give up the spear!"

The harpoon was darted; the stricken whale flew forward; with igniting velocity the line ran through the groove; ran foul. Ahab stooped to clear it; he did clear it; but the flying turn caught him round the neck and, voicelessly as Turkish mutes bowstring their victim, he was shot out of the boat, ere the crew knew he was gone. Next instant, the heavy eyesplice in the rope's final end flew out of the stark-empty tub, knocked down an oarsman, and smiting the sea, disappeared in its depths.

For an instant, the tranced boat's crew stood still; then turned. "The ship? Great God, where is the ship?" Soon they through dim, bewildering mediums saw her sidelong fading phantom, as in the gaseous Fata Morgana,[2] only the uppermost masts out of water; while fixed by infatuation, or fidelity, or fate, to their once lofty perches, the pagan harpooners still maintained their sinking lookouts on the sea. And now, concentric circles

[1] long curling wave   [2] mirage, so-called because once thought the work of the fairy Morgan le Fay, sister of King Arthur in medieval romance

seized the lone boat itself, and all its crew, and each floating oar, and every lance-pole, and spinning, animate and inanimate, all round and round in one vortex, carried the smallest chip of the *Pequod* out of sight.

But as the last whelmings intermixingly poured themselves over the sunken head of the Indian at the mainmast, leaving a few inches of the erect spar yet visible, together with long streaming yards of the flag, which calmly undulated, with ironical coincidings, over the destroying billows they almost touched;—at that instant, a red arm and a hammer hovered backwardly uplifted in the open air, in the act of nailing the flag faster and yet faster to the subsiding spar. A skyhawk that tauntingly had followed the maintruck downwards from its natural home among the stars, pecking at the flag, and incommoding Tashtego there; this bird now chanced to intercept its broad fluttering wing between the hammer and the wood; and simultaneously feeling that ethereal thrill, the submerged savage beneath, in his death-gasp, kept his hammer frozen there; and so the bird of heaven, with archangelic shrieks, and his imperial beak thrust upwards, and his whole captive form folded in the flag of Ahab, went down with his ship, which, like Satan, would not sink to hell till she had dragged a living part of heaven along with her, and helmeted herself with it.

Now small fowls flew screaming over the yet yawning gulf; a sullen white surf beat against its steep sides; then all collapsed, and the great shroud of the sea rolled on as it rolled five thousand years ago.   1851

1807 -- *Henry Wadsworth Longfellow* -- 1882

LONGFELLOW was influential in widening the American outlook and taste. He has been termed an inaugurator of the so-called "New England Renaissance of arts and letters." He did much to domesticate foreign literature and the cosmopolitan spirit, following Irving in popularizing antique legend and in interpreting to the

New World the mellow twilight of the European past. He also deserves credit for popularizing American themes in poetry, from his boyish verses on "The Battle of Lovell's Pond" to *The New England Tragedies* of his later life. Beyond question, he was the best-loved American man of letters of his day, partly because he was the interpreter of the life and emotions of the average man. No other poet has contributed so many favorite pieces to our literature, and no other has been translated into so many foreign languages. His range and variety as a narrative poet, his moral idealism and sentiment, and his gentle didacticism may not appeal to critics today, but they appealed to the generation of readers he addressed, the generation emerging from Calvinism. Longfellow is often called the "most national of our poets," not because he is the best interpreter of our national life, for he is not, but because he was and remains our leading household poet and because of the world-wide acceptance of his verse. His life was a fortunate one, for he enjoyed every advantage of culture, leisure, travel, social intercourse, and contemporary recognition.

Henry Wadsworth Longfellow was born in Portland, Maine, February 27, 1807. His mother came from an army and navy family, and on her side he was of Mayflower stock, descending from John Alden and Priscilla Mullins. His father was a leading citizen, a Harvard graduate, a judge, a man of affairs, a member of Congress. The youth grew up in a home atmosphere of refinement. His father's library contained many books. He knew Dante early and Cowper and Ossian. The appearance of Irving's *Sketch Book* and Bryant's "Thanatopsis" influenced him to write *Outre-Mer* and verses. His first poem was published when he was thirteen, in the Portland *Gazette*. He was educated in private schools, and at fifteen entered Bowdoin, of which his father was a trustee, attending it from 1822 till he was graduated in 1825. Hawthorne was a classmate. While at Bowdoin he became confirmed in his wish to become a man of letters. He is described as a modest boy, well-balanced and amiable, without self-righteousness, and with excellent manners. Along with these virtues he made an exceptional record as a scholar, especially in language and literature.

His father wished him to study law, and he did so half-heartedly for a year. Then at twenty he was offered and accepted a newly founded chair of modern languages at his Alma Mater, on the condition that he visit Europe. The college paid him $600 a year to do so, and he was gone three years, 1826–29, for study in France, Spain, Italy, and Germany, winning a reading knowledge of their languages. He was also in England. Returning to Bowdoin, he occupied the chair of Professor of Modern Languages and served also as Librarian. In September, 1831, he married Miss Mary Potter. In the six years that he remained at Bowdoin his interest turned to prose rather than verse. He published textbooks and magazine articles on European lands and literatures. In the fourth year of his professorship, 1833, he issued his first volume, *Outre-Mer*, a book of sketches and travel first written for the *New England*

Magazine. This book was not of a new type, and it was not on native themes. His early residence abroad, his professorial duties, and his later trips, though excellent for his teaching, made his mind run along traditional lines. Throughout his life his work was to rely chiefly on literary inspiration and to have a decidedly bookish flavor.

A year later, when he was twenty-seven, Longfellow was called to succeed George Ticknor as Professor of Modern Languages at Harvard. He spent another year and a half in Europe, 1835–36, visiting England, Scandinavia, Holland, Germany, Switzerland, France. After the death of his wife at Rotterdam, in 1835, he proceeded to Heidelberg and stayed there seven or eight months, absorbed in the European past and yielding to German romanticism, with its love of sadness, night, and susceptibility to sentiment and dreams. On his return to America he took up his residence in Cambridge, in the days when it was the chief center of culture for the country. He lived at Craigie House, once Washington's headquarters, which was to be his home for the rest of his life. He remained on the Harvard faculty, teaching foreign languages for the eighteen years 1836–54. In his thirty-second year, 1839, Longfellow published *Hyperion*, a prose romance of travel. He next gave increasing attention to poetry, issuing in the same year his first volume of verse, *Voices of the Night*. It appealed to the mood of his time and made its way at once to popularity. Two years later he published *Ballads and Other Poems*, containing many of his successful pieces.

At thirty-five, in 1842, Longfellow went again to Europe, visiting during his leave of absence Belgium, the Rhine, and England. He wrote his *Poems of Slavery* on the return voyage, poems that seemed rather bookish and perfunctory when compared with Whittier's. Shortly afterwards he married Miss Frances Appleton, and her father bought Craigie House for them. His salary as a professor, the profits from his work, and her property made them well-to-do. His first play, *The Spanish Student*, not intended for the stage, was published in 1843, the year of his marriage. During 1845–47 he edited several collections of verse, and in 1845 published his *The Belfry of Bruges and Other Poems*, a volume including many of his best-liked poems. When the poet was forty-seven he composed, from a tale told to Hawthorne, *Evangeline*, which became at once popular for its story, its background of American natural scenery, and its meter, adapted from the classic hexameter. Henceforth he was recognized as a national figure. He published *Kavanagh, a Tale*, a dreamy, not very successful prose work, in 1849, and soon after *The Seaside and the Fireside*, a collection of poems which included "The Building of the Ship." In 1854, at the age of forty-seven, Longfellow resigned his professorship, believing that teaching hampered his poetic inspiration. James Russell Lowell was appointed to succeed him. The rest of his life is mainly a record of successive books and continuing popularity.

After he resigned from Harvard he published *Hiawatha* (1855), expressed in the rhythm of an old Finnish epic; *Drift Wood*, a volume of essays, in 1857; and the next year his third long poem upon an American theme, *The Courtship of Miles Standish*, narrating the wooing of his Puritan ancestors. In 1859 Harvard gave him an LL.D. In 1861 his second wife was accidentally burned to death. For consolation he turned to translation, completing his version of Dante's *Divine Comedy*, which was published 1865–67. During and after these years he issued along with other poems the three parts of the *Tales of a Wayside Inn*, including some of his best-known poems such as "Paul Revere's Ride." The larger part of his sixty-first and sixty-second years, 1868–69, the poet spent with his daughter, traveling in Italy, France, and England, everywhere receiving an admiring welcome. Cambridge and Oxford gave him honorary degrees. After his return he finished *Christus, a Mystery* (1872), his largest and most ambitious work, made up of *The Golden Legend* of 1851, to which he added for completion two long pieces, *The New England Tragedies* (1868) and *The Divine Tragedy* (1871). Also in dramatic form were *Judas Maccabaeus* (1871), *The Masque of Pandora* (1875), and *Michael Angelo*, left unfinished at his death and printed in 1883. No one of his dramas attained the popularity of his narratives and lyrics. His later poems showed no flagging of his powers. Among them were "Aftermath" (1873); "The Hanging of the Crane" (1874); "Morituri Salutamus" (1875), written for the fiftieth anniversary of his college class; and "Kéramos" (1877). His last volume, *Ultima Thule*, appeared in 1880. A rough grouping of his works shows five chief classes, of which the first and second were the most successful: ballads and lyrics of moral inspiration or sentiment, long narrative pieces, dramas, prose, and translations.

Longfellow died March 24, 1882, shortly after his seventy-fifth birthday. He and Lowell are the only American men of letters who are commemorated in Westminster Abbey. His bust was placed there not because English critical opinion thinks him our greatest poet but rather as an expression of the feeling that he had entered into the general stream of life abroad and had become more widely influential than any other American author.

Longfellow's reading was wide and discursive. He knew Shakespeare, Milton, Goethe, Carlyle, and Ruskin, but these authors had no deep influence on him. His debt was greater to Chaucer, Gray, Burns, the German romantic poets, and the works of essayists and travelers. His teaching of foreign languages familiarized him with French, German, Italian, and Spanish classics, especially with Dante, whom he translated. A lay acquaintance with science such as Emerson's, or Whittier's concern with the living issues of his own time, he does not exhibit. He thought of the poet as standing apart from the outer world of toil and action, preferring remote themes; he liked the effect of romantic distance. His primary wish, however, was to be fundamentally ethical, to inspire faith in an ideal, to soothe, to edify, and to instruct.

Art is the gift of God and must be used
Unto his glory. That art is highest
Which aims at this.

His own religious faith was simple and unquestioning, without incertitude or struggle. Longfellow early remarked that he was "better pleased with those pieces which touch the feelings and improve the heart." In 1832 he wished our poets to be "more original and national." He praised Hawthorne in 1837 for dealing with the American romantic past. By 1849 he did not care whether the past was American or European. "Nationality is a good thing to a certain extent, but universality is better." Ultimately he turned to "the conflict between good and evil" in the spirit of the individual man as his preferred theme. Though it is lacking in his own poetry, he thought "the tragic element in poetry" its fundamental. He remained the poet of reverie, of sentiment, and of preference for the bygone; but he gave America what it needed, more respect for the past, for tradition, for the artist, and for the beautiful.

Part of Longfellow's success was owing to the simple sincere feeling of his poetry. He was the poet of the masses in their better moods, the laureate of the common aspirations and sorrows of life. He was also the poet of good manners, dignity, and culture. A fluent craftsman, he tried a great variety of verse forms, exhibiting considerable skill and grace and a sense of melody. He was at his best as a narrator in verse, and he was an excellent sonneteer. Among his limitations were his lack of dramatic vigor, of profound notes, of intensity and ardor. His poems rarely need a second or third reading. His morality often seems stock and his thought and moods are restricted. There is no essential Americanism in his verse. He was somewhat aloof from the forces working in his own time, religious, political, economic, or social. He never liked to cross public opinion but rather to fall in with it. He shrank from controversy as he shrank from violence.

Like Tennyson, Longfellow has suffered from reaction and the growing popularity of verse of other types than his. He has been attacked for sentimentality, bookishness, leaning on European models, lack of originality, commonplace moralizing, and didacticism. He is now dealt with more fairly, however. It is recognized that, though he is indebted to foreign models, he never followed them slavishly. It is recognized, too, that he stimulated the popular taste for poetry, stimulated culture, and was an American poet who could reach the world.

The standard collected edition of Longfellow's work is the *Complete Works*, Riverside Edition (11 vols., 1886). The best one-volume edition of the poems is H. E. Scudder's *Complete Poetical Works*, Cambridge Edition (1893). A more recent collection, *Longfellow's Boyhood Poems* (1925), edited by R. W. Pettengill, makes available some early poems not included in preceding collections.

Samuel Longfellow, a brother of the poet, published *The Life of Henry Wadsworth Longfellow*

(2 vols., 1885–86). A third volume, *Final Memorials*, added in 1887, concerns the poet's last fifteen years. Among other biographies are E. S. Robertson's *The Life of Henry Wadsworth Longfellow*, in the Great Writers Series (1887), a dependable and discerning piece of work; G. R. Carpenter's *Henry Wadsworth Longfellow*, in the Beacon Biography Series (1901), a good succinct account; T. W. Higginson's *Henry Wadsworth Longfellow*, in the American Men of Letters Series (1902); C. E. Norton's *Henry Wadsworth Longfellow, A Sketch of His Life* (1907); and H. S. Gorman's *A Victorian American, Henry Wadsworth Longfellow* (1926), somewhat disparaging but dependable as to facts. W. C. Bronson wrote of him in *DAB*, XI. Lawrance Thompson has given an interesting account of Longfellow's earlier years in *Young Longfellow* (1938).

Criticism concerning Longfellow is readily available. Some of it takes a deprecatory tone, although two more recent writers, G. R. Elliott and H. M. Jones, defend the poet. See Barrett Wendell in *A Literary History of America* (1900); Paul Elmer More, "The Centenary of Longfellow," in *Shelburne Essays, Fifth Series* (1908); Bliss Perry, "The Centenary of Longfellow," in *Park Street Papers* (1908); W. P. Trent, *Longfellow and Other Essays* (1908), who also has the section on Longfellow in *CHAL*, II (1917); Alfred Noyes, "Longfellow and Modern Critics," in *Some Aspects of Modern Poetry* (1924); and G. R. Elliott, "The Gentle Shades of Longfellow," in *The Cycle of Modern Poetry* (1929). Some more recent criticisms are H. M. Jones's "Longfellow," in *American Writers on American Literature*, edited by John Macy (1931); James T. Hatfield's valuable *New Light on Longfellow, with Special Reference to His Relations to Germany* (1933); Odell Shepherd's sound introduction to his *Longfellow*, in American Writers Series (1934); and Gay W. Allen's study of Longfellow's verse form, in *American Prosody*, Chap. VI (1935).

Bibliographies for Longfellow may be found in *CHAL*, II (1917), by H. W. L. Dana; in L. S. Livingston's *A Bibliography of the First Editions in Book Form of the Writings of Henry Wadsworth Longfellow* (1908); and in W. F. Taylor's *A History of American Letters* (1936).

THE SPIRIT OF POETRY

This early piece in blank verse, showing the influence of Bryant or Wordsworth, was composed by Longfellow soon after he left college, in the autumn of 1825. It was published in the *Atlantic Souvenir* for 1828.

THERE is a quiet spirit in these woods,
That dwells where'er the gentle south-wind
    blows;
Where, underneath the white-thorn in the
    glade,
The wild flowers bloom, or, kissing the soft
    air,
The leaves above their sunny palms out-
    spread.
With what a tender and impassioned voice
It fills the nice and delicate ear of thought,
When the fast ushering star of morning comes
O'er-riding the gray hills with golden scarf;
Or when the cowled and dusky-sandalled
    Eve,   10

In mourning weeds, from out the western
    gate,
Departs with silent pace! That spirit moves
In the green valley, where the silver brook,
From its full laver, pours the white cascade;
And, babbling low amid the tangled woods,
Slips down through moss-grown stones with
    endless laughter.
And frequent, on the everlasting hills,
Its feet go forth, when it doth wrap itself
In all the dark embroidery of the storm,
And shouts the stern, strong wind. And here,
    amid   20
The silent majesty of these deep woods,
Its presence shall uplift thy thoughts from
    earth,
As to the sunshine and the pure, bright air
Their tops the green trees lift. Hence gifted
    bards
Have ever loved the calm and quiet shades.
For them there was an eloquent voice in all
The sylvan pomp of woods, the golden sun,

The flowers, the leaves, the river on its way,
Blue skies, and silver clouds, and gentle winds,
The swelling upland, where the sidelong
   sun   30
Aslant the wooded slope, at evening, goes,
Groves, through whose broken roof the sky
   looks in,
Mountain, and shattered cliff, and sunny vale,
The distant lake, fountains, and mighty trees,
In many a lazy syllable, repeating
Their old poetic legends to the wind.

And this is the sweet spirit, that doth fill
The world; and, in these wayward days of
   youth,
My busy fancy oft embodies it,
As a bright image of the light and beauty   40
That dwell in nature; of the heavenly forms
We worship in our dreams, and the soft hues
That stain the wild bird's wing, and flush the
   clouds
When the sun sets. Within her tender eye
The heaven of April, with its changing light,
And when it wears the blue of May, is hung,
And on her lip the rich, red rose. Her hair
Is like the summer tresses of the trees,
When twilight makes them brown, and on her
   cheek
Blushes the richness of an autumn sky,   50
With ever-shifting beauty. Then her breath,
It is so like the gentle air of Spring,
As, from the morning's dewy flowers, it comes
Full of their fragrance, that it is a joy
To have it round us, and her silver voice
Is the rich music of a summer bird,
Heard in the still night, with its passionate
   cadence.

1825   *1828*

A PSALM OF LIFE

WHAT THE HEART OF THE YOUNG MAN
SAID TO THE PSALMIST

Written July 26, 1838; published anonymously
in the *Knickerbocker Magazine*, October, 1838;
included in *Voices of the Night* (1839). The poet
read it to his class of Harvard students at the
close of an hour given to Goethe's *Wilhelm
Meister*. Its leading doctrine is that of the German
novel. Longfellow said of it, "I kept it some time
in manuscript, unwilling to show it to anyone, it

being a voice from my inmost heart, at a time
when I was rallying from depression." He thought
of it as a call to reality from his own nature,
answering and refuting his despondency. In 1929
a poll of many thousands of newspaper readers
over the United States was made to determine
"America's favorite poem." It resulted, according
to an announcement made on March 20, in the
selection of "A Psalm of Life." Bryant's "Thanatopsis" and two other poems by Longfellow,
"Evangeline" and "The Village Blacksmith,"
ranked high.

TELL me not, in mournful numbers,
   Life is but an empty dream!—
For the soul is dead that slumbers,
   And things are not what they seem.

Life is real! Life is earnest!
   And the grave is not its goal;
Dust thou art, to dust returnest,
   Was not spoken of the soul.

Not enjoyment, and not sorrow,
   Is our destined end or way;   10
But to act, that each to-morrow
   Find us farther than to-day.

Art is long, and Time is fleeting,
   And our hearts, though stout and brave,
Still, like muffled drums, are beating
   Funeral marches to the grave.

In the world's broad field of battle,
   In the bivouac of Life,
Be not like dumb, driven cattle!
   Be a hero in the strife!   20

Trust no Future, howe'er pleasant!
   Let the dead Past bury its dead!
Act,—act in the living Present!
   Heart within, and God o'erhead!

Lives of great men all remind us
   We can make our lives sublime,
And, departing, leave behind us
   Footprints on the sands of time;

Footprints, that perhaps another,
   Sailing o'er life's solemn main,   30
A forlorn and shipwrecked brother,
   Seeing, shall take heart again.

Let us, then, be up and doing,
  With a heart for any fate;
Still achieving, still pursuing,
  Learn to labor and to wait.

                                        1838

THE VILLAGE BLACKSMITH

Written in 1839. Published in the *Knicker-bocker Magazine*, November, 1840. Included in *Ballads and Other Poems* (1841). Longfellow wrote to his father that he could consider it as a song in praise of his ancestor, the first Stephen Long-fellow of Cambridge, who was a blacksmith. It was suggested by a smithy which stood beneath a horse chestnut tree on Brattle Street near Long-fellow's home in Cambridge. The tree was cut down in 1876 for the widening of the street, despite the poet's protest. Three years later the schoolchildren of Cambridge, on Longfellow's seventy-second birthday, gave him a chair made from the wood of the tree. See his poem, "From My Arm Chair."

UNDER a spreading chestnut-tree
  The village smithy stands;
The smith, a mighty man is he,
  With large and sinewy hands;
And the muscles of his brawny arms
  Are strong as iron bands.

His hair is crisp, and black, and long,
  His face is like the tan;
His brow is wet with honest sweat,
  He earns whate'er he can,   10
And looks the whole world in the face,
  For he owes not any man.

Week in, week out, from morn till night,
  You can hear his bellows blow;
You can hear him swing his heavy sledge,
  With measured beat and slow,
Like a sexton ringing the village bell,
  When the evening sun is low.

And children coming home from school
  Look in at the open door;   20
They love to see the flaming forge,
  And hear the bellows roar,
And catch the burning sparks that fly
  Like chaff from a threshing-floor.

He goes on Sunday to the church,
  And sits among his boys;
He hears the parson pray and preach,
  He hears his daughter's voice,
Singing in the village choir,
  And it makes his heart rejoice.   30

It sounds to him like her mother's voice,
  Singing in Paradise!
He needs must think of her once more,
  How in the grave she lies;
And with his hard, rough hand he wipes
  A tear out of his eyes.

Toiling,—rejoicing,—sorrowing,
  Onward through life he goes;
Each morning sees some task begin,
  Each evening sees it close;   40
Something attempted, something done,
  Has earned a night's repose.

Thanks, thanks to thee, my worthy friend,
  For the lesson thou hast taught!
Thus at the flaming forge of life
  Our fortunes must be wrought;
Thus on its sounding anvil shaped
  Each burning deed and thought.

1839   1840

THE WRECK OF THE HESPERUS

Originally published in Park Benjamin's *The New World*. Longfellow wrote his narrative in the form of the English and Scottish traditional bal-lads, reproducing from them such characteristics of their technique as the light accent on the last syllables of "daughter" and "sailor," their han-dling of narrative and dialogue, and a stock manner of closing, as well as the staple four-line ballad stanza. The fourth and fifth stanzas echo a passage in a text of "Sir Patrick Spens." In all but its ostensible localization the ballad is more an Old World than an American piece. Longfellow en-tered in his journal, December 30, 1839, "I wrote last evening a notice of Allston's poems. After which I sat till twelve o'clock by my fire smoking, when suddenly it came into my mind to write 'The Ballad of the Schooner Hesperus,' which I accordingly did. Then I went to bed but could not sleep. New thoughts were running in my mind, and I got up to add them to the ballad. . . . I feel pleased with the ballad. It hardly cost me an effort. It did not come into my mind by lines, but by stanzas." He had written in his journal for December 17, "News of shipwrecks horrible on the coast. Twenty bodies washed ashore near Gloucester, one lashed to a piece of the wreck. There is a reef called Norman's Woe where many of these took place; among others the schooner *Hesperus*. Also the *Sea-flower* on Black Rock. I must write a ballad upon this." Norman's Woe is a rock about 200 feet long, jutting out into the sea off Gloucester harbor.

H. Beston wrote of "The Real Wreck of the Hesperus" in the *Bookman*, 1925.

It was the schooner *Hesperus*,
  That sailed the wintry sea;
And the skipper had taken his little daughtèr,
  To bear him company.

Blue were her eyes as the fairy-flax,
  Her cheeks like the dawn of day,
And her bosom white as the hawthorn buds,
  That ope in the month of May.

The skipper he stood beside the helm,
  His pipe was in his mouth,   10
And he watched how the veering flaw did blow
  The smoke now West, now South.

Then up and spake an old Sailòr,
  Had sailed to the Spanish Main,[1]
"I pray thee, put into yonder port,
  For I fear a hurricane.

"Last night, the moon had a golden ring,
  And to-night no moon we see!"
The skipper, he blew a whiff from his pipe,
  And a scornful laugh laughed he.   20

Colder and louder blew the wind,
  A gale from the Northeast,
The snow fell hissing in the brine,
  And the billows frothed like yeast.

Down came the storm, and smote amain
  The vessel in its strength;
She shuddered and paused, like a frighted steed,
  Then leaped her cable's length.

[1] the northern coast of South America, or the adjoining waters

"Come hither! come hither! my little daughtèr,
  And do not tremble so;   30
For I can weather the roughest gale
  That ever wind did blow."

He wrapped her warm in his seaman's coat
  Against the stinging blast;
He cut a rope from a broken spar,
  And bound her to the mast.

"O father! I hear the church-bells ring,
  Oh say, what may it be?"
"'Tis a fog-bell on a rock-bound coast!"—
  And he steered for the open sea.   40

"O father! I hear the sound of guns,
  Oh say, what may it be?"
"Some ship in distress, that cannot live
  In such an angry sea!"

"O father! I see a gleaming light,
  Oh say, what may it be?"
But the father answered never a word,
  A frozen corpse was he.

Lashed to the helm, all stiff and stark,
  With his face turned to the skies,   50
The lantern gleamed through the gleaming snow
  On his fixed and glassy eyes.

Then the maiden clasped her hands and prayed
  That savèd she might be;
And she thought of Christ, who stilled the wave,
  On the Lake of Galilee.

And fast through the midnight dark and drear,
  Through the whistling sleet and snow,
Like a sheeted ghost, the vessel swept
  Tow'rds the reef of Norman's Woe.   60

And ever the fitful gusts between
  A sound came from the land;
It was the sound of the trampling surf
  On the rocks and the hard sea-sand.

The breakers were right beneath her bows,
  She drifted a dreary wreck,
And a whooping billow swept the crew
  Like icicles from her deck.

She struck where the white and fleecy waves
  Looked soft as carded wool,   70
But the cruel rocks, they gored her side
  Like the horns of an angry bull.

Her rattling shrouds, all sheathed in ice,
  With the masts went by the board;
Like a vessel of glass, she stove and sank,
  Ho! ho! the breakers roared!

At daybreak, on the bleak sea-beach,
  A fisherman stood aghast,
To 'see the form of a maiden fair,
  Lashed close to a drifting mast.   80

The salt sea was frozen on her breast,
  The salt tears in her eyes;
And he saw her hair, like the brown sea-
    weed,
  On the billows fall and rise.

Such was the wreck of the *Hesperus*,
  In the midnight and the snow!
Christ save us all from a death like this,
  On the reef of Norman's Woe!

1839   1841

THE SKELETON IN ARMOR

First published in the *Knickerbocker Magazine*,
January, 1841. Reprinted in *Ballads and Other
Poems*, 1841. The stanza form and meter are derived from Michael Drayton's poem on the battle
of Agincourt. Longfellow wrote, December, 1840,
to his father, "Have . . . prepared for the press
another original ballad, which has been lying by
me for some time. It is called 'The Skeleton in
Armor,' and is connected with the old Round
Tower at Newport. The skeleton in armor really
exists. It was dug up near Fall River, where I saw
it some two years ago. I suppose it to be the remains of one of the old Northern sea-rovers, who
came to this country in the tenth century. Of
course I make the tradition myself; and I think I
have succeeded in giving the whole a Northern
air." It was believed in 1840 that the Vikings
under Leif Ericsson had visited the New World,
a belief later given up and now held again. Probably it was southern Nova Scotia that Ericsson
might have visited, hardly a region farther south.
Longfellow had the idea of connecting the old
round stone tower at Newport, generally known
as the Old Windmill, with the skeleton bearing a
breastplate of brass in Massachusetts. The skeleton was buried in an upright position and it is
now believed that it was that of an Indian. Poe
praised this poem highly in his review of Longfellow in *Graham's Magazine*, April, 1842.

"Speak! speak! thou fearful guest!
Who, with thy hollow breast,
Still in rude armor drest,
  Comest to daunt me!
Wrapt not in Eastern balms,[1]
But with thy fleshless palms
Stretched, as if asking alms,
  Why dost thou haunt me?"

Then from those cavernous eyes
Pale flashes seemed to rise,   10
As when the Northern skies
  Gleam in December;
And, like the water's flow
Under December's snow,
Came a dull voice of woe
  From the heart's chamber.

"I was a Viking old!
My deeds, though manifold,
No Skald in song has told,
  No Saga taught thee!   20
Take heed that in thy verse
Thou dost the tale rehearse,
Else dread a dead man's curse;
  For this I sought thee.

"Far in the Northern Land,
By the wild Baltic's strand,
I, with my childish hand,
  Tamed the gerfalcon;
And, with my skates fast-bound,
Skimmed the half-frozen Sound,   30
That the poor whimpering hound
  Trembled to walk on.

"Oft to his frozen lair
Tracked I the grisly bear,
While from my path the hare
  Fled like a shadow;
Oft through the forest dark
Followed the were-wolf's bark,
Until the soaring lark
  Sang from the meadow.   40

[1] a reference to the ancient methods of preserving
the dead, particularly in Egypt

"But when I older grew,
Joining a corsair's crew,
O'er the dark sea I flew
   With the marauders.
Wild was the life we led;
Many the souls that sped,
Many the hearts that bled,
   By our stern orders.

"Many a wassail-bout
Wore the long winter out;   50
Often our midnight shout
   Set the cocks crowing,
As we the Berserk's tale
Measured in cups of ale,
Draining the oaken pail
   Filled to o'erflowing.

"Once as I told in glee
Tales of the stormy sea,
Soft eyes did gaze on me,
   Burning yet tender;   60
And as the white stars shine
On the dark Norway pine,
On that dark heart of mine
   Fell their soft splendor.

"I wooed the blue-eyed maid,
Yielding, yet half afraid,
And in the forest's shade
   Our vows were plighted.
Under its loosened vest
Fluttered her little breast,   70
Like birds within their nest
   By the hawk frighted.

"Bright in her father's hall
Shields gleamed upon the wall,
Loud sang the minstrels all,
   Chanting his glory;
When of old Hildebrand
I asked his daughter's hand,
Mute did the minstrels stand
   To hear my story.   80

"While the brown ale he quaffed,
Loud then the champion laughed,
And as the wind-gusts waft
   The sea-foam brightly,
So the loud laugh of scorn
Out of those lips unshorn,
From the deep drinking-horn
   Blew the foam lightly.

"She was a Prince's child,
I but a Viking wild,   90
And though she blushed and smiled,
   I was discarded!
Should not the dove so white
Follow the sea-mew's flight?
Why did they leave that night
   Her nest unguarded?

"Scarce had I put to sea,
Bearing the maid with me,
Fairest of all was she
   Among the Norsemen!   100
When on the white sea-strand,
Waving his armèd hand,
Saw we old Hildebrand,
   With twenty horsemen.

"Then launched they to the blast,
Bent like a reed each mast,
Yet we were gaining fast,
   When the wind failed us;
And with a sudden flaw
Came round the gusty Skaw,[1]   110
So that our foe we saw
   Laugh as he hailed us.

"And as to catch the gale
Round veered the flapping sail,
'Death!' was the helmsman's hail,
   'Death without quarter!'
Midships with iron keel
Struck we her ribs of steel;
Down her black hulk did reel
   Through the black water!   120

"As with his wings aslant,
Sails the fierce cormorant,
Seeking some rocky haunt,
   With his prey laden,—
So toward the open main,
Beating to sea again,
Through the wild hurricane,
   Bore I the maiden.

"Three weeks we westward bore,
And when the storm was o'er,   130
Cloud-like we saw the shore
   Stretching to leeward;

[1] English name for Cape Skagen, the northern tip of
Jutland in Denmark

There for my lady's bower
Built I the lofty tower,
Which, to this very hour,
  Stands looking seaward.

"There lived we many years;
Time dried the maiden's tears;
She had forgot her fears,
  She was a mother;   140
Death closed her mild blue eyes;
Under that tower she lies;
Ne'er shall the sun arise
  On such another!

"Still grew my bosom then,
Still as a stagnant fen!
Hateful to me were men,
  The sunlight hateful!
In the vast forest here,
Clad in my warlike gear, .   150
Fell I upon my spear,
  Oh, death was grateful!

"Thus, seamed with many scars,
Bursting these prison bars
Up to its native stars
  My soul ascended!
There from the flowing bowl
Deep drinks the warrior's soul,
Skoal! [1] to the Northland! skoal!"
  Thus the tale ended.   160

1840   *1841*

THE SLAVE'S DREAM

When Longfellow was returning from Germany
in 1842 the voyage was stormy and he was confined to his berth for fifteen days. He wrote to a
friend that during this time he composed seven
poems on slavery. They were published in the
same year, receiving praise or criticism according
to the anti- or pro-slavery sentiments of his readers. They lack Whittier's intensity, but show that
Longfellow was willing to take a stand on a burning question.

BESIDE the ungathered rice he lay,
  His sickle in his hand;

His breast was bare, his matted hair
  Was buried in the sand.
Again, in the mist and shadow of sleep,
  He saw his Native Land.

Wide through the landscape of his dreams
  The lordly Niger flowed;
Beneath the palm-trees on the plain
  Once more a king he strode;   10
And heard the tinkling caravans
  Descend the mountain road.

He saw once more his dark-eyed queen
  · Among her children stand;
They clasped his neck, they kissed his cheeks,
  They held him by the hand!—
A tear burst from the sleeper's lids
  And fell into the sand.

And then at furious speed he rode
  Along the Niger's bank;   20
His bridle-reins were golden chains,
  And, with a martial clank,
At each leap he could feel his scabbard of steel
  Smiting his stallion's flank.

Before him, like a blood-red flag,
  The bright flamingoes flew;
From morn till night he followed their flight,
  O'er plains where the tamarind grew,
Till he saw the roofs of Caffre huts,
  And the ocean rose to view.   30

At night he heard the lion roar,
  And the hyena scream,
And the river-horse, as he crushed the reeds
  Beside some hidden stream;
And it passed, like a glorious roll of drums,
  Through the triumph of his dream.

The forests, with their myriad tongues,
  Shouted of liberty;
And the Blast of the Desert cried aloud,
  With a voice so wild and free,   40
That he started in his sleep and smiled
  At their tempestuous glee.

He did not feel the driver's whip,
  Nor the burning heat of day;
For Death had illumined the Land of Sleep,
  And his lifeless body lay
A worn-out fetter, that the soul
  Had broken and thrown away!

1842

THE WARNING

BEWARE! The Israelite of old, who tore
  The lion in his path,—when, poor and
    blind,
He saw the blessed light of heaven no more,
  Shorn of his noble strength and forced to
    grind
In prison, and at last led forth to be
A pander to Philistine revelry,—

Upon the pillars of the temple laid
  His desperate hands, and in its overthrow
Destroyed himself, and with him those who
    made
  A cruel mockery of his sightless woe;   10
The poor blind Slave, the scoff and jest of all,
Expired, and thousands perished in the fall!

There is a poor blind Samson in this land,
  Shorn of his strength and bound in bonds
    of steel,
Who may, in some grim revel, raise his hand,
  And shake the pillars of this Commonweal,
Till the vast Temple of our liberties
A shapeless mass of wreck and rubbish lies.

                1842

MEZZO CAMMIN

WRITTEN AT BOPPARD ON THE RHINE
AUGUST 25, 1842, JUST BEFORE
LEAVING FOR HOME

Suggested by the first line of Dante's *Inferno:*
Nel mezzo del cammin di nostra vita ("In midway
of the road of our life").

HALF of my life is gone, and I have let
  The years slip from me and have not ful-
    filled
  The aspiration of my youth, to build
Some tower of song with lofty parapet.
Not indolence, nor pleasure, nor the fret
  Of restless passions that would not be
    stilled,
  But sorrow, and a care that almost killed,
Kept me from what I may accomplish yet;
Though, halfway up the hill, I see the Past
  Lying beneath me with its sounds and
    sights,—   10
  A city in the twilight dim and vast,
With smoking roofs, soft bells, and gleam-
    ing lights,—

And hear above me on the autumnal blast
The cataract of Death far thundering from
  the heights.

1842   1886

NUREMBERG

Written in the spring of 1844. Published in
Graham's Magazine, June, 1844. Included in the
Belfry of Bruges volume, 1845. Longfellow visited
Nuremberg, a romantic old city in Bavaria, in
1842, and his poem for American readers emerged
from his memories of it. He wrote from the town
(*Life*, I, 436) to Freiligrath, telling of his enthu-
siasm for the place.

IN the valley of the Pegnitz, where across
  broad meadow-lands
Rise the blue Franconian mountains, Nuremberg, the ancient, stands.

Quaint old town of toil and traffic, quaint old
  town of art and song,
Memories haunt thy pointed gables, like the
  rooks that round them throng:

Memories of the Middle Ages, when the emperors, rough and bold,
Had their dwelling in thy castle, time-defying,
  centuries old;

And thy brave and thrifty burghers boasted,
  in their uncouth rhyme,
That their great imperial city stretched its
  hand through every clime.

In the courtyard of the castle, bound with
  many an iron band,
Stands the mighty linden planted by Queen
  Cunigunde's hand;   10

On the square the oriel window, where in old
  heroic days
Sat the poet Melchior singing Kaiser Maximilian's praise.[1]

Everywhere I see around me rise the wondrous world of Art:
Fountains wrought with richest sculpture
  standing in the common mart;

[1] "Melchior Pfinzing was one of the most celebrated
German poets of the sixteenth century. The hero of his
Teuerdank was the reigning Emperor, Maximilian; and
the poem was to the Germans of that day what the
Orlando Furioso was to the Italians." [*Longfellow's note.*]

And above cathedral doorways saints and
    bishops carved in stone,
By a former age commissioned as apostles to
    our own.

In the church of sainted Sebald sleeps en-
    shrined his holy dust,[1]
And in bronze the Twelve Apostles guard
    from age to age their trust;

In the church of sainted Lawrence stands a
    pix of sculpture rare,[2]
Like the foamy sheaf of fountains, rising
    through the painted air.   20

Here, when Art was still religion, with a
    simple, reverent heart,
Lived and labored Albrecht Dürer, the
    Evangelist of Art;

Hence in silence and in sorrow, toiling still
    with busy hand,
Like an emigrant he wandered, seeking for
    the Better Land.

Emigravit is the inscription on the tombstone
    where he lies;
Dead he is not, but departed,—for the
    artist never dies.

Fairer seems the ancient city, and the sun-
    shine seems more fair,
That he once has trod its pavement, that he
    once has breathed its air!

Through these streets so broad and stately,
    these obscure and dismal lanes,
Walked of yore the Mastersingers, chanting
    rude poetic strains.   30

[1] "The tomb of Saint Sebald, in the church which
bears his name, is one of the richest works of art in
Nuremberg. It is of bronze, and was cast by Peter
Vischer and his sons, who labored upon it thirteen years.
It is adorned with nearly one hundred figures, among
which those of the Twelve Apostles are conspicuous
for size and beauty." [*Longfellow' note.*]   [2] "This
pix, or tabernacle for the vessels of the sacrament,
is by the hand of Adam Kraft. It is an exquisite piece
of sculpture in white stone, and rises to the height of
sixty-four feet. It stands in the choir, whose richly
painted windows cover it with varied colors." [*Longfellow's note.*]

From remote and sunless suburbs came they
    to the friendly guild,
Building nests in Fame's great temple, as in
    spouts the swallows build.

As the weaver plied the shuttle, wove he too
    the mystic rhyme,
And the smith his iron measures hammered to
    the anvil's chime;

Thanking God, whose boundless wisdom
    makes the flowers of poesy bloom
In the forge's dust and cinders, in the tissues
    of the loom.

Here Hans Sachs, the cobbler-poet, laureate
    of the gentle craft,
Wisest of the Twelve Wise Masters,[1] in huge
    folios sang and laughed.

But his house is now an alehouse, with a
    nicely sanded floor,
And a garland in the window, and his face
    above the door;   40

Painted by some humble artist, as in Adam
    Puschman's song,
As the old man gray and dove-like, with his
    great beard white and long.

And at night the swart mechanic comes to
    drown his cark and care,
Quaffing ale from pewter tankards, in the
    master's antique chair.

Vanished is the ancient splendor, and before
    my dreamy eye
Wave these mingled shapes and figures, like a
    faded tapestry.

Not thy Councils, not thy Kaisers, win for
    thee the world's regard;
But thy painter, Albrecht Dürer, and Hans
    Sachs thy cobbler bard.

[1] "The Twelve Wise Masters was the title of the
original corporation of the Mastersingers. Hans Sachs,
the cobbler of Nuremberg, though not one of the
original twelve, was the most renowned of the Mastersingers, as well as the most voluminous. He flourished
in the sixteenth century; and left behind him thirty-
four folio volumes of manuscript, containing two
hundred and eight plays, one thousand and seven
hundred comic tales, and between four and five thousand lyric poems." [*Longfellow's note.*]

Thus, O Nuremberg, a wanderer from a
    region far away,
As he paced thy streets and courtyards, sang
    in thought his careless lay: 50

Gathering from the pavement's crevice, as a
    floweret of the soil,
The nobility of labor,—the long pedigree of
    toil.

              1844

THE DAY IS DONE

Composed as a proem to a volume of selected
minor poems (*The Waif*) assembled and edited by
Longfellow in 1845.

THE day is done, and the darkness
    Falls from the wings of Night,
As a feather is wafted downward
    From an eagle in his flight.

I see the lights of the village
    Gleam through the rain and the mist,
And a feeling of sadness comes o'er me
    That my soul cannot resist:

A feeling of sadness and longing,
    That is not akin to pain,   10
And resembles sorrow only
    As the mist resembles the rain.

Come, read to me some poem,
    Some simple and heartfelt lay,
That shall soothe this restless feeling,
    And banish the thoughts of day.

Not from the grand old masters,
    Not from the bards sublime,
Whose distant footsteps echo
    Through the corridors of Time.   20

For, like strains of martial music,
    Their mighty thoughts suggest
Life's endless toil and endeavor;
    And to-night I long for rest.

Read from some humbler poet,
    Whose songs gushed from his heart,
As showers from the clouds of summer,
    Or tears from the eyelids start;

Who, through long days of labor,
    And nights devoid of ease,   30
Still heard in his soul the music
    Of wonderful melodies.

Such songs have power to quiet
    The restless pulse of care,
And come like the benediction
    That follows after prayer.

Then read from the treasured volume
    The poem of thy choice,
And lend to the rhyme of the poet
    The beauty of thy voice.   40

And the night shall be filled with music,
    And the cares, that infest the day,
Shall fold their tents, like the Arabs,
    And as silently steal away.

              1844

THE ARSENAL AT SPRINGFIELD

Published in *Graham's Magazine*, April, 1844.
Reprinted in *The Belfry of Bruges and Other
Poems* (1845). In the summer of 1843, accompanied by his close friend Charles Sumner, Longfellow and his wife visited the United States
Arsenal at Springfield, Massachusetts. Samuel
Longfellow, the biographer of his brother, relates
that "While Mr. Sumner was endeavoring to impress upon the attendant that the money expended
upon these weapons of war would have been much
better spent upon a great library, Mrs. Longfellow
pleased her husband by remarking how like an
organ looked the ranged and shining gun-barrels
which covered the walls from floor to ceiling, and
suggesting what mournful music Death would
bring from them. 'We grew quite warlike against
war,' she wrote, 'and I urged H. to write a peace
poem.'" The poem was written some months
later.

THIS is the Arsenal. From floor to ceiling,
    Like a huge organ, rise the burnished
      arms;
But from their silent pipes no anthem
      pealing
    Startles the villages with strange alarms.

Ah! what a sound will rise, how wild and
      dreary,
    When the death-angel touches those swift
      keys!

What loud lament and dismal Miserere
  Will mingle with their awful sympho-
    nies!

I hear even now the infinite fierce chorus,
  The cries of agony, the endless groan,   10
Which, through the ages that have gone
    before us,
  In long reverberations reach our own.

On helm and harness rings the Saxon ham-
    mer,
  Through Cimbric forest roars the Norse-
    man's song,
And loud, amid the universal clamor,
  O'er distant deserts sounds the Tartar
    gong.

I hear the Florentine, who from his palace
  Wheels out his battle-bell with dreadful din,
And Aztec priests upon their teocallis[1]
  Beat the wild war-drum made of ser-
    pent's skin;   20

The tumult of each sacked and burning
    village;
  The shout that every prayer for mercy
    drowns;
The soldiers' revels in the midst of pillage;
  The wail of famine in beleaguered towns;

The bursting shell, the gateway wrenched
    asunder,
  The rattling musketry, the clashing blade;
And ever and anon, in tones of thunder,
  The diapason of the cannonade.

Is it, O man, with such discordant noises,
  With such accursed instruments as these, 30
Thou drownest Nature's sweet and kindly
    voices,
  And jarrest the celestial harmonies?

Were half the power, that fills the world with
    terror,
  Were half the wealth, bestowed on camps
    and courts,
Given to redeem the human mind from error,
  There were no need of arsenals or forts:

[1] mounds of pyramid shape on which temples were
built

The warrior's name would be a name ab-
    horrèd!
  And every nation, that should lift again
Its hand against a brother, on its forehead
  Would wear forevermore the curse of
    Cain!   40

Down the dark future, through long gen-
    erations,
  The echoing sounds grow fainter and then
    cease;
And like a bell, with solemn, sweet vibra-
    tions,
  I hear once more the voice of Christ say,
    "Peace!"

Peace! and no longer from its brazen por-
    tals
  The blast of War's great organ shakes the
    skies!
But beautiful as songs of the immortals,
  The holy melodies of love arise.

1844   1845

From THE BELFRY OF BRUGES

CARILLON

Composed in 1842, and included in *The Belfry
of Bruges* volume (1845) as a prelude. An entry in
Longfellow's diary for May 30, 1842, notes that
he stopped at the Fleur-de-Blé, attracted by the
name, and an entry for the next day describes the
carillon. In a letter to the German poet, Ferdinand
Freiligrath, Longfellow tells of his pleasure in this
old city. His interest in bells is shown in many
poems in which they figure: "The Bells of Lynn"
(1859), "Christmas Bells" (1864), "The Bell of
Atri" (1870), "The Chimes" (1879), "The Bells
of San Blas" (1882).

In the ancient town of Bruges,
  In the quaint old Flemish city,
As the evening shades descended,
  Low and loud and sweetly blended,
Low at times and loud at times,
  And changing like a poet's rhymes,
Rang the beautiful wild chimes
  From the Belfry in the market
Of the ancient town of Bruges.

Then, with deep sonorous clangor   10
  Calmly answering their sweet anger,

When the wrangling bells had ended,
Slowly struck the clock eleven,
And, from out the silent heaven,
Silence on the town descended.
Silence, silence everywhere,
On the earth and in the air,
Save the footsteps here and there
Of some burgher home returning,
By the street lamps faintly burning,   20
For a moment woke the echoes
Of the ancient town of Bruges.

But amid my broken slumbers
Still I heard those magic numbers,
As they loud proclaimed the flight
And stolen marches of the night;
Till their chimes in sweet collision
Mingled with each wandering vision,
Mingled with the fortune-telling
Gypsy-bands of dreams and fancies,   30
Which amid the waste expanses
Of the silent land of trances
Have their solitary dwelling;
All else seemed asleep in Bruges,
In the quaint old Flemish city.

And I thought how like these chimes
Are the poet's airy rhymes,
All his rhymes and roundelays,
His conceits, and songs, and ditties,
From the belfry of his brain,   4^
Scattered downward, though in vain,
On the roofs and stones of cities!
For by night the drowsy ear
Under its curtains cannot hear,
And by day men go their ways,
Hearing the music as they pass,
But deeming it no more, alas!
Than the hollow sound of brass.

Yet perchance a sleepless wight,
Lodging at some humble inn   50
In the narrow lanes of life,
When the dusk and hush of night
Shut out the incessant din
Of daylight and its toil and strife,
May listen with a calm delight
To the poet's melodies,
Till he hears, or dreams he hears,
Intermingled with the song,
Thoughts that he has cherished long;

Hears amid the chime and singing   60
The bells of his own village ringing,
And wakes, and finds his slumberous eyes
Wet with most delicious tears.

Thus dreamed I, as by night I lay
In Bruges, at the Fleur-de-Blé,[1]
Listening with a wild delight
To the chimes that, through the night,
Rang their changes from the Belfry
Of that quaint old Flemish city.

1842   1845

SEAWEED

The first four stanzas of this poem have had
very high praise. The later stanzas may have appealed to readers of the poet's time, but today the
analogy they elaborate seems forced and the expression commonplace.

WHEN descends on the Atlantic
      The gigantic
Storm-wind of the equinox,
Landward in his wrath he scourges
      The toiling surges,
Laden with seaweed from the rocks:

From Bermuda's reefs; from edges
      Of sunken ledges,
In some far-off, bright Azore;
From Bahama, and the dashing,   10
      Silver-flashing
Surges of San Salvador;

From the tumbling surf, that buries
      The Orkneyan skerries,
Answering the hoarse Hebrides;
And from wrecks of ships, and drifting
      Spars, uplifting
On the desolate, rainy seas;—

Ever drifting, drifting, drifting
      On the shifting   20
Currents of the restless main;
Till in sheltered coves, and reaches
      Of sandy beaches,
All have found repose again.

1 "Flower-of-Grain," the name of an inn

So when storms of wild emotion
   Strike the ocean
Of the poet's soul, erelong
From each cave and rocky fastness,
   In its vastness,
Floats some fragment of a song: 30

From the far-off isles enchanted,
   Heaven has planted
With the golden fruit of Truth;
From the flashing surf, whose vision
   Gleams Elysian
In the tropic clime of Youth;

From the strong Will, and the Endeavor
   That forever
Wrestle with the tides of Fate;
From the wreck of Hopes far-scattered, 40
   Tempest-shattered,
Floating waste and desolate;—

Ever drifting, drifting, drifting
   On the shifting
Currents of the restless heart;
Till at length in books recorded,
   They, like hoarded
Household words, no more depart.

            1845

THE OLD CLOCK ON THE STAIRS

An entry in Longfellow's journal for November 12, 1845, reads, "Began a poem on a clock with the words 'forever, never' as the burden; suggested by the words of Bridaine, the old French missionary, who said of eternity, 'It is a clock whose pendulum utters and repeats without ceasing these two words only, in the silence of the tomb—Forever, never! Never, forever!'" Jacques Bridaine, a noted Catholic preacher, lived 1710–1767.

L'éternité est une pendule, dont le balancier dit et redit sans cesse ces deux mots seulement, dans le silence des tombeaux, "Toujours, jamais! Jamais, toujours!"

                  JACQUES BRIDAINE

SOMEWHAT back from the village street
Stands the old-fashioned country-seat.
Across its antique portico
Tall poplar-trees their shadows throw,

And from its station in the hall
An ancient timepiece says to all,—
   "Forever—never!
   Never—forever!"

Half-way up the stairs it stands,
And points and beckons with its hands   10
From its case of massive oak,
Like a monk, who, under his cloak,
Crosses himself, and sighs, alas!
With sorrowful voice to all who pass,—
   "Forever—never!
   Never—forever!"

By day its voice is low and light;
But in the silent dead of night,
Distinct as a passing footstep's fall
It echoes along the vacant hall,   20
Along the ceiling, along the floor,
And seems to say, at each chamber-door,—
   "Forever—never!
   Never—forever!"

Through days of sorrow and of mirth,
Through days of death and days of birth,
Through every swift vicissitude
Of changeful time, unchanged it has stood,
And as if, like God, it all things saw,
It calmly repeats those words of awe,—   30
   "Forever—never!
   Never—forever!"

In that mansion used to be
Free-hearted Hospitality;
His great fires up the chimney roared;
The stranger feasted at his board;
But, like the skeleton at the feast,
That warning timepiece never ceased,—
   "Forever—never!
   Never—forever!"   40

There groups of merry children played,
There youths and maidens dreaming strayed.
O precious hours! O golden prime,
And affluence of love and time!
Even as a miser counts his gold,
Those hours the ancient timepiece told,—
   "Forever—never!
   Never—forever!"

From that chamber, clothed in white,
The bride came forth on her wedding night;
There, in that silent room below,   51
The dead lay in his shroud of snow;
And in the hush that followed the prayer,
Was heard the old clock on the stair,—
    "Forever—never!
    Never—forever!"

All are scattered now and fled,
Some are married, some are dead;
And when I ask, with throbs of pain,
"Ah! when shall they all meet again?"   60
As in the days long since gone by,
The ancient timepiece makes reply,—
    "Forever—never!
    Never—forever!"

Never here, forever there,
Where all parting, pain, and care,
And death, and time, shall disappear,—
Forever there, but never here!
The horologe of Eternity
Sayeth this incessantly,—   70
    "Forever—never!
    Never—forever!"

    1845

THE BRIDGE

First entitled "The Bridge over the Charles
River." The Charles River runs between Boston
and Cambridge. Published in *The Belfry of Bruges*
volume. Longfellow wrote in a journal entry for
March 15, 1838, that when walking from Boston
to Cambridge "I always stop on the bridge; tide-
waters are beautiful. From the ocean up into the
land they go, like messengers, to ask why tribute
has not been paid."

I stood on the bridge at midnight,
    As the clocks were striking the hour,
And the moon rose o'er the city,
    Behind the dark church-tower.

I saw her bright reflection
    In the waters under me,
Like a golden goblet falling
    And sinking into the sea.

And far in the hazy distance
    Of that lovely night in June,   10
The blaze of the flaming furnace
    Gleamed redder than the moon.

Among the long, black rafters
    The wavering shadows lay,
And the current that came from the ocean
    Seemed to lift and bear them away;

As, sweeping and eddying through them,
    Rose the belated tide,
And, streaming into the moonlight,
    The seaweed floated wide.   20

And like those waters rushing
    Among the wooden piers,
A flood of thoughts came o'er me
    That filled my eyes with tears.

How often, oh how often,
    In the days that had gone by,
I had stood on that bridge at midnight
    And gazed on that wave and sky!

How often, oh how often,
    I had wished that the ebbing tide   30
Would bear me away on its bosom
    O'er the ocean wild and wide!

For my heart was hot and restless,
    And my life was full of care,
And the burden laid upon me
    Seemed greater than I could bear.

But now it has fallen from me,
    It is buried in the sea;
And only the sorrow of others
    Throws its shadow over me.   40

Yet whenever I cross the river
    On its bridge with wooden piers,
Like the odor of brine from the ocean
    Comes the thought of other years.

And I think how many thousands
    Of care-encumbered men,
Each bearing his burden of sorrow,
    Have crossed the bridge since then.

I see the long procession
    Still passing to and fro,   50
The young heart hot and restless,
    And the old subdued and slow!

And forever and forever,
    As long as the river flows,
As long as the heart has passions,
    As long as life has woes;

The moon and its broken reflection
 And its shadows shall appear,
As the symbol of love in heaven,
 And its wavering image here.   60

1845

KING WITLAF'S DRINKING-HORN

Written September 30, 1848. Longfellow quoted
in his diary the part of the charter granted by
King Witlaf (Wichtlaf) of Mercia to the Abbey of
Croyland relating to his drinking horn, cited in
Maitland's *The Dark Ages* (1844): "I also offer to
the refectory at Croyland the horn of my table,
that the elders of the monastery may drink out of
it on the festivals of the Saints, and may sometimes amid their benedictions remember the soul
of the donor, Witlaf."

WITLAF, a king of the Saxons,
 Ere yet his last he breathed,
To the merry monks of Croyland
 His drinking-horn bequeathed,—

That, whenever they sat at their revels
 And drank from the golden bowl,
They might remember the donor,
 And breathe a prayer for his soul.

So sat they once at Christmas,
 And bade the goblet pass;   10
In their beards the red wine glistened
 Like dewdrops in the grass.

They drank to the soul of Witlaf,
 They drank to Christ the Lord,
And to each of the Twelve Apostles,
 Who had preached his holy word.

They drank to the Saints and Martyrs
 Of the dismal days of yore,
And as soon as the horn was empty
 They remembered one Saint more.   20

And the reader droned from the pulpit,
 Like the murmur of many bees,
The legend of good Saint Guthlac,
 And Saint Basil's homilies;

Till the great bells of the convent,
 From their prison in the tower,
Guthlac and Bartholomaeus,
 Proclaimed the midnight hour.

And the Yule-log cracked in the chimney,
 And the Abbot bowed his head,   30
And the flamelets flapped and flickered,
 But the Abbot was stark and dead.

Yet still in his pallid fingers
 He clutched the golden bowl,
In which, like a pearl dissolving,
 Had sunk and dissolved his soul.

But not for this their revels
 The jovial monks forbore,
For they cried, "Fill high the goblet!
 We must drink to one Saint more!"   40

1848

RESIGNATION

THERE is no flock, however watched and
 tended,
 But one dead lamb is there!
There is no fireside, howsoe'er defended,
 But has one vacant chair!

The air is full of farewells to the dying,
 And mournings for the dead;
The heart of Rachel for her children crying,[1]
 Will not be comforted!

Let us be patient! These severe afflictions
 Not from the ground arise,   10
But oftentimes celestial benedictions
 Assume this dark disguise.

We see but dimly through the mists and
 vapors;
 Amid these earthly damps
What seem to us but sad, funereal tapers
 May be heaven's distant lamps.

There is no Death! What seems so is transi-
 tion;
 This life of mortal breath
Is but a suburb of the life elysian,[2]
 Whose portal we call Death.   20

She is not dead,—the child of our affection,—
 But gone unto that school
Where she no longer needs our poor protec-
 tion,
 And Christ himself doth rule.

[1] Jeremiah 31:15   [2] pertaining to Elysium, the
dwelling place, in classic myth, of happy souls after death

In that great cloister's stillness and seclusion,
  By guardian angels led,
Safe from temptation, safe from sin's pollution,
  She lives, whom we call dead.

Day after day we think what she is doing
  In those bright realms of air;   30
Year after year, her tender steps pursuing,
  Behold her grown more fair.

Thus do we walk with her, and keep unbroken
  The bond which nature gives,
Thinking that our remembrance, though unspoken,
  May reach her where she lives.

Not as a child shall we again behold her;
  For when with raptures wild
In our embraces we again enfold her,
  She will not be a child;   40

But a fair maiden, in her Father's mansion,[1]
  Clothed with celestial grace;
And beautiful with all the soul's expansion
  Shall we behold her face.

And though at times impetuous with emotion
  And anguish long suppressed,
The swelling heart heaves moaning like the ocean,
  That cannot be at rest,—

We will be patient, and assuage the feeling
  We may not wholly stay;   50
By silence sanctifying, not concealing,
  The grief that must have way.

1848   1849

From EVANGELINE
A Tale of Acadie

Written 1845–47; published October 30, 1847.
Many think the poem Longfellow's masterpiece.
The story it develops was told at the poet's dinner
table by the Reverend H. L. Conolly of Boston,
who had it in turn from a French Canadian.
Conolly offered it to Hawthorne. When the latter
did not adopt it for a tale, Longfellow asked if he

[1] John 14:2

might not have it for a poem. Many criticized the
verse form of the narrative, an American experiment in hexameter, as unlike the Greek; but it
proved to be a popular and successful venture.
Longfellow's chief source for the setting and events
of the first part was T. C. Haliburton's *An Historical and Statistical Account of Nova Scotia*
(1829), which in turn relied heavily upon the
Abbé Raynal's biased account, from the French
side, of the deportation. Acadie, called Nova
Scotia after 1621, was colonized in 1604 and ceded
to Britain in 1713 by the treaty of Utrecht, and
the cession was later confirmed by the treaty of
Aix-la-Chapelle. Yet the settlement remained the
seat of plots and raids by the French and the
Indians. History somewhat vindicates the British.
The inhabitants had the choice of taking an oath
of allegiance or of expatriation. The embarkation
of 1755 was not a wild scramble but really occupied two weeks. The British commander tried
hard to carry out his painful task humanely, especially to place members of the same family on
the same transport. Some 6000 French inhabitants
were deported.

Longfellow never visited Nova Scotia or the
Mississippi or Louisiana. For his scenes and descriptions he relied on Banvard's diorama of the
Mississippi, which he saw in Boston, December
17 and 19, 1846, and on such guidebooks as
Darby's *Guide to Louisiana* and Watson's *Annals
of Philadelphia*. His chief literary model for the
poem, in general character and form, was Goethe's
Hermann und Dorothea (1798), a story of expulsion
and wandering told in hexameter lines.

This is the forest primeval. The murmuring
    pines and the hemlocks,
Bearded with moss, and in garments green,
    indistinct in the twilight,
Stand like Druids of eld, with voices sad and
    prophetic,
Stand like harpers hoar, with beards that rest
    on their bosoms.
Loud from its rocky caverns, the deep-voiced
    neighboring ocean
Speaks, and in accents disconsolate answers
    the wail of the forest.

This is the forest primeval; but where are
    the hearts that beneath it
Leaped like the roe, when he hears in the
    woodland the voice of the huntsman?
Where is the thatch-roofed village, the home
    of Acadian farmers,—

Men whose lives glided on like rivers that
   water the woodlands,   10
Darkened by shadows of earth, but reflecting an image of heaven?
Waste are those pleasant farms, and the
   farmers forever departed!
Scattered like dust and leaves, when the
   mighty blasts of October
Seize them, and whirl them aloft, and sprinkle
   them far o'er the ocean.
Naught but tradition remains of the beautiful
   village of Grand-Pré.

Ye who believe in affection that hopes, and
   endures, and is patient,
Ye who believe in the beauty and strength of
   woman's devotion,
List to the mournful tradition, still sung by
   the pines of the forest;
List to a Tale of Love in Acadie, home of the
   happy.

PART THE FIRST

I

In the Acadian land, on the shores of the
   Basin of Minas,   20
Distant, secluded, still, the little village of
   Grand-Pré
Lay in the fruitful valley. Vast meadows
   stretched to the eastward,
Giving the village its name, and pasture to
   flocks without number.
Dikes, that the hands of the farmers had
   raised with labor incessant,
Shut out the turbulent tides; but at stated
   seasons the flood-gates
Opened, and welcomed the sea to wander at
   will o'er the meadows.
West and south there were fields of flax, and
   orchards and cornfields
Spreading afar and unfenced o'er the plain;
   and away to the northward
Blomidon rose, and the forests old, and aloft
   on the mountains
Sea-fogs pitched their tents, and mists from
   the mighty Atlantic   30
Looked on the happy valley, but ne'er from
   their station descended.
There, in the midst of its farms, reposed the
   Acadian village.

Strongly built were the houses, with frames
   of oak and of hemlock,
Such as the peasants of Normandy built in
   the reign of the Henries.
Thatched were the roofs, with dormer-win-
   dows; and gables projecting
Over the basement below protected and
   shaded the doorway.
There in the tranquil evenings of summer,
   when brightly the sunset
Lighted the village street, and gilded the
   vanes on the chimneys,
Matrons and maidens sat in snow-white caps
   and in kirtles
Scarlet and blue and green, with distaffs spinning the golden   40
Flax for the gossiping looms, whose noisy
   shuttles within doors
Mingled their sound with the whir of the
   wheels and the songs of the maidens.
Solemnly down the street came the parish
   priest, and the children
Paused in their play to kiss the hand he extended to bless them.
Reverend walked he among them; and up
   rose matrons and maidens,
Hailing his slow approach with words of
   affectionate welcome.
Then came the laborers home from the field,
   and serenely the sun sank
Down to his rest, and twilight prevailed. Anon
   from the belfry
Softly the Angelus sounded, and over the
   roofs of the village
Columns of pale blue smoke, like clouds of
   incense ascending,   50
Rose from a hundred hearths, the homes of
   peace and contentment.
Thus dwelt together in love these simple
   Acadian farmers,—
Dwelt in the love of God and of man. Alike
   were they free from
Fear, that reigns with the tyrant, and envy,
   the vice of republics.
Neither locks had they to their doors, nor
   bars to their windows;
But their dwellings were open as day and the
   hearts of the owners;
There the richest was poor, and the poorest
   lived in abundance.

Somewhat apart from the village, and
　　nearer the Basin of Minas,
Benedict Bellefontaine, the wealthiest farmer
　　of Grand-Pré,
Dwelt on his goodly acres; and with him,
　　directing his household,　　　　60
Gentle Evangeline lived, his child, and the
　　pride of the village.
Stalwart and stately in form was the man of
　　seventy winters;
Hearty and hale was he, an oak that is covered
　　with snow-flakes;
White as the snow were his locks, and his
　　cheeks as brown as the oak-leaves.
Fair was she to behold, that maiden of seven-
　　teen summers;
Black were her eyes as the berry that grows
　　on the thorn by the wayside,
Black, yet how softly they gleamed beneath
　　the brown shade of her tresses!
Sweet was her breath as the breath of kine
　　that feed in the meadows.
When in the harvest heat she bore to the
　　reapers at noontide
Flagons of home-brewed ale, ah! fair in sooth
　　was the maiden.　　　　70
Fairer was she when on Sunday morn, while
　　the bell from its turret
Sprinkled with holy sounds the air, as the
　　priest with his hyssop
Sprinkles the congregation, and scatters bless-
　　ings upon them,
Down the long street she passed, with her
　　chaplet of beads and her missal,
Wearing her Norman cap and her kirtle of
　　blue, and the earrings
Brought in the olden time from France, and
　　since, as an heirloom,
Handed down from mother to child, through
　　long generations.
But a celestial brightness—a more ethereal
　　beauty—
Shone on her face and encircled her form,
　　when, after confession,
Homeward serenely she walked with God's
　　benediction upon her.　　　　80
When she had passed, it seemed like the
　　ceasing of exquisite music.

Firmly builded with rafters of oak, the
　　house of the farmer

Stood on the side of a hill commanding the
　　sea; and a shady
Sycamore grew by the door, with a wood-
　　bine wreathing around it.
Rudely carved was the porch, with seats
　　beneath; and a footpath
Led through an orchard wide, and disappeared
　　in the meadow.
Under the sycamore-tree were hives over-
　　hung by a penthouse,
Such as the traveler sees in regions remote by
　　the roadside,
Built o'er a box for the poor, or the blessed
　　image of Mary.
Farther down, on the slope of the hill, was the
　　well with its moss-grown　　　　90
Bucket, fastened with iron, and near it a
　　trough for the horses.
Shielding the house from storms, on the
　　north, were the barns and the farmyard.
There stood the broad-wheeled wains and
　　the antique plows and the harrows;
There were the folds for the sheep; and there,
　　in his feathered seraglio,
Strutted the lordly turkey, and crowed the
　　cock, with the selfsame
Voice that in ages of old had startled the
　　penitent Peter.[1]
Bursting with hay were the barns, themselves
　　a village. In each one
Far o'er the gable projected a roof of thatch;
　　and a staircase,
Under the sheltering eaves, led up to the
　　odorous corn-loft.
There too the dove-cot stood, with its meek
　　and innocent inmates　　　　100
Murmuring ever of love; while above in the
　　variant breezes
Numberless noisy weathercocks rattled and
　　sang of mutation.

　　Thus, at peace with God and the world,
　　　　the farmer of Grand-Pré
Lived on his sunny farm, and Evangeline
　　governed his household.
Many a youth, as he knelt in the church and
　　opened his missal,
Fixed his eyes upon her as the saint of his
　　deepest devotion;

[1] Matthew 26:74-75

Happy was he who might touch her hand or
the hem of her garment!

Many a suitor came to her door, by the darkness befriended,

And, as he knocked and waited to hear the
sound of her footsteps,

Knew not which beat the louder, his heart or
the knocker of iron; 110

Or, at the joyous feast of the Patron Saint of
the village,

Bolder grew, and pressed her hand in the
dance as he whispered

Hurried words of love, that seemed a part of
the music.

But among all who came young Gabriel only
was welcome;

Gabriel Lajeunesse, the son of Basil the
blacksmith,

Who was a mighty man in the village, and
honored of all men;

For, since the birth of time, throughout all
ages and nations,

Has the craft of the smith been held in repute
by the people.

Basil was Benedict's friend. Their children
from earliest childhood

Grew up together as brother and sister; and
Father Felician, 120

Priest and pedagogue both in the village, had
taught them their letters

Out of the selfsame book, with the hymns of
the church and the plain-song.

But when the hymn was sung, and the daily
lesson completed,

Swiftly they hurried away to the forge of
Basil the blacksmith.

There at the door they stood, with wondering
eyes to behold him

Take in his leathern lap the hoof of the horse
as a plaything,

Nailing the shoe in its place; while near him
the tire of the cart-wheel

Lay like a fiery snake, coiled round in a circle
of cinders.

Oft on autumnal eves, when without in the
gathering darkness

Bursting with light seemed the smithy,
through every cranny and crevice, 130

Warm by the forge within they watched the
laboring bellows,

And as its panting ceased, and the sparks expired in the ashes,

Merrily laughed, and said they were nuns
going into the chapel.

Oft on sledges in winter, as swift as the swoop
of the eagle,

Down the hillside bounding, they glided
away o'er the meadow.

Oft in the barns they climbed to the populous
nests on the rafters,

Seeking with eager eyes that wondrous stone,
which the swallow

Brings from the shore of the sea to restore the
sight of its fledglings;[1]

Lucky was he who found that stone in the
nest of the swallow!

Thus passed a few swift years, and they no
longer were children. 140

He was a valiant youth, and his face, like the
face of the morning,

Gladdened the earth with its light, and ripened thought into action.

She was a woman now, with the heart and
hopes of a woman.

"Sunshine of Saint Eulalie,"[2] was she called;
for that was the sunshine

Which, as the farmers believed, would load
their orchards with apples;

She too would bring to her husband's house
delight and abundance,

Filling it with love and the ruddy faces of
children.

II

Now had the season returned, when the
nights grow colder and longer,

And the retreating sun the sign of the Scor-
pion enters.

Birds of passage sailed through the leaden air,
from the ice-bound, 150

---

[1] French folklore belief that if the eyes of a fledgling
swallow be put out the mother bird will bring from the
seashore a little stone that will restore the sight. When
found in the swallow's nest such stones were supposed
to work wonderful cures. Longfellow had his French
folklore from the citations from Pluquet's *Contes
Populaires* included in Thomas Wright's *Essays on
Subjects Connected with the Literature, Popular Superstitions, and History of England in the Middle Ages*
(1846).   [2] an allusion to the folk-saying that if the
sun shone on Saint Eulalie's Day (February 12) there
would be apples and cider in abundance

Desolate northern bays to the shores of
  tropical islands.
Harvests were gathered in; and wild with
  the winds of September
Wrestled the trees of the forest, as Jacob of
  old with the angel.[1]
All the signs foretold a winter long and in-
  clement.
Bees, with prophetic instinct of want, had
  hoarded their honey
Till the hives overflowed; and the Indian
  hunters asserted
Cold would the winter be, for thick was the
  fur of the foxes.
Such was the advent of autumn. Then fol-
  lowed that beautiful season,
Called by the pious Acadian peasants the
  Summer of All-Saints!
Filled was the air with a dreamy and magical
  light; and the landscape   160
Lay as if new-created in all the freshness of
  childhood.
Peace seemed to reign upon earth, and the
  restless heart of the ocean
Was for a moment consoled. All sounds were
  in harmony blended.
Voices of children at play, the crowing of
  cocks in the farm-yards,
Whir of wings in the drowsy air, and the
  cooing of pigeons,
All were subdued and low as the murmurs of
  love, and the great sun
Looked with the eye of love through the
  golden vapors around him;
While arrayed in its robes of russet and
  scarlet and yellow,
Bright with the sheen of the dew, each glittering tree of the forest
Flashed like the plane-tree the Persian adorned
  with mantles and jewels.[2]   170

Now recommenced the reign of rest and
  affection and stillness.
Day with its burden and heat had departed,
  and twilight descending
Brought back the evening star to the sky,
  and the herds to the homestead.

Pawing the ground they came, and resting
  their necks on each other,
And with their nostrils distended inhaling
  the freshness of evening.
Foremost, bearing the bell, Evangeline's
  beautiful heifer,
Proud of her snow-white hide, and the ribbon
  that waved from her collar,
Quietly paced and slow, as if conscious of
  human affection.
Then came the shepherd back with his bleating flocks from the seaside,
Where was their favorite pasture. Behind
  them followed the watchdog,   180
Patient, full of importance, and grand in the
  pride of his instinct,
Walking from side to side with a lordly air,
  and superbly
Waving his bushy tail, and urging forward
  the stragglers;
Regent of flocks was he when the shepherd
  slept; their protector,
When from the forest at night, through the
  starry silence, the wolves howled.
Late, with the rising moon, returned the
  wains from the marshes,
Laden with briny hay, that filled the air with
  its odor.
Cheerily neighed the steeds, with dew on
  their manes and their fetlocks,
While aloft on their shoulders the wooden
  and ponderous saddles,
Painted with brilliant dyes, and adorned with
  tassels of crimson,   190
Nodded in bright array, like hollyhocks
  heavy with blossoms.
Patiently stood the cows meanwhile, and
  yielded their udders
Unto the milkmaid's hand; whilst loud and
  in regular cadence
Into the sounding pails the foaming streamlets descended.
Lowing of cattle and peals of laughter were
  heard in the farmyard,
Echoed back by the barns. Anon they sank
  into stillness;
Heavily closed, with a jarring sound, the
  valves of the barn-doors,
Rattled the wooden bars, and all for a season
  was silent.

[1] Genesis 32:24–30   [2] Herodotus (VII, 31) tells
that Xerxes so admired a plane tree that he gave it
golden ornaments and left a soldier to guard it.

In-doors, warm by the wide-mouthed fireplace, idly the farmer
Sat in his elbow-chair, and watched how the
flames and the smoke-wreaths 200
Struggled together like foes in a burning
city. Behind him,
Nodding and mocking along the wall, with
gestures fantastic,
Darted his own huge shadow, and vanished
away into darkness.
Faces, clumsily carved in oak, on the back of
his arm-chair
Laughed in the flickering light, and the
pewter plates on the dresser
Caught and reflected the flame, as shields of
armies the sunshine.
Fragments of song the old man sang, and
carols of Christmas,
Such as at home, in the olden time, his fathers
before him
Sang in their Norman orchards and bright
Burgundian vineyards.
Close at her father's side was the gentle
Evangeline seated, 210
Spinning flax for the loom that stood in the
corner behind her.
Silent awhile were its treadles, at rest was
its diligent shuttle,
While the monotonous drone of the wheel,
like the drone of a bagpipe,
Followed the old man's song, and united the
fragments together.
As in a church, when the chant of the choir
at intervals ceases,
Footfalls are heard in the aisles, or words of
the priest at the altar,
So, in each pause of the song, with measured
motion the clock clicked.

Thus as they sat, there were footsteps heard,
and, suddenly lifted,
Sounded the wooden latch, and the door
swung back on its hinges.
Benedict knew by the hobnailed shoes it was
Basil the blacksmith, 220
And by her beating heart Evangeline knew
who was with him.
"Welcome!" the farmer exclaimed, as their
footsteps paused on the threshold,
"Welcome, Basil, my friend! Come, take thy
place on the settle

Close by the chimney-side, which is always
empty without thee;
Take from the shelf overhead thy pipe and the
box of tobacco;
Never so much thyself art thou as when,
through the curling
Smoke of the pipe or the forge, thy friendly
and jovial face gleams
Round and red as the harvest moon through
the mist of the marshes."
Then, with a smile of content, thus answered
Basil the blacksmith,
Taking with easy air the accustomed seat
by the fireside:— 230
"Benedict Bellefontaine, thou hast ever thy
jest and thy ballad!
Ever in cheerfullest mood art thou, when
others are filled with
Gloomy forebodings of ill, and see only ruin
before them.
Happy art thou, as if every day thou hadst
picked up a horseshoe."
Pausing a moment, to take the pipe that
Evangeline brought him,
And with a coal from the embers had lighted,
he slowly continued:—
"Four days now are passed since the English
ships at their anchors
Ride in the Gaspereau's mouth, with their
cannon pointed against us.
What their design may be is unknown; but
all are commanded
On the morrow to meet in the church, where
his Majesty's mandate 240
Will be proclaimed as law in the land. Alas!
in the mean time
Many surmises of evil alarm the hearts of the
people."
Then made answer the farmer:—"Perhaps
some friendlier purpose
Brings these ships to our shores. Perhaps the
harvests in England
By untimely rains or untimelier heat have been
blighted,
And from our bursting barns they would feed
their cattle and children."
"Not so thinketh the folk in the village," said
warmly the blacksmith,
Shaking his head as in doubt; then, heaving a
sigh, he continued:—

"Louisburg is not forgotten, nor Beau Séjour,
nor Port Royal.
Many already have fled to the forest, and lurk
on its outskirts,   250
Waiting with anxious hearts the dubious fate
of tomorrow.
Arms have been taken from us, and warlike
weapons of all kinds;
Nothing is left but the blacksmith's sledge
and the scythe of the mower."
Then with a pleasant smile made answer the
jovial farmer:—
"Safer are we unarmed, in the midst of our
flocks and our cornfields,
Safer within these peaceful dikes besieged by
the ocean,
Than our fathers in forts, besieged by the
enemy's cannon.
Fear no evil, my friend, and tonight may no
shadow of sorrow
Fall on this house and hearth; for this is the
night of the contract.
Built are the house and the barn. The merry
lads of the village   260
Strongly have built them and well; and, breaking the glebe round about them,
Filled the barn with hay, and the house with
food for a twelvemonth.
René Leblanc will be here anon, with his
papers and inkhorn.
Shall we not then be glad, and rejoice in the
joy of our children?"
As apart by the window she stood, with her
hand in her lover's,
Blushing Evangeline heard the words that her
father had spoken,
And, as they died on his lips, the worthy
notary entered.

III

Bent like a laboring oar, that toils in the
surf of the ocean,
Bent, but not broken, by age was the form of
the notary public;
Shocks of yellow hair, like the silken floss of
the maize, hung   270
Over his shoulders; his forehead was high;
and glasses with horn bows
Sat astride on his nose, with a look of wisdom
supernal.

Father of twenty children was he, and more
than a hundred
Children's children rode on his knee, and
heard his great watch tick.
Four long years in the times of the war had
he languished a captive,
Suffering much in an old French fort as the
friend of the English.
Now, though warier grown, without all guile
or suspicion,
Ripe in wisdom was he, but patient, and
simple, and childlike.
He was beloved by all, and most of all by the
children;
For he told them tales of the Loup-garou in
the forest,   280
And of the goblin that came in the night to
water the horses,
And of the white Létiche, the ghost of a child
who unchristened
Died, and was doomed to haunt unseen the
chambers of children;
And how on Christmas eve the oxen talked in
the stable,
And how the fever was cured by a spider shut
up in a nutshell,
And of the marvelous powers of four-leaved
clover and horseshoes,
With whatsoever else was writ in the lore of
the village.
Then up rose from his seat by the fireside
Basil the blacksmith,
Knocked from his pipe the ashes, and slowly
extending his right hand,
"Father Leblanc," he exclaimed, "thou hast
heard the talk in the village,   290
And, perchance, canst tell us some news of
these ships and their errand."
Then with modest demeanor made answer the
notary public,—
"Gossip enough have I heard, in sooth, yet
am never the wiser;
And what their errand may be I know not
better than others.
Yet am I not of those who imagine some evil
intention
Brings them here, for we are at peace; and
why then molest us?"
"God's name!" shouted the hasty and somewhat irascible blacksmith;

"Must we in all things look for the how, and
the why, and the wherefore?
Daily injustice is done, and might is the right
of the strongest!"
But, without heeding his warmth, continued
the notary public,—   300
"Man is unjust, but God is just; and finally
justice
Triumphs; and well I remember a story that
often consoled me,
When as a captive I lay in the old French fort
at Port Royal."
This was the old man's favorite tale, and he
loved to repeat it
When his neighbors complained that any in-
justice was done them.
"Once in an ancient city, whose name I no
longer remember,
Raised aloft on a column, a brazen statue of
Justice
Stood in the public square, upholding the
scales in its left hand,
And in its right a sword, as an emblem that
justice presided
Over the laws of the land, and the hearts and
homes of the people.   310
Even the birds had built their nests in the
scales of the balance,
Having no fear of the sword that flashed in
the sunshine above them.
But in the course of time the laws of the land
were corrupted;
Might took the place of right, and the weak
were oppressed, and the mighty
Ruled with an iron rod. Then it chanced in a
nobleman's palace
That a necklace of pearls was lost, and ere
long a suspicion
Fell on an orphan girl who lived as maid in
the household.
She, after form of trial condemned to die on
the scaffold,
Patiently met her doom at the foot of the
statue of Justice.
As to her Father in heaven her innocent spirit
ascended,   320
Lo! o'er the city a tempest rose; and the bolts
of the thunder
Smote the statue of bronze, and hurled in
wrath from its left hand

Down on the pavement below the clattering
scales of the balance,
And in the hollow thereof was found the nest
of a magpie,
Into whose clay-built walls the necklace of
pearls was inwoven."
Silenced, but not convinced, when the story
was ended, the blacksmith
Stood like a man who fain would speak, but
findeth no language;
All his thoughts were congealed into lines on
his face, as the vapors
Freeze in fantastic shapes on the window-
panes in the winter.

Then Evangeline lighted the brazen lamp
on the table,   330
Filled, till it overflowed, the pewter tankard
with home-brewed
Nut-brown ale, that was famed for its strength
in the village of Grand-Pré;
While from his pocket the notary drew his
papers and inkhorn,
Wrote with a steady hand the date and the
age of the parties,
Naming the dower of the bride in flocks of
sheep and in cattle.
Orderly all things proceeded, and duly and
well were completed,
And the great seal of the law was set like a sun
on the margin.
Then from his leathern pouch the farmer threw
on the table
Three times the old man's fee in solid pieces
of silver;
And the notary rising, and blessing the bride
and the bridegroom,   340
Lifted aloft the tankard of ale and drank to
their welfare.
Wiping the foam from his lip, he solemnly
bowed and departed,
While in silence the others sat and mused by
the fireside,
Till Evangeline brought the draught-board
out of its corner.
Soon was the game begun. In friendly contention the old men
Laughed at each lucky hit, or unsuccessful
maneuver,
Laughed when a man was crowned, or a
breach was made in the king-row.

Meanwhile apart, in the twilight gloom of a
    window's embrasure,
Sat the lovers and whispered together, be-
    holding the moon rise
Over the pallid sea and the silvery mist of the
    meadows.   350
Silently one by one, in the infinite meadows
    of heaven,
Blossomed the lovely stars, the forget-me-
    nots of the angels.

   Thus was the evening passed. Anon the bell
    from the belfry
Rang out the hour of nine, the village curfew,
    and straightway
Rose the guests and departed; and silence
    reigned in the household.
Many a farewell word and sweet good-night
    on the doorstep
Lingered long in Evangeline's heart, and filled
    it with gladness.
Carefully then were covered the embers that
    glowed on the hearthstone,
And on the oaken stairs resounded the tread
    of the farmer.
Soon with a soundless step the foot of
    Evangeline followed.   360
Up the staircase moved a luminous space in
    the darkness,
Lighted less by the lamp than the shining face
    of the maiden.
Silent she passed the hall, and entered the door
    of her chamber.
Simple that chamber was, with its curtains
    of white, and its clothespress
Ample and high, on whose spacious shelves
    were carefully folded
Linen and woollen stuffs, by the hand of
    Evangeline woven.
This was the precious dower she would bring
    to her husband in marriage,
Better than flocks and herds, being proofs of
    her skill as a housewife.
Soon she extinguished her lamp, for the
    mellow and radiant moonlight
Streamed through the windows, and lighted
    the room, till the heart of the maiden
Swelled and obeyed its power, like the trem-
    ulous tides of the ocean.   371
Ah! she was fair, exceeding fair to behold, as
    she stood with

Naked snow-white feet on the gleaming floor
    of her chamber!
Little she dreamed that below, among the
    trees of the orchard,
Waited her lover and watched for the gleam
    of her lamp, and her shadow.
Yet were her thoughts of him, and at times a
    feeling of sadness
Passed o'er her soul, as the sailing shade of
    clouds in the moonlight
Flitted across the floor and darkened the room
    for a moment.
And, as she gazed from the window, she saw
    serenely the moon pass
Forth from the folds of a cloud, and one star
    follow her footsteps,   380
As out of Abraham's tent young Ishmael
    wandered with Hagar![1]

          1847

THE BUILDING OF THE SHIP

   Composed June–September, 1849, twelve years
before the Civil War; published as the leading
poem in the *Seaside and Fireside* volume, 1849.
Although it is a thoroughly American poem in
content, it owes much in pattern and handling to
Schiller's *Das Lied von der Glocke* (1799), in which
the poet follows with technical details the casting
of the bell and the hanging of it in a tower, and so
treats it that it becomes a symbol of humanity.
Longfellow's technical interest in shipbuilding
came no doubt from his boyhood in Portland.
The poem had no little influence in arousing support of the Union. The conclusion that Longfellow
substituted for the originally weaker ending was
recited and quoted far and wide. Longfellow
records, February 12, 1850, hearing the famous
actress Fanny Kemble read the poem "before the
Mercantile Library Association, to an audience
of more than three thousand . . . standing out
upon the platform, book in hand, trembling, palpitating, and weeping, and giving every word its
true weight and emphasis." Noah Brooks tells
(in *Scribner's Monthly*, August, 1879) of reading
the poem to President Lincoln. "He did not speak
for some minutes, but finally said, 'It is a wonderful gift to be able to stir men like that.' "

"BUILD me straight, O worthy Master!
   Stanch and strong, a goodly vessel,
That shall laugh at all disaster,
   And with wave and whirlwind wrestle!"

[1] Genesis 21:14–22

The merchant's word
Delighted the Master heard;
For his heart was in his work, and the heart
Giveth grace unto every Art.
A quiet smile played round his lips,
As the eddies and dimples of the tide   10
Play round the bows of ships
That steadily at anchor ride.
And with a voice that was full of glee,
He answered, "Erelong we will launch
A vessel as goodly, and strong, and stanch,
As ever weathered a wintry sea!"
And first with nicest skill and art,
Perfect and finished in every part,
A little model the Master wrought,
Which should be to the larger plan   20
What the child is to the man,
Its counterpart in miniature;
That with a hand more swift and sure
The greater labor might be brought
To answer to his inward thought.
And as he labored, his mind ran o'er
The various ships that were built of yore,
And above them all, and strangest of all
Towered the Great Harry,[1] crank and tall,
Whose picture was hanging on the wall,   30
With bows and stern raised high in air,
And balconies hanging here and there,
And signal lanterns and flags afloat,
And eight round towers, like those that frown
From some old castle, looking down
Upon the drawbridge and the moat.
And he said with a smile, "Our ship, I wis,
Shall be of another form than this!"
It was of another form, indeed;
Built for freight, and yet for speed,   40
A beautiful and gallant craft;
Broad in the beam, that the stress of the
        blast,
Pressing down upon sail and mast,
Might not the sharp bows overwhelm;
Broad in the beam, but sloping aft
With graceful curve and slow degrees,
That she might be docile to the helm,
And that the currents of parted seas,

Closing behind, with mighty force,
Might aid and not impede her course.   50

In the shipyard stood the Master,
With the model of the vessel,
That should laugh at all disaster,
And with wave and whirlwind wrestle!

Covering many a rood of ground,
Lay the timber piled around;
Timber of chestnut, and elm, and oak,
And scattered here and there, with these,
The knarred and crooked cedar knees;
Brought from regions far away,   60
From Pascagoula's sunny bay,
And the banks of the roaring Roanoke!
Ah! what a wondrous thing it is
To note how many wheels of toil
One thought, one word, can set in motion!
There's not a ship that sails the ocean,
But every climate, every soil,
Must bring its tribute, great or small,
And help to build the wooden wall![1]

The sun was rising o'er the sea,   70
And long the level shadows lay,
As if they, too, the beams would be
Of some great, airy argosy,
Framed and launched in a single day.
That silent architect, the sun,
Had hewn and laid them every one,
Ere the work of man was yet begun.
Beside the Master, when he spoke,
A youth, against an anchor leaning,
Listened, to catch his slightest meaning,   80
Only the long waves, as they broke
In ripples on the pebbly beach,
Interrupted the old man's speech.

Beautiful they were, in sooth,
The old man and the fiery youth!
The old man, in whose busy brain

---

[1] A famous three-masted, two-decked warship
ordered for the English navy by Henry VII in 1488, but
not completed until 1509 at the beginning of the reign
of Henry VIII. The word "crank" as applied to a ship
usually means top-heavy, or easily inclined by the force
of wind or wave, but Longfellow may use the word in
its archaic sense of sturdy or vigorous.

[1] The "wooden wall" metaphor of the ship is an
echo of a famous utterance of the Delphic oracle in
reply to the question of the Greeks as to how they
might best defend themselves against the invading
Persians under Xerxes. The reply was:

" Zeus the sire of all
    Hath safety promised in a wooden wall."

The Greeks interpreted this to mean that they should
depend upon their ships, and by doing so they defeated
the Persians in the sea battle of Salamis.

Many a ship that sailed the main
Was modelled o'er and o'er again;
The fiery youth, who was to be
The heir of his dexterity,   90
The heir of his house, and his daughter's hand,
When he had built and launched from land
What the elder head had planned.

"Thus," said he, "will we build this ship!
Lay square the blocks upon the slip,
And follow well this plan of mine.
Choose the timbers with greatest care;
Of all that is unsound beware;
For only what is sound and strong
To this vessel shall belong.   100
Cedar of Maine and Georgia pine
Here together shall combine.
A goodly frame, and a goodly fame,
And the UNION be her name!
For the day that gives her to the sea
Shall give my daughter unto thee!"

The Master's word
Enraptured the young man heard;
And as he turned his face aside,
With a look of joy and a thrill of pride   110
Standing before
Her father's door,
He saw the form of his promised bride.
The sun shone on her golden hair,
And her cheek was glowing fresh and fair,
With the breath of morn and the soft sea air.
Like a beauteous barge was she,
Still at rest on the sandy beach,
Just beyond the billow's reach;
But he   120
Was the restless, seething, stormy sea!
Ah, how skilful grows the hand
That obeyeth Love's command!
It is the heart, and not the brain,
That to the highest doth attain,
And he who followeth Love's behest
Far excelleth all the rest!

Thus with the rising of the sun
Was the noble task begun,
And soon throughout the shipyard's bounds
Were heard the intermingled sounds   131
Of axes and of mallets, plied
With vigorous arms on every side;
Plied so deftly and so well,
That, ere the shadows of evening fell,

The keel of oak for a noble ship,
Scarfed and bolted, straight and strong,
Was lying ready, and stretched along
The blocks, well placed upon the slip.
Happy, thrice happy, every one   140
Who sees his labor well begun,
And not perplexed and multiplied,
By idly waiting for time and tide!

And when the hot, long day was o'er,
The young man at the Master's door
Sat with the maiden calm and still,
And within the porch, a little more
Removed beyond the evening chill,
The father sat, and told them tales
Of wrecks in the great September gales,   150
Of pirates coasting the Spanish Main,
And ships that never came back again,
The chance and change of a sailor's life,
Want and plenty, rest and strife,
His roving fancy, like the wind,
That nothing can stay and nothing can bind,
And the magic charm of foreign lands,
With shadows of palms, and shining sands,
Where the tumbling surf,
O'er the coral reefs of Madagascar,   160
Washes the feet of the swarthy Lascar,[1]
As he lies alone and asleep on the turf.
And the trembling maiden held her breath
At the tales of that awful, pitiless sea,
With all its terror and mystery,
The dim, dark sea, so like unto Death,
That divides and yet unites mankind!
And whenever the old man paused, a gleam
From the bowl of his pipe would awhile
     illume
The silent group in the twilight gloom,   170
And thoughtful faces, as in a dream;
And for a moment one might mark
What had been hidden by the dark,
That the head of the maiden lay at rest,
Tenderly, on the young man's breast!

Day by day the vessel grew,
With timbers fashioned strong and true,
Stemson and keelson and sternson-knee,
Till, framed with perfect symmetry,
A skeleton ship rose up to view!   180
And around the bows and along the side
The heavy hammers and mallets plied,
Till after many a week, at length,

[1] an East Indian sailor

Wonderful for form and strength,
Sublime in its enormous bulk,
Loomed aloft the shadowy hulk!
And around it columns of smoke, upwreath-
     ing,
Rose from the boiling, bubbling, seething
Caldron, that glowed,
And overflowed   190
With the black tar, heated for the sheathing.
And amid the clamors
Of clattering hammers,
He who listened heard now and then
The song of the Master and his men:—

"Build me straight, O worthy Master,
   Stanch and strong, a goodly vessel,
That shall laugh at all disaster,
   And with wave and whirlwind wrestle!"

With oaken brace and copper band,   200
Lay the rudder on the sand,
That, like a thought, should have control
Over the movement of the whole;
And near it the anchor, whose giant hand
Would reach down and grapple with the land,
And immovable and fast
Hold the great ship against the bellowing
     blast!
And at the bows an image stood,
By a cunning artist carved in wood,
With robes of white, that far behind   210
Seemed to be fluttering in the wind.
It was not shaped in a classic mould,
Not like a Nymph or Goddess of old,
Or Naiad rising from the water,
But modelled from the Master's daughter!
On many a dreary and misty night,
'Twill be seen by the rays of the signal light,
Speeding along through the rain and the dark,
Like a ghost in its snow-white sark,
The pilot of some phantom bark,   220
Guiding the vessel, in its flight,
By a path none other knows aright!

Behold, at last,
Each tall and tapering mast
Is swung into its place;[1]

Shrouds and stays
Holding it firm and fast!

Long ago,
In the deer-haunted forests of Maine,
When upon mountain and plain   230
Lay the snow,
They fell,—those lordly pines!
Those grand, majestic pines!
'Mid shouts and cheers
The jaded steers,
Panting beneath the goad,
Dragged down the weary, winding road
Those captive kings so straight and tall,
To be shorn of their streaming hair,
And naked and bare,   240
To feel the stress and the strain
Of the wind and the reeling main,
Whose roar
Would remind them forevermore
Of their native forests they should not see
     again.

And everywhere
The slender, graceful spars
Poise aloft in the air,
And at the mast-head,
White, blue, and red,   250
A flag unrolls the stripes and stars.
Ah! when the wanderer, lonely, friendless,
In foreign harbors shall behold
That flag unrolled,
'Twill be as a friendly hand
Stretched out from his native land,
Filling his heart with memories sweet and
     endless!

All is finished! and at length
Has come the bridal day
Of beauty and of strength.   260
Today the vessel shall be launched!
With fleecy clouds the sky is blanched,
And o'er the bay,
Slowly, in all his splendors dight,

[1] "I wish to anticipate a criticism on this passage, by stating that sometimes, though not usually, vessels are launched fully sparred and rigged. I have availed myself of the exception as better suited to my purposes than the general rule; but the reader will see that it is neither a blunder nor a poetic license. On this subject a friend in Portland, Maine, writes me thus: 'In this state, and also, I am told, in New York, ships are sometimes rigged upon the stocks, in order to save time, or to make a show. There was a fine large ship launched last summer at Ellsworth, fully sparred and rigged. Some years ago a ship was launched here, with her rigging, spars, sails, and cargo aboard. She sailed the next day and—was never heard of again! I hope this will not be the fate of your poem!' " [*Longfellow's note.*]

The great sun rises to behold the sight.
The ocean old,
Centuries old,
Strong as youth, and as uncontrolled,
Paces restless to and fro,
Up and down the sands of gold.　　270
His beating heart is not at rest;
And far and wide,
With ceaseless flow,
His beard of snow
Heaves with the heaving of his breast.
He waits impatient for his bride.
There she stands,
With her foot upon the sands,
Decked with flags and streamers gay,
In honor of her marriage day,　　280
Her snow-white signals fluttering, blending,
Round her like a veil descending,
Ready to be
The bride of the gray old sea.

On the deck another bride
Is standing by her lover's side.
Shadows from the flags and shrouds,
Like the shadows cast by clouds,
Broken by many a sudden fleck,
Fall around them on the deck.　　290
The prayer is said,
The service read,
The joyous bridegroom bows his head;
And in tears the good old Master
Shakes the brown hand of his son,
Kisses his daughter's glowing cheek
In silence, for he cannot speak,
And ever faster
Down his own the tears begin to run.
The worthy pastor—　　300
The shepherd of that wandering flock,
That has the ocean for its wold,
That has the vessel for its fold,
Leaping ever from rock to rock—
Spake, with accents mild and clear,
Words of warning, words of cheer,
But tedious to the bridegroom's ear.
He knew the chart
Of the sailor's heart,
All its pleasures and its griefs,　　310
All its shallows and rocky reefs,
All those secret currents, that flow
With such resistless undertow,
And lift and drift, with terrible force,

The will from its moorings and its course.
Therefore he spake, and thus said he:—
"Like unto ships far off at sea,
Outward or homeward bound, are we.
Before, behind, and all around,
Floats and swings the horizon's bound,　　320
Seems at its distant rim to rise
And climb the crystal wall of the skies,
And then again to turn and sink,
As if we could slide from its outer brink.
Ah! it is not the sea,
It is not the sea that sinks and shelves,
But ourselves
That rock and rise
With endless and uneasy motion,
Now touching the very skies,　　330
Now sinking into the depths of ocean.
Ah! if our souls but poise and swing
Like the compass in its brazen ring,
Ever level and ever true
To the toil and the task we have to do,
We shall sail securely, and safely reach
The Fortunate Isles, on whose shining beach
The sights we see, and the sounds we hear,
Will be those of joy and not of fear!"

Then the Master,　　340
With a gesture of command,
Waved his hand;
And at the word,
Loud and sudden there was heard,
All around them and below,
The sound of hammers, blow on blow,
Knocking away the shores and spurs.
And see! she stirs!
She starts,—she moves,—she seems to feel
The thrill of life along her keel,　　350
And, spurning with her foot the ground,
With one exulting, joyous bound,
She leaps into the ocean's arms!

And lo! from the assembled crowd
There rose a shout, prolonged and loud,
That to the ocean seemed to say,
"Take her, O bridegroom, old and gray,
Take her to thy protecting arms,
With all her youth and all her charms!"

How beautiful she is! How fair　　360
She lies within those arms, that press
Her form with many a soft caress
Of tenderness and watchful care!

Sail forth into the sea, O ship!
Through wind and wave, right onward steer!
The moistened eye, the trembling lip,
Are not the signs of doubt or fear.

Sail forth into the sea of life,
O gentle, loving, trusting wife,
And safe from all adversity   370
Upon the bosom of that sea
Thy comings and thy goings be!
For gentleness and love and trust
Prevail o'er angry wave and gust;
And in the wreck of noble lives
Something immortal still survives!

Thou, too, sail on, O Ship of State!
Sail on, O UNION, strong and great!
Humanity with all its fears,
With all the hopes of future years,   380
Is hanging breathless on thy fate!
We know what Master laid thy keel,
What Workmen wrought thy ribs of steel,
Who made each mast, and sail, and rope,
What anvils rang, what hammers beat,
In what a forge and what a heat
Were shaped the anchors of thy hope!
Fear not each sudden sound and shock,
'Tis of the wave and not the rock;
'Tis but the flapping of the sail,   390
And not a rent made by the gale!
In spite of rock and tempest's roar,
In spite of false lights on the shore,
Sail on, nor fear to breast the sea!
Our hearts, our hopes, are all with thee,
Our hearts, our hopes, our prayers, our tears,
Our faith triumphant o'er our fears,
Are all with thee,—are all with thee!

1849

MY LOST YOUTH

Written in 1855; published in *Putnam's
Monthly*, August, 1855; reprinted in the *Courtship
of Miles Standish and Other Poems* (1858). Highly
praised by Alfred Noyes, *Some Aspects of Modern
Poetry*, pp. 256–257. The ultimate source of
the refrain is *Lapponia* (1673), a Latin treatise
on Finland by Johannes Scheffer, Professor at
Upsala. Longfellow, however, took his refrain
from the translation of the Lapland song made by
Herder and included in his *Stimmen der Völker
in Liedern* (1778–1779) of which Longfellow owned
a copy. The American poet literally translates—

"*Knabenwille ist Windeswille,
Jünglingsgedanken lange Gedanken.*"

See J. T. Hatfield's "Longfellow's Lapland Song,"
in *Publications of the Modern Language Association
of America*, XLV, 1188–92, and his "Longfellow
a Transmitter of German Culture," in *German
Culture in the United States* (1936).

OFTEN I think of the beautiful town [1]
   That is seated by the sea;
Often in thought go up and down
The pleasant streets of that dear old town,
   And my youth comes back to me.
      And a verse of a Lapland song
      Is haunting my memory still:
      "A boy's will is the wind's will,
And the thoughts of youth are long, long
      thoughts."

I can see the shadowy lines of its trees,   10
   And catch, in sudden gleams,
The sheen of the far-surrounding seas,
And islands that were the Hesperides [2]
   Of all my boyish dreams.
      And the burden of that old song,
      It murmurs and whispers still:
      "A boy's will is the wind's will,
And the thoughts of youth are long, long
      thoughts."

I remember the black wharves and the slips,
   And the sea-tides tossing free;   20
And Spanish sailors with bearded lips,
And the beauty and mystery of the ships,
   And the magic of the sea.
      And the voice of that wayward song
      Is singing and saying still:
      "A boy's will is the wind's will,
And the thoughts of youth are long, long
      thoughts."

I remember the bulwarks by the shore,
   And the fort upon the hill;
The sunrise gun, with its hollow roar,   30
The drumbeat repeated o'er and o'er,
   And the bugle wild and shrill.
      And the music of that old song
      Throbs in my memory still:
      "A boy's will is the wind's will,
And the thoughts of youth are long, long
      thoughts."

[1] Portland, Maine, the poet's birthplace   [2] island
home of the mythological Hesperides, the nymphs who
guarded the garden of the golden apples

I remember the sea-fight[1] far away,
  How it thundered o'er the tide!
And the dead captains, as they lay
In their graves, o'erlooking the tranquil
    bay   40
  Where they in battle died.
    And the sound of that mournful song
    Goes through me with a thrill:
    "A boy's will is the wind's will,
And the thoughts of youth are long, long
    thoughts."

I can see the breezy dome of groves,
  The shadows of Deering's Woods;
And the friendships old and the early loves
Come back with a Sabbath sound, as of doves
  In quiet neighborhoods.   50
    And the verse of that sweet old song,
    It flutters and murmurs still:
    "A boy's will is the wind's will,
And the thoughts of youth are long, long
    thoughts."

I remember the gleams and glooms that dart
  Across the schoolboy's brain;
The song and the silence in the heart,
That in part are prophecies, and in part
  Are longings wild and vain.
    And the voice of that fitful song   60
    Sings on, and is never still:
    "A boy's will is the wind's will,
And the thoughts of youth are long, long
    thoughts."

There are things of which I may not speak;
  There are dreams that cannot die;
There are thoughts that make the strong
    heart weak,
And bring a pallor into the cheek,
  And a mist before the eye.
    And the words of that fatal song
    Come over me like a chill: 70
    "A boy's will is the wind's will,
And the thoughts of youth are long, long
    thoughts."

Strange to me now are the forms I meet,
  When I visit the dear old town;

But the native air is pure and sweet,
And the trees that o'ershadow each well-
    known street,
  As they balance up and down,
  Are singing the beautiful song,
  Are sighing and whispering still:
  "A boy's will is the wind's will,   80
And the thoughts of youth are long, long
    thoughts."

And Deering's Woods are fresh and fair,
  And with joy that is almost pain
My heart goes back to wander there,
And among the dreams of the days that were,
  I find my lost youth again.
    And the strange and beautiful song,
    Sings on, and is never still:
    "A boy's will is the wind's will,
And the thoughts of youth are long, long
    thoughts."   90
1855   1855, 1858

From THE SONG OF HIAWATHA

Begun June 25, 1854, and finished March 29,
1855; published November 10, 1855, in twenty-
two parts with an introduction. It was popular at
once and has remained so, although its romantic
anthropology is not admired by the learned.
Children like it for its vividness and simplicity of
expression, and the mature like it for its ethnic
significance as preserving, however idealized, some
of the traditions of a vanishing race.

One of Longfellow's notes accompanying the
poem reads: "This Indian Edda—if I may so call
it—is founded on a tradition, prevalent among
the North American Indians, of a personage of
miraculous birth, who was sent among them to
clear their rivers, forests, and fishing-grounds,
and to teach them the arts of peace. He was
known among different tribes by the several names
of Michabou, Chiabo, Manabozho, Tarenya-
wagon, and Hiawatha. Mr. Schoolcraft gives an
account of him in his *Algic Researches*, Vol. I,
p. 134; and in his *History, Condition, and Prospects
of the Indian Tribes of the United States*, Part III,
p. 314, may be found the Iroquois form of the
tradition, derived from the verbal narrations of an
Onondaga chief. Into this old tradition I have
woven other curious Indian legends, drawn
chiefly from the various and valuable writings of
Mr. Schoolcraft, to whom the literary world is
greatly indebted for his indefatigable zeal in

rescuing from oblivion so much of the legendary lore of the Indians. The scene of the poem is among the Ojibways on the southern shore of Lake Superior, in the region between the Pictured Rocks and the Grand Sable."

In addition to the works of Henry Rowe Schoolcraft (1794–1863), Longfellow relied, like Cooper, on that of the Rev. John Gottlieb Ernestus Heckewelder (1743–1825), Moravian missionary among the Delaware Indians, whose book he read in his college days; on *The Narrative of the Adventures of John Tanner* (1830); on Mary Eastman's *Dakotah, or Life and Legends of the Sioux around Fort Snelling* (1847), and other works. Following a blunder of Schoolcraft, he confused the historic Hiawatha of the Iroquois tribe and Manabozho, an Algonquin or Chippewa deity. See A. Keiser, *The Indian in Literature* (1933), pp. 189–208; also Stith Thompson, "The Indian Legend of Hiawatha," *Publications of the Modern Language Association*, XXXVII (1922). Longfellow acknowledged that the metrical form of the poem (unrhymed trochaic tetrameter) was suggested to him by the Finnish *Kalevala*, a collection of heroic poetry, the originals dating from the Middle Ages, which was organized into a national epic by Elias Lönnrot and published in 1849.

XVI

Pau-Puk-Keewis

You shall hear how Pau-Puk-Keewis,
He, the handsome Yenadizze,
Whom the people called the Storm-Fool,
Vexed the village with disturbance;
You shall hear of all his mischief,
And his flight from Hiawatha,
And his wondrous transmigrations,
And the end of his adventures.

On the shores of Gitche Gumee,
On the dunes of Nagow Wudjoo, 10
By the shining Big-Sea-Water
Stood the lodge of Pau-Puk-Keewis.
It was he who in his frenzy
Whirled these drifting sands together,
On the dunes of Nagow Wudjoo,
When, among the guests assembled,
He so merrily and madly
Danced at Hiawatha's wedding,
Danced the Beggar's Dance to please them.

Now, in search of new adventures, 20
From his lodge went Pau-Puk-Keewis,
Came with speed into the village,

Found the young men all assembled
In the lodge of old Iagoo,
Listening to his monstrous stories,
To his wonderful adventures.

He was telling them the story
Of Ojeeg, the Summer-Maker,
How he made a hole in heaven,
How he climbed up into heaven, 30
And let out the summer-weather,
The perpetual, pleasant Summer;
How the Otter first essayed it;
How the Beaver, Lynx, and Badger
Tried in turn the great achievement,
From the summit of the mountain
Smote their fists against the heavens,
Smote against the sky their foreheads,
Cracked the sky, but could not break it;
How the Wolverine, uprising, 40
Made him ready for the encounter,
Bent his knees down, like a squirrel,
Drew his arms back, like a cricket.

"Once he leaped," said old Iagoo,
"Once he leaped, and lo! above him
Bent the sky, as ice in rivers
When the waters rise beneath it;
Twice he leaped, and lo! above him
Broke the shattered sky asunder,
And he disappeared within it, 50
And Ojeeg, the Fisher Weasel,
With a bound went in behind him!"

"Hark you!" shouted Pau-Puk-Keewis
As he entered at the doorway;
"I am tired of all this talking,
Tired of old Iagoo's stories,
Tired of Hiawatha's wisdom.
Here is something to amuse you,
Better than this endless talking."

Then from out his pouch of wolfskin 60
Forth he drew, with solemn manner,
All the game of Bowl and Counters,[1]
Pugasaing, with thirteen pieces.
White on one side were they painted,
And vermilion on the other;
Two Kenabeeks or great serpents,
Two Ininewug or wedge-men,
One great war-club, Pugamaugun,
And one slender fish, the Keego,
Four round pieces, Ozawabeeks, 70
And three Sheshebwug or ducklings.

[1] the principal game of hazard among the northern Indians, according to Schoolcraft

All were made of bone and painted,
All except the Ozawabeeks;
These were brass, on one side burnished,
And were black upon the other.

In a wooden bowl he placed them,
Shook and jostled them together,
Threw them on the ground before him,
Thus exclaiming and explaining:
"Red side up are all the pieces,   80
And one great Kenabeek standing
On the bright side of a brass piece,
On a burnished Ozawabeek;
Thirteen tens and eight are counted."

Then again he shook the pieces,
Shook and jostled them together,
Threw them on the ground before him,
Still exclaiming and explaining:
"White are both the great Kenabeeks,
White the Ininewug, the wedge-men,   90
Red are all the other pieces;
Five tens and an eight are counted."

Thus he taught the game of hazard,
Thus displayed it and explained it,
Running through its various chances,
Various changes, various meanings:
Twenty curious eyes stared at him,
Full of eagerness stared at him.

"Many games," said old Iagoo,
"Many games of skill and hazard   100
Have I seen in different nations,
Have I played in different countries.
He who plays with old Iagoo
Must have very nimble fingers;
Though you think yourself so skilful,
I can beat you, Pau-Puk-Keewis,
I can even give you lessons
In your game of Bowl and Counters!"

So they sat and played together,
All the old men and the young men,   110
Played for dresses, weapons, wampum,
Played till midnight, played till morning,
Played until the Yenadizze,
Till the cunning Pau-Puk-Keewis,
Of their treasures had despoiled them,
Of the best of all their dresses,
Shirts of deerskin, robes of ermine,
Belts of wampum, crests of feathers,
Warlike weapons, pipes and pouches.
Twenty eyes glared wildly at him,   120
Like the eyes of wolves glared at him.

Said the lucky Pau-Puk-Keewis:

"In my wigwam I am lonely,
In my wanderings and adventures
I have need of a companion,
Fain would have a Meshinauwa,
An attendant and pipe-bearer.
I will venture all these winnings,
All these garments heaped about me,
All this wampum, all these feathers,   130
On a single throw will venture
All against the young man yonder!"
'Twas a youth of sixteen summers,
'Twas a nephew of Iagoo;
Face-in-a-Mist, the people called him.

As the fire burns in a pipe-head
Dusky red beneath the ashes,
So beneath his shaggy eyebrows
Glowed the eyes of old Iagoo.
"Ugh!" he answered very fiercely;   140
"Ugh!" they answered all and each one.

Seized the wooden bowl the old man,
Closely in his bony fingers
Clutched the fatal bowl, Onagon,
Shook it fiercely and with fury,
Made the pieces ring together
As he threw them down before him.

Red were both the great Kenabeeks,
Red the Ininewug, the wedge-men,
Red the Sheshebwug, the ducklings,   150
Black the four brass Ozawabeeks,
White alone the fish, the Keego;
Only five the pieces counted!

Then the smiling Pau-Puk-Keewis
Shook the bowl and threw the pieces;
Lightly in the air he tossed them,
And they fell about him scattered;
Dark and bright the Ozawabeeks,
Red and white the other pieces,
And upright among the others   160
One Ininewug was standing,
Even as crafty Pau-Puk-Keewis
Stood alone among the players,
Saying, "Five tens! mine the game is!"

Twenty eyes glared at him fiercely,
Like the eyes of wolves glared at him,
As he turned and left the wigwam,
Followed by his Meshinauwa,
By the nephew of Iagoo,
By the tall and graceful stripling,   170
Bearing in his arms the winnings,
Shirts of deerskin, robes of ermine,
Belts of wampum, pipes and weapons.

"Carry them," said Pau-Puk-Keewis,
Pointing with his fan of feathers,
"To my wigwam far to eastward,
On the dunes of Nagow Wudjoo!"

Hot and red with smoke and gambling
Were the eyes of Pau-Puk-Keewis
As he came forth to the freshness 180
Of the pleasant Summer morning.
All the birds were singing gayly,
All the streamlets flowing swiftly,
And the heart of Pau-Puk-Keewis
Sang with pleasure as the birds sing,
Beat with triumph like the streamlets,
As he wandered through the village,
In the early gray of morning,
With his fan of turkey-feathers,
With his plumes and tufts of swan's down, 190
Till he reached the farthest wigwam,
Reached the lodge of Hiawatha.

Silent was it and deserted;
No one met him at the doorway,
No one came to bid him welcome;
But the birds were singing round it,
In and out and round the doorway,
Hopping, singing, fluttering, feeding,
And aloft upon the ridgepole
Kahgahgee, the King of Ravens, 200
Sat with fiery eyes, and, screaming,
Flapped his wings at Pau-Puk-Keewis.

"All are gone! the lodge is empty!"
Thus it was spake Pau-Puk-Keewis,
In his heart resolving mischief;—
"Gone is wary Hiawatha,
Gone the silly Laughing Water,
Gone Nokomis, the old woman,
And the lodge is left unguarded!"

By the neck he seized the raven, 210
Whirled it round him like a rattle,
Like a medicine-pouch he shook it,
Strangled Kahgahgee, the raven,
From the ridgepole of the wigwam
Left its lifeless body hanging,
As an insult to its master,
As a taunt to Hiawatha.

With a stealthy step he entered,
Round the lodge in wild disorder
Threw the household things about him, 220
Piled together in confusion
Bowls of wood and earthen kettles,
Robes of buffalo and beaver,
Skins of otter, lynx, and ermine,

As an insult to Nokomis,
As a taunt to Minnehaha.

Then departed Pau-Puk-Keewis,
Whistling, singing through the forest,
Whistling gayly to the squirrels,
Who from hollow boughs above him 230
Dropped their acorn-shells upon him,
Singing gayly to the wood birds,
Who from out the leafy darkness
Answered with a song as merry.

Then he climbed the rocky headlands,
Looking o'er the Gitche Gumee,
Perched himself upon their summit,
Waiting full of mirth and mischief
The return of Hiawatha.

Stretched upon his back he lay there; 240
Far below him plashed the waters,
Plashed and washed the dreamy waters;
Far above him swam the heavens,
Swam the dizzy, dreamy heavens;
Round him hovered, fluttered, rustled
Hiawatha's mountain chickens,
Flock-wise swept and wheeled about him,
Almost brushed him with their pinions.

And he killed them as he lay there,
Slaughtered them by tens and twenties, 250
Threw their bodies down the headland,
Threw them on the beach below him,
Till at length Kayoshk, the sea-gull,
Perched upon a crag above them,
Shouted: "It is Pau-Puk-Keewis!
He is slaying us by hundreds!
Send a message to our brother,
Tidings send to Hiawatha!"

XVII

The Hunting of Pau-Puk-Keewis

Full of wrath was Hiawatha
When he came into the village,
Found the people in confusion,
Heard of all the misdemeanors,
All the malice and the mischief,
Of the cunning Pau-Puk-Keewis.

Hard his breath came through his nostrils,
Through his teeth he buzzed and muttered
Words of anger and resentment,
Hot and humming, like a hornet.
"I will slay this Pau-Puk-Keewis, 10
Slay this mischief-maker!" said he.
"Not so long and wide the world is,

Not so rude and rough the way is,
That my wrath shall not attain him,
That my vengeance shall not reach him!"

Then in swift pursuit departed
Hiawatha and the hunters
On the trail of Pau-Puk-Keewis,
Through the forest, where he passed it,　20
To the headlands where he rested;
But they found not Pau-Puk-Keewis,
Only in the trampled grasses,
In the whortleberry-bushes,
Found the couch where he had rested,
Found the impress of his body.

From the lowlands far beneath them,
From the Muskoday, the meadow,
Pau-Puk-Keewis, turning backward,
Made a gesture of defiance,　30
Made a gesture of derision;
And aloud cried Hiawatha,
From the summit of the mountains:
"Not so long and wide the world is,
Not so rude and rough the way is,
But my wrath shall overtake you,
And my vengeance shall attain you!"

Over rock and over river,
Thorough bush, and brake, and forest,
Ran the cunning Pau-Puk-Keewis;　40
Like an antelope he bounded,
Till he came unto a streamlet
In the middle of the forest,
To a streamlet still and tranquil,
That had overflowed its margin,
To a dam made by the beavers,
To a pond of quiet water,
Where knee-deep the trees were standing,
Where the water-lilies floated,
Where the rushes waved and whispered.　50
On the dam stood Pau-Puk-Keewis,
On the dam of trunks and branches,
Through whose chinks the water spouted,
O'er whose summit flowed the streamlet.
From the bottom rose the beaver,
Looked with two great eyes of wonder,
Eyes that seemed to ask a question,
At the stranger, Pau-Puk-Keewis.

On the dam stood Pau-Puk-Keewis,
O'er his ankles flowed the streamlet,　60
Flowed the bright and silvery water,
And he spake unto the beaver,
With a smile he spake in this wise:
"O my friend Ahmeek, the beaver,

Cool and pleasant is the water;
Let me dive into the water,
Let me rest there in your lodges;
Change me, too, into a beaver!"

Cautiously replied the beaver,
With reserve he thus made answer:　70
"Let me first consult the others,
Let me ask the other beavers."
Down he sank into the water,
Heavily sank he, as a stone sinks,
Down among the leaves and branches,
Brown and matted at the bottom.

On the dam stood Pau-Puk-Keewis,
O'er his ankles flowed the streamlet,
Spouted through the chinks below him,
Dashed upon the stones beneath him,　80
Spread serene and calm before him,
And the sunshine and the shadows
Fell in flecks and gleams upon him,
Fell in little shining patches,
Through the waving, rustling branches.

From the bottom rose the beavers,
Silently above the surface
Rose one head and then another,
Till the pond seemed full of beavers,
Full of black and shining faces.　90
To the beavers Pau-Puk-Keewis
Spake entreating, said in this wise:
"Very pleasant is your dwelling,
O my friends! and safe from danger;
Can you not, with all your cunning,
All your wisdom and contrivance,
Change me, too, into a beaver?"

"Yes!" replied Ahmeek, the beaver,
He the King of all the beavers,
"Let yourself slide down among us,　100
Down into the tranquil water."

Down into the pond among them
Silently sank Pau-Puk-Keewis;
Black became his shirt of deerskin,
Black his moccasins and leggings,
In a broad black tail behind him
Spread his foxtails and his fringes;
He was changed into a beaver.

"Make me large," said Pau-Puk-Keewis,
"Make me large and make me larger,　110
Larger than the other beavers."
"Yes," the beaver chief responded,
"When our lodge below you enter,
In our wigwam we will make you
Ten times larger than the others."

Thus into the clear, brown water
Silently sank Pau-Puk-Keewis:
Found the bottom covered over
With the trunks of trees and branches,
Hoards of food against the winter, 120
Piles and heaps against the famine;
Found the lodge with arching doorway,
Leading into spacious chambers.

Here they made him large and larger,
Made him largest of the beavers,
Ten times larger than the others.
"You shall be our ruler," said they;
"Chief and King of all the beavers."

But not long had Pau-Puk-Keewis
Sat in state among the beavers, 130
When there came a voice of warning
From the watchman at his station
In the water-flags and lilies,
Saying, "Here is Hiawatha!
Hiawatha with his hunters!"

Then they heard a cry above them,
Heard a shouting and a tramping,
Heard a crashing and a rushing,
And the water round and o'er them
Sank and sucked away in eddies, 140
And they knew their dam was broken.

On the lodge's roof the hunters
Leaped, and broke it all asunder;
Streamed the sunshine through the crevice,
Sprang the beavers through the doorway,
Hid themselves in deeper water,
In the channel of the streamlet;
But the mighty Pau-Puk-Keewis
Could not pass beneath the doorway;
He was puffed with pride and feeding, 150
He was swollen like a bladder.

Through the roof looked Hiawatha,
Cried aloud, "O Pau-Puk-Keewis!
Vain are all your craft and cunning,
Vain your manifold disguises!
Well I know you, Pau-Puk-Keewis!"
With their clubs they beat and bruised him,
Beat to death poor Pau-Puk-Keewis,
Pounded him as maize is pounded,
Till his skull was crushed to pieces. 160

Six tall hunters, lithe and limber,
Bore him home on poles and branches,
Bore the body of the beaver;
But the ghost, the Jeebi in him,
Thought and felt as Pau-Puk-Keewis,
Still lived on as Pau-Puk-Keewis.

And it fluttered, strove, and struggled,
Waving hither, waving thither,
As the curtains of a wigwam
Struggle with their thongs of deerskin, 170
When the wintry wind is blowing;
Till it drew itself together,
Till it rose up from the body,
Till it took the form and features
Of the cunning Pau-Puk-Keewis
Vanishing into the forest.

But the wary Hiawatha
Saw the figure ere it vanished,
Saw the form of Pau-Puk-Keewis
Glide into the soft blue shadow 180
Of the pine-trees of the forest;
Toward the squares of white beyond it,
Toward an opening in the forest,
Like a wind it rushed and panted,
Bending all the boughs before it,
And behind it, as the rain comes,
Came the steps of Hiawatha.

To a lake with many islands
Came the breathless Pau-Puk-Keewis,
Where among the water-lilies 190
Pishnekuh, the brant, were sailing;
Through the tufts of rushes floating,
Steering through the reedy islands.
Now their broad black beaks they lifted,
Now they plunged beneath the water,
Now they darkened in the shadow,
Now they brightened in the sunshine.

"Pishnekuh!" cried Pau-Puk-Keewis,
"Pishnekuh! my brothers!" said he,
"Change me to a brant with plumage, 200
With a shining neck and feathers,
Make me large, and make me larger,
Ten times larger than the others."

Straightway to a brant they changed him,
With two huge and dusky pinions,
With a bosom smooth and rounded,
With a bill like two great paddles,
Made him larger than the others,
Ten times larger than the largest,
Just as, shouting from the forest, 210
On the shore stood Hiawatha.

Up they rose with cry and clamor,
With a whir and beat of pinions,
Rose up from the reedy islands,
From the water-flags and lilies,
And they said to Pau-Puk-Keewis:
"In your flying, look not downward,

Take good heed and look not downward,
Lest some strange mischance should happen,
Lest some great mishap befall you!"   220
    Fast and far they fled to northward,
Fast and far through mist and sunshine,
Fled among the moors and fen-lands,
Slept among the reeds and rushes.
    On the morrow as they journeyed,
Buoyed and lifted by the South-wind,
Wafted onward by the South-wind,
Blowing fresh and strong behind them,
Rose a sound of human voices,
Rose a clamor from beneath them,   230
From the lodges of a village,
From the people miles beneath them.
    For the people of the village
Saw the flock of brant with wonder,
Saw the wings of Pau-Puk-Keewis
Flapping far up in the ether,
Broader than two doorway curtains.
    Pau-Puk-Keewis heard the shouting,
Knew the voice of Hiawatha,
Knew the outcry of Iagoo,   240
And, forgetful of the warning,
Drew his neck in, and looked downward,
And the wind that blew behind him
Caught his mighty fan of feathers,
Sent him wheeling, whirling downward!
    All in vain did Pau-Puk-Keewis
Struggle to regain his balance!
Whirling round and round and downward,
He beheld in turn the village
And in turn the flock above him,   250
Saw the village coming nearer,
And the flock receding farther,
Heard the voices growing louder,
Heard the shouting and the laughter;
Saw no more the flocks above him,
Only saw the earth beneath him;
Dead out of the empty heaven,
Dead among the shouting people,
With a heavy soul and sullen,
Fell the brant with broken pinions.   260
    But his soul, his ghost, his shadow,
Still survived as Pau-Puk-Keewis,
Took again the form and features
Of the handsome Yenadizze,
And again went rushing onward,
Followed fast by Hiawatha,
Crying: "Not so wide the world is,
Not so long and rough the way is,

But my wrath shall overtake you,
But my vengeance shall attain you!"   270
    And so near he came, so near him,
That his hand was stretched to seize him,
His right hand to seize and hold him,
When the cunning Pau-Puk-Keewis
Whirled and spun about in circles,
Fanned the air into a whirlwind,
Danced the dust and leaves about him,
And amid the whirling eddies
Sprang into a hollow oak-tree,
Changed himself into a serpent,   280
Gliding out through root and rubbish.
    With his right hand Hiawatha
Smote amain the hollow oak-tree,
Rent it into shreds and splinters,
Left it lying there in fragments.
But in vain; for Pau-Puk-Keewis,
Once again in human figure,
Full in sight ran on before him,
Sped away in gust and whirlwind,
On the shores of Gitche Gumee,   290
Westward by the Big-Sea-Water,
Came unto the rocky headlands,
To the Pictured Rocks of sandstone,
Looking over lake and landscape.
    And the Old Man of the Mountain,
He the Manito of Mountains,
Opened wide his rocky doorways,
Opened wide his deep abysses,
Giving Pau-Puk-Keewis shelter
In his caverns dark and dreary,   300
Bidding Pau-Puk-Keewis welcome
To his gloomy lodge of sandstone.
    There without stood Hiawatha,
Found the doorways closed against him,
With his mittens, Minjekahwun,
Smote great caverns in the sandstone,
Cried aloud in tones of thunder,
"Open! I am Hiawatha!"
But the Old Man of the Mountain
Opened not, and made no answer   310
From the silent crags of sandstone,
From the gloomy rock abysses.
    Then he raised his hands to heaven,
Called imploring on the tempest,
Called Waywassimo, the lightning,
And the thunder, Annemeekee;
And they came with night and darkness,
Sweeping down the Big-Sea-Water
From the distant Thunder Mountains;

And the trembling Pau-Puk-Keewis 320
Heard the footsteps of the thunder,
Saw the red eyes of the lightning,
Was afraid, and crouched and trembled.

Then Waywassimo, the lightning,
Smote the doorways of the caverns,
With his war-club smote the doorways,
Smote the jutting crags of sandstone,
And the thunder, Annemeekee,
Shouted down into the caverns,
Saying, "Where is Pau-Puk-Keewis!" 330
And the crags fell, and beneath them
Dead among the rocky ruins
Lay the cunning Pau-Puk-Keewis,
Lay the handsome Yenadizze,
Slain in his own human figure.

Ended were his wild adventures,
Ended were his tricks and gambols,
Ended all his craft and cunning,
Ended all his mischief-making,
All his gambling and his dancing, 340
All his wooing of the maidens.

Then the noble Hiawatha
Took his soul, his ghost, his shadow,
Spake and said: "O Pau-Puk-Keewis,
Never more in human figure
Shall you search for new adventures;
Never more with jest and laughter
Dance the dust and leaves in whirlwinds;
But above there in the heavens
You shall soar and sail in circles; 350
I will change you to an eagle,
To Keneu, the great war-eagle,
Chief of all the fowls with feathers,
Chief of Hiawatha's chickens."

And the name of Pau-Puk-Keewis
Lingers still among the people,
Lingers still among the singers,
And among the storytellers;
And in Winter, when the snowflakes
Whirl in eddies round the lodges, 360
When the wind in gusty tumult
O'er the smoke-flue pipes and whistles,
"There," they cry, "comes Pau-Puk-Keewis;
He is dancing through the village,
He is gathering in his harvest!"

1854-1855   1855

THE CHILDREN'S HOUR

First published in the *Atlantic Monthly*, September, 1860. Though it is a poem of Longfellow's own home in Cambridge, the imagery from the fifth stanza onward takes the reader to the feudal past. The poet perhaps had in mind, in the seventh stanza, Southey's poem "God's Judgment on a Wicked Bishop"; he knew, however, from his stay in Germany, the legend of Archbishop Hatto of the tenth century, who built a high tower on the Rhine for protection against mice, yet was eaten by them as a punishment for his cruelty to the common people who stole grain during a famine.

BETWEEN the dark and the daylight,
    When the night is beginning to lower,
Comes a pause in the day's occupations,
    That is known as the Children's Hour.

I hear in the chamber above me
    The patter of little feet,
The sound of a door that is opened,
    And voices soft and sweet.

From my study I see in the lamplight,
    Descending the broad hall stair,   10
Grave Alice, and laughing Allegra,
    And Edith with golden hair.

A whisper, and then a silence:
    Yet I know by their merry eyes
They are plotting and planning together
    To take me by surprise.

A sudden rush from the stairway,
    A sudden raid from the hall!
By three doors left unguarded
    They enter my castle wall!   20

They climb up into my turret
    O'er the arms and back of my chair;
If I try to escape, they surround me;
    They seem to be everywhere.

They almost devour me with kisses,
    Their arms about me entwine,
Till I think of the Bishop of Bingen
    In his Mouse-Tower on the Rhine!

Do you think, O blue-eyed banditti,
    Because you have scaled the wall,   30
Such an old mustache as I am
    Is not a match for you all!

I have you fast in my fortress,
  And will not let you depart,
But put you down into the dungeon
  In the round-tower of my heart.

And there will I keep you forever,
  Yes, forever and a day,
Till the walls shall crumble to ruin,
  And molder in dust away.   40

1859   1860

From TALES OF A WAY-
SIDE INN

First entitled "The Sudbury Tales." The Wayside Inn was the old Red Horse Inn at Sudbury,
Massachusetts, about twenty miles from Boston.
Members of the Howe family, from England, had
kept the inn for a hundred and seventy-five years.
After the death of Lyman Howe, a personal friend
of Longfellow, the inn was closed until 1897, when
E. R. Lemon restored and reopened it. It was
bought in 1923 by Henry Ford to preserve it as a
memorial. The *Tales* are in three parts, the first
published November 25, 1863. The second part
appeared in *Three Books of Song* (1872), and the
last series in *Aftermath* (1873). The collection of
tales and the manner of their telling is modeled
somewhat upon Chaucer's *Canterbury Tales*. The
poet gathered together at the Red Horse Inn a
group of friends, much as Chaucer gathered his
pilgrims at the Tabard Inn. The musician was Ole
Bull, the Norwegian violinist; the student, Henry
Ware Wales; the Sicilian, Luigi Monti; the Spanish
Jew, Israel Edrehi, a Boston merchant; the theologian, Professor Daniel Treadwell of Harvard;
the poet, T. W. Parsons.

PRELUDE

The Wayside Inn

ONE autumn night, in Sudbury town,
Across the meadows bare and brown,
The windows of the wayside inn
Gleamed red with firelight through the
  leaves
Of woodbine, hanging from the eaves
Their crimson curtains rent and thin.

As ancient is this hostelry
As any in the land may be,
Built in the old Colonial day,
When men lived in a grander way,   10
With ampler hospitality;

A kind of old Hobgoblin Hall,
Now somewhat fallen to decay,
With weather-stains upon the wall,
And stairways worn, and crazy doors,
And creaking and uneven floors,
And chimneys huge, and tiled and tall.

A region of repose it seems,
A place of slumber and of dreams,
Remote among the wooded hills!   20
For there no noisy railway speeds,
Its torch-race scattering smoke and gleeds;
But noon and night, the panting teams
Stop under the great oaks, that throw
Tangles of light and shade below,
On roofs and doors and window-sills.
Across the road the barns display
Their lines of stalls, their mows of hay,
Through the wide doors the breezes blow,
The wattled cocks strut to and fro,   30
And, half effaced by rain and shine,
The Red Horse prances on the sign.
Round this old-fashioned, quaint abode
Deep silence reigned, save when a gust
Went rushing down the county road,
And skeletons of leaves, and dust,
A moment quickened by its breath,
Shuddered and danced their dance of death,
And through the ancient oaks o'erhead
Mysterious voices moaned and fled.   40

But from the parlor of the inn
A pleasant murmur smote the ear,
Like water rushing through a weir:
Oft interrupted by the din
Of laughter and of loud applause,
And, in each intervening pause,
The music of a violin.
The firelight, shedding over all
The splendor of its ruddy glow,
Filled the whole parlor large and low;   50
It gleamed on wainscot and on wall,
It touched with more than wonted grace
Fair Princess Mary's pictured face;
It bronzed the rafters overhead,
On the old spinet's ivory keys
It played inaudible melodies,
It crowned the somber clock with flame,
The hands, the hours, the maker's name,
And painted with a livelier red
The Landlord's coat-of-arms again;   60
And, flashing on the window-pane,

Emblazoned with its light and shade
The jovial rhymes, that still remain,
Writ near a century ago
By the great Major Molineaux,
Whom Hawthorne has immortal made.[1]

Before the blazing fire of wood
Erect the rapt musician stood;
And ever and anon he bent
His head upon his instrument, 70
And seemed to listen, till he caught
Confessions of its secret thought,—
The joy, the triumph, the lament,
The exultation and the pain;
Then, by the magic of his art,
He soothed the throbbings of its heart,
And lulled it into peace again.

Around the fireside at their ease
There sat a group of friends, entranced
With the delicious melodies; 80
Who from the far-off noisy town
Had to the wayside inn come down,
To rest beneath its old oak trees.
The firelight on their faces glanced,
Their shadows on the wainscot danced,
And, though of different lands and speech,
Each had his tale to tell, and each
Was anxious to be pleased and please.
And while the sweet musician plays,
Let me in outline sketch them all, 90
Perchance uncouthly as the blaze
With its uncertain touch portrays
Their shadowy semblance on the wall.

But first the Landlord will I trace;
Grave in his aspect and attire;
A man of ancient pedigree,
A Justice of the Peace was he,
Known in all Sudbury as "The Squire."
Proud was he of his name and race,
Of old Sir William and Sir Hugh, 100
And in the parlor, full in view,
His coat-of-arms, well framed and glazed,
Upon the wall in colors blazed;
He beareth gules upon his shield,[2]
A chevron argent in the field,

With three wolf's heads, and for the crest
A Wyvern part-per-pale addressed
Upon a helmet barred; below
The scroll reads, "By the name of Howe."
And over this, no longer bright, 110
Though glimmering with a latent light,
Was hung the sword his grandsire bore
In the rebellious days of yore,
Down there at Concord in the fight.

A youth was there, of quiet ways,
A Student of old books and days,
To whom all tongues and lands were known,
And yet a lover of his own;
With many a social virtue graced,
And yet a friend of solitude; 120
A man of such a genial mood
The heart of all things he embraced,
And yet of such fastidious taste,
He never found the best too good.
Books were his passion and delight,
And in his upper room at home
Stood many a rare and sumptuous tome,
In vellum bound, with gold bedight,
Great volumes garmented in white,
Recalling Florence, Pisa, Rome. 130
He loved the twilight that surrounds
The borderland of old romance;
Where glitter hauberk, helm, and lance,
And banner waves, and trumpet sounds,
And ladies ride with hawk on wrist,
And mighty warriors sweep along,
Magnified by the purple mist,
The dusk of centuries and of song.
The chronicles of Charlemagne,
Of Merlin and the Mort d'Arthure,[1] 140
Mingled together in his brain
With tales of Flores and Blanchefleur,
Sir Ferumbras, Sir Eglamour,
Sir Launcelot, Sir Morgadour,
Sir Guy, Sir Bevis, Sir Gawain.

A young Sicilian, too, was there;
In sight of Etna born and bred,
Some breath of its volcanic air
Was glowing in his heart and brain,
And, being rebellious to his liege, 150
After Palermo's fatal siege,
Across the western seas he fled,
In good King Bomba's[2] happy reign.

[1] in "My Kinsman, Major Molineux," in *The Snow Image and Other Twice-Told Tales* (1851)   [2] For an account of the details of the science of Heraldry, see the illustrated articles on the subject in the *Encyclopædia Britannica* or in the *New International Encyclopædia*.

[1] "Death of Arthur"   [2] familiar name of Ferdinand II, King of the Two Sicilies

His face was like a summer night,
All flooded with a dusky light;
His hands were small; his teeth shone white
As sea-shells, when he smiled or spoke;
His sinews supple and strong as oak;
Clean shaven was he as a priest,
Who at the mass on Sunday sings,   160
Save that upon his upper lip
His beard, a good palm's length at least,
Level and pointed at the tip,
Shot sideways, like a swallow's wings.
The poets read he o'er and o'er,
And most of all the Immortal Four
Of Italy; and next to those,
The story-telling bard of prose,
Who wrote the joyous Tuscan tales
Of the *Decameron*, that make   170
Fiesole's green hills and vales
Remembered for Boccaccio's sake.
Much too of music was his thought;
The melodies and measures fraught
With sunshine and the open air,
Of vineyards and the singing sea
Of his beloved Sicily;
And much it pleased him to peruse
The songs of the Sicilian muse,—
Bucolic songs by Meli sung   180
In the familiar peasant tongue,
That made men say, "Behold! once more
The pitying gods to earth restore
Theocritus of Syracuse!"

A Spanish Jew from Alicant
With aspect grand and grave was there;
Vender of silks and fabrics rare,
And attar of rose from the Levant.
Like an old Patriarch he appeared,
Abraham or Isaac, or at least   190
Some later Prophet or High-Priest;
With lustrous eyes, and olive skin,
And, wildly tossed from cheeks and chin,
The tumbling cataract of his beard.
His garments breathed a spicy scent
Of cinnamon and sandal blent,
Like the soft aromatic gales
That meet the mariner, who sails
Through the Moluccas and the seas
That wash the shores of Celebes.   200
All stories that recorded are
By Pierre Alphonse he knew by heart,
And it was rumored he could say

The Parables of Sandabar,
And all the Fables of Pilpay,
Or if not all, the greater part!
Well versed was he in Hebrew books
Talmud and Targum, and the lore
Of Kabala; and evermore
There was a mystery in his looks;   210
His eyes seemed gazing far away,
As if in vision or in trance
He heard the solemn sackbut play,
And saw the Jewish maidens dance.

A Theologian, from the school
Of Cambridge, on the Charles was there;
Skilful alike with tongue and pen,
He preached to all men everywhere
The Gospel of the Golden Rule,
The New Commandment given to men,   220
Thinking the deed, and not the creed,
Would help us in our utmost need.
With reverent feet the earth he trod,
Nor banished nature from his plan,
But studied still with deep research
To build the Universal Church,
Lofty as in the love of God,
And ample as the wants of man.

A Poet, too, was there, whose verse
Was tender, musical, and terse;   230
The inspiration, the delight,
The gleam, the glory, the swift flight,
Of thoughts so sudden, that they seem
The revelations of a dream,
All these were his; but with them came
No envy of another's fame;
He did not find his sleep less sweet
For music in some neighboring street,
Nor rustling hear in every breeze
The laurels of Miltiades.[1]   240
Honor and blessings on his head
While living, good report when dead,
Who, not too eager for renown,
Accepts, but does not clutch, the crown!

Last the Musician, as he stood
Illumined by that fire of wood;
Fair-haired, blue-eyed, his aspect blithe,
His figure tall and straight and lithe,

[1] According to Plutarch, the Athenian general
Themistocles was envious of the successes of Miltiades,
the famous commander of the Greeks at the Battle of
Marathon.

And every feature of his face
Revealing his Norwegian race; 250
A radiance, streaming from within,
Around his eyes and forehead beamed,
The Angel with the violin,
Painted by Raphael, he seemed.
He lived in that ideal world
Whose language is not speech, but song;
Around him evermore the throng
Of elves and sprites their dances whirled;
The Strömkarl[1] sang, the cataract hurled
Its headlong waters from the height; 260
And mingled in the wild delight
The scream of sea-birds in their flight,
The rumor of the forest trees,
The plunge of the implacable seas,
The tumult of the wind at night,
Voices of eld, like trumpets blowing,
Old ballads, and wild melodies
Through mist and darkness pouring forth,
Like Elivagar's river flowing
Out of the glaciers of the North. 270

The instrument on which he played
Was in Cremona's workshops made,
By a great master of the past,
Ere yet was lost the art divine;
Fashioned of maple and of pine,
That in Tyrolian forests vast
Had rocked and wrestled with the blast:
Exquisite was it in design,
Perfect in each minutest part,
A marvel of the lutist's art; 280
And in its hollow chamber, thus,
The maker from whose hands it came
Had written his unrivaled name,—
"Antonius Stradivarius."

And when he played, the atmosphere
Was filled with magic, and the ear
Caught echoes of that Harp of Gold,
Whose music had so weird a sound,
The hunted stag forgot to bound,
The leaping rivulet backward rolled, 290
The birds came down from bush and tree,
The dead came from beneath the sea,
The maiden to the harper's knee!

The music ceased; the applause was loud,
The pleased musician smiled and bowed;
The wood-fire clapped its hands of flame,

[1] river spirit

The shadows on the wainscot stirred,
And from the harpsichord there came
A ghostly murmur of acclaim,
A sound like that sent down at night 300
By birds of passage in their flight,
From the remotest distance heard.

Then silence followed; then began
A clamor for the Landlord's tale,—
The story promised them of old,
They said, but always left untold;
And he, although a bashful man,
And all his courage seemed to fail,
Finding excuse of no avail,
Yielded; and thus the story ran. 310
1862   1863

THE LANDLORD'S TALE
Paul Revere's Ride

"Paul Revere's Ride" stands first in the series of *Tales*. Its source may be Revere's own account in a letter to Dr. Jeremy Belknap (*Massachusetts Historical Society Collections*, V). Revere rode from Boston to Lexington in Middlesex County on the night of April 18, 1775, to summon the militia. There is some question concerning the church from which the lanterns were hung, signals that the British had left Boston for Concord, and concerning the identity of the "friend." Longfellow believed the church to be the Old North Church. The signals may rather have been hung in the North Meeting House, in North Square, which was destroyed in the siege of Boston, 1775–76. According to his diary, Longfellow climbed the tower of the Old North Church April 5, 1860.

Listen, my children, and you shall hear
Of the midnight ride of Paul Revere,
On the eighteenth of April, in Seventy-five;
Hardly a man is now alive
Who remembers that famous day and year.

He said to his friend, "If the British march
By land or sea from the town tonight,
Hang a lantern aloft in the belfry arch
Of the North Church tower as a signal light,—
One, if by land, and two, if by sea; 10
And I on the opposite shore will be,
Ready to ride and spread the alarm
Through every Middlesex village and farm,
For the country folk to be up and to arm."

Then he said, "Good night!" and with muf-
    fled oar
Silently rowed to the Charlestown shore,
Just as the moon rose over the bay,
Where swinging wide at her moorings lay
The *Somerset*, British man-of-war;
A phantom ship, with each mast and spar   20
Across the moon like a prison bar,
And a huge black hulk that was magnified
By its own reflection in the tide.

Meanwhile, his friend, through alley and
    street,
Wanders and watches with eager ears,
Till in the silence around him he hears
The muster of men at the barrack door,
The sound of arms, and the tramp of feet,
And the measured tread of the grenadiers,
Marching down to their boats on the shore.

Then he climbed the tower of the Old North
    Church,   31
By the wooden stairs, with stealthy tread,
To the belfry chamber overhead,
And startled the pigeons from their perch
On the somber rafters, that round him made
Masses and moving shapes of shade,—
By the trembling ladder, steep and tall,
To the highest window in the wall,
Where he paused to listen and look down
A moment on the roofs of the town,   40
And the moonlight flowing over all.

Beneath, in the churchyard, lay the dead,
In their night-encampment on the hill,
Wrapped in silence so deep and still
That he could hear, like a sentinel's tread,
The watchful night-wind, as it went
Creeping along from tent to tent,
And seeming to whisper, "All is well!"
A moment only he feels the spell
Of the place and the hour, and the secret
    dread   50
Of the lonely belfry and the dead;
For suddenly all his thoughts are bent
On a shadowy something far away,
Where the river widens to meet the bay,—
A line of black that bends and floats
On the rising tide, like a bridge of boats.

Meanwhile, impatient to mount and ride,
Booted and spurred, with a heavy stride

On the opposite shore walked Paul Revere.
Now he patted his horse's side,   60
Now gazed at the landscape far and near,
Then, impetuous, stamped the earth,
And turned and tightened his saddle-girth;
But mostly he watched with eager search
The belfry-tower of the Old North Church,
As it rose above the graves on the hill,
Lonely and spectral and somber and still.
And lo! as he looks, on the belfry's height
A glimmer, and then a gleam of light!   69
He springs to the saddle, the bridle he turns,
But lingers and gazes, till full on his sight
A second lamp in the belfry burns!

A hurry of hoofs in a village street,
A shape in the moonlight, a bulk in the dark,
And beneath, from the pebbles, in passing, a
    spark
Struck out by a steed flying fearless and fleet:
That was all! And yet, through the gloom and
    the light,
The fate of a nation was riding that night;
And the spark struck out by that steed, in his
    flight,
Kindled the land into flame with its heat.   80

He has left the village and mounted the steep,
And beneath him, tranquil and broad and
    deep,
Is the Mystic, meeting the ocean tides;
And under the alders, that skirt its edge,
Now soft on the sand, now loud on the ledge,
Is heard the tramp of his steed as he rides.

It was twelve by the village clock
When he crossed the bridge into Medford
    town.
He heard the crowing of the cock,
And the barking of the farmer's dog,   90
And felt the damp of the river fog,
That rises after the sun goes down.

It was one by the village clock
When he galloped into Lexington.
He saw the gilded weathercock
Swim in the moonlight as he passed,
And the meetinghouse windows, blank and
    bare,
Gaze at him with a spectral glare,
As if they already stood aghast
At the bloody work they would look upon.

It was two by the village clock   101
When he came to the bridge in Concord
    town.
He heard the bleating of the flock,
And the twitter of birds among the trees,
And felt the breath of the morning breeze
Blowing over the meadows brown.
And one was safe and asleep in his bed [1]
Who at the bridge would be first to fall,
Who that day would be lying dead,
Pierced by a British musket-ball.   110

You know the rest. In the books you have
    read,
How the British Regulars fired and fled,—
How the farmers gave them ball for ball,
From behind each fence and farmyard wall,
Chasing the red-coats down the lane,
Then crossing the fields to emerge again
Under the trees at the turn of the road,
And only pausing to fire and load.

So through the night rode Paul Revere;
And so through the night went his cry of
    alarm   120
To every Middlesex village and farm,—
A cry of defiance and not of fear,
A voice in the darkness, a knock at the door,
And a word that shall echo forevermore!
For, borne on the night-wind of the Past,
Through all our history, to the last,
In the hour of darkness and peril and need,
The people will waken and listen to hear
The hurrying hoof-beats of that steed,   129
And the midnight message of Paul Revere.

1860   *1861*

HAWTHORNE

MAY 23, 1864

How beautiful it was, that one bright day
    In the long week of rain!
Though all its splendor could not chase away
    The omnipresent pain.

The lovely town was white with apple-blooms,
    And the great elms o'erhead
Dark shadows wove on their aërial looms,
    Shot through with golden thread.

[1] Captain Isaac Davis of Acton

Across the meadows, by the gray old manse,
    The historic river flowed: 10
I was as one who wanders in a trance,
    Unconscious of his road.

The faces of familiar friends seemed strange;
    Their voices I could hear,
And yet the words they uttered seemed to
    change
    Their meaning to my ear.

For the one face I looked for was not there,
    The one low voice was mute;
Only an unseen presence filled the air,
    And baffled my pursuit.   20

Now I look back, and meadow, manse, and
    stream
    Dimly my thought defines;
I only see—a dream within a dream—
    The hilltop hearsed with pines.

I only hear above his place of rest
    Their tender undertone,
The infinite longings of a troubled breast,
    The voice so like his own.

There in seclusion and remote from men
    The wizard hand lies cold,   30
Which at its topmost speed let fall the pen,
    And left the tale half told. [1]

Ah! who shall lift that wand of magic power,
    And the lost clew regain?
The unfinished window in Aladdin's tower [2]
    Unfinished must remain!

1864

DANTE

TUSCAN, that wanderest through the realms
    of gloom,
    With thoughtful pace, and sad, majestic
    eyes,
    Stern thoughts and awful from thy soul
    arise,
    Like Farinata from his fiery tomb. [3]

[1] Two romances, *Septimius Felton* and *Dr. Grimshawe's Secret*, were left unfinished by Hawthorne.
[2] One of the windows was left unfinished in the tower built by magic by Aladdin in *The Arabian Nights*.
[3] See *Inferno*, X.

Thy sacred song is like the trump of doom;
Yet in thy heart what human sympathies,
What soft compassion glows; as in the skies
The tender stars their clouded lamps relume!
Methinks I see thee stand with pallid cheeks
By Fra Hilario in his diocese,   10
As up the convent-walls, in golden streaks,
The ascending sunbeams mark the day's de-
    crease;
And, as he asks what there the stranger
    seeks,
Thy voice along the cloister whispers,
    "Peace!"

1843   *1845*

DIVINA COMMEDIA

These six sonnets were written during the time
that Longfellow was making his translation of
Dante's *Divina Commedia*. They were first published in the *Atlantic Monthly* at various times
from December, 1864, to November, 1866. The
first and second sonnets were then used to preface
the *Inferno*, the third and fourth to preface the
Purgatorio, and the fifth and sixth to preface the
Paradiso.

I

OFT have I seen at some cathedral door
A laborer, pausing in the dust and heat,
Lay down his burden, and with reverent
    feet
Enter, and cross himself, and on the floor
Kneel to repeat his paternoster o'er;
Far off the noises of the world retreat;
The loud vociferations of the street
Become an undistinguishable roar.
So, as I enter here from day to day,
And leave my burden at this minster gate,   10
Kneeling in prayer, and not ashamed to
    pray,
The tumult of the time disconsolate
To inarticulate murmurs dies away,
While the eternal ages watch and wait.

1864

II

How strange the sculptures that adorn these
    towers!
This crowd of statues, in whose folded
    sleeves
Birds build their nests; while canopied with
    leaves

Parvis[1] and portal bloom like trellised
    bowers,
And the vast minster seems a cross of flowers!
But fiends and dragons on the gargoyled
    eaves
Watch the dead Christ between the living
    thieves,
And, underneath, the traitor Judas lowers!
Ah! from what agonies of heart and brain,
What exultations trampling on despair,   10
What tenderness, what tears, what hate of
    wrong,
What passionate outcry of a soul in pain,
Uprose this poem of the earth and air,
This mediæval miracle of song!

1864   *1866*

III

I enter, and I see thee in the gloom
Of the long aisles, O poet saturnine!
And strive to make my steps keep pace
    with thine.
The air is filled with some unknown per-
    fume;
The congregation of the dead make room
For thee to pass; the votive tapers shine;
Like rooks that haunt Ravenna's groves
    of pine
The hovering echoes fly from tomb to
    tomb.
From the confessionals I hear arise
Rehearsals of forgotten tragedies,   10
And lamentations from the crypts below;
And then a voice celestial that begins
With the pathetic words, "Although your
    sins
As scarlet be," and ends with "as the
    snow."

1865   *1866*

IV

With snow-white veil and garments as of
    flame,
She stands before thee, who so long ago
Filled thy young heart with passion and
    the woe
From which thy song and all its splendors
    came;
And while with stern rebuke she speaks thy
    name,

[1] courtyard before a church

The ice about thy heart melts as the snow
  On mountain heights, and in swift overflow
  Comes gushing from thy lips in sobs of
    shame.
Thou makest full confession; and a gleam,
  As of the dawn on some dark forest cast,   10
  Seems on thy lifted forehead to increase;
Lethe and Eunoë [1]—the remembered dream
And the forgotten sorrow—bring at last
That perfect pardon which is perfect peace.

1867

V

I lift mine eyes, and all the windows blaze
  With forms of Saints and holy men who
    died,
  Here martyred and hereafter glorified;
And the great Rose [2] upon its leaves displays
Christ's Triumph, and the angelic rounde-
    lays,
  With splendor upon splendor multiplied;
  And Beatrice again at Dante's side
No more rebukes, but smiles her words
    of praise.
And then the organ sounds, and unseen choirs
  Sing the old Latin hymns of peace and love
  And benedictions of the Holy Ghost;   11
And the melodious bells among the spires
  O'er all the housetops and through heaven
    above
  Proclaim the elevation of the Host!

1866

VI

O star of morning and of liberty!
  O bringer of the light, whose splendor
    shines
  Above the darkness of the Apennines,
  Forerunner of the day that is to be!
The voices of the city and the sea,
  The voices of the mountains and the pines,
  Repeat thy song, till the familiar lines
  Are footpaths for the thought of Italy!
Thy flame is blown abroad from all the
    heights,
  Through all the nations, and a sound is
    heard,   10
  As of a mighty wind, and men devout,

Strangers of Rome, and the new proselytes,
  In their own language hear the wondrous
    word,
  And many are amazed and many doubt.

1866

GIOTTO'S TOWER

How many lives, made beautiful and sweet
  By self-devotion and by self-restraint,
  Whose pleasure is to run without complaint
  On unknown errands of the Paraclete,[1]
Wanting the reverence of unshodden feet,
  Fail of the nimbus which the artists paint
  Around the shining forehead of the saint,
  And are in their completeness incomplete!
In the old Tuscan town stands Giotto's tower,
  The lily of Florence blossoming in stone,—
  A vision, a delight, and a desire,—   11
The builder's perfect and centennial flower,
  That in the night of ages bloomed alone,
  But wanting still the glory of the spire.[2]

1866

THE THREE SILENCES OF MOLINOS

TO JOHN GREENLEAF WHITTIER

THREE Silences there are: the first of speech,
  The second of desire, the third of thought;
  This is the lore a Spanish monk, distraught
  With dreams and visions, was the first to
    teach.
These Silences, commingling each with each,
  Made up the perfect Silence that he sought
  And prayed for, and wherein at times he
    caught
  Mysterious sounds from realms beyond
    our reach.
O thou, whose daily life anticipates
  The life to come, and in whose thought
    and word   10
  The spiritual world preponderates,
Hermit of Amesbury! thou too hast heard
  Voices and melodies from beyond the gates,
  And speakest only when thy soul is stirred!

1877   1878

---

[1] the rivers of forgetfulness and remembrance   [2] See the mystic celestial rose in *Paradiso*, XXX–XXXI. A conventionalized stained-glass rose design was often placed in Gothic churches.

[1] comforter or intercessor   [2] The tower was to have a 100-foot spire, but when the structure was completed after Giotto's death, the spire was not added.

MORITURI SALUTAMUS

Written in 1874, when the poet was sixty-seven, for the fiftieth anniversary of the class of 1825 of Bowdoin College, the reunion to be held the next summer. The idea and name of the poem came from a famous picture, "Gladiators Saluting Caesar," 1859, by the noted French artist, Jean Léon Gérôme (1824–1904). The gladiators, about to enter mortal combat, salute the emperor. Below it the artist placed their legendary words: *Ave, Caesar Imperator, Morituri Te Salutant* ("Hail, imperial Caesar, they who are about to die salute thee").

"O Caesar, we who are about to die
Salute you!" was the gladiators' cry
In the arena, standing face to face
With death and with the Roman populace.

O ye familiar scenes,—ye groves of pine,
That once were mine and are no longer
    mine,—
Thou river, widening through the meadows
    green
To the vast sea, so near and yet unseen,—
Ye halls, in whose seclusion and repose
Phantoms of fame, like exhalations, rose   10
And vanished,—we who are about to die,
Salute you; earth and air and sea and sky,
And the Imperial Sun that scatters down
His sovereign splendors upon grove and
    town.

Ye do not answer us! ye do not hear!
We are forgotten; and in your austere
And calm indifference, ye little care
Whether we come or go, or whence or where.
What passing generations fill these halls,
What passing voices echo from these walls,
Ye heed not; we are only as the blast,   21
A moment heard, and then forever past.

Not so the teachers who in earlier days
Led our bewildered feet through learning's
    maze;
They answer us—alas! what have I said?
What greetings come there from the voiceless
    dead?
What salutation, welcome, or reply?
What pressure from the hands that lifeless lie?
They are no longer here; they all are gone
Into the land of shadows,—all save one.   30
Honor and reverence, and the good repute

That follows faithful service as its fruit,
Be unto him, whom living we salute.[1]

The great Italian poet, when he made
His dreadful journey to the realms of shade,
Met there the old instructor of his youth,
And cried in tone of pity and of ruth:[2]
"Oh, never from the memory of my heart
Your dear, paternal image shall depart,
Who while on earth, ere yet by death sur-
    prised,   40
Taught me how mortals are immortalized;
How grateful am I for that patient care
All my life long my language shall declare."

Today we make the poet's words our own,
And utter them in plaintive undertone;
Nor to the living only be they said,
But to the other living called the dead,
Whose dear, paternal images appear
Not wrapped in gloom, but roped in sunshine
    here;
Whose simple lives, complete and without
    flaw,   50
Were part and parcel of great Nature's law;
Who said not to their Lord, as if afraid,
"Here is thy talent in a napkin laid,"
But labored in their sphere, as men who live
In the delight that work alone can give.
Peace be to them; eternal peace and rest,
And the fulfilment of the great behest:
"Ye have been faithful over a few things,
Over ten cities shall ye reign as kings."

And ye who fill the places we once filled,   60
And follow in the furrows that we tilled,
Young men, whose generous hearts are beat-
    ing high,
We who are old, and are about to die,
Salute you; hail you; take your hands in ours,
And crown you with our welcome as with
    flowers!

How beautiful is youth! how bright it gleams
With its illusions, aspirations, dreams!
Book of Beginnings, Story without End,
Each maid a heroine, and each man a friend!

[1] Professor A. S. Packard, who died a few years afterward   [2] Dante, to his friend and teacher Brunetto Latini. Lines 38–43 are a free translation of the *Inferno*, I, 82–87.

Aladdin's Lamp, and Fortunatus' Purse,[1] 70
That holds the treasures of the universe!
All possibilities are in its hands,
No danger daunts it, and no foe withstands;
In its sublime audacity of faith,
"Be thou removed," it to the mountain saith,
And with ambitious feet, secure and proud,
Ascends the ladder leaning on the cloud!

As ancient Priam at the Scæan gate[2]
Sat on the walls of Troy in regal state
With the old men, too old and weak to fight,
Chirping like grasshoppers in their delight 81
To see the embattled hosts, with spear and
    shield,
Of Trojans and Achaians in the field;
So from the snowy summits of our years
We see you in the plain, as each appears,
And question of you; asking, "Who is he
That towers above the others? Which may be
Atreides, Menelaus, Odysseus,
Ajax the great, or bold Idomeneus?"

Let him not boast who puts his armor on 90
As he who puts it off, the battle done.
Study yourselves; and most of all note well
Wherein kind Nature meant you to excel.
Not every blossom ripens into fruit;
Minerva, the inventress of the flute,
Flung it aside, when she her face surveyed
Distorted in a fountain as she played;
The unlucky Marsyas found it, and his fate
Was one to make the bravest hesitate. 99
Write on your doors the saying wise and old,
"Be bold! be bold!" and everywhere, "Be bold;
Be not too bold!" Yet better the excess
Than the defect; better the more than less;
Better like Hector in the field to die,
Than like a perfumed Paris turn and fly.

And now, my classmates; ye remaining few
That number not the half of those we knew,
Ye, against whose familiar names not yet
The fatal asterisk of death is set,[4]

[1] In a popular European tale, Fortunatus received
from Fortune an inexhaustible purse, and from the
Sultan a magic wishing cap.   [2] This incident is in
Homer's *Iliad*, III.   [3] Marsyas was flayed alive for
his presumption in daring to compete with Apollo in
a musical contest.   [4] allusion to the custom of marking with an asterisk the names of deceased persons
on a membership roll

Ye I salute! The horologe of Time 110
Strikes the half-century with a solemn chime,
And summons us together once again,
The joy of meeting not unmixed with pain.

Where are the others? Voices from the deep
Caverns of darkness answer me: "They
    sleep!"
I name no names; instinctively I feel
Each at some well-remembered grave will
    kneel,
And from the inscription wipe the weeds and
    moss,
For every heart best knoweth its own loss.
I see their scattered gravestones gleaming
    white 120
Through the pale dusk of the impending
    night;
O'er all alike the impartial sunset throws
Its golden lilies mingled with the rose;
We give to each a tender thought, and pass
Out of the graveyards with their tangled grass,
Unto these scenes frequented by our feet
When we were young, and life was fresh and
    sweet.

What shall I say to you? What can I say
Better than silence is? When I survey
This throng of faces turned to meet my own,
Friendly and fair, and yet to me unknown, 131
Transformed the very landscape seems to be;
It is the same, yet not the same to me.
So many memories crowd upon my brain,
So many ghosts are in the wooded plain,
I fain would steal away, with noiseless tread,
As from a house where some one lieth dead.
I cannot go;—I pause;—I hesitate;
My feet reluctant linger at the gate;
As one who struggles in a troubled dream 140
To speak and cannot, to myself I seem.

Vanish the dream! Vanish the idle fears!
Vanish the rolling mists of fifty years!
Whatever time or space may intervene,
I will not be a stranger in this scene.
Here every doubt, all indecision, ends;
Hail, my companions, comrades, classmates,
    friends!

Ah me! the fifty years since last we met
Seem to me fifty folios bound and set
By Time, the great transcriber, on his shelves,

Wherein are written the histories of our-
        selves.   151
What tragedies, what comedies, are there;
What joy and grief, what rapture and despair!
What chronicles of triumph and defeat,
Of struggle, and temptation, and retreat!
What records of regrets, and doubts, and
        fears!
What pages blotted, blistered by our tears!
What lovely landscapes on the margin shine,
What sweet, angelic faces, what divine
And holy images of love and trust,   160
Undimmed by age, unsoiled by damp or dust!

Whose hand shall dare to open and explore
These volumes, closed and clasped forever-
        more?
Not mine. With reverential feet I pass;
I hear a voice that cries, "Alas! alas!
Whatever hath been written shall remain,
Nor be erased nor written o'er again;
The unwritten only still belongs to thee:
Take heed, and ponder well what that shall
        be."

As children frightened by a thunder-cloud 170
Are reassured if some one reads aloud
A tale of wonder, with enchantment fraught,
Or wild adventure, that diverts their thought,
Let me endeavor with a tale to chase
The gathering shadows of the time and place,
And banish what we all too deeply feel
Wholly to say, or wholly to conceal.

In mediaeval Rome, I know not where,[1]
There stood an image with its arm in air,
And on its lifted finger, shining clear,   180
A golden ring with the device, "Strike here!"
Greatly the people wondered, though none
        guessed
The meaning that these words but half ex-
        pressed,
Until a learned clerk, who at noonday
With downcast eyes was passing on his way,
Paused, and observed the spot, and marked it
        well,
Whereon the shadow of the finger fell;

---

[1] The source of this story is the famous medieval
collection of short tales in Latin, the *Gesta Romanorum*
(CVII, "Of Remembering Death and Forgetting
Things Temporal").

And, coming back at midnight, delved, and
        found
A secret stairway leading underground.
Down this he passed into a spacious hall, 190
Lit by a flaming jewel on the wall;
And opposite, in threatening attitude,
With bow and shaft a brazen statue stood.
Upon its forehead, like a coronet,
Were these mysterious words of menace set:
"That which I am, I am; my fatal aim
None can escape, not even yon luminous
        flame!"

Midway the hall was a fair table placed,
With cloth of gold, and golden cups enchased
With rubies, and the plates and knives were
        gold,   200
And gold the bread and viands manifold.
Around it, silent, motionless, and sad,
Were seated gallant knights in armor clad,
And ladies beautiful with plume and zone,
But they were stone, their hearts within were
        stone;
And the vast hall was filled in every part
With silent crowds, stony in face and heart.

Long at the scene, bewildered and amazed,
The trembling clerk in speechless wonder
        gazed;
Then from the table, by his greed made
        bold,   210
He seized a goblet and a knife of gold,
And suddenly from their seats the guests up-
        sprang,
The vaulted ceiling with loud clamors rang,
The archer sped his arrow, at their call,
Shattering the lambent jewel on the wall,
And all was dark around and overhead;—
Stark on the floor the luckless clerk lay dead.

The writer of this legend then records
Its ghostly application in these words:
The image is the Adversary old,   220
Whose beckoning finger points to realms of
        gold;
Our lusts and passions are the downward stair
That leads the soul from a diviner air;
The archer, Death; the flaming jewel, Life;
Terrestrial goods, the goblet and the knife;
The knights and ladies, all whose flesh and
        bone

By avarice have been hardened into stone;
The clerk, the scholar whom the love of pelf
Tempts from his books and from his nobler
    self.

The scholar and the world! The endless
    strife,   230
The discord in the harmonies of life!
The love of learning, the sequestered nooks,
And all the sweet serenity of books;
The market-place, the eager love of gain,
Whose aim is vanity, and whose end is pain!

But why, you ask me, should this tale be told
To men grown old, or who are growing old?
It is too late! Ah, nothing is too late
Till the tired heart shall cease to palpitate.
Cato learned Greek at eighty; Sophocles   240
Wrote his grand Œdipus, and Simonides
Bore off the prize of verse from his compeers,
When each had numbered more than four-
    score years,
And Theophrastus, at fourscore and ten,
Had but begun his "Characters of Men."
Chaucer, at Woodstock with the nightin-
    gales,
At sixty wrote the Canterbury Tales;
Goethe at Weimar, toiling to the last,
Completed Faust when eighty years were past.
These are indeed exceptions; but they show
How far the gulf-stream of our youth may
    flow   251
Into the arctic regions of our lives,
Where little else than life itself survives.

As the barometer foretells the storm
While still the skies are clear, the weather
    warm,
So something in us, as old age draws near,
Betrays the pressure of the atmosphere.
The nimble mercury, ere we are aware,
Descends the elastic ladder of the air;
The telltale blood in artery and vein   260
Sinks from its higher levels in the brain;
Whatever poet, orator, or sage
May say of it, old age is still old age.
It is the waning, not the crescent moon;
The dusk of evening, not the blaze of noon;
It is not strength, but weakness; not desire,
But its surcease; not the fierce heat of fire,
The burning and consuming element,

But that of ashes and of embers spent,   269
In which some living sparks we still discern,
Enough to warm, but not enough to burn.

What then? Shall we sit idly down and say
The night hath come; it is no longer day?
The night hath not yet come; we are not quite
Cut off from labor by the failing light;
Something remains for us to do or dare;
Even the oldest tree some fruit may bear;
Not Œdipus Coloneus, or Greek Ode,
Or tales of pilgrims that one morning rode
Out of the gateway of the Tabard Inn,   280
But other something, would we but begin;
For age is opportunity no less
Than youth itself, though in another dress,
And as the evening twilight fades away
The sky is filled with stars, invisible by day.
1874   *1875*

VICTOR AND VANQUISHED

As one who long hath fled with panting breath
    Before his foe, bleeding and near to fall,
    I turn and set my back against the wall,
    And look thee in the face, triumphant
        Death.
I call for aid, and no one answereth;
    I am alone with thee, who conquerest all;
    Yet me thy threatening form doth not ap-
        pall,
    For thou art but a phantom and a wraith.
Wounded and weak, sword broken at the
        hilt,
    With armor shattered, and without a
        shield,   10
    I stand unmoved; do with me what thou
        wilt;
I can resist no more, but will not yield.
    This is no tournament where cowards tilt;
    The vanquished here is victor of the field.
                                            1876

NATURE

As a fond mother, when the day is o'er,
    Leads by the hand her little child to bed,
    Half willing, half reluctant to be led,
    And leave his broken playthings on the
        floor,
Still gazing at them through the open door,

Nor wholly reassured and comforted
By promises of others in their stead,
Which, though more splendid, may not
   please him more;
So Nature deals with us, and takes away
Our playthings one by one, and by the
   hand   10
Leads us to rest so gently, that we go
Scarce knowing if we wish to go or stay,
Being too full of sleep to understand
How far the unknown transcends the what
   we know.   1877

THE CROSS OF SNOW

In the long, sleepless watches of the night,
   A gentle face—the face of one long dead—
Looks at me from the wall, where round
   its head
The night-lamp casts a halo of pale light.
Here in this room she died; and soul more
   white
Never through martyrdom of fire was led
To its repose; nor can in books be read
The legend of a life more benedight.
There is a mountain in the distant West,[1]
   That, sun-defying, in its steep ravines 10
Displays a cross of snow upon its side.
Such is the cross I wear upon my breast

[1] probably the Mount of the Holy Cross in the Rocky Mountains near Red Cliff, Eagle County, Colorado

These eighteen years, through all the changing scenes
And seasons, changeless since the day she
   died.[1]

1879   1886

JUGURTHA

Composed in 1879; published in the *Ultima Thule* volume, 1880. The poet's source was Plutarch's life of Marius. Jugurtha, a captive king of Numidia, after a triumphal procession, was thrown into a Roman prison and died there of starvation, B.C. 104. Longfellow changed Hercules, addressed in Plutarch's story, to Apollo, as more suitable.

How cold are thy baths, Apollo!
   Cried the African monarch, the splendid,
As down to his death in the hollow
   Dark dungeons of Rome he descended,
   Uncrowned, unthroned, unattended;
How cold are thy baths, Apollo!

How cold are thy baths, Apollo!
   Cried the Poet, unknown, unbefriended,
As the vision that lured him to follow
   With the mist and the darkness blended, 10
   And the dream of his life was ended;
How cold are thy baths, Apollo!

              1880

[1] reference to the tragic death of the second Mrs. Longfellow in 1861

1809 ~ *Oliver Wendell Holmes* ~ 1894

HOLMES was, even more unmistakably than Longfellow or Bryant or Hawthorne, the son and laureate of New England, and his and Lowell's were the last of its noted literary names. He was conscious of his distinguished ancestry and his connection with families prominent in colonial and Revolutionary days. He was a lineal descendant of Anne Bradstreet, the Phillips family, the Wendells, an old Dutch family, the Quincys, and the Hancocks, one of whom married Dorothy Quincy, the daughter of "Dorothy Q." Wendell Phillips was his cousin. His grandfather, David Holmes, of Connecticut Puritan stock, supposed to be the original of the deacon who built the "one-hoss shay," served in the Revolutionary army. His father, the Reverend Abiel Holmes, a Yale graduate, had a good library and was a writer of both verse and prose. A man of the strict Edwardian Calvinistic faith, pastor for forty years of the first church, Cambridge, he brought up his son in a religious, bookish atmosphere.

Holmes had a happy, successful life, without handicaps or tragedies. He was born in Cambridge, August 29, 1809, in the "house with the gambrel roof" near the old Harvard gymnasium, the house in which the Bunker Hill fight was planned. He was fond of remarking that Lincoln, Gladstone, Darwin, Tennyson, Poe, Chopin, and Mendelssohn were born in the same year. After youthful schooling at Cambridge he attended for one year the orthodox Phillips Academy at Andover, where he made a translation in heroic couplets of the first book of Virgil's *Æneid*. He described himself as a boy who liked to think and read, though he did not often read a book through. Among his early friends were Richard H. Dana and Margaret Fuller.

At the age of sixteen Holmes entered Harvard, and four years later was graduated with the famous class of 1829, for the anniversary of which he wrote many poems, the last in 1888. Besides his own classmates who later became illustrious, James Freeman Clark, writer and clergyman, and Samuel F. Smith, author of "America," he knew in college Charles Sumner of the class of 1830 and J. L. Motley of the class of 1831. At Harvard he came under Unitarian influence and belonged to a rather gay dramatic club, the Hasty Pudding. He made a good record, and like Emerson and Lowell was class poet. He remained a skipping reader, trying many books but rarely going through them as wholes. He showed his tendency toward literary expression by his connection with a college periodical and by the conscious literary form of his early letters. He liked especially the English classics, Pope's Homer, and the Encyclopaedia, then a comparative novelty.

After graduation he spent a year in the Law School but, disliking law, gave it up to study medicine. It was while he was studying law, in 1830, that he wrote "Old Ironsides," as well as some twenty other poems, humorous and sentimental, for the *Harvard Collegian*. After studying medicine in a private school in Boston, he went abroad in April, 1833, and studied for a year in Paris, traveling a little also in England, Germany, and Italy. Holmes's stay in Paris is thought to have increased the natural vivacity of his disposition and to have enhanced his "sparkle."

The next year he began the practice of medicine in Boston and published some creditable medical essays and presented discoveries of some importance. He was not of imposing presence, did not have the professional look or manner, and seemed too literary, or perhaps too given to levity, to acquire a large practice. Appointed professor of anatomy and physiology at Dartmouth College, he did not remain there but soon returned to Boston. In 1840 he married Amelia Lee Jackson.

He became Parkman Professor of anatomy and physiology in the medical school of Harvard in 1847, a post that he held for thirty-five years, delivering four lectures a week. He could enliven any subject he treated and even had a successful course at five in the afternoon. A considerable part of his time was devoted to lecturing about the country, for which he was in demand. Holmes achieved his literary reputation late, his place as a writer being established after 1857. In that year he began a series in the *Atlantic Monthly* through the influence of Lowell, who assumed the editorship on the condition that Holmes contribute. *The Autocrat of the Breakfast-Table* appeared in 1857–58 in that periodical, and *The Professor at the Breakfast-Table* in 1859–60. *The Poet at the Breakfast-Table* came next, in 1872, and *Over the Teacups* in 1891, when the poet was over eighty. Many of his best poems appeared in these series. His series of class poems, more than forty, were written from 1851 onward. At the age of seventy-seven he visited England and Europe, and honorary degrees were conferred on him by Oxford, Cambridge, and Edinburgh. He remained at Harvard as professor and professor emeritus for forty-seven years.

Holmes's three novels are concerned with problems of moral responsibility, especially with accountability for crime. They deal with inherited tendencies. *Elsie Venner* was published in 1861, *The Guardian Angel* in 1867, and *A Mortal Antipathy* in 1885. His friends called these books "medicated novels," and Holmes conceded the justness of the epithet. They impress their readers as thought out by a physician and written by an essayist. They lack close-knit structure and often plausibility. Holmes also wrote two biographies, a life of Motley in 1879 and a life of Emerson in 1885. As his life went on, his time went more and more to literary pursuits and less to medicine. He died October 7, 1894.

Holmes's ideas concerning prosody may be found in his essay, "The Physiology of Versification," in *Pages from an Old Volume of Life* (1892). He finds a physiological connection between the laws of versification and the respiration and the pulse. Holmes believed the octosyllabic couplet singularly easy to read aloud because "it follows more exactly than any other measure the natural rhythm of expiration." His views of poetry may be found here and there in his verse ("The Voiceless," "At the Saturday Club," "Poetry: a Metrical Essay," and pieces concerning various poets) and in stray passages from the volumes of the *Breakfast-Table* series. He believed in the association of sentiment and humor in a poem, and insisted on the distinction between scientific truth and imaginative truth, the latter the province of the poet. He dealt with his own thoughts and emotions, but felt that the true poet should try to penetrate through his subjectivity to "the bedrock of human nature which he has." H. H. Clark writes of him (*Major American Poets*, p. 892): "As a scientist and religious thinker, Holmes was radically hostile toward European traditionalisms and radiantly optimistic about the possibilities of the New World and of Boston. . . . As a literary theorist, however, he held that, 'aesthetically speaking, America is after all a penal colony,' that our writers can profit not only by our 'couple of centuries of half-starved civilization' but also by the rich literary tradition of Europe extending back to the ancients such as his favorite Horace, a tradition that he likened to 'a still lakelet, a mountain tarn, fed by springs that never fail.' Ultimately, then, although Holmes's literary theory is touched by some of the current romantic doctrines, it has an interesting kinship with that of such neoclassicists as Pope and the Augustans, of whose urbanity and cheer Holmes is our most eminent spokesman.'"

Holmes was almost as versatile as Lowell. He was a man of science, physician, poet, professor, essayist, and novelist, had many social interests, and was personally very popular. He experimented with the microscope before this was held necessary in the study of anatomy, and he liked amateur photography. He was hardly a genuine investigator, yet he invented several useful instruments. Theology was another of his especial interests. His favorite subject was moral responsibility for sin, in the light of determining influences of environment and heredity. In all but religion he was a conservative. Here he was a militant Unitarian, in reaction from the strictness of his father. Boston he thought of as the home of free thought and speech and the intellectual center of the America of his day, and he had the highest confidence in his own caste, the "Brahmins." He expected Boston to retain its dominating position in the future.

Holmes's best prose appears in the *Breakfast-Table* series. He wrote light prose with facility and finish and made his papers both entertaining and instructive. The advantage of the method he employed, that of the monologist, enabled him to treat topics briefly and informally and from the point of view of both the literary man and the scientist. Gifted in delivery, bubbling with vivacity, and accounted the chief wit of Boston, he preserved in his series the talk of his city's stellar conversationalist. He treats a variety of subjects whimsically and discursively, and his topics have been little touched by time. If he left followers, they are the newspaper columnists of today, writing verse and prose for daily entertainment.

Much of his verse was made to order for occasions; for his muse was very facile and it was available for inaugurations, commemorative services, dedications of public buildings, anniversary meetings, dinners, the arrivals and departures of celebrities, birthdays, elegies, and tributes. His favorite forms are the couplet and the quatrain. Unlike other poets of his time, he did not write of the Old World or the past or of nature or contemporary public topics. He was less an admirer of the romantic themes that attracted Longfellow and Lowell than he was of eighteenth-century wit and satire. His was chiefly rationalistic verse coming from observation and experience: serious lyrical poems, seriocomic and comic poems, narrative poems, and occasional poems. Those that began gravely might end in jest, and those that began in jest might end in pathos. Holmes's speeches or recitals are said to have been almost a dramatic entertainment in which his whole personality expressed and interpreted what he presented. Read, instead of heard as he delivered them, his verses seem thinner and less vital; but many of them have lasting popular appeal and he has won himself a secure niche in American literature.

The standard collected edition of Holmes's works is the Riverside (13 vols., 1891–1892). The addition of J. T. Morse's *Life and Letters* increased it to 15 vols. in 1896. Horace E. Scudder edited Holmes's *Complete Poetical Works*, Cambridge Edition (1895).

Biographies are J. T. Morse, Jr., *Life and Letters of Oliver Wendell Holmes* (1896), and L. W. Townsend, *Oliver Wendell Holmes* (1907). Among articles may be mentioned E. E. Hale's "Some Personal Recollections of Oliver Wendell Holmes," in the *Arena*, XV (Dec., 1895), and J. T. Trowbridge's "Recollections," in the *Atlantic*, XCI (May, 1903). M. A. De Wolfe Howe wrote of Holmes in the *DAB*, IX (1932).

For critical discussion see E. C. Stedman, in *Poets of America* (1885); Edmund Gosse, "An English View of the Autocrat," in *Critic*, XXII (Dec. 1, 1894); G. W. Curtis, in *Literary and Social Essays* (1895); Sir Leslie Stephen," The Life and Works of Holmes," in *Studies of a Biographer*, II (1898); W. D. Howells, in *Harper's Magazine*, XCIV (Dec., 1896); Samuel M. Crothers, "The Autocrat and His Fellow Boarders," in *Atlantic*, CIV (August, 1909); John Macy, in *The Spirit of American Literature* (1913); A. H. Strong, in *American Poets and Their Theology* (1916); E. J. Bailey, in *Religious Thought in the Greater American Poets* (1922); Brander Matthews, in *CHAL*, II (1918); C. H. Grattan, in *American Mercury*, IV (Jan., 1925); V. L. Parrington, in *Main Currents in American Thought*, II (1927); Alfred Kreymborg, in *Our Singing Strength* (1929); H. S. Canby, *Classic Americans* (1931); R. Brenner, in *Twelve American Poets before 1900* (1933); H. H. Clark, "Dr. Holmes: a Reinterpretation," in *New England Quarterly*, XII (March, 1939); and S. I. Hayakawa and H. M. Jones, *Holmes*, in the American Writers Series (1939).

George B. Ives published *A Bibliography of Oliver Wendell Holmes* (1907), listing his contributions to periodicals.

OLD IRONSIDES

When the secretary of the navy proposed, in September, 1830, that the naval ship *Constitution*, popularly called *Old Ironsides*, which had done remarkable historic service, be broken up and sold, Holmes, then a student in law school, wrote this impromptu outburst. Feeling was aroused, and the ship was saved. As late as 1931, rebuilt by the pennies of schoolchildren, the old ship (it was begun in 1794 and launched in 1797) revisited many American ports.

Aye, tear her tattered ensign down!
  Long has it waved on high,
And many an eye has danced to see
  That banner in the sky;
Beneath it rung the battle shout,
  And burst the cannon's roar;—
The meteor of the ocean air
  Shall sweep the clouds no more!

Her deck, once red with heroes' blood,
  Where knelt the vanquished foe,   10
When winds were hurrying o'er the flood
  And waves were white below,
No more shall feel the victor's tread,
  Or know the conquered knee;—
The harpies of the shore shall pluck
  The eagle of the sea!

O better that her shattered hulk
  Should sink beneath the wave;
Her thunders shook the mighty deep,
  And there should be her grave;   20
Nail to the mast her holy flag,
  Set every threadbare sail,
And give her to the god of storms,—
  The lightning and the gale!

                                    1830

THE LAST LEAF

The old man of this poem was Major Thomas Melville, called the "last of the cocked hats," who was a participant in the "Boston Tea Party." He was the grandfather of Herman Melville. In old age he still wore the colonial costume described in the poem, and was a well-known figure about the streets of Boston. President Lincoln greatly liked this poem, especially the fourth stanza.

I SAW him once before,
As he passed by the door,
   And again
The pavement stones resound
As he totters o'er the ground
   With his cane.

They say that in his prime
Ere the pruning-knife of Time
   Cut him down,
Not a better man was found   10
By the Crier on his round
   Through the town.

But now he walks the streets,
And looks at all he meets
   Sad and wan,
And he shakes his feeble head,
That it seems as if he said,
   "They are gone."

The mossy marbles rest
On the lips that he has prest   20
   In their bloom,
And the names he loved to hear
Have been carved for many a year
   On the tomb.

My grandmamma has said,—
Poor old lady, she is dead
   Long ago,—
That he had a Roman nose,
And his cheek was like a rose
   In the snow;   30

But now his nose is thin,
And it rests upon his chin
   Like a staff,
And a crook is in his back,
And a melancholy crack
   In his laugh.

I know it is a sin
For me to sit and grin
   At him here;
But the old three-cornered hat,   40
And the breeches, and all that,
   Are so queer!

And if I should live to be
The last leaf upon the tree
   In the spring,
Let them smile, as I do now,
At the old forsaken bough
   Where I cling.

                        1831

MY AUNT

First printed in the *New England Magazine*, October, 1831. Light is thrown in this poem on the educational methods, fortunately now long outdated, in the girls' "finishing schools" of Holmes's day.

My aunt! my dear unmarried aunt!
   Long years have o'er her flown,
Yet still she strains the aching clasp
   That binds her virgin zone;
I know it hurts her, though she looks
   As cheerful as she can;
Her waist is ampler than her life,
   For life is but a span.

My aunt! my poor deluded aunt!
   Her hair is almost gray;   10
Why will she train that winter curl
   In such a spring-like way?
How can she lay her glasses down
   And say she reads as well,
When through a double convex lens
   She just makes out to spell?

Her father—grandpapa! forgive
   This erring lip its smiles—
Vowed she should make the finest girl
   Within a hundred miles;   20
He sent her to a stylish school—
   'Twas in her thirteenth June—
And with her, as the rules required,
   "Two towels and a spoon."

They braced my aunt against a board,
   To make her straight and tall;
They laced her up, they starved her down,
   To make her light and small;

They pinched her feet, they singed her hair,
  They screwed it up with pins;—   30
Oh, never mortal suffered more
  In penance for her sins.

So when my precious aunt was done,
  My grandsire brought her back
(By daylight, lest some rabid youth
  Might follow on the track).
"Ah!" said my grandsire as he shook
  Some powder in his pan,
"What could this lovely creature do
  Against a desperate man?"   40

Alas! nor chariot, nor barouche,
  Nor bandit cavalcade,
Tore from the trembling father's arms
  His all-accomplished maid.
For her how happy had it been!
  And Heaven had spared to me
To see one sad, ungathered rose
  On my ancestral tree.

               1831

ON LENDING A PUNCH-BOWL

"This 'punch-bowl' was, according to old
family tradition, a *caudle-cup*. It is a massive
piece of silver, its cherubs and other ornaments
of coarse repoussé work, and has two handles like
a loving-cup, by which it was held, or passed
from guest to guest." [*Holmes's note.*]

THIS ancient silver bowl of mine, it tells of
  good old times,
Of joyous days, and jolly nights, and merry
  Christmas chimes;
They were a free and jovial race, but honest,
  brave, and true,
That dipped their ladle in the punch when this
  old bowl was new.

A Spanish galleon brought the bar,—so runs
  the ancient tale;
'Twas hammered by an Antwerp smith, whose
  arm was like a flail;
And now and then between the strokes, for
  fear his strength should fail,
He wiped his brow, and quaffed a cup of good
  old Flemish ale.

'Twas purchased by an English squire to
  please his loving dame,
Who saw the cherubs, and conceived a longing
  for the same;   10

And oft as on the ancient stock another twig
  was found,
'Twas filled with caudle spiced and hot, and
  handed smoking round.

But, changing hands, it reached at length a
  Puritan divine,
Who used to follow Timothy, and take a
  little wine,
But hated punch and prelacy; and so it was,
  perhaps,
He went to Leyden, where he found con-
  venticles and schnapps.

And then, of course, you know what's next,
  —it left the Dutchman's shore
With those that in the *Mayflower* came,—a
  hundred souls and more,—
Along with all the furniture, to fill their new
  abodes,—
To judge by what is still on hand, at least a
  hundred loads.   20

'Twas on a dreary winter's eve, the night was
  closing dim,
When brave Miles Standish took the bowl,
  and filled it to the brim;
The little Captain stood and stirred the posset
  with his sword,
And all his sturdy men-at-arms were ranged
  about the board.

He poured the fiery Hollands in,—the man
  that never feared,—
He took a long and solemn draught, and wiped
  his yellow beard;
And one by one the musketeers—the men
  that fought and prayed—
All drank as 'twere their mother's milk, and
  not a man afraid.

That night, affrighted from his nest, the
  screaming eagle flew,
He heard the Pequot's ringing whoop, the
  soldier's wild halloo;   30
And there the sachem learned the rule he
  taught to kith and kin,
"Run from the white man when you find he
  smells of Hollands gin!"

A hundred years, and fifty more, had spread
  their leaves and snows,
A thousand rubs had flattened down each
  little cherub's nose;

When once again the bowl was filled, but not
    in mirth or joy,—
'Twas mingled by a mother's hand to cheer
    her parting boy.

"Drink, John," she said, " 'twill do you good,
    —poor child, you'll never bear
This working in the dismal trench, out in the
    midnight air;
And if—God bless me!—you were hurt,
    'twould keep away the chill";
So John *did* drink,—and well he wrought
    that night at Bunker's Hill!   40

I tell you, there was generous warmth in good
    old English cheer;
I tell you, 'twas a pleasant thought to bring
    its symbol here.
'Tis but the fool that loves excess; hast thou a
    drunken soul?
Thy bane is in thy shallow skull, not in my
    silver bowl!

I love the memory of the past,—its pressed
    yet fragrant flowers,—
The moss that clothes its broken walls,—the
    ivy on its towers;—
Nay, this poor bauble it bequeathed,—my
    eyes grow moist and dim,
To think of all the vanished joys that danced
    around its brim.

Then fill a fair and honest cup, and bear it
    straight to me;
The goblet hallows all it holds, whate'er the
    liquid be;   50
And may the cherubs on its face protect me
    from the sin,
That dooms one to those dreadful words,—
"My dear, where *have* you been?"

1848   1849

THE DEACON'S MASTERPIECE;

OR, THE WONDERFUL "ONE-HOSS SHAY."

A LOGICAL STORY

From *The Autocrat of the Breakfast-Table*, No.
XI, printed in the *Atlantic Monthly*, September,
1858. Professor Barrett Wendell interpreted the
poem as a satirical allegory of Calvinism and its
breakdown, an explanation that would be much
clearer to hearers when Holmes recited it than
to readers now. All that logic could compass went

into the making of the "wonderful one-hoss shay";
yet finally, all of a sudden, it went to pieces.

Have you heard of the wonderful one-hoss
    shay,
That was built in such a logical way
It ran a hundred years to a day,
And then, of a sudden, it—ah, but stay,
I'll tell you what happened without delay,
Scaring the parson into fits,
Frightening people out of their wits,—
Have you ever heard of that, I say?

Seventeen hundred and fifty-five.
Georgius Secundus was then alive,—   10
Snuffy old drone from the German hive!
That was the year when Lisbon-town
Saw the earth open and gulp her down,
And Braddock's army was done so brown,
Left without a scalp to its crown.
It was on the terrible Earthquake-day
That the Deacon finished the one-hoss shay.

Now in building of chaises, I tell you what,
There is always *somewhere* a weakest spot,—
In hub, tire, felloe, in spring or thill,   20
In panel, or crossbar, or floor, or sill,
In screw, bolt, thoroughbrace,—lurking still,
Find it somewhere you must and will,—
Above or below, or within or without,—
And that's the reason, beyond a doubt,
That a chaise *breaks down*, but doesn't *wear
    out*.

But the Deacon swore (as Deacons do,
With an "I dew vum," or an "I tell *yeou*")
He would build one shay to beat the taown
'N' the keounty 'n' all the kentry raoun';   30
It should be so built that it *couldn'* break
    daown:
—"Fur," said the Deacon, "'t's mighty plain
Thut the weakes' place mus' stan' the strain;
'N' the way t' fix it, uz I maintain,
    Is only jest
T' make that place uz strong uz the rest."

So the Deacon inquired of the village folk
Where he could find the strongest oak,
That couldn't be split nor bent nor broke,—
That was for spokes and floor and sills;   40
He sent for lancewood to make the thills;
The crossbars were ash, from the straightest
    trees;

The panels of white-wood, that cuts like
    cheese,
But lasts like iron for things like these;
The hubs of logs from the "Settler's ellum,"—
Last of its timber,—they couldn't sell 'em,
Never an axe had seen their chips,
And the wedges flew from between their lips,
Their blunt ends frizzled like celery-tips;
Step and prop-iron, bolt and screw,   50
Spring, tire, axle, and linchpin too,
Steel of the finest, bright and blue;
Thoroughbrace bison-skin, thick and wide;
Boot, top, dasher, from tough old hide
Found in the pit when the tanner died.
That was the way he "put her through."
"There!" said the Deacon, "naow she'll dew!"

Do! I tell you, I rather guess
She was a wonder, and nothing less!
Colts grew horses, beards turned gray,   60
Deacon and deaconess dropped away,
Children and grandchildren—where were
    they?
But there stood the stout old one-hoss shay
As fresh as on Lisbon-earthquake-day!

EIGHTEEN HUNDRED;—it came and found
The Deacon's masterpiece strong and sound.
Eighteen hundred increased by ten;—
"Hahnsum kerridge" they called it then.
Eighteen hundred and twenty came;—
Running as usual; much the same.   70
Thirty and forty at last arrive,
And then come fifty, and FIFTY-FIVE.

Little of all we value here
Wakes on the morn of its hundredth year
Without both feeling and looking queer.
In fact, there's nothing that keeps its youth,
So far as I know, but a tree and truth.
(This is a moral that runs at large;
Take it.—You're welcome.—No extra charge.)

FIRST OF NOVEMBER,—the Earthquake-day.—
There are traces of age in the one-hoss shay,
A general flavor of mild decay,   82
But nothing local, as one may say.
There couldn't be,—for the Deacon's art
Had made it so like in every part
That there wasn't a chance for one to start.
For the wheels were just as strong as the thills,
And the floor was just as strong as the sills,

And the panels just as strong as the floor,
And the whippletree neither less nor more,   90
And the back crossbar as strong as the fore,
And spring and axle and hub *encore*.
And yet, *as a whole*, it is past a doubt
In another hour it will be *worn out!*

First of November, 'Fifty-five!
This morning the parson takes a drive.
Now, small boys, get out of the way!
Here comes the wonderful one-hoss shay,
Drawn by a rat-tailed, ewe-necked bay.
"Huddup!" said the parson.—Off went
    they.   100
The parson was working his Sunday's text,—
Had got to *fifthly*, and stopped perplexed
At what the—Moses—was coming next.
All at once the horse stood still,
Close by the meet'n'-house on the hill.
—First a shiver, and then a thrill,
Then something decidedly like a spill,—
And the parson was sitting upon a rock,
At half-past nine by the meet'n'-house
    clock,—
Just the hour of the Earthquake shock!   110
—What do you think the parson found,
When he got up and stared around?
The poor old chaise in a heap or mound,
As if it had been to the mill and ground!
You see, of course, if you're not a dunce,
How it went to pieces all at once,—
All at once and nothing first,—
Just as bubbles do when they burst.

End of the wonderful one-hoss shay.
Logic is logic. That's all I say.   120

                                   1858

THE VOICELESS

In an introductory paragraph to this poem
in the *Autocrat*, Holmes said, "Read what the
singing-women—one to ten thousand of the suffering women—tell us, and think of the griefs
that die unspoken! Nature is in earnest when she
makes a woman; and there are women enough
lying in the next churchyard with very commonplace blue slate-stones at their head and feet, for
whom it was just as true that 'all sounds of life
assumed one tone of love,' as for Letitia Landon,
of whom Elizabeth Browning said it; but she
could give words to her grief, and they could
not."

WE count the broken lyres that rest
  Where the sweet wailing singers slumber,
But o'er their silent sister's breast
  The wild flowers who will stoop to number?
A few can touch the magic string,
  And noisy Fame is proud to win them:—
Alas for those that never sing,
  But die with all their music in them!

Nay, grieve not for the dead alone
  Whose song has told their hearts' sad
    story,—   10
Weep for the voiceless, who have known
  The cross without the crown of glory!
Not where Leucadian breezes [1] sweep
  O'er Sappho's memory-haunted billow,
But where the glistening night-dews weep
  On nameless sorrow's churchyard pillow.

O hearts that break and give no sign
  Save whitening lip and fading tresses,
Till Death pours out his longed-for wine
  Slow-dropped from Misery's crushing
    presses,—   20
If singing breath or echoing chord
  To every hidden pang were given,
What endless melodies were poured,
  As sad as earth, as sweet as heaven!

1858

THE BOYS

Read by Holmes at the thirtieth reunion of
the class of 1829 of Harvard, held January 6,
1859. Published as part of *The Professor at the
Breakfast-Table* in the *Atlantic Monthly*, February, 1859. Some of the classmates alluded to were
George T. Davis (the member of Congress),
James Freeman Clarke (the "Reverend"), B. R.
Curtis (the "Judge"), George T. Bigelow (the
"Justice"), Benjamin Peirce (the Harvard mathematician), the Reverend S. F. Smith (the author
of "America"), and the Reverend Samuel May
(the abolitionist). For a complete roll call of this
distinguished class at Harvard, see the Cambridge edition of Holmes's poems, p. 340.

HAS there any old fellow got mixed with the
    boys?
If there has, take him out, without making a
    noise.

[1] According to legend, the Greek poet Sappho
(about B.C. 600) threw herself into the sea from a cliff
in Leucadia, one of the Ionian Islands.

Hang the Almanac's cheat and the Catalogue's
    spite!
Old Time is a liar! We're twenty tonight!

We're twenty! We're twenty! Who says we are
    more?
He's tipsy,—young jackanapes!—show him
    the door!
"Gray temples at twenty?"—Yes! *white* if we
    please;
Where the snowflakes fall thickest there's
    nothing can freeze!

Was it snowing I spoke of? Excuse the mis-
    take!
Look close,—you will see not a sign of a
    flake;   10
We want some new garlands for those we
    have shed,—
And these are white roses in place of the red!

We've a trick, we young fellows, you may
    have been told,
Of talking (in public) as if we were old:—
That boy we call "Doctor," and this we call
    "Judge";
It's a neat little fiction,—of course it's all
    fudge.

That fellow's the "Speaker,"—the one on the
    right;
"Mr. Mayor," my young one, how are you
    tonight?
That's our "Member of Congress," we say
    when we chaff;
There's the "Reverend" What's his name?
    —don't make me laugh.   20

That boy with the grave mathematical look
Made believe he had written a wonderful book,
And the ROYAL SOCIETY thought it was *true!*
So they chose him right in; a good joke it was,
    too!

There's a boy, we pretend, with a three-
    decker brain,
That could harness a team with a logical chain;
When he spoke for our manhood in syllabled
    fire,
We called him "The Justice," but now he's
    "The Squire."

And there's a nice youngster of excellent
    pith,—
Fate tried to conceal him by naming him
    Smith;   30
But he shouted a song for the brave and the
    free,—
Just read on his medal, "My country," "of
    thee!"

You hear that boy laughing?—You think he's
    all fun;
But the angels laugh, too, at the good he has
    done;
The children laugh loud as they troop to his
    call,
And the poor man that knows him laughs
    loudest of all!

Yes, we're boys,—always playing with tongue
    or with pen,—
And I sometimes have asked,—Shall we ever
    be men?
Shall we always be youthful and laughing and
    gay,
Till the last dear companion drops smiling
    away?   40

Then here's to our boyhood, its gold and its
    gray!
The stars of its winter, the dews of its May!
And when we have done with our life-lasting
    toys,
Dear Father, take care of thy children, THE
    Boys!

                                               1859

BROTHER JONATHAN'S LAMENT
FOR SISTER CAROLINE

Occasioned by the secession of South Carolina,
December 20, 1860. Compare Lowell's "Jonathan
to John" in the *Biglow Papers*. Holmes dated his
poem March 25, 1861; it was written shortly before the bombardment of Fort Sumter.

SHE has gone,—she has left us in passion and
    pride.—
Our stormy-browed sister, so long at our side!
She has torn her own star from our firma-
    ment's glow,
And turned on her brother the face of a foe!

Oh, Caroline, Caroline, child of the sun,
We can never forget that our hearts have been
    one,—
Our foreheads both sprinkled in Liberty's
    name,
From the fountain of blood with the finger of
    flame!

You were always too ready to fire at a
    touch;
But we said, "She is hasty,—she does not
    mean much."   10
We have scowled, when you uttered some
    turbulent threat;
But Friendship still whispered, "Forgive and
    forget!"

Has our love all died out? Have its altars
    grown cold?
Has the curse come at last which the fathers
    foretold?
Then Nature must teach us the strength of the
    chain
That her petulant children would sever in
    vain.

They may fight till the buzzards are gorged
    with their spoil,
Till the harvest grows black as it rots in the
    soil,
Till the wolves and the catamounts troop
    from their caves,
And the shark tracks the pirate, the lord of the
    waves: 20

In vain is the strife! When its fury is past,
Their fortunes must flow in one channel at
    last,
As the torrents that rush from the mountains
    of snow
Roll mingled in peace through the valleys
    below.

Our Union is river, lake, ocean, and sky:
Man breaks not the medal, when God cuts the
    die!
Though darkened with sulphur, though cloven
    with steel,
The blue arch will brighten, the waters will
    heal!

Oh, Caroline, Caroline, child of the sun,
There are battles with Fate that can never be
　　won! 30
The star-flowering banner must never be
　　furled,
For its blossoms of light are the hope of the
　　world!

Go, then, our rash sister! afar and aloof,
Run wild in the sunshine away from our roof;
But when your heart aches and your feet have
　　grown sore,
Remember the pathway that leads to our door!
　　1861

DOROTHY Q.

A FAMILY PORTRAIT

　　Holmes's great-grandmother was a niece of
Josiah Quincy, Jr., father of the statesman, orator,
and historian, Josiah Quincy of the post-Revo-
lutionary period. Holmes is concerned in this
poem with the question, "What should I have
been if one of my great-grandmothers had married another man?"

GRANDMOTHER's mother: her age, I guess,
Thirteen summers, or something less;
Girlish bust, but womanly air;
Smooth, square forehead with uprolled hair;
Lips that lover has never kissed;
Taper fingers and slender wrist;
Hanging sleeves of stiff brocade;
So they painted the little maid.

On her hand a parrot green
Sits unmoving and broods serene. 10
Hold up the canvas full in view,—
Look! there's a rent the light shines through,
Dark with a century's fringe of dust,—
That was a Red-Coat's rapier-thrust!
Such is the tale the lady old,
Dorothy's daughter's daughter, told.

Who the painter was none may tell,—
One whose best was not over well;
Hard and dry, it must be confessed,
Flat as a rose that has long been pressed; 20
Yet in her cheek the hues are bright,
Dainty colors of red and white,
And in her slender shape are seen
Hint and promise of stately mien.

Look not on her with eyes of scorn,—
Dorothy Q. was a lady born!
Ay! since the galloping Normans came,
England's annals have known her name;
And still to the three-hilled rebel town
Dear is that ancient name's renown, 30
For many a civic wreath they won,
The youthful sire and the gray-haired son.

O Damsel Dorothy! Dorothy Q.!
Strange is the gift that I owe to you;
Such a gift as never a king
Save to daughter or son might bring,—
All my tenure of heart and hand,
All my title to house and land;
Mother and sister and child and wife
And joy and sorrow and death and life! 40

What if a hundred years ago
Those close-shut lips had answered No,
When forth the tremulous question came
That cost the maiden her Norman name,
And under the folds that look so still
The bodice swelled with the bosom's thrill?
Should I be I, or would it be
One tenth another, to nine tenths me?

Soft is the breath of a maiden's YES:
Not the light gossamer stirs with less; 50
But never a cable that holds so fast
Through all the battles of wave and blast,
And never an echo of speech or song
That lives in the babbling air so long!
There were tones in the voice that whispered
　　then
You may hear today in a hundred men.

O lady and lover, how faint and far
Your images hover,—and here we are,
Solid and stirring in flesh and bone,—
Edward's and Dorothy's—all their own,— 60
A goodly record for Time to show
Of a syllable spoken so long ago!—
Shall I bless you, Dorothy, or forgive
For the tender whisper that bade me live?

It shall be a blessing, my little maid!
I will heal the stab of the Red-Coat's blade,
And freshen the gold of the tarnished frame,
And gild with a rhyme your household name
So you shall smile on us brave and bright
As first you greeted the morning's light, 70

And live untroubled by woes and fears
Through a second youth of a hundred years.

1871   1871

AT THE SATURDAY CLUB

The Saturday Club came to life in the late
1850's. Its members dined together once a month
at the Parker House. Holmes was deeply attached to it and attended it regularly. He wrote
of it: "The Saturday Club was founded, or rather
found itself in existence without any organization, almost without parentage. It was natural
enough that such men as Emerson, Longfellow,
Agassiz, Peirce, with Hawthorne, Motley, Sumner
when within reach, and others who would be good
company for them, should meet and dine together
once in a while, as they did, in point of fact. . . .
The club deserves being remembered for having
no constitution, or by-laws, for making no
speeches, reading no papers, observing no ceremonies, coming and going at will without remark,
and acting out, though it did not proclaim the
motto, 'Shall I not take mine ease in mine inn?'"

THIS is our place of meeting: opposite
That towered and pillared building: look at
    it;
King's Chapel in the Second George's day,
Rebellion stole its regal name away,—
Stone Chapel sounded better; but at last
The poisoned name of our provincial past
Had lost its ancient venom; then once more
Stone Chapel was King's Chapel as before.
(So let rechristened North Street, when it
    can,
Bring back the days of Marlborough and
    Queen Anne!)   10
  Next the old church your wandering eye
    will meet—
A granite pile that stares upon the street—
Our civic temple; slanderous tongues have
    said
Its shape was modelled from St. Botolph's
    head,
Lofty, but narrow; jealous passers-by
Say Boston always held her head too high.
  Turn halfway round, and let your look
    survey
The white façade that gleams across the way,—
The many-windowed building, tall and wide,
The palace-inn that shows its northern
    side   20

In grateful shadow when the sunbeams beat
The granite wall in summer's scorching heat.
This is the place; whether its name you spell
Tavern, or caravansera, or hotel.
Would I could steal its echoes! you should find
Such store of vanished pleasures brought to
    mind:
Such feasts! the laughs of many a jocund hour
That shook the mortar from King George's
    tower;
Such guests! What famous names its record
    boasts,
Whose owners wander in the mob of ghosts!
Such stories! Every beam and plank is filled 31
With juicy wit the joyous talkers spilled,
Ready to ooze, as once the mountain pine
The floors are laid with oozed its turpentine!

  A month had flitted since The Club had
    met;
The day came round; I found the table set,
The waiters lounging round the marble stairs,
Empty as yet the double row of chairs.
I was a full half hour before the rest,
Alone, the banquet-chamber's single guest. 40
So from the table's side a chair I took,
And having neither company nor book
To keep me waking, by degrees there crept
A torpor over me,—in short, I slept.
  Loosed from its chain, along the wreck-
    strown track
Of the dead years my soul goes travelling
    back;
My ghosts take on their robes of flesh; it seems
Dreaming is life; nay, life less life than dreams,
So real are the shapes that meet my eyes.
They bring no sense of wonder, no sur-
    prise,   50
No hint of other than an earth-born source;
All seems plain daylight, everything of course.
  How dim the colors are, how poor and faint
This palette of weak words with which I paint!
Here sit my friends; if I could fix them so
As to my eyes they seem, my page would glow
Like a queen's missal, warm as if the brush
Of Titian or Velasquez brought the flush
Of life into their features. *Ay de mi!* [1]
If syllables were pigments, you should see 60
Such breathing portraitures as never man
Found in the Pitti or the Vatican.

[1] Spanish for "Alas, poor me!"

Here sits our POET, Laureate, if you will.
Long has he worn the wreath, and wears it
  still.
Dead? Nay, not so; and yet they say his bust
Looks down on marbles covering royal dust,
Kings by the Grace of God, or Nature's grace;
Dead? No! Alive! I see him in his place,
Full-featured, with the bloom that heaven
  denies
Her children, pinched by cold New England
  skies,   70
Too often, while the nursery's happier few
Win from a summer cloud its roseate hue.
Kind, soft-voiced, gentle, in his eye there
  shines
The ray serene that filled Evangeline's.

Modest he seems, not shy; content to wait
Amid the noisy clamor of debate
The looked-for moment when a peaceful word
Smooths the rough ripples louder tongues
  have stirred.
In every tone I mark his tender grace
And all his poems hinted in his face;   80
What tranquil joy his friendly presence gives!
How could I think him dead? He lives! He
  lives!

There, at the table's further end I see
In his old place our Poet's *vis-à-vis*,
The great PROFESSOR, strong, broad-shoul-
  dered, square,
In life's rich noontide, joyous, debonair.
His social hour no leaden care alloys,
His laugh rings loud and mirthful as a boy's,—
That lusty laugh the Puritan forgot,—
What ear has heard it and remembers not? 90
How often, halting at some wide crevasse
Amid the windings of his Alpine pass,
High up the cliffs, the climbing mountaineer,
Listening the far-off avalanche to hear,
Silent, and leaning on his steel-shod staff,
Has heard that cheery voice, that ringing
  laugh,
From the rude cabin whose nomadic walls
Creep with the moving glacier as it crawls!
How does vast Nature lead her living train
In ordered sequence through that spacious
  brain,   100
As in the primal hour when Adam named
The new-born tribes that young creation
  claimed!—

How will her realm be darkened, losing thee,
Her darling, whom we call *our* AGASSIZ!

But who is he whose massive frame belies
The maiden shyness of his downcast eyes?
Who broods in silence till, by questions
  pressed,
Some answer struggles from his laboring
  breast?
An artist Nature meant to dwell apart,
Locked in his studio with a human heart, 110
Tracking its caverned passions to their lair,
And all its throbbing mysteries laying bare.
Count it no marvel that he broods alone
Over the heart he studies,—'tis his own;
So in his page, whatever shape it wear,
The Essex wizard's shadowed self is there,—
The great ROMANCER, hid beneath his veil
Like the stern preacher of his somber tale;
Virile in strength, yet bashful as a girl,
Prouder than Hester, sensitive as Pearl. 120

From his mild throng of worshippers re-
  leased,
Our Concord Delphi sends its chosen priest,
Prophet or poet, mystic, sage, or seer,
By every title always welcome here.
Why that ethereal spirit's frame describe?
You know the race-marks of the Brahmin
  tribe,—
The spare, slight form, the sloping shoulders'
  droop,
The calm, scholastic mien, the clerkly stoop,
The lines of thought the sharpened features
  wear,
Carved by the edge of keen New England
  air.   130
List! for he speaks! As when a king would
  choose
The jewels for his bride, he might refuse
This diamond for its flaw,—find that less
  bright
Than those, its fellows, and a pearl less white
Than fits her snowy neck, and yet at last,
The fairest gems are chosen, and made fast
In golden fetters; so, with light delays
He seeks the fittest word to fill his phrase;
Nor vain nor idle his fastidious quest, 139
His chosen word is sure to prove the best.
Where in the realm of thought, whose air is
  song,
Does he, the Buddha of the West, belong?

He seems a wingèd Franklin, sweetly wise,
Born to unlock the secrets of the skies;
And which the nobler calling,—if 'tis fair
Terrestrial with celestial to compare,—
To guide the storm-cloud's elemental flame,
Or walk the chambers whence the lightning
    came,
Amidst the sources of its subtile fire,
And steal their effluence for his lips and lyre?

If lost at times in vague aerial flights,   151
None treads with firmer footstep when he lights;
A soaring nature, ballasted with sense,
Wisdom without her wrinkles or pretence,
In every Bible he has faith to read,
And every altar helps to shape his creed.

Ask you what name this prisoned spirit
    bears
While with ourselves this fleeting breath it
    shares?
Till angels greet him with a sweeter one
In heaven, on earth we call him EMERSON.   160

I start; I wake; the vision is withdrawn;
Its figures fading like the stars at dawn;
Crossed from the roll of life their cherished
    names,
And memory's pictures fading in their frames;
Yet life is lovelier for these transient gleams
Of buried friendships; blest is he who dreams!

1884

From THE AUTOCRAT OF THE BREAKFAST-TABLE

EVERY MAN HIS OWN BOSWELL

The first number of the *Autocrat* series appeared in the *Atlantic Monthly*, November, 1857. Holmes had published two essays under this title in the *New England Magazine* in 1831 and 1832, and reverted to these as he opened his series. The "table talk" of the Autocrat, a monologue with the occasional effect of a dialogue, is supposed to take place in a Boston boardinghouse, where boarders representing a diversity of interests gather. This enables a miscellany of topics to be brought up for brief treatment, and any method of approach.

I

I WAS just going to say, when I was interrupted, that one of the many ways of classifying minds is under the heads of arithmetical and algebraical intellects. All economical and practical wisdom is an extension or variation of the following arithmetical formula: $2 + 2 = 4$. Every philosophical proposition has the more general character of the expression $a + b = c$. We are mere operatives, empirics, and egotists, until we learn to think in letters instead of figures.

They all stared. There is a divinity student lately come among us to whom I commonly address remarks like the above, allowing him to take a certain share in the conversation, so far as assent or pertinent questions are in-

volved. He abused his liberty on this occasion by presuming to say that Leibnitz had the same observation.—No, sir, I replied, he has not. But he said a mighty good thing about mathematics, that sounds something like it, and you found it, *not in the original*, but quoted by Dr. Thomas Reid. I will tell the company what he did say, one of these days.

—If I belong to a Society of Mutual Admiration?—I blush to say that I do not at this present moment. I once did, however. It was the first association to which I ever heard the term applied; a body of scientific young men in a great foreign city who admired their teacher, and to some extent each other. Many of them deserved it; they have become famous since. It amuses me to hear the talk of one of those beings described by Thackeray—

"Letters four do form his name"—

about a social development which belongs to the very noblest stage of civilization. All generous companies of artists, authors, philanthropists, men of science, are, or ought to be, Societies of Mutual Admiration. A man of genius, or any kind of superiority, is not debarred from admiring the same quality in another, nor the other from returning his admiration. They may even associate together and continue to think highly of each other. And so of a dozen such men, if any one place is fortunate enough to hold so many.

The being referred to above assumes several false premises. First, that men of talent necessarily hate each other. Secondly, that intimate knowledge or habitual association destroys our admiration of persons whom we esteemed highly at a distance. Thirdly, that a circle of clever fellows, who meet together to dine and have a good time, have signed a constitutional compact to glorify themselves and to put down him and the fraction of the human race not belonging to their number. Fourthly, that it is an outrage that he is not asked to join them.

Here the company laughed a good deal, and the old gentleman who sits opposite said: "That's it! that's it!"

I continued, for I was in the talking vein. As to clever people's hating each other, I think *a little* extra talent does sometimes make people jealous. They become irritated by perpetual attempts and failures, and it hurts their tempers and dispositions. Unpretending mediocrity is good, and genius is glorious; but a weak flavor of genius in an essentially common person is detestable. It spoils the grand neutrality of a commonplace character, as the rinsings of an unwashed wineglass spoil a draught of fair water. No wonder the poor fellow we spoke of, who always belongs to this class of slightly flavored mediocrities, is puzzled and vexed by the strange sight of a dozen men of capacity working and playing together in harmony. He and his fellows are always fighting. With them familiarity naturally breeds contempt. If they ever praise each other's bad drawings, or broken-winded novels, or spavined verses, nobody ever supposed it was from admiration; it was simply a contract between themselves and a publisher or dealer.

If the Mutuals have really nothing among them worth admiring, that alters the question. But if they are men with noble powers and qualities, let me tell you, that, next to youthful love and family affections, there is no human sentiment better than that which unites the Societies of Mutual Admiration. And what would literature or art be without such associations? Who can tell what we owe to the Mutual Admiration Society of which Shakspere, and Ben Jonson, and Beaumont and Fletcher were members?[1] Or to that of which Addison and Steele formed the center,[2] and which gave us the Spectator? Or to that where Johnson, and Goldsmith, and Burke, and Reynolds, and Beauclerk, and Boswell,[3] most admiring among all admirers, met together? Was there any great harm in the fact that the Irvings and Paulding wrote in company[4]? or any unpardonable cabal in the literary union of Verplanck and Bryant and Sands,[5] and as many more as they chose to associate with them?

The poor creature does not know what he is talking about when he abuses this noblest of institutions. Let him inspect its mysteries through the knot-hole he has secured, but not use that orifice as a medium for his popgun. Such a society is the crown of a literary metropolis; if a town has not material for it, and spirit and good feeling enough to organize it, it is a mere caravansary, fit for a man of genius to lodge in, but not to live in. Foolish people hate and dread and envy such an association of men of varied powers and influence, because it is lofty, serene, impregnable, and, by the necessity of the case, exclusive. Wise ones are prouder of the title M.S.M.A. than of all their other honors put together.

. . . . . .

II

. . . . . .

—Have I ever acted in private theatricals? Often. I have played the part of the "Poor Gentleman," before a great many audiences, —more, I trust, than I shall ever face again. I did not wear a stage-costume, nor a wig, nor mustaches of burnt cork; but I was placarded and announced as a public performer, and at the proper hour I came forward with the ballet-dancer's smile upon my countenance, and made my bow and acted my part. I have seen my name stuck up in letters so big that I was ashamed to show myself in the place by daylight. I have gone to a town with a sober

[1] The Elizabethan dramatists met at the Mermaid, a London tavern. [2] This group met at a coffee house (Button's). [3] This group formed the famous Literary Club. [4] They were the authors of *Salmagundi*. [5] These three produced *The Talisman*, an annual of which three volumes were published, 1828–1830.

literary essay in my pocket, and seen myself everywhere announced as the most desperate of *buffos*,[1]—one who was obliged to restrain himself in the full exercise of his powers, from prudential considerations. I have been through as many hardships as Ulysses, in the pursuit of my histrionic vocation.[2] I have traveled in cars until the conductors all knew me like a brother. I have run off the rails, and stuck all night in snowdrifts, and sat behind females 10 that would have the window open when one could not wink without his eyelids freezing together. Perhaps I shall give you some of my experiences one of these days;—I will not now, for I have something else for you.

Private theatricals, as I have figured in them in country lyceum-halls, are one thing,—and private theatricals, as they may be seen in certain gilded and frescoed saloons of our metropolis, are another. Yes, it is pleasant to 20 see real gentlemen and ladies, who do not think it necessary to mouth, and rant, and stride, like most of our stage heroes and heroines, in the characters which show off their graces and talents; most of all to see a fresh, unrouged, unspoiled, highbred young maiden, with a lithe figure, and a pleasant voice, acting in those love-dramas which make us young again to look upon, when real youth and beauty will play them for us. 30

—Of course I wrote the prologue I was asked to write. I did not see the play, though. I knew there was a young lady in it, and that somebody was in love with her, and she was in love with him, and somebody (an old tutor, I believe) wanted to interfere, and, very naturally, the young lady was too sharp for him. The play of course ends charmingly; there is a general reconciliation, and all concerned form a line and take each other's hands, 40 as people always do after they have made up their quarrels,—and then the curtain falls,— if it does not stick, as it commonly does at private theatrical exhibitions, in which case a boy is detailed to pull it down, which he does, blushing violently.

Now, then, for my prologue. I am not

---

going to change my cæsuras and cadences for anybody; so if you do not like the heroic, or iambic trimeter brachycatalectic,[1] you had better not wait to hear it.

This Is It

A Prologue? Well, of course the ladies know;—
I have my doubts. No matter,—here we go!
What is a Prologue? Let our Tutor teach:
Pro means beforehand; *logos* stands for speech.
'Tis like the harper's prelude on the strings,
The prima donna's courtesy ere she sings;—
Prologues in meter are to other *pros*
As worsted stockings are to engine-hose.

"The world's a stage,"—as Shakespeare said, one day;
The stage a world—was what he meant to say.
The outside world's a blunder, that is clear;
The real world that Nature meant is here.
Here every foundling finds its lost mamma;
Each rogue, repentant, melts his stern papa;
Misers relent, the spendthrift's debts are paid,
The cheats are taken in the traps they laid;
One after one the troubles all are past
Till the fifth act comes right side up at last,
When the young couple, old folks, rogues, and all,
Join hands, *so* happy at the curtain's fall.
—Here suffering virtue ever finds relief,
And black-browed ruffians always come to grief,
—When the lorn damsel, with a frantic speech,
And cheeks as hueless as a brandy-peach,
Cries, "Help, kyind Heaven!" and drops upon her knees
On the green—baize,—beneath the (canvas) trees,—
See to her side avenging Valor fly:—
"Ha! Villain! Draw! Now, Terraitorr, yield or die!"
—When the poor hero flounders in despair,
Some dear lost uncle turns up millionaire,—
Clasps the young scapegrace with paternal joy,
Sobs on his neck, "*My boy!* My boy!! My boy!!!"

Ours, then, sweet friends, the real world to-night
Of love that conquers in disaster's spite.

---

[1] comic actors in Italian opera   [2] Holmes was a very popular lecturer in the Lyceums of his day and (like Ulysses in his twenty years of wandering) knew the inconveniences of travel.

[1] a technical description of blank verse

Ladies, attend! While woful cares and doubt
Wrong the soft passion in the world without,
Though fortune scowl, though prudence inter-
 fere,
One thing is certain: Love will triumph here!

Lords of creation, whom your ladies rule,—
The world's great masters, when you're out of
 school,—
Learn the brief moral of our evening's play:
Man has his will,—but woman has her way!
While man's dull spirit toils in smoke and
 fire,
Woman's swift instinct threads the electric
 wire,—
The magic bracelet stretched beneath the
 waves
Beats the black giant with his score of slaves.
All earthly powers confess your sovereign
 art
But that one rebel,—woman's wilful heart.
All foes you master; but a woman's wit
Lets daylight through you ere you know
 you're hit.
So, just to picture what her art can do,
Hear an old story made as good as new.

Rudolph, professor of the headsman's trade,
Alike was famous for his arm and blade.
One day a prisoner Justice had to kill
Knelt at the block to test the artist's skill.
Bare-armed, swart-visaged, gaunt, and shaggy-
 browed,
Rudolph the headsman rose above the crowd.
His falchion lightened with a sudden gleam,
As the pike's armor flashes in the stream.
He sheathed his blade; he turned as if to
 go;
The victim knelt, still waiting for the blow.
"Why strikest not? Perform thy murderous
 act,"
The prisoner said. (His voice was slightly
 cracked.)
"Friend, I *have* struck," the artist straight
 replied;
"Wait but one moment, and yourself decide."

He held his snuffbox,—"Now then, if you
 please!"
The prisoner sniffed, and, with a crashing
 sneeze,
Off his head tumbled,—bowled along the
 floor,—
Bounced down the steps;—the prisoner said
 no more!

Woman! thy falchion is a glittering eye;
If death lurks in it, oh, how sweet to die!
Thou takest hearts as Rudolph took the
 head;
We die with love, and never dream we're
 dead!

The prologue went off very well, as I hear.
No alterations were suggested by the lady to
whom it was sent, so far as I know. Sometimes people criticize the poems one sends
them, and suggest all sorts of improvements.
Who was that silly body that wanted Burns
to alter "Scots wha hae," so as to lengthen the
last line, thus?—

"*Edward!*" Chains and slavery!

Here is a little poem I sent a short time since
to a committee for a certain celebration. I
understood that it was to be a festive and convivial occasion, and ordered myself accordingly. It seems the president of the day was
what is called a "teetotaller." I received a note
from him in the following words, containing
the copy subjoined, with the emendations
annexed to it.

"Dear Sir,—Your poem gives good satisfaction to the committee. The sentiments
expressed with reference to liquor are not,
however, those generally entertained by this
community. I have therefore consulted the
clergyman of this place, who has made some
slight changes, which he thinks will remove
all objections, and keep the valuable portions
of the poem. Please to inform me of your
charge for said poem. Our means are limited,
etc., etc., etc.

"Yours with respect."

Here it is,—with the slight alterations.

Come! fill a fresh bumper,—for why should
 we go
  logwood
While the ~~nectar~~ still reddens our cups as
 they flow!
  decoction
Pour out the ~~rich juices~~ still bright with the
 sun,
  dye-stuff
Till o'er the brimmed crystal the ~~rubies~~ shall
 run.

half-ripened apples
The ~~purple-globed clusters~~ their life-dews have
bled;

    taste   sugar of lead
How sweet is the ~~breath~~ of the ~~fragrance they~~
~~shed!~~

    rank poisons   *wines !!!*
For summer's ~~last roses~~ lie hid in the ~~wines~~
              stable-boys smok-
That were garnered by ~~maidens who laughed~~
ing long-nines.
~~through the vines.~~

    scowl   howl   scoff
Then a ~~smile,~~ and a ~~glass,~~ and a ~~toast,~~ and a
sneer
~~cheer,~~
    strychnine and whisky, and ratsbane and
For ~~all the good wine, and we've some of it~~
beer
~~here~~
In cellar, in pantry, in attic, in hall,
    Down, down, with the tyrant that masters
~~Long live the gay servant that laughs for us~~
us all!
~~all!~~

The company said I had been shabbily
treated, and advised me to charge the committee double,—which I did. But as I never
got my pay, I don't know that it made much
difference. I am a very particular person about
having all I write printed as I write it. I require to see a proof, a revise, a re-revise, and a
double re-revise, or fourth-proof rectified impression of all my productions, especially
verse. A misprint kills a sensitive author. An
intentional change of his text murders him.
No wonder so many poets die young!

I have nothing more to report at this time,
except two pieces of advice I gave to the
young women at table. One relates to a vul-
garism of language, which I grieve to say is
sometimes heard even from female lips. The
other is of more serious purport, and applies to such as contemplate a change of condition,—matrimony, in fact.

—The woman who "calc'lates" is lost.

—Put not your trust in money, but put
your money in trust.

III

.   .   .   .   .

—You need not get up a rebellion against
what I say, if you find everything in my sayings is not exactly new. You can't possibly
mistake a man who means to be honest for a
literary pickpocket. I once read an introductory lecture that looked to me too learned
for its latitude. On examination, I found all
its erudition was taken ready-made from
D'Israeli. If I had been ill-natured, I should
have shown up the little great man, who had
once belabored me in his feeble way. But one
can generally tell these wholesale thieves easily
enough, and they are not worth the trouble of
putting them in the pillory. I doubt the entire
novelty of my remarks just made on telling
unpleasant truths, yet I am not conscious of
any larceny.

Neither make too much of flaws and occasional overstatements. Some persons seem to
think that absolute truth, in the form of
rigidly stated propositions, is all that conversation admits. This is precisely as if a
musician should insist on having nothing but
perfect chords and simple melodies,—no diminished fifths, no flat sevenths, no flourishes,
on any account. Now it is fair to say, that,
just as music must have all these, so conversation must have its partial truths, its embel-
lished truths, its exaggerated truths. It is in
its higher forms an artistic product, and admits
the ideal element as much as pictures or statues.
One man who is a little too literal can spoil
the talk of a whole tableful of men of *esprit*.—
"Yes," you say, "but who wants to hear
fanciful people's nonsense? Put the facts to it,
and then see where it is!"—Certainly, if a man
is too fond of paradox,—if he is flighty and
empty,—if instead of striking those fifths and
sevenths, those harmonious discords, often
so much better than the twinned octaves, in
the music of thought,—if, instead of striking
these, he jangles the chords, stick a fact into
him like a stiletto. But remember that talking
is one of the fine arts,—the noblest, the most
important, and the most difficult,—and that
its fluent harmonies may be spoiled by the
intrusion of a single harsh note. Therefore
conversation which is suggestive rather than
argumentative, which lets out the most of
each talker's results of thought, is commonly
the pleasantest and the most profitable. It is
not easy, at the best, for two persons talking
together to make the most of each other's
thoughts, there are so many of them.

[The company looked as if they wanted an explanation.]

When John and Thomas, for instance, are talking together, it is natural enough that among the six there should be more or less confusion and misapprehension.

[Our landlady turned pale;—no doubt she thought there was a screw loose in my intellects,—and that involved the probable loss of a boarder. A severe-looking person, who wears a Spanish cloak and a sad cheek, fluted by the passions of the melodrama, whom I understand to be the professional ruffian of the neighboring theater, alluded, with a certain lifting of the brow, drawing down of the corners of the mouth, and somewhat rasping *voce di petto*,[1] to Falstaff's nine men in buckram.[2] Everybody looked up. I believe the old gentleman opposite was afraid I should seize the carving-knife; at any rate, he slid it to one side, as it were carelessly.]

I think, I said, I can make it plain to Benjamin Franklin here, that there are at least six personalities distinctly to be recognized as taking part in that dialogue between John and Thomas.

Three Johns
{
1. The real John; known only to his Maker.
2. John's ideal John; never the real one, and often very unlike him.
3. Thomas's ideal John; never the real John, nor John's John, but often very unlike either.
}

Three Thomases
{
1. The real Thomas.
2. Thomas's ideal Thomas.
3. John's ideal Thomas.
}

Only one of the three Johns is taxed; only one can be weighed on a platform-balance; but the other two are just as important in the conversation. Let us suppose the real John to be old, dull, and ill-looking. But as the Higher Powers have not conferred on men the gift of seeing themselves in the true light, John very possibly conceives himself to be youthful, witty, and fascinating, and talks from the point of view of this ideal. Thomas,

again, believes him to be an artful rogue, we will say; therefore he *is*, so far as Thomas's attitude in the conversation is concerned, an artful rogue, though really simple and stupid. The same conditions apply to the three Thomases. It follows, that, until a man can be found who knows himself as his Maker knows him, or who sees himself as others see him, there must be at least six persons engaged in every dialogue between two. Of these, the least important, philosophically speaking, is the one that we have called the real person. No wonder two disputants often get angry, when there are six of them talking and listening all at the same time.

[A very unphilosophical application of the above remarks was made by a young fellow answering to the name of John, who sits near me at table. A certain basket of peaches, a rare vegetable, little known to boarding-houses, was on its way to me *viâ* this unlettered Johannes. He appropriated the three that remained in the basket, remarking that there was just one apiece for him. I convinced him that his practical inference was hasty and illogical, but in the meantime he had eaten the peaches.]

. . . . . .

IV

. . . . . .

So you will not think I mean to speak lightly of old friendships, because we cannot help instituting comparisons between our present and former selves by the aid of those who were what we were, but are not what we are. Nothing strikes one more, in the race of life, than to see how many give out in the first half of the course. "Commencement day" always reminds me of the start for the "Derby," when the beautiful highbred three-year-olds of the season are brought up for trial. That day is the start, and life is the race. Here we are at Cambridge, and a class is just "graduating." Poor Harry! he was to have been there too, but he has paid forfeit; step out here into the grass back of the church; ah! there it is:—

"HUNC LAPIDEM POSUERUNT
SOCII MŒRENTES."[1]

---

[1] Italian for "chest tone" [2] For the Falstaff story, see I Henry IV, II, iv.

[1] "His mourning comrades placed this stone."

But this is the start, and here they are,—coats bright as silk, and manes as smooth as *eau lustrale*[1] can make them. Some of the best of the colts are pranced round, a few minutes each, to show their paces. What is that old gentleman crying about? and the old lady by him, and the three girls, what are they all covering their eyes for? Oh, that is *their* colt which has just been trotted up on the stage. Do they really think those little thin legs can do anything in such a slashing sweepstakes as is coming off in these next forty years? Oh, this terrible gift of second-sight that comes to some of us when we begin to look through the silvered rings of the *arcus senilis!*[2]

Ten years gone. First turn in the race. A few broken down; two or three bolted. Several show in advance of the ruck. *Cassock,* a black colt, seems to be ahead of the rest; those black colts commonly get the start, I have noticed, of the others, in the first quarter. *Meteor* has pulled up.

Twenty years. Second corner turned. *Cassock* has dropped from the front, and *Judex,* an iron-gray, has the lead. But look! how they have thinned out? Down flat—five,—six,—how many? They lie still enough! they will not get up again in this race, be very sure! And the rest of them, what a "tailing off!" Anybody can see who is going to win,—perhaps.

Thirty years. Third corner turned. *Dives,* bright sorrel, ridden by the fellow in a yellow jacket, begins to make play fast; is getting to be the favorite, with many. But who is that other one that has been lengthening his stride from the first, and now shows close up to the front? Don't you remember the quiet brown colt *Asteroid,* with the star in his forehead? That is he; he is one of the sort that lasts; look out for him! The black "colt," as we used to call him, is in the background, taking it easily in a gentle trot. There is one they used to call *the Filly,* on account of a certain feminine air he had; well up, you see; the Filly is not to be despised, my boy!

Forty years. More dropping off,—but places much as before.

Fifty years. Race over. All that are on the course are coming in at a walk; no more running. Who is ahead? Ahead? What! and the winning-post a slab of white or gray stone standing out from that turf where there is no more jockeying or straining for victory! Well, the world marks their places in its betting-book; but be sure that these matter very little, if they have run as well as they knew how!

—Did I not say to you a little while ago that the universe swam in an ocean of similitudes and analogies? I will not quote Cowley, or Burns, or Wordsworth, just now, to show you what thoughts were suggested to them by the simplest natural objects, such as a flower or a leaf; but I will read you a few lines, if you do not object, suggested by looking at a section of one of those chambered shells to which is given the name of Pearly Nautilus. We need not trouble ourselves about the distinction between this and the Paper Nautilus, the *Argonauta*[1] of the ancients. The name applied to both shows that each has long been compared to a ship, as you may see more fully in Webster's Dictionary, or the "Encyclopædia," to which he refers. If you will look into Roget's Bridgewater Treatise, you will find a figure of one of these shells and a section of it. The last will show you the series of enlarging compartments successively dwelt in by the animal that inhabits the shell, which is built in a widening spiral. Can you find no lesson in this?

THE CHAMBERED NAUTILUS

This is the ship of pearl, which, poets feign,
  Sails the unshadowed main,—
  The venturous bark that flings
On the sweet summer wind its purpled wings
In gulfs enchanted, where the siren sings,
  And coral reefs lie bare,
Where the cold sea-maids rise to sun their
    streaming hair.

Its webs of living gauze no more unfurl;
  Wrecked is the ship of pearl!

[1] I have now and then found a naturalist who still worried over the distinction between the Pearly Nautilus and the Paper Nautilus, or Argonauta. As the stories both are mere fables, attaching to the Physalia, or Portuguese man-of-war, as well as to these two molluscs, it seems over-nice to quarrel with the poetical handling of a fiction sufficiently justified by the name commonly applied to the ship of pearl as well as the ship of paper. [*Holmes's note.*]

[1] water for purification [2] a whitish ring in the cornea of the eye which comes with old age

And every chambered cell,
Where its dim dreaming life was wont to
     dwell,
As the frail tenant shaped his growing shell,
     Before thee lies revealed,—
Its irised ceiling rent, its sunless crypt un-
     sealed!

Year after year beheld the silent toil
     That spread his lustrous coil;
     Still, as the spiral grew,
He left the past year's dwelling for the new,
Stole with soft step its shining archway
     through,
     Built up its idle door,
Stretched in his last-found home, and knew
     the old no more.

Thanks for the heavenly message brought by
     thee,
     Child of the wandering sea,
     Cast from her lap forlorn!
From thy dead lips a clearer note is born
Than ever Triton blew from wreathèd horn!
     While on mine ear it rings,
Through the deep caves of thought I hear a
     voice that sings:—

Build thee more stately mansions, O my soul,
     As the swift seasons roll!
     Leave thy low-vaulted past!
Let each new temple, nobler than the last,
Shut thee from heaven with a dome more vast,
     Till thou at length art free,
Leaving thine outgrown shell by life's unrest-
     ing sea!

VI

. . . .

—Every person's feelings have a front-door
and a side-door by which they may be entered.
The front-door is on the street. Some keep it
always open; some keep it latched; some,
locked; some, bolted,—with a chain that will
let you peep in, but not get in; and some nail
it up, so that nothing can pass its threshold.
This front-door leads into a passage which
opens into an anteroom and this into the
interior apartments. The side-door opens at
once into the sacred chambers.

There is almost always at least one key to
this side-door. This is carried for years hidden
in a mother's bosom. Fathers, brothers, sisters,
and friends, often, but by no means so universally, have duplicates of it. The wedding-
ring conveys a right to one; alas, if none is
given with it!

If nature or accident has put one of these
keys into the hands of a person who has the
torturing instinct, I can only solemnly pronounce the words that Justice utters over its
doomed victim—*The Lord have mercy on
your soul!* You will probably go mad within a
reasonable time,—or, if you are a man, run
off and die with your head on a curb-stone, in
Melbourne or San Francisco,—or, if you are
a woman, quarrel and break your heart, or
turn into a pale, jointed petrifaction that moves
about as if it were alive, or play some real life-
tragedy or other.

Be very careful to whom you trust one of
these keys of the side-door. The fact of possessing one renders those even who are dear
to you very terrible at times. You can keep
the world out from your front-door, or receive visitors only when you are ready for
them; but those of your own flesh and blood,
or of certain grades of intimacy, can come in
at the side-door, if they will, at any hour and
in any mood. Some of them have a scale of
your whole nervous system, and can play all
the gamut of your sensibilities in semitones,—
touching the naked nerve-pulps as a pianist
strikes the keys of his instrument. I am satisfied that there are as great masters of this
nerve-playing as Vieuxtemps[1] or Thalberg[2] in
their lines of performance. Married life is the
school in which the most accomplished artists
in this department are found. A delicate
woman is the best instrument; she has such a
magnificent compass of sensibilities! From the
deep inward moan which follows pressure on
the great nerves of right, to the sharp cry as
the filaments of taste are struck with a crashing sweep, is a range which no other instrument possesses. A few exercises on it daily at
home fit a man wonderfully for his habitual
labors, and refresh him immensely as he returns from them. No stranger can get a great
many notes of torture out of a human soul;
it takes one that knows it well,—parent, child,
brother, sister, intimate. Be very careful to
whom you give a side-door key; too many
have them already.

[1] a Belgian violinist   [2] a Swiss pianist

From ELSIE VENNER

Elsie Venner was written, Holmes said, "to test the doctrine of 'original sin' and human responsibility." It was published as *The Professor's Story* in the *Atlantic Monthly*, beginning January, 1860. When it was republished it was given its present title. Elsie's mother was bitten by a rattlesnake before the birth of her daughter, and Elsie had serpent-woman characteristics, against which she struggled and was humanized; but the struggle was too much for her and she died. She stands, then, for those who "receive a moral poison from a remote ancestor, and should be objects of pity."

The first chapter, given here, is an essay on New England aristocracy. Brahmins are members of the highest sacerdotal caste among the Hindus. Originally they were individuals distinguished for wisdom and sanctity, but ultimately they became a strictly hereditary caste. At the present time "Brahmin" is used satirically of highly cultured or intellectual persons, with an implication of exclusiveness and perhaps of superciliousness. The second chapter "introduces a youth belonging to the Brahmin caste of New England," who is to be a leading character.

I

The Brahmin Caste of New England

THERE is nothing in New England corresponding at all to the feudal aristocracies of the Old World. Whether it be owing to the stock from which we were derived, or to the practical working of our institutions, or to the abrogation of the technical "law of honor," which draws a sharp line between the personally responsible class of "gentlemen" and the unnamed multitude of those who are not expected to risk their lives for an abstraction, —whatever be the cause, we have no such aristocracy here as that which grew up out of the military systems of the Middle Ages.

What our people mean by "aristocracy" is merely the richer part of the community, that live in the tallest houses, drive real carriages (not "kerridges"), kid-glove their hands, and French-bonnet their ladies' heads, give parties where the persons who call them by the above title are not invited, and have a provokingly easy way of dressing, walking, talking, and nodding to people, as if they felt entirely at home, and would not be embarrassed in the least, if they met the Governor, or even the President of the United States, face to face. Some of these great folks are really well-bred, some of them are only purse-proud and assuming,—but they form a class, and are named as above in the common speech.

It is in the nature of large fortunes to diminish rapidly, when subdivided and distributed. A million is the unit of wealth, now and here in America. It splits into four handsome properties; each of these into four good inheritances; these, again, into scanty competences for four ancient maidens,—with whom it is best the family should die out, unless it can begin again as its great-grandfather did. Now a million is a kind of golden cheese, which represents in a compendious form the summer's growth of a fat meadow of craft or commerce; and as this kind of meadow rarely bears more than one crop, it is pretty certain that sons and grandsons will not get another golden cheese out of it, whether they milk the same cows or turn in new ones. In other words, the millionocracy, considered in a large way, is not at all an affair of persons and families, but a perpetual fact of money with a variable human element, which a philosopher might leave out of consideration without falling into serious error. Of course, this trivial and fugitive fact of personal wealth does not create a permanent class, unless some special means are taken to arrest the process of disintegration in the third generation. This is so rarely done, at least successfully, that one need not live a very long life to see most of the rich families he knew in childhood more or less reduced, and the millions shifted into the hands of the country-boys who were sweeping stores and carrying parcels when the now decayed gentry were driving their chariots, eating their venison over silver chafing-dishes, drinking Madeira chilled in embossed coolers, wearing their hair in powder, and casing their legs in white-topped boots with silken tassels.

There is, however, in New England, an aristocracy, if you choose to call it so, which has a far greater character of permanence. It has grown to be a *caste*,—not in any odious sense,—but, by the repetition of the same influences, generation after generation, it has acquired a distinct organization and physiognomy, which not to recognize is sheer stupidity, and not to be willing to describe would show a distrust of the good-nature and intelligence of our readers, who like to have us see all we can and tell all we see.

If you will look carefully at any class of students in one of our colleges, you will have no difficulty in selecting specimens of two different aspects of youthful manhood. Of course I shall choose extreme cases to illustrate the contrast between them. In the first, the figure is perhaps robust, but often otherwise,—inelegant, partly from careless attitudes, partly from ill-dressing,—the face is uncouth in feature, or at least common,—the mouth coarse and unformed,—the eye unsympathetic, even if bright,—the movements of the face are clumsy, like those of the limbs, —the voice unmusical,—and the enunciation as if the words were coarse castings, instead of fine carvings. The youth of the other aspect is commonly slender,—his face is smooth, and apt to be pallid,—his features are regular and of a certain delicacy,—his eye is bright and quick,—his lips play over the thought he utters as a pianist's fingers dance over their music,—and his whole air, though it may be timid, and even awkward, has nothing clownish. If you are a teacher, you know what to expect from each of these young men. With equal willingness, the first will be slow at learning; the second will take to his books as a pointer or a setter to his field-work.

The first youth is the common country-boy, whose race has been bred to bodily labor. Nature has adapted the family organization to the kind of life it has lived. The hands and feet by constant use have got more than their share of development,—the organs of thought and expression less than their share. The finer instincts are latent and must be developed. A youth of this kind is raw material in its first stage of elaboration. You must not expect too much of any such. Many of them have force of will and character, and become distinguished in practical life; but very few of them ever become great scholars. A scholar is, almost always, the son of scholars or scholarly persons.

That is exactly what the other young man is. He comes of the *Brahmin caste of New England*. This is the harmless, inoffensive,

untitled aristocracy to which I have referred, and which I am sure you will at once acknowledge. There are races of scholars among us, in which aptitude for learning, and all these marks of it I have spoken of, are congenital and hereditary. Their names are always on some college catalogue or other. They break out every generation or two in some learned labor which calls them up after they seem to have died out. At last some newer name takes their place, it may be,—but you inquire a little and you find it is the blood of the Edwardses or the Chaunceys or the Ellerys or some of the old historic scholars, disguised under the altered name of a female descendant.

I suppose there is not an experienced instructor anywhere in our Northern States who will not recognize at once the truth of this general distinction. But the reader who has never been a teacher will very probably object, that some of our most illustrious public men have come direct from the homespun-clad class of the people,—and he may, perhaps, even find a noted scholar or two whose parents were masters of the English alphabet, but of no other.

It is not fair to pit a few chosen families against the great multitude of those who are continually working their way up into the intellectual classes. The results which are habitually reached by hereditary training are occasionally brought about without it. There are natural filters as well as artificial ones; and though the great rivers are commonly more or less turbid, if you will look long enough, you may find a spring that sparkles as no water does which drips through your apparatus of sands and sponges. So there are families which refine themselves into intellectual aptitude without having had much opportunity for intellectual acquirements. A series of felicitous crosses develops an improved strain of blood, and reaches its maximum perfection at last in the large uncombed youth who goes to college and startles the hereditary class-leaders by striding past them all. That is Nature's republicanism; thank God for it, but do not let it make you illogical. The race of the hereditary scholar has exchanged a certain portion of its animal vigor for its new instincts, and it is hard to lead men without a good deal of animal vigor. The scholar who comes by Nature's special grace from an unworn stock of broad-chested sires and deep-bosomed mothers must always overmatch an equal intelligence with a compromised and lowered vitality. A man's breathing and digestive apparatus (one is tempted to add *muscular*) are just as important to him on the floor of the Senate as his thinking organs. You broke down in your great speech, did you? Yes, your grandfather had an attack of dyspepsia in '82, after working too hard on his famous Election Sermon. All this does not touch the main fact: our scholars come chiefly from a privileged order, just as our best fruits come from well-known grafts,—though now and then a seedling apple, like the Northern Spy, or a seedling pear, like the Seckel, springs from a nameless ancestry and grows to be the pride of all the gardens in the land.

1860

1809 ~ *Abraham Lincoln* ~ 1865

A FEW supplementary details will complete the account of Lincoln's life sketched below in his "Autobiography." In 1860 the Republicans nominated him for President, and he was elected in November. He passed the next four difficult years in the White House, giving his best efforts to the preservation of the Union. He was re-elected to the Presidency in 1864, and a little more than a month after his second inauguration he was shot by John Wilkes Booth, during a performance in a Washington theater. His successful leadership of the country in its time of crisis and the tragic circumstances of his death combined to make him a heroic figure in American history.

Although, like Franklin, Lincoln had no formal education or stimulus to learn, he early had a zest for reading and study. He amassed from books a body of exact general information. He knew Shakespeare, and he had favorite authors and poems. The humor of P. V. Nasby and Artemus Ward attracted him and doubtless influenced him. He could think clearly and express himself clearly, organize his material logically, and adapt his style to those he addressed, whether a bereaved mother, his townsfolk in Springfield, or the cultivated audiences of the East. His grasp of a situation was sure, and he was rich in ideas. He wrote and spoke in direct and vigorous idiom, often the homely idiom of farm life, and sometimes he relied on shrewd anecdote; but he could rise to dignity, sometimes to poetry of expression. His style had terseness, emotional appeal, and strength. The matter was more important to him than the manner, but his manner was effective. Time has awarded him a permanent place among the great writers of American prose.

The best collected edition of Lincoln's works is the *Complete Works of Abraham Lincoln*, edited by J. G. Nicolay and John Hay (12 vols., 1905). There are innumerable studies and reminiscences of special phases of his career. Some leading biographies are *Abraham Lincoln: A*

History, by J. G. Nicolay and John Hay (10 vols., 1890); and *Herndon's Lincoln: The True Story of a Great Life*, by W. H. Herndon and J. W. Weik, edited by P. M. Angle (1930). Other biographical works are Ida M. Tarbell, *The Life of Abraham Lincoln* (2 vols., 1900, 1917); Brand Whitlock, *Abraham Lincoln* (1909, 1916); Lord Charnwood, *Abraham Lincoln* (1917); N. W. Stephenson, *Lincoln: an Account of His Personal Life* (1924); C. Sandburg, *Abraham Lincoln: The Prairie Years* (2 vols., 1926), and *Abraham Lincoln: The War Years* (2 vols., 1939), a somewhat pictorial and imaginative account; L. A. Warren, *Lincoln's Parentage and Childhood* (1926); Albert J. Beveridge, *Abraham Lincoln, 1809–1858* (2 vols., 1928); and E. L. Masters, *Lincoln the Man* (1931), one of few adverse, disparaging treatments of Lincoln. N. W. Stephenson treated Lincoln as an author in *CHAL*, III (1921), and J. G. Randall wrote the account in *DAB* (1933). L. E. Robinson wrote *Abraham Lincoln as a Man of Letters* (1923), and D. K. Dodge, *Lincoln, Master of Words* (1924). Daniel Fish made a *Lincoln Bibliography* (1906), included in *Complete Works*, XI.

AUTOBIOGRAPHY

I was born February 12, 1809, in Hardin County, Kentucky. My parents were both born in Virginia, of undistinguished families —second families, perhaps I should say. My mother, who died in my tenth year, was of a family of the name of Hanks, some of whom now reside in Adams, and others in Macon County, Illinois. My paternal grandfather, Abraham Lincoln, emigrated from Rockingham County, Virginia, to Kentucky about 1781 or 1782, where a year or two later he was killed by the Indians, not in battle but by stealth, when he was laboring to open a farm in the forest. His ancestors, who were Quakers, went to Virginia from Berks County, Pennsylvania. An effort to identify them with the New England family of the same name ended in nothing more definite than a similarity of Christian names in both families, such as Enoch, Levi, Mordecai, Solomon, Abraham, and the like.

My father, at the death of his father, was but six years of age, and he grew up literally without education. He removed from Kentucky to what is now Spencer County, Indiana, in my eighth year. We reached our new home about the time the state came into the Union. It was a wild region, with many bears and other wild animals still in the woods. There I grew up. There were some schools, so called, but no qualification was ever required of a teacher beyond "readin', writin', and cipherin'," to the rule of three. If a straggler supposed to understand Latin happened to

sojourn in the neighborhood, he was looked upon as a wizard. There was absolutely nothing to excite ambition for education. Of course, when I came of age I did not know much. Still, somehow, I could read, write, and cipher to the rule of three, but that was all. I have not been to school since. The little advance I now have upon this store of education, I have picked up from time to time under the pressure of necessity.

I was raised to farm work, which I continued till I was twenty-two. At twenty-one I came to Illinois, Macon County. Then I got to New Salem, at that time in Sangamon, now in Menard County, where I remained a year as a sort of clerk in a store. Then came the Black Hawk War; and I was elected a captain of volunteers, a success which gave me more pleasure than any I have had since. I went the campaign, was elated, ran for the legislature the same year (1832), and was beaten—the only time I ever have been beaten by the people. The next and three succeeding biennial elections I was elected to the legislature. I was not a candidate afterward. During this legislative period I had studied law, and removed to Springfield to practice it. In 1846 I was once elected to the lower House of Congress. Was not a candidate for re-election. From 1849 to 1854, both inclusive, practiced law more assiduously than ever before. Always a Whig in politics; and generally on the Whig electoral tickets, making active canvasses. I was losing interest in politics when the repeal of the Missouri Compromise aroused me again. What I have done since that is pretty well known.

If any personal description of me is thought desirable, it may be said I am, in height, six feet four inches, nearly; lean in flesh, weighing on an average one hundred and eighty pounds; dark complexion, with coarse black hair and gray eyes. No other marks or brands recollected.

THE GETTYSBURG ADDRESS

FOUR score and seven years ago our fathers brought forth on this continent a new nation, conceived in liberty, and dedicated to the proposition that all men are created equal.

Now we are engaged in a great civil war, testing whether that nation, or any nation so conceived and so dedicated, can long endure. We are met on a great battlefield of that war. We have come to dedicate a portion of that field as a final resting-place for those who here gave their lives that that nation might live. It is altogether fitting and proper that we should do this.

But in a larger sense we cannot dedicate, we cannot consecrate, we cannot hallow this ground. The brave men, living and dead, who struggled here have consecrated it, far above our poor power to add or detract. The world will little note, nor long remember what we say here, but it can never forget what they did here. It is for us, the living, rather, to be dedicated here to the unfinished work which they who fought here have thus far so nobly advanced. It is rather for us to be here dedicated to the great task remaining before us,—that from these honored dead we take increased devotion to that cause for which they gave the last full measure of devotion; that we here highly resolve that these dead shall not have died in vain; that this nation, under God, shall have a new birth of freedom; and that government of the people, by the people, and for the people, shall not perish from the earth.

1863

THE SECOND INAUGURAL ADDRESS

FELLOW-COUNTRYMEN: At this second appearing to take the oath of the presidential office, there is less occasion for an extended address than there was at the first. Then a statement, somewhat in detail, of a course to be pursued, seemed fitting and proper. Now, at the expiration of four years, during which public declarations have been constantly called forth on every point and phase of the great contest which still absorbs the attention and engrosses the energies of the nation, little that is new could be presented. The progress of our arms, upon which all else chiefly depends, is as well known to the public as to myself; and it is, I trust, reasonably satisfactory and encouraging to all. With high hope for the future, no prediction in regard to it is ventured.

On the occasion corresponding to this four years ago, all thoughts were anxiously directed to an impending civil war. All dreaded it—all sought to avert it. While the inaugural address was being delivered from this place, devoted altogether to saving the Union without war, insurgent agents were in the city seeking to destroy it without war—seeking to dissolve the Union, and divide effects, by negotiation. Both parties deprecated war; but one of them would make war rather than let the nation survive; and the other would accept war rather than let it perish. And the war came.

One eighth of the whole population were colored slaves, not distributed generally over the Union, but localized in the southern part of it. These slaves constituted a peculiar and powerful interest. All knew that this interest was, somehow, the cause of the war. To strengthen, perpetuate, and extend this interest was the object for which the insurgents would rend the Union, even by war; while the government claimed no right to do more than to restrict the territorial enlargement of it.

Neither party expected for the war the magnitude or the duration which it has already attained. Neither anticipated that the cause of the conflict might cease with, or even before, the conflict itself should cease. Each looked for an easier triumph and a result less fundamental and astounding. Both read the same Bible, and pray to the same God; and each invokes his aid against the other. It may seem strange that any men should dare to ask a just God's assistance in wringing their bread from the sweat of other men's faces; but let us judge not, that we be not judged. The prayers of both could not be answered—that of neither has been answered fully.

The Almighty has his own purposes. "Woe unto the world because of offenses! for it must needs be that offenses come; but woe to that man by whom the offense cometh." If we shall suppose that American slavery is one of those offenses which in the providence of God, must needs come, but which, having continued through his appointed time, he now wills to 10 remove, and that he gives to both North and South this terrible war, as the woe due to those by whom the offense came, shall we discern therein any departure from those divine attributes which the believers in a living God always ascribe to him? Fondly do we hope —fervently do we pray—that this mighty scourge of war may speedily pass away. Yet, if

God wills that it continue until all the wealth piled by the bondman's two hundred and fifty years of unrequited toil shall be sunk, and until every drop of blood drawn with the lash shall be paid by another drawn with the sword, as was said three thousand years ago, so still it must be said, "The judgments of the Lord are true and righteous altogether."

With malice toward none; with charity for all; with firmness in the right, as God gives us to see the right, let us strive on to finish the work we are in; to bind up the nation's wounds; to care for him who shall have borne the battle, and for his widow and his orphan— to do all which may achieve and cherish a just and lasting peace among ourselves, and with all nations.

1865

Civil War Songs and Lyrics

MANY LITERARY lyrics and popular songs emerged from the long, intense struggle of the Civil War period. There were more of them, and they were of better literary quality than those of the Revolution and most of those of World War days, with which it is of interest to compare them. They were published in magazines and newspapers, and were circulated as broadsides and in paper-covered "songsters." Many were sung by the soldiers, comic songs as well as serious pieces, and entered widely into popular tradition.

Stephen Collins Foster (1826–1864), a Pennsylvanian, was the most gifted song writer of his period. He wrote for Christy's Minstrels and other troupes in the days when Negro minstrels were in vogue as entertainers, and his songs were more widely sung than those of any other composer. He was addicted to drink, and, despite his popularity and his unceasing composition, he died in poverty and obscurity. Mainly his songs are of Negro life, some humorous but the majority touched with melancholy. The best known are "O Susanna" (1848), "The Old Folks at Home" (1851), "Massa's in the Cold, Cold Ground" (1852), "My Old Kentucky Home" (1853), and "Old Black Joe" (1860).

James Ryder Randall (1839–1908), a native of Baltimore, when a teacher of literature in a college in Louisiana, composed "My Maryland" at white heat, on reading the news of the attack upon Massachusetts troops passing through Baltimore. The Cary sisters, Jennie and Hetty, of Baltimore, adapted the words to the music of the German college tune "Lauriger Horatius," which was itself based on the older "Tannenbaum, O Tannenbaum." It was so effective when sung that the South adopted it as its war song. Randall tried to enlist in the Civil War, but his health was not adequate. Later he was a successful journalist and remained in newspaper work till the end of his life.

Henry Timrod (1828–1867) of Charleston, South Carolina, was the ablest Southern poet of the time between Poe and Lanier. With his friend Paul Hamilton Hayne, he joined the group of young writers who gathered about William Gilmore Simms, wrote verses, and contributed to magazines. A small collection of his poems appeared in 1860. Reduced to dire straits when his property was swept away in the War, he continued to fight poverty and illness till his death. His early pieces were conventional, mostly love poems marked by sentimentalism. His "Spring" and "The Cotton Boll" were nature pieces, and in 1861 he wrote the ode "Ethnogenesis." These were followed by a series of war poems which are his best. "A Cry to Arms" and "Charleston" show fire and force as well as clear thought. Timrod left but a small body of work, restricted in range, but of fine taste, delicacy of feeling, and often of lyrical power. His poems were collected and published by P. H. Hayne in 1873.

Julia Ward Howe (1819–1910), author, reformer, and lecturer of distinction, was a native of New York City who lived mostly in Boston. She was of distinguished colonial family and well educated. She early allied herself with the abolitionists, afterwards supported woman's suffrage and other reform movements, and showed herself to be a gifted organizer. She wrote "The Battle Hymn of the Republic" to furnish more worthy words to the melody of "John Brown's Body." It appeared in the *Atlantic Monthly*, February, 1862. Her first volume of lyrics was published in 1854, and her *Poems Old and New* in 1898. She wrote many volumes of prose essays, travel sketches, and addresses.

Francis Orray Ticknor (1822–1874) was a country physician and poet in Georgia. He contributed verse to newspapers and minor periodicals. "Little Giffen" was composed during his supervision of Confederate hospital work at Columbus, Georgia. It was based on the true story of a lad he and his wife nursed back to life. His collected verse, *Poems of Frank O. Ticknor, M.D.*, was not published in book form till 1879. An appreciative sketch by Paul Hamilton Hayne was prefixed.

The minor lyric poet Paul Hamilton Hayne (1830–1886) was a native of Charleston and came from an old Southern family. He was graduated at the University of South Carolina, and like Timrod he drifted into the group about William Gilmore Simms. He tried law and then gave himself to journalism and poetry. He published three volumes of verse before the War. During the War period he served as a newspaper writer and wrote patriotic wartime pieces. When Charleston was burned and his property swept away, he retired to a cottage in the pine barrens of Georgia, depending on poetry for his meager income. His best volume, *Legends and Lyrics*, appeared in 1872. His *Collected Poems* was published in 1882. Hayne edited Timrod's poems before he collected his own. His carefully polished pieces show grace of craftsmanship and a lyric sweetness that sometimes becomes sentimentalism, but they display no marked originality. His reputation rests on a few poems.

Thomas Buchanan Read (1822–1872), painter, poet, and lecturer, was a Pennsylvanian of Scotch-Irish descent. After 1846 he lived in Philadelphia. Alongside his career as a painter he wrote many volumes of verse. These he gathered into three volumes in 1866. He wrote with facility, but imitatively and uncritically. His most popular poem, almost the only one that has lasted, was "Sheridan's Ride." Read was a major in the Union army during the War.

Francis Miles Finch (1827–1907) was a native of Ithaca, New York, of New England stock. He was educated at Yale and became associate judge of the New York Court of Appeals. He was active in founding Cornell University, was a trustee, a nonresident lecturer in the Law School, and later dean of the Law School. He composed "The Blue and the Gray," published in the *Atlantic* for September, 1867, on hearing that the women of Columbus, Mississippi, had "strewn flowers alike on the graves of the Confederate and the National soldiers." The poem is said to have done much to allay partisan feeling and bring reconciliation. At the end of his life he collected his verse, and it was published after his death as *The Blue and the Gray and Other Verses* (1909).

For collections of lyrics and songs of the Civil War period, see the four books edited by Frank Moore, *Songs of the Soldiers*, *Lyrics of Loyalty*, *Personal and Political Ballads* (all 1864), and *Songs and Ballads of the Southern People*, *1861–1865* (1886); R. G. White, *Poetry, Lyrical, Narrative, and Satirical of the Civil War* (1866); William Gilmore Simms, *War Poetry of the South* (1867); F. F. Browne, *Bugle Echoes, a Collection of Poems of the Civil War, Northern and Southern* (1886); G. E. Eggleston, *American War Ballads and Lyrics* (2 vols., 1889); Esther P. Ellinger, *Southern Poetry of the Civil War* (1918). The music as well as the texts may be found in "*Sound Off*": *Soldier Songs*, by E. A. Dolph (1929), pp. 226–367. *Southern Poets* (1936), edited by E. W. Parks, contains selections from Southern poets of the Civil War period, with an introduction and bibliography.

Sketches of most of the lyrists and song writers of the period may be found in *DAB*. For Stephen C. Foster, consult Morrison Foster's *Biography, Songs, and Musical Compositions of Stephen C. Foster* (1896) and H. V. Milligan's *Stephen Collins Foster* (1920). G. C. Perine treated James Ryder Randall in *The Poets and Verse-Writers of Maryland* (1898), and M. P. Andrews edited *The Poems of James Ryder Randall* (1910); see also Brander Matthews, "The Songs of the Civil War," in *Pen and Ink* (1888), pp. 172 ff. For Timrod, see H. T. Thompson, *Henry Timrod, Laureate of the Confederacy* (1928), which has a bibliography; and G. A. Wauchope, *Henry Timrod: Man and Poet* (1915). For Julia Ward Howe consult L. E. Richards and M. H. Elliott, *Julia Ward Howe* (2 vols., 1915). There is no good biography of Paul Hamilton Hayne; material concerning him may be found in S. A. Link's *Pioneers of Southern Literature* (1903), in C. W. Hubner's *Representative Southern Poets* (1906), and in

The Library of Southern Literature (1909). For Thomas Buchanan Read, see H. C. Townsend and Others, *A Memoir of T. Buchanan Read* (1889); and R. H. Stoddard, *Recollections, Personal and Literary* (1903), Chapter XIV. There is an account of Francis Miles Finch in A. P. Stokes's *Memorials of Eminent Yale Men* (2 vols., 1914).

MY MARYLAND

By James Ryder Randall

The despot's heel is on thy shore,
    Maryland!
His torch is at thy temple door,
    Maryland!
Avenge the patriotic gore
That flecked the streets of Baltimore,
And be the battle queen of yore,
    Maryland, my Maryland!

Hark to an exiled son's appeal,
    Maryland!   10
My Mother State, to thee I kneel,
    Maryland!
For life and death, for woe and weal,
Thy peerless chivalry reveal,
And gird thy beauteous limbs with steel,
    Maryland, my Maryland!

Thou wilt not cower in the dust,
    Maryland!
Thy beaming sword shall never rust,
    Maryland!   20
Remember Carroll's [1] sacred trust,
Remember Howard's warlike thrust,
And all thy slumberers with the just,
    Maryland, my Maryland!

Come! 'tis the red dawn of the day,
    Maryland!
Come with thy panoplied array,
    Maryland!
With Ringgold's [2] spirit for the fray,
With Watson's blood at Monterey,   30
With fearless Lowe and dashing May,
    Maryland, my Maryland!

Dear Mother, burst the tyrant's chain,
    Maryland!
Virginia should not call in vain,
    Maryland!
She meets her sisters on the plain,—
"*Sic semper!*" [1] 'tis the proud refrain
That baffles minions back amain,
    Maryland!   40
Arise in majesty again,
    Maryland, my Maryland!

Come! for thy shield is bright and strong,
    Maryland!
Come! for thy dalliance does thee wrong,
    Maryland!
Come to thine own heroic throng,
Stalking with Liberty along,
And chant thy dauntless slogan-song,
    Maryland, my Maryland!   50

I see the blush upon thy cheek,
    Maryland!
For thou wast ever bravely meek,
    Maryland!
But lo! there surges forth a shriek,
From hill to hill, from creek to creek,
Potomac calls to Chesapeake,
    Maryland, my Maryland!

Thou wilt not yield the Vandal toil,
    Maryland!   60
Thou wilt not crook to his control,
    Maryland!
Better the fire upon thee roll,
Better the shot, the blade, the bowl,
Than crucifixion of the soul,
    Maryland, my Maryland!

I hear the distant thunder-hum,
    Maryland!
The Old Line's bugle, fife, and drum,
    Maryland!   70

[1] Charles Carroll of Carrollton was the last surviving signer of the Declaration of Independence. John Eager Howard was a prominent military leader in the Revolution, and afterwards U.S. Senator and Federalist candidate for the vice-presidency.   [2] The four names mentioned in this stanza are those of Marylanders who were soldiers in the Mexican War.

[1] the first words of the motto of Virginia's coat of arms, *Sic semper tyrannis* ("Thus always to tyrants")

She is not dead, nor deaf, nor dumb;
Huzza! she spurns the Northern scum!
She breathes! she burns! she'll come! she'll
    come!
  Maryland, my Maryland!

                                1861

CHARLESTON [1]

By Henry Timrod

CALM as that second summer which precedes
  The first fall of the snow,
In the broad sunlight of heroic deeds,
  The city bides the foe.

As yet, behind their ramparts, stern and proud,
  Her bolted thunders sleep,—
Dark Sumter, like a battlemented cloud,
  Looms o'er the solemn deep.

No Calpe [2] frowns from lofty cliff or scar
  To guard the holy strand;   10
But Moultrie holds in leash her dogs of war
  Above the level sand.

And down the dunes a thousand guns lie
    couched,
  Unseen, beside the flood—
Like tigers in some Orient jungle crouched
  That wait and watch for blood.

Meanwhile, through streets still echoing with
    trade,
  Walk grave and thoughtful men,
Whose hands may one day wield the patriot's
    blade
  As lightly as the pen.   20

And maidens, with such eyes as would grow
    dim
  Over a bleeding hound,
Seem each one to have caught the strength of
    him
  Whose sword she sadly bound.

Thus girt without and garrisoned at home,
  Day patient following day,
Old Charleston looks from roof and spire and
    dome,
  Across her tranquil bay.

[1] Here began the Civil War, April 12, 1861. Forts
Sumter and Moultrie are in Charleston harbor.   [2] old
name for the rock of Gibraltar

Ships, through a hundred foes, from Saxon
    lands
  And spicy Indian ports,   30
Bring Saxon steel and iron to her hands,
  And summer to her courts.

But still, along yon dim Atlantic line,
  The only hostile smoke
Creeps like a harmless mist above the brine,
  From some frail floating oak.

Shall the spring dawn, and she, still clad in
    smiles,
  And with an unscathed brow,
Rest in the strong arms of her palm-crowned
    isles,
  As fair and free as now?   40

We know not; in the temple of the Fates
  God has inscribed her doom;
And, all untroubled in her faith, she waits
  The triumph or the tomb.

1861–1862?   1863

BATTLE–HYMN OF THE REPUBLIC

By Julia Ward Howe

MINE eyes have seen the glory of the coming
    of the Lord:
He is trampling out the vintage where the
    grapes of wrath are stored;
He hath loosed the fateful lightning of his
    terrible swift sword;
  His truth is marching on.

I have seen him in the watch-fires of a hundred
    circling camps;
They have builded him an altar in the evening
    dews and damps;
I can read his righteous sentence by the dim
    and flaring lamps:
  His day is marching on.

I have read a fiery gospel, writ in burnished
    rows of steel:
"As ye deal with my contemners, so with you
    my grace shall deal;   10
Let the Hero, born of woman, crush the
    serpent with his heel,
  Since God is marching on."

He has sounded forth the trumpet that shall
never call retreat;
He is sifting out the hearts of men before his
judgment-seat;
Oh, be swift, my soul, to answer him! be
jubilant, my feet!
Our God is marching on.

In the beauty of the lilies Christ was born
across the sea,
With a glory in his bosom that transfigures
you and me:
As he died to make men holy, let us die to
make men free,
While God is marching on.   20

1861   1862

LITTLE GIFFEN

By Francis Orray Ticknor

OUT of the focal and foremost fire,
Out of the hospital walls as dire;
Smitten of grape-shot and gangrene,
(Eighteenth battle, and *he* sixteen!)
Specter! such as you seldom see,
Little Giffen, of Tennessee!

"Take him and welcome!" the surgeons said;
Little the doctor can help the dead!
So we took him; and brought him where
The balm was sweet in the summer air;   10
And we laid him down on a wholesome bed,—
Utter Lazarus, heel to head!

And we watched the war with bated breath,—
Skeleton Boy against skeleton Death.
Months of torture, how many such?
Weary weeks of the stick and crutch;
And still a glint of the steel-blue eye
Told of a spirit that wouldn't die,

And didn't. Nay, more! in death's despite
The crippled skeleton "learned to write."   20
"Dear mother," at first, of course; and then
"Dear captain," inquiring about the men.
Captain's answer: "Of eighty-and-five,
Giffen and I are left alive."

Word of gloom from the war, one day;
Johnston pressed at the front, they say.
Little Giffen was up and away;

A tear—his first—as he bade good-by,
Dimmed the glint of his steel-blue eye.
"I'll write, if spared!" There was news of the
fight;   30
But none of Giffen.—He did not write.

I sometimes fancy that, were I king
Of the princely Knights of the Golden Ring,[1]
With the songs of the minstrel in mine ear,
And the tender legend that trembles here,
I'd give the best on his bended knee,
The whitest soul of my chivalry,
For "Little Giffen," of Tennessee.

1863

SHERIDAN'S RIDE

By Thomas Buchanan Read

UP from the South at break of day,
Bringing to Winchester fresh dismay,
The affrighted air with a shudder bore,
Like a herald in haste, to the chieftain's door,
The terrible grumble, and rumble, and roar,
Telling the battle was on once more,
And Sheridan twenty miles away.

And wider still those billows of war,
Thundered along the horizon's bar;
And louder yet into Winchester rolled   10
The roar of that red sea uncontrolled,
Making the blood of the listener cold,
As he thought of the stake in that fiery fray,
And Sheridan twenty miles away.

But there is a road from Winchester town,
A good broad highway leading down;
And there, through the flush of the morning
light,
A steed as black as the steeds of night,
Was seen to pass, as with eagle flight,
As if he knew the terrible need;   20
He stretched away with his utmost speed;
Hills rose and fell; but his heart was gay,
With Sheridan fifteen miles away.

Still sprung from those swift hoofs, thundering south,
The dust, like the smoke from the cannon's
mouth;

[1] evidently alluding to King Arthur and his Knights
of the Round Table

Or the trail of a comet, sweeping faster and
    faster,
Foreboding to traitors the doom of disaster.
The heart of the steed, and the heart of the
    master
Were beating like prisoners assaulting their
    walls,
Impatient to be where the battlefield calls; 30
Every nerve of the charger was strained to
    full play,
With Sheridan only ten miles away.

Under his spurning feet the road
Like an arrowy Alpine river flowed,
And the landscape sped away behind
Like an ocean flying before the wind;
And the steed, like a bark fed with furnace
    ire,
Swept on, with his wild eye full of fire.
But lo! he is nearing his heart's desire;
He is snuffing the smoke of the roaring fray,
With Sheridan only five miles away.   41

The first that the general saw were the groups
Of stragglers, and then the retreating troops,
What was done? What to do? A glance told
    him both,
Then striking his spurs, with a terrible oath,
He dashed down the line, 'mid a storm of
    huzzas,
And the wave of retreat checked its course
    there, because
The sight of the master compelled it to
    pause.
With foam and with dust, the black charger
    was gray;
By the flash of his eye, and the red nostril's
    play,   50
He seemed to the whole great army to say,
"I have brought you Sheridan all the way
From Winchester, down to save the day!"

Hurrah, hurrah, for Sheridan!
Hurrah, hurrah, for horse and man!
And when their statues are placed on high,
Under the dome of the Union sky
(The American soldiers' Temple of Fame),
There with the glorious general's name,
Be it said, in letters both bold and bright, 60
  "Here is the steed that saved the day

By carrying Sheridan into the fight,
  From Winchester, twenty miles away!"
                     1865

THE BLUE AND THE GRAY

By Francis Miles Finch

By the flow of the inland river,
  Whence the fleets of iron have fled,
Where the blades of the grave grass quiver,
  Asleep are the ranks of the dead:
    Under the sod and the dew,
      Waiting the judgment day;
    Under the one, the Blue,
      Under the other, the Gray.

These in the robings of glory,
  Those in the gloom of defeat,   10
All with the battle-blood gory,
  In the dusk of eternity meet:
    Under the sod and the dew,
      Waiting the judgment day;
    Under the laurel, the Blue,
      Under the willow, the Gray.

From the silence of sorrowful hours
  The desolate mourners go,
Lovingly laden with flowers
  Alike for the friend and the foe: 20
    Under the sod and the dew,
      Waiting the judgment day;
    Under the roses, the Blue,
      Under the lilies, the Gray.

So with an equal splendor,
  The morning sun-rays fall,
With a touch impartially tender,
  On the blossoms blooming for all:
    Under the sod and the dew,
      Waiting the judgment day;   30
    Broidered with gold, the Blue,
      Mellowed with gold, the Gray.

So, when the summer calleth,
  On forest and field of grain,
With an equal murmur falleth
  The cooling drip of the rain:
    Under the sod and the dew,
      Waiting the judgment day;
    Wet with the rain, the Blue,
      Wet with the rain, the Gray.   40

Sadly, but not with upbraiding,
    The generous deed was done,
In the storm of the years that are fading
    No braver battle was won:
        Under the sod and the dew,
            Waiting the judgment day;
        Under the blossoms, the Blue,
            Under the garlands, the Gray.

No more shall the war cry sever,
    Or the winding rivers be red;   50
They banish our anger forever
    When they laurel the graves of our dead!
        Under the sod and the dew,
            Waiting the judgment day:
        Love and tears for the Blue,
            Tears and love for the Gray.

1867

1819 -- *Walt Whitman* -- 1892

WHITMAN thought his chief mission was to be the spokesman and champion
of democratic nationalism. He was a contemporary of Lowell but contrasted strongly with Lowell in temperament, in ideals, and in his attitude toward
the past. America seemed to him a new and free place with boundless opportunities for development, and he had optimistic faith in the new race which should
emerge from its equalitarian conditions. An apostle of American cultural independence, he strove to give expression to the collective attainments, institutions,
and destiny of the new democracy.

Whitman was born May 31, 1819, at the hamlet of West Hills, Huntington,
Long Island, of English and Dutch ancestry. He was early called "Walt" to distinguish him from his father Walter, a farmer, carpenter, and builder. His parents
had Quaker leanings, and were somewhat under the influence of the unorthodox
Quaker preacher Elias Hicks. The family moved to Brooklyn when Walt was about
five years of age. He had only a few years of formal schooling, worked as office boy
for a lawyer, then for a doctor, and when about thirteen began work as a printer.
For several years he worked here and there in newspaper offices as typesetter and
occasional contributor, and taught several brief terms in country schools.

Whitman engaged in journalism as reporter and editor in New York and Brooklyn from 1842 to 1851. His most important position was as editor of the *Brooklyn
Eagle* from 1846 to 1848. On losing this position, partly for political reasons, he
was appointed by chance to an editorial job on the recently founded New Orleans
Daily Crescent and made the long journey there by rail, stage, and steamboat. The
next year he was back in Brooklyn, still in newspaper work and writing for periodicals. Metropolitan life fascinated him, and he took deep interest in the stage, in
concerts, in operatic and orchestral music, and in the human life of the streets
and the ferries. In 1852 he followed his father's occupation of building and
selling houses in Brooklyn. He must have had in mind for some years the com-

position of *Leaves of Grass,* which he published in 1855 when he was thirty-six, setting up the type for it himself. It had no sale, but a gift copy sent to Emerson brought a personal letter recognizing it as a revolutionary book. "I am not blind to the worth of the wonderful gift of *Leaves of Grass.* I find it the most extraordinary piece of wit and wisdom that America has yet contributed . . . I greet you at the beginning of a great career"—a statement that Whitman printed across the back of the next edition, somewhat perhaps to Emerson's embarrassment.

The decade from 1863 to 1873 Whitman spent mostly in Washington. On hearing that his brother George, who had enlisted in the Union army, had been wounded in Virginia, he went South to him. Next he served as a volunteer nurse to the wounded and sick in the Washington hospitals. He made hundreds of visits trying to help the soldiers. His personal experiences are set forth in *Specimen Days* (1882), the oftenest reprinted of his prose works. At the close of the War he had a clerkship in the Department of the Interior, but lost it when his superior officer came upon a copy of *Leaves of Grass* which he was revising, and thought it an objectionable book. His friends came to his defense and obtained for him another position in the office of the Attorney General, but for a long time his reputation was clouded by this happening.

His volume of poems on the Civil War, *Drum Taps,* appeared in 1866, and the fourth edition of *Leaves of Grass* in 1867. Publication of selections from his poetry by William Rossetti aroused interest in him in England. His prose work, *Democratic Vistas,* setting forth his main theses of democracy and individualism, appeared in 1871.

The twenty years from 1872 to 1892 he spent mainly as an invalid or semi-invalid with his brother George at Camden, New Jersey, at first nearly in poverty. Though Europe had welcomed him with appreciation and fame, in his own country recognition of him as one of the most original and stimulating of poets came mainly after the 1880's, when his books began to bring him an income and the number of his friends and admirers increased. His influence was not striking till after 1900, and was at its height in the World War period. He made a leisurely excursion to Denver and the Rocky Mountains in 1877, went to Canada to visit his friend Dr. R. M. Bucke in 1880, revisited Long Island and New York City, and went to Boston in 1881. He died in Camden in 1892 at the age of seventy-three. The last of successively enlarged editions of *Leaves of Grass* was published in 1891–92 and the *Complete Prose Works* in 1892.

Whitman was the last of the major poets emerging from the period of romantic idealism in America. Many of its doctrines—such as faith in the goodness of man, worship of nature as a benign influence, belief in the leadership of the poet—and something of its mysticism appear in his pages. But in much he broke away from European models and existing literary forms and vogues. He thought our literature too imitative and discarded elegance and sentiment, themes of love and war, and legends of old heroes. Some of the ideas he reiterates are that the poet who glorifies himself glorifies everybody; that there is divinity in all created things, hence everything is suitable material for poetry, the body as well as the soul; and that death is to be welcomed as leading to a new and more spiritual existence. To fit the matter of his verse, he sought to create a new kind of poetical manner, rejecting metrical form and rhyme and conventional stanzaic structure. Many writers in the succeeding age were to follow him. They imitated his loose form, free verse, linguistic audacities, and long catalogues and detailed lists, and went further than he in the cult of informality and the free admission to poetry of all topics, ugly as well as beautiful, physical as well as spiritual.

Whitman's poetical expression seems to have been influenced by his love of music, especially his intense devotion to Italian opera. He thought of poetry as a kind of musical utterance. He describes it as "vocalism" and "recitatif." He speaks of "uttering" his verse, of "caroling," "warbling," "trilling" his "songs," and he refers to himself as a "chansonnier." He seems to have wished to reach his readers with his voice, like singers at the opera, or like actors or orators. His pages are sprinkled with Italian, French, and Spanish terms. There is even some resemblance between the look of his verse on a page and operatic librettos.

Whitman's prose is not wide in range, but it serves as a key to his poetry and supplements it. *Specimen Days*, made up of notebook jottings, reads quickly and easily. *Democratic Vistas*, his most ambitious prose work, because of its more abstract subject matter and loose structure and its long repetitional and parenthetical periods, is less easy to follow.

Although Whitman thought himself the poet of the common people and tried to live out his doctrines of equality, sympathy, and comradeship with all human beings, he was first recognized by the sophisticated, and it is to them that he still has the strongest appeal. The position of popular poet was retained by Longfellow. Whitman's verse has been translated into many languages, and European recognition of American poets has gone chiefly to him and to Poe. He proved to be an original and vital force, a major dominating influence in the decades that succeeded him, and he will endure probably as the best poetic interpreter of the American nineteenth-century democratic dream.

Whitman had an unexpectedly extensive and various background of reading. Homer and Shakespeare were his favorites in youth. He had some knowledge of the major classics of Greece and Rome, and of Dante, the *Arabian Nights*, and Cervantes. In German literature he knew Goethe and was interested in the idealistic philosophers of the eighteenth century, especially Hegel. Among French authors he showed acquaintance with Rousseau and Voltaire, and he praised Dumas and George Sand. To the latter he seems to have owed some of his democratic ideas, his pose as a workingman's poet, and his borrowings of vocabulary from the French language. Among English writers he singled out for special discussion Shakespeare, Tennyson, Scott, Dickens, Carlyle, and Burns, and among American writers Emerson, Bryant, Longfellow, and Whittier. He expressed distaste for Poe and Henry James, and strangely enough left no references to Mark Twain. Of Whitman as a critic, M. O. Johnson says: "In every piece of literature Whitman looked for artistic excellence, but he also looked for democratic purpose. If he found a combination of the two, as he almost never did, then the work deserved praise with reservation. For great literature Whitman prescribed restraint, originality, purpose, optimism, universality, concern with nature, concern with contemporary life, and emphasis upon democracy. In the main, they are the essentials of literature of which Whitman spoke in his preface and elsewhere." Whitman held the literary belief that all literature of the past was the expression of "feudalism" and "superstition." He expected the literature of the dawning new day to be the greatest because it emerged from the forces of Democracy, or faith in the self-reliant spirituality of the individual, and of science, with its exaltation of the physical. For such a literature he thought new forms of expression necessary and inevitable.

The standard edition of the complete writings of Whitman is the Camden (10 vols., 1902), edited by R. M. Bucke, H. L. Traubel, and O. L. Triggs. Emory Holloway edited *The Uncollected Poetry and Prose of Walt Whitman* (2 vols., 1921), an inclusive edition of *Leaves of Grass* (1924), and a convenient *Walt Whitman's Complete Poetry and Selected Prose and Letters* (1938). Other Whitman material may be found in *The Gathering of the Forces* (2 vols., 1920), edited by Cleveland Rodgers and John Black; in *Walt Whitman's Workshop, A Collection of Unpublished Manuscripts* (1928), edited by C. J. Furness; and in *Walt Whitman and the Civil War* (1933), by C. I. Glicksberg. The first edition of *Leaves of Grass* has been edited for the Facsimile Text Society (1939) by C. J. Furness.

Biographies include *With Walt Whitman in Camden* (3 vols., 1906–14), an intimate account of the poet's later years, presented in diary form, by his friend and disciple, Horace Traubel; R. M. Bucke, *Walt Whitman* (1883), with the help of Whitman himself; and Bliss Perry, *Walt Whitman, His Life and Work*, in the American Men of Letters Series (1906). The English Men of Letters Series devotes two volumes to Whitman, by G. R. Carpenter (1909) and by John Bailey (1926). A French life by Léon Balzagette, *Walt Whitman and His Work*, was abridged and translated into English by Ellen Fitzgerald in 1920. E. Holloway's *Whitman, an Interpretative Narrative* received the Pulitzer prize for biography in 1926. Floyd Stovall's *Whitman* (revised, 1939), in American Writers Series, has an admirable introduction.

Of an immense number of critical books and articles, only a few may be mentioned. J. A. Symonds's laudatory *Walt Whitman: a Study* (1893) did much to arouse interest in the poet, as did the critical study, *Whitman: a Study* (1896), written by his friend, John Burroughs. In contrast to these complimentary views is George Santayana's hostile "The Poetry of Barbarism," in *Interpretations of Poetry and Religion* (1900). P. E. More wrote of Whitman in the *Shelburne Essays*, 4th series (1906). Other commentators are John Macy, in *The Spirit of American Literature* (1908); Basil de Sélincourt, in *Walt Whitman: a Critical Study* (1914); E. Holloway, in his chapter on Whitman in *CHAL*, II (1918); and Stuart Pratt Sherman, in

Americans (1922). Norman Foerster treated Whitman in both his *Nature in American Literature* (1923) and *American Criticism* (1928). A discussion of Whitman by V. L. Parrington is included in his *Main Currents in American Thought*, III (1927). A recent treatment is by Louise Pound in the introduction to Whitman's *Specimen Days, Democratic Vistas and Other Prose* (1935). Edgar Lee Masters published a study of Whitman (1937), of especial interest as relating Whitman to American history. Esther Shepherd, in *Walt Whitman's Pose* (1938), indicates his indebtedness to George Sand. Maurice O. Johnson treats Whitman's critical views in *Walt Whitman as a Critic* (1938). Newton Arvin's *Whitman* (1938) is concerned with the social implications of his poetry. G. W. Allen deals with Whitman's verse technique in *American Prosody* (1935). Bibliographies of Walt Whitman are by E. Holloway, in *CHAL*, II; Frank Shay, *The Bibliography of Walt Whitman* (1920), which includes no criticism but lists only the works of Whitman himself; O. L. Triggs, in *The Complete Writings of Walt Whitman*, X; and Carolyn Wells and A. F. Goldsmith, *A Concise Bibliography of Walt Whitman* (1922).

From SONG OF MYSELF

This is the first and longest poem in *Leaves of Grass* (1858). It was preceded by a ten-page Preface treating of the nature of poetry and extolling the inspiration which America offers to the poet. Neither this poem nor the eleven that followed had headings. The title "Song of Myself" was given it later. Underlying it is the cult of self of Rousseau and the transcendentalists. The Song reflects Whitman's experiences, his zest for the spectacles of cities and for the out-of-doors, and many of the larger questions of life, faith, death, immortality, and happiness. It is better when read in detached passages than consecutively. Later, Whitman became less crude and incoherent as an artist. He realized the individual character of his work. "I know perfectly well my road is different. Most of the great poets are impersonal; I am personal. They portray characters, events, passions, but never mention themselves. In my poems, all revolves round, concentrates in, radiates from myself. But my book compels, absolutely necessitates, every reader to transpose himself or herself into the central position and become the living fountain, actor, experiencer himself or herself of every page, every aspiration, every line."

I

I CELEBRATE myself, and sing myself,
And what I assume you shall assume,
For every atom belonging to me as good belongs to you.

I loafe and invite my soul,
I lean and loafe at my ease observing a spear of summer grass.

My tongue, every atom of my blood, form'd from this soil, this air,
Born here of parents born here from parents the same, and their parents the same,
I, now thirty-seven years old in perfect health begin,
Hoping to cease not till death.

Creeds and schools in abeyance,
Retiring back a while sufficed at what they are, but never forgotten,
I harbor for good or bad, I permit to speak at every hazard,
Nature without check with original energy.

10

Alone far in the wilds and mountains I hunt,
Wandering amazed at my own lightness and glee,
In the late afternoon choosing a safe spot to pass the night,
Kindling a fire and broiling the fresh-kill'd game,
Falling asleep on the gather'd leaves with my dog and gun by my side.

The Yankee clipper is under her sky-sails, she cuts the sparkle and scud,
My eyes settle the land, I bend at her prow or shout joyously from the deck.
The boatmen and clam-diggers arose early and stopt for me,
I tuck'd my trowser-ends in my boots and went and had a good time;
You should have been with us that day round the chowder-kettle. 10

I saw the marriage of the trapper in the open air in the far west, the bride was a red girl,
Her father and his friends sat near cross-legged and dumbly smoking, they had moccasins to their feet and large thick blankets hanging from their shoulders,
On a bank lounged the trapper, he was drest mostly in skins, his luxuriant beard and curls protected his neck, he held his bride by the hand,
She had long eyelashes, her head was bare, her coarse straight locks descended upon her voluptuous limbs and reach'd to her feet.

The runaway slave came to my house and stopt outside,
I heard his motions crackling the twigs of the woodpile,
Through the swung half-door of the kitchen I saw him limpsy [1] and weak,
And went where he sat on a log and led him in and assured him,
And brought water and fill'd a tub for his sweated body and bruis'd feet,
And gave him a room that enter'd from my own, and gave him some coarse clean clothes, 20
And remember perfectly well his revolving eyes and his awkwardness,
And remember putting plasters on the galls of his neck and ankles;
He staid with me a week before he was recuperated and pass'd north,
I had him sit next me at table, my fire-lock lean'd in the corner.

16

I am of old and young, of the foolish as much as the wise,
Regardless of others, ever regardful of others,
Maternal as well as paternal, a child as well as a man,
Stuff'd with the stuff that is coarse and stuff'd with the stuff that is fine,
One of the Nation of many nations, the smallest the same and the largest the same,
A Southerner soon as a Northerner, a planter nonchalant and hospitable down by the Oconee I live,
A Yankee bound my own way ready for trade, my joints the limberest joints on earth and the sternest joints on earth,
A Kentuckian walking the vale of the Elkhorn in my deer-skin leggings, a Louisianian or Georgian,
A boatman over lakes or bays or along coasts, a Hoosier, Badger, Buckeye;
At home on Kanadian snow-shoes or up in the bush, or with fishermen off Newfoundland, 10
At home in the fleet of ice-boats, sailing with the rest and tacking.
At home on the hills of Vermont or in the woods of Maine, or the Texan ranch,
Comrade of Californians, comrade of free North-Westerners, (loving their big proportions,)
Comrade of raftsmen and coalmen, comrade of all who shake hands and welcome to drink and meat,
A learner with the simplest, a teacher of the thoughtfullest,
A novice beginning yet experient of myriads of seasons,
Of every hue and caste am I, of every rank and religion,
A farmer, mechanic, artist, gentleman, sailor, quaker,
Prisoner, fancy-man, rowdy, lawyer, physician, priest.
I resist any thing better than my own diversity, 20

[1] dialectal or colloquial for the adjective "limp"

Breathe the air but leave plenty after me,
And am not stuck up, and am in my place.
(The moth and the fish-eggs are in their place,
The bright suns I see and the dark suns I cannot see are in their place,
The palpable is in its place and the impalpable is in its place.)

21

I am the poet of the Body and I am the poet of the Soul,
The pleasures of heaven are with me and the pains of hell are with me,
The first I graft and increase upon myself, the latter I translate into a new tongue.

I am the poet of the woman the same as the man,
And I say it is as great to be a woman as to be a man,
And I say there is nothing greater than the mother of men.

I chant the chant of dilation or pride,
We have had ducking and deprecating about enough,
I show that size is only development.

Have you outstript the rest? are you the President?   10
It is a trifle, they will more than arrive there every one, and still pass on.

I am he that walks with the tender and growing night,
I call to the earth and sea half-held by the night.

Press close bare-bosom'd night—press close magnetic nourishing night!
Night of south winds—night of the large few stars!
Still nodding night—mad naked summer night!

Smile O voluptuous cool-breath'd earth!
Earth of the slumbering and liquid trees!
Earth of the departed sunset—earth of the mountains misty-topt!
Earth of the vitreous pour of the full moon just tinged with blue!   20
Earth of shine and dark mottling the tide of the river!
Earth of the limpid gray of clouds brighter and clearer for my sake!
Far-swooping elbow'd earth—rich apple-blossom'd earth!
Smile, for your lover comes.

Prodigal, you have given me love—therefore I to you give love!
O unspeakable passionate love.

31

I believe a leaf of grass is no less than the journey-work of the stars,
And the pismire is equally perfect, and a grain of sand, and the egg of the wren,
And the tree-toad is a chef-d'œuvre for the highest,
And the running blackberry would adorn the parlors of heaven,
And the narrowest hinge in my hand puts to scorn all machinery,
And the cow crunching with depress'd head surpasses any statue,
And a mouse is miracle enough to stagger sextillions of infidels.

I find I incorporate gneiss, coal, long-threaded moss, fruits, grains, esculent roots,
And am stucco'd with quadrupeds and birds all over,
And have distanced what is behind me for all good reasons,   10
But call any thing back again when I desire it.

In vain the speeding or shyness,
In vain the plutonic rocks send their old heat against my approach,
In vain the mastodon retreats beneath its own powder'd bones,
In vain objects stand leagues off and assume manifold shapes,
In vain the ocean settling in hollows and the great monsters lying low,
In vain the buzzard houses herself with the sky,
In vain the snake slides through the creepers and logs,
In vain the elk takes to the inner passes of the woods,
In vain the razor-bill'd auk sails far north to Labrador,
I follow quickly, I ascend to the next in the fissure of the cliff.   20

33

Space and Time! now I see it is true, what I guess'd at,
What I guess'd when I loaf'd on the grass,
What I guess'd while I lay alone in my bed,
And again as I walk'd the beach under the paling stars of the morning.

My ties and ballasts leave me, my elbows rest in sea-gaps,
I skirt sierras, my palms cover continents,
I am afoot with my vision.

By the city's quadrangular houses—in log huts, camping with lumbermen,
Along the ruts of the turnpike, along the dry gulch and rivulet bed,
Weeding my onion-patch or hoeing rows of carrots and parsnips, crossing savannas, trailing in
    forests,   10
Prospecting, gold-digging, girdling the trees of a new purchase,
Scorch'd ankle-deep by the hot sand, hauling my boat down the shallow river,
Where the panther walks to and fro on a limb overhead, where the buck turns furiously at the
    hunter,
Where the rattlesnake suns his flabby length on a rock, where the otter is feeding on fish,
Where the alligator in his tough pimples sleeps by the bayou,
Where the black bear is searching for roots or honey, where the beaver pats the mud with his
    paddle-shaped tail;
Over the growing sugar, over the yellow-flower'd cotton plant, over the rice in its low moist
    field,
Over the sharp-peak'd farm house, with its scallop'd scum and slender shoots from the gutters,
Over the western persimmon, over the long-leav'd corn, over the delicate blue-flower flax,
Over the white and brown buckwheat, a hummer and buzzer there with the rest,   20
Over the dusky green of the rye as it ripples and shades in the breeze;
Scaling mountains, pulling myself cautiously up, holding on by low scragged limbs,
Walking the path worn in the grass and beat through the leaves of the brush,
Where the quail is whistling betwixt the woods and the wheat-lot,
Where the bat flies in the Seventh-month eve, where the great gold-bug drops through the
    dark,
Where the brook puts out of the roots of the old tree and flows to the meadow,
Where cattle stand and shake away flies with the tremulous shuddering of their hides,
Where the cheese-cloth hangs in the kitchen, where andirons straddle the hearth-slab, where cob-
    webs fall in festoons from the rafters;
Where trip-hammers crash, where the press is whirling its cylinders,
Wherever the human heart beats with terrible throes under its ribs,   30

Where the pear-shaped balloon is floating aloft, (floating in it myself and looking composedly down,)

Where the life-car [1] is drawn on the slip-noose, where the heat hatches pale-green eggs in the dented sand,

Where the she-whale swims with her calf and never forsakes it,

Where the steam-ship trails hind-ways its long pennant of smoke,

Where the fin of the shark cuts like a black chip out of the water,

Where the half-burn'd brig is riding on unknown currents,

Where shells grow to her slimy deck, where the dead are corrupting below;

Where the dense-starr'd flag is borne at the head of the regiments,

Approaching Manhattan up by the long-stretching island,

Under Niagara, the cataract falling like a veil over my countenance,   40

Upon a door-step, upon the horse-block of hard wood outside,

Upon the race-course, or enjoying picnics or jigs or a good game of base-ball,

At he-festivals, with blackguard gibes, ironical license, bull-dances, drinking, laughter,

At the cider-mill tasting the sweets of the brown mash, sucking the juice through a straw,

At apple-peelings wanting kisses for all the red fruit I find,

At musters, beach-parties, friendly bees, huskings, house-raisings;

Where the mocking-bird sounds his delicious gurgles, cackles, screams, weeps,

Where the hay-rick stands in the barn-yard, where the dry-stalks are scatter'd, where the brood-cow waits in the hovel,

Where the bull advances to do his masculine work, where the stud to the mare, where the cock is treading the hen,

Where the heifers browse, where geese nip their food with short jerks,   50

Where sun-down shadows lengthen over the limitless and lonesome prairie,

Where herds of buffalo make a crawling spread of the square miles far and near,

Where the humming-bird shimmers, where the neck of the long-lived swan is curving and winding,

Where the laughing-gull scoots by the shore, where she laughs her near-human laugh,

Where bee-hives range on a gray bench in the garden half hid by the high weeds,

Where band-neck'd partridges roost in a ring on the ground with their heads out,

Where burial coaches enter the arch'd gates of a cemetery,

Where winter wolves bark amid wastes of snow and icicled trees,

Where the yellow-crown'd heron comes to the edge of the marsh at night and feeds upon small crabs,

Where the splash of swimmers and divers cools the warm noon,   60

Where the katy-did works her chromatic reed on the walnut-tree over the well,

Through patches of citrons and cucumbers with silver-wired leaves,

Through the salt-lick or orange glade, or under conical firs,

Through the gymnasium, through the curtain'd saloon, through the office or public hall;

Pleas'd with the native and pleas'd with the foreign, pleas'd with the new and old,

Pleas'd with the homely woman as well as the handsome,

Pleas'd with the quakeress as she puts off her bonnet and talks melodiously,

Pleas'd with the tune of the choir of the whitewash'd church,

Pleas'd with the earnest words of the sweating Methodist preacher, impress'd seriously at the camp-meeting;

Looking in at the shop-windows of Broadway the whole forenoon, flatting the flesh of my nose on the thick plate-glass,   70

Wandering the same afternoon with my face turn'd up to the clouds, or down a lane or along the beach,

[1] watertight boat or chamber traveling on a rope

My right and left arms round the sides of two friends, and I in the middle;
Coming home with the silent and dark-cheek'd bush-boy, (behind me he rides at the drape of the day,)
Far from the settlements studying the print of animals' feet, or the moccasin print,
By the cot in the hospital reaching lemonade to a feverish patient,
Nigh the coffin'd corpse when all is still, examining with a candle;
Voyaging to every port to dicker and adventure,
Hurrying with the modern crowd as eager and fickle as any,
Hot toward one I hate, ready in my madness to knife him,
Solitary at midnight in my back yard, my thoughts gone from me a long while,   80
Walking the old hills of Judæa with the beautiful gentle God by my side,
Speeding through space, speeding through heaven and the stars,
Speeding amid the seven satellites and the broad ring, and the diameter of eighty thousand miles,
Speeding with tail'd meteors, throwing fire-balls like the rest,
Carrying the crescent child that carries its own full mother in its belly,
Storming, enjoying, planning, loving, cautioning,
Backing and filling, appearing and disappearing,
I tread day and night such roads.

I visit the orchards of spheres and look at the product,
And look at quintillions ripen'd and look at quintillions green.   90

I fly those flights of a fluid and swallowing soul,
My course runs below the soundings of plummets.

I help myself to material and immaterial,
No guard can shut me off, no law prevent me.

I anchor my ship for a little while only,
My messengers continually cruise away or bring their returns to me.

I go hunting polar furs and the seal, leaping chasms with a pike-pointed staff, clinging to topples of brittle and blue.

I ascend to the foretruck,
I take my place late at night in the crow's-nest,
We sail the arctic sea, it is plenty light enough,   100
Through the clear atmosphere I stretch around on the wonderful beauty,
The enormous masses of ice pass me and I pass them, the scenery is plain in all directions,
The white-topt mountains show in the distance, I fling out my fancies toward them,
We are approaching some great battle-field in which we are soon to be engaged,
We pass the colossal outposts of the encampment, we pass with still feet and caution,
Or we are entering by the suburbs some vast and ruin'd city,
The blocks and fallen architecture more than all the living cities of the globe.

I am a free companion, I bivouac by invading watchfires,
I turn the bridegroom out of bed and stay with the bride myself,
I tighten her all night to my thighs and lips.   110

My voice is the wife's voice, the screech by the rail of the stairs,
They fetch my man's body up dripping and drown'd.

I understand the large hearts of heroes,
The courage of present times and all times,
How the skipper saw the crowded and rudderless wreck of the steam-ship, and Death chasing it
    up and down the storm,
How he knuckled tight and gave not back an inch, and was faithful of days and faithful of nights,
And chalk'd in large letters on a board, *Be of good cheer, we will not desert you;*
How he follow'd with them and tack'd with them three days and would not give it up,
How he saved the drifting company at last,   119
How the lank loose-gown'd women look'd when boated from the side of their prepared graves,
How the silent old-faced infants and the lifted sick, and the sharp-lipp'd unshaven men;
All this I swallow, it tastes good, I like it well, it becomes mine,
I am the man, I suffer'd, I was there.

The disdain and calmness of martyrs,
The mother of old, condemn'd for a witch, burnt with dry wood, her children gazing on,
The hounded slave that flags in the race, leans by the fence, blowing, cover'd with sweat,
The twinges that sting like needles his legs and neck, the murderous buckshot and the bullets,
All these I feel or am.

I am the hounded slave, I wince at the bite of the dogs,
Hell and despair are upon me, crack and again crack the marksmen,   130
I clutch the rails of the fence, my gore dribs, thinn'd with the ooze of my skin,
I fall on the weeds and stones,
The riders spur their unwilling horses, haul close,
Taunt my dizzy ears and beat me violently over the head with whip-stocks.

Agonies are one of my changes of garments,
I do not ask the wounded person how he feels, I myself become the wounded person,
My hurts turn livid upon me as I lean on a cane and observe.

I am the mash'd fireman with breast-bone broken,
Tumbling walls buried me in their debris,
Heat and smoke I inspired, I heard the yelling shouts of my comrades,   140
I heard the distant click of their picks and shovels,
They have clear'd the beams away, they tenderly lift me forth.

I lie in the night air in my red shirt, the pervading hush is for my sake,
Painless after all I lie exhausted but not so unhappy,
White and beautiful are the faces around me, the heads are bared of their fire-caps,
The kneeling crowd fades with the light of the torches.

Distant and dead resuscitate,
They show as the dial or move as the hands of me, I am the clock myself.

I am an old artillerist, I tell of my fort's bombardment,
I am there again.   150

Again the long roll of the drummers,
Again the attacking cannon, mortars,
Again to my listening ears the cannon responsive.

I take part, I see and hear the whole,
The cries, curses, roar, the plaudits for well-aim'd shots,

The ambulanza [1] slowly passing trailing its red drip,
Workmen searching after damages, making indispensable repairs,
The fall of grenades through the rent roof, the fan-shaped explosion,
The whizz of limbs, heads, stone, wood, iron, high in the air.

Again gurgles the mouth of my dying general, he furiously waves with his hand,   160
He gasps through the clot *Mind me not—mind—the entrenchments.*

35

Would you hear of an old-time sea-fight?
Would you learn who won by the light of the moon and stars?
List to the yarn, as my grandmother's father the sailor told it to me.

Our foe was no skulk in his ship I tell you, (said he,)
His was the surly English pluck, and there is no tougher or truer, and never was, and never will
    be;
Along the lower'd eve he came horribly raking us.

We closed with him, the yards entangled, the cannon touch'd,
My captain lash'd fast with his own hands.

We had receiv'd some eighteen pound shots under the water,
On our lower-gun-deck two large pieces had burst at the first fire, killing all around and blowing
    up overhead.   10

Fighting at sun-down, fighting at dark,
Ten o'clock at night, the full moon well up, our leaks on the gain, and five feet of water reported,
The master-at-arms loosing the prisoners confined in the afterhold to give them a chance for
    themselves.

The transit to and from the magazine is now stopt by the sentinels,
They see so many strange faces they do not know whom to trust.

Our frigate takes fire,
The other asks if we demand quarter?
If our colors are struck and the fighting done?

Now I laugh content, for I hear the voice of my little captain,
We have not struck, he composedly cries, *we have just begun our part of the fighting.*   20

Only three guns are in use,
One is directed by the captain himself against the enemy's mainmast,
Two well serv'd with grape and canister silence his musketry and clear his decks.

The tops alone second the fire of this little battery, especially the main-top,
They hold out bravely during the whole of the action.

Not a moment's cease,
The leaks gain fast on the pumps, the fire eats toward the powder-magazine.

One of the pumps has been shot away, it is generally thought we are sinking.
Serene stands the little captain,
He is not hurried, his voice is neither high nor low,
His eyes give more light to us than our battle-lanterns.   30

Toward twelve there in the beams of the moon they surrender to us.

[1] ambulance, an example of Whitman's fondness for Italian forms

36

Stretch'd and still lies the midnight,
Two great hulls motionless on the breast of the darkness,
Our vessel riddled and slowly sinking, preparations to pass to the one we have conquer'd,
The captain on the quarter-deck coldly giving his orders through a countenance white as a sheet,
Near by the corpse of the child that serv'd in the cabin,
The dead face of an old salt with long white hair and carefully curl'd whiskers,
The flames spite of all that can be done flickering aloft and below,
The husky voices of the two or three officers yet fit for duty,
Formless stacks of bodies and bodies by themselves, dabs of flesh upon the masts and spars,
Cut of cordage, dangle of rigging, slight shock of the soothe of waves,   10
Black and impassive guns, litter of powder-parcels, strong scent,
A few large stars overhead, silent and mournful shining,
Delicate sniffs of sea-breeze, smells of sedgy grass and fields by the shore, death-messages given in
        charge to survivors,
The hiss of the surgeon's knife, the gnawing teeth of his saw,
Wheeze, cluck, swash of falling blood, short wild scream, and long, dull, tapering groan,
These so, these irretrievable.

43

I do not despise you priests, all time, the world over,
My faith is the greatest of faiths and the least of faiths,
Enclosing worship ancient and modern and all between ancient and modern,
Believing I shall come again upon the earth after five thousand years,
Waiting responses from oracles, honoring the gods, saluting the sun,
Making a fetich of the first rock or stump, powowing with sticks in the circle of obis,
Helping the lama or brahmin as he trims the lamps of the idols,
Dancing yet through the streets in a phallic procession, rapt and austere in the woods a gymnoso-
        phist,
Drinking mead from the skull-cup, to Shastas and Vedas admirant, minding the Koran,
Walking the teokallis, spotted with gore from the stone and knife, beating the serpent-skin
        drum,   10
Accepting the Gospels, accepting him that was crucified, knowing assuredly that he is divine,
To the mass kneeling or the puritan's prayer rising, or sitting patiently in a pew,
Ranting and frothing in my insane crisis, or waiting dead-like till my spirit arouses me,
Looking forth on pavement and land, or outside of pavement and land,
Belonging to the winders of the circuit of circuits.

One of that centripetal and centrifugal gang I turn and talk like a man leaving charges before a
        journey.

Down-hearted doubters dull and excluded,
Frivolous, sullen, moping, angry, affected, dishearten'd, atheistical,
I know every one of you, I know the sea of torment, doubt, despair and unbelief.

How the flukes splash!   20
How they contort rapid as lightning, with spasms and spouts of blood!

Be at peace bloody flukes of doubters and sullen mopers,
I take my place among you as much as among any,
The past is the push of you, me, all, precisely the same,
And what is yet untried and afterward is for you, me, all, precisely the same.

I do not know what is untried and afterward,
But I know it will in its turn prove sufficient, and cannot fail.
Each who passes is consider'd, each who stops is consider'd, not a single one can it fail.

It cannot fail the young man who died and was buried,
Nor the young woman who died and was put by his side,   30
Nor the little child that peep'd in at the door, and then drew back and was never seen again,
Nor the old man who has lived without purpose, and feels it with bitterness worse than gall,
Nor him in the poor-house tubercled by rum and the bad disorder,
Nor the numberless slaughter'd and wreck'd, nor the brutish koboo call'd the ordure of humanity,
Nor the sacs merely floating with open mouths for food to slip in,
Nor any thing in the earth, or down in the oldest graves of the earth,
Nor any thing in the myriads of spheres, nor the myriads of myriads that inhabit them,
Nor the present, nor the least whisp that is known.

47

I am the teacher of athletes,
He that by me spreads a wider breast than my own proves the width of my own,
He most honors my style who learns under it to destroy the teacher.

The boy I love, the same becomes a man not through derived power, but in his own right,
Wicked rather than virtuous out of conformity or fear,
Fond of his sweetheart, relishing well his steak,
Unrequited love or a slight cutting him worse than sharp steel cuts,
First-rate to ride, to fight, to hit the bull's eye, to sail a skiff, to sing a song or play on the banjo,
Preferring scars and the beard and faces pitted with small-pox over all latherers,
And those well-tann'd to those that keep out of the sun.   10

I teach straying from me, yet who can stray from me?
I follow you whoever you are from the present hour,
My words itch at your ears till you understand them.

I do not say these things for a dollar or to fill up the time while I wait for a boat,
(It is you talking just as much as myself, I act as the tongue of you,
Tied in your mouth, in mine it begins to be loosen'd.)

I swear I will never again mention love or death inside a house,
And I swear I will never translate myself at all, only to him or her who privately stays with me in
      the open air.

If you would understand me go to the heights or water-shore,
The nearest gnat is an explanation, and a drop or motion of waves a key,   20
The maul, the oar, the hand-saw, second my words.

No shutter'd room or school can commune with me,
But roughs and little children better than they.

The young mechanic is closest to me, he knows me well,
The woodman that takes his axe and jug with him shall take me with him all day,
The farm-boy ploughing in the field feels good at the sound of my voice,
In vessels that sail my words sail, I go with fishermen and seamen and love them.

The soldier camp'd or upon the march is mine,
On the night ere the pending battle many seek me, and I do not fail them,
On that solemn night (it may be their last) those that know me seek me.   30

My face rubs to the hunter's face when he lies down alone in his blanket,
The driver thinking of me does not mind the jolt of his wagon,
The young mother and old mother comprehend me,
The girl and the wife rest the needle a moment and forget where they are,
They and all would resume what I have told them.

48

I have said that the soul is not more than the body,
And I have said that the body is not more than the soul,
And nothing, not God, is greater to one than one's self is,
And whoever walks a furlong without sympathy walks to his own funeral drest in his shroud,
And I or you pocketless of a dime may purchase the pick of the earth,
And to glance with an eye or show a bean in its pod confounds the learning of all times,
And there is no trade or employment but the young man following it may become a hero,
And there is no object so soft but it makes a hub for the wheel'd universe,
And I say to any man or woman, Let your soul stand cool and composed before a million universes.

And I say to mankind, Be not curious about God,   10
For I who am curious about each am not curious about God,
(No array of terms can say how much I am at peace about God and about death.)

I hear and behold God in every object, yet understand God not in the least,
Nor do I understand who there can be more wonderful than myself.

Why should I wish to see God better than this day?
I see something of God each hour of the twenty-four, and each moment then,
In the faces of men and women I see God, and in my own face in the glass,
I find letters from God dropt in the street, and every one is sign'd by God's name,
And I leave them where they are, for I know wheresoe'er I go,
Others will punctually come for ever and ever.   20

52

The spotted hawk swoops by and accuses me, he complains of my gab and my loitering.

I too am not a bit tamed, I too am untranslatable,
I sound my barbaric yawp over the roofs of the world.

The last scud of day holds back for me,
It flings my likeness after the rest and true as any on the shadow'd wilds,
It coaxes me to the vapor and the dusk.

I depart as air, I shake my white locks at the runaway sun,
I effuse my flesh in eddies, and drift it in lacy jags.

I bequeath myself to the dirt to grow from the grass I love,
If you want me again look for me under your boot-soles.   10

You will hardly know who I am or what I mean,
But I shall be good health of you nevertheless,
And filter and fibre your blood.

Failing to fetch me at first keep encouraged,
Missing me one place search another,
I stop somewhere waiting for you.

1855, 1881

MIRACLES

WHY, who makes much of a miracle?
As to me I know of nothing else but miracles,
Whether I walk the streets of Manhattan,
Or dart my sight over the roofs of houses toward the sky,
Or wade with naked feet along the beach just in the edge of the water,
Or stand under trees in the woods,
Or talk by day with any one I love, or sleep in the bed at night with any one I love,
Or sit at table at dinner with the rest,
Or look at strangers opposite me riding in the car,
Or watch honey-bees busy around the hive of a summer forenoon,   10
Or animals feeding in the fields,
Or birds, or the wonderfulness of insects in the air,
Or the wonderfulness of the sundown, or of stars shining so quiet and bright,
Or the exquisite delicate thin curve of the new moon in spring;
These with the rest, one and all, are to me miracles,
The whole referring, yet each distinct and in its place.
To me every hour of the light and dark is a miracle,
Every cubic inch of space is a miracle,
Every square yard of the surface of the earth is spread with the same,
Every foot of the interior swarms with the same.   20

To me the sea is a continual miracle,
The fishes that swim—the rocks—the motion of the waves—the ships with men in them,
What stranger miracles are there?

1856

CROSSING BROOKLYN FERRY

1

FLOOD-TIDE below me! I see you face to face!
Clouds of the west—sun there half an hour high—I see you also face to face.

Crowds of men and women attired in the usual costumes, how curious you are to me!
On the ferry-boats the hundreds and hundreds that cross, returning home, are more curious to me
    than you suppose,
And you that shall cross from shore to shore years hence are more to me, and more in my medita-
    tions, than you might suppose.

2

The impalpable sustenance of me from all things at all hours of the day,
The simple, compact, well-join'd scheme, myself disintegrated, every one disintegrated yet part of
    the scheme,
The similitudes of the past and those of the future,
The glories strung like beads on my smallest sights and hearings, on the walk in the street and the
    passage over the river,
The current rushing so swiftly and swimming with me far away,   10
The others that are to follow me, the ties between me and them,
The certainty of others, the life, love, sight, hearing of others.

Others will enter the gates of the ferry and cross from shore to shore,
Others will watch the run of the flood-tide,
Others will see the shipping of Manhattan north and west, and the heights of Brooklyn to the south and east,
Others will see the islands large and small;
Fifty years hence, others will see them as they cross, the sun half an hour high,
A hundred years hence, or ever so many hundred years hence, others will see them,
Will enjoy the sunset, the pouring-in of the flood-tide, the falling-back to the sea of the ebb-tide.

3

It avails not, time nor place—distance avails not,   20
I am with you, you men and women of a generation, or ever so many generations hence,
Just as you feel when you look on the river and sky, so I felt,
Just as any of you is one of a living crowd, I was one of a crowd,
Just as you are refresh'd by the gladness of the river and the bright flow, I was refresh'd,
Just as you stand and lean on the rail, yet hurry with the swift current, I stood yet was hurried,
Just as you look on the numberless masts of ships and the thick-stemm'd pipes of steamboats, I look'd.
I too many and many a time cross'd the river of old,
Watched the Twelfth-month sea-gulls, saw them high in the air floating with motionless wings, oscillating their bodies,
Saw how the glistening yellow lit up parts of their bodies and left the rest in strong shadow,
Saw the slow-wheeling circles and the gradual edging toward the south,   30
Saw the reflection of the summer sky in the water,
Had my eyes dazzled by the shimmering track of beams,
Look'd at the fine centrifugal spokes of light round the shape of my head in the sunlit water,
Look'd on the haze on the hills southward and south-westward,
Look'd on the vapor as it flew in fleeces tinged with violet,
Look'd toward the lower bay to notice the vessels arriving,
Saw their approach, saw aboard those that were near me,
Saw the white sails of schooners and sloops, saw the ships at anchor,
The sailors at work in the rigging or out astride the spars,
The round masts, the swinging motion of the hulls, the slender serpentine pennants,   40
The large and small steamers in motion, the pilots in their pilot-houses,
The white wake left by the passage, the quick tremulous whirl of the wheels,
The flags of all nations, the falling of them at sunset,
The scallop-edged waves in the twilight, the ladled cups, the frolicsome crests and glistening,
The stretch afar growing dimmer and dimmer, the gray walls of the granite storehouses by the docks,
On the river the shadowy group, the big steam-tug closely flank'd on each side by the barges, the hay-boat, the belated lighter,
On the neighboring shore the fires from the foundry chimneys burning high and glaringly into the night,
Casting their flicker of black contrasted with wild red and yellow light over the tops of houses, and down into the clefts of streets.

4

These and all else were to me the same as they are to you,
I loved well those cities, loved well the stately and rapid river,   50
The men and women I saw were all near to me,

Others the same—others who look back on me because I look'd forward to them,
(The time will come, though I stop here today and tonight.)

5

What is it then between us?
What is the count of the scores or hundreds of years between us?

Whatever it is, it avails not—distance avails not, and place avails not,
I too lived, Brooklyn of ample hills was mine,
I too walk'd the streets of Manhattan island, and bathed in the waters around it,
I too felt the curious abrupt questionings stir within me,
In the day among crowds of people sometimes they came upon me,   60
In my walks home late at night or as I lay in my bed they came upon me,
I too had been struck from the float forever held in solution,
I too had receiv'd identity by my body,
That I was I knew was of my body, and what I should be I knew I should be of my body.

6

It is not upon you alone the dark patches fall,
The dark threw its patches down upon me also,
The best I had done seem'd to me blank and suspicious,
My great thoughts as I supposed them, were they not in reality meager?
Nor is it you alone who know what it is to be evil,
I am he who knew what it was to be evil,   70
I too knitted the old knot of contrariety,
Blabb'd, blush'd, resented, lied, stole, grudg'd,
Had guile, anger, lust, hot wishes I dared not speak,
Was wayward, vain, greedy, shallow, sly, cowardly, malignant,
The wolf, the snake, the hog, not wanting in me,
The cheating look, the frivolous word, the adulterous wish, not wanting,
Refusals, hates, postponements, meanness, laziness, none of these wanting,
Was one with the rest, the days and haps of the rest,
Was call'd by my nighest name by clear loud voices of young men as they saw me approaching or
     passing,
Felt their arms on my neck as I stood, or the negligent leaning of their flesh against me as I sat,   80
Saw many I loved in the street or ferry-boat or public assembly, yet never told them a word,
Lived the same life with the rest, the same old laughing, gnawing, sleeping,
Play'd the part that still looks back on the actor or actress,
The same old role, the role that is what we make it, as great as we like,
Or as small as we like, or both great and small.

7

Closer yet I approach you,
What thought you have of me now, I had as much of you—I laid in my stores in advance,
I consider'd long and seriously of you before you were born.

Who was to know what should come home to me?
Who knows but I am enjoying this?
Who knows, for all the distance, but I am as good as looking at you now, for all you cannot see   90
     me?

8

Ah, what can ever be more stately and admirable to me than mast-hemm'd Manhattan?
River and sunset and scallop-edg'd waves of flood-tide?
The sea-gulls oscillating their bodies, the hay-boat in the twilight, and the belated lighter?

What gods can exceed these that clasp me by the hand, and with voices I love call me promptly
    and loudly by my nighest name as I approach?

What is more subtle than this which ties me to the woman or man that looks in my face?
Which fuses me into you now, and pours my meaning into you?

We understand then do we not?
What I promis'd without mentioning it, have you not accepted?
What the study could not teach—what the preaching could not accomplish is accomplish'd, is
    it not?   100

9

Flow on, river! flow with the flood-tide, and ebb with the ebb-tide!
Frolic on, crested and scallop-edg'd waves!
Gorgeous clouds of the sunset! drench with your splendor me, or the men and women generations
    after me!
Cross from shore to shore, countless crowds of passengers!
Stand up, tall masts of Mannahatta! stand up, beautiful hills of Brooklyn!
Throb, baffled and curious brain! throw out questions and answers!
Suspend here and everywhere, eternal float of solution!
Gaze, loving and thirsting eyes, in the house or street or public assembly!
Sound out, voices of young men! loudly and musically call me by my nighest name!
Live, old life! play the part that looks back on the actor or actress!   110
Play the old role, the role that is great or small according as one makes it!
Consider, you who peruse me, whether I may not in unknown ways be looking upon you;
Be firm, rail over the river, to support those who lean idly, yet haste with the hasting current;
Fly on, sea-birds! fly sideways, or wheel in large circles high in the air;
Receive the summer sky, you water, and faithfully hold it till all downcast eyes have time to take it
    from you!
Diverge, fine spokes of light, from the shape of my head, or any one's head, in the sunlit water!
Come on, ships from the lower bay! pass up or down, white-sail'd schooners, sloops, lighters!
Flaunt away, flags of all nations! be duly lower'd at sunset!
Burn high your fires, foundry chimneys! cast black shadows at nightfall! cast red and yellow light
    over the tops of the houses!
Appearances, now or henceforth, indicate what you are,   120
You necessary film, continue to envelop the soul,
About my body for me, and your body for you, be hung our divinest aromas,
Thrive, cities—bring your freight, bring your shows, ample and sufficient rivers,
Expand, being than which none else is perhaps more spiritual,
Keep your places, objects than which none else is more lasting.

You have waited, you always wait, you dumb, beautiful ministers,
We receive you with free sense at last, and are insatiate henceforward,
Not you any more shall be able to foil us, or withhold yourselves from us,
We use you, and do not cast you aside—we plant you permanently within us,
We fathom you not—we love you—there is perfection in you also,   130
You furnish your parts toward eternity,
Great or small, you furnish your parts toward the soul.   1856

THERE WAS A CHILD WENT FORTH

There was a child went forth every day,
And the first object he look'd upon, that object he became,
And that object became part of him for the day or a certain part of the day,
Or for many years or stretching cycles of years.

The early lilacs became part of this child,
And grass and white and red morning-glories, and white and red clover, and the song of the
phœbe-bird,
And the Third-month lambs and the sow's pink-faint litter, and the mare's foal and the cow's calf,
And the noisy brood of the barnyard or by the mire of the pond-side,
And the fish suspending themselves so curiously below there, and the beautiful curious liquid,
And the water-plants with their graceful flat heads, all became part of him.   10

The field-sprouts of Fourth-month and Fifth-month became part of him,
Winter-grain sprouts and those of the light-yellow corn, and the esculent roots of the garden,
And the apple-trees cover'd with blossoms and the fruit afterward, and wood-berries, and the
commonest weeds by the road,
And the old drunkard staggering home from the outhouse of the tavern whence he had lately risen,
And the schoolmistress that pass'd on her way to the school,
And the friendly boys that pass'd, and the quarrelsome boys,
And the tidy and fresh-cheek'd girls, and the barefoot Negro boy and girl,
And all the changes of city and country wherever he went.

His own parents, he that had father'd him and she that had conceiv'd him in her womb and birth'd
him,
They gave this child more of themselves than that,   20
They gave him afterward every day, they became part of him.

The mother at home quietly placing the dishes on the supper-table,
The mother with mild words, clean her cap and gown, a wholesome odor falling off her person
and clothes as she walks by,
The father, strong, self-sufficient, manly, mean, anger'd, unjust,
The blow, the quick loud word, the tight bargain, the crafty lure,
The family usages, the language, the company, the furniture, the yearning and swelling heart,
Affection that will not be gainsay'd, the sense of what is real, the thought if after all it should prove
unreal,
The doubts of day-time and the doubts of night-time, the curious whether and how,
Whether that which appears so is so, or is it all flashes and specks?
Men and women crowding fast in the streets, if they are not flashes and specks what are they?   30
The streets themselves and the façades of houses, and goods in the windows,
Vehicles, teams, the heavy-plank'd wharves, the huge crossing at the ferries,
The village on the highland seen from afar at sunset, the river between,
Shadows, aureola and mist, the light falling on roofs and gables of white or brown two miles off,
The schooner near by sleepily dropping down the tide, the little boat slack-tow'd astern,
The hurrying tumbling waves, quick-broken crests, slapping,
The strata of color'd clouds, the long bar of maroon-tint away solitary by itself, the spread of
purity it lies motionless in,
The horizon's edge, the flying sea-crow, the fragrance of salt marsh and shore mud,
These became part of that child who went forth every day, and who now goes, and will always go
forth every day.

1855

OUT OF THE CRADLE ENDLESSLY ROCKING

A man's reverie over a boy's experience. A new kind of elegy discarding preceding patterns, and making older bird poetry with its usual assumption of the unalloyed happiness of birds compared with the tragedies of human beings seem hollow make-believe and convention. (See L. Pound, "Whitman and Bird Poetry," *English Journal*, XIX, January, 1930.) Interwoven are a trio of themes, the bird's lament (one of the most poignant songs of loss ever written), the accompanying surge of the sea "endlessly rocking," and the boy's questioning soul, bringing him a realization of death and starting his poetic spirit. The bird is his genius of song. The poem is mannered in form, marked especially by incessant dangling present participles and suspended, or periodic, sentences.

Out of the cradle endlessly rocking,
Out of the mocking-bird's throat, the musical shuttle,
Out of the Ninth-month midnight,
Over the sterile sands and the fields beyond, where the child leaving his bed wander'd
    alone, bareheaded, barefoot,
Down from the shower'd halo,
Up from the mystic play of shadows twining and twisting as if they were alive,
Out from the patches of briers and blackberries,
From the memories of the bird that chanted to me,
From your memories sad brother, from the fitful risings and fallings I heard,
From under that yellow half-moon late-risen and swollen as if with tears,   10
From those beginning notes of yearning and love there in the mist,
From the thousand responses of my heart never to cease,
From the myriad thence-arous'd words,
From the word stronger and more delicious than any,
From such as now they start the scene revisiting,
As a flock, twittering, rising, or overhead passing,
Borne hither, ere all eludes me, hurriedly,
A man, yet by these tears a little boy again,
Throwing myself on the sand, confronting the waves,
I, chanter of pains and joys, uniter of here and hereafter,   20
Taking all hints to use them, but swiftly leaping beyond them,
A reminiscence sing.

Once Paumanok,[1]
When the lilac-scent was in the air and Fifth-month grass was growing,
Up this seashore in some briers,
Two feather'd guests from Alabama, two together,
And their nest, and four light-green eggs spotted with brown,
And every day the he-bird to and fro near at hand,
And every day the she-bird crouch'd on her nest, silent, with bright eyes,
And every day I, a curious boy, never too close, never disturbing them,   30
Cautiously peering, absorbing, translating.

Shine! shine! shine!
Pour down your warmth, great sun!
While we bask, we two together,

Two together!
Winds blow south, or winds blow north,
Day come white, or night come black,

[1] the Indian name for Long Island

Home, or rivers and mountains from home,
Singing all time, minding no time,
While we two keep together.   40

Till of a sudden,
May-be kill'd, unknown to her mate,
One forenoon the she-bird crouch'd not on the nest,
Nor return'd that afternoon, nor the next,
Nor ever appear'd again.

And thenceforward all summer in the sound of the sea,
And at night under the full of the moon in calmer weather,
Over the hoarse surging of the sea,
Or flitting from brier to brier by day,
I saw, I heard at intervals the remaining one, the he-bird,   50
The solitary guest from Alabama.

Blow! blow! blow!
Blow up sea-winds along Paumanok's shore;
I wait and I wait till you blow my mate to me.

Yes, when the stars glisten'd,
All night long on the prong of a moss-scallop'd stake,
Down almost amid the slapping waves,
Sat the lone singer wonderful causing tears.
He call'd on his mate,
He pour'd forth the meanings which I of all men know.   60

Yes my brother I know,
The rest might not, but I have treasur'd every note,
For more than once dimly down to the beach gliding,
Silent, avoiding the moonbeams, blending myself with the shadows,
Recalling now the obscure shapes, the echoes, the sounds and sights after their sorts,
The white arms out in the breakers tirelessly tossing,
I, with bare feet, a child, the wind wafting my hair,
Listen'd long and long.

Listen'd to keep, to sing, now translating the notes,
Following you my brother.   70

Soothe! soothe! soothe!
Close on its wave soothes the wave behind,
And again another behind embracing and lapping, every one close,
But my love soothes not me, not me.

Low hangs the moon, it rose late,
It is lagging—O I think it is heavy with love, with love.

O madly the sea pushes upon the land,
With love, with love.

O night! do I not see my love fluttering out among the breakers?
What is that little black thing I see there in the white?   80

Loud! loud! loud!
Loud I call to you, my love!
High and clear I shoot my voice over the waves,
Surely you must know who is here, is here,
You must know who I am, my love.

Low-hanging moon!
What is that dusky spot in your brown yellow?
O it is the shape, the shape of my mate!
O moon do not keep her from me any longer.

Land! land! O land!
Whichever way I turn, O I think you could give me my mate back again if you only would,
For I am almost sure I see her dimly whichever way I look.

90

O rising stars!
Perhaps the one I want so much will rise, will rise with some of you.

O throat! O trembling throat!
Sound clearer through the atmosphere!
Pierce the woods, the earth,
Somewhere listening to catch you must be the one I want.

Shake out carols!
Solitary here, the night's carols!
Carols of lonesome love! death's carols!
Carols under that lagging, yellow, waning moon!
O under that moon where she droops almost down into the sea!
O reckless despairing carols.

100

But soft! sink low!
Soft! let me just murmur,
And do you wait a moment you husky-nois'd sea,
For somewhere I believe I heard my mate responding to me,
So faint, I must be still, be still to listen,
But not altogether still, for then she might not come immediately to me.

110

Hither my love!
Here I am! here!
With this just-sustain'd note I announce myself to you,
This gentle call is for you my love, for you.

Do not be decoy'd elsewhere,
That is the whistle of the wind, it is not my voice,
That is the fluttering, the fluttering of the spray,
Those are the shadows of leaves.

O darkness! O in vain!
O I am very sick and sorrowful.

120

O brown halo in the sky near the moon, drooping upon the sea!
O troubled reflection in the sea!
O throat! O throbbing heart!
And I singing uselessly, uselessly all the night.

O past! O happy life! O songs of joy!
In the air, in the woods, over fields,
Loved! loved! loved! loved! loved!
But my mate no more, no more with me!
We two together no more.

The aria sinking,
All else continuing, the stars shining,
The winds blowing, the notes of the bird continuous echoing,
With angry moans the fierce old mother incessantly moaning,
On the sands of Paumanok's shore gray and rustling,
The yellow half-moon enlarged, sagging down, drooping, the face of the sea almost touching,
The boy ecstatic, with his bare feet the waves, with his hair the atmosphere dallying,
The love in the heart long pent, now loose, now at last tumultuously bursting,
The aria's meaning, the ears, the soul, swiftly depositing,
The strange tears down the cheeks coursing,
The colloquy there, the trio, each uttering,
The undertone, the savage old mother incessantly crying,
To the boy's soul's questions sullenly timing, some drown'd secret hissing,
To the outsetting bard.

Demon or bird (said the boy's soul,)
Is it indeed toward your mate you sing? or is it really to me?
For I, that was a child, my tongue's use sleeping, now I have heard you,
Now in a moment I know what I am for, I awake,
And already a thousand singers, a thousand songs, clearer, louder and more sorrowful than yours,
A thousand warbling echoes have started to life within me, never to die.

O you singer solitary, singing by yourself, projecting me,
O solitary me listening, never more shall I cease perpetuating you,
Never more shall I escape, never more the reverberations,
Never more the cries of unsatisfied love be absent from me,
Never again leave me to be the peaceful child I was before what there in the night,
By the sea under the yellow and sagging moon,
The messenger there arous'd, the fire, the sweet hell within,
The unknown want, the destiny of me.

O give me the clew! (it lurks in the night here somewhere,)
O if I am to have so much, let me have more!

A word then, (for I will conquer it,)
The word final, superior to all,
Subtle, sent up—what is it?—I listen;
Are you whispering it, and have been all the time, you sea waves?
Is that it from your liquid rims and wet sands?

Whereto answering, the sea,
Delaying not, hurrying not,
Whisper'd me through the night, and very plainly before daybreak,
Lisp'd to me the low and delicious word death,
And again death, death, death, death,

130

140

150

160

Hissing melodious, neither like the bird nor like my arous'd child's heart,   170
But edging near as privately for me rustling at my feet,
Creeping thence steadily up to my ears and laving me softly all over,
Death, death, death, death, death.

Which I do not forget,
But fuse the song of my dusky demon and brother,
That he sang to me in the moonlight on Paumanok's gray beach,
With the thousand responsive songs at random,
My own songs awaked from that hour,
And with them the key, the word up from the waves,
The word of the sweetest song and all songs,   180
That strong and delicious word which, creeping to my feet,
(Or like some old crone rocking the cradle, swathed in sweet garments, bending aside,)
The sea whisper'd me.

   1859

ME IMPERTURBE

ME imperturbe,[1] standing at ease in Nature,
Master of all or mistress of all, aplomb in the midst of irrational things,
Imbued as they, passive, receptive, silent as they,
Finding my occupation, poverty, notoriety, foibles, crimes, less important than I thought,
Me toward the Mexican sea, or in the Mannahatta or the Tennessee, or far north or inland,
A river man, or a man of the woods or of any farm-life of these States or of the coast, or the lakes or Kanada,
Me wherever my life is lived, O to be self-balanced for contingencies,
To confront night, storms, hunger, ridicule, accidents, rebuffs, as the trees and animals do.

   1860

FOR YOU O DEMOCRACY

COME, I will make the continent indissoluble,
I will make the most splendid race the sun ever shone upon,
I will make divine magnetic lands,
   With the love of comrades,
     With the life-long love of comrades.

I will plant companionship thick as trees along all the rivers of America, and along
   the shores of the great lakes, and all over the prairies,
I will make inseparable cities with their arms about each other's necks,
   By the love of comrades,
     By the manly love of comrades.

For you these from me, O Democracy, to serve you *ma femme!*   10
For you, for you I am trilling these songs.

   1860

I SAW IN LOUISIANA A LIVE–OAK GROWING

I SAW in Louisiana a live-oak growing,
All alone stood it and the moss hung down from the branches,
Without any companion it grew there uttering joyous leaves of dark green,

[1] undisturbed, calm—one of Whitman's coinages

And its look, rude, unbending, lusty, made me think of myself,
But I wonder'd how it could utter joyous leaves standing alone there without its friend near, for
    I knew I could not,
And I broke off a twig with a certain number of leaves upon it, and twined around it a little
    moss,
And brought it away, and I have placed it in sight in my room,
It is not needed to remind me as of my own dear friends,
(For I believe lately I think of little else than of them,)
Yet it remains to me a curious token, it makes me think of manly love;   10
For all that, and though the live-oak glistens there in Louisiana solitary in a wide flat space,
Uttering joyous leaves all its life without a friend, a lover near,
I know very well I could not.

                                          1860

I HEAR AMERICA SINGING

I HEAR America singing, the varied carols I hear,
Those of mechanics, each one singing his as it should be blithe and strong,
The carpenter singing his as he measures his plank or beam,
The mason singing his as he makes ready for work, or leaves off work,
The boatman singing what belongs to him in his boat, the deck-hand singing on the steamboat
    deck,
The shoemaker singing as he sits on his bench, the hatter singing as he stands,
The wood-cutter's song, the plowboy's on his way in the morning, or at noon intermission or at
    sundown,
The delicious singing of the mother, or of the young wife at work, or of the girl sewing or
    washing,
Each singing what belongs to him or her and to none else,
The day what belongs to the day—at night the party of young fellows, robust, friendly,   10
Singing with open mouths their strong melodious songs.

                                          1860

POETS TO COME

POETS to come! orators, singers, musicians to come!
Not today is to justify me and answer what I am for,
But you, a new brood, native, athletic, continental, greater than before known,
Arouse! for you must justify me.

I myself but write one or two indicative words for the future,
I but advance a moment only to wheel and hurry back in the darkness.

I am a man who, sauntering along without fully stopping, turns a casual look upon
    you and then averts his face,
Leaving it to you to prove and define it,
Expecting the main things from you.

                                          1860

FROM PAUMANOK STARTING I FLY LIKE A BIRD

    FROM Paumanok starting I fly like a bird,
    Around and around to soar to sing the idea of all,
    To the north betaking myself to sing there arctic songs,

To Kanada till I absorb Kanada in myself, to Michigan then,
To Wisconsin, Iowa, Minnesota, to sing their songs (they are inimitable);
Then to Ohio and Indiana to sing theirs, to Missouri and Kansas and Arkansas to sing theirs,
To Tennessee and Kentucky, to the Carolinas and Georgia to sing theirs,
To Texas and so along up toward California, to roam accepted everywhere;
To sing first (to the tap of the war-drum if need be),
The idea of all, of the Western world one and inseparable,   10
And then the song of each member of these States.

                                                                    1865

BIVOUAC ON A MOUNTAIN SIDE

I SEE before me now a traveling army halting,
Below a fertile valley spread, with barns and the orchards of summer,
Behind, the terraced sides of a mountain, abrupt, in places rising high,
Broken, with rocks, with clinging cedars, with tall shapes dingily seen,
The numerous camp-fires scatter'd near and far, some away up on the mountain,
The shadowy forms of men and horses, looming, large-sized, flickering,
And over all the sky—the sky! far, far out of reach, studded, breaking out, the eternal stars.

                                                                    1865

AN ARMY CORPS ON THE MARCH

WITH its cloud of skirmishers in advance,
With now the sound of a single shot snapping like a whip, and now an irregular volley,
The swarming ranks press on and on, the dense brigades press on,
Glittering dimly, toiling under the sun—the dust-cover'd men,
In columns rise and fall to the undulations of the ground,
With artillery interspers'd—the wheels rumble, the horses sweat,
As the army corps advances.

                                                                    1865–1866

RECONCILIATION

WORD over all, beautiful as the sky,
Beautiful that war and all its deeds of carnage must in time be utterly lost,
That the hands of the sisters Death and Night incessantly softly wash again, and
        ever again, this soil'd world;
For my enemy is dead, a man divine as myself is dead,
I look where he lies white-faced and still in the coffin—I draw near,
Bend down and touch lightly with my lips the white face in the coffin.

                                                                    1865

CAVALRY CROSSING A FORD

A LINE in long array where they wind betwixt green islands,
They take a serpentine course, their arms flash in the sun—hark to the musical clank,
Behold the silvery river, in it the splashing horses loitering stop to drink,
Behold the brown-faced men, each group, each person a picture, the negligent rest on the saddles,
Some emerge on the opposite bank, others are just entering the ford—while,
Scarlet and blue and snowy white,
The guidon flags flutter gayly in the wind.

                                                                    1865

COME UP FROM THE FIELDS FATHER

COME up from the fields father, here's a letter from our Pete,
And come to the front door mother, here's a letter from thy dear son.

Lo, 'tis autumn,
Lo, where the trees, deeper green, yellower and redder,
Cool and sweeten Ohio's villages with leaves fluttering in the moderate wind,
Where apples ripe in the orchards hang and grapes on the trellis'd vines,
(Smell you the smell of the grapes on the vines?
Smell you the buckwheat where the bees were lately buzzing?)

Above all, lo, the sky so calm, so transparent after the rain, and with wondrous clouds,
Below too, all calm, all vital and beautiful, and the farm prospers well.   10

Down in the fields all prospers well,
But now from the fields come father, come at the daughter's call,
And come to the entry mother, to the front door come right away.

Fast as she can she hurries, something ominous, her steps trembling,
She does not tarry to smooth her hair nor adjust her cap.

Open the envelope quickly,
O this is not our son's writing, yet his name is sign'd,
O a strange hand writes for our dear son, O stricken mother's soul!
All swims before her eyes, flashes with black, she catches the main words only,
Sentence broken, *gunshot wound in the breast, cavalry skirmish, taken to hospital,*   20
At present low, but will soon be better.

Ah now the single figure to me,
Amid all teeming and wealthy Ohio with all its cities and farms,
Sickly white in the face and dull in the head, very faint,
By the jamb of a door leans.

Grieve not so, dear mother (the just-grown daughter speaks through her sobs,
The little sisters huddle around speechless and dismay'd),
See, dearest mother, the letter says Pete will soon be better.

Alas poor boy, he will never be better (nor may-be needs to be better, that brave and simple
     soul),
While they stand at home at the door he is dead already,
The only son is dead.   30

But the mother needs to be better,
She with thin form presently drest in black,
By day her meals untouched, then at night fitfully sleeping, often waking,
In the midnight waking, weeping, longing with one deep longing,
O that she might withdraw unnoticed, silent from life escape and withdraw,
To follow, to seek, to be with her dear dead son.

PIONEERS! O PIONEERS!

COME my tan-faced children,
Follow well in order, get your weapons ready,
Have you your pistols? have you your sharp-edged axes?
    Pioneers! O pioneers!

For we cannot tarry here,
We must march my darlings, we must bear the brunt of danger,
We the youthful sinewy races, all the rest on us depend,
    Pioneers! O pioneers!

O you youths, Western youths,
So impatient, full of action, full of manly pride and friendship,   10
Plain I see you Western youths, see you tramping with the foremost,
    Pioneers! O pioneers!

Have the elder races halted?
Do they droop and end their lesson, wearied over there beyond the sea?
We take up the task eternal, and the burden and the lesson,
    Pioneers! O pioneers!

All the past we leave behind,
We debouch upon a newer mightier world, varied world,
Fresh and strong the world we seize, world of labor and the march,
    Pioneers! O pioneers!   20

We detachments steady throwing,
Down the edges, through the passes, up the mountain steep,
Conquering, holding, daring, venturing as we go the unknown ways,
    Pioneers! O pioneers!

We primeval forests felling,
We the rivers stemming, vexing we and piercing deep the mines within,
We the surface broad surveying, we the virgin soil upheaving,
    Pioneers! O pioneers!

Colorado men are we,
From the peaks gigantic, from the great sierras and the high plateaus,   30
From the mine and from the gully, from the hunting trail we come,
    Pioneers! O pioneers!

From Nebraska, from Arkansas,
Central inland race are we, from Missouri, with the continental blood intervein'd,
All the hands of comrades clasping, all the Southern, all the Northern,
    Pioneers! O pioneers!

O resistless restless race!
O beloved race in all! O my breast aches with tender love for all!
O I mourn and yet exult, I am rapt with love for all,
    Pioneers! O pioneers!   40

Raise the mighty mother mistress,
Waving high the delicate mistress, over all the starry mistress (bend your heads all),
Raise the fang'd and warlike mistress, stern, impassive, weapon'd mistress,
    Pioneers! O pioneers!

See my children, resolute children,
By those swarms upon our rear we must never yield or falter,
Ages back in ghostly millions frowning there behind us urging,
    Pioneers! O pioneers!

On and on the compact ranks,
With accessions ever waiting, with the places of the dead quickly fill'd,
Through the battle, through defeat, moving yet and never stopping,
    Pioneers! O pioneers!

O to die advancing on!
Are there some of us to droop and die? has the hour come?
Then upon the march we fittest die, soon and sure the gap is fill'd,
    Pioneers! O pioneers!

All the pulses of the world,
Falling in they beat for us, with the Western movement beat,
Holding single or together, steady moving to the front, all for us,
    Pioneers! O pioneers!

Life's involv'd and varied pageants,
All the forms and shows, all the workmen at their work,
All the seamen and the landsmen, all the masters with their slaves,
    Pioneers! O pioneers!

All the hapless silent lovers,
All the prisoners in the prisons, all the righteous and the wicked,
All the joyous, all the sorrowing, all the living, all the dying,
    Pioneers! O pioneers!

I too with my soul and body,
We, a curious trio, picking, wandering on our way,
Through these shores amid the shadows, with the apparitions pressing,
    Pioneers! O pioneers!

Lo, the darting bowling orb!
Lo, the brother orbs around, all the clustering suns and planets,
All the dazzling days, all the mystic nights with dreams,
    Pioneers! O pioneers!

These are of us, they are with us,
All for primal needed work, while the followers there in embryo wait behind,
We to-day's procession heading, we the route for travel clearing,
    Pioneers! O pioneers!

O you daughters of the West!
O you young and elder daughters! O you mothers and you wives!
Never must you be divided, in our ranks you move united,
　　　Pioneers! O pioneers!

Minstrels latent on the prairies!
(Shrouded bards of other lands, you may rest, you have done your work,)
Soon I hear you coming warbling, soon you rise and tramp amid us,
　　　Pioneers! O pioneers!

Not for delectations sweet,
Not the cushion and the slipper, not the peaceful and the studious,　　　90
Not the riches safe and palling, not for us the tame enjoyment,
　　　Pioneers! O pioneers!

Do the feasters gluttonous feast?
Do the corpulent sleepers sleep? Have they lock'd and bolted doors?
Still be ours the diet hard, and the blanket on the ground,
　　　Pioneers! O pioneers!

Has the night descended?
Was the road of late so toilsome? did we stop discouraged nodding on our way?
Yet a passing hour I yield you in your tracks to pause oblivious,
　　　Pioneers! O pioneers!　　　100

Till with sound of trumpet,
Far, far off the daybreak call—hark! how loud and clear I hear it wind,
Swift! to the head of the army!—swift! spring to your places,
　　　Pioneers! O pioneers!

　　　　　　　　　　　　　　　　　　　　　　　　　1865

TO A CERTAIN CIVILIAN

DID you ask dulcet rimes from me?
Did you seek the civilian's peaceful and languishing rimes?
Did you find what I sang erewhile so hard to follow?
Why I was not singing erewhile for you to follow, to understand—nor am I now;
(I have been born of the same as the war was born,
The drum-corps' rattle is ever to me sweet music, I love well the martial dirge,
With slow wail and convulsive throb leading the officer's funeral;)
What to such as you anyhow such a poet as I? therefore leave my works,
And go lull yourself with what you can understand, and with piano tunes,
For I lull nobody, and you will never understand me.　　　10

　　　　　　　　　　　　　　　　　　　　　　　　　1865

BEAT! BEAT! DRUMS!

BEAT! beat! drums!—blow! bugles! blow!
Through the windows—through doors—burst like a ruthless force,
Into the solemn church, and scatter the congregation,
Into the school where the scholar is studying;
Leave not the bridegroom quiet—no happiness must he have now with his bride,
Nor the peaceful farmer any peace, plowing his field or gathering his grain,
So fierce you whirr and pound you drums—so shrill you bugles blow.

Beat! beat! drums!—blow! bugles! blow!
Over the traffic of cities—over the rumble of wheels in the streets;
Are beds prepared for sleepers at night in the houses? no sleepers must sleep in those beds,   10
No bargainers' bargains by day—no brokers or speculators—would they continue?
Would the talkers be talking? would the singer attempt to sing?
Would the lawyer rise in the court to state his case before the judge?
Then rattle quicker, heavier drums—you bugles wilder blow.

Beat! beat! drums!—blow! bugles! blow!
Make no parley—stop for no expostulation,
Mind not the timid—mind not the weeper or prayer,
Mind not the old man beseeching the young man,
Let not the child's voice be heard, nor the mother's entreaties,
Make even the trestles to shake the dead where they lie awaiting the hearses,   20
So strong you thump O terrible drums—so loud you bugles blow.

                                                                                1865

THE WOUND-DRESSER

1

An old man bending I come among new faces,
Years looking backward resuming in answer to children,
Come tell us old man, as from young men and maidens that love me,
(Arous'd and angry, I'd thought to beat the alarum, and urge relentless war,
But soon my fingers fail'd me, my face droop'd and I resign'd myself,
To sit by the wounded and soothe them, or silently watch the dead;)
Years hence of these scenes, of these furious passions, these chances,
Of unsurpass'd heroes, (was one side so brave? the other was equally brave;)
Now be witness again, paint the mightiest armies of earth,
Of those armies so rapid so wondrous what saw you to tell us?   10
What stays with you latest and deepest? of curious panics,
Of hard-fought engagements or sieges tremendous what deepest remains?

2

O maidens and young men I love and that love me,
What you ask of my days those the strangest and sudden your talking recalls,
Soldier alert I arrive after a long march cover'd with sweat and dust,
In the nick of time I come, plunge in the fight, loudly shout in the rush of successful charge,
Enter the captur'd works—yet lo, like a swift-running river they fade,
Pass and are gone, they fade—I dwell not on soldiers' perils or soldiers' joys,
(Both I remember well—many the hardships, few the joys, yet I was content.)

But in silence, in dreams' projections,
While the world of gain and appearance and mirth goes on,   20
So soon what is over forgotten, and waves wash the imprints off the sand,
With hinged knees returning I enter the doors, (while for you up there,
Whoever you are, follow without noise and be of strong heart.)

Bearing the bandages, water and sponge,
Straight and swift to my wounded I go,
Where they lie on the ground after the battle brought in,
Where their priceless blood reddens the grass the ground,

Or to the rows of the hospital tent, or under the roof'd hospital,
To the long rows of cots up and down each side I return,   30
To each and all one after another I draw near, not one do I miss,
An attendant follows holding a tray, he carries a refuse pail,
Soon to be fill'd with clotted rags and blood, emptied, and fill'd again.

I onward go, I stop,
With hinged knees and steady hand to dress wounds,
I am firm with each, the pangs are sharp yet unavoidable,
One turns to me his appealing eyes—poor boy! I never knew you,
Yet I think I could not refuse this moment to die for you, if that would save you.

3

On, on I go, (open doors of time! open hospital doors!)
The crush'd head I dress, (poor crazed hand tear not the bandage away,)   40
The neck of the cavalry-man with the bullet through and through I examine,
Hard the breathing rattles, quite glazed already the eye, yet life struggles hard,
(Come sweet death! be persuaded O beautiful death!
In mercy come quickly.)

From the stump of the arm, the amputated hand,
I undo the clotted lint, remove the slough, wash off the matter and blood,
Back on his pillow the soldier bends with curv'd neck and side-falling head,
His eyes are closed, his face is pale, he dares not look on the bloody stump,
And has not yet look'd on it.

I dress a wound in the side, deep, deep,   50
But a day or two more, for see the frame all wasted and sinking,
And the yellow-blue countenance see.

I dress the perforated shoulder, the foot with the bullet-wound,
Cleanse the one with a gnawing and putrid gangrene, so sickening, so offensive,
While the attendant stands behind aside me holding the tray and pail.

I am faithful, I do not give out,
The fractur'd thigh, the knee, the wound in the abdomen,
These and more I dress with impassive hand, (yet deep in my breast a fire, a burning flame).

4

Thus in silence in dreams' projections,
Returning, resuming, I thread my way through the hospitals,   60
The hurt and wounded I pacify with soothing hand,
I sit by the restless all the dark night, some are so young,
Some suffer so much, I recall the experience sweet and sad,
(Many a soldier's loving arms about this neck have cross'd and rested,
Many a soldier's kiss dwells on these bearded lips).

                                                                       1865

O CAPTAIN! MY CAPTAIN!

O Captain! my Captain! our fearful trip is done,
The ship has weather'd every rack, the prize we sought is won,
The port is near, the bells I hear, the people all exulting,
While follow eyes the steady keel, the vessel grim and daring;

But O heart! heart! heart!
  O the bleeding drops of red,
    Where on the deck my Captain lies,
      Fallen cold and dead.

O Captain! my Captain! rise up and hear the bells;
Rise up—for you the flag is flung—for you the bugle trills,   10
For you bouquets and ribbon'd wreaths—for you the shores a-crowding,
For you they call, the swaying mass, their eager faces turning;
    Here Captain! dear father!
      This arm beneath your head!
        It is some dream that on the deck,
          You've fallen cold and dead.

My Captain does not answer, his lips are pale and still,
My father does not feel my arm, he has no pulse nor will,
The ship is anchor'd safe and sound, its voyage closed and done,
From fearful trip the victor ship comes in with object won;   20
    Exult O shores, and ring O bells!
      But I with mournful tread,
        Walk the deck my Captain lies,
          Fallen cold and dead.

1865–1866

WHEN LILACS LAST IN THE DOORYARD BLOOM'D

An elegy, or burial hymn, composed in a manner independent of all earlier models, this ranks as our best poem on President Lincoln. Some, indeed, have termed it "the high-water mark of American poetry." It lacks clear structure and finish, but is perhaps the more powerful emotionally because of this, as though the poet's grief was too intense for concern with expression. As in "Out of the Cradle Endlessly Rocking," there are interwoven motives. Three accidental experiences, the scent of the lilac, the solitary night song of the wood thrush, and the symbolical falling star, seem to Whitman to associate themselves with the time of Lincoln's death. Other striking features of the poem are the account of the progress of the funeral train, the unique apostrophe to death, and the sense conveyed of the grief of the whole nation.

1

When lilacs last in the dooryard bloom'd,
And the great star early droop'd in the western sky in the night,
I mourn'd, and yet shall mourn with ever-returning spring.

Ever-returning spring, trinity sure to me you bring,
Lilac blooming perennial and drooping star in the west,
And thought of him I love.

2

O powerful western fallen star!
O shades of night—O moody, tearful night!
O great star disappear'd—O the black murk that hides the star!
O cruel hands that hold me powerless—O helpless soul of me!   10
O harsh surrounding cloud that will not free my soul.

3

In the dooryard fronting an old farm-house near the white-wash'd palings,
Stands the lilac-bush, tall-growing with heart-shaped leaves of rich green,

With many a pointed blossom rising delicate, with the perfume strong I love,
With every leaf a miracle—and from this bush in the dooryard,
With delicate-color'd blossoms and heart-shaped leaves of rich green,
A sprig with its flower I break.

4

In the swamp in secluded recesses,
A shy and hidden bird is warbling a song.

Solitary the thrush,   20
The hermit withdrawn to himself, avoiding the settlements,
Sings by himself a song.

Song of the bleeding throat,
Death's outlet song of life (for well dear brother I know,
If thou wast not granted to sing thou would'st surely die).

5

Over the breast of the spring, the land, amid cities,
Amid lanes and through old woods, where lately the violets peep'd from the ground, spotting
    the gray débris,
Amid the grass in the fields each side of the lanes, passing the endless grass;
Passing the yellow-spear'd wheat, every grain from its shroud in the dark-brown fields uprisen,
Passing the apple-tree blows of white and pink in the orchards,   30
Carrying a corpse to where it shall rest in the grave,
Night and day journeys a coffin.

6

Coffin that passes through lanes and streets,
Through day and night with the great cloud darkening the land,
With the pomp of the inloop'd flags with the cities draped in black,
With the show of the States themselves as of crape-veil'd women standing,
With processions long and winding and the flambeaus of the night,
With the countless torches lit, with the silent sea of faces and the unbared heads,
With the waiting depot, the arriving coffin, and the somber faces,
With dirges through the night, with the thousand voices rising strong and solemn,   40
With all the mournful voices of the dirges pour'd around the coffin,
The dim-lit churches and the shuddering organs—where amid these you journey,
With the tolling tolling bells' perpetual clang,
Here, coffin that slowly passes,
I give you my sprig of lilac.

7

(Nor for you, for one alone,
Blossoms and branches green to coffins all I bring.
For fresh as the morning, thus would I carol a song to you O sane and sacred death.

All over bouquets of roses,
O death, I cover you over with roses and early lilies,   50
But mostly and now the lilac that blooms the first,
Copious I break, I break the sprigs from the bushes.
With loaded arms I come, pouring for you,
For you and the coffins all of you O death.)

8

O western orb sailing the heaven,
Now I know what you must have meant as a month since I walk'd,
As I walk'd in silence the transparent shadowy night,
As I saw you had something to tell as you bent to me night after night,
As you droop'd from the sky low down as if to my side (while the other stars all look'd on),
As we wander'd together the solemn night (for something I know not what kept me from sleep),
As the night advanced, and I saw on the rim of the west how full you were of woe,   61
As I stood on the rising ground in the breeze in the cold transparent night,
As I watch'd where you pass'd and was lost in the netherward black of the night,
As my soul in its trouble dissatisfied sank, as where you sad orb,
Concluded, dropt in the night, and was gone.

9

Sing on there in the swamp,
O singer bashful and tender, I hear your notes, I hear your call,
I hear, I come presently, I understand you,
But a moment I linger, for the lustrous star has detain'd me,
The star my departing comrade holds and detains me.   70

10

O how shall I warble myself for the dead one there I loved?
And how shall I deck my song for the large sweet soul that has gone?
And what shall my perfume be for the grave of him I love?

Sea-winds blown from east and west,
Blown from the Eastern sea and blown from the Western sea till there on the prairies meeting:
These and with these and the breath of my chant,
I'll perfume the grave of him I love.

11

O what shall I hang on the chamber walls?
And what shall the pictures be that I hang on the walls,
To adorn the burial-house of him I love?   80

Pictures of growing spring and farms and homes,
With the Fourth-month eve at sundown, and the gray smoke lucid and bright,
With floods of the yellow gold of the gorgeous, indolent, sinking sun, burning, expanding the air,
With the fresh sweet herbage under foot, and the pale green leaves of the trees prolific,
In the distance the flowing glaze, the breast of the river, with a wind-dapple here and there;
With ranging hills on the banks, with many a line against the sky, and shadows;
And the city at hand with dwellings so dense, and stacks of chimneys,
And all the scenes of life and the workshops, and the workmen homeward returning.

12

Lo, body and soul—this land,
My own Manhattan with spires, and the sparkling and hurrying tides, and the ships,   90
The varied and ample land, the South and the North in the light—Ohio's shores and flashing
    Missouri,
And ever the far-spreading prairies cover'd with grass and corn.
Lo, the most excellent sun so calm and haughty,
The violet and purple morn with just-felt breezes,

The gentle soft-born measureless light,
The miracle spreading bathing all, the fulfill'd noon,
The coming eve delicious, the welcome night and the stars,
Over my cities shining all, enveloping man and land.

13

Sing on, sing on you gray-brown bird,
Sing from the swamps, the recesses, pour your chant from the bushes; 100
Limitless out of the dusk, out of the cedars and pines.

Sing on dearest brother, warble your reedy song,
Loud human song, with voice of uttermost woe.

O liquid and free and tender!
O wild and loose to my soul—O wondrous singer!
You only I hear—yet the star holds me (but will soon depart,)
Yet the lilac with mastering odor holds me.

14

Now while I sat in the day and look'd forth,
In the close of the day with its light and the fields of spring, and the farmers preparing their crops,
In the large unconscious scenery of my land with its lakes and forests, 110
In the heavenly aerial beauty (after the perturb'd winds and the storms,)
Under the arching heavens of the afternoon swift passing, and the voices of children and women,
The many-moving sea-tides, and I saw the ships how they sail'd,
And the summer approaching with richness, and the fields all busy with labor,
And the infinite separate houses, how they all went on, each with its meals and minutia of daily usages;
And the streets how their throbbings throbb'd, and the cities pent—lo, then and there,
Falling upon them all and among them all, enveloping me with the rest,
Appear'd the cloud, appear'd the long black trail;
And I knew death, its thought, and the sacred knowledge of death.

Then with the knowledge of death as walking one side of me, 120
And the thought of death close-walking the other side of me,
And I in the middle as with companions, and as holding the hands of companions,
I fled forth to the hiding receiving night that talks not,
Down to the shores of the water, the path by the swamp in the dimness,
To the solemn shadowy cedars and ghostly pines so still.

And the singer so shy to the rest receiv'd me,
The gray-brown bird I know receiv'd us comrades three,
And he sang the carol of death, and a verse for him I love.

From deep secluded recesses,
From the fragrant cedars and the ghostly pines so still, 130
Came the carol of the bird.

And the charm of the carol rapt me,
As I held as if by their hands my comrades in the night;
And the voice of my spirit tallied the song of the bird.

Come lovely and soothing death,
Undulate round the world, serenely arriving, arriving,
In the day, in the night, to all, to each,
Sooner or later delicate death.

Prais'd be the fathomless universe,
For life and joy, and for objects and knowledge curious,
And for love, sweet love—but praise! praise! praise!
For the sure-enwinding arms of cool-enfolding death.

Dark mother always gliding near with soft feet,
Have none chanted for thee a chant of fullest welcome?
Then I chant it for thee, I glorify thee above all,
I bring thee a song that when thou must indeed come, come unfalteringly.

Approach strong deliveress,
When it is so, when thou hast taken them, I joyously sing the dead,
Lost in the loving floating ocean of thee,
Laved in the flood of thy bliss O death.

From me to thee glad serenades,
Dances for thee I propose saluting thee, adornments and feastings for thee,
And the sights of the open landscape and the high-spread sky are fitting,
And life and the fields, and the huge and thoughtful night.

The night in silence under many a star,
The ocean shore and the husky whispering wave whose voice I know,
And the soul turning to thee O vast and well-veil'd death,
And the body gratefully nestling close to thee.

Over the tree-tops I float thee a song,
Over the rising and sinking waves, over the myriad fields and the prairies wide,
Over the dense-pack'd cities all and the teeming wharves and ways,
I float this carol with joy, with joy to thee O death!

15

To the tally of my soul.
Loud and strong kept up the gray-brown bird,
With pure, deliberate notes spreading filling the night.

Loud in the pines and cedars dim,
Clear in the freshness moist and the swamp-perfume,
And I with my comrades there in the night.

While my sight that was bound in my eyes unclosed,
As to long panoramas of visions.

I saw askant the armies;
And I saw as in noiseless dreams hundreds of battle-flags,
Borne through the smoke of the battles and pierc'd with missiles I saw them,
And carried hither and yon through the smoke, and torn and bloody,
And at last but a few shreds left on the staffs (and all in silence,)
And the staffs all splinter'd and broken.

I saw battle-corpses, myriads of them,
And the white skeletons of young men, I saw them,
I saw the débris and débris of all the slain soldiers of the war,
But I saw they were not as was thought,   180
They themselves were fully at rest, they suffer'd not,
The living remain'd and suffer'd, the mother suffer'd,
And the wife and the child and the musing comrade suffer'd,
And the armies that remain'd suffer'd.

16

Passing the visions, passing the night,
Passing, unloosing the hold of my comrades' hands,
Passing the song of the hermit bird and the tallying song of my soul,
Victorious song, death's outlet song, yet varying ever-altering song,
As low and wailing, yet clear the notes, rising and falling, flooding the night,
Sadly sinking and fainting, as warning and warning, and yet again bursting with joy,   190
Covering the earth and filling the spread of the heaven,
As that powerful psalm in the night I heard from recesses,
Passing, I leave thee lilac with heart-shaped leaves,
I leave thee there in the dooryard blooming, returning with spring.

I cease from my song for thee,
From my gaze on thee in the west, fronting the west, communing with thee,
O comrade lustrous with silver face in the night.

Yet each I keep and all, retrievements out of the night,
The song, the wondrous chant of the gray-brown bird,
The tallying chant, the echo arous'd in my soul,   200
With the lustrous and drooping star with the countenance full of woe,
With the holders holding my hand hearing the call of the bird,
Comrades mine and I in the midst, and their memory ever to keep, for the dead I loved so well,
For the sweetest, wisest soul of all my days and lands—and this for his dear sake;
Lilac and star and bird twined with the chant of my soul,
There in the fragrant pines and the cedars dusk and dim.

1865–1866

VIGIL STRANGE I KEPT ON THE FIELD ONE NIGHT

VIGIL strange I kept on the field one night;
When you my son and my comrade dropt at my side that day,
One look I but gave which your dear eyes return'd with a look I shall never forget,
One touch of your hand to mine O boy, reach'd up as you lay on the ground,
Then onward I sped in the battle, the even-contested battle,
Till late in the night reliev'd to the place at last again I made my way,
Found you in death so cold dear comrade, found your body son of responding kisses, (never again
    on earth responding,)
Bared your face in the starlight, curious the scene, cool blew the moderate night-wind,
Long there and then in vigil I stood, dimly around me the battle-field spreading,
Vigil wondrous and vigil sweet there in the fragrant silent night,   10
But not a tear fell, not even a long-drawn sigh, long, long I gazed,
Then on the earth partially reclining sat by your side leaning my chin in my hands,
Passing sweet hours, immortal and mystic hours with you dearest comrade—not a tear, not a
    word,

Vigil of silence, love and death, vigil for you my son and my soldier,
As onward silently stars aloft, eastward new ones upward stole,
Vigil final for you brave boy, (I could not save you, swift was your death,
I faithfully loved you and cared for you living, I think we shall surely meet again,)
Till at latest lingering of the night, indeed just as the dawn appear'd,
My comrade I wrapt in his blanket, envelop'd well his form,
Folded the blanket well, tucking it carefully over head and carefully under feet,   20
And there and then and bathed by the rising sun, my son in his grave, in his rude-dug grave I
    deposited,
Ending my vigil strange with that, vigil of night and battle-field dim,
Vigil for boy of responding kisses, (never again on earth responding,)
Vigil for comrade swiftly slain, vigil I never forget, how as day brighten'd,
I rose from the chill ground and folded my soldier well in his blanket,
And buried him where he fell.

1865

ONE'S–SELF I SING

ONE'S-SELF I sing, a simple separate person,
Yet utter the word Democratic, the word En-Masse.

Of physiology from top to toe I sing,
Not physiognomy alone nor brain alone is worthy for the Muse, I say the Form complete is
    worthier far,
The Female equally with the Male I sing.

Of Life immense in passion, pulse, and power,
Cheerful, for freest action form'd under the laws divine,
The Modern Man I sing.

1867

DAREST THOU NOW O SOUL

DAREST thou now O soul,
Walk out with me toward the unknown region,
Where neither ground is for the feet nor any path to follow?

No map there, nor guide,
Nor voice sounding, nor touch of human hand,
Nor face with blooming flesh, nor lips, nor eyes, are in that land.

I know it not O soul,
Nor dost thou, all is a blank before us,
All waits undream'd of in that region, that inaccessible land.

Till when the ties loosen,   10
All but the ties eternal, Time and Space,
Nor darkness, gravitation, sense, nor any bounds bounding us.

Then we burst forth, we float,
In Time and Space O soul, prepared for them,
Equal, equipt at last, (O joy! O fruit of all!) them to fulfil O soul.

1870

PASSAGE TO INDIA

The Atlantic cable was laid in 1866, in 1869 the Suez Canal was completed, and also in 1869 the tracks of the Union Pacific extending westward from Omaha were connected with the Central Pacific built eastward from San Francisco. Whitman thought of the crossing of the American continent as completing a world circuit, starting eastward from India, and this brought him a vision of world unity. Bret Harte curtly rejected this poem when it was submitted to the *Overland Monthly*.

1

SINGING my days,
Singing the great achievements of the present,
Singing the strong, light works of engineers,
Our modern wonders, (the antique ponderous Seven outvied,)
In the Old World, the east, the Suez canal,
The New by its mighty railroad spann'd,
The seas inlaid with eloquent, gentle wires,
I sound, to commence, the cry, with thee, O soul,
The Past! the Past! the Past!

The Past! the dark, unfathom'd retrospect!   10
The teeming gulf! the sleepers and the shadows!
The past! the infinite greatness of the past!
For what is the present, after all, but a growth out of the past?
(As a projectile, form'd, impell'd, passing a certain line, still keeps on,
So the present, utterly form'd, impell'd by the past.)

2

Passage, O soul, to India!
Eclaircise [1] the myths Asiatic—the primitive fables.

Not you alone, proud truths of the world!
Nor you alone, ye facts of modern science!
But myths and fables of eld—Asia's, Africa's fables!   20
The far-darting beams of the spirit!—the unloos'd dreams!
The deep diving bibles and legends;
The daring plots of the poets—the elder religions;
—O you temples fairer than lilies, pour'd over by the rising sun!
O you fables, spurning the known, eluding the hold of the known, mounting to heaven!
You lofty and dazzling towers, pinnacled, red as roses, burnish'd with gold!
Towers of fables immortal, fashion'd from mortal dreams!
You too I welcome, and fully, the same as the rest;
You too with joy I sing.

3

Passage to India!   30
Lo, soul! seest thou not God's purpose from the first?
The earth to be spann'd, connected by net-work,
The people to become brothers and sisters,
The races, neighbors, to marry and be given in marriage,
The oceans to be cross'd, the distant brought near,
The lands to be welded together.

[1] Make clear. Whitman likes to borrow or to manipulate French words.

(A worship new, I sing;
You captains, voyagers, explorers, yours!
You engineers! you architects, machinists, yours!
You, not for trade or transportation only,
But in God's name, and for thy sake, O soul.)

4

Passage to India!
Lo, soul, for thee, of tableaus twain,
I see, in one, the Suez canal initiated, open'd,
I see the procession of steamships, the Empress Eugenie's leading the van;
I mark, from on deck, the strange landscape, the pure sky, the level sand in the distance;
I pass swiftly the picturesque groups, the workmen gather'd,
The gigantic dredging machines.

In one, again, different, (yet thine, all thine, O soul, the same,)
I see over my own continent the Pacific Railroad, surmounting every barrier;
I see continual trains of cars winding along the Platte, carrying freight and passengers;
I hear the locomotives rushing and roaring, and the shrill steam-whistle,
I hear the echoes reverberate through the grandest scenery in the world;
I cross the Laramie plains—I note the rocks in grotesque shapes—the buttes;
I see the plentiful larkspur and wild onions—the barren, colorless, sage-deserts;
I see in glimpses afar, or towering immediately above me, the great mountains—I see the Wind
    River and the Wahsatch mountains;
I see the Monument mountain and the Eagle's Nest—I pass the Promontory—I ascend the
    Nevadas;
I scan the noble Elk mountain, and wind around its base;
I see the Humboldt range—I thread the valley and cross the river,
I see the clear waters of Lake Tahoe—I see forests of majestic pines,
Or, crossing the great desert, the alkaline plains, I behold enchanting mirages of waters and
    meadows;
Marking through these, and after all, in duplicate slender lines,
Bridging the three or four thousand miles of land travel,
Tying the Eastern to the Western sea,
The road between Europe and Asia.

(Ah Genoese, thy dream! thy dream!
Centuries after thou art laid in thy grave,
The shore thou foundest verifies thy dream!)

5

Passage to India!
Struggles of many a captain—tales of many a sailor dead!
Over my mood, stealing and spreading they come,
Like clouds and cloudlets in the unreach'd sky.

Along all history, down the slopes,
As a rivulet running, sinking now, and now again to the surface rising,
A ceaseless thought, a varied train—Lo, soul! to thee, thy sight, they rise,
The plans, the voyages again, the expeditions:
Again Vasco da Gama sails forth;
Again the knowledge gain'd, the mariner's compass,
Lands found, and nations born—thou born, America, (a hemisphere unborn,)

For purpose vast, man's long probation fill'd, 80
Thou, rondure of the world, at last accomplish'd.

6

O, vast Rondure, swimming in space!
Cover'd all over with visible power and beauty!
Alternate light and day, and teeming, spiritual darkness;
Unspeakable, high processions of sun and moon, and countless stars, above;
Below, the manifold grass and waters, animals, mountains, trees;
With inscrutable purpose—some hidden, prophetic intention;
Now, first, it seems, my thought begins to span thee.

Down from the gardens of Asia, descending, radiating,
Adam and Eve appear, then their myriad progeny after them, 90
Wandering, yearning, curious—with restless explorations,
With questionings, baffled, formless, feverish—with never-happy hearts,
With that sad, incessant refrain, *Wherefore, unsatisfied Soul?* and *Whither, O mocking Life?*

Ah, who shall soothe these feverish children?
Who justify these restless explorations?
Who speak the secret of impassive Earth?
Who bind it to us? What is this separate Nature, so unnatural?
What is this Earth, to our affections? (unloving earth, without a throb to answer ours;
Cold earth, the place of graves.)

Yet, soul, be sure the first intent remains—and shall be carried out; 100
(Perhaps even now the time has arrived.)

After the seas are all cross'd, (as they seem already cross'd,)
After the great captains and engineers have accomplish'd their work,
After the noble inventors—after the scientists, the chemist, the geologist, ethnologist,
Finally shall come the Poet, worthy that name;
The true Son of God shall come, singing his songs.

Then, not your deeds only, O voyagers, O scientists and inventors, shall be justified,
All these hearts, as of fretted children, shall be sooth'd,
All affection shall be fully responded to—the secret shall be told;
All these separations and gaps shall be taken up, and hook'd and link'd together; 110
The whole Earth—this cold, impassive, voiceless Earth, shall be completely justified;
Trinitas divine shall be gloriously accomplish'd and compacted by the true Son of God, the poet,
(He shall indeed pass the straits and conquer the mountains,
He shall double the Cape of Good Hope to some purpose;)
Nature and Man shall be disjoin'd and diffused no more,
The true Son of God shall absolutely fuse them.

7

Year at whose open'd, wide-flung door I sing!
Year of the purpose accomplish'd!
Year of the marriage of continents, climates and oceans!
(No mere Doge of Venice now, wedding the Adriatic;) [1] 120

[1] In the great days of Venice, it was the custom for the Doge, or chief magistrate, to throw a golden ring yearly into the Adriatic to symbolize the wedding of Venice to the sea that had enriched it.

I see, O year, in you, the vast terraqueous globe, given, and giving all,
Europe to Asia, Africa join'd, and they to the New World;
The lands, geographies, dancing before you, holding a festival garland,
As brides and bridegrooms hand in hand.

8

Passage to India!
Cooling airs from Caucasus far, soothing cradle of man,
The river Euphrates flowing, the past lit up again.

Lo, soul, the retrospect, brought forward;
The old, most populous, wealthiest of Earth's lands,
The streams of the Indus and the Ganges, and their many affluents;   130
(I, my shores of America walking to-day, behold, resuming all,)
The tale of Alexander, on his warlike marches, suddenly dying,
On one side China, and on the other side Persia and Arabia,
To the south the great seas, and the Bay of Bengal;
The flowing literatures, tremendous epics, religions, castes,
Old occult Brahma, interminably far back—the tender and junior Buddha,
Central and southern empires, and all their belongings, possessors,
The wars of Tamerlane, the reign of Aurungzebe,
The traders, rulers, explorers, Moslems, Venetians, Byzantium, the Arabs, Portuguese,
The first travelers, famous yet, Marco Polo, Batouta the Moor,   140
Doubts to be solv'd, the map incognita, blanks to be fill'd,
The foot of man unstay'd, the hands never at rest,
Thyself, O soul, that will not brook a challenge.

9

The medieval navigators rise before me,
The world of 1492, with its awaken'd enterprise;
Something swelling in humanity now like the sap of the earth in spring,
The sunset splendor of chivalry declining,

And who art thou, sad shade?
Gigantic, visionary, thyself a visionary,
With majestic limbs, and pious, beaming eyes,   150
Spreading around, with every look of thine, a golden world,
Enhuing it with gorgeous hues.

As the chief histrion,
Down to the footlights walks, in some great scena,
Dominating the rest, I see the Admiral himself,
(History's type of courage, action, faith;)
Behold him sail from Palos, leading his little fleet;
His voyage behold—his return—his great fame,
His misfortunes, calumniators—behold him a prisoner, chain'd,
Behold his dejection, poverty, death.   160

(Curious, in time, I stand, noting the efforts of heroes;
Is the deferment long? bitter the slander, poverty, death?
Lies the seed unreck'd for centuries in the ground? Lo! to God's due occasion,
Uprising in the night, it sprouts, blooms.
And fills the earth with use and beauty.)

Passage indeed, O soul, to primal thought!
Not lands and seas alone—thy own clear freshness,
The young maturity of brood and bloom;
To realms of budding bibles.

O soul, repressless, I with thee, and thou with me,   170
Thy circumnavigation of the world begin;
Of man, the voyage of his mind's return,
To reason's early paradise,
Back, back to wisdom's birth, to innocent intuitions,
Again with fair Creation.

11

O we can wait no longer!
We too take ship, O soul!
Joyous, we too launch out on trackless seas!
Fearless, for unknown shores, on waves of ecstasy to sail,
Amid the wafting winds, (thou pressing me to thee, I thee to me, O soul,)   180
Caroling free—singing our song of God,
Chanting our chant of pleasant exploration.

With laugh, and many a kiss,
(Let others deprecate—let others weep for sin, remorse, humiliation;)
O soul, thou pleasest me—I thee.

Ah, more than any priest, O soul, we too believe in God;
But with the mystery of God we dare not dally.

O soul, thou pleasest me—I thee;
Sailing these seas, or on the hills, or waking in the night,
Thoughts, silent thoughts, of Time, and Space, and Death, like waters flowing,   190
Bear me, indeed, as through the regions infinite,
Whose air I breathe, whose ripples hear—lave me all over;
Bathe me, O God, in thee—mounting to thee,
I and my soul to range in range of thee.

O Thou transcendent!
Nameless—the fibre and the breath!
Light of the light—shedding forth universes—thou centre of them!
Thou mightier centre of the true, the good, the loving!
Thou moral, spiritual fountain! affection's source! thou reservoir!
(O pensive soul of me! O thirst unsatisfied! waitest not there?   200
Waitest not haply for us, somewhere there, the Comrade perfect?)
Thou pulse! thou motive of the stars, suns, systems,
That, circling, move in order, safe, harmonious,
Athwart the shapeless vastnesses of space!
How should I think—how breathe a single breath—how speak—if, out of myself,
I could not launch, to those, superior universes?

Swiftly I shrivel at the thought of God,
At Nature and its wonders, Time and Space and Death,
But that I, turning, call to thee, O soul, thou actual Me,
And lo! thou gently masterest the orbs,
Thou matest Time, smilest content at Death,
And fillest, swellest full, the vastnesses of Space.

210

Greater than stars or suns,
Bounding, O soul, thou journeyest forth;
—What love, than thine and ours could wider amplify?
What aspirations, wishes, outvie thine and ours, O soul?
What dreams of the ideal? what plans of purity, perfection, strength?
What cheerful willingness, for others' sake, to give up all?
For others' sake to suffer all?

Reckoning ahead, O soul, when thou, the time achiev'd, 220
(The seas all cross'd, weather'd the capes, the voyage done,)
Surrounded, copest, frontest God, yieldest, the aim attain'd,
As, fill'd with friendship, love complete, the Elder Brother found,
The Younger melts in fondness in his arms.

12

Passage to more than India!
Are thy wings plumed indeed for such far flights?
O Soul, voyagest thou indeed on voyages like these?
Disportest thou on waters such as these?
Soundest below the Sanscrit and the Vedas?
Then have thy bent unleash'd.

230

Passage to you, your shores, ye aged fierce enigmas!
Passage to you, to mastership of you, ye strangling problems!
You, strew'd with the wrecks of skeletons, that, living, never reach'd you.

13

Passage to more than India!
O secret of the earth and sky!
Of you, O waters of the sea! O winding creeks and rivers!
Of you, O woods and fields! Of you, strong mountains of my land!
Of you, O prairies! Of you, gray rocks!
O morning red! O clouds! O rain and snows!
O day and night, passage to you! 240

O sun and moon, and all you stars! Sirius and Jupiter!
Passage to you!

Passage—immediate passage! the blood burns in my veins!
Away, O soul! hoist instantly the anchor!
Cut the hawsers—haul out—shake out every sail!
Have we not stood here like trees in the ground long enough?
Have we not grovell'd here long enough, eating and drinking like mere brutes?
Have we not darken'd and dazed ourselves with books long enough?

Sail forth! steer for the deep waters only!
Reckless, O soul, exploring, I with thee, and thou with me;   250

For we are bound where mariner has not yet dared to go,
And we will risk the ship, ourselves and all.

O my brave soul!
O farther, farther sail!
O daring joy, but safe! Are they not all the seas of God?
O farther, farther, farther sail!   1871

THOU MOTHER WITH THY EQUAL BROOD

1

Thou Mother with thy equal brood,
Thou varied chain of different States, yet one identity only,
A special song before I go I'd sing o'er all the rest,
For thee, the future.
I'd sow a seed for thee of endless Nationality,
I'd fashion thy ensemble including body and soul,
I'd show away ahead thy real Union, and how it may be accomplish'd.

The paths to the house I seek to make,
But leave to those to come the house itself.
Belief I sing, and preparation;   10
As Life and Nature are not great with reference to the present only,
But greater still from what is yet to come,
Out of that formula for thee I sing.

2

As a strong bird on pinions free,
Joyous, the amplest spaces heavenward cleaving,
Such be the thought I'd think of thee America,
Such be the recitative I'd bring for thee.

The conceits of the poets of other lands I'd bring thee not,
Nor the compliments that have served their turn so long,
Nor rhyme, nor the classics, nor perfume of foreign court or indoor library;   20
But an odor I'd bring as from forests of pine in Maine, or breath of an Illinois prairie,
With open airs of Virginia or Georgia or Tennessee, or from Texas uplands, or Florida's glades,
Or the Saguenay's black stream, or the wide blue spread of the Huron,
With presentment of Yellowstone's scenes, or Yosemite,
And murmuring under, pervading all, I'd bring the rustling sea-sound,
That endlessly sounds from the two Great Seas of the world.

And for thy subtler sense subtler refrains dread Mother,
Preludes of intellect tallying these and thee, mind-formulas for thee, real and sane and large as
    these and thee,
Thou! mounting higher, diving deeper than we knew, thou transcendental Union!
By thee fact to be justified, blended with thought,   30
Thought of man justified, blended with God,
Through thy idea, lo, the immortal reality!
Through thy reality, lo, the immortal idea!

3

Brain of the New World, what a task is thine,
To formulate the Modern—out of the peerless grandeur of the modern,
Out of thyself, comprising science, to recast poems, churches, art,
(Recast, may-be discard them, end them—may-be their work is done, who knows?)
By vision, hand, conception, on the background of the mighty past, the dead,
To limn with absolute faith the mighty living present.

And yet thou living present brain, heir of the dead, the Old World brain,
Thou that lay folded like an unborn babe within its folds so long,   40
Thou carefully prepared by it so long—haply thou but unfoldest it, only maturest it,
It to eventuate in thee—the essence of the by-gone time contain'd in thee,
Its poems, churches, arts, unwitting to themselves, destined with reference to thee;
Thou but the apples, long, long, long a-growing,
The fruit of all the Old ripening to-day in thee.

4

Sail, sail thy best, ship of Democracy,
Of value is thy freight, 'tis not the Present only,
The Past is also stored in thee,
Thou holdest not the venture of thyself alone, not of the Western continent alone,
Earth's *résumé* entire floats on thy keel O ship, is steadied by thy spars,   50
With thee Time voyages in trust, the antecedent nations sink or swim with thee,
With all their ancient struggles, martyrs, heroes, epics, wars, thou bear'st the other continents,
Theirs, theirs as much as thine, the destination-port triumphant;
Steer then with good strong hand and wary eye O helmsman, thou carriest great companions,
Venerable priestly Asia sails this day with thee,
And royal feudal Europe sails with thee.

5

Beautiful world of new superber birth that rises to my eyes,
Like a limitless golden cloud filling the western sky,
Emblem of general maternity lifted above all,
Sacred shape of the bearer of daughters and sons,   60
Out of thy teeming womb thy giant babes in ceaseless procession issuing,
Acceding from such gestation, taking and giving continual strength and life,
World of the real—world of the twain in one,
World of the soul, born by the world of the real alone, led to identity, body, by it alone,
Yet in beginning only, incalculable masses of composite precious materials,
By history's cycles forwarded, by every nation, language, hither sent,
Ready, collected here, a freer, vast, electric world, to be constructed here,
(The true New World, the world of orbic science, morals, literatures to come,)
Thou wonder world yet undefined, unform'd, neither do I define thee,   70
How can I pierce the impenetrable blank of the future?
I feel thy ominous greatness evil as well as good,
I watch thee advancing, absorbing the present, transcending the past,
I see thy light lightning, and thy shadow shadowing, as if the entire globe,
But I do not undertake to define thee, hardly to comprehend thee,
I but thee name, thee prophesy, as now,
I merely thee ejaculate!
Thee in thy future,

Thee in thy only permanent life, career, thy own unloosen'd mind, thy soaring spirit,
Thee as another equally needed sun, radiant, ablaze, swift-moving, fructifying all,   80
Thee risen in potent cheerfulness and joy, in endless great hilarity,
Scattering for good the cloud that hung so long, that weigh'd so long upon the mind of man,
The doubt, suspicion, dread, of gradual, certain decadence of man;
Thee in thy larger, saner brood of female, male—thee in thy athletes, moral, spiritual, South,
    North, West, East,
(To thy immortal breasts, Mother of All, thy ever daughter, son, endear'd alike, forever equal,)
Thee in thy own musicians, singers, artists, unborn yet, but certain,
Thee in thy moral wealth and civilization, (until which thy proudest material civilization must
    remain in vain,)
Thee in thy all-supplying, all-enclosing worship—thee in no single bible, saviour, merely,
Thy saviours countless, latent within thyself, thy bibles incessant within thyself, equal to any,
    divine as any,
(Thy soaring course thee formulating, not in thy two great wars, nor in thy century's visible
    growth,   90
But far more in these leaves and chants; thy chants, great Mother!)
Thee in an education grown of thee, in teachers, studies, students, born of thee,
Thee in thy democratic fêtes en-masse, thy high original festivals, operas, lecturers, preachers,
Thee in thy ultimata, (the preparations only now completed, the edifice on sure foundations tied,)
Thee in thy pinnacles, intellect, thought, thy topmost rational joys, thy love and godlike aspira-
    tion,
In thy resplendent coming literati, thy full-lung'd orators, thy sacerdotal bards, kosmic savans,
These! these in thee, (certain to come,) to-day I prophesy.

    6

Land tolerating all, accepting all, not for good alone, all good for thee,
Land in the realms of God to be a realm unto thyself,
Under the rule of God to be a rule unto thyself.   100

(Lo, where arise three peerless stars,
To be thy natal stars my country, Ensemble, Evolution, Freedom,
Set in the sky of Law.)

Land of unprecedented faith, God's faith,
Thy soil, thy very subsoil, all upheav'd,
The general inner earth so long so sedulously draped over, now hence for what it is boldly laid
    bare,
Open'd by thee to heaven's light for benefit or bale.

Not for success alone,
Not to fair-sail unintermitted always,
The storm shall dash thy face, the murk of war and worse than war shall cover thee all over,
(Wert capable of war, its tug and trials? be capable of peace its trials,   III
For the tug and mortal strain of nations come at last in prosperous peace, not war;)
In many a smiling mask death shall approach beguiling thee, thou in disease shalt swelter,
The livid cancer spread its hideous claws, clinging upon thy breasts, seeking to strike thee deep
    within,
Consumption of the worst, moral consumption, shall rouge thy face with hectic,
But thou shalt face thy fortunes, thy diseases, and surmount them all,
Whatever they are to-day and whatever through time they may be,

They each and all shall lift and pass away and cease from thee,
While thou, Time's spirals rounding, out of thyself, thyself still extricating, fusing,
Equable, natural, mystical Union thou, (the mortal with immortal blent,)   120
Shalt soar toward the fulfilment of the future, the spirit of the body and the mind,
The soul, its destinies.

The soul, its destinies, the real real,
(Purport of all these apparitions of the real;)
In thee America, the soul, its destinies,
Thou globe of globes! thou wonder nebulous!
By many a throe of heat and cold convuls'd, (by these thyself solidifying,)
Thou mental, moral orb—thou New, indeed new, Spiritual World!
The Present holds thee not—for such vast growth is thine,
For such unparallel'd flight as thine, such brood as thine,   130
The FUTURE only holds thee and can hold thee.

1872

A PRAIRIE SUNSET

SHOT gold, maroon and violet, dazzling silver, emerald, fawn,
The earth's whole amplitude and Nature's multiform power consign'd for once to colors;
The light, the general air possess'd by them—colors till now unknown,
No limit, confine—not the Western sky alone—the high meridian—North, South, all,
Pure luminous color fighting the silent shadows to the last.

1888

GOOD-BYE MY FANCY!

GOOD-BYE my Fancy!
Farewell dear mate, dear love!
I'm going away, I know not where,
Or to what fortune, or whether I may ever see you again,
So Good-bye my Fancy.

Now for my last—let me look back a moment;
The slower fainter ticking of the clock is in me,
Exit, nightfall, and soon the heart-thud stopping.
Long have we lived, joy'd, caress'd together;
Delightful!—now separation—Good-bye my Fancy.   10

Yet let me not be too hasty,
Long indeed have we lived, slept, filter'd, become really blended into one;
Then if we die we die together (yes, we'll remain one),
If we go anywhere we'll go together to meet what happens,
May-be we'll be better off and blither, and learn something,
May-be it is yourself now really ushering me to the true songs, (who knows?)
May-be it is you the mortal knob really undoing, turning—so now finally,
Good-bye—and hail! my Fancy.

1891

From DEMOCRATIC VISTAS

I SAY that democracy can never prove itself beyond cavil, until it founds and luxuriantly grows its own forms of art, poems, schools, theology, displacing all that exists, or that has been produced anywhere in the past, under opposite influences. It is curious to me that while so many voices, pens, minds, in the press, lecture-rooms, in our Congress, &c., are discussing intellectual topics, pecuniary dangers, legislative problems, the suffrage, tariff and labor questions, and the various business and benevolent needs of America, with propositions, remedies, often worth deep attention, there is one need, a hiatus the profoundest, that no eye seems to perceive, no voice to state. Our fundamental want to-day in the United States, with closest, amplest reference to present conditions, and to the future, is of a class, and the clear idea of a class, of native authors, literatuses, far different, far higher in grade than any yet known, sacerdotal, modern, fit to cope with our occasions, lands, permeating the whole mass of American mentality, taste, belief, breathing into it a new breath of life, giving it decision, affecting politics far more than the popular superficial suffrage, with results inside and underneath the elections of Presidents or Congresses—radiating, begetting appropriate teachers, schools, manners, and, as its grandest result, accomplishing, (what neither the schools nor the churches and their clergy have hitherto accomplish'd, and without which this nation will no more stand, permanently, soundly, than a house will stand without a substratum,) a religious and moral character beneath the political and productive and intellectual bases of the States. For know you not, dear, earnest reader, that the people of our land may all read and write, and may all possess the right to vote—and yet the main things may be entirely lacking?—(and this to suggest them.)

View'd, to-day, from a point of view sufficiently over-arching, the problem of humanity all over the civilized world is social and religious, and is to be finally met and treated by literature. The priest departs, the divine literatus comes. Never was anything more wanted than, to-day, and here in the States, the poet of the modern is wanted, or the great literatus of the modern. At all times, perhaps, the central point in any nation, and that whence it is itself really sway'd the most, and whence it sways others, is its national literature, especially its archetypal poems. Above all previous lands, a great original literature is surely to become the justification and reliance, (in some respects the sole reliance,) of American democracy.

Few are aware how the great literature penetrates all, gives hue to all, shapes aggregates and individuals, and, after subtle ways, with irresistible power, constructs, sustains, demolishes at will. Why tower, in reminiscence, above all the nations of the earth, two special lands, petty in themselves, yet unexpressibly gigantic, beautiful, columnar? Immortal Judah lives, and Greece immortal lives, in a couple of poems.

Nearer than this. It is not generally realized, but it is true, as the genius of Greece, and all the sociology, personality, politics and religion of those wonderful states, resided in their literature or esthetics, that what was afterwards the main support of European chivalry, the feudal, ecclesiastical, dynastic world over there—forming its osseous structure, holding it together for hundreds, thousands of years, preserving its flesh and bloom, giving it form, decision, rounding it out, and so saturating it in the conscious and unconscious blood, breed, belief, and intuitions of men, that it still prevails powerful to this day, in defiance of the mighty changes of time— was its literature, permeating to the very marrow, especially that major part, its enchanting songs, ballads, and poems.

To the ostent [1] of the senses and eyes, I know, the influences which stamp the world's history are wars, uprisings or downfalls of dynasties, changeful movements of trade, important inventions, navigation, military or civil governments, advent of powerful personalities, conquerors, &c. These of course play their part; yet, it may be, a single new thought, imagination, abstract principle, even literary style, fit for the time, put in shape by some great literatus, and projected among

[1] manifestation, appearance

mankind, may duly cause changes, growths, removals, greater than the longest and bloodiest war, or the most stupendous merely political, dynastic, or commercial overturn.

In short, as, though it may not be realized, it is strictly true, that a few first-class poets, philosophs,[1] and authors, have substantially settled and given status to the entire religion, education, law, sociology, &c., of the hitherto civilized world, by tinging and often creating the atmospheres out of which they have arisen, such also must stamp, and more than ever stamp, the interior and real democratic construction of this American continent, to-day, and days to come. Remember also this fact of difference, that, while through the antique and through the mediæval ages, highest thoughts and ideals realized themselves, and their expression made its way by other arts, as much as, or even more than by, technical literature, (not open to the mass of persons, or even to the majority of eminent persons,) such literature in our day and for current purposes, is not only more eligible than all the other arts put together, but has become the only general means of morally influencing the world. Painting, sculpture, and the dramatic theatre, it would seem, no longer play an indispensable or even important part in the workings and mediumship of intellect, utility, or even high esthetics. Architecture remains, doubtless with capacities, and a real future. Then music, the combiner, nothing more spiritual, nothing more sensuous, a god, yet completely human, advances, prevails, holds highest place; supplying in certain wants and quarters what nothing else could supply. Yet in the civilization of to-day it is undeniable that, over all the arts, literature dominates, serves beyond all—shapes the character of church and school—or, at any rate, is capable of doing so. Including the literature of science, its scope is indeed unparallel'd.

Before proceeding further, it were perhaps well to discriminate on certain points. Literature tills its crops in many fields, and some may flourish, while others lag. What I say in these Vistas has its main bearing on imaginative literature, especially poetry, the stock of

[1] Whitman's variant of "philosophers"

all. In the department of science, and the specialty of journalism, there appear, in these States, promises, perhaps fulfilments, of highest earnestness, reality, and life. These, of course, are modern. But in the region of imaginative, spinal and essential attributes, something equivalent to creation is, for our age and lands, imperatively demanded. For not only is it not enough that the new blood, new frame of democracy shall be vivified and held together merely by political means, superficial suffrage, legislation, &c., but it is clear to me that, unless it goes deeper, gets at least as firm and as warm a hold in men's hearts, emotions and belief, as, in their days, feudalism or ecclesiasticism, and inaugurates its own perennial sources, welling from the centre forever, its strength will be defective, its growth doubtful, and its main charm wanting. I suggest, therefore, the possibility, should some two or three really original American poets, (perhaps artists or lecturers,) arise, mounting the horizon like planets, stars of the first magnitude, that, from their eminence, fusing contributions, races, far localities, &c., together, they would give more compaction and more moral identity, (the quality to-day most needed,) to these States, than all its Constitutions, legislative and judicial ties, and all its hitherto political, warlike, or materialistic experiences. As, for instance, there could hardly happen anything that would more serve the States, with all their variety of origins, their diverse climes, cities, standards, &c., than possessing an aggregate of heroes, characters, exploits, sufferings, prosperity or misfortune, glory or disgrace, common to all, typical of all—no less, but even greater would it be to possess the aggregation of a cluster of mighty poets, artists, teachers, fit for us, national expressers, comprehending and effusing for the men and women of the States, what is universal, native, common to all, inland and seaboard, northern and southern. The historians say of ancient Greece, with her ever-jealous autonomies, cities, and states, that the only positive unity she ever own'd or receiv'd, was the sad unity of a common subjection, at the last, to foreign conquerors. Subjection, aggregation of that sort, is impossible to America; but the fear of conflicting and irreconcilable interiors, and the lack of a common skeleton, knitting all close, continually haunts me. Or, if it does not, nothing is plainer than the need, a long period to come, of a fusion of the States into the only reliable identity, the moral and artistic one. For, I say, the true nationality of the States, the genuine union, when we come to a mortal crisis, is, and is to be, after all, neither the written law, nor, (as is generally supposed,) either self-interest, or common pecuniary or material objects—but the fervid and tremendous IDEA, melting everything else with resistless heat, and solving all lesser and definite distinctions in vast, indefinite, spiritual, emotional power.

It may be claim'd, (and I admit the weight of the claim,) that common and general worldly prosperity, and a populace well-to-do, and with all life's material comforts, is the main thing, and is enough. It may be argued that our republic is, in performance, really enacting to-day the grandest arts, poems, &c., by beating up the wilderness into fertile farms, and in her railroads, ships, machinery, &c. And it may be ask'd, Are these not better, indeed, for America, than any utterances even of greatest rhapsode,[1] artist, or literatus?

I too hail those achievements with pride and joy: then answer that the soul of man will not with such only—nay, not with such at all—be finally satisfied; but needs what, (standing on these and on all things, as the feet stand on the ground,) is address'd to the loftiest, to itself alone.

1871

From SPECIMEN DAYS

My Passion for Ferries

Living in Brooklyn or New York city from this time forward, my life, then, and still more the following years, was curiously identified with Fulton ferry, already becoming the greatest of its sort in the world for general importance, volume, variety, rapidity, and picturesqueness. Almost daily, later, ('50 to '60,) I cross'd on the boats, often up in the pilot-houses where I could get a full sweep, absorbing shows, accompaniments, surround-

[1] professional reciter of poetry in ancient Greece

ings. What oceanic currents, eddies, underneath—the great tides of humanity also, with ever-shifting movements. Indeed, I have always had a passion for ferries; to me they afford inimitable streaming, never-failing, living poems. The river and bay scenery, all about New York Island, any time of a fine day—the hurrying, splashing sea-tides—the changing panorama of steamers, all sizes, often a string of big ones outward bound to distant ports—the myriads of white-sail'd schooners, sloops, skiffs, and the marvellously beautiful yachts—the majestic sound boats as they rounded the Battery and came along towards five, afternoon, eastward bound—the prospect off towards Staten island, or down the Narrows, or the other way up the Hudson—what refreshment of spirit such sights and experiences gave me years ago (and many a time since.) My old pilot friends, the Balsirs, Johnny Cole, Ira Smith, William White, and my young ferry friend, Tom Gere—how well I remember them all.

Broadway Sights

Besides Fulton ferry, off and on for years, I knew and frequented Broadway—that noted avenue of New York's crowded and mixed humanity, and of so many notables. Here I saw, during those times, Andrew Jackson, Webster, Clay, Seward, Martin Van Buren, filibuster Walker, Kossuth, Fitz Greene Halleck, Bryant, the Prince of Wales, Charles Dickens, the first Japanese ambassadors, and lots of other celebrities of the time. Always something novel or inspiriting; yet mostly to me the hurrying and vast amplitude of those never-ending human currents. I remember seeing James Fenimore Cooper in a court-room in Chambers street, back of the city hall, where he was carrying on a law case (I think it was a charge of libel he had brought against some one). I also remember seeing Edgar A. Poe, and having a short interview with him, (it must have been in 1845 or '6,) in his office, second storey of a corner building, (Duane or Pearl street.) He was editor and owner or part owner of *The Broadway Journal*. The visit was about a piece of mine he had publish'd. Poe was very cordial, in a quiet way, appear'd well in person, dress, etc. I have a distinct and pleasing remembrance of his looks, voice, manner and matter; very kindly and human but subdued, perhaps a little jaded.

For another of my reminiscences, here on the west side, just below Houston street, I once saw (it must have been about 1832, of a sharp bright January day) a bent, feeble but stout-built very old man, bearded, swathed in rich furs, with a great ermine cap on his head, led and assisted, almost carried down the steps of his high front stoop (a dozen friends and servants, emulous, carefully holding, guiding him) and then lifted and tuck'd in a gorgeous sleigh, envelop'd in other furs, for a ride. The sleigh was drawn by as fine a team of horses as I ever saw. (You needn't think all the best animals are brought up nowadays; never was such horseflesh as fifty years ago on Long Island, or south, or in New York City; folks look'd for spirit and mettle in a nag, not tame speed merely.) Well, I, a boy of perhaps thirteen or fourteen, stopp'd and gazed long at the spectacle of that fur-swathed old man, surrounded by friends and servants, and the careful seating of him in a sleigh. I remember the spirited, champing horses, the driver with his whip, and a fellow-driver by his side, for extra prudence. The old man, the subject of so much attention, I can almost see now. It was John Jacob Astor.

The years 1846, '47, and there along, see me still in New York city, working as writer and printer, having my usual good health, and a good time generally.

Omnibus Jaunts and Drivers

One phase of those days must by no means go unrecorded—namely, the Broadway omnibuses, with their drivers. The vehicles still (I write this paragraph in 1881) give a portion of the character of Broadway—the Fifth avenue, Madison avenue, and Twenty-third street lines yet running. But the flush days of the old Broadway stages, characteristic and copious, are over. The Yellow-birds, the Red-birds, the original Broadway, the Fourth avenue, the Knickerbocker, and a dozen others of twenty or thirty years ago, are all gone.

And the men specially identified with them, and giving vitality and meaning to them—the drivers—a strange, natural, quick-eyed and wondrous race—(not only Rabelais and Cervantes would have gloated upon them, but Homer and Shakspere would)—how well I remember them, and must here give a word about them. How many hours, forenoons and afternoons—how many exhilarating night-times I have had—perhaps June or July, in cooler air—riding the whole length of Broadway, listening to some yarn, (and the most vivid yarns ever spun, and the rarest mimicry) —or perhaps I declaiming some stormy passage from Julius Cæsar or Richard, (you could roar as loudly as you chose in that heavy, dense, uninterrupted street-bass.) Yes, I knew all the drivers then, Broadway Jack, Dressmaker, Balky Bill, George Storms, Old Elephant, his brother Young Elephant, (who came afterward,) Tippy, Pop Rice, Big Frank, Yellow Joe, Pete Callahan, Patsy Dee, and dozens more; for there were hundreds. They had immense qualities, largely animal—eating, drinking, women—great personal pride, in their way—perhaps a few slouches here and there, but I should have trusted the general run of them, in their simple good-will and honor, under all circumstances. Not only for comradeship, and sometimes affection—great studies I found them also. (I suppose the critics will laugh heartily, but the influence of those Broadway omnibus jaunts and drivers and declamations and escapades undoubtedly enter'd into the gestation of *Leaves of Grass*.)

Some Specimen Cases

June 18. In one of the hospitals I find Thomas Haley, company M, 4th New York cavalry—a regular Irish boy, a fine specimen of youthful physical manliness—shot through the lungs—inevitably dying—came over to this country from Ireland to enlist—has not a single friend or acquaintance here—is sleeping soundly at this moment, (but it is the sleep of death)—has a bullet-hole straight through the lung. I saw Tom when first brought here, three days since, and didn't suppose he could live twelve hours—(yet he looks well enough in the face to a casual observer). He lies there with his frame exposed above the waist, all naked, for coolness—a fine built man, the tan not yet bleach'd from his cheeks and neck. It is useless to talk to him, as with his sad hurt, and the stimulants they give him, and the utter strangeness of every object, face, furniture, etc., the poor fellow, even when awake, is like some frighten'd, shy animal. Much of the time he sleeps, or half sleeps. (Sometimes I thought he knew more than he show'd.) I often come and sit by him in perfect silence; he will breathe for ten minutes as softly and evenly as a young babe asleep. Poor youth, so handsome, athletic, with profuse beautiful shining hair. One time as I sat looking at him while he lay asleep, he suddenly, without the least start, awaken'd, open'd his eyes, gave me a long steady look, turning his face very slightly to gaze easier—one long, clear, silent look—a slight sigh—then turn'd back and went into his doze again. Little he knew, poor death-stricken boy, the heart of the stranger that hover'd near.

W. H. E., Co. F., 2nd N. J. His disease is pneumonia. He lay sick at the wretched hospital below Aquia creek, for seven or eight days before brought here. He was detail'd from his regiment to go there and help as nurse, but was soon taken down himself. Is an elderly, sallow-faced, rather gaunt, grey-hair'd man, a widower, with children. He express'd a great desire for good, strong green tea. An excellent lady, Mrs. W., of Washington, soon sent him a package; also a small sum of money. The doctor said give him the tea at pleasure; it lay on the table by his side, and he used it every day. He slept a great deal; could not talk much, as he grew deaf. Occupied bed 15, ward I, Armory. (The same lady above, Mrs. W., sent the men a large package of tobacco.)

J. G. lies in bed 52, ward I; is of company B, 7th Pennsylvania. I gave him a small sum of money, some tobacco, and envelopes. To a man adjoining also gave twenty-five cents; he flush'd in the face when I offer'd it—refused at first, but as I found he had not a cent, and was very fond of having the daily papers to read, I pressed it on him. He was evidently very grateful, but said little.

J. T. L., of company F., 9th New Hampshire, lies in bed 37, ward I. Is very fond of tobacco. I furnish him some; also with a little money. Has gangrene of the feet; a pretty bad case; will surely have to lose three toes. Is a regular specimen of an old-fashion'd, rude, hearty, New England countryman, impressing me with his likeness to that celebrated singed cat, who was better than she look'd.

Bed 3, ward E, Armory, has a great hankering for pickles, something pungent. After consulting the doctor, I gave him a small bottle of horse-radish; also some apples; also a book. Some of the nurses are excellent. The woman-nurse in this ward I like very much. (Mrs. Wright—a year afterwards I found her in Mansion house hospital, Alexandria—she is a perfect nurse.)

In one bed a young man, Marcus Small, company K, 7th Maine—sick with dysentery and typhoid fever—pretty critical case—I talk with him often—he thinks he will die—looks like it indeed. I write a letter for him home to East Livermore, Maine—I let him talk to me a little, but not much; advise him to keep very quiet—do most of the talking myself—stay quite a while with him, as he holds on to my hand—talk to him in a cheering, but slow, low and measured manner—talk about his furlough, and going home as soon as he is able to travel.

Thomas Lindly, 1st Pennsylvania cavalry, shot very badly through the foot—poor young man he suffers horribly, has to be constantly dosed with morphine, his face ashy and glazed, bright young eyes—I give him a large handsome apple, lay it in sight, tell him to have it roasted in the morning, as he generally feels easier then, and can eat a little breakfast. I write two letters for him.

Opposite, an old Quaker lady is sitting by the side of her son, Amer Moore, 2nd U.S. artillery—shot in the head two weeks since, very low, quite rational—from hips down paralyzed—he will surely die. I speak a very few words to him every day and evening—he answers pleasantly—wants nothing—(he told me soon after he came about his home affairs: his mother had been an invalid, and he fear'd to let her know his condition). He died soon after she came.   1882–1883

1842 ~ *Sidney Lanier* ~ 1881

THE LITERARY life of Sidney Lanier is associated with Baltimore, but by birth and bringing up he belongs to Georgia. He takes a leading rank among the distinguished writers of the South after the Civil War, and next to Whitman and Emily Dickinson, is the most important poet of the seventies.

Lanier was born at Macon, Georgia, in 1842, descended from a family of musicians of Huguenot stock. The poet's branch of the family, which had settled first in Virginia, removed to Alabama and Georgia, where his father practiced law in Macon. His mother had come to Georgia from Virginia. As a child Lanier is said to have been able to learn readily any musical instrument. He could play the flute, violin, organ, piano, and guitar, as early as he could read. He cared most for the violin, but was persuaded by his father to devote himself chiefly to the flute, since "the tones of the violin brought over-excitement to his sensitive, responsive nature."

At the age of fourteen Lanier entered the sophomore class of Oglethorpe University, a small sectarian institution at Midway, Georgia. After spending a year in outside work he was graduated at eighteen, standing highest, with one of his classmates, in scholarship. In 1860, the year of his graduation, he was made tutor. He was ambitious to study in Germany and become a professor, as had Longfellow and Lowell, but was swerved from his normal development by the outbreak of the Civil War. In 1861 he gave up his profession to enlist at the first call as a private in the Confederate army. His younger brother also volunteered, and to remain together they both refused promotions, serving in the line as scouts and then in the signal service. Lanier was finally captured with his vessel in blockade-running and was imprisoned at Point Lookout. He was released in 1865 and returned to Georgia, weakened from a dangerous illness of six weeks. His mother had died shortly before of consumption, and the beginning of that disease was already upon Lanier.

Now, at twenty-three, he served as clerk in a hotel and finished a novel, *Tiger Lilies*, begun while he was in the army. After its failure he taught school, becoming principal of an academy. In 1867 he was married to Mary Day of Macon, and from 1868 to 1872 he was an assistant in his father's law office. During these years he wrote verse but no great quantity of it. In the winter of 1872–73 he decided to give up the law, especially since he wished to devote himself to music and literature and to live in an atmosphere of culture. He went to New York but finally settled in Baltimore in December, 1873, having attained the position of first flute in the Peabody Symphony Orchestra. Music was his most dependable means of support, and he was in great demand for extra local engagements. At Baltimore he had the opportunity he craved to hear good music and to have access to large libraries—the Peabody library and that of the newly organized Johns Hopkins University. "Corn" was written in 1874 and published in 1875. Soon after, he began and finished "The Symphony," published, as was "Corn," in *Lippincott's Magazine.* It was a poem of "real harmonic structure" and better sustained than "Corn." Through Bayard Taylor he received the invitation to write the words of the cantata for the opening of the Centennial Exposition in 1876, the music for which was composed by Dudley Buck. In this year he wrote also his "Evening Song" and in 1878 "The Revenge of Hamish," an excellent narrative poem produced at a time when there was little of this type of verse.

Meanwhile he was struggling against illness, and was forced to interrupt his work to seek health in Florida or Pennsylvania or the mountains of North Carolina, and to do hack work for a living. He was also lecturing for schools and for private classes of ladies. In 1879 he was appointed lecturer in English literature in Johns Hopkins University. This brought him the assurance of a fixed though small income. He planned more scholarly works, of which but one, *The Science of English Verse* (1880), was issued. Unripe and hastily written, it is nonetheless one of the most suggestive books yet published on the subject. Its main thesis—that English verse has strict quantity like music and may be scanned on the basis of time, not accent—is, however, probably not sound. Lanier died in 1881, his final years being a race with death to see how much he could produce before the end came. The poem "Sunrise" was penciled at a fever temperature of 104. Lanier was an author who could not complete his work. He was fundamentally an artist, endowed with an artist's imagination and ambition. His talent was growing when he died.

Lanier was especially concerned with commercialism, with religion, and with the worth of human aspiration. He had wide interests and sympathies, and he responded to contemporary influences, such as that of scientific thought, then not strong in American verse. As a nature poet he was original and a regionalist. Nature was, for him, bound up with a feeling of lofty pantheism; it was not merely a pretty background but a passion. He made much of the Southern scene, the corn, the cotton, the marshes, the Georgia hills. Trees especially were his delight; the forest inspired him to rhapsodies.

Poetry, to Lanier, was invested with the sacredness of religion. His passion for music, stronger even than his passion for books, inspired him to give us verse richer in music than that of any other poet except Poe. Lanier was an investigator of artistic technique and the author of a treatise on prosody in which he tried to explain English versification by the principles of musical composition. He thought that music and poetry were closely related, that they follow the same general laws, and that poetry appeals chiefly to the emotional nature, depending on sound rather than sense for its impression. His work is intricate, full of ingenious devices, literary allusions, and archaic forms. He experimented with "tone color," rhythm, alliteration, and phrasing. In trying to obtain effects belonging to music, he did not sharply sever these arts, and he sacrificed lucidity and ease. Yet, though he deliberately sought effects of sound in his poetry, he held that "wherever there is a contest as between artistic and moral beauty, unless the moral side prevail, all is lost." In 1880 he wished "the sharpest distinction . . . between Technique and Inspiration." In theory he was devoted to the "beauty of holiness" and the traditional unity of beauty, truth, and goodness. His most cherished aim was to be a thinker, moralist, and social reformer.

Although Lanier had great ethical earnestness and fervor, he was not a guiding influence in his own time. Fired with the romantic spirit, he came late, in a post-war, unromantic age. He achieved a distinctive manner; but his technique was too refined, his verse somehow lacked vitality, and the more virile Whitman, not Lanier, was to sway and inspire a generation. Yet an unusual interest attaches to him. His letters reveal a pleasing personality and his last years testify to his ambition and fortitude. A recent biographer describes him as fastidious, dreamlike, and high-minded, and makes much of his manliness, his charm, his antagonism to all that he thought despicable, and his courage in the face of poverty.

The inclusive edition of Lanier's poems is that edited by his wife, with a brief memorial by W. H. Ward (1884; later edition, 1916). M. Callaway, Jr. edited *Select Poems of Sidney Lanier* (1895). *The Letters of Sidney Lanier: Selections from His Correspondence, 1866–1881* was edited by H. W. Lanier (1899). D. C. Gilman published "Sidney Lanier: Reminiscences and Letters" in the *South Atlantic Quarterly*, IV, April, 1905; M. H. Northup, "Sidney Lanier: Recollections and Letters" in *Lippincott's Magazine*, LXXV, March, 1905; and G. H. Clarke, *Some Reminiscences and Early Letters of Sidney Lanier* (pamphlet, 1907).

The best biography of Lanier is that by A. H. Starke, *Sidney Lanier: A Biography and Critical Study* (1933). W. P. Woolf contributed "Sidney Lanier as Revealed in His Letters" to the *Sewanee Review*, VIII, July, 1900. Edwin Mims's *Sidney Lanier*, in the American Men of Letters Series (1905), was the best biography before Starke's; Mims also wrote of Lanier in *DAB*, X (1933). L. Lorenz issued a sympathetic *Life of Sidney Lanier* (1935).

Among critical articles may be noted: C. W. Kent, "A Study of Lanier's Poems," in *PMLA*, VII, April–June, 1892; C. Furst, "Concerning Sidney Lanier," in *Modern Language Notes*, XIV, Nov., 1899; P. Graham, "Lanier's Reading," in *University of Texas Studies in English*, No. 11, 1931; W. M. Baskervill, in *Southern Writers: Biographical and Critical Studies*, I (1896–97); J. Macy, in *The Spirit of American Literature* (1913); F. W. Cady, "Sidney Lanier," in the *South Atlantic Quarterly*, III, April, 1914; A. H. Strong, in *American Poets and Their Theology* (1916); Evander Miles, in *CHAL*, III (1918); Norman Foerster, in *Nature in American Literature* (1923); H. C. Thorpe, "Sidney Lanier—a Poet for Musicians," in *Musical Quarterly*, X, July, 1925; Alfred Kreymborg, in *Our Singing Strength* (1929); V. L. Parrington in *Main Currents in American Thought*, III (1930); S. T. Williams, in Macy's *American Writers on American Literature* (1931);

N. B. Fagin, "Sidney Lanier: Poet of the South," in *Johns Hopkins Alumni Magazine*, XX, March, 1932; R. Brenner, in *Twelve American Poets before 1900* (1933); G. W. Allen, in *American Prosody* (1935).

The best bibliographies of Lanier may be found in A. H. Starke's *Life*, and by H. Hartwick in W. F. Taylor's *A History of American Letters* (1936).

THAR'S MORE IN THE MAN THAN THAR IS IN THE LAND

Composed in 1866, and said to have been printed first in a Georgia newspaper. The first of Lanier's dialect poems, it teaches that it is the efforts of the individual, not external conditions, that bring success or failure. Lanier was much concerned about the overproduction of cotton in the South and the consequent bankruptcy of the farmers. He wished them to cultivate the land more intelligently.

I KNOWED a man, which he lived in Jones,
Which Jones is a country of red hills and
    stones,
And he lived pretty much by gittin' of loans,
And his mules was nuthin' but skin and bones,
And his hogs was flat as his corn-bread pones,
And he had 'bout a thousand acres o' land.

This man—which his name it was also Jones—
He swore that he'd leave them old red hills
    and stones,
Fur he couldn't make nuthin' but yallerish
    cotton,
And little o' *that*, and his fences was rotten,   10
And what little corn he had, *hit* was boughten
And dinged ef a livin' was in the land.

And the longer he swore the madder he got,
And he riz and he walked to the stable lot,
And he hollered to Tom to come thar and
    hitch
Fur to emigrate somewhar whar land was rich,
And to quit raisin' cock-burrs, thistles and
    sich,
And a wastin' ther time on the cussed land.

So him and Tom they hitched up the mules,
Pertestin' that folks was mighty big fools   20
That 'ud stay in Georgy ther lifetime out,
Jest scratchin' a livin' when all of 'em mought
Git places in Texas whar cotton would sprout
By the time you could plant it in the land.

And he driv by a house whar a man named
    Brown
Was a livin', not fur from the edge o' town,
And he bantered Brown fur to buy his place,
And said that bein' as money was skace,
And bein' as sheriffs was hard to face,
Two dollars an acre would git the land.   30

They closed at a dollar and fifty cents,
And Jones he bought him a waggin and tents,
And loaded his corn, and his wimmin, and
    truck,
And moved to Texas, which it tuck
His entire pile, with the best of luck,
To git thar and git him a little land.

But Brown moved out on the old Jones farm,
And he rolled up his breeches and bared his
    arm,
And he picked all the rocks from off'n the
    groun',
And he rooted it up and he plowed it down,   40
Then he sowed his corn and his wheat in the
    land.

Five years glid by, and Brown, one day,
(Which he's got so fat that he wouldn't
    weigh),
Was a settin' down, sorter lazily,
To the bulliest dinner you ever see,
When one of the children jumped on his knee
And says, "Yan's Jones, which you bought his
    land."

And thar was Jones, standin' out at the fence,
And he hadn't no waggin, nor mules, nor
    tents,
For he had left Texas afoot and cum   50
To Georgy to see if he couldn't git sum
Employment, and said he was lookin' as
    hum-
Ble as ef he had never owned any land.

But Brown he axed him in, and he sot
Him down to his vittles smokin' hot,

And when he had filled hisself and the floor
Brown looked at him sharp and riz and swore
That, "whether men's land was rich or poor
Thar was more in the *man* than thar was in the
land."

1866   1869?, 1884

CORN

Published in *Lippincott's Magazine*, February,
1875. A succession of pictures, it opens with a
forest rhapsody, touched with the mystical
("faint bridal-sighs of brown and green," "vague
purports sweet") and expressing Lanier's strong,
ecstatic love of trees. There follows the description of corn, with two elaborated analogies, that
of the poet who, following the romantic tradition,
is viewed as the prophet and leader of his day, and
that of the "home-fond heart." The third picture is that of the worn-out hill, associated with
the story of the unthrifty cotton-grower who spent
his money before his crop was raised and borrowed
at heavy interest. The poem ends as a sermon on
Georgia agriculture. W. D. Howells did not accept "Corn" for the *Atlantic Monthly*, remarking
that there was no "connection between the apostrophe at the beginning and the bit of narrative
at the close," and adding that "neither was striking enough to stand alone." Yet it was "Corn"
that brought Lanier recognition as a poet, and it
has held its popularity well.

TODAY the woods are trembling through and
through
With shimmering forms, that flash before my
view,
Then melt in green as dawn-stars melt in blue.
The leaves that wave against my cheek
caress
Like women's hands; the embracing boughs
express
A subtlety of mighty tenderness;
The copse-depths into little noises start,
That sound anon like beatings of a heart,
Anon like talk 'twixt lips not far apart.
The beech dreams balm, as a dreamer hums
a song;   10
Through that vague wafture, expirations
strong
Throb from young hickories breathing deep
and long
With stress and urgence bold of prisoned
spring
And ecstasy of burgeoning.

Now, since the dew-plashed road of morn
is dry,
Forth venture odors of more quality
And heavenlier giving. Like Jove's locks
awry,
Long muscadines
Rich-wreathe the spacious foreheads of great
pines,
And breathe ambrosial passion from their
vines.   20
I pray with mosses, ferns and flowers shy
That hide like gentle nuns from human
eye
To lift adoring perfumes to the sky.
I hear faint bridal-sighs of brown and green
Dying to silent hints of kisses keen
As far lights fringe into a pleasant sheen.
I start at fragmentary whispers, blown
From undertalks of leafy souls unknown,
Vague purports sweet, of inarticulate tone.

Dreaming of gods, men, nuns and brides,
between   30
Old companies of oaks that inward lean
To join their radiant amplitudes of green
I slowly move, with ranging looks that pass
Up from the matted miracles of grass
Into yon veined complex of space,
Where sky and leafage interlace
So close, the heaven of blue is seen
Inwoven with a heaven of green.

I wander to the zigzag-cornered fence
Where sassafras, intrenched in brambles
dense,   40
Contests with stolid vehemence
The march of culture, setting limb and thorn
As pikes against the army of the corn.

There, while I pause, my fieldward-faring eyes
Take harvests, where the stately corn-
ranks rise
Of inward dignities
And large benignities and insights wise,
Graces and modest majesties.
Thus, without theft, I reap another's field;
Thus, without tilth, I house a wondrous
yield,   50
And heap my heart with quintuple crops con-
cealed.

Look, out of line one tall corn-captain stands
Advanced beyond the foremost of his bands,
  And waves his blades upon the very edge
  And hottest thicket of the battling hedge.
Thou lustrous stalk, that ne'er mayst walk nor
    talk,
  Still shalt thou type the poet-soul sublime
  That leads the vanward of his timid time
  And sings up cowards with commanding
    rhyme—
Soul calm, like thee, yet fain, like thee, to
    grow   60
  By double increment, above, below;
  Soul homely, as thou art, yet rich in grace
    like thee,
  Teaching the yeomen selfless chivalry
  That moves in gentle curves of courtesy;
Soul filled like thy long veins with sweetness
    tense,
  By every godlike sense
Transmuted from the four wild elements.
    Drawn to high plans,
    Thou lift'st more stature than a mortal
      man's,
Yet ever piercest downward in the mold   70
    And keepest hold
  Upon the reverend and steadfast earth
    That gave thee birth;
  Yea, standest smiling in thy future grave,
    Serene and brave,
  With unremitting breath
  Inhaling life from death,
Thine epitaph writ fair in fruitage eloquent,
    Thyself thy monument.

    As poets should   80
Thou hast built up thy hardihood
With universal food,
    Drawn in select proportion fair
    From honest mold and vagabond air;
From darkness of the dreadful night,
    And joyful light;
  From antique ashes, whose departed flame
  In thee has finer life and longer fame;
From wounds and balms,
From storms and calms,   90
    From potsherds and dry bones
    And ruin-stones.
Into thy vigorous substance thou hast wrought
Whate'er the hand of Circumstance hath
    brought;

Yea, into cool solacing green hast spun
  White radiance hot from out the sun.
So thou dost mutually leaven
Strength of earth with grace of heaven;
  So thou dost marry new and old
  Into a one of higher mold;   100
  So thou dost reconcile the hot and cold,
    The dark and bright,
And many a heart-perplexing opposite:
    And so,
  Akin by blood to high and low,
Fitly thou playest out thy poet's part,
Richly expending thy much-bruisèd heart
  In equal care to nourish lord in hall
    Or beast in stall:
  Thou took'st from all that thou might'st
    give to all.   110

O steadfast dweller on the selfsame spot
Where thou wast born, that still repinest not—
Type of the home-fond heart, the happy lot!—
  Deeply thy mild content rebukes the land
  Whose flimsy homes, built on the shifting
    sand
Of trade, forever rise and fall
With alternation whimsical,
    Enduring scarce a day,
    Then swept away
By swift engulfments of incalculable tides
Whereon capricious Commerce rides.   121
Look, thou substantial spirit of content!
Across this little vale, thy continent,
    To where, beyond the moldering mill,
    Yon old deserted Georgian hill
Bares to the sun his piteous aged crest
    And seamy breast,
  By restless-hearted children left to lie
  Untended there beneath the heedless sky,
  As barbarous folk expose their old to die.
Upon that generous-rounding side,   131
    With gullies scarified
    Where keen Neglect his lash hath plied,
Dwelt one I knew of old, who played at toil,
And gave to coquette Cotton soul and soil.
    Scorning the slow reward of patient grain,
    He sowed his heart with hopes of swifter
      gain,
    Then sat him down and waited for the rain.
He sailed in borrowed ships of usury—
A foolish Jason on a treacherous sea,   140
Seeking the Fleece and finding misery.

Lulled by smooth-rippling loans, in idle
    trance
He lay, content that unthrift Circumstance
Should plow for him the stony field of
    Chance.
Yea, gathering crops whose worth no man
    might tell,
He staked his life on games of Buy-and-Sell,
And turned each field into a gambler's hell.
    Aye, as each year began,
    My farmer to the neighboring city ran;
Passed with a mournful anxious face   150
Into the banker's inner place;
Parleyed, excused, pleaded for longer grace;
    Railed at the drought, the worm, the rust,
        the grass;
    Protested ne'er again 'twould come to pass;
    With many an *oh* and *if* and *but alas*
Parried or swallowed searching questions
    rude,
And kissed the dust to soften Dives's mood.
At last, small loans by pledges great renewed,
    He issues smiling from the fatal door,
    And buys with lavish hand his yearly
        store   160
    Till his small borrowings will yield no more.
Aye, as each year declined,
With bitter heart and ever-brooding mind
He mourned his fate unkind.
    In dust, in rain, with might and main,
    He nursed his cotton, cursed his grain,
    Fretted for news that made him fret again,
Snatched at each telegram of Future Sale,
And thrilled with Bulls' or Bears' alternate
    wail—
In hope or fear alike forever pale.   170
    And thus from year to year, through hope
        and fear,
    With many a curse and many a secret tear,
    Striving in vain his cloud of debt to clear,
        At last
He woke to find his foolish dreaming past,
    And all his best-of-life the easy prey
    Of squandering scamps and quacks that
        lined his way
        With vile array,
From rascal statesman down to petty knave;
Himself, at best, for all his bragging brave, 180
A gamester's catspaw and a banker's slave.
    Then, worn and gray, and sick with deep
        unrest,

He fled away into the oblivious West,
Unmourned, unblest.

Old hill! old hill! thou gashed and hairy Lear
Whom the divine Cordelia of the year,
E'en pitying Spring, will vainly strive to
    cheer—
    King, that no subject man nor beast may
        own,
    Discrowned, undaughtered and alone—
Yet shall the great God turn thy fate,   190
And bring thee back into thy monarch state
        And majesty immaculate.
    Lo, through hot waverings of the August
        morn,
    Thou givest from thy vasty sides forlorn
    Visions of golden treasuries of corn—
Ripe largesse lingering for some bolder heart
That manfully shall take thy part,
        And tend thee,
        And defend thee,
With antique sinew and with modern art.   200
1874   1875

THE SYMPHONY

In this poem Lanier turns again to social questions. He arraigns Trade, i.e., commercialism and
industrialism, and praises the Music Master Love.
He voices his condemnation and encomium through
the personified musical instruments of an orchestra:
the violins (ll. 15 ff.); the flute (ll. 86 ff.); the
clarionet (ll. 216 ff.); the horn (ll. 253 ff.); the
hautboy (ll. 325 ff.). The last line has been widely
quoted.

"O Trade! O Trade! would thou wert dead!
The Time needs heart—'tis tired of head:
We're all for love," the violins said.
"Of what avail the rigorous tale
Of bill for coin and box for bale?
Grant thee, O Trade! thine uttermost hope:
Level red gold with blue sky-slope,
And base it deep as devils grope:
When all's done, what hast thou won
Of the only sweet that's under the sun?   10
Ay, canst thou buy a single sigh
Of true love's least, least ecstasy?"
Then, with a bridegroom's heart-beats trem-
    bling,
All the mightier strings assembling
Ranged them on the violins' side

As when the bridegroom leads the bride,
And, heart in voice, together cried:
"Yea, what avail the endless tale
Of gain by cunning and plus by sale?
Look up the land, look down the land,   20
The poor, the poor, the poor, they stand
Wedged by the pressing of Trade's hand
Against an inward-opening door
That pressure tightens evermore:
They sigh a monstrous foul-air sigh
For the outside leagues of liberty,
Where Art, sweet lark, translates the sky
Into a heavenly melody.
'Each day, all day' (these poor folks say),
'In the same old year-long, drear-long way,   30
We weave in the mills and heave in the
        kilns,
We sieve mine-meshes under the hills,
And thieve much gold from the Devil's bank
        tills,
To relieve, O God, what manner of ills?—
The beasts, they hunger, and eat, and die;
And so do we, and the world's a sty;
Hush, fellow-swine: why nuzzle and cry?
Swinehood hath no remedy
Say many men, and hasten by,
Clamping the nose and blinking the eye.   40
But who said once, in the lordly tone,
Man shall not live by bread alone
But all that cometh from the Throne?
        Hath God said so?
        But Trade saith *No:*
And the kilns and the curt-tongued mills say
        Go!
There's plenty that can, if you can't: we know.
Move out, if you think you're underpaid.
The poor are prolific; we're not afraid;
        Trade is trade.'"   50
Thereat this passionate protesting
Meekly changed, and softened till
It sank to sad requesting
And suggesting sadder still:
"And oh, if men might some time see
How piteous-false the poor decree
That trade no more than trade must be!
Does business mean, *Die, you—live, I?*
Then 'Trade is trade' but sings a lie:
'Tis only war grown miserly.   60
If business is battle, name it so:
War-crimes less will shame it so,
And widows less will blame it so.

Alas, for the poor to have some part
In yon sweet living lands of Art,
Makes problem not for head, but heart.
Vainly might Plato's brain revolve it:
Plainly the heart of a child could solve it."

And then, as when from words that seem but
        rude
We pass to silent pain that sits abroad   70
Back in our heart's great dark and solitude,
So sank the strings to gentle throbbing
Of long chords change-marked with sob-
        bing—
Motherly sobbing, not distinctlier heard
Than half wing-openings of the sleeping bird,
Some dream of danger to her young hath
        stirred.
Then stirring and demurring ceased, and lo!
Every least ripple of the strings' song-flow
Died to a level with each level bow
And made a great chord tranquil-surfaced
        so,   80
As a brook beneath his curving bank doth go
To linger in the sacred dark and green
Where many boughs the still pool overlean
And many leaves make shadow with their
        sheen.
        But presently
A velvet flute-note fell down pleasantly
Upon the bosom of that harmony,
And sailed and sailed incessantly,
As if a petal from a wild-rose blown
Had fluttered down upon that pool of tone
And boatwise dropped o' the convex side   91
And floated down the glassy tide
And clarified and glorified
The solemn spaces where the shadows bide.
From the warm concave of that fluted note
Somewhat, half song, half odor, forth did
        float,
As if a rose might somehow be a throat:
"When Nature from her far-off glen
Flutes her soft messages to men,
        The flute can say them o'er again;   100
        Yea, Nature, singing sweet and lone,
Breathes through life's strident polyphone
The flute-voice in the world of tone.
        Sweet friends,
        Man's love ascends
To finer and diviner ends
Than man's mere thought e'er comprehends:

For I, e'en I,
As here I lie,
A petal on a harmony,　　　　　　110
Demand of Science whence and why
Man's tender pain, man's inward cry,
When he doth gaze on earth and sky?
I am not overbold:
　　I hold
Full powers from Nature manifold.
I speak for each no-tonguèd tree
That, spring by spring, doth nobler be,
And dumbly and most wistfully
His mighty prayerful arms outspreads　120
Above men's oft-unheeding heads,
And his big blessing downward sheds.
I speak for all-shaped blooms and leaves,
Lichens on stones and moss on eaves,
Grasses and grains in ranks and sheaves;
Broad-fronded ferns and keen-leaved canes,
And briery mazes bounding lanes,
And marsh-plants, thirsty-cupped for rains,
And milky stems and sugary veins;
For every long-armed woman-vine　　130
That round a piteous tree doth twine;
For passionate odors, and divine
Pistils, and petals crystalline;
All purities of shady springs,
All shynesses of film-winged things
That fly from tree-trunks and bark-rings;
All modesties of mountain-fawns
That leap to covert from wild lawns,
And tremble if the day but dawns;
All sparklings of small beady eyes　　140
Of birds, and sidelong glances wise
Wherewith the jay hints tragedies;
All piquancies of prickly burs,
And smoothnesses of downs and furs
Of eiders and of minevers;
All limpid honeys that do lie
At stamen-bases, nor deny
The humming-birds' fine roguery,
Bee-thighs, nor any butterfly;
All gracious curves of slender wings,　150
Bark-mottlings, fiber-spiralings,
Fern-wavings and leaf-flickerings;
Each dial-marked leaf and flower-bell
Wherewith in every lonesome dell
Time to himself his hours doth tell;
All tree-sounds, rustlings of pine-cones,
Wind-sighings, doves' melodious moans,
And night's unearthly under-tones;

All placid lakes and waveless deeps,
All cool reposing mountain-steeps,　　160
Vale-calms and tranquil lotos-sleeps;—
Yea, all fair forms, and sounds, and lights,
And warmths, and mysteries, and mights,
Of Nature's utmost depths and heights,
—These doth my timid tongue present,
Their mouthpiece and leal instrument
And servant, all love-eloquent.
I heard, when '*All for love*' the violins cried:
So, Nature calls through all her system wide,
Give me thy love, O man, so long denied.　170
Much time is run, and man hath changed his
　　ways,
Since Nature, in the antique fable-days,
Was hid from man's true love by proxy fays,
False fauns and rascal gods that stole her
　　praise.
The nymphs, cold creatures of man's colder
　　brain,
Chilled Nature's streams till man's warm heart
　　was fain
Never to lave its love in them again.
Later, a sweet Voice *Love thy neighbor* said;
Then first the bounds of neighborhood out-
　　spread
Beyond all confines of old ethnic dread.　180
Vainly the Jew might wag his covenant head:
'*All men are neighbors,*' so the sweet Voice
　　said.
So, when man's arms had circled all man's race,
The liberal compass of his warm embrace
Stretched bigger yet in the dark bounds of
　　space;
With hands a-grope he felt smooth Nature's
　　grace,
Drew her to breast and kissed her sweet-
　　heart face:
Yea, man found neighbors in great hills and
　　trees
And streams and clouds and suns and birds and
　　bees,
And throbbed with neighbor-loves in loving
　　these.　　190
But oh, the poor! the poor! the poor!
That stand by the inward-opening door
Trade's hand doth tighten ever more,
And sigh their monstrous foul-air sigh
For the outside hills of liberty,
Where Nature spreads her wild blue sky
For Art to make into melody!

Thou Trade! thou king of the modern days!
    Change thy ways,
    Change thy ways;   200
Let the sweaty laborers file
    A little while,
    A little while,
Where Art and Nature sing and smile.
Trade! is thy heart all dead, all dead?
And hast thou nothing but a head?
I'm all for heart," the flute-voice said,
And into sudden silence fled,
Like as a blush that while 'tis red
Dies to a still, still white instead.   210

    Thereto a thrilling calm succeeds,
Till presently the silence breeds
A little breeze among the reeds
That seems to blow by sea-marsh weeds:
Then from the gentle stir and fret
Sings out the melting clarionet,
Like as a lady sings while yet
Her eyes with salty tears are wet.
"O Trade! O Trade!" the Lady said,
"I too will wish thee utterly dead   220
If all thy heart is in thy head.
For O my God! and O my God!
What shameful ways have women trod
At beckoning of Trade's golden rod!
Alas when sighs are traders' lies,
And heart's-ease eyes and violet eyes
    Are merchandise!
O purchased lips that kiss with pain!
O cheeks coin-spotted with smirch and stain!
O trafficked hearts that break in twain!   230
—And yet what wonder at my sisters' crime?
So hath Trade withered up Love's sinewy prime,
Men love not women as in olden time.
Ah, not in these cold merchantable days
Deem men their life an opal gray, where plays
The one red Sweet of gracious ladies'-praise.
Now, comes a suitor with sharp prying eye—
Says, *Here, you Lady, if you'll sell, I'll buy:*
Come, heart for heart—a trade? What! weeping?
    why?
Shame on such wooers' dapper mercery!   240
I would my lover kneeling at my feet
In humble manliness should cry, *O sweet!*
I know not if thy heart my heart will greet:
I ask not if thy love my love can meet:
Whate'er thy worshipful soft tongue shall say,
I'll kiss thine answer, be it yea or nay:

I do but know I love thee, and I pray
To be thy knight until my dying day.
Woe him that cunning trades in hearts con-
    trives!
Base love good women to base loving drives.
If men loved larger, larger were our lives;   251
And wooed they nobler, won they nobler
    wives."

There thrust the bold straightforward horn
To battle for that lady lorn,
With heartsome voice of mellow scorn,
Like any knight in knighthood's morn.
    "Now comfort thee," said he,
        "Fair Lady.
For God shall right thy grievous wrong,
And man shall sing thee a true-love song,
Voiced in act his whole life long,   261
    Yea, all thy sweet life long,
        Fair Lady.
Where's he that craftily hath said,
The day of chivalry is dead?
I'll prove that lie upon his head,
    Or I will die instead,
        Fair Lady.
Is Honor gone into his grave?
Hath Faith become a caitiff knave,
And Selfhood turned into a slave   270
    To work in Mammon's cave,
        Fair Lady?
Will Truth's long blade ne'er gleam again?
Hath Giant Trade in dungeons slain
All great contempts of mean-got gain
    And hates of inward stain,
        Fair Lady?
For aye shall name and fame be sold,
And place be hugged for the sake of
    gold,
And smirch-robed Justice feebly scold   281
    At Crime all money-bold,
        Fair Lady?
Shall self-wrapt husbands aye forget
Kiss-pardons for the daily fret
Wherewith sweet wifely eyes are wet—
    Blind to lips kiss-wise set—
        Fair Lady?
Shall lovers higgle, heart for heart,
Till wooing grows a trading mart   290
Where much for little, and all for part,
    Make love a cheapening art,
        Fair Lady?

Shall woman scorch for a single sin
That her betrayer may revel in,
And she be burnt, and he but grin
   When that the flames begin,
      Fair Lady?
Shall ne'er prevail the woman's plea,
We maids would far, far whiter be   300
If that our eyes might sometimes see
   Men maids in purity,
      Fair Lady?
Shall Trade aye salve his conscience-aches
With jibes at Chivalry's old mistakes—
The wars that o'erhot knighthood makes
   For Christ's and ladies' sakes,
      Fair Lady?
Now by each knight that e'er hath prayed
To fight like a man and love like a maid, 310
Since Pembroke's life, as Pembroke's blade,
  I' the scabbard, death, was laid,
      Fair Lady,
I dare avouch my faith is bright
That God doth right and God hath might.
Nor time hath changed His hair to white,
   Nor His dear love to spite,
      Fair Lady.
I doubt no doubts: I strive, and shrive my
   clay,
And fight my fight in the patient modern
   way   320
For true love and for thee! ah me! and pray
   To be thy knight until my dying day,
      Fair Lady."
Made end that knightly horn, and spurred
   away
Into the thick of the melodious fray.

And then the hautboy played and smiled,
And sang like any large-eyed child,
Cool-hearted and all undefiled.
   "Huge Trade!" he said,
"Would thou wouldst lift me on thy head
And run where'er my finger led!   331
Once said a Man—and wise was He—
Never shalt thou the heavens see,
Save as a little child thou be."
Then o'er sea-lashings of commingling tunes
The ancient wise bassoons,
   Like weird
   Gray-beard
Old harpers sitting on the high sea-dunes,
   Chanted runes: 340

"Bright-waved gain, gray-waved loss,
The sea of all doth lash and toss,
One wave forward and one across:
But now 'twas trough, now 'tis crest,
And worst doth foam and flash to best,
   And curst to blest.

"Life! Life! thou sea-fugue, writ from east to
   west,
   Love, Love alone can pore
   On thy dissolving score
   Of harsh half-phrasings,   350
     Blotted ere writ,
   And double erasings
     Of chords most fit.
Yea, Love, sole music-master blest,
May read thy weltering palimpsest.
To follow Time's dying melodies through,
And never to lose the old in the new,
And ever to solve the discords true—
   Love alone can do.
And ever Love hears the poor-folks' cry-
   ing,   360
And ever Love hears the women's sighing,
And ever sweet knighthood's death-defying,
And ever wise childhood's deep implying,
But never a trader's glozing and lying.

"And yet shall Love himself be heard,
Though long deferred, though long deferred:
O'er the modern waste a dove hath whirred:
Music is Love in search of a word."
                    1875

FROM THE FLATS

What heartache—ne'er a hill!
Inexorable, vapid, vague and chill
The drear sand-levels drain my spirit low.
With one poor word they tell me all they
   know;
Whereat their stupid tongues, to ease my pain,
Do drawl it o'er again and o'er again.
They hurt my heart with griefs I cannot name:
   Always the same, the same.

Nature hath no surprise,
No ambuscade of beauty 'gainst mine eyes 10
From brake or lurking dell or deep defile;
No humors, frolic forms—this mile, that mile;

No rich reserves or happy-valley hopes
Beyond the bend of roads, the distant slopes.
Her fancy fails, her wild is all run tame:
    Ever the same, the same.

    Oh might I through these tears
But glimpse some hill my Georgia high up-
    rears,
Where white the quartz and pink the pebble
    shine,
The hickory heavenward strives, the musca-
    dine   20
Swings o'er the slope, the oak's far-falling
    shade
Darkens the dogwood in the bottom-glade,
And down the hollow from a ferny nook
    Bright leaps a living brook!

1876   1877

EVENING SONG

LOOK off, dear Love, across the sallow sands,
    And mark yon meeting of the sun and sea,
How long they kiss in sight of all the lands.
    Ah! longer, longer, we.

Now in the sea's red vintage melts the sun,
    As Egypt's pearl dissolved in rosy wine,
And Cleopatra night drinks all. 'Tis done,
    Love, lay thine hand in mine.

Come forth, sweet stars, and comfort heaven's
    heart;
    Glimmer, ye waves, round else-unlighted
        sands.   10
O night! divorce our sun and sky apart
    Never our lips, our hands.

1876   1877

THE STIRRUP-CUP

This poem was written in Florida, where Lanier
had gone for his health. A stirrup-cup is a drink
taken by a rider before his departure; hence a
farewell or parting cup.

DEATH, thou'rt a cordial old and rare:
Look how compounded, with what care!
Time got his wrinkles reaping thee
Sweet herbs from all antiquity.

David to thy distilling went,
Keats and Gotama excellent,
Omar Khayyám, and Chaucer bright,
And Shakespere for a king-delight.

Then, Time, let not a drop be spilt:
Hand me the cup whene'er thou wilt;   10
'Tis thy rich stirrup-cup to me;
I'll drink it down right smilingly.

                                              1877

THE REVENGE OF HAMISH

Lanier's most ambitious narrative poem. It is
told with dramatic intensity and effectiveness.
Professor Morgan Callaway, Jr., pointed out
sources for the poem. One is an inserted tale,
nearly identical in incident, in the third chapter
of William Black's *McLeod of Dare*. There is much
greater indebtedness, however, to Charles Mackay's dramatic ballad in quatrain form, "Ma-
claine's Child, a Legend of Lochbuy-Mull," included in his *Egeria and Other Poems* (1850).
Lanier's Hamish corresponds to Mackay's Evan.

IT was three slim does and a ten-tined buck
    in the bracken lay;
    And all of a sudden the sinister smell of a
        man,
    Awaft on a wind-shift, wavered and ran
Down the hill-side, and sifted along through
    the bracken and passed that way.

Then Nan got a-tremble at nostril; she was
    the daintiest doe;
    In the print of her velvet flank on the
        velvet fern
    She reared, and rounded her ears in turn.
Then the buck leaped up, and his head as a
    king's to a crown did go

Full high in a breeze, and he stood as if
    Death had the form of a deer;
    And the two slim does long lazily stretch-
        ing arose,   10
    For their day-dream slowlier came to a
        close,
Till they woke and were still, breath-bound
    with waiting and wonder and fear.

Then Alan the huntsman sprang over the
    hillock, the hounds shot by,
    The does and the ten-tined buck made a
        marvelous bound,
    The hounds swept after with never a sound,
But Alan loud winded his horn in sign that
    the quarry was nigh.

For at dawn of that day proud Maclean of
    Lochbuy to the hunt had waxed wild,
And he cursed at old Alan till Alan fared
    off with the hounds
For to drive him the deer to the lower glen-
    grounds:
"I will kill a red deer," quoth Maclean, "in
    the sight of the wife and the child."   20

So gayly he paced with the wife and the child
    to his chosen stand;
But he hurried tall Hamish the henchman
    ahead: "Go turn,"—
Cried Maclean—"if the deer seek to cross
    to the burn,
Do thou turn them to me: nor fail, lest thy
    back be red as thy hand!"

Now hard-fortuned Hamish, half blown of
    his breath with the height of the hill,
Was white in the face when the ten-tined
    buck and the does
Drew leaping to burn-ward; huskily rose
His shouts, and his nether lip twitched, and
    his legs were o'er-weak for his will.

So the deer darted lightly by Hamish and
    bounded away to the burn.
But Maclean never bating his watch tarried
    waiting below.   30
Still Hamish hung heavy with fear for to
    go
All the space of an hour; then he went, and
    his face was greenish and stern,

And his eye sat back in the socket, and
    shrunken the eyeballs shone,
As withdrawn from a vision of deeds it
    were shame to see.
"Now, now, grim henchman, what is't
    with thee?"
Brake Maclean, and his wrath rose red as a
    beacon the wind hath upblown.

"Three does and a ten-tined buck made out,"
    spoke Hamish, full mild,
"And I ran for to turn, but my breath it
    was blown, and they passed;
I was weak, for ye called ere I broke me
    my fast."
Cried Maclean: "Now a ten-tined buck in the
    sight of the wife and the child   40

I had killed if the gluttonous kern had not
    wrought me a snail's own wrong!"
Then he sounded, and down came kinsmen
    and clansmen all:
"Ten blows, for ten tine, on his back let
    fall,
And reckon no stroke if the blood follow not
    at the bite of the thong!"

So Hamish made bare, and took him his
    strokes; at the last he smiled.
"Now I'll to the burn," quoth Maclean,
    "for it still may be
If a slimmer-paunched henchman will
    hurry with me,
I shall kill me the ten-tined buck for a gift
    to the wife and the child!"

Then the clansmen departed, by this path and
    that; and over the hill
Sped Maclean with an outward wrath for
    an inward shame;   50
And that place of the lashing full quiet be-
    came;
And the wife and the child stood sad; and
    bloody-backed Hamish sat still.

But look! red Hamish has risen; quick about
    and about turns he.
"There is none betwixt me and the crag-
    top!" he screams under breath.
Then, livid as Lazarus lately from death,
He snatches the child from the mother, and
    clambers the crag toward the sea.

Now the mother drops breath; she is dumb,
    and her heart goes dead for a space,
Till the motherhood, mistress of death,
    shrieks, shrieks through the glen,
And that place of the lashing is live with
    men,
And Maclean, and the gillie that told him, dash
    up in a desperate race.   60

Not a breath's time for asking; an eye-glance
    reveals all the tale untold.
They follow mad Hamish afar up the crag
    toward the sea,
And the lady cries: "Clansmen, run for a
    fee!—
Yon castle and lands to the two first hands
    that shall hook him and hold

Fast Hamish back from the brink!"—and
    ever she flies up the steep,
And the clansmen pant, and they sweat,
    and they jostle and strain.
But, mother, 'tis vain; but, father, 'tis vain;
Stern Hamish stands bold on the brink, and
    dangles the child o'er the deep.

Now a faintness falls on the men that run, and
    they all stand still.
And the wife prays Hamish as if he were
    God, on her knees,   70
Crying: "Hamish! O Hamish! but please,
    but please
For to spare him!" and Hamish still dangles
    the child, with a wavering will.

On a sudden he turns; with a sea-hawk
    scream, and a gibe, and a song,
Cries: "So; I will spare ye the child if, in
    sight of ye all,
Ten blows on Maclean's bare back shall fall,
And ye reckon no stroke if the blood follow
    not at the bite of the thong!"

Then Maclean he set hardly his tooth to his
    lip that his tooth was red,
Breathed short for a space, said: "Nay, but
    it never shall be!
Let me hurl off the damnable hound in the
    sea!"
But the wife: "Can Hamish go fish us the
    child from the sea, if dead?   80

Say yea!—Let them lash *me*, Hamish?"—
"Nay!"—"Husband, the lashing will
    heal;
But, oh, who will heal me the bonny sweet
    bairn in his grave?
Could ye cure me my heart with the death
    of a knave?
Quick! Love! I will bare thee—so—kneel!"
Then Maclean 'gan slowly to kneel

With never a word, till presently downward
    he jerked to the earth.
Then the henchman—he that smote Hamish
    —would tremble and lag;
"Strike, hard!" quoth Hamish, full stern,
    from the crag;
Then he struck him, and "One!" sang
    Hamish, and danced with the child in
    his mirth.

And no man spake beside Hamish; he counted
    each stroke with a song.
When the last stroke fell, then he moved
    him a pace down the height,   90
And he held forth the child in the heart-
    aching sight
Of the mother, and looked all pitiful grave,
    as repenting a wrong.

And there as the motherly arms stretched out
    with the thanksgiving prayer—
And there as the mother crept up with a
    fearful swift pace,
Till her finger nigh felt of the bairnie's
    face—
In a flash fierce Hamish turned round and
    lifted the child in the air,

And sprang with the child in his arms from
    the horrible height in the sea,
Shrill screeching, "Revenge!" in the wind-
    rush; and pallid Maclean,
Age-feeble with anger and impotent pain,
Crawled up on the crag, and lay flat, and
    locked hold of dead roots of a tree—

And gazed hungrily o'er, and the blood from
    his back drip-dripped in the brine,   101
And a sea-hawk flung down a skeleton fish
    as he flew,
And the mother stared white on the waste
    of blue,
And the wind drove a cloud to seaward, and
    the sun began to shine.'

                                1878

SONG OF THE CHATTAHOOCHEE

The best known of Lanier's poems. Its successful onomatopœia, or echoism, recalls Tennyson's
"The Brook" of more than twenty years before
(1855). The Chattahoochee passes through Habersham and Hall counties of Georgia. The second
stanza is notable for its ingenious effects of rhyme,
meter, changing length of line, alliteration, assonance, and skillful use of vowels and liquids and
of stop consonants. The last stanza, stressing the
River's response to the call of duty, shows the
poem to be one of conscience and purpose.

Out of the hills of Habersham,
    Down the valleys of Hall,
I hurry amain to reach the plain,
Run the rapid and leap the fall,

Split at the rock and together again,
Accept my bed, or narrow or wide,
And flee from folly on every side
With a lover's pain to attain the plain
  Far from the hills of Habersham,
  Far from the valleys of Hall.   10

  All down the hills of Habersham,
  All through the valleys of Hall,
The rushes cried *Abide, abide,*
The wilful water weeds held me thrall,
The laving laurel turned my tide,
The ferns and the fondling grass said *Stay,*
The dewberry dipped for to work delay,
And the little reeds sighed *Abide, abide,*
  Here in the hills of Habersham,
  Here in the valleys of Hall.   20

  High o'er the hills of Habersham,
  Veiling the valleys of Hall,
The hickory told me manifold
Fair tales of shade, the poplar tall
Wrought me her shadowy self to hold,
The chestnut, the oak, the walnut, the pine,
Overleaning, with flickering meaning and
  sign,
Said, *Pass not, so cold, these manifold*
  Deep shades of the hills of Habersham,
  These glades in the valleys of Hall.   30

  And oft in the hills of Habersham,
  And oft in the valleys of Hall,
The white quartz shone, and the smooth
  brook-stone
Did bar me of passage with friendly brawl,
And many a luminous jewel lone
—Crystals clear or a-cloud with mist,
Ruby, garnet, and amethyst—
Made lures with the lights of streaming stone
  In the clefts of the hills of Habersham,
  In the beds of the valleys of Hall.   40

  But oh, not the hills of Habersham,
  And oh, not the valleys of Hall
Avail: I am fain for to water the plain.
Downward the voices of Duty call—
Downward, to toil and be mixed with the main,
The dry fields burn, and the mills are to turn,
And a myriad flowers mortally yearn,
And the lordly main from beyond the plain
  Calls o'er the hills of Habersham,
  Calls through the valleys of Hall.   50
        1877

THE MARSHES OF GLYNN

The theme is the influence of the marshes on the spirit. Lanier's overwrought feeling for trees appears in the first fifty lines, celebrating the live-oak woods. Towards sunset he leaves their "green colonnades" for the marshes, and from these he derives a sense of freedom and faith.

GLOOMS of the live-oaks, beautiful-braided
  and woven
With intricate shades of the vines that
  myriad-cloven
  Clamber the forks of the multiform
    boughs,—
      Emerald twilights,—
      Virginal shy lights,
  Wrought of the leaves to allure to the
    whisper of vows,
When lovers pace timidly down through the
  green colonnades
Of the dim sweet woods, of the dear dark
  woods,
  Of the heavenly woods and glades,
That run to the radiant marginal sand-beach
  within   10
      The wide sea-marshes of Glynn;—
Beautiful glooms, soft dusks in the noon-day
  fire,—
Wildwood privacies, closets of lone desire,
Chamber from chamber parted with wavering
  arras of leaves,—
Cells for the passionate pleasure of prayer to
  the soul that grieves,
Pure with a sense of the passing of saints
  through the wood,
Cool for the dutiful weighing of ill with
  good;—
O braided dusks of the oak and woven shades
  of the vine,
While the riotous noon-day sun of the June-
  day long did shine
Ye held me fast in your heart and I held you
  fast in mine;   20
But now when the moon is no more, and riot
  is rest,
And the sun is a-wait at the ponderous gate
  of the West,
And the slant yellow beam down the wood-
  aisle doth seem
Like a lane into heaven that leads from a
  dream,—

Ay, now, when my soul all day hath drunken
    the soul of the oak,
And my heart is at ease from men, and the
    wearisome sound of the stroke
Of the scythe of time and the trowel of trade
    is low,
And belief overmasters doubt, and I know
    that I know,
And my spirit is grown to a lordly great com-
    pass within,
That the length and the breadth and the sweep
    of the marshes of Glynn   30
Will work me no fear like the fear they have
    wrought me of yore
When length was fatigue, and when breadth
    was but bitterness sore,
And when terror and shrinking and dreary
    unnamable pain
Drew over me out of the merciless miles of
    the plain,—
Oh, now, unafraid, I am fain to face
The vast sweet visage of space.
To the edge of the wood I am drawn, I am
    drawn,
Where the gray beach glimmering runs, as a
    belt of the dawn,
    For a mete and a mark
    To the forest-dark:—   40
      So:
Affable live-oak, leaning low,—
Thus—with your favor—soft, with a reverent
    hand,
(Not lightly touching your person, Lord of
    the land!)
Bending your beauty aside, with a step I
    stand
On the firm-packed sand,
    Free
By a world of marsh that borders a world of
    sea.
Sinuous southward and sinuous northward
    the shimmering band
Of the sand-beach fastens the fringe of the
    marsh to the folds of the land.   50
Inward and outward to northward and
    southward the beach-lines linger and
    curl
As a silver-wrought garment that clings to
    and follows the firm sweet limbs of a
    girl.

Vanishing, swerving, evermore curving again
    into sight,
Softly the sand-beach wavers away to a dim
    gray looping of light.
And what if behind me to westward the wall
    of the woods stands high?
The world lies east: how ample, the marsh
    and the sea and the sky!
A league and a league of marsh-grass, waist-
    high, broad in the blade,
Green, and all of a height, and unflecked with
    a light or a shade,
Stretch leisurely off, in a pleasant plain,
To the terminal blue of the main.   60

Oh, what is abroad in the marsh and the
    terminal sea?
Somehow my soul seems suddenly free
From the weighing of fate and the sad dis-
    cussion of sin,
By the length and the breadth and the sweep
    of the marshes of Glynn.

Ye marshes, how candid and simple and
    nothing-withholding and free
Ye publish yourselves to the sky and offer
    yourselves to the sea!
Tolerant plains, that suffer the sea and the
    rains and the sun,
Ye spread and span like the catholic man
    who hath mightily won
God out of knowledge and good out of
    infinite pain
And sight out of blindness and purity out of
    a stain.   70

As the marsh-hen secretly builds on the
    watery sod,
Behold I will build me a nest on the greatness
    of God:
I will fly in the greatness of God as the
    marsh-hen flies
In the freedom that fills all the space 'twixt
    the marsh and the skies:
By so many roots as the marsh-grass sends in
    the sod
I will heartily lay me a-hold on the greatness
    of God:
Oh, like to the greatness of God is the great-
    ness within
The range of the marshes, the liberal marshes
    of Glynn.

And the sea lends large, as the marsh: lo, out
    of his plenty the sea
Pours fast: full soon the time of the flood-tide
    must be: 80
Look how the grace of the sea doth go
About and about through the intricate chan-
    nels that flow
        Here and there, ·
            Everywhere,
Till his waters have flooded the uttermost
    creeks and the low-lying lanes,
)And the marsh is meshed with a million veins,
That like as with rosy and silvery essences
    flow
  In the rose-and-silver evening glow.
        Farewell, my lord Sun!
The creeks overflow: a thousand rivulets
    run   90
'Twixt the roots of the sod; the blades of the
    marsh-grass stir;
Passeth a hurrying sound of wings that west-
    ward whir;
Passeth, and all is still; and the currents cease
    to run;
And the sea and the marsh are one.

How still the plains of the waters be!
The tide is in his ecstasy.
The tide is at his highest height:
    And it is night.

And now from the Vast of the Lord will the
    waters of sleep
Roll in on the souls of men,   100
But who will reveal to our waking ken
The forms that swim and the shapes that
    creep
        Under the waters of sleep?
And I would I could know what swimmeth
    below when the tide comes in
On the length and the breadth of the mar-
    velous marshes of Glynn.
                        1878

A BALLAD OF TREES AND THE MASTER

INTO the woods my Master went,
Clean forspent, forspent.
Into the woods my Master came,
Forspent with love and shame.
But the olives they were not blind to Him,
The little gray leaves were kind to Him:
The thorn-tree had a mind to Him
When into the woods he came.

Out of the woods my Master went,
And He was well content.   10
Out of the woods my Master came,
Content with death and shame.
When Death and Shame would woo Him
    last,
From under the trees they drew Him last:
'Twas on a tree they slew Him—last
When out of the woods he came.
                        1880

MARSH SONG—AT SUNSET

OVER the monstrous shambling sea,
  Over the Caliban sea,
Bright Ariel-cloud, thou lingerest:
Oh wait, oh wait, in the warm red West,—
  Thy Prospero I'll be.

Over the humped and fishy sea,
  Over the Caliban sea
O cloud in the West, like a thought in the
    heart
Of pardon, loose thy wing, and start,
  And do a grace for me.   10

Over the huge and huddling sea,
  Over the Caliban sea
Bring hither my brother Antonio,—
  Man,—
My injurer: night breaks the ban:
  Brother, I pardon thee.
1879–1880   1882

1830 ~ *Emily Dickinson* ~ 1886

EMILY DICKINSON, the chief woman poet of America, was born in Amherst, Massachusetts, December 10, 1830. The belated publication of her poems— until 1914 less than half of her work was available to the public—has tended to obscure the facts that she was sixteen when Emerson's first volume of poems was published; that her poetry was written during the same period with Longfellow's *Tales of a Wayside Inn*, Whittier's *Snow-Bound*, Lowell's *Commemoration Ode*, Holmes's *Breakfast-Table* series, and Whitman's successive editions of *Leaves of Grass;* and that all these writers except Longfellow survived her. She was thus a slightly younger contemporary of these men, and any estimate of nineteenth-century New England literature must take her and her work into consideration.

Her geographical background was the same Massachusetts county of Hampshire in which Bryant had spent his youth and young manhood; and her family background was colored by a Calvinism somewhat less liberal and more genteel than his. If her father, the Honorable Edward Dickinson, treasurer of Amherst College and once Member of Congress, dominated the household with his austere dignity, Emily was clearly its chief ornament. As a girl she was rather vivacious and not averse to social life, with talents which early aroused the interest and encouragement of her teacher at Amherst Academy and other young men friends. The early deaths of two of these in 1851 intensified in her a sense of tragedy in life and a preoccupation with the subject of death that recur throughout her work. After a year at the rather severely religious South Hadley Female Seminary, near by, she spent the spring of 1854 with her father in Washington. On a visit to Philadelphia at this time she met a young Presbyterian minister, the Reverend Charles Wadsworth, for whom she conceived a devoted affection which according to her closest contemporaries was mutual and which was to be a dominating motive in much of her poetry. He probably called on her at least twice at Amherst but in 1862 removed with his family to remote California. The general trend of her emotional experience seems to be reflected in the concluding series of verses in the volume of *Further Poems* (1929). The remainder of her life was spent in increasing seclusion at her home in Amherst, with the exception of a few months in Boston for treatments for her eyes. During the latter years, shadowed by the deaths of close relatives and friends and the long illness of her mother, she kept herself to her house and garden, but maintained a correspondence with neighbors and young kinsfolk by little gifts of flowers or preserves, accompanied by verses. Though a dozen or so of her poems have been identified as written before 1860, the great bulk of her work belongs to the 1860's. Some of her verses were scribbled as notes for relatives and friends, but no such casual origin can account for those which reflect most poignantly her mind and experiences. Though her life was outwardly devoid of exciting incident, it is clear that in the comradeship of her flowers, the day's weather, and her round of household duties, she was constantly encountering adventures which filled her moments with wonder, delight, or a sense of tragedy, reflected in her verses. "If I feel physically as if the top of my head were taken off," she wrote, "I know this is poetry." This emotional intensity, perhaps, is responsible for the fact that only three of her poems were printed, without her consent or knowledge, during her lifetime. For understanding and criticism as a poet, she turned to her brother's wife, Susan Gilbert Dickinson, to whom her verses were usually sent as soon as written; to her girlhood friend Helen Hunt Jackson; and to three appreciative critics, Samuel Bowles of the *Springfield Republican*, Josiah G. Holland, poet and novelist, and Colonel Thomas Wentworth Higginson, whose advice and judgment she courted and disregarded. Her letters to these and other friends are a delightful compound of quizzical whimsey, hyperbole, and self-revelation, unreliable for factual biography but invaluable for an understanding of her personality. She was a semi-invalid from 1884 to her death, May 16, 1886.

Her literary reputation has been a posthumous one, a circumstance which has produced the strange impression that her own time neglected or failed to appreciate her verse. As a matter of fact the first fragmentary selection of her poetry, published in 1890, called for six reprintings and for two further selections in 1891 and 1896. These, however, and a volume of her *Letters*, edited by Mabel Loomis Todd, in 1894, were too slight a basis for permanent fame, and by 1912 the *Forum* could refer to her as "a forgotten poet." The release of a large body of new poems as *The Single Hound* in 1914, at the height of the "New Poetry" movement, followed by the *Further Poems* (1929) and *Unpublished Poems* (1936), gave to our generation the first opportunity to know her full output. In the meantime, also, her niece, Martha Dickinson Bianchi, through her biographical works named below, and especially the more than one hundred and fifty additional letters and notes made available in *Emily Dickinson Face to Face* (1932), has presented an adequate basis for study and appreciation.

The chief literary influences upon her seem to have been those of Emerson, Shakespeare, and Robert and Elizabeth Browning. In the lives and novels of the Brontë sisters she also felt certain parallels to her own experiences and thoughts. Emerson she resembles in ecstatic love of nature, electric sharpness of phrase, effective use of homely metaphor, and oracular brevity. Like Browning's, her thinking leaps from idea to idea—

> . . . I only said the syntax,
> And left the verb and the pronoun out,

—leaving slow readers perplexedly fumbling for omitted connections. Essentially her own, however, are her whimsical, almost perverse play of fancy and humor, the inevitableness of her descriptive terms—*e.g.*, "the distance on the look of death,"—the feminineness of her point of view, her jestingly reverent intimacy with God and the universe, and the poignancy, intensified by innate reserve, of her personal feelings.

Certain critics who have not understood the technique which she consciously or unconsciously evolved have been annoyed by her "carelessness of rhyme" and "lapses of grammar." With Emily Dickinson, rhyming is the gesture of a magnanimous spirit acknowledging an indebtedness which she has no intention of actually paying. What she found in Emerson as an occasional impatience or fault of ear became with her often an obvious technique of eye-rhyme or assonance, as in "I Like to See It Lap the Miles," whose eight "rhymes" are *up–step, peer–pare, while–hill,* and *star–door*— not one of them a genuine rhyme. No allowance for fault or carelessness can account for such totality of irregularity. Moreover, easily nine-tenths of her supposed lapses of grammar are to be accounted for by a stenographic terseness of expression which eliminates customary connectives and suffixes, as in her poem about a secret,

> Better of it
> Continual be afraid
> Than it and whom
> You told it to, beside.

(note the carefully grammatical accuracy of *whom*); and by a habitual subjunctive or optative use of the verb in oblique or concessive senses no longer common in our speech. Thus in her self-revealing quatrain

> Publication is the auction
> Of the mind of man,
> Poverty be justifying
> For so foul a thing,

the sensitive reader will naturally expand the third line to the full interpretation which a Henry James might express as "Let the pressure of poverty, to be sure, in some instances be allowed as a sort of justification."

Such preliminary explanations are perhaps necessary to the appreciation of a poet the full wealth of whose thought is not to be gained by a superficial reading. Let the reader, however, remember that, as she herself wrote,

> The thought beneath so slight a film
> Is more distinctly seen,—
> As laces just reveal the surge
> Or mists the Apennine.

All the successive editions of Miss Dickinson's published poems are included in *The Collected Poems of Emily Dickinson* (1937), edited by the poet's niece, Martha Dickinson Bianchi, and Alfred Leete Hampson; six "Unfinished Poems" were printed in the *New England Quarterly*, IV, 217–220. The letters may best be studied in Martha Dickinson Bianchi's *Emily Dickinson Face to Face*, with a Foreword by Alfred Leete Hampson (1932), and her *Life and Letters of Emily Dickinson* (new revised and expanded edition, in preparation); see also Mabel Loomis Todd's *Letters of Emily Dickinson* (revised edition, 1931). Biographical studies include Martha Dickinson Bianchi's indispensable *Life and Letters of Emily Dickinson* (1924), *Emily Dickinson Face to Face* (1932), and preface to *The Single Hound* (1914); Alfred Leete Hampson's introduction to the *Collected Poems* (1937); Josephine Pollitt's *Emily Dickinson: The Human Background of Her Poetry;* Genevieve Taggard's *The Life and Mind of Emily Dickinson;* George F. Whicher's *This Was a Poet* (1938); and MacGregor Jenkins's *Emily Dickinson, Friend and Neighbor* (revised edition, 1939, with Introductory Note by Alfred Leete Hampson). Separate bibliographies are those of Alfred Leete Hampson (1930) and G. F. Whicher (revised edition, 1931), both entitled *Emily Dickinson: a Bibliography*. Helpful brief articles of biography or criticism are Conrad Aiken, preface to *Selected Poems of Emily Dickinson* (1924); G. W. Allen, *American Prosody* (1935), 307–320; P. H. Boynton, *Literature and American Life* (1936), 690–691; Katherine Brégy, "Emily Dickinson: a New England Anchoress," *Catholic World*, December, 1924; Gamaliel Bradford, *Portraits of American Women* (1919), 229–257; R. W. Brown, *Lonely Americans* (1929), 235–257; H. H. Clark, *Major American Poets* (1936), 893–902; T. W. Higginson, *Carlyle's Laugh and Other Surprises* (1900), 249–283; W. D. Howells, "Poems of Emily Dickinson," *Harper's*, January, 1891 (important contemporary criticism); Ludwig Lewisohn, *Expression in America* (1932), 356–363; Sydney R. McLean, "Emily Dickinson at Mount Holyoke," *New England Quarterly*, VII, 25–42; Grace B. Sherrer, "Unusual Verb Constructions in the Poems of Emily Dickinson," *American Literature*, VII, 37–46; Carl van Doren, *American Literature, An Introduction* (1933), 67–70; and Anna M. Wells, "Early Criticism of Emily Dickinson," *American Literature*, I, 243–259.

From THE POEMS OF EMILY DICKINSON

[Success]

Success is counted sweetest
By those who ne'er succeed.
To comprehend a nectar
Requires sorest need.

Not one of all the purple host
Who took the flag today
Can tell the definition,
So clear, of victory,

As he, defeated, dying,
On whose forbidden ear   10
The distant strains of triumph
Break, agonized and clear.   1866

[The Snake]

A NARROW fellow in the grass
Occasionally rides;
You may have met him,—did you not?
His notice sudden is.

The grass divides as with a comb,
A spotted shaft is seen;
And then it closes at your feet
And opens further on.

He likes a boggy acre,
A floor too cool for corn.   10
Yet when a child, and barefoot,
I more than once, at morn,

Have passed, I thought, a whiplash
Unbraiding in the sun,—
When, stooping to secure it,
It wrinkled, and was gone.

Several of nature's people
I know, and they know me;
I feel for them a transport
Of cordiality;   20

But never met this fellow,
Attended or alone,
Without a tighter breathing,
And zero at the bone.   1878

[Much Madness Is Divinest Sense] [1]

MUCH madness is divinest sense
To a discerning eye;
Much sense the starkest madness.
'Tis the majority
In this, as all, prevails.
Assent, and you are sane;
Demur,—you're straightway dangerous,
And handled with a chain.

[The Soul Selects Her Own Society]

THE soul selects her own society,
Then shuts the door;
On her divine majority
Obtrude no more.

Unmoved, she notes the chariot's pausing
At her low gate;
Unmoved, an emperor is kneeling
Upon her mat.

I've known her from an ample nation
Choose one;   10
Then close the valves of her attention
Like stone.

[To Fight Aloud Is Very Brave]

To fight aloud is very brave,
But gallanter, I know,
Who charge within the bosom,
The cavalry of woe.

Who win, and nations do not see,
Who fall, and none observe,
Whose dying eyes no country
Regards with patriot love.

[1] This and all the following poems from Emily
Dickinson are reprinted from *The Poems of Emily
Dickinson*, Centenary Edition (1930), edited by Martha Dickinson Bianchi and Alfred Leete Hampson, by
permission of Little, Brown & Company, publishers.

We trust, in plumed procession,
For such the angels go,   10
Rank after rank, with even feet
And uniforms of snow.

[The Show Is Not the Show]

THE show is not the show,
But they that go.
Menagerie to me
My neighbor be.
Fair play—
Both went to see.

[Inebriate of Air]

I TASTE a liquor never brewed,
From tankards scooped in pearl;
Not all the vats upon the Rhine
Yield such an alcohol!

Inebriate of air am I,
And debauchee of dew,
Reeling, through endless summer days,
From inns of molten blue.

When landlords turn the drunken bee
Out of the foxglove's door,   10
When butterflies renounce their drams,
I shall but drink the more!

Till seraphs swing their snowy hats,
And saints to windows run,
To see the little tippler
Leaning against the sun!

[The Brain]

THE brain within its groove
Runs evenly and true;
But let a splinter swerve,
'Twere easier for you
To put the water back
When floods have slit the hills,
And scooped a turnpike for themselves,
And blotted out the mills!

[The Locomotive]

I LIKE to see it lap the miles,
And lick the valleys up,
And stop to feed itself at tanks;
And then, prodigious, step

Around a pile of mountains,
And, supercilious, peer
In shanties by the sides of roads;
And then a quarry pare

To fit its sides, and crawl between,
Complaining all the while   10
In horrid, hooting stanza;
Then chase itself down hill

And neigh like Boanerges; [1]
Then, punctual as a star,
Stop—docile and omnipotent—
At its own stable door.

[A Thought Went Up My Mind Today]

This is Emily Dickinson's characteristic treatment of the same experience that forms the basis for Wordsworth's "Ode on the Intimations of Immortality."

A THOUGHT went up my mind today
That I have had before,
But did not finish,—some way back,
I could not fix the year,

Nor where it went, nor why it came
The second time to me,
Nor definitely what it was,
Have I the art to say.

But somewhere in my soul, I know
I've met the thing before;   10
It just reminded me—'twas all—
And came my way no more.

[Hunger]

I HAD been hungry all the years;
My noon had come, to dine;
I, trembling, drew the table near,
And touched the curious wine.

'Twas this on tables I had seen,
When turning, hungry, lone,
I looked in windows, for the wealth
I could not hope to own.

[1] literally "sons of thunder," a nickname applied by Jesus to two vociferous preachers among his followers

I did not know the ample bread,
'Twas so unlike the crumb   10
The birds and I had often shared
In Nature's dining-room.

The plenty hurt me, 'twas so new,—
Myself felt ill and odd,
As berry of a mountain bush
Transplanted to the road.

Nor was I hungry; so I found
That hunger was a way
Of persons outside windows,
The entering takes away.   20

[Just Lost When I Was Saved]

JUST lost when I was saved!
Just felt the world go by!
Just girt me for the onset with eternity,
When breath blew back,
And on the other side
I heard recede the disappointed tide!

Therefore, as one returned, I feel,
Odd secrets of the Line to tell!
Some sailor, skirting foreign shores
Some pale reporter from the awful doors
Before the seal!   11

Next time, to stay!
Next time, the things to see
By ear unheard,
Unscrutinized by eye.

Next time, to tarry,
While the ages steal,—
Slow tramp the centuries,
And the cycles wheel.

[There Is No Frigate Like a Book]

THERE is no frigate like a book
    To take us lands away,
Nor any coursers like a page
    Of prancing poetry.

This traverse may the poorest take
    Without oppress of toll;
How frugal is the chariot
    That bears a human soul!

[Self-Reliance]

WE never know how high we are
  Till we are called to rise;
And then, if we are true to plan,
  Our statures touch the skies.

The heroism we recite
  Would be a daily thing,
Did not ourselves the cubits warp
  For fear to be a king.

[Disillusioned]

IT dropped so low in my regard
  I heard it hit the ground,
And go to pieces on the stones
  At bottom of my mind;

Yet blamed the fate that fractured, less
  Than I reviled myself
For entertaining plated wares
  Upon my silver shelf.

[What Soft, Cherubic Creatures]

WHAT soft, cherubic creatures
  These gentlewomen are!
One would as soon assault a plush
  Or violate a star.

Such dimity convictions,
  A horror so refined
Of freckled human nature,
  Of Deity ashamed,—

It's such a common glory,
  A fisherman's degree!   10
Redemption, brittle lady,
  Be so ashamed of thee.

[To Hear an Oriole Sing]

To hear an oriole sing
  May be a common thing,
  Or only a divine.

It is not of the bird
Who sings the same, unheard,
  As unto crowd.

The fashion of the ear
Attireth that it hear
  In dun or fair.

So whether it be rune,   10
Or whether it be none,
  Is of within;

The "tune is in the tree,"
The sceptic showeth me;
  "No, sir! In thee!"

[The Hummingbird]

A ROUTE of evanescence
With a revolving wheel;
A resonance of emerald,
A rush of cochineal;
And every blossom on the bush
Adjusts its tumbled head,—
The mail from Tunis, probably,
An easy morning's ride.

[A Bird Came Down the Walk]

A BIRD came down the walk:
He did not know I saw;
He bit an angle-worm in halves
And ate the fellow, raw.

And then he drank a dew
From a convenient grass,
And then hopped sidewise to the wall
To let a beetle pass.

He glanced with rapid eyes
That hurried all abroad,—   10
They looked like frightened beads, I thought
He stirred his velvet head

Like one in danger; cautious,
I offered him a crumb,
And he unrolled his feathers
And rowed him softer home

Than oars divide the ocean,
Too silver for a seam,
Or butterflies, off banks of noon,
Leap, plashless, as they swim.   20

[Keeping the Sabbath]

SOME keep the Sabbath going to church;
I keep it staying at home,
With a bobolink for a chorister,
And an orchard for a dome.

Some keep the Sabbath in surplice;
I just wear my wings,
And instead of tolling the bell for church,
Our little sexton sings.

God preaches,—a noted clergyman,—
And the sermon is never long;   10
So instead of getting to heaven at last,
I'm going all along!

[The Frost]

APPARENTLY with no surprise
To any happy flower,
The frost beheads it at its play
In accidental power.

The blond assassin passes on,
The sun proceeds unmoved
To measure off another day
For an approving God.

[Indian Summer]

THESE are the days when birds come back,
A very few, a bird or two,
To take a backward look.

These are the days when skies put on
The old, old sophistries of June,—
A blue and gold mistake.

Oh, fraud that cannot cheat the bee,
Almost thy plausibility
Induces my belief,

Till ranks of seeds their witness bear,   10
And softly through the altered air
Hurries a timid leaf!

Oh, sacrament of summer days,
Oh, last communion in the haze,
Permit a child to join,

Thy sacred emblems to partake,
Thy consecrated bread to break,
Taste thine immortal wine!

[The Sky Is Low]

THE sky is low, the clouds are mean,
A travelling flake of snow
Across a barn or through a rut
Debates if it will go.

A narrow wind complains all day
How some one treated him;
Nature, like us, is sometimes caught
Without her diadem.

[To Make a Prairie]

To make a prairie it takes a clover and one
    bee,—
And revery.
The revery alone will do
If bees are few.

[Elysium Is as Far]

ELYSIUM is as far as to
The very nearest room,
If in that room a friend await
Felicity or doom.

What fortitude the soul contains,
That it can so endure
The accent of a coming foot,
The opening of a door!

[Going to Him! Happy Letter!]

"GOING to him! Happy letter! Tell him—
Tell him the page I didn't write;
Tell him I only said the syntax,
And left the verb and the pronoun out.
Tell him just how the fingers hurried,
Then how they waded, slow, slow, slow;
And then you wished you had eyes in your
    pages,
So you could see what moved them so.

"Tell him it wasn't a practised writer,   9
You guessed, from the way the sentence toiled;
You could hear the bodice tug, behind you,
As if it held but the might of a child;

You almost pitied it, you, it worked so.
Tell him—No, you may quibble there,
For it would split his heart to know it,
And then you and I were silenter.

"Tell him night finished before we finished,
And the old clock kept neighing 'Day!'
And you got sleepy and begged to be ended—
What could it hinder so, to say?   20
Tell him just how she sealed you, cautious,
But if he ask where you are hid
Until to-morrow,—happy letter!
Gesture, coquette, and shake your head!"

[*A Letter Received*]

THE way I read a letter's this:
'Tis first I lock the door,
And push it with my fingers next,
For transport it be sure.

And then I go the furthest off
To counteract a knock;
Then draw my little letter forth
And softly pick its lock.

Then, glancing narrow at the wall,
And narrow at the floor,   10
For firm conviction of a mouse
Not exorcised before,

Peruse how infinite I am
To—no one that you know!
And sigh for lack of heaven,—but not
The heaven the creeds bestow.

[*Exultation Is the Going*]

EXULTATION is the going
Of an inland soul to sea,—
Past the houses, past the headlands,
Into deep eternity!

Bred as we, among the mountains,
Can the sailor understand
The divine intoxication
Of the first league out from land?

[*I Never Saw a Moor*]

I NEVER saw a moor,
I never saw the sea;
Yet know I how the heather looks,
And what a wave must be.

I never spoke with God,
Nor visited in heaven;
Yet certain am I of the spot
As if the chart were given.

[*The Last Night That She Lived*]

THE last night that she lived,
It was a common night,
Except the dying; this to us
Made nature different.

We noticed smallest things,—
Things overlooked before,
By this great light upon our minds
Italicized, as 'twere.

That others could exist
While she must finish quite,   10
A jealousy for her arose
So nearly infinite.

We waited while she passed;
It was a narrow time,
Too jostled were our souls to speak,
At length the notice came.

She mentioned, and forgot;
Then lightly as a reed
Bent to the water, shivered scarce,
Consented, and was dead.   20

And we, we placed the hair,
And drew the head erect;
And then an awful leisure was,
Our faith to regulate.

[*The Bustle in a House*]

THE bustle in a house
The morning after death
Is solemnest of industries
Enacted upon earth,—

The sweeping up the heart,
And putting love away
We shall not want to use again
Until eternity.

[If I Shouldn't Be Alive]

If I shouldn't be alive
When the robins come,
Give the one in red cravat
A memorial crumb.

If I couldn't thank you,
Being just asleep,
You will know I'm trying
With my granite lip!

[I Heard a Fly Buzz When I Died]

I heard a fly buzz when I died;
The stillness round my form
Was like the stillness in the air
Between the heaves of storm.

The eyes beside had wrung them dry,
And breaths were gathering sure
For that last onset, when the king
Be witnessed in his power.

I willed my keepsakes, signed away
What portion of me I   10
Could make assignable,—and then
There interposed a fly,

With blue, uncertain, stumbling buzz,
Between the light and me;
And then the windows failed, and then
I could not see to see.

[For Charlotte Brontë]

All overgrown by cunning moss,
All interspersed with weed,
The little cage of "Currer Bell,"
In quiet Haworth laid.

This bird, observing others,
When frosts too sharp became,
Retire to other latitudes,
Quietly did the same.

But differed in returning;
Since Yorkshire hills are green,   10
Yet not in all the nests I meet
Can nightingale be seen.

Gathered from any wanderings,
Gethsemane can tell
Through what transporting anguish
She reached the asphodel!

Soft fall the sounds of Eden
Upon her puzzled ear;
Oh, what an afternoon for heaven,
When Brontë entered there!   20

[Publication Is the Auction]

This poem gives her reason for not allowing her
verses to be printed. See also the letter to T. W.
Higginson dated April 26, 1862, below.

Publication is the auction
Of the mind of man,
Poverty be justifying
For so foul a thing.

Possibly,—but we would rather
From our garret go
White unto the White Creator,
Than invest our snow.

Thought belongs to Him who gave it—
Then to him who bear   10
Its corporeal illustration.
Sell the royal air

In the parcel,—be the merchant
Of the Heavenly Grace,
But reduce no human spirit
To disgrace of price!

[A Secret]

A secret told
Ceases to be a secret then.
A secret kept—
That can appal but one.

Better of it
Continual be afraid
Than it and whom
You told it to, beside.

[Revolution]

Revolution is the pod
Systems rattle from
When the winds of Will are stirred.
Excellent is bloom,

But except its russet base,
Every summer be
The entomber of itself.
So of Liberty:

Left inactive on the stalk,
All its purple fled,   10
Revolution shakes it
For test if it be dead.

[The Tint I Cannot Take Is Best]

THE tint I cannot take is best,
The color too remote
That I could show it in bazaar
A guinea at a sight—

The fine impalpable array
That swaggers on the eye
Like Cleopatra's company
Repeated in the sky—

The moments of dominion
That happen on the Soul   10
And leave it with a discontent
Too exquisite to tell—

The eager look in the landscapes
As if they just repressed
Some secret that was pushing,
Like chariots, in the breast—

The pleasing of the Summer,
That other prank of snow
That covers mystery with tulle
For fear the squirrels know—   20

Their graspless manners mock us,
Until the cheated eye
Shuts arrogantly in the grave,
Another way to see.

[I Took One Draught of Life]

The remaining poems, mostly taken from *Further Poems* (1929), form a unit, dealing with the central and motivating experience in Emily Dickinson's life.

I TOOK one draught of life,
I'll tell you what I paid,
Precisely an existence—
The market price, they said.

They weighed me, dust by dust,
They balanced film with film,
Then handed me my being's worth—
A single dram of Heaven.

[So the Eyes Accost and Sunder]

So the eyes accost and sunder
In an audience,
Stamped in instances forever,
So may countenance
Entertain without addressing
Countenance of One
In a neighboring horizon,
Gone as soon as known.

[It Was a Quiet Way]

IT was a quiet way
He asked if I was his.
I made no answer of the tongue
But answer of the eyes.

And then he bore me high
Before this mortal noise,
With swiftness as of chariots
And distance as of wheels.

The world did drop away
As countries from the feet   10
Of him that leaneth in the balloon
Upon an ether street.

The gulf behind was not—
The continents were new.
Eternity it was—before
Eternity was due.

No seasons were to us—
It was not night nor noon,
For sunrise stopped upon the place
And fastened it in dawn.   20

[I Make His Crescent Fill or Lack]

I MAKE his crescent fill or lack,
His nature is at full
Or quarter—as I signify,
His tides do I control.

He holds superior in the sky
Or gropes at my command
Behind inferior clouds,
Or round a mist's slow colonnade.

But since we hold a mutual disc
And front a mutual day,   10
Which is the despot neither knows—
Nor whose the tyranny.

[Forever at His Side to Walk]

FOREVER at his side to walk,
The smaller of the two,
Brain of his brain, blood of his blood,
Two lives, one Being, now.

Forever of his fate to taste,
If grief, the largest part—
If joy, to put my piece away
For that beloved heart.

All life to know each other—
Whom we can never learn,   10
And by and by a change called "Heaven"—
Rapt neighborhood of men,
Just finding out what puzzled us
Without the lexicon.

[Why Do I Love Thee?]

WHY do I love thee, Sir?
Because—
The wind does not
Require the grass
To answer wherefore, when
He pass,
She cannot keep her place.

The lightning never asked
An eye
Wherefore she shut   10
When he was by—
Because he knows
She cannot speak,
And reasons not contained
Of talk
There be—preferred by daintier folk.

[Although I Put Away His Life]

ALTHOUGH I put away his life,
An ornament too grand
For forehead low as mine to wear,
This might have been the hand

That sowed the flowers he preferred,
Or smoothed a homely pain—
Or pushed the pebble from his path,
Or played his chosen tune

On lute the least, the latest,
But just his ear could know   10
That what soe'er delighted it
I never would let go.

The foot to bear his errand,
A little boot I know
Would leap abroad like antelope
With just the grant to do.

His weariest commandment
A sweeter to obey
Than "Hide and Seek," or skip to flutes,
Or all day chase the bee.   20

Your servant, Sir, will weary,
The surgeon will not come,
The world will have its own to do,
The dust will vex your fame.

The cold will force your tightest door
Some February day,
But say my apron bring the sticks
To make your cottage gay,

That I may take that promise
To Paradise with me—   30
To teach the angels avarice
Your kiss taught to me.

[So Well That I Can Live Without]

So well that I can live without—
I love Thee;
Then how well is that?
As well as Jesus?
Prove it me
That He loved men
As I love Thee.

[*Bereaved*]

If he were living—dare I ask?
And how if he were dead?
And so around the words I went,
Of meeting them afraid.

I hinted changes, lapse of time;
The surfaces of years
I touched with caution, lest they slit
And show me to my fears;

Reverted to adjoining lives,
Adroitly turning out
Wherever I suspected graves—
'Twas prudenter, I thought.

And He—I rushed with sudden force
In face of the suspense—
"Was buried"—"Buried!" He!
My life just holds the trench.

[*After Great Pain a Formal Feeling Comes*]

After great pain a formal feeling comes—
The nerves sit ceremonious like tombs;
The stiff Heart questions—was it He that bore?
And yesterday—or centuries before?

The feet mechanical
Go round a wooden way
Of ground or air or Ought, regardless grown,
A quartz contentment like a stone.

This is the hour of lead
Remembered if outlived,
As freezing persons recollect the snow—
First chill, then stupor, then the letting go.

[*I Got So I Could Hear His Name*]

I got so I could hear his name
Without—
Tremendous gain!—
That stop-sensation in my soul,
And thunder in the room.

I got so I could walk across
That angle in the floor
Where he turned—so—and I turned how—
And all our sinew tore.

I got so I could stir the box
In which his letters grew—
Without that forcing in my breath
As staples driven through.

Could dimly recollect a Grace—
I think they called it "God,"
Renowned to ease extremity
When formula had failed—

And shape my hands petition's way—
Tho' ignorant of word
That Ordination utters—
My business with the cloud.

If any Power behind it be
Not subject to despair,
To care in some remoter way
For so minute affair
As misery—
Itself too vast for interrupting more,
Supremer than—
Superior to—

["*Till Death" Is Narrow Loving*]

"Till death" is narrow loving;
The scantiest heart extant
Will hold you, till your privilege
Of finiteness be spent.

But he whose loss procures you
Such destination that
Your life, too abject for itself,
Thenceforward imitate—

Until, resemblance perfect,
Yourself for his pursuit
Delight of nature abdicate,
Exibit love somewhat.

[*Savior! I've No One Else to Tell*]

Savior! I've no one else to tell
And so I trouble Thee,
I am the one forgot Thee so.
Dost Thou remember me?

Not for myself I came so far,
That were the little load—
I brought Thee the imperial heart
I had not strength to hold—

The heart I carried in my own,
Till mine too heavy be,   10
Yet strangest—*heavier* since it went—
Is it too large for Thee?

[*A Wife at Daybreak I Shall Be*]

This poem will repay comparison and contrast
in theme and imagery with Browning's "Prospice."

A WIFE at daybreak I shall be;
Sunrise, hast thou a flag for me?
At midnight I am yet a maid—
How short it takes to make it bride!
Then, Midnight, I have passed from thee
Unto the East and Victory.

LETTERS TO T. W. HIGGINSON

[APRIL 16, 1862]

MR. HIGGINSON,—Are you too deeply occupied to say if my verse is alive?[1]

The mind is so near itself it cannot see distinctly, and I have none to ask.

Should you think it breathed, and had you
the leisure to tell me, I should feel quick gratitude.

If I make the mistake, that you dared to tell
me would give me sincerer honor toward you.

I enclose my name, asking you, if you
please, sir, to tell me what is true?

That you will not betray me it is needless to
ask, since honor is its own pawn.

[APRIL 26, 1862]

MR. HIGGINSON,—Your kindness claimed   20
earlier gratitude, but I was ill, and write today
from my pillow.

Thank you for the surgery; it was not so
painful as I supposed. I bring you others, as
you ask, though they might not differ. While
my thought is undressed, I can make the distinction; but when I put them in the gown,
they look alike and numb.

You asked how old I was? I made no verse,
but one or two, until this winter, sir.   30

I had a terror since September, I could tell
to none; and so I sing, as the boy does of the
burying ground, because I am afraid.

[1] Emily's first request for Higginson's criticism of
her poetry

Midnight, "Good night!"
I hear them call.
The Angels bustle in the hall,
Softly my Future climbs the stair,   10
I fumble at my childhood's prayer—
So soon to be a child no more!
Eternity, I'm coming, Sir,—
Master, I've seen that face before.

[*Not What We Did Shall Be the Test*]

NOT what we did shall be the test
When act and will are done,
But what our Lord infers we *would*—
Had we diviner been.

You inquire my books. For poets, I have
Keats, and Mr. and Mrs. Browning. For prose,
Mr. Ruskin, Sir Thomas Browne, and the
Revelations. I went to school, but in your
manner of the phrase, had no education. When
a little girl, I had a friend who taught me Immortality; but venturing too near, himself, he
never returned. Soon after my tutor died, and
for several years my lexicon was my only
companion. Then I found one more, but he
was not contented I be his scholar, so he left
the land.

You ask of my companions. Hills, sir, and
the sundown, and a dog large as myself, that
my father bought me. They are better than
beings because they know, but do not tell;
and the noise in the pool at noon excels my
piano.

I have a brother and sister; my mother does
not care for thought, and father, too busy with
his briefs to notice what we do. He buys me
many books, but begs me not to read them,
because he fears they joggle the mind. They
are religious, except me, and address an eclipse,
every morning, whom they call their "Father."

But I fear my story fatigues you. I would
like to learn. Could you tell me how to grow,
or is it unconveyed, like melody or witchcraft?

You speak of Mr. Whitman. I never read his
book, but was told that it was disgraceful.

I read Miss Prescott's *Circumstance*, but it
followed me in the dark, so I avoided her.

Two editors of journals came to my father's
house this winter, and asked me for my mind,

and when I asked them "why" they said I was penurious, and they would use it for the world.

I could not weigh myself, myself. My size felt small to me. I read your chapters in the *Atlantic*, and experienced honor for you. I was sure you would not reject a confiding question.

Is this, sir, what you asked me to tell you?

Your friend,
E. Dickinson

[JULY, 1862]

Could you believe me without? I had no portrait, now, but am small like the wren; and my hair is bold, like the chestnut burr; and my eyes, like the sherry in the glass the guest leaves. Would this do just as well?

It oftens alarms father. He says death might occur, and he has moulds of all the rest, but has no mould of me; but I noticed the quick wore off those things in a few days, and forestall the dishonor. You will think no caprice of me.

You said "dark." I know the butterfly, and the lizard, and the orchis. Are not those *your* countrymen?

I am happy to be your scholar, and will deserve the kindness I cannot repay.

If you truly consent, I recite now. Will you tell me my fault, frankly, as to yourself, for I had rather wince than die. Men do not call the surgeon to commend the bone, but to set it, sir, and fracture within is more critical. And for this, preceptor, I shall bring you obedience, the blossom from my garden, and every gratitude I know.

Perhaps you smile at me. I could not stop for that. My business is circumference. An ignorance, not of customs, but if caught with the dawn, or the sunset see me, myself the only kangaroo among the beauty, sir, if you please, it afflicts me, and I thought that instruction would take it away.

Because you have much business, beside the growth of me, you will appoint, yourself, how often I shall come without your inconvenience.

And if at any time you regret you received me, or I prove a different fabric to that you supposed, you must banish me.

When I state myself, as the representative of the verse, it does not mean me, but a supposed person.

You are true about the "perfection." Today makes yesterday mean.

You spoke of *Pippa Passes*. I never heard anybody speak of *Pippa Passes* before. You see my posture is benighted.

To thank you baffles me. Are you perfectly powerful? Had I a pleasure you had not, I could delight to bring it.

YOUR SCHOLAR

1836 ~ *Bret Harte* ~ 1902

BRET HARTE is best remembered as the author of stories of the Far West and the Gold Rush era. He broke away from the literature of the Atlantic coast and helped to bring the transition from the legendary material of the stories of Irving and Hawthorne to the more realistic matter to come and to such story writers as O. Henry. A pioneer in "local-color" fiction, he started the "Wild West" vogue which has persisted in cheap popular fiction and in the "westerns" of the films.

Francis Brett Harte (later he signed himself Bret), though writing of California most of his life, was born in 1836 at Albany, New York, of English, Dutch, and

Hebrew ancestry. His father tried teaching, lecturing, and translating, but was never prosperous, and died leaving a widow and four children in 1845. He had a large library, however, and the young Harte, described as a studious, precocious boy, had a cultivated background and early literary interests. He read Froissart, Shakespeare, Fielding, Cervantes, Irving, and Dickens, who was his favorite. The family was provided for by relatives for a while, but at the age of thirteen Harte entered a lawyer's office and helped a merchant, so that before he was seventeen he supported himself. In 1853 his mother married, going to Oakland, California, and in 1854 Harte and a sister followed her there. He remained in California from 1854 till 1871, and most of his literary work is based on these years. Much of his earlier life there is obscure. He seems to have drifted into several employments, teaching or tutoring, like his father, perhaps trying placer mining, serving as a clerk in a drug store, and as an express messenger. He set type on the *Golden Era* of San Francisco, and later wrote articles for that periodical. In 1863 he was given a secretarial post in the branch mint, a position with few duties, which left him time for writing. He next became a contributor to the *Californian*, established in 1864, and wrote for it an amusing series of parodies of the narratives and the styles of such fiction writers as Cooper, Dickens, Hugo, and Dumas. These he published in 1867 under the title *Condensed Novels*. In 1868 he became the first editor of the newly established *Overland Monthly*, and his best stories are associated with this publication. "The Luck of Roaring Camp" was printed in the second issue, "The Outcasts of Poker Flat" in 1869; and these and "Plain Language from Truthful James" ("The Heathen Chinee") of 1870 brought him immediate fame. They were not approved by some Californians, who thought they were "likely to discourage immigration" by their reflections on the region and its morals; but they were received with zest in the East. The author was made professor of recent literature at the University of California. The *Atlantic Monthly* offered him ten thousand dollars for twelve contributions, his output for the coming year. He went east in 1871 and the rest of his work was written on the Atlantic coast or abroad. His later life has little literary significance. He continued to write of California but had exhausted the freshness of his material, and his many later volumes are relatively unimportant. He attempted a novel, *Gabriel Conroy* (1876), and several dramas, and did much work as a hack writer for magazines. He lived expensively, made debts, and tried lecturing, but he had done his best work. In 1878 he was appointed consul to Crefeld in Rhenish Prussia and went abroad, discouraged, leaving his family in America. Though he continued to send back money, he never returned. He became consul at Glasgow (1880–1885), but was supplanted there by a change in administration. The next years he lived chiefly in London until his death in 1902 of cancer of the throat. He is described as of slender, stylish appearance, unlike the frontiersmen that he painted.

Harte wrote in the days of the vogue of Dickens and in a weak period for American fiction. The Dickens strand in his work is strong. Like the English novelist he blends theatrically human sentiment, pathos, and humor, and he likes to depict human oddities in situations of emotional appeal. He brings together a strange medley of characters often speaking in a dialect of provincialisms, and displays them like a showman, with an eye to drama. In technique he is the finished artist, striving for a unique effect and writing fastidiously. He owes something to Poe and to the French school of story writers. Perhaps most effective in his work is the California background he establishes, with its human diversity, incongruities, and strong contrasts—Spaniards, native Indians, Chinese, miners, and adventurers, good and bad, cultivated and ignorant. He writes of them with realism, yet creates an atmosphere of romance. If fiction depicting the westward movement began with Cooper, it reached its final goal with Harte.

Harte wrote a few short essays on literary figures, none very important. He praised Artemus Ward for the "Americanism" of his type of humor, that is, for its "audacious exaggeration," and he mentioned with approval that its real strength did not lie merely in grotesque spellings. In an essay on "American Humor" he expressed the view that characteristic American humor did not derive from "Sam Slick" or from Lowell's *Biglow Papers* but arose in the South and West. Mark Twain he termed "the most original humorist that America has yet produced." Of Dickens he said that "no other writer, living or dead, ever transfused fiction with so much vitality." He admired Dickens's "sense of fun," his "wonderful spontaneity," his portrayal of social wrong, and his tenderness in writing of childhood. When, however, he was asked to write an article on "My Favorite Author and His Best Book," he named not Dickens but the elder Alexander Dumas and *The Count of Monte Cristo*. He stated that "the primary function of the novel is to interest the reader in its story—in the progress of some well-developed plot to a well-defined climax. . . . *Monte Cristo* is *romance*, and, as I am told, of a very antiquated type." The main thing, he thought, is for readers to be lifted "temporarily out of their commonplace surroundings and limited horizon by some specious tale of heroism, endeavor, wrongs redressed and faith rewarded." From youth onward romance was his preference.

The standard edition of Harte's works is *The Writings of Bret Harte* (19 vols., 1896–1903). His *Novels and Stories* (10 vols.) were published in 1910. There is a one-volume Household Edition of his *Poems* (1902). *Letters of Bret Harte* was edited by Geoffrey Bret Harte (1926). Of value also are C. M. Kozlay's *Lectures of Bret Harte* (1909) and *Stories and Poems and Other Uncollected Writings of Bret Harte* (1914). *Sketches of the Sixties*, by Bret Harte and Mark Twain, was published in San Francisco, 1927.

Biographies of Harte include those of T. E. Pemberton (1903), H. W. Boynton (1903), and H. C. Merwin (1911). Noah Brooks wrote of "Bret Harte in California," *Century Magazine*, LVIII, July, 1899. Of especial importance is *Bret Harte, Argonaut and Exile* (1931), by G. R.

Stewart, Jr., who also wrote of Harte in *DAB*, VIII (1932). See also Hamlin Garland, in *Roadside Meetings* (1930) and in *Companions on the Trail* (1931).

For criticism consult H. C. Vedder, in *American Writers Today* (1894); G. K. Chesterton, in *Varied Types* (1903); John Erskine, in *Leading American Novelists* (1910); E. W. Bowen, "Francis Bret Harte," in *Sewanee Review*, XXIV, July, 1916; F. L. Pattee, in *CHAL*, II (1918), and in *The Development of the American Short Story* (1923).

There is a bibliography by G. R. Stewart, Jr. in his *Bret Harte*, and also by Stewart, "A Bibliography of the Writings of Francis Bret Harte in the Magazines and Newspapers of California," in *University of California Publications in English*, III, 1933.

PLAIN LANGUAGE FROM TRUTHFUL JAMES

(Table Mountain, 1870)

Printed first in September, 1870; popularly known as "The Heathen Chinee." "Truthful James," whose experiences with a Chinese card player are related, was the narrator in Harte's poem "The Society upon the Stanislaus." Curiously, Harte modeled the verse of "Plain Language" on the antiphonal dirge at the end of Swinburne's *Atalanta in Calydon*. The poem had unparalleled success and circulated everywhere. Harte himself never liked it and could not understand its enthusiastic reception.

WHICH I wish to remark,
  And my language is plain,
That for ways that are dark
  And for tricks that are vain,
The heathen Chinee is peculiar,
  Which the same I would rise to explain.

Ah Sin was his name;
  And I shall not deny,
In regard to the same,
  What the name might imply;   10
But his smile it was pensive and childlike,
  As I frequent remarked to Bill Nye.

It was August the third,
  And quite soft was the skies;
Which it might be inferred
  That Ah Sin was likewise;
Yet he played it that day upon William
  And me in a way I despise.

Which we had a small game,
  And Ah Sin took a hand;   20
It was Euchre. The same
  He did not understand;
But he smiled as he sat by the table,
  With the smile that was childlike and bland.

Yet the cards they were stocked
  In a way that I grieve,
And my feelings were shocked
  At the state of Nye's sleeve,
Which was stuffed full of aces and bowers,
  And the same with intent to deceive.   30

But the hands that were played
  By that heathen Chinee,
And the points that he made,
  Were quite frightful to see,—
Till at last he put down a right bower,
  Which the same Nye had dealt unto me.

Then I looked up at Nye,
  And he gazed upon me;
And he rose with a sigh,
  And said, "Can this be?   40
We are ruined by Chinese cheap labor,"—
  And he went for that heathen Chinee.

In the scene that ensued
  I did not take a hand,
But the floor it was strewed
  Like the leaves on the strand
With the cards that Ah Sin had been hiding,
  In the game "he did not understand."

In his sleeves which were long,
  He had twenty-four packs,—   50
Which was coming it strong,
  Yet I state but the facts;
And we found on his nails, which were taper,
  What is frequent in tapers,—that's wax.

Which is why I remark,
  And my language is plain,
That for ways that are dark
  And for tricks that are vain,
The heathen Chinee is peculiar,—
  Which the same I am free to maintain.   60

1870

HER LETTER

I'm sitting alone by the fire,
  Dressed just as I came from the dance,
In a robe even *you* would admire,—
  It cost a cool thousand in France;
I'm be-diamonded out of all reason,
  My hair is done up in a cue:
In short, sir, "the belle of the season"
  Is wasting an hour upon you.

A dozen engagements I've broken;
  I left in the midst of a set;   10
Likewise a proposal, half spoken,
  That waits—on the stairs—for me yet.
They say he'll be rich,—when he grows up,—
  And then he adores me indeed;
And you, sir, are turning your nose up,
  Three thousand miles off as you read.

"And how do I like my position?"
  "And what do I think of New York?"
"And now, in my higher ambition,
  With whom do I waltz, flirt, or talk?"   20
"And isn't it nice to have riches,
  And diamonds and silks, and all that?"
"And aren't they a change to the ditches
  And tunnels of Poverty Flat?"

Well, yes,—if you saw us out driving
  Each day in the Park, four-in-hand,—
If you saw poor dear mamma contriving
  To look supernaturally grand,—
If you saw papa's picture, as taken
  By Brady, and tinted at that,—   30
You'd never suspect he sold bacon
  And flour at Poverty Flat.

And yet, just this moment, when sitting
  In the glare of the grand chandelier,—
In the bustle and glitter befitting
  The "finest *soirée* of the year,"
In the mists of a *gaze de Chambéry*,
  And the hum of the smallest of talk,—
Somehow, Joe, I thought of the "Ferry,"
  And the dance that we had on "The Fork";

Of Harrison's barn, with its muster   41
  Of flags festooned over the wall;
Of the candles that shed their soft luster
  And tallow on head-dress and shawl;
Of the steps that we took to one fiddle;
  Of the dress of my queer *vis-à-vis;*
And how I once went down the middle
  With the man that shot Sandy McGee;

Of the moon that was quietly sleeping
  On the hill, when the time came to go; 50
Of the few baby peaks that were peeping
  From under their bedclothes of snow;
Of that ride,—that to me was the rarest;
  Of—the something you said at the gate.
Ah, Joe, then I wasn't an heiress
  To "the best-paying lead in the State."

Well, well, it's all past; yet it's funny
  To think, as I stood in the glare
Of fashion and beauty and money,
  That I should be thinking, right there, 60
Of some one who breasted high water,
  And swam the North Fork, and all that,
Just to dance with old Folinsbee's daughter,
  The Lily of Poverty Flat.

But goodness! what nonsense I'm writing!
  (Mamma says my taste still is low),
Instead of my triumphs reciting,
  I'm spooning on Joseph,—heigh-ho!
And I'm to be "finished" by travel,—
  Whatever's the meaning of that.   70
Oh! why did papa strike pay gravel
  In drifting on Poverty Flat?

Good night!—here's the end of my paper;
  Good night!—if the longitude please,—
For may be, while wasting my taper,
  Your sun's climbing over the trees.
But know, if you haven't got riches,
  And are poor, dearest Joe, and all that,
That my heart's somewhere there in the ditches, 79
  And you've struck it,—on Poverty Flat.

1871

THE LUCK OF ROARING CAMP

Published anonymously in the *Overland Monthly* for August, 1868. This sentimental story of an abandoned baby and its influence on rough miners of the early days of California mining camps was fresh and original and opened up a new vein in short fiction. It barely reached print, however, for the proofreader was shocked by it and the printer doubtful; but Harte insisted on its appearance and it had at once extraordinary success.

THERE was commotion in Roaring Camp. It could not have been a fight, for in 1850 that was not novel enough to have called together the entire settlement. The ditches and claims were not only deserted, but "Tuttle's grocery" had contributed its gamblers, who, it will be remembered, calmly continued their game the day that French Pete and Kanaka Joe shot each other to death over the bar in the front room. The whole camp was collected before a rude cabin on the outer edge of the clearing. Conversation was carried on in a low tone, but the name of a woman was frequently repeated. It was a name familiar enough in the camp,—"Cherokee Sal."

Perhaps the less said of her the better. She was a coarse, and it is to be feared, a very sinful woman. But at that time she was the only woman in Roaring Camp, and was just then lying in sore extremity, when she most needed the ministration of her own sex. Dissolute, abandoned, and irreclaimable, she was yet suffering a martyrdom hard enough to bear even when veiled by sympathizing womanhood, but now terrible in her loneliness. The primal curse had come to her in that original isolation which must have made the punishment of the first transgression so dreadful. It was, perhaps, part of the expiation of her sin, that, at a moment when she most lacked her sex's intuitive tenderness and care, she met only the half-contemptuous faces of her masculine associates. Yet a few of the spectators were, I think, touched by her sufferings. Sandy Tipton thought it was "rough on Sal," and, in the contemplation of her condition, for a moment rose superior to the fact that he had an ace and two bowers in his sleeve.

It will be seen, also, that the situation was novel. Deaths were by no means uncommon in Roaring Camp, but a birth was a new thing. People had been dismissed the camp effectively, finally, and with no possibility of return; but this was the first time that anybody had been introduced *ab initio*. Hence the excitement.

"You go in there, Stumpy," said a prominent citizen known as "Kentuck," addressing one of the loungers. "Go in there, and see what you kin do. You've had experience in them things."

Perhaps there was a fitness in the selection. Stumpy, in other climes, had been the putative head of two families; in fact, it was owing to some legal informality in these proceedings that Roaring Camp—a city of refuge—was indebted to his company. The crowd approved the choice, and Stumpy was wise enough to bow to the majority. The door closed upon the extempore surgeon and midwife, and Roaring Camp sat down outside, smoked its pipe, and awaited the issue.

The assemblage numbered about a hundred men. One or two of these were actual fugitives from justice, some were criminal, and all were reckless. Physically, they exhibited no indication of their past lives and character. The greatest scamp had a Raphael face, with a profusion of blond hair; Oakhurst, a gambler, had the melancholy air and intellectual abstraction of a Hamlet; the coolest and most courageous man was scarcely over five feet in height, with a soft voice and an embarrassed, timid manner. The term "roughs" applied to them was a distinction rather than a definition. Perhaps in the minor details of fingers, toes, ears, etc., the camp may have been deficient, but these slight omissions did not detract from their aggregate force. The strongest man had but three fingers on his right hand; the best shot had but one eye.

Such was the physical aspect of the men that were dispersed around the cabin. The camp lay in a triangular valley, between two hills and a river. The only outlet was a steep trail over the summit of a hill that faced the cabin, now illuminated by the rising moon. The suffering woman might have seen it from the rude bunk whereon she lay,—seen it winding like a silver thread until it was lost in the stars above.

A fire of withered pine boughs added sociability to the gathering. By degrees the natural levity of Roaring Camp returned. Bets were freely offered and taken regarding the result. Three to five that "Sal would get through with it"; even, that the child would survive; side bets as to the sex and complexion of the coming stranger. In the midst of an excited discussion an exclamation came from those nearest the door, and the camp stopped to listen. Above the swaying and moaning of the pines, the swift rush of the river, and the crackling of the fire rose a sharp, querulous cry—a cry unlike anything heard before in the camp. The pines stopped moaning, the river ceased to rush, and the fire to crackle. It seemed as if Nature had stopped to listen too.

The camp rose to its feet as one man! It was proposed to explode a barrel of gunpowder, but, in consideration of the situation of the mother, better counsels prevailed, and only a few revolvers were discharged; for, whether owing to the rude surgery of the camp, or some other reason, Cherokee Sal was sinking fast. Within an hour she had climbed, as it were, that rugged road that led to the stars, and so passed out of Roaring Camp, its sin and shame forever. I do not think that the announcement disturbed them much, except in speculation as to the fate of the child. "Can he live now?" was asked of Stumpy. The answer was doubtful. The only other being of Cherokee Sal's sex and maternal condition in the settlement was an ass. There was some conjecture as to fitness, but the experiment was tried. It was less problematical than the ancient treatment of Romulus and Remus, and apparently as successful.

When these details were completed, which exhausted another hour, the door was opened, and the anxious crowd, who had already formed themselves into a queue, entered in single file. Beside the low bunk or shelf, on which the figure of the mother was starkly outlined below the blankets, stood a pine table. On this a candle-box was placed, and within it, swathed in staring red flannel, lay the last arrival at Roaring Camp. Beside the candle-box was placed a hat. Its use was soon indicated.

"Gentlemen," said Stumpy, with a singular mixture of authority and *ex officio* complacency —"Gentlemen will please pass in at the front door, round the table, and out at the back door. Them as wishes to contribute anything toward the orphan will find a hat handy." The first man entered with his hat on; he uncovered, however, as he looked about him, and so, unconsciously, set an example to the next. In such communities good and bad actions are catching. As the procession filed in, comments were audible,—criticisms addressed, perhaps, rather to Stumpy, in the character of showman,—"Is that him?" "Mighty small specimen"; "Hasn't more'n got the color"; "Ain't bigger nor a derringer." The contributions were as characteristic: A silver tobacco box; a doubloon; a navy revolver, silver mounted; a gold specimen; a very beautifully embroidered lady's handkerchief (from Oakhurst the gambler); a diamond breastpin, a diamond ring (suggested by the pin, with the remark from the giver that he "saw that pin and went two diamonds better"); a slung shot; a Bible (contributor not detected); a golden spur; a silver teaspoon (the initials, I regret to say, were not the giver's); a pair of surgeon's shears; a lancet; a Bank of England note for £5; and about $200 in loose gold and silver coin. During these proceedings Stumpy maintained a silence as impassive as the dead on his left—a gravity as inscrutable as that of the newly-born on his right. Only one incident occurred to break the monotony of the curious procession. As Kentuck bent over the candle-box half curiously, the child turned, and, in a spasm of pain, caught at his groping finger, and held it fast for a moment. Kentuck looked foolish and embarrassed. Something like a blush tried to assert itself in his weather-beaten cheek. "The d—d little cuss!" he said, as he extricated his finger, with, perhaps, more tenderness and care than he might have been deemed capable of showing. He held that finger a little apart from its fellows as he went out, and examined it curiously. The examination provoked the same original remark in regard to the child. In fact, he seemed to enjoy repeating it. "He rastled with my finger," he remarked to Tipton, holding up the member, "the d—d little cuss!"

It was four o'clock before the camp sought repose. A light burnt in the cabin where the watchers sat, for Stumpy did not go to bed that night. Nor did Kentuck. He drank quite freely and related with great gusto his experience, invariably ending with his characteristic condemnation of the newcomer. It seemed to relieve him of any unjust implication of sentiment, and Kentuck had the weaknesses of the nobler sex. When everybody else had gone to bed, he walked down to the river, and whistled reflectingly. Then he walked up the gulch, past the cabin, still whistling with demonstrative unconcern. At a large redwood tree he paused and retraced his steps, and again passed the cabin. Halfway down to the river's bank he again paused, and then returned and knocked at the door. It was opened by Stumpy. "How goes it?" said Kentuck, looking past Stumpy toward the candle-box. "All serene," replied Stumpy. "Anything up?" "Nothing." There was a pause—an embarrassing one—Stumpy still holding the door. Then Kentuck had recourse to his finger, which he held up to Stumpy. "Rastled with it,—the d—d little cuss," he said, and retired.

The next day Cherokee Sal had such rude sepulture as Roaring Camp afforded. After her body had been committed to the hillside, there was a formal meeting of the camp to discuss what should be done with her infant. A resolution to adopt it was unanimous and enthusiastic. But an animated discussion in regard to the manner and feasibility of providing for its wants at once sprung up. It was remarkable that the argument partook of none of those fierce personalities with which discussions were usually conducted at Roaring Camp. Tipton proposed that they should send the child to Red Dog—a distance of forty miles— where female attention could be procured. But the unlucky suggestion met with fierce and unanimous opposition. It was evident that no plan which entailed parting from their new acquisition would for a moment be entertained. "Besides," said Tom Ryder, "them fellows at Red Dog would swap it, and ring in somebody else on us." A disbelief in the honesty of other camps prevailed at Roaring Camp as in other places.

The introduction of a female nurse in the camp also met with objection. It was argued that no decent woman could be prevailed to accept Roaring Camp as her home, and the speaker urged that "they didn't want any more of the other kind." This unkind allusion to the defunct mother, harsh as it may seem, was the first spasm of propriety—the first symptom of the camp's regeneration. Stumpy advanced nothing. Perhaps he felt a certain delicacy in interfering with the selection of a possible successor in office. But when questioned, he averred stoutly that he and "Jinny"—the mammal before alluded to—could manage to rear the child. There was something original, independent, and heroic about the plan that pleased the camp. Stumpy was retained. Certain articles were sent for to Sacramento. "Mind," said the treasurer, as he pressed a bag of gold-dust into the expressman's hand, "the best that can be got—lace, you know, and filigree-work and frills,—d—n the cost!"

Strange to say, the child thrived. Perhaps the invigorating climate of the mountain camp was compensation for material deficiencies. Nature took the foundling to her broader breast. In that rare atmosphere of the Sierra foothills—that air pungent with balsamic odor, that ethereal cordial, at once bracing and exhilarating, he may have found food and nourishment, or a subtle chemistry that transmuted asses' milk to lime and phosphorus. Stumpy inclined to the belief that it was the latter and good nursing. "Me and that ass," he would say, "has been father and mother to him! Don't you," he would add, apostrophizing the helpless bundle before him, "never go back on us."

By the time he was a month old, the necessity of giving him a name became apparent. He had generally been known as "the Kid," "Stumpy's boy," "the Cayote" (an allusion to his vocal powers) and even by Kentuck's endearing diminutive of "the d—d little cuss." But these were felt to be vague and unsatisfactory, and were at last dismissed under another influence. Gamblers and adventurers are generally superstitious, and Oakhurst one day declared that the baby had brought "the luck" to Roaring Camp. It was certain that of late they had been successful. "Luck" was the name agreed upon, with the prefix of Tommy for greater convenience. No allusion was made to the mother, and the father was unknown. "It's better," said the philosophical Oakhurst, "to take a fresh deal all round. Call him Luck, and start him fair." A day was accordingly set apart for the christening. What was meant by this ceremony the reader may imagine, who has already gathered some idea of the reckless irreverence of Roaring Camp. The master of ceremonies was one "Boston," a noted wag, and the occasion seemed to promise the greatest facetiousness. This ingenious satirist had spent two days in preparing a burlesque of the church service, with pointed local allusions. The choir was properly trained, and Sandy Tipton was to stand godfather. But after the procession had marched to the grove with music and banners, and the child had been deposited before a mock altar, Stumpy stepped before the expectant crowd. "It ain't my style to spoil fun, boys," said the little man, stoutly, eyeing the faces around him, "but it strikes me that this thing ain't exactly on the squar. It's playing it pretty low down on this yer baby to ring in fun on him that he ain't goin' to understand. And ef there's going to be any godfathers round, I'd like to see who's got any better rights than me." A silence followed Stumpy's speech. To the credit of all humorists be it said that the first man to acknowledge its justice was the satirist, thus stopped of his fun. "But," said Stumpy, quickly, following up his advantage, "we're here for a christening, and we'll have it. I proclaim you Thomas Luck, according to the laws of the United States and the State of California, so help me God." It was the first time that the name of the Deity had been uttered otherwise but profanely in the camp. The form of christening was perhaps even more ludicrous than the satirist had conceived; but strangely enough, nobody saw it and nobody laughed. "Tommy" was christened as seriously as he would have been under a Christian roof, and cried and was comforted in as orthodox fashion.

And so the work of regeneration began in Roaring Camp. Almost imperceptibly a change came over the settlement. The cabin assigned to "Tommy Luck"—or "The Luck," as he was more frequently called—first showed signs of improvement. It was kept scrupulously clean and whitewashed. Then it was boarded, clothed and papered. The rosewood cradle—packed eighty miles by mule—had, in Stumpy's way of putting it, "sorter killed the rest of the furniture." So the rehabilitation of the cabin became a necessity. The men who were in the habit of lounging in at Stumpy's to see "how The Luck got on" seemed to appreciate the change, and, in self-defense, the rival establishment of "Tuttle's grocery" bestirred itself, and imported a carpet and mirrors. The reflections of the latter on the appearance of Roaring Camp tended to produce stricter habits of personal cleanliness. Again Stumpy imposed a kind of quarantine upon those who aspired to the honor and privilege of holding "The Luck." It was a cruel mortification to Kentuck—who, in the carelessness of a large nature and the habits of frontier life, had begun to regard all garments as a second cuticle, which, like a snake's, only sloughed off through decay—to be debarred this privilege from certain prudential reasons. Yet such was the subtle influence of innovation that he thereafter appeared regularly every afternoon in a clean shirt, and face still shining from his ablutions. Nor were moral and social sanitary laws neglected. "Tommy," who was supposed to spend his whole existence in a persistent attempt to repose, must not be disturbed by noise. The shouting and yelling which had gained the camp its felicitous title were not permitted within hearing distance of Stumpy's. The men conversed in whispers, or smoked with Indian gravity. Profanity was tacitly given up in these sacred precincts, and throughout the camp a popular form of expletive, known as "D—n the luck!" and "Curse the luck!" was abandoned, as having a new personal bearing. Vocal music was not interdicted, being supposed to have a soothing, tranquilizing quality, and one song, sung by "Man-o'-War Jack," an English sailor from Her Majesty's Australian colonies, was quite popular as a lullaby. It was a lugubrious recital of the exploits of "the *Arethusa*, Seventy-four," in a muffled minor, ending with a prolonged dying fall at the burden of each verse, "On b-o-o-o-ard of the *Arethusa*." It was a fine sight to see Jack holding The Luck, rocking from side to side as if with the motion of a ship, and crooning forth this naval ditty. Either through the peculiar rocking of Jack or the length of his song—it contained ninety stanzas, and was continued with conscientious deliberation to the bitter end—the lullaby generally had the desired effect. At such times the men would lie at full length under the trees, in the soft summer twilight, smoking their pipes and drinking in the melodious utterances. An indistinct idea that this was pastoral happiness pervaded the camp. "This 'ere kind o' think," said the Cockney Simmons, meditatively reclining on his elbow, "is 'evingly." It reminded him of Greenwich.

On the long summer days The Luck was usually carried to the gulch, from whence the golden store of Roaring Camp was taken. There, on a blanket spread over pine boughs, he would lie while the men were working in the ditches below. Latterly, there was a rude attempt to decorate this bower with flowers and sweet-smelling shrubs, and generally some one would bring him a cluster of wild honeysuckles, azaleas, or the painted blossoms of Las Mariposas. The men had suddenly awakened to the fact that there were beauty and significance in these trifles, which they had so long trodden carelessly beneath their feet. A flake of glittering mica, a fragment of variegated quartz, a bright pebble from the bed of the creek, became beautiful to eyes thus cleared and strengthened, and were invariably put aside for "The Luck." It was wonderful how many treasures the woods and hillsides yielded that "would do for Tommy." Surrounded by playthings such as never child out of fairyland had before, it is to be hoped that Tommy was content. He appeared to be serenely happy, albeit there was an infantine gravity about him, a contemplative light in his round gray eyes, that sometimes worried Stumpy. He was always tractable and quiet, and it is recorded that once, having crept beyond his "corral"—a hedge of tessellated pine boughs, which surrounded his bed—he dropped over the bank on his head in the soft earth, and remained with his mottled legs in the air in that position for at least five minutes with unflinching gravity. He was extricated without a murmur. I hesitate to record the many other instances of his sagacity, which rest, unfortunately, upon the statements of prejudiced friends. Some of them were not without a tinge of superstition. "I crep' up the bank just now," said Kentuck one day, in a breathless state of excitement, "and dern my skin if he wasn't a talking to a jaybird as was a-sittin on his lap. There they was, just as free and sociable as anything you please, a-jawin at each other just like two cherrybums." Howbeit, whether creeping over the pine boughs or lying lazily on his back, blinking at the leaves above him, to him the birds sang, the squirrels chattered, and the flowers bloomed. Nature was his nurse and playfellow. For him she would let slip between the leaves golden shafts of sunlight that fell just within his grasp; she would send wandering breezes to visit him with the balm of bay and resinous gums; to him the tall redwoods nodded familiarly and sleepily, the bumblebees buzzed, and the rooks cawed a slumbrous accompaniment.

Such was the golden summer of Roaring Camp. They were "flush times"—and the Luck was with them. The claims had yielded enormously. The camp was jealous of its privileges and looked suspiciously on strangers. No encouragement was given to immigration, and, to make their seclusion more perfect, the land on either side of the mountain wall that surrounded the camp they duly pre-empted. This, and a reputation for singular proficiency with the revolver, kept the reserve of Roaring Camp inviolate. The expressman—their only connecting link with the surrounding world—sometimes told wonderful stories of the camp. He would say, "They've a street up there in 'Roaring,' that would lay over any street in Red Dog. They've got vines and flowers round their houses, and they wash themselves twice a day. But they're mighty rough on strangers, and they worship an Ingin baby."

With the prosperity of the camp came a desire for further improvement. It was proposed to build a hotel in the following spring, and to invite one or two decent families to reside there for the sake of "The Luck," who might perhaps profit by female companionship. The sacrifice that this concession to the sex cost these men, who were fiercely skeptical in regard to its general virtue and usefulness, can only be accounted for by their affection for Tommy. A few still held out. But the resolve could not be carried into effect for three months, and the minority meekly yielded in the hope that something might turn up to prevent it. And it did.

The winter of '51 will long be remembered in the foothills. The snow lay deep on the Sierras, and every mountain creek became a river, and every river a lake. Each gorge and gulch was transformed into a tumultuous watercourse that descended the hillsides, tearing down giant trees and scattering its drift and débris along the plain. Red Dog had been twice under water, and Roaring Camp had been forewarned. "Water put the gold into them gulches," said Stumpy; "it's been here once and will be here again!" And that night the North Fork suddenly leaped over its banks, and swept up the triangular valley of Roaring Camp.

In the confusion of rushing water, crashing trees, and crackling timber, and the darkness which seemed to flow with the water and blot out the fair valley, but little could be done to collect the scattered camp. When the morning broke, the cabin of Stumpy nearest the river-bank was gone. Higher up the gulch they found the body of its unlucky owner; but the pride—the hope—the joy—the Luck—of Roaring Camp had disappeared. They were returning with sad hearts, when a shout from the bank recalled them.

It was a relief-boat from down the river. They had picked up, they said, a man and an infant, nearly exhausted, about two miles below. Did anybody know them, and did they belong here?

It needed but a glance to show them Kentuck lying there, cruelly crushed and bruised, but still holding The Luck of Roaring Camp in his arms. As they bent over the strangely assorted pair, they saw that the child was cold and pulseless. "He is dead," said one. Kentuck opened his eyes. "Dead?" he repeated feebly. "Yes, my man, and you are dying too." A smile lit the eyes of the expiring Kentuck. "Dying!" he repeated, "he's a-taking me with him—tell the boys I've got the Luck with me now"; and the strong man, clinging to the frail babe as a drowning man is said to cling to a straw, drifted away into the shadowy river that flows forever to the unknown sea.

1868

THE OUTCASTS OF POKER FLAT

As Mr. John Oakhurst, gambler, stepped into the main street of Poker Flat on the morning of the 23d of November, 1850, he was conscious of a change in its moral atmosphere since the preceding night. Two or three men, conversing earnestly together, ceased as he approached, and exchanged significant glances. There was a Sabbath lull in the air, which, in a settlement unused to Sabbath influences, looked ominous.

Mr. Oakhurst's calm, handsome face betrayed small concern in these indications. Whether he was conscious of any predisposing cause was another question. "I reckon they're after somebody," he reflected; "likely it's me." He returned to his pocket the handkerchief with which he had been whipping away the red dust of Poker Flat from his neat boots, and quietly discharged his mind of any further conjecture.

In point of fact, Poker Flat was "after somebody." It had lately suffered the loss of several thousand dollars, two valuable horses, and a prominent citizen. It was experiencing a spasm of virtuous reaction, quite as lawless and ungovernable as any of the acts that had provoked it. A secret committee had determined to rid the town of all improper persons. This was done permanently in regard of two men who were then hanging from the boughs of a sycamore in the gulch, and temporarily in the banishment of certain other objectionable characters. I regret to say that some of these were ladies. It is but due to the sex, however, to state that their impropriety was professional, and it was only in such easily established standards of evil that Poker Flat ventured to sit in judgment.

Mr. Oakhurst was right in supposing that he was included in this category. A few of the committee had urged hanging him as a possible example and a sure method of reimbursing themselves from his pockets of the sums he had won from them. "It's agin justice," said Jim Wheeler, "to let this yer young man from Roaring Camp—an entire stranger—

carry away our money." But a crude sentiment of equity residing in the breasts of those who had been fortunate enough to win from Mr. Oakhurst overruled this narrower local prejudice.

Mr. Oakhurst received his sentence with philosophic calmness, none the less coolly that he was aware of the hesitation of his judges. He was too much of a gambler not to accept fate. With him life was at best an uncertain game, and he recognized the usual percentage in favor of the dealer.

A body of armed men accompanied the deported wickedness of Poker Flat to the outskirts of the settlement. Besides Mr. Oakhurst, who was known to be a coolly desperate man, and for whose intimidation the armed escort was intended, the expatriated party consisted of a young woman familiarly known as "The Duchess"; another who had won the title of "Mother Shipton"; and "Uncle Billy," a suspected sluice-robber and confirmed drunkard. The cavalcade provoked no comments from the spectators, nor was any word uttered by the escort. Only when the gulch which marked the uttermost limit of Poker Flat was reached, the leader spoke briefly and to the point. The exiles were forbidden to return at the peril of their lives.

As the escort disappeared, their pent-up feelings found vent in a few hysterical tears from the Duchess, some bad language from Mother Shipton, and a Parthian volley of expletives from Uncle Billy. The philosophic Oakhurst alone remained silent. He listened calmly to Mother Shipton's desire to cut somebody's heart out, to the repeated statements of the Duchess that she would die in the road, and to the alarming oaths that seemed to be bumped out of Uncle Billy as he rode forward. With the easy good humor characteristic of his class, he insisted upon exchanging his own riding-horse, "Five-Spot," for the sorry mule which the Duchess rode. But even this act did not draw the party into any closer sympathy. The young woman readjusted her somewhat draggled plumes with a feeble, faded coquetry; Mother Shipton eyed the possessor of "Five-Spot" with malevolence, and Uncle Billy included the whole party in one sweeping anathema.

The road to Sandy Bar—a camp that, not having as yet experienced the regenerating influences of Poker Flat, consequently seemed to offer some invitation to the emigrants—lay over a steep mountain range. It was distant a day's severe travel. In that advanced season the party soon passed out of the moist, temperate regions of the foothills into the dry, cold, bracing air of the Sierras. The trail was narrow and difficult. At noon the Duchess, rolling out of her saddle upon the ground, declared her intention of going no farther, and the party halted.

The spot was singularly wild and impressive. A wooded amphitheatre, surrounded on three sides by precipitous cliffs of naked granite, sloped gently towards the crest of another precipice that overlooked the valley. It was, undoubtedly, the most suitable spot for a camp, had camping been advisable. But Mr. Oakhurst knew that scarcely half the journey to Sandy Bar was accomplished, and the party were not equipped or provisioned for delay. This fact he pointed out to his companions curtly, with a philosophic commentary on the folly of "throwing up their hand before the game was played out." But they were furnished with liquor, which in this emergency stood them in place of food, fuel, rest, and prescience. In spite of his remonstrances, it was not long before they were more or less under its influence. Uncle Billy passed rapidly from a bellicose state into one of stupor, the Duchess became maudlin, and Mother Shipton snored. Mr. Oakhurst alone remained erect, leaning against a rock, calmly surveying them.

Mr. Oakhurst did not drink. It interfered with a profession which required coolness, impassiveness, and presence of mind, and, in his own language, he "couldn't afford it." As he gazed at his recumbent fellow exiles, the loneliness begotten of his pariah trade, his habits of life, his very vices, for the first time seriously oppressed him. He bestirred himself in dusting his black clothes, washing his hands and face, and other acts characteristic of his studiously neat habits, and for a moment forgot his annoyance. The thought of deserting his weaker and more pitiable companions never perhaps occurred to him. Yet he could not help feeling the want of that excitement which, singularly enough, was most conducive to that calm equanimity for which he was notorious. He looked at the gloomy walls that rose a thousand feet sheer above the circling pines around him, at the sky ominously clouded, at the valley below, already deepening into shadows; and, doing so, suddenly he heard his own name called.

A horseman slowly ascended the trail. In the fresh, open face of the newcomer Mr. Oakhurst recognized Tom Simson, otherwise known as "The Innocent," of Sandy Bar. He had met him some months before over a "little game," and had, with perfect equanimity, won the entire fortune—amounting to some forty dollars—of that guileless youth. After the game was finished, Mr. Oakhurst drew the youthful speculator behind the door and thus addressed him: "Tommy, you're a good little man, but you can't gamble worth a cent. Don't try it over again." He then handed him his money back, pushed him gently from the room, and so made a devoted slave of Tom Simson.

There was a remembrance of this in his boyish and enthusiastic greeting of Mr. Oakhurst. He had started, he said, to go to Poker Flat to seek his fortune. "Alone?" No, not exactly alone; in fact (a giggle), he had run away with Piney Woods. Didn't Mr. Oakhurst remember Piney? She that used to wait on the table at the Temperance House? They had been engaged a long time, but old Jake Woods had objected, and so they had run away, and were going to Poker Flat to be married, and here they were. And they were tired out, and how lucky it was they had found a place to camp, and company. All this the Innocent delivered rapidly, while Piney, a stout, comely damsel of fifteen, emerged from behind the pine-tree, where she had been blushing unseen, and rode to the side of her lover.

Mr. Oakhurst seldom troubled himself with sentiment, still less with propriety; but he had a vague idea that the situation was not fortunate. He retained, however, his presence of mind sufficiently to kick Uncle Billy, who was about to say something, and Uncle Billy was sober enough to recognize in Mr. Oakhurst's kick a superior power that would not bear trifling. He then endeavored to dissuade Tom Simson from delaying further, but in vain. He even pointed out the fact that there was no provision, nor means of making a camp. But, unluckily, the Innocent met this objection by assuring the party that he was provided with an extra mule loaded with provisions, and by the discovery of a rude attempt at a log house near the trail. "Piney can stay with Mrs. Oakhurst," said the Innocent, pointing to the Duchess, "and I can shift for myself."

Nothing but Mr. Oakhurst's admonishing foot saved Uncle Billy from bursting into a roar of laughter. As it was, he felt compelled to retire up the cañon until he could recover his gravity. There he confided the joke to the tall pine-trees, with many slaps of his leg, contortions of his face, and the usual profanity. But when he returned to the party, he found them seated by a fire—for the air had grown strangely chill and the sky overcast—in apparently amicable conversation. Piney was actually talking in an impulsive girlish fashion to the Duchess, who was listening with an interest and animation she had not shown for many days. The Innocent was holding forth, apparently with equal effect, to Mr. Oakhurst and Mother Shipton, who was actually relaxing into amiability. "Is this yer a d—d picnic?" said Uncle Billy, with inward scorn, as he surveyed the sylvan group, the glancing firelight, and the tethered animals in the foreground. Suddenly an idea mingled with the alcoholic fumes that disturbed his brain. It was apparently of a jocular nature, for he felt impelled to slap his leg again and cram his fist into his mouth.

As the shadows crept slowly up the mountain, a slight breeze rocked the tops of the pine-trees and moaned through their long and gloomy aisles. The ruined cabin, patched and covered with pine boughs, was set apart for the ladies. As the lovers parted, they unaffectedly exchanged a kiss, so honest and sincere that it might have been heard above the swaying pines. The frail Duchess and the malevolent Mother Shipton were probably too stunned to remark upon this last evidence of simplicity, and so turned without a word to the hut. The fire was replenished, the men lay down before the door, and in a few minutes were asleep.

Mr. Oakhurst was a light sleeper. Toward morning he awoke benumbed and cold. As he stirred the dying fire, the wind, which was now blowing strongly, brought to his cheek that which caused the blood to leave it,— snow!

He started to his feet with the intention of awakening the sleepers, for there was no time to lose. But turning to where Uncle Billy had been lying, he found him gone. A suspicion leaped to his brain, and a curse to his lips. He ran to the spot where the mules had been tethered—they were no longer there. The tracks were already rapidly disappearing in the snow.

The momentary excitement brought Mr. Oakhurst back to the fire with his usual calm. He did not waken the sleepers. The Innocent slumbered peacefully, with a smile on his good-humored, freckled face; the virgin Piney slept beside her frailer sisters as sweetly as though attended by celestial guardians; and Mr. Oakhurst, drawing his blanket over his shoulders, stroked his mustaches and waited for the dawn. It came slowly in a whirling mist of snowflakes that dazzled and confused the eye. What could be seen of the landscape appeared magically changed. He looked over the valley, and summed up the present and future in two words, "Snowed in!"

A careful inventory of the provisions, which, fortunately for the party, had been stored within the hut, and so escaped the felonious fingers of Uncle Billy, disclosed the fact that with care and prudence they might last ten days longer. "That is," said Mr. Oakhurst *sotto voce* to the Innocent, "if you're willing to board us. If you ain't—and perhaps you'd better not—you can wait till Uncle Billy gets back with provisions." For some occult reason, Mr. Oakhurst could not bring himself to disclose Uncle Billy's rascality, and so offered the hypothesis that he had wandered from the camp and had accidentally stampeded the animals. He dropped a warning to the Duchess and Mother Shipton, who of course knew the facts of their associate's defection. "They'll find out the truth about us *all* when

they find out anything," he added significantly, "and there's no good frightening them now."

Tom Simson not only put all his worldly store at the disposal of Mr. Oakhurst, but seemed to enjoy the prospect of their enforced seclusion. "We'll have a good camp for a week, and then the snow'll melt, and we'll all go back together." The cheerful gayety of the young man and Mr. Oakhurst's calm infected the others. The Innocent, with the aid of pine boughs, extemporized a thatch for the roofless cabin, and the Duchess directed Piney in the rearrangement of the interior with a taste and tact that opened the blue eyes of that provincial maiden to their fullest extent. "I reckon now you're used to fine things at Poker Flat," said Piney. The Duchess turned away sharply to conceal something that reddened her cheeks through their professional tint, and Mother Shipton requested Piney not to "chatter." But when Mr. Oakhurst returned from a weary search for the trail, he heard the sound of happy laughter echoed from the rocks. He stopped in some alarm, and his thoughts first naturally reverted to the whiskey, which he had prudently cachéd. "And yet it don't somehow sound like whiskey," said the gambler. It was not until he caught sight of the blazing fire through the still blinding storm, and the group around it, that he settled to the conviction that it was "square fun."

Whether Mr. Oakhurst had cachéd his cards with the whiskey as something debarred the free access of the community, I cannot say. It was certain that, in Mother Shipton's words, he "didn't say 'cards' once" during that evening. Haply the time was beguiled by an accordion, produced somewhat ostentatiously by Tom Simson from his pack. Notwithstanding some difficulties attending the manipulation of this instrument, Piney Woods managed to pluck several reluctant melodies from its keys, to an accompaniment by the Innocent on a pair of bone castanets. But the crowning festivity of the evening was reached in a rude camp-meeting hymn, which the lovers, joining hands, sang with great earnestness and vociferation. I fear that a certain defiant tone and Covenanter's swing to its chorus, rather than any devotional quality, caused it speedily to infect the others, who at last joined in the refrain:

"I'm proud to live in the service of the Lord,
And I'm bound to die in His army."

The pines rocked, the storm eddied and whirled above the miserable group, and the flames of their altar leaped heavenward, as if in token of the vow.

At midnight the storm abated, the rolling clouds parted, and the stars glittered keenly above the sleeping camp. Mr. Oakhurst, whose professional habits had enabled him to live on the smallest possible amount of sleep, in dividing the watch with Tom Simson some-how managed to take upon himself the greater part of that duty. He excused himself to the Innocent by saying that he had "often been a week without sleep." "Doing what?" asked Tom. "Poker!" replied Oakhurst senten-tiously. "When a man gets a streak of luck, —nigger-luck,—he don't get tired. The luck gives in first. Luck," continued the gambler reflectively, "is a mighty queer thing. All you know about it for certain is that it's bound to change. And it's finding out when it's going to change that makes you. We've had a streak of bad luck since we left Poker Flat,—you come along, and slap you get into it, too. If you can hold your cards right along you're all right. For," added the gambler with cheer-ful irrelevance—

" 'I'm proud to live in the service of the Lord,
And I'm bound to die in His army.' "

The third day came, and the sun, looking through the white-curtained valley, saw the outcasts divide their slowly decreasing store of provisions for the morning meal. It was one of the peculiarities of that mountain climate that its rays diffused a kindly warmth over the wintry landscape, as if in regretful commiseration of the past. But it revealed drift on drift of snow piled high around the hut,—a hopeless, uncharted, trackless sea of white lying below the rocky shores to which the castaways still clung. Through the marvel-ously clear air the smoke of the pastoral village of Poker Flat rose miles away. Mother Ship-ton saw it, and from a remote pinnacle of her rocky fastness hurled in that direction a final malediction. It was her last vituperative at-tempt, and perhaps for that reason was in-vested with a certain degree of sublimity. It did her good, she privately informed the Duchess. "Just you go out there and cuss, and see." She then set herself to the task of amusing "the child," as she and the Duchess were pleased to call Piney. Piney was no chicken, but it was a soothing and original theory of the pair thus to account for the fact that she didn't swear and wasn't improper.

When night crept up again through the gorges, the reedy notes of the accordion rose and fell in fitful spasms and long-drawn gasps by the flickering campfire. But music failed to fill entirely the aching void left by insuf-ficient food, and a new diversion was proposed by Piney,—story-telling. Neither Mr. Oak-hurst nor his female companions caring to relate their personal experiences, this plan would have failed too, but for the Innocent. Some months before he had chanced upon a stray copy of Mr. Pope's ingenious transla-tion of the Iliad. He now proposed to narrate the principal incidents of that poem—having thoroughly mastered the argument and fairly forgotten the words—in the current vernacu-lar of Sandy Bar. And so for the rest of that night the Homeric demigods again walked the earth. Trojan bully and wily Greek wrestled in the winds, and the great pines in the cañon seemed to bow to the wrath of the son of Peleus. Mr. Oakhurst listened with quiet satisfaction. Most especially was he in-terested in the fate of "Ash-heels" as the Innocent persisted in denominating the "swift-footed Achilles."

So, with small food and much of Homer and the accordion, a week passed over the heads of the outcasts. The sun again forsook them, and again from leaden skies the snow-flakes were sifted over the land. Day by day closer around them drew the snowy circle, until at last they looked from their prison over drifted walls of dazzling white, that towered twenty feet above their heads. It be-came more and more difficult to replenish their fires, even from the fallen trees beside them, now half hidden in the drifts. And yet no one complained. The lovers turned from the dreary prospect and looked into each other's eyes, and were happy. Mr. Oakhurst settled himself coolly to the losing game before him. The Duchess, more cheerful than she had been, assumed the care of Piney. Only Mother Shipton—once the strongest of the party—seemed to sicken and fade. At midnight on the tenth day she called Oakhurst to her side. "I'm going," she said, in a voice of querulous weakness, "but don't say anything about it. Don't waken the kids. Take the bundle from under my head, and open it." Mr. Oakhurst did so. It contained Mother Shipton's rations for the last week, untouched. "Give 'em to the child," she said, pointing to the sleeping Piney. "You've starved yourself," said the gambler. "That's what they call it," said the woman querulously, as she lay down again, and, turning her face to the wall, passed quietly away.

The accordion and the bones were put aside that day, and Homer was forgotten. When the body of Mother Shipton had been committed to the snow, Mr. Oakhurst took the Innocent aside, and showed him a pair of snowshoes, which he had fashioned from the old pack-saddle. "There's one chance in a hundred to save her yet," he said, pointing to Piney; "but it's there," he added, pointing toward Poker Flat. "If you can reach there in two days she's safe." "And you?" asked Tom Simson. "I'll stay here," was the curt reply.

The lovers parted with a long embrace. "You are not going, too?" said the Duchess, as she saw Mr. Oakhurst apparently waiting to accompany him. "As far as the cañon," he replied. He turned suddenly and kissed the Duchess, leaving her pallid face aflame, and her trembling limbs rigid with amazement.

Night came, but not Mr. Oakhurst. It brought the storm again and the whirling snow. Then the Duchess, feeding the fire, found that some one had quietly piled beside the hut enough fuel to last a few days longer. The tears rose to her eyes, but she hid them from Piney.

The women slept but little. In the morning, looking into each other's faces, they read their fate. Neither spoke, but Piney, accepting the position of the stronger, drew near and placed her arm around the Duchess's waist. They kept this attitude for the rest of the day. That night the storm reached its greatest fury, and, rending asunder the protecting vines, invaded the very hut.

Toward morning they found themselves unable to feed the fire, which gradually died away. As the embers slowly blackened, the Duchess crept closer to Piney, and broke the silence of many hours: "Piney, can you pray?" "No, dear," said Piney simply. The Duchess, without knowing exactly why, felt relieved, and, putting her head upon Piney's shoulder, spoke no more. And so reclining, the younger and purer pillowing the head of her soiled sister upon her virgin breast, they fell asleep.

The wind lulled as if it feared to waken them. Feathery drifts of snow, shaken from the long pine boughs, flew like white-winged birds, and settled about them as they slept. The moon through the rifted clouds looked down upon what had been the camp. But all human stain, all trace of earthly travail, was hidden beneath the spotless mantle mercifully flung from above.

They slept all that day and the next, nor did they waken when voices and footsteps broke the silence of the camp. And when pitying fingers brushed the snow from their wan faces, you could scarcely have told from the equal peace that dwelt upon them which was she that had sinned. Even the law of Poker Flat recognized this, and turned away, leaving them still locked in each other's arms.

But at the head of the gulch, on one of the largest pine-trees, they found the deuce of clubs pinned to the bark with a bowie-knife. It bore the following, written in pencil in a firm hand:

†

BENEATH THIS TREE
LIES THE BODY
OF

JOHN OAKHURST,

WHO STRUCK A STREAK OF BAD LUCK
ON THE 23D OF NOVEMBER 1850,
AND

HANDED IN HIS CHECKS
ON THE 7TH DECEMBER, 1850.

‡

And pulseless and cold, with a Derringer by his side and a bullet in his heart, though still calm as in life, beneath the snow lay he who at once was the strongest and yet the weakest of the outcasts of Poker Flat.

1868   1869

1838 ~ *John Hay* ~ 1905

THIS AMERICAN author, diplomat, and statesman was born in Indiana. After graduating from Brown University in 1858 he studied law in the office of Abraham Lincoln, whom he also served as private secretary during his presidency. He held minor diplomatic posts at Paris, Vienna, and Madrid, and in 1870 joined the staff of the New York *Tribune* in an editorial capacity. During a ten-year residence in Cleveland he had ample opportunity to see the disastrous results of the struggle between capital and labor, which focused his thinking upon one of the most besetting problems in American life. In 1897 President McKinley appointed him ambassador to Great Britain, from which post he resigned a year later to become Secretary of State, an office which he held until his death.

Although Hay achieved fame as one of the great statesmen of his time, he was widely known as an author before he entered public service as a definite career. With the exception of the monumental life of Lincoln, written in collaboration with John G. Nicolay, the literary work upon which his reputation rests had been completed by the time he was forty years old. *Pike County Ballads* and *Castilian Days* came out in 1871, and *The Bread-Winners*, the authorship of which Hay persistently refused to admit, was published in the *Century* in 1883.

Pike County Ballads (1871) is a significant work, having both historical and intrinsic value. In this work Hay joins Lowell (*The Biglow Papers*) and Bret Harte in releasing poetry from conventional subject matter, and in showing its possibilities in the regional representation of life. The poems are written in dialect, treating homely themes, yet with a dignity and high moral elevation that make them impressive. He has proved that there is real poetry in the routine lives and experiences of ordinary people, as well as in those more fortunate in their culture and refinement. At one time rather savagely attacked in certain quarters, poems like "Jim Bludso" and "Little Breeches" have become part of our accepted American heritage. George Eliot called the former one of the gems in the language. *Castilian Days* (1871) is a study of social and political conditions in Spain, able but occasionally rather too polemical. *The Bread-Winners* (1884) deals with the conflict between capital and labor. It received wide recognition in this country and abroad in spite of faults in treatment and structure. Favoring, as he did, the side of capital, Hay could scarcely be expected to treat his theme with impartial sympathy. It is generally conceded that his greatest work is *Abraham Lincoln: A History*, written in collaboration with John Nicolay. Although superseded by later biographies, this monumental study of the man and his times can be ignored by no student of Lincoln in the future.

Hay's poetry is collected in the Household Edition. L. Sears, *John Hay, Author and Statesman* (1914); W. R. Thayer, *The Life and Letters of John Hay* (2 vols., 1915); T. Dennett, *John Hay: From Poetry to Politics* (1933), are extensive biographies. His early letters are published in C. Ticknor, ed., *A Poet in Exile* (1910). For briefer studies and criticism see *DAB*, VIII; B. Adams, "John Hay," *McClure's*, June, 1902; J. B. Moore, "John Hay: an Estimate," *Saturday Review of Literature*, Nov. 11, 1933; W. D. Howells, "John Hay in Literature," *North American Review*, Sept., 1905; G. Hicks, "The Conversion of John Hay," *New Republic*, June 10, 1931; A. S. Chapman, "The Boyhood of John Hay," *Century*, July, 1909; J. B. Bishop, "A Friendship with John Hay," *Century*, March, 1906; T. Stanton, "John Hay and the Bread-Winners," *Nation*, Aug. 10, 1916; J. L. and J. B. Gilder, *Authors at Home* (1902).

LITTLE BREECHES

I DON'T go much on religion,
  I never ain't had no show;
But I've got a middlin' tight grip, sir,
  On the handful o' things I know.
I don't pan out on the prophets
  And free-will, and that sort of thing,—
But I b'lieve in God and the angels,
  Ever sence one night last spring.

I come into town with some turnips,
  And my little Gabe come along,—   10
No four-year-old in the county
  Could beat him for pretty and strong,
Peart and chipper and sassy,
  Always ready to swear and fight,—
And I'd larnt him to chaw terbacker
  Jest to keep his milk-teeth white.

The snow come down like a blanket
  As I passed by Taggart's store;
I went in for a jug of molasses
  And left the team at the door.   20
They scared at something and started,—
  I heard one little squall,
And hell-to-split over the prairie
  Went team, Little Breeches, and all.

Hell-to-split over the prairie!
  I was almost froze with skeer;
But we rousted up some torches,
  And sarched for 'em far and near.
At last we struck hosses and wagon,
  Snowed under a soft white mound,   30
Upsot, dead beat,—but of little Gabe
  No hide nor hair was found.

And here all hope soured on me,
  Of my fellow-critter's aid,—
I jest flopped down on my marrow-bones,
  Crotch-deep in the snow, and prayed.

. . . .

By this, the torches was played out,
  And me, and Isrul Parr
Went off for some wood to a sheepfold
  That he said was somewhar thar.   40

We found it at last, and a little shed
  Where they shut up the lambs at night.
We looked in and seen them huddled thar,
  So warm and sleepy and white;
And thar sot Little Breeches and chirped,
  As peart as ever you see,
"I want a chaw of terbacker,
  And that's what's the matter of me."

How did he git thar? Angels.
  He could never have walked in that storm;
They jest scooped down and toted him   51
  To whar it was safe and warm.
And I think that saving a little child,
  And fotching him to his own,
Is a derned sight better business
  Than loafing around the Throne.

           1870

JIM BLUDSO

OF THE PRAIRIE BELLE

A vivid rendering of an episode from the romantic era of the Mississippi steamboat.

WALL, no! I can't tell whar he lives,
  Becase he don't live, you see;
Leastways, he's got out of the habit
  Of livin' like you and me.

Whar have you been for the last three year
   That you haven't heard folks tell
How Jimmy Bludso passed in his checks
   The night of the Prairie Belle?

He weren't no saint,—them engineers
   Is all pretty much alike,—   10
One wife in Natchez-under-the-Hill
   And another one here, in Pike;
A keerless man in his talk was Jim,
   And an awkward hand in a row,
But he never flunked, and he never lied,—
   I reckon he never knowed how.

And this was all the religion he had,—
   To treat his engine well;
Never be passed on the river;
   To mind the pilot's bell;   20
And if ever the Prairie Belle took fire,—
   A thousand times he swore,
He'd hold her nozzle agin the bank
   Till the last soul got ashore.

All boats has their day on the Mississip,
   And her day come at last,—
The Movastar was a better boat,
   But the Belle she *wouldn't* be passed.
And so she come tearin' along that night—
   The oldest craft on the line—   30
With a nigger squat on her safety-valve,
   And her furnace crammed, rosin and pine.

The fire bust out as she clared the bar,
   And burnt a hole in the night,
And quick as a flash she turned, and made
   For that willer-bank on the right.
There was runnin' and cursin', but Jim yelled
      out,
   Over all the infernal roar,
"I'll hold her nozzle agin the bank
   Till the last galoot's ashore."   40

Through the hot, black breath of the burnin'
      boat
   Jim Bludso's voice was heard,
And they all had trust in his cussedness,
   And knowed he would keep his word.
And, sure's you're born, they all got off
   Afore the smokestacks fell,—
And Bludso's ghost went up alone
   In the smoke of the Prairie Belle.

He weren't no saint,—but at jedgment
   I'd run my chance with Jim,   50
'Longside of some pious gentlemen
   That wouldn't shook hands with him.
He seen his duty, a dead-sure thing,
   And went for it thar and then;
And Christ ain't a-going to be too hard
   On a man that died for men.

                                                     1871

1835 -- *Mark Twain* -- 1910

S AMUEL LANGHORNE CLEMENS (Mark Twain), who now ranks among our major
   writers, brought humor, realism, and western local color to American fiction.
The first author to emerge from beyond the Mississippi, he discarded eastern backgrounds and wrote of the West intimately and authentically. He was, indeed, the
man that Whitman prophesied and awaited, and his picturesque personality and
individual manner of writing gave him world-wide popularity.

   Clemens led an interesting and varied life. He was born on the west bank of the
Mississippi River at Florida, Missouri, on November 30, 1835. His boyhood was
spent in Hannibal, a little slaveholding town about 100 miles above St. Louis. His
father, a lawyer and storekeeper, had moved westward from Virginia to Tennessee,
and thence to Missouri. His mother was a Kentuckian. Young Clemens had little

schooling. On the death of his father in 1847, he was apprenticed to his brother Orion to learn printing. His principal service, however, was running errands and delivering papers. He grew tired of Hannibal, and in 1853 went to St. Louis, Chicago, New York, and Philadelphia, working at the printing trade, and then back to Keokuk. He took passage at Cincinnati in 1857 and went by steamboat down the Mississippi to New Orleans. On this trip he met the pilot, Horace Bixby, and for fifteen months he tried the life of a "cub pilot" in the Golden Age of steamboat navigation. He committed to memory all the turns and all the shallows and shoals for the 1200 miles from St. Louis to New Orleans, along one of the greatest of American waterways. The romantic spell of the river and the pride and responsibilities of the pilots are reflected in some of his best books. He made a fine record, but the pilot's life ended for him when, at the outbreak of the Civil War, the river was closed to navigation. He enlisted as a Confederate soldier, but his company was disbanded in a few weeks and he did not re-enlist.

In 1861, Clemens' brother Orion was made private secretary to the governor of the Territory of Nevada. Samuel followed him there, and for six years entered into the life of the frontier region. He later recorded his experiences as a prospector and journalist in camps and boom towns in *Roughing It* (1872). When the Comstock Lode excitement was at its height, he was at Virginia City on a newspaper. Here he met Artemus Ward, one of the journalistic group of humorists who were his nearest predecessors in his field. By 1863 he had discovered that he could write and began to use the pen name of Mark Twain, a term employed in his piloting experience to register depths of water. In another year he had given up mining for journalism, although he remained in the West. He worked for a while on a newspaper in San Francisco. It was here that he came to know Bret Harte. In 1865 he published "The Celebrated Jumping Frog of Calaveras County" in the New York *Saturday Press*. The following year he visited the Sandwich Islands as a news correspondent, and upon his return he convulsed a San Francisco audience with an account of his experiences, in the first of his many popular humorous lectures. In 1867 he left San Francisco and went to New York, where he published his first book, *The Jumping Frog of Calaveras County and Other Sketches*. *Innocents Abroad* (1869) was the result of a commission given him by a California newspaper to join a European tour to the Holy Land and send home letters concerning it. The accounts were written from the standpoint of how a Westerner might see Europe. It was a new kind of travel book, and it made him a national figure. In 1870 he married Olivia Langdon of Elmira, New York, who exerted a strong and lasting influence over him. The following year he moved from Elmira to Hartford, Connecticut, which he made his permanent home. For most of the next forty years he lived there, a noted man of letters, the center of a literary group. In 1873 he published *The Gilded Age*, written in collaboration with Charles Dudley Warner.

Tom Sawyer, another landmark in American literature, was published in 1876. It was Clemens's desire to picture a real boy instead of another youthful model of all virtue as described by the Sunday-school stories for juveniles. In it he blends romantic and realistic material. *The Adventures of Huckleberry Finn* (1884) has much the same quality as *Tom Sawyer*. It is something of a social study of the midwestern frontier; it deals again with the romance of steamboat days on the river and touches on the problem of slavery. In 1889 came his famous travesty of chivalric romances, the mock-heroic *A Connecticut Yankee in King Arthur's Court*.

Successful though Clemens was as a man of letters, he twice found himself in serious financial straits because of bad speculative investments. In 1895 his publishing house failed, and he lost the fortune he had made from lecturing and writing. Like Sir Walter Scott, he assumed all legal and moral obligations incurred by this failure and wrote copiously in order to pay the indebtedness. He also made a triumphal lecture tour over the world. He not only paid all debts, but retained, in the main, his health. He became a familiar and popular figure with his white clothes, white hair, and rolling gait. His life was not without tragedy, however; his wife died in 1904 and three of his children had also died. In 1907 he was given the honorary degree of Doctor of Letters from Oxford. His death occurred three years later, on April 21, 1910, at Redding, Connecticut.

While Mark Twain drew largely upon his own wide experience and the American frontier scene, recent studies of his reading have made it apparent that he was also strongly influenced by literary tradition and that he had sharply defined literary theories. These are to be found chiefly in his essays on "How to Tell a Story," "Fenimore Cooper's Literary Offences," "In Defence of Harriet Shelley," "Howells," "Is Shakespeare Dead?" "English as She Is Taught," and "What Paul Bourget Thinks of Us," and in passages throughout his works, notably in Chapter XLVI of *Life on the Mississippi*, where he compares Scott unfavorably with his idol Cervantes. As a determinist, Mark Twain sought to rely on "the slow accumulation of *unconscious* observation—absorption," on "years and years of intercourse with the life concerned"; he sought not to present characters in a vacuum but rather to show the interpenetration of character and environment, of ideals and the physical history of the race. Revolting against the uniformity of book-English of earlier novelists such as Scott, Cooper, and Hawthorne, he stressed the need for fidelity to the rich varieties of the speech of different levels of societies, of different races, and of the same people under different emotional influences. As DeVoto says, he made "the vernacular a perfect instrument for all the necessities of fiction." After the transcendental idealism, we find Mark Twain seeking everywhere a simple and intimate recording of the life of the senses; he deplored the vogue of "a sad, false delicacy" as making literature insipid and untrue to life. He once insisted that "to simply amuse" the masses "would have satisfied my dearest ambition at any time," and in

"How to Tell a Story" he shows that he was a highly conscious craftsman in writing the humorous story and in testing the psychological effectiveness of his literary *manner* directly on countless audiences simply by watching their faces and their reactions. "To string incongruities and absurdities together in a wandering and sometimes purposeless way, and seem innocently unaware that they are absurdities, is the basis of the American art." Yet elsewhere he sought, as a believer in rationalism and humanitarian democracy, to pry "up to a higher level of manhood" those Europeans addicted to a feudalistic caste system; this didactic purpose is illustrated, of course, in *A Connecticut Yankee* and in *The Prince and the Pauper*. He attacked Scott not only for his "chivalry-silliness" but for his bookish style, urging as his own ideal "a strong, compact, direct, unflowery style [which] wastes no words, and does not gush." He also attacked Dowden's style as "a literary cake-walk," full of "bowings and smirkings" and distortions of fact. He thought his friend Howells unexcelled "in the sustained exhibition of certain great qualities—clearness, compression, verbal exactness, and unforced and seemingly unconscious felicity of phrasing," as well as for his mastery of "the right word," "cadenced and undulating rhythm," and "architectural felicities of construction." Mark Twain summarized his "nineteen rules governing literary art in the domain of romantic fiction" in the beginning of his satiric essay on Cooper, whom he finds violating all of them. It is instructive to approach the study of Mark Twain's own fiction by ascertaining to what extent he himself succeeded in practicing each of his own "rules."

Mark Twain is one of few writers who have made the world laugh. His humor lies largely in his burlesque exaggeration and his skillful use of anticlimaxes, hoax passages, and humorous incidents. But he had a serious side also. A moralist at heart, he was a man of thought as well as laughter. He protested against sham and hypocrisy, insincerity and sentimentality, and he had a keen sense of the tragic incongruities of life. He wrote with colloquial ease and vigor. His faculty of description and his skillful use of words made him an excellent narrator and a romancer of distinction. His works are genuinely American, and the best of them have the flavor of the Mississippi.

The best edition of Clemens's work is the Definitive (35 vols., 1922). *The Writings of Mark Twain*, Collected Edition (25 vols., 1899–1910), does not include "The Mysterious Stranger" (1916) and "What Is Man?" (1917), or the *Autobiography*, which was edited by Albert Bigelow Paine (2 vols., 1924). Paine also edited *Mark Twain's Letters* (2 vols., 1917) and *Mark Twain's Notebook* (1935). A translation from the German by Clemens of *Struwelpeter* (Slovenly Peter) was first printed in 1935.

The authorized biography is by Paine (2 vols., 1912), now included in the Definitive Edition. *My Mark Twain*, by W. D. Howells, a personal friend, appeared in 1910. *The Life and Letters of W. D. Howells* (2 vols., 1928), edited by Mildred Howells, contains Clemens material.

Other accounts are Van Wyck Brooks's *The Ordeal of Mark Twain* (1920; revised edition, 1933), which leans heavily on Freudian psychology; Mary Lawton's *A Life-Time with Mark Twain* (1925); Carl Van Doren in *DAB*, IV (1930); Bernard De Voto's *Mark Twain's America* (1932); Minnie M. Brashear's excellent *Mark Twain, Son of Missouri* (1934); Edward Wagenknecht's sane and useful *Mark Twain: The Man and His Work* (1935); and Ivan Benson's *Western Years* (1939).

F. G. Meine's *Tall Tales from the Southwest* (1930) affords a good background for Clemens's humor. For general critical discussion of Clemens, see P. Carus, "Mark Twain's Philosophy," in the *Monist*, XXIII, April, 1913; John Macy, in *The Spirit of American Literature* (1913); S. P. Sherman, in *CHAL*, III (1921); Brander Matthews, "Mark Twain and the Art of Writing," in *Essays on English* (1921); Carl Van Doren, in *The American Novel* (1921); Lucy Hazard, in *The Frontier in American Literature* (1927); many papers in the *Missouri Historical Review*, 1927–30; V. L. Parrington in *Main Currents in American Thought*, III (1930); V. R. West, *Folklore in the Works of Mark Twain*, in *University of Nebraska Studies in Language, Literature, and Criticism*, No. 10 (1930); C. H. Grattan, in Macy's *American Writers on American Literature* (1931); Constance Rourke, in *American Humor* (1931); L. Lewisohn, in *Expression in America* (1932); F. G. Emberson, *Mark Twain's Vocabulary*, in *University of Missouri Studies*, June, 1935. Robert L. Ramsay and Frances G. Emberson have published *A Mark Twain Lexicon* (1938).

There is a bibliography of Mark Twain in A. B. Paine's biography, and one by Clarissa Rinaker in *CHAL*, III (1921). See also Brashear's and De Voto's works. M. DeV. Johnson issued *A Bibliography of the Works of Mark Twain* (1910; 1935), and J. K. Potter, *Samuel L. Clemens: First Editions and Values* (1932).

THE CELEBRATED JUMPING FROG OF CALAVERAS COUNTY

Originally entitled "Jim Smiley and His Jumping Frog" in the New York *Saturday Press*, Nov. 18, 1865. Clemens retells in this story an older "tall tale," possibly Negro lore, known along the Mississippi.

IN compliance with the request of a friend of mine, who wrote me from the East, I called on good-natured, garrulous old Simon Wheeler, and inquired after my friend's friend, *Leonidas W.* Smiley, as requested to do, and I hereunto append the result. I have a lurking suspicion that *Leonidas W.* Smiley is a myth; that my friend never knew such a personage; and that he only conjectured that, if I asked old Wheeler about him, it would remind him of his infamous *Jim* Smiley, and he would go to work and bore me nearly to death with some infernal reminiscence of him as long and tedious as it should be useless to me. If that was the design, it certainly succeeded.

I found Simon Wheeler dozing comfortably by the bar-room stove of the old, dilapidated tavern in the ancient mining camp of Angel's,

and I noticed that he was fat and bald-headed, and had an expression of winning gentleness and simplicity upon his tranquil countenance. He roused up and gave me good-day. I told him a friend of mine had commissioned me to make some inquiries about a cherished companion of his boyhood named *Leonidas W.* Smiley—*Rev. Leonidas W.* Smiley—a young minister of the Gospel, who he had heard was at one time a resident of Angel's Camp. I added that, if Mr. Wheeler could tell me anything about this Rev. Leonidas W. Smiley, I would feel under many obligations to him.

Simon Wheeler backed me into a corner and blockaded me there with his chair, and then sat me down and reeled off the monotonous narrative which follows this paragraph. He never smiled, he never frowned, he never changed his voice from the gentle-flowing key to which he tuned the initial sentence, he never betrayed the slightest suspicion of enthusiasm; but all through the interminable narrative there ran a vein of impressive earnestness and sincerity, which showed me plainly that, so far from his imagining that there was anything ridiculous or funny about his story, he regarded it as a really important matter, and admired its two heroes as men of transcendent genius in *finesse*. To me, the spectacle of a man drifting serenely along through such a queer yarn without ever smiling, was exquisitely absurd. As I said before, I asked him to tell me what he knew of Rev. Leonidas W. Smiley, and he replied as follows. I let him go on in his own way, and never interrupted him once:

There was a feller here once by the name of *Jim* Smiley, in the winter of '49—or may be it was the spring of '50—I don't recollect exactly, somehow, though what makes me think it was one or the other is because I remember the big flume wasn't finished when he first came to the camp; but any way, he was the curiousest man about always betting on any thing that turned up you ever see, if he could get any body to bet on the other side; and if he couldn't, he'd change sides. Any way that suited the other man would suit him—any way just so's he got a bet, *he* was satisfied. But still he was lucky, uncommon lucky; he most always come out winner. He was always ready and laying for a chance; there couldn't be no solitary thing mentioned but that feller'd offer to bet on it, and take any side you please, as I was just telling you. If there was a horse-race, you'd find him flush, or you'd find him busted at the end of it; if there was a dog-fight, he'd bet on it; if there was a cat-fight, he'd bet on it; if there was a chicken-fight, he'd bet on it; why, if there was two birds setting on a fence, he would bet you which one would fly first; or if there was a camp-meeting, he would be there reg'lar, to bet on Parson Walker, which he judged to be the best exhorter about there, and so he was, too, and a good man. If he even seen a straddle-bug start to go anywheres, he would bet you how long it would take him to get wherever he was going to, and if you took him up, he would follow that straddle-bug to Mexico but what he would find out where he was bound for and how long he was on the road. Lots of the boys here has seen that Smiley, and can tell you about him. Why, it never made no difference to *him*—he would bet on *any* thing—the dangdest feller. Parson Walker's wife laid very sick once, for a good while, and it seemed as if they warn't going to save her; but one morning he come in, and Smiley asked how she was, and he said she was considerable better—thank the Lord for his inf'nit mercy—and coming on so smart that, with the blessing of Prov'dence, she'd get well yet; and Smiley, before he thought, says, "Well, I'll risk two-and-a-half that she won't, any way."

Thish-yer Smiley had a mare—the boys called her the fifteen-minute nag, but that was only in fun, you know, because, of course, she was faster than that—and he used to win money on that horse, for all she was so slow and always had the asthma, or the distemper, or the consumption, or something of that kind. They used to give her two or three hundred yards start, and then pass her under way; but always at the fag-end of the race she'd get excited and desperate-like, and come cavorting and straddling up, and scattering her legs around limber, sometimes in the air, and sometimes out to one side amongst the fences, and kicking up m-o-r-e dust, and raising m-o-r-e racket with her coughing and sneezing and blowing her nose—and always fetch up at the stand just about a neck ahead, as near as you could cypher it down.

And he had a little small bull pup, that to look at him you'd think he wa'n't worth a cent, but to set around and look ornery, and lay for a chance to steal something. But as soon as money was up on him, he was a different dog; his under-jaw'd begin to stick out like the fo'castle of a steamboat, and his teeth would uncover, and shine savage like the furnaces. And a dog might tackle him, and bully-rag him, and bite him, and throw him over his shoulder two or three times, and Andrew Jackson—which was the name of the pup—Andrew Jackson would never let on but what *he* was satisfied, and hadn't expected nothing else—and the bets being doubled and doubled on the other side all the time, till the money was all up; and then all of a sudden he would grab that other dog jest by the j'int of his hind leg and freeze to it—not chaw, you understand, but only jest grip and hang on till they throwed up the sponge, if it was a year. Smiley always come out winner on that pup, till he harnessed a dog once that didn't have no hind legs, because they'd been sawed off by a circular saw, and when the thing had gone along far enough, and the money was all up, and he come to make a snatch for his pet holt, he saw in a minute how he'd been imposed on, and how the other dog had him in the door, so to speak, and he 'peared surprised, and then he looked sorter discouraged-like, and didn't try no more to win the fight, and so he got shucked out bad. He give Smiley a look, as much as to say his heart was broke, and it was *his* fault, for put-10 ting up a dog that hadn't no hind legs for him to take holt of, which was his main dependence in a fight, and then he limped off a piece and laid down and died. It was a good pup, was that Andrew Jackson, and would have made a name for hisself if he'd lived, for the stuff was in him, and he had genius—I know it, because he hadn't had no opportunity to speak of, and it don't stand to reason that a dog could make such a fight as he could under them circum-20 stances, if he hadn't no talent. It always makes me feel sorry when I think of that last fight of his'n, and the way it turned out.

Well, thish-yer Smiley had rat-tarriers, and chicken cocks, and tom-cats, and all them kind of things, till you couldn't rest, and you couldn't fetch nothing for him to bet on but he'd match you. He ketched a frog one day, and took him home, and said he cal'klated to edercate him; and so he never done nothing 30 for three months but set in his back yard and learn that frog to jump. And you bet he *did* learn him, too. He'd give him a little punch behind, and the next minute you'd see that frog whirling in the air like a doughnut—see him turn one summerset, or may be a couple, if he got a good start, and come down flat-footed and all right, like a cat. He got him up so in the matter of catching flies, and kept him in prac-tice so constant, that he'd nail a fly every time 40 as far as he could see him. Smiley said all a frog wanted was education, and he could do most anything—and I believe him. Why, I've seen him set Dan'l Webster down here on this floor —Dan'l Webster was the name of the frog— and sing out, "Flies, Dan'l, flies!" and quicker'n you could wink, he'd spring straight up, and snake a fly off'n the counter there, and flop down on the floor again as solid as a gob of mud, and fall to scratching the side of his head 50 with his hind foot as indifferent as if he hadn't

no idea he'd been doin' any more'n any frog might do. You never see a frog so modest and straightfor'ard as he was, for all he was so gifted. And when it come to fair and square jumping on a dead level, he could get over more ground at one straddle than any animal of his breed you ever see. Jumping on a dead level was his strong suit, you understand; and when it come to that, Smiley would ante up money on him as long as he had a red. Smiley 10 was monstrous proud of his frog, and well he might be, for fellers that had traveled and been everywheres, all said he laid over any frog that ever *they* see.

Well Smiley kept the beast in a little lattice box, and he used to fetch him down town sometimes and lay for a bet. One day a feller— a stranger in the camp, he was—come across him with his box, and says:

"What might it be that you've got in the 20 box?"

And Smiley says, sorter indifferent like, "It might be a parrot, or it might be a canary, may be, but it ain't—it's only just a frog."

And the feller took it, and looked at it care-ful, and turned it round this way and that, and says, "H'm—so 'tis. Well, what's *he* good for?"

"Well," Smiley says, easy and careless, "he's good enough for *one* thing, I should 30 judge—he can outjump any frog in Calaveras county."

The feller took the box again, and took an-other long, particular look, and give it back to Smiley, and says, very deliberate, "Well, I don't see no p'ints about that frog that's any better'n any other frog."

"May be you don't," Smiley says. "May be you understand frogs, and may be you don't understand 'em; may be you've had experi-40 ence, and may be you an't only a amature, as it were. Anyways, I've got *my* opinion, and I'll risk forty dollars he can outjump any frog in Calaveras county."

And the feller studied a minute, and then says, kinder sad like, "Well, I'm only a stran-ger here, and I an't got no frog, but if I had a frog, I'd bet you."

And then Smiley says, "That's all right— that's all right—if you'll hold my box a min-50 ute, I'll go and get you a frog." And so the feller took the box, and put up his forty dollars along with Smiley's, and set down to wait.

So he set there a good while thinking and thinking to hisself, and then he got the frog out and prized his mouth open and took a teaspoon and filled him full of quail shot—filled him pretty near up to his chin—and set him on the floor. Smiley he went to the swamp and slopped around in the mud for a long time, and finally he ketched a frog, and fetched him in, and give him to this feller, and says:

"Now, if you're ready, set him alongside of Dan'l, with his fore-paws just even with Dan'l, and I'll give the word." Then he says, "one—two—three—jump!" and him and the feller touched up the frogs from behind, and the new frog hopped off, but Dan'l give a heave, and hysted up his shoulders—so—like a Frenchman, but it want no use—couldn't budge; he was planted as solid as an anvil, and he couldn't no more stir than if he was anchored out. Smiley was a good deal surprised, and he was disgusted too, but he didn't have no idea what the matter was, of course.

The feller took the money and started away; and when he was going out of the door, he sorter jerked his thumb over his shoulders—this way—at Dan'l, and says again, very deliberate, "Well, *I* don' see no p'ints about that frog that's any better'n any other frog."

Smiley he stood scratching his head and looking down at Dan'l a long time, and at last he says, "I do wonder what in the nation that frog throw'd off for—I wonder if there ain't something the matter with him—he 'pears to look mighty baggy, somehow." And he ketched Dan'l by the nap of the neck, and lifted him up and says, "Why, blame my cats, if he don't weigh five pound!" and turned him upside down, and he belched out a double handful of shot. And then he see how it was, and he was the maddest man—he set the frog down and took out after that feller, but he never ketched him. And—

[Here Simon Wheeler heard his name called from the front yard, and got up to see what was wanted.] And turning to me as he moved away, he said: "Just set where you are, stranger, and rest easy—I an't going to be gone a second."

But, by your leave, I did not think that a continuation of the history of the enterprising vagabond *Jim* Smiley would be likely to afford me much information concerning the Rev. *Leonidas W.* Smiley, and so I started away.

At the door I met the sociable Wheeler returning, and he buttonholed me and recommenced:

"Well, thish-yer Smiley had a yaller one-eyed cow that didn't have no tail, only jest a short stump like a bannanner, and—"

"Oh! hang Smiley and his afflicted cow!" I muttered, good-naturedly, and bidding the old gentleman good-day, I departed.

1865

From THE GILDED AGE

Mark Twain said (*Autobiography*, I, 89–92) that Colonel Mulberry Sellers, the visionary Southern speculator, was not modeled on his father, as many thought, but was his mother's favorite cousin, James Lampton. "I merely put him on paper; he was not a person who could be exaggerated." The novel was dramatized in 1876, and the play had great success, with John T. Raymond in the role of Colonel Sellers.

CHAPTER VIII

[Colonel Sellers, Financial Wizard]

THE supper at Col. Sellers's was not sumptuous, in the beginning, but it improved on acquaintance. That is to say, that what Washington regarded at first sight as mere lowly potatoes, presently became awe-inspiring agricultural productions that had been reared in some ducal garden beyond the sea, under the sacred eye of the duke himself, who had sent them to Sellers; the bread was from corn which could be grown in only one favored locality in the earth and only a favored few could get it; the Rio coffee, which at first seemed execrable to the taste, took to itself an improved flavor when Washington was told to drink it slowly and not hurry what should be a lingering luxury in order to be fully appreciated—it was from the private stores of a Brazilian nobleman with an unrememberable name. The Colonel's tongue was a magician's wand that turned dried apples into figs and water into wine as easily as it could change a hovel into a palace and present poverty into imminent future riches.

Washington slept in a cold bed in a carpetless room and woke up in a palace in the morning; at least the palace lingered during the moment that he was rubbing his eyes and getting his bearings—and then it disappeared and he recognized that the Colonel's inspiring talk had been influencing his dreams. Fatigue had made him sleep late; when he entered the sitting room he noticed that the old haircloth sofa was absent; when he sat down to breakfast the Colonel tossed six or seven dollars in bills on the table, counted them over, said he was a little short and must call upon his banker; then returned the bills to his wallet with the indifferent air of a man who is used to money. The breakfast was not an improvement upon the supper, but the Colonel talked it up and transformed it into an oriental feast. Bye and bye, he said:

"I intend to look out for you, Washington, my boy. I hunted up a place for you yesterday, but I am not referring to that, now—that is a mere livelihood—mere bread and butter; but when I say I mean to look out for you I mean something very different. I mean to put things in your way that will make a mere livelihood a trifling thing. I'll put you in a way to make more money than you'll ever know what to do with. You'll be right here where I can put my hand on you when anything turns up. I've got some prodigious operations on foot; but I'm keeping quiet; mum's the word; your old hand don't go around powwowing and letting everybody see his k'yards and find out his little game. But all in good time, Washington, all in good time. You'll see. Now there's an operation in corn that looks well. Some New York men are trying to get me to go into it— buy up all the growing crops and just boss the market when they mature—ah I tell you it's a great thing. And it only costs a trifle; two millions or two and a half will do it. I haven't exactly promised yet—there's no hurry—the more indifferent I seem, you know, the more anxious those fellows will get. And then there is the hog speculation—that's bigger still. We've got quiet men at work," [he was very impressive here,] "mousing around, to get propositions out of all the farmers in the whole west and northwest for the hog crop, and other agents quietly getting propositions and terms out of all the manufactories—and don't you see, if we can get all the hogs and all the slaughter houses into our hands on the dead quiet—whew! it would take three ships to carry the money.—I've looked into the thing—calculated all the chances for and all the chances against, and though I shake my head and hesitate and keep on thinking, apparently, I've got my mind made up that if the thing can be done on a capital of six millions, that's the horse to put up money on! Why Washington—but what's the use of talking about it— any man can see that there's whole Atlantic oceans of cash in it, gulfs and bays thrown in. But there's a bigger thing than that, yet—a bigger———"

"Why Colonel, you can't want anything bigger!" said Washington, his eyes blazing. "Oh, I wish I could go into either of those speculations—I only wish I had money—I wish I wasn't cramped and kept down and fettered with poverty, and such prodigious chances lying right here in sight! Oh, it is a fearful thing to be poor. But don't throw away those things—they are so splendid and I can see how sure they are. Don't throw them away for something still better and maybe fail in it! I wouldn't, Colonel. I would stick to these. I wish father were here and were his old self again—Oh, he never in his life had such chances as these are. Colonel, you *can't* improve on these—no man can improve on them!"

A sweet, compassionate smile played about the Colonel's features, and he leaned over the table with the air of a man who is "going to show you" and do it without the least trouble:

"Why Washington, my boy, these things are nothing. They *look* large—of course they look large to a novice, but to a man who has been all his life accustomed to large operations—shaw! They're well enough to while away an idle hour with, or furnish a bit of employment that will give a trifle of idle capital a chance to earn its bread while it is waiting for something to *do*, but—now just listen a moment—just let me give you an idea of what we old veterans of commerce call 'business.' Here's the Rothschild's proposition—this is between you and me, you understand———"

Washington nodded three or four times impatiently, and his glowing eyes said, "Yes, yes—hurry—I understand———"

———"for I wouldn't have it get out for a fortune. They want me to go in with them on the sly—agent was here two weeks ago about it—go in on the sly" [voice down to an impressive whisper, now,] "and buy up a hundred and thirteen wild-cat banks in Ohio, Indiana, Kentucky, Illinois and Missouri— notes of these banks are at all sorts of discount now—average discount of the hundred and thirteen is forty-four per cent—buy them all up, you see, and then all of a sudden let the cat out of the bag! Whiz! the stock of every one of those wild-cats would spin up to a tremendous premium before you could turn a handspring—profit on the speculation not a dollar less than forty millions!" [An eloquent pause, while the marvelous vision settled into W.'s focus.] "Where's your hogs now! Why my dear innocent boy, we would just sit down on the front doorsteps and peddle banks like lucifer matches!"

Washington finally got his breath and said:

"Oh, it is perfectly wonderful! Why couldn't these things have happened in father's day? And I—it's of no use—they simply lie before my face and mock me. There is nothing for me but to stand helpless and see other people reap the astonishing harvest."

"Never mind, Washington, don't you worry. I'll fix you. There's plenty of chances. How much money have you got?"

In the presence of so many millions, Washington could not keep from blushing when he had to confess that he had but eighteen dollars in the world.

"Well, all right—don't despair. Other people have been obliged to begin with less. I have a small idea that may develop into something for us both, all in good time. Keep your money close and add to it. I'll make it breed. I've been experimenting (to pass away the time,) on a little preparation for curing sore eyes—a kind of decoction nine-tenths water and the other tenth drugs that don't cost more than a dollar a barrel; I'm still experimenting; there's one ingredient wanted yet to perfect the thing, and somehow I can't just manage to hit upon the thing that's necessary, and I don't dare talk

with a chemist, of course. But I'm progressing, and before many weeks I wager the country will ring with the fame of Beriah Sellers' Infallible Imperial Oriental Optic Liniment and Salvation for Sore Eyes—the Medical Wonder of the Age! Small bottles fifty cents, large ones a dollar. Average cost, five and seven cents for the two sizes. The first year sell, say, ten thousand bottles in Missouri, seven thousand in Iowa, three thousand in Arkansas, four thousand in Kentucky, six thousand in Illinois, and say twenty-five thousand in the rest of the country. Total, fifty-five thousand bottles; profit clear of all expenses, twenty thousand dollars at the very lowest calculation. All the capital needed is to manufacture the first two thousand bottles—say a hundred and fifty dollars—then the money would begin to flow in. The second year, sales would reach 200,000 bottles—clear profit, say, $75,000—and in the meantime the great factory would be building in St. Louis, to cost, say, $100,000. The third year we could easily sell 1,000,000 bottles in the United States and———"

"O, splendid!" said Washington. "Let's commence right away—let's———"

"———1,000,000 bottles in the United States—profit at least $350,000—and *then* it would begin to be time to turn our attention toward the *real* idea of the business."

"The *real* idea of it! Ain't $350,000 a year a pretty real———"

"Stuff! Why what an infant you are, Washington—what a guileless, short-sighted, easily-contented innocent you are, my poor little country-bred know-nothing! Would I go to all that trouble and bother for the poor crumbs a body might pick up in *this* country? Now do I look like a man who—does my history suggest that I am a man who deals in trifles, contents himself with the narrow horizon that hems in the common herd, sees no further than the end of his nose? Now *you* know that that is not me—couldn't *be* me. *You* ought to know that if I throw my time and abilities into a patent medicine, it's a patent medicine whose field of operations is the solid earth! its clients the swarming nations that inhabit it! Why what is the republic of America for an eye-water country? Lord bless you, it is nothing but a barren highway that you've got to cross to get *to* the true eye-water market! Why, Washington, in the Oriental countries people swarm like the sands of the desert; every square mile of ground upholds its thousands upon thousands of struggling human creatures—and every separate and individual devil of them's got the ophthalmia! It's as natural to them as noses are—and sin. It's born with them, it stays with them, it's all that some of them have left when they die. Three years of introductory trade in the Orient and what will be the result? Why, our headquarters would be in Constantinople and our hindquarters in Further India! Factories and warehouses in Cairo, Ispahan, Bagdad, Damascus, Jerusalem, Yedo, Peking, Bangkok, Delhi, Bombay and Calcutta! Annual income—well, God only knows how many millions and millions apiece!"

Washington was so dazed, so bewildered— his heart and his eyes had wandered so far away among the strange lands beyond the seas, and such avalanches of coin and currency had fluttered and jingled confusedly down before him, that he was now as one who has been whirling round and round for a time, and, stopping all at once, finds his surroundings still whirling and all objects a dancing chaos. However, little by little the Sellers family cooled down and crystallized into shape, and the poor room lost its glitter and resumed its poverty. Then the youth found his voice and begged Sellers to drop everything and hurry up the eye-water; and he got his eighteen dollars and tried to force it upon the Colonel— pleaded with him to take it—implored him to do it. But the Colonel would not; said he would not need the capital (in his native magnificent way he called that eighteen dollars Capital) till the eye-water was an accomplished fact. He made Washington easy in his mind, though, by promising that he would call for it just as soon as the invention was finished, and he added the glad tidings that nobody but just they two should be admitted to a share in the speculation.

When Washington left the breakfast table he could have worshiped that man. Washington was one of that kind of people whose hopes are in the very clouds one day and in the gutter the next. He walked on air, now. The Colonel was ready to take him around and introduce

him to the employment he had found for him, but Washington begged for a few moments in which to write home; with his kind of people, to ride today's new interest to death and put off yesterday's till another time, is nature itself. He ran up stairs and wrote glowingly, enthusiastically, to his mother about the hogs and the corn, the banks and the eye-water— and added a few inconsequential millions to each project. And he said that people little dreamed what a man Col. Sellers was, and that the world would open its eyes when it found out. And he closed his letter thus:

"So make yourself perfectly easy, mother— in a little while you shall have everything you want, and more. I am not likely to stint *you* in anything, I fancy. This money will not be for me, alone, but for all of us. I want all to share alike; and there is going to be far more for each than one person can spend. Break it to father cautiously—you understand the need of that—break it to him cautiously, for he has had such cruel hard fortune, and is so stricken by it that great good news might prostrate him more surely than even bad, for he is used to the bad but is grown sadly unaccustomed to the other. Tell Laura—tell all the children. And write to Clay about it if he is not with you yet; You may tell Clay that whatever I get he can freely share in—freely. He knows that that is true—there will be no need that I should swear to that to make him believe it. Good-bye—and mind what I say: Rest perfectly easy, one and all of you, for our troubles are nearly at an end."

Poor lad, he could not know that his mother would cry some loving, compassionate tears over his letter and put off the family with a synopsis of its contents which conveyed a deal of love to them but not much idea of his prospects or projects. And he never dreamed that such a joyful letter could sadden her and fill her night with sighs, and troubled thoughts, and bodings of the future, instead of filling it with peace and blessing it with restful sleep.

When the letter was done, Washington and the Colonel sallied forth, and as they walked along Washington learned what he was to be. He was to be a clerk in a real estate office. Instantly the fickle youth's dreams forsook the magic eye-water and flew back to the Tennessee Land. And the gorgeous possibilities of that great domain straightway began to occupy his imagination to such a degree that he could scarcely manage to keep even enough of his attention upon the Colonel's talk to retain the general run of what he was saying. He was glad it was a real estate office—he was a made man now, sure.

The Colonel said that General Boswell was a rich man and had a good and growing business; and that Washington's work would be light and he would get forty dollars a month and be boarded and lodged in the General's family—which was as good as ten dollars more; and even better, for he could not live as well even at the "City Hotel" as he would there, and yet the hotel charged fifteen dollars a month where a man had a good room.

General Boswell was in his office; a comfortable looking place, with plenty of outline maps hanging about the walls and in the windows, and a spectacled man was marking out another one on a long table. The office was in the principal street. The General received Washington with a kindly but reserved politeness. Washington rather liked his looks. He was about fifty years old, dignified, well preserved and well dressed. After the Colonel took his leave, the General talked a while with Washington—his talk consisting chiefly of instructions about the clerical duties of the place. He seemed satisfied as to Washington's ability to take care of the books, he was evidently a pretty fair theoretical bookkeeper, and experience would soon harden theory into practice. By and by dinnertime came, and the two walked to the General's house; and now Washington noticed an instinct in himself that moved him to keep not in the General's rear, exactly, but yet not at his side—somehow the old gentleman's dignity and reserve did not inspire familiarity.

1873

From LIFE ON THE MISSISSIPPI

CHAPTER VI

A Cub-Pilot's Experience

WHAT with lying on the rocks four days at Louisville, and some other delays, the poor old *Paul Jones* fooled away about two weeks in making the voyage from Cincinnati to New Orleans. This gave me a chance to get acquainted with one of the pilots, and he taught me how to steer the boat, and thus made the fascination of river life more potent than ever for me.

It also gave me a chance to get acquainted with a youth who had taken deck passage—more's the pity; for he easily borrowed six dollars of me on a promise to return to the boat and pay it back to me the day after we should arrive. But he probably died or forgot, for he never came. It was doubtless the former, since he had said his parents were wealthy, and he only traveled deck passage because it was cooler.

I soon discovered two things. One was that a vessel would not be likely to sail for the mouth of the Amazon under ten or twelve years; and the other was that the nine or ten dollars still left in my pocket would not suffice for so impossible an exploration as I had planned, even if I could afford to wait for a ship. Therefore it followed that I must contrive a new career. The *Paul Jones* was now bound for St. Louis. I planned a siege against my pilot, and at the end of three hard days he surrendered. He agreed to teach me the Mississippi River from New Orleans to St. Louis for five hundred dollars, payable out of the first wages I should receive after graduating. I entered upon the small enterprise of "learning" twelve or thirteen hundred miles of the great Mississippi River with the easy confidence of my time of life. If I had really known what I was about to require of my faculties, I should not have had the courage to begin. I supposed that all a pilot had to do was to keep his boat in the river, and I did not consider that that could be much of a trick, since it was so wide.

The boat backed out from New Orleans at four in the afternoon, and it was "our watch" until eight. Mr. Bixby, my chief, "straightened her up," plowed her along past the sterns of the other boats that lay at the Levee, and then said, "Here, take her; shave those steamships as close as you'd peel an apple." I took the wheel, and my heartbeat fluttered up into the hundreds; for it seemed to me that we were about to scrape the side off every ship in the line, we were so close. I held my breath and began to claw the boat away from the danger; and I had my own opinion of the pilot who had known no better than to get us into such peril, but I was too wise to express it. In half a minute I had a wide margin of safety intervening between the *Paul Jones* and the ships; and within ten seconds more I was set aside in disgrace, and Mr. Bixby was going into danger again and flaying me alive with abuse of my cowardice. I was stung, but I was obliged to admire the easy confidence with which my chief loafed from side to side of his wheel, and trimmed the ships so closely that disaster seemed ceaselessly imminent. When he had cooled a little he told me that the easy water was close ashore and the current outside, and therefore we must hug the bank, upstream, to get the benefit of the former, and stay well out, downstream, to take advantage of the latter. In my own mind I resolved to be a downstream pilot and leave the upstreaming to people dead to prudence.

Now and then Mr. Bixby called my attention to certain things. Said he, "This is Six-Mile Point." I assented. It was pleasant enough information, but I could not see the bearing of it. I was not conscious that it was a matter of any interest to me. Another time he said, "This is Nine-Mile Point." Later he said, "This is Twelve-Mile Point." They were all about level with the water's edge; they all looked about alike to me; they were monotonously unpicturesque. I hoped Mr. Bixby would change the subject. But no; he would crowd up around a point, hugging the shore with affection, and then say: "The slack water ends here, abreast this bunch of China trees; now we cross over." So he crossed over. He gave me the wheel once or twice, but I had no luck. I either came near chipping off the edge of a sugar-plantation, or I yawed too far from shore, and so dropped back into disgrace again and got abused.

The watch was ended at last, and we took supper and went to bed. At midnight the glare of a lantern shone in my eyes, and the night watchman said:

"Come, turn out!"

And then he left. I could not understand this extraordinary procedure; so I presently gave up trying to, and dozed off to sleep. Pretty soon the watchman was back again, and this time he was gruff. I was annoyed. I said:

"What do you want to come bothering around here in the middle of the night for? Now, as like as not, I'll not get to sleep again tonight."

The watchman said:

"Well, if this ain't good, I'm blessed."

The "off-watch" was just turning in, and I heard some brutal laughter from them, and such remarks as "Hello, watchman! ain't the new cub turned out yet? He's delicate, likely. Give him some sugar in a rag, and send for the chambermaid to sing 'Rock-a-by Baby,' to him."

About this time Mr. Bixby appeared on the scene. Something like a minute later I was climbing the pilot-house steps with some of my clothes on and the rest in my arms. Mr. Bixby was close behind, commenting. Here was something fresh—this thing of getting up in the middle of the night to go to work. It was a detail in piloting that had never occurred to me at all. I knew that boats ran all night, but somehow I had never happened to reflect that somebody had to get out of a warm bed to run them. I began to fear that piloting was not quite so romantic as I had imagined it was; there was something very real and worklike about this new phase of it.

It was a rather dingy night, although a fair number of stars were out. The big mate was at the wheel, and he had the old tub pointed at a star and was holding her straight up the middle of the river. The shores on either hand were not much more than half a mile apart, but they seemed wonderfully far away and ever so vague and indistinct. The mate said:

"We've got to land at Jones's plantation, sir."

The vengeful spirit in me exulted. I said to myself, "I wish you joy of your job, Mr. Bixby; you'll have a good time finding Mr. Jones's plantation such a night as this; and I hope you never *will* find it as long as you live."

Mr. Bixby said to the mate:

"Upper end of the plantation, or the lower?"

"Upper."

"I can't do it. The stumps there are out of water at this stage. It's no great distance to the lower, and you'll have to get along with that."

"All right, sir. If Jones don't like it, he'll have to lump it, I reckon."

And then the mate left. My exultation began to cool and my wonder to come up. Here was a man who not only proposed to find this plantation on such a night, but to find either end of it you preferred. I dreadfully wanted to ask a question, but I was carrying about as many short answers as my cargo-room would admit of, so I held my peace. All I desired to ask Mr. Bixby was the simple question whether he was ass enough to really imagine he was going to find that plantation on a night when all plantations were exactly alike and all of the same color. But I held in. I used to have fine inspirations of prudence in those days.

Mr. Bixby made for the shore and soon was scraping it, just the same as if it had been daylight. And not only that, but singing:

"Father in heaven, the day is declining," etc. It seemed to me that I had put my life in the keeping of a peculiarly reckless outcast. Presently he turned on me and said:

"What's the name of the first point above New Orleans?"

I was gratified to be able to answer promptly, and I did. I said I didn't know.

"Don't *know?*"

This manner jolted me. I was down at the foot again, in a moment. But I had to say just what I had said before.

"Well, you're a smart one!" said Mr. Bixby. "What's the name of the *next* point?"

Once more I didn't know.

"Well, this beats anything. Tell me the name of *any* point or place I told you."

I studied awhile and decided that I couldn't.

"Look here! What do you start out from, above Twelve-Mile Point, to cross over?"

"I—I—don't know."

"You—you—don't know?" mimicking my drawling manner of speech. "What *do* you know?"

"I—I—nothing, for certain."

"By the great Caesar's ghost, I believe you! You're the stupidest dunderhead I ever saw or ever heard of, so help me Moses! The idea of *you* being a pilot—*you!* Why, you don't know enough to pilot a cow down a lane."

Oh, but his wrath was up! He was a nervous man, and he shuffled from one side of his wheel to the other as if the floor was hot. He would boil awhile to himself, and then overflow and scald me again.

"Look here! What do you suppose I told you the names of those points for?"

I tremblingly considered a moment, and then the devil of temptation provoked me to say:

"Well to—to—be entertaining, I thought."

This was a red rag to the bull. He raged and stormed so (he was crossing the river at the time) that I judged it made him blind, because he ran over the steering-oar of a trading scow. Of course the traders sent up a volley of red-hot profanity. Never was a man so grateful as Mr. Bixby was; because he was brimful, and here were subjects who could *talk back.* He threw open a window, thrust his head out, and such an irruption followed as I never had heard before. The fainter and farther away the scowmen's curses drifted, the higher Mr. Bixby lifted his voice and the weightier his adjectives grew. When he closed the window he was empty. You could have drawn a seine through his system and not caught curses enough to disturb your mother with. Presently he said to me in the gentlest way:

"My boy, you must get a little memorandum-book; and every time I tell you a thing, put it down right away. There's only one way to be a pilot, and that is to get this entire river by heart. You have to know it just like A B C."

That was a dismal revelation to me; for my memory was never loaded with anything but blank cartridges. However, I did not feel discouraged long. I judged that it was best to make some allowances, for doubtless Mr. Bixby was "stretching." Presently he pulled a rope and struck a few strokes on the big bell. The stars were all gone now, and the night was as black as ink. I could hear the wheels churn along the bank, but I was not entirely certain that I could see the shore. The voice of the invisible watchman called up from the hurricane-deck:

"What's this, sir?"

"Jones's plantation."

I said to myself, "I wish I might venture to offer a small bet that it isn't." But I did not chirp. I only waited to see. Mr. Bixby handled the engine-bells, and in due time the boat's nose came to the land, a torch glowed from the forecastle, a man skipped ashore, a darky's voice on the bank said: "Gimme de k'yarpet-bag, Mass' Jones," and the next moment we were standing up the river again, all serene. I reflected deeply awhile, and then said—but not aloud—"Well, the find of that plantation was the luckiest accident that ever happened; but it couldn't happen again in a hundred years." And I fully believed it *was* an accident, too.

By the time we had gone seven or eight hundred miles up the river, I had learned to be a tolerably plucky upstream steersman, in daylight; and before we reached St. Louis I had made a trifle of progress in night work, but only a trifle. I had a notebook that fairly bristled with the names of towns, "points," bars, islands, bends, reaches, etc.; but the information was to be found only in the note-book—none of it was in my head. It made my heart ache to think I had only got half of the river set down; for as our watch was four hours off and four hours on, day and night, there was a long four-hour gap in my book for every time I had slept since the voyage began.

My chief was presently hired to go on a big New Orleans boat, and I packed my satchel and went with him. She was a grand affair. When I stood in her pilot-house I was so far above the water that I seemed perched on a mountain; and her decks stretched so far away, fore and aft, below me, that I wondered how I could ever have considered the little *Paul Jones* a large craft. There were other differences, too. The *Paul Jones's* pilot-house was a cheap, dingy, battered rattletrap, cramped for room; but here was a sumptuous glass temple; room enough to have a dance in; showy red and gold window-curtains; an imposing sofa; leather cushions and a back to the high bench where visiting pilots sit, to spin yarns and "look at the river"; bright, fanciful "cuspidores," instead of a broad wooden box filled with sawdust; nice new oilcloth on the floor; a hospitable big stove for winter; a wheel as high as my head, costly with inlaid work; a wire tiller-rope; bright brass knobs for the bells; and a tidy, white-aproned, black "texas-tender," to bring up tarts and ices and coffee during mid-watch, day and night. Now this was "something like"; and so I began to take heart once more to believe that piloting was a romantic sort of occupation after all. The moment we were under way I began to prowl about the great steamer and fill myself with joy. She was as clean and as dainty as a drawing-room; when I looked down her long, gilded saloon, it was like gazing through a splendid tunnel; she had an oil-picture, by some gifted sign-painter, on every stateroom door; she glittered with no end of prism-fringed chandeliers; the clerk's office was elegant, the bar was marvelous, and the barkeeper had been barbered and upholstered at incredible cost. The boiler-deck (*i.e.*, the second story of the boat, so to speak) was as spacious as a church, it seemed to me; so with the forecastle; and there was no pitiful handful of deck-hands, firemen, and roustabouts down there, but a whole battalion of men. The fires were fiercely glaring from a long row of furnaces, and over them were eight huge boilers! This was unutterable pomp. The mighty engines —but enough of this. I had never felt so fine before. And when I found that the regiment of natty servants respectfully "sir'd" me, my satisfaction was complete.

CHAPTER VII

A Daring Deed

WHEN I returned to the pilot-house St. Louis was gone, and I was lost. Here was a piece of river which was all down in my book, but I could make neither head nor tail of it; you understand, it was turned around. I had seen it when coming upstream, but I had never faced about to see how it looked when it was behind me. My heart broke again, for it was plain that I had got to learn this troublesome river both ways.

The pilot-house was full of pilots, going down to "look at the river." What is called the "upper river" (the two hundred miles between St. Louis and Cairo, where the Ohio comes in) was low; and the Mississippi changes its channel so constantly that the pilots used to always find it necessary to run down to Cairo to take a fresh look, when their boats were to lie in port a week; that is, when the water was at a low stage. A deal of this "looking at the river" was done by poor fellows who seldom had a berth, and whose only hope of getting one lay in their being always freshly posted and therefore ready to drop into the shoes of some reputable pilot, for a single trip, on account of such pilot's sudden illness, or some other necessity. And a good many of them constantly ran up and down inspecting the river, not because they ever really hoped to get a berth, but because (they being guests of the boat) it was cheaper to "look at the river" than stay ashore and pay board. In time these fellows grew dainty in their tastes, and only infested boats that had an established reputation for setting good tables. All visiting pilots were useful, for they were always ready and willing, winter or summer, night or day, to go out in the yawl and help buoy the channel or assist the boat's pilot in any way they could. They were likewise welcome because all pilots are tireless talkers, when gathered together, and as they talk only about the river they are always understood and are always interesting. Your true pilot cares nothing about anything on earth but the river, and his pride in his occupation surpasses the pride of kings.

We had a fine company of these river inspectors along this trip. There were eight or ten, and there was abundance of room for them in our great pilot-house. Two or three of them wore polished silk hats, elaborate shirt-fronts, diamond breastpins, kid gloves, and patent-leather boots. They were choice in their English, and bore themselves with a dignity proper to men of solid means and prodigious reputation as pilots. The others were more or less loosely clad, and wore upon their heads tall felt cones that were suggestive of the days of the Commonwealth.

I was a cipher in this august company, and felt subdued, not to say torpid. I was not even of sufficient consequence to assist at the wheel when it was necessary to put the tiller hard down in a hurry; the guest that stood nearest did that when occasion required—and this was pretty much all the time, because of the crookedness of the channel and the scant water. I stood in a corner; and the talk I listened to took the hope all out of me. One visitor said to another:

"Jim, how did you run Plum Point, coming up?"

"It was in the night, there, and I ran it the way one of the boys on the *Diana* told me; started out about fifty yards above the woodpile on the false point, and held on the cabin under Plum Point till I raised the reef—quarter less twain—then straightened up for the middle bar till I got well abreast the old one-limbed cottonwood in the bend, then got my stern on the cottonwood, and head on the low place above the point, and came through a-booming—nine and a half."

"Pretty square crossing, ain't it?"

"Yes, but the upper bar's working down fast."

Another pilot spoke up and said:

"I had better water than that, and ran it lower down; started out from the false point —mark twain—raised the second reef abreast the big snag in the bend, and had quarter less twain."

One of the gorgeous ones remarked:

"I don't want to find fault with your leadsmen, but that's a good deal of water for Plum Point, it seems to me."

There was an approving nod all around as this quiet snub dropped on the boaster and "settled" him. And so they went on talk-talk-talking. Meantime, the thing that was running in my mind was, "Now, if my ears hear aright, I have not only to get the names of all the towns and islands and bends, and so on, by heart, but I must even get up a personal acquaintanceship with every old snag and one-limbed cottonwood and obscure woodpile that ornaments the banks of this river for twelve hundred miles; and more than that, I must actually know where these things are in the dark, unless these guests are gifted with eyes that can pierce through two miles of solid blackness. I wish the piloting business was in Jericho and I had never thought of it."

At dusk, Mr. Bixby tapped the big bell three times (the signal to land), and the captain emerged from his drawing-room in the forward end of the "texas," and looked up inquiringly. Mr. Bixby said:

"We will lay up here all night, captain."

"Very well, sir."

That was all. The boat came to shore and was tied up for the night. It seemed to me a fine thing that the pilot could do as he pleased, without asking so grand a captain's permission. I took my supper and went immediately to bed, discouraged by my day's observations and experiences. My late voyage's note-booking was but a confusion of meaningless names. It had tangled me all up in a knot every time I had looked at it in the daytime. I now hoped for respite in sleep; but no, it reveled all through my head till sunrise again, a frantic and tireless nightmare.

Next morning I felt pretty rusty and low-spirited. We went booming along, taking a good many chances, for we were anxious to "get out of the river" (as getting on to Cairo was called) before night should overtake us. But Mr. Bixby's partner, the other pilot, presently grounded the boat, and we lost so much time getting her off that it was plain the darkness would overtake us a good long way above the mouth. This was a great misfortune, especially to certain of our visiting pilots, whose boats would have to wait for their return, no matter how long that might be. It sobered the pilot-house talk a good deal. Coming upstream, pilots did not mind low water or any kind of darkness; nothing stopped them but fog. But downstream work was different; a boat was too nearly helpless, with a stiff current pushing behind her; so it was not customary to run downstream at night in low water.

There seemed to be one small hope, however. If we could get through the intricate and dangerous Hat Island crossing before night, we could venture the rest, for we would have plainer sailing and better water. But it would be insanity to attempt Hat Island at night. So there was a good deal of looking at watches all the rest of the day, and a constant ciphering upon the speed we were making; Hat Island was the eternal subject; sometimes hope was high and sometimes we were delayed in a bad crossing, and down it went again. For hours all hands lay under the burden of this suppressed excitement; it was even communicated to me, and I got to feeling so solicitous about Hat Island, and under such an awful pressure of responsibility, that I wished I might have five minutes on shore to draw a good, full, relieving breath, and start over again. We were standing no regular watches. Each of our pilots ran such portions of the river as he had run when coming upstream, because of his greater familiarity with it; but both remained in the pilot-house constantly.

An hour before sunset Mr. Bixby took the wheel, and Mr. W. stepped aside. For the next thirty minutes every man held his watch in his hand and was restless, silent, and uneasy. At last somebody said, with a doomful sigh:

"Well, yonder's Hat Island—and we can't make it."

All the watches closed with a snap, everybody sighed and muttered something about its being "too bad, too bad—ah, if we could only have got here half an hour sooner!" and the place was thick with the atmosphere of disappointment. Some started to go out, but loitered, hearing no bell-tap to land. The sun dipped behind the horizon, the boat went on. Inquiring looks passed from one guest to another; and one who had his hand on the door-knob and had turned it, waited, then presently took away his hand and let the knob turn back again. We bore steadily down the bend. More looks were exchanged, and nods of surprised admiration—but no words. Insensibly the men drew together behind Mr. Bixby, as the sky darkened and one or two dim stars came out. The dead silence and sense of waiting became oppressive. Mr. Bixby pulled the cord, and two deep, mellow notes from the big bell floated off on the night. The watchman's voice followed, from the hurricane deck:

"Labboard lead, there! Stabboard lead!"

The cries of the leadsmen began to rise out

of the distance, and were gruffly repeated by the word-passers on the hurricane deck.

"M-a-r-k three! M-a-r-k three! Quarter-less-three! Half twain! Quarter twain! M-a-r-k twain! Quarter-les——"

Mr. Bixby pulled two bell-ropes, and was answered by faint jinglings far below in the engine-room, and our speed slackened. The steam began to whistle through the gauge-cocks. The cries of the leadsmen went on—10 and it is a weird sound, always, in the night. Every pilot in the lot was watching now, with fixed eyes, and talking under his breath. Nobody was calm and easy but Mr. Bixby. He would put his wheel down and stand on a spoke, and as the steamer swung into her (to me) utterly invisible marks—for we seemed to be in the midst of a wide and gloomy sea—he would meet and fasten her there. Out of the murmur of half-audible talk, one caught a co-20 herent sentence now and then—such as:

"There; she's over the first reef all right!"

After a pause, another subdued voice:

"Her stern's coming down just exactly right, by George!"

"Now she's in the marks; over she goes!"

Somebody else muttered:

"Oh, it was done beautiful—beautiful!"

Now the engines were stopped altogether, and we drifted with the current. Not that I 30 could see the boat drift, for I could not, the stars being all gone by this time. The drifting was the dismalest work; it held one's heart still. Presently I discovered a blacker gloom than that which surrounded us. It was the head of the island. We were closing right down upon it. We entered its deeper shadow, and so imminent seemed the peril that I was likely to suffocate; and I had the strongest impulse to do something, anything, to save the vessel. But 40 still Mr. Bixby stood by his wheel, silent, intent as a cat, and all the pilots stood shoulder to shoulder at his back.

"She'll not make it!" somebody whispered.

The water grew shoaler and shoaler, by the leadsmen's cries, till it was down to:

"Eight-and-a-half! E-i-g-h-t feet! E-i-g-h-t feet!"

"Seven-and——"

Mr. Bixby said warningly through his speak-50 ing tube to the engineer:

"Stand by, now!"

"Ay, ay, sir!"

"Seven-and-a-half! Seven feet! Six-and——"

We touched bottom! Instantly Mr. Bixby set a lot of bells ringing, shouted through the tube, "Now, let her have it—every ounce you've got!" Then to his partner, "Put her hard down! snatch her! snatch her!" The boat rasped and ground her way through the sand, hung upon the apex of disaster a single tremendous instant, and then over she went! And such a shout as went up at Mr. Bixby's back never loosened the roof of a pilot-house before!

There was no more trouble after that. Mr. Bixby was a hero that night; and it was some little time, too, before his exploit ceased to be talked about by the river men.

Fully to realize the marvelous precision required in laying the great steamer in her marks in that murky waste of water, one should know that not only must she pick her intricate way through snags and blind reefs, and then shave the head of the island so closely as to brush the overhanging foliage with her stern, but at one place she must pass almost within arm's reach of a sunken and invisible wreck that would snatch the hull timbers from under her if she should strike it, and destroy a quarter million dollars' worth of steamboat and cargo in five minutes, and maybe a hundred and fifty human lives into the bargain.

The last remark I heard that night was a compliment to Mr. Bixby uttered in soliloquy and with unction by one of our guests. He said:

"By the Shadow of Death, but he's a lightning pilot!"

1875

CHAPTER VIII
Perplexing Lessons

At the end of what seemed a tedious while, I had managed to pack my head full of islands, towns, bars, "points," and bends; and a curiously inanimate mass of lumber it was, too. However, inasmuch as I could shut my eyes and reel off a good long string of these names without leaving out more than ten miles of river in every fifty, I began to feel that I could take a boat down to New Orleans if I could make her skip those little gaps. But of course my complacency could hardly get start enough to lift my nose a trifle into the air, before Mr. Bixby would think of something to fetch it down again. One day he turned on me suddenly with this settler:

"What is the shape of Walnut Bend?"

He might as well have asked me my grandmother's opinion of protoplasm. I reflected respectfully, and then said I didn't know it had any particular shape. My gun-powdery chief went off with a bang, of course, and then went on loading and firing until he was out of adjectives.

I had learned long ago that he only carried just so many rounds of ammunition, and was sure to subside into a very placable and even remorseful old smoothbore as soon as they were all gone. That word "old" is merely affectionate; he was not more than thirty-four. I waited. By and by he said:

"My boy, you've got to know the *shape* of the river perfectly. It is all there is left to steer by on a very dark night. Everything else is blotted out and gone. But mind you, it hasn't the same shape in the night that it has in the daytime."

"How on earth am I ever going to learn it, then?"

"How do you follow a hall at home in the dark? Because you know the shape of it. You can't see it."

"Do you mean to say that I've got to know all the million trifling variations of shape in the banks of this interminable river as well as I know the shape of the front hall at home?"

"On my honor, you've got to know them *better* than any man ever did know the shapes of the halls in his own house."

"I wish I was dead!"

"Now I don't want to discourage you, but—"

"Well, pile it on me; I might as well have it now as another time."

"You see, this has got to be learned; there isn't any getting around it. A clear starlight night throws such heavy shadows that, if you didn't know the shape of a shore perfectly, you would claw away from every bunch of timber, because you would take the black shadow of it for a solid cape; and you see you would be getting scared to death every fifteen minutes by the watch. You would be fifty yards from shore all the time when you ought to be within fifty feet of it. You can't see a snag in one of those shadows, but you know exactly where it is, and the shape of the river tells you when you are coming to it. Then there's your pitch-dark night; the river is a very different shape on a pitch-dark night from what it is on a starlight night. All shores seem to be straight lines, then, and mighty dim ones, too; and you'd *run* them for straight lines, only you know better. You boldly drive your boat right into what seems to be a solid, straight wall (you knowing very well that in reality there is a curve there), and that wall falls back and makes way for you. Then there's your gray mist. You take a night when there's one of these grisly, drizzly, gray mists, and then there isn't *any* particular shape to a shore. A gray mist would tangle the head of the oldest man that ever lived. Well, then, different kinds of *moonlight* change the shape of the river in different ways. You see——"

"Oh, don't say any more, please! Have I got to learn the shape of the river according to all these five hundred thousand different ways? If I tried to carry all that cargo in my head it would make me stoop-shouldered."

"*No!* you only learn *the* shape of the river; and you learn it with such absolute certainty that you can always steer by the shape that's *in your head*, and never mind the one that's before your eyes."

"Very well, I'll try it; but, after I have learned it, can I depend on it? Will it keep the same form and not go fooling around?"

Before Mr. Bixby could answer, Mr. W. came in to take the watch, and he said:

"Bixby, you'll have to look out for President's Island, and all that country clear away up above the Old Hen and Chickens. The banks are caving and the shape of the shores changing like everything. Why, you wouldn't know the point above 40. You can go up inside the old sycamore snag, now."

So that question was answered. Here were leagues of shore changing shape. My spirits were down in the mud again. Two things seemed pretty apparent to me. One was, that in order to be a pilot a man had got to learn more than any one man ought to be allowed to know; and the other was, that he must learn it all over again in a different way every twenty-four hours.

That night we had the watch until twelve. Now it was an ancient river custom for the two pilots to chat a bit when the watch changed. While the relieving pilot put on his gloves and lit his cigar, his partner, the retiring pilot, would say something like this:

"I judge the upper bar is making down a little at Hale's Point; had quarter twain with the lower lead and mark twain with the other."

"Yes, I thought it was making down a little, last trip. Meet any boats?"

"Met one abreast the head of 21, but she was away over hugging the bar, and I couldn't make her out entirely. I took her for the *Sunny South*—hadn't any skylights forward of the chimneys."

And so on. And as the relieving pilot took the wheel his partner would mention that we were in such-and-such a bend, and say we were abreast of such-and-such a man's woodyard or plantation. This was courtesy; I supposed it was *necessity*. But Mr. W. came on watch full twelve minutes late on this particular night—a tremendous breach of etiquette; in fact, it is the unpardonable sin among pilots. So Mr. Bixby gave him no greeting whatever, but simply surrendered the wheel and marched out of the pilot-house without a word. I was appalled; it was a villainous night for blackness, we were in a particularly wide and blind part of the river, where there was no shape or substance to anything, and it seemed incredible that Mr. Bixby should have left that poor fellow to kill the boat, trying to find out where he was. But I resolved that I would stand by him anyway. He should find that he was not wholly friendless. So I stood around, and waited to be asked where we were. But Mr. W. plunged on serenely through the solid firmament of black cats that stood for an atmosphere, and never opened his mouth. "Here is a proud devil!" thought I; "here is a limb of Satan that would rather send us all to destruction than put himself under obligations to me, because I am not yet one of the salt of the earth and privileged to snub captains and lord it over everything dead and alive in a steamboat." I presently climbed up on the bench; I did not think it was safe to go to sleep while this lunatic was on watch.

However, I must have gone to sleep in the course of time, because the next thing I was aware of was the fact that day was breaking, Mr. W. gone, and Mr. Bixby at the wheel again. So it was four o'clock and all well—but me; I felt like a skinful of dry bones, and all of them trying to ache at once.

Mr. Bixby asked me what I had stayed up there for. I confessed that it was to do Mr. W. a benevolence—tell him where he was. It took five minutes for the entire preposterousness of the thing to filter into Mr. Bixby's system, and then I judge it filled him nearly up to the chin; because he paid me a compliment—and not much of a one either. He said:

"Well, taking you by and large, you do seem to be more different kinds of an ass than any creature I ever saw before. What did you suppose he wanted to know for?"

I said I thought it might be a convenience to him.

"Convenience! D——nation! Didn't I tell you that a man's got to know the river in the night the same as he'd know his own front hall?"

"Well, I can follow the front hall in the dark if I know it *is* the front hall; but suppose you set me down in the middle of it in the dark and not tell me which hall it is; how am *I* to know?"

"Well, you've *got* to, on the river!"

"All right. Then I'm glad I never said anything to Mr. W."

"I should say so! Why, he'd have slammed you through the window and utterly ruined a hundred dollars' worth of window-sash and stuff."

I was glad this damage had been saved, for it would have made me unpopular with the owners. They always hated anybody who had the name of being careless and injuring things.

I went to work now to learn the shape of the river; and of all the eluding and ungraspable objects that ever I tried to get mind or hands on, that was the chief. I would fasten my eyes upon a sharp, wooded point that projected far into the river some miles ahead of me, and go to laboriously photographing its shape upon my brain; and just as I was beginning to succeed to my satisfaction, we would draw up toward it and the exasperating thing would begin to melt away and fold back into the bank! If there had been a conspicuous dead tree standing upon the very point of the cape, I would find that tree inconspicuously merged into the general forest, and occupying the middle of a straight shore, when I got abreast of it! No prominent hill would stick to its shape long enough for me to make up my mind what its form really was, but it was as dissolving and changeful as if it had been a mountain of butter in the hottest corner of the tropics. Nothing ever had the same shape when I was coming downstream that it had borne when I went up. I mentioned these little difficulties to Mr. Bixby. He said:

"That's the very main virtue of the thing. If the shapes didn't change every three seconds they wouldn't be of any use. Take this place where we are now, for instance. As long as that hill over yonder is only one hill, I can boom right along the way I'm going; but the moment it splits at the top and forms a V, I know I've got to scratch to starboard in a hurry, or I'll bang this boat's brains out against a rock; and then the moment one of the prongs of the V swings behind the other, I've got to waltz to larboard again, or I'll have a misunderstanding with a snag that would snatch the keelson out of this steamboat as neatly as if it were a sliver in your hand. If that hill didn't change its shape on bad nights there would be an awful steamboat graveyard around here inside of a year."

It was plain that I had got to learn the shape of the river in all the different ways that could be thought of—upside down, wrong end first, inside out, fore-and-aft, and "thort-

ships"—and then know what to do on gray nights when it hadn't any shape at all. So I set about it. In the course of time I began to get the best of this knotty lesson, and my self-complacency moved to the front once more. Mr. Bixby was all fixed, and ready to start it to the rear again. He opened on me after this fashion:

"How much water did we have in the middle crossing at Hole-in-the-Wall, trip before last?"

I considered this an outrage. I said:

"Every trip, down and up, the leadsmen are singing through that tangled place for three-quarters of an hour on a stretch. How do you reckon I can remember such a mess as that?"

"My boy, you've got to remember it. You've got to remember the exact spot and the exact marks the boat lay in when we had the shoalest water, in every one of the five hundred shoal places between St. Louis and New Orleans; and you mustn't get the shoal soundings and marks of one trip mixed up with the shoal soundings and marks of another, either, for they're not often twice alike. You must keep them separate."

When I came to myself again, I said:

"When I get so that I can do that, I'll be able to raise the dead, and then I won't have to pilot a steamboat to make a living. I want to retire from this business. I want a slush-bucket and a brush; I'm only fit for a roust-about. I haven't got brains enough to be a pilot; and if I had I wouldn't have strength enough to carry them around, unless I went on crutches."

"Now drop that! When I say I'll learn a man the river, I mean it. And you can depend on it, I'll learn him or kill him."

1883

WILLIAM DEAN HOWELLS was a leader in championing realism during the latter part of the nineteenth century. Like Jane Austen, whom he greatly admired, he preferred the realism of the commonplace and believed that fiction should deal with ordinary persons, everyday happenings, and well-known scenes. He disapproved of the romantic, the sensational, and the exaggerated, and desired the actual rather than an idealized presentation of life.

Howells was born on March 1, 1837, at Martin's Ferry, Ohio. His grandfather on his paternal side was of Welsh-Quaker strain and his mother of Pennsylvania-German and Irish. His father, a country printer and druggist and a follower of Swedenborg, had tried with no great success to make a living in various places. The family moved to Hamilton, Ohio, in 1840, and later to Dayton. Periods of residence in Columbus, Ashtabula, and Jefferson followed. At one time the family lived in a log cabin on the Little Miami River. At the age of nine, Howells began to set type for his father. He had little of the conventional schooling, and no college experience, but was largely self-educated. This was not an insurmountable handicap for him, however, for, as he tells in *My Literary Passions* (1895), he read extensively in the classics and knew Chaucer, Shakespeare, Cervantes, Pope, Goldsmith, Macaulay, Dickens, Thackeray, Tennyson, Longfellow, and Hawthorne. He also mastered a number of languages, Latin, Greek, Spanish, French, Italian, and German.

In 1851 Howells was a compositor and reporter in Columbus. The next year he worked on a Cincinnati newspaper, but left it to return to Columbus as the editor of the *Ohio State Journal*. In these years he won recognition for his literary promise. Poetry was his first ambition, and he wrote it in the eighteenth-century tradition of Pope. He contributed verse to the *Atlantic Monthly* in 1860 and with J. J. Piatt published *Poems of Two Friends*. That same year he made a trip to Boston, where he became acquainted with Lowell, Emerson, Holmes, and Hawthorne. As a journalist in Columbus he was called upon to write a campaign life of Lincoln, published in 1860. It was so well received that he was given the political appointment of Consul to Venice, 1861–65. In Venice he studied the Italian language and read European literature extensively. He still wrote verses for the Boston newspapers.

In 1862 Howells married Elinor Mead of Brattleboro, Vermont, whom he had met in Columbus. For a few months in 1865, he acted as editorial assistant on the *Nation* and then went to the *Atlantic* under James T. Fields. His experiences in Europe furnished him the material for *Venetian Life* and *Italian Journeys*, published in 1866 and 1867. At thirty-five he was made editor in chief of the *Atlantic*, a connection he retained until 1881. Among the contributors he enlisted as editor were the contrasting literary figures, Mark Twain and Henry James. He wrote many essays for the magazine himself, and in these was apparent a growing tendency toward realism. His book, *Their Wedding Journey*, partly fiction and partly a travel book, was published in 1872. Thenceforward many novels and essays and a few farces followed, such as *A Foregone Conclusion* (1875), *The Lady of the Aroostook* (1879), *Dr. Breen's Practice* (1881), and *A Modern Instance* (1881). The last-named, *The Rise of Silas Lapham* (1884), and *A Hazard of New Fortunes* (1890) are usually thought to be his strongest novels.

In May, 1885, he moved to New York City, where he was at first on the staff of the *Century Magazine* and then of *Harper's*, for which he conducted "The Editor's Study," 1886–91. He was editor of the *Cosmopolitan* for about half a year, 1891–92. He renewed his connection with *Harper's* in 1900 and for twenty years conducted "The Editor's Easy Chair." A keen sense of political injustice, enhanced by the reading of Tolstoi and a realization of the failings of democracy, developed within him. His growing socialism is apparent in such books as *The Quality of Mercy* (1892), *The World of Chance* (1893), and *A Traveler in Altruria* (1894), a romance depicting an Utopian age of social equality and happiness. *The Eye of the Needle*, a sequel to the latter book, appeared in 1907. Howells was made president of the American Academy of Arts and Letters. He was given honorary degrees by Yale, Columbia, Harvard, Princeton, and Oxford. He died, May 11, 1920, but not before he had seen realism triumph far beyond his conception of it.

Howells's long series of works reflect with meticulous accuracy phases of American life during the years from 1870 to 1920. His was a very gentle realism, however, for he omitted the rougher aspects of existence. There is neither misery nor despair in his books, and he turned away from the sordid and neurotic that have so attracted a later generation. There are no breaches of decorum, no crimes or violence in his pages, for though he was regarded as a radical, he was fastidious about the material he used. A democrat in provenience and socialistic in his sympathies, he was an aristocrat in matters of taste. He wrote for parlor reading in a light, friendly manner, and with a steady flow that sometimes has a sparkle or touch of humor. Today his part in the socialistic literature of the nineties and appreciation of his contributions to technique have restored to him something of his old recognition. As a critic he was even-tempered and discriminating, never self-assertive or Olympian. The general function of criticism, he held, should be to "place a book in such a light that the reader should know its class, its function, its character." Many present-day literary historians think that he did his finest work as a critic, and that his best and most lasting book is *Criticism and Fiction*.

Though Howells wrote several works of a critical nature, it was chiefly in *Criticism and Fiction* (1891) that he dealt with literary theories and abstractions. His creed as a novelist was simple. He believed in the supremacy of truth in fiction. The characters and the settings should be from actuality. They must be true to the author's day and place and true to normal conditions, and the events must be such as might happen to an average person. He stood for an exact depiction of conduct and motive; he observed the life of his time and tried to transfer it to his pages. The everyday and commonplace is not, he thought, either trivial or insignificant. The charge that realism sacrifices distinction and heroism irked him. He engaged in considerable ethical discussion here and there in his works; but his position was that though fiction must be moral, the author must not moralize. He was little influenced by the French realists, for whose subject matter he had an intense dislike. Romanticism he steadily denounced.

Howells left mainly a detailed record of the surface externals of his time, although in *The Rise of Silas Lapham* he does approach an inward conflict. It is partly because of his abundant description that his narratives move slowly. Some think his particularizing excessive. The story element in his earlier books became less prominent in the later, and scientific purpose loomed larger. And as time passed, he became more impatient of conscious art and style. The mechanics of fiction, the construction, the point of view, and problems of expression, did not much interest him. Nor did he care greatly for the plot itself, though his books show rounded structure, for he felt, as did Henry James, that "plot does not characterize." He preferred to "portray human nature" rather than to "warm up old stories." There is more characterization, more analysis, more talk in his maturer books. Howells's handling of dialogue shows great technical skill. Through it he develops his characters and carries on his story. Indeed, though this was contrary to his literary tenets, the talk of his characters is on a higher level than would be true of such persons in real life. Mainly, Howells wished his books to rely on fidelity alone, and through this fidelity to serve as socializing instruments. He had extensive influence in his day, both as a writer of fiction and as an editor. Among the young realists he sponsored were Frank Norris, Stephen Crane, and Hamlin Garland.

There is no complete collected edition of Howells's works. His daughter Mildred Howells edited his *Life in Letters* (2 vols., 1928). Many of his works contain autobiographic material: *A Boy's Town* (1890), *My Year in a Log Cabin* (1893), *Impressions and Experiences* (1896), *Literary Friends and Acquaintance* (1900), *New Leaf Mills* (1913), *The Leatherwood God* (1916), and *Years of My Youth* (1916). O. W. Firkins wrote of Howells in *DAB*, IX (1932). See also Hamlin Garland, *Roadside Meetings* (1930) and *Friendly Contemporaries* (1932). For valuable discussions consult Henry James, "W. D. Howells," *Harper's Weekly*, XXX, June 19, 1886; J. M. Robertson, *Essays toward a Critical Method* (1889); J. Macy, *The Spirit of American Literature* (1913); A. Harvey, *W. D. Howells* (1917); H. T. and W. Follett, *Some Modern Novelists* (1919); W. L. Phelps, "W. D. Howells," *Yale Review*, X, Oct., 1920; Carl Van Doren, *The American Novel* (1921); D. G. Cooke, *W. D. Howells: a Critical Study* (1922); O. W. Firkins, *W. D. Howells, a Study* (1924); V. L. Parrington in *Main Currents in American Thought*, III (1930); H. Garland, in Macy's *American Writers on American Literature* (1931); G. E. De Mille, *Literary Criticism in America*

(1931). Bibliographies are included in the *CHAL*, III (1921), and in the books by D. G. Cooke and O. W. Firkins. The most recent bibliography is by Harry Hartwick, in W. F. Taylor's *A History of American Letters* (1936).

From THE RISE OF SILAS LAPHAM

Silas Lapham is a self-made paint manufacturer, and the new-rich Lapham family is ambitious socially. The novel deals with the contrast between the two social worlds, that of the rather rustic Laphams and that of the Coreys, Boston aristocrats, whose only son Tom is supposed to be interested in Irene, the beautiful younger daughter of the Laphams, but who is really in love with the older daughter, Penelope. Ultimately Lapham has business difficulties and loses his fortune; but in the meantime he develops moral strength and proves himself to be a man of sterling integrity.

XIV

A Dinner Party

. . . THE Coreys were one of the few old families who lingered in Bellingham Place, the handsome, quiet old street which the sympathetic observer must grieve to see abandoned to boardinghouses. The dwellings are stately and tall, and the whole place wears an air of aristocratic seclusion, which Mrs. Corey's father might well have thought assured when he left her his house there at his death. It is one of two evidently designed by the same architect who built some houses in a characteristic taste on Beacon Street opposite the Common. It has a wooden portico, with slender fluted columns, which have always been painted white, and which, with the delicate mouldings of the cornice, form the sole and sufficient decoration of the street front; nothing could be simpler, and nothing could be better. Within, the architect has again indulged his preference for the classic; the roof of the vestibule, wide and low, rests on marble columns, slim and fluted like the wooden columns without, and an ample staircase climbs in a graceful, easy curve from the tessellated pavement. Some carved Venetian *scrigni* stretched along the wall; a rug lay at the foot of the stairs; but otherwise the simple adequacy of the architectural intention had been respected, and the place looked bare to the eyes of the Laphams when they entered. The Coreys had once kept a man, but when young Corey

began his retrenchments the man had yielded to the neat maid who showed the Colonel into the reception-room and asked the ladies to walk up two flights.

He had his charges from Irene not to enter the drawing-room without her mother, and he spent five minutes in getting on his gloves, for he had desperately resolved to wear them at last. When he had them on, and let his large fists hang down on either side, they looked, in the saffron tint which the shopgirl said his gloves should be of, like canvased hams. He perspired with doubt as he climbed the stairs, and while he waited on the landing for Mrs. Lapham and Irene to come down from above before going into the drawing-room, he stood staring at his hands, now open and now shut, and breathing hard. He heard quiet talking beyond the *portière* within, and presently Tom Corey came out.

"Ah, Colonel Lapham! Very glad to see you."

Lapham shook hands with him and gasped, "Waiting for Mis' Lapham," to account for his presence. He had not been able to button his right glove, and he now began, with as much indifference as he could assume, to pull them both off, for he saw that Corey wore none. By the time he had stuffed them into the pocket of his coat-skirt his wife and daughter descended.

Corey welcomed them very cordially too, but looked a little mystified. Mrs. Lapham knew that he was silently inquiring for Penelope, and she did not know whether she ought to excuse her to him first or not. She said nothing, and after a glance toward the regions where Penelope might conjecturably be lingering, he held aside the *portière* for the Laphams to pass, and entered the room with them.

Mrs. Lapham had decided against low-necks on her own responsibility, and had entrenched herself in the safety of a black silk, in which she looked very handsome. Irene wore a dress of one of those shades which only a woman or an artist can decide to be green or blue, and which to other eyes looks both or neither, according to their degrees of ignorance. If it was more like a ball dress than a dinner dress, that might be excused to the exquisite effect. She trailed, a delicate splendor, across the carpet in her mother's somber wake, and the consciousness of success brought a vivid smile to her face. Lapham, pallid with anxiety lest he should somehow disgrace himself, giving thanks to God that he should have been spared the shame of wearing gloves where no one else did, but at the same time despairing that Corey should have seen him in them, had an unwonted aspect of almost pathetic refinement.

Mrs. Corey exchanged a quick glance of surprise and relief with her husband as she started across the room to meet her guests, and in her gratitude to them for being so irreproachable, she threw into her manner a warmth that people did not always find there. "General Lapham?" she said, shaking hands in quick succession with Mrs. Lapham and Irene, and now addressing herself to him.

"No, ma'am, only Colonel," said the honest man, but the lady did not hear him. She was introducing her husband to Lapham's wife and daughter, and Bromfield Corey was already shaking his hand and saying he was very glad to see him again, while he kept his artistic eye on Irene, and apparently could not take it off. Lily Corey gave the Lapham ladies a greeting which was physically rather than socially cold, and Nanny stood holding Irene's hand in both of hers a moment, and taking in her beauty and her style with a generous admiration which she could afford, for she was herself faultlessly dressed in the quiet taste of her city, and looking very pretty. The interval was long enough to let every man present confide his sense of Irene's beauty to every other; and then, as the party was small, Mrs. Corey made everybody acquainted. When Lapham had not quite understood, he held the person's hand, and leaning urbanely forward, inquired, "What name?" He did that because a great man to whom he had been presented on the platform at a public meeting had done so to him, and he knew it must be right.

A little lull ensued upon the introductions, and Mrs. Corey said quietly to Mrs. Lapham, "Can I send any one to be of use to Miss Lapham?" as if Penelope must be in the dressing-room.

Mrs. Lapham turned fire-red, and the graceful forms in which she had been intending to excuse her daughter's absence went out of her head. "She isn't upstairs," she said, at her bluntest, as country people are when embarrassed. "She didn't feel just like coming tonight. I don't know as she's feeling very well."

Mrs. Corey emitted a very small "O!"—very small, very cold,—which began to grow larger and hotter and to burn into Mrs. Lapham's soul before Mrs. Corey could add, "I'm very sorry. It's nothing serious, I hope?"

Robert Chase, the painter, had not come, and Mrs. James Bellingham was not there, so that the table really balanced better without Penelope; but Mrs. Lapham could not know this, and did not deserve to know it. Mrs. Corey glanced round the room, as if to take account of her guests, and said to her husband, "I think we are all here, then," and he came forward and gave his arm to Mrs. Lapham. She perceived then that in their determination not to be the first to come they had been the last, and must have kept the others waiting for them.

Lapham had never seen people go down to dinner arm-in-arm before, but he knew that his wife was distinguished in being taken out by the host, and he waited in jealous impatience to see if Tom Corey would offer his arm to Irene. He gave it to that big girl they called Miss Kingsbury, and the handsome old fellow whom Mrs. Corey had introduced as her cousin took Irene out. Lapham was startled from the misgiving in which this left him by Mrs. Corey's passing her hand through his arm, and he made a sudden movement forward, but felt himself gently restrained. They went out the last of all; he did not know why, but he submitted, and when they sat down he saw that Irene, although she had come in with that Mr. Bellingham, was seated beside young Corey, after all.

He fetched a long sigh of relief when he sank into his chair and felt himself safe from error if he kept a sharp lookout and did only what the others did. Bellingham had certain habits which he permitted himself, and one of these was tucking the corner of his napkin into his collar; he confessed himself an uncertain shot with a spoon, and defended his practice on the ground of neatness and commonsense. Lapham put his napkin into his collar too, and then, seeing that no one but Bellingham did it, became alarmed and took it out again slyly. He never had wine on his table at home, and on principle he was a prohibitionist; but now he did not know just what to do about the glasses at the right of his plate. He had a notion to turn them all down, as he had read of a well-known politician's doing at a public dinner, to show that he did not take wine; but, after twiddling with one of them a moment, he let them be, for it seemed to him that would be a little too conspicuous, and he felt that everyone was looking. He let the servant fill them all, and he drank out of each, not to appear odd. Later, he observed that the young ladies were not taking wine, and he was glad to see that Irene had refused it, and that Mrs. Lapham was letting it stand untasted. He did not know but he ought to decline some of the dishes, or at least leave most of some on his plate, but he was not able to decide; he took everything and ate everything.

He noticed that Mrs. Corey seemed to take no more trouble about the dinner than anybody, and Mr. Corey rather less; he was talking busily to Mrs. Lapham, and Lapham caught a word here and there that convinced him she was holding her own. He was getting on famously himself with Mrs. Corey, who had begun with him about his new house; he was telling her all about it, and giving her his ideas. Their conversation naturally included his architect across the table; Lapham had been delighted and secretly surprised to find the fellow there; and at something Seymour said the talk spread suddenly, and the pretty house he was building for Colonel Lapham became the general theme. Young Corey testified to its loveliness, and the architect said laughingly that if he had been able to make a nice thing of it, he owed it to the practical sympathy of his client.

"Practical sympathy is good," said Bromfield Corey; and, slanting his head confidentially to Mrs. Lapham, he added, "Does he bleed your husband, Mrs. Lapham? He's a terrible fellow for appropriations!"

Mrs. Lapham laughed, reddening consciously, and said she guessed the Colonel knew how to take care of himself. This struck Lapham, then draining his glass of sauterne, as wonderfully discreet in his wife.

Bromfield Corey leaned back in his chair a moment. "Well, after all, you can't say, with all your modern fuss about it, that you do much better now than the old fellows who built such houses as this."

"Ah," said the architect, "nobody can do better than well. Your house is in perfect taste; you know I've always admired it; and I don't think it's at all the worse for being old-fashioned. What we've done is largely to go back of the hideous style that raged after they forgot how to make this sort of house. But I think we may claim a better feeling for structure. We use better material, and more wisely; and by and by we shall work out something more characteristic and original."

"With your chocolates and olives, and your clutter of bric-à-brac?"

"All that's bad, of course, but I don't mean that. I don't wish to make you envious of Colonel Lapham, and modesty prevents my saying that his house is prettier,—though I may have my convictions,—but it's better built. All the new houses are better built. Now, your house—"

"Mrs. Corey's house," interrupted the host, with a burlesque haste in disclaiming responsibility for it that made them all laugh. "*My* ancestral halls are in Salem, and I'm told you couldn't drive a nail into their timbers; in fact, I don't know that you would want to do it."

"I should consider it a species of sacrilege," answered Seymour, "and I shall be far from pressing the point I was going to make against a house of Mrs. Corey's."

This won Seymour the easy laugh, and Lapham silently wondered that the fellow never got off any of those things to him.

"Well," said Corey, "you architects and the musicians are the true and only artistic creators. All the rest of us, sculptors, painters, novelists, and tailors, deal with forms that we have before us; we try to imitate, we try to represent. But you two sorts of artists create form. If you represent, you fail. Somehow or other you do evolve the camel out of your inner consciousness."

"I will not deny the soft impeachment," said the architect, with a modest air.

"I dare say. And you'll own that it's very handsome of me to say this, after your unjustifiable attack on Mrs. Corey's property."

Bromfield Corey addressed himself again to Mrs. Lapham, and the talk subdivided itself as before. It lapsed so entirely away from the subject just in hand, that Lapham was left with rather a good idea, as he thought it, to perish in his mind, for want of a chance to express it. The only thing like a recurrence to what they had been saying was Bromfield Corey's warning Mrs. Lapham, in some connection that Lapham lost, against Miss Kingsbury. "She's worse," he was saying, "when it comes to appropriations than Seymour himself. Depend upon it, Mrs. Lapham, she will give you no peace of your mind, now she's met you, from this out. Her tender mercies are cruel; and I leave you to supply the context from your own scriptural knowledge. Beware of her, and all her works. She calls them works of charity, but heaven knows whether they are. It don't stand to reason that she gives the poor *all* the money she gets out of people. I have my own belief"—he gave it in a whisper for the whole table to hear—"that she spends it for champagne and cigars."

Lapham did not know about that kind of talking; but Miss Kingsbury seemed to enjoy the fun as much as anybody, and he laughed with the rest.

"You shall be asked to the very next debauch of the committee, Mr. Corey; then you won't dare expose us," said Miss Kingsbury.

"I wonder you haven't been down upon Corey to go to the Chardon Street home and talk with your indigent Italians in their native tongue," said Charles Bellingham. "I saw in the *Transcript* the other night that you wanted some one for the work."

"We did think of Mr. Corey," replied Miss Kingsbury; "but we reflected that he probably wouldn't talk with them at all; he would make them keep still to be sketched, and forget all about their wants."

Upon the theory that this was a fair return for Corey's pleasantry, the others laughed again.

"There is one charity," said Corey, pretending superiority to Miss Kingsbury's point, "that is so difficult, I wonder it hasn't occurred to a lady of your courageous invention."

"Yes?" said Miss Kingsbury. "What is that?"

"The occupation, by deserving poor of neat habits, of all the beautiful, airy, wholesome houses that stand empty the whole summer long, while their owners are away in their lowly cots beside the sea."

"Yes, that is terrible," replied Miss Kingsbury, with quick earnestness, while her eyes grew moist. "I have often thought of our great, cool houses standing useless here, and the thousands of poor creatures stifling in their holes and dens, and the little children dying for wholesome shelter. How cruelly selfish we are!"

"That is a very comfortable sentiment, Miss Kingsbury," said Corey, "and must make you feel almost as if you had thrown open No. 31 to the whole North End. But I am serious about this matter. I spend my summers in town, and I occupy my own house, so that I can speak impartially and intelligently; and I tell you that in some of my walks on the Hill and down on the Back Bay, nothing but the surveillance of the local policeman prevents my offering personal violence to those long rows of close-shuttered, handsome, brutally insensible houses. If I were a poor man, with a sick child pining in some garret or cellar at the North End, I should break into one of them, and camp out on the grand piano."

"Surely, Bromfield," said his wife, "you don't consider what havoc such people would make with the furniture of a nice house!"

"That is true," answered Corey, with meek conviction. "I never thought of that."

"And if you were a poor man with a sick child, I doubt if you'd have so much heart for burglary as you have now," said James Bellingham.

"It's wonderful how patient they are," said the minister. "The spectacle of the hopeless comfort the hard-working poor man sees must be hard to bear."

Lapham wanted to speak up and say that

he had been there himself, and knew how such a man felt. He wanted to tell them that generally a poor man was satisfied if he could make both ends meet; that he didn't envy any one his good luck, if he had earned it, so long as he wasn't running under himself. But before he could get the courage to address the whole table, Sewell added, "I suppose he don't always think of it."

"But some day he *will* think about it," said Corey. "In fact, we rather invite him to think about it, in this country."

"My brother-in-law," said Charles Bellingham, with the pride a man feels in a mentionably remarkable brother-in-law, "has no end of fellows at work under him out there at Omaha, and he says it's the fellows from countries where they've been kept from thinking about it that are discontented. The Americans never make any trouble. They seem to understand that so long as we give unlimited opportunity, nobody has a right to complain."

"What do you hear from Leslie?" asked Mrs. Corey, turning from these profitless abstractions to Mrs. Bellingham.

"You know," said that lady in a lower tone, "that there is another baby?"

"No! I hadn't heard of it!"

"Yes; a boy. They have named him after his uncle."

"Yes," said Charles Bellingham, joining in. "He is said to be a noble boy, and to resemble me."

"All boys of that tender age are noble," said Corey, "and look like anybody you wish them to resemble. Is Leslie still homesick for the bean-pots of her native Boston?"

"She is getting over it, I fancy," replied Mrs. Bellingham. "She's very much taken up with Mrs. Blake's enterprises, and leads a very exciting life. She says she's like people who have been home from Europe three years; she's past the most poignant stage of regret, and hasn't reached the second, when they feel that they *must* go again."

Lapham leaned a little toward Mrs. Corey, and said of a picture which he saw on the wall opposite, "Picture of your daughter, I presume?"

"No; my daughter's grandmother. It's a Stewart Newton; he painted a great many Salem beauties. She was a Miss Polly Burroughs. My daughter *is* like her, don't you think?" They both looked at Nanny Corey and then at the portrait. "Those pretty oldfashioned dresses are coming in again. I'm not surprised you took it for her. The others"—she referred to the other portraits more or less darkling on the walls—"are my people; mostly Copleys."

These names, unknown to Lapham, went to his head like the wine he was drinking; they seemed to carry light for the moment, but a film of deeper darkness followed. He heard Charles Bellingham telling funny stories to Irene and trying to amuse the girl; she was laughing, and seemed very happy. From time to time Bellingham took part in the general talk between the host and James Bellingham and Miss Kingsbury and the minister, Mr. Sewell. They talked of people mostly; it astonished Lapham to hear with what freedom they talked. They discussed these persons unsparingly; James Bellingham spoke of a man known to Lapham for his business success and great wealth as not a gentleman; his cousin Charles said he was surprised that the fellow had kept from being governor so long.

When the latter turned from Irene to make one of these excursions into the general talk, young Corey talked to her; and Lapham caught some words from which it seemed that they were speaking of Penelope. It vexed him to think she had not come; she could have talked as well as any of them; she was just as bright; and Lapham was aware that Irene was not as bright, though when he looked at her face, triumphant in its young beauty and fondness, he said to himself that it did not make any difference. He felt that he was not holding up his end of the line, however. When some one spoke to him he could only summon a few words of reply, that seemed to lead to nothing; things often came into his mind appropriate to what they were saying, but before he could get them out they were off on something else; they jumped about so, he could not keep up; but he felt, all the same, that he was not doing himself justice.

At one time the talk ran off upon a subject that Lapham had never heard talked of before; but again he was vexed that Penelope was not there, to have her say; he believed that her say would have been worth hearing.

Miss Kingsbury leaned forward and asked Charles Bellingham if he had read *Tears, Idle Tears*, the novel that was making such a sensation; and when he said no, she said she wondered at him. "It's perfectly heartbreaking, as you'll imagine from the name; but there's such a dear old-fashioned hero and heroine in it, who keep dying for each other all the way through, and making the most wildly satisfactory and unnecessary sacrifices for each other. You feel as if you'd done them yourself."

"Ah, that's the secret of its success," said Bromfield Corey. "It flatters the reader by painting the characters colossal, but with his limp and stoop, so that he feels himself of their supernatural proportions. You've read it, Nanny?"

"Yes," said his daughter. "It ought to have been called *Slop, Silly Slop*."

"Oh, not quite *slop*, Nanny," pleaded Miss Kingsbury.

"It's astonishing," said Charles Bellingham, "how we do like the books that go for our heartstrings. And I really suppose that you can't put a more popular thing than self-sacrifice into a novel. We do like to see people suffering sublimely."

"There was talk some years ago," said James Bellingham, "about novels going out."

"They're just coming in!" cried Miss Kingsbury.

"Yes," said Mr. Sewell, the minister. "And I don't think there ever was a time when they formed the whole intellectual experience of more people. They do greater mischief than ever."

"Don't be envious, parson," said the host.

"No," answered Sewell. "I should be glad of their help. But those novels with old-fashioned heroes and heroines in them—excuse me, Miss Kingsbury—are ruinous!"

"Don't you feel like a moral wreck, Miss Kingsbury?" asked the host.

But Sewell went on: "The novelists might be the greatest possible help to us if they painted life as it is, and human feelings in their true proportion and relation, but for the most part they have been and are altogether noxious."

This seemed sense to Lapham; but Bromfield Corey asked: "But what if life as it is isn't amusing? Aren't we to be amused?"

"Not to our hurt," sturdily answered the minister. "And the self-sacrifice painted in most novels like this—"

"*Slop, Silly Slop?*" suggested the proud father of the inventor of the phrase.

"Yes—is nothing but psychical suicide, and is as wholly immoral as the spectacle of a man falling upon his sword."

"Well, I don't know but you're right, parson," said the host; and the minister, who had apparently got upon a battle-horse of his, careered onward in spite of some tacit attempts of his wife to seize the bridle.

"Right? To be sure I am right. The whole business of love, and love-making and marrying, is painted by the novelists in a monstrous disproportion to the other relations of life. Love is very sweet, very pretty—"

"Oh, *thank* you, Mr. Sewell," said Nanny Corey, in a way that set them all laughing.

"But it's the affair, commonly, of very young people, who have not yet character and experience enough to make them interesting. In novels it's treated, not only as if it were the chief interest of life, but the sole interest of the lives of two ridiculous young persons; and it is taught that love is perpetual, that the glow of a true passion lasts for ever; and that it is sacrilege to think or act otherwise."

"Well, but isn't that true, Mr. Sewell?" pleaded Miss Kingsbury.

"I have known some most estimable people who had married a second time," said the minister, and then he had the applause with him. Lapham wanted to make some open recognition of his good sense, but could not.

"I suppose the passion itself has been a good deal changed," said Bromfield Corey, "since the poets began to idealize it in the days of chivalry."

"Yes; and it ought to be changed again," said Mr. Sewell.

"What! Back?"

"I don't say that. But it ought to be recognized as something natural and mortal, and divine honors, which belong to righteousness alone, ought not to be paid it."

"Oh, you ask too much, parson," laughed

his host, and the talk wandered away to something else.

It was not an elaborate dinner; but Lapham was used to having everything on the table at once, and this succession of dishes bewildered him; he was afraid perhaps he was eating too much. He now no longer made any pretence of not drinking his wine, for he was thirsty, and there was no more water, and he hated to ask for any. The ice-cream came, and then the fruit. Suddenly Mrs. Corey rose, and said across the table to her husband, "I suppose you will want your coffee here." And he replied, "Yes; we'll join you at tea."

The ladies all rose, and the gentlemen got up with them. Lapham started to follow Mrs. Corey, but the other men merely stood in their places, except young Corey, who ran and opened the door for his mother. Lapham thought with shame that it was he who ought to have done that; but no one seemed to notice, and he sat down again gladly, after kicking out one of his legs which had gone to sleep.

They brought in cigars with coffee, and Bromfield Corey advised Lapham to take one that he chose for him. Lapham confessed that he liked a good cigar about as well as anybody, and Corey said: "These are new. I had an Englishman here the other day who was smoking old cigars in the superstition that tobacco improved with age, like wine."

"Ah," said Lapham, "anybody who had ever lived off a tobacco country could tell him better than that." With the fuming cigar between his lips he felt more at home than he had before. He turned sidewise in his chair and, resting one arm on the back, intertwined the fingers of both hands, and smoked at large ease.

James Bellingham came and sat down by him. "Colonel Lapham, weren't you with the 96th Vermont when they charged across the river in front of Pickensburg, and the rebel battery opened fire on them in the water?"

Lapham slowly shut his eyes and slowly dropped his head for assent, letting out a white volume of smoke from the corner of his mouth.

"I thought so," said Bellingham "I was with the 85th Massachusetts, and I sha'n't forget that slaughter. We were all new to it still. Perhaps that's why it made such an impression."

"I don't know," suggested Charles Bellingham. "Was there anything much more impressive afterward? I read of it out in Missouri, where I was stationed at the time, and I recollect the talk of some old army men about it. They said that death-rate couldn't be beaten. I don't know that it ever was."

"About one in five of us got out safe," said Lapham, breaking his cigar-ash off on the edge of a plate. James Bellingham reached him a bottle of Apollinaris. He drank a glass, and then went on smoking.

They all waited, as if expecting him to speak, and then Corey said: "How incredible those things seem already! You gentlemen *know* that they happened; but are you still able to believe it?"

"Ah, nobody *feels* that anything happened," said Charles Bellingham. "The past of one's experience doesn't differ a great deal from the past of one's knowledge. It isn't much more probable; it's really a great deal less vivid than some scenes in a novel that one read when a boy."

"I'm not sure of that," said James Bellingham.

"Well, James, neither am I," consented his cousin, helping himself from Lapham's Apollinaris bottle. "There would be very little talking at dinner if one only said the things that one was sure of."

The others laughed, and Bromfield Corey remarked thoughtfully, "What astonishes the craven civilian in all these things is the abundance—the superabundance—of heroism. The cowards were the exception; the men that were ready to die, the rule."

"The woods were full of them," said Lapham, without taking his cigar from his mouth.

"That's a nice little touch in *School*," interposed Charles Bellingham, "where the girl says to the fellow who was at Inkerman, 'I should think you would be so proud of it,' and he reflects a while, and says, 'Well, the fact is, you know, there were so many of us.'"

"Yes, I remember that," said James Bellingham, smiling for pleasure in it. "But I don't see why you claim the credit of being a craven civilian, Bromfield," he added, with a friendly glance at his brother-in-law, and with the willingness Boston men often show to turn one another's good points to the light in company; bred so intimately together at school and college and in society, they all know these points. "A man who was out with Garibaldi in '48," continued James Bellingham.

"Oh, a little amateur red-shirting," Corey interrupted in deprecation. "But even if you choose to dispute my claim, what has become of all the heroism? Tom, how many club men do you know who would think it sweet and fitting to die for their country?"

"I can't think of a great many at the moment, sir," replied the son, with the modesty of his generation.

"And I couldn't in '61," said his uncle. "Nevertheless they were there."

"Then your theory is that it's the occasion that is wanting," said Bromfield Corey. "But why shouldn't civil service reform, and the resumption of specie payment, and a tariff for revenue only, inspire heroes? They are all good causes."

"It's the occasion that's wanting," said James Bellingham, ignoring the *persiflage*. "And I'm very glad of it."

"So am I," said Lapham, with a depth of feeling that expressed itself in spite of the haze in which his brain seemed to float. There was a great deal of the talk that he could not follow; it was too quick for him; but here was something he was clear of. "I don't want to see any more men killed in my time." Something serious, something somber must lurk behind these words, and they waited for Lapham to say more; but the haze closed round him again, and he remained silent, drinking Apollinaris.

"We noncombatants were notoriously reluctant to give up fighting," said Mr. Sewell, the minister; "but I incline to think Colonel Lapham and Mr. Bellingham may be right. I dare say we shall have the heroism again if we have the occasion. Till it comes, we must content ourselves with the everyday generosities and sacrifices. They make up in quantity what they lack in quality, perhaps."

"They're not so picturesque," said Bromfield Corey. "You can paint a man dying for his country, but you can't express on canvas a man fulfilling the duties of a good citizen."

"Perhaps the novelists will get at him by and by," suggested Charles Bellingham. "If I were one of these fellows, I shouldn't propose to myself anything short of that."

"What? the commonplace?" asked his cousin.

"Commonplace? The commonplace is just that light, impalpable, aërial essence which they've never got into their confounded books yet. The novelist who could interpret the common feelings of commonplace people would have the answer to 'the riddle of the painful earth' on his tongue."

"Oh, not so bad as that, I hope," said the host; and Lapham looked from one to the other, trying to make out what they were at. He had never been so up a tree before.

"I suppose it isn't well for us to see human nature at white heat habitually," continued Bromfield Corey, after a while. "It would make us vain of our species. Many a poor fellow in that war and in many another has gone into battle simply and purely for his country's sake, not knowing whether, if he laid down his life, he should ever find it again, or whether, if he took it up hereafter, he should take it up in heaven or hell. Come, parson!" he said, turning to the minister, "what has ever been conceived of omnipotence, of omniscience, so sublime, so divine as that?"

"Nothing," answered the minister quietly. "God has never been imagined at all. But if you suppose such a man as that was Authorized, I think it will help you to imagine what God must be."

"There's sense in that," said Lapham. He took his cigar out of his mouth, and pulled his chair a little toward the table, on which he placed his ponderous forearms. "I want to tell you about a fellow I had in my own company when we first went out. We were all privates to begin with; after a while they elected me captain—I'd had the tavern stand, and most of 'em knew me. But Jim Millon never got to be anything more than corporal; corporal when he was killed." The others arrested themselves in various attitudes of attention, and remained listening to Lapham with an interest that profoundly flattered him. Now, at last, he felt that he was holding up his end of the rope. "I can't say he went into the thing from the highest motives, altogether; our motives are always pretty badly mixed, and when there's such a hurrah-boys as there was then, you can't tell which is which. I suppose Jim Millon's wife was enough to account for his going, herself. She was a pretty bad assortment," said Lapham, lowering his voice and glancing round at the door to make sure that it was shut, "and she used to lead Jim *one* kind of life. Well, sir," continued Lapham, synthetizing his auditors in that form of address, "that fellow used to save every cent of his pay and send it to that woman. Used to get me to do it for him. I tried to stop him. 'Why, Jim,' said I, 'you know what she'll do with it.' 'That's so, Cap,' says he, 'but I don't know what she'll do without it.' And it did keep her straight—straight as a string—as long as Jim lasted. Seemed as if there was something mysterious about it. They had a little girl,—about as old as my oldest girl,—and Jim used to talk to me about her. Guess he done it as much for her as for the mother; and he said to me before the last action we went into, 'I should like to turn tail and run, Cap. I ain't comin' out o' this one. But I don't suppose it would do.' 'Well, not for you, Jim,' said I. 'I want to live,' he says; and he bust out crying right there in my tent. 'I want to live for poor Molly and Zerilla'—that's what they called the little one; I dunno where they got the name. 'I ain't ever had half a chance; and now she's doing better, and I believe we should get along after this.' He set there cryin' like a baby. But he wan't no baby when he went into action. I hated to look at him after it was over, not so much because he'd got a ball that was meant for me by a sharpshooter—he saw the devil takin' aim, and he jumped to warn me—as because he didn't look like Jim; he looked like—fun; all desperate and savage. I guess he died hard."

The story made its impression, and Lapham saw it. "Now I say," he resumed, as if he felt that he was going to do himself justice, and say something to heighten the effect his story had produced. At the same time he was aware of a certain want of clearness. He had the idea, but it floated vague, elusive, in his brain. He looked about as if for something to precipitate it in tangible shape.

"Apollinaris?" asked Charles Bellingham, handing the bottle from the other side. He had drawn his chair closer than the rest to Lap-

ham's, and was listening with great interest. When Mrs. Corey asked him to meet Lapham, he accepted gladly. "You know I go in for that sort of thing, Anna. Since Leslie's affair we're rather bound to do it. And I think we meet these practical fellows too little. There's always something original about them." He might naturally have believed that the reward of his faith was coming.

"Thanks, I will take some of this wine," said Lapham, pouring himself a glass of Madeira from a black and dusty bottle caressed by a label bearing the date of the vintage. He tossed off the wine, unconscious of its preciousness, and waited for the result. That cloudiness in his brain disappeared before it, but a mere blank remained. He not only could not remember what he was going to say, but he could not recall what they had been talking about. They waited, looking at him, and he stared at them in return. After a while he heard the host saying, "Shall we join the ladies?"

Lapham went, trying to think what had happened. It seemed to him a long time since he had drunk that wine.

Miss Corey gave him a cup of tea, where he stood aloof from his wife, who was talking with Miss Kingsbury and Mrs. Sewell; Irene was with Miss Nanny Corey. He could not hear what they were talking about; but if Penelope had come, he knew that she would have done them all credit. He meant to let her know how he felt about her behavior when he got home. It was a shame for her to miss such a chance. Irene was looking beautiful, as pretty as all the rest of them put together, but she was not talking, and Lapham perceived that at a dinner-party you ought to talk. He was himself conscious of having talked very well. He now wore an air of great dignity, and, in conversing with the other gentlemen, he used a grave and weighty deliberation. Some of them wanted him to go into the library. There he gave his ideas of books. He said he had not much time for anything but the papers; but he was going to have a complete library in his new place. He made an elaborate acknowledgment to Bromfield Corey of his son's kindness in suggesting books for his library; said that he had ordered them all, and that he meant to have pictures. He asked Mr. Corey who was about the best American painter going now. "I don't set up to be a judge of pictures, but I know what I like," he said. He lost the reserve which he had maintained earlier, and began to boast. He himself introduced the subject of his paint, in a natural transition from pictures; he said Mr. Corey must take a run up to Lapham with him some day, and see the Works; they would interest him, and he would drive him round the country; he kept most of his horses up there, and he could show Mr. Corey some of the finest Jersey grades in the country. He told about his brother William, the judge at Dubuque; and a farm he had out there that paid for itself every year in wheat. As he cast off all fear, his voice rose, and he hammered his arm-chair with the thick of his hand for emphasis. Mr. Corey seemed impressed; he sat perfectly quiet, listening, and Lapham saw the other gentlemen stop in their talk every now and then to listen. After this proof of his ability to interest them, he would have liked to have Mrs. Lapham suggest again that he was unequal to their society, or to the society of anybody else. He surprised himself by his ease among men whose names had hitherto overawed him. He got to calling Bromfield Corey by his surname alone. He did not understand why young Corey seemed so preoccupied, and he took occasion to tell the company how he had said to his wife the first time he saw that fellow that he could make a man of him if he had him in the business; and he guessed he was not mistaken. He began to tell stories of the different young men he had had in his employ. At last he had the talk altogether to himself; no one else talked, and he talked unceasingly. It was a great time; it was a triumph.

He was in this successful mood when word came to him that Mrs. Lapham was going; Tom Corey seemed to have brought it, but he was not sure. Anyway, he was not going to hurry. He made cordial invitations to each of the gentlemen to drop in and see him at his office, and would not be satisfied till he had exacted a promise from each. He told Charles Bellinghim that he liked him, and assured James Bellingham that it had always been his ambition to know him, and that if any one had said when he first came to Boston that in less than

ten years he should be hobnobbing with Jim Bellingham, he should have told that person he lied. He would have told anybody he lied that had told him ten years ago that a son of Bromfield Corey would have come and asked him to take him into the business. Ten years ago he, Silas Lapham, had come to Boston a little worse off than nothing at all, for he was in debt for half the money that he had bought out his partner with, and here he was now worth a million, and meeting you gentlemen like one of you. And every cent of that was honest money,—no speculation,—every copper of it for value received. And here, only the other day, his old partner, who had been going to the dogs ever since he went out of the business, came and borrowed twenty thousand dollars of him! Lapham lent it because his wife wanted him to: she had always felt bad about the fellow's having to go out of the business.

He took leave of Mr. Sewell with patronizing affection, and bade him come to him if he ever got into a tight place with his parish work; he would let him have all the money he wanted; he had more money than he knew what to do with. "Why, when your wife sent to mine last fall," he said, turning to Mr. Corey, "I drew my cheque for five hundred dollars, but my wife wouldn't take more than one hundred; said she wasn't going to show off before Mrs. Corey. I call that a pretty good joke on Mrs. Corey. I must tell her how Mrs. Lapham done her out of a cool four hundred dollars."

He started toward the door of the drawing-room to take leave of the ladies; but Tom Corey was at his elbow, saying, "I think Mrs. Lapham is waiting for you below, sir," and in obeying the direction Corey gave him toward another door he forgot all about his purpose, and came away without saying good-night to his hostess.

Mrs. Lapham had not known how soon she ought to go, and had no idea that in her quality of chief guest she was keeping the others. She stayed till eleven o'clock, and was a little frightened when she found what time it was; but Mrs. Corey, without pressing her to stay longer, had said it was not at all late. She and Irene had had a perfect time. Everybody had been very polite; on the way home they celebrated the amiability of both the Miss Coreys and of Miss Kingsbury. Mrs. Lapham thought that Mrs. Bellingham was about the pleasantest person she ever saw; she had told her all about her daughter who had married an inventor and gone to live in Omaha—a Mrs. Blake.

"If it's that car-wheel Blake," said Lapham proudly, "I know all about him. I've sold him tons of the paint."

"Pooh, papa! How you do smell of smoking!" cried Irene.

"Pretty strong, eh?" laughed Lapham, letting down a window of the carriage. His heart was throbbing wildly in the close air, and he was glad of the rush of cold that came in, though it stopped his tongue, and he listened more and more drowsily to the rejoicings that his wife and daughter exchanged. He meant to have them wake Penelope up and tell her what she had lost; but when he reached home he was too sleepy to suggest it. He fell asleep as soon as his head touched the pillow, full of supreme triumph.

But in the morning his skull was sore with the unconscious, nightlong ache; and he rose cross and taciturn. They had a silent breakfast. In the cold grey light of the morning the glories of the night before showed poorer. Here and there a painful doubt obtruded itself and marred them with its awkward shadow. Penelope sent down word that she was not well, and was not coming to breakfast, and Lapham was glad to go to his office without seeing her.

He was severe and silent all day with his clerks and peremptory with customers. Of Corey he was slyly observant, and as the day wore away he grew more restively conscious. He sent out word by his office-boy that he would like to see Mr. Corey for a few minutes after closing. The typewriter girl had lingered too, as if she wished to speak with him, and Corey stood in abeyance as she went toward Lapham's door.

"Can't see you tonight, Zerilla," he said bluffly, but not unkindly. "Perhaps I'll call at the house, if it's important."

"It is," said the girl, with a spoiled air of insistence.

"Well," said Lapham, and, nodding to Corey to enter, he closed the door upon her.

Then he turned to the young man and demanded: "Was I drunk last night?"   1885

From CRITICISM AND FICTION [1]

XV

[Jane Austen]

WHICH brings us again, after this long way about, to the divine Jane and her novels, and that troublesome question about them. She was great and they were beautiful, because she and they were honest, and dealt with nature nearly a hundred years ago as realism deals with it today. Realism is nothing more and nothing less than the truthful treatment of material, and Jane Austen was the first and the last of the English novelists to treat material with entire truthfulness. Because she did this, she remains the most artistic of the English novelists, and alone worthy to be matched with the great Scandinavian and Slavic and Latin artists. It is not a question of intellect, or not wholly that. The English have mind enough; but they have not taste enough; or, rather, their taste has been perverted by their false criticism, which is based upon personal preference, and not upon principle; which instructs a man to think that what he likes is good, instead of teaching him first to distinguish what is good before he likes it. The art of fiction, as Jane Austen knew it, declined from her through Scott, and Bulwer, and Dickens, and Charlotte Brontë, and Thackeray, and even George Eliot, because the mania of romanticism had seized upon all Europe, and these great writers could not escape the taint of their time; but it has shown few signs of recovery in England, because English criticism, in the presence of the Continental masterpieces, has continued provincial and special and personal, and has expressed a love and a hate which had to do with the quality of the artist rather than the character of his work. It was inevitable that in their time the English romanticists should treat, as Señor Valdés says, "the barbarous customs of the Middle Ages, softening and disfiguring them, as Walter Scott and his kind did"; that they should "devote themselves to falsifying nature, refining and subtilizing sentiment, and modifying psychology after their own fancy," like Bulwer and Dickens, as well as like Rousseau and Madame de Staël, not to mention Balzac, the worst of all that sort at his worst. This was the natural course of the disease; but it really seems as if it were their criticism that was to blame for the rest: not, indeed, for the performance of this writer or that, for criticism can never affect the actual doing of a thing; but for the esteem in which this writer or that is held through the perpetuation of false ideals. The only observer of English middle-class life since Jane Austen worthy to be named with her was not George Eliot, who was first ethical and then artistic, who transcended her in everything but the form and method most essential to art, and there fell hopelessly below her. It was Anthony Trollope who was most like her in simple honesty and instinctive truth, as unphilosophized as the light of common day; but he was so warped from a wholesome ideal as to wish at times to be like the caricaturist Thackeray, and to stand about in his scene, talking it over with his hands in his pockets, interrupting the action, and spoiling the illusion in which alone the truth of art resides. Mainly, his instinct was too much for his ideal, and with a low view of life in its civic relations and a thoroughly bourgeois soul, he yet produced works whose beauty is surpassed only by the effect of a more poetic writer in the novels of Thomas Hardy. Yet if a vote of English criticism even at this late day, when all continental Europe has the light of aesthetic truth, could be taken, the majority against these artists would be overwhelming in favor of a writer who had so little artistic sensibility, that he never hesitated on any occasion, great or small, to make a foray among his characters, and catch them up to show them to the reader and tell him how beautiful or ugly they were; and cry out over their amazing properties.

Doubtless the ideal of those poor islanders will be finally changed. If the truth could become a fad it would be accepted by all their "smart people," but truth is something rather too large for that; and we must await the gradual advance of civilization among them. Then they will see that their criticism had misled them; and that it is to this false guide they owe, not precisely the decline of fiction among them, but its continued debasement as an art.

XXIV

[Decency in American Fiction]

One of the great newspapers the other day invited the prominent American authors to speak their minds upon a point in the theory and practice of fiction which had already vexed some of them. It was the question of how much or how little the American novel ought to deal with certain facts of life which are not usually talked of before young people, and especially young ladies. Of course the question was not decided, and I forget just how far the balance inclined in favor of a larger freedom in the matter. But it certainly inclined that way; one or two writers of the sex which is somehow supposed to have purity in its keeping (as if purity were a thing that did not practically concern the other sex, preoccupied with serious affairs) gave it a rather vigorous tilt to that side. In view of this fact it would not be the part of prudence to make an effort to dress the balance; and indeed I do not know that I was going to make any such effort. But there are some things to say, around and about the subject, which I should like to have some one else say, and which I may myself possibly be safe in suggesting.

One of the first of these is the fact, generally lost sight of by those who censure the Anglo-Saxon novel for its prudishness, that it is really not such a prude after all; and that if it is sometimes apparently anxious to avoid those experiences of life not spoken of before young people, this may be an appearance only. Sometimes a novel which has this shuffling air, this effect of truckling to propriety, might defend itself, if it could speak for itself, by saying that such experiences happened not to come within its scheme, and that, so far from maiming or mutilating itself in ignoring them, it was all the more faithfully representative of the tone of modern life in dealing with love that was chaste, and with passion so honest that it could be openly spoken of before the tenderest society bud at dinner. It might say that the guilty intrigue, the betrayal, the extreme flirtation even, was the exceptional thing in life, and unless the scheme of the story necessarily involved it, that it would be bad art to lug it in, and as bad taste as to introduce such topics in a mixed company. It could say very justly that the novel in our civilization now always addresses a mixed company, and that the vast majority of the company are ladies, and that very many, if not most, of these ladies are young girls. If the novel were written for men and for married women alone, as in continental Europe, it might be altogether different. But the simple fact is that it is not written for them alone among us, and it is a question of writing, under cover of our universal acceptance, things for young girls to read which you would be put out-of-doors for saying to them, or of frankly giving notice of your intention, and so cutting yourself off from the pleasure—and it is a very high and sweet one—of appealing to these vivid, responsive intelligences, which are none the less brilliant and admirable because they are innocent.

One day a novelist who liked, after the manner of other men, to repine at his hard fate, complained to his friend, a critic, that he was tired of the restriction he had put upon himself in this regard; for it is a mistake, as can be readily shown, to suppose that others impose it. "See how free those French fellows are!" he rebelled. "Shall we always be shut up to our tradition of decency?"

"Do you think it's much worse than being shut up to their tradition of indecency?" said his friend.

Then that novelist began to reflect, and he remembered how sick the invariable motive of the French novel made him. He perceived finally that, convention for convention, ours was not only more tolerable, but on the whole was truer to life, not only to its complexion, but also to its texture. No one will pretend that there is not vicious love beneath the surface of our society; if he did, the fetid explosions of the divorce trials would refute him; but if he pretended that it was in any just sense characteristic of our society, he could be still more easily refuted. Yet it exists, and it is unquestionably the material of tragedy, the stuff from which intense effects are wrought. The question, after owning this fact, is whether these intense effects are not rather cheap effects. I incline to think they are, and I will try to say why I think so, if I may do so without offense. The material itself, the mere mention of it, has an instant fascination; it arrests, it detains, till the last word is said, and while there is anything to be hinted. This is what makes a love intrigue of some sort all but essential to the popularity of any fiction. Without such an intrigue the intellectual equipment of the author must be of the highest, and then he will succeed only with the highest class of readers. But any author who will deal with a guilty love intrigue holds all readers in his hand, the highest with the lowest, as long as he hints the slightest hope of the smallest potential naughtiness. He need not at all be a great author; he may be a very shabby wretch, if he has but the courage or the trick of that sort of thing. The critics will call him "virile" and "passionate"; decent people will be ashamed to have been limed by him; but the low average will only ask another chance of flocking into his net. If he happens to be an able writer, his really fine and costly work will be unheeded, and the lure to the appetite will be chiefly remembered. There may be other qualities which make reputations for other men, but in his case they will count for nothing. He pays this penalty for his success in that kind; and every one pays some such penalty who deals with some such material. It attaches in like manner to the triumphs of the writers who now almost form a school among us, and who may be said to have established themselves in an easy popularity simply by the study of erotic shivers and fervors. They may find their account in the popularity, or they may not; there is no question of the popularity.

But I do not mean to imply that their case covers the whole ground. So far as it goes, though, it ought to stop the mouths of those who complain that fiction is enslaved to propriety among us. It appears that of a certain kind of impropriety it is free to give us all it will, and more. But this is not what serious men and women writing fiction mean when they rebel against the limitations of their art in our civilization. They have no desire to deal with nakedness, as painters and sculptors freely do in the worship of beauty; or with certain facts of life, as the stage does, in the service of sensation. But they ask why, when the conventions of the plastic and histrionic arts liberate their followers to the portrayal of almost any phase of the physical or of the emotional nature, an American novelist may not write a story on the lines of *Anna Karenina* or *Madame Bovary*. Sappho they put aside, and from Zola's work they avert their eyes. They do not condemn him or Daudet, necessarily, or accuse their motives; they leave them out of the question; they do not want to do that kind of thing. But they do sometimes wish to do another kind, to touch one of the most serious and sorrowful problems of life in the spirit of Tolstoi and Flaubert, and they ask us why they may not. At one time, they remind us, the Anglo-Saxon novelist did deal with such problems—De Foe in his spirit, Richardson in his, Goldsmith in his. At what moment did our fiction lose this privilege? In what fatal hour did the Young Girl arise and seal the lips of Fiction, with a touch of her finger, to some of the most vital interests of life?

Whether I wished to oppose them in their aspiration for greater freedom, or whether I wished to encourage them, I should begin to answer them by saying that the Young Girl had never done anything of the kind. The manners of the novel have been improving with those of its readers; that is all. Gentlemen no longer swear or fall drunk under the table, or abduct young ladies and shut them up in lonely country-houses, or so habitually set about the ruin of their neighbors' wives, as they once did. Generally, people now call a spade an agricultural implement; they have not grown decent without having also grown a little squeamish, but they have grown comparatively decent; there is no doubt about that. They require of a novelist whom they respect unquestionable proof of his seriousness, if he proposes to deal with certain phases of life; they require a sort of scientific decorum. He can no longer expect to be received on the ground of entertainment only; he assumes a higher function, something like that of a physician or a priest, and they expect him to be bound by laws as sacred as those of such pro-

fessions; they hold him solemnly pledged not to betray them or abuse their confidence. If he will accept the conditions, they give him their confidence, and he may then treat to his greater honor, and not at all to his disadvantage, of such experiences, such relations of men and women as George Eliot treats in *Adam Bede*, in *Daniel Deronda*, in *Romola*, in almost all her books; such as Hawthorne treats in *The Scarlet Letter;* such as Dickens treats in *David Copperfield;* such as Thackeray treats in *Pendennis*, and glances at in every one of his fictions; such as most of the masters of English fiction have at some time treated more or less openly. It is quite false or quite mistaken to suppose that our novels have left untouched these most important realities of life. They have only not made them their stock in trade; they have kept a true perspective in regard to them; they have relegated them in their pictures of life to the space and place they occupy in life itself, as we know it in England and America. They have kept a correct proportion, knowing perfectly well that unless the novel is to be a map, with everything scrupulously laid down in it, a faithful record of life in far the greater extent could be made to the exclusion of guilty love and all its circumstances and consequences.

I justify them in this view not only because I hate what is cheap and meretricious, and hold in peculiar loathing the cant of critics who require "passion" as something in itself admirable and desirable in a novel, but because I prize fidelity in the historian of feeling and character. Most of these critics who demand "passion" would seem to have no conception of any passion but one. Yet there are several other passions: the passion of grief, the passion of avarice, the passion of pity, the passion of ambition, the passion of hate, the passion of envy, the passion of devotion, the passion of friendship; and all these have a greater part in the drama of life than the passion of love, and infinitely greater than the passion of guilty love. Wittingly or unwittingly, English fiction and American fiction have recognized this truth, not fully, not in the measure it merits, but in greater degree than most other fiction.

1891

1843 -- *Henry James* -- 1916

IT IS NOT certain that Henry James really belongs to American literature, for he resided in Europe and preferred it to America. But it is also doubtful whether he should be termed British, although he became a British citizen. James won distinction as a psychological novelist of fine artistry. He was interested in the leisurely analysis of character and fastidious craftsmanship rather than in incident and action. He concerned himself with spiritual values, aesthetic and intellectual problems, and fine instincts.

The life of Henry James shows no striking outer events. He lived as a spectator who observed but who did not enter into active life. He was not forced to earn his own living, for he was financially independent and had leisure and advantages that other writers were not able to enjoy. He was free to give to the world his best. James's grandfather was an Albany merchant of Irish stock who became a millionaire and could bequeath a fortune to his descendants. His father, Henry James, Sr., was a philosopher and writer and a close friend of Emerson. The older brother, William James, became professor of philosophy and psychology at Harvard.

At the age of twelve, the future novelist went to Europe, where he studied under private tutors at Geneva, London, and Paris. Later he was at Bonn. This cosmopolitan education served to make him European in temperament. In 1860, the family removed to Newport, and in 1862–63, James attended the Harvard Law School, although he did not intend to practice law. His health kept him out of the Civil War. Influenced by friends, he became interested in literary pursuits and writing. He had early been an admirer of Hawthorne, of George Eliot, who, followed by George Meredith, inaugurated the psychological novel, and of Balzac; and these writers left their imprint upon him. From 1864 to 1868 he lived at Cambridge and Boston and contributed stories and reviews to several periodicals. His first volume of fiction, *A Passionate Pilgrim and Other Tales*, appeared in 1871; and his first long novel, *Roderick Hudson*, which had been issued serially in the *Atlantic*, was reprinted in book form in 1876.

The years between 1876 and 1881 were prolific. While living in Massachusetts, James had made several trips to Europe, and in 1876 he resolved to establish his residence abroad. He was an aristocrat by temperament, and he thought American life thin and crude. It was poor in history, its civilization new, and its culture derivative. He was fond of intellectual society and he seemed to find that society only in Europe. He settled first in Paris, where he met Turgenev and Flaubert, but later gave it up for London. His books of this period deal especially with transplanted Americans and their conduct in the trying situation of finding themselves in an older and more sophisticated society. This was the beginning of the International Novel, a field in which he pioneered, its scenes London, Paris, Rome, New York. To this group belong *The American* (1877), *The Europeans* (1878), *Daisy Miller*, his only genuine "hit" (1879), *The International Episode* (1879), and *Portrait of a Lady* (1881). Later James lost interest in depicting contrasting cultures and the types they foster. His later novels were hardly successful either in the United States or in England, and he gave up expectation of popularity and began to compose in his own way. The last two decades of his life, 1896–1916, were spent at Rye, on the southeast coast of England, where he lived happily a life of considerable seclusion, although he kept his apartment in London. He had by this time changed his manner of writing from one of direct treatment to an involved style that the public found baffling. He gave much thought to intricacies of method and craftsmanship. His sentences were so filled with parenthetical explanations and qualifications that they became tedious and stultifying. Yet fiction writers abroad and in his own country acknowledge that his ideas of structure have had an unmistakable influence on certain groups of writers. Edith Wharton in this country and Marcel Proust in France have been termed his disciples. He remained prolific in his output, for he was able to dictate his involved sentences. The three later books that he thought his best were *Wings of the Dove* (1902), *The Ambassadors* (1903), and *The Golden Bowl* (1904).

After 1914, his work was affected by the World War. He had been virtually a British citizen for many years, and when America did not enter the war following the sinking of the *Lusitania*, he took out his naturalization papers in England. He was awarded the high honor of the Order of Merit by King George early in 1916. He died that same year, February 28, in his apartment in London.

James wrote travel books and was a keen and urbane critic, but he is better remembered as a novelist and story writer, whose method is that of the psychological clinic. He sets forth in minute shades the intangible qualities of the soul. His books contain little action or violence and because of the absence of dramatic happenings in them are often said to lack virility. A recurrent theme is that of renunciation. He deals with a restricted area of life. His characters are of one class, well-bred occupationless men and women who lead a sheltered life of leisure and fashion, and who are concerned with the fine art of living, its decorum and problems of taste. To many it seems that the fastidious culture and subtle mental powers of certain European circles he paints existed only in his imagination. James was perhaps the last embodiment of the genteel tradition. The world of which he wrote, a prewar world, has now passed, if it ever existed, in both the Old World and the New.

The literary theories of Henry James deserve attention, partly because of the care with which he recorded them and partly because of the influence he hoped they might have. His earlier stories were commonplace in method, told in bald, straightforward manner by a narrator. Some were realistic American and some had European backgrounds. The novels of his middle period, *Roderick Hudson*, *The American*, *The Portrait of a Lady*, *The Princess Cassamassima*, and *The Tragic Muse*, show great growth. For a time he wished to "dramatize" his themes, and relied on abundance of dialogue, with his characters in confrontation. He reached his distinctive method with *The Spoils of Poynton* (1896), in which are to be found nearly all the characteristic marks of his procedure. He wished a "central subject" and tried to bring out his basic "idea" by focusing on some intelligent, sensitive, and "aware" central person interposed between the reader and the story, who plays the part of a conscious interpreter for the reader. The "central idea" may be the opposition of new and old world ways of living, an abstraction, a situation, a psychological predicament, a single person or an aspect of a person, or a human relationship. His novels are concerned with pivotal facts or episodes in the lives of his characters, and the action is confined to the consciousness of these characters. The novelist does not tell as an author what he wishes his readers to see. The character or situation is set forth within the story itself, through the mind of someone watching the characters, or through the central character. The reader is on the inside. Who is to see and tell the story, who is to be the "center" or dramatic focus, whose is to be the "point of view," are among the questions James asked himself first. A few critics see in this method the beginning of the subjective "stream of consciousness" movement. James prided himself on the "economy" and "elimination" of his mode of presentation, and he believed that it promoted intensity. In *What Maisie Knew* he registers the impressions of a child. He conveys the whole story, his subject and his personages, through her juvenile intelligence, supplying no other information. Occasionally he makes use of an observer who is only slightly involved in the story, and often a confidant is needed. He never shifts carelessly from the point of view of one person to that of another, in the usual fashion of novelists. Sometimes, however, instead of the restricted point of view of a single character, there are given in contrast the views of other characters in alternation. These he terms a series of "centers," "mirrors," "lighters," "reflectors," or "lamps," each of which sets forth one of the main aspects of the central character or situation.

James often uses the word "picture" when speaking of his fiction, meaning thereby the restricted area through which his idea is developed. He likes a "scene" method of presentation. He relies on dialogue, but it is never to depart from what is "immediately to the purpose." He seeks "unity or pictorial fusion." He speaks of "foreshortening" and the desirability of achieving "balance" between the halves of either side of the "center of structure." There is elimination not only of all official explanation and formal introduction of characters but usually too of description of scenes and other settings. Since the "picture" is there from the start, and there is often no incident, the story seems to make little progress. His process is rather that of unfolding by bits, by gradual revelation, and from a consistent point of view. Indeed, he does not tell a story at all but gives the subjective concomitants of it. The emphasis is on interior states, and the sense of a rounded narrative with a clear ending is slight. He found "no endings in life" and some of his stories seem not to end at all.

James's critical essays have been collected in some six volumes. As a critic he was chiefly influenced by Sainte-Beuve, and in maturity he developed a method of subtle and sensitive impressionism resembling to some extent that of Walter Pater. His critical principles are set forth in his essay called "Criticism" in his volume *Essays in London and Elsewhere* (1893).

The best edition of James's works is the New York Edition (26 vols., 1907–17). In this he included his prefaces and critical theories. P. Lubbock edited the *Letters of Henry James* (2 vols., 1920). No standard life has yet appeared. Autobiographical works by James are *A Small Boy and Others* (1913), *Notes of a Son and Brother* (1914), and *The Middle Years* (1917, unfinished). See Edith Wharton, "Henry James in His Letters," *Quarterly Review*, CCXXXIV, July, 1920; and Hamlin Garland in *Roadside Meetings* (1930) and *Companions on the Trail* (1931).

For critical articles and studies see H. C. Vedder, in *American Writers of To-Day* (1894); E. L. Cary, *The Novels of Henry James* (1905); W. C. Brownell, in *American Prose Masters* (1909); Oliver Elton, in *Modern Studies* (1907); J. Macy, in *The Spirit of American Literature* (1913); F. M. Hueffer, *Henry James, a Critical Study* (1915); Rebecca West, *Henry James* (1916); S. P. Sherman, in *On Contemporary Literature* (1917); J. W. Beach, *The Method of Henry James* (1918), also in *The Twentieth Century Novel* (1932), and an article in *CHAL*, III (1921); H. T. and W. Follett, in *Some Modern Artists* (1919); Carl Van Doren, in *The American Novel* (1921), and in *DAB;* T. Bosanquet, *Henry James at Work* (1924); H. L. Hughes, *Theory and Practice in Henry James* (1926); P. Edgar, *Henry James, Man and Author* (1927); Marie-Reine Garnier, *Henry James et la France* (1927); M. Roberts, *Henry James's Criticism* (1929); V. L. Parrington in *Main Currents in American Thought*, III (1930); C. P. Kelley, *The Early Development of Henry James*, in *University of Illinois Studies in Language and Literature* (1930); Robert Herrick, in Macy's *American Writers on American Literature* (1931); G. E. De Mille, in *Literary Criticism in America* (1931); C. H. Grattan, in *The Three Jameses* (1932); H. Hartwick, in *The Foreground of American Fiction* (1932).

L. R. Phillips published *A Bibliography of the Writings of Henry James* (enlarged edition 1930). See also that by Hartwick in W. F. Taylor's *A History of American Letters* (1935).

GREVILLE FANE

James wrote a number of tales dealing with writers of fiction, among them "The Death of the Lion," "The Figure in the Carpet," "The Coxon Fund," and "The Author of Beltraffio." The latter, a novelette, is an excellent example of James's skill and subtlety in this special field. In most of these tales, the authors are presented as men of talents, somehow frustrated in the quality of their work, or in its reception, or in their life 10 experiences.

COMING in to dress for dinner, I found a telegram: "Mrs. Stormer dying; can you give us half a column for tomorrow evening? Let her off easy, but not too easy." I was late; I was in a hurry; I had very little time to think, but at a venture I dispatched a reply: "Will do what I can." It was not till I had dressed and was rolling away to dinner that, in the hansom, I bethought myself of the difficulty of the condition attached. The difficulty was not of course in letting her off easy but in qualifying that indulgence. "I simply won't qualify it," I said to myself. I didn't admire her, but I liked her, and I had known her so long that I almost felt heartless in sitting down at such an hour to a feast of indifference. I must have seemed abstracted, for the early years of my acquaintance with her came back to me. I spoke of her to the lady I had taken down, but the lady I had taken down had never heard of Greville Fane. I tried my other neighbor, who pronounced her books "too vile." I had never thought them very good, but I should let her off easier than that.

I came away early, for the express purpose of driving to ask about her. The journey took time, for she lived in the northwest district, in the neighborhood of Primrose Hill. My apprehension that I should be too late was justified in a fuller sense than I had attached to it—I had only feared that the house would be shut up. There were lights in the windows, and the temperate tinkle of my bell brought a servant immediately to the door, but poor Mrs. Stormer had passed into a state in which the resonance of no earthly knocker was to be feared. A lady, in the hall, hovering behind the servant, came forward when she heard my voice. I recognized Lady Luard, but she had mistaken me for the doctor.

"Excuse my appearing at such an hour," I said; "it was the first possible moment after I heard."

"It's all over," Lady Luard replied. "Dearest mamma!"

She stood there under the lamp with her eyes on me; she was very tall, very stiff, very cold, and always looked as if these things, and some others beside, in her dress, her manner and even her name, were an implication that she was very admirable. I had never been able to follow the argument, but that is a detail. I expressed briefly and frankly what I felt, while the little mottled maidservant flattened herself against the wall of the narrow passage and tried to look detached without looking indifferent. It was not a moment to make a visit, and I was on the point of retreating when Lady Luard arrested me with a queer, casual, drawling "Would you—a—would you, perhaps, be *writing* something?" I felt for the instant like an interviewer, which I was not. But I

pleaded guilty to this intention, on which she rejoined: "I'm so very glad—but I think my brother would like to see you." I detested her brother, but it wasn't an occasion to act this out; so I suffered myself to be inducted, to my surprise, into a small back room which I immediately recognized as the scene, during the later years, of Mrs. Stormer's imperturbable industry. Her table was there, the battered and blotted accessory to innumerable literary lapses, with its contracted space for the arms (she wrote only from the elbow down) and the confusion of scrappy, scribbled sheets which had already become literary remains. Leolin was also there, smoking a cigarette before the fire and looking impudent even in his grief, sincere as it well might have been.

To meet him, to greet him, I had to make a sharp effort; for the air that he wore to me as he stood before me was quite that of his mother's murderer. She lay silent forever upstairs—as dead as an unsuccessful book, and his swaggering erectness was a kind of symbol of his having killed her. I wondered if he had already, with his sister, been calculating what they could get for the poor papers on the table; but I had not long to wait to learn, for in reply to the scanty words of sympathy I addressed him he puffed out: "It's miserable, miserable, yes; but she has left three books complete." His words had the oddest effect; they converted the cramped little room into a seat of trade and made the "book" wonderfully feasible. He would certainly get all that could be got for the three. Lady Luard explained to me that her husband had been with them but had had to go down to the House. To her brother she explained that I was going to write something, and to me again she made it clear that she hoped I would "do mamma justice." She added that she didn't think this had ever been done. She said to her brother: "Don't you think there are some things he ought thoroughly to understand?" and on his instantly exclaiming "Oh, thoroughly—thoroughly!" she went on, rather austerely: "I mean about mamma's birth."

"Yes, and her connections," Leolin added.

I professed every willingness, and for five minutes I listened, but it would be too much to say that I understood. I don't even now, but it is not important. My vision was of other matters than those they put before me, and while they desired there should be no mistake about their ancestors I became more and more lucid about themselves. I got away as soon as possible, and walked home through the great dusky, empty London—the best of all conditions for thought. By the time I reached my door my little article was practically composed —ready to be transferred on the morrow from the polished plate of fancy. I believe it attracted some notice, was thought "graceful" and was said to be by someone else. I had to be pointed without being lively, and it took some tact. But what I said was much less interesting than what I thought—especially during the half-hour I spent in my arm-chair by the fire, smoking the cigar I always light before going to bed. I went to sleep there, I believe; but I continued to moralize about Greville Fane. I am reluctant to lose that retrospect altogether, and this is a dim little memory of it, a document not to "serve." The dear woman had written a hundred stories, but none so curious as her own.

When first I knew her she had published half-a-dozen fictions, and I believe I had also perpetrated a novel. She was more than a dozen years older than I, but she was a person who always acknowledged her relativity. It was not so very long ago, but in London, amid the big waves of the present, even a near horizon gets hidden. I met her at some dinner and took her down, rather flattered at offering my arm to a celebrity. She didn't look like one, with her matronly, mild, inanimate face, but I supposed her greatness would come out in her conversation. I gave it all the opportunities I could, but I was not disappointed when I found her only a dull, kind woman. This was why I liked her—she rested me so from literature. To myself literature was an irritation, a torment; but Greville Fane slumbered in the intellectual part of it like a Creole in a hammock. She was not a woman of genius, but her faculty was so special, so much a gift out of hand, that I have often wondered why she fell below that distinction. This was doubtless because the transaction, in her case, had remained incomplete; genius always pays for the gift, feels the debt, and she was placidly unconscious of obliga-

tion. She could invent stories by the yard, but she couldn't write a page of English. She went down to her grave without suspecting that though she had contributed volumes to the diversion of her contemporaries she had not contributed a sentence to the language. This had not prevented bushels of criticism from being heaped upon her head; she was worth a couple of columns any day to the weekly papers, in which it was shown that her pictures of life were dreadful but her style really charming. She asked me to come and see her, and I went. She lived then in Montpellier Square; which helped me to see how dissociated her imagination was from her character.

An industrious widow, devoted to her daily stint, to meeting the butcher and baker and making a home for her son and daughter, from the moment she took her pen in her hand she became a creature of passion. She thought the English novel deplorably wanting in that element, and the task she had cut out for herself was to supply the deficiency. Passion in high life was the general formula of this work, for her imagination was at home only in the most exalted circles. She adored, in truth, the aristocracy, and they constituted for her the romance of the world or, what is more to the point, the prime material of fiction. Their beauty and luxury, their loves and revenges, their temptations and surrenders, their immoralities and diamonds were as familiar to her as the blots on her writing-table. She was not a belated producer of the old fashionable novel, she had a cleverness and a modernness of her own, she had freshened up the fly-blown tinsel. She turned off plots by the hundred and—so far as her flying quill could convey her—was perpetually going abroad. Her types, her illustrations, her tone were nothing if not cosmopolitan. She recognized nothing less provincial than European society, and her fine folk knew each other and made love to each other from Doncaster to Bucharest. She had an idea that she resembled Balzac, and her favorite historical characters were Lucien de Rubempré and the Vidame de Pamiers. I must add that when I once asked her who the latter personage was she was unable to tell me. She was very brave and healthy and cheerful, very abundant and innocent and wicked. She was clever and vulgar and snobbish, and never so intensely British as when she was particularly foreign.

This combination of qualities had brought her early success, and I remember having heard with wonder and envy of what she "got," in those days, for a novel. The revelation gave me a pang: it was such a proof that, practicing a totally different style, I should never make my fortune. And yet when, as I knew her better she told me her real tariff and I saw how rumor had quadrupled it, I liked her enough to be sorry. After a while I discovered too that if she got less it was not that *I* was to get any more. My failure never had what Mrs. Stormer would have called the banality of being relative—it was always admirably absolute. She lived at ease however in those days —ease is exactly the word, though she produced three novels a year. She scorned me when I spoke of difficulty—it was the only thing that made her angry. If I hinted that a work of art required a tremendous licking into shape she thought it a pretension and a *pose*. She never recognized the "torment of form"; the furthest she went was to introduce into one of her books (in satire her hand was heavy) a young poet who was always talking about it. I couldn't quite understand her irritation on this score, for she had nothing at stake in the matter. She had a shrewd perception that form, in prose at least, never recommended anyone to the public we were condemned to address, and therefore she lost nothing (putting her private humiliation aside) by not having any. She made no pretense of producing works of art, but had comfortable tea-drinking hours in which she freely confessed herself a common pastrycook, dealing in such tarts and puddings as would bring customers to the shop. She put in plenty of sugar and of cochineal, or whatever it is that gives these articles a rich and attractive color. She had a serene superiority to observation and opportunity which constituted an inexpugnable strength and would enable her to go on indefinitely. It is only real success that wanes, it is only solid things that melt. Greville Fane's ignorance of life was a resource still more unfailing than the most approved receipt. On her saying once that the day would come when she should have written herself out I

answered: "Ah, you look into fairyland, and the fairies love you, and *they* never change. Fairyland is always there; it always was from the beginning of time, and it always will be to the end. They've given you the key and you can always open the door. With me it's different; I try, in my clumsy way, to be in some direct relation to life." "Oh, bother your direct relation to life!" she used to reply, for she was always annoyed by the phrase—which would not in the least prevent her from using it when she wished to try for style. With no more prejudices than an old sausage-mill, she would give forth again with patient punctuality any poor verbal scrap that had been dropped into her. I cheered her with saying that the dark day, at the end, would be for the like of *me;* inasmuch as, going in our small way by experience and observation, we depended not on a revelation, but on a little tiresome process. Observation depended on opportunity, and where should we be when opportunity failed?

One day she told me that as the novelist's life was so delightful and during the good years at least such a comfortable support (she had these staggering optimisms) she meant to train up her boy to follow it. She took the ingenious view that it was a profession like another and that therefore everything was to be gained by beginning young and serving an apprenticeship. Moreover the education would be less expensive than any other special course, inasmuch as she could administer it herself. She didn't profess to keep a school, but she could at least teach her own child. It was not that she was so very clever, but (she confessed to me as if she were afraid I would laugh at her) that *he* was. I didn't laugh at her for that, for I thought the boy sharp—I had seen him at sundry times. He was well grown and good-looking and unabashed, and both he and his sister made me wonder about their defunct papa, concerning whom the little I knew was that he had been a clergyman. I explained them to myself by suppositions and imputations possibly unjust to the departed; so little were they—superficially at least—the children of their mother. There used to be, on the easel in her drawing-room, an enlarged photograph of her husband, done by some horrible posthumous "process" and draped, as to its florid frame, with a silken scarf, which testified to the candor of Greville Fane's bad taste. It made him look like an unsuccessful tragedian; but it was not a thing to trust. He may have been a successful comedian. Of the two children the girl was the elder, and struck me in all her younger years as singularly colorless. She was only very long, like an undecipherable letter. It was not till Mrs. Stormer came back from a protracted residence abroad that Ethel (which was this young lady's name) began to produce the effect, which was afterwards remarkable in her, of a certain kind of high resolution. She made one apprehend that she meant to do something for herself. She was long-necked and near-sighted and striking, and I thought I had never seen sweet seventeen in a form so hard and high and dry. She was cold and affected and ambitious, and she carried an eyeglass with a long handle, which she put up whenever she wanted not to see. She had come out, as the phrase is, immensely; and yet I felt as if she were surrounded with a spiked iron railing. What she meant to do for herself was to marry, and it was the only thing, I think, that she meant to do for anyone else; yet who would be inspired to clamber over that bristling barrier? What flower of tenderness or of intimacy would such an adventurer conceive as his reward?

This was for Sir Baldwin Luard to say; but he naturally never confided to me the secret. He was a joyless, jokeless young man, with the air of having other secrets as well, and a determination to get on politically that was indicated by his never having been known to commit himself—as regards any proposition whatever—beyond an exclamatory "Oh!" His wife and he must have conversed mainly in prim ejaculations, but they understood sufficiently that they were kindred spirits. I remember being angry with Greville Fane when she announced these nuptials to me as magnificent; I remember asking her what splendor there was in the union of the daughter of a woman of genius with an irredeemable mediocrity. "Oh! he's awfully clever," she said; but she blushed for the maternal fib. What she meant was that though Sir Baldwin's estates

were not vast (he had a dreary house in South Kensington and a still drearier "Hall" somewhere in Essex, which was let), the connection was a "smarter" one than a child of hers could have aspired to form. In spite of the social bravery of her novels she took a very humble and dingy view of herself, so that of all her productions "my daughter Lady Luard" was quite the one she was proudest of. That personage thought her mother very vulgar and was distressed and perplexed by the occasional license of her pen, but had a complicated attitude in regard to this indirect connection with literature. So far as it was lucrative her ladyship approved of it, and could compound with the inferiority of the pursuit by doing practical justice to some of its advantages. I had reason to know (my reason was simply that poor Mrs. Stormer told me) that she suffered the inky fingers to press an occasional bank-note into her palm. On the other hand she deplored the "peculiar style" to which Greville Fane had devoted herself, and wondered where an author who had the convenience of so ladylike a daughter could have picked up such views about the best society. "She might know better, with Leolin and me," Lady Luard had been known to remark; but it appeared that some of Greville Fane's superstitions were incurable. She didn't live in Lady Luard's society, and the best was not good enough for her—she must make it still better.

I could see that this necessity grew upon her during the years she spent abroad, when I had glimpses of her in the shifting sojourns that lay in the path of my annual ramble. She betook herself from Germany to Switzerland and from Switzerland to Italy; she favored cheap places and set up her desk in the smaller capitals. I took a look at her whenever I could, and I always asked how Leolin was getting on. She gave me beautiful accounts of him, and whenever it was possible the boy was produced for my edification. I had entered from the first into the joke of his career—I pretended to regard him as a consecrated child. It had been a joke for Mrs. Stormer at first, but the boy himself had been shrewd enough to make the matter serious. If his mother accepted the principle that the intending novelist cannot begin too early to see life, Leolin was not interested in hanging back from the application of it. He was eager to qualify himself, and took to cigarettes at ten, on the highest literary grounds. His poor mother gazed at him with extravagant envy and, like Desdemona, wished heaven had made *her* such a man. She explained to me more than once that in her profession she had found her sex a dreadful drawback. She loved the story of Madame George Sand's early rebellion against this hindrance, and believed that if she had worn trousers she could have written as well as that lady. Leolin had for the career at least the qualification of trousers, and as he grew older he recognized its importance by laying in an immense assortment. He grew up in gorgeous apparel, which was his way of interpreting his mother's system. Whenever I met her I found her still under the impression that she was carrying this system out and that Leolin's training was bearing fruit. She was giving him experience, she was giving him impressions, she was putting a *gagne-pain* into his hand. It was another name for spoiling him with the best conscience in the world. The queerest pictures come back to me of this period of the good lady's life and of the extraordinarily virtuous, muddled, bewildering tenor of it. She had an idea that she was seeing foreign manners as well as her petticoats would allow; but, in reality she was not seeing anything, least of all fortunately how much she was laughed at. She drove her whimsical pen at Dresden and at Florence, and produced in all places and at all times the same romantic and ridiculous fictions. She carried about her box of properties and fished out promptly the familiar, tarnished old puppets. She believed in them when others couldn't, and as they were like nothing that was to be seen under the sun it was impossible to prove by comparison that they were wrong. You can't compare birds and fishes; you could only feel that, as Greville Fane's characters had the fine plumage of the former species, human beings must be of the latter.

It would have been droll if it had not been so exemplary to see her tracing the loves of the duchesses beside the innocent cribs of her children. The immoral and the maternal lived together in her diligent days on the most comfortable terms, and she stopped curling the mustaches of her Guardsmen to pat the heads of her babes. She was haunted by solemn spinsters who came to tea from continental *pensions*, and by unsophisticated Americans who told her she was just loved in *their* country. "I had rather be just paid there," she usually replied; for this tribute of transatlantic opinion was the only thing that galled her. The Americans went away thinking her coarse; though as the author of so many beautiful love-stories she was disappointing to most of these pilgrims, who had not expected to find a shy, stout, ruddy lady in a cap like a crumbled pyramid. She wrote about the affections and the impossibility of controlling them, but she talked of the price of *pension* and the convenience of an English chemist. She devoted much thought and many thousands of francs to the education of her daughter, who spent three years at a very superior school at Dresden, receiving wonderful instruction in sciences, arts and tongues, and who, taking a different line from Leolin, was to be brought up wholly as a *femme du monde*. The girl was musical and philological; she made a specialty of languages and learned enough about them to be inspired with a great contempt for her mother's artless accents. Greville Fane's French and Italian were droll; the imitative faculty had been denied her, and she had an unequaled gift, especially pen in hand, of squeezing big mistakes into small opportunities. She knew it, but she didn't care; correctness was the virtue in the world that, like her heroes and heroines, she valued least. Ethel, who had perceived in her pages some remarkable lapses, undertook at one time to revise her proofs; but I remember her telling me a year after the girl had left school that this function had been very briefly exercised. "She can't read me," said Mrs. Stormer; "I offend her taste. She tells me that at Dresden—at school—I was never allowed." The good lady seemed surprised at this, having the best conscience in the world about her lucubrations. She had never meant to fly in the face of anything, and considered that she groveled before the Rhadamanthus of the English literary tribunal, the celebrated and awful Young Person. I assured her, as a joke, that she was frightfully indecent (she hadn't in fact that reality any more than any other) my purpose being solely to prevent her from guessing that her daughter had dropped her not because she was immoral but because she was vulgar. I used to figure her children closeted together and asking each other while they exchanged a gaze of dismay: "Why should she *be* so—and so *fearfully* so—when she has the advantage of our society? Shouldn't *we* have taught her better?" Then I imagined their recognizing with a blush and a shrug that she was unteachable, irreformable. Indeed she was, poor lady; but it is never fair to read by the light of taste things that were not written by it. Greville Fane had, in the topsy-turvy, a serene good faith that ought to have been safe from allusion, like a stutter or a *faux pas*.

She didn't make her son ashamed of the profession to which he was destined, however; she only made him ashamed of the way she herself exercised it. But he bore his humiliation much better than his sister, for he was ready to take for granted that he should one day restore the balance. He was a canny and far-seeing youth, with appetites and aspirations, and he had not a scruple in his composition. His mother's theory of the happy knack he could pick up deprived him of the wholesome discipline required to prevent young idlers from becoming cads. He had, abroad, a casual tutor and a snatch or two of a Swiss school, but no consecutive study, no prospect of a university or a degree. It may be imagined with what zeal, as the years went on, he entered into the pleasantry of there being no manual so important to him as the massive book of life. It was an expensive volume to peruse, but Mrs. Stormer was willing to lay out a sum in what she would have called her *premiers frais*. Ethel disapproved—she thought this education far too unconventional for an English gentleman. Her voice was for Eton and Oxford, or for any public school (she would have resigned herself) with the army to follow. But Leolin never was afraid of his sister, and they visibly disliked, though they sometimes agreed to assist, each other. They could combine to work the oracle—to keep their mother at her desk.

When she came back to England, telling me she had got all the continent could give her, Leolin was a broad-shouldered, red-faced young man, with an immense wardrobe and an extraordinary assurance of manner. She was fondly obstinate about her having taken the right course with him, and proud of all that he knew and had seen. He was now quite ready to begin, and a little while later she told me he *had* begun. He had written something tremendously clever, and it was coming out in the *Cheapside*. I believe it came out; I had no time to look for it; I never heard anything about it. I took for granted that if this contribution had passed through his mother's hands it had practically become a specimen of her own genius, and it was interesting to consider Mrs. Stormer's future in the light of her having to write her son's novels as well as her own. This was not the way she looked at it herself; she took the charming ground that he would help her to write hers. She used to tell me that he supplied passages of the greatest value to her own work—all sorts of technical things, about hunting and yachting and wine—that she couldn't be expected to get very straight. It was all so much practice for him and so much alleviation for her. I was unable to identify these pages, for I had long since ceased to "keep up" with Greville Fane; but I was quite able to believe that the wine-question had been put, by Leolin's good offices, on a better footing, for the dear lady used to mix her drinks (she was perpetually serving the most splendid suppers) in the queerest fashion. I could see that he was willing enough to accept a commission to look after that department. It occurred to me indeed, when Mrs. Stormer settled in England again, that by making a shrewd use of both her children she might be able to rejuvenate her style. Ethel had come back to gratify her young ambition, and if she couldn't take her mother into society she would at least go into it herself. Silently, stiffly, almost grimly, this young lady held up her head, clenched her long teeth, squared her lean elbows and made her way up the staircases she had elected. The only communication she ever made to me, the only effusion of confidence with which she ever honored me, was when she said: "I don't want to know the people mamma knows; I mean to know others." I took due note of the remark, for I was not one of the "others." I couldn't trace therefore the steps of her process;

I could only admire it at a distance and congratulate her mother on the results. The results were that Ethel went to "big" parties and got people to take her. Some of them were people she had met abroad, and others were people whom the people she had met abroad had met. They ministered alike to Miss Ethel's convenience, and I wondered how she extracted so many favors without the expenditure of a smile. Her smile was the dimmest thing in the world, diluted lemonade, without sugar, and she had arrived precociously at social wisdom, recognizing that if she was neither pretty enough nor rich enough nor clever enough, she could at least in her muscular youth be rude enough. Therefore if she was able to tell her mother what really took place in the mansions of the great, give her notes to work from, the quill could be driven at home to better purpose and precisely at a moment when it would have to be more active than ever. But if she did tell, it would appear that poor Mrs. Stormer didn't believe. As regards many points this was not a wonder; at any rate I heard nothing of Greville Fane's having developed a new manner. She had only one manner from start to finish, as Leolin would have said.

She was tired at last, but she mentioned to me that she couldn't afford to pause. She continued to speak of Leolin's work as the great hope of their future (she had saved no money) though the young man wore to my sense an aspect more and more professional if you like, but less and less literary. At the end of a couple of years there was something monstrous in the impudence with which he played his part in the comedy. When I wondered how she could play *her* part I had to perceive that her good faith was complete and that what kept it so was simply her extravagant fondness. She loved the young imposter with a simple, blind, benighted love, and of all the heroes of romance who had passed before her eyes he was by far the most brilliant. He was at any rate the most real—she could touch him, pay for him, suffer for him, worship him. He made her think of her princes and dukes, and when she wished to fix these figures in her mind's eye she thought of her boy. She had often told me she was carried away by her own creations, and she was sertainly carried away by Leolin. He vivified,

by potentialities at least, the whole question of youth and passion. She held, not unjustly, that the sincere novelist should feel the whole flood of life; she acknowledged with regret that she had not had time to feel it herself, and it was a joy to her that the deficiency might be supplied by the sight of the way it was rushing through this magnificent young man. She exhorted him, I suppose, to let it rush; she wrung her own flaccid little sponge into the torrent. I knew not what passed between them in her hours of tuition, but I gathered that she mainly impressed on him that the great thing was to live, because that gave you material. He asked nothing better; he collected material, and the formula served as a universal pretext. You had only to look at him to see that, with his rings and breastpins, his cross-barred jackets, his early *embonpoint*, his eyes that looked like imitation jewels, his various indications of a dense, full-blown temperament, his idea of life was singularly vulgar; but he was not so far wrong as that his response to his mother's expectations was not in a high degree practical. If she had imposed a profession on him from his tenderest years it was exactly a profession that he followed. The two were not quite the same, inasmuch as *his* was simply to live at her expense; but at least she couldn't say that he hadn't taken a line. If she insisted on believing in him he offered himself to the sacrifice. My impression is that her secret dream was that he should have a *liaison* with a countess, and he persuaded her without difficulty that he had one. I don't know what countesses are capable of, but I have a clear notion of what Leolin was.

He didn't persuade his sister, who despised him—she wished to work her mother in her own way, and I asked myself why the girl's judgment of him didn't make me like her better. It was because it didn't save her after all from a mute agreement with him to go halves. There were moments when I couldn't help looking hard into his atrocious young eyes, challenging him to confess his fantastic fraud and give it up. Not a little tacit conversation passed between us in this way, but he had always the best of it. If I said: "Oh, come now, with *me* you needn't keep it up; plead guilty, and I'll let you off," he wore the most in genuous, the most candid expression, in the depths of which I could read: "Oh, yes, I know it exasperates you—that's just why I do it." He took the line of earnest inquiry, talked about Balzac and Flaubert, asked me if I thought Dickens *did* exaggerate and Thackeray *ought* to be called a pessimist. Once he came to see me, at his mother's suggestion he declared, on purpose to ask me how far, in my opinion, in the English novel, one really might venture to "go." He was not resigned to the usual pruderies—he suffered under them already. He struck out the brilliant idea that nobody knew how far we might go, for nobody had ever tried. Did I think *he* might safely try —would it injure his mother if he did? He would rather disgrace himself by his timidities than injure his mother, but certainly someone ought to try. Wouldn't *I* try—couldn't I be prevailed upon to look at it as a duty? Surely the ultimate point ought to be fixed—he was worried, haunted by the question. He patronized me unblushingly, made me feel like a foolish amateur, a helpless novice, inquired into my habits of work and conveyed to me that I was utterly *vieux jeu* and had not had the advantage of an early training. I had not been brought up from the germ, I knew nothing of life—didn't go at it on *his* system. He had dipped into French feuilletons and picked up plenty of phrases, and he made a much better show in talk than his poor mother, who never had time to read anything and could only be vivid with her pen. If I didn't kick him downstairs it was because he would have alighted on her at the bottom.

When she went to live at Primrose Hill I called upon her and found her weary and wasted. It had waned a good deal, the elation caused the year before by Ethel's marriage; the foam on the cup had subsided and there was a bitterness in the draught. She had had to take a cheaper house and she had to work still harder to pay even for that. Sir Baldwin was obliged to be close; his charges were fearful, and the dream of her living with her daughter (a vision she had never mentioned to me) must be renounced. "I would have helped with things, and I could have lived perfectly in one room," she said; "I would have paid for everything, and—after all—I'm someone, ain't I? But I

don't fit in, and Ethel tells me there are tiresome people she *must* receive. I can help them from here, no doubt, better than from there. She told me once, you know, what she thinks of my picture of life. 'Mamma, your picture of life is preposterous!' No doubt it is, but she's vexed with me for letting my prices go down; and I had to write three novels to pay for all her marriage cost me. I did it very well —I mean the outfit and the wedding; but that's why I'm here. At any rate she doesn't want a dingy old woman in her house. I should give it an atmosphere of literary glory, but literary glory is only the eminence of nobodies. Besides, she doubts my glory—she knows I'm glorious only at Peckham and Hackney. She doesn't want her friends to ask if I've never known nice people. She can't tell them I've never been in society. She tried to teach me better once, but I couldn't learn. It would seem too as if Peckham and Hackney had had enough of me; for (don't tell anyone!) I've had to take less for my last than I ever took for anything." I asked her how little this had been, not from curiosity, but in order to upbraid her, more disinterestedly than Lady Luard had done, for such concessions. She answered "I'm ashamed to tell you," and then she began to cry.

I had never seen her break down, and I was proportionately moved; she sobbed, like a frightened child, over the extinction of her vogue and the exhaustion of her vein. Her little workroom seemed indeed a barren place to grow flowers, and I wondered, in the after years (for she continued to produce and publish) by what desperate and heroic process she dragged them out of the soil. I remember asking her on that occasion what had become of Leolin, and how much longer she intended to allow him to amuse himself at her cost. She rejoined with spirit, wiping her eyes, that he was down at Brighton hard at work—he was in the midst of a novel—and that he *felt* life so, in all its misery and mystery, that it was cruel to speak of such experiences as a pleasure. "He goes beneath the surface," she said, "and he *forces* himself to look at things from which he would rather turn away. Do you call that amusing yourself? You should see his face sometimes! And he does it for me as much as for himself. He tells me everything—he comes home to me with his *trouvailles*. We are artists together, and to the artist all things are pure. I've often heard you say so yourself." The novel that Leolin was engaged in at Brighton was never published, but a friend of mine and of Mrs. Stormer's who was staying there happened to mention to me later that he had seen the young apprentice to fiction driving, in a dogcart, a young lady with a very pink face. When I suggested that she was perhaps a woman of title with whom he was conscientiously flirting my informant replied: "She is indeed, but do you know what her title is?" He pronounced it—it was familiar and descriptive—but I won't reproduce it here. I don't know whether Leolin mentioned it to his mother: she would have needed all the purity of the artist to forgive him. I hated so to come across him that in the very last years I went rarely to see her, though I knew that she had come pretty well to the end of her rope. I didn't want her to tell me that she had fairly to give her books away—I didn't want to see her cry. She kept it up amazingly, and every few months, at my club, I saw three new volumes, in green, in crimson, in blue, on the booktable that groaned with light literature. Once I met her at the Academy soirée, where you meet people you thought were dead, and she vouchsafed the information, as if she owed it to me in candor, that Leolin had been obliged to recognize insuperable difficulties in the question of *form*, he was so fastidious; so that she

had now arrived at a definite understanding with him (it was such a comfort) that *she* would do the form if he would bring home the substance. That was now his position—he foraged for her in the great world at a salary. "He's my 'devil,' don't you see? as if I were a great lawyer: he gets up the case and I argue it." She mentioned further that in addition to his salary he was paid by the piece: he got so much for a striking character, so much for a pretty name, so much for a plot, so much for an incident, and had so much promised him if he would invent a new crime.

"He *has* invented one," I said, "and he's paid every day of his life."

"What is it?" she asked, looking hard at the picture of the year, "Baby's Tub," near which we happened to be standing.

I hesitated a moment. "I myself will write a little story about it, and then you'll see."

But she never saw; she had never seen anything, and she passed away with her fine blindness unimpaired. Her son published every scrap of scribbled paper that could be extracted from her table-drawers, and his sister quarreled with him mortally about the proceeds, which showed that she only wanted a pretext, for they cannot have been great. I don't know what Leolin lives upon, unless it be on a queer lady many years older than himself, whom he lately married. The last time I met him he said to me with his infuriating smile: "Don't you think we can go a little further still—just a little?" *He* really goes too far.

1893

~~IV~~

Literature

of the

Twentieth

Century

Literature of the Twentieth Century

I

SOURCES AND BEGINNINGS

i

Much of the creative energy of early twentieth-century America was consumed by controversies over Darwin and Spencer, and by attempts to form a naturalistic theory of writing from the suggestions offered by those two British theorists of science. The philosophy and psychology of Herbert Spencer was especially adapted to American business apologetics; Spencer was also reassuring to those who wished to combine evolutionary theories with a theory of progress. "The ultimate development of the ideal man is logically certain," he said in *Social Statics* (1850), "as certain as any conclusion in which we place the most explicit faith. . . . Progress, therefore, is not an accident, but a necessity." In his interpretation of that progress, Spencer clearly indicated that the doctrine of evolution involved also a business philosophy of laissez-faire, and vigorously opposed socialist and humanitarian ideals. The captains of industry found in Spencer's reading of Darwin justification and flattery for themselves. "It would be strange," wrote C. R. Henderson in *The American Journal of Sociology* in 1896, "if the 'captain of the industry' did not sometimes manifest a militant spirit, for he has risen from the ranks largely because he was a better fighter than most of us. Competitive commercial life is not a flowery bed of ease, but a battle field where the 'struggle for existence' is defining the industrially 'fittest to survive.'"

The titans and the financiers were quick to take up the refrain. "The growth of a large business is merely a survival of the fittest," said John D. Rockefeller. "The American Beauty rose can be produced in the splendor and fragrance which bring cheer to its beholder only by sacrificing the early buds which grow up around it." This is not an evil thing, but "merely the working out of a law of nature and a law of God." Andrew Carnegie, perhaps Spencer's closest American friend, also saw "the light" when he "had found the truth of evolution." The Christian socialists, some members of the ministry, and such journalists as Edward Bellamy thought otherwise. "I assert that the injustice of society, not the niggardliness of nature, is the cause of the want and misery which the current theory [Spencer's adaptation of Malthus] attributes to overpopulation," said Henry George at the end of Book Two of *Progress and Poverty* (1879). To the "selfishness" of late nineteenth-century capitalism, Bellamy's Dr. Leete (of *Looking Backward*, 1888) opposed "combination," or "The Brotherhood of Humanity," as "the secret of efficient production." So long as competition, "simply the application of the brutal law of the survival of the strongest and most cunning," persists in the American economy, "the highest development of the individual cannot be reached, the loftiest aims of humanity cannot be realized."

At the beginning of the century, these points of view stood as representative expressions of American thought. Darwin's evolutionary theories had been variously interpreted, at first by Spencer and later by Benjamin Kidd, whose *Social Evolution* (1894) was eagerly seized upon as a decisive indication that social reform and Darwinism were not irreconcilable. These theories dominated the intellectual life of a country which had just recently finished the Spanish-American War and emerged with colonial possessions and mandates spread over half the globe. The attitude of American thinkers was dominated by the effort to explain American greatness and bigness; its second concern was to find a philosophical position which would somehow account for the enormous strategic advantage which science had assumed since the end of the Civil War. Northern industrialism, having conquered the South in a test of material strength, now pushed forward and westward. Inventions, scientific discoveries, refinements of efficiency brought into business, above all the presence of the dynamo—these were the order of the day. But, although the writers of the twentieth century could not deny the physical strength of these things and the physical energy of those who exploited them, they were not satisfied with a mere acceptance or an easy explanation in terms of material progress, or in Darwinian catch phrases.

Naturalism in American literature was an expression of the scientific condition of the age. The writers of fiction in the late nineteenth century were aware of both the need and the opportunity to justify their work in terms of a philosophical theory which was certainly not perfectly adjusted to their own tempers but seemed to reflect quite satisfactorily the temper of the times. American naturalism had its European sources in Emile Zola's "experimental novel," in George Moore's *Esther Waters*, in the novels of Thomas Hardy. Zola had said in 1880, "In one word, we should operate on the characters, the passions, on the human and social data, in the same way that the chemist and the physicist operate on inanimate beings and as the physiologist operates on living beings. Determinism dominates everything." Such an approach to literature, while it was seldom used without qualification or reservation, appealed to the novelists of the late nineteenth and the early twentieth centuries. While William Dean Howells had insisted upon "truth" in fiction and described the realist as one who "cannot look upon human life and declare this thing or that thing unworthy of notice, any more than the scientist can declare a fact of the material world beneath the dignity of his inquiry," he had also set limits upon the practice of realism, had in his writings presented for the most part a selectively realistic portrait of certain areas of American and social life. "The manners of the novel have been improving with those of its readers; that is all," he said in answer to critics who would have wanted the novelist to "tell all." "Generally, people now call a spade an agricultural implement; they have not grown decent without having also grown a little squeamish, but they have grown comparatively decent; there is no doubt about that. They require of a novelist whom they respect unquestionable proof of his seriousness, if he proposes to deal with certain phases of life; they require a sort of scientific decorum."

This was polite realism, which, in the opinion of younger writers, could not go far enough or soil its hands enough. The naturalism of Stephen Crane, Frank Norris, Jack London, and Theodore Dreiser was far less "squeamish" and selective. Or, if one of them did follow a principle of selection, it was not Howells's "Young Girl" they had in mind. This is not to say that they followed consistently any philosophy of behavior, or stayed scrupulously and objectively outside their work, as Zola had counseled. Briefly, naturalism, as these writers saw it, did accept, at least in spirit, Zola's belief in "scientific objectivity," which inclined them to the representation of all the crudities of dialect and style implicit in their subjects. On the question of the dominating and controlling causes of the human behavior they were to describe so objectively, they alternated between universal and environmental determinism: fate or society, or society as a passive demonstration of fate, were variously blamed for the behavior of their creatures. Whichever the cause, man seems to act in a blind obedience to his passions and impulses; he is possessed of no free will; he is generally a passive servant of an indifferent universe and acts in terms of "natural law" as expressed either in his own biological condition or in his environment. All of this is oversimplified. Into the history of American fiction went a great number of other determining influences: the Nietzschean idea of the superman, very badly misinterpreted and disarranged, affected the writing of Norris (in *A Man's Woman* and *Moran of the Lady Letty*) and of Jack London; socialist reactions against the convenient Spencerian reading of Darwin qualified and directed the realism of many progressive, "muckraking" novelists of the first two decades; the attention to regional detail, careful and repetitious in the work of Sara Orne Jewett, Mary Wilkins Freeman, and others, continued to dominate the fictional attitudes of Ellen Glasgow, Willa Cather, and Elizabeth Madox Roberts, and much later to contribute to the most effective devices of John Steinbeck and of Katherine Anne Porter; the late nineteenth century celebrations of the men of industry were subsequently to be modified into "naturalistic" accountings for their greatness (as in Norris's *The Pit* and Dreiser's *The Financier* and *The Titan*); melodrama in various forms was to enliven and occasionally to direct the course of such novels as Norris's *The Octopus*. In other words, naturalism, a theory imperfectly understood, was even more imperfectly followed. It led to a great variety of literary practices. But much of the fiction that appeared from 1890 to 1925 represented either an attempt to explain or an effort to escape what in the mind of the American writer was "the dilemma of naturalism."

The effect upon the styles in American fiction was varied. In many cases, naturalism seemed to require, or at the least to excuse, serious weaknesses of style. The effort to imitate the language of the subject led often to a surrender to its manner; the desire to escape selective discrimination led to huge, sprawling, novelistic extensions of the worst vices of journalism; the not infrequent giving in to the temptation for editorializing often revealed appalling sins against good taste. If we will examine a few examples of what might be called "the naturalistic style," we shall be able to note the several manners this fiction assumed. The first is from Stephen Crane's *Maggie: A Girl of the Streets* (1892), stylistically an extremely poor novel. There are only occasional flashes of Crane's descriptive excellence (which in *The Red Badge of Courage*, 1895, proved to be great indeed). The short novel is marked by a painstaking attempt to reproduce the letter of New York slum life. The exposition is given in an awkward, often ponderous, manner.

> As he became aware that she was listening closely, he grew still more eloquent in his description of various happenings in his career. It appeared that he was invincible in fights. "Why," he said, referring to a man with whom he had had a misunderstanding, "dat mug scrapped like a dago. Dat's right. He was dead easy. See? He t'ought he was a scrapper. But he foun' out diff'ent. Hully gee!"

Another passage, from Crane's *The Open Boat* (1898), one of his better works, demonstrates the use made of naturalist despair, together with the author's occasional exploitation of the irony of circumstance, so often and so easily employed by naturalist writers. The men who have survived the wreck of their ship move slowly and uncertainly in their boat toward the Florida shore; at times they are heartened, at times depressed, by signs or imagined signs from the shore. The reflections of the men, as given by their author, read as follows:

> "If I am going to be drowned—if I am going to be drowned—if I am going to be drowned, why, in the name of the seven mad gods who rule the sea, was I allowed to come thus far and contemplate sand and trees? Was I brought here merely to have my nose dragged away as I was about to nibble the sacred cheese of life? It is preposterous. If this old ninny-woman, Fate, cannot do better than this, she should be deprived of the management of men's fortunes. She is an old hen who knows not her intention. If she has decided to drown me, why did she not do it in the beginning and save me all this trouble? The whole affair is absurd.—But no; she cannot mean to drown me. Not after all this work."

The last, melodramatic struggle in Frank Norris's *McTeague* (1899) illustrates once again the rather clumsy consciousness on the part of these writers of the necessity openly and circumstantially to prove the rigors of fate and the impotence of man. McTeague has been fighting with his enemy Marcus Schouler and has managed to kill him:

> As McTeague rose to his feet, he felt a pull at his right wrist; something held it fast. Looking down, he saw that Marcus in that last struggle had found strength to handcuff their wrists to-

gether. Marcus was dead now; McTeague was locked to the body. All about him, vast, interminable, stretched the measureless leagues of Death Valley.

McTeague remained stupidly looking around him, now at the distant horizon, now at the ground, now at the half-dead canary chittering feebly in its little gilt prison.

Here is a final example, this time to illustrate not so much the naturalist's obedience to Zola's call for objectivity as the anxiety of one naturalist author to provide editorial comment, to support overtly what the subject is supposed to demonstrate intrinsically. This is from Theodore Dreiser's *Sister Carrie* (1900), one of a few landmarks in the history of naturalist writing. It is a comment upon Hurstwood's resolve to steal the money and escape Chicago with Carrie. He has just returned the money to the safe, in a moment of wavering. A minute later he takes it once again, and the safe door is accidentally locked against any further weakening of his will. The occasion is a convenient one for the author's comment:

We must remember that it may not be a knowledge of right, for no knowledge of right is predicated of the animal's instinctive recoil at evil. Men are still led by instinct before they are regulated by knowledge. It is instinct which recalls the criminal—it is instinct (where highly organised reasoning is absent) which gives the criminal his feeling of danger, his fear of wrong.

And so on. The patterns of Dreiser's novels are thus broken in upon, again and again, by the author's unhesitating and unfortunate resolve to provide commentary where exposition, however crude, might have sufficed. As R. P. Blackmur has said about another writer, Dreiser's novels can be described as that kind in which "everything is undertaken with seriousness except the writing."

The very complex picture of naturalism in our literature from 1890 to 1925, suggests several comments upon it:

1. It was the reaction of writers to the domination of science over the national scene. As such, it often borrowed suggestions from the scientists and theorists themselves, but with a variety of reinterpretations and "unscientific" uses.

2. It did not mean the abandonment of Howells's kind of realism, which, as a mild form of anti-romanticism, encouraged local color and regional fiction on the one hand, and on the other provided (in *A Traveler from Altruria*, 1894, and in *Through the Eye of the Needle*, 1907) examples and guidance for the social realism of our century. The progressive muckrakers and social novelists of the first two decades were not so much naturalists as social reformists who used the novel as a means of suggesting improvements in a society which the naturalists believed generally to be beyond or beneath improvement. On some occasions, the naturalists themselves left their philosophic positions to assert some kind of social or socialist doctrine, or at least to suggest that the environment might be changed, and men with it.

3. It was often accompanied by contemporary ideas and theories, which yielded such strange results as Jack London's socialism and primitive Nietzscheanism.

4. It was closely associated, and indeed concurrent, with the American confusion

regarding the place of science in the national life. The confused attitude toward the machine in American literature, vacillating between worshipful admiration and hatred, is a reflection of the wider confusion in the American feeling toward theoretic and applied science.

5. Finally, it provided incentives at times, at least precedent, for certain stylistic developments in the fiction of America after World War I. The beginnings of naturalist frankness meant the fairly general defeat of Victorian reticence, and psychoanalysis provided a scientific means of rationalizing postwar frankness. The attack upon war heroics in literature is at least partly traceable to the precedent established by Crane's *The Red Badge of Courage*, though it was by no means the only, or the first, work to treat war in this fashion. It is probable that James T. Farrell, John Dos Passos, Sherwood Anderson, and Ernest Hemingway began their writing in a manner already prepared for them, and with the assurance of a public accustomed to the kind of writing they were to follow. It is a mistake, however, to suggest that these men were predominantly influenced by the earlier naturalists. In a number of ways, the postwar fictionalists belonged to another school of writing, which will be discussed in another section of this essay.

ii

With the exception of the work of Edwin Arlington Robinson, some of whose best poetry was published in the 1890's and 1900's, American poetry could scarcely be called distinguished at the beginning of the twentieth century. The impressive figures of the nineteenth, Walt Whitman and Emily Dickinson, had left the scene; and Stephen Crane's small poetic testimony to Miss Dickinson's manner (*The Black Riders*, 1895, and *War Is Kind*, 1899) was scarcely sufficient in quantity or excellence to disturb or challenge the literary world. American poetry was fairly well held in subjection to the late and last Victorian Englishmen. Robinson himself had rather bitterly complained over the product of "the little sonnet men" and appealed for

> a poet—for a beacon bright
> To rift this changeless glimmer of dead gray;
> To spirit back the Muses, long astray,
> And flush Parnassus with a newer light;
>
> ...

"What does it mean, this barren age of ours?" he asked: everything exists, as it always has, for the poet to put to his uses; yet there is no poet competent enough to take advantage:

> ... Shall there not one arise
> To wrench one banner from the western skies,
> And mark it with his name forevermore?

The "Sonnet" spoke with some bitterness about observable fact. Robinson's early poems, published in 1896, 1897, 1902, and 1910, were brilliant exceptions to the custom. There were the very slender talents of Richard Hovey (1864–1900) and Bliss Carman (1861–1929), the slightly more impressive work of William Vaughn Moody (1869–1910) and Trumbull Stickney (1874–1904); but for the most part poetry can scarcely be said to have given America a reputation to equal that which Gerard Hopkins, Robert Bridges, and Thomas Hardy had given and were giving England. Poetry needed a radical revision; poets needed to be reminded of the special nature of their art; and, not less important, they needed an opportunity, or as many opportunities as they could get, to be published. Robinson's early difficulty and poverty and Frost's move to England testify to the unfavorable climate which American poets had to endure.

One opportunity appeared in 1912, when Harriet Monroe started her *Poetry* magazine in Chicago. Marion Reedy, who in 1913 took over the St. Louis *Mirror* and renamed it *Reedy's Mirror*, also published new poetry by new and inconspicuous talents—especially the poems from *The Spoon River Anthology* by "Webster Ford," who toward the end of his tenure in the *Mirror* announced himself as Edgar Lee Masters. Margaret Anderson's *The Little Review*, begun in Chicago in 1914, published, often in competition with Miss Monroe, poetry by the new poets; but her influence was very small in the first years.

The beginnings of twentieth-century poetry in America would have been impressive enough, although scarcely revolutionary, without the assistance of Ezra Pound, who had found his way to Europe late in 1907, and who became a "foreign correspondent" for *Poetry* through most of the 1910's, and for *The Little Review* toward the end of that decade. While Miss Monroe demonstrated a fine, strong editorial personality, hers was scarcely the discrimination to bring such talent as found its way into the earliest issues of *Poetry*, without the aid of Pound and his fellows in London. "Can you teach the American poet that poetry *is* an art, an art with a technique, with media—an art that must be in constant flux, a constant change of manner, if it is to live?" Pound asked her in an early letter. "Can you teach him it is not a pentametric echo of the sociological dogma printed in last year's magazines?" The work of Pound and his fellow exiles and contemporary English writers in London was dedicated to the elimination of the "dull and interminable effusions" of contemporary versifiers, to the reinstatement of poetry as a valid art, and to the inclusion of at least some of the results of the discussions which had been taking place among men like T. E. Hulme, F. S. Flint, Pound, T. S. Eliot, and Richard Aldington.

The first American poet to be introduced as an Imagist was Hilda Doolittle, who went to Europe in 1911 and whose first contributions to *Poetry* (January, 1913) were signed "H. D., Imagiste." Other poems subsequently published in America included some by her English husband, Richard Aldington, some of Pound's early poems, T. S. Eliot's "Preludes" and "The Love Song of J. Alfred Prufrock," and even a few of D. H. Lawrence's poems. The first Imagist anthology, called *Des Imagistes*, was issued in 1914 from London. Three others were published in the United States—in 1915, in 1916, and in 1917—under the supervision of Amy Lowell and each time with the title *Some Imagist Poets*.

The principles which the Imagists stated and restated were such as any really conscientious poet might have followed without having to be told about them. But they were a refreshing challenge to the poetry of the day and were quite seriously needed as a reminder of the function of poetry. T. E. Hulme, whose influence on the group was great, had said, in speaking of what he wished known as "the new classicism" in literature:

> The essence of poetry to most people is that it must lead them to a beyond of some kind. Verse strictly confined to the earthly and definite (Keats is full of it) might seem to them to be excellent writing, excellent craftsmanship, but not poetry. So much has romanticism debauched us that, without some form of vagueness, we deny the highest.

To eliminate all forms of vagueness, the first set of Imagist principles struck at the vital necessity for poetic economy and insisted upon the "hard core of objectivity," which was crucial to the Imagist strategy. These principles were published in the January, 1913, issue of *Poetry* in an article by F. S. Flint; they are, however, part of Pound's exposition of Imagist theory:

> 1. "Direct treatment of the 'thing,' whether subjective or objective."
> 2. "To use absolutely no word that does not contribute to the presentation."
> 3. "As regards rhythm, to compose in sequence of the musical phrase, not in sequence of a metronome."
> 4. To conform to the "doctrine of the image"—which Pound later defined as "an intellectual and emotional complex in an instant of time."

This was substantially the statement of Imagism during the early years. In 1914 Pound disassociated himself from the group, and his work is not found in the 1915 anthology. "Imagism was a point on the curve of my development. Some people remained at that point. I moved on," he said to Glenn Hughes by way of explaining his break. What he had called "Amygism" continued; and Amy Lowell, having rescued it from Pound, brought it with her to America and proceeded to exhibit, advertise, and defend it in American lecture halls and magazines and in her anthologies and criticism. The revised list of principles, attached to the 1915 anthology, was done principally by Aldington and introduced only a few new ideas to the already established list: for one thing, it emphasized free verse and recommended it by saying that "we believe the individuality of a poet may often be better expressed in free verse than in conventional forms. In poetry, a new cadence means a new idea." It talked also about "the language of common speech" but meant nothing more than the earlier statement had intended. It spoke of the need for "absolute freedom in the choice of subject" but concluded by reiterating the original views of poetry, that it be hard and clear and free of the "vagueness" of which both Hulme and Pound had spoken.

Imagist theory, as it has been summarized, was a necessary and disciplinary step in the development of modern American poetry. The poetry it gave rise to was not often distinguished, and it certainly did not follow consistently the principles as set down. But it impressed, perhaps by virtue of stark contrast with the sadly deficient character of much contemporary verse. In many respects, Imagism was quite consistent with the realism of American fiction. Imagists enjoyed or pretended to an obsessive preoccupation with the hard, objective, irreducible minimum of real fact. The image was designed as the most honest, the most practicable, the least cluttered evidence of reality which poetry was capable of representing. Certainly very little poetry produced since the period of Imagist ferment has failed to reflect in one way or another its elementary and elemental concerns with the language and the technique of poetry.

From 1910 to the present day there have existed at least two major traditions in American poetry. The first of these stems from the Imagist ideas of the second decade; it includes as demonstration and result the poetry of H. D., John Gould Fletcher, Glenway Westcott, Amy Lowell; the early poetry of T. S. Eliot and Ezra Pound; and the work of Wallace Stevens, Marianne Moore, and William Carlos Williams. The second is a nativist tradition, belonging to those poets who followed either the practice of Walt Whitman or his challenging statements concerning the role of the poet in American society. For the most part these poets stayed at home, did not consult French poetics and poetry (from which the Imagists took varied encouragement and aid), were satisfied with American subjects; and they often borrowed from Whitman his expansive, cumulative, catalogic, loose rhythms, his tendency to allow a multitude of impressions to stand as a substitute for tightness of structure and integration of subject matter. They did not often adopt the nationalist optimism of *Leaves of Grass*, although Sandburg's *The People, Yes*, and Stephen Vincent Benét's *John Brown's Body* do in one way or another manage to try for his inclusiveness of vision and subject matter; and Hart Crane (who belongs in both traditions, and in a sense in neither) reflects vividly and earnestly Whitman's attempt to make a kind of mystic order out of the chaos of impressions with which both were supplied and cursed.

iii

The Imagist discussions and debates also produced the beginnings of one of the most important developments in modern American criticism: formalism. Ezra Pound's ceaseless argument for exactness in poetry, and for its declaration of independence from broad, vague, moral generalizations and sentimentalities, provided the first step in formalist criticism. What Pound did was to point to an obvious although neglected fact: the responsibility which an artist owes to his art, to his craft. Bad art, he said, is "immoral art," and explained:

> Bad art is inaccurate art. It is art that makes false reports. If a scientist falsifies a report either deliberately or through negligence we consider him as either a criminal or a bad scientist according to the enormity of his offence, and he is punished or despised accordingly.

More particularly, the responsibilities of the good artist are a truthful and exact rendering of the particulars of his experience, the constant working over of the language and rhythm until it exactly and without consequent confusion or vagueness meets the needs of and corresponds to the nature of his sensibility. Attention to form (to an exact determination of what it is and of how it might best be served) is a primary principle of formalist criticism. Another serves both artist and reader as a protection against what the British critic I. A. Richards was to call the "stock response." Modern poetry and formalist criticism have both fought strenuously against the cliché and have often gone to extremes to avoid even the slightest suggestion of it. In the service of this attack, critics like Pound and Eliot spoke of the necessary impersonality of the artist and of his freedom from such sentiment or emotion as might too easily lead to stock or familiar responses. "Poetry is not a turning loose of emotion, but an escape from emotion," said Eliot in 1917; "it is not the expression of personality, but an escape from personality. But, of course, only those who have personality and emotions know what it means to want to escape from these things." In 1919, in an essay called "Hamlet and His Problems," Eliot stated what is one of the most important definitions of modern poetics. The "objective correlative," as he called it in this essay, is simply a means of describing what the poet uses as a dramatic or "external" equivalent of the emotion which lies at the source of his poem. The "artistic inevitability" (he is speaking here parenthetically of *Macbeth*) consists of the "complete adequacy of the external to the emotion." The only way of finding such an exact correspondence is to give to emotion its "objective correlative": "in other words, a set of objects, a situation, a chain of events which shall be the formula of that *particular* emotion; such that when the external facts, which must terminate in sensory experience, are given, the emotion is immediately invoked."

In no area of American criticism have the admonitions of exactness and formal accuracy been so freely applied as in the development of poetic theory. The tradition of formalist criticism, and the practice of formal analysis to which it has given rise, began with the work of Pound and Eliot (who studied French critics and artists and were both strongly attracted to T. E. Hulme), and with other spokesmen for Imagism. Eliot was also interested in the place and use of tradition in the body of contemporary criticism and literature. He was not committed, however, to the critical position of the Humanists, whose work held the stage for many years of the second and third decades. The publication of Paul Elmer More's *Shelburne Essays* began in 1904 and continued until 1936. With Irving Babbitt and such other Humanists as Stuart Pratt Sherman and W. C. Brownell, More advocated adherence to the classical training and tradition of an earlier academic world. The Humanists considered their major foes to be the science and naturalism of their time, and especially the literature which denied "that element in man which is outside of nature and is denoted by consciously directive purpose. . . ." More and Babbitt insisted that all men have standards, that those standards are best preserved in the literature that has endured the test of time, and that man distinguishes himself from animals by the possession of an "inner check." The major controversy which the Humanists encountered occurred in the late 1920's, and was effectively summarized in two symposia: *Humanism and America*, edited by Norman Foerster (1930), and *The Critique of Humanism*, edited by C. H. Grattan (1930). Though Eliot has several times critically explored the Humanist position, he has not repudiated it entirely. He finds his quarrel chiefly with its rather vague definitions. Humanism "bears the print of the academic man of letters," he said in 1929. The real Humanist, he insisted, is the man of classical and other training who does not force his views into a dogmatic frame. Eliot also discovered a distressing lack of knowledge of and interest in the formal aspects of art; this ignorance, he said, usually led to a rather uncertain and often vague judgment of tradition. In short, humanism for Eliot is culture, "not any subscription to a common programme or platform, which binds [the Humanists] together."

Humanism, in its various forms, was a strong counterirritant to the progress of theory and the Theory of Progress in the second and third decades. It was essentially moral in its judgment of literature (in More's writings, strongly religious as well), much opposed to experimenting in literature, and inclined to dismiss most new writing as trifling. Another critical development in the first two decades of our century was the impressionism of James Gibbons Huneker. Huneker was a superior journalist, whose principal interest was music and whose chief service to American culture was that of bringing to Americans his versions of foreign artists and philosophers and of insisting upon their value—in short, of at least attempting to give American culture a cosmopolitan air. But his writings were so deliberately forced into a mode of day-to-day cleverness, so poorly informed by inadequate training and capricious understanding, and so often vitiated by strange Laokoön analogies of literature with music, that his value to American criticism was limited. One final critical development was provided by Joel Spingarn, of Columbia University, an adaptation of Croce's expressionism, which allowed for a thorough and undiscriminating democracy of expression. "Poets do not really write epics, pastorals, lyrics, however much they may be deceived by these false abstractions; they express themselves, and this expression is their only form," Spingarn said in "The New Criticism" (1910); and there are as many forms as there are individual poets. Spingarn's expressionism disposed of the Humanist's moral judgment of literature, the formalist's analysis of it, the academic's classification of it. What is left is the assertion that "aesthetic judgment and artistic creation are instinct with the same vital life," that we are all creators, and each of us is distinct and unique in his expression.

iv

The years of our century which preceded World War I were years of expansionism and imperialism in politics, naturalism in fiction, scientism in thought. They carried on the political and economic developments of the post-Civil War years, adapted the ready interpretations of Darwin to an expanding business world. They were also crucial years for the development of twentieth-century literature. Beginnings were made in the establishment of American fictional styles which were to be elaborated upon and refined in subsequent years. An aesthetic of poetry, however unoriginal, was suggested and developed, to prepare the way for the much more elaborate and successful criticism which followed the end of the war.

The war itself brought several changes to the American scene. For one thing, it took many of the young men and transferred them to a foreign, an older, culture, which was to have much to do with the changing literary world in the 1920's. The rather easy and haphazard mixture of socialism, anarchism, Nietzscheanism, and liberalism, which is found in the early years, was to be dissipated with the conclusion of the war. The effects of the war upon such writers as Cummings, Hemingway, and Dos Passos, while not as violent as they seem on the surface, are considerable.

While America enjoyed a fairly consistent prosperity and seized one opportunity after another for extending its influence and increasing its strength, writers spoke of the melancholy naturalistic prison of the human soul, of the environment created by business for its own advantage, or of the impossibility of an art in a completely materialistic civilization. Woodrow Wilson's liberalism turned out eventually to have been a continuation of the naïve American feeling that its notions of right need only to be expressed to be accepted. The disillusionment over the results of the war was implicit in the war's failure to convince young intellectuals of its nobility of purpose or its justice. The popularity among business apologists of the Spencerian view of evolution did not last Spencer's own lifetime. The inferences made by the literary naturalists did survive the war years, however. And a conviction not altogether new to American culture, but still strange enough to be startling, was born of the literary debates and theorizing in London and in American magazines: the conviction that art both possesses intrinsic value and involves special obligations for the artist.

II

WORLD WAR I AND AFTER

i

When World War I started, Ernest Hemingway was sixteen years old; John Dos Passos, eighteen; E. E. Cummings, twenty; William Faulkner, seventeen. All of these young men volunteered some time before America joined the Allies. One glance at their ages will suggest that they had had scarcely any opportunity for learning about their own country before they arrived in another. They matured, not in the relatively prosperous and at least superficially stable world of prewar America, but in the ambulance corps, in the Red Cross, or in the first World War's equivalent of the concentration camp.

In his *Exile's Return* (1934), Malcolm Cowley described the condition which made this generation of writers what Gertrude Stein called "the lost generation."

Whatever the doctrines we adopted during our college years, whatever the illusions we had of growing toward culture and self-sufficiency, the same process of deracination was continuing for all of us. . . . Normally the deracination would have ended when we were graduated; outside in the practical world we should have been forced to acquire new roots in order to survive. But we weren't destined to have the fate of the usual college generation, and instead of ceasing, the process would be intensified. . . .

The ambulance corps and the French military transport constituted what Cowley termed "college-extension courses for a generation of writers." What they taught was chiefly the advantage of being near danger and violence; the ambulance service "instilled into us what might be called a *spectatorial* attitude." Some of these young men had more immediate contact with danger and discomfort than others. Hemingway joined the Italian army and was severely wounded on the Italian-Austrian front; Faulkner joined the British air force and experienced direct and dangerous contact with the enemy; Cummings was placed in a French detention camp for three months because of an error of the military censor. The experiences of these men definitely affected their attitudes toward the postwar world. It was with a sense of having been uprooted, of having to return to a country they did not quite understand, that they viewed the end of the war. "School and college had uprooted us in spirit," Cowley said; "now we were physically uprooted. . . . All our roots were dead now, even the Anglo-Saxon tradition of our literary ancestors, even the habits of slow thrift that characterized our social class."

The feeling of deracination, of having had no training in any culture, of having participated in a war which had little meaning for them, contributed much to the formation and the strengthening of postwar attitudes. What the war did to them, the economy and politics of the 1920's enforced and encouraged. Wilson came back from Paris a defeated man; his time had run out. The era of Republican prosperity began with the election of Warren G. Harding in 1920, continued under Calvin Coolidge, and came to an end only in 1932, after Herbert Hoover had failed to convince the electorate that the depression was only a temporary inconvenience. Added to the superficial prosperity which the American economy enjoyed during these years was the chaotic condition of the European exchange. The American dollar bought excitement, comfort, and a home-away-from-America in almost any part of Continental Europe. Having no fear of economic collapse, confident in the continuing prosperity of America, the postwar intellectuals and artists, together with hundreds of men and women who affected to be both but were neither, traveled freely between New York or Boston and Le Havre, France. They indulged themselves and criticized the land of their origin; they studied and imitated the literature of their adopted country; they published magazines, in which they printed their work and editorially praised it. In spite of the chaos and purposelessness of their Paris life (as it is described in the first half of Hemingway's *The Sun Also Rises*), they often learned something of the craft of writing and occasionally produced creditable works of literature.

The immediate result was the production of war books. John Dos Passos' *One Man's Initiation*—1917 (1919) was the first of these. A crude, autobiographical first novel, it described the career of an American ambulance driver in France. E. E. Cummings's *The Enormous Room* followed in 1922—a story, half autobiographical, of Cummings's internment in La Ferté Macé, a hundred miles west of Paris. In 1923 came Dos Passos' second novel about the War, *Three Soldiers*, which was chiefly the story of John Andrews, a soldier who wished to become a composer, who deserted the army and withdrew to the French countryside to write his music, and who was finally arrested for desertion. In 1925 *What Price Glory?* by Maxwell Anderson and Laurence Stallings was produced on Broadway; with frankness of setting and language, it described the lives of several U.S. Marines in the war. At the end of the decade, Ernest Hemingway's *A Farewell to Arms* (1929) was published. It was not only the best of the war novels; it stated quite clearly the general effect of the war upon the generation which had experienced it. From England came Ford Madox Ford's Tietjens novels (published between 1924 and 1928) and Richard Aldington's *Death of a Hero* (1929); and from Germany, at the end of the decade, Erich Remarque's *All Quiet on the Western Front* (1929).

All this work described a fairly general attitude toward the war: it was called an unfortunate, purposeless, cruel, and disillusioning experience. Taking them together, the reader will discover the reasons for the 1920's criticism of American culture, tradition, and institutions. More specifically, he will discover several statements concerning postwar skepticism and the attack not only upon the behavior of the middle class but also upon the language it had used to defend and explain that behavior. Their attitude was a practical "nominalism," which distrusted both political generalities and sentimental clichés. It defended and encouraged the literary economy of the Hemingway school, called much of the philosophical writing of the time a kind of spirited "faking," and insisted upon a reworking in every individual of standards of conduct. The best statement of this postwar nominalism is found in *A Farewell to Arms*, the passage which comes just before the retreat from Caporetto. Lieutenant Henry has just finished talking with Gino, an Italian patriot; as Gino finishes, Henry thinks over certain words he has used: the words *sacred, glorious,* and *sacrifice*. He cannot associate them with any experience they can accurately be said to describe. "There were many words that you could not stand to hear and finally only the names of places had dignity." Besides this distrust of abstract words, there was a rather general suspicion regarding the names of philosophers and scientists who had been held up to the young men as bearers of our tradition. Dos Passos' John Andrews, lying on a hospital cot, "thought of all the long procession of men who had been touched by the unutterable futility of the lives of men, who had tried by phrases to make things otherwise, who had taught unworldliness . . . they had wept, some of them, and some of them had laughed, and their phrases had risen glittering, soap bubbles to dazzle men for a moment, and had shattered." And E. E. Cummings, who in *The Enormous Room* had spoken in undisguised scorn of officialdom which held the keys to a prison for all men of good will, spoke in his poems of the 1920's of the indestructibility of the "sweet spontaneous earth," which resists all efforts of "prurient philosophers" to label and classify it:

(but

true

to the incomparable

couch of death thy

rhythmic

lover

thou answerest

them only with

spring)

The work of Ernest Hemingway is the best source of information concerning this postwar attitude and its literature. In it one may discover the principal points of view of the 1920's. His disposal of the substance of cultural statement (the abstract, "glory" words which belong to an established and trusted world) has already been mentioned. From this point, he has offered us some suggestion of what postwar man may accept as an alternative to a fixed philosophy of life:

1. Man's moral sense was closely related to his immediate experience; morality was tested in terms of immediate consequences: what made you feel good after it was moral; what made you feel disgusted was immoral. In any event, you "paid" for what you got: "No idea of retribution or punishment. Just exchange of values. You gave up something and got something else."

2. Social criteria were also applicable only to immediate circumstances. The test of a man's

character was the way in which he "got along," the way he fitted, most of all the manner in which he assumed his position in a group. Poorly adjusted persons reacted openly to their experiences and exaggerated them or sentimentalized over them. Well-adjusted persons understated their reactions. They were uneasy in the presence of displays of rhetoric or sentiment. One oughtn't to waste too much time trying to explain, even to himself, the meaning of his life.

3. Experiences after the war, especially those of men who had participated, are likely to be violent. This violence cannot be calmed by soothing and vague generalities. Hemingway sought in two ways for a suitable pattern of adjustment to this violence: the first is a kind of primitive idyll, such as the Burguete interlude of *The Sun Also Rises:* when conditions are "right" and you are with men who share your feeling and your interests, the problem of adjustment seems automatically, if temporarily, to have been solved. The second is a statement of an "aesthetic of violence," by which a pattern is imposed upon it and it is subdued. This is what the art of bull-fighting means to him. It is an aesthetic formalization of native courage, which Hemingway has noted in many other situations as well, and approved of.

Finally, in the course of this statement, Hemingway was to develop a literary style which he thought suitable to it. It is, in one respect, a simple reduction of language and syntax to their essentials. The forceful simplicity of the uncomplicated sentence—or of a series of "and clauses"—the absence of excessive explanation or of any attempt to point out "significance," the sparseness of dialogue, the half-shy withdrawal from generalizations, the attention to simple description of concrete facts: all of these characteristics of Hemingway's style impressed his readers and were borrowed and imitated by many writers of the twenties and subsequent decades. A few passages from several writers will illustrate that influence:

It was baking hot in the square when we came out after lunch with our bags and the rod-case to go to Burguete. People were on top of the bus, and others were climbing up a ladder. Bill went up and Robert sat beside Bill to save a place for me, and I went back in the hotel to get a couple of bottles of wine to take with us. When I came out the bus was crowded. Men and women were sitting on all the baggage and boxes on top, and the women all had their fans going in the sun. It certainly was hot. Robert climbed down and I fitted into the place he had saved on the one wooden seat that ran across the top. (*The Sun Also Rises*, 1926)

Mac touched Jim on the arm, and they went out and shut the door. They didn't bother to look around when they went out the gate. Mac set out so rapidly that Jim had to stretch his stride to keep up. The sun was cutting downward now, and the wind was stirring in the branches, so that both trees and ground seemed to quiver nervously. (John Steinbeck, *In Dubious Battle*, 1936)

The man on the load of cotton jumped to the ground, tied the reins to the wagon wheel, and pushed through the crowd to the car where all the swearing was being done. After listening for a while he came back to the street, called a Negro who was standing with the other colored men on the corner, and handed him the reins. The Negro drove off with the cotton towards the gin, and the man went back into the crowd. (Erskine Caldwell, "Daughter," 1935)

Callahan got Pinkman out of his chair, and the two retrieved their hats and went down the dark stairs and out of the Opera House into the blacked-out street. The snow came down thicker than ever, but melted as it fell. (Robert Lowry, *Casualty*, 1946) *ii*

The 1920's have been described by such phrases as "The Jazz Age" and "The Era of Wonderful Nonsense." Frederick Lewis Allen's *Only Yesterday* (1931), Mark Sullivan's *The Twenties* (volume six of *Our Times*, 1935), and Irene and Allen Cleaton's *Books and Battles* (1937) have tried to give the social history of the decade. All these books describe what is substantially true of the decade, but the details are either overstated or superficial. Perhaps the best portrait of the times is found in the fiction of F. Scott Fitzgerald. His first novel, *This Side of Paradise* (1920), gave him enough money for his marriage and for a move to New York, from which most of his subsequent observations of "The Jazz Age" were issued. It was a time of Prohibition and bootleggers, a time of easy money and reckless spending, a period during which many sins against taste were committed in the name of unfettered adolescence. Fitzgerald's novels and short stories underscore several characteristics of the decade: its devotion to the cause of the free and independent woman; the phenomenon of the newly rich, and the protection their wealth afforded them; the search for new physical and social experiences, which proved so often to be simply an acceleration of familiar ones; in general, the psychological tensions endured by a generation which failed to find stability in ways enjoyed in previous times.

The Great Gatsby (1925) is at once the best social portrait of the 1920's and one of the best of modern American novels. In it Fitzgerald achieved a remarkable economy of form, through the use of a narrator who is sufficiently of the cast of characters to know it and to interpret it intelligently, but not so deeply involved in its world as to lose his talent for judging it. He offered a portrait of postwar "magnificence" by means of glimpses of Gatsby's incredible Long Island parties. He presented the postwar flapper, so often inadequately understood in his other work and in numerous cheap imitations of it, in the characters of Daisy Buchanan and Jordan Baker. Finally, he analyzed the psychological effect of wealth upon the American personality: the quick wealth of Jay Gatsby, gained in the Prohibition underworld and serving the one consistent illusion observable in the world described in the book; and the wealth of the Buchanans, which seems to have provided them an immunity from all social and moral responsibility. Fitzgerald was an extremely uneven writer; in this one book, however, he managed to avoid all his excesses and to stay close to the pattern he had originally selected.

The popular intellectual "tone" of the 1920's was that of a cultivated disrespect for the conventions. Young people enjoyed laughing at their elders and didn't mind laughing at themselves. The more cutting the criticism, the more lavish of clever invective, the more popular it became. The pseudo-sophistication of *Vanity Fair* magazine shared popularity with that of a newer arrival on the scene, *The New Yorker*. H. L. Mencken's *American Mercury*, of which he was editor from 1923 to

1933, offered much entertainment to its subscribers and an abundance of data concerning the world of the middle class and its institutions. Mencken's favorite objects of attack were Prohibition, American politics, the clergy, one-hundred-percent patriotism, the "pedagogues," and the cultural ambitions of the middle class. In his *Prejudices*, of which there were six volumes, published from 1919 to 1927, Mencken inveighed against all of these, acknowledged his America as an immensely amusing place, dismissed the popular literature and defended the work of the less favored novelists, condemned the professorial style, fought a battle with the Humanists (especially with Stuart Pratt Sherman), and in general behaved himself in a manner which gave his readers the considerable pleasure of laughing at their elders and guardians and the institutions they were pledged to uphold.

Mencken's journalism was directed chiefly against the American middle class (the "booboisie," as he called it). Sinclair Lewis's success as a novelist came from the same activity. His was a gift of parody, mimicry, and satirical realism which made his novels of the 1920's successes from the start. Lewis attacked the middle class for many of the same reasons which motivated the attacks of Mencken. But he was at the same time committed to liking the American bourgeoisie in a way quite alien to Mencken's taste. The merciless parody of middle-class hypocrisy and pretense continued throughout the 1920's; only the dedicated scientists of *Arrowsmith* (1925) escaped it. But in *Dodsworth* (1929), while he heaped his reproaches upon the idle, foolish wife, Lewis was to suggest that the citizens of the city of Zenith and the state of Winnemac would survive their serious deficiencies—that they were very good people after all, a little unsure of themselves, perhaps, but fundamentally sound. Before he was finished with them, however, Lewis had given all their weaknesses a thorough going over.

iii

As the 1920's were known to the general reader for Lewis's *Main Street* and *Babbitt*, they were known to a smaller audience for the publication (in *The Dial* of November, 1922) of T. S. Eliot's *The Waste Land*. The poem was much discussed and often misunderstood. It was intended not exclusively as a portrait of contemporary life but as an expression of the adventure of one soul in a world unsupported by faith. The journey of the protagonist through the wasteland to "The Chapel Perilous" is finally rewarded not by a redeeming key to a solution of the modern dilemma of the wasteland but only by a few "fragments" which, he says, "I have shored against my ruins." *The Waste Land*, together with "Gerontion" (in *Poems*, 1920) and *The Hollow Men* (1925), provided the intellectuals of the 1920's with a definitive statement regarding the spiritual weaknesses of the postwar world. In the latter half of the decade, Eliot was to search for and to express more directly a statement of a redeeming faith. *Ash-Wednesday* (1930) is a description of that search, of the road to conversion; in his critical essays of the decade, Eliot was to remark upon his explorations of other literatures and of theology, steps on the way to his own clarification of principle. His poetry provided the matter and the style for numerous imitations, until many American poets have finally to acknowledge him as the most important influence upon their work.

The publication in 1923 of Wallace Stevens's *Harmonium* announced the arrival of another important poet. Stevens had shared indirectly in the general excitement provoked by Imagism, but his poems were not limited by any theory or practice but his own. Nevertheless, he shows the great influence of Imagism in his highly original use of language and color and his constant preoccupation with the art of poetry. The work of Marianne Moore demonstrates another individual and unique talent, once more fortifying and illustrating the values of the Imagist influence on American verse. William Carlos Williams contributed to the poetry of the 1920's what are perhaps the most objective and "visual" of all poems within the Imagist tradition.

From April, 1922, to December, 1925, a magazine called *The Fugitive* was published in Nashville, Tennessee. The editorial board included several of our most important poets and critics: John Crowe Ransom, Allen Tate, and Robert Penn Warren especially. Their production of poetry was not great, but it was substantial enough. Although the opening editorial of *The Fugitive* had called its contributors "self-convicted experimentalists," they did not belong to any of the experimental "schools" of poetry of the postwar years. They exercised the classical restraint of traditional forms and demonstrated especially a skill in the use of language and metaphor which recalled and proved their intense interest in the metaphysical poetry of England's seventeenth century. All three of them also made substantial contributions to criticism, and Ransom's book *The New Criticism* (1941) is the best description of modern formalism.

iv

The 1920's were also rich in achievements in the drama. Eugene O'Neill, whose first one-act plays had been produced by the Provincetown Players on Cape Cod, Massachusetts, and in Greenwich Village, offered a considerable number of experiments in the theater, borrowing as he developed from the expressionists of Germany and France, and introducing more innovations to the American theater than its entire previous history had seen. *The Emperor Jones* was produced in 1920; *The Hairy Ape*, in 1923; *The Great God Brown*, in 1926; *Strange Interlude*, in 1928. All these, and a number of others, introduced expressionist and symbolist devices as means of extending the function and the scope of the stage. Another expressionist drama, Elmer Rice's *The Adding Machine*, appeared on Broadway in 1923. His *Street Scene* (1929), a more conventional play, was also highly successful. Other plays of the 1920's included the expressionist comedy by George S. Kaufman and Marc Connelly, *Beggar on Horseback* (1924), George Kelly's comedies, *The Show-Off* (1924) and *Craig's Wife* (1925), and such leftist examples of theatrical expressionism as John Howard Lawson's *Processional* (1925) and *The International* (1927).

American drama of the decade can claim considerable progress over the rather pale, pleasant "entertainments" of the early part of the century. It improved in content, expanded greatly in variety of subject, and proceeded, with a remarkable talent for adaptation, to assimilate a great number of suggestions offered it from abroad. In some respects it also solved the problem of the influence of Broadway; at the very least, experimental dramas were produced, first in the independent "little" theaters and then on Broadway itself.

Meanwhile, aside from the war and postwar fiction previously discussed, the most important novels of earlier traditions were written by women. In 1925, Ellen Glasgow published what is perhaps her best novel, *Barren Ground*, and followed it with *The Romantic Comedians* (1926) and *They Stooped to Folly* (1929). Willa Cather's career as a novelist, which had begun quite promisingly in the second decade with *O Pioneers!* (1913), *The Song of the Lark* (1915), and *My Antonia* (1918), continued in the twenties with *A Lost Lady* (1923), *The Professor's House* (1925), and *Death Comes for the Archbishop* (1927). The fiction of these two novelists can for the most part be said to follow a regionalism earlier practiced by such writers as Sara Orne Jewett and Mary Wilkins Freeman; but both Miss Glasgow and Miss Cather are better artists than their predecessors. Both also show some suggestion of the influence of Henry James in their efforts to subtilize their style. In the list of regionalist novels, Elizabeth Madox Roberts's *The Time of Man* (1926) occupies an important position; it is one of the best examples of its kind.

The fiction of Sherwood Anderson is as much a part of the twenties as is Hemingway's. Although two of his novels appeared before the war, the bulk of Anderson's best work was brought out in the postwar decade. Anderson is concerned chiefly with the problem of the human personality in an age increasingly dominated by industry and the machine. Much of his fiction has the small town for a setting and attempts to show the villager's groping for some kind of articulation or expression. In the preface to *Winesburg, Ohio* (1919), his characters are called "grotesques"; they are exceptional in their strenuous essays at personal definition. *Poor White* (1920), in some respects at least his best novel, pictures the confusion of Hugh McVey, who, in his pity for cabbage planters, invents a cabbage-planting machine and lives to see the damage done to his fellows by modern business methods and the disastrous effects of a machine-dominated community. *Dark Laughter* (1925), like Waldo Frank's *Holiday* (1923), opposes the white and the Negro civilizations, demonstrating the great advantage of the simpler, more primitive society over the repressed and artificial whites. *Many Marriages* (1923) is an inferior attempt to illustrate the repressions caused by modern business and to describe one man's revolt against them. Anderson's best work is to be found in his collections of short stories (*The Triumph of The Egg* and *Horses and Men* are especially noteworthy). He has proved himself eventually to be a rather groping, undisciplined artist, almost as confused about life as are his characters; but at times he is a writer of considerable talent and insight.

v

The 1920's were a decade rich in literary achievement. The literature produced in the years before the financial crash of October, 1929, demonstrates a varied assortment of talents and a correspondingly wide variety of literary experiments. It was an unsettled period but an extremely lively and fruitful one. American literature became more clearly conscious of its native value than it had ever been before. The talent was not always disciplined, and some of it was wasted. But important advances were made.

The most interesting characteristic of the decade was its naïve but genuine willingness to risk statement and argument. Not seriously attached to any single dogma, the writers of the time were willing to experiment with many. Since they had witnessed the successful fight for changes in literary styles and fashions in an earlier decade, they continued to experiment with many of their own.

In matters of politics and economics, these writers were often quite immature and generally ignorant; they took for granted the words of Republican presidents and ignored social and political problems. For the most part, they were satisfied to accept the legend of continuing prosperity, of which their political spokesmen had assured them; while they accepted the financial advantages of this prosperity, they devoted much of their time to ridiculing the social pretensions of the men who worked to provide these advantages. The events of October, 1929, were to change all of that. Writers who had idled away the decade in Paris or Berlin or Rome hurried back to America. There was a sudden renewal of interest in economic questions, and a large percentage of writers flocked to the leftist standard. The 1930's were to see the resurgence of "politically responsible" writing, of dialectically narrow criticism, and of social melodrama.

III

THE NINETEEN THIRTIES

i

The end of the prosperous twenties occurred in the month of October, 1929. In spite of small recoveries in Wall Street and reassurances from the White House, the stock-market collapse was the beginning of one of the severest depressions in American history. The leftists, who had persisted through the twenties in such magazines as *The Liberator* (1918–1924) and *The New Masses* (1926–1947), saw their opportunity; and many uncommitted or only casually committed writers turned leftward with the first definite signs of a crack in the American economy. In many respects, then, the 1930's were the decade of proletarian literature and criticism. John Reed Clubs, designed as cultural centers of leftist activity, were begun in Chicago, Boston, New York, Los Angeles, and other cities. *Partisan Review* was started in 1934 as an organ of the New York John Reed Club. *The New Masses* began its period of greatest ideological prosperity. The leftist cause in America was aided and encouraged by British radical activity and literature: Britain's best young poets, W. H. Auden, Stephen Spender, C. Day Lewis, Louis MacNeice, identified themselves in one way or another with the leftist cause; and such British magazines as *The Left Review* (1934–1938) published them and acted as a center of leftist critical activity.

In the interests of the leftist cause, the naturalist and realist fiction of the early part of our century was imitated by most writers of fiction. Granville Hicks, for a time the most articulate of leftist spokesmen, asserted that our fiction had proved almost always to have been "on the side of the exploited." He suggested that American fiction would find its most successful means of expression in the proletarian novel:

> Long experience shows that for the artist there is no health in the bourgeois way of life. If, then, the issue is clearly presented, if it is fully realized that in this war [the class struggle], as in any war, there is no such thing as neutrality, can artists hesitate to ally themselves with the proletariat?

Many of them did so ally themselves; the pages of new and revived little magazines were filled with proletarian fiction and poetry, the Broadway stage often displayed proletarian drama, the strike novel became a literary staple, and literary criticism (often even in rather conservative magazines) emphasized content over form in its evaluation of the new literature. The short fiction of the time employed both the regional detail with which our literary history was long familiar and the Hemingway kind of underwriting. Dialogue became increasingly important, not only as the key expression of the peculiarities of a region, but also as a means of drawing the lines of proletarian heroism. What Hemingway had done with his dialogue in "The Killers" and in other stories, the proletarian writers exploited in the interests of implicit message. The class-war lines of proletarian literature were often very clearly drawn. Detail no longer served a neutral or aesthetic purpose; it was designed cumulatively to document the facts of exploitation and oppression. In the drama, the class war made for a new kind of social melodrama, with the hero and the villain often very clearly identified with economic classes. Poetry was generally written in free verse, which galloped roughly but vigorously to the aid of the oppressed or celebrated elegiacally the early leaders of the Russian revolution.

Proletarian fiction of the 1930's now seems undistinguished and crude. It was often written hastily and according to a half-understood formula, which required that the writer follow certain lines of characterization and plot. There were a few writers who gained distinction either within or in spite of the formula. Of the sixteen contributors whose short stories are included in the anthology, *Proletarian Literature in the United States* (1935), Albert Maltz, Albert Halper, Erskine Caldwell, Robert Cantwell, James T. Farrell, Josephine Herbst, and John Dos Passos contributed the best work. Of these, only Maltz, Halper, Cantwell, and Miss Herbst belonged strictly and entirely in the proletarian mold. James Farrell's lengthy sociological studies of life in Chicago's lower middle class support rather than provide primary evidence of the leftist revolt. John Dos Passos, who had acquired a reputation long before 1930, published his trilogy of American life, *U.S.A.* (*The 42nd Parallel*, *1919*, and *The Big Money*) in the 1930's; and his sympathies can be said to have touched the leftist interests of the time. At any rate, like Farrell's, his work offered what leftist critics described as "documentary evidence" of oppression. But Dos Passos was scarcely ever comfortable in plain Marxist clothes. In the early years of *The New Masses*, he had asked for an independent, native radicalism, free of Russian directives and taboos; and in *Adventures of a Young Man* (1939), a novel in general quite undistinguished and mediocre, he pointed to the confusion and abuse in leftist political ranks.

Not directly allied with the extreme leftists—in fact, on several occasions rebuked by them—but sympathetically attracted to the underprivileged and concerned over their welfare, John Steinbeck produced fiction in the 1930's which influenced and excited the general reading public much more effectively than that of any Marxist writer. *In Dubious Battle* (1936) is undoubtedly the best strike novel of its time and the most readable today. This is primarily because, like his Doc Burton, Steinbeck did something other than "use" the strikers as a mechanism or formula of leftist polemic; he studied them and at the same time considered them as individuals. *The Grapes of Wrath* (1939), his most successful novel, considers the dispossessed farmers of Oklahoma from a point of view which is substantially democratic and is leftist only because the democratic temper of the times was so. When Tom Joad leaves his family for the last time, it is as an individual who "wants to know," wants "to figure this whole thing out." There is a likelihood that his quest will include some association with Marxist activities, but this is not an exclusive doctrinal message which Steinbeck is trying to offer; rather, Tom Joad sets forth on a journey of democratic inquiry into the evils and inequalities of an abused and misshapen democratic world.

For most leftists of the decade, the Spanish Civil War (1936–1939) was a crucial event. Young men and women of the United States, England, and other countries went to Spain, to serve in the International Brigade or in other ways. The literature reflecting this dress rehearsal for World War II is an important phase of leftist writing. The impact was strongest upon the British poets; or, at least, their poems concerning the event have proved to be the most valuable and lasting. Even a superficial glance at Hemingway's work would have led one to suspect that he too would write of the Civil War. But it was his interest in Spain and in Spaniards rather than any attachment to Marxist ideology which prompted the writing of *For Whom the Bell Tolls* (1940). The novel poses a moral rather than a political problem. Robert Jordan is not the pasteboard hero of the conventional Marxist melodrama. His joining with the Loyalists is personally motivated, a test of private bravery and conviction. It is of course true that Jordan is a Hemingway character quite different from Nick Adams, Jake Barnes, or Lieutenant Henry. He has acquired a sense of responsibility which is lacking in the early characters—which some of them make a point of denying and rejecting. Jordan speaks to himself of this responsibility:

> It was a feeling of consecration to a duty toward all of the oppressed of the world which would be as difficult and embarrassing to speak about as religious experience and yet it was authentic as the feeling you had when you heard Bach, or stood in Chartres Cathedral or the Cathedral at Léon and saw the light coming through the great windows; or when you saw Mantegna and Greco and Breughel in the Prado.

Coming as it did in the latter half of the decade, the Spanish Civil War served in many cases to call attention to the need for "a cause." It was felt that the United States would itself be involved in some form of war against Fascism and Nazism; and when World War II finally did arrive, such writers as Archibald MacLeish and Maxwell Anderson wrote with a view to lining up American literature in a cultural defense against alien social doctrines.

The drama of the left was most effectively forwarded by Clifford Odets. *Waiting for Lefty* (1935) proved the most impressive piece of theatrical propaganda produced in the decade. The play used the setting, the audience, the stage of the union hall. Its spotlights glaringly illuminated fragments of the lives of exploiter and exploited. And the crescendo of strike calls at the finish was designed to provide the shortest route from literature to action ever found on a literary map. Other dramatists, while less explicit and certainly not as fully committed, did reflect the general social interests of the decade. Perhaps the best of the plays was Anderson's *Winterset* (1935), a verse-drama based upon the Sacco-Vanzetti executions of 1927, but not, like the author's earlier *Gods of the Lightning* (1928), committed either factually or doctrinally to that event. It is Anderson's best attempt to write tragedy on a contemporary theme. As the decade moved toward World War II, such writers as Archibald MacLeish were concerned with the problem of pointing forcibly to the menace of war and totalitarianism in the world. MacLeish's *Air Raid* (1938) and his *The Fall of the City* (1937), radio-dramas, are his principal contributions to this literature.

The 1930's represent a decade much more sharply political in its literature than that preceding it. Much of the writing of the time is now interesting chiefly to the social and political historian, who will find in it a great variety of responses to the call for political responsibility. He will find too that the definition of that responsibility took many devious turns and caused much bitter debate and an apparently endless and complex explication of Marx's intentions, Lenin's actions, and Stalin's right of succession. The controversies over Russian political affairs clouded the leftist air in American criticism. Radicals had come a long way and over a very complicated road since the comparatively placid days of Upton Sinclair's Helicon Hall.

ii

In 1930 twelve Southerners published a symposium called *I'll Take My Stand.* All the articles, said the introductory "Statement of Principles," "tend to support a Southern way of life against what may be called the American or prevailing way; and all as much as agree that the best terms in which to represent the distinction are contained in the phrase, Agrarian *versus* Industrial." Briefly, the symposium opposed the industrial advance of America since the Civil War as a damaging progress toward mechanization, which would eventually mean the end of any definable tradition in the country. The principal villain was, of course, the industrialist himself; but, behind him, providing him with his means and offering a philosophy and method alien to man's best instincts, was the scientist. "The capitalization of the applied sciences has now become extravagant and uncritical; it has enslaved our human energies to a degree now clearly felt to be burdensome." The complaint extended also to theoretical science; and it was this criticism of science which marked much of the work of the Agrarians in American criticism.

The South had remained continuously in the background of our national life. It was a defeated region and presumably also a backward one. Material progress had been a gift of Northern industrialists; the philosophy most people knew as American was pragmatism, suited to the expenditure of creative energies in the application of science either to society or to a series of liberal reforms directly related to an optimistic reading of science. The literature of the early part of the century was a product of this thinking over scientific law and its operation in society. But, as we look back upon the first half of our century, we find that many of the best novelists, some of the most excellent of our poets, and certainly our finest critics have been not only geographically, but culturally and traditionally, of the South.

William Faulkner began his career as a writer in the 1920's, but his best work was published from 1929 on. His novels and short stories treat with a tortured sense of responsibility the problems of Southern life from the early nineteenth century to the latest years of our own. Faulkner's Yoknapatawpha County, a place of his own creation and one which he has brilliantly and painstakingly described in a number of his works, provides a locale for a thorough sociological study of the South. As Robert Penn Warren has said, "no land in all fiction is more painstakingly analyzed from the sociological standpoint. . . . Nature and sociology, geography and human geography, are scrupulously though effortlessly presented in Faulkner's work, and their significance for his work is very great; but the significance is of a conditioning order. They are, as it were, aspects of man's 'doom'—a word of which Faulkner is very fond—but his manhood in the face of that doom is what is important."

It was Faulkner's intention to tell the story of the South; and, by the way, to give the fullest analysis of all its social types, all its personalities, and all its social and moral problems. The violence of his novels is a part of the post-Civil War psychology of a defeated nation: the erratic and often unfortunate means by which the South tried to get back upon its feet; the introduction of new social classes, with a code and a manner opportunistically at variance with the old; the tortured sensibility of the descendants of a Southern aristocracy, now helpless to reassert its position but holding perilously to the memory of it; the raw demonstrations of elemental forces, twisted and misshapen by circumstance. In his novels and short stories, Faulkner has explained the South to an American public.

The complex world of the South and the personality of the Southerner have been subjects for other significant writing. "What shall this land produce?" asks John Crowe Ransom, in "Antique Harvesters":

> A meager hill of kernels, a runnel of juice;
> Declension looks from our land, it is old

The land itself, "Of the Mississippi the bank sinister, and of the Ohio the bank sinister," has been depleted, worked over and over until it has become "barren ground." The tobacco crops are in the control of corporations which regulate the sales price. The people adjust themselves to such economic circumstance in their own way. The Southern sharecropper received attention in the 1930's from such novelists as Erskine Caldwell, whose *Tobacco Road* (1932), adapted to the stage, turned into one of the less savory jokes of modern literature. The life of the marginal worker, whether on the farms or in the cities, was treated in other Caldwell novels, such as *God's Little Acre* (1933) and *Journeyman* (1935). Caldwell exploited the sensational and the degenerate; and though he did underscore the injustices and inequalities in the economy which affected the people of his novels, his treatment of poor whites leaves them almost wholly without claim to respect or sympathy. Faulkner's *As I Lay Dying* (1930) and *Sanctuary* (1931) are far more effective treatments of the subject.

The moral and political problems encountered by Southerners as a result of the North's corporate use of their industry and agriculture are given a sensitive reading in Robert Penn Warren's first novel, *Night Rider* (1939); in it, the tobacco farmers of Tennessee combine against the great tobacco companies of the South. The development of that combination from its innocent beginnings to the time of its dissolution is told masterfully, with penetration and great psychological acuteness. The novel points more effectively than any other by Warren to the complex nature of evil, its association with good, and the manner in which earnest men of good intention are led toward first the sanctioning, then the commission, of violence. Unlike *All the King's Men* (1946), *Night Rider* is not overwritten; and it endures a careful second reading much better than does the more popular recent novel.

From the South have come also such excellent writers of shorter fiction as Katherine Anne Porter and Eudora Welty. Miss Porter's fiction is contained in three collections: *Flowering Judas* (1935), *Pale Horse, Pale Rider* (1939), and *The Leaning Tower* (1944); Miss Welty's, in two collections of short stories, *A Curtain of Green* (1943) and *The Wide Net* (1943), and two novels, *The Robber Bridegroom* (1942) and *Delta Wedding* (1945). Miss Porter's themes have been those of Southern life and of life in New York and Connecticut. The title story of her latest volume concerns the life of an American student in pre-Hitler Germany. She has generally written with a sure sense of style and a control of form which contrast with the often excessive and overflowing rhetoric of Faulkner, Thomas Wolfe, and often also of Warren. Miss Welty's writing is uneven; her best work to date is found in *A Curtain of Green*, notably in such stories as "Petrified Man," "Why I Live at the P.O.," "Clytie," and "Old Mr. Marblehall." Two other Southern women who have published work of value or promise are Caroline Gordon and Carson McCullers.

Next to Faulkner, the best known of Southern novelists is Thomas Wolfe. The first of his Eugene Gant-George Webber novels, *Look Homeward, Angel*, was published in 1929. Three others followed in the 1930's, as did two collections of shorter fiction and a brief discussion by him of the writing of his first novel. Wolfe's writing is marked by a strenuous abundance and richness. His characters assume gigantic size; their appetites are huge, their desires enormous and confused, their lives tortured and effusive. Over all of them hangs the pall of their author's rhetoric, imperative, clamorous, and demanding. More typical than fortunate is this example, from *Look Homeward, Angel:*

[Oliver Gant's] life was like that river, rich with its own deposited and onward-borne agglutinations, fecund with its sedimental accretions, filled exhaustlessly by life in order to be more richly itself, and this life, with the great purpose of a river, he emptied now into the harbor of his house, the sufficient haven of himself, for whom the gnarled vines wove round him thrice, the earth burgeoned with abundant fruit and blossom, the fire burnt madly.

iii

The most satisfactory statements of the Agrarian-Fugitive group have appeared in their criticism. Several of the men who supervised the publication of *The Fugitive* magazine in the 1920's subsequently became associated with universities and colleges. John Crowe Ransom went to Kenyon College in 1937, where in 1939 he founded the *Kenyon Review*, which he later edited. Allen Tate has been associated with several colleges and universities. In 1941 and 1942, Cleanth Brooks and Robert Penn Warren edited the brilliant *Southern Review* at the Louisiana State University; Brooks has since gone to Yale University and Warren to the University of Minnesota. Not associated with the Southern group in terms of geographical origin, but a critic joined to them by virtue of his talent and his interests, Richard P. Blackmur has also contributed important collections of critical essays; he is now associated with the Institute for Advanced Study, at Princeton University.

Briefly, the criticism of these men marks a continuation of the formalist methods initially sponsored by Ezra Pound and T. S. Eliot in the second decade of our century. To the original insistence upon careful analytic attention to poetic form, some of these critics (noticeably Tate) have added a concern with tradition as a necessary background of literary excellence. But a major concern is the identification of poetry as a discipline distinct from that of science, with its own objectives, forms, and meanings. "Art arises in particulars," said Allen Tate in a *New Republic* essay, "and it arrives at order at the point of impact between the new particulars and whatever organized experience the poet has been able to acquire." In his preface to *The New Criticism* (1941), Ransom said that "The sciences deal almost entirely with structures, which are scientific structures; but poetic structures differ radically from these, and it is that difference which defines them." The distinction is also one between poetry and prose, and it leads these critics to the careful, acute, and rewarding analyses of poetry which have fortunately become an increasingly significant part of American criticism.

In fiction, poetry, and criticism, the Southerners provide an important share of the literature of the 1930's. Generally undisturbed by the immediate and provoking political and economic issues of the decade, they went about their business with a thoroughness which in its own way has been as great as the preoccupation of the leftists with extra-literary meanings in literature. The result has been twofold: an awakening attention to the South as a region prolific of first-rate literary talent, and a gratifying progress in the development of literary criticism.

IV

THE NINETEEN FORTIES

i

In 1940, when World War II had been several months old, Archibald MacLeish issued "a declaration" called *The Irresponsibles*. The writers of the 1920's, including MacLeish, had not only been guilty of self-indulgence but had threatened American culture by ignoring it. "What matters now," MacLeish asserted, "is the defense of culture—the defense truly, and in the most literal terms, of civilization as men have known it for the last two thousand years. . . . [But] neither the modern scholar nor the modern writer admits responsibility for the defense. They assert on the contrary, each in his particular way, an irresponsibility as complete as it is singular."

This was one voice in a chorus of objection and denunciation. Van Wyck Brooks, in *On Literature Today* (1941) and *Opinions of Oliver Alston* (1941), and Bernard De Voto, in *The Literary Fallacy* (1944), added their voices. It was something of a cultural panic; American civilization was being threatened, and we were not ready. We could not, after the iconoclasm of the twenties and the thirties, convince our people that our culture was worth defending, for the writers of these decades had laughed it out of countenance. The early years of World War II saw a sort of desperate scrambling for evidences of an American tradition which might stand up to that of other nations. They saw a revival of Walt Whitman, a search for "primary" writers, a denunciation of obscurity and preciousness, an appeal to our writers to be "political," socially aware and socially responsible.

The best poetry of the war—and the best of its literature has been its poetry—scarcely reflects any disturbance over what might justly be termed an inflated issue. The work of our young poets during the war continued to announce itself as poetry, continued to reflect the influences which had been there for twenty or more years, and can withstand analysis as the literary work of individual artists. The poetry of Karl Jay Shapiro, Stanley Kunitz, Randall Jarrell, Robert Lowell, and other new poets was often on the subject of the war. "We know very well that the most resounding slogans ring dead after a few years, and that it is not for poetry to keep pace with public speeches and the strategy of events," said Shapiro in his introduction to *V-Letter and Other Poems* (1944). Oscar Williams, introducing an anthology of new poetry in 1943, said that "this is an anthology of war poetry, not of propaganda to arouse patriotism. It is the current work of poets who have intensely felt the fact of war, whether their subject matter be swans or strawberries, rifles or love. They write, not of the movement of troops, the horror of the enemy, or the mechanism of the tank, but of the state of the human organism in the emotion of now living."

ii

Literature of the 1940's has developed generally along the lines suggested in these remarks. Writers may be said, perhaps, to be more specifically aware of events than they were in the 1920's; but the awareness has not meant an exclusive commitment to the immediate present. Nor have these writers felt the urgent pressure of any one ideology such as haunted the consciences of their fellows in the 1930's. Indeed, one important fact about the forties is the decline of Marxism as a major factor in literary thinking. The literary discipline worked out by Hemingway in the twenties continues quietly to affect the writing of fiction in the forties. As his style proved more than equal to the task of describing war and battle, so its adaptations have proved the best way of describing combat scenes in World War II. The best-selling fiction of the decade continues to use historical, costume romance and simplifications of psychoanalysis. The fiction which may endure, for a little while at least, draws upon the examples of Henry James, Edith Wharton, and Ernest Hemingway. The work and example of T. S. Eliot continue to affect the writing of the young poets. In addition there is a growing body of critical work, much of it appearing in critical magazines which are associated in one way or another with American universities.

In its August, 1948, issue, *Partisan Review* published a collection of answers to several questions, under the general title of "The State of American Writing, 1948." The answers were generally either uncertain or critical. "It has been a bad decade so far" said John Berryman. "If the twenties were Eliot's decade, and the thirties Auden's, this has been simply the decade of Survival." We have, according to R. P. Blackmur, "a growing literary expertness in the techniques of expressing the experience of dismay, and the general techniques for creating the conditions of trouble." Clement Greenberg pointed to the stabilization of the literary economy: "The avantgarde has been professionalized, so to speak, organized into a field for careers; it is no longer the adventure beyond ratified norms, the refusal in the name of truth and excellence to abide by the categories of worldly success and failure." John Crowe Ransom pointed to the abundance of what he called "aesthetic theorizing by amateurs. It is a period of Reviews, of Little Magazines, of very serious critical books, which achieve publication on an unprecedented scale because for once there are readers enough to want them."

While such a symposium is scarcely a reliable guide to prediction, it does almost consistently point up the fact of an unsettled condition in the arts. The 1940's have produced no great work because five of their years have been taken up by another kind of activity; they have not produced or sanctioned any philosophy touching upon literature chiefly because writers find themselves exhausted by the release from the Marxist pressures of the 1930's and wary of any subsequent commitment which might lead to further disillusionment. What is mainly happening (outside, and occasionally even inside, the circle of best sellers) is an unceasing attention to the craft of writing—in the universities and in the magazines: a study of it that has led to an enormous increase of interest in the work of Henry James and a continuing attention to the analytics of the new criticism.

The major tendencies in the literary history of our century have made for an American literature genuinely equal to the demands made upon it. Much of the literature written in the name of naturalism, Imagism, expressionism, Marxism, has been crude and naïve; there is a part of it, however, which survives and continues to belong to our cultural life, as testimony to its slow but certain development toward maturity.

1871 -- *Stephen Crane* -- 1900

STEPHEN CRANE was born in Newark, New Jersey, the fourteenth child in a Methodist minister's family. The boy showed early signs of revolt against the confining atmosphere of the parsonage, as well as against the genteel family traditions which generations of Cranes, prominent in state and nation, had built up. He shocked his family by announcing his disbelief in hell, and his schoolmasters by condemning Tennyson's poetry as "swill." Although he studied at Lafayette College and Syracuse University, he did not complete the course at either institution, and was more interested in baseball than in academic distinction. His efforts in journalism were unsuccessful because impressions seemed more important than facts. Commissioned by the Bacheller Syndicate, he traveled through the West and Southwest and into Mexico to write a series of sketches, and was sent by the New York *Journal* as a war correspondent to Greece. He settled in England where, with the exception of several months in America reporting the Spanish-American War, he lived until his premature death in 1900.

Crane was one of the leaders of the realistic revolt against the saccharine insincerity of the time. The chief tenet in his literary theory was the demand for sincerity. Of his first book, *Maggie: A Girl of the Streets* (1893), he said, "I had no other purpose . . . than to show people to people as they seem to me. If this be evil make the best of it." Inasmuch as man is born with his eyes he cannot be held responsible for his vision—"he is merely responsible for his quality of personal honesty. To keep close to this personal honesty is my supreme ambition." Life is represented without comment, as it appears to him. Critical values are left to the reader. Thus it is clear that he is a naturalist by virtue of this impersonal and detached treatment, as well as by his refusal to give expression to moral judgments. He is also a determinist, for both Maggie and the recruit in *The Red Badge of Courage* (1895) are in their respective spheres of the Bowery and war the victims of circumstances over which they had no control. The impressionistic phase of his art is seen in the discarding of detail, and achieving descriptive effect through "snapshot" economy. To be a great artist one must see clearly, and have the gift and inclination to report honestly and sincerely what has been seen.

Although Crane's complete works fill twelve volumes, the two books by which he will be known to posterity are *Maggie* and *The Red Badge of Courage*. The former is a short episodic novel, virile, outspoken, almost brutal, in which is recorded the degeneration of a young Irish girl, a habitué of the Bowery, the life of which Crane came to know intimately during his reporting days. Subject matter like this was not considered respectable, and it was three years after the book was privately printed that a publisher was found to sponsor it. In *The Red Badge of Courage* Crane dealt the death blow to the romantic treatment of war. As a young boy he had listened to Civil War veterans relate experiences when they were not on dress parade, and he came to the conclusion that war was neither glorious nor heroic, but sordid, ghastly, and futile. From this viewpoint he laid bare the soul of the young conscript, the fear, uncertainty, suffering, resentment, and ignorance of everything but the immediate commands of his superiors. Under his hand war became in fiction what it always has been in actuality—a foolish, brutal, ghastly, confused, and unheroic experience. Crane marks the parting of the ways of war and romance.

Crane's poetry anticipated some of the later developments in the new movement. His skill in imagery is unquestioned, although his force is sometimes weakened by a self-conscious effort to say startling things.

Crane's two famous books are *Maggie, a Girl of the Streets* (1893) and *The Red Badge of Courage* (1895). *The Little Regiment* (1896), *The Open Boat and Other Tales of Adventure* (1898), *The Monster and Other Stories* (1899), and *Whilomville Stories* (1900) are collections of short stories. His complete writings are available in W. Follett, ed., *The Work of Stephen Crane* (12 vols., 1925–6). Selections may be found in V. Starrett, ed., *Maggie and Other Stories* (1933); V. Starrett, ed., *Men, Women, and Books* (1921); Henry Hazlitt, *Maggie, Together with George's Mother and The Blue Hotel*, with introduction (1931); Carl Van Doren, ed., *Twenty Stories* (1940). The poetry is available in *The Collected Poems of Stephen Crane* (1930). T. Beer's *Stephen Crane* (1923) is a full-length biography. T. L. Raymond's *Stephen Crane* (1923) is a briefer study. For further biographical information see J. D. Barry, "A Note on Stephen Crane," *Bookman*, April, 1901; C. Bohnenberger and N. M. Hill, eds., "The Letters of Joseph Conrad to Stephen and Cora Crane," *Bookman*, May and June, 1929; J. Conrad, "Stephen Crane: A Note Without Dates," *Bookman*, Feb., 1920; Mrs. J. Conrad, "Recollections of Stephen Crane," *Bookman*, April, 1926; H. R. Crane, "My Uncle, Stephen Crane at College," *American Mercury*, March, 1926; D. C. Seitz, "Stephen Crane: War Correspondent," *Bookman*, Feb., 1933; *DAB*, IV; F. Dell, "Stephen Crane and the Genius Myth," *Nation*, Dec. 10, 1924; R. D. Paine, *Roads to Adventure* (1922); H. Garland, "Stephen Crane as I Knew Him," *Yale Review*, April, 1914; T. Beer, "Mrs. Stephen Crane," *American Mercury*, March, 1934. For critical estimates the following are helpful: C. Van Doren, "Stephen Crane," *American Mercury*, Jan., 1924; H. G. Wells, "Stephen Crane," *North American Review*, Aug., 1900; E. Wyatt, *Great Companions* (1917); W. Follett, "The Second Twenty-Eight Years," *Bookman*, Jan., 1929; H. Hartwick, *The Foreground of American Fiction* (1934); E. Garnett, *Friday Nights* (1922); F. M. Ford, "Stephen Crane," *American Mercury*, Jan., 1936; R. Nye, "Stephen Crane as Social Critic," *Modern Quarterly*, Summer, 1940; A. H. Quinn, *American Fiction* (1936); Alfred Kazin, *On Native Grounds* (1942); George Snell, *The Shapers of American Fiction* (1947).

From THE RED BADGE OF COURAGE

Crane believed that the closer an artist gets to life the greater his art will be. With this as his guiding principle, he undertook to picture war as it really is, stripped of the melodrama, glamour and heroism which characterized many of the romantic war novels. He achieves his purpose by means of a psychological study of the common soldier from the time he enters the army, recording his reactions to his experiences with minute detail. It should be added that from the viewpoint of style the novel is a piece of excellent writing.

CHAPTER V

THERE were moments of waiting. The youth thought of the village street at home before the arrival of the circus parade on a day in the spring. He remembered how he had stood, a small, thrillful boy, prepared to follow the dingy lady upon the white horse, or the band in its faded chariot. He saw the yellow road, the lines of expectant people, and the sober houses. He particularly remembered an old fellow who used to sit upon a cracker box in front of the store and feign to despise such exhibitions. A thousand details of color and form surged in his mind. The old fellow upon the cracker box appeared in middle prominence.

Some one cried, "Here they come!"

There was a rustling and muttering among the men. They displayed a feverish desire to have every possible cartridge ready to their hands. The boxes were pulled around into various positions, and adjusted with great care. It was as if seven hundred new bonnets were being tried on.

The tall soldier, having prepared his rifle, produced a red handkerchief of some kind. He was engaged in knitting it about his throat with exquisite attention to its position, when the cry was repeated up and down the line in a muffled roar of sound.

"Here they come! Here they come!" Gun locks clicked.

Across the smoke-infested fields came a brown swarm of running men who were giving shrill yells. They came on, stooping and swinging their rifles at all angles. A flag, tilted forward, sped near the front.

As he caught sight of them the youth was momentarily startled by a thought that perhaps his gun was not loaded. He stood trying to rally his faltering intellect so that he might recollect the moment when he had loaded, but he could not.

A hatless general pulled his dripping horse to a stand near the colonel of the 304th. He shook his fist in the other's face. "You've got to hold 'em back!" he shouted, savagely; "you've got to hold 'em back!"

In his agitation the colonel began to stammer. "A-all r-right, General, all right, by Gawd! We-we'll do our—we-we'll d-d-do—do our best, General." The general made a passionate gesture and galloped away. The colonel, perchance to relieve his feelings, began to scold like a wet parrot. The youth, turning swiftly to make sure that the rear was unmolested, saw the commander regarding his men in a highly resentful manner, as if he regretted above everything his association with them.

The man at the youth's elbow was mumbling, as if to himself: "Oh, we're in for it now! oh, we're in for it now!"

The captain of the company had been pacing excitedly to and fro in the rear. He coaxed in schoolmistress fashion, as to a congregation of boys with primers. His talk was an endless repetition. "Reserve your fire, boys—don't shoot till I tell you—save your fire—wait till they get close up—don't be damned fools—"

Perspiration streamed down the youth's face, which was soiled like that of a weeping urchin. He frequently, with a nervous movement, wiped his eyes with his coat sleeve. His mouth was still a little way open.

He got the one glance at the foe-swarming field in front of him, and instantly ceased to debate the question of his piece being loaded. Before he was ready to begin—before he had announced to himself that he was about to fight—he threw the obedient, well-balanced rifle into position and fired a first wild shot. Directly he was working at his weapon like an automatic affair.

He suddenly lost concern for himself, and forgot to look at a menacing fate. He became not a man but a member. He felt that something of which he was a part—a regiment, an army, a cause, or a country—was in a crisis. He was welded into a common personality which was dominated by a single desire. For some moments he could not flee no more than a little finger can commit a revolution from a hand.

If he had thought the regiment was about to be annihilated perhaps he could have amputated himself from it. But its noise gave him assurance. The regiment was like a firework that, once ignited, proceeds superior to circumstances until its blazing vitality fades. It wheezed and banged with a mighty power. He pictured the ground before it as strewn with the discomfited.

There was a consciousness always of the presence of his comrades about him. He felt the subtle battle brotherhood more potent even than the cause for which they were fighting. It was a mysterious fraternity born of the smoke and danger of death.

He was at a task. He was like a carpenter who has made many boxes, making still another box, only there was furious haste in his movement. He, in his thought, was careering off in other places, even as the carpenter who as he works whistles and thinks of his friend or his enemy, his home or a saloon. And these jolted dreams were never perfect to him afterward, but remained a mass of blurred shapes.

Presently he began to feel the effects of the war atmosphere—a blistering sweat, a sensation that his eyeballs were about to crack like hot stones. A burning roar filled his ears.

Following this came a red rage. He developed the acute exasperation of a pestered animal, a well-meaning cow worried by dogs. He had a mad feeling against his rifle, which could only be used against one life at a time. He wished to rush forward and strangle with his fingers. He craved a power that would enable him to make a world-sweeping gesture and brush all back. His impotency appeared to him, and made his rage into that of a driven beast.

Buried in the smoke of many rifles his anger was directed not so much against the men who he knew were rushing toward him as against the swirling battle phantoms which were choking him, stuffing their smoke robes down his parched throat. He fought frantically for respite for his senses, for air, as a babe being smothered attacks the deadly blankets.

There was a blare of heated rage mingled with a certain expression of intentness on all faces. Many of the men were making low-toned noises with their mouths, and these subdued cheers, snarls, imprecations, prayers, made a wild, barbaric song that went as an undercurrent of sound, strange and chant-like with the resounding chords of the war march. The man at the youth's elbow was babbling. In it there was something soft and tender like the monologue of a babe. The tall soldier was swearing in a loud voice. From his lips came a black procession of curious oaths. Of a sudden another broke out in a querulous way like a man who has mislaid his hat. "Well, why don't they support us? Why don't they send supports? Do they think——"

The youth in his battle sleep heard this as one who dozes hears.

There was a singular absence of heroic poses. The men bending and surging in their haste and rage were in every impossible attitude. The steel ramrods clanked and clanged with incessant din as the men pounded them furiously into the hot rifle barrels. The flaps of the cartridge boxes were all unfastened, and bobbed idiotically with each movement. The rifles, once loaded, were jerked to the shoulder and fired without apparent aim into the smoke or at one of the blurred and shifting forms which upon the field before the regiment had been growing larger and larger like puppets under a magician's hand.

The officers, at their intervals, rearward, neglected to stand in picturesque attitudes. They were bobbing to and fro roaring directions and encouragements. The dimensions of their howls were extraordinary. They expended their lungs with prodigal wills. And often they nearly stood upon their heads in their anxiety to observe the enemy on the other side of the tumbling smoke.

The lieutenant of the youth's company had encountered a soldier who had fled screaming at the first volley of his comrades. Behind the lines these two were acting a little isolated scene. The man was blubbering and staring with sheeplike eyes at the lieutenant, who had seized him by the collar and was pommeling him. He drove him back into the ranks with many blows. The soldier went mechanically,

dully, with his animal-like eyes upon the officer. Perhaps there was to him a divinity expressed in the voice of the other—stern, hard,
with no reflection of fear in it. He tried to re-
load his gun, but his shaking hands prevented.
The lieutenant was obliged to assist him.

The men dropped here and there like bundles. The captain of the youth's company had
been killed in an early part of the action. His
body lay stretched out in the position of a
tired man resting, but upon his face there was
an astonished and sorrowful look, as if he
thought some friend had done him an ill turn.
The babbling man was grazed by a shot that
made the blood stream widely down his face.
He clapped both hands to his head. "Oh!" he
said, and ran. Another grunted suddenly as if
he had been struck by a club in the stomach.
He sat down and gazed ruefully. In his eyes
there was mute, indefinite reproach. Farther up
the line a man, standing behind a tree, had had
his knee joint splintered by a ball. Immediately
he had dropped his rifle and gripped the tree
with both arms. And there he remained, clinging desperately and crying for assistance that
he might withdraw his hold upon the tree.

At last an exultant yell went along the quivering line. The firing dwindled from an uproar
to a last vindictive popping. As the smoke
slowly eddied away, the youth saw that the
charge had been repulsed. The enemy were
scattered into reluctant groups. He saw a man
climb to the top of the fence, straddle the
rail, and fire a parting shot. The waves had
receded, leaving bits of dark *débris* upon the
ground.

Some in the regiment began to whoop frenziedly. Many were silent. Apparently they
were trying to contemplate themselves.

After the fever had left his veins, the youth
thought that at last he was going to suffocate.
He became aware of the foul atmosphere in
which he had been struggling. He was grimy
and dripping like a laborer in a foundry. He
grasped his canteen and took a long swallow
of the warmed water.

A sentence with variations went up and down
the line. "Well, we've helt 'em back. We've
helt 'em back; derned if we haven't." The men
said it blissfully, leering at each other with
dirty smiles.

The youth turned to look behind him and
off to the right and off to the left. He experienced the joy of a man who at last finds leisure
in which to look about him.

Under foot there were a few ghastly forms
motionless. They lay twisted in fantastic contortions. Arms were bent and heads were turned
in incredible ways. It seemed that the dead
men must have fallen from some great height
to get into such positions. They looked to be
dumped out upon the ground from the sky.

From a position in the rear of the grove a
battery was throwing shells over it. The flash
of the guns startled the youth at first. He
thought they were aimed directly at him.
Through the trees he watched the black figures
of the gunners as they worked swiftly and intently. Their labor seemed a complicated thing.
He wondered how they could remember its
formula in the midst of confusion.

The guns squatted in a row like savage
chiefs. They argued with abrupt violence. It
was a grim pow-wow. Their busy servants ran
hither and thither.

A small procession of wounded men were
going drearily toward the rear. It was a flow
of blood from the torn body of the brigade.

To the right and to the left were the dark
lines of other troops. Far in front he thought
he could see lighter masses protruding in points
from the forest. They were suggestive of un-
numbered thousands.

Once he saw a tiny battery go dashing along
the line of the horizon. The tiny riders were
beating the tiny horses.

From a sloping hill came the sound of cheer-
ings and clashes. Smoke welled slowly through
the leaves.

Batteries were speaking with thunderous
oratorical effort. Here and there were flags, the
red in the stripes dominating. They splashed
bits of warm color upon the dark lines of
troops.

The youth felt the old thrill at the sight of
the emblem. They were like beautiful birds
strangely undaunted in a storm.

As he listened to the din from the hillside,
to a deep pulsating thunder that came from
afar to the left, and to the lesser clamors which
came from many directions, it occurred to him
that they were fighting, too, over there, and

over there, and over there. Heretofore he had supposed that all the battle was directly under his nose.

As he gazed around him the youth felt a flash of astonishment at the blue, pure sky and the sun gleamings on the trees and fields. It was surprising that Nature had gone tranquilly on with her golden process in the midst of so much devilment.

CHAPTER VI

The youth awakened slowly. He came gradually back to a position from which he could regard himself. For moments he had been scrutinizing his person in a dazed way as if he had never before seen himself. Then he picked up his cap from the ground. He wriggled in his jacket to make a more comfortable fit, and kneeling relaced his shoe. He thoughtfully mopped his reeking features.

So it was all over at last! The supreme trial had been passed. The red, formidable difficulties of war had been vanquished.

He went into an ecstasy of self-satisfaction. He had the most delightful sensations of his life. Standing as if apart from himself, he viewed that last scene. He perceived that the man who had fought thus was magnificent.

He felt that he was a fine fellow. He saw himself even with those ideals which he had considered as far beyond him. He smiled in deep gratification.

Upon his fellows he beamed tenderness and good will. "Gee! ain't it hot, hey?" he said affably to a man who was polishing his streaming face with his coat sleeves.

"You bet!" said the other, grinning sociably. "I never seen sech dumb hotness." He sprawled out luxuriously on the ground. "Gee, yes! An' I hope we don't have no more fightin' till a week from Monday."

There were some handshakings and deep speeches with men whose features were familiar, but with whom the youth now felt the bonds of tied hearts. He helped a cursing comrade to bind up a wound of the shin.

But, of a sudden, cries of amazement broke out along the ranks of the new regiment. "Here they come ag'in! Here they come ag'in!" The man who had sprawled upon the ground started up and said, "Gosh!"

The youth turned quick eyes upon the field. He discerned forms begin to swell in masses out of a distant wood. He again saw the tilted flag speeding forward.

The shells, which had ceased to trouble the regiment for a time, came swirling again, and exploded in the grass or among the leaves of the trees. They looked to be strange war flowers bursting into fierce bloom.

The men groaned. The luster faded from their eyes. Their smudged countenances now expressed a profound dejection. They moved their stiffened bodies slowly, and watched in sullen mood the frantic approach of the enemy. The slaves toiling in the temple of this god began to feel rebellion at his harsh tasks.

They fretted and complained each to each. "Oh, say, this is too much of a good thing! Why can't somebody send us supports?"

"We ain't never goin' to stand this second banging. I didn't come here to fight the hull damn' rebel army."

There was one who raised a doleful cry. "I wish Bill Smithers had trod on my hand, insteader me treddin' on his'n." The sore joints of the regiment creaked as it painfully floundered into position to repulse.

The youth stared. Surely, he thought, this impossible thing was not about to happen. He waited as if he expected the enemy to suddenly stop, apologize, and retire bowing. It was all a mistake.

But the firing began somewhere on the regimental line and ripped along in both directions. The level sheets of flame developed great clouds of smoke that tumbled and tossed in the mild wind near the ground for a moment, and then rolled through the ranks as through a gate. The clouds were tinged an earthlike yellow in the sunrays, and in the shadow were a sorry blue. The flag was sometimes eaten and lost in this mass of vapor, but more often it projected, sun-touched, resplendent.

Into the youth's eyes there came a look that one can see in the orbs of a jaded horse. His neck was quivering with nervous weakness and the muscles of his arms felt numb and bloodless. His hands, too, seemed large and awkward as if he was wearing invisible mittens. And there was a great uncertainty about his knee joints.

The words that comrades had uttered previous to the firing began to recur to him. "Oh, say, this is too much of a good thing! What do they take us for—why don't they send supports? I didn't come here to fight the hull damned rebel army."

He began to exaggerate the endurance, the skill, and the valor of those who were coming. Himself reeling from exhaustion, he was astonished beyond measure at such persistency. They must be machines of steel. It was very gloomy struggling against such affairs, wound up perhaps to fight until sundown.

He slowly lifted his rifle and catching a glimpse of the thick-spread field he blazed at a cantering cluster. He stopped then and began to peer as best he could through the smoke. He caught changing views of the ground covered with men who were all running like pursued imps, and yelling.

To the youth it was an onslaught of redoubtable dragons. He became like the man who lost his legs at the approach of the red and green monster. He waited in a sort of a horrified, listening attitude. He seemed to shut his eyes and wait to be gobbled.

A man near him who up to this time had been working feverishly at his rifle suddenly stopped and ran with howls. A lad whose face had borne an expression of exalted courage, the majesty of he who dares give his life, was, at an instant, smitten abject. He blanched like one who has come to the edge of a cliff at midnight and is suddenly made aware. There was a revelation. He, too, threw down his gun and fled. There was no shame in his face. He ran like a rabbit.

Others began to scamper away through the smoke. The youth turned his head, shaken from his trance by this movement as if the regiment was leaving him behind. He saw the few fleeting forms.

He yelled then with fright and swung about. For a moment, in the great clamor, he was like a proverbial chicken. He lost the direction of safety. Destruction threatened him from all points.

Directly he began to speed toward the rear in great leaps. His rifle and cap were gone. His unbuttoned coat bulged in the wind. The flap of his cartridge box bobbed wildly, and his canteen, by its slender cord, swung out behind. On his face was all the horror of those things which he imagined.

The lieutenant sprang forward bawling. The youth saw his features wrathfully red, and saw him make a dab with his sword. His one thought of the incident was that the lieutenant was a peculiar creature to feel interested in such matters upon this occasion.

He ran like a blind man. Two or three times he fell down. Once he knocked his shoulder so heavily against a tree that he went headlong.

Since he had turned his back upon the fight his fears had been wondrously magnified. Death about to thrust him between the shoulder blades was far more dreadful than death about to smite him between the eyes. When he thought of it later, he conceived the impression that it is better to view the appalling than to be merely within hearing. The noises of the battle were like stones; he believed himself liable to be crushed.

As he ran on he mingled with others. He dimly saw men on his right and on his left, and he heard footsteps behind him. He thought that all the regiment was fleeing, pursued by these ominous crashes.

In his flight the sound of these following footsteps gave him his one meager relief. He felt vaguely that death must make a first choice of the men who were nearest; the initial morsels for the dragons would be then those who were following him. So he displayed the zeal of an insane sprinter in his purpose to keep them in the rear. There was a race.

As he, leading, went across a little field, he found himself in a region of shells. They hurtled over his head with long wild screams. As he listened he imagined them to have rows of cruel teeth that grinned at him. Once one lit before him and the livid lightning of the explosion effectually barred the way in his chosen direction. He groveled on the ground and then springing up went careering off through some bushes.

He experienced a thrill of amazement when he came within view of a battery in action. The men there seemed to be in conventional moods, altogether unaware of the impending annihilation. The battery was disputing with a distant antagonist and the gunners were wrapped in admiration of their shooting. They were continually bending in coaxing postures over the guns. They seemed to be patting them on the back and encouraging them with words. The guns, stolid and undaunted, spoke with dogged valor.

The precise gunners were coolly enthusiastic. They lifted their eyes every chance to the smoke-wreathed hillock from whence the hostile battery addressed them. The youth pitied them as he ran. Methodical idiots! Machine-like fools! The refined joy of planting shells in the midst of the other battery's formation would appear a little thing when the infantry came swooping out of the woods.

The face of a youthful rider, who was jerking his frantic horse with an abandon of temper he might display in a placid barnyard, was impressed deeply upon his mind. He knew that he looked upon a man who would presently be dead.

Too, he felt a pity for the guns, standing, six good comrades, in a bold row.

He saw a brigade going to the relief of its pestered fellows. He scrambled upon a wee hill and watched it sweeping finely, keeping formation in difficult places. The blue of the line was crusted with steel color, and the brilliant flags projected. Officers were shouting.

This sight also filled him with wonder. The brigade was hurrying briskly to be gulped into the infernal mouths of the war god. What manner of men were they, anyhow? Ah, it was some wondrous breed! Or else they didn't comprehend—the fools.

A furious order caused commotion in the artillery. An officer on a bounding horse made maniacal motions with his arms. The teams went swinging up from the rear, the guns were whirled about, and the battery scampered away. The cannon with their noses poked slantingly at the ground grunted and grumbled like stout men, brave but with objections to hurry.

The youth went on, moderating his pace since he had left the place of noises.

Later he came upon a general of division seated upon a horse that pricked its ears in an interested way at the battle. There was a great gleaming of yellow and patent leather about the saddle and bridle. The quiet man astride looked mouse-colored upon such a splendid charger.

A jingling staff was galloping hither and thither. Sometimes the general was surrounded by horsemen and at other times he was quite alone. He looked to be much harassed. He had the appearance of a business man whose market is swinging up and down.

The youth went slinking around this spot. He went as near as he dared trying to overhear words. Perhaps the general, unable to comprehend chaos, might call upon him for information. And he could tell him. He knew all concerning it. Of a surety the force was in a fix, and any fool could see that if they did not retreat while they had opportunity—why——

He felt that he would like to thrash the general, or at least approach and tell him in plain words exactly what he thought him to be. It was criminal to stay calmly in one spot and make no effort to stay destruction. He loitered in a fever of eagerness for the division commander to apply to him.

As he warily moved about, he heard the general call out irritably: "Tompkins, go over an' see Taylor, an' tell him not t' be in such an all-fired hurry; tell him t' halt his brigade in th' edge of th' woods; tell him t' detach a reg'ment—say I think th' center'll break if we don't help it out some; tell him t' hurry up."

A slim youth on a fine chestnut horse caught these swift words from the mouth of his superior. He made his horse bound into a gallop almost from a walk in his haste to go upon his mission. There was a cloud of dust.

A moment later the youth saw the general bounce excitedly in his saddle.

"Yes, by heavens, they have!" The officer leaned forward. His face was aflame with excitement. "Yes, by heavens, they've held 'im! They've held 'im!"

He began to blithely roar at his staff: "We'll wallop 'im now. We'll wallop 'im now. We've got 'em sure." He turned suddenly upon an aid: "Here—you—Jones—quick—ride after Tompkins—see Taylor—tell him t' go in—everlastingly—like blazes—anything."

As another officer sped his horse after the first messenger, the general beamed upon the earth like a sun. In his eyes was a desire to chant a paean. He kept repeating, "They've held 'em, by heavens!"

His excitement made his horse plunge, and

he merrily kicked and swore at it. He held a little carnival of joy on horseback.

1895

THE BLUE HOTEL

I

THE Palace Hotel at Fort Romper was painted a light blue, a shade that is on the legs of a kind of heron, causing the bird to declare its position against any background. The Palace Hotel, then, was always screaming and howling in a way that made the dazzling winter landscape of Nebraska seem only a gray swampish hush. It stood alone on the prairie, and when the snow was falling the town two hundred yards away was not visible. But when the traveler alighted at the railway station he was obliged to pass the Palace Hotel before he could come upon the company of low clapboard houses which composed Fort Romper, and it was not to be thought that any traveler could pass the Palace Hotel without looking at it. Pat Scully, the proprietor, had proved himself a master of strategy when he chose his paints. It is true that on clear days, when the great transcontinental expresses, long lines of swaying Pullmans, swept through Fort Romper, passengers were overcome at the sight, and the cult that knows the brown-reds and the subdivisions of the dark greens of the East expressed shame, pity, horror, in a laugh. But to the citizens of this prairie town and to the people who would naturally stop there, Pat Scully had performed a feat. With this opulence and splendor, these creeds, classes, egotisms, that streamed through Romper on the rails day after day, they had no color in common.

As if the displayed delights of such a blue hotel were not sufficiently enticing, it was Scully's habit to go every morning and evening to meet the leisurely trains that stopped at Romper and work his seductions upon any man that he might see wavering, gripsack in hand.

One morning, when a snow-crusted engine dragged its long string of freight cars and its one passenger coach to the station, Scully performed the marvel of catching three men. One was a shaky and quick-eyed Swede, with a great shining cheap valise; one was a tall bronzed cowboy, who was on his way to a ranch near the Dakota line; one was a little silent man from the East, who didn't look it, and didn't announce it. Scully practically made them prisoners. He was so nimble and merry and kindly that each probably felt it would be the height of brutality to try to escape. They trudged off over the creaking board sidewalks in the wake of the eager little Irishman. He wore a heavy fur cap squeezed tightly down on his head. It caused his two red ears to stick out stiffly, as if they were made of tin.

At last, Scully, elaborately, with boisterous hospitality, conducted them through the portals of the blue hotel. The room which they entered was small. It seemed to be merely a proper temple for an enormous stove, which, in the center, was humming with godlike violence. At various points on its surface the iron had become luminous and glowed yellow from the heat. Beside the stove Scully's son Johnnie was playing High-Five with an old farmer who had whiskers both grey and sandy. They were quarreling. Frequently the old farmer turned his face toward a box of sawdust—colored brown from tobacco juice—that was behind the stove, and spat with an air of great impatience and irritation. With a loud flourish of words Scully destroyed the game of cards, and bustled his son upstairs with part of the baggage of the new guests. He himself conducted them to three basins of the coldest water in the world. The cowboy and the Easterner burnished themselves fiery red with this water, until it seemed to be some kind of metal-polish. The Swede, however, merely dipped his fingers gingerly and with trepidation. It was notable that throughout this series of small ceremonies the three travelers were made to feel that Scully was very benevolent. He was conferring great favors upon them. He handed the towel from one to another with an air of philanthropic impulse.

Afterward they went to the first room, and, sitting about the stove, listened to Scully's officious clamor at his daughters, who were preparing the midday meal. They reflected in the silence of experienced men who tread carefully amid new people. Nevertheless, the old farmer, stationary, invincible in his chair near the warmest part of the stove, turned his face from the sawdust-box frequently and addressed a glowing commonplace to the strangers. Usually he was answered in short but adequate sentences by either the cowboy or the Easterner. The Swede said nothing. He seemed to be occupied in making furtive estimates of each man in the room. One might have thought that he had the sense of silly suspicion which comes to guilt. He resembled a badly frightened man.

Later, at dinner, he spoke a little, addressing his conversation entirely to Scully. He volunteered that he had come from New York, where for ten years he had worked as a tailor. These facts seemed to strike Scully as fascinating, and afterward he volunteered that he had lived at Romper for fourteen years. The Swede asked about the crops and the price of labor. He seemed barely to listen to Scully's extended replies. His eyes continued to rove from man to man.

Finally, with a laugh and a wink, he said that some of these Western communities were very dangerous; and after this statement he straightened his legs under the table, tilted his head, and laughed again, loudly. It was plain that the demonstration had no meaning to the others. They looked at him wondering and in silence.

II

As the men trooped heavily back into the front room, the two little windows presented views of a turmoiling sea of snow. The huge arms of the wind were making attempts— mighty, circular, futile—to embrace the flakes as they sped. A gate-post like a still man with a blanched face stood aghast amid this profligate fury. In a hearty voice Scully announced the presence of a blizzard. The guests of the blue hotel, lighting their pipes, assented with grunts of lazy masculine contentment. No island of the sea could be exempt in the degree of this little room with its humming stove. Johnnie, son of Scully, in a tone which defined his opinion of his ability as a card-player, challenged the old farmer of both grey and sandy whiskers to a game of High-Five. The farmer agreed with a contemptuous and bitter scoff. They sat close to the stove, and squared their knees under a wide board. The cowboy and the Easterner watched the game with interest. The Swede remained near the window, aloof, but with a countenance that showed signs of an inexplicable excitement.

The play of Johnnie and the grey-beard was suddenly ended by another quarrel. The old man rose while casting a look of heated scorn at his adversary. He slowly buttoned his coat, and then stalked with fabulous dignity from the room. In the discreet silence of all the other men the Swede laughed. His laughter rang somehow childish. Men by this time had begun to look at him askance, as if they wished to inquire what ailed him.

A new game was formed jocosely. The cowboy volunteered to become the partner of Johnnie, and they all then turned to ask the Swede to throw in his lot with the little Easterner. He asked some questions about the game, and, learning that it wore many names, and that he had played it when it was under an alias, he accepted the invitation. He strode toward the men nervously, as if he expected to be assaulted. Finally, seated, he gazed from face to face and laughed shrilly. This laugh was so strange that the Easterner looked up quickly, the cowboy sat intent and with his mouth open, and Johnnie paused, holding the cards with still fingers.

Afterward there was a short silence. Then Johnnie said, "Well, let's get at it. Come on now!" They pulled their chairs forward until their knees were bunched under the board. They began to play, and their interest in the game caused the others to forget the manner of the Swede.

The cowboy was a board-whacker. Each time that he held superior cards he whanged them, one by one, with exceeding force, down upon the improvised table, and took the tricks with a glowing air of prowess and pride that sent thrills of indignation into the hearts of his opponents. A game with a board-whacker in it is sure to become intense. The countenances of the Easterner and the Swede were miserable whenever the cowboy thundered down his aces and kings, while Johnnie, his eyes gleaming with joy, chuckled and chuckled.

Because of the absorbing play none considered the strange ways of the Swede. They paid strict heed to the game. Finally, during a lull caused by a new deal, the Swede suddenly addressed Johnnie: "I suppose there have been a good many men killed in this room." The jaws of the others dropped and they looked at him.

"What in hell are you talking about?" said Johnnie.

The Swede laughed again his blatant laugh, full of a kind of false courage and defiance. "Oh, you know what I mean all right," he answered.

"I'm a liar if I do!" Johnnie protested. The card was halted, and the men stared at the Swede. Johnnie evidently felt that as the son of the proprietor he should make a direct inquiry. "Now, what might you be drivin' at, mister?" he asked. The Swede winked at him. It was a wink full of cunning. His fingers shook on the edge of the board. "Oh, maybe you think I have been to nowheres. Maybe you think I'm a tenderfoot?"

"I don't know nothin' about you," answered Johnnie, "and I don't give a damn where you've been. All I got to say is that I don't know what you're driving at. There hain't never been nobody killed in this room."

The cowboy, who had been steadily gazing at the Swede, then spoke: "What's wrong with you, mister?"

Apparently it seemed to the Swede that he was formidably menaced. He shivered and turned white near the corners of his mouth. He sent an appealing glance in the direction of the little Easterner. During these moments he did not forget to wear his air of advanced pot-valor. "They say they don't know what I mean," he remarked mockingly to the Easterner.

The latter answered after prolonged and cautious reflection. "I don't understand you," he said, impassively.

The Swede made a movement then which announced that he thought he had encountered treachery from the only quarter where he had expected sympathy, if not help. "Oh, I see you are all against me, I see——"

The cowboy was in a state of deep stupefaction. "Say," he cried, as he tumbled the deck violently down upon the board, "say, what are you gittin' at, hey?"

The Swede sprang up with the celerity of a man escaping from a snake on the floor. "I don't want to fight!" he shouted. "I don't want to fight!"

The cowboy stretched his long legs indolently and deliberately. His hands were in his pockets. He spat into the sawdust-box. "Well, who the hell thought you did?" he inquired.

The Swede backed rapidly toward a corner of the room. His hands were out protectingly in front of his chest, but he was making an obvious struggle to control his fright. "Gentlemen," he quavered, "I suppose I am going to be killed before I can leave this house! I suppose I am going to be killed before I can leave this house!" In his eyes was the dying-swan look. Through the windows could be seen the snow turning blue in the shadow of dusk. The wind tore at the house, and some loose thing beat regularly against the clapboards like a spirit tapping.

A door opened, and Scully himself entered. He paused in surprise as he noted the tragic attitude of the Swede. Then he said, "What's the matter here?"

The Swede answered him swiftly and eagerly: "These men are going to kill me."

"Kill you!" ejaculated Scully. "Kill you! What are you talkin'?"

The Swede made the gesture of a martyr.

Scully wheeled sternly upon his son. "What is this, Johnnie?"

The lad had grown sullen. "Damned if I know," he answered. "I can't make no sense to it." He began to shuffle the cards, fluttering them together with an angry snap. "He says a good many men have been killed in this room, or something like that. And he says he's goin' to be killed here too. I don't know what ails him. He's crazy, I shouldn't wonder."

Scully then looked for explanation to the cowboy, but the cowboy simply shrugged his shoulders.

"Kill you?" said Scully again to the Swede. "Kill you? Man, you're off your nut."

"Oh, I know," burst out the Swede. "I know what will happen. Yes, I'm crazy—yes. Yes, of course, I'm crazy—yes. But I know one thing——" There was a sort of sweat of misery and terror upon his face. "I know I won't get out of here alive."

The cowboy drew a deep breath, as if his mind was passing into the last stages of dissolution. "Well, I'm doggoned," he whispered to himself.

Scully wheeled suddenly and faced his son. "You've been troublin' this man!"

Johnnie's voice was loud with its burden of grievance. "Why, good Gawd, I ain't done nothin' to 'im."

The Swede broke in. "Gentlemen, do not disturb yourselves. I will leave this house. I will go away, because"—he accused them dramatically with his glance—"because I do not want to be killed."

Scully was furious with his son. "Will you tell me what is the matter, you young divil? What's the matter, anyhow? Speak out!"

"Blame it!" cried Johnnie in despair, "don't I tell you I don't know? He—he says we want to kill him, and that's all I know. I can't tell what ails him."

The Swede continued to repeat: "Never mind, Mr. Scully; never mind. I will leave this house. I will go away, because I do not wish to be killed. Yes, of course, I am crazy—yes. But I know one thing! I will go away. I will leave this house. Never mind, Mr. Scully; never mind. I will go away."

"You will not go 'way," said Scully. "You will not go 'way until I hear the reason of this business. If anybody has troubled you I will take care of him. This is my house. You are under my roof, and I will not allow any peaceable man to be troubled here." He cast a terrible eye upon Johnnie, the cowboy, and the Easterner.

"Never mind, Mr. Scully; never mind. I will go away. I do not wish to be killed." The Swede moved toward the door which opened upon the stairs. It was evidently his intention to go at once for his baggage.

"No, no," shouted Scully peremptorily; but the white-faced man slid by him and disappeared. "Now," said Scully severely, "what does this mane?"

Johnnie and the cowboy cried together: "Why, we didn't do nothin' to 'im!"

Scully's eyes were cold. "No," he said, "you didn't?"

Johnnie swore a deep oath. "Why, this is the wildest loon I ever see. We didn't do nothin' at all. We were jest sittin' here playin' cards, and he—"

The father suddenly spoke to the Easterner. "Mr. Blanc," he asked, "what has these boys been doin'?"

The Easterner reflected again. "I didn't see anything wrong at all," he said at last, slowly.

Scully began to howl. "But what does it mane?" He stared ferociously at his son. "I have a mind to lather you for this, me boy."

Johnnie was frantic. "Well, what have I done?" he bawled at his father.

III

"I think you are tongue-tied," said Scully finally to his son, the cowboy, and the Easterner; and at the end of this scornful sentence he left the room.

Upstairs the Swede was swiftly fastening the straps of his great valise. Once his back happened to be half turned toward the door, and, hearing a noise there, he wheeled and sprang up, uttering a loud cry. Scully's wrinkled visage showed grimly in the light of the small lamp he carried. This yellow effulgence, streaming upward, coloured only his prominent features, and left his eyes, for instance, in mysterious shadow. He resembled a murderer.

"Man! man!" he exclaimed, "have you gone daffy?"

"Oh, no! Oh, no!" rejoined the other. "There are people in this world who know pretty nearly as much as you do—understand?"

For a moment they stood gazing at each other. Upon the Swede's deathly pale cheeks were two spots brightly crimson and sharply edged, as if they had been carefully painted. Scully placed the light on the table and sat himself on the edge of the bed. He spoke ruminatively. "By cracky, I never heard of such a thing in my life. It's a complete muddle. I can't, for the soul of me, think how you ever got this idea into your head." Presently he lifted his eyes and asked: "And did you sure think they were going to kill you?"

The Swede scanned the old man as if he wished to see into his mind. "I did," he said at last. He obviously suspected that this answer might precipitate an outbreak. As he pulled on a strap his whole arm shook, the elbow wavering like a bit of paper.

Scully banged his hand impressively on the footboard of the bed. "Why, man, we're goin' to have a line of ilictric street-cars in this town next spring."

" 'A line of electric street-cars,' " repeated the Swede stupidly.

"And," said Scully, "there's a new railroad goin' to be built down from Broken Arm to here. Not to mintion the four churches and the smashin' big brick school-house. Then there's the big factory, too. Why, in two years Romper'll be a met-tro-*pol*-is."

Having finished the preparation of his baggage, the Swede straightened himself. "Mr. Scully," he said, with sudden hardihood, "how much do I owe you?"

"You don't owe me anythin'," said the old man, angrily.

"Yes, I do," retorted the Swede. He took seventy-five cents from his pocket and tendered it to Scully; but the latter snapped his fingers in disdainful refusal. However, it happened that they both stood gazing in a strange fashion at three silver pieces on the Swede's open palm.

"I'll not take your money," said Scully at last. "Not after what's been goin' on here." Then a plan seemed to strike him. "Here," he cried, picking up his lamp and moving toward the door. "Here! Come with me a minute."

"No," said the Swede, in overwhelming alarm.

"Yes," urged the old man. "Come on! I want you to come and see a picter—just across the hall—in my room."

The Swede must have concluded that his hour was come. His jaw dropped and his teeth showed like a dead man's. He ultimately followed Scully across the corridor, but he had the step of one hung in chains.

Scully flashed the light high on the wall of his own chamber. There was revealed a ridiculous photograph of a little girl. She was leaning against a balustrade of gorgeous decoration, and the formidable bang to her hair was prominent. The figure was as graceful as an upright sled-stake, and, withal, it was of the hue of lead. "There," said Scully, tenderly, "that's the picter of my little girl that died. Her name was Carrie. She had the purtiest hair you ever saw! I was that fond of her, she——"

Turning then, he saw that the Swede was not contemplating the picture at all, but, instead, was keeping keen watch on the gloom in the rear.

"Look, man!" cried Scully, heartily. "That's the picter of my little gal that died. Her name was Carrie. And then here's the picter of my oldest boy, Michael. He's a lawyer in Lincoln, an' doin' well. I gave that boy a grand eddication, and I'm glad for it now. He's a fine boy. Look at 'im now. Ain't he bold as blazes, him there in Lincoln, an honored an' respicted gintleman! An honored and respicted gintleman," concluded Scully with a flourish. And, so saying, he smote the Swede jovially on the back.

The Swede faintly smiled.

"Now," said the old man, "there's only one more thing." He dropped suddenly to the floor and thrust his head beneath the bed. The Swede could hear his muffled voice. "I'd keep it under me piller if it wasn't for that boy, Johnnie. Then there's the old woman—— Where is it now? I never put it twice in the same place. Ah, now come out with you!"

Presently he backed clumsily from under the bed, dragging with him an old coat rolled into a bundle. "I've fetched him," he muttered. Kneeling on the floor, he unrolled the coat and extracted from its heart a large yellow-brown whisky-bottle.

His first maneuver was to hold the bottle up to the light. Reassured, apparently, that nobody had been tampering with it, he thrust it with a generous movement toward the Swede.

The weak-kneed Swede was about to eagerly clutch this element of strength, but he suddenly jerked his hand away and cast a look of horror upon Scully.

"Drink," said the old man affectionately. He had risen to his feet, and now stood facing the Swede.

There was a silence. Then again Scully said: "Drink!"

The Swede laughed wildly. He grabbed the bottle, put it to his mouth; and as his lips curled absurdly around the opening and his throat worked, he kept his glance, burning with hatred, upon the old man's face.

IV

After the departure of Scully the three men, with the cardboard still upon their knees, preserved for a long time an astounded silence.

Then Johnnie said: "That's the doddangedest Swede I ever see."

"He ain't no Swede," said the cowboy, scornfully.

"Well, what is he then?" cried Johnnie. "What is he then?"

"It's my opinion," replied the cowboy deliberately, "he's some kind of a Dutchman." It was a venerable custom of the country to entitle as Swedes all light-haired men who spoke with a heavy tongue. In consequence the idea of the cowboy was not without its daring. "Yes, sir," he repeated. "It's my opinion this feller is some kind of a Dutchman."

"Well, he says he's a Swede, anyhow," muttered Johnnie, sulkily. He turned to the Easterner: "What do you think, Mr. Blanc?"

"Oh, I don't know," replied the Easterner.

"Well, what do you think makes him act that way?" asked the cowboy.

"Why, he's frightened." The Easterner knocked his pipe against a rim of the stove. "He's clear frightened out of his boots."

"What at?" cried Johnnie and the cowboy together.

The Easterner reflected over his answer.

"What at?" cried the others again.

"Oh, I don't know, but it seems to me this man has been reading dime novels, and he thinks he's right out in the middle of it—the shootin' and stabbin' and all."

"But," said the cowboy, deeply scandalized, "this ain't Wyoming, ner none of them places. This is Nebrasker."

"Yes," added Johnnie, "an' why don't he wait till he gits *out West?*"

The travelled Easterner laughed. "It isn't different there even—not in these days. But he thinks he's right in the middle of hell."

Johnnie and the cowboy mused long.

"It's awful funny," remarked Johnnie at last.

"Yes," said the cowboy. "This is a queer game. I hope we don't git snowed in, because then we'd have to stand this here man bein' around with us all the time. That wouldn't be no good."

"I wish pop would throw him out," said Johnnie.

Presently they heard a loud stamping on the stairs, accompanied by ringing jokes in the voice of old Scully, and laughter, evidently from the Swede. The men around the stove stared vacantly at each other. "Gosh!" said the cowboy. The door flew open, and old Scully, flushed and anecdotal, came into the room. He was jabbering at the Swede, who followed him, laughing bravely. It was the entry of two roisterers from a banquet hall.

"Come now," said Scully sharply to the three seated men, "move up and give us a chance at the stove." The cowboy and the Easterner obediently sidled their chairs to make room for the new-comers. Johnnie, however, simply arranged himself in a more indolent attitude, and then remained motionless.

"Come! Git over, there," said Scully.

"Plenty of room on the other side of the stove," said Johnnie.

"Do you think we want to sit in the draught?" roared the father.

But the Swede here interposed with a grandeur of confidence. "No, no. Let the boy sit where he likes," he cried in a bullying voice to the father.

"All right! All right!" said Scully deferentially. The cowboy and the Easterner exchanged glances of wonder.

The five chairs were formed in a crescent about one side of the stove. The Swede began to talk; he talked arrogantly, profanely, angrily. Johnnie, the cowboy, and the Easterner maintained a morose silence, while old Scully appeared to be receptive and eager, breaking in constantly with sympathetic ejaculations.

Finally the Swede announced that he was thirsty. He moved in his chair, and said that he would go for a drink of water.

"I'll git it for you," cried Scully at once.

"No," said the Swede, contemptuously. "I'll get it for myself." He arose and stalked with the air of an owner off into the executive parts of the hotel.

As soon as the Swede was out of hearing Scully sprang to his feet and whispered intensely to the others: "Upstairs he thought I was tryin' to poison 'im."

"Say," said Johnnie, "this makes me sick. Why don't you throw 'im out in the snow?"

"Why, he's all right now," declared Scully. "It was only that he was from the East, and he thought this was a tough place. That's all. He's all right now."

The cowboy looked with admiration upon the Easterner. "You were straight," he said. "You were on to that there Dutchman."

"Well," said Johnnie to his father, "he may be all right now, but I don't see it. Other time he was scared, but now he's too fresh."

Scully's speech was always a combination of Irish brogue and idiom, Western twang and idiom, and scraps of curiously formal diction taken from the story-books and newspapers. He now hurled a strange mass of language at the head of his son. "What do I keep? What do I keep? What do I keep?" he demanded, in a voice of thunder. He slapped his knee impressively, to indicate that he himself was going to make reply, and that all should heed. "I keep a hotel," he shouted. "A hotel, do you mind? A guest under my roof has sacred privileges. He is to be intimidated by none. Not one word shall he hear that would prijudice him in favor of goin' away. I'll not have it. There's no place in this here town where they can say they iver took in a guest of mine because he was afraid to stay here." He wheeled suddenly upon the cowboy and the Easterner. "Am I right?"

"Yes, Mr. Scully," said the cowboy, "I think you're right."

"Yes, Mr. Scully," said the Easterner, "I think you're right."

V

At six-o'clock supper, the Swede fizzed like a firewheel. He sometimes seemed on the point of bursting into riotous song, and in all his madness he was encouraged by old Scully. The Easterner was encased in reserve; the cowboy sat in wide-mouthed amazement, forgetting to eat, while Johnnie wrathily demolished great plates of food. The daughters of the house, when they were obliged to replenish the biscuits, approached as warily as Indians, and, having succeeded in their purpose, fled with ill-concealed trepidation. The Swede domineered the whole feast, and he gave it the appearance of a cruel bacchanal. He seemed to have grown suddenly taller; he gazed, brutally disdainful, into every face. His voice rang through the room. Once when he jabbed out harpoon-fashion with his fork to pinion a biscuit, the weapon nearly impaled the hand of the Easterner, which had been stretched quietly out for the same biscuit.

After supper, as the men filed toward the other room, the Swede smote Scully ruthlessly on the shoulder. "Well, old boy, that was a good, square meal." Johnnie looked hopefully at his father; he knew that shoulder was tender from an old fall; and, indeed, it appeared for a moment as if Scully was going to flame out over the matter, but in the end he smiled a sickly smile and remained silent. The others understood from his manner that he was admitting his responsibility for the Swede's new viewpoint.

Johnnie, however, addressed his parent in an aside. "Why don't you license somebody to kick you downstairs?" Scully scowled darkly by way of reply.

When they were gathered about the stove, the Swede insisted on another game of High-Five. Scully gently deprecated the plan at first, but the Swede turned a wolfish glare upon him. The old man subsided, and the Swede canvassed the others. In his tone there was always a great threat. The cowboy and the Easterner both remarked indifferently that they would play. Scully said that he would presently have to go to meet the 6.58 train, and so the Swede turned menacingly upon Johnnie. For a moment their glances crossed like blades, and then Johnnie smiled and said, "Yes, I'll play."

They formed a square, with the little board on their knees. The Easterner and the Swede were again partners. As the play went on, it was noticeable that the cowboy was not board-whacking as usual. Meanwhile, Scully, near the lamp, had put on his spectacles and, with an appearance curiously like an old priest, was reading a newspaper. In time he went out to meet the 6.58 train, and, despite his precautions, a gust of polar wind whirled into the room as he opened the door. Besides scattering the cards, it chilled the players to the marrow. The Swede cursed frightfully. When Scully returned, his entrance disturbed a cozy and friendly scene. The Swede again cursed. But presently they were once more intent, their heads bent forward and their hands moving swiftly. The Swede had adopted the fashion of board-whacking.

Scully took up his paper and for a long time

remained immersed in matters which were extraordinarily remote from him. The lamp burned badly, and once he stopped to adjust the wick. The newspaper, as he turned from page to page, rustled with a slow and comfortable sound. Then suddenly he heard three terrible words: "You are cheatin'!"

Such scenes often prove that there can be little of dramatic import in environment. Any room can present a tragic front; any room can be comic. This little den was now hideous as a torture-chamber. The new faces of the men themselves had changed it upon the instant. The Swede held a huge fist in front of Johnnie's face, while the latter looked steadily over it into the blazing orbs of his accuser. The Easterner had grown pallid; the cowboy's jaw had dropped in that expression of bovine amazement which was one of his important mannerisms. After the three words, the first sound in the room was made by Scully's paper as it floated forgotten to his feet. His spectacles had also fallen from his nose, but by a clutch he had saved them in air. His hand, grasping the spectacles, now remained poised awkwardly and near his shoulder. He stared at the card-players.

Probably the silence was while a second elapsed. Then, if the floor had been suddenly twitched out from under the men they could not have moved quicker. The five had projected themselves headlong toward a common point. It happened that Johnnie, in rising to hurl himself upon the Swede, had stumbled slightly because of his curiously instinctive care for the cards and the board. The loss of the moment allowed time for the arrival of Scully, and also allowed the cowboy time to give the Swede a great push which sent him staggering back. The men found tongue together, and hoarse shouts of rage, appeal, or fear burst from every throat. The cowboy pushed and jostled feverishly at the Swede, and the Easterner and Scully clung wildly to Johnnie; but through the smoky air, above the swaying bodies of the peace-compellers, the eyes of the two warriors ever sought each other in glances of challenge that were at once hot and steely.

Of course the board had been overturned, and now the whole company of cards was scattered over the floor, where the boots of the men trampled the fat and painted kings and queens as they gazed with their silly eyes at the war that was waging above them.

Scully's voice was dominating the yells. "Stop now! Stop, I say! Stop, now—"

Johnnie, as he struggled to burst through the rank formed by Scully and the Easterner, was crying, "Well, he says I cheated! He says I cheated! I won't allow no man to say I cheated! If he says I cheated, he's a —— ——!"

The cowboy was telling the Swede, "Quit, now! Quit, d'ye hear—"

The screams of the Swede never ceased: "He did cheat! I saw him! I saw him—"

As for the Easterner, he was importuning in a voice that was not heeded: "Wait a moment, can't you? Oh, wait a moment. What's the good of a fight over a game of cards! Wait a moment—"

In this tumult no complete sentences were clear. "Cheat"—"Quit"—"He says"—these fragments pierced the uproar and rang out sharply. It was remarkable that, whereas Scully undoubtedly made the most noise, he was the least heard of any of the riotous band.

Then suddenly there was a great cessation. It was as if each man had paused for breath; and although the room was still lighted with the anger of men, it could be seen that there was no danger of immediate conflict, and at once Johnnie, shouldering his way forward, almost succeeded in confronting the Swede. "What did you say I cheated for? What did you say I cheated for? I don't cheat, and I won't let no man say I do!"

The Swede said, "I saw you! I saw you!"

"Well," cried Johnnie, "I'll fight any man what says I cheat!"

"No, you won't," said the cowboy. "Not here."

"Ah, be still, can't you?" said Scully, coming between them.

The quiet was sufficient to allow the Easterner's voice to be heard. He was repeating, "Oh, wait a moment, can't you? What's the good of a fight over a game of cards? Wait a moment!"

Johnnie, his red face appearing above his father's shoulder, hailed the Swede again. "Did you say I cheated?"

The Swede showed his teeth. "Yes."

"Then," said Johnnie, "we must fight."

"Yes, fight," roared the Swede. He was like a demoniac. "Yes, fight! I'll show you what kind of a man I am! I'll show you who you want to fight! Maybe you think I can't fight! Maybe you think I can't! I'll show you, you skin, you card-sharp! Yes, you cheated! You cheated! You cheated!"

"Well, let's go at it, then, mister," said Johnnie, coolly.

The cowboy's brow was beaded with sweat from his efforts in intercepting all sorts of raids. He turned in despair to Scully. "What are you goin' to do now?"

A change had come over the Celtic visage of the old man. He now seemed all eagerness; his eyes glowed.

"We'll let them fight," he answered, stalwartly. "I can't put up with it any longer. I've stood this damned Swede till I'm sick. We'll let them fight."

VI

The men prepared to go out of doors. The Easterner was so nervous that he had great difficulty in getting his arms into the sleeves of his new leather coat. As the cowboy drew his fur cap down over his ears his hands trembled. In fact, Johnnie and old Scully were the only ones who displayed no agitation. These preliminaries were conducted without words.

Scully threw open the door. "Well, come on," he said. Instantly a terrific wind caused the flame of the lamp to struggle at its wick, while a puff of black smoke sprang from the chimney-top. The stove was in mid-current of the blast, and its voice swelled to equal the roar of the storm. Some of the scarred and bedabbled cards were caught up from the floor and dashed helplessly against the farther wall. The men lowered their heads and plunged into the tempest as into a sea.

No snow was falling, but great whirls and clouds of flakes, swept up from the ground by the frantic winds, were streaming southward with the speed of bullets. The covered land was blue with the sheen of an unearthly satin, and there was no other hue save where, at the low, black railway station—which seemed incredibly distant—one light gleamed like a tiny jewel. As the men floundered into a thigh-deep drift, it was known that the Swede was bawling out something. Scully went to him, put a hand on his shoulder, and projected an ear. "What's that you say!" he shouted.

"I say," bawled the Swede again, "I won't stand much show against this gang. I know you'll all pitch on me."

Scully smote him reproachfully on the arm. "Tut, man!" he yelled. The wind tore the words from Scully's lips and scattered them far alee.

"You are all a gang of——" boomed the Swede, but the storm also seized the remainder of this sentence.

Immediately turning their backs upon the wind, the men had swung around a corner to the sheltered side of the hotel. It was the function of the little house to preserve here, amid this great devastation of snow, an irregular V-shape of heavily encrusted grass, which crackled beneath the feet. One could imagine the great drifts piled against the windward side. When the party reached the comparative peace of this spot, it was found that the Swede was still bellowing.

"Oh, I know what kind of a thing this is! I know you'll all pitch on me. I can't lick you all!"

Scully turned upon him panther-fashion. "You'll not have to whip all of us. You'll have to whip my son Johnnie. An' the man what troubles you durin' that time will have me to dale with."

The arrangements were swiftly made. The two men faced each other, obedient to the harsh commands of Scully, whose face, in the subtly luminous gloom, could be seen set in the austere impersonal lines that are pictured on the countenances of the Roman veterans. The Easterner's teeth were chattering, and he was hopping up and down like a mechanical toy. The cowboy stood rocklike.

The contestants had not stripped off any clothing. Each was in his ordinary attire. Their fists were up, and they eyed each other in a calm that had the elements of leonine cruelty in it.

During this pause, the Easterner's mind, like a film, took lasting impressions of three men—the iron-nerved master of the ceremony;

the Swede, pale, motionless, terrible; and Johnnie, serene yet ferocious, brutish yet heroic. The entire prelude had in it a tragedy greater than the tragedy of action, and this aspect was accentuated by the long, mellow cry of the blizzard, as it sped the tumbling and wailing flakes into the black abyss of the south.

"Now!" said Scully.

The two combatants leaped forward and crashed together like bullocks. There was heard the cushioned sound of blows, and of a curse squeezing out from between the tight teeth of one.

As for the spectators, the Easterner's pent-up breath exploded from him with a pop of relief, absolute relief from the tension of the preliminaries. The cowboy bounded into the air with a yowl. Scully was immovable as from supreme amazement and fear at the fury of the fight which he himself had permitted and arranged.

For a time the encounter in the darkness was such a perplexity of flying arms that it presented no more detail than would a swiftly revolving wheel. Occasionally a face, as if illumined by a flash of light, would shine out, ghastly and marked with pink spots. A moment later, the men might have been known as shadows, if it were not for the involuntary utterance of oaths that came from them in whispers.

Suddenly a holocaust of warlike desire caught the cowboy, and he bolted forward with the speed of a broncho. "Go it, Johnnie! go it! Kill him! Kill him!"

Scully confronted him. "Kape back," he said; and by his glance the cowboy could tell that this man was Johnnie's father.

To the Easterner there was a monotony of unchangeable fighting that was an abomination. This confused mingling was eternal to his sense, which was concentrated in a longing for the end, the priceless end. Once the fighters lurched near him, and as he scrambled hastily backward he heard them breathe like men on the rack.

"Kill him, Johnnie! Kill him! Kill him! Kill him!" The cowboy's face was contorted like one of those agony masks in museums.

"Keep still," said Scully, icily.

Then there was a sudden loud grunt, incomplete, cut short, and Johnnie's body swung away from the Swede and fell with sickening heaviness to the grass. The cowboy was barely in time to prevent the mad Swede from flinging himself upon his prone adversary. "No, you don't," said the cowboy, interposing an arm. "Wait a second."

Scully was at his son's side. "Johnnie! Johnnie, me boy!" His voice had a quality of melancholy tenderness. "Johnnie! Can you go on with it?" He looked anxiously down into the bloody, pulpy face of his son.

There was a moment of silence, and then Johnnie answered in his ordinary voice, "Yes, I—it—yes."

Assisted by his father he struggled to his feet. "Wait a bit now till you git your wind," said the old man.

A few paces away the cowboy was lecturing the Swede. "No, you don't! Wait a second!"

The Easterner was plucking at Scully's sleeve. "Oh, this is enough," he pleaded. "This is enough! Let it go as it stands. This is enough!"

"Bill," said Scully, "git out of the road." The cowboy stepped aside. "Now." The combatants were actuated by a new caution as they advanced toward collision. They glared at each other, and then the Swede aimed a lightning blow that carried with it his entire weight. Johnnie was evidently half stupid from weakness, but he miraculously dodged, and his fist sent the overbalanced Swede sprawling.

The cowboy, Scully, and the Easterner burst into a cheer that was like a chorus of triumphant soldiery, but before its conclusion the Swede had scuffled agilely to his feet and come in berserk abandon at his foe. There was another perplexity of flying arms, and Johnnie's body again swung away and fell, even as a bundle might fall from a roof. The Swede instantly staggered to a little wind-waved tree and leaned upon it, breathing like an engine, while his savage and flame-lit eyes roamed from face to face as the men bent over Johnnie. There was a splendour of isolation in his situation at this time which the Easterner felt once when, lifting his eyes from the man on the ground, he beheld that mysterious and lonely figure, waiting.

"Are you any good yet Johnnie?" asked Scully in a broken voice.

The son gasped and opened his eyes languidly. After a moment he answered, "No—I ain't—any good—any—more." Then, from shame and bodily ill, he began to weep, the tears furrowing down through the blood-stains on his face. "He was too—too—too heavy for me."

Scully straightened and addressed the waiting figure. "Stranger," he said, evenly, "it's all up with our side." Then his voice changed into that vibrant huskiness which is commonly the tone of the most simple and deadly announcements. "Johnnie is whipped."

Without replying, the victor moved off on the route to the front door of the hotel.

The cowboy was formulating new and unspellable blasphemies. The Easterner was startled to find that they were out in a wind that seemed to come direct from the shadowed arctic floes. He heard again the wail of the snow as it was flung to its grave in the south. He knew now that all this time the cold had been sinking into him deeper and deeper, and he wondered that he had not perished. He felt indifferent to the condition of the vanquished man.

"Johnnie, can you walk?" asked Scully.

"Did I hurt—hurt him any?" asked the son.

"Can you walk, boy? Can you walk?"

Johnnie's voice was suddenly strong. There was a robust impatience in it. "I asked you whether I hurt him any!"

"Yes, yes, Johnnie," answered the cowboy, consolingly; "he's hurt a good deal."

They raised him from the ground, and as soon as he was on his feet he went tottering off, rebuffing all attempts at assistance. When the party rounded the corner they were fairly blinded by the pelting of the snow. It burned their faces like fire. The cowboy carried Johnnie through the drift to the door. As they entered, some cards again rose from the floor and beat against the wall.

The Easterner rushed to the stove. He was so profoundly chilled that he almost dared to embrace the glowing iron. The Swede was not in the room. Johnnie sank into a chair and, folding his arms on his knees, buried his face in them. Scully, warming one foot and then the other at a rim of the stove, muttered to himself with Celtic mournfulness. The cowboy had removed his fur cap, and with a dazed and rueful air he was running one hand through his tousled locks. From overhead they could hear the creaking of boards, as the Swede tramped here and there in his room.

The sad quiet was broken by the sudden flinging open of a door that led toward the kitchen. It was instantly followed by an inrush of women. They precipitated themselves upon Johnnie amid a chorus of lamentation. Before they carried their prey off to the kitchen, there to be bathed and harangued with that mixture of sympathy and abuse which is a feat of their sex, the mother straightened herself and fixed old Scully with an eye of stern reproach. "Shame be upon you, Patrick Scully!" she cried. "Your own son, too. Shame be upon you!"

"Shame be upon you, Patrick Scully!" The girls, rallying to this slogan, sniffed disdainfully in the direction of those trembling accomplices, the cowboy and the Easterner. Presently they bore Johnnie away, and left the three men to dismal reflection.

VII

"I'd like to fight this here Dutchman myself," said the cowboy, breaking a long silence.

Scully wagged his head sadly. "No, that wouldn't do. It wouldn't be right. It wouldn't be right."

"Well, why wouldn't it?" argued the cowboy. "I don't see no harm in it."

"No," answered Scully, with mournful heroism. "It wouldn't be right. It was Johnnie's fight, and now we mustn't whip the man just because he whipped Johnnie."

"Yes, that's true enough," said the cowboy; "but—he better not get fresh with me, because I couldn't stand no more of it."

"You'll not say a word to him," commanded Scully, and even then they heard the tread of the Swede on the stairs. His entrance was made theatric. He swept the door back with a bang and swaggered to the middle of the room. No one looked at him. "Well," he cried, insolently, at Scully, "I s'pose you'll tell me now how much I owe you?"

The old man remained stolid. "You don't owe me nothin'."

"Huh!" said the Swede, "huh! Don't owe 'im nothin'."

The cowboy addressed the Swede. "Stranger, I don't see how you come to be so gay around here."

Old Scully was instantly alert. "Stop!" he shouted, holding his hand forth, fingers upward. "Bill, you shut up!"

The cowboy spat carelessly into the sawdust-box. "I didn't say a word, did I?" he asked.

"Mr. Scully," called the Swede, "how much do I owe you?" It was seen that he was attired for departure, and that he had his valise in his hand.

"You don't owe me nothin'," repeated Scully in the same imperturbable way.

"Huh!" said the Swede. "I guess you're right. I guess if it was any way at all, you'd owe me somethin'. Thats' what I guess." He turned to the cowboy. " 'Kill him! Kill him! Kill him!' " he mimicked, and then guffawed victoriously. " 'Kill him!' " He was convulsed with ironical humour.

But he might have been jeering the dead. The three men were immovable and silent, staring with glassy eyes at the stove.

The Swede opened the door and passed into the storm, giving one derisive glance backward at the still group.

As soon as the door was closed, Scully and the cowboy leaped to their feet and began to curse. They trampled to and fro, waving their arms and smashing into the air with their fists. "Oh, but that was a hard minute!" wailed Scully. "That was a hard minute! Him there leerin' and scoffin'! One bang at his nose was worth forty dollars to me that minute! How did you stand it, Bill?"

"How did I stand it?" cried the cowboy in a quivering voice. "How did I stand it? Oh!"

The old man burst into sudden brogue. "I'd loike to take that Swade," he wailed, "and hould 'im down on a shtone flure and bate 'im to a jelly wid a shtick!"

The cowboy groaned in sympathy. "I'd like to git him by the neck and ha-ammer him"— he brought his hand down on a chair with a noise like a pistol-shot—"hammer that there Dutchman until he couldn't tell himself from a dead coyote!"

"I'd bate 'im until he—"

"I'd show *him* some things—"

And then together they raised a yearning, fanatic cry—"Oh-o-oh! if we only could—"

"Yes!"

"Yes!"

"And then I'd—"

"O-o-oh!"

VIII

The Swede, tightly gripping his valise, tacked across the face of the storm as if he carried sails. He was following a line of little naked, gasping trees which, he knew, must mark the way of the road. His face, fresh from the pounding of Johnnie's fists, felt more pleasure than pain in the wind and the driving snow. A number of square shapes loomed upon him finally, and he knew them as the houses of the main body of the town. He found a street and made travel along it, leaning heavily upon the wind whenever, at a corner, a terrific blast caught him.

He might have been in a deserted village. We picture the world as thick with conquering and elate humanity, but here, with the bugles of the tempest pealing, it was hard to imagine a peopled earth. One viewed the existence of man then as a marvel, and conceded a glamour of wonder to these lice which were caused to cling to a whirling, fire-smitten, ice-locked, disease-stricken, space-lost bulb. The conceit of man was explained by this storm to be the very engine of life. One was a coxcomb not to die in it. However, the Swede found a saloon.

In front of it an indomitable red light was burning, and the snowflakes were made blood-colour as they flew through the circumscribed territory of the lamp's shining. The Swede pushed open the door of the saloon and entered. A sanded expanse was before him, and at the end of it four men sat about a table drinking. Down one side of the room extended a radiant bar, and its guardian was leaning upon his elbows listening to the talk of the men at the table. The Swede dropped his valise upon the floor and, smiling fraternally upon the barkeeper, said, "Gimmee some whisky, will you?" The man placed a bottle, a whisky-glass, and a glass of ice-thick water upon the bar. The Swede poured himself an abnormal portion of whisky and drank it in three gulps. "Pretty bad night," remarked the bartender, indifferently. He was making the pretension of blindness which is usually a distinction of his class; but it could have been seen that he was furtively studying the half-erased blood-stains on the face of the Swede. "Bad night," he said again.

"Oh, it's good enough for me," replied the Swede, hardily, as he poured himself some more whisky. The barkeeper took his coin and maneuvered it through its reception by the highly nickeled cash-machine. A bell rang; a card labeled "20 cts." had appeared.

"No," continued the Swede, "this isn't too bad weather. It's good enough for me."

"So?" murmured the barkeeper, languidly.

The copious drams made the Swede's eyes swim, and he breathed a trifle heavier. "Yes, I like this weather. I like it. It suits me." It was apparently his design to impart a deep significance to these words.

"So?" murmured the bartender again. He turned to gaze dreamily at the scroll-like birds and bird-like scrolls which had been drawn with soap upon the mirrors in back of the bar.

"Well, I guess I'll take another drink," said the Swede, presently. "Have something?"

"No, thanks; I'm not drinkin'," answered the bartender. Afterward he asked, "How did you hurt your face?"

The Swede immediately began to boast loudly. "Why, in a fight. I thumped the soul out of a man down here at Scully's hotel."

The interest of the four men at the table was at last aroused.

"Who was it?" said one.

"Johnnie Scully," blustered the Swede. "Son of the man what runs it. He will be pretty near dead for some weeks, I can tell you. I made a nice thing of him, I did. He couldn't get up. They carried him in the house. Have a drink?"

Instantly the men in some subtle way encased themselves in reserve. "No, thanks," said one. The group was of curious formation. Two were prominent local business men; one was the district attorney; and one was a professional gambler of the kind known as "square." But a scrutiny of the group would not have enabled an observer to pick the gambler from the men of more reputable pursuits.

He was, in fact, a man so delicate in manner, when among people of fair class, and so judicious in his choice of victims, that in the strictly masculine part of the town's life he had come to be explicitly trusted and admired. People called him a thoroughbred. The fear and contempt with which his craft was regarded were undoubtedly the reason why his quiet dignity shone conspicuous above the quiet dignity of men who might be merely hatters, billiard-markers, or grocery clerks. Beyond an occasional unwary traveler who came by rail, this gambler was supposed to prey solely upon reckless and senile farmers, who, when flush with good crops, drove into town in all the pride and confidence of an absolutely invulnerable stupidity. Hearing at times in circuitous fashion of the despoilment of such a farmer, the important men of Romper invariably laughed in contempt of the victim, and if they thought of the wolf at all, it was with a kind of pride at the knowledge that he would never dare think of attacking their wisdom and courage. Besides, it was popular that this gambler had a real wife and two real children in a neat cottage in a suburb, where he led an exemplary home life; and when anyone even suggested a discrepancy in his character, the crowd immediately vociferated descriptions of this virtuous family circle. Then men who led exemplary home lives, and men who did not lead exemplary home lives, all subsided in a bunch, remarking that there was nothing more to be said.

However, when a restriction was placed upon him—as, for instance, when a strong clique of members of the new Pollywog Club refused to permit him, even as a spectator, to appear in the rooms of the organization—the candor and gentleness with which he accepted the judgment disarmed many of his foes and made his friends more desperately partisan. He invariably distinguished between himself and a respectable Romper man so quickly and frankly that his manner actually appeared to be a continual broadcast compliment.

And one must not forget to declare the fundamental fact of his entire position in Romper. It is irrefutable that in all affairs outside his business, in all matters that occur eternally and commonly between man and man, this thieving card-player was so generous, so just, so moral, that, in a contest, he could have put to flight the consciences of nine tenths of the citizens of Romper.

And so it happened that he was seated in this saloon with the two prominent local merchants and the district attorney.

The Swede continued to drink raw whiskey, meanwhile babbling at the barkeeper and trying to induce him to indulge in potations. "Come on. Have a drink. Come on. What— no? Well, have a little one, then. By gawd, I've whipped a man to-night, and I want to celebrate. I whipped him good, too. Gentlemen," the Swede cried to the men at the table, "have a drink?"

"Ssh!" said the barkeeper.

The group at the table, although furtively attentive, had been pretending to be deep in talk, but now a man lifted his eyes toward the Swede and said, shortly, "Thanks. We don't want any more."

At this reply the Swede ruffled out his chest like a rooster. "Well," he exploded, "it seems I can't get anybody to drink with me in this town. Seems so, don't it? Well!"

"Ssh!" said the barkeeper.

"Say," snarled the Swede, "don't you try to shut me up. I won't have it. I'm a gentleman, and I want people to drink with me. And I want 'em to drink with me now. *Now*—do you understand?" He rapped the bar with his knuckles.

Years of experience had calloused the bartender. He merely grew sulky. "I hear you," he answered.

"Well," cried the Swede, "listen hard then. See those men over there? Well, they're going to drink with me, and don't you forget it. Now you watch."

"Hi!" yelled the barkeeper, "this won't do!"

"Why won't it?" demanded the Swede. He stalked over to the table, and by chance laid his hand upon the shoulder of the gambler. "How about this?" he asked wrathfully. "I asked you to drink with me."

The gambler simply twisted his head and spoke over his shoulder. "My friend, I don't know you."

"Oh, hell!" answered the Swede, "come and have a drink."

"Now, my boy," advised the gambler, kindly, "take your hand off my shoulder and go 'way and mind your own business." He was a little, slim man, and it seemed strange to hear him use this tone of heroic patronage to the burly Swede. The other men at the table said nothing.

"What! You won't drink with me, you little dude? I'll make you, then! I'll make you!" The Swede had grasped the gambler frenziedly at the throat, and was dragging him from his chair. The other men sprang up. The barkeeper dashed around the corner of his bar. There was a great tumult, and then was seen a long blade in the hand of the gambler. It shot forward, and a human body, this citadel of virtue, wisdom, power, was pierced as easily as if it had been a melon. The Swede fell with a cry of supreme astonishment.

The prominent merchants and the district attorney must have at once tumbled out of the place backward. The bartender found himself hanging limply to the arm of a chair and gazing into the eyes of a murderer.

"Henry," said the latter, as he wiped his knife on one of the towels that hung beneath the bar rail, "you tell 'em where to find me. I'll be home, waiting for 'em." Then he vanished. A moment afterward the barkeeper was in the street dinning through the storm for help and, moreover, companionship.

The corpse of the Swede, alone in the saloon, had its eyes fixed upon a dreadful legend that dwelt atop of the cash-machine: "This registers the amount of your purchase."

IX

Months later, the cowboy was frying pork over the stove of a little ranch near the Dakota line, when there was a quick thud of hoofs outside, and presently the Easterner entered with the letters and the papers.

"Well," said the Easterner at once, "the chap that killed the Swede has got three years. Wasn't much, was it?"

"He has? Three years?" The cowboy poised his pan of pork, while he ruminated upon the news. "Three years. That ain't much."

"No. It was a light sentence," replied the Easterner as he unbuckled his spurs. "Seems there was a good deal of sympathy for him in Romper."

"If the bartender had been any good," observed the cowboy, thoughtfully, "he would have gone in and cracked that there Dutchman on the head with a bottle in the beginnin' of it and stopped all this here murderin'."

"Yes, a thousand things might have happened," said the Easterner, tartly.

The cowboy returned his pan of pork to the fire, but his philosophy continued. "It's funny, ain't it? If he hadn't said Johnnie was cheatin' he'd be alive this minute. He was an awful fool. Game played for fun, too. Not for money. I believe he was crazy."

"I feel sorry for that gambler," said the Easterner.

"Oh, so do I," said the cowboy. "He don't deserve none of it for killin' who he did."

"The Swede might not have been killed if everything had been square."

"Might not have been killed?" exclaimed the cowboy. "Everythin' square? Why, when he said that Johnnie was cheatin' and acted like such a jackass? And then in the saloon he fairly walked up to git hurt?" With these arguments the cowboy browbeat the Easterner and reduced him to rage.

"You're a fool!" cried the Easterner, viciously. "You're a bigger jackass than the Swede by a million majority. Now let me tell you one thing. Let me tell you something. Listen! Johnnie *was* cheating!"

" 'Johnnie,' " said the cowboy, blankly. There was a minute of silence, and then he said, robustly, "Why, no. The game was only for fun."

"Fun or not," said the Easterner, "Johnnie was cheating. I saw him. I know it. I saw him. And I refused to stand up and be a man. I let the Swede fight it out alone. And you—you were simply puffing around the place and wanting to fight. And then old Scully himself! We are all in it! This poor gambler isn't even a noun. He is kind of an adverb. Every sin is the result of a collaboration. We, five of us, have collaborated in the murder of this Swede. Usually there are from a dozen to forty women really involved in every murder, but in this case it seems to be only five men—you, I, Johnnie, old Scully; and that fool of an unfortunate gambler came merely as a culmination, the apex of a human movement, and gets all the punishment."

The cowboy, injured and rebellious, cried out blindly into this fog of mysterious theory: "Well, I didn't do anythin', did I?"

1899

From THE BLACK RIDERS

One of the very earliest attempts at writing free verse. As pioneer work it showed the potential possibilities of this literary form which later writers realized more completely.

XXIV

I saw a man pursuing the horizon;
Round and round they sped.
I was disturbed at this;
I accosted the man.
"It is futile," I said,
"You can never—"

"You lie," he cried,
And ran on.

XXXVI

I met a seer.
He held in his hands
The book of wisdom.
"Sir," I addressed him,
"Let me read."
"Child—" he began.
"Sir," I said,
"Think not that I am a child,
For already I know much
Of that which you hold.
Ay, much."
He smiled.
Then he opened the book
And held it before me.—
Strange that I should have grown so suddenly blind.

1895

From WAR IS KIND

I

Do not weep, maiden, for war is kind.
Because your lover threw wild hands toward the sky
And the affrighted steed ran on alone,
Do not weep.
War is kind.

Hoarse, booming drums of the regiment,
Little souls who thirst for fight,
These men were born to drill and die.
The unexplained glory flies above them,
Great is the battle-god, great, and his king-
dom—   10
A field where a thousand corpses lie.

Do not weep, babe, for war is kind.
Because your father tumbled in the yellow
trenches,
Raged at his breast, gulped and died,
Do not weep.
War is kind.

Swift blazing flag of the regiment,
Eagle with crest of red and gold,
These men were born to drill and die.
Point for them the virtue of slaughter,   20
Make plain to them the excellence of killing
And a field where a thousand corpses lie.

Mother whose heart hung humble as a button
On the bright splendid shroud of your son,
Do not weep.
War is kind.

XII

A newspaper is a collection of half-injustices
Which, bawled by boys from mile to mile,
Spreads its curious opinion
To a million merciful and sneering men,
While families cuddle the joys of the fireside
When spurred by tale of dire lone agony.
A newspaper is a court

Where every one is kindly and unfairly tried
By a squalor of honest men.
A newspaper is a market   10
Where wisdom sells its freedom
And melons are crowned by the crowd.
A newspaper is a game
Where his error scores the player victory
While another's skill wins death.
A newspaper is a symbol;
It is feckless life's chronicle,
A collection of loud tales
Concentrating eternal stupidities,
That in remote ages lived unhaltered,   20
Roaming through a fenceless world.

XIII

The wayfarer,
Perceiving the pathway to truth,
Was struck with astonishment.
It was thickly grown with weeds.
"Ha," he said,
"I see that none has passed here
In a long time."
Later he saw that each weed
Was a singular knife.
"Well," he mumbled at last,   10
"Doubtless there are other roads."

XXI

A man said to the universe:
"Sir, I exist!"
"However," replied the universe,
"The fact has not created in me
A sense of obligation."

1899

1870 ~ *Frank Norris* ~ 1902

FRANK NORRIS was one of the leaders in the revolt against the literary fashions of his day. He was born in Chicago, studied art in Paris, and on his return entered the University of California. A year of graduate study at Harvard followed. He served as war correspondent during the Spanish-American War, and in South Africa at the time of the Jameson Raid. A severe attack of fever from which he never fully recovered undoubtedly hastened his premature death. With the exception of journalistic work in San Francisco and a period as a reader for a publishing company, Norris devoted his remaining years to his writing.

The plans he had laid were grandiose and epic in scope. There was to be an epic of wheat, a trilogy dealing with its raising, disposal, and distribution respectively. Only two of the three volumes, *The Octopus* (1901) and *The Pit* (1903), were written. Then there was to be a trilogy about the three days at Gettysburg. This, however, was never even begun.

Unlike Garland, Norris did not approach the problem of revolt through the "local" novel alone. In his *The Responsibilities of the Novelist* (1903), a collection of critical essays, the view is more comprehensive and cosmopolitan. The novelist is confronted with grave responsibilities, for of the three great "molders of public opinion and public morals," the pulpit, the press, and the novel, the novel, he insists, is by far the most powerful. "Every novel," according to his theory, "must do one of three things—it must (1) tell something, (2) show something, or (3) prove something." Obviously a given novel may do all three, and by that token would be superior to others. This also makes it clear that in his judgment any great novel is a purpose novel, that is, "it preaches by telling things and showing things"; in other words it must evaluate what is told and shown, therefore prove something. Yet Norris maintains that as soon as the writer becomes consciously aware of the purpose, the novel will fail, which is another way of saying that the artistic interest must be supreme, a modified version of Shakespeare's suggestion that we may "by indirections find directions out." He laid his plans on a big scale, including the representation of "a whole congeries of forces, social development, race impulses," which opened the way "not to the study of men but of man." He shared the aspirations of one of his characters in *The Octopus*, the poet Presley, who "strove for the diapason, the great song which should embrace in itself a whole epoch, a complete era, the voice of an entire people."

Norris preferred to think of himself as a naturalist, although like Garland he wrote at times in a romantic vein. *McTeague* (1899) and *Vandover and the Brute* (1914), which were begun while he was a student, although not published until later, were written when he was at the height of his rebellion against the literary insincerity of the time, and are outspokenly realistic. The novelettes, *Moran of the Lady Letty* (1898) and *Blix* (1899), are as frankly romantic, insofar, at any rate, as they are unusual, spectacular, and bizarre. *The Octopus* (1901) and *The Pit* (1903) were written under the spell of his critical theory. Although this forced him into his best artistic and creative behavior, there is question whether the process yielded what was hoped for. In *The Octopus* he wrote what Frederic Tabor Cooper called "an example of symbolism pushed to the extreme limit"; in *The Pit* the sociological interest and implications became so absorbing that they victimized Norris the novelist. It is easy to see that Norris was definitely opposed to the ruthlessness and brutality of the capitalistic order, as represented by the railroad, and that his sympathies went out to the "embattled farmers" in their struggle against this powerful force. His realistic novels *McTeague* and *Vandover* have been most influential and possess the most likely guarantee of permanence. The work as a whole leaves the impression of incompleteness, "a rugged torso of a broken statue."

Besides the novels mentioned above, Norris wrote *Yvernelle* (1892) and *A Man's Woman* (1900). His short stories are found in *A Deal in Wheat* (1903); *The Third Circle* (1909); *Frank Norris of "The Wave": Stories and Sketches from the San Francisco Weekly, 1893-1897*, foreword by C. G. Norris (1931). *The Responsibilities of the Novelist* (1903) is a collection of critical essays; see also W. E. Martin, Jr., "Two Uncollected Essays by Frank Norris," *American Literature*, May, 1936. A uniform edition, *The Complete Works of Frank Norris* (1928), is available. The only complete biography is F. Walker, *Frank Norris* (1932). Further information may be found in *DAB*, XIII; H. M. Wright, "In Memoriam—Frank Norris," *University of California Chronicle*, Oct., 1902; C. C. Dobie, "Frank Norris, or Up from Culture," *American Mercury*, April, 1928; H. Garland, *Companions on the Trail* (1931); E. Peixotto, "Romanticist under the Skin: Frank Norris," *Saturday Review of Literature*, May 27, 1933. For criticism the following are helpful: V. L. Parrington, *Main Currents in American Thought*, III (1930); J. C. Underwood, *Literature and Insurgency* (1914); E. Wyatt, *Great Companions* (1917); F. T. Cooper, *Some American Story Tellers* (1911); H. Garland, "The Work of Frank Norris," *Critic*, March, 1903; W. D. Howells, "Frank Norris," *North American Review*, Dec., 1902; W. E. Martin, Jr., "Frank Norris's Reading at Harvard College," *American Literature*, May, 1935; H. Hartwick, *The Foreground of American Fiction* (1934); C. H. Grattan, "Frank Norris," *Bookman*, July, 1929; A. H. Quinn, *American Fiction* (1936); Alfred Kazin, *On Native Grounds* (1942); George Snell, *The Shapers of American Fiction* (1947); Charles C. Walcutt, "The Naturalism of *Vandover and the Brute*," in *Forms of Modern Fiction* (1948); G. W. Meyer, "A New Interpretation of *The Octopus*," *College English*, March, 1943; Charles C. Walcutt, "Frank Norris on Realism and Naturalism," *American Literature*, March, 1941.

From McTEAGUE

Although Norris also wrote romantic novels, *McTeague* and *The Octopus* are realistic in subject matter and treatment. The former is a novel of degeneracy in an adverse environment, the main elements in which are chance and economic pressure. The latter, on the other hand, is built on a larger scale and portrays the losing struggle of the California wheat growers against the economic and political tyranny of the railroads. Norris sought to tell the truth as he saw it with passionate zeal.

CHAPTER X

THAT summer passed, then the winter. The wet season began in the last days of September and continued all through October, November, and December. At long intervals would come a week of perfect days, the sky without a cloud, the air motionless, but touched with a certain nimbleness, a faint effervescence that was exhilarating. Then, without warning, dur-

ing a night when a south wind blew, a gray scroll of cloud would unroll and hang high over the city, and the rain would come pattering down again, at first in scattered showers, then in an uninterrupted drizzle.

All day long Trina sat in the bay window of the sitting-room that commanded a view of a small section of Polk Street. As often as she raised her head she could see the big market, a confectionery store, a bell-hanger's shop, and farther on, above the roofs, the glass skylights and water tanks of the big public baths. In the nearer foreground ran the street itself; the cable cars trundled up and down, thumping heavily over the joints of the rails; market carts by the score came and went, driven at a great rate by preoccupied young men in their shirt sleeves, with pencils behind their ears, or by reckless boys in bloodstained butcher's aprons. Upon the sidewalks the little world of Polk Street swarmed and jostled through its daily round of life. On fine days the great ladies from the avenue, one block above, invaded the street, appearing before the butcher stalls, intent upon their day's marketing. On rainy days their servants—the Chinese cooks or the second girls—took their places. These servants gave themselves great airs, carrying their big cotton umbrellas as they had seen their mistresses carry their parasols, and haggling in supercilious fashion with the market men, their chins in the air.

The rain persisted. Everything in the range of Trina's vision, from the tarpaulins on the market-cart horses to the panes of glass in the roof of the public baths, looked glazed and varnished. The asphalt of the sidewalks shone like the surface of a patent leather boot; every hollow in the street held its little puddle, that winked like an eye each time a drop of rain struck into it.

Trina still continued to work for Uncle Oelbermann. In the mornings she busied herself about the kitchen, the bedroom, and the sitting-room; but in the afternoon, for two or three hours after lunch, she was occupied with the Noah's ark animals. She took her work to the bay window, spreading out a great square of canvas underneath her chair, to catch the chips and shavings, which she used afterwards for lighting fires. One after another she caught up the little blocks of straight-grained pine, the knife flashed between her fingers, the little figure grew rapidly under her touch, was finished and ready for painting in a wonderfully short time, and was tossed into the basket that stood at her elbow.

But very often during that rainy winter after her marriage Trina would pause in her work, her hands falling idly into her lap, her eyes—her narrow, pale blue eyes—growing wide and thoughtful as she gazed, unseeing, out into the rain-washed street.

She loved McTeague now with a blind unreasoning love that admitted of no doubt or hesitancy. Indeed, it seemed to her that it was only *after* her marriage with the dentist that she had really begun to love him. With the absolute final surrender of herself, the irrevocable, ultimate submission, had come an affection the like of which she had never dreamed in the old B Street days. But Trina loved her husband, not because she fancied she saw in him any of those noble and generous qualities that inspire affection. The dentist might or might not possess them, it was all one with Trina. She loved him because she had given herself to him freely, unreservedly; had merged her individuality into his; she was his, she belonged to him forever and forever. Nothing that he could do (so she told herself), nothing that she herself could do, could change her in this respect. McTeague might cease to love her, might leave her, might even die; it would be all the same, *she was his.*

But it had not been so at first. During those long, rainy days of the fall, days when Trina was left alone for hours, at that time when the excitement and novelty of the honeymoon were dying down, when the new household was settling into its grooves, she passed through many an hour of misgiving, of doubt, and even of actual regret.

Never would she forget one Sunday afternoon in particular. She had been married but three weeks. After dinner she and little Miss Baker had gone for a bit of a walk to take advantage of an hour's sunshine and to look at some wonderful geraniums in a florist's window on Sutter Street. They had been caught in a shower, and on returning to the flat the little dressmaker had insisted on fetching Trina up to her tiny room and brewing her a cup of strong tea, "to take the chill off." The two women had chatted over their teacups the better part of the afternoon, then Trina had returned to her rooms. For nearly three hours McTeague had been out of her thoughts, and as she came through their little suite, singing softly to herself, she suddenly came upon him quite unexpectedly. Her husband was in the "Dental Parlors," lying back in his operating chair, fast asleep. The little stove was crammed with coke, the room was overheated, the air thick and foul with the odors of ether, of coke gas, of stale beer and cheap tobacco. The dentist sprawled his gigantic limbs over the worn velvet of the operating chair; his coat and vest and shoes were off, and huge feet, in their thick gray socks, dangled over the edge of the footrest; his pipe, fallen from his half-open mouth, had spilled the ashes into his lap; while on the floor, at his side, stood the half-empty pitcher of steam beer. His head had rolled limply upon one shoulder, his face was red with sleep, and from his open mouth came a terrific sound of snoring.

For a moment Trina stood looking at him as he lay thus, prone, inert, half-dressed, and stupefied with the heat of the room, the steam beer, and the fumes of the cheap tobacco. Then her little chin quivered and a sob rose to her throat; she fled from the "Parlors," locking herself in her bedroom, flung herself on the bed and burst into an agony of weeping. Ah, no, ah, no, she could not love him. It had all been a dreadful mistake, and now it was irrevocable; she was bound to this man for life. If it was as bad as this now, only three weeks after her marriage, how would it be in the years to come? Year after year, month after month, hour after hour, she was to see this same face, with its salient jaw, was to feel the touch of those enormous red hands, was to hear the heavy, elephantine tread of those huge feet—in thick gray socks. Year after year, day after day, there would be no change, and it would last all her life. Either it would be one long continued revulsion, or else—worse than all—she would come to be content with him, would come to be like him, would sink to the level of steam beer and cheap tobacco, and all her pretty ways, her clean, trim little habits, would be forgotten, since they would be thrown away upon her stupid, brutish husband. "Her husband!" *That*, was her husband in there—she could yet hear his snores—for life, for life. A great despair seized upon her. She buried her face in the pillow and thought of her mother with an infinite longing.

Aroused at length by the chittering of the canary, McTeague had awakened slowly. After a while he had taken down his concertina and played upon it the six very mournful airs that he knew.

Face downward upon the bed, Trina still wept. Throughout that little suite could be heard but two sounds, the lugubrious strains of the concertina and the noise of stifled weeping.

That her husband should be ignorant of her distress seemed to Trina an additional grievance. With perverse inconsistency she began to wish him to come to her, to comfort her.

He ought to know that she was in trouble, that she was lonely and unhappy.

"Oh, Mac," she called in a trembling voice. But the concertina still continued to wail and lament. Then Trina wished she were dead, and on the instant jumped up and ran into the "Dental Parlors," and threw herself into her husband's arms, crying: "Oh, Mac, dear, love me, love me *big!* I'm *so* unhappy."

"What—what—what—" the dentist exclaimed starting up bewildered, a little frightened.

"Nothing, nothing, only *love* me, love me always and always."

But this first crisis, this momentary revolt, as much a matter of high-strung feminine nerves as of anything else, passed, and in the end Trina's affection for her "old bear" grew in spite of herself. She began to love him more and more, not for what he was, but for what she had given up to him. Only once again did Trina undergo a reaction against her husband, and then it was but the matter of an instant, brought on, curiously enough, by the sight of a bit of egg on McTeague's heavy mustache one morning just after breakfast.

Then, too, the pair had learned to make concessions, little by little, and all unconsciously they adapted their modes of life to suit each other. Instead of sinking to McTeague's level as she had feared, Trina found that she could make McTeague rise to hers, and in this saw a solution of many a difficult and gloomy complication.

For one thing, the dentist began to dress a little better, Trina even succeeding in inducing him to wear a high silk hat and a frock coat on a Sunday. Next he relinquished his Sunday afternoon's nap and beer in favor of three or four hours spent in the park with her—the weather permitting. So that gradually Trina's misgivings ceased, or when they did assail her, she could at last meet them with a shrug of the shoulders, saying to herself meanwhile, "Well, it's done now and it can't be helped; one must make the best of it."

During the first months of their married life these nervous relapses of hers had alternated with brusque outbursts of affection when her only fear was that her husband's love did not equal her own. Without an instant's warning, she would clasp him about the neck, rubbing her cheek against his, murmuring:

"Dear old Mac, I love you so, I love you so. Oh, aren't we happy together, Mac, just us two and no one else? You love me as much as I love you, don't you, Mac? Oh, if you shouldn't —if you *shouldn't.*"

But by the middle of the winter Trina's emotions, oscillating at first from one extreme to another, commenced to settle themselves to an equilibrium of calmness and placid quietude. Her household duties began more and more to absorb her attention, for she was an admirable housekeeper, keeping the little suite in marvellous good order and regulating the schedule of expenditure with an economy that often bordered on positive niggardliness. It was a passion with her to save money. In the bottom of her trunk, in the bedroom, she hid a brass match-safe that answered the purpose of a savings bank. Each time she added a quarter or a half dollar to the little store she laughed and sang with a veritable childish delight; whereas, if the butcher or milkman compelled her to pay an overcharge she was unhappy for the rest of the day. She did not save this money for any ulterior purpose, she hoarded instinctively, without knowing why, responding to the dentist's remonstrances with:

"Yes, yes, I know I'm a little miser, I know it."

Trina had always been an economical little body, but it was only since her great winning in the lottery that she had become especially penurious. No doubt, in her fear lest their great good luck should demoralize them and lead to habits of extravagance, she had recoiled too far in the other direction. Never, never, never should a penny of that miraculous fortune be spent; rather should it be added to. It was a nest egg, a monstrous, roc-like nest egg, not so large, however, but that it could be made larger. Already by the end of that winter Trina had begun to make up the deficit of two hundred dollars that she had been forced to expend on the preparations for her marriage.

McTeague, on his part, never asked himself now-a-days whether he loved Trina the wife as much as he had loved Trina the young girl. There had been a time when to kiss Trina, to take her in his arms, had thrilled him from head to heel with a happiness that was beyond words; even the smell of her wonderful odorous hair had sent a sensation of faintness all through him. That time was long past now. Those sudden outbursts of affection on the part of his little woman, outbursts that only increased in vehemence the longer they lived together, puzzled rather than pleased him. He had come to submit to them good-naturedly, answering her passionate inquiries with a "Sure, sure, Trina, sure I love you. What— what's the matter with you?"

1899

From ESSAYS IN AUTHORSHIP

The Responsibilities of the Novelist

It is not here a question of the "unarrived," the "unpublished"; these are the care-free irresponsibilities whose hours are halcyon and whose endeavors have all the lure, all the recklessness of adventure. They are not recognized; they have made no standards for themselves, and if they play the *saltimbanque* and the charlatan nobody cares and nobody (except themselves) is affected.

But the writers in question are the successful ones who have made a public and to whom some ten, twenty or a hundred thousand people are pleased to listen. You may believe if you choose that the novelist, of all workers, is independent—that he can write what he pleases, and that certainly, certainly he should never "write down to his readers"—that he should never consult them at all.

On the contrary, I believe it can be proved that the successful novelist should be more than all others limited in the nature and character of his work, more than all others he should be careful of what he says; more than all others he should defer to his audience; more than all others—more even than the minister and the editor—he should feel "his public" and watch his every word, testing carefully his every utterance, weighing with the most relentless precision his every statement; in a word, possess a sense of his responsibilities.

For the novel is the great expression of modern life. Each form of art has had its turn at reflecting and expressing its contemporaneous thought. Time was when the world looked to the architects of the castles and great cathedrals to truly reflect and embody its ideals. And the architects—serious, earnest men—produced such "expressions of contemporaneous thought" as the Castle of Coucy and the Church of Notre Dame. Then with other times came other customs, and the painters had their day. The men of the Renaissance trusted Angelo and Da Vinci and Velasquez to speak for them, and trusted not in vain. Next came the age of drama. Shakespeare and Marlowe found the value of x for the life and the times in which they lived. Later on contemporary life had been so modified that neither painting, architecture nor drama was the best vehicle of expression, the day of the longer poems arrived, and Pope and Dryden spoke for their fellows.

Thus the sequence. Each age speaks with its own peculiar organ, and has left the Word for us moderns to read and understand. The Castle of Coucy and the Church of Notre Dame are the spoken words of the Middle Ages. The Renaissance speaks—and intelligibly—to us through the sibyls of the Sistine chapel and the Mona Lisa. "Macbeth" and "Tamerlane" résumé the whole spirit of the Elizabethan age, while the "Rape of the Lock" is a wireless message to us straight from the period of the Restoration.

Today is the day of the novel. In no other day and by no other vehicle is contemporaneous life so adequately expressed; and the critics of the twenty-second century, reviewing our times, striving to reconstruct our civilization, will look not to the painters, not to the architects nor dramatists, but to the novelists to find our idiosyncrasy.

I think this is true. I think if the matter could in any way be statisticized, the figures would bear out the assumption. There is no doubt the novel will in time "go out" of popular favor as irrevocably as the long poem has gone, and for the reason that it is no longer the right mode of expression.

It is interesting to speculate upon what will take its place. Certainly the coming civilization will revert to no former means of expressing its thought or its ideals. Possibly music will be the interpreter of the life of the twenty-first and twenty-second centuries. Possibly one may see a hint of this in the characterization of Wagner's operas as the "Music of the Future."

This, however, is parenthetical and beside the mark. Remains the fact that today is the day of the novel. By this one does not mean that the novel is merely popular. If the novel was not something more than a simple diversion, a means of whiling away a dull evening, a long railway journey, it would not, believe me, remain in favor another day.

If the novel, then, is popular, it is popular with a reason, a vital, inherent reason; that is to say, it is essential. Essential—to resume once more the proposition—because it expresses modern life better than architecture, better than painting, better than poetry, better than music. It is as necessary to the civilization of the twentieth century as the violin is necessary to Kubelik, as the piano is necessary to Paderewski, as the plane is necessary to the carpenter, the sledge to the blacksmith, the chisel to the mason. It is an instrument, a tool, a weapon, a vehicle. It is that thing which, in the hand of man, makes him civilized and no longer savage, because it gives him a power of durable, permanent expression. So much for the novel—the instrument.

Because it is so all-powerful today, the people turn to him who wield this instrument with every degree of confidence. They expect—and rightly—that results shall be commensurate with means. The unknown archer who grasps the bow of Ulysses may be expected by the multitude to send his shaft far and true. If he is not true nor strong he has no business with the bow. The people give heed to him only because he bears a great weapon. He himself knows before he shoots whether or no he is worthy.

It is all very well to jeer at the People and at the People's misunderstanding of the arts, but the fact is indisputable that no art that is not in the end understood by the People can live or ever did live a single generation. In the larger view, in the last analysis, the People pronounce the final judgment. The People, despised of the artist, hooted, caricatured and vilified, are, after all, and in the main, the real seekers after Truth. Who is it, after all, whose interest is liveliest in any given work of art? It is not now a question of *esthetic* interest—that is, the artist's, the amateur's, the *cognoscente's*.

It is a question of *vital* interest. Say what you will, Maggie Tulliver—for instance—is far more a living being for Mrs. Jones across the street than she is for your sensitive, fastidious, keenly critical artist, literateur, or critic. The People—Mrs. Jones and her neighbors—take the life history of these fictitious characters, these novels, to heart with a seriousness that the esthetic cult have no conception of. The cult consider them almost solely from their artistic sides. The People take them into their innermost lives. Nor do the People discriminate. Omnivorous readers as they are today, they make little distinction between Maggie Tulliver and the heroine of the last "popular novel." They do not stop to separate true from false; they do not care.

How necessary it becomes, then, for those who, by the simple art of writing, can invade the heart's heart of thousands, whose novels are received with such measureless earnestness —how necessary it becomes for those who wield such power to use it rightfully. Is it not expedient to act fairly? Is it not in Heaven's name essential that the People hear, not a lie, but the Truth?

If the novel were not one of the most important factors of modern life; if it were not the completest expression of our civilization; if its influence were not greater than all the pulpits, than all the newspapers between the oceans, it would not be so important that its message should be true.

But the novelist today is the one who reaches the greatest audience. Right or wrong, the People turn to him the moment he speaks, and what he says they believe.

For the Million, Life is a contracted affair, is bounded by the walls of the narrow channel of affairs in which their feet are set. They have no horizon. They look today as they never have looked before, as they never will look again, to the writer of fiction to give them an idea of life beyond their limits, and they believe him as they never have believed before and never will again.

This being so, is it not difficult to understand how certain of these successful writers of fiction—these favored ones into whose hands the gods have placed the great bow of Ulysses —can look so frivolously upon their craft? It is not necessary to specify. One speaks of those whose public is measured by "one hundred and fifty thousand copies sold." We know them, and because the gods have blessed us with wits beyond our deserving we know their work is false. But what of the "hundred and fifty thousand" who are not discerning and who receive this falseness as Truth, who believe this topsy-turvy picture of Life beyond their horizons is real and vital and sane?

There is no gauge to measure the extent of this malignant influence. Public opinion is made no one can say how, by infinitesimal accretions, by a multitude of minutest elements. Lying novels, surely, surely in this day and age of indiscriminate reading, contribute to this more than all other influences or present-day activity.

The Pulpit, the Press and the Novel—these indisputably are the great molders of public opinion and public morals today. But the Pulpit speaks but once a week; the Press is read with lightning haste and the morning news is waste-paper by noon. But the novel goes into the home to stay. It is read word for word; is talked about, discussed; its influence penetrates every chink and corner of the family.

Yet novelists are not found wanting who write for money. I do not think this is an unfounded accusation. I do not think it is asking too much of credulity. This would not matter if they wrote the Truth. But these gentlemen who are "in literature for their own pocket every time" have discovered that for the moment the People have confounded the Wrong with the Right, and prefer that which is a lie to that which is true. "Very well, then," say these gentlemen. "If they want a lie they shall have it"; and they give the People a lie in return for royalties.

The surprising thing about this is that you and I and all the rest of us do not consider this as disreputable—do not yet realize that the novelist has responsibilities. We condemn an editor who sells his editorial columns, and we revile the pulpit attainted of venality. But the venal novelist—he whose influence is greater than either the Press or Pulpit—*him* we greet with a wink and the tongue in the cheek.

This should not be so. Somewhere the protest should be raised, and those of us who see the practice of this fraud should bring home to ourselves the realization that the selling of one hundred and fifty thousand books is a serious business. The People have a right to the Truth as they have a right to life, liberty and the pursuit of happiness. It is *not* right that they be exploited and deceived with false views of life, false characters, false sentiment, false morality, false history, false philosophy, false emotions, false heroism, false notions of self-sacrifice, false views of religion, of duty, of conduct and of manners.

The man who can address an audience of one hundred and fifty thousand people who—unenlightened—*believe what he says*, has a heavy duty to perform, and tremendous responsibilities to shoulder; and he should address himself to his task not with the flippancy of a catchpenny juggler at the county fair, but with earnestness, with soberness, with a sense of his limitations, and with all the abiding sincerity that by the favor and mercy of the gods may be his.

1899

1871 -- *Theodore Dreiser* -- 1945

DREISER was born in Terre Haute, Indiana, of German immigrant parents, the twelfth child in a family of thirteen. His father was given to an intense religiosity almost fanatical in its manifestations, against which the boy rebelled at an early age, and which by its negative influence colored his mature philosophy of life. His mother, on the other hand, was a somewhat dreamy and poetic soul, whose justness and sympathy endeared her to the son. Although the family had to contend with poverty, and unremitting toil and economy were necessary to keep the family larder supplied, young Dreiser made his way through the public schools of his native state, and into the local university, which he left, however, before taking a degree.

Dreiser's ambition led him in 1892 to Chicago, where he secured a position on the staff of the *Chicago Globe*. In search of advancement, he went to St. Louis, and for the next two years he was employed by the *Globe-Democrat* and the *Republican*. Dissatisfied with his prospects and encouraged by friends to seek the larger opportunities in the East, he went to New York, where for a number of years he edited several second-rate magazines and did special editorial work for *Harper's*, *McClure's*, *Century*, *Cosmopolitan*, and *Munsey's*. As editor in chief of all the Butterick publications, a position to which he was appointed in 1907, he achieved signal success both in increasing the subscription lists and in stimulating the intellectual interest of the readers. He retired from editorial work in 1910.

As early as 1900 he had brought out *Sister Carrie*, his first novel, enthusiastically received by Frank Norris, but viewed askance by the critics on account of its extreme frankness, and consequently withdrawn from circulation. The American attitude changed somewhat in the course of the decade, and *Jennie Gerhardt* (1911) was received with less antagonism. *The Financier* (1912) and *The Titan* (1914) deal with big business, while *The "Genius"* (1915) is concerned with the life of an artist, and is largely autobiographical. In 1925 he published *An American Tragedy* in which, against a meticulously drawn background, he portrays what he conceives to be the essentially tragic struggle of the inept and helpless. He also published several volumes of autobiography—*A Traveller at Forty* (1913), *A Hoosier Holiday* (1916), and *A Book About Myself* (1922)—as well as *Plays of the Natural and Supernatural* (1916), *Free and Other Stories* (1918), and *Chains* (1927), collections of "lesser novels and stories." His political views find expression in such books as *Dreiser Looks at Russia* (1928) and *Tragic America* (1932). His solution for the current social ills lies in a socialistic control of the economic system for the benefit of the people.

To understand Dreiser one must have some knowledge of his naturalistic philosophy, inspired, to be sure, by science. In this philosophy, described in *Hey Rub-a-Dub-Dub* (1920), change is the only changeless factor. Life has no significance beyond the limits of experience. Human destiny is determined by environment, a succession of physico-chemical reactions, beyond the control of the individual, and therefore no responsibility of his. Man is swept along by blind forces, apparently causeless, from which he can get no help unless by "accident or per adventure." To him life has neither meaning nor moral purpose; it is merely a "struggle for existence" in various forms, and divides humanity not into the good and the bad, but into the strong and the weak.

In the light of this outlook and philosophy, life becomes for the artist "a thing to be observed, studied, interpreted," "our one great realm of discovery," and art becomes a recording of the facts of life as discovered. Throughout his career Dreiser has manifested the reporter's intense curiosity and passion for fact, unflagging attention to detail—traits which explain at least partially the ponderous quality of the novels. Nothing is allowed to stand between the observing and recording artist and the procession of the changing facts of life; the artist must be free and unhampered in his endeavor "to observe, synchronize, and orientate human knowledge in the most comprehensive form." The novelist is therefore a glorified reporter. Dreiser holds out little hope for great art in America because of the prevailing puritanical attitude and tradesmen's atmosphere. Under these conditions there can be no original thinking, and consequently no leadership (cf. "Life, Art and America," in *Hey Rub-a-Dub-Dub*).

One of the most conspicuous facts of Dreiser's naturalism was that, partly because of ignorance and partly because of temperament, he was not entirely committed to it. His novels do more than report; they interpret, in extremely awkward parentheses, and offer a clumsy, romantic, and sentimental view of events. He is at his best when he reports, though even here he does not wish to, or does not know when to, stop. The most effective single demonstrations of this thoroughness are the description of Cowperwood's trial and imprisonment (*The Financier*) and the story of Hurstwood's decline and fall (*Sister Carrie*).

In the course of the controversies which have raged about Dreiser, he has been subject to savage attacks. His assumption that human conduct revolves rather closely around the focal center of sex and his utter frankness in portraying this conduct aroused violent reactions and opinions. Stuart Pratt Sherman attacked his "representations of animal behavior"; H. L. Mencken and Randolph Bourne rose vehemently to his defense. The controversies have died down, and Dreiser has achieved a definite place in contemporary letters, the acknowledged leader of the "naturalists" in fiction.

Because of the timeliness of his works, the war which raged about them, and the sheer impact of their weighty and bulky analyses of American life, Dreiser achieved a fame which a careful examination of his fiction can scarcely justify. He is one of those novelists in the realist-naturalist tradition who escaped aesthetic censure because of their social importance. The growth of intelligent and careful criticism in twentieth-century America has revised downward the estimate of Dreiser which H. L. Mencken offered to the public in the second and third decades.

Dreiser's novels are *Sister Carrie* (1900); *Jennie Gerhardt* (1911); *The Financier* (1912); *The Titan* (1914); *The "Genius"* (1915); *An American Tragedy* (1925); *The Bulwark* (1946); *The Stoic* (1947). The short stories are collected in *Free* (1918); *Twelve Men* (1919); *Chains* (1927); *A Gallery of Women* (2 vols., 1929); *Selected Short Stories of Theodore Dreiser* (1947). The following are books of travel, description, and social criticism: *A Traveller at Forty* (1913); *A Hoosier Holiday* (1916); *The Color of a Great City* (1923); *Dreiser Looks at Russia* (1928); *Tragic America* (1932). *Moods, Cadenced and Declaimed* (1926) and *Moods, Philosophic and Emotional, Cadenced and Declaimed* (1935) contain his poetry. *Hey Rub-a-Dub-Dub* (1920) is a volume of essays. In the field of the drama he has published *Plays of the Natural and the Supernatural* (1916); *The Hand of the Potter* (1918). *A Book About Myself* (1922 reissued as *Newspaper Days*, 1931) and *Dawn* (1931) are autobiographical. For biographical information see D. Dudley, *Forgotten Frontiers* (1932) re-issued in 1946, with the title, *Dreiser and the Land of the Free*; F. Harris, *Contemporary Portraits* (2nd series, 1919); E. Boyd, *Portraits: Real and Imaginary* (1924); D. Karsner, *Sixteen Authors to One* (1928); E. D. McDonald, "Dreiser Before 'Sister Carrie,'" *Bookman*, June, 1928; *The Intimate Notebooks of George Jean Nathan* (1932); I. Schneider, "Theodore Dreiser," *Saturday Review of Literature*, Mar. 10, 1934. The following provide helpful criticism: T. K. Whipple, *Spokesmen* (1928); C. Van Doren, *Contemporary American Novelists* (1922); S. P. Sherman, *On Contemporary Literature* (1917); S. P. Sherman, *The Main Stream* (1927); V. L. Parrington, *Main Currents in American Thought*, III (1930); B. Rascoe, *Prometheans* (1933); H. L. Mencken, *A Book of Prefaces* (1917); H. Hartwick, *The Foreground of American Fiction* (1934); H. Hatcher, *Creating the Modern American Novel* (1935); P. H. Boynton, *Some Contemporary Americans* (1924); J. B. Cabell, *Some of Us* (1930); E. H. Smith, "Dreiser—After Twenty Years," *American Mercury*, Jan., 1926; R. Michaud, *The American Novel of To-day* (1928); G. B. Munson, *Destinations* (1928); C. R. Walker, "How Big Is Dreiser," *Bookman*, April, 1926; L. Jones, "An American Tragedy," in L. W. Smith, ed., *Current Reviews* (1926); R. Shafer, "An

American Tragedy," in N. Foerster, ed., *Humanism and America* (1930); M. Waldman, "German-American Insurgent," *Living Age*, Oct. 1, 1926; J. C. Squire, *Contemporary American Authors* (1928); Alfred Kazin, *On Native Grounds* (1942); George Snell, *The Shapers of American Fiction* (1947); Malcolm Cowley (ed.), *After the Genteel Tradition* (1937); Charles C. Walcutt, "The Three Stages of Theodore Dreiser's Naturalism," *Publications of the Modern Language Association*, March, 1940; Eliseo Vivas, "Dreiser, an Inconsistent Mechanist," *Ethics*, July, 1938; Robert H. Elias, *Theodore Dreiser: Apostle of Nature* (1949).

THE HAND

"The Hand" is an example of Dreiser's attempt to work in the form of the short story; it differs from much of his other fiction in being a consciously contrived study of a man's sense of guilt and fear.

I

DAVIDSON could distinctly remember that it was between two and three years after the grisly event in the Monte Orte range—the sickening and yet deserved end of Mersereau, his quondam partner and fellow adventurer— that anything to be identified with Mersereau's malice toward him, and with Mersereau's probable present existence in the spirit world, had appeared in his life.

He and Mersereau had worked long together as prospectors, investors, developers of property. It was only after they had struck it rich in the Klondike that Davidson had grown so much more apt and shrewd in all commercial and financial matters, whereas Mersereau had seemed to stand still—not to rise to the splendid opportunities which then opened to him. Why, in some of those later deals it had not been possible for Davidson even to introduce his old partner to some of the moneyed men he had to deal with. Yet Mersereau had insisted, as his right, if you please, on being "in on" everything—everything!

Take that wonderful Monte Orte property, the cause of all the subsequent horror. He, Davidson—not Mersereau—had discovered or heard of the mine, and had carried it along, with old Besmer as a tool or decoy—Besmer being the ostensible factor—until it was all ready for him to take over and sell or develop. Then it was that Mersereau, having been for so long his partner, demanded a full half—a third at least—on the ground that they had once agreed to work together in all these things.

Think of it! And Mersereau growing duller and less useful and more disagreeable day by day, and year by year! Indeed, toward the last he had threatened to expose the trick by which jointly, seven years before, they had possessed themselves of the Skyute Pass Mine; to drive Davidson out of public and financial life, to have him arrested and tried—along with himself, of course. Think of that!

But he had fixed him—yes, he had, damn him! He had trailed Mersereau that night to old Besmer's cabin on the Monte Orte, when Besmer was away. Mersereau had gone there with the intention of stealing the diagram of the new field, and had secured it, true enough. A thief he was, damn him. Yet, just as he was making safely away, as he thought, he, Davidson, had struck him cleanly over the ear with that heavy rail-bolt fastened to the end of a walnut stick, and the first blow had done for him.

Lord, how the bone above Mersereau's ear had sounded when it cracked! And how bloody one side of that bolt was! Mersereau hadn't had time to do anything before he was helpless. He hadn't died instantly, though, but had turned over and faced him, Davidson, with that savage, scowling face of his and those blazing, animal eyes.

Lying half propped up on his left elbow, Mersereau had reached out toward him with that big, rough, bony right hand of his—the right with which he always boasted of having done so much damage on this, that, and the other occasion—had glared at him as much as to say:

"Oh, if I could only reach you just for a moment before I go!"

Then it was that he, Davidson, had lifted the club again. Horrified as he was, and yet determined that he must save his own life, he had finished the task, dragging the body back to an old fissure behind the cabin and covering it with branches, a great pile of pine fronds, and as many as one hundred and fifty boulders, great and small, and had left his victim. It was a sickening job and a sickening sight, but it had to be.

Then, having finished, he had slipped dismally away, like a jackal, thinking of that hand in the moonlight, held up so savagely, and that look. Nothing might have come of that either, if he hadn't been inclined to brood on it so much, on the fierceness of it.

No, nothing had happened. A year had passed, and if anything had been going to turn up it surely would have by then. He, Davidson, had gone first to New York, later to Chicago, to dispose of the Monte Orte claim. Then, after two years, he had returned here to Mississippi, where he was enjoying comparative peace. He was looking after some sugar property which had once belonged to him, and which he was now able to reclaim and put in charge of his sister as a home against a rainy day. He had no other.

But that body back there! That hand uplifted in the moonlight—to clutch him if it could! Those eyes.

II—JUNE, 1905

Take that first year, for instance, when he had returned to Gatchard in Mississippi, whence both he and Mersereau had originally issued. After looking after his own property he had gone out to a tumble-down estate of his uncle's in Issaqueena County—a leaky old slope-roofed house where, in a bedroom on the top floor, he had had his first experience with the significance or reality of the hand.

Yes, that was where first he had really seen it pictured in that curious, unbelievable way; only who would believe that it was Mersereau's hand? They would say it was an accident, chance, rain dropping down. But the hand had appeared on the ceiling of that room just as sure as anything, after a heavy rainstorm—it was almost a cyclone—when every chink in the old roof had seemed to leak water.

During the night, after he had climbed to the room by way of those dismal stairs with their great landing and small glass oil-lamp he carried, and had sunk to rest, or tried to, in the heavy, wide, damp bed, thinking, as he always did those days, of the Monte Orte and Mersereau, the storm had come up. As he had listened to the wind moaning outside he had heard first the scratch, scratch, scratch, of some limb, no doubt, against the wall—sounding, or so it seemed in his feverish unrest, like some one penning an indictment against him with a worn, rusty pen.

And then, the storm growing worse, and in a fit of irritation and self-contempt at his own nervousness, he had gone to the window, but just as lightning struck a branch of the tree nearest the window and so very near him, too —as though some one, something, was seeking to strike him—(Mersereau?) and as though he had been lured by that scratching. God! He had retreated, feeling that it was meant for him.

But that big, knotted hand painted on the ceiling by the dripping water during the night! There it was, right over him when he awoke, outlined or painted as if with wet, gray whitewash against the wretched but normally pale-blue of the ceiling when dry. There it was—a big, open hand just like Mersereau's as he had held it up that night—huge, knotted, rough, the fingers extended as if tense and clutching. And, if you will believe it, near it was something that looked like a pen—an old, long-handled pen—to match that scratch, scratch, scratch!

"Huldah," he had inquired of the old black mammy who entered in the morning to bring him fresh water and throw open the shutters, "what does that look like to you up there—that patch on the ceiling where the rain came through?"

He wanted to reassure himself as to the character of the thing he saw—that it might not be a creation of his own feverish imagination, accentuated by the dismal character of this place.

"'Pears t' me mo' like a big han' 'an anythin' else, Marse Davi'son," commented Huldah, pausing and staring upward. "Mo' like a big fist, kinda. Dat air's a new drip come las' night, I reckon. Dis here old place ain' gonna hang togethah much longah, less'n some repairin' be done mighty quick now. Yassir, dat air's a new drop, sho's yo' bo'n, en it come on'y las' night. I hain't never seed dat befo'."

And then he had inquired, thinking of the fierceness of the storm:

"Huldah, do you have many such storms up this way?"

"Good gracious, Marse Davi'son, we hain't seed no sech blow en—en come three years now. I hain't seed no sech lightnin' en I doan' know when."

Wasn't that strange, that it should all come on the night, of all nights, when he was there? And no such other storm in three years!

Huldah stared idly, always ready to go slow and rest, if possible, whereas he had turned irritably. To be annoyed by ideas such as this! To always be thinking of that Monte Orte affair! Why couldn't he forget it? Wasn't it Mersereau's own fault? He never would have killed the man if he hadn't been forced to it.

And to be haunted in this way, making mountains out of mole-hills, as he thought then! It must be his own miserable fancy—and yet Mersereau had looked so threateningly at him. That glance had boded something; it was too terrible not to.

Davidson might not want to think of it, but how could he stop? Mersereau might not be able to hurt him any more, at least not on this earth; but still, couldn't he? Didn't the appearance of this hand seem to indicate that he might? He was dead, of course. His body, his skeleton, was under that pile of rocks and stones, some of them as big as washtubs. Why worry over that, and after two years? And still—

That hand on the ceiling!

III—DECEMBER, 1905

Then, again, take the matter of meeting Pringle in Gatchard just at that time, within the same week. It was due to Davidson's sister. She had invited Mr. and Mrs. Pringle in to meet him one evening, without telling him that they were spiritualists and might discuss spiritualism.

Clairvoyance, Pringle called it, or seeing what can't be seen with material eyes, and clairaudience, or hearing what can't be heard with material ears, as well as materialization, or ghosts, and table-rapping, and the like. Table-rapping—that damned tap-tapping that he had been hearing ever since!

It was Pringle's fault, really. Pringle had persisted in talking. He, Davidson, wouldn't have listened, except that he somehow became fascinated by what Pringle said concerning what he had heard and seen in his time. Mersereau must have been at the bottom of that, too.

At any rate, after he had listened, he was sorry, for Pringle had had time to fill his mind full of those awful facts or ideas which had since harassed him so much—all that stuff about drunkards, degenerates, and weak people generally being followed about by vile, evil spirits and used to effect those spirits' purposes or desires in this world. Horrible!

Wasn't it terrible? Pringle—big, mushy, creature that he was, sickly and stagnant like a springless pool—insisted that he had even seen clouds of these spirits about drunkards, degenerates, and the like, in street-cars, on trains, and about vile corners at night. Once, he said, he had seen just one evil spirit—think of that!—following a certain man all the time, at his left elbow—a dark, evil, red-eyed thing, until finally the man had been killed in a quarrel.

Pringle described their shapes, these spirits, as varied. They were small, dark, irregular clouds, with red or green spots somewhere for eyes, changing in form and becoming longish or round like a jellyfish, or even like a misshapen cat or dog. They could take any form at will—even that of a man.

Once, Pringle declared, he had seen as many as fifty about a drunkard who was staggering down a street, all of them trying to urge him into the nearest saloon, so that they might re-experience in some vague way the sensation of drunkenness, which at some time or other they themselves, having been drunkards in life, had enjoyed!

It would be the same with a drug fiend, or indeed with any one of weak or evil habits. They gathered about such an one like flies, their red or green eyes glowing—attempting to get something from them perhaps, if nothing more than a little sense of their old earth-life.

The whole thing was so terrible and disturbing at the time, particularly that idea of men being persuaded or influenced to murder, that he, Davidson, could stand it no longer, and got up and left. But in his room upstairs he meditated on it, standing before his mirror. Suddenly—would he ever forget it—as he was taking off his collar and tie, he had heard that queer tap, tap, tap, right on his dressing table or under it, and for the first time, which Pringle said, ghosts made when table-rapping in answer to a call, or to give warning of their presence.

Then something said to him, almost as clearly as if he heard it:

"This is me, Mersereau, come back at last to get you! Pringle was just an excuse of mine to let you know I was coming, and so was that hand in that old house, in Issaqueena County. It was mine! I will be with you from now on. Don't think I will ever leave you!"

It had frightened and made him half sick, so wrought up was he. For the first time he felt cold chills run up and down his spine—the creeps. He felt as if some one were standing over him—Mersereau, of course—only he could not see or hear a thing, just that faint tap at first, growing louder a little later, and quite angry when he tried to ignore it.

People did live, then, after they were dead, especially evil people—people stronger than you, perhaps. They had the power to come back, to haunt, to annoy you if they didn't like anything you had done to them. No doubt Mersereau was following him in the hope of revenge, there in the spirit world, just outside this one, close at his heels, like that evil spirit attending the other man whom Pringle had described.

IV—FEBRUARY, 1906

Take that case of the hand impressed on the soft dough and plaster of Paris, described in an article that he had picked up in the dentist's office out there in Pasadena—Mersereau's very hand, so far as he could judge. How about that for a coincidence, picking up the magazine with that disturbing article about psychic materialization in Italy, and later in Berne, Switzerland, where the scientists were gathered to investigate that sort of thing? And just when he was trying to rid himself finally of the notion that any such thing could be!

According to that magazine article, some old crone over in Italy—spiritualist, or witch or something—had got together a crowd of experimentalists or professors in an abandoned house on an almost deserted island off the coast of Sardinia. There they had conducted experiments with spirits, which they called materialization, getting the impression of the fingers of a hand, or of a whole hand and arm, or of a face, on a plate of glass covered with soot, the plate being locked in a small safe on the center of a table about which they sat!

He, Davidson, couldn't understand, of course, how it was done, but done it was. There in that magazine were half a dozen pictures, reproductions of photographs of a hand, an arm and a face—or a part of one, anyhow. And if they looked like anything, they looked exactly like Mersereau's! Hadn't Pringle, there in Gatchard, Miss., stated spirits could move anywhere, over long distances, with the speed of light. And would it be any trick for Mersereau to appear there at Sardinia, and then engineer this magazine into his presence, here in Los Angeles? Would it? It would not. Spirits were free and powerful *over there*, perhaps.

There was not the least doubt that these hands, these partial impressions of a face, were those of Mersereau. Those big knuckles! That long, heavy, humped nose and big jaw! Whose else could they be?—they were Mersereau's, intended, when they were made over there in Italy, for him, Davidson, to see later here in Los Angeles. Yes, they were! And looking at that sinister face reproduced in the magazine, it seemed to say, with Mersereau's old coarse sneer:

"You see? You can't escape me! I'm showing you how much alive I am over here, just as I was on earth. And I'll get you yet, even if I have to go farther than Italy to do it!"

It was amazing, the shock he took from that. It wasn't just that alone, but the persistence and repetition of this hand business. What could it mean? Was it really Mersereau's hand? As for the face, it wasn't all there—just the jaw, mouth, cheek, left temple, and a part of the nose and eye; but it was Mersereau's, all right. He had gone clear over there into Italy somewhere, in a lone house on an island, to get this message of his undying hate back to him. Or was it just spirits, evil spirits, bent on annoying him because he was nervous and sensitive now?

V—OCTOBER, 1906

Even new crowded hotels and new buildings weren't the protection he had at first hoped and thought they would be. Even there you weren't safe—not from a man like Mersereau. Take that incident there in Los Angeles, and again in Seattle, only two months ago now, when Mersereau was able to make that dreadful explosive or crashing sound, as if one had burst a huge paper bag full of air, or upset a china closet full of glass and broken everything, when as a matter of fact nothing at all had happened. It had frightened him horribly the first two or three times, believing as he did that something fearful had happened. Finding that it was nothing—or Mersereau—he was becoming used to it now; but other people, unfortunately, were not.

He would be—as he had been that first time —sitting in his room perfectly still and trying to amuse himself, or not to think, when suddenly there would be that awful crash. It was astounding! Other people heard it, of course. They had in Los Angeles. A maid and a porter had come running the first time to inquire, and he had had to protest that he had heard nothing. They couldn't believe it at first, and had gone to other rooms to look. When it happened the second time, the management had protested, thinking it was a joke he was playing; and to avoid the risk of exposure he had left.

After that he could not keep a valet or nurse about him for long. Servants wouldn't stay, and managers of hotels wouldn't let him remain when such things went on. Yet he couldn't live in a house or apartment alone, for there the noises and atmospheric conditions would be worse than ever.

VI—JUNE, 1907

Take that last old house he had been in—but never would be in again!—at Anne Haven. There he actually visualized the hand—a thing as big as a washtub at first, something like smoke or shadow in a black room moving about over the bed and everywhere. Then, as he lay there, gazing at it spellbound, it condensed slowly, and he began to feel it. It was now a hand of normal size—there was no doubt of it in the world—going over him softly, without force, as a ghostly hand must, having no real physical strength, but all the time with a strange, electric, secretive something about it, as if it were not quite sure of itself, and not quite sure that he was really there.

The hand, or so it seemed—God!—moved right up to his neck and began to feel over that as he lay there. Then it was that he guessed just what it was that Mersereau was after.

It was just like a hand, the fingers and thumb made into a circle and pressed down over his throat, only it moved over him gently at first, because it really couldn't do anything yet, not having the material strength. But the intention! The sense of cruel, savage determination that went with it!

And yet, if one went to a nerve specialist or doctor about all this, as he did afterward, what did the doctor say? He had tried to describe how he was breaking down under the strain, how he could not eat or sleep on account of all these constant tappings and noises; but the moment he even began to hint at his experiences, especially the hand or the noises, the doctor exclaimed:

"Why, this is plain delusion! You're nervously run down, that's all that ails you—on the verge of pernicious anemia, I should say. You'll have to watch yourself as to this illusion about spirits. Get it out of your mind. There's nothing to it!"

Wasn't that just like one of these nerve specialists, bound up in their little ideas of what they knew or saw, or thought they saw?

VII—NOVEMBER, 1907

And now take this very latest development at Battle Creek recently where he had gone trying to recuperate on the diet there. Hadn't Mersereau, implacable demon that he was, developed this latest trick of making his food taste queer to him—unpalatable, or with an odd odor?

He, Davidson, knew it was Mersereau, for he felt him beside him at the table whenever he sat down. Besides, he seemed to hear something—clairaudience was what they called it, he understood—he was beginning to develop that, too, now! It was Mersereau, of course, saying in a voice which was more like a memory of a voice than anything real—the voice of some one you could remember as having spoken in a certain way, say, ten years or more ago:

"*I've fixed it so you can't eat any more, you—*"

There followed a long list of vile expletives, enough in itself to sicken one.

Thereafter, in spite of anything he could do to make himself think to the contrary, knowing that the food was all right, really, Davidson found it to have an odor or a taste which dis-10 gusted him, and which he could not overcome, try as he would. The management assured him that it was all right, as he knew it was—for others. He saw them eating it. But he couldn't —had to get up and leave, and the little he could get down he couldn't retain, or it wasn't enough for him to live on. God, he would die, this way! Starve, as he surely was doing by degrees now.

And Mersereau always seeming to be stand-20 ing by. Why, if it weren't for fresh fruit on the stands at times, and just plain, fresh-baked bread in bakers' windows, which he could buy and eat quickly, he might not be able to live at all. It was getting to that pass!

VIII—AUGUST, 1908

That wasn't the worst, either, bad as all that was. The worst was the fact that under the strain of all this he was slowly but surely 30 breaking down, and that in the end Mersereau might really succeed in driving him out of life here—to do what, if anything, to him there? What? It was such an evil pack by which he was surrounded, now, those who lived just on the other side and hung about the earth, vile, debauched creatures, as Pringle had described them, and as Davidson had come to know for himself, fearing them and their ways so much, and really seeing them at times.

Since he had come to be so weak and sensitive, he could see them for himself—vile things that they were, swimming before his gaze in the dark whenever he chanced to let himself be in the dark, which was not often—friends of Mersereau, no doubt, and inclined to help him just for the evil of it.

For this long time now Davidson had taken to sleeping with the light on, wherever he was, only tying a handkerchief over his eyes to 50 keep out some of the glare. Even then he could

see them—queer, misshapen things, for all the world like wavy, stringy jellyfish or coils of thick, yellowish-black smoke, moving about, changing in form at times, yet always looking dirty or vile, somehow, and with those queer, dim, reddish or greenish glows for eyes. It was sickening!

IX—OCTOBER, 1908

Having accomplished so much, Mersereau would by no means be content to let him go. Davidson knew that! He could talk to him occasionally now, or at least could hear him and answer back, if he chose, when he was alone and quite certain that no one was listening.

Mersereau was always saying, when Davidson would listen to him at all—which he wouldn't often—that he would get him yet, that he would make him pay, or charging him with fraud and murder.

"*I'll choke you yet!*" The words seemed to float in from somewhere, as if he were remembering that at some time Mersereau had said just that in his angry, savage tone—not as if he heard it; and yet he was hearing it of course.

"*I'll choke you yet! You can't escape! You may think you'll die a natural death, but you won't, and that's why I'm poisoning your food to weaken you. You can't escape! I'll get you, sick or well, when you can't help yourself, when you're sleeping. I'll choke you, just as you hit me with that club. That's why you're always seeing and feeling this hand of mine! I'm not alone. I've nearly had you many a time already, only you have managed to wriggle out so far, jumping up, but some day you won't be able to—see? Then—*"

The voice seemed to die away at times, even in the middle of a sentence, but at the other times—often, often—he could hear it completing the full thought. Sometimes he would 40 turn on the thing and exclaim:

"Oh, go to the devil!" or, "Let me alone!" or, "Shut up!" Even in a closed room and all alone, such remarks seemed strange to him, addressed to a ghost; but he couldn't resist at times, annoyed as he was. Only he took good care not to talk if any one was about.

It was getting so that there was no real place for him outside of an asylum, for often he would get up screaming at night—he had to, 50 so sharp was the clutch on his throat—and then always, wherever he was, a servant would come in and want to know what was the matter. He would have to say that it was a nightmare—only the management always requested him to leave after the second or third time, say, or after an explosion or two. It was horrible!

He might as well apply to a private asylum or sanatorium now, having all the money he had, and explain that he had delusions—delusions. Imagine!—and ask to be taken care of. In a place like that they wouldn't be disturbed by his jumping up and screaming at night, feeling that he was being choked, as he was, or by his leaving the table because he couldn't eat the food, or by his talking back to Mersereau, should they chance to hear him, or by the noises when they occurred.

They could assign him a special nurse and a special room, if he wished—only he didn't wish to be too much alone. They could put him in charge of some one who would understand all these things, or to whom he could explain. He couldn't expect ordinary people, or hotels catering to ordinary people, to put up with him any more. Mersereau and his friends made too much trouble.

He must go and hunt up a good place somewhere where they understood such things, or at least tolerated them, and explain, and then it would all pass for the hallucinations of a crazy man,—though, as a matter of fact, he wasn't crazy at all. It was all too real, only the average or so-called normal person couldn't see or hear as he could—hadn't experienced what he had.

X—DECEMBER, 1908

"The trouble is, doctor, that Mr. Davidson is suffering from the delusion that he is pursued by evil spirits. He was not committed here by any court, but came of his own accord about four months ago, and we let him wander about here at will. But he seems to be growing worse, as time goes on.

"One of his worst delusions, doctor, is that there is one spirit in particular who is trying to choke him to death. Dr. Major, our superintendent, says he has incipient tuberculosis of the throat, with occasional spasmodic contractions. There are small lumps or calluses here

and there as though caused by outside pressure and yet our nurse assures us that there is no such outside irritation. He won't believe that; but whenever he tries to sleep, especially in the middle of the night, he will jump up and come running out into the hall, insisting that one of these spirits, which he insists are after him, is trying to choke him to death. He really seems to believe it, for he comes out coughing and choking and feeling at his neck as if some one has been trying to strangle him. He always explains the whole matter to me as being the work of evil spirits, and asks me to not pay any attention to him unless he calls for help or rings his call-bell; and so I never think anything more of it now unless he does.

"Another of his ideas is that these same spirits do something to his food—put poison in it, or give it a bad odor or taste, so that he can't eat it. When he does find anything he can eat, he grabs it and almost swallows it whole, before, as he says, the spirits have time to do anything to it. Once, he says he weighed more than two hundred pounds, but now he only weighs one hundred and twenty. His case is exceedingly strange and pathetic, doctor!

"Dr. Major insists that it is purely a delusion, that so far as being choked is concerned, it is the incipient tuberculosis, and that his stomach trouble comes from the same thing; but by association of ideas, or delusion, he thinks some one is trying to choke him and poison his food, when it isn't so at all. Dr. Major says that he can't imagine what could have started it. He is always trying to talk to Mr. Davidson about it, but whenever he begins to ask him questions, Mr. Davidson refuses to talk, and gets up and leaves.

"One of the peculiar things about his idea of being choked, doctor, is that when he is merely dozing he always wakes up in time, and has the power to throw it off. He claims that the strength of these spirits is not equal to his own when he is awake, or even dozing, but when he's asleep their strength is greater and that then they may injure him. Sometimes, when he has had a fright like this, he will come out in the hall and down to my desk there at the lower end, and ask if he mayn't sit there by me. He says it calms him. I always tell him yes, but it won't be five minutes before he'll get up and leave again, saying that he's being annoyed, or that he won't be able to contain himself if he stays any longer, because of the remarks being made over his shoulder or in his ear.

"Often he'll say: 'Did you hear that, Miss Liggett? It's astonishing, the low, vile things that man can say at times!' When I say, 'No, I didn't hear,' he always says, 'I'm so glad!'"

"No one has ever tried to relieve him of this by hypnotism, I suppose?"

"Not that I know of, doctor. Dr. Major may have tried it. I have only been here three months."

"Tuberculosis is certainly the cause of the throat trouble, as Dr. Major says, and as for the stomach trouble, that comes from the same thing—natural enough under the circumstances. We may have to resort to hypnotism a little later. I'll see. In the meantime you'd better caution all who come in touch with him never to sympathize, or even to seem to believe in anything he imagines is being done to him. It will merely encourage him in his notions. And get him to take his medicine regularly; it won't cure, but it will help. Dr. Major has asked me to give especial attention to his case, and I want the conditions as near right as possible."

"Yes, sir."

XI—JANUARY, 1909

The trouble with these doctors was that they really knew nothing of anything save what was on the surface, the little they had learned at a medical college or in practice—chiefly how certain drugs, tried by their predecessors in certain cases, were known to act. They had no imagination whatever, even when you tried to tell them.

Take that latest young person who was coming here now in his good clothes and with his car, fairly bursting with his knowledge of what he called psychiatrics, looking into Davidson's eyes so hard and smoothing his temples and throat—massage, he called it—saying that he had incipient tuberculosis of the throat and stomach trouble, and utterly disregarding the things which he, Davidson, could personally see and hear! Imagine the fellow trying to persuade him, at this late date, that all that was wrong with him was tuberculosis, that he didn't see Mersereau standing right beside him at times, bending over him, holding up that hand and telling him how he intended to kill him yet—that it was all an illusion!

Imagine saying that Mersereau couldn't actually seize him by the throat when he was asleep, or nearly so, when Davidson himself, looking at his throat in the mirror, could see the actual finger prints,—Mersereau's,—for a moment or so afterward. At any rate, his throat was red and sore from being clutched, as Mersereau of late was able to clutch him! And that was the cause of these lumps. And to say, as they had said at first, that he himself was making them by rubbing and feeling his throat, and that it was tuberculosis!

Wasn't it enough to make one want to quit the place? If it weren't for Miss Liggett and Miss Koehler, his private nurse, and their devoted care, he would. That Miss Koehler was worth her weight in gold, learning his ways as she had, being so uniformly kind, and bearing with his difficulties so genially. He would leave her something in his will.

To leave this place and go elsewhere, though, unless he could take her along, would be folly. And anyway, where else would he go? Here at least were other people, patients like himself, who could understand and could sympathize with him,—people who weren't convinced as were these doctors that all that he complained of was mere delusion. Imagine! Old Rankin, the lawyer, for instance, who had suffered untold persecution from one living person and another, mostly politicians, was convinced that his, Davidson's, troubles were genuine, and liked to hear about them, just as did Miss Koehler. These two did not insist, as the doctors did, that he had slow tuberculosis of the throat, and could live a long time and overcome his troubles if he would. They were merely companionable at such times as Mersereau would give him enough peace to be sociable.

The only real trouble, though, was that he was growing so weak from lack of sleep and food—his inability to eat the food which his enemy bewitched and to sleep at night on account of the choking—that he couldn't last much longer. This new physician whom Dr. Major had called into consultation in regard to his case was insisting that along with his throat trouble he was suffering from acute anemia, due to long undernourishment, and that only a solution of strychnin injected into the veins would help him. But as to Mersereau poisoning his food—not a word would he hear. Besides, now that he was practically bed-ridden, not able to jump up as freely as before, he was subject to a veritable storm of bedevil-ment at the hands of Mersereau. Not only could he see—especially toward evening, and in the very early hours of the morning—Mer-sereau hovering about him like a black shad-ow, a great, bulky shadow—yet like him in outline, but he could feel his enemy's hand moving over him. Worse, behind or about him he often saw a veritable cloud of evil creatures, companions or tools of Mersereau's, who were there to help him and who kept swimming about like fish in dark waters, and seemed to eye the procedure with satisfaction.

When food was brought to him, early or late, and in whatever form, Mersereau and they were there, close at hand, as thick as flies, pass-ing over and through it in an evident attempt to spoil it before he could eat it. Just to see them doing it was enough to poison it for him. Besides, he could hear their voices urging Mer-sereau to do it.

"*That's right—poison it!*"

"*He can't last much longer!*"

"*Soon he'll be weak enough so that when you grip him he will really die!*"

It was thus that they actually talked—he could hear them.

He also heard vile phrases addressed to him by Mersereau, the iterated and reiterated words "murderer" and "swindler" and "cheat," there in the middle of the night. Often, although the light was still on, he saw as many as seven dark figures, very much like Mersereau's, al-though different, gathered close about him,—like men in consultation—evil men. Some of them sat upon his bed, and it seemed as if they were about to help Mersereau to finish him, adding their hands to his.

Behind them again was a complete circle of all those evil, swimming things with green and red eyes, always watching—helping, prob-ably. He had actually felt the pressure of the hand to grow stronger of late, when they were all there. Only, just before he felt he was going to faint, and because he could not spring up any more, he invariably screamed or gasped a choking gasp and held his finger on the button which would bring Miss Koehler. Then she would come, lift him up, and fix his pillows. She also always assured him that it was only the inflammation of his throat, and rubbed it with alcohol, and gave him a few drops of something internally to ease it.

After all this time, and in spite of anything he could tell them, they still believed, or pre-tended to believe, that he was suffering from tuberculosis, and that all the rest of this was delusion, a phase of insanity!

And Mersereau's skeleton still out there on the Monte Orte!

And Mersereau's plan, with the help of oth-ers, of course, was to choke him to death, there was no doubt of that now; and yet they would believe after he was gone that he had died of tuberculosis of the throat. Think of that.

XII—Midnight of February 10, 1909

THE GHOST OF MERSEREAU (*bending over Davidson*): "Softly! Softly! He's quite asleep! He didn't think we could get him—that I could! But this time,—yes. Miss Koehler is asleep at the end of the hall and Miss Liggett can't come, can't hear. He's too weak now. He can scarcely move or groan. Strengthen my hand, will you! I will grip him so tight this time that he won't get away! His cries won't help him this time! He can't cry as he once did! Now! Now!"

A CLOUD OF EVIL SPIRITS (*swimming about*): "Right! Right! Good! Good! Now! Ah!"

DAVIDSON (*waking, choking, screaming, and feebly striking out*): "Help! Help! H-e-l-p! Miss —Miss—H-e-l-p!"

MISS LIGGETT (*dozing heavily in her chair*): "Everything is still. No one restless. I can sleep." (*Her head nods.*)

THE CLOUD OF EVIL SPIRITS: "Good! Good! Good! His soul at last! Here it comes! He couldn't escape this time! Ah! Good! Good! Now!"

MERSEREAU (*to Davidson*): "You murderer! At last! At last!"

XIII—3 A.M. of February 11, 1909

MISS KOEHLER (*at the bedside, distressed and pale*): "He must have died some time between one and two, doctor. I left him at one o'clock, comfortable as I could make him. He said he was feeling as well as could be expected. He's been very weak during the last few days, taking only a little gruel. Between half past one and two I thought I heard a noise, and came to see. He was lying just as you see here, except that his hands were up to his throat, as if it were hurting or choking him. I put them down for fear they would stiffen that way. In trying to call one of the other nurses just now, I found that the bell was out of order, although I know it was all right when I left, because he always made me try it. So he may have tried to ring."

DR. MAJOR (*turning the head and examining the throat*): "It looks as if he had clutched at his throat rather tightly this time, I must say. Here is the mark of his thumb on this side and of his four fingers on the other. Rather deep for the little strength he had. Odd that he should have imagined that some one else was trying to choke him, when he was always pressing at his own neck! Throat tuberculosis is very painful at times. That would explain the desire to clutch at his throat."

MISS LIGGETT: "He was always believing that an evil spirit was trying to choke him, doctor."

DR. MAJOR: "Yes, I know—association of ideas. Dr. Scain and I agree as to that. He had a bad case of chronic tuberculosis of the throat, with accompanying malnutrition, due to the effect of the throat on the stomach; and his notion about evil spirits pursuing him and trying to choke him was simply due to an innate tendency on the part of the subconscious mind to join things together—any notion, say, with any pain. If he had had a diseased leg, he would have imagined that evil spirits were attempting to saw it off, or something like that. In the same way the condition of his throat affected his stomach, and he imagined that the spirits were doing something to his food. Make out a certificate showing acute tuberculosis of the esophagus as the cause, with delusions of persecution as his mental condition. While I am here we may as well look in on Mr. Baff."

1927

1862 -- *Edith Wharton* -- 1937

BORN IN New York during the Civil War, by birth and breeding belonging to the socially élite, Edith Newbold Jones experienced the changing currents in metropolitan society as they were determined under the impact of post-war influences. On her mother's side she was descended from the Rhinelanders, a family long prominent in the social, civic, and commercial life of New York. Her great-grandfather was a general in the Continental army during the Revolution. She was educated for the most part in Europe, and knew at firsthand the art, literature, and culture of Italy, France, and Germany, a fact which accounts for the reflection of European life in many of her writings. In 1885 she married Edward Wharton, a wealthy banker, established her permanent home in her native city, spending her summers in Newport or Lenox and making frequent trips abroad. After 1906 she lived in Paris. With the exception of the war years, during which she engaged in relief work with whole-hearted devotion, her life is largely a record of publications. In recognition of her war work she was made an Officer of the French Legion of Honor. In 1924 she received the gold medal for literature from the Institute of Arts and Letters.

In *The Writing of Fiction* (1925), a little book which might be used profitably as a text by aspiring writers, Mrs. Wharton states the main principles which she followed as novelist and short-story writer. Art, she maintains at the outset, is still open to countless experiments which will preserve the artist against becoming stereotyped in method and practice. The primary problem in planning a novel is the selection of adequate material, a choice which must be guided, first, by what the material actually contains, and second, by the writer's ability to extract from it what is significant and illuminating. That is, the writer's vision must be commensurate with his capacity to record what he sees; otherwise, the product is marred by a lack of balance and proportion. The novelist must assume a point of view sufficiently removed from the raw material selected for treatment that it can be considered and recorded in an objective manner; to achieve consistency this point of view, once it is chosen, must not be changed lest the singleness of development, both of character and narrative, be broken. Roughly speaking, she recognizes two types of fiction—the novel of manners and the novel of character—but admits that the classification is arbitrary, and that the best novels are a combination of the two types. In the short story, situation is more important than character; in the novel, character is more important, and must change, either develop or decline, with the lapse of time as the narrative progresses. The length of a story will depend entirely upon the nature of the subject. It should stop when it is ended. Brief and inadequate as this summary of her theory is, it does convey the impression that her art is the result of painstaking reflection, and that it rests upon a carefully planned foundation—one reason for the occasional technical excellence of her work.

Like her master, Henry James, Mrs. Wharton achieved distinction in the short story as well as in the novel. She began her career with a collection of short stories under the title of *The Greater Inclination* (1899); it was followed by another volume, *The Descent of Man* (1904), regarded by some as her best work in this field. In later years she published similar collections in *Here and Beyond* (1926), *Human Nature* (1933), and *The World Over* (1936). The list of her novels is so long, and the subject matter and technique so varied, that even a brief characterization of each one is impossible here. The best that one can do is to single out a few more or less typical examples. *The Valley of Decision* (1902), for instance, is a historical novel about Italy in the eighteenth century, based upon such meticulous research that the background becomes more impressive than the narrative. In *The House of Mirth* (1905) she tells the story of Lily Bart and her adventures in exploiting the New York social set. *The Fruit of the Tree* (1907), although unconvincing as a story, illustrates her view of industrialism and social welfare. Critics are practically in unanimous agreement that *Ethan Frome* (1911) is one of her best works. It is a tale of frustrate love set in a Massachusetts countryside, and told with the concentrated austerity of a Greek tragedy. It is only a partial failure, and that because, in restless obedience to the principle of concentration which dominates the story, she so foreshortens her characters as to make them almost stereotypes. The book is too careful, too precise; in her attempt to make a New England tragedy into a universal one, she reduces her story almost to the level of synopsis. The characters do not act freely, or even with a willed constraint; the total effect is too much like that of a mathematical sum. A group of novels including *The Custom of the Country* (1913), *The Children* (1928), *Hudson River Bracketed* (1929), and its sequel, *The Gods Arrive* (1932), deal with divorce and social problems. *A Backward Glance* (1934) is an autobiography treated with the same aloof detachment and objectivity that characterizes her fiction, never very intimate or revealing, and containing, besides personal memoirs, observations on society in New York, London, and Paris, and reminiscences of many noteworthy people whom she met in the course of her life. A chapter is devoted to Henry James.

Mrs. Wharton was a capable and conscientious artist. Her work is marked by painstaking attention to artistic technique, with the result that many of her novels are almost perfect in structure. On the other hand, this self-conscious striving for perfection is at times so obvious that it overshadows the freshness and spontaneity which one expects in art. She is most at home with characters and themes taken from the select and cultured classes of society, and only in *Ethan Frome* and the short story "Bunner Sisters," does she even partially succeed outside her preferred field. In accordance with her principle that the art of fiction is "fluid," she employed a varying technique in her novels, a method by which in spite of certain typical traits she avoided the use of a set and hackneyed formula. Perhaps her greatest success is the novel *The Age of Innocence* (1920). In this portrait of late nineteenth-century New York, her best talents survive her worst defects. The casual irony of circumstance, which all but wrecks *The House of Mirth*, is here brilliantly contained; the characters remain consistent in both exposition and dialogue; and only the conclusion seems musty and dead.

Mrs. Wharton's novels and novelettes include *The Valley of Decision* (1902); *The House of Mirth* (1905); *Madame de Treymes* (1907); *The Fruit of the Tree* (1907); *Ethan Frome* (1911); *The Custom of the Country* (1913); *The Age of Innocence* (1920); *The Old Maid* (1924); *New Year's Day* (1924); *False Dawn* (1924); *The Spark* (1924); *The Children* (1928); *Certain People* (1930); *The Gods Arrive* (1932). Collections of short stories: *The Greater Inclination* (1899); *Crucial Instances* (1901); *The Descent of Man and Other Stories* (1904); *Tales of Men and Ghosts* (1910); *Xingu and Other Stories* (1916); *Here and Beyond* (1926); *Human Nature* (1933). *The Writing of Fiction* (1925) is a critical essay. For biographical information reference is made to her autobiography, *A Backward Glance* (1934); to R. M. Lovett, *Edith Wharton* (1925); to J. Flanner, "Dearest Edith," *The New Yorker*, March 2, 1929; to Percy Lubbock, *A Portrait of Edith Wharton* (1947). The following references will prove helpful for criticism: K. F. Gerould, *Edith Wharton: a Critical*

Study (1922); F. T. Cooper, *Some American Story Tellers* (1911); H. Hartwick, *The Foreground of American Fiction* (1934); H. Hatcher, *Creating the Modern American Novel* (1935); R. Michaud, *The American Novel To-day* (1928); G. Overton, *The Women Who Make Our Novels* (1928); S. P. Sherman, *The Main Stream* (1927); J. C. Underwood, *Literature and Insurgency* (1914); B. C. Williams, *Our Short Story Writers* (1920); H. T. and W. Follett, *Some Modern Novelists* (1919); P. H. Boynton, *Some Contemporary Americans* (1924); E. Björkman, *Voices of To-morrow* (1913); C. Van Doren, *Contemporary American Novelists* (1922); F. T. Russell, "Melodramatic Mrs. Wharton," *Sewanee Review*, Oct.–Dec., 1932; H. James, *Notes on Novelists* (1914); H. D. Sedgwick, *The New American Type and Other Essays* (1908); A. H. Quinn, *American Fiction* (1936); E. K. Brown, "Edith Wharton," *Études Anglaises* (1935); Alfred Kazin, *On Native Grounds* (1942); George Snell, *The Shapers of American Fiction* (1947); Joseph Warren Beach, *The Twentieth Century Novel* (1932); Edmund Wilson, "Justice to Edith Wharton," *The New Republic*, June 29, 1938; Q. D. Leavis, "Henry James's Heiress: The Importance of Edith Wharton," *Scrutiny*, Dec., 1938.

THE OTHER TWO

Taken from *The Descent of Man*. Although written early in her career, "The Other Two" illustrates many of the artistic traits which characterize Mrs. Wharton's later work.

I

WAYTHORN, on the drawing-room hearth, waited for his wife to come down to dinner.

It was their first night under his own roof, and he was surprised at his thrill of boyish agitation. He was not so old, to be sure—his glass gave him little more than the five-and-thirty years to which his wife confessed—but he had fancied himself already in the temperate zone; yet there he was listening for her step with a tender sense of all it symbolised, with some old trail of verse about the garlanded nuptial door-posts floating through his enjoyment of the pleasant room and the good dinner just beyond it.

They had been hastily recalled from their honeymoon by the illness of Lily Haskett, the child of Mrs. Waythorn's first marriage. The little girl, at Waythorn's desire, had been transferred to his house on the day of her mother's wedding, and the doctor, on their arrival, broke the news that she was ill with typhoid, but declared that all the symptoms were favorable. Lily could show twelve years of unblemished health, and the case promised to be a light one. The nurse spoke as reassuringly, and after a moment of alarm Mrs. Waythorn had adjusted herself to the situation. She was very fond of Lily—her affection for the child had perhaps been her decisive charm in Waythorn's eyes—but she had the perfectly balanced nerves which her little girl had inherited, and no woman ever wasted less tissue in unproductive worry. Waythorn was therefore quite prepared to see her come in presently, a little late because of a last look at Lily, but as serene and well-appointed as if her good-night kiss had been laid on the brow of health. Her composure was restful to him; it acted as ballast to his somewhat unstable sensibilities. As he pictured her bending over the child's bed he thought how soothing her presence must be in illness: her very step would prognosticate recovery.

His own life had been a gay one, from temperament rather than circumstance, and he had been drawn to her by the unperturbed gaiety which kept her fresh and elastic at an age when most women's activities are growing either slack or febrile. He knew what was said about her; for, popular as she was, there had always been a faint undercurrent of detraction. When she had appeared in New York, nine or ten years earlier, as the pretty Mrs. Haskett whom Gus Varick had unearthed somewhere—was it in Pittsburg or Utica?—society, while promptly accepting her, had reserved the right to cast a doubt on its own indiscrimination. Enquiry, however, established her undoubted connection with a socially reigning family, and explained her recent divorce as the natural result of a runaway match at seventeen; and as nothing was known of Mr. Haskett it was easy to believe the worst of him.

Alice Haskett's remarriage with Gus Varick was a passport to the set whose recognition she coveted, and for a few years the Varicks were the most popular couple in town. Unfortunately the alliance was brief and stormy, and this time the husband had his champions. Still, even Varick's grievances were of a nature to bear the inspection of the New York courts. A New York divorce is in itself a diploma of virtue, and in the semi-widowhood of this second separation Mrs. Varick took on an air of sanctity, and was allowed to confide her wrongs to some of the most scrupulous ears in town. But when it was known that she was to marry Waythorn there was a momentary reaction. Her best friends would have preferred to see her remain in the role of the injured wife, which was as becoming to her as crape to a rosy complexion. True, a decent time had elapsed, and it was not even suggested that Waythorn had supplanted his predecessor. People shook their heads over him, however, and one grudging friend, to whom he affirmed that he took the step with his eyes open, replied oracularly: "Yes—and with your ears shut."

Waythorn could afford to smile at these innuendoes. In the Wall Street phrase, he had "discounted" them. He knew that society has not yet adapted itself to the consequences of divorce, and that till the adaptation takes place every woman who uses the freedom the law accords her must be her own social justification. Waythorn had an amused confidence in his wife's ability to justify herself. His expectations were fulfilled, and before the wedding took place Alice Varick's group had rallied openly to her support. She took it all imperturbably: she had a way of surmounting obstacles without seeming to be aware of them, and Waythorn looked back with wonder at the trivialities over which he had worn his nerves thin. He had the sense of having found refuge in a richer, warmer nature than his own, and his satisfaction, at the moment, was humorously summed up in the thought that his wife, when she had done all she could for Lily, would not be ashamed to come down and enjoy a good dinner.

The anticipation of such enjoyment was not, however, the sentiment expressed by Mrs. Waythorn's charming face when she presently joined him. Though she had put on her most engaging teagown she had neglected to assume the smile that went with it, and Waythorn thought he had never seen her look so nearly worried.

"What is it?" he asked. "Is anything wrong with Lily?"

"No; I've just been in and she's still sleeping." Mrs. Waythorn hesitated. "But something tiresome has happened."

He had taken her two hands, and now perceived that he was crushing a paper between them.

"This letter?"

"Yes—Mr. Haskett has written—I mean his lawyer has written."

Waythorn felt himself flush uncomfortably. He dropped his wife's hands.

"What about?"

"About seeing Lily. You know the courts ——"

"Yes, yes," he interrupted nervously.

Nothing was known about Haskett in New York. He was vaguely supposed to have remained in the outer darkness from which his wife had been rescued, and Waythorn was one of the few who were aware that he had given up his business in Utica and followed her to New York in order to be near his little girl. In the days of his wooing, Waythorn had often met Lily on the doorstep, rosy and smiling, on her way "to see papa."

"I am so sorry," Mrs. Waythorn murmured. "If Lily could have been moved—"

"That's out of the question," he returned impatiently.

"I suppose so."

Her lip was beginning to tremble, and he felt himself a brute.

"He must come, of course," he said. "When is—his day?"

"I'm afraid—tomorrow."

"Very well. Send a note in the morning."

The butler entered to announce dinner.

Waythorn turned to his wife. "Come—you must be tired. It's beastly, but try to forget about it," he said, drawing her hand through his arm.

"You're so good, dear. I'll try," she whispered back.

Her face cleared at once, and as she looked at him across the flowers, between the rosy candle-shades, he saw her lips waver back into a smile.

"How pretty everything is!" she sighed luxuriously.

He turned to the butler. "The champagne at once, please. Mrs. Waythorn is tired."

In a moment or two their eyes met above the sparkling glasses. Her own were quite clear and untroubled: he saw that she had obeyed his injunction ånd forgotten.

II

Waythorn, the next morning, went down town earlier than usual. Haskett was not likely to come till the afternoon, but the instinct of flight drove him forth. He meant to stay away all day—he had thoughts of dining at his club. As his door closed behind him he reflected that before he opened it again it would have admitted another man who had as much right to enter it as himself, and the thought filled him with a physical repugnance.

He caught the "elevated" at the employes' hour, and found himself crushed between two layers of pendulous humanity. At Eighth Street the man facing him wriggled out, and another took his place. Waythorn glanced up and saw that it was Gus Varick. The men were so close together that it was impossible to ignore the smile of recognition on Varick's handsome overblown face. And after all—why not? They had always been on good terms, and Varick had been divorced before Waythorn's attentions to his wife began. The two exchanged a word on the perennial grievance of the congested trains, and when a seat at their side was miraculously left empty the instinct of self-preservation made Waythorn slip into it after Varick.

The latter drew the stout man's breath of relief. "Lord—I was beginning to feel like a pressed flower." He leaned back, looking unconcernedly at Waythorn. "Sorry to hear that Sellers is knocked out again."

"Sellers?" echoed Waythorn, starting at his partner's name.

Varick looked surprised. "You didn't know he was laid up with the gout?"

"No. I've been away—I only got back last night." Waythorn felt himself reddening in anticipation of the other's smile.

"Ah—yes; to be sure. And Sellers's attack came on two days ago. I'm afraid he's pretty bad. Very awkward for me, as it happens, because he was just putting through a rather important thing for me."

"Ah?" Waythorn wondered vaguely since when Varick had been dealing in "important things." Hitherto he had dabbled only in the shallow pools of speculation, with which Waythorn's office did not usually concern itself.

It occurred to him that Varick might be talking at random, to relieve the strain of their propinquity. That strain was becoming momentarily more apparent to Waythorn, and when, at Cortlandt Street, he caught sight of an acquaintance and had a sudden vision of the picture he and Varick must present to an initiated eye, he jumped up with a muttered excuse.

"I hope you'll find Sellers better," said Varick civilly, and he stammered back: "If I can be of any use to you——" and let the departing crowd sweep him to the platform.

At his office he heard that Sellers was in fact ill with the gout, and would probably not be able to leave the house for some weeks.

"I'm sorry it should have happened so, Mr. Waythorn," the senior clerk said with affable significance. "Mr. Sellers was very much upset at the idea of giving you such a lot of extra work just now."

"Oh, that's no matter," said Waythorn hastily. He secretly welcomed the pressure of additional business, and was glad to think that, when the day's work was over, he would have to call at his partner's on the way home.

He was late for luncheon, and turned in at the nearest restaurant instead of going to his club. The place was full, and the waiter hurried him to the back of the room to capture the only vacant table. In the cloud of cigar-smoke Waythorn did not at once distinguish his neighbors; but presently, looking about him, he saw Varick seated a few feet off. This time, luckily, they were too far apart for conversation, and Varick, who faced another way, had probably not even seen him; but there was an irony in their renewed nearness.

Varick was said to be fond of good living, and as Waythorn sat despatching his hurried luncheon he looked across half enviously at the other's leisurely degustation of his meal. When Waythorn first saw him he had been helping himself with critical deliberation to a bit of Camembert at the ideal point of liquefaction, and now, the cheese removed, he was just pouring his cafe double from its little two-storied earthen pot. He poured slowly, his ruddy profile bent above the task, and one beringed white hand steadying the lid of the coffee-pot; then he stretched his other hand to the decanter of cognac at his elbow, filled a liqueur-glass, took a tentative sip, and poured the brandy into his coffee-cup.

Waythorn watched him in a kind of fascination. What was he thinking of—only of the flavor of the coffee and the liqueur? Had the morning's meeting left no more trace in his thoughts than on his face? Had his wife so completely passed out of his life that even this odd encounter with her present husband, within a week after her remarriage, was no more than an incident in his day? And as Waythorn mused, another idea struck him: had Haskett ever met Varick as Varick and he had just met? The recollection of Haskett perturbed him, and he rose and left the restaurant, taking a circuitous way out to escape the placid irony of Varick's nod.

It was after seven when Waythorn reached home. He thought the footman who opened the door looked at him oddly.

"How is Miss Lily?" he asked in haste.

"Doing very well, sir. A gentleman—"

"Tell Barlow to put off dinner for half an hour," Waythorn cut him off, hurrying upstairs.

He went straight to his room and dressed without seeing his wife. When he reached the drawing-room she was there, fresh and radiant. Lily's day had been good; the doctor was not coming back that evening.

At dinner Waythorn told her of Sellers's illness and of the resulting complications. She listened sympathetically, adjuring him not to let himself be overworked, and asking vague feminine questions about the routine of the of-

fice. Then she gave him the chronicle of Lily's day; quoted the nurse and doctor, and told him who had called to inquire. He had never seen her more serene and unruffled. It struck him, with a curious pang, that she was very happy in being with him, so happy that she found a childish pleasure in rehearsing the trivial incidents of her day.

After dinner they went to the library, and the servant put the coffee and liqueurs on a low table before her and left the room. She looked singularly soft and girlish in her rosy pale dress, against the dark leather of one of his bachelor armchairs. A day earlier the contrast would have charmed him.

He turned away now, choosing a cigar with affected deliberation.

"Did Haskett come?" he asked, with his back to her.

"Oh, yes—he came."

"You didn't see him, of course?"

She hesitated a moment. "I let the nurse see him."

That was all. There was nothing more to ask. He swung round toward her, applying a match to his cigar. Well, the thing was over for a week, at any rate. He would try not to think of it. She looked up at him, a trifle rosier than usual, with a smile in her eyes.

"Ready for your coffee, dear?"

He leaned against the mantelpiece, watching her as she lifted the coffee-pot. The lamplight struck a gleam from her bracelets and tipped her soft hair with brightness. How light and slender she was, and how each gesture flowed into the next! She seemed a creature all compact of harmonies. As the thought of Haskett receded, Waythorn felt himself yielding again to the joy of possessorship. They were his, those white hands with their flitting motions, his the light haze of hair, the lips and eyes . . .

She set down the coffee-pot, and reaching for the decanter of cognac, measured off a liqueur-glass and poured it into his cup.

Waythorn uttered a sudden exclamation.

"What is the matter?" she said, startled.

"Nothing; only—I don't take cognac in my coffee."

"Oh, how stupid of me," she cried.

Their eyes met, and she blushed a sudden agonized red.

III

Ten days later, Mr. Sellers, still house-bound, asked Waythorn to call on his way down town. The senior partner, with his swaddled foot propped up by the fire, greeted his associate with an air of embarrassment.

"I'm sorry, my dear fellow; I've got to ask you to do an awkward thing for me."

Waythorn waited, and the other went on, after a pause apparently given to the arrangement of his phrases: "The fact is, when I was knocked out I had just gone into a rather complicated piece of business for—Gus Varick."

"Well?" said Waythorn, with an attempt to put him at his ease.

"Well—it's this way: Varick came to me the day before my attack. He had evidently had an inside tip from somebody, and had made about a hundred thousand. He came to me for advice, and I suggested his going in with Vanderlyn."

"Oh, the deuce!" Waythorn exclaimed. He saw in a flash what had happened. The investment was an alluring one, but required negotiation. He listened quietly while Sellers put the case before him, and the statement ended, he said: "You think I ought to see Varick?"

"I'm afraid I can't as yet. The doctor is obdurate. And this thing can't wait. I hate to ask you, but no one else in the office knows the ins and outs of it."

Waythorn stood silent. He did not care a farthing for the success of Varick's venture but the honor of the office was to be considered, and he could hardly refuse to oblige his partner.

"Very well," he said, "I'll do it."

That afternoon, apprised by telephone, Varick called at the office. Waythorn, waiting in his private room, wondered what the others thought of it. The newspapers, at the time of Mrs. Waythorn's marriage, had acquainted their readers with every detail of her previous matrimonial ventures, and Waythorn could fancy the clerks smiling behind Varick's back as he was ushered in.

Varick bore himself admirably. He was easy without being undignified, and Waythorn was conscious of cutting a much less impressive figure. Varick had no experience of business, and the talk prolonged itself for nearly an hour while Waythorn set forth with scrupulous precision the details of the proposed transaction.

"I'm awfully obliged to you," Varick said as he rose. "The fact is I'm not used to having much money to look after, and I don't want to make an ass of myself——" He smiled, and Waythorn could not help noticing that there was something pleasant about his smile. "It feels uncommonly queer to have enough cash to pay one's bills. I'd have sold my soul for it a few years ago!"

Waythorn winced at the allusion. He had heard it rumored that a lack of funds had been one of the determining causes of the Varick separation, but it did not occur to him that Varick's words were intentional. It seemed more likely that the desire to keep clear of embarrassing topics had fatally drawn him into one. Waythorn did not wish to be outdone in civility.

"We'll do the best we can for you," he said. "I think this is a good thing you're in."

"Oh, I'm sure it's immense. It's awfully good of you——" Varick broke off, embarrassed. "I suppose the thing's settled now—— but if——"

"If anything happens before Sellers is about, I'll see you again," said Waythorn quietly. He was glad, in the end, to appear the more self-possessed of the two.

* * *

The course of Lily's illness ran smooth, and as the days passed Waythorn grew used to the idea of Haskett's weekly visit. The first time the day came round, he stayed out late, and questioned his wife as to the visit on his return. She replied at once that Haskett had merely seen the nurse downstairs, as the doctor did not wish any one in the child's sick-room till after the crisis.

The following week Waythorn was again conscious of the recurrence of the day, but had forgotten it by the time he came home to dinner. The crisis of the disease came a few days later, with a rapid decline of fever, and the little girl was pronounced out of danger. In the rejoicing which ensued the thought of Haskett passed out of Waythorn's mind, and one afternoon, letting himself into the house with a latch-key, he went straight to his library without noticing a shabby hat and umbrella in the hall.

In the library he found a small effaced-looking man with a thinnish gray beard sitting on the edge of a chair. The stranger might have been a piano-tuner, or one of those mysteriously efficient persons who are summoned in emergencies to adjust some detail of the domestic machinery. He blinked at Waythorn through a pair of gold-rimmed spectacles and said mildly: "Mr. Waythorn, I presume? I am Lily's father."

Waythorn flushed. "Oh——" he stammered uncomfortably. He broke off, disliking to appear rude. Inwardly he was trying to adjust the actual Haskett to the image of him projected by his wife's reminiscences. Waythorn had been allowed to infer that Alice's first husband was a brute.

"I am sorry to intrude," said Haskett, with his over-the-counter politeness.

"Don't mention it," returned Waythorn, collecting himself. "I suppose the nurse has been told?"

"I presume so. I can wait," said Haskett. He had a resigned way of speaking, as though life had worn down his natural powers of resistance.

Waythorn stood on the threshold, nervously pulling off his gloves.

"I'm sorry you've been detained. I will send for the nurse," he said; and as he opened the door he added with an effort: "I'm glad we can give you a good report of Lily." He winced as the we slipped out, but Haskett seemed not to notice it.

"Thank you, Mr. Waythorn. It's been an anxious time for me."

"Ah, well, that's past. Soon she'll be able to go to you." Waythorn nodded and passed out.

In his own room he flung himself down with a groan. He hated the womanish sensibility which made him suffer so acutely from the grotesque chances of life. He had known when he married that his wife's former husbands were both living, and that amid the multiplied contacts of modern existence there were a thousand chances to one that he would run against one or the other, yet he found himself as much disturbed by his brief encounter with Haskett as though the law had not obligingly removed all difficulties in the way of their meeting.

Waythorn sprang up and began to pace the room nervously. He had not suffered half as much from his two meetings with Varick. It was Haskett's presence in his own house that made the situation so intolerable. He stood still, hearing steps in the passage.

"This way, please," he heard the nurse say. Haskett was being taken upstairs, then: not a corner of the house but was open to him. Waythorn dropped into another chair, staring vaguely ahead of him. On his dressing-table stood a photograph of Alice, taken when he had first known her. She was Alice Varick than—how fine and exquisite he had thought her! Those were Varick's pearls about her neck. At Waythorn's instance they had been returned before her marriage. Had Haskett ever given her any trinkets—and what had become of them, Waythorn wondered? He realized suddenly that he knew very little of Haskett's past or present situation; but from the man's appearance and manner of speech he could reconstruct with curious precision the surroundings of Alice's first marriage. And it startled him to think that she had, in the background of her life, a phase of existence so different from anything with which he had connected her. Varick, whatever his faults, was a gentleman, in the conventional, traditional sense of the term: the sense which at that moment seemed, oddly enough, to have most meaning to Waythorn. He and Varick had the same social habits, spoke the same language, understood the same allusions. But this other man . . . it was grotesquely uppermost in Waythorn's mind that Haskett had worn a made-up tie attached with an elastic. Why should that ridiculous detail symbolize the whole man? Waythorn was exasperated by his own paltriness, but the fact of the tie expanded, forced itself on him, became as it were the key to Alice's past. He could see her, as Mrs. Haskett, sitting in a "front parlor" furnished in plush, with a pianola, and a copy of "Ben Hur" on the center-table. He could see her going to the theater with Haskett—or perhaps even to a "Church Sociable"—she in a "picture hat" and Haskett in a black frock-coat, a little creased, with the made-up tie on an elastic. On the way home they would stop and look at the illuminated shop-windows, lingering over the photographs of New York actresses. On Sunday afternoons Haskett would take her for a walk, pushing Lily ahead of them in a white enamelled perambulator, and Waythorn had a vision of the people they would stop and talk to. He could fancy how pretty Alice must have looked, in a dress adroitly constructed from the hints of a New York fashion-paper, and how she must have looked down on the other women, chafing at her life, and secretly feeling that she belonged in a bigger place.

For the moment his foremost thought was one of wonder at the way in which she had shed the phase of existence which her marriage with Haskett implied. It was as if her whole aspect, every gesture, every inflection, every allusion, were a studied negation of that period of her life. If she had denied being married to Haskett she could hardly have stood more convicted of duplicity than in this obliteration of the self which had been his wife.

Waythorn started up, checking himself in the analysis of her motives. What right had he to create a fantastic effigy of her and then pass judgment on it? She had spoken vaguely of her first marriage as unhappy, had hinted, with becoming reticence, that Haskett had wrought havoc among her young illusions. . . . It was a pity for Waythorn's peace of mind that Haskett's very inoffensiveness shed a new light on the nature of those illusions. A man would rather think that his wife has been brutalized by her first husband than that the process had been reversed.

IV

"Mr. Waythorn, I don't like that French governess of Lily's."

Haskett, subdued and apologetic, stood before Waythorn in the library, revolving his shabby hat in his hand.

Waythorn, surprised in his armchair over the evening paper, stared back perplexedly at his visitor.

"You'll excuse my asking to see you," Haskett continued. "But this is my last visit, and I thought if I could have a word with you

it would be a better way than writing to Mrs. Waythorn's lawyer."

Waythorn rose uneasily. He did not like the French governess either; but that was irrelevant.

"I am not so sure of that," he returned stiffly; "but since you wish it I will give your message to—my wife." He always hesitated over the possessive pronoun in addressing Haskett.

The latter sighed. "I don't know as that will help much. She didn't like it when I spoke to her."

Waythorn turned red. "When did you see her?" he asked.

"Not since the first day I came to see Lily —right after she was taken sick. I remarked to her then that I didn't like the governess."

Waythorn made no answer. He remembered distinctly that, after that first visit, he had asked his wife if she had seen Haskett. She had lied to him then, but she had respected his wishes since; and the incident cast a curious light on her character. He was sure she would not have seen Haskett that first day if she had divined that Waythorn would object, and the fact that she did not divine it was almost as disagreeable to the latter as the discovery that she had lied to him.

"I don't like the woman," Haskett was repeating with mild persistency. "She ain't straight, Mr. Waythorn—she'll teach the child to be underhand. I've noticed a change in Lily —she's too anxious to please—and she don't always tell the truth. She used to be the straightest child, Mr. Waythorn——" He broke off, his voice a little thick. "Not but what I want her to have a stylish education," he ended.

Waythorn was touched. "I'm sorry, Mr. Haskett; but frankly, I don't quite see what I can do."

Haskett hesitated. Then he laid his hat on the table, and advanced to the hearth-rug, on which Waythorn was standing. There was nothing aggressive in his manner, but he had the solemnity of a timid man resolved on a decisive measure.

"There's just one thing you can do, Mr. Waythorn," he said. "You can remind Mrs. Waythorn that, by the decree of the courts,

I am entitled to have a voice in Lily's bringing up." He paused, and went on more deprecatingly: "I'm not the kind to talk about enforcing my rights, Mr. Waythorn. I don't know as I think a man is entitled to rights he hasn't known how to hold on to; but this business of the child is different. I've never let go there—and I never mean to."

* * *

The scene left Waythorn deeply shaken. 10 Shamefacedly, in indirect ways, he had been finding out about Haskett; and all that he had learned was favorable. The little man, in order to be near his daughter, had sold out his share in a profitable business in Utica, and accepted a modest clerkship in a New York manufacturing house. He boarded in a shabby street and had few acquaintances. His passion for Lily filled his life. Waythorn felt that this exploration of Haskett was like groping about 20 with a dark-lantern in his wife's past; but he saw now that there were recesses his lantern had not explored. He had never enquired into the exact circumstances of his wife's first matrimonial rupture. On the surface all had been fair. It was she who had obtained the divorce, and the court had given her the child. But Waythorn knew how many ambiguities such a verdict might cover. The mere fact that Haskett retained a right over his daughter implied 30 an unsuspected compromise. Waythorn was an idealist. He always refused to recognize unpleasant contingencies till he found himself confronted with them, and then he saw them followed by a spectral train of consequences. His next days were thus haunted, and he determined to try to lay the ghosts by conjuring them up in his wife's presence.

When he repeated Haskett's request a flame of anger passed over her face; but she subdued 40 it instantly and spoke with a slight quiver of outraged motherhood.

"It is very ungentlemanly of him," she said.

The word grated on Waythorn. "That is neither here nor there. It's a bare question of rights."

She murmured: "It's not as if he could ever be a help to Lily——"

Waythorn flushed. This was even less to his taste. "The question is," he repeated, "what 50 authority has he over her?"

She looked downward, twisting herself a little in her seat. "I am willing to see him—I thought you objected," she faltered.

In a flash he understood that she knew the extent of Haskett's claims. Perhaps it was not the first time she had resisted them.

"My objecting has nothing to do with it," he said coldly; "if Haskett has a right to be consulted you must consult him."

She burst into tears, and he saw that she expected him to regard her as a victim.

Haskett did not abuse his rights. Waythorn had felt miserably sure that he would not. But the governess was dismissed, and from time to time the little man demanded an interview with Alice. After the first outburst she accepted the situation with her usual adaptability. Haskett had once reminded Waythorn of the piano-tuner, and Mrs. Waythorn, after a month or two, appeared to class him with that domestic familiar. Waythorn could not but respect the father's tenacity. At first he had tried to cultivate the suspicion that Haskett might be "up to" something, that he had an object in securing a foothold in the house. But in his heart Waythorn was sure of Haskett's single-mindedness; he even guessed in the latter a mild contempt for such advantages as his relation with the Waythorns might offer. Haskett's sincerity of purpose made him invulnerable, and his successor had to accept him as a lien on the property.

* * *

Mr. Sellers was sent to Europe to recover from his gout, and Varick's affairs hung on Waythorn's hands. The negotiations were prolonged and complicated; they necessitated frequent conferences between the two men, and the interests of the firm forbade Waythorn's suggesting that his client should transfer his business to another office.

Varick appeared well in the transaction. In moments of relaxation his coarse streak appeared, and Waythorn dreaded his geniality; but in the office he was concise and clear-headed, with a flattering deference to Waythorn's judgment. Their business relations being so affably established, it would have been absurd for the two men to ignore each other in society. The first time they met in a drawing-room, Varick took up their intercourse in the same easy key, and his hostess's grateful glance obliged Waythorn to respond to it. After that they ran across each other frequently, and one evening at a ball Waythorn, wandering through the remoter rooms, came upon Varick seated beside his wife. She colored a little, and faltered in what she was saying; but Varick nodded to Waythorn without rising, and the latter strolled on.

In the carriage, on the way home, he broke out nervously: "I didn't know you spoke to Varick."

Her voice trembled a little. "It's the first time—he happened to be standing near me; I didn't know what to do. It's so awkward, meeting everywhere—and he said you had been very kind about some business."

"That's different," said Waythorn.

She paused a moment. "I'll do just as you wish," she returned pliantly. "I thought it would be less awkward to speak to him when we meet."

Her pliancy was beginning to sicken him. Had she really no will of her own—no theory about her relation to these men? She had accepted Haskett—did she mean to accept Varick? It was "less awkward," as she had said, and her instinct was to evade difficulties or to circumvent them. With sudden vividness Waythorn saw how the instinct had developed. She was "as easy as an old shoe"—a shoe that too many feet had worn. Her elasticity was the result of tension in too many different directions. Alice Haskett—Alice Varick—Alice Waythorn—she had been each in turn, and had left hanging to each name a little of her privacy, a little of her personality, a little of the inmost self where the unknown god abides.

"Yes—it's better to speak to Varick," said Waythorn wearily.

V

The winter wore on, and society took advantage of the Waythorns' acceptance of Varick. Harassed hostesses were grateful to them for bridging over a social difficulty, and Mrs. Waythorn was held up as a miracle of good taste. Some experimental spirits could not resist the diversion of throwing Varick and his former wife together, and there were those who thought he found a zest in the propinquity. But Mrs. Waythorn's conduct remained irreproachable. She neither avoided Varick nor sought him out. Even Waythorn could not but admit that she had discovered the solution of the newest social problem.

He had married her without giving much thought to that problem. He had fancied that a woman can shed her past like a man. But now he saw that Alice was bound to hers both by the circumstances which forced her into continued relation with it, and by the traces it had left on her nature. With grim irony Waythorn compared himself to a member of a syndicate. He held so many shares in his wife's personality and his predecessors were his partners in the business. If there had been any element of passion in the transaction he would have felt less deteriorated by it. The fact that Alice took her change of husbands like a change of weather reduced the situation to mediocrity. He could have forgiven her for blunders, for excesses; for resisting Haskett, for yielding to Varick; for anything but her acquiescence and her tact. She reminded him of a juggler tossing knives; but the knives were blunt and she knew they would never cut her.

And then, gradually, habit formed a protecting surface for his sensibilities. If he paid for each day's comfort with the small change of his illusions, he grew daily to value the comfort more and set less store upon the coin. He had drifted into a dulling propinquity with Haskett and Varick and he took refuge in the cheap revenge of satirizing the situation. He even began to reckon up the advantages which accrued from it, to ask himself if it were not better to own a third of a wife who knew how to make a man happy than a whole one who had lacked opportunity to acquire the art. For it was an art, and made up, like all others, of concessions, eliminations and embellishments; of lights judiciously thrown and shadows skilfully softened. His wife knew exactly how to manage the lights, and he knew exactly to what training she owed her skill. He even tried to trace the source of his obligations, to discriminate between the influences which had combined to produce his domestic happiness: he perceived that Haskett's commonness had made Alice worship good breeding, while Varick's liberal construction of the marriage bond had taught her to value the conjugal virtues; so that he was directly indebted to his predecessors for the devotion which made his life easy if not inspiring.

From this phase he passed into that of complete acceptance. He ceased to satirize himself because time had dulled the irony of the situation and the joke lost its humor with its sting. Even the sight of Haskett's hat on the hall table had ceased to touch the springs of epigram. The hat was often seen there now, for it had been decided that it was better for Lily's father to visit her than for the little girl to go to his boarding-house. Waythorn, having acquiesced in this arrangement, had been surprised to find how little difference it made. Haskett was never obtrusive, and the few visitors who met him on the stairs were unaware of his identity. Waythorn did not know how often he saw Alice, but with himself Haskett was seldom in contact.

One afternoon, however, he learned on entering that Lily's father was waiting to see him. In the library he found Haskett occupying a chair in his usual provisional way. Waythorn always felt grateful to him for not leaning back.

"I hope you'll excuse me, Mr. Waythorn," he said rising. "I wanted to see Mrs. Waythorn about Lily, and your man asked me to wait here till she came in."

"Of course," said Waythorn, remembering that a sudden leak had that morning given over the drawing-room to the plumbers.

He opened his cigar-case and held it out to his visitor, and Haskett's acceptance seemed to mark a fresh stage in their intercourse. The spring evening was chilly, and Waythorn invited his guest to draw up his chair to the fire. He meant to find an excuse to leave Haskett in a moment; but he was tired and cold, and after all the little man no longer jarred him.

The two were enclosed in the intimacy of their blended cigar-smoke when the door opened and Varick walked into the room. Waythorn rose abruptly. It was the first time that Varick had come to the house, and the surprise of seeing him, combined with the singular inopportuneness of his arrival, gave a new edge to Waythorn's blunted sensibilities. He stared at his visitor without speaking.

Varick seemed too preoccupied to notice his host's embarrassment.

"My dear fellow," he exclaimed in his most expansive tone, "I must apologize for tumbling in on you in this way, but I was too late to catch you down town, and so I thought——"

He stopped short, catching sight of Haskett, and his sanguine color deepened to a flush which spread vividly under his scant blond hair. But in a moment he recovered himself and nodded slightly. Haskett returned the bow in silence, and Waythorn was still groping for speech when the footman came in carrying a tea-table.

The intrusion offered a welcome vent to Waythorn's nerves. "What the deuce are you bringing this here for?" he said sharply.

"I beg your pardon, sir, but the plumbers are still in the drawing-room, and Mrs. Waythorn said she would have tea in the library." The footman's perfectly respectful tone implied a reflection on Waythorn's reasonableness.

"Oh, very well," said the latter resignedly, and the footman proceeded to open the folding tea-table and set out its complicated appointments. While this interminable process continued the three men stood motionless, watching it with a fascinated stare, till Waythorn, to break the silence, said to Varick: "Won't you have a cigar?"

He held out the case he had just tendered to Haskett, and Varick helped himself with a smile. Waythorn looked about for a match, and finding none, proffered a light from his own cigar. Haskett, in the background, held his ground mildly, examining his cigar-tip now and then, and stepping forward at the right moment to knock its ashes into the fire.

The footman at last withdrew, and Varick immediately began: "If I could just say half a word to you about this business——"

"Certainly," stammered Waythorn; "in the dining-room——"

But as he placed his hand on the door it opened from without, and his wife appeared on the threshold.

She came in fresh and smiling, in her street dress and hat, shedding a fragrance from the boa which she loosened in advancing.

"Shall we have tea in here, dear?" she began; and then she caught sight of Varick. Her smile deepened, veiling a slight tremor of surprise.

"Why, how do you do?" she said with a distinct note of pleasure.

As she shook hands with Varick she saw Haskett standing behind him. Her smile faded for a moment, but she recalled it quickly, with a scarcely perceptible side-glance at Waythorn.

"How do you do, Mr. Haskett?" she said, and shook hands with him a shade less cordially.

The three men stood awkwardly before her, till Varick always the most self-possessed, dashed into an explanatory phrase.

"We—I had to see Waythorn a moment on business," he stammered, brick-red from chin to nape.

Haskett stepped forward with his air of mild obstinacy. "I am sorry to intrude; but you appointed five o'clock——" he directed his re-signed glance to the time-piece on the mantel.

She swept aside their embarrassment with a charming gesture of hospitality.

"I'm so sorry—I'm always late; but the afternoon was so lovely." She stood drawing off her gloves, propitiatory and graceful, diffusing about her a sense of ease and familiarity in which the situation lost its grotesqueness. "But before talking business," she added brightly, "I'm sure every one wants a cup of tea."

She dropped into her low chair by the tea-table, and the two visitors, as if drawn by her smile, advanced to receive the cups she held out.

She glanced about for Waythorn, and he took the third cup with a laugh.

1904

1869 ~ *Edwin Arlington Robinson* ~ 1935

THE STORY of Robinson's life is simple and uneventful. Born of Anglo-Saxon ancestry in Head Tide, Maine, where his father was a grain dealer, he was taken by the family to Gardiner at a very early age. After completing the course in the local high school, he entered Harvard in 1891. He remained only two years, because his father's illness made it necessary for him to be self-supporting. In 1896 a small, privately printed volume appeared under the title of *The Torrent and the Night Before*, to be followed the succeeding year by *The Children of the Night*. Shortly after this he moved to New York in order to be closer to the literary market. The attention of President Roosevelt was drawn to his work by the publication of *Captain Craig and Other Poems* (1902) with the very practical result that he offered Robinson an appointment in the New York Custom House, which he held from 1905 to 1910. Robinson was never married. He spent his winters in Brooklyn and his summers at the MacDowell Colony in Peterborough, New Hampshire, where he did most of his writing. After 1910 he published some twenty volumes of poetry, including *The Man Against the Sky* (1916), *Merlin* (1917), *Lancelot* (1920), *Tristram* (1927), *The Glory of the Nightingales* (1930), and *Matthias at the Door* (1931).

Robinson was shy and retiring. He shrank from dramatizing himself, was averse to lecturing and public reading of his poetry, and did not allow himself to become the victim of press-agent and publicity enterprises. Aside from editing the letters of a friend, he devoted himself exclusively to poetry, accepting the slow but growing recognition of his work with quiet dignity.

Robinson is a poet of considerable talent and insight. His best poems are the shorter ones in which his mastery of technique and language are not interfered with by the need to fill pages and to extend what had best been expressed in concentration. For his early poems he used characters (some imagined, some remembered) from "Tilbury Town"; these characters are presented usually in a moment of crisis to which they react blindly, awkwardly, or despairingly. As the poems demonstrate, Robinson is interested both in emphasizing the futile but intrinsically valuable courage of man and in ridiculing pretense and stupidity. In his best poems, the dramatic burden of the incident is carried competently and made significant by form and language. When his "philosophy," which is at best confused, is expressed directly in his poems (as in the title poem of *The Man Against the Sky* and in "Credo")—that is, not given any or given little dramatic context—the result is very unfortunate. He seems forced to expose the confidence of man, to point to his actual helplessness, and finally to advise a stoicism born of frustration; he is hesitant, vague, tortured, and awkward; his formal excellence collapses under the weight of such necessity. He has given many a cultural historian a field day in these poems, but has scarcely added to his literary importance.

This fondness for the unusual, the eccentric, and the frustrate is paralleled to a degree by the method of artistic treatment. Early in life Robinson came under the enduring influence of Thomas Hardy and George Crabbe. As a result of this influence he stripped poetry of all extraneous adornments, rejected all artistic superfluities, and reduced the matter of presentation to an objectivity of almost steellike hardness. He said he formed the habit, as a young man, of "fishing" for the right word to convey an idea or a mood. He claimed adherence to no literary theory, and endeavored to do "as well as I can what insists on being done." In view of this individualism, it is interesting to note that he avoided free verse, preferring the conventional form, in which he sought to combine the rhythm of speech with that of the verse patterns. The poet must seek the "fearful truth," and present it with utter fearlessness, no matter where it leads. These ideals he steadily pursued; he belonged to no school of poetry, and followed the gleam of his youth irrespective of the bewildering lights of changing poetic fashions. He came upon the scene when poetry in America had become largely a matter of verse-mongering in search of prettiness; naturally, his very austere vigor marked him from the beginning. Indeed, he would have been prominent in any period.

Ultimately, Robinson needs to be judged in terms of his successes, which are as great as his failures, and scarcely less frequent. As such a poem as "Eros Turannos" demonstrates, he is a master of the linguistic and formal disciplines which go into the making of an exact poetry. Although opposed to the experimenting of his contemporaries, he is equally forceful in proving that the traditional poetic forms are alive and worthy of use. He has been his own answer to his appeal (in *The Children of the Night*, 1890–1897) for a poet who would dispel the gloom of mediocrity which covered his own time; he was himself the one

> To put these little sonnet-men to flight
> Who fashion, in a shrewd mechanic way,
> Songs without souls, that flicker for a day,
> To vanish in irrevocable night.

There is a one-volume *Collected Poems of Edwin Arlington Robinson* (1937). More recent individual volumes are *Dionysus in Doubt* (1925); *Tristram* (1927); *Sonnets, 1889–1927* (1928); *Fortunatus* (1928); *Modred, a Fragment* (1929); *The Prodigal Son* (1929); *Cavender's House* (1929); *The Glory of the Nightingales* (1930); *Matthias at the Door* (1931); *Nicodemus* (1932); *Talifer* (1933); *Amaranth* (1934); *King Jasper* (1935). A full-length biography and criticism is Hermann Hagedorn's *Edwin Arlington Robinson* (1938). M. Van Doren's *Edwin Arlington Robinson* (1927) is a biographical and critical study. "Edwin A. Robinson," *Wilson Bulletin*, Nov., 1928, and J. Farrar, ed., *The Literary Spotlight* (1924) are also biographical. See also *Untriangulated Stars: Letters of E. A. Robinson to Harry De Forest Smith*, 1890–1905, ed. Derham Sutcliffe (1947), and R. H. Shauffler, *Edwin Arlington Robinson* (1938). The more extensive critical studies are L. M. Beebe, *Edwin Arlington Robinson and the Arthurian Legend* (1927), and *Aspects of the Poetry of E. A. Robinson* (1928); C. Cestre, *An Introduction to Edwin Arlington Robinson* (1930); B. R. Redman, *Edwin Arlington Robinson* (1926); L. Morris, *The Poetry of Edwin Arlington Robinson* (1923); Emery Neff, *Edwin Arlington Robinson* (1948); Yvor Winters, *Edwin Arlington Robinson* (1946); A. Lowell, *Tendencies in Modern American Poetry* (1917). Briefer discussions may be found in: L. Untermeyer, *American Poetry since 1900* (1923); B. Weirick, *From Whitman to Sandburg in American Poetry* (1924); T. K. Whipple, *Spokesmen* (1928); C. Wood, *Poets of America* (1925); P. H. Boynton, *Some Contemporary Americans* (1924); R. Brenner, *Ten Modern Poets* (1930); J. Drinkwater, *The Muse in Council* (1925); H. Monroe, *Poets & Their Art* (1926); E. E. Pipkin, "The Arthur of Edwin Arlington Robinson," *English Journal*, March, 1930; J. C. Squire and others, *Contemporary American Authors* (1928); T. Maynard, *Our Best Poets* (1922); G. B. Munson, *Destinations* (1928); O. F. Theis, "Edwin Arlington Robinson," *Forum*, Feb., 1914; T. Maynard, "Edwin Arlington Robinson," *Catholic World*, June, 1935; H. Monroe, "Robinson as Man and Poet," *Poetry*, June, 1935; M. D. Zabel, "Edwin Arlington Robinson," *Commonweal*, Feb. 15, 1933; M. D. Zabel, "Robinson in America," *Poetry*, June, 1935; L. Lippincott, *A Bibliography of the Writings and Criticisms of Edwin Arlington Robinson* (1937); L. E. Richards, *E. A. R.* (1936); R. W. Brown, *Next Door to a Poet* (1937); Horace Gregory and Marya Zaturenska, *A History of American Poetry, 1900–1940* (1946); David Brown, "Some Rejected Poems of Edwin Arlington Robinson," *American Literature*, Jan., 1936; H. H. Hudson, "Robinson and Praed," *Poetry*, Feb., 1943; George St. Clair, "E. A. Robinson and Tilbury Town," *New Mexico Quarterly*, May, 1934. For valuable notes and further bibliography, see H. H. Clark, *Major American Poets* (1936).

THE HOUSE ON THE HILL

A villanelle, giving a glimpse of the vanished New England, the same New England described also by Miss Jewett and Mrs. Freeman.

THEY are all gone away,
The House is shut and still,
There is nothing more to say.

Through broken walls and gray
The winds blow bleak and shrill:
They are all gone away.

Nor is there one to-day
To speak them good or ill:
There is nothing more to say.

Why is it then we stray   10
Around that sunken sill?
They are all gone away,

And our poor fancy-play
For them is wasted skill:
There is nothing more to say.

There is ruin and decay
In the House on the Hill:
They are all gone away,
There is nothing more to say.

1897

RICHARD CORY

Robinson's chief interest was in people, as numerous titles of his poems indicate. "Richard Cory" is a sharply etched portrait.

WHENEVER Richard Cory went down town,
We people on the pavement looked at him:
He was a gentleman from sole to crown,
Clean favored, and imperially slim.

And he was always quietly arrayed,
And he was always human when he talked;
But still he fluttered pulses when he said,
"Good-morning," and he glittered when he walked.

And he was rich—yes, richer than a king—
And admirably schooled in every grace: 10
In fine, we thought that he was everything
To make us wish that we were in his place.

So on we worked, and waited for the light,
And went without the meat, and cursed the bread;
And Richard Cory, one calm summer night,
Went home and put a bullet through his head.

1897

CALVARY

FRIENDLESS and faint, with martyred steps and slow,
Faint for the flesh, but for the spirit free,
Stung by the mob that came to see the show,
The Master toiled along to Calvary;
We gibed him, as he went, with houndish glee,
Till his dimmed eyes for us did overflow;
We cursed his vengeless hands thrice wretchedly,—
And this was nineteen hundred years ago.

But after nineteen hundred years the shame
Still clings, and we have not made good the loss   10
That outraged faith has entered in his name.
Ah, when shall come love's courage to be strong!
Tell me, O Lord—tell me, O Lord how long
Are we to keep Christ writhing on the cross!

1897

GEORGE CRABBE

Crabbe was one of Robinson's favorite poets. This chastely wrought sonnet is a sincere tribute to a fellow poet as well as an excellent evaluation of his work and influence.

GIVE him the darkest inch your shelf allows,
Hide him in lonely garrets, if you will,—
But his hard, human pulse is throbbing still
With the sure strength that fearless truth endows.
In spite of all fine science disavows,
Of his plain excellence and stubborn skill
There yet remains what fashion cannot kill,
Though years have thinned the laurel from his brows.

Whether or not we read him, we can feel
From time to time the vigor of his name   10
Against us like a finger for the shame
And emptiness of what our souls reveal
In books that are as altars where we kneel
To consecrate the flicker, not the flame.

1897

CREDO

I CANNOT find my way: there is no star
In all the shrouded heavens anywhere;
And there is not a whisper in the air
Of any living voice but one so far
That I can hear it only as a bar
Of lost, imperial music, played when fair
And angel fingers wove, and unaware,
Dead leaves to garlands where no roses are.

No, there is not a glimmer, nor a call,
For one that welcomes, welcomes when he
    fears,   10
The black and awful chaos of the night;
For through it all—above, beyond it all—
I know the far-sent message of the years,
I feel the coming glory of the Light.

          1897

THE TOWN DOWN THE RIVER

I

SAID the Watcher by the Way
To the young and the unladen,
To the boy and to the maiden,
"God be with you both to-day.
First your song came ringing,
Now you come, you two,—
Knowing naught of what you do,
Or of what your dreams are bringing.

"O you children who go singing
To the Town down the River,   10
Where the millions cringe and shiver,
Tell me what you know to-day;
Tell me how far you are going,
Tell me how you find your way.
O you children who go dreaming,
Tell me what you dream to-day."

"He is old and we have heard him,"
Said the boy then to the maiden;
"He is old and heavy laden
With a load we throw away.   20
Care may come to find us,
Age may lay us low;
Still, we seek the light we know,
And the dead we leave behind us.

"Did he think that he would blind us
Into such a small believing

As to live without achieving,
When the lights have led so far?
Let him watch or let him wither,—
Shall he tell us where we are?   30
We know best who go together,
Downward, onward, and so far."

II

Said the Watcher by the Way
To the fiery folk that hastened,
To the loud and the unchastened,
"You are strong, I see, to-day.
Strength and hope may lead you
To the journey's end,—
Each to be the other's friend
If the Town should fail to need you.   40

"And are ravens there to feed you
In the Town down the River,
Where the gift appalls the giver
And youth hardens day by day?
O you brave and you unshaken,
Are you truly on your way?
And are sirens in the River,
That you come so far to-day?"

"You are old, and we have listened,"
Said the voice of one who halted;   50
"You are sage and self-exalted,
But your way is not our way.
You that cannot aid us
Give us words to eat.
Be assured that they are sweet,
And that we are as God made us.

"Not in vain have you delayed us,
Though the River still be calling
Through the twilight that is falling
And the Town be still so far.   60
By the whirlwind of your wisdom
Leagues are lifted as leaves are;
But a king without a kingdom
Fails us, who have come so far."

III

Said the Watcher by the Way
To the slower folk who stumbled,
To the weak and the world-humbled,
"Tell me how you fare to-day.
Some with ardor shaken,
All with honor scarred,   70

Do you falter, finding hard
The far chance that you have taken?

"Or, do you at length awaken
To an antic retribution,
Goading to a new confusion
The drugged hopes of yesterday?
O you poor mad men that hobble,
Will you not return, or stay?
Do you trust, you broken people,
To a dawn without the day?"   80

"You speak well of what you know not,"
Muttered one; and then a second:
"You have begged and you have beckoned,
But you see us on our way.
Who are you to scold us,
Knowing what we know?
Jeremiah, long ago,
Said as much as you have told us.

"As we are, then, you behold us:
Derelicts of all conditions,   90
Poets, rogues, and sick physicians,
Plodding forward from afar;
Forward now into the darkness
Where the men before us are;
Forward, onward, out of grayness,
To the light that shone so far."

IV

Said the Watcher by the Way
To some aged ones who lingered,
To the shrunken, the claw-fingered,
"So you come for me to-day."—   100
"Yes, to give you warning;
You are old," one said;
"You have old hairs on your head,
Fit for laurel, not for scorning.

"From the first of early morning
We have toiled along to find you;
We, as others, have maligned you,
But we need your scorn to-day.
By the light that we saw shining,
Let us not be lured alway;   110
Let us hear no River calling
When to-morrow is to-day."

"But your lanterns are unlighted
And the Town is far before you:

Let us hasten, I implore you,"
Said the Watcher by the Way.
"Long have I waited,
Longer have I known
That the Town would have its own,
And the call be for the fated.   120

"In the name of all created,
Let us hear no more, my brothers;
Are we older than all others?
Are the planets in our way?"—
"Hark," said one; "I hear the River,
Calling always, night and day."—
"Forward, then! The lights are shining,"
Said the Watcher by the Way.
                                        1908

FLAMMONDE

This is not a mere etching, but a well-rounded
picture, filled in with details and comparable to
a painted portrait.

THE man Flammonde, from God knows where,
With firm address and foreign air,
With news of nations in his talk
And something royal in his walk,
With glint of iron in his eyes,
But never doubt, nor yet surprise,
Appeared, and stayed, and held his head
As one by kings accredited.

Erect, with his alert repose
About him, and about his clothes,   10
He pictured all tradition hears
Of what we owe to fifty years.
His cleansing heritage of taste
Paraded neither want nor waste;
And what he needed for his fee
To live, he borrowed graciously.

He never told us what he was,
Or what mischance, or other cause,
Had banished him from better days
To play the Prince of Castaways.   20
Meanwhile he played surpassing well
A part, for most, unplayable;
In fine, one pauses, half afraid
To say for certain that he played.

For that, one may as well forego
Conviction as to yes or no;

Nor can I say just how intense
Would then have been the difference
To several, who, having striven
In vain to get what he was given,   30
Would see the stranger taken on
By friends not easy to be won.

Moreover, many a malcontent
He soothed and found munificent;
His courtesy beguiled and foiled
Suspicion that his years were soiled;
His mien distinguished any crowd,
His credit strengthened when he bowed;
And women, young and old, were fond
Of looking at the man Flammonde.   40

There was a woman in our town
On whom the fashion was to frown;
But while our talk renewed the tinge
Of a long-faded scarlet fringe,
The man Flammonde saw none of that,
And what he saw we wondered at—
That none of us, in her distress,
Could hide or find our littleness.

There was a boy that all agreed
Had shut within him the rare seed   50
Of learning. We could understand,
But none of us could lift a hand.
The man Flammonde appraised the youth,
And told a few of us the truth;
And thereby, for a little gold,
A flowered future was unrolled.

There were two citizens who fought
For years and years, and over nought;
They made life awkward for their friends,
And shortened their own dividends.   60
The man Flammonde said what was wrong
Should be made right; nor was it long
Before they were again in line,
And had each other in to dine.

And these I mention are but four
Of many out of many more.
So much for them. But what of him—
So firm in every look and limb?
What small satanic sort of kink
Was in his brain? What broken link   70
Withheld him from the destinies
That came so near to being his?

What was he, when we came to sift
His meaning, and to note the drift
Of incommunicable ways
That make us ponder while we praise?
Why was it that his charm revealed
Somehow the surface of a shield?
What was it that we never caught?
What was he, and what was he not?   80

How much it was of him we met
We cannot ever know; nor yet
Shall all he gave us quite atone
For what was his, and his alone;
Nor need we now, since he knew best,
Nourish an ethical unrest:
Rarely at once will nature give
The power to be Flammonde and live.

We cannot know how much we learn
From those who never will return,   90
Until a flash of unforeseen
Remembrance falls on what has been.
We've each a darkening hill to climb;
And this is why, from time to time
In Tilbury Town, we look beyond
Horizons for the man Flammonde.

                                        1915

MINIVER CHEEVY

MINIVER Cheevy, child of scorn,
    Grew lean while he assailed the seasons;
He wept that he was ever born,
    And he had reasons.

Miniver loved the days of old
    When swords were bright and steeds were
        prancing;
The vision of a warrior bold
    Would set him dancing.

Miniver sighed for what was not,
    And dreamed, and rested from his labors; 10
He dreamed of Thebes and Camelot,
    And Priam's neighbors.

Miniver mourned the ripe renown
    That made so many a name so fragrant;
He mourned Romance, now on the town,
    And Art, a vagrant.

Miniver loved the Medici,
   Albeit he had never seen one;
He would have sinned incessantly
   Could he have been one.   20

Miniver cursed the commonplace
   And eyed a khaki suit with loathing:
He missed the mediaeval grace
   Of iron clothing.

Miniver scorned the gold he sought,
   But sore annoyed was he without it:
Miniver thought, and thought, and thought
   And thought about it.

Miniver Cheevy, born too late,   29
   Scratched his head and kept on thinking;
Miniver coughed, and called it fate,
   And kept on drinking.   1907

EROS TURANNOS

SHE fears him, and will always ask
   What fated her to choose him;
She meets in his engaging mask
   All reasons to refuse him;
But what she meets and what she fears
Are less than are the downward years,
Drawn slowly to the foamless weirs
   Of age, were she to lose him.

Between a blurred sagacity
   That once had power to sound him,   10
And Love, that will not let him be
   The Judas that she found him,
Her pride assuages her almost,
As if it were alone the cost.—
He sees that he will not be lost,
   And waits and looks around him.

A sense of ocean and old trees
   Envelops and allures him;
Tradition, touching all he sees,
   Beguiles and reassures him;   20
And all her doubts of what he says
Are dimmed with what she knows of days—
Till even prejudice delays
   And fades, and she secures him.

The falling leaf inaugurates
   The reign of her confusion;

The pounding wave reverberates
   The dirge of her illusion;
And home, where passion lived and died,
Becomes a place where she can hide,   30
While all the town and harbour side
   Vibrate with her seclusion.

We tell you, tapping on our brows,
   The story as it should be—
As if the story of a house
   Were told, or ever could be;
We'll have no kindly veil between
Her visions and those we have seen—
As if we guessed what hers have been,
   Or what they are or would be.   40

Meanwhile we do no harm; for they
   That with a god have striven,
Not hearing much of what we say,
   Take what the god has given;
Though like waves breaking it may be,
Or like a changed familiar tree,
Or like a stairway to the sea
   Where down the blind are driven.
                    1916

LUKE HAVERGAL

Go to the western gate, Luke Havergal,
There where the vines cling crimson on the
   wall,
And in the twilight wait for what will come.
The leaves will whisper there of her, and some,
Like flying words, will strike you as they fall;
But go, and if you listen she will call.
Go to the western gate, Luke Havergal—
Luke Havergal.

No, there is not a dawn in eastern skies
To rift the fiery night that's in your eyes;   10
But there, where western glooms are gathering,
The dark will end the dark, if anything:
God slays Himself with every leaf that flies,
And hell is more than half of paradise.
No, there is not a dawn in eastern skies—
In eastern skies.

Out of a grave I come to tell you this,
Out of a grave I come to quench the kiss
That flames upon your forehead with a glow
That blinds you to the way that you must go.

Yes, there is yet one way to where she is, 21
Bitter, but one that faith may never miss.
Out of a grave I come to tell you this—
To tell you this.

There is the western gate, Luke Havergal,
There are the crimson leaves upon the wall.

Go, for the winds are tearing them away,—
Nor think to riddle the dead words they say,
Nor any more to feel them as they fall;
But go, and if you trust her she will call. 30
There is the western gate, Luke Havergal—
Luke Havergal.

(ca. 1894)

1875 ~ *Robert Frost* ~ ——

ON HIS father's side Frost is of New England ancestry, the family having lived in New Hampshire for seven generations; his mother was a native of Edinburgh, of Lowland Scotch descent. Although he was born, and for ten years lived, in San Francisco, this western environment seems to have made little impression on his mind so far as the subject matter of his work is concerned. On the death of his father, he and his mother moved to Lawrence, Massachusetts, where his paternal grandfather provided a home for them.

Here he was graduated from the local high school, fell in love with Elinor Miriam White, to whom he was later married, and began to write poetry. He entered Dartmouth College, but remained only a few months because the routine pursuit of courses was distasteful to him. At Harvard his venture was scarcely more successful, for he left without a degree at the end of two years. Until 1912 he combined farming, authorship, and teaching, earning very little as a poet, but attracting wide attention through his original methods as a teacher. From 1912 to 1915 he and his family lived in England, where *A Boy's Will* (1913) and *North of Boston* (1914) were published and received with enthusiasm. The University of Michigan offered him an appointment without specified academic duties; later he was on the staff of Amherst College. A number of colleges and universities have conferred honorary degrees upon him, and the Pulitzer prize for poetry was twice awarded to him. His permanent home is in Vermont, where he is a neighbor of Dorothy Canfield Fisher.

Besides *A Boy's Will* and *North of Boston*, issued in America in 1915, he is the author of *Mountain Interval* (1916), *New Hampshire* (1923), *West-Running Brook* (1928), and *A Lone Striker* (1933). Although admittedly one of the most American of our poets, he was in reality "discovered" in England. It was only after assurance came from England that Frost was a poet of high caliber that America became hospitable to him. He is now generally recognized as an important poet; discriminating readers regard him highly, and a few of his poems, like "Mending Wall" and "The Death of the Hired Man," have passed into the common vernacular.

In a sense Frost is a traditionalist, for he writes in the accepted forms and meter, frequently in rhyme, yet allowing himself considerable liberty within them.

Not only is he interested artistically in the present, but in a present of a very limited area. The background of his scene extends from Boston northward and westward some three hundred miles, centering for the most part in New Hampshire, and within the confines of this space he finds the facts of life which he transmutes into art. He is of the soil and loves country life and country people, and in his poetry country people and country scenes predominate. In his choice of subject, one notices a certain exclusiveness, for of the many types that might be found even in so restricted an area as central New England, Frost is concerned primarily with the people of the countryside. Nowhere is there a suggestion of an industrial Manchester or even of his own Lawrence. Only the men and women whose roots extend into the soil intrigue him. Their limited, often frustrate experiences, eccentricities, oddities, tragedies, comedies, passions, and philosophy suggest to him the proper matter for poetry.

In a preface to his *Collected Poems* (1942), Frost describes "The Figure a Poem Makes": "It begins in delight, it inclines to the impulse, it assumes direction with the first line laid down, it runs a course of lucky events, and ends in a clarification of life—not necessarily a great clarification, such as sects and cults are founded on, but in a momentary stay against confusion." The typical Frost poem is written in conventional form (there are really only two meters in English verse, he says: "strict iambic and loose iambic"), treats of native character and landscape, is highly informed with a playful and sometimes a superficial irony, and is sparing in its decorative effects. The "clarification of life" almost never is so explicit as to become didactic; nor is it heavily weighted (as in Robinson at his worst) by a confused philosophic judgment. It is generally implicit and suggested. Often Frost is inclined to a mild form of sentimentality and his exposition is governed by a rather superficial use of his subject.

"The Death of the Hired Man," while it almost deserves its rather extensive reputation, is not altogether successful because of observations bordering on the cliché; "Mending Wall" is similarly afflicted; and there is a playfulness and archness in some of his attitudes that suggest that he is unwilling really to go as far as his subject would seem to warrant. "An Old Man's Winter Night" is almost pure poetry, free of these disturbing and cheapening qualities. "Two Tramps in Mud Time," while sometimes overly "cute," is an excellent and carefully designed poetic organism, in which the conclusion never escapes its dramatic context.

Even at his worst, Frost is a good poet, his eye always aware of concrete detail, his mind almost always in control of structure. His later poetry (beginning, perhaps, with *West-Running Brook*, 1928) is increasingly abstract, skeptical, and personal; fewer and fewer poems imply and suggest by means of economically conceived and objective detail; more and more often a statement is made with little or no genuinely concrete evidence or context. The last poems are good enough for a view of Frost as spokesman of his point-of-view; one uses them to enforce and develop inferences made from his earlier verse.

A Boy's Will (1913); *North of Boston* (1914); *Mountain Interval* (1916); *New Hampshire* (1923); *West-Running Brook* (1928); *A Further Range* (1936); *The Witness Tree* (1942) have been brought together in *Collected Poems of Robert Frost* (1942). In addition he has published *The Lone Striker* (1933); *Three Poems* (1935); *A Masque of Reason* (1945); *A Masque of Mercy* (1947); *Steeple-Bush* (1947). He is the author of a play, *A Way Out* (Seven Arts, Feb., 1917), also included in H. L. Cohen, ed., *More One-Act Plays by Modern Authors* (1927). S. Cox, *Robert Frost, Original "Ordinary Man"* (1929), and G. B. Munson, *Robert Frost* (1927), are biographies. For criticism see Lawrance Thompson, *Fire and Ice* (1942); Horace Gregory and Marya Zaturenska, *A History of American Poetry, 1900–1940* (1946); Malcolm Cowley, "Frost: A Dissenting Opinion," *New Republic*, Sept. 11, 18, 1944; Charles C. Walcutt, "Frost's *Death of the Hired Man*," *Explicator*, October, 1944; Yvor Winters, "Robert Frost: or The Spiritual Drifter as Poet," *The Sewanee Review*, Autumn, 1948. P. H. Boynton, *Some Contemporary Americans* (1924); C. Wood, *Poets of America* (1925); T. K. Whipple, *Spokesmen* (1928); B. Weirick, *From Whitman to Sandburg in American Poetry* (1924); G. R. Elliott, *The Cycle of Modern Poetry* (1929); J. C. Squire and others, *Contemporary American Authors* (1928); A. Lowell, *Tendencies in Modern American Poetry* (1917); A. Kreymborg, *Our Singing Strength* (1929); T. Maynard, *Our Best Poets* (1922); G. B. Munson, "Robert Frost and the Humanistic Temper," *Bookman*, July, 1930; E. S. Sergeant, *Fire Under the Andes* (1927); C. Van Doren, *Many Minds* (1924); L. Untermeyer, *American Poetry since 1900* (1923); R. Brenner, *Ten Modern Poets* (1930); J. Farrar, ed., *The Literary Spotlight* (1924); L. Jones, *First Impressions* (1925); C. Cestre, "*Amy Lowell, Robert Frost, Edwin Arlington Robinson*," *Johns Hopkins Alumni Magazine*, March, 1926; J. McB. Dabbs, "Robert Frost and the Dark Woods," *Yale Review*, March, 1934; E. Garnett, *Friday Nights* (1922); G. O. Akroyed, "The Classical in Robert Frost," *Poet-Lore*, Winter, 1929; C. Ford, *The Less Traveled Road, A Study of Robert Frost* (1935); R. Thornton, *Recognition of Robert Frost* (1937).

THE TRIAL BY EXISTENCE

EVEN the bravest that are slain
  Shall not dissemble their surprise
On waking to find valor reign,
  Even as on earth, in paradise;
And where they sought without the sword
  Wide fields of asphodel fore'er
To find that the utmost reward
  Of daring should be still to dare.

The light of heaven falls whole and white
  And is not shattered into dyes,   10
The light forever is morning light;
  The hills are verdured pasture-wise;
The angel hosts with freshness go,
  And seek with laughter what to brave;—
And binding all is the hushed snow
  Of the far-distant breaking wave.

And from a cliff-top is proclaimed
  The gathering of the souls for birth,
The trial by existence named,
  The obscuration upon earth.   20
And the slant spirits trooping by
  In streams and cross- and counter-
    streams
Can but give ear to that sweet cry
  For its suggestion of what dreams!

And the more loitering are turned
  To view once more the sacrifice
Of those who for some good discerned
  Will gladly give up paradise.
And a white shimmering concourse rolls
  Toward the throne to witness there   30
The speeding of devoted souls
  Which God makes his especial care.

And none are taken but who will,
　Having first heard the life read out
That opens earthward, good and ill,
　Beyond the shadow of a doubt;
And very beautifully God limns,
　And tenderly, life's little dream,
But naught extenuates or dims,
　Setting the thing that is supreme.　40

Nor is there wanting in the press
　Some spirit to stand simply forth,
Heroic in its nakedness,
　Against the uttermost of earth.
The tale of earth's unhonored things
　Sounds nobler there than 'neath the sun;
And the mind whirls and the heart sings,
　And a shout greets the daring one.

But always God speaks at the end:
　"One thought in agony of strife　50
The bravest would have by for friend,
　The memory that he chose the life;
But the pure fate to which you go
　Admits no memory of choice,
Or the woe were not earthly woe
　To which you give the assenting voice."

And so the choice must be again,
　But the last choice is still the same;
And the awe passes wonder then,
　And a hush falls for all acclaim.　60
And God has taken a flower of gold
　And broken it, and used therefrom
The mystic link to bind and hold
　Spirit to matter till death come.

'Tis of the essence of life here,
　Though we choose greatly, still to lack
The lasting memory at all clear,
　That life has for us on the wrack
Nothing but what we somehow chose;
　Thus are we wholly stripped of pride　70
In the pain that has but one close,
　Bearing it crushed and mystified.

1911

MENDING WALL

Stone walls still serve as fences on many New England farms. During the winter so many of the stones become dislodged by the "groundswell" and by thoughtless hunters that it is necessary to mend the wall in the spring. In case the wall separates adjoining properties, the neighbors "walk the line," each one replacing the stones which have fallen on his side. This custom forms the basis of the poem.

SOMETHING there is that doesn't love a wall,
That sends the frozen-ground-swell under it,
And spills the upper boulders in the sun;
And makes gaps even two can pass abreast.
The work of hunters is another thing:
I have come after them and made repair
Where they have left not one stone on a stone,
But they would have the rabbit out of hiding,
To please the yelping dogs. The gaps I mean,
No one has seen them made or heard them
　　made,　10
But at spring mending-time we find them there.
I let my neighbor know beyond the hill;
And on a day we meet to walk the line
And set the wall between us once again.
We keep the wall between us as we go.
To each the boulders that have fallen to each.
And some are loaves and some so nearly balls
We have to use a spell to make them balance:
"Stay where you are until our backs are
　　turned!"
We wear our fingers rough with handling
　　them.　20
Oh, just another kind of out-door game,
One on a side. It comes to little more:
There where it is we do not need the wall:
He is all pine and I am apple orchard.
My apple trees will never get across
And eat the cones under his pines, I tell him.
He only says, "Good fences make good neigh-
　　bors."
Spring is the mischief in me, and I wonder
If I could put a notion in his head:
"*Why* do they make good neighbors? Isn't it
Where there are cows? But here there are no
　　cows.　31
Before I built a wall I'd ask to know
What I was walling in or walling out,
And to whom I was like to give offense.
Something there is that doesn't love a wall,
That wants it down." I could say "Elves" to
　　him,
But it's not elves exactly, and I'd rather
He said it for himself. I see him there
Bringing a stone grasped firmly by the top
In each hand, like an old-stone savage armed.

He moves in darkness as it seems to me,   41
Not of woods only and the shade of trees.
He will not go behind his father's saying,
And he likes having thought of it so well
He says again, "Good fences make good
    neighbors."

                                        1914

THE DEATH OF THE HIRED MAN

MARY sat musing on the lamp-flame at the
    table
Waiting for Warren. When she heard his step,
She ran on tiptoe down the darkened passage
To meet him in the doorway with the news
And put him on his guard. "Silas is back."
She pushed him outward with her through the
    door
And shut it after her. "Be kind," she said.
She took the market things from Warren's
    arms
And set them on the porch, then drew him
    down
To sit beside her on the wooden steps.   10

"When was I ever anything but kind to him?
But I'll not have the fellow back," he said.
"I told him so last haying, didn't I?
'If he left then,' I said, 'that ended it.'
What good is he? Who else will harbor him
At his age for the little he can do?
What help he is there's no depending on.
Off he goes always when I need him most.
'He thinks he ought to earn a little pay,
Enough at least to buy tobacco with,   20
So he won't have to beg and be beholden.'
'All right,' I say, 'I can't afford to pay
Any fixed wages, though I wish I could.'
'Someone else can.' 'Then someone else will
    have to.'
I shouldn't mind his bettering himself
If that was what it was. You can be certain,
When he begins like that, there's someone at
    him
Trying to coax him off with pocket-money,—
In haying time, when any help is scarce.
In winter he comes back to us. I'm done." 30

"Sh! not so loud: he'll hear you," Mary said.

"I want him to: he'll have to soon or late."

"He's worn out. He's asleep beside the stove.
When I came up from Rowe's I found him
    here,
Huddled against the barn-door fast asleep,
A miserable sight, and frightening, too—
You needn't smile—I didn't recognise him—
I wasn't looking for him—and he's changed.
Wait till you see."

        "Where did you say he'd been?"

"He didn't say. I dragged him to the house, 40
And gave him tea and tried to make him smoke.
I tried to make him talk about his travels.
Nothing would do: he just kept nodding off."

"What did he say? Did he say anything?"

"But little."

        "Anything? Mary, confess
He said he'd come to ditch the meadow for
    me."

"Warren!"

        "But did he? I just want to know."

"Of course he did. What would you have him
    say?
Surely you wouldn't grudge the poor old man
Some humble way to save his self-respect.   50
He added, if you really care to know,
He meant to clear the upper pasture, too.
That sounds like something you have heard
    before?
Warren, I wish you could have heard the way
He jumbled everything. I stopped to look
Two or three times—he made me feel so
    queer—
To see if he was talking in his sleep.
He ran on Harold Wilson—you remember—
The boy you had in haying four years since.
He's finished school, and teaching in his
    college.   60
Silas declares you'll have to get him back.
He says they two will make a team for work:
Between them they will lay this farm as
    smooth!
The way he mixed that in with other things.
He thinks young Wilson a likely lad, though
    daft

On education—you know how they fought
All through July under the blazing sun,
Silas up on the cart to build the load,
Harold along beside to pitch it on.''

''Yes, I took care to keep well out of earshot.''

''Well, those days trouble Silas like a dream. 71
You wouldn't think they would. How some
    things linger!
Harold's young college boy's assurance piqued
    him.
After so many years he still keeps finding
Good arguments he sees he might have used.
I sympathize. I know just how it feels
To think of the right thing to say too late.
Harold's associated in his mind with Latin.
He asked me what I thought of Harold's saying
He studied Latin like the violin   80
Because he liked it—that an argument!
He said he couldn't make the boy believe
He could find water with a hazel prong—
Which showed how much good school had
    ever done him.
He wanted to go over that. But most of all
He thinks if he could have another chance
To teach him how to build a load of hay——''

''I know, that's Silas' one accomplishment.
He bundles every forkful in its place,
And tags and numbers it for future reference,
So he can find and easily dislodge it   91
In the unloading. Silas does that well.
He takes it out in bunches like big birds' nests.
You never see him standing on the hay
He's trying to lift, straining to lift himself.''

''He thinks if he could teach him that, he'd be
Some good perhaps to someone in the world.
He hates to see a boy the fool of books.
Poor Silas, so concerned for other folk,
And nothing to look backward to with pride,
And nothing to look forward to with hope, 101
So now and never any different.''

Part of a moon was falling down the west,
Dragging the whole sky with it to the hills.
Its light poured softly in her lap. She saw
And spread her apron to it. She put out her
    hand
Among the harp-like morning-glory strings,

Taut with the dew from garden bed to eaves,
As if she played unheard the tenderness
That wrought on him beside her in the night.
''Warren,'' she said, ''he has come home to
    die: 111
You needn't be afraid he'll leave you this
    time.''

''Home,'' he mocked gently.

        ''Yes, what else but home?
It all depends on what you mean by home.
Of course he's nothing to us, any more
Than was the hound that came a stranger to us
Out of the woods, worn out upon the trail.''

''Home is the place where, when you have to
    go there,
They have to take you in.''

        ''I should have called it
Something you somehow haven't to deserve.''

Warren leaned out and took a step or two, 121
Picked up a little stick, and brought it back
And broke it in his hand and tossed it by.
''Silas has better claim on us, you think,
Than on his brother? Thirteen little miles
As the road winds would bring him to his door.
Silas has walked that far no doubt today.
Why didn't he go there? His brother's rich,
A somebody—director in the bank.''

''He never told us that.''

        ''We know it though.'' 130

''I think his brother ought to help, of course.
I'll see to that if there is need. He ought of right
To take him in, and might be willing to—
He may be better than appearances.
But have some pity on Silas. Do you think
If he'd had any pride in claiming kin
Or anything he looked for from his brother,
He'd keep so still about him all this time?''

''I wonder what's between them.''

        ''I can tell you.
Silas is what he is—we wouldn't mind him—
But just the kind that kinsfolk can't abide. 141

He never did a thing so very bad.
He don't know why he isn't quite as good
As anyone. He won't be made ashamed
To please his brother, worthless though he is."

"*I* can't think Si ever hurt anyone."

"No, but he hurt my heart the way he lay
And rolled his old head on that sharp-edged
    chair-back.
He wouldn't let me put him on the lounge.
You must go in and see what you can do.   150
I made the bed up for him there tonight.
You'll be surprised at him—how much he's
    broken.
His working days are done; I'm sure of it."

"I'd not be in a hurry to say that."

"I haven't been. Go, look, see for yourself.
But, Warren, please remember how it is:
He's come to help you ditch the meadow.
He has a plan. You mustn't laugh at him.
He may not speak of it, and then he may.
I'll sit and see if that small sailing cloud   160
Will hit or miss the moon."

                         It hit the moon.
Then there were three there, making a dim
    row,
The moon, the little silver cloud, and she.
Warren returned—too soon, it seemed to her,
Slipped to her side, caught up her hand and
    waited.
"Warren," she questioned.

                    "Dead," was all he answered.

                                        1914

THE MOUNTAIN

The mountain held the town as in a shadow.
I saw so much before I slept there once:
I noticed that I missed stars in the west,
Where its black body cut into the sky.
Near me it seemed: I felt it like a wall
Behind which I was sheltered from the wind.
And yet between the town and it I found,
When I walked forth at dawn to see new
    things,
Were fields, a river, and beyond, more fields.
The river at the time was fallen away,   10

And made a widespread brawl on cobble-
    stones;
But the signs showed what it had done in
    spring;
Good grassland gullied out, and in the grass
Ridges of sand, and driftwood stripped of bark.
I crossed the river and swung round the
    mountain.
And there I met a man who moved so slow
With white-faced oxen in a heavy cart,
It seemed no harm to stop him altogether.
"What town is this?" I asked.

                         "This? Lunenburg."

Then I was wrong: the town of my sojourn,
Beyond the bridge, was not that of the moun-
    tain,   21
But only felt at night its shadowy presence.
"Where is your village? Very far from here?"
"There is no village—only scattered farms.
We were but sixty voters last election.
We can't in nature grow to many more:
That thing takes all the room!" He moved his
    goad.
The mountain stood there to be pointed at.
Pasture ran up the side a little way,
And then there was a wall of trees and trunks:
After that only tops of trees, and cliffs   31
Imperfectly concealed among the leaves.
A dry ravine emerged from under boughs
Into the pasture.

                 "That looks like a path.
Is that the way to reach the top from here?—
Not for this morning, but some other time:
I must be getting back to breakfast now."
"I don't advise your trying from this side.
There is no proper path, but those that *have*
Been up, I understand, have climbed from
    Ladd's.   40
That's five miles back. You can't mistake the
    place:
They logged it there last winter some way up.
I'd take you, but I'm bound the other way."
"You've never climbed it?"

                          "I've been on the sides
Deer-hunting and trout-fishing. There's a
    brook
That starts up on it somewhere—I've heard say
Right on the top, tip-top—a curious thing.
But what would interest you about the brook,
It's always cold in summer, warm in winter.
One of the great sights going is to see   50

It steam in winter like an ox's breath,
Until the bushes all along its banks
Are inch-deep with the frosty spines and
bristles—
You know the kind. Then let the sun shine
on it!"
"There ought to be a view around the world
From such a mountain—if it isn't wooded
Clear to the top." I saw through leafy screens
Great granite terraces in sun and shadow,
Shelves one could rest a knee on getting up—
With depths behind him sheer a hundred feet;
Or turn and sit on and look out and down, 61
With little ferns in crevices at his elbow.
"As to that I can't say. But there's the spring,
Right on the summit, almost like a fountain.
That ought to be worth seeing."
                                          "If it's there.
You never saw it?"
                          "I guess there's no doubt
About its being there. I never saw it.
It may not be right on the very top:
It wouldn't have to be a long way down
To have some head of water from above, 70
And a good *distance* down might not be no-
ticed
By anyone who'd come a long way up.
One time I asked a fellow climbing it
To look and tell me later how it was."
"What did he say?"
                          "He said there was a lake
Somewhere in Ireland on a mountain top."
"But a lake's different. What about the spring?"
"He never got up high enough to see.
That's why I don't advise your trying this
side.
He tried this side. I've always meant to go 80
And look myself, but you know how it is:
It doesn't seem so much to climb a mountain
You've worked around the foot of all your
life.
What would I do? Go in my overalls,
With a big stick, the same as when the cows
Haven't come down to the bars at milking
time?
Or with a shotgun for a stray black bear?
'Twouldn't seem real to climb for climbing it."
"I shouldn't climb it if I didn't want to—
Not for the sake of climbing. What's its
name?" 90
"We call it Hor: I don't know if that's right."

"Can one walk around it? Would it be too far?"
"You can drive round and keep in Lunenberg,
But it's as much as ever you can do,
The boundary lines keep in so close to it.
Hor is the township, and the township's Hor—
And a few houses sprinkled round the foot,
Like boulders broken off the upper cliff,
Rolled out a little farther than the rest."
"Warm in December, cold in June, you say?"
"I don't suppose the water's changed at all. 101
You and I know enough to know it's warm
Compared with cold, and cold compared with
warm.
But all the fun's in how you say a thing."
"You've lived here all your life?"
                                          "Ever since Hor
Was no bigger than a——" What, I did not
hear.
He drew the oxen toward him with light
touches
Of his slim goad on nose and offside flank,
Gave them their marching orders and was
moving.

                                                    1914

THE BLACK COTTAGE

WE chanced in passing by that afternoon
To catch it in a sort of special picture
Among tar-banded ancient cherry trees,
Set well back from the road in rank lodged
grass,
The little cottage we were speaking of,
A front with just a door between two win-
dows,
Fresh painted by the shower a velvet black.
We paused, the minister and I, to look.
He made as if to hold it at arm's length
Or put the leaves aside that framed it in. 10
"Pretty," he said. "Come in. No one will
care."
The path was a vague parting in the grass
That led us to a weathered window-sill.
We pressed our faces to the pane. "You see,"
he said,
"Everything's as she left it when she died.
Her sons won't sell the house or the things
in it.
They say they mean to come and summer here
Where they were boys. They haven't come
this year.

They live so far away—one is out West—
It will be hard for them to keep their word. 20
Anyway they won't have the place disturbed."
A buttoned hair-cloth lounge spread scrolling
        arms
Under a crayon portrait on the wall
Done sadly from an old daguerreotype.
"That was the father as he went to war.
She always, when she talked about war,
Sooner or later came and leaned, half knelt,
Against the lounge beside it, though I doubt
If such unlifelike lines kept power to stir
Anything in her after all the years.   30
He fell at Gettysburg or Fredericksburg,
I ought to know—it makes a difference which:
Fredericksburg wasn't Gettysburg, of course.
But what I'm getting to is how forsaken
A little cottage this has always seemed;
Since she went more than ever, but before—
I don't mean altogether by the lives
That had gone out of it, the father first,
Then the two sons, till she was left alone.
(Nothing could draw her after those two sons.
She valued the considerate neglect   41
She had at some cost taught them after years.)
I mean by the world's having passed it by—
As we almost got by this afternoon.
It always seems to me a sort of mark
To measure how far fifty years have brought us.
Why not sit down if you are in no haste?
These doorsteps seldom have a visitor.
The warping boards pull out their own old
        nails
With none to tread and put them in their
        place.   50
She had her own idea of things, the old lady.
And she liked talk. She had seen Garrison
And Whittier, and had her story of them.
One wasn't long in learning that she thought
Whatever else the Civil War was for
It wasn't just to keep the States together,
Nor just to free the slaves, though it did both.
She wouldn't have believed those ends enough
To have given outright for them all she gave.
Her giving somehow touched the principle
That all men are created free and equal.   61
And to hear her quaint phrases—so removed
From the world's view today of all those
        things.
That's a hard mystery of Jefferson's.
What did he mean? Of course the easy way

Is to decide it simply isn't true.
It may not be. I heard a fellow say so.
But never mind, the Welshman got it planted
Where it will trouble us a thousand years.
Each age will have to reconsider it.   70
You couldn't tell her what the West was
        saying,
And what the South to her serene belief.
She had some art of hearing and yet not
Hearing the latter wisdom of the world.
White was the only race she ever knew.
Black she had scarcely seen, and yellow never.
But how could they be made so very unlike
By the same hand working in the same stuff?
She had supposed the war decided that.
What are you going to do with such a person?
Strange how such innocence gets its own
        way.   81
I shouldn't be surprised if in this world
It were the force that would at last prevail.
Do you know but for her there was a time
When to please younger members of the
        church,
Or rather say non-members in the church,
Whom we all have to think of nowadays,
I would have changed the Creed a very little?
Not that she ever had to ask me not to;
It never got so far as that; but the bare thought
Of her old tremulous bonnet in the pew,   91
And of her half asleep was too much for me.
Why, I might wake her up and startle her.
It was the words "descended into Hades"
That seemed too pagan to our liberal youth.
You know they suffered from a general on-
        slaught.
And well, if they weren't true why keep right
        on
Saying them like the heathen? We could drop
        them.
Only—there was the bonnet in the pew.
Such a phrase couldn't have meant much to
        her   100
But suppose she had missed it from the Creed
As a child misses the unsaid Good-night,
And falls asleep with heartache—how should
        I feel?
I'm just as glad she made me keep hands off,
For, dear me, why abandon a belief
Merely because it ceases to be true.
Cling to it long enough, and not a doubt
It will turn true again, for so it goes.

Most of the change we think we see in life
Is due to truths being in and out of favor.   110
As I sit here, and oftentimes, I wish
I could be monarch of a desert land
I could devote and dedicate forever
To the truths we keep coming back and back
    to.
So desert it would have to be, so walled
By mountain ranges half in summer snow,
No one would covet it or think it worth
The pains of conquering to force change on.
Scattered oases where men dwelt, but mostly
Sand dunes held closely in tamarisk   120
Blown over and over themselves in idleness.
Sand grains should sugar in the natal dew
The babe born to the desert, the sand storm
Retard mid-waste my cowering caravans——

"There are bees in this wall." He struck the
    clapboards,
Fierce heads looked out; small bodies pivoted.
We rose to go. Sunset blazed on the windows.
                                    1914

AN OLD MAN'S WINTER NIGHT

ALL out of doors looked darkly in at him
Through the thin frost, almost in separate
    stars,
That gathers on the pane in empty rooms.
What kept his eyes from giving back the gaze
Was the lamp tilted near them in his hand.
What kept him from remembering what it was
That brought him to that creaking room was
    age.
He stood with barrels round him—at a loss.
And having scared the cellar under him
In clomping there, he scared it once again   10
In clomping off;—and scared the outer night,
Which has its sounds, familiar, like the roar
Of trees and crack of branches, common
    things,
But nothing so like beating on a box.
A light he was to no one but himself
Where now he sat, concerned with he knew
    what,
A quiet light, and then not even that.
He consigned to the moon, such as she was,
So late-arising, to the broken moon
As better than the sun in any case   20
For such a charge, his snow upon the roof,

His icicles along the wall to keep;
And slept. The log that shifted with a jolt
Once in the stove, disturbed him and he
    shifted,
And eased his heavy breathing, but still slept.
One aged man—one man—can't fill a house,
A farm, a countryside, or if he can,
It's thus he does it of a winter night.
                                    1916

BIRCHES

WHEN I see birches bend to left and right
Across the lines of straighter darker trees,
I like to think some boy's been swinging them.
But swinging doesn't bend them down to
    stay.
Ice-storms do that. Often you must have seen
    them
Loaded with ice a sunny winter morning
After a rain. They click upon themselves
As the breeze rises, and turn many-colored
As the stir cracks and crazes their enamel.
Soon the sun's warmth makes them shed
    crystal shells   10
Shattering and avalanching on the snow-
    crust—
Such heaps of broken glass to sweep away
You'd think the inner dome of heaven had
    fallen.
They are dragged to the withered bracken by
    the load,
And they seem not to break; though once they
    are bowed
So low for long, they never right themselves:
You may see their trunks arching in the woods
Years afterwards, trailing their leaves on the
    ground
Like girls on hands and knees that throw their
    hair   19
Before them over their heads to dry in the sun.
But I was going to say when Truth broke in
With all her matter-of-fact about the ice-
    storm
(Now am I free to be poetical?)
I should prefer to have some boy bend them
As he went out and in to fetch the cows—
Some boy too far from town to learn base-
    ball,
Whose only play was what he found himself,
Summer or winter, and could play alone.

One by one he subdued his father's trees
By riding them down over and over again   30
Until he took the stiffness out of them,
And not one but hung limp, not one was left
For him to conquer. He learned all there
      was
To learn about not launching out too soon
And so not carrying the tree away
Clear to the ground. He always kept his
      poise
To the top branches, climbing carefully
With the same pains you use to fill a cup
Up to the brim, and even above the brim,
Then he flung outward, feet first, with a
      swish,   40
Kicking his way down through the air to the
      ground.
So was I once myself a swinger of birches.
And so I dream of going back to be.
It's when I'm weary of considerations,
And life is too much like a pathless wood
Where your face burns and tickles with the
      cobwebs
Broken across it, and one eye is weeping
From a twig's having lashed across it open.
I'd like to get away from earth awhile
And then come back to it and begin over.   50
May no fate willfully misunderstand me
And half grant what I wish and snatch me
      away
Not to return. Earth's the right place for love:
I don't know where it's likely to go better.
I'd like to go by climbing a birch tree,
And climb black branches up a snow-white
      trunk
Toward heaven, till the tree could bear no
      more,
But dipped its top and set me down again.
That would be good both going and coming
      back.
One could do worse than be a swinger of
      birches.   60
                              1915

THE ROAD NOT TAKEN

Two roads diverged in a yellow wood,
    And sorry I could not travel both
And be one traveler, long I stood
And looked down one as far as I could
To where it bent in the undergrowth;

Then took the other, as just as fair,
And having perhaps the better claim,
Because it was grassy and wanted wear;
Though as for that the passing there
Had worn them really about the same,   10

And both that morning equally lay
In leaves no step had trodden black.
Oh, I kept the first for another day!
Yet knowing how way leads on to way,
I doubted if I should ever come back.

I shall be telling this with a sigh
Somewhere ages and ages hence:
Two roads diverged in a wood, and I—
I took the one less traveled by,
And that has made all the difference.   20
                              1915

A TIME TO TALK

When a friend calls to me from the
      road
And slows his horse to a meaning walk,
I don't stand still and look around
On all the hills I haven't hoed,
And shout from where I am, What is it?
No, not as there is a time to talk.
I thrust my hoe in the mellow ground,
Blade-end up and five feet tall,
And plod: I go up to the stone wall
For a friendly visit.   10
                              1916

STOPPING BY WOODS ON A
SNOWY EVENING

Whose woods these are I think I know.
His house is in the village though;
He will not see me stopping here
To watch his woods fill up with snow.

My little horse must think it queer
To stop without a farmhouse near
Between the woods and frozen lake
The darkest evening of the year.

He gives his harness bells a shake
To ask if there is some mistake.
The only other sound's the sweep   10
Of easy wind and downy flake.

The woods are lovely, dark and deep.
But I have promises to keep,
And miles to go before I sleep,
And miles to go before I sleep.

1923

OUR SINGING STRENGTH

It snowed in spring on earth so dry and warm
The flakes could find no landing place to form.
Hordes spent themselves to make it wet and
    cold,
And still they failed of any lasting hold.
They made no white impression on the black.
They disappeared as if earth sent them back.
Not till from separate flakes they changed at
    night
To almost strips and tapes of ragged white
Did grass and garden ground confess it
    snowed,
And all go back to winter but the road.   10
Next day the scene was piled and puffed and
    dead.
The grass lay flattened under one great tread.
Borne down until the end almost took root,
The rangey bough anticipated fruit
With snowballs cupped in every opening bud.
The road alone maintained itself in mud,
Whatever its secret was of greater heat
From inward fires or brush of passing feet.

In spring more mortal singers than belong
To any one place cover us with song.   20
Thrush, bluebird, blackbird, sparrow, and
    robin throng;
Some to go further north to Hudson's Bay,
Some that have come too far north back away,
Really a very few to build and stay.
Now was seen how these liked belated snow.
The fields had nowhere left for them to go;
They'd soon exhausted all there was in flying;
The trees they'd had enough of with once
    trying
And setting off their heavy powder load.
They could find nothing open but the road.   30
So there they let their lives be narrowed in
By thousands the bad weather made akin.
The road became a channel running flocks
Of glossy birds like ripples over rocks.
I drove them under foot in bits of flight
That kept the ground, almost disputing right

Of way with me from apathy of wing,
A talking twitter all they had to sing.
A few I must have driven to despair
Made quick asides, but having done in air   40
A whir among white branches great and small
As in some too much carven marble hall
Where one false wing beat would have brought
    down all,
Came tamely back in front of me, the Drover,
To suffer the same driven nightmare over.
One such storm in a lifetime couldn't teach
    them
That back behind pursuit it couldn't reach
    them;
None flew behind me to be left alone.

Well, something for a snowstorm to have
    shown
The country's singing strength thus brought
    together,   50
That though repressed and moody with the
    weather
Was none the less there ready to be freed
And sing the wildflowers up from root and
    seed.

1923

TWO LOOK AT TWO

Love and forgetting might have carried them
A little further up the mountain side
With night so near, but not much further up.
They must have halted soon in any case
With thoughts of the path back, how rough
    it was
With rock and washout, and unsafe in dark-
    ness;
When they were halted by a tumbled wall
With barbed-wire binding. They stood facing
    this,
Spending what onward impulse they still had
In one last look the way they must not go,   10
On up the failing path, where, if a stone
Or earthslide moved at night, it moved itself;
No footstep moved it. "This is all," they
    sighed,
"Good-night to woods." But not so; there
    was more.
A doe from round a spruce stood looking at
    them
Across the wall, as near the wall as they.

She saw them in their field, they in hers.
The difficulty of seeing what stood still,
Like some up-ended boulder split in two,
Was in her clouded eyes: they saw no fear
    there.   20
She seemed to think that two thus they were
    safe.
Then, as if they were something that, though
    strange,
She could not trouble her mind with too long,
She sighed and passed unscared along the wall.
"*This*, then, is all. What more is there to ask?"
But no, not yet. A snort to bid them wait.
A buck from round the spruce stood looking
    at them
Across the wall as near the wall as they.
This was an antlered buck of lusty nostril,
Not the same doe come back into her place. 30
He viewed them quizzically with jerks of head,
As if to ask, "Why don't you make some
    motion?
Or give some sign of life? Because you can't.
I doubt if you're as living as you look."
Thus till he had them almost feeling dared
To stretch a proffering hand—and a spell-
    breaking.
Then he too passed unscared along the wall.
Two had seen two, whichever side you spoke
    from.
"This *must* be all." It was all. Still they stood,
A great wave from it going over them,   40
As if the earth in one unlooked-for favor
Had made them certain earth returned their
    love.

            1923

TWO TRAMPS IN MUD TIME, OR A FULL-TIME INTEREST

OUT of the mud two strangers came
And caught me splitting wood in the yard.
And one of them put me off my aim
By hailing cheerily "Hit them hard!"
I knew pretty well why he dropped behind
And let the other go on a way.
I knew pretty well what he had in mind:
He wanted to take my job for pay.

Good blocks of beech it was I split,
As large around as the chopping block; 10
And every piece I squarely hit

Fell splinterless as a cloven rock.
The blows that a life of self-control
Spares to strike for the common good
That day, giving a loose to my soul,
I spent on the unimportant wood.

The sun was warm but the wind was chill.
You know how it is with an April day
When the sun is out and the wind is still,
You're one month on in the middle of May.
But if you so much as dare to speak, 21
A cloud comes over the sunlit arch,
A wind comes off a frozen peak,
And you're two months back in the middle of
    March.

A bluebird comes tenderly up to alight
And fronts the wind to unruffle a plume,
His song so pitched as not to excite
A single flower as yet to bloom.
It is snowing a flake and he half knew
Winter was only playing possum. 30
Except in color he isn't blue,
But he wouldn't advise a thing to blossom.

The water for which we may have to look
In summertime with a witching-wand,
In every wheelrut's now a brook,
In every print of a hoof a pond,
Be glad of water, but don't forget
The lurking frost in the earth beneath
That will steal forth after the sun is set
And show on the water its crystal teeth. 40

The time when most I loved my task
These two must make me love it more
By coming with what they came to ask.
You'd think I never had felt before
The weight of an axe-head poised aloft,
The grip on earth of outspread feet,
The life of muscles rocking soft
And smooth and moist in vernal heat.

Out of the woods two hulking tramps
(From sleeping God knows where last night, 50
But not long since in the lumber camps).
They thought all chopping was theirs of right.
Men of the woods and lumberjacks,
They judged me by their appropriate tool.
Except as a fellow handled an axe,
They had no way of knowing a fool.

Nothing on either side was said.
They knew they had but to stay their stay
And all their logic would fill my head:
As that I had no right to play   60
With what was another man's work for gain.
My right might be love but theirs was need.
And where the two exist in twain
Theirs was the better right—agreed.

But yield who will to their separation,
My object in living is to unite
My avocation and my vocation
As my two eyes make one in sight.
Only where love and need are one,
And the work is play for mortal stakes,   70
Is the deed ever really done
For Heaven and the future's sakes.

1934

THE FIGURE A POEM MAKES

PREFACE TO *Collected Poems*

ABSTRACTION is an old story with the philosophers, but it has been like a new toy in the hands of the artists of our day. Why can't we have any one quality of poetry we choose by itself? We can have in thought. Then it will go hard if we can't in practice. Our lives for it.

Granted no one but a humanist much cares how sound a poem is if it is only *a* sound. The sound is the gold in the ore. Then we will have the sound out alone and dispense with the inessential. We do till we make the discovery that the object in writing poetry is to make all poems sound as different as possible from each other, and the resources for that of vowels, consonants, punctuation, syntax, words, sentences, meter are not enough. We need the help of context—meaning—subject matter. That is the greatest help towards variety. All that can be done with words is soon told. So also with meters—particularly in our language where there are virtually but two, strict iambic and loose iambic. The ancients with many were still poor if they depended on meters for all tune. It is painful to watch our sprung-rhythmists straining at the point of omitting one short from a foot for relief from monotony. The possibilities for tune from the dramatic tones of meaning struck across the rigidity of a limited meter are endless. And we are back in poetry as merely one more art of having something to say, sound or unsound. Probably better if sound, because deeper and from wider experience.

Then there is this wildness whereof it is spoken. Granted again that it has an equal claim with sound to being a poem's better half. If it is a wild tune, it is a poem. Our problem then is, as modern abstractionists, to have the wildness pure; to be wild with nothing to be wild about. We bring up as aberrationists, giving way to undirected associations and kicking ourselves from one chance suggestion to another in all directions as of a hot afternoon in the life of a grasshopper. Theme alone can steady us down. Just as the first mystery was how a poem could have a tune in such a straightness as meter, so the second mystery is how a poem can have wildness and at the same time a subject that shall be fulfilled.

It should be of the pleasure of a poem itself to tell how it can. The figure a poem makes. It begins in delight and ends in wisdom. The figure is the same as for love. No one can really hold that the ecstasy should be static and stand still in one place. It begins in delight, it inclines to the impulse, it assumes direction with the first line laid down, it runs a course of lucky events, and ends in a clarification of life —not necessarily a great clarification, such as sects and cults are founded on, but in a momentary stay against confusion. It has denouement. It has an outcome that though unforeseen was predestined from the first image of the original mood—and indeed from the very mood. It is but a trick poem and no poem at all if the best of it was thought of first and saved for the last. It finds its own name as it goes and discovers the best waiting for it in some final phrase at once wise and sad—the happy-sad blend of the drinking song.

No tears in the writer, no tears in the reader. No surprise for the writer, no surprise for the reader. For me the initial delight is in the surprise of remembering something I didn't know I knew. I am in a place, in a situation, as if I had materialized from cloud or risen out of the ground. There is a glad recognition of the long lost and the rest follows. Step by step the wonder of unexpected supply keeps growing. The impressions most useful to my purpose seem always those I was unaware of and so made no note of at the time when taken, and the conclusion is come to that like giants we are always hurling experience ahead of us to pave the future with against the day when we may want to strike a line of purpose across it for somewhere. The line will have the more charm for not being mechanically straight. We enjoy the straight crookedness of a good walking stick. Modern instruments of precision are being used to make things crooked as if by eye and hand in the old days.

I tell how there may be a better wildness of logic than of inconsequence. But the logic is backward, in retrospect, after the act. It must be more felt than seen ahead like prophecy. It must be a revelation, or a series of revelations, as much for the poet as for the reader. For it to be that there must have been the greatest freedom of the material to move about in it and to establish relations in it regardless of time and space, previous relation, and everything but affinity. We prate of freedom. We call our schools free because we are not free to stay away from them till we are sixteen years of age. I have given up my democratic prejudices and now willingly set the lower classes free to be completely taken care of by the upper classes. Political freedom is nothing to me. I bestow it right and left. All I would keep for myself is the freedom of my material—the condition of body and mind now and then to summon aptly from the vast chaos of all I have lived through.

Scholars and artists thrown together are of-

ten annoyed at the puzzle of where they differ. Both work from knowledge; but I suspect they differ most importantly in the way their knowledge is come by. Scholars get theirs with conscientious thoroughness along projected lines of logic; poets theirs cavalierly and as it happens in and out of books. They stick to nothing deliberately, but let what will stick to them like burrs where they walk in the fields. No acquirement is on assignment, or even self-assignment. Knowledge of the second kind is much more available in the wild free ways of wit and art. A school boy may be defined as one who can tell you what he knows in the order in which he learned it. The artist must value himself as he snatches a thing from some previous order in time and space into a new order with not so much as a ligature clinging to it of the old place where it was organic.

More than once I should have lost my soul to radicalism if it had been the originality it was mistaken for by its young converts. Originality and initiative are what I ask for my country. For myself the originality need be no more than the freshness of a poem run in the way I have described: from delight to wisdom. The figure is the same as for love. Like a piece of ice on a hot stove the poem must ride on its own melting. A poem may be worked over once it is in being, but may not be worried into being. Its most precious quality will remain its having run itself and carried away the poet with it. Read it a hundred times: it will forever keep its freshness as a metal keeps its fragrance. It can never lose its sense of a meaning that once unfolded by surprise as it went.

1942

1879 ~ *Vachel Lindsay* ~ 1931

LIKE SANDBURG, Lindsay was a native of Illinois. His father was a religious evangelist and his mother, an artist—significant facts because the son inherited traits from both. He was born in Springfield, rich in memories of Lincoln, and with the exception of temporary excursions, he lived there throughout his life. After completing high school, he attended Hiram College for three years, where he came under the influence of a strong academic tradition in oratory, and began to write poetry somewhat oratorical in tone and spirit. The influence is noticeable in much of his later work.

He left college without a degree in order to study art, first in Chicago, later in New York under Robert Henri. For four years he was a lecturer for the Y.M.C.A., and for a year served the Illinois Anti-Saloon League in a similar capacity. After the manner of the ancient troubadours he took at various times extensive walking tours, through the West, the Southwest, and the industrial East, for the purpose of preaching the Gospel of Beauty. He traveled alone, carried no baggage or money, avoided cities. He did carry a supply of *Rhymes to Be Traded for Bread*, and received both bread and lodging for them. As his fame and popularity grew, he made extensive tours, giving readings from his works in exchange for greater compensation than bread and lodging. He lived for a short time in the State of Washington, where he was married. Later he returned to Springfield.

General Booth Enters into Heaven (1913) was his first volume of poems. It was followed by *The Congo* (1914), *The Chinese Nightingale* (1917), *Collected Poems* (1923), and *Every Soul Is a Circus* (1929). He also published a number of prose works, chief among which are *Adventures While Preaching the Gospel of Beauty* (1914); *The Art of the Moving Picture* (1915); *The Golden Book of Springfield*, the picture of a Utopia shaped by Art and Beauty; and *The Litany of Washington Street* (1929), which contains an essay on Whitman and voices his political creed.

Lindsay has been variously called "minstrel missionary," "vaudevillian," and "poet of jazz." He was, besides an evangelist crusading for beauty, a political idealist and humanitarian. One of his major passions was to improve men and reform their habits. Although a Campbellite himself, he preached neither sect nor creed, but the religion of Beauty. On his tramping tours he frequently read to his hosts a group of three poems, "The Proud Father," "The Illinois Village," and "On the Building of Springfield," in which he not only expressed, as he said, his theory of American civilization, but described concretely the process of achieving the beautiful life, as he conceived it. As the central function of his gospel, he believed in making one's home community the most beautiful place in the world. This is precisely what he did himself and advised Clement Wood to do—return to Birmingham and join the Salvation Army, a combination of religion and glorified boosting of the home town. In a larger sense he attacked industrialism and preached a militant agrarianism.

His poetic theory may be gathered from *The Gospel of Beauty*, *The Art of the Moving Picture*, the prefaces to his *Collected Poems* and to *Every Soul Is a Circus*, and from "The New Localism, an Illustrated Essay for the Village Statesman." This New Localism is based upon his conception of what he calls the New States' Rights, social rather than political in character, and will reach its consummation in the cities and villages of the future, transformed by a new zeal for beauty, in all its phases. According to Professor H. H. Clark, the theory may be summarized as follows: (1) beauty is the mark of *civic* virtue, while ugliness results from misgovernment; (2) the poet must proceed from the local to the universal; (3) poems are by-products of a happy life and are to be shared with the poet's fellow men; (4) other arts contribute to the creation of perfect poems; (5) poems are to be evaluated on the basis of their broad significance. With similar zeal he strove to bring poetry back to its historic place as a possession of the people as a whole, not only of the esoteric few, to make an appeal to average men as well as to the intellectually and culturally élite.

He wrote in both the traditional form, with stanzaic arrangement and rhyme, as well as in the freer form of the new poetry. For effect he frequently relied upon thumping rhythms and a daring, outspoken style, vocally expressive. To some of the poems he added directions for their proper reading and accompaniment as in "General Booth Enters into Heaven." It was in renderings of poems like this that some critics maintained he became at times a cheap vaudevillian.

Lindsay was, however, more than merely a poet of Middle West localism; in a sense he was representative of the America of his time. "The Congo" is symptomatic of the general interest in the Negro and his early backgrounds; the "Santa Fé Trail" renders forth the raucous noises of our mechanical civilization; "Abraham Lincoln Walks at Midnight" is a pacifist poem of social sympathy and pity; the poems of "Johnny Appleseed" are indicative of the widespread interest in American folklore and its poetic significance.

At his best Lindsay speaks with conviction and authority; at his worst he can be silly and even maudlin. His sense of discrimination seems to have weakened during the later years of his life; at any rate there is a distinct falling off in power and quality. More efficient terminal facilities ready to hand might have saved some otherwise too-thinly expanded pieces.

The successive volumes of Lindsay's poetry are brought together in *Collected Poems* (rev. ed., 1925). Volumes which have appeared since that time are *Going-to-the-Stars* (1926); *The Candle in the Cabin* (1926); *Every Soul Is a Circus* (1929). There is also *Selected Poems*, with introduction by H. Spencer (1931). His prose includes *Adventures While Preaching the Gospel of Beauty* (1914); *A Handy Guide for Beggars* (1916); "Adentures While Preaching Hieroglyphic Sermons" and "Adventures While Singing These Songs" in *Collected Poems; The Art of the Moving Picture* (1915, rev. ed., 1922); *The Golden Book of Springfield* (1920); *The Litany of Washington Street* (1929). E. L. Masters, *Vachel Lindsay: a Poet in America* (1935), is an excellent biography. Other biographical studies are S. Graham, *Tramping With a Poet in the Rockies* (1922); E. L. Masters, "The Tragedy of Vachel Lindsay," *American Mercury*, July, 1933; A. E. Trombly, *Vachel Lindsay, Adventurer* (1929); L. C. Wimberly, "Vachel Lindsay," *Frontier and Midland*, March, 1934. Critical studies are C. Aiken, *Scepticisms* (1919); L. Jones, *First Impressions* (1925); A. Kreymborg, *Our Singing Strength* (1929); C. Wood, *Poets of America* (1925); T. K. Whipple,

Spokesmen (1928); B. Weirick, *From Whitman to Sandburg in American Poetry* (1924); H. Monroe, *Poets & Their Art* (1926); G. B. Munson, *Destinations* (1928); T. Maynard, *Our Best Poets* (1922); L. Untermeyer, *American Poetry since 1900* (1923); H. Spencer, "The Life and Death of a Bard," *Bookman*, April, 1932; J. C. Squire and others, *Contemporary American Authors* (1928); H. S. Canby, "Vachel Lindsay," *Saturday Review of Literature*, Jan. 9, 1932; F. Hackett, "Vachel Lindsay," *New Republic*, Part 2, Nov. 18, 1916; J. B. Rittenhouse, "Vachel Lindsay," *South Atlantic Quarterly*, July, 1933; A. E. Trombly, "Vachel Lindsay's Prose," *Southwest Review*, Summer, 1928; C. Van Doren, *Many Minds* (1924); Austin Warren, "The Case of Vachel Lindsay," *Accent*, Summer, 1946; John Drinkwater, "Two American Lives," *Quarterly Review* (London), Jan., 1936; Hazelton Spencer, "The Life and Death of Vachel Lindsay," *American Mercury*, April, 1932. For helpful notes and bibliography see H. H. Clark, *Major American Poets* (1936).

GENERAL WILLIAM BOOTH ENTERS INTO HEAVEN

Lindsay's popularity began with the publication of this poem in Harriet Monroe's *Poetry* in 1913. Many reviewers praised it, among them William Dean Howells. From this time on he was a prominent figure in the revival of interest in poetry.

———

(To be sung to the tune of "The Blood of the Lamb" with indicated instrument.)

I

(*Brass drum beaten loudly.*)

BOOTH led boldly with his big bass drum—
(Are you washed in the blood of the Lamb?)
The Saints smiled gravely and they said:
    "He's come."
(Are you washed in the blood of the Lamb?)
Walking lepers followed, rank on rank,
Lurching bravos from the ditches dank,
Drabs from the alleyways and drug fiends
    pale—
Minds still passion-riden, soul-powers
    frail:—
Vermin-eaten saints with moldy breath,   9
Unwashed legions with the ways of Death—
(Are you washed in the blood of the Lamb?)

(*Banjos.*)

Every slum had sent its half-a-score
The round world over. (Booth had groaned
    for more.)
Every banner that the wide world flies
Bloomed with glory and transcendent dyes.
Big-voiced lasses made their banjos bang,

Tranced, fanatical they shrieked and sang:—
"Are you washed in the blood of the Lamb?"
Hallelujah! It was queer to see
Bull-necked convicts with that land make
    free.   20
Loons with trumpets blowed a blare, blare,
    blare
On, on upward thro' the golden air!
(Are you washed in the blood of the Lamb?)

II

(*Bass drum slower and softer.*)

Booth died blind and still by faith he trod,
Eyes still dazzled by the ways of God.
Booth led boldly, and he looked the chief
Eagle countenance in sharp relief,
Beard a-flying, air of high command
Unabated in that holy land.

(*Sweet flute music.*)

Jesus came from out the courthouse door,   30
Stretched his hands above the passing poor.
Booth saw not, but led his queer ones there
Round and round the mighty courthouse
    square.
Yet in an instant all that blear review
Marched on spotless, clad in raiment new.
The lame were straightened, withered limbs
    uncurled
And blind eyes opened on a new, sweet world.

(*Bass drum louder.*)

Drabs and vixens in a flash made whole!
Gone was the weasel-head, the snout, the
    jowl!

Sages and sibyls now, and athletes clean,   40
Rulers of empires, and of forests green!

(Grand chorus of all instruments. Tambourines
to the foreground.)

The hosts were sandalled, and their wings
    were fire!
(Are you washed in the blood of the Lamb?)
But their noise played havoc with the angel-
    choir.
(Are you washed in the blood of the
    Lamb?)
Oh, shout Salvation! It was good to see
Kings and Princes by the Lamb set free.

The banjos rattled and the tambourines
Jing-jing-jingled in the hands of Queens.

(Reverently sung, no instruments.)

And when Booth halted by the curb for
    prayer   50
He saw his Master thro' the flag-filled air.
Christ came gently with a robe and crown
For Booth the soldier, while the throng knelt
    down.
He saw King Jesus. They were face to face,
And he knelt a-weeping in that holy place
Are you washed in the blood of the Lamb?
                    1913

From THE CONGO

    Many of Lindsay's poems are built upon impressions of sound. "The Congo" represents phases of life among African Negroes; the "Santa Fé Trail" catches the noise of contemporary industrial civilization.

I. Their Basic Savagery

FAT black bucks in a wine-barrel room,
Barrel-house kings, with feet unstable,
Sagged and reeled and pounded on the table,   *A deep rolling bass.*
Pounded on the table,
Beat an empty barrel with the handle of a broom,
Hard as they were able,
Boom, boom, BOOM,
With a silk umbrella and the handle of a broom.
Boomlay, boomlay, boomlay, BOOM.
THEN I had religion, THEN I had a vision.   10
I could not turn from their revel in derision.
THEN I SAW THE CONGO, CREEPING THROUGH THE BLACK,   *More   deliberate.*
CUTTING THROUGH THE FOREST WITH A GOLDEN TRACK.   *Solemnly chanted.*
Then along that riverbank
A thousand miles
Tattoed cannibals danced in files;
Then I heard the boom of the blood-lust song
And a thigh-bone beating on a tin-pan gong.
And "BLOOD" screamed the whistles and the fifes of the warriors,   *A rapidly*
"BLOOD" screamed the skull-faced, lean witch-doctors,   20   *piling climax*
                                                 of speed and
"Whirl ye the deadly voo-doo rattle,   *racket.*
Harry the uplands,
Steal all the cattle,
Rattle-rattle, rattle-rattle,
Bing!
Boomlay, boomlay, boomlay, BOOM,"
A roaring, epic, rag-time tune   *With   a philo-*
From the mouth of the Congo   *sophic pause.*
To the Mountains of the Moon.
Death is an Elephant,   30

Torch-eyed and horrible,
Foam-flanked and terrible.
BOOM, steal the pygmies,
BOOM, kill the Arabs,
BOOM, kill the white men,
Hoo, Hoo, Hoo.
Listen to the yell of Leopold's ghost
Burning in Hell for his hand-maimed host.
Hear how the demons chuckle and yell
Cutting his hands off, down in Hell.
Listen to the creepy proclamation,
Blown through the lairs of the forest-nation,
Blown past the white-ants' hill of clay,
Blown past the marsh where the butterflies play:—
"Be careful what you do,
Or Mumbo-Jumbo, God of the Congo,
And all of the other
Gods of the Congo,
Mumbo-Jumbo will hoo-doo you,
Mumbo-Jumbo will hoo-doo you,
Mumbo-Jumbo will hoo-doo you."

30

Shrilly and with a heavily accented meter.

40

All the o sounds very golden.

Heavy accents very heavy.

Light accents very light. Last line whispered.

50

II. *Their Irrepressible High Spirits*

WILD crap-shooters with a whoop and a call
Danced the juba in their gambling hall
And laughed fit to kill, and shook the town,
And guyed the policemen and laughed them down
With a boomlay, boomlay, boomlay, BOOM.
THEN I SAW THE CONGO, CREEPING THROUGH THE BLACK,
CUTTING THROUGH THE FOREST WITH A GOLDEN TRACK.
A negro fairyland swung into view,
A minstrel river
Where dreams come true.
The ebony palace soared on high
Through the blossoming trees to the evening sky.
The inlaid porches and casements shone
With gold and ivory and elephant-bone.
And the black crowd laughed till their sides were sore
At the baboon butler in the agate door,
And the well-known tunes of the parrot band
That trilled on the bushes of that magic land.
A troupe of skull-faced witch-men came
Through the agate doorway in suits of flame,
Yea, long-tailed coats with a gold-leaf crust
And hats that were covered with diamond-dust.
And the crowd in the court gave a whoop and a call
And danced the juba from wall to wall.
But the witch-men suddenly stilled the throng
With a stern cold glare, and a stern old song:—
"Mumbo-Jumbo will hoo-doo you." . . .

Rather shrill and high.

Read exactly as in first section.

Lay emphasis on the delicate ideas. Keep as light-footed as possible.

10

20

With pomposity.

With a great deliberation and ghostliness.

Just then from the doorway, as fat as shotes,
Came the cake-walk princes in their long red coats,
Canes with a brilliant lacquer shine,
And tall silk hats that were red as wine.   30
And they pranced with their butterfly partners there,
Coal-black maidens with pearls in their hair,
Knee-skirts trimmed with the jassamine sweet,
And bells on their ankles and little black feet.
And the couples railed at the chant and the frown
Of the witch-men lean, and laughed them down.
(Oh, rare was the revel, and well worth while
That made those glowering witch-men smile.)
The cake-walk royalty then began   40
To walk for a cake that was tall as a man
To the tune of "Boomlay, boomlay, BOOM,"
While the witch-man laughed, with a sinister air,
And sang with the scalawags prancing there:—
"Walk with care, walk with care,
Or Mumbo-Jumbo, God of the Congo,
And all of the other Gods of the Congo,
Mumbo-Jumbo will hoo-doo you.
Beware, beware, walk with care,
Boomlay, boomlay, boomlay, boom.   50
Boomlay, boomlay, boomlay, boom.
Boomlay, boomlay, boomlay, boom.
Boomlay, boomlay, boomlay,
BOOM."
(Oh, rare was the revel, and well worth while
That made those glowering witch-men smile.)

With overwhelming assurance, good cheer, and pomp.

With growing speed and sharply marked dance-rhythm.

With a touch of Negro dialect, and as rapidly as possible toward the end.

Slow philosophic calm.

III. *The Hope of Their Religion*

A good old Negro in the slums of the town
Preached at a sister for her velvet gown.
Howled at a brother for his low-down ways,
His prowling, guzzling, sneak-thief days.
Beat on the Bible till he wore it out
Starting the jubilee revival shout.
And some had visions, as they stood on chairs,
And sang of Jacob and the golden stairs,
And they all repented, a thousand strong
From their stupor and savagery and sin and wrong   10
And slammed with their hymn books till they shook the room
With "glory, glory, glory,"
And "Boom, boom, BOOM."
THEN I SAW THE CONGO, CREEPING THROUGH THE BLACK,
CUTTING THROUGH THE JUNGLE WITH A GOLDEN TRACK.
And the gray sky opened like a new-rent veil
And showed the Apostles with their coats of mail.
In bright white steel they were seated round
And their fire-eyes watched where the Congo wound.

Heavy bass. With a literal imitation of camp-meeting racket, and trance.

Exactly as in the first section. Begin with terror and power, end with joy.

And the twelve Apostles, from their thrones on high 20
Thrilled all the forest with their heavenly cry:—

Sung to the tune of "Hark, ten thousand harps and voices."

"Mumbo-Jumbo will die in the jungle;
Never again will he hoo-doo you,
Never again will he hoo-doo you."
Then along that river, a thousand miles
The vine-snared trees fell down in files.

With growing deliberation and joy.

Pioneer angels cleared the way
For a Congo paradise, for babes at play,
For sacred capitals, for temples clean.
Gone were the skull-faced witch-men lean. 30
There, where the wild ghost-gods had wailed

In a rather high key—as delicately as possible.

A million boats of the angels sailed
With oars of silver, and prows of blue
And silken pennants that the sun shone through.
'Twas a land transfigured, 'twas a new creation.
Oh, a singing wind swept the Negro nation
And on through the backwoods clearing flew:—

To the tune of "Hark, ten thousand harps and voices."

"Mumbo-Jumbo is dead in the jungle.
Never again will he hoo-doo you,
Never again will he hoo-doo you." 40

Redeemed were the forests, the beasts and the men,
And only the vulture dared again
By the far, lone mountains of the moon
To cry, in the silence, the Congo tune:—

Dying down into a penetrating, terrified whisper.

Mumbo-Jumbo will hoo-doo you,
"Mumbo-Jumbo will hoo-doo you.
Mumbo ... Jumbo ... will ... hoo-doo ... you."

1914

THE SANTA-FÉ TRAIL (A HUMORESQUE)

(I asked the old Negro: "What is that bird that sings so well?" He answered: "That is the Rachel-Jane." "Hasn't it another name—lark, or thrush, or the like?" "No. Jus' Rachel-Jane.")

I. In Which a Racing Auto Comes from the East

THIS is the order of the music of the morning:—
First, from the far East comes but a crooning.

To be sung delicately, to an improvised tune.

The crooning turns to a sunrise singing.
Hark to the *calm*-horn, *balm*-horn, *psalm*-horn.
Hark to the *faint*-horn, *quaint*-horn, *saint*-horn. ...

Hark to the *pace*-horn, *chase*-horn, *race*-horn.

To be sung or read with great speed.

And the holy veil of the dawn has gone.
Swiftly the brazen car comes on.
It burns in the East as the sunrise burns.
I see great flashes where the far trail turns. 10
Its eyes are lamps like the eyes of dragons.
It drinks gasoline from big red flagons.

Butting through the delicate mists of the morning,
It comes like lightning, goes past roaring.
It will hail all the windmills, taunting, ringing,
Dodge the cyclones,
Count the milestones,
On through the ranges the prairie-dog tills—
Scooting past the cattle on the thousand hills. . . .
Ho for the *tear*-horn, *scare*-horn, *dare*-horn,
Ho for the *gay*-horn, *bark*-horn, *bay*-horn.
Ho for Kansas, land that restores us
When houses choke us, and great books bore us!
Sunrise Kansas, harvesters' Kansas,
A million men have found you before us.

20 *To be read or sung in a rolling bass, with some deliberation.*

II. In Which Many Autos Pass Westward

I want live things in their pride to remain.
I will not kill one grasshopper vain
Though he eats a hole in my shirt like a door.
I let him out, give him one chance more.
Perhaps, while he gnaws my hat in his whim,
Grasshopper lyrics occur to him.

In an even, deliberate, narrative manner.

30

I am a tramp by the long trail's border,
Given to squalor, rags and disorder.
I nap and amble and yawn and look,
Write fool-thoughts in my grubby book,
Recite to the children, explore at my ease,
Work when I work, beg when I please,
Give crank-drawings, that make folks stare
To the half-grown boys in the sunset glare,
And get me a place to sleep in the hay
At the end of a live-and-let-live day.

40

I find in the stubble of the new-cut weeds
A whisper and a feasting, all one needs:
The whisper of the strawberries, white and red
Here where the new-cut weeds lie dead.
But I would not walk all alone till I die
Without some life-drunk horns going by.
And up round this apple-earth they come
Blasting the whispers of the morning dumb:—
Cars in a plain realistic row.
And fair dreams fade
When the raw horns blow.

50

On each snapping pennant
A big black name:—
The careering city
Whence each car came.
They tour from Memphis, Atlanta, Savannah,

Tallahassee and Texarkana.
They tour from St. Louis, Columbus, Manistee,
They tour from Peoria, Davenport, Kankakee.   60
Cars from Concord, Niagara, Boston,
Cars from Topeka, Emporia, and Austin.
Cars from Chicago, Hannibal, Cairo.
Cars from Alton, Oswego, Toledo.
Cars from Buffalo, Kokomo, Delphi,
Cars from Lodi, Carmi, Loami.
Ho for Kansas, land that restores us
When houses choke us, and great books bore us!
While I watch the highroad
And look at the sky,   70
While I watch the clouds in amazing grandeur
Roll their legions without rain
Over the blistering Kansas plain—
While I sit by the milestone
And watch the sky,
The United States
Goes by.

Like a train-caller in a Union Depot.

Listen to the iron-horns, ripping, racking.
Listen to the quack-horns, slack and clacking.
Way down the road, trilling like a toad,   80
Here comes the *dice*-horn, here comes the *vice*-horn,
Here comes the *snarl*-horn, *brawl*-horn, *lewd*-horn,
Followed by the *prude*-horn, bleak and squeaking:—
(Some of them from Kansas, some of them from Kansas.)
Here comes the *hod*-horn, *plod*-horn, *sod*-horn,
Nevermore-to-*roam*-horn, *loam*-horn, *home*-horn.
(Some of them from Kansas, some of them from Kansas.)

To be given very harshly, with a snapping explosiveness.

> Far away the Rachel-Jane
> Not defeated by the horns
> Sings amid a hedge of thorns:—   90
> "Love and life,
> Eternal youth—
> Sweet, sweet, sweet, sweet,
> Dew and glory,
> Love and truth,
> Sweet, sweet, sweet, sweet."

To be read or sung, well-nigh in a whisper.

WHILE SMOKE-BLACK FREIGHTS ON THE DOUBLE-TRACKED RAIL-
   ROAD,
DRIVEN AS THOUGH BY THE FOUL FIEND'S OX-GOAD,
SCREAMING TO THE WEST COAST, SCREAMING TO THE EAST,
CARRY OFF A HARVEST, BRING BACK A FEAST,   100
AND HARVESTING MACHINERY AND HARNESS FOR THE BEAST,
THE HAND-CARS WHIZ, AND RATTLE ON THE RAILS,
THE SUNLIGHT FLASHES ON THE TIN DINNER-PAILS.

Louder and louder, faster and faster.

And then, in an instant, ye modern men,
Behold the procession once again,
The United States goes by!

In a rolling bass, with increasing deliberation.

Listen to the iron-horns, ripping, racking,
Listen to the *wise*-horn, desperate-to-*advise* horn,
Listen to the *fast*-horn, *kill*-horn, *blast*-horn. . . .

With a snapping explosiveness.

       Far away the Rachel-Jane   110
       Not defeated by the horns
       Sings amid a hedge of thorns:—

To be sung or read well-nigh in a whisper.

       Love and life,
       Eternal youth,
       Sweet, sweet, sweet, sweet,
       Dew and glory,
       Love and truth.
       Sweet, sweet, sweet, sweet.

The mufflers open on a score of cars
With wonderful thunder,   120
Crack, crack, crack,
Crack-crack, crack-crack,
Crack, crack, crack,

To be brawled in the beginning with a snapping explosiveness, ending in a languorous chant.

Listen to the gold-horn . . .
Old-horn . . .
Cold horn . . .
And all of the tunes, till the night comes down
On hay-stack, and ant-hill, and wind-bitten town.
Then far in the west, as in the beginning,
Dim in the distance, sweet in retreating,   130
Hark to the faint-horn, quaint-horn, saint-horn,
Hark to the calm-horn, balm-horn, psalm-horn. . . .

To be sung to exactly the same whispered tune as the first five lines.

They are hunting the goals that they understand:—
San-Francisco and the brown sea-sand.
My goal is the mystery the beggars win.

This section beginning sonorously, ending in a languorous whisper.

I am caught in the web the night-winds spin.
The edge of the wheat-ridge speaks to me.
I talk with the leaves of the mulberry tree.
And now I hear, as I sit all alone
In the dusk, by another big Santa-Fé stone,   140
The souls of the tall corn gathering round
And the gay little souls of the grass in the ground.
Listen to the tale the cottonwood tells.
Listen to the windmills, singing o'er the wells.
Listen to the whistling flutes without price
Of myriad prophets out of paradise.
Harken to the wonder
That the night-air carries. . . .
Listen . . . to . . . the . . . whisper . . .
Of . . . the . . . prairie . . . fairies   150

To the same whispered tune as the Rachel-Jane song . but very slowly.

       Singing o'er the fairy plain:—
       "Sweet, sweet, sweet, sweet.
       Love and glory,
       Stars and rain,
       Sweet, sweet, sweet, sweet. . . ."

1914

ABRAHAM LINCOLN WALKS AT MIDNIGHT

(In Springfield, Illinois)

One of the significant poems called forth by the first World War.

It is portentous, and a thing of state
That here at midnight, in our little town
A mourning figure walks, and will not rest,
Near the old courthouse pacing up and down,

Or by his homestead, or in shadowed yards
He lingers where his children used to play,
Or through the market, on the well-worn
      stones
He stalks until the dawn-stars burn away.

A bronzed, lank man! His suit of ancient
      black,
A famous high top-hat and plain worn shawl
Make him the quaint great figure that men
      love,   11
The prairie-lawyer, master of us all.

He cannot sleep upon his hillside now.
He is among us:—as in times before!
And we who toss and lie awake for long
Breathe deep, and start, to see him pass the
      door.

His head is bowed. He thinks on men and
      kings.
Yea, when the sick world cries, how can he
      sleep?
Too many peasants fight, they know not
      why,
Too many homesteads in black terror weep. 20

The sins of all the war-lords burn his heart.
He sees the dreadnaughts scouring every
      main.
He carries on his shawl-wrapped shoulders
      now
The bitterness, the folly and the pain.

He cannot rest until a spirit-dawn
Shall come;—the shining hope of Europe free:
The league of sober folk, the Workers' Earth,
Bringing long peace to Cornland, Alp and
      Sea.

It breaks his heart that kings must murder
      still,
That all his hours of travail here for men   30
Seem yet in vain. And who will bring white
      peace
That he may sleep upon his hill again?

                                                 1914

THE GHOST OF THE BUFFALOES

A forgotten era in the frontier life on the great plain is here restored and vivified.

Last night at black midnight I woke with a
      cry,
The windows were shaking, there was thunder
      on high,
The floor was a-tremble, the door was a-jar,
White fires, crimson fires, shone from afar.
I rushed to the door yard. The city was gone.
My home was a hut without orchard or lawn.
It was mud-smear and logs near a whispering
      stream,
Nothing else built by man could I see in my
      dream . . .
Then . . .
Ghost-kings came headlong, row upon row,
Gods of the Indians, torches aglow.   11

They mounted the bear and the elk and the
      deer,
And eagles gigantic, aged and sere,
They rode long-horn cattle, they cried "A-la-
      la."
They lifted the knife, the bow, and the spear,
They lifted ghost-torches from dead fires
      below,
The midnight made grand with the cry "A-la-
      la."
The midnight made grand with a red-god
      charge,
A red-god show,
A red-god show,   20
"A-la-la, a-la-la, a-la-la, a-la-la."

With bodies like bronze, and terrible eyes,
Came the rank and the file, with catamount
      cries,
Gibbering, yipping, with hollow-skull clacks,
Riding white bronchos with skeleton backs,
Scalp-hunters, beaded and spangled and bad,
Naked and lustful and foaming and mad,

Flashing primeval demoniac scorn,
Blood-thirst and pomp amid darkness reborn,
Power and glory that sleep in the grass   30
While the winds and the snows and the great
    rains pass.
They crossed the gray river, thousands
    abreast,
They rode in infinite lines to the west,
Tide upon tide of strange fury and foam,
Spirits and wraiths, the blue was their home,
The sky was their goal where the star-flags
    are furled,
And on past those far golden splendors they
    whirled.
They burned to dim meteors, lost in the deep.
And I turned in dazed wonder, thinking of
    sleep.
And the wind crept by   40
Alone, unkempt, unsatisfied,
The wind cried and cried—
Muttered of massacres long past,
Buffaloes in shambles vast . . .
An owl said "Hark, what is a-wing?"
I heard a cricket carolling,
I heard a cricket carolling,
I heard a cricket carolling.
Then . . .
Snuffing the lightning that crashed from on
    high   50
Rose royal old buffaloes, row upon row.
The lords of the prairie came galloping by.
And I cried in my heart "A-la-la, a-la-la,
A red-god show,
A red-god show,
A-la-la, a-la-la, a-la-la, a-la-la."

Buffaloes, buffaloes, thousands abreast,
A scourge and amazement, they swept to the
    west.
With black bobbing noses, with red rolling
    tongues,
Coughing forth steam from their leather-
    wrapped lungs,   60
Cows with their calves, bulls big and vain,
Goring the laggards, shaking the mane,
Stamping flint feet, flashing moon eyes,
Pompous and owlish, shaggy and wise.
Like sea-cliffs and caves resounded their ranks
With shoulders like waves, and undulant
    flanks,
Tide upon tide of strange fury and foam,

Spirits and wraiths, the blue was their home,
The sky was their goal where the star-flags
    are furled,
And on past those far golden splendors they
    whirled.   70
They burned to dim meteors, lost in the deep,
And I turned in dazed wonder, thinking of
    sleep.

I heard a cricket's cymbals play,
A scarecrow lightly flapped his rags,
And a pan that hung by his shoulder rang,
Rattled and thumped in a listless way,
And now the wind in the chimney sang,
The wind in the chimney,
The wind in the chimney,
The wind in the chimney,   80
Seemed to say —
"Dream, boy, dream,
If you anywise can.
To dream is the work
Of beast or man.
Life is the west-going dream-storm's breath,
Life is a dream, the sigh of the skies,
The breath of the stars, that nod on their
    pillows
With their golden hair mussed over their
    eyes."
The locust played on his musical wing,   90
Sang to his mate of love's delight.
I heard the whippoorwill's soft fret.
I heard a cricket carolling,
I heard a cricket carolling,
I heard a cricket carolling,
I heard a cricket say "Good-night, good-
    night,
Good-night, good-night, . . . good-night."

                    1917

From THE BOOKER WASHINGTON TRILOGY

A MEMORIAL TO BOOKER T. WASHINGTON

I. *Simon Legree:—A Negro Sermon*

(To be read in your own variety of Negro dialect.)

LEGREE's big house was white and green.
His cotton-fields were the best to be seen.
He had strong horses and opulent cattle,
And bloodhounds bold, with chains that
    would rattle.

His garret was full of curious things
Books of magic, bags of gold,
And rabbits' feet on long twine strings.
But he went down to the Devil.

Legree he sported a brass-buttoned coat,
A snake-skin necktie, a blood-red shirt.   10
Legree he had a beard like a goat,
And a thick hairy neck, and eyes like dirt.
His puffed-out cheeks were fish-belly white,
He had great long teeth, and an appetite.
He ate raw meat, 'most every meal,
And rolled his eyes till the cat would squeal.

His fist was an enormous size
To mash poor niggers that told him lies
He was surely a witch-man in disguise.
But he went down to the Devil.   20

He wore hip-boots, and would wade all day
To capture his slaves that fled away.
But he went down to the Devil.

He beat poor Uncle Tom to death
Who prayed for Legree with his last breath.
Then Uncle Tom to Eva flew,
To the high sanctoriums bright and new;
And Simon Legree stared up beneath,
And cracked his heels, and ground his teeth:
And went down to the Devil.   30

He crossed the yard in the storm and gloom;
He went into his grand front room.
He said, "I killed him, and I don't care."
He kicked a hound, he gave a swear;
He tightened his belt, he took a lamp,
Went down cellar to the webs and damp.

There in the middle of the mouldy floor
He heaved up a slab, he found a door—
And went down to the Devil.

His lamp blew out, but his eyes burned
    bright.   40
Simon Legree stepped down all night—
Down, down to the Devil.
Simon Legree reached the place,
He saw one half of the human race,
He saw the Devil on a wide green throne,
Gnawing the meat from a big ham-bone,
And he said to Mister Devil:

"I see that you have much to eat—
A red ham-bone is surely sweet.
I see that you have lion's feet;   50
I see your frame is fat and fine,
I see you drink your poison wine—
Blood and burning turpentine."

And the Devil said to Simon Legree:
"I like your style, so wicked and free.
Come sit and share my throne with me,
And let us bark and revel."
And there they sit and gnash their teeth,
And each one wears a hop-vine wreath.
They are matching pennies and shooting
    craps,   60
They are playing poker and taking naps.
And old Legree is fat and fine:
He eats the fire, he drinks the wine—
Blood and burning turpentine—
    Down, down with the Devil;
    Down, down with the Devil;
    Down, down with the Devil.

1917

1878 ~ *Carl Sandburg* ~ —

LIKE HIS contemporary, Lindsay, Sandburg is a product of the Middle West. He
is a native of Galesburg, Illinois, the son of Swedish immigrant parents who
changed their name from Johnson to Sandburg in order to avoid confusion with the
many other Johnsons. The boy contributed to his support by serving in turn as
milk peddler, barbershop porter, sceneshifter in a theater, brickyard laborer, dish-

washer, and harvest hand—employment which undoubtedly gave direction to his later social sympathies. He saw military service in Puerto Rico during the Spanish-American War, and after his discharge entered Lombard College, from which he was graduated in 1902.

Sandburg chose newspaper work as the most likely means of giving expression to his social ideals, which he also translated into more tangible forms as organizer for the Social Democratic party. For two years he was secretary to the Mayor of Milwaukee.

In 1918 he accepted an appointment as editorial writer on the staff of the *Chicago Daily News*, a post which he held for many years. The publication in 1914 of "Chicago," for which he received the Levinson Poetry Prize, marks the definite beginning of his career as a poet.

He has published numerous volumes of poetry, chief of them being *Chicago Poems* (1915), *Cornhuskers* (1918), *Smoke and Steel* (1920), *Slabs of the Sunburnt West* (1922), *Good Morning, America* (1928), and *The People, Yes* (1936). He has also edited *The American Songbag* (1927), a collection of folk ballads and folk tunes on which he is an authority, and which he sings in his platform entertainments. The first two volumes of his monumental study of Lincoln appeared in 1926 under the title of *Abraham Lincoln: The Prairie Years*—a study completed in 1939 by the publication of four more volumes called *Abraham Lincoln: The War Years*.

In *Good Morning, America* Sandburg published thirty-eight "Tentative (First Model) Definitions of Poetry." One gathers from them that Sandburg believes poetry to be expressed in the medium of language, leaving an effect of music, cadence, "wavelengths," and overtones. Inwardly, it seems to be a process of imposing the sublime upon the ridiculous. Its body consists largely of implications, universal deductions from the sphere of the particular. Life is hard, coarse, sometimes brutal; poetry softens it, gives it meaning, beauty, and direction. The most striking characteristic of the definitions is the sharp contrast between the two factors of poetry, as for instance "kinetic arrangement of static syllables," "synthesis of hyacinths and biscuits."

Sandburg is a Socialist, and because he is an insistent pleader for justice to the unfortunate, some have come to regard many of his poems as pieces of propaganda. There can be no question about his sincerity in his sympathy for the downtrodden. The real question is whether the poems are propaganda to the exclusion of art.

In his poetry Sandburg often speaks out openly for "the common man," against the ugliness of industrial America, the venality of the exploiter. He is attracted by the vulgar energy of the industrial city, the factory, and the steel mill. He is like Whitman in often allowing announcement and declamation to substitute for poetic treatment of subject. In some of his shorter poems, his use of imagery suggests an indebtedness to the American and English Imagists who were publishing in Harriet

Monroe's *Poetry* at the same time as he. Sandburg's poetry, however, shows very little of the analytic sense of language, the appreciation of the quality of word and image which characterized the more genuine followers of the Imagist "revolt." He has an enormous "research" energy which he uses to accumulate facts; but these facts are often only superficially organized. One is quite generally led away from the poetry into a consideration of the right or wrong (and the degree or violence of right and wrong) of its subject—forced by a compelling sympathy and sentiment to ignore the serious errors in poetic taste and logical order which he commits.

Sandburg's successive volumes of poetry are *Chicago Poems* (1916); *Cornhuskers* (1918); *Smoke and Steel* (1920); *Slabs of the Sunburnt West* (1922); *Good Morning, America* (1928); *Early Moon* (poems for children) (1930). In biography he has written *Abraham Lincoln: The Prairie Years* (2 vols., 1926); *Abraham Lincoln: The War Years* (4 vols., 1939); and *Mary Lincoln, Wife and Widow* (1932). His only novel, *Remembrance Rock*, appeared in 1948. *Rootabaga Stories* (1922), *Rootabaga Pigeons* (1923), and *Potato Face* (1930) are stories for children. He is also the compiler of *The American Songbag* (1927). Biographical information may be obtained in H. Hansen, *Carl Sandburg: the Man and His Poetry* (1925); D. Karsner, *Sixteen Authors to One* (1928); W. Yust, "Carl Sandburg, Human Being," *Bookman*, Jan., 1921; H. Hansen, "Carl Sandburg—Poet of the Prairie," *Pictorial Review*, Sept. 1925. For criticism the following will be helpful: P. H. Boynton, *Some Contemporary Americans* (1924); H. Hansen, *Midwest Portraits* (1923); L. Jones, *First Impressions* (1925); A. Kreymborg, *Our Singing Strength* (1929); A. Lowell, *Tendencies in Modern American Poetry* (1917); S. P. Sherman, *Americans* (1922); T. K. Whipple, *Spokesmen* (1928); C. Wood, *Poets of America* (1925); L. Untermeyer, *American Poetry since 1900* (1923); H. Monroe, *Poets & Their Art* (1926); C. Van Doren, *Many Minds* (1924); B. Weirick, *From Whitman to Sandburg in American Poetry* (1924); C. H. Compton, "Who Reads Carl Sandburg?", *South Atlantic Quarterly*, April, 1929; C. Aiken, *Scepticisms* (1919); H. M. Jones, "Backgrounds of Sorrow," *Virginia Quarterly Review*, Jan., 1927; R. Brenner, *Ten Modern Poets* (1930); R. West, *Saturday Review of Literature*, Sept. 4, 1926; E. Carnevali, "Our Great Carl Sandburg," *Poetry*, Feb., 1921; Horace Gregory and Marya Zaturenska, *A History of American Poetry* (1946).

CHICAGO

Hog Butcher for the World,
Tool Maker, Stacker of Wheat,
Player with Railroads and the Nation's Freight Handler;
Stormy, husky, brawling,
City of the Big Shoulders:

They tell me you are wicked, and I believe them; for I have seen your painted women under the
    gas lamps luring the farm boys.
And they tell me you are crooked, and I answer: Yes, it is true I have seen the gunman kill and
    go free to kill again.
And they tell me you are brutal, and my reply is: On the faces of women and children I have
    seen the marks of wanton hunger.
And having answered so I turn once more to those who sneer at this my city, and I give them
    back the sneer and say to them:
Come and show me another city with lifted head singing so proud to be alive and coarse and
    strong and cunning.   10

Flinging magnetic curses amid the toil of piling job on job, here is a tall bold slugger set vivid
    against the little soft cities;
Fierce as a dog with tongue lapping for action, cunning as a savage pitted against the wilderness,
        Bareheaded,
        Shovelling,
        Wrecking,
        Planning,
        Building, breaking, rebuilding,
Under the smoke, dust all over his mouth, laughing with white teeth,
Under the terrible burden of destiny laughing as a young man laughs,
Laughing even as an ignorant fighter laughs who has never lost a battle,   20
Bragging and laughing that under his wrist is the pulse, and under his ribs the heart of the people,
    Laughing!
Laughing the stormy, husky, brawling laughter of Youth, half-naked, sweating, proud to be
    Hog Butcher, Tool Maker, Stacker of Wheat, Player with Railroads and Freight Handler to
    the Nation.   1916

THE HARBOR

PASSING through huddled and ugly walls
By doorways where women
Looked from their hunger-deep eyes,
Haunted with shadows of hunger-hands,
Out from the huddled and ugly walls,
I came sudden, at the city's edge,
On a blue burst of lake,
Long lake waves breaking under the sun
On a spray-flung curve of shore;
And a fluttering storm of gulls,   10
Masses of great gray wings
And flying white bellies
Veering and whirling free in the open.

    1916

A TEAMSTER'S FAREWELL

Sobs En Route to a Penitentiary

GOOD-BYE now to the streets and the clash of
  wheels and locking hubs,
The sun coming on the brass buckles and harness knobs,
The muscles of the horses sliding under their
  heavy haunches,
Good-bye now to the traffic policeman and
  his whistle,
The smash of the iron hoofs on the stones,
All the crazy wonderful slamming roar of the
  street—
O God, there's noises I'm going to be hungry
  for.

    1916

TO A CONTEMPORARY BUNKSHOOTER

YOU come along . . . tearing your shirt . . .
  yelling about Jesus.
    Where do you get that stuff?
    What do you know about Jesus,
Jesus had a way of talking soft and outside of
  a few bankers and higher-ups among the
  con men of Jerusalem everybody liked to
  have this Jesus around because he never
  made any fake passes and everything he said
  went and he helped the sick and gave the
  people hope.

You come along squirting words at us, shaking
  your fist and call us all dam fools so fierce
  the froth slobbers over your lips . . . always
  blabbing we're all going to hell straight off
  and you know all about it.

I've read Jesus' words. I know what he said.
  You don't throw any scare into me. I've got
  your number. I know how much you know
  about Jesus.
He never came near clean people or dirty people but they felt cleaner because he came
  along. It was your crowd of bankers and
  business men and lawyers hired the sluggers
  and murderers who put Jesus out of the
  running.
I say the same bunch backing you nailed the
  nails into the hands of this Jesus of Nazareth. He had lined up against him the same

crooks and strong-arm men now lined up with you paying your way.

This Jesus was good to look at, smelled good, listened good. He threw out something fresh and beautiful from the skin of his body and the touch of his hands wherever he passed along.

You slimy bunkshooter, you put a smut on every human blossom in reach of your rotten breath belching about hell-fire and hiccupping about this Man who lived a clean life in Galilee.   10

When are you going to quit making the carpenters build emergency hospitals for women and girls driven crazy with wrecked nerves from your gibberish about Jesus?— I put it to you again: Where do you get that stuff? what do you know about Jesus?

Go ahead and bust all the chairs you want to. Smash a whole wagon-load of furniture at every performance. Turn sixty somersaults and stand on your nutty head. If it wasn't for the way you scare the women and kids I'd feel sorry for you and pass the hat.

I like to watch a good four-flusher work, but not when he starts people puking and calling for the doctors.

I like a man that's got nerve and can pull off a great original performance, but you— you're only a bug-house pedlar of secondhand gospel—you're only shoving out a phoney imitation of the goods this Jesus wanted free as air and sunlight.

You tell people living in shanties Jesus is going to fix it up all right with them by giving them mansions in the skies after they're dead and the worms have eaten 'em.

You tell $6 a week department store girls all they need is Jesus; you take a steel trust wop, dead without having lived, grey and shrunken at forty years of age, and you tell him to look at Jesus on the cross and he'll be all right.

You tell poor people they don't need any more money on pay day and even if it's fierce to be out of a job, Jesus'll fix that up all right,

all right—all they gotta do is take Jesus the way you say.

I'm telling you Jesus wouldn't stand for the stuff you're handing out. Jesus played it different. The bankers and lawyers of Jerusalem got their sluggers and murderers to go after Jesus just because Jesus wouldn't play their game. He didn't sit in with the big thieves.

I don't want a lot of gab from a bunkshooter in my religion.   19

I won't take my religion from any man who never works except with his mouth and never cherishes any memory except the face of the woman on the American silver dollar.

I ask you to come through and show me where you're pouring out the blood of your life.

I've been to this suburb of Jerusalem they call Golgotha, where they nailed Him, and I know if the story is straight it was real blood ran from His hands and the nail-holes, and it was real blood spurted in red drops where the spear of the Roman soldier rammed in between the ribs of this Jesus of Nazareth.
                                                    1916

FOG

The fog comes
on little cat feet.

It sits looking
over harbor and city
on silent haunches
and then moves on.

                                                    1916

NOCTURNE IN A DESERTED BRICKYARD

Stuff of the moon
Runs on the lapping sand
Out to the longest shadows.
Under the curving willows,
And round the creep of the wave line,
Fluxions of yellow and dusk on the waters
Make a wide dreaming pansy of an old pond in the night.

                                                    1916

COOL TOMBS

WHEN Abraham Lincoln was shovelled into
the tombs, he forgot the copperheads and
the assassin . . . in the dust, in the cool
tombs.

And Ulysses Grant lost all thought of con men
and Wall Street, cash and collateral turned
ashes . . . in the dust, in the cool tombs.

Pocahontas' body, lovely as a poplar, sweet
as a red haw in November or a pawpaw in
May, did she wonder? does she remember?
. . . in the dust, in the cool tombs?

Take any streetful of people buying clothes
and groceries, cheering a hero or throwing
confetti and blowing tin horns . . . tell me
if any get more than the lovers . . . in the
dust . . . in the cool tombs.

1916

WORK GANGS

Compare this poem with Markham's "The Man
with the Hoe."

Box cars run by a mile long.
And I wonder what they say to each other
When they stop a mile long on a sidetrack.
Maybe their chatter goes:
I came from Fargo with a load of wheat up
to the danger line.
I came from Omaha with a load of shorthorns
and they splintered my boards.
I came from Detroit heavy with a load of
flivvers.
I carried apples from the Hood river last year
and this year bunches of bananas from Flor-
ida; they look for me with watermelons from
Mississippi next year.

Hammers and shovels of work gangs sleep in
shop corners
when the dark stars come on the sky and the
night watchmen walk and look.   10

Then the hammer heads talk to the handles,
then the scoops of the shovels talk,
how the day's work nicked and trimmed them,
how they swung and lifted all day,
how the hands of the work gangs smelled of
hope

In the night of the dark stars
when the curve of the sky is a work gang
handle,
in the night on the mile long sidetracks,
in the night where the hammers and shovels
sleep in corners,
the night watchmen stuff their pipes with
dreams—   20
and sometimes they doze and don't care for
nothin',
and sometimes they search their heads for
meanings, stories, stars.
     The stuff of it runs like this:
A long way we come; a long way to go; long
rests and long deep sniffs for our lungs on
the way.
Sleep is a belonging of all; even if all songs
are old songs and the singing heart is
snuffed out like a switchman's lantern with
the oil gone, even if we forget our names
and houses in the finish, the secret of sleep
is left us, sleep belongs to all, sleep is the
first and last and best of all.

People singing; people with song mouths connecting with song hearts; people who must
sing or die; people whose song hearts break
if there is no song mouth; these are my
people.

1920

DEATH SNIPS PROUD MEN

DEATH is stronger than all the governments
because the governments are men and men
die and then death laughs: Now you see
'em, now you don't.

Death is stronger than all proud men and so
death snips proud men on the nose, throws
a pair of dice and says: Read 'em and weep.

Death sends a radiogram every day: When I
want you I'll drop in—and then one day
he comes with a master-key and lets himself in and says: We'll go now.

Death is a nurse mother with big arms: 'Twon't
hurt you at all; it's your time now; you just
need a long sleep, child; what have you had
anyhow better than sleep?

1920

FOUR PRELUDES ON PLAYTHINGS OF THE WIND

"The past is a bucket of ashes"

1

THE woman named To-morrow
sits with a hairpin in her teeth
and takes her time
and does her hair the way she wants it
and fastens at last the last braid and coil
and puts the hairpin where it belongs
and turns and drawls: Well, what of it?
My grandmother, Yesterday, is gone.
What of it? Let the dead be dead.

2

The doors were cedar
and the panels strips of gold
and the girls were golden girls
and the panels read and the girls chanted:
    We are the greatest city,
    the greatest nation:
    nothing like us ever was.
The doors are twisted on broken hinges.
Sheets of rain swish through on the wind
    where the golden girls ran and the panels
        read:
    We are the greatest city,
    the greatest nation,
    nothing like us ever was.

3

It has happened before.
Strong men put up a city and got
    a nation together,
And paid singers to sing and women
    to warble: We are the greatest city,
        the greatest nation,
        nothing like us ever was.

And while the singers sang
and the strong men listened
and paid the singers well
and felt good about it all
    there were rats and lizards who listened
    ... and the only listeners left now
    ... are ... the rats ... and the lizards.

And there are black crows
Crying, "Caw, caw,"
bringing mud and sticks
building a nest

over the words carved
on the door where the panels were cedar
and the strips on the panels were gold
and the golden girls came singing:
    We are the greatest city,
    the greatest nation:
    nothing like us ever was.
The only singers now are crows crying, "Caw,
    caw,"
And the sheets of rain whine in the wind and
    doorways.
And the only listeners now are ... the rats
    ... and the lizards.

4

The feet of the rats
scribble on the door sills;
the hieroglyphs of the rat footprints
chatter the pedigrees of the rats
and babble of the blood
and gabble of the breed
of the grandfathers and the great-grand-
    fathers
of the rats.

And the wind shifts
and the wind on the door sill shifts
and even the writing of the rat footprints
tells us nothing, nothing at all
about the greatest city, the greatest nation
where the strong men listened
and the women warbled: Nothing like us
    ever was.
                                    1920

A.E.F.

THERE will be a rusty gun on the wall, sweet-
    heart,
The rifle grooves curling with flakes of rust.
A spider will make a silver string nest in the
    darkest, warmest corner of it.
The trigger and the range-finder, they too will
    be rusty.
And no hands will polish the gun, and it will
    hang on the wall.
Forefingers and thumbs will point absently
    and casually toward it.
It will be spoken among half-forgotten, wished-
    to-be-forgotten things.
They will tell the spider: Go on, you're doing
    good work.
                                    1920

1876 ~ *Willa Cather* ~ 1947

MISS CATHER was born in Virginia, where her great-grandfather had settled after migrating from England by way of Ireland. When she was eight her family moved to a farm in Nebraska. Here she grew up in tomboy enjoyment of the open prairie spaces, the thrills of farm life, and association with persons of varying nationalities. Since there was no available elementary school, she was taught at home, reading the English classics with her grandmother. Later she attended the high school in Red Cloud, and took her B.A. degree at the University of Nebraska at nineteen. During this time she read much French and Russian fiction. Discontented with the meager cultural opportunities of the Middle West, especially the lack of good music, she secured employment on the Pittsburgh *Daily Leader*. From 1901 to 1906 she taught English in the Alleghany High School, at the same time publishing verse and prose in various periodicals. Her work attracted the attention of S. S. McClure, of whose magazine she became in turn associate and later managing editor. This position brought her in contact with many literary people, developed her sense of literary values, and gave her an indication of public taste. The encouragement she received from her friend, Sarah Orne Jewett, whose *Best Stories* she later edited with an admiring introduction, undoubtedly influenced her decision to abandon editorial work. She resigned in 1912 in order to devote herself to creative writing.

In her book of collected essays, *Not Under Forty* (1936), particularly in "The Novel Démeublé" (first published in 1922), she states the general theory of fiction upon which her work is grounded. She distinguishes between novels as entertainment and novels as art. She is interested only in fiction as art. Assuming herself to be a realist, she takes issue with the realistic practice of securing effect by means of piling up details. Realism, in fact, is not at all a matter of recording what one has observed, but a state of mind, an attitude toward one's material. The novel suffers from too many physical properties which clutter up the scene and obscure what is really significant. Her contention is that artistic effects cannot be produced by what is seen or heard, but by what remains unnamed, an overtone, as it were, what she calls "verbal mood, the emotional aura." Her comparison of Balzac with Hawthorne illustrates her point: the former overfurnished his novels, the latter seldom lets the reader see anything; Balzac is the showman who insists on showing all his wares, Hawthorne is indifferent to surroundings, but makes one feel their presence by suggestion. She is a selective realist who insists upon paring down the material properties, indeed the action itself, to the very minimum consistent with the effect she wishes to create. Bare scenes are the ideal setting. Carefully selected properties, wisely chosen action, a minimum of detail, exhibition and suggestion rather than enumeration, and the firm reliance upon the "unnamed thing" as the master key to the finest artistic effects—these are the main principles of her literary creed.

It is precisely this economy and restraint, the refusal to let herself be drawn into emotional debauches, that has led some readers to the conclusion that she is cold and objective, and that her art lacks sympathy. Her very theory of art presupposes a certain sensitiveness to suggestion, for she herself relies upon suggestion instead of veritistic enumeration of details or a mere chronicling of events.

By some critics Miss Cather has been called the novelist of the transplanted European; by others she is associated with those who attack the village and small-town life generally. There is a trace of truth in each suggestion, but neither tells the whole truth. In *O Pioneers!* (1913) and *My Antonia* (1918), for instance, she does write about transplanted Europeans and their bitter struggles for economic security and spiritual integrity; nor can it be denied that in some of her novels she has in mind the cultural shortcomings of the small town. The truth of the matter is that her work must be regarded from a larger point of view. The note that runs through practically all her writings is the struggle that man is compelled to wage against his environment. This may take the form of a positive attack against the barrenness of the typical prairie village, as in *The Sculptor's Funeral* (1920); but it is also true of the professor who was unable to adjust himself when he suddenly found himself in an atmosphere of wealth and luxury, and of Archbishop Latour who after years of labor finally became the victim of life itself. Although she writes against a Midwest background, her theme is universal and limited to no locality. Her backgrounds are so harmonized, almost submerged, that they are absorbed by the personalities of the characters. Her novels are commentaries on the age-old struggle of man against natural and human evils. In *A Lost Lady* (1923), for example, she projects the gradual degeneration of the heroine, Marian Forrester, against the background of the declining West which was losing its heroic qualities.

Throughout her career, Miss Cather worked for an effect of precision and clarity; this effect is most noticeably achieved in such books as *Death Comes for the Archbishop* and *Shadows on the Rock*, books that can scarcely be called novels, so episodic are their contents. Individual sections of them are masterpieces of detail and order, but together they do not enjoy the unity which a novel calls for. Her most successful novels are the two which give most effectively the impression of the plains and prairies: *My Antonia* and *O Pioneers*. *The Professor's House*, sometimes quite satisfactory, is really a collection of unresolved (or arbitrarily resolved) tensions. *The Song of the Lark* is a strenuous book, a heroic effort to describe a heroine, but awkward and artificial in all but the Nebraska scenes.

The principal theme of Miss Cather's novels is the consequence of a dualism in her interests: she wishes at one and the same time to extol the virtues of provincial life and to hope for or insist upon the advantages of sophistication for her characters. Once she has finished with the pioneer phase of her prairie history, she finds serious defects in the life which survives in the small towns. Her characters take refuge, or find expression, in the arts (principally in music), in religion and in one unfortunate case (*One of Ours*) in war and patriotism. Her characters need identification with the land, but they also need what the land apparently cannot give them.

In the matter of style, Miss Cather is often an extremely self-conscious imitator of Henry James. There are echoes of James in the dialogue of many of her novels. But they do not seem more than half appropriate; she has neither James's subject nor his sensitivity to character. Her best writing goes into the development of simple plots and the description of ingenuous persons. When the situation becomes complicated and requires subtle handling, her treatment is naïve and awkward. Perhaps for this reason, she has written most successfully of people whose faith is adequate to their needs: the pioneer woman of Nebraska, the priest and early settler of Canada and the Southwest.

Miss Cather's novels are *Alexander's Bridge* (1912); *O Pioneers!* (1913); *The Song of the Lark* (1915); *My Antonia* (1918); *One of Ours* (1922); *A Lost Lady* (1923); *The Professor's House* (1925); *My Mortal Enemy* (1926); *Death Comes for the Archbishop* (1927); *Shadows on the Rock* (1931); *Lucy Gayheart* (1935); *Sapphira and the Slave Girl* (1940). Her short stories appear in *The Troll Garden* (1905); *Youth and the Bright Medusa* (1920); *Obscure Destinies* (1932); *The Old Beauty and Others* (1948). Her poems are published in *April Twilights* (1903); *April Twilights and Other Poems* (1923). R. Rapin's *Willa Cather* (1930) is a critical and biographical study. Further biographical material may be found in L. Carroll, "Willa Sibert Cather," *Bookman*, May, 1921; W. Tittle, "Glimpses of Interesting Americans," *Century*, July, 1925. For critical estimates and discussion of Miss Cather's work consult P. H. Boynton, *Some Contemporary Americans* (1924); H. Hartwick, *The Foreground of American Fiction* (1934); H. Hatcher, *Creating the Modern American Novel* (1935); G. Hicks, "The Case Against Willa Cather," *English Journal*, Nov., 1933; L. Morris, "Willa Cather," *North American Review*, May, 1924; L. Kronenberger, "Willa Cather," *Bookman*, Oct., 1931; C. Fadiman, "The Past Recaptured," *Nation*, Dec. 7, 1932; R. Michaud, *The American Novel To-day* (1928); T. K. Whipple, *Spokesmen* (1928); E. S. Sergeant, *Fire Under the Andes* (1927); S. P. Sherman, *Critical Woodcuts* (1926); E. Wagenknecht, "Willa Cather," *Sewanee Review*, 1929; C. Van Doren, *Contemporary American Novelists* (1922); H. van Dyke, *The Man Behind the Book* (1929); W. L. Myers, "The Novel Dedicate," *Virginia Quarterly Review*, July, 1932; P. Edgar, *The Art of the Novel from 1700 to the Present Time* (1933); A. R. Marble, *A Study of the Modern Novel* (1928); A. H. Quinn, *American Fiction* (1936); Maxwell Geismar, *The Last of the Provincials* (1947); Alfred Kazin, *On Native Grounds* (1942); George Snell, *The Shapers of American Fiction* (1947); E. K. Brown, "Willa Cather and the West," *University of Toronto Review*, 1936; R. H. Footman, "The Genius of Willa Cather," *American Literature*, May, 1938; Lionel Trilling, "Willa Cather," *New Republic*, Feb. 10, 1937.

THE SCULPTOR'S FUNERAL

Published in *McClure's Magazine*, Jan., 1905. It was issued later in *Youth and the Bright Medusa*. A general favorite with many of Miss Cather's readers, it seems to have caught the essential attitude of the small town and its effect upon the aspiring young mind.

A GROUP of the townspeople stood on the station siding of a little Kansas town, awaiting the coming of the night train, which was already twenty minutes overdue. The snow had fallen thick over everything; in the pale starlight the line of bluffs across the wide, white meadows south of the town made soft, smoke-colored curves against the clear sky. The men on the siding stood first on one foot and then on the other, their hands thrust deep into their trousers pockets, their overcoats open, their shoulders screwed up with the cold; and they glanced from time to time toward the south-east, where the railroad track wound along the river shore. They conversed in low tones and moved about restlessly, seeming uncertain as to what was expected of them. There was but one of the company who looked as if he knew exactly why he was there, and he kept conspicuously apart; walking to the far end of the platform, returning to the station door, then pacing up the track again, his chin sunk in the high collar of his overcoat, his burly shoulders drooping forward, his gait heavy and dogged. Presently he was approached by a tall, spare, grizzled man clad in a faded Grand Army suit, who shuffled out from the group and advanced with a certain deference, craning his neck forward until his back made the angle of a jack-knife three-quarters open.

"I reckon she's a-goin' to be pretty late agin tonight, Jim," he remarked in a squeaky falsetto. "S'pose it's the snow?"

"I don't know," responded the other man with a shade of annoyance, speaking from out an astonishing cataract of red beard that grew fiercely and thickly in all directions.

The spare man shifted the quill toothpick he was chewing to the other side of his mouth. "It ain't likely that anybody from the East will come with the corpse, I s'pose," he went on reflectively.

"I don't know," responded the other, more curtly than before.

"It's too bad he didn't belong to some lodge or other. I like an order funeral myself. They seem more appropriate for people of some repytation," the spare man continued, with an ingratiating concession in his shrill voice, as he carefully placed his toothpick in his vest pocket. He always carried the flag at the G.A.R. funerals in the town.

The heavy man turned on his heel, without replying, and walked up the siding. The spare man rejoined the uneasy group. "Jim's ez full ez a tick, ez ushel," he commented commiseratingly.

Just then a distant whistle sounded, and there was a shuffling of feet on the platform. A number of lanky boys, of all ages, appeared as suddenly and slimily as eels wakened by the crack of thunder; some came from the waiting-room, where they had been warming themselves by the red stove, or half asleep on the slat benches; others uncoiled themselves from baggage trucks or slid out of express wagons. Two clambered down from the driver's seat of a hearse that stood backed up against the siding. They straightened their stooping shoulders and lifted their heads, and a flash of momentary animation kindled their dull eyes at that cold, vibrant scream, the world-wide call for men. It stirred them like the note of a trumpet; just as it had often stirred the man who was coming home tonight, in his boyhood.

The night express shot, red as a rocket, from out the eastward marsh lands and wound along the river shore under the long lines of shivering poplars that sentinelled the meadows, the escaping steam hanging in gray masses against the pale sky and blotting out the Milky Way. In a moment the red glare from the headlight streamed up the snow-covered track before the siding and glittered on the wet, black rails. The burly man with the dishevelled red beard walked swiftly up the platform toward the approaching train, uncovering his head as he went. The group of men behind him hesitated, glanced questioningly at one another, and awkwardly followed his example. The train stopped, and the crowd shuffled up to the express car just as the door was thrown open, the man in the G.A.R. suit thrusting his head forward with curiosity. The express messenger appeared in the doorway, accompanied by a young man in a long ulster and travelling cap.

"Are Mr. Merrick's friends here?" inquired the young man.

The group on the platform swayed uneasily. Philip Phelps, the banker, responded with dignity: "We have come to take charge of the body. Mr. Merrick's father is very feeble and can't be about."

"Send the agent out here," growled the express messenger, "and tell the operator to lend a hand."

The coffin was got out of its rough-box and down on the snowy platform. The townspeople drew back enough to make room for it, and then formed a close semicircle about it, looking curiously at the palm leaf which lay across the black cover. No one said anything. The baggage man stood by his truck, waiting to get at the trunks. The engine panted heavily, and the fireman dodged in and out among the wheels with his yellow torch and long oil-can, snapping the spindle boxes. The young Bostonian, one of the dead sculptor's pupils who had come with the body, looked about him helplessly. He turned to the banker, the only one of that black, uneasy, stoop-shouldered group who seemed enough of an individual to be addressed.

"None of Mr. Merrick's brothers are here?" he asked uncertainly.

The man with the red beard for the first time stepped up and joined the others. "No, they have not come yet; the family is scattered. The body will be taken directly to the house." He stooped and took hold of one of the handles of the coffin.

"Take the long hill road up, Thompson, it will be easier on the horses," called the liveryman as the undertaker snapped the door of the hearse and prepared to mount to the driver's seat.

Laird, the red-bearded lawyer, turned again to the stranger: "We didn't know whether there would be any one with him or not," he explained. "It's a long walk, so you'd better go up in the hack." He pointed to a single battered conveyance, but the young man replied stiffly: "Thank you, but I think I will go up with the hearse. If you don't object," turning to the undertaker, "I'll ride with you."

They clambered up over the wheels and drove off in the starlight up the long, white hill toward the town. The lamps in the still village were shining from under the low, snow-burdened roofs; and beyond, on every side, the plains reached out into emptiness, peaceful and wide as the soft sky itself, and wrapped in a tangible, white silence.

When the hearse backed up to a wooden sidewalk before a naked, weather-beaten frame house, the same composite, ill-defined group that had stood upon the station siding was huddled about the gate. The front yard was an icy swamp, and a couple of warped planks, extending from the sidewalk to the door, made a sort of rickety footbridge. The gate hung on one hinge, and was opened wide with difficulty. Steavens, the young stranger, noticed that something black was tied to the knob of the front door.

The grating sound made by the casket, as it was drawn from the hearse, was answered by a scream from the house; the front door was wrenched open, and a tall, corpulent woman rushed out bareheaded into the snow and flung herself upon the coffin, shrieking: "My boy, my boy! And this is how you've come home to me!"

As Steavens turned away and closed his eyes with a shudder of unutterable repulsion, another woman, also tall, but flat and angular, dressed entirely in black, darted out of the house and caught Mrs. Merrick by the shoulders, crying sharply: "Come, come, mother; you mustn't go on like this!" Her tone changed to one of obsequious solemnity as she turned to the banker: "The parlor is ready, Mr. Phelps."

The bearers carried the coffin along the narrow boards, while the undertaker ran ahead with the coffin-rests. They bore it into a large, unheated room that smelled of dampness and disuse and furniture polish, and set it down under a hanging lamp ornamented with jingling glass prisms and before a "Rogers group" of John Alden and Priscilla, wreathed with smilax. Henry Steavens stared about him with the sickening conviction that there had been a mistake, and that he had somehow arrived at the wrong destination. He looked at the clover-green Brussels, the fat plush upholstery, among the hand-painted china plaques and panels and vases, for some mark of identification,—for something that might once conceivably have belonged to Harvey Merrick. It was not until he recognized his friend in the crayon portrait of a little boy in kilts and curls, hanging above the piano, that he felt willing to let any of these people approach the coffin.

"Take the lid off, Mr. Thompson; let me see my boy's face," wailed the elder woman between her sobs. This time Steavens looked fearfully, almost beseechingly into her face, red and swollen under its masses of strong, black, shiny hair. He flushed, dropped his eyes, and then, almost incredulously, looked again. There was a kind of power about her face—a kind of brutal handsomeness, even; but it was scarred and furrowed by violence, and so colored and coarsened by fiercer passions that grief seemed never to have laid a gentle finger there. The long nose was distended and knobbed at the end, and there were deep lines on either side of it; her heavy black brows almost met across her forehead, her teeth were large and square, and set far apart—teeth that could tear. She filled the room; the men were obliterated, seemed tossed about like twigs in an angry water, and even Steavens felt himself being drawn into the whirlpool.

The daughter—the tall, raw-boned woman in crêpe, with a mourning comb in her hair which curiously lengthened her long face—sat stiffly upon the sofa, her hands, conspicuous for their large knuckles, folded in her lap, her mouth and eyes drawn down, solemnly awaiting the opening of the coffin. Near the door stood a mulatto woman, evidently a servant in the house, with a timid bearing and emaciated face pitifully sad and gentle. She was weeping silently, the corner of her calico apron lifted to her eyes, occasionally suppressing a long, quivering sob. Steavens walked over and stood beside her.

Feeble steps were heard on the stairs, and an old man, tall and frail, odorous of pipe smoke, with shaggy, unkept grey hair and a dingy beard, tobacco stained about the mouth, entered uncertainly. He went slowly up to the coffin and stood rolling a blue cotton handkerchief between his hands, seeming so pained

and embarrassed by his wife's orgy of grief that he had no consciousness of anything else.

"There, there, Annie, dear, don't take on so," he quavered timidly, putting out a shaking hand and awkwardly patting her elbow. She turned and sank upon his shoulder with such violence that he tottered a little. He did not even glance toward the coffin, but continued to look at her with a dull, frightened, appealing expression, as a spaniel looks at the whip. His sunken cheeks slowly reddened and burned with miserable shame. When his wife rushed from the room, her daughter strode after her with set lips. The servant stole up to the coffin, bent over it for a moment, and then slipped away to the kitchen, leaving Steavens, the lawyer, and the father to themselves. The old man stood looking down at his dead son's face. The sculptor's splendid head seemed even more noble in its rigid stillness than in life. The dark hair had crept down upon the wide forehead; the face seemed strangely long, but in it there was not that repose we expect to find in the faces of the dead. The brows were so drawn that there were two deep lines above the beaked nose, and the chin was thrust forward defiantly. It was as though the strain of life had been so sharp and bitter that death could not at once relax the tension and smooth the countenance into perfect peace—as though he were still guarding something precious, which might even yet be wrested from him.

The old man's lips were working under his stained beard. He turned to the lawyer with timid deference: "Phelps and the rest are comin' back to set up with Harve, ain't they?" he asked. "Thank'ee, Jim, thank'ee." He brushed the hair back gently from his son's forehead. "He was a good boy, Jim; always a good boy. He was ez gentle ez a child and the kindest of 'em all—only we didn't none of us ever onderstand him." The tears trickled slowly down his beard and dropped upon the sculptor's coat.

"Martin, Martin! Oh, Martin! come here," his wife wailed from the top of the stairs. The old man started timorously: "Yes, Annie, I'm coming." He turned away, hesitated, stood for a moment in miserable indecision; then reached back and patted the dead man's hair softly, and stumbled from the room.

"Poor old man, I didn't think he had any tears left. Seems as if his eyes would have gone dry long ago. At his age nothing cuts very deep," remarked the lawyer.

Something in his tone made Steavens glance up. While the mother had been in the room, the young man had scarcely seen any one else; but now, from the moment he first glanced into Jim Laird's florid face and blood-shot eyes, he knew that he had found what he had 10 been heartsick at not finding before—the feeling, the understanding, that must exist in some one, even here.

The man was red as his beard, with features swollen and blurred by dissipation, and a hot, blazing blue eye. His face was strained—that of a man who is controlling himself with difficulty—and he kept plucking at his beard with a sort of fierce resentment. Steavens, sitting by the window, watched him turn down the 20 glaring lamp, with its jangling pendants, with an angry gesture, and then stand with his hands locked behind him, staring down into the master's face. He could not help wondering what link there had been between the porcelain vessel and so sooty a lump of potter's clay.

From the kitchen an uproar was sounding; when the dining-room door opened, the import of it was clear. The mother was abusing the maid for having forgotten to make the 30 dressing for the chicken salad which had been prepared for the watchers. Steavens had never heard anything in the least like it; it was injured, emotional, dramatic abuse, unique and masterly in its excruciating cruelty, as violent and unrestrained as had been her grief of twenty minutes before. With a shudder of disgust the lawyer went into the dining-room and closed the door into the kitchen.

"Poor Roxy's getting it now," he remarked 40 when he came back. "The Merricks took her out of the poor-house years ago; and if her loyalty would let her, I guess the poor old thing could tell tales that would curdle your blood. She's the mulatto woman who was standing in here a while ago, with her apron to her eyes. The old woman is a fury; there never was anybody like her. She made Harvey's life a hell for him when he lived at home; he was so sick ashamed of it. I never could see 50 how he kept himself sweet."

"He was wonderful," said Steavens slowly, "wonderful; but until tonight I have never known how wonderful."

"That is the eternal wonder of it, anyway; that it can come even from such a dung heap as this," the lawyer cried, with a sweeping gesture which seemed to indicate much more than the four walls within which they stood.

"I think I'll see whether I can get a little air. The room is so close I am beginning to feel rather faint," murmured Steavens, struggling with one of the windows. The sash was stuck, however, and would not yield, so he sat down dejectedly and began pulling at his collar. The lawyer came over, loosened the sash with one blow of his red fist and sent the window up a few inches. Steavens thanked him, but the nausea which had been gradually climbing into his throat for the last half hour left him with but one desire—a desperate feeling that he must get away from this place with what was left of Harvey Merrick. Oh, he comprehended well enough now the quiet bitterness of the smile that he had seen so often on his master's lips!

Once when Merrick returned from a visit home, he brought with him a singularly feeling and suggestive bas-relief of a thin, faded old woman, sitting and sewing something pinned to her knee, while a full-lipped, full-blooded little urchin, his trousers held up by a single gallows, stood beside her, impatiently twitching her gown to call her attention to a butterfly he had caught. Steavens, impressed by the tender and delicate modelling of the thin, tired face, had asked him if it were his mother. He remembered the dull flush that had burned up in the sculptor's face.

The lawyer was sitting in a rocking-chair beside the coffin, his head thrown back and his eyes closed. Steavens looked at him earnestly, puzzled at the line of the chin, and wondering why a man should conceal a feature of such distinction under that disfiguring shock of beard. Suddenly, as though he felt the young sculptor's keen glance, Jim Laird opened his eyes.

"Was he always a good deal of an oyster?" he asked abruptly. "He was terribly shy as a boy."

"Yes, he was an oyster, since you put it so,"

rejoined Steavens. "Although he could be very fond of people, he always gave one the impression of being detached. He disliked violent emotion; he was reflective, and rather distrustful of himself—except, of course, as regarded his work. He was sure enough there. He distrusted men pretty thoroughly and women even more, yet somehow without believing ill of them. He was determined, indeed, to believe the best; but he seemed afraid to investigate."

"A burnt dog dreads the fire," said the lawyer grimly, and closed his eyes.

Steavens went on and on, reconstructing that whole miserable boyhood. All this raw, biting ugliness had been the portion of the man whose mind was to become an exhaustless gallery of beautiful impressions—so sensitive that the mere shadow of a poplar leaf flickering against a sunny wall would be etched and held there for ever. Surely, if ever a man had the magic word in his finger tips, it was Merrick. Whatever he touched, he revealed its holiest secret; liberated it from enchantment and restored it to its pristine loveliness. Upon whatever he had come in contact with, he had left a beautiful record of the experience—a sort of ethereal signature; a scent, a sound, a color that was his own.

Steavens understood now the real tragedy of his master's life; neither love nor wine, as many had conjectured; but a blow which had fallen earlier and cut deeper than anything else could have done—a shame not his, and yet so unescapably his, to hide in his heart from his very boyhood. And without—the frontier warfare; the yearning of a boy, cast ashore upon a desert of newness and ugliness and sordidness, for all that is chastened and old, and noble with traditions.

At eleven o'clock the tall, flat woman in black announced that the watchers were arriving, and asked them to "step into the dining-room." As Steavens rose, the lawyer said dryly: "You go on—it'll be a good experience for you. I'm not equal to that crowd tonight; I've had twenty years of them."

As Steavens closed the door after him he glanced back at the lawyer, sitting by the coffin in the dim light, with his chin resting on his hand.

The same misty group that had stood before the door of the express car shuffled into the dining-room. In the light of the kerosene lamp they separated and became individuals. The minister, a pale, feeble-looking man with white hair and blond chin-whiskers, took his seat beside a small side table and placed his Bible upon it. The Grand Army man sat down behind the stove and tilted his chair back comfortably against the wall, fishing his quill toothpick from his waistcoat pocket. The two bankers, Phelps and Elder, sat off in a corner behind the dinner-table, where they could finish their discussion of the new usury law and its effect on chattel security loans. The real estate agent, an old man with a smiling, hypocritical face, soon joined them. The coal and lumber dealer and the cattle shipper sat on opposite sides of the hard coal-burner, their feet on the nickel-work. Steavens took a book from his pocket and began to read. The talk around him ranged through various topics of local interest while the house was quieting down. When it was clear that the members of the family were in bed, the Grand Army man hitched his shoulders and, untangling his long legs, caught his heels on the rounds of his chair.

"S'pose there'll be a will, Phelps?" he queried in his weak falsetto.

The banker laughed disagreeably, and began trimming his nails with a pearl-handled pocket-knife.

"There'll scarcely be any need for one, will there?" he queried in his turn.

The restless Grand Army man shifted his position again, getting his knees still nearer his chin. "Why, the ole man says Harve's done right well lately," he chirped.

The other banker spoke up. "I reckon he means by that Harve ain't asked him to mortgage any more farms lately, so as he could go on with his education."

"Seems like my mind don't reach back to a time when Harve wasn't bein' edycated," tittered the Grand Army man.

There was a general chuckle. The minister took out his handkerchief and blew his nose sonorously. Banker Phelps closed his knife with a snap. "It's too bad the old man's sons didn't turn out better," he remarked with reflective authority. "They never hung together. He spent money enough on Harve to stock a dozen cattle-farms, and he might as well have poured it into Sand Creek. If Harve had stayed at home and helped nurse what little they had, and gone into stock on the old man's bottom farm, they might all have been well fixed. But the old man had to trust everything to tenants and was cheated right and left."

"Harve never could have handled stock none," interposed the cattleman. "He hadn't it in him to be sharp. Do you remember when he bought Sander's mules for eight-year olds, when everybody in town knew that Sander's father-in-law give 'em to his wife for a wedding present eighteen years before, an' they was full-grown mules then?"

The company laughed discreetly, and the Grand Army man rubbed his knees with a spasm of childish delight.

"Harve never was much account for anything practical, and he shore was never fond of work," began the coal and lumber dealer. "I mind the last time he was home; the day he left, when the old man was out to the barn helpin' his hand hitch up to take Harve to the train, and Cal Moots was patchin' up the fence; Harve, he come out on the step and sings out, in his ladylike voice: 'Cal Moots, Cal Moots! please come cord my trunk.'"

"That's Harve for you," approved the Grand Army man. "I kin hear him howlin' yet, when he was a big feller in long pants and his mother used to whale him with a rawhide in the barn for lettin' the cows git foundered in the cornfield when he was drivin' 'em home from pasture. He killed a cow of mine that-a-way onct—a pure Jersey and the best milker I had, an' the ole man had to put up for her. Harve, he was watchin' the sun set acrost the marshes when the anamile got away."

"Where the old man made his mistake was in sending the boy East to school," said Phelps, stroking his goatee and speaking in a deliberate, judicial tone. "There was where he got his head full of nonsense. What Harve needed of all people, was a course in some first-class Kansas City business college."

The letters were swimming before Steavens's eyes. Was it possible that these men did not understand, that the palm on the coffin meant nothing to them? The very name of their town would have remained for ever buried in the postal guide had it not been now and again mentioned in connection with Harvey Merrick's. He remembered what his master had said to him on the day of his death, after the congestion of both lungs had shut off any probability of recovery, and the sculptor had asked his pupil to send his body home. "It's not a pleasant place to be lying while the world is moving and doing and bettering," he had said with a feeble smile, "but it rather seems as though we ought to go back to the place we came from, in the end. The townspeople will come in for a look at me; and after they have had their say, I shan't have much to fear from the judgment of God!"

The cattleman took up the comment. "Forty's young for a Merrick to cash in; they usually hang on pretty well. Probably he helped it along with whisky."

"His mother's people were not long lived and Harvey never had a robust constitution," said the minister mildly. He would have liked to say more. He had been the boy's Sunday-school teacher, and had been fond of him; but he felt that he was not in a position to speak. His own sons had turned out badly, and it was not a year since one of them had made his last trip home in the express car, shot in a gambling-house in the Black Hills.

"Nevertheless, there is no disputin' that Harve frequently looked upon the wine when it was red, also variegated, and it shore made an oncommon fool of him," moralized the cattleman.

Just then the door leading into the parlor rattled loudly and every one started involuntarily, looking relieved when only Jim Laird came out. The Grand Army man ducked his head when he saw the spark in his blue, blood-shot eye. They were all afraid of Jim; he was a drunkard, but he could twist the law to suit his client's needs as no other man in all western Kansas could do, and there were many who tried. The lawyer closed the door behind him, leaned back against it and folded his arms, cocking his head a little to one side. When he assumed this attitude in the court-room, ears were always pricked up, as it usually foretold a flood of withering sarcasm.

"I've been with you gentlemen before," he began in a dry, even tone, "when you've sat by the coffins of boys born and raised in this town; and, if I remember rightly, you were never any too well satisfied when you checked them up. What's the matter, anyhow? Why is it that reputable young men are as scarce as millionaires in Sand City? It might almost seem to a stranger that there was some way something the matter with your progressive town. Why did Ruben Sayer, the brightest young lawyer you ever turned out, after he had come home from the university as straight as a die, take to drinking and forge a check and shoot himself? Why did Bill Merrit's son die of the shakes in a saloon in Omaha? Why was Mr. Thomas's son, here, shot in a gambling-house? Why did young Adams burn his mill to beat the insurance companies and go to the pen?"

The lawyer paused and unfolded his arms, laying one clenched fist quietly on the table. "I'll tell you why. Because you drummed nothing but money and knavery into their ears from the time they wore knickerbockers; because you carped away at them as you've been carping here tonight, holding our friends Phelps and Elder up to them for their models, as our grandfathers held up George Washington and John Adams. But the boys were young, and raw at the business you put them to, and how could they match coppers with such artists as Phelps and Elder? You wanted them to be successful rascals; they were only unsuccessful ones—that's all the difference. There was only one boy ever raised in this borderland between ruffianism and civilization who didn't come to grief, and you hated Harvey Merrick more for winning out than you hated all the other boys who got under the wheels. Lord, Lord, how you did hate him! Phelps, here, is fond of saying that he could buy and sell us all out any time he's a mind to; but he knew Harve wouldn't have given a tinker's damn for his bank and all his cattle-farms put together; and a lack of appreciation that way, goes hard with Phelps.

"Old Nimrod thinks Harve drank too much; and this from such as Nimrod and me!

"Brother Elder says Harve was too free with the old man's money—fell short in filial consideration, maybe. Well, we can all remember the very tone in which brother Elder swore his own father was a liar, in the county court; and we all know that the old man came out of that partnership with his son as bare as a sheared lamb. But maybe I'm getting personal, and I'd better be driving ahead at what I want to say."

The lawyer paused a moment, squared his heavy shoulders, and went on: "Harvey Merrick and I went to school together, back East. We were dead in earnest, and we wanted you all to be proud of us some day. We meant to be great men. Even I, and I haven't lost my sense of humor, gentlemen, *I* meant to be a great man. I came back here to practice, and I found you didn't in the least want me to be a great man. You wanted me to be a shrewd lawyer—oh, yes! Our veteran here wanted me to get him an increase of pension, because he had dyspepsia; Phelps wanted a new county survey that would put the widow Wilson's little bottom farm inside his south line; Elder wanted to lend money at 5 per cent a month, and get it collected; and Stark here wanted to wheedle old women up in Vermont into investing their annuities in real estate mortgages that are not worth the paper they are written on. Oh, you needed me hard enough, and you'll go on needing me!

"Well, I came back here and became the damned shyster you wanted me to be. You pretend to have some sort of respect for me; and yet you'll stand up and throw mud at Harvey Merrick, whose soul you couldn't dirty and whose hands you couldn't tie. Oh, you're a discriminating lot of Christians! There have been times when the sight of Harvey's name in some Eastern paper has made me hang my head like a whipped dog, and, again, times when I liked to think of him off there in the world, away from all this hog-wallow, climbing the big, clean up-grade he'd set for himself.

"And we? Now that we've fought and lied and sweated and stolen, and hated as only the disappointed strugglers in a bitter, dead little Western town know how to do, what have we got to show for it? Harvey Merrick wouldn't have given one sunset over your marshes for all you've got put together, and you know it.

It's not for me to say why, in the inscrutable wisdom of God, a genius should ever have been called from this place of hatred and bitter waters; but I want this Boston man to know that the drivel he's been hearing tonight is the only tribute any truly great man could have from such a lot of sidetracked, burnt-dog, land-poor sharks as the here-present financiers of Sand City—upon which town may God have mercy!"

The lawyer thrust out his hand to Steavens as he passed him, caught up his overcoat in the hall and had left the house before the Grand Army man had had time to lift his ducked head and crane his long neck about at his fellows.

Next day Jim Laird was drunk and ⸳ to attend the funeral services. Steavens c twice at his office, but was compelled to sta. East without seeing him. He had a presentiment that he would hear from him again, and left his address on the lawyer's table; but if Laird found it, he never acknowledged it. The thing in him that Harvey Merrick had loved must have gone under ground with Harvey

10 Merrick's coffin; for it never spoke again, and Jim got the cold he died of driving across the Colorado mountains to defend one of Phelps's sons who had got into trouble out there by cutting government timber.

1920

1885 -- *Sinclair Lewis* -- ——

SINCLAIR LEWIS was born on February 7th, 1885, in a small "Main Street" town, Sauk Center, Minnesota. His father and several of his family were physicians, a fact that partially accounts for the respect he held for the medical profession, which comes through with only a small number of scars from the Lewis attack. After six months at Oberlin Academy, he entered Yale in 1903, where he became an editor of the *Yale Literary Magazine* and a contributor to the *Courant*. In one interruption of his college life, he took a position as janitor in Upton Sinclair's socialist enterprise, Helicon Hall, where he met liberal and socialist professors and journalists; he supported himself by editing, translating, and writing. In 1908 he completed his work at Yale and returned to New York, to make his way as a journalist and editor.

Lewis's first novels were potboilers: *Our Mr. Wrenn* (1914), *The Trail of the Hawk* (1915), *The Innocents* (1917), *The Job* (1917), and *Free Air* (1919) all precede and are avowedly inferior to *Main Street* (1920), which had been begun during his Yale years, put aside, and finally considerably changed in style and emphasis. *Main Street* had the advantage of a public anxious to receive it; it described the small town deserted or still lived in, in a way which satisfied their hatred of it and gave good reason for their own "revolt." The success of the novel was due almost entirely to its motif of attack; it joined ranks with Edgar Lee Masters's *Spoon River Anthology* (1915) and Sherwood Anderson's *Winesburg, Ohio* (1919). Lewis became a literary hero. From the small town, he turned to the middle-class industrial city, the city of Zenith in the state of Winnemac. In *Babbitt* (1922) he created an American type; the hustling, frenetic, boastful, but frightened and vaguely, clumsily romantic businessman, George Follansbee Babbitt, realtor extraordinary. The book is an admirable

ribution to the American myth of the all-sufficient world of busi-
ndustry. With impeccable and scathing detail, Lewis described
, his groping attempts at fatherhood, his business life, his errant-
his loneliness. More remarkable is the locale—what Maxwell
most a perfectly conceived poetic vision of a perfectly standardized
money society; it is our native *Inferno* of the mechanized hinterland."

Once established in Zenith, Lewis was scarcely ever to leave it. He saw opportunities for other fantasies of American life, and they followed in fairly regular succession. *Arrowsmith* (1925), which won him a Pulitzer prize he declined, is a more
moderate book, the life of a young doctor, whose career takes him from general
practice in Wheatsylvania to research in the McGurk Institute, and finally to a tragic
but heroic emergency trip to the West Indies, where his wife dies. In addition to the
fairly honest portrait of the dedicated scientist, Lewis offers portraits of such characters as Dr. Almus Pickerbaugh of the Nautilus, Iowa, health department; he refin-
ishes the pictures of *Main Street* and *Babbitt*, and in his characterization of Max
Gottlieb, Arrowsmith's hero at the University of Winnemac, he demonstrates his
whole-hearted approval of the ideals of science.

Elmer Gantry (1927) is a return to the unaffected parody of *Babbitt;* this time the
principal character is a roving evangelist, whose lust for life competes forever with
his desire to influence the crowd. When Elmer Gantry finally settles in Zenith, he
joins the Lewis group already described in detail in earlier novels. With evident
pleasure, and with more venom than he displayed in *Babbitt,* Lewis takes Gantry
through a succession of oily hoaxes, pointing out as he does the unholy alliance of
religion with business, the opportunism of ministers, the callous confidence of busi-
nessmen, and the cultist gullibility of their wives.

The Man Who Knew Coolidge (1928), a series of monologues, portrays the soul
of Lowell Schmaltz, his political opinions, his cultural shallowness, in a series of
bourgeois clichés which have never been equaled either in American literature or in
American life. The book shows the influence of H. L. Mencken, in whose *American
Mercury* appeared the first chapter, in January, 1928. *Dodsworth* (1929) shows Zenith vacationing in Europe. The character of Sam Dodsworth is sympathetically
drawn. His sober virtues and sound views contrast with didactic clarity with the
pale, confused, and superficial quality of his wife's European friends. Ultimately,
the American of Zenith is judged quite competent to stand on his own feet, without
help from Europe, and Dodsworth presents to the Lewis public a Babbitt quite free
of the grotesque inadequacies of the earlier portrait.

Substantially, Lewis is devoted to the American middle class. His most popular
portraits seem to have been those which make the American appear most ridiculous.
He regrets the fact that the American has done so much to spoil his heritage, but he
feels that he is as yet unspoiled by his opportunities. The novels written in the

1930's and 1940's—none of them as good as *Babbitt* or *Main Street*—develop further the positive virtues of the American world, while at the same time continuing to ridicule American pretension and hypocrisy.

Lewis refused the Pulitzer prize for *Arrowsmith* but accepted the Nobel prize (in 1930) for his work in *Babbitt*. In his acceptance speech, he asserted his opposition to the "safe" principle of American literary obedience to a heritage scarcely yet challenged, while at the same time announcing his confidence in the great opportunities open to American writers. As his books continue to appear regularly, the conviction is enforced that Lewis was at his best at the beginning of his popularity: *Main Street* and *Babbitt* are at once his most widely known and his best books. They profit from a freshness of application which the later work does not have. The character of Babbitt is a classic representation of his time and place. His is not a realistic portrait; in the very exaggeration of his behavior and appearance lies the success of the characterization.

Lewis's novels are *Our Mr. Wrenn* (1914); *The Trail of the Hawk* (1915); *The Innocents* (1917); *The Job* (1917); *Free Air* (1919); *Main Street* (1920); *Babbitt* (1922); *Arrowsmith* (1925); *Mantrap* (1926); *Elmer Gantry* (1927); *The Man Who Knew Coolidge* (1928); *Dodsworth* (1929); *Ann Vickers* (1933); *Work of Art* (1934); *It Can't Happen Here* (1935); *The Prodigal Parents* (1938); *Bethel Merriday* (1940); *Gideon Planish* (1943); *Cass Timberlane* (1945); *Kingsblood Royal* (1947); *The God-Seeker* (1949). *Selected Short Stories of Sinclair Lewis* was published in 1935. He has collaborated in the production of two plays: *Jayhawker* (1935), with Lloyd Lewis; and an adaptation of the novel, *It Can't Happen Here* (1938) with John C. Moffit. Most important of his occasional critical pieces is "The American Fear of Literature" (1931), his Nobel prize address. The only biographical study is Carl Van Doren's *Sinclair Lewis, a Biographical Sketch* (1933), with a bibliography by Harvey Taylor. Critical studies include James B. Cabell, *Sinclair Lewis: A Critical Essay* (1932); E. M. Forster, *Sinclair Lewis Interprets America* (1932); Harry Hartwick, *The Foreground of American Fiction* (1934); Harlan Hatcher, *Creating the Modern American Novel* (1935); Annie R. Marble, *The Nobel Prize Winners in Literature, 1901–1931* (1932); Stuart P. Sherman, *The Significance of Sinclair Lewis* (1922); Walter F. Taylor, *A History of American Letters* (1936); Régis Michaud, *The American Novel Today* (1928); Maxwell Geismar, *The Last of the Provincials* (1947); Alfred Kazin, *On Native Grounds* (1942); V. F. Calverton, "Sinclair Lewis, the Last of the Literary Liberals," *Modern Monthly*, March, 1934; T. D. Horton, "Sinclair Lewis: the Symbol of an Era," *North American Review*, Winter, 1939; Lloyd Morris, "Sinclair Lewis—His Critics and the Public," *North American Review*, Summer, 1938. For other titles, see Millett, *Contemporary American Authors* (1940) and Leary, *Articles on American Literature Appearing in Current Periodicals, 1920–1945* (1947); Henry Johnson, *The Other Side of Main Street* (1943).

From BABBITT

CHAPTER I

I

THE TOWERS OF Zenith aspired above the morning mist; austere towers of steel and cement and limestone, sturdy as cliffs and delicate as silver rods. They were neither citadels nor churches, but frankly and beautifully office-buildings.

The mist took pity on the fretted structures of earlier generations: the Post Office with its shingle-tortured mansard, the red brick minarets of hulking old houses, factories with stingy and sooted windows, wooden tenements colored like mud. The city was full of such grotesqueries, but the clean towers were thrusting them from the business center, and on the farther hills were shining new houses, homes—they seemed—for laughter and tranquillity.

Over a concrete bridge fled a limousine of long sleek hood and noiseless engine. These people in evening clothes were returning from an all-night rehearsal of a Little Theater play, an artistic adventure considerably illuminated by champagne. Below the bridge curved a railroad, a maze of green and crimson lights. The New York Flyer boomed past, and twenty lines of polished steel leaped into the glare.

In one of the skyscrapers the wires of the Associated Press were closing down. The telegraph operators wearily raised their celluloid eye-shades after a night of talking with Paris and Peking. Through the building crawled the scrubwomen, yawning, their old shoes slapping. The dawn mist spun away. Cues of men with lunch-boxes clumped toward the immensity of new factories, sheets of glass and hollow tile, glittering shops where five thousand men worked beneath one roof, pouring out the honest wares that would be sold up the Euphrates and across the veldt. The whistles rolled out in greeting a chorus cheerful as the April dawn; the song of labor in a city built—it seemed—for giants.

II

There was nothing of the giant in the aspect of the man who was beginning to awaken on the sleeping-porch of a Dutch Colonial house in that residential district of Zenith known as Floral Heights.

His name was George F. Babbitt. He was forty-six years old now, in April, 1920, and he made nothing in particular, neither butter nor shoes nor poetry, but he was nimble in the calling of selling houses for more than people could afford to pay.

His large head was pink, his brown hair thin and dry. His face was babyish in slumber, despite his wrinkles and the red spectacle-dents on the slopes of his nose. He was not fat but he was exceedingly well fed; his cheeks were pads, and the unroughened hand which lay helpless upon the khaki-colored blanket was slightly puffy. He seemed prosperous, extremely married and unromantic; and altogether unromantic appeared this sleeping-porch, which looked on one sizable elm, two respectable grass-plots, a cement driveway, and a corrugated iron garage. Yet Babbitt was again dreaming of the fairy child, a dream more romantic than scarlet pagodas by a silver sea.

For years the fairy child had come to him. Where others saw but George Babbitt, she discerned gallant youth. She waited for him, in the darkness beyond mysterious groves. When at last he could slip away from the crowded house he darted to her. His wife, his clamoring friends, sought to follow, but he escaped, the girl fleet beside him, and they crouched together on a shadowy hillside. She was so slim, so white, so eager! She cried that he was gay and valiant, that she would wait for him, that they would sail—

Rumble and bang of the milk-truck.

Babbitt moaned, turned over, struggled back toward his dream. He could only see her face now, beyond misty waters. The furnace-man slammed the basement door. A dog barked in the next yard. As Babbitt sank blissfully into a dim warm tide, the paper-carrier went by whistling, and the rolled-up *Advocate* thumped the front door. Babbitt roused, his stomach constricted with alarm. As he relaxed, he was pierced by the familiar and irritating rattle of some one cranking a Ford: snap-ah-ah, snap-ah-ah, snap-ah-ah. Himself a pious motorist, Babbitt cranked with the unseen driver, with him waited through taut hours for the roar of the starting engine, with him agonized as the roar ceased and again began the infernal patient snap-ah-ah—a round, flat sound, a shivering cold-morning sound, a sound infuriating and inescapable. Not till the rising voice of the motor told him that the Ford was moving was he released from the panting tension. He glanced once at his favorite tree, elm twigs against the gold patina of sky, and fumbled for sleep as for a drug. He who had been a boy very credulous of life was no longer greatly interested in the possible and improbable adventures of each new day.

He escaped from reality till the alarm-clock rang, at seven-twenty.

III

It was the best of nationally advertised and quantitatively produced alarm-clocks, with all modern attachments, including cathedral chime, intermittent alarm, and a phosphorescent dial. Babbitt was proud of being awakened by such a rich device. Socially it was almost as creditable as buying expensive cord tires.

He sulkily admitted now that there was no more escape, but he lay and detested the grind of the real-estate business, and disliked his family, and disliked himself for disliking them. The evening before, he had played poker at Vergil Gunch's till midnight, and after such holidays he was irritable before breakfast. It may have been the tremendous home-brewed beer of the prohibition-era and the cigars to which that beer enticed him; it may have been resentment of return from this fine, bold man-world to a restricted region of wives and stenographers, and of suggestions not to smoke so much.

From the bedroom beside the sleeping-porch, his wife's detestably cheerful "Time to get up, Georgie boy," and the itchy sound, the brisk and scratchy sound, of combing hairs out of a stiff brush.

He grunted; he dragged his thick legs, in faded baby-blue pajamas, from under the khaki blanket; he sat on the edge of the cot, running his fingers through his wild hair, while his plump feet mechanically felt for his slippers. He looked regretfully at the blanket—forever a suggestion to him of freedom and heroism. He had bought it for a camping trip which had never come off. It symbolized gorgeous loafing, gorgeous cursing, virile flannel shirts.

He creaked to his feet, groaning at the waves of pain which passed behind his eyeballs. Though he waited for their scorching recurrence, he looked blurrily out at the yard. It delighted him, as always; it was the neat yard of a successful business man of Zenith, that is, it was perfection, and made him also perfect. He regarded the corrugated iron garage. For the three-hundred-and-sixty-fifth time in a year he reflected, "No class to that tin shack. Have to build me a frame garage. But by golly it's the only thing on the place that isn't up-to-date!" While he stared he thought of a community garage for his acreage development, Glen Oriole. He stopped puffing and jiggling. His arms were akimbo. His petulant, sleep-swollen face was set in harder lines. He suddenly seemed capable, an official, a man to contrive, to direct, to get things done.

On the vigor of his idea he was carried down the hard, clean, unused-looking hall into the bathroom.

Though the house was not large it had, like all houses on Floral Heights, an altogether royal bathroom of porcelain and glazed tile and metal sleek as silver. The towel-rack was a rod of clear glass set in nickel. The tub was long enough for a Prussian guard, and above the set bowl was a sensational exhibit of toothbrush holder, shaving-brush holder, soap-dish, sponge-dish, and medicine-cabinet, so glittering and so ingenious that they resembled an electrical instrument-board. But the Babbitt whose god was Modern Appliances was not pleased. The air of the bathroom was thick with the smell of a heathen toothpaste. "Verona been at it again! 'Stead of sticking to Lilidol, like I've re-peat-ed-ly asked her, she's gone and gotten some confounded stinkum stuff that makes you sick!"

The bath-mat was wrinkled and the floor was wet. (His daughter Verona eccentrically took baths in the morning, now and then.) He slipped on the mat, and slid against the tub. He said "Damn!" Furiously he snatched up his tube of shaving-cream, furiously he lathered, with a belligerent slapping of the unctuous brush, furiously he raked his plump cheeks with a safety-razor. It pulled. The blade was dull. He said, "Damn—oh—oh—damn it!"

He hunted through the medicine-cabinet for a packet of new razor-blades (reflecting, as invariably, "Be cheaper to buy one of these dinguses and strop your own blades,") and when he discovered the packet, behind the round box of bicarbonate of soda, he thought ill of his wife for putting it there and very well of himself for not saying "Damn." But he did say it, immediately afterward, when with wet and soap-slippery fingers he tried to remove the horrible little envelope and crisp clinging oiled paper from the new blade.

Then there was the problem, oft-pondered, never solved, of what to do with the old blade, which might imperil the fingers of his young. As usual, he tossed it on top of the medicine-cabinet, with a mental note that some day he must remove the fifty or sixty other blades that were also, temporarily, piled up there. He finished his shaving in a growing testiness increased by his spinning headache and by the emptiness in his stomach. When he was done, his round face smooth and streamy and his eyes stinging from soapy water, he reached for 10 a towel. The family towels were wet, wet and clammy and vile, all of them wet, he found, as he blindly snatched them—his own face-towel, his wife's, Verona's, Ted's, Tinka's, and the lone bath-towel with the huge welt of initial. Then George F. Babbitt did a dismaying thing. He wiped his face on the guest-towel! It was a pansy-embroidered trifle which always hung there to indicate that the Babbitts were in the best Floral Heights society. No one had ever 20 used it. No guest had ever dared to. Guests secretively took a corner of the nearest regular towel.

He was raging, "By golly, here they go and use up all the towels, every doggone one of 'em, and they use 'em and get 'em all wet and sopping, and never put out a dry one for me—of course, I'm the goat!—and then I want one and— I'm the only person in the doggone house that's got the slightest doggone bit of 30 consideration for other people and thoughtfulness and consider there may be others that may want to use the doggone bathroom after me and consider—"

He was pitching the chill abominations into the bathtub, pleased by the vindictiveness of that desolate flapping sound; and in the midst his wife serenely trotted in, observed serenely, "Why Georgie dear, what are you doing? Are you going to wash out the towels? Why, you 40 needn't wash out the towels. Oh, Georgie, you didn't go and use the guest-towel, did you?"

It is not recorded that he was able to answer.

For the first time in weeks he was sufficiently roused by his wife to look at her.

IV

Myra Babbitt—Mrs. George F. Babbitt—was definitely mature. She had creases from the 50 corners of her mouth to the bottom of her chin, and her plump neck bagged. But the thing that marked her as having passed the line was that she no longer had reticences before her husband, and no longer worried about not having reticences. She was in a petticoat now, and corsets which bulged, and unaware of being seen in bulgy corsets. She had become so dully habituated to married life that in her full matronliness she was as sexless as an anemic nun. She was a good woman, a kind woman, a diligent woman, but no one, save perhaps Tinka, her ten-year-old, was at all interested in her or entirely aware that she was alive.

After a rather thorough discussion of all the domestic and social aspects of towels she apologized to Babbitt for his having an alcoholic headache; and he recovered enough to endure the search for a B.V.D. undershirt which had, he pointed out, malevolently been concealed among his clean pajamas.

He was fairly amiable in the conference on the brown suit.

"What do you think, Myra?" He pawed at the clothes hunched on a chair in their bed-room, while she moved about mysteriously adjusting and patting her petticoat and, to his jaundiced eye, never seeming to get on with her dressing. "How about it? Shall I wear the brown suit another day?"

"Well, it looks awfully nice on you."

"I know, but gosh, it needs pressing."

"That's so. Perhaps it does."

"It certainly could stand being pressed, all right."

"Yes, perhaps it wouldn't hurt it to be pressed."

"But gee, the coat doesn't need pressing. No sense in having the whole darn suit pressed, when the coat doesn't need it."

"That's so."

"But the pants certainly need it, all right. Look at them—look at those wrinkles—the pants certainly do need pressing."

"That's so. Oh, Georgie, why couldn't you wear the brown coat with the blue trousers we were wondering what we'd do with them?"

"Good Lord! Did you ever in all my life know me to wear the coat of one suit and the pants of another? What do you think I am? A busted bookkeeper?"

"Well, why don't you put on the dark gray

suit to-day, and stop in at the tailor and leave the brown trousers?"

"Well, they certainly need— Now where the devil is that gray suit? Oh, yes, here we are."

He was able to get through the other crises of dressing with comparative resoluteness and calm.

His first adornment was the sleeveless dimity B.V.D. undershirt, in which he resembled a small boy humorlessly wearing a cheesecloth tabard at a civic pageant. He never put on B.V.D.'s without thanking the God of Progress that he didn't wear tight, long, old-fashioned undergarments, like his father-in-law and partner, Henry Thompson. His second embellishment was combing and slicking back his hair. It gave him a tremendous forehead, arching up two inches beyond the former hairline. But most wonder-working of all was the donning of his spectacles.

There is character in spectacles—the pretentious tortoise-shell, the meek pince-nez of the school teacher, the twisted silver-framed glasses of the old villager. Babbitt's spectacles had huge, circular, frameless lenses of the very best glass; the ear-pieces were thin bars of gold. In them he was the modern business man; one who gave orders to clerks and drove a car and played occasional golf and was scholarly in regard to Salesmanship. His head suddenly appeared not babyish but weighty, and you noted his heavy, blunt nose, his straight mouth and thick, long upper lip, his chin overfleshy but strong; with respect you beheld him put on the rest of his uniform as a Solid Citizen.

The gray suit was well cut, well made, and completely undistinguished. It was a standard suit. White piping on the V of the vest added a flavor of law and learning. His shoes were black laced boots, good boots, honest boots, standard boots, extraordinarily uninteresting boots. The only frivolity was in his purple knitted scarf. With considerable comment on the matter to Mrs. Babbitt (who, acrobatically fastening the back of her blouse to her skirt with a safety-pin, did not hear a word he said), he chose between the purple scarf and a tapestry effect with stringless brown harps among blown palms, and into it he thrust a snake-head pin with opal eyes.

A sensational event was changing from the brown suit to the gray the contents of his pockets. He was earnest about these objects. They were of eternal importance, like baseball or the Republican Party. They included a fountain pen and a silver pencil (always lacking a supply of new leads) which belonged in the right-hand upper vest pocket. Without them he would have felt naked. On his watch-chain were a gold penknife, silver cigar-cutter, seven keys (the use of two of which he had forgotten), and incidentally a good watch. Depending from the chain was a large, yellowish elk's-tooth—proclamation of his membership in the Benevolent and Protective Order of Elks. Most significant of all was his loose-leaf pocket notebook, that modern and efficient note-book which contained the addresses of people whom he had forgotten, prudent memoranda of postal money-orders which had reached their destinations months ago, stamps which had lost their mucilage, clippings of verses by T. Cholmondeley Frink and of the newspaper editorials from which Babbitt got his opinions and his polysyllables, notes to be sure and do things which he did not intend to do, and one curious inscription—D.S.S.D.M.Y.P.D.F.

But he had no cigarette-case. No one had ever happened to give him one, so he hadn't the habit, and people who carried cigarette-cases he regarded as effeminate.

Last, he stuck in his lapel the Boosters' Club button. With the conciseness of great art the button displayed two words "Boosters—Pep!" It made Babbitt feel loyal and important. It associated him with Good Fellows, with men who were nice and human, and important in business circles. It was his V.C., his Legion of Honor ribbon, his Phi Beta Kappa key.

With the subtleties of dressing ran other complex worries. "I feel kind of punk this morning," he said. "I think I had too much dinner last evening. You oughtn't to serve those heavy banana fritters."

"But you asked me to have some."

"I know, but— I tell you, when a fellow gets past forty he has to look after his digestion. There's a lot of fellows that don't take proper care of themselves. I tell you at forty a man's a fool or his doctor—I mean, his own doctor. Folks don't give enough attention to this matter of dieting. Now I think— Course a man ought to have a good meal after the day's work, but it would be a good thing for both of us if we took lighter lunches."

"But Georgie, here at home I always do have a light lunch."

"Mean to imply I make a hog of myself, eating downtown? Yes, sure! You'd have a swell time if you had to eat the truck that new steward hands out to us at the Athletic Club! But I certainly do feel out of sorts, this morning. Funny, got a pain down here on the left side—but no, that wouldn't be appendicitis, would it? Last night, when I was driving over to Verg Gunch's, I felt a pain in my stomach, too. Right here it was—kind of a sharp shooting pain. I— Where'd that dime go to? Why don't you serve more prunes at breakfast? Of course I eat an apple every evening—an apple a day keeps the doctor away—but still, you ought to have more prunes, and not all these fancy doodads."

"The last time I had prunes you didn't eat them."

"Well, I didn't feel like eating 'em, I suppose. Matter of fact, I think I did eat some of 'em. Anyway— I tell you it's mighty important to— I was saying to Verg Gunch, just last evening, most people don't take sufficient care of their diges—"

"Shall we have the Gunches for our dinner, next week?"

"Why sure; you bet."

"Now see here, George: I want you to put on your nice dinner-jacket that evening."

"Rats! The rest of 'em won't want to dress."

"Of course they will. You remember when you didn't dress for the Littlefields' supper-party, and all the rest did, and how embarrassed you were."

"Embarrassed, hell! I wasn't embarrassed. Everybody knows I can put on as expensive a Tux. as anybody else, and I should worry if I don't happen to have it on sometimes. All a darn nuisance, anyway. All right for a woman, that stays around the house all the time, but when a fellow's worked like the dickens all day, he doesn't want to go and hustle his head off getting into the soup-and-fish for a lot of folks that he's seen in just reg'lar ordinary clothes that same day."

"You know you enjoy being seen in one. The other evening you admitted you were glad I'd insisted on your dressing. You said you felt a lot better for it. And oh, Georgie, I do wish you wouldn't say 'Tux.' It's 'dinner-jacket.'"

"Rats, what's the odds?"

"Well, it's what all the nice folks say. Suppose Lucile McKelvey heard you calling it a 'Tux.'"

"Well, that's all right now! Lucile McKelvey can't pull anything on me! Her folks are common as mud, even if her husband and her dad are millionaires! I suppose you're trying to rub in *your* exalted social position! Well, let me tell you that your revered paternal ancestor, Henry T., doesn't even call it a 'Tux.'! He calls it a 'bobtail jacket for a ringtail monkey,' and you couldn't get him into one unless you chloroformed him!"

"Now don't be horrid, George."

"Well, I don't want to be horrid, but Lord! you're getting as fussy as Verona. Ever since she got out of college she's been too rambunctious to live with—doesn't know what she wants—well, I know what she wants!—all she wants is to marry a millionaire, and live in Europe, and hold some preacher's hand, and simultaneously at the same time stay right here in Zenith and be some blooming kind of a socialist agitator or boss charity-worker or some damn thing! Lord, and Ted is just as bad! He wants to go to college, and he doesn't want to go to college. Only one of the three that knows her own mind is Tinka. Simply can't understand how I ever came to have a pair of shilly-shallying children like Rone and Ted. I may not be any Rockefeller or James J. Shakespeare, but I certainly do know my own mind, and I do keep right on plugging along in the office and— Do you know the latest? Far as I can figure out, Ted's new bee is he'd like to be a movie actor and— And here I've told him a hundred times, if he'll go to college and law-school and make good, I'll set him up in business and— Verona's just exactly as bad. Doesn't know what she wants. Well, well, come on! Aren't you ready yet? The girl rang the bell three minutes ago."

V

Before he followed his wife, Babbitt stood at the westernmost window of their room. This residential settlement, Floral Heights, was on a rise; and though the center of the city was three miles away—Zenith had between three and four hundred thousand inhabitants now—he could see the top of the Second National Tower, an Indiana limestone building of thirty-five stories.

Its shining walls rose against April sky to a simple cornice like a streak of white fire. Integrity was in the tower, and decision. It bore its strength lightly as a tall soldier. As Babbitt stared, the nervousness was soothed from his face, his slack chin lifted in reverence. All he articulated was "That's one lovely sight!" but he was inspired by the rhythm of the city; his love of it renewed. He beheld the tower as a temple-spire of the religion of business, a faith passionate, exalted, surpassing common men; and as he clumped down to breakfast he whistled the ballad, "Oh, by gee, by gosh, by jingo" as though it were a hymn melancholy and noble.

1922

1876 ～ *Sherwood Anderson* ～ 1941

ANDERSON, like his contemporary, Dreiser, hails from the Middle West, having been born in Camden, Ohio, the third of five children. His father, a veteran of the Civil War, popularly known as the colonel, the major, or the captain, lover of fine clothes and good food, was notorious for his thriftlessness and his irrepressible tendency for storytelling. The mother, partly of Italian descent, practical, resourceful, and warmhearted, was the mainstay of the family until her death when Sherwood was fourteen.

Young Anderson, whose education was at best desultory, left school about this time and earned a livelihood in a variety of odd enterprises—hostler, mechanic's apprentice, factory worker, and hobo. He answered the call for volunteers at the outbreak of the Spanish-American War because enlistment offered an avenue of escape from the drab and sordid life which he had been leading. After demobilization he married, settled down, and rose to the presidency of a paint-manufacturing company, well on the way to becoming a prosperous, successful businessman.

But neither business success nor prosperity had any fascination for him. He began to sense what the oncoming industrialism, with its standardization, was doing to society and feared what it would do to him. In a sudden move he left his business and his home to seek the life of his choice in Chicago. Here he wrote advertisements for business concerns, and in his leisure time composed *Windy McPherson's Son*, (1916), his first novel, which at forty launched him upon a literary career. From this time on, his life was for the most part the record of his books, which appeared with almost annual regularity. In his later years Anderson published a small-town newspaper in Virginia.

His career divides itself into three periods. To the first belong *Windy McPherson's Son* (1916) and *Marching Men* (1917), dominated by a "defeated romanticism."

Then came the Freudian influence shown in *Winesburg, Ohio* (1919), *Poor White* (1920), *The Triumph of the Egg* (1921), and *Many Marriages* (1923). The more recent books, such as *Dark Laughter* (1925) and *Death in the Woods* (1933), constitute a third, and more sensual, group. He has also published several volumes of verse and autobiography.

In *A Story Teller's Story* (1924) he states clearly the theory with which he approached the business of writing. To begin with, he set himself deliberately to restore the intimate relation of life and art between which he felt there had grown an ever-widening breach. Artists had drifted into the habit of doctoring life to fit the conveniences of their art. He objected to the plotted story because it enabled writers to take liberties which transcend the bounds of common sense, as for instance, the transformation of villains into saints, a common American trick. "It was certain there were no plot stories ever lived in any life I had known anything about." In the second place, he would dissociate art and morality, rebelling with equal vehemence against "that absurd Anglo-Saxon notion that they [stories] must point a moral, uplift the people, make better citizens, etc." He insisted that "In the life of the fancy there is no such thing as good or bad," and that morality is, as far as the artist is concerned, a matter of aesthetics. The third point in his theory dealt with the matter of language. Here too he found fault with earlier practices which made average Americans feel and talk in a manner utterly out of harmony with real life. He set himself, therefore, to find the medium of expression which would convey the artist's ideas without violence to his subject.

Anderson is one of the stout rebels against village life, its narrowness, provincialism, frustration, and prejudice, especially as it is changed by growing industrialism. Like Dreiser he was a naturalist, at any rate to the extent of his belief in environmental determinism, but he insisted upon probing beyond the merely physical for an explanation of life. The fact that he experienced difficulty in reaching a satisfactory explanation caused him to brood with melancholy disillusionment, and drove him to employ a symbolism which is at times far from apparent, and to seek refuge in an "intuitive mysticism" which lacks both definition and clarity.

Furthermore, a society dominated by lust for material gain, gradually regimented by a growing standardizing industrialism, presented a spectacle beyond which he saw little hope. His concern for an American civilization built on intellectual and cultural interests is especially noticeable in his earlier novels. Then came the period dominated by the Freudian pre-occupation with sex, as the core and center of all human motives. To the frustration of sex impulses he traced most of the ills and griefs of life. He capitalized it in *Winesburg, Ohio*, a collection of short stories, as well as in some of his novels. His persistent quarrel with society, indeed with life itself, is its emphasis upon inhibitions rather than unhindered self-expression. His success lay in his short stories rather than the novels, for the sharp and vivid impression of the short story was better suited to his genius than the sustained interest of the novels.

As novelist Anderson wrote *Windy McPherson's Son* (1916); *Marching Men* (1917); *Poor White* (1920); *Many Marriages* (1925); *Dark Laughter* (1925); *Tar* (1926); *Beyond Desire* (1932); *Kit Brandon* (1936). His short stories are in *Winesburg, Ohio* (1919); *The Triumph of the Egg* (1921); *Horses and Men* (1923); *Death in the Woods* (1933). His essays and sketches are collected in *The Modern Writer* (1925); *Sherwood Anderson's Notebook* (1926); *Hello Towns!* (1929); *Puzzled America* (1935). *Mid-American Chants* (1918) and *A New Testament* (1927) contain his poetry. *Perhaps Women* (1931) is a book of social criticism. *A Story Teller's Story* (1924) is autobiography. *Tar* (1926) is likewise autobiographic. For biography and criticism consult D. Karsner, *Sixteen Authors to One* (1928); T. K. Whipple, *Spokesmen* (1928); S. P. Sherman, *Critical Woodcuts* (1926); C. Van Doren, "Sinclair Lewis and Sherwood Anderson," *Century*, July, 1925; H. Hartwick, *The Foreground of American Fiction* (1934); H. Hatcher, *Creating the Modern American Novel* (1935); R. Michaud, *The American Novel To-day* (1928); P. Rosenfeld, *Port of New York* (1924); J. Collins, *Taking the Literary Pulse* (1924); V. F. Calverton, "Sherwood Anderson," *Modern Quarterly*, Fall, 1924; P. H. Boynton, *More Contemporary Americans* (1927); N. B. Fagin, *The Phenomenon of Sherwood Anderson* (1927); H. Hansen, *Midwest Portraits* (1923); C. B. Chase, *Sherwood Anderson* (1927); H. Wickham, *The Impuritans* (1929); C. Fadiman, "Sherwood Anderson: the Search for Salvation," *Nation*, Nov. 9, 1932; E. J. O'Brien, *The Advance of the American Short Story* (rev. ed., 1931); A. H. Quinn, *American Fiction* (1936); Maxwell Geismar, *The Last of the Provincials* (1947); Alfred Kazin, *On Native Grounds* (1942); Lionel Trilling, "Sherwood Anderson," *Kenyon Review*, Summer, 1941; Irving Howe, "Sherwood Anderson: The Unavailable Self," *Partisan Review*, April, 1948; F. J. Hoffman, *Freudianism and the Literary Mind* (1945).

THE EGG

MY FATHER was, I am sure, intended by nature to be a cheerful, kindly man. Until he was thirty-four years old he worked as a farmhand for a man named Thomas Butterworth whose place lay near the town of Bidwell, Ohio. He had then a horse of his own, and on Saturday evenings drove into town to spend a few hours in social intercourse with other farmhands. In town he drank several glasses of beer and stood about in Ben Head's saloon—crowded on Saturday evenings with visiting farmhands. Songs were sung and glasses thumped on the bar. At ten o'clock father drove home along a lonely country road, made his horse comfortable for the night, and himself went to bed, quite happy in his position in life. He had at that time no notion of trying to rise in the world.

It was in the spring of his thirty-fifth year that father married my mother, then a country schoolteacher, and in the following spring I came wriggling and crying into the world. Something happened to the two people. They became ambitious. The American passion for getting up in the world took possession of them.

It may have been that mother was responsible. Being a schoolteacher she had no doubt read books and magazines. She had, I presume, read of how Garfield, Lincoln, and other Americans rose from poverty to fame and greatness, and as I lay beside her—in the days of her lying-in—she may have dreamed that I would some day rule men and cities. At any rate she induced father to give up his place as a farmhand, sell his horse, and embark on an independent enterprise of his own. She was a tall silent woman with a long nose and troubled gray eyes. For herself she wanted nothing. For father and myself she was incurably ambitious.

The first venture into which the two people went turned out badly. They rented ten acres of poor stony land on Grigg's Road, eight miles from Bidwell, and launched into chicken-raising. I grew into boyhood on the place and got my first impressions of life there. From the beginning they were impressions of disaster, and if, in my turn, I am a gloomy man inclined to see the darker side of life, I attribute it to the fact that what should have been for me the happy joyous days of childhood were spent on a chicken farm.

One unversed in such matters can have no notion of the many and tragic things that can happen to a chicken. It is born out of an egg, lives for a few weeks as a tiny fluffy thing such as you will see pictured on Easter cards, then becomes hideously naked, eats quantities of corn and meal bought by the sweat of your father's brow, gets diseases called pip, cholera, and other names, stands looking with stupid eyes at the sun, becomes sick and dies. A few hens and now and then a rooster, intended to serve God's mysterious ends, struggle through to maturity. The hens lay eggs out of which come other chickens and the dreadful cycle is thus made complete. It is all unbelievably complex. Most philosophers must have been raised on chicken farms. One hopes for so much from a chicken and is so dreadfully disillusioned. Small chickens, just setting out on the journey of life, look so bright and alert and they are in fact so dreadfully stupid. They are so much like people they mix one up in one's judgments of life. If disease does not kill them, they wait until your expectations are thoroughly aroused and then walk under the wheels of a wagon—to go squashed and dead back to their maker. Vermin infest their youth, and fortunes must be spent for curative powders. In later life I have seen how a literature has been built up on the subject of fortunes to be made out of the raising of chickens. It is intended to be read by the gods who have just eaten of the tree of the knowledge of good and evil. It is a hopeful literature and declares that much may be done by simple, ambitious people who own a few hens. Do not be led astray by it. It was not written for you. Go hunt for gold on the frozen hills of Alaska, put your faith in the honesty of a politician, believe if you will that the world is daily growing better and that good will triumph over evil, but do

not read and believe the literature that is written concerning the hen. It was not written for you.

I, however, digress. My tale does not primarily concern itself with the hen. If correctly told it will center on the egg. For ten years my father and mother struggled to make our chicken farm pay, and then they gave up that struggle and began another. They moved into the town of Bidwell, Ohio, and embarked in the restaurant business. After ten years of worry with incubators that did not hatch, and with tiny—and in their own way lovely—balls of fluff that passed on into semi-naked pullethood and from that into dead henhood, we threw all aside and, packing our belongings on a wagon, drove down Griggs's Road toward Bidwell, a tiny caravan of hope looking for a new place from which to start on our upward journey through life.

We must have been a sad-looking lot, not, I fancy, unlike refugees fleeing from a battlefield. Mother and I walked in the road. The wagon that contained our goods had been borrowed for the day from Mr. Albert Griggs, a neighbor. Out of its sides stuck the legs of cheap chairs, and at the back of the pile of beds, tables, and boxes filled with kitchen utensils was a crate of live chickens, and on top of that the baby carriage in which I had been wheeled about in my infancy. Why we stuck to the baby carriage I don't know. It was unlikely other children would be born, and the wheels were broken. People who have few possessions cling tightly to those they have. That is one of the facts that make life so discouraging.

Father rode on top of the wagon. He was then a baldheaded man of forty-five, a little fat, and from long association with mother and the chickens he had become habitually silent and discouraged. All during our ten years on the chicken farm he had worked as a laborer on neighboring farms, and most of the money he had earned had been spent for remedies to cure chicken diseases, on Wilmer's White Wonder Cholera Cure or Professor Bidlow's Egg Producer or some other preparations that mother found advertised in the poultry papers. There were two little patches of hair on father's head just above his ears. I remember that as a child

I used to sit looking at him when he had gone to sleep in a chair before the stove on Sunday afternoons in the winter. I had at that time already begun to read books and have notions of my own, and the bald path that led over the top of his head was, I fancied, something like a broad road, such a road as Caesar might have made on which to lead his legions out of Rome and into the wonders of an unknown world. The tufts of hair that grew above father's ears were, I thought, like forests. I fell into a half-sleeping, half-waking state and dreamed I was a tiny thing going along the road into a far beautiful place where there were no chicken farms and where life was a happy eggless affair.

One might write a book concerning our flight from the chicken farm into town. Mother and I walked the entire eight miles—she to be sure that nothing fell from the wagon and I to see the wonders of the world. On the seat of the wagon beside father was his greatest treasure. I will tell you of that.

On a chicken farm, where hundreds and even thousands of chickens come out of eggs, surprising things sometimes happen. Grotesques are born out of eggs as out of people. The accident does not often occur—perhaps once in a thousand births. A chicken is, you see, born that has four legs, two pairs of wings, two heads, or what not. The things do not live. They go quickly back to the hand of their maker that has for a moment trembled. The fact that the poor little things could not live was one of the tragedies of life to father. He had some sort of notion that if he could but bring into henhood or roosterhood a five-legged hen or a two-headed rooster his fortune would be made. He dreamed of taking the wonder about to county fairs and of growing rich by exhibiting it to other farmhands.

At any rate, he saved all the little monstrous things that had been born on our chicken farm. They were preserved in alcohol and put each in its own glass bottle. These he had carefully put into a box, and on our journey into town it was carried on the wagon seat beside him. He drove the horses with one hand and with the other clung to the box. When we got to our destination, the box was taken down at once and the bottles removed. All during our days as keepers of a restaurant in the town of Bidwell, Ohio, the grotesques in their little glass bottles sat on a shelf back of the counter. Mother sometimes protested, but father was a rock on the subject of his treasure. The grotesques were, he declared, valuable. People, he said, liked to look at strange and wonderful things.

Did I say that we embarked in the restaurant business in the town of Bidwell, Ohio? I exaggerated a little. The town itself lay at the foot of a low hill and on the shore of a small river. The railroad did not run through the town, and the station was a mile away to the north at a place called Pickleville. There had been a cider mill and pickle factory at the station, but before the time of our coming they had both gone out of business. In the morning and in the evening busses came down to the station along a road called Turner's Pike from the hotel on the main street of Bidwell. Our going to the out-of-the-way place to embark in the restaurant business was mother's idea. She talked of it for a year and then one day went off and rented an empty store building opposite the railroad station. It was her idea that the restaurant would be profitable. Traveling men, she said, would be always waiting around to take trains out of town, and town people would come to the station to await incoming trains. They would come to the restaurant to buy pieces of pie and drink coffee. Now that I am older I know that she had another motive in going. She was ambitious for me. She wanted me to rise in the world, to get into a town school and become a man of the towns.

At Pickleville father and mother worked hard, as they always had done. At first there was the necessity of putting our place into shape to be a restaurant. That took a month. Father built a shelf on which he put tins of vegetables. He painted a sign on which he put his name in large red letters. Below his name was the sharp command—"EAT HERE"— that was so seldom obeyed. A showcase was bought and filled with cigars and tobacco. Mother scrubbed the floor and the walls of the room. I went to school in the town and was glad to be away from the farm and from the presence of the discouraged, sad-looking chickens. Still I was not very joyous. In the evening I walked home from school along

Turner's Pike and remembered the children I had seen playing in the town schoolyard. A troop of little girls had gone hopping about and singing. I tried that. Down along the frozen road I went hopping solemnly on one leg. "Hippity Hop To The Barber Shop," I sang shrilly. Then I stopped and looked doubtfully about. I was afraid of being seen in my gay mood. It must have seemed to me that I was doing a thing that should not be done by one who, like myself, had been raised on a chicken farm where death was a daily visitor.

Mother decided that our restaurant should remain open at night. At ten in the evening a passenger train went north past our door followed by a local freight. The freight crew had switching to do in Pickleville, and when the work was done they came to our restaurant for hot coffee and food. Sometimes one of them ordered a fried egg. In the morning at four they returned north-bound and again visited us. A little trade began to grow up. Mother slept at night and during the day tended the restaurant and fed our boarders while father slept. He slept in the same bed mother had occupied during the night, and I went off to the town of Bidwell and to school. During the long nights, while mother and I slept, father cooked meats that were to go into sandwiches for the lunch baskets of our boarders. Then an idea in regard to getting up in the world came into his head. The American spirit took hold of him. He also became ambitious.

In the long nights when there was little to do, father had time to think. That was his undoing. He decided that he had in the past been an unsuccessful man because he had not been cheerful enough and that in the future he would adopt a cheerful outlook on life. In the early morning he came upstairs and got into bed with mother. She woke and the two talked. From my bed in the corner I listened.

It was father's idea that both he and mother should try to entertain the people who came to eat at our restaurant. I cannot now remember his words, but he gave the impression of one about to become in some obscure way a kind of public entertainer. When people, particularly young people from the town of Bidwell, came into our place, as on very rare occasions they did, bright entertaining conversation was to be made. From father's words I gathered that something of the jolly innkeeper effect was to be sought. Mother must have been doubtful from the first, but she said nothing discouraging. It was father's notion that a passion for the company of himself and mother would spring up in the breasts of the younger people of the town of Bidwell. In the evening bright happy groups would come singing down Turner's Pike. They would troop shouting with joy and laughter into our place. There would be song and festivity. I do not mean to give the impression that father spoke so elaborately of the matter. He was, as I have said, an uncommunicative man. "They want some place to go. I tell you they want some place to go," he said over and over. That was as far as he got. My own imagination has filled in the blanks.

For two or three weeks this notion of father's invaded our house. We did not talk much, but in our daily lives tried earnestly to make smiles take the place of glum looks. Mother smiled at the boarders and I, catching the infection, smiled at our cat. Father became a little feverish in his anxiety to please. There was, no doubt, lurking somewhere in him, a touch of the spirit of the showman. He did not waste much of his ammunition on the railroad men he served at night, but seemed to be waiting for a young man or woman from Bidwell to come in to show what he could do. On the counter in the restaurant there was a wire basket kept always filled with eggs, and it must have been before his eyes when the idea of being entertaining was born in his brain. There was something pre-natal about the way eggs kept themselves connected with the development of his idea. At any rate, an egg ruined his new impulse in life. Late one night I was awakened by a roar of anger coming from father's throat. Both mother and I sat upright in our beds. With trembling hands she lighted a lamp that stood on a table by her head. Downstairs the front door of our restaurant went shut with a bang and in a few minutes father tramped up the stairs. He held an egg in his hand, and his hand trembled as though he were having a chill. There was a half-insane light in his eyes. As he stood glaring at us I was sure he intended throwing the egg at either mother or me. Then he laid it gently on the table beside the lamp and dropped on his knees beside mother's bed. He began to cry like a boy, and I, carried away by his grief, cried with him. The two of us filled the little upstairs room with our wailing voices. It is ridiculous, but of the picture we made I can remember only the fact that mother's hand continually stroked the bald path that ran across the top of his head. I have forgotten what mother said to him and how she induced him to tell her of what had happened downstairs. His explanation also has gone out of my mind. I remember only my own grief and fright and the shiny path over father's head glowing in the lamplight as he knelt by the bed.

As to what happened downstairs. For some unexplainable reason I know the story as well as though I had been a witness to my father's discomfiture. One in time gets to know many unexplainable things. On that evening young Joe Kane, son of a merchant of Bidwell, came to Pickleville to meet his father, who was expected on the ten o'clock evening train from the South. The train was three hours late and Joe came into our place to loaf about and to wait for its arrival. The local freight train came in and the freight crew were fed. Joe was left alone in the restaurant with father.

From the moment he came into our place the Bidwell young man must have been puzzled by my father's actions. It was his notion that father was angry at him for hanging around. He noticed that the restaurant-keeper was apparently disturbed by his presence and he thought of going out. However, it began to rain and he did not fancy the long walk to town and back. He bought a five-cent cigar and ordered a cup of coffee. He had a newspaper in his pocket and took it out and began to read. "I'm waiting for the evening train. It's late," he said apologetically.

For a long time father, whom Joe Kane had never seen before, remained silently gazing at his visitor. He was no doubt suffering from an attack of stage fright. As so often happens in life he had thought so much and so often of the situation that now confronted him that he was somewhat nervous in its presence.

For one thing, he did not know what to do with his hands. He thrust one of them nervously over the counter and shook hands with Joe Kane. "How-de-do," he said. Joe Kane put his newspaper down and stared at him. Father's eyes lighted on the basket of eggs that sat on the counter and he began to talk. "Well," he began hesitatingly, "well, you have heard of Christopher Columbus, eh?" He seemed to be angry. "That Christopher Columbus was a cheat," he declared emphatically. "He talked of making an egg stand on its end. He talked, he did, and then he went and broke the end of the egg."

My father seemed to his visitor to be beside himself at the duplicity of Christopher Columbus. He muttered and swore. He declared it was wrong to teach children that Christopher Columbus was a great man when, after all, he cheated at the critical moment. He had declared he would make an egg stand on end and then, when his bluff had been called, he had done a trick. Still grumbling at Columbus, father took an egg from the basket on the counter and began to walk up and down. He rolled the egg between the palms of his hands. He smiled genially. He began to mumble words regarding the effect to be produced on an egg by the electricity that comes out of the human body. He declared that, without breaking its shell and by virtue of rolling it back and forth in his hands, he could stand the egg on its end. He explained that the warmth of his hands and the gentle rolling movement he gave the egg created a new center of gravity, and Joe Kane was mildly interested. "I have handled thousands of eggs," father said. "No one knows more about eggs than I do."

He stood the egg on the counter and it fell on its side. He tried the trick again and again, each time rolling the egg between the palms of his hands and saying the words regarding the wonders of electricity and the laws of gravity. When after a half-hour's effort he did succeed in making the egg stand for a moment, he looked up to find that his visitor was no longer watching. By the time he had succeeded in calling Joe Kane's attention to the success of his effort, the egg had again rolled over and lay on its side.

Afire with the showman's passion and at the same time a good deal disconcerted by the failure of his first effort, father now took the bottles containing the poultry monstrosities down from their place on the shelf and began to show them to his visitor. "How would you like to have seven legs and two heads like this fellow," he asked, exhibiting the most remarkable of his treasures. A cheerful smile played over his face. He reached over the counter and tried to slap Joe Kane on the shoulder as he had seen men do in Ben Head's saloon when he was a young farmhand and drove to town on Saturday evenings. His visitor was made a little ill by the sight of the body of the terribly deformed bird floating in the alcohol in the bottle and got up to go. Coming from behind the counter, father took hold of the young man's arm and led him back to his seat. He grew a little angry and for a moment had to turn his face away and force himself to smile. Then he put the bottles back on the shelf. In an outburst of generosity he fairly compelled Joe Kane to have a fresh cup of coffee and another cigar at his expense. Then he took a pan and filling it with vinegar, taken from a jug that sat beneath the counter, he declared himself about to do a new trick. "I will heat this egg in this pan of vinegar," he said. "Then I will put it through the neck of a bottle without breaking the shell. When the egg is inside the bottle it will resume its normal shape and the shell will become hard again. Then I will give the bottle with the egg in it to you. You can take it about with you wherever you go. People will want to know how you got the egg in the bottle. Don't tell them. Keep them guessing. That is the way to have fun with this trick."

Father grinned and winked at his visitor. Joe Kane decided that the man who confronted him was mildly insane but harmless. He drank the cup of coffee that had been given him and began to read his paper again. When the egg had been heated in vinegar, father carried it on a spoon to the counter and going into a back room got an empty bottle. He was angry because his visitor did not watch him as he began to do his trick, but nevertheless went cheerfully to work. For a long time he struggled, trying to get the egg to go through the neck of the bottle. He put the pan of vinegar back on the stove, intending to reheat the egg, then picked it up and burned his fingers. After a

second bath in the hot vinegar, the shell of the egg had been softened a little, but not enough for his purpose. He worked and worked and a spirit of desperate determination took possession of him. When he thought that at last the trick was about to be consummated, the delayed train came in at the station and Joe Kane started to go nonchalantly out at the door. Father made a last desperate effort to conquer the egg and make it do the thing that would establish his reputation as one who knew how to entertain guests who came into his restaurant. He worried the egg. He attempted to be somewhat rough with it. He swore and the sweat stood out on his forehead. The egg broke under his hand. When the contents spurted over his clothes, Joe Kane, who had stopped at the door, turned and laughed.

A roar of anger rose from my father's throat. He danced and shouted a string of inarticulate words. Grabbing another egg from the basket on the counter, he threw it, just missing the head of the young man as he dodged through the door and escaped.

Father came upstairs to mother and me with an egg in his hand. I do not know what he intended to do. I imagine he had some idea of destroying it, of destroying all eggs, and that he intended to let mother and me see him begin. When, however, he got into the presence of mother, something happened to him. He laid the egg gently on the table and dropped on his knees by the bed as I have already explained. He later decided to close the restaurant for the night and to come upstairs and get into bed. When he did so, he blew out the light and after much muttered conversation both he and mother went to sleep. I suppose I went to sleep also, but my sleep was troubled. I awoke at dawn and for a long time looked at the egg that lay on the table. I wondered why eggs had to be and why from the egg came the hen who again laid the egg. The question got into my blood. It has stayed there, I imagine, because I am the son of my father. At any rate, the problem remains unsolved in my mind. And that, I conclude, is but another evidence of the complete and final triumph of the egg—at least as far as my family is concerned.

1921

1896 ~ *F. Scott Fitzgerald* ~ 1940

F. SCOTT FITZGERALD was born in Saint Paul, Minnesota, on September 24, 1896. He was educated at the Newman School, in New Jersey, and at Princeton, which he entered in 1913. While in college, he was active in local literary and dramatic circles, helping to edit *The Princeton Tiger* and the *Nassau Literary Magazine*. In 1917 he left college to join the army; but his army career, all of it spent in the United States, proved dull and tedious, and he began work on his first novel, which he called at the time *The Romantic Egoist*. The novel, much rejected and much revised, but still inexpertly done, was finally published by Scribners in 1920, as *This Side of Paradise*.

The publication of *This Side of Paradise* marked the beginning of Fitzgerald's role as the interpreter and spokesman of postwar American youth. He married and began living in the city of New York from the receipts of his first novel, plus a number of short stories, some of them slick and smooth as polished glass, sold to *The Saturday Evening Post* and other commercial magazines. *The Beautiful and Damned*, his second novel (1922), better but still immature and overly contrived, continued and encouraged his success. Two volumes of short stories, *Flappers and Philosophers* and *Tales of the Jazz Age*, were also published in these years.

Fitzgerald's real merit as a writer was not clearly demonstrated until the publication of *The Great Gatsby*, in 1925. Within a very short space, Fitzgerald captured many of the characteristics of the 1920's: the shady and shadowy path to quick wealth followed by those who took advantage of Prohibition's continuing failure, the frenetic pursuit of entertainment and debauch, the sense of social irresponsibility of the rich, as demonstrated by the Buchanans, and finally the unsteady foundation in a world of unreal values of Gatsby's pathetic but persistent romantic illusion. The story is told with remarkable and compelling economy and grace. Nick Carraway, the narrator, belongs to the cast of characters but is sufficiently isolated from them in spirit to tell it objectively. Fitzgerald's fondness for the glittering phrase is held in restraint; his control of the novel's pace and unity is extremely good. If there are weaknesses, they lie in the author's failure to consider Gatsby objectively; he is deluded almost as much as is his hero.

Another collection of short stories, *All the Sad Young Men*, followed in 1926. In 1934 appeared *Tender Is the Night*, a story of Dick Diver's attempt to combine the roles of husband and of psychiatrist. The novel is crowded with characters and incidents which do not always succeed in proving their relevance, but the main line of story is clear enough. In selecting psychiatry as a principal carrier of the plot, Fitzgerald was simply acknowledging the tremendous importance of that science for postwar Americans. A second theme is that of the wealthy expatriate, and Fitzgerald offers a generous number of examples of the Americans who, as he said, for a decade "had wanted only to be entertained."

Another collection of short stories, *Taps at Reveille*, appeared in 1935, containing one of his best stories, "Babylon Revisited." In his last years, Fitzgerald lived and worked in Hollywood, fighting both debts and illness, and restless under the commercial demands of the film center. He died of a heart attack on December 21, 1940. A few months later, Edmund Wilson published *The Last Tycoon*, an unfinished novel concerning the film industry, together with notes which suggested the way in which it might have been finished. As it stands, *The Last Tycoon* shows little advance over *Tender Is the Night;* the finished portion is chaotic and disorderly, with an added tendency toward sensationalism that had previously been exhibited only in Fitzgerald's slickest satevepost products. His fame rests chiefly upon the accomplishment of *The Great Gatsby* and several excellent short stories. Beyond that, he can be credited with a remarkable idea, in *Tender Is the Night*, several fine scenes in that novel, and a number of illuminating sketches of his own life and his times, preserved for us in *The Crack-Up* (edited in 1945 by Edmund Wilson).

Fitzgerald's novels are *This Side of Paradise* (1920); *The Beautiful and Damned* (1922); *The Great Gatsby* (1925); *Tender Is the Night* (1934); and *The Last Tycoon* (1941). Short story collections are found in *Flappers and Philosophers* (1920); *Tales of the Jazz Age* (1922); *All the Sad Young Men* (1926); and *Taps at Reveille* (1935). One play, *The Vegetable, or From President to Postman*, was published in 1923. *The Crack-Up*, edited by Edmund Wilson (1945), contains some sketches, many of them autobiographical, selections from Fitzgerald's notebooks, and some letters. It also includes critical estimates by Wilson, Paul Rosenfeld, Glenway Westcott, John Dos Passos, and others. The most convenient anthology of Fitzgerald's work, *The Viking Portable Fitzgerald*, contains *The Great Gatsby, Tender Is the Night*, and a selection of short stories. Critical discussions of Fitzgerald can be found in Paul Rosenfeld, *Men Seen* (1925); Harlan Hatcher, *Creating the Modern American Novel* (1935); Maxwell Geismar, *The Last of the Provincials* (1947); Alfred Kazin, *On Native Grounds* (1942); John Berryman, "F. Scott Fitzgerald," *Kenyon Review*, Winter, 1946; William Troy, "Scott Fitzgerald: The Authority of Failure," *Accent*, Autumn, 1945 (also in *Forms of Modern Fiction*, ed. W. V. O'Connor, 1948); Arthur Mizener, "Scott Fitzgerald and the Imaginative Possession of American Life," *Sewanee Review*, Winter, 1946.

THE RICH BOY

I

BEGIN with an individual, and before you know it you find that you have created a type; begin with a type, and you find that you have created—nothing. That is because we are all queer fish, queerer behind our faces and voices than we want any one to know or than we know ourselves. When I hear a man proclaiming himself an "average, honest, open fellow," I feel pretty sure that he has some definite and perhaps terrible abnormality which he has agreed to conceal—and his protestation of being average and honest and open is his way of reminding himself of his misprision.

There are no types, no plurals. There is a rich boy, and this is his and not his brothers' story. All my life I have lived among his brothers but this one has been my friend. Besides, if I wrote about his brothers I should have to begin by attacking all the lies that the poor have told about the rich and the rich have told about themselves—such a wild structure they have erected that when we pick up a book about the rich, some instinct prepares us for unreality. Even the intelligent and impassioned reporters of life have made the country of the rich as unreal as fairy-land.

Let me tell you about the very rich. They are different from you and me. They possess and enjoy early, and it does something to them, makes them soft where we are hard, and cynical where we are trustful, in a way that, unless you were born rich, it is very difficult to understand. They think, deep in their hearts, that they are better than we are because we had to discover the compensations and refuges of life for ourselves. Even when they enter deep into our world or sink below us, they still think that they are better than we are. They are different. The only way I can describe young Anson Hunter is to approach him as if he were a foreigner and cling stubbornly to my point of view. If I accept his for a moment I am lost—I have nothing to show but a preposterous movie.

II

Anson was the eldest of six children who would some day divide a fortune of fifteen million dollars, and he reached the age of reason—is it seven?—at the beginning of the century when daring young women were already gliding along Fifth Avenue in electric "mobiles." In those days he and his brother had an English governess who spoke the language very clearly and crisply and well, so that the two boys grew to speak as she did—their words and sentences were all crisp and clear and not run together as ours are. They didn't talk exactly like English children but acquired an accent that is peculiar to fashionable people in the city of New York.

In the summer the six children were moved from the house on Seventy-first Street to a big estate in northern Connecticut. It was not a fashionable locality—Anson's father wanted to delay as long as possible his children's knowledge of that side of life. He was a man somewhat superior to his class, which composed New York society, and to his period, which was the snobbish and formalized vulgarity of the Gilded Age, and he wanted his sons to learn habits of concentration and have sound constitutions and grow up into right-living and successful men. He and his wife kept an eye on them as well as they were able until the two older boys went away to school, but in huge establishments this is difficult—it was much simpler in the series of small and medium-sized houses in which my own youth was spent—I was never far out of the reach of my mother's voice, of the sense of her presence, her approval or disapproval.

Anson's first sense of his superiority came to him when he realized the half-grudging American deference that was paid to him in the Connecticut village. The parents of the boys he played with always inquired after his father and mother, and were vaguely excited when their own children were asked to the Hunters' house. He accepted this as the natural state of things, and a sort of impatience with all groups of which he was not the center —in money, in position, in authority—remained with him for the rest of his life. He disdained to struggle with other boys for precedence—he expected it to be given him freely, and when it wasn't he withdrew into his family. His family was sufficient, for in the East money is still a somewhat feudal thing, a clan-forming thing. In the snobbish West, money separates families to form "sets."

At eighteen, when he went to New Haven, Anson was tall and thick-set, with a clear complexion and a healthy color from the ordered life he had led in school. His hair was yellow and grew in a funny way on his head, his nose was beaked—these two things kept him from being handsome—but he had a confident charm and a certain brusque style, and the upper-class men who passed him on the street knew without being told that he was a rich boy and had gone to one of the best schools. Nevertheless, his very superiority kept him from being a success in college—the independence was mistaken for egotism, and the refusal to accept Yale standards with the proper awe seemed to belittle all those who had. So, long before he graduated, he began to shift the center of his life to New York.

He was at home in New York—there was his own house with "the kind of servants you can't get any more"—and his own family, of which, because of his good humor and a certain ability to make things go, he was rapidly becoming the centre, and the débutante parties, and the correct manly world of the men's clubs, and the occasional wild spree with the gallant girls whom New Haven only knew from the fifth row. His aspirations were conventional enough —they included even the irreproachable shadow he would some day marry, but they differed from the aspirations of the majority of young men in that there was no mist over them, none of that quality which is variously known as "idealism" or "illusion." Anson accepted without reservation the world of high finance and high extravagance, of divorce and dissipation, of snobbery and of privilege. Most of our lives end as a compromise—it was as a compromise that his life began.

He and I first met in the late summer of 1917 when he was just out of Yale, and, like the rest of us, was swept up into the systematized hysteria of the war. In the blue-green uniform of the naval aviation he came down to Pensacola, where the hotel orchestras played "I'm sorry, dear," and we young officers danced with the girls. Every one liked him, and though he ran with the drinkers and wasn't an especially good pilot, even the instructors treated him with a certain respect. He was always having long talks with them in his confident, logical voice —talks which ended by his getting himself, or, more frequently, another officer, out of some impending trouble. He was convivial, bawdy, robustly avid for pleasure, and we were all surprised when he fell in love with a conservative and rather proper girl.

Her name was Paula Legendre, a dark, serious beauty from somewhere in California. Her family kept a winter residence just outside of town, and in spite of her primness she was enormously popular; there is a large class of men whose egotism can't endure humor in a woman. But Anson wasn't that sort, and I couldn't understand the attraction of her "sincerity"—that was the thing to say about her— for his keen and somewhat sardonic mind.

Nevertheless, they fell in love—and on her terms. He no longer joined the twilight gathering at the De Sota bar, and whenever they were seen together they were engaged in a long, serious dialogue, which must have gone on several weeks. Long afterward he told me that it was not about anything in particular but was composed on both sides of immature and even meaningless statements—the emotional content that gradually came to fill it grew up not out of the words but out of its enormous seriousness. It was a sort of hypnosis. Often it was interrupted, giving way to that emasculated humor we call fun; when they were alone it was resumed again, solemn, low-keyed, and pitched so as to give each other a sense of unity in feeling and thought. They came to resent any interruptions of it, to be unresponsive to facetiousness about life, even to the mild cynicism of their contemporaries. They were only happy when the dialogue was going on, and its seriousness bathed them like the amber glow of an open fire. Toward the end there came an interruption they did not resent—it began to be interrupted by passion.

Oddly enough, Anson was as engrossed in the dialogue as she was and as profoundly affected by it, yet at the same time aware that on his side much was insincere, and on hers much was merely simple. At first, too, he despised her emotional simplicity as well, but with his love her nature deepened and blossomed, and he could despise it no longer. He felt that if he could enter into Paula's warm safe life he would be happy. The long preparation of the dialogue removed any constraint—he taught her some of what he had learned from more adventurous women, and she responded with a rapt holy intensity. One evening after a dance they agreed to marry, and he wrote a long letter about her to his mother. The next day Paula told him that she was rich, that she had a personal fortune of nearly a million dollars.

III

It was exactly as if they could say "Neither of us has anything: we shall be poor together" —just as delightful that they should be rich instead. It gave them the same communion of adventure. Yet when Anson got leave in April, and Paula and her mother accompanied him North, she was impressed with the standing of his family in New York and with the scale on which they lived. Alone with Anson for the first time in the rooms where he had played as a boy, she was filled with a comfortable emotion, as though she were pre-eminently safe and taken care of. The pictures of Anson in a skull cap at his first school, of Anson on horseback with the sweetheart of a mysterious forgotten summer, of Anson in a gay group of ushers and bridesmaids at a wedding, made her jealous of his life apart from her in the past, and so completely did his authoritative person seem to sum up and typify these possessions of his that she was inspired with the idea of being married immediately and returning to Pensacola as his wife.

But an immediate marriage wasn't discussed —even the engagement was to be secret until after the war. When she realized that only two days of his leave remained, her dissatisfaction crystallized in the intention of making him as unwilling to wait as she was. They were driving to the country for dinner, and she determined to force the issue that night.

Now a cousin of Paula's was staying with them at the Ritz, a severe, bitter girl who loved Paula but was somewhat jealous of her impressive engagement, and as Paula was late in dressing, the cousin, who wasn't going to the party, received Anson in the parlor of the suite.

Anson had met friends at five o'clock and drunk freely and indiscreetly with them for an hour. He left the Yale Club at a proper time, and his mother's chauffeur drove him to the Ritz, but his usual capacity was not in evidence, and the impact of the steam-heated sitting-room made him suddenly dizzy. He knew it, and was both amused and sorry.

Paula's cousin was twenty-five, but she was exceptionally naïve, and at first failed to realize what was up. She had never met Anson before, and she was surprised when he mumbled strange information and nearly fell off his chair, but until Paula appeared it didn't occur to her that what she had taken for the odor of a dry-cleaned uniform was really whisky. But Paula understood as soon as she appeared; her only thought was to get Anson away before her mother saw him, and at the look in her eyes the cousin understood too.

When Paula and Anson descended to the limousine they found two men inside, both asleep; they were the men with whom he had been drinking at the Yale Club, and they were also going to the party. He had entirely forgotten their presence in the car. On the way to Hempstead they awoke and sang. Some of the songs were rough, and though Paula tried to reconcile herself to the fact that Anson had few verbal inhibitions, her lips tightened with shame and distaste.

Back at the hotel the cousin, confused and agitated, considered the incident, and then walked into Mrs. Legendre's bedroom, saying: Isn't he funny?"

"Who is funny?"

"Why—Mr. Hunter. He seemed so funny." Mrs. Legendre looked at her sharply.

"How is he funny?"

"Why, he said he was French. I didn't know he was French."

"That's absurd. You must have misunderstood." She smiled: "It was a joke."

The cousin shook her head stubbornly.

"No. He said he was brought up in France. He said he couldn't speak any English, and that's why he couldn't talk to me. And he couldn't!"

Mrs. Legendre looked away with impatience just as the cousin added thoughtfully, "Perhaps it was because he was so drunk," and walked out of the room.

This curious report was true. Anson, finding his voice thick and uncontrollable, had taken the unusual refuge of announcing that he spoke no English. Years afterward he used to tell that part of the story, and he invariably communicated the uproarious laughter which the memory aroused in him.

Five times in the next hour Mrs. Legendre tried to get Hempstead on the phone. When she succeeded, there was a ten-minute delay before she heard Paula's voice on the wire.

"Cousin Jo told me Anson was intoxicated."

"Oh, no. . . ."

"Oh, yes. Cousin Jo says he was intoxicated. He told her he was French, and fell off his chair and behaved as if he was very intoxicated. I don't want you to come home with him."

"Mother, he's all right! Please don't worry about——"

"But I do worry. I think it's dreadful. I want you to promise me not to come home with him."

"I'll take care of it, mother. . . ."

"I don't want you to come home with him."

"All right, mother. Good-by."

"Be sure now, Paula. Ask some one to bring you."

Deliberately Paula took the receiver from her ear and hung it up. Her face was flushed with helpless annoyance. Anson was stretched asleep out in a bedroom upstairs, while the dinner-party below was proceeding lamely to-ward conclusion.

The hour's drive had sobered him some-what—his arrival was merely hilarious—and Paula hoped that the evening was not spoiled, after all, but two imprudent cocktails before dinner completed the disaster. He talked bois-terously and somewhat offensively to the party at large for fifteen minutes, and then slid si-lently under the table; like a man in an old print—but, unlike an old print, it was rather horrible without being at all quaint. None of the young girls present remarked upon the in-cident—it seemed to merit only silence. His uncle and two other men carried him upstairs, and it was just after this that Paula was called to the phone.

An hour later Anson awoke in a fog of ner-vous agony, through which he perceived after a moment the figure of his uncle Robert stand-ing by the door.

". . . I said are you better?"

"What?"

"Do you feel better, old man?"

"Terrible," said Anson.

"I'm going to try you on another Bromo-seltzer. If you can hold it down, it'll do you good to sleep."

With an effort Anson slid his legs from the bed and stood up.

"I'm all right," he said dully.

"Take it easy."

"I thin' if you gave me a glass brandy I could go downstairs."

"Oh, no——"

"Yes, that's the only thin'. I'm all right now. . . . I suppose I'm in dutch dow' there."

"They know you're a little under the wea-ther," said his uncle deprecatingly. "But don't worry about it. Schuyler didn't even get here. He passed away in the locker-room over at the Links."

Indifferent to any opinion, except Paula's, Anson was nevertheless determined to save the débris of the evening, but when after a cold bath he made his appearance most of the party had already left. Paula got up imme-diately to go home.

In the limousine the old serious dialogue began. She had known that he drank, she ad-mitted, but she had never expected anything like this—it seemed to her that perhaps they were not suited to each other, after all. Their ideas about life were too different, and so forth. When she finished speaking, Anson spoke in turn, very soberly. Then Paula said she'd have to think it over; she wouldn't decide tonight; she was not angry but she was terrible sorry. Nor would she let him come into the hotel with her, but just before she got out of the car she leaned and kissed him unhappily on the cheek.

The next afternoon Anson had a long talk with Mrs. Legendre while Paula sat listening in silence. It was agreed that Paula was to brood over the incident for a proper period and then, if mother and daughter thought it best, they would follow Anson to Pensacola. On his part he apologized with sincerity and dignity—that was all; with every card in her hand Mrs. Legendre was unable to establish any advantage over him. He made no prom-ises, showed no humility, only delivered a few serious comments on life which brought him off with rather a moral superiority at the end. When they came South three weeks later, neither Anson in his satisfaction nor Paula in her relief at the reunion realized that the psy-chological moment had passed forever.

IV

He dominated and attracted her, and at the same time filled her with anxiety. Confused by his mixture of solidity and self-indulgence, of sentiment and cynicism—incongruities which her gentle mind was unable to resolve—Paula grew to think of him as two alternating per-sonalities. When she saw him alone, or at a formal party, or with his casual inferiors, she felt a tremendous pride in his strong, attractive presence, the paternal, understanding stature of his mind. In other company she became un-easy when what had been a fine imperviousness to mere gentility showed its other face. The other face was gross, humorous, reckless of everything but pleasure. It startled her mind temporarily away from him, even led her into a short covert experiment with an old beau, but it was no use—after four months of Anson's enveloping vitality there was an anæmic pallor in all other men.

In July he was ordered abroad, and their tenderness and desire reached a crescendo. Paula considered a last-minute marriage—decided against it only because there were always cocktails on his breath now, but the parting itself made her physically ill with grief. After his departure she wrote him long letters of regret for the days of love they had missed by waiting. In August Anson's plane slipped down into the North Sea. He was pulled onto a destroyer after a night in the water and sent to hospital with pneumonia; the armistice was signed before he was finally sent home.

Then, with every opportunity given back to them, with no material obstacle to overcome, the secret weavings of their temperaments came between them, drying up their kisses and their tears, making their voices less loud to one another, muffling the intimate chatter of their hearts until the old communication was only possible by letters, from far away. One afternoon a society reporter waited for two hours in the Hunters' house for a confirmation of their engagement. Anson denied it; nevertheless an early issue carried the report as a leading paragraph—they were "constantly seen together at Southampton, Hot Springs, and Tuxedo Park." But the serious dialogue had turned a corner into a long-sustained quarrel, and the affair was almost played out. Anson got drunk flagrantly and missed an engagement with her, whereupon Paula made certain behavioristic demands. His despair was helpless before his pride and his knowledge of himself: the engagement was definitely broken.

"Dearest," said their letters now, "Dearest, Dearest, when I wake up in the middle of the night and realize that after all it was not to be, I feel that I want to die. I can't go on living any more. Perhaps when we meet this summer we may talk things over and decide differently— we were so excited and sad that day, and I don't feel that I can live all my life without

you. You speak of other people. Don't you know there are no other people for me, but only you. . . . ."

But as Paula drifted here and there around the East she would sometimes mention her gaieties to make him wonder. Anson was too acute to wonder. When he saw a man's name in her letters he felt more sure of her and a little disdainful—he was always superior to such things. But he still hoped that they would some day marry.

Meanwhile he plunged vigorously into all the movement and glitter of post-bellum New York, entering a brokerage house, joining half a dozen clubs, dancing late, and moving in three worlds—his own world, the world of young Yale graduates, and that section of the half-world which rests one end on Broadway. But there was always a thorough and infractible eight hours devoted to his work in Wall Street, where the combination of his influential family connection, his sharp intelligence, and his abundance of sheer physical energy brought him almost immediately forward. He had one of those invaluable minds with partitions in it; sometimes he appeared at his office refreshed by less than an hour's sleep, but such occurrences were rare. So early as 1920 his income in salary and commissions exceeded twelve thousand dollars.

As the Yale tradition slipped into the past he became more and more of a popular figure among his classmates in New York, more popular than he had ever been in college. He lived in a great house, and had the means of introducing young men into other great houses. Moreover, his life already seemed secure, while theirs, for the most part, had arrived again at precarious beginnings. They commenced to turn to him for amusement and escape, and Anson responded readily, taking pleasure in helping people and arranging their affairs.

There were no men in Paula's letters now, but a note of tenderness ran through them that had not been there before. From several sources he heard that she had "a heavy beau," Lowell Thayer, a Bostonian of wealth and position, and though he was sure she still loved him, it made him uneasy to think that he might lose her, after all. Save for one unsatisfactory day she had not been in New York for almost five months, and as the rumors multiplied he became increasingly anxious to see her. In February he took his vacation and went down to Florida.

Palm Beach sprawled plump and opulent between the sparkling sapphire of Lake Worth, flawed here and there by houseboats at anchor, and the great turquoise bar of the Atlantic Ocean. The huge bulks of the Breakers and the Royal Poinciana rose as twin paunches from the bright level of the sand, and around them clustered the Dancing Glade, Bradley's House of Chance, and a dozen modistes and milliners with goods at triple prices from New York. Upon the trellissed veranda of the Breakers two hundred women stepped right, stepped left, wheeled, and slid in that then celebrated calisthenic known as the double-shuffle, while in half-time to the music two thousand bracelets clicked up and down on two hundred arms.

At the Everglades Club after dark Paula and Lowell Thayer and Anson and a casual fourth played bridge with hot cards. It seemed to Anson that her kind, serious face was wan and tired—she had been around now for four, five, years. He had known her for three.

"Two spades."

"Cigarette? . . . Oh, I beg your pardon. By me."

"By."

"I'll double three spades."

There were a dozen tables of bridge in the room, which was filling up with smoke. Anson's eyes met Paula's, held them persistently even when Thayer's glance fell between them. . . .

"What was bid?" he asked abstractedly.

"*Rose of Washington Square*"
sang the young people in the corners:
"*I'm withering there
In basement air——*"
The smoke banked like fog, and the opening of a door filled the room with blown swirls of ectoplasm. Little Bright Eyes streaked past the tables seeking Mr. Conan Doyle among the Englishmen who were posing as Englishmen about the lobby.

"You could cut it with a knife."

". . . cut it with a knife."

". . . a knife."

At the end of the rubber Paula suddenly got up and spoke to Anson in a tense, low voice. With scarcely a glance at Lowell Thayer, they walked out the door and descended a long flight of stone steps—in a moment they were walking hand in hand along the moonlit beach.

"Darling, darling. . . ." They embraced recklessly, passionately, in a shadow . . . Then Paula drew back her face to let his lips say what she wanted to hear—she could feel the words forming as they kissed again. . . . Again she broke away, listening, but as he pulled her close once more she realized that he had said nothing—only *"Darling! Darling!"* in that deep, sad whisper that always made her cry. Humbly, obediently, her emotions yielded to him and the tears streamed down her face, but her heart kept on crying: "Ask me—oh, Anson, dearest, ask me!"

"Paula. . . . *Paula!*"

The words wrung her heart like hands, and Anson, feeling her tremble, knew that emotion was enough. He need say no more, commit their destinies to no practical enigma. Why should he, when he might hold her so, biding his own time, for another year—forever? He was considering them both, her more than himself. For a moment, when she said suddenly that she must go back to her hotel, he hesitated, thinking, first, "This is the moment, after all," and then: "No, let it wait—she is mine. . . ."

He had forgotten that Paula too was worn away inside with the strain of three years. Her mood passed forever in the night.

He went back to New York next morning filled with a certain restless dissatisfaction. Late in April, without warning, he received a telegram from Bar Harbor in which Paula told him that she was engaged to Lowell Thayer, and that they would be married immediately in Boston. What he never really believed could happen had happened at last.

Anson filled himself with whisky that morning, and going to the office, carried on his work without a break—rather with a fear of what would happen if he stopped. In the evening he went out as usual, saying nothing of what had occurred; he was cordial, humorous, unabstracted. But one thing he could not help

—for three days, in any place, in any company, he would suddenly bend his head into his hands and cry like a child.

V

In 1922 when Anson went abroad with the junior partner to investigate some London loans, the journey intimated that he was to be taken into the firm. He was twenty-seven now, a little heavy without being definitely stout, and with a manner older than his years. Old people and young people liked him and trusted him, and mothers felt safe when their daughters were in his charge, for he had a way, when he came into a room, of putting himself on a footing with the oldest and most conservative people there. "You and I," he seemed to say, "we're solid. We understand."

He had an instinctive and rather charitable knowledge of the weaknesses of men and women, and, like a priest, it made him the more concerned for the maintenance of outward forms. It was typical of him that every Sunday morning he taught in a fashionable Episcopal Sunday school—even though a cold shower and a quick change into a cutaway coat were all that separated him from the wild night before.

After his father's death he was the practical head of his family, and, in effect, guided the destinies of the younger children. Through a complication his authority did not extend to his father's estate, which was administrated by his Uncle Robert, who was the horsy member of the family, a good-natured, hard-drinking member of that set which centers about Wheatley Hills.

Uncle Robert and his wife, Edna, had been great friends of Anson's youth, and the former was disappointed when his nephew's superiority failed to take a horsy form. He backed him for a city club which was the most difficult in America to enter—one could only join if one's family had "helped to build up New York (or, in other words, were rich before 1880)—and when Anson, after his election, neglected it for the Yale Club, Uncle Robert gave him a little talk on the subject. But when on top of that Anson declined to enter Robert Hunter's own conservative and somewhat neglected brokerage house, his manner grew cooler. Like a primary teacher who has taught all he knew, he slipped out of Anson's life.

There were so many friends in Anson's life—scarcely one for whom he had not done some unusual kindness and scarcely one whom he did not occasionally embarrass by his bursts of rough conversation or his habit of getting drunk whenever and however he liked. It annoyed him when any one else blundered in that regard—about his own lapses he was always humorous. Odd things happened to him and he told them with infectious laughter.

I was working in New York that spring, and I used to lunch with him at the Yale Club, which my university was sharing until the completion of our own. I had read of Paula's marriage, and one afternoon, when I asked him about her, something moved him to tell me the story. After that he frequently invited me to family dinners at his house and behaved as though there was a special relation between us, as though with his confidence a little of that consuming memory had passed into me.

I found that despite the trusting mothers, his attitude toward girls was not indiscriminately protective. It was up to the girl—if she showed an inclination toward looseness, she must take care of herself, even with him.

"Life," he would explain sometimes, "has made a cynic of me."

By life he meant Paula. Sometimes, especially when he was drinking, it became a little twisted in his mind, and he thought that she had callously thrown him over.

This "cynicism," or rather his realization that naturally fast girls were not worth sparing, led to his affair with Dolly Karger. It wasn't his only affair in those years, but it came nearest to touching him deeply, and it had a profound effect upon his attitude toward life.

Dolly was the daughter of a notorious "publicist" who had married into society. She herself grew up into the Junior League, came out at the Plaza, and went to the Assembly; and only a few old families like the Hunters could question whether or not she "belonged," for her picture was often in the papers, and she had more enviable attention than many girls who undoubtedly did. She was dark-haired, with carmine lips and a high, lovely color,

which she concealed under pinkish-gray powder all through the first year out, because high
color was unfashionable—Victorian-pale was
the thing to be. She wore black, severe suits
and stood with her hands in her pockets leaning a little forward, with a humorous restraint
on her face. She danced exquisitely—better
than anything she liked to dance—better than
anything except making love. Since she was ten
she had always been in love, and usually with
some boy who didn't respond to her. Those
who did—and there were many—bored her
after a brief encounter, but for her failures she
reserved the warmest spot in her heart. When
she met them she would always try once
more—sometimes she succeeded, more often
she failed.

It never occurred to this gypsy of the unattainable that there was a certain resemblance
in those who refused to love her—they
shared a hard intuition that saw through to
her weakness, not a weakness of emotion but
a weakness of rudder. Anson perceived this
when he first met her, less than a month after
Paula's marriage. He was drinking rather
heavily, and he pretended for a week that he
was falling in love with her. Then he dropped
her abruptly and forgot—immediately he took
up the commanding position in her heart.

Like so many girls of that day Dolly was
slackly and indiscreetly wild. The unconven-
tionality of a slightly older generation had been
simply one facet of a post-war movement to
discredit obsolete manners—Dolly's was both
older and shabbier, and she saw in Anson the
two extremes which the emotionally shiftless
woman seeks, an abandon to indulgence alternating with a protective strength. In his character she felt both the sybarite and the solid
rock, and these two satisfied every need of her
nature.

She felt that it was going to be difficult, but
she mistook the reason—she thought that
Anson and his family expected a more spectacular marriage, but she guessed immediately
that her advantage lay in his tendency to drink.

They met at the large débutante dances, but
as her infatuation increased they managed to be
more and more together. Like most mothers,
Mrs. Karger believed that Anson was exceptionally reliable, so she allowed Dolly to go
with him to distant country clubs and suburban houses without inquiring closely into
their activities or questioning her explanations
when they came in late. At first these explanations might have been accurate, but Dolly's
worldly ideas of capturing Anson were soon
engulfed in the rising sweep of her emotion.
Kisses in the back of taxis and motor-cars were
no longer enough; they did a curious thing:

They dropped out of their world for a while
and made another world just beneath it where
Anson's tippling and Dolly's irregular hours
would be less noticed and commented on. It
was composed, this world, of varying elements
—several of Anson's Yale friends and their
wives, two or three young brokers and bond
salesmen and a handful of unattached men,
fresh from college, with money and a propensity to dissipation. What this world lacked in
spaciousness and scale it made up for by allowing them a liberty that it scarcely permitted
itself. Moreover, it centered around them and
permitted Dolly the pleasure of a faint condescension—a pleasure which Anson, whose
whole life was a condescension from the certi-
tudes of his childhood, was unable to share.

He was not in love with her, and in the long
feverish winter of their affair he frequently told
her so. In the spring he was weary—he wanted
to renew his life at some other source—moreover, he saw that either he must break with
her now or accept the responsibility of a definite seduction. Her family's encouraging attitude precipitated his decision—one evening
when Mr. Karger knocked discreetly at the
library door to announce that he had left a
bottle of old brandy in the dining-room, Anson felt that life was hemming him in. That
night he wrote her a short letter in which he
told her that he was going on his vacation,
and that in view of all the circumstances they
had better meet no more.

It was June. His family had closed up the
house and gone to the country, so he was living temporarily at the Yale Club. I had heard
about his affair with Dolly as it developed—
accounts salted with humor, for he despised
unstable women, and granted them no place in
the social edifice in which he believed—and
when he told me that night that he was definitely breaking with her I was glad. I had seen

Dolly here and there, and each time with a feeling of pity at the hopelessness of her struggle, and of shame at knowing so much about her that I had no right to know. She was what is known as "a pretty little thing," but there was a certain recklessness which rather fascinated me. Her dedication to the goddess of waste would have been less obvious had she been less spirited—she would most certainly throw herself away, but I was glad when I heard that the sacrifice would not be consummated in my sight.

Anson was going to leave the letter of farewell at her house next morning. It was one of the few houses left open in the Fifth Avenue district, and he knew that the Kargers, acting upon erroneous information from Dolly, had foregone a trip abroad to give their daughter her chance. As he stepped out the door of the Yale Club into Madison Avenue the postman passed him, and he followed back inside. The first letter that caught his eye was in Dolly's hand.

He knew what it would be—a lonely and tragic monologue, full of the reproaches he knew, the invoked memories, the "I wonder if's"—all the immemorial intimacies that he had communicated to Paula Legendre in what seemed another age. Thumbing over some bills, he brought it on top again and opened it. To his surprise it was a short, somewhat formal note, which said that Dolly would be unable to go to the country with him for the week-end, because Perry Hull from Chicago had unexpectedly come to town. It added that Anson had brought this on himself: "—if I felt that you loved me as I love you I would go with you at any time, any place, but Perry is *so* nice, and he so much wants me to marry him—"

Anson smiled contemptuously—he had had experience with such decoy epistles. Moreover, he knew how Dolly had labored over this plan, probably sent for the faithful Perry and calculated the time of his arrival—even labored over the note so that it would make him jealous without driving him away. Like most compromises, it had neither force nor vitality but only a timorous despair.

Suddenly he was angry. He sat down in the lobby and read it again. Then he went to the phone, called Dolly and told her in his clear, compelling voice that he had received her note and would call for her at five o'clock as they had previously planned. Scarcely waiting for the pretended uncertainty of her "Perhaps I can see you for an hour," he hung up the receiver and went down to his office. On the way he tore his own letter into bits and dropped it in the street.

He was not jealous—she meant nothing to him—but at her pathetic ruse everything stubborn and self-indulgent in him came to the surface. It was a presumption from a mental inferior and it could not be overlooked. If she wanted to know to whom she belonged she would see.

He was on the door-step at quarter past five. Dolly was dressed for the street, and he listened in silence to the paragraph of "I can only see you for an hour," which she had begun on the phone.

"Put on your hat, Dolly," he said, "we'll take a walk."

They strolled up Madison Avenue and over to Fifth while Anson's shirt dampened upon his portly body in the deep heat. He talked little, scolding her, making no love to her, but before they had walked six blocks she was his again, apologizing for the note, offering not to see Perry at all as an atonement, offering anything. She thought that he had come because he was beginning to love her.

"I'm hot," he said when they reached 71st Street.

"This is a winter suit. If I stop by the house and change, would you mind waiting for me downstairs? I'll only be a minute."

She was happy; the intimacy of his being hot, of any physical fact about him, thrilled her. When they came to the iron-grated door and Anson took out his key she experienced a sort of delight.

Downstairs it was dark, and after he ascended in the lift Dolly raised a curtain and looked out through opaque lace at the houses over the way. She heard the lift machinery stop, and with the notion of teasing him pressed the button that brought it down. Then on what was more than an impulse she got into it and sent it up to what she guessed was his floor.

"Anson," she called, laughing a little.

"Just a minute," he answered from his bedroom . . . then after a brief delay: "Now you can come in."

He had changed and was buttoning his vest. "This is my room," he said lightly. "How do you like it?"

She caught sight of Paula's picture on the wall and stared at it in fascination, just as Paula had stared at the pictures of Anson's childish sweethearts five years before. She knew something about Paula—sometimes she tortured herself with fragments of the story.

Suddenly she came close to Anson, raising her arms. They embraced. Outside the area window a soft artificial twilight already hovered, though the sun was still bright on a back roof across the way. In half an hour the room would be quite dark. The uncalculated opportunity overwhelmed them, made them both breathless, and they clung more closely. It was eminent, inevitable. Still holding one another, they raised their heads—their eyes fell together upon Paula's picture, staring down at them from the wall.

Suddenly Anson dropped his arms, and sitting down at his desk tried the drawer with a bunch of keys.

"Like a drink?" he asked in a gruff voice.

"No, Anson."

He poured himself half a tumbler of whisky, swallowed it, and then opened the door into the hall.

"Come on," he said.

Dolly hesitated.

"Anson—I'm going to the country with you tonight after all. You understand that, don't you?"

"Of course," he answered brusquely.

In Dolly's car they rode on to Long Island, closer in their emotions than they had ever been before. They knew what would happen —not with Paula's face to remind them that something was lacking, but when they were alone in the still, hot Long Island night they did not care.

The estate in Port Washington where they were to spend the week-end belonged to a cousin of Anson's who had married a Montana copper operator. An interminable drive began at the lodge and twisted under imported poplar saplings toward a huge, pink, Spanish house. Anson had often visited there before.

After dinner they danced at the Linx Club. About midnight Anson assured himself that his cousins would not leave before two—then he explained that Dolly was tired; he would take her home and return to the dance later. Trembling a little with excitement, they got into a borrowed car together and drove to Port Washington. As they reached the lodge he stopped and spoke to the night-watchman.

"When are you making a round, Carl?"

"Right away."

"Then you'll be here till everybody's in?"

"Yes, sir."

"All right. Listen: if any automobile, no matter whose it is, turns in at this gate, I want you to phone the house immediately." He put a five-dollar bill into Carl's hand. "Is that clear?"

"Yes, Mr. Anson." Being of the Old World, he neither winked nor smiled. Yet Dolly sat with her face turned slightly away.

Anson had a key. Once inside he poured a drink for both of them—Dolly left hers untouched—then he ascertained definitely the location of the phone, and found that it was within easy hearing distance of their rooms, both of which were on the first floor.

Five minutes later he knocked at the door of Dolly's room.

"Anson?" He went in, closing the door behind him. She was in bed, leaning up anxiously with elbows on the pillow; sitting beside her he took her in his arms.

"Anson, darling."

He didn't answer.

"Anson. . . . Anson! I love you. . . . Say you love me. Say it now—can't you say it now? Even if you don't mean it?"

He did not listen. Over her head he perceived that the picture of Paula was hanging here upon this wall.

He got up and went close to it. The frame gleamed faintly with thrice-reflected moonlight—within was a blurred shadow of a face that he saw he did not know. Almost sobbing, he turned around and stared with abomination at the little figure on the bed.

"This is all foolishness," he said thickly. "I don't know what I was thinking about. I don't love you and you'd better wait for somebody that loves you. I don't love you a bit, can't you understand?"

His voice broke, and he went hurriedly out. Back in the salon he was pouring himself a drink with uneasy fingers, when the front door opened suddenly, and his cousin came in.

"Why, Anson, I hear Dolly's sick," she began solicitously. "I hear she's sick. . . ."

"It was nothing," he interrupted, raising his voice so that it would carry into Dolly's room. "She was a little tired. She went to bed."

For a long time afterward Anson believed that a protective God sometimes interfered in human affairs. But Dolly Karger, lying awake and staring at the ceiling, never again believed in anything at all.

VI

When Dolly married during the following autumn, Anson was in London on business. Like Paula's marriage, it was sudden, but it affected him in a different way. At first he felt that it was funny, and had an inclination to laugh when he thought of it. Later it depressed him—it made him feel old.

There was something repetitive about it— why, Paula and Dolly had belonged to different generations. He had a foretaste of the sensation of a man of forty who hears that the daughter of an old flame has married. He wired congratulations and, as was not the case with Paula, they were sincere—he had never really hoped that Paula would be happy.

When he returned to New York, he was made a partner in the firm, and, as his responsibilities increased, he had less time on his hands. The refusal of a life-insurance company to issue him a policy made such an impression on him that he stopped drinking for a year, and claimed that he felt better physically, though I think he missed the convivial recounting of those Celliniesque adventures which, in his early twenties, had played such a part of his life. But he never abandoned the Yale Club. He was a figure there, a personality, and the tendency of his class, who were now seven years out of college, to drift away to more sober haunts was checked by his presence.

His day was never too full nor his mind too weary to give any sort of aid to any one who asked it. What had been done at first through pride and superiority had become a habit and a passion. And there was always something—a younger brother in trouble at New Haven, a quarrel to be patched up between a friend and his wife, a position to be found for this man, an investment for that. But his specialty was the solving of problems for young married people. Young married people fascinated him and their apartments were almost sacred to him—he knew the story of their love-affair, advised them where to live and how, and remembered their babies' names. Toward young wives his attitude was circumspect: he never abused the trust which their husbands—strangely enough in view of his unconcealed irregularities— invariably reposed in him.

He came to take a vicarious pleasure in happy marriages, and to be inspired to an almost equally pleasant melancholy by those that went astray. Not a season passed that he did not witness the collapse of an affair that perhaps he himself had fathered. When Paula was divorced and almost immediately remarried to another Bostonian, he talked about her to me all one afternoon. He would never love any one as he had loved Paula, but he insisted that he no longer cared.

"I'll never marry," he came to say; "I've seen too much of it, and I know a happy marriage is a very rare thing. Besides, I'm too old."

But he did believe in marriage. Like all men who spring from a happy and successful marriage, he believed in it passionately—nothing he had seen would change his belief, his cynicism dissolved upon it like air. But he did really believe he was too old. At twenty-eight he began to accept with equanimity the prospect of marrying without romantic love; he resolutely chose a New York girl of his own class, pretty, intelligent, congenial, above reproach —and set about falling in love with her. The things he had said to Paula with sincerity, to other girls with grace, he could no longer say at all without smiling, or with the force necessary to convince.

"When I'm forty," he told his friends, "I'll be ripe. I'll fall for some chorus girl like the rest."

Nevertheless, he persisted in his attempt. His mother wanted to see him married, and he could now well afford it—he had a seat on the

Stock Exchange, and his earned income came to twenty-five thousand a year. The idea was agreeable: when his friends—he spent most of his time with the set he and Dolly had evolved—closed themselves in behind domestic doors at night, he no longer rejoiced in his freedom. He even wondered if he should have married Dolly. Not even Paula had loved him more, and he was learning the rarity, in a single life, of encountering true emotion.

Just as this mood began to creep over him a disquieting story reached his ear. His aunt Edna, a woman just this side of forty, was carrying on an open intrigue with a dissolute, hard-drinking young man named Cary Sloane. Every one knew of it except Anson's Uncle Robert, who for fifteen years had talked long in clubs and taken his wife for granted.

Anson heard the story again and again with increasing annoyance. Something of his old feeling for his uncle came back to him, a feeling that was more than personal, a reversion toward that family solidarity on which he had based his pride. His intuition singled out the essential point of the affair, which was that his uncle shouldn't be hurt. It was his first experiment in unsolicited meddling, but with his knowledge of Edna's character he felt that he could handle the matter better than a district judge or his uncle.

His uncle was in Hot Springs. Anson traced down the sources of the scandal so that there should be no possibility of mistake and then he called Edna and asked her to lunch with him at the Plaza next day. Something in his tone must have frightened her, for she was reluctant, but he insisted, putting off the date until she had no excuse for refusing.

She met him at the appointed time in the Plaza lobby, a lovely, faded, gray-eyed blonde in a coat of Russian sable. Five great rings, cold with diamonds and emeralds, sparkled on her slender hands. It occurred to Anson that it was his father's intelligence and not his uncle's that had earned the fur and the stones, the rich brilliance that buoyed up her passing beauty.

Though Edna scented his hostility, she was unprepared for the directness of his approach.

"Edna, I'm astonished at the way you've been acting," he said in a strong, frank voice. "At first I couldn't believe it."

"Believe what?" she demanded sharply.

"You needn't pretend with me, Edna. I'm talking about Cary Sloane. Aside from any other consideration, I didn't think you could treat Uncle Robert——"

"Now look here, Anson——" she began angrily, but his peremptory voice broke through hers:

"—and your children in such a way. You've been married eighteen years, and you're old enough to know better."

"You can't talk to me like that! You——"

"Yes, I can. Uncle Robert has always been my best friend." He was tremendously moved. He felt a real distress about his uncle, about his three young cousins.

Edna stood up, leaving her crab-flake cocktail untasted.

"This is the silliest thing——"

"Very well, if you won't listen to me I'll go to Uncle Robert and tell him the whole story—he's bound to hear it sooner or later. And afterward I'll go to old Moses Sloane."

Edna faltered back into her chair.

"Don't talk so loud," she begged him. Her eyes blurred with tears. "You have no idea how your voice carries. You might have chosen a less public place to make all these crazy accusations."

He didn't answer.

"Oh, you never liked me, I know," she went on. "You're just taking advantage of some silly gossip to try and break up the only interesting friendship I've ever had. What did I ever do to make you hate me so?"

Still Anson waited. There would be the appeal to his chivalry, then to his pity, finally to his superior sophistication—when he had shouldered his way through all these there would be admissions, and he could come to grips with her. By being silent, by being impervious, by returning constantly to his main weapon, which was his own true emotion, he bullied her into frantic despair as the luncheon hour slipped away. At two o'clock she took out a mirror and a handkerchief, shined away the marks of her tears and powdered the slight hollows where they had lain. She had agreed to meet him at her own house at five.

When he arrived she was stretched on a chaise longue which was covered with cretonne for the summer, and the tears he had called up at luncheon seemed still to be standing in her eyes. Then he was aware of Cary Sloane's dark anxious presence upon the cold hearth.

"What's this idea of yours?" broke out Sloane immediately. "I understand you invited Edna to lunch and then threatened her on the basis of some cheap scandal."

Anson sat down.

"I have no reason to think it's only scandal."

"I hear you're going to take it to Robert Hunter, and to my father."

Anson nodded.

"Either you break it off—or I will," he said.

"What God damned business is it of yours, Hunter?"

"Don't lose your temper, Cary," said Edna nervously. "It's only a question of showing him how absurd——"

"For one thing, it's my name that's being handed around," interrupted Anson. "That's all that concerns you, Cary."

"Edna isn't a member of your family."

"She most certainly is!" His anger mounted. "Why—she owes this house and the rings on her fingers to my father's brains. When Uncle Robert married her she didn't have a penny."

They all looked at the rings as if they had a significant bearing on the situation. Edna made a gesture to take them from her hand.

"I guess they're not the only rings in the world," said Sloane.

"Oh, this is absurd," cried Edna. "Anson, will you listen to me? I've found out how the silly story started. It was a maid I discharged who went right to the Chilicheffs—all these Russians pump things out of their servants and then put a false meaning on them." She brought down her fist angrily on the table: "And after Tom lent them the limousine for a whole month when we were South last winter ——"

"Do you see?" demanded Sloane eagerly. "This maid got hold of the wrong end of the thing. She knew that Edna and I were friends, and she carried it to the Chilicheffs. In Russia they assume that if a man and a woman——"

He enlarged the theme to a disquisition upon social relations in the Caucasus.

"If that's the case it better be explained to Uncle Robert," said Anson dryly, "so that

when the rumors do reach him he'll know they're not true."

Adopting the method he had followed with Edna at luncheon he let them explain it all away. He knew that they were guilty and that presently they would cross the line from explanation into justification and convict themselves more definitely than he could ever do. By seven they had taken the desperate step of telling him the truth—Robert Hunter's neglect, Edna's empty life, the casual dalliance that had flamed up into passion—but like so many true stories it had the misfortune of being old, and its enfeebled body beat helplessly against the armor of Anson's will. The threat to go to Sloane's father sealed their helplessness, for the latter, a retired cotton broker out of Alabama, was a notorious fundamentalist who controlled his son by a rigid allowance and the promise that at his next vagary the allowance would stop forever.

They dined at a small French restaurant, and the discussion continued—at one time Sloane resorted to physical threats, a little later they were both imploring him to give them time. But Anson was obdurate. He saw that Edna was breaking up, and that her spirit must not be refreshed by any renewal of their passion.

At two o'clock in a small night-club on 53d Street, Edna's nerves suddenly collapsed, and she cried to go home. Sloane had been drinking heavily all evening, and he was faintly maudlin, leaning on the table and weeping a little with his face in his hands. Quickly Anson gave them his terms. Sloane was to leave town for six months, and he must be gone within forty-eight hours. When he returned there was to be no resumption of the affair, but at the end of a year Edna might, if she wished, tell Robert Hunter that she wanted a divorce and go about it in the usual way.

He paused, gaining confidence from their faces for his final word.

"Or there's another thing you can do," he said slowly, "if Edna wants to leave her children, there's nothing I can do to prevent your running off together."

"I want to go home!" cried Edna again. "Oh, haven't you done enough to us for one day?"

Outside it was dark, save for a blurred glow

from Sixth Avenue down the street. In that light those two who had been lovers looked for the last time into each other's tragic faces, realizing that between them there was not enough youth and strength to avert their eternal parting. Sloane walked suddenly off down the street and Anson tapped a dozing taxi-driver on the arm.

It was almost four; there was a patient flow of cleaning water along the ghostly pavement of Fifth Avenue, and the shadows of two night women flitted over the dark façade of St. Thomas's church. Then the desolate shrubbery of Central Park where Anson had often played as a child, and the mounting numbers, significant as names, of the marching streets. This was his city, he thought, where his name had flourished through five generations. No change could alter the permanence of its place here, for change itself was the essential substratum by which he and those of his name identified themselves with the spirit of New York. Resourcefulness and a powerful will— for his threats in weaker hands would have been less than nothing—had beaten the gathering dust from his uncle's name, from the name of his family, from even this shivering figure that sat beside him in the car.

Cary Sloane's body was found next morning on the lower shelf of a pillar of Queensboro Bridge. In the darkness and in his excitement he had thought that it was the water flowing black beneath him, but in less than a second it made no possible difference—unless he had planned to think one last thought of Edna, and call out her name as he struggled feebly in the water.

VII

Anson never blamed himself for his part in this affair—the situation which brought it about had not been of his making. But the just suffer with the unjust, and he found that his oldest and somehow his most precious friendship was over. He never knew what distorted story Edna told, but he was welcome in his uncle's house no longer.

Just before Christmas Mrs. Hunter retired to a select Episcopal heaven, and Anson became the responsible head of his family. An unmarried aunt who had lived with them for years ran the house, and attempted with helpless inefficiency to chaperone the younger girls. All the children were less self-reliant than Anson, more conventional both in their virtues and in their shortcomings. Mrs. Hunter's death had postponed the début of one daughter and the wedding of another. Also it had taken something deeply material from all of them, for with her passing the quiet, expensive superiority of the Hunters came to an end.

For one thing, the estate, considerably diminished by two inheritance taxes and soon to be divided among six children, was not a notable fortune any more. Anson saw a tendency in his youngest sisters to speak rather respectfully of families that hadn't "existed" twenty years ago. His own feeling of precedence was not echoed in them—sometimes they were conventionally snobbish, that was all. For another thing, this was the last summer they would spend on the Connecticut estate; the clamor against it was too loud: "Who wants to waste the best months of the year shut up in that dead old town?" Reluctantly he yielded— the house would go into the market in the fall, and next summer they would rent a smaller place in Westchester County. It was a step down from the expensive simplicity of his father's idea, and, while he sympathized with the revolt, it also annoyed him; during his mother's lifetime he had gone up there at least every other week-end—even in the gayest summers.

Yet he himself was part of this change, and his strong instinct for life had turned him in his twenties from the hollow obsequies of that abortive leisure class. He did not see this clearly—he still felt that there was a norm, a standard of society. But there was no norm, it was doubtful if there had ever been a true norm in New York. The few who still paid and fought to enter a particular set succeeded only to find that as a society it scarcely functioned—or, what was more alarming, that the Bohemia from which they fled sat above them at table.

At twenty-nine Anson's chief concern was his own growing loneliness. He was sure now that he would never marry. The number of weddings at which he had officiated as best man or usher was past all counting—there was a drawer at home that bulged with the official neckties of this or that wedding-party, neckties standing for romances that had not endured a year, for couples who had passed completely from his life. Scarfpins, gold pencils, cuff-buttons, presents from a generation of grooms had passed through his jewel-box and been lost—and with every ceremony he was less and less able to imagine himself in the groom's place. Under his hearty good-will toward all those marriages there was despair about his own.

And as he neared thirty he became not a little depressed at the inroads that marriage, especially lately, had made upon his friendships. Groups of people had a disconcerting tendency to dissolve and disappear. The men from his own college—and it was upon them he had expended the most time and affection—were the most elusive of all. Most of them were drawn deep into domesticity, two were dead, one lived abroad, one was in Hollywood writing continuities for pictures that Anson went faithfully to see.

Most of them, however, were permanent commuters with an intricate family life centering around some suburban country club, and it was from these that he felt his estrangement most keenly.

In the early days of their married life they had all needed him; he gave them advice about their slim finances, he exorcised their doubts about the advisability of bringing a baby into two rooms and a bath, especially he stood for the great world outside. But now their financial troubles were in the past and the fearfully expected child had evolved into an absorbing family. They were always glad to see old Anson, but they dressed up for him and tried to impress him with their present importance, and kept their troubles to themselves. They needed him no longer.

A few weeks before his thirtieth birthday the last of his early and intimate friends was married. Anson acted in his usual rôle of best man, gave his usual silver tea-service, and went down to the usual *Homeric* to say good-by. It was a hot Friday afternoon in May, and as he walked from the pier he realized that Saturday closing had begun and he was free until Monday morning.

"Go where?" he asked himself.

The Yale Club, of course; bridge until dinner, then four or five raw cocktails in somebody's room and a pleasant confused evening. He regretted that this afternoon's groom wouldn't be along—they had always been able to cram so much into such nights: they knew how to attach women and how to get rid of them, how much consideration any girl deserved from their intelligent hedonism. A party was an adjusted thing—you took certain girls to certain places and spent just so much on their amusement; you drank a little, not much, more than you ought to drink, and at a certain time in the morning you stood up and said you were going home. You avoided college boys, sponges, future engagements, fights, sentiment, and indiscretions. That was the way it was done. All the rest was dissipation.

In the morning you were never violently sorry—you made no resolutions, but if you had overdone it and your heart was slightly out of order, you went on the wagon for a few days without saying anything about it, and waited until an accumulation of nervous boredom projected you into another party.

The lobby of the Yale Club was unpopulated. In the bar three very young alumni looked up at him, momentarily and without curiosity.

"Hello there, Oscar," he said to the bartender. "Mr. Cahill been around this afternoon?"

"Mr. Cahill's gone to New Haven."

"Oh . . . that so?"

"Gone to the ball game. Lot of men gone up."

Anson looked once again into the lobby, considered for a moment, and then walked out and over to Fifth Avenue. From the broad window of one of his clubs—one that he had scarcely visited in five years—a gray man with watery eyes stared down at him. Anson looked quickly away—that figure sitting in vacant resignation, in supercilious solitude, depressed him. He stopped and, retracing his steps, started over 47th Street toward Teak Warden's apartment. Teak and his wife had once been his most familiar friends—it was a household where he and Dolly Karger had been used to go in the days of their affair. But Teak had taken to drink, and his wife had remarked publicly that Anson was a bad influence on him. The remark reached Anson in an exaggerated form—when it was finally cleared up, the delicate spell of intimacy was broken, never to be renewed.

"Is Mr. Warden at home?" he inquired.

"They've gone to the country."

The fact unexpectedly cut at him. They were gone to the country and he hadn't known. Two years before he would have known the date, the hour, come up at the last moment for a final drink, and planned his first visit to them. Now they had gone without a word.

Anson looked at his watch and considered a week-end with his family, but the only train was a local that would jolt through the aggressive heat for three hours. And tomorrow in the country, and Sunday—he was in no mood for porch-bridge with polite undergraduates, and dancing after dinner at a rural road-house, a diminutive of gaiety which his father had estimated too well.

"Oh, no," he said to himself. . . . "No."

He was a dignified, impressive young man, rather stout now, but otherwise unmarked by dissipation. He could have been cast for a pillar of something—at times you were sure it was not society, at others nothing else—for the law, for the church. He stood for a few minutes motionless on the sidewalk in front of a 47th Street apartment-house; for almost the first time in his life he had nothing whatever to do.

Then he began to walk briskly up Fifth Avenue, as if he had just been reminded of an important engagement there. The necessity of dissimulation is one of the few characteristics that we share with dogs, and I think of Anson on that day as some well-bred specimen who had been disappointed at a familiar back door. He was going to see Nick, once a fashionable bartender in demand at all private dances, and now employed in cooling non-alcoholic champagne among the labyrinthine cellars of the Plaza Hotel.

"Nick," he said, "what's happened to everything?"

"Dead," Nick said.

"Make me a whisky sour." Anson handed a pint bottle over the counter. "Nick, the girls

are different; I had a little girl in Brooklyn and she got married last week without letting me know."

"That a fact? Ha-ha-ha," responded Nick diplomatically. "Slipped it over on you."

"Absolutely," said Anson. "And I was out with her the night before."

"Ha-ha-ha," said Nick, "ha-ha-ha!"

"Do you remember the wedding, Nick, in Hot Springs where I had the waiters and the musicians singing 'God save the King'?"

"Now where was that, Mr. Hunter?" Nick concentrated doubtfully. "Seems to me that was——"

"Next time they were back for more, and I began to wonder how much I'd paid them," continued Anson.

"——seems to me that was at Mr. Trenholm's wedding."

"Don't know him," said Anson decisively. He was offended that a strange name should intrude upon his reminiscences; Nick perceived this.

"Naw—aw—" he admitted, "I ought to know that. It was one of *your* crowd—Brakins. . . . Baker——"

"Bicker Baker," said Anson responsively. "They put me in a hearse after it was over and covered me up with flowers and drove me away."

"Ha-ha-ha," said Nick. "Ha-ha-ha."

Nick's simulation of the old family servant paled presently and Anson went upstairs to the lobby. He looked around—his eyes met the glance of an unfamiliar clerk at the desk, then fell upon a flower from the morning's marriage hesitating in the mouth of a brass cuspidor. He went out and walked slowly toward the blood-red sun over Columbus Circle. Suddenly he turned around and, retracing his steps to the Plaza, immured himself in a telephone-booth.

Later he said that he tried to get me three times that afternoon, that he tried every one who might be in New York—men and girls he had not seen for years, an artist's model of his college days whose faded number was still in his address book—Central told him that even the exchange existed no longer. At length his quest roved into the country, and he held brief disappointing conversations with emphatic butlers and maids. So-and-so was out, riding, swimming, playing golf, sailed to Europe last week. Who shall I say phoned?

It was intolerable that he should pass the evening alone—the private reckonings which one plans for a moment of leisure lose every charm when the solitude is enforced. There were always women of a sort, but the ones he knew had temporarily vanished, and to pass a New York evening in the hired company of a stranger never occurred to him—he would have considered that that was something shameful and secret, the diversion of a traveling salesman in a strange town.

Anson paid the telephone bill—the girl tried unsuccessfully to joke with him about its size—and for the second time that afternoon started to leave the Plaza and go he knew not where. Near the revolving door the figure of a woman, obviously with child, stood sideways to the light—a sheer beige cape fluttered at her shoulders when the door turned and, each time, she looked impatiently toward it as if she were weary of waiting. At the first sight of her a strong nervous thrill of familiarity went over him, but not until he was within five feet of her did he realize that it was Paula.

"Why, Anson Hunter!"

His heart turned over.

"Why, Paula——"

"Why, this is wonderful. I can't believe it, *Anson!*"

She took both his hands, and he saw in the freedom of the gesture that the memory of him had lost poignancy to her. But not to him—he felt that old mood that she evoked in him stealing over his brain, that gentleness with which he had always met her optimism as if afraid to mar its surface.

"We're at Rye for the summer. Pete had to come East on business—you know of course I'm Mrs. Peter Hagerty now—so we brought the children and took a house. You've got to come out and see us."

"Can I?" he asked directly. "When?"

"When you like. Here's Pete." The revolving door functioned, giving up a fine tall man of thirty with a tanned face and a trim mustache. His immaculate fitness made a sharp contrast with Anson's increasing bulk, which was obvious under the faintly tight cut-away coat.

"You oughtn't to be standing," said Hagerty to his wife. "Let's sit down here." He indicated lobby chairs, but Paula hesitated.

"I've got to go right home," she said. "Anson, why don't you—why don't you come out and have dinner with us tonight? We're just getting settled, but if you can stand that——"

Hagerty confirmed the invitation cordially. "Come out for the night."

Their car waited in front of the hotel, and Paula with a tired gesture sank back against silk cushions in the corner.

"There's so much I want to talk to you about," she said, "it seems hopeless."

"I want to hear about you."

"Well"—she smiled at Hagerty—"that would take a long time too. I have three children—by my first marriage. The oldest is five, then four, then three." She smiled again. "I didn't waste much time having them, did I?"

"Boys?"

"A boy and two girls. Then—oh, a lot of things happened, and I got a divorce in Paris a year ago and married Pete. That's all—except that I'm awfully happy."

In Rye they drove up to a large house near the Beach Club, from which there issued presently three dark, slim children who broke from an English governess and approached them with an esoteric cry. Abstractedly and with difficulty Paula took each one into her arms, a caress which they accepted stiffly, as they had evidently been told not to bump into Mummy. Even against their fresh faces Paula's skin showed scarcely any weariness—for all her physical languor she seemed younger than when he had last seen her at Palm Beach seven years ago.

At dinner she was preoccupied, and afterward, during the homage to the radio, she lay with closed eyes on the sofa, until Anson wondered if his presence at this time were not an intrusion. But at nine o'clock, when Hagerty rose and said pleasantly that he was going to leave them by themselves for a while, she began to talk slowly about herself and the past.

"My first baby," she said—"the one we call Darling, the biggest little girl—I wanted to die when I knew I was going to have her, because Lowell was like a stranger to me. It didn't seem as though she could be my own. I wrote you a letter and tore it up. Oh, you were *so* bad to me, Anson."

It was the dialogue again, rising and falling. Anson felt a sudden quickening of memory.

"Weren't you engaged once?" she asked— "a girl named Dolly something?"

"I wasn't ever engaged. I tried to be engaged, but I never loved anybody but you, Paula."

"Oh," she said. Then after a moment: "This baby is the first one I ever really wanted. You see, I'm in love now—at last."

He didn't answer, shocked at the treachery of her remembrance. She must have seen that the "at last" bruised him, for she continued:

"I was infatuated with you, Anson—you could make me do anything you liked. But we wouldn't have been happy. I'm not smart enough for you. I don't like things to be complicated like you do." She paused. "You'll never settle down," she said.

The phrase struck at him from behind—it was an accusation that of all accusations he had never merited.

"I could settle down if women were different," he said, "If I didn't understand so much about them, if women didn't spoil you for other women, if they had only a little pride. If I could go to sleep for a while and wake up into a home that was really mine—why, that's what I'm made for, Paula, that's what women have seen in me and liked in me. It's only that I can't get through the preliminaries any more."

Hagerty came in a little before eleven; after a whisky Paula stood up and announced that she was going to bed. She went over and stood by her husband.

"Where did you go, dearest?" she demanded.

"I had a drink with Ed Saunders."

"I was worried. I thought maybe you'd run away."

She rested her head against his coat.

"He's sweet, isn't he, Anson?" she demanded.

"Absolutely," said Anson, laughing.

She raised her face to her husband.

"Well, I'm ready," she said. She turned to Anson: "Do you want to see our family gymnastic stunt?"

"Yes," he said in an interested voice.

"All right. Here we go!"

Hagerty picked her up easily in his arms.

"This is called the family acrobatic stunt," said Paula. "He carries me upstairs. Isn't it sweet of him?"

"Yes," said Anson.

Hagerty bent his head slightly until his face touched Paula's.

"And I love him," she said. "I've just been telling you, haven't I, Anson?"

"Yes," he said.

"He's the dearest thing that ever lived in this world; aren't you, darling? . . . Well, good night. Here we go. Isn't he strong?"

"Yes," Anson said.

"You'll find a pair of Pete's pajamas laid out for you. Sweet dreams—see you at breakfast."

"Yes," Anson said.

VIII

The older members of the firm insisted that Anson should go abroad for the summer. He had scarcely had a vacation in seven years, they said. He was stale and needed a change. Anson resisted.

"If I go," he declared, "I won't come back any more."

"That's absurd, old man. You'll be back in three months with all this depression gone. Fit as ever."

"No." He shook his head stubbornly. "If I stop, I won't go back to work. If I stop, that means I've given up—I'm through."

"We'll take a chance on that. Stay six months if you like—we're not afraid you'll leave us. Why, you'd be miserable if you didn't work."

They arranged his passage for him. They liked Anson—every one liked Anson—and the change that had been coming over him cast a sort of pall over the office. The enthusiasm that had invariably signaled up business, the consideration toward his equals and his inferiors, the lift of his vital presence—within the past four months his intense nervousness had melted down these qualities into the fussy pessimism of a man of forty. On every transaction in which he was involved he acted as a drag and a strain.

"If I go I'll never come back," he said.

Three days before he sailed Paula Legendre Hagerty died in childbirth. I was with him a great deal then, for we were crossing together, but for the first time in our friendship he told me not a word of how he felt, nor did I see the slightest sign of emotion. His chief preoccupation was with the fact that he was thirty years old—he would turn the conversation to the point where he could remind you of it and then fall silent, as if he assumed that the state- ment would start a chain of thought sufficient to itself. Like his partners, I was amazed at the change in him, and I was glad when the *Paris* moved off into the wet space between the worlds, leaving his principality behind.

"How about a drink?" he suggested.

We walked into the bar with that defiant feeling that characterizes the day of departure and ordered four Martinis. After one cock- tail a change came over him—he suddenly reached across and slapped my knee with the first joviality I had seen him exhibit for months.

"Did you see that girl in the red tam?" he demanded, "the one with the high color who had the two police dogs down to bid her good- by."

"She's pretty," I agreed.

"I looked her up in the purser's office and found out that she's alone. I'm going down to see the steward in a few minutes. We'll have dinner with her tonight."

After a while he left me, and within an hour he was walking up and down the deck with her, talking to her in his strong, clear voice. Her red tam was a bright spot of color against the steel-green sea, and from time to time she looked up with a flashing bob of her head, and smiled with amusement and interest, and an- ticipation. At dinner we had champagne, and were very joyous—afterward Anson ran the pool with infectious gusto, and several people who had seen me with him asked me his name. He and the girl were talking and laughing to- gether on a lounge in the bar when I went to bed.

I saw less of him on the trip than I had hoped. He wanted to arrange a foursome, but there was no one available, so I saw him only at meals. Sometimes, though, he would have a cocktail in the bar, and he told me about the girl in the red tam, and his adventures with her, making them all bizarre and amusing, as he had a way of doing, and I was glad that he was himself again, or at least the self that I knew, and with which I felt at home. I don't think he was ever happy unless some one was in love with him, responding to him like filings to a magnet, helping him to explain himself, prom- ising him something. What it was I do not know. Perhaps they promised that there would always be women in the world who would spend their brightest, freshest, rarest hours to nurse and protect the superiority he cherished in his heart.

1926

1898 ~ *Ernest Hemingway* ~

HEMINGWAY was born in the Chicago suburban town of Oak Park. He was edu- cated in the public schools, where he distinguished himself as a football player and boxer. Upon graduation (1917) from Oak Park High School he accepted a post as reporter on the staff of a Kansas City newspaper. Before the United States entered World War I, Hemingway served in a French ambulance unit, later enlist- ing in the Italian army. He saw active service on the Austrian front, where he was severely wounded and twice decorated for bravery in action.

After the armistice he resumed his newspaper work, first in the Middle East with the Toronto *Star*, and later as Paris correspondent for a Hearst syndicate. During this European stay he continued his active participation in sports, especially tennis, boxing, and fishing, and developed an eager interest in bullfighting, later to figure prominently in one of his novels.

In Europe he began seriously his training for the career of writer. He met Gertrude Stein, Ezra Pound, and Ford Madox Ford; for a while, he helped Ford edit the *Transatlantic Review*. Miss Stein and Pound were especially important to him as teachers of writing. From each he learned much, and he was independent enough of them to retain his own style, free of any excesses of imitation.

Aside from a few rather immature things which he published in high-school papers, *Poetry*, and *The Double Dealer*, Hemingway's career as a published writer began in Europe. He had some pieces published in a German magazine, *Der Querschnitt*, in 1923. In the same year *Three Stories & Ten Poems* was published in Dijon, France, by The Contact Publishing Company. In 1924, *in our time* appeared in Paris; it consisted only of the "chapters," the running commentary of the later (capitalized) version, issued in New York in 1925. *The Torrents of Spring*, which began as a parody of Sherwood Anderson's *Dark Laughter*, appeared (Paris) in 1926.

With the publication of *The Sun Also Rises* (October, 1926) in New York, Hemingway established himself as a writer; his apprenticeship was over, and he became the object of controversy and the leader of a group of writers, many of them expatriates, which was to grow in succeeding years. *Men Without Women*, another collection of short stories, appeared in 1927; *A Farewell to Arms*, his most popular novel until *For Whom the Bell Tolls*, was published first in *Scribner's Magazine*, then in book form, in September of 1929. In 1932 his long interest in bullfighting and his great and accurate knowledge of the sport received treatment in *Death in the Afternoon*. Another collection of short stories, *Winner Take Nothing*, appeared in 1933. The story of one of his hunting expeditions in Africa, *The Green Hills of Africa*, was published in 1935. *To Have and Have Not*, his first novel in eight years, came out in 1937. This was followed by *The Fifth Column and the First Forty-Nine Stories* (1938) and *For Whom the Bell Tolls* (1940).

Hemingway has acquired a fabulous reputation in his own time. He has had numerous imitators, and has appealed both to the literary *avant-garde* and to the general public. Several of his stories have already been adapted to the screen, one or two of them with considerable success. He is one of a few primary American influences upon the literature and philosophy of the French existentialists; articles on his work continue to appear in the literary reviews of England and of Continental Europe. In short, he has become a classic in his own lifetime.

Perhaps the most important principle which governs his taste and his writing is the need of simplicity, of absolute candidness, of complete freedom from abstraction or mystification. "If a man writes clearly enough any one can see if he fakes," he said in *Death in the Afternoon*. It is bad taste, in Hemingway's opinion, to over-emotionalize a situation, to take advantage of facts and to make them serve vague generalizations. Hemingway is the leading exponent of "postwar nominalism"; the lesson of World War I was that the "glory words" mean nothing, are disgusting because they mislead, force men into awkward and artificial situations, make them suffer and die for causes they do not understand, which are remote from their personal lives. "I was always embarrassed by the words *sacred, glorious*, and *sacrifice* and the expression *in vain*," his Lieutenant Henry says in *A Farewell to Arms*.

Along with such abstract words (only things, and the names of places, have dignity), he condemned obscure, involuted, complicated style, the use of elaborate syntax to confuse or over-extend an impression. Hemingway's style is consistent with his views of writing. The simple sentence, the compound sentence, individual clauses brought together by a series of "and's," flat statement free of what he would call extraneous interpretation or "setting," understatement: all of these are found in most of his writing. The dialogue is sparse, clean, and unexcessive; description is pared to an appropriate minimum; he does not seek "the essential" at the sacrifice of detail.

These characteristics of his style are closely linked with Hemingway's general approach to the postwar world. The "glory words" no longer attract; philosophy confuses and evades responsibility. What is left is the discrete moment of sensation, the isolated demonstration of physical courage, whatever one can clearly identify as an authentic act or gesture. His novels and short stories extol the genuine, discard the artificial, the self-consciously histrionic. Robert Cohn of *The Sun Also Rises* fails to adjust to the group of Jake's friends because his gestures are unnatural and vague; he dramatizes excessively his self-consciousness. The best aesthetic demonstration of the "clean line" of behavior is to be found in sports: at first fishing, hunting, boxing, whenever they are free of commercialism, are genuine exercises; then, the greatest of them all, bullfighting. Bullfighting provides an aesthetic of action; it is an external demonstration of the Hemingway style—that is, when it is practiced cleanly, without deception, as it is by Pedro Romero, of *The Sun Also Rises*:

> Romero never made any contortions, always it was straight and pure and natural in line. The others twisted themselves like corkscrews, their elbows raised, and leaned against the flanks of the bull after his horns had passed, to give a faked look of danger.

Beginning with *To Have and Have Not*, Hemingway was slowly to abandon the point of view which his style suggested, and in some respects also to change his style. *To Have and Have Not* is a poor novel, lacking the tightness and simplicity of design of his early work, and in many respects demonstrating a new kind of affectation, scarcely ever before noticeable in his work. *For Whom the Bell Tolls*, a crashing success at the box-office, presents a more complicated style, manifests an anxiety on the author's part to "use" his material rather than simply to state it. The book is dominated by the necessity of proof, by the need for attachment to "a cause"; while many incidents are superbly told, and the Spanish character is not unintelligibly remote from his cousins of *The Sun Also Rises*, Hemingway's wall of defense against doctrine has been broken. It is quite possible that he has gone as far as he can with the early manner and is in process of abandoning it.

Hemingway's novels are *Torrents of Spring* (1926); *The Sun Also Rises* (1926); *A Farewell to Arms* (1929); *To Have and Have Not* (1937); *For Whom the Bell Tolls* (1940). His short stories appear in *In Our Time* (1925); *Men Without Women* (1927); *Winner Take Nothing* (1933); *The Fifth Column* (a play) *and the First Forty-Nine Stories* (1938). A collection of *The Short Stories of Ernest Hemingway* appeared in 1942. *Death in the Afternoon* (1932) is for the most part a factual account (history and description) of bullfighting. *Green Hills of Africa* (1935) is a book of travel and description. For biographical and critical studies consult H. S. Canby, "Farewell to the Nineties," *Saturday Review of Literature*, Oct. 28, 1933; A. Dewing, "The Mistake About Hemingway," *North American Review*, Oct., 1931; H. Hartwick, *The Foreground of American Fiction* (1934); H. Hatcher, *Creating the Modern American Novel* (1935); E. Wilson, "The Sportsman's Tragedy," *New Republic*, Dec. 14, 1927; E. J. O'Brien, *The Advance of the American Short Story* (rev. ed., 1931); R. M. Lovett, "Ernest Hemingway," *English Journal*, Oct., 1932; W. Lewis, *Men Without Art* (1934); E. Hemingway, "Monologue to the Maestro," *Esquire*, Oct., 1935; C. Fadiman, "Ernest Hemingway: an American Byron," *Nation*, Jan. 18, 1933; L. Leighton, "An Autopsy and a Prescription," *Hound and Horn*, July–Sept., 1932; T. S. Matthews, "Nothing Ever Happens to the Brave," *New Republic*, Oct. 9, 1929; M. Eastman, *Art and the Life of Action* (1934); G. Stein, *The Autobiography of Alice B. Toklas* (1933); R. Herrick, "What Is Dirt?," *Bookman*, Nov., 1929; L. Kirstein, "The Canon of Death," *Hound and Horn*, Jan.–March, 1933; C. J. McCole, "Ernest Hemingway, Spokesman for His Generation," *Lucifer at Large* (1937); Joseph Warren Beach, *American Fiction, 1920-1940* (1941); Alfred Kazin, *On Native Grounds* (1942); George Snell, *The Shapers of American Fiction* (1947); Mawxell Geismar, *Writers in Crisis* (1942); Malcolm Cowley, Introduction to *The Viking Portable Hemingway* (1944); Ray B. West Jr., "Ernest Hemingway: The Failure of Sensibility," in *Forms of Modern Fiction*, ed. W. V. O'Connor (1948); Edwin Berry Burgum, *The Novel and the World's Dilemma* (1947); Robert Penn Warren, "Hemingway," *Kenyon Review*, Winter, 1947; Cleanth Brooks and R. P. Warren, "The Killers," *American Prefaces*, Spring, 1942 (also in *Understanding Fiction*, 1946); Elliott Paul, "Hemingway and the Critics," *Saturday Review of Literature*, Nov. 6, 1937; Delmore Schwartz, "Ernest Hemingway's Literary Situation," *Southern Review*, April, 1938.

THE KILLERS

THE DOOR of Henry's lunch-room opened and two men came in. They sat down at the counter.

"What's yours?" George asked them.

"I don't know," one of the men said. "What do you want to eat, Al?"

"I don't know," said Al. "I don't know what I want to eat."

Outside it was getting dark. The street-light came on outside the window. The two men at the counter read the menu. From the other end of the counter Nick Adams watched them. He had been talking to George when they came in.

"I'll have a roast pork tenderloin with apple sauce and mashed potatoes," the first man said.

"It isn't ready yet."

10

"What the hell do you put it on the card for?"

"That's the dinner," George explained. "You can get that at six o'clock."

George looked at the clock on the wall behind the counter.

"It's five o'clock."

"The clock says twenty minutes past five," the second man said.

"It's twenty minutes fast."

"Oh, to hell with the clock," the first man said. "What have you got to eat?"

"I can give you any kind of sandwiches," George said. "You can have ham and eggs, bacon and eggs, liver and bacon, or a steak."

"Give me chicken croquettes with green peas and cream sauce and mashed potatoes."

"That's the dinner."

"Everything we want's the dinner, eh? That's the way you work it."

"I can give you ham and eggs, bacon and eggs, liver——"

"I'll take ham and eggs," the man called Al said. He wore a derby hat and a black overcoat buttoned across the chest. His face was small and white and he had tight lips. He wore a silk muffler and gloves.

"Give me bacon and eggs," said the other man. He was about the same size as Al. Their faces were different, but they were dressed like twins. Both wore overcoats too tight for them. They sat leaning forward, their elbows on the counter.

"Got anything to drink?" Al asked.

"Silver beer, bevo, ginger-ale," George said.

"I mean you got anything to *drink?*"

"Just those I said."

"This is a hot town," said the other. "What do they call it?"

"Summit."

"Ever hear of it?" Al asked his friend.

"No," said the friend.

"What do you do here nights?" Al asked.

"They eat the dinner," his friend said. "They all come here and eat the big dinner."

"That's right," George said.

"So you think that's right?" Al asked George.

"Sure."

"You're a pretty bright boy, aren't you?"

"Sure," said George.

"Well, you're not," said the other little man. "Is he, Al?"

"He's dumb," said Al. He turned to Nick. "What's your name?"

"Adams."

"Another bright boy," Al said. "Ain't he a bright boy, Max?"

"The town's full of bright boys," Max said.

George put the two platters, one of ham and eggs, the other of bacon and eggs, on the counter. He set down two side-dishes of fried potatoes and closed the wicket into the kitchen.

"Which is yours?" he asked Al.

"Don't you remember?"

"Ham and eggs."

"Just a bright boy," Max said. He leaned forward and took the ham and eggs. Both men ate with their gloves on. George watched them eat.

"What are *you* looking at?" Max looked at George.

"Nothing."

"The hell you were. You were looking at me."

"Maybe the boy meant it for a joke, Max," Al said.

George laughed.

"*You* don't have to laugh," Max said to him. "*You* don't have to laugh at all, see?"

"All right," said George.

"So he thinks it's all right." Max turned to Al. "He thinks it's all right. That's a good one."

"Oh, he's a thinker," Al said. They went on eating.

"What's the bright boy's name down the counter?" Al asked Max.

"Hey, bright boy," Max said to Nick. "You go around on the other side of the counter with your boy friend."

"What's the idea?" Nick asked.

"There isn't any idea."

"You better go around, bright boy," Al said. Nick went around behind the counter.

"What's the idea?" George asked.

"None of your damn business," Al said. "Who's out in the kitchen?"

"The nigger."

"What do you mean the nigger?"

"The nigger that cooks."

"Tell him to come in."

"What's the idea?"

"Tell him to come in."

"Where do you think you are?"

"We know damn well where we are," the man called Max said. "Do we look silly?"

"You talk silly," Al said to him. "What the hell do you argue with this kid for? Listen," he said to George, "tell the nigger to come out here."

"What are you going to do to him?"

"Nothing. Use your head, bright boy. What would we do to a nigger?"

George opened the slit that opened back into the kitchen. "Sam," he called. "Come in here a minute."

The door to the kitchen opened and the nigger came in. "What was it?" he asked. The two men at the counter took a look at him.

"All right, nigger. You stand right there," Al said.

Sam, the nigger, standing in his apron, looked at the two men sitting at the counter. "Yes, sir," he said. Al got down from his stool.

"I'm going back to the kitchen with the nigger and bright boy," he said. "Go on back to the kitchen, nigger. You go with him, bright boy." The little man walked after Nick and Sam, the cook, back into the kitchen. The door shut after them. The man called Max sat at the counter opposite George. He didn't look at George but looked in the mirror that ran along back of the counter. Henry's had been made over from a saloon into a lunch-counter.

"Well, bright boy," Max said, looking into the mirror, "why don't you say something?"

"What's it all about?"

"Hey, Al," Max called, "bright boy wants to know what it's all about."

"Why don't you tell him?" Al's voice came from the kitchen.

"What do you think it's all about?"

"I don't know."

"What do you think?"

Max looked into the mirror all the time he was talking.

"I wouldn't say."

"Hey, Al, bright boy says he wouldn't say what he thinks it's all about."

"I can hear you, all right," Al said from the kitchen. He had propped open the slit that dishes passed through into the kitchen with a catsup bottle. "Listen, bright boy," he said from the kitchen to George. "Stand a little further along the bar. You move a little to the left, Max." He was like a photographer arranging for a group picture.

"Talk to me, bright boy," Max said. "What do you think's going to happen?"

George did not say anything.

"I'll tell you," Max said. "We're going to kill a Swede. Do you know a big Swede named Ole Andreson?"

"Yes."

"He comes here to eat every night, don't he?"

"Sometimes he comes here."

"He comes here at six o'clock, don't he?"

"If he comes."

"We know all that, bright boy," Max said. "Talk about something else. Ever go to the movies?"

"Once in a while."

"You ought to go to the movies more. The movies are fine for a bright boy like you."

"What are you going to kill Ole Andreson for? What did he ever do to you?"

"He never had a chance to do anything to us. He never even seen us."

"And he's only going to see us once," Al said from the kitchen.

"What are you going to kill him for, then?" George asked.

"We're killing him for a friend. Just to oblige a friend, bright boy."

"Shut up," said Al from the kitchen. "You talk too goddam much."

"Well, I got to keep bright boy amused. Don't I, bright boy?"

"You talk too damn much," Al said. "The nigger and my bright boy are amused by themselves. I got them tied up like a couple of girl friends in the convent."

"I suppose you were in a convent?"

"You never know."

"You were in a kosher convent. That's where you were."

George looked up at the clock.

"If anybody comes in you tell them the cook is off, and if they keep after it, you tell them you'll go back and cook yourself. Do you get that, bright boy?"

"All right," George said. "What you going to do with us afterward?"

"That'll depend," Max said. "That's one of those things you never know at the time."

George looked up at the clock. It was a quarter past six. The door from the street opened. A street-car motorman came in.

"Hello, George," he said. "Can I get supper?"

"Sam's gone out," George said. "He'll be back in about half an hour."

"I'd better go up the street," the motorman said. George looked at the clock. It was twenty minutes past six.

"That was nice, bright boy," Max said. "You're a regular little gentleman."

"He knew I'd blow his head off," Al said from the kitchen.

"No," said Max. "It ain't that. Bright boy is nice. He's a nice boy. I like him."

At six-fifty-five George said: "He's not coming."

Two other people had been in the lunch-room. Once George had gone out to the kitchen and made a ham-and-egg sandwich "to go" that a man wanted to take with him. Inside the kitchen he saw Al, his derby hat tipped back, sitting on a stool beside the wicket with the muzzle of a sawed-off shotgun resting on the ledge. Nick and the cook were back to back in the corner, a towel tied in each of their mouths. George had cooked the sandwich, wrapped it up in oiled paper, put it in a bag, brought it in, and the man had paid for it and gone out.

"Bright boy can do everything," Max said. "He can cook and everything. You'd make some girl a nice wife, bright boy."

"Yes?" George said. "Your friend, Ole Andreson, isn't going to come."

"We'll give him ten minutes," Max said.

Max watched the mirror and the clock. The hands of the clock marked seven o'clock, and then five minutes past seven.

"Come on, Al," said Max. "We better go. He's not coming."

"Better give him five minutes," Al said from the kitchen.

In the five minutes a man came in, and George explained that the cook was sick.

"Why the hell don't you get another cook?" the man asked. "Aren't you running a lunch-counter?" He went out.

"Come on, Al," Max said.

"What about the two bright boys and the nigger?"

"They're all right."

"You think so?"

"Sure. We're through with it."

"I don't like it," said Al. "It's sloppy. You talk too much."

"Oh, what the hell," said Max. "We got to keep amused, haven't we?"

"You talk too much, all the same," Al said. He came out from the kitchen. The cut-off barrels of the shotgun made a slight bulge under the waist of his too tight-fitting overcoat. He straightened his coat with his gloved hands.

"So long, bright boy," he said to George. "You got a lot of luck."

"That's the truth," Max said. "You ought to play the races, bright boy."

The two of them went out the door. George watched them, through the window, pass under the arc-light and cross the street. In their tight overcoats and derby hats they looked like a vaudeville team. George went back through the swinging-door into the kitchen and untied Nick and the cook.

"I don't want any more of that," said Sam, the cook. "I don't want any more of that."

Nick stood up. He had never had a towel in his mouth before.

"Say," he said. "What the hell?" He was trying to swagger it off.

"They were going to kill Ole Andreson," George said. "They were going to shoot him when he came in to eat."

"Ole Andreson?"

"Sure."

The cook felt the corners of his mouth with his thumbs.

"They all gone?" he asked.

"Yeah," said George. "They're gone now."

"I don't like it," said the cook. "I don't like any of it at all."

"Listen," George said to Nick. "You better go see Ole Andreson."

"All right."

"You better not have anything to do with it at all," Sam, the cook, said. "You better stay way out of it."

"Don't go if you don't want to," George said.

"Mixing up in this ain't going to get you anywhere," the cook said. "You stay out of it."

"I'll go see him," Nick said to George. "Where does he live?"

The cook turned away.

"Little boys always know what they want to do," he said.

"He lives up at Hirsch's rooming-house," George said to Nick.

"I'll go up there."

Outside the arc-light shone through the bare branches of a tree. Nick walked up the street beside the car-tracks and turned at the next arc-light down a side-street. Three houses up the street was Hirsch's rooming-house. Nick walked up the two steps and pushed the bell. A woman came to the door.

"Is Ole Andreson here?"

"Do you want to see him?"

"Yes, if he's in."

Nick followed the woman up a flight of stairs and back to the end of a corridor. She knocked on the door.

"Who is it?"

"It's somebody to see you, Mr. Andreson," the woman said.

"It's Nick Adams."

"Come in."

Nick opened the door and went into the room. Ole Andreson was lying on the bed with all his clothes on. He had been a heavyweight prizefighter and he was too long for the bed. He lay with his head on two pillows. He did not look at Nick.

"What was it?" he asked.

"I was up at Henry's," Nick said, "and two fellows came in and tied up me and the cook, and they said they were going to kill you."

It sounded silly when he said it. Ole Andreson said nothing.

"They put us out in the kitchen," Nick went on. "They were going to shoot you when you came in to supper."

Ole Andreson looked at the wall and did not say anything.

"George thought I better come and tell you about it."

"There isn't anything I can do about it," Ole Andreson said.

"I'll tell you what they were like."

"I don't want to know what they were like," Ole Andreson said. He looked at the wall. "Thanks for coming to tell me about it."

"That's all right."

Nick looked at the big man lying on the bed.

"Don't you want me to go and see the police?"

"No," Ole Andreson said. "That wouldn't do any good."

"Isn't there something I could do?"

"No. There ain't anything to do."

"Maybe it was just a bluff."

"No. It ain't just a bluff."

Ole Andreson rolled over toward the wall.

"The only thing is," he said, talking toward the wall, "I just can't make up my mind to go out. I been in here all day."

"Couldn't you get out of town?"

"No," Ole Andreson said. "I'm through with all that running around."

He looked at the wall.

"There ain't anything to do now."

"Couldn't you fix it up some way?"

"No. I got in wrong." He talked in the same flat voice. "There ain't anything to do. After a while I'll make up my mind to go out."

"I better go back and see George," Nick said.

"So long," said Ole Andreson. He did not look toward Nick. "Thanks for coming around."

Nick went out. As he shut the door he saw Ole Andreson with all his clothes on, lying on the bed looking at the wall.

"He's been in his room all day," the landlady said down-stairs. "I guess he don't feel well. I said to him: 'Mr. Andreson, you ought to go out and take a walk on a nice fall day like this,' but he didn't feel like it."

"He doesn't want to go out."

"I'm sorry he don't feel well," the woman said. "He's an awfully nice man. He was in the ring, you know."

"I know it."

"You'd never know it except from the way his face is," the woman said. They stood talking just inside the street door. "He's just as gentle."

"Well, good-night, Mrs. Hirsch," Nick said.

"I'm not Mrs. Hirsch," the woman said.

"She owns the place. I just look after it for her. I'm Mrs. Bell."

"Well, good-night, Mrs. Bell," Nick said.

"Good-night," the woman said.

Nick walked up the dark street to the corner under the arc-light, and then along the car-tracks to Henry's eating-house. George was inside, back of the counter.

"Did you see Ole?"

"Yes," said Nick. "He's in his room and he won't go out."

The cook opened the door from the kitchen when he heard Nick's voice.

"I don't even listen to it," he said and shut the door.

"Did you tell him about it?" George asked.

"Sure. I told him but he knows what it's all about."

"What's he going to do?"

"Nothing."

"They'll kill him."

"I guess they will."

"He must have got mixed up in something in Chicago."

"I guess so," said Nick.

"It's a hell of a thing."

"It's an awful thing," Nick said.

They did not say anything. George reached down for a towel and wiped the counter.

"I wonder what he did?" Nick said.

"Double-crossed somebody. That's what they kill them for."

"I'm going to get out of this town," Nick said.

"Yes," said George. "That's a good thing to do."

"I can't stand to think about him waiting in the room and knowing he's going to get it. It's too damned awful."

"Well," said George, "you better not think about it."

1927

IN ANOTHER COUNTRY

IN THE fall the war was always there, but we did not go to it any more. It was cold in the fall in Milan and the dark came very early. Then the electric lights came on, and it was pleasant along the streets looking in the windows. There was much game hanging outside the shops, and the snow powdered in the fur of the foxes and the wind blew their tails. The deer hung stiff and heavy and empty, and small birds blew in the wind and the wind turned their feathers. It was a cold fall and the wind came down from the mountains.

We were all at the hospital every afternoon, and there were different ways of walking across the town through the dusk to the hospital. Two of the ways were alongside canals, but they were long. Always, though, you crossed a bridge across a canal to enter the hospital. There was a choice of three bridges. On one of them a woman sold roasted chestnuts. It was warm, standing in front of her charcoal fire, and the chestnuts were warm afterward in your pocket. The hospital was very old and very beautiful, and you entered through a gate and walked across a courtyard and out a gate on the other side. There were usually funerals starting from the courtyard. Beyond the old hospital were the new brick pavilions, and there we met every afternoon and were all very polite and interested in what was the matter, and sat in the machines that were to make so much difference.

The doctor came up to the machine where I was sitting and said: "What did you like best to do before the war? Did you practise a sport?"

I said: "Yes, football."

"Good," he said. "You will be able to play football again better than ever."

My knee did not bend and the leg dropped straight from the knee to the ankle without a calf, and the machine was to bend the knee and make it move as in riding a tricycle. But it did not bend yet, and instead the machine lurched when it came to the bending part. The doctor said: "That will all pass. You are a fortunate young man. You will play football again like a champion."

In the next machine was a major who had a little hand like a baby's. He winked at me when the doctor examined his hand, which was between two leather straps that bounced up and down and flapped the stiff fingers, and said: "And will I too play football, captain-doctor?" He had been a very great fencer, and before the war the greatest fencer in Italy.

The doctor went to his office in a back room and brought a photograph which showed a hand that had been withered almost as small as the major's, before it had taken a machine course, and after was a little larger. The major held the photograph with his good hand and looked at it very carefully. "A wound?" he asked.

"An industrial accident," the doctor said.

"Very interesting, very interesting," the major said, and handed it back to the doctor.

"You have confidence?"

"No," said the major.

There were three boys who came each day who were about the same age I was. They were all three from Milan, and one of them was to be a lawyer, and one was to be a painter, and one had intended to be a soldier, and after we were finished with the machines, sometimes we walked back together to the Café Cova, which was next door to the Scala. We walked the short way through the communist quarter because we were four together. The people hated us because we were officers, and from a wine-shop some one called out, "A basso gli ufficiali!" as we passed. Another boy who walked with us sometimes and made us five wore a black silk handkerchief across his face because he had no nose then and his face was to be rebuilt. He had gone out to the front from the military academy and been wounded within an hour after he had gone into the front line for the first time. They rebuilt his face, but he came from a very old family and they could never get the nose exactly right. He went to South America and worked in a bank. But this was a long time ago, and then we did not any of us know how it was going to be afterward. We only knew then that there was always the war, but that we were not going to it any more.

We all had the same medals, except the boy with the black silk bandage across his face, and he had not been at the front long enough to get any medals. The tall boy with a very pale face who was to be a lawyer had been a lieutenant of Arditi and had three medals of the sort we each had only one of. He had lived a very long time with death and was a little detached. We were all a little detached, and there was nothing that held us together except that we met every afternoon at the hospital. Although, as we walked to the Cova through the tough part of town, walking in the dark, with light and singing coming out of the wine-shops, and some-times having to walk into the street when the men and women would crowd together on the sidewalk so that we would have had to jostle them to get by, we felt held together by there being something that had happened that they, the people who disliked us, did not understand.

We ourselves all understood the Cova, where it was rich and warm and not too brightly lighted, and noisy and smoky at certain hours, and there were always girls at the tables and the illustrated papers on a rack on the wall. The girls at the Cova were very patriotic, and I found that the most patriotic people in Italy were the café girls—and I believe they are still patriotic.

The boys at first were very polite about my medals and asked me what I had done to get them. I showed them the papers, which were written in very beautiful language and full of *fratellanza* and *abnegazione*, but which really said, with the adjectives removed, that I had been given the medals because I was an American. After that their manner changed a little toward me, although I was their friend against outsiders. I was a friend, but I was never really one of them after they had read the citations, because it had been different with them and they had done very different things to get their medals. I had been wounded, it was true; but we all knew that being wounded, after all, was really an accident. I was never ashamed of the ribbons, though, and sometimes, after the cocktail hour, I would imagine myself having done all the things they had done to get their medals; but walking home at night through the empty streets with the cold wind and all the shops closed, trying to keep near the street lights, I knew that I would never have done such things, and I was very much afraid to die, and often lay in bed at night by myself, afraid to die and wondering how I would be when I went back to the front again.

The three with the medals were like hunting-hawks; and I was not a hawk, although I might seem a hawk to those who had never hunted; they, the three, knew better and so we drifted apart. But I stayed good friends with the boy who had been wounded his first day at the front, because he would never know now how he would have turned out; so he could never be accepted either, and I liked him because I thought perhaps he would not have turned out to be a hawk either.

The major, who had been the great fencer, did not believe in bravery, and spent much time while we sat in the machines correcting my grammar. He had complimented me on how I spoke Italian, and we talked together very easily. One day I had said that Italian seemed such an easy language to me that I could not take a great interest in it; everything was so easy to say. "Ah, yes," the major said. "Why, then, do you not take up the use of grammar?" So we took up the use of grammar, and soon Italian was such a difficult language that I was afraid to talk to him until I had the grammar straight in my mind.

The major came very regularly to the hospital. I do not think he ever missed a day, although I am sure he did not believe in the machines. There was a time when none of us believed in the machines, and one day the major said it was all nonsense. The machines were new then and it was we who were to prove them. It was an idiotic idea, he said, "a theory, like another." I had not learned my grammar, and he said I was a stupid impossible disgrace, and he was a fool to have bothered with me. He was a small man and he sat straight up in his chair with his right hand thrust into the machine and looked straight ahead at the wall while the straps thumped up and down with his fingers in them.

"What will you do when the war is over if it is over?" he asked me. "Speak grammatically!"

"I will go to the States."

"Are you married?"

"No, but I hope to be."

"The more of a fool you are," he said. He seemed very angry. "A man must not marry."

"Why, Signor Maggiore?"

"Don't call me 'Signor Maggiore.' "

"Why must not a man marry?"

"He cannot marry. He cannot marry," he said angrily. "If he is to lose everything, he should not place himself in a position to lose that. He should not place himself in a position to lose. He should find things he cannot lose."

He spoke very angrily and bitterly, and looked straight ahead while he talked.

"But why should he necessarily lose it?"

"He'll lose it," the major said. He was looking at the wall. Then he looked down at the machine and jerked his little hand out from between the straps and slapped it hard against his thigh. "He'll lose it," he almost shouted. "Don't argue with me!" Then he called to the attendant who ran the machines. "Come and turn this damned thing off."

He went back into the other room for the light treatment and the massage. Then I heard him ask the doctor if he might use his telephone and he shut the door. When he came back into the room, I was sitting in another machine. He was wearing his cape and had his cap on, and he came directly toward my machine and put his arm on my shoulder.

"I am sorry," he said, and patted me on the shoulder with his good hand. "I would not be rude. My wife has just died. You must forgive me."

"Oh—" I said, feeling sick for him. "I am so sorry."

He stood there biting his lower lip. "It is very difficult," he said. "I cannot resign myself."

He looked straight past me and out through the window. Then he began to cry. "I am utterly unable to resign myself," he said and choked. And then crying, his head up looking at nothing, carrying himself straight and soldierly, with tears on both his cheeks and biting his lips, he walked past the machines and out the door.

The doctor told me that the major's wife, who was very young and whom he had not married until he was definitely invalided out of the war, had died of pneumonia. She had been sick only a few days. No one expected her to die. The major did not come to the hospital for three days. Then he came at the usual hour, wearing a black band on the sleeve of his uniform. When he came back, there were large framed photographs around the wall, of all sorts of wounds before and after they had been cured by the machines. In front of the machine the major used were three photographs of hands like his that were completely restored. I do not know where the doctor got them. I always understood we were the first to use the machines. The photographs did not make much difference to the major because he only looked out of the window.

1927

1888 ~ *Eugene O'Neill* ~ ——

O'NEILL laid the foundations of his work as a dramatic artist during years of uncertainty, varied occupations, and vagabonding. He was born on Broadway, the son of the prominent American actor James O'Neill and his wife Ella Quinlan O'Neill. From the former he probably inherited his inclination toward the drama, from the latter his mysticism and love of beauty. For a number of years he accompanied his parents on their theatrical tours. He was educated in private schools and entered Princeton in 1906, but was suspended before the year was out and never returned. After serving as secretary of a mail-order house, he began in 1909 a series of wanderings which in the course of two years took him to Honduras in search of gold, on two theatrical tours as assistant manager and member of his father's troupe, on voyages to Buenos Aires, and back to New York. His experiences as a sailor, his association with the waterfront hangers-on, and his destitute condition and reckless living made a deep impression on his mind, and are reflected in some of the plays he wrote later. After a brief period of newspaper work his health broke, and he was threatened with tuberculosis, the result of excessive strain on his physique.

The months he spent recuperating in a sanatorium mark the turning point in his life. It was during this period that he felt the urge to write, and tried his hand at verse and plays. For a year or more he lived on the shore of Long Island Sound where he carefully built up his health through exercise and regulated routine, read classic and modern drama, wrote more than a dozen plays, and published in 1914 *Thirst and Other One-Act Plays* at his father's expense. After studying playwriting at Harvard under Professor Baker, from whom he received much encouragement, he became associated with the Provincetown Players, who produced many of his early plays. Feeling that the one-act play was too limited in scope, he brought out his first long play, *Beyond the Horizon*, in 1920, and was awarded the Pulitzer prize. Later his *Anna Christie* (1922) and *Strange Interlude* (1928) were similarly rewarded. The year 1920 marked the end of his apprentice period. Since that time he has been constantly in the public eye, and has brought out many plays of startling originality.

Negatively O'Neill represents a definite reaction against the romantic glitter-and-tinsel dramatics of the time. On the positive side, the rise and development of the art theater, which freed writers and producers from the inhibiting demands of the commercial theater, made it possible for him to bring new content and form to the contemporary stage. He had seen the seamier, coarser, and more tragic aspects of life, and found in them dramatic possibilities which for the most part had been ignored. Nor was he satisfied with the current stage effects. Thus, with the support of the Provincetown Players and their theaters, he was enabled to experiment in subject and form, thereby introducing many innovations in practical stagecraft. His place therefore is at the very heart of the revolt in the American drama.

Through the success of *Bound East for Cardiff* (1916) and *The Moon of the Caribbees* (1919) he gave distinct impetus to the one-act play as a dramatic medium. His fame rests, however, on the impressive list of long plays, beginning with *Beyond the Horizon* (1920) and containing such well-known titles as *The Emperor Jones* (1921), *The Hairy Ape* (1922), *All God's Chillun Got Wings* (1924), *Desire Under the Elms* (1925), *Strange Interlude* (1928), and *Mourning Becomes Electra* (1931).

He shared with his contemporaries the tendencies of his time; he was a realist in *Beyond the Horizon*, a naturalist in *Desire Under the Elms*, a symbolist in *The Great God Brown* (1926), an expressionist in *The Emperor Jones* (1921). The main points in O'Neill's literary theory appear in various statements and letters quoted in Clark's *Eugene O'Neill: The Man and His Plays*, and may be briefly summarized. In preparation for his work he read widely in dramatic literature, including the Greeks, the Elizabethans, Ibsen, and "especially Strindberg," who influenced him very strongly. He determined early to avoid conventional dramatic technique, and expressed dissatisfaction with his *In the Zone* because it is theatrical sentimentalism. He has been a lifelong experimenter, avoiding mechanistic methods of plot construction, and trying in each case to adapt the technique to the peculiar demands of the theme. Some critics, who did not realize what his plan and purpose were, felt that he was "bungling through ignorance."

As far as the treatment of his material is concerned, he was not satisfied with mere surface realism, and resorted to what he called super-naturalism, for "the old 'naturalism'—or 'realism,' if you prefer . . .—no longer applies." He portrayed phases of life which to many seemed questionable as dramatic or literary subject-matter. His primary interest lay in the representation of character, but that did not prevent him from striving for a symbolism which extends beyond the individual. In *The Hairy Ape*, for instance, the hero is not merely a specific human being but the symbol of mankind in general. In this way he achieves a universality which transcends the ordinary type of realism.

O'Neill's world is a world of tragedy, somber and unrelieved, the result for the most part of frustration and the ironical tricks which fate plays on man. Many of his characters are dreamers who are forced to battle maladjustment in a limited, material world, and become victims of circumstances. Many of them suffer from the negative ills of spiritual starvation, while others are subject to a more positive inability to shape and control their lives. Incidental to his essentially tragic conception of life, he offers criticism of current tendencies in the larger national life, especially in *The Great God Brown*, *Marco Millions*, and *The Hairy Ape*; but it would be straining the point to say that he is a social critic. His primary purpose is to show the transforming power of tragedy, tragedy as it enters into the lives of people apparently at the very bottom of the scale of existence, but tragedy which through its purgation of the emotions, somewhat in the Greek sense, ennobles and purifies the soul.

O'Neill has been the most ambitious, and the most pretentious, dramatist of the contemporary American scene. He has progressively experimented with varieties of stagecraft and playwrighting. The more complicated the theatrical idea, the longer the play, until it might be said that technique almost takes the place of literary insight. His most brilliant stage successes have been scored, in *Strange Interlude* and *Mourning Becomes Electra*, at the expense of clarity and cleanness of conception. But he remains an exciting playwright, as much for his failures as for his successes. The failures are chiefly the result of his inadequacy as a writer; his dialogue is often flat and spiritless; one is attracted by the design more than by the matter. His last play, *The Ice-Man Cometh* (1946), betrays a muzzy sentimentality, which to this time seems rather to have been the prerogative of William Saroyan. In many respects, the early sea plays remain the most satisfactory; their authenticity (so brilliantly demonstrated in John Ford's film-version, *The Long Voyage Home*) is unimpaired. Of the experimental plays, *The Emperor Jones* appears to have a good chance of surviving the later, more ambitious plays.

Only a limited number of O'Neill's long list of plays can be noted: *Thirst and Other One-Act Plays* (1914); *Before Breakfast* (1916); *Bound East for Cardiff* (1916); *The Moon of the Caribbees, and Six Other Plays of the Sea* (1919); *Beyond the Horizon* (1920); *Gold* (1920); *The Emperor Jones, Diff'rent, The Straw* (1921); *The Hairy Ape, Anna Christie, The First Man* (1922); *All God's Chillun Got Wings, Welded* (1924); *Desire Under the Elms* (1925); *The Great God Brown* (1926); *Strange Interlude* (1928); *Mourning Becomes Electra* (1931); *Ah, Wilderness!* (1933); *Days Without End* (1934); *The Ice-Man Cometh* (1946). The best collected edition is *The Plays of Eugene O'Neill* (12 vols., 1934-35). There are also *The Complete Works of Eugene O'Neill* (2 vols., 1924), *Collected Plays* (4 vols., 1925), and *Collected Plays* (1943). For biography of O'Neill consult B. H. Clark, *Eugene O'Neill; the Man and His Plays* (1933); D. Karsner, *Sixteen Authors to One* (1928); B. Mantle, *American Playwrights of To-day* (1921); M. B. Mullet, "The Extraordinary Story of Eugene O'Neill," *American Magazine*, Nov., 1922; G. J. Nathan, *The Intimate Notebooks of George Jean Nathan* (1932); J. Janney, "Perfect Ending," *American Magazine*, April, 1934. For criticism of his work see R. D. Skinner, *Eugene O'Neill* (1935); T. H. Dickinson, *Playwrights of the New American Theater* (1925); J. T. Shipley, *The Art of Eugene O'Neill* (1928); T. K. Whipple, *Spokesmen* (1928); A. Woollcott, *Shouts and Murmurs* (1922); W. P. Eaton, *The Drama in English* (1930); I. Goldberg, *The Drama of Transition* (1922); H. G. Kemelman, "Eugene O'Neill and the Highbrow Melodrama," *Bookman*, Sept., 1932; M. J. Moses, *The American Dramatist* (1925); A. H. Quinn, *A History of the American Drama from the Civil War to the Present Day* (1926); V. Geddes, *The Melodramadness of Eugene O'Neill* (1934); B. H. Clark, "Aeschylus and O'Neill," *English Journal*, Nov., 1932; P. Loving, "Eugene O'Neill," *Bookman*, Aug., 1921; S. K. Winther, *Eugene O'Neill* (1934); E. S. Sergeant, *Fire Under the Andes* (1927); A. R. Thompson, "The Dilemma of Modern Tragedy," in N. Foerster, ed., *Humanism in America* (1930); E. W. Parks, "O'Neill's Symbolism," *Sewanee Review*, Oct.–Dec., 1935;

Edmond Gagey, *Revolution in American Drama* (1947); Clara Blackburn, "Continental Influences on Eugene O'Neill's Expressionistic Dramas," *American Literature*, May, 1941; Francis Fergusson, "Eugene O'Neill," *Hound and Horn*, Jan.–March, 1930.

THE EMPEROR JONES

CHARACTERS

BRUTUS JONES . . . . *Emperor*
HENRY SMITHERS . . . . . *A Cockney Trader*
AN OLD NATIVE WOMAN
LEM . . . . *A Native Chief*
SOLDIERS . . . . *Adherents of Lem*
*The Little Formless Fears; Jeff; The Negro Convicts;
The Prison Guard; The Planters; The Auctioneer;
The Slaves; The Congo Witch-Doctor; The Croco-
dile God.*
*The action of the play takes place on an island in the
West Indies as yet not self-determined by White Marines.
The form of native government is, for the time being,
an Empire.*

SCENE ONE

SCENE. *The audience chamber in the palace of the Emperor — a spacious, high-ceilinged room with bare, white-washed walls. The floor is of white tiles. In the rear, to the left of center, a wide archway giving out on a portico with white pillars. The palace is evidently situated on high ground, for beyond the portico nothing can be seen but a vista of distant hills, their summits crowned with thick groves of palm trees. In the right wall, center, a smaller arched doorway leading to the living quarters of the palace. The room is bare of furniture with the exception of one huge chair made of uncut wood which stands at center, its back to rear. This is very apparently the Emperor's throne. It is painted a dazzling, eye-smiting scarlet. There is a brilliant orange cushion on the seat and another smaller one is placed on the floor to serve as a footstool. Strips of matting, dyed scarlet, lead from the foot of the throne to the two entrances.*

It is late afternoon but the sunlight still blazes yellowly beyond the portico and there is an oppressive burden of exhausting heat in the air.

As the curtain rises, a native Negro woman sneaks in cautiously from the entrance on the right. She is very old, dressed in cheap calico, bare-footed, a red bandana handkerchief covering all but a few stray wisps of white hair. A bundle bound in colored cloth is carried over her shoulder on the end of a stick. *She hesitates beside the doorway, peering back as if in extreme dread of being discovered. Then she begins to glide noiselessly, a step at a time, toward the doorway in the rear. At this moment,* SMITHERS *appears beneath the portico.*

SMITHERS *is a tall, stoop-shouldered man about forty. His bald head, perched on a long neck with an enormous Adam's apple, looks like an egg. The tropics have tanned his naturally pasty face with its small, sharp features to a sickly yellow, and native rum has painted his pointed nose to a startling red. His little, wash-blue eyes are red-rimmed and dart about him like a ferret's. His expression is one of unscrupulous meanness, cowardly and dangerous. He is dressed in a worn riding suit of dirty white drill, puttees, spurs, and wears a white cork helmet. A cartridge belt with an automatic revolver is around his waist. He carries a riding whip in his hand. He sees the woman and stops to watch her suspiciously. Then, making up his mind, he steps quickly on tiptoe into the room. The woman, looking back over her shoulder continually, does not see him until it is too late. When she does* SMITHERS *springs forward and grabs her firmly by the shoulder. She struggles to get away, fiercely but silently.*

SMITHERS (*Tightening his grasp —roughly*). Easy! None o' that, me birdie. You can't wriggle out now. I got me 'ooks on yer.

WOMAN (*Seeing the uselessness of struggling, gives way to frantic terror, and sinks to the ground embracing his knees supplicatingly*). No tell him! No tell him, Mister!

SMITHERS (*With great curiosity*). Tell 'im? (*Then scornfully*) Oh, you mean 'is bloomin' Majesty. What's the gaime, any'ow? What are you sneakin' away for? Been stealin' a bit, I s'pose. (*He taps her bundle with his riding whip significantly.*)

WOMAN (*Shaking her head vehemently*). No, me no steal.

SMITHERS. Bloody liar! But tell me what's up. There's somethin' funny goin' on. I smelled it in the air first thing I got up this mornin'. You blacks are up to some devilment. This palace of 'is is like a bleedin' tomb. Where's all the 'ands? (*The woman keeps sullenly silent.* SMITHERS *raises his whip threateningly.*) Ow, yer won't, won't yer? I'll show yer wot's what.

WOMAN (*Coweringly*). I tell, Mister. You no hit. They go—all go. (*She makes a sweeping gesture toward the hills in the distance.*)

SMITHERS. Run away—to the 'ills?

WOMAN. Yes, Mister. Him Emperor— Great Father. (*She touches her forehead to the floor with a quick mechanical jerk.*) Him sleep after eat. Then they go—all go. Me old woman. Me left only. Now me go too.

SMITHERS (*His astonishment giving way to an immense, mean satisfaction*). Ow! So that's the ticket! Well, I know bloody well wot's in the air—when they runs orf to the 'ills. The tomtom'll be thumping out there bloomin' soon. (*With extreme vindictiveness.*) And I'm bloody glad of it, for one! Serve 'im right! Puttin' on airs, the stinkin' nigger! 'Is Majesty! Gawd blimey! I only 'opes I'm there when they takes 'im out to shoot 'im. (*Suddenly.*) 'E's still 'ere all right, ain't 'e?

WOMAN. Yes. Him sleep.

SMITHERS. 'E's bound to find out soon as 'e wakes up. 'E's cunnin' enough to know when 'is time's come. (*He goes to the doorway on right and whistles shrilly with his fingers in his mouth. The old woman springs to her feet and runs out of the doorway, rear.* SMITHERS *goes after her, reaching for his revolver.*) Stop or I'll shoot! (*Then stopping—indifferently.*) Pop orf then, if yer like, yer black cow. (*He stands in the doorway, looking after her.*)

(JONES *enters from the right. He is a tall, powerfully-built, full-blooded Negro of middle age. His features are typically Negroid, yet there is something decidedly distinctive about his face—an underlying strength of will, a hardy, self-reliant confidence in himself that inspires respect. His eyes are alive with a keen, cunning intelligence. In manner he is shrewd, suspicious, evasive. He wears a light blue uniform coat, sprayed with brass buttons, heavy gold chevrons on his shoulders, gold braid on the collar, cuffs, etc. His pants are bright red with a light blue stripe down the side. Patent leather laced boots with brass spurs, and a belt with a long-barreled, pearl-handled revolver in a holster complete his* make-up. *Yet there is something not altogether ridiculous about his grandeur. He has a way of carrying it off.*)

JONES (*Not seeing anyone—greatly irritated and blinking sleepily—shouts*). Who dare whistle dat way in my palace? Who dare wake up de Emperor? I'll git de hide frayled off some o' you niggers sho'!

SMITHERS (*Showing himself—in a manner half-afraid and half-defiant*). It was me whistled to yer. (*As* JONES *frowns angrily.*) I got news for yer.

JONES (*Putting on his suavest manner, which fails to cover up his contempt for the white man*). Oh, it's you, Mister Smithers. (*He sits down on his throne with easy dignity.*) What news you got to tell me?

SMITHERS (*Coming close to enjoy his discomfiture*). Don't yer notice nothin' funny today?

JONES (*Coldly*). Funny? No. I ain't perceived nothin' of de kind!

SMITHERS. Then yer ain't so foxy as I thought yer was. Where's all your court? (*Sarcastically*) the Generals and the Cabinet Ministers and all?

JONES (*Imperturbably*). Where dey mostly runs to minute I close my eyes—drinkin' rum and talkin' big down in de town. (*Sarcastically.*) How come you don't know dat? Ain't you sousin' with 'em most every day?

SMITHERS (*Stung but pretending indifference— with a wink*). That's part of the day's work. I got ter—ain't I—in my business?

JONES (*Contemptuously*). Yo' business!

SMITHERS (*Imprudently enraged*). Gawd blimey, you was glad enough for me ter take yer in on it when you landed here first. You didn't 'ave no 'igh and mighty airs in them days!

JONES (*His hand going to his revolver like a flash—menacingly*). Talk polite, white man! Talk polite, you heah me! I'm boss heah now, is you forgettin'? (*The Cockney seems about to challenge this last statement with the facts but something in the other's eyes holds and cows him.*)

SMITHERS (*In a cowardly whine*). No 'arm meant, old top.

JONES (*Condescendingly*). I accepts yo' apology. (*Lets his hand fall from his revolver.*) No use'n you rakin' up ole times. What I was den is one thing. What I is now's another. You didn't let me in on yo' crooked work out o' no kind feelin's dat time. I done de dirty work fo' you—and most o' de brain work, too, fo' dat matter—and I was wu'th money to you, dat's de reason.

SMITHERS. Well, blimey, I give yer a start, didn't I—when no one else would. I wasn't afraid to 'ire yer like the rest was—'count of the story about your breakin' jail back in the States.

JONES. No, you didn't have no s'cuse to look down on me fo'dat. You been in jail you'self more'n once.

SMITHERS (*Furiously*). It's a lie! (*Then trying to pass it off by an attempt at scorn.*) Garn! Who told yer that fairy tale?

JONES. Dey's some tings I ain't got to be tole. I kin see 'em in folks' eyes. (*Then after a pause—meditatively.*) Yes, you sho' give me a start. And it didn't take long from dat time to git dese fool, woods' niggers right where I wanted dem. (*With pride.*) From stowaway to Emperor in two years! Dat's goin some!

SMITHERS (*With curiosity*). And I bet you got yer pile o' money 'id safe some place.

JONES (*With satisfaction*). I sho' has! And it's in a foreign bank where no pusson don't ever git it out but me no matter what come. You didn't s'pose I was holdin' down dis Emperor job for de glory in it, did you? Sho'! De fuss and glory part of it, dat's only to turn de heads o' de low-flung, bush niggers dat's here. Dey wants de big circus show for deir money. I gives it to 'em an' I gits de money. (*With a grin.*) De long green, dat's me every time! (*Then rebukingly.*) But you ain't got no kick agin me, Smithers. I'se paid you back all you done for me many times. Ain't I per-tected you and winked at all de crooked tradin' you been doin' right out in de broad day? Sho' I has—and me makin' laws to stop it at de same time! (*He chuckles.*)

SMITHERS (*Grinning*). But, meanin' no 'arm, you been grabbin' right and left yourself, ain't yer? Look at the taxes you've put on 'em! Blimey! You've squeezed 'em dry!

JONES (*Chuckling*). No, dey ain't *all* dry yet. I'se still heah, ain't I?

SMITHERS (*Smiling at his secret thought*). They're dry right now, you'll find out.

(*Changing the subject abruptly.*) And as for me breakin' laws, you've broke 'em all yerself just as fast as yer made 'em.

JONES. Ain't I de Emperor? De laws don't go for him. (*Judicially.*) You heah what I tells you, Smithers. Dere's little stealin' like you does, and dere's big stealin' like I does. For de little stealin' dey gits you in jail soon or late. For de big stealin' dey makes you Emperor and puts you in de Hall o' Fame when you croaks. (*Reminiscently.*) If dey's one thing I learns in ten years on de Pullman ca's listenin' to de white quality talk, it's dat same fact. And when I gits a chance to use it I winds up Emperor in two years.

SMITHERS (*Unable to repress the genuine admiration of the small fry for the large*). Yes, yer turned the bleedin' trick, all right. Blimey, I never seen a bloke 'as 'ad the bloomin' luck you 'as.

JONES (*Severely*). Luck? What you mean —luck?

SMITHERS. I suppose you'll say as that swank about the silver bullet ain't luck— and that was what first got the fool blacks on yer side of the revolution, wasn't it?

JONES (*With a laugh*). Oh, dat silver bullet! sho was luck! But I makes dat luck, you heah? I loads de dice! Yessuh! When dat murderin' nigger ole Lem hired to kill me takes aim ten feet away and his gun misses fire and I shoots him dead, what you heah me say?

SMITHERS. You said yer'd got a charm so's no lead bullet'd kill yer. You was so strong only a silver bullet could kill yer, you told 'em. Blimey, wasn't that swank for yer—and plain, fat-'eaded luck?

JONES (*Proudly*). I got brains and I use 'em quick. Dat ain't luck.

SMITHERS. Yer know they wasn't 'ardly liable to get no silver bullets. And it was luck 'e didn't 'it you that time.

JONES (*Laughing*). And dere all dem fool, bush niggers was kneelin' down and bumpin' deir heads on de ground like I was a miracle out o' de Bible. Oh Lawd, from dat time on I has dem all eatin' out of my hand. I cracks de whip and dey jumps through.

SMITHERS (*With a sniff*). Yankee bluff done it.

JONES. Ain't a man's talkin' big what makes him big—long as he makes folks believe it? Sho', I talks large when I ain't got nothin' to back it up, but I ain't talkin' wild just de same. I knows I kin fool 'em—I *knows* it—and dat's backin' enough fo' my game. And ain't I got to learn deir lingo and teach some of dem English befo' I kin talk to 'em? Ain't dat wuk? You ain't never learned any word er it, Smithers, in de ten years you been heah, dough you know it's money in yo' pocket tradin' wid 'em if you does. But you'se too shiftless to take de trouble.

SMITHERS (*Flushing*). Never mind about me. What's this I've 'eard about yer really 'avin' a silver bullet moulded for yourself?

JONES. It's playin' out my bluff. I has de silver bullet moulded and I tells 'em when de time comes I kills myself wid it. I tells 'em dat's 'cause I'm de on'y man in de world big enuff to get me. No use'n deir tryin'. And dey falls down and bumps deir heads. (*He laughs.*) I does dat so's I kin take a walk in peace widout no jealous nigger gunnin' at me from behind de trees.

SMITHERS (*Astonished*). Then you 'ad it made—'onest?

JONES. Sho' did. Heah she be. (*He takes out his revolver, breaks it, and takes the silver bullet out of one chamber.*) Five lead an' dis silver baby at de last. Don't she shine pretty? (*He holds it in his hand, looking at it admiringly, as if strangely fascinated.*)

SMITHERS. Let me see. (*Reaches out his hand for it.*)

JONES (*Harshly*). Keep yo' hands whar dey b'long, white man. (*He replaces it in the chamber and puts the revolver back on his hip.*)

SMITHERS (*Snarling*). Gawd blimey! Think I'm a bleedin' thief, you would.

JONES. No, 'tain't dat. I knows you'se scared to steal from me. On'y I ain't 'lowin' nary body to touch dis baby. She's my rabbit's foot.

SMITHERS (*Sneering*). A bloomin' charm, wot? (*Venomously.*) Well, you'll need all the bloody charms you 'as before long, s' 'elp me!

JONES (*Judicially*). Oh, I'se good for six months yit 'fore dey gits sick o' my game. Den, when I sees trouble comin,' I makes my getaway.

SMITHERS. Ho! You got it all planned, ain't yer?

JONES. I ain't no fool. I know dis Emperor's time is sho't. Dat why I make hay when de sun shine. Was you thinkin' I'se aimin to hold down dis job for life? No, suh! What good is gettin' money if you stays back in dis raggedy country? I wants action when I spends. And when I sees dese niggers gittin' up deir nerve to tu'n me out, and I'se got all de money in sight, I resigns on de spot and beats it quick.

SMITHERS. Where to?

JONES. None o' yo' business.

SMITHERS. Not back to the bloody States, I'll lay my oath.

JONES (*Suspiciously*). Why don't I? (*Then with an easy laugh.*) You mean 'count of dat story 'bout me breakin' from jail back dere? Dat's all talk.

SMITHERS (*Skeptically*). Ho, yes!

JONES (*Sharply*). You ain't 'sinuatin' I'se a liar, is you?

SMITHERS (*Hastily*). No, Gawd strike me! I was only thinkin' o' the bloody lies you told the blacks 'ere about killin' white men in the States.

JONES (*Angered*). How come dey're lies?

SMITHERS. You'd 'ave been in jail if you 'ad, wouldn't yer then? (*With venom.*) And from what I've 'eard, it ain't 'ealthy for a black to kill a white man in the States. They burns 'em in oil, don't they?

JONES (*With cool deadliness*). You mean lynchin' 'd scare me? Well, I tells you, Smithers, maybe I does kill one white man back dere. Maybe I does. And maybe I kills another right heah 'fore long if he don't look out.

SMITHERS (*Trying to force a laugh*). I was on'y spoofin' yer. Can't yer take a joke? And you was just sayin' you'd never been in jail.

JONES (*In the same tone—slightly boastful*). Maybe I goes to jail dere for gettin' in an argument wid razors ovah a crap game. Maybe I gits twenty years when dat colored man die. Maybe I gits in 'nother argument wid de prison guard was overseer ovah us when we're wukin' de roads. Maybe he hits me wid a whip and I splits his head wid a shovel and runs away and files de chain off my leg and gits away safe. Maybe I does all dat an' maybe I don't. It's a story I tells you so's you knows I'se de kind of man dat if you evah repeats one word of it, I ends yo' stealin' on dis yearth mighty damn quick!

SMITHERS (*Terrified*). Think I'd peach on yer? Not me! Ain't I always been yer friend?

JONES (*Suddenly relaxing*). Sho' you has— and you better be.

SMITHERS (*Recovering his composure—and with it his malice*). And just to show yer I'm yer friend, I'll tell yer that bit o' news I was goin' to.

JONES. Go ahead! Shoot de piece. Must be bad news from de happy way you look.

SMITHERS (*Warningly*). Maybe it's gettin' time for you to resign—with that bloomin' silver bullet, wot? (*He finishes with a mocking grin.*)

JONES (*Puzzled*). What's dat you say? Talk plain.

SMITHERS. Ain't noticed any of the guards or servants about the place today, I 'aven't.

JONES (*Carelessly*). Dey're all out in de garden sleepin' under de trees. When I sleeps, dey sneaks a sleep, too, and I pretends I never suspicions it. All I got to do is to ring de bell and dey come flyin', makin' a bluff dey was wukin' all de time.

SMITHERS (*In the same mocking tone*). Ring the bell now an' you'll bloody well see what I means.

JONES (*Startled to alertness, but preserving the same careless tone*). Sho' I rings. (*He reaches below the throne and pulls out a big, common dinner bell which is painted the same vivid scarlet as the throne. He rings this vigorously—then stops to listen. Then he goes to both doors, rings again, and looks out.*)

SMITHERS (*Watching him with malicious satisfaction, after a pause—mockingly*). The bloody ship is sinkin' an' the bleedin' rats 'as slung their 'ooks.

JONES (*In a sudden fit of anger flings the bell clattering into a corner*). Low-flung, woods' niggers! (*Then catching Smithers' eye on him, he controls himself and suddenly bursts into a low chuckling laugh.*) Reckon I overplays my hand dis once! A man can't take de pot on a bob-tailed flush all de time. Was I sayin' I'd sit in six months mo'? Well, I'se changed my mind den. I cashes in and resigns de job of Emperor right dis minute.

SMITHERS (*With real admiration*). Blimey, but you're a cool bird, and no mistake.

JONES. No use'n fussin'. When I knows de game's up I kisses it good-bye widout no long waits. Dey've all run off to de hills, ain't dey?

SMITHERS. Yes—every bleedin' man jack of 'em.

JONES. Den de revolution is at de post. And de Emperor better git his feet smokin' up de trail. (*He starts for the door in rear.*)

SMITHERS. Goin' out to look for your 'orse? Yer won't find any. They steals the 'orses first thing. Mine was gone when I went for 'im this mornin'. That's wot first give me a suspicion of wot was up.

JONES (*Alarmed for a second, scratches his head, then philosophically*). Well, den I hoofs it. Feet, do yo' duty! (*He pulls out a gold watch and looks at it.*) Three-thuty. Sundown's at six-thuty or dere-abouts. (*Puts his watch back —with cool confidence.*) I got plenty o' time to make it easy.

SMITHERS. Don't be so bloomin' sure of it. They'll be after you 'ot and 'eavy. Ole Lem is at the bottom o' this business an' 'e 'ates you like 'ell. 'E'd rather do for you than eat 'is dinner, 'e would!

JONES (*Scornfully*). Dat fool no-count nigger! Does you think I'se scared o' him? I stands him on his thick head more'n once befo' dis, and I does it again if he come in my way . . . (*Fiercely.*) And dis time I leave him a dead nigger fo' sho'!

SMITHERS. You'll 'ave to cut through the big forest—an' these blacks 'ere can sniff and follow a trail in the dark like 'ounds. You'd 'ave to 'ustle to get through that forest in twelve hours even if you knew all the bloomin' trails like a native.

JONES (*With indignant scorn*). Look-a-heah, white man! Does you think I'se a natural bo'n fool? Give me credit fo' havin' some sense, fo' Lawd's sake! Don't you s'pose I'se looked ahead and made sho' of all de chances? I'se gone out in dat big forest, pretendin' to hunt, so many times dat I knows it high an' low like a book. I could go through on dem trails wid my eyes shut. (*With great contempt.*) Think dese ign'rent bush niggers dat ain't got brains enuff to know deir own names even can catch Brutus Jones? Huh, I s'pects not! Not on yo' life! Why, man, de white men went after me wid bloodhounds where I come from an' I jes' laughs at 'em. It's a shame to fool dese black trash around heah, dey're so easy. You watch me, man. I'll make dem look sick, I will. I'll be 'cross de plain to de edge of de forest by time dark comes. Once in de woods in de night, dey got a swell chance o' findin' dis baby! Dawn tomorrow I'll be out at de oder side and on de coast whar dat French gunboat is stayin'. She picks me up, take me to Martinique when she go dar, and dere I is safe wid a mighty big bankroll in my jeans. It's easy as rollin' off a log.

SMITHERS (*Maliciously*). But s'posin' some-thin' 'appens wrong an' they do nab yer?

JONES (*Decisively*). Dey don't—dat's de answer.

SMITHERS. But, just for argyment's sake—what'd you do?

JONES (*Frowning*). I'se got five lead bullets in dis gun good enuff fo' common bush nig-gers—and after dat I got de silver bullet left to cheat 'em out o' gittin' me.

SMITHERS (*Jeeringly*). Ho, I was fergettin' that silver bullet. You'll bump yourself orf in style, won't yer? Blimey!

JONES (*Gloomily*). You kin bet yo' whole roll on one thing, white man. Dis baby plays out his string to de end and when he quits, he quits wid a bang de way he ought. Silver bullet ain't none too good for him when he go, dat's a fac'! (*Then shaking off his nervousness—with a confident laugh.*) Sho'! What is I talkin' about? Ain't come to dat yit and I never will—not wid trash niggers like dese yere. (*Boastfully.*) Silver bullet bring me luck anyway. I kin out-guess, outrun, outfight, an' outplay de whole lot o' dem all ovah de board any time o' de day er night! You watch me! (*From the distant hills comes the faint, steady thump of a tom-tom, low and vibrating. It starts at a rate exactly corres-ponding to normal pulse beat—72 to the minute —and continues at a gradually accelerating rate from this point uninterruptedly to the very end of the play.*)

(JONES *starts at the sound. A strange look of apprehension creeps into his face for a moment as he listens. Then he asks, with an attempt to re-gain his most casual manner.*) What's dat drum beatin' fo'?

SMITHERS (*With a mean grin*). For you. That means the bleedin' ceremony 'as started. I've 'eard it before and I knows.

JONES. Cer'mony? What cer'mony?

SMITHERS. The blacks is 'oldin' a bloody meetin', 'avin' a war dance, gettin' their cour-age worked up b'fore they starts after you.

JONES. Let dem! Dey'll sho' need it!

SMITHERS. And they're there 'oldin' their 'eathen religious service—makin' no end of devil spells and charms to 'elp 'em against your silver bullet. (*He guffaws loudly.*) Blimey, but they're balmy as 'ell!

JONES (*A tiny bit awed and shaken in spite of himself*). Huh! Takes more'n dat to scare dis chicken!

SMITHERS (*Scenting the other's feeling—malic-iously*). Ternight when it's pitch black in the forest, they'll 'ave their pet devils and ghosts 'oundin' after you. You'll find yer bloody 'air 'll be standin' on end before termorrow mor-nin'. (*Seriously.*) It's a bleedin' queer place, that stinkin' forest, even in daylight. Yer don't know what might 'appen in there, it's that rotten still. Always sends the cold shivers down my back minute I gets in it.

JONES (*With a contemptuous sniff*). I ain't no chicken-liver like you is. Trees an' me, we'se friends, and dar's a full moon comin' bring me light. And let dem po' niggers make all de fool spells dey'se a min' to. Does yo' s'pect I'se silly enuff to b'lieve in ghosts an' ha'nts an' all dat ole women's talk? G'long, white man! You ain't talkin' to me. (*With a chuckle.*) Doesn't you know dey's got to do wid a man was mem-ber in good standin' o' de Baptist Church? Sho' I was dat when I was porter on de Pull-mans, befo' I gits into my little trouble. Let dem try deir heathen tricks. De Baptist Church done pertect me and land dem all in hell. (*Then with more confident satisfaction.*) And I'se got little silver bullet o' my own, don't forgit.

SMITHERS. Ho! You 'aven't give much 'eed to your Baptist Church since you been down 'ere. I've 'eard myself you 'ad turned yer coat an' was takin' up with their blarsted witch-doctors, or whatever the 'ell yer calls the swine.

JONES (*Vehemently*). I pretends to! Sho' I pretends! Dat's part o' my game from de fust. If I finds out dem niggers believes dat black is white, den I yells it out louder 'n deir loudest.

It don't git me nothin' to do missionary work for de Baptist Church. I'se after de coin, an' I lays my Jesus on de shelf for de time bein'. (*Stops abruptly to look at his watch—alertly.*) But I ain't got de time to waste no more fool talk wid you. I'se gwine away from heah dis secon'. (*He reaches in under the throne and pulls out an expensive Panama hat with a bright multi-colored band and sets it jauntily on his head.*) So long, white man! (*With a grin.*) See you in jail 10 sometime, maybe!

SMITHERS. Not me, you won't. Well, I wouldn't be in yer bloody boots for no bloomin' money, but 'ere's wishin' yer luck just the same.

JONES (*Contemptuously*). You're de frightenedest man evah I see! I tells you I'se safe's 'f I was in New York City. It takes dem niggers from now to dark to git up de nerve to start somethin'. By dat time, I'se got a head start 20 dey never kotch up wid.

SMITHERS (*Maliciously*). Give my regards to any ghosts yer meets up with.

JONES (*Grinning*). If dat ghost got money, I'll tell him never ha'nt you less'n he wants to lose it.

SMITHERS(*Flattered*). Garn!(*Then curiously.*) Ain't yer takin' no luggage with yer?

JONES. I travels light when I wants to move fast. And I got tinned grub buried on de edge 30 o' de forest. (*Boastfully.*) Now say dat I don't look ahead an' use my brains! (*With a wide, liberal gesture.*) I will all dat's left in de palace to you—and you better grab all you kin sneak away wid befo' dey gits here.

SMITHERS (*Gratefully*). Righto—and thanks ter yer. (*As* JONES *walks toward the door in rear —cautioningly.*) Say! Look 'ere, you ain't goin' out that way, are yer?

JONES. Does you think I'd slink out de back 40 door like a common nigger? I'se Emperor yit, ain't I? And de Emperor Jones leaves de way he comes, and dat black trash don't dare stop him—not yit, leastways. (*He stops for a moment in the doorway, listening to the far-off but insistent beat of the tom-tom.*) Listen to dat roll-call, will you? Must be mighty big drum carry dat far. (*Then with a laugh.*)Well, if dey ain't no whole brass band to see me off, I sho' got de drum part of it. So long, white man. (*He puts 50 his hands in his pockets and with studied careless-*

ness, *whistling a tune, he saunters out of the doorway and off to the left.*)

SMITHERS (*Looks after him with a puzzled admiration*). 'E's got 'is bloomin' nerve with 'im, s'elp me! (*Then angrily.*) Ho—the bleedin' nigger—puttin' on 'is bloody airs! I 'opes they nabs 'im an' gives 'im what's what! (*Then putting business before the pleasure of this thought, looking around him with cupidity.*) A bloke ought to find a 'ole lot in this palace that'd go for a bit of cash. Let's take a look, 'Arry, me lad. (*He starts for the doorway on right as*

(*The curtain falls.*)

SCENE TWO

SCENE—*Nightfall. The end of the plain where the Great Forest begins. The foreground is sandy, level ground dotted by a few stones and clumps of stunted bushes cowering close against the earth to escape the buffeting of the trade wind. In the rear the forest is a wall of darkness dividing the world. Only when the eye becomes accustomed to the gloom can the outlines of separate trunks of the nearest trees be made out, enormous pillars of deeper blackness. A somber monotone of wind lost in the leaves moans in the air. Yet this sound serves but to intensify the impression of the forest's relentless immobility, to form a background throwing into relief its brooding, implacable silence.*

(JONES *enters from the left, walking rapidly. He stops as he nears the edge of the forest, looks around him quickly, peering into the dark as if searching for some familiar landmark. Then, apparently satisfied that he is where he ought to be, he throws himself on the ground, dog-tired.*)

Well, heah I is. In de nick o' time, too! Little mo' an' it'd be blacker'n de ace of spades heah-abouts. (*He pulls a bandana handkerchief from his hip pocket and mops off his perspiring face.*) Sho'! Gimme air! I'se tuckered out sho' 'nuff. Dat soft Emperor job ain't no trainin' for a long hike ovah dat plain in de brilin' sun. (*Then with a chuckle.*) Cheah up, nigger, de worst is yet to come. (*He lifts his head and stares at the forest. His chuckle peters out abruptly. In a tone of awe.*) My goodness, look at dem woods, will you? Dat no-count Smithers said dey'd be black an' he sho' called de turn. (*Turning away from them quickly and looking down at his feet, he snatches at a chance to change the subject—solicitously.*) Feet, you is holdin' up yo' end fine an' I sutinly hopes you ain't blisterin' none. It's time you git a rest. (*He takes off his shoes, his eyes studiously avoiding the forest. He feels of the soles of his feet gingerly.*) You is still in de pink—on'y a little mite feverish. Cool yo'selfs. Remember you done got a long journey yit befo' you. (*He sits in a weary attitude, listening to the rhythmic beating of the tom-tom. He grumbles in a loud tone to cover up a growing uneasiness.*) Bush niggers! Wonder dey wouldn't git sick o' beatin' dat drum. Sound louder, seem like. I wonder if dey's startin' after me? (*He scrambles to his feet, looking back across the plain.*) Couldn't see dem now, nohow, if dey was hundred feet away. (*Then shaking himself like a wet dog to get rid of these depressing thoughts.*) Sho', dey's miles an' miles behind. What you gittin' fidgety about? (*But he sits down and begins to lace up his shoes in great haste, all the time muttering reassuringly.*) You know what? Yo' belly is empty, dat's what's de matter wid you. Come time to eat! Wid nothin' but wind on yo' stumach, o' course you feels jiggedy. Well, we eats right heah an' now soon's I gits dese pesky shoes laced up! (*He finishes lacing up his shoes.*) Dere! Now le's see. (*Gets on his hands and knees and searches the ground around him with his eyes.*) White stone, white stone, where is you? (*He sees the first white stone and crawls to it—with satisfaction.*) Heah you is! I knowed dis was de right place. Box of grub, come to me. (*He turns over the stone and feels in under it—in a tone of dismay.*) Ain't heah! Gorry, is I in de right place or isn't I? Dere's 'nother stone. Guess dat's it. (*He scrambles to the next stone and turns it over.*) Ain't heah, neither! Grub, whar is you? Ain't heah. Gorry, has I got to go hungry into dem woods—all de night? (*While he is talking he scrambles from one stone to another, turning them over in frantic haste. Finally, he jumps to his feet excitedly.*) Is I lost de place? Must have! But how dat happen when I was followin' de trail across de plain in broad daylight? (*Almost plaintively.*) I'se hungry, I is! I gotta git my feed. What's my strength gonna come from if I doesn't? Gorry, I gotta find dat grub high an' low somehow! Why it come dark so quick like dat? Can't see nothin'. (*He scratches a match on his trousers*

and peers about him. The rate of the beat of the far-off tom-tom increases perceptibly as he does so. He mutters in a bewildered voice.) How come all dese white stones come heah when I only remembers one? (*Suddenly, with a frightened gasp, he flings the match on the ground and stamps on it.*) Nigger, is you gone crazy mad? Is you lightin' matches to show dem whar you is? Fo' Lawd's sake, use yo' haid. Gorry, I'se got to be careful! (*He stares at the plain behind him apprehensively, his hand on his revolver.*) But how come all dese white stones? And whar's dat tin box o' grub I hid all wrapped up in oil cloth?

(*While his back is turned, the* LITTLE FORMLESS FEARS *creep out from the deeper blackness of the forest. They are black, shapeless, only their glittering little eyes can be seen. If they have any describable form at all, it is that of a grubworm about the size of a creeping child. They move noiselessly, but with deliberate, painful effort, striving to raise themselves on end, failing and sinking prone again.* JONES *turns about to face the forest. He stares up at the tops of the trees, seeking vainly to discover his whereabouts by their conformation.*)

Can't tell nothin' from dem trees! Gorry, nothin' round heah look like I evah seed it befo'. I'se done lost de place sho' 'nuff! (*With mournful foreboding.*) It's mighty queer! It's mighty queer! (*With sudden forced defiance—in an angry tone.*) Woods, is you tryin' to put somethin' ovah on me?

(*From the formless creatures on the ground in front of him comes a tiny gale of low mocking laughter like a rustling of leaves. They squirm upward toward him in twisted attitudes.* JONES *looks down, leaps backward with a yell of terror, yanking out his revolver as he does so—in a quavering voice.*) What's dat? Who's dar? What is you? Git away from me befo' I shoots you up! You don't? . . .

(*He fires. There is a flash, a loud report, then silence broken only by the far-off, quickened throb of the tom-tom. The formless creatures have scurried back into the forest.* JONES *remains fixed in his position, listening intently. The sound of the shot, the reassuring feel of the revolver in his hand, have somewhat restored his shaken nerve. He addresses himself with renewed confidence.*)

Dey're gone. Dat shot fix 'em. Dey was

only little animals—little wild pigs, I reckon. Dey've maybe rooted out yo' grub an' eat it. Sho', you fool nigger, what you think dey is—ha'nts? (*Excitedly.*) Gorry, you give de game away when you fire dat shot. Dem niggers heah dat fo' su'tin! Time you beat it in de woods widout no long waits. (*He starts for the forest—hesitates before the plunge—then urging himself in with manful resolution.*) Git in, nigger! What you skeered at? Ain't nothin' dere but de trees! Git in! (*He plunges boldly into the forest.*)

SCENE THREE

Scene—*Nine o'clock. In the forest. The moon has just risen. Its beams, drifting through the canopy of leaves, make a barely perceptible, suffused, eerie glow. A dense low wall of under-brush and creepers is in the nearer foreground, fencing in a small triangular clearing. Beyond this is the massed blackness of the forest like an encompassing barrier. A path is dimly discerned leading down to the clearing from left, rear, and winding away from it again toward the right. As the scene opens nothing can be distinctly made out. Except for the beating of the tom-tom, which is a trifle louder and quicker than in the previous scene, there is silence, broken every few seconds by a queer, clicking sound. Then gradually the figure of the Negro,* JEFF, *can be discerned crouching on his haunches at the rear of the tri-angle. He is middle-aged, thin, brown in color, is dressed in a Pullman porter's uniform, cap, etc. He is throwing a pair of dice on the ground before him, picking them up, shaking them, casting them out with the regular, rigid, mechanical movements of an automaton. The heavy, plodding foot-steps of someone approaching along the trail from the left are heard and* JONES' *voice, pitched in a slightly higher key and strained in a cheering effort to overcome its own tremors.*

De moon's rizen. Does you heah dat, nigger? You gits more light from dis out. No mo' buttin' yo' fool head agin' de trunks an' scratchin' de hide off yo' legs in de bushes. Now you sees whar yo'se gwine. So cheer up! From now on you has a snap. (*He steps just to the rear of the triangular clearing and mops off his face on his sleeve. He has lost his Pana-ma hat. His face is scratched, his brilliant uni-form shows several large rents.*) What time's it

gittin' to be, I wonder? I dassent light no match to find out. Phoo'. It's wa'm an' dat's a fac'! (*Wearily.*) How long I been makin' tracks in dese woods? Must be hours an' hours. Seems like fo'evah! Yit can't be, when de moon's jes' riz. Dis am a long night fo' yo', yo' Majesty! (*With a mournful chuckle.*) Maj-esty! Der ain't much majesty 'bout dis baby now. (*With attempted cheerfulness.*) Never min'. It's all part o' de game. Dis night come to an end like everything else. And when you gits dar safe and has dat bankroll in yo' hands you laughs at all dis. (*He starts to whistle but checks himself abruptly.*) What yo' whistlin' for, you po' dope! Want all de worl' to heah you? (*He stops talking to listen.*) Heah dat ole drum! Sho' gits nearer from de sound. Dey're packin' it along wid 'em. Time fo' me to move. (*He takes a step forward, then stops—worriedly.*) What's dat odder queer clickety sound I heah? Dere it is! Sound close! Sound like—sound like—Fo' God sake, sound like some nigger was shootin' crap! (*Frightenedly.*) I better beat it quick when I gits dem notions. (*He walks quickly into the clear space—then stands transfixed as he sees* JEFF—*in a terrified gasp.*) Who dar? Who dat? Is dat you, Jeff? (*Start-ing toward the other, forgetful for a moment of his surroundings and really believing it is a living man that he sees—in a tone of happy relief.*) Jeff! I'se sho' mighty glad to see you! Dey tol' me you done died from dat razor cut I gives you. (*Stopping suddenly, bewilderedly.*) But how you come to be heah, nigger? (*He stares fascinatedly at the other who continues his mechanical play with the dice.* JONES' *eyes begin to roll wildly. He stutters.*) Ain't you gwine—look up—can't you speak to me? Is you—is you—a ha'nt? (*He jerks out his revolver in a frenzy of terrified rage.*) Nigger, I kills you dead once. Has I got to kill you agin? You take it den. (*He fires. When the smoke clears away* JEFF *has disappeared.* JONES *stands trem-bling—then with a certain reassurance.*) He's gone, anyway. Ha'nt or no ha'nt, dat shot fix him. (*The beat of the far-off tom-tom is percep-tibly louder and more rapid.* JONES *becomes con-scious of it—with a start, looking back over his shoulder.*) Dey's gittin' near! Dey's comin fast! And I is shootin' shots to let 'em know jes' whar I is. Oh, Gorry, I'se got to run.

(*Forgetting the path he plunges wildly into the underbrush in the rear and disappears in the shadow.*)

SCENE FOUR

SCENE—*Eleven o'clock. In the forest. A wide dirt road runs diagonally from right, front, to left, rear. Rising sheer on both sides the forest walls it in. The moon is now up. Under its light the road glimmers ghastly and unreal. It is as if the forest had stood aside momentarily to let the road pass through and accomplish its veiled purpose. This done, the forest will fold in upon itself again and the road will be no more.* JONES *stumbles in from the forest on the right. His uniform is ragged and torn. He looks about him with numbed surprise when he sees the road, his eyes blinking in the bright moonlight. He flops down exhaustedly and pants heavily for a while. Then with sudden anger.*

I'm meltin' wid heat! Runnin' an' runnin' an' runnin'! Damn dis heah coat! Like a strait-jacket! (*He tears off his coat and flings it away from him, revealing himself stripped to the waist.*) Dere! Dat's better! Now I kin breathe! (*Looking down at his feet, the spurs catch his eye.*) And to hell wid dese high-fangled spurs. Dey're what's been a-trippin' me up an' breakin' my neck. [*He unstraps them and flings them away disgustedly.*) Dere—I gits rid o' dem frippety Emperor trappin's an' I travels lighter. Lawd! I'se tired! (*After a pause, listening to the insistent beat of the tom-tom in the distance.*) I must 'a put some distance between myself an' dem —runnin' like dat—and yit—dat damn drum sound jes' de same—nearer, even. Well, I guess I a'most holds my lead anyhow. Dey won't never catch up. (*With a sigh.*) If on'y my fool legs stand up. Oh, I'se sorry I evah went in for dis. Dat Emperor job is sho' hard to shake. (*He looks around him suspiciously.*) How'd dis road evah git heah? Good level road, too. I never remembers seein' it befo'. (*Shaking his head apprehensively.*) Dese woods is sho' full o' de queerest things at night. (*With a sudden terror.*) Lawd God, don't let me see no more o' dem ha'nts! Dey gits my goat! (*Then trying to talk himself into confidence.*) Ha'nts! You fool nigger, dey ain't no such things! Don't de Baptist parson tell you dat many time? Is you civilized, or is you like dese

ign'rent black niggers heah? Sho'! Dat was all in yo' own head. Wasn't nothin' dere. Wasn't no Jeff! Know what? You jus' get seein' dem things 'cause yo' belly's empty and you's sick wid hunger inside. Hunger 'fects yo' head and yo' eyes. Any fool know dat. (*Then pleading fervently.*) But bless God, I don't come across no more o' dem, whatever dey is! (*Then cautiously.*) Rest! Don't talk! Rest! You needs it. Den you gits on yo' way again. (*Looking at the moon.*) Night's half gone a'most. You hits de coast in de mawnin'! Den you'se all safe.

(*From the right forward a small gang of Negroes enter. They are dressed in striped convict suits, their heads are shaven, one leg drags limpingly, shackled to a heavy ball and chain. Some carry picks, the others shovels. They are followed by a white man dressed in the uniform of a prison guard. A Winchester rifle is slung across his shoulders and he carries a heavy whip. At a signal from the* GUARD *they stop on the road opposite where* JONES *is sitting.* JONES, *who has been staring up at the sky, unmindful of their noiseless approach, suddenly looks down and sees them. His eyes pop out, he tries to get to his feet and fly, but sinks back, too numbed by fright to move. His voice catches in a choking prayer.*)

Lawd Jesus!

(*The* PRISON GUARD *cracks his whip—noiselessly—and at that signal all the convicts start to work on the road. They swing their picks, they shovel, but not a sound comes from their labor. Their movements, like those of* JEFF *in the preceding scene, are those of automatons,— rigid, slow, and mechanical. The* PRISON GUARD *points sternly at* JONES *with his whip, motions him to take his place among the other shovelers.* JONES *gets to his feet in a hypnotized stupor. He mumbles subserviently.*)

Yes, suh! Yes, suh! I'se comin'.

(*As he shuffles, dragging one foot, over to his place, he curses under his breath with rage and hatred.*)

God damn yo' soul, I gets even wid you yit, sometime.

(*As if there were a shovel in his hands he goes through weary, mechanical gestures of digging up dirt, and throwing it to the roadside. Suddenly the* GUARD *approaches him angrily, threateningly. He raises his whip and lashes* JONES *viciously* across the shoulders with it. JONES winces with pain and cowers abjectly. The GUARD turns his back on him and walks away contemptuously. Instantly JONES straightens up. With arms upraised as if his shovel were a club in his hands, he springs murderously at the unsuspecting GUARD. In the act of crashing down his shovel on the white man's skull, JONES suddenly becomes aware that his hands are empty. He cries despairingly.)

Whar's my shovel? Gimme my shovel 'till I splits his damn head! (Appealing to his fellow convicts.) Gimme a shovel, one o' you, fo' God's sake!

(They stand fixed in motionless attitudes, their eyes on the ground. The GUARD seems to wait expectantly, his back turned to the attacker. JONES bellows with baffled, terrified rage, tugging frantically at his revolver.)

I kills you, you white debil, if it's de last thing I evah does! Ghost or debil, I kill you again!

(He frees the revolver and fires point-blank at the GUARD'S back. Instantly the walls of the forest close in from both sides, the road and the figures of the convict gang are blotted out in an enshrouding darkness. The only sounds are a crashing in the underbrush as JONES leaps away in mad flight and the throbbing of the tom-tom still far distant, but increased in volume of sound and rapidity of beat.)

SCENE FIVE

SCENE—One o'clock. A large circular clearing, enclosed by the serried ranks of gigantic trunks of tall trees whose tops are lost to view. In the center is a big dead stump worn by time into a curious resemblance to an auction block. The moon floods the clearing with a clear light. JONES forces his way in through the forest on the left. He looks wildly about the clearing with hunted, fearful glances. His pants are in tatters, his shoes cut and misshapen, flapping about his feet. He slinks cautiously to the stump in the center and sits down in a tense position, ready for instant flight. Then he holds his head in his hands and rocks back and forth, moaning to himself miserably.)

Oh Lawd, Lawd! Oh Lawd, Lawd! (Suddenly he throws himself on his knees and raises his clasped hands to the sky—in a voice of agonized pleading.) Lawd Jesus, heah my prayer! I'se a po' sinner, a po' sinner! I knows I done wrong, I knows it! When I cotches Jeff cheatin' wid loaded dice my anger overcomes me and I kills him dead! Lawd, I done wrong! When dat guard hits me wid de whip, my anger overcomes me, and I kills him dead. Lawd, I done wrong! And down heah whar dese fool bush niggers raises me up to the seat o' de mighty, I steals all I could grab. Lawd, I done wrong! I knows it! I'se sorry! Forgive me, Lawd! Forgive dis po' sinner! (Then beseeching terrifiedly.) And keep dem away, Lawd! Keep dem away from me! And stop dat drum soundin' in' in my ears! Dat begin to sound ha'nted, too. (He gets to his feet, evidently slightly reassured by his prayer—with attempted confidence.) De Lawd'll preserve me from dem ha'nts after dis. (Sits down on the stump again.) I ain't skeered o' real men. Let dem come. But dem odders . . . (He shudders—then looks down at his feet, working his toes inside the shoes—with a groan.) Oh, my po' feet! Dem shoes ain't no use no more 'ceptin' to hurt. I'se better off without dem. (He unlaces them and pulls them off—holds the wrecks of the shoes in his hands and regards them mournfully.) You was real, A-one patin' leather, too. Look at you now. Emperor, you'se gittin' mighty low!

(He sits dejectedly and remains with bowed shoulders, staring down at the shoes in his hands as if reluctant to throw them away. While his attention is thus occupied, a crowd of figures silently enter the clearing from all sides. All are dressed in Southern costumes of the period of the fifties of the last century. There are middle-aged men who are evidently well-to-do planters. There is one spruce, authoritative individual—the AUCTIONEER. There is a crowd of curious spectators, chiefly young belles and dandies who have come to the slave-market for diversion. All exchange courtly greetings in dumb show and chat silently together. There is something stiff, rigid, unreal, marionettish about their movements. They group themselves about the stump. Finally a batch of slaves are led in from the left by an attendant—three men of different ages, two women, one with a baby in her arms, nursing. They are placed to the left of the stump, beside JONES.

The white planters look them over appraisingly as if they were cattle, and exchange judgments on each. The dandies point with their fingers and make witty remarks. The belles titter bewitchingly. All this in silence save for the ominous throb of the tom-tom. The AUCTIONEER *holds up his hand, taking his place at the stump. The groups strain forward attentively. He touches* JONES *on the shoulder peremptorily motioning for him to stand on the stump—the* 10 *auction block.*

JONES *looks up, sees the figures on all sides, looks wildly for some opening to escape, sees none, screams and leaps madly to the top of the stump to get as far away from them as possible. He stands there, cowering, paralyzed with horror. The* AUCTIONEER *begins his silent spiel. He points to* JONES, *appeals to the planters to see for themselves. Here is a good field hand, sound in wind and limb as they can see. Very strong* 20 *still in spite of his being middle-aged. Look at that back. Look at those shoulders. Look at the muscles in his arms and his sturdy legs. Capable of any amount of hard labor. Moreover, of a good disposition, intelligent and tractable. Will any gentleman start the bidding? The* PLANTERS *raise their fingers, make their bids. They are apparently all eager to possess* JONES. *The bidding is lively, the crowd interested. While this has been going on,* JONES *has been seized by the* 30 *courage of desperation. He dares to look down and around him. Over his face abject terror gives way to mystification, to gradual realization— stutteringly.*)

What you all doin', white folks? What's all dis? What you all lookin' at me fo'? What you doin' wid me, anyhow? (*Suddenly convulsed with raging hatred and fear.*) Is dis a auction? Is you sellin' me like dey uster befo' de war? (*Jerking out his revolver just as the* 40 AUCTIONEER *knocks him down to one of the planters—glaring from him to the purchaser.*) And *you* sells me? And *you* buys me? I shows you I'se a free nigger, damn yo' souls! (*He fires at the* AUCTIONEER *and at the* PLANTER *with such rapidity that the two shots are almost simultaneous. As if this were a signal the walls of the forest fold in. Only blackness remains and silence broken by* JONES *as he rushes off, crying with fear—and by the quickened, ever louder beat of* 50 *the tom-tom.*)

SCENE SIX

SCENE. *Three o'clock. A cleared space in the forest. The limbs of the trees meet over it forming a low ceiling about five feet from the ground. The interlocked ropes of creepers reaching upward to entwine the tree trunks give an arched appearance to the sides. The space thus enclosed is like the dark, noisome hold of some ancient vessel. The moonlight is almost completely shut out and only a vague, wan light filters through. There is the noise of someone approaching from the left, stumbling and crawling through the undergrowth.* JONES' *voice is heard between chattering moans.*

Oh, Lawd, what I gwine do now? Ain't got no bullet left on'y de silver one. If mo' o' dem ha'nts come after me, how I gwine skeer dem away? Oh, Lawd, on'y de silver one left—an' I gotta save dat fo' luck. If I shoots dat one I'm a goner sho'! Lawd, it's black heah! Whar's de moon? Oh, Lawd, don't dis night evah come to an end? (*By the sounds, he is feeling his way cautiously forward.*) Dere! Dis feels like a clear space. I gotta lie down an' rest. I don't care if dem niggers does cotch me. I gotta rest.

(*He is well forward now where his figure can be dimly made out. His pants have been so torn away that what is left of them is no better than a breech cloth. He flings himself full length, face downward on the ground, panting with exhaustion. Gradually it seems to grow lighter in the enclosed space and two rows of seated figures can be seen behind* JONES. *They are sitting in crumpled, despairing attitudes, hunched, facing one another with their backs touching the forest walls as if they were shackled to them. All Negroes, naked save for loin cloths. At first they are silent and motionless. Then they begin to sway slowly forward toward each and back again in unison, as if they were laxly letting themselves follow the long roll of a ship at sea. At the same time, a low, melancholy murmur rises among them, increasing gradually by rhythmic degrees which seem to be directed and controlled by the throb of the tom-tom in the distance, to a long, tremulous wail of despair that reaches a certain pitch, unbearably acute, then falls by* 50 *slow gradations of tone into silence and is taken up again.* JONES *starts, looks up, sees the figures,* and throws himself down again to shut out the sight. A shudder of terror shakes his whole body as the wail rises up about him again. But the next time, his voice, as if under some uncanny compulsion, starts with the others. As their chorus lifts he rises to a sitting posture similar to the others, swaying back and forth. His voice reaches the highest pitch of sorrow, of desolation. The light fades out, the other voices cease, and only darkness is left. JONES can be heard scrambling to his feet and running off, his voice sinking down the scale and receding as he moves farther and farther away in the forest. The tom-tom beats louder, quicker, with a more insistent, triumphant pulsation.)

SCENE SEVEN

SCENE. *Five o'clock. The foot of a gigantic tree by the edge of a great river. A rough structure of boulders, like an altar, is by the tree. The raised river bank is in the nearer background. Beyond this the surface of the river spreads out, brilliant and unruffled in the moonlight, blotted out and merged into a veil of bluish mist in the distance.* JONES' *voice is heard from the left rising and falling in the long, despairing wail of the chained slave, to the rhythmic beat of the tom-tom. As his voice sinks into silence, he enters the open space. The expression of his face is fixed and stony, his eyes have an obsessed glare, he moves with a strange deliberation like a sleepwalker or one in a trance. He looks around at the tree, the rough stone altar, the moonlit surface of the river beyond, and passes his hand over his head with a vague gesture of puzzled bewilderment. Then, as if in obedience to some obscure impulse, he sinks into a kneeling, devotional posture before the altar. Then he seems to come to himself partly, to have an uncertain realization of what he is doing, for he straightens up and stares about him horrifiedly—in an incoherent mumble.*

What—what is I doin? What is—dis place? Seems like—seems like I know dat tree—an' dem stones—an' de river. I remember—seems like I been heah befo'.(*Tremblingly.*)Oh, Gorry, I'se skeered in dis place! I'se skeered! Oh, Lawd, pertect dis sinner!

(*Crawling away from the altar, he cowers close to the ground, his face hidden, his shoulders heaving with sobs of hysterical fright. From behind the trunk of the tree, as if he had sprung out of it, the figure of the* CONGO WITCH-DOCTOR *appears. He is wizened and old, naked except for the fur of some small animal tied about his waist, its bushy tail hanging down in front. His body is stained all over a bright red. Antelope horns are on each side of his head, branching upward. In one hand he carries a bone rattle, in the other a charm stick with a bunch of white cockatoo feathers tied to the end. A great number of glass beads and bone ornaments are about his neck, ears, wrists, and ankles. He struts noiselessly with a queer prancing step to a position in the clear ground between* JONES *and the altar. Then with a preliminary, summoning stamp of his foot on the earth, he begins to dance and to chant. As if in response to his summons the beating of the tom-tom grows to a fierce, exultant boom whose throbs seem to fill the air with vibrating rhythm.* JONES *looks up, starts to spring to his feet, reaches a half-kneeling, half-squatting position and remains rigidly fixed there, paralyzed with awed fascination by this new apparition. The* WITCH-DOCTOR *sways, stamping with his foot, his bone rattle clicking the time. His voice rises and falls in a weird, monotonous croon, without articulate word divisions. Gradually his dance becomes clearly one of a narrative in pantomime, his croon is an incantation, a charm to allay the fierceness of some implacable deity demanding sacrifice. He flees, he is pursued by devils, he hides, he flees again. Even wilder and wilder becomes his flight, nearer and nearer draws the pursuing evil, more and more the spirit of terror gains possession of him. His croon, rising to intensity, is punctuated by shrill cries.* JONES *has become completely hypnotized. His voice joins in the incantation, in the cries, he beats time with his hands and sways his body to and fro from the waist. The whole spirit and meaning of the dance has entered into him, has become his spirit. Finally the theme to the pantomime halts on a howl of despair, and is taken up again in a note of savage hope. There is a salvation. The forces of evil demand sacrifice. They must be appeased. The* WITCH-DOCTOR *points with his wand to the sacred tree, to the river beyond, to the altar, and finally to* JONES *with a ferocious command.* JONES *seems to sense the meaning of this. It is he who must offer himself for sacrifice. He beats his forehead abjectly to the ground, moaning hysterically.*)

Mercy, Oh Lawd! Mercy! Mercy on dis po' sinner.

(*The* WITCH-DOCTOR *springs to the river bank. He stretches out his arms and calls to some God within its depths. Then he starts backward slowly, his arms remaining out. A huge head of a crocodile appears over the bank, and its eyes, glittering greenly, fasten upon* JONES. *He stares into them fascinatedly. The* WITCH-DOCTOR *prances up to him, touches him with his wand, motions him with hideous command toward the waiting monster.* JONES *squirms on his belly nearer and nearer, moaning continually.*)

Mercy, Lawd! Mercy!

(*The crocodile heaves more of his enormous hulk onto the land.* JONES *squirms toward him. The* WITCH-DOCTOR'S *voice shrills out in furious exaltation, the tom-tom beats madly.* JONES *cries out in a fierce, exhausted spasm of anguished pleading.*)

Lawd, save me! Lawd Jesus, heah my prayer!

(*Immediately, in answer to his prayer, comes the thought of the one bullet left him. He snatches at his hip, shouting defiantly.*)

De silver bullet! You don't get me yit!

(*He fires at the green eyes in front of him. The head of the crocodile sinks back behind the river bank, the* WITCH-DOCTOR *springs behind the sacred tree and disappears.* JONES *lies with his face to the ground, his arms outstretched, whimpering with fear as the throb of tom-tom fills the silence about him with a somber pulsation, a baffled but revengeful power.*)

SCENE EIGHT

SCENE. *Dawn. Same as Scene Two. The dividing line of forest and plain. The nearest tree trunks are dimly revealed but the forest behind them is still a mass of glooming shadow. The tom-tom seems on the very spot, so loud and continuously vibrating are its beats.* LEM *enters from the left, followed by a small squad of his soldiers, and by the Cockney trader,* SMITHERS. LEM *is a heavy-set, ape-faced old savage of the extreme African type, dressed only in a loin cloth. A revolver and cartridge belt are about his waist. His soldiers are in different degrees of rag-concealed nakedness. All wear broad palm-leaf hats. Each one carries a rifle.* SMITHERS *is the same as in Scene One. One of the soldiers, evidently a*

tracker, is peering about keenly on the ground. He grunts and points to the spot where JONES *entered the forest.* LEM *and* SMITHERS *come to look.*

SMITHERS (*After a glance, turns away in disgust*). That's where'e went in right enough. Much good it'll do yer. 'E's miles orf by this an' safe to the Coast, damn 'is 'ide! I tole yer yer'd lose 'im, didn't I?—wastin' the 'ole bloomin' night beatin' yer bloody drum and castin' yer silly spells! Gawd blimey, wot a pack!

LEM (*Gutturally*). We cotch him. You see. (*He makes a motion to his soldiers who squat down on their haunches in a semicircle.*)

SMITHERS (*Exasperatedly*). Well, ain't yer goin' in an' 'unt 'im in the woods? What the 'ell's the good of waitin'?

LEM (*Imperturbably—squatting down himself*). We cotch him.

SMITHERS (*Turning away from him contemptuously*). Aw! Garn! 'E's a better man than the lot o' you put together. I 'ates the sight o' 'im but I'll say that for 'im. (*A sound of snapping twigs comes from the forest. The soldiers jump to their feet, cocking their rifles alertly.* LEM *remains sitting with an imperturbable expression, but listening intently. The sound from the woods is repeated.* LEM *makes a quick signal with his hand. His followers creep quickly but noiselessly into the forest, scattering so that each enters a different spot.*)

SMITHERS (*In the silence that follows—in a contemptuous whisper*). You ain't thinkin' that would be 'im I 'ope?

LEM (*Calmly*). We cotch him.

SMITHERS. Blarsted fat 'eads! (*Then after a second's thought—wonderingly.*) Still an' all, it might 'appen. If 'e lost 'is bloody way in these stinkin' woods 'e'd likely turn in a circle without 'is knowin' it. They all does.

LEM (*Peremptorily*). Sssh! (*The reports of several rifles sound from the forest, followed a second later by savage, exultant yells. The beating of the tom-tom abruptly ceases.* LEM *looks up at the white man with a grin of satisfaction.*) We cotch him. Him dead.

SMITHERS (*With a snarl*). 'Ow d'yer know it's 'im an' 'ow d'yer know 'e's dead?

LEM: My mens dey got 'um silver bullets. Dey kill him shore.

SMITHERS (*Astonished*). They got silver bullets?

Lem. Lead bullet no kill him. He got um strong charm. I cook um money, make um silver bullet, make um strong charm, too.

Smithers (*Light breaking upon him*). So that's wot you was up to all night, wot? You was scared to put after 'im till you'd molded silver bullets, eh?

Lem (*Simply stating a fact*). Yes. Him got strong charm. Lead no good.

Smithers (*Slapping his thigh and guffawing*). 10 Haw-haw! If yer don't beat all 'ell! (*Then recovering himself—scornfully.*) I'll bet yer it ain't 'im they shot at all, yer bleedin' looney!

Lem (*Calmly*). Dey come bring him now. (*The soldiers come out of the forest, carrying* Jones' *limp body. There is a little reddish-purple hole under his left breast. He is dead. They carry him to* Lem, *who examines his body with great satisfaction.*)

Smithers (*leans over his shoulder—in a tone of frightened awe*). Well, they did for yer right enough, Jonesey, me lad! Dead as a 'erring! (*Mockingly.*) Where's yer 'igh an' mighty airs now, yer bloomin' Majesty? (*Then with a grin.*) Silver bullets! Gawd blimey, but yer died in the 'eight o' style, any'ow! (Lem *makes a motion to the soldiers to carry the body out left.* Smithers *speaks to him sneeringly.*)

Smithers. And I s'pose you think it's yer bleedin' charms and yer silly beatin' the drum that made 'im run in a circle when 'e'd lost 'imself, don't yer? (*But* Lem *makes no reply, does not seem to hear the question, walks out left after his men.* Smithers *looks after him with contemptuous scorn.*) Stupid as 'ogs, the lot of 'em! Blarsted niggers!

(*Curtain falls.*)

1921

1874 ~ *Amy Lowell* ~ 1925

Miss Lowell came from a distinguished New England family and numbered among her ancestors famous statesmen, educators, writers, and diplomats. Her grandfather was a cousin of James Russell Lowell, and her brothers were Percival Lowell, the astronomer, and Abbott Lawrence Lowell, for many years president of Harvard University. She was a native of Brookline, Massachusetts, where she made her home to the end of her life. Born to great wealth, she had the advantage of private education and much foreign travel. At thirteen, it is said, she began to write verse, but it was not until she was twenty-eight that she made up her mind to make poetry her profession. At thirty-eight she published her first book. Although known primarily as a poet, she also achieved distinction as a critic and biographer. By some it is believed that the unremitting work on her life of Keats, one of her masters, hastened her death.

During her lifetime she published eight volumes of poetry, and three others appeared after her death. Of these *Sword Blades and Poppy Seed* (1914) and *Can Grande's Castle* (1918) are representative of her most original and best work. *A Critical Fable* (1922) tries to do for her contemporaries what James Russell Lowell did earlier in his *A Fable for Critics*. *Six French Poets* (1915) and *Tendencies in Modern American Poetry* (1917) are critical studies variously estimated as to their ultimate value. There are differing opinions about her biography of *John Keats* (1925), but it is safe to say that she brought together the greatest amount of material concerning Keats ever assembled, and that all future biographers and interpreters will be indebted to her.

In view of Miss Lowell's staid New England ancestry and background it would have been natural for her to become a poet in the classical tradition. Indeed, her first volume, *A Dome of Many-Colored Glass* (1912), seemed to confirm this anticipation, for most of the poems in it were written in more or less stereotyped forms. Two forces, however, united to change the current of her development. During recent years America with its youthful instability and passion for change had become interested in a changing form of poetic art, referred to in such terms as "new poetry," *vers libre*, and Imagism. A woman of boundless energy, with a good deal of the pugnacious and belligerent in her nature, she seized the opportunity to make herself the promoter, leader, spokesman, and interpreter of the small group of poets who were struggling to arrive at a new medium of poetic expression. And in her own creative work she began to experiment with new forms in accordance with their *Credo*, the change being definitely noticeable in *Sword Blades and Poppy Seed*.

The chief articles in the new creed to which the Imagists subscribed are: (1) to use only the *exact* word; (2) to substitute cadence for meter; (3) to have free choice of subject matter; (4) to create definite and concrete images that are hard and clear; and (5) to strive for concentration.

Some of the precepts Miss Lowell followed, and others she ignored. She chose her subject matter rather promiscuously from human experience past and present, actual as well as imagined (one of her volumes is entitled *Legends*); in her development of polyphonic prose as a medium of expression she probably went further than was originally anticipated. On the other hand the exact word, the hard poetic effect, and the clear image are seldom absent.

One wonders why the creed of the Imagists, on the surface harmless enough, should have precipitated discussion and controversy. Some of the suggestions had been followed by poets from time immemorial. Yet controversy did rage as to whether this new thing was actually poetry, and stirred up anew the age-old problem of the relation of prose to poetry. To a certain degree it was undoubtedly due to the aggressive tactics of Miss Lowell, who throve on argument and loved a fight. While she lived the Imagists were active and aggressive; since her death the movement has declined.

Her poetry, widely experimental, sometimes graceful and rich, is still neither representative of what the Imagists wanted modern poetry to be nor wholly successful intrinsically. Her poems have almost always the character of cold preciousness, of self-conscious experiments, and often of show-pieces or bric-a-brac. She is often quite happy in her effects (as in "Patterns") experimenting with slant rhymes, internal rhyming, and alliteration. But in the main she is valuable chiefly as a saleswoman for "the new poetry," and her poems fill well the role of sample pieces of what might be done with the principles which she preached. She was able to do what Pound could not: she had the money, the patience, and the vigor to help young poets to a hearing. Many of these poets have survived the rather thorough eclipse of her own reputation as a poet.

Miss Lowell's writings include poetry, criticism, and biography. The volumes of her poems are *A Dome of Many-Colored Glass* (1912); *Sword Blades and Poppy Seed* (1914); *Men, Women and Ghosts* (1916); *Can Grande's Castle* (1918); *Pictures of the Floating World* (1919); *Legends* (1921); *A Critical Fable* (1922); *What's O'Clock* (1925); *East Wind* (1926); *Ballads for Sale* (1927); *The Madonna of Carthagena* (1927); selections from her poetry are published in J. L. Lowes, ed., *Selected Poems of Amy Lowell* (1928). In criticism she has written *Six French Poets* (1915); *Tendencies in Modern American Poetry* (1917); *Poetry and Poets* (1930). Her biographical work is *John Keats* (2 vols., 1925). S. F. Damon, *Amy Lowell* (1935), is a definitive biography. Briefer accounts are found in R. Hunt and R. H. Snow, *Amy Lowell: a Sketch of Her Life and Her Place in Contemporary American Literature* (1917); E. S. Sergeant, *Fire Under the Andes* (1927); H. B. Kizer, "Amy Lowell, a Personality," *North American Review*, Jan., 1918; H. Monroe, *Poets & Their Art* (1926). For critical estimates and interpretation consult C. Wood, *Amy Lowell* (1926); P. H. Boynton, *Some Contemporary Americans* (1924); L. Untermeyer, *American Poetry Since 1900* (1923); J. W. Tupper, "The Poetry of Amy Lowell," *Sewanee Review*, Jan., 1920; R. Brenner, *Ten Modern Poets* (1930); C. Cestre, "Amy Lowell, Robert Frost, and Edwin Arlington Robinson," *Johns Hopkins Alumni Magazine*, March, 1926; J. Farrar, ed., *The Literary Spotlight* (1924); T. Maynard, *Our Best Poets* (1922); W. T. Scott, "Amy Lowell and the Art of Poetry," *North American Review*, March, 1925; A. Kreymborg, *Our Singing Strength* (1929); G. Hughes, *Imagism and the Imagists* (1931); B. Weirick, *From Whitman to Sandburg in American Poetry* (1924); C. Aiken, *Scepticisms* (1919); W. L. Schwartz, "A Study of Amy Lowell's Far Eastern Verse," *Modern Language Notes*, March, 1928; J. Kilmer, *Literature in the Making* (1917); J. G. Fletcher, "Living History: Amy Lowell's *Men, Women and Ghosts*," *Poetry*, June, 1917; J. G. Fletcher, "Miss Lowell's Discovery: Polyphonic Prose," *Poetry*, April, 1915; F. Ayscough, "Amy Lowell and the Far East," *Bookman*, March, 1926; W. M. Patterson, "New Verse and New Prose," *North American Review*, Feb., 1918; Horace Gregory and Marya Zaturenska, *A History of American Poetry, 1900-1940* (1946).

PATTERNS

I WALK down the garden-paths,
And all the daffodils
Are blowing, and the bright blue squills.
I walk down the patterned garden-paths
In my stiff, brocaded gown.
With my powdered hair and jewelled fan,
I too am a rare
Pattern. As I wander down
The garden-paths.
My dress is richly figured,   10
And the train
Makes a pink and silver stain
On the gravel, and the thrift

Of the borders.
Just a plate of current fashion,
Tripping by in high-heeled, ribboned shoes.
Not a softness anywhere about me,
Only whalebone and brocade.
And I sink on a seat in the shade
Of a lime-tree. For my passion   20
Wars against the stiff brocade.
The daffodils and squills
Flutter in the breeze
As they please.
And I weep;
For the lime-tree is in blossom
And one small flower has dropped upon my
          bosom.

And the plashing of waterdrops
In the marble fountain
Comes down the garden-paths,   30
The dripping never stops.
Underneath my stiffened gown
Is the softness of a woman bathing in a marble
        basin,
A basin in the midst of hedges grown
So thick, she cannot see her lover hiding,
But she guesses he is near,
And the sliding of the water
Seems the stroking of a dear
Hand upon her.
What is Summer in a fine brocaded gown! 40
I should like to see it lying in a heap upon the
        ground.
All the pink and silver crumpled up on the
        ground.

I would be the pink and silver as I ran along
        the paths,
And he would stumble after,
Bewildered by my laughter.
I should see the sun flashing from his sword-
        hilt and the buckles on his shoes.
I would choose
To lead him in a maze along the patterned
        paths,
A bright and laughing maze for my heavy-
        booted lover.
Till he caught me in the shade,   50
And the buttons of his waistcoat bruised my
        body as he clasped me
Aching, melting, unafraid.
With the shadows of the leaves and the sun-
        drops,
And the plopping of the waterdrops,
All about us in the open afternoon—
I am very like to swoon
With the weight of this brocade,
For the sun sifts through the shade.
Underneath the fallen blossom
In my bosom,   60
Is a letter I have hid.
It was brought to me this morning by a rider
        from the Duke.
"Madam, we regret to inform you that Lord
        Hartwell
Died in action Thursday se'nnight."
As I read it in the white, morning sunlight,
The letters squirmed like snakes.

"Any answer, Madam," said my footman.
"No," I told him.
"See that the messenger takes some refresh-
        ment.
No, no answer."   70
And I walked into the garden,
Up and down the patterned paths,
In my stiff, correct brocade.
The blue and yellow flowers stood up proudly
        in the sun,
Each one.
I stood upright too,
Held rigid to the pattern
By the stiffness of my gown.
Up and down I walked,
Up and down.   80

In a month he would have been my hus-
        band.
In a month, here, underneath this lime,
We would have broke the pattern;
He for me, and I for him,
He as Colonel, I as Lady,
On this shady seat.
He had a whim
That sunlight carried blessing.
And I answered, "It shall be as you have
        said."
Now he is dead.   90

In Summer and in Winter I shall walk
Up and down
The patterned garden paths
In my stiff, brocaded gown.
The squills and daffodils
Will give place to pillared roses, and to asters,
        and to snow.
I shall go
Up and down,
In my gown.
Gorgeously arrayed,   100
Boned and stayed.
And the softness of my body will be guarded
        from embrace
By each button, hook, and lace.
For the man who should loose me is dead,
Fighting with the Duke in Flanders,
In a pattern called a war.
Christ! What are patterns for?

                                                     1915

1886 ~ *H(ilda) D(oolittle)* ~ ——

HILDA DOOLITTLE was born in Bethlehem, Pennsylvania, spent two years at Bryn Mawr College, and in 1911 went to Europe, where later she married the British poet, Richard Aldington. While in London, H. D. became acquainted with the group of writers who were interested in new poetic theories and practices, and joined enthusiastically with them. It is said that Pound started the Imagist movement to give her poetry a hearing. Even after discounting the claim, one has to admit that H. D.'s verse does preserve more successfully than most the qualities which the Imagists admired. Her writing is clear and objective, sparing but precise in imagery, concentrated and intense. Withal, it is often slight and always limited. Ultimately it demonstrates, better than does the poetry of other Imagists, both the gains made by the school and the limitations which poetry that follows its principles too narrowly suffers.

H.D.'s verse has been published as follows: *Sea Garden* (1916); *The Tribute and Circe* (1917); *Hymen* (1921); *Heliodora and Other Poems* (1924); *Red Roses for Bronze* (1931); *The Walls Do Not Fall* (1944). *Collected Poems* was published in 1925. She has written one play, *Hippolytus Temporizes* (1927); translations or adaptations from the Greek include *Choruses from Iphigeneia* (1916); and *Euripides Ion* (1936). Critical studies of her work include Babette Deutsch, *This Modern Poetry* (1935); Glenn Hughes, *Imagism and the Imagists* (1931); Alfred Kreymborg, *Our Singing Strength* (1929); Amy Lowell, *Tendencies in Modern American Poetry* (1917); Horace Gregory and Marya Zaturenska, *A History of American Poetry, 1900-1940* (1946); R. P. Blackmur, "The Lesser Satisfactions," *Poetry*, Nov., 1932; May Sinclair, "The Poems of H.D.," *Fortnightly Review*, March, 1927.

THE GARDEN

I

You are clear,
O rose, cut in rock.

I could scrape the colour
From the petals,
Like spilt dye from a rock.

If I could break you
I could break a tree.

If I could stir
I could break a tree,
I could break you.

10

II

O wind, rend open the heat,
Cut apart the heat,
Slit it to tatters.

Fruit cannot drop
Through this thick air;
Fruit cannot fall into heat
That presses up and blunts
The points of pears,
And round grapes.

Cut the heat;
Plough through it,
Turning it on either side
Of your path.

20

1916

SONG

You are as gold
As the half-ripe grain
That merges to gold again,
As white as the white rain
That beats through
The half-opened flowers
Of the great flower tufts
Thick on the black limbs
Of an Illyrian apple bough.

Can honey distil such fragrance   10
As your bright hair—
For your face is as fair as rain,
Yet as rain that lies clear
On white honey-comb,
Lends radiance to the white wax,
So your hair on your brow
Casts light for a shadow.

                                        1921

ORCHARD

I saw the first pear
as it fell—
the honey-seeking, golden banded,
the yellow swarm,
was not more fleet than I,

(spare us from loveliness!)
and I fell prostrate,
crying:
you have flayed us with your blossoms,
spare us the beauty   10
of fruit-trees!

The honey-seeking
paused not;
the air thundered their song,
and I alone was prostrate.

O rough-hewn
god of the orchard,
I bring you an offering—
do you, alone unbeautiful,
son of the god,   20
spare us from loveliness:
these fallen hazel-nuts,
stripped late of their green sheaths,
grapes, red-purple,
their berries
dripping with wine;
pomegranates already broken,
and shrunken figs,
and quinces untouched,
I bring you as offering.   30

                                        1916

1888 ~ *T. S. Eliot* ~ ——

Born in Saint Louis, Missouri, Thomas Stearns Eliot was educated at Smith Academy in that city, Harvard (1906–1910), the Sorbonne, Paris (1910–1911), and Merton College, Oxford (1914–1915). At Harvard he was an editor of *The Advocate*, to which he contributed some poems; and, after finishing his undergraduate course, he remained for one year as a graduate student in philosophy. He continued indulging his philosophical interests at the Sorbonne and at Oxford; in Paris he attended lectures given by Henri Bergson; at Oxford he studied chiefly Greek philosophy. From 1911 to 1914 he was again at Harvard, studying philosophy and philology (including Sanskrit); he was made an assistant in philosophy in 1913–1914.

It is barely possible that, had Eliot not become acquainted with T. E. Hulme and Ezra Pound, he would not have turned to poetry at all. The poems in *The*

Harvard Advocate are interesting college products; but his interests were predominantly in philosophy and theology. For this latter he had the precedent of New England and Saint Louis ministers among his ancestry. Through Pound, Hulme, F. S. Flint, and other young men in the Harold Monro and *Egoist* circles, Eliot became acquainted with French poetry, French poetic theory, and the first stirrings of Imagism. Most important was Pound, *"il miglior fabbro"* as he called him in the dedication of *The Waste Land* in 1922.

The early poems reflect these interests and influences: "The Love Song of J. Alfred Prufrock" appeared in Harriet Monroe's *Poetry*, April-Sept., 1915; "Preludes" and "Rhapsody on a Windy Night" in Wyndham Lewis's "vorticist" magazine, *Blast*, July, 1915. In 1915, Eliot contributed to Pound's *Catholic Anthology*, "Prufrock," "Portrait of a Lady," and several other poems. There is no doubt that these poems (and others, brought together under the title of *Prufrock and Other Observations*, 1917) reflect the interest of the group in French poetry, French criticism (especially that of Rémy de Gourmont), and the preoccupation of the Imagists with objective representation. Added to these, however, was the interest in the "self-conscious irony" of Jules Laforgue and the rough ironic sketches of urban life in Tristan Corbière's poetry. These early poems of Eliot, brilliantly independent of all of these influences, however noticeable their effect is, reflect Eliot's early thinking upon the facts of modern civilization and its impact upon the modern personality. The setting is often urban; the details, offered sparingly but with penetration, are those of city streets which seem to give tangible evidence of spiritual desolation. Both Prufrock and the Lady are contemporary types, which can be matched in Pound's poetry. Their hesitation, unhappiness, fear, lack of moral incentive are portrayed by means of objective detail and allusion. The Sweeney poems offer another character: the modern vulgarian, obtuse, straightforward, lusty and lustful. The contrast with earlier cultures is much more obvious, much less skillful or subtle, than in the later poems.

"Gerontion," published in *Poems*, 1920, is a first view of *The Waste Land*. In 1923, Eliot became editor of *The Criterion*, a position he held until 1939. The poems written at this time reflect a much wider use of sources; the Jacobin dramatists, Dante's *Divine Comedy*, and other sources begin to manifest themselves. The wasteland situation, while dramatized in simple form in the early poems, is more fully and more solidly characterized in "Gerontion," *The Waste Land* (1922) and "The Hollow Men" (in *Poems, 1909-1925*). By the use of the myth of the Fisherking, which he first studied in Jessie Weston's *From Ritual to Romance*, and of other themes and legends, Eliot presented, in *The Waste Land*, a theme poignantly applicable to contemporary society. The protagonist of *The Waste Land* moves through the dry, sterile, desert land of modern life in search of a clue to his personal salvation. "I had not thought death had undone so many," he says, paraphrasing

Dante's *Inferno*; and the waste land is a composite drawn from Dante's hell, Baudelaire's "unreal city," Paris, and modern London. The point is not that modern civilization is necessarily inferior to that of other times, but that all peoples who lack spiritual resources, who have been led to denounce faith, are doomed to an ugly and hysterical kind of sterility. The protagonist does find some clues to his spiritual progress (they are drawn from Hindu scriptures and given in Sanskrit), but they are for him, not for the others. The waste land remains, but "These fragments I have shored against my ruins."

After the postlude called "The Hollow Men," Eliot turned to what may more literally be called religious poetry. In addition to such religious poems as "Journey of the Magi," "A Song for Simeon," and "Animula," he was working in the late 1920's on *Ash Wednesday*, which finally appeared in book form in 1930. It is a poem which quite literally conveys the hesitations, the alternations of fear and ecstasy, of religious conversion; the source continues to be Dante, but to him are added such religious mystics as St. John of the Cross. In 1927 Eliot became a British citizen, and announced his affiliation with the Anglo-Catholic church. "The World is trying the experiment of attempting to form a civilized but non-Christian mentality," he said in 1931. "The experiment will fail; but we must be very patient in awaiting its collapse; meanwhile redeeming the time: so that the Faith may be preserved alive through the dark ages before us; to renew and rebuild civilization, and save the World from suicide."

If it is true that Eliot's poetry shows a continuous progress toward a more exact and a more positive definition of man's spiritual condition, it is also true that his latest work, while not abandoning the interest in the world of Prufrock and Aunt Helen, is primarily concerned not only with presenting a religious search but also with underscoring the positive attributes of a specific faith. *Four Quartets* (1943) (besides offering some of the most interesting poetry of our time) is marked by a religious confidence that overcomes in each case the disciplinary (and often rather factitious) despair expressed by the poet. The Quartets are infinitely more subtle, more complex poetry than *Ash Wednesday*; they are also a completion of the work begun by the protagonist of *The Waste Land*, in the last section of that poem.

Eliot is by all odds the most significant poet of our century. In training, discipline, equipment, he excels all of his contemporaries. His poetry offers technical skills in a new context of language and allusion. From Pound to the Anglo-Catholic divines, he has run the gamut of sources and influences, borrowing and reshaping whatever his eclectic taste has seized upon. Yet he is a highly personal poet; surprising though it may seem, in view of his enormous influence upon young contemporaries, his poetry reflects an individual search for, then an enforcement of, a personal salvation. His followers have admired him for his skill, his mastery of form and language; they have often been mistaken about his meaning, or imitated one level of meaning (as in Archibald MacLeish's *Pot of Earth*) in ignorance of the other. He remains, however, the most stimulating and challenging of literary personalities.

See below, page 1076, for a brief summary of Eliot's criticism.

Eliot's poems have been published as follows: *Prufrock and Other Observations* (1917); *Ara Vos Prec* (1919); *Poems* (1919); *Poems* (1920); *The Waste Land* (1922); *Poems, 1909-1925* (1925); *Journey of the Magi* (1927); *A Song for Simeon* (1928); *Animula* (1929); *Ash Wednesday* (1930); *Marina* (1930); *Triumphal March* (1931); *Sweeney Agonistes, Fragments of an Aristophanic Melodrama* (1932); *Collected Poems, 1909-1935* (1936); *Four Quartets* (1943). He has published three dramatic pieces: *The Rock* (1934); *Murder in the Cathedral* (1935); *The Family Reunion* (1939); and one translation, that of St. J. Perse's *Anabasis* (1930). For a list of his critical works, see below, p. 1078. The best of many critical studies of Eliot is F. O. Matthiessen's *The Achievement of T. S. Eliot* (second edition, 1947); collections of criticism include B. Rajan (ed.) *T. S. Eliot: A Study of His Writings by Several Hands* (1947) and Leonard Unger (ed.) *T. S. Eliot: A Selected Critique* (1948). See also Cleanth Brooks, *Modern Poetry and the Tradition* (1939); Elizabeth Drew, *Directions in Modern Poetry* (1940); David Daiches, *Poetry and the Modern World* (1940); Ruth Bailey, *A Dialogue on Modern Poetry* (1929); R. P. Blackmur, *The Double Agent* (1935) and *The Expense of Greatness* (1940); Maud Bodkin, *The Quest for Salvation in an Ancient and a Modern Play* (1941); Geoffrey Bullough, *The Trend of Modern Poetry* (1934); J. R. Daniells, "T. S. Eliot and His Relationship to T. E. Hulme," *The University of Toronto Quarterly*, 1933; Ramon Fernandez, *Messages* (1927); Louis Grudin, *Mr. Eliot Among the Nightingales* (1932); Peter Monro Jack, "A Review of Reviews of T. S. Eliot's *Four Quartets*," *American Bookman*, 1944; F. R. Leavis, *New Bearings in English Poetry* (1932); Theodore Morrison, "Ash Wednesday: A Religious History," *New England Quarterly*, 1938; Ferner Nuhn, *The Wind Blew from the East* (1942); Ezra Pound, "T. S. Eliot," *Poetry*, 1917; Mario Praz, "T. S. Eliot and Dante," *The Southern Review*, 1937; Raymond Preston, *Four Quartets Rehearsed* (1946); John Crowe Ransom, *The World's Body* (1938); Philip Blair Rice, "Out of the Waste Land," *Symposium*, 1932; H. Ross Williamson, *The Poetry of T. S. Eliot* (1933); D. S. Savage, *The Personal Principle* (1944); Edith Sitwell, *Aspects of Modern Poetry* (1934); Stephen Spender, *The Destructive Element* (1936); Eliseo Vivas, "The Objective Correlative of T. S. Eliot," *The American Bookman*, 1944; W. B. Yeats, *The Oxford Book of Modern Verse* (1936).

THE LOVE SONG OF J. ALFRED PRUFROCK

S'io credesse che mia risposta fosse
A persona che mai tornasse al mondo,
Questa fiamma staria senza piu scosse.
Ma perciocche giammai di questo fondo
Non torno vivo alcun, s'i'odo il vero,
Senza tema d'infamia ti rispondo.

LET us go then, you and I,
When the evening is spread out against the
    sky
Like a patient etherised upon a table;
Let us go, through certain half-deserted
    streets,
The muttering retreats

Of restless nights in one-night cheap hotels
And sawdust restaurants with oyster-shells:
Streets that follow like a tedious argument
Of insidious intent
To lead you to an overwhelming question . . .
Oh, do not ask, "What is it?" 11
Let us go and make our visit.

In the room the women come and go
Talking of Michelangelo.

The yellow fog that rubs its back upon the
    window-panes,
The yellow smoke that rubs its muzzle on the
    window-panes

Licked its tongue into the corners of the eve-
    ning,
Lingered upon the pools that stand in drains,
Let fall upon its back the soot that falls from
    chimneys,
Slipped by the terrace, made a sudden leap, 20
And seeing that it was a soft October night,
Curled once about the house, and fell asleep.

And indeed there will be time
For the yellow smoke that slides along the
    street,
Rubbing its back upon the window-panes;
There will be time, there will be time
To prepare a face to meet the faces that you
    meet;
There will be time to murder and create,
And time for all the works and days of hands
That lift and drop a question on your plate;
Time for you and time for me,   31
And time yet for a hundred indecisions,
And for a hundred visions and revisions,
Before the taking of a toast and tea.

In the room the women come and go
Talking of Michelangelo.

And indeed there will be time
To wonder, "Do I dare?" and, "Do I dare?"
Time to turn back and descend the stair,
With a bald spot in the middle of my hair—
(They will say: "How his hair is growing
    thin!")   41
My morning coat, my collar mounting firmly
    to the chin,
My necktie rich and modest, but asserted by
    a simple pin—
(They will say: "But how his arms and legs
    are thin!")
Do I dare
Disturb the universe?
In a minute there is time
For decisions and revisions which a minute
    will reverse.

For I have known them all already, known
    them all:—
Have known the evenings, mornings, after-
    noons,   50
I have measured out my life with coffee
    spoons;

I know the voices dying with a dying fall
Beneath the music from a farther room.
    So how should I presume?

And I have known the eyes already, known
    them all—
The eyes that fix you in a formulated phrase,
And when I am formulated, sprawling on a pin,
When I am pinned and wriggling on the wall,
Then how should I begin
To spit out all the butt-ends of my days and
    ways?   60
    And how should I presume?

And I have known the arms already, known
    them all—
Arms that are braceleted and white and bare
(But in the lamplight, downed with light
    brown hair!)
Is it perfume from a dress
That makes me so digress?
Arms that lie along a table, or wrap about a
    shawl.
    And should I then presume?
    And how should I begin?

   .   .   .   .   .

Shall I say, I have gone at dusk through narrow
    streets   70
And watched the smoke that rises from the
    pipes
Of lonely men in shirt-sleeves, leaning out of
    windows? . . .

I should have been a pair of ragged claws
Scuttling across the floors of silent seas.

   .   .   .   .   .

And the afternoon, the evening, sleeps so
    peacefully!
Smoothed by long fingers,
Asleep . . . tired . . . or it malingers,
Stretched on the floor, here beside you and me.
Should I, after tea and cakes and ices,
Have the strength to force the moment to its
    crisis?   80
But though I have wept and fasted, wept and
    prayed,
Though I have seen my head (grown slightly
    bald) brought in upon a platter,
I am no prophet—and here's no great matter;
I have seen the moment of my greatness flicker,
And I have seen the eternal Footman hold my

coat, and snicker,
And in short, I was afraid.

And would it have been worth it, after all,
After the cups, the marmalade, the tea,
Among the porcelain, among some talk of you
    and me,
Would it have been worth while,   90
To have bitten off the matter with a smile,
To have squeezed the universe into a ball
To roll it toward some overwhelming question,
To say: "I am Lazarus, come from the dead,
Come back to tell you all, I shall tell you all"—
If one, settling a pillow by her head,
    Should say: "That was not what I meant
        at all;
That is not it, at all."

And would it have been worth it, after all,
Would it have been worth while,   100
After the sunsets and the dooryards and the
    sprinkled streets,
After the novels, after the teacups, after the
    skirts that trail along the floor—
And this, and so much more?—
It is impossible to say just what I mean!
But as if a magic lantern threw the nerves in
    patterns on a screen:
Would it have been worth while
If one, settling a pillow or throwing off a
    shawl,
And turning toward the window, should say:
    "That is not it at all,
    That is not what I meant at all."   110

   .   .   .   .   .

No! I am not Prince Hamlet, nor was meant
    to be;
Am an attendant lord, one that will do
To swell a progress, start a scene or two,
Advise the prince; no doubt, an easy tool,
Deferential, glad to be of use,
Polite, cautious, and meticulous;
Full of high sentence, but a bit obtuse;
At times, indeed, almost ridiculous—
Almost, at times, the Fool.

I grow old . . . I grow old . . .   120
I shall wear the bottoms of my trousers rolled.

Shall I part my hair behind? Do I dare to eat
    a peach?

I shall wear white flannel trousers, and walk
    upon the beach.
I have heard the mermaids singing, each to
    each.

I do not think that they will sing to me.

I have seen them riding seaward on the waves
Combing the white hair of the waves blown
    back
When the wind blows the water white and
    black.

We have lingered in the chambers of the sea
By sea-girls wreathed with seaweed red and
    brown   130
Till human voices wake us, and we drown.
                     1917

PRELUDES

I

THE winter evening settles down
With smell of steaks in passageways.
Six o'clock.
The burnt-out ends of smoky days.
And now a gusty shower wraps
The grimy scraps
Of withered leaves about your feet
And newspapers from vacant lots;
The showers beat
On broken blinds and chimney-pots,   10
And at the corner of the street
A lonely cab-horse steams and stamps.
And then the lighting of the lamps.

II

The morning comes to consciousness
Of faint stale smell of beer
From the sawdust-trampled street
With all its muddy feet that press
To early coffee-stands.
With the other masquerades
That time resumes,
One thinks of all the hands
That are raising dingy shades
In a thousand furnished rooms.   10

III

You tossed a blanket from the bed,
You lay upon your back, and waited;

You dozed, and watched the night reveal-
    ing
The thousand sordid images
Of which your soul was constituted;
They flickered against the ceiling.
And when all the world came back
And the light crept up between the shutters
And you heard the sparrows in the gutters,
You had such a vision of the street   10
As the street hardly understands;
Sitting along the bed's edge, where
You curled the papers from your hair,
Or clasped the yellow soles of feet
In the palms of both soiled hands.

IV

His soul stretched tight across the skies
That fade behind a city block,
Or trampled by insistent feet
At four and five and six o'clock;
And short square fingers stuffing pipes,
And evening newspapers, and eyes
Assured of certain certainties,
The conscience of a blackened street
Impatient to assume the world.

I am moved by fancies that are curled   10
Around these images, and cling:
The notion of some infinitely gentle
Infinitely suffering thing.

Wipe your hand across your mouth, and
    laugh;
The worlds revolve like ancient women
Gathering fuel in vacant lots.

                        1917

MORNING AT THE WINDOW

THEY are rattling breakfast plates in basement
    kitchens,
And along the trampled edges of the street
I am aware of the damp souls of housemaids
Sprouting despondently at area gates.

The brown waves of fog toss up to me
Twisted faces from the bottom of the street,
And tear from a passer-by with muddy
    skirts
An aimless smile that hovers in the air
And vanishes along the level of the roofs.

GERONTION

    Thou hast nor youth nor age
    But as it were an after dinner sleep
    Dreaming of both.

HERE I am, an old man in a dry month,
Being read to by a boy, waiting for rain.
I was neither at the hot gates
Nor fought in the warm rain,
Nor knee deep in the salt marsh, heaving a
    cutlass,
Bitten by flies, fought.
My house is a decayed house,
And the jew squats on the window sill, the
    owner,
Spawned in some estaminet of Antwerp,
Blistered in Brussels, patched and peeled in
    London.   10
The great coughs at night in the field over-
    head;
Rocks, moss, stonecrop, iron, merds.
The woman keeps the kitchen, makes tea,
Sneezes at evening, poking the peevish gutter.
                       I an old man,
A dull head among windy spaces.

Signs are taken for wonders. "We would see
    a sign"!
The word within a word, unable to speak a
    word,
Swaddled with darkness. In the juvescence of
    the year
Came Christ the tiger   20
In depraved May, dogwood and chestnut,
    flowering judas,
To be eaten, to be divided, to be drunk
Among whispers; by Mr. Silvero
With caressing hands, at Limoges
Who walked all night in the next room;

By Hakagawa, bowing among the Titians;
By Madame de Tornquist, in the dark room
Shifting the candles; Fräulein von Kulp
Who turned in the hall, one hand on the door.
           Vacant shuttles   30
Weave the wind. I have no ghosts,
An old man in a draughty house
Under a windy knob.
After such knowledge, what forgiveness?
    Think now
History has many cunning passages, contrived
    corridors

And issues, deceives with whispering ambi-
tions,
Guides us by vanities. Think now
She gives when our attention is distracted
And what she gives, gives with such supple
confusions
That the giving famishes the craving. Gives
too late   40
What's not believed in, or if still believed,
In memory only, reconsidered passion. Gives
too soon
Into weak hands, what's thought can be dis-
pensed with
Till the refusal propagates a fear. Think
Neither fear nor courage saves us. Unnatural
vices
Are fathered by our heroism. Virtues
Are forced upon us by our impudent crimes.
These tears are shaken from the wrathbearing
tree.

The tiger springs in the new year. Us he de-
vours. Think at last
We have not reached conclusion, when I   50
Stiffen in a rented house. Think at last
I have not made this show purposelessly
And it is not by any concitation
Of the backward devils.
I would meet you upon this honestly.
I that was near your heart was removed there-
from
To lose beauty in terror, terror in inquisi-
tion.
I have lost my passion: why should I need to
keep it
Since what is kept must be adulterated?
I have lost my sight, smell, hearing, taste and
touch: 60
How should I use it for your closer contact?

These with a thousand small deliberations
Protract the profit of their chilled delirium,
Excite the membrane, when the sense has
cooled,
With pungent sauces, multiply variety
In a wilderness of mirrors. What will the
spider do,
Suspend its operations, will the weevil
Delay? De Bailhache, Fresca, Mrs. Cammel,
whirled
Beyond the circuit of the shuddering Bear

In fractured atoms. Gull against the wind, in
the windy straits   70
Of Belle Isle, or running on the Horn,
White feathers in the snow, the Gulf claims,
And an old man driven by the Trades
To a sleepy corner.

               Tenants of the house
Thoughts of a dry brain in a dry season.

                     1920

JOURNEY OF THE MAGI

"A COLD coming we had of it,
Just the worst time of the year
For a journey, and such a long journey:
The ways deep and the weather sharp,
The very dead of winter."
And the camels galled, sore-footed, refractory,
Lying down in the melting snow.
There were times we regretted
The summer palaces on slopes, the terraces,
And the silken girls bringing sherbet.   10
Then the camel men cursing and grumbling
And running away, and wanting their liquor
and women,
And the night-fires going out, and the lack of
shelters,
And the cities hostile and the towns unfriendly
And the villages dirty and charging high
prices:
A hard time we had of it.
At the end we preferred to travel all night,
Sleeping in snatches,
With the voices singing in our ears, saying
That this was all folly.   20

Then at dawn we came down to a temperate
valley,
Wet, below the snow line, smelling of vege-
tation;
With a running stream and a water-mill beat-
ing the darkness,
And three trees on the low sky,
And an old white horse galloped away in the
meadow.
Then we came to a tavern with vine-leaves
over the lintel,
Six hands at an open door dicing for pieces of
silver,
And feet kicking the empty wine-skins.

But there was no information, and so we continued
And arriving at evening, not a moment too
soon   30
Finding the place; it was (you may say) satisfactory.

All this was a long time ago, I remember,
And I would do it again, but set down
This set down
This: were we led all that way for
Birth or Death? There was a Birth, certainly,

We had evidence and no doubt. I had seen
birth and death,
But had thought they were different; this
Birth was
Hard and bitter agony for us, like Death, our
death.
We returned to our places, these Kingdoms, 40
But no longer at ease here, in the old dispen-
sation,
With an alien people clutching their gods.
I should be glad of another death.

1927

1879 -- *Wallace Stevens* -- —

WALLACE STEVENS' career as poet thus far divides itself into four periods.
From 1914 to 1923 he wrote such poems as "Sunday Morning" and "Peter
Quince at the Clavier" and published them in little magazines such as *Others* and
Poetry. In these years he was interested in French symbolism, notably Mallarmé,
and in certain contributions which the Imagists made to contemporary poetry. His
description of beauty is given in "Sunday Morning":

> Death is the mother of beauty, mystical,
> Within whose burning bosom we devise
> Our earthly mothers waiting, sleeplessly.

In 1923 his first volume of poems, *Harmonium*, appeared. In it was the long
narrative poem, "The Comedian as the Letter C," whose hero moves away from
romanticism to objective realism. The intention of the poem is ironical, but as a
whole it suggests a change from Stevens' early preoccupation with symbolist
poetry. Except for "Sea-Surface Full of Clouds," published in *The Dial* of July,
1924, and a few other poems, Stevens published nothing until 1931, when the revised and enlarged edition of *Harmonium* appeared. In 1935 *Ideas of Order* was
published, and it was followed by *Owl's Clover* (1936) and *The Man with the Blue
Guitar* (1937). The principal emphasis in these three volumes is upon the human
imagination as a faculty for bringing order to reality, which is otherwise chaotic.
The song of the girl in "The Idea of Order at Key West," for example, provides
the means by which the sea can be known.

> It was her voice that made
> The sky acutest at its vanishing.
> She measured to the hour its solitude.

She was the single artificer of the world
In which she sang. . . .

In the most recent development of Stevens' poetry, he has set about the task of presenting a clarified and definitive exposition of the imagination as "The Supreme Fiction" by which we know reality. *Notes Toward a Supreme Fiction* (1942) and *Ésthetique du Mal* (1944), both of them included in *Transport to Summer* (1947), his most recent collection, are key poems in this development. Suggestions also appear in *The Man with the Blue Guitar* and *Parts of a World* (1942). The "supreme fiction" (that is, the imaginative form of the world) must be abstract; one must become "an ignorant man again," must see reality pure; the idea must also allow for change, for the introduction of many particulars which are characteristic only of the moment and the place. Finally, the "fiction" must give pleasure, must always be available to new and interesting impressions. This theory, of the imagination as providing a workable order for reality, Stevens has continued to define, explain, and defend. In his essay, "The Noble Rider and the Sound of Words," included in *The Language of Poetry* (1942), he explains what he means by imagination's role: "The imagination loses vitality as it ceases to adhere to what is real. When it adheres to the unreal and intensifies what is unreal, while its effect may be extraordinary, that effect is the maximum effect that it will ever have."

Stevens has been a vice-president of the Hartford Accident and Indemnity Company for many years. His poetry continues to appear regularly in magazines and in collections; and there is apparently a complete separation between his life as poet and his life as businessman. He has lately taken to prose more often than previously; his name has appeared in several symposia, honoring such contemporaries as Marianne Moore and John Crowe Ransom. His recent poetry contains flatter, more direct statement, less of the purely sensory detail which characterized his early work. He can be said to have inherited many of the interests of the Imagist group but to have developed quite independently of them.

Stevens' poetry has been published in the following volumes: *Harmonium* (1923; revised and enlarged in 1931); *Ideas of Order* (1935); *Owl's Clover* (1936); *The Man with the Blue Guitar* (1937); *Parts of a World* (1942); *Notes Toward a Supreme Fiction* (1942); *Ésthetique du Mal* (1944); *Transport to Summer* (1947); *A Primitive Like an Orb* (1948). His most important prose writing is the essay, "The Noble Rider and the Sound of Words," in *The Language of Poetry*, ed. Allen Tate (1942). The December, 1940, issue of *The Harvard Advocate* contains some biographical information provided by Hi Simons, and several critical estimates, by Theodore Spencer, Morton Zabel, and others. Other criticisms can be found in R. P. Blackmur, *The Double Agent* (1935); Paul Rosenfeld, *Men Seen* (1925); Gorham Munson, *Destinations* (1928); Yvor Winters, *The Anatomy of Nonsense* (1943); Horace Gregory and Marya Zaturenska, *A History of American Poetry, 1900–1940* (1946); R. P. Blackmur, "An Abstraction Blooded," *Partisan Review*, May-June, 1943; Wm. V. O'Connor, "Wallace Stevens and Imagined Reality," *Western Review*, Spring, 1948; H. R. Hays, "Laforgue and Wallace Stevens," *Romantic Review*, July-Sept., 1934; Hi Simons, "Wallace Stevens and Mallarmé," *Modern Philology*, May, 1946.

SUNDAY MORNING

I

COMPLACENCIES of the peignoir, and late
Coffee and oranges in a sunny chair,
And the green freedom of a cockatoo
Upon a rug mingle to dissipate
The holy hush of ancient sacrifice.
She dreams a little, and she feels the dark
Encroachment of that old catastrophe,
As a calm darkens among water-lights.
The pungent oranges and bright, green wings
Seem things in some procession of the dead,   10
Winding across wide water, without sound.
The day is like wide water, without sound,
Stilled for the passing of her dreaming feet
Over the seas, to silent Palestine,
Dominion of the blood and sepulchre.

II

Why should she give her bounty to the dead?
What is divinity if it can come
Only in silent shadows and in dreams?
Shall she not find in comforts of the sun,
In pungent fruit and bright, green wings, or
      else   20
In any balm or beauty of the earth,
Things to be cherished like the thought of
      heaven?
Divinity must live within herself:
Passions of rain, or moods in falling snow;
Grievings in loneliness, or unsubdued
Elations when the forest blooms; gusty
Emotions on wet roads on autumn nights;
All pleasures and all pains, remembering
The bough of summer and the winter branch.
These are the measures destined for her soul.

III

Jove in the clouds had his inhuman birth. 31
No mother suckled him, no sweet land gave
Large-mannered motions to his mythy mind.
He moved among us, as a muttering king,
Magnificent, would move among his hinds,
Until our blood, commingling, virginal,
With heaven, brought such requital to desire
The very hinds discerned it, in a star.
Shall our blood fail? Or shall it come to be
The blood of paradise? And shall the earth 40
Seem all of paradise that we shall know?
The sky will be much friendlier then than now,

A part of labor and a part of pain,
And next in glory to enduring love,
Not this dividing and indifferent blue.

IV

She says, "I am content when wakened birds,
Before they fly, test the reality
Of misty fields, by their sweet questionings;
But when the birds are gone, and their warm
      fields
Return no more, where, then, is paradise?" 50
There is not any haunt of prophecy,
Nor any old chimera of the grave,
Neither the golden underground, nor isle
Melodious, where spirits gat them home,
Nor visionary south, nor cloudy palm
Remote on heaven's hill, that has endured
As April's green endures; or will endure
Like her remembrance of awakened birds,
Or her desire for June and evening, tipped 59
By the consummation of the swallow's wings.

V

She says, "But in contentment I still feel
The need of some imperishable bliss."
Death is the mother of beauty; hence from her,
Alone, shall come fulfilment to our dreams
And our desires. Although she strews the leaves
Of sure obliteration on our paths,
The path sick sorrow took, the many paths
Where triumph rang its brassy phrase, or love
Whispered a little out of tenderness,
She makes the willow shiver in the sun 70
For maidens who were wont to sit and gaze
Upon the grass, relinquished to their feet.
She causes boys to pile new plums and pears
On disregarded plate. The maidens taste
And stray impassioned in the littering leaves.

VI

Is there no change of death in paradise?
Does ripe fruit never fall? Or do the boughs
Hang always heavy in that perfect sky,
Unchanging, yet so like our perishing earth,
With rivers like our own that seek for seas
They never find, the same receding shores 81
That never touch with inarticulate pang?
Why set the pear upon those river-banks
Or spice the shores with odors of the plum?
Alas, that they should wear our colors there,
The silken weavings of our afternoons,

And pick the strings of our insipid lutes!
Death is the mother of beauty, mystical,
Within whose burning bosom we devise
Our earthly mothers waiting, sleeplessly. 90

VII

Supple and turbulent, a ring of men
Shall chant in orgy on a summer morn
Their boisterous devotion to the sun,
Not as a god, but as a god might be,
Naked among them, like a savage source.
Their chant shall be a chant of paradise,
Out of their blood, returning to the sky;
And in their chant shall enter, voice by voice,
The windy lake wherein their lord delights,
The trees, like serafim, and echoing hills, 100
That choir among themselves long afterward.
They shall know well the heavenly fellowship
Of men that perish and of summer morn.
And whence they came and whither they shall go
The dew upon their feet shall manifest.

VIII

She hears, upon that water without sound,
A voice that cries, "The tomb in Palestine
Is not the porch of spirits lingering.
It is the grave of Jesus, where he lay."
We live in an old chaos of the sun, 110
Or old dependency of day and night,
Or island solitude, unsponsored, free,
Of that wide water, inescapable.
Deer walk upon our mountains, and the quail
Whistle about us their spontaneous cries;
Sweet berries ripen in the wilderness;
And, in the isolation of the sky,
At evening, casual flocks of pigeons make
Ambiguous undulations as they sink, 119
Downward to darkness, on extended wings.

1915

SEA SURFACE FULL OF CLOUDS

I

In that November off Tehuantepec,
The slopping of the sea grew still one night
And in the morning summer hued the deck

And made one think of rosy chocolate
And gilt umbrellas. Paradisal green
Gave suavity to the perplexed machine

Of ocean, which like limpid water lay.
Who, then, in that ambrosial latitude
Out of the light evolved the moving blooms,

Who, then, evolved the sea-blooms from the
clouds 10
Diffusing balm in that Pacific calm?
C'était mon enfant, mon bijou, mon âme.

The sea-clouds whitened far below the calm
And moved, as blooms move, in the swimming
green
And in its watery radiance, while the hue

Of heaven in an antique reflection rolled
Round those flotillas. And sometimes the
sea
Poured brilliant iris on the glistening blue.

II

In that November off Tehuantepec
The slopping of the sea grew still one night. 20
At breakfast jelly yellow streaked the deck

And made one think of chop-house chocolate
And sham umbrellas. And a sham-like green
Capped summer-seeming on the tense ma-
chine

Of ocean, which in sinister flatness lay.
Who, then, beheld the rising of the clouds
That strode submerged in that malevolent
sheen,

Who saw the mortal massives of the blooms
Of water moving on the water-floor?
C'était mon frère du ciel, ma vie, mon or. 30

The gongs rang loudly as the windy booms
Hoo-hooed it in the darkened ocean-blooms.
The gongs grew still. And then blue heaven
spread

Its crystalline pendentives on the sea
And the macabre of the water-glooms
In an enormous undulation fled.

III

In that November off Tehuantepec,
The slopping of the sea grew still one night
And a pale silver patterned on the deck

And made one think of porcelain chocolate 40
And pied umbrellas. An uncertain green,
Piano-polished, held the tranced machine

Of ocean, as a prelude holds and holds.
Who, seeing silver petals of white blooms
Unfolding in the water, feeling sure

Of the milk within the saltiest spurge, heard,
    then,
The sea unfolding in the sunken clouds?
Oh! C'était mon extase et mon amour.

So deeply sunken were they that the shrouds,
The shrouding shadows, made the petals black
Until the rolling heaven made them blue, 51

A blue beyond the rainy hyacinth,
And smiting the crevasses of the leaves
Deluged the ocean with a sapphire blue.

IV

In that November off Tehuantepec
The night-long slopping of the sea grew still.
A mallow morning dozed upon the deck

And made one think of musky chocolate
And frail umbrellas. A too-fluent green
Suggested malice in the dry machine 60

Of ocean, pondering dank stratagem.
Who then beheld the figures of the clouds
Like blooms secluded in the thick marine?

Like blooms? Like damasks that were shaken off
From the loosed girdles in the spangling must.
C'était ma foi, la nonchalance divine.

The nakedness would rise and suddenly turn
Salt masks of beard and mouths of bellow-
    ing,
Would—But more suddenly the heaven rolled

Its bluest sea-clouds in the thinking green, 70
And the nakedness became the broadest blooms,
Mile-mallows that a mallow sun cajoled.

V

In that November off Tehuantepec
Night stilled the slopping of the sea. The day
Came, bowing and voluble, upon the deck,

Good clown . . . . One thought of Chinese
    chocolate
And large umbrellas. And a motley green
Followed the drift of the obese machine

Of ocean, perfected in indolence.
What pistache one, ingenious and droll, 80
Beheld the sovereign clouds as jugglery

And the sea as turquoise-turbaned Sambo, neat
At tossing saucers—cloudy-conjuring sea?
C'était mon esprit bâtard, l'ignominie.

The sovereign clouds came clustering. The
    conch
Of loyal conjuration trumped. The wind
Of green blooms turning crisped the motley
    hue

To clearing opalescence. Then the sea
And heaven rolled as one and from the two
Came fresh transfigurings of freshest blue. 90
                                          1924

1894 -- *E. E. Cummings* -- —

THE LITERARY CAREER of Edward Estlin Cummings began as a result of his war
experiences. Confined for three months in a French detention camp because
of the error of a military censor, he returned to America, to write his account of
that experience, *The Enormous Room* (1922). In this novelized version of autobiography one can discover all of the points of view and biases which Cummings was to

show in his poetry and other writings: specifically, his abhorrence of officialdom, which he considers brutal, inefficient, and stupid; his love of the exceptional human being, the eccentric, the people whom he called "The Delectable Mountains" in *The Enormous Room;* and, less certainly in that book than in later ones, his primary opposition of love and war as antipodal circumstances.

Cummings had already (in 1917) contributed to a volume of *Eight Harvard Poets;* after his return from the war he produced small volumes of poems almost annually, which were brought together in *Collected Poems* (1938); since that date he has published 50 *Poems* (1940) and *1 × 1* (1944). He has written two plays: *Him* (1927) and *Santa Claus: A Morality* (1946). His account of his journey to the Soviet Union, *Eimi,* was published in 1933.

Cummings' views are those of a Bohemian (he has continued to live in Greenwich Village), an unreconstructed poet-anarchist. He is one of a very few writers of the 1920's who have remained quite consistent in their opposition to organized society, their sympathy for the neglected and the ignored portions of our society. He refuses (rather sadly) to subscribe to any revolutionary views, and has quite tellingly denounced the Russian "experiment," preferring to be in what he calls "beautiful hideous imperfection": "I'd just as soon be imprisoned in freedom than free in a jail." To the monster called organized society, its officers and guides, and its military end-product, Cummings opposes love, in all its forms, sacred and profane. His love poetry ranges from the frankly obscene to the quite simply lyrical: "feeling is first," he says, and the beauty of nature and its simple creatures will never be either defined or destroyed by the "doting/fingers of/prurient philosophers" or "the naughty thumb/of science." His satirical attacks upon American institutions and pretensions are gay, witty, and telling: the Cambridge ladies, the patriotic orator, the writer of modern advertising, the politician. He believes that "this monster manunkind" fears knowledge of himself and prefers living in an "Ever-Ever land," and believing that "nothing really exists."

Cummings achieves his effects through methods that are quite unorthodox. He often uses a single grammatical peculiarity to stress and repeat a point: the prefix "un," attached to nouns and adjectives, for example, to suggest the negative character of the mass. More ambitious is his attempt to make the poem force the reader into an almost kinetic appreciation of its subject. By quite unusual uses of punctuation, typography, and syllabification, he regulates the pace of the poem in the reader's mind, creates simultaneous effects (the use of parentheses is especially striking), delays or prolongs impressions, and in general makes of the reading a motor as well as an imaginative exercise.

Cummings' method is unique and inimitable. It is also in danger of being "used up." Once one gets used to the tricks, he may lose interest in the matter, which continues however to be clever and not irrelevant in his latest poems. He has done some especially interesting things with the sonnet form (which was his favorite form in his Harvard years) and has enlivened others. He has been taken too seriously by some critics (who have denounced him as obscene and unintelligible) and not seriously enough by others (who enjoy the typographic exploits without attending the meaning for which they occasionally strive).

Cummings' poems have appeared in *Eight Harvard Poets* (1917); *Tulips and Chimneys* (1923); *&* (1925); *XLI Poems* (1925); *Is 5* (1926); *Christmas Tree* (1928); *W* (1931); *No Thanks* (1935); *1/20 Poems* (1937); *Collected Poems* (1938); *50 Poems* (1940); *1 × 1* (1944). Two plays and one ballet have been published: *Him* (1927); *Santa Claus, a Morality* (1946); and *Tom* (1935). *Eimi* (1933) is a record of Cummings' trip to the USSR. The Spring, 1946, issue of *The Harvard Wake* is dedicated to Cummings, and contains (in addition to the first publication of *Santa Claus*) a number of biographical and critical studies by Allen Tate, Paul Rosenfeld, Karl Shapiro, Theodore Spencer, Lionel Trilling, and others. See also R. P. Blackmur, *The Double Agent* (1935); Babette Deutsch, *This Modern Poetry* (1935); Allen Tate, *Reactionary Essays in Poetry and Ideas* (1936); John P. Bishop, "The Poems and Prose of E. E. Cummings," *Southern Review*, Summer, 1938; S. I. Hayakawa, "Is Indeed 5," *Poetry*, Aug., 1938; John Arthos, "The Poetry of E. E. Cummings," *American Literature*, January, 1943.

ALL IN GREEN
WENT MY LOVE RIDING

ALL in green went my love riding
on a great horse of gold
into the silver dawn.

four lean hounds crouched low and smiling
the merry deer ran before.

Fleeter be they than dappled dreams
the swift sweet deer
the red rare deer.

Four red roebuck at a white water
the cruel bugle sang before.   10

Horn at hip went my love riding
riding the echo down
into the silver dawn.

four lean hounds crouched low and smiling
the level meadows ran before.

Softer by they than slippered sleep
the lean lithe deer
the fleet flown deer.

Four fleet does at a gold valley
the famished arrow sang before.   20

Bow at belt went my love riding
riding the mountain down
into the silver dawn.

four lean hounds crouched low and smiling
the sheer peaks ran before.

Paler be they than daunting death
the sleek slim deer
the tall tense deer.

Four tall stags at a green mountain
the lucky hunter sang before.   30

All in green went my love riding
on a great horse of gold
into the silver dawn.

four lean hounds crouched low and smiling
my heart fell dead before.

1923

ALWAYS BEFORE YOUR
VOICE MY SOUL

ALWAYS before your voice my soul
half-beautiful and wholly droll
is as some smooth and awkward foal,
whereof young moons begin
the newness of his skin,

so of my stupid sincere youth
the exquisite failure uncouth
discovers a trembling and smooth
Unstrength, against the strong
silences of your song;   10

or as a single lamb whose sheen
of full unsheared fleece is mean
beside its lovelier friends, between
your thoughts more white than wool
My thought is sorrowful:

but my heart smote in trembling thirds
of anguish quivers to your words,
As to a flight of thirty birds
shakes with a thickening fright
the sudden fooled light.   20

it is the autumn of a year:
When through the thin air stooped with fear,
across the harvest whitely peer
empty of surprise
death's faultless eyes

(whose hand my folded soul shall know
while on faint hills do frailly go
The peaceful terrors of the snow,
and before your dead face
which sleeps, a dream shall pass)   30

and these my days their sounds and flowers
Fall in a pride of petaled hours,
like flowers at the feet of mowers
whose bodies strong with love
through meadows hugely move.

yet what am i that such and such
mysteries very simply touch
me, whose heart-wholeness overmuch
Expects of your hair pale,
a terror musical?   40

while in an earthless hour my fond
soul seriously yearns beyond
this fern of sunset frond on frond
opening in a rare
Slowness of gloried air . . .

The flute of morning stilled in noon—
noon the implacable bassoon—
now Twilight seeks the thrill of moon,

washed with a wild and thin
despair of violin   50
                                                  1923

BUFFALO BILL

BUFFALO Bill's
defunct
        who used to
        ride a watersmooth-silver
                                stallion
and break
    onetwothreefourfive pigeonsjustlikethat
                                        Jesus
he was a handsome man
                        and what i want to know is
how do you like your blueeyed boy
Mister Death

                                                  1923

THE CAMBRIDGE LADIES

the Cambridge ladies who live in furnished souls
are unbeautiful and have comfortable minds
(also, with the church's protestant blessings
daughters, unscented shapeless spirited)
they believe in Christ and Longfellow, both dead,
are invariably interested in so many things—
at the present writing one still finds
delighted fingers knitting for the is it Poles?
perhaps. While permanent faces coyly bandy
scandal of Mrs. N and Professor D   10
. . . . the Cambridge ladies do not care, above
Cambridge if sometimes in its box of
sky lavender and cornerless, the
moon rattles like a fragment of angry candy
                                                  1923

PITY THIS BUSY MONSTER, MANUNKIND

PITY this busy monster, manunkind,

not. Progress is a comfortable disease:
your victim (death and life safely beyond)

plays with the bigness of his littleness
—electrons deify one razorblade
into a mountainrange; lenses extend

unwish through curving wherewhen till unwish
returns on its unself.

A world of made   ultraomnipotence. We doctors know
is not a world of born—pity poor flesh   10

and trees, poor stars and stones, but never this   a hopeless case if—listen: there's a hell
fine specimen of hypermagical   of a good universe next door; let's go

                                                                                1944

1899 ~ (Harold) Hart Crane ~ 1932

THE SHORT LIFE and the poetry of Hart Crane have already provided the subject of two book-length studies and numerous critical essays. His is primarily the story of a failure of discipline which prevented an intrinsically great talent from realizing itself. Born in a town near Cleveland, Ohio, Crane early rebelled against his father, a prosperous candy manufacturer. For some years he tried to adjust himself to the needs of business, but failed to do so, and alternated between Bohemian life in New York and business life in Ohio. In Greenwich Village he made the acquaintance of many young writers and editors, secured publication of his early (rather poor) romantic poems in *Bruno's Bohemian* and *The Pagan* (he was an associate editor of the latter for a short while). He began reading widely and without particular order in the metaphysicals, Rimbaud, Eliot, such Americans as Whitman and Melville, and Sherwood Anderson. In 1925, Crane wrote to Otto Kahn outlining the theme of his major poem, *The Bridge*, and asking for financial aid, which he received. *White Buildings* was published in 1926. He traveled restlessly in England and France in 1928 and 1929; in this latter year he finally finished *The Bridge*. On April 26, 1932, returning from Mexico where he had gone on a Guggenheim fellowship, he committed suicide by jumping from the steamship into the Gulf of Mexico.

That life, described brilliantly in Philip Horton's *Hart Crane, The Life of an American Poet* (1937), is in itself worthy of examination in the light of what he tried to do in his poetry. *White Buildings* contains the six "Voyages," remarkable and obscure evocations in the manner of Rimbaud, and other short poems. The major effort, the "myth of America," was *The Bridge*. As Crane planned the poem, the Brooklyn Bridge was to be its central symbol, representing both the mechanical ingenuity of modern man and (through its design) the bridge to infinity. The poem was to touch simultaneously upon America's present and past, to cover its industrial strength, its machinery, its fertile plains. What was finally published as *The Bridge* contains some of the most remarkable verse in modern American literature, but the major design, as Crane explained it to Otto Kahn, is inadequately executed, and there are sections of the poem which have little or no relevance to the plan. The "Cape Hatteras" section attempts to incorporate the spirit and idiom of modern machinery as poetic subject; the effect is sometimes good, often merely absurd. While *The Bridge* must be marked finally as a conspicuous failure, it is important as one of a few serious attempts by modern American poets to pursue and complete an ambitious plan for the integration of American life and culture in one definite design. That the poem remains interesting is due to Crane's great talent; that it did not fulfill its original purpose is due to his lack of discipline, his very spotty knowledge of the subject, and the erratic character of its composition.

Crane's poems (*White Buildings*, 1926, and *The Bridge*, 1930) have been brought together in *The Collected Poems of Hart Crane*, edited and introduced by Waldo Frank (1933); this collection contains a number of poems not published in the two volumes. His critical point of view is to be found in essays published as appendices in *The Collected Poems* and in Philip Horton's *Hart Crane, The Life of an American Poet* (1937); the latter is also the best biography of Hart Crane available. Brom Weber's *Hart Crane: A Biographical and Critical Study* (1948) contains new biographical material, as well as an explication of *The Bridge*. For other criticism, see R. P. Blackmur, *The Double Agent* (1935); Allen Tate, *Reactionary Essays on Poetry and Ideas* (1936); Yvor Winters, *In Defense of Reason* (1947); Horace Gregory and Marya Zaturenska, *A History of American Poetry, 1900–1940* (1946); Babette Deutsch, *This Modern Poetry* (1935); H. H. Waggoner, "Hart Crane and the Broken Parabola," *University of Kansas City Review*, Summer, 1945. For other titles, see Millett, *Contemporary American Authors* (1940) and Leary, *Articles on American Literature Appearing in Current Periodicals, 1920–1945* (1947).

THE RIVER

from The Bridge

STICK your patent name on a signboard
brother—all over—going west—young man
Tintex—Japalac—Certain-teed Overalls ads
and lands sakes! under the new playbill ripped
in the guaranteed corner—see Bert Williams
   what?
Minstrels when you steal a chicken just
save me the wing for if it isn't
Erie it ain't for miles around a
Mazda—and the telegraphic night coming on
   Thomas

a Ediford—and whistling down the tracks 10
a headlight rushing with the sound—can you
imagine—while an EXPRESS makes time like
SCIENCE—COMMERCE and the HOLYGHOST
RADIO ROARS IN EVERY HOME WE HAVE THE
   NORTHPOLE
WALLSTREET AND VIRGINBIRTH WITHOUT STONES
   OR
WIRES OR EVEN RUNning brooks connecting ears
and no more sermons windows flashing roar
Breathtaking—as you like it. . . eh?

So the 20th Century—so
whizzed the Limited—roared by and left 20
three men, still hungry on the tracks, plod-
   dingly
watching the tail lights wizen and converge,
   slip-
ping gimleted and neatly out of sight.

The last bear, shot drinking in the Dakotas,
Loped under wires that span the mountain
   stream.
Keen instruments, strung to a vast precision
Bind town to town and dream to ticking dream.
But some men take their liquor slow—and
   count
—Though they'll confess no rosary nor clue—
The river's minute by the far brook's year. 30
Under a world of whistles, wires and steam
Caboose-like they go ruminating through
Ohio, Indiana—blind baggage—
To Cheyenne tagging . . . Maybe Kalamazoo.

Time's rendings, time's blendings they con-
   strue
As final reckonings of fire and snow;
Strange bird-wit, like the elemental gist

Of unwalled winds they offer, singing low
My Old Kentucky Home and *Casey Jones,*
Some Sunny Day. I heard a road-gang chant-
    ing so.   40
And afterwards, who had a colt's eyes—one
    said,
"Jesus! Oh I remember watermelon days!"
    And sped
High in a cloud of merriment, recalled
"—And when my Aunt Sally Simpson
    smiled," he drawled—
"It was almost Louisiana, long ago."

"There's no place like Booneville though,
    Buddy,"
One said, excising a last burr from his vest,
"—For early trouting." Then peering in
    the can,
"—But I kept on the tracks." Possessed,
    resigned,
He trod the fire down pensively and grinned, 50
Spreading dry shingles of a beard. . . .

                        Behind
My father's cannery works I used to see
Rail-squatters ranged in nomad raillery,
The ancient men—wifeless or runaway
Hobo-trekkers that forever search
An empire wilderness of freight and rails.
Each seemed a child, like me, on a loose
    perch,
Holding to childhood like some termless
    play.
John, Jake or Charley, hopping the slow
    freight   60
—Memphis to Tallahassee—riding the rods,
Blind fists of nothing, humpty-dumpty clods.

Yet they touch something like a key perhaps.
From pole to pole across the hills, the
    states
—They know a body under the wide rain;
Youngsters with eyes like fjords, old repro-
    bates
With racetrack jargon,—dotting immensity
They lurk across her, knowing her yonder
    breast
Snow-silvered, sumac-stained or smoky blue—
Is past the valley-sleepers, south or west. 70
—As I have trod the rumorous midnights,
    too

And past the circuit of the lamp's thin flame
(O Nights that brought me to her body
    bare!)
Have dreamed beyond the print that bound
    her name.
Trains sounding the long blizzards out—I
    heard
Wail into distances I knew were hers.
Papooses crying on the wind's long mane
Screamed redskin dynasties that fled the
    brain,
—Dead echoes! But I knew her body there,
Time like a serpent down her shoulder,
    dark,   80
And space, an eaglet's wing, laid on her hair.

Under the Ozarks, domed by Iron Mountain,
The old gods of the rain lie wrapped in pools
Where eyeless fish curvet a sunken fountain
And re-descend with corn from querulous
    crows.
Such pilferings make up their timeless eatage,
Propitiate them for their timber torn
By iron, iron—always the iron dealt cleavage!
They doze now, below axe and powder horn.

And Pullman breakfasters glide glistening
    steel   90
From tunnel into field—iron strides the dew—
Straddles the hill, a dance of wheel on wheel.
You have a half-hour's wait at Siskiyou,
Or stay the night and take the next train
    through.
Southward, near Cairo passing, you can see
The Ohio merging,—borne down Tennessee;
And if it's summer and the sun's in dusk
Maybe the breeze will lift the River's musk
—As though the waters breathed that you
    might know
Memphis Johnny, Steamboat Bill, Missouri
    Joe.   100
Oh, lean from the window, if the train slows
    down,
As though you touched hands with some
    ancient clown,
—A little while gaze absently below
And hum *Deep River* with them while they go.

Yes, turn again and sniff once more—look
    see,
O Sheriff, Brakeman and Authority—

Hitch up your pants and crunch another
    quid,
For you, too, feed the River timelessly.
And few evade full measure of their fate;
Always they smile out eerily what they
    seem.   110
I could believe he joked at heaven's gate—
Dan Midland—jolted from the cold brake-
    beam.

Down, down—born pioneers in time's
    despite,
Grimed tributaries to an ancient flow—
They win no frontier by their wayward
    plight,
But drift in stillness, as from Jordan's brow.

You will not hear it as the sea; even stone
Is not more hushed by gravity . . . But
    slow,
As loth to take more tribute—sliding prone
Like one whose eyes were buried long ago.

The River, spreading, flows—and spends
    your dream.   121
What are you, lost within this tideless spell?
You are your father's father, and the stream—
A liquid theme that floating niggers swell. '

Damp tonnage and alluvial march of days—
Nights turbid, vascular with silted shale
And roots surrendered down of moraine clays:
The Mississippi drinks the farthest dale.

O quarrying passion, undertowed sunlight!
The basalt surface drags a jungle grace   130
Ochreous and lynx-barred in lengthening
    might;
Patience! and you shall reach the biding place!

Over De Soto's bones the freighted floors
Throb past the City storied of three thrones.
Down two more turns the Mississippi pours
(Anon tall ironsides up from salt lagoons)

And flows within itself, heaps itself free.
All fades but one thin skyline 'round . . .
    Ahead
No embrace opens but the stinging sea;
The River lifts itself from its long bed,   140

Poised wholly on its dream, a mustard glow
Tortured with history, its one will—flow!
—The Passion spreads in wide tongues,
    choked and slow,
Meeting the Gulf, hosannas silently below.
                                             1930

1892 ~ *Archibald MacLeish* ~ —

BORN IN ILLINOIS, MacLeish was educated in Glencoe, Illinois, at Hotchkiss
School in Connecticut, and at Yale. At Yale he joined such Eli celebrities as
Thornton Wilder and Stephen Vincent Benét, edited and contributed to the Yale
Literary Magazine, and began writing poetry. He entered the Harvard Law School
in 1915 and in 1917 went to France with a hospital unit. In this same year the Yale
University Press issued a volume of his poems. Upon his return from the wars, he
practiced law in Boston for three years; then, in an effort to find more time for his
writing, he sailed with his family to Paris. In 1928 he returned to America and continued writing; he traveled in 1929 to Mexico, at work on *Conquistador*. He took up
journalism in the 1930's, working for *Fortune* magazine and traveling in America,
Europe, and Japan, as a journalist. During the Spanish Civil War, he took up the
Loyalist cause, and collaborated with Ernest Hemingway and two others on the

film *The Spanish Earth*. He joined the government service in 1939 as Librarian of Congress, and later in other government posts.

MacLeish is a weather vane for contemporary American poetry. During the 1920's, and especially during the Paris years, he wrote chiefly in imitation of Eliot and of the metaphysicals, in whom Eliot was also interested. His poetry of *The Pot of Earth* (1925), *The Hamlet of A. MacLeish* (1928), and other volumes of this decade reflects a preoccupation with the wasteland theme, the manner, the style, the pose, of Eliot's followers. He tried his hand at all manners and all styles, and showed great versatility and a remarkable ability to skim the surface from the talent of his mentors. In the 1930's, he turned to free verse commentary, sometimes satirical, sometimes frankly leftist. *Conquistador* (1932), for which he won the Pulitzer prize, is a long, elaborate, and often effective account of the conquest of Mexico by Cortez. *Land of the Free* (1938) is a commentary upon many photographs of the American scene, identifying the social inequalities in the country with the broad irony characteristic of leftist accounts. His verse plays of this decade are attempts to underscore the Nazi-Fascist menace by pointing up the disastrous consequences of our failure to prepare and pointing to the devastation our modern weapons of war might cause. Two of these plays (*The Fall of the City*, 1937, and *Air Raid*, 1938) make use of radio techniques, somewhat after the manner of W. H. Auden, but without Auden's subtlety.

In 1940 MacLeish published an essay called "The Irresponsibles," in which he addressed himself to a review of the 1920's and the 1930's, condemning the intellectuals in America and elsewhere for having deliberately closed their eyes to the advance of evil in the world, for their failure of responsibility in a developing world crisis. This was the first of a series of essays and addresses to which MacLeish has since devoted himself. Except for a slender volume of poems (*Act Five and Other Poems*, 1948) he has confined his writing to occasional public addresses and articles.

MacLeish's poetry at its best is a convenient means of studying the currents and cross-currents of modern American poetry. It is facile, versatile, almost always derivative. His *tours de force* are clever and have a popular appeal which sends them into and keeps them in the anthologies.

MacLeish's volumes of poetry include *Tower of Ivory* (1917); *The Happy Marriage and Othe Poems* (1924); *The Pot of Earth* (1925); *Streets in the Moon* (1926); *The Hamlet of A. MacLeish* (1928); *Einstein* (1929); *New Found Land* (1930); *Conquistador* (1932); *Frescoes for Mr. Rockefeller's City* (1933); *Public Speech* (1936); *Land of the Free* (1938); *Act Five and Other Poems* (1948). A collection, *Poems, 1924–1933*, was published in 1933. His plays are *Nobodaddy* (1926); *Panic* (1935); *The Fall of the City* (1937); *Air Raid* (1938). *A Time to Speak* (1941) is a selection from his prose. It includes "The Irresponsibles," which also appeared in separate publication, in 1940. For biographical and critical studies, consult Allen Tate, *Reactionary Essays in Poetry and Ideas* (1936); Llewelyn Jones, "Archibald MacLeish, a Modern Metaphysical," *English Journal*, June, 1935; Arthur Mizener, "The Poetry of Archibald MacLeish," *Sewanee Review*, Oct.-Dec.,

1938; Mason Wade, "The Anabasis of Archibald MacLeish," *North American Review*, Summer, 1937; Edmund Wilson, "The Omelet of A. MacLeish," *New Yorker*, Jan. 14, 1939 (a parody); Morton D. Zabel, "The Poet on Capitol Hill," *Partisan Review*, Jan.-March, 1941; E. M. Sickels, "Archibald MacLeish and American Democracy," *American Literature*, Nov., 1943. For other titles, see Millett, *Contemporary American Authors* (1940) and Leary, *Articles on American Literature in Current Periodicals, 1920–1945* (1947).

YOU, ANDREW MARVELL

AND here face down beneath the sun
And here upon earth's noonward height
To feel the always coming on
The always rising of the night

To feel creep up the curving east
The earth chill of dusk and slow
Upon those under lands the vast
And everclimbing shadow grow

And strange at Ecbatan the trees
Take leaf by leaf the evening strange   10
The flooding dark about their knees
The mountains over Persia change

And now at Kermanshah the gate
Dark empty and the withered grass
And through the twilight now the late
Few travellers in the westward pass

And Baghdad darken and the bridge
Across the silent river gone
And through Arabia the edge
Of evening widen and steal on   20

And deepen on Palmyra's street
The wheel rut in the ruined stone
And Lebanon fade out and Crete
High through the clouds and overblown

And over Sicily the air
Still flashing with the landward gulls
And loom and slowly disappear
The sails above the shadowy hulls

And Spain go under and the shore
Of Africa the gilded sand   30
And evening vanish and no more
The low pale light across that land

Nor now the long light on the sea

And here face downward in the sun
To feel how swift, how secretly
The shadow of the night comes on. . . .

   1930

MEMORIAL RAIN

AMBASSADOR PUSER the ambassador
Reminds himself in French, felicitous tongue,
What these (young men no longer) lie here for
In rows that once, and somewhere else, were
   young—

   All night in Brussels the wind had tugged
     at my door:
   I had heard the wind at my door and the
     trees strung
   Taut, and to me who had never been before
   In that country it was a strange wind blow-
     ing
   Steadily, stiffening the walls, the floor,
   The roof of my room. I had not slept for
     knowing   10
   He too, dead, was a stranger in that land
   And felt beneath the earth in the wind's
     flowing
   A tightening of roots and would not un-
     derstand,
   Remembering lake winds in Illinois,
   That strange wind. I had felt his bones in
     the sand
   Listening.

      —Reflects that these enjoy
Their country's gratitude, that deep repose,
That peace no pain can break, no hurt destroy,
That rest, that sleep—   20

      At Ghent the wind rose.
There was a smell of rain and a heavy drag
Of wind in the hedges but not as the wind
   blows
Over fresh water when the waves lag

Foaming and the willows huddle and it will
    rain:
I felt him waiting.

        —Indicates the flag
Which (may he say) enisles in Flanders' plain
This little field these happy, happy dead
Have made America—   30

          In the ripe grain
The wind coiled glistening, darted, fled,
Dragging its heavy body: at Waereghem
The wind coiled in the grass above his head:
Waiting—listening—

        —Dedicates to them
This earth their bones have hallowed, this last
    gift
A grateful country—

          Under the dry grass stem
The words are blurred, are thickened, the
    words sift   40
Confused by the rasp of the wind, by the
    thin grating
Of ants under the grass, the minute shift
And tumble of dusty sand separating
From dusty sand. The roots of the grass
    strain,
Tighten, the earth is rigid, waits—he is
    waiting—

And suddenly, and all at once, the rain!

The people scatter, they run into houses,
    the wind
Is trampled under the rain, shakes free, is
    again
Trampled. The rain gathers, running in
    thinned
Spurts of water that ravel in the dry sand 50
Seeping in the sand under the grass roots,
    seeping

Between cracked boards to the bones of a
    clenched hand:
The earth relaxes, loosens; he is sleeping,
He rests, he is quiet, he sleeps in a strange
    land.
                  1926

... & FORTY-SECOND STREET

BE proud New-York of your prize domes
And your docks & the size of your doors &
    your dancing
Elegant clean big girls & your
Niggers with narrow heels & the blue on their
Bad mouths & your bars & your automobiles
    in the struck steel light & your
Bright Jews & your sorrow-sweet singing
Tunes & your signs wincing out in the wet
Cool shine & the twinges of
Green against evening. . .

    When the towns go down there are stains
        of   10
Rust on the stone shores and illegible
Coins and a rhyme remembered of
                swans say
Or birds or leaves or a horse or fabulous
Bull forms or a falling of gold upon
Softness

    Be proud City of Glass of your
Brass roofs & the bright peaks of your
    Houses
    Town that stood to your knees in the
Sea water be proud be proud   20
Of your high gleam on the sea

            Do they think
They must rhyme your name with the name of a
              Town
Talking beast that the place of your walls be
    remembered
                  1933

1892 ~ *Edna St. Vincent Millay* ~ ——

MISS MILLAY was born in Rockland, Maine, and received her early education in Camden. As a schoolgirl she wrote verses, some of which were printed in magazines. When she was nineteen her "Renascence" was published. After her schooldays she continued the study of literature and music, was for a time a student at Barnard College, and then entered Vassar, from which she was graduated in 1917. In college she took part in dramatic performances, in her senior year playing the leading role in *The Princess Marries the Page*, a verse drama of her own composition. For several years she was associated with the Greenwich Village and Provincetown Players as playwright and actress. In 1923 she won the Pulitzer prize for poetry and married Eugene Jan Boissevain, an importer.

Since Miss Millay's first book, *Renascence and Other Poems* (1917), she has published numerous volumes, the most widely known of which are *Second April* (1921), *The Ballad of the Harp-Weaver* (1922), *Fatal Interview* (1931), *Wine from These Grapes* (1934), and *Huntsman, What Quarry?* (1939). Among her short plays are *Two Slatterns and a King* (1921), and *The Lamp and the Bell* (1921). *The King's Henchman* (1927), a poetic drama, was written as an opera for which Deems Taylor, an American musician, composed the music.

Miss Millay's verse is found in *Renascence* (1917); *A Few Figs from Thistles* (1920); *Second April* (1921); *The Ballad of the Harp-Weaver* (1922); *The Harp-Weaver and Other Poems* (1923); *Distressing Dialogues* (1924); *The Buck in the Snow and Other Poems* (1928); *Fatal Interview* (1931); *Wine from These Grapes* (1934); *Conversation at Midnight* (1937); and *Huntsman, What Quarry?* (1939). Collections of her poetry are *The Collected Sonnets of Edna St. Vincent Millay* (1941) and *The Collected Lyrics of Edna St. Vincent Millay* (1943). Her plays are: *Aria da Capo* (1921); *The Lamp and the Bell* (1921); *Two Slatterns and a King* (1921); *The King's Henchman* (1927); *The Princess Marries the Page* (1932). Biographical accounts: J. Beatty, " 'Best Sellers' in Verse: the Story of Edna St. Vincent Millay," *American Magazine*, Jan., 1932; E. Breuer, "Edna St. Vincent Millay," *Pictorial Review*, Nov., 1931. For criticism, see R. Brenner, *Ten Modern Poets* (1930); E. Davidson, "Edna St. Vincent Millay," *English Journal*, Nov., 1927; A. E. DuBois, "Edna St. Vincent Millay," *Sewanee Review*, Jan.–Mar., 1935; J. H. Preston, "Edna St. Vincent Millay," *Virginia Quarterly Review*, April, 1927; H. Monroe, *Poets and Their Art* (1926); C. Wood, *Poets of America* (1925); L. Untermeyer, *American Poetry since 1900* (1923); L. Simonson, *Minor Prophecies* (1927); C. Van Doren, *Many Minds* (1924); J. Farrar, ed., *The Literary Spotlight* (1924); T. Maynard, *Our Best Poets* (1922); E. W. Parks, "Edna St. Vincent Millay," *Sewanee Review*, Jan.–Mar., 1930; P. B. Rice, "Edna Millay's Maturity," *Nation*, Nov. 14, 1934; E. Atkins, *Edna St. Vincent Millay and Her Times* (1936); John Crowe Ransom, "The Poet as Woman," in *The World's Body* (1938).

GOD'S WORLD

O WORLD, I cannot hold thee close enough!
  Thy winds, thy wide grey skies!
  Thy mists, that roll and rise!
Thy woods, this autumn day, that ache and
    sag
And all but cry with colour! That gaunt
    crag
To crush! To lift the lean of that black bluff!
World, World, I cannot get thee close
    enough!

Long have I known a glory in it all,
  But never knew I this;
  Here such a passion is   10
As stretcheth me apart,—Lord I do fear
Thou'st made the world too beautiful this
    year;
My soul is all but out of me,—let fall
No burning leaf; prithee, let no bird call.

                                  1913

JUSTICE DENIED IN
MASSACHUSETTS

This poem was suggested by the case of Saccho
and Vanzetti, who after repeated and prolonged
trials were finally convicted of murder. On the
night of their execution Miss Millay joined a
peaceful parade in protest.

LET us abandon then our gardens and go home
And sit in the sitting-room.
Shall the larkspur blossom or the corn grow
    under this cloud?
Sour to the fruitful seed
Is the cold earth under this cloud,
Fostering quack and weed, we have marched
    upon but cannot conquer;
We have bent the blades of our hoes against
    the stalks of them.

Let us go home, and sit in the sitting-room.
Not in our day
Shall the cloud go over and the sun rise as
    before,   10
Beneficent upon us
Out of the glittering bay,
And the warm winds be blown inward from
    the sea
Moving the blades of corn

With a peaceful sound.
Forlorn, forlorn,
Stands the blue hay-rack by the empty
    mow.
And the petals drop to the ground,
Leaving the tree unfruited.
The sun that warmed our stooping backs and
    withered the weed uprooted—   20
We shall not feel it again.
We shall die in darkness, and be buried in the
    rain.
What from the splendid dead
We have inherited—
Furrows sweet to the grain, and the weed
    subdued—
See now the slug and the mildew plunder.
Evil does overwhelm
The larkspur and the corn;
We have seen them go under.

Let us sit here, sit still,   30
Here in the sitting-room until we die;
At the step of Death on the walk, rise and
    go;
Leaving to our children's children this beauti-
    ful doorway,
And this elm,
And blighted earth to till
With a broken hoe.

                                  1928

SONNET TO GATH

COUNTRY of hunchbacks!—where the strong,
    straight spine,
Jeered at by crooked children, makes his way
Through by-streets at the kindest hour of
    day,
Till he deplore his stature, and incline
To measure manhood with a gibbous line;
Till out of loneliness, being flawed with
    clay,
He stoop into his neighbor's house and say,
"Your roof is low for me—the fault is mine."
Dust in an urn long since, dispersed and dead
Is great Apollo; and the happier he;   10
Since who amongst you all would lift a head
At a god's radiance on the mean door-tree,
Saving to run and hide your dates and bread,
And cluck your children in about your knee.

                                  1928

1885 ~ *Elinor Hoyt Wylie* ~ 1928

ELINOR HOYT was born in Rosemont, Pennsylvania, the daughter of Henry Martyn and Anne Hoyt. She attended private schools in ·Bryn Mawr and in Washington, where her father held a government post. Her education was continued through foreign travel. An unhappy marital venture and *ennui* over the activities of capital society induced her to leave Washington. In 1919 she made her home in New York, where in 1925 she married the poet William Rose Benét. For a time she was associate editor of *Vanity Fair* and at the time of her death was a contributing editor on the staff of *The New Republic*. She published four novels and four volumes of poetry in the short period of eight years, which, in view of her careful workmanship, is an almost unparalleled achievement.

Elinor Wylie's poetry was not received with the wide acclaim that greeted some of her contemporaries. Her work does not have inherent popular appeal but has been praised highly by discriminating readers. Some critics have suggested comparison with Emily Dickinson. She belonged to no school, took part in no movement, was apparently unmindful of contemporary currents and popular taste, but like Emily Dickinson, perfected and practiced her art in a way that was satisfying to her own ideals. Her work is carefully wrought and trimmed, abounds in compact phrasing, with an occasional telling epigram, and all in all is characterized by a beauty which is crystalline and often colorful.

Mrs. Wylie's poetry appeared in *Nets to Catch the Wind* (1921); *Black Armour* (1923); *Trivial Breath* (1928); *Angels and Earthly Creatures* (1929). These, together with hitherto uncollected poems, are available in *Collected Poems of Elinor Wylie*, foreword by W. R. Benét (1932). Her novels, *Jennifer Lorn, The Venetian Glass Nephew, The Orphan Angel*, and *Mr. Hodge and Mr. Hazard*, together with some fugitive prose, were issued in *Collected Prose of Elinor Wylie*, prefaces by C. Van Doren, C. Van Vechten, S. V. Benét, I. Patterson, and W. R. Benét (1933). For criticism consult W. R. Benét, *The Prose and Poetry of Elinor Wylie* (1934); J. B. Cabell, *One of Us* (1930); E. S. Sergeant, *Fire Under the Andes* (1927); E. Clark, *Innocence Abroad* (1927); N. Hoyt, *Elinor Wylie: the Portrait of an Unknown Lady* (1935); A. Kreymborg, *Our Singing Strength* (1929); H. Gorman, "Daughter of Donne," *North American Review*, May, 1924; C. Wood, *Poets of America* (1925); L. Untermeyer, *American Poetry since 1900* (1923); M. M. Colum, "O Virtuous Light!", *Saturday Review of Literature*, May 25, 1929; E. Wilson and M. M. Colum, "In Memory of Elinor Wylie," *New Republic*, Feb. 6, 1929; M. D. Zabel, "The Pattern of the Atmosphere," *Poetry*, Aug., 1932; L. Untermeyer, "Elinor Wylie's Poetry," *Saturday Review of Literature*, May 21, 1932; C. Van Doren, *Three Worlds* (1936); Horace Gregory and Marya Zaturenska, *A History of American Poetry, 1900–1940* (1946); Julia Cluck, "Elinor Wylie's Shelley Obsession," *Publications of the Modern Language Association*, Sept., 1941.

THE LION AND THE LAMB

I saw a Tiger's golden flank,
I saw what food he ate,
By a desert spring he drank;
The Tiger's name was Hate.

Then I saw a placid Lamb
Lying fast asleep;
Like a river from its dam
Flashed the Tiger's leap.

I saw a Lion tawny-red,
Terrible and brave;   10
The Tiger's leap overhead
Broke like a wave.

In sand below or sun above
He faded like a flame.
The Lamb said, "I am Love;
Lion, tell your name."

The Lion's voice thundering
Shook his vaulted breast,
"I am Love. By this spring,
Brother, let us rest."   20
                                          1921

SUNSET ON THE SPIRE

All that I dream
    By day or night
Lives in that stream
    Of lovely light.
Here is the earth,
    And there is the spire;
This is my hearth,
    And that is my fire.
From the sun's dome
    I am shouted proof   10
That this is my home,
    And that is my roof.

Here is my food,
    And here is my drink,
And I am wooed
    From the moon's brink.
And the days go over,
    And the nights end;
Here is my lover,
    Here is my friend.   20
All that I

Could ever ask
Wears that sky
Like a thin gold mask.
                                          1921

HEROICS

Though here and there a man is left
Whose iron thread eludes the shears,
The martyr with his bosom cleft
Is dead these seven heavy years.

Does he survive whose tongue was slit,
To slake some envy of a king's?
Sportive silver cried from it
Before the savage cut the strings.

The rack has crumpled up the limb
Stretched immediate to fly;   10
Never ask the end of him
Stubborn to outstare the sky.

Assuming an heroic mask,
He stands a tall derisive tree,
While servile to the speckled task
We move devoted hand and knee.

It is no virtue, but a fault
Thus to breathe ignoble air,
Suffering unclean assault
And insult dubious to bear.   20
                                          1922

KING HONOR'S ELDEST SON

His father's steel, piercing the wholesome fruit
Of his mother's flesh, wrought acidly to mar
Its own Damascus, staining worse than war
A purity intense and absolute;

While her clean stock put forth a poisoned
        shoot,
In likeness of a twisted scimitar,
Sleek as a lovelock, ugly as a scar,
Wrong as the firstborn of a mandrake root.

There was a waning moon upon his brow,
A fallen star upon his pointed chin;   10
He mingled Ariel with Caliban;
But such a blossom upon such a bough
Convinced his poor progenitors of sin
In having made a something more than man.
                                          1923

THE EAGLE AND THE MOLE

AVOID the reeking herd,
Shun the polluted flock,
Live like that stoic bird,
The eagle of the rock.

The huddled warmth of crowds
Begets and fosters hate;
He keeps, above the clouds,
His cliff inviolate.

When flocks are folded warm
And herds to shelter run,   10
He sails above the storm,
He stares into the sun.

If in the eagle's track
Your sinews cannot leap,
Avoid the lathered pack,
Turn from the steaming sheep.

If you would keep your soul
From spotted sight or sound,
Live like the velvet mole;
Go burrow underground.   20

And there hold intercourse
With roots of trees and stones,
With rivers at their source
And disembodied bones.

                              1921

UNFINISHED PORTRAIT

MY love, you know that I have never used
That fluency of colour smooth and rich
Could cage you in enamel for the niche
Whose heart-shape holds you; I have been accused
Of gold and silver trickery, infused
With blood of meteors, and moonstones which
Are cold as eyeballs in a flooded ditch;
In no such goblin smithy are you bruised.

I do not glaze a lantern like a shell
Inset with stars, nor make you visible   10
Through jewelled arabesques which adhere to clothe
The outline of your soul; I am content
To leave you an uncaptured element;
Water, or light, or air that's stained by both.

                              1923

NAMELESS SONG

MY heart is cold and weather-worn,
  A musical and hollow shell:
The winds have blown it like a horn,
  The waves have rung it like a bell.

The waves have whirled it round and round,
  The winds have worn it thin and fine:
It is alive with a singing sound:
  Whose Voice is that? It is not mine.

                              1932

1887 ~ *Robinson Jeffers* ~ ──

JEFFERS, a native of western Pennsylvania, has spent his working years on the Pacific coast. His father was a Presbyterian clergyman and professor of theology, his mother a woman of high character, fine education, and a lover of music. As a boy, Jeffers had the advantage of extensive European travel as well as early training in European schools. While he was a student at Occidental College in California, from which he was graduated in 1905, he contributed verse to campus publications, and developed a passion for poetry which became a determining factor in his life. After completing his course, he pursued at various times graduate study in literature, medicine, and forestry. By 1911 he was convinced that poetry was his primary interest, and withdrew to Hermosa Beach where he spent a year in writing. *Flagons and Apples*, his first volume, appeared in 1912. Since 1914 he has made his home on the California coast near Carmel-by-the-Sea. He does his writing in the tiny top room of Hawk's Tower which he erected close to his home. He has published numerous volumes, among them being *Tamar and Other Poems* (1924), *Roan Stallion* (1925), *Cawdor and Other Poems* (1928), *Thurso's Landing and Other Poems* (1932), *Give Your Heart to the Hawks* (1933), and *Solstice and Other Poems* (1935).

The early work of Jeffers attracted scarcely any attention, and it was not until 1924 when *Tamar* appeared that he began to be recognized. Behind the framework of gray landscape, stark tragedies, neurotic characters obsessed by sex and an abounding love of nature, a definite purpose is steadily unfolding, the search for fundamental and ultimate reality. He does not tell tragic stories merely for their own sakes, but as a way of seeking, as it were, the primal irreducible force in the universe. Having revolted early from the Calvinistic theology of his forebears, he set out on an independent quest to find, if possible, a rational theory more satisfying than their explanations. Upon the results of his scientific study, and upon his observations of the Carmel landscape, of which he has grown to be an indigenous poet, he trained the sharp focus of his imagination to see what light there might be on the eternal problems of living.

But the light he sought turned to darkness. Science led him to see man as merely another phenomenon of nature at one with the pounding surf, the stars, and the Carmel landscape, essentially ignorant and helpless as far as his questing is concerned, still held in the clutches of this blind force. He found the world of the twenties a hopeless world. This explains, in a measure at least, his primitivistic treatment of man in his most elemental relations, far removed from the culture and sophistication of the city and the fatalistic mysticism with which he accepts his unhappy fate.

On the other hand, certain very definite characteristics of a more positive nature tend to offset the negative quality of his gloom, hopelessness, and depression. These equalities are found in Jeffers the poet rather than in Jeffers the thinker. Chief of these are his penetrating imagination, which finds poetry in even the most tragic phases of life, and the remarkably original style in which he writes, a style which is personal and unique, and does not seem to fit into any of the accepted categories. On the surface it seems to be formless and uncontrolled, but closer study shows in the apparent formlessness a definite plan in the use of stresses and syllabic quantity which reveals new rhythmic possibilities of the language. He startles and refreshes by his originality of treatment and expression.

Jeffers has published many volumes; of the more important are *Tamar and Other Poems* (1924); *Roan Stallion, Tamar and Other Poems* (1925); *The Women at Point Sur* (1927); *Poems* (1928); *Cawdor and Other Poems* (1928); *Dear Judas and Other Poems* (1929); *Descent to the Dead* (1931);

Thurso's Landing and Other Poems (1932); *Give Your Heart to the Hawks and Other Poems* (1933); *Solstice and Other Poems* (1935). *The Selected Poetry of Robinson Jeffers* was published in 1938. The most extensive critical and biographical study of Jeffers is L. C. Powell, *Robinson Jeffers: the Man and His Work* (1934). There is a briefer account in L. Adamic, *Robinson Jeffers: a Portrait* (1929). Helpful critical discussions and estimates are J. G. Fletcher, "The Dilemma of Robinson Jeffers," *Poetry*, March, 1934; H. Hatcher, "The Torches of Violence," *English Journal*, Feb., 1934; G. Sterling, *Robinson Jeffers: the Man and the Artist* (1926); A. Kreymborg, *Our Singing Strength* (1929); H. L. Davis, "Jeffers Denies Us Twice," *Poetry*, Feb., 1928; B. H. Lehman, "The Most Significant Tendency in Modern Poetry," *Scripps College Papers*, No. 2, 1929; Y. Winters, "Robinson Jeffers," *Poetry*, Feb., 1930; H. S. Canby, "North of Hollywood," *Saturday Review of Literature*, Oct. 7, 1933; B. DeCasseres, "Robinson Jeffers: Tragic Error," *Bookman*, Nov., 1927; R. Humphries, "Robinson Jeffers," *Modern Monthly*, Jan., 1935; H. Gorman, "Jeffers, Metaphysician," *Saturday Review of Literature*, Sept. 17, 1927; H. H. Waggoner, "Science and the Poetry of Robinson Jeffers," *American Literature*, Nov., 1938; E. K. Brown, "Robinson Jeffers: The Tower beyond Tragedy," *Manitoba Arts Review*, Spring, 1939—an especially fine interpretation.

SCIENCE

MAN, introverted man, having crossed
In passage and but a little with the nature of things this latter century
Has begot giants; but being taken up
Like a maniac with self-love and inward conflicts cannot manage his hybrids.
Being used to deal with edgeless dreams,
Now he's bred knives on nature turns them also inward: they have thirsty points though.
His mind forebodes his own destruction;
Actaeon who saw the goddess naked among leaves and his hounds tore him.
A little knowledge, a pebble from the shingle,
A drop from the oceans: who would have dreamed this infinitely little too much?   10

1925

TO A YOUNG ARTIST

IT is good for strength not to be merciful
To its own weakness, good for the deep urn to run over, good to explore
The peaks and the deeps, who can endure it,
Good to be hurt, who can be healed afterward: but you that have whetted consciousness
Too bitter an edge, too keenly daring,
So that the color of a leaf can make you tremble, and your own thoughts like harriers
Tear the live mind: were your bones mountains,
Your blood rivers to endure it? and all that labor of discipline labors to death.
Delight is exquisite, pain is more present;
You have sold the armor, you have bought shining with burning, one should be stronger than strength   10
To fight baresark in the stabbing field
In the rage of the stars: I tell you unconsciousness is the treasure, the tower, the fortress;
Referred to that one may live anything;
The temple and the tower: poor dancer on the flints and shards in the temple porches, turn home.

1928

HURT HAWKS

I

The broken pillar of the wing jags from the clotted shoulder,
The wing trails like a banner in defeat,
No more to use the sky forever but live with famine
And pain a few days: cat nor coyote
Will shorten the week of waiting for death, there is game without talons.
He stands under the oak-bush and waits
The lame feet of salvation; at night he remembers freedom
And flies in a dream, the dawns ruin it.
He is strong and pain is worse to the strong, incapacity is worse.
The curs of the day come and torment him   10
At distance, no one but death the redeemer will humble that head,
The intrepid readiness, the terrible eyes.
The wild God of the world is sometimes merciful to those
That ask mercy, not often to the arrogant,
You do not know him, you communal people, or you have forgotten him;
Intemperate and savage, the hawk remembers him;
Beautiful and wild, the hawks, and men that are dying, remember him.

II

I'd sooner, except the penalties, kill a man than a hawk; but the great redtail
Had nothing left but unable misery
From the bone too shattered for mending, the wing that trailed under his talons when he moved.
We had fed him six weeks, I gave him freedom,   21
He wandered over the foreland hill and returned in the evening, asking for death,
Not like a beggar, still eyed with the old
Implacable arrogance. I gave him the lead gift in the twilight. What fell was relaxed,
Owl-downy, soft feminine feathers; but what
Soared: the fierce rush: the night-herons by the flooded river cried fear at its rising
Before it was quite unsheathed from reality.

1928

1897 ~ *William Faulkner* ~ —

WILLIAM FAULKNER was born in Mississippi, and has lived, with a few interruptions, in Oxford, Mississippi, all of his life. His major preoccupation has been with the South of his great-grandfather's time and of his own. His fiction has created a Mississippi county, Yoknapatawpha County, described its history and explained its people. During the first World War Faulkner served with the British Royal Air Force in France and was wounded in an airplane accident. His war experiences are reflected in stories in *These 13* (1931), and in the novel *Sartoris* (1929); his interest in aviation appears in these works, and in the novel *Pylon* (1935). After the war, he spent some little time in New Orleans, where he met and discussed writing with Sherwood Anderson. From this experience came the mediocre "lost generation" novel, *Mosquitoes* (1927).

But his major concern has been with Yoknapatawpha County. As Malcolm Cowley has pointed out, nine of his books are devoted to that mythical county and its people, "who also appear in parts of three others and in thirty or more uncollected stories." The range of his treatment in these works is as varied as the subject matter. *Sartoris* (1929) is a fairly conventional novel; *The Unvanquished* (1938) is a series of sketches and stories, held together by the Sartoris theme, and concluding on a note of naïve romanticism rare in Faulkner's work; *As I Lay Dying* (1930) and *The Sound and the Fury* (1929) (the latter Faulkner considers his best book) work several remarkable changes upon the stream-of-consciousness method; *Absalom, Absalom!* (1936) is a tortured, complex history of the Sutpen family, as told by Quentin Compson, hero of another Faulkner novel, to his roommate at Harvard; *Sanctuary* (1931) is a tale of unrelieved violence in which are also found grotesquely humorous passages of great effectiveness.

Faulkner's themes, which become what can almost be called obsessions, have been acutely analyzed by Malcolm Cowley (in his introduction to the *Viking Portable Faulkner*, 1946) and Robert Penn Warren (in a *New Republic* essay, 1946). His primary concern is with the South, its tradition, and the decay of that tradition in the years following the Civil War. It is not only that the land has been "deswamped and denuded and derivered in two generations," as Ike McCaslin puts it; it is also the responsibility, the sense of guilt, which the Southerner feels for the decline. To quote Cowley's succinct summary:

> The Deep South was settled partly by aristocrats like the Sartoris clan and partly by new men like Colonel Sutpen. Both types of planters were determined to establish a lasting social order on the land they had seized from the Indians (that is, to leave sons behind them). They had the virtue of living single-mindedly by a fixed code; but there was also an inherent guilt in their "design," their way of life; it was slavery that put a curse on the land and brought about the Civil War. After the War was lost, partly as a result of their own mad heroism ... they tried to restore "the design" by other methods. But they no longer had the strength to achieve more than a partial success ... [and they had also] to fight a new exploiting class descended from the landless whites of slavery days.

It was convenient for Faulkner to invent a county for his people, to give the history of that county as typical of the Deep South, and to create typical figures to represent the peoples of that South: the Sartorises, who carried the burden of tradition and whose attachment to "the code" accelerated their downfall; the poor whites of *As I Lay Dying;* the Snopeses, who represented the rising class of commercial opportunists of carpet-bagging days and land failures. To these groups Faulkner adds memorable characters who writhe in prolonged, rhetorical debate over the moral issues involved in the South's decline, portraits of idiocy and psychological decay, and crudely brutal and harshly vital characters (like Popeye, of *Sanctuary*). The collection is astonishing and depressing, but there is no simple view of it. Faulkner has done more than any other writer to convince the reading public of the very complex culture of the South, of the varied and difficult reasons for its difference from Northern culture.

Faulkner's style is often tortured, involved, and needlessly polysyllabic. Usually the involution is an integral and necessary part of the subject; often, however, the lack of discipline shows in his failure to economize, to write cleanly, and without excessive qualification. His experiments (especially with stream of consciousness) are brilliant; his humor, often gargantuan and grotesque, is admirable; his preoccupation with characterization ultimately leads to a complex, rather thick, clarity of outline and depth of portrait. To take a single instance, where Erskine Caldwell (in *Trouble in July*) is shoddy and sensationalistic, Faulkner (in "Dry September") presents the same situation (a lynching) with a definitive clarity and precision. Faulkner's weaknesses are those of an inadequately disciplined talent, which is great enough to more than survive its occasional abuse and misuse.

Faulkner's novels are *Soldier's Pay* (1926); *Mosquitoes* (1927); *Sartoris* (1929); *The Sound and the Fury* (1929); *As I Lay Dying* (1930); *Sanctuary* (1931); *Light in August* (1933); *Pylon* (1935); *Absalom, Absalom!* (1936); *The Unvanquished* (1938); *The Wild Palms* (1939); *The Hamlet* (1941); *Intruder in the Dust* (1948). Collections of short stories include *Idyll in the Desert* (1931); *These 13* (1931); *Doctor Martino and Other Stories* (1934); *Go Down, Moses* (1942). There are two volumes of poems: *The Marble Faun* (1924) and *A Green Bough* (1933). For criticism consult Pelham Edgar, *The Art of the Novel from 1700 to the Present Time* (1933); Alfred Kazin, *On Native Grounds* (1942); J. W. Beach, *American Fiction, 1920–1940* (1941); Maxwell Geismar, *Writers in Crisis* (1942); George Snell, *The Shapers of American Fiction* (1947); E. B. Burgum, *The Novel and the World's Dilemma* (1947); Malcolm Cowley, Introduction to *The Viking Portable Faulkner* (1946); Robert Penn Warren, "William Faulkner," in *Forms of Modern Fiction*, ed. W. V. O'Connor (1948); Wyndham Lewis "A Moralist with a Corn-Cob: A Study of William Faulkner," *Life and Letters*, June, 1934; Conrad Aiken, "William Faulkner: The Novel as Form," *Atlantic Monthly*, Nov., 1939; Warren Beck, "Faulkner's Point of View," *College English*, May, 1941; A. W. Green, "William Faulkner at Home," *Sewanee Review*, July–Sept., 1932; J. M. Machlachlan, "William Faulkner and the Southern Folk," *Southern Folklore Quarterly*, Sept., 1945; G. M. O'Donnell, "Faulkner's Mythology," *Kenyon Review*, Summer, 1939; Delmore Schwartz, "The Fiction of William Faulkner," *Southern Review*, Summer, 1941. For other titles, see Fred B. Millett, *Contemporary American Authors* (1940) and Leary, *Articles on American Literature Appearing in Current Periodicals, 1920–1945* (1947).

A ROSE FOR EMILY

I

WHEN Miss Emily Grierson died, our whole town went to her funeral: the men through a sort of respectful affection for a fallen monument, the women mostly out of curiosity to see the inside of her house, which no one save an old manservant—a combined gardener and cook—had seen in at least ten years.

It was a big, squarish frame house that had once been white, decorated with cupolas and spires and scrolled balconies in the heavily lightsome style of the seventies, set on what had once been our most select street. But garages and cotton gins had encroached and obliterated even the august names of that neighborhood; only Miss Emily's house was left, lifting its stubborn and coquettish decay above the cotton wagons and the gasoline pumps—an eyesore among eyesores. And now Miss Emily had gone to join the representatives of those august names where they lay in the cedar-bemused cemetery among the ranked and anonymous graves of Union and Confederate soldiers who fell at the battle of Jefferson.

Alive, Miss Emily had been a tradition, a duty, and a care; a sort of hereditary obligation upon the town, dating from that day in 1894 when Colonel Sartoris, the mayor—he who fathered the edict that no Negro women should appear on the streets without an apron—remitted her taxes, the dispensation dating from the death of her father on into perpetuity. Not that Miss Emily would have accepted charity. Colonel Sartoris invented an involved tale to the effect that Miss Emily's father had loaned money to the town, which the town, as a matter of business, preferred this way of repaying. Only a man of Colonel Sartoris' generation and thought could have invented it, and only a woman could have believed it.

When the next generation, with its more modern ideas, became mayors and aldermen, this arrangement created some little dissatisfaction. On the first of the year they mailed her a tax notice. February came, and there was no reply. They wrote her a formal letter, asking her to call at the sheriff's office at her convenience. A week later the mayor wrote her himself, offering to call or to send his car for her, and received in reply a note on paper of an archaic shape, in a thin, flowing calligraphy in faded ink, to the effect that she no longer went out at all. The tax notice was also enclosed, without comment.

They called a special meeting of the Board of Aldermen. A deputation waited upon her, knocked at the door through which no visitor had passed since she ceased giving china-painting lessons eight or ten years earlier. They were admitted by the old Negro into a dim hall from which a stairway mounted into still more shadow. It smelled of dust and disuse—a close, dank smell. The Negro led them into the parlor. It was furnished in heavy, leather-covered furniture. When the Negro opened the blinds of one window, they could see that the leather was cracked; and when they sat down, a faint dust rose sluggishly about their thighs, spinning with slow motes in the single sun-ray. On a tarnished gilt easel before the fireplace stood a crayon portrait of Miss Emily's father.

They rose when she entered—a small, fat woman in black, with a thin gold chain descending to her waist and vanishing into her belt, leaning on an ebony cane with a tarnished gold head. Her skeleton was small and spare; perhaps that was why what would have been merely plumpness in another was obesity in her. She looked bloated, like a body long submerged in motionless water, and of that pallid hue. Her eyes, lost in the fatty ridges of her face, looked like two small pieces of coal pressed into a lump of dough as they moved from one face to another while the visitors stated their errand.

She did not ask them to sit. She just stood in the door and listened quietly until the spokesman came to a stumbling halt. Then they could hear the invisible watch ticking at the end of the gold chain.

Her voice was dry and cold. "I have no taxes in Jefferson. Colonel Sartoris explained it to me. Perhaps one of you can gain access to the city records and satisfy yourselves."

"But we have. We are the city authorities, Miss Emily. Didn't you get a notice from the sheriff, signed by him?"

"I received a paper, yes," Miss Emily said. "Perhaps he considers himself the sheriff . . . I have no taxes in Jefferson."

"But there is nothing on the books to show that, you see. We must go by the—"

"See Colonel Sartoris. I have no taxes in Jefferson."

"But, Miss Emily—"

"See Colonel Sartoris." (Colonel Sartoris had been dead almost ten years.) "I have no taxes in Jefferson. Tobe!" The Negro appeared. "Show these gentlemen out."

II

So she vanquished them, horse and foot, just as she had vanquished their fathers thirty years before about the smell. That was two years after her father's death and a short time after her sweetheart—the one we believed would marry her—had deserted her. After her father's death she went out very little; after her sweetheart went away, people hardly saw her at all. A few of the ladies had the temerity to call, but were not received, and the only sign of life about the place was the Negro man—a young man then—going in and out with a market basket.

"Just as if a man—any man—could keep a kitchen properly," the ladies said; so they were not surprised when the smell developed. It was another link between the gross, teeming world and the high and mighty Griersons.

A neighbor, a woman, complained to the mayor, Judge Stevens, eighty years old.

"But what will you have me do about it, madam?" he said.

"Why, send her word to stop it," the woman said. "Isn't there a law?"

"I'm sure that won't be necessary," Judge Stevens said. "It's probably just a snake or a rat that nigger of hers killed in the yard. I'll speak to him about it."

The next day he received two more complaints, one from a man who came in diffident deprecation. "We really must do something about it, Judge. I'd be the last one in the world to bother Miss Emily, but we've got to do something." That night the Board of Aldermen met—three graybeards and one younger man, a member of the rising generation.

"It's simple enough," he said. "Send her word to have her place cleaned up. Give her a certain time to do it in, and if she don't . . ."

"Dammit, sir," Judge Stevens said, "will you accuse a lady to her face of smelling bad?"

So the next night, after midnight, four men crossed Miss Emily's lawn and slunk about the house like burglars, sniffing along the base of the brickwork and at the cellar openings while one of them performed a regular sowing motion with his hand out of a sack slung from his shoulder. They broke open the cellar door and sprinkled lime there, and in all the outbuildings. As they recrossed the lawn, a window that had been dark was lighted and Miss Emily sat in it, the light behind her, and her upright torso motionless as that of an idol. They crept quietly across the lawn and into the shadow of the locusts that lined the street. After a week or two the smell went away.

That was when people had begun to feel really sorry for her. People in our town, remembering how old lady Wyatt, her great-aunt, had gone completely crazy at last, believed that the Griersons held themselves a little too high for what they really were. None of the young men were quite good enough to Miss Emily and such. We had long thought of them as a tableau; Miss Emily a slender figure in white in the background, her father a spraddled silhouette in the foreground, his back to her and clutching a horsewhip, the two of them framed by the back-flung front door. So when she got to be thirty and was still single, we were not pleased exactly, but vindicated; even with insanity in the family she wouldn't have turned down all of her chances if they had really materialized.

When her father died, it got about that the house was all that was left to her; and in a way, people were glad. At last they could pity Miss Emily. Being left alone, and a pauper, she had become humanized. Now she too would know the old thrill and the old despair of a penny more or less.

The day after his death all the ladies prepared to call at the house and offer condolence and aid, as is our custom. Miss Emily met them at the door, dressed as usual and with no trace of grief on her face. She told them that her father was not dead. She did that for three days, with the ministers calling on her, and the doctors, trying to persuade her to let them dispose of the body. Just as they were about to resort to law and force, she broke down, and they buried her father quickly.

We did not say she was crazy then. We believed she had to do that. We remembered all the young men her father had driven away, and we knew that with nothing left, she would have to cling to that which had robbed her, as people will.

III

She was sick for a long time. When we saw her again, her hair was cut short, making her look like a girl, with a vague resemblance to those angels in colored church windows—sort of tragic and serene.

The town had just let the contracts for paving the sidewalks, and in the summer after her father's death they began the work. The construction company came with niggers and mules and machinery, and a foreman named Homer Barron, a Yankee—a big, dark, ready man, with a big voice and eyes lighter than his face. The little boys would follow in groups to hear him cuss the niggers, and the niggers singing in time to the rise and fall of picks. Pretty soon he knew everybody in town. Whenever you heard a lot of laughing anywhere about the square, Homer Barron would be in the center of the group. Presently we began to see him and Miss Emily on Sunday afternoons driving in the yellow-wheeled buggy and the matched team of bays from the livery stable.

At first we were glad that Miss Emily would have an interest, because the ladies all said, "Of course a Grierson would not think seriously of a Northerner, a day laborer." But there were still others, older people, who said that even grief could not cause a real lady to forget *noblesse oblige*—without calling it *noblesse oblige*. They just said, "Poor Emily. Her kinsfolk should come to her." She had some kin in Alabama; but years ago her father had fallen out with them over the estate of old lady Wyatt, the crazy woman, and there was no communication between the two families. They had not even been represented at the funeral.

And as soon as the old people said, "Poor Emily," the whispering began. "Do you suppose it's really so?" they said to one another. "Of course it is. What else could . . ." This behind their hands; rustling of craned silk and satin behind jalousies closed upon the sun of Sunday afternoon as the thin, swift clop-clop-clop of the matched team passed: "Poor Emily."

She carried her head high enough—even when we believed that she was fallen. It was as if she demanded more than ever the recognition of her dignity as the last Grierson; as if it had wanted that touch of earthiness to reaffirm her imperviousness. Like when she bought the rat poison, the arsenic. That was over a year after they had begun to say "Poor Emily," and while the two female cousins were visiting her.

"I want some poison," she said to the druggist. She was over thirty then, still a slight woman, though thinner than usual, with cold, haughty black eyes in a face the flesh of which was strained across the temples and about the eye-sockets as you imagine a lighthousekeeper's face ought to look. "I want some poison," she said.

"Yes, Miss Emily. What kind? For rats and such? I'd recom—"

"I want the best you have. I don't care what kind."

The druggist named several. "They'll kill anything up to an elephant. But what you want is—"

"Arsenic," Miss Emily said. "Is that a good one?"

"Is . . . arsenic? Yes, ma'am. But what you want—"

"I want arsenic."

The druggist looked down at her. She looked back at him, erect, her face like a strained flag. "Why, of course," the druggist said. "If that's what you want. But the law requires you to tell what you are going to use it for."

Miss Emily just stared at him, her head tilted back in order to look him eye for eye, until he looked away and went and got the arsenic and wrapped it up. The Negro delivery boy brought her the package; the druggist didn't come back. When she opened the package at home there was written on the box, under the skull and bones: "For rats."

IV

So the next day we all said, "She will kill herself"; and we said it would be the best thing. When she had first begun to be seen with Homer Barron, we had said, "She will marry him." Then we said, "She will persuade him yet," because Homer himself had remarked—he liked men, and it was known that he drank with the younger men in the Elk's Club—that he was not a marrying man. Later we said, "Poor Emily" behind the jalousies as they passed on Sunday afternoon in the glittering buggy, Miss Emily with her head high and Homer Barron with his hat cocked and a cigar in his teeth, reins and whip in a yellow glove.

Then some of the ladies began to say that it was a disgrace to the town and a bad example to the young people. The men did not want to interfere, but at last the ladies forced the Baptist minister—Miss Emily's people were Episcopal—to call upon her. He would never divulge what happened during that interview, but he refused to go back again. The next Sunday they again drove about the streets, and the following day the minister's wife 10 wrote to Miss Emily's relations in Alabama.

So she had blood-kin under her roof again and we sat back to watch developments. At first nothing happened. Then we were sure that they were to be married. We learned that Miss Emily had been to the jeweler's and ordered a man's toilet set in silver, with the letters H. B. on each piece. Two days later we learned that she had bought a complete outfit of men's clothing, including a nightshirt, and 20 we said, "They are married." We were really glad. We were glad because the two female cousins were even more Grierson than Miss Emily had ever been.

So we were not surprised when Homer Barron—the streets had been finished some time since—was gone. We were a little disappointed that there was not a public blowing-off, but we believed that he had gone on to prepare for Miss Emily's coming, or to give 30 her a chance to get rid of the cousins. (By that time it was a cabal, and we were all Miss Emily's allies to help circumvent the cousins.) Sure enough, after another week they departed. And, as we had expected all along, within three days Homer Barron was back in town. A neighbor saw the Negro man admit him at the kitchen door at dusk one evening.

And that was the last we saw of Homer Barron. And of Miss Emily for some time. The 40 Negro man went in and out with the market basket, but the front door remained closed. Now and then we would see her at a window for a moment, as the men did that night when they sprinkled the lime, but for almost six months she did not appear on the streets. Then we knew that this was to be expected too; as if that quality of her father which had thwarted her woman's life so many times had been too virulent and too furious to die. 50

When we next saw Miss Emily, she had grown fat and her hair was turning gray. During the next few years it grew grayer and grayer until it attained an even pepper-and-salt iron-gray, when it ceased turning. Up to the day of her death at seventy-four it was still that vigorous iron-gray, like the hair of an active man.

From that time on her front door remained closed, save for a period of six or seven years, when she was about forty, during which she gave lessons in china-painting. She fitted up a studio in one of the downstairs rooms, where the daughters and granddaughters of Colonel Sartoris' contemporaries were sent to her with the same regularity and in the same spirit that they were sent to church on Sundays with a twenty-five cent piece for the collection plate. Meanwhile her taxes had been remitted.

Then the newer generation became the backbone and the spirit of the town, and the painting pupils grew up and fell away and did not send their children to her with boxes of color and tedious brushes and pictures cut from the ladies' magazines. The front door closed upon the last one and remained closed for good. When the town got free postal delivery, Miss Emily alone refused to let them fasten the metal numbers above her door and attach a mailbox to it. She would not listen to them.

Daily, monthly, yearly we watched the Negro grow grayer and more stooped, going in and out with the market basket. Each December we sent her a tax notice, which would be returned by the post office a week later, unclaimed. Now and then we would see her in one of the downstairs windows—she had evidently shut up the top floor of the house—like the carven torso of an idol in a niche, looking or not looking at us, we could never tell which. Thus she passed from generation to generation—dear, inescapable, impervious, tranquil, and perverse.

And so she died. Fell ill in the house filled with dust and shadows, with only a doddering Negro man to wait on her. We did not even know she was sick; we had long since given up trying to get any information from the Negro. He talked to no one, probably not even to her, for his voice had grown harsh and rusty, as if from disuse.

She died in one of the downstairs rooms, in a heavy walnut bed with a curtain, her gray head propped on a pillow yellow and moldy with age and lack of sunlight.

V

The Negro met the first of the ladies at the front door and let them in, with their hushed, sibilant voices and their quick, curious glances, and then he disappeared. He walked right through the house and out the back and was not seen again.

The two female cousins came at once. They held the funeral on the second day, with the town coming to look at Miss Emily beneath a mass of bought flowers, with the crayon face of her father musing profoundly above the bier and the ladies sibilant and macabre; and the very old men—some in their brushed Confederate uniforms—on the porch and the lawn, talking of Miss Emily as if she had been a contemporary of theirs, believing that they had danced with her and courted her perhaps, confusing time with its mathematical progression, as the old do, to whom all the past is not a diminishing road but, instead, a huge meadow which no winter ever quite touches, divided from them now by the narrow bottle-neck of the most recent decade of years.

Already we knew that there was one room in that region above stairs which no one had seen in forty years, and which would have to be forced. They waited until Miss Emily was decently in the ground before they opened it.

The violence of breaking down the door seemed to fill this room with pervading dust. A thin, acrid pall as of the tomb seemed to lie everywhere upon this room decked and furnished as for a bridal: upon the valence curtains of faded rose color, upon the rose-shaded lights, upon the dressing table, upon the delicate array of crystal and the man's toilet things backed with tarnished silver, silver so tarnished that the monogram was obscured. Among them lay a collar and tie, as if they had just been removed, which, lifted, left upon the surface a pale crescent in the dust. Upon a chair hung the suit, carefully folded; beneath it the two mute shoes and the discarded socks.

The man himself lay in the bed.

For a long while we just stood there, looking down at the profound and fleshless grin. The body had apparently once lain in the attitude of an embrace, but now the long sleep that outlasts love, that conquers even the grimace of love, had cuckolded him. What was left of him, rotted beneath what was left of the nightshirt, had become inextricable from the bed in which he lay; and upon him and upon the pillow beside him lay that even coating of the patient and biding dust.

Then we noticed that in the second pillow was the indentation of a head. One of us lifted something from it, and leaning forward, that faint and invisible dust dry and acrid in the nostrils, we saw a long strand of iron-gray hair.

1931

1900 -- *Thomas Wolfe* -- 1938

THE MAJOR SETTINGS of Thomas Wolfe's novels are the hills of North Carolina and the city of New York. He was born in Asheville, North Carolina, went to the state university at Chapel Hill (1916–1920), where he studied playwriting and edited the college paper and magazine. He took a Master's degree at Harvard in 1922; here he studied under Professor Baker and continued writing plays. After some travel in Europe he became an instructor in English at Washington Square College of New York University, a position he held from 1924 to early 1930. In 1930 and 1931 he again traveled abroad, this time on a Guggenheim fellowship.

The publication, in 1929, of *Look Homeward, Angel*, began eight years of writing, revising, cutting, quarreling with editors, and publishing the endless story of Eugene Gant—George Webber, continued in *Of Time and the River* (1935); *The Web and the Rock* (1939), and *You Can't Go Home Again* (1940). *The Hills Beyond* (1941) is still another version of the story to which are added several short stories, some of them touching upon similar themes. In 1936 appeared a short critical and autobiographical piece, *The Story of a Novel*. In response to favorable and shocked reactions to his first novel, Wolfe attempted to defend the autobiographical character of his work by saying that "my conviction is that all serious creative work must be at bottom autobiographical, and that a man must use the material of his own life if he is to create anything that has substantial value." Use it he did, and in abundance. The hundreds of MS sheets cluttering his apartment, piled into his trunk, and finding their way to editorial cutting rooms point extensively and repeatedly to Wolfe's voluminous concern over the personal and family matters that were to crowd his novels. Much of the order one finds in his work is a gift of his editors (all but the first two of his novels and one of his collections of short stories were published posthumously). Wolfe provided the vigor, the verbiage, the color; his editors (Maxwell Perkins and Edward C. Aswell), the form. What has attracted Wolfe's large following to him is his exuberance, the vigor which he put into the release of his creative energies, the very strong fondness for cumulative detail, and the rhetoric which makes bad writing momentarily seem good, or at least exciting. As Edward Aswell has explained, "Being a Southerner, with a Southerner's innate love of rhetoric, he would often be swept away by the cadence of his own words. Sometimes, more especially in his younger writing, he attached so much importance to the measured flow of his sentences that he might sacrifice his meaning to his music." Aswell goes on, to defend Wolfe's formal failures, by insisting that Wolfe followed but one form—that of the flow of the stream of life; his writing, Aswell says, "has a natural form, an elemental form, the form of which all other forms are but variations on a theme—the form of life itself." However well or poorly such an explanation may hold, Wolfe's novels did have an enormous attraction for readers in the thirties. There are genuine values, and many untutored skills, in the work.

Thomas Wolfe believed that in his later writing he had achieved greater objectivity and a more careful organization of his work. Writing to his editors about "the book" (by which term he meant his manuscript, which he left at his death), he said that it "marks not only a turning away from the books he has written in the past, but a genuine spiritual and artistic change. . . . [he] hoped to obtain, through free creation, a release of his inventive power which the shackling limitations of identifiable autobiography do not permit." He changed the name of his hero from Eugene Gant to George Webber, introduced new scenes and new persons, experimented with social satire and criticism; but the result was not an "objective" account so much as it was a reshaping of the same materials. The last three books do, however, show the effects of his attempts to write objectively, and in some respects at least the characters, released from their author's tight hold upon them, do seem to have more clarity of outline than do those of the Eugene Gant novels.

It is true that Wolfe's theme is that of an American's search for definition: in some respects, like that of Joyce's Stephen Dedalus, it is a search for a spiritual father, but generally it is an attempt to break through the jungle of multiplicity into some cleared spade of spiritual and cultural meaning. Wolfe's characters are tortured persons, whose gusto and appetite lead either to frustration or to confusion. Their appetite consumes them; their rhetoric attempts endlessly and futilely to explain the appetite. The very multitude of impressions offered by locale leads to formlessness and confusion which are not so much corrected in his work as they are demonstrated and commented upon.

The merits of Wolfe's fiction come from these defects. His characters are bloated by over-explanation, but they remain exceptional, striking personalities through many ordeals by rhetoric. His power of social burlesque and parody is enormously effective, and the passages which treat so vigorously of the commercialization of America survive as excellent contributions to social criticism. Finally, Wolfe's great appetite for sensory detail leads often to amazing results. He has been praised for his affirmation of American democracy, which transcends its weaknesses (much of this praise is due to the appearance of Wolfe's posthumous works at the beginning of World War II); and this praise is merited, though the impact of affirmation is too often made, in Wolfe's case, at the expense of clarity and formal excellence.

Wolfe's novels are *Look Homeward, Angel* (1929); *Of Time and the River* (1935); *The Web and the Rock* (1939); *You Can't Go Home Again* (1940). Collections of short stories are found in *From Death to Morning* (1935); *The Hills Beyond* (1941). Excerpts from his work have been collected and arranged in *The Face of a Nation* (1939) and *A Stone, A Leaf, A Door*, sel. by John S. Barnes (1945). *The Story of a Novel* (1936) is partly autobiographical, partly critical. Biographical and autobiographical materials include *Thomas Wolfe's Letters to His Mother*, ed. John Skally Terry (1943) and Hayden Norwood's *The Marble Man's Wife: Thomas Wolfe's Mother* (1947). Other biographical and critical studies include H. J. Muller, *Thomas Wolfe* (1947); Pamela H. Johnson, *Hungry Gulliver* (1948); J. W. Beach, *American Fiction, 1920–1940* (1941); Alfred Kazin, *On Native Grounds* (1942); Maxwell Geismar, *Writers in Crisis* (1942); E. B. Burgum, *The Novel and the World's Dilemma* (1947); H. J. Muller, *Modern Fiction* (1937); John Peale Bishop, "The Sorrows of Thomas Wolfe," *Kenyon Review*, Winter, 1939; Henry T. Volkering, "Tom Wolfe, Penance No More," *Virginia Quarterly Review*, Apr., 1939; Robert Penn Warren, "A Note on the Hamlet of Thomas Wolfe," *American Review*, May, 1935; Carlos Baker, "Thomas Wolfe's Apprenticeship," *Delphian Quarterly*, Jan., 1940; E. K. Brown, "Thomas Wolfe: Realist and Symbolist," *University of Toronto Quarterly*, Jan., 1941; Malcolm Cowley, "Profiles," *New Yorker*, Apr. 8, 1944; Bella Kussy, "The Vitalist Trend and Thomas Wolfe," *Sewanee Review*, July–Sept., 1942; C. M. Simpson, "Thomas Wolfe: A Chapter in His

Biography," *Southwest Review*, Apr., 1940. For other titles, see Millett, *Contemporary American Authors* (1940) and Leary, *Articles on American Literature Appearing in Current Periodicals*, *1920–1945* (1947).

From LOOK HOMEWARD, ANGEL

CHAPTER VI

* * *

The death of Grover gave Eliza the most terrible wound of her life: her courage was snapped, her slow but powerful adventure toward freedom was abruptly stopped. Her flesh seemed to turn rotten when she thought of the distant city and the Fair: she was appalled before the hidden adversary who had struck her down.

With desperate sadness she encysted herself within her house and her family, reclaimed that life she had been ready to renounce, lived laborious days and tried to drink, in toil, oblivion. But the dark lost face gleamed like a sudden and impalpable faun within the thickets of memory: she thought of the mark on his brown neck and wept.

During the grim winter the shadows lifted slowly. Gant brought back the roaring fires, the groaning succulent table, the lavish and explosive ritual of the daily life. The old gusto surged back in their lives.

And, as the winter waned, the interspersed darkness in Eugene's brain was lifted slowly, days, weeks, months began to emerge in consecutive brightness; his mind came from the confusion of the Fair: life opened practically.

Secure and conscious now in the guarded and sufficient strength of home, he lay with well-lined belly before the roasting vitality of the fire, poring insatiably over great volumes in the bookcase, exulting in the musty odor of the leaves, and in the pungent smell of their hot hides. The books he delighted in most were three huge calf-skin volumes called *Ridpath's History of the World*. Their numberless pages were illustrated with hundreds of drawings, engravings, wood-cuts: he followed the progression of the centuries pictorially before he could read. The pictures of battle delighted him most of all. Exulting in the howl of the beaten wind about the house, the thunder of

great trees, he committed himself to the dark storm, releasing the mad devil's hunger all men have in them, which lusts for darkness, the wind, and incalculable speed. The past unrolled to him in separate and enormous visions; he built unending legends upon the pictures of the kings of Egypt, charioted swiftly by soaring horses, and something infinitely old and recollective seemed to awaken in him as he looked on fabulous monsters, the twined beards and huge beast-bodies of Assyrian kings, the walls of Babylon. His brain swarmed with pictures—Cyrus directing the charge, the spear-forest of the Macedonian phalanx, the splintered oars, the numberless huddle of the ships at Salamis, the feasts of Alexander, the terrific melée of the knights, the shattered lances, the axe and the sword, the massed pikemen, the beleaguered walls, the scaling ladders heavy with climbing men hurled backward, the Swiss who flung his body on the lances, the press of horse and foot, the gloomy forests of Gaul and Caesarean conquests. Gant sat farther away, behind him, swinging violently back and forth in a stout rocker, spitting clean and powerful spurts of tobacco-juice over his son's head into the hissing fire.

Or again, Gant would read to him with sonorous and florid rhetoric passages from Shakespeare, among which he heard most often Marc Antony's funeral oration, Hamlet's soliloquy, the banquet scene in Macbeth, and the scene between Desdemona and Othello before he strangles her. Or, he would recite or read poetry, for which he had a capacious and retentive memory. His favorites were: "O why should the spirit of mortal be proud" ("Lincoln's favorite poem," he was fond of saying); "'We are lost,' the captain shouted, As he staggered down the stairs"; "I remember, I remember, the house where I was born"; "Ninety and nine with their captain, Rode on the enemy's track, Rode in the gray light of morning, Nine of the ninety came back"; "The boy stood on the burning deck"; and

"Half a league, half a league, half a league on-ward."

Sometimes he would get Helen to recite "Still sits the schoolhouse by the road, a ragged beggar sunning; Around it still the sumachs grow, and blackberry vines are running."

And when she had told how grasses had been growing over the girl's head for forty years, and how the gray-haired man had found in life's harsh school how few hated to go above him, because, you see, they love him, Gant would sigh heavily, and say with a shake of his head:

"Ah me! There was never a truer word spoken than that."

The family was at the very core and ripeness of its life together. Gant lavished upon it his abuse, his affection, and his prodigal provisioning. They came to look forward eagerly to his entrance, for he brought with him the great gusto of living, of ritual. They would watch him in the evening as he turned the corner below with eager strides, follow carefully the processional of his movements from the time he flung his provisions upon the kitchen table to the re-kindling of his fire, with which he was always at odds when he entered, and on to which he poured wood, coal and kerosene lavishly. This done, he would remove his coat and wash himself at the basin vigorously, rubbing his great hands across his shaven, tough-bearded face with the cleansing and male sound of sand paper. Then he would thrust his body against the door jamb and scratch his back energetically by moving it violently to and fro. This done he would empty another half can of kerosene on the howling flame, lunging savagely at it, and muttering to himself.

Then, biting off a good hunk of powerful apple tobacco, which lay ready to his use on the mantel, he would pace back and forth across his room fiercely, oblivious of his grinning family who followed these ceremonies with exultant excitement, as he composed his tirade. Finally, he would burst in on Eliza in the kitchen, plunging to the heart of denunciation with a mad howl.

His turbulent and undisciplined rhetoric had acquired, by the regular convention of its usage, something of the movement and directness of classical epithet: his similes were preposterous, created really in a spirit of vulgar mirth, and the great comic intelligence that was in the family—down to the youngest—was shaken daily by it. The children grew to await his return in the evening with a kind of exhilaration. Indeed, Eliza herself, healing slowly and painfully her great hurt, got a certain stimulation from it; but there was still in her a fear of the periods of drunkenness, and latently, a stubborn and unforgiving recollection of the past.

But, during that winter, as death, assaulted by the quick and healing gaiety of children, those absolute little gods of the moment, lifted itself slowly out of their hearts, something like hopefulness returned to her. They were a life unto themselves—how lonely they were they did not know, but they were known to every one and friended by almost no one. Their status was singular—if they could have been distinguished by caste, they would probably have been called middle-class, but the Duncans, the Tarkintons, all their neighbors, and all their acquaintances throughout the town, never drew in to them, never came into the strange rich color of their lives, because they had twisted the design of all orderly life, because there was in them a mad, original, disturbing quality which they did not suspect. And companionship with the elect—those like the Hilliards—was equally impossible, even if they had had the gift or the desire for it. But they hadn't.

Gant was a great man, and not a singular one, because singularity does not hold life in unyielding devotion to it.

As he stormed through the house, unleashing his gathered bolts, the children followed him joyously, shrieking exultantly as he told Eliza he had first seen her "wriggling around the corner like a snake on her belly," or, as coming in from freezing weather he had charged her and all the Pentlands with malevolent domination of the elements.

"We will freeze," he yelled, "we will freeze in this hellish, damnable, cruel and God-forsaken climate. Does Brother Will care? Does Brother Jim care? Did the Old Hog, your miserable old father, care? Merciful God! I have fallen into the hands of fiends incarnate, more savage, more cruel, more abominable than the beasts of the field. Hellhounds that they are, they will sit by and gloat at my agony until I am done to death."

He paced rapidly about the adjacent wash-room for a moment, muttering to himself, while grinning Luke stood watchfully near.

"But they can eat!" he shouted, plunging suddenly at the kitchen door. "They can eat —when some one else will feed them. I shall never forget the Old Hog as long as I live. Cr-unch, Cr-unch, Cr-unch,"—they were all exploded with laughter as his face assumed an expression of insane gluttony, and as he con-tinued, in a slow, whining voice intended to represent the speech of the late Major: "'Eliza, if you don't mind I'll have some more of that chicken,' when the old scoundrel had shovelled it down his throat so fast we had to carry him away from the table.'"

As his denunciation reached some high ex-travagance the boys would squeal with laugh-ter, and Gant, inwardly tickled, would glance around slyly with a faint grin bending the corners of his thin mouth. Eliza herself would laugh shortly, and then exclaim roughly: "Get out of here! I've had enough of your goings-on for one night."

Sometimes, on these occasions, his good humor grew so victorious that he would at-tempt clumsily to fondle her, putting one arm stiffly around her waist, while she bridled, be-came confused, and half-attempted to escape, saying: "Get away! Get away from me! It's too late for that now." Her white embarrassed smile was at once painful and comic: tears pressed closely behind it. At these rare, un-natural exhibitions of affection, the children laughed with constraint, fidgeted restlessly, and said: "Aw, papa, don't."

Eugene, when he first noticed an occurrence of this sort, was getting on to his fifth year: shame gathered in him in tangled clots, aching in his throat; he twisted his neck about con-vulsively, smiling desperately as he did later when he saw poor buffoons or mawkish scenes in the theatre. And he was never after able to see them touch each other with affection, with-out the same inchoate and choking humilia-tion: they were so used to the curse, the clamor, and the roughness, that any variation into ten-derness came as a cruel affectation.

But as the slow months, gummed with sor-row, dropped more clearly, the powerful germinal instinct for property and freedom began to reawaken in Eliza, and the ancient submerged struggle between their natures be-gan again. The children were growing up— Eugene had found playmates—Harry Tark-inton and Max Isaacs. Her sex was a fading coal.

Season by season, there began again the old strife of ownership and taxes. Returning home, with the tax-collector's report in his hand, Gant would be genuinely frantic with rage.

"In the name of God, Woman, what are we coming to? Before another year we'll all go to the poorhouse. Ah, Lord! I see very well where it will all end. I'll go to the wall, every penny we've got will go into the pockets of those accursed swindlers, and the rest will come under the sheriff's hammer. I curse the day I was ever fool enough to buy the first stick. Mark my words, we'll be living in soup-kitchens before this fearful, this awful, this hellish and damnable winter is finished."

She would purse her lips thoughtfully as she went over the list, while he looked at her with a face of strained agony.

"Yes, it does look pretty bad," she would remark. And then: "It's a pity you didn't listen to me last summer, Mr. Gant, when we had a chance of trading in that worthless old Owenby place for those two houses on Carter Street. We could have been getting forty dol-lars a month rent on them ever since."

"I never want to own another foot of land as long as I live," he yelled. "It's kept me a poor man all my life, and when I die they'll have to give me six feet of earth in Pauper's Field." And he would grow broodingly phil-osophic, speaking of the vanity of human ef-fort, the last resting-place in earth of rich and poor, the significant fact that we could "take none of it with us," ending perhaps with "Ah me! It all comes to the same in the end, any-way."

Or, he would quote a few stanzas of Gray's *Elegy*, using that encyclopaedia of stock mel-ancholy with rather indefinite application:

"—Await alike th' inevitable hour,
The paths of glory lead but to the grave."

But Eliza sat grimly on what they had.

Gant, for all his hatred of land ownership, was proud of living under his own shelter, and indeed proud in the possession of anything that was sanctified by his usage, and that gave him comfort. He would have liked ready and unencumbered affluence—the possession of huge sums of money in the bank and in his pocket, the freedom to travel grandly, to go before the world spaciously. He liked to carry large sums of money in his pocket, a practice of which Eliza disapproved, and for which she reprimanded him frequently. Once or twice, when he was drunk, he had been robbed: he would brandish a roll of bills about under the stimulation of whiskey, and dispense large sums to his children—ten, twenty, fifty dollars to each, with maudlin injunctions to "take it all! Take it all, God damn it!" But next day he was equally assiduous in his demands for its return: Helen usually collected it from the sometimes unwilling fingers of the boys. She would give it to him next day. She was fifteen or sixteen years old, and almost six feet high: a tall thin girl, with large hands and feet, big-boned, generous features, behind which the hysteria of constant excitement lurked.

The bond between the girl and her father grew stronger every day: she was nervous, intense, irritable, and abusive as he was. She adored him. He had begun to suspect that this devotion, and his own response to it, was a cause more and more of annoyance to Eliza, and he was inclined to exaggerate and emphasize it, particularly when he was drunk, when his furious distaste for his wife, his obscene complaint against her, was crudely balanced by his maudlin docility to the girl.

And Eliza's hurt was deeper because she knew that just at this time, when her slightest movement goaded him, did what was most rawly essential in him reveal itself. She was forced to keep out of his way, lock herself in her room, while her young daughter victoriously subdued him.

The friction between Helen and Eliza was often acute: they spoke sharply and curtly to each other, and were painfully aware of the other's presence in cramped quarters. And, in addition to the unspoken rivalry over Gant, the girl was in the same way, equally, rasped by the temperamental difference of Eliza—driven to fury at times by her slow, mouth-pursing speech, her placidity, the intonations of her voice, the deep abiding patience of her nature.

They fed stupendously. Eugene began to observe the food and the seasons. In the autumn, they barrelled huge frosty apples in the cellar. Gant bought whole hogs from the butcher, returning home early to salt them, wearing a long work-apron, and rolling his sleeves half up his lean hairy arms. Smoked bacons hung in the pantry, the great bins were full of flour, the dark recessed shelves groaned with preserved cherries, peaches, plums, quinces, apples, pears. All that he touched waxed in rich pungent life: his Spring gardens, wrought in the black wet earth below the fruit trees, flourished in huge crinkled lettuces that wrenched cleanly from the loamy soil with small black clots stuck to their crisp stocks; fat red radishes; heavy tomatoes. The rich plums lay bursted on the grass; his huge cherry trees oozed with heavy gum jewels; his apple trees bent with thick green clusters. The earth was spermy for him like a big woman.

Spring was full of cool dewy mornings, spurting winds, and storms of intoxicating blossoms, and in this enchantment Eugene first felt the mixed lonely ache and promise of the seasons.

In the morning they rose in a house pungent with breakfast cookery, and they sat at a smoking table loaded with brains and eggs, ham, hot biscuit, fried apples seething in their gummed syrups, honey, golden butter, fried steak, scalding coffee. Or there were stacked battercakes, rum-colored molasses, fragrant brown sausages, a bowl of wet cherries, plums, fat juicy bacon, jam. At the mid-day meal, they ate heavily: a huge hot roast of beef, fat buttered lima-beans, tender corn smoking on the cob, thick red slabs of sliced tomatoes, rough savory spinach, hot yellow corn-bread, flaky biscuits, a deep-dish peach and apple cobbler spiced with cinnamon, tender cabbage, deep glass dishes piled with preserved fruits—cherries, pears, peaches. At night they might eat fried steak, hot squares of grits fried in egg and butter, pork-chops, fish, young fried chicken.

For the Thanksgiving and Christmas feasts four heavy turkeys were bought and fattened for weeks: Eugene fed them with cans of shelled corn several times a day, but he could not bear to be present at their executions, because by that time their cheerful excited gobbles made echoes in his heart. Eliza baked for weeks in advance: the whole energy of the family focussed upon the great ritual of the feast. A day or two before, the auxiliary dainties arrived in piled grocer's boxes—the magic of strange foods and fruits was added to familiar fare: there were glossed sticky dates, cold rich figs, cramped belly to belly in small boxes, dusty raisins, mixed nuts—the almond, the pecan, the meaty nigger-toe, the walnut, sacks of assorted candies, piles of yellow Florida oranges, tangerines, sharp, acrid, nostalgic odors.

Seated before a roast or a fowl, Gant began a heavy clangor on his steel and carving knife, distributing thereafter Gargantuan portions to each plate. Eugene feasted from a high chair by his father's side, filled his distending belly until it was drum-tight, and was permitted to stop eating by his watchful sire only when his stomach was impregnable to the heavy prod of Gant's big finger.

"There's a soft place there," he would roar, and he would cover the scoured plate of his infant son with another heavy slab of beef. That their machinery withstood this hammer-handed treatment was a tribute to their vitality and Eliza's cookery.

Gant ate ravenously and without caution. He was immoderately fond of fish, and he invariably choked upon a bone while eating it. This happened hundreds of times, but each time he would look up suddenly with a howl of agony and terror, groaning and crying out strongly while a half-dozen hands pounded violently on his back.

"Merciful God!" he would gasp finally, "I thought I was done for that time."

"I'll vow, Mr. Gant," Eliza was vexed. "Why on earth don't you watch what you're doing? If you didn't eat so fast you wouldn't always get choked."

The children, staring, but relieved, settled slowly back in their places.

He had a Dutch love of abundance: again and again he described the great stored barns, the groaning plenty of the Pennsylvanians.

On his journey to California, he had been charmed in New Orleans by the cheapness and profusion of tropical fruits: a peddler offered him a great bunch of bananas for twenty-five cents, and Gant had taken them at once, wondering desperately later, as they moved across the continent, why, and what he was going to do with them.

1929

From OF TIME AND THE RIVER

CHAPTER VII

THE train rushed on across the brown autumnal land, by wink of water and the rocky coasts, the small white towns and flaming colors and the lonely, tragic and eternal beauty of New England. It was the country of his heart's desire, the dark Helen in his blood forever burning—and now the fast approach across October land, the engine smoke that streaked back on the sharp gray air that day!

The coming on of the great earth, the new lands, the enchanted city, the approach, so smoky, blind and stifled, to the ancient web, the old grimed thrilling barricades of Boston. The streets and buildings that slid past that day with such a haunting strange familiarity, the mighty engine steaming to its halt, and the great train-shed dense with smoke and acrid with its smell and full of the slow pantings of a dozen engines, now passive as great cats, the mighty station with the ceaseless throngings of its illimitable life, and all of the murmurous, remote and mighty sounds of time forever held there in the station, together with a tart and nasal voice, a hand'sbreadth off that said: "There's hahdly time, but try it if you want."

He saw the narrow, twisted, age-browned streets of Boston, then, with their sultry fragrance of fresh-roasted coffee, the sight of the man-swarm passing in its million-footed weft, the distant drone and murmur of the great mysterious city all about him, the shining water of the Basin, and the murmur of the harbor and its ships, the promise of glory and of a thousand secret, lovely and mysterious women that were waiting somewhere in the city's web.

He saw the furious streets of life with their unending flood-tide of a million faces, the enormous library with its million books; or was it just one moment in the flood-tide of the city, at five o'clock, a voice, a face, a brawny lusty girl with smiling mouth who passed him in an instant at the Park Street station, stood printed in the strong October wind a moment —breast, belly, arm, and thigh, and all her brawny lustihood—and then had gone into 10 the man-swarm, lost forever, never found?

Was it at such a moment—engine-smoke, a station, a street, the sound of time, a face that came and passed and vanished, could not be forgot—*here* or *here* or *here*, at such a moment of man's unrecorded memory, that he breathed fury from the air, that fury came?

He never knew; but now mad fury gripped his life, and he was haunted by the dream of time. Ten years must come and go without a 20 moment's rest from fury, ten years of fury, hunger, all of the wandering in a young man's life. And for what? For what?

What is the fury which this youth will feel, which will lash him on against the great earth forever? It is the brain that maddens with its own excess, the heart that breaks from the anguish of its own frustration. It is the hunger that grows from everything it feeds upon, the thirst that gulps down rivers and remains in- 30 satiate. It is to see a million men, a million faces and to be a stranger and an alien to them always. It is to prowl the stacks of an enormous library at night, to tear the books out of a thousand shelves, to read in them with the mad hunger of the youth of man.

It is to have the old unquiet mind, the famished heart, the restless soul; it is to lose hope, heart, and all joy utterly, and then to have them wake again, to have the old feeling re- 40 turn with overwhelming force that he is about to find the thing for which his life obscurely and desperately is groping—for which all men on this earth have sought—one face out of the million faces, a wall, a door, a place of certitude and peace and wandering no more. For what is it that we Americans are seeking always on this earth? Why is it we have crossed the stormy seas so many times alone, lain in a thousand alien rooms at night hearing the 50 sounds of time, dark time, and thought until

heart, brain, flesh and spirit were sick and weary with the thought of it; "Where shall I go now? What shall I do?"

He did not know the moment that it came, but it came instantly, at once. And from that moment on mad fury seized him, from that moment on, his life, more than the life of any one that he would ever know, was to be spent in solitude and wandering. Why this was true, or how it happened, he would never know; yet it was so. From this time on—save for two intervals in his life—he was to live about as solitary a life as a modern man can have. And it is meant by this that the number of hours, days, months, and years—the actual time he spent alone—would be immense and extraordinary.

And this fact was all the more astonishing because he never seemed to seek out solitude, nor did he shrink from life, or seek to build himself into a wall away from all the fury and the turmoil of the earth. Rather, he loved life so dearly that he was driven mad by the thirst and hunger which he felt for it. Of this fury, which was to lash and drive him on for fifteen years, the thousandth part could not be told, and what is told may seem unbelievable, but it is true. He was driven by a hunger so literal, cruel and physical that it wanted to devour the earth and all the things and people in it, and when it failed in this attempt, his spirit would drown in an ocean of horror and desolation, smothered below the overwhelming tides of this great earth, sickened and made sterile, hopeless, dead by the stupefying weight of men and objects in the world, the everlasting flock and flooding of the crowd.

Now he would prowl the stacks of the library at night, pulling books out of a thousand shelves and reading in them like a madman. The thought of these vast stacks of books would drive him mad: the more he read, the less he seemed to know—the greater the number of the books he read, the greater the immense uncountable number of those which he could never read would seem to be. Within a period of ten years he read at least 20,000 volumes—deliberately the number is set low— and opened the pages and looked through many times that number. This may seem unbelievable, but it happened. Dryden said this about Ben Jonson: "Other men read books but he read libraries"—and so now was it with this boy. Yet this terrific orgy of the books brought him no comfort, peace, or wisdom of the mind and heart. Instead, his fury and despair increased from what they fed upon, his hunger mounted with the food it ate.

He read insanely, by the hundreds, the thousands, the ten thousands, yet he had no desire to be bookish; no one could describe this mad assault upon print as scholarly: a ravening appetite in him demanded that he read everything that had ever been written about human experience. He read no more from pleasure—the thought that other books were waiting for him tore at his heart forever. He pictured himself as tearing the entrails from a book as from a fowl. At first, hovering over book stalls, or walking at night among the vast piled shelves of the library, he would read, watch in hand, muttering to himself in triumph or anger at the timing of each page: "Fifty seconds to do that one. Damn you, we'll see! You will, will you?"—and he would tear through the next page in twenty seconds.

This fury which drove him on to read so many books had nothing to do with scholarship, nothing to do with academic honors, nothing to do with formal learning. He was not in any way a scholar and did not want to be one. He simply wanted to know about everything on earth; he wanted to devour the earth, and it drove him mad when he saw he could not do this. And it was the same with everything he did. In the midst of a furious burst of reading in the enormous library, the thought of the streets outside and the great city all around him would drive through his body like a sword. It would now seem to him that every second that he passed among the books was being wasted—that at this moment something priceless, irrecoverable was happening in the streets, and that if he could only get to it in time and see it, he would somehow get the knowledge of the whole thing in him—the source, the well, the spring from which all men and words and actions, and every design upon this earth proceeds.

And he would rush out in the streets to find it, be hurled through the tunnel into Boston and then spend hours in driving himself savagely through a hundred streets, looking into the faces of a million people, trying to get an instant and conclusive picture of all they did and said and were, of all their million destinies, and of the great city and the everlasting earth, and the immense and lonely skies that bent above them. And he would search the furious streets until bone and brain and blood could stand no more—until every sinew of his life and spirit was wrung, trembling, and exhausted, and his heart sank down beneath its weight of desolation and despair.

Yet a furious hope, a wild extravagant belief, was burning in him all the time. He would write down enormous charts and plans and projects of all that he proposed to do in life—a program of work and living which would have exhausted the energies of 10,000 men. He would get up in the middle of the night to scrawl down insane catalogs of all that he had seen and done:—the number of books he had read, the number of miles he had travelled, the number of people he had known, the number of women he had slept with, the number of meals he had eaten, the number of towns he had visited, the number of states he had been in.

And at one moment he would gloat and chuckle over these stupendous lists like a miser gloating over his hoard, only to groan bitterly with despair the next moment, and to beat his head against the wall, as he remembered the overwhelming amount of all he had not seen or done, or known. Then he would begin another list filled with enormous catalogs of all the books he had not read, all the food he had not eaten, all the women that he had not slept with, all the states he had not been in, all the towns he had not visited. Then he would write down plans and programs whereby all these things must be accomplished, how many years it would take to do it all, and how old he would be when he had finished. An enormous wave of hope and joy would surge up in him, because it now looked easy, and he had no doubt at all that he could do it.

He never asked himself in any practical way how he was going to live while this was going on, where he was going to get the money for this gigantic adventure, and what he was going to do to make it possible. If he thought about it, it seemed to have no importance or reality whatever—he just dismissed it impatiently, or with a conviction that some old man would die and leave him a fortune, that he was going to pick up a purse containing hundreds of thousands of dollars while walking in the Fenway, and that the reward would be enough to keep him going, or that a beautiful and rich young widow, true-hearted, tender, loving, and voluptuous, who had carrot-colored hair, little freckles on her face, a snub nose and luminous gray-green eyes with something wicked, yet loving and faithful in them, and one gold filling in her solid little teeth, was going to fall in love with him, marry him, and be forever true and faithful to him while he went reading, eating, drinking, whoring, and devouring his way around the world; or finally that he would write a book or play every year or so, which would be a great success, and yield him fifteen or twenty thousand dollars at a crack. Thus, he went storming away at the whole earth about him, sometimes mad with despair, weariness, and bewilderment; and sometimes wild with a jubilant and exultant joy and certitude as the conviction came to him that everything would happen as he wished. Then at night he would hear the vast sounds and silence of the earth and of the city, he would begin to think of the dark sleeping earth and of the continent of night, until it seemed to him it all was spread before him like a map—rivers, plains, and mountains and 10,000 sleeping towns; it seemed to him that he saw everything at once.

1935

1896 ~ *John Dos Passos* ~ —

JOHN DOS PASSOS was born in Chicago and educated at Harvard (1912–1916). He traveled in Spain to study architecture, while in Europe enlisted in the Volunteer Ambulance Service and served in that and the Red Cross and the American Medical Corps. His first novel, *One Man's Initiation—1917* (1920), is a crude autobiographical comment upon war experiences. His next novel, *Three Soldiers* (1921), is also about the war. *Streets of Night* (1923) is a novel about adolescent intellectuals.

Dos Passos' real contribution to American fiction began with the publication of *Manhattan Transfer* (1925). In this novel of New York City from 1890 to 1925, he begins the use of his "collectivist" technique: the book is a collection of fragmentary impressions of and bits of information about a number of New York characters chosen from various classes. There is no settled progression, only biographical and sociological data; and the novel holds to a kind of sociological objectivity, designed to underplay significance and dimension. The newspaperman, Jimmy Herf, may be an exception to this impartiality of treatment; if he is, as so many critics insist, he escapes it by the narrowest of margins. The object is to give information, to provide flesh-and-blood statistics for a sociology and an economics of modern industrial civilization as it is seen in the largest urban monster created by it.

The celebrated and remarkable trilogy began with *42nd Parallel* (1930), continued with *1919* (1932), and was completed in *The Big Money* (1936). Since then, Dos Passos has published *Adventures of a Young Man* (1939), a story of a young radical and his unhappiness under leftist discipline; and *Number One* (1943), a novel on the Huey Long theme, describing power politics in the South. In addition, there have been three nonfiction books, collections of essays (*In All Countries*, 1934; *Journeys between Wars*, 1938) and a commentary upon America's political inheritance (*The Ground We Stand On*, 1941).

The trilogy of novels is Dos Passos' most extreme attempt to reform and reshape the structure of the novel. *Manhattan Transfer* tried to reflect an unsettled world, what might almost be called social chaos. The three novels which followed extend and elaborate upon the form of the earlier one. They are composed of many individual biographies of persons drawn from several classes and covering the United States and its political fortunes from the beginning of the twentieth century to the end of the 1920's. Individual biographical sketches of American heroes and rascals are provided at convenient places; the "Newsreel" offers fragments of appropriate news at each stage of the accumulated narratives; "The Camera Eye" is pointed at Dos Passos himself and provides a series of views of the author's life in terms of the events narrated. The total effect is that of attempted objectivity—a vast collection of interrelated biographical and social data—which is quite definitely slanted to provide an expression of its author's view, and is also arranged to demonstrate over and over again a thesis concerning the overwhelming domination of American life by materialism, the desire above all and at all costs to gain financial security, and, beyond that, affluence. Dos Passos' favorites among the biographies (Thorstein Veblen, Eugene Debs, Robert M. LaFollette, Sr.) underscore this thesis; the objects of his satire (Carnegie, Rockefeller, Hearst, Frederick Taylor, author of speed-ups in assembly-line production) emphasize it further. And the substance of the trilogy, what these devices are designed merely to highlight, is a series of portraits of the consequences for the American personality of American materialism. Only a few characters escape the vulgarity, the selfishness, or the neuroticism which seems the end of man and woman. And the novels do not by any means try to demonstrate a leftist thesis; they are quite free of the Marxist intellectual gymnastics which were practiced by Dos Passos' contemporaries. The Communists are no more intelligent in the trilogy, and they are in many ways more pathetic.

When considered in terms other than the rather ingenious devices Dos Passos has used, his fiction seems shallow and his characters lacking in dimension, as though they were all riding along an immense assembly line of sociological proof. Their behavior is almost entirely external; little attention is paid to motive beyond the obvious, and they are made to act hastily and frantically. Only the camera eye gets beneath the surface, and it not very far. Occasionally, as in the case of Charley Anderson, sheer persistence and accumulation of detail make a character interesting beyond his role as demonstration; at times also, the humorous parody of American life (a result of extravagance in illustration) creates notable effects. *U.S.A.* (as the trilogy was eventually called) is a monument to a persistent strategy and painstaking labor. It is interesting as social document and, structurally, as formal experiment.

Dos Passos' novels are *One Man's Initiation—1917* (1920); *Three Soldiers* (1921); *Streets of Night* (1923); *Manhattan Transfer* (1925); *The 42nd Parallel* (1930); *1919* (1932); *The Big Money* (1936); these last three published as *U.S.A.* in 1938; *Adventures of a Young Man* (1939); *Number One* (1943); *The Grand Design* (1949). His poems appeared in *Eight Harvard Poets* (1917) and in *A Pushcart at the Curb* (1922). Plays include *The Garbage Man* (1926); *Airways, Inc.* (1928); and *Three Plays* (1934; the two above plus *Fortune Heights*). Books of travel and social comment are *Rosinante to the Road Again* (1922); *Orient Express* (1927); *In All Countries* (1934); *Journeys between Wars* (1938). *The Ground We Stand On* (1941) is a study of American political principles and their historical sources. Biographical and critical comment is found in Pelham Edgar, *The Art of the Novel from 1700 to the Present Time* (1933); Harlan Hatcher, *Creating the Modern American Novel* (1935); J. W. Beach, *American Fiction, 1920–1940* (1941); Alfred Kazin, *On Native Grounds* (1942); Maxwell Geismar, *Writers in Crisis* (1942); George Snell, *The Shapers of American Fiction* (1947); Alan Calmer, "John Dos Passos," *Sewanee Review*, July–Sept., 1932; R. H. Footman, "John Dos Passos," *Sewanee Review*, July, 1939; Margaret Marshall, "John Dos Passos," *Nation*, Jan. 6, 1940; Milton Rugoff, "Dos Passos, Novelist of Our Time," *Sewanee Review*, Oct.–Dec., 1941; Delmore Schwartz, "John Dos Passos and the Whole Truth," *Southern Review*, Oct., 1938. For other titles, see Millett, *Contemporary American Authors* (1940), and Leary, *Articles on American Literature Appearing in Current Periodicals, 1920–1945* (1947).

From U.S.A.

THE PROLOGUE

THE young man walks fast by himself through the crowd that thins into the night streets; feet are tired from hours of walking; eyes greedy for warm curve of faces, answering flicker of eyes, the set of a head, the lift of a shoulder, the way hands spread and clench; blood tingles with wants; mind is a beehive of hopes buzzing and stinging; muscles ache for the knowledge of jobs, for the roadmender's pick and shovel work, the fisherman's knack with a hook when he hauls on the slithery net from the rail of the lurching trawler, the swing of the bridgeman's arm as he slings down the whitehot rivet, the engineer's slow grip wise on the throttle, the dirtfarmer's use of his whole body when, whoaing the mules, he yanks the plow from the furrow. The young man walks by himself searching through the crowd with greedy eyes, greedy ears taut to hear, by himself, alone.

The streets are empty. People have packed into subways, climbed into streetcars and buses; in the stations they've scampered for suburban trains; they've filtered into lodgings and tenements, gone up in elevators into apartmenthouses. In a showwindow two sallow windowdressers in their shirtsleeves are bringing out a dummy girl in a red evening dress, at a corner welders in masks lean into sheets of blue flame repairing a cartrack, a few drunk bums shamble along, a sad streetwalker fidgets under an arclight. From the river comes the deep rumbling whistle of a steamboat leaving dock. A tug hoots far away.

The young man walks by himself, fast but not fast enough, far but not far enough (faces slide out of sight, talk trails into tattered scraps, footsteps tap fainter in alleys); he must catch the last subway, the streetcar, the bus, run up the gangplanks of all the steamboats, register at all the hotels, work in the cities, answer the wantads, learn the trades, take up the jobs, live in all the boardinghouses, sleep in all the beds. One bed is not enough, one job is not enough, one life is not enough. At night, head swimming with wants, he walks by himself alone.

No job, no woman, no house, no city.

Only the ears busy to catch the speech are not alone; the ears are caught tight, linked tight by the tendrils of phrased words, the

turn of a joke, the singsong fade of a story,
the gruff fall of a sentence; linking tendrils of
speech twine through the city blocks, spread
over pavements, grow out along broad parked
avenues, speed with the trucks leaving on their
long night runs over roaring highways, whisper down sandy byroads past wornout farms,
joining up cities and fillingstations, round-
houses, steamboats, planes groping along airways; words call out on mountain pastures, 10
drift slow down rivers widening to the sea and
the hushed beaches.

It was not in the long walks through jostling
crowds at night that he was less alone, or in
the training camp at Allentown, or in the day
on the docks at Seattle, or in the empty reek
of Washington City hot boyhood summer
nights, or in the meal on Market Street, or in
the swim off the red rocks at San Diego, or in
the bed full of fleas in New Orleans, or in the 20
cold razorwind off the lake, or in the gray faces
trembling in the grind of gears in the street
under Michigan Avenue, or in the smokers of
limited expresstrains, or walking across country, or riding up the dry mountain canyons,
or the night without a sleepingbag among
frozen beartracks in the Yellowstone, or ca-
noeing Sundays on the Quinnipiac;

but in his mother's words telling about
longago, in his father's telling about when I 30
was a boy, in the kidding stories of uncles, in
the lies the kids told at school, the hired man's
yarns, the tall tales the doughboys told after
taps;

it was the speech that clung to the ears, the
link that tingled in the blood; U.S.A.

U.S.A. is the slice of a continent. U.S.A.
is a group of holding companies, some aggre-
gations of trade unions, a set of laws bound in
calf, a radio network, a chain of moving pic- 40
ture theatres, a column of stockquotations
rubbed out and written in by a Western Union
boy on a blackboard, a publiclibrary full of
old newspapers and dogeared historybooks
with protests scrawled on the margins in pencil. U.S.A. is the world's greatest rivervalley
fringed with mountains and hills, U.S.A. is a
set of bigmouthed officials with too many
bankaccounts. U.S.A. is a lot of men buried
in their uniforms in Arlington Cemetery. 50
U.S.A. is the letters at the end of an address

when you are away from home. But mostly
U.S.A. is the speech of the people.

1938

From THE 42nd PARALLEL

LOVER OF MANKIND

DEBS was a railroad man, born in a weather-
boarded shack at Terre Haute.

He was one of ten children.

His father had come to America in a sailing-
ship in '49,

an Alsatian from Colmar; not much of a
moneymaker, fond of music and reading,

he gave his children a chance to finish public school and that was about all he could
do.

At fifteen Gene Debs was already working
as a machinist on the Indianapolis and Terre
Haute Railway.

He worked as locomotive fireman,

clerked in a store

joined the local of the Brotherhood of Locomotive Firemen, was elected secretary, traveled all over the country as organizer.

He was a tall shamblefooted man, had a sort
of gusty rhetoric that set on fire the railroad
workers in their pineboarded halls

made them want the world he wanted,

a world brothers might own

where everybody would split even:

*I am not a labor leader. I don't want you to
follow me or anyone else. If you are looking for
a Moses to lead you out of the capitalist wilderness you will stay right where you are. I would
not lead you into this promised land if I could,
because if I could lead you in, someone else would
lead you out.*

That was how he talked to freighthandlers
and gandywalkers, to firemen and switchmen
and engineers, telling them it wasn't enough
to organize the railroadmen, that all workers
must be organized, that all workers must be
organized in the workers' cooperative commonwealth.

Locomotive fireman on many a long night's
run,

under the smoke a fire burned him up,
burned in gusty words that beat in pineboarded
halls; he wanted his brothers to be free men.

That was what he saw in the crowd that met

him at the Old Wells Street Depot when he came out of jail after the Pullman strike,

those were the men that chalked up nine hundred thousand votes for him in nineteen twelve and scared the frockcoats and the tophats and diamonded hostesses at Saratoga Springs, Bar Harbor, Lake Geneva with the bogy of a socialist president.

But where were Gene Debs' brothers in nineteen eighteen when Woodrow Wilson had him locked up in Atlanta for speaking against war,

where were the big men fond of whisky and fond of each other, gentle rambling tellers of stories over bars in small towns in the Middle West,

quiet men who wanted a house with a porch to putter around and a fat wife to cook for them, a few drinks and cigars, a garden to dig in, cronies to chew the rag with

and wanted to work for it

and others to work for it;

where were the locomotive firemen and engineers when they hustled him off to Atlanta Penitentiary?

And they brought him back to die in Terre Haute

to sit on his porch in a rocker with a cigar in his mouth,

beside him American Beauty roses his wife fixed in a bowl;

and the people of Terre Haute and the people in Indiana and the people of the Middle West were fond of him and afraid of him and thought of him as an old kindly uncle who loved them, and wanted to be with him and to have him give them candy,

but they were afraid of him as if he had contracted a social disease, syphilis or leprosy, and thought it was too bad,

but on account of the flag

and prosperity

and making the world safe for democracy,

they were afraid to be with him,

or to think much about him for fear they might believe him;

for he said:

While there is a lower class I am of it, while there is a criminal class I am of it, while there is a soul in prison I am not free.

1930

From THE BIG MONEY

THE AMERICAN PLAN

FREDERICK Winslow Taylor (they called him Speedy Taylor in the shop) was born in Germantown, Pennsylvania, the year of Buchanan's election. His father was a lawyer, his mother came from a family of New Bedford whalers; she was a great reader of Emerson, belonged to the Unitarian Church and the Browning Society. She was a fervent abolitionist and believed in democratic manners; she was a housekeeper of the old school, kept everybody busy from dawn till dark. She laid down the rules of conduct:

selfrespect, selfreliance, selfcontrol and a cold long head for figures.

But she wanted her children to appreciate the finer things so she took them abroad for three years on the Continent, showed them cathedrals, grand opera, Roman pediments, the old masters under their brown varnish in their great frames of tarnished gilt.

Later Fred Taylor was impatient of these wasted years, stamped out of the room when people talked about the finer things; he was a testy youngster, fond of practical jokes and a great hand at rigging up contraptions and devices.

At Exeter he was head of his class and captain of the ballteam, the first man to pitch overhand. (When umpires complained that overhand pitching wasn't in the rules of the game, he answered that it got results.)

As a boy he had nightmares, going to bed was horrible for him; he thought they came from sleeping on his back. He made himself a leather harness with wooden pegs that stuck into his flesh when he turned over. When he was grown he slept in a chair or in bed in a sitting position propped up with pillows. All his life he suffered from sleeplessness.

He was a crackerjack tennisplayer. In 1881, with his friend Clark, he won the National Doubles Championship. (He used a spoonshaped racket of his own design.)

At school he broke down from overwork, his eyes went back on him. The doctor suggested manual labor. So instead of going to

Harvard he went into the machineshop of a small pumpmanufacturing concern, owned by a friend of the family's, to learn the trade of patternmaker and machinist. He learned to handle a lathe and to dress and cuss like a workingman.

Fred Taylor never smoked tobacco or drank liquor or used tea or coffee; he couldn't understand why his fellowmechanics wanted to go on sprees and get drunk and raise Cain Saturday nights. He lived at home, when he wasn't reading technical books he'd play parts in amateur theatricals or step up to the piano in the evening and sing a good tenor in *A Warrior Bold* or *A Spanish Cavalier*.

He served his first year's apprenticeship in the machineshop without pay; the next two years he made a dollar and a half a week, the last year two dollars.

Pennsylvania was getting rich off iron and coal. When he was twentytwo, Fred Taylor went to work at the Midvale Iron Works. At first he had to take a clerical job, but he hated that and went to work with a shovel. At last he got them to put him on a lathe. He was a good machinist, he worked ten hours a day and in the evenings followed an engineering course at Stevens. In six years he rose from machinist's helper to keeper of toolcribs to gangboss to foreman to mastermechanic in charge of repairs to chief draftsman and director of research to chief engineer of the Midvale Plant.

The early years he was a machinist with the other machinists in the shop, cussed and joked and worked with the rest of them, soldiered on the job when they did. Mustn't give the boss more than his money's worth. But when he got to be foreman he was on the management's side of the fence, *gathering in on the part of those on the management's side all the great mass of traditional knowledge which in the past has been in the heads of the workmen and in the physical skill and knack of the workman.* He couldn't stand to see an idle lathe or an idle man.

Production went to his head and thrilled his sleepless nerves like liquor or women on a Saturday night. He never loafed and he'd be damned if anybody else would. Production was an itch under his skin.

He lost his friends in the shop; they called him niggerdriver. He was a stockily built man with a temper and a short tongue.

I was a young man in years but I give you my word I was a great deal older than I am now, what with the worry, meanness and contemptibleness of the whole damn thing. It's a horrid life for any man to live not being able to look any workman in the face without seeing hostility there, and a feeling that every man around you is your virtual enemy.

That was the beginning of the **Taylor** System of Scientific Management.

He was impatient of explanations, he didn't care whose hide he took off in enforcing the laws he believed inherent in the industrial process.

When starting an experiment in any field question everything, question the very foundations upon which the art rests, question the simplest, the most selfevident, the most universally accepted facts; prove everything,

except the dominant Quaker Yankee (the New Bedford skippers were the greatest niggerdrivers on the whaling seas) rules of conduct. He boasted he'd never ask a workman to do anything he couldn't do.

He devised an improved steamhammer; he standardized tools and equipment, he filled the shop with college students with stop-watches and diagrams, tabulating, standardizing. *There's the right way of doing a thing and the wrong way of doing it; the right way means increased production, lower costs, higher wages, bigger profits:* the American plan.

He broke up the foreman's job into separate functions, speedbosses, gangbosses, timestudy men, orderofwork men.

The skilled mechanics were too stubborn for him, what he wanted was a plain handyman who'd do what he was told. If he was a firstclass man and did firstclass work Taylor was willing to let him have firstclass pay; that's where he began to get into trouble with the owners.

At thirtyfour he married and left Midvale and took a flyer for the big money in connection with a pulpmill started in Maine by some admirals and political friends of Grover Cleveland's;

the panic of '93 made hash of that enterprise,
so Taylor invented for himself the job of Consulting Engineer in Management and began to build up a fortune by careful investments.

The first paper he read before the American Society of Mechanical Engineers was anything but a success, they said he was crazy. *I have found*, he wrote in 1909, *that any improvement is not only opposed but aggressively and bitterly opposed by the majority of men.*

He was called in by Bethlehem Steel. It was in Bethlehem he made his famous experiments with handling pigiron; he taught a Dutchman name Schmidt to handle fortyseven tons instead of twelve and a half tons of pigiron a day and got Schmidt to admit he was as good as ever at the end of the day.

He was a crank about shovels, every job had to have a shovel of the right weight and size for that job alone; every job had to have a man of the right weight and size for that job alone; but when he began to pay his men in proportion to the increased efficiency of their work,

the owners who were a lot of greedy smalleyed Dutchmen began to raise Hail Columbia;
when Schwab bought Bethlehem Steel in 1901
Fred Taylor
inventor of efficiency
who had doubled the production of the stampingmill by speeding up the main lines of shafting from ninetysix to twohundred and twentyfive revolutions a minute
was unceremoniously fired.

After that Fred Taylor always said he couldn't afford to work for money.

He took to playing golf (using golfclubs of his own design), doping out methods for transplanting huge boxtrees into the garden of his home.

At Boxly in Germantown he kept open house for engineers, factorymanagers, industrialists;

he wrote papers,
lectured,
appeared before a congressional committee,
everywhere preached the virtues of scientific management and the Barth slide rule, the

cutting down of waste and idleness, the substitution for skilled mechanics of the plain handyman (like Schmidt the pigiron handler) who'd move as he was told

and work by the piece:
production;
more steel rails more bicycles more spools of thread more armorplate for battleships more bedpans more barbedwire more needles more lightningrods more ballbearings more dollarbills;

(the old Quaker families of Germantown were growing rich, the Pennsylvania millionaires were breeding billionaires out of iron and coal)

production would make every firstclass American rich who was willing to work at piecework and not drink or raise Cain or think or stand mooning at his lathe.

Thrifty Schmidt the pigiron handler can invest his money and get to be an owner like Schwab and the rest of the greedy smalleyed Dutchmen and cultivate a taste for Bach and have hundredyearold boxtrees in his garden at Bethlehem or Germantown or Chestnut Hill,

and lay down the rules of conduct;
the American plan.

But Fred Taylor never saw the working of the American plan;

in 1915 he went to the hospital in Philadelphia suffering from a breakdown.

Pneumonia developed; the nightnurse heard him winding his watch;

on the morning of his fiftyninth birthday, when the nurse went into his room to look at him at fourthirty,

he was dead with his watch in his hand.

1936

NEWSREEL LXVI

HOLMES DENIES STAY

A better world's in birth

Tiny Wasps Imported from Korea In Battle
To Death With Asiatic Beetle

BOY CARRIED MILE DOWN SEWER; SHOT OUT
ALIVE

CHICAGO BARS MEETINGS

For justice thunders condemnation
Washington Keeps Eye On Radicals

Arise rejected of the earth
PARIS BRUSSELS MOSCOW GENEVA ADD THEIR
VOICES

It is the final conflict
Let each stand in his place
Geologist Lost in Cave Six Days

The International Party

SACCO AND VANZETTI MUST DIE

Shall be the human race.

Much I thought of you when I was lying in the death house — the singing, the kind tender voices of the children from the playground where there was all the life and the joy of liberty — just one step from the wall that contains the buried agony of three buried souls. It would remind me so often of you and of your sister and I wish I could see you every moment, but I feel better that you will not come to the death house so that you could not see the horrible picture of three living in agony waiting to be electrocuted.

1936

THE CAMERA EYE (50)

they have clubbed us off the streets they are stronger they are rich they hire and fire the politicians the newspapereditors the old judges the small men with reputations the college-presidents the wardheelers (listen business men collegepresidents judges America will not forget her betrayers) they hire the men with guns the uniforms the policecars the patrol wagons

all right you have won you will kill the brave men our friends tonight

there is nothing left to do we are beaten we the beaten crowd together in these old dingy schoolrooms on Salem Street shuffle up and down the gritty creaking stairs sit hunched with bowed heads on benches and hear the old words of the haters of oppression made new in sweat and agony tonight

our work is over the scribbled phrases the nights typing releases the smell of the print-shop the sharp reek of newprinted leaflets the rush for Western Union stringing words into wires the search for stinging words to make you feel who are your oppressors America

America our nation has been beaten by strangers who have turned our language inside out who have taken the clean words our fathers spoke and made them slimy and foul

their hired men sit on the judge's bench they sit back with their feet on the tables under the dome of the State House they are ignorant of our beliefs they have the dollars the guns the armed forces the powerplants

they have built the electricchair and hired the executioner to throw the switch

all right we are two nations

America our nation has been beaten by strangers who have bought the laws and fenced off the meadows and cut down the woods for pulp and turned our pleasant cities into slums and sweated the wealth out of our people and when they want to they hire the executioner to throw the switch

but do they know that the old words of the immigrants are being renewed in blood and agony tonight do they know that the old American speech of the haters of oppression is new tonight in the mouth of an old woman from Pittsburgh of a husky boilermaker from Frisco who hopped freights clear from the Coast to come here in the mouth of a Back Bay socialworker in the mouth of an Italian printer of a hobo from Arkansas the language of the beaten nation is not forgotten in our ears tonight

the men in the death house made the old words new before they died

If it had not been for these things, I might have lived out my life talking at streetcorners to scorning men. I might have died unknown, unmarked, a failure. This is our career and our triumph. Never in our full life can we hope to do such work for tolerance, for justice, for man's understanding of man as how we do by an accident.

now their work is over the immigrants haters of oppression lie quiet in black suits in the little undertaking parlor in the North End the city is quiet the men of the conquering nation are not to be seen on the streets

they have won why are they scared to be

seen on the streets? on the streets you see only the downcast faces of the beaten the streets belong to the beaten nation all the way to the cemetery where the bodies of the immigrants are to be burned we line the curbs in the driz-

zling rain we crowd the wet sidewalks elbow to elbow silent pale looking with scared eyes at the coffins

    we stand defeated America

1936

1902 ~ *John Steinbeck* ~ ─

BORN IN Salinas, California, Steinbeck attended California schools and spent some years (1919–1925) as a special student at Stanford University, leaving without a degree. He went to New York on a freight boat, worked in New York City for a while, then returned to California. As a winter watchman in the Sierra mountains, Steinbeck spent the very considerable leisure time in writing his first novel, *The Cup of Gold*, which was published in 1929 but caused no stir in literary circles and made no money. The next two novels, *The Pastures of Heaven* (1932) and *To a God Unknown* (1933), also failed to bring him either fame or fortune.

The publication of *Tortilla Flat*, in 1935, brought Steinbeck popularity, which increased steadily with the subsequent appearance of *In Dubious Battle* (1936) and *Of Mice and Men* (1937), and reached its peak with the publication of *The Grapes of Wrath* (1939). Steinbeck also wrote a considerable number of short stories, of which the collection *The Long Valley* (1938) and the story *The Red Pony* (first published in 1937 and often reprinted) are the best known.

Steinbeck's principal concern is for "the little man"—the exploited laborer, the independent, the paisano of the hills near Monterey. Though he was taken up by the leftists in the 1930's as a champion of the proletariat, *In Dubious Battle* is a strike novel not quite appropriate to the Marxist cause. It is the most objective and the most penetrating of the many leftwing novels which were produced in the decade. The characters of Mac, Jim, and Doc represent respectively the hard, practical, Communist organizer, the enthusiastic and eager neophyte who eventually goes beyond his mentor in self-sacrifice, and the objective scientist who looks upon strikes as another activity of man in the mass, available for investigation. "Why do you hang around with us if you aren't for us?" Mac asks Doc in one of the several conversations Steinbeck provides for purposes of ideological statement. "I want to *see*," Doc answers, and goes on to explain: "A man in a group isn't himself at all, he's a cell in an organism that isn't like him any more than the cells in your body are like you."

However much Steinbeck shared Doc's views, his sponsorship of the workers and of the "little man" generally continued to dominate his writings. *Of Mice and Men* is a highly contrived, theatrically planned short novel about the migrant workers in California wheat fields. His greatest success, *Grapes of Wrath*, describes the travels of the Joad family, from drouth-stricken Oklahoma to vigilante and police-controlled California. Throughout, the simplest and crudest gestures of these dispossessed people are endowed with a dignity and purpose which suggest Steinbeck's supreme confidence in them. "We ain't gonna die out," says Ma Joad to her son, Tom. "People is goin' on—changin' a little, maybe, but goin' right on." This speech suggests another affirmative statement, by Carl Sandburg, who in his *The People, Yes* expressed in poetry what Steinbeck attempted to say in his fiction:

> The people will live on.
> The learning and blundering people will live on.
>   . . . . .
> The people so peculiar in renewal and comeback,
> You can't laugh off their capacity to take it.
> The mammoth rests between his cyclonic dramas.

Steinbeck's major themes are thus concerned with the people who have been abused and exploited, and at crucial times deprived of their land or of their means of livelihood. He is especially interested in the simple, naïve souls—small children, old men, the feeble-minded (as in *The Pastures of Heaven* and *Of Mice and Men*) and quaint, clever, and eccentric persons who elude social responsibility and thus make a gesture of protest against organized society. *Tortilla Flat, Cannery Row* (1945), and several of the short stories play up these characters in a manner reminiscent of the treatment Saroyan gives their cousins in his plays.

Steinbeck's literary manner varies from the hard kind of understatement and simple style which is Hemingway's contribution, to the semi-poetic, panoramic sweep of the inter-chapters of *Grapes of Wrath*. This novel is a curious mixture of simple, effective writing and the strangely didactic, pseudo-epic style of these inter-chapters. The success of the book was at least partly due to the immediate need for a statement such as it provided concerning the vast and obviously oppressive inequalities existing in the national economy. His latest books have steadily declined in effectiveness.

Steinbeck's novels are *Cup of Gold, A Life of Henry Morgan, Buccaneer* (1929); *The Pastures of Heaven* (1932); *To a God Unknown* (1933); *Tortilla Flat* (1935); *In Dubious Battle* (1936); *Of Mice and Men* (1937); *The Grapes of Wrath* (1939); *The Moon Is Down* (1943); *The Wayward Bus* (1947); *The Pearl* (1947). Short stories include *Saint Katy the Virgin* (1936); *The Red Pony* (1937); *The Long Valley* (1938). He has also written a dramatic version of *Of Mice and Men* (1937), and three books of travel and social comment, *The Forgotten Village* (1941), *Sea of Cortez* (with Edward F. Ricketts) (1941), and *A Russian Journal* (with pictures by Robert Capa) (1948). Harry Thornton Moore's *The Novels of John Steinbeck* (1939) is a full-length critical study. See also Edmund Wilson, *The Boys in the Back Room* (1941); J. W. Beach, *American Fiction 1920–1940* (1941); Alfred Kazin, *On Native Grounds* (1942); Maxwell Geismar, *Writers in Crisis* (1942);

Harry Slochower, *No Voice Is Wholly Lost* (1945); Leo Gurko, *The Angry Decade* (1947); Lewis Gannett, Introduction to *The Viking Portable Steinbeck* (1946); Burton Rascoe, "John Steinbeck," *English Journal*, Mar., 1938; T. K. Whipple, "Steinbeck Through a Glass, Though Brightly," *New Republic*, Oct. 12, 1938; F. I. Carpenter, "The Philosophical Joads," *College English*, Jan., 1941; L. R. Gibbs, "John Steinbeck, Moralist," *Antioch Review*, Summer, 1942; C. E. Jones, "Proletarian Writing and John Steinbeck," *Sewanee Review*, Oct., 1940; Frederick Bracher, "Steinbeck and the Biological View of Man," *The Pacific Spectator*, Winter, 1948. For other titles, see Millett, *Contemporary American Authors* (1940), and Leary, *Articles on American Literature Appearing in Current Periodicals, 1920–1945* (1947).

THE CHRYSANTHEMUMS

THE high gray-flannel fog of winter closed the Salinas Valley from the sky and from all the rest of the world. On every side it sat like a lid on the mountains and made of the great valley a closed pot. On the broad, level land floor the gang plows bit deep and left the black earth shining like metal where the shares had cut. On the foothill ranches across the Salinas River the yellow stubble fields seemed to be bathed in pale cold sunshine; but there was no sunshine in the valley now in December. The thick willow scrub along the river flamed with sharp and positive yellow leaves.

It was a time of quiet and of waiting. The air was cold and tender. A light wind blew up from the southwest so that the farmers were mildly hopeful of a good rain before long; but fog and rain do not go together.

Across the river, on Henry Allen's foothill ranch there was little work to be done, for the hay was cut and stored and the orchards were plowed up to receive the rain deeply when it should come. The cattle on the higher slopes were becoming shaggy and rough-coated.

Elisa Allen, working in her flower garden, looked down across the yard and saw Henry, her husband, talking to two men in business suits. The three of them stood by the tractor shed, each man with one foot on the side of the Little Fordson. They smoked cigarettes and studied the machine as they talked.

Elisa watched them for a moment and then went back to her work. She was thirty-five. Her face was lean and strong and her eyes were as clear as water. Her figure looked blocked and heavy in her gardening costume, a man's black hat pulled low down over her eyes, clodhopper shoes, a figured print dress almost completely covered by a big corduroy apron with four big pockets to hold the snips, the trowel and scratcher, the seeds and the knife she worked with. She wore heavy leather gloves to protect her hands while she worked.

She was cutting down the old year's chrysanthemum stalks with a pair of short and powerful scissors. She looked down toward the men by the tractor shed now and then. Her face was eager and mature and handsome; even her work with the scissors was overeager, overpowerful. The chrysanthemum stems seemed too small and easy for her energy.

She brushed a cloud of hair out of her eyes with the back of her glove, and left a smudge of earth on her cheek in doing it. Behind her stood the neat white farmhouse with red geraniums close-banked round it as high as the windows. It was a hard-swept-looking little house, with hard-polished windows, and a clean mat on the front steps.

Elisa cast another glance toward the tractor shed. The stranger men were getting into their Ford coupé. She took off a glove and put her strong fingers down into the forest of new green chrysanthemum sprouts that were growing round the old roots. She spread the leaves and looked down among the close-growing stems. No aphids were there, no sow bugs nor snails nor cutworms. Her terrier fingers destroyed such pests before they could get started.

Elisa started at the sound of her husband's voice. He had come near quietly and he leaned over the wire fence that protected her flower garden from cattle and dogs and chickens.

"At it again," he said. "You've got a strong new crop coming."

Elisa straightened her back and pulled on

the gardening glove again. "Yes. They'll be strong this coming year." In her tone and on her face there was a little smugness.

"You've got a gift with things," Henry observed. "Some of those yellow chrysanthemums you had last year were ten inches across. I wish you'd work out in the orchard and raise some apples that big."

Her eyes sharpened. "Maybe I could do it too. I've a gift with things all right. My mother had it. She could stick anything in the ground and make it grow. She said it was having planter's hands that knew how to do it."

"Well, it sure works with flowers," he said.

"Henry, who were those men you were talking to?"

"Why, sure, that's what I came to tell you. They were from the Western Meat Company. I sold those thirty head of three-year-old steers. Got nearly my own price too."

"Good," she said. "Good for you."

"And I thought," he continued, "I thought how it's Saturday afternoon, and we might go into Salinas for dinner at a restaurant and then to a picture show—to celebrate, you see."

"Good," she repeated. "Oh, yes. That will be good."

Henry put on his joking tone. "There's fights to-night. How'd you like to go to the fights?"

"Oh, no," she said breathlessly. "No, I wouldn't like fights."

"Just fooling, Elisa. We'll go to a movie. Let's see. It's two now. I'm going to take Scotty and bring down those steers from the hill. It'll take us maybe two hours. We'll go in town about five and have dinner at the Cominos Hotel. Like that?"

"Of course I'll like it. It's good to eat away from home."

"All right, then. I'll go get up a couple of horses."

She said, "I'll have plenty of time to transplant some of these sets, I guess."

She heard her husband calling Scotty down by the barn. And a little later she saw the two men ride up the pale-yellow hillside in search of the steers.

There was a little square sandy bed kept for rooting the chrysanthemums. With her trowel she turned the soil over and over and smoothed it and patted it firm. Then she dug ten parallel trenches to receive the sets. Back at the chrysanthemum bed she pulled out the little crisp shoots, trimmed off the leaves of each one with her scissors, and laid it on a small orderly pile.

A squeak of wheels and plod of hoofs came from the road. Elisa looked up. The country road ran along the dense bank of willows and cottonwoods that bordered the river, and up this road came a curious vehicle, curiously drawn. It was an old springwagon, with a round canvas top on it like the cover of a prairie schooner. It was drawn by an old bay horse and a little gray-and-white burro. A big stubble-bearded man sat between the cover flaps and drove the crawling team. Underneath the wagon, between the hind wheels, a lean and rangy mongrel dog walked sedately. Words were painted on the canvas in clumsy, crooked letters. "Pots, pans, knives, scissors, lawn mowers, Fixed." Two rows of articles, and the triumphantly definitive "Fixed" below. The black paint had run down in little sharp points beneath each letter.

Elisa, squatting on the ground, watched to see the crazy loose-jointed wagon pass by. But it didn't pass. It turned into the farm road in front of her house, crooked old wheels skirling and squeaking. The rangy dog darted from beneath the wheels and ran ahead. Instantly the two ranch shepherds flew out at him. Then all three stopped, and with stiff and quivering tails, with taut straight legs, with ambassadorial dignity, they slowly circled, sniffing daintily. The caravan pulled up to Elisa's wire fence and stopped. Now the newcomer dog, feeling outnumbered, lowered his tail and retired under the wagon with raised hackles and bared teeth.

That man on the wagon seat called out, "That's a bad dog in a fight when he gets started."

Elisa laughed. "I see he is. How soon does he generally get started?"

The man caught up her laughter and echoed it heartily. "Sometimes not for weeks and weeks," he said. He climbed stiffly down over the wheel. The horse and the donkey drooped like unwatered flowers.

Elisa saw that he was a very big man. Although his hair and beard were graying, he did not look old. His worn black suit was wrinkled and spotted with grease. The laughter had disappeared from his face and eyes the moment his laughing voice ceased. His eyes were dark and they were full of the brooding that gets in the eyes of teamsters and of sailors. The calloused hands he rested on the fence were cracked, and every crack was a black line. He took off his battered hat.

"I'm off my general road, ma'am," he said. "Does this dirt road cut over across the river to the Los Angeles highway?"

Elisa stood up and shoved the thick scissors in her apron pocket. "Well, yes, it does, but it winds around and then fords the river. I don't think your team could pull through the sand."

He replied with some asperity, "It might surprise you what them beasts can pull through."

"When they get started?" she asked.

He smiled for a second. "Yes. When they get started."

"Well," said Elisa. "I think you'll save time if you go back to the Salinas road and pick up the highway there."

He drew a big finger down the chicken wire and made it sing. "I ain't in any hurry, ma'am. I go from Seattle to San Diego and back every year. Takes all my time. About six months each way. I aim to follow nice weather."

Elisa took off her gloves and stuffed them in the apron pocket with the scissors. She touched the under edge of her man's hat, searching for fugitive hairs. "That sounds like a nice kind of a way to live," she said.

He leaned confidentially over the fence. "Maybe you noticed the writing on my wagon. I mend pots and sharpen knives and scissors. You got any of them things to do?"

"Oh, no," she said quickly. "Nothing like that." Her eyes hardened with resistance.

"Scissors is the worst thing," he explained. "Most people just ruin scissors trying to sharpen 'em, but I know how. I got a special tool. It's a little bobbit kind of thing and patented. But it sure does the trick."

"No. My scissors are all sharp."

"All right, then. Take a pot," he continued earnestly, "a bent pot or a pot with a hole. I can make it like new so you don't have to buy no new ones. That's a saving for you."

"No," she said shortly. "I tell you I have nothing like that for you to do."

His face fell to an exaggerated sadness. His voice took on a whining undertone. "I ain't had a thing to do to-day. Maybe I won't have no supper to-night. You see I'm off my regular road. I know folks on the highway clear from Seattle to San Diego. They save their things for me to sharpen up because they know I do it so good and save them money."

"I'm sorry," Elisa said irritably. "I haven't anything for you to do."

His eyes left her face and fell to searching the ground. They roamed about until they came to the chrysanthemum bed where she had been working. "What's them plants, ma'am?"

The irritation and resistance melted from Elisa's face. "Oh, those are chrysanthemums, giant whites and yellows. I raise them every year, bigger than anybody around here."

"Kind of a long-stemmed flower? Looks like a quick puff of colored smoke?" he asked.

"That's it. What a nice way to describe them."

"They smell kind of nasty till you get used to them," he said.

"It's a good bitter smell," she retorted, "not nasty at all."

He changed his tone quickly. "I like the smell myself."

"I had ten-inch blooms this year," she said.

The man leaned farther over the fence. "Look. I know a lady down the road a piece has got the nicest garden you ever seen. Got nearly every kind of flower but no chrysanthemums. Last time I was mending a copper-bottom washtub for her (that's a hard job but I do it good), she said to me, 'If you ever run acrost some nice chrysanthemums I wish you'd try to get me a few seeds.' That's what she told me."

Elisa's eyes grew alert and eager. "She couldn't have known much about chrysanthemums. You *can* raise them from seed, but it's much easier to root the little sprouts you see there."

"Oh," he said. "I s'pose I can't take none to her, then."

"Why, yes, you can," Elisa cried. "I can put some in damp sand, and you can carry them right along with you. They'll take root in the pot if you keep them damp. And then she can transplant them."

"She'd sure like to have some, ma'am. You say they're nice ones?"

"Beautiful," she said. "Oh, beautiful." Her eyes shone. She tore off the battered hat and shook out her dark pretty hair. "I'll put them in a flower pot, and you can take them right with you. Come into the yard."

While the man came through the picket gate Elisa ran excitedly along the geranium-bordered path to the back of the house. And she returned carrying a big red flower pot. The gloves were forgotten now. She kneeled on the ground by the starting bed and dug up the sandy soil with her fingers and scooped it into the bright new flower pot. Then she picked up the little pile of shoots she had prepared. With her strong fingers she pressed them into the sand and tamped round them with her knuckles. The man stood over her. "I'll tell you what to do," she said. "You remember so you can tell the lady."

"Yes, I'll try to remember."

"Well, look. These will take root in about a month. Then she must set them out, about a foot apart in good rich earth like this, see?" She lifted a handful of dark soil for him to look at. "They'll grow fast and tall. Now remember this. In July tell her to cut them down, about eight inches from the ground."

"Before they bloom?" he asked.

"Yes, before they bloom." Her face was tight with eagerness. "They'll grow right up again. About the last of September the buds will start."

She stopped and seemed perplexed. "It's the budding that takes the most care," she said hesitantly. "I don't know how to tell you." She looked deep into his eyes searchingly. Her mouth opened a little, and she seemed to be listening. "I'll try to tell you," she said. "Did you ever hear of planting hands?"

"Can't say I have, ma'am."

"Well, I can only tell you what it feels like. It's when you're picking off the buds you don't want. Everything goes right down into your fingertips. You watch your fingers work.

They do it themselves. You can feel how it is. They pick and pick the buds. They never make a mistake. They're with the plant. Do you see? Your fingers and the plant. You can feel that, right up your arm. They know. They never make a mistake. You can feel it. When you're like that, you can't do anything wrong. Do you see that? Can you understand that?"

She was kneeling on the ground looking up at him. Her breast swelled passionately.

The man's eyes narrowed. He looked away self-consciously. "Maybe I know," he said. "Sometimes in the night in the wagon there ——"

Elisa's voice grew husky. She broke in on him. "I've never lived as you do, but I know what you mean. When the night is dark—the stars are sharp-pointed, and there's quiet. Why, you rise up and up!"

Kneeling there, her hand went out toward his legs in the greasy black trousers. Her hesitant fingers almost touched the cloth. Then her hand dropped to the ground.

He said, "It's nice, just like you say. Only when you don't have no dinner it ain't."

She stood up, then, very straight, and her face was ashamed. She held the flower pot out to him and placed it gently in his arms. "Here. Put it in your wagon, on the seat, where you can watch it. Maybe I can find something for you to do."

At the back of the house she dug in the can pile and found two old and battered aluminum saucepans. She carried them back and gave them to him. "Here, maybe you can fix these."

His manner changed. He became professional. "Good as new I can fix them." At the back of his wagon he set a little anvil, and out of an oily tool box dug a small machine hammer. Elisa came through the gate to watch him while he pounded out the dents in the kettles. His mouth grew sure and knowing. At a difficult part of the work he sucked his under-lip.

"You sleep right in the wagon?" Elisa asked.

"Right in the wagon, ma'am. Rain or shine I'm dry as a cow in there."

"It must be nice," she said. "It must be very nice. I wish women could do such things."

"It ain't the right kind of a life for a woman."

Her upper lip raised a little, showing her teeth. "How do you know? How can you tell?" she said.

"I don't know, ma'am," he protested. "Of course I don't know. Now here's your kettles, done. You don't have to buy no new ones."

"How much?"

"Oh, fifty cents'll do. I keep my prices down and my work good. That's why I have all them satisfied customers up and down the highway."

Elisa brought him a fifty-cent piece from the house and dropped it in his hand. "You might be surprised to have a rival sometime. I can sharpen scissors too. And I can beat the dents out of little pots. I could show you what a woman might do."

He put his hammer back in the oily box and shoved the little anvil out of sight. "It would be a lonely life for a woman, ma'am, and a scary life, too, with animals creeping under the wagon all night." He climbed over the singletree, steadying himself with a hand on the burro's white rump. He settled himself in the seat, picked up the lines. "Thank you kindly, ma'am," he said. "I'll do like you told me; I'll go back and catch the Salinas road."

"Mind," she called, "if you're long in getting there, keep the sand damp."

"Sand, ma'am—sand? Oh, sure. You mean around the chrysanthemums. Sure I will." He clucked his tongue. The beasts leaned luxuriously into their collars. The mongrel dog took his place between the back wheels. The wagon turned and crawled out the entrance road and back the way it had come, along the river.

Elisa stood in front of her wire fence watching the slow progress of the caravan. Her shoulders were straight, her head thrown back, her eyes half-closed, so that the scene came vaguely into them. Her lips moved silently, forming the words "Good-by—good-by." Then she whispered, "That's a bright direction. There's a glowing there." The sound of her whisper startled her. She shook herself free and looked about to see whether anyone had been listening. Only the dogs had heard. They lifted their heads toward her from their sleeping in the dust, and then stretched out their chins and settled asleep again. Elisa turned and ran hurriedly into the house.

In the kitchen she reached behind the stove and felt the water tank. It was full of hot water from the noonday cooking. In the bathroom she tore off her soiled clothes and flung them into the corner. And then she scrubbed herself with a little block of pumice, legs and thighs, loins and chest and arms, until her skin was scratched and red. When she had dried herself she stood in front of a mirror in her bedroom and looked at her body. She tightened her stomach and threw out her chest. She turned and looked over her shoulder at her back.

After a while she began to dress slowly. She put on her newest underclothing and her nicest stockings and the dress which was the symbol of her prettiness. She worked carefully on her hair, pencilled her eyebrows, and rouged her lips.

Before she was finished, she heard the little thunder of hoofs and the shouts of Henry and his helper as they drove the red steers into the corral. She heard the gate bang shut and set herself for Henry's arrival.

His step sounded on the porch. He entered the house, calling, "Elisa, where are you?"

"In my room, dressing. I'm not ready. There's hot water for your bath. Hurry up. It's getting late."

When she heard him splashing in the tub, Elisa laid his dark suit on the bed, and shirt and socks and tie beside it. She stood his polished shoes on the floor beside the bed. Then she went to the porch and sat primly and stiffly down. She looked toward the river road where the willow-line was still yellow with frosted leaves so that under the high gray fog they seemed a thin band of sunshine. This was the only color in the gray afternoon. She sat unmoving for a long time.

Henry came banging out of the door, shoving his tie inside his vest as he came. Elisa stiffened and her face grew tight. Henry stopped short and looked at her. "Why—why, Elisa. You look so nice!"

"Nice? You think I look nice? What do you mean by 'nice'?"

Henry blundered on. "I don't know. I mean you look different, strong and happy."

"I am strong? Yes, strong. What do you mean 'strong'?"

He looked bewildered. "You're playing

some kind of a game," he said helplessly. "It's a kind of a play. You look strong enough to break a calf over your knee, happy enough to eat it like a watermelon."

For a second she lost her rigidity. "Henry! Don't talk like that. You didn't know what you said." She grew complete again. "I am strong," she boasted. "I never knew before how strong."

Henry looked down toward the tractor shed, and when he brought his eyes back to her, they were his own again. "I'll get out the car. You can put on your coat while I'm starting."

Elisa went into the house. She heard him drive to the gate and idle down his motor, and then she took a long time to put on her hat. She pulled it here and pressed it there. When Henry turned the motor off she slipped into her coat and went out.

The little roadster bounced along on the dirt road by the river, raising the birds and driving the rabbits into the brush. Two cranes flapped heavily over the willow-line and dropped into the river-bed.

Far ahead on the road Elisa saw a dark speck in the dust. She suddenly felt empty. She did not hear Henry's talk. She tried not to look; she did not want to see the little heap of sand and green shoots, but she could not help herself. The chrysanthemums lay in the road close to the wagon tracks. But not the pot; he had kept that. As the car passed them, she remembered the good bitter smell, and a little shudder went through her. She felt ashamed of her strong planter's hands, that were no use, lying palms up in her lap.

The roadster turned a bend and she saw the caravan ahead. She swung full round toward her husband so that she could not see the little covered wagon and the mismatched team as the car passed.

In a moment they had left behind them the man who had not known or needed to know what she said, the bargainer. She did not look back.

To Henry she said loudly, to be heard above the motor, "It will be good, to-night, a good dinner."

"Now you're changed again," Henry complained. He took one hand from the wheel and patted her knee. "I ought to take you in to dinner oftener. It would be good for both of us. We get so heavy out on the ranch."

"Henry," she said, "could we have wine at dinner?"

"Sure. Say! That will be fine."

She was silent for a while; then she said, "Henry, at those prize-fights do the men hurt each other very much?"

"Sometimes a little, not often. Why?"

"Well, I've read how they break noses, and blood runs down their chests. I've read how the fighting gloves get heavy and soggy with blood."

He looked round at her. "What's the matter, Elisa? I didn't know you read things like that." He brought the car to a stop, then turned to the right over the Salinas River bridge.

"Do any women ever go to the fights?" she asked.

"Oh, sure, some. What's the matter, Elisa? Do you want to go? I don't think you'd like it, but I'll take you if you really want to go."

She relaxed limply in the seat. "Oh, no. No. I don't want to go. I'm sure I don't." Her face was turned away from him. "It will be enough if we can have wine. It will be plenty." She turned up her coat collar so he could not see that she was crying weakly—like an old woman.

1938

1913 ~ *Karl Jay Shapiro* ~ ——

KARL SHAPIRO is one of the most promising of the younger poets who began their careers in the middle and late thirties. Educated at the Johns Hopkins University, Shapiro was first introduced to the public as one of New Directions' *Five Young American Poets*, in 1941. In 1942 his *Person, Place and Thing* appeared and established him as a poet of great gifts, one whose mastery of form and whose satirical talent were destined to give him an important position in the newer American poetry. He served in the Pacific area during the war; while there, his *V-Letter and Other Poems*, collected and edited by his wife, appeared (1944) and was awarded the Pulitzer prize. It is a collection of poems written, with few exceptions, in Australia and New Guinea. A number of them are on war themes, but Shapiro does not wish to be known as a "war poet"; as he says in the introduction to that volume: "I have not written these poems to accord with any doctrine or system of thought or even a theory of composition. I have nothing to offer in the way of beliefs or challenges or prosody. I try to write freely, one day as a Christian, the next as a Jew, the next as a soldier who sees the gigantic slapstick of modern war. .... Certainly our contemporary man should feel divested of the stock attitudes of the last generation, the stance of the political intellectual, the proletarian, the expert, the salesman, the world-traveler, the pundit-poet."

In 1945 appeared Shapiro's *Essay on Rime*, which had been begun as a verse letter from New Guinea to a friend of his in Baltimore, and was expanded as a critical statement regarding the "three major confusions" in modern poetry, "In Prosody, in Language, and in Belief." Shapiro's most recent volume, *Trial of a Poet* (1947) contains much of his magazine verse written since 1945, some excerpts from an Australian volume, called *The Place of Love*, and a verse-and-prose drama from which the book takes its title. Since his return from the war, Shapiro has taught and lectured at several universities and currently is an associate professor at the Johns Hopkins University.

Shapiro's poems are in *Five Young American Poets* (1941); *Person, Place and Thing* (1942); *The Place of Love* (1943); *V-Letter and Other Poems* (1944); *Trial of a Poet* (1947). He has written several critical essays, notably "A Farewell to Criticism," published in *Poetry*, Jan., 1948; a collection of his essays is due to appear in 1949. For critical comment, see W. V. O'Connor, "Shapiro on Rime," *Kenyon Review*, Winter, 1946; William Carlos Williams, "Shapiro Is All Right," *Kenyon Review*, Winter, 1946; David Daiches, "The Poetry of Karl Shapiro," *Poetry*, Aug., 1945; W. V. O'Connor, *Sense and Sensibility in Modern Poetry* (1948).

UNIVERSITY

To hurt the Negro and avoid the Jew
Is the curriculum. In mid-September
The entering boys, identified by hats,
Wander in a maze of mannered brick
    Where boxwood and magnolia brood
    And columns with imperious stance
    Like rows of ante-bellum girls
        Eye them, outlanders.

In white cells, on lawns equipped for peace,
Under the arch, and lofty banister,   10
Equals shake hands, unequals blankly pass;
The exemplary weather whispers, 'Quiet,
    quiet'
    And visitors on tiptoe leave
    For the raw North, the unfinished
        West,
    As the young, detecting an advantage,
        Practice a face.

Where, on their separate hill, the colleges,
Like manor houses of an older law,
Gaze down embankments on a land in fee,
The Deans, dry spinsters over family
    plate,   20
    Ring out the English name like coin,
    Humor the snob and lure the lout.
    Within the precincts of this world
        Poise is a club.

But on the neighboring range, misty and
    high,
The past is absolute: some luckless race
Dull with inbreeding and conformity
Wears out its heart, and comes barefoot and
    bad
    For charity or jail. The scholar
    Sanctions their obsolete disease;   30
    The gentleman revolts with shame
        At his ancestor.

And the true nobleman, once a democrat,
Sleeps on his private mountain. He was
    one
Whose thought was shapely and whose dream
    was broad;
This school he held his art and epitaph.
    But now it takes from him his name,
    Falls open like a dishonest look,

And shows us, rotted and endowed,
    Its senile pleasure.   40
                                              1942

BUICK

As a sloop with a sweep of immaculate wing
    on her delicate spine
And a keel as steel as a root that holds in the
    sea as she leans,
Leaning and laughing, my warm-hearted
    beauty, you ride, you ride,
You tack on the curves with parabola speed
    and a kiss of goodbye,
Like a thoroughbred sloop, my new high-
    spirited spirit, my kiss.

As my foot suggests that you leap in the air
    with your hips of a girl,
My finger that praises your wheel and an-
    nounces your voices of song,
Flouncing your skirts, you blueness of joy,
    you flirt of politeness,
You leap, you intelligence, essence of wheel-
    ness with silvery nose,
And your platinum clocks of excitement stir
    like the hairs of a fern.   10

But how alien you are from the booming belts
    of your birth and the smoke
Where you turned on the stinging lathes of
    Detroit and Lansing at night
And shrieked at the torch in your secret parts
    and amorous tests,
But now with your eyes that enter the future
    of roads you forget;
You are all instinct with your phosphorous
    glow and your streaking hair.

And now when we stop it is not as the bird
    from the shell that I leave
Or the leathery pilot who steps from his bird
    with a sneer of delight,
And not as the ignorant beast do you squat
    and watch me depart,
But with exquisite breathing you smile, with
    satisfaction of love,
And I touch you again as you tick in the si-
    lence and settle in sleep.   20
                                              1942

THE FLY

O HIDEOUS little bat, the size of snot,
With polyhedral eye and shabby clothes,
To populate the stinking cat you walk
The promontory of the dead man's nose,
Climb with the fine leg of a Duncan-Phyfe
 The smoking mountains of my food
  And in a comic mood
 In mid-air take to bed a wife.

Riding and riding with your filth of hair
On gluey foot or wing, forever coy, 10
Hot from the compost and green sweet
 decay,
Sounding your buzzer like an urchin toy —
You dot all whiteness with diminutive stool,
 In the tight belly of the dead
  Burrow with hungry head
 And inlay maggots like a jewel.

At your approach the great horse stomps and
 paws
Bringing the hurricane of his heavy tail;
Shod in disease you dare to kiss my hand
Which sweeps against you like an angry flail;
Still you return, return, trusting your wing 21
 To draw you from the hunter's reach
  That learns to kill to teach
 Disorder to the tinier thing.

My peace is your disaster. For your death
Children like spiders cup their pretty hands
And wives resort to chemistry of war.
In fens of sticky paper and quicksands
You glue yourself to death. Where you are
 stuck
 You struggle hideously and beg 30
  You amputate your leg
 Imbedded in the amber muck.

But I, a man, must swat you with my hate,
Slap you across the air and crush your flight
Must mangle with my shoe and smear your
 blood,
Expose your little guts pasty and white,
Knock your head sidewise like a drunkard's
 hat,
 Pin your wings under like a crow's,
  Tear off your flimsy clothes
 And beat you as one beats a rat. 40

Then like Gargantua I stride among
The corpses strewn like raisins in the dust,
The broken bodies of the narrow dead
That catch the throat with fingers of disgust.
I sweep. One gyrates like a top and falls
 And stunned, stone blind, and deaf
  Buzzes its frightful F
 And dies between three cannibals. 1942

1865 ~ *Irving Babbitt* ~ 1933

W RITER, teacher, and admittedly the leader of the New Humanist movement, Babbitt hailed from the Middle West, his native city being Dayton, Ohio. After his graduation from Harvard he spent two years studying at the Sorbonne. In 1893-1894 he was an instructor in Romance languages at Williams College, returning to Harvard the following year as instructor in French. In 1902 he was promoted to an assistant professorship, and in 1912 to a full professorship, a position which he held until his death. He achieved fame through his writings, lectured extensively before college audiences throughout the United States, and in 1923 served as the Harvard exchange professor at the Sorbonne. The American Academy of Arts and Letters elected him to membership in 1930. Besides his original writings, he edited for college classes books by Renan, Taine, Voltaire, and Racine.

Probably few Americans of modern times have stirred up as much discussion and controversy as Babbitt has in his books, all of which treat some phase or other of his humanistic doctrine. In his first book, *Literature and the American College* (1908), he describes Humanism as the search for individual perfection through selective discipline. It is aristocratic in temper, and concerns itself only with the individual as against society as a whole. The unique purpose of it is to help man overcome his natural propensity to one-sidedness, as manifested, for instance, in modern educational emphasis upon specialization, or in the human tendency to let one or another aspect of personality, such as the emotions, dominate and control conduct. Babbitt had as his ideal a man who could harmonize within himself all the qualities of his nature, what he calls the opposite virtues, through obedience to the law of measure, which in turn saved him from excesses. This ideal man is characterized by a poised equilibrium of all his powers in which the extremes of the opposing virtues, as seen in the ideas of unity and plurality, or as Plato expresses it, the combination of the "one with the many," are held in balance. Only such a balance can preserve mental sanity. As far as Babbitt is concerned, this ideal, based upon the classical tradition, can stem the tide of excessive sympathy, primitivism, and emotionalism let loose by Rousseau and appropriated by the Romantics. The remainder of the book is a discussion of the educational problems as affected by this approach.

The New Laokoön (1910), an essay in comparative aesthetics, is a study of the confusion of the arts as a result of the Romantic movement. In *The Masters of Modern French Criticism* (1912) he investigates nineteenth-century French critics to ascertain the movement of thought represented by them, as well as to erect a background against which the anti-intellectual revolt of the day can be studied and understood. The problem of critical standards is involved, and so is the philosophical problem of finding a unifying principle in the flux of life, as against the intuitive sense of change proposed and accepted by some of the newer philosophers. Babbitt returns to the Platonic "one and the many" as the core of the critical and philosophical attitude. *Rousseau and Romanticism* (1919) attacks the ideals of the Romanticists and the baneful effects, which in his estimation they have had on modern civilization. *Democracy and Leadership* (1924) is a searching analysis of democratic society in reference to its ability to set up standards for its own development. His last book, *On Being Creative* (1932), is a collection of miscellaneous essays unified by their general bearing on literary criticism.

Babbitt believed with Arnold that criticism had a determining influence upon creative literature. With that constantly in mind he sought for a philosophy of life in which he could find the necessary critical standards of judgment, and which would point the way for the future development of literature. The entire body of his work is a protest and reaction against many of the younger critics who flouted the ap-

critic remarks, was a home thrust that one of Molière's soubrettes could not have improved upon. The claim of Rousseau and his earlier followers was to be not simply unique, but unique in feeling. This sentiment of uniqueness in feeling speedily became that of uniqueness in suffering—on the familiar principle, no doubt, that life, which is a comedy for those who think, is a tragedy for those who feel. Hence arose in the romantic school a somewhat theatrical affectation of grief. Byron was far from being the first who paraded before the public "the pageant of his bleeding heart." Chateaubriand especially nourished in himself the sense of fated and preëminent sorrow, and was ready to exclaim at the most ordinary mischance: "Such things happen only to me!" Sainte-Beuve makes an interesting comparison between Chateaubriand and another native of Brittany, the author of *Gil Blas*. "A book like *René*," says Sainte-Beuve, "encourages a subtle spiritual pride. A man seeks in his imagination some unique misfortune to which he may abandon himself and which he may fold about him in solitude. He says to himself that a great soul must contain more sorrow than a little one; and adds in a whisper that he himself may be this great soul. *Gil Blas*, on the other hand, is a book that brings you into full contact with life and the throng of your fellow creatures. When you are very gloomy and believe in fatality and imagine that certain extraordinary things happen to you alone, read *Gil Blas*, and you will find that he had that very misfortune or one just like it, and that he took it as a simple mishap and got over it."

The same contrast might be brought out by comparing Montaigne and Rousseau, the two writers who, in a broad sense, are the masters respectively of Lesage and Chateaubriand. This contrast is easily missed, because at first glance Montaigne seems an arch-egotist like Rousseau, and is almost equally ready to bestow his own idiosyncrasies on the reader. Yet in the final analysis Montaigne is interested in Montaigne because he is a human being; Rousseau is interested in Rousseau because he is Jean-Jacques. Montaigne observes himself impartially as a normal specimen of the genus homo. Rousseau, as we have seen,

positively gloats over his own otherwiseness. Montaigne aims to be the average, or, it would be less misleading to say, the representative man; Rousseau's aim is to be the extraordinary man, or original genius. Rousseau is an eccentric, Montaigne a concentric individualist. The sentence of Montaigne that sums him up is, "Every man bears within him the entire image of the human lot." Rousseau is rather summed up in his phrase, "There are souls that are too privileged to follow the common path," with its corollary that he is himself one of these privileged souls.

The nineteenth century saw the rise of a race of eccentric individualists, especially in art and literature, who, like Rousseau scorned the common path and strove to distinguish themselves from the bourgeois and philistine in everything, from the details of their dress to the refinements of their sensations. In this quest of the rare and the original they attained to a departure from the norm that was not only eccentric, but pathological. Every man was to have the right to express not only his own particular vision of life, but his own particular nightmare. We finally come to a writer like Baudelaire, who builds himself a "little strangely scented and strangely colored kiosk on the extreme tip of the romantic Kamchatka" and "cultivates his hysteria with delight and terror"; who, instead of being true to the human heart, as the old-fashioned classicist would say, makes it his ambition to create a "new shudder." All the modern writer cares for, says M. Anatole France, is to be thought original. In his fear of becoming commonplace he prides himself, like Victor Hugo, on reading only those books that other men do not read, or else he does not read at all, and so comes to resemble that eighteenth-century Frenchwoman who was said to have "respected in her ignorance the active principle of her originality." The danger of the man who is too assimilative, who possesses too perfectly the riches of tradition, is to feel that originality is henceforth impossible. It is related of a French critic that he used to turn away wearily from every new volume of poetry that was submitted to him, with the remark: "All the verses are written."

Genuine originality, however, is a hardy

growth, and usually gains more than it loses by striking deep root into the literature of the past. La Bruyère begins his *Characters* by observing that "Everything has been said," and then goes on to write one of the most original books in French. Montaigne wrote a still more original book which often impresses the reader as a mere cento of quotations. An excessive respect for the past is less harmful than the excess from which we are now suffering. For example, one of our younger writers is praised in a review for his "stark freedom from tradition . . . as though he came into the world of letters without ever a predecessor. He is the expression in literary art of certain enormous repudiations." It is precisely this notion of originality that explains the immense insignificance of so much of our contemporary writing. The man who breaks with the past in this way will think that he is original when he is in reality merely ignorant and presumptuous. He is apt to imagine himself about a century ahead of his age when he is at least four or five centuries behind it. "He comes to you," as Bagehot puts it, "with a notion that Noah discarded in the ark, and attracts attention to it as if it were a stupendous novelty of his own."

We may be sure that the more enlightened of the Cave Dwellers had already made deeper discoveries in human nature than many of our modern radicals. Goethe said that if as a young man he had known of the masterpieces that already existed in Greek he would never have written a line. Goethe carries his modesty too far; but how grateful just a touch of it would be in the average author of today! With even a small part of Goethe's knowledge and insight, he would no longer go on serving up to us the dregs and last muddy lees of the romantic and naturalistic movements as originality and genius. He would see that his very paradoxes were stale. Instead of being a half-baked author, he would become a modest and at the same time judicious reader; or, if he continued to write, he would be less anxious to create and more anxious to humanize his creations. Sooner or later every author, as well as the characters he conceives, will have to answer the question that was the first addressed to any one who designed to enter the Buddhist church: "Are you a human being?" The world's suffrage will go in the long run to the writer or artist who dwells habitually in the center and not on the remote periphery of human nature. Gautier paid a doubtful compliment to Victor Hugo when he said that Hugo's works seemed to proceed not from a man, but an element, that they were Cyclopean, "as it were, the works of Polyphemus." Hugo remained the original genius to the end, in contrast with Goethe, who attained humane restraint after having begun as a Rousseauist.

Romanticism from the very beginning tended to become eccentric through over-anxiety to be original; and romanticism is now running to seed. Many of our contemporary writers are as plainly in an extreme as the most extreme of the neo-classicists. They think that to be original they need merely to arrive at self-expression without any effort to be representative. The neo-classicist, on the other hand, strove so hard to be representative that he often lost the personal flavor entirely and fell into colorless abstraction. Both extremes fail equally of being humane. For, to revert to our fundamental principle, the humanist must combine opposite extremes and occupy all the space between them. Genuine originality is so immensely difficult because it imposes the task of achieving work that is of general human truth and at the same time intensely individual. Perhaps the best examples of this union of qualities are found in Greek. The original man for the Greek was the one who could create in the very act of imitating the past. Greek literature at its best is to a remarkable degree a creative imitation of Homer.

The modern does not, like the Greek, hope to become original by assimilating tradition, but rather by ignoring it, or, if he is a scholar, by trying to prove that it is mistaken. We have been discussing thus far almost entirely the originality of the Rousseauist or sentimental naturalist; but we should not fail to note the curious points of contact here as elsewhere between sentimental and scientific naturalism. The Baconian aims less at the assimilation of past wisdom than at the advancement of learning. With him too the prime stress is on the new and the original.

Formerly there was a pedantry of authority and prescription. As a result of the working together of Rousseauist and Baconian there has arisen a veritable pedantry of originality. The scientific pedant who is entirely absorbed in his own bit of research is first cousin to the artistic and literary pedant who is entirely absorbed in his own sensation. The hero of modern scholarship is not the humanist, but the investigator. The man who digs up an unpublished document from some musty archive outranks the man who can deal judiciously with the documents already in print. His glory will be all the greater if he can make the new document a pretext for writing a book, for attempting a rehabilitation. The love of truth shades imperceptibly into the love of paradox; and Rousseauist and Baconian often coexist in the same person.

A royal road to a reputation for originality is to impugn the verdicts of the past,—to whitewash what is traditionally black or to blackwash what is traditionally white. Only the other day one of the English reviews published the "Blackwashing of Dante." A still better example is Renan's blackwashing of King David, which concludes as follows: "Pious souls, when they take delight in the sentiments filled with resignation and tender melancholy contained in the most beautiful of the liturgical books, will imagine that they are in communion with this bandit. Humanity will believe in final justice on the testimony of David, who never gave it a thought and of the Sibyl, who never existed," etc. The whitewashings have been still more numerous. Rehabilitations have appeared of Tiberius, the Borgias, and Robespierre. A book has also been written to prove that the first Napoleon was a man of an eminently peace-loving disposition. Mr. Stephen Phillips undertakes to throw a poetical glamour over the character of Nero, that amiable youth, who, as the versifier in *Punch* observes,—

"would have doubtless made his mark,
Had he not, in a mad, mad, boyish lark,
Murdered his mother!"

If this whitewashing and blackwashing goes on, the time will soon come when the only way left to be original will be to make a modest plea for the traditional good sense of the world. This traditional good sense was never treated with an easier contempt than at present. A writer named Bax, who recently published a volume rehabilitating the revolutionary monster Marat, says in his preface: "It is in fact a fairly safe rule to ascertain for oneself what most people think on such questions" (*i.e.* as the character of Marat), "and then assume the exact opposite to be true." Of most books of this kind we may say what FitzGerald said when Henry Irving made himself up in the rôle of Shylock to look like the Saviour: "It is an attempt to strike out an original idea in the teeth of common sense and tradition." Of course there are in every age and individual, as we have said elsewhere, elements that run counter to the main tendency. One of the regular recipes for writing German doctors' theses is to seize on one of these elements, exaggerate it, and take it as a point of departure for refuting the traditional view. Thus Rousseau says in one place that he has always detested political agitators. We may be sure in advance that some German will start from this to prove that Rousseau has been cruelly maligned in being looked on as a revolutionist.

Even our more serious scholars are finding it hard to resist that something in the spirit of the age which demands that their results be not only just, but novel. Even our older universities are becoming familiar with the professor who combines in about equal measure his love of research and his love of the limelight. In public opinion, the perfection of the type is the Chicago professor whose originality has become the jest of the cheap newspapers. Here are a few Chicago "discoveries," selected almost at random from the many that have been announced from time to time in the daily press:—

Kissing causes lockjaw.

The Pennsylvanians are turning into Indians.

A man does not need to take exercise after the age of thirty-five.

Music is antiseptic.

A dog will not follow an uneducated man.

Marriage is a form of insanity.

Americans are incapable of friendship.

Boccaccio was a Swede.

John D. Rockefeller is as great a man as Shakespeare.

Some day a wounded or even worn-out heart of a human may be replaced by a healthy heart from a living monkey, etc.

The Chicago professors would say, and no doubt rightly, that they are misrepresented by these newspaper statements. But we are only giving the general impression. Even the utterance of Dr. Osler that at once gave him such a start over all his academic rivals in the race for notoriety becomes comparatively unsensational when read in its context. The professor with an itch for the limelight has only to pattern himself on Rousseau, the great master of paradox. Rousseau's method has been compared to that of a man who fires off a pistol in the street to attract a crowd. When Rousseau has once drawn his crowd, he may proceed to attenuate his paradox, until sometimes it is in danger of dwindling into a commonplace.

Most good observers would probably agree that contemporary scholarship and literature are becoming too eccentric and centrifugal; they would agree that some unifying principle is needed to counteract this excessive striving after originality. For example, Professor Gummere, who is one of the most distinguished representatives of the scholarly tradition that ultimately goes back to Herder and the Grimm brothers, diagnoses our present malady with great clearness in a recent article on "Originality and Convention in Literature." The higher forms of poetry and creative art, he says, are being made impossible by the disintegrating influences at work in modern life, and by an excess of analysis. He suggests as remedy that we jettison this intellectual and analytical element, and seek to restore once more the bond of communal sympathy. This remedy betrays at once its romantic origin. It is only one form of Rousseau's assumption that an unaided sympathy will do more to draw men together than the naked forces of egoism and self-assertion will do to drive them asunder. Even in his studies

of the beginnings of poetry Professor Gummere should, perhaps, have insisted more on communal discipline as a needful preliminary to communal sympathy. However that may be, our present hope does not seem to lie in the romanticist's attempt to revert to the unity of instinct and feeling that he supposes to have existed in primitive life. We need to commune and unite in what is above rather than in what is below our ordinary selves, and the pathway to this higher unity is not through sympathy, communal or otherwise, but through restraint. If we have got so far apart, it is because of the lack, not of sympathy, but of humane standards.

Without trying to enter fully into so large a topic as the impressionism of our modern society, its loss of traditional standards, and its failure as yet to find new, we may at least point out that education should be less infected than it is with a pedantic straining after originality. In general, education should represent the conservative and unifying element in our national life. The college especially must maintain humane standards, if it is to have any reason at all for existing as something distinct from university and preparatory school. Its function is not, as is so often assumed merely to help its students to self-expression, but even more to help them to become humane. In the words of Cardinal Newman, the college is "the great ordinary means to a great but ordinary end"; this end is to supply principles of taste and judgment and train in sanity and centrality of view; to give background and perspective, and inspire, if not the spirit of conformity, at least a proper respect for the past experience of the world. Most of us have heard of Mrs. Shelley's reply when advised to send her boy to a school where he would be taught to think for himself: "My God! teach him rather to think like other people." Mrs. Shelley had lived with a man who was not only a real genius, but also an original genius in the German sense, and knew whereof she spoke. Now the college should not necessarily teach its students to think like other people, but it should teach them to distinguish between what is original and what is merely odd and eccentric, both in themselves and others. According to Lowell this is a distinction that Wordsworth could never make, and Wordsworth is not alone in this respect among the romantic leaders. We must insist, at the risk of causing scandal, that the college is not primarily intended to encourage originality and independence of thought as these terms are often understood. The story is told of a professor in one of our Eastern colleges that he invariably gave a high mark to the undergraduates who contradicted the received opinions in his subjects; but the highest mark here served for the undergraduate who in addition to contradicting the traditional view set up a new view of his own. As this fact became known, the professor was gratified by a rapid growth among his students of independent and original thinking.

The college should guard against an undue stress on self-expression and an insufficient stress on human assimilation. This danger is especially plain in the teaching of English composition. A father once said to me of a "daily theme" course that it had at least set his son's wits to working. But what if it set them to working in the void? The most that can be expected of youths who are put to writing with little or no background of humane assimilation is a clever impressionism. They will be fitted, not to render serious service to literature, but at most to shine in the more superficial kinds of journalism. It is still an open question whether any direct method of teaching English really takes the place of the drill in the niceties of style that can be derived from translation, especially the translation of Latin; whether a student, for example, who rendered Cicero with due regard for the delicate shades of meaning would not gain more mastery of English (to say nothing of Latin) than a student who devoted the same amount of time to daily themes and original composition. We must, however, be fair to our departments of English. They have to cope with conditions not entirely of their own making, of which the most serious is something approaching illiteracy in many of the students that are forced upon them from the preparatory schools. In practice they have to devote most of their time to imparting, not the elegancies, but the simplest decencies of the English language. Ultimately a great deal of what goes on in the more elementary college courses in English may well be relegated to the lower schools,—and the home,—and the work that is done in the advanced courses in composition will probably either be omitted entirely, or else done, as it is in France, in connection with the reading and detailed study of great writers. Assimilation will then keep pace as it should with expression.

Spinoza says that a man should constantly keep before his eye a sort of exemplar of human nature (*idea hominis, tamquam naturae humanae exemplar*). He should, in other words, have a humane standard to which he may defer, and which will not proscribe originality but will help him to discriminate between what is original and what is merely freakish and abnormal in himself and others. Now this humane standard may be gained by a few through philosophic insight, but in most cases it will be attained, if at all, by a knowledge of good literature—by a familiarity with that golden chain of masterpieces which links together into a single tradition the more permanent experience of the race; books which so agree in essentials that they seem, as Emerson puts it, to be the work of one all-seeing, all-hearing gentleman. In short, the most practical way of promoting humanism is to work for a revival of the almost lost art of reading. As a general rule, the humane man will be the one who has a memory richly stored with what is best in literature, with the sound sense perfectly expressed that is found only in the masters. Conversely, the decline of humanism and the growth of Rousseauism have been marked by a steady decay in the higher uses of the memory. For the Greeks the Muses were not the daughters of Inspiration or of Genius, as they would be for a modern, but the daughters of Memory. Sainte-Beuve says that "from time to time we should raise our eyes to the hill-tops to the group of revered mortals, and ask ourselves: What would they say of us?" No one whose memory is not enriched in the way we have described can profit by this advice. Sainte-Beuve himself in giving it was probably only remembering Longinus.

1908

1880 -- *Henry Louis Mencken* --

ENCKEN is a native of Baltimore and has lived in that city all his life. He was educated in private schools and the Baltimore Polytechnic Institute, but looked upon college as a waste of time, inasmuch as he was expected to join his father in the tobacco business. After the latter's death he secured a position on the Baltimore *Morning Herald*, and served on various papers until 1914, when he became co-editor of *The Smart Set* with George Jean Nathan. From 1924 to 1933 he edited *The American Mercury*.

To begin with, Mencken maintains that criticism must be emancipated from the mistaken notion that it deals with ideas at second hand. Criticism is an art, the critic an artist who seeks self-expression as does the poet, painter, novelist, or musician, the only difference being that he proceeds from the vantage point of another's ideas, rather than his own. He has the same desire for the free play of his powers, the same zeal to give permanent form to ideas, and the same hope to draw to himself the attention of thinking people. But the final product is therefore primarily the expression of the critic's ideas. For that reason Mencken approves of the methods of the earlier reviewers who wrote lengthy treatises on subjects suggested by the work or works under consideration. And in whatever he has written, his personality colors and dominates the scene.

Though he is not a scholar in the technical or professional sense of the term, the range of his interests and information is amazing, and he has explored many areas in the world's intellectual and artistic geography. The mere titles of his books convey an idea of this range—*The Philosophy of Friedrich Nietzsche* (1908), *In Defense of Women* (1918), *Prejudices* (six series, 1919–1927), *Notes on Democracy* (1926), *Treatise on the Gods* (1930), *Treatise on Right and Wrong* (1934), and *The American Language* (which has gone through four revisions, the last in 1936, and has acquired two supplements, each as long as the last version of the original book). He has entered the fields of philosophy, literature and art, linguistics, politics, economics, ethics, and religion.

In method he is iconoclastic and destructive. He rather frowns upon so-called constructive criticism as futile. By some he has been called the debunker of American literature, for many established reputations have fallen under his sturdy hammer strokes. But he is not entirely negative in his thought; he was instrumental in helping to establish reputations, as in the cases of Dreiser and Cabell. To him nothing is sacred, he bows before no idol or standard, feels no reverence for tradition or accepted usage, and belabors Bryan and God with equal vehemence. In philosophy he was in some respects a disciple of Nietzsche; in religion he owes much to Darwin, Spencer, and Huxley.

Besides dullness and stupidity the chief objects of his venom are sham, pretense, and hypocrisy, in whatever form they may appear. He would have human beings emerge from under the dead weight of the past, assert their dignity and power in the light of growing knowledge and intelligence, and achieve their destiny through urges from within rather than through inspiration from without. An American Nietzschean, he is an enemy of both democracy and socialism, and an upholder of the doctrine of *laissez-faire*. "I am in many fields a flouter of the accepted revelation and hence immoral, but the field of economics is not one of them. Here, indeed, I know of no man who is more orthodox than I am. I believe that the present organization of society, as bad as it is, is better than any other that has ever been proposed. I reject all the sure cures in current agitation from government ownership to the single tax. I am in favor of free competition in all human enterprises, and to the utmost limit."

Mencken wrote against the background of a changing America; ideas, standards, and authority were tested, found wanting, and discarded. In *The American Mercury*, Mencken appealed to postwar attitudes and, to the great evident enjoyment of the magazine's growing list of subscribers, struck out at conventional stupidities and barbarities, which he collected and arranged with a scholar's zeal. Yet his criticism is chiefly that of a journalist, momentary, clever, typed, and only superficially provided with intellectual background. For all Mencken's intellectual interests (and they were many) he is not a great critic, but rather one who caught the attention of a public which liked whole-hearted and clever attacks upon its scarcely cherished institutions.

Since most of Mencken's books are of a critical nature no attempt will be made to classify them. Representative titles will be listed chronologically as follows: *George Bernard Shaw: His Plays* (1905); *The Philosophy of Friedrich Nietzsche* (1908); *A Little Book in C Major* (1916); *A Book of Prefaces* (1917); *In Defense of Women* (1918); *The American Language* (1919, rev. 1921, 1923, 1935); *Prejudices* (6 vols., 1919–27); *The American Credo*, introduction by G. J. Nathan (1920, rev. 1921); *Notes on Democracy* (1926); *James Branch Cabell* (1927); *Treatise on the Gods* (1930); *Treatise on Right and Wrong* (1934). I. Goldberg, *The Man Mencken* (1925), is a full-length biographical study. Briefer accounts are available in J. Farrar, ed., *The Literary Spotlight* (1924); G. J. Nathan, *The Intimate Notebooks of George Jean Nathan* (1932); E. Clark, *Innocence Abroad* (1931); O. Hatteras, *Pistols for Two* (1917), said to have been written by Nathan and Mencken under a pseudonym. Available critical studies are J. W. Beach, *The Outlook for American Prose* (1926); E. Boyd, *H. L. Mencken* (1925); J. B. Cabell, *Some of Us* (1930); V. F. Calverton, *The Newer Spirit* (1925); H. S. Canby, *American Estimates* (1929); B. DeCasseres, *Mencken and Shaw* (1930); C. Van Doren, *Many Minds* (1924); S. P. Sherman, *Critical Woodcuts* (1926); S. P. Sherman, *Americans* (1922); F. L. Pattee, *Side-Lights on American Literature* (1922); H. Wickham, *The Impuritans* (1929); Van W. Brooks, *Sketches in Criticism* (1932); R. Forsythe, *Redder Than the Rose* (1935); F. Harris, *Contemporary Portraits* (4th ser., 1923); E. S. Sergeant, *Fire Under the Andes* (1927); H. M. Parshley, "H. L. Mencken: an Appreciation," *American Review*, Jan.–Feb., 1925; W. Lippmann, *Men of Destiny* (1927); B. Rascoe and others, *H. L. Mencken* (1920); J. B. Harrison, *A Short View of Menckenism in Menckenese* (1927); *Menckeniana: a Schimpf-lexikon* (1928); T. Maynard, "Mencken Leaves 'The American Mercury'," *Catholic World*, April, 1934; S. Collins, "Criticism in America," *Bookman*, June, 1930; C. Van Doren, "Smartness and Light. H. L. Mencken: A Gadfly for Democracy," *Century*, March, 1923; I. Babbitt, "The Critic and American Life," *Forum*, Feb., 1928; G. K. Chesterton, "The Skeptic as Critic," *Forum*, Feb., 1929; C. F. Glicksberg, "H. L. Mencken: The Dean of Iconoclasts," *Calcutta Review*, April, 1938.

FOOTNOTE ON CRITICISM

From *Prejudices: Third Series* (1922).

NEARLY all the discussions of criticism that I am acquainted with start off with a false assumption, to wit, that the primary motive of the critic, the impulse which makes a critic of him instead of, say, a politician, or a stock-broker, is pedagogical—that he writes because he is possessed by a passion to advance the enlightenment, to put down error and wrong, to disseminate some specific doctrine: psycho-logical, epistemological, historical, or aes-thetic. This is true, it seems to me, only of bad critics, and its degree of truth increases in direct ratio to their badness. The motive of the critic who is really worth reading—the only critic of whom, indeed, it may be said truthfully that it is at all possible to read him, save as an act of mental discipline—is some-thing quite different. That motive is not the motive of the pedagogue, but the motive of the artist. It is no more and no less than the simple desire to function freely and beauti-fully, to give outward and objective form to ideas that bubble inwardly and have a fas-cinating lure in them, to get rid of them dramatically and make an articulate noise in the world. It was for this reason that Plato wrote the "Republic," and for this reason that Beethoven wrote the Ninth Symphony, and it is for this reason, to drop a million miles, that I am writing the present essay. Everything else is afterthought, mock-mod-esty, messianic delusion—in brief, affectation and folly. Is the contrary conception of criti-cism widely cherished? Is it almost uni-versally held that the thing is a brother to jurisprudence, advertising, laparotomy, chau-tauqua lecturing and the art of the school-marm? Then certainly the fact that it is so held should be sufficient to set up an over-whelming probability of its lack of truth and sense. If I speak with some heat, it is as one who has suffered. When, years ago, I devoted myself diligently to critical pieces upon the writings of Theodore Dreiser, I found that practically every one who took any notice of my proceedings at all fell into either one of two assumptions about my underlying pur-pose: (*a*) that I had a fanatical devotion for Mr. Dreiser's ideas and desired to propagate them, or (*b*) that I was an ardent patriot, and yearned to lift up American literature. Both assumptions were false. I had then, and I have now, very little interest in many of Mr. Dreiser's main ideas; when we meet, in fact, we usually quarrel about them. And I am wholly devoid of public spirit, and haven't the least lust to improve American literature; if it ever came to what I regard as perfection my job would be gone. What, then, was my motive in writing about Mr. Dreiser so co-piously? My motive, well known to Mr. Dreiser himself and to every one else who knew me as intimately as he did, was simply and solely to sort out and give coherence to the ideas of Mr. Mencken, and to put them into suave and ingratiating terms, and to dis-charge them with a flourish, and maybe with a phrase of pretty song, into the dense fog that blanketed the Republic.

The critic's choice of criticism rather than of what is called creative writing is chiefly a matter of temperament—perhaps, more ac-curately of hormones—with accidents of edu-cation and environment to help. The feelings that happen to be dominant in him at the moment the scribbling frenzy seizes him are feelings inspired, not directly by life itself, but by books, pictures, music, sculpture, architecture, religion, philosophy—in brief, by some other man's feelings about life. They are thus, in a sense, secondhand, and it is no wonder that creative artists so easily fall into the theory that they are also second-rate. Perhaps they usually are. If, indeed, the critic continues on this plane—if he lacks the intellectual agility and enterprise needed to make the leap from the work of art to the vast and mysterious complex of phenomena behind it —then they *always* are, and he remains no more than a fugelman or policeman to his betters. But if a genuine artist is concealed within him—if his feelings are in any sense profound and original, and his capacity for self-expression is above the average of educated men—then he moves inevitably from the work of art to life itself, and begins to take on a dignity that he formerly lacked. It is impossible to think of a man of any actual force and originality, universally recognized as having those qualities, who spent his whole life appraising and describing the work of other men. Did Goethe, or Carlyle, or Matthew Arnold, or Sainte-Beuve, or Macaulay, or even, to come down a few pegs, Lewes, or Lowell, or Hazlitt? Certainly not. The thing that becomes most obvious about the writings of all such men, once they are examined carefully, is that the critic is always being swallowed up by the creative artist—that what starts out as the review of a book, or a play, or other work of art, usually develops very quickly into an independent essay upon the theme of that work of art, or upon some theme that it suggests—in a word, that it becomes a fresh work of art, and only indirectly related to the one that suggested it. This fact, indeed, is so plain that it scarcely needs statement. What the pedagogues always object to in, for example, the *Quarterly* reviewers is that they forgot the books they were supposed to review, and wrote long papers—often, in fact small books—expounding ideas suggested (or not suggested) by the books under review. Every critic who is worth reading falls inevitably into the same habit. He cannot stick to his task: what is before him is always infinitely less interesting to him than what is within him. If he is genuinely first-rate—if

what is within him stands the test of type, and wins an audience, and produces the reactions that every artist craves—then he usually ends by abandoning the criticism of specific works of art altogether, and setting up shop as a merchant in general ideas, *i.e.*, as an artist working in the materials of life itself.

Mere reviewing, however conscientiously and competently it is done, is plainly a much inferior business. Like writing poetry, it is chiefly a function of intellectual immaturity. The young literatus just out of the university, having as yet no capacity for grappling with the fundamental mysteries of existence, is put to writing reviews of books, or plays, or music, or painting. Very often he does it extremely well; it is, in fact, not hard to do well, for even decayed pedagogues often do it, as such graves of the intellect as the New York *Times* bear witness. But if he continues to do it, whether well or ill, it is a sign to all the world that his growth ceased when they made him *Artium Baccalaureus*. Gradually he becomes, whether in or out of the academic grove, a professor, which is to say, a man devoted to diluting and retailing the ideas of his superiors—not an artist, not even a bad artist, but almost the antithesis of an artist. He is learned, he is sober, he is painstaking and accurate—but he is as hollow as a jug. Nothing is in him save the ghostly echoes of other men's thoughts and feelings. If he were a genuine artist he would have thoughts and feelings of his own, and the impulse to give them objective form would be irresistible. An artist can no more withstand that impulse than a politician can withstand the temptations of a job. There are no mute, inglorious Miltons, save in the hallucinations of poets. The one sound test of a Milton is that he functions as a Milton. His difference from other men lies precisely in the superior vigor of his impulse to self-expression, not in the superior beauty and loftiness of his ideas. Other men, in point of fact, often have the same ideas, or perhaps even loftier ones, but they are able to suppress them, usually on grounds of decorum, and so they escape being artists, and are respected by right-thinking persons, and die with money in the bank, and are forgotten in two weeks.

Obviously, the critic whose performance we are commonly called upon to investigate is a man standing somewhere along the path leading from the beginning that I have described to the goal. He has got beyond being a mere cataloguer and valuer of other men's ideas, but he has not yet become an autonomous artist—he is not yet ready to challenge attention with his own ideas alone. But it is plain that his motion, in so far as he is moving at all, must be in the direction of that autonomy—that is, unless one imagines him sliding backward into senile infantilism: a spectacle not unknown to literary pathology, but too pathetic to be discussed here. Bear this motion in mind, and the true nature of his aims and purposes becomes clear; more, the incurable falsity of the aims and purposes usually credited to him becomes equally clear. He is not actually trying to perform an impossible act of arctic justice upon the artist whose work gives him a text. He is not trying with mathematical passion to find out exactly what was in the artist's mind at the moment of creation, and to display it precisely and in an ecstasy of appreciation. He is not trying to bring the work discussed into accord with some transient theory of aesthetics, or ethics, or truth, or to determine its degree of departure from that theory. He is not trying to lift up the fine arts, or to defend democracy against sense, or to promote happiness at the domestic hearth, or to convert sophomores into right-thinkers, or to serve God. He is not trying to fit a group of novel phenomena into the orderly process of history. He is not even trying to discharge the catalytic office that I myself, in a romantic moment, once sought to force upon him. He is, first and last, simply trying to express himself. He is trying to arrest and challenge a sufficient body of readers, to make them pay attention to him, to impress them with the charm and novelty of his ideas, to provoke them into an agreeable (or shocked) awareness of him, and he is trying to achieve thereby for his own inner ego the grateful feeling of a function performed, a tension relieved, a *katharsis* attained which Wagner achieved when he wrote "Die Walküre," and a hen achieves every time she lays an egg.

Joseph Conrad is moved by that necessity to write romances; Bach was moved to write music; poets are moved to write poetry; critics are moved to write criticism. The form is nothing; the only important thing is the motive power, and it is the same in all cases. It is the pressing yearning of every man who has ideas in him to empty them upon the world, to hammer them into plausible and ingratiating shapes, to compel the attention and respect of his equals, to lord it over his inferiors. So seen, the critic becomes a far more transparent and agreeable fellow than ever he was in the discourses of the psychologists who sought to make him a mere appraiser in an intellectual customs house, a gauger in a distillery of the spirit, a just and infallible judge upon the cosmic bench. Such offices, in point of fact, never fit him. He always bulges over their confines. So labelled and estimated, it inevitably turns out that the specific critic under examination is a very bad one, or no critic at all. But when he is thought of, not as pedagogue, but as artist, then he begins to take on reality, and, what is more, dignity. Carlyle was surely no just and infallible judge; on the contrary, he was full of prejudices, biles, naïvetés, humors. Yet he is read, consulted, attended to. Macaulay was unfair, inaccurate, fanciful, lyrical—yet his essays live. Arnold had his faults too, and so did Sainte-Beuve, and so did Goethe, and so did many another of that line—and yet they are remembered today, and all the learned and conscientious critics of their time, laboriously concerned with the precise intent of the artists under review, and passionately determined to set it forth with god-like care and to relate it exactly to this or that great stream of ideas—all these pedants are forgotten. What saved Carlyle, Macaulay and company is as plain as day. They were first-rate artists. They could make the thing charming, and that is always a million times more important than making it true.

Truth, indeed, is something that is believed in completely only by persons who have never tried personally to pursue it to its fastnesses and grab it by the tail. It is the adoration of second-rate men—men who always receive it at secondhand. Pedagogues believe in immutable truths and spend their lives trying to determine them and propagate them; the intellectual progress of man consists largely of a concerted effort to block and destroy their enterprise. Nine times out of ten, in the arts as in life, there is actually no truth to be discovered; there is only error to be exposed. In whole departments of human inquiry it seems to me quite unlikely that the truth ever *will* be discovered. Nevertheless, the rubber stamp thinking of the world always makes the assumption that the exposure of an error is identical with the discovery of the truth—that error and truth are simple opposites. They are nothing of the sort. What the world turns to when it has been cured of one error, is usually simply another error, and maybe one worse than the first one. This is the whole history of the intellect in brief. The average man of today does not believe in precisely the same imbecilities that the Greek of the fourth century before Christ believed in, but the things that he *does* believe in are often quite as idiotic. Perhaps this statement is a bit too sweeping. There is, year by year, a gradual accumulation of what may be called, provisionally, truths—there is a slow accretion of ideas that somehow manage to meet all practicable human tests, and so survive. But even so, it is risky to call them absolute truths. All that one may safely say of them is that no one, as yet, has demonstrated that they are errors. Soon or late, if experience teaches us anything, they are likely to succumb too. The profoundest truths of the Middle Ages are now laughed at by schoolboys. The profoundest truths of democracy will be laughed at, a few centuries hence, even by schoolteachers.

In the department of aesthetics, wherein critics mainly disport themselves, it is almost impossible to think of a so-called truth that shows any sign of being permanently true. The most profound of principles begins to fade and quiver almost as soon as it is stated. But the work of art, as opposed to the theory behind it, has a longer life, particularly if that theory be obscure and questionable, and so cannot be determined accurately. "Hamlet," the Mona Lisa, "Faust," "Dixie," "Parsifal," "Mother Goose," "Annabel Lee," "Huckle-

berry Finn"—these things, so baffling to pedagogy, so contumacious to the categories, so mysterious in purpose and utility—these things live. And why? Because there is in them flavor of salient, novel and attractive personality, because the quality that shines from them is not that of correct demeanor but that of creative passion, because they pulse and breathe and speak, because they are genuine works of art. So with criticism. Let us forget all the heavy effort to make a science of it; it is a fine art, or nothing, If the critic, retiring to his cell to concoct his treatise upon a book or play or what-not, produces a piece of writing that shows sound structure, and brilliant color, and the flash of new and persuasive ideas, and civilized manners, and the charm of an uncommon personality in free function, then he has given something to the world that is worth having, and sufficiently justified his existence. Is Carlyle's "Frederick" true? Who cares? As well ask if the Parthenon is true, or the C Minor Symphony, or "Wiener Blut." Let the critic who is an artist leave such necropsies to professors of aesthetics, who can no more determine the truth than he can, and will infallibly make it unpleasant and a bore.

It is, of course, not easy to practice this abstention. Two forces, one within and one without, tend to bring even a Hazlitt or a Huneker under the campus pump. One is the almost universal human susceptibility to messianic delusions—the irresistible tendency of practically every man, once he finds a crowd in front of him, to strut and roll his eyes. The other is the public demand, born of such long familiarity with pedagogical criticism that no other kind is readily conceivable, that the critic teach something as well as say something—in the popular phrase, that he be constructive. Both operate powerfully against his free functioning, and especially the former. He finds it hard to resist the flattery of his customers, however little he may actually esteem it. If he knows anything at all, he knows that his following, like that of every other artist in ideas, is chiefly made up of the congenitally subaltern type of man and woman—natural converts, lodge joiners, me-toos, stragglers after circus parades. It is precious seldom that he ever gets a positive idea out of them; what he usually gets is mere unintelligent ratification. But this troop, despite its obvious failings, corrupts him in various ways. For one thing, it enormously reënforces his belief in his own ideas, and so tends to make him stiff and dogmatic—in brief, precisely everything that he ought not to be. And for another thing, it tends to make him (by a curious contradiction) a bit pliant and politic: he begins to estimate new ideas, not in proportion as they are amusing or beautiful, but in proportion as they are likely to please. So beset, front and rear, he sometimes sinks supinely to the level of a professor, and his subsequent proceedings are interesting no more. The true aim of a critic is certainly not to make converts. He must know that very few of the persons who are susceptible to conversion are worth converting. Their minds are intrinsically flabby and parasitical, and it is certainly not sound sport to agitate minds of that sort. Moreover, the critic must always harbor a grave doubt about most of the ideas that they lap up so greedily—it must occur to him not infrequently, in the silent watches of the night, that much that he writes is sheer buncombe. As I have said, I can't imagine any idea—that is, in the domain of aesthetics—that is palpably and incontrovertibly sound. All that I am familiar with, and in particular all that I announce most vociferously, seem to me to contain a core of quite obvious nonsense. I thus try to avoid cherishing them too lovingly, and it always gives me a shiver to see any one else gobble them at one gulp. Criticism, at bottom, is indistinguishable from skepticism. Both launch themselves, the one by aesthetic presentations and the other by logical presentations, at the common human tendency to accept whatever is approved, to take in ideas ready-made, to be responsive to mere rhetoric and gesticulation. A critic who believes in anything absolutely is bound to that something quite as helplessly as a Christian is bound to the Freudian garbage in the Book of Revelation. To that extent, at all events, he is unfree and unintelligent, and hence a bad critic.

The demand for "constructive" criticism is based upon the same false assumption that immutable truths exist in the arts, and that the artist will be improved by being made aware of them. This notion, whatever the form it takes, is always absurd—as much so, indeed, as its brother delusion that the critic, to be competent, must be a practitioner of the specific art he ventures to deal with, *i.e.*, that a doctor, to cure a belly-ache, must have a belly-ache. As practically encountered, it is disingenuous as well as absurd, for it comes chiefly from bad artists who tire of serving as performing monkeys, and crave the greater ease and safety of sophomores in class. They demand to be taught in order to avoid being knocked about. In their demand is the theory that instruction, if they could get it, would profit them—that they are capable of doing better work than they do. As a practical matter, I doubt that this is ever true. Bad poets never actually grow any better; they invariably grow worse and worse. In all history there has never been, to my knowledge, a single practitioner of any art who, as a result of "constructive" criticism, improved his work. The curse of all the arts, indeed, is the fact that they are constantly invaded by persons who are not artists at all—persons whose yearning to express their ideas and feelings is unaccompanied by the slightest capacity for charming expression—in brief, persons with absolutely nothing to say. This is particularly true of the art of letters, which interposes very few technical obstacles to the vanity and garrulity of such invaders. Any effort to teach them to write better is an effort wasted, as every editor discovers for himself; they are as incapable of it as they are of jumping over the moon. The only sort of criticism that can deal with them to any profit is the sort that employs them frankly as laboratory animals. It cannot cure them, but it can at least make an amusing and perhaps edifying show of them. It is idle to argue that the good in them is thus destroyed with the bad. The simple answer is that there *is* no good in them. Suppose Poe had wasted his time trying to dredge good work out of Rufus Dawes, author of "Geraldine." He would have failed miserably—and spoiled a capital essay, still diverting after three quarters of a century. Suppose Beethoven, dealing with Gottfried Weber, had tried laboriously to make an intelligent music critic of him. How much more apt, useful and durable the simple note: "Arch-ass! Double-barrelled ass!" Here was absolutely sound criticism. Here was a judgment wholly beyond challenge. Moreover, here was a small but perfect work of art.

Upon the low practical value of so-called constructive criticism I can offer testimony out of my own experience. My books are commonly reviewed at great length, and many critics devote themselves to pointing out what they conceive to be my errors, both of fact and of taste. Well, I cannot recall a case in which any suggestion offered by a constructive critic has helped me in the slightest, or even actively interested me. Every such wet-nurse of letters has sought fatuously to make me write in a way differing from that in which the Lord God Almighty, in His infinite wisdom, impels me to write—that is, to make me write stuff which, coming from me, would be as false as an appearance of decency in a Congressman. All the benefits I have ever got from the critics of my work have come from the destructive variety. A hearty slating always does me good, particularly if it be well written. It begins by enlisting my professional respect; it ends by making me examine my ideas coldly in the privacy of my chamber. Not, of course, that I usually revise them, but I at least examine them. If I decide to hold fast to them, they are all the dearer to me thereafter, and I expound them with a new passion and plausibility. If, on the contrary, I discern holes in them, I shelve them in a *pianissimo* manner, and set about hatching new ones to take their place. But constructive criticism irritates me. I do not object to being denounced, but I can't abide being school-mastered, especially by men I regard as imbeciles.

I find, as a practicing critic, that very few men who write books are even as tolerant as I am—that most of them, soon or late, show signs of extreme discomfort under criticism, however polite its terms. Perhaps this is why enduring friendships between authors and critics are so rare. All artists, of course, dislike one another more or less, but that dislike seldom rises to implacable enmity, save between opera singer and opera singer, and creative author and critic. Even when the latter two keep up an outward show of good-will, there is always bitter antagonism under the surface. Part of it, I daresay, arises out of the impossible demands of the critic, particularly if he be tinged with the constructive madness. Having favored an author with his good opinion, he expects the poor fellow to live up to that good opinion without the slightest compromise or faltering, and this is commonly beyond human power. He feels that any let-down compromises *him* —that his hero is stabbing him in the back, and making him ridiculous—and this feeling rasps his vanity. The most bitter of all literary quarrels are those between critics and creative artists, and most of them arise in just this way. As for the creative artist, he on his part naturally resents the critic's air of pedagogical superiority and he resents it especially when he has an uneasy feeling that he has fallen short of his best work, and that the discontent of the critic is thus justified. Injustice is relatively easy to bear; what stings is justice. Under it all, of course, lurks the fact that I began with: the fact that the critic is himself an artist, and that his creative impulse, soon or late, is bound to make him neglect the punctilio. When he sits down to compose his criticism, his artist ceases to be a friend, and becomes mere raw material for his work of art. It is my experience that artists invariably resent this cavalier use of them. They are pleased so long as the critic confines himself to the modest business of interpreting them—preferably in terms of their own estimate of themselves— but the moment he proceeds to adorn their theme with variations of his own, the moment he brings new ideas to the enterprise and begins contrasting them with their ideas, that moment they grow restive. It is precisely at this point, of course, that criticism becomes genuine criticism; before that it was mere reviewing. When a critic passes it he loses his friends. By becoming an artist, he becomes the foe of all other artists.

But the transformation, I believe, has good effects upon him: it makes him a better critic. Too much *Gemütlichkeit* is as fatal to criticism as it would be to surgery or politics. When it rages unimpeded it leads inevitably either to a dull professorial sticking on of meaningless labels or to log-rolling, and often it leads to both. One of the most hopeful symptoms of the new *Aufklärung* in the Republic is the revival of acrimony in criticism—the renaissance of the doctrine that aesthetic matters are important, and that it is worth the while of a healthy male to take them seriously, as he takes business, sport and amour. In the days when American literature was showing its first vigorous growth, the native criticism was extraordinarily violent and even vicious; in the days when American literature swooned 10 upon the tomb of the Puritan *Kultur* it became flaccid and childish. The typical critic of the first era was Poe, as the typical critic of the second was Howells. Poe carried on his critical jehads with such ferocity that he often got into law-suits, and sometimes ran no little risk of having his head cracked. He regarded literary questions as exigent and momentous. The lofty aloofness of the don was simply not in him. When he encountered a book that seemed to 20 him to be bad, he attacked it almost as sharply as a Chamber of Commerce would attack a fanatic preaching free speech, or the corporation of Trinity Church would attack Christ. His opponents replied in the same Berserker manner. Much of Poe's surviving ill-fame, as a drunkard and dead-beat, is due to their inordinate denunciations of him. They were not content to refute him; they constantly tried to dispose of him altogether. The very ferocity 30 of that ancient row shows that the native literature, in those days, was in a healthy state. Books of genuine value were produced. Literature always thrives best, in fact, in an atmosphere of hearty strife. Poe, surrounded by admiring professors, never challenged,

never aroused to the emotions of revolt, would probably have written poetry indistinguishable from the hollow stuff of, say, Prof. Dr. George E. Woodberry. It took the persistent (and often grossly unfair and dishonorable) opposition of Griswold *et al* to stimulate him to his highest endeavors. He needed friends, true enough, but he also needed enemies.

Today, for the first time in years, there is strife in American criticism, and the Paul Elmer Mores and Hamilton Wright Mabies are no longer able to purr in peace. The instant they fall into stiff professorial attitudes they are challenged, and often with anything but urbanity. The *ex cathedra* manner thus passes out, and free discussion comes in. Heretics lay on boldly, and the professors are forced to make some defense. Often, going further, they attempt counter-attacks. Ears are bitten off. Noses are bloodied. There are wallops both above and below the belt. I am, I need not say, no believer in any magical merit in debate, no matter how free it may be. It certainly does not necessarily establish the truth; both sides, in fact, may be wrong, and they often are. But it at least accomplishes two important effects. On the one hand, it exposes all the cruder fallacies to hostile examination, and so disposes of many of them. And on the other hand, it melodramatizes the business of the critic, and so convinces thousands of bystanders, otherwise quite inert, that criticism is an amusing and instructive art, and that the problems it deals with are important. What men will fight for seems to be worth looking into.

1922

1888 ~ *T. S. Eliot* ~ ——

FOR a consideration of Eliot as poet, see page 992.
In his valuable book *The New Criticism*, John Crowe Ransom calls Eliot "the Historical Critic," and explains that

> It is Eliot who uses his historical studies for the sake of literary understanding, and therefore might be called a historical critic. . . . I mean the formality to stand for the fact that he is learned in the precise learning of the scholars, a Pharisee of the Pharisees.

Eliot's critical studies of past poetry, theology, and drama have for their purpose the sharpening of present perceptions and the cumulative enrichment of the present by a judicious reading of the past. He is not interested in historical surveys; nor does he always consider all of the work of any man; rather, he seeks out the literary product which is most pertinent and will be most helpful to the development of creative insights. "The critical activity finds its highest, its true fulfilment in a kind of union with creation in the labour of the artist." His critical essays are therefore, in the main, reflections upon his reading in which he has always sought for new insights, confirming views, and perhaps most of all, testimony of a continuing tradition which both fortifies and enriches the literature of the present.

As for his major contributions to modern criticism, these are brilliant asides, or near-asides, found in his "historical" essays. One of these concerns what is called the "objective correlative," a phrase which is found explained in Eliot's essay on Hamlet: speaking there of the inadequacy of Shakespeare's treatment of Hamlet (who he says, is "dominated by an emotion which is inexpressible, because it is in *excess* of the facts as they appear") Eliot defines the "objective correlative" as "a set of objects, a situation, a chain of events which shall be the formula of that *particular* emotion; such that when the external facts, which must terminate in sensory experience, are given, the emotion is immediately evoked." This brilliant generalization, reflecting as it does the very strong impression which Pound made upon him, as well as the degree to which he was to progress beyond Pound, has been an important part of formalist criticism ever since its original appearance, in 1919.

Eliot's critical method is purposefully casual; he very often does not explain so much as he directs the reader to explain for himself. As M. C. Bradbrooke has put it, "The quotations are made to do the critic's work, and the reader is made to work on them. They are more than 'happy quotations' in the usual sense: frequently they constitute Eliot's main statement. Against his reserved and restricted style they stand out, exactly chosen to make the point towards which he has been engaging the reader—but making it because the reader too is compelled to work over these particular lines, to respond actively to them, to relate to them all his own past experience of the writer under discussion."

As Eliot's poetry concerned itself increasingly with religious matters (that is, with the nature of conversion and the documentation of its causes), his critical writing also focussed upon the study of Anglo-Catholic divines and religious mystics. *For Lancelot Andrewes* (1928), *Dante* (1929), *Thoughts After Lambeth* (1931), and *After Strange Gods* (1934) testify to this concentration of interest. He was also to concern himself with the nature and development of culture, and more specifically with a definition of a culture. All of these more recent emphases make Eliot's criticism a rather special thing, nonetheless informed by the same quiet manner and perception as characterized his earlier work.

Eliot's criticism is found in *Ezra Pound: His Metric and Poetry* (1917); *The Sacred Wood* (1921); *Poetry in Prose* (1921); *Homage to John Dryden* (1924); *Shakespeare and the Stoicism of Seneca* (1927); *An Essay of Poetic Drama* (1928); *For Lancelot Andrewes* (1928); *Dante* (1929); *Charles Whibley* (1931); *Thoughts After Lambeth* (1931); *John Dryden* (1932); *The Use of Poetry and the Use of Criticism* (1933); *After Strange Gods* (1934). Three collections of his criticism have so far appeared: *Selected Essays, 1917–1932* (1932); *Essays Ancient and Modern* (1936); and *Points of View* (1941). Studies which concern his criticism include F. O. Matthiessen, *The Achievement of T. S. Eliot* (rev. ed., 1947); M. C. Bradbrooke, "Eliot's Critical Method," in *T. S. Eliot: A Study of His Writing by Several Hands*, ed. B. Rajan (1947); J. C. Ransom, *The New Criticism* (1941); Stanley Edgar Hyman, *The Armed Vision* (1948); Yvor Winters, *The Anatomy of Nonsense* (1943); Leonard Unger (ed.) *T. S. Eliot: A Selected Critique* (1948); J. A. Borey, "The Literary Criticism of T. S. Eliot," *American Prefaces*, 1936; Kenneth Burke, "The Allies of Humanism Abroad," in *The Critique of Humanism*, ed. C. H. Grattan (1930); Harry M. Campbell, "An Examination of Modern Critics: T. S. Eliot," *Rocky Mountain Review*, 1944; W. E. Collin, "T. S. Eliot the Critic," *Sewanee Review* (1931); G. R. Elliott, "T. S. Eliot and Irving Babbitt," *The American Review*, 1936; Francis Fergusson, "T. S. Eliot and His Impersonal Theory of Art," *The American Caravan*, 1927; Ramon Fernandez, *Messages* (1927); Humphrey House, "Mr. Eliot as a Critic," *New Oxford Outlook*, 1933; Ants Oras, "The Critical Ideas of T. S. Eliot," *Tartu*, 1932; Arthur Quiller-Couch, *The Poet as Citizen and Other Papers* (1935); Delmore Schwartz, "*The Criterion, 1922–1939*," *Kenyon Review*, 1939; René Taupin, "The Classicism of T. S. Eliot," *Symposium*, 1932. For additional titles, see Leonard Unger (ed.), *T. S. Eliot: A Selected Critique* (1948); Millett, *Contemporary British Literature* (1935); Leary, *Articles on American Literature Appearing in Current Periodicals, 1920–1945* (1947).

FROM THE SACRED WOOD

TRADITION AND THE INDIVIDUAL TALENT

I

IN English writing we seldom speak of tradition, though we occasionally apply its name in deploring its absence. We cannot refer to "the tradition" or to "a tradition"; at most, we employ the adjective in saying that the poetry of So-and-so is "traditional" or even "too traditional." Seldom, perhaps, does the word appear except in a phrase of censure. If otherwise, it is vaguely approbative, with the implication, as to the work approved, of some pleasing archaeological reconstruction. You can hardly make the word agreeable to English ears without this comfortable reference to the reassuring science of archaeology.

Certainly the word is not likely to appear in our appreciations of living or dead writers. Every nation, every race, has not only its own creative, but its own critical turn of mind; and is even more oblivious of the shortcomings and limitations of its critical habits than of those of its creative genius. We know, or think we know, from the enormous mass of critical writing that has appeared in the French language the critical method or habit of the French; we only conclude (we are such unconscious people) that the French are "more critical" than we, and sometimes even plume ourselves a little with the fact, as if the French were the less spontaneous. Perhaps they are; but we might remind ourselves that criticism is as inevitable as breathing, and that we should be none the worse for articulating what passes in our minds when we read a book and feel an emotion about it, for criticizing our own minds in their work of criticism. One of the facts that might come to light in this process is our tendency to insist, when we praise a poet, upon those aspects of his work in which he least resembles anyone else. In these aspects or parts of his work we pretend to find what is individual, what is the peculiar essence of the man. We dwell with satisfaction upon the poet's difference from his predecessors, especially his immediate predecessors; we endeavour to find something that can be isolated in order to be enjoyed. Whereas if we approach a poet without his prejudice we shall often find that not only the best, but the most individual parts of his work may be those in which the dead poets, his ancestors, assert their immortality most vigorously. And I do not mean the impressionable period of adolescence, but the period of full maturity.

Yet if the only form of tradition, of handing down, consisted in following the ways of the immediate generation before us in a blind or timid adherence to its successes, "tradition" should positively be discouraged. We have seen many such simple currents soon lost in the sand; and novelty is better than repetition. Tradition is a matter of much wider significance. It cannot be inherited, and if you want it you must obtain it by great labour. It involves, in the first place, the historical sense, which we may call nearly indispensable to anyone who would continue to be a poet beyond his twenty-fifth year; and the historical sense involves a perception not only of the pastness of the past, but of its presence; the historical sense compels a man to write not merely with his own generation in his bones, but with a feeling that the whole of the literature of Europe from Homer and within it the whole of the literature of his own country has a simultaneous existence and composes a simultaneous order. This historical sense, which is a sense of the timeless as well as of the temporal and of the timeless and of the temporal together, is what makes a writer traditional. And it is at the same time what makes a writer most acutely conscious of his place in time, of his contemporaneity.

No poet, no artist of any art, has his complete meaning alone. His significance, his appreciation is the appreciation of his relation to the dead poets and artists. You cannot value him alone; you must set him, for contrast and comparison, among the dead. I mean this as a principle of aesthetic, not merely historical, criticism. The necessity that he shall conform, that he shall cohere, is not one-sided; what happens when a new work of art is created is something that happens simultaneously to all the works of art which preceded it. The existing monuments form an ideal order among themselves, which is modified by the introduction of the new (the really new) work of art among them. The existing order is complete before the new work arrives; for order to persist after the supervention of novelty, the *whole* existing order must be, if ever so slightly, altered; and so the relations, proportions, values of each work of art toward the whole are readjusted; and this is conformity between the old and the new. Whoever has approved this idea of order, of the form of European, of English literature, will not find it preposterous that the past should be altered by the present as much as the present is directed by the past. And the poet who is aware of this will be aware of great difficulties and responsibilities.

In a peculiar sense he will be aware also that he must inevitably be judged by the standards of the past. I say judged, not amputated, by them; not judged to be as good as, or worse or better than, the dead; and certainly not judged by the canons of dead critics. It is a judgment, a comparison, in which two things are measured by each other. To conform merely would be for the new work not really to conform at all; it would not be new, and would therefore not be a work of art. And we do not quite say that the new is more valuable because it fits in; but its fitting in is a test of its value— a test, it is true, which can only be slowly and cautiously applied, for we are none of us infallible judges of conformity. We say: it appears to conform, and is perhaps individual, or it appears individual, and may conform; but we are hardly likely to find that it is one and not the other.

To proceed to a more intelligible exposition of the relation of the poet to the past: he can neither take the past as a lump, an indiscriminate bolus, nor can he form himself wholly on one or two private admirations, nor can he form himself wholly upon one preferred period. The first course is inadmissible, the second is an important experience of youth, and the third is a pleasant and highly desirable supplement. The poet must be very conscious of the main current, which does not at all flow invariably through the most distinguished reputations. He must be quite aware of the obvious fact that art never improves, but that the material of art is never quite the same. He must be aware that the mind of Europe—the mind of his own country—a mind which he learns in time to be much more important than his own private mind—is a mind which changes, and that this change is a development which abandons nothing *en route*, which does not superannuate either Shakespeare, or Homer, or the rock drawing of the Magdalenian draughtsmen. That this development, refinement perhaps, complication certainly, is not, from the point of view of the artist, any improvement. Perhaps not even an improvement from the point of view of the psychologist or not to the extent which we imagine; perhaps only in the end based upon a complication in economics and machinery. But the difference between the present and the past is that the conscious present is an awareness of the past in a way and to an extent which the past's awareness of itself cannot show.

Some one said: "The dead writers are remote from us because we *know* so much more than they did." Precisely, and they are that which we know.

I am alive to a usual objection to what is clearly part of my programme for the *metier* of poetry. The objection is that the doctrine requires a ridiculous amount of erudition (pedantry), a claim which can be rejected by appeal to the lives of poets in any pantheon. It will even be affirmed that much learning deadens or perverts poetic sensibility. While, however, we persist in believing that a poet ought to know as much as will not encroach upon his necessary receptivity and necessary laziness, it is not desirable to confine knowledge to whatever can be put into a useful shape for examinations, drawing-rooms, or the still more pretentious modes of publicity. Some can absorb knowledge, the more tardy must sweat for it. Shakespeare acquired more essential history from Plutarch than most men could from the whole British Museum. What is to be insisted upon is that the poet must develop or procure the consciousness of the past and that he should continue to develop this consciousness throughout his career.

What happens is a continual surrender of himself as he is at the moment to something which is more valuable. The progress of an artist is a continual self-sacrifice, a continual extinction of personality.

There remains to define this process of depersonalization and its relation to the sense of tradition. It is in this depersonalization that art may be said to approach the condition of science. I shall, therefore, invite you to consider, as a suggestive analogy, the action which takes place when a bit of finely filiated platinum is introduced into a chamber containing oxygen and sulphur dioxide.

II

Honest criticism and sensitive appreciation is directed not upon the poet but upon the poetry. If we attend to the confused cries of the newspaper critics and the susurrus of popular repetition that follows, we shall hear the names of poets in great numbers; if we seek not Blue-book knowledge but the enjoyment of poetry, and ask for a poem, we shall seldom find it. In the last article I tried to point out the importance of the relation of the poem to other poems by other authors, and suggested the conception of poetry as a living whole of all the poetry that has ever been written. The other aspect of this Impersonal theory of poetry is the relation of the poem to its author. And I hinted, by an analogy, that the mind of the mature poet differs from that of the immature one not precisely in any valuation of "personality," not being necessarily more interesting, or having "more to say," but rather by being a more finely perfected medium in which special, or very varied, feelings are at liberty to enter into new combinations.

The analogy was that of the catalyst. When the two gases previously mentioned are mixed in the presence of a filament of platinum, they form sulphurous acid. This combination takes place only if the platinum is present; nevertheless the newly formed acid contains no trace of platinum, and the platinum itself is apparently unaffected; has remained inert, neutral, and unchanged. The mind of the poet is the shred of platinum. It may partly or exclusively operate upon the experience of the man himself; but, the more perfect the artist, the more completely separate in him will be the man who suffers and the mind which creates; the more perfectly will the mind digest and transmute the passions which are its material.

The experience, you will notice, the elements

which enter the presence of the transforming catalyst, are of two kinds: emotions and feelings. The effect of a work of art upon the person who enjoys it is an experience different in kind from any experience not of art. It may be formed out of one emotion, or may be a combination of several; and various feelings, inhering for the writer in particular words or phrases or images, may be added to compose the final result. Or great poetry may be made without the direct use of any emotion whatever: composed out of feelings solely. Canto XV of the *Inferno* (Brunetto Latini) is a working up of the emotion evident in the situation; but the effect, though single as that of any work of art, is obtained by considerable complexity of detail. The last quatrain gives an image, a feeling attaching to an image, which "came," which did not develop simply out of what precedes, but which was probably in suspension in the poet's mind until the proper combination arrived for it to add itself to. The poet's mind is in fact a receptacle for seizing and storing up numberless feelings, phrases, images, which remain there until all the particles which can unite to form a new compound are present together.

If you compare several representative passages of the greatest poetry you see how great is the variety of types of combination, and also how completely any semi-ethical criterion of "sublimity" misses the mark. For it is not the "greatness," the intensity, of the emotions, the components, but the intensity of the artistic process, the pressure, so to speak, under which the fusion takes place, that counts. The episode of Paolo and Francesca employs a definite emotion, but the intensity of the poetry is something quite different from whatever intensity in the supposed experience it may give the impression of. It is no more intense, furthermore, than Canto XXVI, the voyage of Ulysses, which has not the direct dependence upon an emotion. Great variety is possible in the process of transmutation of emotion: the murder of Agamemnon, or the agony of Othello, gives an artistic effect apparently closer to a possible original than the scenes from Dante. In the *Agamemnon*, the artistic emotion approximates to the emotion of an actual spectator; in *Othello* to the emotion of

the protagonist himself. But the difference between art and the event is always absolute; the combination which is the murder of Agamemnon is probably as complex as that which is the voyage of Ulysses. In either case there has been a fusion of elements. The ode of Keats contains a number of feelings which have nothing particular to do with the nightingale, but which the nightingale, partly, perhaps, because of its attractive name, and partly because of its reputation, served to bring together.

The point of view which I am struggling to attack is perhaps related to the metaphysical theory of the substantial unity of the soul: for my meaning is, that the poet has, not a "personality" to express, but a particular medium, which is only a medium and not a personality, in which impressions and experiences combine in peculiar and unexpected ways. Impressions and experiences which are important for the man may take no place in the poetry, and those which become important in the poetry may play quite a negligible part in the man, the personality.

I will quote a passage which is unfamiliar enough to be regarded with fresh attention in the light—or darkness—of these observations:

And now methinks I could e'en chide myself
For doting on her beauty, though her death
Shall be revenged after no common action.
Does the silkworm expend her yellow labours
For thee? For thee does she undo herself?
Are lordships sold to maintain ladyships
For the poor benefit of a bewildering minute?
Why does yon fellow falsify highways,
And put his life between the judge's lips,
To refine such a thing—keeps horse and men
To beat their valours for her? . . .

In this passage (as is evident if it is taken in its context) there is a combination of positive and negative emotions: an intensely strong attraction toward beauty and an equally intense fascination by the ugliness which is contrasted with it and which destroys it. This balance of contrasted emotion is in the dramatic situation to which the speech is pertinent, but that situation alone is inadequate to it. This is, so to speak, the structural emotion, provided by the drama. But the whole effect, the dominant tone, is due to the fact that a number of floating feelings, having an affinity to this emotion by no means superficially evident, have combined with it to give us a new art emotion.

It is not in his personal emotions, the emotions provoked by particular events in his life, that the poet is in any way remarkable or interesting. His particular emotions may be simple, or crude, or flat. The emotion in his poetry will be a very complex thing, but not [10] with the complexity of the emotions of people who have very complex or unusual emotions in life. One error, in fact, of eccentricity in poetry is to seek for new human emotions to express; and in this search for novelty in the wrong place it discovers the perverse. The business of the poet is not to find new emotions, but to use the ordinary ones and, in working them up into poetry, to express feelings which are not in actual emotions at all. [20] And emotions which he has never experienced will serve his turn as well as those familiar to him. Consequently, we must believe that "emotion recollected in tranquillity" is an inexact formula. For it is neither emotion, nor recollection, nor, without distortion of meaning, tranquillity. It is a concentration, and a new thing resulting from the concentration, of a very great number of experiences which to the practical and active person would not seem [30] to be experiences at all; it is a concentration which does not happen consciously or of deliberation. These experiences are not "recollected," and they finally unite in an atmosphere which is "tranquil" only in that it is a passive attending upon the event. Of course this is not quite the whole story. There is a great deal, in the writing of poetry, which must be conscious and deliberate. In fact, the bad poet is usually unconscious where he ought to be conscious, and conscious where he ought to be unconscious. Both errors tend to make him "personal." Poetry is not a turning loose of emotion, but an escape from emotion; it is not the expression of personality, but an escape from personality. But, of course, only those who have personality and emotions know what it means to want to escape from these things.

III

ὁ δὲ νοῦς, ἴσως, θειότερόν τι καὶ ἀπαθές ἐστιν*

This essay proposes to halt at the frontier of metaphysics or mysticism, and confine itself to such practical conclusions as can be applied by the responsible person interested in poetry. To divert interest from the poet to the poetry is a laudable aim: for it would conduce to a juster estimation of actual poetry, good and bad. There are many people who appreciate the expression of sincere emotion in verse, and there is a smaller number of people who can appreciate technical excellence. But very few know when there is expression of *significant* emotion, emotion which has its life in the poem and not in the history of the poet. The emotion of art is impersonal. And the poet cannot reach this impersonality without surrendering himself wholly to the work to be done. And he is not likely to know what is to be done unless he lives in what is not merely the present, but the present moment of the past, unless he is conscious, not of what is dead, but of what is already living.

1921

*ὁ ... ἐστιν, "Possibly the mind is too divine, and is therefore unaffected," quoted from Aristotle's *On the Soul*, I, iv (translation by W. S. Hett).

1905 ~ *Robert Penn Warren* ~ —

ROBERT PENN WARREN, with Ransom, Tate, and Davidson, a product of the Vanderbilt "Fugitive" group of the early twenties, has not yet published a collected volume of his critical essays. As these essays appear in various literary reviews and symposia, it becomes increasingly obvious that Warren is possessed of an exceptional taste and a shrewd talent for discovering and emphasizing literary essentials. He has taught at Southwestern University, Vanderbilt University, Louisiana State University (where he helped to edit *The Southern Review*), and at the University of Minnesota. The essay on "William Faulkner," printed below, is not only a perceptive study of its subject but a good example of Warren's critical work.

Warren's work includes a biography (*John Brown*, 1929), poetry (*Thirty-six Poems*, 1935; *Selected Poems*, 1944), three novels (*Night Rider*, 1939; *At Heaven's Gate*, 1943; and *All the King's Men*, 1946), and a collection of short stories (*The Circus in the Attic and Other Stories*, 1947). He has contributed, with eleven other Southern writers, to *I'll Take My Stand* (1930), and has written, in collaboration with Cleanth Brooks, two textbooks (*Understanding Poetry*, 1938; and *Understanding Fiction*, 1943). His critical essays include an introduction to Coleridge's "The Rime of the Ancient Mariner," (1946); essays on Katherine Anne Porter (*Kenyon Review*, Winter, 1942), Eudora Welty (*Kenyon Review*, Spring, 1944), Ernest Hemingway (*Kenyon Review*, Winter, 1947), and William Faulkner (in *Forms of Modern Fiction*, ed. W. V. O'Connor, 1948); and an essay on "Pure and Impure Poetry" (*Kenyon Review*, Spring, 1943). For essays on Warren, see Morton D. Zabel, "Problems of Knowledge," *Poetry*, Apr., 1936; Cleanth Brooks and Mark Van Doren, "Modern Poetry; A Symposium," *American Review*, Feb., 1937; Irene Hendry, "Regional Novel: The Example of Robert Penn Warren," *Sewanee Review*, Jan., 1945; W. P. Southard, "The Religious Poetry of Robert Penn Warren," *Kenyon Review*, Autumn, 1945; Eric Bentley, "The Meaning of Robert Penn Warren's Novels," in *Forms of Modern Fiction*, ed. W. V. O'Connor (1948); R. W. Stallman, "The New Criticism and the Southern Critics," in *A Southern Vanguard*, ed. Allen Tate (1947); Stallman, Warren Checklist, *The University of Kansas City Review*, Autumn, 1947; W. V. O'Connor, "Robert Penn Warren: 'Provincial' Poet," in *A Southern Vanguard* (1947).

WILLIAM FAULKNER

Malcolm Cowley's editing of *The Portable Faulkner** is remarkable on two counts. First, the selection from Faulkner's work is made not merely to give a cross section or a group of good examples but to demonstrate one of the principles of integration in the work. Second, the introductory essay is one of the few things ever written on Faulkner which is not hagridden by prejudice or preconception and which really sheds some light on the subject.

The selections here are made to describe the place, Yoknapatawpha County, Mississippi, which is, as Cowley puts it, "Faulkner's mythical kingdom," and to give the history of that kingdom. The place is the locale of most of Faulkner's work. Its 2400 square miles lie between the hills of north Mississippi and the rich, black bottom lands. It has a population

The Portable Faulkner, edited by Malcolm Cowley. New York: Viking Press.

of 15,611 persons, composing a society with characters as different as the Bundrens, the Snopeses, Ike McCaslin, Percy Grimm, Temple Drake, the Compsons, Christmas, Dilsey, and the tall convict of *The Wild Palms*. No land in all fiction lives more vividly in its physical presence than this mythical county—the "pine-winey" afternoons, the nights with "a thin sickle of moon like the heel print of a boot in wet sand," the tremendous reach of the big river in flood, "yellow and sleepy in the afternoon," and the "little piddling creeks, that run backward one day and forward the next and come busting down on a man full of dead mules and hen houses," the ruined plantation which was Popeye's hangout, the swamps and fields and hot, dusty roads of the Frenchman's Bend section, and the remnants of the great original forests, "green with gloom" in summer, "if anything actually dimmer than they had been in November's gray dissolution, where even at noon the sun fell only in windless dappling upon the earth which never completely dried."

And no land in all fiction is more painstakingly analyzed from the sociological standpoint. The descendants of the old families, the descendants of bushwhackers and carpetbaggers, the swamp rats, the Negro cooks and farm hands, bootleggers and gangsters, peddlers, college boys, tenant farmers, country store-keepers, county-seat lawyers are all here. The marks of class, occupation, and history are fully rendered and we know completely their speech, dress, food, houses, manners, and attitudes. Nature and sociology, geography and human geography, are scrupulously though effortlessly presented in Faulkner's work, and their significance for his work is very great; but the significance is of a conditioning order. They are, as it were, aspects of man's "doom" —a word of which Faulkner is very fond—but his manhood in the face of that doom is what is important.

Cowley's selections are made to give the description of the mythical kingdom, but more important, they are made to give its history. Most critics, even those who have most naïvely or deliberately misread the meaning of the fact, have been aware that the sense of the past is crucial in Faulkner's work. Cowley has here set up selections running in date of action from 1820 to 1940. The first, "A Justice," is a story about Ikkemotubbe, the nephew of a Chickasaw chief who went to New Orleans, where he received the name of *du Homme*, which became Doom; who came back to the tribe to poison his way to the Man-ship; and who, in the end (in Faulkner's "history" though not in "A Justice" itself), swaps a mile square of "virgin north Mississippi dirt" for a racing mare owned by Jason Lycurgus Compson, the founder of the Compson family in Mississippi. The last selection, "Delta Autumn," shows us Isaac McCaslin, the man who brings the best of the old order, philosopher, aristocrat, woodsman, into the modern world and who gives the silver-mounted horn which General Compson had left him to a mulatto woman for her bastard son by a relative of McCaslin's. In between "A Justice" and "Delta Autumn" fall such pieces as the magnificent "Red Leaves," the profoundly symbolic story

called "The Bear," the Civil War and Reconstruction stories, "Rain" (from *The Unvanquished*) and "Wash," "Old Man" (the story of the tall convict from *The Wild Palms*), and the often anthologized "That Evening Sun" and "A Rose for Emily," and the brilliant episode of "Percy Grimm" (from *Light in August*). There are other pieces included, but these are the best, and the best for showing the high points in the history of Yoknapatawpha County.

Cowley's introduction undertakes to define the significance of place and history in Faulkner's work, that "labor of imagination that has not been equaled in our time." That labor is, as he points out, a double labor: "first, to invent a Mississippi county that was like a mythical kingdom, but was complete and living in all its details; second, to make his story of Yoknapatawpha County stand as a parable or legend of all the Deep South." The legend —called a legend "because it is obviously no more intended as a historical account of the country south of the Ohio than *The Scarlet Letter* was intended as a history of Massachusetts"—is, as Cowley defines it, this:

The South was settled by Sartorises (aristocrats) and Sutpens (nameless, ambitious men) who, seizing the land from the Indians, were determined to found an enduring and stable order. But despite their strength and integrity their project was, to use Faulkner's word, "accursed" by slavery, which, with the Civil War as instrument, frustrated their design. Their attempt to rebuild according to the old plan and old values was defeated by a combination of forces—the carpetbaggers and Snopeses ("a new exploiting class descended from the landless whites"). Most of the descendants of the old order are in various ways incompetent: They are prevented by their code from competing with the codeless Snopeses, they cling to the letter and forget the spirit of their tradition, they lose contact with the realities of the present and escape into a dream world of alcohol or rhetoric or gentility or madness, they fall in love with defeat or death, they lose nerve and become cowards, or they, like the last Jason in *The Sound and the Fury*, adopt Snopesism and become worse than any Snopes. Figures like Popeye (eyes like "rubber knobs," a creature having "that vicious depthless quality of stamped tin," the man "who made money and had nothing he could do with it, spend it for, since he knew that alcohol would kill him like poison, who had no friends and had never known a woman") are in their dehumanized quality symbols of modernism, for the society of finance capitalism. The violence of some of Faulkner's work is, according to Cowley, "an example of the Freudian method turned backward, being full of sexual nightmares that are in reality social symbols. It is somehow connected in the author's mind with what he regards as the rape and corruption of the South."

This is, in brief, Cowley's interpretation of the legend, and it provides an excellent way into Faulkner; it exactly serves the purpose which an introduction should serve. The interpretation is indebted, no doubt, to that of George Marion O'Donnell (the first and still an indispensable study of Faulkner's theme), but it modifies O'Donnell's tendency to read Faulkner with an allegorical rigidity and with a kind of doctrinal single-mindedness.

It is possible that the present view, however, should be somewhat modified, at least in emphasis. Although no writer is more deeply committed to a locality than Faulkner, the emphasis on the Southern elements may blind us to other elements, or at least other applications, of deep significance. And this is especially true in so far as the work is interpreted merely as Southern apologetics or, as it is by Maxwell Geismar, as the "extreme hallucinations" of a "cultural psychosis."

It is important, I think, that Faulkner's work be regarded not in terms of the South against the North, but in terms of issues which are common to our modern world. The legend is not merely a legend of the South, but is also a legend of our general plight and problem. The modern world is in moral confusion. It does suffer from a lack of discipline, of sanctions, of community of values, of a sense of a mission. It is a world in which self-interest, workability, success, provide the standards. It is a world which is the victim of abstraction and of mechanism, or at least, at moments, feels itself to be. It can look back nostalgically upon the old world of traditional values and feel loss

and perhaps despair—upon the world in which, as one of Faulkner's characters puts it, men "had the gift of living once or dying once instead of being diffused and scattered creatures drawn blindly from a grab bag and assembled"— a world in which men were, "integer for integer," more simple and complete.

If it be objected that Faulkner's view is unrealistic, that had the old order satisfied human needs it would have survived, and that it is sentimental to hold that it was killed from the outside, the answer is clear in the work: the old order did not satisfy human needs—the Southern old order or any other—for it, not being founded on justice, was "accursed" and held the seeds of its own ruin in itself. But even in terms of the curse the old order, as opposed to the new order (in so far as the new is to be equated with Snopesism), allowed the traditional man to define himself as human by setting up codes, concepts of virtue, obligations, and by accepting the risks of his humanity. Within the traditional order was a notion of truth, even if man in the flow of things did not succeed in realizing that truth. Take, for instance, the passage from "The Bear":

"All right," he said. "Listen," and read again, but only one stanza this time and closed the book and laid it on the table. "She cannot fade, though thou hast not thy bliss," McCaslin said: "Forever wilt thou love, she be fair."

"He's talking about a girl," he said.

"He had to talk about something," McCaslin said. Then he said, "He was talking about truth. Truth is one. It doesn't change. It covers all things which touch the heart— honor and pride and pity and justice and courage and love. Do you see now?"

The human effort is what is important, the capacity to make the effort to rise above the mechanical process of life, the pride to endure, for in endurance there is a kind of self-conquest.

When it is said, as it is often said, that Faulkner's work is "backward-looking," the answer is that the constant ethical center is to be found in the glorification of the human effort and of human endurance, which are not in time, even though in modernity they seem to persist most surely among the despised and rejected. It is true that Faulkner's work contains a savage attack on modernity, but it is to be remembered that Elizabethan tragedy, for instance, contained just such an attack on its own special "modernity." (Ambition is the most constant tragic crime, and ambition is the attitude special to an opening society; all villains are rationalists and appeal to "nature" beyond traditional morality for justification, and rationalism is, in the sense implied here, the attitude special to the rise of a secular and scientific order before a new morality can be formulated.)

It is not ultimately important whether the traditional order (Southern or other) as depicted by Faulkner fits exactly the picture which critical historical method provides. Let it be granted, for the sake of discussion, that Faulkner does oversimplify the matter. What is ultimately important, both ethically and artistically, is the symbolic function of that order in relation to the world which is set in opposition to it. The opposition between the old order and the new does not, however, exhaust the picture. What of the order to come? "We will have to wait," old Ike McCaslin says to the mulatto girl who is in love with a white man. A curse may work itself out in time; and in such glimpses, which occur now and then, we get the notion of a grudging meliorism, a practical supplement to the idealism, like Ike McCaslin's, which finds compensation in the human effort and the contemplation of "truth."

The discussion, even at a larger scope and with more satisfactory analysis, of the central theme of Faulkner would not exhaust the interest of his work. In fact, the discussion of this question always runs the risk of making his work appear too schematic, too dry and too complacent when in actual fact it is full of rich detail, of shadings and complexities of attitude, of ironies and ambivalences. Cowley's introduction cautions the reader on this point and suggests various fruitful topics for investigation and thought. But I shall make bold—and in the general barrenness of criticism on Faulkner it does not require excessive boldness—to list and comment on certain topics which seem to me to demand further critical study.

Nature. The vividness of the natural background is one of the impressive features of Faulkner's work. It is accurately observed, but observation only provides the stuff from which the characteristic effects are gained. It is the atmosphere which counts, the poetry, the infusion of feeling, the symbolic weight. Nature provides a backdrop—of lyric beauty (the meadow in the cow episode of *The Hamlet*), of homely charm (the trial scene of the "Spotted Horses" story from the same book), of sinister, brooding force (the river in "Old Man" from *The Wild Palms*), of massive dignity (the forest in "The Bear")—for the human action and passion. The indestructible beauty is there: "God created man," Ike McCaslin says in "Delta Autumn," "and He created the world for him to live in and I reckon He created the kind of world He would have wanted to live in if He had been a man."

Ideally, if man were like God, as Ike McCaslin puts it, man's attitude toward nature would be one of pure contemplation, pure participation in its great forms and appearances; the appropriate attitude is love, for with Ike McCaslin the moment of love is equated with godhood. But since man "wasn't quite God himself," since he lives in the world of flesh, he must be a hunter, user, and violator. To return to McCaslin: God "put them both here: man and the game he would follow and kill, foreknowing it. I believe He said, 'So be it.' I reckon He even foreknew the end. But He said, 'I will give him his chance. I will give him warning and foreknowledge too, along with the desire to follow and the power to slay. The woods and the fields he ravages and the game he devastates will be the consequence and signature of his crime and guilt, and his punishment.'"

There is, then, a contamination implicit in the human condition—a kind of Original Sin, as it were—but it is possible, even in the contaminating act, the violation, for man to achieve some measure of redemption, a redemption through love. For instance, in "The Bear," the great legendary beast which is pursued for years to the death is also an object of love and veneration, and the symbol of virtue, and the deer hunt of "Delta Autumn" is for Ike McCaslin a ritual of renewal. Those who have learned the right relationship to nature—"the

pride and humility" which young Ike Mc-
Caslin learns from the half-Negro, half-Indian
Sam Fathers—are set over against those who
have not. In "The Bear," General Compson
speaks up to Cass McCaslin to defend the wish
of the boy Ike McCaslin to stay an extra week
in the woods: "You got one foot straddled
into a farm and the other foot straddled into
a bank; you ain't even got a good hand-hold
where this boy was already an old man long 10
before you damned Sartorises and Edmondses
invented farms and banks to keep yourselves
from having to find out what this boy was
born knowing and fearing too maybe, but
without being afraid, that could go ten miles
on a compass because he wanted to look at a
bear none of us had ever got near enough to
put a bullet in and looked at the bear and came
the ten miles back on the compass in the dark;
maybe by God that's the why and the where- 20
fore of farms and banks."

Those who have the wrong attitude toward
nature are the pure exploiters, the apostles of
abstractionism, the truly evil men. For instance, the very opening of *Sanctuary* presents
a distinction on this ground between Benbow
and Popeye. While the threat of Popeye keeps
Benbow crouching by the spring, he hears a
Carolina wren sing, and even under these circumstances tries to recall the local name for it. 30
And he says to Popeye: "And of course you
don't know the name of it. I don't suppose
you'd know a bird at all, without it was singing in a cage in a hotel lounge, or cost four
dollars on a plate." Popeye, as we may remember, spits in the spring (he hates nature and
must foul it), is afraid to go through the woods
("Through all them trees?" he demands when
Benbow points out the short cut), and when
an owl whisks past them in the twilight, claws 40
at Benbow's coat with almost hysterical fear
("It's just an owl," Benbow says. "It's nothing
but an owl.").

The pure exploiters, though they may gain
ownership and use of a thing, never really
have it; like Popeye, they are impotent. For
instance, Flem Snopes, the central character
and villain of *The Hamlet*, who brings the exploiter's mentality to Frenchman's Bend, finally marries Eula Varner, a kind of fertility 50
goddess or earth goddess; but his ownership

is meaningless, for she always refers to him as
"that man" (she does not even have a name
for him), and he has only got her after she has
given herself willingly to one of the bold, hot-
blooded boys of the neighborhood. In fact,
nature can't, in one sense, be "owned." Ike
McCaslin, in "The Bear," says of the land
which has come down to him: "It was never
Father's and Uncle Buddy's to bequeath me to
repudiate, because it was never Grandfather's
to bequeath them to bequeath me to repudiate, because it was never old Ikkemotubbe's to
sell to Grandfather for bequeathment and re-
pudiation. Because it was never Ikkemotubbe's
fathers' father's to bequeath Ikkemotubbe to
sell to Grandfather or any man because on the
instant when Ikkemotubbe discovered, realized, that he could sell it for money, on that
instant it ceased ever to have been his forever,
father to father, to father, and the man who
bought it bought nothing."

The right attitude toward nature is, as a
matter of fact, associated with the right attitude toward man, and the mere lust for power
over nature is associated with the lust for power
over other men, for God gave the earth to man,
we read in "The Bear," not "to hold for himself and his descendants inviolable title forever,
generation after generation, to the oblongs and
squares of the earth, but to hold the earth
mutual and intact in the communal anonymity
of brotherhood, and all the fee He asked was
pity and humility and sufferance and endurance and the sweat of his face for bread." It
is the failure of this pity which curses the earth
(the land in Faulkner's particular country is
"accursed" by chattel slavery, but slavery is
simply one of the possible forms of the failure).
But the rape of nature and the crime against
man are always avenged. The rape of nature,
the mere exploitation of it without love, is
always avenged because the attitude which
commits that crime also commits the crime
against men which in turn exacts vengeance,
so that man finally punishes himself. It is only
by this line of reasoning that one can, I think,
read the last page of "Delta Autumn":

This land which man has deswamped and
denuded and derivered in two generations
so that white men can own plantations and

commute every night to Memphis and black men own plantations and ride in Jim Crow cars to Chicago to live in millionaires' mansions on Lake Shore Drive; where white men rent farms and live like niggers and niggers crop on shares and live like animals; where cotton is planted and grows man-tall in the very cracks of the sidewalks, and usury and mortgage and bankruptcy and measureless wealth, Chinese and African and Aryan and Jew, all breed and spawn together until no man has time to say which one is which nor cares. . . . No wonder the ruined woods I used to know don't cry for retribution! he thought: The people who have destroyed it will accomplish its revenge.

The attitude toward nature in Faulkner's work, however, does not involve a sinking into nature. In Faulkner's mythology man has "suzerainty over the earth," he is not of the earth, and it is the human virtues which count —"pity and humility and sufferance and endurance." If we take even the extreme case of the idiot Snopes and his fixation on the cow in *The Hamlet* (a scene whose function in the total order of the book is to show that even the idiot pervert is superior to Flem), a scene which shows the human being as close as possible to the "natural" level, we find that the scene is the most lyrical in Faulkner's work: even the idiot is human and not animal, for only human desires, not animal, clothe themselves in poetry. I think that George Marion O'Donnell is right in pointing to the humanism-naturalism opposition in Faulkner's work, and over and over again we find that the point of some novel or story has to do with the human effort to find or create values in the mechanical round of experience—"not just to eat and evacuate and sleep warm," as Charlotte Rittenmeyer says in *The Wild Palms*, "so we can get up and eat and evacuate in order to sleep warm again," or not just to raise cotton to buy niggers to raise cotton to buy niggers, as it is put in another place. Even when a character seems to be caught in the iron ring of some compulsion, of some mechanical process (the hunted Negro of "Red Leaves," the tall convict of *The Wild Palms*, Christmas of *Light in Au-*

gust), the effort may be discernible. And in Quentin's attempt, in *The Sound and the Fury*, to persuade his sister Caddy, who is pregnant by one of the boys of Jefferson, to confess that she has committed incest with him, we find among other things the idea that "the horror" and "the clean flame" would be preferable to the meaninglessness of the "loud world."

Humor. One of the most important remarks in Cowley's introduction is that concerning humor. There is, especially in the later books, "a sort of homely and sober-sided frontier humor that is seldom achieved in contemporary writing." Cowley continues: "In a curious way, Faulkner combines two of the principal traditions in American letters: the tradition of psychological horror, often close to symbolism, that begins with Charles Brockden Brown, our first professional novelist, and extends through Poe, Melville, Henry James (in his later stories), Stephen Crane and Hemingway; and the other tradition of frontier humor and realism, beginning with Augustus Longstreet's *Georgia Scenes* and having Mark Twain as its best example." The observation is an acute one, for the distortions of humor and the distortions of horror in Faulkner's work are closely akin and frequently, in a given instance, can scarcely be disentangled.

It is true that the most important strain of humor in Faulkner's work is derived from the tradition of frontier humor (though it is probable that he got it from the porches of country stores and the courthouse yards of county-seat towns and not from any book), and it is true that the most spectacular displays of Faulkner's humor are of this order—for example, the "Spotted Horses" episode from *The Hamlet* or the story "Was." But there are other strains which might be distinguished and investigated. For example, there is a kind of Dickensian humor; the scene in the Memphis brothel from *Sanctuary*, which is reprinted here under the title "Uncle Bud and the Three Madams," is certainly more Dickensian than frontier. There is a subdued humor, sometimes shading into pathos, in the treatment of some of the Negro characters and in their dialogue. And there is an irony ranging from that in the scene in *Sanctuary* where Miss Reba, the madam, in offended decency keeps telling Temple,

"Lie down and cover up your nekkidness," while the girl talks with Benbow, to that in the magnificently sustained monologue of Jason at the end of *The Sound and the Fury*.

In any case, humor in Faulkner's work is never exploited for its own sake. It is regularly used as an index, as a lead, to other effects. The humor in itself may be striking, but Faulkner is not a humorist in the sense, say, that Mark Twain is. His humor is but one perspective on the material and it is never a final perspective, as we can see from such an example as the episode of "Spotted Horses." Nothing could be more wide of the point than the remark in Maxwell Geismar's essay on Faulkner to the effect that Faulkner in *The Hamlet* "seems now to accept the antics of his provincial morons, to enjoy the chronicle of their low-grade behavior; he submerges himself in their clownish degradation." All the critic seems to find in Mink Snopes' victim with his lifelong devotion to the memory of his dead wife, and in Ratliff with his good heart and ironical mind and quiet wisdom, is comic "descendants of the gangling and giggling Wash Jones."

The Poor White. The above remark leads us to the not uncommon misconception about the role of the poor white in Faulkner's work. It is true that the Snopeses are poor whites, descendants of bushwhackers (and therefore outside society, as the bushwhacker was outside society, had no "side" in the Civil War but tried to make a good thing of it), and it is true that Snopesism represents a special kind of villainy and degradation, the form that the pure doctrine of exploitation and degradation takes in the society of which Faulkner writes, but any careful reader realizes that a Snopes is not to be equated with a poor white. For instance, the book most fully about the poor white, *As I Lay Dying*, is full of sympathy and poetry. There are a hundred touches like that in Cash's soliloquy about the phonograph: "I reckon it's a good thing we aint got ere a one of them. I reckon I wouldn't never get no work done a-tall for listening to it. I dont know if a little music aint about the nicest thing a fellow can have. Seems like when he comes in tired of a night, it aint nothing could rest him like having a little music played and him resting." Or like the long section toward the middle of the

book devoted to Addie Bundren, a section which is full of eloquence like that of this paragraph: "And then he died. He did not know he was dead. I would lie by him in the dark, hearing the dark land talking of God's love and His beauty and His sin; hearing the dark voicelessness in which the words are the deeds, and the other words that are not deeds, that are just the gaps in peoples' lacks, coming down like the cries of geese out of the wild darkness in the old terrible nights, fumbling at the deeds like orphans to whom are pointed out in a crowd two faces and told, That is your father, your mother." Do these passages indicate a relish in the "antics of his provincial morons"?

The whole of *As I Lay Dying* is based on the heroic effort of the Bundren family to fulfill the promise to the dead mother, to take her body to Jefferson; and the fact that Anse Bundren, after the heroic effort has been completed, immediately gets him a new wife, the "duck-shaped woman" with the "hard-looking pop-eyes," does not negate the heroism of the effort nor the poetry and feeling which give flesh to the book. We are told by one critic that "what should have been the drama of the Bundrens thus becomes in the end a sort of brutal farce," and that we are "unable to feel the tragedy because the author has refused to accept the Bundrens, as he did accept the Compsons, as tragic." Rather, I should say, the Bundrens may come off a little better than the latter-day Compsons, the whining mother, the promiscuous Caddy, the ineffectual Quentin, and the rest. The Bundrens, at least, are capable of the heroic effort, and the promise is fulfilled. What the conclusion indicates is that even such a fellow as Anse Bundren (who is not typical of his family, by the way), in the grip of an idea, in terms of promise or code, is capable of rising out of his ordinary level; Anse falls back at the end, but only after the prop of the idea and obligation have been removed. And we may recall that even the "gangling and giggling Wash Jones" has always been capable of some kind of obscure dream and aspiration (his very attachment to Sutpen indicates that), and that in the end he achieves dignity and manhood.

The final and incontrovertible evidence that Snopes is not to be equated with poor white comes in *The Hamlet* (though actually most of the characters in the book, though they may be poor, are not, strictly speaking, "poor whites" at all, but rather what uninstructed reviewers choose to call by that label). The point of the book is the assault made on a solid community of plain, hard-working small farmers by Snopeses and Snopesism. Ratliff is not rich, but he is not Flem Snopes. And if the corruption of Snopesism does penetrate into the community, there is no one here who can be compared in degradation and vileness to Jason of *The Sound and the Fury*, the Compson who has embraced Snopesism. In fact, Popeye and Flem, Faulkner's best advertised villains, cannot, for vileness and ultimate meanness, touch Jason.

The Negro. In one of Faulkner's books it is said that every white child is born crucified on a black cross. Remarks like this have led to a gross misconception of the place of the Negro in Faulkner's work, to the notion that Faulkner "hates" Negroes. For instance, we find Maxwell Geismar exclaiming what a "strange inversion" it is to take the Negro, who is the "tragic consequence," and to exhibit him as the "evil cause" of the failure of the old order in the South.

This is a misreading of the text. It is slavery, not the Negro, which is defined, quite flatly, as the curse, over and over again, and the Negro is the black cross in so far as he is the embodiment of the curse, the reminder of the guilt, the incarnation of the problem. That is the basic point. But now and then, as a kind of tangential irony, we have the notion, not of the burden of the white on the black, but of the burden of the black on the white, the weight of obligation, inefficiency, and so on, as well as the weight of guilt (the notion we find in the old story of the plantation mistress who, after the Civil War, said: "Mr. Lincoln thought he was emancipating those slaves, but he was really emancipating me").

For instance, we get hints of this notion in "Red Leaves": one of the Indians, sweating in the chase of the runaway Negro who is to be killed for the Man's funeral, says, "Damn that Negro," and the other Indian replies, "Yao. When have they ever been anything but a trial and a care to us?" But the black cross is, funda-

mentally, the weight of the white man's guilt, the white man who now sells salves and potions to "bleach the pigment and straighten the hair of Negroes that they might resemble the very race which for two hundred years had held them in bondage and from which for another hundred years not even a bloody civil war would have set them completely free." The curse is still operative, as the crime is still compounded.

The actual role of the Negro in Faulkner's fiction is consistently one of pathos or heroism. It is not merely, as has been suggested more than once, that Faulkner condescends to the good and faithful servant, the "white folks' nigger." There are figures like Dilsey, but they are not as impressive as the Negro in "Red Leaves" or Sam Fathers, who, with the bear, is the hero of "The Bear." The fugitive, who gains in the course of the former story a shadowy symbolic significance, is told in the end by one of the Indians who overtake him, "You ran well. Do not be ashamed," and when he walks among the Indians, he is "the tallest there, his high, close, mud-caked head looming above them all." And Sam Fathers is the fountainhead of wisdom which Ike McCaslin finally gains, and the repository of the virtues which are central for Faulkner—"an old man, son of a Negro slave and an Indian king, inheritor on the one hand of the long chronicle of a people who had learned humility through suffering and learned pride through the endurance which survived suffering, and on the other side the chronicle of a people even longer in the land than the first, yet who now existed there only in the solitary brotherhood of an old and childless Negro's alien blood and the wild and invincible spirit of an old bear."

Even Christmas, in *Light in August*, though he is sometimes spoken of as a villain, is a mixture of heroism and pathos. He is the lost, suffering, enduring creature (the figure like Sam Fathers, the tall convict of *The Wild Palms*, or Dilsey in *The Sound and the Fury*), and even the murder he commits at the end is a fumbling attempt to define his manhood, is an attempt to break out of the iron ring of mechanism, to lift himself out of "nature," for the woman whom he kills has become a figure of the horror of the human which has surrendered the human attributes. (We may compare Christmas to Mink Snopes in *The Hamlet* in this respect: Mink, mean and vicious as he is, kills out of a kind of warped and confused pride, and by this affirmation is set off against his kinsmen Flem, whose only values are those of pure Snopesism.)

Even such a brief comment on the Negro in Faulkner's work cannot close without this passage from "The Bear":

"Because they will endure. They are better than we are. Stronger than we are. Their vices are vices aped from white men or that white men and bondage have taught them: improvidence and intemperance and evasion —not laziness: evasion: of what white men had set them to, not for their aggrandizement or even comfort but his own—" and McCaslin

"All right. Go on: Promiscuity. Violence. Instability and lack of control. Inability to distinguish between mine and thine—" and he

"How distinguish when for two hundred years mine did not even exist for them?" and McCaslin

"All right. Go on. And their virtues—" and he

"Yes. Their own. Endurance—" and McCaslin

"So have mules: and he

"—and pity and tolerance and forbearance and fidelity and love of children—" and McCaslin

"So have dogs:" and he

"—whether their own or not or black or not. And more: what they got not only from white people but not even despite white people because they had it already from the old free fathers a longer time free than us because we have never been free—"

And there is the single comment under Dilsey's name in the annotated genealogy of the Compsons which Faulkner has prepared for the present volume: "They endured."

Technique. There are excellent comments on this subject by Cowley, Conrad Aiken, Warren Beck, Joseph Warren Beach, and Alfred Kazin, but the subject has not been fully explored. One difficulty is that Faulkner is an incorrigible and restless experimenter, is peculiarly sensitive to the expressive possibilities of shifts in technique and has not developed (like Hemingway or Katherine Anne Porter— lyric rather than dramatic writers, artists with a great deal of self-certainty) in a straight line.

Provisionally, we may distinguish in Faulkner's work three basic methods of handling a narrative. One is best typified in *Sanctuary*, where there is a tightly organized plot, a crisp, laconic style, an objective presentation of character—an impersonal method. Another is best typified by *As I Lay Dying* or *The Sound and the Fury*, where each character unfolds in his own language or flow of being before us—a dramatic method in that the author does not obtrude, but a method which makes the subjective reference of character the medium of presentation. Another is best typified by "Was," "The Bear," or the story of the tall convict in *The Wild Palms*, where the organization of the narrative is episodic and the sense of a voice, a narrator's presence (though not necessarily a narrator in the formal sense), is almost constantly felt—a method in which the medium is ultimately a "voice" as index to sensibility. The assumptions underlying these methods, and the relations among them, would provide a study.

Cowley's emphasis on the unity of Faulkner's work, the fact that all the novels and stories are to be taken as aspects of a single, large design, is very important. It is important, for one thing, in regard to the handling of character. A character, Sutpen, for instance, may appear in various perspectives, so that from book to book we move toward a final definition much as in actual life we move toward the definition of a person. The same principle applies to event, as Conrad Aiken has pointed out, the principle of the spiral method which takes the reader over and over the same event from a different altitude, as it were, and a different angle. In relation to both character and event this method, once it is understood by the reader, makes for a kind of realism and a kind of suspense (in the formal not the factual sense) not common in fiction.

The emphasis on the unity of Faulkner's work may, however, lead to an underrating of the degree of organization within individual works. Cowley is right in pointing out the structural defect in *Light in August*, but he may be putting too much emphasis on the over-all unity and not enough on the organization of the individual work when he says that *The Hamlet* tends to resolve into a "series of episodes resembling beads on a string." I think that in that novel we have a type of organization in which the thematic rather than the narrative emphasis is the basic principle, and once we grasp that fact the unity of the individual work may come clear. In fact, the whole subject of the principle of thematic organization in the novels and long stories, "The Bear," for instance, needs investigation. In pieces which seem disjointed, or which seem to have the mere tale-teller's improvisations, we may sometimes discover the true unity if we think of the line of meaning, the symbolic ordering, and surrender ourselves to the tale-teller's "voice." And it may be useful at times to recall the distinction between the formal, forensic realism of Ibsen as opposed to the fluid, suggestive realism of Chekhov.

Symbol and Image. Cowley and O'Donnell have given acute readings of the main symbolic outline of Faulkner's fiction, but no one has yet devoted himself to the study of symbolic motifs which, though not major, are nevertheless extremely instructive. For instance, the images of the hunt, the flight, the pursuit, such as we have in "Red Leaves," *The Wild Palms*, the episode of "Peter Grimm" in *Light in August*, "The Bear," "Delta Autumn," "Was," and (especially in the hordes of moving Negroes) in *The Unvanquished*. Or there is the important symbolic relationship between man and earth. Or there is the contrast between images of compulsion and images of will or freedom. Or there is the device of what we might call the frozen moment, the arrested action which becomes symbolic, as in the mo-

ment when, in "An Odor of Verbena" (from *The Unvanquished*), Drusilla offers the pistols to the hero.

Polarity. To what extent does Faulkner work in terms of polarities, oppositions, paradoxes, inversions of roles? How much does he employ a line of concealed (or open) dialectic progression as a principle for his fiction? The study of these questions may lead to the discovery of principles of organization in his work not yet defined by criticism.

The study of Faulkner is the most challenging single task in contemporary American literature for criticism to undertake. Here is a novelist who, in mass of work, in scope of material, in range of effect, in reportorial accuracy and symbolic subtlety, in philosophical weight, can be put beside the masters of our own past literature. Yet this accomplishment has been effected in what almost amounts to critical isolation and silence, and when the silence has been broken it has usually been broken by someone (sometimes one of our better critics) whose reading has been hasty, whose analysis unscholarly and whose judgments superficial. The picture of Faulkner presented to the public by such criticism is a combination of Thomas Nelson Page, a fascist and a psychopath, gnawing his nails. Of course, this picture is usually accompanied by a grudging remark about genius.

Cowley's book, for its intelligence, sensitivity, and sobriety in the introduction, and for the ingenuity and judgment exhibited in the selections, would be valuable at any time. But it is especially valuable at this time. Perhaps it can mark a turning point in Faulkner's reputation. That will be of slight service to Faulkner, who, as much as any writer of our place and time, can rest in confidence. He can afford to wait. But can we?

1946

~ General Bibliography ~

I. General Bibliographical References

The student should be acquainted with the following chief sources for finding material on American literary history, biography, and criticism, aside from such general works as the *Cumulative Book Index* and *Readers' Guide to Periodical Literature:*

"American Bibliography," the annual list of books and articles dealing with American literature, in the Supplement to *Publications of the Modern Language Association of America* (*PMLA*), issued in March and compiled at present by Gregory Paine, 1922 to date.

"Articles on American Literature Appearing in Current Periodicals," the quarterly list in each issue of *American Literature*, 1929 to date.

The extensive bibliographies for Volumes I, II, and IV of the *Cambridge History of American Literature*, adequate to the date of compilation, 1917–1921.

Evans, Charles, *American Bibliography*, a list of all American books printed in America since 1639 (compiled to 1820), 1903–1934.

Leisy, E. E., and Hubbell, J. B., *Doctoral Dissertations in American Literature*, 1933.

Manly, J. M., Rickert, Edith, and Millett, F. B., *Contemporary American Literature*, revised edition, 1940.

Van Patten, Nathan, ed., *An Index to Bibliographies . . . . Relating to . . . . American and British Authors, 1923–1932*, 1934.

Extended bibliographical lists are to be found in W. F. Taylor's *A History of American Letters*, pp. 447–664, compiled by Harry Hartwick, 1936; and Warfel, Gabriel, and Williams's *The American Mind*, pp. 1489–1496 (particularly good on historical, social, and economic background), 1937. Excellent period and background, as well as special, bibliographies are included in the several volumes of the American Writers Series, under the direction of H. H. Clark.

II. Biographical Collections

The Dictionary of American Biography (*DAB*), 20 vols., edited by Allen Johnson and Dumas Malone (the standard work), 1928–1937.

Appleton's *Cyclopedia of American Biography*, 12 vols., edited by J. G. Wilson and John Fiske (includes many names not in *DAB*), revised edition, 1914–1931.

The Dictionary of National Biography (*DNB*), 63 vols., edited by Leslie Stephen and Sidney Lee (includes American authors born in Great Britain), 1885–1900; supplements 1901, 1912, 1922.

Kunitz, S. J., ed., *Living Authors: A Book of Biographies*, 1932.

——, and Haycraft, H., eds., *American Authors, 1600–1900: A Biographical Dictionary of American Literature*, 1938.

——, Haycraft, Howard, and Hadden, W. C., eds., *Authors Today and Yesterday: A Companion Volume to Living Authors*, 1933.

Sprague, W. B., *Annals of the American Pulpit*, 9 vols., 1857–1869.

Who's Who in America (a biennial volume of sketches furnished by the persons included), 1899–   .

Who's Who among North American Authors, edited by A. Lowell, 1921–   .

III. General Background

A. Historical

Adams, Henry, *History of the United States during the Administrations of Jefferson and Madison* (an excellent interpretation of an important period), 1921.

Adams, J. T., *The Epic of America* (summarizes well the chief trends in American history), 1931.

Andrews, C. M., *The Colonial Background of the American Revolution*, 1924.

Bassett, J. S., *The Federalist System*, 1906.

Beard, C. A., *The Economic Origins of Jeffersonian Democracy*, 1915.
——, C. A. and M. R., *The Rise of American Civilization* (a clear analysis of forces and motives behind the Revolution), 1933.
Bowers, C. G., *Jefferson and Hamilton*, 1925.
——, *Jefferson in Power*, 1936.
Brawley, B. G., *A Social History of the American Negro*, 1921.
Commons, J. R., *Races and Immigrants in America*, 1920.
Corwin, E. S., *The Constitution and What It Means Today*, 1930.
Couch, W. T., ed., *Culture in the South*, 1934.
De Toqueville, Alexis, *Democracy in America* (a penetrating interpretation by a contemporary French traveler), 1904.
De Voto, B. A., *Mark Twain's America*, 1932.
Dondore, Dorothy, *The Prairie and the Making of Middle America*, 1926.
Gabriel, R. H., ed., *The Pageant of America: A Pictorial History of the United States*, 15 vols., 1925–1929.
Hacker, L. M., and Kendrick, B. B., *The United States since 1865*, 1934.
Hart, A. B., ed., *The American Nation*, 28 vols., 1904–1918.
Jameson, J. F., *The American Revolution Considered as a Social Movement*, 1926.
Johnson, Allen, ed., *The Chronicles of America*, 50 vols., 1918–1921.
Koch, G. A., *Republican Religion: The American Revolution and the Cult of Reason* (deism in American political thought), 1933.
McMaster, J. B., *A History of the People of the U. S. from the Revolution to the Civil War* (personalities and social aspects), 1883–1913.
Mesick, J. L., *The English Traveller in America, 1785–1835*, 1922.
Morison, S. E., *Three Centuries of Harvard, 1636–1936*, 1936.
——, and Commager, H. S., *The Growth of the American Republic*, 2 vols., 1937.
Mumford, Lewis, *The Story of Utopias* (pantisocracy and other idealistic designs for colonization), 1922.
Nevins, Allan, ed., *American Social History as Recorded by British Travellers*, 1923.
Oberholtzer, E. P., *A History of the United States since the Civil War*, 5 vols., 1917–1937.
Ogg, F. A., *The Old Northwest*, 1919.
Paxson, F. L., *The History of the American Frontier, 1763–1893*, 1924.
Phillips, U. B., *Life and Labor in the Old South*, 1929.
Schlesinger, A. M., *The Rise of the City, 1878–1898*, 1933.
——, *New Viewpoints in American History*, 1922.
——, and Fox, D. R., eds., *A History of American Life*, 12 vols., 1927– .
Stephenson, G. M., *A History of American Immigration*, 1926.
Thomas, Isaiah, *History of Printing in America*, 1871.
Turner, F. J., *The Frontier in American History*, 1921.
Van Tyne, C. H., *The Loyalists in the American Revolution*, 1902.
Weeden, W. B., *Economic and Social History of New England, 1620–1789*, 2 vols., 1890.
Wertenbaker, T. J., *The Planters of Colonial Virginia* (valuable), 1922.

B. *Currents of American Thought*

Adams, G. P., and Montague, W. P., eds., *Contemporary American Philosophy*, 1930.
Bailey, E. J., *Religious Thought in the Greater American Poets*, 1922.
Bimba, A., *The History of the American Working Class*, 1927.
Bryce, James, *The American Commonwealth*, 2 vols., 1922–1923.
Butler, H. B., *Industrial Relations in the United States*, 1927.
Cannan, Edwin, *A Review of Economic Theory*, 1929.
Carpenter, W. S., *The Development of American Political Thought*, 1930.
Cobb, S. H., *The Rise of Religious Liberty in America*, 1902.
Coker, F. W., *Recent Political Thought*, 1934.
Commons, J. R., and others, *History of Labour in the United States*, 2 vols., 1921.
Cooke, G. W., *Unitarianism in America*, 1902.

Cubberley, E. P., *Public Education in the United States*, 1934.

Curti, M. E., *The Social Ideas of American Educators*, 1935.

Dewey, John, and others, *Living Philosophies*, 1931.

Dodd, W. E., *The Old South: Struggles for Democracy*, 1937.

Elson, L. C., *The History of American Music*, 1925.

Frothingham, O. B., *Transcendentalism in New England*, 1876.

Gewehr, W. M., *The Great Awakening in Virginia, 1740–1790*, 1930.

Hall, T. C., *The Religious Background of American Culture*, 1930.

Haney, L. H., *History of Economic Thought*, rev. ed., 1936.

Hartmann, Sadakichi, *A History of American Art*, 1934.

Howard, J. T., *Our American Music; Three Hundred Years of It*, 1931.

Jacobson, J. M., *The Development of American Political Thought*, 1932.

Jones, H. M., *The Drift to Liberalism in the American Eighteenth Century* (neo-classicism a liberalizing influence in America from religious domination), 1936.

Jones, R. M., *The Quakers in the American Colonies*, 1921.

Josephson, Matthew, *The Robber Barons: the Great American Capitalists, 1861–1901*, 1934.

Kimball, Fiske, *American Architecture*, 1928.

Knight, E. W., *Education in the United States*, 1929.

Locke, Alain, *Negro Art: Past and Present*, 1936.

Luccock, H. E., *Contemporary American Literature and Religion*, 1934.

Mencken, H. L., *Notes on Democracy*, 1926.

Merriam, C. E., *A History of American Political Theories*, 1920.

——, *American Political Ideas, 1865–1917*, 1920.

Miller, Perry, "The Marrow of Puritan Divinity," in *Publications of the Colonial Society of Massachusetts*, XXXII, pp. 243–300, 1936.

——, *The New England Mind: The Seventeenth Century*, 1939.

——, and Johnson, T. H., *The Puritans* (The introduction is a valuable discussion of Puritanism as a product of its age and the Puritans in literature), 1938.

Monroe, Paul, ed., *Cyclopedia of Education*, 3 vols., 1925.

Morais, H. M., *Deism in Eighteenth Century America* (a useful survey), 1934.

Mumford, Lewis, *Sticks and Stones: A Study of American Architecture and Civilization*, 1924.

——, *The Brown Decades: A Study of the Arts in America, 1865–1895*, 1931.

——, *The Culture of Cities*, 1938.

Parrington, V. L., *Main Currents in American Thought*, 3 vols. (valuable interpretation from point of view of a Jeffersonian agrarian), 1927–1930.

Perry, R. B., *Philosophy of the Recent Past*, 1926.

——, *Recent Social Trends in the United States*, 2 vols., 1933.

Riley, I. W., *American Thought from Puritanism to Pragmatism*, 1915.

Rowe, H. K., *The History of Religion in the United States*, 1924.

Santayana, George, *Winds of Doctrine*, 1926.

Shea, J. D. G., *The Catholic Church in the United States*, 4 vols., 1886–1892.

Shuster, G. N., *The Catholic Church and Current Literature*, 1930.

Sweet, W. W., *The Story of Religions in America*, 1930.

Taft, Lorado, *The History of American Sculpture*, 1930.

Thompson, Oscar, *The American Singer: A Hundred Years of Success in Opera*, 1937.

Thwing, C. F., *A History of Higher Education in America*, 1906.

Turner, L. D., *Antislavery Sentiment in American Literature Prior to 1865*, 1929.

Ware, N. J., *The Labor Movement in the United States, 1860–1895*, 1929.

Wright, F. L., *Modern Architecture*, 1931.

IV. *General Literary History and Criticism*

A. *Periodicals, Collections, and Series*

American Literature, a quarterly magazine, the semi-official organ of the American Literature Group of the Modern Language Association (contains many important articles of current scholarship), 1929– .

The New England Quarterly (contains articles dealing with New England literature), 1928– .

Alderman, E. A., and others, eds., *A Library of Southern Literature*, 17 vols., 1908–1923.

Allibone, S. A., *A Critical Dictionary of English Literature and British and American Authors*, 3 vols., 1858–1871, 2 vols. supplement, 1891.

Blair, Walter, ed., *Native American Humor, 1800–1900* (an excellent history, with selections and extended bibliography), 1937.

Cairns, W. B., ed., *Selections from Early American Writers, 1607–1800* (thirty-nine writers, with brief introductions), 1917.

Clark, H. H., ed., *Major American Poets* (anthology, with annotated bibliographies and notes), 1936.

Duyckinck, E. A. and G. L., *Cyclopedia of American Literature*, 2 vols. (selections and biographical sketches of many American writers prior to 1870), 1875.

Griswold, R. W., *Poets and Poetry of America to the Middle of the Nineteenth Century*, 1852.

——, *The Prose Writers of America*, 1854.

Halline, A. G., ed., *American Plays*, 1935.

Lomax, J. A. and A., comps., *American Ballads and Folk Songs*, 1934.

——, eds., *Cowboy Songs and Other Frontier Ballads*, 1938.

Meine, F. J., ed., *Tall Tales of the Southwest*, 1930.

Moses, M. J., ed., *Representative Plays by American Dramatists*, 3 vols., 1918–1926.

Otis, W. B., *American Verse, 1625–1807*, 1909.

Parrington, V. L., ed., *The Connecticut Wits*, 1926.

Pound, Louise, ed., *American Ballads and Songs*, 1922.

Prescott, F. C., and Nelson, J. H., eds., *Prose and Poetry of the Revolution* (supplements the Trent and Wells collection), 1925.

Quinn, A. H., ed., *Representative American Plays*, 1930.

Sandburg, Carl, *The American Songbag*, 1927.

Stedman, E. C., ed., *An American Anthology, 1787–1900* (an excellent volume of selections of poetry, with brief biographical sketches), 1900.

Trent, W. P., and Wells, B. W., *Colonial Prose and Poetry* (fifty-eight writers, with biographical introductions), single-volume edition, 1903.

Untermeyer, Louis, ed., *Modern American Poetry: A Critical Anthology*, rev. ed., 1930.

The American Authors Series, general editor, Stanley T. Williams, 9 vols., dealing with C. B. Brown, the Connecticut Wits, Cooper, Freneau, Irving, Kennedy, Cotton Mather, Paine, and Poe.

The American Writers Series, general editor, H. H. Clark, 18 vols. to date, with introductions and bibliographies, dealing with Bryant, Clemens, Cooper, Edwards, Emerson, Franklin, Hamilton and Jefferson, Hawthorne, Holmes, Irving, Longfellow, Melville, Motley, Parkman, Poe, the Southern Poets, Thoreau, and Whitman.

The Modern Student's Library, general editor, Will D. Howe (includes several volumes dealing with American authors, notably that on Franklin and Edwards, with a helpful introduction by Carl Van Doren).

B. *History and Criticism*

Allen, G. W., *American Prosody* (a useful study of the versification of the chief poets), 1935.

Babbitt, Irving, and others, *Criticism in America*, 1924.

Baskervill, W. M., *Southern Writers: Biographical and Critical*, 2 vols., 1897–1903.

Beach, J. W., *The Outlook for American Prose*, 1926.

Beer, Thomas, *The Mauve Decade*, 1926.

Blair, Walter, ed., *Native American Humor, 1800–1900*, 1937.

Blankenship, Russell, *American Literature*, 1931.

Bleyer, W. G., *Main Currents in the History of American Journalism*, 1927.

Bowman, J. C., ed., *Contemporary American Criticism*, 1926.

Boynton, P. H., *Literature and American Life* (links the literature and the cultural background), 1936.

——, *Some Contemporary Americans*, 1924.

——, *More Contemporary Americans*, 1927.

Brawley, Benjamin, ed., *Early Negro American Writers*, 1935.

Brenner, Rica, *Twelve American Poets before 1900*, 1933.

Bronson, W. C., *A Short History of American Literature*, 1902.

Brooks, Van Wyck, *America's Coming-of-Age*, 1915.

——, *Letters and Leadership*, 1918.

——, *The Flowering of New England, 1815–1865*, 1936.

Brown, T. A., *History of the New York Stage, from 1730 to 1901*, 3 vols., 1903.

Brownell, W. C., *American Prose Masters*, 1923.

Cairns, W. B., *British Criticisms of American Writings, 1783–1815*, 1918; *1815–1833*, 1922.

Calverton, V. F., *The Liberation of American Literature* (literature from a "class" viewpoint), 1932.

Cambridge History of American Literature (CHAL), 4 vols., W. P. Trent, *et al.*, eds. (some chapters of great merit), 1917–1921.

Canby, H. S., *Definitions: Essays in Contemporary Criticism*, 2 series, 1922 and 1924.

——, *American Estimates*, 1929.

Charvat, William, *The Origins of American Critical Thought, 1810–1835*, 1936.

Clark, H. H., "Nationalism in American Literature," *University of Toronto Quarterly*, II, 492–519 (July, 1933).

Coad, O. S., *William Dunlap* (a good picture of theatrical conditions in New York), 1917.

Cooper, F. T., *Some American Story Tellers*, 1911.

Davidson, L. J., and Bostwick, Prudence, eds., *The Literature of the Rocky Mountain West, 1803–1903*, 1939.

De Mille, G. E., *Literary Criticism in America*, 1931.

Dickinson, T. H., *Playwrights of the New American Theater*, 1925.

——, *The Making of American Literature*, 1932.

Du Breuil, A. J., *The Novel of Democracy in America*, 1923.

Dunlap, G. A., *The City in the American Novel, 1789–1900*, 1934.

Dunlap, William, *History of the American Theatre*, 1832.

Eastman, Max, *The Literary Mind*, 193̇.

Edgar, P., *The Art of the Novel, from 1700 to the Present Time*, 1933.

Emerson, E. W., *The Early Years of the Saturday Club*, 1918.

Erskine, J., *Leading American Novelists*, 1910.

Foerster, N., *Nature in American Literature*, 1923.

——, ed., *The Reinterpretation of American Literature*, 1928.

——, *American Criticism: A Study in Literary Theory from Poe to the Present*, 1928.

——, ed., *Humanism and America*, 1930.

Goddard, H. C., *Studies in New England Transcendentalism*, 1908.

Gohdes, C. L. F., *The Periodicals of American Transcendentalism*, 1931.

Grattan, C. H., ed., *The Critique of Humanism*, 1930.

Hansen, Harry, *Midwest Portraits*, 1923.

Hartwick, Harry, *The Foreground of American Fiction*, 1934.

Hatcher, Harlan, *Creating the Modern American Novel*, 1935.

Hatfield, J. T., *German Culture in the United States*, 1936.

Hazard, L. L., *The Frontier in American Literature*, 1927.

Herron, I. H., *The Small Town in American Literature*, 1939.

Hicks, Granville, *The Great Tradition: An Interpretation of American Literature since the Civil War*, 1933.

Holliday, Carl, *A History of Southern Literature*, 1906.

Hornblow, A., *A History of the Theatre in America from Its Beginnings to the Present Time*, 2 vols., 1919.

Howe, M. A. De W., ed., *Later Years of the Saturday Club*, 1927.

Hudson, A. P., ed., *Humor of the Old Deep South*, 1936.

Hughes, G., *Imagism and the Imagists*, 1931.

Jameson, J. F., *The History of Historical Writing in America*, 1891.

Jones, H. M., "American Prose Style, 1700–1770," *Huntington Library Bulletin*, No. 6, pp. 115–151, 1934.

Jones, H. M., *America and French Culture, 1750–1848*, 1927.

Keiser, A., *The Indian in American Literature*, 1933.

Knight, G. C., *The Novel in English*, 1931.

——, *American Literature and Culture*, 1932.

Krapp, G. P., *The English Language in America*, 1925.

Kreymborg, A., *Our Singing Strength*, 1929.

Krutch, J. W., *The Modern Temper*, 1929.

Lawrence, D. H., *Studies in Classic American Literature*, 1923.

Lee, J. M., *History of American Journalism*, rev. ed., 1923.

Leisy, E. E., *American Literature*, 1929.

Lewisohn, L., *Expression in America*, 1932.

Loggins, V., *The Negro Author: His Development in America*, 1931.

Long, O. W., *Literary Pioneers: Early American Explorers of European Culture*, 1935.

Lowell, Amy, *Tendencies in Modern American Poetry*, 1921.

——, *Poetry and Poets*, 1930.

Lowes, J. L., *Convention and Revolt in Poetry*, 1919.

Macy, J. A., *The Spirit of American Literature*, 1913.

——, ed., *American Writers on American Literature*, 1931.

McWilliams, C., *The New Regionalism in American Literature*, 1930.

Mencken, H. L., *Notes on Democracy*, 1926.

——, *The American Language*, 1919, 1923, rev., 1936.

Merrill, D. K., *The Development of American Biography*, 1932.

Michaud, R., *The American Novel Today*, 1928.

Mims, E., *The Advancing South*, 1926.

——, *Adventurous America; A Study of Contemporary Life and Thought*, 1929.

Morris, L. R., ed., *The Young Idea, an Anthology of Opinion concerning the Spirit and Aims of Contemporary American Literature*, 1917.

Moses, M. J., *The Literature of the South*, 1910.

——, *The American Dramatist*, rev. ed., 1925.

——, and Brown, J. M., eds., *The American Theatre, As Seen by Its Critics, 1752–1934*, 1934.

Mott, F. L., *A History of American Magazines* (Vols. II and III cover the period from 1850 to 1885), 1938.

Moulton, C. W., ed., *The Library of Literary Criticism of English and American Authors*, 8 vols., 1901–1905.

Mumford, Lewis, *The Golden Day: A Study in American Experience and Culture*, 1926.

Munson, G. B., *Destinations: A Canvass of American Literature since 1900*, 1928.

——, *Style and Form in American Prose*, 1929.

Nelson, J. H., *The Negro Character in American Literature*, 1926.

Odell, G. C. D., *Annals of the New York Stage*, 10 vols. to date, 1927–1939.

Onderdonk, J. L., *A History of American Verse, 1610–1897*, 1901.

Painter, F. V. N., *Poets of the South*, 1903.

Pattee, F. L., *Development of the American Short Story*, 1923.

——, *The First Century of American Literature, 1770–1870*, 1935.

——, *A History of American Literature since 1870*, 1915.

Payne, W. M., *Various Views*, 1902.

——, ed., *American Literary Criticism*, 1904.

——, *Leading American Essayists*, 1910.

Pearson, E. L., *Dime Novels*, 1929.

Perry, R. B., *Philosophy of the Recent Past*, 1926.

Phelps, W. L., *The Twentieth Century Theatre*, 1918.

Quinn, A. H., ed., *Contemporary American Plays*, 1923.

——, *A History of the American Drama, from the Civil War to the Present Day*, 2 vols., 1927.

——, *The Soul of America, Yesterday and Today*, 1932.

——, *American Fiction: An Historical and Critical Survey*, 1936.

Regier, C. C., *The Era of the Muckrakers*, 1932.

Richardson, C. F., *American Literature, 1607–1885*, 2 vols., 1887–1889.

Riding, L., and Graves, R., *American Thought, from Puritanism to Pragmatism*, 2d ed., 1923.
Rourke, Constance, *American Humor, a Study of the National Character*, 1931.
Rusk, R. L., *The Literature of the Middle Western Frontier*, 2 vols., 1925.
Sherman, S. P., *On Contemporary Literature*, 1917.
——, *Americans*, 1922.
Smith, Bernard, *Forces in American Criticism*, 1939.
Smith, C. A., *Southern Literary Studies*, 1927.
Smith, L. W., ed., *Current Reviews*, 1926.
Speare, M. E., *The Political Novel: Its Development in England and in America*, 1924.
Stedman, E. C., *Poets of America* (13th edition), 1894.
Sterner, L. G., *The Sonnet in American Literature*, 1930.
Stoddard, R. H., *Recollections, Personal and Literary*, 1903.
Tandy, Jennette R., *Crackerbox Philosophers in American Humor and Satire*, 1925.
Taylor, Bayard, *Critical Essays and Literary Notes*, 1880.
Taylor, W. F., *A History of American Letters* (with extended bibliographies by Harry Hartwick), 1936.
Trent, W. P., and Erskine, J., *Great American Writers*, 1912.
[Twelve Southerners], *I'll Take My Stand: The South and the Agrarian Tradition*, 1930.
Tyler, M. C., *A History of American Literature during the Colonial Time*, 2 vols., 1878.
——, *The Literary History of the American Revolution, 1763–1783*, 2 vols., 1897.
Underwood, J. C., *Literature and Insurgency*, 1914.
Untermeyer, Louis, *The New Era in American Poetry*, 1919.
——, *American Poetry since 1900*, 1923.
Van Doren, Carl, *The American Novel*, 1921.
——, *The Roving Critic*, 1923.
——, ed., *Modern American Prose*, 1934.
Vincent, L. H., *American Literary Masters*, 1906.
Violette, A. G., *Economic Feminism in American Literature Prior to 1848*, 1925.
Ward, A. C., *American Literature, 1880–1930*, 1932.
Weeks, E. A., "Best Sellers since 1875," *Publishers' Weekly*, CXXV, 1503–6 (April 21, 1934).
Weirick, B., *From Whitman to Sandburg in American Poetry: A Critical Survey*, 1924.
Wendell, Barrett, *A Literary History of America* (6th edition), 1911.
Whipple, E. P., *American Literature and Other Papers*, 1887.
Whipple, T. K., *Spokesmen: Modern Writers and American Life*, 1928.
Williams, Blanche Colton, *Our Short Story Writers*, 1920.
Wilt, Napier, *Some American Humorists*, 1929.
Winters, Yvor, *Primitivism and Decadence, a Study of American Experimental Poetry*, 1937.
Wood, Clement, *Poets of America*, 1925.
Woodberry, G. E., *Literary Memoirs of the Nineteenth Century*, 1921.

General Index of Authors and Titles ~

The names of authors are printed in **black type**, the titles of books are printed in *italics*, and the titles of individual poems and prose selections are printed in ordinary roman type.

Abraham Davenport, 379
Abraham Lincoln Walks at Midnight, 904
Advantages of the Union, 102
A.E.F., 912
After Great Pain a Formal Feeling Comes, 712
After the Burial, 403
Al Aaraaf (Song), 444
All in green went my love riding, 1006
All the Sad Young Men, 940
Allen, Ethan (see **Young, Thomas**)
Although I put Away His Life, 711
Always before your voice my soul, 1006
American Democrat, The, 219
American Notebooks, 348
American Plan, The, 1043
American Scholar, The, 241
Among the Hills, 379
. . . & Forty-Second Street, 1014
Anderson, Sherwood, 931
Annabel Lee, 456
Antiquity of Freedom, The, 201
Apology, The, 226
Application, 25
Aristocrat and a Democrat, An, 219
Army Corps on the March, An, 654
Arsenal at Springfield, The, 554
At the Saturday Club, 606
Auf Wiedersehen, 403
Autobiography (Franklin), 52
Autobiography (Lincoln), 619
Autocrat of the Breakfast-Table, The, 608

Babbitt, 925
Babbitt, Irving, 1057
Ballad of Trees and the Master, A, 699
Barefoot Boy, The, 364
Barlow, Joel, 119
Battlefield, The, 201
Battle-Hymn of the Republic, 625
Beat! Beat! Drums! 658
Beauties of Santa Cruz, The, 110
Beauty, 238
Beaver Brook, 402
Belfry of Bruges, The, 555

Bells, The, 454
Bereaved, 712
Big Money, The, 1043
Biglow Papers, First Series, The, 404
Biglow Papers, Second Series, The, 407
Biographical Sketch of Thoreau, 272
Birches, 888
Bird Came Down the Walk, A, 706
Bivouac on a Mountain Side, 654
Black Cottage, The, 886
Black Riders, The, 837
Blue and the Gray, The, 627
Blue Hotel, The, 823
Booker Washington, Trilogy, The, 905
Boyhood Experiences, 19
Boys, The, 603
Bracebridge Hall, 172
Brahma, 236
Brahmin Caste of New England, The, 616
Brain, The, 704
Bridge, The (Crane), 1009
Bridge, The (Longfellow), 558
Broadway Sights, 680
Brother Jonathan's Lament for Sister Caroline, 604
Brute Neighbors, 299
Bryant, William Cullen, 181
Buffalo Bill, 1007
Buick, 1056
Building of the Ship, The, 568
Burns, 361
Bustle in a House, The, 708

Calvary, 874
Cambridge Ladies, The, 1007
Camera Eye, The, 1046
Capture of Fort Christina, The, 157
Carillon, 555
Cask of Amontillado, The, 470
Cather, Willa, 913
Cavalry Crossing a Ford, 654
Celebrated Jumping Frog of Calaveras County, The, 736
Chambered Nautilus, The, 614

Channing, William Ellery, 144
Character, 267
Character of Washington, The, 99
Charleston, 625
Chase—First Day, The, 525
Chase—Second Day, The, 530
Chase—Third Day, The, 534
Chicago, 908
Children's Hour, The, 581
Chrysanthemums, The, 1049
City in the Sea, The, 445
Civil Disobedience, 301
Clemens, Samuel Langhorne (Mark Twain), 732
Collected Poems of Robert Frost, Preface to, 892
Colonel Sellers, Financial Wizard, 739
Columbiad, The, 125
Come Up from the Fields Father, 655
Common Sense, 81
Conclusion (Walden), 300
Concord Hymn, 227
Congo, The, 897
Conqueror Worm, The, 449
Cool Tombs, 911
Cooper, James Fenimore, 205
Corn, 687
Courtin', The, 407
Crane, (Harold) Hart, 1008
Crane, Stephen, 815
Credo, 875
Crèvecœur, Michel-Guillaume Jean de, 37
Crisis, The, 79
Criticism and Fiction, 766
Cross of Snow, The, 594
Crossing Brooklyn Ferry, 643
Cub-Pilot's Experience, A, 743
Cummings, E. E., 1004

Dana, Richard Henry, Jr., 494
Dante, 587
Darest Thou Now O Soul, 667
Daring Deed, A, 746
David Swan, 334
Day Is Done, The, 554
Days, 235
Deacon's Masterpiece, The, 601
Death of Lincoln, The, 203
Death of the Flowers, The, 196
Death of the Hired Man, The, 883
Death Snips Proud Men, 911

Decency in American Fiction, 767
Dedication (Whittier), 358
Democratic Vistas, 678
Dickinson, Emily, 700
Dinner Party, A, 756
Discovery of Land, The, 177
Disillusioned, 706
Divina Commedia, 588
Do Not Weep, Maiden, for War Is Kind, 837
Doolittle, Hilda (H.D.), 991
Dorothy Q., 605
Dos Passos, John, 1039
Dream-Land, 449
Dream within a Dream, A, 444
Dreiser, Theodore, 846
Dr. Heidegger's Experiment, 329

Each and All, 227
Eagle and the Mole, The, 1019
Early Reading and Self-Cultivation, 53
Earth-Song, 232
Economy, 281
Edwards, Jonathan, 16
Egg, The, 933
Eldorado, 455
Eliot, T. S., 992, 1076
Elsie Venner, 616
Elysium Is as Far, 707
Embargo, The, 185
Emerson, Ralph Waldo, 221
Emerson the Lecturer, 426
Emperor Jones, 973
Employed as Printer in Philadelphia, 58
English Traits, 267
English Writers on America, 168
Eros Turannos, 878
Essays in Authorship, 843
Eternal Goodness, The, 382
Ethan Brand, 337
Evangeline, 560
Evening Song, 694
Evening Wind, The, 197
Exile's Departure, The, 353
Exultation Is the Going, 708

Fable for Critics, A, 393
Fall of the House of Usher, The, 456
Faulkner, William, 1022
Federalist, The, 101
Figure a Poem Makes, The, 892
Finch, Francis Miles, 627

First Inaugural Address (Jefferson), 94
Fitzgerald, F. Scott, 939
Flammonde, 876
Fly, The, 1057
Fog, 910
Footnote on Criticism, 1070
For Charlotte Brontë, 709
For You O Democracy, 652
Forbearance, 231
Forest Hymn, A, 195
Forever at His Side to Walk, 711
42nd Parallel, The, 1042
Four Preludes on Playthings of the Wind, 912
Franklin, Benjamin, 49
Freneau, Philip, 106
From Paumanok Starting I Fly Like a Bird,
  653
From the Flats, 693
Frost, Robert, 879
Frost, The, 707

Garden, The, 991
General William Booth Enters into Heaven,
  896
George Crabbe, 874
Gerontion, 998
Gettysburg Address, The, 620
Ghost of the Buffaloes, The, 904
Gilded Age, The, 739
Giotto's Tower, 589
Girl's Education, A, 92
God's World, 1016
Going to Him! Happy Letter! 707
Good-bye, 226
Good-bye My Fancy! 677
Grace, 231
Gray Champion, The, 311
Great Expectations, 62
Green River, 190
Greville Fane, 773

"H.D." (Hilda Doolittle), 991
Hamatreya, 232
Hand, The, 849
Harbor, The, 909
Harmonium, 1002
Harte, Bret, 714
Hasty Pudding, The, 120
Haunted Palace, The, 461
Hawthorne, 587
Hawthorne, Nathaniel, 304

Hawthorne's "Twice-Told Tales," 483
Hay, John, 730
Haze, 280
Hemingway, Ernest, 959
Her Letter, 718
Heroics, 1018
Hints for Stories, 348
History of New York, A, 154
Holmes, Oliver Wendell, 594
House on the Hill, The, 874
Howe, Julia Ward, 625
Howells, William Dean, 753
Hummingbird, The, 706
Hunger, 705
Hunting of Pau-Puk-Keewis, The, 577
Hurricane, The, 113
Hurt Hawks, 1022

I Cannot Forget with What Fervid Devotion,
  190
I Got So I Could Hear His Name, 712
I Hear America Singing, 653
I Heard a Fly Buzz When I Died, 709
I Make His Crescent Fill or Lack, 710
I Met a Seer, 837
I Never Saw a Moor, 708
I Saw a Man Pursuing the Horizon, 837
I Saw in Louisiana a Live-Oak Growing,
  652
I Took One Draught of Life, 710
Ichabod, 360
If I Shouldn't Be Alive, 709
In Another Country, 967
In School-Days, 383
Independence, 281
Indian at the Burial-place of His Fathers, An,
  193
Indian Burying Ground, The, 114
Indian Summer, 707
Inebriate of Air, 704
Inscription for the Entrance to a Wood, 189
Irving, Washington, 150
Israfel, 448
It Was a Quiet Way, 710

James, Henry, 770
Jane Austen, 766
Jeffers, Robinson, 1019
Jefferson, Thomas, 89
Jim Bludso, of the Prairie Belle, 731
Jonathan to John, 408

Journal (Woolman), 31
Journey of the Magi, 999
Journey to Philadelphia, 55
Jugurtha, 594
June, 197
Just Lost When I Was Saved, 705
Justice Denied in Massachusetts, 1016

Kansas Emigrants, The, 361
Keeping the Sabbath, 707
Killers, The, 962
King Honor's Eldest Son, 1018
King Witlaf's Drinking-Horn, 559

Lanier, Sidney, 683
Last Leaf, The, 599
Last Night That She Lived, The, 708
Laus Deo! 369
League of Nations, A, 125
Lenore, 447
Letter from Mr. Ezekiel Biglow, A, 404
Letter of Reconciliation, A, 97
Letter Received, A, 708
Letters (Franklin), 72
Letters from an American Farmer, 38
Letters (Jefferson), 92, 93, 96
Letters to T. W. Higginson, 713
Lewis, Sinclair, 923
*Life and Voyages of Christopher Columbus,
   The*, 177
Life on the Mississippi, 743
Lincoln, Abraham, 618
Lindsay, Vachel, 893
Lion and the Lamb, The, 1018
Little Breeches, 731
Little Giffen, 626
Locomotive, The, 704
Long Valley, The, 1049
Longfellow, Henry Wadsworth, 540
Look Homeward, Angel, 1032
Lost Occasion, The, 384
Love Song of J. Alfred Prufrock, The, 995
Lover of Mankind, 1042
Lowell, Amy, 987
Lowell, James Russell, 385
Luck of Roaring Camp, The, 719
Luke Havergal, 878

MacLeish, Archibald, 1011
Madison, James, 102
Man Said to the Universe, A, 838

Mark Twain (Samuel Langhorne Cle-
   mens), 732
Marsh Song—At Sunset, 699
Marshes of Glynn, The, 697
Masque of the Red Death, The, 466
Massachusetts to Virginia, 355
Maud Muller, 363
Maypole of Merry Mount, The, 323
McTeague, 840
Me Imperturbe, 652
Melville, Herman, 517
Memorial Rain, 1013
Memories, 354
Men Without Women, 962
Mencken, Henry Louis, 1068
Mending Wall, 882
Mezzo Cammin, 552
Millay, Edna St. Vincent, 1015
Miniver Cheevy, 877
Miracles, 643
Moby Dick, 520
Moral Argument against Calvinism, The, 145
Morituri Salutamus, 590
Morning at the Window, 998
Mountain, The, 885
Much Madness Is Divinest Sense, 704
Murdered Traveller, The, 194
Musketaquid, 233
My Aunt, 599
My Lost Youth, 573
My Maryland, 624
My Passion for Ferries, 680
My Playmate, 368

Nameless Song, 1019
Nature (Emerson), 237
Nature (Longfellow), 593
New England Two Centuries Ago, 431
Newspaper Is a Collection of Half-Injustices,
   A, 838
Newsreel LXVI, 1045
Nocturne in a Deserted Brickyard, 910
Norris, Frank, 838
Not What We Did Shall Be the Test, 713
Notes on the State of Virginia, 92
Nuremberg, 552

O Captain! My Captain! 660
O Mother of a Mighty Race, 202
Ode (Freneau), 115
Ode for the Fourth of July, 1876, An, 422

Ode Inscribed to W. H. Channing, 234
Ode Recited at the Harvard Commemoration, 416
Of the Eternity and Infinitude of Divine Providence, 85
Of the Importance of the Exercise of Reason and Practice of Morality, in Order to the Happiness of Mankind, 88
Of Time and the River, 1036
Oh Fairest of the Rural Maids, 191
Old Clock on the Stairs, The, 557
Old Ironsides, 598
Old Man's Winter Night, An, 888
Omnibus Jaunts and Drivers, 681
On a Honey Bee, 117
On Agricultural Education, 96
On Being Original, 1060
On Lending a Punch-Bowl, 600
On Slavery, 92
On the Adoption of the Constitution, 93
On the Anniversary of the Storming of the Bastille, 115
On the Religion of Nature, 118
On the Uniformity and Perfection of Nature, 118
O'Neill, Eugene, 970
One's-Self I Sing, 667
Orchard, 992
Other Two, The, 861
Our Singing Strength, 890
Out of the Cradle Endlessly Rocking, 648
Outcasts of Poker Flat, The, 724
Over-Soul, The, 265

Paine, Thomas, 77
Passage to India, 668
Patterns, 989
Paul Revere's Ride, 585
Pau-Puk-Keewis, 575
Perplexing Lessons, 749
Person, Place and Thing, 1056
Personal Narrative, 19
Philosophy of Composition, The, 487
Pilot, The, 209
Pioneers! Oh Pioneers! 656
Pity this busy Monster, manunkind, 1007
Plain Language from Truthful James, 717
Poe, Edgar Allan, 439
Poet, The, 203
Poets to Come, 653
Pond, The, 291

Power of Fancy, The, 109
Prairie Sunset, A, 677
Prairies, The, 199
Preface to Collected Poems of Robert Frost, 892
Preface to Twice-Told Tales, 346
Prejudices, Third Series, 1070
Prelude (Whittier), 380
Preludes (Eliot), 997
Present Crisis, The, 390
Problem, The, 228
Proem (Whittier), 358
Project of Attaining Moral Perfection, The, 64
Prologue to U.S.A., 1041
Psalm of Life, A, 546
Publication Is the Auction, 709
Public-spirited Projects, 67
Purloined Letter, The, 473

Randall, James Ryder, 624
Raven, The, 450
Read, Thomas Buchanan, 626
Reason the Only Oracle of Man, 85
Reasons for Writing, 52
Reconciliation, 654
Red Badge of Courage, The, 817
Resignation, 559
Responsibilities of the Novelist, The, 843
Revenge of Hamish, The, 694
Revolution, 709
Rhodora, The, 227
Rich Boy, The, 940
Richard Cory, 874
Right of Workmen to Strike, The, 204
Rip Van Winkle, 159
Rise of Silas Lapham, The, 756
River, The, 1009
Road Not Taken, The, 889
Robinson, Edwin Arlington, 871
Romany Girl, The, 236
Rose for Emily, A, 1024
Rounding the Horn, 495

Sacred Wood, The, 1078
Sandburg, Carl, 906
Santa-Fé Trail, The, 900
Sarah Pierrepont, 24
Savior! I've No One Else to Tell, 712
Science, 1021
Sculptor's Funeral, The, 916
Sea Surface Full of Clouds, 1003

Seaweed, 556
Second Inaugural Address, The, 620
Secret, A, 709
Self-Reliance (Dickinson), 706
Self-Reliance (Emerson), 252
Sense of Sinfulness, 23
Shapiro, Karl Jay, 1055
She Came and Went, 402
Sheridan's Ride, 626
Shoemakers, The, 359
Show Is Not the Show, The, 704
Sights from a Steeple, 308
Simon Legree:—A Negro Sermon, 905
Sinners in the Hands of an Angry God, 25
Skeleton in Armor, The, 549
Sketch Book, The, 159
Skipper Ireson's Ride, 366
Sky Is Low, The, 707
Slave's Dream, The, 551
Sleeper, The, 446
Smoke, 280
Snake, The, 703
Snow-Bound, 370
Snow-Storm, The, 231
So the Eyes Accost and Sunder, 710
So Well That I Can Live Without, 711
Solitude, 291
Some Specimen Cases, 681
Song (H.D.), 992
Song of Hiawatha, The, 574
Song of Marion's Men, 198
Song of Myself, 632
Song of the Chattahoochee, 696
Songs of Labor, 358
Sonnet to Gath, 1016
Sonnet—To Science, 445
Sonnets (Lowell), 389
Soul Selects Her Own Society, The, 704
Specimen Days, 680
Spirit of Poetry, The, 545
Stanzas (Freneau), 116
Stanzas on Freedom, 390
Steinbeck, John, 1047
Stevens, Wallace, 1000
Stirrup-Cup, The, 694
Stopping by Woods on a Snowy Evening, 889
Stout Gentleman, The, 172
Success, 703
Sunday Morning, 1002
Sundry Exercises, 31
Sunset on the Spire, 1018

Sunthin' in the Pastoral Line, 410
Symphony, The, 689

Tales of a Wayside Inn, 582
Teamster's Farewell, A, 909
Telling the Bees, 367
Terminus, 236
Thanatopsis, 186
Thar's More in the Man Than Thar Is in the
    Land, 686
There Is No Frigate Like a Book, 705
There Was a Child Went Forth, 647
These 13, 1024
Thoreau, Henry David, 278
Thou Mother with Thy Equal Brood, 674
Thought, 225
Thought Went Up My Mind Today, A, 705
Thoughts in Old Age, 98
Thoughts on the Present State of American
    Affairs, 81
Three Silences of Molinos, The, 589
Ticknor, Francis Orray, 626
"Till Death" Is Narrow Loving, 712
Time to Talk, A, 889
Times That Try Men's Souls, The, 79
Timrod, Henry, 625
Tint I Cannot Take Is Best, The, 710
To a Caty-did, 117
To a Certain Civilian, 658
To a Contemporary Bunkshooter, 909
To a Waterfowl, 188
To a Young Artist, 1021
To an Author, 114
To Ezra Stiles, 76
To Fight Aloud Is Very Brave, 704
To Hear an Oriole Sing, 706
To Helen, 445
To Make a Prairie, 707
To Mason Weems and Edward Gantt, 73
To Mrs. Sarah Bache, 74
To One in Paradise, 448
To Samuel Mather, 72
To Sir Toby, 112
To the Dandelion, 392
To the Fringed Gentian, 198
To the Memory of the Brave Americans, 111
To the Reverend Henry Ware, Jr., 251
To Whittier, 426
To William Lloyd Garrison, 354
Town Down the River, The, 875
Tradition and the Individual Talent, 1078

Trailing Arbutus, The, 383
Transcendent Contemplations, 21
Trial by Existence, The, 881
Trip to Boston and Back, 60
Triumph of the Egg, The, 933
Two Look at Two, 890
Two Rivers, 235
Two Tramps in Mud Time, 891
Two Years Before the Mast, 495

Ulalume, 452
Unanimous Declaration of the Thirteen
    United States of America, The, 91
Unfinished Portrait, 1019
University, 1056
U.S.A., Prologue to, 1041

Victor and Vanquished, 593
Vigil Strange I Kept on the Field One Night,
    666
Village Blacksmith, The, 547
Voiceless, The, 602
Voyage to England, 34

Walden, 281
War Is Kind, 837
Warning, The, 552
Warren, Robert Penn, 1082
Washers of the Shroud, The, 414
Wayfarer, The, 838
Wayside Inn, The, 582

Wharton, Edith, 858
What Is an American? 38
What Soft, Cherubic Creatures, 706
When Lilacs Last in the Dooryard Bloom'd,
    661
Where I Lived and What I Lived For, 288
Whistle, The, 71
Whitman, Walt, 628
Whittier, John Greenleaf, 350
Why Do I Love Thee? 711
Why Franklin Seldom Went to Church Serv-
    ices, 63
Wife at Daybreak I Shall Be, A 713
Wild Honey Suckle, The, 113
William Faulkner, 1083
Winter Piece, A, 191
Wolfe, Thomas, 1029
Woodnotes, 229
Woolman, John, 31
Work Gangs, 911
Wound-Dresser, The, 659
Wouter Van Twiller, 154
Wreck of the Hesperus, The, 547
Written in Naples, 226
Wylie, Elinor, 1017

Yellow Violet, The, 188
You, Andrew Marvell, 1013
Young, Thomas, and Allen, Ethan, 84
Young Goodman Brown, 316
Youth and The Bright Medusa, 916